THE LAW OF REAL PROPERTY

AUSTRALIA
LBC Information Services
Sydney

CANADA and USA
Carswell
Toronto, Ontario

NEW ZEALAND
Brooker's
Auckland

SINGAPORE and MALAYSIA
Sweet & Maxwell Asia
Singapore and Kuala Lumpur

THE LAW
of
REAL PROPERTY

BY

THE RT. HON. SIR ROBERT MEGARRY,
M.A., LL.D. (Cantab.), Hon.LL.D.(Hull, Nottingham,
The Law Society of Upper Canada, and London),
Hon. D.U. (Essex), F.B.A.
*A Bencher of Lincoln's Inn; an Honorary Fellow of Trinity Hall, Cambridge;
formerly the Vice-Chancellor of the Supreme Court*

AND

SIR WILLIAM WADE,
Q.C., M.A., LL.D. Hon. Litt.D. (Cantab.), F.B.A.
*Formerly the Master of Gonville and Caius College, Cambridge;
formerly Rouse Ball Professor of English Law in the
University of Cambridge and Professor of English Law in the
University of Oxford; Honorary Bencher of Lincoln's Inn*

SIXTH EDITION

BY

CHARLES HARPUM
M.A., LL.B. (Cantab.)
*Fellow of Downing College, Cambridge; a Barrister
of Lincoln's Inn; a Law Commissioner*

with

MALCOLM GRANT
LL.D. (Otago); Hon. M.R.T.P.I.; Hon. R.I.C.S.
*Professor of Land Economy in the University of Cambridge;
Fellow of Clare College, Cambridge; a Barrister of the Middle Temple*
(for Chapter 22, Part 2)

and

STUART BRIDGE
M.A. (Cantab.)
*Fellow of Queen's College, Cambridge; Lecturer in Law in the
University of Cambridge; a Barrister of the Middle Temple*
(for Chapter 22, Part 3)

LONDON
SWEET & MAXWELL LIMITED
2000

First Edition	-	-	-	-	1957
Second Impression		-	-	1958
Second Edition	-	-	-	-	1959
Second Impression		-	-	1964
Third Edition	-	-	-	-	1966
Second Impression		-	-	1971
Fourth Edition	-	-	-	-	1975
Second Impression		-	-	1979
Third Impression		-	-	1982
Fifth Edition	-	-	-	-	1984
Sixth Edition	-	-	-	-	2000

Published by
Sweet & Maxwell Limited
100 Avenue Road, Swiss Cottage
London NW3 3PF
(http://www.smlawpub.co.uk)
Computerset by Interactive Sciences Ltd, Gloucester
Printed in Great Britain by
Richard Clay (The Chaucer Press) Limited,
Bungay, Suffolk

A CIP catalogue record for the book is available from the British Library

ISBN 0 421 47460 2
ISBN 0 421 47470 X Pbk

FOREWORD

It is more than forty years since this work first appeared and time, inexorably, has decreed that it should pass into other and younger hands. It is a piece of good fortune that the hands are those of Mr Charles Harpum, who in addition to his learning and expertise has the authority of a Law Commissioner and is thus at the epicentre of the seismic upheavals which have recently occurred in this area of the law. The price that had to be paid for this advantage was an abnormal delay in publication, which we much regret. In our last preface we said that our successive editions had settled down into a life cycle of about nine years and that real property moved at a slower tempo than did some more volatile branches of the law. This edition has proved us wrong on both counts.

As we retire into the shadows among the ghostly figures of former legal authors, we bid a fond farewell to many of the old and classic doctrines which were our companions for so many years and are now reformed—the Statute of Frauds, for example, and its illegitimate offspring the doctrine of part performance. For the Settled Land Act, on the other hand, we retain no sentimental feeling. In our first and all later editions we have advocated its abolition in favour of simpler forms of trust, and we have at least lived to see the day when this wish was fulfilled.

We thank all our readers, colleagues and students who have helped this work on its way into the new millennium.

LINCOLN'S INN   R.E.M.
All Saints Day, 1999   H.W.R.W.

PREFACE

Megarry & Wade's *Law of Real Property*, perhaps more than any other textbook by living authors, is universally accepted to be a work of authority. In the lifetime of the Fifth Edition, it was frequently cited with approbation and seldom disapproved. Its stature is such that the Parliamentary draftsman has drawn on it on at least one occasion in recent years.[1] The opinions expressed in it have frequently been vindicated. When, some seven years ago, Sir William Wade generously invited me on behalf of Sir Robert Megarry and himself to edit the Sixth Edition, I accepted with a very real sense of the daunting task that I was undertaking: I could only make the book worse. Furthermore, I could not have foreseen that, the very next year I would be appointed to be one of the five Law Commissioners for England and Wales. This meant that the work of preparing the new edition had to be fitted into evenings and weekends to the extent that my extensive duties in London would permit. It is a matter of profound regret to me that it has taken so long for the new edition to see the light of day. I am grateful not only to Sir Robert and Sir William for their much-tried patience and forbearance, but also to readers.

The basis on which I agreed to edit the book was that it would be revised in the tradition and style that it had hitherto always had. This I have endeavoured to do, though with what success I leave readers to judge. Although Sir William has read all the Chapters, and Sir Robert some of them, I undertook the task on the basis that editorial reponsibility rested ultimately with me. This absolves Sir Robert and Sir William from any blame for the errors, omissions, infelicities and solecisms that exist and for which I alone am responsible. I am very grateful for their comments on draft chapters. There are few suggestions that they made which I have not adopted. There is one Chapter that I have not edited, namely Chapter 22, *The Social Control of Land*. Professor Malcolm Grant wrote the part of it that is concerned with planning control and Stuart Bridge edited the section on the protection of tenants.

One of the main reasons why the new edition has been so long in its gestation is that since the last edition the law of real property has undergone the most important changes since the reforms of 1925. Previous editions have emphasised the traditional principles of unregistered land. However, the balance has now firmly shifted so that the great majority of titles are registered. The Land Registration Act 1925, imperfect creature that it is, is now the most important part of the property legislation and the new edition has attempted to reflect this. But there have been other profound changes. Not only have there been many important decisions of the House of Lords and Privy Council (particularly in relation to the nature of leases), but there have been major legislative changes. It is no longer possible to create settled land or entails, and in leases granted after 1995, the original tenant who assigns the

---

[1] See *post*, para. 12–080.

lease no longer remains liable for breaches of covenant committed thereafter, except where he guarantees performance by the assignee. The formal requirements for contracts for the sale of land have been made stricter and the doctrine of part performance has been consigned to oblivion. All of these developments are considered in the new edition.[2]

These changes pale into insignificance when compared to those that are expected to occur in the lifetime of the present edition. The existing land registration legislation is likely to be replaced, in part at least to enable electronic conveyancing to be introduced. Today's paper-based conveyancing system is not likely to survive for much longer. It can also be anticipated that the Human Rights Act 1998, which will be brought into force on October 3, 2000, will have a marked impact on the development of property law. Long cherished doctrines and remedies may not withstand its impact.

I wish to record my thanks to Stuart Bridge and Malcolm Grant, not only for their contributions to the new edition but for their support and friendship throughout the time that it has been under preparation. Stuart Bridge read every chapter in draft. He eliminated many errors and made many helpful comments. Having already done so much, he then generously assisted with proof reading. I also owe a profound debt of gratitude to many other friends and colleagues who have not only been kind, patient and supportive over the years, but have also provided great assistance and given unstintingly of their time. They have made a significant contribution to the quality of the new edition. I would particularly like to thank Andrew Burns, Matthew Coggins, Michael Croker, Richard Dew, Dr David Fox, Sir Gavin Lightman, Tony Oakley, Rupert Reed, Christopher West and Derek Wood, Q.C., for the considerable help that each of them gave in different ways, wittingly or unwittingly. I am also grateful to the Trustees of the Yorke Fund of the Faculty of Law of the University of Cambridge for a grant that enabled me to employ a research assistant one summer. Last, but by no means least, I am indebted to the staff of Sweet & Maxwell who have worked on this book over the years. I particularly wish to thank Sarah Lewis, Anne Godfrey, Nick O'Dell and, above all, Tony Hawitt and Helen Vaux, who have carried the burden of seeing the new edition into print. For their unfailing courtesy and enormous patience, I am most appreciative.

The law is stated as at June 30, 1999, though it has been possible to include one or two late developments. There have been some minor changes since that date, for example in the Civil Procedure Rules and the Land Registration Rules.

The views that are expressed in this edition are in my private capacity alone and not as Law Commissioner.

C.H.

DOWNING COLLEGE FALCON CHAMBERS,
CAMBRIDGE LONDON EC4
October 26, 1999

---

[2] The Contracts (Rights of Third Parties) Bill had not cleared all its stages in Parliament at the time of going to press. Some but by no means all of its likely implications for land law are considered in this edition.

PREFACE TO THE FIRST EDITION

THIS is a book in which we have attempted to state the English law of real property within a reasonable compass and in a form which will be both intelligible to students and helpful to practitioners. In some other spheres, the claims of student and practitioner are barely reconcilable, but here we are fortunate in our subject. In the main, the English law of real property rests on the logical development of clear principles, and it is these principles that throughout we have sought to emphasise. There are indeed certain passages in this book which are addressed solely or mainly to the student, and a number of details which, though important to the practitioner, need trouble none save the more zealous students; but for the most part it is our hope to have achieved a work of dual utility.

The book is founded on pre-war manuscript from which *A Manual of the Law of Real Property* has already been drawn. As first conceived, the task was to revise and bring the manuscript up to date; in the outcome most, but by no means all, of that manuscript has found its way into this book, while at the same time much new material has been interwoven with it. For unlike the manuscript and the *Manual*, this is a work of joint authorship, with all the mutual aid that flows from the application of a second mind to that was conceived and in the main executed as a complete entity. Instead of dividing up the subject-matter and each writing the text of part, nearly all of this book has been covered by each of us in close detail, often more than once. It would be too much to hope that even this time-consuming process has extirpated all error, but we hope that the result will be thought to have justified the effort. In addition to this, other factors have combined to delay publication, including our geographical separation, the press of other claims upon our time, difficulties in resolving how much of the original manuscript to omit, and the troubles of the printing industry in 1956. The printers' skill has, however, enabled us to keep the text under constant revision, and although the vicissitudes of publication have made it difficult to ensure that the whole of the text has been brought up to the same date, we hope that in general the law will be found to have been accurately stated down to the beginning of 1957, with such later additions as the state of the proofs admitted.

The publication of this work completes the original scheme for two books of a common design but different scope. Those who in student days have become familiar with the *Manual* should be able to turn with ease to the greater amplitude of this book; and the similarity of design will, we hope, not only assist teachers of law in their tasks, but also make it possible for future editions of the *Manual* to become a little slimmer.

Finally, we have the pleasure of giving thanks where thanks are due. Some of our obligations are general and distributed; we are grateful to many of those whom we have severally sought to teach, for they have themselves taught us more than they are ever likely to realise. Other gratitude is more specific. The publishers and printers have earned more praise than even they are accustomed to; it would be wrong if we did not mention specifically the printers' skill and publishers' generosity which made it possible for the work to proceed when the manuscript and galley proofs had reached a condition more deplorable than any we had seen before. Mr I. Goldsmith also gave invaluable help with the manuscript at that stage, Mr P. V. Baker read the proofs, and Mr R. Higgins prepared the table of cases and table of statutes. To all of them we are grateful.

LINCOLN'S INN,   R. E. M.
New Year's Day, 1957   H. W. R. W.

CONTENTS

APPENDIX

TABLE OF CASES

TABLE OF STATUTES

COMMONWEALTH STATUTES

ALPHABETICAL LIST OF STATUTES

*This list will enable any statute to be found in the chronological
Table of Statutes.*

TABLE OF STATUTORY INSTRUMENTS

2. RULES OF COURT

ABBREVIATIONS

STATUTES, ORDERS AND CASES

A.E.A. - - - - - - - -	Administration of Estates Act
A.H.A. - - - - - - - -	Agricultural Holdings Act
A.J.A. - - - - - - - -	Administration of Justice Act
A.T.A. - - - - - - - -	Agricultural Tenancies Act
B.S. - - - - - - - -	Building Society
C.A. - - - - - - - -	Conveyancing Act
C.C.A. - - - - - - - -	County Courts Act
C.L.P.A. - - - - - - -	Common Law Procedure Act
C.P.R. - - - - - - - -	Civil Procedure Rules
E.C.H.R. - - - - - - -	European Convention on Human Rights
F.L.A. - - - - - - - -	Family Law Act
F.R.A. - - - - - - - -	Fines and Recoveries Act
H.A. - - - - - - - -	Housing Act
I.A. - - - - - - - -	Insolvency Act
I.E.A. - - - - - - - -	Intestates' Estates Act
In. b. - - - - - - - -	(*In bonis*) In the Goods of, In the Estate of
J.A. - - - - - - - -	Judicature Act
L & T.A. - - - - - -	Landlord and Tenant Act
L. & T.C.A. - - - - -	Landlord and Tenant (Covenants) Act
L.A. - - - - - - - -	Limitation Act
L.B.C. - - - - - - -	London Borough Council
L.C.C.P. - - - - - - -	Law Commission Consultation Paper
L.C.A. - - - - - - -	Land Charges Act
L.G.H.A. - - - - - -	Local Government and Housing Act
L.P.A. - - - - - - -	Law of Property Act
L.P.Am.A. - - - - - -	Law of Property (Amendment) Act
L.P.(M.P.)A. - - - - -	Law of Property (Miscellaneous Provisions) Act
L.R. & L.C.A. - - - -	Land Registration and Land Charges Act
L.R.A. - - - - - - -	Land Registration Act
L.R.A. 1967 - - - - -	Leasehold Reform Act 1967
L.R.H.U.D.A. - - - - -	Leasehold Reform, Housing and Urban Development Act
L.R.R. - - - - - - -	Land Registration Rules
L.T.A. 1954 - - - - -	Landlord and Tenant Act 1954
P.A.A. - - - - - - -	Perpetuities and Accumulations Act
P.E.A. - - - - - - -	Protection from Eviction Act
R.A. - - - - - - - -	Rent Act
R.P.A. - - - - - - -	Real Property Act
S.E. - - - - - - - -	Settled Estate(s)
S.I. - - - - - - - -	Statutory Instrument
S.L.A. - - - - - - -	Settled Land Act
S.R. & O. - - - - - -	Statutory Rules and Orders
S.T. - - - - - - - -	Settlement Trusts
T. & C.P.A. - - - - -	Town and Country Planning Act
T.A. - - - - - - - -	Trustee Act
T.I.A. - - - - - - -	Trustee Investments Act
T.L.A.T.A. - - - - - -	Trusts of Land and Appointment of Trustees Act
W.T. - - - - - - - -	Will Trusts

BOOKS, PERIODICALS, ETC.
(Normally recognised abbreviations are not given for law reports,
law reviews and law journals.)

Bailey, *Wills*: S. J. Bailey, The Law of Wills, 7th ed., 1973.

Bl.Comm.: Sir William Blackstone, Commentaries on the Laws of England, 15th ed., by E. Christian, 1809 (first ed. published 1765).

Blount, Frag.: Thomas Blount, Fragmenta Antiquitatis, or Antient Tenures, 2nd ed., 1784.

Bracton: Henry de Bracton, De Legibus et Consuetudinibus Angliae, Rolls ed. by T. Twiss, 1879; G. E. Woodbine's ed., 1915–1942. "Bracton" is thought to have been written in the years prior to 1257.

Challis: H. W. Challis, The Law of Real Property, 3rd ed. by C. Sweet, 1911.

Cole, *Ejectment:* W. R. Cole, The Law of Ejectment, 1857.

Co.Litt.: Coke upon Littleton, 19th ed., with notes by F. Hargrave and C. Butler, 1832 (Littleton's Tenures was first printed in or about 1481; Sir Edward Coke's commentary was first published in 1628).

Conv. Y.B.: Conveyancers' Year Book.

Coote, *Mortgages*: Coote's Law of Mortgages, 9th ed. by R. L. Ramsbotham, 1927.

C.P.L.: Current Property Law.

Cru.Dig: William Cruise, A Digest of the Laws of England, 4th ed. by H. H. White, 1835.

Dart, V. & P.: Dart's Vendors and Purchasers of Real Estate, 8th ed. by E. P. Hewitt and M. R. C. Overton, 1929.

Digby: K. E. Digby, Introduction to the History of the Law of Real Property, 5th ed. by K. E. Digby and W. M. Harrison, 1897.

Elphinstone, *Covenants*: Sir L. H. Elphinstone, Covenants Affecting Land, 1946.

Emmet: Emmet on Title, 19th ed. by J. T. Farrand, 1986, looseleaf.

Farrand, Contract and Conveyance: J. T. Farrand, Contract and Conveyance, 4th ed. 1983.

Farwell, *Powers*: Sir G. Farwell, Powers, 3rd ed. by C. J. W. Farwell and F. K. Archer, 1916.

Fearne: Charles Fearne, Essay on the Learning of Contingent Remainders and Executory Devises, 10th ed., with C. Butler's notes, 1844 (1st ed. published 1772). The second volume of the 10th edition is Josiah W. Smith's Original View of Executory Interests.

Fisher and Lightwood, *Mortgage*: Fisher and Lightwood's Law of Mortgage, 10th ed., by E. L. G. Tyler, 1988.

Fletcher: E. W. S. Fletcher, Contingent and Executory Interests in Land, 1915.

Foa, L. & T.: Edgar Foa, Law of Landlord and Tenant, 8th ed. by H. Heathcote Williams, 1957.

Fry, S. P.: Sir E. Fry, Specific Performance, 6th ed. by G. R. Northcote, 1921.

Gale: C. J. Gale, Law of Easements, 16th ed., by J. Gaunt and P. Morgan, 1996 (1st ed. published 1839).

Gilb. *Uses*: Gilbert on Uses and Trusts, 3rd ed. by E. B. Sugden, 1811.

Gray: J. C. Gray, Perpetuities, 4th ed. by R. Gray, 1942.

Halsb.: Halsbury's Laws of England, 4th ed., 1973—1988; with re-issue volumes 1988—to date.

Hanbury, *Modern Equity*: H. G. Hanbury and J. E. Martin, Modern Equity, 15th ed., by J. E. Martin, 1997.

Hawkins and Ryder: Hawkins and Ryder's The Construction of Wills by E. C. Ryder, 1965 (based on Hawkins on the Construction of Wills, 3rd ed. 1925).

Hayes: William Hayes, An Introduction to Conveyancing, 5th ed. 1840.
   Limitations: William Hayes, Limitations to Heirs of the Body in Devises, 1824.

H.E.L.: Sir W. S. Holdsworth, A History of English Law, 1903–1952; latest editions as in 61 L.Q.R. 346 (1945); also vol. i, 7th ed., 1956; vol. xiii, 1952; vol. xiv, 1964; vol. xv, 1965; vol. xvi, 1966.

Hill & Redman, L. & T.: Hill and Redman's Landlord and Tenant, looseleaf ed., by J. Furber, J. Harper *et al.*

Hood and Challis: Hood and Challis' Property Acts, 8th ed., by J. H. Boraston, 1938.

Jarman: Thomas Jarman, A Treatise on Wills, 8th ed. by R. W. Jennings and J. C. Harper, 1951 (1st ed. published 1841–1843).

Jurid.Soc.Papers: Juridical Society's Papers, 1858–1874.

K. & E.: Key and Elphinstone's Precedents in Conveyancing, 15th ed. by various editors, 1953–1954.

Law Com.: Reports of the Law Commission.

Law Com. W.P.: Law Commission Working Paper.

Lewin: Lewin on Trusts, 16th ed. by W. J. Mowbray, 1964 (1st ed. published 1837).

Lewis, *Perpetuity*: W. D. Lewis, The Law of Perpetuity, 1843.

Littleton: see Co.Litt.

L.J.News.: Law Journal (the weekly periodical, now called the New Law Journal).

L.N.: Law Notes (1882–).

Maitland, *Coll. Pp.*: F. W. Maitland, collected Papers, ed. by H. A. L. Fisher, 1911.

    Equity: F. W. Maitland, Equity, revised ed. by J. W. Brunyate, 1936.

    Forms of Action: F. W. Maitland, Forms of Action at Common Law, ed. by A. H. Chaytor and W. J. Whittaker, 1936 (first printed with *Equity*, 1909).

Marsden: R. G. Marsden, Perpetuities, 1883.

Maudsley: R. H. Maudsley, The Modern Law of Perpetuities, 1979.

Millard, *Tithes*: P. W. Millard, Tithes, 3rd ed., 1938.

Morris and Leach: J. H. C. Morris and W. B. Leach, The Rule against Perpetuities, 2nd ed., 1962, with Supplement, 1964.

Norton, *Deeds*: R. F. Norton, Deeds, 2nd ed. by R. J. A. Morrison and H. J. Goolden, 1928.

O.E.D.: Oxford English Dictionary.

Perk.: Perkins' Profitable Book Touching the Laws of England, 15th ed. by R. J. Greening, 1827 (first ed. published 1530).

Platt on *Leases*: Thomas Platt, Law of Leases, 1847.

P. & M.: Sir F. Pollock and F. W. Maitland, History of English Law before the time of Edward I, 2nd ed., 1898.

Preston: Richard Preston, An Elementary Treatise on Estates, 2nd ed., 1820–1827.

    Abstracts: Richard Preston, Essay on Abstracts of Title, 2nd ed., 1823–1824.

    Conveyancing: Richard Preston, A Treatise on Conveyancing, 3rd ed., 1819–1829.

Prideaux: Prideaux's Forms and Precedents in Conveyancing, 25th ed., 1958–1959. Vol. 1 by T. K. Wigan and I. M. Phillips; Vol. 2 by V. G. H. Hallett, A. P. McNabb and T. A. Blanco White; Vol. 3 by I. M. Phillips, E. H. Scammell and V. G. H. Hallett (1st ed. published 1853).

Rob.Gav.: Thomas Robinson, The Common Law of Kent, or the Custom of Gavelkind, 3rd ed. by J. Wilson, 1822 (this is the edition usually cited; the latest is 5th ed. by C. J. Elton and H. J. H. Mackay, 1897).

Ruoff & Roper: R. G. Roper, E. J. Pryer, C. West *et al.*, The Law and Practice of Registered Conveyancing, looseleaf ed.

Sanders, *Uses*: F. W. Sanders, Uses and Trusts, 5th ed. by G. W. Sanders and J. Warner, 1844.

Scriven: J. Scriven, A Treatise on the Law of Copyholds, 7th ed. by A. Brown, 1896.

Shep.Touch.: Sheppard's Touchstone of Common Assurances, 8th ed. by E. G. Atherley, 1826 (7th ed. (1st ed. published 1641) by R. Preston, 1820, is, however, not superseded).

Smith, *Executory Interests*: see Fearne.

Smith's L.C.: J. W. Smith, Leading Cases, 13th ed. by T. W Chitty, A. T. Denning and C. P. Harvey, 1929.

Snell, *Equity*: Snell's Principles of Equity, 29th ed., by P. V. Baker and P. St.J. Langan, 1990 (1st ed. published 1868).

S.S.: Selden Society's Publications.

Sugden, *Powers*: E. B. Sugden, A Practical Treatise on Powers, 8th ed., 1861.

    V. & P.: E. B. Sugden, The Law of Vendors and Purchasers, 14th ed., 1862.

Tudor L.C.: Tudor's Leading Cases on Real Property, 4th ed. by T. H. Carson and H. B. Bompas, 1898.

Vin.Abr.: Viner's Abridgment of Law and Equity, 2nd ed., 1791–1806.

Waldock, *Mortgages*: C. H. M. Waldock, Mortgages, 2nd ed., 1950.

Wh. & T.: White and Tudor's Leading Cases in Equity, 9th ed. by E. P. Hewitt and J. B. Richardson, 1928.

Williams, *Executors*: Williams, Mortimer and Sunnucks on Executors, Administrators and Probate (which includes the 16th edition of Williams on Executors), by J. H. G. Sunnucks, J. G. R. Martyn and K. M. Garnett, 1982.

Williams, *Statute of Frauds, Section IV*: James Williams, The Statute of Frauds, Section Four, 1932.

Williams, R.P.: Joshua Williams, Principles of the Law of Real Property, 23rd ed. by T. C. Williams, 1920. (This is cited in preference to 24th ed. by R. A. Eastwood, 1926, since Williams is a classic work on the pre-1926 law.)

    Seisin: Joshua Williams, The Seisin of the Freehold, 1878.

GLOSSARY

[The object of this glossary is to provide a ready source of reference to the meanings of some of the more troublesome technical expressions used in the text. For the most part, brief but not necessarily exhaustive definitions have been given, with references to the paragraphs of the text where further information can be obtained and the terms may be seen in their context; references which are essential to a proper understanding of the terms are in heavy type. Where the text contains a convenient collection and explanation of a number of contrasting terms, a simple reference to the appropriate pages is given instead of setting out the definition.]

Absolute: not conditional or determinable (in relation to an estate) (4–039).
Abstract of title: an epitome of documents and facts showing ownership (**5–028**).
Ad hoc settlement or trust for sale: one with special overreaching powers (**8–168**).
Ademption: failure of a testamentary gift, *e.g.* by the testator ceasing to own the property (11–071).
Administrators: persons authorised to administer the estate of an intestate (11–124); compare Executors.
Advancement: gift by parent or husband to provide for child or wife (10–015).
Advowson: a right of presenting a clergyman to a vacant benefice (18–007).
Alienation: the act of disposing of or transferring property.
Ante-nuptial: before marriage.
Appendant: attached to land by operation of law (18–083); compare Appurtenant.
Approvement: appropriation of portion of manorial waste free from rights of common.
Appurtenant: attached to land by act of parties (18–082); compare Appendant.
Assent: an assurance by personal representatives vesting property in the person entitled (11–126).
Assignment: a disposition or transfer, usually of a lease.
Assurance: a disposition or transfer.
Assured tenancy: a residential tenancy with limited statutory protection as to rent and possession (**22–131**).
Attorney, power of: authority to another person to execute deeds or carry out transactions (10–080).

Base fee: a fee simple produced by partially barring an entail (3–083).
Beneficial owner: a person entitled for his own benefit and not, *e.g.*, as trustee.
Beneficiaries: those entitled to benefit under a trust or will.
Bona vacantia: goods without an owner.

Caution: an entry protecting an interest in registered land (6–083).
Cestui que trust: a beneficiary under a trust.
     ”   ”   *vie*: a person for whose life an estate *pur autre vie* lasts (3–095).
Charge: an incumbrance securing the payment of money.
Chattel real: a leasehold interest (1–010).
Codicil: a supplementary will (11–012).
Collaterals: blood relations who are neither ancestors nor descendants.
Commorientes: persons dying at the same time (11–053).
Condition precedent: a condition which must be fulfilled before a disposition can take effect (3–064).
Condition subsequent: a condition which may defeat a gift after it has taken effect (3–064).
Consolidation: a requirement that a mortgagor shall not redeem one mortgage without another (19–096).
Constructive: inferred or implied (5–017, 10–017).
Contingent: operative only upon an uncertain event (**7–001**): compare Vested.
Conversion: a change in the nature of property, either actually or notionally (8–007).
Conveyance: an instrument (other than a will) transferring property.
Copyhold: a form of tenure peculiar to manors (2–034).

Corporeal: admitting of physical possession (18–003).
Covenant: a promise contained in a deed.

Deed: a document signed, sealed and delivered.
Deed poll: a deed with only one party (5–037); compare Indenture.
Defeasance: the determination of an interest on a specified event.
Demise: a transfer, usually by the grant of a lease.
Determine: terminate, come to an end.
Development: altering land or the use of it (22–023).
Devise: a gift of real property by will.
Disentail: to bar an entail (3–088).
Disseisin: dispossession; see Seisin.
Distrain, distress: the lawful extrajudicial seizure of chattels to enforce a right, *e.g.* to the payment of rent (14–253).
Dominant tenement: land to which the benefit of a right is attached (18–044); compare Servient tenement.
Durante viduitate: during widowhood.

Easement: a right over land for the benefit of other land, such as a right of way (**18–042** et seq.).
Ejectment: obsolete action for recovery of land (Appendix).
Emblements: growing crops which an outgoing tenant may take (3–114).
En ventre sa mère: conceived but not born.
Enfranchise: the statutory right of certain lessees to purchase the fee simple (22–228).
Entail: an estate or interest descending only to issue of the grantee.
Equitable easement: a right over land operating in equity only (**5–104**).
Equities: equitable rights.
Equity of redemption: the sum of a mortgagor's rights in the mortgaged property (**19–017**).
Escheat: a lord's right to ownerless realty (2–014).
Escrow: a document which upon delivery will become a deed.
Estate: 1. the *quantum* of an interest in land (2–005): compare Tenure.
       2. an area of land (2–005).
       3. the whole of the property owned by a deceased person (11–122).
Estate contract: a contract for the sale or lease of land (4–025, **5–099**).
Estate rentcharge: a rentcharge created for certain purposes of management (**18–019**).
Estoppel: prohibition of a party from denying facts which he has led another to assume to be true (13–002).
Estovers: wood which a tenant may take for domestic and other purposes (3–105).
Execute: to perform or complete, *e.g.* a deed.
Executors: persons appointed by a testator to administer his estate (11–123); compare Administrators.

Fealty: loyalty due to a feudal lord (2–010).
Fee: base (3–083), conditional (3–064), determinable (3–062), simple (3–005), tail (3–006).
Fee farm rent: a rentcharge payable in lieu of purchase money (4–039, 18–017).
Fine: 1. a collusive action partially barring an entail (3–083); compare Recovery.
      2. a premium or a lump sum payment, *e.g.*, for the grant of a lease.
Foreclosure: proceedings by a mortgagee which free mortgaged property from the equity of redemption (19–049).
Franchise: royal right granted to a subject, e.g. to hold a market (18–013).
Freehold: 1. free tenure (2–016, 2–047).
      2. an estate of uncertain maximum duration (**3–003**).

Gavelkind: a special customary tenure, formerly common in Kent (2–019).
General equitable charge: an equitable charge of a legal estate not protected by a deposit of title deeds (5–098).
Good consideration: natural love and affection for near relatives (5–008).

Hereditaments: inheritable rights in property (18–001).
Heriot: the best beast of a deceased tenant, to which the lord of the manor was entitled (2–032).

In capite: in chief, holding immediately of the Crown (2–003).

In esse: in existence (opposed to *in posse*, not in existence) (15–038).

In gross: existing independently of a dominant tenement.

Incorporeal: not admitting of physical possession (18–003).

Incumbrance: a liability burdening property.

Indenture: a deed between two or more parties (5–037); compare Deed poll.

Inhibition: an order prohibiting dealings with registered land (6–091).

Injunction: an order of a court restraining a breach of obligation, or commanding performance.

Instrument: a legal document.

Interesse termini: the rights of a lessee before entry (14–062).

Intestacy: the failure to dispose of property by will.

Jus accrescendi: right of survivorship (9–003).

Jus tertii: a third party's title (3–124).

Lapse: the failure of a gift, especially by the beneficiary predeceasing the testator (11–045).

Legal memory: any time later than the accession of Richard I in 1189 (18–133).

Letters of administration: an authorisation to persons to administer the estate of a deceased person (11–124).

Licence: a permission, *e.g.* to enter on land (17–001).

Lien: a form of security for unpaid money (19–002).

Limitation of actions: statutory barring of rights of action after a period of years (21–003).

Limitation, words of: words delimiting the estate granted to some person previously mentioned (**3–026, 3–033, 3–039**); compare Purchase, words of.

Limited owner: an owner with an estate less than a fee simple.

Lis pendens: a pending action (5–088).

Mesne: intermediate, middle (2–003).

Minor: a person under 18 years of age.

Minor interest: an interest in registered land which requires protection by an entry on the register (6–075).

Mortgage: transfer of property as security for a loan (19–001).

Notice: knowledge or imputed knowledge (5–005, 5–015).

Nuncupative: oral (of wills) (11–043).

Overreach: to transfer rights from land to the purchase-money paid therefor (4–078—4–080).

Overriding interest: an interest in registered land which binds the proprietor without being entered on the register (6–036).

Parol: word of mouth.

Particular estate: an estate less than a fee simple (7–009).

Periodic tenancy: tenancy from year to year, month to month, etc. (14–064, 14–072).

Perpetuity: undue remoteness of a future gift; excessive inalienability (**7–012**).

Personal chattels: (**11–092**).

Personal representatives: executors or administrators (11–123).

Possibility of reverter: the grantor's right to the land if a determinable fee determines.

Powers: an authority given to a person to dispose of property which is not his (10–077), general (7–103), special (7–103).

Prescription: the acquisition of easements or profits by long user (18–121, 21–002).

Privity of contract: the relation between parties to a contract (15–003).

Privity of estate: the relation of landlord and tenant (15–004).

Probate: the formal confirmation of a will, granted by the court to an executor (558).

Profit *à prendre*: right to take something from another's land (18–079).

Protected tenancy: a contractual tenancy fully protected by the Rent Acts (22–181).

Protector of the settlement: the person able to control the barring of an entail (3–088).

Puisne mortgage: a legal mortgage not protected by a deposit of title deeds (5–096, 19–220).

Pur autre vie: for the life of another person (3–095).

Purchase, words of: words conferring an interest on the person they mention (3–023); compare Limitation, words of.

Que estate: dominant tenement (18–130).

Recovery: a collusive action completely barring an entail (3–081); compare Fine, 1.
Regulated tenancy: a protected or statutory tenancy (**22–180**).
Release: waiver of some right or interest without transfer of possession (9–102) [release].
Remainder: the interest of a grantee subject to a prior particular estate (7–008).
Rent: fee farm rent (4–039, 18–017), ground rent (12–045), rack rent (12–045), rentcharge (18–014).
Restrictive covenant: a covenant restricting the use of land (4–026, 16–032).
Resulting: returning to the grantor, or remaining in him, by implication of law or equity (**10–009**).
Reversion: the interest remaining in a grantor after granting a particular estate (7–008).
Riparian owner: the owner of land adjoining a watercourse (3–055).
Root of title: a document from which ownership is traced (12–076).

Seignory: the rights of a feudal lord.
Seisin: the possession of land by a freeholder (**3–018**).
Servient tenement: land burdened by a right such as an easement (18–044); compare Dominant tenement.
Settlement: provisions for persons in succession (or the instruments making such provisions) (8–018, 8–047).
Severance: the conversion of a joint tenancy into a tenancy in common (9–036).
Severance, words of: words showing that property is to pass in distinct shares (9–017).
Simplified planning zone (S.P.Z.): an area in which it is proposed to authorise specified types of development in advance (22–032).
Socage: freehold tenure (2–018).
Specialty: a contract by deed.
Squatter: a person wrongfully occupying land and claiming title to it (3–117).
Statutory owner: persons with the powers of a tenant for life (8–014).
Statutory tenant: a person holding over under the Rent Acts (22–186).
Statutory trusts: certain trusts imposed by statute (10–004), especially—
    1. the trust of land under co-ownership (9–051).
    2. the trusts for issue on intestacy (11–088).
Subinfeudation: alienation by creating a new tenure (2–039).
Sub-mortgage: a mortgage of a mortgage (19–185).
Sui juris: "of his own right," *i.e.* subject to no disability.
Surrender: the transfer of an interest (*e.g.* for life, or for years) to the person next entitled to the property (14–172).
Survivorship: a surviving joint tenant's right to the whole land (9–003).

Tabula in naufragio: "a plank in a shipwreck" (a form of tacking mortgages) (19–244).
Tacking: extension of a mortgagee's security to cover a later loan (19–243).
Tenement: property held by a tenant.
Tenure: the set of conditions upon which a tenant holds land (2–004); compare Estate, 1.
Term of years: a period with a defined minimum for which a tenant holds land (4–045).
Time immemorial: the time of the accession of Richard I in 1189 (18–133).
Title: the evidence of a person's right to property, or the right itself.
Trust: bare (8–129), completely constituted (10–036), constructive (10–017), executed (10–034), executory (10–034), express (10–005), implied (10–009), incompletely constituted (10–036), resulting (10–013), secret (10–045).
Trust corporation: one of certain companies with a large paid-up capital, or one of certain officials (8–162).
Trust of land: any trust of property which consists of or includes land, whether the interests under that trust are successive, concurrent or otherwise (**8–123**).

Undivided share: the interest of a tenant in common (9–010).
User: use, enjoyment (Note: *not* the person who uses).

Vested: unconditionally owned (**7–001**); compare Contingent.
Vesting assent (8–021), declaration (10–070), deed (8–020), instrument (8–017).

Voluntary conveyance: a conveyance not made for valuable consideration.

Volunteer: a person who takes under a disposition without having given valuable consideration.

Waiver: abandonment of a legal right.

Waste: ameliorating (3–100), equitable (3–103), permissive (3–101), voluntary (3–102).

Chapter 1

INTRODUCTION

Section 1. Real Property in Perspective

ENGLISH real property law has tended to have an unenviable reputation for its **1–001** complexity. Until comparatively recently, that reputation was thoroughly deserved, but that is no longer the case. For 150 years, the objective of reformers has been to make dealings in land as simple as dealings in stocks and shares.[1] As a result of the statutory reforms of real property law,[2] particularly those in 1925[3] and since, the process of dealing in land has been simplified so much that this objective is now close to realisation. More than four-fifths of all titles to land in England and Wales are now registered at HM Land Registry,[4] and most of those titles have been computerised. For the growing number of practitioners who have direct access by computer to the Land Register, the title to a parcel of land can be called up at the press of a button on their own terminals.[5] It seems likely that the electronic transfer of title to land will be possible within a very few years.[6]

Although the content of the law of real property is increasingly statutory, it is however in no sense a statutory code. It is therefore still essential to have an understanding of the substratum of common law and equitable principles upon which the statutory framework has been overlaid,[7] together with some grasp of the way in which the subject has developed historically.[8]

---

[1] For the beginnings of the process and the first proposals for the registration of title to land, see S. J. Anderson, *Lawyers and the Making of English Land Law 1832–1940*, (1992), pp. 63 *et seq.*
[2] The process really began with the Conveyancing Act 1881.
[3] Usually referred to as "the 1925 property legislation". For a brief explanation, see *post*, para. 1–014.
[4] See below, Chap. 6.
[5] Direct access was introduced in 1995.
[6] HM Land Registry plans to introduce electronic conveyancing in the comparatively near future. See (1998) Law Com. 254, proposing a legal framework for its introduction. In this, land would follow the example of stocks and shares. Since July 1996, securities on the London and Dublin Stock Exchanges have been traded electronically under the CREST system. Gilt-edged securities have been traded electronically for over a decade through the Central Gilts Office.
[7] As registered title has gradually become the norm, some of the best-known features of this underlying framework—particularly the difference between legal and equitable interests (explained in Chap. 4)—have declined in importance.
[8] For an outline of the main statutory developments affecting land law, see *post*, paras 1–014–1–015.

1–002   **Scope of the subject.** It is not easy to distinguish accurately between real property and conveyancing. In general, the former is static, and the latter dynamic. Real property deals with the rights and liabilities of land owners, whereas conveyancing is concerned with how rights in land may be created and transferred. The two inevitably overlap and there is no scientific dividing line between them. In reality, real property and conveyancing are not so much separate (but closely related) subjects, but two parts of the one subject of land law.[9]

The material in this book has been arranged in such a way as to minimise the amount of repetition and preliminary explanation. Those topics that can be understood in isolation have been treated in the later chapters. However the main principles are explained first, because they constantly interact. They are not easy to grasp on initial acquaintance. This is due in part to their historical origins and partly to the technical language which is a feature of the subject. The glossary of terms which precedes this chapter may be helpful in relation to the latter.

What follows is intended as a guide to the subjects that are examined in this book. It also gives an idea of the nature of real property and introduces a number of the most important technical terms.

1–003   After this introductory chapter, Chapters 2 and 3 give an account of tenures and estates. *Tenure* means the holding of land on certain terms and conditions. It refers to the *manner* in which the law allows a person to hold land. Points of tenure are extremely rare in practice today[10]; but historically tenure was the fundamental doctrine of land law. It is therefore examined first. *Estates* are of much greater importance in both theory and practice. The term "estate" refers to the duration of a landowner's interest. He may hold his land in fee simple, *i.e.* as absolute owner; or he may hold it for a limited interest—for his life or under a lease for a period of years.[11] He will then be said to have an estate in fee simple, or for life, or for a term of years, as the case may be. After explaining the classification and nature of the various estates, and the rules for their creation, Chapter 3 concludes with an analysis of the nature of estate ownership.

Chapter 4, *Law and Equity*, contains the fundamental doctrine which has given a peculiar dual character to English land law. "Law" and "equity" are used in a technical sense. They correspond to the two systems of justice, "common law" and "equity", which were administered in separate courts until 1875. The character of the law of property has been significantly influenced by their interaction. Equity mitigated the rigour of the ancient common law in the interests of justice and at the expense of tradition and formality. Although the two systems have been administered together for over 120 years, interests in land are still classified as "legal" or "equitable" with consequences that are still important, though much less so than formerly. This

---

[9] Chapter 12 provides an introduction to conveyancing law.

[10] They tend to arise principally in relation to the Crown's rights to land.

[11] One of the three limited forms of estate, the entail, can no longer be created as a result of recent legislation: see *post*, para. 3–037.

is a typical example of a distinction that can only be understood historically, but which nonetheless underpins the 1925 property legislation. In Chapter 4, therefore, a historical account of the development of doctrines of equity is interwoven with a description of the statutory changes that have taken place at various times, most notably in 1925.

Chapter 5, *Unregistered Conveyancing: Titles and Incumbrances*, gives an **1–004** account of the workings of the principles of common law and equity in a practical context. The two systems combined to shape the practice of buying and selling land and to protect a variety of subsidiary interests over it such as mortgages and restrictive covenants. These rules were modified by a statutory requirement that a number of subsidiary rights should be registered if they were to bind third parties. This traditional system of conveyancing is rapidly disappearing and is being replaced by a system of registered title. Most dispositions of unregistered land must now be completed by registering the title. Chapter 6, *Registration of Title*, gives an account of this registered system under which a computerised official register of title is replacing the cumbersome practice of examining title deeds. The whole of England and Wales has been subject to compulsory registration since December 1, 1990, and recent legislation[12] has extended the range of dealings with unregistered land to which the requirement of compulsory registration applies.

Chapter 7, *Perpetuities and Accumulations* is concerned with future interests. If A gives land to B for life and, after B's death, to C in fee simple, C has a future interest for the period of B's life. There are limits to the future interests which the law allows. In particular the period of time during which they can take effect is limited by the rule against perpetuities, now reformed by statute. Its near relation, the rule against accumulations, prevents income from being added to capital for an excessive period.

Prior to 1997, when land had been made subject to successive (*i.e.* both **1–005** present and future) interests, it created what was known as a "settlement". The elaborate rules governing the transfer and management of such land are dealt with in Chapter 8, *Successive Interests: Settlements and Trusts of Land*. After 1996, it has ceased to be possible to create settlements under the Settled Land Act 1925, though existing settlements remain subject to that Act. A settlor who wishes to create successive interests must now employ the new device of the trust of land.[13] This requires the trustees to hold the land on trust for the beneficiaries in succession. The trust of land, as its name suggests, does in fact apply to *all* types of trusts of land, whether the interests are successive or otherwise. Apart from Settled Land Act settlements created before 1997, virtually all other trusts (whenever created) are now trusts of land and subject to the provisions of the Trusts of Land and Appointment of Trustees Act 1996.

In Chapter 9, *Co-ownership*, the subject of concurrent (rather than successive) interests in land is considered. Such interests are very common and they

---

[12] L.R.A. 1997, s.1.
[13] See T.L.A.T.A. 1996, s.1.

arise, for example, where X and Y are entitled to a particular piece of land in equal shares. The share of each is merely a part interest in the whole. The device of the trust of land is employed in virtually all cases of co-ownership as a means of giving effect to the rights of the owners.

1–006 Chapter 10, *Trusts and Powers*, is the first of the chapters on distinct topics. It begins with an explanation of how trusts are classified and the principal features of the different types of trust. One type of trust—the constructive trust—has assumed considerable importance in recent years as a means of accommodating informal arrangements between cohabitants. The second part of the chapter is concerned with powers. A power is a right to dispose of someone else's property, as where A leaves property by will to such of B's children as B may appoint.

Chapter 11, *Wills and Intestacy*, describes the legal machinery for succession on death, both in the case where a person dies leaving a will of his property and in the case where he does not. This is followed in Chapter 12, *Contracts of Sale*, by an account of the rules governing the formation and effect of agreements to sell land. This chapter provides a general introduction to the law of conveyancing. Chapter 13, *Proprietary Estoppel*, is new to this edition, and explains the operation of this ancient doctrine, now much used in relation to informal dealings with land. If an owner of land in some way leads another person to believe that he has or will enjoy some right or benefit over that property, and that person acts to his detriment in that belief, an "equity" is said to arise in favour of the claimant. The court may give effect to that "equity" by granting the claimant some right or redress that is appropriate in the circumstances, whether over the land or otherwise.

1–007 Chapter 14, *Leases and Tenancies*, contains the general law of landlord and tenant, the most litigated area of land law. Two aspects of the subject are *not* found in this chapter. The first is the part of the subject that arises most commonly in practice, namely the collection of statutory controls that fundamentally affect many leases. These controls—which are a statutory system of their own and merit a book to themselves—have in fact been substantially relaxed since the last edition of this work. They are treated separately at the end of the book in Chapter 22, *Social Control of Land*. The second aspect of the law of landlord and tenant that is treated separately is found in Chapter 15, *Leasehold Covenants*. A covenant is a promise made by deed usually in a conveyance or a lease. Most covenants in leases are capable of binding successors in title. The rules which govern the transmission of the benefit and the burden of such covenants differ according to whether the lease was granted before 1996 (when they are a complex amalgam of ancient common law and more modern statute) or after 1995 (when the rules are contained in the Landlord and Tenant (Covenants) Act 1995). Chapter 16, *Freehold Covenants*, explains the very different principles that apply to covenants affecting freehold land. Only the burden of a negative or *restrictive* covenant, such as a covenant not to use a house for business purposes, can pass on the sale of the land affected by it so as to bind the person into whose hands it has come. Although restrictive covenants were part of the law of contract, they have developed into a doctrine of property. Until recently, it was thought that licences—mere permission to go on to or use land—might be in the process of a similar transformation. However, in Chapter 17, *Licences*, where an account is given of the types of licence as they affect real property, it is explained how this transformation was abruptly reversed.

Chapters 18, *Incorporeal Hereditaments*, and 19, *Mortgages*, deal with certain rights over the land of other people. Incorporeal hereditaments comprise a class of rights over land, some of them rather curious. The most important are easements and profits *à prendre*. An easement is a right over a neighbour's land, such as a right of way or a right of light. A profit is similar, except that it is a right to remove something from the land, such as a right to work gravel, graze animals, take game or fish. A mortgage is a conveyance of land for the purpose of securing a loan of money, under which the lender is given power to sell the land or take various other steps in relation to it if the debt, or the interest upon it, is not paid when due. This group of interests, together with restrictive covenants, are collectively called "incumbrances", since they are burdens on the ownership of land. **1–008**

The last part of the book deals with certain miscellaneous (but not unimportant) subjects. Chapter 20, *Disabilities*, examines the position of those, such as minors and mental patients, who are less able to dispose of land than other people. In Chapter 21, *Adverse Possession and Limitation*, an explanation is given as to how a squatter can become the owner of land by (in most cases) 12 years' occupation of it. Finally, in Chapter 22, *Social Control of Land*, the statutory restrictions on an owner's right to do as he wishes with his land are explained, both in relation to its use, and to the letting of it.

Section 2. Meaning of "Real Property"

In common with so many expressions in English law, the explanation of the term "real property" is historical. **1–009**

In early law, property was deemed "real" if the courts would restore to a dispossessed owner the thing itself, the "*res*", and not merely give compensation for the loss. Thus if X forcibly evicted Y from his freehold land, Y could bring a "real" action by which he could obtain an order from the court that X should return the land to him.[14] But if X took Y's sword or glove from him, he could bring only a personal action which gave X the choice of either returning the article to Y or paying him its value. In consequence a distinction was made between real property (or "realty"), which could be specifically recovered, and personal property (or "personalty"), which could not. In making this distinction, English law follows the natural division between immovables (*i.e.* land) and movables, but with one important exception. In general, all interests in land are real property, except leaseholds (or "terms of years") which are classified as personalty.

[14] For real actions, see the Appendix.

1–010   This peculiar exception initially arose because leases fell outside the feudal system of landholding by tenure. Originally leases were treated as personal business arrangements under which one party allowed the other the use of his land for a rent.[15] Such personal contracts did not create rights in the land itself which could attract feudal status. Leases helped to supply a useful form of investment at a time when there was little other. Money either might be employed in buying land and letting it out on lease in order to obtain income from the capital, or in buying a lease for a lump sum which could be recovered with interest out of the produce of the land. Such commercial transactions were more in the sphere of money than of land. The classification of lease-holds as personal property was discovered to be advantageous. Leases were immune from feudal burdens and could be bequeathed by will before wills of freeholds were allowed.[16] In this way the illogical position continued until it became too well settled to alter.

Leaseholds are still, therefore, personalty in law. But having been recog-nised so long as interests in land and not only contractual rights,[17] they have been classed under the paradoxical heading of "chattels real". "Chattels" indicates their personal nature,[18] "real" shows their connection with the land.[19] The three types of property may, therefore, be classified thus:

Land	{	(i) Realty
Personalty	{{	(ii) Chattels real
	{	(iii) Pure personalty

1–011   Although strictly speaking a book on real property should exclude leaseholds, it has long been usual to include them, and this course is adopted here.

The legislation of 1925 abolished many of the remaining differences between the legal principles applicable to realty and personalty respectively.[20] For example, before 1926, if a person died intestate (*i.e.* without a will), all his realty passed to his heir, while his personalty was divided between certain of his relatives. After 1925, however, realty and personalty both pass on intes-tacy to certain relatives. Nevertheless, the distinction may still be important.

Real property is subclassified into corporeal and incorporeal heredita-ments,[21] though this classification is of little practical importance. "Heredita-ment" indicates property which descended to the heir on intestacy before 1926, *i.e.* realty as opposed to personalty. Corporeal hereditaments are lands,

---

[15] *Post*, para. 3–009.
[16] *Post*, para. 3–010.
[17] *Post*, para. 3–015.
[18] Cattle were the most important chattels in early days, hence the name.
[19] See *Smith v. Baker* (1737) 1 Atk. 386 at 385; *Ridout v. Pain* (1747) 3 Atk. 486 at 492, *per* Lord Hardwicke L.C. ("*extradictions* out of the real").
[20] There were other chattels real than leaseholds: see *post*, para. 2–011 and Co.Litt. 118b. But leaseholds are the only chattels real of any importance today.
[21] See further, *post*, para. 18–001.

buildings, minerals, trees and all other things which are part of or are fixed to land. They are the physical matter over which ownership is exercised. By contrast, incorporeal hereditaments are not things at all, but rights. Certain rights were classified as real property, so that on intestacy before 1926 they also descended to the heir, rather than to the relatives entitled to personalty. The most important incorporeal hereditaments are easements and profits,[22] but there are others also.[23]

Section 3. The Basis of the Law of Real Property

1. Common law, equity and statute. The origin of the law of real property is the origin of the common law itself.[24] In this context, "common law" means the law which was applied to the country as a whole by the king's ordinary courts, as opposed to the local feudal and customary laws which varied from place to place and were administered in each locality free from central control until the middle of the twelfth century. The centralised judicial system established in the two centuries after the Norman Conquest—particularly in the region of Henry II—resulted in a body of new and uniform rules, although some of the old customs survived in the form of local variations of common law.[25]   **1–012**

The new rules were laid down and developed by the decisions of the judges in particular cases. Centralised records were kept and a systematic body of doctrine began to develop. "Common law" came to mean the ordinary judge-made law of the three central royal courts.[26] This was then contrasted with statute. Statutory reform of the land law was by no means unknown or insignificant, as the Acts of Edward I attest. With time, these statutes came to be regarded as of a piece with the judge-made rules, and the "common law" might, in a suitable context, include these ancient statutes, for the purposes of contrast with more modern parliamentary legislation.

A third force entered the field in the form of equity. As shall be explained,[27] certain interests in land were not protected by the courts of common law but were protected by the Chancellor, the royal official who dispensed the Crown's residuary powers of redressing wrong. It was the Chancellor who first compelled trustees to carry out their trusts. He also devised remedies for cases where, owing to non-compliance with some formality, the result at common law would not have been equitable. In this context "common law" came to be contrasted with "equity" as well as with statute. Rights which the common law would recognise and enforce were known as rights at common   **1–013**

---

[22] See *ante*, para. 1–008, and *post*, para. 18–040. Rentcharges (*post*, para. 18–014), though formerly important, are in the process of being phased out.

[23] *Post*, para. 8–004.

[24] See the Appendix.

[25] The local courts continued to function, but their jurisdiction came to be limited to small claims, particularly in relation to minor wrongs.

[26] The King's Bench, Common Pleas and Exchequer.

[27] *Post*, para. 4–003 *et seq.*

law, or simply as "legal rights". Rights enforced by the Chancellor, but not at common law, were called rights in equity, or "equitable rights". As the name implies, the Chancellor proceeded on grounds of equity or good conscience. He would grant special remedies where the justice of the case required some tempering of the rigour of common law. In the course of time, equity developed into a separate branch of the legal system. It profoundly modified the common law of real property. The special characteristics of equitable rights led to the fundamental distinction between legal and equitable interests in land which was adopted as the foundation of the reforms of 1925 in relation to land with unregistered title. Although common law and equity are distinct concepts, there is a modern trend to minimise these distinctions.

1–014　　**2. Statutory reform.** The statutory reform of the law of real property began in the nineteenth century, particularly in the periods 1832–45 and 1881–90. However, the most significant changes to the law were made between 1922 and 1925. There were two stages in this legislation. First, by the Law of Property Act 1922, and the Law of Property (Amendment) Act 1924, the necessary changes in the law were made.[28] Secondly, these Acts were for the most part repealed before they could come into force, and were replaced by a series of Acts passed in 1925. The Acts of 1925 consolidated both the changes made by the Acts of 1922 and 1924 together with much of the law laid down by earlier statutes (particularly those of 1881–90), which were also repealed and replaced by the new legislation. The resulting body of law was broken down into six consolidating Acts—

> The Settled Land Act 1925
> The Trustee Act 1925
> The Law of Property Act 1925
> The Land Registration Act 1925
> The Land Charges Act 1925
> The Administration of Estates Act 1925

These Acts, together with those unrepealed parts of the 1922 and 1924 Acts, constitute "the 1925 property legislation" and were all brought into force on January 1, 1926.

1–015　　The form of the legislation can sometimes affect its construction. Because the 1925 Acts are consolidation Acts, they are presumed not to alter the pre-existing law more than their wording necessarily requires. Where the Acts of 1922 and 1924 left the old law unchanged, the presumption is that the Acts of 1925 did not alter it either.[29] But where the Acts of 1922 or 1924 changed the previous law, the presumption is only that the Acts of 1925 have not further

---

[28] It should be noted that the 1924 Act made a number of amendments to the 1922 Act.

[29] See, *e.g. Beswick v. Beswick* [1968] A.C. 58 (L.P.A. 1925, s.56); and see *Re Eichholz* [1959] Ch. 708 (especially at 726, 727), where the presumption was stated but misapplied; see (1960) 76 L.Q.R. 197 (R.E.M.); *Lloyds Bank Ltd. v. Marcan* [1973] 1 W.L.R. 339 at 344 (affirmed at 1387); *Re Dodwell & Co. Ltd's Trust* [1979] Ch. 301 at 308 (L.P.A. 1925, s.164).

modified it.[30] It is therefore sometimes necessary to have recourse to the repealed parts of the Acts of 1922 and 1924 to resolve obscurities in the Acts of 1925.[31]

Since 1925 there has been a steady flow of legislation which, until recently, has been of a piecemeal character for carrying out particular reforms. Over the last few years, however, more sweeping changes have taken place and more may be expected. As a result, significant parts of the 1925 legislation have now been replaced, at least prospectively.[32] The main statutes are—

The Law of Property (Amendment) Act 1926
The Perpetuities and Accumulations Act 1964
The Law of Property (Joint Tenants) Act 1964
The Land Registration and Land Charges Act 1971
The Land Charges Act 1972[33]
The Local Land Charges Act 1975
The Rentcharges Act 1977
The Charging Orders Act 1979
The Land Registration Acts 1986, 1988 and 1997
The Reverter of Sites Act 1987
The Law of Property (Miscellaneous Provisions) Acts 1989 and 1994
The Access to Neighbouring Land Act 1992
The Landlord and Tenant (Covenants) Act 1995
The Trusts of Land and Appointment of Trustees Act 1996

Section 4. The Law in Action

To conclude this introduction, it may be helpful to give an example of a **1–016** typical transaction involving land, namely a sale of a house. The situation envisaged is that V (the vendor) has agreed to sell his house to P (the purchaser) and that their solicitors (or licensed conveyancers) proceed to make the legal arrangements.[34]

Before the parties bind themselves by contract to the transaction, they will usually have to attend to a number of preliminary matters. First, P will commonly purchase the house with the aid of a mortgage and will therefore need to ensure that the necessary financial arrangements are in place. Secondly, it is good practice for P to have the property surveyed. It is for the purchaser to satisfy himself as to the physical state of the property. Thirdly, it

---

[30] See *Grey v. I.R.C.* [1960] A.C. 1 (L.P.A. 1925, s.53); *Re Turner's W.T.* [1937] Ch. 15 (T.A. 1925, s.31).
[31] *cf. State Bank of India v. Sood* [1997] Ch. 276 at 287.
[32] Most notably S.L.A. 1925, which now applies only to settlements in existence before 1997: see T.L.A.T.A. 1996, ss.1, 2.
[33] Another consolidating Act, which replaced L.C.A. 1925.
[34] See further, *post*, Chap. 12.

has become the normal practice for P's solicitor to investigate V's title in advance of the exchange of contracts. This is explained below.

1-017   The parties then enter into a contract by which V agrees to sell and P agrees to buy the house.[35] That contract must be made in writing and must contain all the terms agreed by the parties. The contract must either be contained in one document and signed by both parties or, where contracts are exchanged (as commonly happens), each party must sign one part which is then given to, or held to the order of, the other. The contract does not transfer the full legal ownership from V to P.[36] In the normal case, where the title is registered, V must execute a transfer of the land to P. Title will pass to P when that transfer has been submitted to HM Land Registry, and P registered as owner of the land.[37] P will in turn pay V the purchase price. This final exchange of the transfer for money is called completion. Although the exchange of contracts and completion sometimes occur on the same day, there is normally an interval of a week or two between the two stages.

P will not wish to part with his money without making sure that he will receive what V contracted to sell him, so he (or rather his solicitor) will investigate V's title. If V's title is registered, there is unlikely to be any doubt as to his entitlement to convey the land. Although P will wish to be sure that he is not (for example) merely a tenant who has only a leasehold interest to sell, and that there are no other restrictions on his powers of disposition, all of that will be apparent from the register. There may sometimes be situations where V does not in fact own the land of which he is the registered proprietor. It may be that he has been registered as the owner by mistake and that some third party is the true owner and is also registered as proprietor of the land. Another possibility is that V's title has been barred by lapse of time, and that a squatter who has been in effective adverse possession of the land for 12 years or more is the true owner.

1-018   A far more common source of trouble is incumbrances. V's property may be subject to easements, such as rights to light or rights of way acquired by neighbours, or to restrictive covenants which prevent any occupant from using it in a particular way, for instance, as a shop or for business. V may have mortgaged it as security for a loan, so that the creditor has rights in the land which must be protected. V is required to disclose to P prior to contract any incumbrances that will not be discharged on completion[38] and which are not apparent on an inspection of the land. An inspection of the register will reveal the existence of many incumbrances, but there are some which will bind a

---

[35] Commonly the sale will be one of a chain of sales. Thus P may be selling his house and V may be purchasing another. The exchange of all of the contracts in the chain is usually synchronised by telephone in accordance with a practice devised by The Law Society.

[36] In some continental legal systems the two steps are elided.

[37] Legal title is taken to pass when the application for registration is made. Where the title has not been registered, V executes a deed of conveyance to P. This transfers the legal title to P at once. However, P must apply to have the title registered at the Land Registry within two months: see *post*, para. 6–018.

[38] In practice, where there is a mortgage, the property will not be sold unless the mortgage will be discharged out of the proceeds of sale.

purchaser even though they are not protected by registration, such as certain easements and the proprietary rights of persons in actual occupation. If before completion P discovers an incumbrance that V ought to have disclosed, he will be entitled to terminate the contract and recover damages from V.

Where P purchases the property with the aid of a mortgage from a building society or (as is increasingly the case) some other lending institution, both the transfer of title and the mortgage[39] take effect simultaneously. P will then be able to occupy the house so long as he keeps up the payments due under the loan. The creditor is given an immediate and indefeasible interest in the land as security against non-payment. Until he has repaid the loan, P's position is not unlike that of a tenant, but one who pays mortgage interest instead of rent.

[39] Known as a registered charge where the title to the land is registered.

CHAPTER 2

TENURES

Part 1

TENURES AND ESTATES

2–001   **1. Crown ownership.** Although in practice land is commonly, and correctly, described as owned by its various proprietors, English land law still retains its original basis, that all land in England is owned by the Crown. A small part is in the Crown's own occupation; the rest is occupied by tenants holding either directly or indirectly from the Crown. In England all land is held of a lord,[1] and allodial land (*i.e.* land owned independently and not "held of" some lord) is unknown.[2]

2–002   **2. Feudal structure.** This unusually perfect feudal structure was imposed after the Norman Conquest. William I regarded the whole of England as his by conquest. To reward his followers and those of the English who submitted to him, he granted and confirmed certain lands to be held of him as overlord.[3] These lands were granted not by way of an out-and-out transfer, but to be held from the Crown upon certain conditions. Thus, Blackacre might have been granted to X on the terms that he did homage and swore fealty, that he provided five armed horsemen to fight for the Crown for 40 days in each year. Whiteacre might have been granted to Y on condition that he supported the King's train in his coronation. X and Y might each in turn grant land to other persons to hold of them in return for services, and these others might repeat the process.

2–003   **3. Services.** In this way the feudal pyramid was constructed from the top downwards, with the King at the apex and the actual occupants of the land at the base. In the middle were persons who both rendered and received services, much in the same way as a modern leasehold tenant who has sublet the property. In days when land and its produce constituted nearly the whole

---

[1] Expressed by the maxim, *"nulle terre sans seigneur"*: P. & M. i, 232; H.E.L. ii, 199; Co.Litt. 1b; *Doe d. Hayne v. Redfern* (1810) 12 East 96 at 103; *Att.-Gen. of Ontario v. Mercer* (1883) 8 App.Cas. 767 at 772.

[2] In Scotland there is some allodial land: see W. M. Gordon, *Scottish Land Law*, pp. 40 *et seq.*

[3] Williams R.P. 12.

tangible wealth of a country, it was more usual to secure the performance of services by the grant of land in return for those services than it was to secure them by payment. The whole social organisation was based on landholding in return for service, and for most purposes, such as military service and taxation, government was carried on by devolving upon each lord the control of his immediate tenants. The King need look only to his "tenants in chief", they in their turn to their immediate dependants, and so on downwards if there were further steps in the scale.

Tenants in chief were those who held directly of the King; there were about 1,500 of them in 1086, at the time of Domesday Book. Those who in fact occupied the land were called tenants in demesne. Those who stood between the King and tenants in demesne were called mesne lords or mesnes (mesne, pronounced "mean", meaning intermediate). The King was lord paramount. The status of lordship, including the right to receive the tenant's services, was called seignory.

4. Tenure. Feudal services became to a certain extent standardised. Thus there was one set of services (which included the provision of armed horsemen for battle) which became known as knight's service, and there was another set (which included the performance of some honourable service for the King in person) which was known as grand sergeanty. Each of these sets of services was known as a *tenure*, for it showed upon what terms the land was held (*tenere*, to hold).[4] The commonest type of tenure was that known as socage.[5] **2–004**

5. Estates. Whatever the tenure, the land might be held for different periods of time. It might be granted for life (for so long as the tenant lived), in tail (for so long as the tenant or any of his descendants lived), or in fee simple (for so long as the tenant or any of his heirs, whether descendants or not, were alive).[6] Each of these interests was known as an *estate*, a word derived from *status*.[7] Thus the Crown might grant land to A for an estate in fee simple, and A in turn might grant it to B for life. Both the Crown and A thus retained interests in the land. A man might hold land for one or more estate, yet this was only a qualified form of ownership. **2–005**

The largest estate in land, the fee simple, has come more and more to resemble absolute ownership, and its proprietor is commonly called the owner of the land. This is because the tenurial relationship is now so slender that it can in practice be ignored. But even today it is in one sense true to say that all land in England is vested in the Crown; a subject can hold it only as tenant. When we say "X owns Blackacre in fee simple" we really mean "X holds

---

[4] Co.Litt. 1a.
[5] *Post*, para. 2–016.
[6] Leaseholds (which are now estates: *post*, para. 3–015 fell outside the feudal system, since in early times they were not considered to be estates but merely personal contracts. See Challis 63, 64, *ante*, para. 1–010 and *post*, para. 3–009.
[7] H.E.L. ii, 351, 352; Williams R.P. 7, 8.

Blackacre of Y (his lord) by the tenure of fee and common socage for an estate in fee simple". But the difference in practice is negligible and the full formula is, therefore, not used. It should be noted that both in popular speech and in legal parlance the word "estate" is often used in other senses, for example, as a description of an area of land (as in "The Blank estate is to be sold"), or as a general term meaning property (as in "the deceased's net estate"). The context will usually leave little doubt about which sense is intended.

2–006   **6. Fundamental doctrine.** There are thus two fundamental doctrines in the law of real property—

> (i) the doctrine of tenures: all land is held of the Crown, either directly or indirectly, in one or other of the various tenures; and

> (ii) the doctrine of estates: land held in tenure is also held for an estate, that is to say for some period of time.

In short, the tenure answers the question "upon what terms is it held?"; the estate answers the question "for how long?".

These two doctrines of tenures and estates are considered in greater detail in this chapter and the next.

Part 2

TYPES OF TENURE

2–007   The main tenures which existed at common law may be classified as follows.[8]

> 1. Free tenures: A. Tenures in Chivalry (or Military Tenures).
> B. Tenures in Socage.
> C. Spiritual Tenures.
>
> 2. Unfree tenures.
>
> 3. Miscellaneous tenures.

Leasehold tenure, the one form of tenure which remains familiar today, played no part in this scheme. It stood outside the feudal system, having developed

---

[8] See S. F. C. Milsom, *Historical Foundations of the Common Law* (2nd ed.), chap. 5; A. W. B. Simpson, *A History of the Land Law* (2nd ed.), chap. 1. There were certain ancient tenures which did not fall within this classification, such as homage ancestral and ancient demesne: see the previous edition of this work at pp. 27–28.

relatively late, and it has to be treated as a separate subject, both historically and legally.[9]

Section 1. Free Tenures

A. *Tenures in Chivalry*

There were two tenures in chivalry, grand sergeanty and knight's service.   **2–008**

1. Grand sergeanty. By tenure in grand sergeanty the King provided for his principal servants, holders of high offices and places of honour. The tenant was bound to perform in person some service for the King of an honourable nature, such as carrying his banner, leading his army, or being his chamberlain.[10] There were many grand sergeanties in connection with the coronation.[11] "Honorary services" might extend even to the duties of the royal carver or butler, or to "cornage", alleged to be the duty to guard the Scottish border and "winde a horn" to give warning if "the Scots or other enemies" entered the country.[12] Such services were regarded as personal to the King, and this tenure was ultimately[13] (though not originally[14]) confined to tenants in chief. It followed from this that land could be held in grand sergeanty only by a tenant in chief.

2. Knight's service. By tenure in knight's service the lord provided him-   **2–009**
self with an army. The lord in question was, of course, most commonly the King, but land could be held in knight's service of a mesne lord.[15] Originally the distinguishing feature of this tenure was the obligation of the tenant to provide his lord with a fixed number of fully armed horsemen for 40 days in each year.[16] By the middle of the twelfth century, however, this obligation had in most cases been commuted for a money payment known as escuage or scutage,[17] and by the fourteenth century the levy of scutage had ceased.[18]

Tenures in chivalry were subject to an elaborate catalogue of "incidents", some of which remained important until modern times. The list may be summarised as follows.

---

[9] See *post*, para. 14–002.
[10] Litt. 153; Challis 9.
[11] Blount. Frag., 25, 26. In this work are collected many curious conditions of tenure, not all of which are honourable by modern standards (*e.g.* at p. 60); some of the more remarkable are recounted in Megarry, *Miscellany-at-Law*, pp. 154–157.
[12] Litt. 156. But much more probably cornage was a payment for the right to pasture horned cattle: Maitland, Coll.Pp. ii, 98–100.
[13] Litt. 161.
[14] Bracton 35b; P. & M. i, 285.
[15] *Ante,* para. 2–003, for this term.
[16] P. & M. i, 252 *et seq.*; H.E.L. iii, 37 *et seq.* The last summons of the feudal levy was in 1385; (1958) 73 E.H.R. 1 (N. B. Lewis).
[17] P. & M. i, 266.
[18] H.E.L. iii, 44, 45.

(1) THE HONOURABLE OR MILITARY SERVICE, mentioned above.

2–010   (2) HOMAGE, FEALTY AND SUIT OF COURT. Homage was the spiritual bond created by the tenant swearing to be his lord's man,[19] fealty the temporal link arising from the tenant's oath to perform his feudal obligations faithfully,[20] and suit of court the tenant's obligation to attend his lord's court and assist in its deliberations.[21]

2–011   (3) WARDSHIP AND MARRIAGE. These affected only infant heirs. Wardship was the lord's right to manage for his own profit[22] the lands of a tenant who left as his heir a male under 21 or a female under 14 (or 16, if not married before the land descended to her).[23] The lord was in this way compensated for his tenant's incapacity for service. At the end of the wardship, the lord was entitled to a further half-year's profits of the land as the price of its surrender to the heir ("suing out livery"[24]) or "ouster-le-main"[25] (removing his hand); but the right to levy this additional impost was confined to the King by Magna Carta 1215.[26] Marriage was the lord's right to select a spouse for any tenant whom he had in wardship, and to fine the ward for declining a suitable spouse or for marrying under age without the lord's licence.[27] These rights were often of considerable value; they could be bought, sold, and bequeathed, and came to be classed as chattels real.[28]

2–012   (4) RELIEF AND PRIMER SEISIN. These affected only heirs of full age,[29] and represented the price paid by the heir for the right to succeed as tenant.[30] Relief was the lord's right to a payment, often of one year's value of the land,[31] when an heir of full age succeeded to the land on the death of the tenant. Where the King was the lord he enjoyed also the prerogative right called primer seisin (first seisin), the right to take possession until homage and relief were rendered. This practice entitled the Crown to a further year's profits in addition to the relief.[32]

2–013   (5) AIDS. These were payments which a lord could demand from his tenants on certain occasions involving the lord in expense. Magna Carta 1215 limited

---

[19] Litt. 85; Co.Litt. 64b, 65a.

[20] Litt. 91; Co.Litt. 67b.

[21] Williams R.P. 49.

[22] But he could not commit waste: Magna Carta 1215, cc. 4, 5; P. & M. i, 319. A lord who wasted the land forfeited the wardship: *ibid*. For waste, see *post*, para. 3–098.

[23] Litt. 103.

[24] Bl.Comm. ii, 76; Co.Litt. 77a; H.E.L. iii, 64.

[25] *Anon.* (1559) 2 Dy. 168a.

[26] c. 3; but see *Anon.* (1559) 2 Dy. 168a.

[27] Litt. 103–110; Statute of Merton 1235; Statute of Westminster I, 1275, c.22. The lord might not tender a disparaging marriage (for a catalogue of disparagements, see Co.Litt. 80a, b, and *cf.* Litt. 107–109); but if the ward refused a "convenable" [suitable] marriage, he or she was liable to pay to the lord "the value of the marriage". If the ward married against the lord's consent, this fine was doubled: Litt. 110.

[28] P. & M. i, 322; ii, 116.

[29] Magna Carta 1215, c. 3.

[30] H.E.L. iii, 57.

[31] H.E.L. iii, 60.

[32] Bl.Comm. ii, 66; Cru.Dig. i, 25–26; Statute of Marlbridge 1267, c. 16.

these occasions to three: the ransom of the lord, the knighting of his eldest son, and the marriage of his eldest daughter.[33] The last two aids did not, however, apply to grand sergeanty.[34]

(6) ESCHEAT AND FORFEITURE. Unlike the previous incidents, escheat and **2–014** forfeiture retained their importance until comparatively recent years. One was an essential part of the feudal structure, the other was valuable to the State. Escheat occurred on the extinction of a tenancy: the immediate lord became tenant in demesne[35] and entitled to occupy the land. Thus was preserved the principle that some person must always be in possession (or "seised"). Escheat always took place when a tenancy came to an end, for whatever cause,[36] but only two types of escheat were common—

> (i) *propter defectum sanguinis* (for failure of blood): if a tenant died without heirs, the land escheated to the lord from whom he held it[37]; and

> (ii) *propter delictum tenentis* (for the tenant's crime).[38] If a tenant was attainted of felony[39] (*i.e.* convicted and sentenced to death, and not merely convicted[40]), his land escheated to his lord subject to the Crown's right to "year, day and waste", which was a right to hold the land for a year and a day and commit waste (such as cutting down trees).[41] The attainder related back to the time when the felony was committed, and so invalidated intermediate dealings.[42]

Forfeiture was a right of the Crown, dependent upon the Royal Prerogative **2–015** and not upon tenure, to seize and keep the lands of any person attainted of high treason, whether he held of the Crown or some mesne lord.[43] For while felony was, in its earliest sense, a breach of homage, treason was a breach of allegiance. As with felony, the attainder related back to the time when the

---

[33] Magna Carta 1215, cc. 12, 15; the amounts leviable for the last two were fixed by the Statute of Westminster I, 1275, c. 36, and 25 Edw. 3, st. 5, c. 11, 1351; H.E.L. iii, 66.

[34] Co.Litt. 105b.

[35] For this term, see *ante*, para. 2–003.

[36] See, *e.g. British General Insurance Co. Ltd v. Att.-Gen.* [1945] L.J. N.C.C.R. 113; *post*, para. 2–052, n. 99.

[37] Co.Litt. 13a; Williams R.P. 49.

[38] Co.Litt. 13a.

[39] Felony included certain serious crimes such as murder, suicide, arson, robbery, and almost all kinds of larceny. Many other felonies were created by statute. Almost all felonies were punishable with death until the law was reformed in the first half of the nineteenth century. See Radzinowicz, *History of English Criminal Law*, i, 3–5, 578–607.

[40] See *R. v. Wilks* (1820) 3 B. & Ald. 510; and see *R. v. Kelly* [1950] 1 K.B. 164.

[41] Challis R.P. 34, 35; Williams R.P. 49. For waste, see *post*, para. 3–098. The usual practice was for the lord to compound with the Exchequer for year, day and waste, and take the land at once.

[42] H.E.L. iii, 69; see Co.Litt. 390b, 391a.

[43] P. & M. i, 351; H.E.L. iii, 70.

treason was committed.[44] A tenant might also forfeit his land to his lord if he failed to perform his feudal services, either by virtue of an express right of forfeiture reserved by the lord,[45] or under statute. The primary remedy for default in services was distress, *i.e.* the lord's right to seize chattels on the land and hold them until the services were performed. This, however, was often unsatisfactory, and the Statute of Gloucester 1278[46] gave the lord an action for forfeiture if services were two years in arrear and there were no distrainable goods on the land; and this action was made effective against third parties who acquired the land.[47]

B. Tenures in Socage

2–016   There were other tenures, less exalted than tenures in chivalry, where the tenants were nevertheless free tenants. We must now consider petty sergeanty and socage. Each is, strictly speaking, a distinct variety of tenure, but they are much alike and can both be correctly classed as socage.[48] In general, these socage tenures were subject to all the incidents of tenures in chivalry except homage,[49] the honourable or military service, wardship and marriage.[50] Relief, however, was normally one year's rent (not one year's profits), and so was payable only where an annual money rent was reserved.[51] Nor was there any legal necessity for any incident but fealty.[52]

2–017   **1. Petty sergeanty.** The tenant was bound to perform for the King some service of a non-personal nature, such as supplying him with footmen, arrows, or straw for his bed.[53] After the fifteenth century it could exist only as a tenure in chief.[54]

2–018   **2. Socage.** This was the commonest form of socage tenure and ultimately became the commonest tenure of all. All free tenure was common socage[55]

---

[44] *Pimbs Case* (1585) Moo.K.B. 196; P. & M. i, 352–355; H.E.L. iii, 70.

[45] P. & M. i, 352.

[46] c. 4. The writ employed was the writ *cessavit per biennium*.

[47] Statute of Westminster II, 1285, c. 21.

[48] Litt. 118, 160, 162.

[49] Litt. 118, 131.

[50] In socage tenure the place of wardship and marriage was taken by guardianship. The lord had no right to be guardian and the guardian's rights and duties were fiduciary: P. & M. i, 321; H.E.L. iii, 65.

[51] Co.Litt. 93a, Hargrave's note.

[52] Litt. 131.

[53] Blount, Frag. 73–184. For other more comical services listed by Blount (including that of the unfortunate tenant who had to make "a leap, a whistle and a fart" on Christmas Day in the presence of his lord), see A. W. B. Simpson, *A History of the Land Law* (2nd ed.), p. 6. The dividing line between sergeanty and other tenures, and between grand and petty sergeanty, was shadowy: P. & M. i, 287, 323, *cf.* Litt. 159, 160.

[54] Litt. 161.

[55] The word "socage" is probably derived from the Saxon "soc", meaning "seek", for the tenant had to seek his lord's "soke" or court: H.E.L. iii, 51; formerly it was thought to be derived from the French "soc", a plough-share, on account of the usual agricultural service: *ibid.*; Litt. 119.

unless proved to be one of the others, and it is defined not by what it is but by what it is not. Any type of service might be reserved,[56] though generally it was some agricultural service which was fixed both as to nature and amount, *e.g.* so many days' ploughing each year.[57] By the end of the fifteenth century most of these services had been commuted for money payments, often known as "quit rents", for the tenant thereby went quit, or free, from his services.

The conditions of socage tenure might vary from place to place according to local custom.[58] In contrast to "common socage" (the ordinary type) there were customary variations which were particularly important, gavelkind and borough English. Their peculiarities relate more to the law of inheritance[59] and alienation than to the law of tenure, but it is convenient to collect them together here.

(a) Gavelkind.[60] The custom of gavelkind (from the Saxon "gafol", or "gavel", a rent[60]) applied to all land in Kent unless the contrary was shown.[61] It could apply to land outside Kent (there were variants in different parts of the country[62]) but in that case the burden of proof was on the person who alleged that it applied.[62] The chief feature of the custom was *partibility*, whereby on intestacy the land descended to all males of the same degree equally, instead of to the eldest male in accordance with the ordinary rule.[63] Thus, if a tenant died leaving five sons, the five took in equal shares if the land was gavelkind, but the eldest took to the exclusion of the others if the land was held in common socage. This rule was not confined to descendants, but applied also to collaterals,[64] such as brothers,[65] cousins[66] or great nephews[67]; and it applied to entails as well as to fees simple.[68]

2–019

In the case of gavelkind land in Kent, certain other peculiarities were attached by immemorial custom. Even where a statute had disgavelled land (*i.e.* converted the tenure into common socage and so abolished partibility),[69] these other peculiarities usually continued.[70] They were as follows.

---

[56] *e.g.* to be a hangman, "the worst tenure that I have read of": Co.Litt. 86a. The question whether the services must be certain in amount, or whether they might be variable at the lord's discretion, was raised but not decided in *Att.-Gen. for Alberta v. Huggard Assets Ltd* [1953] A.C. 420.

[57] H.E.L. iii, 52.

[58] For the principle that ancient custom can produce local variations in the common law, see *post*, para. 18–078.

[59] See the previous edition of this work at p. 542. Customary variations in conditions of tenure were often called "tenures": see P. & M. i, 239, 240, 293, 294.

[60] Rob.Gav. 3.

[61] *ibid.* 48; Bl.Comm. ii, 84; H.E.L. iii, 262.

[62] *e.g.* in Kentish Town in London, in Wales and in Ireland: Rob.Gav. 22, 43; Co.Litt. 176a, n. 1.

[63] For the ordinary rule of primogeniture, see the previous edition of this work at p. 540.

[64] *Re Chenoweth* [1902] 2 Ch. 488.

[65] Co.Litt. 140a.

[66] *Re Fullager* (1812) Rob.Gav. 117.

[67] *Hook v. Hook* (1862) 1 H. & M. 43.

[68] See, *e.g. Doe d. Bosnall v. Harvey* (1825) 4 B. & C. 610.

[69] *e.g.* Statute of Wales 1543, which disgavelled all land in Wales.

[70] *Wiseman v. Cotten* (1663) 1 Sid. 135.

2–020   (1) DEVISES. From the earliest times, the land might be devised (*i.e.* disposed of by will),[71] whereas by the end of the thirteenth century it had been settled that other land was not devisable.[72]

2–021   (2) NO ESCHEAT. Upon the tenant being attainted of felony, the land did not escheat to the lord, nor was the Crown entitled to year, day and waste: "The father to the bough, the son to the plough."[73] But gavelkind land was subject to forfeiture for high treason.[74]

2–022   (3) INFANT'S CONVEYANCE. An infant of 15 years of age or more could make a binding conveyance of his land if the conveyance was made for full value and was in the form known as a feoffment (pronounced feffment).[75] The parties to a feoffment were called the feoffer and the feoffee, the former being the person making the conveyance and the latter the recipient. In the case of other land, any feoffment made by an infant was liable to be set aside by him at or soon after his majority.[76]

2–023   (4) DOWER. When a tenant died leaving a widow, she was entitled to dower, which in common socage land was a life interest in one-third of her husband's realty. But dower in gavelkind was in one-half of the realty,[77] though it only lasted *dum casta et sola, i.e.* while she remained chaste and unmarried.[78] It was benevolently held that for this purpose unchastity could be established only by the birth of a child[79]; but the widow could not waive her right to one-half of gavelkind land *dum casta et sola* and choose to take one-third without these restrictions.[80]

2–024   (5) CURTESY. When a tenant died leaving a widower, he was entitled to curtesy, which in common socage land was a life interest in all his wife's realty, but could be claimed only if issue capable of inheriting the land had been born of the marriage. Curtesy in gavelkind land, however, was in only one-half and lasted only until remarriage, although it could be claimed even if no issue was born.[81]

These five collateral customs were primarily customs annexed to gavelkind land in Kent, but some or all of them might apply to land elsewhere if their existence could be proved. Unlike partibility, they were not essential to the existence of gavelkind.[82]

---

[71] Rob.Gav. 298 *et seq.*
[72] *Post*, para. 3–043.
[73] *Brook v. Ward* (1572) 3 Dy. 310b.
[74] *Case of Tanistry* (1608) Dav.Ir. 28 at 37.
[75] *Re Maskell & Goldfinch's Contract* [1895] 2 Ch. 525; Rob.Gav. 248, 249.
[76] *Post*, para. 20–012.
[77] *e.g. Re Wilson* [1916] 1 Ch. 220.
[78] *Cobham v. Tomlinson* (1672) T.Jo. 6.
[79] Rob.Gav. (5th ed.) 142–144.
[80] *Davies v. Selby* (1601) Cro.Eliz. 825.
[81] Rob.Gav. 183–201.
[82] Rob.Gav. 51–53.

(b) Borough English. This was a custom existing in many parts of the **2–025** country, principally Sussex and Surrey,[83] whereby land descended on intestacy to the youngest son instead of the eldest.[84] The custom applied only to sons; thus if a tenant died leaving only brothers, the elder brother was preferred to the younger unless a special custom extending to remoter relatives could be proved.[85] The name "borough English" seems to have originated in Nottingham, where the custom applied in the English part of the town but not in the French,[86] though it was mainly a rural custom and originally more widespread in villein tenure than in socage.[87] Its origins are obscure and few of the suggested explanations are neither lame nor fanciful.[88] The least improbable perhaps is that which links the custom with "that pastoral state of our British and German ancestors, which Caesar and Tacitus describe".[89] In such times, it is said, the eldest sons might be endowed out of their father's flocks and migrate, while the youngest would remain at home to help his father, and so naturally inherited his house.

Other customs attaching to socage land were sometimes called tenures, as if they were distinct. An example is tenure in burgage,[90] which was "only a kind of town socage".[91] In boroughs where this prevailed there were usually special local customs, such as the power to devise the land, or the widow's dower being in the whole of the land; and money rents generally took the place of all other services.

C. Spiritual Tenures

In ancient times much monastic and ecclesiastical land was held in spiritual **2–026** tenure.[92] The two spiritual tenures were frankalmoign and divine service. If land was granted to an ecclesiastical corporation, whether a corporation sole such as a bishop, or a corporation aggregate such as a monastery,[93] tenure in frankalmoign ("free alms") arose if no fealty was demanded and no specific services were reserved.[94] In that case the tenant's sole obligation was to pray for the repose of the grantor's soul, and even this could be enforced only by

---

[83] Kenny, *Primogeniture*, 30; Rob.Gav. (5th ed.) 238.
[84] *Weeks v. Carvel* (1602) Noy 106; *Lutwyche v. Lutwyche* (1735) Ca.t.Talb. 276. Maitland calls this custom "ultimogeniture": P. & M. ii, 279.
[85] Rob.Gav. 390, 391; *Re Smart* (1881) 18 Ch.D. 165.
[86] Y.B. 1 Edw. 3, f. 12, pl. 38 (1327).
[87] P. & M. ii, 279.
[88] *e.g.* Litt. 211; and the imaginative association with the *jus primae noctis*: Bl.Comm. ii, 82.
[89] Bl.Comm. ii, 83; *cf.* P. & M. ii, 280–283. A similar custom was certainly widespread in Germany.
[90] Litt. 162–167. For borough customs generally, see H.E.L. iii, 269–275. For an example, see *Busher v. Thompson* (1846) 4 C.B. 47.
[91] Bl.Comm. ii, 82; *cf.* P. & M. i, 295.
[92] But Magna Carta 1217, c. 43; and the Statutes of Mortmain 1279 and 1290, forbade the conveyance of land to religious bodies, since this led to loss of feudal dues. If land was conveyed "into mortmain", the "dead hand" of the corporation meant that there would be no reliefs, wardships, marriages or escheats: Williams R.P. 54. For the mortmain legislation, now repealed, see the previous edition of this work at p. 1027.
[93] For corporation sole and aggregate, see *post*, paras 3–028, 3–029.
[94] H.E.L. iii, 35.

complaint to the ecclesiastical powers.[95] Tenure in divine service, on the other hand, was tenure subject to definite spiritual services, such as singing mass every Friday or giving a certain sum of money to the poor.[96] Fealty was then due, and the lord could enforce the service in the ordinary way by distraint or forfeiture.[97]

Spiritual tenures could exist only between the grantor (or his heirs) and the grantee; if the tenant disposed of the land or there was an escheat of the lord's seignory (*i.e.* his right to the feudal services)[98] such tenures usually became socage subject to the sole incident of fealty.[99]

Section 2. Unfree Tenures

2–027   The great unfree tenure was villeinage, later called copyhold. There was also a variety known as customary freehold. Generally speaking, one may say that free tenure was the tenure of landed proprietors and independent farmers, while unfree tenure was the tenure of common labourers. In law they were contrasted as follows.

2–028   (1) NO SEISIN. In the case of free tenures, the tenant had seisin, which meant that for feudal purposes he was deemed to be the lawful tenant of the land, and the King's courts would protect him against ejectment, even by his lord.[1] In the case of unfree tenure, the seisin was deemed to be in the lord and the tenant merely occupied on his behalf; the King's courts originally would not recognise any claim by the tenant, whose only recourse was to the court of his lord.[2] At first, therefore, the villein had no place in the feudal scale.

2–029   (2) UNCERTAIN SERVICES. The services of a freeholder were fixed both as to quantity and quality, whereas the services of an unfree tenant, although fixed as to quantity, were unfixed as to quality, and often more onerous. The freeholder might have to do so much ploughing or so much reaping for his lord each year, but these were "certain services".[3] The villein would have to work so many days a week at whatever his lord required. When villeins "go to bed on Sunday night they do not know what Monday's work will be"[4]; it might be ditching, it might be threshing, it might be driving a cart. A free tenant, on the other hand, was less a servant and more an independent contractor[5]; either he had a set task which he carried out in the way he thought best, or he merely paid a fixed rent in money or in kind.

---

[95] Litt. 135, 136: *R. v. Brockham* (1628) Litt.R. 105 at 109.
[96] Litt. 137.
[97] *Ante*, para. 2–015, Litt. 137. There was writ *cessavit de cantaria*: P. & M. i, 240.
[98] *Ante*, para. 2–004.
[99] Litt. 139, 141.
[1] H.E.L. iii, 30. For seisin, see *post*, para. 3–018.
[2] P. & M. i, 361.
[3] Litt. 117; P. & M. i, 364.
[4] P. & M. i, 371.
[5] H.E.L. iii, 31.

(3) SERVILE STATUS. All land held in free tenure was held by tenants who **2–030** were personally free. Until the fourteenth and fifteenth centuries, however, many but not all tenants of land held in unfree tenure were themselves personally unfree. Villein status must thus be distinguished from villein tenure[6]; if a man of villein status held land, the tenure was necessarily villein tenure, whereas land of villein tenure might be held by a free man.

1. Villeinage

(a) Origin. A large proportion of England after the Conquest was held in **2–031** villein tenure, and most agricultural labour was done by villein tenants.[7] This tenure was closely connected with that important feudal unit, the manor. A manor usually consisted of:

> (i) the lord's demesne, comprising the manor house and the cultivable land which the lord himself occupied;
>
> (ii) the land held by tenants, in either free or unfree tenure; and
>
> (iii) the waste, on which the tenants could pasture their beasts.[8]

The cultivation of the lord's demesne was ensured by the services owed by the tenants. Each manor had its own courts in which disputes were settled and land transferred. There was a Court Baron for the free tenants, and a Customary Court for the unfree tenants.[9]

The dependence of the villein tenants upon the manor is shown by the development of villein tenure. At first, the villein tenant was literally a tenant "at the will of the lord",[10] who could at any time evict him: the King's courts would not protect him, and he could not sue his lord in the manor court.[11] Yet his tenure, precarious in theory, came in practice to be well enough protected, for customs arose in each manor that tenants should not lose their lands unless they had done some act which was recognised as meriting forfeiture. The "custom of the manor" became the recognised "law" of the manor court, and

---

[6] See P. & M. i, 414–420; H.E.L. ii, 491 *et seq.* The villein was protected in life and limb, but had few other rights against his lord. He could be sold, leased or recovered, but gained his freedom if not captured within four days. Against third parties he had all the rights of a free man, so that his status was not that of slavery (P. & M. i, 415). Villeins were later classified as either "in gross" or "regardant to a manor", *i.e.* either as separate property or as part of a manor; unless sold separately villeins would pass with a conveyance of the manor: see Litt. 181; P. & M. i, 413; H.E.L. iii, 509. Villeins were corporeal hereditaments. In many colonies statutes declared slaves to be real property: see Burton's *Compendium* (8th ed., 1856), Appendix.

[7] H.E.L. iii, 198; *Heydon's Case* (1584) 3 Co.Rep. 7a at 8b.

[8] For the manor, see P. & M. i, 594 *et seq.*; H.E.L. ii, 375 *et seq.*; iii, 32, 33, 491, 492; *Baxendale v. Instow Parish Council* [1982] Ch. 14 at 26.

[9] Co.Litt. 58a. If the number of free tenants fell below two, the Court Baron ceased to exist (*Tonkin v. Croker* (1700) 2 Ld.Raym. 860 at 864), and the manor became a "reputed manor" (Scriven 3).

[10] P. & M. i, 360.

[11] *ibid.* And see at pp. 377, 379, 382.

although there was no means of enforcing it against the lord, he normally (as was natural) observed it.[12] The villein was therefore said to hold "at the will of the lord and according to the custom of the manor". In practice the second condition counted for most, though only the first was admitted by the common law.

2–032   (b) *Incidents*. The principal incidents of villein tenure were as follows.

(i) Agricultural services. These have been mentioned above. During the fourteenth and fifteenth centuries, as we shall see,[13] most of them were commuted for money payments.

(ii) Fealty and suit of court.[14]

(iii) Reliefs in some cases.[15]

(iv) Escheat and forfeiture. Since the villein had no tenure recognised outside the manor, these were always in favour of the lord; the Crown had no claim even in the case of treason.[16]

(v) Heriots.[17] By a very general custom, which occasionally applied even to freehold land,[18] the lord was entitled to take the tenant's best beast or other chattel on the tenant's death.[19] This was a relic of times when the lord furnished each new villein tenant with cattle and farming implements, and on the tenant's death took back his own.

(vi) Fines, payable to the lord on alienation of the land. Originally these were at the discretion of the lord; but ultimately two years' improved value of the land (*i.e.* the annual value of the land together with all increases in its value due to improvements) was regarded as the ordinary maximum.[20]

2–033   (c) *Transition from villein tenure to copyhold*. Great changes were wrought in villein tenure in the fourteenth and fifteenth centuries and they were accelerated by the Black Death of 1349 and 1361, and the Peasants' Revolt of 1381.[21] The Black Death greatly reduced the number of labourers and strengthened their bargaining power. It became common to commute villein services for fixed money rents. Just as in the twelfth and thirteenth centuries

---

[12] *ibid.*, 361, 376, 377.
[13] *Infra*.
[14] Williams R.P. 519.
[15] *ibid.*
[16] *ibid.*
[17] For derivation, see P. & M. i, 312–314, 316, 317.
[18] See, *e.g. Copestake v. Hoper* [1908] 2 Ch. 10.
[19] See, *e.g. Western v. Bailey* [1897] 1 Q.B. 86 (immaterial that beast had never been in the manor).
[20] Scriven 182.
[21] H.E.L. iii, 203–205.

the feudal levy was turned into a paid army, and military service into scutage,[22] so in the fourteenth and fifteenth centuries was labour service replaced by hired labour, and the serf by a rent-paying, wage-earning tenant. This process in turn hastened the disappearance of villein status; and in 1618 the last case on villein status was fought and decided against the lord.[23]

Meanwhile, as the old system of manorial agriculture changed, and as public policy demanded better control over feudal powers, the royal courts took the important step of protecting tenants of villein land against their lords.[24] The Chancery made the first move in 1439, and by the end of the fifteenth century, it seems, the common law courts were ready to assist any tenant ejected by his lord otherwise than in accordance with the custom of the manor.[25] No change, however, was made in the rule that the lord, not the tenant, had the legal seisin of the land.

At law, therefore, as well as by custom, the villein tenant held "at the will of the lord according to the custom of the manor",[26] with the emphasis upon the latter words. Everything was regulated by the custom of the particular manor in question, which, when proved, would be enforceable at common law. This change was marked by a change in name: "tenure in villeinage" became known as "tenure by copy of the court roll" or "copyhold", and the term "villein" was reserved for the few remaining persons whose status was still unfree.[27]

(d) Copyhold

(1) CONVEYANCE. The name "copyhold" is derived from the way in which **2–034** such land was conveyed. In the case of free tenures (after 1290) a conveyance could be made without reference to the lord[28]; copyholds, however, could be transferred only by a surrender and admittance made in the lord's court. The transferor surrendered his land to the lord, who then admitted as tenant the person nominated by the transferor. In practice, the lord's steward or bailiff conducted the business of the manor court for the lord; and sometimes there was a symbolic surrender and delivery of a small rod or verge, whence the term "tenant by the verge".[29] In the days of villeinage the lord had some discretion in controlling such transfers. After the transition to copyhold he had none; he was merely "custom's instrument".[30] The transaction was recorded on the court rolls and the transferee had a copy of the entry to prove his title; he thus held "by copy of the court roll".

---

[22] *Ante*, para. 2–009.
[23] *Pigg v. Caley* (1618) Noy 27; H.E.L. iii, 508 ("sixty" in line 1 of the note on p. 509 is a slip for "six").
[24] H.E.L. iii, 206–209.
[25] Litt. 77, 82; H.E.L. iii, 208, 209. The remedy was by the action of ejectment (*post*, Appendix); H.E.L. vii, 9.
[26] *Brown's Case* (1581) 4 Co.Rep. 21a.
[27] H.E.L. iii, 206.
[28] *Post*, para. 2–041.
[29] Litt. 78.
[30] H.E.L. iii, 247, 248.

2–035 (2) SURRENDER AND ADMITTANCE. Surrenders could be made in or out of court; if made out of court, due "presentment" (*i.e.* mention) of this at the next court was necessary.[31] Admittances could be made only in court[32] unless made by the lord himself.[33] But after the Copyhold Act 1841 presentment became unnecessary and admittances could be made out of court even by the steward.[34] The substantial part of a transfer was the surrender; the admittance was a mere form.[35] Nevertheless, until admittance the legal estate remained in the transferor, and the transferee's title was incomplete. But the admittance, when made, related back to the time of the surrender as against all save the lord,[36] and so invalidated any intermediate dealings inconsistent with the surrender.[37]

2–036 (3) CUSTOM. By the end of the sixteenth century the legal position of the copyholder had become substantially settled. But, of course, the custom of the manor in which the land lay was all-important: "the custom of the manor is the soul and life of copyhold".[38] Yet all customs were required to be reasonable.[39] Gavelkind and borough English might be found among copyhold customs, as well as in free tenure[40]; and entails,[41] life interests and leases[42] could exist also. Copyhold lost its taint of servility, and became merely a form—indeed, one of the commonest forms—of tenure. Since rents could not be increased as the value of money fell, copyhold lands became valuable inheritances to their tenants, and permanently ceased to be a source of much profit to their lords.[43]

2–037 (4) RIGHTS OF THE LORD. History, nevertheless, left enduring marks on this tenure. First, despite the loosening of the communal bonds within the manor, the method of conveyance prevented the lord from losing touch with his tenants, and so preserved the feudal incidents. Fines, reliefs and heriots, for example, were taken as before. Freehold tenants, on the other hand, could convey their land without reference to their lords, who sooner or later found it hardly worth while to trace their tenants in order to collect feudal dues which had greatly diminished in value. Secondly, the lord had valuable timber and mineral rights, the rules for which were the same.[44] The ownership of all

---

[31] Williams R.P. 527.
[32] *Doe d. Gutteridge v. Sowerby* (1860) 7 C.B.(N.S.) 599.
[33] *Melwich v. Luter* (1588) 4 Co.Rep. 26a.
[34] ss.88, 90.
[35] *Baddeley v. Leppingwell* (1764) 3 Burr. 1533 at 1543.
[36] *Holdfast d. Woollams v. Clapham* (1787) 1 T.R. 600.
[37] Scriven 97, 130; Williams R.P. 529; see, *e.g. Doe d. Wheeler v. Gibbons* (1835) 7 C. & P. 161.
[38] *Brown's Case* (1581) 4 Co.Rep. 21a.
[39] Scriven 313.
[40] Scriven 19–20, 172–174; H.E.L. vii, 300. For gavelkind and borough English, see *ante*, paras 2–019–2–025.
[41] See the previous edition of this work at p. 86.
[42] See *Re Broxhead Common, Whitehill, Hampshire* (1977) 3 P. & C.R. 451 at 458.
[43] H.E.L. iii, 212.
[44] *Lewis v. Branthwaite* (1831) 2 B. & Ad. 437 at 443.

timber and minerals was vested in the lord,[45] but as they were in the possession of the tenant, it was a trespass for the lord to enter to take them without the tenant's consent.[46] Both these rules were subject to any custom to the contrary, but in the absence of any such custom, the trees and minerals could not be dealt with except by agreement between lord and tenant.[47] Copyhold tenants therefore rarely thought it worth while to cultivate timber; "the oak scorns to grow except on free land".[48] Further, the lord had no right to use the space left by minerals which had been extracted (*e.g.* for transporting minerals from another mine), for the space belonged to the tenant.[49]

2. Customary freehold. "Customary freehold" was the name given to copyhold where the tenant was expressed to hold "according to the custom of the manor", but not "at the will of the lord".[50] A conveyance of such land might be made by surrender and admittance, by an ordinary conveyance followed by admittance, or by an ordinary conveyance coupled with surrender and admittance. In other respects, customary freehold was no different from ordinary copyhold, so that its title was misleading. Seisin was in the lord,[51] and the lord was entitled to the timber and minerals.[52] A more apt name for customary freehold was "privileged copyhold".[53]

 2–038

Part 3

REDUCTION IN THE NUMBER OF TENURES

Section 1. Prohibition of New Tenures After 1290

1. Before 1290. In early times there was no theoretical limit to the number of intervening tenures between the King and the tenant in occupation of the land. A new rung could always be added at the bottom of the feudal ladder by the creation of a further tenure. This process was called subinfeudation. It was popular in an age where land was almost the only form of capital wealth, for then the seller of land preferred to take payment in the form of a continuing right to rent or services charged on the land. For example, the King might grant to A, A might grant to B and B might grant to C. A and B would then be mesne lords,[54] and if A (for example) was not rendered his services by B,

 2–039

[45] *Eardley v. Earl Granville* (1876) 3 Ch.D. 826 at 832.
[46] *Bourne v. Taylor* (1808) 10 East 189 (minerals); *Whitechurch v. Holworthy* (1815) 4 M. & S. 340 (trees).
[47] *Commissioners of Inland Revenue v. Joicey (No. 2)* [1913] 2 K.B. 580 at 586.
[48] Williams R.P. 506.
[49] *Eardley v. Earl Granville* (1876) 3 Ch.D. 826.
[50] Scriven 14–19. Distinguish "ancient freeholds" (*ibid.*, p. 19), which were a species of free tenure subject to manorial customs: see *Passingham v. Pitty* (1855) 17 C.B. 299.
[51] *Doe d. Cook v. Danvers* (1806) 7 East 299; *Thompson v. Hardinge* (1845) 1 C.B. 940.
[52] *Bishop of Winchester v. Knight* (1717) 1 P. Wms. 406.
[53] *Duke of Portland v. Hill* (1866) L.R. 2 Eq. 765 at 776.
[54] See *ante*, para. 2–003.

he could proceed against the land. *i.e.* distrain on C. C in turn had a remedy against B, the writ of mesne.[55] But for obvious reasons this system was excessively cumbrous and inconvenient, particularly as the value of seignories came to lie in incidents rather than in services.[56] "Suppose that A enfeoffed B to hold by knight's service, and that B enfeoffed C to hold at a rent of a pound of pepper; B dies leaving an heir within age; A is entitled to a wardship; but it will be worth very little: instead of being entitled to enjoy the land itself until the heir is of age, he will get a few annual pounds of pepper. And so in case of an escheat, instead of enjoying the land for ever he may have but a trifling rent."[57] Further, if B disappeared, A would be ignorant of the occasions on which the benefits of escheat, marriage and wardship arose.

The alternative to subinfeudation was substitution. B might grant to C not by creating a new tenure but by letting C step into his shoes so that C became, and B ceased to be, tenant of A. But could A be compelled to take C for his tenant at B's instance? "If a new is substituted for an old tenant, a poor may take the place of a rich, a dishonest that of an honest man, a foe that of a friend, and the solemn bond of homage will be feeble if the vassal has a free power of putting another man in his room."[58] There was a further objection if B alienated only a part of his land by substitution: the lord would have to look to two tenants instead of one for the services. Nevertheless, and despite the personal character of the feudal bond, it appears to have become the general rule in the thirteenth century that tenants could alienate by substitution without their lords' consent. In that period freedom of alienation was in the ascendant as a principle of public policy.[59]

2. The Statute *Quia Emptores* 1290

2–040   (a) *The statute.* Magna Carta 1217, c. 39, had attempted to meet the lords' objections by prohibiting alienations which left insufficient security for the services. But dissatisfaction continued until a revolutionary settlement was made by the statute *Quia Emptores* 1290.[60] The effect of this was as follows.

---

[55] P. & M. i, 238.
[56] H.E.L. ii, 348, 349, iii, 80.
[57] P. & M. i, 330.
[58] *ibid.*
[59] P. & M. i, 344.
[60] An abbreviated version of the first chapter may be given as follows: "Whereas purchasers of lands and tenements have many times heretofore entered into their fees, to be holden in fee of their feoffors and not of the chief lords of the fees, whereby the said chief lords have many times lost their escheats, marriages and wardships; which things seemed very hard and extreme unto those lords and other great men: our lord the king has granted, provided and ordained that henceforth it shall be lawful for every freeman to sell at his own pleasure his lands and tenements, or part of them; so nevertheless that the feoffee shall hold the same lands or tenements of the chief lord of the same fee, by such service and customs as his feoffor held before." For the historical and legal background to the statute, see S. F. C. Milsom, *Historical Foundations of the Common Law* (2nd ed.), p. 113; J. M. W. Bean, *The Decline of English Feudalism*, p. 79.

(i) Alienation by subinfeudation was prohibited (c. 1).

(ii) All free tenants were authorised to alienate the whole or part of their land by substitution, without the lord's consent, the new tenant to hold by the same services as the old (c. 1).

(iii) On alienation of part of the land by substitution, the feudal services were to be apportioned (c. 2).

(iv) The statute applied only to grants in fee simple (c. 3).

(b) Effect of the statute. *Quia Emptores* marked the victory of the modern   **2–041**
concept of land as alienable property over the more restrictive principles of feudalism. For no new tenures in fee simple could thenceforth be created except by the Crown. Existing tenures could be freely transferred from hand to hand, and they could be extinguished as before by escheat or forfeiture. The network of tenures could therefore no longer grow; it could only contract. Every conveyance of land in fee simple by a subject after 1290 was bound to be an out-and-out transfer and could not create the relationship of lord and tenant between the parties. On such a conveyance no services could be reserved; any rights reserved, such as a rent, must be rights existing independently of the relationship of lord and tenant. Nor could any fines for alienation be lawfully demanded by any subject.[61]

(c) Limits of statute. Since the statute was expressly confined to alienations   **2–042**
in fee simple, it did not prevent a tenant in fee simple from granting a life estate or a fee tail to another to hold of him as lord.[62] Further, as it did not mention the Crown either expressly or by necessary implication, the Crown was not bound by it.[63] Consequently the statute conferred no right of free alienation upon tenants in chief, and an Ordinance of 1256 forbidding them to alienate without a royal licence remained effective. However, in 1327 tenants in chief were given a right of free alienation, subject only to the payment of a reasonable fine in some cases,[64] and the Tenures Abolition Act 1660 abolished this fine.[65] Nor did the Statute prevent the Crown from granting land to be held of the Crown; but the Tenures Abolition Act 1660 provided that such grants could be made only in common socage.[66]

(d) Effect today. *Quia Emptores* 1290 is still in force today and may be   **2–043**
regarded as one of the pillars of the law of real property. It operates every time that a conveyance in fee simple is executed, automatically shifting the status of tenant from grantor to grantee and fulfilling the rule that all land held by a subject shall be held in tenure of the Crown either mediately or immediately.

[61] See, *e.g. Merttens v. Hill* [1901] 1 Ch. 842.
[62] Challis 22.
[63] Litt. 140. See H.E.L. iii, 84, i, 473. But tenants in chief were prevented from subinfeudating: *Re Holliday* [1922] 2 Ch. 698.
[64] 1 Edw. 3, st. 2, cc. 12, 13, 1327; *cf.* 34 Edw. 3, c. 15, 1360, confirming alienations made be 1272.
[65] s.1. For this statute, see below.
[66] s.4.

The lord of the fee is the successor in title to the person who was lord in 1290, for there can have been no change in the tenure since then.[67] But it is rare for records of a mesne lordship to have been preserved for so long, except in the case of manors where mesne tenure remained of importance until 1925 and later.[68] Other cases are governed by the presumption that, if no mesne lord appears, the land is held immediately of the Crown.[69] Innumerable mesne lordships came to be forgotten as, with the passage of time and the inflation of the currency, the ancient services or commutation rents ceased to be worth collecting. After 1290 the feudal pyramid began to crumble. The number of mesne lordships could not be increased, evidence of existing mesne lordships gradually disappeared with the passing of time, and so most land came to be held directly from the Crown.

Section 2. The Tenures Abolition Act 1660

2–044   **1. Tenures.** The system of landholding in return for services fell into decay long before the most onerous incidents of tenure were legally abolished. In particular, the incidents of military tenure, such as wardships, marriages and aids, were zealously preserved by the Crown for the sake of revenue.[70] The King, who was always lord and never tenant, was the only proprietor who had all to gain and nothing to lose by preserving these feudal imposts. But, like certain other items of unparliamentary revenue, they were swept away in the seventeenth century. The Tenures Abolition Act 1660, confirming a resolution of the Long Parliament of 1646, converted all tenures into free and common socage with the exception of frankalmoign and copyhold.[71]

2–045   **2. Incidents.** The statute also abolished many burdensome incidents, including aids for the knighting of the lord's eldest son and the marriage of his eldest daughter, wardships, marriages, primer seisin, *ouster le main*, and most fines for alienation; and it abolished the Court of Wards and Liveries which the Crown had set up to enforce some of these incidents against tenants *in capite*. The Crown was compensated for its loss of revenue by the imposition of a tax on beer and other beverages. Fixed rents, heriots and suit of court were expressly saved, and reliefs were restricted to those payable for land of socage tenure, *i.e.* one year's rent. Since it was uncommon for military tenure to be subject to rent, relief in effect disappeared with the other incidents.

---

[67] But it is possible that a subinfeudation in fee simple can be brought about (since 1881) by the enlargement of a long lease: see *post*, para. 14–178.

[68] See *post*, para. 2–047.

[69] Williams R.P. 58; Challis 33; and see *Re Lowe's W.T.* [1973] 1 W.L.R. 882.

[70] Bl.Comm. ii, 69, 76. There was also the lucrative prerogative right to compel military tenants in chief to assume knighthood: *ibid.*

[71] For criticisms of the drafting of this statute, see Co.Litt. 108a, n. 1, and Challis 23.

3. Summary. The principal results of the Act may be summarised thus.   2–046

(*a*) Nearly all burdensome incidents were abolished for all land of free tenure. Escheat and forfeiture survived as the only important incidents of free tenure. Fealty survived, but was of no importance.

(*b*) All free tenures were converted into free and common socage and no other type of tenure might be created in future. But the Act preserved, *inter alia*, (i) copyhold, (ii) frankalmoign, (iii) the honorary incidents of grand sergeanty, and (iv) services incident to socage (*e.g.* those of petty sergeanty[72]). Customs such as gavelkind and borough English, and the peculiarities of ancient demesne, continued unaltered.

Section 3. The 1925 Legislation

A. Tenures

1. Before 1926. From 1645 until 1926 the two surviving tenures held the   2–047
field: socage (often called freehold) and copyhold. Frankalmoign, since it could not survive alienation at any time after 1290, had become obsolete.[73] This dual system of tenure was an impediment to conveyancing. Copyhold had the great merit that the books of the manor were a register of title,[74] whereas freehold titles had mostly to be proved in the traditional way by investigating past transactions recorded in the title deeds.[75] But copyhold had disadvantages. Its peculiar mode of conveyance (surrender and admittance) made it impossible to convey freeholds and copyholds by a single deed. It was subject both to customary incidents which might vary from manor to manor and also the lord's rights to timber and minerals. Accordingly provision was made by statute for the enfranchisement of copyholds, *i.e.* the conversion of land of copyhold tenure into socage. The Copyhold Acts of 1841, 1843 and 1844 provided for voluntary enfranchisement, *i.e.* enfranchisement where both lord and tenant agreed. The Copyhold Acts of 1852, 1858 and 1887 (consolidated in the Copyhold Act 1894) enabled either lord or tenant to secure compulsory enfranchisement. But apart from any proceedings taken under these Acts, tenures remained substantially unaltered until the legislation of 1922–1925 came into force.

2. After 1925. By the Law of Property Act 1922 (which took effect at the   2–048
beginning of 1926) all copyhold land was enfranchised, *i.e.* made land of

---

[72] Despite the sweeping words of the statute, it has been asserted that the actual tenure of petty sergeanty continued in being, and not merely the incidents: see Co.Litt. 108a, n. 1; Cru.Dig. i, 41.

[73] *Ante*, para. 2–041.

[74] Williams, *Seisin*, 41.

[75] *Post*, para. 12–067.

freehold (socage) tenure.[76] Freehold and copyhold incidents were dealt with as explained below. At the same time frankalmoign was formally abolished.[77] A new system of intestate succession was introduced whereby all special customs of descent, including gavelkind and borough English, were superseded.[78] The only remaining traces of special types of freehold tenure are now the services incident to grand and petty sergeanty, which were left untouched by the Acts.[79] The result was that as from the beginning of 1926 (when these provisions all took effect) all land has been held in freehold, the modern name for free and common socage.

B. Incidents

2–049   **1. Freehold.** Quit rents, reliefs, fealty, suit of court and occasional escheats were the only feudal incidents ordinarily existing in freehold land in 1925. Most of the money payments had ceased to be payable; the value of money had fallen so much that the payments were not worth collecting, and after non-payment for 12 years they were barred by statute.[80] Manorial incidents affecting freeholds (*e.g.* freeholds within manors or enfranchised copyholds) were dealt with in the same way as copyhold incidents.[81] Fealty and suit of court, although abolished in the case of copyholds, have been left in existence in the case of freeholds. This is probably accidental but quite unimportant.

Escheat *propter defectum sanguinis* (on death of the tenant intestate and without heirs) was often the one valuable right of the lord still in existence in 1925. In most cases it was impossible for the mesne lord to prove his lordship, for freeholders could alienate their land without reference to the lord and thus for many years no act to mark the lordship might occur.[82] The Administration of Estates Act 1925 abolished this form of escheat and provided that if a person died leaving property not disposed of by will, that property should pass to the Crown[83] in default of any of the limited class of relatives set out in the Act.[84] Escheat *propter delictum tenentis* (for felony) no longer existed in 1925. The Corruption of Blood Act 1814 had restricted it to cases of *petit treason and murder*, and the Forfeiture Act 1870 completely abolished it, together with the Crown's prerogative right of forfeiture for high treason. No

---

[76] s.128 and 12th Sched., para. (1), A.E.A. 1925, 2nd Sched., Pt I, also repealed the saving words of the Tenures Abolition Act 1660, s.7.

[77] A.E.A. 1925, 2nd Sched., Pt I. This repeals the words in the Tenures Abolition Act 1660, s.7, which saved frankalmoign from destruction by s.1 of that Act, whereby all tenures as from February 24, 1646, "and for ever thereafter" were to be "turned into free and common socage". In the face of these words and s.7, the suggestion that frankalmoign still survives because it is not mentioned in s.1 seems unsound. See, however, Co.Litt. 100b, n. 1.

[78] A.E.A. 1925, s.45(1), 2nd Sched., Pt I; *post*, para. 11–088. Infants' power to convey gavelkind land was abolished by L.P.A. 1925, ss.1(6), 51(1).

[79] L.P.A. 1922, s.136.

[80] *Post*, para 21–034. *De Beauvoir v. Owen* (1850) 5 Exch. 166 (freehold); *Howitt v. Harrington* [1893] 2 Ch. 497 (copyhold).

[81] L.P.A. 1922, s.138(1); and see *post*, para. 2–053.

[82] *Ante*, para. 2–043.

[83] Or Duchy of Lancaster or Duke of Cornwall.

[84] ss.45, 46; and see Crown Estate Act 1961, s.8(3).

longer, therefore, can there be an escheat of either of the two principal kinds.

Nevertheless, in certain cases, the possibility of escheat remains. Escheat is **2–050** a principle inseparable from tenure which ensures that land will never be without an owner,[85] for if there is no tenant and no mesne lord it will return to the Crown. Escheat will still take place where a landowner's trustee in bankruptcy or liquidator (if it is a corporation) exercises his statutory power[86] to disclaim the land.[87] Escheat takes place automatically, and the freehold is extinguished.[88] On the dissolution of a company governed by the Companies Acts, statute vests its property in the Crown[89] as *bona vacantia*.[90] Although in those circumstances, the Crown may disclaim the freehold,[91] this has a "boomerang effect", because the land then escheats to the Crown.[92] The object of these statutory provisions is not therefore easy to see in so far as they concern freeholds.[93] Where the corporation dissolved is not governed by the Companies Acts, there will be an escheat of its real property.[94] Leases owned by such a corporation, on the other hand, will pass to the Crown under the Crown's prerogative right to *bona vacantia, i.e.* personal property without an owner.[95] Escheat does not determine any subordinate interest in the land in question, such as a mortgage or lease. The Crown takes the land subject to such rights.[96]

2. Copyhold. In the case of copyholds, the incidents were in most cases **2–051** still fully effective in 1925. The Law of Property Act 1922 divided them into three classes.

(a) Those abolished forthwith.[97] As soon as the Act came into force (on **2–052** January 1, 1926), the following incidents were abolished subject to a single payment of compensation.[98]

---

[85] See *Ho Young v. Bess* [1995] 1 W.L.R. 350 at 355.

[86] I.A. 1986, ss.315 and 178 respectively.

[87] *Scmlla Properties Ltd v. Gesso Properties (B.V.I.) Ltd* [1995] B.C.C. 793 (the leading modern case, which contains a perceptive and illuminating discussion of the issues). See too *British General Insurance Co. Ltd v. Att.-Gen.* [1945] L.J.N.C.C.R. 113, discussed (1946) 62 L.Q.R. 223 (R.E.M.); and also (1931) 75 S.J. 843 (T.C. Williams).

[88] *Scmlla Properties Ltd v. Gesso Properties (B.V.I.) Ltd, supra.* It is clear from that case, that escheat applies as much to registered land as it does to unregistered: *ibid.*, at 802.

[89] Or Duchy of Lancaster or Duke of Cornwall.

[90] Companies Act 1985, s.654.

[91] *ibid.*, ss.656, 657.

[92] *Scmlla Properties Ltd v. Gesso Properties (B.V.I.) Ltd, supra*, at 805, *per* Burnton, Q.C.

[93] *ibid.* See too (1954) 70 L.Q.R. 25 (D. W. Elliott).

[94] *Re Wells* [1933] Ch. 29 at 54, approving Challis 467; *Re Strathblaine Estates Ltd* [1948] Ch. 228. Previously it had been doubtful whether there was escheat, or reverter to the donor: Co.Litt. 13b; Preston ii, 50; Challis 65, 66, 226; (1933) 49 L.Q.R. 160 (Sir W. S. Holdsworth), 240 (F. E. Farrer); (1935) 51 L.Q.R. 347 (M. W. Hughes), 361 (F. E. Farrer). See also *post*, para. 7–091.

[95] *Re Wells, supra* (equitable interest in leaseholds).

[96] *Att.-Gen. of Ontario v. Mercer* (1883) 8 App. Cas. 767 at 772; *Scmlla Properties Ltd v. Gesso Properties (B.V.I.) Ltd, supra*, at 806–808.

[97] 12th Sched., para. (1).

[98] 13th Sched., Pt II, para. 13, as amended by L.P.Am.A. 1924, 2nd Sched., para. 4(3), and L.P.Am.A. 1926, Sched. (usually 20% of the annual value of the land).

(i) Forfeiture for alienation in freehold (*i.e.* for purporting to convey the land as freehold) or without licence.

(ii) Fealty and customary suits and services.

(iii) Escheat for want of heirs.[99]

(iv) Special customs of descent (*e.g.* gavelkind and borough English), dower, freebench (the usual name for dower in copyhold land) and curtesy.

2–053   *(b) Those preserved until 1936.*[1] This class automatically disappeared after December 31, 1935, unless previously extinguished either voluntarily or compulsorily. Until 1936 the parties could extinguish them at any time voluntarily, or either party could serve a notice on the other requiring the amount of compensation to be ascertained.[2] Immediately on service of the notice the incidents ceased, and compensation became payable as fixed by the Minister of Agriculture according to a scale. If the compensation was £20 or less it was payable by the tenant as a debt. If it was more than £20 it took the form of a rentcharge running with the land and spread over 20 years.[3]

So long as any incidents in this class existed, no conveyance of the land would pass the legal estate unless it was produced to the steward of the manor within six months and indorsed by him with a certificate that all payments due on the transfer had been duly made. This provision was necessary since the land, being freehold, became transferable without reference to the lord, and thus the lord might not know that there had been a conveyance entitling him to a fine or some other payment.

Even though the incidents ceased at the end of 1935 (and thus production of a conveyance made after 1935 was unnecessary), the lord was enabled to claim compensation, originally up to 1941, and later, by a war-time extension, up to the end of October 1950.[4]

The incidents in this class are as follows.

(i) Quit rents, chief rents and other similar payments.

(ii) Fines, reliefs, heriots and dues (including fees payable to stewards).

(iii) Forfeitures other than for alienation in freehold or without licence.

---

[99] In *British General Insurance Co. Ltd v. Att.-Gen.* [1945] L.J.N.C.C.R. 113 at 125 it was said that all kinds of escheat were abolished for enfranchised land by L.P.A. 1922, 12th Sched., para. (1)(c). But the more natural interpretation is that escheat is excluded only where the Crown takes as *bona vacantia* under the A.E.A. 1925 (replacing Pt VIII of the L.P.A. 1922).

[1] ss.128, 129, 138, 140, 13th Sched., Pt II.

[2] In order to give the tenant time to raise the money the lord was prohibited from serving a notice until 1931: L.P.A. 1922, s.138(1)(b).

[3] s.139(1)(v).

[4] Postponement of Enactments (Miscellaneous Provisions) Act 1939, s.3; S.I. 1949 No. 836.

(iv) Timber rights.

As mentioned above,[5] these provisions for extinguishment apply also to the few cases where incidents of manorial origin were attached to freehold land.

(c) Those preserved indefinitely.[6] The rights and liabilities which continue **2–054** indefinitely unless abolished by written agreement between lord and tenant are as follows.

(i) Any rights of the lord or tenant to mines[7] and minerals.

(ii) Any rights of the lord in respect of fairs, markets and sporting.

(iii) Any tenant's rights of common (*e.g.* to pasture beasts on the waste land of the manor). A statutory scheme for registration of these rights was introduced in 1965.[8]

(iv) Any liability of lord or tenant for the upkeep of dykes, ditches, sea walls, bridges, and the like.

Only by the existence of these rights and duties is land which was formally copyhold now distinguishable from other land as regards the conditions of tenure.

Lordships of manors continue to exist, representing mesne tenure between the Crown and the freeholders. Since they carry the right to the manorial records, there is a market for them for historical or antiquarian purposes. Often also they carry the right to hold a court baron and sometimes also a court leet, though in nearly all cases such courts have lost all legal jurisdiction.[9]

Part 4

TENURE AND OWNERSHIP TODAY

There is only one feudal tenure left today, namely socage, now called free- **2–055** hold. Feudal incidents have in practice disappeared,[10] except for land formerly held in grant sergeanty, petty sergeanty or copyhold, where some traces of the

---

[5] *Ante,* para. 2–049.
[6] L.P.A. 1922, ss.128(2), 138, 12th Sched., paras (4)–(6).
[7] "Mines" is a more comprehensive term than "minerals", for it relates not only to the minerals but also to the passages in the mine: *Batten Pooll v. Kennedy* [1907] 1 Ch. 256.
[8] See *post,* para. 18–181.
[9] Various obsolete jurisdictions were extinguished by A.J.A. 1977, s.23 and 4th Sched., as recommended by Law Com. No. 72 (1976). For courts leet, see H.E.L. i, 135.
[10] For a Crown grant in 1913 of Canadian land in socage in fee simple subject to rent service (a royalty), see *Att.-Gen. for Alberta v. Huggard Assets Ltd* [1953] A.C. 420. In principle there is nothing to prevent the Crown reserving services upon such grants.

former tenure remain. Except in the case of land formerly copyhold, mesne lordships are nearly all untraceable, for it is many years since there were any enforceable rights to preserve evidence of the relationship of lord and tenant; consequently the courts are ready to act on the presumption that the land is held directly of the Crown, *e.g.* for the purposes of escheat.[11]

Yet despite the sweeping changes made by statute, "the fundamental principles of the law of ownership of land remain the same as before the legislation of 1925. Land is still the object of feudal tenure; the Sovereign remains the lord paramount of all the land within the realm; every parcel of land is still held of some lord . . . and the greatest interest which any subject can have in land is still an estate in fee simple and no more".[12] The title "tenant in fee simple" is still the technically correct description of the person who is popularly regarded as the owner of land, and every conveyance in fee simple substitutes the new tenant for the old as provided by the statute *Quia Emptores* 1290. Nevertheless, as will be seen, for all practical purposes ownership in fee simple "differs from the absolute dominion of a chattel in nothing except the physical indestructibility of its subject".[13] Our law has preferred to suppress one by one the practical consequences of tenure rather than to strike at the root of the theory of tenure itself. It remains possible, therefore, that in rare cases not covered by the statutory reforms recourse may have to be had to the feudal principles which still underlie our land law.[14]

The one field in which rules derived from tenure remain of practical importance is, paradoxically, leasehold ("landlord and tenant"). Leasehold developed independently of the feudal system, and although it became a genuine tenure, it was never part of the network of tenures which connected land ownership with the Crown. It forms a separate branch of the law which in due course will be explained at length.[15]

For practical purposes, therefore, the law of tenure is no longer of assistance in solving problems about rights over land. The owner in fee simple is regarded as absolute owner, and the fundamentals of his title depend on principles which have nothing to do with tenure. The basis of land ownership is the system of estates, which is the subject of the following chapter. The final part of that chapter will elucidate what ownership really means in modern land law.

---

[11] See, *e.g. Re Lowe's W.T.* [1973] 1 W.L.R. 882 at 886.
[12] Cyprian Williams, 75 S.J. 848 ("The fundamental principles of the present law of ownership of land", 1931).
[13] Challis 218; and see *post*, para. 3–041 but compare *post*, para. 3–001, n. 2.
[14] *e.g.* in the still possible cases of escheat: *ante*, para. 2–050.
[15] *Post*, Chap. 14.

Chapter 3

ESTATES

Part 1

CLASSIFICATION

The term "estate", as we have seen,[1] indicates an interest in land of some particular duration. It is now necessary to consider the different kinds of estate, *i.e.* the various possible interests in land classified according to their duration.

It is the doctrine of estates, coupled with the permanence of land as opposed to destructible chattels, which makes the law relating to land so much more complex than the law governing chattels.[2] At common law it can in general be said that only two distinct legal rights can exist at the same time in chattels, namely, possession and ownership. If A lends his watch to B, the ownership of the watch remains vested in A, while B has possession of it. But in the case of land, a large number of legal rights could and still can exist at the same time. Thus the position of Blackacre today may be that A is entitled to the land for life, B to a life interest in remainder (*i.e.* after A's death), and C to the fee simple in remainder. At the same time, D may own a lease for 99 years, subject to a sub-lease in favour of E for 21 years, and the land may be subject to a mortgage in favour of F, a profit *à prendre* in favour of G, easements such as rights of way in favour of H, J and K, and so on indefinitely. Before 1926 all these estates and interests could exist as legal rights. Some, but not all, can exist as legal rights today.

In the case of a chattel, ownership is absolute. It is either owned outright by one person (or by several persons jointly or in common with each other) or it is not owned at all. However there is in law, at least in theory, no absolute ownership of land. The land is held in tenure and there is a presumption that it is held directly of the Crown.[3] It may so be held for various different estates, *i.e.* for a greater or less period of time. In popular speech one may refer to X's ownership of Blackacre; but technically one should speak of X holding Blackacre for an estate in fee simple in socage tenure or for a term of years,

3–001

3–002

---

[1] *Ante*, para. 2–005.

[2] Land is not always indestructible, *e.g.* an upper floor of a house: *post*, para. 3–041.

[3] See *Re Lowe's W.T.* [1973] 1 W.L.R. 882 at 886, *per* Russell L.J., where "the theoretical possibility" of an escheat to a mesne lord was considered to be "so remote that it may be wholly ignored". *Ante*, Chap. 2.

and subject perhaps to easements, mortgages, and the like, which give other people limited rights of property in the land. Land law, therefore, has to concern itself with many varieties of qualified ownership.

3–003   The system of estates is of vital importance, but since it was radically amended in 1925, the past tense will be used in much of the discussion. The present law can be understood only by reference to the old.

Estates were divided into two classes:

1. Freehold estates;

2. Leasehold estates.

It should be noted that "freehold" here has nothing to do with freehold (or socage) tenure; it is merely that the same word is used sometimes to express the quality of the tenure, and sometimes the quantity of the estate. "Freehold" is normally used by the man in the street as combining these senses; thus when a house agent advertises "a desirable freehold residence", he may be taken to refer to a fee simple estate in land of freehold tenure.

Section 1. Estates of Freehold

3–004   **1. The three estates.** There were three estates of freehold:

    (i) fee simple;

    (ii) fee tail; and

    (iii) life estate.[4]

The fee simple and the life estate have always existed in English law. The fee tail was introduced by statute in 1285, but can no longer be created. Before considering the estates in any detail a brief account of each must be given.

3–005   *(a) Fee simple.* Originally this was an estate which endured for so long as the original tenant or any of his heirs (blood relations, and their heirs, and so on)[5] survived. Thus at first a fee simple would terminate if the original tenant died without leaving any descendants or collateral blood relations (*e.g.* brothers or cousins), even if before his death the land had been conveyed to another tenant who was still alive.[6] But by 1306 it was settled that where a tenant in fee simple alienated the land, the fee simple would continue as long as there were heirs of the new tenant, and so on, irrespective of any failure of the original tenant's heirs.[7] From that time onwards a fee simple was virtually

---

[4] Co.Litt. 43b.
[5] For the exact meaning of "heir", see the previous edition of this work at p. 540.
[6] H.E.L. iii, 106; P. & M. ii, 14.
[7] Y.B. 33–35 Edw. 1 (R.S.) 362; H.E.L. iii, 106, 107.

perpetual. It would terminate only if the tenant for the time being died leaving no heir, when it would escheat to his lord.[8]

(b) Fee tail. This was an estate which continued for so long as the original tenant or any of his lineal descendants survived. Thus if the original tenant died leaving no relatives except a brother, a fee simple would continue, but a fee tail would come to an end. The terms "fee tail", "estate tail", "entail" and "entailed interest" are often used interchangeably; but "fee tail" is the correct expression for a legal entail,[9] and "entailed interest" is usually reserved for an equitable entail.[10]

3–006

(c) Life estate. As its name indicates, this lasted for life only. The name "life estate" usually denoted that the measuring life was that of the tenant himself, *e.g.* when the grant was to A for life. The form of life estate where the measuring life was that of some person was known as an estate *"pur autre vie"* (for the life of another), *e.g.* to A for so long as B lives.

3–007

2. "Freehold". A common feature of all estates of freehold was that the duration of the estate, though limited, was uncertain. Nobody could say when the death would occur of a particular person and all his future heirs, or of a person and all his descendants, or of a person alone. Nor was it certain that the duration would be perpetual. The estate was always liable to determine if some event occurred. In the case of the fee simple and the fee tail, the word "fee" denoted (i) that the estate was an estate of inheritance, *i.e.* an estate which, on the death of the tenant, was capable of descending to his heir[11]; and (ii) that the estate was one which might continue for ever.[12] The words "simple" and "tail" distinguished the classes of heirs who could inherit. A fee simple descended to the heirs general, including collaterals.[13] A fee tail descended to heirs special, *i.e.* to lineal descendants only.

3–008

A life estate, on the other hand, was not a fee. It was not an estate of inheritance and it could not continue for ever. On the death of the tenant an ordinary life estate determined, and an estate *pur autre vie* did not descend to the tenant's heir, but passed under the special rules of occupancy.[14] Life estates were sometimes called "mere freeholds" or simply "freeholds", as opposed to "freeholds of inheritance".[15]

Each estate of freehold could exist in a number of varied forms which will be considered in due course.

---

[8] *Ante*, p. 17, and see T.C. Williams, 69 L.J.News. 369, 385; 70 L.J.News. 4, 20; 75 S.J. 847.
[9] Challis 60. A legal entail can no longer exist: *post*, para. 4–035.
[10] *Post*, para. 4–038.
[11] Litt. 1, 9; Preston i, 262; Challis 218.
[12] Preston i, 419, 480.
[13] Preston i, 428. Formerly the word "simple" also signified "absolute", as opposed to "conditional"; Co.Litt. 1b; Challis 218; *post*, para. 3–060, n.63.
[14] *Post*, para. 3–095.
[15] Co.Litt. 266b, n.1; Preston i, 214; Challis 99.

Section 2. Leaseholds

3–009   **1. Nature of leases.** At first the three estates of freehold were the sole estates recognised by law; the only other lawful right to the possession of land was known as a tenancy at will, under which the tenant could be ejected at any time, and which therefore gave him no estate at all.[16] Terms of years grew up outside this system of estates. Originally they were regarded not as property (as object of ownership) but as personal contracts binding only on the parties. The leaseholder was not fully protected against other persons until the end of the fifteenth century, and the nature of the remedy (the action of ejectment) marked off leaseholds from the other estates.[17] When they became fully protected by the law of property they became estates,[18] but it was too late for them to be classified with the others.

3–010   **2. "Less than freehold".** Leaseholds have long been denominated "estates less than freehold", and in theory they are inferior. "In law the duration of a term is immaterial, and a term for 21 years is as great an estate as one for 21,000 years. The distinction is between a chattel interest, which is a term for years, and a freehold interest. A freehold interest of the smallest duration is greater in the contemplation of law than the longest term."[19] Nevertheless, their inferiority exists only in history and in theory. A rent-free lease for 3,000 years may be as secure and as valuable as any freehold estate.[20] It is true that the early attitude towards leases led to their being classified as personal and not as real property, and that this distinction, which is still law, remains of some importance even after 1925.[21] It is also true that before 1926 leasehold property could not be entailed or granted by deed for life.[22] On the other hand, leases in early times had the important advantage that since they were personalty they could be devised, while wills of freehold land were not allowed before 1540.[23]

3–011   **3. Categories of leaseholds.** Today the various forms of leasehold estates are of the first importance. Their distinguishing characteristic, by contrast with freehold estates, is that their maximum duration is fixed in time. The principal categories, which are dealt with more fully later, are as follows.[24]

3–012   *(a) Fixed term of certain duration.* The tenant may hold the land of a fixed term of certain duration,[25] as under a lease for 99 years. The possibility of the term being curtailed (*e.g.* by forfeiture for non-payment of rent) under some

---

[16] *Post*, para. 3–014.
[17] *Post*, Appendix; H.E.L. iii, 213–217; iv, 486.
[18] Litt. 58.
[19] *Re Russell Road Purchase-Moneys* (1871) L.R. 12 Eq. 78 at 84, *per* Malins V.-C.
[20] *cf. post*, para. 19–020, in regard to mortgages.
[21] *Ante*, para. 1–019.
[22] *Post*, paras 3–087.
[23] *Post*, para. 3–043.
[24] *Post*, paras. 14–001 *et seq.*
[25] Bracton Bk. iv, c. 28, f. 207; Preston i, 203.

provision to this effect in the lease does not affect the basic conception, which is one of certainty of duration in the absence of steps being taken for extension or curtailment. A lease for "99 years if X so long lives" also fell under this head; it was not an estate of freehold,[26] for although X might well die before the 99 years had run, the maximum duration of the lease was fixed. Even if there was no chance of X outliving the 99 years, so that the duration of the lease would be the same as an estate granted "to X for life", yet in law the former was leasehold and the latter freehold. Partly as a result of the intervention of statute, such leases are comparatively rare today.[27]

(b) Fixed term with duration capable of being rendered certain. A lease of   **3–013** land "to A from year to year", with no other provision as to its duration, will continue indefinitely unless either landlord or tenant takes some step to determine it. But either party can give half a year's notice to determine it at the end of a year of the tenancy, and thus ensure its determination on a fixed date. "The term continues until determined as if both parties made a new agreement at the end of each year for a new term for the ensuing year."[28] At any given moment, therefore, the tenant's estate has a fixed term set to it, though it may later be extended if no notice is given. The same applies to quarterly, monthly, weekly and other periodical tenancies. A term of years accompanied by an option for either party to renew the lease is, on similar principles, regarded as a lease for a term certain.

(c) Tenancies at will and at sufferance. Tenancies at will and tenancies at   **3–014** sufferance,[29] which are generally treated as part of the law relating to leasehold estates,[30] require special explanation,[31] as they are "unlike any other tenancy".[32] A tenancy at will is a tenancy which may continue indefinitely or may be determined by either party at any time.[33] This involves tenure[34] (*i.e.* a relationship of landlord and tenant) but no definite estate,[35] for there is no defined duration of the interest. The tenant has nothing which he can alienate.[36] T holds of L, but not for any appointed period. This resembles the earliest type of precarious tenure (*precarium*), which perhaps existed before estates were granted at all.[37]

---

[26] Cru.Dig. i, 47.

[27] *Post*, para. 14–086.

[28] *Prudential Assurance Co. Ltd v. London Residuary Body* [1992] 2 A.C. 386 at 394, *per* Lord Templeman. See *post*, para. 14–064.

[29] For these interests, see *post*, paras 14–075, 14–079.

[30] Preston i, 25, 28, 29, etc., speaks of an "estate at will". *cf.* Co.Litt. 55a, n.3; Bl.Comm. ii, 144; Cru.Dig. i, 242; Tudor L.C. 11.

[31] And see *post*, paras 14–075 *et seq.*

[32] *Wheeler v. Mercer* [1957] A.C. 416 at p. 427, *per* Viscount Simonds.

[33] *Post*, para. 14–078.

[34] Litt. 460; Co.Litt. 270b, n.1. Despite the tenure, a tenant at will was absolved from fealty because he had no estate: Litt. 132, Co.Litt. 63a.

[35] Litt. 68 ("no certain nor sure estate"); *cf.* Litt. 132.

[36] Bl.Comm. ii, 144.

[37] Bracton Bk. ii, c. 9, f. 27 (Digby, 178); Co.Litt. 55a, 266b, n.1; Bl.Comm. ii, 55.

A tenancy at sufferance arises where a tenancy has terminated but the tenant "holds over" (*i.e.* remains in possession) without the landlord's assent or dissent.[38] Such a tenant differs from a trespasser only in that his original entry was not wrongful and the landlord must re-enter before he can sue for trespass.[39] His "estate" in the land[40] is no true estate, and there is no real tenure[41]; the "tenancy" seems to have originated as a pretext for preventing the occupation being regarded as "adverse possession", which in time could bar the landlord's title altogether.[42] The old rules as to adverse possession have long disappeared,[43] and this "tenancy" might be permitted to go with them. Neither tenancies at will nor tenancies at sufferance, therefore, need be classified as additions to the catalogue of estates. If they are excluded, the classification can be simplified into freeholds and leaseholds.

3–015   **4. Leasehold tenure and estates.** In early times, when leaseholds were regarded as mere contractual rights to occupy land,[44] they were hardly estates at all. But in time, when the law came to give them full protection as proprietary interests,[45] they were added to the list of recognised legal estates. They always remained outside the feudal system of land-holding, but when they became a new type of estate it was impossible to deny that they were also a new type of tenure; for every tenant must hold by tenure of some sort if he is to hold an estate at all.[46]

This position has been recognised since the time of Littleton[47] (c. 1480), and is still recognised today; tenure is essential between landlord and tenant,[48] and leaseholds are within the statutory term[49] "land of any tenure".[50] By a paradox of history the relationship of landlord and tenant, originally no tenure at all, is now the only tenure which has any practical importance. It is non-feudal tenure and is not, of course, touched by the statute *Quia Emptores* 1290, which applies only to fees simple,[51] and so does not prevent the grant of sub-leases. The one remaining feudal tenure, socage, has been shorn of all the incidents of any consequence, whereas in the case of leaseholds a valuable

---

[38] See *post*, para. 14–079.
[39] See Co.Litt. 57b, 270b, n.1; *Land v. Sykes* [1992] 1 E.G.L.R. 1 at 4.
[40] So called: Cru.Dig. i, 249; Tudor L.C. 7.
[41] See Co.Litt. 270b, n.1.
[42] *Remon v. City of London Real Property Co. Ltd* [1921] 1 K.B. 49 at 58: Tudor L.C. 9.
[43] *Post*, para. 21–016.
[44] *Ante*, para. 3–009.
[45] *Post*, Appendix.
[46] *Ante*, para. 2–007.
[47] Litt. 132, saying that a tenant for years owes fealty to his landlord because of the tenure subsisting between them. Challis (65, 424–427) was unwilling to admit that terms of years were held in tenure; but his criticisms cannot be reconciled with the authorities (*ante*, para. 3–014, n. 34).
[48] *Milmo v. Carreras* [1946] K.B. 306 at 310, 311; *Parc Battersea Ltd v. Hutchinson* [1999] 22 E.G. 149 at 151.
[49] L.P.A. 1925, s.205(1)(ix).
[50] *Re Brooker* [1926] W.N. 93; *Re Berton* [1939] Ch. 200 at 203; *cf.* Hood & Challis 333; *post*, para. 14–002.
[51] *Ante*, para. 2–040.

rent (called rent-*service* because of the tenure[52]) is nearly always payable, and the lord, in addition to his tenurial remedy of distress,[53] usually has power to determine the lease if the tenant does not fulfil his obligations. In all these ways it appears that leases imply tenure. A lease is still personalty, as opposed to realty, but the most important differences to which this technicality gave rise have now been abolished.[54]

5. Interests in leaseholds. At common law a freehold estate could not be created out of a leasehold estate, for the obvious reason that a disposition by a leaseholder was only a disposition of personalty and he could give no seisin. The estates of freehold were peculiar to the land law and there was no corresponding system for personalty. But when other methods of conveyance not dependent upon seisin were introduced (for example, wills and trusts), these technical difficulties were overcome. Thus, if A held Blackacre for a term of 200 years, at common law he could not effectively assign the lease to X for life with remainder to Y absolutely. This would merely give the whole lease to X outright[55]; since limited estates in personalty could not be created, a limited gift was an absolute gift. But when, in due course, wills and settlements by way of trust were invented, A could carry out his design by employing one or other of the new kinds of disposition. Even when a trust was employed, however, it was impossible to create an entailed interest in personalty. It was only after 1925 that leasehold property could be entailed.[56] After 1996, it has not been possible to create an entail of either real or personal property.[57]

3–016

Section 3. Remainders and Reversions

An estate in land may exist in one of three different ways: in possession, in remainder or in reversion.[58] An estate in possession gives an immediate right to possession and enjoyment of the land. Estates in remainder or reversion, on the other hand, are future interests, and meanwhile some other person is usually entitled in possession. "Remainder" signifies a future gift to some person not previously entitled to the land. "Reversion" signifies the residue of an owner's interest after he has granted away some lesser estate in possession to some other person.[59]

3–017

[52] *Post*, para. 14–245.
[53] *Post*, para. 14–253.
[54] *Post*, para. 11–082.
[55] *Woodcock v. Woodcock* (1600) Cro.Eliz. 795; *Anon* (1552) 1 Dy. 74a: *North v. Butts* (1557) 2 Dy. 139b at 140b; "The gift of a term (like any other chattel) for an hour was good for ever"; *Wright d. Plowden v. Cartwright* (1757) 1 Burr. 282 at 284, *per* Lord Mansfield C.J.
[56] *Post*, para. 3–087.
[57] T.L.A.T.A. 1996, Sched. 1, para. 5; *post*, para. 3–037.
[58] Bl.Comm. ii, 163.
[59] "Reversion, reversio, commeth of the Latine word *revertor*, and signifieth a returning againe": Co.Litt. 142b.

Reversions and remainders are fully treated in Chapter 7, but at this point the general meaning of the terms may be made clear by examples. If A owns land in fee simple, and makes a grant "to B for life and thereafter to C in fee simple", B has a life estate in possession and so long as that estate continues C has a fee simple estate in remainder. When B dies, C has the fee simple in possession. A, having granted away his whole interest, has nothing. But if A had granted the land "to B for life and thereafter to C for life (or in tail)", B would have had a life estate in possession, C would have had a life estate (or estate tail) in remainder, and A would have retained the fee simple in reversion. So too if A had merely granted the land "to B for life", A would have had the fee simple in reversion while B had his life estate in possession. A reversion will thus be found in every case where the owner has made a grant which does not exhaust the whole of his own interest.[60]

Similarly, if A wishes to grant his land to B for life and thereafter to C in fee simple, and does so by single deed, C's estate is a remainder. But if the transaction is carried out in two steps by two successive grants, C's estate is a reversion, for he has acquired the reversion which was left in A after his initial grant to B. If A grants to B a lease, A is likewise said to retain the reversion; and if B grants a sub-lease to C both A and B have reversions. In the eye of the law a lease is always a lesser estate than a freehold,[61] so that if a tenant for life grants a lease for 100 years (for example) he retains a life estate in reversion expectant upon the lease.

Section 4. Seisin

3–018 **1. Meaning of seisin.** One very important distinction between freeholders and leaseholders was that only a freeholder had seisin. Seisin has nothing to do with the word "seizing", with its implication of violence. To medieval lawyers, as Maitland said, it suggested the very opposite—peace and quiet.[62] A man who was put in seisin of land was "set" there and continued to "sit" there.[62] Seisin thus denotes quiet possession of land,[63] but of a particular kind. Although at first the term was applied to the possession of a leaseholder as well as that of a freeholder,[64] during the fifteenth century it became confined to those who held an estate of freehold.[65] A leaseholder merely had possession; his landlord, as the freeholder, was seised.[66] And since, as we shall see, it was essential that someone should always have seisin, it followed that a freeholder remained seised even after he had granted a term of years and given

---

[60] See *post*, para. 7–008.
[61] *Ante*, para. 3–010.
[62] P. & M. ii, 30. Originally seisin had a specific feudal meaning, namely the possession of a tenant with his lord's authority: S.F.C. Milsom, *Historical Foundations of the Common Law* (2nd ed.), p. 120.
[63] Co.Litt. 153a; *Brediman's Case* (1607) 6 Co.Rep. 56b at 57b.
[64] Williams, *Seisin*, 4.
[65] Maitland, Coll.Pp. i, 359; Challis 99.
[66] Litt. 324; Co.Litt. 17a, 200b.

up physical possession of the land. Receipt of rent was evidence of seisin,[67] but a mere right to recover possession was not by itself seisin.[68] Further, only land of freehold tenure carried seisin with it. A copyholder could not be seised, even if he held a fee simple[69]; seisin in that case was in the lord of the manor.

2. Elements of seisin. From this it will be seen that a person was seised   **3–019** only if—

(i) he held an estate in freehold,

(ii) the land was of freehold tenure, and

(iii) either he had physical possession of the land, or a leaseholder or copyholder held the land from him.

Seisin, therefore, was a word which reflected the historical differences between the two main types of tenure and estates. It meant possession of land, disregarding those interests (leaseholds and copyholds) which the King's courts did not at first protect as property.[70] But the attribution of seisin to lords of manors and landlords, who had not possession, made it difficult to define seisin concisely. "Possession by a freeholder" embodies the fundamental idea.

3. Nature of seisin. Seisin was a characteristic product of the feudal   **3–020** system, and the three following rules help to explain its nature.

(i) Someone must always be seised. The person seised was the person against whom any default of feudal services had to be enforced,[71] and if seisin could be in abeyance the feudal system could not work. The common law abhorred an abeyance of seisin.[72]

(ii) The person seised must be a person with a status in the feudal scale, *i.e.* a person who held in free tenure for an estate of freehold. The person at the bottom of the scale was seised of the land. A mesne lord was seised of a seignory, *i.e.* the right to the tenant's services.[73]

---

[67] See *De Grey v. Richardson* (1747) 3 Atk. 469 at 472.

[68] *Leach v. Jay* (1878) 9 Ch.D. 42.

[69] Preston i, 212, 213. But occasionally copyholders were said to be seised: *e.g. Chudleigh's Case* (1595) 1 Co.Rep. 113b at 117a, explained in *Wade v. Bache* (1668) 1 Wms.Saund. 144 at 147.

[70] See *post*, Appendix.

[71] *Ante*, para. 2–039.

[72] For this principle and for exceptional cases, some common law and some statutory, see Challis 100, 101; C.A. 1881, s.30; *Re Pilling's Trusts* (1884) 26 Ch.D. 432 at 433.

[73] P. & M. ii, 38, 39.

    (iii) Seisin was a fact, not a right. If A, a freeholder, was dispossessed by B, B acquired seisin and A was disseised. A could, of course, recover the land from B, and be put back into seisin. But until he did so B claimed the freehold and, having actual possession, was seised in the eye of the law.

3–021   **4. Importance of seisin.** Seisin is no longer of importance, for the distinctions which gave it its peculiar meaning no longer exist. But it was the key to many of the mysteries of our land law before the statutory reforms of the 1830s and later.[74] In general it was the person seised—and he alone—who could exercise an owner's rights over the land. It did not matter whether his seisin was rightful or wrongful, or subject to the right of some other person to recover the land. Only the person seised could convey, for only he could give livery of seisin. Only the heir of the person seised could succeed to the land at that person's death. The fact of seisin, irrespective of the strength of the title of the person seised, used to be of greater technical importance than it is today.[75] Possession is still, of course, of great importance, but it is usually no longer necessary to distinguish it from seisin.

Part 2

ESTATES OF FREEHOLD

3–022   The two main branches of the law concerning estates of freehold relate to—

    (1) the words required to create each of the estates, and

    (2) the characteristics of each estate.

It should be noted that after 1996 it has not been possible to create an entail, though existing entails remain unaffected.[76]

Section 1. Words of Limitation

3–023   **1. Meaning.** In a conveyance *inter vivos* (*i.e.* a transfer of land between living persons) or in a will, the "words of limitation" are the words which limit (*i.e.* define or mark out) the estate to be taken. They do not confer an estate on any person. That is effected by "words of purchase".[77] In this

---

[74] For examples, see the previous edition of this work at p. 47.
[75] H.E.L. iii, 91, 92. For discussion of seisin, possession and ownership, see *post*, paras 3–115 *et seq.*
[76] *Post*, para. 3–037.
[77] For this distinction, see Fearne 79, 80.

technical sense a "purchaser" is a person who takes property by grant (*e.g.* by gift or sale) and not by operation of law (*e.g.* by intestacy[78]). In a conveyance today "to A in fee simple", the words "in fee simple" are words of limitation, because they "measure out the quantity of estate"[79] that A is to have, and the words "to A" are words of purchase that actually confer the estate on A.

2. *Inter vivos.* At common law, a freehold estate of inheritance[80] could be created in a conveyance *inter vivos* only by a phrase that included the word "heirs".[81] An attempt to grant a freehold estate in other terms (as "to A", or "to A in fee simple") gave A merely a life estate.[82] This incongruous rule survived until 1925, with only a minor mitigation in 1881. 3–024

3. In wills. In the case of gifts by will, the attitude of the courts was different. Conveyances *inter vivos* were originally accompanied by a solemn ceremony using a precise form of words. Later, as conveyances became more complex, professional assistance was usually sought. For these reasons and because any flaw in the transaction could normally be rectified if the grantor was still alive, such conveyances were construed strictly. Most wills of land were first enforced by the Court of Chancery, which looked to the intent of any transaction rather than the form. When the Statute of Wills 1540 first compelled common law courts to give effect to wills, they followed the same practice of liberal construction.[83] Wills were often home-made, and since they were operative only on the testator's death, mistakes could not be rectified.[84] Effect would therefore be given to the testator's intention provided that it was clear.[85] Strict words of limitation were not required. 3–025

The detailed rules will now be considered, taking the fee simple, fee tail and life estate in turn and dealing separately under each head with conveyances *inter vivos* and wills.[86]

A. Words of Limitation for a Fee Simple

I. CONVEYANCES *INTER VIVOS*

1. At common law

(1) *(a) Natural persons.* At common law the proper expression to employ was "and his heirs" following the grantee's name, *e.g.* "to A and his heirs".[87] 3–026

---

[78] *Post*, para. 11–087.

[79] *Goodright v. Wright* (1717) 1 P.Wms. 397, *per* Parker C.J.

[80] *i.e.* a fee simple or a fee tail.

[81] Litt. 1; Co.Litt. 20a. Even analogous expressions such as "relatives", "issue", "descendants", "assigns", "for ever", or "in tail" were ineffective: *ibid.*

[82] Litt. 1; Co.Litt. 20a.

[83] *Post*, para. 11–060.

[84] Testators' "ignorance and simplicity demands a favourable interpretation of their words": *Paramour v. Yardley* (1579) 2 Plowd. 539 at 540, in argument; *cf. Newis v. Lark* (1571) 2 Plowd. 403 at 413.

[85] *Throckmerton v. Tracy* (1555) 1 Plowd. 145 at 162, 163; Perkins, s.555.

[86] This is a shortened version of the text in the previous edition of this work at pp. 49–58.

[87] Preston ii, 1. For a solemn consideration of the apt words for monsters and hermaphrodites, see Co.Litt. 8a.

"Heir" in the singular did not suffice.[88] If "or" was used in place of "and",[89] or if any expression not containing the word "heirs" was employed,[90] a mere life estate was given. The words "and his heirs" were words of limitation not words of purchase.[91] They conferred no estate on any child of A who happened to be alive at the date of the conveyance, because a living person has no heir.[92] Only on A's death could his heir be ascertained.[93] However, a conveyance to "the heirs of A", A being dead at the time of the conveyance, gave a fee simple to the person who was A's heir.[94]

(b) Corporations

3–027   (1) TYPES. Different rules governed conveyances to corporations, which are themselves legal persons, distinct from the individuals who represent them. This artificial personality may be created by royal charter,[95] by statute, or by some rule of law. Corporations are usually classified as of two kinds, aggregate and sole. A corporation aggregate is made up of two or more individuals acting under a corporate name, *e.g.* the mayor and corporation of a borough, a dean and chapter, or a limited company. A corporation sole consists of a single individual holding an office which has a perpetual succession. Few corporations sole are known to the law: examples are (at common law) the Crown,[96] a bishop, a parson; and (by statute) the Treasury Solicitor and the Secretary of State for Defence.[97]

3–028   (2) CORPORATIONS AGGREGATE. A conveyance of land to a corporation aggregate by its corporate name has always given it a fee simple without any special words of limitation.[98] For since such a corporation neither died nor had heirs, it could take no other estate, apart from a lease.

---

[88] Co.Litt. 8b; Preston ii, 397; Challis 221, 222; *cf. Re Davison's Settlement* [1913] 2 Ch. 498.
[89] Co.Litt. 8b; Preston ii, 11; *Mallory's Case* (1601) 5 Co.Rep. 111b at 112a; contrast *Wright v. Wright* (1750) 1 Ves.Sen. 409 at 411.
[90] *e.g.* "to A and his successors": *Bankes v. Salisbury Diocesan Council of Education Inc.* [1960] Ch. 631 at 644; "to A for ever", or "to A in fee simple": Litt. 1.
[91] *Doe d. Long v. Laming* (1760) 2 Burr. 1100 at 1106.
[92] Co.Litt. 8b; (1300) Y.B. 2 Edw. 2. Mich. (S.S.) 70. Prior to A's death, any such child had only a *spes successionis* (a hope of succeeding) to the fee simple if A died without having otherwise disposed of it: *Re Parsons* (1890) 45 Ch.D. 51 at 55. Descent of real property to the heir on intestacy has been abolished: A.E.A. 1925, s.45(1); *post*, para. 11–087.
[93] *Re Parsons, supra,* at 63.
[94] For this and other exceptional cases, see the previous edition of this work at p. 50.
[95] The Crown has the prerogative power of incorporation.
[96] There has been some confusion as to the status of the Crown caused principally by misleading statements in *Town Investments Ltd v. Department of the Environment* [1978] A.C. 359. However it has now been held that "at least for some purposes, the Crown has a legal personality. It can be appropriately described as a corporation sole of a corporation aggregate . . . The Crown can hold property and enter into contracts": *Re M* [1994] 1 A.C. 377 at 424, *per* Lord Woolf. In fact, the Crown has long been recognised to be a corporation sole: see *e.g.* Bl.Comm. i, 469; *Att.-Gen v. Köhler* (1861) 9 H.L.C. 654 at 670; *Re Mason* [1928] Ch. 385 at 401; (1992) 108 L.Q.R. 173; (1992) 142 N.L.J. 1315 at 1317 (H.W.R.W.).
[97] C.T. Carr, *Corporations*, 15, 23–25; Defence (Transfer of Functions) Act 1964, s.2(1).
[98] *Re Woking U.D.C. (Basingstoke Canal) Act 1911* [1914] 1 Ch. 300 at 312; Co.Litt. 94b.

(3) CORPORATIONS SOLE. Corporations sole, on the other hand, were mortal **3–029** men, and died.[99] The general rule at common law for corporations sole was that land would pass with the office only if limited to the holder "and his successors".[1] A conveyance in fee simple to the See of Ely would therefore have to be phrased "to the Bishop of Ely and his successors".

At common law (as also by statute) ecclesiastical corporations had restricted powers of alienation.[2] A person could not prejudice the rights of his successors, so that any rights which he attempted to grant in the church lands, except as empowered by statute,[3] would terminate at his death.[4] It was sometimes said therefore that he had only a life interest and that the fee was in abeyance.[5] But it seems more probable that the corporation sole possessed a qualified fee[6] to which special restrictions attached, and which was in abeyance only when the office was vacant.[7] Where the vacancy exists at the time of the conveyance, statute has retrospectively provided that the property is to vest in the successor as soon as the vacancy is filled, without prejudice to his right to disclaim the property.[8]

A conveyance to a corporation sole without any words of limitation would give the incumbent merely a life estate. But a conveyance to him "and his heirs" would give him a fee simple in his private capacity, under the ordinary rule,[9] for the person of the grantee was clearly described[10] and the proper words of limitations were used.

2. By statute. After 1881 it became possible to convey a fee simple by **3–030** using the words "in fee simple" as an alternative to the words "and his

---

[99] Maitland, Coll.Pp., iii, 240. In his essay "The Corporation Sole" (*ibid.* p. 210; (1900) 16 L.Q.R. 335) Maitland demonstrated that a corporation sole was never a true legal person at all, since it lacked immortality; it was either "natural man or juristic abortion". A corporation sole could not convey to himself as an individual (*Salter v. Grosvenor* (1724) 8 Mod. 303; and see *Howley v. Knight* (1849) 14 Q.B. 240); but he could be tenant in common with himself as individual (Co.Litt. 190a) which implies two distinct legal persons. Probably no explanation will fit all the facts.

[1] Co.Litt. 8b, 94b; *Ex p. Vicar of Castle Bytham* [1895] 1 Ch. 348 at 354; but consider *Bentley v. Bishop of Ely* (1732) Fitz. 305; Co.Litt. 94b, n.5. Grants to the Crown were an exception to this rule and did not require the words "and his successors": Co.Litt. 9b; Preston ii, 50.

[2] Co.Litt. 44a, 341b; Challis 225.

[3] See Halsb. vol. 14, para. 1153.

[4] See n.2, *supra.*

[5] *St. Gabriel, Fenchurch Street (Rector) v. City of London Real Property Co. Ltd* [1896] P. 95 at 101; *Re. St. Paul's Covent Garden* [1974] Fam. 1 at 4; *cf.* Litt. 648.

[6] Co.Litt. 341b. Co.Litt. 44a says that with the consent of the patron and ordinary a parson could make a grant in fee at common law. See also Cru.Dig. i, 114.

[7] Litt. 647; Challis 101; and see *St. Edmundsbury and Ipswich Diocesan Board of Finance v. Clark (No. 2)* [1973] 1 W.L.R. 1572 at 1580.

[8] L.P.A. 1925, s.180(2).

[9] See Shep. Touch. 237. The contrary suggestion that these words create a life estate (see Norton, *Deeds* 333) is not supported by the authorities cited.

[10] It would seem from the discussion of the *Chantry Priest's Case* in Co.Litt. 9a, and from Preston ii, 48, 49, that it did not matter whether the private or official title of the grantee was used; but contrast Co.Litt. 94b, n.5. Normally, both would be used together, *e.g.* to A, Bishop of Ely. If the grant was to him, "his heirs and successors", the title used might help to resolve the ambiguity: Co.Litt. 9a.

heirs".[11] The necessity for words of limitation in creating a fee simple was finally abolished by the Law of Property Act 1925,[12] in the case of all deeds executed after 1925. The grantee now takes "the fee simple or other the whole interest which the grantor had power to convey in such land unless a contrary intention appears in the conveyance". The same is true of a conveyance to a corporation sole by its corporate designation. It is no longer necessary to indicate a grant to a corporation as such by using the word "successors".[13] The rule formerly applicable to grants has now been reversed. A conveyance without words of limitation passes the largest, and not the smallest, of the possible freehold estates. In practice, the words "in fee simple" are always inserted to make it clear that there is no contrary intention.[14]

II. GIFTS BY WILL

3–031   **1. Before 1838.** Before 1838 no formal words of limitation were required in a will, but it was necessary for the will to show an intent to pass the fee simple.[15] Thus "to A for ever", or "to A and his heir", or "to A to dispose at will and pleasure" all sufficed to pass the fee simple.[16] But it was for the devisee to show from the terms of the will (read as a whole) that a fee simple was intended to pass; a devise "to A" prima facie passed merely a life estate.[17]

3–032   **2. After 1837.** By the Wills Act 1837,[18] any devise of land passes the fee simple or other the whole interest of which the testator has power to dispose unless a contrary intention is apparent from the will. This provision reverses the onus of proof, so that a devise "to A" passes the fee simple unless a contrary intention is shown.[19] As the same rule was extended to deeds in 1925,[20] there is now no longer any difference between the rule for deeds and the rule for wills.

---

[11] C.A. 1881, s.51.

[12] s.60(1). As to rentcharges, see *post*, para. 18–024. As to easements, see *post*, para. 18–092.

[13] s.60(2). A conveyance by both personal and corporate designations, *e.g.* "to A, Bishop of Ely", is now even more ambiguous than before, since in most cases under the previous law the necessary words of limitation made the matter plain.

[14] There was formerly an important conveyancing reason for including these words: *post*, para. 5–048.

[15] Preston ii, 68; *ante*, para. 3–025.

[16] *Chamberlayne v. Turner* (1628) Cro.Car. 129; *Countess of Bridgwater v. Duke of Bolton* (1704) 6 Mod. 106 at 111; Gilb. *Uses*. 24. For other examples, see Cru.Dig. vi. Chap. 11.

[17] Preston ii, 78; Cru.Dig. vi, 259–274.

[18] s.28. The Act applies to any will made or confirmed after 1837: s.34.

[19] The rule applies to the transfer of existing interests and not to the creation of new ones to which the old rule still applies: *Nicholls v. Hawkes* (1853) 10 Hare 342. In practice this can seldom occur now; *e.g.* it is only in very rare cases that a perpetual rentcharge can be granted: *post*, para. 18–018. A grant of such a rentcharge "to A" by will will take effect as grant for A's lifetime in the absence of contrary intention.

[20] *Supra.*

B. Words of Limitation for a Fee Tail

I. CONVEYANCES *INTER VIVOS*

1. At common law

(a) "Heirs" with words of procreation. The expression required to create a **3–033**
fee tail was the word "heirs" followed by some words of procreation, *i.e.*
words which confined "heirs" to descendants of the original grantee.[21] An
example is "to X and the heirs of his body". The word "heirs" was essential,[22] but any words of procreation sufficed.[23] Words of procreation were
required to restrict the word "heirs", which extended to all the "heirs general", including relatives other than descendants of the grantee, such as his
brothers, uncles or cousins. An entail, however, was an interest that could pass
only to lineal descendants of the original grantee, who were known as "heirs
special".[24]

(b) Restricted entails. By the addition of suitable words an entail could be **3–034**
further restricted so that it descended only to a particular class of descendants.[25] There were thus the following types of entail:

(i) a tail general, *e.g.* "to A and the heirs of his body", where any
descendants of A, male or female, could inherit;

(ii) a tail male, *e.g.* "to A and the heirs male of his body", in which
case only male descendants of A who could trace an unbroken
descent from him through males could inherit, and not, *e.g.* a son
of A's daughter[26];

(iii) a tail female, *e.g.* "to A and the heirs female of his body", where
corresponding rules applied.[27]

In addition, a "special tail" could be created, confining the heirs entitled to
those descended from a specified spouse, such as "to A and the heirs of his
body begotten upon Mary", when only issue of A and Mary could inherit;

---

[21] Preston ii, 477, 478.

[22] Therefore phrases such as "to A and his issue" or "to A and his seed" when used in a deed
would not create an entail: *Wheeler v. Duke* (1832) 1 Cr. & M. 210; Co.Litt. 20b. A and any
issue alive would probably have taken joint life estates: see (1936) 6 C.L.J. 67 at 81 (S. J.
Bailey).

[23] *e.g.* "to A and the heirs of his flesh" or "to A and the heirs from him proceeding": *Idle v. Cook*
(1705) 1 P.Wms. 70 at 73; 2 Ld.Raym. 1144 at 1153; *Beresford's Case* (1607) 7 Co.Rep. 41a
at 42a.

[24] See *Doe d. Littledale v. Smeddle* (1818) 2 B. & Ald. 126; *Galley v. Barrington* (1824) 2 Bing.
387.

[25] See Challis 294.

[26] Litt. 21. 24.

[27] Litt. 22.

Mary, of course, took nothing.[28] A special tail could exist in any of the three above forms: special tail general, special tail male, special tail female. The unrestricted types of entail could by contrast be called "general tail": general tail, general tail male, general tail female.

3–035 *(c) Limitation not purchase.* In a conveyance "to A and the heirs of his body", the words following A's name were words of limitation and not purchase. They conferred no estate on A's heir presumptive or heir apparent but merely a *spes successionis*. However, a conveyance of land "to the heirs of the body of A", made after A's death, gave a fee tail to the heir of A's body.[29]

3–036 **2. By statute.** After 1881, by provisions similar to those enacted for the creation of a fee simple, it became possible to create a fee tail by using the words "in tail" as an alternative to "heirs" plus words of procreation.[30] Thus "to X in tail" would create a fee tail.[31] These rules were preserved by the Law of Property Act 1925[32] and the law thus remained unchanged. The policy of the Act of 1925 was to maintain the strict rules for limitation of entails. In this way, entails could not arise unintentionally but had to be deliberately created. Expressions intended to create entails that would not have created them before 1926 would not therefore have created them after 1925.[33]

3–037 **3. No entails can be created after 1996.** Entails became virtually obsolete[34] and their prospective abolition was recommended by the Law Commission.[35] Parliament has now implemented that recommendation. Under the Trusts of Land and Appointment of Trustees Act 1996,[36] where after 1996 a person purports by an instrument[37]—

> (i) to grant to another an entailed interest in real or personal property, the instrument operates not to create an entail, but as a declaration that the property is held absolutely for the person to whom the interest was granted; and

---

[28] Litt. 29; Preston ii, 488.

[29] *Mandeville's Case* (1328) Y.B. 2 Edw. 3, Hil. pl. 1 and 2; Co.Litt. 26b. A conveyance after A's death "to the heir of the body of A" passed a mere life estate to such an heir: *Chambers v. Taylor* (1837) 2 My. & Cr. 376; but see *Marshall v. Peascod* (1861) 2 J. & H. 73 at 75. For other special cases, see the previous edition of this work at p. 56.

[30] C.A. 1881, s.51.

[31] The entail could be restricted, *e.g.* "to A in tail male".

[32] ss.60(4)(b), (c); 130(1), now repealed by T.L.A.T.A. 1996 s.25(2), Sched. 4.

[33] For the effect of such expressions, see L.P.A. 1925, s.130(2); *post*, para. 3–038.

[34] It appears that they were still sometimes created in certain parts of the country, notably in the north east of England.

[35] (1989) Law Com. No. 181, para. 16.1.

[36] Sched. 1, para. 5. The Act came into force on January 1, 1997.

[37] An entail, whether of real or personal property, could only be created by an instrument: see L.P.A. 1925, ss.130(6), 205(1)(xxvi); S.L.A. 1925, ss.1, 117(1)(xxiv).

(ii) to declare himself to be a tenant in tail of real or personal property, the instrument is not effective to create an entailed interest.

Thus, for example, if A purports to create a settlement of Blackacre under which B is to be a tenant in tail,[38] B will be absolutely entitled to the property. Similarly if A declares himself trustee of Whiteacre for B for life, thereafter to himself in tail, the attempt to create an entail in reversion will be ineffective and A will have a fee simple in reversion instead. The Act has no effect on entails created before 1997.[39]

II. GIFTS BY WILL

The rule before 1926 was that any words showing an intention to create an entail were sufficient in a will, even if no technical expressions were used.[40] The Law of Property Act 1925[41] made the rules for the creation of entails more rigid than before. It laid down that informal expressions would no longer suffice to create an entail by will, but that expressions that would have been effective to create an entail in a deed before 1926 must be employed. This reflected the policy already mentioned and made the creation of an entail a matter of technical words rather than a matter of intention. The same rules therefore applied to both deeds and wills, but in contrast to the position of the fee simple, it was the restrictive rules applicable to deeds rather than the more liberal rules for wills that were extended.

3–038

Special provision was made for expressions that could formerly have created an entail in a will but could no longer do so.[42] Such expressions, in both deeds and wills, and for both realty and personality, operated to create "absolute, fee simple or other interests corresponding to those which, if the property affected had been personal estate, would have been created therein by similar expressions before [1926]".[43] The effect of this provision was (and is likely to remain) uncertain. It has been the subject of some comment[44] but no reported decision. It is at least clear that no entail could arise in such cases because personality could not be entailed before 1926.[45]

The prohibition on the creation of entails after 1996 applies as much to wills as it does to any other form of instrument. The effect of a purported grant of an entail by will is therefore to confer on the grantee an absolute interest in the property.

---

[38] Whether in possession or in reversion.

[39] Although this is not explicitly stated in the Act, it is implicit: *cf.* T.L.A.T.A. 1996, s.2.

[40] *e.g.* "to A and his seed": Co.Litt. 9b; "to A and his descendants": *Re Sleeman* [1929] W.N. 16; "to A and his issue": *Slater v. Dangerfield* (1846) 15 M. & W. 263 at 272. See Preston ii, 534 *et seq.*

[41] s.130(1).

[42] L.P.A. 1925, s.130(2).

[43] *ibid.*

[44] See (1936) 6 C.L.J. 67; (1949) 9 C.L.J. 185 (S.J. Bailey), and contrast (1945) 9 C.L.J. 46 (R.E.M.).

[45] *Post*, para. 3–087.

C. *Words of Limitation for a Life Estate*

I. CONVEYANCES *INTER VIVOS*

3–039   A life estate was created before 1926 either by words showing an intention to create a life estate, such as "to A for life", or by using expressions insufficient to create a fee simple of fee tail, such as "to A", or "to A for ever". The rule that a life estate was created by such imperfect expressions has already been explained.[46] A tenancy for an indefinite period more than from year to year was usually construed as a tenancy for life.[47]

After 1925, a fee simple (or the whole of the interest the grantor has power to convey, if it is less than a fee simple) passes unless a contrary intention is shown.[48] Thus in order to create a life interest words showing an intention to do so must normally be used, *e.g.* "to A for life".

II. WILLS

3–040   Before the Wills Act 1837 a devise passed only a life estate unless an intention to create a fee simple or fee tail was shown.[49] Section 28 of the Act provided, as has already been noticed,[50] that the fee simple passes unless a contrary intention is shown. The rule for wills therefore anticipated the modern rule for deeds, and they are now the same. Some words of limitation are therefore equally necessary in order to create a life interest by will.

Section 2. Nature of the Estates of Freehold

A. *The Fee Simple*

3–041   The fee simple is the most substantial estate which can exist in land.[51] Although strictly speaking it is still held in tenure and therefore falls short of absolute ownership, in practice it is absolute ownership,[52] for nearly all traces of the old feudal burdens have disappeared. "A tenant in fee simple enjoys all the advantages of absolute ownership, except the form."[53] His powers of "enjoying, using and abusing" his land are indeed limited in many ways by statute and by the rights of his neighbours, but they are not limited by any inherent narrowness in the concept of property in land. A fee simple may exist

---

[46] *Ante*, para. 3–024.
[47] *Re Coleman's Estate* [1907] 1 I.R. 488 at 492; and see *post*, para. 14–055.
[48] *Ante*, para. 3–030.
[49] *Ante*, para. 3–031.
[50] *Ante*, para. 3–032.
[51] Litt. 11; Williams R.P. 6.
[52] See Challis 218; and as to the possible effect of the 1925 legislation, see 70 L.J.News. 4, 20 (T.C. Williams).
[53] 75 S.J. 843 (T.C. Williams). To Joshua Williams' statement that "the first thing the student has to do is to get rid of the idea of absolute ownership", Maitland added "and the next thing the student has to do is painfully to reacquire it" (*ibid.*).

in an upper storey of a building, separately from the rest[54]; and it may even also be made movable, so as to shift from plot to plot within a defined area,[55] or so as to vary with changes of a boundary such as the foreshore.[56]

Pre-eminent among a fee simple owner's rights are his right of alienation (the right to transfer to another the whole or any part of his interest in the land) and his right to everything in, on, or over the land. These will be considered in turn, and will be followed by a discussion of the various types of fee simple.

I. RIGHT OF ALIENATION

Today a tenant in fee simple may dispose of his estate in whatever way he **3–042** thinks fit, either by will[57] or *inter vivos*.[58] This has not always been so. Before the Norman Conquest much land seems to have been freely alienable,[59] but under the universal feudalism of the Normans the tendency at first was to restrict alienation.[60] Two people might suffer if a tenant was able to dispose of his land: his heir and his lord.

1. Rights of the heir. In early law the heir apparent or heir presumptive was **3–043** regarded as having a definite interest in the land, so that the tenant could not dispose of the land without his consent; and as subsequent events might show that the prospective heir was not the person who would have succeeded to the land had it not been alienated, it was not unusual to get the consent of as many near relatives as possible.[61]

By about 1200 this doctrine had disappeared, and a tenant in fee simple was able to alienate his land *inter vivos* so as to defeat all claims by his heirs.[62] Thereafter the prospective heir was regarded as having no estate or interest in

---

[54] "A man may have an inheritance in an upper chamber though the lower buildings and soil be in another": Co.Litt. 48b. There have long been so-called "flying freeholds" in New Square, Lincoln's Inn, which statute regulated: see Lincoln's Inn Act 1860; (1977) 41 Conv.(N.S.) 11 (M. Vitoria). See too *Sovmots Investments Ltd v. Secretary of State for the Environment* [1979] A.C. 114, *e.g.* at 179, 184. For a claim to a "subterranean flying freehold" see *Grigsby v. Melville* [1974] 1 W.L.R. 80 at 83, *per* Russell L.J. For a period in the late 1950s and early 1960s, it was common to create freehold flats to escape the provisions of the Rent Acts, but this practice has been discontinued. For the possibility of a system of flying freeholds to be called "commonhold", see *post*, para. 16–029.

[55] *Weldon v. Bridgewater* (1595) Cro. Eliz. 421; Co.Litt. 4a, 48b; 1 Preston 258; Challis, 54. In earlier times such estates were commonly held in the open fields, strips being allotted annually in rotation. Examples may still be found, *e.g.* a fee simple in such part of a specified area as may be allocated in an annual drawing of lots (the "lot meadows" at Yarnton, Oxfordshire): see (1936) 1 Conv. (N.S.) 53 (F.E. Farrer); (1978) 122 S.J. 723 (W.A. Greene); [1982] Conv. 208 (R.E. Annand).

[56] *Baxendale v. Instow Parish Council* [1982] Ch. 14.

[57] Subject to proper provision being made for near relatives in certain cases: *post*, para. 11–004.

[58] Subject to the law against racial discrimination in dispositions of land: Race Relations Act 1976, ss.21–24.

[59] H.E.L. ii, 68, iii, 73.

[60] Williams R.P. 68; Cru. Dig. iv, 3.

[61] P. & M. ii, 309, 310.

[62] *ibid.*, 311, 313; (1976) 92 L.Q.R. 108 (J.L. Barton).

the land but only a mere hope of succeeding to it, a *spes successionis*.[63] And it was then clear that the words "and his heirs" in a conveyance were words of limitation, not words of purchase.[64] By the beginning of the fourteenth century the existence of a fee simple had ceased to be in any way dependent upon the existence of heirs of the original owner. Strictly, if land were given "to A and his heirs", the fee simple should have determined as soon as A and all his heirs were dead, even if A had alienated the land. But a fee simple became potentially eternal when the courts decided that if a fee simple was alienated it continued to exist so long as there was no failure of heirs of the owner for the time being.[65]

Although after the twelfth century a tenant in fee simple could alienate his land *inter vivos* and so defeat the expectations of his relatives, he could not dispose of it by will. In some cases devises were permitted as late as the latter half of the thirteenth century, but from the end of that century the rule was settled that land was not devisable. Any land not disposed of before death must descend to the heir and to no one else: for, said Glanville, "only God can make an heir".[66] This remained law until wills of land were made possible by uses[67] and later by the Statute of Wills 1540.[68]

3–044 **2. Rights of the lord.** The feudal aspects of alienation, the two methods of subinfeudation and substitution, and the final prohibition of the former by the Statute *Quis Emptores* 1290, have already been discussed.[69] Both methods of alienation could work to the disadvantage of the lord. By *Quia Emptores* all land held in fee simple became freely alienable by substitution but by substitution only: the grantee became tenant of the grantor's lord, not of the grantor. From this time onwards no feudal restrictions hampered the alienability of the fee simple, except that fines were sometimes payable on alienation of land held directly of the Crown until 1660,[70] and of copyhold land until 1926.[71]

II. RIGHT TO EVERYTHING IN, ON OR OVER THE LAND

3–045 **1. General rule.** There is an ancient maxim: *cujus est solum, ejus est usque ad coelum et ad inferos*,[72] meaning that the owner of the soil is presumed to

---

[63] This was not an assignable interest at common law, but "an absolutely bare possibility": Challis 76.

[64] *Ante*, para. 3–023.

[65] Y.B. 33–35 Edw. 1 (R.S.) 362 (1306); H.E.L. iii, 106, 107.

[66] P. & M. ii, 325; H.E.L. iii, 75, 76. But customs to devise were admitted, *e.g.* under the customs of gavelkind or burgage, *ante*, paras 2–019–2–025.

[67] See the previous edition of this work at p. 1165.

[68] *ibid.*, at p. 1168.

[69] *Ante.*, para. 2–041.

[70] *Ante*, para. 2–044. In other cases fines upon alienation were illegal, as being contrary to *Quia Emptores*: *Merttens v. Hill* [1901] 1 Ch. 842.

[71] *Ante*, para. 2–051.

[72] *Mitchell v. Moseley* [1914] 1 Ch. 438 at 450.

own everything "up to the sky and down to the centre of the earth".[73] But this is inaccurate as regards the right to airspace, which extends only to such height as is necessary for the ordinary use and enjoyment of the land and structures upon it.[74] As regards the land itself, the owner in fee simple is prima facie in possession of, and therefore entitled to, any chattel not the property of any known person which is found under or attached to his land,[75] *e.g.* in a field[76] or in the bed of a canal.[77] This rule also applies to any unattached chattel found on the land if, but only if, before the chattel is found, the owner has manifested an intention to exercise control over things which may be upon the land.[78] Otherwise the finder is prima facie entitled as against the land-owner, though not against the true owner of the chattel, if any.[79] All of these rules are now qualified by the provisions of the Treasure Act 1996 which is explained later.[80]

The owner is also entitled to land added by gradual accretion, as where his territory is extended by deposits caused by currents in the sea or in a lake or by the action of winds, or even by human action, provided that it is not the deliberate action of the claimant himself.[81] Conversely the owner may lose part of his land from erosion, sometimes called avulsion or diluvion, brought about by similar causes. The doctrine of accretion requires that the process should be gradual and imperceptible, but the fact that movement could occasionally be detected by an observer may not be fatal. Where the land affected is subject to a lease, the tenant obtains the benefit of the accretion and the terms of the lease apply to it. But a conveyance or lease of land may be

---

[73] "A colourful phrase often upon the lips of lawyers since it was first coined by Accursius in Bologna in the 13th Century": *Bernstein of Leigh (Baron) v. Skyviews & General Ltd* [1978] Q.B. 479 at 485, *per* Griffiths J. And see *Corbett v. Hill* (1870) L.R. 9 Eq. 671 at 673; *Wandsworth Board of Works v. United Telephone Co.* (1884) 13 Q.B.D. 904 at 915 ("fanciful phrases"); *Commissioner for Railways v. Valuer-General* [1974] A.C. 328 at 351 ("this brocard"). For a critique, see [1991] C.L.J. 252 at 253 *et seq.* (K.J. Gray).

[74] *Bernstein of Leigh (Baron) v. Skyviews & General Ltd, supra* (aircraft taking photographs: no trespass). However, it is well settled that "a party is not entitled to swing his crane over neighbouring land without the consent of the neighbouring owner": *London & Manchester Assurance Co. Ltd v. O. & H. Construction Ltd* [1989] 2 E.G.L.R. 185 at 186, *per* Harman J. See too *Anchor Brewhouse Developments Ltd v. Berkley House (Docklands Developments) Ltd* [1987] 2 E.G.L.R. 173; and *post,* para. 3–051.

[75] *Elwes v. Brigg Gas Co.* (1886) 33 Ch. D. 562 (prehistoric boat excavated by tenant held property of landlord); *South Staffordshire Water Co. v. Sharman* [1896] 2 Q.B. 44 (gold rings found by workmen in pool held property of landowner); *Waverley Borough Council v. Fletcher* [1996] Q.B. 334 (medieval gold brooch excavated by member of the public using metal detector in recreation ground); [1996] Conv. 216 (J. Stevens).

[76] *Att.-Gen. of the Duchy of Lancaster v. G.E. Overton (Farms) Ltd* [1982] Ch. 277.

[77] *R. v. Rowe* (1859) 28 L.J.M.C. 128.

[78] *Parker v. British Airways Board* [1982] Q.B. 1004 (gold bracelet found in airport lounge; no claim by owner: finder entitled). Trespassers cannot claim as finders: *ibid.*

[79] *Bridges v. Hawkesworth* (1851) 15 Jur. 1079; *Hannah v. Peel* [1945] K.B. 509; see Goodhart, *Essays in Jurisprudence and the Common Law,* 75–90.

[80] *Post,* para. 3–053.

[81] *Southern Centre of Theosophy Inc. v. South Australia* [1982] A.C. 706, containing a full discussion of the authorities including Bracton bk. 2, ch. 2, f.9; Bl. Comm. ii, 262; *R. v. Lord Yarborough* (1828) 2 Bli. (N.S.) 147; *Att.-Gen. v. M'Carthy* [1911] 2 I.R. 260; *Att.-Gen. of Southern Nigeria v. John Holt & Co. (Liverpool) Ltd* [1915] A.C. 599.

so worded as to exclude accretions or movements of boundaries altogether.[82] Sudden accretions of substantial size belong to the Crown, as also do islands which arise in the sea.[83] The foreshore (the land between high and low water[84]) is the property of the Crown, unless the Crown has parted with its rights in any particular place.[85]

3–046 An owner can, if he wishes, divide his land horizontally or in any other way. He can dispose of minerals under the surface, or the top floor of a building,[86] so as to make them separate properties. But unless some contrary intention is shown[87] a grant will normally pass the owner's whole interest in the space above and below the land, so that, for example, a lease will give the tenant the right to the airspace above the land let.[88] The owner may in general use his property in the natural course of user in any way he thinks fit.[89] He may waste or despoil the land as he pleases, and he is not normally liable merely because he neglects it.[90] He can sue for damages or injunctions against those who commit trespass or nuisance.[91] It sometimes happens that a landowner wishes to undertake works on his property that can be carried out only by going on to his neighbour's land. If the neighbour refuses his consent, the landowner may apply to the court for an "access order" to enable him to do works that are reasonably necessary for the preservation of all or any part of his land. This will be granted only if those works cannot be carried out (or would be substantially more difficult to carry out) without entry on to the neighbour's land.[92]

3–047   **2. Qualifications.** The absolute freedom of the owner is qualified in many ways.

3–048   *(a) Other rights over his land.* He is naturally subject to such rights as others have over his land, such as rights of way, the rights of tenants under leases, and the rights of mortgagees.

---

[82] As in *Baxendale v. Instow Parish Council* [1982] Ch. 14 (conveyance of foreshore).

[83] Bl. Comm. ii, 262, discussing also (at 261) islands which arise in rivers.

[84] On the meaning of "the low water line", see *Anderson v. Alnwick D.C.* [1993] 1 W.L.R. 1156.

[85] Halsb. vol. 8, para. 1418.

[86] *Ante*, para. 3–041; and see L.P.A. 1925, s.205(1)(ix).

[87] *Truckell v. Stock* [1957] 1 W.L.R. 161.

[88] *Kelsen v. Imperial Tobacco Co. (of Great Britain and Ireland) Ltd* [1957] 2 Q.B. 334; *Grigsby v. Melville* [1974] 1 W.L.R. 80; *Davies v. Yadegar* [1990] 1 E.G.L.R. 71; *Haines v. Florensa* [1990] 1 E.G.L.R. 73.

[89] *Wilson v. Waddell* (1876) 2 App. Cas. 95 at 99; (1895) 11 L.Q.R. 225 (T.C. Williams).

[90] *Giles v. Walker* (1890) 24 Q.B.D. 656 (thistles); *Brady v. Warren* [1900] 2 I.R. 632 (rabbits). But see *Davey v. Harrow Corporation* [1958] 1 Q.B. 60.

[91] Even after parting with the land; *G.U.S. Property Management Ltd v. Littlewoods Mail Order Stores Ltd* 1982 S.C. 157 at 177 (H.L.) Abatement by means of self-redress can only be employed in simple cases (such as lopping branches that overhang from a neighbour's tree) or in cases or urgency: *Burton v. Winters* [1993] 1 W.L.R. 1077 at 1080 *et seq.*

[92] Access to Neighbouring Land Act 1992, considered *post*, para. 18–255. For the Party Walls, etc., Act, see *post*, para. 9–109.

(b) Statute. In the last century, and particularly during the last 70 years, **3–049**
there has been much legislation imposing on landowners restrictions and
liabilities in the public interest and subjecting them to interference by public
authorities. It was said more than half a century ago that "the fundamental
assumption of modern statute law is that the landowner holds his land for the
public good".[93]

These statutes are of great importance but they do not, generally speaking,
affect the principles of the law of real property. They restrict the liberties of
great numbers of landowners and so many affect, among other things, the
prices at which they can sell their land and the terms of sale. But the substance
of the various possible transactions in land is not thereby altered: sales,
settlements, leases, mortgages, and so on, continue as before. These statutes
form a body of regulatory or administrative law which stands apart from
property law. The statutes that regulate planning[94] and provide protection for
tenants[95] are treated concisely in this book. But those statutes that govern
housing[96] and public health[97] are not considered, since they lie outside the
subject. The same applies to the law about compulsory purchase of land and
compensation,[98] under which many public authorities have power to acquire
land for public purposes, subject to compensation. The Leasehold Reform Act
1967 and the Leasehold Reform, Housing and Urban Development Act 1993
are in a class by themselves. They provide a mechanism by which certain
categories of tenant are able to purchase the freehold from their landlords for
their own private purposes and without payment of full compensation. These
remarkable statutes are explained alongside the legislation that protects
tenants.[99]

(c) Liability in tort. A landowner may be liable in tort for injuries caused to **3–050**
third parties by his acts and omissions, *e.g.* if he withdraws support to which
his neighbour is entitled,[1] or if water in a reservoir escapes,[2] or if a lamp
projecting over a highway gets into a dangerous state of repair and injuries a
passer-by.[3] In the same way he may be liable for nuisance, *e.g.* if he makes an
unusual and excessive collection of manure which attracts flies and causes a
smell,[4] or if he permits go-kart racing on his land that causes excessive
noise.[5]

---

[93] (1936) 49 Harv.L.R. 426 at p. 436 (W. I. Jennings).
[94] *Post*, para. 22–009.
[95] *Post*, para. 22–062.
[96] Housing Acts 1985 and 1988, and Local Government and Housing Act 1989.
[97] See the Public Health Acts 1875 to 1961, the Building Act 1984, and Environmental Protection
Act 1990.
[98] The principal statutes are the Acquisition of Land Act 1981, Compulsory Purchase Act 1965,
Land Compensation Acts 1961 and 1973, and the Planning and Compensation Act 1991.
[99] *Post*, para. 22–232.
[1] See *post*, para. 18–061.
[2] *Rylands v. Fletcher* (1868) L.R. 3 H.L. 330; and see Reservoirs Act 1975.
[3] *Tarry v. Ashton* (1876) 1 Q.B.D. 314.
[4] *Bland v. Yates* (1914) 58 S.J. 612.
[5] *Tetley v. Chitty* [1986] 1 All E.R. 663.

3–051   *(d) Airspace.* The owner's rights over the airspace above his land and buildings are limited to the height necessary for their ordinary use and enjoyment.[6] Within this limit he can take proceedings for trespass, and often also for nuisance, if his airspace is invaded by a tree, a crane, a cornice or telephone wires,[7] or if projectiles are fired over it.[8] Damages may be claimed for any injury, but the most important remedy is an injunction to prevent the wrong continuing. A land owner has a prima facie right to an injunction to restrain any trespass on his land whether or not the trespass harms him.[9] It will be granted almost invariably for a violation of his airspace,[10] and refused only in exceptional circumstances.[11] In such a case the court will not grant an injunction and then suspend its operation.[12]

Aircraft enjoy a wide dispensation under the Civil Aviation Act 1982[13] which provides that no action shall lie in respect of trespass or nuisance by reason only of the flight of aircraft over property at a height which is reasonable under the circumstances, provided the proper regulations are observed.

3–052   *(e) Minerals.* Although prima facie a tenant in fee simple is entitled to all mines and minerals[14] under his land,[15] this is subject to some exceptions. Thus at common law, as modified by statute, the Crown is entitled to all gold and silver in gold and silver mines[16]; and under the Petroleum Act 1998 petroleum

---

[6] *Ante*, para. 3–045.

[7] *Fay v. Prentice* (1845) 1 C.B. 828 at 835; *Lemmon v. Webb* [1895] A.C. 1; *Gifford v. Dent* [1926] W.N. 336; 71 S.J. 83; *Kelsen v. Imperial Tobacco Co. (of Great Britain and Ireland) Ltd* [1957] 2 Q.B. 334; *Anchor Brewhouse Developments Ltd v. Berkley House (Docklands Developments) Ltd* [1987] 2 E.G.L.R. 173; *London & Manchester Assurance Co. Ltd v. O. & H. Construction Ltd* [1989] 2 E.G.L.R. 185. But see McNair, *Law of the Air* (3rd ed.), chap. 3.

[8] *Clifton v. Viscount Bury* (1887) 4 T.L.R. 8.

[9] *Patel v. W.H. Smith (Eziot) Ltd* [1987] 1 W.L.R. 853; *Anchor Brewhouse Developments Ltd v. Berkley House (Docklands Developments) Ltd* [1987] 2 E.G.L.R. 173; and see *Lovett v. Fairclough* (1990) 61 P. & C.R. 385 at 403 (trespass by casting a fishing line from Scotland into England).

[10] *Trenberth (John) Ltd v. National Westminster Bank Ltd* (1979) 39 P. & C.R. 104 (projecting crane).

[11] *Behrens v. Richards* [1905] 2 Ch. 614; *Patel v. W.H. Smith (Eziot) Ltd, supra,* at 859, 863; *Gooden v. Ketley* [1996] E.G.C.S. 47; *Anchor Brewhouse Developments Ltd v. Berkley House (Docklands Developments) Ltd, supra,* at 177. Where a landowner seeks a mandatory injunction requiring his neighbour to remove part of a structure that intrudes into his airspace, relief is never granted as a matter of course: see, *e.g. Tollemache & Cobbold Breweries Ltd v. Reynolds* [1983] 2 E.G.L.R. 158 (protruding eaves: injunction refused).

[12] *Jaggard v. Sawyer* [1995] 1 W.L.R. 269, disapproving *Woollerton & Wilson Ltd v. Richard Costain Ltd* [1970] 1 W.L.R. 411 (where an injunction was suspended in such circumstances).

[13] s.76(1), replacing earlier legislation. See *Bernstein of Leigh (Baron) v. Skyviews & General Ltd* [1978] Q.B. 479 (aircraft taking photographs protected).

[14] For the meaning of "mines and minerals" in a lease, see *Lonsdale (Earl) v. Att.-Gen.* [1982] 1 W.L.R. 887 (on facts, oil and natural gas not included).

[15] *Mitchell v. Mosley* [1941] 1 Ch. 438 at p. 450.

[16] *The Case of Mines* [1568] 1 Plowd. 310; Royal Mines Acts 1688, 1693; and see *Att.-Gen. v. Morgan* [1891] 1 Ch. 432.

existing in its natural condition in strata is vested in the Crown.[17] Under the Coal Act 1938 all interests in coal (except interests arising under a coal-mining lease) were vested in the Coal Commission in return for compensation. These interests (including coal-mining leases) were vested subsequently in the National Coal Board,[18] then in the British Coal Corporation,[19] and finally, (following the privatisation of the coal industry) in the Coal Authority.[20] That body has extensive powers to licence coal mining operations.[21]

(f) Treasure. Under the Treasure Act 1996,[22] all treasure is vested in the   **3–053**
Crown or its franchisee,[23] and the old law on treasure trove is abolished.[24]
Treasure is elaborately defined[25] and includes—

(a)   certain coin and other objects[26] at least 300 years old when found;

(b)   any object at least 200 years old when found and of a class designated by the Secretary of State[27] as being of outstanding historical, archaeological or cultural importance;

(c)   any object which before the Act came into force would have been treasure trove[28]; or

(d)   an object found with any of (a)–(c).

The title that vests in the Crown or its franchisee is however subject to any prior interests or rights in the property.[29]

(g) Wild animals. Wild animals are not the subject of ownership.[30] But a   **3–054**
landowner has what is sometimes called a "qualified property" in them, consisting of the exclusive right to catch, kill and appropriate the animals on

---

[17] ss.1, 2. The Act consolidates earlier legislation. On the previous and related legislation see *Lonsdale (Earl) v. Att.-Gen., supra.*

[18] Coal Nationalisation Act 1946.

[19] Coal Industry Act 1987.

[20] Coal Industry Act 1994, ss.7, 8. The Authority is not the servant or agent of the Crown and does not enjoy any status, immunity or privilege of the Crown: *ibid.,* s.1(5).

[21] *ibid.* Pt II.

[22] See (1996) 146 N.L.J. 1346 (C. MacMillan); [1997] Conv. 273 (J. Marston and L. Ross). The Act provides a more rational system for the preservation of historical artefacts than the law of treasure trove, a royal prerogative of profit that was never intended for that purpose. The Act was brought into force on September 27, 1997: S.I. 1997 No. 1977. For the Code of Practice made under Treasure Act 1996, s.11, see [1998] Conv. 252 (J. Marston and L. Ross).

[23] s.4. For the franchisee, see *ibid.,* s.5.

[24] *ibid.,* s.4(3).

[25] *ibid.,* ss.1, 3.

[26] The objects and the coin (unless one of at least 10) must have a content of at least 10% by weight gold or silver.

[27] See Treasure Act 1996, s.2.

[28] For the old law of treasure trove, see the previous edition of this work at p. 64.

[29] Treasure Act 1996, s.4(2).

[30] *The Case of Swans* (1592) 7 Co.Rep. 15b at 17b.

his land, unless they are protected by law; and as soon as the animals are killed, they fall into the ownership of the landowner, even if killed by a trespasser.[31]

3–055   *(h) Water.* A landowner has no property in water which either percolates through his land[32] or flows through it in a defined channel.[33] In the case of percolating water, at common law the landowner could draw any or all of it off without regard to the claims of neighbouring owners[34]; but now, by statute, he normally cannot do so without a licence granted by a river authority unless the water is taken for the domestic purposes of his household.[35]

In the case of water flowing through a defined channel, even at common law the riparian owner (the owner of the land through which the water flows) could not always take all the water[36]; but he has certain valuable rights.

3–056   (1) FISHING. As part of his natural right of ownership,[37] he has the sole right to fish in the water.[38] Except in tidal waters,[39] the public has no right of fishing even if there is a public right of navigation.[40] For although a public right of navigation on a river may be acquired in much the same way as a public right of way over land can be acquired,[41] this no more entitles the public to fish in the stream than a right of way entitles the public to shoot on the highway[42]: the public's right is merely a right of passage.

3–057   (2) FLOW. He is entitled to the flow of water through the land unaltered in volume or quantity,[43] subject to ordinary and reasonable use by the upper riparian owners,[44] though he has no right to object to the level of the water

---

[31] *Blades v. Higgs* (1865) 11 H.L.C. 621; *R. v. Townley* (1871) L.R. 1 C.C.R. 315.

[32] *Ballard v. Tomlinson* (1885) 29 Ch.D. 115 at 121. Where the water percolates from higher to lower ground, the owner of the lower property is under no obligation to receive it and may erect barriers to pen it back, provided that, in so doing, he does not act unreasonably: *Home Brewery Co. Ltd v. William Davis & Co. (Leicester) Ltd* [1987] Q.B. 339.

[33] *Mason v. Hill* (1833) 5 B. & Ad. 1 at 24. See generally W. Howarth, *Wisdom's Law of Watercourses* (5th ed., 1992).

[34] *Chasemore v. Richards* (1859) 7 H.L.C. 349; *Langbrook Properties Ltd. v. Surrey C.C.* [1970] 1 W.L.R. 161; *Thomas v. Gulf Oil Refining Ltd* (1979) 123 S.J. 787; and see *Bradford Corpn. v. Pickles* [1895] A.C. 587; *Stephens v. Anglian Water Authority* [1987] 1 W.L.R. 1381.

[35] Water Resources Act 1991, ss.24, 27.

[36] As to the right to divert water, see (1958) 74 L.Q.R. 361 (D.P. Derham).

[37] See *Cooper v. Phibbs* (1867) L.R. 2 H.L. 149 at 165.

[38] *Eckroyd v. Coulthard* [1898] 2 Ch. 358 at 366.

[39] *Malcomson v. O'Dea* (1863) 10 H.L.C. 593; *Alfred F. Beckett Ltd v. Lyons* [1967] Ch. 449 (coal on sea shore). The right to fish in tidal waters includes the ancillary right to dig for bait, provided that the taking of bait is directly related to an actual or intended exercise of the right to fish: *Anderson v. Alnwick D.C.* [1993] 1 W.L.R. 1156 at 1166 *et seq.*

[40] *Pearce v. Scotcher* (1882) 9 Q.B.D. 162; *Blount v. Layard* [1891] 2 Ch. 681 at 689, 690.

[41] *Post*, para. 18–065. The Rights of Way Act 1932. s.1 (now replaced in an amended form by the Highways Act 1980, s.31), does not apply to public rights of navigation: *Att-Gen. ex re. Yorkshire Derwent Trust Ltd v. Brotherton* [1992] 1 A.C. 425; *post*, para. 18–069.

[42] *Smith v. Andrews* [1891] 2 Ch. 678 a 695, 696. But local inhabitants may sometimes acquire fishing rights: *post*, para. 18–078.

[43] See *Scott-Whitehead v. N.C.B.* (1985) 53 P. & C.R. 263; [1987] Conv. 368 (S. Tromans).

[44] See *John Young & Co. v. The Bankier Distillery Co.* [1893] A.C. 691 at 698.

being lowered unless this causes damage or a nuisance.[45] He is bound by corresponding obligations to the lower riparian owners.

(3) ABSTRACTION. The ordinary and reasonable use which at common law a riparian owner was entitled to make of the water flowing through his land was— **3–058**

> (i) the right to take and use all water necessary for ordinary purposes[46] connected with his riparian tenement (such as for watering his cattle[47] or for domestic purposes,[48] or, possibly, in some manu-facturing districts, for manufacturing purposes[49]), even though this completely exhausted the stream[50]; and

> (ii) the right to use the water for extraordinary purposes connected with his riparian tenement, provided the use was reasonable[51] and the water was restored substantially undiminished in volume and unaltered in character.[52] Such purposes included irrigation[53] and (in all districts[54]) manufacturing purposes,[55] such as for cooling apparatus.[56] The amount by which the flow might be diminished was a question of degree in each case.[57]

Statute has now severely curtailed these rights, so that in most cases a riparian owner cannot take any water without a licence granted by a water authority. The two main exceptions are where the water is taken for use on a holding comprising the riparian land and any other land held with it, and the use is for either—

> (i) the domestic purposes of the occupier's household, or

> (ii) agricultural purposes other than "spray irrigation" (*i.e.* watering land by jets or sprays from hoses and the like).

---

[45] *Tate & Lyle Industries Ltd v. Greater London Council* [1983] 2 A.C. 509 (ferry terminals caused silting at plaintiffs' jetty: claim of riparian right failed, but claim for special damage for public nuisance succeeded).

[46] *Miner v. Gilmour* (1858) 12 Moo.P.C. 131 at 156.

[47] *McCartney v. Londonderry and Lough Swilly Ry* [1904] A.C. 301 at 306.

[48] *Kensit v. Great Eastern Ry* (1883) 23 Ch.D. 566 at 574.

[49] See *Ormerod v. Todmorton Joint Stock Mill Co. Ltd* (1883) 11 Q.B.D. 155 at 168. *Sed quaere:* such a rule would enable an upper riparian owner, by starting a factory on his land, to take all the water previously enjoyed by factories lower down; and compare *McIndoe v. Jutland Flat (Waipori) Gold Mining Co. Ltd* (1893) 12 N.Z.L.R. 226 at 238. See generally (1959) 22 M.L.R. 35 (A.H. Hudson).

[50] *McCartney v. Londonderry and Lough Swilly Ry, supra,* at 307.

[51] See *Sharp v. Wilson, Rotheray & Co.* (1905) 93 L.T. 155.

[52] *McCartney v. Londonderry and Lough Swilly Ry, supra,* at 307; *Rugby Joint Water Board v. Walters* [1967] Ch. 397 (spray irrigation).

[53] See *Embrey v. Owen* (1851) 6 Exch. 353; *Rugby Joint Water Board v. Walters, supra.*

[54] *Semble,* despite the language in *Elmhurst v. Spencer* (1849) 2 Mac. & G. 45 at 50.

[55] *Swindon Waterworks Co. Ltd v. Wilts and Berks Canal Navigation Co.* (1875) L.R. 7 H.L. 697 at 704.

[56] *Kensit v. Great Eastern Ry* (1883) 23 Ch.D. 566.

[57] *Embrey v. Owen, supra,* at 372.

If a licence is granted, it constitutes a defence to any action (*e.g.* by a lower riparian owner) in respect of the abstraction of any water in accordance with it.[58]

3–059   Apart from these rights a riparian owner cannot take water from a stream at all; thus without statutory authority a waterworks company owning land on the bank of a stream cannot take water to supply a neighbouring town.[59] The owner of only one bank of a non-tidal stream is prima facie entitled to exercise riparian rights up to the middle of the stream.[60] But when the waters are tidal, prima facie the Crown is entitled to the foreshore (*i.e.* the land between ordinary high and low water marks) and there are no private riparian rights,[61] though it is possible for them to be created.[62]

III. TYPES OF FEE SIMPLE

3–060   A fee simple may be absolute or modified; a modified fee simple (sometimes called a modified fee) is any fee simple except a fee simple absolute. There are three main types of fee simple.[63]

3–061   **1. Fee simple absolute.** This is the type most frequently encountered in practice, and is an estate which continues indefinitely. "Fee" and "simple" have already been explained. "Absolute" means perpetual, *i.e.* not determinable by any special event.[64]

3–062   **2. Determinable fee.** A determinable fee is a fee simple which will automatically determine on the occurrence of some specified event which may never occur.[65] If the event is bound to happen at some time, the estate created is not a determinable fee; for it is said to be an essential characteristic of every fee that it may possibly last for ever.[66] Thus a grant "to A until the death of B" gives A a life estate *pur autre vie*,[67] but a grant to X "as long as the church of St Paul shall stand", creates a determinable fee simple.[68] In the latter case, X's estate may continue for ever, but if the specified state of affairs comes

---

[58] Water Resources Act 1991, ss.24, 27, 48, 70. See *Cargill v. Gotts* [1981] 1 W.L.R. 441; (1981) 97 L.Q.R. 382 (P. Jackson). Drought restrictions may also be imposed under the provisions of Pt II, Chap. III of the Act.

[59] See the *Swindon* case, *supra*.

[60] *Micklethwait v. Newlay Bridge Co.* (1886) 33 Ch.D. 133.

[61] *Ante*, para. 3–045.

[62] *Gann v. Free Fishers of Whitstable* (1865) 11 H.L.C. 192; *Loose v. Castleton* (1978) 41 P. & C.R. 19; *post*, para. 18–086.

[63] "Fee simple" has sometimes been used to mean "fee simple absolute" only: Co.Litt. 1b; Preston i, 428–431; Challis 438; but here the term is used in its wider and more usual sense. And "fee" by itself is sometimes used for "fee simple absolute": see Litt. 293; Challis 438.

[64] See *post*, paras 4–039–4–043.

[65] Preston i, 419, 431, 479; Challis 251.

[66] Challis 251.

[67] Challis 252; Litt. 740. Compare *Vernon v. Gatacre* (1564) 3 Dy. 253a; *Gawen v. Ramtes* (1600) Cro.Eliz. 804.

[68] *Walsingham's Case* (1573) 2 Plowd. 547 at 557; and see *Idle v. Cook* (1705) 1 P.Wms. 70 at 75 ("so long as such a tree stands"); see also the catalogue of examples given by Challis, 225–260.

about, the fee determines and the land reverts to the original grantor or his estate. The grantor's interest is called a possibility of reverter, *i.e.* a possibility of having an estate at a future time.[69] If the occurrence of the determining event becomes impossible, the possibility of reverter is destroyed and the fee simple becomes absolute, *e.g.* if land is given "to A until B marries" and B dies a bachelor.[70]

It has been suggested that the Statute *Quia Emptores* 1290 made it impossible to create determinable fees at common law[71] but there are dicta,[72] assumptions[73] and a decision[74] to the contrary, and the suggestion seems unsound in principle.[75] In any case, whatever doubts there may be about determinable fees created by direct grant (which are rarely encountered in practice), it has long been generally accepted that such fees can be created by means of trusts.[76]

3–063

3. A fee simple upon condition.[77] Akin to but distinct from a determinable fee is a fee simple which has some condition attached to it by which the estate given to the grantee may be cut short. A grant of land "to X in fee simple on condition that he does not marry Y", for example, will give X a fee simple, which is liable to forfeiture if the forbidden marriage takes place. This type of condition is sometimes called a condition subsequent, in order to distinguish it from a condition precedent relating to the beginning of the estate, *e.g.* "to X in fee simple when he reaches 21". Conditions precedent are dealt with later.[78]

3–064

The difference between a determinable fee and a fee simple defeasible by condition subsequent is not always easy to discern.[79] The essential distinction is that the determining event in a determinable fee itself sets the limit for the estate first granted. A condition subsequent, on the other hand, is an independent clause added to a limitation of a complete fee simple absolute which operates so as to defeat it. Thus a devise to a school in fee simple "until it

[69] Preston i, 441; Fearne 381; Challis 83; and see *Re Rowhook Mission Hall, Horsham* [1985] Ch. 62 at 74.

[70] Preston i, 440; Challis 254; and see *Re Leach* [1912] 2 Ch. 422 at 429.

[71] See the authorities cited in *Hopper v. Corporation of Liverpool* (1944) 88 S.J. 213 and *Third Report of Real Property Commissioners* (1832) 36; Marsden, *Perpetuities*, 71; Sweet's note in Challis 439.

[72] See Challis 251–262, 437–439; 23 Col.L.R. 207 (R.R.B. Powell).

[73] See *Re Leach* [1912] 2 Ch. 422; contrast *Re Chardon* [1928] Ch. 464 at 469, treating the question as open.

[74] *Hopper v. Corporation of Liverpool, supra,* analysed in 1945 Conv.Y.B. 203 and noted at (1946) 62 L.Q.R. 222 (R.E.M.). See also *Re Rowhook Mission Hall, Horsham, supra,* at 74.

[75] See Morris and Leach, 209, 210. For this debate, see the previous edition of this work at p. 68, n.90.

[76] An example, once common, was the usual provision of a marriage settlement whereby the settlor granted land to himself until the solemnisation of the marriage: see the previous edition of this work at p. 411.

[77] Commonly called a conditional fee. But there has been much confusion of language over determinable and conditional fees. "Conditional fee" was often used for both (see, *e.g.* Challis 261, 262), and "determinable fee" may cover both: S.L.A. 1925, s.117(1)(iv).

[78] *Post,* para. 7–094.

[79] See *Re Moore* (1888) 39 Ch.D. 116.

ceases to publish its accounts" creates a determinable fee, whereas a devise to the school in fee simple "on condition that the accounts are published annually" creates a fee simple defeasible by condition subsequent.[80] Words such as "while", "during", "as long as", "until" and so on are apt for the creation of a determinable fee,[81] whereas words which form a separate clause of defeasance, such as "provided that", "on condition that", "but if", or "if it happen that", operate as a condition subsequent.[82]

3–065   [The distinction is therefore really one of words.[83] [The determining event can be incorporated into the limitation in such a way as to create either a determinable fee or a fee simple defeasible by condition subsequent, which-ever the grantor wishes. The estate is determinable if the words limit the maximum period of time that it can endure. The limitation marks its bounds or compass. If the words define the event that will, if it happens, cut short the estate before it attains its boundary, they take effect as a condition.[84]

The distinction has been called "little short of disgraceful to our jurispru-dence".[85] It is sometimes a fine one, but it is important, since there are differences between the two forms of fee. These are set out here, although this requires a number of references to later parts of the book.

3–066   *(a) Determination*: a determinable fee automatically determines when the specified event occurs,[86] for the natural limits of its existence have been reached and the land reverts to the grantor or, if the grantor is dead, to the person entitled under his will or intestacy.[87] A fee simple upon condition merely gives the grantor (or whoever is entitled to his interest in the land, if the grantor is dead)[87] a right to enter and determine the estate when the event occurs[88]; unless and until entry is made, the fee simple continues.[89] The *possibility of reverter* after a determinable fee therefore operates automat-ically. The *right of entry* arising on a breach of condition is exercisable at the option of the grantor or his successor. These two special rights must be carefully distinguished.[90]

As a condition subsequent thus gives rise to a right of forfeiture, the courts continue it strictly, and require precise wording; such a condition is void

---

[80] *Re Da Costa* [1912] 1 Ch. 337.
[81] *Newis v. Lark* (1571) 2 Plowd. 403 at 413; *Mary Portington's Case* (1613) 10 Co.Rep. 35b at 41b; Challis 252.
[82] *Mary Portington's Case, supra*, at 42a; Litt. 328–330; Shep. 121; and see *Sifton v. Sifton* [1938] A.C. 656 at 677. Technically such words reserve a right of entry (*post*, para. 4–040) to the grantor. This is a reservation out of the grant, which is quite distinct from a limitation. *cf. Brandon v. Robinson* (1811) 18 Ves. 429 at 432, 433.
[83] *Dean v. Dean* [1891] 3 Ch. 150 at 155.
[84] Preston i, 49; see *Re Moore, supra*.
[85] *Re King's Trusts* (1892) 29 L.R.Ir. 401 at 410, *per* Porter M.R.
[86] Co.Litt. 214b; Challis 252; *Newis v. Lark, supra; Mary Portington's Case, supra*, at 42a.
[87] As to the transferability of possibilities of reverter and rights of entry, see *post*, para. 3–076.
[88] Litt. 331; Co.Litt. 214b; Challis 208, 261.
[89] *Matthew Manning's Case* (1609) 8 Co.Rep. 94b at 95b; Challis 219; *Re Evan's Contract* [1920] 2 Ch. 469 at 472.
[90] Here again, however, there is confusion of terminology, Challis (76 n., 228) uses "possibility of reverter" as meaning "right of entry".

unless it can be seen precisely and distinctly from the moment of its creation what events will cause a forfeiture.[91] Thus conditions subsequent requiring a donee to "continue to reside in Canada",[92] or prohibiting marriage with a person "not of Jewish parentage and of the Jewish faith",[93] have been held insufficiently precise, and so void. But a condition of defeasance if the donee should "be or become a Roman Catholic" has been upheld, as creating no uncertainty.[94] The question is one of certainty of concept and not ease of application, so that a sufficiently certain condition is not invalidated merely by possible difficulties in ascertaining whether events have occurred which give rise to a forfeiture.[95]

These strict rules do not, however, apply to a condition precedent: in order **3–067** to qualify, the claimant need only show that, whatever its possible uncertainty in other cases, he at least has complied with it.[96] A condition against marriage with "a person professing the Jewish faith" may thus be valid as a condition of entitlement but void as a condition of forfeiture.[97]

The court may grant relief against forfeiture where the object of a condition subsequent is to secure the payment of money or the performance of covenants, provided that the breach is not wilful and the default is made good.[98] This equitable jurisdiction, well established in the fields of leases[99] and mortgages,[1] may occasionally be invoked in other cases.

(b) Remoteness: under the rules against remoteness a right of entry was void **3–068** at common law if it might possibly arise at too distant a date. It follows that in such a case a condition subsequent had no effect and the fee simple became absolute.[2] But a determinable limitation could not last beyond the limiting event, no matter how far in the future that event might lie; and this was so even if the possibility of reverter was void for remoteness.[3] Statute has now modified this rule.[4]

---

[91] *Clavering v. Ellison* (1859) 7 H.L.C. 707. A court will however try to uphold the validity of a gift, particularly if it is contained in a will. It will therefore admit evidence as to the meaning which a testator attached to particular words: *Re Tepper's W.T.* [1987] Ch. 358 (condition of defeasance if a recipient married "outside the Jewish faith").

[92] *Sifton v. Sifton* [1938] A.C. 656; *cf. Re Coghlan* [1963] I.R. 246.

[93] *Clayton v. Ramsden* [1943] A.C. 320; *Re Tarnpolsk* [1958] 1 W.L.R. 1157; *Re Krawitz* [1959] 1 W.L.R. 1192.

[94] *Blathwayt v. Baron Cawley* [1976] A.C. 397.

[95] *Re Gape* [1952] Ch. 743.

[96] *Re Allen* [1953] Ch. 810; *Re Abrahams' W.T.* [1969] 1 Ch. 463.

[97] *Re Abrahams' W.T., supra*; *Re Tepper's W.T., supra*. See likewise *Re Tuck's S.T.* [1978] Ch. 49, where Lord Denning M.R. criticises both the distinctions explained above, and holds that the problem can be solved by a clause empowering some other person (such as the Chief Rabbi) to decide disputes. For further criticisms see (1977) 8 Sydney L.R. 400 (P. Butt); (1982) 98 L.Q.R. 551 (C.T. Emery).

[98] See *Shiloh Spinners Ltd v. Harding* [1973] A.C. 691. *cf. Sport Internationaal Bussum B.V. v. Inter-Footwear Ltd* [1984] 1 W.L.R. 776.

[99] *Post*, para. 14–136.

[1] *Post*, para. 19–017.

[2] *Sifton v. Sifton* [1938] A.C. 656.

[3] *Post*, para. 7–089.

[4] *Post*, para. 7–092.

3–069   *(c) Existence at law*: it is probable that a determinable fee cannot exist as a legal estate after 1925, apart from statutory exceptions, but that a fee simple subject to a condition subsequent can do so.[5]

3–070   *(d) Flexibility*: determinable fees are less hampered by restrictions on the events on which they may be made to determine. Conditions subsequent are more jealously regarded by the law and are more readily held to be void (so making the fee simple absolute) as being contrary to public policy. The law of conditions is a large subject and its rules apply to all kinds of dispositions, including trusts, and not only to the rights of entry at common law with which we are here concerned. Taking the authorities together, we find the following general rules.

3–071   (1) ALIENATION. The condition must not take away the power of alienation. One of the incidents of ownership is the right to sell or otherwise dispose of the property.[6] A condition[7] against alienation is said to be repugnant to this right, and contrary to public policy,[8] if is substantially takes away the tenant's power of alienation; and such conditions are void. Examples are conditions prohibiting—

> alienation at any time,[9]
> alienation during a person's life,[10]
> alienation to anyone except X,[11]
> alienation to anyone except a brother of the donee,[12] or
> alienation by mortgage[13] or by will.[14]

The question is, however, one of degree, and it is possible for some kinds of "partial restraint" to be valid. An example, well known but much criticised, is given by a case where land was devised to A "on the condition that he never sells it out of the family". The condition was held valid on the grounds that it did not prohibit any form of alienation except sale, it did not prohibit sales to members of the family, and it bound only A and not subsequent owners of

---

[5] *Post*, para. 4–041.
[6] Litt. 360. *Ante*, para. 2–041 (Statute *Quia Emptores* 1290). But see the position in relation to trusts of land: *post*, para. 8–140.
[7] But not a mere contract or covenant, where breach gives rise to a claim for damages but not to forfeiture of the estate: *Caldy Manor Estate Ltd v. Farrell* [1974] 1 W.L.R. 1303.
[8] (1917) 33 L.Q.R. 11 (E. Jenks).
[9] Co.Litt. 223a; *Hood v. Oglander* (1865) 34 Beav. 513 at 522.
[10] *Re Rosher* (1884) 26 Ch.D. 801; *Corbett v. Corbett* (1888) 14 P.D. 7.
[11] *Re Cockerill* [1929] 2 Ch. 131; *Attwater v. Attwater* (1853) 18 Beav. 330; *cf. Re Elliott* [1896] 2 Ch. 353 (condition that part of proceeds of sale should be paid to X held void).
[12] *Re Brown* [1954] Ch. 39 (holding that the doctrine extends to personalty, *e.g.* to a share under a trust for sale).
[13] *Ware v. Cann* (1830) 10 B. & C. 433.
[14] *Re Jones* [1898] 1 Ch. 438; *Re Dunstan* [1918] 2 Ch. 304.

the land.[15] And a condition that land should not be disposed of except to four sisters or their children has been upheld.[16] But it would not be safe to treat these decisions as examples of the court's normal attitude to restraints on alienation.

It may be mentioned that entails[17] and life interests[18] are in principle **3–072** equally protected against such restraints. But in the case of life interests the court is much readier to find that what appears to be a conditional limitation is intended to be determinable,[19] which makes an important difference.[20] Thus provisos for forfeiture of a life interest upon any attempt at alienation, or upon bankruptcy, are generally upheld.[21]

(2) COURSE OF LAW. The condition must not be directed against a course of **3–073** devolution prescribed by law. A condition rendering a fee simple liable to be defeated if the tenant dies intestate,[22] becomes bankrupt,[23] or has the estate seized in execution,[24] is void; for on each of these events the law prescribes that a fee simple shall devolve in a particular way, and this course of devolution cannot be altered by condition.[25]

(3) PUBLIC POLICY. The condition must not be illegal, immoral or otherwise **3–074** contrary to public policy. The condition most frequently encountered under this head is a condition in restraint of marriage. Partial restraints, for example, prohibiting marriage with a Papist,[26] or a Scotsman,[27] or a person who had been a domestic servant,[28] have been held good.[29] But total restraints (or restraints which are virtually total, *e.g.* against marrying a person who has not freehold property worth £500 per annum[30]) are void unless the intent is not primarily to restrain marriage but simply to provide for the donee until

---

[15] *Re Macleay* (1875) L.R. 20 Eq. 186 (Jessel M.R.). Contrast *Re Rosher, supra; Re McDonnell* [1965] I.R. 354; Gray, *Restraints on the Alienation of Property* (2nd ed.), 28, 43; Jarman 1480. And see discussion by Harman J. in *Re Brown, supra. Re Macleay* was distinguished in *Re Brown* by the fact that in the latter case the permitted class was small and was bound to diminish. See also (1917) 33 L.Q.R. 236, 342 (Sweet); (1954) 70 L.Q.R. 15 (R.E.M.); and see *Petrofina (Gt. Britain) Ltd v. Martin* [1965] Ch. 1073 at 1097 (not reversed on appeal, [1966] Ch. 146).

[16] *Doe d. Gill v. Pearson* (1805) 6 East 173.

[17] See *post*, para. 3–084.

[18] *Brandon v. Robinson* (1811) 18 Ves. 429; *Rochford v. Hackman* (1852) 9 Hare 475 at 480.

[19] *Rochford v. Hackman, supra,* at 480, 482; *Hurst v. Hurst* (1882) 21 Ch. D. 278 at 283.

[20] This is explained *ante*, para. 3–066.

[21] See Jarman 1485, 1496; Lewin 99. The common "protective trusts" set out in T.A. 1925, s.33 include a determinable life interest.

[22] *Re Dixon* [1903] 2 Ch. 458.

[23] *Re Machu* (1882) 21 Ch.D. 838.

[24] *Re Dugdale* (1888) 38 Ch.D. 176 at 182.

[25] *Holmes v. Godson* (1856) 8 De G.M. & G. 152.

[26] *Duggan v. Kelly* (1847) 10 Ir.Eq.R. 295.

[27] *Perrin v. Lyon* (1807) 9 East 170.

[28] *Jenner v. Turner* (1880) 16 Ch.D. 188.

[29] And see *Greene v. Kirkwood* [1895] 1 I.R. 130; but such gifts should be closely scrutinised for sufficient certainty: see *ante*, para. 3–066.

[30] *Keily v. Monck* (1795) 3 Ridg.P.C. 205.

marriage,[31] or unless the donee has already been married once.[32] A condition giving a wife an incentive to cease to cohabit with her husband is bad.[33]

Other conditions which are contrary to public policy, and therefore void, are conditions requiring the donee to acquire a dukedom[34] (as being a title carrying with it legislative rights), or forbidding entry into the naval or military services,[35] or the undertaking of any public office.[36] A donee may be forbidden to dispute a will, but such a condition is void if drawn so widely as to disable the donee from protecting his rights.[37] A condition may forbid a change of religion,[38] but only in the case of an adult: for otherwise it conflicts with the parent's duty to provide proper religious instruction for his child.[39] A condition that X should not be allowed to set foot on the property has been held good.[40]

3–075 (4) DETERMINABLE FEES. A determinable fee, on the other hand, is not so strictly confined,[41] "if the gift is until marriage, and no longer, there is nothing to carry the gift beyond the marriage".[42] A devise of freeholds on trust for X "until he shall assign charge or otherwise dispose of the same or some part thereof or become bankrupt . . . or do something whereby the said annual income or some part thereof would become payable to or vested in some other person" has been held to give X a determinable fee.[43] On any of the events occurring X's estate would determine; if he died before any of them occurred, the fee simple would become absolute, for it ceases to be possible for any of them to occur.[44] But although a fee may thus be made determinable on alienation or on bankruptcy or on similar events, a limitation would probably be void if it were contrary to public policy for the fee to be determinable on the stated event, *e.g.* if the event were the return to her husband of a wife who

---

[31] See *Jones v. Jones* (1876) 1 Q.B.D. 279; *Re Hewett* [1918] 1 Ch. 458 (personalty). The rules as to personalty are "proverbially difficult" (*ibid.*); partial restraints are treated as intended merely *in terrorem* (and so void in law) unless enforced by a gift over or a clear clause of revocation. See *Re Whitting* [1905] 1 Ch. 96; *Re Hanlon* [1933] Ch. 254.

[32] *Newton v. Marsden* (1862) 2 J. & H. 356 (woman); *Allan v. Jackson* (1875) 1 Ch.D. 399 (man).

[33] *Wilkinson v. Wilkinson* (1871) L.R. 12 Eq. 604 (life estate); *Re Johnson's W.T.* [1967] Ch. 387.

[34] *Egerton v. Brownlow* (1853) 4 H.L.C. 1 (fee tail); contrast *Re Wallace* [1920] 2 Ch. 274 (the "barren title" of baronet).

[35] See *Re Beard* [1908] 1 Ch. 383.

[36] *Re Edgar* [1939] 1 All E.R. 635.

[37] *Cooke v. Turner* (1846) 15 M. & W. 727; *Re Boulter* [1922] 1 Ch. 75.

[38] *Hodgson v. Halford* (1879) 11 Ch.D. 959 (life estate). Public policy in relation to religious discrimination may be changing: see *Blathwayt v. Baron Cawley* [1976] A.C. 397 at 425, 426 (*ante*, paras. 3–066–3–067). *cf. Re Remnant's S.T.* [1970] Ch. 560.

[39] *Re Borwick* [1933] Ch. 657 (personalty); *Re Tegg* [1936] 2 all E.R. 878 (personalty).

[40] *Re Talbot-Ponsonby* [1937] 4 All E.R. 309.

[41] *Brandon v. Robinson* (1811) 18 Ves. 429 at 432, 433; *Re Wilkinson* [1926] Ch. 842 at 847.

[42] *Morley v. Rennoldson* (1843) 2 Hare 570 at 580, *per* Wigram V.-C.; and see *Leong v. Chye* [1955] A.C. 648 at 660.

[43] *Re Leach* [1912] 2 Ch. 422; Jenks (1917) 33 L.Q.R. 14. *Re Machu* (1882) 21 Ch.D. 838 does not conflict with this, since the fee simple was subject to a condition, and was not a determinable fee: Challis 261.

[44] *Re Leach* [1912] 2 Ch. 422 at 429.

was separated from him.[45] In such a case the whole gift fails, for there is no proper limitation; whereas a corresponding conditional gift would become absolute, since the fee is properly limited even though the condition fails.[46]

(e) Alienability of the expectant interest. At common law a right of entry **3–076** and a possibility of reverter were descendible but not alienable *inter vivos*, for they were not themselves estates but merely special rights incident to other estates.[47] Nor did they become devisable by the Statute of Wills 1540. But rights of entry for condition broken were made devisable in 1837[48] and alienable *inter vivos* in 1845.[49] They may also now be made exercisable by any person,[50] not merely by the grantor or his successors in title, so that they may now be given to some other person at the moment of their creation. It is not quite so clear that a possibility of reverter is devisable[51] or assignable, but it seems highly probable that it is, at least after 1925.[52]

4. Nature of modified fees. The owner of a modified fee has the same **3–077** rights over the land as the owner of a fee simple absolute: thus the common law refused to restrain him from committing acts of waste,[53] such as opening and working mines. Equity, on the other hand, intervened to prevent the commission of equitable waste, *i.e.* acts of wanton destruction,[54] although the owner of a fee simple absolute is under no such restraint; for where there is a modified fee, there is some other person interested in expectancy whose interest may need protecting.

At common law the owner of a modified fee could not convey a fee simple absolute but merely a fee liable to determination, for a man cannot convey more than he has.[55] But these interests now fall within the statute law dealing with settlements and trusts of land, so that they are now subject to the statutory powers of making sales and other dispositions.[56] A modified fee may, moreover, become enlarged into a fee simple absolute, *e.g.* by the determining event

---

[45] *cf. Re Moore* (1888) 39 Ch.D. 116 (life interest in personalty determinable on wife returning to husband: held void).

[46] Co.Litt. 206a, b; *Re Greenwood* [1903] 1 Ch. 749; *cf. Sifton v. Sifton* [1938] A.C. 656.

[47] Co.Litt. 201a, n.1; Challis 76n. For the unsettled state of the law in the twelfth and thirteenth centuries, see Maitland, "Remainders after Conditional Fees", Coll. Pp. ii, 174; Challis 428.

[48] Wills Act 1837, s.3; *Pemberton v. Barnes* [1899] 1 Ch. 544.

[49] R.P.A. 1845, s.6; L.P.A. 1925, s.4(2); Wolst. & C. i, 60.

[50] L.P.A. 1925, s.4(3). This is subject to the perpetuity rule: *post,* para. 7–089.

[51] Challis 228, 229, where "possibility of reverter" is apparently used to mean "right of entry".

[52] As a "future equitable interest" under L.P.A. 1925, s.4(2), which in any case is not exclusive of any interest of any kind. Only if "interest" is made synonymous with "estate" is there any difficulty in fitting possibilities into it. The only possibility specifically included is "a possibility coupled with an interest", which does not include a possibility of reverter: Challis 76n.

[53] Challis 262; *Lewis Bowles's Case* (1615) 11 Co.Rep. 79b at 81a. For waste, see *post,* para. 3–098.

[54] Williams R.P. 414; *Re Hanbury's S.E.* [1913] 2 Ch. 357 at 365.

[55] Preston i, 435, 436.

[56] *Post,* paras 8–001, 8–048–8–050, 8–137.

becoming impossible[57]; and there are special rules for the enlargement of base fees.[58]

B. The Fee Tail

I. HISTORY

3–078   **1. Origins: the Statute *De Donis Conditionalibus* 1285.** There are few fee tails now in existence and, as already explained, none can now be created.[59] Only a brief account will therefore be given of the history of the entail.[60] Its hallmark was a limitation to a person and the heirs *of his body*, restricting inheritance to his lineal descendants, as opposed to the collateral relations who could inherit the fee simple if there were no issue.[61] The fee tail was not created by, but was the consequence of, the Statute *De Donis Conditionalibus* 1285.[62] Prior to that statute, two types of fee simple were employed to make provision respectively for daughters by way of marriage-gifts[63] and for younger sons. The intention in making such gifts was to ensure that the land would revert to the settlor or his heir on any failure of issue. However, a marriage-gift became absolute after three generations and could then be freely alienated. The gift to a younger son came to be regarded as a fee simple granted conditionally upon the birth of issue: once a child was born, the fee became absolute and the son could then alienate the land.[64] The Statute was passed in response to a baronial petition[65] to give settlors more secure control of the land which they had settled. It provided that in the case of these conditional gifts, the will of the donor should be observed according to the form expressed in the deed of gift. Notwithstanding any alienation by the donee, the land would descend to his issue on his death and would revert to the donor when the donee and all his issue were dead.[66] Although the statute by its terms merely modified the rules relating to conditional fees, this

---

[57] *Ante*, para. 3–066.

[58] *Post*, para. 3–088. A base fee is one form of determinable fee, though it is commonly treated as being a distinct entity.

[59] *Ante*, para. 3–037.

[60] For a fuller account, see the previous edition of this work at pp. 76–87. See too S.F.C. Milsom, *Historical Foundations of the Common Law* (2nd ed.), chap. 8; J. H. Baker, *An Introduction to English Legal History* (3rd ed.) at pp. 307–327.

[61] *Ante*, para. 3–008. For the common law rules of intestate inheritance, see the previous edition of this work at pp. 540–542.

[62] Statute of Westminster II, 1285, c. 1.

[63] Known as the *maritagium*.

[64] See Milsom, *Historical Foundations of the Common Law* at pp. 171–173; Baker, *An Introduction to English Legal History* at pp. 310–311.

[65] For this petition, see J. H. Baker and S. F. C. Milsom, *Sources of English Legal History*, p. 48.

[66] The statute provided for a writ of "formedon in the descender" to enable the donee's issue to claim the land. Reversioners and remaindermen were already protected by writs of formedon in the reverter and formedon in the remainder: H.E.L. iii, 18; P. & M. ii, 28; (1940) 7 C.L.J. 238 (W. H. Humphreys); (1944) 8 C.L.J. 275, n.9 (S. J. Bailey); and occasionally a formedon in the descender had been used before in the statute in cases where a tenant in tail died seised and his heir entitled under the entail was not also the heir general: (1956) 72 L.Q.R. 391 (S. F. C. Milsom). "Formedon" is from *"forma doni"*.

modification was so important that the estate was thereafter renamed "fee tail" or "estate tail". For all practical purposes it was a new estate.[67]

A fee tail, unlike a fee simple, was followed by a reversion or remainder.[68] **3–079** On the failure of the donee's lineal issue the land would still belong to the original donor in fee simple. The fee tail was a lesser estate that did not exhaust his interest. Alternatively he could also alienate this reversionary interest and thereby make someone entitled by way of remainder. The tenant in tail by contrast had in substance only a life estate. If he alienated the land it was recoverable after his death by the heir to the fee tail or (if he died without issue) by the reversioner or remainderman. The Statute therefore gave to landowners what the common law had always denied to them: the power to create a virtually inalienable estate. It "established a general perpetuity by Act of Parliament",[69] and for some 200 years this "common grievance of the realm"[70] continued. However in the fifteenth century the courts, with their accustomed hostility to restraints upon alienation, began to countenance devices by which the Statute could be frustrated.[71]

2. Fee tail barrable by recovery or fine. The two devices were successful. **3–080** These were the common recovery and the fine. Each involved an ingenious abuse of an action at law, and each took advantage of the binding effect of a judgment of the court. It is necessary here only to explain in the barest outline how each worked.[72]

(a) The common recovery. By 1472,[73] it was recognised that a tenant in tail **3–081** in possession could "bar" the entail by means of a collusive action known as a "common recovery". To ensure that the claims of the tenant in tail's heirs and any reversioner or remainderman were barred, there were two elements in this process.

> (i) An accomplice[74] of the tenant in tail would bring an action claiming the fee simple on the basis of a wholly spurious title. The tenant in tail would not contest this suit, but would submit to it, allowing the accomplice to "recover" it. That barred the tenant in tail and his issue.

---

[67] See *Willion v. Berkley* (1561) 1 Plowd. 223 at 248; H.E.L. ii, 350.
[68] Challis 298.
[69] *Mildmay's Case* (1605) 6 Co.Rep. 40a. It has been described as a "juridical monster": Milsom, *Historical Foundations of the Common Law* at p. 177.
[70] Bl.Comm. ii, 116 (where the many inconveniences of entails are bewailed).
[71] H.E.L. iii, 118, 119.
[72] For fuller accounts, see A. W. B. Simpson, *A History of the Land Law* (2nd ed.), chap. 6; and the previous edition of this work at pp. 79 *et seq.*
[73] *Taltarum's Case* (1472) Y.B. 12 Edw. 4, Mich., fo. 14b, pl. 16, fo. 19a, pl. 25; 13 Edw. 4, Mich., fo. 1a, pl. 1. A full translation of the record and reports is in Kiralfy, *Source Book of English Law* (1957) pp. 86–89 (where the name of the case appears as *Talcarn's Case*, or in the modern style *Hunt v. Smyth*); and there is an account of the case in Challis 309.
[74] Who was often a lawyer: Baker, *An Introduction to English Legal History*, at p. 319.

(ii) In order to bar the reversioner or remainderman, the tenant in tail
would in those proceedings "vouch to warranty" some third party.
When one person conveyed land to another, he would "warrant"
the grantee in his holding.[75] By virtue of this warranty, the grantor
agreed to provide the grantee with lands of equivalent value[76] if his
title turned out to be bad. In the collusive recovery, the vouchee to
warranty would in fact be a landless man of straw[77] and he would
always default.

3–082   The effect of this subterfuge was that the accomplice acquired the fee simple
absolute. The other claimants were barred and left to console themselves with
a valueless judgment.[78] The accomplice then either reconveyed the land to the
tenant in tail, or paid him the purchase price if he was himself to buy it. The
entail had been turned into a fee simple.

The common recovery could only be brought against the person seised. It
could not therefore be employed against a tenant in tail in remainder unless
the freeholder in possession would collaborate.[79] It was this limitation that the
second device, the fine, was designed to circumvent.

3–083   *(b) The fine.* A fine was a final compromise of litigation that was entered in
the court's records to show the terms on which, with the court's leave, the
action was discontinued.[80] The practice of "levying a fine" pre-dated the
common recovery. It was commonly employed in early times as a method of
conveyancing because of its sanctity as a compromise approved by the court
and registered in the court records.[81] The Statute expressly prohibited the
barring of entails by fines.[82] However it was held in the Exchequer Chamber
that the law had been changed by virtue of the Statute of Fines 1489, which
dealt with fines generally, and that a fine would bar the issue in tail.[83] The
effect of this decision was subsequently confirmed by statute in 1540.[84]

Although the fine could be levied without the concurrence of the tenant in
possession, it suffered from one serious disadvantage. It barred the rights of
the issue in tail but did not bar the owner of the subsequent remainder,
reversion or other estate.[85] The estate produced by a fine was known as a
"base fee", which was in effect a determinable fee simple. It endured for as

---

[75] This warranty was the predecessor of the modern covenants for title: *post*, para. 5–047.
[76] Known as "*escambium*".
[77] He was in practice the common crier of the Court of Common Pleas who was paid four pence
for his services: Baker, *An Introduction to English Legal History*, at pp. 319–320.
[78] *Capel's Case* (1593) 1 Co.Rep. 61b; *Cholmley's Case* (1597) 2 Co.Rep. 50a at 52a.
[79] Challis, 310; Cru.Dig. v, 274; Williams R.P. 106.
[80] Williams R.P. 73n; H.E.L. iii, 236 *et seq.*
[81] *ibid.* See too C. A. F. Meekings, *The 1235 Surrey Eyre* (1979) 31 Surrey Record Society at
p. 43.
[82] Statute of Westminster II, c. 1, s.4.
[83] *Anon* (1527) 1 Dy. 2b. Blackstone saw the statute as a covert attempt by "that politic prince,
King Henry VII" to provide a means of barring entails: Bl.Comm. ii, 354.
[84] Statute of Fines; 32 Hen.8, c. 36.
[85] *Margaret Podger's Case* (1613) 9 Co.Rep. 104a.

long as the entail would have continued if it had been barred, and determined when the entail would have ended.[86]

To suppress still further the inconveniences of the Statute *De Donis Conditionalibus*, the judges created a rule that the power to suffer recoveries and levy fines was an inseparable incident of every entail. Any attempt to hamper this power in any way was void.[87] It followed therefore that the interests of issue in tail, remaindermen and reversioners were in fact wholly precarious, precisely contrary to the provisions of the Statute.

3–084

Although by the eighteenth century fines and recoveries had become purely formal, they remained dilatory, complicated and expensive. However the barring of entails had come to play a vital part in the system of family settlements.[88] Simpler methods of barring entails were therefore provided by the Fines and Recoveries Act 1833,[89] which was designed to produce almost exactly the same results as the earlier law. As it is still in force today, its provisions can be more conveniently considered with the present law.

II. RIGHTS OF A TENANT IN TAIL

Apart from the peculiar law about alienation a tenant in tail had all the rights of enjoyment of a fee simple owner. He was not liable for waste of any kind, and he could therefore cut timber, open mines or pull down buildings as he pleased,[90] even if some statute restrained him from barring the entail.[91] A statute of 1540 empowered him to grant leases binding on his issue (but not remaindermen or reversioners) for terms of not more than 21 years or a period of three lives.[92] This power remained until superseded by the new law of settlements in the nineteenth century.[93]

3–085

III. PRESENT LAW

1. Existence only in equity. After 1925 it was not possible for an entail to exist as a legal estate.[94] The significance of this is explained in Chapter 4. All entails exist as equitable interests behind trusts. This means that the legal estate must be vested in some trustees or trustee (who may be the tenant in tail himself) on trust for the person entitled in tail and everyone else interested in the land. This does not alter anyone's rights of enjoyment: only the bare legal

3–086

---

[86] On base fees see Challis 325 *et seq.*
[87] See Fearne 256 *et seq.*, where the authorities are collected.
[88] See *post*, para. 8–003.
[89] This statute was drafted by the eminent conveyancer Peter Brodie, who was also one of the Real Property Commissioners. It was highly regarded by many, though some considered that he could have achieved its effect more directly: see J. S. Anderson, *Lawyers and the Making of English Land Law 1832–1940*, p. 7.
[90] Williams R.P. 114, 198; *Lord Glenorchy v. Bosvilie* (1733) Ca.t.Talb. 3 at 16 (not liable for equitable waste).
[91] *Att.-Gen. v. Duke of Marlborough* (1813) 3 Madd. 498.
[92] 32 Hen. 8, c. 28; and see *Att.-Gen. v. Duke of Marlborough, supra*, at 532.
[93] *Post*, chap. 8.
[94] L.P.A. 1925, s.1; *post*, para. 4–034.

ownership is affected.[95] Similarly a "base fee" can no longer exist as a legal estate but only as an equitable interest in the nature of a base fee.

3–087   **2. Personality entailable.** In the period after 1925 and before 1997 any property, real or personal, could be entailed. Before 1926 this had not been the case.

> (i) Statute *De Donis* 1285 applied only to "tenements", *i.e.* property held in tenure, real property.[96]

> (ii) An entail could only subsist in a hereditament, *i.e.* land which was heritable. Thus life estates (which were not inheritable) and leaseholds (which were personalty) could not be entailed.[97]

A purported grant of personalty in tail before 1926 (whether by deed or will) gave the grantee absolute ownership of the property.[98]

After 1925 and before 1997, entails could be created in personalty. All the rules applying to entails of realty (*e.g.* as to words of limitation and barring) applied equally to entails of personalty.[99] It was expressly provided however that if personalty was directed "to be enjoyed or held with, or upon trusts corresponding to trusts affecting" land which was already held in tail, this was sufficient to entail the personalty,[1] provided that the exact wording was used.[2]

3. Barring the entail

3–088   *(a) Barring inter vivos: the Fines and Recoveries Act 1833.*[3] The Act provides that an entail can be barred by any assurance (*i.e.* any conveyance or other transfer) which a fee simple owner can employ, except a will. Such a disentailing assurance passes a fee simple to the transferee. Although an entailed interest is nowadays always equitable, any disentailing assurance must be made or evidenced by deed.[4] A mere declaration that the entail is

---

[95] The correct title for an entail is now "entailed interest" rather than "estate tail" or "fee tail": it is no longer a legal estate for which the land itself is held.

[96] Challis 43, 47, 61.

[97] *Leventhorpe v. Ashbie* (1635) 1 Roll.Abr. 831, pl. 1; *Leonard Lovie's Case* (1614) 10 Co.Rep. 78a; Co.Litt. 20a, n.5.

[98] Norton, *Deeds*, 376 (deed); *Dawson v. Small* (1874) 9 Ch.App. 651 (will); and see *Portman v. Viscount Portman* [1922] 2 A.C. 473. A gift using informal words, such as "to A and his issue" or "to A and his descendants", usually gave the property to A and such of his issue or descendants as were alive at the relevant date: *Re Hammond* [1924] 2 Ch. 276.

[99] L.P.A. 1925, s.130(1) (repealed, T.L.A.T.A. 1996, Sched. 4). An entail of personalty had to be made by instrument: see L.P.A. 1925, ss.130(6); 205(1)(xxvi); S.L.A. 1925, ss.1, 117(1)(xxiv).

[1] L.P.A. 1925, s.130(3) (repealed, T.L.A.T.A. 1996, Sched. 4).

[2] *Re Jones* [1934] Ch. 315 at 321.

[3] The Act remains in force "in regard to dealings with entailed interests as equitable interests": L.P.Am.A. 1924, Sched. 9, para. 4. For a much fuller account of the history and operation of the Act, see the previous edition of this work at pp. 83–85.

[4] F.R.A. 1833, ss.15, 40. In general a disposition of an equitable interest can be made in writing without a deed: L.P.A. 1925, s.53(1)(c); *post*, para. 10–046.

barred will not suffice because it is not an "assurance" as the Act requires.[5]

A disentailing assurance is unlikely to be made nowadays on an *inter vivos* disposition of the land. As entails operate only in equity, it is no longer necessary to bar the entail in order to convey the legal fee simple.[6] When a tenant in tail in possession wishes to bar the entail, he will usually convey his entailed interest to trustees by way of disentailing assurance. They will then reconvey the resulting equitable fee simple back to him.[7] Although in principle a tenant in tail could now execute a disentailing assurance in his own favour,[8] this is not the practice.[9]

If a tenant in tail in remainder wishes to execute a disentailing assurance that will bar the entail, he must obtain the consent of the "protector of the settlement".[10] The protector is normally the person who is entitled to the land in possession.[11] Any disentailing assurance executed without his concurrence will create only a base fee.[12] The interests of the issue in tail will be barred, but not those of the remainderman or reversioner. Base fees are rarely if ever encountered nowadays.[13]

(b) Barring by will. By virtue of section 176 of the Law of Property Act 1925, a tenant in tail can now bar his entail by will, and thus dispose of the fee simple or any other estate. This power is subject to a number of limitations.

    3–089

   (a)   It applies only to entails in possession: there is no power to bar an entail in remainder by will, even if the protector consents.

   (b)   The tenant in tail must be of full age.

   (c)   The will must be either executed after 1925 or confirmed by a codicil executed after 1925.

   (d)   The will must refer specifically either to—

       (i)   the property (*e.g.* "Blackacre"),[14] or

---

[5] A declaration of trust will suffice: *Carter v. Carter* [1896] 1 Ch. 162.

[6] Entailed interests usually take effect under a settlement made under the S.L.A. 1925: *post*, para. 8–049. Under such a settlement, the legal estate and the powers of disposition of the settled land are vested in the life tenant.

[7] For a precedent, see Prideaux, Vol. iii, 415.

[8] A disentailing assurance is a "conveyance": L.P.A. 1925, s.205(1)(ii). Since 1925, it has been possible for a person to convey land to himself: L.P.A. 1925, s.72(3). This subsection is particularly intended to cover conveyances by a person in one capacity to himself in another: *Rye v. Rye* [1962] A.C. 496 at 511, 514.

[9] See the doubt raised in Wolst. & C. i, 151.

[10] F.R.A. 1833, s.34.

[11] *ibid.*, s.22. This follows the position that existed prior to 1833.

[12] F.R.A. 1833, s.34.

[13] For the base fee and the methods by which it may be enlarged into a fee simple, see the previous edition of this work at p. 89.

[14] See *Acheson v. Russell* [1951] Ch. 67 ("all other my estate and interest" in the property held sufficiently specific).

(ii) the instrument under which it was acquired (*e.g.* "all the property to which I succeeded under Uncle Harry's will"), or

(iii) entails generally (*e.g.* "all property to which I am entitled in tail").

This power extends to all entailed property, whether real or personal, whenever the entail was created.

3–090   *(c) Unbarrable entails.* It became a rule, as has been seen, that it was impossible to create an unbarrable entail, and that any attempt to restrain the tenant from barring was ineffective.[15] This rule was not affected by the Fines and Recoveries Act 1833.[16] Despite this general rule there are certain entails which cannot be barred,[17] *e.g.* those made unbarrable by Act of Parliament.[18] Furthermore there are certain persons who are unable to bar an entail, such as mental patients[19] and bankrupts.[20]

3–091   **3. Descent.** The old law of inheritance still applies to entails. They could not exist if it did not.[21] However on the death of a tenant in tail, the entail (if unbarred) descends according to the *general* law that was in force before 1926. Special customs such as gavelkind are excluded.[22]

C. The Life Estate

3–092   After 1925 an interest in land for life can no longer exist as a legal estate but only as an equitable interest.[23] In general, the law of life estates set out below appears to apply equally to the corresponding life interests after 1925; at all events, this is assumed in practice.[24]

I. TYPES OF LIFE ESTATE

3–093   The two types of life estate were the ordinary life estate for the life of the tenant and the estate *pur autre vie.*

---

[15] *Ante*, para. 3–083.

[16] See *Dawkins v. Lord Penrhyn* (1878) 4 App.Cas. 51 at 64.

[17] See the previous edition of this work at p. 91.

[18] These include the entails given by reward to the first Duke of Marlborough (6 Anne, c. 6, 1706, s.5; 6 Anne, c. 7, 1706, s.4) and the first Duke of Wellington (54 Geo. 3, c. 161, 1814, s.28). *cf. Hambro v. Duke of Marlborough* [1994] Ch. 158; *post*, para. 8–087.

[19] But the entail may be barred by an order of the judge or the Court of Protection, *e.g.* by his receiver: Mental Health Act 1983, Pt VII.

[20] The power to bar an entail vests instead in the bankrupt's trustee in bankruptcy: I.A. 1986, s.314(1); Sched. 5, Pt II, para. 13.

[21] A.E.A. 1925, s.45(2). The old rules of inheritance are explained in the previous edition of this work at p. 532.

[22] L.P.A. 1925, s.130(4); *Re Higham* [1937] 2 All E.R. 17 (land disgavelled by A.E.A. 1925, s.51(2)). For gavelkind, see *ante*, para. 2–019.

[23] L.P.A. 1925, s.1; *post*, para. 4–030.

[24] See, *e.g. Re Harker's W.T.* [1938] Ch. 323.

1. Estate for the life of the tenant. This arose either— **3–094**

(i) by express limitation, as by a grant "to A for life"[25]; or

(ii) by operation of law, as in the case of curtesy and dower.[26]

2. Estate *pur autre vie*. An estate *pur autre vie*[27] was an estate which was **3–095**
granted for the life of someone other than the tenant. The person whose life
measured the duration of the estate was called the *"cestui que vie"*. More than
one *cestui que vie* could be named, and the estate could be limited either for
the longest or for the shortest (*i.e.* for the joint lives) of such persons.[28] An
estate *pur autre vie* could arise either—

(i) by the owner of life estate assigning it to another person. As
nobody can give what they do not have,[29] the assignor could create
no interest which would last longer than his own life;

(ii) by express grant, *e.g.* "to A for the life of X".

Both types of life estate were estates of freehold,[30] but neither was a freehold
of inheritance, for neither could descend to the tenant's heir. This was self-
evident in the case of an ordinary life estate. But if A held for the life of B and
predeceased B, what was to happen to the residue of A's estate? It had not yet
ceased,[31] but A's heir could not inherit as such.[32] This problem was solved by
a doctrine, now abolished, known as "occupancy".[33] Since 1925, the tenant's
interest has passed like any other property to his personal representatives, who
hold it in trust for the persons entitled under his will.[34]

Both types of life estate could be made determinable or subject to condi- **3–096**
tions subsequent.[35] Limitations of this kind were often found in settlements,
for example, where a life interest was given to a wife, if she should survive
her husband, "during her widowhood" or to a man "until he may become
bankrupt". The principles governing such determinable or conditional life
interests were probably[36] the same as those governing the corresponding types
of fee simple.[37]

---

[25] *Ante*, para. 3–007.
[26] See the previous edition of this work at p. 543.
[27] More correctly, but less commonly, *"pur auter vie"*: Challis 356. Much of the learning about
this estate will be found in *Doe d. Jeff v. Robinson* (1828) 2 Man. & Ry. 249, and the notes
thereon.
[28] Challis 356.
[29] Commonly expressed in Latin: *"nemo dat quod non habet"*.
[30] Litt. 57.
[31] *Utty Dale's Case* (1590) Cro.Eliz. 182.
[32] If A had alienated before his death to Y, the same problem would arise if Y predeceased A.
[33] For the details, see the previous edition of this work at pp. 93–94.
[34] A.E.A. 1925, s.45(1)(a).
[35] Co.Litt. 42a; *Brandon v. Robinson* (1811) 18 Ves. 429; and see *Re Evans's Contract* [1920] 2
Ch. 469. See also *ante*, para. 3–066.
[36] In *Re Machu* (1882) 21 Ch.D. 838 at 842 the possibility of determinable interests being subject
to special rules was raised but not decided.
[37] *Ante*, paras 3–060 *et seq*.

II. POSITION OF A TENANT FOR LIFE AT COMMON LAW

3–097   A tenant for life at common law was subject to important restrictions imposed by the law of waste (particularly as to timber and minerals), and by the rules relating to emblements and fixtures. These rules still apply to the modern equitable life interests.[38]

Waste

3–098   **1. Function.** "Waste", it has been said, "is a somewhat archaic subject, now seldom mentioned".[39] It can arise in other connections, notably in the law of landlord and tenant,[40] but it is most suitably considered in relation to life interests, where it is applicable both to ordinary life interests and to interests *pur autre vie*.[41] Liability for waste is tortious in character.[42] Its object is to prevent a limited owner, such as a tenant for life or years, despoiling the land to the prejudice of those in reversion or remainder. Their remedy is to bring an action for damages or to apply for an injunction[43]; and if the tenant for life has profited from the waste (*e.g.* by cutting timber), he may be made liable for the money received from the sale, or an account.[44]

There was an ancient writ of waste which gave treble damages and recovery of the place wasted[45]; but as it had serious defects, and could be used only by the owner of a vested estate of inheritance immediately expectant on the estate in possession,[46] it was superseded by the remedies just mentioned,[47] and abolished in 1833.[48]

3–099   **2. Nature.** Technically, waste consists of any act which alters the nature of the land, whether for the better or for the worse, *e.g.* the conversion of arable land into a woodland or vice versa.[49] Four types of waste must be considered: ameliorating, permissive, voluntary and equitable.[50]

---

[38] This was assumed in *Re Harker's W.T.* [1938] Ch. 323, but criticised at (1938) 2 Conv.(N.S.) 233 (H. Potter).

[39] *Mancetter Developments Ltd v. Garmanson Ltd* [1986] Q.B. 1212 at 1218, *per* Dillon L.J.

[40] It is seldom of importance in dealings between landlord and tenant nowadays because actions in respect of disrepair are usually brought on the covenant to repair: *Mancetter Developments Ltd v. Garmanson Ltd, supra,* at pp. 1218, 1223. See *post,* para. 14–274.

[41] See *Edward Seymor's Case* (1612) 10 Co.Rep. 95b at 98a.

[42] *Mancetter Developments Ltd v. Garmanson Ltd, supra,* at 1219, 1222, 1223.

[43] *Woodhouse v. Walker* (1880) 5 Q.B.D. 404 (damages); *Lowndes v. Norton* (1864) 33 L.J.Ch. 583 (injunction).

[44] *Seagram v. Knight* (1867) 2 Ch.App. 628 at 632; *Dashwood v. Magniac* [1891] 3 Ch. 306.

[45] Statute of Gloucester 1278.

[46] But see *Bacon v. Smith* (1841) 1 Q.B. 345.

[47] For the common law, see notes to *Greene v. Cole* (1682) 2 Wms.Saund. 252; for equity, see *Garth v. Cotton* (1750) 1 Ves.Sen. 546; Wh. & T. ii, 927, 962; and see generally Tudor L.C. 147–157.

[48] Along with the real actions: *post,* Appendix.

[49] Co.Litt. 53a, b; *Lord Darcy v. Askwith* (1618) Hob. 234; but see *Jones v. Chappell* (1875) L.R. 20 Eq. 539.

[50] For the common law rules about waste, see (1950) 13 Conv.(N.S.) 278 (M.E. Bathurst).

(a) Ameliorating waste. Alterations which improve the land, such as con- **3–100** verting dilapidated store buildings into dwellings[51] or a farm into a market-garden,[52] constitute what is paradoxically termed ameliorating waste. Claims for this type of waste find little favour in the courts unless the whole character of the property has been changed. Where improvements have been made, an action for damages will fail because no damage has been suffered, and an injunction will be awarded only if the court thinks fit.[53]

(b) Permissive waste. This is failure to do that which ought to be done, as **3–101** by the non-repair of buildings[54] or sea or river walls,[55] or the failure to clean out a ditch or moat so as to prevent foundations becoming rotten.[56] But mere non-cultivation of land is not permissive waste.[57] A tenant for life is not liable for permissive waste unless an obligation to repair is imposed upon him by the terms of the limitation under which he holds.[58] This obligation is as rare in life tenancies as it is common in tenancies for years.

(c) Voluntary waste. This is doing that which ought not to be done. "The **3–102** committing of any spoil or destruction in houses, lands, etc., by tenants, to the damage of the heir, or of him in reversion or remainder"[59] is voluntary waste. Examples of voluntary waste include—

    (i) removal of fixtures that are not tenant's fixtures[60];

    (ii) removal of tenant's fixtures without making good any damage so caused[61];

    (iii) opening and working a mine in the land[62] (but not merely working a mine already open[63]); and

    (iv) cutting timber.[64]

---

[51] *Doherty v. Allman* (1878) 3 App.Cas. 709; and see *Hyman v. Rose* [1912] A.C. 623 (chapel into cinema).
[52] *Meux v. Cobley* [1892] 2 Ch. 253; *cf. Jones v. Chappell* (1875) L.R. 20 Eq. 539 (erection of buildings).
[53] *Doherty v. Allman, supra; Re McIntosh and Pontypridd Improvements Co. Ltd* (1891) 61 L.J.Q.B. 164.
[54] Co.Litt. 53a; *Powys v. Blagrave* (1854) 4 De G.M. & G. 448.
[55] *Anon.* (1564) Moo.K.B. 62; *Griffith's Case* (1564) Moo.K.B. 69.
[56] *Sticklehorne v. Hatchman* (1586) Owen 43.
[57] *Hutton v. Warren* (1836) 1 M. & W. 466 at 472.
[58] *Re Cartwright* (1889) 41 Ch.D. 532.
[59] Bacon's *Abridgement* (7th ed.), viii, 379; and see *Mancetter Developments Ltd v. Garmanson Ltd* [1986] Q.B. 1212 at 1218, 1221.
[60] *Mancetter Developments Ltd v. Garmanson Ltd, supra,* at 1218. For tenant's fixtures, see *post,* paras 14–317 *et seq.*
[61] *Mancetter Developments Ltd v. Garmanson Ltd, supra.* There is no liability for minimal damage: *Re De Falbe* [1901] Ch. 523 at 542.
[62] *Saunders's Case* (1599) 5 Co.Rep. 12A; *Campbell v. Wardlaw* (1883) 8 App.Cas. 641.
[63] *Dashwood v. Magniac* [1891] 3 Ch. 306 at 360.
[64] *Honywood v. Honywood* (1874) L.R. 18 Eq. 306.

Timber consists of oak, ash and elm trees which are at least 20 years old and not too old to have a reasonable quantity of usable wood in them.[65] Other trees may rank as timber by local custom, *e.g.* beech in Buckinghamshire, willow in Hampshire and birch in Yorkshire and Cumberland[66]; and custom may also prescribe some qualification other than an age of 20 years for the trees to be considered timber, *e.g.* an age of 24 years or a specified girth.[67]

A tenant for life is liable for voluntary waste[68] unless his interest was granted to him by an instrument[69] exempting him from liability for voluntary waste, *e.g.* a grant "without impeachment of waste".[70] Where there is such an exemption the tenant is said to be "unimpeachable of waste"; otherwise he is said to be "impeachable of waste". Thus if nothing is said about waste, the tenant is impeachable; in practice, however, he is often made unimpeachable.

3–103   *(d) Equitable waste.* Even where a tenant for life is unimpeachable of waste, it is considered to be inequitable for him to ruin the property by acts of wanton destruction. To prevent this the equitable remedy of an injunction[71] will be granted. "Equitable waste is that which a prudent man would not do in the management of his own property."[72] The term applies to acts such as stripping a house of all its lead, iron, glass, doors, boards, etc., to the value of £3,000,[73] or pulling down houses,[74] or cutting timber planted with the object of providing ornament or shelter[75] (whether or not in fact it does provide it[76]), unless this is necessary for the preservation of part of the timber.[77] These acts are, of course, also voluntary waste, but are not relevant as such where the tenant is unimpeachable. Equitable waste therefore is a peculiarly flagrant branch of voluntary waste, which the ordinary dispensation from waste will not excuse.

There is one exception to the general rule that a tenant for life is liable for equitable waste even though he was granted his interest without impeachment of waste. He will not be liable if it expressly appears from the document that confers his interest upon him that he is to have the right to commit equitable waste as well as voluntary waste.[78]

---

[65] *ibid.*, at 309.
[66] *Aubrey v. Fisher* (1809) 10 East 446 (Bucks); Cru.Dig. i, 117 (Hants); *Countess of Cumberland's Case* (1610) Moo.K.B. 812 (Yorks.); *Pinder v. Spencer* (—) Noy 30 (Cumb.).
[67] *Honywood v. Honywood, supra,* at 309.
[68] *Pardoe v. Pardoe* (1900) 82 L.T. 547; *Re Ridge* (1885) 31 Ch.D. 504 at 507; H.E.L. iii, 121, 122. As to a tenant for life of leaseholds, see *Re Parry and Hopkin* [1900] 1 Ch. 160; *Re Field* [1925] Ch. 636.
[69] See *Dowman's Case* (1583) 9 Co.Rep. 1a at 10b.
[70] *Lewis Bowles's Case* (1616) 11 Co.Rep. 79b at 82b; *Waldo v. Waldo* (1841) 12 Sim. 107.
[71] *Post,* para. 4–015.
[72] *Turner v. Wright* (1860) 2 De G.F. & J. 234 at 243, *per* Lord Campbell, L.C.
[73] *Vane v. Lord Barnard* (1716) 2 Vern. 738.
[74] *Williams v. Day* (1680) 2 Ch.Ca. 32.
[75] *Marker v. Marker* (1851) 9 Hare 1.
[76] *Weld-Blundell v. Wolseley* [1903] 2 Ch. 664.
[77] *Baker v. Sebright* (1879) 13 Ch.D. 179.
[78] L.P.A. 1925, s.135; *Micklethwait v. Micklethwait* (1857) 1 De G. & J. 504 at 524.

Timber and minerals

Although largely governed by the general law of waste, the rights of a tenant **3–104**
for life with regard to timber and minerals are so important as to merit
separate treatment.

1. Timber

(a) Estovers. Whether impeachable of waste or not, a tenant for life can take **3–105**
reasonable estovers (or botes) from the land. These consist of wood and
timber taken as—

> (i) house-bote, for repairing the house or burning in it;
>
> (ii) plough-bote, for making and repairing agricultural implements;
> and
>
> (iii) hay-bote, for repairing fences.[79]

The tenant's right to house-bote does not entitle him to cut down timber in
excess of his present needs in order to use it for any repairs which become
necessary in the future, nor does it authorise him to sell the timber, even if he
employs the proceeds in repairs, or the timber proves unfit for repairs.[80]

(b) Timber estate. If the land is a timber estate (an estate cultivated mainly **3–106**
for the produce of saleable timber which is cut periodically[81]), the tenant can
cut and sell timber according to the rules of proper estate management even
if he is impeachable of waste. The reason for this rule is that the timber
properly cut on such an estate is part of the annual fruits of the land rather than
part of the inheritance.[82]

(c) Timber planted for ornament or shelter. As has been seen,[83] it is **3–107**
equitable waste to cut timber planted for ornament or shelter, and only a tenant
unimpeachable of equitable waste is permitted to do this.

(d) Trees. A tenant for life, even if he is impeachable of waste, may cut **3–108**
dotards (dead trees not fit for use as timber) and all trees which are not timber,
e.g. in most cases larches or willows.[84] But there are a number of exceptions

---

[79] Co.Litt. 41b, 53b; Tudor L.C. 147.
[80] *Gorges v. Stanfield* (1597) Cro.Eliz. 593; *Simmons v. Norton* (1831) 7 Bing. 640; Co.Litt.
53b.
[81] *Honywood v. Honywood* (1874) L.R. 18 Eq. 306 at 309, 310, where "merely" is used in place
of "mainly".
[82] *Honywood v. Honywood, supra,* at 309, 310; *Dashwood v. Magniac* [1891] 3 Ch. 306; *Re
Trevor-Batye* [1912] 2 Ch. 339.
[83] *Ante,* para. 3–103.
[84] *Herlakenden's Case* (1589) 4 Co.Rep. 62a at 63b; *Phillipps v. Smith* (1845) 14 M. & W. 589;
Honywood v. Honywood, supra; Re Harker's W.T. [1938] Ch. 323.

to this. It is voluntary waste to cut trees which would be timber but for their immaturity (unless the cutting is necessary to thin them out and so allow proper development)[85] or to cut fruit trees in a garden or orchard.[86] Further, it is voluntary waste to cut wood which a prudent man would not cut, such as willows which help to hold a river bank together[87]; and it may be equitable waste to cut trees planted for ornament or shelter, or to grub up an entire wood.[88]

3–109 *(e) Normal rules.* Subject to the above special rules, the position is that a tenant for life who is unimpeachable of waste may cut and sell timber and keep all the proceeds.[89] But if the tenant is impeachable of waste, his only right to cut timber is that given to him by statute.[90] This authorises him to cut and sell timber ripe and fit for cutting, provided—

> (i) the consent of the trustees of the settlement under which he holds his life interest, or an order of the court, is obtained; and

> (ii) three-quarters of the proceeds are set aside as capital money. This means that the trustees hold this portion of the price on trust for all persons having any interest in the land, paying only the interest to the tenant for life. The remaining quarter of the proceeds is paid to the tenant for life as income.

3–110 *(f) Ownership of severed timber.* Standing trees are part of the land and do not belong to the tenant for life until properly cut by him. Therefore if the land is sold with the trees standing, the life tenant cannot claim any share of the price even though he could lawfully have cut them.[91] The rule at common law was that severed trees belonged to the life tenant if he had the right to sever them, whether they had been felled by him, by a stranger, or by an act of God (such as a storm).[92] If he was not entitled to sever them, they belonged to the owner of the next vested estate or interest of inheritance.[93] Life estates can now exist only in equity and the equitable rules are less stringent. A court of equity has sometimes been willing to declare the proceeds of timber wrongfully cut to be part of the settled property, to be held for the benefit of all

[85] *Phillipps v. Smith, supra,* at 594; *Bagot v. Bagot* (1863) 32 Beav. 509 at 518; *Earl Cowley v. Wellesey* (1866) L.R. 1 Eq. 656.
[86] Co.Litt. 53a; *Kaye v. Banks* (1770) Dick. 431.
[87] *Stripping's Case* (1621) Winch 15.
[88] *Lord Tamworth v. Lord Ferrers* (1801) 6 Ves. 419; *Aston v. Aston* (1749) 1 Ves.Sen. 264 at 265.
[89] *Lewis Bowles's Case* (1615) 11 Co.Rep. 79b; Cru.Dig. i, 127.
[90] S.L.A. 1925, s.66, applicable only to settled land. This is one of the many statutory powers of a tenant for life under the settled land legislation. See notes in Wolst. & C. iii, 145.
[91] *Re Llewellin* (1887) 37 Ch.D. 317; *Re Londesborough* [1923] 1 Ch. 500.
[92] *Anon.* (1729) Mos. 237 at 238; *Lewis Bowles's Case, supra,* at 84a.
[93] *Paget's Case* (1593) 5 Co.Rep. 76b; *Bewick v. Whitfield* (1734) 3 P.Wms. 267; *Honywood v. Honywood* (1874) L.R. 18 Eq. 306; but see *Tooker v. Annesley* (1832) 5 Sim. 235 at 240.

parties other than the wrongdoer.[94] The tenant for life may also be allowed to take the income if the court would have authorised the cutting.[95]

2. Minerals. The mineral rights of a tenant for life depend on two factors, namely, whether the mine was already open when his tenancy began, and whether he is impeachable of waste. **3–111**

(a) Right to work mines. A tenant for life may work a mine and take all the proceeds unless— **3–112**

> (i) he is impeachable of waste, and

> (ii) the mine was not open when his tenancy began.

Where both these conditions are satisfied, he cannot work the mine at all, for to open and work an unopened mine is voluntary waste.[96] But it is not waste to continue working a mine already open[97] even if new pits are made on different parts of the same plot of land to pursue the same or a new vein, for the grantor, by opening or allowing the opening of the mines, has shown an intent that the minerals should be treated as part of the profits of the land.[98] Minerals improperly mined are dealt with in the same way as timber wrongfully cut.[99]

(b) Right to lease mines. The Settled Land Act 1925[1] authorises a tenant for life to grant mining leases for 100 years or less, whether the mine is open or not and whether or not the tenant is impeachable of waste. Leases granted under this power are binding on those in remainder or reversion. In each case the tenant for life is entitled to three-quarters of the rent, except that if he is impeachable of waste and the mine is unopened, he is entitled to only one-quarter of the rent under any lease granted by him and not by any previous owner or tenant for life.[2] The balance of rent is capital money and held for the benefit of all those interested under the settlement. But the whole of the rent will be paid to the tenant for life if the settlement shows such an intention. The powers conferred upon tenants for life by the settled land legislation are treated more fully later.[3] **3–113**

---

[94] *Lushington v. Boldero* (1851) 15 Beav. 1; *Honywood v. Honywood, supra*; Tudor L.C. 155.

[95] *Tooker v. Annesley, supra*; *Waldo v. Waldo* (1835) 7 Sim. 261; (1841) 12 Sim. 107; *Bateman v. Hotchkin (No. 2)* (1862) 31 Beav. 486; compare *Re Harrison's Trusts* (1884) 28 Ch.D. 220 at 228 (larches: trust for sale).

[96] *Ante*, para. 3–102. As to the meaning of "open", see *Greville-Nugent v. Mackenzie* [1900] A.C. 83; *Re Morgan* [1914] 1 Ch. 910 at 919, 920; *Elias v. Snowdon Slate Quarries Co.* (1879) 4 App.Cas. 454 at 465.

[97] *Viner v. Vaughan* (1840) 2 Beav. 466 at 469.

[98] *Re Hall* [1916] 2 Ch. 488 at 493; *Spencer v. Scurr* (1862) 31 Beav. 334; *cf. Re Ridge* (1885) 31 Ch. 504 at 508 and contrast *Re Maynard* [1899] 2 Ch. 347.

[99] *Re Barrington* (1886) 33 Ch.D. 523 at 527; *supra*.

[1] ss.41, 42, 45–47.

[2] S.L.A. 1925, s.47; *Re Fitzwalter* [1943] Ch. 285.

[3] *Post*, para. 8–079.

Emblements and fixtures

3–114   A tenant for life cannot foresee the date on which his estate will determine. In order to encourage him to cultivate his land by assuring him of the fruits of his labour, the law gives him a right to emblements.[4] This means that the tenant's personal representatives, or in the case of an estate *pur autre vie* the tenant himself,[5] may enter the land after the life estate has determined and reap the crops which the tenant has sown.[6] This applies only to cultivated crops such as corn, hemp, and flax, and not to things such as fruit trees and timber; and it extends only to the crops actually sown by the tenant for life[7] and growing at the determination of the tenancy.[8] Where the end of the tenancy is brought about by the tenant's own act (*e.g.* where a life estate is granted to a widow until remarriage and she remarries) there is no right to emblements.[9]

Prima facie any fixtures attached to the land by a tenant for life must be left after his death for the person next entitled to the land; but trade fixtures and ornamental and domestic fixtures are excepted. This is explained in greater detail later.[10]

Part 3

OWNERSHIP, POSSESSION AND TITLE

3–115   **1. Estate ownership.** Ownership in its fullest sense means, as already explained, that the owner holds the land in tenure (now universally socage) for an estate in fee simple absolute.[11] Tenure is an unimportant element in this formula of ownership: the vital element is the estate. The nature of estate ownership will to a large extent have become obvious from the preceding parts of this chapter. But the picture is not complete without some investigation of the theory of ownership which was developed by the common law, under which "absolute ownership" turns out to contain an unexpected measure of relativity.

It is natural to assume that the nature of title to an estate in land at common law is entirely derivative. Discussion proceeds as if the fee simple absolute is obtainable only by some kind of transfer from its previous owner, either by grant *inter vivos* or under his will or through the law of intestate succession. He can transmit no greater estate than he owned himself; and since the same was necessarily true of his own predecessors in title, the fee simple absolute

---

[4] *Graves v. Weld* (1833) 5 B. & Ad. 105 at 107.
[5] *Kelly v. Webber* (1860) 3 L.T. 124.
[6] Co.Litt. 55b.
[7] *Grantham v. Hawley* (1615) Hob. 132.
[8] *Graves v. Weld, supra,* at 119.
[9] *Oland's Case* (1602) 5 Co.Rep. 116a; Williams R.P. 135.
[10] *Post,* para. 14–323.
[11] *Ante,* para. 3–005.

which he owned must have had a continuous history going back to the year 1189, the limit of legal memory.[12] It is true that in earlier times the law allowed "tortious assurances" under which a tenant in tail or for life could convey a fee simple, due to the almost magical efficacy of the ancient forms of conveyance, feoffments, fines and recoveries. But all such possibilities were finally terminated in 1845.[13] From then on there was no exception, save only where provided by statute, to the principle *nemo dat quod non habet*: no one can convey what he does not own. It is possible, as will be seen in the next chapter, for a purchaser to take a title free from some incumbrance which was binding on the vendor, so that in one sense he may obtain more than the vendor had himself. But as regards the vendor's own estate in the land, the principle is fundamental.

There is then a clear contrast between ownership at common law and registered ownership under the modern system of registration of title. Under that system the estate of the registered proprietor is determined by what is shown on the register rather than by the estate of his predecessor. There is nevertheless some connection between these two things, so that even registered titles are to some extent derivative.[14] But in principle the registered system is not governed by the maxim *nemo dat quod non habet*, which for centuries dominated conveyancing at common law and which still does so where registration of title does not yet operate.   **3–116**

2. Possessory title. Title to land at common law is not invariably derivative; for it is sometimes possible for an entirely fresh title to be created, conferring a new fee simple estate. This can be made clear by looking at the remedies which were available to dispossessed owners and the time limits for those remedies imposed by various Acts of Parliament, of which the latest is the Limitation Act 1980.[15] All that need be assumed at this point is that under that Act, as under several of its predecessors, the remedy of a dispossessed owner is normally extinguished after the land has been in adverse possession for 12 years. Where the title to the land is unregistered the Act does not in any way transfer the dispossessed owner's estate to the adverse possessor. It merely extinguishes the earlier title, leaving the adverse possessor free from any claims under it. He then has a new and independent title, based upon his own possession.[15a] Here therefore is an example of a non-derivative title, based primarily on the fact of possession, but protected by statute against the former owner. An investigation of this phenomenon, and of its history, will serve to explain the essential nature of title, the strong links between possession and ownership, and the legal foundations of the fee simple estate.   **3–117**

---

[12] For this see *post*, para. 18–133.

[13] R.P.A. 1845, s.4, providing simply that a feoffment "shall not have any tortious operation". From then on all forms of conveyance were "innocent", *i.e.* subject to the *nemo dat* rule. Fines and recoveries had been abolished in 1833; *ante*, para. 3–084.

[14] See *post*, paras 3–126, n.53, 6–004, 6–028.

[15] For details see *post*.

[15a] The position is different where title is registered: *post*, para. 6–116.

3–118   For example, if S (squatter) wrongfully takes possession of land belonging to O (owner), O immediately acquires a right of action against S for recovery of the land.[16] If O takes no action, in 12 years (normally) his right of action becomes barred and his title extinguished by limitation. S can no longer be disturbed by O, and as against the rest of the world S is protected by the fact of his possession. Possession by itself gives a good title against all the world, except someone having a better legal right to possession.[17]

This last proposition is fundamental to our concept of title to land. If the occupier's possession is disturbed, for example by trespass or nuisance, he can sue on the strength of his possession and does not have to prove his title. It follows that the person disturbing the occupier's possession cannot attack his title, if he admits his possession; in the language of pleading, a defendant sued for trespass in such a case cannot plead *jus tertii* (that the land belongs to some third party, not to the plaintiff[18]). As against a defendant having no title to the land, the occupier's possession is in itself a title.[19] But if the defendant himself lays claim to the land by a title of his own, he may of course plead his own title and so put the plaintiff's title in issue; for then he is alleging a title not in a third party but in himself.[20] Accordingly he may show title in a third party if he himself claims through the third party, *e.g.* as purchaser, tenant or licensee.[21]

3. History

3–119   *(a) Proprietary and possessory actions.* This essentially possessory character of title to land is a product of historical evolution and, in particular, of the old forms of action. For some time after the middle of the twelfth century

---

[16] O may re-enter, but if resisted he may be guilty of an offence under the Criminal Law Act 1977, replacing the Statutes of Forcible Entry, 1381–1623, O will therefore be put to an action if S refuses to give up possession, though CPR Sched. 1, RSC O. 113 provides a speedy means of recovering it: *post*, Appendix.

[17] *Asher v. Whitlock* (1865) L.R. 1 Q.B. 1. This is the leading decision on the principle in modern times. H enclosed manorial land, and died in 1860 leaving the land by his will to his widow for life or until remarriage, remainder to his daughter in fee simple. The widow remarried, and two years after her death in 1863 the daughter's heir successfully claimed the land from the husband. The reason was that the heir had succeeded to H's possessory rights, and that these were good against the husband since his was a later possession. The lord of the manor was not a party to the proceedings, and it was not shown that his title was barred; and see *Perry v. Clissold* [1907] A.C. 73.

[18] "It is well settled that in an action of trespass a defendant may not set up a *jus tertii*. He may set up a title in himself, or show that he acted on the authority of the real owner, but he cannot set up a mere *jus tertii*": *Nicholls v. Ely Beet Sugar Factory (No. 1)* [1931] 2 Ch. 84 at 86, *per* Farwell J. *cf. Lall v. Lall* [1965] 1 W.L.R. 1249.

[19] It is however essential that possession should be taken. In *Marsden v. Miller* (1992) 64 P. & C.R. 239, two neighbours each made use of a piece of land of unknown ownership. One of them then erected a fence around the strip that was removed by the other within 24 hours. The erection of the fence in those circumstances was not such an assumption of control of the land by the former that he could bring trespass proceedings against his neighbour.

[20] See n.18 above.

[21] "If possession be shown, the defendant is not at liberty to set up the title of a third party unless he justifies what he has done under a licence from such third party": *Lord Fitzhardinge v. Purcell* [1908] 2 Ch. 139 at 145, *per* Parker J.

there were (at least in name) both proprietary and possessory actions, the former asserting title and the latter asserting possessory rights.[22] Thus if S disseised O of a piece of land, O could recover the land by a possessory action, showing merely the fact of dispossession. But this did not prejudice the question of title, and if S claimed title he might still recover the land again from O by a proprietary action. Originally the possessory actions were speedy and temporary remedies introduced in the king's courts for the purpose of preserving the peace and preventing forcible dispossessions, whether rightful or wrongful. But they were extended so fast and so far that they soon came to cover almost all claims, and superseded the ancient proprietary actions which lay only in the feudal courts.[23]

(b) Title based on seisin. Title to land therefore depended on the better right   **3–120** to possession (seisin) rather than vice versa. The concept of ownership was never really disentangled from that of possession.[24] As between two rival claimants, the land belonged to him who could lay claim to the earlier and therefore the better seisin, whether that seisin was his own or that of some person to whose rights he had succeeded, *e.g.* as heir or feoffee. Seisin was thus the root of all titles. When in the seventeenth century the action of ejectment[25] had been perfected as a general action for the recovery of land, it shifted the basis of title from the technical seisin of feudal law to the simple fact of possession.[26] This was because the action of ejectment was a branch of the action of trespass, which lay for a wrongful disturbance of possession, whereas the older possessory actions belonged to the family of the "real actions" which were peculiar to real property and were available only for claims based on seisin.[27]

(c) Possession as a root of title. The real actions were abolished in 1833[28]   **3–121** and the action of ejectment in 1852.[29] But our substantive law is still that

---

[22] See *post*, Appendix. Even the proprietary ("droitural") actions had a strong possessory flavour: Litt. 478; H.E.L. iii, 89, 90: Lightwood, *Possession of Land*, 71–75.

[23] H.E.L. iii, 8–14; *post*, Appendix.

[24] H.E.L. ii, 88 *et seq.*, and *ante*, para. 3–018, for the pre-eminence of seisin in medieval law. An owner disseised had a mere right of entry or action, which at common law was not assignable; he could not convey (being unable to deliver seisin); neither curtesy nor dower could be taken at his death; his death without heirs caused no escheat. Rights of entry did not become assignable at law until the R.P.A. 1845; *ante*, para. 3–076.

[25] *Post*, Appendix.

[26] In *Doe d. Crisp v. Barber* (1788) 2 T.R. 749 and *Doe d. Carter v. Barnard* (1849) 13 Q.B. 945 it was laid down that mere possession (*i.e.* possession unaccompanied by any other interest) would not support an action of ejectment. But this doctrine was wrong: see *Asher v. Whitlock*, *supra*, *Perry v. Clissold* [1907] A.C. 73 at 79, 80; *Hawdon v. Khan* (1920) 20 S.R. (N.S.W.) 703 at 707, 712; *Allen v. Roughley* (1955) 94 C.L.R. 98, noted in [1956] C.L.J. 177 (H.W.R.W.); *Oxford Meat Co. Pty Ltd v. McDonald* [1963] S.R. (N.S.W.) 423; *Nair Service Society Ltd v. K.C. Alexander* A.I.R. 1968 S.C. 1165; *Spark v. Whale Three Minute Car Wash (Cremorne Junction) Pty Ltd* (1970) 92 W.N. (N.S.W.) 1087; *Marsden v. Miller* (1992) 64 P. & C.R. 239 at 242–243; Lightwood, *Time Limit on Actions*, pp. 120–126; and see *Davison v. Gent* (1857) 1 H. & N. 744. The shift towards mere possession as the basis of title was further assisted by the Real Property Limitation Act 1833; see Lightwood, *Possession of Land*, pp. 123, 124.

[27] *Post*, Appendix.

[28] Real Property Limitation Act 1833, s.36.

[29] Common Law Procedure Act 1852, s.3.

developed from the action of ejectment,[30] so that today it is still true that possession is a root of title.[31] Any distinction between seisin and possession as the basis of title is obscured by the well-established rule that possession of land, if exclusive of other claimants[32] and not otherwise explained, is evidence of seisin in fee simple.[33] Naturally possession by a tenant or an agent is no foundation for a title against the landlord or the principal, for the possession is not adverse. Where the possession is truly adverse, there is little merit today in preserving for this purpose any distinction between seisin and possession; it is possession that forms the recognised root of title.[34] Ownership, as between two rival claimants, is the better right to possession.

4. Titles relative

3–122   *(a) Relativity of titles.* "At common law . . . there is no such concept as an 'absolute' title. Where questions of title to land arise in litigation the court is concerned only with the relative strengths of the titles proved by the rival claimants. If party A can prove a better title than party B he is entitled to succeed notwithstanding that C may have a better title than A, if C is neither a party to the action nor a person by whose authority B is in possession or occupation of the land."[35]

---

[30] See *Bristow v. Cormican* (1878) 3 App. Cas. 641 at 661. At one time an order for possession could not be made in *ex parte* proceedings. However since the introduction in 1970 of summary possession proceedings (CPR Sched. 1, RSC O. 113; Sched. 2, CCR O. 24; *post*, Appendix), the courts have been willing in wholly exceptional cases to make such an order where there is a real danger to life, limb or property: *Re Milward and Sons Ltd* (1980, unreported). Once an order for possession has been made the consequent writ or warrant of possession (CPR Sched. 1, RSC O. 45, rr. 3,12; Forms 66, 66A; Sched. 2, CCR O. 26, r. 17) operates *in rem*, since it requires the sheriff to enter the land and "cause" the plaintiff "to have possession of it". The writ thus takes effect against all persons there, whether or not they were defendants: *R. v. Wandsworth County Court, ex p. Wandsworth L.B.C.* [1975] 1 W.L.R. 1314. If after entry by the sheriff the defendant wrongfully resumes possession, the plaintiff may seek a writ of restitution to restore him to possession. This can be enforced even if there are new unlawful occupiers who have come on to the land since the original writ was issued: *Wiltshire C.C. v. Frazer (No. 2)* [1986] 1 W.L.R. 109.

[31] See (1940) 56 L.Q.R. 376, where in a valuable article A.D. Hargreaves maintained that seisin is still the basis; see esp. the summary at p. 397.

[32] Where the alleged trespasser is not a claimant (*i.e.* where he is merely disputing the plaintiff's actual possession), the plaintiff need show only slight evidence of possession: *Wuta-Ofei v. Danquah* [1961] 1 W.L.R. 1238; and acts of possession are strengthened by a claim of right: *Fowley Marine (Emsworth) Ltd v. Gafford* [1968] 2 Q.B. 618 (exclusive possession of tidal creek successfully shown); *Ocean Estates Ltd v. Pinder* [1969] 2 A.C. 19 (acts of possession strengthened by documentary title); and see *post*, para. 21–016.

[33] *Peaceable d. Uncle v. Watson* (1811) 4 Taunt. 16 at 17; *Jayne v. Price* (1814) 5 Taunt. 326; *Jones v. Smith* (1841) 1 Hare 43 at 60; *Re Atkinson & Horsell's Contract* [1912] 2 Ch. 1 at 9; Lightwood, *Possession of Land*, 114–121; (1940) 56 L.Q.R. 376 at 381, 382 (A.D. Hargreaves).

[34] See Lightwood, *Possession of Land*, pp. 124, 126; Pollock & Wright, *Possession*, 93–96; *Re Atkinson & Horsell's Contract*, *supra*, at p. 9. Holdsworth in H.E.L. vii, 62–68, and in (1940) 56 L.Q.R. 479 maintains that the action of ejectment, instead of making title more possessory, introduced a concept of absolute ownership and enabled the defendant to plead *jus tertii*. This theory is refuted by A.D. Hargreaves, *supra*, conflicts with *Asher v. Whitlock* and *Perry v. Clissold*, *supra*, n.26, and is treated as wrong in the later cases there cited.

[35] *Ocean Estates Ltd v. Pinder*, *supra*, at 24, 25, *per* Lord Diplock.

Some examples will illustrate this fundamental doctrine and the right and wrong occasions for the plea of *jus terii*. If last year S dispossessed O of land which had hitherto belonged to O, and O is taking no action, there are now two incompatible titles to the land: as between O and S, O is the owner, for he can recover the land by bringing an action; but as between S and the rest of the world (except O and persons claiming through him) S is owner, for he is in possession and that is equivalent to ownership as against all persons who have no better right.[36] Thus S can sue strangers for trespass or nuisance, just as O could before.[37] Furthermore, S can convey the land, or make any other disposition which an owner can make.[38] If S dies, the land will pass under his will or intestacy.[39] But all such rights derived through S are subject to O's (or his successor in title's) paramount right to recover the land. S's possession at once[40] gives him all the rights and powers of ownership, at least for the purposes of the civil law.[41] S has, in fact, a legal estate, a fee simple absolute in possession.[42] But so also has O, until such time as his title is extinguished by limitation.

(b) The better title. There is thus no absurdity in speaking of two or more **3–123** adverse estates in the land, for their validity is relative. If O allows his title to become barred by lapse of time. S's title becomes the better, and S then becomes "absolute owner". But if O brings his action within the time allowed,

---

[36] *Doe d. Hughes v. Dyeball* (1829) Moo. & M. 346; 3 C. & P. 610 (one year's possession held a good title as against a stranger); *Doe d. Humphrey v. Martin* (1841) Car. & M. 32; *Asher v. Whitlock* (1865) L.R. 1 Q.B. 1 (*ante*, para. 3–117).

[37] *Graham v. Peat* (1801) 1 East 244; *Chambers v. Donaldson* (1809) 11 East 65; *Nicholls v. Ely Beet Sugar Factory (No. 1)* [1931] 2 Ch. 84 at 86 (*post*, para. 18–175). Similarly if A supports his house on B's land (having no right), he cannot sue if B removes the support, but he can sue if C does: *Jeffries v. Williams* (1850) 5 Exch. 792 at 800; and see *Laing v. Whaley* (1858) 3 H. & N. 675. Again, if A uses B's road for access to his house he cannot sue if B obstructs the road, but he can if C does: *Beckett v. Midland Ry* (1867) L.R. 3 C.P. 82 at 103. But contrast *post*, para. 18–175.

[38] See Litt. 472, 474, 476, 477. But compare *R. v. Edwards* [1978] Crim.L.R. 49, where a squatter was convicted of obtaining by deception. She had received rent from a tenant to whom she had let part of the property. The court considered that she was never more than a trespasser and that "the one thing she was not entitled to do was to let". It is not apparent why she should not have had the power to let or why the Crown was able to rely on the *jus tertii*.

[39] Litt. 385 (intestacy); *Asher v. Whitlock*, *supra* (will and intestacy: two stages of devolution); *Allen v. Roughley*, *supra*, n.26 (will).

[40] The statement in H.E.L. vii, 64 that S has no title until the limitation period has run is erroneous: see cases cited *supra*, n.26.

[41] *cf. R. v. Edwards*, *supra*.

[42] *Rosenberg v. Cook* (1881) 8 Q.B.D. 162 at 165; *Central London Commercial Estates Ltd v. Kato Kagaku Ltd* [1998] 4 All E.R. 948 at 951. The old maxim was that a wrongdoer could not qualify his wrong, *i.e.* he was taken to claim the largest possible interest: Co.Litt. 271a. "For a disseisor, abator, intruder, usurper, etc., have a fee simple, but it is not a lawful fee": Co.Litt. 2a; and see *ibid.* p. 297a; Litt. 519, 520; Williams, *Seisin*, p. 7, cited with approval by Dixon J. in *Wheeler v. Baldwin* (1934) 52 C.L.R. 609 at 632; *Leach v. Jay* (1878) 9 Ch.D. 42 at 44, 45; *Spark v. Meers* [1971] 2 N.S.W.L.R. 1 at 12. Thus if S is a leasehold tenant his encroachments are presumed to enure to the benefit of his landlord: *post*, paras. 18–129, 21–027. See also *post*, para. 21–061. For the context of modern legislation, see (1964) 80 L.Q.R. 63 (B. Rudden).

he can successfully assert his better title based on his prior possession; as against O, S's legal estate is nothing.[43]

3–124   *(c) Jus tertii.* We have already seen that other persons who have themselves no title cannot exploit the relative weakness of S's title by pleading *jus tertii.* If X (a stranger) takes possession of the land from S, S or his successors can recover it within the limitation period and X cannot plead that the land is not in fact S's but O's.[44] This is self-evident, for otherwise anyone could help himself to the land.[45] If X claims the land, he must do so on the strength of some title of his own, not on the weakness of S's.[46]

On the other hand, suppose that, while S is still in undisturbed possession, O dies and by his will leaves all his land to X. If X acts in time he can obtain the land by asserting O's superior title. But here S, who is in possession, can compel X to prove his title, and if X's title, as derived from O, is subject to a *jus tertii* then S can plead it. If, for example, S can prove that O revoked the will in favour of X by a later will in favour of Y, S can plead that the land is not X's but Y's; and therefore, since Y's title shows X to be a mere stranger, S's possession is a good title against X. This again is self-evident, for otherwise S would have no protection against anyone purporting to claim though O. S can plead *jus tertii* against O himself if O has conveyed or demised the land to Z, for then the right to possession can be shown to be in Z, not in O.[47] It is only the title behind O's original possession that S is not allowed to dispute.[48]

3–125   Where one party has obtained possession by permission of the other, he naturally cannot use that possession to support a plea of *jus tertii* against that

---

[43] "When any man is disseised, the disseisor has only the naked possession, because the disseisee may enter and evict him; but against all other persons the disseisor has a right, and in this respect only can be said to have the right of possession, for in respect to the disseisee he has no right at all": Gilbert, *Tenures*, p. 21, cited in Butler's note to Co.Litt. 238a.

[44] *Asher v. Whitlock* (1865) L.R. 1 Q.B. 1, *ante*, para. 3–117; *Spark v. Whale Three Minute Car Wash (Cremorne Junction) Pty. Ltd* (1970) 92 W.N. (N.S.W.) 1087. It makes no difference that O's title may be registered and "indefeasible": *ibid.*

[45] "Can it be at the mere will of any stranger to disturb the person in possession?": *Asher v. Whitlock, supra,* at 6, *per* Cockburn C.J.

[46] *Martin d. Tregonwell v. Strachan* (1743) 5 T.R. 107n., affd. (1744) Willes 444; *Roe d. Haldane v. Harvey* (1769) 4 Burr. 2484; *Bristow v. Cormican* (1878) 3 App.Cas. 641 at 661.

[47] *Roe d. Haldane v. Harvey, supra* (the defendant, being in possession, proved that the plaintiff Haldane had conveyed the land to another person, and so had no title); *Doe d. Wawn v. Horn* (1838) 3 M. & W. 333 (defendant in possession proved that plaintiff had demised the land, so the proper plaintiff was the tenant); *Culley v. Doe d. Taylerson* (1840) 3 Per. & D. 539 at 552, 557 (defendant in possession proved that plaintiff's claim as heir to A was bad because A had devised the land to B); *cf. Doe d. Lloyd v. Passingham* (1827) 6 B. & C. 305 (defendant in possession proved that legal estate was outstanding in a trustee). The many cases in which actions of ejectment failed for want of the immediate legal title are in fact cases of *jus tertii* properly pleaded. For modern examples see *ante*, para. 3–120, n.26 and *Wirral B.C. v. Smith* (1982) 43 P. & C.R. 312.

[48] "Possession gives the defendant a right against every man who cannot show a good title": *Roe d. Haldane v. Harvey, supra,* at 2487, *per* Lord Mansfield C.J. See [1956] C.L.J. 177 (H.W.R.W.). For the same principle applied to personalty (a motor car), see *Wilson v. Lombank Ltd* [1963] 1 W.L.R. 1294.

other. This explains why a tenant or licensee is estopped from denying the title of his lessor or licensor.[49]

Sometimes neither party may be able to show possession in fact, and the question then is which of them can show possession in law, *i.e.* the better right to possession. This is a straight contest of documentary titles, and either can defend an action of trespass by showing that the plaintiff is not the true owner.[50]

5. Ownership. Although the person with the best ascertained right to   **3–126**
possession is often called the "absolute owner", it is clear from the foregoing analysis that English law knows no abstract ownership, as opposed to the right to recover possession, unless perhaps the Crown's universal seignorial rights should be so classified.[51] O may be "owner" of Blackacre, but it is always theoretically possible for someone to come forward and prove a better title, as by proving that he owns the reversion on a long term of years which has now expired, or by finding a lost will which alters the devolution of the property.

This "possessory ownership" is well illustrated by the ordinary procedure for proving title to a purchaser of unregistered land.[52] "The standing proof that English law regards, and has always regarded, Possession as a substantive root of title, is the standing usage of English lawyers and landowners. With very few exceptions, there is only one way in which an apparent owner of English land who is minded to deal with it can show his right so to do; and that way is to show that he and those through whom he claims have possessed the land for a time sufficient to exclude any reasonable probability of a superior adverse claim."[53] It is by limitation that any such superior claim will have been excluded. Adverse possession and limitation together are therefore the foundations of a good title; if this is understood, the nature of a title acquired by limitation becomes plain. Where title is unregistered there is no "parliamentary conveyance"[54] from the one party to the other; one title is

---

[49] See *post*, para. 14–097.
[50] *Lord Fitzhardinge v. Purcell* [1908] 2 Ch. 139 at 145.
[51] As they are in Scottish law: see W. M. Gordon, *Scottish Land Law*, pp. 40–41. For the Crown's seignorial rights, see *ante*, para. 2–001.
[52] *Post*, paras. 12–072 *et seq.*
[53] Pollock and Wright, *Possession*, p. 94. Even under the system of registration of title (*post*, para. 6–001) titles are still relative, although the mode of proof is different. A person claiming a better title than that of the registered owner can sue for rectification of the register: *post*, para. 6–119.
[54] This expression attained some currency (see *Scott v. Nixon* (1843) 3 Dr. & War. 388 at 407; *Doe d. Jukes v. Sumner* (1845) 14 M. & W. 39 at 42; and see *Dawkins v. Lord Penrhyn* (1877) 6 Ch.D. 318 at 323), but it is now established that it is erroneous: see *Tichborne v. Weir* (1892) 67 L.T. 735; *Re Atkinson & Horsell's Contract* [1912] 2 Ch. 1 at 9. Thus the possessor is not entitled to any right that depends on the making of a grant, *e.g.* a way of necessity: *Wilkes v. Greenway* (1890) 6 T.L.R. 449. For such easements, see *post*, para. 18–098. Where title is registered, adverse possession *does* operate as a "parliamentary conveyance": see *post*, para. 21–056.

extinguished altogether and a new one arises. The new title is, however, subject to the rights of third parties, whether legal or equitable,[55] unless they too have been barred by limitation.[56]

CHAPTER 4

LAW AND EQUITY

Part 1

GENERAL PRINCIPLES

A fundamental distinction in the law of real property is that between legal and **4–001** equitable interests in land. This was a product of the history of the courts. The judges in the courts of common law were concerned with legal interests, the Chancellor in his Court of Chancery with equitable interests. Although these rival jurisdictions were amalgamated in 1873, the dual system which they produced remains firmly embedded in the law. The importance of the distinction has been much reduced by the 1925 legislation, particularly in relation to the system of registered title.[1]

Section 1. The Historical Basis of Equity

1. Common law: the writ system

(a) The writs. In order to commence an action in any of the common law **4–002** courts (King's Bench, Common Pleas and Exchequer) normally a writ had first to be issued under the seal of the Chancellor, the keeper of the Great Seal. Each different kind of action had its own writ, often with its own special procedure.[2] If an heir was claiming land from a dispossessor after his father's death, the action had to be started by a writ of *mort d'ancestor*; if he was the grandfather of the heir, a writ of *aiel* had to be used, and if he was the great-grandfather, a writ of *besaiel*.[3] No action could succeed unless the correct writ was chosen.[4] There was, therefore, a strictly *formulary* legal system: a plaintiff would succeed only if some writ provided a formula to fit his case. England was no exception to the rule that in early law justice was dominated by procedure.[5]

---

[1] *Post*, para. 6–001.
[2] Maitland, *Forms of Action*, 2. For a discussion of actions for the recovery of land, see *post*, Appendix; J. H. Baker, *An Introduction to English Legal History* (3rd ed.), 63.
[3] Maitland, *Forms of Action*, 31.
[4] *ibid.*, 4; H.E.L. ix. 245.
[5] Maine, *Early Law and Custom*, 389; Maitland, *Forms of Action*, 1, 6.

4–003   *(b) New writs.* At first new writs were invented with comparative freedom for cases not covered by existing writs, though some were disallowed by the courts.[6] They were severely restricted by the Provisions of Oxford 1258, in which the Chancellor swore that he would seal no new form of writ without the command of the King and his Council.[7] But the Statute of Westminster II, 1285, provided in the famous Chapter 24, *In Consimili Casu*, that the clerks in Chancery should have a limited power to invent new writs. If there already existed one writ, and in a like case *(in consimili casu)*, falling under like law and requiring like remedy, there was none, the clerks in Chancery might make a suitable writ, or else refer the matter to the next Parliament. The result, nevertheless, was to stunt the growth of the writ system,[8] and to leave many cases without remedy.

4–004   **2. Petitions to the King and Chancellor.** Suitors therefore turned to the King, as the fountain of justice. Their petitions were heard by the King's Council, of which the Chancellor was an important member.[9] After the reign of Edward III petitions were often addressed to the Chancellor alone, and in this way he acquired a regular and expanding judicial business. At first the decisions upon the petitions were made either in the name of the King's Council or else with the advice of the serjeants and judges. During the course of the fifteenth century the Chancellor began to make decrees on his own authority, and his decrees thereafter became frequent.[10]

3. The Court of Chancery

4–005   *(a) The Chancellor.* In this way there gradually came into existence a Court of Chancery in which the Chancellor, acting independently of the King's Council, sat as a judge administering a system of justice called equity.[11] Although prior to the appointment of Sir Thomas More in 1529 the Chancellor

---

[6] Maitland, *Forms of Action*, 41.

[7] *ibid.*, 41, 46, 51; H.E.L. i, 398.

[8] There was a widespread belief from the sixteenth century onwards that this statute was the origin of the action on the case: [1971] C.L.J. 213 at 217 (J. H. Baker). In fact very few new writs were created under the statute and all were concerned with real property: (1931) 31 Columbia L.R. 778 (T. F. T. Plucknett). It is now known that the action on the case derived from certain types of trespass action: S. F. C. Milsom, *Historical Foundations of the Common Law* (2nd ed.), chap. 11.

[9] H.E.L. i, 400.

[10] See (1969) 42 *Bulletin of the Institute of Historical Research* 129; (1970) 86 L.Q.R. 84 (M. E. Avery). For early reports of decisions by the Chancellor, see *Cardinal Beaufort's Case* (1453), J. H. Baker and S. F. C. Milsom, *Sources of English Legal History*, 95; *Anon.* (1467), *ibid.*, 98.

[11] The Chancery was not the only court which exercised an equity jurisdiction. Not only were there a number of local conciliar courts with an equity jurisdiction during the Tudor and Stuart period (see J. H. Baker, *An Introduction to English Legal History*, 139), but the Court of Exchequer had an equity side until 1842 (see W. H. Bryson, *The Equity Side of Exchequer*); and in the Law Journal Reports there was a separate series of Exchequer Equity reports. *cf. Billson v. Residential Apartments Ltd* [1992] 1 A.C. 494 at 512, where Browne-Wilkinson V.-C. said that it had not been explained "how, in 1816, the Court of Exchequer came to be ruling upon equitable doctrines".

had sometimes been a layman, he was usually a senior clergyman. After the 1550s however a lawyer was normally appointed.[12] Equity, which had varied with the ideas of each Chancellor, began with Lord Ellesmere (1596–1617) to develop into a code of principles, and the work of Lord Nottingham (1673–1682) in systematising the rules earned him the title of the Father of Equity.[13] When Lord Eldon retired in 1827 the rules of equity were as well settled as those of the common law; a "*rigor aequitatis*" had developed, and he could safely say "nothing would inflict on me greater pain, in quitting this place, than the recollection that I had done anything to justify the reproach that the equity of this court varies like the Chancellor's foot".[14] But equity, although it followed the inevitable course towards fixity and dogma, remained in general a more modern and flexible system than the common law. Originally it provided the means, needed in every legal system, of adapting general rules to particular cases, and this character was never entirely lost.

(b) A court of conscience. In the course of time various subsidiary officials **4–006** were appointed to assist the Chancellor, a system of appeals grew up, and finally in 1875 the Chancery system was merged with the common law courts to form the present Supreme Court of Judicature.[15] In short, the practice of petitioning the King for justice in exceptional cases gradually opened the way to a supplementary system of law administered regularly by a court, but by a court quite different and separate from the courts of common law. The latter decided cases according to the strict common law rules, and with much fondness for technicality. Chancery, on the other hand, deliberately mitigated the rigour of the common law, tempering its rules to the needs of particular cases on principles which seemed just and equitable to generations of Chancellors, and technical pleas were usually unsuccessful. The common law courts were mainly concerned with enforcing the strict rights of the parties regardless of their merits, whereas Chancery was a court of conscience where remedies would be withheld from a party guilty of sharp practice or any kind of unconscionable conduct.

(c) Conflict. The decrees of the Chancellor would often, therefore, conflict **4–007** with judgments obtained at common law. A party who had lost his case because of some trickery or accident, for example, could obtain in Chancery an injunction forbidding his opponent to execute the common law judgment. This power to interrupt the common law process was used so often that this type of injunction was called a "common injunction". The Chancellor's

---

[12] J. H. Baker, *An Introduction to English Legal History*, 125.

[13] *Kemp v. Kemp* (1801) 5 Ves. 849 at 858.

[14] *Gee v. Pritchard* (1818) 2 Swans. 402 at 414. Selden had complained (*Table Talk*, 31b) that equity varied with the conscience of each Chancellor, and that this was as absurd as making the measurement known as a foot vary with each Chancellor's foot.

[15] *Post*, para. 4–017. For the reorganisation of the Court of Chancery in the nineteenth century, see H.E.L. i, 442 *et seq.*

jurisdiction to issue it was clearly established after the decision of James I in the celebrated dispute between Coke C.J. and Lord Ellesmere L.C.[16]

4–008   *(d) Equity acts in personam.* A peculiarity of equity was that it acted *in personam*, "on the person". The Chancellor's ultimate sanction was to imprison for contempt anyone who disobeyed his decree. He could not, as could the common law courts, award damages enforceable by a sheriff's execution against the defendant's property. But he could decree that the defendant should pay a sum of money, and imprison him if he would not, or that he should do or abstain from doing something on pain of imprisonment for disobedience.[17]

Section 2. The Nature of Equitable Rights

4–009   **1. Legal and equitable ownership.** The essential difference between legal and equitable rights is best understood by comparing absolute ownership with trusts. Trusts were not enforceable at common law but only by the Chancellor.[18] If land was conveyed to A in fee simple upon trust for B in fee simple, the common law courts regarded A as absolute owner and would not recognise any rights in B. But the Chancellor would enforce trusts, as matters of conscience, and compel A to hold the land on B's behalf and to allow B to enjoy it. In such a case A is the "legal owner", B is the "equitable owner". The land is vested in A, but since he is trustee of it he is not the beneficial owner: he has only the "bare legal estate", and the beneficial interest belongs to B.

Now legal ownership confers rights *in rem*, rights of property in the land itself, which can be enforced against anyone. Equitable ownership conferred at first only a right *in personam*, a right to compel the trustee personally to perform his trust. But what should happen if the trustee died or disposed of the land? Trusts would have been hopelessly insecure if means had not been found to protect them from such events.

4–010   **2. Extent of enforcement.** The Chancellors solved this problem by extending the categories of persons upon whom performance of the trust would be enjoined. As case followed case the extensions became very wide. In 1465 it was laid down that a trust would be enforced against anyone who took a conveyance of the land *with notice of the trust.*[19] In 1483 the Chancellor said

---

[16] It is often said that the dispute was resolved in *Earl of Oxford's Case* (1615) 1 Ch.Rep. 1, but this was not in fact the case: see (1969) 4 *Irish Jurist*, 368 (J. H. Baker). For the legal background to the dispute, see (1976) 20 *American Journal of Legal History*, 192 (C. M. Gray).

[17] Maitland, *Equity*, 9; H.E.L. i, 458.

[18] For the history of trusts, see the previous edition of this work, Appendix 3, and S. F. C. Milsom, *Historical Foundations of the Common Law* (2nd ed.), p. 233.

[19] Y.B. 5 Edw. 4, Mich. pl. 16.

that he would enforce a trust against the trustee's heir.[20] In 1522 it was said that a trust would be enforced against anyone to whom the land had been conveyed as a gift.[21] It was later decided that others such as the executors and execution creditors of the trustees would be bound by the trust.[22]

3. The purchaser without notice. Two equitable principles explain these developments. First, a person who takes the land without giving value in exchange (such as an heir, executor or donee) must take it with all its burdens, equitable as well as legal: trusts bind volunteers. Secondly, even a person who has given value will be bound if before he obtained the land he knew of the trust: trusts bind all who take with notice. Both these principles are summed up in the cardinal maxim in which is expressed the true difference between legal and equitable rights:

Legal rights are good against all the world; equitable rights are good against all persons except a bona fide purchaser of a legal estate for value without notice, and those claiming under such a purchaser.[23]

Such as purchaser is often referred to, somewhat inappropriately, as "equity's darling".[24]

4. Equitable interests. This rule runs right though the law of property; it has been called "the polar star of equity".[25] Its detailed anatomy will be investigated later,[26] and it will be shown that it has only a residual role in relation to real property. Its general meaning is that equitable rights advanced almost to the status of legal rights, but not quite. Equity always stopped short of enforcing a trust against a person who had bought the land from the legal owner in genuine ignorance of the existence of the trust. An equitable owner was therefore never quite in the impregnable position of a legal owner: he never had an absolutely indefeasible title. But the rules relating to notice and the system of conveyancing founded upon them protected equitable interests, as we shall see, for nearly all practical purposes, so that for the sake of their other advantages they were very much used. They became much more than rights *in personam* against trustees: they were a new species of property right, really rights *in rem*,[27] but exceptional because of their peculiar infirmity, that

4–011

4–012

---

[20] Y.B. 22 Edw. 4, Pasch. pl. 18.

[21] Y.B. 14 Hen. 8, Mich. pl. 5, fo. 7. See *Chudleigh's Case* (1595) 1 Co.Rep. 113b at 122b.

[22] For accounts of these developments, see Maitland, *Equity*, 112; and A. W. B. Simpson, *A History of the Land Law* (2nd ed.), p. 179.

[23] Maitland, *Equity*, pp. 114, 115; *cf.* L.P.A. 1925, s.2(5). Where the title to land is registered, the doctrine of notice has no role to play: *post*, para. 5–006.

[24] Maitland, *Coll. Pp.*, iii, 350. The appellation is inappropriate because if the defence of bona fide purchase is established, an encumbrance will have been defeated and the proper working of the system of conveyancing will have failed.

[25] *Stanhope v. Earl Verney* (1761) 2 Eden 81 at 85, *per* Lord Henley L.C.

[26] *Post*, para. 5–005.

[27] Maitland laid stress on the personal nature of equitable rights, for historical and other good reasons: *Equity*, 23, 29, 107, 117. If by rights *in rem* is meant (as normally) rights enforceable against third parties generally, as opposed to rights *in personam* which are enforceable only against specified persons (*e.g.* contractual rights), then equitable rights to property are unquestionably rights *in rem*, though somewhat different from legal rights to property.

they would be lost if the legal title came to a bona fide purchaser without notice. They are therefore commonly called"equitable interests" (*sc.* in property); for "equity has modelled them into the shape and quality of real estates".[28]

4–013   **5. Persons bound.** The wide, proprietary character of equitable interests is shown by the modern form of the fundamental rule. Instead of enumerating all the classes of persons bound in addition to trustees themselves, the rule lays down in the first place that equities bind *all* persons, and then gives a single but very important exception. This change of form marks an increase in scope. In 1905 the question arose whether a squatter (a person who had obtained title to land by long occupation uncontested by the previous owner[29]) was bound by an equitable interest created by the previous owner. A squatter was not among the classes of persons held liable in the line of cases which led to the rule. But he was not a purchaser for value; and the rule was so well established in its wide form that there was no difficulty in deciding that the squatter was bound.[30]

This special characteristic of equitable rights may be made clearer by an illustration. Suppose that in 1920[31] A was legal owner of Blackacre, holding it upon trust for B absolutely, and that Blackacre was subject to a legal lease to a tenant T, to a legal right of way owned by R, to a legal mortgage in favour of L and an equitable mortgage[32] in favour of E. If in 1921 A succeeded in selling Blackacre to a purchaser P who had no notice of any of the other interests, P's position would be as follows. On taking a conveyance of the legal estate he would still be bound by T's lease, R's right of way and L's legal mortgage, since these belong to the class of legal estates and interests which bind all comers. But B's trust and E's equitable mortgage would be defeated by the purchase of the legal estate without notice: B and E would lose their rights over the land, and their only remedies would be against A personally.

Section 3. Equitable Remedies

4–014   **1. Discretionary nature of equitable remedies.** A further distinction between law and equity lay in the matter of remedies. In general, if a legal

---

[28] *Burgess v. Wheate* (1759) 1 Eden 177 at 149, *per* Henley L.K.

[29] *Ante*, para. 3–117; *post*, para. 21–001.

[30] *Re Nisbet and Potts' Contract* [1906] 1 Ch. 386 (squatter held liable to restrictive covenant); followed in *Ashe v. Hogan* [1920] 1 I.R. 159. Contrast *Bolling v. Hobday* (1882) 31 W.R. 9 (squatter held free from trust for sale), and see 51 S.J. 141, 155 (T. C. Williams). The Limitation Act 1980, s.18 (*post*, para. 21–038) makes provision for land held upon trust which alters the principle in *Bolling v. Hobday*. The difficulty which was felt was that a squatter acquired a new legal estate (*post*, para. 21–055), and not the legal estate which was subject to the trust. But in reality it is the land, not the estate, which is affected.

[31] This date is chosen because if created after 1925, the equitable mortgage would probably have been registrable: see *post*, para. 19–218.

[32] A less formal type of mortgage: *post*, para. 19–039.

right was infringed, the person injured was entitled as of right to a legal remedy, either an order for the recovery of his land or damages. Thus, if A trespassed on X's land X had a legal right to sue him for damages and, on proving his case, he was entitled to damages as of right. If the trespass was trivial the damages might be nominal (*e.g.* £2) or contemptuous (*e.g.* 1p) and X might be ordered to pay the costs; but he had a right to judgment. A plaintiff seeking an equitable remedy, on the other hand, had no right to anything at all; equitable remedies were discretionary, and even if the plaintiff proved his case, equity might refuse to give him any assistance if, for example, his claim was trivial or it would be inconvenient or unconscionable to grant an equitable remedy. This discretion was exercised not arbitrarily according to the whim of the judge but "judicially", according to settled principles, so that a plaintiff could succeed in equity only if, in addition to a right having been infringed, there was no equitable principle which prevented him from being granted a remedy.[33]

2. The remedies. The principal remedies given by equity were specific **4–015** performance (an order to a person to carry out his obligations) and injunction (an order to a person to refrain from doing some act in the future or, more rarely, to put right something already done). These remedies were evolved from the forms of decree acting *in personam*. Equity would also make orders for money payments either where no remedy existed at law, as, for example, where a trustee had dissipated trust moneys, or as an adjunct to equitable relief.[34] It would on occasions even award damages, though the limits of the jurisdiction were ill-defined.[35] The Court of Chancery was finally given a statutory power to award damages by the Chancery Amendment Act 1958. That Act provided that in any case where the Chancery had power to entertain an application for an injunction or specific performance, it could award damages either in addition to or in substitution for such injunction or specific performance.[36] This did not alter the rule that equitable remedies were discretionary, nor did it enable the court to award damages in all cases. The Chancery could award damages only where it had jurisdiction to grant specific performance or an injunction, and in no other case.[37]

In the same way that the Chancery was originally unable to give the legal remedy of damages, the common law courts were unable to give the equitable remedies of specific performance and injunction. Consequently a plaintiff who

---

[33] Snell, *Equity*, 652–654.

[34] For example, specific performance with compensation: [1981] C.L.J. 48 (C.H.); and damages when relief was granted against a penalty of forfeiture: S. Goldstein, ed., *Equity and Contemporary Legal Developments* (C.H.), p. 829.

[35] See (1992) 108 L.Q.R. 652 (P. McDermott).

[36] The provision is now to be found in the Supreme Court Act 1981, s.50.

[37] *Lavery v. Pursell* (1889) 39 Ch.D. 508; *Proctor v. Bayley* (1889) 42 Ch.D. 390; *Wroth v. Tyler* [1974] Ch. 30; *Johnson v. Agnew* [1980] A.C. 367 at 400; *Jaggard v. Sawyer* [1995] 1 W.L.R. 269; *post*, para. 12–118; Wh. & T. ii, 399 *et seq.*; [1975] C.L.J. 224 (J. A. Jolowicz); [1977] C.L.J. 369 (P. H. Pettit); [1981] Conv. 286 (T. Ingman and J. Wakefield). The measure of damages is the same as at common law: *Johnson v. Agnew, supra*.

wanted, say, damages for past trespasses, and an injunction to restrain future trespasses, formerly had to take proceedings both in one of the common law courts and in Chancery.

4–016   **3. Relationship with law.** The manner in which the courts of common law and of Chancery used to operate side by side, with mutually exclusive but complementary jurisdictions, cannot here be explained at length.[38] But it may be illustrated by the fourfold classification of the jurisdiction in equity. This comprised—

  (i)   the exclusive jurisdiction, dealing with matters which the common law totally ignored, such as trusts;

  (ii) the concurrent jurisdiction, where equity offered remedies better suited to some cases than damages at common law, as, for example, specific performance of contracts for the sale of land, and injunctions against trespass or breach of covenant;

  (iii) the auxiliary jurisdiction, where equity assisted common law procedure, for example, by decrees for discovery of documents; and

  (iv) the overriding jurisdiction, interrupting common law process in the manner already explained.[39]

In all these ways equity supplied or corrected deficiencies of the common law. But until 1875 equity was administered in its own separate court. To put an end to multiplicity of proceedings where both legal and equitable issues arose in the same case was one of the principal objects of the Judicature Acts 1873 and 1875.

Section 4. The Judicature Acts: Union of the Courts of Law and Equity

4–017   **1. Union of courts.** By the Judicature Act 1873[40] the superior courts of law and equity were united into one Supreme Court, divided into a High Court and Court of Appeal. All parts of the Supreme Court were given full jurisdiction both in law and in equity without any distinction of subject-matter. For convenience the High Court was divided into five Divisions, each of which had certain matters assigned to it. In 1880[41] the Common Pleas Division and Exchequer Division were merged into the Queen's Bench Division, and in

---

[38] Maitland, *Equity*, 17; Ashburner, *Equity* (2nd ed.), 10; Snell, *Equity* 11.

[39] *Ante*, para. 4–007. This classification of equitable jurisdictions was rendered obsolete by the Judicature Act 1873.

[40] This came into force on November 1, 1875 (Supreme Court of Judicature (Commencement) Act 1874, s.2). The Judicature Acts 1873 and 1875 were replaced by the J.A. 1925, now in turn replaced by the Supreme Court Act 1981.

[41] Order in Council of December 16, 1880, made under J.A. 1873, s.32.

1972 the Probate, Divorce and Admiralty Division was re-named the Family Division,[42] with some adjustments of jurisdiction. There are now three Divisions[43]:

the Chancery Division,
the Queen's Bench Division, and
the Family Division.

2. Jurisdiction of Divisions. It is important to notice that these are only **4–018** divisions of one court, the High Court, and not separate courts having distinct jurisdiction[44]; each Division of the High Court has the same jurisdiction and can enforce both legal and equitable rights and give both legal and equitable remedies. This means that it is no longer necessary to go to two separate courts to enforce legal and equitable rights or to obtain legal and equitable remedies. If a point of equity arises in an action in the Queen's Bench Division, for example, the court can deal with it; and it will not be fatal to an action if it is started in the wrong Division, for the case may be transferred to the proper Division if it is not decided in the Division in which it was started.[45] The allocation of business between the three Divisions cannot therefore affect any question of law: it is so arranged merely for administrative convenience.

3. Law and equity still distinct. Law and equity nevertheless remain **4–019** distinct.[46] The two bodies of law have not been altered, although they are now both administered by the same court.[47] A legal right is still enforceable against a purchaser of a legal estate without notice, while an equitable right is not. Equitable rights are still enforceable only by equitable remedies, subject to the statutory jurisdiction to award damages in addition to or in substitution for an injunction or a decree of specific performance. The so-called "fusion of law and equity"[48] has not in fact altered the substance of any person's rights, duties or remedies: it has altered only the courts which enforce them. The reform was therefore primarily a reform of procedure, providing new judicial machinery for the enforcement of the settled rules of law and equity.[49] Under the current procedural rules, for example, an equitable owner can bring proceedings to assert his title and recover land in the same way as a legal

---

[42] Administration of Justice Act 1970.
[43] Supreme Court Act 1981, s.5.
[44] *Serrao v. Noel* (1885) 15 Q.B.D. 549 at 558.
[45] Supreme Court Act 1981, s.65; and see s.61(3) and *Practice Direction* [1973] 1 W.L.R. 627.
[46] *Salt v. Cooper* (1880) 16 Ch.D. 544 at 549.
[47] *Clements v. Matthews* (1883) 11 Q.B.D. 808 at 814.
[48] Supreme Court Act 1981, s.50; *ante*, para. 4–015.
[49] See *United Scientific Holdings Ltd v. Burnley B.C.* [1978] A.C. 904 at 925, 945, emphasising the extent of fusion. Contrast (1954) 70 L.Q.R. 326 at 327 (Sir R. Evershed); (1977) 93 L.Q.R. 529 (P. V. Baker).

owner, whereas previously only a legal owner could use the action at law for the recovery of land.[50]

4–020   **4. Conflict.** The continuing distinction between the two systems is emphasised by the provision that where there is any conflict or variance between the rules of law and those of equity, the rules of equity shall prevail.[51] This effectively preserves the established relationship between law and equity, by which equitable principles can modify common law rules. Before the Judicature Acts equity asserted itself, when in conflict with common law, by the overriding jurisdiction and the common injunction.[52] The Judicature Acts abolished both this special machinery and the need for it. In practice, of course, these cases of conflict were not fought out because of equity's acknowledged right to the last word. Common law and equity have been harmoniously administered side by side for centuries.

Much therefore still depends upon the division between legal and equitable interests. Our property law is as much founded upon it now as it was before the Judicature Acts. The Court of Chancery is a ghost, but like many other English legal ghosts, its influence can be felt on every side.

Part 2

EQUITABLE RIGHTS BEFORE 1926

4–021   Equitable rights may be divided into two classes: those modelled upon common law rights; and those invented by equity independently.

4–022   **1. "Equity follows the law".** The device of the trust brought into being a large family of equitable interests closely corresponding to the analogous legal estates. The legal fee simple could, for example, be held by trustees upon trust for A for life with remainder to B in tail with remainder to C in fee simple; or upon trust for A for 99 years; or upon trust for A until he should die or become bankrupt. Equitable life interests, entails, leases, reversions and remainders, and any other interest corresponding to an interest recognised at common law, could thus be created under trusts. The maxim was "Equity follows the law".[53]

This was carried to great lengths. An equitable fee simple, for example, descended on intestacy to the heirs general, an equitable entail descended to the heirs of the body. Even the common law's mysterious methods of barring entails[54] were adopted in due course, so that there were equitable fines and

---

[50] See *post*, Appendix.
[51] J.A. 1873, s.25(11), now Supreme Court Act 1981, s.49(1). For a leading illustration, see *post*, para. 14–041; and see generally Snell, *Equity*, 15–17.
[52] *Ante*, para. 4–007.
[53] Snell, *Equity*, 29.
[54] *Ante*, paras 3–080 *et seq.*

recoveries.[55] And for the creation of this type of equitable interest equity adopted many of the common law rules as to words of limitation. It is true that there were exceptions, as mentioned below. "But", as a great authority wrote, "the cases, where the analogy fails, are not numerous; and there scarcely is a rule of law or equity, of a more ancient origin, or which admits of fewer exceptions, than the rule, that equity followeth the law".[56]

2. Equity corrects the law. Equity did not, of course, follow the law in matters where it was concerned to amend it. The maxim means rather that equity was content to adopt much common law doctrine without modification for the purpose of developing the trust. In particular the fundamental rules as to the possible estates, devolution on intestacy and words of limitation were followed respectfully.[57]

4–023

3. New equitable interests. Quite apart from those equitable interests which corresponded in a general way with the comparable common law estates, equity devised certain interests in land which had no common law equivalents. These were therefore additions made by equity to the limited number of interests in land which the law permits.[58] They were few in number, for the law was slow to extend the species of property rights (rights *in rem*) which could be created by private transactions.[59] Personal rights and duties of almost any kind can be created by contract as rights *in personam*. But rights *in rem*, binding not only the parties but other persons generally, can exist only in the form approved by the law and not in any novel form desired by the parties creating them. Yet equity did make possible certain dispositions of property which were impossible at common law. Some of these could exist only under trusts, where the interests affected were equitable in any case; these included executory interests[60] (which by statute became capable of existing at law[61]), and life interests, remainders and reversions (but not entails) in leaseholds and other personalty.[62] But apart from trusts of the ordinary kind, equity introduced three important new interests in property: estate contracts, restrictive covenants, and the mortgagor's equity of redemption. These property rights, which are distinct from "mere equities",[63] require brief explanation.

4–024

[55] *Kirkham v. Smith* (1749) Amb. 518; Lewin, *Trusts* (15th ed.), 631, 632; Bayley, *Fines and Recoveries* (1828) 254.

[56] Co.Litt. 290b, n. 1 (xvi) by Butler.

[57] Even in these regions however there were exceptions: see the previous edition of this work at p. 120.

[58] Called "nondescript equities" by Challis 183.

[59] It is questionable whether it is now possible to create novel equitable rights in land: see L.P.A. 1925, s.4(1); *post*, para. 4–090.

[60] *Ante*, para. 4–023; and see the previous edition of this work at p. 1179.

[61] See the previous edition of this work at p. 1179.

[62] *Ante*, para. 3–016; and see the previous edition of this work at pp. 815, 1169.

[63] See *post*, para. 5–012.

4–025   *(a) Estate contracts.* Equity would decree specific performance of certain contracts which were remediable only by damages at common law. Of these the most important were contracts for the sale or lease of land, now called estate contracts.[64] A purchaser under contract to buy land had therefore at common law only a right to damages if his vendor broke the contract. But in equity he had a right to compel his vendor to convey the land itself. This right to specific performance created a right in the land, a species of equitable property right. Therefore, if A agreed to sell land to B, but instead later sold and conveyed it to C, B could recover the land from C if C had notice of B's contract when he obtained the land. B was equitable owner from the time of the contract, and could enforce his equitable right to the land against anyone except a bona fide purchaser of a legal estate without notice of the contract.

4–026   *(b) Restrictive covenants.* A landowner selling a plot of land will often wish to restrict its use if he has other land adjoining. He may make his purchaser contract accordingly, but a simple contract will bind only the parties and not other future owners. Equity allowed covenants restrictive of the use of land (for example, covenants not to build, or not to use the property otherwise than as a private dwelling) to run with the land[65] so as to bind all future owners except a bona fide purchaser of a legal estate without notice of the covenant. The benefit of such a covenant, belonging to the original vendor, was thus a new kind of property right created by equity.

4–027   *(c) Mortgagor's equity of redemption.* If A conveyed his land to B as security for a loan, equity would allow A at any time, after repayment of the loan fell due, and despite any contrary provisions in the mortgage, to recover his land by paying to B what was due to him under the loan. This was the equitable right to redeem. Taken together with the other rights of the mortgagor, the mortgagor thus had an "equity of redemption", which was in effect ownership of the property subject to the rights of the mortgagee.[66] A could so recover the land not only from B but from anyone to whom B had conveyed it, saving only a bona fide purchaser of a legal estate without notice of the mortgage. Equity thus gave the mortgagor a right of property which was valuable if, as is usual, the land was worth more than the amount of the debt.

4–028   **4. Separation of legal and equitable interests.** Often the legal estate in land carries with it the beneficial interest, and no separate equitable interest exists.[67] If Blackacre is merely conveyed to X in fee simple, X takes it beneficially, for his own enjoyment.[68] But although in the case of a beneficial

---

[64] For fuller explanation, see *post*, paras. 5–099, 12–050.

[65] For fuller explanation, see *post*, para. 16–030.

[66] For fuller explanation, see *post*, para. 19–017.

[67] See *Selby v. Aston* (1797) 3 Ves. 339.

[68] See *Sammes's Case* (1609) 13 Co.Rep. 54 at 56; Co.Ltt. 23a; *Commissioner of Stamp Duties (Queensland) v. Livingston* [1965] A.C. 694 at 712.

legal owner there is no need to consider separately the legal and equitable estate in land, in other cases this is the only way to arrive at a proper understanding of the law. The ability of the beneficial owner of a legal estate to separate the equitable from the legal interest, so that the legal owner becomes a mere trustee for the equitable owner, is one of the fundamentals of English law.[69] The way in which equity sometimes protects a person's rights in property without conferring any equitable interest in it upon him is considered further on.[70]

Part 3

THE 1925 LEGISLATION

Section 1. Policy of the Legislation

It has been seen that where the title to land is unregistered, a purchaser who **4–029** buys without notice of some adverse right is bound by that right if it is legal and takes free from it if it is equitable. Consequently, the fewer legal estates and interests which can exist in land, the less precarious is the position of a purchaser. But conversely, the more equitable interests which can exist in land the more precarious are rights in real property generally, for all such equitable interests lie open to the risk that the legal estate may be bought without notice. The property legislation of 1925 radically altered the system of legal and equitable interests in order to simplify the law, to protect purchasers from interests of which they had no notice, and at the same time to protect equitable owners. A description must be given of three of the principal measures of this policy—

    (i) the reduction of legal estates to two;

    (ii) the protection of certain equitable interests by registration in the register of land charges; and

    (iii) the extension of registration of title.

Section 2. Reduction of Legal Estates to Two

A. *The General Scheme*

1. Two estates. The scheme of the Acts is to provide that after 1925 only **4–030** two kinds of legal estate can exist, the fee simple absolute in possession and the lease. Apart from leases, therefore, all interests derived out of the fee

---

[69] See *Abbot v. Burton* (1708) 1 Mod. 181 at 182; Challis 385.
[70] *Post*, paras 4–094, 11–130.

simple must now be equitable: life interests, entails,[71] and the remainders or reversions (even though in fee simple) expectant upon them, determinable fees, base fees, and so on, must all now be mere equitable interests. That is to say, in any such case the fee simple absolute in possession, the legal estate, is held upon trust to give effect to the lesser interest in equity.

4–031   **2. The indivisible fee.** Conveyancing is materially assisted by this uniform system of allowing life interests and the like to exist only behind trusts of the legal estate. Before 1926 it was always possible for a fee simple owner to make a settlement (for example, on A for life with remainder to B in fee simple) by which the legal estate was split up into portions. In the above example there would be no immediate fee simple owner during A's life: the absolute owner had temporarily disappeared. The present scheme ensures that he can never disappear. The legal estate, the fee simple absolute in possession, cannot be split up into derivative interests: derivative interests can be created only as trusts of the fee simple, which itself remains inviolate. Therefore in conveyancing the title to the fee simple will now always have a continuous history. It cannot be lost among the fragments of life or other lesser interests.

4–032   **3. Leases.** Leases may still exist as legal estates, but they stand on a different footing from the interests mentioned above. A lease is generally a business transaction for which the mechanism of trusts is inapposite. Leases as legal estates were no serious danger to purchasers since the possession of the tenant was usually self-evident. Leases therefore may, and ordinarily do, still take effect as legal estates.

4–033   **4. "Family" and "commercial" interests.** The key to the present arrangement of legal and equitable interests is the distinction between what may loosely be described as "family" and "commercial" transactions.[72] Life interests and determinable fees, for example, are typically found in family settlements made by deed or will. To these the machinery of a trust is natural and convenient. The design is therefore to make all such interests equitable, under trusts of the legal estate. On the other hand, leases, easements, profits and similar interests (often generically called incumbrances) are generally granted for money or other valuable consideration on a commercial basis. For these the machinery of a trust is out of place. The purchaser expects a legal estate and, as will be seen, the scheme of the Act ensures that he may still get one.

---

[71] Such interests can no longer be created: T.L.A.T.A. 1996, Sched. 1, para. 5; *ante*, para. 3–037.

[72] These terms must not be interpreted literally. Trusts are often set up nowadays for purposes which are unconnected with the family. Equally, there are some "commercial" interests, which are concerned solely with family rights, such as a spouse's matrimonial home rights under the Family Law Act 1996: *post*, para. 17–022.

5. Section 1. Section 1 of the Law of Property Act 1925, must now be **4–034** looked at more closely. The terms of the first three subsections of this section are as follows.

"1.—(1) The only estates in land which ar capable of subsisting or of being conveyed or created at law are—

(a)   An estate in fee simple absolute in possession;

(b)   A term of years absolute.

(2) The only interests or charges in or over land which are capable of subsisting or of being conveyed or created at law are—

(a)   An easement, right, or privilege in or over land for an interest equivalent to an estate in fee simple absolute in possession or a term of years absolute;

(b)   A rentcharge in possession issuing out of or charged on land being either perpetual or for a term of years absolute;

(c)   A charge by way of legal mortgage;

(d)   Land tax, tithe rentcharge,[73] and any other similar charge on land which is not created by an instrument;

(e)   Rights of entry exercisable over or in respect of a legal term of years absolute, or annexed, for any purpose, to a legal rentcharge.

(3) All other estates, interests, and charges in or over land take effect as equitable interests."

6. Existence at law. It should first be noted that the section does not **4–035** provide that the estates and interests mentioned in subsections (1) and (2) are *necessarily* legal, but merely that they alone *can* be legal. For example, a life interest or an entail[74] cannot be legal estates after 1925, for they are not included in section 1. On the other hand, a lease for a term of years is included in section 1 and so may exist either as a legal estate, as it normally does, or as an equitable interest under a trust. A leasehold is "land" for the purposes of the Act.[75] This means that an interest for life or in tail in leasehold land must be equitable, for it is governed by section 1(1). Previously it was possible to create a legal life interest in leasehold land by will, but no entail in leasehold could be created at all.[76]

---

[73] These four words have been repealed: see *post*, para. 4–053.
[74] After 1996, entails, whether of freehold or leasehold land, can no longer be created: T.L.A.T.A. 1996, Sched. 1, para. 5; *ante*, paras 3–037, 3–078.
[75] *Ante*, para. 3–015.
[76] *Ante*, paras 3–016, 3–087.

4–036   **7. Incidents.** The incidents of equitable interests are in general similar to those attaching to corresponding legal estates before 1926. Thus the position of a tenant for life as regards waste seems to have remained unchanged despite the conversion of his legal life estate into an equitable life interest at the beginning of 1926. There is no express provision on this point but "equity follows the law".[77]

4–037   **8. Rights over other land.** The general scheme of the section is to deal with the legal rights of ownership in the land itself in subsection (1), and with legal rights over the land of another in subsection (2). Subsection (2) contains an important list of charges or incumbrances which can still be legal and of which purchasers must therefore still beware. This list is modelled on the traditional definition of real property,[78] which includes not only physical land (corporal hereditaments) but also certain rights over land such as easements, profits (covered by subsection (2)(a)) and rentcharges (incorporeal hereditaments).[79] Any of these, being real property, can be held for any estate or interest known to the law.[80] For this reason they are included within the meaning of "land" for the purposes of the Law of Property Act 1925.[81] A rentcharge, for example, can be held in fee simple, for a term of years, or for life. In the first two cases, but not in the third, it may still be a legal incumbrance, either under subsection (1) as "land" held for a permissible legal estate, or in its own rights under subsection (2)(b). There are other incorporeal hereditaments which rank as real property in our law and which may be held for either of the two possible legal estates although they are not mentioned in subsection (2), such as an advowson (the right to present a clergyman to a living).[82] These curiously assorted interests all fall within the statutory definition of "land" mentioned above.

4–038   **9. Estates and interests.** It will be noted that the rights mentioned in subsection (1) are called legal estates and those mentioned in subsection (2) are called legal interests or charges. This is a convenient distinction between rights over a person's own land and rights over the land of another, but both types of rights are referred to in the Act as "legal estates", and have the same incidents attached to them as attached to legal estates before 1926.[83] The title of "estate owner" is given to the owner of a legal estate.[83] Before 1926 equitable rights in land were frequently and properly called equitable estates, but they should now be called equitable interests, the name "estate" being reserved for legal rights.

---

[77] *Ante*, para. 4–022.
[78] See *ante*, para. 1–099.
[79] For incorporeal hereditaments, see *ante*, para. 1–011, *post*, para. 18–001.
[80] *Post*, para. 18–002. It will be remembered that only a "tenement" could be held in tail before 1926: *ante*, para. 3–087.
[81] L.P.A. 1925, s.205(1)(ix).
[82] *Post*, para. 18–007. Advowsons are no longer "land" for the purposes of L.R.A. 1925: see Patronage (Benefices) Measure 1986, s.6.
[83] s.1(4).

The various legal estates and interests must now be examined more closely.

B. *The Estates and Interests*

1(a). "Fee simple absolute in possession". The meaning of *"fee simple"* has already been considered.[84]   **4–039**

"Absolute" is used in its accustomed sense to distinguish a fee simple which will continue for ever[85] from a modified fee, such as a determinable fee or a base fee.[86] The policy of the Act requires that any such interest, being less than a fee simple absolute, should take effect only in equity, under a trust of the legal estate. A fee simple defeasible by condition subsequent would also necessarily be equitable but for the Law of Property (Amendment) Act 1926.[87] By this Act an amendment was made to meet an unforeseen difficulty connected with rentcharges. In some parts of the country, particularly Manchester and the north, it has been a common practice to sell a fee simple not for a capital sum, but for an income in the form of a perpetual rentcharge (an annual sum charged on the land).[88] Rentcharges of this kind are commonly called "fee farm rents". A scheme for their commutation and extinguishment was enacted in 1977, but this will not be completed until 2037.[89]

The remedies for non-payment of a rentcharge include a right to enter on the land temporarily to collect rents and profits.[90] Further, in a number of cases an express right of re-entry is reserved by the conveyance, entitling the grantor to enter and determine the fee simple and thus regain his old estate if any payment is a specified number of days in arrear. The reservation of a right of re-entry clearly made the fee simple less than absolute, and it was thought by some that even a temporary right of entry might have this effect.[91] This meant that those who had purchased land in this way before 1926 and had obtained legal estates suddenly found that their estates might no longer be legal and that it was doubtful who had the legal estate. Further, the complicated provisions of the Settled Land Act 1925 probably applied.[92]   **4–040**

To remedy these difficulties the Schedule to the Law of Property (Amendment) Act 1926 added a clause to the Law of Property Act 1925, s.7(1), providing that "a fee simple subject to a legal or equitable right of entry or re-entry is for the purposes of this Act a fee simple absolute". This amendment thus allows a fee simple to remain a legal estate even though it is subject to a right of entry. It ruled out any possible complication with the Settled Land   **4–041**

[84] *Ante*, para. 3–005.
[85] See *Edward Seymor's Case* (1612) 10 Co.Rep. 95b at 97b.
[86] *Ante*, para. 3–060.
[87] Sched.
[88] For rentcharges, see *post*, paras 4–048, 8–014.
[89] *ibid.*
[90] *Post*, para. 18–030.
[91] See 61 L.J.News. 50, 145, 167, 501.
[92] *Post*, para. 8–048.

Act 1925 before 1997[93] where land was subject to a legal rentcharge such as a fee farm rent. But the exception is so widely drawn that it affects all conditional fees; for the effect of a condition subsequent annexed to the fee simple is to give rise to a right of re-entry exercisable on breach of the condition, and until this right of re-entry is exercised, the fee simple continues.[94] Consequently, by virtue of the Amendment Act any fee simple defeasible by condition subsequent appears able to rank as a legal estate if limited to take effect as such, even though it is far from being "absolute" in the ordinary sense of the word. It is now clear that any fee simple that was absolute by virtue of section 7(1) of the Law of Property Act 1925 could not create a settlement under the Settled Land Act 1925.[95]

Two other statutory exceptions to the meaning of *absolute* are to be found in section 7 of the Law of Property Act 1925. These relate to fees simple liable to be divested by statute, and to the property of corporations.

4–042

(i) By subsection (1)[96] a fee simple may be absolute for the purposes of the Act although liable to be divested "by virtue of the Land Clauses Acts, or any similar statute".[97] Such Acts provide that land granted or acquired for various public purposes shall re-vest in the grantor, his successors, or some other person if the purpose is not carried out, or if use for that purpose ceases in the future. Thus a highway authority, in which the surface of the highway is vested until the land ceases to be used as a highway, has a legal estate.[98] The exception contained in section 7 used to be considerably wider. As originally drafted, it also included cases of divestment under certain statutes where land had been conveyed to trustees for the purpose of providing a school, museum, church or chapel, and the building ceased to be required for that purpose.[99] There was a conflict of authority as to whether the legal estate vested in the revertee[1] or whether the trustees held it on a bare trust for him.[2] In the former case, if the trustees remained in adverse possession for 12 years after the building ceased to be used for its original purpose the rights of the revertee would be barred under the

---

[93] Subject to two minor exceptions, it ceased to be possible to create settlements under the Settled Land Act 1925 after 1996: *post*, para. 8–001.

[94] *Ante*, para. 3–064.

[95] S.L.A. 1925, s.1(1)(ii)(c) (as amended by T.L.A.T.A. 1996, s.25(1), Sched. 3, para. 2); *post*, para. 8–049.

[96] As amended by Reverter of Sites Act 1987, s.8(3), Sched.

[97] See, *e.g. Re Cawston's Conveyance* [1940] Ch. 27; *Pickin v. British Railways Board* [1974] A.C. 765.

[98] *Tithe Redemption Commission v. Runcorn U.D.C.* [1954] Ch. 383, holding the Local Government Act 1929 to be a "similar statute".

[99] The relevant statutes were the School Sites Act 1841, the Literary and Scientific Institutions Act 1854 and the Places of Worship Act 1873.

[1] As to who constitutes the revertee, see *Marchant v. Onslow* [1995] Ch. 1.

[2] *Re Clayton's Deed Poll* [1980] Ch. 99 favoured the latter view, but Nourse J. declined to follow it in *Re Rowhook Mission Hall, Horsham* [1985] Ch. 62, preferring the former: see (1984) 100 L.Q.R. 527 (C. E. Evans).

Limitation Act 1980, but in the latter case they would not.[3] However the Reverter of Sites Act 1987 provides that trustees hold the legal estate on trust for the revertee with a power to sell the land but without the need to consult him.[4] They may therefore sell the land even if they cannot ascertain his identity. If it proves impossible for the trustees to find the revertee,[5] they may apply to the Charity Commissioners to have both his interest extinguished and a scheme drawn up for the property to be applied for other charitable purposes.[6]

(ii) By subsection (2) similar provision is made for a fee simple vested in a corporation, so that even if it were argued that a corporation's fee simple is determinable on its dissolution,[7] the fee would not be less than absolute.

4–043

The three exceptions made by section 7 (as amended) are, of course, exceptions only for the purposes of the Act, that is to say, for the purpose of allowing those interests to be legal estates. Section 7 in no way alters the conditions attached to them.

"*In possession*" means that the estate must be immediate, and not in remainder or reversion.[8] Remainders and reversions are now equitable interests, taking effect behind a trust of the legal estate. But, in order to prevent temporary interests such as leases from disturbing the legal ownership, "possession" is defined so as to include not only physical possession of the land but also the receipt of rents and profits or the right to receive them, if any.[9] Thus fee simple is still "in possession" even though the owner has granted a lease, for he is entitled to the rent reserved by the lease, and even if the land has also been mortgaged, for he is entitled to the rents and profits, if any, in excess of any interest payable to the mortgagee.[10] But if land has been granted "to A for life, remainder to B in fee simple", the interests of both A and B are necessarily equitable, for a life interest cannot now be legal and B's fee simple is not in possession. These words therefore signify that future estates of freehold cannot be legal after 1925.[11]

4–044

---

[3] *Post*, para. 21–039.
[4] s.1 (as amended by T.L.A.T.A. 1996, Sched. 2, para. 6). But for the amendments made by the 1996 Act, the revertee, as a beneficiary under a trust of land, would have had a right to be consulted about any sale, and might have been entitled to occupy the land: see T.L.A.T.A. 1996, ss.11, 12; *post*, paras 8–147 *et seq*. Quite apart from the practical difficulties that this would have created, it often takes some time to determine who is entitled to the land. For commentary on the Reverter of Sites Act 1987 (as originally enacted) see [1987] *Current Law Statutes* 15–1 (J. Hill); and [1987] Conv. 408 (D. E. Evans).
[5] For the steps which the trustees must take to find the revertee, see s.3.
[6] s.2.
[7] A view rejected in *Re Strathblaine Estates Ltd* [1948] Ch. 228; and see *ante*, para. 3–063.
[8] See *District Bank Ltd v. Webb* [1958] 1 W.L.R. 148.
[9] L.P.A. 1925, s.205(1)(xix): and see s.95(4).
[10] *Post*, para. 19–069.
[11] For a very limited exception, see Welsh Church (Burial Grounds) Act 1945, s.1(2).

4–045 **1(b). "Term of years absolute".** *"Term of years"* is defined as including a term of less than a year, or for a year or years and a fraction of a year, or from year to year.[12] It means any term for any period having a fixed and certain maximum duration.[13] Thus in addition to a tenancy for a specified number of years (*e.g.* "to X for 99 years"), such tenancies as a yearly tenancy or a weekly tenancy are "terms of years" within the definition. In law the term is considered to be for a period of a year or a week respectively. Although in practice such terms continue to run on until determined, the parties are notionally treated as making a new agreement for a fresh term at the end of every period.[14] But a lease "for the life of X" cannot exist as a legal estate, for it is limited by the uncertain duration of X's life and not by a term of years.[15]

Tenancies at will and at sufferance are perhaps best regarded as not being estates or interests within the meaning of the Act, but as being bare tenure and mere occupation respectively.[16] If this view is legitimate it avoids the absurdity of turning these special types of tenancy into equitable interests. It would be strange if a fee simple owner became trustee for a tenant for years holding over after expiry of the lease, and stranger still if he became trustee for his tenant at sufferance, holding over without his consent.

4–046 *"Absolute".* This word is here used in no intelligible sense, for it is provided that a term of years is not prevented from being absolute merely by being "liable to determination by notice, re-entry, operation of law, or by a provision for cesser on redemption, or in any other event (other than the dropping of a life, or the determination of a determinable life interest)".[17] This means that a term of years may be absolute even if it contains a clause enabling either party to determine it by giving notice,[18] or if it provides (as is almost always the case) that the landlord may recover the land if the rent is not paid or a covenant is broken.[19] "Operation of law" is illustrated by a proviso for cesser on redemption under the law of mortgages.[20]

It will be seen from this that by the express provisions of the Act a term of years absolute may consist of a tenancy which is neither a "term of years" nor "absolute" according to the natural meaning of the words, *e.g.* a monthly tenancy liable to be forfeited for non-payment of rent.

It should be noted that, unlike a fee simple absolute, a term of years absolute may be a legal estate even though not "in possession". A lease

---

[12] L.P.A. 1925, s.205(1)(xxvii); *post*, para. 14–007; for an analogy *cf.* Litt. 67. See also *Re Land and Premises at Liss, Hants.* [1971] Ch. 986 at 990. *cf. E.W.P. Ltd v. Moore* [1992] QB 460.

[13] *Prudential Assurance Co. Ltd v. London Residuary Body* [1992] 2 A.C. 386.

[14] *ibid.*, at 394.

[15] For terms of years determinable on life, see *post*, para. 14–086.

[16] *Ante*, para. 3–014, *post*, para. 14–075.

[17] L.P.A. 1925, s.205(1)(xxvii).

[18] Consider *Simons v. Associated Furnishers Ltd* [1931] 1 Ch. 379.

[19] See *post*, para. 14–118.

[20] *Post*, para. 19–020.

granted now but to commence in five years' time may thus be legal, although there is a limit to the length of time which may elapse between the grant of a lease and the commencement of the term.[21] There is no limit to the length of a term of years absolute: terms of 3,000 years are common in the case of mortgages.[22] But there is no such thing as a lease in perpetuity, for that is not a "term" at all.[23]

2(a). "An easement, right, or privilege in or over land for an interest equivalent to an estate in fee simple absolute in possession or a term of years absolute". This head includes both easements and profits *à prendre*.[24] An easement confers the right to use the land of another in some way, or to prevent it from being used for certain purposes. Thus rights of way, rights of water and rights of light may exist as easements. A profit *à prendre* gives the right to take something from the land of another, *e.g.* peat, fish or wood. "Right or privilege" means only rights in property known to the law, such as profits or other incorporeal hereditaments[25] (not being rentcharges, which are separately dealt with next). Rights such as a franchise to wrecks[26] or treasure trove[27] can thus apparently still exist at law. Under this head rights can be legal only if they are held for interests equivalent to one of the two legal estates; thus a right of way for 21 years may be legal but a right of way for life must be equitable.

4–047

2(b). "A rentcharge in possession issuing out of or charged on land being either perpetual or for a term of years absolute". A "rentcharge" is a right which, independently of any lease or mortgage, gives the owner the right to a periodical sum of money secured on land, as where the fee simple owner of Blackacre charges the land with a payment of £50 per annum to X.[28] The rentcharge is a burden on the land since the free-holder is personally liable to pay it, and if payment is in arrear the beneficiary has a right of entry on the land.[29] With certain exceptions, as from July 22, 1977, no new rentcharge can be created; and most existing rentcharges will be extinguished 60 years later, *i.e.* on July 22, 2037.[30]

4–048

"*In possession*". Under the subsection a rentcharge to start at a date subsequent to that on which it is granted cannot be legal, whether it is perpetual or for a term of years absolute. But the Law of Property (Entailed

4–049

[21] *Post*, para. 14–061.
[22] *Post*, para. 19–020.
[23] *Post*, paras 14–005 *et seq. cf. Prudential Assurance Co. Ltd v. London Residuary Body* [1992] 2 A.C. 386 at 394.
[24] For these interests, see *post*, paras 18–040 *et seq.*
[25] See *post*, para. 18–001.
[26] *R. v. Forty-Nine Casks of Brandy* (1836) 3 Hagg.Adm. 257.
[27] *Att.-Gen. v. Trustees of the British Museum* [1903] 2 Ch. 598 at 612. For franchises, see *post*, para. 18–013.
[28] For rentcharges, see *post*, para. 18–014.
[29] *Post*, para. 18–030.
[30] Rentcharges Act 1977, ss.2, 3; *post*, para. 18–018.

Interests) Act 1932[31] provided that a rentcharge was "in possession" notwith-standing that the payments were limited to commence or accrue at a date subsequent to its creation, unless the rentcharge was limited to take effect in remainder after or expectant on the failure or determination of some other interest.

4–050   *"Issuing out of or charged on land"*. "Land" includes another rentcharge.[32] Thus if P charged his fee simple estate in Blackacre with the payment to Q of £100 per annum in perpetuity, Q could create a legal rentcharge of £50 per annum in favour of R, charged on his rentcharge of £100.

4–051   *"Being either perpetual or for a term of years absolute"*. "Perpetual" is used here in place of "fee simple absolute" used in 2(a) above. but there seems to be no practical importance in this difference of wording.

4–052   2(c). **"A charge by way of legal mortgage"**. This must be explained later.[33] It is one of the ways of creating a legal mortgage after 1925, and is similar in effect to the ordinary form of mortgage made by grant of a long term of years. This type of interest in land was created by the Law of Property Act 1925.

4–053   2(d). **"Land tax, tithe rentcharge, and any other similar charge on land which is not created by an instrument"**. This group comprises periodical payments with which land is burdened by law and not by some conveyance or other voluntary act of parties. "Instrument" is so defined as to exclude statute[34] and the charges covered in this group are statutory. In fact the three main charges that fell within this paragraph, land tax, tithe rentcharge and tithe redemption annuity, have all been abolished[35] and the first four words have been repealed.[36] The unrepealed remnant still has some effect, even though it is no longer grammatical and lacks any point of reference for "similar".

4–054   2(e). **"Rights of entry exercisable over or in respect of a legal term of years absolute, or annexed, for any purpose, to a legal rentcharge"**. As already mentioned,[37] a legal term of years absolute is usually made subject to the right of the landlord to re-enter if the tenant fails to pay rent or comply

---

[31] s.2. The Act takes its name from another matter.

[32] L.P.A. 1925, ss.122, 205(1)(ix); *post*, para. 18–032.

[33] *Post*, para. 19–025.

[34] L.P.A. 1925, s.205(1)(viii).

[35] See Finance Act 1963, Pt V, Sched. 14 (land tax); Tithe Act 1936, s.1 (tithe rentcharge); Finance Act 1977, s.56 (tithe redemption annuity). For further details of these charges, see the previous edition of this work at p. 132.

[36] Tithe Act 1936, s.48, Sched. 9 (tithe rentcharge); Finance Act 1963, s.73, Sched. 14 (land tax).

[37] *Ante*, para. 4–046.

with the covenants.[38] A right of entry is itself an interest in land[39] and in the cases mentioned it may still be a legal right. The statutory language seems wide enough to cover any right of entry affecting a legal lease. But it has been held that the scheme of the Act requires the right to be merely equitable if it is created on the assignment of the lease (rather than, as normally, on its grant), and it is limited to an uncertain period instead of being perpetual or for a term of years.[40]

A right of entry or re-entry is often attached to a legal rentcharge in order to secure the due payment of the rent.

Concurrent legal estates. Any number of legal estates may exist con- **4–055** currently in the same piece of land.[41] Thus A may have the legal fee simple in Blackacre, subject to a legal mortgage in favour of B, a legal rentcharge in favour of C, a legal lease in favour of D, and so on. The legal fee simple is often referred to as *the* legal estate because of its paramount importance. Legal leases, mortgages, rentcharges, easements and the like are regarded as incumbrances upon it.

Section 3. Extension of System of Registration of Charges for Unregistered Land

1. Registration. The greatest risk of disaster in transactions in land is the **4–056** possibility that some interest may not be discovered at the proper time. If the interest is legal an innocent purchaser will find himself bound by it; if it is equitable, its owner may lose it to a purchaser without notice. Registration of interests, particularly of those which are least likely to appear in a routine investigation of title, is one obvious solution to such problems. It was in use before 1926, but it was greatly extended by the 1925 legislation. Registration of pending actions relating to land was introduced in 1839,[42] and was extended to certain annuities and rentcharges in 1855.[43] The system was further extended by the Land Charges Registration and Searches Act 1888 and the Land Charges Act 1900. But even then the interests which were registrable were comparatively few and unimportant. By the Land Charges Act 1925 (now replaced by the Land Charges Act 1972), a large body of important interests became registrable, and for the first time registration of land charges

---

[38] The right of entry "is what gives value and substance" to the freehold reversion: *Cowan v. Department of Health* [1992] Ch. 286 at 295, *per* Mummery J.

[39] *Cowan v. Department of Health, supra*, at 295. For the alienability of a right of entry, see *ante*, para. 3–076.

[40] *Shiloh Spinners, Ltd v. Harding* [1973] A.C. 691. The exercise of such a right will not put an end to the lease, but there is no reason in principle or in the language of the Act why this should matter.

[41] L.P.A. 1925, s.1(5).

[42] Judgments Act 1839.

[43] Judgments Act 1855.

became a fundamental part of the general system of unregistered conveyancing.

Under this system of registration the doctrine of notice has been profoundly changed; indeed, in substance it has been abandoned. If the right in issue is registrable, the question is whether it is registered rather than whether the purchaser knows or should have known of it. This is a sharp departure from equity in the sense of fairness, but a gain in practical convenience.

The elements of the system of registration of land charges, which for many years has formed part of the system of unregistered conveyancing, can be briefly explained here as part of the general strategy of the 1925 reforms. The system is treated in detail in the following chapter.

4–057   2. **Principles of registration.** The two cardinal principles of the registration of land charges are—

> (i) failure to register makes the interest *void against a purchaser*[44]; and

> (ii) registration is deemed to constitute *actual notice to all persons for all purposes* connected with the land.[45]

It is a corollary of (i) that if an interest is registrable but unregistered a purchaser is unaffected by notice obtained through other channels: even though he knew of the interest, he will take free from it.[46] The doctrine of notice thus exists in name only. It has been mechanised by statute. The test is now the state of the register, not the state of the purchaser's mind. It is therefore best not to try to translate this system of registration into terms of the equitable rules about a purchaser without notice, but to treat it as a separate system. There are two reasons for this.

4–058   (i) Certain legal rights[47] are registrable, and if not registered are void against a purchaser. Registration thus deprives these legal rights of some of the security against purchasers which they formerly enjoyed. This cannot be explained by reference to the doctrine of notice, which had no application to legal rights.

4–059   (ii) Under the rules of equity a purchaser without notice took free from equities if he gave *value* and acquired a *legal estate*. An unregistered right is in some cases void against a purchaser if he gave *value* and acquired *any*

---

[44] See L.C.A. 1972, s.4; *post*, para. 5–117.

[45] L.P.A. 1925, s.198.

[46] By L.P.A. 1925, s.199(1)(i), a purchaser is not to be prejudicially affected by notice of any registrable land charge which is void against him for want of registration. The purchaser will take free of the unregistered incumbrance even though the incumbrancer is in possession of the land: *post*, para. 5–119. Because notice is irrelevant, the ancient rule that the fact of possession constitutes notice of the rights of the possessor (*post*, para. 5–020) does not apply.

[47] *Post*, para. 4–063.

estate, legal or equitable, and in other cases void against a purchaser only if he gave *money or money's worth* and acquired a *legal estate.*[48]

3. Unregistered interests. In cases not covered by the provisions as to registration the ordinary legal and equitable rules still apply. Where an equitable interest is registrable but has not been registered the position is as follows. **4–060**

> (i) It will be binding on any person who takes the land by way of gift.

> (ii) A charge which is void for non-registration only as against a purchaser of the legal estate for money or money's worth, will not necessarily bind any other type of purchaser. If the legal estate is conveyed to a person in consideration of marriage, he will take free of the charge if he has no notice of it.[49]

The legislation is concerned with the protection of purchasers, and registrable interests remain valid for all other purposes despite non-registration.

4. Summary. The position created by the extension of registration is therefore best described as follows. **4–061**

> (i) Most legal rights are not registrable; these continue to be good against the whole world.

> (ii) Some equitable rights are not registrable; these continue to be good against the whole world except a bona fide purchaser for value of a legal estate without notice or someone claiming through such a person.

> (iii) A few legal rights and many equitable rights are registrable. If these are not registered, they will be void for non-registration against certain purchasers, irrespective of any question of notice. If they are registered, they bind every purchaser, again irrespective of notice. Whether they are legal or equitable no longer makes any difference.

5. Classification of rights. The following is a summary of the most important rights which are registrable after 1925. These rights are not self-explanatory but they will be dealt with in detail later.[50] **4–062**

(a) Legal interests **4–063**

> (i) A charge on land imposed by certain statutes such as the Agricultural Holdings Act 1986.

---

[48] L.C.A. 1972, s.4; *post*, para. 5–117.
[49] *Post*, para. 5–117.
[50] *Post*, paras 5–087 *et seq.*

    (ii) A puisne (pronounced "puny") mortgage, defined as a legal mortgage not protected by a deposit of title deeds. This covers most second, third or later legal mortgages.

    (iii) An Inland Revenue charge for inheritance tax.[51]

4–064   *(b) Equitable interests*

    (i) A limited owner's charge. This includes a charge on land acquired by some limited owner, such as a tenant for life, who pays out of his own pocket capital transfer tax (*e.g.* on the death of the previous owner) which should have been borne by the estate. Security for the debt from the estate to the tenant for life is provided by the charge.

    (ii) A general equitable charge, defined as an equitable charge which affects a legal estate in land but does not arise under a trust and is not secured by a deposit of title deeds. This class covers many equitable mortgages and annuities. It is a residuary class into which equitable interests may fall if not registrable under other heads.

    (iii) An estate contract,[52] defined as a contract to convey or create a legal estate. This includes every contract for the sale or lease of a legal estate.

    (iv) A restrictive covenant,[53] provided that it is made after 1925 and is not made between lessor and lessee.

    (v) An equitable easement, or similar right, provided that it is created after 1925. An easement held for life would be an example, but in practice this class is narrowly confined.

4–065   **6. Operation of the system.** The heterogeneous nature of this catalogue makes it difficult to describe the registration machinery in simple terms. The design of the Land Charges Acts can be perceived only after study of many different interests. But four clues may be given in advance.

    (i) Interests of a "family" type found under settlements and trusts of land are not registrable. These are sufficiently protected by the provisions briefly described in the next section.

    (ii) Mortgages have special peculiarities, particularly in the device of protection by a deposit of title deeds. This protection makes registration unnecessary and explains the reservations as to title deeds in (a)(ii) and (b)(ii) above.

---

[51] *Post*, para. 5–102.
[52] *Ante*, para. 4–025.
[53] *Ante*, para. 4–026.

(iii) It will be noticed that the list includes two of the interests invented by equity[54] other than trusts, namely, estate contracts and restrictive covenants (there are special reasons for excluding the mortgagor's equity of redemption). These are the best examples to observe and bear in mind as registrable interests. They are the commonest of the interests which became registrable in 1926 and they represent the most important extension of the field of registration.

(iv) Registrable interests are a miscellaneous collection because they comprise only such interests as are not sufficiently protected by other means. Registration has been introduced only where it was thought necessary to strengthen the weak points of the existing system of conveyancing, not as a comprehensive system. Thus there is no presumption that equitable interests which cannot be overreached (as explained below) are registrable.[55]

Section 4. Registration of Title

1. Registration of title. The system of unregistered conveyancing is being rapidly replaced by registration of title under the Land Registration Act 1925. Under the latter system,[56] not only are third party rights over land recorded on the register, but the title is itself registered. When registered land is sold, the legal title to the land does not pass to the purchaser when the vendor executes the transfer (which is the equivalent of a deed of conveyance in unregistered conveyancing) but only when that transfer is registered.[57] Although the registered proprietor is given a land certificate as his proof of his ownership of the land,[58] the register alone is conclusive as to the state of the title.[59] The register may be rectified in certain circumstances, but a registered proprietor who suffers loss in consequence is entitled to an indemnity from the Land Registry.[60]

4–066

The introduction of registration of title in England and Wales was a protracted affair.[61] The first serious proposals for title registration were made in the 1840s,[62] and the first legislation was enacted in 1862.[63] The legislation

4–067

[54] *Ante*, paras 4–024 *et seq.*
[55] *Post*, para. 4–073. See *Shiloh Spinners Ltd v. Harding* [1973] A.C. 691. Examples which fall into neither category include an equitable right of entry (*post*, para. 5–104); and probably an equity arising by estoppel (*post*, Chap. 13).
[56] *Post*, para. 6–001.
[57] L.R.A. 1925, ss.19(1), 22(1).
[58] *ibid.*, s.63(1).
[59] The register is not required to be in documentary form and is indeed now computerised: L.R.A. 1925, s.1(2) (as substituted by A.J.A. 1982, s.66(1)).
[60] For rectification and indemnity, see *post*, para. 6–118.
[61] For an admirable account of the history, see J. S. Anderson, *Lawyers and the Making of English Land Law 1832–1940.*
[62] Anderson, *op. cit.*, 63–73.
[63] Land Registry Act 1862.

was not a success. Not only was registration not compulsory, but it was only possible to register a title that was in all respects sound.[64] The registry was little used and there was further legislation in both 1875[65] and 1897.[66] Except in London, effective compulsory registration was not introduced until the enactment of the Land Registration Act 1925, but even then its implementation was postponed for 10 years.[67] The areas of compulsory registration were gradually extended to the whole of England and Wales.[68] Furthermore, the dispositions of unregistered land which are required to be registered has been considerably extended.[69] This means that any of the following dispositions, if made for valuable consideration, by way of gift, or pursuant to an order of the court, must now be completed by registration even though the title has hitherto been unregistered—

　(i)　the conveyance of a freehold;

　(ii)　the grant of a lease for more than 21 years; or

　(iii)　the assignment of a lease with more than 21 years to run;

　(iv)　the transfer of a freehold or assignment of a lease with more than 21 years to run by an assent (including a vesting assent) or a vesting deed.[70]

Furthermore, on a legal mortgage of a freehold or of a lease having more than 21 years to run, which is protected by documents of title, the legal estate mortgaged must be registered.[71]

4–068　　**2. Principles of registration.** The most fundamental principle of registered conveyancing is that a purchaser of registered land takes it subject only to—

　(i)　the incumbrances and other entries appearing on the register;

---

[64] The title had to be what the Court of Chancery would have regarded as a good marketable title, which was at that time a remarkably difficult standard to achieve.

[65] L.T.A. 1875. This relaxed the requirement of a marketable title as a pre-condition for registration.

[66] L.T.A. 1897. Under this Act it became possible for the first time for registration to be made compulsory in a county by Order in Council. Compulsory registration could not be introduced, however, if the county council voted to oppose it at a meeting attended by two-thirds of its members: *ibid.*, s.20.

[67] L.R.A. 1925, s.120. Even after the 10-year period had elapsed, the Lord Chancellor might be compelled by a county council or local law society to hold a public inquiry into whether compulsory registration should be introduced into a particular county: *ibid.*, s.122 (repealed by L.R.A. 1966, s.2(3), Sched.). By January 1, 1937, only Eastbourne, Hastings and Middlesex had joined London as areas of compulsory registration.

[68] *Post*, paras 5–001, 6–014. In areas of compulsory registration, certain dispositions of unregistered land are required to be registered: see *infra*.

[69] See L.R.A. 1997, s.1, replacing L.R.A. 1925, s.123, and inserting a new s.123A.

[70] L.R.A. 1925, s.123(1), (6) (as substituted), *post*, paras 5–001, 6–015.

[71] L.R.A. 1925, s.123(2) (as substituted).

(ii) what are called "overriding interests"; and

(iii) where the property transferred is leasehold, all implied covenants, obligations and liabilities incident to the estate transferred or created.[72]

Most incumbrances, whether legal or equitable, should be protected by registration,[73] and the methods by which this is done are explained later.[74] Certain rights which are listed in the Land Registration Act 1925[75] do not require registration but take effect as overriding interests. The most important of these include—

(i) certain easements[76] and profits, particularly those which have not been expressly granted or reserved,[77] but which arise by implied grant or reservation or have been acquired by prescription[78];

(ii) rights acquired or in the course of being acquired under the Limitation Acts[79];

(iii) the rights of every person who is either in actual occupation or in receipt of the rents and profits of the land, except where enquiry is made of such persons and their rights are not disclosed[80];

(iv) local land charges[81]; and

(v) leases for a term not exceeding 21 years.[82]

3. The effects of non-registration. As regards the effects of non-registration, it is convenient to consider separately: (i) dispositions of registered land which are required to be completed by registration; and (ii) "minor interests" which may be protected by an appropriate entry on the register.   **4–069**

(a) Registered dispositions. Certain dispositions of the registered land are required by the Act to be completed by registration.[83] All of these dispositions involve the transfer or creation of a legal estate or interest. Examples include   **4–070**

---

[72] *ibid.*, ss.20(1), 23(1).

[73] A lease of 21 years or less is not capable of substantive registration and takes effect as an overriding interest: L.R.A. 1925, ss.19(2), 22(2), 48(1), 70(1)(k).

[74] *Post*, para. 6–075.

[75] s.70(1); *post*, para. 6–036.

[76] Including some equitable easements: *post*, paras 6–033, 6–042.

[77] Such easements and profits should be completed by registration: *post*, para. 6–031, but see *post*, paras 6–033, 6–042.

[78] L.R.A. 1925, s.70(1)(a). Although easements and profits which have been expressly granted or reserved should be registered (*ibid.*, ss.18(1), 19(2), 21(1), 22(2)), some may take effect (illogically) as overriding interests: see *post*, para. 6–033. For the implied grant and reservation of easements, see *post*, para. 18–097; and for prescription, see *post*, para. 18–121.

[79] L.R.A. 1925, s.70(1)(f).

[80] *ibid.*, s.70(1)(g).

[81] *ibid.*, s.70(1)(i). For local land charges, see *post*, para. 5–132.

[82] *ibid.*, s.70(1)(k) as substituted by L.R.A. 1986, s.4(1).

[83] See L.R.A. 1925, s.3(xxii).

the transfer of the fee simple, the assignment of a lease with more than 21 years to run, the grant of a lease or sub-lease for a term of more than 21 years, the grant or reservation of an easement and the creation and transfer of a registered charge.[84] An unregistered disposition transfers no legal estate or interest to the grantee but operates only in equity as a minor interest.[85] As such it will be overridden by any registered disposition of the property for valuable consideration[86] unless it happens to fall within one of the categories of overriding interest and is therefore protected as such. Thus if the grantee is either in actual occupation of the land or in receipt of its rents and profits, then his interest will bind any purchaser of the property notwithstanding the lack of registration because it will take effect as an overriding interest.[87]

4–071   *(b) Minor interests.* The definition of minor interests is complex.[88] It is a residual category which includes all equitable interests in or rights over land unless they are overriding interests. Thus the following are all minor interests—

(i) beneficial interests under any trust of land; and

(ii) rights which, if the title were unregistered, would either be registrable as land charges or are amongst the category of interests which still depend for their protection on the doctrine of notice.

Minor interests should be protected by an appropriate entry in the register.[89] If they are not, they will be overridden by a registered disposition for valuable consideration.[90] Once again, if the grantee is either in actual occupation or in receipt of the rents and profits of the land, his failure to register his right will be immaterial because it will take effect as an overriding interest.[91] Thus if under a lease of registered land a tenant is given an option to purchase the freehold reversion, that option will bind any purchaser of the reversion even if it has not been protected by registration.[92]

---

[84] *ibid.*, ss.18, 21, 33, 34.

[85] *ibid.*, ss.19, 22, 101; Ruoff & Roper, 8–03. For minor interests, see *infra*.

[86] L.R.A. 1925, ss.20(1), 23(1), 101(3). Thus if a registered proprietor charges his property but the chargee fails to register it, and the proprietor then makes a subsequent registered disposition of the property, the subsequent disponee will take free of the unregistered charge.

[87] L.R.A. 1925, s.70(1)(g), *supra*. For example, A grants B a 99-year lease of Blackacre by deed which B fails to register. B enters into possession. A sells the freehold reversion to C, who is registered as proprietor of the land. C will be bound by B's lease, which will take effect as an overriding interest because B is in actual occupation of the property. *cf. Strand Securities Ltd v. Caswell* [1965] Ch. 958.

[88] L.R.A. 1925, s.3(xv); *post*, para. 6–075.

[89] *Post*, para. 6–078.

[90] L.R.A. 1925, s.101(2). "Valuable consideration" includes marriage, but not a nominal consideration in money: *ibid.*, s.3(xxxi). Any disposition that is not made for value takes effect subject to all minor interests, whether protected by registration or not: *ibid.* ss.20(4), 23(5).

[91] L.R.A. 1925, s.70(1)(g); *post*, para. 6–047.

[92] *Webb v. Pollmount Ltd* [1966] Ch. 584. In unregistered land, a purchaser would take free of the option for want of registration: *Midland Bank Trust Co. Ltd v. Green* [1981] A.C. 513; *post*, para. 5–119.

4. The irrelevance of the doctrine of notice. The doctrine of notice has no **4–072** place in registered conveyancing.[93] "The only kind of notice recognised is by entry on the register."[94] If a right is capable of registration but has not been registered, it will not bind a purchaser unless it takes effect as an overriding interest. Furthermore, where title is registered, the distinction between legal and equitable interests is much reduced. Thus if a registered proprietor grants a 99-year legal lease of his property and also enters into a restrictive covenant for the benefit of his neighbour's land, both incumbrances will be protected by the same type of entry on the register of his title.[95]

Section 5. Extension of Overreaching Provisions

1. Methods of holding land on trust

(a) Introduction. Land may be held on trust by trustees in a number of **4–073** different ways:

(i) for persons who are entitled to the land successively, as where A by his will leaves property to his widow, B, for life and after her death to his children;

(ii) for persons who are concurrently entitled to the land, as where land is held for A and B jointly; or

(iii) for A absolutely, a type of trust known as a "bare trust".

(b) Successive interests. Prior to 1997,[96] successive interests in land might **4–074** take effect either as settled land (often called a "strict settlement"[97]) or under a trust for sale. In a strict settlement (which was governed by the Settled Land Act 1925), the land itself was given to the beneficiaries, *e.g.* "to A for life with remainder to B in fee simple".[98] In a trust for sale the land was given to trustees who were instructed to sell it, invest the proceeds of sale, and hold the trust fund, perhaps again for A for life with remainder to B absolutely.

Whether the land was held in strict settlement or on trust for sale, the land could be sold. From the moment of sale the trusts attached to the proceeds of sale and not to the land. The trusts were said to be *overreached, i.e.* transferred

---

[93] " . . . the doctrine of purchaser for value without notice has no application to registered land": *Barclays Bank plc. v. Boulter* [1998] 1 W.L.R. 1 at 11, *per* Mummery L.J. *cf. Frazer v. Walker* [1967] 1 A.C. 569 at 582 (a decision on the New Zealand Land Transfer Act 1952).

[94] *Williams & Glyn's Bank Ltd v. Boland* [1981] A.C. 487 at 504, *per* Lord Wilberforce; *post*, para. 5–006.

[95] *Post*, para. 6–080.

[96] When the Trusts of Land and Appointment of Trustees Act 1996 came into force.

[97] The term "strict settlement" primarily meant a marriage settlement in the usual form. However, in the absence of a better term it was often used to describe any settlement, in whatever form, that fell within the Settled Land Acts.

[98] The Settled Land Act settlement was the traditional means employed by settlors who wished to keep land in the family. The provisions of the Settled Land Act 1925 ensured that such land was not inalienable, even though it was held in settlement.

from the land to the purchase-money. The land was in either case freed from
the trusts by the sale and the purchaser took the full beneficial interest in the
land.[99]

Since 1996, no further settlements can be created under the Settled Land
Act 1925, though existing ones continue to be governed by its provisions.[1]
When a settlor or testator now creates successive interests in land, they take
effect under a trust of land,[2] the effect of which is briefly explained below.
Although it remains possible to create trusts for sale of land expressly, and
certain consequences still follow from so doing,[3] there will usually be no
reason to do so. This is because—

(i) all trusts for sale—whether created before 1997 or after
1996—take effect as trusts of land[4]; and

(ii) there is implied into every trust for sale, despite any provision to
the contrary in the disposition creating it, a power for the trustees
to postpone sale.[5]

4–075   *(c) Concurrent interests.* Before 1997, concurrent interests in land usually
took effect behind a trust for sale,[6] express or implied. Land might be
conveyed to A and B to hold on an express trust for sale for C and D jointly
or in common,[7] or it might simply be conveyed to A and B jointly or in
common. In the latter case, there was a trust for sale implied by statute[8] and
A and B held the property on a trust for themselves as joint tenants or tenants
in common. The trustees had a duty to sell, but in the absence of a contrary
intention, this was coupled with an implied power to postpone sale,[9] which in
practice was commonly exercised. Since 1996, concurrent interests in land,
whenever created, take effect behind trusts of land.[10]

4–076   *(d) Bare trusts.* A bare trust arises where a trustee is to hold or manage the
land for the sole benefit of one beneficiary who is of full age.[11] The trustee is,
in effect, a nominee, who holds the land at the direction of the beneficiary.
Before 1997, such trusts took effect neither as settlements under the Settled
Land Act 1925 nor (in the absence of an express provision) as trusts for sale.
There was some uncertainty as to the powers of a bare trustee and whether

---

[99] For overreaching, see *infra.*
[1] T.L.A.T.A. 1996, s.2(1).
[2] *ibid.,* s.1.
[3] *Post,* para. 8–126.
[4] T.L.A.T.A. 1996, s.1(2).
[5] *ibid.,* s.4(1). The trustees are under no liability if, in the exercise of their discretion, they choose
to postpone sale of the land for an indefinite period: *ibid.*
[6] Concurrent interests could sometimes arise under Settled Land Act settlements, as where two
persons were entitled to land for their joint lives: *post,* para. 9–089.
[7] For the differences between joint tenancies and tenancies in common, see *post,* Chap. 9.
[8] L.P.A. 1925, ss.34 and 36; *post,* para. 9–051. Those sections have now been amended by
T.L.A.T.A. 1996, Sched. 2, paras 3, 4.
[9] L.P.A. 1925, s.25, repealed by T.L.A.T.A. 1996, Sched. 4.
[10] T.L.A.T.A. 1996, s.1. See *infra.*
[11] For a fuller consideration of the nature of bare trusts, see *post,* para. 8–129.

such a trustee could ever make a disposition of the land which would overreach the interest under the trust.[12] These uncertainties no longer exist. Bare trusts, whenever created, now take effect as trusts of land.[13]

2. Trusts of land. Any trust of property which consists of or includes land   **4–077**
is a trust of land except for settled land (which is confined to settlements created prior to 1997) and land to which the Universities and College Estates Act 1925 applies.[14] Trustees of land hold the property on trust for the beneficiaries and are under no obligation to sell it. For the purposes of exercising their functions as trustees, they have in relation to the land held in trust all the powers of an absolute owner.[15] Provided that certain conditions are satisfied, trustees of land may make a disposition that will overreach all interests under the trust.[16] The details of trusts of land are fully explained later.[17]

3. Overreaching. Overreaching is the necessary corollary of a trust or   **4–078**
power of disposition.[18] The term is nowadays understood in two distinct senses.

(a) Subordination of one interest to another. In its traditional meaning,[19]   **4–079**
overreaching is the process whereby existing proprietary interests, whether legal or equitable, are subordinated to or "overridden" by[20] some later interest or estate created pursuant to a trust or power.[21] Thus under a mortgage, a mortgagor in possession has a statutory power to grant certain leases of the land. If he grants such a lease, it will bind the mortgagee, thereby subordinating the mortgagee's interest to the lessee's and so overreaching it, without transferring it to other property.[22] A mortgagee in possession has a similar power to grant certain leases which will bind the mortgagor's interest in the land, and so overreach that interest.[23] Overreaching in this broad sense was well-known by the early years of the nineteenth century.[24]

---

[12] *ibid.*
[13] T.L.A.T.A. 1996, s.1(2).
[14] *ibid.*, s.1.
[15] *ibid.*, s.6(1). The instrument creating the trust may provide that this provision should not apply: *ibid.*, s.8(1).
[16] *Post*, para. 8–165.
[17] *Post*, Chaps 8 and 9.
[18] Sugden, *Powers*, 483; *State Bank of India v. Sood* [1997] Ch. 276.
[19] See Sugden, *Powers*, 482, 483; [1987] Conv. 451 at 453 (W. J. Swadling). This meaning has now been accepted by the Court of Appeal: *State Bank of India v. Sood, supra.*
[20] Prior to 1926 at least, the terms "overreach" and "override" were often used interchangeably: see Farwell, *Powers*, 581. An interest in unregistered land can probably be overridden however (but not overreached) in cases where the disposition is not within the powers of the grantor, but where the purchaser takes in good faith and without notice of the irregularity: *cf. State Bank of India v. Sood* [1997] Ch. 276 at 281.
[21] [1990] C.L.J. 277 (C.H.).
[22] See *post*, paras 4–082, 19–114.
[23] *ibid.*
[24] See *e.g.*, *Wheate v. Hall* (1809) 17 Ves. 80 at 86.

4–080   *(b) Transfer of an interest in property to its proceeds.* Overreaching has tended to be used in a narrower sense to mean the process by which an interest in land is transferred from the land to the purchase money or other property acquired in exchange for it, leaving the land free from that interest. Thus where, under a settlement created before 1997, land is settled on A for life, with remainder to B in fee simple, A has a statutory power to sell the land (in fee simple), and when he does so, B's interest will be transferred from the land to the purchase money.[25] It is clear, however, that even in the context of dispositions of land held in trust, there has been a reversion to the wider traditional understanding of overreaching. Thus where trustees for sale mortgaged a property in consideration of an existing indebtedness, the interests of the beneficiaries were overreached by that mortgage and thereafter bound the equity of redemption.[26]

The draftsman of the 1925 property legislation placed statutory restrictions on the circumstances in which interests under both trusts for sale[27] and strict settlements could be overreached, thereby providing greater protection for the beneficiaries.[28] Overreaching applies to trusts of both registered and unregistered land,[29] and to all types of property, not merely land.

Interests under both trusts of land and strict settlements may all be overreached if the disposition is one which is within the powers of the trustees,[30] whether those powers are conferred by statute or by the trust itself.[31] Overreaching is therefore a valuable means of preventing interests of the "family" type from inconveniencing purchasers. It is inappropriate for rights of a "commercial" character such as estate contracts or restrictive covenants which cannot readily be converted into money. These are better protected by registration.

4–081   **4. Extent of overreaching.** Overreaching, like registration, can be applied, and has been applied, to legal interests as well as to certain types of equitable interests. Before 1926 the rights of beneficiaries under a settlement might be either legal (if the legal estate had been conveyed to them) or equitable (if it had been conveyed to trustees on trust from them). In either case the rights could be overreached—

---

[25] See *post*, paras 8–158–8–164. In such a situation, B's interest can be said to be both "overreached and overridden": see *City of London Building Society v. Flegg* [1988] A.C. 73, 74, *per* Lord Templeman (a case concerned with an overreaching disposition by trustees for sale).

[26] *State Bank of India v. Sood* [1997] Ch. 276.

[27] Which are now trusts of land.

[28] *Post*, paras 8–162 *et seq.*

[29] *City of London Building Society v. Flegg, supra.* See *post*, para. 6–093.

[30] For the limits on the dispositive powers of life tenants under a strict settlement, see *post*, para. 8–071. Trustees of land will normally have in relation to the land subject to the trust all the powers of an absolute owner, so that all dispositions will be within their powers: see *post*, para. 8–137.

[31] For a more detailed treatment of the overreaching provisions applicable to strict settlements and trusts of land, see *post*, para. 8–157.

(i) under an express power contained in the settlement, or

(ii) under the Settled Land Act 1882.

Since 1925 no legal life estate, entail or remainder is possible. A power to overreach legal estates under settlements is therefore no longer needed. However, overreaching is now far more important than it was prior to 1926 because of the statutory extension of what are now trusts of land[32] to certain situations where they did not exist before, *e.g.* under an intestacy, or in the case of concurrent interests.[33]

5. Other overreaching conveyances. Although settlements and trusts of **4–082** land are the most important sources of overreaching conveyances, they are not the only sources. Thus, if X has mortgaged his land to M, and then fails to keep up the payments due, M has a statutory power to sell the land free from X's equitable right to redeem it. X's rights will then be transferred to the purchase-money in M's hands, for M is a trustee for X of any surplus after paying off the mortgage debt.[34] Again, a conveyance by the personal representatives of a deceased person will overreach the claims of the beneficiaries under the will or intestacy; the purchaser gets a clear title, and the beneficiaries are satisfied out of the purchase-money.[35] A list of overreaching conveyances is to be found in section 2(1) of the Law of Property Act 1925,[36] though it is not comprehensive. This section and others in the 1925 property legislation[37] regulate the manner in which overreaching can take place in those situations specifically listed in section 2(1), but they do not preclude it in other cases.[38] Thus mortgagors or mortgagees, if in possession, have statutory powers to grant leases which will overreach both the rights of the other party, and those of other prior parties.[39]

In general, it is only equitable rights that need now to be overreached. There are however a few exceptional cases where there is a statutory power to overreach legal rights. These include—

(a) a mortgagee's power to overreach the mortgagor's legal estate on sale[40];

---

[32] What were trusts for sale prior to 1997.

[33] See *post*, paras 9–051 (concurrent interests), 11–088 (intestacy). See too para. 8–135. For the special overreaching powers applicable to *ad hoc* trusts of land or settlements, see the previous edition of this work at pp. 405 *et seq.*

[34] *Post*, para. 19–063.

[35] *Post*, para. 11–127.

[36] As amended by T.L.A.T.A. 1996, Sched. 3, para. 4.

[37] See, *e.g.* S.L.A. 1925, s.94(1).

[38] This is clear from the history of the 1925 property legislation: [1990] C.L.J. 277, 287–304 (C.H.). What is now L.P.A. 1925, s.2(1) differs markedly from its precursor, L.P.A. 1922, s.3(2). See *State Bank of India v. Sood* [1997] Ch. 276 at 287.

[39] L.P.A. 1925, s.99; *post*, para. 19–114.

[40] L.P.A. 1925, ss.101, 103, 104; *post*, para. 19–059.

(b) a mortgagor's right to grant a lease that is binding on the mortgagee[41]; and

(c) a mortgagee's corresponding right to grant a lease that is binding on
the mortgagor.[42]

Section 6. Effect of a Sale on Legal and Equitable Rights

4–083 The operation of the provisions set out above on a sale of land subject to legal
and equitable rights may be summarised and illustrated as follows.

1. Summary

(a) Where the title is unregistered.

4–084 (1) The purchaser takes subject to all legal rights.
Exceptions: He takes free from—

>   (i) the few legal rights which are void against him for want of
>   registration; and
>
>   (ii) the few legal rights which are overreached.

4–085 (2) The purchaser takes subject to all equitable rights.
Exceptions: He takes free from—

>   (i) equitable rights which are void against him for want of registra-
>   tion: notice is irrelevant;
>
>   (ii) the many equitable rights which are overreached, *e.g.* under a
>   settlement or trust of land: notice is irrelevant; and
>
>   (iii) unregistrable and non-overreachable equitable rights in respect of
>   which he can show either that he is a bona fide purchaser of a legal
>   estate for value without notice, or else that he claims through such
>   a person.

4–086 *(b) Where the title is registered.* The purchaser takes subject to all entries
on the register and any overriding interests, but free from all other rights.
Notice is irrelevant. It is immaterial for this purpose whether a right is legal
or equitable.

4–087 **2. Example.** An example may be of assistance in understanding the above
summary. A has bought land from trustees of land, and at the time of the sale
the land was subject to—

---

[41] L.P.A. 1925, s.99; *post*, para. 19–114.
[42] *ibid.*

(i) the rights of the beneficiaries under the trust of land,

(ii) a restrictive covenant imposed before 1926,

(iii) a binding contract of sale made by the trustees with X shortly before they offered the land to A (an estate contract), and

(iv) a lease to Y (a legal estate).

A's position is as follows.

(a) Where the title is unregistered.

(i) A is not bound by the rights of the beneficiaries (class (2)(ii) above).

(ii) He is bound by the pre-1926 restrictive covenant only if he had notice of it at the time of completing his purchase (class (2)(iii) above).

(iii) He is bound to give up the land to X, the earlier purchaser, only if X registered his estate contract before A completed his purchase (class (2)(i) above).

(iv) He is in any event bound by the lease.

(b) Where the title is registered.   **4-088**

(i) A is not bound by the rights of the beneficiaries: they will be overreached in the same way as when the title is unregistered.

(ii) He is bound by the pre-1926 restrictive covenant only if it was protected by an appropriate entry on the register.[43]

(iii) He is bound to give up the land to X, the earlier purchaser, only if X either protected his estate contract by an entry on the register before A was registered as proprietor of the land, or was for some reason in actual occupation of the land at the time of A's purchase so that the right was an overriding interest.

(iv) He is bound by the lease either because it is protected by an entry on the register or because it takes effect as an overriding interest.

3. Legal and equitable rights. The classical doctrine that legal rights bind   **4-089**
all the world while equitable rights do not bind a bona fide purchaser of a legal estate without notice is now of only residual importance in dealings with unregistered land. It has no role to play in the scheme of registered conveyancing. Indeed where title is registered the difference between legal and equitable rights is now much diminished. It is relevant only to the remedies

---

[43] In practice, such an entry would have been made at the time when the title was first registered or not at all.

that exist to enforce the right and to the nature of any entry that is made on
the register to protect the right.

Section 7. New Equitable Interests?

4–090 It is often said that the category of equitable interests is not closed and that
new ones may therefore be created.[44] However this ignores the Delphic
proviso to section 4(1) of the Law of Property Act 1925 by which "after the
commencement of this Act (and save as hereinafter expressly enacted), an
equitable interest in land shall only be capable of being validly created in any
case in which an equivalent equitable interest in property real or personal
could have been validly created before such commencement". This proviso
has tended to be overlooked and has never been judicially considered.[45] There
appear to be three elements in it.

> (i) It makes it clear that equitable interests in land can be created in
> any case in which such interests could have existed in real or
> personal property prior to 1926.[46] It is therefore one of the provi-
> sions of the 1925 legislation that assimilate the rules applicable to
> real and personal property.

> (ii) That general rule is subject to the qualification that some interests
> cannot be created after 1925 because of certain provisions of the
> Law of Property Act 1925 itself.[47]

> (iii) It appears to preclude the creation of novel forms of equitable
> interest after 1925. This would seem to follow from the use in the
> proviso of the word "only".

4–091 It is this third element that is the most important, and the history of the proviso
tends to confirm that it was intended to have this effect.[48] In its final form, the
draftsman's scheme for the protection of equitable interests in unregistered
land appears to have been based on the assumption that, as far as possible, all

---

[44] Harman J. is reputed to have said that "Equity is not presumed to be of an age past
childbearing", but was unable to recall the context: see Megarry, *Miscellany-at-Law* (1955),
p. 142; *A Second Miscellany-at-Law* (1973), p. 293. See too *Pennine Raceway Ltd v. Kirklees
Metropolitan B.C.* [1983] QB 382 at 392. *cf. Western Fish Products Ltd v. Penwith D.C.* (1978)
[1981] 2 All E.R. 204 at 218, where Megaw L.J. observed that "the system of equity has
become a very precise one. The creation of new rights and remedies is a matter for Parliament,
not the judges".

[45] *cf. E.R. Ives Investment Ltd v. High* [1967] 2 QB 379 at 395; and see (1937) 59 L.Q.R. 259 at
260 (C. V. Davidge).

[46] Wolst. & C. i. 60.

[47] There were a number of such provisions: see, *e.g.* L.P.A. 1925, s.130(2) (*ante*, para. 3–038).
That section was recently repealed: see T.L.A.T.A. 1996, Sched. 4.

[48] See J. S. Anderson, *Lawyers and the Making of English Land Law 1832–1940*, at p. 309.
Section 4 was first introduced by the L.P.Am.A. 1924, together with both the final version of
the overreaching provisions and the extension of the system of registration of land charges.

equitable interests should be either overreachable or registrable as land charges, and that the doctrine of notice should pay only a residual role.[49] The draftsman did not lay down a general rule that all equitable rights over land which were incapable of being overreached should be registrable. Instead he specifically listed the charges that could be registered in the Land Charges Act 1925.[50] The creation of new equitable interests would necessarily defeat the draftsman's purpose because it would increase the number of rights which would depend for their protection on the doctrine of notice. No new kinds of equitable interest have in fact been created since 1925.[51] However it has become clear that the list of registrable rights is incomplete. A number of equitable rights have arisen that do not fall within it and these are therefore protected by the doctrine of notice.[52] It may be noted that the practical objection to the creation of new types of equitable interest does not apply where the title is registered. Any minor interest can be protected by an entry on the register.[53]

Section 8. Personal Rights which May Affect Third Parties

Although legislation would probably now be required to create new equitable proprietary interests, rights of a purely personal character affecting land may sometimes be enforced indirectly by or against third parties either under the law of tort or by means of a constructive trust. The availability of such remedies is most likely to be important where the right in issue is— **4–092**

(i) contractual and therefore only binding on the parties to it[54];

(ii) a mere licence[55]; or

(iii) a property right which is not binding on a purchaser of the land because it has not been registered.[56]

---

[49] He originally intended that all equitable interests should be overreachable, whether of a family or of a commercial character: J. S. Anderson, *op. cit.*, at 296.

[50] Now replaced by L.C.A. 1972.

[51] Though there have been unsuccessful attempts to do so: *post*, paras 17–017 (contractual licences), 17–022 (deserted wife's equity). If it had been cited, the proviso might have provided another ground for rejecting the deserted wife's equity.

[52] *Post*, paras 5–104, 5–105.

[53] See Ruoff & Roper, 8–02; 35–33.

[54] The so-called privity rule. When the Contracts (Rights of Third Parties) Bill, presently before Parliament, is enacted, a contract made for the benefit of a third party in accordance with the Bill will be enforceable by him. The Bill implements the recommendations in (1996) Law Com. No 242. See *post*, para. 10–022.

[55] It seems probable that licences are merely personal rights which donot create interests in land: *post*, Chap. 17.

[56] *Post*, paras 5–115 (unregistered land); 6–032 (registered land).

4–093   **1. Remedies in tort.** There is no doubt that "on ordinary principles" the
tort of wrongful interference with a contract is applicable to contracts concerning land,[57] though many uncertainties remain as to its application.[58] The
tort is committed when C interferes deliberately in the performance of a
contract made between A and B,[59] either by inducing or procuring its breach
or by preventing or hindering its performance.[60] To be liable, C must have
actual knowledge of the contract (though not necessarily of its contents).[61]
Constructive notice of the agreement,[62] or honest doubts as to its existence or
validity,[63] are not enough. In one remarkable case,[64] B Ltd, which owned a
garage, covenanted that it would buy petrol only from A, and that if it sold the
garage, it would obtain a similar covenant from the purchaser. A "solus
agreement" of this kind is personal to the parties to it and does not create a
property right. C Ltd acquired the shares in B Ltd, procured the transfer of the
garage to one of its subsidiary companies in order to defeat the solus tie, and
started to sell petrol from a different supplier. Even though the subsidiary had
been registered as proprietor of the garage, the court granted a mandatory
injunction in interlocutory proceedings requiring it to reconvey the property to
B Ltd.[65] In this way, a mere contractual right was enforced against a third
party who had brought about its breach. In another case,[66] B granted A a
contractual licence to live in a cottage for her lifetime. B then sold the cottage
to C expressly subject to A's rights. C attempted to evict A. One ground for
dismissing C's claim, was that it amounted to an interference with B's
contractual rights with A. In effect therefore, C was held to be bound by B's
licence.

---

[57] *Binions v. Evans* [1972] Ch. 359 at 371, *per* Megaw L.J. See too *Sefton v. Tophams Ltd* [1965]
Ch. 1140 at 1160–1162, 1187. Other economic torts, such as conspiracy, also apply to dealings
with real property: *Midland Bank Trust Co. Ltd v. Green (No. 3)* [1982] Ch. 529; *Hemingway
Securities Ltd v. Dunraven Ltd* [1995] 1 E.G.L.R. 61.

[58] See (1977) 41 Conv. (N.S.) 318 (R. J. Smith).

[59] For the essentials of the tort, see *Greig v. Insole* [1978] 1 W.L.R. 302 at 332.

[60] *Torquay Hotel Co. Ltd v. Cousins* [1969] 2 Ch. 106 at 138. There is no tort however where D
knowingly deprives A of his claim to a remedy against C for interference with A's contract
with B: *Law Debenture Trust Corporation v. Ural Caspian Oil Corporation Ltd* [1995] Ch.
152. But *cf.* (1995) 111 L.Q.R. 400 (P. Cane).

[61] *Greig v. Insole, supra,* at 336.

[62] *Swiss Bank Corporation v. Lloyds Bank Ltd* [1979] Ch. 548 at 575 (reversed on other grounds
[1982] A.C. 584).

[63] *Smith v. Morrison* [1974] 1 W.L.R. 659 at 677, 678.

[64] *Esso Petroleum Co. Ltd v. Kingswood Motors (Addlestone) Ltd* [1974] QB 142. The case has
been criticised: see (1977) 41 Conv. (N.S.) 318 (R. J. Smith). However, not only has it been
applied (see *Hemingway Securities Ltd v. Dunraven Ltd* [1995] 1 E.G.L.R. 61), but its
correctness was not doubted by the Court of Appeal in *Law Debenture Trust Corporation v.
Ural Caspian Oil Corporation Ltd, supra.*

[65] *A fortiori,* A could have obtained an injunction restraining the transfer of the property to the
subsidiary if he had acted sooner: *cf. Smith v. Morrison, supra.* See too *Hemingway Securities
Ltd v. Dunraven Ltd* [1995] 1 E.G.L.R. 61. In that case, a tenant sublet without the landlord's
consent in breach of covenant. The subtenant was considered to have induced or assisted that
brech and was ordered to surrender the sublease. *cf.* [1995] Conv. 416 (P. Luxton and M.
Wilkie); *post,* para. 14–146.

[66] *Binions v. Evans, supra.*

Justification is a defence to the tort of wrongful interference. In particular, C may plead that his conduct was justified by some equal or superior right.[67] Thus if A contracted to sell Blackacre to C, and then subsequently contracted to sell it to B, C would be entitled to require A to fulfil his contract even though he knew that he would thereby procure a breach of A's contract with B.[68] Similarly, if A had mortgaged his land to C, C could exercise his paramount power of sale even though in so doing he might bring about a breach of some contract relating to the land which A had made with B and of which C was aware.[69] It is less clear whether C would be justified in interfering in a contract just because it was not binding on him for want of registration. There is some authority which suggests that he would.[70] However, in another case, C was held liable in the tort of conspiracy where land was transferred to her by B in order to defeat A's unregistered option to purchase it.[71] This was so even though C took the land free of the option.[72]

2. Constructive trusts.[73] In certain circumstances, if B grants A a right   **4–094** over his land and then transfers the property to C expressly subject to that right, the court may impose a constructive trust on C, requiring him to give effect to the right, even though it is not binding on him as a matter of property law.[74] In such a case, the court imposes a new liability on C rather than holding him bound by an existing interest.[75] It will do so only if it would be unconscionable for him to deny A the right.[76] If there is no contract between A and B, no tortious remedy is likely to be available to A and a constructive trust of this kind may provide the only possible form of relief.

[67] *Read v. Friendly Society of Operative Stonemasons* [1902] 2 K.B. 88 at 96, 97.
[68] *Pritchard v. Briggs* [1980] Ch. 338 at 415.
[69] *Edwin Hill v. First National Finance Corporation Plc* [1989] 1 W.L.R. 225 at 229. For a mortgagee's power of sale, see *post*, para. 19–056.
[70] *cf. Miles v. Bull (No. 2)* [1969] 3 All E.R. 1585 at 1590.
[71] *Midland Bank Trust Co. Ltd v. Green (No. 3)* [1982] Ch. 529 (where the point was not expressly argued). Justification is a defence to the tort of conspiracy: *Crofter Hand Woven Harris Tweed Co. Ltd v. Veitch* [1942] A.C. 435 at 476.
[72] *Midland Bank Trust Co. Ltd v. Green* [1981] A.C. 513; *post*, para. 5–119.
[73] *Post*, paras 10–017 *et seq.* For the possible effect of the Contracts (Rights of Third Parties) Bill (when enacted) on such trusts, see *post*, para. 10–022.
[74] *e.g.* because it is a personal right such as a licence or is a property right which is void against C for non-registration.
[75] *IDC Group Ltd v. Clark* [1992] 1 E.G.L.R. 187 at 190.
[76] *ibid.*; *Ashburn Anstalt v. Arnold* [1989] Ch. 1 at 22, 25.

CHAPTER 5

UNREGISTERED CONVEYANCING: TITLES AND INCUMBRANCES

Part 1

THE UNREGISTERED SYSTEM IN DECLINE

5–001   In the previous chapter it was explained that there were two systems of conveyancing, unregistered and registered.[1] Unregistered conveyancing is applicable where the title is not yet registered. It is the traditional practice of investigating the title to land on sale, so as to make sure that the purchaser really becomes owner and does not find himself burdened with unsuspected liabilities. This practice, developed and refined over the centuries, eventually became unduly troublesome, despite the reforms of 1925. It is being rapidly replaced by a system of registration of title, which is based upon quite different principles. Since 1990, registration of title on dispositions of unregistered land has been compulsory throughout England and Wales.[2] After March 1998, the range of transactions that must be completed by registration has been significantly increased.[3] Compulsory registration now applies to the following dispositions[4]:

(i) conveyances of the freehold[5];

(ii) the grant of leases or underleases for a term of more than 21 years[6];

(iii) the assignment of any lease or underlease having more than 21 years to run[7]; and

(iv) a disposition by assent or vesting deed of a freehold, or of a lease or underlease having more than 21 years to run.

---

[1] *Ante* para. 4–066.
[2] S.I. 1989 No. 1347.
[3] By L.R.A. 1997, s.1; subsisting a new L.R.A. 1925, s.123, and adding L.R.A. 1925, s.123A; see *post*, para. 6–014.
[4] L.R.A. 1925, s.123(1), (6), as substituted by L.R.A. 1997, s.1.
[5] Whether for valuable consideration, by way of gift, or pursuant to a court order: L.R.A. 1925, s.123(6).
[6] *ibid.*
[7] *ibid.*

Furthermore, where there is a legal mortgage protected by the deposit of documents of title[8] of a freehold, or of a lease or underlease having more than 21 years to run, the title to the freehold or leasehold must now be registered.[9] It follows that most common dealings with unregistered land will trigger its compulsory registration. Unregistered conveyancing is therefore quickly disappearing. However, an understanding of it is still important in any study of land law, because it demonstrates the working and interaction of legal and equitable interests in their classic form and in the context of everyday transactions.

The central dilemma of land law is how to reconcile security of title with ease of transfer. The law permits a wide variety of incumbrances and charges such as leases, easements, restrictive covenants, estate contracts and mortgages, as already explained in outline. The owners of these interests are concerned that the land should not be transferred in any manner which might defeat them. A purchaser of the land, on the other hand, is concerned that he should not be bound by any interest not fully known to him in advance. The solution adopted in 1925 in relation to unregistered conveyancing was to require the registration of those third party interests which were likely to be the most elusive. Prior to that time, the protection of incumbrances had been achieved by imposing a high duty of care upon the purchaser. He was expected to make full and detailed investigation of his vendor's title so that, barring accidents, he would be bound to find out all the facts. The law's principal instrument for this purpose was the equitable doctrine of notice. **5–002**

Legal estates and interests would of course bind the purchaser in any event, and for them he had to inquire at his peril. But many equitable incumbrances could exist, and from them he would be safe only if he could show that he was a bona fide purchaser of a legal estate without notice. It was in order that he might, if necessary, be in a position to defend himself with this plea that he would undertake the elaborate inquiries required by the old system. These inquiries had to be repeated upon every purchase, so that the same title might be investigated again and again at quite short intervals, wasteful of effort though that was. Before Parliament came to his assistance with statutory reforms, a purchaser investigating title often had to make elaborate investigations into family settlements, joint ownership and other complexities, with the result that the intricacies of conveyancing became an obstacle to the ready marketability of land. **5–003**

The reformers of 1925 put their faith primarily in a modification of the old system of conveyancing. This was achieved, as already described, by the reorganisation of legal and equitable interests, by the system of overreaching, and by the extended use of registration of land charges. By these means it was given a further lease of life.[10] At the same time, provision was made for its progressive replacement by registration of title, described in the following **5–004**

---

[8] Which means, in practice, a first legal mortgage.
[9] L.R.A. 1925, s.123(2) (as substituted).
[10] See (1977) 40 M.L.R. 505 (A. Offer); and J. S. Anderson, *Lawyers and the Making of English Land Law 1832–1940.*

chapter. Although these two radically different systems still operate side by side, they are both based on the same general structure of estates and interests. The detailed rules about leases, mortgages, easements, settlements and so forth are in general the same under both systems, subject to some significant exceptions. The transition from unregistered to registered conveyancing can therefore be made smoothly. It is now questionable whether the development of registered conveyancing should be constrained by the principles of unregistered land, and the two systems may be expected to develop separately in future.

Unregistered conveyancing as it has operated since 1925 is comprised of three disparate elements:

1. The doctrine of the purchaser without notice.

2. The procedure followed on a sale of land and of the form and effect of the conveyance.

3. The system of registration of land charges.

Part 2

THE PURCHASER WITHOUT NOTICE

5–005   It is a fundamental rule that a purchaser of a legal estate for value without notice is "an absolute, unqualified, unanswerable defence"[11] against the claims of any prior equitable owner or incumbrancer. The onus of proof lies on the person putting forward this plea[12]: it is a single plea, and is not sufficiently made out by proving purchase for value and leaving it to the plaintiff to prove notice if he can.[13] The scope of the rule is explained, and then its elements are analysed.

5–006   **1. The Scope of the Rule.** Subject to two minor statutory exceptions,[14] the doctrine of notice has no role to play in registered conveyancing.[15] In unregistered conveyancing, notice will continue to be relevant in two situations. The

---

[11] *Pilcher v. Rawlins* (1872) 7 Ch. App. 259 at 269, James L.J.
[12] *Re Nisbett and Pott's Contract* [1906] 1 Ch. 386 at 404, 409, 410; *Barclays Bank Plc v. Boulter* [1998] 1 W.L.R. 1 at 8.
[13] *Re Nisbett and Potts' Contract* [1905] 1 Ch. 391 at 402 (on appeal, [1906] 1 Ch. 386); *Wilkes v. Spooner* [1911] 2 K.B. 473 at 486.
[14] L.R.A. 1925, ss.33(3) (a transferee of a registered charge for valuable consideration will be affected by any irregularity in the charge if he had notice of the irregularity at the time of the transfer); 61(6) (purchaser of a registered estate bound if he has notice of the vendor's bankruptcy, even if that bankruptcy has not been entered in the appropriate manner on the register).
[15] *Williams & Glyn's Bank Ltd v. Boland* [1981] A.C. 487 at 503–4; *Barclays Bank Plc v. Boulter* [1998] 1 W.L.R. 1 at 11. An earlier decision suggesting that notice might be relevant (*Peffer v. Rigg* [1977] 1 W.L.R. 285) must be regarded as incorrect. There are certain statutory provisions which protect purchasers without notice of factors which might lead to the setting aside of a disposition of land: *post,* para. 5–078. These provisions apply even if the land is registered: *Kemmis v. Kemmis* [1988] 1 W.L.R. 1307.

first is in relation to those dispositions for value of unregistered land that are not required to be completed by registration.[16] In practice this is likely to be confined to—

(i) the grant of leases for 21 years or less; and

(ii) the assignment or mortgage of existing leases of unregistered land having 21 years or less to run.

The second situation is on application for first registration following a conveyance that is required to be registered.[17] The issue of whether the purchaser (or some person through whom he derived title) took free of a right over the land because he was a bona fide purchaser will have to be determined by the registrar when he registers the title because it will affect the entries he makes on the register.

2. Bona fide. The purchaser must act in good faith. Any sharp practice or unconscionable conduct may forfeit the privileges of a purchaser in the eyes of equity in accordance with general principles. But although good faith is traditionally mentioned as "a separate test which may have to be passed even though absence of notice is proved",[18] there are no clear examples of it operating independently in that way.[19] It therefore serves mainly to emphasise that the purchaser must be innocent as to notice, and this is considered in detail below.

5–007

3. Purchaser for value. The words "for value" are included to show that value must have been given, because "purchaser" in its technical sense does not necessarily imply this.[20] "Value" does not necessarily mean full value.[21] It means any consideration in money, money's worth (*e.g.* other land, or stocks and shares, or services) or marriage.[22] "Money's worth" extends to all forms of non-monetary consideration in the sense used in the law of contract, but it also includes the satisfaction of an existing debt.[23] "Marriage", however, extends only to a future marriage: an ante-nuptial agreement (*i.e.* a promise made in consideration of future marriage) is deemed to have been made for value as regards both the spouses and the issue of the marriage[24]; but a promise made in respect of a past marriage (a post-nuptial agreement) is not.[25] "Good consideration" (the natural love and affection which a person

5–008

---

[16] *Ante*, para. 5–001.
[17] *ibid.*
[18] *Midland Bank Trust Co. Ltd v. Green* [1981] A.C. 513 at 528, *per* Lord Wilberforce.
[19] Though it is easy to imagine such cases, *e.g.* if a purchaser induced a vendor by fraud or coercion to sell land to him at an undervalue.
[20] *cf. ante*, para. 3–023.
[21] *Basset v. Nosworthy* (1673) Rep.t.Finch 102; Wh. & T. ii, 138, 140.
[22] See, *e.g. Wormald v. Maitland* (1866) 35 L.J.Ch. 69 at 73; *Salih v. Atchi* [1961] A.C. 778.
[23] *Thorndike v. Hunt* (1859) 3 De G. & J. 563; Maitland, *Equity*, 134; (1943) 59 L.Q.R. 208 (R.E.M.).
[24] *Att.-Gen. v. Jacobs Smith* [1895] 2 Q.B. 341.
[25] Wh. & T. ii, 791.

has for his near relatives) is of small importance and does not amount to value.[26] "Purchaser" is not confined to someone who acquires a fee simple; it includes, for example, mortgagees and lessees, who are purchasers *pro tanto* (to the extent of their interests).[27]

If the purchase is for money consideration, the purchaser must actually pay all the money before receiving notice of the equitable interest; and if such notice is received before the money is paid, no obligation or security for its payment will be enforceable.[28] The mere execution of a conveyance of a legal estate before notice is received, without payment of the money, will not suffice.[29]

5–009   **4. Of a legal estate.** This element is most important. The immunity from equities enjoyed by the purchaser without notice is founded on equity's deference to the legal estate. "As courts of equity break in upon the common law, when necessity and conscience require it, still they allow superior force and strength to a legal title to estates."[30] Unless he is a volunteer or has notice the legal owner cannot be interfered with by merely equitable claimants.

A purchaser of an equitable interest, even without notice, is in an entirely different position.[31] If A and B hold land on trust for X, and X sells his equitable interest to Y, Y takes subject to any other prior equitable interests there may be in the land, whether or not he has notice of them. The owner of an equitable interest can prima facie convey only what is vested in him, so that if part of his equitable interest has already been conveyed away, a subsequent purchaser can take only so much of it as remains.[32] The rule is thus that "where the equities are equal, the first in time prevails".[33] It is only acquisition of the legal estate for value and without notice which will reverse the natural order of priority. A neat illustration is provided by a case where land held upon trust was fraudulently mortgaged first to legal and later to equitable mortgagees, none of whom had notice of the trust. It was held that the legal mortgagee took priority over the beneficiaries under the trust, but that the equitable mortgagees did not.[34]

5–010   The purchaser must have the legal estate properly vested in him (by a conveyance[35]) before he will be safe. If he has paid the purchase-money, but

---

[26] *Goodright d. Humphreys v. Moses* (1774) 2 Wm.Bl. 1019.

[27] *ibid.; Brace v. Duchess of Marlborough* (1728) 2 P.Wms. 491; *Re King's Leasehold Estates* (1873) L.R. 16 Eq. 521 at 525.

[28] *Tourville v. Naish* (1734) 3 P.Wms. 307; *Taylor Barnard v. Tozer* [1984] 1 E.G.L.R. 21 at 22; Wh. & T. ii, 140.

[29] *Story v. Windsor* (1743) 2 Atk. 630. For the converse case, see below.

[30] *Wortley v. Birkhead* (1754) 2 Ves.Sen. 571 at 574, *per* Lord Hardwicke L.C.; and see *Pilcher v. Rawlins* (1872) 72 Ch.App. 259 at 268, 269; *L. & S. W. Ry. v. Gomm* (1882) 20 Ch.D. 562 at 586.

[31] *Phillips v. Phillips* (1862) 4 De G.F. & J. 208.

[32] See *Phillips v. Phillips, supra,* at 215.

[33] Snell, *Equity,* 47.

[34] *Cave v. Cave* (1880) 15 Ch.D. 639. And see *post,* para. 5–012, n.49.

[35] But an imperfect conveyance operating by estoppel may suffice: *Sharpe v. Foy* (1868) 4 Ch. App. 35.

then gets notice of a prior equitable interest before the purchase is completed by the conveyance of the legal estate, he will take subject to the equity.[36] But this does not apply to a subsequent equitable interest. A purchaser who takes a conveyance of the legal estate with notice of an equitable interest created after he contracted to buy the land takes free from it; for his equitable interest under the contract[37] has priority over the later equity, and the conveyance merely carries out the contract.[38]

The rule that the purchaser must take a legal estate before receiving notice is subject to two qualifications, or perhaps three.

(a) Superior right to legal estate. A purchaser without notice who acquires **5–011** only an equitable interest can defeat a prior equity if his equitable interest gives him a superior right to the legal estate. This rule is thus consistent with the principle that the legal estate must prevail. The simplest example is where the purchaser procures a conveyance not to himself but to some person who is trustee for him, and neither purchaser nor trustee has notice of the equity at the time of the conveyance.[39] An analogous but less obvious case could arise before 1926 where the legal estate was outstanding, *i.e.* was held by some third person who had no knowledge of the equity and who, before having notice of it, declared himself trustee for a purchaser who also had no notice.[40] This situation rarely occurred, but when it did the later purchaser took precedence. Since 1925 the priority of equitable claimants to an outstanding legal estate is governed by different rules which must be explained later, in connection with mortgages.[41]

This exception does not alter the general rule that a purchaser of an equitable interest who purchases it from the owner of the legal estate, but does not obtain the legal estate, is bound by all previous equitable interests affecting the land, whether or not he has notice of them. Nor is a superior right to a legal estate any shield against the legal estate itself; a purchaser of a legal estate without notice of a prior equitable interest takes free from it in accordance with the basic rule, even though the equitable interest conferred an equitable right to call for a legal estate.[42] Thus, if A holds land upon trust to

[36] *Wigg v. Wigg* (1739) 1 Atk. 382 at 384. For this rule as applied to mortgages, see *Saunders v. Dehew* (1692) 2 Vern. 271; *Allen v. Knight* (1846) 5 Hare 272, affirmed 16 L.J.Ch. 370; *Mumford v. Stohwasser* (1874) L.R. 18 Eq. 556; *cf. McCarthy & Stone Ltd v. Julian S. Hodge & Co. Ltd* [1971] 1 W.L.R. 1547 (equity registered before legal estate vested in mortgagee). In *Mumford v. Stohwasser* the *obiter dicta* of Jessel M.R. at 562–563 are not clear.

[37] See *ante*, para. 4–025.

[38] An example similar in principle is *Barclays Bank Ltd v. Bird* [1954] Ch. 274.

[39] *Stanhope v. Earl Verney* (1761) 2 Eden 81; "the *cestuy que trust* and trustees are one": *ibid.*, at 85, *per* Lord Henley L.C.

[40] *Wilkes v. Bodington* (1707) 2 Vern. 599; *Wilmot v. Pike* (1845) 5 Hare 14 at 21, 22; *Rooper v. Harrison* (1855) 2 K. & J. 86; *Taylor v. London & County Banking Co.* [1901] 2 Ch. 231 at 262, 263; *Assaf v. Fuwa* [1955] A.C. 215, noted in [1955] C.L.J. 32 (H.W.R.W.). These examples (except the last) are complicated, and are best studied as part of the law of priority of mortgages, *post*, paras 19–194, *et seq.* (esp. para. 19–205, n.25).

[41] *Post*, paras 19–205, 19–206, 19–232. The rule since 1925 is that the first interest of which the trustees get notice prevails.

[42] *Garnham v. Skipper* (1885) 55 L.J.Ch. 263; 53 L.T. 940 (contract to grant legal mortgage to A followed by grant of legal mortgage to B. B, having no notice, prevailed).

convey the legal estate to B, but then wrongfully conveys it to C, a purchaser without notice, C's title, of course, prevails.

5-012   *(b) Mere equities.* A purchaser without notice does not have to take a legal estate in order to take free from a "mere equity", *i.e.* an equitable right which falls short of an equitable interest in land.[43] There are a number of such "equities", arising out of special forms of equitable relief which the court will normally enforce against successors in title. Examples are the right of a party to a deed to have the deed set aside on account of fraud[44] or undue influence[45] and the right to have a document rectified for mutual mistake,[46] as where a lease stated the rent to be £130 but £230 was the figure to which the parties had in fact agreed.[47] The right of a mortgagor to reopen a foreclosure is probably in the same category.[48] On the other hand the rights of beneficiaries under a trust,[49] and a vendor's lien for unpaid purchase-money,[50] are equitable interests in land as opposed to mere equities; thus they will obey the general rule and bind a purchaser without notice unless he obtains the legal estate. The same is presumably true of estate contracts and restrictive covenants.[51]

5-013   The courts have not explained precisely where the dividing line between equitable interests and mere equities lies. All that can be said is that mere equities which may affect a purchaser are essentially rights which are ancillary

[43] *Phillips v. Phillips* (1862) 4 De G.F. & J. 208 at 218; *Westminster Bank Ltd v. Lee* [1956] Ch. 7; *Mid-Glamorgan County Council v. Ogwr B.C.* (1993) 68 P. & C.R. 1 at 9.

[44] *Bowen v. Evans* (1844) 1 Jo. & Lat. 178 at 263, 264; *Phillips v. Phillips, supra; Ernest v. Vivian* (1863) 33 L.J.Ch. 513; *Latec Investments Ltd v. Hotel Terrigal Pty Ltd* (1965) 113 C.L.R. 265; and see *Cloutte v. Storey* [1911] 1 Ch. 18 at 24, 25. For setting aside conveyances, see *post,* para. 5–078.

[45] *Bainbrigge v. Browne* (1881) 18 Ch.D. 188 (charge of equitable interest, executed under undue influence, held binding only upon volunteers and purchasers with notice, and so not upon chargee who took without notice; but the case contains no mention of "mere equities" or of the importance of the legal estate).

[46] See, *e.g. Blacklocks v. J.B. Developments (Godalming) Ltd* [1982] Ch. 183; *Taylor Barnard v. Tozer* [1984] 1 E.G.L.R. 21 at 22. For rectification, see *post,* para. 12–122.

[47] *Garrard v. Frankel* (1862) 30 Beav. 445 (which must now be read subject to the doubts expressed upon it in *Riverlate Properties Ltd v. Paul* [1975] Ch. 133; *post,* para. 12–122). *Smith v. Jones* [1954] 2 All E.R. 823 is evidently a case of a purchaser of a *legal* estate without notice: the report in [1954] 1 W.L.R. 1089 is not clear on the point.

[48] For this right, see *post,* para. 19–055.

[49] *Cave v. Cave* (1880) 15 Ch.D. 639; *cf. Re Vernon, Ewens & Co.* (1886) 33 Ch.D. 402. But *Cave v. Cave* has not been followed in Ireland: *Re Ffrench's Estate* (1887) 21 L.R. Ir. 283; *Re Sloane's Estate* [1895] 1 I.R. 146; and see (1958) 21 Conv. (N.S.) 195 (V.T.H. Delany). In the Irish cases it was held that beneficiaries under a trust had "mere equities" which would not bind a later equitable mortgagee who had no notice; and *Scott v. Scott* [1924] 1 I.R. 141 applied the same doctrine to assets improperly applied by an administrator. These decisions are strongly tinged with the old idea that equitable interests under trusts are primarily rights *in personam* against the trustee, and that any right "to follow the trust property" is less substantial and a mere equity: see especially *Scott v. Scott, supra,* at 150, 151. But in England the courts have tended rather to treat equitable interests as fully developed rights *in rem* (*ante,* para. 4–012) and rights under trusts should really be the equitable interests *par excellence.* The English doctrine is both simpler and more consistent with the paramount necessity of making the trust a secure form of property.

[50] *Mackreth v. Symmons* (1808) 15 Ves. 329; *Rice v. Rice* (1853) 2 Drew. 73; *Kettlewell v. Watson* (1882) 21 Ch.D. 685 at 711 (on appeal, (1884) 26 Ch.D. 501); *Cave v. Cave* (1880) 15 Ch. D. 639 at 648, 649. For this lien, see *post,* paras 12–054, 19–003.

[51] *National Provincial Bank Ltd v. Ainsworth* [1965] A.C. 1175 at 1238, *per* Lord Upjohn.

to or dependent upon some interest in the land which that purchaser takes.[52] There is thus a parallel with the ordinary rule relating to the purchaser of a legal estate without notice. Just as that purchaser takes the estate free from any equitable interests which affect it (and *a fortiori* any mere equities), so a purchaser of an equitable interest takes it entire and free from any mere equities affecting it of which he has no notice.[53]

Underlying the whole subject is the principle that it is only *where the equities are equal* that the first in time prevails[54]; and sometimes the balance between competing equities may be too delicate to be settled by rigid rules. Even an equitable interest may lose priority to a later equity if there has been negligence or fraud on the part of the equitable owner.[55] A "mere equity" has the additional weakness that it is more at the discretion of the court; and the court may naturally be loath to exercise its discretion against an innocent purchaser without notice, even though he is not clad in the armour of the legal estate, and even though the person entitled to the earlier equity cannot be accused of misconduct.[56]

(c) Subsequent acquisition of legal estate. A purchaser of an equitable **5–014** interest who pays the purchase-money without notice of a prior equity has been held to be protected if he later acquires a legal estate, even with notice, provided it is not conveyed to him in breach of trust.[57] Yet this supposed exception may be merely a corollary of the general rule. For if the legal estate is subject to a prior equity inconsistent with the purchaser's title, it will necessarily be a breach of trust to convey it to him,[58] whether or not the facts are known to the person conveying it. If the prior equity is consistent with the

---

[52] *ibid.* The benefit of a mere equity passes with the land that it affects under the "all estate" clause (L.P.A. 1925, s.63(1)): *Boots the Chemist Ltd v. Street* [1983] 2 E.G.L.R. 51. See too *Berkeley Leisure Group Ltd v. Williamson* [1996] E.G.C.S. 18. For the "all estate" clause, see *post*, para 5–044.

[53] See (1955) 71 L.Q.R. 481, 482 (R.E.M.), approved in *National Provincial Bank Ltd v. Ainsworth, supra,* at 1238, *per* Lord Upjohn.

[54] *Rice v. Rice, supra,* contains a classic discussion of this principle by Kindersley V.-C.

[55] *Rice v. Rice, supra* (lien of unpaid vendor postponed to equitable mortgage because vendor had signed receipt for the purchase-money); *Re King's Settlement* [1931] 2 Ch. 294. And even a legal estate may lose its priority for similar reasons: see the cases on mortgages cited *post*, para. 19–203.

[56] See [1955] C.L.J. at 160 (H.W.R.W.); (1955) 19 Conv.(N.S.) 343 (F. R. Crane); (1957) 21 Conv.(N.S.) at 201 (V. T. H. Delany); (1976) 40 Conv.(N.S.) 209 (A. R. Everton).

[57] *Bailey v. Barnes* [1894] 1 Ch. 25 at 36; *cf. Powell v. London and Provincial Bank* [1893] 1 Ch. 610, affirmed [1893] 2 Ch. 555. In *Bailey v. Barnes* property subject to equitable claims by creditors was first mortgaged to A (legal estate) and then sold to B (equity of redemption). Neither A (it seems) nor B had notice. B later got notice, paid off A and acquired the legal estate. *Held*, the equity did not bind B. As A, it seems, had no notice himself, B, as successor in title to A, would not in any case have been bound: *post*, para. 5–025. But the Court of Appeal invoked the principle of tacking mortgages (*post*, para. 19–243), though this seems inapplicable to the facts since the legal estate was from the first subject to the equity and not paramount to it, as was requisite for tacking: *post*, para. 19–248. The same difficulty arises in *McCarthy & Stone Ltd v. Julian S. Hodge & Co. Ltd* [1971] 1 W.L.R. 1547, although the purchaser had constructive notice at the outset and therefore failed. See *Macmillan Inc. v. Bishopsgate Investment Trust Plc* [1995] 1 W.L.R. 978 at 1002–1005.

[58] See *Mumford v. Stohwasser* (1874) L.R. 18 Eq. 566; *McCarthy & Stone Ltd v. Julian S. Hodge & Co. Ltd, supra* (breach of trust no mortgage land already subject to contract of sale).

purchaser's title, as where it is a mere incumbrance such as a restrictive covenant, the "breach of trust" exception probably does not apply at all; for it is founded on rules devised for competing mortgages,[59] which are wholly inapplicable to consistent titles. Those rules were abolished as regards mortgages in 1925,[60] being "technical and not satisfactory".[61] They would be best abandoned altogether.

5–015   **5. Without notice.** There are three kinds of notice.[62]

5–016   *(a) Actual notice.* Strictly speaking there is a distinction between knowledge and notice. A person may be regarded as having notice of a fact not because he knows it, but because for legal purposes he is to be taken to know it.[63] In practice, however, this distinction is not always observed.[64] The term "actual notice" has been used in at least three different senses:

    (i) A person is commonly said to have "actual notice" of a fact where he subjectively knows of it, regardless of how that knowledge was acquired.[65]

    (ii) There is some authority for the view that a person is considered to have actual notice of a matter of which he had once known but has since forgotten.[66] Certainly a court would be likely to scrutinise with care a purchaser's assertion of forgetfulness.[67] However it has been suggested that a purchaser will not be fixed with notice of

---

[59] Explained *post*, para. 19–243.

[60] L.P.A. 1925, s.94(3); *post*, para. 12–257. Apparently the provision applies only to mortgages: *McCarthy & Stone Ltd v. Julian S. Hodge & Co. Ltd, supra*, at 1556; contrast (1957) 21 Conv. (N.S.) at 196 (V. H. T. Delany).

[61] *Bailey v. Barnes* (1894) 1 Ch. 25 at 36.

[62] The fullest modern discussions of notice are found in the context of liability for intermeddling with trusts: see, *e.g. Baden Delvaux v. Société General* (1983) [1993] 1 W.L.R. 509n. at 575, 576; and (1986) 102 L.Q.R. 114 at 120–127 (C.H.). *cf. Royal Brunei Airlines Sdn. Bhd. v. Tan* [1995] 2 A.C. 378 at 392.

[63] *Ashburner's Principles of Equity* (2nd ed.), 59. See too *Rignall Developments Ltd v. Halil* [1988] Ch. 190, at 200–202; and *post*, para. 5–109.

[64] Though in certain contexts it can be of considerable importance: see *post*, paras 5–109, 12–082.

[65] *Lloyd v. Banks* (1868) 3 Ch. App. 488. He is not however regarded as having notice of facts which have come to his ears only in the form of vague rumours: *Barnhart v. Greenshields* (1853) 9 Moo. P.C. 18 at 36, explained in *Reeves v. Pope* [1914] 2 K.B. 284.

[66] See dicta in *Rignall Developments Ltd v. Halil* [1988] Ch. 190 at 201–202; *Eagle Trust Plc v. SBC Securities Ltd* [1993] 1 W.L.R. 484 at 494; *Polly Peck International Plc v. Nadir (No. 2)* [1992] 4 All E.R. 769 at 781. None of these decisions was concerned with whether a purchaser of land was bound by an incumbrance.

[67] Where in the course of a purchase, a matter is brought to the knowledge of the purchaser's agent, that knowledge is imputed to the purchaser: L.P.A. 1925, s.199(1)(ii)(b); *post*, para. 5–023. This will be so even if the agent has failed to read the document: *cf. Rignall Developments Ltd v. Halil, supra*, at 198. In principle therefore if a matter has been brought to the purchaser's own attention in the course of the purchase, a court should not entertain an assertion that he has forgotten it.

something which he has genuinely forgotten.[68] This view is supported by the statutory provision that such a purchaser is not to be "prejudicially affected" by notice of anything unless it "is within his own knowledge", because it is unlikely that "is" will be taken to mean "is or ever has been".[69] The point remains an open one.

(iii) By statute a number of rights have become registrable in the Land Charges Register, and it has been provided that registration of such rights constitutes actual notice.[70] This subject is considered below.[71]

(b) Constructive notice

(1) DUTY OF DILIGENCE. Equitable interests would have been entirely insecure if it had been made easy for purchasers to acquire the legal estate without notice, as by merely asking no questions. Accordingly the Court of Chancery insisted that purchasers should inquire about equitable interests with no less diligence than about legal interests, which they could ignore only at their own peril. The motto of English conveyancing is *caveat emptor*[72]: the risk of incumbrances is on the purchaser, who must satisfy himself by a full investigation of title before completing his purchase.[73]   **5–017**

(2) STANDARD REQUIRED. By the doctrine of constructive notice equity adopted a similar principle and adapted itself to the ordinary conveyancing practice. A purchaser would be able to plead absence of notice only if he had made all usual and proper inquiries, and had still found nothing to indicate the equitable interest.[74] If he fell short of this standard he could not plead that he had no notice of rights which proper diligence would have discovered. Of these he was said to have "constructive notice". A purchaser accordingly has constructive notice of a fact if he—   **5–018**

(i) had actual notice that there was some incumbrance and a proper inquiry would have revealed what it was, or

---

[68] *Re Montagu's S.T.* [1987] Ch. 264 at 284; *El Ajou v. Dollar Land Holdings Plc* [1993] 3 All E.R. 717 at 743.

[69] L.P.A. 1925, s.199(1)(ii)(a); *Re Montagu's S.T., supra.* It also seems improbable that a solicitor who buys a house for himself would be affected by notice of all that he had discovered and forgotten in a lifetime of conveyancing, especially as such notice would not be imputed to his clients: see *post*, para. 5–023.

[70] L.P.A. 1925, s.198(1). A person may be fixed with actual notice of a land charge by reason of this subsection even though he could not have discovered its existence: *post*, para. 5–112; and see *Eagle Trust Plc v. SBC Securities Ltd, supra*, at 494.

[71] *Post*, para. 5–109.

[72] Let a purchaser beware.

[73] It should be noted however that the courts have frequently warned against the extension of the doctrine of constructive notice into commercial transactions unconnected with dispositions of land: see, *e.g. Eagle Trust Plc v. SBC Securities Ltd* [1993] 1 W.L.R. 484 at 504–506.

[74] *Bailey v. Barnes, supra*, C.A. 1882, s.3(1)(i), replaced by L.P.A. 1925, s.199(1)(ii).

(ii) deliberately abstained from inquiry in an attempt to avoid having notice, or

(iii) omitted by carelessness or for any other reason to make an inquiry which a purchaser acting on skilled advice ought to make and which would have revealed the incumbrance.[75]

A purchaser's ordinary duties fall into two main categories: inspection of the land, and investigation of the vendor's title.

5–019   (3) INSPECTION OF LAND. A purchaser is expected to inspect the land and make inquiry as to anything which appears inconsistent with the title offered by the vendor.

It is an ancient rule that the fact of possession constitutes notice of the rights of the possessor.[76] Two reasons have been given for this. First, occupation of the premises by a person whose presence is inconsistent with the vendor's title places any purchaser on inquiry as to the occupier's rights.[77] Secondly, and in the alternative, it is said that as possession is prima facie evidence of title,[78] a purchaser is deemed to have notice of the rights of any person in possession.[79] There is an important distinction between these two explanations. If the latter is correct, a purchaser will have notice of the rights of the possessor, even though his possession is not immediately apparent.[80] Modern authority tends to confirm the latter view.[81] A purchaser should therefore—

(i) ascertain whether there is anybody in possession or occupation of the land apart from the vendor, at least if there are any circumstances from which a reasonable person might infer this[82]; and

(ii) make inquiry of any such person.[83]

---

[75] See *Jones v. Smith* (1841) 1 Hare 43 at 55; *Kemmis v. Kemmis* [1988] 1 W.L.R. 1307; Snell, *Equity*, 51–55; Maitland, *Equity*, 118, 119.

[76] See [1990] C.L.J. 277 at 315–320 (C.H.).

[77] *Barnhart v. Greenshields* (1853) 9 Moo. P.C. 18 at 32.

[78] *Jones v. Smith* (1841) 1 Hare 43 at 60. *Ante*, para. 3–121.

[79] *Holmes v. Powell* (1856) 8 De G.M. & G. 572 at 580, 581. This is in accordance with the protection which the law gives to persons in possession: *ante*, para. 3–122. It is clear that a person may be in possession of land even though he is not in occupation of it, *e.g.* where the land consists of fields or woodland.

[80] *Holmes v. Powell, supra*, at 581.

[81] *Kingsnorth Finance Co. Ltd v. Tizard* [1986] 1 W.L.R. 783.

[82] *ibid.* The case has been criticised for imposing an excessive burden of inquiry on any purchaser: All E.R. Rev. 1986, 181–184 (P. J. Clarke); [1986] Conv. 283 (M. P. Thompson). It is, however, in accordance with earlier authority. In practice, the first of these inquiries will usually be necessary only where the vendor is mortgaging the property. If he is leasing the land or assigning an existing lease, the purchaser will not complete unless vacant possession can be given. See *Northern Bank Ltd v. Henry* [1981] I.R. 1 at 9, 10.

[83] The purchaser should make inquiry of the occupier or possessor personally, since "the untrue *ipse dixit* of the vendor will not suffice": *Hodgson v. Marks* [1971] Ch. 892 at 932, *per* Russell L.J. Although that was a decision on registered land, the rules for unregistered land were also expounded.

The mere fact that there is on the land a person, such as a spouse, whose presence is not inconsistent with that of the vendor does not obviate the need for the purchaser to make inquiry of them.[84] The old view to the contrary has now been discredited.[85] If, for example, a husband is sole legal owner of land, but his wife has an equitable interest in the property by reason of some contribution to the cost of its acquisition, any purchaser will be bound by her interest unless it was not disclosed after proper inquiry by her.[86] There may of course be circumstances in which a person in possession of land is estopped from asserting any interest in it.[87]

Occupation by a tenant is notice of the interest of the tenant,[88] the terms of his tenancy[89] and his other rights,[90] though not of any right not apparent from the lease, such as a right to have it rectified[91] on account of a mistake. But a purchaser is under no duty to find out to whom a tenant pays rent or otherwise to investigate the tenant's title, so that failure to make such inquiries does not give him constructive notice of any rights of the tenant's landlord, who may be a different person from the vendor.[92] **5–020**

Notice resulting from occupation extends in general to all equitable rights which the occupier may have in the land.[93] Notice that property is subject to trusts is notice of all the trusts to which it is subject in the hands of the trustees[94] and notice of the existence of a document that might be expected to be relevant[95] is notice of its contents.[96]

(4) INVESTIGATION OF TITLE. A purchaser has constructive notice of all rights which he would have discovered[97] had he investigated the vendor's title to the land for the period allowed by law in ordinary cases where the parties make no special agreement as to length of title. Investigation of title means the **5–021**

---

[84] *Kingsnorth Finance Co. Ltd v. Tizard, supra.*

[85] See *Williams & Glyn's Bank Ltd v. Boland* [1981] A.C. 487, a case on registered land, in which earlier authorities on unregistered land such as *Caunce v. Caunce* [1969] 1 W.L.R. 286 were disapproved. The decision in *Williams & Glyn's Bank v. Boland* caused concern to the conveyancing world and led to a report by the Law Commission recommending that the equitable interests of all co-owners should be made registrable and so eliminated from the doctrine of notice: (1982) Law Com. No. 115. These proposals were however never implemented: see [1983] Conv. 87 (J. T. Farrand).

[86] *Kingnorth Finance Co. Ltd v. Tizard, supra.* For interests obtained by contribution, see *post,* para. 10–016.

[87] For example, an agent who negotiates a sale or mortgage on behalf of his principal impliedly represents to the purchaser that the property is free from any undisclosed interest of the agent's: *Midland Bank Ltd v. Farmpride Hatcheries Ltd* [1981] 2 E.G.L.R. 147 (directors residing in their company's property).

[88] *Daniels v. Davison* (1809) 16 Ves. 249; *Allen v. Anthony* (1816) 1 Mer. 282: *Mumford v. Stohwasser* (1874) L.R. 18 Eq. 556; *Hunt v. Luck* [1902] 1 Ch. 428.

[89] *Taylor v. Stibbert* (1794) 2 Ves. Jun. 437.

[90] *Barnhart v. Greenshields* (1853) 9 Moo. P.C. 18.

[91] *Smith v. Jones* [1954] 1 W.L.R. 1089.

[92] *Hunt v. Luck, supra.*

[93] *Jones v. Smith* (1841) 1 Hare 43; *Barnhart v. Greenshields, supra.*

[94] *Perham v. Kempster* [1907] 1 Ch. 373.

[95] *Re Valletort Sanitary Steam Laundry Co.* [1903] 2 Ch. 654; Snell, *Equity,* 52.

[96] *Bisco v. Earl of Banbury* (1676) 1 Ch. Ca. 287.

[97] See *Carter v. Williams* (1870) L.R. 9 Eq. 678.

examination of documents relating to transactions in the land during the period immediately prior to the purchase.[98] This period used by convention to be at least 60 years, but by the Vendor and Purchaser Act 1874 it was reduced to at least 40 years, and by the Law of Property Act 1925 to at least 30 years. Under the Law of Property Act 1969 it is now at least 15 years.[99] The period is "at least" 15 years, for the purchaser can call for a good root of title which is at least 15 years old, and see all subsequent documents which trace the dealing with the property.[1] A good root of title may be, for example, a conveyance or a mortgage, provided that it offers a clear starting point for the title. To do this it must be a document which deals with the whole legal and equitable interest in the land, describes the property adequately, and contains nothing to throw any doubt on the title.[1a]

5–022   For example, if the title consists of a series of conveyances respectively 5, 14, 25 and 48 years old, as well as older deeds, a purchaser is entitled to production of the conveyance 25 years old and all subsequent conveyances. If in fact he fails to investigate the title at all,[2] or else investigates it for only part of this period (*e.g.* because he has agreed to accept a shorter title, or to make no objection to some dubious transaction),[3] he is fixed with constructive notice of everything that he would have discovered had he investigated the whole title for the full statutory period. With transactions prior to the root of title a purchaser need have no concern. He may be affected by notice if he actually investigates them or inquires about them, but not otherwise.[4] A purchaser who, having notice of relevant title deeds, inquires for them, and is met with a reasonable excuse for their non-production is (by an exceptional rule) free from notice of their contents.[5] But this does not alter the rule as to notice by failing to inquire at all[6] even if an inquiry would probably have been met by some false but apparently reasonable excuse.[7]

5–023   (c) *Imputed notice.* If a purchaser employs an agent, such as a solicitor, any actual or constructive[8] notice which the agent receives is imputed to the purchaser.[9] The basis of this doctrine is that a person who empowers an agent

---

[98] For a fuller account of proof of title, see *post*, para. 12–072.

[99] L.P.A. 1969, s.23. See *post*, para. 12–075, for these periods. For the interrelationship between periods of limitation and the period for which title has to be investigated, see [1985] Conv. 272 (M. Dockray).

[1] *Post*, paras 12–075–12–076.

[1a] *ibid.*

[2] *Worthington v. Morgan* (1849) 16 Sim. 547.

[3] *Re Cox & Neve's Contract* [1891] 2 Ch. 109 at 117, 118; *Re Nisbett and Potts' Contract* [1906] 1 Ch. 386.

[4] *Post*, para. 12–078.

[5] *Hewitt v. Loosemore* (1851) 9 Hare 449 at 458; *Espin v. Pemberton* (1859) 3 De G. & J. 547; Williams, V. & P 309, criticised *post*, para. 19–206.

[6] *Peto v. Hammond* (1861) 30 Beav. 495.

[7] *Jones v. Williams* (1857) 24 Beav. 47.

[8] *Re The Alms Corn Charity* [1901] 2 Ch. 750.

[9] In a conveyancing transaction, a solicitor has authority to receive communications for his client from the other party. It is his duty to pass them on to his principal. Even if this does not happen, then in the absence of fraud by the agent, the client will be estopped from denying that he received the information: *Strover v. Harrington* [1988] Ch. 390 at 409, 410.

to act for him is not allowed to plead ignorance of his agent's dealings.[10] Thus where a solicitor discovered an equitable mortgage on the title and was deceived by a forged receipt into believing that the mortgage had been discharged, the purchaser had imputed notice of the mortgage and was bound by it.[11] Since solicitors are usually employed to investigate title this branch of the doctrine of notice is essential. But, in order to check its extension, it is confined by statute to notice which the agent acquires acting as such in the same transaction.[12] Where the same solicitor acts for both parties, there is a conflict of authority as to whether any notice that he acquires will be imputed to both parties.[13] The older cases tended to favour the view that it would,[14] but in more recent decisions, the courts have held that what the solicitor learns when acting for one party, he does not learn while acting as agent for the other.[15] Notice will not be imputed to a party just because the solicitor knows that another member of his firm acted for the other party in an earlier transaction, unless the facts are so compelling as to put him on inquiry.[16] Nor will a purchaser be fixed with notice if he employed the vendor's solicitor not generally but merely to draw up the conveyance.[17] Because imputed notice rests upon a person's presumed knowledge of his agent's dealings, an exception also arises where the agent deliberately defrauds the principal.[18]

(d) *Extent of doctrine of notice.* The tendency of the Court of Chancery was constantly to extend and refine the doctrines of constructive and imputed notice. So much property was held under trusts and other equitable dispositions that the frequent appearance of the bona fide purchaser of the legal estate without notice would have been intolerable. Equity's ambition was to eliminate him, so far as possible, by ensuring that it should be almost impossible to escape notice of any equity properly created and recorded. In so far as he could be excluded, equitable rights were as secure as legal rights. Equity's policy was in the main successful, as may be judged from the rarity and

5–024

---

[10] Williams, V. & P. 306.

[11] *Jared v. Clements* [1903] 1 Ch. 428.

[12] L.P.A. 1925, s.199(1)(ii)(b); replacing C.A. 1882, s.3(1)(ii); *Thorne v. Marsh* [1895] A.C. 495 at 501.

[13] A party could certainly plead that he purchased without notice if the solicitor had entered into a conspiracy with the vendor to conceal something from the purchaser: *Sharpe v. Foy* (1868) 4 Ch.App. 35; *Cave v. Cave* (1880) 15 Ch.D. 639.

[14] *Dryden v. Frost* (1838) 3 My. & Cr. 670; *Meyer v. Chartres* (1918) 34 T.L.R. 589; and see *Kennedy v. Green* (1834) 3 My. & Cr. 699; *Lloyds Bank Ltd v. Marcan* [1973] 1 W.L.R. 339 at 348 (affd. [1973] 1 W.L.R. 1387); but see *Bateman v. Hunt* [1904] 2 K.B. 530.

[15] *Halifax Mortgage Services Ltd v. Stepsky* [1996] Ch. 207; *Birmingham Midshires Mortgage Services v. Mahal* (1996) 73 P. & C.R. D7; *Barclays Bank Plc v. Thomson* [1997] 4 All E.R. 816 at 828, 829; *National Westminster Bank Plc v. Beaton* (1997) 30 H.L.R. 99; *Leamington Spa B.S. v. Verdi* (1997) 75 P. & C.R. D16; *post*, para. 19–170. In each of these cases, a solicitor acting for a creditor also gave advice in an independent capacity to a surety prior to her agreeing to guarantee her husband's debts. The earlier authorities were not cited, but some of them pre-date what is now L.P.A. 1925, s.199(1)(ii)(b).

[16] *B. v. B. (P Ltd Intervening) (No. 2)* [1995] 1 F.L.R. 374; [1995] Fam. Law 244 (S. Cretney).

[17] *Kettlewell v. Watson* (1882) 21 Ch.D. 685; (1884) 26 Ch.D. 639.

[18] Williams V. & P., 306, 307.

abstruseness of the cases in which the defence of purchaser without notice has been made out. Even today, when the doctrine of notice has such a limited role to play, there are still situations in which it can pose a threat to a purchaser.[19]

The Conveyancing Act 1882 is regarded as closing the period in which the rules relating to notice were widely extended. Apart from the change in the law about imputed notice, mentioned above, the Act merely stated that a purchaser should not be affected by notice unless he had failed to make "such inquiries and inspections as ought reasonably to have been made by him".[20] This, it has been said, "really does no more than state the law as it was before, but its negative form shows that a restriction rather than an extension of the doctrine of notice was intended by the legislature[21]."

5–025   **6. Successor in title.** The protection of the doctrine of purchaser without notice also extends to any purchaser claiming through such a purchaser,[22] even though he took with notice of the equity.[23] Similarly, a mere volunteer, if he claims through a purchaser without notice, can presumably claim freedom from the equity, for the principle is that once a legal estate has passed into the hands of a purchaser without notice of the equity, that equity ceases to be enforceable against that estate, and cannot be revived.[24] Unless this were so, the owner of the equity could, by widely advertising his claim, make it difficult for the purchaser without notice to dispose of the land for the price that he gave for it.[24]

The only qualification to this rule is based on the principle that a man cannot take advantage of his own wrong. If a trustee disposes of trust property to a purchaser without notice, and later reacquires the property, he will again hold it subject to the trusts, and not free from them.[25]

Part 3

CONVEYANCING PRACTICE

5–026   The procedure followed on an ordinary sale of unregistered land will now be described in outline, together with some details about the form and effect of the conveyance. Almost all conveyances of unregistered land must now be

---

[19] Most notably where A, the sole legal owner of unregistered land, holds the property on trust for himself and B, and then mortgages it: see *post*, para. 10–032.

[20] s.3(1)(i), replaced by L.P.A. 1925, s.199(1)(ii). See Maitland, *Equity*, 120, 121.

[21] *Bailey v. Barnes* [1894] 1 Ch. 25 at 35, *per* Lindley L.J.; and see *Caunce v. Caunce* [1969] 1 W.L.R. 286 at 293. *cf. Northern Bank Ltd v. Henry* [1981] I.R. 1 at 15–17.

[22] *Sweet v. Southcote* (1786) 2 Bro. C.C. 66; *Wilkes v. Spooner* [1911] 2 K.B. 473; Wh. & T. ii, 110.

[23] See, *e.g. Harrison v. Forth* (1695) Prec. Ch. 51; *Wilkes v. Spooner, supra*.

[24] Maitland, *Equity*, 117.

[25] *Re Stapleford Colliery Co.* (1880) 14 Ch.D. 432 at 445; *Gordon v. Holland* (1913) 82 L.J.P.C. 81; and contrast *Piggott v. Stratton* (1859) 1 De G.F. & J. 33 with *Wilkes v. Spooner, supra*.

completed by registration.[26] However, in such circumstances, the sale is still conducted according to the principles of unregistered conveyancing. It is only when the land has been conveyed that an application for registration of the title can be made. All the conveyancing documents (including the conveyance itself) must then accompany that application.[27]

Section 1. From Contract to Completion

1. The contract. First of all the parties will have made a contract in writing. Contracts for the sale of land are subject to many rules both as to formalities and as to their effect, but this subject is largely unaffected by the differences between registered and unregistered conveyancing, and is therefore treated independently in Chapter 12.   **5–027**

There have been some changes in standard conveyancing practice following the introduction of the National Conveyancing Protocol by The Law Society in 1990.[28] The Protocol provides a code of practice that is appropriate for sales of domestic property by private treaty (rather than by auction) and has been introduced in order to streamline such transactions. Quite apart from this Protocol, it has long been normal to incorporate into contracts for the sale of land standard sets of conditions of sale which regulate the conduct of the transaction. There is now just one set, the Standard Conditions of Sale.[29] In practice, whether the National Protocol is used or not, much of the legal work associated with the purchase of land is nowadays conducted before contract.

Prior to the exchange of written contracts, a purchaser will normally search the local land charges register[30] and will make certain other inquiries of the relevant local authorities[31] on matters not registrable as local land charges.[32] Where the National Protocol is not employed, he will submit to the vendor a series of written preliminary inquiries which are intended to clear up doubts concerning the state of the property. Such inquiries are now much more limited in their scope than was formerly the case, and are confined to matters not otherwise readily ascertainable.[33] They are unnecessary where the National Protocol is employed, as it commonly will be in domestic sales,

---

[26] See *ante*, para. 5–001.

[27] L.R.R. 1925, rr. 19–21; Ruoff & Roper, 12–03–12–07.

[28] The 3rd edition of the Protocol appeared in 1994. The Protocol sets out the steps which a vendor of land should take to provide the purchaser with as much information as possible at the commencement of the transaction. Use of the Protocol is entirely voluntary. For a discussion, see M. P. Thompson, *Barnsley's Conveyancing Law and Practice* (4th ed.), p. 188.

[29] 3rd ed., 1995.

[30] For local land charges, see *post*, para. 5–132.

[31] It will not always be possible to make such inquiries, *e.g.* if the property is purchased at auction.

[32] Such inquiries relate to matters such as roads, sewers, drains and, above all, planning.

[33] Following guidelines given by the Conveyancing Standing Committee of the Law Commission: *Preliminary Enquiries: House Purchase. A Practice Recommendation* (1987).

because the vendor will supply the purchaser with the information by means of a completed questionnaire.[34]

5–028   **2. Delivery of the abstract.** The vendor is under an obligation to prove that he has a good title. Whether the title is deduced before or after contracts have been exchanged, the first stage in this process is for the vendor (V) to deliver to the purchaser (P) the abstract of title.[35] This document consists in part of an epitome of the various documents, and in part of a recital of the relevant events, such as births, deaths and marriages, which affect the title. The abstract starts with a good root of title and traces the devolution of the property down to V. Thus a very simple abstract might consist of—

    (i) an epitome of a conveyance by A to B;

    (ii) a recital of B's death;

    (iii) a recital of probate of B's will being granted to X and Y;

    (iv) an epitome of the assent by X and Y in favour of V.

Today, photocopies of the documents usually take the place of epitomes.

5–029   **3. Consideration of abstract.** P then peruses the abstract of title, considers the validity of the title shown, and checks the abstract against V's title deeds, grants of probate, and other papers which prove the statements made in the abstract.

5–030   **4. Requisitions on title.** P's examination of the abstract usually discloses a number of points upon which he requires further information. This further explanation is obtained by means of "requisitions on title", a series of written questions which P delivers to V. Requisitions usually consist of a mixture of requests for information genuinely needed (*e.g.* as to the date of a death not revealed by the abstract, or as to some incumbrance which the abstract mentions but does not explain), statements of the obvious (*e.g.* that V, having agreed to sell free from incumbrances, must discharge the mortgage or obtain the concurrence of his mortgagee to the sale of the property free from the mortgage), and general inquiries designed to make V commit himself to a definite statement (*e.g.* whether there are any incumbrances other than those specifically mentioned). In addition to dealing with matters disclosed in the

---

[34] The vendor's solicitor will send the purchaser's solicitor a package of documents containing all the necessary information about both the title and the property, other than matters covered by local searches.

[35] This is part of the package provided under the National Protocol.

abstract of title, requisitions cover most or all of the points raised in preliminary inquiries.

5. Replies to requisitions. V then answers the requisitions within the agreed time; if his answers are unsatisfactory on any point, P may make further requisitions.

5–031

6. Draft conveyance. P next prepares a draft conveyance in the form which he thinks it should take. He sends this draft to V for his approval; V makes any emendations he considers necessary, returns it to P, who makes any further amendments, and so on until the conveyance is agreed. P then prepares an engrossment (fair copy) of the conveyance and sends it to V for execution.

5–032

7. Searches. A few days before the day fixed for completion, P makes his searches. Normally this will be limited to searching the Land Charges Register and the Register of Local Land Charges.[36]

5–033

8. Completion. Completion then takes place, usually at the office of V's solicitor. V delivers to P the conveyance duly executed; only if P is entering into some obligation towards V, as by binding himself to observe restrictive covenants, will P have to execute the conveyance as well, though even if he does not do so he will still be bound by the covenants if he takes possession under the deed.[37] In addition to receiving the conveyance, P is entitled to receive the title deeds. This is more than a contractual right, for the owner of land has a right to the title deeds under a general rule.[38] However, V may retain any deed which—

5–034

(i) relates to other land retained by him; or

(ii) creates a trust which is still subsisting; or

(iii) relates to the appointment or discharge of trustees of a subsisting trust.[39]

If V retains any deeds, he must give P an acknowledgement of P's right to production of the deeds and, unless V is a mortgagee or trustee of the land, an

---

[36] See *post,* paras 5–127, 5–132. Where the National Protocol is employed, the vendor will conduct the searches of the Land Charges Register (but not the Register of Local Land Charges).

[37] Litt. 374; Dart, V. & P. 507; and see *post,* para. 16–025.

[38] Co. Litt. 6a ("the purchaser shall have all the charters, deeds and evidences, as incident to the lands . . . for the evidences are, as it were, the sinews of the land".); *Harrington v. Price* (1832) 3 B. & Ad. 170; *Loosemore v. Radford* (1842) 9 M. & W. 657; *cf. Re Knight's Question* [1958] Ch. 381. And see Halsb., vol. 39, para. 388, where special rules as to tenants for life, mortgagees, etc., are stated.

[39] L.P.A. 1925, s.45(9).

undertaking for their safe custody.[40] In return P pays V the purchase-money either in cash or by banker's draft. The exact amount due is settled by the "completion statement" which apportions the outgoings up to the day of completion. It is for the purchaser to have the conveyance duly stamped, which is usually done after completion. Most conveyances will now require registration under the Land Registration Act 1925.[41]

Section 2. The Conveyance

A. Precedent of a Conveyance

5–035   Commencement and date.

THIS CONVEYANCE is made the 1st day of June, 1998,

Parties.

BETWEEN Victor Vendor of No. 1 Smith Street Dorking in the County of Surrey Computer Engineer (hereinafter called "the vendor") of the one part and Percy Purchaser of No. 2 Brown Street Lewes in the County of Sussex Auctioneer (hereinafter called "the purchaser") of the other part

WHEREAS—

Recitals.

(1) The vendor is the estate owner in respect of the fee simple of the property hereby assured for his own use and benefit absolutely free from incumbrances

(2) The vendor has agreed with the purchaser to sell to him the said property free from incumbrances for the price of £100,000

Testatum.
Consideration.
Receipt clause.
Operative words.

NOW THIS DEED WITNESSETH that in consideration of the sum of £100,000 now paid by the purchaser to the vendor (the receipt whereof the vendor acknowledges) the vendor hereby conveys to the purchaser

Parcels.

ALL THAT messuage or dwelling house with the yard gardens offices and outbuildings thereto belonging known as 703 Robinson Street Ashford in the County of Kent which premises are more particularly delineated and coloured pink on the plan annexed hereto

---

[40] As to the effect of such acknowledgements and undertakings see L.P.A. 1925, s.64, and notes thereto in Wolst. & C. The benefit of these covenants runs with the land at common law (*post*, para. 16–011), the burden runs with the deeds by L.P.A. 1925, s.64(2), (9).
[41] L.R.A. 1925, s.123(1) (as substituted by L.R.A. 1997, s.1). See *ante*, paras 5–001, 5–026.

Habendum.

Covenants for
title

TO HOLD the same unto the purchaser in fee simple
THE PROPERTY is conveyed with full title guarantee

Testimonium.

IN WITNESS WHEREOF the parties to these presents have
hereunto set their hands the day and year first written above

Attestation
Clause

Signed as a deed by the
vendor in the presence
of Charles Brown clerk to   VICTOR VENDOR
Argue and Phibbs solicitors

CHARLES BROWN

B. *Details of the Conveyance*

In the very simple form of conveyance set out above, the following matters **5–036**
should be noticed. The titles refer to the side-notes to its various parts.

1. Commencement. The old practice was for the initial words to be "This **5–037**
Indenture". An indenture was a deed made in two counterparts, each having
an indented or irregular edge. The deed was written out twice on a single sheet
of parchment, which was then severed by cutting it with an irregular edge; the
two halves of the parchment thus formed two separate deeds which could be
fitted together to show their genuineness. This contrasted with a "deed poll",
a deed to which there was only one party, which at the top had been polled,
or shaved even.[42] The modern practice is for the commencement to describe
the general nature of the document, *e.g.* "This Conveyance", or "This
Mortgage".[43]

2. Date. Whatever date is in fact inserted in the conveyance, the document **5–038**
when executed[44] takes effect from the date upon which it was delivered by the
parties to it.[45] A deed which has been executed but not delivered is ineffective.[46] Delivery is effected formally by doing some act showing that the deed
is intended to be operative. When a company executes a deed in accordance
with the provisions of the Companies Act 1985,[47] there is in favour of a

---

[42] Norton, *Deeds*, 27.
[43] See L.P.A. 1925, s.57.
[44] The different methods of executing a deed are considered *post*, para. 5–073. Since July 31,
1990 a seal has not been required for a deed executed by an individual or by a company: *post*,
paras 5–074, 5–075.
[45] Norton, *Deeds*, 189; *Bentray Investments Ltd v. Venner Time Switches Ltd* [1985] 1 E.G.L.R.
39 at 43.
[46] Co.Litt. 35b, 171b; Norton, *Deeds*, 10.
[47] s.36A(4), inserted by the Companies Act 1989, s.130(2).

purchaser[48] a statutory presumption of delivery on execution.[49] By contrast, where a corporation aggregate which is not a company executes a deed, there is no such presumption.[50] A deed may be delivered in escrow, *i.e.* delivered on the condition that it is not to become operative until some stated event occurs,[51] in which case it takes effect as soon as the event occurs; it is not revocable in the meantime.[52] Usually a vendor of land will execute the conveyance some days before completion. It had become the practice for him to deliver it to his solicitor in escrow, the condition being the completion of the purchase by the purchaser; and delivery on this condition will be inferred without proof.[53] The deed then took effect when the solicitor delivered it to the purchaser (or his solicitor) on completion; but the grantee's title, as against the grantor but not third parties, appeared to operate from the date of the earlier delivery in escrow.[54] This practice developed because of the old rule that a deed was itself required to authorise an agent to deliver a deed.[55] That rule has now been abrogated,[56] and in a conveyancing transaction, a solicitor or licensed conveyancer is conclusively presumed in favour of a purchaser to have authority to deliver the deed.[57] In the light of this, when a vendor gives his solicitor an executed conveyance in advance of completion, he should no longer be regarded as delivering it in escrow. The most natural interpretation of his conduct is that he is authorising his solicitor to deliver the deed on completion.[58]

---

[48] In other cases, there is merely a rebuttable presumption of delivery: Companies Act 1985, s.36A(5).

[49] Companies Act 1985, s.36A(6), inserted by the Companies Act 1989, s.130(2). It is unclear whether the irrebuttable presumption applies to all deeds executed by a company or whether it only applies to those which are not executed under the common seal pursuant to the Companies Act 1985, s.36A(4). In the only case to consider these provisions, *Johnsey Estates (1990) Ltd v. Newport Marketworld Ltd* (May 10, 1996, unreported), Judge Moseley, Q.C. held that it was the former. *Sed quaere.* The provisions governing execution and the presumptions of delivery are unsatisfactory. The Law Commission has recently made proposals to rationalise them, including the repeal of s.36A(6): see (1998) Law Com. No. 253.

[50] *Longman v. Viscount Chelsea* (1989) 58 P. & C.R. 189 at 199, rejecting the view that L.P.A. 1925, s.74(1) created a presumption of delivery on the execution of a deed by a corporation aggregate.

[51] Norton, *Deeds,* 18 *et seq.*

[52] *Beesly v. Hallwood Estates Ltd* [1961] Ch. 105; *Kingston v. Ambrian Investment Co. Ltd* [1975] 1 W.L.R. 161; *Venetian Glass Gallery Ltd v. Next Properties Ltd* [1989] 2 E.G.L.R. 42.

[53] *Glessing v. Green* [1975] 1 W.L.R. 863; *Bentray Investments Ltd v. Venner Time Switches Ltd* [1985] 1 E.G.L.R. 39. *cf. Longman v. Viscount Chelsea* (1989) 58 P. & C.R. 189 where it was held on such facts that there had been no delivery in escrow because the parties had negotiated "subject to the completion of the lease". *Sed quaere:* see [1991] L.M.C.L.Q. 209 at 219–222 (G. Virgo and C.H.).

[54] Preston, *Abstracts,* iii, 65; *Alan Estates Ltd v. W.G. Stores Ltd* [1982] Ch. 511, a case on a lease in which opinions in the Court of Appeal were divided.

[55] Co.Litt, 52a; *Powell v. London and Provincial Bank* [1893] 2 Ch. 555.

[56] L.P.(M.P.)A. 1989, s.1(1)(c).

[57] *ibid.,* s.1(5).

[58] There are, however, difficulties with this view where a company executes a deed, because of the irrebuttable presumption of delivery on execution in favour of a purchaser contained in the Companies Act 1985, s.36A(6), *supra*: see (1998) Law Com. No. 253, para. 6.12. The Law Commission has recommended the repeal of s.36A(6).

3. Parties. If any other person is an essential party to the transaction, such **5–039** as a mortgagee who is releasing the property from his mortgage, he will be included as a party.

4. Recitals. These are of two types: **5–040**

(a) *Narrative recitals*, which deal with such matters as how the vendor became entitled to the land; and

(b) *Introductory recitals*, which explains how and why the existing state of affairs is to be altered, *e.g.* that the parties have agreed on the sale of the property.

These recitals can create estoppels. For example, the common form of recital of ownership set out above will estop the vendor from denying that he owns the legal estate. If at the time of the conveyance he does not own the legal estate but later acquires it, it will in effect pass to the purchaser under the doctrine of "feeding the estoppel" (explained elsewhere[59]) as against the vendor and persons claiming through him.[60]

5. Testatum. This is the beginning of the operative part of the conveyance. **5–041** Since the Law of Property (Miscellaneous Provisions) Act 1989 came into force on July 31, 1990, the testatum has acquired added importance. An instrument will not now be a deed unless it is clear on its face that it is intended to be so by the person making or the parties to it.[61] Two obvious methods are for the instrument to describe itself as a deed or to be signed as a deed.[62] The words of the testatum, "Now this deed witnesseth . . . " meet this requirement.

6. Consideration. The consideration is stated to show (*inter alia*) that the **5–042** transaction is not a voluntary one.[63]

7. Receipt clause. This is inserted to save a separate receipt being given. **5–043** A solicitor who produces a conveyance containing such a clause which has been executed by the vendor thereby shows the purchaser that he has authority from the vendor to receive the purchase-money.[64]

8. Operative words. These effect the actual conveyance of the property. **5–044** Formerly they included an "all estate clause" declaring that the conveyance passed the whole estate, title and interest which the vendor had in the land or had power to convey. But statute has rendered that superfluous by providing

---

[59] *Post*, para. 14–098.
[60] *Cumberland Court (Brighton) Ltd v. Taylor* [1964] Ch. 29.
[61] L.P.(M.P.)A. 1989, s.1(2)(a).
[62] *ibid.* Other methods may of course be used.
[63] See *post*, paras 5–081, 10–011.
[64] L.P.A. 1925, s.69.

that every conveyance shall have this effect unless a contrary intention is expressed in it.[65] If the vendor purports to convey as legal owner but proves only to have an equitable interest, that interest will accordingly pass to the purchaser.[66]

5–045   **9. Parcels.** This is the description of the property. Description by reference to an annexed plan is a common alternative, but is not essential if an accurate verbal description can be given.[67] Very often a conveyance both describes the property verbally and also includes a plan. In that case it is advisable to provide that one or other shall prevail in case of inconsistency. For example, if the plan is expressed to be included "for the purposes of facilitating identification only" the verbal description will prevail.[68] However, if the property is said to be "more particularly described in the plan", then the plan will prevail.[69] If the verbal description is insufficient, as by failing to indicate a boundary, the court may have recourse to the plan, even though it is "by way of identification only".[70] In such a case, the court adopts an objective test. Taking into account the surrounding circumstances, the language of the conveyance and the representation of the plan, what would the reasonable lay person think that they were buying?[71]

A common defect of conveyances is that boundaries are inadequately defined.[72] In that case extrinsic evidence is admissible to establish the true intent of the parties, which may be clear from other documents, such as auction particulars.[73] But if the location of boundaries is clear from the conveyance, neither extrinsic evidence nor any presumptions can be used to contradict it, save only in proceedings for rectification.[74] These are general

---

[65] L.P.A. 1925, s.63.

[66] *Thellusson v. Liddard* [1900] 2 Ch. 635. A legal charge by husband and wife as co-onwers which is ineffective at law because her signature is forged nevertheless creates an equitable charge on his beneficial interest (*First National Securities Ltd v. Hegarty* [1985] Q.B. 850 at 854; *Ahmed v. Kendrick* (1987) 56 P. & C.R. 120).

[67] *Re Sharman's Contract* [1936] Ch. 755.

[68] See *Hopgood v. Brown* [1955] 1 W.L.R. 213.

[69] *Eastwood v. Ashton* [1915] A.C. 900; for other examples, see Lord Sumner's speech at 914 and *Norton on Deeds*; 237, 238, 243; and see *Wallington v. Townsend* [1939] 2 All E.R. 225. See, however, *Truckell v. Stock* [1957] 1 W.L.R. 161, and contrast *Grigsby v. Melville* [1974] 1 W.L.R. 80. If both phrases are used, they are "mutually stultifying": *Neilson v. Poole* (1968) 20 P. & C.R. 909 at 916, *per* Megarry J. See *Alan Wibberley Buildings Ltd v. Insley* [1999] 1 W.L.R. 894 at 899.

[70] *Wigginton & Milner Ltd v. Winster Engineering Ltd* [1978] 1 W.L.R. 1462; and see *Hatfield v. Moss* [1988] 2 E.G.L.R. 58; *Targett v. Ferguson* (1996) 72 P. & C.R. 106; *Affleck v. Shorefield Holidays Ltd* [1997] E.G.C.S. 159.

[71] *Toplis v. Green* (unreported, CA; February 14, 1992); *Targett v. Ferguson, supra* at 114.

[72] It is particularly undesirable to use small-scale plans taken from Ordnance Survey maps: *Mayer v. Hurr* (1983) 49 P. & C.R. 56; *Clarke v. O'Keefe* (1997) 75 P. & C.R. D18.

[73] *Scarfe v. Adams* [1981] 1 All E.R. 843. See too *Spall v. Owen* (1981) 44 P. & C.R. 36; *Mayer v. Hurr, supra*; and *Re St. Clement's Leigh-on-Sea* [1988] 1 W.L.R. 720.

[74] *Scarfe v. Adams, supra*, at 851; *Clarke v. O'Keefe, supra*; *cf. Alan Wibberley Buildings Ltd v. Insley* [1999] 1 W.L.R. 894, where the so-called "hedge and ditch" presumption overrode the the wording of a conveyance which defined the boundary by reference to an Ordnance Survey map, but where the two properties separated by that boundary had never been in common ownership.

rules which apply to other obscurities in the definition of the land or of the interest granted.[75]

The conveyance will pass all fixtures without mention, for they are part of the land and pass with it.[76] But it will not pass removable chattels such as movable greenhouses.[77] The purchaser is entitled on completion to all fixtures attached to the land at the date of the contract.[78]

10. Habendum. This shows that the purchaser is to hold the land for his own benefit and not upon trust for a third party. It also contains the usual words of limitation.[79] It is followed by the acknowledgement and undertaking where these are to be included.[80]   **5–046**

11. Covenants for title. The words "with full title guarantee" are important and their effect must be explained in detail. They imply covenants for title, which are the nearest thing to a guarantee that the purchaser receives from the vendor.[81] They have their origins in the old system of warranties[82] which was replaced by the practice of giving express covenants for title.[83] The remedy for their breach is damages. The law was reformed by the Law of Property (Miscellaneous Provisions) Act 1994,[84] and it is necessary to examine conveyances executed both before July 1, 1995 when the Act was brought into force, and those made thereafter, to which the new rules apply.[85] There are likely to be cases for a number of years to come where the old form of covenants are in issue. In conveyances prior to July 1, 1995, the covenants for title were implied by the words "as Beneficial Owner" which were invariably included in the operative words of the conveyance.[86–87]   **5–047**

---

[75] *Scarfe v. Adams, supra*; *Spall v. Owen, supra*.

[76] Although L.P.A. 1925, s.62, expressly includes "building, erections, fixtures", fixtures would pass as part of the land even if s.62 were expressly excluded.

[77] *H. E. Dibble Ltd v. Moore* [1970] 2 Q.B. 181; *Deen v. Andrews* (1985) 52 P. & C.R. 17; *post*, para. 14–325.

[78] For discussion of fixtures, see *post*, para. 14–311.

[79] *Ante*, para. 3–023.

[80] *Ante*, para. 5–034.

[81] A vendor is of course under an obligation to deduce a title in accordance with the terms of the contract of sale. This obligation, like most others under the contract, is merged in the deed of conveyance and no action lies for its breach thereafter: see generally *Knight Sugar Co. Ltd v. The Alberta Railway & Irrigation Co.* [1938] 1 All E.R. 266 at 269. For the doctrine of merger, see *post*, para. 12–099.

[82] See the previous edition of this work at p. 159.

[83] The invention of the modern form of covenants is attributed to Sir O. Bridgeman (1606–1674): see Platt, *Covenants*, 304.

[84] Implementing in amended form the recommendations of the Law Commission: see (1991) Law Com. No. 199.

[85] The covenants will be implied into a conveyance of unregistered land even though the disposition is one which must now be completed by registration. For the implication of the covenants for title on a transfer of registered land, see *post*, para. 6–102.

[86–87] Typically the operative words were: "the vendor As Beneficial Owner hereby conveys to the purchaser".

(a) Conveyances prior to July 1995

5–048   (1) WHEN THE COVENANTS WOULD BE IMPLIED. In conveyances made prior to July 1995, the covenants for title were implied by the Law of Property Act 1925, s.76 and Sched. 2. They were implied if the following conditions were satisfied:

> (i) the conveyance was for valuable consideration; and

> (ii) the vendor conveyed and was expressed to convey as beneficial owner. The conveyance must therefore have stated in terms that he conveyed "as beneficial owner". It was held that the inept statutory formula[88] required in addition that the vendor should in fact have been a beneficial owner.[89] This would deprive the purchaser of the protection of the covenants in exactly the case where he ought to have it, namely, where the vendor's title was not as represented, *e.g.* where the vendor was not a beneficial owner but a trustee.

The covenants would be implied into the conveyance only "as far as regards the subject-matter . . . expressed to be conveyed".[90] If the vendor's title subsequently proved to be defective, he would incur no liability on the covenants for title he had conveyed the land—

> (i) only with such title as he had,[91] or

> (ii) if the land were freehold, without words of limitation.[92]

5–049   (2) THE COVENANTS. The implied covenants were set out in the lengthy and long-settled but "extremely difficult"[93] form of words that were formerly inserted in full by conveyancers. They may be summarised as follows.

---

[88] Contrast L.P.A. 1925, s.77, which used instead the formula "conveys *or* is expressed to convey" rather than the words "conveys *and* is expressed to convey" employed in s.76. The drafting seems to have been quite indiscriminate.

[89] *Fay v. Miller, Wilkins & Co.* [1941] Ch. 360. See too *Pilkington v. Wood* [1953] Ch. 770 at 777; and *Re Robinson's Application* [1969] 1 W.L.R. 109 at 112. This interpretation conflicted with the policy of the Act, with conveyancing practice, and with previous decisions which implied that the nature of the vendor's actual interest was irrelevant, as it ought to be: *David v. Sabin* [1893] 1 Ch. 523; *Re Ray* [1896] 1 Ch. 468; *Parker v. Judkin* [1931] 1 Ch. 475. See M. P. Thompson, *Barnsley's Conveyancing Law and Practice* (4th ed.), p. 665; (1968) 32 Conv.(N.S.) 123 (M. J. Russell). It was also illogical: if the vendor did not own the land at all, the covenants would nonetheless have been implied if he had conveyed as beneficial owner: *Conodate Investments Ltd v. Bentley Quarry Engineering Co. Ltd* (1970) 216 E.G. 1407; *Jackson v. Bishop* (1979) 48 P. & C.R. 57; *A. J. Dunning & Sons (Shopfitters) Ltd v. Sykes & Son (Poole) Ltd* [1987] Ch. 287. A nominee could quite properly convey "as beneficial owner" if authorised to make the disposition: *Harwood v. Harwood* [1991] 2 F.L.R. 274 at 286.

[90] L.P.A. 1925, s.76(1).

[91] *May v. Platt* [1900] 1 Ch. 616 at 619.

[92] Such a conveyance would pass "the fee simple or other the whole interest which the grantor had power to convey": L.P.A. 1925, s.60(1). See *ante*, para. 3–030; and (1991) Law Com. No. 199, paras 2.18, 2.19.

[93] *Pilkington v. Wood* [1953] Ch. 770 at 777, *per* Harman J.

(i) Full power to convey: the vendor had a good right to convey the whole property and interest agreed to be sold.

(ii) Quiet enjoyment: the purchaser should have quiet enjoyment of the land.[94]

(iii) Freedom from incumbrances: the land should be enjoyed free from any incumbrances other than those subject to which the conveyance was expressly made. This covenant applied even to incumbrances known to the purchaser, unless the conveyance was expressed to be subject to them.[95]

(iv) Further assurance: the vendor would execute such assurances and do such things as were necessary to cure any defect in the conveyance.[96]

(3) LEASEHOLDS. In the case of a sale of leaseholds, the following additional covenants were implied on such a conveyance.[97] **5–050**

(v) That the lease was valid and in full force.

(vi) That the rent had been paid and the covenants in the lease duly performed.

It should be noted that this set of covenants applied only when an existing lease was assigned, and not on its grant. The covenants arose between vendor and purchaser and not between landlord and tenant.[98]

(4) LIMITED COVENANTS. Where a person conveyed and was expressly to convey "as settlor" the only covenant implied was one for further assurance, binding that person and those claiming under him.[99] This applied whether the settlement was voluntary or for value. On the other hand, where a person conveyed (whether or not for value) "as trustee", "as mortgagee", "as personal representative",[1] or "under an order of the court" the only covenant implied was that the grantor had not himself incumbered the land.[2] Where the vendor sold in any such capacity the purchaser was entitled only to covenants limited accordingly. Where, in any case, the vendor's liability for the state of **5–051**

---

[94] *cf. post*, para. 14–196.
[95] *Page v. Midland Ry.* [1894] 1 Ch. 11; *Great Western Ry v. Fisher* [1905] 1 Ch. 316. Contrast the rule for contracts, *post*, para. 12–080.
[96] See [1985] Conv. 398 (M. J. Russell).
[97] L.P.A. 1925, s.76(1)(B) and Sched. 2, Pt II. The implication only occurred if the conveyance was for "valuable consideration". This requirement was fulfilled in most cases where a lease was assigned, because the assignee normally assumed primary responsibility for the performance of the covenants in the lease: L.P.A. 1925, s.77(1)(C); *Johnsey Estates Ltd v. Lewis and Manley (Engineering) Ltd* (1987) 54 P. & C.R. 296.
[98] For the covenants implied on the *grant* of a lease, see *post*, para. 14–195. In relation to leases granted after June 1995, there may be implied covenants for title: see *post*, para. 14–205.
[99] s.76(1)(E) and Sched. 2, Pt V.
[1] The covenant might be implied in an assent as well as in a deed: L.P.A. 1925, s.76(1).
[2] s.76(1)(F) and Sched. 2, Pt VI, as amended by the Mental Health Act 1959, Sched. 8, Pt 1.

the title was limited by the contract, the vendor might insert corresponding limitations in the conveyance.[3] If the purchaser had agreed to buy subject to rights such as a mortgage or a right of way, the effect of conveying expressly subject to them was the automatic exclusion of liability for them.

5–052   (5) ENFORCEABILITY OF THE COVENANTS. The rules for enforcing covenants of title are as follows.

5–053   (I) *Benefit.* The benefit of the covenants runs with the land, so that each person in whom the land is for the time being vested is entitled to enforce them.[4] Thus, if V entered into the covenants with P and later P sold the land to Q, Q is entitled to enforce the covenants against V, even though Q was not a party to the conveyance from V to P which created the obligations.

5–054   (II) *Burden.* As regards the burden of the covenants, the person liable is the individual who gave them. The obligation is a purely personal one which does not run with the land. The vendor who conveyed "as beneficial owner" personally guaranteed the title. However, as will be seen from the full form of the covenants, his liability is limited to the consequences of the conduct of certain persons. This is a very important restriction on the scope of the covenants. They are not a warranty of title, but qualified covenants only. The general rule is that they extend only to the lawful acts and omissions of—

(i) the covenantor himself, and

(ii) anyone claiming through, under, or in trust for him, and

(iii) anyone through whom he claims otherwise than by purchase for money or money's worth, and

(iv) anyone claiming through or under those in class (iii).[5]

Thus if prior to July 1995, V had conveyed land to P for value "as beneficial owner" and P subsequently discovers undisclosed incumbrances, he can sue V on the covenants for title if those incumbrances were created by V, or by V's tenant, mortgagee, or trustee (all examples of class (ii)); or by a person who left the hand to V by will, or gave it to him by deed of gift or marriage settlement (class (iii)). Class (iv) extends class (iii) in the same way as class (ii) extends class (i).

5–055   (III) *Example.* A simple example will show how these qualified covenants operate. Suppose that V had allowed his neighbour X to acquire a right of way over V's land by prescription. V then sold and conveyed the land to P "as beneficial owner". P in turn sold the land in the same way to Q.[6] Finally X

---

[3] Williams, V. & P. 662–665.
[4] L.P.A. 1925, s.76(6). As to the position of mortgagees, see (1964) 28 Conv.(N.S.) 205 (A. M. Prichard).
[5] See, *e.g. David v. Sabin* [1893] 1 Ch. 523 at 532, 542.
[6] It is to be assumed that both conveyances occurred prior to July 1995.

asserted his rights against Q. For this defect in title and disturbance of quiet enjoyment Q may sue V, for Q obtains the benefit of V's covenants with P, which run with the land. Q cannot sue P, because P is not responsible for incumbrances created by V, who sold to him for value. But if the land had passed from V to P under V's will, Q could then sue P, for P's covenants would extend to V's acts. Q could not sue V, because V would have given no covenant at all.

(IV) *Mortgages.* Where a person created a mortgage "as beneficial owner", **5–056** the covenants for title implied were absolute.[7] The mortgagor therefore made himself responsible for the acts of everyone, and gave a complete warranty that his title was good. This is because it had long been the practice for mortgagees to insist on these unqualified covenants, and this situation was recognised by statute. As stated under (4) above, the liability on the covenants implied by using phrases other than "as beneficial owner" is limited to the grantor's own acts.[8]

(V) *Gifts.* Even where the phrase "as beneficial owner" was used, it implied **5–057** covenants only where the conveyance was made for valuable consideration, *e.g.* by way of sale or marriage settlement.[9] In a deed of gift therefore, it had no effect. The phrase "as settlor", if used, would have given the limited covenant already mentioned in (4) above. If more extensive covenants were required, they had to be set out expressly.

(6) LIMITATION. The covenants are subject to the usual period of limitation **5–058** (12 years).[10] The covenant for full power to convey was broken, if at all, at the movement when the conveyance was made,[11] so that the right to sue on it expires 12 years after that conveyance.[12] The same rule was held to apply to the covenant for freedom from incumbrances.[13] However, it seems more probable that this is merely part of the covenant for quiet enjoyment,[14] and operates not as a separate warranty that the land was free from encumbrances when conveyed, but as a covenant that the purchaser should not be disturbed by incumbrancers.[15] The covenant for quiet enjoyment is not broken until the purchaser is actually dispossessed by someone with a valid prior right, *e.g.* the owner of an easement, so that this covenant can be sued on at any time within

---

[7] s.76(1)(D) and Sched. 2, Pt IV. See (1964) 28 Conv.(N.S.) 205 (A. M. Prichard).

[8] *Ante*, para. 5–051.

[9] s.76(1)(A). For a case where executors conveyed "as beneficial owners", see *Parker v. Judkin* [1931] 1 Ch. 475.

[10] Limitation Act 1980, s.8; *post*, para. 21–006.

[11] *Spoor v. Green* (1874) L.R. 9 Ex. 99 at 110, adopted in *Turner v. Moon* [1901] 2 Ch. 825; and see *Pilkington v. Wood* [1953] Ch. 770 at 777.

[12] See *post*, para. 21–006.

[13] *Turner v. Moon, supra.*

[14] *Nottidge v. Dering* [1909] 2 Ch. 647, affd. [1910] 1 Ch. 297; and see *Vane v. Lord Barnard* (1708) Gilb. Eq. 6 at 8; Williams, V. & P. 1080, 1081; Platt, *Covenants*, 331.

[15] A further argument for this construction is that the general purpose of the covenant is to give an indemnity.

12 years of the disturbance.[16] Although the covenant covers much of the same ground as the other two, it is of particular value for this reason. Similarly the covenant for further assurance is not broken until execution of some necessary document is demanded and refused.[17]

(7) EFFECT OF THE SYSTEM OF VENDOR'S COVENANTS

5–059   (I) *Chain of covenants*. Since the benefit of the covenants runs with the land, but the burden is purely personal, the purchaser normally obtains the benefit of a chain of covenants given by all previous vendors of the land. Each vendor's covenants extend back to the acts of the last previous purchaser, so that the chain is continuous even if between purchases the land passes by will or intestacy, or by deed of gift. "The covenant by a vendor in fee is not understood as extending to acts done previously to the last preceding sale. On each sale the title is investigated, and conveyancers are content with a series of covenants for title each of which covers the time which has elapsed since the last conveyance from a vendor in fee."[18] Therefore, although no one vendor gave a full warranty of title, the various covenants added together amount to a comprehensive guarantee to the purchaser, provided that he sues the proper defendant in each case. However, this rests on the assumption that the full covenants were given on each sale. The chain may have been broken if a vendor sold as trustee or executor,[19] or if a previous vendor sold with limited covenants. Furthermore, the right to sue a previous vendor who is dead may be valueless if his estate has been fully distributed.

5–060   (II) *Acts and omissions*. The covenants extend both to acts and omissions. Thus they cover adverse claims caused not only by the grant of rights (*e.g.* easements) or bankruptcy,[20] but also by the failure to contest a squatter's rights while the period of limitation is running.[21] But only rightful acts are covered: if the purchaser is disturbed by a trespasser or a claimant with no title he has his own remedies and needs no recourse against his vendor.

5–061   (III) *Power to convey*. The first covenant (full power to convey) is qualified even more strictly than the others, despite its somewhat ambiguous language.[22] It makes the vendor liable only in respect of the acts or omissions of himself and persons through whom he claims otherwise than by purchase for money or money's worth. It does not therefore extend to eviction by title paramount. If the vendor was merely a squatter and the purchaser is evicted by the true owner, or if the vendor purported to sell land to which neither he

---

[16] See *Spoor v. Green, supra,* at 111; *Conodate Investments Ltd v. Bentley Quarry Engineering Co. Ltd* (1970) 216 E.G. 1407.

[17] *King v. Jones* (1815) 4 M. & S. 188.

[18] *David v. Sabin* [1893] 1 Ch. 523 at 534, *per* Lindley L.J.

[19] *Ante,* para. 5–051.

[20] *Jenkins v. Jones* (1882) 9 Q.B.D. 128.

[21] *Eastwood v. Ashton* [1915] A.C. 900.

[22] See L.P.A. 1925, Sched. 2, Pt I, "Notwithstanding" (the second word of the covenant) is used in the sense of "to the extent of"; but see (1961) 105 S.J. 743.

nor his predecessors (other than previous vendors) had ever had title at all, then the purchaser has no remedy under the ordinary covenants.

For example, if, owing to a mistake about his boundary, the vendor of a farm had sold and purported to convey a field which was in fact his neighbour's property, the purchaser had no remedy if he failed to detect the flaw in the title before completion.[23] On the other hand the vendor will be liable if the defect in title is one which he had power to remove, for then it subsists because of his omission to remove it. Thus where a tenant in tail purported to dispose of the fee simple, and the purchaser was evicted by the remainderman, the tenant in tail was held liable because he could have barred the entail and so perfected his title.[24] Similarly, as already mentioned, the covenant covers loss of title under the Limitation Acts, for that is caused by omission to eject the squatter while there is yet time. And it covers ejection by anyone claiming through a person who left the land by will to the vendor, as where after the fee simple had been sold and (as it was thought) conveyed, it was discovered that the will gave the vendor only a life interest: for then the remainderman's claim was caused by the act (*i.e.* the will) of a person in class (iii) for whom the vendor was answerable under the covenant.[25] But the burden of proof is on the purchaser, so that if the origin of the adverse claimant's title is uncertain, the vendor is not liable.[26]

(IV) *Predecessors and successors in title.* The meaning of "through" in the phrases "claiming through" and "through whom he claims"[27] is apparently not the same throughout all the covenants. In class (iii) it extends to the vendor's predecessors in title in fee simple if he acquired the land from them without giving money or money's worth for it, whereas in classes (ii) and (iv) the corresponding expression does not extend to successors in title to the fee simple, or whatever else the vendor's whole interest may be. This is best explained by examples.[28] If A granted an easement to X and then devised the fee simple to V, and then V sold and conveyed the land to P with the usual covenants for title, V is liable to P for the easement because V claims through A and is responsible for his act, *viz.*, the granting of the easement. Here

5–062

---

[23] See *Browning v. Wright* (1799) 2 B. & P. 13, and the remarks of Lord Eldon C.J. at 22, 23. Where a tenant for life purported to sell the fee, the purchaser would have no remedy on the covenants unless the vendor (or his ancestor, etc.) himself once had the fee and then disposed of it. In other cases the purchaser bears the risk of the title.

[24] *Cavan v. Pulteney* (1795) 2 Ves. Jun. 544 (a case of landlord and tenant, with an express covenant); *cf. Howes v. Bushfield* (1803) 3 East 491, discussed in Sugden V. & P. 602, 603, where the question is raised whether this principle extends to a mortgage created by an earlier vendor which the latter vendor might have paid off even though he was not responsible for its creation; and see *Stock v. Meakin* [1900] 1 Ch. 683, where a statutory charge for sewers (which the vendor had no power to prevent) was held within the covenant, apparently because the vendor "omitted" to pay it off (see argument at 688, 689). See also *Chivers & Sons Ltd v. Air Ministry* [1955] Ch. 585.

[25] *Page v. Midland Ry* [1894] 1 Ch. 11.

[26] *Howard v. Maitland* (1883) 11 Q.B.D. 695; *Stoney v. Eastbourne R.D.C.* [1927] 1 Ch. 367.

[27] As regards predecessors in title the precise words are "through whom he derives title"; as regards successors they are "claiming through, under or in trust for".

[28] In each case, it should be assumed that the conveyance in which the covenants were implied was made before July 1995.

"claiming through" is used in its widest sense, including all successors in title. But on the other hand if V had sold first to L, then L granted a lease to T, then L resold the fee simple to V and concealed the lease, and V then sold and conveyed to P, V's covenant with P does not make V liable for the lease, even though L derived title through V in the first place.[29] Here, therefore, "claiming through" means claiming a derivative interest (*e.g.* under a lease) and not merely being a successor in title to the fee simple.

5–063   A contrasting case, on the other hand, in which V was held liable, was where V, being fee simple owner, first granted a *lease* to T, then T sub-leased to S, T then surrendered his lease back to V for payment and concealed the sub-lease, and V then sold and conveyed to P.[30] Here T claimed through V in the sense of having a derivative interest carved out of V's fee simple, and the fact that V also claimed through T for value (by the surrender) did not prevent him being liable in his original capacity as a person through whom T claimed, who was therefore answerable for T's sub-lease under the ordinary covenants against incumbrances. In this case it was also held that V was liable under the covenant for full power to convey, because of his own act in granting the lease to T; for "it is a mere conveyancing illusion to suppose that the defendant ever by the so-called surrender . . . got back the term which he had granted so as to extinguish it. He only recovered it mangled by the sub-leases and shorn of all right to possession".[31]

5–064   (8) PURCHASER'S COVENANTS. Where the land sold was leasehold, or was subject to a rentcharge (except as mentioned under (9) below), a conveyance for value implied covenants by the purchaser that he and his successors in title would perform all covenants connected with the lease or rentcharge and would indemnify the vendor against liability.[32] No special words had to be used to imply these covenants. They were designed as a safeguard to vendors who might remain personally liable by privity of contract even after they had parted with the land affected.[33]

5–065   (9) FAMILY CHARGES. Where land was subject to a rentcharge of the "family" type created after July 22, 1977[34] and was sold subject to the rentcharge in the manner explained later,[35] the conveyance implied a covenant that the vendor would pay the rentcharge and indemnify the purchaser and his successors against liability.[36] Any agreement to the contrary was void.[37] This

---

[29] Based on an example given by Romer J. in *David v. Sabin* [1893] 1 Ch. 523 at 530 and approved by A. L. Smith L.J. at 544; *cf. Steping v. Gladding* (1671) 1 Free K.B. 18 at 20; *Butler v. Swinerton* (1623) Palm. 339; Cru. Dig. iv, 386.

[30] *David v. Sabin* [1893] 1 Ch. 523 (the leading case on covenants for title).

[31] *ibid.*, at 538, *per* Bowen L.J.

[32] L.P.A. 1925, s.77 and Sched. 2, Pts VII–X.

[33] See *post*, para. 15–008. The lease to which the old covenants for title apply are unaffected in this regard by L. & T.C.A. 1995, *post*, para. 15–064.

[34] See *post*, para. 18–019.

[35] *Post*, para. 18–093.

[36] Rentcharges Act 1977, s.11.

[37] *ibid.*

implied covenant is unaffected by the Law of Property (Miscellaneous Provisions) Act 1994, and continues to apply.

(b) Conveyances after June 1995

(1) THE REASONS FOR REFORM. The Law of Property (Miscellaneous Provisions) Act 1994[38] was enacted to remedy a number of defects in the previous law.[39] These included—   **5–066**

(i) the qualified nature of the covenants: the vendor was only responsible for the acts and omissions of specified persons, and the onus lay on the purchaser to show that the act or omission complained of was one for which the vendor was responsible[40];

(ii) the obscure language of the covenants, which gave rise to a number of difficulties[41];

(iii) the direct relevance of the grantor's capacity to the covenants that were implied: if he covenanted in the wrong capacity some authority suggested that no covenants would be implied[42]; and

(iv) the lack of comprehensive cover afforded by the covenants: if a defect in title was imposed at common law or by statute rather than by the act of any person, there was no liability on the covenants.[43]

(2) WHEN THE COVENANTS WILL BE IMPLIED. Under the 1994 Act, covenants for title may be implied into any instrument made after June 1995, effecting or purporting to effect a disposition of property, whether or not for valuable consideration.[44] For these purposes, "disposition" expressly includes the grant of a lease,[45] but it will also include, *e.g.* the grant of an easement. The new covenants (unlike the old) may therefore apply where a landlord grants a lease.[46] They may also apply to dispositions of property other than land, including assignments of choses in action.[47] Covenants for title will be implied only if the disposition is expressed to be made with either full or   **5–067**

---

[38] This implemented (with some changes) the recommendations in (1991) Law Com. No. 199.
[39] See *ibid.*, paras 3.13–3.35.
[40] For the difficulties to which this could give rise see, *e.g. Stoney v. Eastbourne R.D.C.* [1927] 1 Ch. 367; *ante*, para. 5–061.
[41] See *ante*, para. 5–049.
[42] See *ante*, para. 5–048.
[43] See (1991) Law Com. No. 199, para. 2.5; *Chivers & Sons Ltd v. Air Ministry* [1955] Ch. 585 (covenantor not liable for obligation to pay for repair of church chancel which was imposed by a combination of common law and statute).
[44] L.P.(M.P.)A. 1994, s.1(2).
[45] *ibid.* s.1(4).
[46] See *post*, para. 14–205.
[47] L.P.(M.P.)A. 1994, s.1(4).

limited title guarantee.[48] These are a matter for negotiation between the parties to the disposition. They are not a consequence of the capacity of the person making the disposition. A feature of the new covenants is that they are all expressed in plain and straightforward language.

5–068   (3) THE COVENANTS: FULL TITLE GUARANTEE. Where a disposition is made with full title guarantee, the person making the disposition[49] impliedly covenants[50] that—

    (i) he has the right[51] to dispose of the property as he purports to[52];

    (ii) he will at his own cost do all that he reasonably can to give the disponee the title he purports to give[53];

    (iii) the property is free from all charges, incumbrances and third party rights other than those of which the disponer neither knew nor could reasonably be expected to know[54]; and

    (iv) where the disposition is of a leasehold, the lease is subsisting at the time of the disposition and that there are no subsisting breaches of the tenant's obligations that would render the lease liable to forfeiture.[55]

As regards (i), (iii) and (iv), the disponer is not liable for any matter to which the disposition is expressly made subject,[56] or for anything actually known by the disponee or which was a necessary consequence of facts of which he actually knew.[57] Where the disposition is of an existing legal estate in

---

[48] *ibid.*, s.1(2). For the Welsh equivalents, see s.8(4). For the transitional provisions, see *ibid.*, ss.11, 12.

[49] Where a disposition is expressed to be made at the direction of a person (as where a nominee conveys at the direction of the beneficial owner, or a vendor conveys to a third party at the direction of the purchaser), the implied covenants apply to him as if he were the person making the disposition: *ibid.*, s.8(3).

[50] *ibid.*, s.1(2)(a).

[51] With the concurrence of any other person conveying the property.

[52] L.P.(M.P.)A. 1994, s.2(1).

[53] *ibid.*, Where, as will now usually be the case, a disposition of unregistered land is required to be registered (see *ante*, para. 5–001), this obligation requires the disponer to give all reasonable assistance to establish to the satisfaction of the Chief Land Registrar the right of the disponee to be registered as proprietor of the land: *ibid.*, s.2(2)(b).

[54] *ibid.*, s.3(1). There is no liability under this covenant in respect of liabilities and third party rights imposed by statute which are merely potential (such as a power for a body compulsorily to acquire property), or which are imposed in relation to property generally (such as a liability to pay council tax): *ibid.*, s.3(2).

[55] *ibid.*, s.4(1).

[56] *ibid.*, s.6(1).

[57] *ibid.*, s.6(2). *cf. Yandle & Sons v. Sutton* [1922] 2 Ch. 199 at 210; *post*, para. 12–068 (from which this provision is derived). In determining the disponee's actual knowledge, L.P.A. 1925, s.198 (deemed notice by virtue of registration as a land charge: *post*, para. 5–109) is disregarded: L.P.(M.P.)A. 1994, s.6(3).

unregistered land, then subject to the terms of the instrument, it is presumed that if the property is a leasehold the disponer purports to dispose of the unexpired portion of the lease. In any other case, the presumption is that the property disposed of is the fee simple.[58]

Where the disposition is a mortgage either of property subject to rentcharge, **5–069** or of a lease, the mortgagor impliedly covenants, in addition to the covenants set out above, that he will fully and promptly observe and perform all the obligations—

(v) imposed by the rentcharge that are enforceable by the owner of it as such; or (as the case may be)

(vi) under the lease that are imposed on him in his capacity as tenant.[59]

The operation of any of the implied covenants may be either limited or extended by a term of the instrument making the disposition,[60] and in practice often is.

(4) THE COVENANTS: LIMITED TITLE GUARANTEE. Where a disposition is **5–070** made with limited title guarantee, the position is the same as where full title guarantee is given, subject to one important exception. To the extent that they are applicable, the disponee impliedly enters into covenants (i), (ii) and (iv)–(vi) set out in the two preceding paragraphs, but not (iii).[61] He covenants instead that he has not, since the last disposition for value, either charged or incumbered the property by means of any charge or incumbrance which subsists at the time when the disposition is made, or allowed the property to become charged or incumbered in that way,[62] and that he is not aware that anyone else has done so.[63]

It will be noted that the new covenants do not include a covenant for quiet enjoyment, as did the old covenants. The Law Commission considered that such a covenant was inappropriate, because it related not to the title to the property but to the enjoyment of the land granted.[64] If a vendor retained land adjoining the part which he had sold, the objective of the covenant for quiet enjoyment could be better achieved by the use of restrictive covenants. In practice, covenants for quiet enjoyment are rarely enforced except by tenants

---

[58] *ibid.*, s.2(3)(b). These presumptions are intended to avoid the difficulties that could arise under the old covenants: see *ante*, para. 5–048; and (1991) Law Com. No. 199, paras 2.18, 2.19, 4.20.

[59] L.P.(M.P.)A. 1994, s.5.

[60] *ibid.*, s.8(1).

[61] *ibid.*, s.1(2)(b).

[62] *e.g.* by allowing a third party to acquire title to part of the land by adverse possession.

[63] L.P.(M.P.)A. 1994, s.3(3).

[64] (1991) Law Com. No. 199, para. 4.33.

against their landlords.[65] A covenant for quiet enjoyment is (and continues to be) implied at common law on the grant of a lease.[66]

5–071   (5) ENFORCEABILITY OF THE COVENANTS. The benefit of the new covenants runs with the disponee's estate or interest in the land.[67] They may therefore be enforced by any person in whom that estate or interest (in whole or in part) is for the time being vested.[68] As regards the burden of the covenant, the disponer's liability is absolute. It is not limited (as it is under the old covenants) to the conduct or certain persons for whom he is held responsible.[69] The disponer's liability is therefore more extensive than under the old covenants, and this was undoubtedly the objective of the legislation.

Of the six covenants, set out above, for which a disponer may be liable,[70] (i),[71] (iii)[72] and (iv)[73] will necessarily be broken (if at all) at the time of the disposition and the right to sue on them will expire 12 years thereafter. That is not the case in relation to the other covenants. For example, breach of covenant (ii)[74] would not occur until the disponer had refused to take the necessary steps to give the disponee the title which he had purported to give. The limitation period would run from that date.

5–072   12. Testimonium, and

5–073   13. Attestation clause. At common law, a deed had to be sealed.[75] The method of attestation that must now be employed depends upon the legal status of the party who is making the deed. Since July 31, 1990 the law has been as follows.[76]

5–074   *(a) Individuals.* A seal is no longer required for the valid execution of a deed by an individual.[77] To be a deed, an instrument must be signed either by the maker in the presence of an attesting witness, or at the maker's direction in his presence and in the presence of two attesting witnesses.[78]

---

[65] *ibid.*, para 4.35.
[66] *Post*, para. 14–196.
[67] L.P.(M.P.)A. 1994, s.7 (a provision added in the course of the passage of the legislation through Parliament under an amendment proposed by Lord Brightman). *cf.* (1991) Law Com. No. 199, para. 4.9.
[68] L.P. (M.P.)A. 1994, s.7.
[69] *Ante*, paras 5–054, 5–062, 5–063.
[70] *Ante*, paras 5–068, 5–069.
[71] Power to dispose.
[72] Freedom from incumbrances.
[73] Lease subsisting and not liable to forfeiture.
[74] Further assurance.
[75] *Goddard's Case* (1584) 2 Co. Rep. 4b at 5a. The two other essentials of a deed were that it should be written on paper or parchment and delivered. The requirement of paper or parchment has been abrogated by L.P.(M.P.)A. 1989, s.1(1)(a). There is now no restriction on the substance upon which a deed may be written.
[76] For the previous law, see the 5th edition of this work at p. 167.
[77] L.P.(M.P.)A. 1989, s.1(1)(b).
[78] *ibid.*, s.1(3). For these purposes, the signing of a document "includes making one's mark on the instrument": s.1(4).

(b) Companies. A company may execute a deed by affixing its common **5–075** seal.[79] However, as it is no longer necessary that a company should have a common seal,[80] the deed may instead be signed by a director and the secretary of the company, or by two company directors.[81] It will take effect as the company's deed if it makes it clear on its face that it is intended to be a deed.[82]

(c) Other corporations aggregate. A deed made by a corporation aggregate **5–076** which is not a company within the Companies Act 1985, such as a Cambridge college, must be sealed with the corporation's common seal. In practice, that sealing is likely to be attested by "its clerk, secretary or other permanent officer or his deputy, and a member of the board of directors".[83]

(d) Corporations sole. The common law requirement of sealing still **5–077** applies.[84]

C. Setting Aside and Modification of Conveyances

An executed conveyance may be avoided, set aside or modified by the court[85] **5–078** in various cases of fraud, undue influence, or mistake; and where this occurs the court may order the document to be delivered up for cancellation.[86] The jurisdiction is either equitable or statutory. In either case the conveyance is not void but voidable. Where the jurisdiction is equitable, the right to set aside the instrument is a mere equity.[87] If therefore the property comes into the hands of an innocent purchaser (including a purchaser of an equitable interest[88]) without notice of the vitiating facts, his title will be unimpeachable. If the right is statutory, provision is normally made for the protection of purchasers. The extent of that protection depends upon the wording of the statute and may override the proprietary principles that would otherwise apply.[89]

---

[79] Companies Act 1985, s.36A(2) (s.36A was inserted by the Companies Act 1989, s.130(2)). For a recent review of the formal requirements for deeds and documents made by and on behalf of corporations, see (1998) Law Com. No. 253.

[80] Companies Act 1985, s.36A(3).

[81] *ibid.*, s.36A(4).

[82] *ibid.*, s.36A(5).

[83] L.P.A. 1925, s.74(1). This subsection raises a presumption of due execution in favour of a purchaser.

[84] None of the statutory provisions which now regulate attestation apply to corporations sole. L.P.(M.P.)A. 1989, s.1 expressly does not: s.1(10). L.P.A. 1925 s.74(1) applies only to a corporation aggregate. The Companies Act 1985, s.36A applies only to companies formed or registered under that Act, to companies that existed in 1985, and to unregistered companies: see s.735(1); Companies (Unregistered Companies) Regulations 1985 (S.I. 1985 No. 680) (as amended).

[85] For minors' dispositions, see *post*, para. 20–012.

[86] See Snell, *Equity*, 624.

[87] *Ante*, para. 5–012.

[88] *ibid.*

[89] This point is of some importance. Even where title to land is registered, the transaction may be set aside against a purchaser with notice, even though under the provisions of the Land Registration Act 1925, he would otherwise take free of the claimant's right: *Kemmis v. Kemmis* [1988] 1 W.L.R. 1307 (a case on M.C.A. 1973, s.37).

5–079   1. Misrepresentation. The court has an inherent jurisdiction to set aside a conveyance induced by fraudulent misrepresentation,[90] and may also set aside a conveyance induced by innocent misrepresentation under the Misrepresentation Act 1967.[91]

5–080   2. Conveyances made with intent to defraud creditors. Where, after December, 28 1986,[92] a transaction (including a conveyance[93]) was entered into at an undervalue and was made for the purpose of putting assets beyond the reach of the creditors of the transferor[94] or otherwise prejudicing them, the court has a power to make such order as it thinks fit for restoring the position to what it would have been had the transaction not been entered into, and for protecting the interests of persons who are victims of the transaction.[95] No order will be made against a purchaser in good faith who acquires any interest in property for value and without notice of the relevant circumstances.[96]

5–081   3. Voluntary conveyances made with intent to defraud a subsequent purchaser. Every voluntary disposition of land made with intent to defraud a subsequent purchaser is by statute voidable at the instance of that purchaser.[97] A subsequent conveyance for value is not *per se* evidence of fraudulent intent.[98]

5–082   4. Conveyances made at an undervalue by a person subsequently declared bankrupt or by a company which becomes insolvent. Where an individual is adjudged bankrupt and has "at the relevant time" entered into a transaction with any person at an undervalue, his trustee in bankruptcy may apply to the court for such order as it thinks fit for restoring the position to

---

[90] See, *e.g. Brownlie v. Campbell* (1880) 5 App. Cas. 925 at 937; *post*, para. 12–112. For the position of a co-owner who is induced by the fraud of the other to agree to a mortgage of the property, see *post*, para. 19–159.

[91] s.1(b). This reverses the former common law rule: see *Angel v. Jay* [1911] 1 K.B. 666; *post*, para. 12–112.

[92] For the law prior to that date, see Snell, *Equity*, 128.

[93] I.A. 1986, s.425(1).

[94] See, *e.g. Midland Bank Plc v. Wyatt* [1995] 1 F.L.R. 696 (declaration of trust of matrimonial home to safeguard it from commercial risk, not to benefit daughters).

[95] I.A. 1986, ss.423–425; see Snell, *Equity*, 130. A transaction is at an undervalue if it is a gift or a transaction in consideration of marriage or for a value that is significantly less than that of the property transferred: I.A. 1986, s.423(1). See, *e.g. Re Kumar* [1993] 1 W.L.R. 224 (transfer to co-owner on assumption of sole liability on a joint mortgage a transfer at an undervalue); *Agricultural Mortgage Corporation Plc v. Woodward* [1995] 1 B.C.L.C. 1; *Barclays Bank Plc v. Eustice* [1995] 1 W.L.R. 1238 (grants of tenancies which had a greater surrender value that the consideration given for them). *cf. Pinewood Joinery v. Starelm Properties Ltd* [1994] 2 B.C.L.C. 412 (transfer for £1 of property worth £0.75 million but mortgaged for £2.65 million not at an undervalue). For those who may apply to have the transaction set aside, see I.A. 1986, s.424. For the orders which the court may make, see *ibid.* s.425(1). The court's powers are not limited to setting the transaction aside, but to restoring and protecting so far as is practicable: see *Chohan v. Saggar* [1994] 1 B.C.L.C. 706.

[96] *ibid.*, s.425(2).

[97] L.P.A. 1925, s.173(1). See generally Snell, *Equity*, 132.

[98] L.P.A. 1925, s.173(2).

what it would have been had the transaction not been entered into.[99] The "relevant time" means any time within the five years preceding the presentation of the bankruptcy petition.[1] However, if the transaction was entered into between two and five years prior to that petition, the transaction will be set aside only if the individual was insolvent at the time or became so in consequence of the transaction.[2] The court can make an order against someone other than the transferee.[3] However, it will not make an order against a purchaser who in good faith and for value acquired any interest in property that was formerly the bankrupt's from anybody other than the bankrupt.[4] There are analogous provisions which apply to transactions by a company which goes into liquidation or against which an administration order is made.[5]

5. Conveyances made to defeat a spouse's claim for financial relief in matrimonial proceedings. The court may set aside any disposition made with the intention of defeating a claim for financial relief by a spouse in matrimonial proceedings.[6] However, the court will not do so in favour of a purchaser for valuable consideration (other than marriage) who acted in good faith and without notice of any intention on the part of the transferor to defeat the spouse's claim.[7]   **5–083**

6. Conveyances induced by undue influence or unconscionability. Conveyances made under undue influence may be set aside under the court's equitable jurisdiction.[8] A distinction is drawn between—   **5–084**

> (i) actual undue influence, in which such influence has to be affirmatively proved; and

---

[99] I.A. 1986, ss.339, 342 (as amended by the Insolvency (No. 2) Act 1994, s.2). The meaning of "undervalue" in s.339 is the same as in I.A. 1986, s.423 (*supra*): s.339(3). The Insolvency (No. 2) Act 1994 was enacted to remedy perceived drafting errors in I.A. 1986, ss.241 (*infra*), 342.

[1] I.A. 1986, s.341(1).

[2] *ibid.*, s.341(2). See s.341(3) for the definition of insolvency.

[3] *ibid.*, s.342(1).

[4] *ibid.*, s.342(2) (as amended by the Insolvency (No. 2) Act 1994, s.2). For the circumstances in which such a purchaser will be rebuttably presumed to have acquired an interest from such a third party otherwise than in good faith, see I.A. 1986, s.342(2A), (4), (5) (inserted by the Insolvency (No. 2) Act 1994, s.2).

[5] *ibid.*, ss.238, 240, 241 (as amended by the Insolvency (No. 2) Act 1994, s.1). A transaction is at an undervalue for these purposes if it is a gift, or for a value that is significantly less than that of the property transferred: *ibid.*, s.238(4).

[6] M.C.A. 1973, s.37(2). "Disposition" includes a conveyance: s.37(6). The concept of "defeating a claim" is widely defined: s.37(1). The presentation of a petition for bankruptcy by a spouse does not fall within s.37: *Woodley v. Woodley (No. 2)* [1994] 1 W.L.R. 1167. For a full discussion of these provisions, see *Kemmis v. Kemmis* [1988] 1 W.L.R. 1307 and *Sherry v. Sherry* [1991] 1 F.L.R. 307.

[7] M.C.A. 1973, s.37(4). "Notice" in this context includes "constructive notice": *Kemmis v. Kemmis* [1988] 1 W.L.R. 1307. *cf.* Inheritance (Provision for Family and Dependants) Act 1975, s.10, *post*, para. 11–004.

[8] See, *e.g. Cheese v. Thomas* [1994] 1 W.L.R. 129; *Langton v. Langton* [1995] 3 F.C.R. 521; and *post*, para. 19–159.

(ii) presumed undue influence in which the relationship between the
parties will lead the court to presume such influence in the absence
of evidence to the contrary.[9]

Although the courts have refused to define the limits of presumed undue
influence, there are a number of well-known categories of relationship, such
as doctor and patient[10] and solicitor and client, to which the presumption
applies.[11] It is now established that these do not include husband and wife or
banker and customer.[12] However, it has been recognised that the presumption
can apply to any relationship[13] if one party has reposed a sufficient degree of
trust and confidence in the other.[14] Where undue influence is presumed, it is
necessary for the party alleging it to prove that the transaction was to his
"manifest disadvantage".[15] This test has been much criticised,[16] and has
occasioned some difficulty in practice.[17] In cases of actual undue influence,
proof of manifest disadvantage is not required.[18]

There is a developing jurisdiction under which the court may set aside a
conveyance on grounds of unconscionability.[19] Furthermore, as will be seen,[20]
in some cases conveyances may be rectified, set aside or modified for mutual
mistake.

---

[9] *Bank of Credit and Commerce International S.A. v. Aboody* [1900] 1 Q.B. 923 at 953;
Goldsworthy v. Brickell [1987] Ch. 378 at 400; *Barclays Bank Plc v. O'Brien* [1994] 1 A.C. 180
at 189, 190.

[10] For a recent example, see *Knapton's Trustee in Bankruptcy v. Price* (1997) 74 P. & C.R.
D15.

[11] *Barclays Bank Plc v. O'Brien, supra*, at 189.

[12] *Bank of Montreal v. Stuart* [1911] A.C. 120 (husband and wife); *National Westminster Bank Plc
v. Morgan* [1985] A.C. 686 (banker and customer).

[13] Including that of husband and wife: *Barclays Bank Plc v. O'Brien, supra*, at 190; wife and
husband: *Simpson v. Simpson* [1992] 1 F.L.R. 601 (husband dependent on wife through age and
infirmity); employer and employee: *Steeples v. Lea* [1998] 1 F.L.R. 138; and banker and
customer: *National Westminster Bank Plc v. Morgan, supra*, at 708; *Petrou v. Woodstead
Finance Ltd* [1986] F.L.R. 158 at 169, 170 (where the banker acquires "a dominating
influence" over the customer).

[14] *Goldsworthy v. Brickell, supra*, at 401. Whether or not this is so is an issue of fact: compare
Avon Finance Co. Ltd v. Bridger [1985] 2 All E.R. 281 with *Forsdike v. Forsdike* (1997) 74 P.
& C.R. D4 (both cases involving a son and an elder parent: undue influence was established in
the former but not the latter).

[15] *National Westminster Bank Plc v. Morgan, supra*.

[16] See, *e.g.* (1985) 48 M.L.R. 579 (D. Tiplady). *cf. C.I.B.C. Mortgages Plc v. Pitt* [1994] 1 A.C.
200 at 209 (indicating doubts about the decision in *National Westminster Bank Plc v. Morgan,
supra*.

[17] Compare *Barclays Bank Plc v. Kennedy* [1989] 1 F.L.R. 356 with *Bank of Credit and
Commerce International S.A. v. Aboody, supra*. The disadvantageous nature of the transaction
must be obvious and not such as arises after a "fine and close evaluation of its various
beneficial and detrimental features": *C.I.B.C. Mortgages Plc v. Pitt* (1993) 25 H.L.R. 439 at
451, *per* Neill L.J.

[18] *C.I.B.C. Mortgages Plc v. Pitt* [1994] 1 A.C. 200, HL, overruling on this point *Bank of Credit
and Commerce International S.A. v. Aboody, supra*.

[19] See *Boustany v. Pigott* (1993) 69 P. & C.R. 298 (where the Privy Council set aside a lease on
this ground). Unconscionability is subsuming some of the older grounds of relief (such as
purchase from a poor and ignorant person, as in *Fry v. Lane* (1888) 40 Ch.D. 312). See [1995]
L.M.C.L.Q. 538 (N. Bamforth).

[20] *Post*, para. 12–122.

Part 4

REGISTRATION OF LAND CHARGES

The system of unregistered conveyancing is reinforced by a limited system for the registration of land charges.[21] This is to be distinguished from registration of title which is rapidly superseding the unregistered system and is the subject of the next chapter.

5–085

Section 1. Land Charges

The object of the registration of land charges is to simplify traditional conveyancing by eliminating the doctrine of notice and the elaborate inquiries which it necessitated. If the incumbrance is registrable and duly registered, its owner is protected and the purchaser can ascertain it without trouble. If it is not registered, the purchaser takes free from it and the owner's rights against the land are defeated. But the system will only work satisfactorily if owners of incumbrances realise that they must take a positive step to protect themselves. Experience shows that even professional lawyers sometimes neglect to register.[22] Furthermore, the mechanics of the system have some serious defects.

5–086

Before 1926 only a few special imcumbrances were registrable, and they did not include the most common kinds such as mortgages and restrictive covenants. The underlying policy was to require registration only of somewhat unusual charges which a purchaser might fail to discover in an ordinary investigation of title. Under the Land Charges Registration and Searches Act 1888 these charges were (in terms of the catalogue given below) pending actions, annuities, writs and orders affecting land, deeds of arrangement, and land charges of Class A. Pending actions had been registrable since 1839 and certain annuities and rentcharges since 1855, as mentioned earlier.[23]

The legislation of 1925 extended the system widely (in some respects too widely[24]) by applying it to numerous everyday transactions also. It thus became an important part of the system of unregistered conveyancing. Two different classes of registers are in operation: the central Land Charges Register and the various Local Land Charges Registers.

---

[21] There was an older system of registration, the registration of deeds. This was introduced by statute in Yorkshire and Middlesex in the early eighteenth century, but suffered from serious drawbacks. The Middlesex and the Yorkshire Deeds Registers were closed in 1940 and 1976 respectively: see the previous edition of this work at p. 169 for a fuller discussion.

[22] The extension of registered conveyancing has sharpened the awareness of the legal profession to the importance of registration.

[23] *Ante*, para. 4–056.

[24] See *post*, para. 5–112.

Section 2. Land Charges Register

A. Registrable Interests

5–087   The Land Charges Act 1925 was the primary statute governing the registration of incumbrances. Although to some extent it reproduced earlier statutes, it revolutionised the system by making many interests registrable for the first time. This was an important part of the policy of the 1925 legislation.[25] The Act has now been consolidated, with later amendments, in the Land Charges Act 1972,[26] and references in this chapter are to the latter Act. The Land Charges Rules 1974[27] regulate the procedure, and prescribe the contents of the registers and the forms.

The five registers[28] under the Act are kept in the Land Charges Department of the Land Registry at Plymouth, and searches are now carried out with the aid of a computer.[29] One of the five registers—the annuities register—is now obsolete, and will not be considered.[30] Of the remainder—land charges, pending actions; writs and orders; deeds of arrangement—the most important is land charges, which will be considered last.

Registration must be "in the name of the estate owner or other person whose estate or interest is intended to be affected", save that for land charges only the estate owner suffices.[31] Registration is accordingly an adverse entry against the owner for the time being of the burdened land, recording the interest claimed and the name of the claimant. There is no investigation or guarantee of the claim by the registrar. All that the applicant need do is fill in a form with the necessary particulars and submit it in the appropriate registry, usually by post.

5–088   **1. Pending actions.** The register of pending actions contains pending actions, and petitions in bankruptcy.[32] A "pending land action" (often called by its old name of *lis pendens*) is "any action or proceeding pending in court relating to land or any interest in or charge on land".[33] The words "relating to

---

[25] See the general discussion in the Report of the Committee on Land Charges, 1956, Cmd. 9825; Law Commission Report 1969 (Law Com. No. 18).

[26] Except as regards local land charges: *post*, para. 5–132.

[27] S.I. 1974 No. 1286.

[28] As required by L.C.A. 1972, s.1.

[29] Application for a search may now be made by fax: Land Charges (Amendment) Rules 1990 (S.I. 1990 No. 485), and for those who have direct access under the Land Registry's Direct Access Service (*post*, para. 6–106), by direct computer link: see Ruoff & Roper, F-11.

[30] For an account, see the previous edition of this work at p. 172.

[31] L.C.A. 1972, ss.3(1), 5(4); and see *post*, paras 5–100, 5–110.

[32] L.C.A. 1972, s.5 (replacing earlier legislation).

[33] *ibid.*, s.17(1). It is expressly provided by statute that certain applications to the court are pending land actions for these purposes. The relevant applications are for: (i) a restraint order to prohibit dealings with property in connection with certain criminal proceedings (see Criminal Justice Act 1988, s.77(12)(b); Drug Trafficking Act 1994, s.26(12)(b); (ii) an access order under the Access to Neighbouring Land Act 1992 (L.C.A. 1972, s.6(1)(d), inserted by Access to Neighbouring Land Act 1992, s.5(6); and see *post*, para. 18–227; (iii) an acquisition order under the Landlord and Tenant Act 1987 (L. & T.A. 1987, s.28(5)); and (iv) a vesting order under the Leasehold Reform, Housing and Urban Development Act 1993, s.97(2)(b). See Ruoff & Roper, 36–06.

land" are of wide and indefinite meaning, but in this context they mean that the claim must affect the title to the land by asserting some claim to it or to some proprietary right over it.[34] They do not, however, include the following claims—

(i) to prevent the land from being sold until some matter has been dealt with[35];

(ii) to a declaration that no contract affecting the land exists[36];

(iii) by a creditor in a company's liquidation[37];

(iv) for damages for breach of a repairing covenant in a lease[38]; or

(v) for a sum of money and a charge on the land if the claim succeeds.[39]

Prior to 1997, a claim to share in the proceeds of sale of land held on trust for sale was not a pending land action: because of the doctrine of conversion, such a share was not regarded as an interest in land, but in the notional proceeds of sale.[40] However, trusts for sale are now included within the definition of a trust of land,[41] and the doctrine of conversion has been retrospectively abolished.[42] Notwithstanding this change, it remains the case that a claim to an undivided share in land cannot be registered as a pending land action.[43] "If they were made registrable as land charges the effect would be to bring onto the Land Charges Register orders affecting only beneficial interests, which under normal conveyancing procedure now take effect only behind a trust, and

---

[34] As in *Whittingham v. Whittingham* [1979] Fam. 9 (wife's claim to house in divorce proceedings); *Greenhi Builders Ltd v. Allen* [1979] 1 W.L.R. 156 (claim to easement); *Selim Ltd v. Bickenhall Engineering Ltd* [1981] 1 W.L.R. 1318 (application for leave to bring proceedings under Leasehold Property (Repairs) Act 1938. A claim for a property adjustment order in matrimonial proceedings will be registrable even though the land has not been specifically identified in those proceedings but only in the application for registration: *Perez-Adamson v. Perez-Rivas* [1987] Fam. 89.

[35] *Calgary and Edmonton Land Co. Ltd v. Dobinson* [1974] Ch. 102.

[36] *Heywood v. B.D.C. Properties Ltd (No. 2)* [1964] 1 W.L.R. 971.

[37] *Calgary and Edmonton Land Co. Ltd v. Dobinson, supra.*

[38] *Regan & Blackburn Ltd v. Rogers* [1985] 1 W.L.R. 870; *13–20 Embankment Gardens Ltd v. Coote* (1997) 74 P. & C.R. D6.

[39] *Haslemere Estates Ltd v. Baker* [1982] 1 W.L.R. 1109.

[40] See *Taylor v. Taylor* [1968] 1 W.L.R. 378, where a wife claimed beneficial co-ownership of the home but sought an order for sale and a share of the proceeds. For the former doctrine of conversion, see *post*, para. 8–118.

[41] T.L.A.T.A. 1996, s.1(2).

[42] *ibid.*, s.3(1), (3).

[43] The definition of "land" in L.C.A. 1972, s.17(1) still excludes "an undivided share in land" (*i.e.* an interest under a tenancy in common). Prior to 1997, the reason for this exclusion was the now-abolished doctrine of conversion. Elsewhere in the property legislation, the exclusion of undivided shares from the definition of land was removed by T.L.A.T.A. 1996. It was decided to retain it in the legislation on land charges to ensure that claims concerning beneficial interests were kept off the title.

do not appear on the title to the land".[44] There are other types of claim by beneficiaries under trust of land that *will* be registrable as pending land actions.[45]

5–089   The court has a wide discretion to order the removal of an unjustified entry.[46] Registration ensures that if the owner disposes of the land before the action is decided the new owner will be bound by the claim.[47] For equitable claims, registration has the advantage of ensuring that third parties have notice, and for legal and equitable claims alike it avoids the penalties of non-registration.[48]

Registration lasts for five years. If the case has not then been decided, registration may be renewed for successive periods of five years.[49]

5–090   **2. Writs and orders affecting land.** The register of writs and orders is for writs and orders *enforcing* judgments and orders of the court. It does not include writs employed to *commence* an action relating to land which come under the head of pending land actions. The chief items are as follows.[50]

> (i) Writs or orders affecting land issued or made by a court for the purpose of enforcing a judgment or recognisance, *e.g.* an order of the court charging the land of a judgment debtor with payment of the money due,[51] or an access order.[52] No writ or order affecting an interest under a trust of land may be registered in this register.[53] Nor is a *Mareva injunction*[54] registrable, because it merely prevents a litigant from disposing of his assets pending the trial of some claim against him.[55]

> (ii) An order appointing a receiver or sequestrator of land.[56]

---

[44] *Perry v. Phoenix Assurance Plc* [1988] 1 W.L.R. 940 at 945, *per* Browne-Wilkinson V.-C. That case was concerned with the registration of a writ or order under L.C.A. 1972, s.6; see *infra*.

[45] A claim for an order relating to the exercise of the powers by trustee under T.L.A.T.A. 1996, s.14 (*post*, paras 8–142, 9–064), would be registrable if it was an action or proceeding pending in court relating to land or any interest in or charge on land, *e.g.* a claim to be entitled to occupy the premises under *ibid.*, s.12.

[46] See *post*.

[47] If registered, the charge will bind a purchaser even if he had no express notice of the action: *Perez-Adamson v. Perez-Rivas* [1987] Fam. 89; and see L.C.A. 1972, s.5(7).

[48] See *post*, para. 5–131.

[49] L.C.A. 1972, s.8.

[50] *ibid.*, s.6.

[51] Charging Orders Act 1979.

[52] L.C.A. 1972, s.6(1)(d), inserted by Access to Neighbouring Land Act 1992, s.5(1). For these orders, see *post*, paras 18–225 *et seq*.

[53] L.C.A. 1972, s.6(1A), inserted by T.L.A.T.A. 1996, s.25(1), Sched. 3, para. 12(1), (3). This restriction preserves the rule that charging orders over an undivided share in land are incapable of registration: see *Perry v. Phoenix Assurance Plc* [1988] 1 W.L.R. 940, *supra*.

[54] *Mareva Compania Naviera S.A. v. International Bulk Carriers S.A.* [1975] 2 Ll.Rep. 509.

[55] *Stockler v. Fourways Estates Ltd* [1984] 1 W.L.R. 25.

[56] Such an order may be registered even though the receivership does not create an interest in land: *Clayhope Properties Ltd v. Evans* [1986] 1 W.L.R. 1223 (receiver appointed because of a landlord's failure to observe a repairing covenant: *post*, para. 14–283).

(iii) A bankruptcy order, whether or not the bankrupt's estate is known to include land.[57]

Registration remains effective for five years, but may be renewed for successive periods of five years.[58]

3. Deeds of arrangement. The Deeds of Arrangement Act 1914, elaborately defines deeds of arrangement, and the definition applies to this register.[59] For the present purpose a deed of arrangement may be taken as any document whereby control over a debtor's property is given for the benefit of his creditors generally, or, if he is insolvent, for the benefit of three or more of his creditors. A common example arises when a debtor, seeking to avoid bankruptcy, assigns all his property to a trustee for all his creditors.

Registration is effective for five years and may be renewed for successive periods of five years.[60] The registration may be effected by the trustee of the deed or by any creditor assenting to or taking the benefit of the deed.[61]

5–091

4. Land charges. This is the most important register. Land charges are divided into six classes, A, B, C, D, E and F.[62] The most important classes, D and C, are sub-divided.

5–092

Class A consists of charges imposed on land by some statute, but which comes into existence only when some person makes an application. Thus, where a landlord who is not entitled to land for his own benefit (such as a life tenant under the Settled Land Act 1925), has to pay compensation to an agricultural tenant or a tenant holding under a farm business tenancy, the landlord is entitled to a charge on the land for the amount of such compensation.[63] A Class A charge should be registered as soon as it arises.[64]

5–093

Class B consists of charges which are similar to those in Class A except that they are not created on the application of any person, but are imposed automatically by statute.[65] Most charges thus imposed appear to be local land charges, and as these are registrable in a separate register, few charges are registrable in Class B. An example is a charge on land recovered or preserved for an assisted litigant under the Legal Aid Act 1988 in respect of unpaid

5–094

---

[57] L.C.A. 1972, s.6(1)(c), as substituted by I.A. 1985, s.235(1), Sched. 8, para. 21.
[58] L.C.A. 1972, s.8.
[59] L.C.A. 1972, ss.7, 17(1).
[60] L.C.A. 1972, s.8.
[61] *ibid.*, s.7(1).
[62] *ibid.*, s.2.
[63] Agricultural Holdings Act 1986, s.86(1)–(3) (such a charge requires an application to the Minister of Agriculture, Fisheries and Food); Agricultural Tenancies Act 1995, s.33(2) (no ministerial consent required).
[64] L.C.A. 1972, s.4(2).
[65] L.C.A. 1972, s.2(3).

contributions to the legal aid fund.[66] Such a charge should be registered as soon as it is created.[67]

5–095   *Class C* land charges are divided into four categories.[68]

5–096   C (i): A PUISNE MORTGAGE. This is a legal mortgage not protected by a deposit of documents relating to the legal estate affected.[69]

5–097   C (ii): A LIMITED OWNER'S CHARGE. This is an equitable charge which a tenant for life or statutory owner acquires under any statute by discharging inheritance tax or other liabilities,[70] and to which the statute gives special priority. Thus on the death of a tenant for life of settled land, inheritance tax must be paid. If a succeeding tenant for life finds the money out of his own pocket instead of leaving the burden on the settled property itself, he is entitled to a charge on the land in the same way as if he had lent money to the estate on mortgage.[71] Such a charge arises automatically[72] and, being equitable,[73] is registrable in Class C (ii).[74]

5–098   C (iii): A GENERAL EQUITABLE CHARGE. This is any equitable charge on land which—

> (i) is not included in any other class of land charge;
>
> (ii) is not secured by a deposit of documents relating to the legal estate affected[75]; and
>
> (iii) does not arise, or affect an interest arising, under a trust of land or settlement.[76]

This is a residuary class which catches equitable charges not registrable elsewhere. It includes equitable annuities, *e.g.* rentcharges for life, if created after 1925,[77] and equitable mortgages of a legal estate if not protected by a

---

[66] Legal Aid Act 1988, s.16(6); S.I. 1989 No. 339, r. 95.
[67] L.C.A. 1972, s.4(5).
[68] *ibid.*, s.2(4).
[69] "Puisne" is pronounced "puny".
[70] If a tenant for life pays off a mortgage on the settled property he may keep it alive and enforce his rights as mortgagee: *Lord Gifford v. Lord Fitzhardinge* [1899] 2 Ch. 32; see *post*, para. 19–143.
[71] Inheritance Tax Act 1984, s.212(2).
[72] *Lord Advocate v. Countess of Moray* [1905] A.C. 531 at 539.
[73] L.P.A. 1925, s.1(3).
[74] L.C.A. 1972, s.2(4)(ii) as amended by the Inheritance Tax Act 1984, s.276, Sched. 8, para. 3.
[75] This excludes "protected" mortgages of a legal estate as explained *post*, para. 19–218.
[76] L.C.A. 1972, s.2(4), as amended by T.L.A.T.A. 1996, s.25(1), Sched. 3, para. 12(1), (2).
[77] Annuities created prior to 1926 were registrable under the now obsolete register of annuities: see *ante*, para. 5–087.

deposit of title deeds[78] and if not limited owner's charges. It also includes an unpaid vendor's lien.[79] It specifically excludes a charge given by way of indemnity against rents equitably apportioned or charged exclusively on land in exoneration of other land and against the breach or non-observance of covenants or conditions.[80] Equitable mortgages of an equitable interest under a settlement or a trust of land are excluded, as they are overreached on a conveyance to a purchaser, and therefore no question of enforcing them against him can arise.[81] The same applies to other charges on the proceeds of sale of land, as opposed to charges on the land itself, such as an agreement to share the proceeds of sale,[82] or an estate agent's charge on them for commission.[83]

C (iv): AN ESTATE CONTRACT. This is a "contract by an estate owner" (*i.e.*   **5–099** the owner of a legal estate[84]) "or by a person entitled at the date of the contract to have a legal estate conveyed to him to convey or create a legal estate". The contract must be made in writing, contain all the terms expressly agreed and be signed by both parties.[85] A notice to treat served under a compulsory purchase order is not a contract and cannot be registered.[86] The definition expressly includes "a contract conferring either expressly or by statutory implication a valid option to purchase, a right of pre-emption or any other like right".[87] The definition applies both to ordinary contracts for the sale, sub-sale,[88] lease,[89] or mortgage[90] of a legal estate, whether unconditional or conditional,[91] and also to unilateral contracts such as an option to renew a

---

[78] Equitable mortgages protected by a deposit of title deeds can now only take effect if there is a binding contract to create a mortgage: see *United Bank of Kuwait Plc v. Sahib* [1997] Ch. 107; *post*, paras 12–043, 19–039. It remains an open question whether such a mortgage should now be registered as an estate contract: *post*, para. 19–222.

[79] *Uziell-Hamilton v. Keen* (1971) 22 P. & C.R. 655. See [1997] Conv. 336 at 342 (D. G. Barnsley).

[80] L.P.(Am.)A. 1926, Sched.

[81] *Post*, paras 8–157 *et seq.* where it is also explained how a number of land charges (including general equitable charges) may be overreached even though created prior to the trust for sale or settlement.

[82] *Thomas v. Rose* [1968] 1 W.L.R. 1797.

[83] *Georgiades v. Edward Wolfe & Co. Ltd* [1965] Ch. 487.

[84] L.C.A. 1972, s.17(1); L.P.A. 1925, s.205(1)(v); *ante.*

[85] L.P.(M.P.)A. 1989, s.2, *post*, para. 12–018.

[86] *Capital Investments Ltd v. Wednesfield U.D.C.* [1965] Ch. 774.

[87] For options as interests in land, see *post*, para. 12–061.

[88] *i.e.* a resale by a purchaser before the land has been conveyed to him. *cf. Barrett v. Hilton Developments Ltd* [1975] Ch. 237; *post*, para. 5–100.

[89] See *Blamires v. Bradford Corporation* [1964] Ch. 585, where a testamentary option to occupy land for life at a rent had been exercised.

[90] Equitable mortgages by deposit of title deeds can only take effect as contracts to grant a mortgage: see *United Bank of Kuwait Plc v. Sahib* [1997] Ch. 107; *post*, paras 12–043, 19–039. It has not been decided whether such mortgages are required to be registered as estate contracts. Although the wording of L.C.A. 1972, s.2(4) suggests that they should, in principle this seems unnecessary: see *post*, para. 19–222.

[91] At any rate if the condition is extraneous to the parties themselves (*Haslemere Estates Ltd v. Baker* [1982] 1 W.L.R. 1109), and probably if it is not: see *Williams v. Burlington Investments Ltd* (1977) 121 S.J. 424 (agreement to grant mortgage of unsold land on demand).

lease,[92] to purchase the reversion,[93] or to require a tenant to surrender his lease instead of assigning it.[94] However, it does not apply to such contracts at one remove (*i.e.* a contract authorising an agent to make such a contract),[95] nor to a contract to sell an interest under a trust of land,[96] nor to a boundary agreement unless it clearly involves the transfer of land.[97] Registration of a right of pre-emption is held, anomalously, to take effect only from the time when the right becomes exercisable.[98] Where an option which has been registered is then exercised, it is unnecessary to register additionally the resultant contract of sale.[99]

5–100   If V contracts to sell land to P, who then contracts to sell it to Q, it is against V, the estate owner,[1] and not P, that Q must register his estate contract; registration against P will not be effective even if P later acquires the legal estate.[2] This is a trap for sub-purchasers, who often will not know that the sub-vendor is not an estate owner. But when a yearly tenant agreed that if he acquired the freehold he would grant his sub-tenant a lease for 10 years, the contract was somewhat surprisingly held to be registrable as an estate contract because even though the tenant had only a hope of acquiring the freehold, his yearly tenancy made him an estate owner.[3]

It has also been held that a contract by a landowner with an agent to convey the land to such persons as the agent should direct is registrable.[4] Yet here it seems that the contract created no specifically enforceable rights in the land, for the agent's interest was merely financial, and damages would have been an adequate remedy.

There are certain rights which, by statute, are registrable as if they were contracts, namely—

---

[92] *Phillips v. Mobil Oil Co. Ltd* [1989] 1 W.L.R. 888; and see *Markfaith Investment Ltd v. Chiap Hua Flashlights Ltd* [1991] 2 A.C. 43. As a matter of literal interpretation, this seems correct, though the practical need to register such covenants is not apparent: see [1990] Conv. 168 and 250 (J. Howell). An assignee of the reversion prior to 1926 would have been bound by such a covenant regardless of notice because it touched and concerned the land: *post*, para. 15–026. The requirement of registration may have been due to a mistake in drafting: *post*, para. 5–121.

[93] *Midland Bank Trust Co. Ltd v. Green* [1981] A.C. 513; *post*, para. 5–119.

[94] *Greene v. Church Commissioners for England* [1974] Ch. 467.

[95] *Thomas v. Rose* [1968] 1 W.L.R. 1797.

[96] It is not a contract "to convey or create a legal estate" within L.C.A. 1972, s.2(4): *cf. Re Rayleigh Weir Stadium* [1954] 1 W.L.R. 786.

[97] *Neilson v. Poole* (1969) 20 P. & C.R. 909.

[98] *Pritchard v. Briggs* [1980] Ch. 339, *post*, para. 12–062.

[99] *Armstrong and Holmes Ltd v. Holmes* [1993] 1 W.L.R. 1482.

[1] L.C.A. 1972 ss.3(1), 17(1). Contrast s.5(4), which is not confined to estate owners: *ante*, para. 5–087.

[2] *Barrett v. Hilton Developments Ltd* [1975] Ch. 237, a decision strengthened by the contrast mentioned in n. 1 above; *Property Discount Corporation Ltd v. Lyon Group Ltd* [1981] 1 W.L.R. 300.

[3] *Sharp v. Coates* [1949] 1 K.B. 285. A legal estate in *other* land is of course irrelevant: see at 294. Such a contract should be registered against the freeholder: *ante*, para. 5–087.

[4] *Turley v. Mackay* [1944] Ch. 37, questioned in *Thomas v. Rose, supra*; and see *Re Rayleigh Weir Stadium, supra*, at 791.

(i) a tenant's notice to purchase the freehold or take an extended lease under the Leasehold Reform Act 1967[5];

(ii) certain notices given under the Leasehold Reform, Housing and Urban Development Act 1993[6]; and

(iii) a request for an overriding lease under the Landlord and Tenant (Covenants) Act 1995.[7]

Class D land charges are divided into three categories.[8] **5–101**

D (i) INLAND REVENUE CHARGES. These are statutory charges in favour of **5–102**
the Board of Inland Revenue which arise automatically when inheritance tax is unpaid.[9] Inheritance tax is levied primarily on the estate of a deceased person but a liability to tax may also arise on certain gifts made *inter vivos*. Where the charge affects land it is registrable under this head,[10] but in practice this precaution is rarely taken. Formerly there were similar rules for securing the payment of death duties (estate duty) and subsequently capital transfer tax.[11]

D (ii): RESTRICTIVE COVENANTS. Under this head any covenant or agreement **5–103**
restrictive of the user of land[11a] may be registered provided it—

(i) was entered into after 1925, and

(ii) is not "between a lessor and a lessee".

Thus restrictive covenants in leases are never registrable, even where they relate not to the land demised but to adjoining land of the lessor[12]; the normal rules as to privity of contract and privity of estate apply and where there is neither of these the question is one of notice.[13] Similarly restrictive covenants made before 1926 still depend upon the doctrine of notice for their effect against purchasers, since they are enforceable against everyone except a purchaser for value of a legal estate without notice.

D (iii): EQUITABLE EASEMENTS. Any "easement, right or privilege over or **5–104**
affecting land" is registrable under this head, provided—

---

[5] Leasehold Reform Act 1967, s.5(5); *post*, para. 22–239.
[6] Leasehold Reform, Housing and Urban Development Act 1993, s.97(1).
[7] L. & T.C.A. 1995, s.20(6); *post*, para. 15–019.
[8] L.C.A. 1972, s.2(5).
[9] Inheritance Tax Act 1984, s.237.
[10] Land Charges Act 1972, s.2(5), as amended by the Inheritance Tax Act 1984, s.276, Sched. 8, para. 3(1). Inheritance tax was introduced by the Finance Act 1986. The Capital Transfer Tax Act 1984 was renamed the Inheritance Tax Act by the Finance Act 1986, s.100(1)(b).
[11] Death duties date back to Legacy Duty Act 1796, Succession Duty Act 1853 and Finance Act 1894 (estate duty). Legacy and succession duties were abolished in 1949. Registration of death duty charges was introduced by L.C.A. 1925, s.10, replaced by L.C.A. 1972, s.2(5).
[11a] *cf. Langevad v. Chiswick Quay Freeholds Ltd* [1999] 1 E.G.L.R. 61 at 62.
[12] *Darstone Ltd v. Cleveland Petroleum Co. Ltd* [1969] 1 W.L.R. 1807.
[13] *Post*, para. 15–004.

  (i) it is merely equitable, and

  (ii) it was created or arose after 1925.

An example would be an easement granted after 1925 merely by contract, or only for life.[14]

Much trouble has been caused both by the vagueness of this definition and by the injustice of applying it to informal arrangements, such as agreements between neighbours as to rights of way, which the dominant owner pardonably omits to register. These defects have caused the Court of Appeal to hold, at one extreme, that it does not include an equitable right of way arising by acquiescence or estoppel,[15] and, at the other extreme, that it includes the whole residue of equitable proprietary rights capable of binding a purchaser. The latter decision was reversed by the House of Lords, which held that the definition should be given "its plain prima facie meaning".[16] This meaning, though not precisely explained, is evidently narrow. It is probably confined to rights in the nature of easements and profits.[17] Accordingly the House of Lords held that it does not extend to an equitable right of entry.[18] Nor does it extend to a right to remove fixtures at the end of a lease,[19] or to the interest of public authority requisitioning land under Defence Regulations.

5–105   The courts have therefore rejected the contention[20–21] that the policy of 1925 was to require registration of all equitable interests in land which were not protected by deposit of title deeds and not overreachable.[22] An example of an unregistrable interest that is not overreachable is an equity arising by estoppel.[23] The defects of the legislation are now so obvious that the advantage lies in giving it the narrowest possible scope. It has indeed been suggested that the whole class of equitable easements might be abolished.[24] It was one of the mistakes of the reformers of 1925.[25]

5–106   *Class E* consists of annuities created before 1926 but not registered until after 1925. They are, in practice, obsolete.[26]

---

[14] *Post*, para. 18–092.

[15] *E.R. Ives Investment Ltd v. High* [1967] 2 Q.B. 379, holding that the equitable grounds on which the purchaser (with notice) was bound were unaffected by the Land Charges Act 1925: see *post*, para. 13–006. For a discussion of this very difficult case, see (1995) 58 M.L.R. 637 at 643 (G. Battersby).

[16] *Shiloh Spinners Ltd v. Harding* [1973] A.C. 691 at 721, *per* Lord Wilberforce; and see *Poster v. Slough Estates Ltd* [1968] 1 W.L.R. 1515 at 1520, 1521.

[17] See (1937) 53 L.Q.R. 259 (C. V. Davidge); (1948) 12 Conv.(N.S.) 202 (J. F. Garner); [1986] Conv. 31 (M. P. Thompson).

[18] *Shiloh Spinners Ltd v. Harding*, *supra*.

[19] *Poster v. Slough Estates Ltd*, *supra*.

[20–21] *Lewisham Borough Council v. Maloney* [1948] 1 K.B. 50.

[22] Contrast the policy for registered land: *post*, para. 6–077.

[23] *Post*, Chap. 13.

[24] Report of the Committee on Land Charges, 1956, Cmd. 9825, para. 16.

[25] See *Poster v. Slough Estates Ltd*, *supra*, at 1521, *per* Cross J.; *cf. post*, para. 5–110.

[26] Prior to 1926, they would have been registered in the old register of annuities: see *ante*, para. 5–087.

Class F consists of charges affecting any land by virtue of Part IV of the **5–107** Family Law Act 1996. These "matrimonial home rights"[27] are explained later.[28]

Companies. Most charges on land created by a company for securing **5–108** money (including a charge created by a deposit of title deeds[29]) require registration within 21 days in the Companies Register maintained under the Companies Act 1985.[30] For floating charges this suffices in place of registration in the Land Charges Register, and has the same effect.[31] For other charges, this suffices if the charge was created before 1970[32] but otherwise the charge requires registration on both registers. The two systems of registration do not fit together neatly, and so it has proved necessary to adopt the cumbersome system of double registration.[33]

B. Effects of Registration and Non-Registration

1. Effect of registration

(a) Actual notice. By the Law of Property Act 1925,[34] registration under **5–109** the Land Charges Act of any instrument or matter required or authorised to be registered under the Act[35] is deemed to constitute actual notice of the interest registered "to all persons and for all purposes[36] connected with the land affected, as from the date of registration or other prescribed date and so long

---

[27] F.L.A. 1996, s.30(2).

[28] *Post*, para. 17–023.

[29] *Re Wallis & Simmonds (Builders) Ltd* [1974] 1 W.L.R. 391. To be enforceable, such charges must now be binding contracts to mortgage: see *post*, paras 12–043, 19–039.

[30] ss.395, 396. Should it ever be brought into force (which is unlikely) the Companies Act 1989, s.93 will replace these provisions, renaming the register as the "Companies Charges Register".

[31] L.C.A. 1972, s.3(7), as amended by the Companies Consolidation (Consequential Provisions) Act 1985, s.30, Sched. 2; see *Re Molton Finance Ltd* [1968] Ch. 325. There will be a further amendment should the Companies Act 1989, s.93 ever be brought into force: see s.107, Sched. 16, para. 1.

[32] Even if the company's name differed from the estate owner's and did not appear on the title, thereby creating a trap: *Property Discount Corporation Ltd v. Lyon Group Ltd* [1981] 1 W.L.R. 300.

[33] See [1982] Conv. 43 (D. M. Hare and T. Flanagan).

[34] s.198.

[35] Thus registration of a covenant in a lease, or of any other non-registrable interest, is nugatory.

[36] These words mean "for all purposes *for which notice is material*, that is to say for the purpose of the enforcement of third parties' rights against the land affected": *Rignall Developments Ltd v. Halil* [1988] Ch. 190 at 202, *per* Millett J. (*cf.* p. 180 of the 5th edition of this work). "Notice" has a technical meaning that is not synonymous with "knowledge": *ante*, para. 5–016. Thus a person who is deemed to have actual notice of a matter under s.198 will not thereby have the *mens rea* for the commission of a criminal offence (*Wrekin D.C. v. Shah* (1985) 150 J.P. 22), nor lose a right to rescind for misrepresentation in respect of that matter: *Coles v. White City (Manchester) Greyhound Association Ltd* (1928) 45 T.L.R. 125 at 127, affirmed *ibid.*, at 230. A purchaser may terminate a contract for the sale of land on grounds of non-disclosure of a land charge even though he has actual notice of it under s.198: *Rignall Developments Ltd v. Halil, supra*: see *post*, para. 12–082.

as the registration continues in force". There are exceptions to this rule,[37] but in general it prevents any person claiming to be a purchaser without notice of a registered interest.

5–110   *(b) Names register.* Registration is effected against the name of the estate owner at the time.[38] An error in the name registered does not invalidate the registration if the name given may fairly be called a version of the true name (*e.g.* "Frank" or "Francis"); but a person who makes an official search in the correct name is protected even if it fails to reveal the entry.[39]

This system of registration against names is seriously defective from the point of view of a purchaser. There is no map or plan enabling him to search against the land itself: he must search against the names of all previous owners of the land, as ascertained from the title deeds. The rights most likely to concern a purchaser, namely Classes C and D, only became registrable after 1925, but in the course of time the cost of searches may become considerable. It has been said that "this system will end in chaos if it is perpetuated",[40] and that "it is obvious that such a register must in time sink under its own weight".[41] Trouble can be saved if each purchaser preserves the certificate of the search which he made when purchasing the land, handing the certificate on with the title deeds so that subsequent owners can rely upon it. But there is no means of enforcing this practice.

5–111   A further difficulty formerly arose where the estate owner died before the land charge had been registered. Because the charge had to be registered "in the name of the estate owner whose estate is intended to be affected",[42] it was questionable whether registration could validly be made in the deceased's name.[43] To resolve this difficulty, the Law Commission recommended that such registration after death should be effective,[44] and this has been implemented.[45] It is now provided in relation respectively to the registers of land charges, of pending actions, and of writs and orders affecting land, that where a person has died and at the time of his death—

(i) a land charge had been created; or

(ii) there was a pending land action; or

[37] *Post*, paras 19–094, 19–260.
[38] See L.C.A. 1972, ss.3(1), 17(1); Land Charges Rules 1974, r. 5, Sched. 1.
[39] *Oak Co-operative B.S. v. Blackburn* [1968] Ch. 730; for searches, see *post*, para. 5–127.
[40] (1940) 56 L.Q.R. 373 (D. W. Logan); and see Sir J. Stewart-Wallace, *Principles of Land Registration* (1937) pp. 83–84.
[41] (1931) 75 S.J. 807. For an account of the mechanism, see *Oak Co-operative B.S. v. Blackburn*, *supra*.
[42] L.C.A. 1972, s.3(1).
[43] Because he was no longer the estate owner: see generally [1979] Conv. 249 (A. M. Prichard).
[44] (1989) Law Com. No. 184, para. 2.7.
[45] By L.P.(M.P.)A. 1994, s.15.

(iii) there was a writ or order affecting land;

that would, apart from his death, have been registrable against his name, it may be so registered notwithstanding his death.[46]

(c) Names behind the root of title. In 1955, when 30 years had elapsed since 1925, the time arrived when the names of persons against whom charges were registered might lie behind the root of title; and this possibility became much more serious in 1969 when the period for title was reduced to 15 years.[47] A purchaser may be unable to discover the relevant names, but none the less he will be deemed to have actual notice of the charges because they are in fact registered. A problem of this kind had already arisen in the case of leases, owing to an intending tenant's inability to inspect the freehold title or a superior leasehold title.[48] These are grave difficulties, and a Committee[49] which studied them despaired of finding any satisfactory solution except by abandoning name registration and pressing on with the registration of title throughout the country. "We are the inheritors of a transitory system which was bound to disclose this defect after 30 years, and it seems too late to disclaim our inheritance."[50]

5–112

(d) Compensation scheme. In 1969 a palliative was provided in the form of financial compensation at public expense for purchasers affected by undiscoverable land charges.[51] The compensation is recoverable by action in the High Court against the Chief Land Registrar.[52] There are two main requirements. First, at the date of completion (which must be after 1969) neither the purchaser nor any agent of his, acting as such in the transaction, must have had any "actual knowledge" of the charge; and for this purpose, contrary to the general rule, registration is to be disregarded.[53] Secondly, the charge must be registered against the name of an owner of an estate in the land who was not, as such, a party to any transaction in the relevant title, or concerned in any event in it.[54] The "relevant title" means the full title as under an open contract, together with any additional title contracted to be shown; and if a document in the title expressly provided that it was to take effect subject to some

5–113

---

[46] See respectively L.C.A. 1972, ss.3(1A), 5(4A), 6(2A) (as inserted).
[47] *Post*, para. 12–075.
[48] This is explained *post*, para. 14–295.
[49] Report of the Committee on Land Charges 1956 (Cmd. 9825), discussed in [1956] C.L.J. 215 (H.W.R.W.).
[50] Report of the Committee on Land Charges, *supra*, at 8.
[51] L.P.A. 1969, s.25, implementing recommendations made in (1969) Law Com. No. 18.
[52] *ibid.*, s.25(4), (6).
[53] L.P.A. 1969, s.25(1), (2), (11).
[54] *ibid.*, s.25(1). The wording of this section could create a difficulty in one situation. Suppose a charge was registered against the name of a landowner, Joan Smith. She subsequently changed her name by deed poll or marriage to Joan Jones. She then conveyed the land to a purchaser. If at some future date that conveyance became the root of title in a conveyancing transaction, could the purchaser claim an indemnity if he failed to discover the land charge registered against Joan Smith? The wording of the section suggests that he could not.

registrable interest (*e.g.* a restrictive covenant), the title includes the transaction creating that interest.[55] The scheme avoids the problem of leases by excluding grants and mortgages of leases derived out of the freehold; but, with no apparent logic, it extends to sub-leases,[56] and it extends generally to sales, exchanges, mortgages and compulsory purchases.

The compensation scheme has to date generated just two claims,[57] and may not have been strictly necessary. This is because of the practice of carrying forward with the title deeds the results of previous searches of the land charges register, thereby overcoming the difficulty of discovering the names of the owners of the land prior to the root of title.[58]

5–114   (*e*) *Transactions on the title.* Name registration is not only inherently defective; it has also been applied too widely. Its utility is greatest where it brings to a purchaser's notice, and so also protects, some equitable incumbrance which the purchaser might otherwise miss when investigating title, such as a prior contract for sale to another person (an estate contract).[59] But where the transaction normally appears or is mentioned in the title deeds, as for example does a restrictive covenant in a conveyance or an option in a lease, there is no risk of the purchaser overlooking it; yet there is a considerable risk of its owner failing to register it, so that it will be defeated by a purchase of a legal estate. To require registration in such cases merely creates insecurity of property. The difficulties in requiring registration of equitable easements have already been noted.[60]

These unsuitable requirements have been aggravated by errors of drafting. Registration was not intended to apply to covenants in leases, including options to renew the lease or to purchase the reversion, since all such obligations are self-evident from the lease itself; and the Law of Property Act 1922 provided accordingly.[61] But when the saving clause was transposed to the Law of Property Act 1925 it remained confined to "this Part of this Act" although "this Part" no longer contained the provisions about registration, as

---

[55] L.P.A. 1969, s.25(3), (10). Where compensation has been so claimed, the registrar may make additions or alterations to the registers and index so as to facilitate disclosure: S.I. 1970 No. 136.

[56] L.P.A. 1969, s.25(9). It appears that a sub-lessee can claim compensation for, *e.g.* a registered restrictive covenant on the freehold title but that a lessee cannot. This discrimination seems inexplicable.

[57] For £20,000 (1988: see HM Land Registry, *Annual Report 1988–1989*, para. 56) and for £375 (1990: see HM Land Registry, *Annual Report 1989–1990*, p. 11). The Law Commission had in fact predicted that such cases were likely to be rare: see (1969) Law Com. No. 18, para. 32.

[58] See *ante*, para. 5–110, where it is pointed out that there is no legal sanction to enforce this practice.

[59] Curiously enough, it is the practice of some solicitors not to register ordinary contracts of sale, though they are ideally suited for protection by a names register.

[60] *Ante*, para. 5–104.

[61] s.28(4), expressly providing that no registration of any land charge should be necessary. L.P.(Am.)A. 1924, Sched. 3, Pt II, para. 4, amended this into the weak and defective form of L.P.A. 1925, s.6.

the corresponding part of the Act of 1922 had done.[62] The legal profession, misguided by the author of the legislation himself,[63] acted on the assumption that options in leases were exempt from registration until this was shown to be wrong.[64]

2. Effect of non-registration

(a) Persons affected. It is only as against third parties, *i.e.* successors in **5–115** title, that non-registration may invalidate a registrable interest. Failure to register is immaterial as between the original parties to the transaction, *e.g.* as between the vendor and the purchaser under an estate contract, or as between the covenantor and the covenantee in the case of a restrictive covenant. A registrable transaction, even though not registered, remains valid in every respect except as against certain purchasers.[65]

(b) Categories of purchaser. If a registrable incumbrance is not registered, **5–116** the consequences fall into two main categories:

(i) the incumbrance may be void against a purchaser for value of any interest in the land; or

(ii) the incumbrance may be void against a purchaser for money or money's worth of a legal estate in the land.

One difference between (i) and (ii) is that a purchaser of an equitable interest is protected in case (i) but not in case (ii); and a purchaser of an equitable interest does not come within (ii) even if the legal estate which is subject to the incumbrance is specifically declared to be held in trust for him.[66] Another difference is that marriage is "value" but is not "money or money's worth",[67] so that in the case of land settled by an ante-nuptial marriage settlement, the spouses and issue will be protected in case (i) but not in case (ii). In both cases "purchaser" has an extended meaning and includes a lessee, mortgagee or other person taking an interest in land for value.[68] The crucial time in every case is the completion of the transaction, *i.e.* the actual transfer of the legal

---

[62] For another mistake of this kind, see *post*, para. 5–121.

[63] Wolst & C., 12th ed., i, 246, explaining that "the lease is the charter of the title". See *Taylors Fashions Ltd v. Liverpool Victoria Trustees Co. Ltd* [1982] Q.B. 133 at 143.

[64] In *Beesly v. Hallwood Estates Ltd* [1960] 1 W.L.R. 549. That decision has since been approved by the Court of Appeal: *Phillips v. Mobil Oil Co. Ltd* [1989] 1 W.L.R. 888.

[65] *Lloyds Bank Plc v. Carrick* [1996] 4 All E.R. 630 at 642. Thus on a compulsory acquisition the statutory right to compensation is not prejudiced by non-registration: *Blamires v. Bradford Corporation* [1964] Ch. 585.

[66] *McCarthy & Stone Ltd v. Julian S. Hodge & Co. Ltd* [1971] 1 W.L.R. 1547. See *ante*, para. 5–014.

[67] *Ante*, para. 5–008.

[68] L.C.A. 1972, s.17(1).

estate or the equitable interest, as the case may be[69]; subsequent registration cannot impose any burden on the purchaser.

5–117   *(c) Effect.* The effect of non-registration may be expressed as follows.

(i) In general, whichever register is concerned, failure to register any registrable matter in the appropriate register[70] makes it void against a purchaser for value of any interest in the land.[71]

(ii) But in the case of a post-1925 estate contract, restrictive covenant, equitable easement or inland revenue charge[72] (*i.e.* charges within Class C(iv) or Class D) non-registration makes it void against a purchaser of a legal estate for money or money's worth.[73]

(iii) Bankruptcy petitions (registrable as pending actions) and the title of the trustees in bankruptcy under bankruptcy orders (registrable as writs and orders) are void only against a bona fide purchaser of a legal estate for money or money's worth.[74]

(iv) Any other pending land action is void against a purchaser for value of any interest in the land, unless he has express notice of it.[75]

Where an interest is void for non-registration, any right that depends upon or is a consequence of that interest will also be void. Thus, where a purchaser under an unregistered estate contract had paid the entire price, so that the vendor held it on a bare trust for her, a subsequent legal mortgagee took free not only of her estate contract but her interest under the bare trust as well.[76]

5–118   *(d) Exclusion of the doctrine of notice.* It should be noted that with the comparatively unimportant exception of (iv) above, the equitable doctrine of

---

[69] L.C.A. 1972, s.4, makes unregistered land charges void unless registered "before the completion of the purchase". The corresponding provisions for other registers are less specific, but "purchaser" means a person who "takes" an interest for value (s.17(1)), so that the moment of taking is presumably the critical moment.

[70] *i.e.* under L.C.A. 1972: *Kitney v. M.E.P.C. Ltd* [1977] 1 W.L.R. 981 (entry in Middlesex deeds register insufficient).

[71] L.C.A. 1972, ss.4–7.

[72] In the case of inland revenue charges the purchaser must be in good faith and nominal consideration does not count: Inheritance Tax Act 1984, ss.238, 272. This provides that such a charge, if unregistered, and so void against a purchaser, is attached to the proceeds of sale, so that it is not destroyed but overreached.

[73] L.C.A. 1972, s.4(6). It does not follow that an unregistered charge in this category will necessarily be valid as against any other form of purchaser. It could be defeated by a bona fide purchaser of a legal estate made in consideration of marriage who had no notice of the charge: see *ante*, para. 4–060.

[74] L.C.A. 1972, ss.5(8), 6(5), as amended by I.A. 1985, s.235, Sched. 8, para. 21, and Sched. 10, Pt III.

[75] L.C.A. 1972, s.5(7). This does not prevent a fresh action being brought against the purchaser if there is some charge or interest which is enforceable against him.

[76] *Lloyds Bank Plc v. Carrick* [1996] 4 All E.R. 630; criticised (1996) 112 L.Q.R. 549 (P. Ferguson). For the bare trust which arises where a purchaser has paid the whole purchase price, see *post*, para. 12–055.

notice is wholly excluded. Under the Land Charges Act 1972[77] the purchaser is not required to act in good faith, except under (iii) above: the unregistered interest is simply void against him. He does not need to rely upon the provision (seemingly redundant) of the Law of Property Act 1925[78] that he is not to be prejudiced by notice of any interest which is void against him under the Land Charges Acts, which in any case is narrower in scope since under that Act good faith is necessary.[79] In the result, therefore, it is quite immaterial that the purchaser was not diligent in investigating title[80] or had actual knowledge of the interest,[81] or deliberately intended to defeat it,[82] or that the owner of the interest was in possession of the land.[83] It has even been held that where land is granted expressly subject to another person's interest, the grantee is not subject to that interest if it is registrable but unregistered.[84] It is possible that in that situation, the court would now in appropriate circumstances impose a constructive trust upon the grantee,[85] though it will not do so merely because a conveyance is made "subject to" an unregistered land charge. If such a trust can be imposed at all, it will only be where the circumstances make it unconscionable for the grantee to refuse to give effect to the unregistered charge.[86] It is possible also, in special circumstances, for

---

[77] s.17(1) defines "purchaser" as "any person (including a mortgagee or lessee) who, for valuable consideration, takes any interest in land or in a charge on land". "Valuable consideration" may, in this context, include nominal consideration: see *Midland Bank Trust Co. Ltd v. Green* [1981] A.C. 513 at 532.

[78] s.199(1).

[79] s.205(1)(xxi) defines "purchaser" as "a purchaser in good faith for valuable consideration . . ." except in Part I of the Act, not here relevant. "Nominal consideration" is, however, expressly excluded. Nominal consideration is a sum that "can be mentioned as consideration but is not necessarily paid": *Midland Bank Trust Co. Ltd v. Green* [1981] A.C. 513 at 532, *per* Lord Wilberforce. *cf. Nurdin & Peacock Plc v. D. B. Ramsden & Co. Ltd* [1999] 1 E.G.L.R. 119 at 123.

[80] In *Sharp v. Coates* [1949] 1 K.B. 285 (*ante*, para. 5–100), the owner of the defeated interest was in possession, so that the purchaser had at least constructive notice of it.

[81] *Coventry Permanent Economic B.S. v. Jones* [1951] 1 All E.R. 901 at 904; *Hollington Bros. Ltd v. Rhodes* [1951] 2 T.L.R. 691 at 696; and see *ante*, para. 4–057. Registered land is similar: *post*, para. 6–105.

[82] *Midland Bank Trust Co. Ltd v. Green*, *post*, para. 5–119.

[83] *Hollington Bros. Ltd v. Rhodes*, *supra*. The opinion to the contrary in *Bendall v. McWhirter* [1952] 2 Q.B. 466 at 483 must be regarded as erroneous, being based on L.P.A. 1925, s.14, which is inapplicable, as explained below. See (1952) 68 L.Q.R. at 384, 385 (R.E.M.); *Westminster Bank Ltd v. Lee* [1956] Ch. 7 at 21.

[84] *Hollington Bros Ltd v. Rhodes* [1951] 2 T.L.R. 691 (assignee of leasehold "subject to . . . such leases and tenancies as may affect the premises" held free from prior agreement for an underlease to another person who had taken possession but had not registered an estate contract); *Markfaith Investment Ltd v. Chiap Hua Flashlights Ltd* [1991] 2 A.C. 43.

[85] *Ashburn Anstalt v. Arnold* [1989] Ch. 1 at 22–26. That case was concerned with the situation where there was a sale of land subject to a contractual licence rather than to an unregistered land charge. It is not therefore necessarily conclusive, but see *Lyus v. Prowsa Developments Ltd* [1982] 1 W.L.R. 1044, *post*, paras 6–105, 10–022. When enacted, the Contract (Rights of Third Parties) Bill may overcome these difficulties in some cases: see *post*, para. 10–022.

[86] *Ashburn Anstalt v. Arnold*, *supra*, at 25. In the *Hollington* case, *supra*, at 696, Harman J. said: "I do not see how that which is void and which is not to prejudice the purchaser can be validated by some equitable doctrine". But in the *Lyus* case the contract was equally void against the purchaser without the aid of the clause making the sale subject to it. *cf. Markfaith Investment Ltd v. Chiap Hua Flashlights Ltd*, *supra*, where on facts "indistinguishable" from

a party to be estopped from asserting that an unregistered charge is ineffective.[87] But in general the penalties for non-registration are inexorable.

5–119   *(e) A notable illustration.* The rigour of these rules is exemplified by *Midland Bank Trust Co. Ltd v. Green.*[88] In this case a husband and wife arranged a collusive sale for the purpose of defeating a land charge which they knew to be unregistered. The husband had granted to his son, who occupied a farm as his tenant, a 10-year option to purchase the farm at a price of £22,500. Wishing to revoke the option six years later, and ascertaining that it was unregistered, he conveyed the farm, then worth about £40,000, to his wife for £500. The House of Lords held that the wife took the farm free from the option.[89] It was held that the conveyance to the wife was a genuine sale to a purchaser for money or money's worth; that a party was entitled to take deliberate advantage of non-registration; and that the clear words of the Land Charges Act 1972 could not be qualified by any requirement of good faith. That requirement was conspicuously absent from the definition of "purchaser" in the Land Charges Act 1972,[90] in contrast with the definition in the Law of Property Act 1925,[91] the presumed reason being to eliminate the necessity of inquiring into the purchaser's motives and state of mind where there is a failure to register. Lord Wilberforce said that the terms of the Land Charges Act 1972 were clear and definite, that the Act was intended to provide a simple and understandable system for the protection of title to land, and that to read it down or gloss it would destroy its usefulness.[92] The answer to any complaint of injustice is that the Act provides a simple and effective protection: registration.

5–120   *(f) The change of policy.* The illustrations in (d) and (e) above bring out the profound change in the policy of the law which was effected by the legislation of 1925 and later. For centuries the courts had developed a policy based upon good faith and fair dealing under the doctrine of notice, the reasons for which were primarily ethical. Its refinements having grown too great for practical convenience, they were largely swept away in favour of a mechanical system from which the ethical element was eliminated.[93] Convenience was bought at

---

the *Hollington* case, the Privy Council did not consider the possibility of imposing a constructive trust.

[87] As in *Taylors Fashions Ltd v. Liverpool Victoria Trustees Co. Ltd* [1982] Q.B. 133. He may also be bound if he fails to plead non-registration when sued: *Balchin v. Buckle* (1982) 126 S.J. 412.

[88] [1981] A.C. 513.

[89] The son had remedies in damages against the husband for breach of contract and against his solicitors for negligence and perhaps against the husband and wife for conspiracy: *Midland Bank Trust Co. Ltd v. Green (No. 2)* [1979] 1 W.L.R. 460; *(No. 3)* [1982] Ch. 529; *Midland Bank Trust Co. Ltd v. Hett, Stubbs & Kemp* [1979] Ch. 384. This mass of litigation was all caused by the failure to register.

[90] See n. 77, *supra.*

[91] See n. 79, *supra.*

[92] *Midland Bank Trust Co. Ltd v. Green, supra,* at 528.

[93] Bankruptcy petitions apart: *ante,* para. 5–117.

the price of injustice in cases where the owners of registrable interests did not realise that they should register them (their solicitors usually making the omission) and so suffered loss. To allow the defeat of a prior interest by a later transaction is a failure on the part of the law, and a natural reluctance to enforce it has sometimes tempted judges to resist the policy of the legislation, clear-cut though it is. In the case of the collusive sale of the farm in the *Green* case,[94] the majority of the Court of Appeal, in order to prevent the defeat of the option, held that the sale price of £500 was not "money or money's worth" within the meaning of the Act, on the ground that it was a gross undervalue and the true character of the transaction was that of a gift, not a sale; and it was said that the transaction was vitiated by fraud, namely dishonest dealing designed to deprive the unwary of their rights.[95] The House of Lords has now reasserted the stark policy of 1925, unethical and uncompromising but clear and simple, at least for those who are aware of it.

(g) Persons in possession or occupation. In one important respect the **5–121** policy of 1925 appears to have been made even more rigorous than intended. Where the owner of the interest is in occupation of the land the obvious fact of his occupation ought to protect his rights against any later purchaser, just as under the doctrine of notice.[96] In the case of land with registered title that principle was respected by the Land Registration Act 1925, under which actual occupation confers an overriding interest which does not require to be protected on the register.[97] In the case of unregistered titles it was apparently also intended that actual occupation or possession should give protection, since the Law of Property Act 1922[98] provided:

> "This Part of this Act shall not prejudicially affect the interest of any person in possession or in actual occupation of land to which he may be entitled in virtue of such possession or occupation."

The same part of the Act of 1922 contained the amendments extending the scheme for the registration of land charges.[99] But when that Act was later broken up into the 1925 legislation, and the provisions for registration were moved to the Land Charges Act 1925, the section quoted was carried without amendment into Part I of the Law of Property Act 1925.[1] In that position it has minimal effect since it can no longer govern the provisions about registration.

---

[94] *Supra*, para. 5–119.
[95] [1980] Ch. 590. For other examples see *ante*, para. 5–118.
[96] *Ante*, para. 5–019.
[97] *Post*, para. 6–047.
[98] s.33. The wording was not very apt for this purpose, but probably sufficient. It reads as if its primary purpose may have been to prevent the interests of adverse possessors from being turned into equitable interests.
[99] s.14 and Sched. 7.
[1] s.14.

So it may be due to a blunder of draftsmanship that the interest of a person in actual occupation can be defeated by a later purchase.[2] It is an indefensible anomaly that a tenant in possession under an agreement for a lease, for example, who excusably fails to register, may be ejected by a later purchaser with notice to whom the landlord may have been able to sell or let the land more profitably. If the title is registered there is no such injustice.[3]

5–122   *(h) No duty to register.* Although in his own interests the owner of a registrable land charge obviously ought to register it, he is under no duty to anyone else to do so. This has a notable effect on the measure of damages for breach of contract. If V contracts to sell land to P, who fails to register the estate contract, and V conveys the land to X in breach of contract, P can recover full damages from V (or the full amount paid by X to V[4]), even though P, had he registered, could have enforced his equitable interest against X and so would have suffered no loss.[5]

5–123   **3. Companies.** If a charge registrable in the Companies Register[6] is not duly registered there within 21 days of its creation, it is, in addition to any consequences of not being registered in the Land Charges Register, void as a security as against the liquidator and all creditors of the company, and the money becomes immediately payable.[7]

5–124   **4. Unregistrable interests.** Unregistrable equitable interests, *e.g.* pre-1926 restrictive covenants and pre-1926 equitable mortgages where there is either a deposit of title deeds or there has been no transfer since 1925, are still governed by the old doctrine of notice.

---

[2] See (1977) 41 Conv.(N.S.) 415 at 419; [1990] C.L.J. 277 at 315–320 (C.H.); [1982] Conv. 213 (M. Friend and J. Newton). The point was left open in *Lloyds Bank Plc v. Carrick* [1996] 4 All E.R. 630 at 642, but Morritt L.J. observed that "what is now s.14 of the Law of Property Act 1925 does not achieve for unregistered land that which s.70(1)(g) of the Land Registration Act 1925 achieves for registered land".

[3] In *Midland Bank Trust Co. Ltd v. Green, supra,* the son was in occupation of the farm as a tenant. If the title to the land had been registered, his option would have been protected as an overriding interest under L.R.A. 1925, s.70(1)(g): *Webb v. Pollmount Ltd* [1966] Ch. 584; *post,* para. 6–052. For another striking example, see *Lloyds Bank Plc v. Carrick, supra.*

[4] *Lake v. Bayliss* [1974] 1 W.L.R. 1073 (since V is a qualified trustee for P: *post,* para. 12–052).

[5] *Wright v. Dean* [1948] Ch. 686 (unregistered option for tenant to purchase freehold); *Hollington Bros Ltd v. Rhodes* [1951] 2 T.L.R. 691 (unregistered contract to grant underlease). See [1956] C.L.J. 227, n. 57 (H.W.R.W.).

[6] See *ante,* para. 5–108.

[7] Companies Act 1985, s.395; *Capital Finance Co. Ltd v. Stokes* [1969] 1 Ch. 261. Delay in registration will be cured by the registrar's certificate of registration: *Re C.L. Nye Ltd* [1971] Ch. 442. His decision in this regard is not subject to judicial review: Companies Act 1985, s.401; *R. v. Registrar of Companies, ex p. Central Bank of India* [1986] Q.B. 1114. Should the Companies Act 1989, s.93 ever be brought into force, it will replace the Companies Act 1985 ss.395–409 with new provisions concerning the registration of charges. Non-registration of a charge within 21 days would no longer make a charge automatically invalid but only potentially so: see the new ss.399, 400.

C. Differences Between Class C and Class D Land Charges

1. Date of creation. The main difference between Class C and Class D land **5–125**
charges is that a Class C land charge can be registered if it is either created or
transferred after 1925, but a Class D land charge can be registered only if it
is created after 1925.[8]

2. Non-registration. A further difference between Class C and Class D **5–126**
land charges is the effect of non-registration considered above.[9] This, however, is a qualified distinction, since estate contracts (Class C(iv)) created after
1925 fall into the same category for this purpose as Class D.[10]

D. Operation of the Register

1. Searches. The means by which an intending purchaser of land can **5–127**
discover registrable incumbrances is by a search. This may be made in
person,[11] but it is advisable to obtain an official search.[12] An official certificate
of search has three advantages.

(i) It is conclusive in favour of a purchaser or intending purchaser,[13]
provided that his application correctly specified the persons[14] and
the land[15]; it therefore frees him from any liability in respect of
rights which it fails to disclose.[16] The correct name is that which
appears on the title deeds.[17]

(ii) It protects a solicitor or trustee who makes the official search from
liability for any error in the certificate.[18]

(iii) It provides protection against incumbrances registered in the interval between search and completion.[19] If a purchaser completes his
transaction before the expiration of the 15th day after the date
of the certificate[20] (excluding days when the registry is not open to

---

[8] *ibid.*, s.4(6), (7).
[9] *ante*, para. 5–117.
[10] *ibid.*
[11] L.C.A. 1972, s.9. "Anyone who nowadays is foolish enough to search personally deserves what
he gets": *Oak Co-operative B.S. v. Blackburn* [1968] Ch. 730 at 743. *per* Russell L.J.
[12] L.C.A. 1972, s.10, providing also for enquiry by telephone. Inquiry may also be made both by
fax (see Land Charges (Amendment) Rules 1990 (S.I. 1990 No. 485)) and, for those who have
direct access under the Land Registry's Direct Access Service (*post*, para. 6–106), by direct
computer link: see Ruoff & Roper, F-11.
[13] L.C.A. 1972, s.10(4). *cf. Re C.L. Nye Ltd* [1971] Ch. 442.
[14] A trivial error may be fatal: *Oak Co-operative B.S. v. Blackburn* [1968] Ch. 730 (Francis Davis
Blackburn specified by mistake for Francis David Blackburn: purchaser not protected); and see
ante, para. 5–110.
[15] *Du Sautoy v. Simes* [1967] Ch. 1146; the application must give "no reasonable scope for
misunderstanding" in the Registry: see at 1168.
[16] See *Stock v. Wanstead and Woodford B.C.* [1962] 2 Q.B. 469 (local land charges).
[17] *Standard Property Investment Plc v. British Plastics Federation* (1985) 53 P. & C.R. 25.
[18] L.C.A. 1972, s.12.
[19] *ibid.*, s.11(5), (6), replacing L.P.(Am.)A, 1926, s.4.
[20] Defined by Land Charges Rules 1974, r. 17(2).

the public), he is not affected by any entry made after the date of the certificate and before completion, unless it is made pursuant to a priority notice[21] entered on the register on or before the date of the certificate.[22]

5–128 If the official certificate of search mistakenly fails to mention an incumbrance duly registered before the purchaser's search, the owner of the incumbrance is unjustly deprived of his rights over the land, since the certificate is conclusive. Parliament made no provision for compensation, but the court will award damages for negligence against the public authority responsible,[23] which in the case of the central register is the Crown.

A single search is effective for all divisions of all registers.

5–129 **2. Priority notices.** Special provision had to be made to provide for a rapid sequence of transactions, such as the creation of a restrictive covenant followed immediately by the creation of a mortgage before there has been time to register the covenant. Thus, if V is selling land to P, who is raising the purchase-money by means of a loan on mortgage from M, and is to enter into a restrictive covenant with V, the conveyance from V to P creating the restrictive covenant will be simultaneous with the creation of the mortgage by P to M, which enables P to pay V. In such a case, V's restrictive covenant could not be registered before the simultaneous execution of the mortgage, and so it will be void against M, a purchaser for money or money's worth of a legal estate, unless V has availed himself of the machinery of the priority notice. To do this he must give a priority notice to the registrar at least 15 days before the creation of the restrictive covenant, and then, if he registers his charge within 30 days of the entry of the priority notice in the register, the registration dates back to the moment of the creation of the restrictive covenant, *i.e.* to the execution of the conveyance from V to P.[24] Days on which the registry is not open to the public are again excluded in the computation of these periods. The requirement of 15 days' advance notice is to allow the expiry of the 15 days' period of protection given to those who made official searches before the priority notice was lodged.[25] Priority notices

---

[21] *Infra.*
[22] L.C.A. 1972, s.11(5), (6).
[23] *Ministry of Housing and Local Government v. Sharp* [1970] 2 Q.B. 223 (damages awarded against local authority for overlooking entry on register of local land charges); *Coats Patons (Retail) Ltd v. Birmingham Corporation* (1971) 69 L.G.R. 356 (exemption clause ineffective). *cf.* L.C.A. 1972, s.10(6) (enacted after the *Sharp* decision), which provides that in the absence of fraud nobody employed in the registry is liable for any loss suffered by reason of any discrepancy between the particulars stated in the certificate as being those for which the search was being made and those in the request for a search, or in any communication of the result of a search except in a certificate. If the clerk cannot be personally liable for his negligence, presumably his employers cannot be liable vicariously. For local land charges: *post*, para. 5–132.
[24] L.C.A. 1972, s.11; Land Charges Rules 1974 (S.I. 1974 No. 1286), rr. 4, 7, 8.
[25] See *supra*, para. 5–127.

are not, of course, confined to restrictive covenants, but apply to all charges governed by the Land Charges Act 1972.

Where another charge is created simultaneously with a charge which is **5–130** protected by a priority notice, and that other charge is subject to or dependent on the protected charge, the other charge is deemed to have been created after the protected charge.[26] Thus time is notionally allowed for the priority notice to operate.

3. Vacation of registration. The court has a wide jurisdiction, both statu- **5–131** tory[27] and inherent,[28] to order the vacation of any registration, *i.e.* that the entry be removed from the register. The owner of the land affected thus has a means of clearing off an unjustified blot on his title, *e.g.* where an estate contract is registered against him but the contract never existed,[29] or has been terminated.[30] In a proper case this power will be exercised speedily on motion, and with a certain robustness,[31] without awaiting the trial of any action, thereby preventing the entry from improperly inhibiting dealings with the land. Where the registration is only arguably correct, a motion to vacate the entry will usually be dismissed only on terms. The party seeking vacation will normally be required to give an undertaking to pay the landowner damages if at trial it is held that the entry was wrongly made.[32]

Section 3. Local Land Charges Registers

1. The registers. In addition to the registers kept by the Land Charges **5–132** Department of the Land Registry, registers of local land charges are kept in London, by each London borough (or the City of London), and elsewhere by each district council.[33] These registers were introduced by the Land Charges Act 1925 and were reorganised by the Local Land Charges Act 1975, which came into force on August 1, 1977.[34] Their purpose is to enable purchasers to

---

[26] L.C.A. 1972, s.11(4). For an example, see Wolst & C. ii, 102.
[27] L.C.A. 1972, s.1(6). See *Northern Developments (Holdings) Ltd v. U.D.T. Securities Ltd* [1976] 1 W.L.R. 1230 (entries of pending land actions vacated).
[28] *Heywood v. B.D.C. Properties Ltd (No. 2)* [1964] 1 W.L.R. 267; *Calgary and Edmonton Land Co. Ltd v. Dobinson* [1974] Ch. 102; but see *Norman v. Hardy* [1974] 1 W.L.R. 1048, not followed in *Northern Developments (Holdings) Ltd v. U.D.T. Securities Ltd, supra.*
[29] *Heywood v. B.D.C. Properties Ltd (No. 2), supra:* and see *Rawlplug Co. Ltd v. Kamvale Properties Ltd,* (1968) 20 P. & C.R. 32 at 40.
[30] *Hooker v. Wyle* [1974] 1 W.L.R. 235. See also *post,* para. 6–089.
[31] *Rawlplug Co. Ltd v. Kamvale Properties Ltd, supra.*
[32] See *Tucker v. Hutchinson* (1987) 54 P. & C.R. 106 at 112 where the Court of Appeal expressed a preference for *Northern Developments (Holdings) Ltd v. U.D.T. Securities Ltd, supra,* over *Norman v. Hardy, supra.*
[33] Local Land Charges Act 1975, replacing the Land Charges Act 1925, s.15 and other legislation; Local Land Charges Rules 1977 (S.I. 1977 No. 985) amended by the Local Land Charges (Amendment) Rules 1978 (S.I. 1978 No. 1638) and 1989 (S.I. 1989 No. 951). See generally Report of Law Commission on Local Land Charges, 1974 (Law Com. No. 62), on which the Act of 1975 was based; J. E. Boothroyd, *Garner's Local Land Charges* (12th ed.).
[34] S.I. 1977 No. 984.

discover the numerous charges and restrictions which public authorities, both central and local, may impose upon land under statutory powers, for example under the legislation governing public health, housing, highways and town and country planning. These liabilities may be of great importance, particularly since statutory charges may have overriding effect and prevail over pre-existing incumbrances such as mortgages.[35] Local land charges, almost without exception,[36] are governmental in character, as contrasted with ordinary land charges, which are mostly matters of private right.[37]

5–133   The machinery of local registration has an important advantage over that operated centrally at the Land Registry in that the charges are registered against the land itself and not against the owner of it.[38] Thus a series of searches against successive owners is unnecessary, and there are no problems of discovering names. Since these registers are public, a purchaser can and normally does search the registers (which are public) before contract.[39]

In other respects, and subject to certain requirements of the statutory rules, the local authority may keep the register in such form as it thinks fit. In particular, it need not be kept in documentary form, so that it may be kept by computer.[40] The same applies to the index to the register which the local authority must also keep.

It is important to note that the system of local land charges applies as much to registered land as it does to unregistered. Where title to the land is registered, local land charges still have to be registered in local authority registers as they are seldom registrable at the Land Registry.[41]

5–134   **2. Registration of charges.** Before the Act of 1975 came into force there was some overlap between local land charges and ordinary land charges registrable at the central land registry. A local authority which sold land subject to a restrictive covenant might register the covenant either as a local land charge or as an ordinary land charge, or as both, though either would

---

[35] See *Westminster City Council v. Haymarket Publishing Ltd* [1981] 1 W.L.R. 677 (rating surcharge on unoccupied premises, registered as local land charge, held to prevail over prior mortgage). This doctrine does not apply to inland revenue charges: Finance Act 1975, Sched. 4, para. 20(5).

[36] For one exception see *post*, para. 18–170 (notice in lieu of obstruction of light).

[37] Though inland revenue charges are an exception: *ante*, para. 5–102.

[38] Registration must be "by reference to the land affected": Local Land Charges Act 1975, s.5(3); and it must show the situation and extent of the land: Local Land Charges Rules 1977 (S.I. 1977 No. 985), r. 6.

[39] A vendor is in fact obliged to disclose to the purchaser prior to the contract those local land charges wich amount to latent defects in title (as many will): *post*, para. 12–068. The view to the contrary expressed obiter in *Re Forsey and Hollebone's Contract* [1927] 2 Ch. 379 (*post*, para. 12–082) has at last been disapproved: *Rignall Developments Ltd v. Halil* [1988] Ch. 190. A purchaser will not always be able to search the register prior to contract, *e.g.* if he buys at auction. Furthermore, in recent years some local authorities have become dilatory in replying to local searches: *Rignall Developments Ltd v. Halil*, *supra* at 194. There is currently a pilot scheme in Bristol to test computerised searches of local land charges registers.

[40] Local Government (Miscellaneous Provisions) Act 1982, s.34.

[41] Such charges take effect as overriding interests: L.R.A. 1925, s.70(1)(i), *post*, para. 6–065.

suffice by itself.[42] The Act of 1975 has made the two systems mutually exclusive by providing that local land charges are no longer registrable under the Land Charges Act 1972[43]; this is necessary because the effects of non-registration now differ.[44]

The Act of 1975 gives local land charges a wide definition which is then cut down by exclusions.[45] The definition, briefly summarised, comprises any charge acquired by a local authority, water authority or new town development corporation under public health or highways legislation "or any similar charge acquired by a local authority under any other Act", if binding on successive owners of the land affected; positive or negative obligations or restrictions imposed or enforceable by ministers, government departments or local authorities, if binding on successors[46]; and any other matter expressly made a local land charge by statute or regulation. Among the exclusions are covenants or agreements between lessor and lessee; restrictions which bind successive owners because made for the benefit of the authority's land (thus excluding ordinary restrictive covenants, which are registrable as land charges); restrictions in by-laws; conditions in planning permissions granted before August 1977; and forestry dedication covenants.

The great majority of local land charges are expressly declared to be such **5–135** by some statute.[47] Examples are charges recoverable to local authorities for works required for drainage and sewerage works, for repairing or demolishing dangerous buildings, for cleansing filthy premises or for providing dustbins; charges levied for the making up of roads or for coast protection works; numerous items under the town and country planning legislation, including enforcement notices, tree preservation orders, building preservation notices, conditions in planning permissions granted after July 1977,[48] and potential claims for repayment of compensation money paid on refusal of planning permission, in case permission should later be given.[49] A few compulsory purchase orders are expressly made local land charges,[50] but in general compulsory purchase orders do not appear to be registrable. One particular species of local land charge is a "general charge" which may be registered by a local authority which has incurred expenditure which will in due course give

---

[42] L.C.A. 1925, s.21.

[43] s.17.

[44] *Post*, para. 5–136.

[45] ss.1, 2.

[46] The terms of s.1(1)(d) ("any positive obligation affecting land enforceable by a Minister of the Crown, government department or local authority under any covenant or agreement") would seem to include ordinary contracts of purchase or options enforceable by the authority. Positive covenants may be binding on successors under local Acts of Parliament: see Law Com. No. 62 (1974), para. 87.

[47] For a table of these, see Halsb. 26, para. 574.

[48] The Law Commission (*supra*, para. 38) recommended against inclusion of these conditions, since they are fully available in the public registers maintained by planning authorities (under the Town and Country Planning Act 1990, s.69) and regularly inspected by purchasers.

[49] See *Ministry of Housing and Local Government v. Sharp* [1970] 2 Q.B. 223; *ante*, para. 5–128.

[50] *e.g.* under the New Towns Act 1981, s.12.

rise to a local land charge in their favour, thus protecting their claim in advance.[51]

5–136   **3. Non-registration.** Formerly, failure to register a local land charge had an effect similar to that of failure to register an ordinary land charge: the charge was void against a purchaser for money or money's worth of a legal estate in the land affected who completed his purchase before the charge was registered.[52]

The Local Land Charges Act 1975 made a radical change. Failure to register no longer affects the enforceability of the charge, but a purchaser suffering loss thereby is entitled to compensation.[53] The new rule expresses the principle that charges imposed in the public interest ought to be enforced, but that compensation should be paid by public authorities who fail to give warning of them.[54] The right to compensation is conditional on a proper search, whether personal or official, having been made with negative results. Compensation is payable in all cases by the authority maintaining the register, but that authority can recover it from the authority which ought to have registered it, if the loss is due to their default.[55] Compensation is also payable where an official search fails to disclose an existing local land charge, whether registered or not.[56]

5–137   There are facilities for personal and official searches, with due provision for computerised registers, which are generally similar to those of the Land Charges Act 1972, except that priority notices are not available, and searches do not give a period of protection.[57] The court has power to order the cancellation of the registration of a local land charge.[58]

---

[51] L.L.C.A. 1975, s.6.
[52] L.C.A. 1925, s.15(1).
[53] L.L.C.A. 1975, s.10.
[54] There is a statutory duty to register: s.5.
[55] s.10(4), (5).
[56] s.10(1)(b). Contrast land charges: *ante*, para. 5–128.
[57] These procedures proved unsuitable for local land charges and were discontinued: see (1974) Law Com. No. 62, para. 70.
[58] L.L.C.A. 1975, s.5(5).

CHAPTER 6

REGISTRATION OF TITLE

Part 1

HISTORY AND BACKGROUND

1. The nature of land registration. Registration of title is a system of **6–001** conveyancing that is based upon different principles from the traditional unregistered system which it is intended to replace in its entirety. Its principal object is to substitute a single established title, guaranteed by the State, in place of the traditional title which must be separately investigated on every purchase at the purchaser's own risk. In the case of unregistered land, a purchaser must satisfy himself from the abstract of title, the deeds, his requisitions on title, his searches and his inspection of the land that the vendor has power to sell the land and that it is subject to no undisclosed incumbrances. This investigation must be repeated in full by every subsequent purchaser. This wasteful re-examination of the same title is eliminated in the case of registered land. The purchaser can discover from the mere inspection of the register whether the vendor has power to sell the land. The register also discloses many important incumbrances, though certain other incumbrances must be investigated in much the same way as in the case of unregistered land. The complexity of rights in land makes it impossible for the transfer of registered land to be as simple as the transfer of shares in a company, but the present system of registration of title attempts to follow the analogy so far as is practicable.[1] Conveyancing accordingly becomes easier, quicker and cheaper. Registration of title is a fundamental departure from the traditional system by which the title is deduced historically. Instead the register provides a statement of the title as it stands at any given time. Where the register has been computerised (as is now almost always the case),[2] it is not in fact possible to discern from the register who the previous owners of the land were.[3]

---

[1] On registration of title, see generally Ruoff & Roper. The analogy with transfers of stock was suggested in one of the earliest proposals for title registration, made in 1844 by a solicitor, Robert Wilson: see J. S. Anderson, *Lawyers and the Making of English Land Law 1832–1940*, pp. 62–68.

[2] *Post*, para. 6–011.

[3] It was not always possible to trace the record of title even when the register was kept in materialised form, because the registrar could (and did) issue new editions of the register from time to time, so that the earlier transactions were removed: see L.R.R. 1925, r. 4. Where the register is computerised, the registrar does in fact keep a historical record of title, though it is

Registration of title is a great improvement on the old-fashioned system of unregistered conveyancing, and is destined to supplant it in England as it has done in many other countries.[4] As has already been explained, the whole of England and Wales has been subject to compulsory registration since December 1, 1990.[5]

6–002 **2. Open register.**[6] Prior to December 3, 1990, the land register (unlike the land charges register) was not open to public inspection,[7] though an Index Map and a Parcels Index could (and still can) be searched by the public.[8] From these indexes it is possible to determine whether any particular parcel of land has been registered, but no details of the registration are given. The secrecy of the land registration system was much criticised, and the Law Commission recommended that the register should be open to public inspection.[9] That recommendation was implemented by the Land Registration Act 1988. Since December 3, 1990 (when the Act came into force[10]), any person may, subject to prescribed conditions[11] and on payment of a fee, inspect and make copies of and extracts from both entries on the register and documents referred to in the register which are in the custody of the registrar (other than leases or charges or copies of leases or charges).[12] Other documents in the custody of the registrar (*i.e.* leases and charges and documents not referred to on the register) may be inspected as of right in certain prescribed cases,[13] and at his discretion in all other instances.[14]

The existence of the open register has important implications of which two may be mentioned here. First, it provides a greater security of title in many conveyancing transactions. Thus under a contract to grant a lease or sub-lease, the purchaser has no right to call for the title to the freehold or to the superior lease.[15] If the superior title is registered, however, the purchaser can now inspect it and so discover any incumbrances which may affect the property.

---

not part of the register and will not be disclosed except at the registrar's discretion: see L.R.A. 1925, s.112(2). See *post*, para. 6–002.

[4] For comparative treatment, see S. Rowton Simpson, *Land Law and Registration* (1976); Ruoff & Roper, 2–02–2–05.

[5] *Ante*, para. 5–001; S.I. 1989 No. 1347.

[6] See Ruoff & Roper, 3–28, 30–21.

[7] In general no person could inspect the register without the authority of the registered proprietor: see the previous edition of this work at p. 195.

[8] L.R.R. rr. 8, 10; Ruoff & Roper, 4–06, 4–07, 12–43.

[9] (1986) Law Com. No. 148.

[10] By S.I. 1990 No. 1359.

[11] Land Registration (Open Register) Rules 1991 (S.I. 1992 No. 122) (as amended).

[12] L.R.A. 1925, s.112(1) (substituted by L.R.A. 1988). "Documents" include things kept otherwise than in documentary form (such as material held on computer): L.R.A. 1925, s.112(3) (substituted by L.R.A. 1988). Documents which may be inspected must however be made available for inspection in a visible and legible form: *ibid* s.113A (inserted by A.J.A. 1982, s.66(2)).

[13] L.R.A. 1925, s.112(2)(a) (substituted by L.R.A. 1988). The special cases concern criminal proceedings, receivership and insolvency: Land Registration (Open Register) Rules 1991, r. 6(1); Ruoff & Roper, 30–25.

[14] L.R.A. 1925, s.112(2)(b) (substituted by L.R.A. 1988).

[15] L.P.A. 1925, s.44(2), (3); *post*, para. 14–295.

Secondly, the register provides the basis of an authoritative public land record which may in time provide the necessary information to develop a national land information system.[16]

3. Development. Registration of title has a long history.[17] The first terri- **6–003**
tory in the British Empire to adopt it was South Australia, where it was introduced by Sir Robert Torrens in 1858.[18] The "Torrens system" has been followed in many other countries, but it differs materially from the system eventually adopted in England. Torrens' objective was to "escape from the grievous yoke of the English property law"[19] by making radical changes in it. The English policy, on the other hand, was to simplify the machinery of conveyancing without altering the substantive rules of law. Neither of these policies was wholly successful, but the two systems remained distinct.[20]

The first English measures were the Land Registry Act 1862 and the Land Transfer Act 1875. These provided for voluntary registration of title, but few titles were registered until the Land Transfer Act 1897 made registration of title compulsory on dealings with land in the County of London. The present Acts are the Land Registration Acts 1925, 1936, 1986, 1988 and 1997, and the Land Registration and Land Charges Act 1971.[21] These are supplemented by the Land Registration Rules 1925, as amended, and numerous other statutory rules.[22]

4. Character. Although the aim is simplicity, the scheme of the Land **6–004**
Registration Act 1925 is complicated and obscure.[23] First, its primary policy is unclear. The traditional view is that it is supposed to improve the machinery of conveyancing and not to change the substantive law.[24] In fact it has made

---

[16] See *Completing The Land Register in England & Wales* (Land Registry Consultation Paper, 1992), Pt II.

[17] *Ante*, para. 4–067. For a full account, see J. S. Anderson, *Lawyers and the Making of English Land Law 1832–1940.* See too Ruoff & Roper, Chapter 1; A. W. B. Simpson, *A History of the Land Law* (2nd ed.), pp. 280–283. Registration of title was proposed as long ago as 1652: Ruoff & Roper, 6–02.

[18] S. Rowton Simpson, *Land Law and Registration*, p. 68.

[19] Torrens, *South Australian Registration of Title* (1859), p. 44.

[20] For a comparison of them, see Ruoff & Roper, 2–04. Contrasting features of the Torrens system are that boundaries are officially surveyed ("guaranteed boundaries"), rectification and indemnity are less freely available, there are no overriding interests, and the Torrens caveat is more efficient than the English caution.

[21] L.R.A. 1966, which restricted the right to apply for first registration of title in non-compulsory registration areas, was repealed after the whole of England and Wales became subject to compulsory registration.

[22] For the extensive powers conferred on the Lord Chancellor to make rules, see L.R.A. 1925, s.144(1). Any rules made under that section have the same force as if enacted in the Act: *ibid.*, s.144(2).

[23] "The Act has not had a good press": *Central London Commercial Estates Ltd v. Kato Kagaku Co. Ltd* [1998] 4 All E.R. 948 at 953, *per* Sedley J.

[24] J. S. Stewart-Wallace, *Principles of Land Registration*, p. 33; Ruoff & Roper, 2–06; (1983) Law Com. No. 125, para. 1.5; (1987) Law Com. No. 158, para. 1.2. See too *City of London B.S. v. Flegg* [1988] A.C. 54 at 84; *Abbey National B.S. v. Cann* [1991] 1 A.C. 56 at 77.

striking changes in the rights of owners, purchasers and incumbrancers, and its system of priorities is radically different.[25] It abandons the fundamental principle that no one can pass a better title than he has (*nemo dat quod non habet*), and substitutes for it, though only by implication, the so-called principle of indefeasibility of the registered title. There is a growing recognition that the registered and unregistered systems are not the same and that no good purpose is served by attempting to keep them in step.[26] It seems likely that in future the registered system will be developed in ways that exploit its particular advantages.

Secondly, on the technical plane, the principles of the legislation are sometimes equally obscure, its definitions are often confusing, and by no means all the rules are meritorious. It can produce "difficulties and pitfalls in the way of comparatively simple transactions which would not have arisen with unregistered land".[27]

6–005   It is only in the last quarter of a century that the legislation has received much judicial interpretation. Even with increasing judicial guidance, however, much still depends upon the practice of the Land Registry.[28] The Registry has to handle great numbers of transactions and enquiries[29] and at the same time must provide a prompt and reliable service to the public. The system is therefore a branch of public administration as well as of property law.[30] In view of the deficiencies of the Act, it is not surprising that the courts have on occasions held that the Registry has not interpreted its provisions correctly.[31] Everyday conveyancing requires clear and rapid guidance, even where the law lacks clarity. The Registry has succeeded in constructing a smooth-running machine out of opaque legislation of exceptionally low quality which is in need of a thorough overhaul.[32] Following an extensive review by HM Land Registry and the Law Commission, there is a prospect that such an overhaul will happen in the near future, prompted by the need for legislation to introduce electronic conveyancing.[33]

---

[25] See *post*, para. 6–105. Other salient differences are noted *post*, paras 6–047 (rights of persons in occupation); 6–116 (right of squatter who bars tenant); and 6–132 (right to compensation for defeated claimant). See too (1977) 41 Conv. (N.S.) 405 (J. G. Riddall).

[26] See (1987) Law Com. No. 158, para. 2.5; (1998) Law Com. No. 254, para. 1.5.

[27] *Re White Rose Cottage* [1965] Ch. 940 at 952, *per* Harman L.J.

[28] For this, Ruoff & Roper, the work of three Land Registrars, is particularly authoritative. But Registry practice does not make law: *Strand Securities Ltd v. Caswell* [1965] Ch. 958 at 977.

[29] In 1997–98, it received over 12 million applications and enquiries: see HM Land Registry, *Annual Report and Accounts* 1997–98.

[30] For the administration of the Land Registry, see Ruoff & Roper, 1–13. The Chief Land Registrar is no longer required to be (and is not in fact) a barrister or solicitor of 10 years' standing: Courts and Legal Services Act 1990, s.125(7); Sched. 20, repealing A.J.A. 1956, s.53.

[31] See *Strand Securities Ltd v. Caswell, supra*, at 977, 978; *cf.* Ruoff & Roper, 3–30(4); *Barclays Bank Ltd v. Taylor* [1973] Ch. 63 at 73.

[32] See *Clark v. Chief Land Registrar* [1994] Ch. 370 at 382; *Central London Commercial Estates Ltd v. Kato Kagaku Co. Ltd* [1998] 4 All E.R. 948 at 953.

[33] See (1998) Law Com. No. 254; and *post*, para. 6–101.

Registration of title is in essentials a good system that is burdened with much more difficulty and technicality than seems necessary.[34] Its great merits are that it eliminates repetitive and unproductive work in conveyancing, and provides financial compensation in cases where otherwise an innocent party would suffer loss.

Part 2

PRINCIPLES OF REGISTRATION

1. Classification of rights. Three classes of rights in registered land must be distinguished.   **6–006**

(a) Registered interests. These are rights in respect of which a title has been granted by the registrar. It is fundamental that the only estates in respect of which a proprietor can be registered are legal estates.[35] Thus a legal fee simple absolute in possession and (subject to certain significant exceptions[36]) a legal term of years absolute are registrable interests. The Crown cannot register any land which it holds in absolute ownership,[37] because it has no estate in the land.[38] No equitable estate can be registered with its own title,[39] and all references to trusts are, so far as is possible, excluded from the register.[40]   **6–007**

(b) Overriding interests. These are rights which do not appear on the register, but which will nonetheless bind any purchaser.[41] They include rights acquired or in the course of being acquired under the Limitation Act 1980, the rights of persons in actual occupation of land, and leases of 21 years or less.   **6–008**

(c) Minor interests. These are rights which will bind a purchaser only if protected by some entry on the register. They include all equitable rights and interests (including both interests under trusts and rights over land such as   **6–009**

---

[34] The Law Commission has published six reports on Land Registration: Law Com. Nos 125 (1983: see L.R.A. 1986), 148 (1985: see L.R.A. 1988); 158 (1987), 173 (1988), 235 (1995: see L.R.A. 1997) and 254 (1998). The last two of these were published jointly with HM Land Registry. A seventh report, following on Law Com. No. 254 and consisting of a draft Land Registration Bill (which is intended to replace the existing Land Registration Acts *in toto*), is likely to be published in the autumn of 1999.

[35] L.R.A. 1925, s.2.

[36] *Post*, para 6–015.

[37] See *ante*, para. 2–001. This will be the case where the land is part of the ancient estates of the Crown that it has never granted away, or has escheated to the Crown. For escheat, see *ante*, para. 2–050.

[38] *Scmlla Properties Ltd v. Gesso Properties (B.V.I.) Ltd* [1995] B.C.C. 793 at 798. See *ante*, para. 2–050.

[39] This is implicit: see L.R.A. 1925, ss 4(b); 8(1)(b); Ruoff & Roper, 9–12.

[40] L.R.A. 1925, s.74.

[41] *ibid.*, s.3(xiv).

restrictive covenants) and many legal ones, such as leases over 21 years[42] or easements which have been expressly granted.

The categories of overriding interests and minor interests are not mutually exclusive. A right which is capable of registration as a minor interest but which is not registered, may nonetheless take effect as an overriding interest in certain circumstances.[43]

Before dealing with these rights in detail, it should be made clear that if the title to land is registered, there is no question of registration in the Land Charges Registry, for entries on the Land Register take the place of this. However, entries must still be made in local land charges registers.[44] So far as possible, dealings with registered land must be carried out as provided by the Act and the rules, and duly registered.[45] The prescribed forms, adapted as necessary, must be used for such dealings.[46]

2. The register. The register itself is divided into three parts.[47]

6–010   *(a) The property register.* This describes the land and the estate for which it is held, refers to a map or plan showing the land, and contains notes of interests held for the benefit of the land, such as easements and restrictive covenants of which the registered land is the dominant tenement.[48] Except where the register notes the boundaries shown on the map or plan as being "fixed", they are "general boundaries" only, so that the exact line of the boundary is left undetermined.[49] Fixing boundaries involves serving notice on neighbours and determining any disputes judicially, a process that is so contentious and expensive that it is rarely used.[50]

6–011   *(b) The proprietorship register.* This states the nature of the title (*i.e.* whether it is absolute, good leasehold, qualified or possessory[51]), states the name, address and description of the registered proprietor, and sets out any cautions, inhibitions and restrictions[52] which affect his right to deal with the land.[53]

---

[42] Although such leases will be separately registered with their own title, they should be noted on the register of the superior title: *post*, para. 6–080.

[43] *Post*, paras 6–036 *et seq.*

[44] L.R.A. 1925, ss.59, 110(7); and see *ibid.*, s.50(1) (restrictive covenants).

[45] L.R.A. 1925, ss.39, 109.

[46] L.R.R. 1925, rr. 74, 75. Provision is made for the forms to be in the Welsh language: *ibid.*, r. 74A. For the forms see the Schedules to the Rules.

[47] L.R.R. 1925, r. 2.

[48] *ibid.*, r. 3.

[49] See *ibid.*, rr. 276–278; *Lee v. Barrey* [1957] Ch. 251; (1983) Law Com. No. 125, Pt II; Ruoff & Roper, 4–17–4–21.

[50] Only nine cases were recorded between 1937 and 1972: (1972) Law Commission W.P. No. 45, para. 34. See Ruoff & Roper, 4–22.

[51] See *post*, paras 6–022–6–026.

[52] See *post*, paras 6–083 *et seq.*

[53] L.R.R. 1925, r. 6.

(c) The charges register. This contains entries relating to rights adverse to the land, such as mortgages or restrictive covenants, neighbours' easements over the land, and in general all notices[54] protecting rights over the land.[55]

The register is not immutable. Although it is a fundamental principle of title registration that the proprietor's title is normally indefeasible, the Act makes provision for the rectification of the register in certain circumstances.[56] As a corollary, it is also provided that a person who suffers loss by reason of the rectification or non-rectification of the register is usually entitled to an indemnity from the Consolidated Fund.[57]

The register is kept at the Land Registry in London[58] and in 22 District Registries.[59] Most of the register[60] has now been computerised, replacing the original card index system.[61] A copy of the three parts of the register is included in the land certificate which is issued to every registered proprietor as his document of title.[62] The old title deeds, stamped with a notice of registration,[63] are usually returned when the title is first registered. However the registered proprietor's proof of title is the register itself and not the land certificate, which may be out of date if entries have been made on the register since the certificate was last in the registry.[64]

2. The duties and powers of the Chief Land Registrar. It is the statutory duty of the Chief Land Registrar to keep a register of title.[65] He also has the responsibility for the conduct of the whole business of registration under the Land Registration Act 1925.[66] Both that Act[67] and the Land Registration Rules 1925[68] confer judicial and quasi-judicial powers on him,[69] though these have now been delegated to the Solicitor to HM Land Registry.[70] Any person aggrieved by an order or decision of the registrar may appeal to the Chancery

6–012

---

[54] *Post*, para. 6–079.

[55] L.R.R. 1925, r. 7.

[56] *Post*, para. 6–119.

[57] *Post*, para. 6–132.

[58] See L.R.A. 1925, s.126(1). The headquarters are in Lincoln's Inn Fields. The Land Registry has been a self-financing Executive Agency since July 2, 1990: Ruoff & Roper, 1–13.

[59] S.I. 1998 No. 140 (defining the areas). For the creation and powers of District Registries, see L.R.A. 1925, ss.132–134.

[60] Some 92% of all registered titles by April 1998: See HM Land Registry, *Annual Report and Accounts 1997–98.*

[61] Since 1993 a computerised system has been operating in all District Registries: Ruoff & Roper, 1–11. The register is no longer required to be kept in documentary form: L.R.A. 1925, s.1(2) (substituted by A.J.A. 1982, s.66).

[62] See L.R.A. 1925, s.63; L.R.R. 1925, r. 261; Sched 2, Form 78; Ruoff & Roper, 3–16.

[63] See L.R.A. 1925, s.16.

[64] See *Strand Securities Ltd v. Caswell* [1965] Ch. 958.

[65] L.R.A. 1925, s.1(1).

[66] *ibid.*, s.127.

[67] ss.13, 15, 17, 82, 83(5).

[68] rr. 131, 158, 220, 230(2), 298, 321.

[69] See Ruoff & Roper, Chap 41.

[70] This post was created in 1990 when the requirement that the Chief Land Registrar should be a lawyer was abrogated (*ante*, para. 6–005, n. 30): see L.R.A. 1925, s.126(6A) (inserted by the Courts and Legal Services Act 1990, s.135(2); Sched. 17, para. 2); S.I. 1997 No. 913; Ruoff & Roper, 1–15.

Division of the High Court.[71] However this right is confined to matters heard and determined by the registrar.[72] No appeal lies against decisions of a purely administrative character,[73] though they may be subject to judicial review.[74]

4. Compulsory and voluntary registration

6–013   *(a) Background.* Whether or not a transfer of land must be completed by registration now depends upon the nature of the transaction. There was formerly a further factor. Compulsory registration applied only where the land was in an area declared to be one of compulsory registration by Order in Council.[75] The designation of areas of compulsory registration proceeded very slowly prior to 1965, but accelerated rapidly thereafter.[76] The process was completed on December 1, 1990[77]: since that date the whole of England and Wales has been subject to compulsory registration.

6–014   *(b) Compulsory registration.* The transactions involving unregistered land that require registration have been considerably extended by the Land Registration Act 1997[78] with effect from April 1, 1998.[79] This, together with fee incentives to encourage voluntary first registration,[80] are intended to expedite the speed at which unregistered land is brought onto the register.

6–015   (1) DISPOSITIONS REQUIRING REGISTRATION. The dispositions of unregistered land that are required to be registered fall into three categories.[81]

> (a)   Certain conveyances, grants and assignments, whether made for valuable or other consideration,[82] by way of gift,[83] or pursuant to an order of the court,[84] namely—

---

[71] L.R.R. 1925, r. 299; Ruoff & Roper, 41–11.

[72] *i.e.* those matters listed in L.R.R. 1925, r. 298: *Quigly v. Chief Land Registrar* [1993] 1 W.L.R. 1435.

[73] *e.g.* whether to allow inspection of documents that the Registrar is not required to produce: L.R.A. 1925, s.112(2)(b); *ante*, para. 6–002.

[74] *Quigly v. Chief Land Registrar, supra,* at 1438, 1439. See too *Dennis v. Malcolm* [1934] Ch. 244 at 252, 253.

[75] L.R.A. 1925, s.120(1) (now repealed).

[76] See Ruoff & Roper, 1–06–1–08.

[77] S.I. 1989 No. 1347.

[78] Implementing the recommendations in (1995) Law Com. No. 235, published jointly by HM Land Registry and the Law Commission. The opportunity was taken to clarify and modernise the legislation governing first registrations.

[79] See L.R.A. 1997, s.1, substituting and inserting respectively L.R.A. 1925, ss.123, 123A. The new triggers were brought into force by S.I. 1997 No. 3036.

[80] See L.R.A. 1925, s.145(3), (3A) (substituted by L.R.A. 1997, s.3).

[81] See Ruoff & Roper, 11–03.

[82] This includes a conveyance of property (i) for a nominal consideration; and (ii) with a negative value (such as an assignment of a lease for what is sometimes called a "reverse premium"): L.R.A. 1925, s.123(6).

[83] It is thought that "gift" will include a conveyance: (i) to trustees to hold on trust (other than as nominees for the transferee); and (ii) by trustees to a beneficiary (other than the settlor or his estate) who becomes absolutely entitled to it under the trust. By contrast, where trustees hold unregistered land as nominees and transfer the land to the person absolutely entitled to it, there is no element of gift and the transfer is not required to be registered.

[84] See L.R.A. 1925, s.123(1), (6).

(i) a conveyance of the freehold estate;

(ii) a grant of a term of years absolute of more than 21 years from the date of the grant; and

(iii) an assignment on sale of leasehold land having more than 21 years to run from the date of delivery of the assignment.[85]

This considerably extends the range of dispositions subject to compulsory registration. Prior to April 1998, it included (ii) above, but was confined to conveyances and assignments of leases *on sale* only.

(b) Any disposition that is made by way of an assent[86] (including a vesting assent[87]) or a vesting deed[88] of a freehold estate of a lease having more than 21 years to run on the date of the disposition.[89] This means that where such estates pass on death, whether of an absolute owner or of a tenant for life under the Settled Land Act 1925, the title will be subject to compulsory registration. The same will be the case where the interest of a tenant for life under a strict settlement terminates other than on his death.

(c) In certain cases where there is a legal mortgage of a freehold estate or of a lease having more than 21 years to run on the date of the mortgage, there is a requirement to register the estate which is mortgaged. This will be the case where the mortgage takes effect as a mortgage to be protected by a deposit of documents of title and has priority ahead of any other mortgages (if any) affecting the property.[90] Thus if the owner of an unregistered freehold executes a first legal mortgage over the property, the requirement of compulsory registration applies to the freehold title.

There is a power, exercisable by statutory instrument, by which the Lord Chancellor may add to the dispositions that trigger compulsory registration.[91] It should be noted that this power is confined to dispositions. It could not be employed to introduce compulsory registration of title in other circumstances.

---

[85] For certain exceptional cases where the assignment of a lease having 21 years or less to run must be completed by registration, see H.A. 1985, s.154; and s.171G and Sched. 9A (inserted by the Housing and Planning Act 1986, s.8; Sched. 2); Ruoff & Roper, 11–04.

[86] For assents, see *post*, para. 11–126.

[87] For vesting assents, see L.R.A. 1925, s.3(xxvi); S.L.A. 1925, s.117(1)(xxxi); *post*, para. 8–021.

[88] For vesting deeds, see L.R.A. 1925, s.3(xxvi); S.L.A. 1925, s.117(1)(xxxi); *post*, para. 8–020.

[89] L.R.A. 1925, s.123(1)(d).

[90] *ibid.*, s.123(2).

[91] L.R.A. 1925, s.123(4), (5).

6–016 (2) DISPOSITIONS THAT ARE NOT REQUIRED TO BE REGISTERED.[92] The dispositions of unregistered land that do not fall within the requirement of compulsory registration[93] include the following—

(i) a transfer of land to a nominee or by that nominee to the transferor: the transfer is made neither as a gift nor for any consideration;

(ii) a conveyance which gives effect to the appointment of a new trustee of a trust of land[94];

(iii) the surrender of a lease which merges in the immediate reversion[95];

(iv) the grant of an incorporeal hereditament, such as an easement, a *profit à prendre* or a manor[96];

(v) a conveyance of mines and minerals apart from the surface[97];

(vi) a conveyance of corporeal hereditaments which are part of a manor and are included in the sale of the manor as such[98]; and

(vii) a disposition of land within an area designated as souvenir land.[99]

All or any of these exceptions could be removed through the exercise of the power to extend the triggers for compulsory registration explained above.[1]

6–017 (3) LEASEHOLDS. Prior to 1987 the provisions governing leases were needlessly complex.[2] They have however been much more simplified as regards any term of years granted or assigned after January 1, 1987.[3] As has been explained above, the grant or assignment of a lease which has more than 21

---

[92] See Ruoff & Roper, 11–05, 11–06.
[93] Including those that are expressly excluded from it by statute.
[94] See T.A. 1925, s.40; *post*, para. 10–070.
[95] L.R.A. 1925, s.123(6)(c).
[96] *ibid.* s.123(3)(a). A manor may be registered with its own title voluntarily, but easements and profits cannot: see *post*, para. 6–035.
[97] L.R.A. 1925, s.123(3)(b).
[98] *ibid.*, s.123(3)(c). The reason for this exception appears to be that as the manor (meaning the incorporeal lordship of the manor) is itself not subject to compulsory registration, nor should a sale of the lands of the manor together with it.
[99] The Registrar has power to exclude areas from compulsory registration where numerous small plots are sold as "souvenir land": L.R. & L.C.A. 1971, s.4; S.I. 1972 No. 985. In practice these provisions are seldom used.
[1] For a recommendation that (vi) should be abrogated, see (1998) Law Com. No. 254, para. 3.23.
[2] See the previous edition of this work at pp. 199, 200.
[3] See L.R.A. 1986, s.2.

years to run must be completed by registration.[4] This is so, even though the lease contains a prohibition or restriction on any dealings with it,[5] provided that such prohibition is protected by an entry on the register.[6] Once a lease has been registered, any subsequent assignment of it must be completed by registration whether or not the unexpired term then exceeds 21 years.[7]

(4) THE EFFECT OF NON-REGISTRATION.[8] Registration is "compulsory" only **6–018** in the sense that there is a statutory sanction that applies in cases of non-registration. This sanction was recast by the Land Registration Act 1997[9] to make good the shortcomings of the previous legislation.[10] In the case of a conveyance, grant, assignment, assent, vesting or vesting deed which is subject to the requirement of compulsory registration,[11] the person entitled to the legal estate that has been transferred or created by the disposition[12] must apply to be registered as first proprietor of the estate within the period specified.[13] Where it is a legal mortgage that triggers the requirement of compulsory registration,[14] it is not the mortgagee[15] but the owner of the estate mortgaged[16] who must apply to be registered within the period specified.[17] That period is, in either case, two months beginning with the date of the disposition. However, the registrar has power to extend the period if he is satisfied that there is a good reason for doing so, in which case it is the extended period which applies.[18] During the two-month or other extended period, the disposition is effective according to its terms to transfer or grant a legal estate or to create a legal mortgage.[19] Once the period has elapsed and the title has not been registered, the disposition becomes void as regards the transfer or creation of a legal estate or mortgage. In the case of a transfer of the freehold or an assignment of a lease, the legal estate reverts to the

---

[4] The lease may be registered if it had more than 21 years to run at the time of the grant or assignment, even though at the time of registration the unexpired term was 21 years or less, provided that application for registration is made within the period allowed by L.R.A. 1925, s.123A (*infra*), or any authorised extension of that period: L.R.A. 1925, s.8(1A) (substituted by L.R.A. 1997, s.4(1)): see Ruoff & Roper, 9–07.

[5] Prior to 1987 such leases could not be registered: Ruoff & Roper, 9–08.

[6] L.R.A. 1925, s.8(2) (substituted by L.R.A. 1986, s.3(1)). For the appropriate form of notice that should be entered on the charges register in such cases, see L.R.R. 1925, r. 45 (substituted by L.R.R. 1986, r. 3).

[7] L.R.A. 1925, s.22(1).

[8] See Ruoff & Roper, 11–08–11.11.

[9] s.1, inserting a new L.R.A. 1925, s.123A.

[10] Which had been much criticised: see, *e.g.* (1968) 32 Conv. (N.S.) 391 (D. G. Barnsley).

[11] Under L.R.A. 1925, s.123(1); *ante*, para 6–015.

[12] Or his successor in title or assign.

[13] L.R.A. 1925, s.123A(2). If he is not a person in a fiduciary position, he may have his nominee registered as proprietor instead: *ibid.*

[14] Under L.R.A. 1925, s.123(2); *ante*, para. 6–015.

[15] The registrar will, however, accept an application for registration from the mortgagee: see L.R.A. 1925, s.123A(10)(b); L.R.R. 1925, r. 73(1). See Ruoff & Roper, 11–11.

[16] Or his successor in title or assign.

[17] L.R.A. 1925, s.123A(2). Again, if he is not a person in a fiduciary position, he may have his nominee registered as proprietor instead: *ibid.*

[18] L.R.A. 1925, s.123A(3). In practice, such extensions are quite common.

[19] L.R.A. 1925, s.123A(4).

transferor who then holds it on a bare trust for the transferee.[20] In the case of a grant of a lease or the creation of a mortgage, the disposition takes effect as if it were a contract to grant the estate or mortgage for valuable consideration.[21] In either case, the interest of the transferee, grantee or mortgagee could be at risk if there were a disposition of the legal estate. This is particularly so in the case of a mortgage, because the mortgagee is unlikely to be in possession and his notional estate contract is registerable as a land charge.[22] If it is not registered,[23] it will not bind a purchaser of the legal estate for money or money's worth.[24]

6–019 Even if the disposition has become void for non-registration in the manner explained above, the registrar may grant an extension of the period in which the application can be made.[25] On granting such an extension, the disposition is effective once again to transfer or grant a legal estate or to create a legal mortgage for the duration of the extended period.[26] The legal estate or interest may in this way "oscillate" between the parties to the disposition.[27] In the rare cases in which registration is not made within the specified period and no extension is granted, the disposition has to be replicated at the expense of the transferee, grantee or mortgagor who failed to apply to be registered.[28] Any such replicated disposition is itself subject to the requirement of compulsory registration and an application must be made to register it within two months or such extended period as the registrar may order.[29]

For the statutory sanctions to apply, there must be a "total failure" to apply for registration of a transaction.[30] There is no such failure merely because the application contains a misdescription of the land or omits part of it from the filed plan.[31]

6–020 (5) VOLUNTARY REGISTRATION. Except where registration is prohibited (*e.g.* in the case of a lease for 21 years or less), the owner of a legal estate may always apply for his title to be registered, whether or not any transaction is being effected.[32] There were formerly restrictions on voluntary registration in areas which were not subject to compulsory registration,[33] but these have been repealed because the whole country is included within the compulsory area.

---

[20] *ibid.*, s.123A(5)(a).
[21] *ibid.*, s.123A(5)(b). This will be so even though (i) it was *not* made for valuable consideration; or (ii) it did not satisfy the formal requirements for such a contract: *ibid.* For the formal requirements for a contract for the sale or other disposition of an interest in land, see *post*, para. 12–018.
[22] Under L.C.A. 1972, s.2(4)(iv); *ante*, para. 5–099.
[23] It is unlikely to be.
[24] L.C.A. 1972, s.4(6); *ante*, para. 5–117.
[25] This situation is not uncommon.
[26] L.R.A. 1925, s.123A(6).
[27] For the effect of such oscillations on the transmission of leasehold covenants, see Ruoff & Roper, 11–10.
[28] L.R.A. 1925, s.123A(8), (9).
[29] *ibid.*, s.123A(7).
[30] *Proctor v. Kidman* (1985) 51 P. & C.R. 67 at 72, *per* Croom-Johnson L.J.
[31] *ibid.*
[32] L.R.A. 1925, ss.4, 8.
[33] L.R.A. 1966, s.1(2).

Since April 1, 1999, there are fee incentives to encourage voluntary first registration.[34]

5. Titles. There are four titles with which an applicant for registration may be registered.   **6–021**

(a) Absolute. In the case of freeholds, this vests in the first registered proprietor the fee simple in possession together with the benefit of all the rights, privileges and appurtenances that go with the land,[35] subject only—   **6–022**

    (i) to entries on the register, so far as they are valid[36];

    (ii) to overriding interests, except so far as the register states that the land is free from them;

    (iii) as between himself and those entitled to minor interests, to minor interests of which he has notice, if he is not entitled to the land for his own benefit[37];

but "free from all other estates and interests whatsoever".[38] In principle, first registration should therefore vest both the legal and equitable fee simple in the proprietor because only in this way can effect be given to the words of the statute.[39]

In the case of leaseholds, registration with an absolute title vests the leasehold in the first registered proprietor[40] subject to the rights set out above and subject also—

    (iv) to all the implied and express covenants, obligations and liabilities incident to the leasehold.

An absolute title in this case of leaseholds guarantees not only that the registered proprietor is the owner of the lease but also that the lease was validly granted. Any restrictive covenants, easements and other incumbrances (except mortgages or charges) which affect the superior title will be registered against the leasehold title.[41] In sharp contrast to the position in unregistered   **6–023**

---

[34] See S.I. 1998 No. 3199, made pursuant to L.R.A. 1925, s.145(3), (3A) (substituted by L.R.A. 1925, s.3).

[35] L.R.A. 1925, s.5, discussed at (1974) 38 Conv. (N.S.) 236 (S.N.L. Palk).

[36] *Kitney v. M.E.P.C. Ltd* [1977] 1 W.L.R. 981.

[37] Thus trustees of land who are registered as proprietors will still hold subject to the claims of the beneficiaries.

[38] L.R.A. 1925, s.5; *post,* para. 6–029.

[39] In *Epps v. Esso Petroleum Co. Ltd* [1973] 1 W.L.R. 1071, 1075, 1077, 1078, Templeman J. appears to have assumed that where A was mistakenly registered as first proprietor of B's land, A held it on a bare trust for B. However this seems unsound: see (1974) 38 Conv. (N.S.) 236 at 250 (S.N.L. Palk).

[40] L.R.A. 1925, s.9, which in terms merely vests "the possession of the leasehold interest": but the meaning appears to be stated as in the text.

[41] Ruoff & Roper, 5–09.

land,[42] any subsequent assignee of the lease can therefore be confident that he will not find himself bound by an undisclosed incumbrance, even if the superior title (or some part of it) is not registered.[43] A leasehold will be registered with absolute title only if the superior title is itself registered, or if the tenant, with the consent and assistance of the lessor, is able to deduce that superior title.[44]

6–024   *(b) Qualified.* In the case of freeholds, this has the same effect as an absolute title except that the property is held subject to any estate, right or interest arising before a specified date, or under a specified instrument, or otherwise specified in the register.[45] This title is granted when an application has been made for an absolute title but the registrar has been unable to grant it. A qualified title to leaseholds has the same effect as an absolute or good leasehold title, as the case may be, except for the specified defect.[46]

6–025   *(c) Possessory.* In the case of either freeholds or leaseholds, first registration with possessory title has the same effect as registration with an absolute title, except that the title is subject to all estates, rights and interests adverse to the first registered proprietor, and subsisting or capable of arising at the time of first registration.[47] In other words, the title is guaranteed as far as dealings after the date of registration are concerned. However, no guarantee is given as to the title prior to first registration, which must accordingly be investigated by a purchaser in the same way as if the land were not registered.

6–026   *(d) Good leasehold.* This is applicable only to leaseholds. It is the same as an absolute title, except that registration does not "affect or prejudice the enforcement of any estate, right or interest affecting or in derogation of the title of the lessor to grant the lease".[48] In other words, the lessor's right to grant the lease is not guaranteed. Thus, should it appear that the lessor was never entitled to grant the lease, the lessee is protected if he has an absolute title, but unprotected if he has a good leasehold title. Since a lessee cannot investigate the freehold title unless he stipulates for this in his contract,[49] he cannot give the registrar evidence of the freehold title (unless it is registered), and so he can apply only for a good leasehold. In practice, contractual stipulations providing for the investigation of the superior title are increasingly common.[50]

---

[42] *Ante, post,* para. 5–112; *post,* para. 14–296.
[43] If the superior title is registered, any intending assignee may now inspect the register of that title as of right: L.R.A. 1925, s.112(1); *ante,* para. 6–002.
[44] Ruoff & Roper, 5–09.
[45] L.R.A. 1925, s.7.
[46] *ibid.,* s.12.
[47] *ibid.,* ss.6, 11. See *Re King* [1962] 1 W.L.R. 632 (on appeal on other points, [1963] Ch. 459); *Spectrum Investment Co. v. Holmes* [1981] 1 W.L.R. 221.
[48] L.R.A. 1925, ss.8(1), 10.
[49] *Post,* para. 14–295; L.P.A. 1925, s.44.
[50] *cf.* Standard Conditions of Sale (3rd ed.), c.8.2.4.

Application can be made for any of the titles explained above except a qualified title.[51]

6. Conversion of titles. Where land has been registered with a good   **6–027**
leasehold, possessory or qualified title, that title may be converted subsequently to a superior form of title, either on an application by the proprietor or by the registrar on his own initiative.[52] Prior to 1987 the provisions that governed conversion were complex, but they have been much simplified.[53] The registrar may convert—

   (i) a good leasehold title to an absolute title if he is satisfied as to the title to the freehold and to any intermediate leasehold;

  (ii) a possessory title to an absolute title (if freehold) or to a good leasehold (if leasehold) if he is satisfied as to the title, or if the land has been registered with possessory title for at least 12 years and he is satisfied that the proprietor is in possession; and

 (iii) a qualified title to an absolute title (if freehold) or to a good leasehold (if leasehold) if he is satisfied as to the title.[54]

If any claim adverse to the title has been made, it must be disposed of before the registrar can convert the title.[55] Any person (other than the proprietor) who suffers loss by reason of the conversion of any title is entitled to be indemnified as if a mistake had been made in the register.[56]

7. Application for first registration. Where the estate is one which may   **6–028**
be registered,[57] an application for registration may be made by—

  (i) any estate owner, including those holding a legal estate as a trustee; or

 (ii) any person entitled to call for a legal estate to be vested in him (except a mortgagee or a mere purchaser under a contract).[58]

---

[51] See L.R.A. 1925, s.7(1).

[52] Application is usually by the proprietor, but there may be occasions on which it is convenient for the registrar to convert a title, *e.g.* when he wishes to amalgamate several titles and they are not all of the same class: Ruoff & Roper, 14–07. For the procedure on an application for conversion, see L.P.R. 1925, r. 48; Ruoff & Roper, 14–06.

[53] See L.R.A. s.77, inserted by L.R.A. 1986, s.1(1). This provision, which came into force on January 1, 1987, gives effect to proposals in (1983) Law Com. No. 125, Pt III.

[54] L.R.A. 1925, s.77(1)–(3).

[55] *ibid.*, s.77(4).

[56] *ibid.*, s.77(6); *post*, para. 6–135.

[57] *Ante*, para. 6–015.

[58] L.R.A. 1925, ss.4, 8(1) (as amended by T.L.A.T.A. 1996, s.25(1); Sched. 3, para. 5).

Thus if A holds land on a bare trust for B, B can apply for registration without first requiring a conveyance to be executed in his favour. Either the applicant or (where the applicant is not in a fiduciary position) his nominee may be registered as proprietor.[59]

The procedure for applications is prescribed by the Act and the Rules,[60] which provide, *inter alia*, for the hearing of objections made by third parties.[61] The documents which an applicant should submit are prescribed, and the registrar has jurisdiction to call for such other evidence of title as he may consider necessary.[62] The registrar is expressly empowered to approve a title that is open to objection but is one "the holding under which will not be disturbed".[63] In practice he will inquire whether there is anybody who could impugn the title even though it is defective.[64] He will therefore often grant an absolute title despite a technical flaw such as the absence of an assent by personal representatives in favour of themselves, it being his policy to cure defective titles so far as possible.[65] There is a right of appeal to the Chancery Division of the High Court by any person aggrieved by an order or decision made by the registrar.[66] A refusal by him to register a property with absolute title is not regarded as a decision for these purposes, but as a mere administrative act from which no appeal lies.[67] However it may be subject to judicial review.[68]

6–029   **8. Ownership.** It is fundamental to the system of registered title that the legal estate is vested in the registered proprietor for the time being.[69] This is a statutory title which is quite independent of legal ancestry or legitimacy: if a person is in fact registered as proprietor, he is owner of the land and all its appurtenances.[70] He may have obtained registration by fraud or by mistake,

---

[59] *ibid.*

[60] *ibid.*, ss.13–17; L.R.R. 1925, rr. 19–42. See Ruoff & Roper, chap. 12.

[61] L.R.A. 1925, s.13; L.R.R. 1925, rr. 34, 35.

[62] L.R.A. 1925, ss.14, 15; L.R.R. 1925, rr. 20, 21, 27, 29, 37.

[63] L.R.A. 1925, s.13(c).

[64] Ruoff & Roper, 12–47.

[65] *ibid.* Although this practice has been criticised as a matter of law (see (1976) 40 Conv. (N.S.) 122 (C. T. Emery)), it has much to commend it from a conveyancer's standpoint.

[66] L.R.A. 1925, s.13(b); L.R.R. 1925, r. 299. See too L.R.A. 1925, s.15(2) (right of appeal by a person aggrieved by an order of the registrar that he produce "deeds, instruments, or evidences of title").

[67] *Dennis v. Malcolm* [1934] Ch. 244 at 252, 253. *cf. Quigly v. Chief Land Registrar* [1992] 1 W.L.R. 834 at 836 (on appeal [1993] 1 W.L.R. 1435).

[68] *Dennis v. Malcolm, supra,* at 252, 253. See too *Quigly v. Chief Land Registrar* [1993] 1 W.L.R. 1435.

[69] L.R.A. 1925, s.69(1).

[70] This is so whether the benefit of the appurtenant right was acquired before first registration or subsequently, and whether or not there is anything on the proprietorship register to indicate its existence: see L.R.A. 1925, s.72; L.R.R. 1925, r. 251; *Re Evans' Contract* [1970] 1 W.L.R. 583. It is open to a registered proprietor to seek the registration of the benefit of any appurtenant right that is capable of subsisting as a legal estate, such as the benefit of a legal easement: L.R.R. 1925, r. 252.

and according to the law of unregistered land he may have no title at all.[71] None of this will prevent him from holding the legal estate if he is the registered proprietor[72]: he does so simply by reason of the "statutory magic" of the Act.[73] But fraud, mistake, etc., may provide grounds for rectifying the register against him.[74]

It is fundamental also that the first registered proprietor holds the legal estate subject only to the various interests and liabilities explained above, and "free from all other estates and interests whatsoever".[75] Registration thus has a curative effect on the title, exonerating the proprietor from other defects in it,[76] though again subject to the possibility of rectification.

9. Dealings.[77]

(a) Powers of disposition. The registered proprietor's power to deal with **6–030** the legal estate is put on an exclusively statutory basis. The way in which this is done is unsatisfactory: the Land Registration Act 1925 sets out those powers in various places rather than according to any clear or coherent principles. However, the overall effect of the provisions is that any registered proprietor does in fact have unfettered powers of disposition in the absence of an entry on the register in some way restricting them.[78] Although the proprietor has such powers, he may only dispose of or deal with his estate in the manner authorised by the Land Registration Act 1925.[79] The dispositions which he may make are of two kinds[80]—

  (i) registered dispositions which transfer or create a legal estate or interest and which should normally be completed by substantive registration; and

---

[71] See, *e.g. Hounslow L.B.C. v. Hare* (1990) 24 H.L.R. 9 (void disposition by charity); *Hayes v. Nwajiaku* [1994] E.G.C.S. 106 (forged transfer). *Cf. British American Cattle Co. v. Caribe Farm Industries Ltd* [1998] 1 W.L.R. 1529 at 1532, a case on Torrens title, where Lord Browne-Wilkinson commented that "a registered proprietor may obtain absolute title to land or an interest in land by registration even though there was no title in the person who granted him those rights".

[72] See *post*, para. 6–097.

[73] *Argyle B.S. v. Hammond* (1984) 49 P. & C.R. 148 at 153, *per* Slade L.J.; Ruoff & Roper, 2–08 (in the present edition more prosaically rendered as "automatic vesting"). See too *Kitney v. M.E.P.C. Ltd* [1977] 1 W.L.R. 981, where it was held that no such magic would revive a third party right (an option to renew a lease) which had become void before registration of the title.

[74] See *post*, para. 6–119.

[75] L.R.A. 1925, s.5.

[76] Ruoff & Roper, 2–10, also discussed in *Kitney v. M.E.P.C. Ltd, supra.*

[77] For fuller consideration, see *post*, para. 6–096.

[78] See Ruoff & Roper, 7–05, 15–01; and see *State Bank of India v. Sood* [1997] Ch. 276 at 284. For such entries, see *post*, paras 6–083 (cautions); 6–092 (restrictions); and 6–091 (inhibitions). A registered proprietor enjoys the statutory powers of disposition even if the transfer to him was a nullity because it was a forgery: *Argyle B.S. v. Hammond* (1984) 49 P. & C.R. 148 at 156.

[79] L.R.A. 1925, s.69(4); *Spectrum Investment Co. Ltd v. Holmes* [1981] 1 W.L.R. 221 at 228; Ruoff & Roper, 8–04. See too L.R.A. 1925, s.39.

[80] See Ruoff & Roper, 15–03, 15–04.

(ii) dispositions which create minor interests and which take effect in equity only.

Minor interests are considered later in this chapter,[81] but something must be said here of registered dispositions.

6–031   *(b) Registered dispositions.* Under the Land Registration Act 1925, registered dispositions enjoy two advantages once they have been registered—

(1) they are given "special effect or priority"[82]; and

(2) the validity of them is guaranteed by the registry, so that if they turn out to be invalid for some reason, any person suffering loss as a result will be entitled to an indemnity.[83]

The dispositions that take effect as registered dispositions include[84]—

(i) the transfer of a registered estate or charge[85];

(ii) the grant of an easement, right or privilege in, over or derived from the land[86];

(iii) the grant of a lease or underlease[87];

(iv) the grant of a rentcharge[88]; and

(v) a charge on the land by way of legal mortgage or by demise or subdemise.[89]

To take effect as registered dispositions, such dispositions must be completed by registration,[90] with the exception of a lease or underlease granted for a term of 21 years or less.[91] Although such a lease is an overriding interest,[92] it takes effect as if it were a registered disposition immediately on being granted.[93] As

---

[81] *Post*, para. 6–075.

[82] L.R.A. 1925, s.3(xxii). See further *ibid*., ss.20, 23; *post*, para. 6–105.

[83] For rectification and indemnity, see *post*, paras 6–119, 6–133. The validity of minor interests is not similarly guaranteed: *cf.* L.R.A. 1925, s.52.

[84] See Ruoff & Roper, 15–03.

[85] L.R.A. 1925, ss.18(1) (freeholds), 21 (leaseholds), 33 (charges). The surrender of a lease is a transfer for these purposes: *Spectrum Investment Co. Ltd v. Holmes, supra*, at 228.

[86] L.R.A. 1925, ss.18(1), 21(1). There is also a power to reserve an easement on the transfer of the registered estate or on the grant of any lease or underlease: *ibid*.

[87] L.R.A. 1925, ss.18(1), 21(1).

[88] *ibid*. There is also a power to reserve a rentcharge on the transfer of the registered estate or on the grant of any lease or underlease: *ibid*.

[89] *ibid*., ss.25–27.

[90] *ibid*., ss.19, 23, 26, 33.

[91] *ibid*., ss.19(2); 22(2).

[92] *ibid*., s. 70(1)(k); *post*, para. 6–066. The exception appears to apply not only to leases or underleases which take effect in possession, but also to those granted to take effect within one year of the date thereof: *ibid*. ss.18(3), 21(3).

[93] L.R.A. 1925, ss.19(2); 22(2).

a result, it enjoys the "special effect or priority"[94] that is given to registered dispositions.[95] However, its validity is not guaranteed by the registry.[96]

(c) Effect of failure to register

(1) TRANSFERS. Unless and until a transfer of a registered estate or charge **6–032** is completed by registration the transferor remains the proprietor of the registered estate or charge.[97] In consequence the transferee cannot normally[98] exercise any of the powers of a registered proprietor.[99] Conversely, the transferor may still be able to, at least in some circumstances.[1] Such a transfer is however effective in equity,[2] and takes effect as a minor interest.[3] As such, the rights of the transferee will be defeated by a disposition of the registered land for value unless it is either—

    (i) protected by an entry on the register; or

    (ii) an overriding interest.[4]

Thus if A grants B a 99-year lease, that lease will take effect as a minor interest until B secures his registration as proprietor of that lease. If, as is likely, B is in actual occupation of the land, the lease will be an overriding interest.[5] Although B's rights will thereby be binding on any third party who acquires A's land or any interest in it, there is a strong incentive for B to register his lease, because he will be unable to exercise his powers of disposition over the property until then.[6]

(2) OTHER DISPOSITIONS. Other registered dispositions will also operate in **6–033** equity as minor interests until they are registered. This is expressly so in relation to registered charges,[7] and is implicitly the case as regards other

---

[94] *Supra.*

[95] See *Barclays Bank Plc v. Zaroovabli* [1997] Ch. 321 at 327.

[96] Because such leases are not registrable, the jurisdiction to rectify the register has no application to them.

[97] L.R.A. 1925, ss.19(1); 22(1); 33(2).

[98] For an exception, see L.R.A. 1925, s.37, *post*, para. 6–107.

[99] *Lever Finance Ltd v. Needleman's Trustee* [1956] Ch. 375 (transferee of charge unable to exercise power to appoint receiver).

[1] Thus after an assignment of a registered lease which had not yet been registered, the assignor was able to terminate the lease validly by exercising a break clause that was personal to him: *Brown & Root Technology Ltd v. Sun Alliance & London Assurance Co. Ltd* (1996) 75 P. & C.R. 223. The case turned on the meaning of "assignment" for the purposes of the break clause: see *post*, para. 14–108.

[2] *E. S. Schwab & Co. Ltd v. McCarthy* (1975) 31 P. & C.R. 196 at 201; *Mascall v. Mascall* (1984) 50 P. & C.R. 119 (gift of registered land complete in equity once the transferor had executed the transfer and handed over the land certificate to the transferee).

[3] L.R.A. 1925, s.2; Ruoff & Roper, 8–03.

[4] L.R.A. 1925, ss.3(xv); 20(1); 23(1).

[5] *ibid.*, s.70(1)(g); *post*, para. 6–047.

[6] *cf.* L.R.A. 1925, s.69(4); *Spectrum Investment Co. Ltd v. Holmes* [1981] 1 W.L.R. 221 at 228.

[7] L.R.A. 1925, s.106(2) (as substituted by A.J.A. 1977, s.26(1)).

registered dispositions.[8] It is less certain whether such a disposition could, until registered, take effect as an overriding interest. The matter could arise in relation to the grant of an easement, right or privilege. Easements may take effect as overriding interests in certain circumstances.[9] Until 1984, it was thought that only legal easements fell within this category,[10] so that easements which had been expressly granted but not registered could never be overriding interests. However, in a controversial decision,[11] since approved by the Court of Appeal,[12] it was held that equitable easements that were openly exercised and enjoyed with land could also be overriding interests. If this is correct, there is little incentive for the grantee of an easement to register his grant.[13]

Part 3

CLASSIFICATION OF INTERESTS

Section 1. Registered Interests

6–034 It has been explained above,[14] that the only estates in respect of which a proprietor can be registered are "estates capable of subsisting as legal estates".[15] The following legal estates may be registered with their own title[16]—

(a) a fee simple absolute in possession[17]; and

(b) a term of years, which at the time when it was first registered was either—

(i) granted for a term of more than 21 years[18]; or

---

[8] Ruoff & Roper, 8–03; M. P. Thompson, *Barnsley's Conveyancing Law and Practice* (4th ed.), p. 70.

[9] L.R.A. 1925, s.70(1)(a); *post*, para. 6–040.

[10] See, *e.g.* J. S. Stewart-Wallace, *Brickdale and Stewart-Wallace's Land Registration Act, 1925* (4th ed.), p. 191; D. J. Hayton, *Registered Land* (3rd ed.), p. 84.

[11] *Celsteel Ltd v. Alton House Holdings Ltd* [1985] 1 W.L.R. 204; applying L.R.R. 1925, r. 258; *post*, para. 6–042.

[12] *Thatcher v. Douglas* (1996) 146 N.L.J. 282.

[13] The Law Commission has recommended that easements and profits expressly granted or reserved should not be capable of taking effect as overriding interests: (1998) Law Com. No. 254, para. 5.14.

[14] See *ante*, para. 6–007.

[15] L.R.A. 1925, s.2(1). See *State Bank of India v. Sood* [1997] Ch. 276 at 283, 284.

[16] L.R.A. 1925, ss.2, 3(xxiii).

[17] *ibid.*, s.4.

[18] Subject to certain statutory exceptions concerning a tenant's right to buy a lease under H.A. 1985, Pt V: see H.A. 1985, s.154(6), and s.171G and Sched. 9A, para. 3 (substituted by the Housing and Planning Act 1986, s.8; Sched. 2); L.R.A. 1925, s.8(1A) (inserted by L.R.A. 1997, s.4(1); Sched. 1); Ruoff & Roper, 9–07.

(ii) was assigned and had more than 21 years to run.[19]

Of the four principal legal interests that may now exist over land[20]—   **6–035**

(a) the benefit of an easement, right or privilege cannot be registered with its own title but only as appurtenant to a registered estate[21];

(b) a rentcharge is registered with its own title[22];

(c) a charge by way of legal mortgage is protected by the registration of the chargee as proprietor of the registered charge against the title of the property charged,[23] but without a separate title of its own[24]; and

(d) the benefit of a right of entry exercisable over or in respect of a legal term of years, or annexed to a legal rentcharge will vest automatically in the registered proprietor of the lessor's estate or the rentcharge as appurtenances and without the need for registration.[25]

Because of the applicable definition of "legal estate",[26] a manor may also be registered with its own title.[27] There can be no registration of a right of common over land which is capable of being registered under the Commons Registration Act 1965.[28]

Section 2. Overriding Interests

1. Nature. Overriding interests[29] are, by definition, rights which are not   **6–036** protected on the register.[30] Nevertheless they bind any proprietor of registered land even though he has no knowledge of them.[31] In general, and subject to

---

[19] L.R.A. 1925, s.8(1). Once a lease has been registered it must be dealt with thereafter as a registered estate, even though it has less than 21 years to run: *ibid.*, s.22(1).

[20] See L.P.A. 1925, s.1(2); *ante*, paras 4–047 *et seq.* That subsection lists five legal interests, but the fourth (certain charges on land created other than by an instrument) is virtually obsolete: *ante*, para. 4–053.

[21] L.R.R. 1925, r. 257. The effect of this is that neither *profits à prendre* in gross (*post*, para. 18–079), nor franchises (*post*, para. 18–013) can be registered with their own titles.

[22] L.R.R. 1925, rr. 50, 107, 108, The registered proprietor will either be the grantee of the rentcharge or the transferor of the land in consideration of a rent. For the categories of rentcharge that are registrable, see Ruoff & Roper, 26–03.

[23] L.R.A. 1925, s.26(1). For registered charges, see *post*, para. 6–074.

[24] L.R.A. 1925, s.8(1)(a); Ruoff & Roper, 9–15.

[25] L.R.A. 1925, ss.5, 9; L.R.R. 1925, r. 251; Ruoff & Roper, 9–16.

[26] See L.R.A. 1925, s.3(xi); L.P.A. 1925, ss. 1(4), 205(1)(ix).

[27] *cf.* L.R.R. 1925, rr. 50, 51. See Ruoff & Roper, 12–32.

[28] Commons Registration Act 1965, s.1(1); Ruoff & Roper, 6–05, 12–33. Rights of common take effect as overriding interests under L.R.A. 1925, s.70(1)(a); *post*, para. 6–040. For the Commons Registration Act 1965, see *post*, para. 18–179.

[29] L.R.A. 1925, s.70(1).

[30] *ibid.*, s.3(xvi).

[31] *ibid.*, ss. 5, 9, 20(1), 23(1).

one significant exception,[32] they are the kind of rights which a purchaser of unregistered land would not expect to discover from a mere examination of the abstract and title deeds, but for which he would make inquiries and inspect the land.[33] The traditional view has been that the register is a substitute for the title deeds, but not for those other inquiries and inspections which a purchaser should make. However this analogy is not an exact one. Rights which in unregistered land would require registration as land charges may sometimes take effect as overriding interests in registered land. They will therefore bind any purchaser even though careful inspection and inquiry would not have revealed their existence.[34] Furthermore, the traditional view of overriding interests is now being questioned. If the system of registered title is to be wholly effective, the register should be an accurate reflection of the state of the title, and the range of inquiries beyond the register should be kept to a minimum.[35]

Many (but not all) overriding interests are legal rights. However, it must be emphasised that as far as incumbrances on registered land are concerned, the issue in deciding whether a purchaser is bound irrespective of any entry on the register is not whether the rights are legal or equitable but whether they are overriding interests or minor interests. The doctrine of notice has no part to play,[36] so that the difference between legal and equitable interests largely disappears.

6–037   The term "overriding interests" is employed in at least two different ways in the Act. First, it is sometimes used in a general sense to describe those rights which, although not registered, have priority over the proprietor's registered estate, such as charges which he has himself created over the land.[37] Secondly, it is defined by the Act in a technical sense to mean those interests which—

   (a)   are made overriding by the Act; and

   (b)   are not entered on the register.[38]

The first of those requirements is circular[39] and it is necessary to look to other provisions in the Act (and indeed elsewhere) to determine which rights are

---

[32] The rights of persons in occupation: *ibid.* s.70(1)(g); *post*, para. 6–047.

[33] Ruoff & Roper, 6–04; *Lloyds Bank Plc. v. Rosset* [1989] Ch. 350 at 371, 372 (on appeal [1991] 1 A.C. 107).

[34] *Kling v. Keston Properties Ltd* (1983) 49 P. & C.R. 212 at 222; *post*, para. 6–054.

[35] See (1998) Law Com. No. 254, Pt IV.

[36] *Post*, paras 6–077, 6–105.

[37] See L.R.A. 1925, s.69(1); Ruoff & Roper, 6–01. *cf. Abbey National B.S. v. Cann* [1991] 1 A.C. 56 at 85, where Lord Oliver appears to have assumed that the term always has this broad meaning. *Sed quaere.*

[38] L.R.A. 1925, s.3(xvi).

[39] See *Abbey National B.S. v. Cann, supra,* at 84.

regarded as overriding.[40] An overriding interest ceases to be such if, as is often the case, it is entered on the register. It then becomes a minor interest.[41]

2. Reform. Overriding interests are the most unsatisfactory feature of the Land Registration Act 1925. They constitute a major flaw in the registration scheme.[42] They do not appear on the register, they may not always be readily discoverable, and yet they will bind any purchaser.[43] Furthermore, if the register is subsequently rectified to give effect to an overriding interest, the purchaser will be unable to obtain an indemnity.[44] These consequences are exacerbated because of the breadth of some categories of overriding interests and the uncertain ambit of others.[45] A reform of the system of overriding interests has been recommended by the Law Commission and HM Land Registry.[46]

6–038

3. Categories of overriding interests. The interests which can exist as overriding interests in the technical sense given above are—

6–039

(a) those which are listed in section 70(1) of the Land Registration Act 1925[47]; and

(b) one further interest which has since been added.[48]

A right cannot be an overriding interest within section 70(1) unless it subsists in reference to the registered land.[49] The only interests which may be overriding interests are therefore property rights and not merely personal rights.[50] However, there remains some uncertainty as to whether some rights are capable of falling within section 70(1).[51] The date at which the overriding

---

[40] *Williams & Glyn's Bank Ltd v. Boland* [1981] A.C. 487 at 503.

[41] *Post*, para. 6–071.

[42] See (1998) Law Com. No. 254, paras 4.11–4.16.

[43] *cf. Overseas Investment Ltd v. Simcobuild Construction Ltd* (1995) 70 P. & C.R. 322 at 327, where Peter Gibson L.J. commented that "the register of title is not a perfect mirror of the title to a registered property. It is not possible to rely on entries on the register as the complete record of everything that affects the title".

[44] *Post*, para. 6–133.

[45] The courts will "not be astute to give a wide meaning to any item constituting an overriding interest": *Overseas Investment Ltd v. Simcobuild Construction Ltd, supra* at 327, *per* Peter Gibson L.J. See too Staughton L.J. at 330, 331.

[46] (1998) Law Com. No. 254, Pt V.

[47] Described as a "somewhat inconsequential and jumbled" list: Ruoff & Roper, 6–01.

[48] Appurtenances (*post*, para. 6–040).

[49] *Williams & Glyn's Bank Ltd v. Boland, supra; City of London B.S. v. Flegg* [1988] A.C. 54 at 91.

[50] *Ashburn Anstalt v. Arnold* [1989] Ch. 1 at 8; *Nationwide Anglia B.S. v. Ahmed* (1995) 70 P. & C.R. 381 at 387. It has been said that "[s]ection 70 in all its parts is dealing with rights in reference to land which have the quality of being capable of enduring through different ownerships of the land, according to normal conceptions of title to real property": *National Provincial Bank Ltd v. Hastings Car Mart Ltd* [1964] Ch. 665 at 696, *per* Russell L.J.; approved on appeal: [1965] A.C. 1175 at 1226, 1228, 1261, 1262. See too *Hodges v. Jones* [1935] Ch. 657 at 670.

[51] See [1998] C.L.J. 328 (L. Tee); and see *post*, para. 6–050.

interest must exist if it is to bind any purchaser is the date of the registration of the disposition.[52] It is not the date upon which the transaction is completed by the execution of the transfer.[53] This means that a purchaser will be bound by overriding interests, such as local land charges, which arise between transfer and registration, as indeed he should be.[54] It does however give rise to the "theoretical possibility" that the transferor might create an overriding interest, such as a lease, in the period between completion and the registration of the transferee as proprietor, but the likelihood of his so doing is remote.[55]

The principal categories of overriding interest must now be considered.[56]

6–040   *(a) Easements, profits and analogous rights.* Section 70(1) of the Act lists two categories of rights which fall within this description—

> "(a) Rights of common, drainage rights, customary rights (until extin-
> guished), public rights, *profits à prendre*, rights of sheepwalk, rights
> of way, watercourses, rights of water, and other easements not being
> equitable easements required to be protected by notice on the regis-
> ter;" and

> (j) Rights of fishing and sporting,[57] seigniorial and manorial rights of
> all descriptions (until extinguished), and franchises."

In addition, rule 258 of the Land Registration Rules 1925 provides that "rights, privileges, and appurtenances appertaining or reputed to appertain to land or demised, occupied, or enjoyed therewith or reputed or known as part or parcel of or appurtenant thereto, which adversely affect registered land are overriding interests within section 70 of the Act". These three provisions are unsatisfactory and give rise to a number of difficulties.

---

[52] Registration takes effect on the day on which the application for registration is delivered to the registry: L.R.R. 1925, rr. 83–85 (as amended); *Lloyds Bank Plc. v. Rosset* [1989] Ch. 350 at 371 (on appeal [1991] 1 A.C. 107).

[53] *Abbey National B.S. v. Cann, supra.* See (1990) 106 L.Q.R. 545 (R. J. Smith). This result follows from the wording of L.R.A. 1925, ss.20(1), 23(1).

[54] *Lloyds Bank Plc v. Rosset, supra,* at 373; *Abbey National B.S. v. Cann, supra.* at 85.

[55] *Abbey National B.S. v. Cann, supra,* at 87, *per* Lord Oliver. For the converse possibility of overriding interests created between completion and registration by the transferee or those whom he allows into occupation, see *post,* para. 6–049.

[56] In addition to the categories of overriding interests discussed below, see the following paragraphs of L.R.A. 1925, s.70(1): (b) tenurial rights (now largely obsolete: see (1998) Law Com. No. 254, paras 5.32–5.36,); (d) liability in respect of embankments, and sea and river walls (see Ruoff & Roper, 6–12; (1998) Law Com. No. 254, paras 5.38, 5.39); (e) certain statutory annuities (obsolete except for corn rents: see (1998) Law Com. No. 254, paras 5.40, 5.41); and (l) certain old mineral rights (see Ruoff & Roper, 6–26; (1998) Law Com. No. 254, paras 5.95, 5.96).

[57] This reference is not to *profits à prendre* (which fall within paragraph (a)), but to those seigniorial rights that were not included within the general enfranchisement of manorial rights in 1926: Ruoff & Roper, 6–24.

(1) SUPERFLUOUS WORDS. The list of rights contained in section 70(1)(a) **6–041** and (j) is unnecessarily verbose and encompasses just six types of right of which the others are no more than examples[58]:

(a) easements;

(b) *profits à prendre*;

(c) public rights;

(d) customary rights; and

(e) manorial rights; and

(f) franchises.[59]

(2) RIGHTS INCLUDED. The provisions as to the rights included are unsat- **6–042** isfactory. First, the extent of the rights which fall within them is, in some cases, obscure. Thus there is no doubt as to what constitutes a "customary right",[60] and there was some uncertainty as to which rights were considered to be "public rights", though this has now been resolved.[61] It is clear that they are present (and not future) rights which can be exercised by any member of the public, such as a right of passage along a highway, or the right to discharge into a public sewer. Secondly, it might have been expected (by analogy with unregistered land) that only legal rights, such as easements or profits arising by prescription,[62] could be overriding interests. The wording of section 70(1)(a), although badly drafted,[63] appears to exclude equitable easements.[64] Had it been so interpreted, easements, rights and privileges expressly granted over registered land[65] could never have been overriding interests because they require registration and so take effect only in equity as minor interests in the interim.[66] However, as has already been explained,[67] it has now been held that

---

[58] See (1998) Law Com. No. 254, paras 5.3, 5.84–5.86.

[59] See *ante*, para. 2–054 (manorial rights); *post*, paras 18–013 (franchises); 18–040 (easements); 18–064 (public rights); 18–078 (customary rights); 18–079 (*profits à prendre*). In practice manorial rights should be apparent from the title deeds, and will therefore be entered on the register should the land come to be registered: Ruoff & Roper, 6–24.

[60] See (1998) Law Com. No. 254, paras 5.25–5.29.

[61] *Overseas Investment Services Ltd v. Simcobuild Construction Ltd* (1995) 70 P. & C.R. 322.

[62] Such rights are clearly overriding interests: see L.R.A. 1925, s.75(5); L.R.R. 1925, r. 250.

[63] The wording of the exception, "not being equitable easements required to be protected by notice on the register", is inappropriate because such easements are not "required" by the Act to be so protected. It has been held that "required to be protected" means "which need to be protected": *Celsteel Ltd v. Alton House Holdings Ltd* [1985] 1 W.L.R. 204 at 220.

[64] See D. J. Hayton, *Registered Land* (3rd ed.), p. 84.

[65] On first registration, the registrar is under a mandatory duty to note on the register those easements, rights, privileges, or benefits appearing on the title which adversely affect the title of the land: L.R.A. 1925, s.70(2). In cases where the existence of the adverse rights does not appear on the title, registration is discretionary: L.R.R. 1925, r. 41: see *Re Dances Way, West Town, Hayling Island* [1962] Ch. 490 at 508; Ruoff & Roper, 6–28. Any rights not so noted will be legal and will take effect as overriding interests within s.70(1)(a).

[66] See *ante*, para. 6–033.

[67] *Ante*, para. 6–033.

certain easements may exist as overriding interests.[68] They can only fall within section 70(1)(a) if they do not need to be registered as minor interests but can be protected by some other statutory provision or rule of law.[69] However the scope of this exception is apparently very wide, for it has been held that any "right privilege or appurtenance" that is "openly exercised and enjoyed" with land and which adversely affects registered land does not need to be registered, but can exist as an overriding interest by reason of rule 258 of the Land Registration Rules 1925.[70] If this is correct—and the decision has been approved by the Court of Appeal[71]—most expressly granted easements, rights or privileges will take effect as overriding interests even if unregistered,[72] and the provisions of the Act requiring their registration are undermined.[73]

6–043   (3) APPURTENANCES. The registration of a person as the proprietor of land vests in him not only the registered estate but all appurtenant rights.[74] Such rights will now take effect as overriding interests by virtue of rule 258 of the Land Registration Rules 1925 provided that they are openly exercised and enjoyed.[75] The wording of the rule suggests that it was intended to be confined to certain easements arising by implied grant on a transfer of the legal estate.[76] It is not however expressly so limited, and may include easements and rights expressly granted. Thus where an equitable lease of a garage was granted, the right of access to it (which, like the lease, had not been protected by registration) was held to be an appurtenant right within the rule. As such it had the status of an overriding interest and bound a subsequent purchaser of the servient tenement.[77]

6–044   (4) REFORM. The Law Commission and HM Land Registry have recommended the following reforms.

---

[68] *Celsteel Ltd v. Alton House Holdings Ltd, supra* (reversed in part on appeal, but without affecting this point: [1986] 1 W.L.R. 512). For comment, see [1985] All E.R. Annual Review 199 (P. J. Clarke); [1986] Conv. 31 (M. P. Thomson); (1999) 115 L.Q.R. 89 (D. G. Barnsley).

[69] *Celsteel Ltd v. Alton House Holdings Ltd* [1985] 1 W.L.R. 204 at 220. In this context, Scott J. held that "equitable easement" does not have the narrow meaning that it has sometimes been given in the context of the Land Charges Act 1972, s.4(5) (*ante*, para. 5–104): *ibid.*

[70] *Celsteel Ltd v. Alton House Holdings Ltd, supra* at 221, *per* Scott J. Rule 258 is considered *infra.*

[71] *Thatcher v. Douglas* (1996) 146 N.L.J. 204.

[72] In a number of recent decisions it appears to have been assumed that an easement that had been expressly granted or reserved could take effect as an overriding interest: see *Abbey National B.S. v. Cann* [1991] 1 A.C. 56 at 87; *Willies-Williams v. National Trust* (1993) 65 P. & C.R. 359 at 363. *Sed quaere.*

[73] *Ante*, para. 6–033.

[74] L.R.A. 1925, ss.5, 9, 20, 23.

[75] *Celsteel Ltd v. Alton House Holdings Ltd, supra*, at 221. It has been held that r. 258 is not *ultra vires: ibid.*, at 221.

[76] The wording is similar to L.P.A. 1925, s.62, by which easements and analogous right may sometimes be impliedly granted on a conveyance of a legal estate; *post*, para. 18–108. See Ruoff & Roper, 6–07.

[77] *Celsteel Ltd v. Alton House Holdings Ltd, supra*, at 221.

(i) The only easements and *profits à prendre* that should be capable of existing as overriding interests over registered land are those that have not been expressly granted by the registered proprietor or do not arise from a contract by him to grant such rights.[78] The only easements and profits that would be overriding interests would be—

   (a) those arising by implied grant or reservation;

   (b) those that are acquired or are in the course of acquisition by prescription;

   (c) those to which the property was subject at the time of first registration but which were not then noted on the register; and

   (d) those which are appurtenant to an overriding interest.[79]

(ii) Customary rights that are exercisable by all or some of the inhabitants of a particular locality should take effect as overriding interests.[80]

(iii) Only those rights which are lawfully exercisable by any member of the public over any land should take effect as overriding interests as public rights.[81]

(b) Liability to repair the chancel of any church. The liability of certain **6–045** landowners to repair the chancel of a church is one of the few remaining relics of the old law of tithes.[82] Its incidence is both capricious and anomalous. It is provided by section 70(1)(c) that this liability is an overriding interest. The Law Commission recommended that it should either be abolished after a period of 10 years or become registrable as a local land charge if this could not be done.[83] However, this recommendation was rejected by the government because of fears that it might contravene the European Convention on Human Rights.[84] The Law Commission and HM Land Registry have recommended that such rights should remain as overriding interests.[85]

(c) The rights of adverse possessors.[86] Section 70(1)(f) of the Act provides **6–046** that rights acquired or in course of being acquired under the Limitation Acts

---

[78] (1998) Law Com. No. 254, paras 5.6–5.24. This would have the effect of reversing the decision in *Celsteel Ltd v. Alton House Holdings Ltd, supra. cf.* [1987] Conv. 328 (A. M. Pritchard).

[79] Such as those enjoyed with a lease granted for a term of 21 years or less. See L.R.A. 1925, s.70(1)(k); *post*, para. 6–066.

[80] (1998) Law Com. No. 254, paras 5.25–5.29. Customary rights having their origin in tenure are obsolete.

[81] (1998) Law Com. No. 254, paras 5.30–5.31.

[82] *Post*, para. 18–008.

[83] (1985) Law Com. No. 152, Pt VII.

[84] See Article 1 of the First Protocol; and *post*, para. 18–010.

[85] (1998) Law Com. No. 254, para. 5.37.

[86] For the application of the Limitation Act 1980 to registered land, see *post*, paras 6–116, 21–056, 21–058.

take effect as overriding interests. A purchaser of registered land will there-fore acquire the land subject to the rights of such a squatter,[87] even though—

   (i) those rights may not be apparent[88]; or

   (ii) the squatter has abandoned the land since he acquired the right to be registered as proprietor by virtue of 12 years' adverse possession,[89] and the registered proprietor has resumed possession and is the apparent owner in possession of the land.[90]

The reference in the paragraph to rights in course of acquisition is intended to make it clear that time continues to run even if there is a change in the registered proprietor during the period of adverse possession. The Law Commission and HM Land Registry have recommended that such rights should cease to be overriding interests and that a squatter should only be able to protect his rights as an overriding interest if he is in actual occupation.[91]

6–047   *(d) The rights of persons in actual occupation.* The most sweeping and most often litigated category of overriding interests is found in the now notorious section 70(1)(g) of the Land Registration Act 1925—

> "The rights of every person in actual occupation of the land or in receipt of the rents and profits thereof, save where enquiry is made of such person and the rights are not disclosed".[92]

6–048   (1) BACKGROUND.[93] It was explained in the previous chapter that where title is unregistered, the fact of possession constitutes notice of the rights of the possessor,[94] though this rule has been qualified by statute.[95] Although section 70(1)(g) provides an analogue to that rule in relation to registered land,[96] it does not exactly reproduce it. Indeed the range of rights that may be protected by actual occupation is significantly wider where the title is registered than where it is unregistered.

---

[87] *Bridges v. Mees* [1957] Ch. 475.
[88] *cf. Chowood Ltd v. Lyall* [1930] 2 Ch. 156.
[89] *Post*, para. 6–116.
[90] See R. J. Smith, *Property Law* (2nd ed.), p. 229.
[91] (1998) Law Com. No. 254, paras 5.42–5.55. For the overriding status of the rights of persons in actual occupation, see L.R.A. 1925, s.70(1)(g); *infra.*
[92] The breadth of the paragraph was deliberate and the intention behind it was to limit claims for indemnity: J. S. Anderson, *Lawyers and the Making of English Land Law 1832–1940*, pp. 277–280.
[93] See [1990] C.L.J. 277 at 315–320 (C.H.); (1998) Law Com. No. 254, paras 5.57–5.58.
[94] *Ante*, paras 5–019, 5–121.
[95] In particular by the requirement that land charges should be protected by registration: *ante*, paras 5–086, 5–118.
[96] It has been described as being "similar to" the common law rule: *Woolwich Equitable B.S. v. Marshall* [1951] 2 All E.R. 769 at 773, *per* Danckwerts J. (the report of the case in the Law Reports omits these words and appears to equate the two rules: [1952] Ch. 1 at 9).

(a) Where the title to land is registered, a purchaser may be bound by the rights of an occupier even though the most searching enquiries fail to reveal his occupation.[97] This is because the fact of actual occupation is all important[98] and the doctrine of notice is irrelevant.[99]

(b) Where a person who has the benefit of a right which is registrable as a minor interest is in actual occupation, that right will bind any purchaser even though it has not been so registered.[1] By contrast, where the title is unregistered, a land charge can only be protected by registration and not by actual occupation.[2]

(c) A purchaser of registered land will be bound by the rights not only of the occupier of the land but also of any person who is "in receipt of the rents and profits thereof".[3] This means, *e.g.* that—

(i) an assignee of any lease will be bound by the landlord's rights to have that lease rectified for mistake[4]; and

(ii) if a sub-tenant is in actual occupation, any purchaser will be bound by the rights of any intermediate landlord.

A purchaser of unregistered land is not fixed with notice of the rights of an occupier's landlord.[5]

(2) RELEVANT DATE. Because most dispositions of registered land should be registered,[6] there will necessarily be a period of time between the completion of a transaction and its registration.[7] Any purchaser will inspect the land and make his inquiries of those in occupation immediately prior to completion rather than between completion and registration, for once completion has

6–049

---

[97] *Kling v. Keston Properties Ltd* (1983) 49 P. & C.R. 212 at 222. There is a doubt about this, however, and some authorities suggest that the actual occupation must be apparent, see *post*, para. 6–054.

[98] "The statute has substituted a plain factual situation for the uncertainties of notice, actual or constructive as the determinant of an overriding interest": *Williams & Glyn's Bank Ltd v. Boland* [1981] A.C. 487 at 511, *per* Lord Scarman. *cf. Lloyds Bank Plc v. Rosset* [1989] Ch. 350 at 403 (on appeal [1991] 1 A.C. 107) where Purchas L.J. suggested that "the provisions of the section clearly were intended to import into the law relating to registered land the equitable concept of constructive notice". This is plainly incorrect.

[99] *Williams & Glyn's Bank Ltd v Boland, supra,* at 508. See too *Lloyds Bank Plc. v. Rosset, supra,* at 396, *per* Mustill L.J.

[1] *Bridges v. Mees* [1957] Ch. 475 at 487; *Webb v. Pollmount Ltd* [1966] Ch. 584; *Williams & Glyn's Bank Ltd v. Boland, supra, Kling v. Keston Properties Ltd, supra,* at 221, 222.

[2] *Midland Bank Trust Co. Ltd v. Green* [1981] A.C. 513. This fundamental distinction between registered and unregistered conveyancing may have arisen because of a draftsman's error: *ante,* para. 5–121.

[3] See *Strand Securities Ltd v. Caswell* [1965] Ch. 958 at 980, 983.

[4] *Nurdin & Peacock Plc v. D. B. Ramsden & Co. Ltd* [1999] 1 E.G.L.R. 119 at 124–126. For subsequent proceedings, see *Nurdin & Peacock Plc v. D. B. Ramsden & Co. Ltd (No. 2)* [1999] 1 W.L.R. 1249 (recovery of rent overpaid by mistake).

[5] *Hunt v. Luck* [1902] 1 Ch. 428; *ante,* para. 5–020. There is no apparent reason for this distinction between registered and unregistered land; [1990] C.L.J. 277 at 317, 318 (C.H.).

[6] *Ante,* para. 6–030.

[7] The so-called "registration gap": see (1998) Law Com. No. 254, para. 5.112.

taken place he will be bound by the transaction, even though it has not yet been registered.[8] But a purchaser takes the land subject to any overriding interests which exist at the date of registration,[9] and there was a danger therefore that he might find himself bound by the rights of an occupier who moves into the property after completion but before registration.[10] However, that danger has been removed. It has been held that a person claiming to have an overriding interest under section 70(1)(g) must be in actual occupation on the date on which the transaction is completed.[11] It is uncertain whether the person claiming the overriding interest must be in actual occupation on the date of registration as well as on the completion date.[12] However, once such an overriding interest has crystallised,[13] the owner of the right may continue to enforce it even though he subsequently goes out of occupation.[14]

6–050   (3) RIGHTS. It is not every right enjoyed by the occupier that can be protected by his actual occupation. First, as section 70(1) itself provides, the right must be one which subsists "in reference to" the land. This restricts the ambit of paragraph (g) in at least three respects.

>   (a)   Only property rights may be overriding interests.[15] Purely personal rights, such as licences,[16] mere contractual rights,[17] a right of set-off[18]; the benefit of a promissory estoppel,[19] or a tenant's right to recover a security deposit from his landlord,[20] will not therefore bind a purchaser.

>   (b)   Any rights or interests under a trust of land which are overreached on a disposition for value do not subsist in reference to land and are not therefore within the paragraph.[21] Thus where A and B held land upon trust for sale[22] for A, B, C and D, all of whom were in

---

[8] *Lloyds Bank Plc v. Rosset* [1989] Ch. 350 at 372.

[9] L.R.A. 1925, ss.20, 23.

[10] See *Re Boyle's Claim* [1961] 1 W.L.R. 339 at 344; *Kling v. Keston Properties Ltd* (1983) 49 P. & C.R. 212 at 218.

[11] *Lloyds Bank Plc v. Rosset, supra,* at 370–375, 393, 402; *Abbey National B.S. v. Cann* [1991] 1 A.C. 56 at 88, 106.

[12] See *Abbey National B.S. v. Cann, supra,* at 104 (where Lord Jauncey appears to suggest that there must be actual occupation on both dates); (1990) 106 L.Q.R. 545 (R. J. Smith); Ruoff & Roper, 6–19.

[13] Which will occur, at latest, when the transaction in favour of the purchaser is registered.

[14] *London and Cheshire Insurance Co. Ltd v. Laplagrene Property Co. Ltd* [1971] Ch. 499 at 504, 505.

[15] *Ante,* para. 6–039. See [1998] C.L.J. 328 (L. Tee).

[16] *Ashburn Anstalt v. Arnold* [1989] Ch. 1 at 22; *Canadian Imperial Bank of Commerce v. Bello* (1991) 64 P. & C.R. 48 at 51. For licences, see *post,* Chap. 17.

[17] *cf. Lynton International Ltd v. Noble* (1991) 63 P. & C.R. 452; *Gracegrove Estates Ltd v. Boateng* [1997] E.G.C.S. 103.

[18] *Mortgage Corporation Ltd v. Ubah* (1996) 73 P. & C.R. 500 at 506–508.

[19] *Canadian Imperial Bank of Commerce v. Bello, supra,* at 52.

[20] *Eden Park Estates Ltd v. Longman* (unreported, CA), noted in [1982] Conv. 239 (P. H. Kenny). For such security deposits, see *Hua Chiao Commercial Bank Ltd v. Chiaphua Industries Ltd* [1987] A.C. 99, *post,* para. 15–024.

[21] *City of London B.S. v. Flegg* [1988] A.C. 54.

[22] Which would now take effect as a trust of land: see T.L.A.T.A. 1996, s.1; *post,* para. 8–126.

occupation of the property, and A and B mortgaged the property, the mortgagee took free of the interests of C and D, which were overreached on payment to the two trustees.[23] The rights of a beneficiary in actual occupation which are not overreached will however take effect as an overriding interest.[24] Where a husband, who held the matrimonial home on trust for sale[25] for himself and his wife, mortgaged the house to a bank to secure an advance that had been made to him alone, the bank was bound by the wife's beneficial interest.[26] A single trustee could not make an over-reaching conveyance.[27]

(c) The rights must be such as to give the person asserting them priority over any purchaser. A person whose rights are subordinated to those of the purchaser under the general law cannot claim an overriding interest.[28] Thus if A holds a property on a trust of land for himself and B and then mortgages the property to C with B's acquiescence, B cannot assert his interest against C, even though it has not been overreached.[29]

Secondly, it is expressly provided that certain rights cannot be overriding **6–051** interests but can exist only as minor interests.[30] These include—

(i) the "successive or other interests created by or arising under a settlement"[31];

(ii) a spouse's matrimonial home rights under the Family Law Act 1996[32];

(iii) rights under a mortgage which is not a registered charge[33];

(iv) the rights of a leaseholder who has given notice of his intention to acquire the freehold or an extended lease[34];

[23] *City of London B.S. v. Flegg, supra.* For overreaching, see *ante*, para. 4–078; *post*, para. 8–157.
[24] *Williams & Glyn's Bank Ltd v. Boland* [1981] A.C. 487.
[25] Which would now take effect as a trust of land: *supra.*
[26] *Williams & Glyn's Bank Ltd v. Boland, supra.*
[27] See *City of London B.S. v. Flegg, supra* at 74, 89, 90.
[28] *Paddington B.S. v. Mendelsohn* (1985) 50 P. & C.R. 244 at 248.
[29] *ibid.*, at 247, 248; *Abbey National B.S. v. Cann* [1991] 1 A.C. 56 at 94; *Skipton B.S. v. Clayton* (1993) 66 P. & C.R. 223 at 229; *post*, para. 10–032.
[30] See Ruoff & Roper, 6–20.
[31] L.R.A. 1925, s.86(2). At first sight this exception is anomalous because beneficial interests under a trust of land may be overriding interests within section 70(1)(g). However, in practice, when a settlement was created under the Settled Land Act 1925, an appropriate restriction was normally entered on the register: see L.R.R. 1925, rr. 56–58; Sched. 2, Forms 9–11; *post*, para. 8–022.
[32] F.L.A. 1996, s.31(10)(b); *post*, para. 17–023.
[33] L.R.A. 1925, s.106(2); *post*, para. 6–113.
[34] Leasehold Reform Act 1967, s.5(5); Leasehold Reform, Housing and Urban Development Act 1993, s.97(1).

(v) the "preserved right to buy" of a public sector tenant[35];

(vi) the rights conferred on a person under an access order made under the Access to Neighbouring Land Act 1992[36]; and

(vii) a right to call for an overriding lease under the Landlord and Tenant (Covenants) Act 1995.[37]

Apart from these exceptional cases, however, the fact that a proprietary right is registrable as a minor interest does not preclude its protection under section 70(1)(g) in the absence of such registration.[38] Furthermore, there is no requirement that the right claimed should in any way be linked to the capacity in which a person occupies.[39]

6–052   The range of proprietary rights that has been held to fall within the paragraph is very wide indeed, and includes—

(i) a term of years[40];

(ii) an option to purchase or a right of pre-emption in respect of the freehold reversion vested in an occupying lessee[41];

(iii) the benefit of an estate contract[42];

(iv) an unpaid vendor's lien for the purchase price where he occupies as tenant under a lease-back transaction[43];

(v) the right to rectification of a conveyance which mistakenly included land which the grantor[44] continued to occupy[45] and of a lease which incorrectly recorded the provisions as to rent[46];

---

[35] Housing Act 1985, Sched. 9A, para. 6(1)(b) (inserted by Housing and Planning Act 1986, s.8(2), Sched. 2).

[36] Access to Neighbouring Land Act 1992, s.5(5); *post*, para. 18–225.

[37] L. & T.C.A. 1995, s.20(6); *post*, para. 15–019.

[38] *Williams & Glyn's Bank Ltd v. Boland* [1981] A.C. 487.

[39] *Ferrishurst Ltd v. Wallcite Ltd* [1999] 2 W.L.R. 667 at 681.

[40] *Ashburn Anstalt v. Arnold* [1989] Ch. 1 at 27; *Canadian Imperial Bank of Commerce v. Bello* (1991) 64 P. & C.R. 48. Normally it will only be equitable leases that require protection under s.70(1)(g): *post*, para. 6–068.

[41] *Webb v. Pollmount Ltd* [1966] Ch. 584 (option); *Kling v. Keston Properties Ltd* (1983) 49 P. & C.R. 212 (pre-emption).

[42] *Bridges v. Mees* [1957] Ch. 475; *Ashburn Anstalt v. Arnold, supra,* at 28.

[43] *London and Cheshire Insurance Co. Ltd v. Laplagrene Property Co. Ltd* [1971] Ch. 499. See too *Nationwide Anglia B.S. v. Ahmed* (1995) 70 P. & C.R. 381 at 386, *cf. U.C.B. Bank Plc v. Beasley & France* [1995] N.P.C. 144; [1997] Conv. 336 at 344 (D. G. Barnsley).

[44] Or his successor in title, as in *Goodger v. Willis* [1999] E.G.C.S. 32.

[45] *Blacklocks v. J. B. Developments (Godalming) Ltd* [1982] Ch. 183 (rectification ordered). For the view that what was in issue in that case was a right to rectify *the register*, see [1983] Conv. 361 (D. G. Barnsley). See too *Goodger v. Willis, supra. Cf. Re Leighton's Conveyance* [1936] 1 All E.R. 667.

[46] *Nurdin & Peacock Plc v. D. B. Ramsden & Co. Ltd* [1999] 1 E.G.L.R. 119 at 124–126 (where the claim to rectification failed on the facts).

(vi) an equity arising by estoppel or acquiescence[47]; and

(vii) unless overreached, beneficial interests under a trust of land.[48]

Furthermore, the rights of a person in actual occupation may include appurtenant rights. Thus where a tenant under an equitable lease of a garage had a right of way to the building over his landlord's property, that right of way was part of the tenant's overriding interest and so binding on a purchaser of the reversion.[49] Derivative interests (such as leases) granted by a person having an overriding interest under section 70(1)(g), enjoy the same protection as the interests out of which they are created.[50]

(4) ACTUAL OCCUPATION. Whether or not a person is in actual occupation of land is a question of fact,[51] and the courts are unwilling to "lay down a code or catalogue of situations" in which such occupation will be established.[52] " 'Occupation' is a concept which may have different connotations according to the nature and purpose of the property which is claimed to be occupied."[53] However the cases do provide some guidance. First, there must be some physical presence (and not merely some legal entitlement to occupy),[54] but this does not mean that the person claiming the overriding interest must reside or work on the premises.[55] Thus it is possible to be in actual occupation of a garage by parking a car in it regularly.[56] Secondly, occupation does not necessarily require the personal presence of the person claiming the right.[57] An employee, agent or a contractor (such as a caretaker or a builder) who is specifically employed for a purpose that entails his being in occupation, can

6–053

---

[47] *Semble*: see *Lee-Parker v. Izzett (No. 2)* [1972] 1 W.L.R. 775 at 780; *Singh v. Sandhu* (unreported, May 4, 1995, CA); *Locobail (U.K.) Ltd v. Bayfield Properties Ltd* (unreported, March 9, 1999, Lawrence Collins, Q.C.). The point was left open in *Habermann v. Koehler* (1996) 73 P. & C.R. 515: *post*, para. 13–022.

[48] *Williams & Glyn's Bank Ltd v. Boland* [1981] A.C. 487; *Hodgson v. Marks* [1971] Ch. 892; *Goodger v. Willis, supra*.

[49] *Celsteel Ltd v. Alton House Holdings Ltd* [1985] 1 W.L.R. 204 at 219; *ante*, para. 6–042.

[50] *Marks v. Attallah* (1966) 110 S.J. 709 (lease granted by a beneficiary under a bare trust who was in occupation of the land).

[51] *Williams & Glyn's Bank Ltd v. Boland, supra*, at 504, 506, 511.

[52] *Hodgson v. Marks, supra*, at 932, *per* Russell L.J.

[53] *Abbey National B.S. v. Cann* [1991] 1 A.C. 56 at 93, *per* Lord Oliver. See too *Lloyds Bank Plc v. Rosset* [1989] Ch. 350 at 377, 394 (on appeal [1991] 1 A.C. 107, where no question on s.70(1)(g) arose).

[54] *Williams & Glyn's Bank Ltd v. Boland, supra*, at 505. For the old suggestion that a lodger is not a person in actual occupation, see *Hodgson v. Marks, supra*, at 932. *Sed quaere*.

[55] *Lloyds Bank Plc v. Rosset, supra*, at 377.

[56] *Kling v. Keston Properties Ltd* (1983) 49 P. & C.R. 212 at 219 (where the car was trapped in the garage due to the defendant's conduct, but where the result would probably have been the same if the garage had been used for its ordinary purpose). See too *Re Boyle's Claim* [1961] 1 W.L.R. 339 at 345 (person in actual occupation of a garage but not of a hedge). *cf. Epps v. Esso Petroleum Co. Ltd* [1973] 1 W.L.R. 1071 at 1079, 1080 (no actual occupation where a car was parked on an open strip of land).

[57] *Abbey National B.S. v. Cann, supra*, at 93.

occupy on behalf of his employer.[58] However, occupation by a friend or relative for his own purposes (rather than for the person claiming the right) will not suffice.[59] Thirdly, actual occupation involves some degree of permanence and continuity.[60] Mere fleeting presence, as where a prospective purchaser or tenant is allowed on to the premises to plan decorations, measure for furnishings, or undertake acts preparatory to moving in, will not suffice.[61] If a person normally resides or works in a property, he will not cease to be in actual occupation merely because he is temporarily absent (as where he spends a period in hospital), even if he is away on a regular and repeated basis,[62] at least if there is some evidence of his presence on the land, such as his furniture or belongings.[63] Fourthly, a person can be in actual occupation of land—

   (i) simultaneously with another, including the vendor or mortgagor whose disposition of the land has put the occupier's rights in issue[64]; or

   (ii) even if he merely occupies a part of it.[65]

In those cases where occupation is shared with the vendor or mortgagor, the occupier's presence need not be inconsistent with or adverse to his.[66] Inquiry must therefore be directed to any adult members of his family (and indeed to anyone else) who happens to be in occupation with him.[67] The view once current that a wife's occupation could be attributed to her husband,[68] has now been decisively rejected.[69] However, notwithstanding this rejection, it has

---

[58] *Strand Securities Ltd v. Caswell* [1965] Ch. 958 at 981, 984; *Lloyds Bank Plc v. Rosset, supra,* at 377, 397; *Abbey National B.S. v. Cann, supra,* at 93. It is controversial whether a person can be in actual occupation when he is not himself present on the premises but is employing builders to carry out work on them. In *Lloyds Bank Plc v. Rosset, supra,* Nicholls and Purchas L.JJ. held that he could, but *cf.* Mustill L.J. at 397 *et seq.* See (1988) 104 L.Q.R. 507 at 510 (R. J. Smith).

[59] *Strand Securities Ltd v. Caswell, supra,* at 984; *Lloyds Bank Plc v. Rosset, supra,* at 405.

[60] *Abbey National B.S. v. Cann, supra,* at 93.

[61] *ibid.,* at 93, 94. Similarly, a builder who comes on to the premises to carry out renovation work is not himself thereby in actual occupation: *Canadian Imperial Bank of Commerce v. Bello* (1991) 64 P. & C.R. 48 at 51.

[62] *Kingsnorth Finance Ltd v. Tizard* [1986] 1 W.L.R. 783 at 788 (wife separated from husband, but visited the house every day to look after the children).

[63] *Chhokar v. Chhokar* [1984] F.L.R. 313 at 317. See too in the analogous context of what is now F.L.A. 1996, s.30, *Hoggett v. Hoggett* (1979) 39 P. & C.R. 121 at 127, 128; *post,* para. 17–024. Actual occupation will not be established merely because a person keeps some of his furniture on the property: *Strand Securities Ltd v. Caswell, supra,* at 985.

[64] *Williams & Glyn's Bank Ltd v. Boland* [1981] A.C. 487 at 505; *Lloyds Bank Plc v. Rosset, supra,* at 394.

[65] *Hodgson v. Marks* [1971] Ch. 892 at 916, 931.

[66] *Williams & Glyn's Bank Ltd v. Boland, supra,* at 505, 506, 511.

[67] *ibid.,* at 508.

[68] See *Caunce v. Caunce* [1969] 1 W.L.R. 440; *Bird v. Syme-Thomson* [1979] 1 W.L.R. 440.

[69] *Williams & Glyn's Bank Ltd v. Boland, supra,* at 505, 506, 511. At 505, Lord Wilberforce described such a view as "heavily obsolete".

been held that children are not in actual occupation in their own right, but merely "as shadows of occupation of their parents".[70]

There is some doubt as to whether the occupation of the person claiming the **6–054** right must be apparent.[71] The weight of authority is at present probably against any such limitation.[72] As the law now stands, the principle embodied in section 70(1)(g) is not one of constructive notice.[73] Where a person is in actual occupation, a purchaser will take free of his rights only if he makes inquiry of him and his interest is not revealed.[74] Even if the existence of the occupier is undiscoverable, a purchaser who makes no inquiry will be bound by his rights, and this is so whether or not they would have been elicited by inquiry.[75] However this narrow approach may require reconsideration. It has been suggested that "even if constructive notice no longer applies in this field, the old law still gives a flavour" to the words of section 70(1)(g).[76] The paragraph expressly visualises that inquiry will be made of the occupier, and this would be meaningless "if actual occupier embraced those whose existence it would be impractical to detect".[77] This approach, which has much to commend it (and is perfectly consistent with the wording of the paragraph), suggests that even if occupation need not be immediately apparent, it should at least be reasonably discoverable.[78]

(5) OCCUPATION OF PART. Although it had been held that an overriding **6–055** interest under section 70(1)(g) "will relate to the land occupied but not anything further",[79] this view has not prevailed. Where a person is in occupation of part of a piece of land but has property rights relating to the whole, those rights are enforceable against any purchaser who acquires the whole.[80] This places a heavy burden of inquiry on the purchaser, particularly where the property is in multiple occupation. He must make inquiry of every occupant

---

[70] *Hypo-Mortgage Services Ltd v. Robinson* [1997] 2 F.C.R. 422 at 426, *per* Nourse L.J. (applying *Bird v. Syme-Thomson, supra*). *cf.* [1998] Fam. Law 349 (E. Cooke).

[71] There is in fact a similar uncertainty as to the basis of the analogous rule which applies to unregistered land: compare *Holmes v. Powell* (1856) 8 De G.M. & G. 572 at 581 with *Cavander v. Bulteel* (1873) 9 Ch. App. 79 at 82. See *ante*, para. 5–019.

[72] *Kling v. Keston Properties Ltd* (1983) 49 P. & C.R. 212 at 222. See too *Hodgson v. Marks, supra*, at 932, where Russell L.J. considered that the law would protect the rights of an occupier even though a "wise purchaser" might be unable to discover them. For a full discussion, see [1989] Conv. 342 (P. Sparkes).

[73] See *Lloyds Bank Plc v. Rosset* [1989] Ch. 350 at 396; *Ferrishurst Ltd v. Wallcite Ltd* [1999] 2 W.L.R. 667 at 681. *cf.* [1989] Conv. 342 at 349 (P. Sparkes).

[74] *Ante*, para. 6–047.

[75] *Williams & Glyn's Bank Ltd v. Boland* [1981] A.C. 487 at 504, 511. *Contrà: Lloyds Bank Plc v. Rosset, supra*, at 404, criticised (1988) 104 L.Q.R. 507 at 511 (R. J. Smith).

[76] *Lloyds Bank Plc v. Rosset, supra*, at 397, *per* Mustill L.J.

[77] *ibid.* See too *Hodgson v. Marks, supra*, at 915, 916; *Abbey National B.S. v. Cann* (1989) 57 P. & C.R. 381 at 394.

[78] *Lloyds Bank Plc v. Rosset, supra*, at 394.

[79] *Ashburn Anstalt v. Arnold* [1989] Ch. 1 at 28, *per* Fox L.J.

[80] *Ferrishurst Ltd v. Wallcite Ltd* [1999] 2 W.L.R. 667. The conclusion in that case that *Ashburn Anstalt v. Arnold, supra*, is inconsistent with *Williams & Glyn's Bank Ltd v. Boland, supra*, is questionable.

as to his rights in relation to all or any part of the land and not just to the part which he occupies.[81]

6–056   (6) RECEIPT OF RENTS AND PROFITS. It has been explained that a purchaser of registered land (in contrast to a purchaser of unregistered land[82]) will be bound by the rights not only of the occupier but also of any person who is in receipt of the rents and profits of the land.[83] Inquiry must therefore be made of any person in occupation as to whom he pays his rent.[84] To fall within the paragraph however, the intermediate landlord must actually be in receipt of rent.[85] If he either takes no steps to enforce its payment,[86] or allows a person (such as a relative) to live on the premises rent-free,[87] he will not be protected.

6–057   (7) INQUIRY. A purchaser will not be bound by the rights of a person in actual occupation if he makes inquiry of him and his rights are not disclosed.[88] Inquiry must however be directed to the occupier, for "reliance upon the untrue *ipse dixit* of the vendor will not suffice".[89] No inquiry of the kind contemplated by section 70(1)(g) can be made of children, who are not regarded as being in actual occupation in any event.[90] However, it is unclear what a purchaser should do in the case of an occupier who is unable to comprehend any inquiry by reason of his mental incapacity. Because the relevant date at which actual occupation must exist is the date of the completion of the transaction,[91] inquiry should be made at or immediately before that time.[92]

6–058   (8) OPERATION OF THE PARAGRAPH. The operation of section 70(1)(g) can be illustrated by four examples.

6–059   (i) *The sale of land subject to tenancies.* A purchaser of registered land subject to a lease will be bound by the rights of the tenant who is in actual occupation, such as an option to purchase the freehold, even though those rights have not been protected as minor interests by registration.[93] Similarly, where the tenant holds under a mere agreement for a lease which he has failed

---

[81] *Ferrishurst Ltd v. Wallcite Ltd, supra,* at 680, instancing a tenant of one flat in a block who had an option to purchase the whole block. *cf. ante,* para. 6–038, n.45.

[82] See *Hunt v. Luck* [1902] 1 Ch. 428; *ante,* para. 5–020.

[83] *Ante,* para. 6–048.

[84] Indeed the same inquiry should also be made of any intermediate landlord.

[85] A token payment will, it seems, suffice: *Strand Securities Ltd v. Caswell* [1965] Ch. 958 at 981.

[86] *E. S. Schwab & Co. Ltd v. McCarthy* (1975) 31 P. & C.R. 196.

[87] *Strand Securities Ltd v. Caswell, supra.*

[88] In substance this qualification operates as a form of estoppel.

[89] *Hodgson v. Marks, supra,* at 932, *per* Russell L.J.

[90] *Hypo-Mortgage Services Ltd v. Robinson* [1997] 2 F.C.R. 422; *ante,* para. 6–053.

[91] *Ante,* para. 6–049.

[92] *Lloyds Bank Plc v. Rosset* [1989] Ch. 350 at 374; *Abbey National B.S. v. Cann* [1991] 1 A.C. 56 at 88.

[93] *Webb v. Pollmount Ltd* [1966] Ch. 584.

to protect by registration, he can still enforce it against the purchaser of the reversion.[94] This is in sharp contrast to the position in unregistered land where the unregistered rights of the tenant are void for non-registration in such circumstances,[95] even though he is in actual occupation and the purchaser of the reversion is fully aware of them (as will almost always be the case).[96] The rule in registered land is more satisfactory.[97]

(ii) *The sale of land with vacant possession.*[98] Where a vendor contracts to **6–060** sell (or to lease) land with vacant possession, the rights of occupiers seldom cause difficulty. The sale is unlikely to be completed unless vacant possession can be given.[99] As the vendor will be liable to pay damages if he fails to complete or if completion is delayed because of the rights of an occupier,[1] he is unlikely to contract to sell the property until he is sure that any occupant is willing to leave. In practice therefore a purchaser will be bound by the rights of an occupier in such cases only where completion has been possible notwithstanding his actual occupation, as where his presence was undiscoverable,[2] or where he was temporarily absent from the property.[3]

(iii) *Mortgage by sole trustee of land.* Where a registered proprietor, who **6–061** holds the property on trust for himself and a person with whom he cohabits (typically but not necessarily his spouse), mortgages the property to a bank as security for an advance made to him alone, the beneficial interest of the co-owner will not be overreached, because payment is not made to two trustees.[4] In *Williams & Glyn's Bank Ltd v. Boland*[5] the House of Lords held that because the co-owner is in actual occupation, the bank will be bound by her beneficial interest as an overriding interest. The House criticised the "easy-going practice of dispensing with enquiries as to occupation beyond that of the vendor", which was at variance with "the widespread development

---

[94] *ibid.*, at 602, 603. See too *City Permanent B.S. v. Miller* [1952] Ch. 840 at 854; *Bridges v. Mees* [1957] Ch. 475 at 486.

[95] *Ante*, para. 5–119; *post*, para. 14–048.

[96] A vendor is under a duty to disclose to a purchaser prior to contract the details of any tenancies affecting the property: *Caballero v. Henty* (1874) 9 Ch. App. 447. For the modern practice see the Standard Conditions of Sale (3rd ed.), c.3.3.

[97] See [1956] C.L.J. 215 at 227, 228 (H.W.R.W.); [1981] C.L.J. 213 at 216, 217 (C.H.) and *ante*, para. 5–120.

[98] See [1990] C.L.J. 277 at 324 (C.H.). For the obligation to give vacant possession, see *post*, para. 12–088.

[99] For a case where a purchaser was unwise enough to complete without insisting that the vendor vacate the property, see *Hodgson v. Marks* [1971] Ch. 892.

[1] *Sharneyford Supplies Ltd v. Edge* [1987] Ch. 305 (vendor unable to complete sale of maggot farm because tenant refused to vacate); *post*, para. 12–090. For delay in completion, see *post*, para. 12–092.

[2] *Kling v. Keston Properties Ltd* (1983) 49 P. & C.R. 212 (person in actual occupation of garage had a right of pre-emption).

[3] *Chhokar v. Chhokar* [1984] F.L.R. 313 (husband deliberately tried to defeat wife's beneficial interest by selling house to accomplice at an undervalue while she was in hospital).

[4] For overreaching, see *ante*, para. 4–078; *post*, para. 8–157.

[5] [1981] A.C. 487; see [1980] C.L.J. 243 (M. J. Prichard); (1981) 97 L.Q.R. 12 (R. J. Smith).

of shared interests of ownership".[6] Although the decision caused consternation amongst bankers and conveyancers when it first appeared,[7] they soon adjusted to it.[8] This is hardly surprising. The problem is in practice usually confined to cases where the registered proprietor already owns the land, requires the mortgage for some purpose unconnected with its acquisition, and therefore seeks to capitalise some part of his "equity" in the property.[9] It is now the usual practice to require all adult occupants to be joined as parties to the transaction or to sign a waiver of their rights in the property.[10]

In any event it has also been held by the House of Lords that where the mortgagee makes the advance to two or more registered proprietors, the interests of any beneficial co-owners in actual occupation will be overreached, and the mortgagee will then take free of their interests.[11] This is because once overreaching has taken place, "there is no longer an interest in the land to which the occupation can be referred or which it can protect".[12]

6–062   (iv) *Purchase of land with the aid of a mortgage.* The problem which arose in the *Boland* case has no application in the common case where a property is purchased with the aid of a mortgage. An example will demonstrate why this is so. A contracts to purchase a house. Both he and his wife, B, contribute part of the price and the balance is provided by a bank mortgage. A alone is the registered proprietor. The purchaser allows A and B to move their belongings onto the premises one hour before the transaction is completed. The bank's registered charge takes priority to B's beneficial interest in the property to which she is entitled by reason of her contribution,[13] and she cannot claim an overriding interest. There are three reasons for this.

> (i) B was not in actual occupation at the time of completion, because the acts which she undertook prior to completion were merely of a "preparatory character carried out by courtesy of the vendor".[14]

---

[6] [1981] A.C. 487 at 508, 509, *per* Lord Wilberforce.

[7] The implications of the *Boland* case were considered by the Law Commission: See Law Com. No. 115, where the conveyancing difficulties are fully rehearsed. For its recommendations (which have since been abandoned by the Commission), see *post*, para. 9–083.

[8] As Lord Hailsham L.C. observed, "conveyancers have come to terms with it—and come to terms with it fairly well. Contrary to their predictions, the world has not come to an end as a result of the decision": *Hansard* (HL), December 15, 1982, vol. 437, col. 662. Lord Scarman considered that the conveyancing difficulties were "exaggerated": *Williams & Glyn's Bank Ltd v. Boland, supra,* at 510.

[9] See [1987] Conv. 334 at 343 (R. J. Smith); [1990] C.L.J. 277 at 312–314, 324 (C.H.).

[10] This is not always effective however: see *post*, para. 10–031.

[11] *City of London B.S. v. Flegg* [1988] A.C. 54. The same will be true where there are two trustees and the mortgage is executed in respect of pre-existing indebtedness: see *State Bank of India v. Sood* [1997] Ch. 276.

[12] *City of London B.S. v. Flegg, supra,* at 91, *per* Lord Oliver.

[13] B has an interest under a presumed resulting trust: *post*, para. 10–016.

[14] *Abbey National B.S. v. Cann* [1991] 1 A.C. 56 at 94, *per* Lord Oliver.

(ii) A's acquisition of the legal estate and the execution of the charge in favour of the bank took effect simultaneously. There is not (as there was once thought to be) a notional moment of time (*scintilla temporis*) between the transfer of the legal title and the mortgage in which B could acquire an equitable interest in the land (by reason of her contribution to the price) that would take priority over the bank's charge.[15]

(iii) B consented to the bank's charge and is therefore estopped from asserting the priority of her interest over it.[16]

(9) REFORM. The Law Commission and HM Land Registry have proposed **6–063** that section 70(1)(g) should be retained in a modified form.[17] Although the rights of persons in actual occupation would continue to be protected as overriding interests, the rights of those who were merely in receipt of the rents and profits of the land would not. The fact of occupation would have to be apparent on a reasonable inspection of land. Occupation of part of the land would only protect the occupier's rights in relation to that part.[18] However, the real limitation on the rights of occupiers will come when the system of electronic conveyancing proposed by the Law Commission and HM Land Registry is fully implemented.[19] It will then only be possible to create many rights in or over registered land by registering them.[20] It follows that the range of rights that could be protected under section 70(1)(g) would be considerably limited. It would exclude expressly created incumbrances but would continue to include interests under trusts of land.[21]

(e) *Rights excepted from the effect of registration.* In those cases where the **6–064** title is not absolute,[22] all estates, rights, interests, and powers excepted from the effect of registration take effect as overriding interests.[23] It is not clear why these excepted rights (the nature of which has already been explained[24]) need to be overriding interests. Where a registered proprietor has a title that is less than absolute, that fact is stated on the proprietorship register, and the rights which are excepted from registration take effect as if the land were unregistered (and are therefore outside the scope of the Act). Because this category of overriding interests is unnecessary, the Law Commission has recommended

---

[15] *Abbey National B.S. v. Cann, supra,* overruling *Church of England B.S. v. Piskor* [1954] Ch. 553; *post,* para. 14–102. See (1990) 106 L.Q.R. 545 (R. J. Smith).

[16] *Skipton B.S. v. Clayton* (1993) 66 P. & C.R. 223 at 229; *post,* para. 10–032.

[17] See (1998) Law Com. No. 254, paras 5.56–5.77.

[18] Thereby reversing the decision in *Ferrishurst Ltd v. Wallcite Ltd* [1999] 2 W.L.R. 667; *ante,* para. 6–055 (decided after Law Com. No. 254 had been published).

[19] See *post,* para. 6–101.

[20] See (1998) Law Com. No. 254, paras 4.35, 11.24, 11.25.

[21] See *ibid.,* paras 11.10–11.12.

[22] *i.e.* where it is possessory, qualified, or good leasehold title.

[23] L.R.A. 1925, s.70(1)(h); Ruoff & Roper, 6–22.

[24] *Ante,* paras 6–024–6–026.

its abolition.[25] In any event such titles are often converted to absolute titles within a comparatively short time.[26]

6–065   *(f) Local land charges.*[27] By section 70(1)(i) of the Act, "rights under local land charges unless and until registered or protected on the register[28] in the prescribed manner", are overriding interests. The general principle applicable to local land charges (whether the title to the land is registered or unregistered) is that they are—

> (i) registrable at the local land charges register for the area in which the land in question is situated[29]; but

> (ii) enforceable against any purchaser of the land affected even if they have not been so registered.[30]

To give effect to this principle where the title is registered, local land charges have the status of overriding interests under section 70(1)(i), whether or not they have been registered at the local land charges register. Although every local land charge will in consequence *bind* any purchaser of the land, some charges will not be *enforceable* against him until they have been registered as registered charges on the Land Register under the Land Registration Act 1925. This applies only to those which are charges to secure money.[31] Until the charge is registered in this way, the chargee will be unable to exercise his powers (*e.g.* of sale).[32]

6–066   *(g) Leases granted for a term not exceeding 21 years.* By section 70(1)(k) of the Land Registration Act 1925,[33] such leases are overriding interests.[34] They take effect however as if they were registered dispositions.[35] The grantee therefore acquires a legal estate and takes the land subject only to entries on

---

[25] (1998) Law Com. No. 254, para. 5.79.

[26] *Ante*, para. 6–027.

[27] For local land charges, see *ante*, para. 5–132. Such charges are now governed by L.L.C.A. 1975. Prior to its enactment, they were governed by L.C.A. 1925, s.15. For the operation of that section in relation to registered land, see *Abbey National B.S. v. Cann* [1991] 1 A.C. 56 at 105, 106.

[28] The "register" referred to in the paragraph is the Land Register and not the local land charges register: *Abbey National B.S. v. Cann, supra*, at 85.

[29] L.L.C.A. 1975, s.4.

[30] If a charge has not been registered, however, a purchaser who has made a proper search of the register will be entitled to compensation: L.L.C.A. 1975, s.10; *ante*, para. 5–136.

[31] L.R.A. 1925, s.59(2); L.R.R. 1925, r. 155; Ruoff & Roper, 6–23, 23–33.

[32] Ruoff & Roper, 23–33. The date at which the charge is registered will not affect its priority: L.R.A. 1925, s.59(2); Ruoff & Roper, 23–34.

[33] As substituted by L.R.A. 1986, s.4(1). Prior to 1987, such leases fell within the paragraph only if they were granted at a rent without taking a fine.

[34] The paragraph is subject to certain exceptions arising out of a public sector tenant's right to buy: see H.A. 1985, s.154(7) (inserted by L.R.A. 1986, s.2(4)), Sched. 9A, para. 3 (inserted by the Housing and Planning Act 1986, s.8; Sched. 2); Ruoff & Roper, 6–25.

[35] L.R.A. 1925, ss.19(2), 22(2); *Barclays Bank Plc v. Zaroovabli* [1997] Ch. 321 at 327. The status of an assignment of such a lease has been described as "obscure": M. P. Thompson, *Barnsley's Conveyancing Law and Practice*, (4th ed.), p. 482; but see (1998) Law Com. No. 254, para. 7.11.

the register and overriding interests.[36] Such leases can never take effect as minor interests.[37]

(1) LEASES WITHIN THE PARAGRAPH. The paragraph applies only to legal leases. An agreement for a lease is excluded because it is not "granted" as the paragraph requires.[38] There is no requirement that the lease should take effect in possession. A term of years that is granted from some future date will fall within the paragraph provided that it complies with the restrictions on such reversionary leases.[39] Nor is it necessary that the lessee should be in occupation. He could, for example, hold a lease of the reversion,[40] or he might allow a relative or friend to live on the premises rent-free. In principle the paragraph should also include a discontinuous term of years where the total period granted does not exceed 21 years, such as a time-share agreement whereby the tenant is granted the right to occupy a property for one week each year for 80 years.[41]

6–067

(2) CONTRAST WITH RIGHTS OF OCCUPIERS. In many cases a lease that has not been completed by registration may take effect as an overriding interest under either paragraph (g) (the rights of persons in actual occupation of the land or in receipt of the rents and profits thereof)[42] or (k) of section 70(1). A tenant will have to rely on paragraph (g) if—

6–068

(i) he holds under an agreement for a lease; or

(ii) his lease was granted for more than 21 years but has not been completed by registration.[43]

By contrast, he will have to rely on paragraph (k) if he is neither in actual occupation nor in receipt of the rents and profits of the land. In certain cases, a lease which a tenant fails to protect by registration will fall within neither paragraph, so that a purchaser will take free of it. Examples include—

(i) an agreement for a lease where the tenant has not entered into actual occupation of the land[44]; and

---

[36] L.R.A. 1925, s.20(1). If the lease granted is a sub-lease, the grantee also takes subject to covenants and other liabilities incident to the estate created: *ibid.*, s.23(1). A lease or sub-lease granted for a term not exceeding 21 years, to take effect in possession or within one year of its grant, may be granted notwithstanding that there is on the register (*inter alia*) a caution, restriction or an inhibition (other than a bankruptcy inhibition), but subject to the interests intended to be protected by such entry: *ibid.*, ss.18(3), 21(3).

[37] L.R.A. 1925, ss.19(2), 22(2), 48(1).

[38] *City Permanent B.S. v. Miller* [1952] Ch. 840.

[39] *Post*, para. 14–061. For the distinction between reversionary leases and leases of the reversion, see *post*, para. 14–103.

[40] *Post*, para. 14–103.

[41] In *Cottage Holiday Associates Ltd v. Customs and Excise Commissioners* [1983] Q.B. 735, it was held that such a lease was not "a term certain exceeding 21 years" for the purposes of the legislation on value added tax.

[42] *Ante*, para. 6–047.

[43] For the drawbacks of non-registration, see *ante*, para. 6–032.

[44] *City Permanent B.S. v. Miller, supra.*

(ii) a lease granted for more than 21 years where the tenant is not himself in actual occupation of the premises but allows some other person to reside there without payment.[45]

6–069   (3) REFORM. The Law Commission and HM Land Registry have recommended that the scope of section 70(1)(k) should be narrowed.[46] First, reversionary leases would cease to be included (except for those which would take effect within three months of their grant) because they are not readily discoverable by inspection or inquiry.[47] Secondly, it should be confined to leases granted for a continuous term, so that time-share arrangements would be excluded and would require registration.[48]

6–070   *(h) Rights to coal.*[49] All the rights and title to coal that are by statute vested in what is now the Coal Authority, together with all ancillary rights, take effect as overriding interests.[50] The reason for the overriding status of these rights is wholly pragmatic: the extent and complexity of such rights would make it virtually impossible to register them. The Law Commission and Land Registry have therefore recommended that such rights should continue to be overriding interests.[51]

6–071   **4. Entries on register.** The registrar has a discretion to make entries on the register stating that the land is free from or subject to certain overriding interests.[52] This is a helpful practice since it brings third party rights onto the registered title, or clears them off, as the case may be.[53] The registrar is also under a mandatory duty to enter a notice of the existence of any easement, right privilege or benefit created by an instrument (and not, for example, an easement acquired by prescription) which appears on the title at the time of first registration.[54] Interests so registered cease to be overriding interests since the definition of that term excludes them.[55]

---

[45] *Strand Securities Ltd v. Caswell* [1965] Ch. 958.
[46] (1998) Law Com. No. 254, paras 5.87–5.94.
[47] *ibid.*, para. 5.91.
[48] *ibid.*, para. 5.92.
[49] Ruoff & Roper, 6–27.
[50] L.R.A. 1925, s.70(1)(m) (inserted by Coal Industry Act 1994, s.67(1); Sched. 9, para. 1(2)); and see Coal Industry Act 1994, Sched. 9, para. 1(1).
[51] (1998) Law Com. No. 254, paras 5.97–5.98.
[52] L.R.A. 1925, ss.5, 9, 20(1), 23(1), 70(3); L.R.R. 1925, r. 197; Ruoff & Roper, 6–29, 6–30. Application for an entry that a title is free from an overriding interest must be specific as to the interest in question. There can be no entry that the land is free from overriding interests generally: L.R.R. 1925, r. 197; Ruoff & Roper, 12–37. In *Re Dances Way, West Town, Hayling Island* [1962] Ch. 490 at 510, Diplock L.J. suggested than an entry of freedom from an overriding interest could be made only where there had been a previous entry of such an interest. This view is wholly unsupported by r. 197, and must be doubted.
[53] In practice, an entry stating that the land is free from an overriding interest would only be made if a specific overriding interest were determined: see Ruoff & Roper, 6–29. Such entries are not common.
[54] L.R.A. 1925, s.70(2). L.R.R. 1925, r. 41 does not qualify the mandatory nature of this duty: *Re Dances Way, West Town, Hayling Island, supra,* at 508.
[55] L.R.A. 1925, s.3(xvi).

5. Power to dispose of overriding interests. The Land Registry Act 1925 **6–072** does not expressly define the powers of disposition of a person having the benefit of an overriding interest (such as a person in actual occupation under an agreement for a lease). However, it is clear that both he and any person (such as a mortgagee) who has paramount powers in relation to that interest, may deal with or dispose of it in the same way as if the land were unregistered.[56] Although interests and rights created in this way normally take effect as minor interests which are capable of being overridden by registered dispositions for valuable consideration,[57] this does not apply to the disposition or creation of overriding interests.[58] Thus a tenant under a 21-year lease can assign it or grant a sub-lease in the same manner as if the title were unregistered, and the assignee or grantee will thereby also have an overriding interest.[59]

6. Priority of overriding interests. The priority of overriding interests has **6–073** attracted little attention. The Land Registration Act 1925 makes express provision for one type of overriding interest—the grant of a lease or underlease for a term not exceeding 21 years—to have the same priority as if it were a registered disposition.[60] Although the position is nowhere stated in relation to the grant or assignment of other overriding interests, it seems probable that they take subject to existing overriding interests and minor interests.[61] The Law Commission and HM Land Registry have recommended that this rule should be set out in legislative form.[62]

Section 3. Registered Charges

If a registered proprietor wishes to charge his land by way of legal mortgage **6–074** he must create a registered charge by deed.[63] That charge should be completed by registration,[64] and normally takes effect as a charge by way of legal mortgage.[65] The registered chargee is not a registered proprietor and is issued not with a land certificate, but with a charge certificate.[66] The proprietor of a registered charge has power to transfer it,[67] and (in the absence of any entry

---

[56] *ibid.*, s.101(1).
[57] *ibid.*, s.101(2).
[58] *ibid.*, s.101(6).
[59] Ruoff & Roper, 8–05. Presumably if the tenant merely granted a third party an option to purchase his lease, that would take effect as a minor interest under L.R.A. 1925, s.101(2).
[60] L.R.A. 1925, ss.19(2), 22(2); *Barclays Bank Plc v. Zaroovabli* [1997] Ch. 321 at 327; *ante*, para. 6–031.
[61] See the discussion in (1998) Law Com. No. 254, paras 7.12–7.14.
[62] *ibid.*, para. 7.35.
[63] L.R.A. 1925, s.25.
[64] *ibid.*, s.26.
[65] *ibid.*, s.27(1). For charges by way of legal mortgage, see *post*, para. 19–025.
[66] L.R.A. 1925, s.63(1). The land certificate has to be deposited at the registry until the charge is cancelled: *ibid.*, s.65.
[67] *ibid.*, s.33.

to the contrary on the register) has and may exercise all the powers conferred by law on a legal mortgagee.[68] The charge will be protected by an entry on the charges register of the land charged.[69] Registered charges are therefore *sui generis*. The proprietor does not have a registered estate.[70] The charge is not an overriding interest because it is completed by registration, whereas an overriding interest is "not entered on the register".[71] It differs from a minor interest in that it is created by a registered disposition.[72] Registered charges are considered more fully later in this chapter.[73]

Section 4. Minor Interests

1. Definition

6–075   (1) RESIDUAL NATURE. The Act defines minor interests elaborately and rather confusingly in negative terms.[74] They are interests which are incapable of being disposed of or created by registered disposition and which are not overriding interests. In the scheme of registered land, minor interests therefore constitute a residual category. Registrable interests are protected by the grant of registered title; overriding interests need no protection; registrable charges are a special case; and all other interests fall into the class of minor interests. These take effect in equity[75] and require protection by some entry on the register, for otherwise they will not bind a purchaser for valuable consideration under a registered disposition, whether or not he has notice of them.[76] Even though a minor interest has not been protected by registration, it may still take effect as an overriding interest in appropriate circumstances and so bind a purchaser of the land. This has already been explained.[77]

6–076   (2) CLASSES OF MINOR INTERESTS. Although minor interests are a residual category, it is possible to define them with some precision. The principal classes of minor interests are as follows.[78]

---

[68] *ibid.*, s.34(1). He may not have these powers where the owner of the estate concerned has not executed a valid charge: see *Halifax Mortgage Services Ltd v. Muirhead* (1997) 76 P. & C.R. 418 at 428.

[69] *ibid.*, s.26(1); L.R.R. 1925, r. 7.

[70] L.R.A. 1925, s.3(xxiii).

[71] *ibid.*, s.3(xvi).

[72] *ibid.*, s.3(xxii). A minor interest cannot be so created: *ibid.* s.3(xv).

[73] *post*, para. 6–112.

[74] L.R.A. 1925, s.3(xv).

[75] L.R.A. 1925, ss.2, 101(3).

[76] *Post*, para. 6–105. It is in fact possible to create minor interests which are incapable of registration under L.R.A. 1925, as where a tenant holding under a lease not exceeding 21 years contracts to assign it. There is no title against which such an estate contract can be registered. Such leases are treated as if they were unregistered land, and the estate contract is registered as a land charge under L.C.A 1972, s.2 (para. 5–099), against the name of the tenant. See (1998) Law Com. No. 254, para. 7.11.

[77] *Ante*, para. 6–047. Some minor interests cannot be overriding interests: *ante*, para. 6–051.

[78] In addition to the interests listed, leases granted prior to 1987 which either contain an absolute prohibition on dealings, or were granted at a premium for a term not exceeding 21 years can only be minor interests. As regards leases granted since 1986, the former category are now registrable, and the latter take effect as overriding interests: see L.R.A. 1925, ss.8(2), 70(1)(k) (as amended in each case by L.R.A. 1986).

(i) Matters which in unregistered land are capable of protection as land charges under the Land Charges Act 1972.[79] Because not all such matters are interests in land, there may be minor interests which are not interests in land,[80] such as rights of pre-emption when they are first granted,[81] or some receivership orders.[82] In such cases the purpose of registration may be to ensure that an interested person is notified of a proposed dealing rather than to make a property right binding on any purchaser.[83]

(ii) Interests under a trust of land or settlement which are capable of being overridden on a disposition by the trustees of land, life tenant or statutory owner (as the case may be).[84] Even though such interests may be overreached, they should be protected by the appropriate form of registration. Indeed the function of registration in such cases is to facilitate overreaching and to ensure that a purchaser takes free of such interests.

(iii) All other equitable rights. These will include the residual category of rights which in unregistered land are not registrable under the Land Charges Act 1972 but are protected by the doctrine of notice.[85]

(iv) Interests created by registered dispositions in the period between their execution and their completion by registration.[86]

Minor interests are created in the same way as they would be if the title to the land were not registered.[87]

(3) POLICY OF THE ACT. The policy of the Act is twofold. First, the purpose **6–077** of making an entry on the register in respect of a minor interest is not only to ensure that purchasers are made aware of and take subject to equitable rights over property. Registration is also employed to facilitate conveyancing (by

---

[79] Ruoff & Roper, 7–08.
[80] *Clayhope Properties Ltd v. Evans* [1986] 1 W.L.R. 1223 at 1229; *post*, para. 00. *cf. Elias v. Mitchell* [1972] Ch. 652 at 659; *Lynton International Ltd v. Noble* (1991) 63 P. & C.R. 452 at 455.
[81] A right of pre-emption is initially a contractual right, but becomes an option when the grantor decides to sell: *Pritchard v. Briggs* [1980] Ch. 338; criticised *post*, paras 12–062, 12–063. It may be registered as a minor interest as soon as it is created, but takes its priority from the time when it becomes an option: Ruoff & Roper, 35–18. The suggestion in K. J. Gray, *Elements of Land Law* (2nd ed.), p. 146, that a right of pre-emption is registrable only when it becomes an option is not thought to be correct.
[82] *Clayhope Properties Ltd v. Evans*, *supra* (receiver appointed to manage a block of flats where the landlord was allegedly in breach of his repairing obligations).
[83] *Clayhope Properties Ltd v. Evans*, *supra*, at 1231.
[84] L.R.A. 1925, s.3(xv).
[85] *Ante*, para. 5–124.
[86] *Ante*, paras 6–032, 6–033.
[87] L.R.A. 1925, s.101(1).

ensuring that beneficial interests under trusts will be overreached),[88] to fore-warn interested parties of dealings with registered land,[89] and (in appropriate cases) to prevent fraudulent dealings with the property.[90] Secondly, and following from this, minor interests form a comprehensive residual class, which necessarily comprises all interests in and certain rights relating to land not otherwise provided for.[91] No residual class of interests or equities can bind purchasers under the doctrine of notice, "which has no application to registered conveyancing".[92] Indeed, for reasons already explained, minor interests are "a far more comprehensive substitute for notice than the Land Charges Act 1972".[93] Unless a minor interest takes effect as an overriding interest, it must either be protected on the register, or else be defeasible by a purchaser. This undoubtedly weakens the security of those interests which it is unreasonable to expect their owners to register, and which the doctrine of notice more suitably protects in unregistered land.[94] However, as has already been explained, the rigour of the registration requirements is tempered by the protection that is given to overriding interests.[95] There can be little doubt that if the Land Registration Act 1925 is considered as a whole, third party rights are much better protected where title is registered than where it is unregistered.

6–078   **2. Protection of minor interests.** A minor interest may be protected by a notice, a caution, an inhibition, or a restriction.[96] There are two main factors which determine the appropriate form of protection. First, each of the four forms of protection fulfils a different function: this is explained below. Secondly, as a general rule, a notice or a restriction can only be entered on the register if the registered proprietor's land certificate is either produced to the registrar,[97] or is already deposited with him, as will be the case where the registered land is subject to a subsisting registered charge.[98] The entry of a notice or restriction generally requires the co-operation of or has to be made

---

[88] *Post*, para. 6–092.

[89] *Post*, para. 6–083.

[90] *Post*, para. 6–091.

[91] Ruoff & Roper, 7–07. Contrast the policy of the L.C.A. 1925 (now L.C.A. 1972) as interpreted in *Shiloh Spinners Ltd v. Harding* [1973] A.C. 691: *ante*, para. 5–104.

[92] *Williams & Glyn's Bank Ltd v. Boland* [1981] A.C. 487 at 508, *per* Lord Wilberforce. "One of the essential features of registration of title is to substitute a system of registration of rights for the doctrine of notice": *Parkash v. Irani Finance Ltd* [1970] Ch. 101 at 109, *per* Plowman J. See too *Barclays Bank Plc v. Boulter* [1998] 1 W.L.R. 1 at 11.

[93] (1987) Law Com. No. 158, para. 4.09.

[94] This is particularly so as regards an equity arising by estoppel. Estoppel is now the most important way in which the law accommodates informal transactions: see *post*, chap. 13.

[95] *Ante*, para. 6–047.

[96] L.R.A. 1925, s.101(3); Ruoff & Roper, 7–01.

[97] L.R.A. 1925, s.64(1). This subsection applies only where the land certificate is "outstanding".

[98] L.R.A. 1925, s.65. In this situation, the land certificate is not "outstanding": Ruoff & Roper, 3–29. The registry will however notify the registered proprietor of the application for registration to give him an opportunity to object to the entry: Ruoff & Roper, 35–36.

by the registered proprietor and is not therefore "hostile" unlike the registration of a caution or inhibition.[99] If the registered proprietor objects to the entry on the register, then unless the court or registrar orders it,[1] the party seeking to register the right will have to lodge a caution instead. In an increasing number of situations statute specifically provides that a notice may be registered even though the land certificate is not produced.[2] This applies to the registration of—

(i) a lease at a rent without taking a fine[3];

(ii) a creditor's notice[4];

(iii) a notice of a charge for inheritance tax[5];

(iv) a spouse's charge in respect of matrimonial home rights under the Family Law Act 1996[6];

(v) a notice of any variation of a lease of a flat under the Landlord and Tenant Act 1987[7];

(vi) a notice of a public sector tenant's preserved right to buy under the Housing Act 1985 (as amended)[8]; and

(vii) a notice in respect of an access order under the Access to Neighbouring Land Act 1992.[9]

It should be noted that a purchaser of registered land always takes it subject to "the incumbrances and other entries, if any, appearing on the register".[10] The priority of minor interests *inter se* is considered later in this chapter.[11]

Each of the four methods of protecting a minor interest must now be considered.

---

[99] Ruoff & Roper, 35–36. *cf.* (1998) Law Com. No. 254, paras 6.8, 6.32.

[1] As it may, as where the proprietor has granted the right, but refuses to produce his land certificate: see L.R.A. 1925, s.48(2); L.R.R. 1925, r. 298.

[2] Ruoff & Roper, 3–33.

[3] L.R.A. 1925, s.64(1)(c); *Strand Securities Ltd v. Caswell* [1965] Ch. 958 (disapproving the practice of the Land Registry which had previously required the production of the certificate in such cases). The logic of this exception is not apparent, because leases granted at a premium can be registered only on production of the land certificate: see Ruoff & Roper, 21–14.

[4] L.R.A. 1925, s.64(1)(c).

[5] *ibid.* (as amended by the Finance Act 1975, s.52(1), Sched. 12, and Finance Act 1986, s.100).

[6] L.R.A. 1925, s.64(5) (inserted by the Matrimonial Homes and Property Act 1981, s.4(1); amended by M.H.A. 1983, s.12, Sched. 2; and the Family Law Act 1996, s.66(1); Sched. 8).

[7] L.R.A. 1925, s.64(6) (inserted by the Landlord and Tenant Act 1987, s.61(1), Sched. 4).

[8] H.A. 1985, Sched. 9A, para. 5(3) (inserted by the Housing and Planning Act 1986, s.8(2), Sched. 2).

[9] L.R.A. 1925, s.65(7) (inserted by the Access to Neighbouring Land Act 1992, s.5(3)).

[10] L.R.A. 1925, ss.20(1), 23(1); *post*, para. 6–105.

[11] *Post*, para. 6–094.

(a) Notices

6–079   (1) EFFECT. A notice is the most effective method of protecting a right over land. In most cases the registered proprietor must agree to its registration and therefore the existence or validity of the right is not normally in issue.[12] Notice of a right or incumbrance is entered on the charges register,[13] and once registered—

> (i) the proprietor of the land and those deriving title under him are deemed to be fixed with notice of it[14]; and

> (ii) any disposition of the land made thereafter takes effect subject to the right so far as it is valid and is not (apart from the Act) overridden by the disposition.[15]

A purchaser will be bound by any right that is properly protected by a notice even if it is not disclosed on a search of the register.[16] It should be noted that registration of a notice neither validates the right nor gives it a priority that it would not otherwise have.[17] Unlike a registered disposition,[18] the validity of a minor interest protected by the registration of a notice is not therefore guaranteed by the registry.

6–080   (2) REGISTRABLE RIGHTS. The Act provides neither a general principle for determining which rights can be protected by means of a notice nor any comprehensive list of such rights.[19] Instead they have to be ascertained by reference to numerous provisions in both the Act and the Land Registration Rules 1925. It is possible to summarise the effects of these provisions as follows.

> (i) Where a registered disposition creates an adverse right over registered land,[20] a notice of that right will be entered automatically against the title of

---

[12] See (1998) Law Com. No. 254, paras 6.8. 6.9.

[13] L.R.R 1925, r. 7. The entry on the register gives details of the right protected: see (1998) Law Com. No. 254, para. 2.29; and L.R.R. 1925, rr. 188, 190.

[14] L.R.A. 1925, ss.48(1), 49(1), 50(2); L.R.R. r. 190; *Re White Rose Cottage* [1965] Ch. 940 at 949; *Clark v. Chief Land Registrar* [1993] Ch. 294 at 310; *Mortgage Corporation Ltd v. Nationwide Credit Corporation Ltd* [1994] Ch. 49 at 54. Registration of a notice, unlike the registration of a land charge in unregistered land, is not notice to all persons for all purposes, but only to the proprietor and those deriving title under him: *cf. ante.* paras 4–057, 5–019.

[15] L.R.A. 1925, s.52. See *Mortgage Corporation Ltd v. Nationwide Credit Corporation Ltd, supra* at 56; *Clark v. Chief Land Registrar* [1994] Ch. 370 at 382.

[16] This may be inferred from *Clark v. Chief Land Registrar* [1993] Ch. 294 at 313, 314; [1994] Ch. 370 at 385.

[17] "Notice is indeed notice, but it does not give validity, if validity is not otherwise there, and it does not give priority which would not, apart from the Act, have been there": *Mortgage Corporation Ltd v. Nationwide Credit Corporation Ltd, supra,* at 56, *per* Dillon L.J. For the priority of minor interests, see *post,* paras 6–094, 6–095.

[18] *Ante,* para. 6–031.

[19] The suggestion in Ruoff & Roper, 36–05, that L.R.A. 1925, s.49(1) provides a "definitive list" of such interests is misleading.

[20] For registered dispositions, see *ante,* para. 6–031.

the property in question when that transaction is completed by registration in the proper way,[21] as where a registered proprietor grants a lease for a term exceeding 21 years,[22] or an easement, right or privilege.[23] It should be emphasised that the entry of a notice in this situation is a means of protecting a *registered disposition* and not a mere minor interest.

(ii) The Act lists certain rights which can be protected by notice where an application is made specifically for that purpose.[24] That list includes certain registered dispositions,[25] which for the reasons explained above, require no such specific application in fact, including the grant of legal annuities or rentcharges.[26] Of the remaining rights which can only be registered on a specific application, the following are the most important:

(i) all land charges under the Land Charges Act 1972[27] (*e.g.* estate contracts[28] and restrictive covenants[29]);

(ii) charging orders under the Charging Orders Act 1979, the Criminal Justice Act 1988 and the Drug Trafficking Act 1994[30];

(iii) acquisition orders under the Landlord and Tenant Act 1987[31];

(iv) access orders under the Access to Neighbouring Land Act 1992[32]; and

(v) "creditors notices and any other right, interest or claim which it may be deemed expedient to protect by notice instead of by caution, inhibition, or restriction".[33]

---

[21] Ruoff & Roper, 35–05.

[22] L.R.R. 1925, r. 46; Ruoff & Roper, 21–12. Where the lease contains a prohibition against dealing, the notice is in the form prescribed by L.R.R. 1925, r. 45 (as substituted).

[23] L.R.A. 1925, s.144(1)(xviii); Ruoff & Roper, 17–47.

[24] L.R.A. 1925, ss.48–51.

[25] Including leases which are not overriding interests: *ibid.*, s.48(1); L.R.R. 1925, r. 186. However, these provisions are now obsolete. Their former function was as follows. Prior to 1987, leases which contained an absolute prohibition against dealings were incapable of substantive registration and could only be protected by a notice under those provisions: Ruoff & Roper, 21–18; *ante*, para. 6–017. Since 1986 all leases granted for a term exceeding 21 years, whether containing such a prohibition or not, can and should be completed by registration: see L.R.A. 1925, ss.8(2) (as substituted by L.R.A. 1986, s.3(1)), 19(2), 22(2) (as amended by L.R.A. 1986, s.4(3)).

[26] L.R.A. 1925, s.49(1)(a). When the disposition was completed, a notice would be entered automatically under L.R.R. r. 40.

[27] L.R.A. 1925, s.49(1)(c).

[28] Where a purchaser contracts to sub-sell the land, the sub-purchaser can register his estate contract against the registered proprietor's title provided that the land certificate is produced: Ruoff & Roper, 35–15. *cf. ante*, para. 5–100.

[29] L.R.A. 1925, s.50(1). See, *e.g. Re Stone and Saville's Contract* [1963] 1 W.L.R. 163.

[30] L.R.A. 1925, s.49(1)(g) (inserted by the Charging Orders Act 1979, s.3(3), as amended by Criminal Justice Act 1988, s.170(1), Sched. 15, para. 6; Drug Trafficking Act 1994, s.65(1), Sched. 1, para. 1).

[31] L.R.A. 1925, s.49(1)(h) (inserted by the Landlord and Tenant Act 1987, s.61(1), Sched. 4, para. 1).

[32] L.R.A. 1925, s.49(1)(j) (inserted by the Access to Neighbouring Land Act 1992, s.5(2)).

[33] L.R.A. 1925, s.49(1)(f).

Under the last of these categories, rights which in unregistered land are still governed by the doctrine of notice (such as an equity arising by estoppel),[34] may be protected by the registration of a notice.[35]

6–081 (iii) There is an important limitation on the registration of notices which provides a clue as to their nature. A notice cannot be registered in respect of any estate, right, or interest which (independently of the Act) is capable of being both—

> (i) overridden by the proprietor under a trust for sale, the powers of the Settled Land Act 1925 or any other statute, or of a settlement; and
>
> (ii) protected by a restriction.[36]

A notice is not therefore an appropriate method of protecting interests under trusts, which should be done instead by entering a restriction on the register.[37]

> (iv) Leases of 21 years or less take effect as overriding interests and cannot be protected by the entry of a notice.[38]

The function of a notice is to protect rights over and incumbrances upon land. Of the four methods of protecting minor interests, registration of a notice is the closest in concept to the registration of a land charge in unregistered land, though (as will be apparent) it differs from the latter in many respects.

6–082 (3) DISCHARGE OF NOTICES. The registrar is empowered to cancel a notice which he is satisfied has determined, ceased or been discharged or for any other reason no longer affects the registered land.[39] While a caution may be cancelled without necessarily destroying the interest which it protects, a notice can be cancelled only where the right ceases to exist.[40]

(b) Cautions

6–083 (1) NATURE AND EFFECT. It has been said that a caution "is essentially a procedure . . . not an interest in land".[41] It entitles the cautioner to be warned of any proposed dealing with the property, and to be given an opportunity to

---

[34] See *ante*, para. 5–105.
[35] Ruoff & Roper, 35–33.
[36] L.R.A. 1925, s.49(2). There is however a curious but seldom used power for a beneficiary to register a notice to ensure that there are always two trustees of a settlement or trust of land: *ibid.*, s.49(1)(d). In practice a restriction is normally used: Ruoff & Roper, 35–29.
[37] But see L.R.A. 1925, s.49(2) (proviso).
[38] L.R.A. 1925, ss.19(2), 22(2), 48(1).
[39] L.R.R. 1925, r. 16; Ruoff & Roper, 35–35.
[40] *Holmes v. Kennard & Son* (1984) 49 P. & C.R. 202 at 209 (where solicitors were held liable in negligence for failing to appreciate this distinction).
[41] *Clark v. Chief Land Registrar* [1993] Ch. 294 at 314, *per* Ferris J. (aff'd [1994] Ch. 370).

assert priority for his interest,[42] but it does no more than that.[43] While it remains on the register, no such transaction can be completed.[44] By contrast, where there is a notice on the register, that entry does not prevent the sale or other disposition of the property, but instead the purchaser or chargee takes the land subject to the right so protected.[45] The function of registering a caution (unlike that of registering a notice) has therefore been described as "very largely a purpose of obtaining notice of proposed dealings rather than a purpose of overriding purchasers".[46]

A caution lodged under the Act does not prejudice the claim or title of any person and has only such effect as the Act gives to it.[47] Unlike a notice, it confers no priority on the cautioner's interest, but merely gives him the right to be notified of the transaction.[48] The effects of this are as follows.

(i) The lodgement of a caution has no relevance to the priority of competing equitable interests. It will not give a later equitable interest priority over an earlier one.[49]

(ii) A purchaser who acquires title under a registered disposition[50] will not always be bound by an interest even it is protected by a caution.[51] This will be the case where, due to an error at the registry, the cautioner is not notified of the proposed transaction.[52] As the transaction is thereby completed without the cautioner being notified, he is unable to assert his right against the purchaser.[53] If the cautioner suffers loss in such circumstances, he will be entitled to an indemnity because of the error on the part of the registry.[54]

---

[42] *Clark v. Chief Land Registrar* [1994] Ch. 370 at 383.

[43] *Clark v. Chief Land Registrar* [1993] Ch. 294 at 314.

[44] L.R.A. 1925, ss.53(3), 55(1); *Willies-Williams v. National Trust* (1993) 65 P. & C.R. 359 at 362. See too *Abigail v. Lapin* [1934] A.C. 491 at 500 (explaining the effect of the similar but not identical procedure of entering a *caveat* under the Australian Torrens system of land registration).

[45] *Ante*, para. 6–079.

[46] *Clayhope Properties Ltd v. Evans* [1986] 1 W.L.R. 1223 at 1231, *per* Dillon L.J.

[47] L.R.A. 1925, s.56(2).

[48] *Clark v. Chief Land Registrar* [1994] Ch. 370.

[49] *Barclays Bank Ltd v. Taylor* [1974] Ch. 137; *post*, para. 6–095.

[50] This includes the grant of a lease for 21 years or less and which therefore takes effect as an overriding interest: *ante*, para. 6–031. The Act provides that such a lease takes effect subject to the interest intended to be protected by any caution: L.R.A. 1925, ss.18(3), 21(3).

[51] *Clark v. Chief Land Registrar* [1993] Ch. 294 at 312, 313 (disapproving a statement to the contrary in the previous edition of this work at p. 213); [1994] Ch. 370 at 384, 385 (not following *Parkash v. Irani Finance Ltd* [1970] Ch. 101 at 110). A purchaser is, in any event, not concerned with any matter (not being an overriding interest) "which is not protected by a caution or other entry on the register": L.R.A. 1925, s.59(6).

[52] *Clark v. Chief Land Registrar* [1993] Ch. 294 at 311–314; [1994] Ch. 370 at 385.

[53] *Clark v. Chief Land Registrar* [1994] Ch. 370 (following *Barclays Bank Ltd v. Taylor, supra,* and distinguishing *Parkash v. Irani Finance Ltd, supra*). In no case has there been any discussion of L.R.A. 1925, s.79(4) (purchaser not to be affected by omission to send notice or by non-receipt thereof), the effect of which is obscure.

[54] See L.R.A. 1925, s.83(2), (3); *post*, para. 6–136; *Clark v. Chief Land Registrar* [1994] Ch. 370.

(iii) Where a cautioner consents to the creation of a later charge, that charge takes priority over the rights of the cautioner.[55]

6–084 Cautions against dealings tend to be lodged in three circumstances. The first is when the registered proprietor refuses to co-operate in the registration of a notice. It is a "hostile" form of registration that does not require the production of the proprietor's land certificate. Secondly, the precarious and impermanent nature of a caution[56] makes it appropriate where only temporary protection is required, as in the case of an estate contract. Thirdly, where the parties to a transaction wish to keep its details confidential, they may employ a caution because the entry on the register gives no indication of the ground on which the caution is lodged.[57]

There are two different types of caution, a caution against first registration and a caution against dealings. As the first relates to unregistered land and the second to registered land, the term "caution" *simpliciter*, when used in relation to registered land, means a caution against dealings. In each case a statutory declaration in prescribed form must be made in support of the application for the caution.[58] The normal period of notice of any transaction to which the cautioner is entitled is 14 days.[59]

6–085 (2) CAUTIONS AGAINST FIRST REGISTRATION.[60] Any person having or claiming to have an interest in land such that he may object to any disposition of it, may lodge with the registrar a caution against its first registration.[61] Thus a person who has contracted to purchase the land or who claims a beneficial interest in it may lodge a caution to ensure that the owner does not dispose of the property without the cautioner's knowledge. No registration can then be made of that estate until notice has been served on the cautioner to appear and oppose such registration (if he thinks fit) and either the period of notice has elapsed, or the cautioner has before that time entered an appearance.[62] If the cautioner contests the registration, a hearing will take place before the Chief Land Registrar.[63] He will then order that—

(i) the caution be continued and the application for registration be cancelled; or

---

[55] *Chancery Plc. v. Ketteringham* (1993) 69 P. & C.R. 426; aff'd [1994] Ch. 370.
[56] *Post*, para. 6–088.
[57] See (1998) Law Com. No. 254, para. 2.29.
[58] L.R.A. 1925, ss.53(2), 54(2); L.R.R. 1925, rr. 64, 215; Sched. 1, Form CT1; Sched. 2, Form 14.
[59] L.R.R. 1925, rr. 67, 218. For notices served by post, L.R.A. 1925, s.79(2) in effect makes the 14 days 22: Ruoff & Roper, 36–17.
[60] See Ruoff & Roper, 13–03–13–09.
[61] L.R.A. 1925, s.53(1). For the form of the caution, see L.R.R. 1925, r. 64; Sched. 1, Form CT1.
[62] L.R.A. 1925, s.53(3).
[63] Or rather the Solicitor to HM Land Registry to whom the Registrar's judicial functions have now been delegated: *ante*, para. 6–012. For the Registrar's right to hear and determine the matter, see L.R.R. 1925, r. 298: *ante*, para. 6–012. Any person aggrieved by any act done by the registrar may appeal to the court: L.R.A. 1925, s.56(1).

(ii) the application for registration be granted (conditionally[64] or unconditionally) and the caution cancelled.[65]

It is normally only on an application to register that a caution against registration can be contested. There is no machinery for "warning off" such a caution before that time.[66]

(3) CAUTIONS AGAINST DEALINGS. Although the Act contains no compre- **6–086** hensive list of rights which may be protected by a caution against dealings, it lays down a general principle upon which such cautions may be registered.[67] Any person interested under any unregistered instrument, or as a judgment creditor, or "otherwise howsoever, in any land or charge registered in the name of any other person", whose interest has not been registered or protected by a notice or restriction, may lodge a caution against any dealing with the land or charge.[68] Thereafter no entry in respect of any dealing with that land or charge may be made on the register until notice has been served on the cautioner and has expired.[69] To fall within this provision, the intending cautioner must have an interest in land.[70] Thus a caution may be lodged in respect of an interest under a trust of land, as where property is held on a constructive trust for the claimant.[71] By contrast, it has been held that a person with the benefit of a contractual right to a share of profits on the resale of a property does not have a sufficient interest for these purposes.[72] Nor can a caution be lodged in respect of a party wall award.[73]

The Act also provides for the specific protection of particular rights and **6–087** interests by means of a caution, some of which do not fall within the general principle explained above. Of these the most important[74] are writs, orders, deeds of arrangement, pending actions or other similar interests which may be protected by registration under the Land Charges Act 1972.[75] These must be protected by lodging a caution (or, where relevant, a creditor's notice or a

---

[64] He might (for example) order that the cautioner's right be protected as a notice.
[65] Ruoff & Roper, 13–09.
[66] *ibid.*, 13–07. Contrast the position with cautions against dealings, *infra*.
[67] See Ruoff & Roper, 36–05 *et seq.*
[68] L.R.A. 1925, s.54(1). A spouse's matrimonial home rights must now be registered as a notice and cannot be protected by a caution: F.L.A. 1996, s.31(10), (11); *post*, para. 17–025.
[69] L.R.A. 1925, s.55(1).
[70] *Elias v. Mitchell* [1972] Ch. 652 at 659.
[71] *Carlton v. Halestrap* (1988) 4 B.C.C. 538. The allegation had not yet been proved in that case, but the caution was allowed to remain pending trial of the issue. An example would be where an agent buys land purchased with a bribe: *cf. Att-Gen. for Hong Kong v. Reid* [1994] 1 A.C. 324.
[72] *Lynton International Ltd v. Noble* (1991) 63 P. & C.R. 452.
[73] *Observatory Hill Ltd v. Camtel Investments S.A.* [1997] 1 E.G.L.R. 140; see *post*, para. 9–109.
[74] See too Ruoff & Roper, 36–11, for other miscellaneous examples, including mortgages which are not registered charges and which may be protected by notice or caution: L.R.A. 1925, s.106(3) (as substituted by A.J.A. 1977, s.26(1)); *post*, para. 6–113.
[75] See L.C.A. 1972, ss.5, 6 and 7; *ante*, paras 5–088–5–091.

bankruptcy inhibition).[76] Such a caution can be registered in respect of a pending land action only if it involves a claim to the land or to some proprietary right in or over it,[77] or where statute expressly so provides.[78] There will be such a claim however where a landlord seeks to forfeit a lease for breach of covenant,[79] or where a landowner seeks a declaration that his property is no longer subject to an easement.[80] By contrast, a writ or order may be protected by a caution even though it does not involve the creation of any interest in land, provided that it is of the kind that is required to be registered under the Land Charges Act 1972.[81] Thus a caution may be lodged where a receiver is appointed to manage a block of flats because the landlord fails to meet his repairing obligations.[82]

A caution cannot be granted in support of a *Mareva* injunction[83] in so far as it relates to land owned by the party injuncted. The grant of such relief is merely ancillary to the claimant's pecuniary claims against the defendant.[84] The claimant is neither a judgment creditor nor in any other way a "person interested" in such land.[85] Furthermore, such an injunction is not registrable as a writ or order affecting land.[86]

6–088   (4) PROCEDURE. Any caution is registered on the proprietorship register.[87] Once registered, a notice will be served on the cautioner either—

> (i) when a dealing with the registered land (or charge) is brought in for registration without the consent of the cautioner;

> (ii) at any time, on the written application of the proprietor of the land or charge.[88]

---

[76] L.R.A. 1925, s.59(1); Ruoff & Roper, 36–06, 36–07.
[77] *Calgary and Edmonton Land Co. Ltd v. Dobinson* [1974] Ch. 102; *Whittingham v. Whittingham* [1979] Fam. 9; *ante*, para. 5–088.
[78] For the relevant statutory provisions, see *ante*, para. 5–088, n.33.
[79] *Selim Ltd v. Bickenhall Engineering Ltd* [1981] 1 W.L.R. 1318.
[80] *Willies-Williams v. National Trust* (1993) 65 P. & C.R. 359.
[81] *Clayhope Properties Ltd v. Evans* [1986] 1 W.L.R. 1223.
[82] *ibid.*, The registration of a caution in such a case "is not without an underlying sensible and reasonable basis": *ibid.*, at 1229, *per* Nicholls L.J. Any attempt by the landlord to interfere with the work of the receiver (as by attempting to grant a lease at a premium) will be frustrated. For the appointment of a receiver in such situations, see *post*, para. 14–283. *cf.* L. & T.A. 1987, s.24(8).
[83] That is an interlocutory injunction "restraining a party to any proceedings from removing from the jurisdiction of the High Court, or otherwise dealing with assets located within that jurisdiction": Supreme Court Act 1981, s.37(3), so called after *Mareva Compania Naviera S.A. v. International Bulk Carriers S.A.* [1975] 2 Lloyd's Rep. 509.
[84] For the characteristics of such injunctions, see *Z Ltd v. A-Z* [1982] QB 558.
[85] As required by L.R.A. 1925, s.54(1), *supra*.
[86] *Stockler v. Fourways Estates Ltd* [1984] 1 W.L.R. 25; *ante*, para. 5–090. The Law Commission and HM Land Registry have recommended that such an injunction should be registrable as a restriction: (1998) Law Com. No. 254, paras 6.58–6.59.
[87] L.R.R. 1925, r. 6.
[88] *ibid.*, r. 218.

The availability of the latter procedure enables the registered proprietor to have the caution "warned off" before he enters into any transaction concerning the land. On receipt of the notice,[89] the cautioner may—

    (i) allow the caution to be cancelled[90];

    (ii) agree to its withdrawal, whether conditionally[91] or unconditionally; or

    (iii) object to its cancellation.[92]

If he objects to its cancellation, he is required to show cause before the expiry of the notice why the caution should remain or why the dealing should not be registered.[93] If the cautioner shows prima facie grounds for his objection, the matter will then be determined by the Chief Land Registrar[94] at a hearing, and he will make such order in the matter as he shall think just.[95] The caution will usually be cancelled in any event, because it is not appropriate to allow "hostile claims to be indefinitely prolonged".[96] Amongst the orders that the Registrar may make[97] are that—

    (i) the registration of any dealing be refused[98]; or

    (ii) the dealing be completed by registration[99]; or

    (iii) some other entry be made to protect the rights of a cautioner.

The great merit of this procedure is that it enables the rights of the parties to be resolved swiftly and cheaply. However, the Chief Land Registrar will not resolve the dispute between the parties if it raises issues unconnected with registered land which are more appropriately determined by the court, such as a claim to an interest in the matrimonial home.[1] In any event, any person aggrieved by any act done by the registrar in relation to a caution may appeal to the court.[2]

---

[89] If a warning-off notice is lost in the post, the cautioner would seem to have no protection under L.R.A. 1925, s.79(4), which only avails purchasers.

[90] Which will happen if he fails to show cause before it expires: L.R.R. 1925, r. 221.

[91] *e.g.* where his consent is conditional on the protection of his interest by the entry of a notice.

[92] Ruoff & Roper, 36–18.

[93] L.R.R. 1925, rr. 219, 220(1).

[94] Or, in practice, the Solicitor to HM Land Registry: *ante*, para. 6–012.

[95] L.R.R. 1925, r. 220(2), (3).

[96] Ruoff & Roper, 36–20. It is only cautions in respect of writs, orders and pending actions that may be continued.

[97] See Ruoff & Roper, 36–20.

[98] An inhibition may also be granted against any future dealings.

[99] Which will commonly be conditional, *e.g.* on the registration of some entry (such as a notice) in favour of the cautioner.

[1] Ruoff & Roper, 36–21.

[2] L.R.A. 1925, s.56(1).

6–089 (5) DISCHARGE OF CAUTIONS. The consequences of registering a caution are often serious.[3] Because the registration of a caution prevents any dealings with land until the caution is either withdrawn or the issue between the cautioner and the registered proprietor is resolved, its practical effect may be to prevent the completion of a transaction. It therefore has "considerable nuisance value".[4] The purchaser may be unwilling or unable to await the resolution of that issue even though he might have been content to complete subject to the rights of the cautioner.[5] Abuse of the procedure is discouraged by provisions whereby any person who causes damage to another by lodging either form of caution without reasonable cause[6] is liable to pay him compensation.[7] Furthermore, as with unregistered land,[8] the court has an inherent jurisdiction,[9] which in a proper case will be exercised speedily and if necessary, robustly, to order the vacation of cautions[10] and, perhaps other entries as well.[11] Such an order should be made on interlocutory motion if there is no fair arguable case to go to trial.[12] A caution may be vacated even where the cautioner can show a triable issue, but he may then be granted an interim injunction against dealings, subject to his giving an undertaking in damages so as to protect the registered owner, *e.g.* if he loses the sale in the meantime.[13] In fact the more common practice now is not to vacate the caution, but only on terms that the cautioner gives a cross-undertaking in damages to pay the proprietor any damages suffered as a consequence of the continuance of the caution.[14]

---

[3] Ruoff & Roper, 36–01. For the hardship that it may cause to a registered proprietor who has contracted to sell his land, see *Clearbrook Property Holdings Ltd v. Verrier* [1974] 1 W.L.R. 243 at 245.

[4] *Rawlplug Co. Ltd v. Kamvale Properties Ltd* (1968) 20 P. & C.R. 32 at 40, *per* Megarry J. For a case in which a purchaser registered a caution in an attempt to force an abatement of the price, see *Hynes v. Vaughan* (1985) 50 P. & C.R. 444 at 461, 462.

[5] *Willies-Williams v. National Trust* (1993) 65 P. & C.R. 359 at 362, 363.

[6] *cf. Clearbrook Property Holdings Ltd v. Verrier, supra,* at 246.

[7] L.R.A. 1925, s.56(3); Ruoff & Roper, 36–01. This is another example of the superiority of registered land over unregistered land. There is no provision for any form of compensation for the improper registration of a land charge under the Land Charges Act 1972.

[8] *Northern Developments (Holdings) Ltd v. U.D.T. Securities Ltd* [1976] 1 W.L.R. 1230.

[9] See *ante*, para. 5–131. The court may also vacate a caution under its statutory jurisdiction to rectify the register: *Price Bros (Somerford) Ltd v. J. Kelly Homes (Stoke-on-Trent) Ltd* [1975] 1 W.L.R. 1512; *Hynes v. Vaughan, supra,* at 462; *post,* para. 6–122.

[10] *Rawlplug Co. Ltd v. Kamvale Properties Ltd, supra; Calgary & Edmonton Land Co. Ltd v. Discount Bank (Overseas) Ltd* [1971] 1 W.L.R. 81; *Lester v. Burgess* (1973) 26 P. & C.R. 536; *Calgary & Edmonton Land Co. Ltd v. Dobinson* [1974] Ch. 102; *Alpenstow Ltd v. Regalian Properties Plc* [1985] 1 W.L.R. 721; *Clowes Developments (U.K.) Ltd v. Mulchinock* [1998] 1 W.L.R. 42.

[11] This is unlikely to occur in relation to other forms of entry except those where a notice can be registered without the consent of the registered proprietor. Special provision is made for the cancellation of inhibitions, *post,* para. 6–091. In other cases, the correct procedure would normally be to seek rectification of the register: L.R.A. 1925, s.82(1)(b); *post,* para. 6–122.

[12] *Alpenstow Ltd v. Regalian Properties Plc, supra,* at 728; *Woolf Project Management Ltd v. Woodtrek Ltd* (1987) 56 P. & C.R. 134 at 140, 141.

[13] *Clearbrook Property Holdings Ltd v. Verrier, supra; Carlton v. Halestrap* (1988) 4 B.C.C. 538 at 541.

[14] *Tiverton Estates Ltd v. Wearwell Ltd* [1975] Ch. 146 at 161, 172; *Alpenstow Ltd v. Regalian Properties Plc, supra,* at 726; *Tucker v. Hutchinson* (1987) 54 P. & C.R. 106.

A caution can be cancelled at any time on the application of the cautioner, but without prejudice to any liability to indemnify or compensate the registered proprietor which he may already have incurred.[15] The withdrawal of a caution in this way does not necessarily destroy the interest which it protects.[16]

(6) REFORM. The advantage of cautions from the point of view of registered proprietors, purchasers and incumbrancers alike is that they provide a speedy, simple and cheap procedure for resolving disputed rights without the necessity in most cases of having to go to court. Furthermore, registration of a caution without reasonable cause is discouraged by the liability in such cases to pay compensation—a feature that is absent from the legislation governing land charges in unregistered land. However, it is now clear[17] that cautions suffer from a serious weakness. They do not confer priority on property rights so as to make them binding on third parties but merely provide a means by which the cautioner is warned of any dealing that may affect his rights. In consequence, the Law Commission and HM Land Registry have recommended that cautions against dealings should be abolished[18] and that there should instead be two forms of notice.[19] Consensual notices would be employed in much the same circumstances as notices are at present. Unilateral notices would replace cautions. They would give priority to the right protected in the same way as a consensual notice, but would be capable of being warned off. There would be a liability in damages for lodging a unilateral notice without reasonable cause. It would not be possible to protect an interest under a trust by means of a notice, but only by restriction.

6–090

(c) *Inhibitions.* An inhibition is an order of the court or registrar which forbids any dealings with the land, either absolutely or until a certain time or event.[20] The court or registrar may impose an inhibition on the application of "any person interested",[21] and annex to it such terms or conditions as the court or the registrar thinks fit, and discharge or cancel the order, and generally act "in such manner as the justice of the case requires".[22] This is therefore a provision of last resort, intended for use only where there is no other way of protecting the claim. Thus inhibitions have been issued where the land certificate has been stolen,[23] and where some dealing with the land has

6–091

---

[15] L.R.R. 1925, r. 222; Sched. 2, Form 71.
[16] *Holmes v. Kennard & Son* (1984) 49 P. & C.R. 202 at 209.
[17] Following the decision in *Clark v. Chief Land Registrar* [1994] Ch. 370.
[18] But not cautions against first registration.
[19] See (1998) Law Com. No. 254, paras 6.50–6.54.
[20] L.R.A. 1925, s.57(1).
[21] *ibid.* Although a registered proprietor cannot apply for a caution in respect of his own land, he may seek an inhibition: Ruoff & Roper, 37–05. There are a number of statutory provisions which expressly provide that a specific person is a person interested for these purposes, *e.g.* a prosecutor seeking a restraint order under either Criminal Justice Act 1988, s.77, or Drug Trafficking Act 1994, s.26(13). See Ruoff & Roper, 37–05.
[22] L.R.A. 1925, s.57(2).
[23] Ruoff & Roper, 37–03.

involved forgery or fraud.[24] In a few cases the issue of an inhibition is used as a matter of routine without the need for an application.[25] Thus where a bankruptcy order is registered as a land charge, a "bankruptcy inhibition" must be entered in the Land Register preventing the registered proprietor from disposing of the land.[26] Any person aggrieved by an inhibition may apply to the registrar for its discharge or cancellation, unless the entry was originally made by court order.[27]

The Law Commission and HM Land Registry have recommended that inhibitions should be abolished and that a modified form of restriction should be employed instead.[28]

6–092   *(d) Restrictions.* A restriction is similar to an inhibition in that it prevents any dealing with the land until some condition has been complied with.[29] It differs in that it is entered on the proprietorship register on the application of the registered proprietor himself or with his consent.[30] A restriction is therefore normally a friendly and not a hostile entry. Its function is to ensure that limitations upon a registered proprietor's power to deal with or dispose of the registered land or charge are observed.[31] A restriction is not therefore intended to make an incumbrance binding on a third party. Examples of restrictions include[32]—

> (i) where the registered proprietor is a tenant for life of settled land, that no disposition shall be registered unless—
>
> > (a) the capital money which arises is paid to the trustees of the settlement, being at least two in number or a trust corporation, or into court; and
> >
> > (b) it is authorised by the Settled Land Act 1925[33];
>
> (ii) where the registered proprietors are trustees of land (except where they hold on trust for themselves as beneficial joint tenants), that no disposition by a sole proprietor of the land (not being a trust corporation) under which capital money arises is to be registered[34];
>
> (iii) where the registered proprietor is a charity,[35] that no disposition shall be registered unless the instrument giving effect to it contains

---

[24] *Ahmed v. Kendrick* (1987) 56 P. & C.R. 120 (husband forged estranged wife's signature on transfer of the matrimonial home which they jointly owned).
[25] Ruoff & Roper, 37–03.
[26] L.R.A. 1925, s.61(3) (as amended by I.A. 1985, s.235(1), Sched. 8, para. 5(3)).
[27] L.R.R. 1925, r. 231.
[28] (1998) Law Com. No. 254, paras 6.55–6.57.
[29] L.R.A. 1925, s.58(1).
[30] *ibid.*; L.R.R. 1925, r. 235.
[31] Ruoff & Roper, 38–01.
[32] *ibid.*, 38–15–38–18 (where other examples are given).
[33] L.R.A. 1925, s.86(3); L.R.R. 1925, rr. 56–58; *post*, para. 8–022.
[34] L.R.A. 1925, s.58(3); L.R.R. 1925, r. 213; Sched. 2, Form 62; *post*, paras 8–166, 9–053.
[35] Other than an exempt charity. For dispositions by charities, see *post*, para. 20–029.

a certificate complying with the relevant provisions of the Charities Act 1993[36];

(iv) where the dispositionary powers of the registered proprietor are limited, whether by statute, by its public documents (in the case of a corporation) or by the terms of his grant (in the case of a personal representative), a restriction to reflect the limitation[37]; and

(v) where the registered proprietors are the officers of a club, that no disposition shall be registered unless authorised by the rules of the club.[38]

Restrictions are particularly important in protecting beneficial interests under trusts.[39] They can be used to ensure that such interests are overreached, that a life tenant under a settlement does not act outside his powers, or that any requisite consent to a disposition is obtained.[40] Beneficial interests under a trust of land will be overreached even in the absence of such restriction, provided that the purchaser pays any capital money to two or more registered proprietors or to a trust corporation (where it is the registered proprietor).[41] Where an interest under a trust is not protected by an entry on the register, any purchaser of the land will take free of it unless, by reason of the beneficiary's actual occupation, it constitutes an overriding interest.[42]

In many cases, the entry of a restriction is either voluntary[43] or at the discretion of the registrar,[44] but in some instances either the Act or the Land Registration Rules 1925[45] impose a mandatory duty on the registrar to make it.[46] Of the above examples, (i)–(iii) are cases where the registrar is under such a duty. An obligatory restriction differs from a voluntary one in two respects. First, it will be cancelled as a matter of course on the completion of a transaction in accordance with the restriction.[47] Where the restriction is

6–093

---

[36] L.R.R. 1925, r. 123; Sched. 2, Form 12. For this and other forms of restriction applicable to charities, see Ruoff & Roper, 33–09.

[37] L.R.R. 1925, r. 236A; Ruoff & Roper, 38–16.

[38] Ruoff & Roper, 32–13, 38–15; *post*, para. 9–096.

[39] The Land Registration Act 1925 has the same philosophy as the Law of Property Act 1925 "of keeping behind the curtain those interests which are overreached by dispositions by the registered owner": *City of London B.S. v. Flegg* [1988] A.C. 54 at 85, *per* Lord Oliver. See L.R.A. 1925, ss.3(xv), 74.

[40] The advantage of the registered system over the unregistered is that it provides a more effective means of ensuring that these objectives are achieved. The purchaser knows what has to be done from a clear statement on the register.

[41] *City of London B.S. v. Flegg, supra; ante*, para. 6–050; *post*, para. 8–166. The interests of beneficiaries under a will will also be overreached where the disposition is made in consideration of pre-existing indebtedness by the trustees: see *State Bank of India v. Sood* [1997] Ch. 276.

[42] Under L.R.A. 1925, s.70(1)(g); *ante*, paras 6–047, 6–052. An interest under a settlement cannot be so protected.

[43] *e.g.* example (v), *supra*.

[44] *e.g.* example (iv) *supra*.

[45] See, *e.g.* L.R.A. 1925, s.58(3); L.R.R. 1925, r. 213.

[46] These situations are listed in Ruoff & Roper, 38–17.

[47] *ibid.*, 38–12.

voluntary, application has to be made for its withdrawal if it is not intended to continue after the particular disposition.[48] Secondly, although a voluntary restriction can at any time be withdrawn by the registered proprietor,[49] an obligatory one cannot.[50]

The Law Commission and H M Land Registry have recommended that the entry of a restriction should be the only method of restricting the powers of a registered proprietor.[51] Under their proposals for reform a restriction might be entered—

(i) by or with the consent of the registered proprietor;

(ii) by order of the court or registrar; or

(iii) by a person with an interest that should be protected by a restriction (such as a beneficiary under a trust of land).[52]

In (iii), the registered proprietor would have an opportunity to object to the entry.

3. Priorities between minor interests

6–094   *(a) Interests under trusts.*[53] When beneficial interests under a trust of land are assigned or mortgaged, the assignees or mortgagees preserve priority by giving written notice of their interests to the trustees under the rule in *Dearle v. Hall*[54] as applied by the Law of Property Act 1925.[55] This rule now applies to both registered and unregistered land. Prior to 1987, however, in the case of registered land, priorities between assignees and incumbrancers of such beneficial interests were regulated by the order in which the assignments or mortgages were protected by priority inhibitions or cautions entered in the Minor Interests Index.[56] This index was outside the register of title and its operation was unsatisfactory. It was abolished by the Land Registration Act 1986.[57]

6–095   *(b) Other interests.*[58] The Land Registration Act 1925 provides no guidance as to the priority of competing minor interests other than interests under trusts. In default of statutory guidance the courts have fallen back on the

[48] *ibid.*, 38–05.
[49] L.R.A. 1925, s.58(4); L.R.R. 236B; Sched. 2, Form 77.
[50] L.R.A. 1925, s.58(4).
[51] (1998) Law Com. No. 254, paras 6.56, 6.57.
[52] *ibid.*, paras 6.58, 6.59.
[53] See [1993] Conv. 22 at 36 (J. Howell).
[54] (1828) 3 Russ. 1.
[55] s.137; *post*, para. 19–223.
[56] L.R.A. 1925, s.102(2) (repealed by L.R.A. 1986, s.5(1)); see the previous edition of this work at p. 223.
[57] s.5(1), implementing the recommendations in (1983) Law Com. No. 125, Pt V.
[58] See (1977) 93 L.Q.R. 541 (R. J. Smith). This article must now be read in the light of the decisions in *Mortgage Corporation Ltd v. Nationwide Credit Corporation Ltd* [1994] Ch. 49 and *Freeguard v. Royal Bank of Scotland* (1998) 95/13 L.S.Gaz. 29. For the problems of priorities under Australian Torrens systems, see (1994) 68 A.L.J. 143 (T. D. Castle).

general principle that as minor interests take effect in equity only,[59] they must obey the classical rule that where the equities are equal, the first in time prevails.[60] The order of priorities is thus the order of creation, subject to the usual exception in cases of gross carelessness or inequitable conduct.[61] A legal mortgage not entered on the register, and therefore a minor interest, accordingly takes priority over a later contract of sale protected by a caution. Both are equitable interests, and the caution merely entitles the cautioner to be warned of later dealings, without affecting existing priorities.[62]

The same rule applies where the later interest is protected by a notice rather than by a caution.[63] Even where an unregistered minor interest takes effect as an overriding interest,[64] it will not take priority over an earlier unregistered minor interest.[65]

The Law Commission and HM Land Registry have recommended the retention of the present rules as to the priority of minor interests and that they should be set out in statutory form.[66] However, this recommendation has to be read in conjunction with others. It is intended that one feature of electronic conveyancing would be that most estates, rights and interests in registered land would only be capable of creation by entering them on the register. The effect of this would be that the priority of most minor interests would be apparent from the register.[67]

Part 4

CERTAIN DEALINGS WITH REGISTERED LAND

A. Transfer Inter Vivos

I. THE TRANSFER

1. Transfer. A freehold conveyance of registered land *inter vivos* is **6–096** effected by a simple statutory form of transfer[68] which must be lodged at the

---

[59] L.R.A. 1925, ss.2(1), 101(3).

[60] *Barclays Bank Ltd v. Taylor* [1974] Ch. 137 at 146, 147; *Mortgage Corporation Ltd v. Nationwide Credit Corporation Ltd, supra,* at 56.

[61] *Ante,* para. 5–013; *post,* para. 19–207. Failure to protect a minor interest by registration is not regarded as gross carelessness for these purposes and will not deprive the party having the interest of his priority: *Mortgage Corporation Ltd v. Nationwide Credit Corporation Ltd, supra,* at 56. See too *Freeguard v. Royal Bank of Scotland, supra,* where the claimants failed to prove that their later minor interest should prevail.

[62] *Barclays Bank Ltd v. Taylor, supra.* See too *E. S. Schwab & Co. Ltd v. McCarthy* (1975) 31 P. & C.R. 196 at 208; *Watts v. Waller* [1973] Q.B. 153.

[63] *Mortgage Corporation Ltd v. Nationwide Credit Corporation Ltd, supra,* at 55, 56, interpreting L.R.A. 1925, s.52.

[64] It should be noted that a lease for 21 years or less, although an overriding interest, is not a minor interest. When granted, it takes effect as if it were a registered disposition, and therefore free of any unregistered minor interests: *ante,* para. 6–031.

[65] *E. S. Schwab & Co. Ltd v. McCarthy, supra,* at 208.

[66] (1998) Law Com. No. 254, paras 7.32, 7.34.

[67] *ibid.,* paras 7.28–7.30.

[68] An example is given, *infra.*

appropriate District Land Registry[69] together with the land certificate.[70] The registrar makes the necessary entries on the register and the land certificate,[71] and returns the latter to the proprietor if the whole of the land has been sold.[72] If part only has been transferred, the original certificate is amended and returned to the transferor, and a new certificate for the part sold is issued to the transferee.[73]

Leases, unlike transfers of freehold land, may be granted in any form, provided that the land is identified by its title number and, where part only is let, by a plan.[74] The same applies to the grant and transfer of easements.[75] However transfers of leasehold land do have to be in a prescribed form.[76]

6–097   **2. Title.** As between the parties the transfer takes effect from the date when it is executed.[77] However, the transferee acquires no legal estate until the transfer is registered,[78] though registration is deemed to occur when the transferee delivers the relevant documents to the appropriate District Land Registry.[79] The disposition, when registered, confers the legal estate "expressed to be created" on the transferee.[80] It is immaterial that the transferor may have had no power to convey the land.[81] Even a forged transfer from an impostor will, if registered, make the transferee the legal owner.[82] Registration itself confers the legal title,[83] and there is no room for the principle *nemo dat quod non habet*.[84] It scarcely matters for this purpose therefore that the Act provides that a disposition which would be fraudulent and void in the case of unregistered land shall be fraudulent and void likewise,[85] though this may well be relevant for the purpose of rectification, as explained below.[86]

As with unregistered land, the transfer passes with all its appurtenances, such as easements and quasi-easements.[87]

---

[69] L.R.R. 1925, rr. 74, 74A, 83, 98, Sched. 1. Registration cures any irregularity in the form of transfer: *ibid.*, r. 322; *Morelle Ltd v. Wakeling* [1955] 2 Q.B. 379.

[70] L.R.A. 1925, s.64(1); L.R.R. 1925, r. 266.

[71] *cf.* L.R.A. 1925, s.64(2).

[72] L.R.A. 1925, s.64(3).

[73] *ibid.*; Ruoff & Roper, 3–36.

[74] L.R.A. 1925, ss.18, 21; L.R.R. 1925, r. 113(1).

[75] *ibid.*

[76] L.R.R. 1925, r. 98.

[77] "Once the transfer . . . has been executed the die has been cast": *Lloyds Bank Plc v. Rosset* [1989] Ch. 350 at 372, *per* Nicholls L.J. (on appeal) [1991] 1 A.C. 107). See too *Abbey National B.S. v. Cann* [1991] 1 A.C. 56 at 84.

[78] L.R.A. 1925, s.19(1).

[79] L.R.R. 1925, r. 83.

[80] L.R.A. 1925, s.20(1).

[81] *Hounslow L.B.C. v. Hare* (1990) 24 H.L.R. 9 at 23 (void disposition by charity).

[82] Ruoff & Roper, 2–18; *Argyle B.S. v. Hammond* (1984) 49 P. & C.R. 148 at 156. For the problems created by forged transfers, see (1985) 101 L.Q.R. 79 (R. J. Smith).

[83] L.R.A. 1925, s.69(1); *Morelle Ltd v. Wakeling* [1955] 2 Q.B. 379 at 411.

[84] *Argyle B.S. v. Hammond, supra*, at 156.

[85] L.R.A. 1925, s.114.

[86] *Post*, para. 6–124.

[87] L.R.A. 1925, s.20(1) (freeholds), 23(1) (leaseholds).

II. PRECEDENT OF A TRANSFER

The forms of transfer have recently been recast.[88] The following is a transfer   **6–098**
of the whole of a registered title.[89]

Transfer of whole of registered title	**HM Land Registry**	**TR1**

1. Stamp duty[90]

2. Title Number of the Property

K 098765

3. Property

13, Wood Street, West Croker, Kent, TX99 0ZZ

4. Date

29 March 1999

5. Transferor

Theodore Ruoff

6. Transferee **for entry on the register**

John Brickdale and Helen Brickdale

---

[88] By L.R.R. 1997, amending L.R.R. 1925 and introducing a new Sched. 1 into the latter.
[89] See L.R.R. 1925, r. 98, Sched. 1, Form TR1.
[90] The first part dealing with stamp duty has not been completed.

---

7. The transferee's intended **address for service in the U.K.** (including postcode) **for entry on the register**

13, Wood Street, West Croker, Kent, TX99 0ZZ[91]

---

8. The Transferor transfers the property to the Transferee

---

9. Consideration

☒   The Transferor has received from the Transferee for the property the sum of one hundred thousand pounds (£100,000)[92]

☐   (*insert other receipt as appropriate*)

☐   The Transfer is not for money or anything which has a money value

---

10. The Transferor transfers with

☒   full title guarantee[93]   ☐   limited title guarantee

---

11. Declaration of trust[94]

☒   The transferees are to hold the property on trust for themselves as joint tenants[95]

☐   The transferees are to hold the property on trust for themselves as tenants in common in equal shares[96]

☐   The transferees are to hold the property (*complete as necessary*)

---

[91] The transferee will usually insert his new address here. However, he may instead wish to give the address of an agent, such as his solicitor.

[92] The consideration is stated to indicate that the transaction is not a voluntary one. For the effect of a voluntary transfer of registered land, see *post*, para. 6–105.

[93] This imports the covenants for title: *post*, para. 6–102.

[94] For the significance of this declaration, see *post*, para. 9–026.

[95] For joint tenancy, see *post*, para. 9–002.

[96] For tenancy in common, see *post*, para. 9–009.

12. Additional Provision(s) *Insert here any required or permitted statement, certificate or application and any agreed covenants, declarations, etc.*

---

13. The Transferors and all other necessary parties should execute this transfer as a deed using the space below.

Signed as a deed by the said Theodore Ruoff in the presence of Charles Brown, legal executive, Messrs Argue and Phibbs, Solicitors, 53 Wide Way, Ashford, Kent

---

THEODORE RUOFF

CHARLES BROWN

Signed as a deed by the said John Brickdale in the presence of Thelma Green, secretary, of 8, The Grove, West Croker, Kent,

JOHN BRICKDALE

THELMA GREEN

Signed as a deed by the said Helen Brickdale in the presence of Thelma Green, secretary, of 8, The Grove, West Croker, Kent,

HELEN BRICKDALE

THELMA GREEN

---

3. Electronic conveyancing. The Law Commission and HM Land Registry have recommended that legislation should be introduced to enable conveyancing to be conducted electronically.[97] It is envisaged that conveyancing would be conducted in a paperless form, and that both the creation and disposition of estates, rights and interests in registered land would be entered

6–101

---

[97] See (1998) Law Com. No. 254, Pt XI. A pilot scheme for a system of electronic requests for the discharge of mortgages is already under way.

directly on to the register by solicitors and licensed conveyancers, instead of sending in a transfer or other document to a District Land Registry for registration. The intended outcome is that many dispositions of estates, rights and interests in or over registered land would not be capable of being effected *except* by entering them on the register.[98] In other words, registration would become the means by which the disposition was made or the right created.[99]

III. COVENANTS FOR TITLE

6–102 The Act makes provision for rules to be made for prescribing the effect of covenants for title in dispositions of registered land.[1] Although it was once thought that the covenants for title had little if any role to play where the land conveyed was registered with absolute title,[2] it is now clear that this is not so.[3]

6–103 **1. Transfers made prior to July 1995.** In a transfer made before July 1995,[4] the covenants were imported if the transferor was expressed to execute, transfer or charge "as beneficial owner, as settlor, as trustee, as mortgagee, as personal representative of a deceased person, or under an order of the court".[5] The capacity in which the transferor executed the transfer determined the covenants which he undertook.[6] Thus on the normal sale of freehold land, the words "as beneficial owner" imported what were then the four usual covenants for title,[7] namely full power to convey, quiet enjoyment, freedom from incumbrances and further assurance.[8] Any implied covenant was annexed to the proprietor's registered estate[9] and took effect as though the disposition was expressly made subject to—

> (i) charges or interests protected on the register at the time of the execution of the disposition; and

---

[98] (1998) Law Com. No. 254, para. 11.9. This would not apply to all transactions. For example, those arising without any express grant or reservation or by operation of law, would still be capable existing off the register. Trusts would not require registration either. See *ibid.* para. 11.12.

[99] This would eliminate the "registration gap": see *ante*, para. 6–049.

[1] L.R.A. 1925, s.38(2) (as amended by L.P.(M.P.)A. 1994, s.21(1); Sched. 1). For covenants for title, see *ante*, para. 5–047.

[2] See, *e.g. Re King* [1963] 1 W.L.R. 632 at 651.

[3] See *infra*.

[4] *Ante*, para. 5–048.

[5] L.R.R. 1925, r. 76 (now revoked).

[6] *Ante*, paras 5–048, 5–051.

[7] *Ante*, para. 5–049.

[8] *A. J. Dunning & Sons (Shopfitters) Ltd v. Sykes & Son (Poole) Ltd* [1987] Ch. 287 at 299, 300.

[9] L.R.R. 1925, r. 77(2).

(ii) any overriding interests of which the purchaser had notice[10] and subject to which it would have taken effect, had the land been unregistered.[11]

It was held that the covenants were implied as regards the property which was expressed to be conveyed and not merely as regards that which was actually transferred.[12] Thus a purchaser could for example sue on the covenants for title in respect of—

(i) a piece of land which the vendor purported to include in the transfer, but of which he was not the registered proprietor[13]; or

(ii) an overriding interest to which the land was subject and of which he did not have notice.[14]

2. Transfers made after June 1995. In a transfer made after June 1995, **6–104** the covenants for title will be imported if the transferor makes a disposition with either full or limited guarantee.[15] The covenants are no longer connected to the transferor's capacity in making the disposition.[16] In the usual case, where there is a transfer of a registered freehold or leasehold estate with full title guarantee, that imports the covenants that the transferor has full power to convey, further assurance,[17] freedom from incumbrances, and where the property transferred is leasehold, that the lease is subsisting and there are no breaches of covenant that would render it liable to forfeiture.[18] For the purposes of ascertaining what the transfer comprises, there is a presumption (which may be rebutted by the terms of the instrument) that the disposition of

---

[10] Which appears to include constructive notice: see Ruoff & Roper, 16–11.

[11] L.R.R. 1925, r. 77(1). The wording of this provision was unfortunate in three respects. First, where land is unregistered, a purchaser can enforce the covenants for title even in respect of an interest of which he has notice: *ante*, para. 5–049. It is unclear why the matter should have been different where title was registered. Secondly, the doctrine of notice has no role to play in registered land. Thirdly, some rights may take effect as overriding interests which if the title were unregistered would not bind a purchaser, such as unregistered minor interests which are protected by actual occupation: *ante*, para. 6–048. See M. P. Thompson, *Barnsley's Conveyancing Law and Practice* (4th ed.), pp. 680–682.

[12] *A. J. Dunning & Sons (Shopfitters) Ltd v. Sykes & Son (Poole) Ltd, supra*, at 300. This endorses the view expressed in [1981] Conv. 32 (P. H. Kenny) and [1982] Conv. 145 (M. J. Russell). The contrary view, which would have rendered the provisions of the Act and the Rules nugatory, had formerly enjoyed wide support: see, *e.g.* D. J. Hayton, *Registered Land* (3rd ed.), p. 70.

[13] *A. J. Dunning & Sons (Shopfitters) Ltd v. Sykes & Son (Poole) Ltd, supra*.

[14] The right to sue on the covenants for title in respect of overriding interests is important, because if the register is rectified to give effect to them, the purchaser cannot obtain an indemnity: *post*, para. 6–133.

[15] *Ante*, paras 5–067 *et seq.*

[16] *Ante*, para. 5–067.

[17] This includes an obligation to ensure that the disponee is entitled to be registered as proprietor with at least the same class of title as that registered immediately before the disposition: L.P.(M.P.)A. 1994, s.2(2).

[18] See *ibid.*, ss.2(1), 3(1), 4(1).

an existing legal interest in the land is of the whole of that interest.[19] Any implied covenant is annexed to the proprietor's registered estate.[20]

There is no liability on the implied covenants in respect of any matter to which the disposition is expressly made subject.[21] Furthermore, the disposition shall take effect as if it had been made expressly subject to—

(a) all charges and other interests appearing or protected on the register at the time of the execution of the disposition and affecting the title of the registered proprietor; and

(b) any overriding interest of which the disponee has notice and which will affect the estate created or disposed of when the disposition is registered.[22]

There would, therefore, be no liability in respect of such interests. In this context, "notice" means something which is either within the actual knowledge of the disponee at the time of the disposition or is a necessary consequence of facts that are then within his actual knowledge.[23]

IV. INCUMBRANCES

6–105 The most fundamental principle of land registration[24] is that a transferee of registered land for valuable consideration[25] takes the legal estate specified subject to—

(i) the entries on the register;

(ii) overriding interests; and

(iii) in the case of a disposition of a leasehold, to all implied and express covenants, obligations, and liabilities incident to the estate transferred or created;

"but free from all other estates and interests whatsoever".[26] Even where the interest is one to which the transferee is a party, he will not be bound by it if

---

[19] *ibid.*, s.2(3).
[20] *ibid.*, s.7; L.R.R. 1925, r. 77(2).
[21] L.P.(M.P.) A, 1994, s.6(1).
[22] L.R.R. 1925, r. 77A.
[23] L.P.(M.P.)A. 1994, s.6(2). This accords with the general rule that a purchaser contracts to buy land subject to defects in title of which he actually knows or which are patent: see *post*, paras 12–067, 12–068.
[24] *Ante*, para. 4–068.
[25] This includes marriage but not a nominal consideration in money: L.R.A. 1925, s.3(xxxi). Contrast "money or money's worth", *ante*, para. 5–119.
[26] L.R.A. 1925, ss.20(1) (freeholds), 23(1) (leaseholds); *Miles v. Bull (No. 2)* [1969] 3 All E.R. 1585; *Freer v. Unwins Ltd* [1976] Ch. 288; *Sussex Investments Ltd v. Jackson* [193] E.G.C.S. 152.

it is not registered.[27] It is irrelevant that the transferee knows or has notice of an unregistered incumbrance,[28] for it is an essential feature of the system of registration that the transferee is entitled to act according to the information shown on the register and nothing else.[29] Although there is one contrary decision,[30] not only does it conflict with that essential feature of title registration, but it is based on a construction of the Act that is difficult to defend.[31] It is unlikely to be followed. The Law Commission and HM Land Registry have recommended that the legislation should be recast to ensure that such a decision could not occur in the future.[32]

The position is different in cases where the transferee's conduct has been fraudulent or unconscionable,[33] for the registration provisions do not deprive a claimant of his right to seek relief *in personam* against him.[34] First, the transferee will be unable to rely upon the provisions of the Act where the transaction is a sham. Thus in one case, A contracted to sell land to B and then, pending completion, sold the same land to C Ltd, a company of which he was director and controlling shareholder, which was then registered as proprietor. Specific performance of B's estate contract was decreed against C Ltd even though it had not been protected by registration.[35] Secondly, although a transferee may take free of an unregistered interest, a constructive trust may sometimes be imposed upon him.[36] If A transfers registered land to B expressly subject to the unregistered rights of C, B will take free of them, for it is not fraud for B to avail himself of a statutory right to purchase land free of unregistered rights.[37] However, if B has undertaken to give effect to those rights in circumstances where it would be unconscionable for him not to

---

[27] *Orakpo v. Manson Investments Ltd* [1977] 1 W.L.R. 347 at 360, 369 (affirmed on other grounds, [1978] A.C. 95), holding that an unpaid vendor's lien was not binding on a transferee because it was not registered. For unpaid vendor's liens, see [1997] Conv. 336.

[28] *Hodges v. Jones* [1935] Ch. 657 at 671; *Strand Securities Ltd v. Caswell* [1965] Ch. 373 at 390 (reversed on appeal on other grounds, [1965] Ch. 958); *Miles v. Bull (No. 2), supra,* at 1590; *De Lusignan v. Johnson* (1973) 230 E.G. 499. See too (in the context of the New Zealand Land Transfer Act 1952) *Frazer v. Walker* [1967] 1 A.C. 569 at 582.

[29] *Parkash v. Irani Finance Ltd* [1970] Ch. 101 at 109; *Williams & Glyn's Bank Ltd v. Boland* [1981] A.C. 487 at 504.

[30] *Peffer v. Rigg* [1977] 1 W.L.R. 285; criticised (1977) 93 L.Q.R. 341 (R. J. Smith); [1977] C.L.J. 227 (D. J. Hayton); (1977) 40 M.L.R. 602 (J. S. Anderson). See too (1978) 94 L.Q.R. 239 (D. C. Jackson).

[31] L.R.A. 1925, s.20(1) refers to "transferee" (not "purchaser") and says nothing about the transferee's state of mind. In *Peffer v. Rigg, supra,* at 294, Graham J. held that the section had to be read with L.R.A. 1925, s.59(6), which provides that a "purchaser" is not to be affected by matters which are not protected by an appropriate entry on the register "whether he has or has not notice thereof, express implied or constructive". However, L.R.A. 1925 s.3(xxi) defines "purchaser" as a "purchaser in good faith". Graham J. held that a purchaser with notice would not be in good faith and *would* be concerned with matters not protected by registration (despite the express words of s.59(6) to the contrary).

[32] (1998) Law Com. No. 254, paras 3.39–3.50.

[33] See [1985] C.L.J. 280 (M. P. Thompson).

[34] *Frazer v. Walker, supra,* at 585.

[35] *Jones v. Lipman* [1962] 1 W.L.R. 832.

[36] *Ante,* para. 4–094; *post,* paras 10–017, 10–022.

[37] *Midland Bank Trust Co. Ltd v. Green* [1981] A.C. 513 at 530, (in context of L.C.A. 1925); *ante,* para. 5–119.

do so, that undertaking will be enforced by means of a constructive trust.[38] For the future, these matters are likely to be dealt with as a matter of contract law without the need to have recourse to constructive trusts.[39] Thirdly, the register may be rectified in cases where an entry in the register has been obtained by fraud.[40]

If a transfer is made without valuable consideration, the transferee takes subject to any minor interests which bound the transferor, but otherwise, when registered, the transfer has the same effect as a transfer for value.[41]

V. SEARCHES

6–106 It has been explained that the register is now open to public inspection and may be searched by any person.[42] Although such searches are used primarily in the context of conveyancing, the information available from the register is now often sought for other purposes.[43] The Land Registration (Official Searches) Rules 1993[44] make provision for a number of different types of search. Of these, the most important is the official search with priority,[45] which is the form of search most commonly used in conveyancing transactions.[46] This procedure—

(i) enables a purchaser to check the entries on the register immediately prior to the completion of his purchase; and

(ii) ensures that no entry will be made on the register before the purchaser has had an opportunity to complete the transfer by registration, provided that he does so within the priority period.[47]

For these purposes—

---

[38] *Lyus v. Prowsa Developments Ltd* [1982] 1 W.L.R. 1044; *Ashburn Anstalt v. Arnold* [1989] Ch. 1 at 22 *et seq.*; *Canadian Imperial Bank of Commerce v. Bello* (1991) 64 P. & C.R. 48 at 51; *IDC Group Ltd v. Clark* [1992] 1 E.G.L.R. 187 at 189, 190; *post*, para. 10–022 (where such trusts are criticised).

[39] See the Contracts (Rights of Third Parties) Bill that is presently before Parliament; *post*, para. 10–022. It implements the recommendations of the Law Commission in (1996) Law Com. No. 242.

[40] L.R.A. 1925, s.82(1)(d); *post*, para. 6–124.

[41] L.R.A. 1925, s.20(4).

[42] *ibid.*, s.112(1) (substituted by L.R.A. 1988, s.1(1)); *ante*, para. 6–002.

[43] *e.g.* local political parties sometimes search the register to discover the ownership of derelict land in order to bring pressure to bear for its sale or redevelopment.

[44] S.I. 1993 No. 3276. See generally Ruoff & Roper, chap. 30.

[45] Provision is made whereby a person other than a purchaser may make an official search without priority in order to protect his interest. This may be of value to persons who are not "purchasers" for the purposes of the Land Registration (Official Searches) Rules 1993 (*infra*), such as an equitable mortgagee who intends to protect his interest by entry of a notice: see Ruoff & Roper, 30–12.

[46] See Land Registration (Official Searches) Rules 1993, Pt II.

[47] *Howell v. Montey* (1990) 61 P. & C.R. 18 at 19; Ruoff & Roper, 30–10.

(i) a purchaser means any person (including a lessee or chargee) who in good faith[48] and for valuable consideration acquires or intends to acquire a legal estate in land; and

(ii) the priority period is the period between the day when his application is deemed to have been delivered and the 30th working day thereafter.[49]

If the purchaser's application to register is substantially[50] in order and is delivered to the appropriate office within the priority period, any entries on the register made during that period are postponed to the purchaser's application.[51] If any person suffers loss by reason of an error in any search, he is entitled to be indemnified.[52] A search may be made either in the prescribed documentary form or, in those areas designated by the Chief Land Registrar, in other ways.[53] These other ways are, to date, searches which are made—

(i) orally by a person attending at a District Land Registry[54] or Land Registry Property Centre[55];

(ii) by telephone[56];

(iii) by fax[57]; or

(iv) by direct access.[58]

B. Transfer on Death

On the death of a sole registered proprietor, his personal representatives may either— **6–107**

(i) apply for registration themselves, on producing to the registrar the grant of probate or letters of administration[59]; or

(ii) without being themselves registered, transfer the land direct either to a purchaser or to the person entitled under the will or intestacy. In this case, both the transfer or assent and the probate or letters of

---

[48] *i.e.* one who acts honestly, even though he knows of a competing claim: *Smith v. Morrison* [1974] 1 W.L.R. 659.
[49] Land Registration (Official Searches) Rules 1993, r. 2(1).
[50] *Smith v. Morrison, supra.*
[51] Land Registration (Official Searches) Rules 1993, r. 6. Once the priority period has elapsed, the purchaser loses his priority: *Howell v. Montey, supra,* at 19.
[52] L.R.A. 1925, s.83(3); *post,* para. 6–136.
[53] Land Registration (Official Searches) Rules 1993, rr. 3, 14. See Ruoff & Roper, 30–04–30–06.
[54] Ruoff & Roper, Appendix F–06.
[55] *ibid.,* Appendix F–10.
[56] *ibid.,* Appendix F–05.
[57] *ibid.,* Appendix F–08.
[58] *ibid.,* Appendix F–13.
[59] L.R.A. 1925, s.41(1); L.R.R. 1925, r. 168; *post,* para. 11–126.

administration must be lodged with the application for registration.[60]

If one of two or more joint proprietors dies, his name will be removed from the register on proof of death, or production of probate or letters of administration, together with any further evidence required by the registrar.[61]

C. Settlements and Trusts of Land

6–108   **1. Settlements.** After 1996, it is not possible to create new settlements.[62] Prior to 1997, in a settlement of registered land[63] a vesting transfer in statutory form took the place of a vesting deed,[64] but the trust instrument was made in the ordinary form. In the vesting transfer the settlor or proprietor (normally the tenant for life) had to apply for the entry of suitable restrictions to protect the beneficiaries against dealings not permitted by the Settled Land Act 1925.[65] Since that Act is subject to the Land Registration Act 1925,[66] the principle that the registered title is paramount prevails over the normal rule that unauthorised dealings with settled land are void.[67] However, in general the law of settled land applies to registered land without modification.

6–109   **2. Trusts of land.** Where registered land is held on a trust of land, the land should be registered in the names of the trustees.[68] If there are any limitations on the trustees' powers of disposition, or if any consents are required, the trustees should apply for the entry of an appropriate restriction on the register,[69] and if they do not, any person interested in the land may do so.[70]

D. Transfer on Bankruptcy

6–110   The steps taken on bankruptcy, so far as they affect registered land, are briefly as follows.[71]

(i) A bankruptcy petition is presented. This is protected by the entry of a creditor's notice, which prevents the registered proprietor from selling the land free from the claims of the creditors.[72] In practice, it is often not

---

[60] L.R.A. 1925, s.37(1), (2); L.R.R. 1925, r. 170; *post*, para. 11–126.
[61] L.R.R. 1925, r. 172.
[62] T.L.A.T.A. 1996, s.2(1); *post*, para. 8–001.
[63] See *post*, para. 8–022, where the matter is more fully considered.
[64] L.R.R. 1925, r. 99, prescribing forms.
[65] *Post*, para. 8–022.
[66] S.L.A. 1925, s.119(3).
[67] *Post*, paras 8–042–8–044.
[68] L.R.A. 1925, s.94(1) (as substituted by T.L.A.T.A. 1996, s.25(1), Sched. 3, para. 5). For trusts of land, see *post*, para. 8–123.
[69] See L.R.A. 1925, s.94(4) (as inserted by T.L.A.T.A. 1996, s.25(1), Sched. 3, para. 5); L.R.R. 1925, rr. 59A, 106A; see *post*, paras 8–140, 8–155.
[70] L.R.R. 1925, r. 236(3).
[71] See Ruoff & Roper, chap. 28.
[72] L.R.A. 1925, s.59(1); L.R.R. 1925, r. 179.

known whether a bankrupt owns registered land or not, so the petition is registered as a pending action under the Land Charges Act 1972.[73] The registrar controls both the Land Charges Department and the Land Registry,[74] and is required to register a creditor's notice against the title of any proprietor of any registered land or charge which appears to be affected,[75] as soon as is practicable after registration as a land charge.[76]

(ii) A bankruptcy order is made by which the registered proprietor is adjudicated bankrupt.[77] This order is protected by a bankruptcy inhibition, which prevents the registered proprietor from dealing with the land at all.[78]

(iii) The making of a bankruptcy order will always be followed by the appointment of a trustee in bankruptcy unless it is annulled or discharged in the interim.[79] Once appointed, the trustee[80] is entitled to be registered as proprietor in place of the bankrupt,[81] provided that he produces an office copy of the bankruptcy order; a duly certified copy of his certificate of appointment; and a certificate signed by him that the land or charge is comprised in the bankrupt's estate.[82]

E. Mortgages

There are, in theory, three ways in which a mortgage of registered land may be effected. However, the third is now obsolete. **6–111**

1. By registered charge. A registered charge may be effected by any deed **6–112** charging the land in a way making it identifiable without reference to any other document.[83] The charge must not refer to any other interest or charge which would have priority over it and is not registered or protected on the register, or which is not an overriding interest.[84] The deed must be registered. This is done by an entry in the Charges Register giving details of the charge.[85]

---

[73] s.5(1)(b), (3)(b).
[74] L.C.A. 1972, ss.1(1), 17.
[75] This is ascertained by reference to the register of proprietors' names: L.R.R. 1925, r. 9.
[76] L.R.A. 1925, s.61(1); Ruoff & Roper, 28–08.
[77] I.A. 1986, ss.274(3)(b), 278(a).
[78] L.R.A. 1925, s.61(3), (4); L.R.R. 1925, r. 180. In practice the order will be registered first as a land charge in the same way as a bankruptcy petition: L.C.A. 1972, s.6(1)(c) (as substituted by I.A. 1985, s.235(1), Sched. 8, para. 21(3)).
[79] *Re Palmer* [1994] Ch. 316 at 324.
[80] Who in certain circumstances will or may be the official receiver: see Ruoff & Roper, 28–19. It is no longer the case that a bankrupt's estate vests in the official receiver pending the appointment of a trustee in bankruptcy, as it was under the Bankruptcy Act 1914, s.53(1).
[81] L.R.A. 1925, s.42(1) (as amended by I.A. 1985, s.235(1), Sched. 8, para. 5(2)).
[82] L.R.R. 1925, r. 176(1).
[83] L.R.A. 1925, s.25(1), (2).
[84] *ibid.*, s.25(2)(b).
[85] *ibid.*, s.26(1).

A legal estate does not arise until the charge is registered.[86] As the charge is entered on the register it cannot be an overriding interest.[87] The land certificate must be deposited at the registry for as long as a registered charge exists,[88] and a charge certificate is issued to the chargee as his document of title.[89]

A registered chargee has all the powers of a legal mortgagee, unless the register otherwise provides.[90] Any provision purporting to interfere with the registered chargee's power of transferring the charge by registered disposition is void.[91] The priority of registered charges is governed by the order of entry in the register, subject to any entry to the contrary.[92] As regards tacking, section 94 of the Law of Property Act 1925[93] does not apply to registered land. However, further advances may be tacked only if—

> (i) they are made by a chargee under an obligation to do so which has been entered on the register; or

> (ii) the charge was made for securing further advances, and the advance was made before notice of the intervening incumbrance (which the registrar must send to the chargee) ought to have reached the chargee in due course of post.[94]

A right to consolidate may, it seems, be reserved as in the case of unregistered land.[95]

A sub-mortgage is made by means of a charge of the mortgage or charge by way of sub-charge.[96]

6–113   **2. By unregistered mortgage.** Unless the register otherwise indicates, registered land may be mortgaged in the same way as if it were unregistered.[97] Such a mortgage may be dealt with in the same manner as if the land had not been registered.[98] Until it has been duly protected by entry on the register of

---

[86] *Grace Rymer Investments Ltd v. Waite* [1958] Ch. 831; *E. S. Schwab & Co. Ltd v. McCarthy* (1975) 31 P. & C.R. 196.

[87] L.R.A. 1925, s.3(xvi). Neither is it a registered interest under s.2 or a minor interest under s.3(xv), since it is created by registered disposition. It is therefore *sui generis*.

[88] L.R.A. 1925, s.65.

[89] L.R.R. 1925, r. 262.

[90] L.R.A. 1925, ss.27(1), 34(1).

[91] *ibid.*, s.25(3).

[92] *ibid.*, s.29; *cf. post*, para. 19–263.

[93] *Post*, para. 19–258.

[94] L.R.A. 1925, s.30(1), (3); L.R.R. 1925, r. 139A; Ruoff & Roper, 23–40. See *Lloyd v. Nationwide Anglia B.S.* [1996] E.G.C.S. 80. L.R.A. 1925, s.30(2) provides for compensation if any failure by the post office or registrar causes loss to the registered chargee in respect of a further advance.

[95] See (1950) 100 L.J.News. 353; (1952) 214 L.T.News 305; Ruoff & Roper, 23–41. For consolidation, see *post*, paras 19–096 *et seq.*

[96] L.R.A. 1925, s.36; L.R.R. 1925. rr. 163–166.

[97] L.R.A. 1925, s.106 (as substituted by A.J.A. 1977, s.26).

[98] *ibid.*, s.106(4).

a notice or caution, such a mortgage takes effect only in equity as a minor interest.[99]

It is also possible to create an equitable charge corresponding to a general equitable charge upon unregistered land. Like other land charges within the meaning of the Land Charges Act 1972, this is a minor interest, and can be protected by a notice or caution.[1]

3. By deposit of the land certificate. The land certificate takes the place   **6–114**
of title deeds. Prior to April 3, 1995, it was possible to create a lien by deposit of the land certificate with the lender.[2] A chargee could similarly create a lien on his charge by deposit of his charge certificate.[3] Such a lien was a contract to create a charge,[4] and it could be protected by a notice of deposit.[5] However, if such a deposit was made after September 26, 1989, it was valid only if it complied with the formal requirements that now apply to such contracts.[6] Since April 2, 1995, it has ceased to be possible to protect a lien by notice of deposit.[7] The lien may now be protected by the entry of a notice on the register.[8] This had in fact been a common practice because it avoided the payment of fees payable on registration of the charge. However, in order to exercise his power of sale, the mortgagee will be obliged to obtain registration of his charge, which will then take priority from the date of the notice.[9]

4. Company charges. Where a company creates a charge by way of   **6–115**
security over its land (other than a charge for rent or other periodical payment),[10] it is required[11] to register it within 21 days in the Companies Register or it will be void against the liquidator and any creditor of the company.[12] A

---

[99] *ibid.*, s.106(2).

[1] L.R.A. 1925, ss.49(1)(c), 59(2).

[2] L.R.A. 1925, s.66. See *Thames Guaranty Ltd v. Campbell* [1985] Q.B. 210 at 232.

[3] L.R.A. 1925, s.66.

[4] *Birch v. Ellames* (1794) 2 Anst. 427 at 431; *Carter v. Wake* (1877) 4 Ch.D. 605 at 606; *Re Wallis & Simmonds (Builders) Ltd* [1974] 1 W.L.R. 391 at 395; *Swiss Bank Corporation v. Lloyds Bank Ltd* [1982] A.C. 584 at 594, 595; *Thames Guaranty Ltd v. Campbell, supra,* at 232, 233; *Re Alton Corporation* [1985] B.C.L.C. 27 at 33.

[5] L.R.R. 1925, rr. 239–243.

[6] *United Bank of Kuwait Plc v. Sahib* [1997] Ch. 107. Formerly the agreement to charge would be implied from the mere fact that title deeds or a land certificate were deposited by a debtor with a creditor. Such a contract was enforceable without writing because the deposit of the deeds or certificate was considered to be an act of part performance: see the previous edition of this work at pp. 927, 928. The doctrine of part performance has now been abolished however and contracts for the sale or other disposition of an interest in land must be made in writing: L.P.(M.P.)A. 1989, s.2; *post,* para. 12–042.

[7] L.R.R. 1925, rr. 240–243 were revoked, and a new r. 239 substituted, by L.R.R. 1995, S.I. 1995 No. 140, in response to the decision in *United Bank of Kuwait Plc v. Sahib, supra.*

[8] See Ruoff & Roper, 25–07.

[9] *ibid.*, 28–33(4).

[10] Companies Act 1985, s.396(1)(d). If Pt IV of the Companies Act 1989 is ever brought into force (which is unlikely), the existing provisions on company charges will be replaced. See *ante,* para. 5–108.

[11] Companies Act 1985, s.399.

[12] *ibid.*, s.395(1).

certificate is issued on registration.[13] However, the Land Registration Act 1925 provides that the registrar is not concerned with any company charge, whether registered on the Companies Register or not, unless it is also protected in the appropriate way at the Land Registry.[14] Any purchaser of registered land from a company need not search the Companies Register therefore but only the register of title.[15] If the company charge has been registered on the Companies Register, the certificate of registration must be produced when that charge is registered at the Land Registry.[16]

F. Limitation and Prescription

6–116   **1. The present law.** A title to registered land may be acquired under the Limitation Act 1980 by adverse possession in the same way as in the case of unregistered land.[17] However, in the case of registered land no legal title can vest in the adverse possessor until he has been registered as proprietor. In the meantime he is protected by the provision that the registered proprietor's estate is not extinguished but is held by the proprietor upon trust for the adverse possessor.[18] This reveals another contrast with the law of unregistered land, under which the dispossessed owner's estate is extinguished and the adverse possessor obtains a wholly new estate.[19]

The statutory trust has been described as "a conveyancing device"[20] designed to fill the gap until the squatter registers his own possessory title. Once he has done so he becomes the registered proprietor of the very estate which he has barred[21] so that, in contrast to the law of unregistered land, he acquires that estate by a "parliamentary conveyance".[22] The squatter is, in the true sense, a successor in title to the former registered proprietor.[23] If it is a leasehold estate, he cannot be defeated by a surrender by the former leasehold proprietor to the freeholder, since the former proprietor no longer has the power of disposition.[24] The result is the same if the surrender is made before

---

[13] *ibid.*, s.401(2).

[14] L.R.A. 1925, s.60(1). Charges created by companies are protected in the same manner as those created by individuals. For floating charges, see Ruoff & Roper, 34–07.

[15] Ruoff & Roper, 23–11–23–12.

[16] L.R.R. 1925, r. 145(1); Ruoff & Roper, 34–08. A charge can be registered at the Land Registry even though it has not been registered at the Companies Register: L.R.R. 1925, r. 145(2).

[17] *Post*, para. 21–056. For the complexities of applying the principles of limitation to registered land, see (1994) 14 L.S. 1 (E. Cooke); and (1998) Law Com. No. 254, paras 10.27–10.39. Both of these commentaries must now be read subject to the important decision in *Central London Commercial Estates Ltd v. Kato Kagaku Co. Ltd* [1998] 4 All E.R. 948; noted (1999) 115 L.Q.R. 187 (C.H.); [1999] Conv. 136 (E. Cooke).

[18] L.R.A. 1925, s.75(1); *Central London Commercial Estates Ltd v. Kato Kagaku Co. Ltd, supra.*

[19] *Ante*, para. 3–118; *post*, para. 21–002.

[20] *Jessamine Investment Co. v. Schwartz* [1978] Q.B. 264 at 275, *per* Sir John Pennycuick.

[21] L.R.A. 1925, s.75(2); *Central London Commercial Estates Ltd v. Kato Kagaku Co. Ltd, supra.*

[22] *Central London Commercial Estates Ltd v. Kato Kagaku Co. Ltd, supra,* at 959, 960.

[23] For the implications of this, see *post*, paras 14–143, 16–063, 21–064, 21–066, 21–068.

[24] *Spectrum Investment Co. v. Holmes* [1981] 1 W.L.R. 221.

the squatter's title is registered, since his rights are an overriding interest.[25] The landlord therefore takes the lease impressed with the trust in favour of the squatter.[26] This result accords with principle much better than does the rule for unregistered land.[27]

Registration of the squatter's title may be made with absolute, qualified, good leasehold or possessory title as the case may be. This has the effect of first registration, though interests not extinguished by the adverse possession are not affected.[28]

Easements and profits may similarly be acquired by prescription against registered land in the same way as if it were not registered.[29]

2. Reform. In a number of states which have a Torrens system of title **6–117** registration,[30] the principles of adverse possession are either inapplicable to land with registered title,[31] or have been modified.[32] The basis of registered title is not possession (as it is with unregistered land) but registration,[33] and there can never be any doubt as to the ownership of the land. Nor is adverse possession needed to cure defects in title and so facilitate conveyancing, which is its most important role in relation to unregistered land.[34] The Law Commission and HM Land Registry have recommended the introduction of a new system of adverse possession applicable only to registered land, which would reflect the different principles applicable to such land.[35] This would make it considerably more difficult to acquire title to registered land by adverse possession. A squatter would be able to apply to be registered as proprietor after 10 years' adverse possession. The existing registered proprietor[36] would have the opportunity to object. If he did, the application would fail unless the squatter could bring himself within a number of limited exceptions.[37] The registered proprietor would then have two years either to commence proceedings to evict the squatter or regularise his position, as by

[25] Under L.R.A. 1925, s.70(1)(f) and (g); *ante*, paras 6–046, 6–047.
[26] *Central London Commercial Estates Ltd v. Kato Kagaku Co. Ltd*, *supra*, at 960, not following rather obscure dicta in *St. Marylebone Property Co. Ltd v. Fairweather* [1963] A.C. 510 at 542; and *Jessamine Investment Co. v. Schwartz*, *supra* at 275.
[27] Explained, *post*, para. 21–064.
[28] L.R.A. 1925, s.75(3). See (1963) 27 Conv. (N.S.) 353 (T. B. F. Ruoff).
[29] L.R.A. 1925, s.75(5); L.R.R. 1925, r. 250.
[30] *Ante*, para. 6–003.
[31] *e.g.* Australian Capital Territories, Northern Territories (Australia), Brunei and Alberta (Canada). From 1875 until 1925 there was no adverse possession of registered land in England: see Land Transfer Act 1875, s.21.
[32] *e.g.* New South Wales, Queensland, South Australia (Australia), British Columbia (Canada) and New Zealand.
[33] *cf.* L.R.A. 1925, s.69(1); *ante*, para. 6–029.
[34] See *post*, para. 21–001.
[35] See (1998) Law Com. No. 254, Pt X. The proposed scheme was developed from that which applies in Queensland. For the details of the scheme, see *ibid.*, paras 10.44–10.69.
[36] And any other person with a right, actual or contingent, to possession, such as a registered chargee or, where the property was leasehold, the landlord.
[37] *e.g.* that the registered proprietor was estopped from denying the squatter possession, or that the squatter had some other right to the land, as where he was a purchaser who was in possession.

granting him a lease or a licence. If after two years the proprietor had done neither, a squatter who remained in adverse possession would be entitled to be registered as proprietor instead. The effect of the scheme would be that, if land had been abandoned and the proprietor had disappeared, the squatter would obtain title. Where that was not the case, the proprietor would have an opportunity to terminate the adverse possession, but not an indefinite one. Analogous principles would apply to possession proceedings brought against a squatter.

The Law Commission and HM Land Registry have also recommended the abolition of the trust as a mechanism for giving effect to adverse possession in registered land.[38]

Part 5

INDEFEASIBILITY

6–118   **1. The principle.** One of the attractions of registration of title is the general principle (nowhere made explicit in the Act) that the registered proprietor has a title which is indefeasible without compensation. In other words, there is a State guarantee of title, so that the registered proprietor and those dealing with him may rely upon his title being as it appears on the register, and will normally be able to claim compensation if it is not. But the principle, as it emerges from the Act, is a principle of partial compensation rather than of indefeasibility.[39] Although there is a wide jurisdiction to rectify the register, the right to compensation is by no means automatic.

2. Rectification

6–119   *(a) The nature of rectification.* Rectification "is used to denote any amendment to the register . . . for the purpose of putting right any substantive error of omission or commission, or any legally recognised grievance".[40] The term is not employed to describe those cases where the registrar is under a mandatory duty to amend the register, and where no question of indemnity can arise, such as where registered land is compulsorily acquired and the registered proprietor refuses to execute a transfer,[41] or where a squatter has acquired title by adverse possession and is entitled to be registered as proprietor.[42] There is a threefold jurisdiction to rectify the register. First, the court has

---

[38] See (1998) Law Com. No. 254, paras 10.70–10.78.
[39] The legislation on rectification and indemnity has been amended twice, first by A.J.A. 1977, s.24 (following criticism of the legislation and its interpretation: see (1968) 84 L.Q.R. 528 (S. M. Cretney and G. Dworkin) and (1972) Law Com. W.P. No. 45); and secondly by L.R.A. 1997, s.2 (implementing the recommendations of the Law Commission and HM Land Registry in (1995) Law Com. No. 235).
[40] Ruoff & Roper, 40–04.
[41] Ruoff & Roper, 29–15. The registrar acts pursuant to L.R.R. 1925, r. 131. For other examples, see Ruoff & Roper, 29–11–29–20.
[42] L.R.A. 1925, s.75(3); *ante*, para. 6–116.

an inherent jurisdiction to order the vacation of cautions and perhaps other entries from the register. This has already been explained.[43] Secondly, the Act confers powers to rectify in specified instances either on the court alone,[44] or on the court or registrar.[45] These are explained below. Thirdly, the Land Registration Rules 1925 confer powers on the registrar to rectify the register in a number of cases, of which the most important[46] are where—

(i) there has been a clerical error or error of like nature[47]; or

(ii) the proprietor has in error been registered as owner of land which he does not own.[48]

The availability of rectification emphasises the principle that titles are relative, not absolute, and that no title is completely free from the danger that some better right to the land may be established.[49]

(b) Statutory power to rectify. The Act confers a power to rectify the register[50] which can only be exercised if the circumstances fall within one of eight specified grounds.[51] Those grounds are not mutually exclusive, and the same facts may fall within more than one of them.[52] There is no general residual power to rectify the register because it may appear just to do so.[53] Even if one of the grounds is established, rectification is always discretionary,[54] and there are limitations on the circumstances in which the register may be rectified against "the proprietor who is in possession".[55] The power to rectify extends to each part of the register, and one part of the register may be rectified even when another is not.[56] Each of the grounds of rectification must be considered.[57]

6–120

---

[43] *Ante*, para. 6–089.

[44] L.R.A. 1925, s.82(1) (paras (a) and (b)).

[45] *ibid.* (paras (c)–(h)).

[46] See too r. 283 (amendment of addresses where street names and numbers are changed); r. 284 (revision and correction of plans); and r. 285 (resolving conflicts between verbal particulars and filed plan). See *Proctor v. Kidman* (1985) 51 P. & C.R. 67.

[47] r.13. This rule applies only where the correction can be made without detriment to any registered interest.

[48] r.14 ("the whole of the land comprised in the title, or too large a part" to be dealt with as a clerical error). This power is a sweeping one and is apparently unlimited: *Chowood Ltd v. Lyall (No. 2)* [1930] 1 Ch. 426 at 438 (on appeal [1930] 2 Ch. 156).

[49] *Ante*, para. 3–122.

[50] L.R.A. 1925, s.82(1).

[51] For an analysis, see (1998) Law Com. No. 254, paras 8.9.–8.22.

[52] See, *e.g. Chowood Ltd v. Lyall (No. 2)* [1930] 2 Ch. 156.

[53] *Norwich & Peterborough B.S. v. Steed* [1993] Ch. 116 at 138.

[54] "The register may be rectified . . . ": L.R.A. 1925, s.82(1). See, *e.g. Epps v. Esso Petroleum Co. Ltd* [1973] 1 W.L.R. 1071 at 1078, 1079; *Argyle B.S. v. Hammond* (1984) 49 P. & C.R. 148 at 158; *Norwich & Peterborough B.S. v. Steed, supra,* at 132; *Clark v. Chief Land Registrar* [1993] Ch. 294 at 318.

[55] L.R.A. 1925, s.82(3); *post*, para. 6–130.

[56] See, *e.g. Re Leighton's Conveyance* [1936] 1 All E.R. 667; *Norwich & Peterborough B.S. v. Steed, supra* (A entered as proprietor in place of B on the proprietorship register, but subject to incumbrances on the charges register created by B).

[57] See (1993) 109 L.Q.R. 187 (R. J. Smith).

6–121   (1) TO GIVE EFFECT TO COURT ORDER. The register may be rectified where a court determines as a matter of substantive law that a person is entitled to an estate, right or interest in or to any registered land or charge and, in consequence, considers that rectification of the register is required.[58] The basis of this form of rectification is that the claimant has established some proprietary right to the land in court proceedings,[59] as where a squatter successfully asserts a possessory title,[60] or a disposition of the property is set aside on the ground of fraud, misrepresentation or undue influence.[61] Rectification on this ground is appropriate only where the rights of the parties have been finally adjudicated. A court will not order the vacation of a caution in interlocutory proceedings under this head.[62]

6–122   (2) PERSON AGGRIEVED BY ENTRY. A court may order rectification of the register on the application of any person who is aggrieved by the making, delay in making, or omission of any entry in the register.[63] In practice, this ground of rectification is often used as an alternative to the inherent jurisdiction to vacate a caution,[64] and it may be used in interlocutory proceedings.[65] To rectify on this ground, there must be some substantive ground for the removal of the entry because it "provides a remedy but does not create any new substantive rights or causes of action".[66]

It may be doubted whether these first two grounds are true instances of rectification. It is improbable that where a court has established the substantive rights of the parties it would then exercise its discretion to refuse to rectify the register to give effect to them.[67]

---

[58] L.R.A. 1925, s.82(1)(a).

[59] *Norwich & Peterborough B.S. v. Steed, supra* at 132, 133. See too *Proctor v. Kidman* (1985) 51 P. & C.R. 67 at 73.

[60] *Chowood Ltd v. Lyall (No. 2)* [1930] 2 Ch. 156. In that case a purchaser acquired land to part of which a squatter had acquired title by adverse possession. The register did not therefore reflect the true state of the title. *cf.* (1998) Law Com. No. 254, para. 8.13, and see L.R.A. 1925, s.75(3); *ante*, para. 6–116.

[61] *Norwich & Peterborough B.S. v. Steed, supra*, at 132, 133.

[62] The court must have "decided" that a person is entitled to a property right: L.R.A. 1925, s.82(1)(a); *Lester v. Burgess* (1973) 26 P. & C.R. 536 at 541. *cf. Tiverton Estates Ltd v. Wearwell Ltd* [1975] Ch. 146 at 156.

[63] L.R.A. 1925, s.82(1)(b).

[64] *Lester v. Burgess, supra; Price Bros (Somerford) Ltd v. J. Kelly Homes (Stoke-on-Trent) Ltd* [1975] 1 W.L.R. 1512; *Hynes v. Vaughan* (1985) 50 P. & C.R. 444 at 462; *Chancery Lane Developments Ltd v. Wades Departmental Stores Ltd* (1986) 53 P. & C.R. 306 at 310. It should be noted that an order under s.82(1)(b) is necessarily *in rem* because it has to be obeyed by the registrar, whereas an order under the inherent jurisdiction may either be directed *in personam* solely against the cautioner, or be impersonal so that the registrar may safely act upon it as well by removing the caution from the register: see *Lester v. Burgess, supra*, at 543; *Calgary & Edmonton Land Co. Ltd v. Dobinson* [1974] Ch. 102 at 111.

[65] *Lester v. Burgess, supra; Chancery Developments Ltd v. Wades Departmental Stores Ltd, supra*, at 310.

[66] *Norwich & Peterborough B.S. v. Steed* [1993] Ch. 116 at 133, *per* Scott L.J. See (1993) 109 L.Q.R. 187 at 188 (R. J. Smith).

[67] See *Norwich & Peterborough B.S. v. Steed, supra*, at 139. See (1998) Law Com. No. 254, para. 8.13 (explaining the anomalies that would result if rectification were truly discretionary in such cases).

(3) BY CONSENT. The register may be rectified "in any case and at any time" with the consent of all persons interested.[68] In practice, most cases of rectification are effected on this ground. This provision is not unlimited however. A transfer of title or other disposition cannot be effected as a rectification by consent.[69] In practice, consent is by far the commonest ground for rectification. **6–123**

(4) ENTRY OBTAINED BY FRAUD. Rectification of the register may be ordered if the court or registrar is satisfied that any entry in the register has been obtained by fraud.[70] This provision has been held to apply only where fraud is practised upon the Land Registry in order to obtain the entry in question, as where a forged transfer is presented for registration.[71] It does not apply (contrary to the suggestion in earlier authority[72]) in the more usual case where the transfer was procured by fraud.[73] If therefore A induces B by fraud to execute a transfer in his favour which is then registered, and A then charges the land to C (a mortgagee acting in good faith) before B can take steps to set aside the transfer to A, B will be able to seek rectification of the proprietorship register against A,[74] but not of the charges register against C.[75] B will therefore be bound by C's mortgage just as he would if the title were unregistered.[76] **6–124**

(5) CASES OF MISTAKEN REGISTRATION. Rectification may be ordered by the court or registrar— **6–125**

(i) if two or more persons are, by mistake, registered as proprietors of the same charge[77]; or

(ii) where a mortgagee has been registered as proprietor of the land instead of as proprietor of a charge and a right of redemption is subsisting.[78]

(6) PROPRIETOR NOT ESTATE OWNER. The court or registrar may order rectification of the register where a legal estate has been registered in the name of a person who if the land had not been registered would not have been the estate owner.[79] It has been explained that registration will vest a legal estate in the proprietor even though the transfer to him was wholly void, *e.g.* in cases **6–126**

[68] L.R.A. 1925, s.82(1)(c).
[69] See (1998) Law Com. No. 254, para. 8.14.
[70] L.R.A. 1925, s.82(1)(d).
[71] *Norwich & Peterborough B.S. v. Steed, supra,* at 134.
[72] See *Re Leighton's Conveyance* [1936] 1 All E.R. 667; *Argyle B.S. v. Hammond* (1984) 49 P. & C.R. 148.
[73] See [1992] Conv. 293 at 297 (C. Davis); (1993) 109 L.Q.R. 187 at 188 (R. J. Smith).
[74] Under L.R.A. 1925, s.82(1)(a).
[75] *Norwich & Peterborough B.S. v. Steed, supra.* If C was implicated in the fraud, rectification *could* also be ordered against him under L.R.A. 1925, s.82(1)(a).
[76] See *ante*, paras 5–011–5–013.
[77] L.R.A. 1925, s.82(1)(e).
[78] *ibid.*, s.82(1)(f).
[79] *ibid.*, s.82(1)(g).

of forgery or *non est factum*, or where the transferor either had no title to the property, or no power to convey it.[80] Where there is such a void transfer, the register may be rectified on this ground.[81] Examples of its application have included—

(i) cases of double conveyancing, where A conveyed unregistered land to B, and subsequently conveyed the same land to C, who was then registered as proprietor of it[82];

(ii) where D was registered as proprietor of land, to one part of which E had acquired title by adverse possession[83]; and

(iii) where a charity conveyed land to a purchaser when it had no power to do so.[84]

This ground for rectification has been criticised because it is defined by reference to principles of unregistered land.[85] The concern is that it may have the effect "of re-introducing much of the old unregistered law (including the doctrine of notice) by the back door of rectification".[86] In practice, however, this has not happened.[87]

6–127   (7) OTHER CASES OF ERRORS, OMISSIONS AND MISTAKES. There is a residual power to rectify in other cases where, by reason of—

(i) any error or omission in the register; or

(ii) any entry made under a mistake[88];

it may be deemed just to rectify the register.[89] This power does not confer a general discretion to rectify because it seems just but applies only in the circumstances listed.[90] Examples of rectification of the register on this ground include where—

---

[80] *Ante*, paras 6–029, 6–097.
[81] *Norwich & Peterborough B.S. v. Steed* [1993] Ch. 116 at 132; *Hayes v. Nwajiaku* [1994] E.G.C.S. 106.
[82] *Re Seaview Gardens* [1967] 1 W.L.R. 134; *Epps v. Esso Petroleum Co. Ltd* [1973] 1 W.L.R. 1071. If both B and C had been registered as proprietors of the same land, L.R.A. s.82(1)(e) rather than s.82(1)(g) would be the appropriate ground of rectification.
[83] *Chowood Ltd v. Lyall (No. 2)* [1930] 2 Ch. 156.
[84] *Hounslow L.B.C. v. Hare* (1990) 24 H.L.R. 9.
[85] See D. J. Hayton, *Registered Land* (3rd ed.), p. 169.
[86] (1993) 109 L.Q.R. 187 at 188 (R. J. Smith). See too [1987] Conv. 334 at 340 (R. J. Smith).
[87] See (1998) Law Com. No. 254, para. 8.18.
[88] "Mistake" is widely interpreted: *Chowood Ltd v. Lyall (No. 2), supra*, at 168. See *Clark v. Chief Land Registrar* [1993] Ch. 294 at 315 (registration of charge where the land was subject to a caution and the cautioner was not notified) (not considered on appeal: [1994] Ch. 370).
[89] L.R.A. 1925, s.82(1)(h).
[90] *Norwich & Peterborough B.S. v. Steed, supra*, at 135.

(i) a purchaser, on being registered as proprietor, claimed to take free of an unpaid vendor's lien which had not been registered[91];

(ii) restrictive covenants on the register of title were no longer enforceable[92]; and

(iii) an easement had been erroneously noted on the title.[93]

(c) The effect of rectification.[94] The effect of rectification depends on its nature. If the name of one registered proprietor is removed from the register and another is substituted, the legal estate vests in the new proprietor.[95] If the register is rectified by deleting some other entry upon it, "the effect of the deleted entry is thereupon destroyed".[96] Conversely, where the register is rectified by the addition of some entry on the charges register, the proprietor will thereafter be bound by the right.[97] It is not possible to rectify the register retrospectively.[98] However, rectification may be ordered even though it may affect any estates, rights, charges, or interests which are protected either by registration or as overriding interests.[99] But a party seeking rectification against any such derivative interest must bring his claim within one of the eight grounds for rectification.[1] The benefit of a claim to rectification passes on a transfer of registered land.[2]

6–128

(d) The effect of non-rectification. Where as a matter of discretion the register is not rectified even though a ground for doing so exists, there may be situations where in consequence it is necessary or desirable to make a corresponding amendment to another title.[3] This commonly happens where, for example, both A and B are registered as proprietors of the same piece of land. If the court decides not to rectify A's title, it must rectify B's. A more difficult case would be if the extent of an easement was inaccurately described on the register of the dominant land but it was decided not to rectify the register. It would then be necessary to amend the servient title, even though it was not erroneous. However, the extent to which the court can order such

6–129

---

[91] *Orakpo v. Manson Investments Ltd* [1977] 1 W.L.R. 347 (on appeal [1978] A.C. 95). It was not the vendor who was seeking to enforce the lien, but a moneylender who had been subrogated to his rights. For criticism see (1978) 94 L.Q.R. 239 (D. C. Jackson).

[92] *Re Sunnyfield* [1932] 1 Ch. 79.

[93] *Re Dances Way, West Town, Hayling Island* [1962] Ch. 490.

[94] See Ruoff & Roper, 40–15.

[95] L.R.A. 1925, s.69(1).

[96] *Lester v. Burgess* (1973) 26 P. & C.R. 536 at 540, *per* Goulding J.

[97] *Freer v. Unwins Ltd* [1976] Ch. 288; (1976) 92 L.Q.R. 338 (R. J. Smith).

[98] *Freer v. Unwins Ltd, supra* (where prospective rectification of the freehold title did not affect a lease, even though the omission which was rectified pre-dated the grant of that lease); *Clark v. Chief Land Registrar* [1993] Ch. 294 at 315–317 (not considered on appeal: [1994] Ch. 370).

[99] L.R.A. 1925, s.82(2); *Argyle B.S. v. Hammond* (1984) 49 P. & C.R. 148 at 157.

[1] *Norwich & Peterborough B.S. v. Steed* [1993] Ch. 116 at 138.

[2] *Berkeley Leisure Group Ltd v. Williamson* [1996] E.G.C.S. 18 (holding that the right to rectification of the register passes under the all estate clause, L.P.A. 1925, s.63; *ante*, para. 5–044).

[3] See (1998) Law Com. No. 254, para. 8.44.

correlative amendments to a title which contains no mistake because it declines to rectify one that does, has not been explored in this country.[4]

6–130   *(e) Registered proprietor in possession.* The Act contains provisions "which restrict, though they do not eliminate"[5] the jurisdiction to rectify the register against "the proprietor who is in possession".[6] Although there is some uncertainty as to the meaning of this phrase,[7] the principle behind it appears to be to protect a registered proprietor who is in physical possession of the land and at least some other persons who either have an interest in the property or are in possession with the consent of the registered proprietor. It has been held to include the case where the proprietor has granted a lease[8] because "possession" includes the receipt of rents and profits or the right to receive the same.[9] Furthermore, where a person is in possession in right of a minor interest (as where a beneficiary under a trust occupies the premises), he is deemed to be in possession as agent for the registered proprietor.[10] Conversely, where the party seeking rectification of the register is in physical possession, the proprietor will not be "in possession" for these purposes.[11] Nor will he be where a registered chargee has exercised his right to take possession of the premises.[12] It should be noted that the wider the ambit given to the phrase "the proprietor who is in possession", the greater the security of title enjoyed by a registered proprietor.

Rectification can be ordered against a proprietor who is in possession in just four situations,[13] namely the following.

(i)   Where the purpose is to give effect to an overriding interest.[14] Since the registered title is in any event subject to overriding interests, this head does not affect the registered owner's rights.

(ii) Where the registered proprietor "has caused or substantially contributed to the error or omission by fraud or lack of proper care". Under this amended wording[15] the proprietor no longer loses his

---

[4] But see *Racoon Ltd v. Turnbull* [1997] A.C. 158 (Registered Land Ordinance 1970, British Virgin Islands).

[5] *Argyle B.S. v. Hammond, supra,* at 158, *per* Slade L.J.

[6] L.R.A. 1925, s.82(3) as amended by A.J.A. 1977, s.24.

[7] See Ruoff & Roper, 40–10.

[8] *Freer v. Unwins Ltd* [1976] Ch. 288 at 294. *cf. Racoon Ltd v. Turnbull, supra,* at 164 (citing the British Virgin Islands' Registered Land Ordinance 1970, s.140).

[9] L.R.A. 1925, s.3(xviii).

[10] *ibid.*, s.82(4).

[11] *Chowood Ltd v. Lyall (No. 2)* [1930] 1 Ch. 156 at 162, 166, 167 (proprietor not "in possession" where squatter was). See too *Epps v. Esso Petroleum Co. Ltd* [1973] 1 W.L.R. 1071 at 1080.

[12] *Hayes v. Nwajiaku* [1994] E.G.C.S. 106. *Sed quaere.*

[13] L.R.A. 1925, s.82(3) as amended by A.J.A. 1977, s.24.

[14] In many such cases the proprietor will not in fact be "in possession" within L.R.A. 1925, s.82(3) because the person having the benefit of the overriding interest will be: see *Chowood Ltd v. Lyall (No. 2)* [1930] 2 Ch. 156 (squatter in possession); *Bridges v. Mees* [1957] Ch. 475; *Goodger v. Willis* [1999] E.G.C.S. 32 (contractual purchaser in actual occupation).

[15] Substituted by A.J.A. 1977, s.24(b).

protection on account of some innocent act such as submitting an erroneous description of the property for registration.[16] It now accords with the corresponding rule for compensation.[17]

(iii) Where the purpose is to give effect to an order of the court. This provision, also introduced by amendment,[18] was intended to ensure that rectification could be ordered even against a proprietor in possession, if the transfer to him had been made to defeat the rights of the transferor's creditors.[19] Its wording is however unfortunate. If read literally it renders nugatory the intended protection for proprietors in possession against rectification: one order which a court can make is for rectification of the register.[20]

(iv) Where "for any other reason, in any particular case, it is considered that it would be unjust not to rectify the register against him". In the last resort, accordingly, the court may always be guided by the justice of the case in the light of all the facts. Thus, if the proprietor has innocently spent money on the land, this will weigh against rectification.[21] The relative blameworthiness of the parties in relation to the ground of rectification may be relevant.[22] The court may also take account of the fact that rectification would entitle the losing party to indemnity, while non-rectification would not,[23] or that the measure of indemnity will be different according to whether the register is rectified or not.[24] Rectification may still be refused however if the indemnity will not be adequate compensation for loss of the land.[25]

(f) Reform. The Law Commission and HM Land Registry have recommended a clarification of the present law governing rectification rather than a fundamental revision of it.[26] The legislation would make it clear that rectification was available only in cases where there was an error or omission in the **6–131**

---

[16] As in *Chowood Ltd v. Lyall (No. 2), supra; Re 139 High Street Deptford* [1951] Ch. 884; *Re Sea View Gardens* [1967] 1 W.L.R. 134.

[17] *Post*, para. 6–137.

[18] A.J.A. 1977, s.24(a).

[19] See now I.A. 1986, s.339.

[20] See (1987) Law Com. No. 158, para. 3.13.

[21] *Re 139 High Street Deptford, supra*, at 892; *Re Sea View Gardens, supra*, at 141.

[22] *Hounslow L.B.C. v. Hare* (1990) 24 H.L.R. 9 at 26. See too *Horrill v. Cooper* [1998] E.G.C.S. 151 (where a purchaser was fully alive to a defect not recorded on the register and had apparently taken it into account in the price he was prepared to pay).

[23] But see *Norwich & Peterborough B.S. v. Steed* [1993] Ch. 116 at 138.

[24] *Hounslow L.B.C. v. Hare, supra*, at 25.

[25] *Epps v. Esso Petroleum Co. Ltd* [1973] 1 W.L.R. 1071, another case of "double conveyancing" where rectification against the registered proprietor was refused since he was in possession and refusal was not unjust, even though he was second in time and the land was conveyed to him by mistake.

[26] (1998) Law Com. No. 254, Pt VIII.

register.[27] The present limitations on rectification against a proprietor in possession would apply in all cases where there was lawful physical possession under the proprietor's registered title.

6–132   **3. Compensation.** In registered conveyancing, as in all conveyancing, ease of transfer can be bought only at some risk to titles and third parties. An element of insurance is therefore provided in the form of monetary compensation for losses that arise from errors and omissions in the register or by the registry. These have been creditably small.[28] Only once have claims exceeded £2,000,000 and that was due to one particular fraud.[29] Both the entitlement and the amount of any indemnity are determinable by the court in proceedings against the Chief Land Registrar.[30] The provisions governing indemnity were reformed by the Land Registration Act 1997[31] to give effect to recommendations made by the Law Commission and HM Land Registry.[32] They are as follows.

(a) Right to indemnity. There are four main heads.[33]

6–133   (1) RECTIFICATION. There are three distinct provisions governing the award of indemnity where the register is rectified. First, "any person suffering loss by reason of the rectification shall be entitled to be indemnified".[34] This protection is not so wide as it seems. Any transferee of registered land takes it subject to overriding interests,[35] such as the rights of a squatter.[36] Rectification of the register therefore is no more than formal recognition of the true state of affairs. Any "loss" occurred when the land was purchased.[37] Similarly where a boundary is rectified in favour of an adjacent owner the registered proprietor suffers no "loss" as regards any part of the land which the adjacent owner actually occupied at the time of the registration.[38] However the registered proprietor is entitled to indemnity in respect of any other land affected by rectification, because it was subject to no overriding interest, and the registered title has proved to be defective.[39]

---

[27] L.R.A. 1925, s.82(1)(a) and (b) would not therefore be replicated.
[28] The figures for 1996–97 were £1.93 million (563 claims) and for 1997–98, £1.68 million (646 claims). See Ruoff & Roper, 40–32.
[29] 1992–93: when claims amounted to £5.09 million, with a single claim for £3.65 million.
[30] L.R. & L.C.A. 1971, s.2.
[31] s.2, substituting a new L.R.A. 1925, s.83. All references given *infra*, are to s.83 as amended.
[32] See (1995) Law Com. No. 235.
[33] See Ruoff & Roper, 40–16.
[34] L.R.A. s.83(1)(a).
[35] L.R.A. 1925, ss.20, 23; *ante*, para. 6–105.
[36] L.R.A. 1925, s.70(1)(f); *ante*, para. 6–046.
[37] *Re Chowood's Registered Land* [1933] Ch. 574. See too *Hodgson v. Marks* [1971] Ch. 892 (overriding interest of occupying beneficiary under bare trust).
[38] *Re Boyle's Claim* [1961] 1 W.L.R. 339.
[39] *ibid.*

Secondly, if the title of a registered proprietor claiming in good faith under a forged disposition is rectified, he is deemed to have suffered loss by reason of the rectification.[40]

Thirdly, "if, notwithstanding the rectification of the register, the person in whose favour the register is rectified suffers loss by reason of an error or omission in the register in respect of which it is so rectified, he also shall be entitled to be indemnified".[41] This provision was introduced by the Land Registration Act 1997 to remedy a shortcoming in the law. As explained above,[42] rectification is only prospective in its effect. As a result, there may be cases where a person suffers loss notwithstanding that he obtains rectification of the register.[43]

(2) NON-RECTIFICATION. Where an error or omission has occurred in the register, but it is not rectified, any person suffering loss by reason of the error or omission is entitled to indemnity.[44] A classic example occurred when the murderer of a registered proprietor forged a transfer to himself, obtained registration, and sold the land to an innocent purchaser. Rectification was not available, because the purchaser was the registered proprietor in possession, and so the victim's personal representative was indemnified for the loss to the estate.[45] **6–134**

(3) CONVERSION OF TITLE. Any person except the registered proprietor who suffers loss by reason of any entry made on the register on the conversion of a title into absolute or good leasehold is entitled to indemnity.[46] **6–135**

(4) ERRORS. A person is entitled to indemnity if he suffers loss from— **6–136**

    (i) any error in an official search[47];

    (ii) any loss or destruction of documents lodged at the registry[48];

    (iii) any inaccuracy in an office copy of the register or of any filed document or plan, or any extracts from such copy or extract[49];

---

[40] L.R.A. 1925, s.83(4).

[41] *ibid.*, s.83(1)(b).

[42] See para. 6–128.

[43] The defect in the law was revealed in *Freer v. Unwins Ltd* [1976] Ch. 288. When land which was burdened by a restrictive covenant was registered, the covenant was, by mistake, not entered on the register. A 21-year lease was then granted, and the lessee, who was not bound by the unregistered covenant, conducted a business that was prohibited by the covenant. The register was rectified (though the grounds for doing so are not apparent). The rectification could not affect the tenant, whose lease took effect as an overriding interest and could not, therefore, be rectified: see *ibid.*, 299. As a result, the person having the benefit of the covenant continued to suffer loss notwithstanding rectification in his favour: *ibid.*, 295.

[44] L.R.A. 1925, s.83(2).

[45] Related in Ruoff & Roper, 40–13 (the *Haigh* or acid bath case); D. J. Hayton, *Registered Land* (3rd ed.), 185. *cf. Frazer v. Walker* [1967] 1 A.C. 569.

[46] L.R.A. 1925, s.77(6).

[47] *ibid.*, s.83(3).

[48] *ibid.*

[49] *ibid.*, s.113.

    (iv)　any error or omission in any filed abstract or copy of any document, or from any extract from such abstract or copy, to which the register refers[50]; and

    (v)　in certain other cases where there has been an error or omission.[51]

6–137　　*(b) Fraud and lack of care.*[52] No indemnity is payable on account of any loss suffered by the claimant either—

    (i)　wholly or partly as a result of his own fraud; or

    (ii)　wholly as a result of his own lack of proper care.[53]

Where, however, the loss incurred by the claimant is suffered partly as a result of his own lack of proper care, any indemnity will be reduced to such extent as is just and equitable having regard to his share in the responsibility.[54] These principles also apply where the fraud or negligence was not that of the claimant, but of a predecessor in title through whom he claims otherwise than by a registered disposition for valuable consideration.[55]

6–138　　*(c) Amount of indemnity.* The claimant is normally entitled to indemnity for the amount of his loss, together with reasonable costs and expenses properly incurred.[56] However an indemnity for rectification is limited to the value of the lost interest immediately before rectification; and an indemnity for non-rectification is limited to the value of the lost interest at the time when the mistake was made.[57] The latter restriction is not as harsh as it might appear to be. This is because the registry pays interest on the sum from the time when the mistake is made.[58]

---

[50] *ibid.*, s.110(4).

[51] See *ibid.*, s.30(2) (further advances under a registered charge: *ante*, para. 6–112, n.94; s.61(3) (failure to register a creditor's notice or bankruptcy inhibition: *ante*, para. 6–110; s.61(7) (trustee in bankruptcy: creditor's notice or bankruptcy inhibition). See Ruoff & Roper, 40–16.

[52] See Ruoff & Roper, 40–23B.

[53] L.R.A. 1925, s.83(5)(a).

[54] L.R.A. 1925, s.83(6). This principle of contributory negligence was introduced by L.R.A. 1997, s.2. Previously *any* negligence by the claimant barred his claim: see the previous edition of this work at p. 229. *cf.* the Land Registration (Scotland) Act 1979, s.13(4), which contains a similar provision.

[55] L.R.A. 1925, s.83(7).

[56] L.R.A. 1925, s.83(9). No indemnity is recoverable on account of costs and expenses incurred by the claimant without the registrar's consent, unless by reason of urgency it was not practicable to apply for his consent before they were incurred and he subsequently approves them: see *ibid.*, s.83(5)(c). This restriction does not apply to an application to the court to determine the applicant's entitlement to indemnity: L.R. & L.C.A. 1971, s.2(2).

[57] L.R.A. 1925, s.83(8).

[58] This practice apparently rests on L.R. & L.C.A. 1971, s.2(5) (power for the registrar to settle claims for indemnity by agreement).

(d) Time-limits. A liability to pay indemnity is deemed to be a simple **6–139** contract debt, so that it is barred after six years. However, time does not begin to run until the claimant knows, or but for his own default might have known, of the existence of his claim.[59]

(e) Rights of recourse.[60] Where the registrar has paid an indemnity, he is **6–140** entitled to recover the amount paid from any person who has caused or substantially contributed to the loss by his fraud.[61] Furthermore, for the purpose of recovering the amount paid, he is entitled to enforce any right of action (of whatever nature and however arising) which the claimant would have been entitled to enforce if indemnity had not been paid.[62] Where the register has been rectified, he may also enforce any right of action (of whatever nature and however arising) which the person in whose favour the register has been rectified would have been entitled to enforce had it not been rectified.[63] These rights of recourse are likely to be most commonly employed in cases where a solicitor has been negligent, and has, for example, lodged inaccurate documents or has failed to verify the identity of the person who has purported to instruct him.[64] The registrar has certain additional statutory rights of recoupment under other legislation.[65]

(f) Comparison with unregistered land. It will be evident from the account **6–141** given above that the compensation scheme provides a solution in some cases where otherwise one of two innocent parties would have to bear the loss, *e.g.* where by forgery or fraud a false title has been marketed, or where by some mistake there has been "double conveyancing" of the same piece of land to two different purchasers.[66] This is a notable advantage as compared with dealings in unregistered land, where the weaker of two conflicting titles merely fails and the loss must be borne by the loser.[67] Furthermore, because rectification is discretionary and there are limitations on its availability against a proprietor who is in possession, a purchaser of registered land may obtain a good title when he would not have done had the title been unregistered.[68]

---

[59] L.R.A. 1925, s.83(12). Formerly there were significant qualifications to this provision which led to injustice: see, *e.g. Epps v. Esso Petroleum Co. Ltd* [1973] 1 W.L.R. 1071; and the previous edition of this work at pp. 229, 230. These qualifications were removed by L.R.A. 1997, s.2.

[60] See Ruoff & Roper, 40–30.

[61] L.R.A. 1925, s.83(10)(a).

[62] *ibid.*, s.83(10)(b)(i). For an example of where this was actually done under the analogous (but more limited) provision prior to amendment by L.R.A. 1997, see Ruoff & Roper, 40–30.

[63] L.R.A. 1925, s.83(10)(b)(ii).

[64] Cases of personation are becoming regrettably common: see, *e.g. Midland Bank Plc. v. Cox McQueen* (1999) 149 N.L.J. 164.

[65] See *e.g.* Housing Act 1985, s.154(5); Ruoff & Roper, 40–31. The exercise of rights of recourse under L.R.A. 1925, s.83(10) does not prejudice such statutory rights of recovery: *ibid.* s.83(11).

[66] Ruoff & Roper, 40–33.

[67] Subject to possibility of compensation under L.P.A. 1969, s.25: *ante*, para. 5–113. As explained there, such claims are virtually never made.

[68] See, *e.g. Hounslow L.B.C. v. Hare* (1990) 24 H.L.R. 9 at 22 *et seq.* (void lease granted by charity, but register not rectified against the grantee).

6–142   **4. The limits of indefeasibility.** The first English Act for the registration of title proclaimed its intention "to give certainty to the title to real property".[69] However, the reality is that registration does not confer an indefeasible title, for there is a discretion to rectify the register in cases of error, omission or mistake.[70] The "state guarantee of title" is not comprehensive. There are cases where the true owner or an innocent purchaser may be left with neither the property nor compensation, though the recent reforms of indemnity have considerably reduced these. Overriding interests remain the principal defect in the land registration system. However, if implemented, the reforms recently proposed by the Law Commission and HM Land Registry,[71] and in particular the recommendations to restrict the scope of overriding interests, to introduce electronic conveyancing, to make registration the means of creating most rights, and to strengthen the indefeasibility of the title of a registered proprietor against rectification, will make the register conclusive as to title in most respects.

---

[69] Land Registry Act 1862, preamble.
[70] *Norwich & Peterborough B.S. v. Steed* [1993] Ch. 116.
[71] In (1998) Law Com. No. 254.

CHAPTER 7

PERPETUITIES AND ACCUMULATIONS

Part 1

VESTED AND CONTINGENT FUTURE INTERESTS

1. Classification of future interests. A future interest in land is an interest   **7–001**
which confers a right to the enjoyment of the land at a future time, such as a
right to land by way of remainder after the death of a living person. A
distinction which has always been of fundamental importance is that between
vested and contingent remainders, which is vital in particular to the subject of
perpetuities. "Perpetuities" are contingent interests which may take effect at
too remote a date in the future. Any future interest may be either vested or
contingent, and vested interests may be either "vested in interest" or "vested
in possession". An interest is "vested in possession" when it gives the right
of present enjoyment[1]; but of course it is not then a future interest. If it is
vested in interest but not in possession (for which situation the term "vested"
is ordinarily used by itself) it is a "future interest", since the right of
enjoyment is postponed, yet it is also an already subsisting right in property
vested in its owner: it is a present right to future enjoyment.[2] By contrast with
a vested interest, a contingent interest is one which will give no right at all
unless or until some future event happens. So if land is transferred to trustees
to hold on trust for A, B and C, all living persons, as follows—

> "to A for life, remainder to B for life, remainder to C in fee simple if he
> survives B",

then A's interest is vested in possession, B's is vested in interest but not in
possession (a vested remainder) and C's is contingent. If B dies first, C's
remainder will vest; and on A's death it will fall into possession.

2. Conditions of vesting. A remainder is vested if two requirements are   **7–002**
satisfied:

---

[1] See Fearne, *Contingent Remainders*, 2. Fearne's treatise (10th ed., 1844, with notes by Butler)
is the classic work on the whole subject of future interests. The other leading works are *Gray
on Perpetuities* (4th ed., 1942); Morris and Leach, *The Rule against Perpetuities* (2nd ed.,
1962; supp. 1964); Maudsley, *The Modern Law of Perpetuities* (1979).
[2] Fearne 2.

(i) the person or persons entitled to it must be ascertained[3]; and

(ii) it must be ready to take effect in possession forthwith, and be prevented from doing so only by the existence of some prior interest or interests.[4]

If either requirement is not satisfied, the remainder is contingent.

To return to the example—

"to A for life, remainder to B for life, remainder to C in fee simple if he survives B",

it has been seen that B's interest is vested and C's is contingent. Neither is vested in possession, for A has the only interest which is vested both in interest and in possession. And C's interest is bound to remain contingent during B's life, even if A is already dead, since it depends not only upon the determination of B's life interest but upon the further contingency of C outliving B. B's interest is vested because, if A's life interest were to terminate forthwith, an ascertained person, B, is already entitled to the land, subject only to A's prior interest. Even if A is aged 23 and B 97, so that it is improbable that B's interest will ever vest in possession, B nevertheless has a vested interest[5]; for an interest may be vested even if there is no certainty of it taking effect in possession at any time,[6] otherwise no future life interest or entail could be vested.[7] If land is given to X in tail, remainder to Y in fee simple, Y's remainder is vested, not because X's entail is bound to determine at some time (for this is not the case[8]) but because Y has been at once *invested* with the fee simple, subject only to X's entail.[9] On the other hand, an interest is not necessarily vested because it is bound to take effect at some time. For example, if property is given—

"to A and B for their joint lives, with remainder to the survivor",

the death of one before the other is bound to occur at some time[10]; yet since it is uncertain which will be the survivor, the remainder is contingent, whether the remainder is in fee simple[11] or for life.[12]

---

[3] Fearne 9: *Re Legh's S.T.* [1938] Ch. 39 at 52.

[4] *cf.* Fearne 3–9, 216; Gray, ss.101, 108; (1913) 29 L.Q.R. 290 (H. T. Tiffany).

[5] Fearne 216.

[6] *Smith d. Dormer v. Packhurst* (1740) 3 Atk. 135.

[7] Fearne 216.

[8] *Contra*, Smith, *Executory Interests*, p. 67 (this work forms Vol. ii of the 10th ed. of Fearne, *Contingent Remainders, supra*).

[9] Hawkins & Ryder 282. Entails can no longer be created: *ante*, para. 3–037.

[10] See *post*, para. 11–053, as to L.P.A. 1925, s.184, which deals with the ascertainment of the survivor in doubtful cases.

[11] *Biggot v. Smyth* (1628) Cro.Car. 102; *Quarm v. Quarm* [1892] 1 QB 184.

[12] *Whitby v. Von Luedecke* [1906] 1 Ch. 783; *Re Legh's S.T.* [1938] Ch. 39.

Other examples of contingent interests occur where there is a gift to the heir **7–003** of a living person (for until that person dies, his heir cannot be ascertained),[13] or where although the gift is in favour of a specified person, it is made contingent upon some event occurring, *e.g.*—

"to A upon attaining 25 or marrying",[14] or
"to B if he returns to England".[15]

In such cases, the interests of A and B are contingent until the event occurs, whereupon they become vested.[16]

There are no restrictions on the kinds of conditions to which gifts can be made subject, provided that they do not offend against public policy[17] or against the rules explained in this chapter.

3. Concealed vestings and contingencies. It is in most cases obvious **7–004** whether or not a remainder is made subject to a contingency; but there are some apparently conditional phrases which do not create legal contingencies, and some apparently unconditional remainders which are nevertheless contingent. For example, a limitation made prior to 1997[18]—

"To A in tail, but if A's issue should at any time fail then to B in fee simple",

would have given B a vested remainder, for the phrase beginning "but if" adds no contingency other than the inevitable possibility that A's entail may come to its natural end; it can be read as being merely the equivalent of "subject to the prior interest".[19] The limitation in effect is simply to A in tail with remainder to B in fee simple, giving B a vested remainder. Similarly a limitation—

"To A (a bachelor) for life, remainder to his eldest son for life, but in default of such issue then to B in fee simple",

gives B a vested remainder, for the contingency expressed is merely the non-existence of a preceding life interest on the failure of which B stands ready to take.[20] But if the gift had been—

---

[13] Challis 75. *cf. post*, para. 11–120.
[14] *Leake v. Robinson* (1817) 2 Mer. 363.
[15] *Re Arbib and Class's Contract* [1891] 1 Ch. 601.
[16] Preston i, 88.
[17] See *ante*, para. 3–074.
[18] Entails cannot be created after 1996: see *ante*, para. 3–037.
[19] See *Maddison v. Chapman* (1858) 4 K. & J. 709 at 719 (affd. (1859) 3 De G. & J. 536); *Permanent Trustee Co. of New South Wales Ltd v. d'Apice* (1968) 118 C.L.R. 105.
[20] For the effect of expressions such as "in default of such issue", see *White v. Summers* [1908] 2 Ch. 256 at 271 *et seq.*

"To A (a bachelor) for life, remainder to his eldest son (if any) in fee simple, remainder to B in fee simple",

B's remainder would have been contingent, for there was a rule that no interest which followed a contingent fee simple could be vested.[21] This was because although a grantor can create any number of successive life interests or entails (limited interests) and vest them in living persons, he can part with the fee simple (an absolute interest) only once; so that any two limitations of the fee simple are not successive but alternative, and if one is contingent the other must depend on the converse contingency.[22] For somewhat similar reasons a gift which follows a determinable or conditional fee simple is regarded as contingent, as for example B's interest in a limitation—

"To A in fee simple until he ceases to reside in the family home, remainder to B in fee simple".[23]

7–005   **4. Size of beneficiary's interest.** An interest may be vested although the size of the beneficiary's interest is not finally ascertained. For example, where land is devised—

"to A for life, remainder to all his children who shall attain the age of 21 years",

each child obtains a vested interest on attaining his majority[24]; but these vested interests are liable to open to let in each child who subsequently attains full age.[25] Thus if X and Y are the only children who have attained their majority, they each have a vested interest in one-half of the property, but that interest may later be partially divested in favour of subsequent children[26]; the divesting affects only the *quantum* of the interest vested in each beneficiary.[27] When Z becomes 21, the shares of X and Y each fall to one-third and Z has the other third; and so on for the other children.[28] X and Y can dispose of their vested shares either *inter vivos* or by will,[29] although even in the hands of the transferee the shares will be liable to be diminished by other children attaining

---

[21] *Loddington v. Kime* (1697) 1 Ld.Raym. 203; 1 Salk. 199; Fearne 225, 374–377; Gray, s.112, who is hesitant. The rule is disputed by Hayes, *Limitations*, pp. 81 *et seq.*; (1913) 29 L.Q.R. 296 (H. T. Tiffany). But the authorities in favour of the rule seem sufficient, and its principle seems sound.

[22] See 1 Ld.Raym. at p. 208.

[23] Gray, s.114, n. 3.

[24] *Brackenbury v. Gibbons* (1876) 2 Ch.D. 417 at 419; *Randoll v. Doe d. Roake* (1817) 5 Dow 202.

[25] *Re Lechmere and Lloyd* (1881) 18 Ch.D. 524 at 529; *Baldwin v. Rogers* (1853) 3 De G.M. & G. 649 at 657.

[26] *Cattlin v. Brown* (1853) 11 Hare 372 at 379; *Holmes v. Prescott* (1864) 10 Jur. (N.S.) 507 at 510.

[27] *Matthews v. Temple* (1699) Comb. 467; *Stanley v. Wise* (1788) 1 Cox Eq. 432 at 433.

[28] *Doe d. Comberbach v. Perryn* (1789) 3 T.R. 484 at 493, 495.

[29] *Oppenheim v. Henry* (1853) 10 Hare 441. For the alienability of contingent interests, see *post*, para. 7–007.

full age. But any child of A who dies under 21 has no interest in the property at all[30]; for the contingent interest which he had while alive has failed to vest.

5. Vested interest subject to divesting. A remainder may also be vested   **7–006** and yet subject to a possibility of its being divested, not only partially but completely. For example, if land is held in trust for A for life, remainder to such of A's issue as A shall appoint, and in default of appointment among all A's children in equal shares, the remainders to the children in equal shares are vested, subject to being divested to the extent of any appointment made by A.[31] In cases of doubt the law favours early vesting, and every interest is construed as being vested forthwith if that is possible; if not, it is treated as becoming vested as soon as possible.[32]

6. Assignability. It is in reference to futurity of possession that vested and   **7–007** contingent remainders are classed as future interests. In one sense a vested remainder is an existing interest, and therefore not future. And in one sense a contingent remainder is future, but is not an interest: it is only a possibility that an interest may arise if some contingency happens. Contingent remainders were so regarded by the common law,[33] and were therefore inalienable by conveyance[34]; for there was no subsisting estate which could be granted. But, exceptionally, they were able to pass by inheritance,[35] *e.g.* where land was limited to A in tail, but in case A inherited Blackacre then to B and his heirs. If B died and then A inherited Blackacre, B's heir would take the land.[36] But equity would enforce assignments of contingent remainders[37] by compelling the assignor to convey the property to the assignee when it fell into possession[38]; and in this way contingent remainders could in practice be sold. Statutes gave further assistance. By a liberal interpretation of the Statute of Wills 1540, it was held that contingent interests could be devised[39]; and this was confirmed by the Wills Act 1837.[40] Finally, by the Real Property Act

---

[30] *Rhodes v. Whitehead* (1865) 2 Dr. & Sm. 532.

[31] *Cunningham v. Moody* (1748) 1 Ves.Sen. 174; *Doe d. Willis v. Martin* (1790) 4 T.R. 39; *Lambert v. Thwaites* (1866) L.R. 2 Eq. 151; *Re Master's Settlement* [1911] 1 Ch. 321; Fearne 226 *et seq.*; Farwell, *Powers*, 310 *et seq.*; Challis 75. For a classification of vested remainders, see *Restatement of the Law of Property*, § 157.

[32] Smith, *Executory Interests*, 73; Hawkins & Ryder 302; Jarman 1365 *et seq.*

[33] Challis 76, 77; Williams R.P. 398, 400.

[34] *Lampet's Case* (1612) 10 Co. Rep. 46b. But they could be released, *i.e.* waived in favour of the holder of a prior vested estate (*ibid.*); and until the F.R.A. 1833, they could to some extent be alienated by fine or recovery operating by estoppel: Fearne 365, 366; Cru.Dig. ii, 333; Williams R.P. 398.

[35] *Weale v. Lower* (1672) Pollexf. 54; *Goodright d. Larmer v. Searle* (1756) 2 Wils.K.B. 29.

[36] Fearne 364 *et seq.*; Challis 76n.

[37] *Wright v. Wright* (1750) 1 Ves.Sen. 409; *Crofts v. Middleton* (1856) 8 De G.M. & G. 192.

[38] Fearne 548 *et seq.*

[39] *Jones v. Roe d. Perry* (1789) 3 T.R. 88; Fearne 368 (discussing earlier authorities to the contrary, *e.g. Bishop v. Fountaine* (1695) 3 Lev. 427).

[40] s.3.

1845,[41] they became fully alienable at law. Although a right does not necessarily become an interest in land merely because statute has made it alienable, it now seems proper to regard such contingent interests as interests in land rather than mere possibilities; but the difference between vested and contingent interests is of course unaffected. Where the contingency is as to the person entitled, as in the case of a limitation to the heir of a living person,[42] or the survivor of two living persons,[43] there is still no transmissible interest vested in anyone.[44]

Part 2

REVERSIONS

7–008　**1. Nature of reversions.** So far the nature of reversions and remainders has been only briefly explained.[45] A reversion is such part of a grantor's interest as is not disposed of by his grant; a remainder is such part as is disposed of, provided that it is postponed to some estate in possession created at the same time. Thus if a tenant in fee simple grants a life interest, the fee simple which he retains is a reversion. His estate in fee simple in possession has become a fee simple in reversion. If, on the other hand, he creates a lesser estate and by the same instrument disposes of some or all of the residue of his estate to one or more other persons, the interests of those other persons are not reversions but remainders. In the case of a reversion, the land reverts to the grantor when the lesser estate determines; in the case of a remainder, it remains away from him for the benefit of some third party.[46] It follows that while there may be many remainders created out of one estate, there can be but one reversion. Thus, if prior to 1997, X, a tenant in fee simple, had granted land—

"to A for life, remainder to B for life, remainder to C in tail",[47]

he retained the reversion in fee simple, and yet had created two remainders, namely, those of B and C. It will be seen that a reversion arises by operation of law, a remainder by act of parties.[48] If the estate in possession was created at some earlier time, the grantee takes no remainder but a transfer of the

---

[41] s.6, now replaced by L.P.A. 1925, s.4(2).
[42] Fearne 371.
[43] *Doe d. Calkin v. Tomkinson* (1813) 2 M. & S. 165.
[44] *Re Cresswell* (1883) 24 Ch.D. 102 at 107.
[45] *Ante*, para. 3–017.
[46] See the discussions by Maitland at (1890) 6 L.Q.R. 25 and S.S., Vol. 17, p. xxxviii. In the text, "reversion" is always employed in its correct sense, although in practice the terms "reversions" or "reversionary interests" are often loosely applied to remainders as well as reversions.
[47] Entails cannot be created after 1996: see *ante*, para. 3–037.
[48] Williams R.P. 362.

grantor's reversion or some estate derived out of it. A reversion therefore need not necessarily be owned by the person who created the antecedent estate.

Estates less than a fee simple, and upon which therefore remainders or **7–009** reversions (or both) are expectant, are called "particular estates",[49] for such an estate is given for a particular portion of time,[50] and is only a part (*or particula*[51]) of the fee simple. But no fee simple could be a particular estate, even if it was a determinable fee.[52] Future interests expectant on a conditional or determinable fee simple, such as a right of entry or a possibility of reverter, are neither reversions nor remainders, for they exist independently of any estate in their owners. The fee simple has been disposed of, and so there is nothing left of the grantor's estate, even though the fee simple granted is made determinable or subject to conditions. These special interests are best treated in connection with the special types of fee simple to which they attach,[53] and they may here be left out of account.

2. All reversions are vested. From its very nature it follows that a rever- **7–010** sion is a vested interest[54]; for it is the remnant of an estate which has never passed away from the grantor, and he or (if he is dead) his representatives stand ready to receive the land as soon as the particular estate determines. According to feudal principles, moreover, a freehold reversioner on a term of years has an estate which is vested not only in interest but also in possession, for the grant of a lease does not deprive a grantor of seisin,[55] and he therefore has what is properly called a freehold in possession subject to the term.[56] From this point of view a reversion on a lease is not a reversion or, indeed, a future interest at all.[57] This technicality is a relic of the ancient doctrine that leases were not even estates and were to be disregarded for feudal purposes.[58] But, as has been seen, leases have long since achieved the status of estates, and it is therefore common and correct to speak of a landlord's reversion.[59] Although seisin as such is no longer important, a landlord's reversion is still an ambiguous interest, for as explained above, it is regarded as being an estate in possession for the purposes of the Law of Property Act 1925.[60]

3. Reversions after 1925. Before 1926 a reversion might be legal or **7–011** equitable, depending on the estate out of which it was created. After 1925 a reversion upon an entail or life estate is necessarily equitable,[61] for even if it

---

[49] Preston, *Conveyancing*, iii, 169.
[50] *ibid.*
[51] Williams R.P. 361.
[52] Preston, i, 91.
[53] *Ante*, para. 3–060; *post*, para. 7–089.
[54] Cru.Dig. ii, 336; Challis 67.
[55] Challis 233; see *De Grey v. Richardson* (1747) 3 Atk. 469 at 472.
[56] Challis 100.
[57] *Wakefield & Barnsley Union Bank Ltd v. Yates* [1916] 1 Ch. 452 at 460.
[58] *Ante*, para. 3–015.
[59] Challis 80.
[60] *Ante*, para. 4–044; and see *post*, para. 14–008.
[61] L.P.A. 1925, s.1(1), (3).

is a fee simple absolute it is not in possession; the land will be settled land and in accordance with the Settled Land Act 1925, the legal estate will be vested in the tenant for life or statutory owner.[62] A reversion upon a term of years, however, can still exist as a legal estate because—

    (i) if the owner of a legal fee simple absolute in possession grants a lease, his estate remains a legal estate; for "possession" for this purpose is defined by statute so as to include the right to receive the rents and profits, if any[63]; and

    (ii) if the owner of a legal term of years absolute grants a sublease, there is nothing in this to render his estate any the less legal; any number of legal estates can exist concurrently in the same land.[64]

Part 3

PERPETUITIES

Section 1. Introduction

7–012   **1. Policy against perpetuities.** It has commonly been the ambition of landowners to dictate to posterity how their land is to devolve in the future, and so to fetter the powers of alienation of those to whom they may give it[65]; and it has always been the purpose of the courts, as a matter of public policy, to confine such settlements within narrow limits and to frustrate them when they attempt to reach too far into the future. We have already seen how the courts in time circumvented the designs of the barons who had obtained by the Statute *De Donis* 1285 the power to create an inalienable estate tail.[66] For similar reasons the courts later laid down that all unduly remote future interests were void as "perpetuities"; for, as Lord Nottingham L.C. observed in 1681, "the law hath so long laboured to defeat perpetuities, that now it is become a sufficient reason of itself against any settlement to say it tends to a perpetuity ... such perpetuities fight against God, by affecting a stability

---

[62] *Post*, para. 8–013. Neither entails nor strict settlements can be created after 1996, *ante*, para. 3–037; *post*, para. 8–001.

[63] L.P.A. 1925, s.205(1)(xix); *ante*, para. 4–044.

[64] *ibid.*, s.1(5); *ante*, para. 4–055.

[65] "*Te teneam moriens* is the dying lord's apostrophe to his manor, for which he is forging these fetters, that seem, by restricting the dominion of others, to extend his own": Jarman, *Wills* (1st ed.), i. 196.

[66] *Ante*, paras 3–079, 3–080.

which human providence can never attain to, and are utterly against the reason and policy of the common law".[67]

2. Rules against perpetuities. All types of future interests have therefore been made subject to important rules limiting the period for which a settlor can exercise control over property. A settlor cannot render property for ever inalienable, nor can he settle it so that it may vest an inordinate number of years in the future. The following rules must be distinguished.

    7–013

    (i) The rules of common law which governed contingent remainders and executory interests. Those rules finally became obsolete in 1926.[68]

    (ii) The rule in *Whitby v. Mitchell*,[69] sometimes called the old rule against perpetuities, or the rule against double possibilities. That rule was abolished in 1925.[70]

    (iii) The rule against perpetuities. This is sometimes referred to as the modern rule against perpetuities to distinguish it from the rule in *Whitby v. Mitchell*.

    (iv) The rule against inalienability or perpetual trusts.

    (v) The rule against accumulations.

Rules (iii), (iv) and (v) are still in force and are explained in this chapter.

3. Origin of the rules. The old contingent remainder rules were of medieval origin, and were later complicated by the invention of executory interests under the Statute of Uses 1535 and the Statute of Wills 1540. The rule in *Whitby v. Mitchell* dated from the sixteenth century, but it was of uncertain scope and was complicated by technicalities of the old law of future interests. A clearer and more comprehensive rule was needed, and this was eventually evolved in the form known as the modern rule against perpetuities. Its general outline first emerged in 1685, when the House of Lords settled the great legal controversy which arose in the *Duke of Norfolk's Case*.[71] The new principle was that the vesting of an interest must not be capable of exceeding a period based upon an existing lifetime. It was developed step by step[72] until it reached its final form in 1833.[73] The rule against inalienability is also based on decided cases of respectable antiquity. The rule against accumulations, on

    7–014

---

[67] *Duke of Norfolk's Case* (1681) 2 Swans. 454 at 460.
[68] See Appendix 4 of the previous edition of this work.
[69] (1890) 44 Ch.D. 85.
[70] See Appendix 4 of the previous edition of this work.
[71] (1681) 2 Swans 454; (1685) 3 Ch.Ca. 1; H.E.L. vii, 223–225. The development of the modern rule is well explained in H.E.L. vii, 215–238.
[72] H.E.L. vii, 226, 227; *post*, para. 7–015.
[73] *Cadell v. Palmer* (1833) 1 Cl. & F. 372 (also a decision of the House of Lords).

the other hand, has a statutory and comparatively modern origin, the Accumulations Act 1800.

Section 2. The Rule against Perpetuities

A. History

7–015   **1. Origin.** The combined effect of the Statute of Uses 1535 and the Statute of Wills 1540 was to bring into existence a whole new family of future interests which were free from the strict rules which governed remainders at common law. These "executory interests" were obnoxious to the law's policy against perpetuities, since they could be used to make gifts take effect at remote future dates, so that the ultimate ownership and right of alienation of the fee simple absolute might be put into abeyance for a long time. A comprehensive rule was needed to keep all such interests within reasonable limits, while at the same time enabling landowning families to retain their land in their families from generation to generation. The rule eventually devised allowed settlors to leave the ultimate ownership uncertain for a maximum period of one subsisting lifetime and a further 21 years. This rule was modelled upon the period for which the power of alienation could normally be restrained in settlements operating at common law[74]: land could be settled upon A for life with remainder to his son in tail, so that the maximum period which could elapse before the entail could effectively be barred was A's lifetime plus the son's minority, *i.e.* 21 years.

7–016   **2. Development.** It was many years before the rule was finally settled.[75] In 1662 the limitation of a term of years to several living persons in succession was held good[76]; and so in 1678 was an executory devise which might not have vested until the expiration of a lifetime plus 21 years.[77] But the rule became firmly established only by later stages. The *Duke of Norfolk's Case*[78] in 1685 settled beyond doubt that a shifting use bound to take effect, if at all, during a life in being was valid. In 1697 a life in being plus one year was held valid[79]; and in 1736 this was extended to a life in being plus a minority, *i.e.* plus a maximum period of 21 years.[80]

In 1797 it was settled that a child *en ventre sa mère* (conceived but not born) might be treated as a life in being,[81] thus extending the period by a possible

---

[74] As explained *post*, para. 8–003. See *Long v. Blackall* (1797) 7 T.R. 100 at 102; Hargrave, p. 518; Butler's notes to Co.Litt. 20(a), note (5); Fearne 444, 566.
[75] See H.E.L. vii, 215 *et seq.*; Morris & Leach, chap. 1 (dealing both with the history of the rule and its general place in the legal system); (1977) 126 U. Penn L.R. 19 (G. L. Haskins, discussing the historical, social and legal background).
[76] *Goring v. Bickerstaffe*, Pollexf. 31.
[77] *Taylor d. Smith v. Biddall*, 2 Mod. 289.
[78] 3 Ch.Ca. 1.
[79] *Lloyd v. Carew*, Show. P.C. 137.
[80] *Stephens v. Stephens*, Ca.t.Talb. 228.
[81] *Long v. Blackall*, 7 T.R. 100.

further nine months; and by then it had also become accepted that the period of 21 years after the life in being also might be extended to cover a further period of gestation if it existed.[82] In 1805 it was finally settled that the lives in being might be chosen at random and be unconnected with the property[83]; and in 1833 the rule was completed by the decision of the House of Lords in *Cadell v. Palmer*[84] that the period of 21 years was an absolute period without reference to any minority, but that the periods of gestation could be added only if in fact gestation existed. These two last decisions show that the analogy with common law limitations was not followed very far.

3. Reform. The invention of this rule provided a general solution to the problem of perpetuity. Subject to a few exceptions the courts applied it to all contingent interests in property, whether in realty or personalty and whether created by deed, will, contract or otherwise. It is a striking example of wholly new law created judicially. It was amended in minor respects by the Law of Property Act 1925, and then much more extensively by the Perpetuities and Accumulations Act 1964.[85] It is unlikely that this will be the end of the process of reform, particularly in view of both the complexity and artificiality of the present law. The Law Commission has recently reviewed the rule against perpetuities, and has made radical proposals for its simplification, which are explained in this chapter.[86] Manitoba has gone still further and has already abolished the rule.[87] The function of the rule is no longer perceived to be that of ensuring that land is freely alienable,[88] but to "strike a balance between on the one hand the freedom of the present generation and, on the other, that of future generations to deal as they wish with property in which they have interests".[89] The trend of modern legislation is to prolong the period in which a gift may vest,[90] thereby achieving more exactly the settlor's objectives. The Law Commission has recommended that there should be one statutory perpetuity period of 125 years.[91]

7–017

---

[82] Lewis, *Perpetuity*, p. 149. These extensions were assisted by a statute of 1698 (10 Will. 3, c. 22; Ruff. 10 & 11 Will. 3, c. 16) which enacted that a child born after the father's death should be deemed to be born in his lifetime for purposes of succession: *ibid.*

[83] *Thellusson v. Woodford*, 11 Ves. 112.

[84] 1 Cl. & F. 372.

[85] For the P.A.A. 1964 see Elphinstone, *Perpetuities and Accumulations Act 1964*; Morris & Leach, 1964 Supp.; Maudsley, *The Modern Law of Perpetuities*.

[86] (1998) Law Com. No. 251.

[87] Perpetuities and Accumulations Act 1983 (S.M. 1982–83, c.43); (1984) 4 O.J.L.S. 454 (R. Deech). There was considerable opposition to abolition in England and Wales, even though the Law Commission considered it as an option: see, *e.g.* (1994) 57 M.L.R. 602 (C. T. Emery); [1995] Conv. 212 (P. Sparkes).

[88] This objective has now been achieved by means of conferring an unfetterable right of alienation on a tenant for life under the Settled Land Act 1925 and by the imposition of a trust with a power of sale in most cases of co-ownership: *post*, Chap. 8.

[89] The so-called "Dead Hand Rationale": (1981) 97 L.Q.R. 593 at 594 (R. Deech).

[90] By the principle of "wait and see": *post*, para. 7–030. See (1984) 4 O.J.L.S. 454 at 459 (R. Deech).

[91] (1998) Law Com. No. 251; *post*, para. 7–136.

Statutory reform in this country has proceeded hitherto in the usual way by building on the old law. An understanding of the old law is still the first essential, both because it still governs future interests taking effect under past dispositions, and also because the new law applies for the most party only where a disposition would fail under the old law. It is a typical case of reform by supplementation rather than by replacement.

B. Statement of the Rule

7–018　The rule in its classical form, as it existed before the reforms of 1964, may be epitomised in two propositions.[92]

> (i) Any future interest in any property, real or personal,[93] is void from the outset if it may possibly vest after the perpetuity period has expired.
>
> (ii) The perpetuity period consists of any life or lives in being[94] together with a further period of 21 years[95] and any period of gestation.

The Perpetuities and Accumulations Act 1964[96] has introduced two important modifications.

> (i) Instead of being void because it may possibly vest outside the perpetuity period, the interest is void only where it must so vest, if it is to vest at all.
>
> (ii) The perpetuity period may, alternatively, be a fixed period not exceeding 80 years.

The first of these modifications alters the character and application of the rule fundamentally. The Act of 1964 (as it will be called) applies however, only to interests arising under instruments[97] taking effect after July 15, 1964. Great care must therefore be taken for many years to come to ascertain whether or not the Act of 1964 applies. The following discussion accordingly deals separately with—

---

[92] For the classical definitions, see *Re Thompson* [1906] 2 Ch. 199 at 202; Gray, § 201; Morris & Leach 1; Lewis, *Perpetuity*, p. 164.

[93] Marsden, *Perpetuities*, 4; Morris & Leach 12.

[94] *Lord Dungannon v. Smith* (1846) 12 Cl. & F. 546 at 563.

[95] This is unaffected by the reduction of the age of majority to 18 under the Family Law Reform Act 1969 (*post*, para. 20–002).

[96] The Act is based on the Fourth Report of the Law Reform Committee, Cmnd. 18 (1956) which was first acted on in Western Australia: see the Law Reform (Property, Perpetuities and Succession) Act 1962, of that State, now replaced by the Property Law Act 1969, Pt xi. The Perpetuities Act (Northern Ireland) 1966 avoids some of the drafting defects of the English Act.

[97] See *Re Holt's Settlement* [1969] 1 Ch. 100 (order of court).

(i) the rule at common law,[98] and

(ii) the rule as amended by statute;

but in discussing the elements of the rule the corresponding common law and statutory principles will be treated together so far as possible.

1. The meaning of "vest".

(a) Vest in interest. The rule does not require that an interest should be incapable of vesting *in possession* after the period has run, but only that it should be incapable of becoming vested *in interest* outside the period.[99] This distinction has already been explained.[1] Thus if land is devised on trust for X for life with remainder to his first and other sons successively for life, the limitations are valid even if X was a bachelor at the time of the gift. Each of X's sons obtains a vested interest at birth, and these interests are not invalidated by the fact that some of the sons may not be entitled to possession of the property until after the period has run. It is thus immaterial that if X was a bachelor at the time of the gift and his eldest son outlives him by 50 years, the interest of the second son will not vest in possession until 29 years after the perpetuity period has expired.[2]

7–019

(b) Test. For the purposes of the perpetuity rule, however, an interest will rank as vested only if it satisfies a particularly stringent test. The two usual requirements[3] must be satisfied:

7–020

(i) the person or persons entitled must be ascertained; and

(ii) the interest must be ready to take effect in possession forthwith, subject only to any prior interests.

But there is also a third requirement:

(iii) the size of the benefit must be known.

The importance of this third requirement will be seen in connection with class gifts, discussed below. If there is any possibility that a person's share of the property given may vary according to some future event, the whole gift will fail for remoteness if that event might possibly happen outside the perpetuity period.[4] Thus in a gift "to such of A's grandchildren as attain 21", where A

---

[98] And also, of course, in equity: for brevity, the phrase "at common law" is used for the rule as unamended by statute.

[99] *Evans v. Walker* (1876) 3 Ch.D. 211.

[1] *Ante*, para. 7–001.

[2] *Re Hargreaves* (1890) 43 Ch.D. 401.

[3] *Ante*, paras 7–002, 7–003.

[4] *Jee v. Audley* (1787) 1 Cox Eq. 324; *Leake v. Robinson* (1817) 2 Mer. 363; *Cattlin v. Brown* (1853) 11 Hare 372; *Pearks v. Moseley* (1880) 5 App.Cas. 714; *Re Whiteford* [1915] 1 Ch. 347 at 352. See Morris & Leach, p. 38.

is alive at the date of the gift and none of his grandchildren have yet come of age, the whole gift must fail under the perpetuity rule at common law, even as regards any grandchildren of X who were alive at the date of the gift, and so were bound to attain 21 (if at all) during their own lifetimes.[5] Until it is known exactly how many grandchildren will ultimately attain 21, the size of each grandchild's interest will necessarily remain uncertain, and its final determination may well occur outside the perpetuity period. In other words, the possibility that the size of a person's share may vary is treated as a contingency (as indeed it is[6]) for perpetuity purposes.

7–021   If the size of a person's interest is known, it is immaterial that its amount or value may fluctuate. Thus an annuity or rentcharge is not void for perpetuity merely because it is made to vary with the total rent and outgoings of a house[7] or its rating assessment,[8] and this may occur outside the period. But it is otherwise if the annuity or rentcharge may not arise until the period has run.[9]

7–022   *(c) Leaning towards vesting.* In doubtful cases the court, as already explained,[10] leans in favour of vesting. A natural inclination to save gifts from the perpetuity rule sometimes leads to fine distinctions. For example, a bequest to an unborn person "at 21", or "when he attains 21", is clearly contingent.[11] But it may be held that "to B, to be paid at 21" gives B an immediately vested interest, with a postponed right of enjoyment.[12] It may also be held that "to A at 21, but if A dies under that age, to B" gives A a vested interest, subject to being divested in favour of B if the contingency occurs.[13] In this class of case the words of contingency are treated as governing the gift to B but not the gift to A.

7–023   *(d) Interests within the rule.* The rule applies to all types of proprietary interests. Thus an easement in fee simple to use all drains "hereafter to pass" under the grantor's adjacent land is void for perpetuity for it might first arise in favour of a successor in title to the grant at an indefinitely future date.[14]

---

[5] *cf. Boreham v. Bignall* (1850) 8 Hare. 131.

[6] Gray, § 110.1 and note. *cf.* the expression "absolute vesting" in L.P.A. 1925, s.163, explained *post*, para. 7–071.

[7] *Re Cassel* [1926] Ch. 358.

[8] *Beachway Management Ltd v. Wisewell* [1971] Ch. 610.

[9] *Re Whiteford* [1915] 1 Ch. 347; *Re Johnson's S. T.* [1943] Ch. 341 (trust to make up unborn beneficiary's income to a given amount). A discretionary trust will similarly fail: *post*, para. 7–094.

[10] *Ante*, para. 7–006. See *Duffield v. Duffield* (1829) 3 Bli (N.S.) 260 at 331; *Re Petrie* [1962] Ch. 355 (realisation of estate: executor's year taken).

[11] *Stapleton v. Cheales* (1711) Prec.Ch. 317; *Hanson v. Graham* (1801) 6 Ves. 239; *cf. Re Blackwell* [1926] Ch. 223 ("upon attaining 21").

[12] *Re Couturier* [1907] 1 Ch. 470.

[13] *Phipps v. Ackers* (1842) 9 Cl. & F. 583; *Re Heath* [1936] Ch. 259; *Re Mallinson's Trusts* [1974] 1 W.L.R. 1120. See Jarman 1388 *et seq.* for a variety of special cases, in particular as to the effect of an ultimate gift over on the construction of the prior gift. See also Morris & Leach 44.

[14] *Dunn v. Blackdown Properties Ltd* [1961] Ch. 433. *cf. S.E. Ry v. Associated Portland Cement Manufacturers (1900) Ltd* [1910] 1 Ch. 12; *Sharpe v. Durrant* (1911) 55 S.J. 423; *Smith v. Colbourne* [1914] 2 Ch. 533.

2. No "wait and see" at common law

(a) Possibilities. The cardinal doctrine of the rule at common law is that **7–024** everything depends upon possibilities, not probabilities or actual events.[15] Every interest must be considered at the time when the instrument creating it takes effect. Thus a deed must be considered at the time when it is executed, while a will must be considered at the moment of the testator's death.[16] If at the relevant moment there is the slightest possibility that the perpetuity period may be exceeded,[17] the limitation is void *ab initio*, even if it is most improbable that this in fact will happen and even if, as events turn out, it does not.[18] For example, if property is given—

"to the first son of A who may marry",

the gift must fail at common law if A is alive and has no married son at the time of the gift. For all existing sons of A may die unmarried, then A may have another son (not a life in being at the time of the gift), then A may die, and finally the last-born son may marry more than 21 years after the death of A, the last surviving life in being. This possibility may be exceedingly remote, as where a son of A is to be married within the next week, or where A is a woman past the age of child-bearing. But the degree of improbability is immaterial.[19]

Similarly in the case of a gift— **7–025**

"to A (a bachelor) for life, remainder to his widow for life, remainder to the eldest of his brothers living at the widow's death",

the remainder to the brother is bad if A's parents are alive. Even if A already has brothers living, they may predecease him, and another brother may be born later. It is then just possible that A will marry someone who was not alive at the time of the gift, so that if A's wife survived him for more than 21 years, the property might become vested outside the period in a brother born after the date of the gift. This possibility renders the gift to the brother void, even if A is old and unlikely to marry or in fact later marries someone alive at the time of the gift,[20] and even if A's parents are so old that they are most unlikely to have more children.[21]

---

[15] Morris & Leach 70.

[16] *Vanderplank v. King* (1843) 3 Hare 1 at 17; *Re Mervin* [1891] 3 Ch. 197 at 204: Lewis, *Perpetuity*, 171. Suppt. 64; Gray, § 231; Morris & Leach 56.

[17] Ambiguity may be resolved in favour of validity: see *Re Deeley's Settlement* [1974] Ch. 454.

[18] This sentence was approved in *Re Watson's S.T.* [1959] 1 W.L.R. 732 at 739.

[19] See nn. 20 and 21, *infra*.

[20] See *Hodson v. Ball* (1845) 14 Sim. 558; *Lett v. Randall* (1855) 3 Sm. & Giff. 83; Gray, § 214; Morris & Leach 72.

[21] *Ward v. Van de Loeff* [1924] A.C. 653 (persons aged 66); *Jee v. Audley* (1787) 1 Cox Eq. 324 (persons aged 70); *cf.* Co.Litt. 40a. For recent discussion in the Privy Council, see *Air Jamaica Ltd v. Charlton* [1999] 1 W.L.R. 1399 at 1408.

7–026   *(b) Impossibility.* Even where it can be proved that the birth of further children is a physical impossibility, the rule at common law maintains the same stubborn disregard for the facts of life.[22] But it respects the legal proprieties, and so will disregard what can only be done in breach of trust.[23] In one case[24] the gift was made—

> "to such of the grandchildren of G, living at the testatrix's death or born within five years thereafter, who should attain 21 or being female marry under that age".

The perpetuity period could have been exceeded only if a child of G born after the testatrix's death (and so not a life in being) had had a child within the prescribed period of five years after the testatrix's death. This was rejected as being not merely physically but legally impossible, for no legitimate child can be born to a person under the age of 16[25]; and so the gift was good.

7–027   Much care is therefore necessary to detect any possibility, however remote and in whatever improbable circumstances that a gift may transgress the rule. A gift "to the first son of A to be called to the Bar" is similarly void if A is alive, however old A may be, and even if he has a son who is due to be called to the Bar the next day; for it is possible that this son may never be called, and A may have another son (not a life in being at the time of the gift) who may be called to the Bar more than 21 years after the death of his father and his elder brothers.

Similarly, a gift of property to certain persons "if the minerals under the said farm should be worked" offends the perpetuity rule and is void because of the possibility that the minerals will first be worked outside the perpetuity period.[26]

7–028   *(c) Gifts which may never vest.* It is immaterial that the gift may never vest at all; the question is whether, if it does vest, it is capable of vesting outside the period. A gift to the first son of X, a bachelor, may never vest at all, for X may never have a son. But this possibility does not render the gift void

---

[22] *Jee v. Audley, supra; Re Dawson* (1888) 39 Ch.D. 155; *Re Deloitte* [1926] Ch. 56; *Figg v. Clarke* [1997] 1 W.L.R. 603. For reforms made by P.A.A. 1964, see *post*, para. 7–035. In Eire the courts have rejected the doctrine as absurd: *Exham v. Beamish* [1939] I.R. 336.

[23] *Re Atkin's W.T.* [1974] 1 W.L.R. 761 (postponing sale).

[24] *Re Gaite's W.T.* [1949] 1 All E.R. 459.

[25] Marriage Act 1949, s.2 (replacing Age of Marriage Act 1929, s.1), invalidating any marriage by a person under the age of 16. Had the gift extended to illegitimate grandchildren (*post*, para. 11–061), it might have been void. And in any case it is arguable that legitimate grandchildren might have qualified outside the perpetuity period under foreign law: see Morris & Leach 85, 86; J. H. C. Morris (1949) 13 Conv. (N.S.) 289; W. B. Leach (1952) 68 L.Q.R. 35, 46. Professor Leach's article is an entertaining attack on many developments of the perpetuity rule, particularly on the "fertile octogenarian" cases, and foreshadows the reforms of 1964. The law admits the physical impossibility of child-bearing for other purposes: see *e.g. Re Widdow's Trusts* (1871) L.R. 11 Eq. 408; *Re Millner's Estate* (1872) L.R. 14 Eq. 245; *Re White* [1901] 1 Ch. 570; *Re Tennant's Settlement* [1959] Ir.Jur.Rep. 76; *Re Westminster Bank Ltd's Declaration of Trusts* [1963] 1 W.L.R. 820; *Re Pettifor's W.T.* [1966] 1 W.L.R. 778; and contrast *Croxton v. May* (1878) 9 Ch.D. 388.

[26] *Thomas v. Thomas* (1902) 87 L.T. 58.

for perpetuity. The gift is incapable of vesting outside the perpetuity period, for if X does have a son, the son must be born or conceived during X's lifetime and X is a life in being. The rule requires, therefore, that the gift shall be bound to vest, *if it vests at all*, within the perpetuity period. Again, a gift by will—

"to the first of my daughters to marry after my death"

is valid, even though no daughter may marry; for if any daughter does marry, she must do so in her own lifetime, and since the testator is dead when the gift takes effect, no further daughters can be born and all those who are alive or *en ventre sa mère* rank as lives in being. Had the gift been made by deed, it would have been void, for the donor might have had further daughters after the date of the gift (who would not have been lives in being) and one of these might have been the first to qualify for the gift by marrying more than 21 years after the death of the donor and all his other daughters.

To this rule against "wait and see" there are two special exceptions which are considered below under the respective headings of "alternative contingencies" and "powers of appointment".[27]

(d) Express clauses. A gift which would otherwise be too remote may be **7–029** validated by the insertion of an express clause confining its vesting to the proper period. Thus a gift by a testator to such of his issue as shall be living when certain gravel pits become exhausted is void as it stands, even if it is highly probable that the pits will be worked out in five or six years.[28] The gift would have been valid, however, if worded "to such of my issue as shall be living 21 years after my death or when the gravel pits are exhausted, whichever first happens",[29] or "to such of my children and grandchildren as shall be living when the gravel pits are exhausted, provided that no grandchild aged 21 or over shall participate". But a clause seeking to confine the vesting within the period must do so sufficiently explicitly; the addition of words providing that the vesting shall be postponed only "so far as the rules of law and equity will permit" will not validate a void gift,[30] though "within the limitations prescribed by law" may suffice.[31]

---

[27] *Post*, paras 7–086, 7–110.
[28] *Re Wood* [1894] 3 Ch. 381.
[29] See (1938) 51 Harv.L.R. 638 at 645 (W. B. Leach).
[30] *Portman v. Viscount Portman* [1922] A.C. 473. But such words may be effective in a contract or in an executory trust (*post*, para. 10–034) where the settlor has not "been his own conveyancer" and set out all the trusts explicitly, but has merely given a general indication of how the settlement is to be made. In such cases the trusts will be "moulded so as to carry out the intentions of the testator so far as the rules of law permit" (*Christie v. Gosling* (1866) L.R. 1 H.L. 279 at 290, *per* Lord Chelmsford L.C.), so confining the limitations within the permitted boundaries, unless the settlor has clearly intended them to be exceeded: *Lyddon v. Ellison* (1854) 19 Beav. 565. See also *Re Hooper* [1932] 1 Ch. 38.
[31] *Re Vaux* [1939] Ch. 465, on which see *I.R.C. v. Williams* [1969] 1 W.L.R. 1197; and contrast *Re Abrahams' W.T.* [1969] 1 Ch. 463.

3. "Wait and see" under the Act of 1964.

7–030   *(a) Operation of the new rule.* The absolute certainty required by the rule at common law was convenient in that it enabled the validity of contingent gifts to be determined at the outset. But this convenience was bought at too high a price: the rule defeated many gifts which might well have vested within the permitted period, and which in any case could have been validated by an express clause of the kind mentioned in the previous paragraph. In order to stop this "slaughter of the innocents"[32] the Act of 1964 has now introduced the principle of "wait and see". The Act provides that a gift is to fail only if and when "it becomes established that the vesting must occur, if at all, after the end of the perpetuity period"; and until that time arrives the Act requires the disposition to be treated as if it were not subject to the rule.[33] Corresponding provision is made for powers and rights (for example, an option[34]) which do not so much "vest" as become exercisable in the future, and accordingly any power, option or other right is to be void for perpetuity only if and so far as it is not fully exercised within the period.[35] Thus the new principle extends to all classes of proprietary interests, powers and rights. But it has two most important limitations:

(i) it applies only to instruments taking effect after July 15, 1964; and

(ii) it applies only to dispositions which would be void at common law.

Even where the gift is made after July 15, 1964, therefore, the first step must always be to apply the old rule, *i.e.* the rule at common law. For only if the gift fails to satisfy the rule at common law will it fall within the scope of the Act. Instead of replacing the old rule, the Act merely supplements it by coming to the rescue when needed, but not otherwise.

7–031   *(b) Impossibility of vesting in time.* A gift which would be void for perpetuity at common law, therefore, is now to be void only if and when circumstances make it clear that it can only vest outside the perpetuity period. If circumstances make this clear at the outset, the gift is void from the beginning. In other cases its validity depends on later events which actually happen, as opposed to depending on events which might happen, as at common law. Thus where land is devised—

"to A's first son to marry",

and A is a bachelor at the testator's death, it is clear that the gift would be void at common law, and equally clear that the first son to marry might be a son

---

[32] Leach (1952) 68 L.Q.R. 35.
[33] s.3(1).
[34] For options, etc., see *post*, para. 7–118.
[35] P.A.A. 1964, s.3(2), (3).

who marries in A's lifetime or within 21 years of A's death. The Act therefore allows us to wait and see whether this happens; and if it does, the gift is good. But if A dies before any of his sons has married, and none of them marry during the next 21 years, it then "becomes established" that the gift is incapable of vesting within the perpetuity period, and thereupon it fails. In effect, it operates like a gift "to A's first son to marry before the expiration of 21 years from A's death", which of course is valid at common law, and involves a similar period of waiting to see whether any son of A becomes entitled. Had A died before the testator, the gift would in any case have been valid at common law, and the Act would have no application.

As another illustration we may take a devise—   **7–032**

> "to A for life, remainder to his eldest son for life, remainder to the eldest of A's issue living at the son's death".

At common law the final remainder would be void. But under the Act we may wait and see whether in fact it vests (a) in a person who was alive at the date of the gift or (b) in a person born later, where not more than 21 years have elapsed since the death of the last survivor of A and any of his issue who were alive at the date of the gift (why these are the lives in being is explained below[36]). If (a) or (b) in fact occurs, the final remainder is good; but as soon as the facts show that neither (a) nor (b) can occur, it fails.

Similarly, in the case of a gift to such of the testator's issue as are alive when certain gravel pits become exhausted,[37] the gift will be valid if the pits are exhausted within 21 years of the death of the survivor of those of the issue who were alive at the testator's death. In the case of a grant of the right to use all drains "hereafter to pass" under certain land, the grant will be valid in respect of all drains constructed within 21 years of the death of the survivor of the grantor and the grantee.[38]

In all these cases it will be seen that the perpetuity periods made available by the Act of 1964 are such as the donor could himself have validly used at common law, had he been well advised. Although, therefore, the change to "wait and see" is in one sense revolutionary, in another sense it is merely a reframing of the gift so as to give it the best possible chance of satisfying the rule at common law.

(c) Relation to other rules. Where other provisions of the Act of 1964   **7–033**
(explained later) may save a gift by reducing an excessive age, or by excluding members of a class, or by accelerating vesting during the life of a surviving spouse, the Act requires the "wait and see" rule to be applied first.[39] Only if and when it becomes apparent that "wait and see" by itself will not

---

[36] *cf. post*, para. 7–043.
[37] *cf. ante*, para. 7–029.
[38] This is under s.3(3). *cf. ante*, para. 7–023. For explanation of the choice of lives in being, which is governed by P.A.A. 1964, see *post*, para. 7–047.
[39] This is the effect of the opening words of s.3, excluding ss.4 and 5.

save the gift will these other provisions come into play. It is important to observe that this is the order of priority of these various gift-saving provisions. In applying them the motto is "first wait and see". This embodies the policy that the gift should be given every opportunity to take effect as the donor intended, and that only as a last resort should his dispositions be modified by statute.

7–034   *(d) Maintenance and advancement.* While the validity of a gift remains in suspense under the "wait and see" provisions trustees have their usual powers of maintenance and advancement, which enable them to use income and capital for the benefit of contingent beneficiaries, subject to certain restrictions.[40] It if turns out that a contingent beneficiary who has been assisted in this way fails to qualify for the gift, *e.g.* by failing to attain 21 or marry, the validity of the trustees' action is unaffected.[41] It is thus possible for a substantial part of a gift to be used for the benefit of someone who never becomes entitled to take, at the expense of the one who does become entitled.

7–035   *(e) Future parenthood.* Statutory presumptions as to "future parenthood" have also been enacted, in order to remedy the absurdities which can occur under the rule at common law.[42] Where the gift is made after July 15, 1964, the Act of 1964 requires it to be presumed that—

> (i) a male can have a child at the age of 14 years or over, but not under that age; and

> (ii) a female can have a child at the age of 12 years or over but not under that age, or over the age of 55 years.[43]

But these presumptions are rebuttable; evidence may be given to show that a living person will or will not be able to have a child at the time in question.[44] Thus, medical evidence of a person's incapacity may be given, and may be contradicted by evidence of capacity.

The above provisions apply only where a perpetuity question arises "in any proceedings", meaning legal proceedings[45]; if necessary, a declaratory judgment can be sought.[46] Once the question is decided, the decision will govern any future proceedings concerning the same gift for perpetuity purposes.[47]

7–036   For the purposes of the Act, "having a child" extends not only to natural birth but to "adoption, legitimation or other means".[48] It is obviously possible

---

[40] Trustee Act 1925, ss.31, 32.
[41] P.A.A. 1964, s.3(1). See (1964) 80 L.Q.R. at 494 (Morris and Wade).
[42] *Ante*, para. 7–026.
[43] s.2(1)(a).
[44] s.2(1)(b).
[45] s.2(1).
[46] CPR, Sched. 1, O.15, r.16.
[47] s.2(3).
[48] s.2(4). For the right of such children to take, see *post*, para. 11–062.

that a child may be legitimated or adopted after the date of the gift by a woman over 55, thus falsifying the statutory presumption. To deal with this, and also with any cases of freak births inconsistent with the statutory ages or evidence of incapacity, the High Court is given discretion to make such order as it thinks fit for placing the persons interested in the property, so far as may be just, in the position they would have held had the statutory provisions not been applied.[49] The Act therefore contemplates the possibility that it may not be right to order full restitution by those who had previously taken the property, or expected to take it.

4. Lives in being at common law

(a) Relevant lives. Any living person or persons may be used as lives in being, since for a gift to be valid at common law it is only necessary to demonstrate that it must necessarily vest, if at all, within the period of a (meaning "any") life in being plus 21 years. In the literal sense, everyone alive at the time of the gift is a life in being.[50] Nevertheless, the only lives in being which can be of assistance for the purposes of the perpetuity rule are those which in some way other can govern the time when the gift is to vest. The only lives worth considering are thus those which are implicated in the contingency upon which the vesting has been made to depend.[51]

    7–037

(b) Lives mentioned in gift. It follows that the life or lives in being must be mentioned in the gift either expressly or by implication. In the great majority of cases the only lives which can possibly be of use are those of the persons expressly mentioned in the gift. Any or all of them may be used to demonstrate, if possible, that the gift must vest, if at all, within the permitted period. There is therefore no difficulty in ascertaining the relevant lives. But sometimes lives which are relevant to the period of vesting are brought in by implication, without express mention. If a testator gives property to such of his grandchildren as attain the age of 21, his children's lives clearly help to confine the period of time which the gift can vest; therefore his children can be taken as lives in being. They are all bound to have been born[52] by the time of the testator's death, and a gift to grandchildren presupposes the existence of children. The gift is therefore good,[53] for no grandchild can take longer than 21 years from its parent's death to reach the age of 21. But a gift to the grandchildren of a living person is of course bad,[54] unless the class is restricted in some way, *e.g.* to those living at the death of a life in being[55]; for the living person might have another child after the date of the gift and then,

    7–038

[49] P.A.A. 1964, s.2(2).
[50] See *Pownall v. Graham* (1863) 33 Beav. 242 at 246, 247.
[51] *cf.* Morris & Leach 62.
[52] Or about to be born: see *post*, para. 7–057; Morris & Leach 65.
[53] Gray, §§ 220, 370; *cf. Blagrove v. Hancock* (1848) 16 Sim. 371 (where, however, the excessive age of 25 was specified); *Re Lodwig* [1916] 2 Ch. 26.
[54] *Seaman v. Wood* (1856) 22 Beav. 591 at 594.
[55] *Wetherell v. Wetherell* (1863) 1 De G.J. & S. 134 at 139, 140.

more than 21 years after all those alive at the date of the gift had died, that child might have a child.

7–039   Consequently it can be said that everyone who—

(i) is alive at the time of the gift, and

(ii) is mentioned in it either expressly or by implication

should be considered as a possible life in being. But it does not follow that everyone so mentioned will be an effective life in being, for the life of the person in question may have no connection with the contingency which governs the vesting and thus set no limit to the time within which it must occur. If A grants B the right in fee simple "to use all drains hereafter to pass under Blackacre", both A and B are mentioned in the gift, but neither of their lives has any bearing on the fact that no such drain may be built until long after the perpetuity period, when some successor of B might claim to use it; and so the gift is void.[56] For similar reasons all persons not mentioned in the gift must be ignored, since the length or shortness of their lives can have no bearing on the vesting of the gift.

7–040   *(c) Time for ascertaining lives.* In the case of gifts made *inter vivos*, the date of the instrument, and, in the case of wills, the date of the testator's death is the time when the period starts running and the facts must be ascertained; to be a life in being a person must be alive at that moment.[57]

7–041   *(d) Choice of lives.* For a person to be a life in being for the purposes of the rule, it is unnecessary that he should receive any benefit from the gift or that he should be related in any special way to the beneficiaries.[58] Nor is there any restriction upon the number of lives selected provided that it is reasonably possible to ascertain who they are, "for let the lives be never so many, there must be a survivor, and so it is but the length of that life".[59] "If a term be limited to one for life, with twenty several remainders for lives to other persons successively, who are all alive and in being, so that all the candles are lighted together, this is good enough."[60]

For example, gifts by a testator to such of his descendants as are living 21 years after the death of the last survivor of the members of a given school

---

[56] *Dunn v. Blackdown Properties Ltd* [1961] Ch. 433; *ante*, para. 7–023. It is otherwise under the P.A.A. 1964; *post*, para. 7–054.

[57] See *ante*, para. 7–024.

[58] *Cadell v. Palmer* (1833) 1 Cl. & F. 372. This was said to be a mistaken doctrine (*Cole v. Sewell* (1848) 2 H.L.C. 186 at 233), and Lewis, *Perpetuity*, p. 167, calls it "a flagrant abuse of the spirit of the Rule". But the law had generally been supposed to be thus for some time (see, *e.g.* *Goodman v. Goodright* (1759) 2 Burr. 873 at 879); and it was settled beyond question by the House of Lords' decision first cited.

[59] *Scatterwood v. Edge* (1697) 1 Salk. 229. ("The candles were all lighted at once", as Twisden J. used to say: see *Love v. Wyndham* (1670) 1 Mod. 50 at 54).

[60] *Howard v. Duke of Norfolk* (1681) 2 Swans 454 at 458, *per* Lord Nottingham L.C. And see *Low v. Burron* (1734) 3 P. Wmns. 262 at 265; *Robinson v. Hardcastle* (1786) 2 Bro.C.C. 22 at 30; *Thellusson v. Woodford* (1805) 11 Ves. 112 at 136.

living at the testator's death,[61] or 20 years after the death of the last survivor of all the lineal descendants of Queen Victoria living at the testator's death,[62] have been held valid. In the latter case the testator died in 1926, when there were 120 lives in being and it was reasonably possible to follow the duration of their lives; a similar limitation today might well be void for uncertainty, and so should preferably be made by reference to a smaller class, such as the descendants of King George V.[63] The clearest possible case of uncertainty occurred where a testatrix chose the period "until 21 years from the death of the last survivor of all persons who shall be living at my death".[64]

The lives must be human lives, and not the lives of animals.[65]

5. Alternative fixed period under the Act of 1964. "Royal lives clauses", **7–042** of the type just discussed, have been much used as a draftsman's device for providing a long perpetuity period when required for any purpose under the rule at common law.[66] In order to provide a more straightforward substitute the Act of 1964 has made available an alternative perpetuity period consisting of a fixed period of years not exceeding 80.[67] Although this period is to be "specified in that behalf" in the instrument,[68] it probably suffices if, without expressly stating it to be the perpetuity period, the limitation specifies a period of years within which vesting must occur. Thus a gift by will "to my first descendant to marry within 80 years of my death" seems to fall within the provision. Yet it would be safer to specify the perpetuity period in terms, as by framing gifts by will—

(i) "To A's first son to marry within eighty years of my death, which period I hereby specify as the perpetuity period for this gift"; or

(ii) "To A's first son to marry. I hereby specify the period of eighty years from my death as the perpetuity period for this gift".

The difference in effect should be noticed. Example (i) is a straightforward case of a valid gift, which is bound to vest, if at all, within the specified statutory period. The gift in example (ii) is not so confined, and it may or may not vest within that period (assuming A to be alive and without a married son

---

[61] *Pownall v. Graham* (1863) 33 Beav. 242 at 245, 247.

[62] *Re Villar* [1929] 1 Ch. 243.

[63] See *Re Leverhulme (No. 2)* [1943] 2 All E.R. 274.

[64] *Re Moore* [1901] 1 Ch. 936.

[65] For remarks on this, see *Re Kelly* [1932] I.R. 255 at 260, 261. *Re Dean* (1889) 41 Ch.D. 552 is probably incorrect on this point. See Gray, § 896, and *post*, para. 7–143, n. 4. See also *post*, para. 7–140, as to the necessity for a beneficiary able to enforce the trust.

[66] *e.g.* to confine a discretionary trust within legal limits. See Fourth Report of the Law Reform Committee, 1956, Cmnd. 18, p. 6.

[67] s.1. A period "from the date of my death to the 1st day of January 2020" which was specified as the perpetuity period in a will has been held to fall within this section: *Re Green's W.T.* [1985] 3 All E.R. 455.

[68] *ibid.*

at the testator's death); the "wait and see" provisions therefore apply, and the period of waiting in such a case is the specified statutory period.[69]

Nothing in the Act of 1964 affects the validity of an ordinary "royal lives clause" or similar perpetuity clause where the gift must vest, if at all, within the specified period.

6. Lives in being under the Act of 1964

7–043   *(a) Effect of the introduction of "wait and see".* It is a controversial question whether the introduction of the "wait and see" principle called for any special provisions for restricting the persons who could be used as lives in being. The policy of the "wait and see" provisions of the Act of 1964 is not to alter the length of the perpetuity period,[70] but to provide that gifts shall be valid if they do in fact vest within it rather than be void if they might by possibility vest outside it. The perpetuity period itself remains unchanged, and the lives in being which determine the period in any given case ought likewise to remain unchanged. This was assumed (correctly, it is submitted) by the Law Reform Committee when they recommended the change to "wait and see".[71]

7–044   According to the school of thought which the Act has followed, however, an unconfined "wait and see" provision would enable a contingent gift to remain in suspense for 21 years beyond the life of anyone in the world who could be shown to have been alive at the date of the gift.[72] This startling proposition is deduced from the fallacious hypothesis that the common law rule identifies only lives which validate a gift; on this footing, in every case where the gift fails no relevant lives exist at all. This reasoning disregards the fact, already explained, that the only lives in being which are significant under the rule at common law are those which in some way restrict the time within which the gift can vest, and which are expressly or impliedly connected with the gift by the donor's directions. The available perpetuity period must always be ascertained before it can be said whether the gift succeeds or fails. The conditions governing the vesting of the gift, and the lives implicated in those conditions, necessarily remain the same, whether or not the conditions are ultimately satisfied. It cannot therefore be right to suppose that an unconfined "wait and see" rule would make the lives of all or any other people in the world relevant in any way. If we contrast two gifts such as

> "To A for life, remainder to his first son to attain 21", and
> "To A for life, remainder to his first son to attain 25"

---

[69] See P.P.A. 1964, s.3(4).
[70] Except by introducing the alternative fixed period under s.1, above.
[71] Fourth Report, Cmnd. 18 (1956), paras 17, 18.
[72] Allan (1963) 6 U. of W.A.L.Rev. 27, 43–46, (1965) 81 L.Q.R. 106; Maudsley (1970) 86 L.Q.R. 357, (1975) 60 Cornell L.R. 355, *The Modern Law of Perpetuities*, 5, 94; and see Simes (1963) 6 U. of W.A.L.R. 21, 22–25; Fetters (1975) 60 Cornell L.R. 381; Deech (1981) 97 L.Q.R. 593; Dukeminier (1986) 102 L.Q.R. 250.

we see at once that the lives of A and his sons are in both cases equally related to the time of vesting of the remainder, and that all other lives are in both cases equally irrelevant. The fact that in the second case the remainder would have failed at common law cannot bring other lives into the picture since they cannot affect the time of vesting. Under a "wait and see" system the only possible question in that case would be whether a son of A did in fact attain 25 within the lifetime of A plus 21 years.

In order to introduce the "wait and see" principle, therefore, the most that was required was to enact that no extension of the familiar category of lives should be implied.[73] Instead, it was thought necessary to insert in the Act of 1964 a detailed definition of the lives in being which are to be used for the purposes of its "wait and see" provisions. It is both more complex and less rational in operation than the reforming statutes of many other countries, which have followed simpler and sounder principles.[74] The definition is a fertile source of problems and obscurities. As compared with the rule at common law, it sometimes allows different lives in being to be used; and it is sometimes more indulgent than the common law and sometimes less so. Although in many cases there will be no discrepancy and little difficulty, this cannot be taken for granted. **7–045**

(b) Conditions for the use of statutory lives in being. It is only for the purpose of its "wait and see" provisions that the Act of 1964 defines the lives in being.[75] A gift which is valid at common law (*e.g.* one confined by a conventional "royal lives clause") is unaffected, as also is a gift made before July 16, 1964. Where the donor has chosen the alternative of appointing a fixed statutory perpetuity period, of course no lives in being can be used.[76] **7–046**

In all other cases where "wait and see" applies, the Act provides that the perpetuity period shall be determined by reference to the lives of certain categories of persons and no others. The definition is therefore both imperative and exclusive. The persons concerned must, of course, be in being at the relevant time. In addition, they must satisfy two requirements—

    (i) they must be ascertainable at the commencement of the perpetuity period, and

---

[73] For fuller discussion see Morris and Wade (1964) 80 L.Q.R. 486, 495–501; *cf.* Elphinstone, *Perpetuities and Accumulations Act 1964*, 14.

[74] *e.g.* Perpetuities Act 1966 (Ontario); Property Law Act 1969 (Western Australia); Property Law Act 1974 (Queensland); Perpetuities and Accumulations Act 1968, s.6(4) (Victoria). The Victorian statute is especially interesting, since its "wait and see" provision initially follows the wording of the U.K. Act but rejects its definition of lives in being in favour of a simple and accurate formula indicating the same lives as at common law. If the theory criticised above were correct, this and similar statutes would be unworkable. For details of legislation in the British Commonwealth and U.S.A. see Maudsley, *The Modern Law of Perpetuities*, Appendix D.

[75] s.3(4).

[76] *ibid.*

(ii) if a "description of persons", they must not be so numerous as to render it impracticable to ascertain the date of death of the survivor.[77]

The second of these requirements is in conformity with the rule at common law, as already explained.[78] The first requirement is new, and is a restriction of the rule at common law. For example, in a gift by will—

"to A's first grandchild to marry a woman born before my death" (A being alive at the testator's death),

the gift is presumably valid at common law because it must vest during the lifetime of the potential wife, who is by definition a life in being. It does not matter that the wife is not ascertainable at the commencement of the perpetuity period, *i.e.* at the testator's death. But in cases where the "wait and see" provisions of the Act apply, such a life may not be used, for it is unascertainable at the outset.

7–047   *(c) Statutory categories of lives in being.* Where the above-mentioned conditions are satisfied, the Act of 1964 provides that four categories of lives in being are to be used.[79] If none of these are in fact available, the perpetuity period for "wait and see" purposes is 21 years only.[80] The four statutory categories are as follows.[81]

7–048   (a) THE DONOR: "the person by whom the disposition was made".

7–049   (b) A DONEE: "a person to whom or in whose favour the disposition was made, that is to say—

(i) in the case of a disposition to a class of persons, any member or potential member of the class;

(ii) in the case of an individual disposition to a person taking only on certain conditions being satisfied, any person as to whom some of the conditions are satisfied and the remainder may in time be satisfied";

(iii) and (iv) (these concern special powers of appointment, discussed separately below);

(v) "in the case of any power, option or other right, the person on whom the right is conferred".

7–050   (c) A DONEE'S PARENT OR GRANDPARENT: "a person having a child or grandchild within sub-paragraphs (i) or (iv) of paragraph (b) above, or any of whose

---

[77] s.3(4); see *Re Thomas Meadows & Co. Ltd* [1971] Ch. 278.
[78] *Ante,* para. 7–041.
[79] s.3(5).
[80] s.3(4)(b).
[81] s.3(5).

children or grandchildren, if subsequently born, would by virtue of his or her descent fall within those sub-paragraphs".

(d) THE OWNER OF A PRIOR INTEREST: "any person on the failure or determi- **7–051**
nation of whose prior interest the disposition is limited to take effect".[82]

(d) "The disposition". Each of these categories, it will be noticed, is **7–052**
defined in relation to "the disposition"[83]; and it is plain from the Act that each
distinct gift counts as a distinct disposition. Thus, in a gift by will—

> "To A's first son to marry, and, in default of any son of A marrying, then
> to B's first son to marry" (A and B being alive and without married sons
> at the testator's death),

there are two separate dispositions. Any son of A alive at the testator's death
is a life in being under (b) for the purposes of the first gift, and under (d) for
the purposes of the second gift. Any such son of B is a life in being under (b)
for the purposes of the second gift, but not a life in being at all for the purposes
of the first gift. A is also a life in being under (c) for the purposes of the first
gift, but not the second; and B is a life in being under (c) for the purposes of
the second gift, but not the first. The scheme is thus both more complicated
and more restrictive than that under the rule at common law. At common law
royal lives, or any other lives, may be specified by the settlor. But such lives
are now useless for statutory "wait and see" purposes.

A class gift is a single "disposition" to which the Act applies as explained
below.[84]

(e) Examples. Some further examples will illustrate the operation of the **7–053**
statutory rules, and what seems to be their pointless divergence from the
principle of the rule at common law.

Suppose that a settlement made *inter vivos* in 1975 gives property "to A's
first grandchild to attain 21" and that A is then alive and without such a
grandson. The gift would be void at common law, and therefore "wait and
see" applies. The possible lives in being are the settlor (under (a)), A and any
existing children of A (under (c)), any existing grandsons of A (under (b)(ii)),
and also it seems A's spouse, the spouses of A's children, and the parents of
the latter spouses.[85] The validity of the gift may therefore remain in suspense
until 21 years after the death of the last of these persons who was alive at the
date of the settlement. Here the Act goes much further than the rule at
common law: for the life of the settlor has nothing to do with the conditions
for vesting, nor has the life of an existing child of A as regards anyone but that
child's own son or sons; nor has the life of an existing grandson of A, except

---

[82] See *Re Thomas Meadows & Co. Ltd* [1971] Ch. 278.
[83] Registration of a member of a pension scheme may be "the disposition": *Re Thomas Meadows & Co. Ltd, supra*.
[84] *Post*, para. 7–068.
[85] Unless excluded by the words "by virtue of his or her descent". For this and other obscurities see [1969] C.L.J. 284 (M. J. Prichard).

as regards himself; nor have the lives of the above-mentioned spouses and parents. A grandson may thus be allowed to "wait and see" for the duration of several lives which are irrelevant to his interest and so operate fortuitously. If, for example, he happens to have an uncle or a cousin born before the settlement, his chances of taking may be greatly extended. The complexity of this new law is evident.

7–054   Suppose that a testator dying in 1975 leaves property "to A's first son to marry, but if there is no such son, to B". Here the eligible lives are, for the first disposition, A and A's spouse (under (c)) and any existing sons of A (under (b)(ii)); but for the second disposition, the only available lives are any existing sons of A (under (d)) and perhaps[86] B himself (under (b)(ii)); A's life will not count. Here the Act is more restrictive than the common law, for plainly the life of A may affect the period of time within which the gift to B may vest. If A has no son and survives B for more than 21 years, B's gift will therefore fail to vest within the statutory perpetuity period, and B's estate will take nothing, although, in fact, the period is not extended beyond the lifetime of a living person, namely, A.

Suppose, finally, that A grants to B the right to use "all drains hereafter to be constructed under Blackacre". Here the Act allows the use of A (under (a)) and B (under (b)(v)) as lives in being, so that B or his successors in title will be entitled to use all such drains in fact constructed within 21 years of the death of the survivor of A and B. Here the Act goes further than the rule at common law, for the lives of A and B have no necessary effect on the time within which the right may become exercisable: A and B might die or sell their interests long before that time, yet their lives will continue to be important to their successors. If A and B are both corporations, the period is 21 years only.

7–055   *(f) Comparison with common law lives.* It will be observed that, as a general rule, the Act allows a greater number of lives in being to be used than could be used at common law. But the Act is more restrictive than the common law in two situations—

   (i) where a life in being is not an ascertainable person at the time of the gift; and

   (ii) where there is a gift over and the donee dies more than 21 years before the gift is to vest.

7–056   **7. Perpetuity period without lives in being.** If no lives in being are available, the perpetuity period is 21 years only. This is equally true at

---

[86] Is B a person "as to whom some of the conditions are satisfied"? His mere identity can hardly count, since an immediate gift "to B" is vested and not conditional at all. Benevolent construction may solve this problem.

common law[87] and under the Act of 1964,[88] unless, of course, the alternative statutory perpetuity period (not exceeding 80 years)[89] has been used.

At common law, for example, a gift by a testator to all his issue living 50 years after his death,[90] or to all the children of X (who is alive) living 28 years after the testator's death,[91] is void. The difficulty is that neither the lives of the testator's children in the first case nor X's life in the second case have any bearing on the time of vesting: it is a period of years quite unconnected with any lifetimes, so that all available lives might fail more than 21 years before its termination. There are therefore no effective lives in being and the perpetuity period is 21 years only. This is sometimes called a period in gross. A gift to all the children of X living 30 years after the testator's death is of course good if X is dead, for all the beneficiaries are lives in being.[92]

The Act of 1964, as explained above, has abandoned the principle that lives in being must be connected with the time of vesting. All the persons mentioned in the above two examples of void gifts would, if the Act of 1964 applied, be within the new statutory categories of lives in being, and "wait and see" would operate during the period of their lives plus 21 years. An example of a gift without lives in being under the Act of 1964 is a devise to the first woman to land on the moon. Here "wait and see" will operate, but only during the period of 21 years.

8. Children *en ventre sa mère*. For the purpose of the perpetuity rule, a child *en ventre sa mère*[93] is treated as if it had been born,[94] even if the child does not benefit from the gift.[95] Two cases can arise.   **7–057**

> (i) A child may be *en ventre sa mère* at the beginning of the period, *i.e.* at the time of the gift. In this case the child is treated as a life in being.[96] Thus if a testator gives property for life to the child with which the wife is enceinte, with remainder contingent upon certain circumstances existing at that child's death, or bound to occur within 21 years thereof, the remainder is good, for the contingency must be resolved within the permissible period.[97]

---

[87] Marsden 34.
[88] s.3(4)(b). This applies only in cases of "wait and see". In other cases the Act leaves the common law unchanged.
[89] *Ante*, para. 7–042.
[90] *Speakman v. Speakman* (1850) 8 Hare 180.
[91] *Palmer v. Holford* (1828) 4 Russ. 403.
[92] *Lachlan v. Reynolds* (1852) 9 Hare 796.
[93] "In simple English it is an unborn child inside the mother's womb": *Royal College of Nursing v. Dept of Health and Social Security* [1981] A.C. 800 at 802, *per* Lord Denning M.R. On the perpetuity aspects of delayed posthumous births by means of sperm banks or other devices, see (1979) 53 A.L.J. 311 (C. Sappideen).
[94] *Thellusson v. Woodford* (1805) 11 Ves. 112 at 141.
[95] *Re Wilmer's Trusts* [1903] 2 Ch. 411.
[96] *Thellusson v. Woodford, supra*, at 143; *Re Wilmer's Trusts, supra*, at 421.
[97] *Long v. Blackall* (1797) 7 T.R. 100.

(ii) A child may be *en ventre sa mère* during the period. In this case the period is extended so far as is necessary to include the period of gestation.[98] Thus if property is given to the first of A's sons to reach 21 years, the gift is valid even if A's only son was unborn at A's death; the perpetuity period in such a case is A's lifetime plus the period of gestation and 21 years.

It will be seen from this that two periods of gestation may arise in the same case; both are then allowed.[99] If property is given to Jane's eldest child for life, with remainder to the first son of that child to be 21 and Jane is pregnant with her first child at the time of the gift, the remainder does not infringe the perpetuity rule even though Jane's child may be a son who dies leaving his wife enceinte of an only son. Jane's child is treated as a life in being and the perpetuity period will be extended to cover the period of gestation of the child's son.[1] In exceptional cases. there may even be three periods of gestation.[2]

These rules do not allow the addition of any period or periods of nine months or so for all cases; they apply only where gestation actually exists, and where the date of the subsequent birth affects the period chosen.[3]

The Act of 1964 makes no change to these rules.

7-058   **9. "Surviving spouse" conditions.** Donors often made gifts to such children as might be living at the death of their last-surviving parent. Such gifts often failed at common law where one parent was not a life in being, and so the Act of 1964 has made special provision for preventing this particular disaster. Where a gift is made by will—

"to A (a bachelor) for life, with remainder to any wife of A for life, with remainder to such of their children as survive them both",

the remainder to the children is, as we have seen, void at common law if A is alive at the same time of the gift.[4] But if the gift is made after July 15, 1964, the Act of 1964 now saves the remainder to the children. This it does by providing that, subject to the "wait and see" rule, "where a disposition is limited by reference to the time of death of the survivor of a person in being at the commencement of the perpetuity period and any spouse of that person, and that time has not arrived at the end of the perpetuity period, the disposition shall be treated for all purposes, where to do so would save it from being void

---

[98] Gray, § 221; Morris and Leach 65; Jarman 305, 306.
[99] *Thellusson v. Woodford* (1805) 11 Ves. 112 at 143, 149, 150.
[1] See *Gulliver v. Wickett* (1745) 1 Wils.K.B. 105; *Thellusson v. Woodford, supra*, at 149, 150.
[2] *Smith v. Farr* (1838) 3 Y. & C. Ex. 328; Gray, § 222.
[3] *Cadell v. Palmer* (1833) 1 Cl. & F. 372 at 421, 422.
[4] *Ante*, paras 7–024, 7–025.

for remoteness, as if it had instead been limited by reference to the time immediately before the end of that period".[5] In such cases, therefore, under the "wait and see" rule no change in the time of vesting is required if the survivor of the parents in fact dies within the perpetuity period (A's lifetime plus 21 years). But if A's widow survives him for 21 years, the "wait and see" rule can do no more, and the Act then converts the gift into a gift to the children then living, even if some of them predecease the widow and so fall outside the class which the testator intended to benefit.

10. Class gifts

(a) At common law

(1) NATURE OF CLASS GIFTS. A class gift is a gift of property to all who come within some description, the property being divisible in shares varying according to the number of persons in the class.[6] Thus gifts of property—   **7–059**

> "to my children who shall live to be 25",[7] or
> "to all the nephews and nieces of my late husband who were living at his death, except A and B",[8] or
> "to my children A, B, C, D, and E, and such of my children hereafter to be born as shall attain the age of 21 years or marry",[9] or
> "to A, B, C, D and E if living",[10]

are class gifts. The essence of the matter in each case is the intention that if one member of the class is subtracted the shares of the others will be increased. But gifts of property to be equally divided between—

> "the five daughters of X",[11] or
> "my nine children",[12]

or a gift of £2,000—

> "to each of my daughters",[13]

---

[5] s.5.
[6] See Gray, § 369n.; *Pearks v. Moseley* (1880) 5 App.Cas. 714 at 723; *Kingsbury v. Walter* [1901] A.C. 187 at 192; Jarman 341, 348.
[7] *Boreham v. Bignall* (1850) 8 Hare 131.
[8] *Dimond v. Bostock* (1875) 10 Ch.App. 358.
[9] *Re Jackson* (1883) 25 Ch.D. 162.
[10] *Re Hornby* (1859) 7 W.R. 729.
[11] *Re Smith's Trusts* (1878) 9 Ch.D. 117.
[12] *Re Stansfield* (1880) 15 Ch.D. 84.
[13] *Wilkinson v. Duncan* (1861) 30 Beav. 111; *Rogers v. Mutch* (1878) 10 Ch.D. 25.

are not class gifts, for a distinct one-fifth or one-ninth share or the sum of £2,000 is given to each child, exactly as if he or she had been named[14]; and these shares cannot vary according to the number of the recipients. It is therefore necessary to distinguish class gifts, where the ultimate shares are at first uncertain in amount, from groups of independent gifts, where the shares are quantified from the beginning.

7–060   (2) APPLICATION OF RULE. At common law the perpetuity rule applies to class gifts in the following way. If a single member of the class might possibly take a vested interest outside the period, the whole gift fails, even as regards those members of the class who have already satisfied any required contingency.[15] A class gift cannot be good as to part and void as to the rest: "the vice of remoteness affects the class as a whole, if it may affect an unascertained number of its members".[16] Until the total number of members of the class has been ascertained, it cannot be said what share any member of the class will take, and this state of affairs will continue so long as it is possible for any alteration in the number to be made. Commonly the offending possibility is that the number may be increased; but the possibility that it may be decreased is equally fatal. Even though in such a case the minimum amount of each share is fixed within the period, the whole gift is void if the shares could be augmented by an event which is too remote.[17]

Thus if before 1926[18] personalty was given—

> "to A for life and after her death to be equally divided between all her children who shall attain the age of 25",

an intent being shown to include every child of A, the remainder was void even as regards children alive at the time of the gift, who were thus lives in being.[19] This was so even if A was in fact many years past the age of child-bearing, for in theory other children might be born[20]; and since one of these might not be 25 until more than 21 years after the death of all lives in being at the time of the gift, the period might be exceeded. However, a gift to a class as joint tenants, if otherwise complying with the rule, is not invalidated merely

---

[14] Similarly, a gift to "each child that may be born to either of the children of either of my brothers": *Storrs v. Benbow* (1853) 3 De G.M. & G. 390.

[15] Thus even a vested share can fail for perpetuity, for although vested in the ordinary sense it is not vested in the special perpetuity sense (*ante*, para. 7–020): *Leake v. Robinson* (1817) 2 Mer. 363. See criticism of this rule by Leach in (1938) 51 Harv.L.R. 1328 and (1952) 68 L.Q.R. 35 at 50; Morris & Leach, 125; *Re Drummond* [1988] 1 W.L.R. 233 at 240, 241.

[16] *Pearks v. Moseley* (1880) 5 App.Cas. 714 at 723, *per* Lord Selborne L.C.; and see *Re Lord's Settlement* [1947] 2 All E.R. 685; *Re Hooper's S.T.* [1948] Ch. 586.

[17] *Smith v. Smith* (1870) 5 Ch.App. 342; *Hale v. Hale* (1876) 3 Ch.D. 643; *Re Hooper's S.T.* [1948] Ch. 586.

[18] After 1925 the gift will be saved by L.P.A. 1925, s.163; and see P.A.A. 1964: *post*, para. 7–073.

[19] *Leake v. Robinson* (1817) 2 Mer. 363.

[20] *Ante*, para. 7–026.

because the joint tenancy gives a right of survivorship[21] which may operate outside the period.[22]

(3) GIFTS NOT SEVERABLE. At common law class gifts are not, of course, **7–061** severable, since it is the essence of the rule that any taint of remoteness affects the whole class. But what appears at first sight to be a gift to a class may in truth be two gifts to separate classes, so that the first may be valid even if the second is void. The usual test must be applied: if the size of the shares given to members of a class cannot be affected by some further contingent gift which is too remote, the class gift may stand although the further gift cannot. For example, suppose land to be settled on A (a bachelor) for life, remainder for life to any wife he may marry, remainder in fee simple to their children in equal shares, with a proviso that if any such child dies before A or his wife, leaving children who survive A and his wife, these children shall take their parent's share. In this case each child's share vests at birth, subject to being divested by the proviso if the contingency occurs. And if a child of A dies before A or his wife and leaves no children who survive A and his wife, that child's vested share passes under his will or intestacy. Whatever happens, therefore, the size of the shares given to A's children is unaffected, and their vested interests are not invalidated by the proviso, which is a separate gift and void for perpetuity at common law.[23]

Contrast with this the all too common form of gift "to all the children of A who attain 21, provided that if any child of A dies under 21 leaving children who attain 21 such children shall take the share which their parent would have taken had he attained 21". If A is alive, this is wholly void at common law, since the size of all the shares may possibly be varied according to the age attained by some grandchild of A outside the perpetuity period.[24] If the gift were instead "to the children of A, provided that" (etc.), at least the gift to the children would be valid, since their interests would vest at birth and the provision for a possible divesting at an unduly remote time would be void for perpetuity.[25]

(4) ACT OF 1964. The Act of 1964 has mitigated the severity of the common **7–062** law rule as applied to class gifts. But before the Act is explained it is necessary to notice the judge-made rules which govern the closing of classes. These rules are an essential part of the common law as to class gifts, and have to be applied before it can be determined whether the Act is applicable.

---

[21] For joint tenancy and survivorship, see *post*, para. 9–003.

[22] See *Re Roberts* (1881) 19 Ch.D. 520; Gray, § 232.1.

[23] See *Goodier v. Johnson* (1881) 18 Ch.D. 441 (a somewhat tangled case).

[24] *Pearks v. Moseley* (1880) 5 App.Cas. 714; *Re Lord's Settlement* [1947] 2 All E.R. 685; *Re Hooper's S.T.* [1948] Ch. 586. The question has been thought to be one of construction, the question being whether the final gift was or was not "substitutional": Jarman 344, 345; Gray, §§ 386–388. But it is submitted that the question is really one of law, as stated in the text, depending not upon the testator's supposed intention of making one gift or two, but upon the possible effect of his directions on the size of the individual shares: see especially *Re Hooper's S.T.*, *supra*, at 590, 591; *cf.* Morris & Leach 104–106.

[25] *cf. Re Hooper's S.T.*, *supra*, at 590, 591.

(b) Rules of construction as to closing of classes

7–063   (1) THE RULE IN ANDREWS v. PARTINGTON. For the sake of convenience the courts have laid down the rule, often called the Rule in *Andrews v. Partington*,[26] that a numerically uncertain class of beneficiaries normally closes when the first member becomes entitled to claim his share.[27] If this were not so, it would be impossible to give him his portion without waiting until there could be no more members of the class. Therefore the settlor is presumed to have intended that the class should close as soon as the first share vests in possession[28]; no one born subsequently can enter the class, but any potential member of it already born is included. Thus by closing the class against those born later, the maximum number of shares is fixed and the first taker can receive his share.[29]

7–064   (2) OPERATION. If the gift is contingent, *e.g.* upon the members of the class attaining 21, the class will close when the first member attains 21, if he is then entitled in possession. Any others who are then in existence but under age will take their shares if they attain 21; but any not yet born will be excluded, in order that the minimum size of the shares may be fixed. If such a gift is preceded by a life interest, the class will not close until the death of the tenant for life at the earliest, since not before then can any share vest in possession; and if there is then no member aged 21, the class will remain open until there is such a member, whereupon it will close, so as to exclude any person then unborn.[30] For no obvious reason there is an exception where the members of the class are to take vested interests at birth and no member exists at the time when the property is available for distribution: in such cases the class remains open indefinitely, *i.e.* no special rule applies.[31]

7–065   (3) EXAMPLES. This doctrine is important here because by limiting a class it may save a gift which at common law would otherwise be void for perpetuity.[32] Some examples will explain its operation.

> (i) Devise "to all A's grandchildren", where A is living at the testator's death and has a living grandchild. The class closes at once, since one share is already vested in possession, and includes only

---

[26] (1791) 3 Bro.C.C. 401.

[27] See *post*, para. 11–073, where this rule is further explained. For valuable accounts of it for the purposes of the perpetuity rule, see Morris & Leach 109 *et seq.*; (1954) 70 L.Q.R. 61 (J. H. C. Morris, dealing especially with the perpetuity rule); [1958] C.L.J. 39 (S. J. Bailey, dealing especially with the rule against accumulations). See also the discussions of the rule in two cases not concerned with perpetuities, *Re Bleckly* [1951] Ch. 740; and *Re Tom's Settlement* [1987] 1 W.L.R. 1021.

[28] *Barrington v. Tristram* (1801) 6 Ves. 345 at 348; Jarman 1660, 1671.

[29] If any other potential member of the class dies without having become entitled, those who do become entitled, those who be become entitled will receive accrued shares in addition.

[30] *Post*, para. 11–075; *Re Bleckly* [1951] Ch. 740.

[31] *Shepherd v. Ingram* (1764) Amb. 448; (1954) 70 L.Q.R. 66, 67 (J. H. C. Morris).

[32] See *Picken v. Matthews* (1878) 10 Ch.D. 264.

grandchildren who are already lives in being.[33] Therefore the gift, which would otherwise be void for perpetuity, is saved. But if A had no grandchildren living at the testator's death, the gift would fail,[34] for the class might remain open beyond the perpetuity period.

(ii) Devise "to A for life, with remainder to all the grandchildren of B in equal shares", where B is living at the testator's death. Here the class will close at A's death, if a grandchild is born to B before that moment.[35] But the perpetuity rule at common law will not allow us to wait and see whether this happens: the matter must be settled on the facts as they stand at the *testator's* death. Therefore if B has a grandchild living at the testator's death, the remainder is saved; for one share has vested, and even if that grandchild dies before A, someone will be entitled (by succession) to call for that share at A's death.[36] But if B has no grandchild living at the testator's death, the remainder fails; for there is then no certainty that the class will close at A's death, since no grandchild will necessarily be born in A's lifetime.

(ii) If the gifts to the grandchildren in the above examples had been contingent on some further event (*e.g.* on attaining 21 or previously marrying), it would have been necessary for a grandchild to have fulfilled the condition before the testator's death in order to save the class gift. This again follows from the requirements of the perpetuity rule at common law. Were it not for the perpetuity rule the class could remain open until the first grandchild reached 21 or married, or (in example (ii)) until the life tenant died, whichever was the later.

(4) INTENTION. The doctrine applies both to deeds[37] and wills, but is most commonly met with in construing wills. In connection with wills it is explained more generally below.[38] Being a rule of construction, it will yield to any expression of contrary intention. If therefore it is apparent from the document that the draftsman has specifically considered the date on which the class is to close, the rule will be excluded.[39] But expressions like "all or any", and "born or to be born", may not by themselves prevent the class being prematurely closed for the sake of convenience, at least where the gift is to

7–066

---

[33] *cf. Warren v. Johnson* (1673) 2 Rep.Ch. 69.
[34] Jarman 1683; (1954) 70 L.Q.R. 66 (J. H. C. Morris); *Shepherd v. Ingram* (1764) Amb. 448. This would be the exceptional case where the special rule does not apply. But even if it did, the gift would be equally void for perpetuity.
[35] *Ayton v. Ayton* (1787) 1 Cox Eq. 327; (1954) 70 L.Q.R. at 67 (J. H. C. Morris).
[36] *Re Chartres* [1927] 1 Ch. 466.
[37] *Re Knapp's Settlement* [1895] 1 Ch. 91.
[38] *Post*, para. 11–073.
[39] *Re Tom's Settlement* [1987] 1 W.L.R. 1021 at 1026.

take effect in the future.[40] Where the language is ambiguous and one interpretation makes the gift void for perpetuity, the court may prefer the interpretation which will save the gift[41]; and there are certain other class gifts
which, even though outside the rule of construction, have been construed as
confining the gift to those living at the testator's death.[42]

7–067   (5) CLASS CLOSING DURING THE PERIOD OF "WAIT AND SEE".[43] A question that
has not been addressed in any decision hitherto is whether the rule in *Andrews
v. Partington* will be applied to a gift that is void at common law during the
"wait and see" period. An example would be a gift by will—

> "to A's grandchildren who attain 25",

where at the date of the testator's death A is alive and there is just one
grandchild aged 24. If the rule applies, and the grandchild lives for one more
year, he can call for the distribution to him of the trust property. If it does not,
the trustees will have to wait until the end of the perpetuity period before
making a distribution. The only logical reason why the rule should not apply
is because it is implicitly excluded by the provisions for class reduction that
are contained in the Act of 1964.[44] However the function of these statutory
provisions is quite different from the class closing rules at common law. Class
closing enables class gifts to vest at the earliest possible date, whereas the
class reduction rules may save such a gift at the end of the period of wait and
see if it would otherwise fail for perpetuity.[45]

7–068   *(c) Class-reduction under the Act of 1964.* Even where a class gift is made
after July 15, 1964, and so is subject to the Act of 1964, the first necessity is
to construe it, taking account of the class-closing rules where applicable, and
then to determine whether it is valid or void at common law. If it is valid, the
Act will not apply. But if it would be void the Act will save some or all of it,
if that can be done by eliminating offending members of the class. The
principle that a class gift cannot be partially good and partially bad has been
abandoned, and it is thus no longer true that any taint of remoteness affects the
whole class.

    The Act provides that where the inclusion of potential members of a class
would cause the disposition to fail for remoteness, those persons shall, unless
their exclusion would exhaust the class, be deemed for all the purposes of the

---

[40] See *post*, para. 11–073.
[41] *Pearks v. Moseley* (1880) 5 App.Cas. 714 at 719; *Re Mortimer* [1905] 2 Ch. 502 at 506; *Re
Hume* [1912] 1 Ch. 693; *Re Deeley's Settlement* [1974] Ch. 454.
[42] See, *e.g. Elliott v. Elliott* (1841) 12 Sim. 276 (to the children of A at 22); *Re Coppard's Estate*
(1887) 35 Ch.D. 350 (similar, but at 25); see also *Re Barker* (1905) 92 L.T. 831 at 834;
Wetherell v. Wetherell (1863) 1 De G.J. & S. 134; *Re Powell* [1898] 1 Ch. 227 (gift to
grandchildren of a living person held valid). In principle these decisions are doubtful: see
Jarman 1676; Gray, §§ 634–642; Morris & Leach 113, 250.
[43] See Maudsley, *The Modern Law of Perpetuities* 145; [1988] Conv. 339 (P. Sparkes and R.
Snape).
[44] Considered *infra*.
[45] [1988] Conv. 339, *supra*, at 344.

disposition to be excluded.[46] This provision comes into play whenever it "becomes apparent" that inclusion of the potential members would be fatal.[47] But, following its policy of allowing the donor's intentions to take effect if possible, the Act requires the "wait and see" rule to be applied first. Only if that fails to save the gift will the question of class-reduction arise.[48]

For example, take the case of a gift by will—

"to all the children of A who marry".

If A has predeceased the testator, the gift is valid at common law and the Act does not apply. If A survives the testator, so that the gift would be void at common law, the "wait and see" rule protects the whole class so long as any member may marry within the perpetuity period (the lifetimes of A, and of any children of A born before the testator's death, plus 21 years). If all A's children marry within this period, there is no question of excluding members of the class. But if at the end of the period unmarried children of A are living, it then becomes apparent that the whole class gift would be void at common law, even as modified by "wait and see". Thereupon the Act excludes those unmarried children, provided that they are not the only members of the class, thus saving the gift to the other members. The practical effect of these two rules ("wait and see" and class-reduction) is that the Act treats a class gift as a gift to those members of the class who do in fact comply with the perpetuity rule.

7–069

The Act makes special provision for cases where class-reduction has to be combined with age-reduction.[49] This is explained below.[50]

11. Reduction of excessive ages. At common law gifts frequently failed because they were made contingent upon the beneficiary attaining an age greater then 21. Thus property might be given—

7–070

"to the first of A's children to attain the age of 25".

In certain circumstances the gift would be good: if A was dead at the time of the gift, he could have no further children and since every possible claimant was a life in being, the gift would be valid.[51] Even if A was then alive, the gift would be valid if one of his children was already aged 25 or over, so that the gift would vest at once.[52] But if A was alive and no child had attained the age of 25, the gift was bad.[53] This was so even if a child had attained the age of 24, for there was no certainty that he would not die before his 25th birthday,

---

[46] s.4(4).

[47] *ibid.*

[48] *Ante*, para. 7–033.

[49] s.4(3).

[50] *Post*, para. 7–079.

[51] *Southern v. Wollaston (No. 2)* (1852) 16 Beav. 276; *ante*, para. 7–056.

[52] *Picken v. Matthews* (1878) 10 Ch.D. 264.

[53] *Merlin v. Blagrave* (1858) 25 Beav. 125.

so that a child born after the date of the gift and shortly before the death of A might be the first child to reach the age of 25.[54]

Both the Law of Property Act 1925 and the Perpetuities and Accumulations Act 1964 contain provisions for substituting lower ages in such cases, so that the gift may comply with the perpetuity rule. These are respectively as follows.

(a) Under the Law of Property Act 1925

7–071   (1) SUBSTITUTING 21. The 1925 Act, s.163, introduced the principle that in certain circumstances the age of 21 may be substituted for the offending age.[55] This may be done only if—

  (i) the limitation is contained in an instrument executed after 1925, or in the will of a testator dying after 1925[56]; and

  (ii) the limitation would otherwise be void[57]; and

  (iii) the excess is in the age of the beneficiary or class of beneficiaries.[58]

The first point needs no illustration; the second may be illustrated by considering the limitation mentioned above, namely, "to the first of A's children to attain the age of 25". Before 1926, if A was alive and no child had reached the age of 25, the gift failed; if made after 1925, section 163 substitutes "21" for "25" and the gift is good, the first child to attain the age of 21 taking the property at that age. If the section applies, therefore, it not only saves but accelerates the gift. But if A had been dead, the gift would have been valid without the aid of section 163 and so "25" would be left undisturbed. In the result, if A's eldest child is aged 19 at the time of the gift, he must wait either two years or six before becoming entitled, according to whether A is alive or dead.

7–072   (2) ACCELERATION. Where section 163 applies it can both save and accelerate a remainder or gift over limited to take effect upon the failure of the gift to the first beneficiary. For example, in a gift "to the first of A's children to attain 25, but if no such child attains 25 then to the eldest of B's children living at the date of B's death", the section will validate the first part of the gift and thereby also save the gift over in case all A's children die in infancy.[59] Furthermore, the section will operate equally well where there are several contingencies, as for example in a gift "to the first of A's children to attain 25

---

[54] See *e.g. Re Finch* (1881) 17 Ch.D. 211, where the child was 19.
[55] As suggested by the Third Report of the Real Property Commissioners (1832), p. 41. But no action was taken until 1925.
[56] L.P.A. 1925, s.163(2).
[57] *ibid.*, subs. (1).
[58] *ibid.*
[59] This is a "dependent" limitation as explained below.

or marry under that age". The condition as to marriage is unaffected, so that a child who marries at 20 takes immediately.[60]

The third point may be illustrated by cases where vesting is postponed for a fixed period of years. A gift to the testator's issue living 50 years after his death was void before 1926 and is equally void under section 163; for the "50" is not the age of a beneficiary.

(b) Under the Act of 1964. The Act of 1964, where it applies, has replaced **7–073** the Law of Property Act 1925, s.163, by an amended provision. Section 163 is repealed but only as regards instruments taking effect after July 15, 1964.[61] Where the instrument took effect after 1925 but before July 16, 1964, section 163 still applies.

(1) CONDITIONS. The Act of 1964 provides for age-reduction where the **7–074** following conditions are all satisfied:

    (i) the instrument takes effect after July 15, 1964;

    (ii) the disposition is not saved by the "wait and see" rule[62];

    (iii) "the disposition is limited by reference to the attainment by any person or persons of a specified age exceeding 21 years"; and

    (iv) it is apparent when the disposition is made, or becomes apparent later—

        (1) that the disposition would otherwise be void for remoteness, but

        (2) that it would not be thus void if the specified age had been 21 years.

In such cases the disposition is treated for all purposes as if in place of the age specified there had been specified the nearest age which would prevent the disposition from being void for remoteness.[63] The Act thus differs from section 163 both in that the reduction in age is not necessarily to 21 years, and also in that it applies even if the offending age is not that of a beneficiary, as when the gift is to A's eldest descendant living when B's first son attains 25 years.

(2) EXAMPLES. Thus in the case of a gift by will— **7–075**

    "to the first of A's children to attain the age of 25",

where A is alive and unmarried at the testator's death, the first necessity is to wait and see whether a child of A in fact attains 25 during A's lifetime or

---

[60] s.163(3).
[61] P.A.A. 1964, ss.4(6), 15(5); see *post*, para. 7–111.
[62] For this principle, see *ante*, para. 7–033.
[63] s.4(1).

within 21 years of A's death. If so, the child will take at 25. But if at A's death his only child is aged three, it is apparent that the child cannot take at age 25 within the perpetuity period. The qualifying age is therefore reduced to 24, being the nearest age at which the gift could be good. If A left three children aged three, two and one at A's death, the problem is more difficult. Is the qualifying age first to be reduced to 24, and then successively to 23 and 22 in case the two elder children die prematurely? Or is there to be a single reduction to 22, so as to eliminate perpetuity trouble once and for all? Since the Act requires reduction to the *nearest* age which prevents the gift being void, and since it intends that "wait and see" shall continue to operate, the former solution may be right. In that case no reduction is required if the eldest child is aged six or more at A's death, unless and until that child dies under 25. A case can, however, be made for a once-for-all reduction to an age which will protect all the children.[64]

7–076 The same dilemma presents itself where the gift is to a class, as in a gift by will—

"to all A's children who attain the age of 25".

Suppose that A is alive at the testator's death but dies 10 years later leaving children aged three, two and one. Here there is a stronger case for once-for-all reduction to 22. Although 24 would be the *nearest* age at which "wait and see" could continue, it would require the assumption that the younger children might die, leaving only the eldest child to take. But the gift is to the children as a class, and to preserve it as such requires reduction to an age which will protect them all. Here again a case can be made for the alternative solution, *i.e.* for age-reduction by stages.[65] The departure from the sound 1925 policy of reducing excessive ages uniformly to 21 has produced a crop of doubts and difficulties.

7–077 (3) DEFECTIVE REPEAL OF SECTION 163. The evident intention of the Act of 1964, as explained above, is that the "wait and see" rule shall operate before age-reduction comes into play. Owing to a flaw in drafting, the Act originally failed to effect its intention,[66] since it required the repeal of section 163 of the Law of Property Act 1925 to be ignored in applying the "wait and see" test of whether the gift would otherwise be void for remoteness.[67] The mistake was corrected by the Children Act 1975,[68] so that the rules for age-reduction

---

[64] See [1969] C.L.J. 286 (M. J. Prichard).

[65] *ibid.*, 290.

[66] See (1965) 81 L.Q.R. 346 (J. D. Davies); and see the draftsman's confession in (1976) 120 S.J. 498 (F. A. R. Bennion).

[67] This was because the repeal of s.163 was contained in s.4, and under s.3 "wait and see" operates only where the gift would be void "apart from . . . sections 4 and 5 of this Act". Gifts would thus be saved by the imaginary s.163, so preventing "wait and see". For the same reason they would not be void "apart from this section" under s.4(1)(a). Yet in the end they would fail, since s.163 was in fact repealed and none of the saving provisions would apply.

[68] Sched. 3, para. 43, providing that for questions arising under ss.3 and 4(1)(a) the repeal of s.163 takes effect as if contained in a separate section.

will operate as intended, *i.e.* only after the "wait and see" rule has failed to save the gift.

(4) DIFFERENTIAL AGES. The Act of 1964 (unlike section 163) also makes **7–078** provision for differential ages, as, for example, in a gift—

> "to all the children of A who being sons attain 25 or being daughters attain 30".

Where the above-mentioned conditions for the application of the Act are satisfied the effect is to reduce each such age so far as its necessary to save the gift.[69]

(5) CLASS-REDUCTION. The Act allows age-reduction to be combined with **7–079** class-reduction, where this would save a gift which neither form of reduction would by itself suffice to save. An example is a gift by will—

> "to such of A's children as attain 25 together with such children as attain 25 of any children of A who may die under 25".[70]

If A is unmarried at the time of the gift, and at his death his only two children are aged three and one, it is plain that no grandchildren can attain 25 within the perpetuity period, even if their qualifying age is reduced to 21. The grandchildren are therefore excluded from the class, and the qualifying age for A's children is then reduced as already explained.[71]

The effect of age-reduction under the Act of 1964 in saving and accelerating a remainder or gift over is the same as under section 163, explained above.

12. Gifts which follow void gifts. The general rule is that where there are **7–080** successive limitations in one instrument of gift, the perpetuity rule must be applied to each limitation separately. Thus if there is a gift—

> "to A for life, remainder to his eldest son for life, remainder to B's eldest grandson in fee simple"

there are three distinct gifts, each of which must by itself pass the test of the rule. Where all the gifts are valid, no difficulty arises. But where one of the gifts is void, this may sometimes invalidate another gift. The rules are as follows.

(a) No limitation is void merely because it is followed by a void limita- **7–081** *tion.*[72] A gift "to A for life" standing by itself is clearly good, and it is not

---

[69] s.4(2).
[70] For this form of gift, see *ante*, para. 7–061.
[71] s.4(3).
[72] *Garland v. Brown* (1864) 10 L.T. 292. But see *Re Abraham's W.T.* [1969] 1 Ch. 463, where valid and void limitations were so intermixed as to vitiate the whole settlement.

invalidated merely because a limitation which infringes the rule is added, *e.g.* "to A for life, remainder to the first of his descendants to marry a Latvian". In such a case A takes a life interest and after his death the property reverts to the grantor or, if the grantor is dead, passes under his will or intestacy.[73]

(b) At common law a limitation which is subsequent to and dependent upon a void limitation is itself void, even though it must itself vest (if at all) within the perpetuity period.[74]

7–082
(1) THE RULE. It will be noticed that a limitation is not void merely because it follows a void limitation; it is invalidated by the rule only if in addition to following the void limitation it is also dependent upon it. A "dependent" limitation for this purpose is one intended to take effect only if the prior gift does, or (as the case may be) does not, itself take effect. By contrast, an independent limitation is one intended to take effect in any case, whether the prior gift takes effect or not.[75] The vesting of a dependent limitation therefore remains uncertain until the fate of the prior gift can be seen; an independent limitation vests (in interest) at its own separate time, and the fate of the prior gift, to which it is subject, affects only the date at which it finally takes effect in possession. It follows that a gift made "subject to" a prior void gift will often nevertheless be independent of it as regards the all-important moment of vesting[76]; and, on the other hand, that where the prior void gift is a gift in fee simple, the subsequent gift will always be dependent, since it must be contingent upon the prior gift failing.[77]

If, for example, a testator devises property in fee simple—

> "to the first of X's sons to become a clergyman, but if X has no such son, to Y for life",

and when the testator dies X is alive, the first part of the gift is clearly void at common law since the required event might occur more than 21 years after the death of lives in being. The gift to Y is, equally clearly, subsequent to and dependent upon this void limitation; for its vesting depends entirely upon the gift to X's son not taking effect. It therefore makes no difference that it is itself bound to vest (if at all) within Y's lifetime and so within the perpetuity period.[78]

---

[73] *Stuart v. Cockerell* (1870) 5 Ch.App. 713.

[74] *Proctor v. Bishop of Bath and Wells* (1794) 2 Hy.Bl. 358; *Re Abbott* [1893] 1 Ch. 54 at 57; *Re Hubbard's W.T.* [1963] Ch. 275; *Re Leek* [1967] Ch. 1061.

[75] J. H. C. Morris in (1950) 10 C.L.J. 392 criticises the rule about "dependent" gifts as meaningless. But its principle seems clear from the authorities next cited and from the initial classification of contingent remainders by Fearne 5. See also Morris & Leach 173; (1950) 14 Conv. (N.S.) 148 (A. K. R. Kiralfy).

[76] See *Re Canning's W.T.* [1936] Ch. 309.

[77] As explained *ante*, para. 7–004.

[78] *Proctor v. Bishop of Bath and Wells* (1794) 2 Hy.Bl. 358. See also *Re Hubbard's W.T.* [1963] Ch. 275; *Re Buckton's S.T.* [1964] Ch. 497 (good examples of the settled rules); contrast *Re Robinson* [1963] 1 W.L.R. 628; and see (1964) 80 L.Q.R. 323 (R.E.M.).

(2) CLASSES OF LIMITATION. Limitations which follow void limitations can **7–083** accordingly be divided into three classes for the purposes of the rule at common law.

> (i) *Vested.* These are always safe from the perpetuity rule.[79] Example: gift to A for life, remainder for life to A's first son to marry, remainder to B in fee simple. If A is alive and has no married son at the time of the gift, the second gift is void; but the remainder to B is valid, for since it is ready to take effect in possession at any time, whether the prior interests determine naturally or fail, it must be vested from the beginning.[80]

> (ii) *Contingent, but independent.* This class will be valid if its own contingency does not infringe the perpetuity rule, and it will make no difference that some prior gift fails for perpetuity.[81] Example: gift to A for life, remainder for life to A's first son to marry, remainder in fee simple to B (an infant) at 21. Here again, unless A already has a married son, the first remainder will be void. But B's remainder is still valid, for the only contingency is that B shall attain 21, an event which has nothing to do with the possible events which make the prior gift void.

> (iii) *Contingent, but dependent.* In this case the ulterior gift fails, even though itself bound to vest (if at all) within the perpetuity period.[82] Example: gift to A for life, remainder in fee simple to A's first son to marry, but if there is no such son then remainder to B for life. Here, unless A already has a married son, both remainders are void. B's remainder, although itself confined to the period of a life in being (B), is a contingent interest, for it follows a gift in fee simple[83]; and the contingency is that no son of A shall marry. Since B's remainder depends upon precisely the converse contingency to that which invalidates the prior gift, it is dependent upon that gift not taking effect and is therefore void. It would make no difference if the words "but if there is no such son" were omitted, since the contingency which they express is inherent in any gift which

---

[79] See *Re Allan* [1958] 1 W.L.R. 220. So far as *Re Backhouse* [1921] 2 Ch. 51 invalidates vested interests, it is probably wrong in principle and contrary to authorities cited under the next class: see Morris & Leach 175–179.

[80] *Lewis v. Waters* (1805) 6 East 336; *Re Hubbard's W.T.* [1963] Ch. 275; Fearne 222; Jarman 366. To the same class belong cases where there is a void appointment and a vested gift in default of appointment: Jarman 364. *cf.* (1944) 60 L.Q.R. 297, 298 (R.E.M.).

[81] *Re Abbott* [1893] 1 Ch. 54; *Re Canning's W.T.* [1936] Ch. 309; *Re Coleman* [1936] Ch. 528; *Re Hubbard's W.T., supra.*

[82] *Re Thatcher* (1859) 26 Beav. 365 at 369; *Re Hewitt's Settlement* [1915] 1 Ch. 810; *Re Ramadge* [1919] 1 I.R. 205; *Re Hubbard's W.T., supra.*

[83] As explained *ante,* para. 7–004.

follows a gift in fee simple.[84] If the final remainder had been to B in fee simple, it would have failed on its own account, quite apart from its dependence on the prior gift, for there would have been nothing to confine it within the perpetuity period: the contingency itself is unduly remote, since some successor in title to B could have taken at a distant time in the future.[85]

7-084   (3) CONSTRUCTION. The dependence or independence of a gift is a question of construction, for it is governed by the donor's intention so far as it can be collected from the terms of the gift. In one much criticised line of decision,[86] the courts appear to have forsaken their usual presumption in favour of early vesting, and to have held cases of the type of class (i) to belong to class (iii). The argument runs that "the persons entitled under the subsequent limitation are not intended to take unless and until the prior limitation is exhausted; and as the prior limitation which is void for remoteness can never come into operation, much less be exhausted, it is impossible to give effect to the intentions of the settlor in favour of the beneficiaries under the subsequent limitation".[87] This reasoning could perhaps apply to cases where the only prior interest is void, *e.g.* to a devise for life to A's first son to marry, remainder to B in fee simple; for there B is evidently not intended to take at once, and the remainder cannot, in Lord St Leonards' words, "dovetail in and accord with previous limitations which are valid".[88] But even in that kind of case the construction put upon the gift seems to be hostile to the testator's wishes[89]; and in some of the cases it seems to be directly contrary to the principle which requires gifts to be construed as vested wherever possible.[90]

7-085   *(c) Where the Act of 1964 applies, a gift cannot fail merely because it is dependent upon a prior void gift.* If the gift is made after July 15, 1964, so that it is governed by the Perpetuities and Accumulations Act 1964, it will no longer fail merely because it is "ulterior to and dependent upon" another gift

---

[84] *Proctor v. Bishop of Bath and Wells* (1794) 2 Hy.Bl. 358; *Palmer v. Holford* (1828) 4 Russ. 403 (decided on this ground alone without mention of "dependence"); *cf.* The remarks of Jessel M.R. in *Miles v. Harford* (1879) 12 Ch.D. 691 at 703. *Re Mill's Declaration of Trust* [1950] 1 All E.R. 789, [1950] 2 All E.R. 292 is a case of this type, although the judgments proceed upon the alternative (but logically posterior) ground that the ultimate gift was dependent. For the rule under which B's successors can take, see Jarman 1342.

[85] See previous note.

[86] *Robinson v. Hardcastle* (1788) 2 T.R. 241 at 251; *Brudenell v. Elwes* (1801) 1 East 442 at 454; *Beard v. Westcott* (1822) 5 B. & Ald. 801, as explained by Lord St Leonards in *Monypenny v. Dering* (1852) 2 De G.M. & G. 145 at 182 (though see Jarman 368, n. (*q*)). For criticism, see Gray, § 254; Jarman 365, 366; (1950) 10 C.L.J. at 396 (J. H. C. Morris); Morris & Leach 179–181.

[87] *Re Abbott* [1893] 1 Ch. 54 at 57, *per* Stirling J.; he also cites *Routledge v. Dorril* (1794) 2 Ves.Jun. 357, but that case was apparently within class (iii) for other reasons (see p. 363).

[88] *Monypenny v. Dering* (1852) 2 De G.M. & G. 145 at 182.

[89] Nor is it assisted by words such as "and after his death" before the remainder: (1950) 10 C.L.J. at 396 (J. H. C. Morris).

[90] *Ante*, para. 7–006.

which is void.[91] Where the Act applies, therefore, all the complications of the law about dependent gifts disappear: each distinct gift must stand or fall by itself, and the perpetuity rule must be applied to each in isolation.

It is also provided that the vesting of an interest shall not be prevented from being accelerated on the failure of a prior interest merely because the failure is caused by remoteness.[92] This eliminates the questionable reasoning mentioned in paragraph 7–084 above, and removes any obstacle to the acceleration of the ulterior gift, if valid, to fill the vacuum left by the failure of the preceding gift. But any contingency specifically applicable to the ulterior gift must, of course, be fulfilled before it can vest.[93] These rules under the Act of 1964 operate *ab initio*, and are not dependent upon the "wait and see" rule.

13. Alternative contingencies

(a) "Wait and see" at common law. Where a gift expresses two alternative   **7–086**
contingencies upon which the property may vest, and one contingency is too remote and one is not, the gift is good at common law if in fact the valid contingency occurs.[94] This is one of the rare occasions when even the common law will allow "wait and see".[95] Thus in one case[96] a testator gave property to his grandchildren and issue of his grandchildren living—

> "on the decease of my last surviving child or on the death of the last surviving widow or widower of my children as the case may be whichever shall last happen".

It was held that this gift did not necessarily infringe the perpetuity rule as it stood, and that if in fact one of the testator's children outlived all the other children and their spouses, the gift would be valid. There were two alternatives:

(i) that one of the testator's children (a life in being) would be the last survivor, or

(ii) that the spouse of one of the testator's children (not necessarily a life in being) would be the last survivor.

If the former alternative actually occurred, the gift did not infringe the rule. If the latter in fact occurred, it did, and must fail. Whether it was to fail or not could only be told by events.

---

[91] s.6.
[92] *ibid.*
[93] See *Re Edwards' W.T.* [1948] Ch. 440; *Re Allan* [1958] 1 W.L.R. 220; *Re Hubbard's W.T.* [1963] Ch. 275.
[94] *Longhead d. Hopkins v. Phelps* (1770) 2 Wm.Bl. 704; *Hodgson v. Halford* (1879) 11 Ch.D. 959.
[95] For the other case, see *post* para. 7–110 (powers of appointment).
[96] *Re Curryer's W.T.* [1938] Ch. 952.

(b) Implicit alternatives. This benignant principle applies only if the two alternative contingencies are expressed in the gift.[97] If only one contingency is expressed in the gift and that may be too remote, the gift fails even if there are in fact two contingencies. Thus in *Proctor v. Bishop of Bath and Wells*[98] only one contingency was expressed, namely, that if no son of A became a clergyman, B should be entitled. In fact, two contingencies were implicit in the gift, namely,

> (i) A might leave no son; this must be known at A's death, which would be within the period;

> (ii) A might leave one or more sons, who might become clergymen more than 21 years after A's death, which would be outside the period.

Nevertheless, the gift to B was void *ab initio*, for the only contingency expressed was a void one. Had the gift over been worded—

> "but if no son of A shall become a clergyman, or if A shall leave no son, to B in fee simple",

the gift to B would have been valid if A had died leaving no son, *i.e.* if the valid contingency had occurred.[99]

7–088		*(c) Act of 1964.* The Act of 1964 has made no change in this rule. But where the Act applies, the "wait and see" rule will now operate in its normal way if the unduly remote contingency occurs or if only one contingency is expressed. In the example in (a), above, the "surviving spouse" rule[1] may also assist.

14. Determinable and conditional interests

(a) Determinable interests[2]

7–089		(1) THE RULE AT COMMON LAW. "The rule against perpetuities is not dealing with the duration of interests but with their commencement, and so long as the interest vests within lives in being and 21 years it does not matter how long that interest lasts".[3] That is to say, the perpetuity rule does not invalidate a limitation merely because it provides that an interest shall cease at some future date outside the perpetuity period. Accordingly where property is given to an unborn person—

---

[97] *Re Harvey* (1888) 39 Ch.D. 289; *Re Bence* [1891] 3 Ch. 242.
[98] See *ante*, paras 7–081, 7–082.
[99] *Miles v. Harford* (1879) 12 Ch.D. 691 at p. 703.
[1] *Ante*, para. 7–058.
[2] For these, see *ante*, para. 3–062.
[3] *Re Chardon* [1928] Ch. 464 at 468, *per* Romer J.; see Gray, §§ 41, 603.9.

"for life or until she becomes a member of the Roman Catholic Church",[4]

or—

"for life or until marriage",[5]

the specified event may occur outside the perpetuity period but at common law the limitation is nevertheless valid. The better view is that it is immaterial that the determinable interest is a free simple and the event on which it will determine may not happen for centuries,[6] *e.g.* where property is conveyed to the X Co. Ltd in fee simple until the premises are used otherwise than as a biscuit factory, or to trustees "for so long as the premises are used for the purpose of a public library".[7] In certain circumstances these interests may cease at any time in the future, and the perpetuity rule will not prolong them.

(2) POSSIBILITY OF REVERTER. The grantor's possibility of reverter is, it **7–090** seems, exempt from the perpetuity rule at common law, and so always able to take effect. On the face of it this is anomalous. A possibility of reverter was not a reversion (and so vested) but a "bare possibility" that an interest might vest in the future,[8] and so necessarily contingent.[9] Being a potential fetter on property, such an interest ought to be subject to the perpetuity rule,[10] and in one modern case (of a conveyance *inter vivos* before 1926) it has been held that it is.[11] But weightier authorities indicate that there can be a valid reverter or resulting trust[12] after an interest which terminates, even where an express gift after that interest would be void for perpetuity.

Thus, on a direct devise of land to a school "so long as it shall continue to be endowed with charity", Lord Hardwicke L.C. held that the testator's heir

---

[4] *Wainwright v. Miller* [1897] 2 Ch. 255.

[5] *Re Gage* [1898] 1 Ch. 498. And see *Re Randell* (1888) 38 Ch.D. 213; *Re Blunt's Trusts* [1904] 2 Ch. 767.

[6] See *Att.-Gen. v. Pyle* (1738) 1 Atk. 435; *Boughton v. James* (1844) 1 Coll.C.C. 26 at 46; Tiffany, *Real Property*, 603.

[7] *Hopper v. Corporation of Liverpool* (1944) 88 S.J. 213; *ante*, para. 3–063.

[8] *Ante*, para. 3–062.

[9] Jarman 289; Tudor L.C. 702; *cf.* Challis 76n, classifying possibilities as one degree more remote than contingent remainders, since there is merely a chance that upon a certain contingency an interest may arise; and *cf. ante*, para. 3–062. Gray, §§ 113, 312, maintains that they are vested interests, though a "vested possibility" seems a contradiction in terms.

[10] See Fourth Report of the Law Reform Committee (1956, Cmnd. 18), para. 39; Morris & Leach 213; and the Real Property Commissioners (Third Report (1832), p. 36) would have been of the same view had they not supposed possibilities of reverter to be extinct at law: *ante*, para. 3–063. The view that the perpetuity rule was inapplicable for historical reasons (powerfully championed by Palles C.B. in *Att.-Gen. v. Cummins* (1895) [1906] 1 I.R. 406) has been rejected in England: *post*, para. 7–096, n.29.

[11] *Hooper v. Corporation of Liverpool* (1944) 88 S.J. 213 (Vice-Chancellor of Lancaster); see (1946) 62 L.Q.R. 222 (R.E.M.); 1945 Conv. Y.B. 203; (1957) 21 Conv. (N.S.) 213 (P. H. Pettit).

[12] For resulting trusts, see para. 10–009.

had a valid possibility of reverter.[13] In a similar modern case land was conveyed to trustees in fee simple upon trust for an orphan's home, and upon failure of that trust then upon trust for other purposes. The latter trust was clearly void for perpetuity; nevertheless it was held not only that the trust for the orphans' home duly determined in accordance with the donor's intention,[14] but also that there was a valid resulting trust for the donor's estate.[15]

7–091   (3) RESULTING TRUSTS. The equitable doctrine is that any beneficial interest of which the settlor fails to dispose remains in him under a resulting trust,[16] and that this interest is vested *ab initio* even if it is uncertain when, if ever, it will become effective.[17] Even if before 1926 the perpetuity rule applied to legal possibilities of reverter, such interests are necessarily equitable after 1925,[18] and as such should be free from any difficulty arising from the common law objection to any vested interest following a determinable fee.[19] There is also the problem of finding an owner for the land if the right of reverter is void. The determinable interest will not become absolute, for the problem arises only when that interest has first terminated independently for reasons of its own. An equitable interest in land does not escheat,[20] nor does it pass to the Crown as *bona vacantia* since that prerogative right appears to apply only to personalty[21]; and it would ill accord with modern equitable principles to allow the trustees to take beneficially. The only solutions left are to make the determinable interest absolute, as the Act of 1964 has now done, or to allow a resulting trust for the grantor, which may be said to correspond with the escheat of legal estates (where the seignory is vested) and to be equally outside the perpetuity rule.

7–092   (4) ACT OF 1964. In cases of dispositions made after July 15, 1964, the Act of 1964 has applied the perpetuity rule to possibilities of reverter and resulting

---

[13] *Att.-Gen. v. Pyle* (1738) 1 Atk. 435; *sub nom. Att.-Gen. v. Montague* (1738) Westt.Hard 587 (an authority merely *sub silentio*: the brief reports disclose no express consideration of the rule against perpetuities); *Re Tilbury West Public School Board and Hastie* (1966) 55 D.L.R. (2d) 407, considering the rule and holding it inapplicable to possibilities of reverter.

[14] Had no such intention appeared, the limitation would have created a fee simple absolute.

[15] *Re Cooper's Conveyance Trusts* [1956] 1 W.L.R. 1096; *cf. Gibson v. South American Stores (Gath and Chaves) Ltd* [1950] Ch. 177. See also similar decisions on bequests of personalty: *Re Randell* (1888) 38 Ch.D. 213; *Re Blunt's Trusts* [1904] 2 Ch. 767; *Re Chardon* [1928] Ch. 464. These three cases also appear to hold that property can fall into residue and so benefit a residuary legatee at any future time, even though a remainder to that legatee would be void for perpetuity; and consider para. 7–090, n. 13, *supra*. But this distinction is difficult to analyse satisfactorily. On the problematical case of *Re Chardon* and the use of "vested" therein, see (1938) 54 L.Q.R. 264 (M. J. Albery) and contrast *Re Wightwick's W.T.* [1950] Ch. 260 at 265, 266.

[16] *Post*, para. 10–009.

[17] See cases in n. 15, *supra*.

[18] Under L.P.A. 1925, s.1; *ante*, paras 4–030 *et seq*.

[19] See *ante*, para. 3–002.

[20] See the previous edition of this work at p. 120.

[21] See *Re Wells* [1933] Ch. 29 at 57, 58, discussed in B.V. Ing, *Bona Vacantia* (1971) pp. 172–179, contending for the Crown's right to an equitable interest in freeholds as *bona vacantia*.

trusts arising on the termination of any other determinable interest in property.[22] The anomaly of their exemption at common law is thus removed. And, as is logically necessary, the preceding determinable interest is made absolute in cases where the possibility of reverter or resulting trust fails.[23] If today a testator leaves property to an orphans' home for so long as it exists, with a gift over to A in case the prior gift terminates, the first step is to apply the "wait and see" rule: if the orphans' home ceases to exist within 21 years (there are no lives in being), A can take. But after the 21 years neither A nor the testator's successors can take, and the property belongs to the home absolutely.

The Act of 1964 achieves this result by requiring the possibility of reverter or resulting trust to be treated as if it were a condition subsequent created by a separate disposition.[24] Conditions subsequent are discussed below. The rules for determinable and conditional interests have thus been assimilated.

(b) Conditional interests. A condition may be either precedent or subsequent.[25]   **7–093**

(1) CONDITIONS PRECEDENT. A condition precedent is one which must be fulfilled before the beneficiary is entitled to a vested interest. It is of course to conditions of this type that the perpetuity rule most commonly applies, and many examples have already been given, such as "to A at 21", and "to A if he survives B". A less obvious but similar type of case is a discretionary trust, as where land is given to trustees upon trust to apply the rents and profits for the benefit of an unborn person in the trustees' absolute discretion. Since the trustees need not necessarily pay the beneficiary any particular sum within the perpetuity period, at common law the whole gift fails[26]; no ascertainable interest ever vests at all, even though the beneficiary must be born within the period. Some decision by the trustees is a condition precedent to every payment.   **7–094**

(2) ACT OF 1964. Where the Act of 1964 applies, conditions precedent are now of course subject to the "wait and see" principle. For the purposes of the Act discretionary trusts rank as powers of appointment,[27] which are discussed below.   **7–095**

(3) CONDITIONS SUBSEQUENT. A condition subsequent, as already explained,[28] is one which authorises the grantor or his representatives to determine an existing interest. It will be remembered that a gift of land to trustees in fee simple—   **7–096**

---

[22] s.12.
[23] *ibid.*
[24] *ibid.*
[25] *Ante,* para. 3–064.
[26] *Re Blew* [1906] 1 Ch. 624; *Re Coleman* [1936] Ch. 528; *Re Leek* [1967] Ch. 1061; *ante,* para. 7–020, n. 6; and see, *e.g. Pickford v. Brown* (1856) 2 K. & J. 426.
[27] s.15(2). See *post,* para. 7–104.
[28] *Ante,* para. 3–064.

"on condition that it shall always be used for the purposes of a hospital only"

gives the grantor and his successors in title a right of re-entry if the condition is broken. If such a condition infringes the perpetuity rule the right of re-entry, being of course contingent, is void.[29] The interest which it was intended to defeat is not invalidated[30]; rather, it becomes an absolute interest, since the condition subsequent can defeat it only if re-entry is actually made,[31] and the right of re-entry is void. A determinable interest, on the other hand, determines automatically at common law, as explained above, whether the possibility of reverter is void or not.[32]

Thus, if there is a valid gift by a testator to his grandchildren followed by a provision for the forfeiture of the interest of any grandchild who forsakes the Jewish faith or marries outside that faith, the provision might not take effect until the perpetuity period had run. It is accordingly void, and can neither carry the property to any other person[33] nor determine the interests of the grandchildren, despite any intention to do so[34]; the grandchildren accordingly take absolute interests.

7–097   (4) ACT OF 1964. No change in these rules has been made by the Act of 1964, apart from the introduction of the "wait and see" principle. As already explained,[35] the Act has extended the law governing conditions subsequent so that it now also governs possibilities of reverter and resulting trusts.

15. Powers and duties

(a) Powers, duties and trusts generally

7–098   (1) PERPETUITY RULE APPLIES. Settlements often authorise persons to do things which they would otherwise have no legal ability to do. Such provisions create *powers*.[36]

The exercise of a power creates or alters an interest, and accordingly it is the general rule at common law that a power which is exercisable outside the

---

[29] *Re the Trustees of Hollis' Hospital and Hague's Contract* [1889] 2 Ch. 440 (criticised, Challis 207; not followed, *Walsh v. Wightman* [1927] N.I. 1); *Re Da Costa* [1912] 1 Ch. 337; *Re Macleay* (1875) L.R. 20 Eq. 186; *Dunn v. Flood* (1883) 25 Ch.D. 629; 28 Ch.D. 586 at 592; *Imperial Tobacco Co. Ltd v. Wilmott* [1964] 1 W.L.R. 902. See now L.P.A. 1925, s.4(3).

[30] *Blease v. Burgh* (1840) 2 Beav. 221; *Ring v. Hardwick* (1840) 2 Beav. 352.

[31] *Ante*, para. 3–066.

[32] For this distinction generally, see *ante*, paras 3–064, 3–065; for its application here, see *Re Talbot* [1933] Ch. 895 and cases there cited.

[33] *Re Brown and Sibly's Contract* (1876) 3 Ch.D. 156; *Re Spitzel's W.T.* [1939] 2 All E.R. 266; *Re Pratt's S.T.* [1943] Ch. 356.

[34] *Re Pratt's S.T.* [1943] Ch. 356, confirming Jarman (now p. 1425); and see *Harding v. Nott* (1857) 7 E. & B. 650. If a gift over is void not for perpetuity but for some other reason, then if such an intention appears the condition may defeat the first gift even though the gift over is void: *Doe d. Blomfield v. Eyre* (1848) 5 C.B. 713.

[35] *Ante*, para. 7–092.

[36] For powers, see *post*, para. 10–077.

perpetuity period is void. A power given to trustees to lease[37] or to sell[38] which may be exercisable during the lifetime of an unborn person is therefore void *ab initio* at common law. The same principle applies *a fortiori* to duties, for a duty to do something of course includes a power to do it: thus a trust for sale which may be exercised outside the perpetuity period will be void, even though it may be for the benefit of living persons whose equitable interests in the property vest at once and so are valid.[39] But it is unnecessary to set a separate time-limit to trusts and powers if they are incidental to an interest which will keep them within due bounds,[40] as for example where powers are given to a tenant for life who is a life in being. Where a power of sale is limited to come into existence at the end of a life in being, the court may find an intention in the will or settlement that the power should be exercised, if at all, within a reasonable period, and since 21 years is more than a reasonable period for this purpose, the power will be held valid[41]; and a trust to sell at the "expiration" of a term of 21 years arises *eo instanti* with the expiration of the term, and so does not exceed the period.[42]

(2) STATUTORY POWERS. The perpetuity rule may also apply to statutory powers. Many powers which used to be conferred on trustees and beneficiaries by lengthy clauses in settlements are now, for the sake of convenience, embodied in statutes. For example, trustees have statutory power to advance capital to a potential beneficiary[43]; and if they do so by making a settlement on him and his children, this is analogous to a power of appointment and therefore subject to the special perpetuity rules discussed below.[44] Statutory powers of sale, leasing and management, on the other hand, which Parliament intends all owners to have as a matter of policy and which themselves create no beneficial interest, are in a different category. Thus it is assumed that the various powers given to tenants for life by the Settled Land Act 1925 can be exercised at any time,[45] as where land was settled prior to 1997[46] on A (a bachelor) for life with remainder to his widow for life. The same is presumably true of trusts of land (where the trustees normally have the powers of a beneficial owner).[47]

7–099

---

[37] *Re Allott* [1924] 2 Ch. 498 (power exercisable during the lifetime of an unborn person and so void); *Air Jamaica Ltd v. Charlton* [1999] 1 W.L.R. 1399 at 1408, 1409.

[38] *Re Daveron* [1893] 3 Ch. 421 (trust to sell in 49 years' time held void); *Goodier v. Johnson* (1881) 18 Ch.D. 441 at 446 (trust to sell during the lifetime of an unborn person held void); *Re Wood* [1894] 3 Ch. 381 (trust to sell gravel pits when they were worked out held void).

[39] *Goodier v. Edmunds* [1893] 3 Ch. 455 at 461; and see preceding note.

[40] *Peters v. Lewes & East Grinstead Ry.* (1881) 18 Ch.D. 429 at 433, 434; *Re Wills' W.T.* [1959] Ch. 1; *cf. Pilkington v. I.R.C.* [1964] A.C. 612.

[41] See *Peters v. Lewes & East Grinstead Ry.*, *supra*, at 434; *Re Lord Sudeley and Baines & Co.* [1894] 1 Ch. 334; and as to construction of powers, Jarman 319.

[42] *English v. Cliff* [1914] 2 Ch. 376.

[43] T.A. 1925, s.32. This power does not extend to land (unless held on trust for sale) or to trust property representing land.

[44] *Pilkington v. I.R.C.* [1964] 1 Ch. 612; *Re Abraham's W.T.* [1969] 1 Ch. 463.

[45] Wolst. & C. iii; *post*, para. 8–071.

[46] No new settlements can be created after 1996: *post*, para. 8–001.

[47] *Post*, para. 8–137.

7–100   (3) ACT OF 1964. The Act of 1964 has extended its "wait and see" principle to powers, provided that the instrument creating the power takes effect after July 15, 1964. A power is no longer void, in a case governed by the Act, merely because it might be exercised outside the perpetuity period: it will be void only if so far as it is not in fact fully exercised during the period.[48] The person on whom the power is conferred counts as a life in being.[49] These rules have already been explained.[50] Similarly other provisions of the Act, for example for reducing excessive ages, may apply to grants of powers in the same way as to other grants. Presumably all these provisions extend also to duties, for the reasons given in the previous paragraph, although duties do not so easily fit within the statutory words "any power, option or other right".

7–101   (4) ADMINISTRATIVE POWERS. Further indulgence towards special classes of powers is shown by the Act of 1964. It is provided that the perpetuity rule shall not invalidate a power conferred on trustees or other persons to dispose of property for full consideration or to do any other act in the administration (as opposed to the distribution) of any property.[51] The Act thus makes a distinction between administrative (or ancillary) powers and beneficial powers. A power to sell or let for full value, or to make or vary investments, is accordingly exempted from the perpetuity rule, but a power to sell at an undervalue is not, because it contains an element of gift. The Act also protects powers to pay reasonable remuneration for services, *e.g.* those of trustees or agents.[52] Furthermore, and exceptionally, the Act protects these various powers if they are exercised after July 15, 1964, even if the instrument conferring them took effect before that date.[53] This reflects the opinion that the application of the perpetuity rule to such powers was a mistake.[54]

(b) Powers of appointment and analogous powers

7–102   (1) CLASSIFICATION. The powers which most frequently have to be considered in relation to the perpetuity rule are powers of appointment.[55] A power of appointment is a power for the person to whom it is given ("the donee of the power") to appoint property to such persons ("the objects of the power") as he may select. The power is known as a "special power" if the donee's choice is restricted to a limited class of objects, such as X's children, and as a "general power" if his choice is unrestricted. Special powers are very common in settlements, as where land is given "to A for life, and after his death to his surviving children in such shares as he may be deed or will appoint". The distinction between general and special powers is important

---

[48] s.3(3).
[49] s.3(5)(b)(v).
[50] *Ante*, paras 7–030, 7–047.
[51] s.8(1).
[52] *ibid.*
[53] ss.8(2), 15(5).
[54] See Fourth Report of the Law Reform Committee, Cmnd. 18, 1956, para. 34, comparing the rule to an unruly dog wandering into the wrong places.
[55] Considered *post*, para. 10–081.

here because special powers to some extent restrict disposal of the property, so that the rule applies to their exercise, whereas general powers do not, and are therefore unobjectionable.

The rules now to be explained also apply in principle to powers which are analogous to powers of appointment, such as a trustee's power of advancement, even if statutory,[56] and a discretionary trust.[57] Any power to create or alter a beneficial interest deriving from a settlor by way of gift will fall within these rules.

(2) GENERAL OR SPECIAL. For the purposes of the perpetuity rule, a power to appoint with the consent of X is a special power,[58] unless the court can find grounds for holding that the donee was in substance the owner of the property and free to deal with it at will.[59] A power exercisable jointly by two or more persons has also been held to be special,[60] and probably a power for the donee to appoint to anyone except himself would also be held to be special.[61] On the other hand, a power for the donee to appoint to himself or anyone else except X,[62] or to a class of people including himself,[63] would probably be held to be general. For where the donee may at once appoint to himself he can, by doing so, obtain unfettered powers of disposition. An unrestricted power to appoint by will only is the subject of a distinction. It has been held to be special for the purpose of deciding the validity of the power,[64] but general for the purpose of determining the validity of the appointment[65]; for such a power fetters the property during the donee's life but leaves him an unrestricted choice in his will.

7–103

(3) ACT OF 1964. The Act of 1964 in effect confirms the above distinctions in cases where it applies, and provides for the resolution of doubtful cases. For the purposes of the rule against perpetuities a power of appointment is to be treated as a special power unless it satisfies two conditions:

7–104

    (i) it is expressed to be exercisable by one person only; and

    (ii) it empowers the donee to transfer the whole property to himself immediately at all times when he is himself of full age and

---

[56] *Pilkington v. I.R.C., supra.*

[57] *Ante*, para. 7–099.

[58] *Re Watts* [1931] 2 Ch. 302.

[59] *Re Dilke* [1921] 1 Ch. 34; *Re Phillips* [1931] 1 Ch. 347.

[60] *Re Churston S.E.* [1954] Ch. 334 (criticised at (1955) 71 L.Q.R. 242 (A. H. Droop); supported by Morris & Leach 137; *Re Earl of Coventry's Indentures* [1974] Ch. 77. *Sed quaere*: like an estate held jointly, any restriction flows not from the power or estate itself but merely from the form of ownership of it. Contrast the case when one of the donees of the power is a trustee of it, and so is restricted in exercising it.

[61] See *Re Park* [1932] 1 Ch. 500; (1937) 1 Conv. (N.S.) 198 (F. E. Farrer).

[62] Consider *Platt v. Routh* (1841) 3 Beav. 257; affirmed *sub nom. Drake v. Att.-Gen.* (1843) 10 Cl. & F. 257; and see (1932) 48 L.Q.R. 475 (H.P.). Compare *Re Triffitt's Settlement* [1958] Ch. 852 at 860, 861 (exclusion of two persons, and requirement of consent of trustees: a special power for perpetuity purposes).

[63] *cf. Re Penrose* [1933] Ch. 793.

[64] *Wollaston v. King* (1868) L.R. 8 Eq. 165; *Morgan v. Gronow* (1873) L.R. 16 Eq. 1.

[65] *Rous v. Jackson* (1885) 29 Ch.D. 521; *Re Flower* (1885) 55 L.J.Ch. 200.

capacity without the consent of any other person or compliance with any other condition (not being a mere formal condition as to its mode of exercise).[66]

It will be seen that these conditions determine the character of the power from the outset. If a power is exercisable by A and B jointly, or by A with the consent of B, the subsequent death of B will not make it a general power for the purposes of the Act. As regards powers exercisable by will only, the Act confirms the previous case-law by providing that for the purpose of applying the perpetuity rule to an appointment made under such a power, the power shall be treated as general if it would have been so treated had it been exercisable by deed.[67]

7–105   (4) EXERCISE OF SPECIAL POWERS. In general, the Act of 1964 applies to powers of appointment (including for this purpose discretionary trusts[68]) in the same way as it applies to other transactions. The conferring of a power and the exercise of a power are both "dispositions" within the meaning of the Act.[69] The "wait and see" principle applies, and both the donee and the objects or potential objects of the power may count as lives in being.[70] But there are two special provisions.

(i) In the case of a special power (as determined according to the foregoing rules, whenever it was created), the Act applies only when both the creation and the exercise of the power were under instruments taking effect after July 15, 1964.[71] Thus the governing date is the date of the original settlement, not the date of the exercise of the special power.

(ii) The alternative fixed perpetuity period (not exceeding 80 years) cannot be used in the *exercise* of a special power.[72] But it can be used in the *creation* of a special power, and in that case it will of course govern the exercise of the power also. In other words, the alternative fixed period can apply to a special power only if it is specified in the original settlement. If it is not so specified, the donee of the power cannot prolong the perpetuity period by invoking it.

7–106   (c) *Application of the rule to powers of appointment.* The application of the perpetuity rule to powers of appointment can be clarified by dealing separately with the two questions:

[66] s.7.
[67] *ibid.*
[68] s.15(2) includes any discretionary power to transfer a beneficial interest without valuable consideration.
[69] s.15(2).
[70] s.3(2), (3), (5)(b)(iii)–(v).
[71] s.15(5).
[72] s.1(2).

(i) Does the power itself infringe the rule?

(ii) If it does not, does the appointment made under the power infringe the rule?

(1) VALIDITY OF THE POWER

(i) A special power. A special power of appointment is subject to the **7–107** ordinary rule relating to powers and is thus void at common law if it could be exercised outside the period. Time runs from the date when the instrument creating the power took effect.[73] Thus, if the donee of the power will not necessarily be ascertained within the period (if at all)[74] or is capable of exercising the power when the period has expired,[75] it is bad. But a power given exclusively to a person living when it was created can never be void for remoteness,[76] unless it allows only appointments that would necessarily be void.[77]

If a power complies with these conditions, it is not void merely because an appointment which offends the rule might be made under it.[78] For example, where a living person is given the power to appoint to his issue, he might make an appointment to his great-great-grandchildren; but this possibility does not invalidate the power itself or an appointment which in fact complies with the rule.[79]

If the power is created by an instrument taking effect after July 15, 1964, it will no longer be void *ab initio* merely because it could be exercised outside the perpetuity period. The "wait and see" principle of the Act of 1964 will apply, and the power will be void only in so far as it is not in fact fully exercised within the period.[80] If, for example, property is given by will—

"to A for life, with remainder for life to any widow A may leave, with remainder to such of their issue as the survivor of them may appoint",

and A is unmarried at the testator's death, the power is valid during A's lifetime and for 21 years thereafter (assuming A's widow to be still living) but then becomes void.

If a power is void for remoteness, a gift in default of appointment (*e.g.* "but if no appointment shall be made, to X and Y equally") is not thereby invalidated; provided it does not itself infringe the rule, it is valid.[81]

---

[73] *Re De Sommery* [1912] 2 Ch. 622; *Re Watson's S.T.* [1959] 1 W.L.R. 732.
[74] See *Re Hargreaves* (1890) 43 Ch.D. 401.
[75] *Re Abbott* [1893] 1 Ch. 54 (power exercisable by the survivor of X and her husband: X might have married someone not born when the power was given, and so it was void).
[76] Jarman 329.
[77] *Bristow v. Boothby* (1826) 2 Sim. & St. 465; Gray, § 476.
[78] *Slark v. Dakyns* (1874) 10 Ch.App. 35.
[79] See *Routledge v. Dorrill* (1794) 2 Ves.Jun. 357.
[80] s.3(3).
[81] *Re Abbott* [1893] 1 Ch. 54. Such gifts may be vested: *ante*, para. 7–002.

7–108   *(ii) A general power.* For the purposes of the perpetuity rule, a general power to appoint by deed or will is so nearly akin to absolute ownership that the time and manner of its exercise are irrelevant[82]: the perpetuity rule is satisfied if the power must be acquired (if at all) within the period.[83] But if the power is exercisable by will only, it ranks for this purpose as a special power, as already explained, and is subject to the rules stated above.

The Act of 1964 applies its "wait and see" principle in the usual way, so that a general power created by an instrument taking effect after July 15, 1964, is not void merely because it might be acquired at too remote a time: it is valid unless and until it becomes established that it will not be exercisable within the perpetuity period.[84]

7–109   (2) VALIDITY OF APPOINTMENTS MADE UNDER A VALID POWER. If the power itself is void, clearly no valid appointment can be made under it. But even if the power itself is valid, an appointment made under it may nevertheless be too remote.

7–110   *(i) A special power.* In the case of a special power of appointment, the property is fettered from the moment the power is created. If an appointment is made, it will carry the property to one or more persons designated by the original settlor who is in reality the true donor. The perpetuity period therefore starts to run from the creation of the power.[85] But, as has been seen,[86] the mere fact that the power authorises the making of an appointment which may be too remote does not invalidate it, and until the appointment is in fact made, it cannot be said whether it is too remote. Even at common law, therefore, "the principle seems to be to wait and see".[87] The rule at common law is that when the appointment is ultimately made, it must be examined to see whether the interests appointed are bound to vest (if at all) within 21 years of the dropping of lives which were in being (or *en ventre sa mère*[88]) *when the power was created* and ascertainable from the instrument creating it. Facts existing at the time of the *appointment*, although irrelevant for ascertaining the perpetuity period, must be taken into account in order to find the true nature of the appointment itself, before it can be referred back to the date of the original instrument and tested by the facts existing at that time.[89]

7–111   Some examples may make this clearer.

(i) Devise to A for life with power to appoint to his children: A appoints to his son B "'when he is 23": B was unborn at the

---

[82] See *Re Fane* [1913] 1 Ch. 404 at 413.
[83] *Bray v. Hammersley* (1830) 3 Sim. 513; 2 Cl. & F. 453.
[84] s.3(2).
[85] *Re Brown and Sibley's Contract* (1876) 3 Ch.D. 156; *Re Thompson* [1906] 2 Ch. 199.
[86] *Ante*, para. 7–107.
[87] *Re Witty* [1913] 2 Ch. 666 at 673, *per* Cozens-Hardy M.R.
[88] *Re Stern* [1962] Ch. 732.
[89] It is therefore inaccurate to say (see *Duke of Marlborough v. Lord Godolphin* (1750) 2 Ves.Sen. 61 at 78; *Harvey v. Stracey* (1852) 1 Drew. 73 at 134) that the appointment must be looked at as if it were contained in the instrument creating the power: see *Re Thompson* [1906] 2 Ch. 199 at 205; *Gray,* § 515.

testator's death (in 1950) but aged three at the time of the appointment. A is the only life in being, but since the property is bound to vest (if at all) within 20 years of his death, the appointment is good.[90] The facts existing at the time of the appointment show that it is really an appointment "to B in 20 years' time, if he is then living". That is to say, the maximum possible postponement of vesting is, in truth, 20 years from A's death. Had B been aged one at the time of the appointment, then if it had been made before 1926 it would have been void; if it had been made after 1925, B would have taken when he was 21,[91] unless the testator died after July 15, 1964, in which case B would have taken when he was 23 if in fact he attained that age within the perpetuity period, and if he could not do so he would take at 22.[92]

(ii) Marriage settlement, made in 1930, upon C for life, remainder as he should appoint among his issue: C appoints in favour of his daughter D, postponing the vesting of her interest until her marriage; D is unmarried at the date of the appointment. The appointment is void.[93] A few years later D marries and C then executes a document confirming the void appointment. D is entitled to the property, since the confirmation operates as a fresh appointment, and in the light of the facts existing at the time of the appointment the property can be said to have vested during the lifetime of a person alive at the date of the settlement, namely, C.[94] Had the settlement been made in 1965, the first appointment would have been valid unless and until it appeared that D would not marry within the perpetuity period,[95] which runs from the date of the settlement.

(iii) Deed, made in 1940, giving property to F for life with power to appoint to his issue: F appoints by his will in favour of his grandchildren G and H (neither of whom was alive at the date of the gift) for their joint lives as tenants in common, with remainder to the survivor. The interest for their joint lives is valid but the remainder is void.[96] Had the deed been made in 1965, the remainder would be valid if in fact it vested within the perpetuity period. The period would run from the date of the deed and the lives in

---

[90] This example is suggested by *Peard v. Kekewich* (1852) 15 Beav. 166.

[91] L.P.A. 1925, s.163; *ante*, para. 7–071. The statements in Wolst. & C. i, 293, ii, 141, that neither s.163 nor P.A.A. 1964 applies if the appointment but not the settlement is made after July 15, 1964, appears to overlook P.A.A. 1964, s.15(5), which leaves, s.163 unrepealed in such a case.

[92] P.A.A. 1964, s.4(1); *ante*, para. 7–074. This is subject to the difficulty mentioned *ante*, para. 7–077 (defective repeal of s.163).

[93] This example is based on *Morgan v. Gronow* (1873) L.R. 16 Eq. 1.

[94] See previous note.

[95] P.A.A. 1964, s.3(1); *ante*, para. 7–030.

[96] *Re Legh's S.T.* [1938] Ch. 39.

being would be the donor, F, and any of F's issue living at the date of the deed.[97]

As will be evident from these examples, the provisions of the Act of 1964 (*e.g.* the provisions for "wait and see", age-reduction and class-reduction) apply to an appointment made under a special power in the same way as they apply to gifts generally, provided only that the instrument creating the power took effect after July 15, 1964.[98]

7–112   (*ii*) *A general power.* Since the property is unfettered until the appointment has been made and the donee of the power is able to deal with it as he wishes, the perpetuity period does not begin to run until the date of the appointment[99]; and this is so even if the power is exercisable by deed only[1] or by will only.[2] Thus, for the purposes of the perpetuity rule there is no difference between the exercise of a general power and a conveyance by an absolute owner.

The difference between appointments under general and special powers may be summarised thus. In both cases, the relevant facts are those existing at the time of the appointment; but the time from which the perpetuity period runs, and at which the lives in being must be ascertained, is the creation of the power in the case of a special power, and the exercise of the power in the case of a general power.

7–113   **16. Contractual interests, obligations, covenants and options.** The perpetuity rule was devised in order to control interests in property, not mere personal obligations. Here we reach the boundary between property and contract. Here, also, the Act of 1964 has made important changes.

(*a*) *Personal obligations (at common law)*

7–114   (1) CONTRAST WITH PROPRIETARY INTERESTS. The perpetuity rule was never applied to mere personal obligations created by contract, *e.g.* to pay money,[3] or to buy stone exclusively from a particular quarry.[4] The rule is directed against the tying up of property by granting interests in it which may vest at too remote a date. By "interests" is meant rights *in rem*, rights of property, enforceable against other persons generally according to the principles governing legal and equitable interests.[5] Contracts, on the other hand, primarily

---

[97] *Ante*, paras 7–047 *et seq.*
[98] s.15(5).
[99] *Re Thompson* [1906] 2 Ch. 199 at 202.
[1] Consider *Re Phillips* [1931] 1 Ch. 347.
[2] *Ante*, para. 7–103. Contrast the rule as to the power itself, *ante* para. 7–107.
[3] *Walsh v. H.M. Sec. of State for India* (1863) 10 H.L.C. 367; *Witham v. Vane* (1883) reported in Challis 440; *Borland's Trustee v. Steel Brothers & Co. Ltd* [1901] 1 Ch. 279; see Challis 440.
[4] *Keppell v. Bailey* (1834) 2 My. & K. 517 at 527; *South Eastern Ry. v. Associated Portland Cement Manufacturers (1900) Ltd* [1901] 1 Ch. 12 (allowing landowner to make a tunnel under ajoining land); see 54 S.J. 471, 501; *Sharpe v. Durrant* (1911) 55 S.J. 423; [1911] W.N. 158 (allowing landowner to make crossings over a tramway); (1911) 27 L.Q.R. 151; Challis 184.
[5] The true character of equitable interests as rights *in rem* clearly emerges here: see *ante*, para. 4–102.

create personal obligations between the contracting parties; and therefore between the parties themselves (and their respective personal representatives, who can sue and be sued on a deceased person's contract) the rule against perpetuities, in its classical common law form, has no application[6]: a contracting party may be made liable on any contingency, however remote, so that, *e.g.* an option given by one corporation to another in (say) 1800 or 1950 may remain enforceable for ever.[7]

(2) SPECIFIC PERFORMANCE. It makes no difference that the contract is **7–115** specifically enforceable (as for example a contract for the sale of land), and thus gives one party a right to obtain specific property; for the rights of the parties *inter se* are personal as well as proprietary, and "specific performance is merely an equitable mode of enforcing a personal obligation with which the rule against perpetuities has nothing to do".[8] If the vendor, for instance, has parted with the land contracted to be sold, it is useless to decree specific performance against him when he can no longer perform his obligations. The property itself, therefore, is not fettered by the vendor's obligations in so far as they are personal to him. "The real answer to the argument founded on the inconvenience of tying up land is that the action upon the covenant sounds in damages only unless the defendant has still got the land to which the covenant relates."[9]

(3) ASSIGNMENT. Since it is the general rule that the benefit, but not the **7–116** burden, of a contract is assignable,[10] an assignee of a contractual right can enforce it against the original promisor personally, or his estate if he is dead, at any time regardless of the perpetuity rule.[11] But the assignment itself, which is proprietary in nature and so resembles a conveyance rather than a contract, must take effect within the period, running from the date when it is made.[12]

(b) Proprietary interests (at common law)

(1) PERSONAL AND PROPRIETARY RIGHTS. Many contracts create not only **7–117** personal obligations but interests in property as well. Contracts for the sale or lease of land, if specifically enforceable, are binding as equitable interests (estate contracts) not only upon the original promisor but also upon his successors in title, subject to the reservations which must always be remembered.[13] Against such successors in title, who are not parties to the contract, the contract can be enforced only in so far as it creates an interest in land, a

---

[6] Challis 184n. But restrictive covenants create property rights: see *ante*, para. 4–026.
[7] Challis 184n.
[8] *Hutton v. Watling* [1948] Ch. 26 at 36, *per* Jenkins J.
[9] *South Eastern Ry v. Associated Portland Cement Manufacturers (1900) Ltd* [1910] 1 Ch. 12 at 34, *per* Farwell L.J.
[10] *cf. post*, para. 14–051.
[11] *South Eastern Ry v. Associated Portland Cement Manufacturers (1900) Ltd* [1910] 1 Ch. 12.
[12] Gray, § 329, n. 1.
[13] *Ante*, paras 4–009 *et seq.* As to estate contracts, see *ante*, para. 4–025; *post*, paras 12–050 *et seq.*

right *in rem*; and to this element of it the perpetuity rule naturally applies.[14] At common law, therefore, although a contract creating an interest in property which may arise outside the perpetuity period is valid as against the original promisor, or his estate, at the suit of anyone entitled to the benefit of it, it is void as against third parties. Probably a firm contract (as opposed to a mere option) for sale "in 25 years' time" would also be void against a third party, for the purchaser's equitable interest, though it arises at once,[15] cannot be truly vested until the time has expired.[16]

7–118		(2) OPTIONS. The contracts which most commonly produce contingent interests in property, capable of arising after an extended period of time, are options.[17] At common law these must obey the above rules, and since the time for exercising the option usually has no connection with lives in being (unless, for example, a "royal lives clause" is used), the perpetuity period is normally 21 years only.

Options occur particularly commonly in leases, both in the form of options to purchase the reversion (*i.e.* the freehold, or some superior lease) and in the form of options for the renewal of the lease. Options *to purchase the reversion* are likewise subject to the above rules at common law.[18] But options *to renew a lease* enjoy a special exemption from the perpetuity rule.[19] This is because options to renew a lease, unlike options to purchase a freehold, are among the recognised leasehold covenants which "run with the land",[20] and if long leases are to be allowed this class of covenant must, in general, be allowed to run with them. But statute has provided that a contract to renew a lease for more than 60 years is void if made after 1925.[21] Even covenants which made leases perpetually renewable were exempt from the perpetuity rule[22]; but now perpetually renewable leases can no longer exist.[23]

7–119		*(c) Statutory changes.* The Act of 1964 has made three changes in the law in the case of instruments taking effect after July 15, 1964.

			(i) An option to acquire for value any interest in land is subject to a perpetuity period of 21 years only.[24] No period based on lives in

---

[14] *L. & S.W. Ry v. Gomm* (1882) 20 Ch.D. 562; *Woodall v. Clifton* [1905] 2 Ch. 257; *Worthing Corpn. v. Heather* [1906] 2 Ch. 532. And see the illuminating judgment of Jenkins J. in *Hutton v. Watling* [1948] Ch. 26, not challenged on this point on appeal: [1948] Ch. 398.

[15] *Post*, para. 12–051.

[16] See Gray, § 330, n. 2. Ordinary contracts for sale are safe because even if no date is fixed for completion there is an implied term that completion shall take place within a reasonable time.

[17] For options see *post*, para. 12–061.

[18] *Woodall v. Clifton* [1905] 2 Ch. 257.

[19] *L. & S.W. Ry. v. Gomm* (1882) 20 Ch.D. 562 at 579; *Woodall v. Clifton, supra*, at 265, 268; *Weg Motors Ltd v. Hales* [1962] Ch. 49; Gray § 230.

[20] *Post*, para. 15–026; *Muller v. Trafford* [1901] 1 Ch. 54 at 61. This in itself is somewhat anomalous.

[21] *Post*, para. 14–093.

[22] *Hare v. Burges* (1857) 4 K. & J. 45 at 57.

[23] *Post*, para. 14–089.

[24] s.9(2).

being and no alternative fixed statutory period may be used. (An exception is made in favour of certain rights of pre-emption conferred on public or local authorities in respect of land devoted to religious use which ceases to be used thus.[25]) The "wait and see" principle also applies.[26] As against a successor in title of the person who gave the option, therefore, the option is valid for 21 years from the date of the instrument creating it (assuming that it was duly registered) and thereafter is void.

(ii) A contract or other disposition *inter vivos* which creates an interest in property is void even between the original contracting parties whenever it would have been void for remoteness as against a third party.[27]

(iii) The perpetuity rule does not apply to an option for a lessee (whether under a lease or an agreement for a lease) to purchase the freehold or a superior leasehold reversion, provided that it is exercisable only by the lessee or his successors in title and that it ceases to be exercisable not later than one year after the end of the lease.[28]

The reason underlying (iii) is that an option for a tenant to purchase the reversion is not an objectionable fetter on the property, for it encourages the tenant to maintain the property and make improvements. It is, in fact, merely a means of prolonging the ownership which he already has. Options unconnected with leases (options in gross) have the opposite effect, for they put it into the power of a stranger to take the benefit of any increase in the value of the land. This is the reason underlying (ii), although this goes beyond the subject of perpetuity and represents an interference with freedom of contract.[29] **7–120**

Changes (i) and (ii) above do not, as will be seen, fit together neatly, since (i) is confined to options relating to land whereas (ii) operates more widely. This difference will be brought out in the examples which follow, in which it must also be remembered that the option or contract may need to be registered as an estate contract if it is to be valid against a later purchaser from the grantor.[30]

(*d*) *Examples* (*common law and statute*). The effect of the common law rules and of the Act of 1964 may be seen from the following examples. **7–121**

---

[25] *ibid.*
[26] s.3(1), (3).
[27] s.10. The language of this provision is curious. See (1964) 80 L.Q.R. 486 at 525.
[28] s.9(1).
[29] See Fourth Report of the Law Reform Committee, Cmnd. 18, 1956, paras 35–38.
[30] *Ante*, para. 5–099 (unregistered land). Where title is registered, the estate contract should be protected by the entry of either a notice (*ante*, para. 6–079) or a caution (*ante*, para. 6–083).

(i) Contract made between A and B giving B the option to purchase Blackacre from A for £5,000 "at any future date". If the contract was made before July 16, 1964, the option is enforceable by B (and also by B's personal representatives and assignees from B) against A and A's personal representatives. If they still have the land, specific performance or damages may be awarded against them.[31] If A sold the land to C, A may also be liable in damages for non-performance of the contract.[32] But as against C the option is void for perpetuity because it might be exercised more than 21 years after its creation. It would be equally void against C if he had taken the land under A's will.

If the contract was made after July 15, 1964, it would have been valid for 21 years both against A and against any of A's successors in title. But if not in fact exercised within that time it became equally void against all of them.

7–122 *(ii) Contract made between A and B by which A is to sell Blackacre to B for £5,000 if and when it is possible to obtain planning permission to build on the land.* If the contract was made before July 16, 1964, the common law rules apply as in example (i) above. If the contract was made on or after that date, it will apparently be valid (both against A and against A's successors in title) if in fact permission is obtainable within 21 years of the death of the survivor of A and B,[33] but otherwise the contract will be void (against all of them). The difference between this and example (i) is that the special 21-year perpetuity period applies only to an "option", meaning presumably a contract which only one party can insist upon enforcing.

(iii) Lease for 99 years made in 1910 between L and T giving to T (the tenant) the option to purchase the freehold at a stated price at any time during the term. During the term L assigns the reversion to X and T assigns the lease to Y. If Y or his successor in title wishes to exercise the option, he can recover damages from L's personal representatives if any of L's assets remain unadministered. But he cannot obtain either the property or damages from X or his successors in title,[34] for the option is void except in its purely contractual aspect.

If the lease had been made in 1965, the option would be valid against X and his successors in title as well as against L.[35]

(iv) Lease for 50 years made in 1930 between L and T giving to T (the tenant) the option to renew the lease, at its expiry, for a further 50 years. This option is valid at common law both against L and against L's successors in title to the reversion. It would be equally valid if the lease had been made in 1965.

---

[31] *Hutton v. Watling* [1948] Ch. 26.
[32] See *ante*, para. 5–122.
[33] They are lives in being under s.3(5)(a) and (b) respectively: *ante*, paras 7–048–7–049.
[34] *Woodall v. Clifton* [1905] 2 Ch. 257. On this case, see (1955) 19 Conv. (N.S.) 255–257.
[35] See *post*, para. 15–063.

C. *Exceptions to the Perpetuity Rule*

1. **Certain limitations after entails**

(a) Power to bar. Remainders following upon entails have been recognised **7–123** as valid since early times.[36] As a consequence of the Statute *De Donis*, 1285,[37] they became indefeasible interests; but when entails later became barrable[38] they were left in a precarious state, and thenceforth were liable to be destroyed if at any time the entail was barred. When, later still, the modern rule against perpetuities was devised, the courts did not apply it to these well-recognised interests,[39] since the prior tenant in tail was potentially an absolute owner and his power to alienate the land was in no way fettered by any remainder.[40]

(b) Vesting before entail determines. Interests limited to take effect after **7–124** entails may be either vested or contingent. If contingent, they will be exempt from the perpetuity rule only if they are certain to vest, if at all, during the continuance of the entail or at the moment of its determination.[41] Thus a gift to X in tail, with remainder to such of Y's issue as are alive when the entail determines, is valid, even though the persons entitled to take the remainder may not be ascertained for several hundred years.[42] Similarly a devise to Y in tail, with a gift over to other persons if Y or the heirs of his body should become seised of certain land, is valid; for this event could occur only while Y or an heir of his body was alive, *i.e.* during the period for which the entail, if unbarred, would endure.

(c) Possible vesting later. This exception, however, does not protect limita- **7–125** tions which might possibly vest at some time later than the moment of the natural determination of the entail.[43] If property is given to trustees in trust for A in tail, remainder to the first son of B to marry, A's entail is valid but the remainder is void at common law, for it might vest after the period had run and the entail determined.[44] Again, in a limitation in trust for X in tail male with a gift over to Y's oldest descendant living when all X's issue fail, the gift over is void at common law, since the existence of female issue of X might postpone its vesting until some date later than the end of the tail male.[45]

(d) Act of 1964. The Act of 1964 makes no change in the above rules, since **7–126** its "wait and see" provisions operate only by reference to the regular perpe-tuity periods[46] and the Act does not allow "wait and see" during the con-tinuance of an entail. But, of course, gifts following entails which do in fact

---

[36] *Ante*, para. 3–078.
[37] *Ante*, para. 3–080.
[38] *Ante*, para. 3–079.
[39] *Nicholls v. Sheffield* (1787) 2 Bro.C.C. 215.
[40] See, *e.g. Newell v. Crayford Cottage Society* [1922] 1 K.B. 656 at 663.
[41] Morris & Leach 195.
[42] See *Heaseman v. Pearse* (1871) 7 Ch.App. 275 at 282, 283.
[43] Morris & Leach 195.
[44] See Marsden 147; and see authorities quoted in Halsb. Vol. 35, para. 1050, n. 1.
[45] See *Bristow v. Boothby* (1826) 2 Sim. & St. 465.
[46] *i.e.* lives in being plus 21 years; or 21 years only; or a fixed term not exceeding 80 years; s.3(4); *ante*, paras 7–042, 7–056.

vest during the regular perpetuity periods will be saved by the Act, where it applies, in the normal way.

7–127 **2. Certain gifts to charities.** The general rule is that a gift to a charity[47] is subject to the rule in the same way as any other gift.[48] If there is a gift to a private person with a gift over to a charity, the gift over is void for perpetuity if it is capable of vesting outside the period.[49] Similarly a charitable gift which is to take effect on the appointment of the next lieutenant-colonel of a volunteer corps is void.[50] But if there is a gift to one charity followed by a gift over to another charity on a certain event, the gift over is not void merely because the event may occur outside the perpetuity period.[51] Thus if property is given to Charity A with a proviso that it shall go to Charity B if Charity A fails to keep the testator's tomb in repair, the gift over is valid.[52] To this extent alone are charities exempted from the rule against perpetuities[53]; thus a gift to a natural person is not validated merely because it is preceded by a gift to charity.[54]

3. Certain contracts and covenants.

7–128 *(a) Personal obligations.* The exemption of personal obligations created by contract or covenant, and the changes made by the Act of 1964, have already been explained.[55]

7–129 *(b) Options in leases.* The exemptions allowed for options to renew leases (at common law) and for options to acquire the reversion (under the Act of 1964) have also already been explained.[56]

7–130 *(c) Restrictive covenants.* A restrictive covenant (whether affecting freehold or leasehold land) creates an equitable interest in the land[57] which is enforceable against future occupiers at any distance in time. It is not subject to the perpetuity rule, because a future breach of the covenant does not bring

---

[47] For charities, see *post*, para. 20–028.
[48] *Chamberlayne v. Brockett* (1872) 8 Ch.App. 206 at 211; *Re Bowen* [1893] 2 Ch. 491 at 494; dicta to the contrary (*e.g. Goodman v. The Mayor and Free Burgesses of the Borough of Saltash* (1882) 2 App.Cas. 633 at 650; *Re St. Stephen, Coleman Street* (1888) 39 Ch.D. 492 at 501; *Re Rymer* [1895] 1 Ch. 19 at 25) are concerned with "inalienability" (*post*, para. 7–137) rather than "perpetuity".
[49] *Att.-Gen. v. Gill* (1726) 2 P. Wms. 369; *Re Johnson's Trusts* (1866) L.R. 2 Eq. 716; and see *Re Bushnell* [1975] 1 W.L.R. 1596.
[50] *Re Lord Stratheden & Campbell* [1894] 3 Ch. 265.
[51] *Christ's Hospital v. Grainger* (1849) 1 Mac. & G. 460.
[52] *Re Tyler* [1891] 3 Ch. 252 (doubted in *R.S.P.C.A. of N.S.W. v. Benevolent Society of N.S.W.* (1960) 102 C.L.R. 629); contrast *Re Dalziel* [1943] Ch. 277. This is so even if the maintenance of the tomb will leave no surplus for Charity A: *Re Davies* [1915] 1 Ch. 543. The gift to Charity A is also valid, even though it may continue indefinitely: see *ante*, para. 7–089.
[53] But for their exception from the rule against inalienability, see *post*, para. 7–151.
[54] *Re Bowen* [1893] 2 Ch. 491.
[55] *Ante*, paras 7–113 *et seq.*
[56] *ibid.*
[57] *Ante*, para. 4–026, *post*, para. 16–030 *et seq.*

about the vesting of any interest in the land.[58] This is not, therefore, a genuine exception.

4. Forfeiture of leases and enforcement of rentcharges. Leases often contain a forfeiture clause, by which the tenant agrees that if at any time he breaks the terms of the lease the landlord may re-enter and put an end to the lease.[59] This contingent liability to re-entry runs with the land demised and is a proprietary interest.[60] But since it is a recognised incident of leases it is exempt from the perpetuity rule.[61] For similar reasons statutory exemption was given in 1925 to certain rights of entry reserved to secure payment of rentcharges, whether such rights were given by contract or by statute[62]; and for rentcharges created after July 15, 1964, the exemption has now been extended to all powers and remedies for enforcing rentcharges.[63] A right to redeem a rentcharge for, *e.g.* 500 years, on payment of a fixed sum at any time, is not invalidated by the perpetuity rule.[64] It will be remembered, on the other hand, that rights of entry or re-entry reserved on the grant of a conditional fee simple in corporeal land are subject to the perpetuity rule[65]; they are contingent rights to substantial ownership, not rights incidental to some other legitimately vested interest such as is conferred by a lease or rentcharge.

7–131

5. Resulting trusts. The exception permitted by the common law and abolished by the Act of 1964 has been explained above.[66]

7–132

6. Mortgages. "The rule has never been applied to mortgages", and thus a clause postponing the mortgagor's right to redeem the property is not invalid merely because the right is postponed for longer than the perpetuity period.[67]

7–133

7. Right of survivorship. As already mentioned,[68] a joint tenant's right of survivorship[69] is exempt from the rule.[70] Since it can always be destroyed by

7–134

---

[58] *Mackenzie v. Childers* (1889) 43 Ch.D. 265 at 279; *Marten v. Flight Refuelling Ltd* [1962] Ch. 115 at 136; Gray, § 280. Contrast *Halsall v. Brizell* [1957] Ch. 169 (positive covenant).
[59] See *post*, para. 14–122.
[60] L.P.A. 1925, s.1(2)(e); *ante*, para. 4–054.
[61] *Re Tyrrell's Estate* [1907] 1 I.R. 292 at 298; Gray, § 303; Challis 186 and see *Re Garde Browne* [1911] 1 I.R. 205 at 210; *Woodall v. Clifton* [1905] 2 Ch. 257 at 279.
[62] L.P.A. 1925, s.121(6) (contrast s.4(3)); *post*, para. 18–031.
[63] P.A.A. 1964, ss.11(1), 15(5); see (1964) 80 L.Q.R. 486 at 528.
[64] *Switzer & Co. Ltd v. Rochford* [1906] 1 I.R. 399.
[65] *Ante*, para. 7–096.
[66] See *ante*, para. 7–091.
[67] *Knightsbridge Estates Trust Ltd v. Byrne* [1939] Ch. 441 at 463, *per* Greene M.R. (affirmed on another ground, [1940] A.C. 613).
[68] *Ante*, para. 7–060.
[69] *Post*, para. 9–003.
[70] *Re Roberts* (1881) 19 Ch.D. 520; Gray § 232.1.

severance by the other joint tenant,[71] it is no more objectionable than a remainder after an entail.[72]

7–135   **8. Miscellaneous.** The Law of Property Act 1925[73] sets out a list of certain special rights exempted from the rule both for the future and retrospectively. These rights relate to rentcharges,[74] minerals, timber, and repair or maintenance of land, building, sewers, and other things. The general effect of the exemptions is to enable rights which are merely ancillary to other valid interests to be exercised outside the perpetuity period.[75] Registered pension funds for employees have also been given exemption by statute, subject to certain conditions.[76]

D. Proposals for Further Reform of the Perpetuity Rule

7–136   The Law Commission has recommended a radical simplification of the law governing perpetuities.[77] It would for the most part be prospective in effect and there would therefore be a further set of perpetuity rules applying to dispositions made after any legislation was brought into force. The main features of the scheme which has been proposed are as follows. First, the rule against perpetuities would apply only to interests under wills and trusts.[78] It would not therefore apply to easements or restrictive covenants granted to take effect at a future date, nor to options or rights of pre-emption.[79] There would be one fixed and overriding perpetuity period of 125 years,[80] and the "wait and see" principle would apply.[81] As one of the limited exceptions to the otherwise prospective application of the proposals, trustees of existing trusts would be permitted to elect for the 125-year perpetuity period if the trust contained an express perpetuity period of lives in being plus 21 years and the trustees believed that it was difficult or impracticable to ascertain the existence or whereabouts of the measuring lives in being.[82] This is intended to assist the trustees where there is a large class of lives in being, as where a royal lives clause has been employed.[83]

---

[71] *Post*, para. 9–036.

[72] *Ante*, para. 7–123.

[73] s.162.

[74] See also *ante*, para. 7–131.

[75] *Dunn v. Blackdown Properties Ltd* [1961] Ch. 433. *cf. ante*, para. 7–023.

[76] Pension Schemes Act 1993, s.163 (replacing earlier legislation). For the rule against perpetuities and pension trusts, see (1998) Law Com. No. 251, paras 3.52–3.62; and [1995] Private Client Business 133 and 223 (G. Thomas); approved in *Air Jamaica Ltd v. Charlton* [1999] 1 W.L.R. 1399 at 1409. The Privy Council there held that a defined benefit pension scheme consisted of a series of individual settlements created in relation to each employee within the scheme. Each employee was therefore a life in being for the purposes of the rule.

[77] (1998) Law Com. No. 251. See (1998) 12 T.L.I. 148 (P. Sparlies).

[78] *ibid.*, paras 7.29–7.32.

[79] *ibid.*, para. 7.35. All pension schemes would be excluded from the rule: *ibid.*, para. 7.36. This would resolve an uncertainty in the present law.

[80] Law Com. No. 251, para. 8.13.

[81] *ibid.*, para. 8.25.

[82] *ibid.*, paras 8.19, 8.20.

[83] *Ante*, para. 7–041. But see *post*, para. 8–140.

Section 3. The Rule against Inalienability

1. "Perpetual trusts"

(a) The principle. It is a fundamental principle of English law that property **7–137** must not be rendered inalienable.[84] It is therefore necessary to prohibit not only indefeasible future interests which are unduly remote, but immediate gifts which are subject to some permanent restraint upon alienation. The two principles are often confused, but need to be considered separately. Restraints upon alienation attached to direct gifts of property are generally invalid on their face, as repugnant to the interest granted.[85] But if a trust is employed, the donor's intention may be that the capital shall be held indefinitely, or that some beneficial interest given to a club or other permanent institution shall continue indefinitely so that it is, in effect, inalienable. The rule now to be explained is therefore sometimes also called "the rule against perpetual trusts",[86] although the rule against such trusts is only part of a wider rule against inalienability.

(b) Trusts for non-charitable purposes. The trusts in question are the **7–138** so-called non-charitable purpose trusts, by which the trust property is to be applied to promote some particular purpose rather than to benefit some individual or a class. Such trusts have been held void for two reasons.

(1) PERPETUAL DURATION. Where the trust is for purposes, the ordinary **7–139** perpetuity rule cannot prevent the property from being tied up indefinitely, since there are no individual beneficiaries in whom successive interests are to vest. Such trusts will however fail if they may be of perpetual duration.[87] However, although property cannot be rendered inalienable for ever, or for a period to which no clear and definite limit is set,[88] it seems that alienation may be validly restricted for a period which cannot exceed a life or lives in being at the time of the gift, and further 21 years.[89] This period is borrowed from the rule against perpetuities,[90] and as under that rule, probably the lives must be human lives.[91] A purpose trust "for so long as the law permits" will be valid for a period of 21 years.[92]

---

[84] *cf. ante,* para. 3–071 (conditions in restraint of alienation); and see *Carne v. Long* (1860) 2 De G.F. & J. 75 at 80.

[85] *ibid.*

[86] See Gray, § 909.1.

[87] *Leahy v. Att.-Gen. for New South Wales* [1959] A.C. 457; *Re Bushnell* [1975] 1 W.L.R. 1596 at 1602. "Wait and see" under P.A.A. 1964 does not apply to purpose trusts: s.15(4). Charitable trusts may be and often are of perpetual duration.

[88] *Kennedy v. Kennedy* [1914] A.C. 215; *Re Wightwick's W.T.* [1950] Ch. 260.

[89] See *Thellusson v. Woodford* (1805) 11 Ves. 112 at 135, 146; *Carne v. Long* (1860) 2 De G.F. & J. 75 at 80; *Re Dean* (1889) 41 Ch.D. 552 at 557. See too *Re Denley's Trust Deed* [1969] 1 Ch. 373.

[90] *Ante,* para. 7–018.

[91] *Re Dean* (1889) 41 Ch.D. 552 (upholding a trust for dogs and horses for their lives) is probably wrong; see *ante,* para. 7–042.

[92] *Pirbright v. Salwey* [1896] W.N. 86; *Re Hooper* [1932] 1 Ch. 38.

In cases involving purpose trusts, it would seem desirable that a settlor should be able to specify a perpetuity period of a fixed number of years whether greater or less than 21 and unconnected with any lives in being. However, the Act of 1964 expressly refrains from making any change in the law where property is to be applied for purposes.[93] While this is generally thought to preclude the employment of the fixed perpetuity period provided for by the Act, this is by no means a certainty.[94]

7–140   (2) UNENFORCEABILITY. Even if a valid perpetuity period has been speci- fied, a purpose trust may be held to be void because there is no one who can enforce it and because the court cannot control its execution.[95] This is the so-called "beneficiary principle". The rule that such trusts are invalid is applied inflexibly. Even if the trustees are willing to carry out a purpose trust, it will fail because of the court's inability to control its performance.[96] Although this rule has often been criticised, there is a good reason for it. "It is not possible to contemplate with equanimity the creation of large funds devoted to non-charitable purposes which no court and no department of state can control, or in the case of maladministration reform".[97]

7–141   (c) *Cases in which non-charitable purposes have been upheld.* In a number of cases trusts for non-charitable purposes have been upheld. These have been described as "concessions to human weakness or sentiment",[98] "when Homer has nodded", which will not be extended.[99] These cases fall into three main categories of which the first two are anomalous, whereas the third is consistent with principle.

7–142   (1) TRUSTS FOR TOMBS AND MONUMENTS. A trust to erect a tomb or funerary monument will be valid provided that the executors or trustees are willing to carry out the wishes of the testator or settlor.[1] However a trust for the upkeep of a grave or monument will be valid only if it is confined to a perpetuity period.[2] It is now provided by statute that a burial or local authority may enter

---

[93] s.15(4).
[94] See Maudsley, *The Modern Law of Perpetuities* 177.
[95] *Morice v. Bishop of Durham* (1804) 9 Ves. 399; (1805) 10 Ves. 522; *Re Astor's S.T.* [1952] Ch. 534; *Re Endacott* [1960] Ch. 232. This rule applies only to non-charitable purpose trusts: trusts for charitable purposes are enforceable by the Attorney-General.
[96] *Re Shaw* [1957] 1 W.L.R. 729 at 745.
[97] *Re Astor's S.T.* [1952] Ch. 534 at 542, *per* Roxburgh J. See too *R. v. District Auditor, ex p. West Yorkshire Metropolitan County Council* [1986] R.V.R. 24; [1986] C.L.J. 391 (C.H.). For a possible solution to this problem, see the Bermudan Trusts (Special Provisions) Act 1989.
[98] *Re Astor's S.T.* [1952] Ch. 534 at 547.
[99] *Re Endacott* [1960] Ch. 232 at 250. Some of the exceptional cases are clearly incorrect, see *e.g. Re Thompson* [1934] Ch. 342 (trust for the furtherance of fox-hunting, where the validity of the gift was not challenged by the remainderman).
[1] *Trimmer v. Danby* (1856) 25 L.J.Ch. 424 (bequest by the painter Turner for the erection of a monument to his own memory in St Paul's Cathedral "among those of my brothers in art"). The monument need not be for the testator himself: *Mussett v. Bingle* [1876] W.N. 170 (bequest for a monument to the testator's wife's first husband).
[2] *Mussett v. Bingle* [1876] W.N. 170; *Re Hooper* [1932] 1 Ch. 38. If such trusts are set up in perpetuity they will be void: *Rickard v. Robson* (1862) 31 Beav. 244; *Yeap Cheah Neo v. Ong Cheng Neo* (1875) L.R. 6 P.C. 381.

into an agreement with any person on payment of a sum of money to maintain a grave, tombstone or other memorial for a period of up to 99 years.[3]

(2) TRUSTS FOR THE UPKEEP OF ANIMALS. There is some authority which **7–143** suggests that trusts for the maintenance of animals may be validly created. The authority for this supposed exception is very weak,[4] and some of the cases can be better explained in other ways.[5]

(3) PURPOSE TRUSTS FOR THE BENEFIT OF A PERSON OR PERSONS. A trust for **7–144** a purpose which benefits directly or indirectly a person or persons will be valid provided that it is confined to a perpetuity period.[6] Such trusts do not offend the beneficiary principle because any person who benefits, although having no beneficial interest in the property, has *locus standi* to enforce the trust.[7] If the purpose for which the trust was set up comes to an end, the property passes on a resulting trust to the settlor or donor.[8] It does not become the absolute property of those who have benefited from the trust.[9]

(d) Cases in which gifts for purposes are interpreted as absolute gifts. In **7–145** some situations a gift that is expressed to be for a purpose will be construed as an outright gift to a person. The rule, which is one of construction of the instrument creating the gift, applies where the primary reason for the gift is to benefit a named individual and the expressed purpose is merely the motive for making it.[10] Even if the purpose is fulfilled or cannot be carried out, the donee takes absolutely.[11] It is often difficult to distinguish gifts of this kind from trusts for purposes which benefit persons directly or indirectly (considered *supra*).[12]

(e) Gifts to unincorporated associations. An unincorporated association, **7–146** such as a club or society, consists of two or more persons contractually bound together for common purposes other than for business, each having mutual duties and obligations, in an organisation having rules regulating such matters as membership and control of funds.[13] Such a body is regarded in law as no

---

[3] Parish Councils and Burial Authorities (Miscellaneous Provisions) Act 1970, s.1.

[4] *Re Dean* (1889) 41 Ch.D. 552 (the testator left his horses and hounds to his trustees with an annuity for up to 50 years for the maintenance of the animals). See *ante*, para. 7–041.

[5] See, *e.g. Pettingall v. Pettingall* (1842) 11 L.J.Ch. 176 (gift of £50 *per annum* to an executor conditional upon his maintaining out of it the testator's favourite black mare).

[6] *Re Sanderson's Trust* (1854) 3 K. & J. 497; *Re the Trusts of the Abbott Fund* [1900] 2 Ch. 326; *Re Denley's Trust Deed* [1969] 1 Ch. 373. See too *Re Northern Developments Holdings Ltd* (unreported, October 6, 1978, Megarry V.-C.); *Carreras Rothermans Ltd v. Freeman Mathews Treasure Ltd* [1985] Ch. 207 at 223.

[7] *Re Denley's Trust Deed*, *supra* (trust of sports ground for use by employees of a company).

[8] *Re the Trusts of the Abbott Fund*, *supra* (fund subscribed for the upkeep of two deaf and dumb ladies; surplus returned to the subscribers on the death of the ladies).

[9] *Re Sanderson's Trust*, *supra*.

[10] *Re Sanderson's Trust*, *supra*, at 503; *Re Andrew's Trust* [1905] 2 Ch. 48; *Re Lipinski's W.T.* [1976] Ch. 235; *Re Osoba* [1979] 1 W.L.R. 247.

[11] *e.g. Re Osoba* (gift to daughter for her training "up to university grade" held to be an absolute one).

[12] Compare *Re the Trusts of the Abbott Fund*, *supra*, with *Re Andrew's Trust*, *supra*.

[13] *Conservative and Unionist Central Office v. Burrell* [1982] 1 W.L.R. 522 at 525.

more than the aggregate of its members.[14] At one time it was thought that a gift to an unincorporated association could be valid only if it took effect as a gift to the then members as joint tenants or as tenants in common. If it was in the nature of an endowment, it was void for perpetuity.[15] Neither of these alternatives was satisfactory and such gifts are now wherever possible construed as a gift to the members of the association subject to their contractual rights *inter se*.[16] Provided that the rules do not prevent the distribution of the association's assents amongst its members on dissolution, the gift will be valid.[17]

Where an *inter vivos* gift is made for the purposes of a more amorphous body that is not an unincorporated association, the person who receives it on behalf of that body undertakes to apply it for those purposes as agent for the contributor.[18] It is unclear whether a gift of this kind could be validly made by will, because an agency could not be set up at the moment of death.[19]

7–147   **2. Protective trusts.** Another form of limitation that can offend against the rule against inalienability is the protective trust.[20] This may be created by directing any life or lesser interest to be held "on protective trusts" thereby incorporating statutory forms of trust,[21] or by setting out express trusts. Such trusts provide for the income to be paid to the principal beneficiary during his life (or lesser period) under a determinable limitation, *i.e.* until he attempts any alienation, or any other event occurs whereby he might be deprived of any of the income; and thereafter the property is held on discretionary trusts for a number of persons, including the principal beneficiary.

If such a trust is created in favour of, for example, an unborn child of a living person, to vest at birth, it seems that at common law it is partly valid and partly void. On the principle that the perpetuity rule is not concerned with the determination of interests,[22] the determinable interest will duly terminate whenever the specified event occurs, even if it is outside the perpetuity period; but the discretionary trust, since it may arise at too remote a date, would plainly be void at common law.[23] Where the Act of 1964 applies, the result

---

[14] *Leahy v. Att.-Gen. for New South Wales* [1959] A.C. 457 at 477.
[15] *ibid.*, at 478.
[16] *Neville Estates Ltd v. Madden* [1962] Ch. 832 at 849; *Re Recher's W.T.* [1972] Ch. 526; *Conservative and Unionist Central Office v. Burrell* [1982] 1 W.L.R. 522 at 529; *News Group Newspapers Ltd v. S.O.G.A.T. 1982* [1986] I.C.R. 716. A gift expressed to be for a purpose that is for the benefit of the members of the association will also be construed in this manner: *Re Lipinski's W.T.* [1976] Ch. 235. See *post*, para. 9–093.
[17] *Re Recher's W.T., supra.* Even if the rules as they stand do preclude the members from dividing the assets amongst themselves, the gift should be valid provided that the rules can be changed by the association. For the position where the rules are controlled by an outside body, see *Re Grant's W.T.* [1980] 1 W.L.R. 360.
[18] *Conservative and Unionist Central Office v. Burrell, supra.*
[19] In the *Burrell* case, *supra*, at 530, Brightman L.J. considered that the answer to this problem was "not difficult to find" but unfortunately all commentators have found it so.
[20] See generally Snell, *Equity*, 274.
[21] See T.A. 1925, s.33; Family Law Reform Act 1969, s.14(3).
[22] *Ante*, para. 7–089.
[23] And see para. 7–092.

will be different: if the determinable interest in fact outlasts the perpetuity period, it will become absolute and the discretionary trust will be void[24]; but otherwise the discretionary trust will be valid up to the end of the perpetuity period, and thereafter void.[25]

3. Capital and income

(a) Inalienable capital. If the beneficial interest, *i.e.* the right to the income, is itself free from any trust or restraint and so is freely assignable, it does not matter that the capital may be vested inalienably in trustees. Thus, a life interest in a trust fund may be given to an unborn person, provided of course that it must vest within the perpetuity period, even though the capital of the fund must be held by the trustees until the beneficiary's death, which may be more than 21 years from the end of lives in being at the date of the gift.[26] The same principle has been applied even to the case of a determinable interest in the income of a trust fund,[27] analogous to a determinable fee in real property, where the capital might have remained in the hands of the trustees for ever.

7–148

(b) Alienable income. If this is correct it would seem that a gift to trustees upon trust "to apply the income to the upkeep of my grave" is bad, since both capital and income are tied up indefinitely by the trust[28]; but a trust "to pay the income to X during such time as my grave is properly tended" is good, for X can dispose of his determinable interest in the income without any breach of trust; and the fact that the capital is to be held upon trust meanwhile is held to be immaterial, for the person able to dispose of the income and the persons entitled on the determination of the interest[29] could at any time combine and put an end to the trust.[30]

7–149

(c) Settled land and land held on a trust of land. From the enactment of the Settled Land Act 1882 until 1997,[31] land held upon trust for limited interests was alienable, and it was only a beneficial interest in land which could be made inalienable. This remains the case in relation to land that was settled prior to 1997. However, where land is held on a trust of land, it is now open

7–150

---

[24] *Ante*, para. 7–092.
[25] s.3(3), s.15(2) treats discretionary trusts as powers of appointment: *ante*, para. 7–095.
[26] *Wainwright v. Miller* [1897] 2 Ch. 255; *Re Gage* [1898] 1 Ch. 498.
[27] *Re Chardon* [1928] Ch. 464, followed in *Re Chambers' W.T.* [1950] Ch. 267. The criticisms excited by *Re Chardon* (*ante*, para. 7–090, n. 15) mainly relate to the gift over, not to the determinable interest: see (1937) 53 L.Q.R. 24; (1938) 54 L.Q.R. 258; Tudor, *Charities* (5th ed.), p. 701 (not included in the present 8th ed.); Jarman p. 288. But if the determining event is so vague that the time of its happening could never be proved by evidence, the capital is perpetually tied up and the gift is void: *Re Wightwick's W.T.* [1950] Ch. 260 (abolition of vivisection by law "in the United Kingdom of Great Britain and Ireland, on the continent of Europe and elsewhere").
[28] See, *e.g. Re Dalziel* [1943] Ch. 277.
[29] Probably only residuary legatees may be so entitled (*ante*, para. 7–091, n. 15); and the P.A.A. 1964, where it applies, may affect their interests: *ante*.
[30] *Re Chardon* [1928] Ch. 464 at 470; *Re Wightwick's W.T.* [1950] Ch. 260 at 264, 265; *Re Chambers' W.T.* [1950] Ch. 267.
[31] When T.L.A.T.A. 1996 came into force: *post*, para. 8–001.

to a settlor to restrict or exclude the trustees' powers of disposition.[32] In this way, it is possible that land may be made inalienable for the duration of the trust.[33]

7–151   **4. Exemption of charities.** Charities are exempt from the rule against inalienability; no gift for charitable purposes is void merely because it renders property inalienable in perpetuity.[34] Were this not so it would be virtually impossible to make gifts to charity, since the income, if not also the capital, would almost always be confined by some trust for use for the purposes of the charity only.

Part 4

ACCUMULATIONS

7–152   The rule against accumulations resembles the rule against inalienability in that it is directed against remoteness of control over property, whether or not vested in a beneficiary, rather than against remoteness of vesting. The principle at common law was that accumulations of income could validly be directed only for so long as property might validly be rendered inalienable.[35] These two restrictions therefore originally went hand in hand. But they parted company when the Accumulations Act 1800 drastically cut down the period allowed for accumulation, without affecting the rest of the law about inalienability. The Act was the sequel to the famous case of *Thellusson v. Woodford*.[36] The "Thellusson Act", as it was often called, bore the stigma of being "one perhaps of the most ill-drawn Acts to be found in our statute book".[37] Mr Thellusson had by his will directed that the income of his property should be accumulated at compound interest during the lives of his sons, grandsons and great-grandchildren living at his death, and that on the death of the survivor the accumulated fund should be divided among certain of his descendants. This direction, being confined to lives in being, was held valid, but as it was calculated that the accumulated fund would probably amount to many millions of pounds,[38] Parliament intervened to prevent other testators or

---

[32] T.L.A.T.A. 1996, s.8(1); *post*, para. 8–140.

[33] But see *post*, para. 8–140.

[34] *Chamberlayne v. Brockett* (1872) 8 Ch.App. 206 at 211. A charitable trust established in 1585 was upheld in *Att.-Gen. v. Webster* (1875) L.R. 20 Eq. 483.

[35] See *Thellusson v. Woodford* (1799) 4 Ves. 227 at 317, 318, 338, 339; (1805) 11 Ves. 112 at 146, 147.

[36] (1799) 4 Ves. 227; (1805) 11 Ves. 112. See the discussion of Thellusson and his will at (1974) 118 S.J. 544, 560.

[37] *Tench v. Cheese* (1855) 6 De G.M. & G. 453 at 460 *per* Lord Cranworth L.C.; and see *Edwards v. Tuck* (1853) 3 De G.M. & G. 40 at 55 ("Lord Loughborough's Act").

[38] Challis 201; Marsden 321. Under favourable circumstances less than £750,000 might have produced over £100,000,000 by the end of the period. In fact, owing to mismanagement and the costs of litigation, the fund actually accumulated was comparatively small: H.E.L. vii, 230; and see (1965) 62 L.S.Gaz. 613; (1970) 21 N.I.L.Q. 131 (G. W. Keeton); (1994) 45 N.I.L.Q. 13 (P. Polden).

settlors afflicting their successors with compulsory hoarding upon this scale.[39]

The common law rule was that a direction to accumulate was valid if it was confined to the perpetuity period,[40] so that in theory Mr Thellusson might have effectively directed accumulation for a further 21 years; but at that time the principle that an extra 21 years is always available had not been firmly settled.[41] The normal perpetuity period was therefore excessively long in the case of accumulations, and the statutory rules cut it down severely.

A. The Statutory Periods

1. The periods. The present law is contained in the Law of Property Act 1925[42] and the Perpetuities and Accumulations Act 1964. If the disposition took effect before July 16, 1964, so that only the Act of 1925 applies, accumulation of income may not be directed by any person,[43] either expressly or impliedly,[44] for longer than one (not more[45]) of the following periods.

7–153

    (i) The life of the grantor or settlor.

    (ii) 21 years from the death of the grantor, settlor or testator.

    (iii) The minority or respective minorities only of any person or persons living or *en ventre sa mère* at the death of the grantor, settlor or testator.

    (iv) The minority or respective minorities only of any person or persons who under the limitations of the instrument directing accumulation would for the time being, if of full age, be entitled to the income directed to be accumulated.[46]

The Act of 1964 has now added two further periods in the case of dispositions taking effect after July 15, 1964.

    (v) 21 years from the making of the disposition.

    (vi) The minority or respective minorities of any person or persons in being at that date.[47]

---

[39] See *Re Earl of Berkeley* [1968] Ch. 744 at 780, approving this statement.

[40] *Harrison v. Harrison* (1786) cited 4 Ves. 338; *Wilson v. Wilson* (1851) 1 Sim. (N.S.) 288 at 298; Marsden 314; Challis 201.

[41] *Ante*, para. 7–016; Challis 201.

[42] ss.164–166, replacing with amendments the Accumulations Acts 1800 and 1892.

[43] This means a natural person not a corporation: *Re Dodwell & Co. Ltd's Trust* [1979] Ch. 301, holding that the Act of 1800 was framed in terms of natural persons only and that the Act of 1925, being a consolidating Act, did not alter the law. This does not necessarily mean that the Act can be evaded merely by interposing a company as the nominal settlor (see at 311). Yet in a settlement created prior to 1997 under the Settled Land Act 1925 a company may be a "tenant for life": *post*, para. 8–062 and see [1979] Conv. 319 (J.T.F.).

[44] See *Re Rochford's S.T.* [1965] Ch. 111.

[45] *Re Errington* (1897) 76 L.T. 616.

[46] L.P.A. 1925, s.164(1).

[47] s.13.

In other words, where the Act of 1964 applies, it allows periods (ii) and (iii) to run from the date of a settlement *inter vivos*, as well as from the death of the settlor. Previously it appeared arbitrary that those periods could run only from the date of death.[48]

7–154   **2. Choice of periods.** The question which period has been chosen in any particular case is one of construction.[49] The first two periods cause little difficulty. Of the first it should be noted that it is the only period of a life available for accumulation, and that it must be the life of the grantor or settlor himself and not of some other person.[50] The second period is a fixed term of years which starts to run at the beginning of the day after the testator's death and expires at the end of the 21st anniversary of his death.[51] Thus if a testator directs accumulation to start at the end of an interval after his death and continue for 21 years, he has exceeded the second period.[52]

7–155   **3. The periods of minorities.** The third, fourth and sixth periods are all minorities. Minority now ends at the age of 18.[53] But this does not affect the validity of directions for accumulation in dispositions made before 1970 with reference to the earlier period of minority ending at 21.[54]

The third period and (where it applies) the sixth period differ from the fourth period in the following respects.

7–156   *(a) Living minors.* The third and sixth periods are confined to the minorities of persons alive or *en ventre sa mère* at the death of the settlor or at the date of the settlement, as the case may be. The fourth period is not so confined.[55]

7–157   *(b) Beneficiaries.* The third and sixth periods are not confined to the minorities of those who are prospectively entitled to any benefit under the gift, whereas the fourth period is confined to the minorities of those who can say "but for my minority I should be entitled to the income which is being accumulated".[56]

7–158   *(c) Successive minorities.* The third and sixth periods can never exceed a single minority; for even if accumulation is directed during a large number of minorities, the period is in effect merely the longest of these minorities. Nor can any accumulation continue under them for longer than the second period,

---

[48] See *e.g. Re Bourne's S.T.* [1946] 1 All E.R. 411 at 415, 416; *Jagger v. Jagger* (1883) 25 Ch.D. 729 at 733.

[49] *Jagger v. Jagger* (1883) 25 Ch.D. 729; see *e.g. Re Watt's W.T.* [1936] 2 All E.R. 1555.

[50] *Re Lady Rosslyn's Trust* (1848) 16 Sim. 391.

[51] *Gorst v. Lowndes* (1841) 11 Sim. 434; *Att.-Gen. v. Poulden* (1844) 3 Hare 555.

[52] *Webb v. Webb* (1840) 2 Beav. 493.

[53] Family Law Reform Act 1969, s.1. The Act does not change the second and fifth periods of 21 years but only the meaning of "minority", "infancy", "full age" and similar expressions.

[54] *ibid.*, Sched. 3, para. 7; S.I. 1969 No. 1140.

[55] See *Sidney v. Wilmer* (1863) 4 De.G.J. & S. 84.

[56] See *Jagger v. Jagger* (1883) 25 Ch.D. 729 at 733, as corrected in *Re Cattell* [1914] 1 Ch. 177 at 189.

except where a child is *en ventre sa mère* at the relevant time. Under the fourth period, on the other hand, accumulation is possible during the minorities of persons unborn at the time of the gift[57]; and these minorities may be successive, for any beneficiary's interest may be made subject to accumulation during his own minority. For example, before 1970 property could be settled upon A for life with remainder to his eldest son at 21, with a direction to accumulate income meanwhile if A dies leaving such son under age. If the settlement was made after 1969, accumulation could continue only until the son was 18.

Successive accumulations may be illustrated by the following example.[58] A testator devises the residue of his property to all the children of his sons, whether born before or after his death, the income of their shares to be accumulated during their respective minorities. At the testator's death there is only one child of his sons alive, and she is a minor named D. The whole of the income must be accumulated during this minority, the direction to accumulate falling within the fourth period; for if she was of full age she would for the time being be entitled to the whole of the income. After D attains her majority, a child C is born to one of the testator's sons. C becomes entitled to one-half of the estate, subject to the same liability, *i.e.* that his share may be partially divested by the birth of other children. During the minority of C, the income from his share must be accumulated, even though the income from the whole of the residuary estate has already been accumulated once. If D had not been born until after the testator's death, there could have been no accumulation under the fourth period until her birth, for not until then would her minority have begun.[59]

7–159

(d) Purchase of land. Where accumulation is directed for the sole[60] purpose of purchasing land, only the fourth period may be selected.[61] But this restriction does not apply to accumulations to be held as capital money under the Settled Land Act 1925 or any of the Acts which it replaces.[62]

7–160

4. Application of rules. These rules apply whether the limitations are contained in a deed or a will,[63] whether the accumulation is at simple or compound interest,[64] whether there is a positive direction or a mere power to

7–161

---

[57] See *Re Cattell, supra,* at 189.
[58] See *Re Cattell, supra.*
[59] *Ellis v. Maxwell* (1841) 3 Beav. 587 at 596. The income meanwhile would have fallen into residue or (if there was no residuary gift) would have gone as on intestacy: *post,* para. 11–088.
[60] *Re Knapp* [1929] 1 Ch. 341.
[61] L.P.A. 1925, s.166.
[62] *Supra.*
[63] *Re Lady Rosslyn's Trust* (1848) 16 Sim. 391.
[64] *Re Hawkins* [1916] 2 Ch. 570 at 577; *Re Garside* [1919] 1 Ch. 132 at 137; Marsden 325; *contra, Re Pope* [1901] 1 Ch. 64 at 69, 70 and authorities there cited (and see *Union Bank of Scotland v. Campbell* 1929 S.C. 143) for the opinion that only accumulations at compound interest are prohibited. There would seem to be little justification in principle for this opinion. The P.A.A. 1964, where it applies, rejects it: s.13(2).

accumulate,[65] and whether the whole or any part of the income of a fund is to be accumulated.[66]

B. Excessive Accumulation

7–162   **1. Exceeding perpetuity period.** If the period for which accumulation is directed may possibly exceed the perpetuity period, the direction to accumulate is totally void.[67] This is the original common law rule, and it still operates. Thus where accumulation was directed until a lease with over 60 years to run had "nearly expired", no accumulation at all was permissible.[68] This applies even to accumulations for the benefit of charities.[69]

The Act of 1964 appears to leave this rule of common law unaltered. One might expect that the "wait and see" principle would be applied, but the Act apparently makes no such provision.[70] It is possible that the "wait and see" provisions governing "any power, option or other right"[71] might extend to accumulations, on the reasoning (explained above) that duties are subject to the same rules as apply to powers.[72] This would be straining the language of the Act; but it would perhaps best fulfil its general policy, and may therefore possibly find favour.

2. Exceeding accumulation period

7–163   *(a) Excess void.* If the period for which accumulation is directed cannot exceed the perpetuity period but exceeds the relevant accumulation period, the direction to accumulate is good *pro tanto* and only the excess over the appropriate accumulation period is void[73]; for the statutory provisions merely cut down the wider powers permitted by common law.[74]

7–164   *(b) Appropriate period.* In determining the appropriate period, the starting point is to ascertain which of the periods the testator or settlor seemingly had in mind,[75] if, indeed, he had any in mind.[76] Thus, where accumulation is directed by a deed made *inter vivos* for the lifetime of someone other than the settlor, accumulation takes place during the first of the periods, *i.e.* during the period common to the lives of the settlor and the named person.[77] But the first period is clearly inapplicable to accumulations directed by will, and in a case

---

[65] *Re Robb* [1953] Ch. 459; *Baird v. Lord Advocate* [1979] A.C. 666; P.A.A. 1964, s.13(2).
[66] *Re Travis* [1900] 2 Ch. 541 (surplus income).
[67] *Marshall v. Holloway* (1820) 2 Swans. 432; *Boughton v. James* (1844) 1 Coll.C.C. 26 at 45.
[68] *Curtis v. Lukin* (1842) 5 Beav. 147.
[69] *Martin v. Maugham* (1844) 14 Sim. 230.
[70] s.3(1) applies only where an interest may vest too remotely, and remote vesting is not the basis of the rule against accumulations: *ante*, para. 7–152.
[71] s.3(3).
[72] *Ante*, para. 7–098. *cf.* P.A.A. 1964, s.13(2).
[73] Challis 202, 203; *Griffiths v. Vere* (1803) 9 Ves. 127; *Eyre v. Marsden* (1838) 2 Keen 564 (affirmed 4 My. & Cr. 231).
[74] *Leake v. Robinson* (1817) 2 Mer. 363 at 389.
[75] *Re Watt's W.T.* [1936] 2 All E.R. 1555 at 1562.
[76] See *Re Ransome* [1957] Ch. 348 at 361.
[77] *Re Lady Rosslyn's Trust* (1848) 16 Sim. 391.

such as the above arising under a will, the second period is the most appropriate; accumulation will thus take place for 21 years from the testator's death if the named person so long lives.[78] The second period is also the most appropriate where a will directs accumulation for a period of years,[79] or, until X is 25,[80] or from the time Y remarries until her death,[81] or from the death of either A or B until the death of the survivor,[82] or, in some cases, during an inappropriate minority.[83] In each of these cases, if accumulation is still continuing 21 years after the death of the settlor or testator, it must cease forthwith even if it has been proceeding for only a short period, *e.g.* two years.[84]

(c) Minorities. If property is given by will to all the children of X (a living person) who attain their majority, and accumulation of the whole fund is directed while any child of X is a minor, the first two periods are clearly not intended and the fourth is not appropriate, for the accumulation is directed to continue for as long as *any* child is a minor even if some of the children are of full age; even though the latter children are of full age, they are not entitled to the income to be accumulated within the wording of the fourth period. Consequently the third period is the most appropriate, and so far as it is exceeded the direction is void; accumulation will therefore cease as soon as all children living at the testator's death are of full age.[85] **7–165**

(d) The Act of 1964. In the case of settlements made *inter vivos* after July 15, 1964, the fifth or sixth periods may be appropriate. **7–166**

C. Surplus Income

1. Person entitled. Where a direction to accumulate is void, either wholly or partially, the income so released passes to the persons who would have been entitled had no such accumulation been directed.[86] Thus if a beneficiary is entitled in possession to the enjoyment of the property or to its income, subject only to an excessive trust for accumulation, that beneficiary will be entitled to any income not validly accumulated.[87] For example, where property is given by will to X, subject to a direction that the income exceeding a certain figure is to be accumulated during X's life for the benefit of Y, the accumulation must cease 21 years after the testator's death and the surplus income will go **7–167**

---

[78] *Griffiths v. Vere* (1803) 9 Ves. 127; *Talbot v. Jevers* (1875) L.R. 20 Eq. 255 (for A's life or such portion of it as the rules of law will permit).

[79] *Longdon v. Simson* (1806) 12 Ves. 295 at 298.

[80] *Crawley v. Crawley* (1835) 7 Sim. 427; and see *Carey's Trustees v. Rose* 1957 S.C. 252 (trust for unborn person on attaining full age).

[81] *Weatherall v. Thornburgh* (1878) 8 Ch.D. 261.

[82] *Webb v. Webb* (1840) 2 Beav. 493.

[83] *Re Ransome* [1957] Ch. 348.

[84] *Shaw v. Rhodes* (1836) 1 My. & Cr. 135.

[85] *Re Watt's W.T.* [1936] 2 All E.R. 1555.

[86] L.P.A. 1925, s.164(1); *Green v. Gascoyne* (1865) 4 De G.J. & S. 565.

[87] *Combe v. Hughes* (1865) 2 De G.J. & S. 657.

to X.[88] But if there is no such person, as, for example, if X is given a mere annuity of a certain sum and excessive accumulation of the surplus is directed, the surplus after 21 years reverts to the settlor or his estate,[89] or in the case of a will may pass under a residuary gift,[90] or, in default, go to the persons entitled on intestacy.[91]

7–168   **2. No acceleration.** There is no acceleration of subsequent interests.[92] Thus a remainderman whose interest is not to fall into possession until the death of a life annuitant cannot claim surplus income arising before the annuitant's death.[93] The statutory rules do not alter any disposition made by the testator except his direction to accumulate.[94]

D. The Rule in Saunders v. Vautier[95]

7–169   **1. The rule.** Under this rule a beneficiary of full age who has an absolute, vested and indefeasible interest in property may at any time, notwithstanding any direction to accumulate, require the transfer of the property to him and terminate any accumulation. A man may do as he likes with his own, and the court will not enforce a mere restraint on his enjoyment of the property if that restraint cannot benefit any other person.[96] Thus if property is given absolutely to A, aged 10, with a direction to accumulate the income for his benefit until he is 24, A can demand payment of both the original property and the accumulations as soon as he is of full age.[97]

7–170   **2. Operation.** The rule applies equally where a number of adult beneficiaries seeking to put an end to an accumulation together comprise every person who has any vested or contingent interest in the property[98]; and it applies to charities.[99] But it will not apply if there is a gift to a class of persons[1] or charities[2] not yet determined. This remains true, at common law,

---

[88] *Trickey v. Trickey* (1832) 3 My. & K. 560.

[89] *Re O'Hagen* [1932] W.N. 188.

[90] *O'Neill v. Lucas* (1838) 2 Keen 313; *Ellis v. Maxwell* (1841) 3 Beav. 587; *Re Ransome* [1957] Ch. 348. The income is treated as income of the residue, not as capital, as between tenant for life and remainderman: *Morgan v. Morgan* (1851) 4 De G. & Sm. 164; *Re Garside* [1919] 1 Ch. 132; and see [1979] Conv. 423 (J. G. Riddall).

[91] *Mathews v. Keble* (1868) 3 Ch.App. 691; *Re Walpole* [1933] Ch. 431.

[92] *Green v. Gascoyne* (1865) 4 De G.J. & S. 565 at 569; see *Re Parry* (1889) 60 L.T. 489.

[93] See *Weatherall v. Thornburgh* (1878) 8 Ch.D. 261 at 269, 271, 272; *Berry v. Geen* [1938] A.C. 575; *Re Robb* [1953] Ch. 459.

[94] *Eyre v. Marsden* (1838) 2 Keen. 564 at 574, affirmed 4 My. & Cr. 231.

[95] (1841) 4 Beav. 115, affirmed Cr. & Ph. 240.

[96] See *Gosling v. Gosling* (1859) Johns. 265 at 272.

[97] *Josselyn v. Josselyn* (1837) 9 Sim. 63.

[98] See *Berry v. Geen* [1938] A.C. 575 at 582.

[99] *Wharton v. Masterman* [1895] A.C. 186.

[1] *Green v. Gascoyne* (1865) 4 De G.J. & S. 565.

[2] *Re Jefferies* [1936] 2 All E.R. 626; there is no such entity as "charity": *ibid.*

even if an increase in the class is most improbable, *e.g.* dependant on a woman of 65 having another child.[3] But the Act of 1964 applies its presumptions as to "future parenthood", already explained,[4] in cases where the disposition took effect after July 15, 1964.[5] An accumulation cannot be terminated at the sole request of a beneficiary whose interest is future, contingent or in any way limited, for in all such cases there are bound to be other persons interested in the accumulation, either actually or potentially.[6] It will be seen that the rule, where it does apply, makes the trust for accumulation precarious whether or not it is confined to one of the permitted periods.[7]

E. Exceptions from the Rule against Accumulations

There are the following exceptions from the rule against accumulations.   **7–171**

1. Payment of debts: a provision for accumulation for the payment of the   **7–172** debts of any person.[8] By the terms of the Act this exception includes an accumulation directed for the payment of any debts, whether of the settlor or testator, or any other person.[9] Indeed, an accumulation for the payment of the debts of the settlor or testator is valid even if it may exceed the perpetuity period[10]; such a direction can cause little mischief, for the creditors may terminate the accumulation at any time by demanding payment.[11] But an accumulation to pay the debts of any other person (though not the National Debt[12]) must be confined within the perpetuity period.[13]

The exception extends only to debts deriving from an existing source of obligation[14]; and the accumulation must be directed bona fide for their payment.[15] Subject to this, it may extend both to existing and to contingent

---

[3] *Re Deloitte* [1926] Ch. 56. This may one day be reconsidered by the House of Lords: *Berry v. Geen* [1938] A.C. 575 at 584.

[4] *Ante*, para. 7–035.

[5] s.14.

[6] See *Eyre v. Marsden* (1839) 4 My. & Cr. 231; *M'Donald v. Bryce* (1838) 2 Keen 276. As to determination of an accumulation of surplus income subject to an annuity (which may raise difficult questions as to the precise rights of the annuitant, who may have an interest in the accumulation if a deficiency of income in any year may be made up out of the accumulated fund), see *Re Travis* [1900] 2 Ch. 541 at 548; *Wharton v. Masterman* [1895] A.C. 186; *Harbin v. Masterman* [1896] 1 Ch. 351; *Berry v. Geen* [1938] A.C. 575; *Re Coller's Deed Trusts* [1939] Ch. 277.

[7] *Wharton v. Masterman* [1895] A.C. 186 at 200.

[8] L.P.A. 1925, s.164(2)(i).

[9] *Viscount Barrington v. Liddell* (1852) 2 De G.M. & G. 480 at 497, 498.

[10] *Lord Southampton v. Marquis of Hertford* (1813) 2 V. & B. 54 at 65; *Bateman v. Hotchkin* (1847) 10 Beav. 426.

[11] Gray, § 676.

[12] Superannuation and other Trust Funds (Validation) Act 1927, s.9.

[13] See *Viscount Barrington v. Liddell* (1852) 2 De G.M. & G. 480 at 498; Marsden 344.

[14] *Re Rochford's S.T.* [1965] Ch. 111 (accumulation for paying estate duty on deaths of living persons not exempted).

[15] *Mathews v. Keble* (1868) 3 Ch.App. 691 at 697.

debts,[16] as where the object of the accumulation is to discharge a mortgage[17] or to provide for liability under a leasehold covenant not yet broken.[18]

7–173   **2. Portions:** a provision for accumulation for raising portions for any legitimate[19] issue (even if unborn[20]) of the grantor, settlor or testator or any person to whom an interest is limited under the settlement.[21] This is a statutory exception from the rule against accumulations only; such accumulations must be confined to the perpetuity period. The meaning of "portions" here is not clear.[22] It is not confined to sums raised out of real estate,[23] nor to provisions for the benefit of the younger children of a marriage[24]; and it applies equally to portions created by the instrument directing accumulation[25] or any other instrument.[26] It does not, however, extend to a direction to accumulate the income from the whole of,[27] or the bulk of,[28] a testator's estate, for "it is not raising a portion at all, it is giving everything".[29] An accumulation for raising portions for the unborn children of X, a beneficiary, and in default of such children for Y, depends upon the event; if X has children it is within the exceptions, otherwise it is not.[30]

7–174   **3. Timber or wood:** a provision for accumulation of the produce of timber or wood.[31] Although expressly excepted from the statutory accumulation rules, such a direction will be void if it can exceed the perpetuity period.[32]

7–175   **4. Minority:** accumulations made during a minority under the general law or any statutory power.[33] While the person entitled to any trust property is a minor, a statutory power is given to the trustees to apply the income for his maintenance; subject thereto, they are bound to accumulate the residue of the

[16] *Varlo v. Faden* (1859) 1 De. G.F. & J. 211 at 224, 225.
[17] *Bateman v. Hotchkin* (1847) 10 Beav. 426 at 433.
[18] *Re Hurlbatt* [1910] 2 Ch. 553.
[19] *Shaw v. Rhodes* (1836) 1 My. & Cr. 135 at 159 (on appeal *sub nom. Evans v. Hellier* (1837) 5 Cl. & F. 114). But see now Family Law Reform Act 1969, s.15; Family Law Reform Act 1987, ss.1, 19.
[20] *Beech v. Lord St Vincent* (1850) 3 De G. & Sm. 678.
[21] L.P.A. 1925, s.164(2)(ii).
[22] See *Watt v. Wood* (1862) 2 Dr. & Sm. 56 at 60.
[23] *Re Elliott* [1918] 2 Ch. 150 at 153.
[24] *Re Stephens* [1904] 1 Ch. 322.
[25] *Beech v. Lord St Vincent* (1850) 3 De G. & Sm. 678.
[26] *Halford v. Stains* (1849) 16 Sim. 488 at 496.
[27] *Wildes v. Davies* (1853) 1 Sm. & G. 475.
[28] *Bourne v. Buckton* (1851) 2 Sim. (N.S.) 91.
[29] *Edwards v. Tuck* (1853) 3 De G.M. & G. 40 at 58, *per* Lord Cranworth L.C.; but see the next sentence in his judgment.
[30] *Re Clulow's Trust* (1859) 1 J. & H. 639.
[31] L.P.A. 1925, s.164(2)(iii). This exception is said to be due to the need for naval timber in 1800: Marsden, *Perpetuities*, p. 346, who also cites Pepys's dictum that "timber is an excrescence of the earth, provided by God for the payment of debts".
[32] *Ferrand v. Wilson* (1845) 4 Hare 344.
[33] L.P.A. 1925, s.165.

income.[34] Since 1925 it is expressly provided that the period of such accumulation is to be disregarded when determining the period for which accumulations are permitted.[35] Thus if a testator directs accumulation for 21 years after his death and the beneficiary at the end of this period is a minor, the accumulations both for the 21 years and during the minority are valid.[36]

5. Maintenance of property: a provision for maintaining property at its present value.[37] If the property is of a wasting nature, it may be kept up out of income; this is not "accumulation" within the meaning of the Act, for the property is never augmented, even though income is added to capital.[38] This head is accordingly not a true exception to the rule but merely a case in which there is no real accumulation. Thus directions to devote surplus income to maintaining buildings in a proper state of repair[39] (as distinct from building new houses[40]), or to apply a fixed annual sum to keep up a "sinking fund" insurance policy to replace the capital lost by the expiry of leaseholds,[41] are outside the statutory rules against accumulations.[42] But an accumulation for replacing the capital lost in payment of estate duty is not within this exception, at any rate if it extends to more than a reasonable proportion of the income.[43]

7–176

Dispositions falling within this exception must be confined to the perpetuity period.[44]

6. Certain commercial contracts: transactions which cannot fairly be described as settlements or dispositions. The Act merely provides that no person may "settle or dispose"[45] of property in breach of the restrictions against accumulations, and there are many commercial transactions involving accumulation which are not properly within these terms, *e.g.* partnership agreements providing for the accumulation of certain profits,[46] certain policies of life insurance,[47] and investment trusts which capitalise part of their income.[48] Such transactions, and provisions for making payments (*e.g.* of

7–177

---

[34] T.A. 1925, s.31. They had to do so in any case, unless othewise empowered, owing to the inability of a minor to give a binding receipt (as to minor's disabilities, see *post*, para. 20–002). A *married* minor may now give a valid receipt under L.P.A. 1925, s.21; but this does not, it seems, apply to a minor who is a widow or a widower.

[35] See n. 34, *supra*.

[36] *Re Maber* [1928] Ch. 88.

[37] *Re Gardiner* [1901] 1 Ch. 697 at 699, 700.

[38] *ibid. A fortiori* if surplus income is not added to capital but is merely retained to meet possible future deficiencies of income for paying annuities: *Re Earl of Berkeley* [1968] Ch. 744.

[39] *Vine v. Raleigh* [1891] 2 Ch. 13; *Re Mason* [1891] 3 Ch. 467.

[40] *Vine v. Raleigh, supra*, at 26.

[41] *Re Gardiner* [1901] 1 Ch. 697.

[42] For other examples, see *Bassil v. Lister* (1851) 9 Hare 177 at 184.

[43] *Re Rochford's S.T.* [1965] Ch. 111.

[44] *Curtis v. Lukin* (1842) 5 Beav. 147.

[45] L.P.A. 1925, s.164(1).

[46] See *Bassil v. Lister, supra*, at 184.

[47] *ibid.*

[48] *Re A.E.G. Unit Trust (Managers) Ltd's Deed* [1957] Ch. 415.

premiums) in respect of them, are accordingly outside the rule; and most of them also fall outside the perpetuity rule as being mere personal obligations sounding in contract.[49]

F. Proposals for further reform of the Rule against Accumulations

7–178   There can be little doubt that the present law on accumulations is unsatisfactory.[50] Few other jurisdictions have adopted a rule against excessive accumulations even though most have a rule against perpetuities. The operation of the rule is needlessly complicated and its application can be capricious. It is a cause of considerable difficulty in the administration of many trusts, including in particular pension trusts. The Law Commission has recommended that it should be abolished[51] except in relation to charitable trusts. Because such trusts, unlike private trusts, may be perpetual, the Commission considered that it was necessary to have some restriction on them.[52] It therefore recommended that there should be a 21-year limit on any power to accumulate conferred by the trust.[53]

---

[49] See *ante*, para. 7–114.
[50] See the discussion at (1998) Law Com. No. 251, paras 10.5–10.14.
[51] *ibid.*, para. 10.15. Accumulation would therefore be possible for the duration of the trust. That duration is necessarily limited because any disposition under it must vest within the perpetuity period.
[52] It should be noted that the Charity Commission may sanction the retention of income by charities for specific purpose provided that there are reasonable grounds for doing so. Administrative retention of this kind is not accumulation. The income remains income and is not regarded as capital.
[53] Law Com. No. 251, paras 10.18–10.21.

CHAPTER 8

SUCCESSIVE INTERESTS:
SETTLED LAND AND TRUSTS OF LAND

THIS chapter explains the law which governs successive interests in land. It **8–001** has been conventional to explain this subject historically and to give an account of the development of what is called a "settlement"—the name traditionally given to arrangements by which property is given to particular persons in succession. However, the law which governs successive interests has recently undergone a fundamental reform through the Trusts of Land and Appointment of Trustees Act 1996. This marks a significant break with the past by introducing a unitary system of trusts of land, which applies whatever form the beneficial interests may take. The emphasis of this chapter reflects that change.

The chapter begins with an account of the traditional method of settling land by means of a strict settlement. Such settlements were governed by the Settled Land Act 1925. Subject to certain minor exceptions, it ceased to be possible to create any new settlements after 1996. Although existing settlements remain subject to the 1925 Act, any new ones are governed by the Trusts of Land and Appointment of Trustees Act 1996.[1] This Act is explained later in the chapter.[2] The new trust of land and its legal framework owe little, if anything, to the old settlement. It is instead a development of the trust for sale. The trust for sale could be employed as an alternative means of creating successive interests in land prior to 1997 (and often was). As is explained in the next chapter, it was also the device adopted in the Law of Property Act 1925 to regulate the co-ownership of land. As all trusts for sale now take effect as trusts of land,[3] only a summary of the law which previously governed them is given as a necessary introduction to trusts of land.[4]

---

[1] See T.L.A.T.A. 1996, s.2. There are two exceptions to this: see *ibid.* s.2(2); *post*, para. 8–070.

[2] *Post*, para. 8–123.

[3] T.L.A.T.A. 1996, s.1(2).

[4] *Post*, para. 8–109. For a detailed treatment of trusts for sale reference should be made to the previous edition of this work at p. 385.

Part 1

SETTLEMENTS AND TRUSTS FOR SALE PRIOR TO 1926

Section 1. Introduction

8–002 Traditionally, the word "settlement" has been employed in a general sense for all kinds of arrangement by which property was given to particular persons in succession. If A by his will left property to B for life with remainder to C in fee simple, that was a simple type of settlement. Whenever a donor created a limited interest (an interest less than a fee simple absolute) there was usually a settlement, since someone would or might be entitled in succession after the limited interest.[5] The essence of a settlement was a series of interests created by a single gift, whether by deed or will. Almost all of the examples given in the previous chapter on perpetuities were also examples of settlements. In that chapter the question was whether certain remainders and other rights could exist at all. In the first part of this chapter, the concern is with the rights and powers of those who have interests in the land under a settlement, particularly the person in actual possession, who is usually the tenant for life.

The more elaborate types of settlement, such as the old-fashioned marriage settlement,[6] were the product of the settlor's desire to keep his land in the family and to make appropriate provision for the various members of the family. Such transactions had long ago become fiscally disadvantageous and were very uncommon by the time that settlements were prospectively abolished by the Trusts of Land and Appointment of Trustees Act 1996.

In the course of time two distinct methods of settling land had come into general use: the strict settlement and the trust for sale. The term "strict settlement" was an appropriate description of the complicated type of family settlement which flourished before statute intervened. The term "settlement" came to be used in a special sense to mean any settlement which was not made by way of trust for sale.

Section 2. The Strict Settlement

8–003 **1. Evils of settlements.**[7] The classical strict settlement was devised to preserve a family estate intact through succeeding generations. In its simplest form, a testator granted the land to A (his eldest son) for life, with remainder to A's eldest son in tail.[8] The settlement would also commonly contain

---

[5] Leases were an exception, and did not normally give rise to settlements: *post*, para. 8–060.

[6] See the previous edition of this work at p. 411.

[7] For a fuller account, see the previous edition of this work at p. 312; and B. English and J. Saville, *Strict Settlement*, chap. 1.

[8] Further more restrictive limitations would violate the perpetuity rules: *ante*, paras 7–015, 7–123.

provision for other members of the family[9] which was usually raised by mortgaging the land, thereby burdening the property with debt. A's eldest son could not alienate the land until he came of age, when he might bar the entail. If A were still alive, his consent to the barring was required, otherwise the son could create no more than a base fee. In practice, this consent would not be forthcoming and, as the son usually needed ready money, he would come to an agreement with A. A would grant his son some immediate share (perhaps an annual income) in return for the resettlement of the land on A for life, remainder to the son for life, remainder to the son's eldest son in tail.

So long as this process of settlement and resettlement continued, no person of full age ever had more than a life estate. The life tenant could alienate his own life interest but had no power to sell or lease the land. Any improvements to the land had to be met out of his own pocket. Although extensive powers of management and even of sale might be conferred by the settlement, the practice was not universal. In the absence of such powers, the land might be rendered both unmanageable and inalienable. During the course of the nineteenth century, the fetters were gradually removed from settled land by a series of statutes. These culminated in the Settled Land Act 1882.[10]

Prior to 1926, the legal estate in settled land might either be split up between beneficiaries or vested in trustees according to the way in which the settlement was made.

2. The Settled Land Act 1882. The general scheme of the Settled Land Act 1882[11] was to give the tenant for life under the settlement wide powers of dealing with the land free from the trusts of the settlement without the consent of the other beneficiaries, or application to the court, just as if he were owner in fee simple. The rights of beneficiaries were protected in the case of a sale by shifting the settlement from the land to the purchase-money, which had to be paid to the trustees or into court. The purchaser would have no concern with the trusts of the settlement.   **8–004**

The main features of the Act were as follows:

(i) It applied to any land or estate or interest in land, which under any document stood for the time being limited to, or in trust for, any persons by way of succession.[12] It was immaterial whether the interests were legal or equitable.

(ii) Wide powers of sale, exchange, leasing, mortgaging and otherwise dealing with the land were given to the tenant for life or other limited owner in possession.[13] In exercising those powers, the life

---

[9] *e.g.* annuities for widows ("jointures") and lump sums for younger children ("portions").

[10] For an excellent account of the changes in the law of settled land, see A. Underhill's lecture, printed in *A Century of Law Reform* (1901), pp. 281–297, and *Select Essays in Anglo-American Legal History* (1909) III, pp. 674–686.

[11] There is a full account of the Act in the previous edition of this work at pp. 317–324.

[12] S.L.A. 1882, s.2. It also applied to land held by, or in trust for, infants; *ibid.,* s.59.

[13] S.L.A. 1882, ss.3(i), 3(iii), 6, 18, and 2(5) respectively.

tenant was deemed to be in the position of a trustee and was required to "have regard to the interests of all parties entitled under the settlement".[14]

(iii) Although additional powers could be conferred on the life tenant by the settlement, any provision in it which purported to take away or cut down his statutory powers, either directly or indirectly, was void.[15]

(iv) There was an elaborate definition of the persons who were to be the trustees of the settlement.[16] Normally they consisted of the persons expressly appointed as trustees. Although the legal estate might in certain circumstances be vested in them,[17] they had no real control over the land. Their main function was to receive and hold any capital, *e.g.* when land was sold.

(v) When the life tenant exercised his powers, and the settled land was for example sold, the rights of the beneficiaries were overreached (*i.e.* transferred from the land to the proceeds of sale), provided that the money was paid to the trustees (of whom there had to be not less than two), or into court.[18] It was immaterial for these purposes whether the legal estate was vested in the life tenant or in the trustees. Capital money in the hands of the trustees (which had to be invested in the manner provided for by the Act[19]) was treated as if it were the land "for all purposes of disposition, transmission, and devolution".[20] It made no difference that the purchaser had notice of the interests under the settlement. The statute provided that they were to be overreached, whether they were legal or equitable.[21]

Section 3. Trusts for Sale

8–005   **1. Objects of trusts for sale.** A trust for sale was a trust which directed the trustees to sell the trust property, invest the proceeds, and hold the resulting fund upon the trusts declared by the settlor.[22] Its objects and operation were therefore quite different from those of a strict settlement. Instead of aiming to preserve a family estate intact, as did the old strict settlement, the trust for sale

---

[14] *ibid.*, s.53.

[15] *ibid.*, s. 51.

[16] *ibid.*, s.2(8); S.L.A. 1890, s.16.

[17] This depended upon how the settlement was created.

[18] S.L.A. 1882, ss.20, 22(1), 39(1).

[19] *ibid.*, s.21.

[20] *ibid.*, s.22(5).

[21] *ibid.*, s.20(2).

[22] It is still possible to create a trust for sale: T.L.A.T.A. 1996, s.1(2). However, it takes effect as a trust of land: *ibid.* There will therefore normally be little point in creating such a trust now. *cf. post*, para. 8–126.

set out by treating the property as so much potential money. Dividing it among the family was therefore easy, and there was the convenience that a mixed fund of land and personalty could be disposed of under the same set of trusts. This form of settlement was ideal for settling fortunes made in commerce, and for this reason, trusts for sale were sometimes called "traders' settlements".[23] They were of more recent origin than strict settlements.[24]

2. Position pending sale. In a trust for sale the legal estate was vested in   **8–006** the trustees upon trust to sell the land and hold the income until sale and the proceeds thereafter upon specified trusts for the beneficiaries. The trustees were usually given power to postpone sale in their discretion, and to manage the land until sale. It followed that the trustees did not have to sell until market conditions were suitable. Often the consent of the beneficiaries entitled in possession was made a prerequisite to a sale, and in the meantime they could usually have the benefit of the property itself if they wished, whether by living in a house, or by enjoying the rents if it was let. The purchase-money arising on a sale was usually directed to be invested in stocks, shares and other securities,[25] and then held upon trusts for the members of the family. These trusts would often provide for life interests, widows' annuities, remainders to children, and so on, in much the same way as a strict settlement. There was one significant difference: until 1926 no entail could be created under a trust for sale.[26]

3. The doctrine of conversion. The effect of creating a trust for sale was   **8–007** that even before sale the rights of beneficiaries were for certain purposes deemed to be rights in personalty. Equity treated as done that which ought to be done.[27] As soon as there was a binding obligation to sell, the interests of the beneficiaries were notionally converted into the money into which the land was destined to be converted. This was the equitable doctrine of conversion. Although its consequences were often followed out logically (there could, for example, be no entail under a trust for sale made before 1926 because personalty was not entailable[28]) it was never an absolute rule to be applied in all circumstances.[29] The doctrine was a source of considerable difficulty and has now been abolished with retrospective effect.[30]

---

[23] For other situations in which trusts for sale were employed, see (1984) 100 L.Q.R. 86 at 87 (J. S. Anderson).

[24] See the previous edition of this work at p. 314.

[25] See Davidson, *Precedents in Conveyancing* (3rd ed.), III, pp. 711, 712, 868.

[26] See *infra*.

[27] See, *e.g. Lechmere v. Earl of Carlisle* (1733) 3 P. Wms. 211 at 215; *Guidot v. Guidot* (1745) 3 Atk. 254 at 256.

[28] *Ante*, para. 3–087.

[29] For a review of the substantial and often contradictory body of authority, see (1984) 100 L.Q.R. 86 (J. S. Anderson).

[30] See T.L.A.T.A. 1996, s.3(1), (3), subject to certain exceptions: *ibid.* ss.3(2), 18(3); *post*, para. 8–127.

8–008   **4. The Settled Land Acts 1882 and 1884.** The Settled Land Act 1882 applied to land held upon trust for sale for the benefit of a person with a life or other limited interest.[31] The apparent effect was that all the powers, including that of sale, belonged to the life beneficiary and not to the trustees. The courts interpreted the legislation very narrowly,[32] and consternation among conveyancers led to a change in the law in the Settled Land Act 1884.[33] This provided that in the case of trusts for sale the tenant for life should be unable to exercise the powers of the Act of 1882 without an order of the court, and that until such an order was made, the trustees could sell without the consent of the tenant for life.[34] A purchaser could safely deal with the trustees for sale unless such an order had been registered as a *lis pendens* (pending action).[35]

Although the Act of 1884 restored the trustees' power of sale it did not equip them with other powers of management (*e.g.* of leasing) which they might need if sale was postponed. Nor was this the only disadvantage of trusts for sale: they were unsatisfactory from a conveyancer's point of view.[36] In consequence, the practice developed towards the end of the nineteenth century of keeping trusts off the face of the title by making the trustees appear as absolute owners.[37] The device did not prove to be wholly successful, however.[38]

8–009   **5. Trust for sale or power of sale.** After the Act of 1884 it was essential for conveyancing purposes to distinguish between a trust for sale and other forms of settlement. If there was a trust for sale and no order of the court had been made, a purchaser could get a good title only from the trustees. In any other case he could obtain a good title only from the tenant for life. The distinction was not always a clear one. A mere *power* of sale given to trustees was not a *trust* for sale: there had to be an imperative obligation upon the trustees to sell and not merely a discretionary power. But trusts and powers often shade into one another, and a *trust* to sell with a *power* to postpone sale had to be distinguished from a *trust* to retain with a *power* to sell; even words such as "upon trust to sell" might not create a trust for sale if from the context it was clear that a mere power was intended.[39] A trust "to retain or sell the land" was a borderline case: it might or might not be construed as a trust for

---

[31] s.63. This section was not included in the original Bill but was added during the passage through Parliament: 27 S.J. 113; 28 S.J. 703.

[32] See *Taylor v. Poncia* (1884) 25 Ch.D. 646.

[33] s.7.

[34] S.L.A. 1884, s.6(1).

[35] *ibid.,* s.7(vi); *ante,* para. 5–088.

[36] For example, the beneficiaries might have elected to take the land as land, so that the trustees could no longer sell. For this and other drawbacks, see J. S. Anderson, *Lawyers and the Making of English Land Law 1832–1940*, pp. 269–273; and [1990] C.L.J. 277 at 283–286 (C.H.).

[37] See, *e.g. Re Chafer and Randall's Contract* [1916] 2 Ch. 258; *Re Soden and Alexander's Contract* [1918] 2 Ch. 258.

[38] J. S. Anderson, *op. cit.* p. 271.

[39] *Re Hotchkys* (1886) 32 Ch.D. 408; *Re Newbould* (1913) 110 L.T. 6.

sale, depending upon whether the general intention of the settlement was that the land should be sold[40] or that it should be retained as land.[41]

6. Bare trusts. The Settled Land Acts never applied to a trust where one or   **8–010**
more persons of full age were entitled in possession absolutely and there was no element of succession, whether there was a trust for sale or not.[42] Thus a conveyance "to A in fee simple in trust for B in fee simple" created a bare trust which was not within the Acts.[43] Bare trusts remained outside the provisions of the 1925 property legislation which govern trusts for sale and settled land. However, after 1996, they take effect as a trust of land whenever created.[44]

Part 2

THE SETTLED LAND ACT 1925

The Settled Land Act 1925 continued the policy of the Act of 1882, making   **8–011**
certain extensions and alterations of the statutory powers. In substance the position of a tenant for life was little changed. The powers contained in the 1882 Act (as amended) were repeated in the Act of 1925. However, as part of the wider design of the 1925 legislation to improve the system of conveyancing, important changes were made in the legal machinery by which settlements were made and settled land was disposed of. In the following account of the 1925 Act these changes will be considered first. It should be emphasised that, subject to certain minor exceptions,[45] it has not been possible to create new settlements after 1996.[46] References to settlements under the 1925 Act are therefore to settlements created after 1925 but before 1997.

Section 1. Principal Alterations Made by the Settled Land Act 1925

A. *Trusts for Sale were Excluded from the Act*

Land subject to "an immediate binding trust for sale"[47] was expressly   **8–012**
excluded from the definition of settled land.[48] If a trust for sale arose, the

---

[40] *Re Johnson* [1915] 1 Ch. 435; and see *Re Crisp* (1907) 95 L.T. 865.
[41] *Re White's Settlement* [1930] 1 Ch. 179.
[42] See, *e.g. Re Earle and Webster's Contract* (1883) 24 Ch.D. 144.
[43] See, *e.g. Re British Land Co. and Allen's Contract* (1900) 44 S.J. 593.
[44] T.L.A.T.A. 1996, s.1(2).
[45] *Post*, para. 8–070.
[46] *Ante*, para. 8–001.
[47] S.L.A. 1925, s.117(1)(xxx), referring to L.P.A. 1925, s.205(1)(xxix). The meaning of this phrase gave rise to some difficulty: see the previous edition of this work at p. 386.
[48] S.L.A. 1925, s.1(7), added by L.P.(Am.)A. 1926, Sched. For a detailed account of trusts for sale (which were governed by L.P.A. 1925), see the previous edition of this work at p. 385. See too *post*, para. 8–126.

Settled Land Act 1925 could not apply, even if the land was previously settled.[49]

B. *The Legal Estate was Normally in the Tenant for Life*

8–013 Before 1926 the legal estate in settled land was either vested in trustees or split between the beneficiaries. This depended on how the settlement was made.[50] In either case, the tenant for life was able to deal with it by his statutory powers. After 1925, apart from the exception stated below, the whole legal estate will always have been vested in the tenant for life; and that legal estate will usually have been a fee simple absolute in possession.[51] This has been given to the tenant for life not for his personal benefit (because he is a trustee of it, as he is of the other statutory privileges[52]) but to make the system of conveyancing more logical. Instead of being endowed with a power to sell or administer a legal fee simple which was held by the trustees, the tenant for life has been given the legal fee simple itself. But since he must be prevented from taking advantage of it except for proper purposes, his powers as fee simple owner are still restricted.[53] The result of these changes has been to make it easier to trace the title to the legal estate (where it is unregistered), thereby improving the position of a purchaser.[54]

Where a settlement was made after 1925, the legal estate had to be conveyed to the life tenant, unless, of course, it was already vested in him,[55] as where the owner of property settled it upon himself as tenant for life, with remainders over ("with remainders over" is a concise way of referring to the remainders following the life interest without setting them out in detail).

8–014 Any tenant for life is therefore not only a trustee of the statutory powers, as he was before 1926, but is also a trustee of the legal estate. Both the powers[56] and the estate[57] are vested in him for himself and the other beneficiaries under the settlement. The tenant for life's trusteeship is however a "highly interested" one.[58] On the one hand, he must have regard to the interests of all parties under the settlement. The court can therefore intervene if he seeks to sell at a price well below the value of the property,[59] or effect any transaction

---

[49] *e.g.* where land was left to A for life thereafter to trustees for sale. The land ceased to be settled on A's death.

[50] *Ante*, para. 8–004.

[51] *Ante*, para. 4–034. Other interests in land (*e.g.* leaseholds) could also be settled, but they were less common.

[52] *Post*, para. 8–093.

[53] *Post*, para. 8–042.

[54] *Post*, paras 8–031 *et seq.*

[55] S.L.A. 1925, s.4(2).

[56] S.L.A. 1925, s.107(1).

[57] S.L.A. 1925, s.16(1); see *Re Boston's W.T.* [1956] Ch. 395 (esp. at 405); (1956) 72 L.Q.R. 328 (R.E.M.). For the power of a tenant for life to acquire the settled land or part of it, see *post*, para. 8–095.

[58] *Re Earl of Stamford and Warrington* [1916] 1 Ch. 404 at 420, *per* Younger J.

[59] *Wheelwright v. Walker (No. 1)* (1883) 23 Ch.D. 752 at 762.

which, although within his powers, will prejudice other beneficiaries.[60] Furthermore, any exercise of his powers which is not made bona fide will be restrained even though it may cause no pecuniary loss.[61] Against this, however, the tenant for life's fiduciary position is necessarily qualified by the fact that he is also a beneficiary, so that "he can legitimately exercise his powers with some, but not, of course, an exclusive, regard for his own personal interests, wishes and tastes".[62] The inherent conflict of interest in the tenant for life's position is one of the principal reasons why settlements were prospectively abolished by the Trusts of Land and Appointment of Trustees Act 1996.[63]

There are two cases in which the legal and statutory powers under a settlement are not vested in the tenant for life, but in the "statutory owner". They are as follows.

1. Tenant for life a minor. A legal estate cannot be vested in a minor after 1925[64] and it would be undesirable to give him the statutory powers. Consequently where the person who would otherwise be the tenant for life is a minor, the legal estate and the statutory powers are vested in the statutory owner who is—   **8–015**

    (i) any personal representative in whom the land is vested, providing no vesting instrument[65] has been executed[66]; but otherwise,

    (ii) the trustees of the settlement.[67]

2. No tenant for life. Where under a settlement there is no tenant for life,[68] the legal estate and statutory powers are vested in the statutory owner, who is—   **8–016**

    (i) any person of full age upon whom the settlement expressly confers the powers[69]; but if there is none,

---

[60] See *Hampden v. Earl of Buckinghamshire* [1893] 2 Ch. 531 at 544; and by way of example, *Re Earl Somers* (1895) 11 T.L.R. 567 (life tenant, who was a total abstainer, restrained from leasing a public house on terms that no intoxicating liquor should be sold there).

[61] *Middlemas v. Stevens* [1901] 1 Ch. 574; and see *Dowager Duchess of Sutherland v. Duke of Sutherland* [1893] 3 Ch. 169.

[62] *Re Boston's W.T.* [1956] Ch. 395 at 405, *per* Vaisey J.; and see (1956) 72 L.Q.R. 327 (R.E.M.). See too *Cardigan v. Curzon-Howe* (1885) 30 Ch.D. 531 at 540.

[63] *Post*, para. 8–124.

[64] L.P.A. 1925, s.1(6); *post*, para. 20–003.

[65] *Post*, para. 8–017.

[66] Such cases will now be rare. It used to arise, *e.g.* where the settlement had been made by the will of a testator who had just died.

[67] S.L.A. 1925, ss.26 (powers) and 117(xxvi); *ibid.*, s.4(2). Where a personal representative is the statutory owner, he must follow the directions of the trustees of the settlement: S.L.A. 1925, s.26(2).

[68] See *post*, para. 8–064.

[69] See, *e.g. Re Craven S.E.* [1926] Ch. 985; *Re Norton* [1929] 1 Ch. 84.

(ii) the trustees of the settlement.[70]

Although there is usually a tenant for life, there are situations where there is not, *e.g.* where the first life interest is not to begin until marriage, or until after a period of accumulation.[71] The provisions of the 1925 Act—

(i) ensure that the land can always be dealt with[72]; and

(ii) preserve the principle that the legal estate and the managerial powers should not be separated.

The legal estate is never vested in the trustees of the settlement as such, but in some other capacity, such as statutory owner,[73] or special personal representatives.[74]

C. *All Settlements Had to be Made by Two Documents*

8–017 Before 1926 a settlement was usually made by one document. If the settlement was made by will, the will constituted the settlement. A settlement *inter vivos* was made by deed. This considerably complicated conveyancing transactions.[75] The Settled Land Act 1925 met these difficulties by adopting what had long been the practice of conveyancers in cases of trust for sale made *inter vivos*.[76] This was to draw two separate deeds (each referring to the other), a *conveyance* to the trustees upon trust to sell, and a *trust instrument* declaring the trusts of the proceeds of sale. When the land was sold, the purchaser took the conveyance and the trustees retained the trust instrument.

The two documents made necessary by the Act were a vesting instrument or, where the title was registered, a transfer in lieu of a vesting instrument,[77] and a trust instrument.[78] The vesting instrument contained all the information to which a purchaser was entitled. The trust instrument set out the details of the settlement and any purchaser is not normally concerned with them. The trusts are said to be "behind the curtain" formed by the vesting instrument, and the purchaser is not entitled to look behind the curtain.[79] These provisions must now be examined in greater detail.

---

[70] S.L.A. 1925, ss.23 (powers) and 117(xxvi) (definition); *ibid.*, s.4(2). For a further case of a statutory owner, see S.L.A. 1925, s.23(2); *post*, para. 8–058, n. 55.

[71] *Post.*

[72] Which was not always the case prior to 1926: see, *e.g. Re Horne's S.E.* (1888) 39 Ch.D. 84; *Re Astor* [1922] 1 Ch. 364.

[73] *Supra.*

[74] *Post*, para. 8–035.

[75] See the previous edition of this work at p. 327.

[76] See J. M. Lightwood (1927) 3 C.L.J. 62, 63; S. J. Bailey (1942) 8 C.L.J. 43, 44.

[77] *Post*, para. 8–022.

[78] S.L.A. 1925, ss.4(1), 6, 8(1).

[79] *ibid.*, s.110(2); but in four cases a purchaser *is* concerned to see the trust instrument: see *post*, paras 8–026, 8–030.

1. Settlements of unregistered land made after 1925 and before 1997.   8–018

(a) Settlements made inter vivos. Any settlement of a legal estate in unregistered land made *inter vivos* after 1925 and before 1997,[80] had to be made by two deeds: a principal vesting deed and a trust instrument.[81] The contents of those two documents were as follows.

(1) TRUST INSTRUMENT

The trust instrument[82]—   8–019

    (i) declared the trusts affecting the settled land;

    (ii) bore any *ad valorem* stamp duty payable in respect of the settlement;

    (iii) appointed trustees of the settlement;

    (iv) contained the power, if any, to appoint new trustees of the settlement; and

    (v) set out, either expressly or by reference, any powers intended to be conferred by the settlement in extension of those conferred by the Act.

(2) PRINCIPAL VESTING DEED

The principal vesting deed[83]—   8–020

    (i) described the settled land, either specifically or generally[84];

    (ii) declared that the settled land was vested in the person or persons to whom it was conveyed or in whom it was declared to be vested upon the trusts from time to time affecting the settled land;

    (iii) stated the names of the trustees of the settlement;

    (iv) stated the names of any persons empowered to appoint new trustees of the settlement; and

    (v) stated any additional or larger powers conferred by the trust instrument.

The last three particulars of both documents were similar. The vesting deed acted as a précis of those parts of the trust instrument which are of concern to a purchaser, so that he need inquire no further. The first and second parts of

---

[80] It has not been possible to create new settlements after 1996: *ante*, para. 8–001.
[81] S.L.A. 1925, s.4(1).
[82] *ibid.*, s.4(3).
[83] *ibid.*, s.5(1).
[84] See *ibid.*, s.5(2).

the vesting deed were the operative parts, and vested the legal estate in the tenant for life. The second part was worded so as to cover two cases—

(1) where the vesting deed acted as a conveyance from the settlor to the tenant for life or statutory owner, as where X settled property on A for life with remainders over; and

(2) where the same person was both settlor and tenant for life, so that there was no transfer of the legal estate, as where Z on his marriage settled property on himself for life with remainders over.

A vesting deed was not invalidated merely because of some mistake in the statutory particulars.[85] It was, however, inoperative if it had some fundamental defect, *e.g.* if the wrong person executed it.[86]

8–021   *(b) Settlements made by will.* Where land was settled by the will of a testator dying after 1925 and before 1997, the will was treated as the trust instrument.[87] The legal estate, by the ordinary law, vested immediately in the testator's personal representatives.[88] They were subject to a trust under the Act to transfer the legal estate to the tenant for life by means of a proper vesting instrument.[89] Since personal representatives can convey land by means of a simple assent in writing,[90] a vesting assent could be employed instead of a vesting deed. A vesting assent had to contain the same particulars as a vesting deed.[91]

8–022   **2. Settlements of registered land made after 1925 and before 1997.**[92] The provisions of the Settled Land Act 1925 apply as much to registered land as to unregistered. To create a settlement of registered land, there had to be a trust instrument in the usual way. It was the duty of the registered proprietor (or if he was dead, his personal representatives) to execute an appropriate vesting transfer in statutory form[93] in favour of the tenant for life or statutory owner,[94] and to procure the registration of the necessary restrictions on the

---

[85] S.L.A. 1925, s.5(3).
[86] *Re Cayley and Evans' Contract* [1930] 2 Ch. 143; *cf. Re Curwen* [1931] 2 Ch. 341.
[87] S.L.A. 1925, s.6(a).
[88] *Post*, para. 11–125.
[89] S.L.A. 1925, ss.6(b), 8(4).
[90] *Post*, para. 11–126.
[91] S.L.A. 1925, s.8(1), (4).
[92] The creation of a settlement of unregistered land was not, as the law stood, an occasion on which the title to the land was required to be registered (though it could be registered voluntarily): see Ruoff & Roper, 31–07. However, since April 1998, a vesting deed or assent triggers compulsory registration: see L.R.A. 1925, s.123(1) (as substituted by L.R.A. 1997, s.1). Although this is irrelevant as regards the *creation* of settlements (as none can now be created), it *is* relevant to dispositions of the settled land during the life of the settlement.
[93] Which took the place of and contained the same information as a vesting instrument.
[94] See L.R.A. 1925, s.86(1).

register.[95] Where the proprietor was himself the life tenant, the vesting transfer was merely declaratory.[96]

The interests of the beneficiaries under the settlement take effect only as minor interests and cannot be overriding interests.[97] They should therefore be protected by the entry of a restriction on the register.[98] When the tenant for life is registered as proprietor, the restriction will provide that[99]—

(i) except under an order of the registrar, no disposition will be registered unless it is authorised either by the Settled Land Act 1925 or under any additional powers conferred by the settlement; and

(ii) no disposition under which capital money arises is to be registered unless the money is paid to the trustees of the settlement (of which there must be two and not more than four, or a trust corporation), or into court.

It follows that the registrar cannot register any transaction that is on its face outside the powers of the tenant for life.[1] The restrictions entered on the register, although binding on the tenant for life, do not restrain or in any other way affect a disposition made by his personal representatives.[2]

3. Section 13. Some provision had to be made to prevent evasion of the requirement that there should be a vesting instrument. The policy of the Act was therefore to make it impossible to deal with the land in any case where a vesting instrument ought to have existed but did not. First, a settlement of a legal estate in land made by a single document could not transfer or create a legal estate.[3] The tenant for life or statutory owner can require the trustees of the settlement (not the settlor) to remedy matters by executing a vesting deed.[4] Secondly, section 13 of the Settled Land Act 1925[5] (sometimes called the "paralysing section") in effect provides that where a tenant for life or statutory owner has become entitled to have a vesting instrument executed in his favour, no disposition of a legal estate can be made until a vesting instrument has been executed in accordance with the Act. Until this has been done, any purported disposition of the land *inter vivos* by any person operates

8–023

---

[95] L.R.R. 1925, rr. 99, 104, 170; and Sched. 2, Forms 21, 22, 56, 57: see Ruoff & Roper, 31–06.

[96] L.R.R. 1925, r. 100; and Sched. 2, Form 23.

[97] L.R.A. 1925, s. 86(2); *ante*, para. 6–051.

[98] *ibid.*, s.86(3); L.R.R. 1925, rr. 56, 57.

[99] L.R.R. 1925, r. 58; Sched., Form 9. See Ruoff & Roper, 31–02; 38–17.

[1] See Ruoff & Roper, 31–06.

[2] L.R.A. 1925, s.86(3).

[3] S.L.A. 1925, ss.4(1), (6).

[4] *ibid.*, ss.4, 9.

[5] As amended by L.P.(Am.)A. 1926, s.6 and Sched.

only as a contract for valuable consideration[6] to carry out the transaction after the necessary vesting deed has been executed. In effect this forced the tenant for life to obtain a proper vesting instrument before he could exercise his dispositive powers under the Act. The section does not appear to affect any disposition not made under the Act.[7] Nor does it prevent the tenant for life from disposing of his equitable interest or exercising any equitable powers given to him by the trust instrument.[8] Although it has not been possible to create new settlements after 1996,[9] it is conceivable that section 13 may not yet be spent. There could still be situations where a settlement was made prior to 1997 but where a vesting instrument has still to be executed.

To this rule against premature disposal of a legal estate there are certain exceptions which may be briefly considered.

8–024   *(a) Dispositions by personal representatives.* The section does not apply where the disposition was made by a personal representative.[10] This preserves the usual powers of personal representatives to deal freely with the land in the due course of administering the estate and to make title to a purchaser by virtue of their office.[11]

8–025   *(b) Purchaser without notice of the settlement.* The section does not apply where the disposition is made to a purchaser of a legal estate without notice of the tenant for life or statutory owner having become entitled to a vesting instrument.[12] This might happen if, *e.g.* a settlor declared himself trustee of land for A for life with remainders over, and then sold the land to B, apparently as beneficial owner.

8–026   *(c) Settlement at an end.* The section does not apply where the settlement has come to an end before a vesting instrument has been executed.[13] The settlement ends when one person becomes solely and absolutely entitled, and the trusts of the trust instrument are otherwise exhausted. When the land ceases to be settled, the fetters of section 13 fall away.[14]

---

[6] Registrable (where the title was unregistered) as an estate contract, and, if not registered, void against a purchaser of a legal estate for money or money's worth: *ante*, para. 5–099. Where the title was registered, the estate contract should have been protected as a minor interest by registration of a notice or caution (*ante*, paras 6–079, 6–083). It could, however, take effect as an overriding interest if the purchaser were in actual occupation: *ante*, para. 6–047.

[7] S.L.A. 1925, s.112(2); *Re Alefounder's W.T.* [1927] 1 Ch. 360; but consider Wolst. & C. ii, 55; *Weston v. Henshaw* [1950] Ch. (on s.18; see *post*, para. 8–042).

[8] S.L.A. 1925, s.13.

[9] *Ante*, para. 8–001.

[10] S.L.A. 1925, s.13.

[11] See *post*, para. 11–127.

[12] S.L.A. 1925, s.13, as amended by L.P.(Am.)A. 1926, Sched. If title to the land is registered, the interests under the settlement will not be binding on any purchaser, regardless of notice, unless protected as minor interests: L.R.A. 1925, s.86(2): *ante*, para. 6–051.

[13] *Re Alefounder's W.T.* [1927] 1 Ch. 360, applying S.L.A. 1925, s.112(2).

[14] See, *e.g. Re Alefounder's W.T.*, *supra* (tenant in tail in possession barred his entail thereby causing the settlement to end: no vesting instrument was required).

The operation of these provisions may be illustrated by the example of a case where, prior to 1997, a settlor attempted to make a settlement *inter vivos* in favour of his son and family by means of a single document. This was an imperfect settlement, and—

(i) the document was ineffective to transfer or create any legal estate, which therefore remained vested in the settlor[15];

(ii) the document was treated as the trust instrument[16];

(iii) the trustees of the settlement might either have executed a principal deed on their own initiative, or have been required to execute one by the tenant for life. This would have transferred the legal estate from the settlor to the tenant for life[17];

(iv) until the trustees had duly executed the vesting deed, section 13 would operate to prevent any disposition of the land being made. It was *only* the trustees of the settlement who could execute a vesting deed[18];

(v) even after a vesting deed had been executed the settlement would not have been as convenient as one made in the proper manner. This was because the document which created the settlement, although treated as the trust instrument, was not behind the curtain.[19] This is the most important exception to the rule that a purchaser is not concerned with the trust instrument.[20] A settlement *inter vivos* which was wrongly made in the first place must be investigated by any purchaser to make sure that the vesting deed, executed at a later date, really contained the true particulars about the land, the tenant for life, and the trustees.

4. Subsidiary vesting deed. Where unregistered land is brought into an existing settlement, it must be conveyed to the tenant for life or statutory owner by a vesting deed.[21] This requires a subsidiary vesting deed.[22] This must be done in the following cases. **8–027**

---

[15] S.L.A. 1925, s.4(1).

[16] *ibid.*, s.9(1)(iii).

[17] *ibid.*, s.9(2). If the legal estate was already vested in the life tenant (*e.g.* because he was the settlor), the vesting deed would have been merely declaratory.

[18] If there were no trustees and no person able and willing to appoint them, it would have been necessary to make an application to the court for the appointment of trustees: S.L.A. 1925, s.9(3).

[19] *ibid.*, s.110(2).

[20] For the other (less important) exceptions, see s.110(2) and *post*, para. 8–030.

[21] S.L.A. 1925, s.10(1). It should be noted that if there ceases to be any land or heirlooms subject to the settlement, but merely capital money, the settlement comes to an end: see T.L.A.T.A. 1996, s.2(4): *post*, para. 8–041.

[22] S.L.A. 1925, s.10(1) proviso.

(i) Where land is acquired with capital money or in exchange for settled land.[23]

(ii) Where capital money has been lent on mortgage and the mortgagor's right to redeem has become barred (*e.g.* by limitation or foreclosure). In this case the trustees at first hold the land on a trust of land, but at the request of the tenant for life or statutory owner they must execute a subsidiary vesting deed.[24]

Since April 1998, a subsidiary vesting deed of unregistered land is a disposition that triggers the requirement of compulsory registration. The tenant for life must therefore be registered as proprietor of the land subject to the entry of the usual restrictions.[25]

A subsidiary vesting deed, in addition to conveying the land to the tenant for life or statutory owner (if it is not already vested in him), must contain the following particulars[26]—

(i) particulars of the last or only principal vesting deed affecting the land subject to the settlement;

(ii) a statement that the land conveyed is to be held upon and subject to the same trusts and powers as the land comprised in the principal vesting deed;

(iii) the names of the trustees of the settlement;

(iv) the name of any person entitled to appoint new trustees of the settlement.

It is unnecessary to refer to the trust instrument or to any additional powers which it confers.[27]

Where registered land is brought into the settlement, the transfer to the life tenant must be made by a specially prescribed form of transfer.[28] This is deemed to fulfil the requirements of the Settled Land Act 1925 for vesting deeds.[29]

D. A Purchaser May Not Go Behind the Vesting Deed

8–028   **1. The curtain.** The objects of having a separate vesting deed (where the title is unregistered) or a vesting transfer and the entry on the register of

---

[23] *ibid.* Another case is the reservation of a rentcharge on the sale of settled land; but after the Rentcharges Act 1977 (see *post*, para. 18–018), such cases can only rarely arise.

[24] L.P.A. 1925, s.31 (as amended by T.L.A.T.A. 1996, s.5(1); Sched. 2, para. 1).

[25] See *ante*, para. 8–022.

[26] S.L.A. 1925, s.10(2).

[27] Wolst. & C. ii, 51.

[28] L.R.A. 1925, s.86(4); L.R.R. 1925, r. 101; Sched. 2, Form 24: see Ruoff & Roper, 31–08. The application must both state the names of the trustees of the settlement and seek the entry of restrictions in the form usual for settled land: *ante*, para. 8–022.

[29] L.R.A. 1925, s.86(4).

appropriate restrictions (where the title is registered) may be summarised as follows—

(i) to vest the fee simple in the tenant for life, or declare it to be vested in him;

(ii) to indicate on the face of the title that the legal owner is a tenant for life;

(iii) to define his powers of disposition; and

(iv) to ensure that the trusts of the settlement are overreached by payment of any capital monies to the trustees of the settlement.[30]

In this way the trust instrument is kept off the title: indeed it is a document which no purchaser is entitled to see.[31] Furthermore, the disposition of settled land is facilitated, and the interests of the beneficiaries are protected.

2. Errors. A vesting deed or transfer is not invalidated by any mistake in the particulars required to be contained in it,[32] and it is provided by section 110(2) of the Act[33] that a purchaser of a legal estate in settled land is bound and entitled to assume that those particulars are correct as to the persons who are the tenant for life and the trustees.[34] There is no statutory provision to indicate what is to happen if any of the matters is wrongly stated in the vesting instrument. An example is where, prior to 1997, land was settled on W for life or until remarriage, with remainder to X in fee simple. If W is widowed and secretly remarries, she will cease to be a tenant for life, the land would no longer be settled, and she would hold the property on a bare trust for X; yet this would not be apparent to any person dealing with the land. If W purported as tenant for life to exercise some power of disposition, would P, a purchaser of a legal estate, obtain a good title if he both dealt with W on the assumption that she was a tenant for life and paid any capital monies to the trustees? One view is that because P is not a purchaser of a legal estate in settled land, he is not entitled to treat the vesting deed as conclusive that W is the tenant for life. P purchases the land with notice that the land is held on trust and therefore, it is said, takes the land subject to X's interest. A number of solutions to this problem have been offered.[35] First, both from the wording of

8–029

---

[30] For the overreaching provisions, see, *post*, paras 8–158 *et seq.*

[31] S.L.A., s.110(2); nor may he see any deed appointing trustees, if curtained off by a deed of declaration: *post*, para. 8–107.

[32] S.L.A. 1925, s.5(3). But a vesting deed executed by the wrong person is inoperative: *ante*, para. 8–020.

[33] Subject to certain exceptions considered *infra*.

[34] Where the title is registered, a purchaser will not see the vesting transfer. There is no statutory provision to indicate whether he is bound and entitled to make the same assumptions about the restrictions on the register.

[35] See [1984] Conv. 354 (P. A. Stone); and the previous edition of this work at p. 335. *cf.* [1985] Conv. 377 (R. Warrington).

section 110(2) itself[36] and from other provisions of the Act,[37] there is reason to think that P would in fact be regarded as a purchaser of a legal estate in settled land and could therefore claim the protection of the section. Secondly, although P would have notice that the property was held on trust, there would be nothing to put him on inquiry that the settlement had terminated so that the conveyance to him was in breach of trust.[38]

The spread of registration of title is likely to eliminate such slight risk as there may be that this problem may arise. If the title to the land is registered and the settlement is protected by the usual restriction,[39] W will have all the powers of disposition conferred by the Settled Land Act 1925. Any transaction made by W in exercise of those powers will necessarily confer a good title on P.[40]

8–030   **3. Exceptions.** In four situations, a purchaser is entitled to inspect the trust instrument and should do so.[41] They are—

(i) pre-1926 settlements, whether made by will or deed[42];

(ii) imperfect settlements made *inter vivos* after 1925[43];

(iii) instruments which by the Act are for special reasons "deemed to be settlements"[44]; and

(iv) settlements which are "deemed to have been made by any person".[45]

All four cases are abnormal in that no proper vesting instrument was drawn up in the course of constituting the settlement. The accuracy of a vesting deed executed at a later stage should therefore be checked by reference to the trust instrument.

---

[36] See s.110(2)(e), which provides that a purchaser of a legal estate in settled land is bound and entitled to assume that any statements contained in any deed of discharge are correct. If there is a deed of discharge, the land cannot be settled land: *post*, para. 8–036.

[37] See s.36(1), where "settled land" includes land which is notionally treated as if it were settled: see the previous edition of this work at p. 452. *cf. post*, para. 9–090.

[38] [1984] Conv. 354 at 360 (P. A. Stone).

[39] *Ante*, para. 8–022.

[40] L.R.A. 1925, s.20(1), *ante*, para. 6–105.

[41] S.L.A. 1925, s.110(2).

[42] *ibid.*, Sched. 2.

[43] *Ante*, paras 8–023–8–026.

[44] The principal example of this—S.L.A. 1925, s.29—which deemed land held on trust for charitable, ecclesiastical or public purposes to be settled land, and the instruments creating such trusts to be settlements, has been repealed (except for a limited saving in relation to the Chequers and Chevening Estates: see T.L.A.T.A. 1996, s.25(3)). Such trusts now take effect as trusts of land: see T.L.A.T.A. 1996, s.2(5); *post*, para. 20–029.

[45] *e.g.* under S.L.A. 1925, ss.1(2) (minor entitled under intestacy), 1(3) (dower assigned by metes and bounds), 20(3) (curtesy).

E. The Legal Estate Must be Transferred in Due Form

Because the title to the legal estate is independent of the trust instrument, it remains in the tenant for life until he disposes of it or dies. **8–031**

1. Transfer of the legal estate during the lifetime of the tenant for life. **8–032**

A tenant for life may transfer the legal estate during the course of his life for one of two reasons. First, he may of course sell the land under his statutory power. The legal estate will then pass to the purchaser upon conveyance or registration.[46] Secondly, his interest under the settlement may come to an end because it is determinable upon an event which occurs. If that occurs, he must forthwith convey the land to the new owner in the appropriate manner.[47] The method of conveyance will depend upon whether the land remains settled or not and whether the title to it is registered or unregistered. For example, land is settled on A for life or until she remarries, remainder to B for life, remainder to C in fee simple.

(i) If A remarries during B's lifetime, A is bound to convey the legal estate to B. If the title is unregistered this must be done by a further vesting deed because the land remains settled.[48] If the title is registered, A is required to transfer the land to B. It is then the duty of the trustees of the settlement to apply for such alteration, if any, in the restrictions as may be required for the protection of the minor interests under the settlement.[49]

(ii) If B dies and then A remarries, A must convey the land to C. If the title is unregistered, this should be done by means of an ordinary conveyance, for C is absolutely entitled and the settlement is at an end.[50] Should the title be registered, A must transfer the land to C. The trustees of the settlement should execute a deed declaring that they are discharged from the trust[51] and that deed should be lodged at the Land Registry together with an application to cancel the Settled Land Act restrictions.[52]

If any necessary document is not executed, the court may make a vesting order instead of it.[53]

---

[46] The method will depend upon whether the title is already registered or not. If it is not, the purchaser will have to complete his title by registration: L.R.A. 1925, s.123 (as substituted by L.R.A. 1997, s.1).

[47] S.L.A. 1925, s.7(4). If a paramount right to the legal estate arises (*e.g.* by condition broken and re-entry) the tenant for life must convey accordingly: *ibid.*, s.16(1)(ii).

[48] S.L.A. 1925, s.8(4)(a). That vesting deed will now trigger the requirement to register the title: see L.R.A. 1925, s.123(1) (as substituted).

[49] L.R.A. 1925, s.87(6).

[50] S.L.A. 1925, s.7(5). That conveyance will trigger the requirement to register the title: see L.R.A. 1925, s.123(1) (as substituted).

[51] S.L.A. 1925, s.17.

[52] L.R.A. 1925, s.87(4); L.R.R. 1925, r. 106; Ruoff & Roper, 31–14.

[53] S.L.A. 1925, s.12. See, *e.g. Re Shawdon Estates Settlement* [1930] 2 Ch. 1.

8–033   **2. Death of tenant for life.** Similar principles apply where the tenant for life dies, though they are complicated by special rules for devolution on death. Two possible situations may arise.

8–034   *(a) Land ceases to be settled.* On the death of the tenant for life, the land may cease to be settled, either because the remainderman becomes absolutely entitled to the property or because the land becomes subject to a trust of land. In such circumstances, the legal estate vests in the general personal representatives of the tenant for life in the usual way. They must transmit it to the remainderman or to the trustees of land by means of an ordinary assent or conveyance.[54] Where the title is registered, the personal representatives should lodge an assent in the usual way.[55] If the land is to vest in the remainderman, it is probably not necessary either to seek the removal of the restrictions that had hitherto applied to the tenant for life (because these will be removed) or to execute a deed of discharge.[56] If the land is to vest in trustees of land, this should be made apparent on the application for registration, to ensure that the proper restriction is entered on the register.[57]

8–035   *(b) Land remains settled.* If the land remains settled on the death of the tenant for life, it vests in the trustees of the settlement[58] in the capacity of special personal representatives.[59] They should—

> (i) take out a grant of probate or letters of administration limited to the settled land;
>
> (ii) execute a vesting assent in favour of the next life tenant; and
>
> (iii) whether or not the title is already registered, secure both his registration as registered proprietor and entry on the register of the appropriate restrictions.[60]

---

[54] *Re Bridgett and Hayes' Contract* [1928] Ch. 163. Where title is unregistered, this assent or conveyance will, once again, trigger the requirement to register the title: L.R.A. 1925, s.123 (as substituted). If the life tenant dies intestate his administrator succeeds to the legal estate: see Wolst. & C. v. 26.

[55] L.R.A. 1925, s.41(4); L.R.R. 1925, r. 170; Sched. 2, Form 56.

[56] See Ruoff & Roper, 31–14. Once the restrictions have been removed, a deed of discharge fulfils no practical purpose.

[57] See L.R.R. 1925, r. 213; Sched. 2, Form 62. See Ruoff & Roper, 31–14.

[58] A.E.A. 1925, s.22(1) (will); Supreme Court Act 1981, s.116 (intestacy), under which the court will presumably be guided by the repealed provisions of J.A. 1925, s.162, as amended by the Administration of Justice Act 1928, s.9.

[59] "Special executors" in the case of a will: A.E.A. 1925, s.22. In the case of the intestacy no statutory title is now prescribed (see preceding note). And see *Re Rawlinson* (1934) 78 S.J. 602 (special personal representatives held beneficially entitled); *Re Mortifee* [1948] P. 274.

[60] Where title is already registered, see L.R.R. 1925, r. 170; Ruoff & Roper, 27–14. Where title is unregistered, the assent triggers compulsory registration: L.R.A. 1925, s.123(1) (as substituted by L.R.A. 1997, s.1). On registration the appropriate restrictions will then be entered on the register.

The special and general personal representatives can each deal with the land under their control independently of each other.[61] Accordingly, if the land remains settled, it follows a different course of devolution through special personal representatives.

F. Deed of Discharge as Evidence of End of Settlement

1. Need for deed of discharge. A deed of discharge is the instrument designed by the Act to cancel the effect of the vesting deed when its work has been done. If the land eventually devolves upon someone who is absolutely entitled, he must have some means of proving this to a purchaser without showing him the trust instrument. The Act therefore requires that, when the legal estate is held free from all limitations of a trust instrument, the trustees of the settlement must execute a deed declaring that they are discharged from their duties.[62] In case of difficulty, the court may make an order to the same effect.[63] The deed or order of discharge entitles (and compels[64]) a purchaser to assume that the trusts mentioned in the vesting deed no longer exist. He may then safely pay the money to the vendor, for his notice of the trusts is cancelled by the deed of discharge.

8–036

2. Deed of discharge not required. There are two cases where no deed of discharge is required.

8–037

(a) No vesting instrument executed. The object of a deed of discharge is to neutralise the vesting deed, and so no deed of discharge is needed if the land ceases to be settled before any vesting instrument has been executed. In such circumstances there is no tenant for life or statutory owner, and the land must be dealt with outside the Settled Land Act 1925.[65]

8–038

(b) Disposition of unregistered land under ordinary conveyance or assent on the title. In relation to unregistered land, no deed of discharge is required if, after a vesting assent has been executed, there appears on the title a simple assent or conveyance not referring to the trustees of the settlement. This follows from a provision that if a vesting instrument has been executed, but there is a subsequent conveyance or assent on the title which does not contain a statement of the names of the Settled Land Act trustees, a bona fide purchaser of a legal estate for value[66] is both entitled and bound to assume that every statement in the assent or conveyance is correct and that the person in whom the land was thereby vested holds it free from all rights under the

8–039

---

[61] A.E.A. 1925, s.24.

[62] S.L.A. 1925, s.17 (as amended by T.L.A.T.A. 1996, s.25(1), Sched. 3). There is a proviso for securing interests created by any derivative settlement, *e.g.* where a beneficial interest has itself been settled.

[63] *ibid.*, s.17(2).

[64] *ibid.*, s.110(2)(e).

[65] *cf. Re Alefounder's W.T.* [1927] 1 Ch. 360.

[66] S.L.A. 1925, ss.110(5), 117(1)(xxi): as usual, this includes a lessee or mortgagee: *ibid.*

settlement.[67] For the future, this provision will be of little importance. Since April 1998, any conveyance or assent on the termination of the settlement is now required to be completed by registration.[68] The person entitled to the land will be registered as proprietor without the entry of any restriction, and can therefore transfer a good title.

8–040   **3. Registered land.** We have already seen that where the title is registered, the minor interests under the settlement are protected by restrictions.[69] Once those restrictions are removed, the registered proprietor is free to deal with the land as absolute owner. In practice, the Land Registry requires a deed of discharge before it will remove these restrictions only where the settlement terminates during the lifetime of the tenant for life, *e.g.* where he is a tenant in tail and he disentails.[70] In such circumstances, the trustees should submit the deed together with an application to remove the restrictions.[71]

G. Duration of Settlements

8–041   A settlement created prior to 1997 is deemed to continue for the purposes of the Settled Land Act so long as there is still "relevant property" which is subject to the settlement[72] and—

(i) any limitation, charge or power of charging under the settlement still subsists or is capable of being exercised; or

(ii) the person beneficially entitled in possession is a minor.[73]

For these purposes "relevant property" means land and personal chattels included within the settlement.[74] It follows that, if all the settled property is sold, the settlement ceases, and this is so even if (as they are empowered to do) the trustees subsequently purchase more land with the proceeds of sale. Such new land will be held by the trustees on a trust of land.[75] By contrast, if at a time when there is still relevant property, the trustees of the settlement apply capital money in the purchase of more land, that land will be brought within the settlement, and will be settled land.[76]

A settlement will no longer be deemed to continue when the only subsisting limitation is an absolute interest vested in a person of full age. Even if there

---

[67] S.L.A. 1925, s.110(5).
[68] L.R.A. 1925, s.123 (substituted by L.R.A. 1997, s.1).
[69] See *ante*, para. 8–022.
[70] Ruoff & Roper, 31–14.
[71] L.R.A. 1925, s.87(4); L.R.R. 1925, r. 106.
[72] T.L.A.T.A. 1996, s.2(4).
[73] S.L.A. 1925, s.3 (as amended by T.L.A.T.A. 1996, s.25(1), Sched. 3).
[74] T.L.A.T.A. 1996, s.2(4). For settled chattels, see S.L.A. 1925, s.67; *post*, para. 8–086.
[75] See T.L.A.T.A. 1996, ss.2(6), 6(3), (4), 17; Sched. 1, para. 6.
[76] *Ante*, para. 8–027.

is still a trust in favour of such a person,[77] it is generally assumed that the settlement is nevertheless at an end.[78]

H. While Settlement Continues, No Dealings Except Under Act

1. Unauthorised Dealings. We have already seen how section 13 paralyses **8–042** dealings in the land until there is a vesting instrument.[79] After the vesting instrument has been executed, and for so long as the settlement continues, although the tenant for life or statutory owner has the legal estate, he cannot deal with it freely, but only as allowed by the Act, or any other Act,[80] or by any additional powers conferred by the settlement.[81] By section 18 any disposition by the tenant for life or statutory owner which is not authorised by the Act is void,[82] except for the purpose of binding the tenant for life's own beneficial interest while it continues. In one case,[83] a father sold land to his son and later bought it back again. On his death he settled the land by will upon his son for life with remainder to a grandson. The son mortgaged the land, not under his Settled Land Act powers, but for his own personal needs, showing to the mortgagee only his original title by purchase from his father. Since he was in fact tenant for life and his father's executors had made a vesting assent in his favour, his improper mortgages were held void against the grandson so that the mortgagee lost his security.

2. Scheme of the Act. A sharp contrast is therefore revealed between **8–043** section 13 and section 18. While the settlement is still incipient and there is no vesting instrument, section 13 allows a purchaser of a legal estate without notice of the settlement to obtain a good title.[84] But once there is a vesting instrument, section 18 operates in its full rigour, without any exception in favour of innocent purchasers. The scheme of the Act is that once the legal estate has been vested in the tenant for life as such, he can deal with it only in accordance with the powers conferred upon him by the Act or by the settlement. Although he has a legal estate, he is treated as if he were the mere donee of a power.[85] Any disposition that is *ultra vires* will be void and will not

---

[77] As where the land is still vested in the personal representatives of the last tenant for life on a bare trust for the absolute owner under the final limitation of the final settlement.

[78] Wolst. & C. ii, 34; and see *Re Bridgett and Hayes' Contract* [1928] Ch. 163; *ante*, para. 8–034.

[79] *Ante*, para. 8–023.

[80] *e.g.* L.P.(Am.)A. 1926, s.1.

[81] He can of course dispose of his beneficial interest, if any.

[82] s.18 ceases to apply when the settlement ends, even though no need of discharge has been executed: see s.18(1)(a), (b), (c) (once the settlement is at an end no "tenant for life" or "capital money" can exist: ss.19, 20, 117(1)(ii)).

[83] *Weston v. Henshaw* [1950] Ch. 510. See too *Bevan v. Johnston* [1990] 2 E.G.L.R. 33, where a tenant for life of registered land granted an oral lease not authorised by the Act. The lease was held to be void even though the purchaser could not at that time have inspected the register and discovered the restrictions on the proprietor's powers: see (1991) 107 L.Q.R. 596 at 601 (J. Hill). But now the register is open to all: see *ante*, para. 6–002.

[84] *Ante*, para. 8–023.

[85] For powers, see *post*, para. 10–077.

pass the legal estate.[86] To this extent he remains in the position of a tenant for life at common law, who could give no better title than he had himself.

8–044   **3. Registered Land.** Where the title to settled land is registered, a purchaser will be better protected than if it is not. Provided that the usual restriction has been entered, no transaction will be registered unless it is authorised by either the Act or the settlement.[87] It is only in transactions that are not required to be completed by registration that section 18 can operate to defeat the purchaser's title.[88] If the tenant for life were to forge a deed of discharge so that any restrictions on the register were removed, any *ultra vires* disposition would confer on the purchaser a good title,[89] subject only to the possibility that the register might be rectified against him.[90]

8–045   **4. Protection of Purchasers.** A certain (or perhaps uncertain) measure of protection is nevertheless given to purchasers by section 110(1). This provides that a purchaser dealing in good faith with a tenant for life or statutory owner shall, as against all parties entitled under the settlement, be conclusively taken—

(i) to have given the best consideration reasonably obtainable[91]; and

(ii) "to have complied with all the requisitions of this Act".

This provision which, unlike section 18, derives from the 1882 Act,[92] applies to all kinds of dispositions, including sales, leases, mortgages and contracts to enter into such dispositions.[93] However, it applies only to "transactions under this Act".[94] In a case concerning a lease it was explained that it "confirms the view that in the case of a lessee dealing in good faith the remedy, if any, of the persons entitled under the settlement for any neglect of the provisions of the Act is to be against the tenant for life in his fiduciary character, not against the lessee, and is not to affect the validity of the lease".[95] For this reason, it is difficult to see how section 110 can temper the rigour of section

---

[86] See (1971) 87 L.Q.R. 338 at 341 (D. W. Elliott); [1990] C.L.J. 277 at 280 (C.H.).

[87] *Ante*, para. 8–022.

[88] See *Bevan v. Johnston, supra.*

[89] *cf. Hounslow L.B.C. v. Hare* (1990) 24 H.L.R. 9.

[90] It is suggested that the register might be rectified under L.R.A. 1925, s.82(1)(d), "where . . . any entry in the register has been obtained by fraud", and that those words would include a case where the *deletion* of an entry was obtained by fraud. However, it should be noted that if the purchaser is a proprietor who is in possession (as will often be the case), it will be possible to rectify the register against him only if one of the limited grounds set out in *ibid.*, s.82(3) is established, as where he is a party to the life tenant's fraud. See *ante*, para. 6–130.

[91] See, *e.g. Hurrell v. Littlejohn* [1904] 1 Ch. 689 (where a purchaser who had bought property from a tenant for life for £2,000 and promptly resold it for £3,000 was held to be protected by the section).

[92] S.L.A. 1882, s.54. This explains the uncertain relationship of the section with S.L.A. 1925, s.18.

[93] *Re Morgan's Lease* [1972] Ch. 1 (contract to grant a lease).

[94] S.L.A. 1925, s.112(2).

[95] *Mogridge v. Clapp* [1892] 3 Ch. 382 at 400, *per* Kay L.J. (on S.L.A. 1882, s.54, the precursor to S.L.A. 1925, s.110(1)).

18. It would appear to protect a purchaser only where the transaction is authorised by the Act or settlement,[96] but where there is some peripheral irregularity, such as where a lease was granted at a time when there were no trustees of the settlement,[97] or where the tenant for life exercised a power of disposition for some improper motive.[98] It will have no application where the transaction is wholly outside the powers of the tenant for life.[99] Even in those circumstances, when the transaction is one of leasing, the lease may be validated under the Law of Property Act 1925, provided that the irregularities are of an insubstantial character.[1] However these provisions have sometimes been overlooked.[2]

5. No knowledge of life tenancy. There is a conflict of authority as to　**8–046** whether a purchaser who does not know that he is dealing with a tenant for life can rely upon the protection of section 110(1). Although there is a decision to the contrary,[3] the better view is that he can,[4] because he may have no means of discovering the status of the vendor.[5] Thus in one case, a tenant for life granted a lessee an option to renew a lease at a rent alleged by the remaindermen to be inadequate and therefore a contravention of the Act. He was able to rely upon section 110(1), even though he did not know that the lease had been granted by a tenant for life.[6] If, however, the purchaser knows that the transaction is improper, or if its impropriety is apparent on its face, the purchaser will lose the protection of section 110 since he will not be acting in good faith.[7]

Section 2. Other Provisions Relating to Settled Land

A. Essentials of Settled Land

Land is settled land if "it is or is deemed to be the subject of a settlement".[8]　**8–047** There are three questions of primary importance—

---

[96] *cf. Gilbey v. Rush* (1905) 75 L.J.Ch. 32 at 34 (not included in the report in [1906] 1 Ch. 11).

[97] *Mogridge v. Clapp, supra.*

[98] Wolst. & C. iii, 224. This was evidently the draftsman's intention: *cf. Wolstenholme's Conveyancing Statutes* (10th ed.), p. 456 (commenting on S.L.A. 1882, s.54).

[99] In this way *Weston v. Henshaw* [1950] Ch. 510 (where a mortgage was outside the tenant for life's powers) can be reconciled with *Re Morgan's Lease, supra* (where a contract to grant a lease that was within the tenant for life's powers was upheld).

[1] s.152; *post*, para. 8–078; *Re Morgan's Lease, supra*, at 4; (1971) 87 L.Q.R. 338 (D. W. Elliott).

[2] *cf. Bevan v. Johnston, supra*, where a lease within the tenant for life's powers was held to be void because it had been granted orally instead of by deed. Neither S.L.A. 1925, s.110 nor L.P.A. 1925, s.152 was considered by the court.

[3] *Weston v. Henshaw, supra.*

[4] *Mogridge v. Clapp, supra; Re Morgan's Lease, supra.*

[5] *e.g.* a lessee has no right to see his landlord's title: L.P.A. 1925, s.44; *post*, para. 14–295.

[6] *Re Morgan's Lease, supra.*

[7] *Re Handman and Wilcox's Contract* [1902] 1 Ch. 599; *Gilbey v. Rush, supra; Kisch v. Hawes Bros Ltd* [1935] Ch. 102; *Davies v. Hall* [1954] 1 W.L.R. 855.

[8] S.L.A. 1925, s.2.

(1) whether the land is the subject of a settlement;

(2) who is the tenant for life; and

(3) who are the trustees.

I. DEFINITION OF SETTLEMENT

8–048   **1. "Settlement".** The policy of the Settled Land Act 1925 was to give full powers of management to all limited owners. In general, therefore, any limited interest (*e.g.* for life, or for a determinable fee) created prior to 1997 indicated a settlement. But the statutory definition of "settlement" extended to various other situations and its precise limits were not always clear.

For the purposes of the Act a "settlement" meant either the actual document or documents creating the settlement,[9] or more usually, the state of affairs in relation to certain land brought about by one or more documents.[10] Without a document there could be no "settlement" within the Act.[11] By section 1(1), a settlement was created by any deed, will, agreement, Act of Parliament[12] or other instrument, or any other number of instruments,[13] by which one of the following conditions was satisfied.

8–049   *(a) Succession:* where land stood "for the time being limited in trust for any persons by way of succession".

In addition to cases such as limitations "to A for life, remainder to B in fee simple", this definition seemed to be wide enough to cover the following cases, which were somewhat superfluously set out in the section as independent heads. These were where land was limited in trust for any person in possession—

(i) for an entailed interest, whether or not capable of being barred or defeated;

(ii) for an estate in fee simple or for a term of years absolute subject to an executory gift over (*e.g.* a devise to trustees in trust for "A in fee simple but for B in fee simple when B marries");

(iii) for a base or determinable fee, including a fee determinable by condition,[14] (other than a fee which is a fee simple absolute by

---

[9] See, *e.g.* S.L.A. 1925, ss.1(1), 47, 64.
[10] *Re Ogle's S.E.* [1927] 1 Ch. 229 at 232.
[11] See *Griffiths v. Williams* [1978] 2 E.G.L.R. 121 at 123, revealing an earlier judicial oversight in relation to proprietary estoppel: *post*, para. 8–057.
[12] S.L.A. 1925, s.1(1); see, *e.g. Vine v. Raleigh* [1896] 1 Ch. 37 (settlement composed of a will and a public Act of Parliament, the Accumulations Act 1800). *cf. Talbot v. Scarisbrick* [1908] 1 Ch. 812, where a private Act merely conferred powers and did not directly or indirectly create or incorporate any of the limitations.
[13] *e.g. Re Lord Hereford's S.E.* [1932] W.N. 34 (one private Act of Parliament and three conveyances).
[14] S.L.A. 1925, s.117(1)(iv).

virtue of section 7 of the Law of Property Act 1925)[15] or any corresponding interest in leasehold land.

In all of these cases there was an element of succession sufficient to satisfy the definition in (*a*). Furthermore, all of the interests which were so created are to be treated as subsisting under the settlement,[16] so that they can be overreached by a sale under the statutory power.[17]

(*b*) *Springing interests:* where land was limited in trust for an estate in fee simple or a term of years absolutely contingently on the happening of any event (*e.g.* a devise to trustees on trust for X in fee simple if his brothers died under the age of 21 years[18]). Here too there would usually be an element of succession, although sometimes there might not. It was (and remains) possible for a settlor to direct that the rents and profits should meanwhile be accumulated for the eventual beneficiary,[19] within the limits allowed by the rule against accumulations.[20]   **8–050**

(*c*) *Minors:* where land stood limited in trust for a minor in possession for an estate in fee simple or for a term of years absolute.[21]   **8–051**

(*d*) *Family charges:* where land stood charged, whether voluntarily or in consideration of marriage or by way of family arrangement, with the payment of any sums for the benefit of any persons.[22]   **8–052**

2. "Limited in trust". It will be noted that under heads (*a*) (succession), (*b*) (springing interests) and (*c*) (minors), but not (*d*) (family charges), it was necessary for the land to be "limited in trust" if it was to fall within the definition. However, this requirement was automatically satisfied, since none of the beneficial interests mentioned under heads (*a*), (*b*) and (*c*) could exist as a legal estate.[23] Either the interest was a limited one (*i.e.* less than a fee simple absolute), or it was not yet in possession, or it was held by a minor who since 1925 cannot hold a legal estate.[24] Consequently, on the principle that   **8–053**

---

[15] See *ibid.*, s.1(1)(ii)(c) (as amended by T.L.A.T.A. 1996, s.25(1); Sched. 3, para. 2). The amendment was intended to be no more than declaratory: see (1989) Law Com. No. 181, para. 17.1.

[16] S.L.A. 1925, s.1(4). See *Re Hunter & Hewlett's Contract* [1907] 1 Ch. 46 (on the corresponding provision in S.L.A. 1882, s.2(2)).

[17] For overreaching, see *post*, para. 8–157.

[18] See *Re Bird* [1927] 1 Ch. 210; *Re Walmsley's S.E.* (1911) 105 L.T. 332.

[19] Under a will, this happens in any case, in default of other directions: L.P.A. 1925, s.175.

[20] *Ante*, para. 7–152.

[21] For the position where land is held in trust for a minor after 1996, see *post*, para. 20–011.

[22] For a full discussion of this case, and also of married women subject to restraint upon anticipation, see the previous edition of this work at p. 346. For the effect of family charges created after 1996, see T.L.A.T.A. 1996, s.2(6), Sched. 1, para. 3; *post*, para. 8–125.

[23] L.P.A. 1925, s.1(1), (2); *ante*, paras 4–039 *et seq.* and as to wills, see L.P.(Am.)A. 1924, Sched. 9, para. 3.

[24] L.P.A. 1925, s.1(6); *post*, para. 20–003.

there is usually a trust if the legal estate is in one person and the equitable interest in another,[25] the land would be held upon trust in these cases.[26]

One exception was possible. A fee simple defeasible by condition subsequent might, if so limited, still exist as a legal estate. The reason for this was to ensure that certain types of conditional fees did not fall within the Settled Land Act 1925.[27] It is now clear from an amendment to that Act, which was intended to be no more than declaratory, that there was no settlement, where there was a fee simple which was subject to a legal or equitable right of entry or re-entry.[28] If, however, a trust were employed, the land would have been settled land, as for example where there was, prior to 1997, a devise "to A in fee simple, but if A succeeds to Blackacre then to B" (for wills automatically create a trust[29]) or a grant by deed "to T in fee simple upon trust for A . . . "[30] for a similar interest.

Under head (*d*) no limitation by way of trust was required. Whether the estate which was made subject to the family charges was conveyed directly to the beneficiary or whether it was held in trust for the beneficiary, the land was nevertheless settled land.

8–054 **3. Sale subject to family charges.** There were a number of situations where land which was not settled land before 1926 became so after 1925.[31] One of these caused some difficulty. This was where land was vested in fee simple in a person absolutely entitled, but subject to family charges under the settlement.[32] The owner of such land found that he could only sell it by complying with the troublesome Settled Land Act procedure. To meet this difficulty, it was enacted that a person of full age, who was beneficially entitled to land in fee simple or for a term of years absolute which was settled land solely because it was subject to family charges, might nevertheless create or convey a legal estate subject to the charges in the same way as if the land were not settled land.[33]

---

[25] See *Rayner v. Preston* (1881) 18 Ch.D. 1 at 13; *Hardoon v. Belilos* [1901] A.C. 118 at 123. This will not always be the case: see *Westdeutsche Landesbank Girozentrale v. Islington L.B.C.* [1996] A.C. 669 at 706 at 707.

[26] In *Ungurian v. Lesnoff* [1990] Ch. 206 at 225, Vinelott J. held that land was "limited" in trust if the trust arose by operation of law and not by express limitation (as where land is devised "to A in tail"), notwithstanding earlier remarks to the contrary by Lord Denning M.R. in *Binions v. Evans* [1972] Ch. 359 at 366.

[27] *Ante*, para. 4–041.

[28] See S.L.A. 1925, s.1(1)(ii)(c) (as amended by T.L.A.T.A. 1996, s.25(1); Sched. 3, para. 2); (1989) Law Com. No. 181, para. 17.1.

[29] *Post*, para. 11–125.

[30] A devise in fee simple absolute by the owner of land subject to a fee farm rent (*ante*, para. 4–039) presumably created no settlement (or were it to occur now, a trust of land), since the condition was a legal right attaching to the legal estate itself and was not part of the trusts upon which it was held: *cf.* Wolst. & C. ii, 24.

[31] For a full treatment, see the previous edition of this work at pp. 345–349.

[32] See *ante*, para. 8–052.

[33] L.P.(Am.)A. 1926, s.1. For a fuller treatment, see the previous edition of this work at pp. 346–348.

4. Borderline cases. Prior to the Settled Land Act 1882, a person who was **8–055** given a right to reside in a property for his lifetime or for some lesser determinable period was usually regarded as a mere licensee.[34] However in most cases after 1882 and before 1997, a person with such a right was held to be a tenant for life under the relevant Settled Land Act.[35] This was so, even though the settlor never intended that the person should have the extensive powers which were conferred by statute on a tenant for life.[36] This reflected the policy of the Acts which was "to render land a marketable article notwithstanding the settlement".[37] The fact that a settlement arose in such circumstances gave rise to difficulties in two situations.

(a) Where a settlement inadvertently arose under an order of the court. This **8–056** occurred—

    (i) where a court either sanctioned an agreement made between the parties on divorce by which the wife was allowed to live in a particular house rent free for her lifetime or made such an order itself under the Matrimonial Causes Act 1973[38];

    (ii) where an equity arose by estoppel and the court gave effect to it by granting the claimant a licence to reside on the premises for life or as long as he desired.[39]

In each situation, it would have been open to the court to have made some other order.[40] Thus, in other cases where an equity arising by estoppel might have been satisfied by granting the claimant a right to reside on the property for life, the court has in its discretion granted him some lesser right to ensure that he did not obtain the extensive powers of tenant for life.[41]

---

[34] See, *e.g. Parker v. Parker* (1863) 1 New Rep. 508; *May v. May* (1881) 44 L.T. 412. The right was usually given by will. See generally, B.W. Harvey, *Settlements of Land*, chap. 6.

[35] *Ungurian v. Lesnoff* [1990] Ch. 206 at 226, *per* Vinelott J.; *post*, para. 8–062. See, *e.g. Costello v. Costello* (1994) 27 H.L.R. 12 (where the authorities are reviewed). *cf. Dent v. Dent* [1996] 1 W.L.R. 683, where an undertaking (professionally drawn) that a person could reside on property for her lifetime created a licence. It merely formalised an existing family arrangement and did not involve the creation of any trust or make any disposition of the estate.

[36] *Re Carne's S.E.* [1899] 1 Ch. 324 at 330; *Re Baroness Llanover's Will* [1902] 2 Ch. 679 at 683. *cf. Ayer v. Benton* (1967) 204 E.G. 359, where Buckley J. "found" a trust for sale, quite unwarranted by the facts, to avoid the consequences of an application of the Act.

[37] *Re Mundy & Roper's Contract* [1899] 1 Ch. 275 at 288, *per* Chitty L.J. See too *Lord Henry Bruce v. Marquess of Ailesbury* [1892] A.C. 356 at 361; *Ungurian v. Lesnoff, supra*, at 226.

[38] *Morss v. Morss* [1972] Fam. 264 (but *cf.* Stamp L.J. at 279); *Martin v. Martin* [1978] Fam. 12; and see [1978] Conv. 229 (P. W. Smith).

[39] See, *e.g. Inwards v. Baker* [1965] 2 QB 29; *Williams v. Staite* [1979] Ch. 291. For rights arising by proprietary estoppel, see, *post* para. 13–001.

[40] For the wide powers of the court on divorce, see M.C.A. 1973, ss.24, 24A, 25. The court has a discretion when satisfying an equity arising by estoppel and may ensure that the claimant does not obtain a greater interest than the parties intended. See *post*, para. 13–021.

[41] *Dodsworth v. Dodsworth* (1973) 228 E.G. 1115; *Griffiths v. Williams* [1978] 2 E.G.L.R. 121. *cf. Costello v. Costello* (1994) 27 H.L.R. 12 at 19.

A claimant who became a tenant for life without appreciating that fact was vulnerable because he was unlikely to ensure that a vesting deed or transfer was executed in his favour. There is a risk therefore that his interest might at some stage be defeated by a disposition by the legal owner in favour of a purchaser.[42]

8–057　　*(b) Where the court held that an informal settlement had arisen by estoppel or constructive trust.* In some cases it was held that a settlement had arisen either by proprietary estoppel[43] or under a constructive trust.[44] This appears to be at variance with the requirement of section 1(1) of the Act that the settlement should arise from some document or instrument.[45] Where the interest arose by estoppel, the order of the court giving effect to the equity might itself have been the "instrument".[46] However this reasoning could not apply where a settlement came into being through the imposition of a constructive trust. Such a trust arises either from the common intention of the parties or because it would be inequitable for a landowner to deny a claimant an interest in the property.[47] In such circumstances the claimant's beneficial interest in the property crystallises at the time of his detrimental reliance, not when he seeks to vindicate his rights before a court.[48] It was assumed in such cases that there was a settlement,[49] and that it fell within section 1(1) of the Act because it arose as a result of an "agreement".[50] But this view could not be reconciled with the wording of the Act in cases where the agreement was informal and was not contained in any document.

II. DEFINITION OF TENANT FOR LIFE

1. Tenant for life.

8–058　　*(a) Definition.* The primary definition of "tenant for life" in the Settled Land Act 1925 is "the person of full age who is for the time being entitled under a settlement to possession of settled land for his life".[51] But the

---

[42] *Ante,* para. 8–025.

[43] For proprietary estoppel, see *post,* para. 13–001.

[44] For constructive trusts, see *post,* para. 10–017.

[45] See *Griffiths v. Williams, supra,* at 123; *ante,* para. 8–048.

[46] *Griffiths v. Williams, supra,* at 123.

[47] *Post,* paras 10–022, 10–023.

[48] *Post,* paras 10–030, 13–036.

[49] *Bannister v. Bannister* [1948] 2 All E.R. 133; *Binions v. Evans* [1972] Ch. 359 (Lord Denning dissenting on this point); *Ungurian v. Lesnoff* [1990] Ch. 206. For criticism of these decisions see (1977) 93 L.Q.R. 561 (J. A. Hornby); (1991) 107 L.Q.R. 596 (J. Hill). *cf. Ivory v. Palmer* [1975] I.C.R. 340 (right of occupation granted for the term of the claimant's employment, which was said to be "for life", conferred only a contractual licence); and *Chandler v. Kerley* [1978] 1 W.L.R. 693 at 698.

[50] *Ungurian v. Lesnoff, supra,* at 226. Where A claimed an interest under a constructive trust in land owned by B, the "settlement" could not have been the conveyance of the land to B, because A might have acquired his interest only subsequently: *post,* para. 10–027. *cf.* (1991) 107 L.Q.R. 596 at 599 (J. Hill).

[51] S.L.A. 1925, s.19(1).

definition also includes any person (other than a statutory owner[52]) who has the statutory powers.[53] As those powers are conferred not only on those who have life interests (by section 19), but also on many other persons (under section 20), "tenant for life" has for this purpose an artificially extended meaning. Generally speaking, every limited owner who is of full age and beneficially entitled in possession under the settlement[54] is thus a "tenant for life", so that the definition of tenant for life is complementary to the definition of settled land. A "tenant for life" may thus be a person entitled to a life interest, a tenant in tail,[55] a tenant in fee simple subject to a gift over or to family charges, a tenant for years not at a rent terminable on life,[56] a tenant *pur autre vie*, a person entitled to the income of land for his own or any other life, and others. As explained later,[57] two or more persons entitled jointly may also constitute the tenant for life.

(b) Special cases. Although it is essential that the person claiming to have the powers of tenant for life should fit precisely into one or other of the specified classes, there is usually little difficulty in ascertaining him. The following cases do however require special mention.[58]   **8–059**

(1) TENANTS FOR YEARS. The Settled Land Act 1925 is only concerned with "family" and not "commercial" leases. The definition of tenant for life extends to tenants for years determinable on life,[59] and tenants *pur autre vie*, provided in both cases that they do not hold "merely under a lease at a rent".[60]   **8–060**

(2) PERSONS ENTITLED TO THE INCOME OF THE LAND. If the settlement gave the land to trustees upon trust to pay the income to A for life, all the statutory powers are vested in A and not in the trustees.[61] A can therefore call for a vesting deed in his own favour, and so obtain the right to occupy the land.[62] To fall within this category—   **8–061**

---

[52] *Ante*, para. 8–016.

[53] S.L.A. 1925, s.117(1)(xxvii).

[54] See *post*, para. 8–062.

[55] Even if unable to bar his entail, unless the property was purchased with money provided by Parliament and statute prohibits barring the entail: S.L.A. 1925, s.20(1)(i). But see *Re Duke of Marlborough's Parliamentary Estates* (1891) 8 T.L.R. 179; *Re Duke of Marlborough's Blenheim Estates* (1892) 8 T.L.R. 582; and see S.L.A. 1925, s.23(2).

[56] S.L.A. 1925, s.20(1)(iv). See too *ibid.* s.20(1)(vi) (determinable interests); *Re Boyer's S.E.* [1916] 2 Ch. 404.

[57] *Post*, para. 9–089.

[58] For fuller treatment, see the previous edition of this work at pp. 350–352.

[59] *Re Mundy & Roper's Contract* [1899] 1 Ch. 275 at 298.

[60] s.20(1)(iv), (v). A person who paid a rent of £1 per annum was held not to be the tenant for life: *Re Catling* [1931] 2 Ch. 359.

[61] S.L.A. 1925, s.20(1)(viii); *post*, para. 8–096.

[62] There was no such right to possession prior to 1926, unles the court thought it proper to give it to him: see *Re Bagot's Settlement* [1894] 1 Ch. 177.

(i) the person must be entitled to the whole of the net income of the land,[63] and not merely to some part of it[64]; and

(ii) the right must be for his lifetime, for the life of some other person, or until sale of the land or the determination of his interest.[65]

8–062 *(c) Beneficially entitled in possession.* A tenant for life must, as an additional requirement, be of full age (*i.e.* not a minor[66]) and beneficially entitled in possession under the settlement.[67] A future interest in remainder or reversion will not suffice.[68] However, a right to occupy will suffice, as where, in the will of a testator who died before 1997, the trustees of his settlement are instructed to permit his widow to reside in a specific house for as long as she might wish.[69]

Although the terms "beneficially entitled" and "under the settlement" appear only in section 19 (in relation to a tenant with an actual life interest) and not in section 20 (as regards those with other interests such as a tenant in tail), it is thought that the requirement that the tenant for life should have a beneficial interest is implied in all cases.[70] An executor of a person beneficially entitled is also, exceptionally, regarded as satisfying the words "beneficially entitled".[71] Although he is not entitled for his own benefit, he can represent the deceased's beneficial interest as against others. Where the tenant for life assigns his interest, he remains tenant for life for the purposes of the Act.[72] This is because the assignee is entitled under the assignment and not "under the settlement".[73]

8–063 *(d) Effect of definition.* The practical effect of the definition is that where there is some person of full age beneficially entitled to possess or occupy some specific land or to receive the whole of the income from it, that person will have the statutory powers.

---

[63] It is not enough that he is an object of a power of appointment in respect of such income: *Re Atkinson* (1886) 31 Ch.D. 577; *Re Gallenga W.T.* [1938] 1 All E.R. 106; Wolst. & C. ii, 78, 79.

[64] *Re Frewen* [1926] Ch. 580.

[65] *Re Astor* [1922] 1 Ch. 364.

[66] A corporation may therefore be a life tenant: *Re Earl of Carnarvon's Chesterfield S.E.* [1927] 1 Ch. 138 (limited company).

[67] S.L.A. 1925, ss.19(1), 20(1).

[68] *Re Morgan* (1883) 24 Ch.D. 114 at 116; and see *Re Strangeways* (1886) 34 Ch.D. 423; *Re Martyn* (1900) 69 L.J.Ch. 733; *Re Beauchamp's W.T.* [1914] 1 Ch. 676.

[69] *Re Carne's S.E.* [1899] 1 Ch. 324. See similarly *Re Baroness Llanover's Will* [1903] 2 Ch. 16; *Re Boyer's S.E.* [1916] 2 Ch. 404; *Re Anderson* [1920] 1 Ch. 175; *Re Gibbons* [1920] 1 Ch. 372. A mere right to occupy such one of 14 houses as the beneficiary might choose was not enough: *Re Bond* (1904) 48 S.J. 192.

[70] This was so prior to 1926: see *Re Jemmett & Guest's Contract* [1907] 1 Ch. 629. It is not thought that the comparatively minor changes in drafting made in 1925 have affected this conclusion.

[71] See *Vine v. Raleigh* [1896] 1 Ch. 37; *Re Johnson* [1914] 2 Ch. 134.

[72] *Re Earl of Carnarvon's Chesterfield S.E.* [1927] 1 Ch. 138.

[73] *ibid.* This is also the result of S.L.A. 1925, s.104, explained *post*, para. 8–102.

The position where two or more persons are entitled jointly or in common in this way is explained later.[74]

2. Cases where there is no tenant for life. In some cases there may be a settlement, but no person entitled as tenant for life. Examples include the following[75]:

    (i) Where the person beneficially entitled is a minor.[76]

    (ii) Where no person is entitled to the whole of the net income, as where there is a trust to pay a fixed annuity to X, with a direction to accumulate the balance.[77]

    (iii) Where no person is entitled to the income at all, as where there is a discretionary trust for the trustees to pay the income to such person or persons as they think fit.

    (iv) Where trustees are directed to accumulate the income for a future contingent beneficiary, without any other limitations which create successive interests.[78]

In any case where there is no tenant for life, the legal estate and statutory powers are vested in the statutory owner.[79] A statutory owner is not subject to all the duties and restrictions imposed upon tenants for life, unless they are expressed to apply. The definition of "tenant for life" specifically excludes statutory owners.[80]

III. DEFINITION OF TRUSTEES OF THE SETTLEMENT

1. The definition. The trustees of the settlement are defined by section 30 of the Settled Land Act 1925. There are five heads, which must be applied in turn. If there are trustees under one head, they will exclude any trustees under a subsequent head.[81] The definition is as follows.

    (i) The persons who, under the settlement, are trustees with power to sell the land (even if this power is subject to the consent of anyone, *e.g.* the tenant for life[82]) or with power to consent to or to approve the exercise of a power of sale.[83]

8–064

8–065

---

[74] *Post*, paras 9–089, 9–090.

[75] *cf.* Wolst. & C. iii, 86.

[76] *Ante*, para. 8–015. For the special powers of the statutory owners in such a case, see S.L.A. 1925, s.102.

[77] *Re Jeffreys* [1939] Ch. 205.

[78] In this case too special powers of interim management are conferred by S.L.A. 1925, s.102.

[79] *Ante*, para. 8–016.

[80] S.L.A. 1925, s.117(1)(xxviii); *Re Craven's S.E.* [1926] Ch. 985.

[81] For a list of the trustees' duties and an explanation of the documents used in case of a change of trustees, see *post*, paras 8–107, 8–108.

[82] *Constable v. Constable* (1886) 32 Ch.D. 233.

[83] S.L.A. 1925, s.30(1)(i).

For example, if in a settlement on A for life, with remainders over, there was provision giving X and Y power to sell the land, this made them trustees of the settlement, in preference even to any other persons expressly appointed Settled Land Act trustees. X and Y would in fact have no power to sell, for as will be seen,[84] this power is given to A, the tenant for life.[85] Nevertheless, the attempt to give them the power sufficed to make them trustees of the settlement.[86]

> (ii) The persons declared by the settlement to be trustees thereof for the purposes of the Settled Land Acts 1882 to 1890, or 1925, or any of them.[87]

This is the head under which the trustees of the settlement were usually to be found. To satisfy this head, it was necessary to specify in the settlement that X and Y were appointed not merely trustees or trustees of the settlement, but "for the purposes of the Settled Land Act 1925".[88]

> (iii) Persons who, under the settlement, are trustees with—
>
>   (a) a power or duty to sell; or
>   (b) a power to consent to or approve the exercise of the power of sale of,
>
>   *other* land held under the same settlement and upon the same trusts.[89]
>
> (iv) Persons who, under the settlement, are trustees with—
>
>   (a) a *future* power or duty to sell; or
>   (b) a power of consenting to or approving the exercise of such a future power of sale,
>
>   even if the power or duty does not take effect in all events.[90]

8–066   Thus if there was a settlement of Blackacre and Whiteacre which attempted to give the trustees (albeit ineffectively) a power of sale over Blackacre alone, clause (iii) made those trustees Settled Land Act trustees of both properties.[91] Again, if Greenacre is settled on A for life with remainder to X and Y upon trust to sell the land,[92] clause (iv) made X and Y Settled Land Act trustees.[93]

---

[84] *Post*, para. 8–096.
[85] S.L.A. 1925, s.108(2).
[86] *ibid.*, s.30(2).
[87] *ibid.*, s.30(1)(ii).
[88] See, *e.g. Re Bentley* (1885) 54 L.J.Ch. 782 ("trustees").
[89] S.L.A. 1925, s.30(1)(iii) (as amended by T.L.A.T.A. 1996, s.25(1), Sched. 3, para. 2).
[90] S.L.A. 1925, s.30(1)(iv) (as amended by T.L.A.T.A. 1996, s.25(1), Sched. 2, para. 2).
[91] *Re Moore* [1906] 1 Ch. 789.
[92] Which will now take effect as a trust of land. For the effect of any such duty to sell, see T.L.A.T.A. 1996, s.4; *post*, para. 8–126.
[93] *Re Johnson's S.E.* [1913] W.N. 222. This would not be the case if the trust to sell was void for perpetuity: *Re Davies and Kent's Contract* [1910] 2 Ch. 35 at 45. For the perpetuity rule, see *ante*, para. 7–018.

Under both (iii) and (iv), it is immaterial that the powers given by the settlement are, under the Act, not exercisable by the trustees.[94]

    (v) The persons appointed by deed by those able to dispose of the whole equitable interest in the settled land.[95]

For example, if land is settled on A for life, remainder to B in tail, A and B can appoint trustees of the settlement. B could bar the entail with A's consent, and thus between them they could dispose of the whole interest in the land.[96]

    There is nothing in the Act which prevents the tenant for life himself from being one of the trustees, or even two or more joint tenants for life from being the sole trustees.[97] It is of course the primary duty of the trustees to protect the interests of future beneficiaries against abuse of the tenant for life's powers.

2. Personal representatives. Where a settlement arose under a will or intestacy and there were no trustees under any other provisions, the personal representatives were trustees of the settlement until other trustees were appointed.[98] This provision dealt with the most frequent cause of a lack of trustees, namely a will made without proper legal advice. Where even this provision failed (*e.g.* where there was a home-made settlement created *inter vivos*) the court was empowered to appoint trustees on the application of any person interested under the settlement.[99] Once persons have become trustees, whether by order of the court or otherwise, they or their successors in office remain trustees as long as the settlement subsists.[1]   **8–067**

3. Referential settlements. Special provision was made[2] for referential settlements, that is to say, settlements which referred to earlier settlements, *e.g.* directing Blackacre to be held on the same trusts as Whiteacre, which was already settled.[3] Unless trustees were separately appointed under head (ii) above, the trustees of the earlier settlement became trustees of the later settlement which referred to it.[4]   **8–068**

---

[94] S.L.A. 1925, s.30(2); *post*, para. 8–096.
[95] *ibid.*, s.30(1)(v).
[96] *Re Spearman S.E.* [1906] 2 Ch. 502, *cf. Re Spencer's S.E.* [1903] 1 Ch. 75 (appointment executed by some only of the beneficiaries held invalid).
[97] See *Re Jackson's S.E.* [1902] 1 Ch. 258; *Re Davies and Kent's Contract*, *supra*, at 50, 51; *Re Pennant's W.T.* [1970] Ch. 75; and see S.L.A. 1925, s.68(3).
[98] S.L.A. 1925, s.30(3). If there was only one personal representative, and he was not a trust corporation, he was bound to appoint another trustee to act with him: *ibid*. The section does not empower the personal representatives to retire and appoint new trustees, but they may do so under T.A. 1925, ss.64(1), 68(5); *Re Dark* [1954] Ch. 291.
[99] S.L.A. 1925, s.34.
[1] *ibid.*, s.33. See the example in Wolst. & C. iii, 101. As to appointment, replacement and removal of trustees, see *post*, paras 10–052, 10–056, 10–059, 10–067.
[2] S.L.A. 1925, s.32.
[3] See, *e.g. Re Shelton's S.E.* [1928] W.N. 27.
[4] S.L.A. 1925, s.32(1); see, *e.g. Re Adair* (1927) 71 S.J. 844. For the difficulties to which referential settlements could give rise, see the previous edition of this work at pp. 356, 357.

B. Compound Settlements[5]

8–069   "Compound settlement" is the term used to describe the situation when the trusts affecting the land were created by two or more instruments, as where a settlement was followed by a resettlement. Occasionally it is used to describe a referential settlement.[6] However, it is best confined to two or more sets of trusts applying to one parcel of land rather than two or more parcels of land governed by similar trusts.[7] For example, suppose that land had been settled on A for life with remainder to his son in tail, and that on the son attaining his majority, A and the son barred the entail and resettled the property on A for life, with remainder to the son for life and remainders over. Since a settlement might consist of a single instrument or any number of instruments,[8] there would then be three distinct settlements to consider—

> (i) the original settlement;

> (ii) the resettlement; and

> (iii) the compound settlement, which is a separate entity.[9]

8–070   It should be noted in this context that, although the Trusts of Land and Appointment of Trustees Act 1996 precludes the creation of any new settlements after 1996,[10] that is subject to two exceptions,[11] namely where a settlement is created on the occasion of an alteration in any interest in, or of a person becoming entitled under, a settlement which—

> (i) was in existence on January 1, 1997 (when the Act came into force); or

> (ii) derived from a settlement within (i), or a derivative settlement within (ii).

The effect of (i) is that any resettlement will itself take effect as a settlement under the Settled Land Act 1925, and not as a trust of land. The effect of (ii) is that where a sub-settlement is created under a power of appointment that is contained in a settlement, resettlement or previous sub-settlement, it too will be governed by the Settled Land Act 1925. The reason for these exceptions was to prevent management conflicts that might otherwise have arisen, if the settlement had been governed by the 1925 Act, but any resettlement or sub-settlement had taken effect as a trust of land. Under a trust of land, the legal estate and powers of disposition are vested in the trustees and not in the person

---

[5] For a fuller account, and for the difficulties that sometimes arose before 1926, see the previous edition of this work, p. 357.
[6] See, *e.g. Re Byng's S.E.* [1892] 2 Ch. 219; for such settlements, see the text above.
[7] See *Re Adair, supra.*
[8] S.L.A. 1925, s.1(1).
[9] See *Re Coull's S.E.* [1905] 1 Ch. 712 at 720.
[10] T.L.A.T.A. 1996, s.2(1); *ante,* paras 8–001, 8–011.
[11] T.L.A.T.A. 1996, s.2(2).

beneficially entitled in possession,[12] subject to a power for them to delegate their functions to such person.[13] If the parties to any resettlement or sub-settlement wish it to take effect as a trust for land, they may so provide in the instrument or instruments by which it is created.[14]

Under a compound settlement, the tenant for life can exercise any additional powers conferred by either settlement, and also overreach the rights of the beneficiaries under both the settlement and the resettlement.[15] The trustees of the original settlement (provided it is still subsisting[16]) or, in default,[17] the trustees of the resettlement, will be the trustees of the compound settlement.[18]

C. Powers and Position of a Tenant for Life

I. POWERS OF A TENANT FOR LIFE

A tenant for life can of course deal with his limited interest in the land as he likes, subject only to the law of waste.[19] Therefore he may lease it rent-free, or give away valuable rights over it such as easements. However, these transactions will not bind his successors since they can take effect only out of his interest.[20] His successors will be bound only by transactions authorised by the Act or by any additional powers given by the settlement.[21] For this reason an account of those powers must be given. It should be noted that although the legal estate is vested in the tenant for life, he cannot dispose of any legal estate or interest except as provided by the Act.[22]

8–071

A tenant for life is normally subject to no control in the exercise of his statutory powers.[23] The chief safeguards against abuse are—

(1) his position as trustee for the beneficiaries;

(2) the provision that in the case of the most important powers he must give notice to the trustees of his intention to exercise them; and

(3) the provision that in a few exceptional cases he must not exercise his powers without the leave of the trustees or an order of the court.

---

[12] *ibid.*, s.6; *post*, para. 8–136.

[13] *ibid.*, s.9; *post*, para. 8–145.

[14] *ibid.*, s.2(3).

[15] See *Re Cowley S.E.* [1926] Ch. 725.

[16] *Re Gordon and Adams' Contract* [1914] 1 Ch 110; compare *Re Lord Alington and the L.C.C.'s Contract* [1927] 2 Ch. 253; S.L.A. 1925, ss.3, 33.

[17] *Re Cayley and Evans' Contract* [1930] 2 Ch. 143.

[18] S.L.A. 1925, s.31(1), as amended by L.P.(Am.)A. 1926, Sched. See, *e.g. Re Symons* [1927] 1 Ch. 344.

[19] *Ante*, para. 3–098.

[20] S.L.A. 1925, s.18(1).

[21] *Ante*, para. 8–014.

[22] S.L.A. 1925, s.18; *ante*, para. 8–042. But if the disposition complies with the Act, it need not be intended to be an exercise of the statutory power: *Re Pennant's W.T.* [1970] Ch. 75.

[23] One joint tenant for life cannot force the other to sell: *Re 90 Thornhill Road, Tolworth* [1970] Ch. 261.

The treatment which is given to the powers of a tenant for life (and those of the trustees of the settlement) is, in this edition, considerably more abbreviated than in the previous one.[24] This reflects the diminishing importance of settlements under the Settled Land Act 1925, which were not very common even before their prospective abolition by the Trusts of Land and Appointment of Trustees Act 1996. Furthermore, prior to 1997, both trustees for sale[25] and trustees of charitable and ecclesiastical trusts[26] had, in relation to any land held in trust, the same powers as a tenant for life and the trustees of the settlement under the Settled Land Act 1925. By contrast, after 1996, for the purposes of exercising their functions as trustees, trustees of land[27] have in relation to the land, all the powers of an absolute owner.[28]

8–072   **1. The tenant for life's position as trustee.** This fundamental safeguard has already been explained.[29]

8–073   **2. Powers exercisable upon giving notice.** If the tenant for life intends to make a sale, exchange, lease, mortgage or charge, or to grant an option, he must give notice to the trustees of the settlement and, if known, to the solicitor for the trustees.[30] Trustees who are also the statutory owner are not required to give notice to themselves.[31] The notice must be given by a registered or recorded delivery letter posted at least one calendar[32] month before the transaction or the contract to enter into it.[33] The notice is invalid unless when it is given the trustees consist of two or more persons or a trust corporation.[34] Thus if there are no trustees, a tenant for life is not entitled to exercise these powers,[35] and an injunction may be granted to restrain him from doing so.[36]

The object of this provision for giving notice seems to be to enable the trustees to prevent any improper dealing[37] by applying to the court for an injunction.[38] Furthermore, if the tenant for life fails to give notice, he may be

---

[24] To which reference should be made: see pp. 360–377.

[25] L.P.A. 1925, s.28(1) (repealed by T.L.A.T.A. 1996, s.25(2), Sched. 4).

[26] S.L.A. 1925, s.29 (repealed by T.L.A.T.A. 1996, s.25(2), Sched. 4).

[27] Who include trustees of charitable and ecclesiastical trusts: T.L.A.T.A. 1996, ss.1, 2(5); *post*, para. 20–029.

[28] T.L.A.T.A. 1996, s.6(1); *post*, para. 8–136.

[29] *Ante*, paras 8–093, 8–095.

[30] S.L.A. 1925, s.101(1).

[31] See *Re Countess of Dudley's Contract* (1887) 35 Ch.D. 338 at 342.

[32] Interpretation Act 1978, Sched.

[33] S.L.A. 1925, s.101(1); Recorded Delivery Service Act 1962, s.1, Sched. 1. This provision is cast in an alternative form which seems to be satisfied by a notice given at least a month before the transaction, even if less than a month before the contract: *Duke of Marlborough v. Sartoris* (1886) 32 Ch.D. 616; *sed quaere.*

[34] S.L.A. 1925, s.101(1).

[35] *Re Bentley* (1885) 54 L.J.Ch. 782.

[36] *Wheelwright v. Walker (No. 1)* (1883) 23 Ch.D. 752.

[37] See *Lord Monson's S.E.* [1898] 1 Ch. 427 at 432.

[38] See *Hampden v. Earl of Buckinghamshire* [1893] 2 Ch. 531, where some of the beneficiaries obtained an injunction.

refused the equitable remedy of specific performance against a purchaser.[39] But for general purposes the requirement of notice gives little protection, for—

(i) although the trustees may bring an improper transaction before the court,[40] they are not apparently obliged to do so[41];

(ii) except in the case of a mortgage or charge, a notice in general terms suffices.[42] However, the tenant for life must, at the request of a trustee of the settlement, give reasonable information as to any sales, exchanges or leases effected, in progress or immediately intended[43];

(iii) any trustee may by writing accept less than one month's notice or waive it altogether,[44] even if the contract was made before any trustees had been appointed[45]; and

(iv) a person dealing in good faith with the tenant for life is not concerned to inquire whether notice has been given.[46] Even if there are no trustees, a purchaser in good faith for value of a legal estate gets a good title if the transaction is one on which no capital money is payable,[47] *e.g.* the grant of a lease without a premium.[48]

Each of the powers in respect of which notice is normally required must be explained in outline.[49]

(a) Power to sell. A tenant for life may sell all or part of the settled land, **8–074** or any easement, right or privilege of any kind over the land.[50] The general rule is that he must obtain the best consideration in money that can reasonably be obtained.[51] It follows that, subject to certain exceptions, he cannot give away the land or any rights over it.[52] The sale may be by auction or by private treaty. It may be made in one lot or several lots and free from or subject to

---

[39] Wolst. & C. iii, 204. For a vendor's right to specific performance, see *post*, para. 12–115.
[40] S.L.A. 1925, s.93.
[41] *ibid.*, s.97.
[42] *ibid.*, s.101(2). See *Re Ray's S.E.* (1884) 25 Ch.D. 464.
[43] S.L.A. 1925, s.101(3).
[44] *ibid.*, s.101(4).
[45] *Hatten v. Russell* (1888) 38 Ch.D. 334.
[46] S.L.A. 1925, s.101(5).
[47] *ibid.*, ss.104(4), 117(1)(xxi).
[48] See *Mogridge v. Clapp* [1892] 3 Ch. 382.
[49] For a fuller account, see the previous edition at pp. 360–377.
[50] S.L.A. 1925, s.38(i).
[51] *ibid.*, s.39(1). See *Wheelwright v. Walker (No. 2)* (1883) 31 W.R. 912. *cf. Buttle v. Saunders* [1950] 2 All E.R. 193; (1975) 39 Conv. (N.S.) 177 (A. Samuels).
[52] For these exceptions, see S.L.A. 1925, ss.54 (water rights), 55 (public or charitable purposes— see too *ibid.* s. 57(2)), 56 (dedication of highways and open spaces). Even in these cases, the disposition must be for the general benefit of the settled land.

stipulations as to title or otherwise.[53] If the land is sold at auction, the tenant for life may fix a reserve and buy it in.[54]

8–075 *(b) Power to exchange.* Settled land, or any part of it, or any easement, right or privilege over it, may be exchanged for other land or any easement, right or privilege.[55] For "equality of exchange" (*i.e.* to adjust any difference in value) capital money may be paid or received[56] and every exchange must be for the best consideration obtainable.[57] But settled land in England and Wales may not be given in exchange for land outside England and Wales.[58]

(c) Power to lease

8–076 (1) THE POWER. The settled land, or any part of it, or any easement, right or privilege over it (*e.g.* for shooting or fishing, or to let down the surface by mining[59]) may be leased for any period not exceeding—

(i) 999 years for building or forestry;

(ii) 100 years for mining;

(iii) 50 years for any other purpose.[60]

The Act provides definitions and lays down specific requirements in respect of building, mining and forestry leases.[61] Where land is to be leased in lots there are certain restrictions to ensure an even apportionment of the rent.[62] The tenant for life has no power to lease settled land together with his own land unless the rent is apportioned between the two.[63]

"Lease" includes an agreement for a lease (as it does throughout the Act[64]), but in this context it has been held to include only such tenancy agreements as take effect either in law or in equity as demises.[65] Contracts for the grant of future leases are the subject of different provisions.[66]

8–077 (2) CONDITIONS OF LEASE. Every lease of settled land must comply with the following conditions.

---

[53] S.L.A. 1925, s.39(6).
[54] *ibid.*, s.39(7).
[55] *ibid.*, s.38(iii).
[56] *ibid.*, ss.38(iii), 73(1)(v).
[57] *ibid.*, s.40(1).
[58] *ibid.*, s.40(3).
[59] *Sitwell v. Earl of Londesborough* [1905] 1 Ch. 460.
[60] S.L.A. 1925, s.41. The court may extend the periods (*post*, para. 8–077) and the limits do not apply to mortgage terms: see *post*, para. 8–080.
[61] See S.L.A. 1925, ss.44–48; 117(1)(x). For further details, see the previous edition of this work at p. 362.
[62] S.L.A. 1925, s.44(3); *Re Rycroft's Settlement* [1962] Ch. 263.
[63] *Re Rycroft's Settlement, supra.*
[64] S.L.A. 1925, s.117(1)(x).
[65] *Re Rycroft's Settlement, supra*; but see *Re Morgan's Lease* [1972] Ch. 1, holding that an executory contract is included. For this distinction, see *post*, para. 14–040.
[66] *Post*, para. 8–092.

(i) It must be made by deed.[67]

(ii) It must be made to take effect in possession not more than one year after its date, or in reversion after an existing lease with not more than seven years to run at the date of the new lease.[68] Thus if a tenant for life grants a lease to commence in 14 months' time it is invalid[69] unless it is to commence on the determination of an existing lease.[70] But a *contract* to grant a lease in, say, 10 years' time is valid.[71]

(iii) It must reserve the best rent reasonably obtainable in the circumstances, regard being had to any fine taken, and to any money laid out or to be laid out for the benefit of the land.[72] "Fine" is widely defined as including any premium or fore-gift, and any payment, condition or benefit in the nature of a fine, premium or fore-gift,[73] so that although it usually means a lump sum paid for the grant of the lease, it is not confined to such payments.[74] Any fine is capital money.[75]

(iv) It must contain a covenant by the lessee for payment of rent and a condition of re-entry (*i.e.* a provision for forfeiture of the lease) on rent not being paid within a specified time not exceeding 30 days.[76]

(v) A counterpart (*i.e.* a copy) of the lease must be executed by the lessee and delivered to the tenant for life. It is sufficient evidence that this has been done if the tenant for life duly executes the lease.[77]

The normal rules that a lease must be made by deed and that notice must be given to the trustees is relaxed in certain cases. No notice is required if the lease is not for more than 21 years, but otherwise satisfies the conditions set out above.[78] Furthermore, if the lease is not for more than three years,[79] it may

---

[67] S.L.A. 1925, s.42(1)(i). *cf. Bevan v. Johnston* [1990] 2 E.G.L.R. 33.

[68] S.L.A. 1925, s.42(1)(i).

[69] See *Kisch v. Hawes Bros Ltd* [1935] Ch. 102; but see also L.P.A. 1925, s.152, explained *post*, para. 8–078.

[70] For the general rules about reversionary leases, see *post*, para. 14–061.

[71] See the preceding paragraph.

[72] S.L.A. 1925, s.42(1)(ii).

[73] *ibid.*, s.117(1)(xxii).

[74] *Lloyd-Jones v. Clark-Lloyd* [1919] 1 Ch. 424 at 438; and see *Waite v. Jennings* [1906] 2 K.B. 11; *Comber v. Fleet Electrics Ltd* [1955] 1 W.L.R. 566.

[75] S.L.A. 1925, s.42(4); see *Pumford v. W. Butler & Co. Ltd* [1914] 2 Ch. 353; for certain special rules applicable to building, forestry and mining leases, see the previous edition of this work at p. 363.

[76] S.L.A. 1925, s.42(1)(iii).

[77] *ibid.*, s.42(2).

[78] *ibid.*, s.42(5).

[79] And this appears to include a weekly or other periodic tenancy, even though it may last more than three years: see *Davies v. Hall* [1954] 1 W.L.R. 855.

also be made merely in writing and not by deed, with an agreement, instead of a covenant to pay the rent.[80] In the case of building and mining leases, the court may relax the statutory requirements, including the maximum term, if these conflict with what is customary in the district or make it difficult to grant such leases.[81]

8–078   (3) DEFECTIVE LEASES. A lease which does not comply with the requirements of the Act is void, except so far as it binds the beneficial interest of the tenant for life.[82] But under statutory provisions now contained in the Law of Property Act 1925,[83] leases which are invalid because they fail to comply with the terms of a power may nevertheless be effective in equity at the lessee's option as contracts for leases,[84] subject to such variations as are necessary in order to comply with the power. This saving enactment applies only if the lease was made in good faith and the lessee has taken possession,[85] so that only sitting tenants are benefited. By judicial construction its operation is confined, it seems, to the curing of minor irregularities only, such as the omission of some restriction or condition, or a mistake in form.[86]

Furthermore, the Settled Land Act 1925[87] gives special protection to a purchaser (including a tenant) who deals in good faith with the tenant for life.[88] He is conclusively presumed, as against those entitled under the settlement, to have given the best consideration reasonably obtainable and to have complied with the other requirements of the Act. If the consideration is insufficient, therefore, the title of such tenant is none the worse, and the point can only be disputed as between the beneficiaries under the settlement. If, however, the lease on its face violates the requirements of the Act, the tenant will not be taken to have dealt in good faith and he may have to be prepared to prove that he gave the best consideration reasonably obtainable, or complied with any of the other statutory conditions which are alleged to have been violated.[89]

---

[80] S.L.A. 1925, s.42(5). *cf. Bevan v. Johnston* [1990] 2 E.G.L.R. 33.

[81] S.L.A. 1925, s.46.

[82] *ibid.* s.18(1) (*ante*, para. 8–042); *Bevan v. Johnston, supra.*

[83] s.152. The provisions date back to the Leases Acts 1849, 1850.

[84] Registrable as estate contracts (Wolst. & C. i, 281); but in any case remaindermen or reversioners will be bound since they are not purchasers: L.C.A. 1972, s.4, *ante* para. 5–117. But it is arguable that registration is not required, since L.P.A. 1925, s.152(1), provides that the contract "shall take effect" against successors in title. Where title is registered, the lessee will be protected as he will be in actual occupation, even if registration were otherwise required: see L.R.A. 1925, s.70(1)(g); *ante*, para. 6–047.

[85] See L.P.A. 1925, s.152(1).

[86] *Hallett to Martin* (1883) 24 Ch.D. 624; *Brown v. Peto* [1900] 1 QB 346; *Re Newell* [1900] 1 Ch. 30; Halsb. vol. 27(1), para. 120. This provision appears to have been overlooked in *Bevan v. Johnston* [1990] 2 E.G.L.R. 33, where a weekly tenancy that had been granted orally (rather than in writing as required by S.L.A. 1925, s.42(5)) was held to be void.

[87] s.110(1).

[88] See *ante*, para. 8–045.

[89] *Davies v. Hall* [1954] 1 W.L.R. 855, explaining the dictum of Farwell J. in *Kisch v. Hawes Bros Ltd* [1935] Ch. 102 at 109, 110; and see *Re Morgan's Lease* [1972] Ch. 1, holding that the protection extends to an option to renew a lease. See generally (1971) 87 L.Q.R. 338 (D. W. Elliott).

As a corollary to his power to grant leases, a tenant for life has wide powers of accepting surrenders of leases[90] and of varying or waiving the terms of any lease.[91] These powers are exercisable without notice to the trustees.

(4) RENT FROM LEASES. The normal rule is that the tenant for life is entitled **8–079** to the whole of the rent from leases of the settled land.[92] It has already been noted that this rule does not apply to mining leases, which are subject to special rules.[93]

(d) Power to mortgage. In the absence of a contrary provision in the **8–080** settlement,[94] a tenant for life has no power to mortgage or charge the legal estate for his own benefit. If he wishes to raise money for his own use, he can of course do so by mortgaging his beneficial interest. The legal estate, on the other hand, can be mortgaged or charged for the following purposes only.

   (i) To provide money which is required to be raised under the provisions of the settlement,[95] *e.g.* portions.[96]

   (ii) To provide money where it is reasonably required[97] for certain specified purposes.[98] These are all cases connected with the well-being of the land, and include—

      (a) discharging an incumbrance of a permanent nature (and not, *e.g.* annual sums payable for a life or term of years[99]) on all or part of the land, including such matters as charges for making up streets.[1] Thus it may be possible to pay off two or more mortgages by raising money on a new mortgage at a lower rate of interest,[2] and the whole of the land may be mortgaged in order to pay off a mortgage on part[3];

      (b) paying for authorised improvements[4];

      (c) equality of exchange[5];

---

[90] S.L.A. 1925, s.52.

[91] *ibid.,* s.59. See *Re Saville S.E.* [1931] 2 Ch. 210 (mining lease for 60 years extended to 100 years).

[92] See, *e.g. Re Wix* [1916] 1 Ch. 279.

[93] *Ante,* para. 3–113. See S.L.A. 1925, s.47; and the previous edition of this work at pp. 365, 366. The rules applicable to a tenant for life who works the minerals himself are different from those which are applicable where he leases the land: see *ante,* para. 3–112.

[94] See *Re Egertons' S.E.* [1926] Ch. 357.

[95] S.L.A. 1925, s.16(1): if such sums have already been raised by means of an equitable charge affecting the whole of the land, the tenant for life can replace this charge by a legal mortgage or charge: *ibid.* Whether the money has already been raised or not, on being requested in writing the tenant for life is bound to create the requisite legal mortgage or charge: *ibid.*

[96] For these, see *ante,* para. 7–173.

[97] *Re Clifford* [1902] 1 Ch. 87; *Re Bruce* [1905] 2 Ch. 372 at 376.

[98] S.L.A. 1925, s.71(1).

[99] *ibid.,* s.71(2).

[1] *Re Smith's S.E.* [1901] 1 Ch. 689; and see *Re Pizzi* [1907] 1 Ch. 67.

[2] *More v. More* (1889) 37 W.R. 414.

[3] *Re Lord Monson's S.E.* [1898] 1 Ch. 427.

[4] See *post,* para. 8–088.

[5] *Ante,* para. 8–075.

    (d) extinguishing manorial incidents; and

    (e) paying the costs of the above and certain other transactions, *e.g.* the costs of discharging mortgages.[6]

Since a mortgage overrides the beneficiaries' interests under the settlement,[7] and they do not automatically attach to the money raised by the mortgage, the court will intervene to prevent the power of mortgaging being used to prejudice beneficiaries. It will treat any such inequitable mortgage as a breach of trust.[8] However a mortgagee is not concerned to see—

    (i) that any money advanced by him is wanted for any purpose under the Act, nor

    (ii) that no more than is wanted is raised,

provided that the mortgage monies were received by the trustees of the settlement or paid at their direction.[9]

    A mortgage of the legal estate is required to be a legal mortgage or a charge by way of legal mortgage.[10] But since an equitable mortgage is really a contract to create a legal mortgage,[11] and a tenant for life can make such a contract,[12] it seems that an equitable mortgage would be effective, provided that it was made for one of the permitted purposes.

8–081   *(e) Power to grant options.* A tenant for life may grant an option in writing to purchase or take a lease of all or any part of the settled land or any easement, right or privilege over it.[13] But—

    (i) the price or rent must be the best reasonably obtainable[14] and must be fixed at the time of granting the option[15];

---

[6] *More v. More, supra*; and see *Re Maryon-Wilson's S.E.* [1915] 1 Ch. 29.

[7] See *post*, para. 8–159.

[8] *Hampden v. Earl of Buckinghamshire* [1893] 2 Ch. 531: this is the case "in which the court has gone the furthest in controlling the discretion of the tenant for life": *Re Richardson* [1900] 2 Ch. 778 at 790, *per* Stirling J.

[9] S.L.A. 1925, s.95. This position is the same where title to the land is registered: L.R.A. 1925, s.89; Ruoff & Roper, 31–10.

[10] S.L.A. 1925, ss.16(1), 17(1), 117(1)(xi). s.71(3) expressly empowers the tenant for life to grant the long term of years (*e.g.* 3,000 years) by which legal mortgages are made (*post*, para. 19–020), despite the restrictions on the length of leases imposed in other cases by the Act (*ante*, para. 8–077). For mortgages of registered land, see *ante*, para. 6–111.

[11] *Post*, para. 19–039.

[12] S.L.A. 1925, s.90(1)(i).

[13] *ibid.*, s.51(1).

[14] *ibid.*, s.51(3).

[15] *ibid.*, s.51(1). This is an unfortunate limitation, as it precludes a sale at a market valuation at the time when the option is exercised. It may be based on the view that a trustee has no power to sell at a valuation, because to do so would be a delegation of his discretion to determine the price: *cf. Re Earl of Wilton's S.E.* [1907] 1 Ch. 50 at 55. That view cannot be reconciled with more modern authorities which make it clear that valuation involves no element of discretion: see *Sudbrook Trading Estate Ltd v. Eggleton* [1983] 1 A.C. 444 at 483; [1985] Conv. 44 (G. Lightman).

(ii) the option must be made exercisable within an agreed number of years not exceeding 10[16]; and

(iii) the option may be granted with or without any consideration being paid,[17] but if any is paid, it is capital money.[18]

3. Powers exercisable with consent of the trustees or under an order of the court. In the following cases the tenant for life can exercise his powers only with the consent of the trustees of the settlement or under an order of the court. **8–082**

(a) Power to dispose of the principal mansion house. If the tenant for life wishes to make a disposition[19] of the principal mansion house,[20] if any, and the pleasure grounds and park (whether or not usually occupied therewith), and land, if any, usually occupied therewith, the consent of the trustees or an order of the court is required if the settlement expressly so requires.[21] In other cases, no consent is required, but the usual notice must be given. **8–083**

(b) Power to cut and sell timber. This has already been explained.[22] **8–084**

(c) Power to compromise claims. Subject to the consent in writing of the trustees, the tenant for life has a wide power to compromise and settle disputes relating to all or any part of the settled land.[23] He has a similar power by deed or writing to release, waive or modify rights over other land which benefit the settled land, *e.g.* easements and restrictive covenants, whether or not consideration is given.[24] **8–085**

(d) Power to sell settled chattels. Special provision was made in the Settled Land Act for personal chattels settled so as to devolve with (or as nearly possible with) settled land.[25] The tenant for life is empowered to sell[26] (but not lease[27]) such chattels, provided that he first obtains an order of the court.[28] **8–086**

(e) Power to do anything proper with the court's consent. The court has a statutory jurisdiction to authorise the tenant for life to effect any transaction not otherwise authorised by the Act or the settlement[29] if it affects the settled **8–087**

---

[16] S.L.A. 1925, s.51(2).
[17] *ibid.,* s.51(1).
[18] *ibid.,* s.51(5).
[19] See *ibid.,* s.117(1)(v).
[20] For what does and does not constitute a principal mansion house, see *ibid.,* s.65(2), and the previous edition of this work at pp. 368, 369.
[21] S.L.A. 1925, s.65(1).
[22] *Ante,* para. 3–109.
[23] S.L.A. 1925, s.58(1).
[24] *ibid.,* s.58(2).
[25] *ibid.,* s.67(1). For a fuller account, see the previous edition of this work at pp. 370–371.
[26] S.L.A. 1925, s.67(1).
[27] See *Re Lacon's Settlement* [1911] 1 Ch. 351 at 353, 354; [1911] 2 Ch. 17 at 19.
[28] S.L.A. 1925, s.67(3). There is no provision enabling him to sell with the consent of the trustees.
[29] See *Re Symons* [1927] 1 Ch. 344 at 345.

land, is for the benefit of the land or the beneficiaries,[30] and is a transaction which an absolute owner could validly effect.[31] "Transaction" is widely defined, and includes the application of capital money.[32] The court has, for example, authorised a tenant for life to mortgage the land, and to save himself from bankruptcy, where his debts arose from the expenses of maintaining the land.[33] It has also sanctioned the following schemes—

(i) a transfer of property (made for tax reasons) from one settlement to another in order to establish a maintenance fund[34]; and

(ii) a transfer to trustees to hold the property on trust for sale (and no longer as a settlement).[35]

Furthermore, this jurisdiction allows the court to authorise a scheme which alters the beneficial interests under the settlement, not only on behalf of those who cannot consent (such as minors and unborn persons),[36] but also those of beneficiaries of full age and capacity who did not consent.[37]

4. Other powers of a tenant for life

8–088   (a) *Power to effect improvements.* Improvements have to be distinguished in principle from current repairs. The former are special operations of a capital nature, the latter are ordinary outgoings and must be paid for out of income. A tenant for life may of course make both improvements and repairs at his own expense. Indeed, in the case of repairs, he may have to pay for them himself. In the case of improvements he may be entitled to have the costs borne either temporarily or permanently by capital money, or raised by a mortgage or charge of the settled land.

The Settled Land Act provides that capital money may be applied by the tenant for life in or towards payment for an improvement only if the payment is authorised by that Act and certain specified requirements are satisfied.[38] The

---

[30] See, *e.g. Re Cleveland Literary and Philosophical Society's Land* [1931] 2 Ch. 247.

[31] S.L.A. 1925, s.64, as amended by the Settled Land and Trustee Acts (Court's General Powers) Acts 1943, s.2. See also s.1 of the latter Act, giving power to authorise expenses of management to be treated as capital outgoings.

[32] S.L.A. 1925, s.64(2) (as amended). See *Hambro v. Duke of Marlborough* [1994] Ch. 158 at 164–166. "Capital money" includes capital assets that could be turned into capital money: *Raikes v. Lygon* [1988] 1 W.L.R. 281 at 289.

[33] *Re White-Popham S.E.* [1936] Ch. 725.

[34] *Raikes v. Lygon, supra.*

[35] *Hambro v. Duke of Marlborough, supra* (transfer of the Parliamentary Estates to trustees for sale because of concerns about the heir apparent's "unbusinesslike habits and lack of responsibility").

[36] *Re Simmons* [1956] Ch. 125. Prior to the Variation of Trusts Act 1958, this could not normally be done under the general law: *cf. Chapman v. Chapman* [1954] A.C. 429.

[37] *Hambro v. Duke of Marlborough, supra.* This is now the leading case on S.L.A. 1925, s.64. See [1994] Conv. 492 (E. Cooke); (1996) 47 N.I.L.Q. 63 (J. Howell).

[38] S.L.A. 1925, s.84. These are explained in detail in the previous edition of this work at pp. 373–376, to which reference should be made.

tenant for life can be required to repay the cost of carrying out certain improvements.[39]

(b) Power to select investments for capital money. Capital money must be applied in one or more of the 21 methods specified in the Act.[40] These include investments in trustee securities,[41] discharge of incumbrances,[42] paying for authorised improvements, the purchase of land held in fee simple or on a lease with 60 or more years unexpired,[43] and any other method authorised by the settlement. The tenant for life may select which of these methods of application shall be employed, in default of which the trustees make the choice.[44] If the tenant for life chooses the manner of application, he must of course in so doing act as trustee.[45]

8–089

(c) Power to dedicate highways and open spaces. For the general benefit of the residents on the settled land or any part of it, the tenant for life has wide powers of dedicating land for use as streets, paths, squares, gardens or other open spaces.[46]

8–090

(d) Power to take a lease of other land. There may be practical advantages to the settled land in taking on lease other land, mines, easements, rights or privileges which can conveniently be held or worked with it, and in such cases the lease should devolve with the settled land after the tenant for life's death. A tenant for life is therefore empowered to take such leases.[47] The lease is deemed to be a subsidiary vesting deed and the requisite particulars may be either inserted in it or indorsed on it.[48] No fine may be paid out of capital money.[49]

8–091

(e) Power to contract. Detailed powers are conferred on tenants for life to enter into contracts for sales, leases, mortgages and other dispositions authorised by the Act.[50] Such contracts are enforceable by and against the tenant for

8–092

---

[39] See S.L.A. 1925, Sched. 3, Pts II and III. The tenant for life may be required to repay the cost of improvements in Pt II, and must do so as regards those listed in Pt III.

[40] S.L.A. 1925, s.73(1). In general, the permitted objects are all of a capital nature, *i.e.* including improvements but excluding repairs. But they include payment of costs of exercising any of the powers (s.73(1)(xx)), and although it has been held that this would not cover the costs of granting a short occupation lease (for 14 years, determinable in certain events: *Re Leveson-Gower's S.E.* [1905] 2 Ch. 95), it is not clear how the line is to be drawn.

[41] *i.e.* those which are either specified in T.I.A. 1961, or authorised by the settlement.

[42] See, *e.g.* S.L.A. 1925, s.73(1)(ii). Some of the specific incumbrances provided for in the section are now obsolete.

[43] See *Re Wellsted's W.T.* [1949] Ch. 296. Compare the position where land is held on a trust of land: *post*, para. 8–139.

[44] S.L.A. 1925, s.75(2).

[45] *Re Sir Robert Peel's S.E.* [1910] 1 Ch. 389; *Re Gladwin's Trust* [1919] 1 Ch. 232; *cf. Re Lord Coleridge's Settlement* [1895] 2 Ch. 704; *Re Hotham* [1902] 2 Ch. 575.

[46] S.L.A. 1925, s.56; and see *ante*, para. 8–074, n.52.

[47] S.L.A. 1925, s.53(1).

[48] *ibid.*, s.53(2).

[49] *ibid.*, s.53(1).

[50] *ibid.*, s.90.

life's successors in title,[51] and are subject to any directions by the court.[52] The transaction must be authorised by the Act at the time when the contract comes to be performed, so that in the case of a contract for a lease the rent must be the best rent reasonably obtainable when the lease is finally granted, and the other statutory conditions must also be satisfied then.[53] The powers extend to the variation and rescission of contracts.

II. POSITION OF TENANT FOR LIFE

8–093   **1. The tenant for life is trustee both of the land and of his powers.** This has already been explained in general terms.[54] However, two special aspects of this trusteeship require discussion here.

8–094   *(a) Capital money.* All receipts of a capital nature must be treated as capital money and paid to the trustees of the settlement or into court.[55] The term "capital money" has a broad meaning[56] and includes—

    (i)   the proceeds of sale or mortgage;

    (ii) fines upon the grant of leases;

    (iii) part of the proceeds of mining and timber transactions;

    (iv) money (not being rent) paid by a tenant either as compensation for breach of covenant,[57] or payable as the price of being allowed to surrender his lease[58] (unless in either case the court otherwise directs);

    (v)   insurance money receivable under a policy of insurance kept up under a requirement of the settlement or of the Act, or by a tenant for life impeachable for waste[59];

    (vi) any money arising outside the Act "which ought to be capital money"[60]; and

    (vii) various other specified receipts.[61]

Despite the wide meaning of capital money, tenants for life have been held to be entitled to retain compensation for damage done to property while under

---

[51] *ibid.*, s.90(2).
[52] *ibid.*, s.90(3).
[53] *Re Rycroft's Settlement* [1962] Ch. 263. For these conditions, see *ante*, para. 8–077.
[54] *Ante*, paras 8–013, 8–014.
[55] *Post*, para. 8–162.
[56] *cf.* S.L.A. 1925, s.117(1)(ii).
[57] *ibid.*, s.80(1).
[58] *ibid.*, s.52(7).
[59] T.A. 1925, s.20. See, *e.g. Re Scholfield's Trusts* [1949] Ch. 341.
[60] S.L.A. 1925, s.81; see Wolst. & C. iii, 180, giving examples.
[61] For a list, see Wolst. & C. iii, 156.

requisition,[62] and also income tax allowances resulting from improvements that were carried out with capital money.[63]

(b) Acquisition by tenant for life. The tenant for life is given a special power **8–095** to acquire any or all of the settled land for himself. It is a long-established rule of equity that no trustee may acquire the trust property for himself either directly or indirectly, no matter how fair the transaction may be.[64] The "court will not permit a party to place himself in a situation in which his interest conflicts with his duty".[65] To avoid this difficulty, the Settled Land Act 1925[66] authorises the trustees of the settlement to exercise all the powers of a tenant for life in carrying out any transaction whereby the tenant for life acquires any interest in the settled land. The trustees are empowered to act in the name and on behalf of the tenant for life even if he is one of them, in which case he should join in the transaction with them as a trustee.[67] However, they are not authorised to have any dealings with a body of persons which includes one of the trustees (not being the tenant for life) unless the court approves the transaction.[68] There is a similar power to carry out certain other transactions, such as a purchase from the tenant for life of land to be brought into the settlement.[69]

2. No powers can be given to anyone except the tenant for life. Any **8–096** power, other than a power of revocation or appointment, which the settlement purports to give to anyone except the tenant for life, is exercisable not by that person but by the tenant for life as if it were an additional power conferred by the settlement.[70] This is so whether or not the tenant for life already has such a power under the Act.[71] Thus if in a will of a person dying before 1997, land had been devised "to X and Y in fee simple with power to sell, on trust for A for life and then for B absolutely", X and Y would not have had the power of sale. It would have been given to A, notwithstanding that he already had such a power of sale by statute. However, the abortive attempt to give a power of sale to X and Y might not be wholly without effect. It may have made them Settled Land Act trustees.[72]

---

[62] *Re Pomfret's Settlement* [1952] Ch. 48; contrast *Re Thompson* [1949] Ch. 1.
[63] *Re Pelly's W.T.* [1957] Ch. 1.
[64] *Fox v. Mackreth* (1791) 2 Cox Eq. 320; *Ex p. Hughes* (1802) 6 Ves. 617; *Ex p. Lacey* (1802) 6 Ves. 625; *Ex p. James* (1803) 8 Ves. 337; *Sanderson v. Walker* (1807) 13 Ves. 601; *Whitcomb v. Minchin* (1820) 5 Madd. 91.
[65] *Re Bloye's Trusts* (1849) 1 Mac. & G. 488 at 495, *per* Lord Cottenham L.C.; affirmed *sub nom. Lewis v. Hillman* (1852) 3 H.L.C. 607. *cf. Swain v. The Law Society* [1982] 1 W.L.R. 17 at 36; and see *Sargeant v. National Westminster Bank Plc* (1990) 61 P. & C.R. 518.
[66] s.68.
[67] *Re Pennant's W.T.* [1970] Ch. 75; and see *ante*, para. 8–066.
[68] S.L.A. 1925, s.68(3).
[69] *ibid.*, s.68(1).
[70] *ibid.*, s.108(2).
[71] *ibid.*
[72] *Ante*, para. 8–066.

3. The statutory powers cannot be ousted, curtailed or hampered.

8–097   *(a) The Act prevails.* The settlor may confer additional powers on the tenant for life, and such powers are exercisable in the same way as if they were conferred by the Act.[73] Further, nothing in the Act in any way restricts powers which the settlement gives to the tenant for life or purports to give to the trustees to be exercised with the approval of the tenant for life.[74] The powers given by the Act and the settlement are cumulative.[75] But in other respects, so far as the settlement and the Act conflict in relation to powers exercisable under the Act, the Act prevails.[76] For example, if the settlement provides that no sale shall be made without the consent of some specified person, this provision is inconsistent with the unfettered power of sale given by the Act and the latter prevails.[77]

8–098   *(b) Void provisions.* There is a sweeping section[78] which makes void any provision in any document (*e.g.* another settlement[79]) "as far as it purports, or attempts, or tends, or is intended to have, or would or might have" the effect of preventing or discouraging the tenant for life from exercising his statutory powers or from requiring the land to be vested in him.[80] This applies even when the attempt to restrain the exercise of the powers is made by way of a determinable limitation.[81] A settlement on "Y for life until he attempts to alienate the land" gave Y a life interest which would continue despite any alienation by him.[82] Nevertheless, for the section to operate, there must be someone who, but for the restriction that is in issue, would be the tenant for life under the Act.[83] The section does nothing to enlarge the beneficiary's estate.[84] Finally, it is provided that notwithstanding anything in a settlement, the exercise of a statutory power can never cause a forfeiture.[85]

8–099   *(c) Extent of invalidity.* Provisions for the curtailment or forfeiture of the interest of a tenant for life are not automatically invalidated by these rules. They are affected only so far as they in fact tend to fetter the statutory powers of the tenant for life or statutory owner. This may be illustrated by a condition of residence, *e.g.* a provision in the settlement that the tenant for life shall forfeit his interest on ceasing to reside on the settled land. In such cases, if the tenant for life ceases to reside there for some reason other than the exercise of his statutory powers (as where he prefers to live elsewhere) the proviso for

---

[73] S.L.A. 1925, s.109: see, *e.g. Re The Earl of Egmont's S.E.* (1900) 16 T.L.R. 360; *Re Duke of Westminster's S.E. (No. 2)* [1921] 1 Ch. 585; *Re Cowley's S.E.* [1926] Ch. 725.
[74] Such powers are exercisable by the tenant for life: see above.
[75] S.L.A. 1925, s.108(1); see *Re Jeffreys* [1939] Ch. 205.
[76] S.L.A. 1925, s.108(2).
[77] *Re Jeffreys, supra.*
[78] S.L.A. 1925, s.106(1).
[79] *Re Smith* [1899] 1 Ch. 331; *Re Burden* [1948] Ch. 160.
[80] See *Ungurian v. Lesnoff* [1990] Ch. 206 at 226.
[81] S.L.A. 1925, s.106(2).
[82] *ibid.*
[83] *Re Atkinson* (1886) 31 Ch.D. 577 at 581.
[84] *Re Hazle's S.E.* (1885) 29 Ch.D. 78 at 84.
[85] S.L.A. 1925, s.106(3).

forfeiture is operative and he loses his interest.[86] But if the reason for his ceasing to reside there is that he has exercised his statutory powers, as by leasing[87] or selling[88] the land, or both,[89] there is no forfeiture.[90] He continues to be entitled as tenant for life, receiving the rent from the lease[91] or the income from the purchase-money.[92] Another example to which the same distinction applies is a condition that the tenant for life should provide a home for X on the settled land.[93]

(d) Inoperative fetters. One result of these rules is that a provision which **8–100** attempts to fetter the powers may actually encourage their exercise. If the tenant for life is subject to a condition of residence but wishes to reside elsewhere, he can protect his life interest from the condition by first selling or letting the land. Furthermore, quite apart from these rules—

> (i) provisions of this nature are sometimes void under the doctrine that conditions subsequent will be construed strictly and held to be ineffective unless it can be seen precisely upon what grounds a forfeiture will be incurred[94]; and

> (ii) a minor who cannot control his place of residence cannot be said to "refuse or neglect" to reside on the property so as to incur a forfeiture.[95]

(e) Upkeep of the property. Difficulty sometimes arises over funds provided **8–101** by the settlor for the payment of taxes and other such outgoings during the tenant for life's personal occupation. Here the settlor's object is to enable the tenant for life to live on the property free from the expenses of its upkeep. It has been held that the tenant for life can still claim such payments after letting the land,[96] but not after selling it.[97] There has been some difference of judicial opinion on this difficult subject, which has been fully reviewed by the Court

---

[86] *Re Haynes* (1887) 37 Ch.D. 306; *Re Trenchard* [1902] 1 Ch. 378. As to what constitutes "residence", contrast *Re Moir* (1884) 25 Ch.D. 605 (residence) with *Re Wright* [1907] 1 Ch. 231 (non-residence).

[87] *Re Gibbons* [1920] 1 Ch. 372.

[88] *Re Paget's S.E.* (1885) 30 Ch.D. 161.

[89] *Re Acklom* [1929] 1 Ch. 195.

[90] *Re Orlebar* [1936] Ch. 147; *cf. Re Ames* [1893] 2 Ch. 479.

[91] *Re T. J. Freme* (1912) 56 S.J. 362.

[92] *Re Sarah Dalrymple* (1901) 49 W.R. 627.

[93] *Re Richardson* [1904] 2 Ch. 777 (condition that the life tenant X provide a home for Y void so far as it prevented X from exercising her Settled Land Act powers).

[94] *Ante,* para. 3–066. Contrast *Sifton v. Sifton* [1938] A.C. 656 ("so long as she shall continue to reside in Canada" held too vague) with *Re Gape* [1952] Ch. 743 (condition requiring "permanent residence" in England held effective).

[95] *Partridge v. Partridge* [1894] 1 Ch. 351.

[96] *Re Patten* [1929] 2 Ch. 276.

[97] *Re Simpson* [1913] 1 Ch. 277, not following *Re Trenchard* (1900) 16 T.L.R. 525; *Re Burden* [1948] Ch. 160; *Re Aberconway's S.T.* [1953] Ch. 647. Contrast *Re Ames* [1893] 2 Ch. 479; and *cf. Re Eastman's S.E.* (1898) 68 L.J.Ch. 122 (provision for reduction of annuity).

of Appeal.[98] Further, where the Act gives special powers to the trustees (for example, the powers of management during a minority[99]), the powers are made subject to any contrary intention and are not, therefore, protected like the powers of the tenant for life.

4. The tenant for life cannot assign, release or contract not to exercise his powers[1]

8–102   *(a) Exercise of powers.* A statutory owner can release his powers,[2] but a tenant for life cannot. Once a person has become a tenant for life, he is incapable of divesting himself of his powers, even if he parts with his entire beneficial interest,[3] as he is entitled to do.[4] It is he, and not the assignee of his beneficial interest, who alone can exercise the statutory powers,[5] and this is so whether the disposition was voluntary or involuntary (*e.g.* on bankruptcy), and even if it was made while the life interest was still in remainder.[6] But in three exceptional cases[7] the statutory powers may become exercisable by someone other than the tenant for life.

8–103   (1) EXTINGUISHMENT OF INTEREST. Where the interest of the tenant for life has been assured, with intent to extinguish it, to the person next entitled under the settlement, the statutory powers cease to be exercisable by the tenant for life and become exercisable as if he were dead.[8] For this purpose, an "assurance" is any surrender, conveyance, assignment or appointment which operates in equity to extinguish the interest.[9] A partial surrender is insufficient,[10] and so is a surrender to a later remainderman where some intermediate gift remains capable of taking effect, even though contingently.[11] But it is immaterial that a term of years or charge intervenes between the interest surrendered and that of the person next entitled, or that the latter interest is defeasible, or that the interest surrendered was in remainder at the time.[12]

The provision may be illustrated by a settlement of land on A for life, remainder to B for life, remainder to C in fee simple. If A surrenders his life interest to B, the statutory powers become exercisable by B instead of A, and

---

[98] *Re Aberconway's S.T., supra*; see [1954] C.L.J. 60 (R. N. Gooderson); and *Raikes v. Lygon* [1988] 1 W.L.R. 281 at 288.

[99] S.L.A. 1925, s.102; *ante*, para. 8–015.

[1] S.L.A. 1925, s.104(1), (2); and see s.19(4).

[2] *Re Craven's S.E.* [1926] Ch. 985.

[3] *Re Mundy and Roper's Contract* [1899] 1 Ch. 275; *Re Cope and Wadland's Contract* [1919] 2 Ch. 376.

[4] *Re Trenchard* [1902] 1 Ch. 378 at 384, 385.

[5] *Re Earl of Carnarvon's Chesterfield S.E.* [1927] 1 Ch. 138 at 145, 146; see, *e.g. Earl of Lonsdale v. Lowther* [1900] 2 Ch. 687.

[6] S.L.A. 1925, s.104(1).

[7] See also *ante*, para. 8–095 (acquisition of the settled land).

[8] S.L.A. 1925, s.105(1).

[9] *ibid.*, s.105(2).

[10] *Re Barlow's Contract* [1903] 1 Ch. 382.

[11] *Re Maryon-Wilson's Instrument* [1971] Ch. 789.

[12] S.L.A. 1925, s.105(1).

A must at once convey the legal estate to B by a vesting deed.[13] If A is bankrupt, his trustee in bankruptcy can surrender A's interest with the same effect.[14] If A refuses to execute the necessary vesting deed, the court can instead make a vesting order.[15] If after the surrender of A's interest, B then surrenders his life interest to C, he must convey the legal estate to C.[16] This will be by an ordinary conveyance as the land ceases to be settled land.[17]

(2) ORDER OF COURT. If the tenant for life—   **8–104**

> (i) has ceased to have a substantial interest in the land, whether by bankruptcy, assignment or otherwise; and

> (ii) either consents to an order being made or else has unreasonably refused to exercise his statutory powers,[18]

any person interested in the land may apply to the court for an order authorising the trustees to exercise any or all of the statutory powers in the name and on behalf of the tenant for life.[19] Such an order prevents the tenant for life from exercising any of the powers affected by the order, but until it has been registered[20] the order does not affect persons dealing with the tenant for life.[21] It should be noted that such an order vests neither the legal estate nor the statutory powers in the trustees, who do not become the statutory owners. The order merely authorises the trustees to exercise the powers on behalf of the tenant for life and in his name. Furthermore, the provision is confined to tenants for life, and does not apply to statutory owners.[22] Where the title to the settled land is registered, the trustees of the settlement must file an office copy of the court's order with the Land Registry before they exercise any of the powers that it confers upon them.[23]

(3) MENTAL PATIENT. Where the tenant for life is a mental patient, his   **8–105** statutory powers may be exercised under an order of the judge or Court of Protection, *e.g.* by his receiver.[24] They may also be exercised by a donee of an enduring power of attorney made by the tenant for life prior to his mental incapacity.[25]

---

[13] *ibid.,* ss.7(4), 8(4).

[14] *Re Shawdon Estates Settlement* [1930] 2 Ch. 1.

[15] S.L.A. 1925, s.12(1); see, *e.g. Re Shawdon Estates Settlement, supra.*

[16] S.L.A. 1925, s.7(5).

[17] Wolst. & C. iii, 43; *cf. ante,* para. 8–032.

[18] See *Re Thornhill's Settlement* [1941] Ch. 24 (neglect or failure to exercise powers by a tenant for life is not a ground for making an order under s.24: there must be a refusal to act).

[19] S.L.A. 1925, s.24(1) see, *e.g. Re Cecil's S.E.* [1926] W.N. 262.

[20] As an "order affecting land": see L.C.A. 1972, s.6 (*ante,* para. 5–090); L.R.A. 1925, s.59(1) (*ante,* para. 6–087).

[21] S.L.A. 1925, s.24(2).

[22] *Re Craven's S.E.* [1926] Ch. 985.

[23] L.R.A. 1925, s.87(5).

[24] Mental Health Act 1983, Pt VII. See *post,* para. 20–021.

[25] Enduring Powers of Attorney Act 1985, s.3(3). This subsection will be prospectively repealed when the Trustee Delegation Act 1999 is brought into force: see s.4(1). For transitional provisions in relation to existing powers, see *ibid.,* s.4(2)–(6).

8–106 *(b) Position of assignees.* Usually neither a voluntary assignee of the beneficial interest of a tenant for life, nor his trustee in bankruptcy, who is an assignee by operation of law, has control over the exercise of the tenant for life's powers.[26] Whether or not the assignment was made for money or money's worth, the assignee's consent is not required for the exercise of the statutory powers.[27] However such an assignee does have certain rights of control. For the application of capital money affected by the assignment for any purpose other than for investment in trustee securities, his consent is required if the assignment so provides or if it takes effect by operation of the law of bankruptcy, and the trustees have notice of this.[28] Further, unless the assignment otherwise provides, notice of any intended transaction must be given to the assignee.[29] No period of notice is specified, and a purchaser is not concerned to see or inquire whether notice has been given.[30]

If the land is sold, the rights of the assignee are transferred to the capital money which represents the land,[31] and provision is made for obtaining consents in any cases of difficulty.[32]

D. The Appointment and Functions of Settled Land Act Trustees

8–107 **1. Their appointment.** It has already been explained how the initial trustees of the settlement were to be found.[33] The usual rules for the retirement of existing trustees and the appointment of new ones are then applicable.[34] The number of such trustees should not rise above four or fall below two, or one, if it is a trust corporation.[35]

The curtain principle extends to the appointment and discharge of Settled Land Act trustees, so that a purchaser does not have to investigate such matters. The Settled Land Act 1925 provides for the execution of a "deed of declaration" stating who are the trustees of the settlement after any appointment or discharge.[36] In favour of a purchaser this is conclusive evidence of the matters stated in it.[37] This deed is made supplemental to the principal vesting deed, on which the names of the new trustees are also indorsed.[38] The actual deed of appointment or discharge is kept by the trustees and is not seen by the

---

[26] See S.L.A. 1925, s.104(4), (10).
[27] *ibid.*, s.104(4); and see subss.(10), (11).
[28] *ibid.*, s.104(4).
[29] *ibid.*
[30] *ibid.*
[31] *Post*, para. 8–158.
[32] *Ante*, para. 8–104.
[33] *Ante*, para. 8–065.
[34] *Post*, paras 10–055 *et seq.*, 10–066.
[35] T.A. 1925, ss.34, 39. These rules are applicable to both registered and unregistered land: L.R.A. 1925, s.95.
[36] S.L.A. 1925, s.35(1). Where the title is registered, it is unnecessary to produce this deed to the Registrar: Ruoff & Roper, 31–12. All that is required is an application to modify the existing restriction by substituting the names of the new and continuing trustees: L.R.R. 1925, r. 236B; Sched., Form 77.
[37] S.L.A. 1925, s.35(3).
[38] *ibid.*, s.35(1); T.A. 1925, s.35(2).

purchaser. The deed of declaration provides the necessary link in his title between the old and the new trustees.

2. Their functions. Trustees of the settlement under the Settled Land Act **8–108** 1925 are unusual in that they do not normally hold any property on trust unless and until the settled land is sold. Their principal functions may be summarised as follows.

(i) To receive and hold capital money.[39]

(ii) To receive notice from the tenant for life of his intention to effect certain transactions.[40]

(iii) To give consent to certain transactions.[41]

(iv) To act as special personal representatives on the death of a tenant for life.[42]

(v) To act as statutory owner if the tenant for life is a minor or there is no tenant for life.[43]

(vi) To execute the principal vesting deed in cases where it is not provided in the ordinary case.[44]

(vii) To execute a deed of discharge, when it is necessary, on the determination of the settlement.[45]

(viii) To exercise the powers of the tenant for life if he wishes to acquire the settled land for his own benefit.[46]

(ix) To exercise the powers of the tenant for life where he has no substantial beneficial interest and either consents to such exercise or unreasonably refuses to exercise his powers.[47]

(x) To exercise a general supervision over the well-being of the settled land.[48] They will have to be parties to all litigation concerning the land. If they are not opposed to a transaction for which the tenant for life is seeking the authority of the court, their duty is "to hold an even hand" and refrain from supporting the application.[49]

---

[39] *ibid.*, ss.18(1)(b), 75(1); *ante*, para. 8–094.
[40] *Ante*, para. 8–073.
[41] *Ante*, para. 8–082.
[42] *Ante*, para. 8–035.
[43] *Ante*, para. 8–015.
[44] *Ante*, para. 8–023.
[45] *Ante*, para. 8–036.
[46] *Ante*, para. 8–095.
[47] *Ante*, para. 8–104.
[48] *Ante*, paras 8–013, 8–014; and see *Re Boston's W.T.* [1956] Ch. 395 at 405.
[49] See *Re Hotchkin's S.E.* (1887) 35 Ch.D. 41 at 43; *cf. Re Marquis of Aylesbury's S.E.* [1892] 1 Ch. 506 at 526.

Part 3

TRUSTS FOR SALE AFTER 1925 AND BEFORE 1997

8–109   **1. The nature of a trust for sale.** Prior to 1997 the alternative method of creating a settlement of land was by means of a trust for sale. The nature of a trust for sale has already been explained.[50] Such trusts were subject to provisions of the Law of Property Act 1925, many of which have been amended by the Trusts of Land and Appointment of Trustees Act 1996 so that they apply with necessary modifications to trusts of land. It has been explained that trusts for sale and settlements under the Settled Land Act 1925 were mutually exclusive.[51] If there was an immediate binding trust for sale,[52] there could be no settlement.[53] The main distinction between trusts for sale and settlements was that under a trust for sale all powers of dealing with the land were vested in the trustees, whereas under a settlement they were given to the tenant for life.

8–110   **2. Species of trust for sale.** A trust for sale could arise either expressly, where land was deliberately limited on trust for sale, or by operation of statute. Where trusts for sale were expressly created *inter vivos*, it was the invariable practice[54] to employ two documents—

> (i) a conveyance or, where the land was registered, a transfer, to the trustees on trust for sale; and

> (ii) a trust instrument.

A purchaser was not concerned to see the trust instrument, and it was irrelevant that he had notice of the trust. When the trustees exercised their powers of disposition, the trusts were overreached, provided any capital monies were paid to the trustees, of whom there had to be at least two, except where the trustee was a trust corporation.[55] Testamentary trusts for sale were also created by two documents, the will and the written assent. The will operated as the trust instrument and a purchaser from the trustees for sale was not concerned to see it. The written assent took effect as a conveyance from the deceased's personal representatives which vested the legal estate in the trustees for sale.[56]

---

[50] *Ante*, para. 8–005.
[51] *Ante*, para. 8–012.
[52] L.P.A. 1925, s.205(1)(xxix) (as originally enacted). See the previous edition of this work at p. 386.
[53] S.L.A. 1925, s.1(7).
[54] It was not a legal necessity.
[55] L.P.A. 1925, s.27(2) (this subsection has since been amended to apply to trusts of land). For overreaching, see *post*, paras 8–157, 8–165.
[56] An assent was necessary even if the trustees for sale and the personal representatives were the same persons: see *post*, para. 11–129.

A trust for sale was a convenient device for liquidating and distributing property, and it was employed by statute in a number of cases. In these situations, a trust of land is now imposed[57] and the provisions are considered in the context of such trusts.[58]

3. Position of trustees for sale.

(a) Power to postpone sale. Unless a contrary intention appeared, trustees for sale had an implied power to postpone sale and were not liable even if they did so indefinitely.[59] However, if they refused to sell, the court had power to order a sale at the instance of any person interested, and could make such order as it thought fit.[60] It was the trustees' duty to sell the property unless they unanimously agreed to exercise the power to postpone sale.[61] Nevertheless, many trusts for sale were created with the intention that the land should be retained for specific purposes,[62] and the courts took this into account when a sale was sought. They might in their discretion decline to order a sale. This practice has now been given statutory effect in relation to trusts of land.[63]

8–111

(b) Other powers of trustees for sale. Trustees for sale had all the powers of a tenant for life and the trustees of the settlement under the Settled Land Act 1925.[64] Pending sale, they could (for example) lease or mortgage the land in the same circumstances as a tenant for life under a settlement might have done.[65] Provided that they did not, by selling all the land, cease to be trustees for sale,[66] they could purchase further land with any proceeds of sale in their hands.[67] It was implicit in the Law of Property Act 1925 that a settlor or testator might make the sale by trustees subject to their obtaining the prior consent of one or more persons. This followed from the provision that the exercise of their powers was subject to the consent of any person that was required to a sale.[68]

8–112

---

[57] See T.L.A.T.A. 1996, s.5(1).
[58] *Post*, para. 8–135.
[59] L.P.A. 1925, s.25 (now repealed).
[60] *ibid.*, s.30 (now repealed).
[61] See *Re Mayo* [1943] Ch. 302; Snell, *Equity*, 237. As an exception to the general rule, charity trustees do not have to be unanimous, but may act by a majority.
[62] *e.g.* where a property was purchased jointly as a family home.
[63] See T.L.A.T.A. 1996, ss.14, 15; *post*, paras 8–142 *et seq.*
[64] L.P.A. 1925, s.28(1) (now repealed). These included the powers of management conferred by S.L.A. 1925, s.102, during a minority, even though no minority in fact existed. If land previously settled became subject to a trust for sale, the trustees had any additional powers conferred by the settlement on the tenant for life or trustees of the settlement: L.P.A. 1925, s.28(1). For a fuller account, see the previous edition of this work at p. 392. The application of the provisions of the Settled Land Act 1925 to trusts for sale was not always easy: *cf. State Bank of India v. Sood* [1997] Ch. 276 at 282.
[65] See *ante*, paras 8–076, 8–080.
[66] L.P.A. 1925, s.205(1)(xxix) (as originally enacted); *Re Wakeman* [1945] Ch. 177.
[67] L.P.A. 1925, s.28(1); S.L.A. 1925, s.73(1)(xi); *Re Wellsted's W.T.* [1949] Ch. 296.
[68] L.P.A. 1925, s.28(1). If the consent of more than two persons was required, a bona fide purchaser for value was protected if the consent of any two was obtained: L.P.A. 1925, s.26 (now repealed).

8–113 *(c) Application of income.* Unless there was a contrary provision in the trust for sale, the income from the land until sale was to be applied in the same way as the investments representing the proceeds of sale would be applied.[69]

8–114 *(d) Curtailment of powers.* The extent to which it was possible to curtail the powers of trustees for sale was uncertain. It has been explained above that a trust to sell could be made subject to the prior consent of one or more persons. There was authority which suggested that, in consequence, it was possible to make land held on trust for sale inalienable, despite the obvious paradox of the result. In one case, a testator had directed that the trustees for sale were to sell certain land only with the consent of X. X was a contingent remainderman who was to benefit only if the land was unsold at the death of the life beneficiary.[70] X's consent to a sale was unobtainable for obvious reasons. The question whether the court would dispense with it, or what would happen to X's interest if it did, was not raised.

Apart from the question of consents, it was probably the case that the powers of the trustees for sale could not be cut down[71] except where a particular power was, by statute, expressly subject to a contrary intention.[72] There was no provision corresponding to section 106 of the Settled Land Act 1925.[73] However, it was arguable that that section was imported together with the Settled Land Act powers by section 28 of the Law of Property Act 1925.[74]

4. Position of beneficiaries.

8–115 *(a) Powers in trustees.* Subject to one qualification explained below, all powers of disposition and management were vested in the trustees for sale and not in the beneficiary or beneficiaries who were entitled to an immediate life interest in possession. Such persons either received the net income or they might enjoy the property *in specie* by occupying it pending any sale.[75] Indeed, trusts for sale were often created with the express intention that the beneficiary entitled in possession should occupy the land.

8–116 *(b) Delegation.* Although all the powers were vested in the trustees for sale, they might revocably and in writing delegate certain of them to the person of full age[76] who for the time being was beneficially entitled in possession to the

---

[69] L.P.A. 1925, s.28(2) (now repealed). This was subject to keeping down the cost of repairs and insurance and other outgoings.

[70] *Re Inns* [1947] Ch. 576 at 582.

[71] This followed from the apparently mandatory wording of L.P.A. 1925, s.28(1) (trustees "shall have all" Settled Land Act powers). See the previous edition of this work at p. 395.

[72] *e.g.* the power to postpone sale: see L.P.A. 1925, s.25(1); *ante*, para. 8–111.

[73] *Ante*, para. 8–098.

[74] *cf.* the argument in *Re Davies' W.T.* [1932] 1 Ch. 530 at 532, 533; and see the previous edition of this work at p. 395.

[75] See *City of London B.S. v. Flegg* [1988] A.C. 54 at 81.

[76] Other than an annuitant.

net rents and profits of the land for his life or any less period.[77] The powers
which could be delegated were the powers of, and incidental to, leasing,
accepting surrenders of leases and management.[78] The powers delegated had
to be exercised in the name of and on behalf of the trustees.[79] Liability for
misuse of the power rested with the person exercising it, who was deemed to
be in the position of a trustee.[80]

(c) Consultation. In relation to the exercise of all their powers, the trustees   **8–117**
were required—

> (i) so far as was practicable, to consult the persons of full age for the
> time being beneficially interested in possession in the rents and
> profits of the land; and
>
> (ii) so far as consistent with the general interests of the trust, to give
> effect to their wishes, or the wishes of the majority in terms of
> value.[81]

This provision was confined to trusts for sale which were either created by
statute or showed an intention that the provision was to apply. This had the
effect of excluding most express trusts for sale from its ambit. In any case, a
purchaser was not concerned to see that the trustees had complied with this
requirement,[82] though a beneficiary could restrain a trustee who sought to
breach it.[83]

5. The doctrine of conversion.

(a) The nature and purpose of the doctrine. Reference has already been   **8–118**
made to one aspect of the doctrine of conversion[84] and the difficulties to which
it gave rise.[85] It was long settled that where land was directed to be sold, it was
considered in equity to be money.[86] This doctrine turned on "the maxim that
Equity considers to have been done what ought to have been done pursuant to
the trust".[87] Even if there was a power to invest the proceeds of sale in the
purchase of other land, then unless the settlement otherwise provided, that

---

[77] L.P.A. 1925, s.29(1) (s.29 has now been repealed).
[78] *ibid.*
[79] *ibid.*, s.29(2).
[80] *ibid.*, s.29(3).
[81] *ibid.*, s.26(3) (as amended by L.P.(Am.)A. 1926, Sched.) (now repealed).
[82] *ibid.*
[83] *Waller v. Waller* [1967] 1 W.L.R. 451.
[84] For another aspect of the doctrine of conversion, see *post*, para. 12–052 (vendor trustee for
    purchaser).
[85] *Ante*, para. 8–007.
[86] *Fletcher v. Ashburner* (1779) 1 Bro.C.C. 497.
[87] *Re Walker* [1908] 2 Ch. 705 at 712, *per* Parker J.

land was held on trust for sale[88] and so treated as money. Correspondingly, if money was directed to be laid out in the purchase of land, it was thereafter treated as land.[89] A trust to sell land and purchase other land with the proceeds of sale worked a double conversion, so that the interests of the beneficiaries remained land throughout.[90] Conversion operated from the date on which the trust for sale was created, which was the date either of the conveyance to the trustees for sale, or of the death of the testator if it arose by will.[91]

The doctrine of conversion apparently rested on the principle that it would be wrong that the precise moment at which the trustees carried out their administrative duty of selling should determine whether the rights of the beneficiaries were realty or personalty, especially where a delay in selling might be due to a breach of trust.[92]

(b) Criticisms of the doctrine

8–119   (1) THE RIGHTS OF THE BENEFICIARIES PENDING SALE. If the doctrine of conversion was strictly applied, then no person could have any beneficial interest in the land held on trust pending sale.[93] Yet it was obvious that a beneficiary had such an interest in the sense that, until sale, the land was held for his benefit.[94] This paradox was long appreciated[95] and the courts were unwilling to press the doctrine so far. It was therefore accepted on a number of occasions that pending sale, the beneficiary's interest was an interest in land.[96] This was especially so in cases where a statutory trust for sale was imposed in cases of co-ownership.[97]

It was sometimes said that the doctrine of conversion was essential to ensure that the interests of the beneficiaries were overreached on any sale.[98] However this view must be regarded as questionable[99] for the following reasons.

---

[88] L.P.A. 1925, s.32 (now repealed).

[89] Wh. & T. i, 301; *Re Scarth* (1879) 10 Ch.D. 499.

[90] See Wh. & T. i, 309.

[91] *Clarke v. Franklin* (1858) 4 K. & J. 257; *Re Lord Grimthorpe* [1908] 1 Ch. 666. Where the title to the land was registered it was uncertain whether conversion operated from the execution of the transfer in favour of the trustees for sale or from their registration as proprietors.

[92] *Re Richerson* [1892] 1 Ch. 379 at 383; Maitland, *Equity*, 277.

[93] It was not easy to accept that "all beneficial interest in a parcel of land evaporates (*in nubibus?*)": see [1979] C.L.J. 251 at 253 (M. J. Prichard).

[94] *Irani Finance Ltd v. Singh* [1971] Ch. 59 at 68.

[95] "The equitable interest in that estate must have resided somewhere": *Pearson v. Lane* (1809) 17 Ves. 101 at 104, *per* Grant M.R.

[96] *Franks v. Bollans* (1867) 37 L.J.Ch. 148 at 158. See too the same case on appeal: (1868) 3 Ch.App. 717 at 718, 719.

[97] Particularly of the matrimonial home: see *Williams & Glyn's Bank Ltd v. Boland* [1979] Ch. 312 at 329; [1981] A.C. 487 at 507.

[98] *Irani Finance Ltd v. Singh, supra,* at 80; *City of London Building Society v. Flegg* [1988] A.C. 54 at 82. These remarks could not be readily reconciled with the decision in *Williams & Glyn's Bank Ltd v. Boland, supra.* See [1987] Conv. 451 at 455 (W. J. Swadling); [1988] Conv. 108 at 117 (M. P. Thompson). For overreaching, see *post,* paras 8–157, 8–165.

[99] See [1979] C.L.J. 251 at 253 (M. J. Prichard); (1984) 100 L.Q.R. 86 at 109 (J. S. Anderson); [1990] C.L.J. 277 at 278 (C.H.).

(i) It is now settled that "overreaching is the process whereby existing interests are subordinated to a later interest or estate created pursuant to a trust or power".[1] A disposition under a mere power of sale would therefore have overreached interests under a trust just as much as a disposition under a trust for sale.[2] This was so even though the doctrine of conversion had no application to powers of sale.[3]

(ii) The doctrine of conversion was usually relevant to determine whether beneficial interests under a trust for sale of land were to be regarded as interests in land or in personalty. Overreaching however has no necessary connection with trusts of land. Trustees who have a trust or power of sale can overreach the beneficial interests whatever the nature of the trust property. Thus if trustees sell shares, the equitable interests in them will be overreached and will attach instead to the proceeds of sale.

(iii) When overreaching occurs, the trusts are transferred from the original subject-matter of the trust to the actual proceeds of the sale. By contrast, the effect of the doctrine of conversion was that the beneficial interests of those entitled under a trust for sale of land were regarded as interests in the notional proceeds of sale from the date of the creation of the trust: the doctrine did not turn "sovereigns into acres, or *vice versa*".[4]

(2) APPLICATION UNINTENDED. In many cases, the application of the doctrine **8–120** of conversion did not accord with the intention of the settlor. Trusts for sale were developed in the nineteenth century as a conveyancing device to enable trust property to be sold without the consent of the beneficiaries. Although the same result could be achieved by conferring on the trustees a mere power of sale, any purchaser would in such a case have had to investigate whether the power was exercisable.[5] The mandatory obligation to sell under a trust for sale, coupled as it often was with a power to postpone,[6] was in many cases therefore no more than a fiction intended to achieve a conveyancing purpose. The doctrine of conversion which it necessarily triggered must frequently have been an unintended and unwanted consequence. It is also clear that the imposition of a statutory trust for sale on all legal tenancies in common in existence at the beginning of 1926[7] had the unfortunate effect of frustrating the intentions of a number of testators who failed to amend their wills after the

---

[1] *State Bank of India v. Sood* [1997] Ch. 276 at 281, *per* Peter Gibson L.J.
[2] See, *e.g. Wheate v. Hall* (1809) 17 Ves. 80 at 86; Sugden, *Powers*, 482; Farwell, *Powers*, 581.
[3] See, *e.g.* Farwell, *Powers*, 617; Wh. & T. i, 306.
[4] *Chandler v. Pocock* (1880) 15 Ch.D. 491 at 496, *per* Jessel M.R.
[5] See (1984) 100 L.Q.R. 86 at 89 (J. S. Anderson).
[6] See *ante*, para. 8–009.
[7] L.P.A. 1925, Sched. 1, Pt IV. For discussion of the transitional provisions, see the previous edition of this work at p. 447.

enactment of the Law of Property Act 1925.[8] The courts nevertheless insisted that the doctrine had to be applied.[9]

8–121   (3) APPLICATION UNCERTAIN. The doctrine of conversion was never applied as an absolute rule in all cases where land was held on trust for sale, nor was its application consistent.[10] For example—

    (i) there was a sharp divergence of judicial opinion as to whether the doctrine should always be applied to the beneficial interest of a co-owner under a statutory trust for sale[11] or only where it was essential to the working of the 1925 property legislation[12]; and

    (ii) there was a series of cases in which a court had to consider whether a beneficiary under a trust for sale was to be regarded as having an interest in land for the purposes of a particular statute.[13]

To overcome the latter point, it became the practice for new statutes to deal expressly with their application to interests under a trust for sale.[14]

8–122   **6. Protection of purchasers.** For the protection of any purchaser from the trustees for sale, a trust for sale once created was deemed to subsist until the land had been conveyed either to the beneficiaries themselves or to some other person under their direction.[15]

---

[8] See *Re Price* [1928] Ch. 579; *Re Kempthorne* [1930] 1 Ch. 268; *Re Newman* [1930] 2 Ch. 409. *cf. Re Warren* [1932] 1 Ch. 42.

[9] *Re Newman, supra,* at 417.

[10] [1990] Conv. 12 at 22 (R. J. Smith). For the historical background to the doctrine, see (1984) 100 L.Q.R. 86 (J. S. Anderson). For the later authorities, see [1978] Conv. 194 (H. Forrest); [1986] Conv. 415 (J. Warburton).

[11] See, *e.g. Harman v. Glencross* [1986] Fam. 81 at 94, 95.

[12] See, *e.g. Williams Glyn's Bank Ltd v. Boland* [1979] Ch. 312 at 336, where Ormrod L.J. described the imposition of a trust for sale in such a case as a "legal fiction". One way in which the courts attempted to resolve this uncertainty was by having regard to the purpose for which the trust was set up: see *Barclay v. Barclay* [1970] 2 QB 677; [1971] C.L.J. 44 (M. J. Prichard).

[13] Thus a beneficiary under a trust for sale had a sufficient interest in land to register a caution (L.R.A. 1925, s.54(1); *Elias v. Mitchell* [1972] Ch. 652); to constitute an overriding interest (L.R.A. 1925, s.70(1)(g); *Williams & Glyn's Bank Ltd v. Boland* [1981] A.C. 487); for his equitable interest to pass under the "all estate clause" (L.P.A. 1925, s.63(1); *Ahmed v. Kendrick* (1987) 56 P. & C.R. 120); for any contract to sell his interest to require written evidence (L.P.A. 1925, s.40 (since repealed); see *Cooper v. Critchley* [1955] Ch. 431); and to constitute a "beneficial interest in real estate" (A.E.A. 1925, s.51(2); *Re Bradshaw* [1950] Ch. 582 *cf. Re Donkin* [1948] Ch. 74); but not to register a charging order as a writ or order affecting land (L.C.A. 1972, s.6; see *Perry v. Phoenix Assurance Plc* [1988] 1 W.L.R. 940); or to register as a *lis pendens* a claim to a share of the proceeds of sale of the property held on trust (L.C.A. 1972, s.5 (replacing L.C.A. 1925, s.2); *Taylor v. Taylor* [1968] 1 W.L.R. 378).

[14] See, *e.g.* Limitation Act 1980, s.38(1); L.P.(M.P.)A. 1989, s.2 (in each case as originally enacted: both have since been amended by T.L.A.T.A. 1996); Charging Orders Act 1979, s.2 (which did not require amendment by T.L.A.T.A. 1996).

[15] L.P.A. 1925, s.23 (now repealed). This was to meet the difficulty that if all the beneficiaries were of full age and capacity, they could put an end to the trust for sale by electing to have the land retained. This might have turned the land into settled land.

Part 4

TRUSTS OF LAND AFTER 1996

1. The nature of a trust of land. It has already been explained that the **8–123** Trusts of Land and Appointment of Trustees Act 1996, which came into force on January 1, 1997, introduced a unitary system of trusts of land.[16] The threefold division between settlements, trusts for sale and bare trusts has gone. Subject to two exceptions, explained below, a trust of land is any trust of property which consists of or includes land.[17] It applies to any description of trust including—

    (i) an express, implied, resulting or constructive trust;

    (ii) a trust for sale; and

    (iii) a bare trust.[18]

The trust of land follows the model of the trust for sale. Both the legal estate in the land and all the powers of disposition and management are vested in the trustees of land.[19] Where, as will commonly be the case, the title to the land is registered, it will be registered in the names of the trustees.[20]

The Act is applicable to trusts created or arising before 1997.[21] As a result, trusts for sale (whether express or implied) and bare trusts that were in existence on January 1, 1997, automatically became trusts of land.[22] The two exceptional situations in which the Act does not apply are—

---

[16] *Ante,* para. 8–001. For commentaries on the Act, see [1997] Conv. 401 (A. J. Oakley); 411 (N. Hopkins); (1998) 61 M.L.R. 56 (L. M. Clements).

[17] T.L.A.T.A. 1996, s.1(1). A mixed trust of land and personalty will therefore be a trust of land. However, it is only in relation to the land so held that the trustees of land have the powers conferred by the Act: *ibid.,* s.6(1); *post,* para. 8–136.

[18] T.L.A.T.A. 1996, s.1(2). It appears to have been assumed that where a person grants another a limited interest (as where A grants B an interest in Blackacre for life), only the limited interest takes effect under the trust of land, and that the reversion to the settlor does not: see L.P.A. 1925, s.2(1A) (inserted by T.L.A.T.A. 1996, s.25(1), Sched. 3, para. 4), which provides that such reversionary interests will be overreached as if they were an interest under the trust of land. The provision is puzzling: it is difficult to see how an equitable reversion can exist other than under a trust of land. The provision was introduced on the basis of an analogy with S.L.A. 1925, s.1(4) (which is derived from S.L.A. 1882, s.2(2)). However, the analogy is very questionable. As a settlement had to be created by an instrument (S.L.A. 1925, s.1(1)), it was necessary to make provision for a reversion that was not specifically dealt with by the instrument which created the limited interest. No such need exists in relation to a trust of land which can be created in certain circumstances without any instrument.

[19] Subject to their power to delegate any of their functions to one or more beneficiaries: *ibid.* s.9; *post,* para. 8–145. For the analogous but more limited powers of delegation that were conferred on trustees for sale, see *ante,* para. 8–116.

[20] L.R.A. 1925, s.94(1) (as substituted by T.L.A.T.A. 1996, s.25(1), Sched. 3, para. 5).

[21] T.L.A.T.A. 1996, s.1(2). Many (but not all) of the provisions of the Act of 1996 apply to personal representatives: *ibid.,* s.18(1); see *post,* para. 8–156.

[22] T.L.A.T.A. 1996, s.192); and see s.4. There are however some differences between those trusts of land which were created before 1997 and those created after 1996: see, *e.g. post,* para. 8–147.

(i) in relation to land which was settled land prior to 1997; and

(ii) as regards land which is subject to the Universities and College Estates Act 1925.[23]

8–124   **2. The reasons for the introduction of trusts of land.** Trusts of land were introduced on the recommendation of the Law Commission.[24] Amongst the principal defects in the law identified by the Law Commission which their introduction was intended to remedy were the following.[25]

(i) The continuation of a dual system of settlements and trusts for sale was considered to be unnecessary. One particular difficulty was that successive interests in land created a settlement under the Settled Land Act 1925 unless a trust for sale was expressly imposed. This often led to the creation of inadvertent settlements and this could cause conveyancing difficulties for purchasers where the existence of the settlement was not appreciated.[26]

(ii) A number of specific difficulties existed in relation to settled land, of which three examples may be given. The first was its complexity. The second was the inadequate (and uncertain) protection that was given to purchasers where a life tenant made an unauthorised disposition.[27] The third was the inherent conflict of interest in the position of the tenant for life. He was both a beneficiary and a trustee for the other beneficiaries. However, the courts were in practice remarkably indulgent to such life tenants and did not treat them like ordinary trustees.[28] In reality they were able to give preference to their own personal interests.

(iii) There were also a number of specific problems in relation to trusts for sale. The primary obligation to sell was inconsistent with the normal circumstances of co-ownership in which a trust for sale most commonly arose. The application of the doctrine of conversion had become particularly uncertain and unsatisfactory.[29] There

---

[23] *ibid.,* s.1(3). The Universities and College Estates Act 1925, applies to certain unversities and colleges (Oxford, Cambridge and Durham Universities and their respective colleges, and Eton and Winchester Colleges) and lays down a distinct code of rules applicable to dealings with land which is subject to it. It was considered preferable for those rules to continue to apply rather than imposing the trusts of land scheme, which would have involved some difficult consequential repeals and amendments.

[24] See (1989) Law Com. No. 181; [1990] Conv. 12 (R. J. Smith). The Bill attached to the Law Commission's Report differed substantially from the one that was eventually introduced and enacted. *cf.* [1996] Conv. 411 (N. Hopkins).

[25] They are summarised in Law Com. No. 181; para. 1.3.

[26] *cf. ante*, paras 8–055 *et seq.*

[27] *Ante*, paras 8–042 *et seq.*

[28] See, *e.g. Re Thornhill's Settlement* [1941] Ch. 24 (*ante*, para. 8–104); *England v. Public Trustee* (1968) 112 S.J. 70.

[29] *Ante*, paras 8–118 *et seq.*

were perceived to be uncertainties as to the rights of occupation of a tenant in common.[30]

(iv) Bare trusts were anomalous and were neither settlements nor trusts for sale. There was also uncertainty as to the ability to overreach such trusts.[31]

In addition to these defects a number of others have been identified, of which two may be mentioned. The first was that the powers given to tenants for life and trustees of the settlement under the Settled Land Act 1925 and by reference to trustees for sale were "notoriously restrictive" and had "come to be seen as inappropriate for modern conditions".[32] This was particularly important in relation to charitable trusts. Prior to 1997, in the absence of any extension of their powers by the court or by the Charity Commission, charity trustees had, in relation to any land held in trust, the powers of the tenant for life and the trustees of the settlement under the Settled Land Act 1925.[33] The second was that a tenant for life under the Settled Land Act 1925, unlike any other person in a position of trusteeship, was born to the role and could not be readily removed or replaced if he turned out to be unsuitable.[34]

3. Trusts of land in cases which would formerly have created a settle- 8–125
ment. As has been explained,[35] subject to two exceptions, it is not possible to create any new settlements for the purposes of the Settled Land Act 1925.[36] Specific provision is made for certain situations arising after 1996 which, prior to 1997, would have created a settlement.[37] Two of these situations, namely where land is held either in trust for a minor[38] or on charitable, ecclesiastical or public trusts,[39] are fully explained in a later chapter.[40] A third situation is where, by an instrument, land becomes charged either voluntarily or in consideration of marriage, by way of family arrangement, whether immediately or after an interval, with the payment of—

[30] But see *post*, para. 9–062.
[31] *cf. post*, para. 8–130.
[32] See [1998] Conv. 246 (C. Jessel). This was in fact touched upon by the Law Commission: (1989) Law Com. No. 181, para. 1.5. The Commission's principal reasons for widening the powers of trustees of land were to give them the greatest flexibility and to make the law simpler: *ibid.*, para. 10.5.
[33] S.L.A. 1925, s.29; *ante*, paras 8–030, 8–071. Such trusts now take effect as trusts of land, and the trustees therefore have the beneficial owner powers of such trustees: see *post*, para. 20–029. For the powers of trustees of land, see *post*, para. 8–136.
[34] See, *e.g. Hambro v. Duke of Marlborough* [1994] Ch. 158, *ante*, para. 8–087; and S. Bright and J. Dewar (ed.), *Land Law: Themes and Perspectives*, 151 at 171 (C.H.). Although there are ways of dealing with this problem in the case of settled land (see *ante*, para. 8–136), they are likely to be employed only in extreme cases.
[35] *Ante*, para. 8–070.
[36] T.L.A.T.A. 1996, s.2(1), (2).
[37] *ibid.* s.2(6); Sched. 1.
[38] *ibid.* Sched. 1, paras 1, 2.
[39] *ibid.* para. 4.
[40] Chapter 20 at paras 20–006, 20–029 respectively.

(i) a rentcharge for the life of a person or a shorter period; or

(ii) capital, annual or periodical sums for the benefit of a person.

The instrument takes effect as a trust of land. It operates as a declaration that the land is held in trust for giving effect to the charge.[41]

4. Trusts for sale and trusts of land

8–126   *(a) Express trusts for sale take effect as trusts of land.* Although a trust for sale may still be expressly created,[42] it takes effect as a trust of land. Furthermore, the Act provides in relation to any trust for sale, whenever made, that there is an implied power (which overrides any contrary provision in the disposition creating the trust) for the trustees to postpone sale, and that they are not liable in any way for indefinitely postponing sale in the exercise of their discretion.[43] It remains the case, however, that trustees for sale are under a *duty* to sell. Unless they are charity trustees,[44] they must therefore be unanimous in exercising the power to postpone.[45] However, any person who is a trustee or who has an interest in property subject to a trust of land might in such circumstances apply to the court to stop the sale.[46] The fact that the settlor has expressly imposed a trust *for sale* is a consideration that the court will take into account in making its decision. This is explained more fully later.[47]

8–127   *(b) Abolition of the doctrine of conversion.* The Act abolishes those aspects of the doctrine of conversion[48] by which—

(i) a beneficial interest in land held on trust for sale was regarded as an interest in personalty; and

(ii) a beneficial interest in personal property held on trust for sale to purchase land was regarded as an interest in land.[49]

---

[41] T.L.A.T.A. 1996, Sched. 1, para. 3. *cf.* S.L.A. 1925, s.1(1)(v); *ante*, para. 8–053.

[42] Trusts for sale cannot arise impliedly after 1996, because of amendments to the legislation by which any implied trusts take effect as trusts of land: *post*, para. 8–132. The definition of "trust for sale" in L.P.A. 1925, s.205(1)(xxix) has been amended by T.L.A.T.A. 1996, s.25(2); Sched. 4. It is now "an immediate trust for sale" (*i.e.* not a trust to sell at some future date) and not, as formerly, "an immediate binding trust for sale": *cf. ante*, para. 8–109; and see the previous edition of this work at p. 386.

[43] *ibid.*, s.4(1), (2). Any liability incurred by trustees prior to 1997 is, however, unaffected: *ibid.* s.4(3).

[44] Who may act by majority: see, *e.g. Perry v. Shipway* (1859) 1 Giff. 1 at 9; *Re Whiteley* [1910] 1 Ch. 600 at 607, 608.

[45] See (1997) 113 L.Q.R. 207 at 208 (P. H. Pettit). In this regard, express trustees for sale differ from other trustees for sale, who have a *power* to sell the land, and must therefore be unanimous in its exercise: *post*, para. 8–137.

[46] *ibid.* ss.14, 15; *post*, paras 9–064 *et seq.*

[47] *Post*, para 8–142 *et seq.*

[48] *Ante*, para. 8–118.

[49] T.L.A.T.A. 1996, s.3(1). The criticism of the side note to the section in (1997) 113 L.Q.R. 207 at 209 (P. H. Pettit) appears to be based on a misconception: see S. Bright and J. Dewar (ed.), *Land Law: Themes and Perspectives*, 151 at 173 (C.H.).

The abolition of the doctrine in (ii), necessarily means that it is also abolished where a settlor directs that a sum of money (rather than personalty that must first be sold and converted into money) shall be applied in the purchase of land.[50] Because of the introduction of the trust of land, the effect of abolishing these aspects of the doctrine is likely to be comparatively limited. It will be relevant only to trusts for sale that were in existence when the Trusts of Land and Appointment of Trustees Act 1996 was brought into force on January 1, 1997, or which are expressly created after that date. The latter are unlikely to be common. Where there is a trust of land which is not an express trust for sale, there is no duty to sell. Conversion would therefore have been irrelevant in such cases even if the doctrine had been retained.

A number of the provisions of the Act confer rights on a beneficiary who is "beneficially entitled to an interest in possession in land subject to the trust".[51] As a result of the abolition of the doctrine of conversion, all beneficiaries entitled in possession under a trust of land—including any trust for sale—will have the rights conferred by these provisions.[52]

There are two exceptions to the abolition of the doctrine of conversion **8–128** which will necessarily be short-lived. Where a person died before 1997, the doctrine of conversion continues to apply to—

(i) any trust created by that person's will[53]; or

(ii) the deceased's personal representatives in the administration of his estate (whether he died testate or intestate).[54]

As regards the first of these exceptions, a testator who had died before the 1996 Act came into force would necessarily have made his dispositions on the basis of the previous law. To have applied the abolition of the doctrine of conversion to those dispositions retrospectively, thereby altering their effect, would have defeated the testator's intentions and so caused injustice. The second exception covers the case of personal representatives who, at the time when the Act came into force, were treating the deceased's beneficial interest under a trust for sale as personalty for the purposes of its devolution (as they were bound to do).

---

[50] The suggestion to the contrary in (1996) 10 T.L.I. 97 (P. Matthews) is plainly erroneous: see S. Bright and J. Dewar (ed.), *Land Law: Themes and Perspectives*, 151 at 173 (C.H.).

[51] See, *e.g.* ss.9 (*post*, para. 8–145), 11 (*post*, para. 8–147), 12 (*post*, para. 8–148). An annuitant is not beneficially entitled to an interest in possession: T.L.A.T.A. 1996, s.22(3). Nor, in principle, is the object of a discretionary trust, as he merely has a right to be considered by the trustees and to compel due administration of the trust. For a different view, see C. Whitehouse and N. Hassall, *The Trust of Land and Appointment of Trustees Act 1996*, para. 2.168.

[52] The suggestion in [1996] Current Law Statutes 47–15 (P. Kenny) that beneficiaries under trusts for sale do not have such rights would defeat one of the main reasons for abolishing the doctrine of conversion. *cf.* (1989) Law Com. No. 181, para. 13.6. It has been rejected by most other commentators: see, *e.g.* [1998] C.L.J. 123, 131 (D. G. Barnsley); P. H. Pettit, *Equity and the Law of Trusts* (8th ed.), p. 372.

[53] T.L.A.T.A. 1996, s.3(2).

[54] *ibid.*, s.18(3).

Of the statutory repeals and amendments consequent upon the abolition of the doctrine of conversion, two require specific mention. First, prior to 1997, where trustees of personalty or of land held upon trust for sale had a power to invest money in land, they held any such land on trust for sale unless the settlement otherwise provided.[55] This preserved the character of the investment as personalty. That provision is now repealed as regards land purchased after 1996, whatever the date of the instrument creating the trust.[56] The trustees will hold such land on a trust of land. This is simply a corollary of the definition of a trust of land as one which consists of or includes land.[57] Secondly, where trustees lend money on mortgage and the property becomes vested in them free from the right of repayment (*e.g.* by foreclosure[58]), it is provided that the trustees hold that land on trust—

(i) to apply the income from it in the same manner as the interest paid on the mortgage debt would have been applicable; and

(ii) if the property is sold, to apply the proceeds of sale in the same manner as the repayment of the mortgage debt would have been applicable.[59]

This provision ensures that the character of the money advanced by the trustees as personalty is not affected by the fortuitous circumstance that the mortgagor's interest in the property is extinguished.

5. Bare trusts as trusts of land.

8–129 *(a) The nature of a bare trust.* A bare trust is a trust to hold or manage the land for the sole benefit of one beneficiary who is of full age. Such a trust is called a bare, or simple, trust.[60] It arises when the nature of the trust is not prescribed by the settlor but is left to the ordinary rules of law, as where T purchases land with money provided by A,[61] or X conveys land—

"to T in fee simple on trust for A in fee simple".

Where there is a bare trust T, the trustee, must obey A's instructions about the disposition of the land.[62] A may therefore call for an outright conveyance to

---

[55] L.P.A. 1925, s.32.

[56] T.L.A.T.A. 1996, s.5(1); Sched. 2, para. 2.

[57] *ibid.*, s.1; *ante*, para. 8–123.

[58] *Post*, para. 19–049. Such cases will now be extremely rare: *ibid.*

[59] L.P.A. 1925, s.31 (as amended by T.L.A.T.A. 1996, s.5(1); Sched. 2, para. 1). *cf. ante*, para. 8–027.

[60] *cf. ante*, para. 8–010. The authorities provide only limited guidance as to the meaning of "bare trust", a term which has been described as "ambiguous": *Christie v. Ovington* (1875) 1 Ch.D. 278 at 281, *per* Hall V.-C. The expression was used in a number of statutes, *e.g.* F.R.A. 1833, s.27, but the meaning given to it varied from statute to statute: see *Re Blandy Jenkins' Estate* [1917] 1 Ch. 46 and *Herdegen v. Federal Commissioner of Taxation* (1988) 84 A.L.R. 271 at 281.

[61] See *Dyer v. Dyer* (1788) 2 Cox Eq. 92 at 93; *Finch v. Finch* (1808) 15 Ves. 43 at 50.

[62] Lewin 6; Williams R.P. 191; *Herdegen v. Federal Commissioner of Taxation, supra*, at 281, 282.

him. It is pointless to keep the legal and equitable interests separated where only one person is entitled to the whole beneficial interest. This is equally true if the trustees are expressly given duties to perform, *e.g.* to sell, or to accumulate the income, provided that all such duties are for the benefit of one person only, and that person is of full age. This is the basis of the rule in *Saunders v. Vautier*,[63] which has already been explained.

(b) *The uncertain position of bare trusts prior to 1997.* Prior to 1997, there **8–130** was some uncertainty both as to the powers of disposition that a bare trustee of land had, and (consequent upon this) whether he could make an over-reaching conveyance.[64] Prior to the 1925 legislation, a bare trustee of land had no power of sale and could therefore make title to the property only with the concurrence of the beneficiary.[65] After 1925 and before 1997, the extent of a bare trustee's powers was not clearly settled. However, it appears to have depended on whether the title to the land was registered or unregistered. If a bare trustee was registered as proprietor of the trust property, the Land Registration Act 1925 conferred on him all the powers of disposition of an absolute owner unless a restriction had been entered on the register.[66] By contrast, a bare trustee of unregistered land had no powers of disposition prior to 1961. The Trustee Investments Act 1961, however, conferred on all trustees (including a bare trustee of land) a power to sell the trust property in the absence of an expression of contrary intention in the instrument creating the trust.[67] However, although a bare trustee might by exercising his powers have passed a good title to a purchaser, he was personally liable for breach of trust if he acted contrary to the beneficiary's wishes. In principle, if a bare trustee did have a power of sale, such a sale ought to have overreached the interest of the beneficiary on payment to one trustee alone.[68] However, the contrary was assumed,[69] and the point was never settled.

(c) *Effect as trusts of land.* By bringing bare trusts (including those in **8–131** existence when the Trusts of Land and Appointment of Trustees Act 1996 came into force) within the scope of trusts of land, these uncertainties have been resolved. Both the powers of trustees of land, and the circumstances in

---

[63] (1841) 4 Beav. 115; Cr. & Ph. 240; *ante*, para. 7–169.
[64] Overreaching occurs when a disposition is made pursuant to a trust or power: *post*, para. 8–157.
[65] *Lee v. Soames* (1888) 34 W.R. 884.
[66] L.R.A. 1925, ss.18, 21 and 25; Ruoff & Roper 32–05; [1990] C.L.J. 277 at 310 (C.H.). The register is a public document and the beneficiary may therefore choose not to enter a restriction so as to avoid disclosing the existence of his interest in the property.
[67] s.1(1) provides that "a trustee may invest *any property* in his hands, whether at the time in a state of investment or not . . . ". This gives the trustee power to sell in order to invest (*Re Pratt's W.T.* [1943] Ch. 326), and the words "any property" in place of "any trust fund" (T.A. 1925, s.1(1)) extended the power to land. See [1990] C.L.J. 277 at 303 (C.H.). The change in the law was probably inadvertent.
[68] For overreaching, see *ante*, para. 4–073; and *post*, para. 8–157. Payment to two trustees was only required in relation to trusts for sale and settlements: see T.A. 1925. s.14(1) (as originally enacted).
[69] See *Hodgson v. Marks* [1971] Ch. 892; and Ruoff & Roper 32–05.

which a disposition by trustees of land will overreach the interests of the beneficiaries are explained below.[70]

8-132   **6. Species of trust of land.** A trust of land may arise—

    (a) expressly, where land is deliberately limited on a trust of land;

    (b) impliedly, where through the doctrines of equity there is an implied, resulting or constructive trust; or

    (c) by operation of statute.[71]

8-133   *(a) Express trusts of land.* It has already been explained that, prior to 1997, express trusts for sale were invariably created by two documents—

    (i) in the case of an *inter vivos* trust, a conveyance or transfer to the trustees and a trust instrument[72]; and

    (ii) where the trust was testamentary, the will and a written assent to the trustees for sale.[73]

The same practice now applies to the express creation of trusts of land. Where the title to the land to be held in trust is unregistered and comprises a freehold or a lease having more than 21 years to run, the assent, conveyance or assignment to the trustees, if made after March 1998, must be registered within two months. This is because the requirement of compulsory registration now applies to such assents, and to conveyances or assignments if made for valuable or other consideration (as in the case of a marriage settlement) or by way of gift (in other cases).[74] It should be noted that on the first registration of unregistered land, or on any transfer of registered land,[75] the trusts upon which the land is held must now be set out briefly in the application for registration.[76] It follows that in the case of an *inter vivos* trust, the transfer could itself satisfy the requirement of a trust instrument.[77]

    Where the trust arises by will, the personal representatives must make a written assent in favour of the trustees of land even if they are the same

[70] *Post*, paras 8–136 (powers); 8–165 (overreaching).
[71] See T.L.A.T.A. 1996, s.1.
[72] The use of two documents was a matter of practice rather than legal necessity.
[73] *Ante*, para. 8–110.
[74] L.R.A. 1925, ss.123, 123A (as substituted and inserted by L.R.A. 1997, s.1). See *ante* para. 6–015.
[75] Unless it is merely a transfer of part of the land comprised in a registered title: see L.R.R. 1925, r. 98(3) (as substituted); Sched. 2, Form 20 (as substituted).
[76] L.R.R. 1925, rr. 19(1), 98(1) (as substituted); Sched. 1, Forms FR1, TS1, AS1.
[77] A trust of land may be declared orally, but it is unenforceable in the absence of written evidence: see L.P.A. 1925, s.53(1)(b); *post*, para. 10–039. In the case of first registration the owners of the land (or their agent) must execute the application for registration. In the case of a transfer or assent of registered land, both the transferors and the transferees must execute the instrument.

persons as the personal representatives.[78] Where the assent was made prior to April 1998 and the title to the land is unregistered, a purchaser from the trustees of land may be entitled to require production of such an assent to prove that they had ceased to act as personal representatives if they sell as trustees of land,[79] though not if they sell as personal representatives.[80] As explained above, if the assent was made after March 1998, the title to the land is required to be registered, so that this difficulty should not arise.

(b) *Implied, resulting and constructive trusts.* The circumstances in which implied, resulting and constructive trusts arise or are imposed are explained later.[81] It is provided that such trusts now take effect as trusts of land.[82] This avoids the difficulties that sometimes occurred in the past—   **8–134**

    (i) when successive interests arose under a constructive trust and were held to create a settlement under the Settled Land Act 1925[83]; and

    (ii) when concurrent interests arose which did not fall within the statutory provisions which imposed a trust for sale in many but not all cases of co-ownership.[84]

The trustee or trustees will be the person or persons in whom the legal estate is vested.

(c) *Statutory trusts of land.* A statutory trust is imposed in a number of circumstances, though the reasons for its imposition differ.[85] The situations are as follows.   **8–135**

    (i) Where a person dies intestate, his personal representatives hold all his property, both real and personal, on trust with a power to sell it.[86] Personal representatives must have power to sell the

---

[78] *Re Yerburgh* [1928] W.N. 208; *Re King's W.T.* [1964] Ch. 542; *post*, para. 11–129; *cf. Re Cugny's W.T.* [1931] 1 Ch. 305.

[79] See *Re Hodge* [1940] Ch. 260 at 264. *cf. Re King's W.T.*, *supra.*

[80] See A.E.A. 1925, s.36(4); *Eaton v. Daines* [1894] W.N. 32; *Re Ponder* [1921] 2 Ch. 59; *Re Pitt* (1928) 44 T.L.R. 371; J.M.L. 87 L.J.News. 372.

[81] *Post*, paras 10–009, 10–017.

[82] T.L.A.T.A. 1996, s.1(2)(a). A constructive trust which created a settlement under the Settled Land Act 1925 prior to 1997 is unaffected by this provision: *ibid.* s.1(3). All other implied, resulting and constructive trusts take effect as trusts of land whenever created: *ibid.* s.1(2)(b).

[83] *Ante*, para. 8–057.

[84] *Post*, para. 9–053.

[85] The situations in which a trust is imposed are the same as those where a trust for sale was imposed prior to 1997: *ante*, para. 8–110.

[86] A.E.A. 1925, s.33 (as amended by T.L.A.T.A 1996, s.5(1); Sched. 2, para. 5); *post*, para. 11–088. To the extent that the property is land, there is a trust of land and the personal representatives necessarily have a power of sale: see T.L.A.T.A 1996, s.6(1); *post*, paras 8–136, 8–137. The reference to a power of sale is included to avoid any uncertainty in relation to the deceased's personalty.

deceased's property to enable them to meet his debts and any expenses, and to distribute what remains of the estate.

(ii) If two or more persons are entitled to land as joint tenants or tenants in common, a trust of land is normally imposed by the Law of Property Act 1925[87] (as amended by the Trusts of Land and Appointment of Trustees Act 1996[88]). This is explained more fully later.[89] The use of a trust facilitates both conveyancing and the management of the co-owned property.[90]

(iii) Where land reverts to the grantor's estate under the Reverter of Sites Act 1987,[91] the trustees have a statutory power to sell the land even before they have identified the person or persons entitled to the proceeds.[92] In practice it is often desirable that the land should be sold before the identity of those entitled is established. This can take some time, as many of the grants were made in the nineteenth century.

7. Position of trustees of land.

8–136   *(a) Powers of trustees of land.* It has already been explained that trusts of land follow the model of trusts for sale, rather than that of settlements, in that both the legal estate in the land and the powers of disposition and management are vested in the trustees.[93] Section 6 of the Trusts of Land and Appointment of Trustees Act 1996 confers on trustees of land—

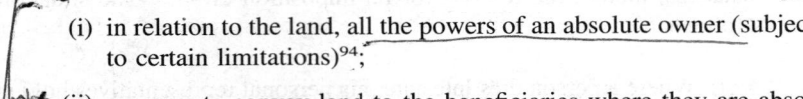

  (i) in relation to the land, all the powers of an absolute owner (subject to certain limitations)[94];

  (ii) a power to convey land to the beneficiaries where they are absolutely entitled to it[95]; and

  (iii) a power to purchase land.[96]

---

[87] ss.34 (tenancy in common), 36 (joint tenancy).

[88] Sched. 2, paras 3 (tenancy in common), 4 (joint tenancy).

[89] *Post*, para. 9–051.

[90] *Post*, para. 9–031. In practice, where the land is to be registered in the name of two or more persons (as will usually be the case), there will have to be a statement in the transfer or application for first registration as to the *express* trusts on which the land is held: see *ante*, para. 8–133. Most cases of co-ownership will therefore take effect as express rather than statutory trusts.

[91] *Ante*, para. 4–042. The Act applies to conveyances made for the purposes of providing a school, museum, church or chapel, where the building has ceased to be required for that purpose.

[92] Reverter of Sites Act 1987, s.1 (as amended by T.L.A.T.A. 1996, Sched. 2, para. 6). The position of the trustees is analogous to that of personal representatives in a case of intestacy in that they do not have to consult the beneficiaries of the trust before exercising the power to sell the land: *ibid.* See *ante*, para. 4–042.

[93] *Ante*, para. 8–123.

[94] s.6(1).

[95] s.6(2).

[96] s.6(3), (4).

Each of these powers is explained in more detail below.[97] They are all, however, subject to the following restrictions.

(a) The trustees must have regard to the rights of the beneficiaries when exercising them.[98]

(b) The powers cannot be exercised by the trustees in contravention of, or of an order made in pursuance of, any other enactment or any rules of law or equity.[99] Thus the trustees are not authorised to act in a breach of trust[1] or to engage in conduct that would in some other way contravene their fiduciary obligations.[2] Nor may they delegate any functions which, as trustees, they could not otherwise delegate.[3]

(c) Where trustees are authorised by any statutory provision[4] to act subject to any restriction, limitation or condition, they cannot exercise the powers given to them by the 1996 Act in any way that it is prevented by those restrictions, limitations or conditions.[5] For example, if trustees of land are minded to exercise their power to invest in the purchase of land, they must first comply with the obligations imposed on all trustees by the Trustee Investments Act 1961 when choosing investments.[6]

(1) TRUSTEES HAVE ALL THE POWERS OF A BENEFICIAL OWNER. Prior to 1997, **8–137** because of the inadequacy of the statutory powers conferred on trustees for sale,[7] it had for some time been the practice of conveyancers, when drafting an express trust for sale, to confer on the trustees all the powers of a beneficial

---

[97] For the trustees' power of partition under s.7; see *post*, para. 9–100.

[98] s.6(5). This is likely to be of particular relevance where trustees exercise their power to purchase land for occupation by a beneficiary.

[99] T.L.A.T.A. 1996, s.6(6). The reference to an "order" includes an order of the court or of the Charity Commissioner: *ibid.*, s.6(7).

[1] One consequence of this limitation is that certain trustees, such as constructive or resulting trustees of land, or nominees who hold land on a bare trust, will not normally be able to make *any* disposition of the trust property except to or with the concurrence of the beneficiary under the trust. This is because any other disposition would be a breach of trust. Such trusts do not necessarily have all the incidents normally associated with the relationship of trustee and beneficiary: *cf. Berkley v. Poulett* [1977] 1 E.G.L.R. 86 at 93; *Target Holdings Ltd v. Redferns* [1996] A.C. 421 at 434–436. For the protection of purchasers, see *post*, paras 8–151 *et seq.*

[2] An obvious example is the rule that a trustee cannot sell trust property to himself. Although such a sale can be set aside at the behest of the beneficiaries, it is not, on present authority, a breach of trust: see *Tito v. Waddell (No. 2)* [1977] Ch. 106 at 248. *cf. ante*, para. 8–095.

[3] See (1989) Law Com. No. 181, para. 10.9. In summary, trustees may delegate ministerial acts, but not their fiduciary powers, such as the power to sell the land: Farwell, *Powers*, p. 498. For a detailed consideration of when trustees may delegate their functions, see (1997) Law Com. C.P. No. 146, Part III; and see (1999) Law Com. No. 260, Part IV.

[4] Other than T.L.A.T.A. 1996, s.6.

[5] *ibid.* s.6(8).

[6] See T.I.A. 1961, s.6. Thus the trustees should, *e.g.* have regard both to the need for diversification of investments so far as that was appropriate to the circumstances of the trust, and to the suitability of the proposed investment.

[7] Trustees for sale had all the powers of the tenant for life and the trustees of the settlement under the Settled Land Act 1925: L.P.A. 1925, s.28(1) (now repealed). See *ante*, para. 8–112.

owner. This practice has now been adopted in the Trusts of Land and Appointment of Trustees Act 1996. It provides that, for the purposes of exercising their functions as trustees, the trustees of land have in relation to the land subject to the trust all the powers of an absolute owner.[8] These powers are not as sweeping as they might at first sight appear to be. In addition to the limitations on the exercise of the powers of trustees of land explained above, there are several important restrictions on these specific powers.

(i) They are given to the trustees only for the purposes of exercising their functions *as trustees*. They are therefore conferred on the trustees in a fiduciary capacity and must be exercised in the best interests of the trust.[9]

(ii) They are applicable only in relation to the *land* held in trust. This is so even though a trust of land is a trust of property which comprises or includes land,[10] and may therefore also include personalty. Thus, while the trustees may (for example) insure the land held in trust against fire or other risks, they cannot insure against any liabilities that they may themselves incur in their capacity as trustees.[11] Furthermore, once the trustees have sold all the land, they cease to have the powers conferred by the 1996 Act, except where it otherwise provides,[12] or where they purchase more land and thereupon become trustees of land once again.[13]

(iii) Subject to certain exceptions, trustees of land[14] are under a duty, in exercising any function in relation to the land, to consult the beneficiaries (so far as is practicable) and to give effect to their wishes to the extent that it is consistent with the general interest of the trust.[15] This obligation is explained later.[16]

---

[8] s.6(1). It should be noted that the Act distinguishes between the trustees' "functions" and their "powers". The former includes the entirety of the trustees' powers and obligations and is therefore much wider than the latter. This distinction, which has been overlooked by some commentators, is of some importance: see *post*, para. 8–144.

[9] *Cowan v. Scargill* [1985] Ch. 270 at 286, 287. See too *Harries v. The Church Commissioners for England* [1992] 1 W.L.R. 1241 at 1246.

[10] T.L.A.T.A. 1996, s.1(1).

[11] The extent of trustees' powers to insure trust property (other than where it is held on a trust of land) is remarkably uncertain. For a full discussion and recommendations for reform, see (1997) Law Com. C.P. No. 146, Part IX; (1999) Law Com. No. 260, Part IV. The only statutory power to insure is very limited: see T.A. 1925, s.19 (as amended by T.L.A.T.A. 1996, s.25(1), Sched. 3, para. 3(4)). One apparently unintended consequence of the amendment of this section is that trustees of the settlement under the Settled Land Act 1925 no longer have a statutory power to insure the settled land. However, there is almost certainly an inherent power to insure which arises from the trustees' duty to act in the best interests of the trust: see Law Com. C.P. No. 146, para. 9.4.

[12] *cf.* T.L.A.T.A. 1996, s.17.

[13] *Post*, para. 8–139.

[14] Other than personal representatives: s.18(1); *post*, para. 8–156.

[15] T.L.A.T.A. 1996, s.11.

[16] *Post*, para. 8–147.

The most important of the powers which are conferred on trustees of land is that of sale. This is most likely to be an issue where land is held on trust for beneficiaries with concurrent interests, and it is therefore considered more fully in that context.[17] However, it should be noted here that, in the absence of a trust for sale,[18] trustees of land will have a mere *power* of sale which, like all powers, can only be exercised by a unanimous decision of the trustees[19] or pursuant to an order of the court.[20]

Although the powers of trustees of land are substantially wider than were those of trustees for sale prior to 1997, it appears, however, that in one minor respect they may be narrower.[21] Amongst the powers conferred on trustees for sale were certain powers of an altruistic character[22] such as a power to grant land for public and charitable purposes,[23] and to sell or lease land for small dwellings and small holdings at less than the best consideration or rent that might be obtained.[24] As trustees have no power to give away trust assets or dispose of them at an undervalue in the absence of express authorisation, it would seem that they can no longer make dispositions of this character.[25]

(2) TRUSTEES MAY REQUIRE BENEFICIARIES TO TAKE A CONVEYANCE OF THE **8–138** LAND. The 1996 Act makes provision for the case where each of the beneficiaries is of full age and capacity and is absolutely entitled either to all or to some particular parcel of the land held on a trust of land. In such a case, the trustees are entitled to convey the land to the beneficiaries, even though they are not required by them to do so.[26] Thus where land is held on trust for A for life, thereafter to B, C and D equally, and A dies, the trustees may convey the land to B, C and D provided that they are of full age and capacity, whether or not the beneficiaries ask them to do so. The object of the provision is to enable the trust to be determined (whether in whole or part) and the trustees discharged.[27] For that reason, the trustees may exercise this power without the need to consult the beneficiaries.[28] Furthermore, the beneficiaries are required

---

[17] *Post*, para. 9–064.
[18] After 1996, there will be a trust for sale only (i) where it was already in existence when T.L.A.T.A. 1996 was brought into force on January 1, 1997; or (ii) where it was expressly created thereafter: *ante*, para. 8–126.
[19] Exceptionally, charity trustees may act by a majority: *ante* para. 8–126. Where a periodic tenancy is vested in two or more joint tenants, the determination of the tenancy is not considered to be the exercise of a power, and can be effected by just one of them. Such an act is not a breach of trust: see *Crawley B.C. v. Ure* [1996] QB 13; see *post*, para. 9–006.
[20] Under T.L.A.T.A. 1996, s.14; *post*, para. 8–142.
[21] See [1998] Conv. 246 (C. Jessel).
[22] See *ante*, paras 8–074, 8–090.
[23] S.L.A. 1925, s.55.
[24] *ibid.*, s.57.
[25] For the future, settlors can of course expressly grant the necessary powers if they are minded to do so.
[26] T.L.A.T.A. 1996, s.6(2).
[27] *cf.* (1989) Law Com. No. 181, para. 14.3.
[28] Something which they are required to do in relation to their other powers: see T.L.A.T.A. 1996, s.11; *post*, para. 8–147.

to do whatever is necessary to secure that the land vests in them,[29] and if they fail to do so, the court may make an order requiring them to do so.[30]

This statutory power is confined to cases where there are two or more beneficiaries. In such circumstances, although the trustees convey the land to persons who are absolutely entitled, the land will remain subject to a trust of land. The provision enables them to transfer their trusteeship (and the obligations that go with it) to the beneficiaries. By contrast, where trustees convey land to a sole beneficiary who is absolutely entitled to it, the trust terminates, and the trustees need no express authority to make the conveyance.

8–139   (3) TRUSTEES MAY PURCHASE LAND. Trustees of land have a power to purchase a legal estate in any land in England and Wales.[31] This power, which applies to trustees not only of land but of the proceeds of sale of land,[32] may be exercised to purchase land

    (a) by way of investment;

    (b) for occupation by any beneficiary; or

    (c) for any other reason.[33]

This is an extension of the powers of trustees holding land. Prior to 1997, trustees for sale could invest or otherwise apply capital money in the purchase of either freehold land or leasehold land held for a term of at least 60 years.[34] However, if the trustees sold all the land held on trust for sale, they ceased to

---

[29] *e.g.* by registering the transfer to them (even if the land is unregistered, the transfer will now trigger the requirement of compulsory registration: see L.R.A. 1925, s.123 (as substituted by L.R.A. 1997, s.1)).

[30] T.L.A.T.A. 1996, s.6(2).

[31] T.L.A.T.A. 1996, s.6(3). The restriction of this power reflects the fact that trusts are not universally recognised and enforced by other states under their conflict of laws rules. *cf.* Recognition of Trusts Act 1987, which implements the Hague Convention on the Law Applicable to Trusts and on Their Recognition. Even where the Convention has been incorporated by a state into its domestic law, it contains wide "let out" provisions, *e.g.* to protect marital property rights and rights of succession: see Arts 15, 16.

[32] T.L.A.T.A. 1996, s.17(1). For these purposes, "proceeds of sale" include any proceeds of a disposition of land held in trust (including settled land), or any property representing any such proceeds: *ibid.*, s.17(3). Thus, if all the land which was held in a Settled Land Act settlement was sold, so that the settlement ceased (see *ibid.*, s.2(4); *ante*, para. 8–041), the trustees would have the power to purchase land conferred by T.L.A.T.A. 1996, s.6(3). If land remains settled land notwithstanding the sale of part of the property, the trustees of the settlement do not have these powers, but only those conferred by the Settled Land Act 1925: T.L.A.T.A. 1996, s.17(5).

[33] *ibid.*, s.6(4). An example of (c) might be where trustees purchased land for a beneficiary to be used for the purposes of his business.

[34] L.P.A. 1925, s.28(1) (now repealed); S.L.A. 1925, s.73(1)(xi). In the case of settled land, the trustees of the settlement continue to have this power. The power is one either to invest *or* otherwise apply capital money and these are distinct: see *Re Duke of Marlborough's Settlement* (1886) 32 Ch.D. 1. The power to apply capital money may be employed to purchase a residence for a beneficiary (whether or not that constitutes an investment). See *infra*.

be trustees for sale, and as trustees of personalty no longer had this power.[35] The present power applies to freeholds and to leaseholds of any duration.[36] It is couched in wide terms to avoid the difficulties that have in the past arisen because of the narrow interpretation given to express powers to purchase land.[37] In exercising this power, the trustees are once again under an obligation to consult the beneficiaries so far as is practicable.[38]

(b) Curtailment of powers

(1) EXCLUSION AND RESTRICTION OF POWERS. The powers conferred on trustees of land by the Trusts of Land and Appointment of Trustees Act 1996 may be restricted or wholly excluded by an express provision in the disposition creating the trust[39] except—   **8–140**

(i) where the property is held on charitable, ecclesiastical or public trusts[40];

(ii) where any enactment prohibits or restricts any such provision[41]; and

(iii) where trustees of land hold the property on trust for sale, the implied power to postpone sale.[42]

The implication of these provisions is that a settlor may now create a trust of land under which the property may be inalienable for the duration of the trust.[43] Where the title to the land held in trust is registered,[44] there is an

---

[35] *Ante*, para. 8–112. In the absence of express provision in the trust instrument, trustees of personalty (except trustees of a pension trust who have the same powers of investment as a beneficial owner: Pensions Act 1995, s.34(1)) have no power to invest in the purchase of land (other than in mortgages of land: see T.I.A. 1961, Sched. 1, Pt II, para. 13). *cf.* (1999) Law Com. No. 260, Part II, recommending that all trustees should have power to invest in the purchase of land.

[36] See (1989) Law Com. No. 181, para. 10.8.

[37] An express power for trustees merely to "invest" in the purchase of land has been held not to authorise the trustees to purchase a residence for a beneficiary: see *Re Power* [1947] Ch. 572; *Re Peczenik's S.T.* [1964] 1 W.L.R. 720 at 723. This narrow view of what constitutes an investment has been criticised: (1947) 63 L.Q.R. 421 (R.E.M.). More recently, it has been held that occupation by a beneficiary is no more than a method of enjoying in specie the rents and profits of the land: *City of London B.S. v. Flegg* [1988] A.C. 54 at 83. See (1997) Law Com. C.P. No. 146, Pt VIII.

[38] T.L.A.T.A. 1996, s.11; *post*, para. 8–147.

[39] T.L.A.T.A. 1996, s.8(1). See too, in relation to trustees' powers of partition (under *ibid.*, s.7), *post*, para. 9–100. The term "disposition" is widely defined: see L.P.A. 1925, s.205(1)(ii) (which is applicable: see T.L.A.T.A. 1996, s.23(2)).

[40] *ibid.*, s.8(3). The reason for this exception (which was introduced by amendment during the passage of the legislation through Parliament) is that trustees must administer a charitable trust as effectively as possible to achieve its objects. This might not be possible if their powers could be excluded or constrained.

[41] *ibid.*, s.8(4). For the reasons for this exception, see *post*, para. 8–141.

[42] T.L.A.T.A. 1996, s.4(1); *ante*, para. 8–126.

[43] Which would necessarily be confined by the rule against perpetuities. *cf. ante*, para. 7–012.

[44] After March 1998, any transfer of unregistered land to trustees of land will have to be registered: see L.R.A. 1925, s.123 (as substituted by L.R.A. 1997, s.1).

obligation to apply for an appropriate restriction to be entered on the register.[45]

The ability of a settlor to restrict the trustees' powers stands in sharp contrast to the position in relation to settled land, where the powers conferred on a tenant for life or statutory owner cannot in any way be excluded or restricted.[46] It has been explained that the extent to which it was possible to curtail the powers of trustees for sale was uncertain, but that there appeared to be ways by which it might be achieved.[47] Furthermore, the courts developed a doctrine by which they would not order a sale of land held on trust for sale where the purposes for which the land was acquired still subsisted, even though the trustees were not unanimous in exercising the power to postpone sale.[48] Although this doctrine was most commonly applied in the context of the family home, it was also employed for other purposes, *e.g.* to preserve land from development.[49]

The Law Commission gave little indication as to why it recommended that settlors should have an unfettered right to restrict the powers of trustees of land.[50] However, this freedom does provide a counterpoise for the much wider powers that trustees of land now enjoy. It gives settlors greater flexibility to make arrangements that are effective to achieve their wishes.[51] A settlor can (for example) provide both for the retention within the family of an ancestral home or estate and for its maintenance.[52] It seems unlikely that many settlors will attempt to create trusts which so restrict the trustees' powers that the evils once associated with settlements are revived.[53] However, if they do, the trustees (or beneficiaries) may not be without remedy.[54] It seems probable that the court has power under the Trusts of Land and Appointment of Trustees Act 1996 to override the restrictions imposed by the settlor to the extent that it is necessary to enable the trustees to exercise their functions.[55] This is explained later.[56] Even if this is not the case, where in the management or administration of any trust property, any disposition is in the court's opinion expedient, but

---

[45] L.R.A. 1925, s.94(4) (substituted by T.L.A.T.A. 1996, s.25(1), Sched. 3, para. 5); L.R.R. 1925, r. 106A; Sched. 2, Form 11A. See too L.R.R. 1925, r. 236(3) (right of beneficiary under a trust of land to apply for entry of restriction in a case where the trustees' powers are limited).

[46] S.L.A. 1925, s.106; *ante*, para. 8–098.

[47] By making the remainderman's interest contingent on the property not being sold and then requiring his consent to its sale: *ante*, para. 8–114.

[48] See *ante*, para. 8–111; and *post*, para. 9–064.

[49] *Re Buchanan-Wollaston's Conveyance* [1939] Ch. 738.

[50] *cf.* (1989) Law Com. No. 181, para. 10.10. A condition which takes away an *absolute* owner's right to alienate the property is normally void as being contrary to public policy, because the right of disposition is an incident of such ownership (see *ante*, para. 3–037). However, this principle may not apply in its full force to property held by trustees in cases where the restraints on alienation are intended by the settlor to preserve the property for the enjoyment of the beneficiaries.

[51] This was not always possible when creating a settlement under the Settled Land Act 1925 because of the prohibition on fettering powers contained in S.L.A. 1925, s.106.

[52] *cf. Raikes v. Lygon* [1988] 1 W.L.R. 281; *ante*, para. 8–087.

[53] See *ante*, para. 8–003; *cf.* [1990] Conv. 12 at 16 (R. J. Smith).

[54] See [1997] Conv. 263 (G. Watt); and see *post*, para. 8–144.

[55] T.L.A.T.A. 1996, s.14(1), (2); *post*, para. 8–142.

[56] *Post*, para. 8–144.

cannot be effected by reason of the absence of any power, it may give the trustees the necessary power, either generally or in the particular instance.[57]

(2) CONSENTS. If the disposition creating a trust of land makes provision requiring any consent to be obtained to the exercise of any power conferred by the Trusts of Land and Appointment of Trustees Act 1996,[58] the power may not be exercised without that consent[59] except where any enactment prohibits or restricts any such provision.[60] Where such a consent requirement exists in relation to a trust of registered land,[61] an application should be made to register an appropriate restriction.[62] The court has power under the Act to relieve trustees of their obligation to obtain the consent of any person.[63] This is explained below.[64] **8–141**

(3) POWERS OF THE COURT. Prior to 1997, where there was a trust for sale and either— **8–142**

> (i) the trustees refused to sell or to exercise any of their other powers; or
>
> (ii) any requisite consent could not be obtained;

any person interested[65] might apply to the court for an order giving effect to the proposed transaction, and the court had power to make such order as it

---

[57] T.A. 1925, s.57. It has never been decided whether the court could confer on trustees a power which the settlor had expressly excluded, but where its absence was disadvantageous to the trust. However, there seems to be no reason to restrict "the absence of any power" to cases where none was conferred. *cf. Re Cockerell's S.T.* [1956] Ch. 372, where the court sanctioned a sale, even though the settlor had provided that a sale should take place only at a later date.

[58] s.6; *ante*, para. 8–136.

[59] T.L.A.T.A. 1996, s.8(2). For the protection of purchasers, see *ibid.*, s.10; *post*, para. 8–151.

[60] *ibid.*, s.8(4). This exception, which was added by amendment during the passage of the legislation through Parliament, arose out of a concern about pension schemes. *cf.* Pensions Act 1995, s.35(4), which prohibits the restriction of the investment powers of pension trustees by reference to the consent of the employer.

[61] Including land which is required to be registered on its transfer to the trustees of land: see L.R.A. 1925, s.123 (as substituted by L.R.A. 1997, s.1).

[62] L.R.A. 1925, s.94(4) (substituted by T.L.A.T.A. 1996, s.25(1), Sched. 3, para. 5); L.R.R. 1925, rr. 106A, 236(3); Sched. 2, Form 11A; *ante*, para. 8–140.

[63] T.L.A.T.A. 1996, s.14(1), (2).

[64] *Infra.*

[65] This term was widely interpreted. It included (i) a trustee for sale (whether or not he was also a beneficiary): *Re Buchanan-Wollaston's Conveyance* [1939] Ch. 738; *Re Mayo* [1943] Ch. 302; (ii) a beneficiary under the trust for sale: *e.g. Jones v. Challenger* [1961] 1 QB 176; (iii) a trustee in bankruptcy of such a beneficiary: *Re Solomon* [1967] Ch. 573 at 586; (iv) a receiver appointed by way of equitable execution to enforce a judgment debt against a beneficiary: *Levermore v. Levermore* [1979] 1 W.L.R. 1277; (v) a judgment creditor who had obtained a charging order against a beneficiary: *First National Securities Ltd v. Hegerty* [1985] QB 850 at 867; *Midland Bank Plc v. Pike* [1988] 2 All E.R. 434; *Lloyds Bank Plc v. Byrne* [1993] 1 F.L.R. 369 at 370; and (vi) a secured creditor, such as a mortgagee, even if his mortgage was not binding on all the beneficiaries under the trust for sale: *Kingsnorth Finance Co. Ltd v. Tizard* [1986] 1 W.L.R. 783 at 795.

thought fit.[66] A considerable body of authority grew up around this provision, particularly in the context of land which was in co-ownership.

The Trusts of Land and Appointment of Trustees Act 1996 contains somewhat similar but wider provisions that are derived in part from the practice that evolved in relation to trusts for sale.[67] The intention of the legislation was that the court should have power to intervene "in any dispute relating to a trust of land",[68] other than as to the appointment or removal of trustees.[69] On an application[70] by any person who is either a trustee of land or has an interest[71] in any property[72] which is subject to either a trust of land[73] or a trust of the proceeds of sale of land,[74] the court is given discretion to make such an order as it thinks fit in relation to two matters—

> (i) the exercise by the trustees of any of their functions,[75] which expressly includes an order to relieve the trustees of the obligation to obtain the consent of, or to consult, any person in connection with the exercise of any of their functions[76]; and

> (ii) the nature or extent of a person's interest in property subject to the trust, which it may declare.[77]

In relation to (i), the power to relieve the trustees of the obligation to obtain a necessary consent to the exercise of some function should, in principle, apply not only where there are practical difficulties in obtaining such consent (as where the relevant person cannot be found), but also where it has been refused.[78] As regards (ii), the element of discretion is intelligible only if it is confined to a decision by the court whether or not to make a declaration as to

---

[66] L.P.A. 1925, s.30(1) (now repealed).

[67] T.L.A.T.A. 1996, ss.14, 15. *cf.* (1989) Law Com. No. 181, paras 12.1–12.13.

[68] (1989) Law Com. No. 181, para. 12.6.

[69] T.L.A.T.A. 1996, s.14(3). For the appointment and removal of trustees, see *post*, paras 10–52–10–67.

[70] Whether that application is made before 1997 or after 1996: *ibid.*, s.14(4).

[71] The expression "interest in property" is likely to be widely interpreted (as was the equivalent expression in L.P.A. 1925, s.30, *supra*). It would probably include an object of a discretionary trust (who has the right to compel the proper administration of the trust).

[72] Including personal property.

[73] T.L.A.T.A. 1996, s.14(1).

[74] *ibid.*, s.17(2). For the meaning of a trust of the proceeds of sale of land, see *ibid.* s.17(3)–(6).

[75] T.L.A.T.A. 1996, s.14(2)(a).

[76] For the obligation of trustees to consult certain beneficiaries in the exercise of any of their functions, see *ibid.*, s.11; *post*, para. 8–147.

[77] T.L.A.T.A. 1996, s.14(2)(b).

[78] This was the case in relation to trusts for sale under the different wording of L.P.A. 1925, s.30: *Re Beale's S.T.* [1932] 2 Ch. 15. The Draft Bill in (1989) Law Com. No. 181 did not specifically mention the issue of consents in its equivalent provision. Although it was added when the Bill was redrafted by the Law Commission, there is no reason to think that there was any intention to change the law.

a person's proprietary rights.[79] It seems improbable that the court was intended to have a discretion to vary such rights.[80]

In exercising its discretion, the matters to which the court is required to **8–143** have regard include the following—

(a) the intentions of the person or persons (if any) who created the trust;

(b) the purposes for which the property subject to the trust is held;

(c) the welfare of any minor who occupies or might reasonably be expected to occupy any land subject to the trust as his home; and

(d) the interests of any secured creditor of any beneficiary.[81]

It should be emphasised both that this list is not an exhaustive one, and that the relevant factors will sometimes conflict, so that the court will have to decide which is to prevail. The court is also required to have regard to certain additional factors in relation to particular functions. First, it must have regard to the circumstances and wishes of any beneficiaries of full age who are entitled to an interest in possession in property[82] subject to the trust or (in case of dispute) of the majority (according to the value of their combined interests).[83] This applies to all applications except those relating to the exercise by the trustees of their powers either—

(i) to convey land to beneficiaries who are absolutely entitled to it[84]; or

(ii) to exclude a beneficiary from occupation of any land held in trust.[85]

Secondly, on an application relating to the exercise of the power to exclude a beneficiary from occupation of any land held in trust,[86] the court must have regard to the circumstances and wishes of each of the beneficiaries who is (or apart from any previous exercise by the trustees of those powers would be) entitled to occupy the land.[87]

---

[79] Compare the provision as originally drafted by the Law Commission, which seems preferable: see (1989) Law Com. No. 181, Draft Bill, cl. 6.

[80] Under the equivalent provision applicable to trusts for sale, L.P.A. 1925, s.30, it was settled that the court had no such power to vary the beneficial interests of the parties: see *Stott v. Ratcliffe* (1982) 126 S.J. 310; *Ahmed v. Kendrick* (1987) 56 P. & C.R. 120 at 127. The circumstances in which the court has a discretion to determine what a person's proprietary rights might be are rare. One example is where proprietary estoppel is alleged (see *post*, Chap. 13).

[81] T.L.A.T.A. 1996, s.15(1). The section is inapplicable where a trustee in bankruptcy applies for an order for sale under *ibid.*, s.14: *ibid.*, s.15(4). see I.A. 1986, s.335A; *post*, para. 9–070.

[82] Whether land or personalty.

[83] T.L.A.T.A. 1996, s.15(3).

[84] See T.L.A.T.A. 1996, s.6(2); *ante*, para. 8–138.

[85] See T.L.A.T.A. 1996, s.13. This is explained, *post*, para. 8–150.

[86] *Post*, para. 8–150.

[87] T.L.A.T.A. 1996, s.15(2).

8–144   Most issues relating to the exercise of the court's discretion are likely to arise in relation to property which is in co-ownership, and they are discussed in that context.[88] However, one matter, already mentioned,[89] must be considered here. This is whether the court may, in the exercise of its statutory discretion, override an express exclusion by the settlor[90] of all or some of the powers conferred on the trustees by the Trusts of Land and Appointment of Trustees Act 1996. It is suggested that there are at least three reasons why it can.

(i)   The court is authorised to make an order "relating to the exercise of the trustees of any of their *functions*".[91] Trustees' functions comprise the totality of their powers and obligations,[92] including their paramount duty to act in the best interests of the beneficiaries and to further the purposes of the trust,[93] and their duty to maintain an even hand between life tenant and remainderman.[94] The exclusion of all or some of the trustees' powers will not therefore deprive them of all of their functions and, in particular, it will not affect their fundamental duties.[95] They should therefore be able to seek the assistance of the court to the extent that the exclusion impedes their performance of any such duty.

(ii)   The settlor's intentions are merely one factor which the court must take into account on an application for an order, and may be outweighed by others.[96]

(iii)   The court is expressly empowered to override any requirement imposed by the settlor that a particular consent be obtained in connection with the exercise of any function.[97] This is closely analogous to the present issue, and there is no obvious reason for adopting a different approach in relation to each.

The example may be given of a settlor who created a trust of land but excluded the trustees' powers to sell, lease or charge the land held in trust. His intention was to ensure the retention of the property in his family for the duration of the trust. If he failed to make proper provision for the maintenance and upkeep of the estate, so that it fell into disrepair, an application by the trustees to the court for power to sell, lease or charge part of the land to the

---

[88] *Post*, para. 9–064.

[89] *Ante*, para. 8–140.

[90] Under T.L.A.T.A. 1996, s.8.

[91] *ibid.*, s.14(2)(a).

[92] *Ante*, para. 8–137.

[93] See *Cowan v. Scargill* [1985] Ch. 270 at 286, 287; *Harries v. The Church Commissioners for England* [1992] 1 W.LR. 1241 at 1246; *ante*, para. 8–137.

[94] See P. D. Finn, *Fiduciary Obligations*, Chap. 13.

[95] This point is overlooked in [1997] Conv. 263, 266 (G. Watt).

[96] T.L.A.T.A. 1996, s.15(1); *ante*, para. 8–143.

[97] T.L.A.T.A. 1996, s.14(2)(a); *ante*, para. 8–142.

extent necessary to maintain as much of the estate as possible should in principle succeed.

8. Position of beneficiaries

(a) Delegation of functions. It has been explained that, under the Settled **8–145** Land Act 1925, where land is settled—

    (i) the powers of disposition and management are normally vested in the tenant for life[98];

    (ii) most such powers are exercisable on notice to the trustees of the settlement,[99] but that some require the consent of the trustees or an order of the court[1]; and

    (iii) any attempt to confer such powers on the trustees of the settlement instead is ineffective.[2]

By contrast, where land was held on trust for sale prior to 1997, the powers of disposition and management were vested in the trustees for sale, subject to a limited power to delegate revocably the exercise of certain powers to the adult beneficiary who was entitled in possession to the net rents and profits of the land.[3]

The Trusts of Land and Appointment of Trustees Act 1996 adopts a middle course between these two positions.[4] Where property is held on a trust of land, all powers and other functions in relation to a trust of land are vested in the trustees.[5] However, they are given authority to delegate for any period or indefinitely[6] *any* of their functions as trustees which relate to the land.[7] This power can only be exercised by a power of attorney[8] given by all the trustees

---

[98] *Ante*, para. 8–071.

[99] *Ante*, para. 8–073.

[1] *Ante*, para. 8–082.

[2] *Ante*, para. 8–096

[3] L.P.A. 1925, s.29 (now repealed); *ante*, para. 8–116. Any such delegation made before 1997 is unaffected by the repeal of L.P.A. 1925, s.29 or the provisions of T.L.A.T.A 1996: see T.L.A.T.A. 1996, s.9(9).

[4] One reason for the prospective abolition of settled land was the inherent conflict of interest in the position of the tenant for life, who is both a beneficiary and a trustee for the other beneficiaries: *ante*, para. 8–124.

[5] *Ante*, para. 8–123.

[6] See T.L.A.T.A. 1996, s.9(5).

[7] T.L.A.T.A. 1996, s.9(1). This power is separate and distinct from the trustees' powers to delegate collectively certain of their functions to an agent (see T.A. 1925, s.23), and the power of an individual trustee to delegate all of his trusts, powers and discretions (see T.A. 1925, s.25 (as amended)). The latter form of delegation can only be made for a period of up to one year: T.A. 1925, s.25(1). It should be noted that T.L.A.T.A 1996, s.9 underwent substantial amendment during its passage through Parliament, mainly because of concerns raised by The Law Society.

[8] Which cannot be an enduring power of attorney within the Enduring Powers of Attorney Act 1985: T.L.A.T.A. 1996, s.9(6). This is because an enduring power of attorney is irrevocable once the donor has lost capacity: see Enduring Powers of Attorney Act 1985, s.2. For the revocability of a power of attorney given under T.L.A.T.A. 1996, s.9(1); see *infra*.

jointly in favour of one or more beneficiaries who are beneficially entitled to an interest in possession in land subject to the trust.[9] Because trustees' powers must be exercised unanimously, the power of attorney—

(i) may be revoked at any time by any one or more of the trustees[10];

(ii) will be revoked by the appointment of a new trustee: in such circumstances, the power must be exercised afresh by all the trustees jointly[11]; but

(iii) will not be revoked where a person ceases to be a trustee whether on death or otherwise: in such a case, the unanimity of the remaining trustees is not affected.[12]

Should a beneficiary to whom the functions are delegated cease to be a person beneficially entitled to an interest in possession in land subject to the trust,[13] the power is revoked if the functions were delegated to him alone. If they were delegated to two or more beneficiaries jointly, they will be revoked only if each of the beneficiaries ceases to be entitled. Otherwise the functions remain exercisable by the remaining beneficiary or beneficiaries. Where the functions were delegated severally, the power is revoked only as regards the beneficiary whose interest has ceased.[14]

8–146   Beneficiaries to whom functions have been delegated are subject to the same duties and liabilities as trustees in relation to their exercise.[15] They are not, however, regarded as trustees for any other purposes, and in particular—

(a) they have no power to sub-delegate those functions[16]; and

(b) if they make a disposition of the trust property, in order to overreach the trusts, any capital money must be paid to the trustees of the land and not to them.[17]

---

[9] T.L.A.T.A 1996, s.9(1), (3). An annuitant is not such a beneficiary: *ibid.*, s.22(3).

[10] *ibid.,* s.9(3). This will not be the case where the power is expressed to be irrevocable and is given by way of security: *ibid.*

[11] *ibid.*

[12] *ibid.*

[13] As where the beneficiary has a determinable interest and the determining event occurs.

[14] T.L.A.T.A. 1996, s.9(4).

[15] *ibid.*, s.9(7).

[16] This is because the reason for allowing trustees to delegate a function to a beneficiary is that he (and not some agent) should exercise it. Contrast the position of a tenant for life under the Settled Land Act 1925. As a trustee he may employ agents whenever a trustee might under T.A. 1925, s.23. He may also delegate all his trusts and discretions by power of attorney under *ibid.* s.25.

[17] T.L.A.T.A. 1996, s.9(7). For overreaching, see *post*, para. 8–157.

A beneficiary to whom some function has been delegated, is not required either to obtain the consent of the trustees or to notify them of his intention to exercise it.[18]

Where trustees have exercised the power to delegate some or all of their functions to one or more beneficiaries, they are jointly and severally liable for the acts or defaults of any such beneficiary in exercising the function if, and only if, the trustees did not exercise reasonable care in deciding to delegate it.[19] This provision, which was the result of an amendment made during the passage of the Trusts of Land and Appointment of Trustees Act 1996 through Parliament,[20] has been criticised because it apparently imposes no duty on the trustees to keep under review a beneficiary's exercise of any function once a delegation has been made.[21] However, trustees are under a paramount duty to act in the best interests of the trust,[22] and it seems likely that they would be in breach of that duty if they failed to revoke a power of attorney once it became apparent that a beneficiary was abusing the functions that had been delegated to him.[23]

It may happen that the trustees delegate their functions under the Act and either that delegation is subsequently revoked or it transpires that the person to whom they purported to delegate, X, was not in fact beneficially entitled to an interest in possession in land subject to the trust, so that the delegation is invalid. X may have dealt with or disposed of that land. There is statutory protection for third parties in the following situations.

(i) Where the delegation has been revoked, and a person, Y, then deals with X without knowledge of the revocation, the transaction is treated as being as valid as it would have been if the delegation had not been revoked.[24]

(ii) Where the delegation was made to the wrong person, and Y deals in good faith with X without knowledge of the mistake, X is deemed to be a person to whom the functions could be delegated.[25]

(iii) Where in any subsequent transaction between Y and a purchaser, Z, Z's interest depends on the validity of the earlier transaction between X and Y, there is a conclusive presumption that Y did not

---

[18] Compare the position of a tenant for life of settled land: *ante*, paras 8–073, 8–082.

[19] T.L.A.T.A. 1996, s.9(8).

[20] As originally drafted, trustees would have been vicariously liable for the acts and defaults of the beneficiary to whom the functions had been delegated, whether or not they had acted with reasonable care. The change was made because of opposition to the provision from The Law Society.

[21] See [1997] Conv. 372 (A. Kenny). *cf.* (1999) Law Com. No. 260, pp. 125, 134, 135.

[22] *Ante*, paras 8–137, 8–144.

[23] In other words they would be in breach of their own *primary* duty, rather than *vicariously* liable for the defaults of the beneficiary. T.L.A.T.A. 1996, s.9(8) is concerned only with the latter form of liability.

[24] Powers of Attorney Act 1971, s.5(2).

[25] T.L.A.T.A. 1996, s.9(2).

know of the revocation or that the delegation to X was mistaken if, within three months after the completion of the purchase Y makes a statutory declaration to that effect,[26] or, in the case of a revocation,[27] if the transaction between X and Y took place within 12 months of the date of the delegation.[28]

8–147   *(b) Consultation.* Prior to 1997, where land was held on trust for sale, trustees for sale were under a limited statutory duty to consult the beneficiaries entitled in possession when exercising their powers. This applied only where the trust for sale was created by statute or showed an intention that the provision was to apply.[29]

The Trusts of Land and Appointment of Trustees Act 1996 imposes a much wider duty of consultation on trustees of land, which applies in relation to the exercise of any function relating to land subject to the trust[30] (with one minor exception[31]). The trustees must—

>   (i) so far as practicable, consult the beneficiaries of full age who are beneficially entitled to an interest in possession in the land; and

>   (ii) so far as consistent with the general interest of the trust, give effect to the wishes of those beneficiaries, or the wishes of the majority according to the value of their combined interests.[32]

This obligation applies to all trusts of land created after 1996 except where the disposition provides to the contrary,[33] or where the trust arises under a will made before 1997 (even if the testator dies after 1996).[34] As regards any trust that was created before 1997 by a disposition,[35] the duty to consult does not apply[36] unless provision that it should is made by a deed executed by the settlor who is of full age and capacity, or where more than one person created the trust, such of them as are alive and of full capacity.[37] It should be noted that this does produce a substantive difference between—

>   (i) those trusts that were created before 1997 but which now take effect as trusts of land; and

---

[26] Powers of Attorney Act 1971, s.5(4)(b); T.L.A.T.A. 1996, s.9(2). In relation to registered land, see too L.R.R. 1925, rr. 82A, 82B; Ruoff & Roper, 15–16, 15–20A.

[27] Z will in practice require Y to make such a statutory declaration. *cf.* L.R.R. 1925, r. 82B.

[28] Powers of Attorney Act 1971, s.5(4)(a). In relation to registered land, see too L.R.R. 1925, r. 82A, Ruoff & Roper, 15–16.

[29] L.P.A. 1925, s.26(3) (as amended by L.P.(Am.)A. 1926, Sched.); *ante*, para. 8–117.

[30] T.L.A.T.A. 1996, s.11.

[31] It does not apply to the power to convey land to beneficiaries who are absolutely entitled to it under s.6(2): see *ibid.*, s.11(2)(c); *ante*, para. 8–138.

[32] T.L.A.T.A. 1996, s.11(1).

[33] Thereby reversing the position that existed in relation to trusts for sale prior to 1997.

[34] T.L.A.T.A. 1996, s.11(2).

[35] Or after 1996 by reference to such a trust, *e.g.* through the exercise of a power of appointment contained in a trust made before 1997.

[36] T.L.A.T.A. 1996, s.11(3).

[37] *ibid.* The deed importing such a duty to consult is irrevocable: *ibid.*, s.11(4).

(ii) trusts of land created after 1996.[38]

As regards the former, the trustees are now under no obligation to consult the beneficiaries about the exercise of their powers, even in relation to those trusts where, prior to 1997, such a duty existed.[39] However, on any application relating to the exercise by the trustees of their functions,[40] the courts must take into account the wishes of the beneficiaries of full age who are entitled to an interest in possession in the property held in trust.[41] In practice therefore, trustees are well advised to consult such beneficiaries—whether or not they are obliged to do so—in order to minimise the risk that one of them may make an application to the court.

(c) The right to occupy

(1) BACKGROUND. Prior to 1997, where land was held in trust, the rights of those entitled in possession to occupy the land (assuming that it was both suitable for that purpose and available) were as follows. **8–148**

    (i) *Settled land.* A tenant for life (or person having the powers of a tenant for life) was entitled to occupy the land as an incident of the legal ownership that was vested in him.

    (ii) *Trust for sale: successive interests.* Where there were successive interests under an express trust for sale, it was a matter for the trustees' discretion whether the beneficiary having the life interest should be permitted to occupy the land.[42]

    (iii) *Trusts for sale: concurrent interests.* Although there had been some uncertainty as to the rights of co-owners entitled in possession under a trust for sale,[43] it had been settled that in the absence of some indicator to the contrary,[44] they would normally have a right to occupy the land pending sale.[45]

    (iv) *Bare trust.* A beneficiary under a bare trust was entitled to occupy the land because the trustees held the land as nominees to his order.

---

[38] This distinction arose as a result of an amendment made during the passage of the Bill through Parliament at the prompting of The Law Society. The concern was that to impose a requirement of consultation on all trusts might run counter to the intentions of the settlor. However, for reasons explained *infra*, this amendment is unlikely to have much practical effect.

[39] L.P.A. 1925, s.26(3) was repealed by T.L.A.T.A. 1996, s.25(2), Sched. 4, without any saving to cover this situation. This was probably due to an oversight.

[40] T.L.A.T.A. 1996, s.14, *ante*, para. 8–142.

[41] T.L.A.T.A. 1996, s.15(3); *ante*, para. 8–143.

[42] *Re Bagot's Settlement* [1894] 1 Ch. 177.

[43] *cf.* (1955) 19 Conv. (N.S.) 146 (F. R. Crane); (1966) 82 L.Q.R. 29 at 33 (R.E.M.).

[44] *e.g.* the terms of an express trust (which commonly place the matter at the discretion of the trustees), or the purpose for which the trust was created.

[45] *City of London B.S. v. Flegg* [1988] A.C. 54 at 81; *post*, para. 9–062.

After 1996, in relation to trusts of land,[46] the Trusts of Land and Appointment of Trustees Act 1996 confers a statutory right of occupation in the circumstances explained below. This right was conferred for two reasons. First, there was thought to be some uncertainty as to the powers of trustees for sale to allow beneficiaries into occupation.[47] Secondly, there was a concern that although trustees of land would have the powers of an absolute owner,[48] it might not be a proper exercise of that power to allow beneficiaries into occupation.[49]

8–149   (2) THE RIGHT. The Trusts of Land and Appointment of Trustees Act 1996 confers a statutory right on a beneficiary who is beneficially entitled to an interest in possession in land to occupy the land at any time.[50] This right continues only so long as certain conditions are satisfied.

> (i) The purposes of the trust must at the time include the making available of the land for occupation either by him specifically or by the beneficiaries (whether in general or of some class of which he is a member).[51] If this is not the case, there is still a right of occupation if the land is in fact held by trustees so as to be available for the beneficiary's occupation.[52]

> (ii) There is no right to occupy land which is at the time either unavailable[53] or unsuitable for occupation by him.[54]

If at any stage these conditions cease to be satisfied—as where land has ceased to be suitable for a beneficiary who is occupying it—the occupation may be terminated by the trustees. The beneficiary's right is also subordinated to the trustees' power, explained below, to exclude or restrict it where two or more beneficiaries are entitled to occupy the land.[55] Furthermore, the trustees may from time to time impose reasonable conditions on the beneficiary in relation to his occupation.[56] These include a requirement that—

> (i) he pay any outgoings or expenses in respect of the land, such as meeting the costs of repairs and decoration; or

---

[46] Which include all trusts for sale and bare trusts that were in existence when the Act came into force.

[47] See (1989) Law Com. No. 181, para. 13.2.

[48] T.L.A.T.A. 1996, s.6(1); *ante*, para. 8–137.

[49] (1989) Law Com. No. 181, para. 13.2. This was presumably because of the decision in *Re Power* [1947] Ch. 572; *ante*, para. 8–139.

[50] T.L.A.T.A. 1996, s.12(1).

[51] *ibid.*, s.12(1)(a).

[52] *ibid.*, s.12(1)(b).

[53] As where the trustees had already let it pursuant to the exercise of their powers of disposition after due consultation with the beneficiaries.

[54] T.L.A.T.A. 1996, s.12(2), as where a beneficiary sought to occupy a farm when he had no farming experience: see [1996] Conv. 411 at 419 (N. Hopkins). *cf.* [1990] Conv. 12 at 18 (R. J. Smith).

[55] T.L.A.T.A. 1996, s.12(3).

[56] *ibid.*, s.13(3). For the factors which the trustees are to take into account in deciding whether or not to impose conditions, see *ibid.*, s.13(4); *post*, para. 8–150.

(ii) he assume any other obligation in relation to the land or to some activity that is (or is to be) carried out on the land, such as obtaining planning permission for a particular purpose, or making changes to the property so that it is fit to be used as a home.[57]

The Act is not explicit as to whether this qualified statutory right to occupy the land is additional to any common law right to occupy the land that the beneficiary might otherwise have, or whether it has wholly replaced it.[58] If, however, the scheme laid down in the Act is to be effective, and in particular, if trustees are to be able to exercise their powers (explained below) to exclude or restrict the right of a beneficiary to occupy the land, then the common law rights must be superseded. This will only be the case in relation to a beneficiary who is beneficially entitled to an interest in possession in land, but who has no other rights. Thus where that beneficiary also holds the legal estate as trustee (as will commonly be the case where the land is held in co-ownership[59]), he has a right at common law to occupy the land by reason of his joint legal ownership of it.[60] There is nothing in the Act to remove that right. Similarly, trustees who hold land as nominees on a bare trust cannot, in practice, impose conditions on the beneficiary's occupancy, because they must act at his direction.

(3) EXCLUSION OR RESTRICTION OF THE RIGHT TO OCCUPY. Where only one beneficiary has a statutory right to occupy the land,[61] the trustees have no power to exclude or restrict that right.[62] However, where two or more beneficiaries are entitled to occupy the land, the trustees may exclude or restrict the entitlement of any one or more (but not all) of them.[63] Any exclusion or restriction must not be unreasonable.[64] Equally, as explained above, the trustees are entitled to impose reasonable conditions on *any* beneficiary in relation to his occupation under the statutory right, and this is so even if he is the only beneficiary with such a right (so that no issue arises of excluding any other beneficiary).[65] Like all powers, the power to exclude or restrict the right to occupy must be exercised by the trustees unanimously.[66]

8–150

In exercising the powers to exclude or restrict beneficiaries, or to impose conditions on an occupying beneficiary, the matters to which the trustees are required to have regard include the intentions of the settlor (or settlors), the purposes for which the land is held and the circumstances and wishes of each of the beneficiaries who has a statutory right to occupy the land.[67] It should be

---

[57] T.L.A.T.A. 1996, s.13(5).
[58] See [1998] C.L.J. 123 (D. G. Barnsley).
[59] For the imposition of a trust of land in cases of co-ownership, see *post*, para. 9–051.
[60] *cf. post*, paras 9–005, 9–062.
[61] *i.e.* where T.L.A.T.A. 1996, s.12(1) is satisfied, and s.12(2) is inapplicable.
[62] This follows from T.L.A.T.A. 1996, ss.12, 13(1).
[63] *ibid.*, s.13(1).
[64] *ibid.*, s.13(2).
[65] *ibid.*, s.13(3).
[66] *Ante*, para. 8–137.
[67] T.L.A.T.A. 1996, s.13(4).

emphasised that the settlor's intentions are merely one factor that the trustees must consider, and will not necessarily be decisive.

The conditions which the trustees may impose[68] on an occupying beneficiary, where they have exercised their power to exclude one or more other beneficiaries, include a requirement that—

> (i) he makes payment by way of compensation to the beneficiary whose entitlement has been excluded or restricted[69]; or

> (ii) he forgoes any payment or other benefit to which he would otherwise be entitled under the trust so as to benefit the excluded or restricted beneficiary.[70]

The Act gives protection to any beneficiary with a statutory right of occupation, and also to any other person occupying the land with him, such as a spouse, partner or relative. It provides that the powers given to exclude or restrict a beneficiary from occupation or to impose conditions on a beneficiary in occupation may not be exercised either so as to prevent *any* person[71] who is in occupation from continuing to occupy the land, or in a manner likely to result in any such person ceasing to occupy the land, unless he either consents or the court has given its approval.[72] It should be noted that, although the beneficiary's occupation cannot be terminated directly or indirectly through the power to exclude, restrict or impose conditions, the trustees are entitled to terminate that occupation if the beneficiary ceases to have a *right* to occupy the land. This may be either because he ceases to be beneficially entitled to an interest in possession of the land,[73] or because the conditions upon which that right depends[74] are no longer satisfied.

9. Protection of purchasers

8–151   *(a) Consent requirements.* It has been explained that a settlor may impose a requirement that the consent of one or more persons be obtained by the trustees of land to the exercise of all or some of their functions.[75] Where such requirements are imposed in relation to land held on charitable, ecclesiastical or public trusts, any purchaser must ensure that all requisite consents are obtained,[76] however many may be necessary.[77] But, in relation to all other trusts of land, if the consent of more than two persons is required, a purchaser

---

[68] Under *ibid.* s.13(3); *supra.* As explained, such conditions must be reasonable.

[69] It should be noted that trustees have a *power* but no *duty* to require this. *cf. post,* para. 9–063.

[70] T.L.A.T.A. 1996, s.13(6).

[71] And not just a person entitled to occupy under T.L.A.T.A. 1996, s.12.

[72] *ibid.* s.13(7). In giving or withholding its approval, the matters to which the court will have regard include those set out in *ibid.,* s.13(4), *supra:* see *ibid.,* s.13(8).

[73] As where he has a determinable interest, and the determining event occurs.

[74] T.L.A.T.A. 1996, s.12(1); *ante,* para. 8–149.

[75] *Ante,* para. 8–141.

[76] Except those of any minor: see *infra.*

[77] T.L.A.T.A. 1996, s.10(2). There was a similar requirement prior to 1997: see S.L.A. 1925, s.29(1) (now repealed).

is protected if he obtains the consent of any two of them.[78] However, this provision operates only for the protection of a purchaser. The trustees will be guilty of a breach of trust if they do not obtain all the stipulated consents. In favour of a purchaser, the consent of a minor is not required to any disposition, but where the trust expresses such a requirement, the trustees must obtain the consent of either a parent who has parental responsibility for the child[79] or a guardian of his.[80] Where the consent of a mental patient is required, it may be given by a receiver appointed on his behalf by the Court of Protection[81] or by an attorney acting under an enduring power of attorney.[82]

(b) Other cases: unregistered land. The Trusts of Land and Appointment of **8–152** Trustees Act 1996 contains a number of provisions which are intended to provide protection for purchasers of unregistered land that is or has been subject to a trust of land.[83]

(1) FAILURE TO COMPLY WITH STATUTORY REQUIREMENTS. The Act makes **8–153** provision for the protection of purchasers without actual notice that the trustees have in some way contravened certain of its requirements. "Actual notice" is not defined, but the context suggests that it means something which either the purchaser or his agent actually knows.[84] In these cases, although a purchaser will be protected, the trustees will be accountable to the beneficiaries for any loss caused by their breach of trust. The provisions may be summarised as follows.

(a) A purchaser is not concerned to see that the trustees of land have, in exercising their powers or functions, complied with their obligations to have regard to the rights of the beneficiaries, or to consult them and to give effect to their wishes.[85] It seems to be clear from this that these obligations are personal to the trustees and do not affect the land as such.[86]

(b) Where trustees[87] convey land to a purchaser in contravention either of some other enactment or rule of law or equity,[88] or of some

---

[78] T.L.A.T.A. 1996, s.10(1) (replicating the effect of L.P.A. 1925, s.26(1) which applied to trusts for sale prior to 1997: see *ante*, para. 8–112).

[79] See Children Act 1989, ss.2, 3.

[80] T.L.A.T.A. 1996, s.10(3).

[81] *Post*, para. 20–022.

[82] *Post*, para. 20–026.

[83] T.L.A.T.A. 1996, s.16. For the protection of those who either deal with, or whose title depends upon an earlier dealing with, a person to whom trustees have delegated all or some of their functions under T.L.A.T.A. 1996, s.9, see *ante*, para. 8–146.

[84] *cf.* [1998] Conv. 168 at 177, 178 (G. Ferris and G. Battersby).

[85] T.L.A.T.A. 1996, s.16(1). For these obligations, see respectively, *ibid.*, ss.6(5), 11(1), *ante*, paras 8–136, 8–147). See too in relation to obtaining the consent of beneficiaries to partition under T.L.A.T.A. 1996, s.7(3), *post*, para. 9–100.

[86] Contrast the requirement that trustees obtain any consent to the exercise of any power: T.L.A.T.A. 1996, s.8(2); *ante*, para. 8–141.

[87] Other than trustees of land which is held on charitable, ecclesiastical or public trusts: T.L.A.T.A. 1996, s.16(6). See *post*, para. 20–028.

[88] *ibid.* s.6(6); *ante*, para. 8–136.

statutory restriction or limitation on the exercise of their powers,[89] the conveyance is not invalidated where that purchaser had no actual notice of the contravention.[90] An example would be where all the beneficiaries under a trust, being of full age and capacity and collectively absolutely entitled to the land, instructed the trustees to convey the land to them jointly,[91] but where the trustees sold the land to a purchaser instead. The purchaser would obtain a good title unless he knew of the trustees' breach of trust.

(c) Where the powers of trustees have been expressly limited,[92] it is the duty of the trustees to bring it to the notice of any purchaser. However, if they make a conveyance that does not comply with that limitation to a purchaser who has no actual notice of it, the conveyance is not invalidated.[93] If, therefore, the trust instrument excluded the trustees' power to mortgage the land held in trust, but the trustees nonetheless did so, the mortgage would be valid, provided that the mortgagee did not know of the restriction on the trustees' powers. This provision does not apply where the land is held on charitable, ecclesiastical or public trusts,[94] because the powers conferred by the 1996 Act on the trustees of such trusts cannot be limited.[95]

8–154   (2) DEED OF DISCHARGE. It has been explained how, in relation to settled land, where the settlement comes to an end, the trustees should execute a deed of discharge to indicate this fact.[96] There was no equivalent provision in relation to land held on trust for sale prior to 1997.[97] However, the Trusts of Land and Appointment of Trustees Act 1996 has introduced such a requirement in relation to trusts of land.[98] Where trustees of land convey land to those of full age and capacity whom they believe to be absolutely entitled to the land under the trust, they must execute a deed of discharge declaring that they are discharged from the trust in relation to that land.[99] It is provided that—

[89] T.L.A.T.A. 1996, s.6(8); *ante*, para. 8–136.
[90] T.L.A.T.A. 1996, s.16(2).
[91] As they are entitled to do under the rule in *Saunders v. Vautier* (1841) 4 Beav. 115; Cr. & Ph. 240; *ante*, para. 7–169.
[92] Under T.L.A.T.A. 1996, s.8; *ante*, para. 8–140.
[93] T.L.A.T.A. 1996, s.16(3). The reason for imposing this positive obligation is to preserve the curtain principle and keep the trust instrument off the title. A conveyance will be invalidated only if a purchaser has *actual* notice of the limitation and not merely *constructive* notice. He is not expected to investigate the trust instrument: see (1989) Law Com. No. 181, para. 10.10.
[94] *ibid.*, s.16(6). See *post*, para. 20–028.
[95] T.L.A.T.A. 1996, s.8(3).
[96] See S.L.A. 1925, s.17; *ante*, para. 8–036.
[97] *cf.* L.P.A. 1925, s.23 (now repealed); *ante*, para. 8–122.
[98] Implementing the recommendation in (1989) Law Com. No. 181, paras 14.1–14.3.
[99] T.L.A.T.A. 1996, s.16(4). If they fail to do so, the court may make an order requiring them to do so: *ibid.*

(i) a subsequent purchaser of the land to which the deed of discharge relates[1]; or

(ii) the registrar on any subsequent application to register the land[2];

is entitled to assume that, as from its date, the land was no longer subject to the trust of land, unless the purchaser or registrar has actual notice that the trustees were mistaken in their belief that the land was conveyed to beneficiaries of full age and capacity who were absolutely entitled to the land under the trust. For the future, this protection will be of most importance to the registrar on an application for first registration rather than to subsequent purchasers.[3] This is because, after March 1998, any conveyance of unregistered land by trustees on the termination of the trust to those absolutely entitled must be completed by registration.[4]

(c) Other cases: registered land. The provisions explained above have no application where the title to the land acquired by the purchaser is registered,[5] as they are not needed.[6] "In registered conveyancing it is fundamental that any registered proprietor can exercise all or any powers of disposition unless some entry on the register exists to curtail or remove those powers."[7] Where there is a trust of land and the title is registered, the Land Registration Act 1925 (as amended) requires the entry on the register of such restrictions as may be either prescribed or expedient, for the protection of those beneficially interested in the land held on trust.[8] If, therefore, the trustees' powers or functions can only be exercised with the consent of some specified person, or have been limited in some way by the instrument creating the trust, the trustees should apply for the entry of a restriction on the register to reflect this.[9] Any

8–155

---

[1] *ibid.*, s.16(5).

[2] L.R.A. 1925, s.94(5) (added by T.L.A.T.A. 1996, s.25(1), Sched. 3, para. 5).

[3] In relation to registered land, if the registrar does have actual notice that the trustees were mistaken, one of two things may happen. First, the registrar will be entitled to refuse to register the transfer. Secondly, if he does register the transfer notwithstanding his actual notice of the mistake, there will be a ground for seeking rectification of the register: see L.R.A. 1925, s.82(1)(h); *ante*, para. 6–127.

[4] L.R.A. 1925, s.123 (as substituted by L.R.A. 1997, s.1). Such a conveyance, being by way of gift, is a "qualifying conveyance" for the purposes of that section: see *ibid.*, s.123(6).

[5] T.L.A.T.A. 1996, s.16(7). For the background to this provision, see (1989) Law Com. No. 181, para. 10.10.

[6] For a contrary view (which, as the authors admit, would have very serious consequences), see [1998] Conv. 168 (G. Ferris and G. Battersby).

[7] *State Bank of India v. Sood* [1997] Ch. 276 at 284, *per* Peter Gibson L.J., quoting with approval a passage that was formerly in Ruoff & Roper, 32–05. For comparable statements, see now Ruoff & Roper, 7–05, 32–07.

[8] L.R.A. 1925, s.94(4) (added by T.L.A.T.A. 1996, s.25(1), Sched. 3, para. 5). Parliament clearly intended this provision to provide protection for purchasers: see the Explanatory Memorandum accompanying the Trusts of Land and Appointment of Trustees Bill at p. iii.

[9] See L.R.R. 1925, rr. 59A, 106A, Sched. 2, Form 11A. A beneficiary (or other person interested in the land) may also apply for a restriction: *ibid.*, r. 236. See *ante*, paras 8–140, 8–141 and Ruoff & Roper, 32–11. For personal representatives, see L.R.R. 1925, r. 169A, Sched. 2. Form 11B.

disposition made by the trustees must be in accordance with these restrictions.[10] A purchaser is not concerned with any limitations on the powers of trustees that are not protected on the register.[11] When the trust comes to an end and the trustees transfer the land to the person beneficially entitled to it, they should apply to the registrar to remove any such restrictions.[12] The transferee can then deal with the land as beneficial owner.

8–156   **10. Application to personal representatives.** Subject to certain exceptions, the provisions of the Trusts of Land and Appointment of Trustees Act 1996 relating to trustees of land, apply equally to personal representatives.[13] However, this is without prejudice to their functions for the purposes of administration,[14] and it is also subject to appropriate modifications.[15] By way of exception,[16] personal representatives (unlike trustees of land) are not obliged to obtain any consents to any disposition[17] or to consult with beneficiaries in relation to the exercise of their powers.[18] Nor is there any power for a person who has an interest in property to apply to the court for an order.[19]

Part 5

OVERREACHING EFFECT OF DISPOSITIONS

8–157   Overreaching occurs when a disposition is made pursuant to a trust or power.[20] A sale or other disposition by trustees of land (who have the

---

[10] No provision is made for the entry of restrictions in relation to the trustees' obligations to have regard to the rights of the beneficiaries, or to consult them and to give effect to their wishes. As explained *ante*, para. 8–153, where title is unregistered, these obligations are treated as purely personal to the beneficiaries and do not create rights that are capable of binding purchasers. It is unclear whether this would preclude a beneficiary under a trust of registered land from lodging a caution to ensure that the trustees complied with these obligations.

[11] Ruoff & Roper, 32–17. There may be situations in which a purchaser, either knowing or (probably) being put upon inquiry that the trustees of land have transferred registered land to him in breach of trust, acquires a good title to it (there being no adverse entry on the register), but is nonetheless *personally* liable in equity to the beneficiaries for what is commonly called "knowing receipt" of trust property: see *post*, para. 10–019

[12] See L.R.R. 1925, rr. 236B; Sched. 2, Form 77; Ruoff & Roper, 32–20; 38–12.

[13] T.L.A.T.A. 1996, s.18(1). One exception of a transitional nature has already been explained: where a person died before 1997, the doctrine of conversion continues to apply to personal representatives in the administration of his estate: *ibid.*, s.18(3); *ante*, para. 8–128

[14] T.L.A.T.A. 1996, s.18(1).

[15] Including the substitution of (i) references to persons interested in the due administration of the estate for references to beneficiaries; and (ii) references to the will for references to the disposition creating the trust: *ibid.*, s.18(2).

[16] *ibid.* s.18(1).

[17] See *ibid.*, s.10; *ante*, paras 8–141, 8–151.

[18] T.L.A.T.A. 1996, s.11; *ante*, para. 8–147

[19] T.L.A.T.A. 1996, s.14; *ante*, para. 8–142.

[20] *State Bank of India v. Sood* [1997] Ch. 276 at 281; *ante*, para. 4–078.

dispositive powers of an absolute owner[21]) will therefore automatically over-reach the interests under the trust.[22] However, dispositions by a life tenant or statutory owner under the Settled Land Act 1925, will overreach the interest under the trust or settlement only if they are made under powers conferred either by statute[23] or by the settlement itself. In relation to both settled land and trusts for sale, the legislation of 1925 extended the device of overreaching and modified its application to provide greater protection for the beneficiaries under the settlement or trust.[24] The overreaching machinery applicable to trusts for sale has now been applied to trusts for land. The law relating to settled land will be considered first, and then trusts of land.

Section 1. Under the Settled Land Act 1925

Section 72 of the Settled Land Act 1925 authorises a tenant for life to effect **8–158** a sale or other transaction by deed. It then goes on to state the overreaching effect of such a deed (a term which here includes any lease authorised by the Act to be made merely in writing[25]). In its policy the section distinguishes between the beneficial interests of the family, which ought to be overreached on sale, and commercial interests which ought not to be overreached. For example, the beneficial interest of a tenant for life is overreachable. However, a lease or easement created by the tenant for life is not. If the land is sold, it must (like any other land) be sold subject to such leases and other interests as have been validly created.

Interests (both family and commercial) which arise under the settlement must be distinguished from interests which affected the land before it was settled, and which therefore have priority to the settlement. The overreaching principle has been extended to some of these prior interests, but only to those of a family character.

Three specific interests which are registrable as land charges under what is now the Land Charges Act 1972[26] may also be overreached under the express terms of section 72. As will be explained,[27] these are all claims to money, and are not prejudiced by being transferred to the proceeds of sale.

Section 72 applies as much where the title to the settled land is registered as it does where it is not. Where the title is registered, the overreaching effect of section 72 is achieved by the entry on the register of appropriate restrictions which are framed to ensure that only family interests under the trust will be overreached.[28] It should be noted that, where title is unregistered, most

---

[21] T.L.A.T.A. 1996, s.6(1); *ante*, para. 8–137.
[22] Provided that the purchaser complies with the requirements as to the payment of capital money: *post*, para. 8–166.
[23] *Ante*, para. 8–071.
[24] See [1990] C.L.J. 277 at 287 *et seq.* (C.H.).
[25] S.L.A. 1925, s.72(4); see *ante*, para. 8–077.
[26] Namely an annuity, a limited owner's charge and a general equitable charge.
[27] *Post*, para. 8–161.
[28] L.R.A. 1925, s.86(3); L.R.R. 1925, rr. 56–58; *ante*, para. 8–022.

dispositions by a tenant for life of the legal estate will now trigger the requirement of compulsory registration.[29]

1. Rights under the settlement

8–159   *(a) Rights overreached.* The rights and interests overreached by the deed are—

> (i) all the limitations, powers, and provisions of the settlement; and

> (ii) all estates, interests, and charges subsisting or to arise under the settlement.[30]

It is immaterial whether or not the purchaser has notice of these rights.[31] He therefore takes the land free from interests under the settlement,[32] and from all other rights created out of them, such as mortgages of beneficial interests.[33]

8–160   *(b) Exceptions.* This general principle, if it stood unqualified, would be too sweeping and would mean that commercial as well as family interests could be overreached. It is therefore subject to a number of qualifications. Certain rights which are prior to the settlement, and numerous commercial interests which have been created under the settlement by the exercise of the Settled Land Act powers, are excepted. These exceptions fall into three categories.

First, a purchaser takes subject to "all legal estates and charges by way of legal mortgage having priority to the settlement".[34] This exception is largely redundant, as there is no power to overreach rights prior to the settlement.[35]

Secondly, a purchaser will be bound by "all legal estates and charges by way of legal mortgage[36] which have been conveyed or created for securing money actually raised at the date of the deed".[37] This is a true exception, for it excludes a commercial interest arising under the settlement which otherwise would have been included in the overreaching provision.[38]

Thirdly, a purchaser will be bound by all leases and grants of other rights which at the date of the deed were—

---

[29] L.R.A. 1925, s.123 L.R.A. 1925 (substituted by L.R.A. 1997, s.1); *ante*, para. 6–015.

[30] S.L.A. 1925, s.72(2).

[31] L.P.A. 1925, s.2(1).

[32] The interests of assignees of the equitable interests are overreached, together with those of the beneficiaries.

[33] *Re Dickin and Kelsall's Contract* [1908] 1 Ch. 213; *Re Davies and Kent's Contract* [1910] 2 Ch. 35.

[34] S.L.A. 1925, s.72(2)(i).

[35] *Re Davies and Kent's Contract, supra*, at 54, 57. *cf.* 77 L.J. News 39 (J. M. Lightwood).

[36] *cf. ante*, para. 8–080.

[37] S.L.A. 1925, s.72(2)(ii). An example would be where the tenant for life had created a legal mortgage of the settled land to pay for improvements.

[38] *Re Dickin and Kelsall's Contract, supra*, at 221.

(i) created for money or money's worth (or agreed so to be) under the settlement or any statutory power, or otherwise made binding on the successors in title of the tenant for life; and

(ii) duly registered, if capable of registration.[39]

This is also a true exception. It means that commercial interests created under the settlement, either in accordance with the directions of the settlor or under the Settled Land Act powers, are not overreached. These include legal estates, rights and interests, such as leases and easements, properly granted by the tenant for life, and equitable rights of a commercial sort, such as options and restrictive covenants.[40] Also protected under this exception are those dispositions which a tenant for life is allowed to make voluntarily, such as gifts of land for public purposes.[41]

2. Rights prior to the settlement. Section 72 provides that certain rights **8–161** will always be overreached, even though they were created prior to the settlement. These rights will therefore be overreachable whether they exist under the settlement or take priority to it. The Act provides that—

(i) an annuity[42];

(ii) a limited owner's charge[43]; and

(iii) a general equitable charge[44]

shall be overreached on a disposition under the Settled Land Act even if they have been duly protected by registration as a land charge.[45] These rights are treated as if they had been created by the settlement even if in fact they arose before it came into existence.[46] Although not exclusively family rights, these are all rights which represent merely claims to money. They will not therefore suffer if they are transferred to the purchase-money. It is therefore convenient to take the opportunity to clear them off the title when an overreaching disposition is made.

---

[39] S.L.A. 1925, s.72(2)(iii).
[40] Though these must be protected by registration, whether as land charges (if title is unregistered) or as minor interests (where title is registered).
[41] See S.L.A. 1925, ss.54–57; *ante*, paras 8–074, 8–090
[42] See the previous edition of this work at p. 172.
[43] *Ante*, para. 5–097.
[44] *Ante*, para. 5–098. A general equitable charge must be prior to the settlement, for, by definition, it cannot exist under the settlement: *ibid.*
[45] Where the title is registered, the annuity, limited owner's charge or general equitable charge cannot be protected by notice, but only by a restriction, so as to ensure that it can be overreached: L.R.A. 1925, s.49(2). There is one exception to this: a notice may be registered pending the appointment of the trustees of the settlement, but it should be replaced by the appropriate restriction when the appointment is made: *ibid.*
[46] S.L.A. 1925, s.72(3).

3. Payment of capital money

8–162   *(a) Payment.* There is one important condition which must be observed if a conveyance or transfer is to take effect under the Act and so have an overreaching effect.[47] This is the rule that any capital money[48] payable in respect of the transaction must be paid either—

> (i) to, or by the direction of, all the trustees of the settlement,[49] who must be either two or more in number or a trust corporation[50]; or
>
> (ii) into court.[51]

This rule applies notwithstanding anything to the contrary in the settlement,[52] so that a provision authorising the tenant for life as sole trustee to give a receipt for capital money is ineffective. A "trust corporation" is elaborately defined, and includes the Public Trustee, Treasury Solicitor, the Official Solicitor, and companies incorporated in the United Kingdom or under the law of any Member State of the European Union to undertake trust business if they have—

> (i) a place of business in the United Kingdom; and
>
> (ii) an issued capital of at least £250,000 of which not less than £100,000 has been paid up in cash.[53]

8–163   *(b) Failure.* If a purchaser fails to pay his money in accordance with these provisions and pays it, for example, to the tenant for life—

> (i) he will not get a good discharge;
>
> (ii) he will not take the land free from beneficial interests[54]; and
>
> (iii) he will be unable to make a good title to a subsequent purchaser.[55]

The tenant for life may choose whether payment should be to the trustees or into court.[56] However, if there are no trustees, he cannot direct payment into court,[57] but if he does so, a purchaser who is unaware that there are no trustees

---

[47] *ibid.*, s.18(1)(b); L.P.A. 1925, s.2(1)(i).
[48] As to what is capital money, see *ante*, para. 8–094.
[49] S.L.A. 1925, s.18(1)(b).
[50] *ibid.*, s.18(1)(c).
[51] *ibid.*, s.18(1)(b).
[52] *ibid.*, s.18(1)(c).
[53] Public Trustee Rules (S.I. 1975 No. 1189; S.I. 1976 No. 836; S.I. 1981 No. 109; S.I. 1985 No. 132; S.I. 1987 No. 1891); L.P.(Am.)A. 1926, s.3; L.P.A. 1925, s.205(1)(xxviii); S.L.A. 1925, s.117(1)(xxx); Charities Act 1993, s.35. For details, see Snell, *Equity*, 199.
[54] S.L.A. 1925, s.18(1)(b); *ante*, para. 8–042.
[55] *Re Norton & Las Casas' Contract* [1909] 2 Ch. 59.
[56] S.L.A. 1925, s.75(1).
[57] *Hatten v. Russell* (1888) 38 Ch.D. 334 at 345.

will get a good discharge.[58] Where no capital money arises on a transaction (as where a lease is granted without taking a premium), a disposition in favour of a bona fide purchaser for value of a legal estate[59] takes effect under the Act and thus has an overreaching effect even though there are no trustees.[60]

(c) Capital money as land. The capital money and any investments repre- **8–164** senting it are for all purposes of disposition, transmission and devolution treated as land. They are held for, and go to, the same persons, in the same manner and for the same estates, interests and trusts, as the land from which they arise would have been held and would have gone under the settlement.[61] The object of this provision is "to preserve the legal character of settled land notwithstanding its conversion into capital money . . . Where you are dealing with a settled freehold which is sold, the capital money would be treated as freehold, and where you have a settled leasehold which is sold, the capital money would be treated as leasehold".[62] Thus an absolute interest in the capital money representing settled freeholds cannot be disposed of by a will that only disposes of personalty.[63] However, for fiscal purposes, the money is not treated as land.[64] In general, the state in which the settled property happens to be at any given moment, whether it is in land, investments or money, cannot affect the rights of the beneficiaries or those claiming under them.

Section 2. Under a Trust of Land

1. Overreaching. Where trustees of land either sell the land or make some **8–165** other disposition of the property, and in consequence capital money is paid to them by the purchaser, the rights of the beneficiaries are transferred from the land to those proceeds. It has already been explained that overreaching is, and has always been, the necessary corollary of the exercise of a trust or power to sell or to make some other disposition.[65] For this reason, the Trusts of Land and Appointment of Trustees Act 1996 makes no express provision for overreaching to take place on dispositions made by trustees of land under their powers.[66]

---

[58] *Re Fisher & Grazebrook's Contract* [1898] 2 Ch. 660 at 662.
[59] S.L.A. 1925, s.117(1)(xxi).
[60] *ibid.*, s.110(4). This provision applies to both registered and unregistered land. It is irrelevant that the purchaser knows or has notice that there are no trustees: *ibid.*, s.110(2).
[61] *ibid.*, s.75(5).
[62] *Re Cartwright* [1939] Ch. 90 at 103, 104, *per* Greene M.R.
[63] *Re Cartwright, supra.*
[64] *Earl of Midleton v. Baron Cottesloe* [1949] A.C. 418.
[65] See *State Bank of India v. Sood* [1997] Ch. 276 at 281; Sugden, *Powers*, 482; Farwell, *Powers*, 581; *ante*, paras 4–078, 8–157.
[66] Nor was there any express provision in L.P.A. 1925 in relation to trusts for sale prior to 1997. It was implicit in L.P.A. 1925, s.28(1) (now repealed) that overreaching took place in relation to capital money arising from the exercise by the trustees of their powers. Unless expressly restricted by the trust, trustees of land have, in relation to the land, all the powers of an absolute owner: T.L.A.T.A. 1996, s.6(1); *ante*, para. 8–137.

8–166   **2. Position of purchaser.** A proper disposition under a trust of land is automatically effective to overreach the rights of the beneficiaries under it, so that the purchaser is not concerned with them. These rights are necessarily equitable. Trustees of land have no power to overreach either legal estates[67] or rights already existing when the trust of land was created.[68] The purchaser's immunity from the rights of the beneficiaries depends, however, upon the sale being made in accordance with the law and the terms of the trust. The Law of Property Act 1925 requires that, notwithstanding anything to the contrary in the trust of land or of any trust affecting the proceeds of sale of the land if sold,[69] the proceeds of sale or other capital money, "shall not be paid to or applied by the direction of fewer than two persons as trustees, except where the trustee is a trust corporation".[70] There is no provision for payment into court. Where no capital money arises (*e.g.* on the grant of a lease without a fine[71]) it is unnecessary to have more than one trustee.[72] Furthermore, a sole personal representative, acting as such, may give a valid receipt even for capital money.[73]

Where two or more persons apply to be registered as proprietors of registered land then, unless they are beneficial joint tenants,[74] a restriction must be entered on the register. This provides that no disposition by a sole proprietor (other than a trust corporation) under which capital money arises shall be registered except under an order of the registrar or of the court.[75]

The Law of Property Act 1925 omits to say what will happen if these directions are not obeyed. The existence of a trust of land will not always appear from the title deeds or the register, as where a house stands in the husband's name but was bought partly with the wife's money, so that she owns a share under a statutory trust of land.[76] It is now clear however that in such circumstances the wife's interest will not be overreached. Where the title is unregistered, the purchaser will obtain a good title only if he is a bona fide purchaser of a legal estate without notice of the trust.[77] If the wife (or other cohabitant) is in possession or occupation of the land, a purchaser is likely to

---

[67] Unlike mortgagees exercising their paramount power of sale: see *post*, para. 19–065.

[68] Except in the special case of an ad hoc trust of land: see *post*, para. 8–168, and the previous edition of this work at p. 407. Such ad hoc trusts have seldom (if ever) been used.

[69] But see *Re Wight & Best's Brewery Co. Ltd's Contract* [1929] W.N. 11.

[70] L.P.A. 1925, ss.2(1)(ii), 27(2), as amended by L.P.(Am)A. 1926, Sched.; and T.L.A.T.A. 1996, s.25(1), Sched. 3, para. 4.

[71] See *Re Myhill* [1928] Ch. 100.

[72] L.P.A. 1925, s.27(2), as amended by L.P.(Am.)A. 1926, Sched; and T.L.A.T.A. 1996, s.25(1), Sched. 3, para. 4.

[73] *ibid.*

[74] Where A and B hold the land on trust for themselves as beneficial joint tenants and A dies, the trust of land terminates and B can pass a good title: *post*, para. 9–055.

[75] L.R.A. 1925, s.58(3); L.R.R. 1925, Sched. 2, Form 62.

[76] See *post*, para. 10–016. Such cases have become much less common over the last 20 years. To avoid the difficulties which they can create, it is now usual for land to be conveyed to both spouses jointly.

[77] *Williams & Glyn's Bank Ltd v. Boland* [1979] Ch. 312 at 330; *Kingsnorth Finance Co. Ltd v. Tizard* [1986] 1 W.L.R. 783. See too *City of London Building Society v. Flegg* [1988] A.C. 54 at 83.

be fixed with notice of her interest.[78] In the usual case where the title is registered, the purchaser will take the land free of any interest unless the wife has protected her minor interest by registration,[79] or is in actual occupation so that she has an overriding interest.[80]

Where the capital money is paid to at least two trustees or to a trust corporation, the interests of the beneficiaries will be overreached even though those beneficiaries may be in occupation of the land and may never have been consulted by the trustees.[81] The same is true where trustees of land mortgage the land held in trust as security for existing and future liabilities.[82]

3. Proposals for reform. In 1989 the Law Commission proposed that a **8–167** conveyance of the legal estate in land by trustees for sale should not overreach the interest of any beneficiary of full age and capacity who had a right to occupy the property and who was in actual occupation of it at the date of the conveyance, unless that person expressly or impliedly consented.[83] At present there is no such requirement of consent and, as explained above, this can on occasions cause considerable hardship.[84] The Commission's proposals were criticised because they went further than was necessary to protect beneficiaries while increasing the burden of inquiries which would have to be made by purchasers.[85] A sale or lease of trust property will in practice require the concurrence of any beneficiary who is in occupation, because without his agreement the trustees cannot convey with vacant possession. It is in relation to mortgages of the property that the interests of beneficiaries most require protection.[86] The Government has decided not to implement the Law Commission's proposals because they were not widely supported.

Section 3. Under Ad Hoc Settlements and Trusts of Land

The original intention of the 1925 legislation was that a conveyance under a **8–168** settlement or trust for sale should overreach not only the interests of the beneficiaries but also prior equities of the kind which can be translated into

---

[78] *ibid.* See *ante*, para. 5–019.

[79] Whether by way of a caution or a restriction: see *ante*, paras 6–086, 6–092.

[80] L.R.A. 1925, s.70(1)(g); *Williams & Glyn's Bank Ltd v. Boland* [1981] A.C. 487. See *ante*, paras 6–047, 6–061.

[81] *City of London Building Society v. Flegg*, *supra*. For the trustees' duty to consult the beneficiaries, see T.L.A.T.A. 1996, s.11, *ante*, para. 00. See too T.L.A.T.A. 1996, s.16(1); *ante*, para. 8–153.

[82] *State Bank of India v. Sood* [1997] Ch. 276.

[83] (1989) Law Com. No. 188, para. 4.15. For criticism, see [1990] C.L.J. 277 at 328 (C.H.).

[84] *City of London Building Society v. Flegg*, *supra*; *State Bank of India v. Sood*; *supra*; *ante*, para. 8–166.

[85] [1990] C.L.J. 277 at 328 (C.H.). See too J. S. Anderson, *Lawyers and the Making of English Land Law*, 332.

[86] *cf. State Bank of India v. Sood*; *supra*, at 290.

money and can conveniently be cleared off the title to the legal estate.[87] This policy was indeed implemented in relation to dispositions under the Settled Land Act 1925.[88] However, because of Parliamentary opposition,[89] it was confined in cases of trusts for sale to cases where the trustees were appointed by the court, or a trust corporation. It was thought that such special trustees would be particularly trustworthy, and that this additional security would compensate those whose interests would otherwise have been charged on the land. In practice, what are now "ad hoc" trusts of land[90] are seldom (if ever) used because the additional overreaching powers which are conferred are both meagre and inappropriate. Still rarer was the ad hoc settlement under the Settled Land Act 1925,[91] which can no longer be created after 1996. This corresponded to what was then the ad hoc trust for sale: there was the same requirement of special trustees, and the special overreaching powers were the same.[92] Ad hoc settlements and trusts of land are both complicated and ineffective.[93] As they are, in practice, obsolete, no further consideration will be given to them.[94]

---

[87] (1927) 3 C.L.J. 67, 68 (J. M. Lightwood). The draftsman's first thoughts were in fact that *all* equitable interests should be overreachable. This was rejected mainly because of the opposition of Viscount Cave: J. S. Anderson, *Lawyers and the Making of English Law 1832–1940*, pp. 296 *et seq.*

[88] *Ante*, para. 8–161.

[89] See 61 L.J. News. 468 (J.M.L.).

[90] See L.P.A. 1925, s.2(2)–(5) (as amended by T.L.A.T.A. 1996, s.25(1), Sched. 3, para. 4).

[91] 71 L.J. News. 341 (J.M.L.).

[92] *ibid.*

[93] It is rather surprising that the opportunity was not taken of abolishing them in T.L.A.T.A. 1996.

[94] Reference should be made to the previous edition of this work, at pp. 405 *et seq.*, for the details of their operation.

CHAPTER 9

CO-OWNERSHIP

Hitherto no consideration has been given to cases where two or more persons have been entitled to the simultaneous enjoyment of land. Two types of such ownership are of primary importance: **9–001**

    (1) joint tenancy;

    (2) tenancy in common.[1]

When used in this context the title "tenancy" means simply co-ownership, and has nothing to do with leases. The terms "co-ownership" and "concurrent interests" may each be used to indicate any of the forms of co-ownership.

Part 1

JOINT TENANCY AND TENANCY IN COMMON

Section 1. Nature of the Tenancies

A. Joint Tenancy

"A gift of lands to two or more persons in joint tenancy is such a gift as imparts to them, with respect to all other persons than themselves, the properties of one single owner."[2] Although as between themselves joint tenants have separate rights, as against everyone else they are in the position of a single owner.[3] The intimate nature of joint tenancy is shown by its two principal features, the right of survivorship and the "four unities". **9–002**

1. The right of survivorship. This is, above all others, the distinguishing feature of a joint tenancy.[4] On the death of one joint tenant, his interest in the **9–003**

---

[1] Two further types of co-ownership used to exist, coparcenary and tenancy by entireties. These are now virtually extinct and need not be considered. See the previous edition of this work at pp. 456 (coparcenary), 460 (tenancy by entireties).
[2] Williams P.R. 143.
[3] *ibid.*, 145; *Hammersmith & Fulham L.B.C. v. Monk* [1992] 1 A.C. 478 at 492.
[4] Preston, *Abstracts*, ii, 57.

land passes to the other joint tenants by the right of survivorship (*jus accrescendi*). This process continues until there is one survivor, who then holds the land as sole owner.[5] A joint tenancy cannot pass under the will[6] or intestacy[7] of a joint tenant. In each case the right of survivorship takes precedence. It is often said therefore that each joint tenant holds nothing by himself and yet holds the whole together with the other.[8] Whether he takes everything or nothing depends upon whether or not he is the last joint tenant to die.[9]

At common law, if there could be no right of survivorship there could be no joint tenancy. A corporation could not therefore be a joint tenant because it could never die.[10] A conveyance to a corporation jointly with another corporation or individual made the grantees tenants in common.[11] However, by statute, a corporation can now acquire and hold any property in joint tenancy in the same manner as if it were an individual.[12] Trustees are always made joint tenants because of the convenience of the trust property passing automatically by the right of survivorship to the other trustees when one trustee dies. If trustees were made tenants in common, a conveyance of the trust property to the surviving trustees by the personal representatives of the deceased trustee would be necessary. The right of survivorship of a joint tenancy is often unsuitable for beneficial owners because it introduces an element of chance. However, it is ideal for trustees.

The right of survivorship does not mean that a joint tenant cannot dispose of an interest in the land independently. He has full power of alienation *inter vivos*, though if, for example, he conveys his interest, he destroys the joint tenancy by severance and turns his interest into a tenancy in common. But he must act in his lifetime, for a joint tenancy cannot be severed by will. These rules are explained later.[13]

9–004   **2. The four unities must be present.** The four unities of a joint tenancy are the unities of possession, interest, title and time.[14]

---

[5] Litt. 280; Co.Litt. 181a; Preston, *Abstracts*, ii, 57.

[6] Litt. 287; Co.Litt. 185b ("*jus accrescendi praefertur ultimae voluntati*"); *Swift d. Neale v. Roberts* (1764) 3 Burr. 1488; *Gould v. Kemp* (1834) 2 My. & K. 304 at 309.

[7] *cf.* A.E.A. 1925, ss.1(1), 3(4).

[8] Co.Litt. 186a.

[9] Where there is a doubt as to who has survived (*e.g.* where all the joint tenants die in an accident), statute usually resolves the question who is deemed to be the survivor: L.P.A. 1925, s.184; *post*, para. 11–053.

[10] Litt. 297; Bl.Comm. ii, 184; Williams R.P. 331; *Bennett v. Holbech* (1671) 2 Wms.Saund. 317, 319; *Law Guarantee & Trust Society Ltd v. Bank of England* (1890) 24 Q.B.D. 406 at 411.

[11] *Fisher v. Wigg* (1700) 1 Ld. Raym. 622 at 627; Litt. 296; Co.Litt. 189b; Cru. Dig. ii, 372.

[12] Bodies Corporate (Joint Tenancy) Act 1899; see *In b. Martin* (1904) 90 L.T. 264; *Re Thompson's S.T.* [1905] 1 Ch. 229. This provision became necessary when banks and other corporations began to act as trustees.

[13] *Post*, paras 9–036 *et seq.*

[14] This analysis appears to have been first made by Blackstone, Comm. ii, 180–182, but it is disparaged by Challis 367, as having a "captivating appearance of symmetry and exactness" rather than any practical utility; yet see Preston, *Abstracts*, ii, 62. It has been accepted in the House of Lords: *A.G. Securities v. Vaughan* [1990] 1 A.C. 417 at 472, 474.

(a) Unity of possession. Unity of possession is common to all forms of **9–005** co-ownership. At common law, each co-owner is as much entitled to posses- sion of any part of the land as the others.[15] He cannot point to any part of the land as his own to the exclusion of the others; if he could, there would be separate ownership and not co-ownership. This doctrine has led to difficulties where one joint tenant (for example) occupies the whole property, or takes the whole of the rents and profits, to the exclusion of the others. No one co-owner (whether a joint tenant or a tenant in common) has a better right to the property than another, so that an action for trespass or for rent or for money had and received or an account will not normally lie.[16] But destruction of part of the subject-matter (*e.g.* by removing soil) is actionable in damages.[17] There is also an equitable jurisdiction to compel a co-owner (whether a joint tenant or a tenant in common[18]) to pay a due proportion of an occupation rent if it is necessary to do equity between the parties.[19] Until recently, the court only decreed such an occupation rent where one co-owner had excluded or evicted the other, as where one co-owner left the home after the breakdown of the relationship and under threats of violence.[20] However, it will now be willing to order such a payment in any case where a marriage breaks down and one of the parties leaves the matrimonial home.[21] Furthermore, a co-owner who has received more than his share can be compelled by the other to account for the surplus. Formerly this was under a statute of 1705, since repealed, which gave the co-owner an action of account.[22] However, since 1925 this obligation to account arises out of the trust that is now imposed in most cases of joint tenancy.[23] If the joint tenants hold the legal estate, they are trustees for, and therefore accountable to, one another. If the legal estate is vested in others (*e.g.* a testator's personal representatives), they are beneficiaries under a trust and a court may hold them accountable *inter se* in administering the trust.[24]

---

[15] Litt. 288; Bl.Comm. ii, 182; *Wiseman v. Simpson* [1988] 1 W.L.R. 35 at 42. In the case of co-ownership in remainder (*e.g.* where land was limited to A for life with remainder to B and C in fee simple) there was a *potential* unity of possession.

[16] *M'Mahon v. Burchell* (1846) 2 Ph. 127; *Kennedy v. De Trafford* [1897] A.C. 180 at 190; *Jones v. Jones* [1977] 1 W.L.R. 438; Co.Litt. 200b.

[17] *Wilkinson v. Haygarth* (1847) 12 Q.B. 837; and see *Martyn v. Knowllys* (1799) 8 T.R. 145 (cutting trees).

[18] *Re Pavlou* [1993] 1 W.L.R. 1046.

[19] *Dennis v. McDonald* [1982] Fam. 63; *Re Pavlou, supra.* See too *Ali v. Hussein* (1974) 231 E.G. 372; *Bernard v. Josephs* [1982] Ch. 391. *cf. Stott v. Radcliffe* (1982) 126 S.J. 310; *Lloyds Bank Plc v. Byrne* [1993] 1 F.L.R. 369 at 374. For a survey of the old equitable practice, see *Dennis v. McDonald, supra,* at pp. 68–71. For the court's jurisdiction to grant an occupation order in matrimonial proceedings, see F.L.A. 1996, s.33; *post,* para. 17–024.

[20] As in *Dennis v. McDonald, supra; Ali v. Hussein, supra.*

[21] *Re Pavlou, supra,* at 1050. It is otherwise if the departure was voluntary.

[22] 4 & 5 Anne, see *Henderson v. Eason* (1851) 17 Q.B. 701. The statute was repealed by L.P.(Am)A. 1924, Sched. 10.

[23] *Post,* paras 9–051—9–053. For equitable accounting between co-owners, see *post,* para. 9–073.

[24] For the statutory right of a beneficiary beneficially entitled to an interest in possession under a trust of land to occupy the land held in trust and for the trustees' power to exclude or restrict that occupation, see T.L.A.T.A. 1996, ss.12, 13; *ante* para. 8–148; *post,* para. 9–062.

9–006 *(b) Unity of interest.* The interest of each joint tenant is the same in extent, nature and duration, for in theory of law they hold just one estate. This has important consequences.

> (i) Although in theory of law each joint tenant has the whole of the property, the rents and profits of the land are to be divided equally between them.

> (ii) There can be no joint tenancy between those with interests of a different nature, *e.g.* a freeholder and a tenant for years, a tenant in possession and tenant in remainder, or a tenant with a vested interest and a tenant with a contingent interest.[25] But personal disability (*e.g.* if a person is a minor or a mental patient) is not inconsistent with a joint tenancy.[26]

> (iii) There can be no joint tenancy between those whose interests are similar but of different duration. Thus before 1926 a tenant in fee simple and a tenant in tail both owned freeholds but the differing durations of the estates prevented them from being held in joint tenancy.[27]

> (iv) Any legal act, *e.g.* a conveyance or lease of the land, or a surrender of a lease,[28] or the exercise of a break clause,[29] or the giving of a notice,[30] requires the participation of all the joint tenants. They cannot be effected by one joint tenant alone because he does not by himself have the whole estate.[31] But exceptions are found in the cases of personal representatives[32] and of the determination of periodic tenancies (*e.g.* weekly or monthly tenancies), which are

---

[25] *Kenworthy v. Ward* (1853) 11 Hare 196 at 198, 199; *M'Gregor v. M'Gregor* (1859) 1 De G.F. & J. 63 at 74; *Ruck v. Barwise* (1865) 2 Dr. & Sm. 510 at 512. See, *e.g. Woodgate v. Unwin* (1831) 4 Sim. 129 (gift to class on attaining 21 cannot create joint tenancy, for some interests would be vested and some contingent: *Ruck v. Barwise, supra,* at 512); *cf. M'Gregor v. M'Gregor, supra,* at 74, showing that the interpretation put on *Woodgate v. Unwin, supra,* in *Booth v. Arlington* (1857) 3 Jur. (N.S.) 835 at 837 is unsound. See also Tudor L.C. 275.

[26] *Re Gardner* [1924] 2 Ch. 243 at 251.

[27] Bl.Comm. ii, 181.

[28] *Leek and Moorlands B.S. v. Clark* [1952] 2 Q.B. 788.

[29] *Hounslow L.B.C. v. Pilling* [1993] 1 W.L.R. 1242. See too *Osei-Bonsu v. Wandsworth LBC* [1999] 1 W.L.R. 101.

[30] *Newman v. Keedwell* (1977) 35 P. & C.R. 393 (a statutory counter-notice under the Agricultural Holdings Act 1948).

[31] Bl.Comm. ii, 183. This rule has assumed some importance in more recent cases. Thus in *Thames Guaranty Ltd v. Campbell* [1985] Q.B. 210, a contract by one joint tenant to grant a mortgage was effective to bind only his own beneficial interest. The lender sought specific performance but it was refused because of the probable hardship to the other joint tenant, the borrower's wife. In *Ashmed v. Kendrick* (1987) 56 P. & C.R. 120, one joint tenant forged the signature of the other on a registered transfer. Only the equitable interest of the party making the transfer passed to the purchaser. *Post,* para. 9–039.

[32] See *post,* para. 11–131.

determinable on the usual notice[33] given by one of joint landlords[34] or one of joint tenants.[35] A periodic tenancy continues only so long as it is the will of both parties that it should continue.[36] This is because there is a notional renewal of the term at the end of each period[37] which requires the consent of all the parties.[38] A co-owner who gives such a notice without the consent of the others does not commit a breach of the trust that applies in cases of co-ownership.[39] This is because the interest which is subject to the trust will in any event terminate at the end of the period of the notice.[40] The notice does not operate as a disposition of the property.[41]

Unity of interest must apply to the estate which is held jointly; but if that requirement is satisfied, it does not matter that one joint tenant has a further and separate interest in the same property.[42] A conveyance "to A and B as joint tenants for lives, remainder to B in fee simple" would make A and B joint tenants for life despite the remainder to B.[43]

(c) *Unity of title.* Each joint tenant must claim his title to the land under the **9–007** same act or document.[44] This requirement is satisfied if all the tenants acquired their rights by the same conveyance[45] or if they simultaneously took possession of land and acquired title to it by adverse possession.[46]

---

[33] See *post*, para. 14–068.

[34] *Doe d. Aslin v. Summersett* (1830) 1 B. & Ad. 135; *Parsons v. Parsons* [1983] 1 W.L.R. 1390. The criticism of these cases in [1983] Conv. 194 (F. Webb) has been rejected by the Court of Appeal: *Hammersmith & Fulham L.B.C. v. Monk* [1991] 1 E.G.L.R. 263 (affirmed on appeal: [1992] 1 A.C. 478).

[35] *Greenwich L.B.C. v. McGrady* (1982) 46 P. & C.R. 223; *Hammersmith & Fulham L.B.C. v. Monk* [1992] 1 A.C. 478; *Newham L.B.C. v. Hill* (1998) 76 P. & C.R. D24. See [1992] Conv. 279 (S. Goulding).

[36] *Hammersmith & Fulham L.B.C. v. Monk* [1991] 1 E.G.L.R. 263 at 269; [1992] 1 A.C. 478 at 484; *A.G. Securities v. Vaughan* [1990] 1 A.C. 417 at 473.

[37] *Prudential Assurance Co. Ltd v. London Residuary Body* [1992] 2 A.C. 386 at 394.

[38] *Hammersmith & Fulham L.B.C. v. Monk, supra.* For telling criticism of this result, see (1992) 108 L.Q.R. 375 (J. Dewar); [1998] Fam. Law 590 (S. Cretney: "One moment you have an apparently secure tenancy; the next minute it has disappeared by the unilateral (and secret) action of your former partner of which you know nothing"). *cf. Hounslow L.B.C. v. Pilling* [1993] 1 W.L.R. 1242 at 1246, 1247.

[39] *Crawley B.C. v. Ure* [1996] Q.B. 13. See too *Harrow L.B.C. v. Johnstone* [1997] 1 W.L.R. 459 (issue of notice not a breach of an ouster order). For the trust of land in cases of co-ownership, see *post*, para. 9–051.

[40] *Hammersmith & Fulham L.B.C. v. Monk, supra,* at 490.

[41] *Newlon Housing Trust v. Alsulaimen* [1999] 1 A.C. 313 (M.C.A. 1973, s.37(2)(b)).

[42] *Burton's Compendium*, 245.

[43] Co.Litt. 182a, b, 184a; *Wiscot's Case* (1599) 2 Co.Rep. 60b; *Quarm v. Quarm* [1892] 1 Q.B. 184. Litt. 285 and Co.Litt. 188a, which speak of joint tenants, one for life and one in fee, must be understood to refer to this situation.

[44] Litt. 278; Co.Litt. 189a, 299b; Bl.Comm. ii, 181; *A.G. Securities v. Vaughan, supra,* at 435, 474.

[45] Cru.Dig. ii, 367.

[46] Litt. 278; *Ward v. Ward* (1871) 6 Ch.App. 789; *post*, para. 21–016.

9–008   *(d) Unity of time.* The interest of each tenant must vest at the same time.[47] This does not necessarily follow from unity of title. For example, if before 1926, land was conveyed "to A for life, remainder to the heirs of B and C", and B and C died at different times in A's lifetime, B's heirs and C's heirs took the fee simple in remainder as tenants in common. The heirs could not take as joint tenants, for although there was unity of title there was no unity of time.[48]

B. Tenancy in Common

9–009   A tenancy in common differs significantly from a joint tenancy.

9–010   **1. The tenants hold in undivided shares.** Unlike joint tenants, tenants in common hold in undivided shares. Each tenant in common has a distinct share in property which has not yet been divided among the co-tenants.[49] Thus tenants in common have quite separate interests. The only fact which brings them into co-ownership is that they both have shares in a single property which has not yet been divided among them. While the tenancy in common lasts, no one can say which of them owns any particular parcel of land.

9–011   **2. There is no right of survivorship.** The size of each tenant's share is fixed once and for all and is not affected by the death of one of his companions. When a tenant in common dies, his interest passes under his will or intestacy, for his undivided share is his to dispose of as he wishes.[50] But rights equivalent to survivorship may be given by express limitation.[51]

The absence of the right of survivorship can create anomalies. Where a husband and wife are beneficial joint tenants and one of the spouses dies intestate, the survivor will acquire the property by right of survivorship and will in addition be entitled to a statutory legacy.[52] If, however, the home is owned by the spouses as tenants in common,[53] the survivor will receive only the statutory legacy, although he may require the personal representatives to apply this sum towards the acquisition of the deceased's interest in the property.[54] Although the Law Commission recommended a change in the law

---

[47] Bl.Comm. ii, 181; *A.G. Securities v. Vaughan, supra,* at 436, 474. For "vest" (in interest), see *ante,* para. 7–001.

[48] Co.Litt 188a; Bl.Comm. ii, 181.

[49] *Fisher v. Wiggs* (1700) 12 Mod. 296 at 302; *Re King's Theatre, Sunderland* [1929] 1 Ch. 483 at 488.

[50] Challis 368.

[51] See *Doe d. Borwell v. Abey* (1813) 1 M. & S. 428; *Haddesley v. Adams* (1856) 22 Beav. 266; *Taafe v. Conmee* (1862) 10 H.L.C. 64.

[52] A.E.A. 1925, s.46; S.I. 1993 No. 2906; *post,* para. 11–088.

[53] Even if the spouses had once been joint tenants, a tenancy in common may have been created by the unilateral act of the first spouse to die: *post,* para. 9–038.

[54] *Post,* para. 11–097.

so that a surviving spouse should in all cases receive the whole estate of the first to die,[55] the government rejected the proposal.[56]

3. Only the unity of possession is essential. Although the four unities of a joint tenancy may be present in a tenancy in common, the only unity which is essential is the unity of possession.[57] In particular, it should be noted that the unity of interest may be absent and the tenants may hold unequal interests, so that one tenant in common may be entitled to a one-fifth share and the other to four-fifths, or one may be entitled for life and another in fee simple.[58]   **9–012**

Section 2. Estates in which the Tenancies could Exist

In general, before 1926, joint tenancies and tenancies in common could exist at law or in equity (*i.e.* as legal estates or as equitable interests), and in possession or in remainder, in any of the estates of freehold or in leasehold.[59] Thus if land was given to A and B as joint tenants for their lives, they enjoyed it jointly for their joint lives, and the survivor enjoyed the whole for the rest of his life,[60] whereas an interest given for their *joint* lives would end as soon as one died.[61] If A and B were made tenants in common for life, the survivor would retain his original share and no more,[62] the deceased's share having passed to the remainderman. Where X and Y were joint tenants for the life of X, if X survived he became sole tenant of the whole for the rest of his life, whereas if Y were the survivor he took nothing. The estate which he acquired by survivorship was one which determined at the moment he received it.[63]   **9–013**

After 1925 the position is substantially the same except that a tenancy in common can no longer exist at law. This is explained below.[64] Further, since life estates and entails can exist only in equity,[65] even a joint tenancy in such interests must also be equitable.

Section 3. Creation of the Tenancies

The key to a proper understanding of joint tenancies and tenancies in common is always to consider the legal estate separately from the equitable interest.   **9–014**

---

[55] (1989) Law Com. No. 187.
[56] The Law Commission's proposals were criticised on the ground that the code of intestate distribution is already generous to a surviving spouse: S. M. Cretney and J. M. Masson, *Principles of Family Law* (6th ed.), 203. See too [1990] Conv. 358 (R. Kerridge).
[57] Co.Litt. 189a; Cru.Dig. ii, 399.
[58] Challis 370; Williams R.P. 148; Bl.Comm. ii, 191; and see *Sturton v. Richardson* (1844) 10 M. & W. 17.
[59] Williams R.P. 143. As to periodic tenancies, see *ante*, para. 9–006.
[60] *Moffat v. Burnie* (1853) 18 Beav. 211; *Jones v. Jones* (1881) 44 L.T. 642 at 644.
[61] *Re Legh's S.T.* [1938] Ch. 39.
[62] Co.Litt 191a; Preston, *Abstracts*, ii, 63.
[63] Challis 366.
[64] *Post*, para. 9–034.
[65] *Ante*, para. 4–030. It ceased to be possible to create entails after 1996: *ante*, para. 3–037.

Thus A and B may be legal joint tenants but equitable tenants in common; that is to say, A and B hold the legal estate jointly upon trust for themselves as tenants in common. Their rights of enjoyment, therefore, are the rights of tenants in common, not the rights of joint tenants. The effect of A's death on the legal joint tenancy is that B is solely entitled. However, A's equitable interest (his undivided share) passes under his will or intestacy. The result is that B holds the legal estate on trust for himself as to his share, and for A's personal representatives as to A's share.

It is always possible for a joint tenant to turn his beneficial interest into a tenancy in common by effecting a severance. The manner in which this may be done is explained later.[66]

The methods of creating joint tenancies and tenancies in common must now be considered. These are the primary rules of common law and equity, on which the statutory reforms of 1925 were later superimposed.

I. AT LAW

9–015 Prior to 1926 there was an ancient presumption that where the legal title to property was vested in two or more persons they were joint tenants and not tenants in common.[67] Joint tenancy had been advantageous to both feudal lords and tenants before feudal tenures were abolished.[68] It was also preferred by conveyancers who had to investigate title. Joint tenants held by a single title, whereas the title of every tenant in common had to be separately examined.[69] If a joint tenant died, there was one less tenant but still one title. If however a tenant in common died and devised his share equally between his 12 children, that would increase by 11 the titles that had to be investigated before the property could be sold as a whole.

Because of the presumption in favour of a joint tenancy, a conveyance of land before 1926 to two or more persons created a joint tenancy of the legal estate unless either—

    (i) one of the unities was absent; or

    (ii) words of severance were employed.

Since 1925 joint tenancy has been the only form of co-ownership of a legal estate.[70] However in either of these two situations an equitable tenancy in

---

[66] *Post*, para. 9–036. Since 1925, it has only been possible to sever a joint tenancy in equity: *post*, para. 9–036.

[67] *Campbell v. Campbell* (1792) 4 Bro.C.C. 15; *Morley v. Bird* (1798) 3 Ves. 628; *Corbett d. Clymer v. Nicholls* (1851) 2 L.M. & P. 87 at 89. "The law loves not fractions of estates, nor to divide and multiply tenures": *Fisher v. Wigg* (1700) 1 Salk. 391 at 392, *per* Holt C.J.

[68] See the previous edition of this work at p. 424. For the abolition of feudal tenures, see *ante*, para. 2–044.

[69] See *Bruerton's Case* (1594) 6 Co.Rep. 1a; *Fisher v. Wigg* (1700) 1 P.Wms. 14 at 21; *Garland v. Jekyll* (1824) 2 Bing. 273.

[70] *Post*, para. 9–034.

common will now be created instead. The common law rules are therefore still applicable and must be considered.

1. Absence of unities. The four unities have already been considered. If **9–016** there is unity of possession but one or more of the other unities is missing, the parties take as tenants in common. If there is no unity of possession, the parties take as separate owners.

2. Words of severance

(a) Express words. Any words in the grant which show that the tenants are **9–017** each to take a distinct share in the property amount to words of severance and thus create a tenancy in common.[71] Words which have been held to have this effect include—

"in equal shares"[72]
"share and share alike"[73]
"to be divided between"[74]
"to be distributed amongst them in joint and equal proportions"[75]
"equally"[76]
"between"[77]
"amongst"[78]
"respectively".[79]

(b) Other provisions. Even if there are no clear words of severance, the gift **9–018** taken as a whole may show that a tenancy in common is intended.[80] Two

---

[71] See *Robertson v. Fraser* (1871) 6 Ch.App. 696 at 699. Decisions on particular expressions (other than those given in the text) are *Marryat v. Townley* (1748) 1 Ves.Sen. 102 ("respective ages") *Sutcliffe v. Howard* (1868) 38 L.J.Ch. 472 ("respective lives"); *Re Atkinson* [1892] 3 Ch. 52 ("respective heirs"); *Sheppard v. Gibbons* (1742) 2 Atk. 441 ("severally"); *Halton v. Finch* (1841) 4 Beav. 186 ("each"); *Liddard v. Liddard* (1860) 28 Beav. 266 and *Robertson v. Fraser* (1871) 6 Ch.App. 696 ("participate"). At one time stronger words were required in deeds than in wills, and in law than in equity, but these differences gradually decreased: see Saunders, *Uses*, i, 130.

[72] *Payne v. Webb* (1874) L.R. 19 Eq. 26.

[73] *Heathe v. Heathe* (1740) 2 Atk. 121; and see *James v. Collins* (1627) Het. 29 ("part and part alike"). Contrast *Re Schofield* [1918] 2 Ch. 64 (mere reference to "share" insufficient).

[74] *Peat v. Chapman* (1750) 1 Ves.Sen. 542; *cf. Askeman v. Burrows* (1814) 3 V. & B. 54 (personalty). For similar expressions, see *Fisher v. Wigg* (1700) 1 P.Wms. 14; *Goodtitle d. Hood v. Stokes* (1753) 1 Wils.K.B. 341; *Bridge v. Yates* (1842) 12 Sim. 645; *Lucas v. Goldsmid* (1861) 29 Beav. 657.

[75] *Ettricke v. Ettricke* (1767) Amb. 656.

[76] *Lewen v. Dodd* (1595) Cro.Eliz. 443; *Lewen v. Cox* (1599) Cro.Eliz. 695; *Denn d. Gaskin v. Gaskin* (1777) 2 Cowp. 657; *Right d. Compton v. Compton* (1808) 9 East 267 at 276.

[77] *Lashbrook v. Cock* (1816) 2 Mer. 70. But "all and every" (introducing members of a class, *e.g.* children) were not normally words of severance: *Stratton v. Best* (1787) 2 Bro.C.C. 233; *Binning v. Binning* (1895) 13 R. 654; but contrast *Re Grove's Trusts* (1862) 3 Gif. 575.

[78] *Richardson v. Richardson* (1845) 14 Sim. 526.

[79] *Stephens v. Hide* (1734) Ca.t.Talb.27.

[80] See, *e.g. Ryves v. Ryves* (1871) L.R. 11 Eq. 539; *Surtees v. Surtees* (1871) L.R. 12 Eq. 400.

examples may be given. First, it has been held that certain provisions for the use of capital or income or both for the maintenance and advancement of those concerned created a tenancy in common.[81] For example, if under a settlement on children containing such provisions an advance was made to one child, it could not be done unless the child was tenant in common and so had a distinct share.[82] Secondly, a bequest to A and B on condition that they should pay the testator's widow an annuity "in equal shares" has been held to create a tenancy in common, since the testator was presumed to have intended that the gift should correspond to the obligation.[83]

9–019   *(c) Words negativing severance.* Expressions which by themselves might create a tenancy in common can be negatived by words showing a clear intention to create a joint tenancy.[84] Contradictory expression such as "jointly and severally" or "as joint tenants in common in equal shares" are nowadays normally resolved by construing the document[85] and without recourse to the quaint rule that the first word prevailed in a deed, but the last in a will.[86]

9–020   *(d) Special cases.* Mention may be made of two special situations. First, under a testamentary gift to a vague class, such as the testator's "relations", the court can sometimes save the gift from uncertainty by restricting the class to those who would take on an intestacy.[87] The class will then take as joint tenants, not as tenants in common in the statutory shares, unless by an express reference to the statutes governing intestacy or otherwise the testator has shown a contrary intention.[88] Secondly, under a substitutionary gift, as where a gift to children in equal shares provides that children of a deceased child are to take that child's share, prima facie those substituted will take as joint tenants unless there are further words of severance; for in a gift to a compound class, compound words of severance are usually required.[89]

---

[81] *Re Ward* [1920] 1 Ch. 334; *Bennett v. Houldsworth* (1911) 104 L.T. 304; *Re Dunn* [1916] 1 Ch. 97.

[82] *L'Estrange v. L'Estrange* [1902] 1 I.R. 467; *cf. Twigg v. Twigg* [1933] I.R. 65. Since 1925 there has been an implied statutory power of advancement: T.A. 1925, s.32. This is applicable to land held upon a trust of land but not to settled land: *ibid.*, s.32(2); *Re Stimpson's Trusts* [1931] 2 Ch. 77. However the power can be exercised only in favour of a person "entitled to the capital of the trust property or of any share thereof". It would probably not be applicable therefore where land was held on trust for joint tenants.

[83] *Re North* [1952] Ch. 397.

[84] See cases collected in Halsb. 4th ed., Vol. 50 (revised ed.), para. 627.

[85] *Martin v. Martin* (1987) 54 P. & C.R. 238 ("beneficial joint tenants in common in equal shares" held to create a tenancy in common). *cf. Joyce v. Barker Bros (Builders) Ltd* (1980) 40 P. & C.R. 512 (where identical words were held to create a joint tenancy): see [1988] Conv. 57 (J. E. Martin).

[86] *Slingby's Case* (1587) 5 Co.Rep. 18b at 19a (deed); *Perkins v. Bayton* (1781) 1 Bro.C.C. 118 (will); contrast *Cookson v. Bingham* (1853) 17 Beav. 262, 3 De G.M. & G. 668 (will: contrary intention). For this rule, see *post*, para. 11–069.

[87] See *post*, para. 11–063.

[88] *Re Ganloser's W.T.* [1952] Ch. 30; and see *Re Kilvert* [1957] Ch. 388; *Re Pulton's W.T.* [1987] 1 W.L.R. 795.

[89] *Re Brooke* [1953] 1 W.L.R. 439; Jarman 1792, 1797; but see *Re Froy* [1938] Ch. 566.

Unlike the common law, equity did not favour joint tenancy.[90] Equity often did not follow the law where it was merely feudal in character, and equity in this case was more concerned to achieve fairness than to simplify the tasks of conveyancers. Equity therefore preferred the certainty and equality of a tenancy in common to the chance of "all or nothing" which arose from the right of survivorship.[91] "Equity leans against joint tenants and favours tenancies in common." This maxim meant that a tenancy in common would exist in equity not only in those cases where it would have existed at law, but also in certain other cases where an intention to create a tenancy in common ought to be presumed. There are several such special cases, in all of which persons who were joint tenants at law were compelled by equity to hold the legal estate upon trust for themselves as equitable tenants in common. These rules, which have not been altered by the 1925 legislation, remain applicable and are stated in their present form.[92] A tenancy in common which arises in one of these ways is classified as a resulting or constructive trust.[93]

9–021

1. Purchase-money provided in unequal shares

(a) The presumptions. If two or more persons together purchase property and provide the money in equal shares they are presumed in equity to be joint tenants.[94] However if their contributions are unequal, the purchasers are presumed to take beneficially as tenants in common in shares proportionate to the sums advanced.[95] Thus if A contributes one-third and B two-thirds of the price, they are presumed to be equitable tenants in common as to one-third and two-thirds respectively. Although this distinction has been criticised,[96] it is long established.[97]

9–022

(b) Rebutting the presumptions. Each of these two presumptions can be rebutted by evidence of contrary intention, whether from the surrounding circumstances,[98] by proof of express agreement between the parties, or from the wording of the conveyance or transfer of the property to the co-owners.

9–023

---

[90] *Burgess v. Rawnsley* [1975] Ch. 429 at 438, *per* Lord Denning M.R.; and see *Gould v. Kemp* (1834) 2 My. & K. 304 at 309.

[91] "Survivorship is looked upon as odious in equity": *R. v. Williams* (1735) Bunb. 342 at 343, *per cur*; and see *Re Woolley* [1903] 2 Ch. 206 at 211.

[92] The list of such special situations is not closed: *Malayan Credit Ltd v. Jack Chia-MPH Ltd* [1986] A.C. 549 at 560.

[93] See *post*, paras 10–009, 10–017.

[94] *Aveling v. Knipe* (1815) 19 Ves. 441 at 445; *Robinson v. Preston* (1858) 4 K. & J. 505 at 510; *Harrison v. Barton* (1860) 1 J. & H. 287 at 292.

[95] *Lake v. Gibson* (1729) 1 Eq.Ca.Abr. 290 at 291; *Robinson v. Preston, supra*, at 510; *Bull v. Bull* [1955] 1 Q.B. 234; *Ulrich v. Ulrich* [1968] 1 W.L.R. 180 at 185; *Crisp v. Mullings* [1976] 2 E.G.L.R. 103; and see *Bernard v. Joseph* [1982] Ch. 391. It seems that originally a tenancy in common would be presumed only if the contributions were unequal and that fact was recited in the conveyance to the purchasers: Sugden, V. & P. 698; [1982] Conv. 213 at 214 (M. Friend and J. Newton); [1990] C.L.J. 297 at 298 (C.H.).

[96] *Jackson v. Jackson* (1804) 9 Ves. 591 at 604n.

[97] Page Wood V.-C. described it as "settled" in *Robinson v. Preston, supra*, at 510.

[98] *Edwards v. Fashion* (1712) Prec. Ch. 332; *Harrison v. Barton, supra*.

9–024   (1) SURROUNDING CIRCUMSTANCES. There are many situations in which these presumptions have been rebutted by evidence or surrounding circumstances. For example, where T devised a mortgage by will to A and B as tenants in common, and A and B then purchased the mortgagor's equity of redemption, they were held to be tenants in common of the property even though each had half the price. The purchase was considered to flow from the devise.[99]

9–025   (2) EXPRESS AGREEMENT. The presumption (whether of joint tenancy or tenancy in common) which arises from the contributions made by the parties to the cost of acquiring the land will be rebutted by proof of an express agreement between them that they should hold the property in some other way. Thus if A and B make unequal contributions to the initial purchase price, the presumption of a tenancy in common will be rebutted if the parties have expressly agreed that they should hold the property as beneficial joint tenants.[1]

9–026   (3) THE WORDING OF THE CONVEYANCE OR TRANSFER. The mere fact that the legal title to the property is conveyed "to A and B jointly" does not rebut the equitable presumption of a tenancy in common because it is silent as to their beneficial interest.[2] However, as a general rule, where the conveyance expressly declares not only in whom the legal title is to vest but also how the beneficial interests are to be held, a court will give effect to that trust.[3] This is subject to two exceptions. The first is where the trust is either set aside on grounds of fraud or mistake or rectified.[4] The second is where the purchasers did not assent to the terms of the declaration.[5] Thus in one case land was conveyed to A and B as joint tenants beneficially, but without the approbation of C and D who had contributed a substantial part of the purchase price. C and D were held to be equitable tenants in common of the property in proportion to their contributions notwithstanding the declaration.[6]

It is likely that, for the future, many of the difficulties that have previously arisen will be obviated because of the introduction of new Land Registry forms.[7] On an application for first registration, to transfer land with registered title, or to assent to the vesting of land in persons entitled under a deceased's

---

[99] *Edwards v. Fashion, supra.*

[1] *Re Densham* [1975] 1 W.L.R. 1519. A common but uncommunicated intention between the parties will not suffice; *Springette v. Defoe* [1992] 1 F.L.R. 388. See *post*, para. 10–025.

[2] *Pettitt v. Pettitt* [1970] A.C. 777 at 813; *Crisp v. Mullings, supra; Walker v. Hall* [1984] F.L.R. 126 at 133; *Huntingford v. Hobbs* [1993] 1 F.L.R. 736 at 744.

[3] *Pettitt v. Pettitt, supra*, at 813; *Gissing v. Gissing* [1971] A.C. at 905; *Pink v. Lawrence* (1977) 36 P. & C.R. 98 at 101; *Goodman v. Gallant* [1986] Fam. 106; *Turton v. Turton* [1988] Ch. 542 at 553; *Huntingford v. Hobbs, supra*, at 753. A party seeking rectification must prove that the terms of the conveyance did not record the true intentions of the parties: see *Roy v. Roy* (1991) [1996] 1 F.L.R. 541.

[4] *Pettitt v. Pettitt, supra*, at 813; *Pink v. Lawrence* (1977) 36 P. & C.R. 98 at 101.

[5] The parties may have assented to the declaration in the conveyance even if they did not execute the instrument: *Re Gorman* [1990] 1 W.L.R. 616, not following *Robinson v. Robinson* [1977] 1 E.G.L.R. 80.

[6] *City of London B.S. v. Flegg* [1988] A.C. 54 at 70.

[7] Under L.R.R. 1997. See *ante*, paras 6–098, 8–133.

estate, the relevant form must set out any declaration of trust affecting the land where it is to vest in joint proprietors.[8] The instrument should state whether the transferees or recipients hold on trust for themselves either as joint tenants or as tenants in common; or, if neither of these, on what trusts.[9] In the case of an assent or transfer of registered land, the instrument must be executed by all necessary parties.[10] Where the application is for first registration, the person lodging the application must confirm that he has authority to do so. In the absence of some vitiating factor, the terms of the assent, transfer or application for registration will be conclusive as to the trusts declared.

(c) Failure of purpose. If the property was acquired for a common purpose which later fails, there is an equitable tenancy in common even where the contributions were equal,[11] as in most cases justice will require.   **9–027**

2. Loan on mortgage. Where two or more persons advance money on mortgage, whether in equal or unequal shares, equity presumes a tenancy in common in the land between the mortgagees.[12] "If two people join in lending money upon a mortgage, equity says, it could not be the intention that the interest in that should survive. Though they take a joint security, each means to lend his own and take back his own."[13] "It is obvious, however, that this proposition cannot be put higher than a presumption capable of being rebutted."[14]   **9–028**

3. Partnership assets and property acquired for business purposes. Where partners acquire land as part of their partnership assets, they are presumed to hold it as beneficial tenants in common.[15] It was an ancient rule   **9–029**

---

[8] L.R.R. 1925, rr. 19, 98; Sched. 1, Forms FR1, TR1 and AS1 (as substituted or inserted by L.R.R. 1997). Most dispositions of unregistered freehold land or of leaseholds with more than 21 years to run must now be completed by registration: see L.R.A. 1925, s.123 (as substituted by L.R.A. 1997, s.1).

[9] For certain difficulties that arose in relation to transfers that were not in a form promulgated by the L.R.R. 1925, see *Harwood v. Harwood* [1991] 2 F.L.R. 275; *Huntingford v. Hobbs* [1993] 1 F.L.R. 736.

[10] *i.e.* both the transferors and transferees.

[11] *Burgess v. Rawnsley* [1975] Ch. 429 (though in that case there was no such failure). See too *Ulrich v. Ulrich* [1968] 1 W.L.R. 180 at 185. For this type of resulting trust see *post*, para. 10–010.

[12] *Petty v. Styward* (1632) 1 Ch.Rep. 57; *Rigden v. Vallier* (1751) 2 Ves.Sen. 252 at 258; *Vickers v. Cowell* (1839) 1 Beav. 529. For a doubt as to the logic of this rule see *Harrison v. Barton* (1860) 1 J. & H. 287 at 292.

[13] *Morley v. Bird* (1798) 3 Ves. 628 at 631, *per* Arden M.R.

[14] *Steeds v. Steeds* (1889) 22 Q.B.D. 537 at 541, *per* Wills J. It should be noted that the "joint account clause" which was normally inserted in a mortgage to make the mortgagees appear as joint tenants to the outside world, and so simplify the mechanism of discharging the mortgage (see *post*, para. 19–181: such a clause is now implied: see L.P.A. 1925, s.111), did not affect this presumption of a tenancy in common in the relationship of mortgagees *inter se: Re Jackson* (1887) 34 Ch.D. 732.

[15] *Jeffreys v. Small* (1683) 1 Vern. 217; *Lake v. Gibson* (1729) 1 Eq.Ca.Abr. 290; *Lake v. Craddock* (1732) 3 P.Wms 158; Sugden, V. & P. 698.

that the right of survivorship had no place in business.[16] The rule extends to
any joint undertaking carried on with a view to profit, even if there is no
formal partnership between the parties,[17] and even if the property has not been
purchased but acquired by inheritance by the persons who use it for business.[18] Thus where premises are held by two joint tenants at law for their
individual business purposes, they will be tenants in common in equity.[19]
Although the partners must hold the legal estate as joint tenants, in equity they
are presumed to be entitled in undivided shares.[20] On the death of a partner,
the surviving partners (or whoever holds the legal estate) will be compelled to
hold the legal estate on trust for those entitled to the property of a deceased
partner as to his share.[21]

The presumption of a tenancy in common may however be rebutted by
evidence of contrary intention. Thus if property is conveyed to two or more
persons as beneficial joint tenants, that declaration will be conclusive in the
absence of any grounds for rectification.[22]

9–030   **4. Contracts and executory trusts.** It sometimes happens that a preliminary contract or declaration of trust is required to be perfected by the
execution of a proper deed of settlement. An example that was formerly
common was a contract to execute a marriage settlement upon certain terms
known as marriage articles. In construing such articles and other executory
transactions[23] the court would readily find that gifts to classes, *e.g.* to the
children of the marriage, were intended to give each child a separate share for
his own family, even though the appropriate words of severance were absent,
and decree accordingly. "Joint tenancy as a provision for the children of a
marriage, is an inconvenient mode of settlement, because during their minorities, no use can be made of their portions for their advancement, as the joint

---

[16] *Hammond v. Jethro* (1611) 2 Brownl. & Golds. 97 at 99; *Buckley v. Barber* (1851) 6 Exch. 164
at 179. The rule "*jus accrescendi inter mercatores pro beneficium commercii locum non habet*"
(Co.Litt. 182a) was applied at law as regards the chattels of merchants and manufacturers:
Buckley v. Barber, supra; but not to land: *cf.* Partnership Act 1890, s.20(2). See Lindley and
Banks, *Partnership* (17th ed.), 18–62, 19–14.

[17] *Lake v. Gibson, supra*; *Lyster v. Dolland* (1792) 1 Ves.Jun. 431; *Dale v. Hamilton* (1846) 5 Hare
369; (1847) 2 Ph. 266; *Darby v. Darby* (1856) 3 Drew 495; *Re Hulton* (1890) 62 L.T. 200.
Contrast *Ward v. Ward* (1871) 6 Ch.App. 789 (farming jointly but not as partners).

[18] *Jackson v. Jackson* (1804) 9 Ves. 591; *cf. Morris v. Barrett* (1829) 3 Y. & J. 384.

[19] *Malayan Credit Ltd v. Jack Chia-MPH Ltd* [1986] A.C. 549.

[20] *Re Fuller's Contract* [1933] Ch. 652. After 1925 and before 1997, the legal estate was held
upon a statutory trust for sale. After 1996, it has been held on a trust of land: see *post*, para.
9–051. For the nature of a partner's equitable interest in the partnership property see *Rodriguez
v. Speyer Brothers* [1919] A.C. 59 at 68; *Burdett-Coutts v. I.R.C.* [1960] 1 W.L.R. 1027;
Lindley and Banks, *Partnership, supra*, 19–03, 19–04.

[21] *Elliott v. Brown* (1791) 3 Swans. 489; *Re Ryan* (1868) 3 Ir.R.Eq. 222 at 232; *Wray v. Wray*
[1905] 2 Ch. 349; Partnership Act 1890, s.20(2).

[22] *Barton v. Morris* [1985] 1 W.L.R. 1257 (mere inclusion of such property in partnership
accounts for tax purposes held to be irrelevant).

[23] See, *e.g. Synge v. Hales* (1814) 2 Ball & B. 499; *Mayn v. Mayn* (1867) L.R. 5 Eq. 150; compare
Re Bellasis' Trust (1871) L.R. 12 Eq. 218.

tenancy cannot be severed."[24] This was not a case where equity enforced a tenancy in common on persons who were joint tenants at law. It was simply an example of the rule that contracts are construed so as to give effect to the true intention of the parties. But the question normally fell to the Chancery side since the remedy sought would be a decree for the execution of a proper settlement by deed, *i.e.* a decree for specific performance.[25]

III. THE EFFECT OF THE 1925 AND SUBSEQUENT LEGISLATION

The mechanisms for the co-ownership of land have been affected both by the 1925 property legislation and, more recently, by the Trusts of Land and Appointment of Trustees Act 1996. Under the law as it stood before 1926, joint tenancy was clearly the convenient form of co-ownership for non-beneficial owners such as trustees, since the right of survivorship prevented the property from becoming entangled with the personal affairs of a deceased trustee. But for beneficial owners tenancy in common was almost always preferable, so that the share of each co-owner would devolve or be disposable just like his other property, free from the right of survivorship. **9–031**

1. The drawbacks of tenancy in common[26]

(a) Investigation of titles. Tenancy in common was a great inconvenience in conveyancing. Whether the tenancy was legal or equitable a purchaser who bought the land as a whole was compelled to investigate the titles of all the co-owners. Since there was no unity of title, the titles to all the separate shares had to be scrutinised and pieced together. **9–032**

(a) Management of land. Even where there was no difficulty in deducing title to land held by tenants in common, its management often proved trouble-some. Thus if a freehold was held in common and the property was leased to tenants, it was necessary to obtain the agreement of all the co-owners to the execution of any improvements or repairs. **9–033**

In order to eliminate such difficulties, four substantial changes were made by the Law of Property Act 1925. These were—

    (i) the abolition of legal tenancies in common;

    (ii) the abolition of the right to sever a legal joint tenancy;

    (iii) the imposition of a trust for sale in most cases of co-ownership; and

---

[24] *Taggart v. Taggart* (1803) 1 Sch. & Lef. 84 at 88, *per* Lord Redesdale L.C. There is now an implied statutory power of advancement where land is held upon a trust of land though not where it is settled: T.A. 1925, s.32. However, it may not apply to beneficial joint tenants: *ante,* para. 9–018.

[25] For this remedy, see *post,* para. 12–115.

[26] See J. S. Anderson, *Lawyers and the Making of English Land Law 1832–1940,* pp. 286–290.

(iv) the conferment of powers of disposition and management on those trustees.

The imposition of a trust for sale—and its more recent replacement by the trust of land—is considered later,[27] but the abolition of legal tenancies in common and of the right to sever a legal joint tenancy must now be explained.

9–034   **2. The abolition of legal tenancies in common.** Even if there are clear words of severance, after 1925 the legal estate cannot be held by tenancy in common.[28] A tenancy in common can now exist only in equity; at law the only form of co-ownership possible after 1925 is a joint tenancy. Thus a conveyance today "to A, B and C in fee simple as tenants in common" (all being of full age) will vest the legal estate in A, B and C as joint tenants, although in equity they will be tenants in common.[29] If any of the co-owners is a minor, he cannot hold a legal estate in land.[30] Therefore if A is a minor, he will be co-owner in equity but the legal estate will vest in B and C alone.[31] B and C will be trustees for A, B and C. If A, B and C are all minors, the legal estate remains in the grantor who holds it on trust for the minors.[32]

9–035   **3. The abolition of the right to sever a legal joint tenancy.** A legal joint tenancy cannot be severed after 1925.[33] This rule is a necessary counterpart of the rule that a legal tenancy in common cannot be created. It does not prevent one joint tenant from releasing his interest to the others, nor does it affect the right to sever a joint tenancy in equity.[34] This is now the only form of severance.

Section 4. The Right of Severance

A. *Severance in equity*

9–036   The common law mitigated the uncertainty of the right of survivorship by enabling a joint tenant to destroy the joint tenancy by severance. In this way it became a tenancy in common. "Severance" is normally used to describe the process whereby a joint tenancy is converted into a tenancy in common.[35] No

---

[27] *Post*, para. 9–051.
[28] L.P.A. 1925, ss.1(6), 34(1), 36(2); S.L.A. 1925, s.36(4).
[29] L.P.A. 1925, s.34(2).
[30] *ibid.*, s.1(6).
[31] T.L.A.T.A. 1996, Sched. 1, para. 1(2); *post*, para. 20–006.
[32] See T.L.A.T.A. 1996, s.2(6); Sched. 1, para. 1(1); and (in relation to registered land) L.R.A. 1925, s.111(1).
[33] L.P.A. 1925, s.36(2).
[34] *ibid.*
[35] Strictly it also includes partition. See *post*, para. 9–098. For proposals as to how the law on severance might be reformed, see [1995] Conv. 105 (L. Tee). Any reform would be controversial.

joint tenant owns any distinct share in the land. However, each has a potential share equal in size to that of the others.[36] The size depends on the number of joint tenants at the time in question. Thus if there are five, each has the right to sever his joint tenancy and become a tenant in common of one undivided fifth share. If one joint tenant dies before severance, each of the survivors has a potential quarter share and so on. It is no bar to severance that the joint tenants are husband and wife.[37]

Where land is conveyed to two or more persons as joint tenants beneficially, each will share equally on severance even though they may have contributed unequally to the purchase price.[38] It may however be possible for a trust to declare expressly that the beneficial interests of two or more parties should be equivalent to those of joint tenants unless and until severed, but that in the event of severance their interests should be in some specified shares other than equal shares.[39]

Before 1926, a joint tenancy could be severed both at law and in equity.[40] It has already been explained that severance is now possible only in equity. Since 1925 a joint tenancy may be severed in equity—

    (i) in the same manner as a joint tenancy of personal estate could have been severed prior to 1926[41];

    (ii) by notice in writing to the other joint tenants[42];

    (iii) by the act of some third party;

    (iv) by the acquisition of another estate in the land; and

    (v) by homicide.

Each of these must now be considered.

---

[36] *Goodman v. Gallant* [1986] Fam. 106 at 118, 119.

[37] *Bedson v. Bedson* [1965] 2 Q.B. 666 at 690; *Radziej v. Radziej* [1967] 1 W.L.R. 659; *Re Draper's Conveyance* [1969] 1 Ch. 486; *Harris v. Goddard* [1983] 1 W.L.R. 1203 at 1208. The contrary view was expressed in *Bedson v. Bedson, supra,* at 678, apparently on the basis of L.P.A. 1925, s.36(1), (3). But the subsections seem to provide no support: see (1966) 82 L.Q.R. 29 (R.E.M.).

[38] *Goodman v. Gallant, supra,* at 117.

[39] *ibid.,* at 119.

[40] The rules of severance prior to 1926 are explained in the previous edition of this work at pp. 430 *et seq.* The old common law methods of severance must be treated with some caution because the equitable rules which now apply lean against joint tenancies: see *Burgess v. Rawnsley* [1975] Ch. 429 at 438.

[41] L.P.A. 1925, s.36(2). However, "the methods of severance of a joint tenancy in personal estate before 1926 were precisely the same as the methods of severance of a joint tenancy in real estate": *Nielson-Jones v. Fedden* [1975] Ch. 222 at 229, *per* Walton J. *cf.* [1975] C.L.J. 28 at 29 (M. J. Pritchard).

[42] L.P.A. 1925, s.36(2).

9–037   1. Methods of severance recognised in equity before 1926. In *Williams v. Hensman*,[43] Page Wood V.-C. listed the three methods by which a joint tenancy of personal estate[44] could be severed before 1926—

(i) "an act of any one of the persons interested operating upon his own share";

(ii) "by mutual agreement";

(iii) "by any course of dealing sufficient to intimate that the interests of all were mutually treated as constituting a tenancy in common".

If any one of these methods is established, the joint tenancy will be severed in equity. The onus of proof rests on the party asserting that severance has occurred.[45]

9–038   *(a) An act operating upon the share of any one of the joint tenants.* At common law, the alienation of property was favoured against the right of survivorship.[46] If therefore a joint tenant alienates his beneficial interest *inter vivos*, his joint tenancy is severed.[47] The person to whom the interest is assigned takes it as a tenant in common with the other joint tenants, because he has no unity of title with them.[48] Any severance must take place during the lifetime of the joint tenant. A joint tenant "cannot make a will of what he holds in jointure",[49] nor can a will sever a joint tenancy.[50]

9–039   1. TOTAL ALIENATION. If A, B and C are beneficial joint tenants and A assigns his interest to X,[51] X will become tenant in common as to one-third with B and C as to two-thirds, but B and C will remain joint tenants of those two-thirds as between themselves.[52] If B then dies, C alone profits by the right of survivorship, X and C being left as tenants in common as to one-third and two-thirds respectively.[53]

---

[43] (1861) 1 J. & H. 546 at 557. This statement of the law is always treated as authoritative: *Burgess v. Rawnsley, supra,* at 438; *Harris v. Goddard, supra,* at 1209; *Hunter v. Babbage* [1994] 2 F.L.R. 806 at 811; *Re Palmer* [1994] Ch. 316 at 341.

[44] Personal estate included leaseholds: *ante,* para. 1–010.

[45] *Re Denny* (1947) 177 L.T. 291 at 293; *Greenfield v. Greenfield* (1979) 38 P. & C.R. 570 at 578.

[46] "*Alienato rei praefertur juri accrescendi*": Co.Litt. 185a. In equity the rule was the same: *Patriche v. Powlett* (1740) 2 Atk. 54 at 55.

[47] *Re Wilks* [1891] 3 Ch. 59 at 61.

[48] Litt. 292; Williams R.P. 147.

[49] *Swift d. Neale v. Roberts* (1764) 3 Burr. 1488 at 1496, *per* Lord Mansfield. Because of the operation of the right of survivorship he has nothing to leave by will: *Gould v. Kemp* (1834) 2 My. & K. 304 at 309; *ante,* para. 9–003.

[50] Cru. Dig. ii, 382. *Aliter* a mutual wills agreement; *post,* para. 9–039.

[51] An assignment or any other disposition of an equitable interest must be made in writing signed by the person disposing of that interest: L.P.A. 1925, s.53(1)(c): see *post,* para. 10–046.

[52] If A had assigned his interest to B, B, like X, would hold A's one-third share as a tenant in common. B's acquisition of A's share would have no effect on his joint tenancy with C of the remaining two-thirds: Litt. 304, 312, *Wright v. Gibbons* (1949) 78 C.L.R. 313 at 324, 332.

[53] See *Philpott v. Dobbinson* (1829) 3 Moo. & P. 320 at 330; *Denne d. Bowyer v. Judge* (1809) 11 East 288; *Williams v. Hensman, supra.*

If one joint tenant forges the signatures of the others on a purported conveyance of the property, that conveyance will not transfer the legal estate, but is effective to pass the forger's beneficial interest to the purchaser, thereby severing the joint tenancy.[54] It has been held that, where the joint tenant and the purchaser act in concert, the transaction is a sham and has no effect on the joint tenancy.[55] However, it is questionable whether such a transaction can in law be regarded as a sham, as the parties plainly did intend it to have legal consequences.[56]

It has long been settled that a contract by one joint tenant to sell his interest effects a severance in equity provided that the contract is specifically enforceable.[57] If, therefore, a joint tenant contracts to sell his interest to X, this causes a severance in equity. The trustees will therefore hold the legal estate subject to X's equitable right to share as tenant in common.[58] It is for this reason that severance was brought about by a covenant in a marriage articles or a marriage settlement to settle property held in joint tenancy.[59] Similarly a mutual wills agreement between two joint tenants will sever the joint tenancy.[60]

A declaration of trust by one joint tenant of his interest in favour of a third party will sever the joint tenancy as regards that share.[61]

2. PARTIAL ALIENATION. Although at common law the right to alienate was preferred to the right of survivorship, the right of survivorship took precedence over mere encumbrances.[62] The distinction lay between acts which were inconsistent with the right of survivorship and those which were not. Thus a rentcharge could be satisfied out of one joint tenant's share of the rents and profits[63] without disturbing the joint tenancy. These distinctions may no

9–040

---

[54] L.P.A. 1925, s.63(1); *Ahmed v. Kendrick* (1987) 56 P. & C.R. 120; *Abbey National Plc v. Moss* (1993) 26 H.L.R. 249; *Bankers Trust Co. v. Namdar* [1997] E.G.C.S. 20. See *post*, para. 10–031.

[55] *Penn v. Bristol & West B.S.* [1995] 2 F.L.R. 938 (not considered on appeal: [1997] 1 W.L.R. 1356).

[56] See [1996] Fam. Law 28 at 29 (S. Cretney).

[57] *Brown v. Raindle* (1796) 3 Ves. 256 at 257; *Re Hewett* [1894] 1 Ch. 362 at 367; *Burgess v. Rawnsley* [1975] Ch. 429 at 443. However no severance occurs if all the joint tenants contract to sell their interests: *Re Hayes' Estate* [1920] 1 I.R. 207.

[58] Such a contract constitutes the vendor a constructive trustee of the equitable interest for the purchaser: see *Neville v. Wilson* [1997] Ch. 144. Once the purchaser has paid the consideration, the vendor will in any event have no equity which he can assert against him: *Rose v. Watson* (1864) 33 L.J.Ch. 385.

[59] *Caldwell v. Fellowes* (1870) L.R. 9 Eq. 410; *Baillie v. Treherne* (1881) 17 Ch.D. 388; *Burnaby v. Equitable Reversionary Interest Society* (1885) 28 Ch.D. 416. In *Re Hewett*, *supra*, it was held that an aptly worded covenant would sever a joint tenancy in property subsequently acquired.

[60] *Re Wilford's Estate* (1879) 11 Ch.D. 267; *In b. Heys* [1914] P. 192; *post*, para. 10–020. In England, there must be a contract between the parties before the mutual wills doctrine will operate. In other jurisdictions the requirements are less exacting: *cf. Szabo v. Boros* (1967) 64 D.L.R. (2d) 48.

[61] See *Re Mee* (1971) 23 D.L.R. (3d) 491; *Re Sorensen and Sorensen* (1977) 90 D.L.R. (3d) 26.

[62] "*Jus accrescendi praefertur oneribus*": Litt. 289; Co.Litt. 185a.

[63] *Ante*, para. 9–006.

longer be strictly applied now that the equitable rules for the severance of interests in personalty prevail.[64] The trend of modern decisions is to treat any partial alienation by a joint tenant as a severance if it can be regarded as an act operating on his share. Thus the following dispositions by a joint tenant have all been held to effect a severance—

> (1) the execution of a mortgage or charge over his interest[65];
>
> (ii) a specifically enforceable contract to grant a charge over his interest[66]; and
>
> (iii) a purported mortgage over the entire property where he has forged the signatures of the other joint tenants.[67]

Although the point is not free from doubt, both principle and judicial opinion suggest that a lease for years granted by one or more (but not all[68]) of the joint tenants will effect a severance of the joint tenancy[69] not just for the duration of the lease but thereafter.[70] A lease for years confers a right to possession of some particular share of the land for a fixed period, and this right arises by a separate title.[71]

By contrast, where a joint tenant creates an encumbrance such as an easement or profit, no estate or interest passes to the grantee. Such a grant destroys none of the four unities and provided that it does not interfere with

---

[64] *cf. Burgess v. Rawsley, supra,* at 438.

[65] *York v. Stone* (1709) 1 Salk. 158; *Williams v. Hensman* (1861) 1 J. & H. 546 at 558; *Re Pollard's Estate* (1863) 3 De G.J. 7 S. 541 at 558; *Re Sharer* (1912) 57 S.J. 60. Before 1926, the execution of a mortgage severed the joint tenancy because it involved an outright transfer of the joint tenant's interest to the mortgagee: see *Lyons v. Lyons* [1967] V.R. 169 at 173. *Quaere* whether since 1925 this is subject to the doubt as regards leases, *infra*, since mortgages are now made by demise: *post*, para. 19–019. In Australia, it has been held that a mortgage under the Torrens system of title registration does not sever a joint tenancy. It operates as a mere security without any transfer or grant of an interest to the mortgagee: *Lyons v. Lyons, supra*.

[66] See *Thames Guaranty Ltd v. Campbell* [1985] Q.B. 210 (where specific performance was in fact refused because of the prejudice it would have caused to the other joint tenant).

[67] *First National Securities Ltd v. Hegerty* [1985] Q.B. 850. *cf. Rogers v. Resi-Statewide Corporation Ltd* (1991) 105 A.L.R. 145 at 150.

[68] See *Palmer v. Rich* [1897] 1 Ch. 134.

[69] *Clerk v. Clerk* (1694) 2 Vern. 323; *Gould v. Kemp* (1834) My. & K. 304 at 310; *Cowper v. Fletcher* (1865) 6 B. & S. 464 at 472; *Re Armstrong* [1920] 1 I.R. 239. *Contra, Harbin v. Loby* (1629) Noy 157 at 158; Co.Litt 185a; Preston, *Abstracts*, ii, 58; Challis 367n. For a full discussion of the authorities, see *Frieze v. Unger* [1960] V.R. 230 at 241 *et seq.*

[70] This was certainly the case where a joint tenant of a lease granted an underlease, whether to a stranger (*Sym's Case* (1584) Cro. Eliz. 33; *Connolly v. Connolly* (1866) 17 Ir.Ch.R. 208 at 233) or to one of his fellow joint tenants (*Pleadal's Case* (1579) 2 Leon. 159; and see Co.Litt. 192a). But a lease for life granted by one joint tenant to another does not effect a severance: *Re Sorensen and Sorensen, supra*.

[71] It has been settled that the rights of a lessee were unaffected by the death of a joint tenant who granted him the lease: *Anon* (1560) 2 Dy. 187a; *Harbin v. Barton* (1595) Moo.K.B. 395; *Whitlock v. Horton* (1605) Cro.Jac. 91; *Lampit v. Starkey* (1612) 2 Brownl. & Golds. 172 at 175; *Smallman v. Agbrow* (1617) Cro.Jac 417; Litt. 289. See too *Frieze v. Unger, supra*, at 244.

the rights of the other joint tenants (and in particular, the right to possession) the joint tenancy will not be severed.[72]

3. OTHER SITUATIONS. Alienation is not the only way in which a joint tenant **9–041** may act upon his own share so as to sever the joint tenancy. Severance may also occur if he enlarges his beneficial interest. Thus where a husband and wife are beneficial joint tenants of the matrimonial home and one of them substantially improves the property, that party's share in the property will thereby be enlarged in the absence of any express or implied agreement to the contrary between them.[73]

It has been suggested that a mere declaration to sever by one joint tenant will effect a severance under this head.[74] However the better view is that such an act is insufficient and that this form of severance occurs only where a joint tenant alienates his interest, or in some other way acts so that there is a change in his equitable interest in the property.[75]

(b) Mutual agreement. A joint tenancy can be severed by the mutual **9–042** agreement of all[76] the joint tenants.[77] Originally such an agreement had to amount to an enforceable contract,[78] so that this form of severance was simply an example of joint tenants acting upon their own share. Furthermore, any such agreement would be invalid if any of the joint tenants lacked capacity.[79] However severance by mutual agreement is now acknowledged to be a distinct category of severance and it is no longer necessary that the agreement should be enforceable as a contract.[80]

(c) Course of dealing. Severance by a course of dealing depends upon **9–043** inferences drawn from conduct where there is no express act of severance. To fall within this head of severance there must be "a course of dealing by which the shares of *all* the parties to the contest have been affected".[81] For this

---

[72] Litt. 286; Co.Litt. 185a; *Lyons v. Lyons, supra*, at 174; *Hedley v. Roberts* [1977] V.R. 282 at 286–289.

[73] Matrimonial Proceedings and Property Act 1970, s.37; *post*, para. 10–025. This is a potential trap of some seriousness. Many married couples own their homes as beneficial joint tenants, with the intention that the survivor takes the property. If one of them substantially improves the property, the tenancy may be severed without either of them realising it, thereby defeating the parties' intentions.

[74] *Hawkesley v. May* [1956] 1 Q.B. 304 at 313; *Re Draper's Conveyance* [1969] 1 Ch. 486 at 491.

[75] *Harris v. Goddard* [1983] 1 W.l.R. 1203 at 1209; *Corin v. Patton* (1990) 169 C.L.R. 540 at 547, 548, 584.

[76] Agreement between some but not all of the joint tenants will not suffice: *Wright v. Gibbons* (1949) 78 C.L.R. 313 at 322.

[77] It is not necessary that all should agree to sever their interests. Thus if A, B and C are joint tenants, the three may agree that A should sever his joint tenancy, leaving B and C as joint tenants *inter se*.

[78] *Frewen v. Relfe* (1787) 2 Bro.C.C. 220; *Wilson v. Bell* (1843) 5 Ir.Eq.R. 501 at 507; *Kingsford v. Ball* (1852) 2 Giff. App. i; *Re Wilford's Estate* (1879) 11 Ch.D. 267 at 269; Cru. Dig. ii, 389; and see *Lyons v. Lyons, supra* at 171.

[79] *Re Wilks* [1891] 3 Ch. 59 at 62 (the joint tenants were minors).

[80] *Burgess v. Rawnsley* [1975] Ch. 429 at 444, 446; *Hunter v. Babbage* [1994] 2 F.L.R. 806 at 812. See [1975] C.L.J. 28 at 30 (M.J. Pritchard).

[81] *Williams v. Hensman* (1861) 1 J. & H. 546 at 558, *per* Page Wood V.-C. (emphasis added).

reason, a unilateral statement of an intention to sever by one joint tenant, whether communicated to the other joint tenants or not, will not constitute a course of dealing,[82] though a written notice to the other joint tenants may sever for reasons considered shortly.[83] Although it is not necessary that the joint tenants should have reached a concluded agreement,[84] the acts and dealings with the property must indicate an intention by them that they should hold in common.[85] Thus periodic distributions of property amongst joint tenants[86] or the apportionment of the profits of trade amongst the joint owners of a business [87] on the assumption that they are tenants in common,[88] has been held to constitute such a course of dealing. However inconclusive negotiations by one joint tenant to purchase the interest of the other,[89] or a mere agreement in principle to do so but without any final commitment will not suffice.[90] Where a house is jointly-owned, the mere conversion of it into two self-contained maisonettes,[91] or its inclusion in partnership accounts purely for tax purposes[92] will not amount to a sufficient course of dealing to effect a severance.

9–044   **2. By notice in writing.** A method of unilateral severance by notice in writing was introduced by the 1925 legislation.[93] It is provided that "where a legal estate (not being settled land) is vested in joint tenants beneficially, and any tenant desires to sever the joint tenancy in equity, he shall give to the other joint tenants a notice in writing[94] of such desire".[95] The wording of this provision suggests that there are significant limitations on this power to sever. First, it applies only to notices in writing given *inter vivos*. There is still no power to sever by will. Secondly, and for no obvious reason, it has no

---

[82] *Burgess v. Rawnsley, supra* at 448. The suggestion to the contrary at 439 cannot be supported: see [1976] C.L.J. 20 at 23 (D.J. Hayton). See too *Harris v. Goddard, supra*, at 1209; *Gore v. Carpenter* (1990) 60 P. & C.R. 456 at 462.

[83] L.P.A. 1925, s.36(2), *infra*. A mere verbal notice can never effect a severance: *Burgess v. Rawnsley, supra*, at 448.

[84] *Burgess v. Rawnsley, supra*; *Greenfield v. Greenfield* (1979) 38 P. &. C.R. 570 at 577.

[85] *Wilson v. Bell* (1843) 5 Ir.Eq.R. 501 at 507.

[86] *Wilson v. Bell, supra, Re Denny* (1947) 177 L.T. 291. There is, however, no severance where the rents of jointly-owned properties are used as a common fund for the maintenance of the joint tenants: *Palmer v. Rich* [1897] 1 Ch. 134 at 143.

[87] *Jackson v. Jackson* (1804) 9 Ves. 591.

[88] *Hunter v. Babbage* [1994] 2 F.L.R. 806 at 812.

[89] *McDowell v. Hirschfield Lipson & Rumney* [1992] 2 F.L.R. 126.

[90] *Gore v. Carpenter, supra.*

[91] *Greenfield v. Greenfield, supra.*

[92] *Barton v. Morris* [1985] 1 W.L.R. 1257.

[93] The suggestion in *Burgess v. Rawnsley, supra*, at 439, 444, that severance by written notice was effective in the case of personalty before 1926 is incorrect; *cf. ibid.*, at 447; and see *Re Wilks* [1891] 3 Ch. 59; *Harris v. Goddard, supra*, at 1209; *Hunter v. Babbage, supra*, at 814, 815.

[94] See L.P.A. 1925, s.196; *Re Berkeley Road, N.W. 9* [1971] Ch. 648 (notice duly posted in accordance with s.196 but not received, held effective); *Kinch v. Bullard* [1999] 1 W.L.R. 423 (wife intercepted and destroyed notice served on her husband on her behalf after it had been delivered, because his death appeared imminent: the notice was held to be effective as it complied with s.196).

[95] L.P.A. 1925, s.36(2), proviso.

application to settled land, nor to personal property[96] other than leaseholds.[97] Thirdly, because the legal estate must be "vested in joint tenants beneficially", it would seem to apply only where the legal and beneficial joint tenants are one and the same. On a strict construction of the section, this method of severance would not therefore be available where A and B held the legal estate on trust either for A, B and C, or for X and Y. It might be possible however to construe the statutory words so as to give them a wider meaning than normally.

The notice in writing need not be in any particular form. A writ or originating summons commencing legal proceedings or an affidavit sworn in those proceedings might suffice,[98] but only if the relief sought would necessarily entail a severance of the joint tenancy. Furthermore, it is essential that the notice should seek an immediate severance and not one at some time in the future.[99] Therefore although a prayer in a divorce petition that the matrimonial home should be sold and the proceeds divided equally will satisfy the requirements of the section,[1] a prayer for the court to grant a property adjustment order at some future time will not.[2] A mere proposal to sever made in the course of negotiations will not constitute a notice within the section.[3]

3. By the act of a third party. In a number of circumstances the interest of a joint tenant will be severed not by his own act but by some form of involuntary alienation. **9–045**

(a) On the bankruptcy of the joint tenant. It has long been settled that where a joint tenant is adjudicated bankrupt, the joint tenancy will be severed when his property is vested in his trustee in bankruptcy.[4] That vesting operates as an involuntary form of alienation. Since the enactment of the Insolvency Act 1986,[5] there has been some uncertainty as to the date upon which severance occurs. At common law, where a person was adjudicated bankrupt, the bankruptcy was deemed to relate back to the commission by him of an act of bankruptcy.[6] It followed that if a joint tenant committed an act of bankruptcy and then died before he had been adjudicated bankrupt, the joint tenancy **9–046**

---

[96] This latter limitation has been criticised: *Nielson-Jones v. Fedden* [1975] Ch. 222 at 229; *Burgess v. Rawnsley, supra* at 447.

[97] Leaseholds fall within s.36(2): L.P.A. 1925, ss.1(1), 205(1)(x).

[98] *Burgess v. Rawnsley, supra*, at 447.

[99] *Harris v. Goddard, supra.*

[1] *Re Draper's Conveyance* [1969] 1 Ch. 486, as explained in *Harris v. Goddard, supra.*

[2] *Harris v. Goddard, supra; Hunter v. Babbage* [1994] 2 F.L.R. 806 at 818. See M.C.A. 1973, s.24. A property adjustment order would not necessarily involve severance of the joint tenancy.

[3] *Gore v. Carpenter, supra.*

[4] *Morgan v. Marquis* (1853) 9 Ex. 145 at 147; *Bedson v. Bedson* [1965] 2 Q.B. 666 at 690; *Re Rushton* [1972] Ch. 197 at 203; *Re Gorman* [1990] 1 W.L.R. 616 at 620.

[5] The Act came into force on December 29, 1986.

[6] See, *e.g. Cooper v. Chitty* (1755) 1 Burr. 20, 31, 32; *Smith v. Stokes* (1801) 1 East 363, 367. Both the concept of an act of bankruptcy and the relation back to the trustee's title were abolished by I.A. 1986: see *Re Dennis* [1996] Ch. 80 at 88.

would be regarded as having been severed prior to his death.[7] The same rule applied under the Bankruptcy Act 1914.[8] Under the Insolvency Act 1986, however, the bankrupt is no longer divested of his property on the making of the bankruptcy order. Instead, his estate (which comprises all property belonging to or vested in him at the commencement of the bankruptcy[9]) vests in the trustee in bankruptcy immediately on the latter's appointment.[10] This will usually occur some time after the making of the bankruptcy order.[11] Although the official receiver acts as the receiver of the bankrupt's estate in the interim,[12] he acquires no title to the property.[13] It is uncertain whether severance takes place at the time of the bankruptcy order or only on the appointment of the trustee in bankruptcy, although in one case it was assumed to occur at the earlier date.[14] The point will be material if A owned property jointly with B, and either A or B died after a bankruptcy order had been made against A but before a trustee had been appointed. If A dies before any bankruptcy order is made, but where an insolvency administration order is subsequently made against his estate,[15] that order relates back to A's death. It has no effect on the joint tenancy therefore and B takes the property by survivorship.[16]

9–047   (b) Other cases. Other situations in which a joint tenancy may be severed by the act of a third party include—

  (i) the imposition of a charging order in respect of a money judgment against one joint tenant[17]; and

  (ii) the imposition of a charge in favour of the Legal Aid Fund under the Legal Aid Act 1988.[18]

9–048   **4. By acquisition of another estate in the land.** It was never fatal to a joint tenancy that one of the joint tenants was initially given some further estate in the land than his joint tenancy.[19] However at common law prior to the Judicature Act 1873, the subsequent acquisition of some further estate in the land by a legal joint tenant destroyed the unity of interest and severed the joint

---

[7] Smith v. Stokes, supra.
[8] Re Dennis, supra.
[9] s.283(1).
[10] s.306(1).
[11] cf. I.A. 1986, ss.287, 293.
[12] ibid., s.287.
[13] The bankrupt is however under a duty to deliver up possession of his estate to him: I.A. 1986, s.291.
[14] Re Pavlou [1993] 1 W.L.R. 1046 at 1048. See however [1993] Fam. Law 196; [1995] All E.R. Rev. 292 (S.M. Cretney) and [1995] C.L.J. 52 at 59 (L. Tee).
[15] Under the Administration of Insolvent Estates of Deceased Persons Order, S.I. 1986 No. 1999.
[16] Re Palmer [1994] Ch. 316; [1995] C.L.J. 52 (L. Tee); [1995] Conv. 68 (M. Haley).
[17] Charging Orders Act 1979, ss.2(1), (2); 3(4); Midland Bank Plc v. Pike [1988] 2 All E.R. 434. See post, para. 9–074.
[18] s.16(6); Bedson v. Bedson [1965] 2 Q.B. 666 at 691.
[19] Ante, para. 9–006.

tenancy.[20] Thus if land was limited to A, B and C as joint tenants for life, with remainder to C in fee simple, the mere existence of C's fee simple remainder did not destroy his joint tenancy for life. However, if A acquired C's fee simple, A's life estate merged in the fee simple and severed his joint tenancy for life.[21] So also if land were held by X for life with remainder to Y and Z in fee simple as joint tenants, and X conveyed his life estate to Y, the joint tenancy was severed.[22] If X had instead surrendered his life estate to Y, this would have extinguished it, and so Y and Z would have benefited from their joint tenancy taking effect in possession.[23]

The basis of this form of severance was the doctrine of merger[24]: "whenever a greater estate and a less coincide and meet in one and the same person, without any intermediate estate, the less is immediately . . . sunk or drowned in the greater."[25] Although the operation of the doctrine at law was automatic, equity by contrast leaned against merger.[26] The intention of the person in whom the interests coalesced determined whether merger occurred.[27] In the absence of evidence of intention, there would be no merger if it was in the interests of the party or consistent with his duty that merger should not take place.[28] Since 1873, the equitable rules of merger have prevailed.[29] As severance of a joint tenancy by the acquisition of another estate operates only if merger takes place, it is no longer automatic, but depends upon the intention of the party who acquires the estate.[30] There is little authority on when a joint tenancy will now be held to have been severed by the operation of the doctrine of merger.[31] In principle however, the acquisition by one equitable joint tenant of the legal estate as trustee should not, without more, sever the joint tenancy.[32]

5. Homicide. One consequence of the rule that no one may benefit in law from his own crime,[33] is that, in general, if one joint tenant criminally kills another, the killer cannot take any beneficial interest by survivorship. This rule of public policy, commonly known as the "forfeiture rule", applies to cases of deliberate and intentional homicide, whether the killing is murder, manslaughter or aiding and abetting a suicide.[34] It has not been conclusively   **9–049**

[20] *Morgan's Case* (t. Eliz. 1) 2 And. 202; *Wiscot's Case* (1599) 2 Co.Rep. 60b.

[21] *ibid.*

[22] Co.Litt. 183a; Preston *Conveyancing*, iii, 24.

[23] See *post*, para. 14–172.

[24] See *post*, para. 14–176.

[25] 2 Bl.Comm. 177.

[26] *Chambers v. Kingham* (1878) 10 Ch.D. 743, 745.

[27] *Forbes v. Moffatt* (1811) 18 Ves. 384 at 390.

[28] *Re Fletcher* [1917] 1 Ch. 339 at 341.

[29] J.A. 1873, s.25(4). See now L.P.A. 1925, s.185.

[30] See (1990) 41 N.I.L.Q. 359 (A. Dowling).

[31] *cf. Nielson-Jones v. Fedden* [1975] Ch. 222 at 228.

[32] The decision to the contrary in *Conolly v. Conolly* (1867) I.R. 1 Eq. 376 is unlikely to be followed in England.

[33] *e.g. In b. Hall* [1914] P. 1. See the general survey by T.G. Youdan (1973) 89 L.Q.R. 235; and see *post*, para. 11–058.

[34] *Dunbar v. Plant* [1998] Ch. 412; [1998] C.L.J. 31 (S. Bridge).

settled in England whether the application of the rule causes the automatic severance of the joint tenancy or whether a constructive trust is imposed to prevent the killer from obtaining any benefit from his crime.[35] Where there are just two joint tenants the answer will be the same on either view. Thus if A and B hold the legal estate on trust for themselves as joint tenants, and A murders B, the legal estate will vest by survivorship in A alone but upon trust for himself and B's estate as equitable tenants in common in equal shares.[36] However, if there is a third joint tenant, C, the two different approaches lead to different results. The legal estate will necessarily vest in A and C jointly. If severance is automatic they will hold it upon trust for A, B's estate and C as tenants in common in equal shares. If a constructive trust is imposed they will hold it for C as to one-third and for A and C as joint tenants as to the remaining two-thirds.[37]

The court now has a statutory power[38] to modify the application of the forfeiture rule in cases where a person has unlawfully killed[39] another (other than where he has been convicted of murder[40]). It may do so only if it is satisfied that, having regard to the conduct of the offender and of the deceased and to such other circumstances as may appear material to it, the justice of the case so requires.[41] In exercise of this power, the court may hold that the right of survivorship applies notwithstanding that one joint tenant killed another.[42]

B. Devolution of the legal estate

9–050	Where a joint tenancy is severed, the co-owner does not cease to be a joint tenant and trustee of the legal estate if that was his position before severance took place. He can divest himself of the legal estate only by retiring from the trust, or by releasing his interest in the legal estate to the other tenants of it. Where the legal title to unregistered land is vested in joint tenants beneficially, and one of them severs his joint tenancy, he should ensure that a memorandum of severance is indorsed on, or annexed to, the conveyance which vested the legal estate in the co-owners. This will ensure that his interest is protected if

---

[35] The remarks in *Re K* [1985] Ch. 85 at 100, suggest that severance is automatic. In Australia, however, the courts impose a constructive trust instead, and there are persuasive reasons for preferring this latter view: see *Rasmanis v. Jurewitsch* (1969) 70 S.R. (N.S.W.) 407; *Public Trustee v. Evans* (1985) 2 N.S.W.L.R. 188; *Re Stone* [1989] 1 Qd.R.351.

[36] *Re K, supra,* at 100; *Re Stone, supra,* at 352–353.

[37] *Rasmanis v. Jurewitsch, supra* at 411–412. See (1974) 37 M.L.R. 481 at 488–492 (T.K. Earnshaw & P.J. Pace); M. Cope, *Constructive Trusts,* 561–56.

[38] Forfeiture Act 1892, s.2(1); see *post,* para. 11–058.

[39] The forfeiture rule may apply even if a person has been acquitted of a charge of murder or manslaughter provided that in civil proceedings the court is satisfied on the balance of probabilities that he was guilty of a killing that fell within the scope of the rule: *Gray v. Barr* [1971] 2 Q.B. 554; *Public Trustee v. Evans, supra,* at 190.

[40] Forfeiture Act 1982, s.5.

[41] *ibid.,* s.2(2).

[42] *ibid.,* s.2(4)(b); *Re K* [1985] Ch. 85; affirmed [1986] Ch. 180.

there is subsequently a conveyance of the legal estate by a sole surviving joint tenant. This is explained later.[43]

Section 5. The Imposition of a Statutory Trust in Cases of Co-ownership

A. *The imposition of a statutory trust of land*

The conversion of tenancies in common into equitable interests would not by itself have simplified the investigation of title. Where the title was unregistered a purchaser would have had notice of the trusts. It was therefore essential to provide overreaching machinery, so that it would be necessary for any purchaser to investigate only the title to the legal estate. Prior to 1997, this was achieved by imposing a statutory trust for sale upon land conveyed to or held by or on behalf of two or more persons beneficially, whether as tenants in common or joint tenants.[44] After 1996, a trust of land is imposed instead in the same circumstances, and all existing trusts for sale have become trusts of land.[45] The trust is imposed whether the co-owners are given interests in the land itself or in the income from it.[46] In the following cases, therefore, the legal estate is subject to a statutory trust of land[47]:   **9–051**

(i) a conveyance or devise to A and B jointly (*i.e.* as beneficial joint tenants);

(ii) a conveyance[48] or devise[49] to A and B as tenants in common;

(iii) a conveyance or devise to X and Y jointly upon trust for A and B either jointly or in common (or upon trust to pay the income to A and B jointly or in common).[50]

In the case of a devise it should be noted that the legal estate vests not in any of the persons named but in the testator's personal representatives,[51] who

---

[43] See *post*, paras 9–056 *et seq.*

[44] This states the combined effect of L.P.A. 1925, ss.34 and 36 (as they had been interpreted), which dealt with the various cases. The machinery is described in more detail below.

[45] T.L.A.T.A. 1996, s.1; *ante*, paras 8–001, 8–123. See L.P.A. 1925, ss.34, 36 (as amended by T.L.A.T.A. 1996, s.5(1); Sched. 2).

[46] *Re House* [1929] 2 Ch. 166.

[47] L.P.A. 1925, s.36(1) (as amended by T.L.A.T.A. 1996, s.5(1); Sched. 2).

[48] L.P.A. 1925, s.34(2) (as amended by T.L.A.T.A. 1996, s.5(1); Sched. 2).

[49] L.P.A. 1925, s.34(3) (as amended by T.L.A.T.A. 1996, ss.5(1), 25(2); Scheds 2, 4).

[50] *Re House, supra* (devise upon trust for tenants in common held to fall within L.P.A. 1925, s.34(3)). The same presumably applies to a conveyance which will then fall within s.34(2), but it is not clear whether the legal estate vests in X and Y or in A and B. The case is even more difficult, on the wording of s.34(2), where there is a conveyance to X (alone) upon trust for A and B in common. Beneficial joint tenancy is clearly dealt with by s.36: the legal estate vests in the trustee or trustees.

[51] L.P.A. 1925, s.34(3) (as amended by T.L.A.T.A. 1996, ss.5(1), 25(2); Scheds 2, 4).

therefore become trustees of land. Since they automatically hold the deceased's property on trust to give effect to the will, there is no point in creating another set of trustees. There are special provisions for settled land, which are explained later.[52]

9–052 The Law of Property Act 1925 had been interpreted in such a way that a trust of land[53] is imposed in all cases of beneficial co-ownership.[54] In the case of joint beneficial interests this is effected in a straightforward way[55] by section 36(1).[56] In the case of beneficial interests in common the position is more difficult. Section 34(1) provides that "an undivided share in land shall not be capable of being created except as provided by the Settled Land Act 1925 or as hereinafter mentioned".[57] The draftsman appears to have contemplated that a tenancy in common could be created in just four situations:

(i) where settled land comes to be held "on trust for persons entitled in possession under a trust instrument in undivided shares"[58];

(ii) where land "is expressed to be conveyed to any persons in undivided shares"[59];

(iii) where land is devised or bequeathed "to two or more persons in undivided shares"[60]; and

(iv) where land is conveyed to trustees to hold on an express trust of land[61] for two or more persons as tenants in common.[62]

If a tenancy in common is created in one of these ways, it will be apparent on the face of the title (if unregistered) that the land is held upon a trust of land. A purchaser will therefore know that any purchase monies must be paid to at least two trustees if the beneficial interests are to be overreached.[63] It is therefore at least possible that the draftsman meant what he said in section

---

[52] *Post*, para. 9–089. No new settlements may be created after 1997: see *ante*, para. 9–089.

[53] And before 1997, a trust for sale.

[54] *Williams & Glyn's Bank Ltd v. Boland* [1981] A.C. 487 at 503; *City of London B.S. v. Flegg* [1988] A.C. 54 at 77.

[55] See however, 62 L.J.News. 437; 64 L.J.News. 66.

[56] As amended by T.L.A.T.A. 1996, s.5(1); Sched. 2.

[57] See too S.L.A. 1925, s.36(4) (as amended by T.L.A.T.A. 1996, s.25(1); Sched. 3). For comment on these provisions, see (1963) 27 Conv. (N.S.) 51 at 53–54 (B. Rudden); [1982] Conv. 213 (M. Friend and J. Newton); [1986] Conv. 379; [1987] Conv. 451 at 454–457; (W. J. Swadling); C.L.J. 277 at 297–302 (C.H.).

[58] S.L.A. 1925, s.36(1); *post*, para. 9–090.

[59] L.P.A. 1925, s.34(2) (see now, as amended by T.L.A.T.A. 1996, s.5(1); Sched. 2).

[60] L.P.A. 1925, s.34(3) (see now, as amended by T.L.A.T.A. 1996, ss.5(1), 25(2); Scheds 2, 4).

[61] Prior to 1997, an express trust for sale.

[62] This is not explicitly covered by the Law of Property Act 1925, but *cf.* L.P.A. 1922, Sched. 3, paras 2(6), (7). See too L.P.A. 1925, s.3(1)(b) (repealed by T.L.A.T.A. 1996, s.25(2); Sched. 4); 73 L.J.News 355 (J. M. Lightwood); [1990] C.L.J. 277 at 299 (C.H.).

[63] L.P.A. 1925, s.27(2) (as amended by L.P.(Am.)A. 1926, Sched; T.L.A.T.A. 1996, s.25(1); Sched. 3); *ante*, para. 8–166. Prior to 1997, the fact that land was held on trust for sale was also relevant because the powers of the trustees were restricted: see L.P.A. 1925, s.28(1) (now repealed; *ante*, para. 8–122). By contrast, trustees of land have the powers of an absolute owner: see T.L.A.T.A. 1996, s.6(1); *ante*, para. 8–137.

34(1) and intended that a tenancy in common should only be created in one of the four ways outlined above.[64] The fundamental weakness of his scheme however is that he failed to provide what was to happen in cases of non-compliance.

There are in fact a number of situations that fall outside the various **9–053** provisions, though some of these could not have been foreseen in 1925.[65] The following are amongst the most important[66]—

(i) a conveyance to A and B as joint tenants, where equity presumes them to take as beneficial tenants in common, *e.g.* because they are partners, or contribute purchase-money in unequal shares[67];

(ii) a conveyance to X, purchasing as trustee for A and B who are equitable owners in common of the purchase money;

(iii) a declaration by A, as sole owner, that he holds on trust for himself and B in equal shares[68];

(iv) where a spouse acquires a shares or an enhanced share in the matrimonial home by virtue of substantial improvement which he has made to the property subsequent to its acquisition[69]; and

(v) where A acquires a beneficial interest under a constructive trust in property belonging to B because he acted to his detriment in reliance on the parties' common intention that he should have such a share.[70]

The courts found a way of escape in section 36(4) of the Settled Land Act 1925[71] which provides that an undivided share in land cannot be created

---

[64] See [1982] Conv. 213 (M. Friend and J. Newton); [1990] C.L.J. 277 at 298 (C.H.). *cf.* J.S. Anderson, *Lawyers and the Making of English Land Law 1832–1940*, pp. 330–331.

[65] See (1944) 9 Conv. (N.S.) 37 *et seq.* For difficulties in applying the provisions to leases, see (1989) 18 *Anglo-American Law Review* 151 (P. Sparkes).

[66] A situation that was a possible cause of difficulty prior to 1997 was a conveyance to A (a minor) and B (an adult) as tenants in common: see the previous edition of this work at p. 438. If they were *joint* tenants, L.P.A. 1925, s.19(2) (repealed by T.L.A.T.A. 1996, s.25(2); Sched. 4) covered the case. It *may* have been wide enough to include tenants in common: see [1990] C.L.J. 277 at 300 (C.H.). For conveyances after 1996 there is no difficulty: see T.L.A.T.A. 1996, s.2(6); Sched. 1, para. 1(2).

[67] *Ante*, para. 9–022. This situation does not fall within L.P.A. 1925, s.34(2), because the land is not *expressed* to be conveyed to A and B in undivided shares. In two such cases (of purchasers contributing unequally) different solutions have been found: that the case falls within L.P.A. 1925, s.36(1), which governs beneficial joint tenancy (*Re Buchanan-Wollaston's Conveyance* [1939] Ch. 217 at 222; [1939] Ch. 738 at 744); and that S.L.A. 1925, s.36(4) governs any case of tenancy in common not otherwise provided for (*Bull v. Bull* [1955] 1 Q.B. 234; *City of London B.S. v. Flegg* [1988] A.C. 54 at 77). *cf.* [1990] C.L.J. 277 at 298–301 (C.H.).

[68] See, *e.g. Re Hind* [1933] Ch. 208; *Jones v. Jones* [1972] 1 W.L.R. 1269.

[69] Matrimonial Proceedings and Property Act 1970, s.37; *post*, para. 10–025.

[70] *Post*, para. 10–023. For a case where the court, in giving effect to an equity by estoppel, declared that A held land upon trust for sale for A and B equally, see *Holiday Inns v. Broadhead* (1974) 232 E.G. 951, 1087. For proprietary estoppel, see *post*, Chap. 13.

[71] As now amended by T.L.A.T.A. 1996, s.25(1); Sched. 3.

"except under a trust instrument or under the Law of Property Act 1925 and shall then only take effect behind a trust of land".[72] Plainly this provision is not well framed to remedy the deficiencies of the Law of Property Act 1925. But to employ it for that purpose is probably a better course than to extend the incomplete provisions of that Act by straining their language.[73] It is perhaps surprising that the opportunity was not taken in the Trusts of Land and Appointment of Trustees Act 1996 to rectify the position.

Most dispositions of either a freehold or a leasehold having more than 21 years to run, or the grant of lease for more than 21 years to two or more persons as tenants in common will now have to be completed by registration, whether or not the title is already registered.[74] The trusts upon which the land is to be held must be set out in the application for first registration (if the title is unregistered) or in the transfer or assent (if title is already registered).[75] Because the transferees are tenants in common, the last survivor of them will be unable to give a valid receipt for capital money arising on any disposition of the land.[76] In those circumstances a restriction will be entered on the register by which no disposition by a sole proprietor of the land under which capital money arises is to be registered except under an order of the registrar or of the court.[77]

9–054   The imposition of a statutory trust of land in all cases where there is tenancy in common is not without its hazards. The existence of the trust may not be apparent on the face of the title. A person who appears to be an absolute owner may turn out to be a trustee of land. Unless a co-trustee is appointed, he will be unable to make an overreaching conveyance. The difficulties which may result from this are explained elsewhere.[78]

Provided that these difficulties can be overcome, the advantages of employing the device of a trust are two-fold.[79] First, it keeps the beneficial interests of the co-owners off the title. A purchaser is not concerned with the beneficial interests in the land, but only with the legal estate vested in the trustees of land. Provided that he pays his purchase-money to trustees of land who are either two or more in number or a trust corporation, he takes free from the rights of the beneficiaries.[80] It will not matter to the purchaser whether there are three or 30 people entitled, or whether they are joint tenants or tenants in

---

[72] See *Bull v. Bull, supra,* at 237; *City of London B.S. v. Flegg, supra,* at 77.

[73] The solution adopted in *Re Buchanan-Wollaston's Conveyance, supra,* is at the expense of the word "beneficially" in L.P.A. 1925, s.36(1).

[74] See L.R.A. 1925, s.123 (as substituted by L.R.A. 1997, s.1).

[75] L.R.R. 1925, rr. 19, 98; (Sched. 1, Forms FR1, TR1 and AS1 (as substituted or inserted by L.R.R. 1997); *ante,* paras 6–098, 8–133, 9–026.

[76] The survivor of beneficial *joint* tenants would be able to give such a valid receipt.

[77] L.R.A. 1925, s.58(3); L.R.R. 1925, r. 213; Sched. 2, Form 62; Ruoff & Roper, 32–09, 32–10.

[78] See *ante,* para. 8–166; *post,* para. 10–031.

[79] English law is unique in having adopted the trust as a device to give effect to co-ownership: see *Land Law: Themes and Perspectives* (eds S. Bright and J. Dewar), 107 (J. S. Anderson).

[80] For this overreaching machinery, see *ante,* para. 8–165.

common.[81] Secondly, the imposition of a trust makes it much easier to administer property that is owned by more than four co-owners. As has been explained, the trustees are, in exercising their functions, obliged to consult the beneficiaries of full age who are entitled to an interest in possession in the land and, so far as consistent with the general interest of the trust, to give effect to the wishes of the majority (according to the value of the combined interests).[82] However—

    (i) such functions can be exercised without the concurrence of *all* such beneficiaries[83];

    (ii) the court may relieve the trustees of the need to obtain consents if, *e.g.* the beneficiaries cannot readily be contacted[84]; and

    (iii) the trustees' overriding concern is to act in the general interest of the trust.[85]

B. Determination of the statutory trust of land

1. Union in sole tenant. Once all the legal and equitable interests in the property have finally vested in one person (*e.g.* where A, B and C were beneficial joint tenants in fee simple and B and C have died), there can no longer be an effective trust and the statutory trust of land therefore ceases.[86] In the example given, A can sell as sole owner and take the purchase-money.[87] Nothing in the Law of Property Act 1925 affects the right of a survivor of joint tenants who is solely and beneficially interested to deal with his legal estate as if it were not held on a trust of land.[88] A surviving joint tenant does not therefore have to go through the pointless procedure of appointing another trustee of a trust under which he is the sole beneficiary.

    9–055

2. Investigation of title: unregistered land

(a) The situation prior to 1964. Prior to 1964, a particular problem existed for a purchaser of unregistered land. He could not tell whether a vendor, who was the surviving owner of the legal estate, was also solely entitled in equity

    9–056

---

[81] The statutory machinery has to apply to a joint tenancy because, as has been explained (see *ante*, para. 9–036) a joint tenancy may be severed, and a purchaser must be absolved from inquiring whether this has happened. See *post*, paras 9–056, 9–057.

[82] T.L.A.T.A. 1996, s.11; *ante*, para. 8–147.

[83] As was required prior to 1926: see *ante*, paras 9–032, 9–033.

[84] T.L.A.T.A. 1996, s.14(2); *ante*, para. 8–142.

[85] T.L.A.T.A. 1996, s.11(1)(b).

[86] *Re Cook* [1948] Ch. 212.

[87] For the protection of purchasers, see *ante* para. 8–154. Where title is registered, any purchaser from A can rely on the absence of any restriction against a disposition by a sole proprietor of the kind that should have been entered if A, B and C had been beneficial tenants in common: see L.R.R. 1925, r. 213(1); Sched. 2, Form 62 (as amended); *ante*, para. 9–053.

[88] L.P.A. 1925, s.36(2) (as amended by L.P.(Am).A. 1926, s.7, Sched.; T.L.A.T.A. 1996, s.5(1); Sched. 2, para. 4).

unless he investigated the beneficial interests. A beneficial joint tenancy, for example, might have been turned into a tenancy in common[89] by some act or event not shown in the title to the legal estate, and perhaps not even known to the vendor, so that A, in the above example, might turn out to be a trustee of land for himself and some other person claiming through B or C. Even in this case the purchaser, if he had made all due inquiries and found no evidence of a tenancy in common, could probably plead that he was a bona fide purchaser of the legal estate for value without notice of the outstanding equitable interest.[90] But no purchaser wishes to be driven to that plea. There was also the practical problem of what proof of a negative (non-severance) could be given.

9–057   *(b) Statements under the Act of 1964.* This situation violated the principle of the 1925 legislation that the purchaser should not be concerned with beneficial interests.[91] It was remedied by the Law of Property (Joint Tenants) Act 1964,[92] though the legislation itself creates a number of problems.[93] This short statute provides that, in favour of a purchaser of a legal estate, a survivor of two or more joint tenants shall "be deemed to be solely and beneficially interested if the conveyance includes a statement that he is so interested".[94] Thus the purchaser of the legal estate will take it without notice of any severance and will defeat the equitable title of any owner of a severed share. Where the survivor has himself died, his personal representatives are given corresponding powers.[95]

9–058   *(c) The exclusion of the Act.* The Act of 1964 does not apply if, before the date of the conveyance by the survivor, a memorandum of severance is indorsed on or annexed to the conveyance which vested the legal estate in the joint tenants. The memorandum must be signed by one or all of them and record the severance on a specified date.[96] Nor does the Act apply where, before the same date, a bankruptcy order has been registered[97] so as to affect the purchaser with actual notice of it,[98] or where the title to the land is registered.[99]

---

[89] *i.e.* severed, *e.g.* by a sale of a share: *ante*, paras 9–038, 9–039.

[90] *Williams & Glyn's Bank Ltd v. Boland* [1979] Ch. 312 at 330, 334.

[91] Purchasers often had to be advised to obtain the appointment of another trustee to join the vendor in receiving the purchase money, in case the land was still held on trust: see 219 L.T.News 217.

[92] The legislation was retrospective. It was deemed to have come into force on January 1, 1926: s.2. It was a Private Member's Bill introduced by Sir Barnett Janner M.P. with the express intention of making it unnecessary for a surviving joint tenant to have to appoint a second trustee when he wished to sell the land.

[93] See M. P. Thompson, *Barnsley's Conveyancing Law and Practice*, 4th ed., p. 316; and *infra*.

[94] s.1(1) (as amended by L.P.(M.P.)A. 1994, s.21; Scheds 1, 2).

[95] s.1(2). See [1977] Conv. 423 (P.W. Smith).

[96] s.1(1).

[97] Under L.C.A. 1972; *ante* para. 5–090.

[98] s.1(1), as amended by I.A. 1985, s.235(1), Sched. 8, para. 13.

[99] See *infra*.

(d) Severance. The Act of 1964 provides more convenient conveyancing **9–059** machinery in the normal case where there has been no severance. But where there has been a severance, which may be unknown to the survivor, the title of the owner of the severed share will be imperilled unless he attaches a memorandum of severance to the document of title. The Act gives him no power to insist upon this, but his powers as co-owner probably suffice. Nor does the Act say what is to happen where the vendor conveys on the basis that he is solely and beneficially interested but the purchaser has notice that there has been severance. On its face, the Act even then protects the purchaser, and this appears to have been Parliament's intention.[1] If this is so, the Act has made the rights of the beneficiaries more vulnerable to fraud than they were hitherto.[2] It is possible that a court would not allow a purchaser to take advantage of the Act in circumstances where he knew of or was a party to the vendor's inequitable conduct.[3]

3. Investigation of title: registered land. It has already been explained **9–060** that where registered land is transferred to co-owners they are required to state in the transfer the trusts upon which they hold the land.[4] If they hold on trust such that the survivor cannot give a valid receipt for capital money on a disposition of the land, a restriction must be entered on the register to that effect.[5] If a beneficial joint tenant of registered land subsequently severs the joint tenancy, he should ensure that a restriction is then placed upon the register to indicate that the survivor can no longer give a valid receipt for capital money.[6] The Law of Property (Joint Tenants) Act 1964 has no application to registered land.[7] This is because those who promoted the Act apparently assumed that if there was no restriction on the register, any purchaser from a surviving joint tenant would obtain a good title even if severance had in fact taken place. It is now clear that this assumption is not always correct. An interest under a trust of land can be an overriding interest if it is supported by actual occupation.[8] If therefore severance took place, and one of the tenants in common died, leaving his share by will to some person who was in occupation of the land, any purchaser of the land from the survivor who completed without being given vacant possession,[9] would take the land subject to the beneficial interest of that occupier unless he had made enquiries

---

[1] See (1966) 30 Conv. (N.S.) 27 at 28 (P. Jackson).
[2] M. P. Thompson, *Barnsley's Conveyancing Law and Practice*, 4th ed., 316.
[3] *cf.* the judicial restriction of the provision protecting purchasers from mortgagees: *post*, para. 19–059.
[4] *Ante*, paras 9–026, 9–053.
[5] L.R.A. 1925, s.58(3); L.R.R. 1925, r. 213; Sched. 2, Form 62 (as amended).
[6] See L.R.R. 1925, r. 213(5).
[7] s.3.
[8] L.R.A. 1925, s.70(1)(g); *Williams & Glyn's Bank Ltd v. Boland* [1981] A.C. 487; *ante*, para. 6–061.
[9] Typically a mortgagee.

of that person and he failed to disclose his rights.[10] A purchaser is not normally at risk if he purchases with vacant possession.

C. Operation of the statutory trust

9–061   The working of the statutory trust imposed by the Trusts of Land and Appointment of Trustees Act 1996 as it applies to cases of co-ownership must now be explained. In relation to many aspects of the law, it is necessary to consider the position prior to 1997 when a trust for sale rather than a trust of land was imposed in such cases. This will make clear the changes that the 1996 Act has brought about. Furthermore, although the statutory provisions prior to 1997 differ significantly from those which now apply, the case law that developed in relation to them is likely to remain relevant as regards some parts of the new law.

1. Rights of beneficiaries

9–062   *(a) The right to occupy.* Prior to 1997 beneficial co-owners of land had a common law right of occupation pending sale.[11] Before 1926 they had been entitled to occupy the land themselves,[12] and it was eventually settled that the imposition of the statutory trust for sale, which was primarily a conveyancing device, did not deprive them of this right.[13] Occupation of the premises by a beneficiary was no more than the enjoyment *in specie* of the rents and profits of the land to which he was entitled,[14] and was not a separate and severable right.[15] The interests of the beneficiaries could therefore be overreached in the usual way on a disposition by the trustees for sale.[16]

It has been explained that after 1997, where land is held on a trust of land, a beneficiary who is beneficially entitled to an interest in possession in land, has a statutory right to occupy it,[17] subject to the trustees' powers to exclude or restrict that right in certain circumstances.[18] This statutory right is unlikely to be in issue in the common case of co-ownership where the legal and beneficial owners of the land are one and the same. In such a situation, the co-owners' right to possession is simply a concomitant of their ownership of the legal estate,[19] and the unity of possession to which all co-owners are entitled at common law.[20]

---

[10] L.R.A. 1925, s.70(1)(g).
[11] *City of London B.S. v. Flegg* [1988] A.C. 54 at 71, 81. *cf. Barclay v. Barclay* [1970] 1 Q.B. 677.
[12] *Ante*, para. 9–005. See [1998] C.L.J. 123 at 127 (D.G. Barnsley).
[13] *Bull v. Bull* [1955] 1 Q.B. 234, approved in *Williams & Glyn's Bank Ltd v. Boland* [1981] A.C. 487; and see *Cook & Cook* [1962] P. 235; *I.R.C. v. Lloyds Private Banking Ltd* [1998] 2 F.C.R. 41 at 49.
[14] *City of London B.S. v. Flegg, supra,* at 81.
[15] *ibid.*
[16] *City of London B.S. v. Flegg, supra,* and see *ante*, para. 8–166.
[17] T.L.A.T.A. 1996, s.12; *ante*, para. 8–149.
[18] T.L.A.T.A. 1996, s.13; *ante*, para. 8–150.
[19] *Ante*, para. 8–149.
[20] *Ante*, para. 9–005.

The statutory right of occupation given to beneficiaries has been criticised on the ground that it has reduced the rights that beneficial co-owners had hitherto enjoyed.[21] This is because the right—

(i) depends upon the purposes of the trust and the availability and suitability of the land for occupation[22]; and

(ii) is subject to the trustees' power to exclude or restrict the beneficiary's right of occupation.[23]

It has been suggested that, in consequence, an equitable co-owner no longer **9–063** enjoys unity of possession as that concept has hitherto been understood.[24] This may be more apparent than real. First, as indicated above, where a person is both a legal and beneficial co-owner, his right to occupy cannot be restricted or excluded without his consent or a court order. This is because he is a trustee, and the power to restrict or exclude must be exercised unanimously.[25] Secondly, even where a beneficiary's entitlement to occupy the land does depend upon the Act, it is suggested that any exercise by the trustees of their power of exclusion will normally be on terms that he is compensated by the beneficiaries who remain in occupation.[26] To deny a beneficiary who is entitled in possession both the right to receive the rents and profits of the land and the right to enjoy it *in specie* by occupation is likely to be regarded as unreasonable in the absence of some compelling circumstance.[27] Notwithstanding the criticisms of the statutory power to exclude a co-owner (whether or not on terms), its availability has a significant advantage. It gives the court greater flexibility in the case where the relationship between co-owners has come to an end, and one of them has applied for an order for sale.[28] In practice, it is in this situation that the power is most likely to be employed.

(b) Disputes between co-owners. Many disputes between co-owners of land **9–064** arise on the termination of the relationship or arrangement between the parties, where one of them wishes to have the property sold but the other does not. The relevant provisions of the Trusts of Land and Appointment of Trustees Act 1996 have already been explained,[29] but their application to such disputes requires more detailed consideration. It will be recalled that under these provisions—

(i) a trustee of land; and

---

[21] See [1998] C.L.J. 123 (D. G. Barnsley).
[22] T.L.A.T.A. 1996, s.12(1), (2); *ante*, para. 8–149.
[23] T.L.A.T.A. 1996, s.13; *ante*, para. 8–150.
[24] [1998] C.L.J. 123 at 137 (D. G. Barnsley).
[25] See *ante*, para. 8–137.
[26] Under T.L.A.T.A. 1996, s.13(6). A beneficiary who is already in occupation can only be excluded by his consent or by court order: s.13(7). See *ante*, para. 8–150.
[27] *cf.* T.L.A.T.A. 1996, s.13(2); *ante*, para. 8–150.
[28] Under T.L.A.T.A. 1996, s.14; *infra*.
[29] ss.14, 15; *ante*, paras 8–142 *et seq.*

(ii) any person who has an interest in any property which is subject to either a trust of land or a trust of the proceeds of sale of land;

may apply to the court, which may make such an order as it thinks fit in relation to the exercise by the trustees of any of their functions.[30] It may, for example, direct or restrain a sale or other disposition by the trustees, or relieve the trustees of the necessity of obtaining any consent to a disposition that would otherwise be needed by them.[31]

Prior to 1997, the courts evolved a number of principles as to how they would exercise their discretion in disputes under the equivalent but narrower provision that was applicable where land was held on trust for sale.[32] The matters to which the court is required to have regard in exercising its discretion under the 1996 Act[33] are intended to be a consolidation and rationalisation of those principles.[34] Although the authorities on the law prior to 1997 will therefore continue to provide guidance,[35] the outcome will not in all cases be the same as it would have been under the previous law. This is because the legislation is much more specific as to the matters which a court is required to take into account on such an application.[36] Six of these matters are expressly mentioned, of which two have already been discussed.[37] The remaining four are considered in detail below.[38] It has been explained[39] that this list is not exhaustive, and that in a given situation not only may there be other considerations, but two or more of the matters specifically listed may conflict, and the court will therefore have to decide which is to be given the greater weight. It should be noted that these factors must be taken into account in all cases, regardless of who the applicant may be, except where a trustee in bankruptcy applies for an order.[40] Rather different principles then govern the application.[41]

9–065   (1) THE INTENTIONS OF THE PERSON WHO CREATED THE TRUST. This is most likely to be relevant in cases where the trust has been expressly created, and there seems no reason why the settlor should not indicate his intentions in the trust instrument expressly or by necessary implication. Thus one reason why

---

[30] T.L.A.T.A. 1996, ss.14(1), (2), 17(2)–(6).

[31] *ibid.*, s.14(2); *Abbey National Mortgages Plc v. Powell* (1999) 78 P. & C.R. D16.

[32] L.P.A. 1925, s.30; *ante*, para. 8–111.

[33] T.L.A.T.A. 1996, s.15(1); *infra*; and see *ante*, para. 8–143.

[34] See (1989) Law Com. No. 181, para. 12.9.

[35] See *TSB Bank Plc v. Marshall* [1998] 3 E.G.L.R. 100 at 102; [1998] Fam. Law 596 at 597 (R. Bailey-Harris).

[36] T.L.A.T.A. 1996, s.15(1).

[37] See *ibid.*, ss.15(2) (views of beneficiaries entitled to occupy on an application relating to the trustees' power to exclude or restrict the right to occupy), 15(3) (circumstances and wishes of the beneficiaries of full age entitled to an interest in possession); *ante*, para. 8–143.

[38] T.L.A.T.A. 1996, s.15(1).

[39] *Ante*, para. 8–143.

[40] T.L.A.T.A. 1996, s.15(4).

[41] *Post*, para. 9–070.

a settlor may choose to create an express trust for sale after 1996,[42] is because he wishes to make it clear that the trustees should sell the land.[43]

(2) THE PURPOSES FOR WHICH THE PROPERTY SUBJECT TO THE TRUST IS HELD. **9–066** Prior to 1997, it had long been the practice on an application for sale by a co-owner[44] for the court to have regard to the underlying purpose of the trust.[45] The court considered whether the object of the trust was indeed to sell the land[46] or to retain it for some secondary or collateral purpose.[47] This practice has now been made statutory. Once again, there seems no reason why a settlor should not set out the purposes of the trust expressly when he creates it.

The cases decided prior to 1997 on trusts for sale provide guidance as to what, in the absence of any express statement, constitutes a purpose and when it is at an end.[48] Many of them arose on the separation of married or unmarried couples. Where there were no children, the underlying purpose of the trust was regarded as the provision of a home for the parties while the relationship subsisted.[49] Neither party had a right to demand a sale until the termination of the relationship.[50] Even when the parties had separated, the court would decline to order a sale in appropriate circumstances,[51] or it might order a sale on terms.[52] Under the previous law,[53] the court had no power to act unless it made an order for sale.[54] However, it might indicate that it would order a sale unless the party in occupation agreed to make some financial adjustment in favour of the other, *e.g.* by offering to pay an occupation rent pending an eventual sale.[55] After 1996, the court has much wider powers and can act directly to achieve such a result. It may make any order relating to the exercise by the trustees of *any* of their functions as it thinks fit.[56] It could (for example) make an order for sale to take effect at some future date, and, in the interim, exclude one of the co-owners on terms that the other compensate him.[57]

---

[42] *cf. ante*, para. 8–126.

[43] *cf. Barclay v. Barclay* [1970] 2 Q.B. 677.

[44] The same was true where the co-owner was a trustee who sought an order for possession: *Bull v. Bull* [1955] 1 Q.B. 234.

[45] *Re Buchanan-Wollaston's Conveyance* [1939] Ch. 738; *Jones v. Challenger* [1961] 1 Q.B. 176; *Re Evers' Trust* [1980] 1 W.L.R. 1327; *Harris v. Harris* (1995) 72 P. & C.R. 408.

[46] Because it was a trust *for sale.*

[47] *Jones v. Challenger, supra, Barclay v. Barclay, supra.*

[48] The issue is one of fact: see, *e.g. Harris v. Harris, supra.*

[49] *Jones v. Challenger, supra,* at 182; *Bernard v. Josephs* [1982] Ch. 391 at 405.

[50] *Jones v. Challenger, supra,* at 182. Where the parties are married, the relationship may be regarded as terminated even if there has been no divorce: *Rawlings v. Rawlings* [1964] P. 398 at 418, 419.

[51] *Bedson v. Bedson* [1965] 2 Q.B. 66; *Hayward v. Hayward* [1976] 1 E.G.L.R. 46 (no sale at behest of deserting spouse).

[52] *Ali v. Hussein* (1974) 231 E.G. 372 (occupying co-owner given opportunity to buy out the other).

[53] *i.e.* where there had been an application to the court under L.P.A. 1925, s.30.

[54] *Bernard v. Josephs, supra,* at 410. See too *Dennis v. McDonald* [1982] Fam. 63 at 73, 74.

[55] *ibid.* See (1982) 98 L.Q.R. 519 (F. Webb); [1984] Conv. 103 (M. P. Thompson).

[56] T.L.A.T.A. 1996, s.14(2).

[57] See *ibid.*, s.13(6).

9–067   Because the court must have regard to the purpose for which the trust was created, a co-owner's right to a sale may be restricted by agreement or by his conduct. If a trustee-beneficiary has covenanted to sell only with another co-owner's consent, the court will not normally assist him to break his contract by forcing a sale against the other co-owner's wishes.[58] Similarly where one co-owner has been induced to move house and contribute to the purchase of a new home in reliance on an assurance that he could remain there, the other co-owner is unlikely to obtain an order for sale.[59] It should be noted, however, that as the purpose for which the property is held is now just one of the factors that a court is required to take into account in exercising its discretion, there might be circumstances where the other factors outweighed the purpose, notwithstanding the co-owner's agreement or conduct.[60]

Where the co-owners are married, and the relationship comes to an end on divorce, any application for sale should be heard by the court that is dealing with any application for ancillary relief under the Matrimonial Causes Act 1973.[61] The court then has extensive discretionary powers and may make a property adjustment order.[62] In practice it will be the exercise of those powers that is determinative.[63]

9–068   (3) THE WELFARE OF ANY MINOR WHO OCCUPIES OR MIGHT REASONABLY BE EXPECTED TO OCCUPY ANY LAND SUBJECT TO THE TRUST AS HIS HOME. Prior to 1997, in cases where the co-owners were either married or lived together as man and wife, there was some uncertainty as to the relevance of any children in determining both the purpose of the trust and whether, on the termination of the couple's relationship, that purpose had come to an end. In some cases it was held that the purpose of the trust was to provide a family home. A sale would not be ordered therefore merely because the relationship between the parents had terminated, but only when accommodation was no longer required for the children.[64] In other cases the court took the view that as the children were not beneficiaries under the trust for sale, their interests could only be taken into account incidentally as a factor which affected the equities between

---

[58] *Re Buchanan-Wollaston's Conveyance, supra.*

[59] *Charlton v. Lester* [1976] 1 E.G.L.R. 131; *Jones v. Jones* [1977] 1 W.L.R. 438.

[60] This might occur where, *e.g.* a creditor of one of the co-owners was seeking a sale.

[61] *Williams v. Williams* [1976] Ch. 278. At p. 286, Roskill L.J. suggested that, "nowadays it is desirable that applications should be made under all the relevant sections of all the modern legislation".

[62] M.C.A. 1973 (as amended by the Matrimonial Homes and Property Act 1981 and the Matrimonial and Family Proceedings Act 1984), ss.24, 24A, 25, 25A (s.24A expressly confers a power of sale, but only when the court has made an order for financial provision of a property adjustment order: see *Wicks v. Wicks* [1999] Fam. 65 at 80). See *Harman v. Glencross* [1986] Fam. 81 at 96. The existence of these statutory powers influenced the manner in which the discretion to order a sale under L.P.A. 1925, s.30 was exercised in cases where M.C.A. 1973 was inapplicable, as where the parties either chose not to divorce or were not married: see *Re Evers' Trust* [1980] 1 W.L.R. 1327 at 1332, 1333; *Dennis v. McDonald, supra,* at 73, 74; *Bernard v. Josephs* [1982] Ch. 391 at 410; [1984] Conv. 103 (M. P. Thompson).

[63] As explained *ante*, para. 8–142, it seems unlikely that T.L.A.T.A. 1996, s.14(2) confers on the court any power to vary beneficial interests under a trust of land.

[64] *Williams v. Williams* [1976] Ch. 278; *Re Evers' Trust, supra.* See too *Rawlings v. Rawlings* [1964] P. 398 at 419.

the two co-owners.[65] This uncertainty has now been resolved by the 1996 Act. In an application made under the Act for an order of sale, the court must take into account the welfare of any minor.

As already explained, where the co-owners are married and the issue of sale arises on divorce, it is likely to be subsumed in any order which the court makes for ancillary relief under the Matrimonial Causes Act 1973. In such proceedings, the court will take into account the welfare of any child who is a minor.[66] Where the co-owners are not married, provision of a home for a child may be obtained in one of two ways, namely under the Children Act 1989 or under the Trusts of Land and Appointment of Trustees Act 1996.[67] Under the Children Act 1989, the court has power to make an order requiring one parent to transfer property either to the other or to the child for the benefit of that child, or to create a settlement for the benefit of that child.[68] However, there are constraints on the court when exercising its discretion in such a case. Commonly it will be the mother who is seeking an order. However, where the parents are unmarried, she has no right to be supported by the other, and in the absence of any interest in the property, "no right in herself to have even a roof over her head".[69] There is therefore a concern that the court's order may be seen to confer a "windfall" on her.[70] The court is likely to restrict the duration of such orders in favour of the children until they have completed their education. Thereafter the property reverts to the father, because the children cease to have any continuing claim on him.[71] Where the mother is a co-owner and seeks an order under the Trusts of Land and Appointment of Trustees Act 1996, she does so on her own behalf, rather than on behalf of the children (as under the Children Act 1989). On such an application the court will have regard to all circumstances, including the interests of the children. In practice, it seems likely that, in many such cases, the court will make an order postponing any sale of the family home during the period of the children's minority, and perhaps not until their education is finished (if that is later). The

---

[65] *Burke v. Burke* [1974] 1 W.L.R. 1063; *Re Densham* [1975] 1 W.L.R. 1519 at 1531; *Re Bailey* [1977] 1 W.L.R. 278; *Re Holliday* [1981] Ch. 405 at 417. For attempts to reconcile the authorities, see *Cousins v. Dzosens, The Times*, December 12, 1981; *Chhokar v. Chhokar* [1984] F.L.R. 313 at 327 (where Cumming-Bruce L.J. suggested that, "as a matter of common sense, the arrangements made by the court should take proper account of the need of the children for accommodation").

[66] M.C.A. 1973, s.25(3) (substituted by the Matrimonial and Family Proceedings Act 1984, s.3).

[67] In practice, applications may be made under both Acts. See [1998] Fam. Law 349 at 350 *et seq.* (E. Cooke). An application will probably be made under the provisions of the Children Act 1989 alone only where the applicant has no interest in the property.

[68] s.15; Sched. 1. These provisions are applicable where the parents are married and in some cases where they are unmarried. Where the parents are unmarried, a claim under the Children Act 1989 will lie only against the biological parent of the child and not against a step-parent even if he treats the child as a child of the family: see *J v. J (A Minor: Property Transfer)* [1993] 2 F.L.R. 56.

[69] *T v. S (Financial Provision for Children)* [1994] 2 F.L.R. 883 at 890, *per* Johnson J.

[70] *ibid. cf. Pearson v. Franklin* [1994] 1 W.L.R. 370 at 375, 376.

[71] *T v. S (Financial Provision for Children), supra,* at 891. See too *A v. A (A Minor: Financial Provision)* [1994] 1 F.L.R. 657.

proceeds of sale will then be split between the parents according to their interests.

9–069   (4) THE INTERESTS OF ANY SECURED CREDITOR OF ANY BENEFICIARY.[72] Prior to 1997, where a secured creditor of a co-owner applied for a sale of property,[73] the principle that the court applied was the same as in cases of insolvency.[74] That principle, explained more fully below,[75] was that the voice of the creditor would normally prevail and a sale would be ordered in the absence of exceptional circumstances.[76] This was held to apply—

   (i) where a creditor obtained a charging order[77] against the beneficial interest of a co-owner[78];

  (ii) where a creditor had a mortgage over a property with a registered title, but that charge was subject to the overriding interest of a co-owner[79];

 (iii) where one co-owner forged the signature of the other on a mortgage of the property which they owned, so that it was binding only on the beneficial interest of the forger[80]; and

 (iv) where although both co-owners had executed a mortgage in favour of a creditor, it was rescinded as against one of them because it had been induced by the fraud or undue influence of the other.[81]

It is by no means certain that these principles still apply after 1996. First, the interests of any secured creditor of any beneficiary are just one factor that a court is now required to take into account[82] on an application for an order under section 14 of the Trusts of Land and Appointment of Trustees Act 1996. Secondly, where such an application is made by the trustee of a bankrupt's estate those factors do not apply.[83] This suggests that the analogy with bankruptcy will no longer be strictly applied, and that the courts may adopt a

---

[72] See (1985) 5 O.J.L.S. 132 (N. P. Gravells); [1995] J.B.L. 384 (S. Cooper). These must now be read subject to T.L.A.T.A. 1996, ss.14, 15.

[73] Under L.P.A. 1925, s.30.

[74] See *Lloyds Bank Plc v. Byrne* [1993] 1 F.L.R. 369; *Zandfarid v. B.C.C.I. International S.A.* [1996] 1 W.L.R. 1420, 1429.

[75] *Post*, para. 9–071.

[76] For a case in which the circumstances were exceptional, see *Halifax Mortgage Services Ltd v. Muirhead* (1997) 76 P. & C.R. 418 (charge in favour of the creditor had not been executed by the debtor, but had been altered by the creditor's solicitors).

[77] Charging Orders Act 1979, s.2; *post*, para. 9–076.

[78] *Lloyds Bank Plc v. Byrne, supra; Barclays Bank Plc v. Hendricks* [1996] 1 F.L.R. 258.

[79] *Bank of Baroda v. Dhillon* [1998] 1 F.L.R. 324. In such circumstances, the creditor could not have obtained an order for possession against the beneficiary having an overriding interest: see *Williams & Glyn's Bank Ltd v. Boland* [1981] A.C. 487; *Kemmis v. Kemmis* [1988] 1 W.L.R. 1307.

[80] *Bankers Trust Co. v. Namdar* [1997] E.G.C.S. 20; [1996] Conv. 371 (A. Dunn); *ante*, para. 9–039.

[81] *Zandfarid v. B.C.C.I. International S.A., supra*, at 1428–1430. See *post*, para. 19–159.

[82] Under T.L.A.T.A. 1996, s.15(1).

[83] *ibid*., s.15(4). The application is then governed by I.A. 1986, s.335A (as inserted by T.L.A.T.A. 1996, s.25(1); Sched. 3); *post*, para. 9–070.

much more flexible approach when a secured creditor's interests are in issue.[84]

(c) *Bankruptcy of a co-owner*

(1) APPLICATIONS TO THE COURT. Where a co-owner of land is bankrupt, his **9–070** trustee in bankruptcy will commonly wish to obtain a sale of the property. In deciding whether or not to exercise his powers, the trustee must not favour the interests of a secured creditor over the unsecured, but must act in the best interests of the bankrupt's estate.[85] Any application by him for an order relating to the exercise by trustees of land of any of their functions[86] must be made to the court having jurisdiction in relation to the bankruptcy.[87] The provisions of the Trusts of Land and Appointment of Trustees Act 1996, explained above,[88] which specify the matters which the court is to take into account in all other such applications[89] are excluded.[90] Instead the court is required to make such order as it thinks just and reasonable having regard to the interests of the bankrupt's creditors[91] and all the circumstances of the case other than the needs of the bankrupt.[92] Furthermore, where the application is made in respect of land which includes a dwelling house which is or has been the home of the bankrupt or his spouse or former spouse,[93] the court must, in addition to these factors, have regard to—

---

[84] In at least one case prior to 1997 the court did adopt a more flexible approach: see *Abbey National Plc v. Moss* (1993) 26 H.L.R. 249. This case was criticised at the time because it could not be reconciled with earlier authorities: see [1994] Fam. Law 255 (S. M. Cretney).

[85] *Re Ng* [1998] 2 F.L.R. 386. The courts view with disfavour applications for sale by a trustee in bankruptcy where the principal creditor is a mortgagee which has chosen not to enforce its security, *e.g.* to avoid bad publicity, as in *Re Ng, supra.* However, trustees in bankruptcy will be assumed to be the best judges of what is in the interests of the creditors in the absence of evidence that they acted to the contrary: *Judd v. Brown* [1999] 1 F.L.R. 1191 at 1198.

[86] Under T.L.A.T.A. 1996, s.14.

[87] I.A. 1986, s.335A(1) (inserted by T.L.A.T.A. 1996, s.25(1), Sched. 3). For the background to the legislation, see (1991) 107 L.Q.R. 177 (S. M. Cretney) (dealing with the precursor to the present provisions).

[88] *Ante*, paras 9–064—9–069.

[89] T.L.A.T.A. 1996, s.15.

[90] *ibid.*, s.15(4). Prior to 1997, it had been suggested that the principle which applied in cases of bankruptcy was not in fact a special one, but was merely an application of the general rule that the court would look to the underlying purpose of the trust in considering whether to order a sale. Where property was acquired for the purpose of joint occupation that purpose came to an end when the interest of one of the co-owners vested in his trustee in bankruptcy: *Abbey National Plc v. Moss* (1993) 26 H.L.R. 249 at 257 (criticised [1994] Fam. Law 255 (S. M. Cretney)). However, this was open to question. The purpose for which the co-owners acquired the property was considered to be irrelevant in relation to the trustee in bankruptcy because it was *res inter alios acta: Re Solomon* [1967] Ch. 573 at 589; *Re Holliday* [1981] Ch. 405 at 419; *Re Citro* [1991] Ch. 142 at 157. By virtue of T.L.A.T.A. 1996, s.15(4), this latter view necessarily prevails.

[91] Whether secured or unsecured: see *Judd v. Brown, supra*, at 1197. Even if there is unlikely to be any surplus on any sale to meet the claims of the creditors after discharging the expenses of the bankruptcy, a sale may still be justified. It is in the interests of the creditors that those expenses should, so far as possible, be discharged out of the bankrupt's assets: see *Trustee of the Estate of Bowe v. Bowe* (1994) [1998] 2 F.L.R. 439.

[92] I.A. 1986, s.335A(2)(a), (c).

[93] The provision does not therefore apply to an unmarried couple: *Re Citro* [1991] Ch. 142 at 159.

(i) the conduct of the spouse or former spouse, to the extent that it contributed to the bankruptcy;

(ii) the needs and financial resources of the spouse or former spouse; and

(iii) the needs of any children.[94]

When the trustee in bankruptcy's application is made more than one year from the date on which the property vested in the trustee in bankruptcy, the court is required to assume, unless the circumstances of the case are exceptional, that the interests of the bankrupt's creditors outweigh all other considerations.[95]

9–071　　(2) THE EXERCISE OF DISCRETION. These statutory provisions are essentially a codification of the rules previously applied at common law. The principle underlying them is the same, namely, that in a case of insolvency an immediate sale of the land should be ordered by the court[96] in the absence of exceptional circumstances, even in the common case where the co-owners are spouses.[97] "A person must discharge his liabilities before there is any room for being generous."[98]

9–072　　(3) EXCEPTIONAL CIRCUMSTANCES. Where exceptional circumstances exist, the court may either refuse a sale altogether[99] or postpone it.[1] What constitutes an exceptional circumstance is a question of fact in any given case as to which the court will not lay down guidelines.[1a] The following are examples of such circumstances which have either arisen, or have been suggested—

(i) where the bankrupt's spouse was seriously ill[2];

(ii) where a house had been specially adapted for a handicapped child[3] or spouse; and

(iii) where the bankrupt was bankrupt on his own petition, was not being pressed by creditors, and the property was occupied by his former wife and his children.[4]

---

[94] I.A. 1986, s.335A(2)(b).

[95] *ibid.*, s.335A(3).

[96] Subject only to a short period of suspension to enable the bankrupt and his family to arrange their affairs: *Re Lowrie* [1981] 3 All E.R. 353 at 355.

[97] See *Re Citro* [1991] Ch. 142 (the leading modern authority in which the earlier decisions were reviewed). *cf.* (1991) 107 L.Q.R. 177 (S. M. Cretney); [1991] C.L.J. 45 (J. C. Hall).

[98] *Re Bailey* [1977] 1 W.L.R. 278 at 283, *per* Walton J.

[99] As in *Judd v. Brown* [1998] 2 F.L.R. 360.

[1] As in *Re Raval* [1998] 2 F.L.R. 718.

[1a] *Claughton v. Charalambous* [1999] 1 F.L.R. 740 at 744.

[2] *Judd v. Brown, supra; Re Raval, supra; Claughton v. Charalambous, supra.*

[3] *Re Bailey, supra,* at 284; *Claughton v. Charalambous, supra,* at 744.

[4] *Re Holliday* [1981] Ch. 405, a decision described as being "very much against the run of the recent authorities": *Harman v. Glencross* [1986] Fam. 81 at 95, *per* Balcombe L.J. See too *Re Citro, supra,* at 157.

However, the court is unlikely to regard as exceptional the displacement of the bankrupt's wife and of any children, or her inability to buy a comparable home elsewhere.[5] Such circumstances are "the melancholy consequences of debt and improvidence with which every civilised society has been familiar".[6]

(d) Equitable accounting after sale.[7] Where property held on a trust of land **9–073** is sold following an application to the court under section 14 of the Trusts of Land and Appointment of Trustees Act 1996, it is often necessary to settle accounts between the co-owners (or if one of them is insolvent, his trustee in bankruptcy). This may be for one of three reasons. First, one of the co-owners may have left the property some time before the sale, and the party who remained may be held liable to pay an occupation rent for the period thereafter.[8] Secondly, one of the co-owners may have expended money on improvements to the premises. Neither party can take the benefit of an increase in the value of the property without making an allowance for what has been expended by the other in order to obtain it.[9] Credit will be given for the actual expenditure or for the amount by which the improvement has increased the value of the property, whichever is the lesser.[10] Thirdly, one of the parties may have paid the whole or a disproportionate part of the mortgage instalments. Credit will always be given for the capital element in such payments. The interest element is often treated as being equal to an occupation rent and so disregarded.[11] This is not a rule of law however and the parties are entitled to insist that the occupation rent and the mortgage interest should each be separately calculated and that any difference between the two should be brought into account.[12]

2. Charging orders. Although charging orders are a form of security over **9–074** property for the payment of a sum of money and therefore more properly belong in a chapter on mortgages, it is convenient to treat them in detail here. This is because the most difficult issues in relation to such orders arise in connection with land held upon trust.[13] These cannot be understood without an explanation of the system of charging orders.

---

[5] *Re Citro, supra.* For discussion see (1992) 55 M.L.R. 284 (D. Brown).

[6] *Re Citro, supra,* at 157, *per* Nourse L.J. See too *Re Lowrie* [1981] 3 All E.R. 353 at 356.

[7] See [1995] Conv. 391 (E. Cooke); and *post,* para. 9–100.

[8] *Re Pavlou* [1993] 1 W.L.R. 1046; *ante,* para. 9–005.

[9] *Leigh v. Dickeson* (1884) 15 Q.B.D. 60 at 65, 67. This rule has its origin in equity practice in a partition suit.

[10] *Re Pavlou, supra,* at 1049. *cf. Bernard v. Josephs* [1982] Ch. 391 at 405, 408 (credit given for actual expenditure without reference to the increase in value of the property).

[11] *Suttill v. Graham* [1977] 1 W.L.R. 819. However, if one party has been ousted by the other, the fact that the remaining co-owner has paid all the mortgage instalments after that ouster will be disregarded and no credit will be given to him for paying the ousted party's share: *Cracknell v. Cracknell* [1971] P. 356; *Shinh v. Shinh* [1977] 1 All E.R. 97. *cf. ante,* para. 9–005.

[12] *Re Gorman* [1990] 1 W.L.R. 616 at 626; *Re Pavlou, supra,* at 1051.

[13] Prior to the abolition of the doctrine of conversion by T.L.A.T.A. 1996, s.3(1) (*ante,* para. 8–127), there were a number of difficulties in relation to charging orders and interests under a trust for sale: see *post,* para. 9–076.

9–075 *(a) The nature of a charging order.* Under the Charging Orders Act 1979,[14] a discretionary power is conferred on the court[15] to impose a charging order on the property of a debtor (including any land or interest in land which he owns[16]) to secure payment of any sum of money that is or will become payable under a judgment.[17] In deciding whether or not to make a charging order the court is required to consider all the circumstances of the case and, in particular, any evidence before it as to the personal circumstances of the debtor, and whether any other creditor of the debtor would be likely to be unduly prejudiced by the making of the order.[18] A charging order, when granted, has the same effect as if it were an equitable charge created by the debtor by writing under hand.[19] As such it may be enforced either by a sale of the property or by the appointment of a receiver.[20]

9–076 *(b) Application to land held upon trust.* Formerly the court could make a charging order on "any land or interest in land".[21] However these words were held not to include the interest of a beneficiary under a trust for sale, which by a strict application of the doctrine of conversion, was considered to be in the proceeds of sale and not in the land itself.[22] By contrast, where A and B held land on trust for themselves as joint tenants and a judgment was obtained against them jointly, a charging order could be imposed on the legal estate in the property.[23] This unsatisfactory situation was remedied by the Charging Orders Act 1979, and the doctrine of conversion has, in any event, been retrospectively abolished.[24] A charging order may now be imposed on—

(i) land or any interest in land which is held by the debtor beneficially[25];

(ii) any interest of the debtor's under any trust of land[26];

(iii) land held on trust where the judgment is against the trustee as such[27];

---

[14] The Act gives effect to the recommendations of the Law Commission: (1976) Law Com. No. 74. It replaces A.J.A. 1956, s.35, which itself replaced L.P.A. 1925, s.195. Charging orders on land were first introduced by the Judgments Act 1838, s.13. See *Irani Finance Ltd v. Singh* [1971] Ch. 59 at 76–78; (1984) 100 L.Q.R. 86 at 90–93 (J.S. Anderson).

[15] For the appropriate court, see the Charging Orders Act 1979, s.1(2).

[16] *ibid.*, s.2; considered *infra*.

[17] *ibid.*, s.1. Charging orders may also be made in certain criminal proceedings: see the Criminal Justice Act 1988; Drug Trafficking Act 1994.

[18] Charging Orders Act 1979, s.1(5).

[19] *ibid.*, s.3(4); *First National Securities Ltd v. Hegerty* [1985] Q.B. 850 at 863.

[20] *Midland Bank Plc v. Pike* [1988] 2 All E.R. 434 at 435.

[21] A.J.A. 1956, s.35.

[22] *Irani Finance Ltd v. Singh, supra,* criticised [1971] C.L.J. 46 (M. J. Pritchard); (1971) 34 M.L.R. 441 (S. M. Cretney); and see *ante,* para. 8–119.

[23] *National Westminster Bank Ltd v. Allen* [1971] 2 Q.B. 718.

[24] T.L.A.T.A. 1996, s.3(1); *ante,* para. 8–127.

[25] Charging Orders Act 1979, s.2(1)(a)(i). A charging order over property held on trust should not be made under this paragraph: *Clark v. Chief Land Registrar* [1993] Ch. 294 at 305 (on appeal, [1994] Ch. 370).

[26] Charging Orders Act 1979, s.2(1)(a)(ii).

[27] *ibid.*, s.2(1)(b)(i).

(iv) land held on a bare trust for the debtor[28]; or

(v) land held on trust for two or more debtors who together hold the whole beneficial interest under the trust unencumbered and for their own benefit.[29]

The Land Charges Act 1972 and the Land Registration Act 1925 apply to charging orders as they apply to other writs or orders for the purpose of enforcing judgments.[30] In the case of land with unregistered title, a charging order can be registered as a land charge only if it is a "writ or order affecting land".[31] A charging order made against the interest of a beneficiary under a trust of land cannot be registered in this way.[32] Where the title is registered, a judgment creditor may lodge a caution in respect of any charging order.[33] This is so even though the charging order relates to an interest under a trust of land.[34] However, where the charging order would in the case of unregistered land have been registrable as a land charge, it may now be protected by the entry of a notice rather than by a caution.[35]

(c) Procedure.[36] On an application for a charging order by a judgment creditor (which is invariably made without notice) the court may make an order *nisi*. The court will direct that a copy of any such order be served on the judgment debtor, and, where it relates to an interest under a trust, on some or all of the trustees. It may direct that a copy should also be served on any other creditor of the debtor or on any other interested person. The matter is then adjourned for further consideration *inter partes*. In those proceedings, the court is required either to make the charging order absolute (with or without modifications[37]) or to discharge it. The court may however order the postponement of the execution of the order.[38] Although the jurisdiction to grant a charging order is discretionary, "a judgment creditor is in general entitled to enforce a money judgement which he has lawfully obtained against a judgment debtor by all or any of the means of execution prescribed by the relevant

9–077

---

[28] *ibid.*, s.2(1)(b)(ii).

[29] *ibid.*, s.2(1)(b)(iii). This paragraph is intended to cover the situation that arose in *National Westminster Bank Ltd v. Allen, supra.*

[30] Charging Orders Act 1979, s.3(2).

[31] L.C.A. 1972, s.6(1)(a).

[32] L.C.A. 1972, s.6(1A) (inserted by T.L.A.T.A. 1996, s.25(1), Sched. 3); *ante*, para. 5–090. This is logical. As beneficial interests under trusts of land are not themselves registrable as land charges but are protected by overreaching, charging orders which bind such interests should be treated in the same manner. *cf. Perry v. Phoenix Assurance Plc* [1988] 1 W.L.R. 940; [1989] Conv. 133 (N.S. Price).

[33] L.R.A. 1925, s.54(1).

[34] Ruoff & Roper, 36–08.

[35] L.R.A. 1925, s.49(1)(g), inserted by the Charging Orders Act 1979, s.3(3). Such a notice can be entered only if the land certificate is produced by the chargee or is deposited with the registry: Ruoff & Roper, 35–32.

[36] For the rules of court see CPR Sched. 1, R50; Sched. 2, C31. The two sets of rules are not identical and the text therefore states their broad effect. See too *Roberts Petroleum Ltd v. Bernard Kenny Ltd* [1983] 2 A.C. 192 at 204.

[37] The court may attach conditions to the order: Charging Orders Act 1979, s.3(1).

[38] *ibid.*; *Austin-Fell v. Austin-Fell* [1990] Fam. 172.

rules of court".[39] The burden of showing cause why a charging order *nisi* should not be made absolute rests on the judgment debtor.[40] The court may decline to make the order absolute on account of events which have occurred subsequent to the order *nisi*, such as supervening insolvency of the debtor,[41] or the sale of the property to a purchaser who acquired it without notice of the order.[42]

The judgment debtor or any person interested in any property to which the charging order relates may apply to the court at any time to have the order discharged or varied.[43] Where a charging order is imposed on the beneficial interest of one co-owner, the other is a person interested for these purposes.[44] This is because a creditor will normally enforce such a charging order by an application to the court for the sale of the property under section 14 of the Trusts of Land and Appointment of Trustees Act 1996.[45] Although the co-owner whose interest is not affected by the charging order would be entitled to his share of the proceeds of any sale, he will commonly not wish to see the property sold.

9–078   *(d) Charging orders and the matrimonial home.* Where a creditor seeks a charging order against the beneficial interest of a co-owner, the court has a discretion not only whether to make the order absolute,[46] but if it does, whether to order an immediate sale to enforce the charge.[47] The exercise of this discretion has caused some difficulty where a husband and wife and joint owners of the matrimonial home and a charging order is sought against the husband's beneficial interest.[48]

9–079   (1) WHERE NO DIVORCE PROCEEDINGS ARE PENDING BETWEEN THE SPOUSES. Prior to 1997, where no divorce proceedings were pending between the spouses and there were no exceptional circumstances, the court normally exercised its discretion in favour of the creditor both in making the charging order absolute[49] and in ordering an immediate sale of the property (subject only to a short postponement) on an application by the creditor under section

---

[39] *Roberts Petroleum Ltd v. Bernard Kenny Ltd* [1982] 1 W.L.R. 301 at 307, *per* Lord Brandon. The House of Lords affirmed this principle but reversed the decision on appeal: [1983] 2 A.C. 192. See *First National Securities Ltd v. Hegerty* [1985] Q.B. 850 at 866, 867.

[40] *Roberts Petroleum Ltd v. Bernard Kenny Ltd* [1982] 1 W.L.R. 301 at 307.

[41] *Roberts Petroleum Ltd v. Bernard Kenny Ltd* [1983] 2 A.C. 192 (where the debtor was a company which went into liquidation).

[42] *Howell v. Montey* (1990) 61 P. & C.R. 18.

[43] Charging Orders Act 1979, s.3(5). Presumably such an application would have to be made before the order was executed.

[44] *Harman v. Glencross* [1986] Fam. 81.

[45] *Ante*, paras 9–064, 9–069.

[46] Charging Orders Act 1979, ss.1(5), 3(1).

[47] T.L.A.T.A. 1996, ss.14, 15; *ante*, para. 9–069; *First National Securities Ltd v. Hegerty, supra*, at 856 (a case on L.P.A. 1925, s.30).

[48] For discussion see [1985] Conv. 129 (P. F. Smith); (1985) 5 O.J.L.S. 132 (N. P. Gravells); [1986] Conv. 218 (J. Warburton); [1989] Fam. Law 438; [1993] Fam. Law 184 (S. M. Cretney). These must now be read subject to T.L.A.T.A. 1996, ss.14, 15.

[49] *First National Securities Ltd v. Hegerty, supra.*

30 of the Law of Property Act 1925.[50] As explained above, this may no longer be the case on an application under section 14 of the Trusts of Land and Appointment of Trustees Act 1996.[51] The interests of any secured creditor are now only one factor that the court is directed to consider even in the absence of exceptional circumstances.

(2) WHERE DIVORCE PROCEEDINGS ARE PENDING BETWEEN THE PARTIES. **9–080** Where divorce proceedings are pending, the court normally directs that the charging order application should be transferred to the Family Division so that both sets of proceedings can be heard together.[52] Even prior to 1997, the court would normally prefer the claims of the wife and any children over those of the husband's creditor[53] and would usually make the charging order absolute but postpone its enforcement until any children of the marriage had reached a specified age.[54] In exceptional circumstances the court might even make a property adjustment order transferring the husband's interest in the home to the wife, which would necessarily defeat any charging order obtained by a creditor.[55] It seems unlikely that the position would be any different after 1996, particularly as a court may no longer be prepared to order a sale almost as a matter of course on the application of a secured creditor.[56]

3. Proposals for reform. It has been explained that the law governing **9–081** co-ownership has been reformed as a result of the introduction of the trust of land and the abolition of the doctrine of conversion as it applied to trusts for sale.[57] Mention should be made of certain earlier proposals for reform made by the Law Commission, none of which has been implemented.

(a) Statutory co-ownership of the matrimonial home. In 1978 the Commis- **9–082** sion recommended that there should be a statutory scheme of co-ownership of the matrimonial home by which married couples would automatically have an equitable half share in the property.[58] A Bill to implement the proposals[59] was introduced into Parliament in 1979 but failed to complete all its stages. In

---

[50] *Lloyds Bank Plc v. Byrne* [1993] 1 F.L.R. 369; *ante*, para. 9–069.
[51] *Ante*, paras 9–068, 9–069.
[52] *Harman v. Glencross* [1986] Fam. 81.
[53] This was controversial: for a different view see *First National Securities Ltd v. Hegerty, supra* at 868, *per* Stephenson L.J. ("the court should not use its powers under Pt II of the Matrimonial Causes Act 1973 to override the claims of a creditor seeking security for a debt by a charging order").
[54] *Harman v. Glencross, supra,* at 99, 104; *Austin-Fell v. Austin-Fell, supra.* For the form of such a *Mesher* order see *Mesher v. Mesher* (1973) [1980] 1 All E.R. 126. Sale is commonly postponed until the children reach the age of 17 or 18.
[55] This was in fact the situation in *Harman v. Glencross, supra.* If the husband is subsequently adjudged bankrupt such a transfer may be challenged as a transaction at an undervalue or as a preference: I.A. 1986, ss.339, 340. But see *Re Abbott* [1983] Ch. 45; *Harman v. Glencross, supra,* at 97.
[56] See *ante*, para. 9–069.
[57] *Ante*, paras 8–124 *et seq.*
[58] (1978) Law Com. No. 86. For criticism see (1978) 94 L.Q.R. 26 (A.A.S. Zuckerman), but *cf.* [1983] J.S.W.L. 67 (A. Evans).
[59] Matrimonial Homes (Co-Ownership) Bill (introduced by Lord Simon of Glaisdale).

1988 the Law Commission proposed a more limited reform. It recommended that the purchase of property by one or both spouses for their joint use or benefit should give rise to joint ownership of that property subject to a contrary intention on the part of the purchasing spouse, known to the other spouse,[60] but this was not accepted by the Government.

9–083   *(b) Registration of the rights of co-owners.* In 1982, in response to the conveyancing problems which arose out of the decision of the House of Lords in *Williams & Glyn's Bank Ltd. v. Boland*,[61] and by way of an addendum to its earlier proposals,[62] the Commission put forward a hybrid scheme by which the rights of co-owners would be both registrable and overreachable. Under this scheme, it would have remained the case that the beneficial interests of any co-owner would have been overreached if a purchaser paid the purchase money to the trustees (of whom there would have to be not less than two) or to a trust corporation. However if the purchaser had failed to comply with these requirements and paid the purchase money to just one trustee, he would not have been bound by the interests of the beneficiaries unless they had been registered either as land charges (where the title was unregistered) or as minor interests (where the title was registered).[63] It was also proposed that the consent of both spouses would have been required to any disposition of the matrimonial home. These proposals were much criticised and were abandoned.[64] A more limited version of the Law Commission's scheme, which would have required co-owners other than spouses to register their beneficial interests to protect them against purchasers in cases where there was only one trustee for sale, was introduced into Parliament in 1985 but withdrawn.[65]

D. The Vesting of the Legal Estate

9–084   The various provisions which impose the statutory trust of land also limit the number of the trustees in accordance with the principle that in settlements and trusts of land there shall not be more than four trustees.[66] The rules are as follows.

1. Unregistered land

9–085   *(a) Tenancies in common.* A conveyance of land to trustees of land on trust for tenants in common is subject to the general rule which limits the number

---

[60] (1988) Law Com. No. 175.
[61] [1981] A.C. 487. See *ante*, paras 5–019, 6–061.
[62] (1978) Law Com. No. 86, *supra.*
[63] (1982) Law Com. No. 115. A new category of land charge, Class G, was proposed. For land charges, see *ante*, para. 5–086. For minor interests, see *ante*, para. 6–075.
[64] See [1982] Conv. 393 (J.T. Farrand); [1983] J.S.W.L. 67 (A. Evans); (1987) Law Com. No. 158, para. 2.7. For the view that, although these proposals were rejected, the courts have since their publication "been pursuing a policy which is in many respects very similar to that of the Commission", see [1993] Fam. Law 231 (J. Dewar).
[65] Land Registration and Law of Property Bill. See (1987) Law Com. No. 158, para. 1.3.
[66] There is no restriction on the number of trustees who may hold land on trust for charitable, ecclesiastical or public purposes: see T.A. 1925, s.34(3).

of trustees of land to four.[67] If the conveyance is made to the tenants in common themselves, and they are of full age, it operates as a conveyance "to the grantees, or if there are more than four grantees, to the first four named in the conveyance, as joint tenants in trust for the persons interested in the land".[68] A gift of land by will to, or on trust for[69] tenants in common operates as a gift to the testator's personal representatives in trust for the persons interested in the land.[70] The number of personal representatives cannot exceed four.[71]

(b) *Joint tenancies.* There are no provisions dealing expressly with the **9–086** number of persons in whom the legal estate can be vested when two or more persons are beneficially entitled as joint tenants.[72] But the trust of land arising in such cases is subject to the general provision that in a disposition of land on trust of land the number of trustees shall not exceed four, and "where more than four persons are named as such trustees, the first four named (who are willing and able to act) shall alone be the trustees".[73] In the case of a devise to joint tenants, the general rules against more than four personal representatives[74] or trustees of land[75] prevent the legal estate from vesting in or being conveyed to more than four persons.

2. Registered land. Where registered land is subject to a trust of land, the **9–087** land is registered in the names of the trustees.[76] The statutory restrictions affecting the number of persons entitled to hold land on a trust of land apply as much to registered land as they do where the title is unregistered.[77]

E. *The Operation of the Present Law*

An example illustrating the present position may be useful. **9–088**

> (i) In 1998 X purported to convey land to A, B, C, D and E in fee simple. All were of full age. The legal estate vested in A, B, C and

---

[67] T.A. 1925, s.34(2) (as amended by T.L.A.T.A. 1996, s.25(2); Sched. 3, para. 3); *post*, para. 10–053.

[68] L.P.A. 1925, s.34(2) (as amended by T.L.A.T.A. 1996, s.5(1), Sched. 2, para. 3).

[69] *Re House* [1929] 2 Ch. 166.

[70] L.P.A. 1925, s.34(3) (as amended by T.L.A.T.A. 1996, ss.5(1), 25(2); Sched. 2, para. 3; Sched. 4).

[71] Supreme Court Act 1981, s.114(1); *post*, para. 11–132.

[72] But see L.P.A. 1925, s.36(1) (as amended by T.L.A.T.A. 1996, s.5(1), Sched. 2 para. 4). This may be intended to apply the mechanism set out in L.P.A. 1925, s.34(2), (3) to land held for beneficial joint tenants.

[73] T.A. 1925, s.34(2) (as amended by T.L.A.T.A 1996, s.25(2); Sched. 3, para. 3). The language is obviously designed to fit express trusts of land and is not very apt for statutory trusts, where no persons are "named as . . . trustees". However it seems probable that it would be held applicable.

[74] *Post*, para. 11–132.

[75] T.A. 1925, s.34(2) (as amended by T.L.A.T.A. 1996, s.25(2); Sched. 3, para. 3); *post*, para. 10–053.

[76] L.R.A. 1925, s.94(1) (as substituted by T.L.A.T.A. 1996, s.25(1); Sched. 3, para. 5).

[77] L.R.A. 1925, s.95 (as amended by T.L.A.T.A. 1996, s.25(1); Sched. 3, para. 5); *post*, para. 10–053.

D on trust. In equity, A, B, C, D and E were tenants in common if there were words of severance or if it was one of equity's special cases, but otherwise joint tenants.

(ii) If they were joint tenants and A died, B, C and D would then hold the legal estate on trust for B, C, D and E as joint tenants. E would not automatically fill the vacancy at law, but could, of course, be appointed a new trustee in place of A.

(iii) If B afterwards sold his interest to P, then B, C and D would continue to hold the legal estate, but on trust for P as tenant in common of a quarter and C, D and E as joint tenants of three-quarters.

(iv) If C then severed his share by agreement[78] with D and E, the legal estate would remain in B, C and D as before, on trust for P and C as tenants in common of one-quarter each, and D and E as joint tenants of half.

(v) On D's death, B and C would hold on trust for P, C and E as tenants in common as to one-quarter, one-quarter and one-half respectively.

Section 6. Position of Settled Land

A. Joint Tenancy

9–089 If two or more persons of full age are entitled to settled land[79] as joint tenants (but not as tenants in common[80]) they together constitute the tenant for life,[81] even, it seems, if they are more than four in number. If any of them are minors, such one or more of them as for the time being is or are of full age constitute the tenant for life.[82] If they are all minors, the legal estate and statutory powers are vested in the statutory owner[83] until one of them is of full age.[84] The land therefore remains settled land, and there is no trust of land.[85]

B. Tenancy in Common

9–090　　**1. Trust of land.** The scheme of the 1925 legislation was that whenever two or more tenants in common became entitled in possession, the land could not

---

[78] Severance by notice may be impossible if L.P.A. 1925, s.36(2) is strictly construed, for the legal estate is not vested in all the joint tenants beneficially: see *ante*, para. 9–044.

[79] No new settlements can be created after 1996: see *ante*, para. 8–001.

[80] Prior to 1926, it was possible for two or more tenants in common to be the tenant for life: see S.L.A. 1882, s.2(6).

[81] S.L.A. 1925, s.19(2). One joint tenant for life cannot force the other to sell: *ante*, para. 8–071.

[82] S.L.A. 1925, s.19(3).

[83] *Ante*, para. 8–015.

[84] S.L.A. 1925, s.26(4), (5).

[85] *cf.* L.P.A. 1925, s.36(1) (as amended by T.L.A.T.A. 1996, s.5(1); Sched. 2, para. 4); *Re Gaul and Houlston's Contract* [1928] Ch. 689.

be settled land and had to be held upon trust for sale. After 1996, a trust of land is imposed instead of a trust for sale.[86] Therefore if A and B are tenants in common for life, the land cannot be settled land but is held on a trust of land.[87] The same is true where, prior to 1997, land was devised to A for life and after his death to his children in equal shares. During A's life the land is settled land but on his death it ceases to be so.

In these situations the person or persons, whoever they may be, in whom the legal estate is vested will hold it upon a trust of land.[88] Any former Settled Land Act trustees are empowered to require the legal estate to be conveyed to them if it is not already vested in them. Although the settlement is superseded by the statutory trust of land, it is appropriate that the same trustees should be able to act, if they wish, in the new trust. If they do, they will hold the land in trust for the persons interested in the land.[89]

2. Devolution on death. A consequential difficulty arises in tracing the devolution of the legal estate on death. We have seen how, in a settlement made prior to 1997 upon A for life with remainder to B in fee simple, the legal estate devolves at A's death upon A's ordinary personal representatives, since the settlement no longer exists.[90] In a settlement on A for life with remainder to his children in equal shares the same rule applies in the first instance. But then (paradoxical as it may seem[91]) section 36 of the Settled Land Act 1925 is also held to apply, so that the trustees of the settlement (which *ex hypothesi* no longer exists) may call upon A's personal representatives to convey the land to them. If they are the same persons, they should assent in favour of themselves as trustees of land.[92] In any case, the land is held on a trust of land, and is not settled land for any purpose other than the interpretation of section 36.

9–091

A similar procedure should presumably be followed in cases where land would, apart from section 36, continue to be settled, *e.g.* where the limitations in an instrument made prior to 1997 are to A for life, remainder to his children as tenants in common for life, remainder to B in fee simple. On A's death, if he leaves children, the land becomes subject to a trust of land, and the former trustees of the settlement will have to call for the legal estate since it will have vested in A's ordinary personal representatives.[93]

---

[86] T.L.A.T.A. 1996, s.1; *ante*, paras 8–123, 8–126.
[87] S.L.A. 1925, s.36(1), (2) (as amended by T.L.A.T.A. 1996, s.25(1), Sched. 3, para. 2). For the difficulties of construction of s.36(1), see the previous edition of this work at p. 452.
[88] S.L.A. 1925, s.36(1), (2) (as amended by T.L.A.T.A. 1996, s.25(1), Sched. 3 para. 2).
[89] S.L.A. 1925, s.36(2), (6) (as amended or substituted by T.L.A.T.A. 1996, s.25(1), Sched. 3, para. 2).
[90] *Ante*, para. 8–034.
[91] See 71 L.J.News. 179.
[92] *Re Cugny's W.T.* [1931] 1 Ch. 305. Despite the dictum at p. 309, this should be an ordinary assent, and not a vesting assent; and see *ante*, para. 8–039.
[93] *Ante*, para. 8–034.

9–092 **4. Registered land.** The provisions of section 36 of the Settled Land Act 1925 apply as much to registered land as they do where the title is unregistered.[94] The former trustees of the settlement may require that the property be transferred to them. That transfer should contain a restriction that, except under an order of the registrar, no disposition is to be registered unless authorised by the Settled Land Act 1925, and except where the sole proprietor is a trust corporation, no disposition under which capital money arises is to be registered unless the money is paid to at least two proprietors.[95]

Section 7. The Special Position of Unincorporated Associations

9–093 **1. Nature of an Unincorporated Association.** An unincorporated association (such as a club or society) is a body of "two or more persons bound together for one or more common purposes, not being business purposes, by mutual undertakings, each having mutual duties and obligations, in an organisation which has rules which identify in whom control of it and its funds rests and upon what terms and which can be joined or left at will".[96] It is now accepted that a body cannot be an unincorporated association unless there is a contractual bond between the members,[97] although at one time it seems to have been assumed that there was no such requirement and that a grouping of persons together for a common purpose was sufficient.[98] It is often said that an unincorporated association is not in law a separate entity but merely the aggregate of its members,[99] but this is not reflected in the manner in which such associations are now taken to hold their property.

2. Method of Property Holding

9–094 *(a) The traditional view.* The legal title to the property of an unincorporated association is usually vested in its officers as trustees. At one time it was thought that the only way in which the trustees could hold the property was on trust for the persons who were members at the time it was acquired, either as joint tenants or as tenants in common.[1] The consequences of this view were inconvenient. If strictly applied, it meant that any member—

> (i) could at any stage demand to sever his share of the association's property;

---

[94] L.R.A. 1925, s.86(2).
[95] L.R.R. r. 58; Sched. 2, Form 10; Ruoff & Roper, 38–10, 38–17.
[96] *Conservative and Unionist Central Office v. Burrell* [1982] 1 W.L.R. 522 at 525, *per* Lawton L.J.; see *ante*, para. 7–146.
[97] *Conservative and Unionist Central Office v. Burrell, supra* at 525.
[98] *cf. Leahy v. Att.-Gen. for New South Wales* [1959] A.C. 457 at 486 (order of nuns assumed to be an unincorporated association).
[99] *Leahy v. Att.-Gen. for New South Wales, supra*, at 477.
[1] *ibid.* Any attempt to create an endowment for an unincorporated association will be void as a non-charitable purpose trust: *Re Grant's W.T.* [1980] 1 W.L.R. 360; *ante*, para. 7–146.

(ii) would retain his share of that property after leaving the association, unless he assigned it in writing to the other members[2];

(iii) could leave his share by will on his death if he was a tenant in common; and

(iv) would only have an interest in those assets of the association which were acquired during the period of his membership.

In practice these rules were unworkable and were disregarded.

(b) Property holding based upon contract. In order to escape from these **9–095** difficulties, the courts developed a new form of property holding by unincorporated associations.[3] It is now accepted that the trustees of such an association hold its property on trust for the members not as joint tenants or as tenants in common, but "subject to their respective contractual rights and liabilities towards one another as members of the association".[4] A characteristic of this novel form of property holding is that a member cannot sever his share.[5] It will accrue to the other members on his death or resignation, even though they may include persons who joined the association after it had acquired the property in question.[6] The interest passes without the need for the member to make any written or (as the case may be) testamentary disposition. The nature of the rights of a member of such an association has never been explained.[7]

This new form of property holding was evolved in a series of decisions concerning the validity of gifts to unincorporated associations. However, its implications are not confined to that issue. One consequence is that on the dissolution of such an association,[8] its assets will commonly be distributed amongst the persons who are then members, in accordance with the rules of the society.[9]

(c) Conveyancing implications. It used to be the practice for land to be **9–096** conveyed to the officers of an unincorporated association on an express trust

---

[2] L.P.A. 1925, s.53(1)(c); *post,* para. 10–046.
[3] *cf. Walker v. Hall* [1984] F.L.R. 126 at 135, *per* Lawton L.J. denying, obiter, that there was any "special law relating to property used in common by . . . members of a club".
[4] *Neville Estates Ltd v. Madden* [1962] Ch. 832 at 849, *per* Cross J. See too *Re Recher's W.T.* [1972] Ch. 526; *Universe Tankships Inc. of Monrovia v. I.T.W.F.* [1981] I.C.R. 129 at 156–159; *Conservative and Unionist Central Office v. Burrell, supra,* at 529; *News Group Newspapers Ltd v. S.O.G.A.T. 1982* [1986] I.C.R. 716.
[5] "The individual members would only have any realisable rights in the property if and when the club was dissolved": *Abbatt v. Treasury Solicitor* [1969] 1 W.L.R. 1575 at 1583, *per* Lord Denning M.R.
[6] *Neville Estates Ltd v. Madden, supra,* at 849.
[7] One view is that it is akin to the rights of a person entitled under the unadministered estate of a deceased person. These are explained, *post,* para. 11–130.
[8] For the circumstances in which an unincorporated association may be dissolved, see *Re GKN Bolts & Nuts Ltd (Automotive Division) Birmingham Works Sports and Social Club* [1982] 1 W.L.R. 774.
[9] *Re Sick and Funeral Society* [1973] Ch. 51. Difficult questions may arise on such a dissolution: see *Davis v. Richards & Wallington Industries Ltd* [1990] 1 W.L.R. 1511 at 1538 *et seq*; [1992] Conv. 41 (S. Gardner).

for sale for the members of the society for the time being.[10] It is now more usual for the property to be held upon a trust of land for the members of the association according to it rules, to be dealt with by the trustees as directed by the managing committee of the society.[11] As the property is not held for the members as joint tenants or as tenants in common, the provisions of the Law of Property Act 1925 which deal with the creation of such tenancies[12] have no application. Where the title to the land is registered, it is the practice to register the trustees as proprietors, but with a restriction that no disposition of the land shall be registered unless authorised by the rules of the association.[13]

Section 8. Determination of Joint Tenancies and Tenancies in Common

9–097   Joint tenancies and tenancies in common may de determined by partition or by union in a sole tenant. As already explained, joint tenancies may also be determined by severance, which converts them into tenancies in common.[14]

A. Partition

9–098   **1. Voluntary partition.** Joint tenants and tenants in common can always make a voluntary partition of the land if all agree.[15] Their co-ownership comes to an end by each of them becoming sole tenant of the piece of land allotted to him. This voluntary partition must be effected by deed.[16]

9–099   **2. Compulsory partition.** Although at common law there was no right to compel a partition,[17] the Partition Acts of 1539 and 1540[18] conferred a statutory right for joint tenants and tenants in common to do so.[19] One tenant was entitled to insist upon a partition[20] however inconvenient it might be.[21]

9–100   **3. Sale.** It was not until the Partition Act 1868[22] that the court was empowered to decree a sale instead of partition, an order which might be

---

[10] See *Abbatt v. Treasury Solicitor* [1969] 1 W.L.R. 1575. This method is still sometimes employed: see Encyclopaedia of Forms and Precedents (5th ed.), vol. 7, p. 351. The trust for sale would now take effect as a trust of land.

[11] Encyclopaedia of Forms and Precedents, vol. 7, pp. 458, 460, 461.

[12] ss.34, 36, *ante*, paras 9–051 *et seq.*

[13] See Ruoff & Roper, 32–13, 38–15.

[14] *Ante*, para. 9–036.

[15] Litt. 290, 318.

[16] L.P.A. 1925, ss.52(1), 205(1)(ii).

[17] Litt. 290, 318. For a fuller account of the history of partition, see the previous edition of this work at p. 454.

[18] 31 Hen. 8, c. 1 (estates of inheritance); 32 Hen. 8, c. 32 (estates for life or years). The procedure was improved by the Partition Act 1697 (8 & 9 Will. 3, c. 31).

[19] See n. (2) to Co.Litt. 169a.

[20] *Parker v. Gerard* (1754) Amb. 236.

[21] *Warner v. Baynes* (1750) Amb. 589; *Baring v. Nash* (1813) 1 V. & B. 551 at 554.

[22] As amended by the Partition Act 1876. See *Pemberton v. Barnes* (1871) 6 Ch.App. 685; *Powell v. Powell* (1874) 10 Ch.App. 130; *Drinkwater v. Ratcliffe* (1875) L.R. 20 Eq. 528.

highly desirable where, for example, the cost of partition proceedings would exceed the value of the property,[23] or where a single house had to be partitioned into thirds, and the owner of two-thirds was given all the chimneys and fireplaces and the only stairs.[24]

The Partition Acts were repealed[25] and replaced in turn by a statutory power for trustees for sale to partition land with the consent of the beneficiaries.[26] After 1996, trustees of land have had similar powers under the Trusts of Land and Appointment of Trustees Act 1996. Where beneficiaries of full age are absolutely entitled in undivided shares to land subject to the trust,[27] the trustees of land have a power to partition all or part of it.[28] They may provide (by way of mortgage or otherwise) for the payment of any equality money.[29] Where trustees exercise their power, they should convey the partitioned land to those entitled whether absolutely or, where the person entitled is a trustee, on trust.[30]

The power to partition can only be exercised with the prior consent of each of those beneficiaries.[31] If the trustees or any of the beneficiaries refuse to consent, any trustee or any person who has an interest in the property subject to the trust of land, may apply to the court for an order under the powers already explained.[32] The court may make such order as it thinks fit,[33] including an order to partition or sell the land.

On a partition of the property, it will often be necessary for accounts to be taken between the former co-owners in the same way as if there were a sale.[34] The guiding principle in such equitable accounting is that neither party can take the benefit of any increase in the value of the property without making an allowance for what has been expended by the other in order to obtain it.[35]

B. *Union in a Sole Tenant*

1. Union. Joint tenancies and tenancies in common may be determined if **9–101** the whole of the land becomes vested in a single beneficial owner. Thus where one of two surviving joint tenants dies, the other becomes sole tenant by right

---

[23] See *Griffies v. Griffies* (1863) 11 W.R. 943.

[24] See *Turner v. Morgan* (1803) 8 Ves. 143, 11 Ves. 157n.

[25] For a retrospective account see [1982] Conv. 415 (R. Cock).

[26] See L.P.A. 1925, s.28(3) (repealed by T.L.A.T.A. 1996, s.25(2); Sched. 4).

[27] This includes the situation where the person absolutely entitled is a trustee or personal representative, who holds the interest on trust for some other person or persons: T.L.A.T.A. 1996, s.22(1).

[28] *ibid.*, s.7(1). The power may either be expressly excluded by a provision in the disposition creating the trust of land, or made subject to the requirement that it be exercised subject to the trustees obtaining some consent: *ibid.*, s.8(1), (2). *cf. ante*, para. 8–140.

[29] T.L.A.T.A. 1996, s.7(1).

[30] *ibid.*, s.7(2). The property transferred may be subject to any mortgage created for raising equality money: *ibid.* If that share is affected by an incumbrance, the trustees may either give effect to it or provide for its discharge as they think fit: *ibid.*, s.7(4).

[31] *ibid.*, s.7(3).

[32] *ibid.*, s.14(1), (2); *ante*, paras 8–142, 9–064.

[33] T.L.A.T.A. 1996, s.14(2).

[34] *Re Pavlou* [1993] 1 W.L.R. 1046 at 1048; *ante*, para. 9–073.

[35] *Re Pavlou, supra*, at 1048. See [1995] Conv. 391 (E. Cooke).

of survivorship and the joint tenancy is at an end. Similarly if one joint tenant or tenant in common acquires the interests of all of the other tenants, *e.g.* by purchasing them, the co-ownership is at an end.[36]

9–102   **2. Release.** Because in theory each joint tenant is seised of the whole of the land, the appropriate way for one joint tenant to transfer his rights to another joint tenant before 1926 was by deed of release, which operated to extinguish his interest.[37] Although it has been retrospectively provided that one co-owner can convey to another by grant,[38] the power of a joint tenant to release his interest has been preserved,[39] so that a joint tenant may still release his legal estate or equitable interest (or both) to his fellow joint tenants. A release resembles a conveyance (and differs from a surrender[40]) in that it benefits only the person in whose favour it is made. Thus if A, B and C are beneficial joint tenants and A releases his beneficial interest to B, B alone acquires A's one-third share as equitable tenant in common. He remains joint tenant with C as to the other two-thirds.[41] Any purported disclaimer to which the other joint tenants are parties will be construed as a release.[42] A tenant in common, on the other hand, cannot release his share to the other tenants for a "release supposes the party to have the thing in demand".[43] As a tenancy in common can only exist in equity,[44] he will therefore have to assign his interest in writing to the other tenants.[45]

9–103   **3. Sale.** Co-ownership in land is also extinguished if the land is duly sold to a purchaser by trustees of land under their powers of disposition.[46] The interests of the co-owners are overreached and attach instead to the proceeds of sale.[47]

Part 2

PARTY WALLS

9–104 Boundary walls dividing one property from another may be in the sole ownership of one owner, free from any rights of the other. But often each of

---

[36] See, *e.g. Burton v. Camden L.B.C.* [1998] 1 F.L.R. 681.
[37] Co.Litt. 9b, 200b; Preston, *Abstracts*, ii, 61; Cru.Dig. ii, 382.
[38] L.P.A. 1925, s.72(4). Prior to 1926 such a grant was inoperative but was construed as a release: *Eustace v. Scawen* (1624) Co.Jac. 696; *Chester v. Willans* (1670) 2 Wms. Saund. 96; Halsb. vol. 39, para. 530.
[39] L.P.A. 1925, s.36(2). See *Burton v. Camden L.B.C., supra*, at 684.
[40] See *ante*, para. 9–048.
[41] See *ante*, para. 9–035; Litt. 304, 305; Co.Litt. 193a.
[42] *Re Schär* [1951] Ch. 280.
[43] Co.Litt 193a, n. (1).
[44] L.P.A. 1925, s.1(6).
[45] See *ibid.*, s.53(1)(c).
[46] See T.L.A.T.A. 1996, s.6(1); *ante*, para. 8–137.
[47] See *ante*, para. 8–165.

the adjoining owners has certain rights over the walls. Such walls are known as party walls, and need special treatment. This is because although party walls used to be subject to the ordinary law as to co-ownership or easements of support, they obviously had to be excepted from the statutory trust for sale that was imposed in cases of co-ownership after 1925. Brief mention must also be made of the provisions of the Party Wall etc. Act 1996, which is concerned to regulate the construction and repair of party walls and not with their ownership.

1. "Party wall". There is no precise definition of the expression "party **9–105** wall".[48] Since 1925 it may mean any one of the following[49]:

    (i) a wall divided longitudinally into strips, one belonging to each of the neighbouring owners[50]; or

    (ii) a wall divided as in (i), but each half being subject to an easement of support in favour of the owner of the other half[51];

    (iii) a wall belonging entirely to one of the adjoining owners, but subject to an easement or right in the other to have it maintained as a dividing wall.[52]

Prior to 1926 there was a fourth category. There could be a party wall of which the two adjoining owners were tenants in common. The disadvantage of such a wall was that either owner could insist upon partition.[53] Had special provision not been made by statute, all party walls in this category would have become subject to a trust for sale after 1925. It was consequently provided that after 1925 all party walls of this kind, whether created before 1926[54] or after 1925,[55] should be deemed to be severed vertically, and that the owner of each part should have such rights of support and user over the rest of the wall as were requisite for giving the parties rights similar to those which they would have enjoyed had they been tenants in common of the wall.[56] The practical effect of this provision was to translate all party walls of this kind into the second category listed above.

The characteristics of each of these categories must now be explained.

---

[48] *Kempston v. Butler* (1861) 12 Ir.C.L.R. 516 at 526. For the meaning of "party wall" in the context of the Party Wall etc. Act 1996, see *post*, para. 9–109.

[49] *Watson v. Gray* (1880) 14 Ch.D. 192 at 194, 195, as modified by L.P.A. 1925, s.38.

[50] *Matts v. Hawkins* (1813) 5 Taunt. 20.

[51] See *Wiltshire v. Sidford* (1827) 1 Man. & Ry. 404 at 408; *Jones v. Pritchard* [1908] 1 Ch. 630.

[52] See *Sheffield Improved Industrial and Provident Society v. Jarvis* [1871] W.N. 208; [1872] W.N. 47.

[53] *Mayfair Property Co. v. Johnston* [1894] 1 Ch. 508. The alternative of a sale (introduced by the Partition Act 1868) was normally unsuitable.

[54] L.P.A. 1925, Sched. 1, Pt V, para. 1.

[55] *ibid.*, s.38(1).

[56] *ibid.*, s.38, Sched. 1, Pt V, para. 1. In case of dispute the court may make an order declaratory of the rights of the parties: *ibid.*

2. Characteristics

9–106   *(a) Longitudinal division into two strips.* As a general rule, ownership of a party wall follows the ownership of the land upon which it is built.[57] There is therefore a presumption that, where a wall between adjacent properties is constructed so that the median line follows the boundary,[58] ownership of the wall is split longitudinally between the two landowners.[59] The presumption is not a strong one and cases of longitudinal division of this kind are in fact rare.[60]

An inconvenient characteristic of this type of party wall is that neither owner has any right of lateral support from the other.[61] Either owner, acting with reasonable care,[62] can remove his half of the wall and leave a structure which may be incapable of standing alone.[63]

9–107   *(b) Longitudinal division with mutual easements of support.* At common law there was a presumption that adjoining owners were tenants in common of a party wall, at all events if evidence was given that each owner had exercised dominion over the entire wall[64] provided that—

(i) the exact boundary could not be shown; or

(ii) the site of the wall could be shown to have been owned in common.[65]

This presumption still applies, but its effect is qualified by the provisions of the Law of Property Act 1925.[66] The party wall is no longer owned in common but longitudinally, with each party having an easement of support over the property of the other.

Neither party is under any positive obligation to repair his half of the wall (though he may if he wishes repair his neighbour's half).[67] However neither

---

[57] *Jones v. Read* (1876) 10 I.R.C.L. 315 at 320. It should be noted however that a wall may be in sole ownership for part of its height and a party wall for the rest: *Weston v. Arnold* (1873) 8 Ch.App. 1084.

[58] This presumption applies even if the middle of the wall is not precisely on the boundary: *Reading v. Barnard* (1827) Moo. & M. 71 at 73, 74.

[59] *Matts v. Hawkins, supra,* at 23; *Kempston v. Butler* (1861) 12 Ir.C.L.R. 516 at 526.

[60] *cf. Cubitt v. Power* (1828) 8 B. & C. 257 at 263, 264; *Mason v. Fulham Corporation* [1910] 1 K.B. 631 at 637.

[61] *Wigford v. Gill* (1592) Cro. Eliz. 269.

[62] See *Bradbee v. Governors of Christ's Hospital* (1842) 4 Man. & G. 714 at 706, 761; *Kempston v. Buller* (1861) 12 Ir.C.L.R. 516. It is desirable (see *Massey v. Goyder* (1829) 4 C. & P. 161) but not essential (*Chadwick v. Trower* (1839) 6 Bing. N.C. 1) to give warning of the intention to pull down the wall.

[63] *Wigford v. Gill, supra, Wiltshire v. Sidford, supra,* at 408; *Cubitt v. Porter, supra,* at 264. See however the Building Act 1984, ss.80–82.

[64] *Wiltshire v. Sidford, supra,* at 407, 408; *Cubitt v. Porter, supra, Jones v. Read, supra, Standard Bank of British South America v. Stokes* (1878) 9 Ch.D. 68 at 71; *Watson v. Gray, supra,* at 194, 195.

[65] *Wiltshire v. Sidford, supra,* at 407, 409.

[66] s.38; *ante,* para. 9–105.

[67] *Jones v. Pritchard, supra,* at 637, 638; *Sack v. Jones* [1925] Ch. 235; *post,* para. 18–209.

owner is entitled to pull down the wall[68] (except for the purpose of rebuilding it with reasonable dispatch[69]), or to demolish his half of it, thereby removing his neighbour's support.[70] Nor can either owner prevent the other from enjoying any part of the wall, as by covering the top with broken glass or replacing it with part of a shed.[71] For these purposes the two owners still enjoy the same rights as if they were tenants in common,[72] and therefore neither can oust the other.[73]

(c) Wall in single ownership subject to easement. Where the party wall is built entirely on the land of one owner, there is a presumption that the wall belongs to that landowner.[74] This category of party wall can be established only on proof that an appropriate easement has either been expressly granted or has been acquired by prescription.[75] The servient owner is under no obligation to repair the wall, though the other party may enter his land to do so.[76] **9–108**

3. The Party Wall, etc., Act 1996. The Party Wall etc. Act 1996 extends to the whole of England and Wales certain provisions that have existed in some form or another in inner London and other parts of the country for many years.[77] The definition of party wall in the Act is not in terms of the ownership but of the function of the wall. A wall will be a party wall in two circumstances— **9–109**

  (a) where a wall forms part of a building, and the wall itself (and not merely its foundations) projects beyond the boundary[78] into the land of the adjoining owner; or

---

[68] *Jones v. Read, supra.*

[69] *Cubitt v. Porter, supra, Standard Bank of British South America v. Stokes, supra,* at 71, 72; *Joliffe v. Woodhouse* (1894) 38 S.J. 578.

[70] *Upjohn v. Seymour Estates Ltd* [1938] 1 All E.R. 614; *Brace v. S.E. Regional Housing Association Ltd* [1984] 1 E.G.L.R. 144. See too *Bradburn v. Lindsay* [1982] 2 All E.R. 408 (owner liable in negligence where local authority demolished his side of a party wall because the property was unsafe due to his neglect).

[71] *Stedman v. Smith* (1857) 8 E. & B. 1 at 6, 7 (construction of wash house roof across the entire width of the party wall).

[72] L.P.A. 1925, s. 38.

[73] *Ante,* para. 9–005.

[74] *Hutchinson v. Mains* (1832) Alc. & N. 155. Similarly if one landowner makes an addition to his neighbour's wall, the addition prima facie belongs to the neighbour: *Waddington v. Naylor* (1889) 60 L.T. 480.

[75] For the creation of easements, see *post,* para. 18–090.

[76] *Jones v. Pritchard, supra,* at 637, 638.

[77] See *e.g.* London Building Acts (Amendment) Act 1939 and Bristol Improvements Act 1847. The relevant parts of this local legislation have now been repealed under the Party Wall, etc., Act 1996, s. 21: see S.I. 1997 No. 671. The Party Wall, etc., Act 1996, which came into force on July 1, 1997, was promoted by the Pyramus and Thisbe Club, a body of surveyors who specialise in party wall matters. For comment on the Act, see S. Bickford-Smith & C. Sydenham, *Party Walls* (1997).

[78] Described as the "line of junction": Party Wall, etc., Act 1996, s. 1.

(b) where the wall is built on the land of one owner but separates buildings belonging to different owners.[79]

The legislation makes provision for the following—

(i) the construction of a new party wall[80];

(ii) the repair of and a wide variety of other works[81] to an existing party wall[82]; and

(iii) any excavation work within a certain distance of any building or structure on the adjacent owner's land.[83]

The Act requires a building owner who intends to carry out any of those works to serve a notice of a specified kind on the adjoining owner.[84] A method of dispute resolution by a form of arbitration by "surveyors"[85] is also specified.[86] The "surveyors" are required in such a case to make an "award".[87] This may determine the right of the building owner to execute any work and the time and manner in which it may be done, together with any incidental matters.[88] There is, surprisingly, no mechanism for the registration of such an award.[89]

Sweeping rights are conferred on a person who is carrying out works under the Act.[90] These include the right to enter any land, remove any furniture or fittings, and even (if accompanied by a police officer) to break open doors or fences to enter the premises.[91] There is a correlative obligation to compensate the adjoining owner or occupier for any loss or damage caused in execution of the works.[92] If a building owner fails to comply with the requirements of the Act in carrying out works that fall within it, he commits a nuisance and is

---

[79] *ibid.*, s. 20. *cf. Knight v. Pursell* (1879) 11 Ch.D. 412.

[80] Party Wall, etc., Act 1996, s. 1.

[81] Such as underpinning, thickening, raising, demolition and replacement of the wall.

[82] Party Wall, etc., Act 1996, s. 2.

[83] *ibid.*, s. 6 (for some purposes the distance is 3 metres, for others, 6).

[84] For the adjoining owner's right to serve a counter-notice and the effect of his failure to do so, see *ibid.*, ss. 4, 5.

[85] Such persons need not be surveyors at all (though in practice they will be): see *ibid.*, s. 20.

[86] *ibid.*, s. 10.

[87] *ibid.*, s. 10(10).

[88] *ibid.*, s. 10(12).

[89] See *Observatory Hill Ltd v. Camtel Investments S.A.* [1997] 1 E.G.L.R. 140 (party wall award in respect of registered land could not be protected by a caution). *cf.* Access of Neighbouring Land Act 1992, s. 4; *post*, para. 18–227.

[90] Party Wall, etc., Act 1996, s. 8. An exercise of rights under s. 8 might contravene Article 8 of the European Convention on Human Rights, which confers (*inter alia*) a right to peaceful enjoyment of the home.

[91] A person may not enter under s. 8 unless he serves a notice of his intention to enter on the owner or occupier of the land at least 14 days in advance of such entry (except in cases of emergency, when he must give such notice as is reasonably practicable): s. 8(3), (4). It is a criminal offence to obstruct a person who is entitled to enter: *ibid.*, s. 15.

[92] *ibid.*, s. 7.

liable as such.[93] In exceptional circumstances, a court may even grant a mandatory injunction requiring the removal or reversal of any unauthorised works.[94]

The rights conferred under the Party Wall etc. Act 1996 are considerably more extensive than those enjoyed by a landowner who needs to enter his neighbour's property in order to carry out works which are reasonably necessary for the preservation of all or part of his own land. These rights, which are given by the Access to Neighbouring Land Act 1992, are explained later.[95] A landowner will therefore rely upon the Act of 1992 only if he cannot bring himself within the provisions of the Act of 1996.[96]

---

[93] See *Louis v. Sadiq* [1997] 1 E.G.L.R. 136, a case on the London Building Acts (Amendment) Act 1939.

[94] *cf. London & Manchester Assurance Co. Ltd v. O & H Construction Ltd* [1989] 2 E.G.L.R. 185 (also a case on the London Buildings Acts (Amendment) Act 1939).

[95] *Post*, para. 18–225.

[96] The Access to Neighbouring Land Act 1992 applies to party walls: see *Dean v. Walker* (1996) 73 P. & C.R. 366; *post*, para. 18–225.

CHAPTER 10

TRUSTS AND POWERS

10–001 The nature of trusts and powers has already been briefly discussed in connection with settlements.[1] The principal distinction is that whereas a trust is normally imperative, binding the trustee to carry out a duty, a power is discretionary, enabling the donee of the power to exercise it if he wishes but not binding him to do so. Much of the law of trusts and powers is more appropriate to textbooks on equity than to a book on real property, but some account must be given here of the points which most concern land law. They will be dealt with under the heads of—

    —(1) Trusts
    —(2) Trustees
    —(3) Powers.

Part 1

TRUSTS

Section 1. Classification

A. Conveyancing Classification

10–002 From the point of view of a conveyancer, land held in trust is either settled land or a trust of land. As has been explained, after 1996 it is no longer possible to create settled land.[2] Wherever land becomes subject to a trust after 1996 there is a trust of land for the purposes of the Trusts of Land and Appointment of Trustees Act 1996. This is so whether the interests of the beneficiaries under that trust are successive, concurrent or absolute.[3]

---

[1] *Ante*, Chap. 8.
[2] *Ante*, para. 8–001.
[3] *i.e.* where there is a bare trust.

B. *Judicial Classification*

The courts have established a general classification of trusts as statutory, **10–003**
express, implied or resulting, and constructive trusts. This is not the only
classification, nor are all categories clearly defined. The terminology is not
used consistently, particularly in relation to implied, resulting and constructive
trusts. The nomenclature is to some extent a matter of convenience.[4]

1. Trusts imposed by statute. Various trusts are imposed by statute. Some **10–004**
are expressly described as "statutory trusts", as with trusts for certain relations on an intestacy.[5] Others, although not given this name, are nevertheless
trusts imposed by statute, *e.g.* the trusts which are—

(a) imposed on the property of an intestate[6];

(b) imposed on property which trustees have obtained by foreclosure[7];
or

(c) created by an attempt to convey a legal estate in land to a minor.[8]

2. Express trusts. These are trusts declared by a settlor. To create an **10–005**
express trust, the "three certainties" of a trust must be present, *i.e.* imperative
words, certainty of subject-matter, and certainty of objects.[9]

(a) Imperative words. The settlor must indicate that a trust is intended. **10–006**
Although at one time words expressing a request (known as precatory words)
such as "in the full confidence", "recommending" or "my dying request"
were construed as creating a trust,[10] that is no longer so. Under the present law
such words create no trust unless the instrument as a whole shows an intention
that they should.[11]

Where the words are not imperative, the donee holds the property beneficially free from any trust.[12]

(b) Certainty of subject-matter. Both the property to be vested in the trustees **10–007**
and the beneficial interest to be taken by each beneficiary must be defined with
sufficient certainty. If there is no certainty as to what is conveyed to the trustees,
the entire transaction is ineffective, *e.g.* if a testator purports to leave "the bulk

---

[4] See Snell, *Equity*, 101.
[5] A.E.A. 1925, ss.46, 47; *post*, para. 11–102.
[6] A.E.A. 1925, s.33 (as amended); *post*, para. 11–088.
[7] L.P.A. 1925, s.31 (as amended by T.L.A.T.A. 1996, s.5(1); Sched. 2, para. 1); *ante*, para.
8–128.
[8] T.L.A.T.A. 1996, s.2(6); Sched. 1, paras 1, 2; *ante*, para. 8–125; *post*, para. 20–006.
[9] Snell, *Equity*, 113 *et seq.*; *Knight v. Knight* (1840) 3 Beav. 148 at 173; (1940) 2 M.L.R. 20
(Glanville Williams).
[10] See, *e.g. Harding v. Glyn* (1739) 1 Atk. 469; Wh. & T. ii, 285.
[11] See *Re Adams and the Kensington Vestry* (1884) 27 Ch.D. 394 at 410; *Re Williams* [1897] 2 Ch.
12; *Cominsky v. Bowring-Hanbury* [1905] A.C. 84; *Re Johnson* [1939] 2 All E.R. 458.
[12] See, *e.g. McCormick v. Grogan* (1869) L.R. 4 H.L. 82.

of my property" to trustees.[13] Examples of uncertainty of beneficial interest occur where defined property is given to X on trust that he should leave to A and B "the bulk" of it[14] or "such parts of my estate as he shall not have sold or disposed of".[15] In such cases the donee holds the property beneficially free from any trust,[16] unless it is clear that the whole of the property was to be held on trust and the only uncertainty is which part was intended for each beneficiary. In that case the donee will hold on a resulting trust for the settlor.[17]

10–008   *(c) Certainty of objects.*[18] The objects (*i.e.* the persons or purposes intended to benefit by the trust) must be defined with sufficient certainty. Where there is a fixed trust for the benefit of individuals, it must be possible to draw up a complete list of the objects.[19] Where there is a discretionary trust (*i.e.* a trust to distribute the property coupled with a power to select which member or members of a class of objects should benefit),[20] it must be possible to say with certainty whether any given individual is or is not a member of the class of objects.[21] A trust for "my old friends" is uncertain as to the concept of who are to be regarded as the donor's "old friends", and so is void.[22] Subject to certain exceptions,[23] trusts for pure purposes that are not exclusively charitable are void.[24] This is sometimes explained on the grounds that such purposes are too vague to be executed.[25] However non-charitable purpose trusts fail not so much because of uncertainty as to their objects, but because there is no beneficiary who can enforce them, and in some cases at least, because they may be perpetual.[26] A trust for charitable purposes will not fail for uncertainty

---

[13] *Palmer v. Simmonds* (1854) 2 Drew. 221; contrast *Bromley v. Tryon* [1952] A.C. 265. Where a settlor purports to create a trust of an undefined part of a homogenous mass, there is some authority that a distinction is to be drawn between tangible and intangible property. A purported declaration of trust of "20 cases of my 80 cases of wine" will fail for uncertainty. The quality of the different cases may vary, so that it is essential to segregate the property: *Re London Wine Co. (Shippers) Ltd* (1975) [1986] P.C.C. 121. A declaration of trust of "50 of my 950 shares in X. Co. Ltd" has been held to be valid however, because no such segregation was required: *Hunter v. Moss* [1994] 1 W.L.R. 452. That decision has been strongly criticised: see (1994) 110 L.Q.R. 335 (D. J. Hayton). It is difficult to reconcile with *Re Goldcorp Exchange Ltd* [1995] 1 A.C. 74.
[14] *Palmer v. Simmonds, supra.*
[15] *Re Jones* [1898] 1 Ch. 438; but see *Re Thomson's Estate* (1879) 13 Ch.D. 144; *Re Sanford* [1901] 1 Ch. 939. As to executory trusts, see *post*, para. 10–034; and see Snell, *Equity*, 118.
[16] See, *e.g. Fox v. Fox* (1859) 27 Beav. 301.
[17] See, *e.g. Boyce v. Boyce* (1849) 16 Sim. 476; *cf. Re Clarke* [1923] 2 Ch. 407.
[18] See (1982) 98 L.Q.R. 551 (C. T. Emery).
[19] *I.R.C. v. Broadway Cottages Trust* [1955] Ch. 20 at 29; *Re Gulbenkian's Settlements* [1970] A.C. 508 at 524.
[20] Discretionary trusts of land are rare but do occasionally occur: see, *e.g. Leahy v. Att.-Gen. (N.S.W.)* [1959] A.C. 457.
[21] *McPhail v. Doulton* [1971] A.C. 424.
[22] *Brown v. Gould* [1972] Ch. 53 at 57.
[23] Considered *ante*, paras 7–141—7–144.
[24] See, *e.g. Chichester Diocesan Fund v. Simpson* [1944] A.C. 341 (a trust for "charitable *or* benevolent" objects held void because not all benevolent objects are charitable).
[25] See, *e.g. Farley v. Westminster Bank* [1939] A.C. 430 at 433 (trust for the churchwardens of St. Cuthbert's Church "for parish work" held to be void because the purpose was not charitable).
[26] *Ante*, paras 7–139, 7–140.

since the Crown in some cases and the court in others will direct a suitable mode of application.[27]

If a trust is void for uncertainty of objects, there is a resulting trust for the settlor.[28]

3. Implied or resulting trusts. An implied or resulting trust[29] is said to exist where, on a conveyance of property, a trust arises by operation of equity.[30] However, the basis for such trusts is the presumed intention of the settlor or of the parties whose conduct leads to their creation. They are not imposed by law.[31] The presumption of a resulting trust can be rebutted by evidence of *any* intention that is inconsistent with such a trust and not merely evidence that there was an intention to make a gift.[32] A number of these trusts are of importance in land law. **10–009**

(a) Trusts not exhaustive. Where a disposition of property is made by the owner, and all or part of the equitable interest is not effectively disposed of, there is normally a resulting trust for the owner. If the property is conveyed expressly on trust, *e.g.* **10–010**

"to X on trust",

there is no difficulty. A trustee can take no benefit from the fact that the declared trusts do not exhaust the beneficial interest. To the extent that the beneficial interest is not disposed of, it results to the grantor.[33] Thus, if G conveys property to X on trust for a beneficiary who is dead, there is a resulting trust of the entire beneficial interest in favour of G.[34] The rule that there is a resulting trust in such circumstances can be rebutted by evidence—

(i) that the trustee was intended to take beneficially[35]; or

(ii) that the settlor had expressly or by necessary implication abandoned any interest in the property: the undisposed of interest will then pass to the Crown as *bona vacantia*.[36]

---

[27] *Morice v. Bishop of Durham* (1804) 9 Ves. 399 at 405.

[28] See, *e.g. Kendall v. Granger* (1842) 5 Beav. 300; *Re Carville* [1937] 4 All E.R. 464.

[29] The terms are generally treated as synonymous. In practice, the term "implied trust" is little used now, and such trusts are invariably referred to as "resulting trusts".

[30] See generally, R. Chambers, *Resulting Trusts*.

[31] See *Westdeutsche Landesbank Girozentrale v. Islington L.B.C.* [1996] A.C. 669 at 708, disapproving suggestions to the contrary in *Re Vandervell's Trusts (No. 2)* [1974] Ch. 269 at 289.

[32] *Westdeutsche Landesbank Girozentrale v. Islington L.B.C., supra,* at 708; (1996) 16 L.S. 110 (W. Swadling). *cf.* [1996] R.L.R. 3 (P. Birks).

[33] See *Merchant Taylors' Co. v. Att.-Gen.* (1871) 6 Ch. App. 512 at 518.

[34] *Re Tilt* (1896) 74 L.T. 163.

[35] See, *e.g. Smith v. Cooke* [1891] A.C. 297.

[36] *Re West Sussex Constabulary's Widows, Children and Benevolent (1930) Fund Trusts* [1971] Ch. 1; *Westdeutsche Landesbank Girozentrale v. Islington L.B.C., supra,* at 708.

One particular example of this type of resulting trust arises where a trust is made for some specific purpose, and later that purpose wholly fails. In such a case, there is a resulting trust for the party who paid for or provided the property: the trusts declared do not exhaust the whole beneficial interests.[37] Thus, where A and B, intending marriage, contribute equally and buy a house as joint tenants, but later decide not to marry, there will be a resulting trust in their favour as tenants in common in equal shares, so that there will be no right of survivorship.[38]

10–011   *(b) Voluntary conveyance.* Where before 1926 property was conveyed without any consideration, but not expressly on trust, difficult questions could arise. Resulting uses and resulting trusts must be distinguished, for after the Statute of Uses 1535 a resulting use would be executed by the statute and so carry the legal estate back to the grantor, whereas a resulting trust was purely equitable, so that the grantor would continue to hold the legal estate as trustee for the grantor.

10–012   (1) RESULTING USES. Before 1535 it had been settled that on a voluntary conveyance in fee simple by A to B in which no use was expressed, there was a presumption of a resulting use to the grantor of the whole estate granted.[39] If it appeared that a gift was intended, as where a use was expressed in the conveyance (*e.g.* in favour of B), that of course prevented a resulting use from being implied. A resulting use was also excluded if the conveyance was made either for valuable consideration (even if nominal[40]) or for good consideration, *e.g.* the "natural love and affection" that indicated a genuine gift if B was a near relation of A.[41] If B held of A in tenure, that also sufficed, so that no resulting use arose on a grant in tail, for life or for years.[42]

10–013   (2) RESULTING TRUSTS. After the Statute of Uses 1535 a resulting use was executed by the Statute, with the result that such a conveyance was totally ineffective, and A was regarded as holding the same estate as before.[43] When trusts later came into use and a grant "unto and to the use of B" became a common form merely for the purpose of vesting the legal estate in B, whether or not upon further trusts, it was arguable that a voluntary grant in such terms raised a resulting trust in equity for the grantor, by analogy with the old doctrine of resulting uses. But, rather curiously, this question was never

---

[37] See *Westdeutsche Landesbank Girozentrale v. Islington L.B.C.*, *supra*, at 715, criticising the reasoning (but not the result) in *Re Ames' Settlement* [1946] Ch. 217.

[38] *Burgess v. Rawnsley* [1975] Ch. 429. If the contributions are unequal, the shares will be in proportion to them.

[39] H.E.L. iv, 424; *Beckwith's Case* (1589) 2 Co.Rep. 56b at 58a; *Armstrong d. Neve v. Wolsey* (1755) 2 Wils.K.B. 19; Sanders, *Uses*, i, 60, 97, 365; Williams R.P. 185, 186; Norton, *Deeds*, 410.

[40] *Case of Sutton's Hospital* (1612) 10 Co.Rep. 1a.

[41] See Sanders, *Uses*, ii, 98–100; Snell, *Equity*, 125; *ante*, para. 5–008.

[42] H.E.L. iv, 429. The statute *Quia Emptores* 1290 prevented tenure arising between grantor and grantee on grants in fee simple (*ante*, paras 2–040, 2–041), but not on grants of lesser estates.

[43] See the authorities cited in n. 39, *supra*, and *Godbold v. Freestone* (1694) 3 Lev. 406 at 407; *Harris v. Bishop of Lincoln* (1723) 2 P. Wms. 135; Preston, *Conveyancing*, ii, 487.

settled. The old authorities seem to show that a resulting trust would arise if circumstances pointed to the conclusion that the grantee was not intended to take beneficially,[44] but that in the absence of such evidence the grantee would take for his own use.[45] Unlike resulting uses, resulting trusts were not excluded merely by the presence of a nominal consideration.[46] In practice it would nearly always be made clear whether a voluntary conveyance was intended as a gift or not, so that the point was never squarely raised in a modern case.[47]

(3) AFTER 1925. The Law of Property Act 1925 has disposed of the difficulty in the case of conveyances executed after 1925. Since uses can no longer be executed and so turned into legal estates, the old form of conveyance "unto and to the use of A" is now obsolete. A conveyance simply "to A" now suffices. However, where this formula was used in a voluntary conveyance a resulting use would still arise in equity, and take effect as a trust, for the repeal of the Statute of Uses does not alter the equitable principle under which the use resulted. This is however prevented by the provision that "in a voluntary conveyance a resulting trust shall not be implied merely by reason that the property is not expressed to be conveyed for the use or benefit of the grantee".[48] Since in a voluntary grant made after 1925 "to A for his own benefit" the last four words would undoubtedly rebut a resulting trust, it follows that a resulting trust cannot now arise merely from the omission of any such formula in a grant made simply "to A", with no indication whether or not A was intended to take for his own benefit. Where there is evidence that A was to take as trustee for the grantor, there will be a resulting trust to that effect.[49]   **10–014**

(4) ADVANCEMENT. One class of case was always outside the doctrine of resulting trusts. Where the grantee was the wife[50] or child of the grantor there was a contrary presumption ("the presumption of advancement") that a   **10–015**

---

[44] *Duke of Norfolk v. Browne* (1697) Prec.Ch. 80; *R. v. Williams* (1735) Bunb. 342.
[45] *Lloyd v. Spillet* (1740) 2 Atk. 148; *Young v. Peachy* (1741) 2 Atk. 254. Lord Hardwicke was clearly of opinion that there was no imperative rule demanding a resulting trust.
[46] See *Hayes v. Kingdome* (1681) 1 Vern. 33 at 34; *Sculthorp v. Burgess* (1790) 1 Ves. Jun. 91 at 92.
[47] Though see the remarks of Jessel M.R. in *Strong v. Bird* (1874) L.R. 18 Eq. 315 at 318; and (in the opposite sense) of James L.J. in *Fowkes v. Pascoe* (1875) 10 Ch.App. 343 at 348. The authorities are collected in the editorial note to Maitland, *Equity*, 1936 ed., 330. Text-writers conflicted equally freely on the question: see Wh. & T. ii, 762. A resulting trust was favoured by Maitland, *Equity*, 77; Williams R.P. 194; Lewin 131; and opposed by Sanders, *Uses*, i, 365; Ashburner, *Equity*, 107.
[48] L.P.A. 1925, s.60(3), (4). cf. *Tinsley v. Milligan* [1994] 1 A.C. 340 at 371; R. Chambers, *Resulting Trusts*, 14–19.
[49] *Hodgson v. Marks* [1971] Ch. 892, admitting evidence of oral agreement not indicated in the grant.
[50] Or (probably) a fiancée: see *Moate v. Moate* [1948] 2 All E.R. 486 at 487 (though it may be conditional on the parties' subsequently marrying). In any event, it has been suggested that the presumption applies in such a case by virtue of the Law Reform (Miscellaneous Provisions) Act 1970, s.2(1) (*post*, para. 10–024), though whether conditionally or unconditionally is uncertain: see *Mossop v. Mossop* [1989] Fam. 77 at 82.

beneficial gift was intended.[51] But other relationships (*e.g.* where the grantee was husband or nephew of the grantor) raised no such presumption.[52] The presumption could always be rebutted by evidence that the wife or child was not intended to take beneficially.[53] The presumption of advancement and, in particular the relationships that give rise to it, are wholly out of date and may lead to arbitrary results.[54] It may be abrogated to enable the United Kingdom to ratify the Seventh Protocol of the European Convention on Human Rights.[55]

10–016　　　　*(c) Purchase with another's money: presumed resulting trusts.* Where land is conveyed to one person, but the purchase-money[56] is provided by another as purchaser,[57] there is presumed to be a resulting trust in favour of the person providing the purchase-money. If V conveys land to P, A being the real purchaser and as such providing the purchase-money, prima facie P holds on a resulting trust for A.[58] Similarly, if A provides part of the purchase-money[59] he acquires a proportionate share in equity.[60] Nevertheless these are only presumptions which can be rebutted either—

---

[51] See Snell, *Equity*, 178. It is doubtful whether there is any presumption of advancement when a mother contributes towards the cost of a property purchased by her son or daughter: Snell, *supra*, 179; *Sekhon v. Alissa* [1989] 2 F.L.R. 94. It has been suggested that even if the presumption survives between husband and wife, it will seldom be decisive if other evidence is available: *Pettitt v. Pettitt* [1970] A.C. 777 at 811; *Gissing v. Gissing* [1971] A.C. 886 at 907. *cf. McHardy & Sons v. Warren* [1994] 2 F.L.R. 338, where a husband paid his earnings into a joint bank account, from which the mortgage on the house was paid. Although the house was in his name alone, it was held that the repayments could be regarded as made jointly. See [1994] Fam. Law 567 (J. Dewar).

[52] The presumption does not apply as between man and mistress: see *Lowson v. Coombes* [1999] 2 W.L.R. 720 at 726, 729. The point had been left open in *Cantor v. Cox* [1976] 2 E.G.L.R. 105.

[53] *Stock v. McAvoy* (1875) L.R. 15 Eq. 55; *Gross v. French* [1976] 1 E.G.L.R. 129 (money provided by mother for daughter's house but without intent to make daughter owner); *Sekhon v. Alissa, supra* (a similar situation); *Simpson v. Simpson* [1992] 1 F.L.R. 601 (transfer of property to a wife by a husband who was seriously ill, simply as a matter of convenience).

[54] See, *e.g. Trends in Contemporary Trust Law* (ed. A. J. Oakley), p. 33 (J. D. Davies); and *infra*.

[55] See *Hansard* (H.L.), April 21, 1998, vol. 588, W.A., col. 197. Article 5 of the 7th Protocol provides for equality of rights and responsibilities between husband and wife.

[56] For these purposes, borrowed money is equated to a cash contribution: *Crisp v. Mullings* [1976] 2 E.G.L.R. 103; *Marsh v. Von Sternberg* [1986] 1 F.L.R. 526; *Springette v. Defoe* [1992] 2 F.L.R. 388; so too is a discount under the "right to buy" legislation (*post*, para. 22–290): *Springette v. Defoe, supra*.

[57] And not, for example, as mortgagee.

[58] *Dyer v. Dyer* (1788) 2 Cox Eq. 92.

[59] It has been held that no interest is acquired from the payment of rent under a tenancy, because this purchases no asset but merely pays for the use of the property: *Savage v. Dunningham* [1974] Ch. 181. This is questionable. The consideration paid under a lease, whether rent or premium, purchases an estate in land: *Malayan Credit Ltd v. Jack Chia-MPH Ltd* [1986] A.C. 549 at 560.

[60] *Wray v. Steele* (1814) 2 V. & B. 388; *Gissing v. Gissing* [1971] A.C. 886 at 897; *Heseltine v. Heseltine* [1971] 1 W.L.R. 342 (money provided by wife); *Dewar v. Dewar* [1975] 1 W.L.R. 1532 (money provided by brother). The quantification of a beneficiary's interest is considered further in relation to constructive trusts, *infra*.

   (i) by evidence that P was intended to benefit, A's money being in effect a gift or loan to P,[61] or

   (ii) by the presumption of advancement which arises if P is the wife or child of A.[62]

It has been explained that the presumption of advancement is itself rebuttable by evidence of contrary intention.[63] This has given rise to some difficulty where A has transferred property to B for some illegal purpose. In a controversial decision, *Tinsley v. Milligan*,[64] the House of Lords held that a claim to a beneficial interest under a presumed resulting trust, made by a person who has contributed to the price, would not fail merely because the property was acquired in the course of an illegal transaction. "A party to an illegality can recover by virtue of a legal or equitable property interest if, but only if, he can establish his title without relying on his own illegality."[65] In that case, two female lovers, A and B, purchased land which was conveyed to B alone to facilitate a social security fraud to which they were both parties. This was held not to bar A's claim to an equitable interest in the property under a presumed resulting trust. A necessary consequence of the decision is that, in a case where the presumption of advancement applies, A will only be able to rebut the presumption of gift in favour of B by relying on the underlying illegality. His claim will therefore fail.[66] Because the relationships to which the presumption of advancement applies have not evolved in line with changing social conditions, this leads to arbitrary results. Thus where A is a male, he will be able to recover property transferred for an illegal purpose to his mistress,[67] but not if it is made to his wife[68] or son.[69] By contrast, where A is female, she should, in principle, succeed in recovering property transferred to

---

[61] *e.g. Fowkes v. Pascoe* (1875) 10 Ch. App. 343; *Standing v. Bowring* (1885) 31 Ch.D. 282; *Dewar v. Dewar, supra* (gift from mother), not mentioning the presumption of advancement. In *Westdeutsche Landesbank Girozentrale v. Islington L.B.C.* [1996] A.C. 669 at 708, Lord Browne-Wilkinson accepted that the presumption of a resulting trust could be rebutted "by evidence of any intention inconsistent with such trust, not only by evidence of an intention to make a gift". See (1996) 16 L.S. 110 (W. Swadling).

[62] *Supra.*

[63] *Ante*, para. 10–015.

[64] [1994] 1 A.C. 340. See (1994) 110 L.Q.R. 3 (R. A. Buckley); (1995) 111 L.Q.R. 135 (N. Enonchong). For the very different approach adopted in Australia, see *Nelson v. Nelson* (1995) 184 C.L.R. 538; (1996) 112 L.Q.R. 386 (F. D. Rose); [1996] R.L.R. 78 (N. Enonchong).

[65] *Tinsley v. Milligan, supra*, at 375, *per* Lord Browne-Wilkinson. See too *Rowan v. Dann* (1991) 64 P. & C.R. 202 at 209 (decided before *Tinsley v. Milligan* had been heard by the House of Lords). Evidence of illegality may be given, however, to rebut a spurious defence by the party resisting the claim: see *Silverwood v. Silverwood* (1997) 74 P. & C.R. 453.

[66] *Tinsley v. Milligan, supra*, at 375.

[67] *Lowson v. Coombes* [1999] 2 W.L.R. 720 (property transferred to defeat any ancillary relief proceedings brought by A's wife), disapproving *Cantor v. Cox* [1976] 2 E.G.L.R. 105 (in which A's claim failed on grounds of illegality).

[68] *Tinker v. Tinker* [1970] P. 136 (property conveyed by a husband to his wife to keep it out of the hands of his creditors in case he should go bankrupt).

[69] *Chettiar v. Chettiar* [1962] A.C. 294 at 302 (transfer to son disguised as a sale to circumvent regulations which restricted rubber planting).

her husband to further an illegal design.[70] The presumption of advancement does not apply to a transfer by a wife to her husband,[71] and she would not, therefore, have to rely on the illegality of the act. The present law has been judicially criticised,[72] and the courts have devised one means of ameliorating its potentially mischievous effects. It has been held that a person may recover property even if he has to lead evidence of an illegal purpose, provided that he withdrew from that purpose before it was wholly or partially executed.[73] The Law Commission has recommended that the courts should be given a structured discretion to deal with illegal transactions, thereby overcoming the difficulties explained above.[74]

10–017   **4. Constructive trusts.** There is no accepted definition of a constructive trust[75] and no single principle which unites the circumstances in which it may be imposed. It is a residual category of trusts. A constructive trustee is subject to some aspect of an express trustee's liability, but not necessarily to all his fiduciary obligations.[76] English law tends to treat constructive trusts as "institutional".[77] The trust "arises by operation of law as from the date of the circumstances which give rise to it: the function of the court is merely to declare that such trust has arisen in the past".[78] In some other jurisdictions the courts will impose a "remedial constructive trust". This is "a judicial remedy giving rise to an enforceable equitable obligation", the retrospectivity of which is a matter for the court's discretion.[79] It remains to be seen whether English law will develop remedial constructive trusts.[80] It is not a pre-requisite to liability that the trustee should ever have received any property.[81] A constructive trustee may be personally liable to account for any improper gain which he has made or for any loss which his acts or omissions have

---

[70] There is no authority directly in point.

[71] See, *e.g. Mercier v. Mercier* [1903] 2 Ch. 98.

[72] See *Tribe v. Tribe* [1996] Ch. 107 at 118, 134; *Silverwood v. Silverwood* (1997) 74 P. & C.R. 453 at 458.

[73] *Tribe v. Tribe, supra.* The court declined to define the limits of this "doctrine of the *locus poenitentiae*", but did comment that "genuine repentance" was not required: *ibid.* at 135, *per* Millett L.J. See [1996] C.L.J. 23 (G. Virgo).

[74] (1999) Law Com. C.P. No. 154.

[75] Snell, *Equity*, 192.

[76] *Lonrho Plc v. Fayed (No. 2)* [1992] 1 W.L.R. 1 at 12. See (1997) 1 E.L.R. 437 (C.H.). *cf.* [1999] C.L.J. 294 (L. Smith).

[77] See *Re Polly Peck International Plc (No. 2)* [1998] 3 All E.R. 812 at 823–827.

[78] *Westdeutsche Landesbank Girozentrale v. Islington L.B.C.* [1996] A.C. 669 at 714, *per* Lord Browne-Wilkinson.

[79] *ibid.* See too *Halifax B.S. v. Thomas* [1996] Ch. 217 at 229.

[80] For differing views, contrast *The Frontiers of Liability* (ed. P. B. H. Birks), vol. ii, 165 (D. W. M. Waters); with (1998) 12 T.L.I. 202 (P. B. H. Birks).

[81] *Selangor United Rubber Estates Ltd v. Cradock (No. 3)* [1969] 1 W.L.R. 1555 at 1582; *Royal Brunei Airlines Sdn. Bhd. v. Tan* [1995] 2 A.C. 378, at 382. But *cf. Westdeutsche Landesbank Girozentrale v. Islington L.B.C.* [1996] A.C. 669 at 705 (treating cases of dishonest assistance in a breach of trust as the only instances where a person might be liable without receipt of trust property: *sed quaere*).

caused, or in appropriate circumstances, he may hold specific property in his hands on trust.

There are a number of well-known situations in which a constructive trust is imposed.

(a) Where there is an existing fiduciary relationship. If by virtue of his position a trustee or other fiduciary obtains any valuable interest in the trust property for himself, the general rule is that he holds it on a constructive trust for the beneficiaries.[82] An example is where a trustee of a lease either obtains a renewal for his own benefit[83] or acquires the freehold reversion.[84]

10–018

(b) Where a stranger intermeddles in a trust.[85] A constructive trust will be imposed on a person who in some way intermeddles in a trust where—

10–019

(i) he acts as a trustee although not so appointed and commits a breach of trust[86];

(ii) he dishonestly procures or assists in a breach of trust[87];

(iii) he receives trust property transferred to him in breach of trust.[88]

The intermeddler's liability is personal and not *in rem*, even if the basis for it is his receipt of trust property.[89]

(c) Where parties enter into an agreement to make mutual wills. If A and B agree to leave their property to the survivor for life with remainder to X, and make mutual wills accordingly, the survivor will hold the property on trust for

10–020

---

[82] *Bray v. Ford* [1896] A.C. 44 at 51.

[83] *Keech v. Sandford* (1726) Sel.Ca.t.King 61; *cf. Re Morgan* (1881) 18 Ch.D. 93. See generally Snell, *Equity*, 246.

[84] *Protheroe v. Protheroe* [1968] 1 W.L.R. 519.

[85] See (1986) 102 L.Q.R. 114, 267; (C.H.); (1991) 107 L.Q.R. 71 at 80 (Sir Peter Millett); *The Frontiers of Liability* (ed. P. B. H. Birks), vol. i, 9 (C.H.); (1996) 112 L.Q.R. 56 (S. Gardner).

[86] *e.g. Pearce v. Pearce* (1856) 25 L.J.Ch. 893.

[87] *Royal Brunei Airlines Sdn. Bhd. v. Tan, supra* (disapproving *Barnes v. Addy* (1874) 9 Ch. App. 244); (1995) 111 L.Q.R. 545 (C.H.); [1995] C.L.J. 505 (R. Nolan). See too *Brinks Ltd v. Abu-Saleh* [1996] C.L.C. 133; [1996] Conv. 447 (J. Stevens). It is questionable whether this form of accessory liability, which is the equitable equivalent of the tort of inducing a breach of contract, should be characterised as a form of constructive trusteeship, nor in *Tan* did the Privy Council do so.

[88] The degree of knowledge or notice required for liability has not been settled: *Polly Peck International Plc v. Nadir (No. 2)* [1992] 4 All E.R. 769 at 777. It now appears that such liability is regarded as restitutionary and is not imposed because of the recipient's wrongdoing: *Royal Brunei Airlines Sdn. Bhd. v. Tan, supra*, at 386. For the view that liability is strict but subject to the defences of change of position and bona fide purchase, see [1989] L.M.C.L.Q. 296 (P. B. H. Birks). This form of liability can apply to a recipient of land: *Cowan de Groot Properties Ltd v. Eagle Trust Plc* [1992] 4 All E.R. 700 at 759–760; *Eagle Trust Plc v. S.B.C. Securities Ltd* [1993] 1 W.L.R. 484 at 503–504.

[89] *Re Montagu's S.T.* [1987] Ch. 264 at 276.

X, so that he will be unable to defeat X's expectations by revoking his will.[90] In this case the constructive trust solves the problem of allowing a third party to sue on a contract.

10–021   *(d) Where a vendor contracts to sell land to a purchaser.* Where a vendor enters into a specifically enforceable contract to sell land, he is regarded for certain purposes as a trustee of the property for the purchaser.[91] The vendor's fiduciary obligations may be regarded as based upon a constructive trust.

10–022   *(e) Where it would be inequitable for a landowner to deny a claimant an interest in land.* Where a person acquires land in circumstances in which it would be inequitable to deny the claimant an interest in the property, a constructive trust will be imposed upon him.[92] Such trusts have been imposed upon a purchaser who—

> (i)   reneged on an informal promise to allow the vendor to remain in a cottage rent-free[93];
>
> (ii) repudiated a contract, not otherwise binding on him, to which a conveyance to him was expressly made subject and which he had undertaken to respect.[94]

It is however clear that a constructive trust will not be imposed on a purchaser merely because he acquires the land "subject to" some third party right that would not otherwise bind him. Such a trust will be created only "where there are very special circumstances showing that the transferee of the property undertook a new liability to give effect to provisions for the benefit of third parties",[95] so that his conscience was affected.[96] The "heresy"[97] that the grantor of an irrevocable contractual licence would in all cases become subject to a constructive trust for the benefit of the licensee, regardless of

---

[90] *Dufour v. Pereira* (1769) Dick. 419; *Re Oldham* [1925] Ch. 75; *Re Hagger* [1930] 2 Ch. 190; *Re Green* [1951] Ch. 148; *Re Cleaver* [1981] 1 W.L.R. 939; *Re Dale* [1994] Ch. 31; Snell, *Equity*, 190. For there to be a valid mutual will, there must be a contract between the parties: see *Re Dale, supra*; *Re Goodchild* [1997] 1 W.L.R. 1216. If, subsequent to the mutual wills agreement, the first testator to die alters his will so that it no longer conforms to it, the agreement is terminated: *Re Hobley, The Times*, May 23, 1997.

[91] *Post*, para. 12–051. See *Lysaght v. Edwards* (1876) 2 Ch.D. 499; A. J. Oakley, *Constructive Trusts* (3rd ed.), p. 282.

[92] *Gissing v. Gissing* [1971] A.C. 886 at 905; *Ashburn Anstalt v. Arnold* [1989] Ch. 1 at 22.

[93] *Bannister v. Bannister* [1948] 2 All E.R. 133.

[94] *Lyus v. Prowsa Developments Ltd* [1982] 1 W.L.R. 1044; [1983] C.L.J. 54 (C.H.). See too *Binions v. Evans* [1972] Ch. 359 at 368. The possibility of a constructive trust does not appear to have been argued in either *Hollington Brothers Ltd v. Rhodes* [1951] 2 T.L.R. 691 or *Markfaith Investment Ltd v. Chiap Hua Flashlights Ltd* [1991] 2 A.C. 43. See *ante*, para. 5–118.

[95] *IDC Group Ltd v. Clark* [1992] 1 E.G.L.R. 187 at 190, *per* Browne-Wilkinson V.-C.; not questioned on appeal: (1992) 65 P. & C.R. 179.

[96] *Ashburn Anstalt v. Arnold, supra*, at 25; *IDC Group Ltd v. Clark, supra*, at 189. No constructive trust will be imposed therefore if the vendor has sold "subject to" the right merely in order to satisfy his duty to disclose any incumbrances known to him.

[97] *IDC Group Ltd v. Clark, supra*, at 189, *per* Browne-Wilkinson V.-C.

whether his conduct was unconscionable,[98] has now been discredited.[99] There must, however, be a serious doubt as to the correctness of these cases. They suggest that a constructive trust can be employed to impose on the trustee the burden of an encumbrance over land[1] rather than one of the incidents of trusteeship, which has been the invariable characteristic of a constructive trust hitherto.[2] As such, they pose a threat to the security of title to land by providing a means of circumventing the policy which underlies the registration of title. If, as seems likely, the Contracts (Rights of Third Parties) Bill,[3] is enacted, these cases may not arise in future. Under the Bill, a person who is not a party to a contract will normally be able to enforce it if there is an express term to that effect, or if the contract purports to confer a benefit on him.[4]

A more conventional example of this type of constructive trust is sufficiently important to merit separate treatment.

(f) Where a party has acted to his or her detriment in reliance upon a **10–023** *common intention that he or she will acquire an interest in a property.*[5] It frequently happens that land is purchased in A's name alone, but B claims an interest in the property by reason either of some contribution direct or indirect to its acquisition or from having made some improvement to it. To succeed, B will have to demonstrate—

(i) a common intention that both parties should have a beneficial interest in the property; and

(ii) that B acted to his (or as is commonly the case, her[6]) detriment on the basis of that common intention so that it would be inequitable for A to deny B an interest.[7]

The House of Lords has now classified this trust as constructive.[8] However, there will be situations where it is indistinguishable from a presumed resulting

---

[98] *D.H.N. Food Distributors Ltd v. Tower Hamlets B.C.* [1976] 1 W.L.R. 852.

[99] *Ashburn Anstalt v. Arnold, supra*, at 22, 24; *Canadian Imperial Bank of Commerce v. Bello* (1991) 64 P. & C.R. 48 at 51. Both decisions remain good authority on this point although they have been overruled on another: *Prudential Assurance Co. Ltd v. London Residuary Body* [1992] 2 A.C. 386.

[1] Such as the burden of an option in *Lyus v. Prowsa Developments Ltd, supra*; or a licence in *Ashburn Anstalt v. Arnold, supra* (where the claim in fact failed).

[2] See (1997) 1 E.L.R. 437 at 451 (C.H.); R. J. Smith, *Property Law* (2nd ed.), p. 458.

[3] The Bill is presently before Parliament and it implements with some modifications the recommendations of the Law Commission in (1996) Law Com. No. 242.

[4] See *post*, para. 10–037.

[5] See [1990] Conv. 370 (D. J. Hayton).

[6] For a case where B was described by Slade L.J as "a kept man", see *Thomas v. Fuller-Brown* [1988] 1 F.L.R. 237. For a case where A and B were female lovers, see *Tinsley v. Milligan* [1994] 1 A.C. 340.

[7] *Gissing v. Gissing* [1971] A.C. 886 at 905; *Grant v. Edwards* [1986] Ch. 638 at 654.

[8] *Lloyds Bank Plc v. Rosset* [1991] 1 A.C. 107 at 132.

trust. This will be the case where B's detrimental act consists of a contribution to the cost of acquiring the property and the common intention of A and B is that B's interest should be commensurate with his contribution.[9] Neither form of trust will arise if B's contribution is by way of gift or loan.[10]

10–024   The existence of this form of constructive trust is important because there is in this country no special doctrine of "family assets", whether in relation to married or merely cohabiting parties.[11] While some jurisdictions, such as California, recognise a common law claim for "palimony" between cohabitants,[12] "English law recognises neither the term nor the obligation to which it gives effect".[13] The trust was initially developed in disputes between spouses on the breakdown of marriage, though it is now seldom necessary to have recourse to it in such circumstances. There is a broad statutory jurisdiction under the Matrimonial Causes Act 1973 to make property adjustment orders either when a court grants a decree of divorce, nullity or judicial separation, or at any time thereafter.[14] Such constructive trusts may however be relevant in a domestic context—

   (i) on the death of a spouse, in deciding what property passes with his or her estate[15];

   (ii) on the insolvency of a spouse, in determining what property is available for his or her creditors[16];

   (iii) where co-owners (whether married or otherwise) mortgage land and the mortgage is held not to be binding on one of them,[17] in

---

[9] *McFarlane v. McFarlane* [1972] N.I. 59 at 67; *Tinsley v. Milligan, supra*, at 371 ("a development of the old law of resulting trusts", *per* Lord Browne-Wilkinson). *cf. Midland Bank Plc v. Cooke* [1995] 4 All E.R. 562.

[10] See in relation to constructive trusts *Spence v. Brown* (1988) 18 Fam. Law 291 (contribution by mother by way of loan to extension to daughter's house). In determining whether a payment was a loan the courts will look to the substance of what happened rather than as to how the parties described the transaction: *Risch v. McFee* [1991] 1 F.L.R. 105; *Stokes v. Anderson* [1991] 1 F.L.R. 391 (in each case a "loan" was found in fact to be a cash contribution). See [1991] Fam. Law 311 (S. M. Cretney).

[11] See *Pettitt v. Pettitt* [1970] A.C. 777 at 795, 801, 810, 817, 820; *Gissing v. Gissing* [1971] A.C. 886 at 899, 904, in relation to spouses. As regards cohabitants, see *Walker v. Hall* [1984] F.L.R. 126 at 135; *Grant v. Edwards* [1986] Ch. 638 at 651; *Windeler v. Whitehall* [1990] 2 F.L.R. 505 at 506, 513 (where Millett J. spoke of "some kind of erroneous belief in a doctrine of community of property without benefit of clergy").

[12] See, *Marvin v. Marvin* 557 P.2d. 957 (1976).

[13] *Windeler v. Whitehall, supra*, at 506, *per* Millett J.

[14] s.24. On remarriage, a party loses the right to obtain such an order: s.28(3) (as amended by the Matrimonial and Family Proceedings Act 1984, s.5).

[15] The surviving spouse may have a claim against the deceased's estate under the Inheritance (Provision for Family and Dependants) Acts 1975: *post*, para. 11–004.

[16] *Midland Bank Plc v. Dobson* [1986] 1 F.L.R. 171; *Lloyds Bank Plc v. Rosset* [1991] 1 A.C. 107.

[17] *e.g.* because his consent to it was obtained as a result of the fraud or undue influence: see *Barclays Bank Plc v. O'Brien* [1994] 1 A.C. 180; *post*, para. 19–159.

determining the extent of the interest that is bound by the mortgage[18]; and

(iv) in cases between unmarried cohabitants, whether engaged or not,[19] and whether on the breakdown of their relationship[20] or on death[21] or insolvency of one of the parties.

It has been accepted by the Privy Council that such a trust may also arise in a commercial transaction.[22]

(1) COMMON INTENTION.[23] It is now clear that common intention is relevant **10–025** both to whether a party has an interest in the property and to the quantum of that share if he does.[24] The latter is considered below.[25]

The common intention that both A and B should have a beneficial interest in the property[26] may be inferred or it may arise by express agreement. It will be inferred only where B contributes directly to the purchase price, whether by a cash contribution or its equivalent, or by paying mortgage instalments.[27] In all other cases express agreement will have to be proved.[28] In three situations in particular it has been held that B's interest is dependent upon proof of such express agreement.

(i) Where, on the acquisition of the property, B has contributed to the purchase price but A and B have agreed that B should have a greater or lesser share than would otherwise be presumed from the

---

[18] *Midland Bank Plc v. Cooke* [1995] 4 All E.R. 562.

[19] Where engaged couples break off their engagement, "any rule of law relating to the rights of husbands and wives in relation to property in which either or both has or have an interest" applies equally to them: Law Reform (Miscellaneous Provisions) Act 1970, s.2(1). However, it has been held that this does not include the property adjustment provisions of M.C.A. 1973: *Mossop v. Mossop* [1989] Fam. 77.

[20] *Eves v. Eves* [1975] 1 W.L.R. 1338; *Grant v. Edwards* [1986] Ch. 638.

[21] *Layton v. Martin* [1986] 2 F.L.R. 227 (where the claim in fact failed). Again, the survivor may have a claim against the deceased's estate under the Inheritance (Provision for Family and Dependants) Acts 1975: *post*, para. 11–005.

[22] See *Austin v. Keele* (1987) 72 A.L.R. 579 where the claim failed on the facts.

[23] See [1992] Fam. Law 72 (P. J. Clarke). *cf.* (1996) 16 L.S. 325 (N. Glover and P. Todd).

[24] *Midland Bank Plc v. Cooke* [1995] 4 All E.R. 562; *Clough v. Killey* (1996) 72 P. & C.R. D22.

[25] *Post*, para. 10–028.

[26] The intention must relate to a specific property: *Layton v. Martin* [1986] 2 F.L.R. 227 at 237.

[27] *Grant v. Edwards, supra*, at 647; *Lloyds Bank Plc v. Rosset* [1991] 1 A.C. 107 at 132. The contributions are taken as evidence of the parties' intentions: *Grant v. Edwards, supra*, at 655. A discount on a sale to a sitting tenant has been treated as equivalent to a direct contribution: *Marsh v. Von Sternberg* [1986] 1 F.L.R. 26; *Springette v. Defoe* [1992] 2 F.L.R. 388; *Evans v. Hayward* [1995] 2 F.L.R. 511. The court may be willing to infer a common intention from a wedding present or loan made to a married couple: *McHardy & Sons v. Warren* [1994] 2 F.L.R. 338; *Midland Bank Plc v. Cooke* [1995] 4 All E.R. 562; *Halifax B.S. v. Brown* [1996] 1 F.L.R. 103. *cf.* [1994] Fam. Law 567 (J. Dewar).

[28] *Lloyds Bank Plc v. Rosset, supra*, at 133; *Burns v. Burns* [1984] Ch. 317.

size of B's contribution.[29] In the absence of express agreement, the normal principles of presumed resulting trust will apply.[30]

(ii) Where B has contributed indirectly to the acquisition of the property by undertaking household expenditure which A would otherwise have had to meet.[31] There can be no presumed resulting trust in respect of such indirect contributions and B's claim to an equitable interest under a constructive trust can be founded only upon some express arrangement between the parties.[32]

(iii) Where B has carried out some improvement to the property (other than work of a trivial kind).[33] The general rule is that where B voluntarily spends money on improving property which belongs either to A alone or to A and B, he or she acquires no interest or increased interest in the property in the absence of express agreement.[34] There is a statutory exception to this rule which applies both to spouses and by extension to engaged couples. The Matrimonial Proceedings and Property Act 1970[35] has "declared" that substantial contributions in money or money's worth by a husband or wife to the improvement of real or personal property[36] belonging beneficially to either or both of them are to entitle the contributor to such share as was agreed or, in default, "as may seem in all the circumstances just". It is clear from the section that the contributing spouse acquires a beneficial interest or an enlarged beneficial interest in the property.[37] A trust of land is presumably imposed to give effect to the spouse's interest in the same way as if it arose under a constructive trust by reason of common intention.[38]

---

[29] *Re Densham* [1975] 1 W.L.R. 1519; *Lloyds Bank Plc v. Rosset, supra*, at 132; *Drake v. Whipp* [1996] 1 F.L.R. 826; *Clough v. Killey* (1996) 72 P. & C.R. D22.

[30] *Springette v. Defoe, supra*.

[31] *Grant v. Edwards* [1986] Ch. 638.

[32] *McFarlane v. McFarlane* [1972] N.I. 59 at 71; *Ivin v. Blake* (1993) 67 P. & C.R. 263. *cf. Burns v. Burns, supra*, at 329.

[33] *Eves v. Eves* [1975] 1 W.L.R. 1338; *Ungurian v. Lesnoff* [1990] Ch. 206. Improvements which are "so trifling as to be almost *de minimis*" will be discounted: *Lloyds Bank Plc v. Rosset* [1991] 1 A.C. 107 at 131, *per* Lord Bridge; *Windeler v. Whitehall* [1990] 2 F.L.R. 505 at 514.

[34] *Pettitt v. Pettitt* [1970] A.C. 777 at 818; *Thomas v. Fuller-Brown* [1988] 1 F.L.R. 237 at 240; *Harwood v. Harwood* [1991] 2 F.L.R. 274 at 294.

[35] s.37, extended to engaged couples as explained above, n. 19. This provision, being declaratory, is retrospective: *Davis v. Vale* [1971] 1 W.L.R. 1022. It reverses *Pettitt v. Pettitt, supra*, where the House of Lords held that improvements made by the husband did not entitle him to a share since no agreement to that effect existed at the time of the improvement.

[36] See *Harnett v. Harnett* [1973] Fam. 156 at 167 (contributions must be identifiable with relevant improvements: not discussed on appeal, [1974] 1 W.L.R. 219); *Re Nicholson* [1974] 1 W.L.R. 476; *Samuels' Trustee v. Samuels* (1973) 233 E.G. 149 (£227 held substantial contribution; Act gives wife no rights against husband's trustee in bankruptcy in respect of post-bankruptcy contributions).

[37] If prior to the improvement the parties are beneficial joint tenants, the operation of the section will presumably sever the joint tenancy. The unfortunate effects of this have already been noted: *ante*, para. 9–041.

[38] Considered *post*, para. 10–027.

Where express common intention is essential to establish a beneficial interest, it must be founded on evidence of "express discussions between the partners, however imperfectly remembered and however imprecise their terms may have been".[39] In determining from such evidence whether there is a common intention, a court will draw the inferences that a reasonable person would have drawn at the relevant time.[40] Such an intention is sufficiently established if A induces B to believe that B will have an interest in the property, even if A does not in fact so intend.[41] Assertions by the parties as to their common intentions which are unsupported by contemporaneous evidence will be treated with caution where they are raised in order to defeat a claim by a creditor.[42]

(2) DETRIMENTAL RELIANCE. A constructive trust "does not come into being merely from a gratuitous intention to transfer or create a beneficial interest",[43] because such an intention would amount to an unenforceable declaration of trust.[44] B must have acted to his detriment in reliance upon the parties' common intention[45] and in the reasonable expectation that he would thereby acquire an interest in the property.[46] It is this detriment that takes the trust outside the formal requirements normally applicable to declarations of trusts of land.[47] The acts of detrimental reliance must amount to "an irrevocable change of legal position"[48] and be of a kind upon which B could not reasonably have been expected to embark unless he or she was to have an interest in the property.[49] B will therefore acquire no interest if the acts are ones which he or she would have undertaken in any event. In consequence, the performance of domestic duties will not suffice.[50] The extent to which acts unrelated to the acquisition or improvement of the property will satisfy the

10–026

---

[39] *Lloyds Bank Plc v. Rosset* [1991] 1 A.C. 107 at 132, *per* Lord Bridge. See too *Hammond v. Mitchell* [1991] 1 W.L.R. 1127 at 1139 (a case which concerned a Bunny Girl and a second hand car salesman), where Waite J. observed that, "the tenderest exchanges of a common law courtship may assume an unforeseen significance many years later when they are brought under equity's microscope". An uncommunicated intention, even if shared by both parties, will not suffice: *Springette v. Defoe* [1992] 2 F.L.R. 388 at 393.

[40] *Gissing v. Gissing* [1971] A.C. 886 at 906; *Burns v. Burns* [1984] Ch. 317 at 336. The subsequent conduct of the parties cannot affect what was originally agreed in the absence of an express or implied variation: *Marsh v. Von Sternberg* [1986] 1 F.L.R. 526 at 533.

[41] *Eves v. Eves* [1975] 1 W.L.R. 1338; *Grant v. Edwards* [1986] Ch. 638. In each of those cases, A provided a specious excuse why the land should not be conveyed to A and B jointly. See too *Lloyds Bank Plc v. Rosset, supra*, at 133. *cf.* (1990) 106 L.Q.R. 539 (J. D. Davies); (1991) 54 M.L.R. 126 (S. Gardner).

[42] *Midland Bank Plc v. Dobson* [1986] 1 F.L.R. 171 at 174.

[43] *Austin v. Keele* (1987) 72 A.L.R. 579 at 587, *per* Lord Oliver.

[44] *Gissing v. Gissing, supra*, at 905; *Midland Bank Plc v. Dobson, supra*, at 175. For the formalities required for the creation of trusts, see *post*, para. 10–039.

[45] The detrimental acts must be referable to that common intention: *Grant v. Edwards, supra*, at 653; *Austin v. Keele, supra*, at 588.

[46] *Gissing v. Gissing, supra*, at 905.

[47] For these, see L.P.A. 1925, s.53(1)(b); *post*, para. 10–039.

[48] *Austin v. Keele, supra*, at 588, *per* Lord Oliver.

[49] *Grant v. Edwards, supra*, at 650.

[50] This is so whether B is A's spouse (*Midland Bank Plc v. Dobson* [1986] 1 F.L.R. 171, where there was express common intention) or not (*Burns v. Burns* [1984] Ch. 317, where there was no such intention).

requirement of detriment has not been finally determined.[51] The House of Lords has held that a payment by B to reduce the overdraft of a company that had purchased a property used by A and B as their matrimonial home was not referable to its acquisition.[52] However, where A promised B that he would provide her with a home for the rest of her life and in reliance upon this B abandoned her flat and a promising academic career in Poland, those acts were considered to be a sufficient detriment to justify the imposition of a constructive trust.[53]

10–027   (3) THE NATURE OF THE TRUST. Although a constructive trust of this kind commonly crystallises at the time when the property is acquired, this need not be so. It may arise subsequently, as where B either improves A's property or discharges the mortgage on it some years after its acquisition.[54]

The trust will give effect to the common intention of the parties, whether express or inferred. After 1996, this will normally mean that A (whether alone or jointly with B) holds the property on a trust of land for himself and B as beneficial joint tenants or tenants in common.[55] There may however be occasions where the parties have expressly agreed that B should be able to live in the house for the rest of his or her lifetime. In such cases, A may hold the property on a trust of land for B for his lifetime. Prior to 1997, it had been held that in such circumstances a settlement under the Settled Land Act 1925 might be created,[56] of which B was the life tenant.[57] However, after 1996, no new settlements can be created.[58]

10–028   (4) QUANTIFYING THE BENEFICIAL INTEREST.[59] Although the proportionate shares of the parties may be determined at the time of the express or implied agreement between them, the valuation of those shares takes place on the

[51] Compare *Grant v. Edwards, supra,* at 656 (where Browne-Wilkinson V.-C. expressly left the question open), with *Layton v. Martin* [1986] 2 F.L.R. 227 at 237 (where Scott J. suggested that "contributions to the acquisition or preservation of specific property" were essential). In cases of inferred common intention the detriment must always be referable to the acquisition of the property: *Winkworth v. Edward Baron Development Co. Ltd* [1986] 1 W.L.R. 1512 at 1515; *Windeler v. Whitehall* [1990] 2 F.L.R. 505 at 514.

[52] *Winkworth v. Edward Baron Development Co. Ltd, supra.*

[53] *Ungurian v. Lesnoff* [1990] Ch. 206; [1990] C.L.J. 25 (M. Oldham). In that case, the facts of which are remarkable, the defendant also carried out substantial improvements to the property. See too *Maharaj v. Chand* [1986] A.C. 898 at 907.

[54] *Bernard v. Josephs* [1982] Ch. 391 at 404; *Grant v. Edwards* [1986] Ch. 638 at 651; *Austin v. Keele* (1987) 72 A.L.R. 579 at 587; *Harwood v. Harwood* [1991] 2 F.L.R. 274 at 294; *Lloyds Bank Plc v. Rosset* [1991] 1 A.C. 107 at 132.

[55] See *e.g. Lloyds Bank Plc v. Rosset* [1989] Ch. 350 (reversed [1991] 1 A.C. 107, but not so as to affect this point).

[56] There must be a "settlement" within S.L.A. 1925, s.1: see *Griffiths v. Williams* [1978] 2 E.G.L.R. 121. This requirement has been overlooked, see *ante,* para. 8–057.

[57] *Ungurian v. Lesnoff, supra.* See too *Bannister v. Bannister* [1948] 2 All E.R. 133; *Binions v. Evans* [1972] Ch. 359; *ante,* para. 8–057. If the title was registered, the finding that B had a life estate could have unfortunate consequences. An interest under a settlement takes effect only as a minor interest and cannot be an overriding interest: L.R.A. 1925, s.86(2). B's interest would therefore require registration if it was to bind purchasers. *Aliter* if B has an interest under a trust of land.

[58] T.L.A.T.A. 1996, s.2; *ante,* para. 8–001.

[59] See (1991) 11 O.J.L.S. 39 (P. Sparkes).

dissolution of the trust.[60] The trust terminates when the parties' interests are realised (whether on sale or when one party purchases the interest of the other),[61] not as was once thought on the date when the parties separated.[62]

Where the parties have expressly agreed the shares in which they are to hold, that will normally be conclusive,[63] and a court will depart from it only if there is good cause to do so.[64] In the absence of such agreement, the position is less clear, and there appears to have been a change in judicial practice from quantification that is determined by reference to the parties' contributions to one that depends upon the common intentions of the parties as deduced from all relevant circumstances.

(i) *By reference to contributions.* Until recently, the court generally looked at the contributions made by the parties to determine their shares.[65] It sought to find out how much of the total outlay had been contributed by each, whether directly, or by the assumption of mortgage commitments. The parties' beneficial interests would be proportionate to their financial contributions.[66] For these purposes, a mortgage advance was considered to be the same as a cash payment.[67] However, the amount of capital repaid would necessarily affect the valuation of the parties' respective shares when they came to be realised on sale.[68] Where A and B had contributed to the mortgage successively, no distinction was drawn between payments of interest and capital in determining the respective shares of the parties *inter se*.[69] Although the quantification of the

---

[60] *Cowcher v. Cowcher* [1972] 1 W.L.R. 425 at 432; *Marsh v. Von Sternberg* [1986] 1 F.L.R. 526 at 533.

[61] *Gordon v. Douce* [1983] 1 W.L.R. 563; *Walker v. Hall* [1988] F.L.R. 126; *Turton v. Turton* [1988] Ch. 542.

[62] *Hall v. Hall* (1981) 3 F.L.R. 379; *Bernard v. Josephs*, *supra*, at 399. This view was illogical because once B acquired an interest in the property it was indefeasible unless and until he or she expressly assigned it: *Brykiert v. Jones* (1981) 2 F.L.R. 373; *Turton v. Turton, supra*, at 552.

[63] *Pettitt v. Pettitt* [1970] A.C. 777 at 813; *Lloyds Bank Plc v. Rosset* [1991] 1 A.C. 107 at 132; *Savill v. Goodall* [1993] 1 F.L.R. 755; *Clough v. Killey* (1996) 72 P. & C.R. D22. This is analogous to the position where the conveyance expressly declares what the respective interests of the parties are to be. This will normally be conclusive: *Goodman v. Gallant* [1986] Fam. 106; *ante*, para. 9–026.

[64] *Clough v. Killey* (1996) 72 P. & C.R. D22 at D24.

[65] *Crisp v. Mullings* [1976] 2 E.G.L.R. 103; *Walker v. Hall* [1984] F.L.R. 126; *Young v. Young* [1984] F.L.R. 375; *Springette v. Defoe* [1992] 2 F.L.R. 388; *Huntingford v. Hobbs* [1993] 1 F.L.R. 736.

[66] *Walker v. Hall, supra*, at 130.

[67] *Marsh v. Von Sternberg* [1986] 1 F.L.R. 526 at 533; *Harwood v. Harwood* [1991] 2 F.L.R. 274 at 292; *Huntingford v. Hobbs, supra*, at 745.

[68] See, *e.g. Re Densham* [1975] 1 W.L.R. 1519.

[69] *Passee v. Passee* [1988] 1 F.L.R. 263 at 267. This is material for instalment mortgages, where, as in that case, the initial payments are largely of interest. There is no authority for an interest-only mortgage under which B pays the interest on the loan and A the premiums on the endowment policy. In principle both premium and interest should be regarded globally as mortgage repayments and it should be irrelevant that, strictly speaking, B made no payments towards the capital cost of acquiring the property.

parties' interests from their contributions was not carried out "as a strict mathematical exercise", it was only in the last resort that the court should "abandon the attempt in favour of applying the presumption of equality".[70] In cases where B's interest arose from an improvement that he or she had made to the property,[71] there was some authority which suggested that B's share would be quantified by having regard to the amount by which the improvement enhanced the value of the property at the time when it was made.[72]

10–029   (ii) *By reference to common intention.* Subsequent authorities suggest a different approach. Where, by reason of a direct contribution to the cost of acquiring the land, the court infers a common intention that the contributor should have an interest in the property, it may then have regard to the whole course of conduct between the parties to determine the shares of the parties.[73]

> "That scrutiny will not confine itself to the limited range of acts of direct contribution of the sort that are needed to found a beneficial interest in the first place. It will take into consideration all conduct which throws light on the question what shares were intended. Only if that search proves inconclusive does the court fall back on the maxim that 'equality is equity'."[74]

This approach does in fact accord with a number of earlier authorities[75] which suggested that the common intention as to the extent of a claimant's beneficial interest did not have to be ascertained "once and for all at the date of its acquisition".[76] In such cases the court determines what in the circumstances is a fair share for each party.[77] Thus in one case, a wife contributed half of the deposit on the common home, which was vested in the husband's name. Although she made no further financial contributions to the cost of acquiring the property, the court held that, having regard to the

---

[70] *Bernard v. Josephs* [1982] Ch. 391 at 404, *per* Griffiths L.J. See too *Gissing v. Gissing* [1971] A.C. 886 at 908. Where B's contributions are of an indirect character, the presumption of equal division may be the only possible solution.

[71] Whether by a constructive trust or under the Matrimonial Proceedings and Property Act 1970, s.37.

[72] *Re Nicholson* [1974] 1 W.L.R. 476 (decided under the Matrimonial Proceedings and Property Act 1970, s.37).

[73] *Midland Bank Plc v. Cooke* [1995] 4 All E.R. 562; (1996) 112 L.Q.R. 378 (S. Gardner); [1996] C.L.J. 194 (M. Oldham); (1996) 8 C.F.L.Q. 261 (G. Battersby); [1996] Fam. Law 298 (D. Wragg); [1997] Conv. 66 (M. J. Dixon). See too *Drake v. Whipp* [1996] I F.L.R. 826; [1997] Conv. 467 (A. Dunn).

[74] *Midland Bank Plc v. Cooke, supra*, at 574, *per* Waite L.J.

[75] See especially *Gissing v. Gissing, supra*, at 909; *Stokes v. Anderson* [1991] 1 F.L.R. 391 at 400.

[76] *Stokes v. Anderson, supra*, at 399, *per* Nourse L.J.

[77] *Gissing v. Gissing, supra*, at 909.

course of dealings between the parties, the wife was entitled to a half share in the property.[78] The odd result of this is that a person who has made a small monetary contribution may end up with a substantial share in the property on the basis of the parties' common intention, whereas one who has made no contribution at all obtains nothing, regardless of any common intention.[79]

(5) COMPARISON WITH PROPRIETARY ESTOPPEL.[80] There are close parallels **10–030** between constructive trusts which arise from the parties' common intention and the doctrine of proprietary estoppel.[81] By that doctrine, if A, by his conduct, encourages B to believe that he has some right in relation to A's property, and B acts in some way to his detriment in reliance upon that belief, an equity arises in B's favour to which the court may give effect in the manner and to the extent that it considers appropriate.[82] In this way B may acquire a proprietary interest in, or right over, A's property. Although these parallels have often been acknowledged,[83] the two doctrines at present remain distinct,[84] though the differences between them are not now substantial.

It is often said that constructive trusts depend upon proof of some bilateral consensus between the parties, whereas estoppel will be established if B unilaterally acts to his detriment on the basis of some express or implied representation by A. However, a representation by A that leads B to believe that he will acquire an interest in the property may be evidence of express common intention.[85] Where a constructive trust is alleged, B must prove that he acted in reliance upon the common understanding with A.[86] However, where the basis of B's claim is proprietary estoppel, he will be presumed to have acted in reliance on A's representation if a reasonable person would have done so.[87] Where a constructive trust arises, the claimant acquires a beneficial interest in the property at the time when he acts to his detriment.[88] In a case

---

[78] *Midland Bank Plc v. Cooke, supra*. Had her share been determined according to her contribution, she would have had a mere 6.47% interest in the property. The fact that the parties were married was a significant factor: see *ibid.*, at 576. *cf. Drake v. Whipp, supra*, where the parties were not married and the claimant, whose monetary contribution was 19.4%, was awarded a one-third share.

[79] *cf. Midland Bank Plc v. Dobson* [1986] I F.L.R. 171. See (1996) 8 C.F.L.Q. 261 at 266 (G. Battersby); [1996] Fam. Law 298 at 299 (D. Wragg).

[80] See [1990] Conv. 370 at 371 (D. J. Hayton) (1993) 109 L.Q.R. 114 (P. Ferguson); and *post*, para. 13–036.

[81] Proprietary estoppel is considered, *post*, para. 13–001.

[82] See, *e.g. Crabb v. Arun D.C.* [1976] Ch. 179 at 193.

[83] *Grant v. Edwards* [1986] Ch. 638 at 656; *Re Basham* [1986] 1 W.L.R. 1498 at 1504; *Austin v. Keele* (1987) 72 A.L.R. 579 at 587; *Lloyds Bank Plc v. Rosset* [1991] 1 A.C. 107 at 132; *Yaxley v. Gott* [1999] E.G.C.S. 92.

[84] *Stokes v. Anderson, supra*, at 399. See too *Maharaj v. Chand* [1986] A.C. 898 at 908. Because of the close similarities between them, constructive trust and proprietary estoppel will nowadays often be pleaded in the alternative.

[85] *Gissing v. Gissing, supra*, at 905; *Lloyds Bank Plc v. Rosset, supra*, at 133.

[86] *Grant v. Edwards, supra*, at 652; *Lloyds Bank Plc v. Rosset, supra*, at 131.

[87] *Greasley v. Cooke* [1980] 1 W.L.R. 1306.

[88] *Turton v. Turton* [1988] Ch. 542 at 555; *Grant v. Edwards, supra*, at 651, 652. The quantum of the claimant's interest will not necessarily be determined at that time: see *ante*, para. 10–029.

of proprietary estoppel, the claimant's detrimental reliance raises only an inchoate "equity" in his favour.[89] The precise nature of the claimant's right remains in limbo until the court determines how best to give effect to it. Although the court will often grant the claimant the interest that he was intended to have, it is not bound to do so and has a discretion as to how the equity should be satisfied.[90] The circumstances may make it inappropriate for the claimant to be granted any interest in the property.[91] An interest arising under a constructive trust is undoubtedly a proprietary right which is capable of binding a third party. Although an equity arising by estoppel probably enjoys the same status, the point cannot be regarded as finally settled.[92] It is however clear in relation both to constructive trusts arising out of common intention and to proprietary estoppel that B's claim may be defeated if it is tainted by unlawful or inequitable conduct.[93]

10–031   (6) THE CONVEYANCING IMPLICATIONS.[94] The imposition of constructive trusts in cases where one cohabitant has acted to his detriment in reliance upon a common intention may jeopardize conveyancing transactions. Proprietary rights arising under such trusts are created informally so that there is no indication of their existence on the title. Without making intimate inquiries a purchaser from one cohabitant will have no means of knowing whether resulting, constructive or statutory trusts exist in favour of another and whether he should comply with the requirements governing the disposition of land held on a trust of land.[95] The judicial reluctance to require such enquiries[96] was reversed in 1980, when the "easy-going practice of dispensing with enquiries as to occupation beyond that of the vendor" was held by the House of Lords to be inadequate.[97] The potential conveyancing difficulties are usually overcome by requiring any cohabitant either to be joined as a party to the conveyance or to sign a waiver of his or her rights in the property.[98] Neither of these methods has proved infallible. In some cases, A has forged B's signature on the conveyance or transfer, so that no legal estate has passed but only A's beneficial interest.[99] In others, A has procured B's signature to

---

[89] *Griffiths v. Williams* [1978] 2 E.G.L.R. 121 at 122.
[90] *Burrows v. Sharp* (1989) 23 H.L.R. 82 at 92.
[91] *Dodsworth v. Dodsworth* (1973) 228 E.G. 1115 (court ordered reimbursement of expenditure).
[92] *cf. Shiloh Spinners Ltd v. Harding* [1973] A.C. 691 at 721; *Williams v. Staite* [1979] Ch. 291. The case for regarding such an equity as a proprietary right is strong: *post*, paras 13–031, 13–032.
[93] See as regards constructive trusts, *Winkworth v. Edward Baron Development Co. Ltd* [1986] 1 W.L.R. 1512 at 1516 (B had acted in breach of her duties as a director of a company and could not claim a beneficial interest in its property in priority to its creditors); and in relation to estoppel, *J. Willis & Son v. Willis* [1986] 1 E.G.L.R. 62 (false claims submitted by B as to his expenditure on the property).
[94] See [1990] C.L.J. 277 at 312 (C.H.); [1993] Fam. Law 231 (J. Dewar).
[95] *Ante*, para. 8–166.
[96] See *Caunce v. Caunce* [1969] 1 W.L.R. 286.
[97] *Williams & Glyn's Bank Ltd v. Boland* [1981] A.C. 487 at 508, *per* Lord Wilberforce.
[98] But compare L.P.A. 1925, s.42.
[99] See, *e.g. Ahmed v. Kendrick* (1987) 56 P. & C.R. 120; *ante*, paras 5–044, 9–039.

a conveyance or waiver by fraud or undue influence in circumstances in which the purchaser has been unable to rely on the instrument.[1]

There have been few cases of sales or leases in which a purchaser has taken **10–032** subject to the rights of a beneficiary, and those which have arisen have been characterised by unusual facts.[2] Property is normally sold or let with vacant possession, and in consequence any dispute between the cohabitants as to whether the land should be sold will usually have been resolved prior to completion. In practice, conveyancing difficulties have most commonly arisen where A has mortgaged a property in which B already has an interest.[3] Where the monies advanced are paid to A alone, B's interest is not overreached.[4] In those circumstances, the mortgage will not be binding on B—

(i) if A's title was unregistered and the mortgagee had notice of B's interest[5]; or

(ii) if A's title was registered and B's interest was protected as an overriding interest because he was in actual occupation of the land.[6]

By contrast, the mortgage will take priority over B's interest if B was either aware of it or must have known that a mortgage would be necessary to finance the balance of the purchase price.[7] In such circumstances he or she will be taken to have impliedly consented to the charge, and will be estopped from asserting his interest.[8] If A subsequently re-mortgages the property for a larger sum without B's consent, B's interest will be subordinated to the new mortgage but only to the extent of the original charge which it replaces. In one case this was explained as an extension of the estoppel principle set out above.[9] However, in a later case the same answer was reached on the more orthodox

---

[1] See, *e.g. Barclays Bank Plc v. O'Brien* [1994] 1 A.C. 180; *post*, para. 19–159. Normally the transaction has been a mortgage or the provision of some other form of security.

[2] See *Hodgson v. Marks* [1971] Ch. 892 (vacant possession was not to be given on completion); *Chhokar v. Chhokar* [1984] F.L.R. 313 (husband connived with purchaser to defeat wife's rights while she was in a maternity hospital); and *Ahmed v. Kendrick, supra* (husband forged wife's name on the transfer after she had ceased to live with him).

[3] Where A mortgages the property at the time of acquisition, B will not gain priority over the mortgagee merely because he or she contributes to the purchase price. The transfer of the legal estate to A and the mortgage are regarded as taking place simultaneously, so that there is no moment of time in which B could gain priority: *Abbey National B.S. v. Cann* [1991] 1 A.C. 56; *post*, para. 14–102.

[4] *Ante*, para. 8–166.

[5] *Kingsnorth Finance Co. Ltd v. Tizard* [1986] 1 W.L.R. 783; *ante*, para. 5–019.

[6] *Williams & Glyn's Bank Ltd v. Boland, supra; ante*, para. 6–061.

[7] *Abbey National B.S. v. Cann, supra*, at 95.

[8] *Bristol and West B.S. v. Henning* [1985] 1 W.L.R. 778; *Paddington B.S. v. Mendelsohn* (1985) 50 P. & C.R. 244; *Skipton B.S. v. Clayton* (1993) 66 P. & C.R. 223 at 229; (1996) 8 C.F.L.Q. 261 at 266 (G. Battersby). This will be so, even though the mortgage is in fact for a sum greater than that to which B had agreed: *Abbey National B.S. v. Cann, supra*.

[9] *Equity & Law Home Loans Ltd v. Prestidge* [1992] 1 W.L.R. 137. Although the decision has been criticised (see [1992] C.L.J. 223 (M. J. Dixon); [1992] Conv. 206 (M. P. Thompson)), the result, if not the reasoning, seems correct: see (1992) 108 L.Q.R. 371 (R. J. Smith).

Trusts and Powers

(and, it is suggested, preferable) basis that the second mortgagee was sub-rogated to the rights of the first.[10]

10–033   (7) CRITICISMS OF THE PRESENT LAW.[11] The constructive trust based upon the common intentions of the parties has not only given rise to conveyancing difficulties, but has also proved to be an unsatisfactory method of adjusting property rights between cohabitants on the breakdown of their relationship.[12] The more closely the relationship resembles marriage, the less likely it is that there will have been a common understanding that the non-owning partner should have an interest in the shared home.[13] In some jurisdictions, a statutory power exists to adjust property rights between unmarried cohabitants on the termination of their relationship in a manner similar to that applicable to spouses in this country.[14] The Scottish Law Commission has recommended the introduction of such a power in Scotland.[15] It has also been suggested that constructive trusts based upon common intention are unnecessary and that the law would be better served if they were subsumed "within the more flexible doctrine of proprietary estoppel".[16]

10–034   **5. Other classifications: completely and incompletely constituted trusts.** In addition to the main classification considered above, equity classified trusts in other ways. One of these must be considered here,[17] namely the distinction between completely and incompletely constituted trusts.

10–035   *(a) Classification.* A trust is completely constituted as soon as the trust property is vested in the trustee. Until this has been done, it is incompletely constituted. The usual example of an incompletely constituted trust is where

---

[10] *Castle Phillips Finance v. Piddington* [1995] 1 F.L.R. 783. *cf. Bankers Trust Co. v. Namdar* [1997] E.G.C.S. 20.

[11] See [1987] Conv. 93 (J. Eekelaar); (1990) 106 L.Q.R. 539 (J. D. Davies); (1993) 109 L.Q.R. 263 (S. Gardner).

[12] For judicial criticism, see *Burns v. Burns* [1984] Ch. 317 at 332, 345. Where A and B cohabit and B dies, A may be in a stronger position than if their relationship had terminated *inter vivos*. This will be so where (i) A and B lived together in the same household for two years as if they were husband and wife; or (ii) A was partly or wholly maintained by B: see the Inheritance (Provision for Family and Dependants) Act 1975, s.1(1)(ba) (as inserted by the Law Reform (Succession) Act 1995, s.2), (e), *post*, para. 11–005; and (1982) 2 O.J.L.S. 277 (C.H.).

[13] "A woman's place is often still in the home, but if she stays there, she will acquire no interest in it": [1987] Conv. 93 at 94 (J. Eekelaar).

[14] See, *e.g.* the New South Wales De Facto Relationships Act 1984; [1992] Fam. Law 72 at 76 (P. J. Clarke).

[15] Scottish Law Com. No. 135 (1992). See [1992] Fam. Law 523 at 525 (L. Clarke and I. R. Edmunds). The Law Commission for England and Wales is at present considering the property rights of homesharers.

[16] [1987] Conv. 93 at 101 (J. Eekelaar). See too [1990] Conv. 370 (D. J. Hayton).

[17] Another distinction, formerly of some significance, is between executed and executory trusts. An executory trust is one which calls for the execution of some further instrument for the purpose of defining the beneficial interests exactly. For example, at one time marriage articles often provided that certain property belonging to one of the parties should be settled upon them and their children. The property was at once subject to a valid trust, but until the settlement was duly executed the trust was executory. The importance of the distinction between executed and executory trusts lies in the more liberal manner in which executory trusts are construed for some purposes: see, *e.g. ante*, para. 9–030; and see Snell, *Equity*, 119.

a settlor covenants with trustees to transfer to them property which he may acquire in the future.

(b) Completely constituted trusts. A trust may be completely constituted in **10–036** one of two circumstances.[18]

(i) Where the trust property is vested in the trustees upon the required trusts.

(ii) Where "a present irrevocable declaration of trust" is made by the settlor.[19] It is not essential that the settlor should use the words "I declare myself a trustee", but he must do something equivalent to this. Thus, where a man cohabiting with a woman authorised her to draw on his bank account and said repeatedly "the money is as much yours as mine", a declaration of trust was found as to a half share of the money.[20]

Although words of direct gift have occasionally been construed as declarations of trust,[21] it is now generally regarded as settled that an imperfect attempt to transfer property to a volunteer[22] (a person who gives no valuable consideration) or to trustees for a volunteer[23] will not be construed as a declaration of trust. Nor will the court compel the settlor to perfect his attempted transfer in proceedings brought by the volunteer, for "there is no equity in this court to perfect an imperfect gift".[24] Thus if A owns leasehold property and, wishing to give it to E, endorses on the lease "This deed and all thereto belonging I give to E from this time forth", neither this endorsement nor the delivery of the lease to E's mother on his behalf (E being an infant) will give E any beneficial interest in the lease. The legal term of years has not been vested in E or his mother, because a deed is required for this,[25] and A's words will not be construed as a declaration of trust.[26]

(c) Volunteers. The importance of the distinction between a completely and **10–037** incompletely constituted trust lies in the fact that if a trust is completely constituted, it can be enforced by the beneficiaries even if they are volunteers.[27] By contrast, if the trust is incompletely constituted, it will be enforced

---

[18] *Milroy v. Lord* (1862) 4 De G.F. & J. 264 at 274; *Richards v. Delbridge* (1874) L.R. 18 Eq. 11 at 14.

[19] *Re Cozens* [1913] 2 Ch. 478 at 486. There is no power of revocation unless it is expressly reserved: *Re Bowden* [1936] Ch. 71.

[20] *Paul v. Constance* [1977] 1 W.L.R. 527. See too *Vandenberg v. Palmer* (1858) 4 K. & J. 204.

[21] See, *e.g. Richardson v. Richardson* (1867) L.R. 3 Eq. 686; and see *Bowman v. Secular Society Ltd* [1917] A.C. 406 at 436, 437.

[22] *Jones v. Lock* (1865) 1 Ch. App. 25; *Re Swinburne* [1926] Ch. 38.

[23] *Jeffreys v. Jeffreys* (1841) Cr. & Ph. 138; *cf. Re Wale* [1956] 1 W.L.R. 1346.

[24] *Milroy v. Lord* (1862) 4 De G.F. & J. 264 at 274, *per* Turner L.J.

[25] *Post*, para. 14–034.

[26] *Richards v. Delbridge* (1874) L.R. 18 Eq. 11.

[27] *Paul v. Paul* (1882) 20 Ch.D. 742.

at the suit of beneficiaries who gave valuable consideration[28] (including those regarded as "within the marriage consideration" under a marriage settlement[29]) but cannot be enforced by volunteers.[30] The difference may be compared with the familiar distinction between grants and contracts at common law. A grant by deed at once vests the property in the grantee, whether or not he gave consideration for it. A contract to make a grant in the future will be enforceable only if supported by valuable consideration. It is therefore in the context of an incompletely constituted trust that the maxim "equity will not assist a volunteer" is applicable. Completely constituted trusts are, of course, enforceable at the suit of volunteer beneficiaries.

In the context of covenants to settle property, the distinction between completely and incompletely constituted trusts is likely to disappear if the Contracts (Rights of Third Parties) Bill, presently before Parliament, is enacted.[31] This will enable a person who is not a party to a contract to enforce it if there is an express term to that effect, or if the contract purports to confer a benefit on him.[32]

Section 2. Formalities Required for the Creation of a Trust

A. Pure Personalty

10–038　An enforceable trust of pure personalty can be validly created by word of mouth, whether the owner is declaring himself a trustee of the property or is transferring it to a third party on trust for the beneficiaries.[33]

B. Land

10–039　**1. The general rule: trusts of land must be evidenced in writing.** Before 1677 a trust of land could be created orally. Thereafter, first by the Statute of Frauds 1677,[34] and after 1925 by the Law of Property Act 1925,[35] a "declaration of trust respecting any land or any interest therein must be manifested and proved by some writing signed by some person who is able to declare such

---

[28] *Pullan v. Koe* [1913] 1 Ch. 9. If they do so, other beneficiaries who are volunteers may also enforce it. *Davenport v. Bishopp* (1843) 2 Y. & C.C.C. 451; (1846) 1 Ph. 698.

[29] *Ante,* para. 5–008.

[30] *Re Plumptre's Marriage Settlement* [1910] 1 Ch. 609; *Re Pryce* [1917] 1 Ch. 234. But see (1975) 91 L.Q.R. 236 (J. L. Barton) and (1976) 92 L.Q.R. 236 (R. P. Meagher and J. R. F. Lehane), criticising *Re Pryce* and decisions following it on the ground that there may be a completely constituted trust of the benefit of the covenant. For the intention necessary to create a trust of the benefit of a covenant, see (1982) 98 L.Q.R. 17 (J. D. Feltham).

[31] The Bill will implement (with some modifications) the recommendations of the Law Commission: see (1996) Law Com. No. 242.

[32] The contract will not be enforceable by the third party, even if it is made for his benefit, if on a proper construction of the contract it appears that the parties did not intend it to be enforceable by him.

[33] *e.g. Harris v. Truman* (1881) 7 Q.B.D. 340 at 356.

[34] ss.7, 8.

[35] s.53(1)(b), (2).

trust or by his will".[36] The chief points to note on this provision are as follows.

(a) "Any land". This includes leaseholds.[37]

10–040

(b) Evidenced. It is settled that the statutory words "manifested and proved" merely require that the trust should be evidenced by writing.[38] The declaration need not be *made* in writing.[39] It suffices if an oral declaration is supported by some signed acknowledgement or declaration[40] in existence when the action is begun,[41] such as a letter[42] or a recital in a deed,[43] even if this was made some time after the trust was declared.[44] The writing must show not only that there is a trust but also what its terms are.[45]

10–041

A trust will never be void for lack of written evidence, but merely unenforceable. It follows that where A transfers property to B who orally agrees to hold it on trust for C, C cannot enforce the trust. However, the trust is not void, and B will not therefore hold it on a resulting trust for A.[46] B will take the property beneficially (because the trust cannot be enforced against him) unless (as would generally be the case in such circumstances) he is estopped from relying on the lack of writing because it would be fraud for him to do so.[47]

(c) "Some person who is able to declare such trust". This means the owner of the beneficial interest, so that if a trust is declared of an equitable interest under an existing trust, the writing must be signed by the beneficiary. The signatures of the trustees are not sufficient.[48]

10–042

(d) "Or by his will". These words allow even an informal will (if valid as such[49]) to suffice.

10–043

2. Exceptions to the general rule. To these requirements there are two important exceptions.

---

[36] Most wills are required to be in writing, but some may be oral: see *post*, para. 11–038.

[37] See *Forster v. Hale* (1798) 3 Ves. 696; affirmed 5 Ves. 308.

[38] This is an exception to the general rule that writing is required for the creation or disposition of an interest in land: L.P.A. 1925, s.53(1)(a).

[39] *Randall v. Morgan* (1805) 12 Ves. 67 at 74.

[40] See *Ambrose v. Ambrose* (1717) 1 P.Wms. 321.

[41] See *Forster v. Hale, supra.*

[42] *Morton v. Tewart* (1842) 2 Y. & C.C.C. 67; *Childers v. Childers* (1857) 1 De G. & J. 482.

[43] See *Deg v. Deg* (1727) 2 P.Wms. 412; and see *Re Holland* [1902] 2 Ch. 360.

[44] *Rochefoucauld v. Boustead* [1897] 1 Ch. 196 at 206; and see *Barkworth v. Young* (1856) 4 Drew. 1.

[45] *Smith v. Matthews* (1861) 19 Beav. 330.

[46] The contrary is suggested in *Hodgson v. Marks* [1971] Ch. 892 at 933. However that case is best explained as one where it would have been fraudulent for B to rely on L.P.A. 1925, s.53(1)(b): see *ibid.* at 908, 909.

[47] *Post*, para. 10–045.

[48] *Tierney v. Wood* (1854) 19 Beav. 330; *Kronheim v. Johnson* (1877) 7 Ch.D. 60.

[49] See *post*, para. 11–038.

10–044   *(a) Resulting, implied or constructive trusts.* They do not affect the creation or operation of resulting, implied or constructive trusts.[50] Thus, for example, if land is conveyed to A in circumstances where A and B have contributed to the purchase price, B will not be precluded from enforcing the trust in his favour because of the lack of written evidence of it.

10–045   *(b) Where it would be fraud for the trustee to rely on the absence of writing.* The court will not permit a statute to be used as an engine of fraud.[51] "It is a fraud on the part of a person to whom land is conveyed, to deny the trust and claim the land himself. Consequently, notwithstanding the statute, it is competent for a person claiming land conveyed to another to prove by parol evidence that it was so conveyed upon trust for the claimant, and that the grantee, knowing the facts, is denying the trust and relying upon the form of conveyance and the statute, in order to keep the land himself."[52]

It is on this principle that secret trusts are enforced.[53] If a testator informs X of his intention to leave property to X to be held on trust for Y, and X acquiesces, whether expressly or by silence, this trust will be enforced even though it is not contained in the will or evidenced by writing.[54] This applies whether the trust is—

    (i) half secret, *i.e.* where the will discloses that the property is held upon trust without disclosing the beneficiary (*e.g.* "to X upon trusts which I have already communicated to him")[55]; or

    (ii) fully secret, *i.e.* where the gift is apparently beneficial (*e.g.* "to X absolutely").[56]

However, in the case of fully secret trusts it suffices if the trusts are communicated at any time before the testator's death.[57] In relation to half secret trusts, there is some rather unsatisfactory authority for saying that the trusts must

---

[50] L.P.A. 1925, s.53(2) (replacing Statute of Frauds 1677, s.8).

[51] *Stickland v. Arlidge* (1804) 9 Ves. 516; *Lincoln v. Wright* (1859) 4 De G. & J. 16; *Re Duke of Marlborough* [1894] 2 Ch. 133; *McGillycuddy of the Reeks v. Joy* [1959] I.R. 189; *Gilmurray v. Corr* [1978] N.I. 99; *cf. Hodgson v. Marks, supra*, at 933. The ambit of this doctrine is uncertain: compare [1984] C.L.J. 306; [1988] Conv. 267 (T. G. Youdan); with [1987] Conv. 246 (J. D. Feltham).

[52] *Rochefoucauld v. Boustead* [1897] 1 Ch. 196 at 206, *per* Lindley L.J.; and see *Haigh v. Kaye* (1872) 7 Ch.App. 469 at 474; *Du Boulay v. Raggett* (1988) 58 P. & C.R. 138 at 150.

[53] See Snell, *Equity*, 108 *et seq.*; *Drakeford v. Wilks* (1747) 3 Atk. 539.

[54] *Jones v. Badley* (1868) 3 Ch.App. 262; *Re Maddock* [1902] 2 Ch. 220; *Re Falkiner* [1924] 1 Ch. 88.

[55] *Blackwell v. Blackwell* [1929] A.C. 318; *Re Colin Cooper* [1939] Ch. 811.

[56] *Re Boyes* (1884) 26 Ch.D. 531. As to the position where only one of several beneficiaries is told of the trust, see *Re Stead* [1900] 1 Ch. 237 at 241, on which see (1972) 88 L.Q.R. 225 (B. Perrins).

[57] *Moss v. Cooper* (1861) 1 J. & H. 352. The trust is destroyed if the trustee predeceases the testator (*Re Maddock* [1902] 2 Ch. 220 at 231) but not if the beneficiary does so: *Re Gardner (No. 2)* [1923] 2 Ch. 230 (*sed quaere*: it is not apparent how a trust can be constituted in favour of a dead person: *cf.*; para. 10–010).

have been declared to and agreed by X before or at the time of making the will,[58] and that the will must show this to be the case.[59]

Section 3. Formalities Required for the Transfer of an Interest under a Trust

1. General rule: dispositions must be made in writing. By the Law of Property Act 1925, "a disposition of an equitable interest or trust subsisting at the time of the disposition, must be in writing signed by the person disposing of the same, or by his agent thereunto lawfully authorised in writing or by will".[60] This provision differs significantly from the Statute of Frauds 1677,[61] from which it derives.[62] The Statute of Frauds applied only to "grants and assignments" of equitable interests, whereas the present provision is broader and applies to any "disposition".[63] Furthermore, the requirements of the Law of Property Act 1925 do not affect the creation or operation of resulting, implied or constructive trusts.[64] There was no such qualification in the Statute of Frauds.[65] The following points should be noted.

10–046

(a) "Disposition". "Disposition" is given a very wide meaning.[66] It includes oral instructions given by a beneficiary to a bare trustee for him to hold the property on trust for other persons,[67] but not instructions to the trustee to transfer both the legal and equitable interests together to others.[68]

10–047

(b) "In writing". An oral disposition supported by evidence of it is not enough. Unlike the rule for the creation of trusts,[69] the rule here requires the disposition itself to be written,[70] and is thus not a mere rule of evidence.[71]

10–048

---

[58] *Johnson v. Ball* (1851) 5 De G. & Sm. 85; *Blackwell v. Blackwell* [1929] A.C. 318 at 339; *Re Colin Cooper* [1939] Ch. 811.

[59] *Re Keen* [1937] Ch. 236.

[60] s.53(1)(c). See [1979] Conv. 17 (G. Battersby); (1984) 47 M.L.R. 385 (B. Green).

[61] s.9. Previously an oral assignment was valid.

[62] The wording was changed by the Law of Property (Amendment) Act 1924, Sched. 3, Pt II, para. 15. The changes may not have been intended: see J. S. Anderson, *Lawyers and the Making of English Land Law 1832–1940*, p. 311.

[63] *Grey v. I.RC.* [1960] A.C. 1.

[64] s.53(2), *ante*, para. 10–044.

[65] s.8 of that Act (the nearest equivalent to L.P.A. 1925, s.53(2)) qualified s.7, but not s.9.

[66] "The wide meaning that it would seem to have in normal everyday usage": *Grey v. I.R.C.* [1958] Ch. 690 at 722, *per* Ormerod L.J. The broad definition of "disposition" found in L.P.A. 1925, s.205(1)(ii) has not always been applied in cases on s.53(1)(c): see *Re Paradise Motor Co. Ltd* [1968] 1 W.L.R. 1125. *cf. Grey v. I.R.C., supra*, at 719.

[67] *Grey v. I.R.C.* [1960] A.C. 1; see (1960) 76 L.Q.R. 197 (R.E.M.).

[68] *Vandervell v. I.R.C.* [1967] 2 A.C. 291.

[69] *Ante*, para. 10–041.

[70] See *Re Tyler* [1967] 1 W.L.R. 1269.

[71] There is an obvious parallel with the requirement that a legal estate can only be transferred by deed. It means that where A makes a disposition of his equitable interest to B, B can prove his title to that interest to the trustees. This may be important because of the rule in *Dearle v. Hall* (1828) 3 Russ. 1; *post*, para. 19–208.

10–049   *(c) "Signed by the person disposing of the same or by his agent thereunto lawfully authorised in writing"*. The disposition must be made by or on behalf of the person having the equitable interest. If a person is divested of his equitable interest through the exercise of a power, that exercise does not fall within the formal requirements of the Law of Property Act 1925 and need not be made in writing.[72]

The fact that a disposition may be made by an agent should be contrasted with—

> (i) the rule for the creation of a trust of land, where the signature of an agent is not enough[73]; and

> (ii) the rule for contracts for the disposition of land, where the signature of an agent suffices even if his authority was given only by word of mouth.[74]

10–050   *(d) The rule applies to pure personalty as well as land.* Although a trust of pure personalty is enforceable even if it is not evidenced in writing,[75] once the trust has been created, a disposition of any interest under it is void unless it is in writing.[76]

10–051   **2. Exception: resulting, implied or constructive trusts.** As mentioned above,[77] the requirement that a disposition of an equitable interest must be made in writing does not apply where that disposition is brought about through the creation or operation of a resulting, implied or constructive trust.[78] The reason for this exception is not apparent and it has led to curious results. It has been held that a specifically enforceable contract to transfer an equitable interest in circumstances where the transferee has furnished the consideration creates a constructive trust in favour of the transferee. This vests the equitable interest in him, without the need for writing.[79] It is not clear why the need for a written disposition of an equitable interest should be obviated simply because the agreement to make it is specifically enforceable and the purchaser has paid the price or met his reciprocal obligations.

---

[72] See *Re Vandervell's Trusts (No. 2)* [1974] Ch. 269, where A, a bare trustee holding on trust for B, had power to declare trusts in favour of C and was held to have done. Although this is probably the most plausible explanation of this difficult case, it may be doubted whether on the facts A's conduct did amount to a declaration of new trusts: see (1975) 38 M.L.R. 557 (J. W. Harris).

[73] *Ante*, para. 10–042.

[74] *Post*, para. 12–041.

[75] *Ante*, para. 10–038.

[76] See *Oughtred v. I.R.C.* [1960] A.C. 206, and the notes of the draftsman in Wolst. & C., 12th ed., i, 321. If L.P.A. 1925, s.53(1)(c) were confined to dispositions of equitable interests in land it would be otiose: see s.53(1)(a).

[77] *Ante*, para. 10–046.

[78] L.P.A. 1925, s.53(2).

[79] *Neville v. Wilson* [1997] Ch. 144; [1996] C.L.J. 436 (R. Nolan); [1996] Conv. 368 (M. P. Thompson).

Part 2

TRUSTEES

Section 1. Appointment of Trustees

A. *Original Appointment*

1. Appointment. Trustees are usually appointed by the settlor when creat- **10–052**
ing the trust. If he neither makes an appointment nor makes any provision for
one, the court may appoint trustees.[80] Once the trust has been created, the
settlor has no power to make an appointment unless he has reserved such a
power. A person appointed trustee need not accept the trust[81] even if he had
agreed to do so before it was created,[82] provided he disclaims the trust before
he has accepted it either expressly or by acting as trustee.[83] A disclaimer is
void if it relates only to part of the trusts.[84] It should preferably be express but
it may be inferred from conduct.[85] Although the presumption is in favour of
acceptance, a person appointed a trustee who is completely inactive in relation
to the trust for a long period (*e.g.* for more than 25 years) may be held thereby
to have disclaimed the trust.[86] Disclaimer operates retrospectively to divest
the person appointed both of his office and the trust property.[87]

2. Maximum number. No more than four trustees of settled land or **10–053**
(subject to one important exception) land held on a trust of land can be
appointed, whether the title is unregistered or registered.[88] If more than four
are named as trustees, the first four named who are able and willing to act
become trustees to the exclusion of the others.[89] These provisions apply only
to private trusts of land.[90] In general there is no limit to the number of trustees
of either—

    (i) land held on trust for charitable, ecclesiastical or public pur-
        poses[91]; or

    (ii) pure personalty.[92]

---

[80] *e.g. Re Smirthwaite* (1871) L.R. 11 Eq. 251.
[81] *Robinson v. Pett* (1734) 3 P.Wms. 249 at 251.
[82] See *Doyle v. Blake* (1804) 2 Sch. & Lef. 231 at 239 (executor).
[83] *Conyngham v. Conyngham* (1750) 1 Ves.Sen. 522; *Noble v. Meymott* (1851) 14 Beav. 471.
[84] *Re Lord and Fullerton's Contract* [1896] 1 Ch. 228.
[85] *Stacey v. Elph* (1833) 1 My. & K. 195. This is so even for freehold land: *Re Gordon* (1877) 6
Ch.D. 531 and *Re Birchall* (1889) 40 Ch.D. 436, ignoring doubts expressed in *Re Ellison's
Trusts* (1856) 2 Jur. (N.S.) 62.
[86] *Jago v. Jago* (1893) 68 L.T. 654; *Re Clout and Frewer's Contract* [1924] 2 Ch. 230.
[87] *Peppercorn v. Wayman* (1852) 2 De G. & Sm. 230; *Re Martinez' Trusts* (1870) 22 L.T. 403.
[88] T.A. 1925, s.34(2) (as amended by T.L.A.T.A. 1996, s.25(1), Sched. 3, para. 3); L.R.A. 1925,
s.95 (as amended by T.L.A.T.A. 1996, s.25(1), Sched. 3, para. 5); *ante*, paras 8–107, 9–084.
[89] T.A. 1925, s.34(2) (as amended by T.L.A.T.A. 1996, s.25(1), Sched. 3, para. 3).
[90] *ibid.*, s.34(3).
[91] *ibid.*
[92] See Lewin 163.

10–054   **3. Minimum number.** There is no minimum number of trustees even in the case of land.[93] However, whether the land is settled or held on a trust of land, then notwithstanding any contrary provision, a sole trustee cannot give a valid receipt for capital money unless that trustee is a trust corporation.[94] This restriction, however, does not affect the right of a sole personal representative acting as such to give valid receipts for purchase-money,[95] *e.g.* where a sole administrator sells under the trust which is imposed on all the property of an intestate.[96]

B. Replacement

10–055   Even if there are properly appointed trustees when the trust is created, it may later become necessary to appoint new trustees, *e.g.* owing to the death of trustees. The events upon which new trustees can be appointed may be specified in the trust instrument. This is not usual however, and reliance is normally placed on certain statutory provisions. The principal provisions are found in the Trustee Act 1925, but these have been supplemented by Part II of the Trusts of Land and Appointment of Trustees Act 1996. These provisions of the 1996 Act owe little to the Law Commission from whose report the remainder of the Act derives, but were for the most part introduced by amendment during the passage of the legislation through Parliament.[97] Part II of the 1996 Act applies to all trusts and not merely to trusts of land.[98]

1. Replacement under the Trustee Act 1925

10–056   *(a) Power to appoint.* By the Trustee Act 1925,[99] a new trustee or trustees[1] may be appointed if a trustee—

> (i) is dead (and this includes a person nominated trustee by a will who predeceases the testator[2]); or
>
> (ii) remains outside the United Kingdom for a continuous[3] period exceeding 12 months; or

---

[93] See *Re Myhill* [1928] Ch. 100; *Re Wight & Best's Brewery Co. Ltd's Contract* [1929] W.N. 11; L.P.A. 1925, s.27(2) (as substituted by L.P.(Am.)A. 1926, s.7; Sched; and amended by T.L.A.T.A. 1996, s.25(1), Sched. 3, para. 4).

[94] S.L.A. 1925, s.18(1); L.P.A. 1925, s.27(2) (as amended); *ante*, paras 8–162, 8–166.

[95] *ibid.*

[96] By A.E.A. 1925, s.33 (as amended by T.L.A.T.A. 1925, s.5(1), Sched. 2, para. 5); *post*, para. 11–088.

[97] Mainly at the behest of The Law Society.

[98] *cf.* (1989) Law Com. No. 181, paras 9.1, 9.2; draft Bill, cl. 18 (under which T.A. 1925, s.36 would have been amended, rather than having free-standing provisions as in T.L.A.T.A. 1996, Pt II).

[99] s.36(1).

[1] Including Settled Land Act trustees: see *Re Dark* [1954] Ch. 291.

[2] T.A. 1925, s.36(8).

[3] See *Re Walker* [1901] 1 Ch. 259 (continuity broken by return for a week).

(iii) desires to be discharged from all or any of his trusts or powers; or

(iv) refuses to act (*e.g.* if he disclaims[4]); or

(v) is unfit to act (*e.g.* if he is bankrupt[5]); or

(vi) is incapable of acting, as by mental disorder,[6] or age and infirmity,[7] or, in the case of a corporation, by dissolution[8]; or

(vii) is a minor[9]; or

(viii) is removed under a power in the trust instrument.[10]

This provision applies notwithstanding any express provision specifying when new trustees may be appointed[11] unless a contrary intention is shown.[12]

(b) Method of appointment. The appointment must be made in writing[13] and **10–057**
must be made—

(i) by the person or persons[14] nominated by the trust instrument for the purpose of appointing trustees, *i.e.* nominated generally[15] and not merely in certain stated events[16]; in default of there being any such person able and willing to act (as where the person nominated cannot be found,[17] or disagrees[18]), the appointment may be made,

(ii) by the "surviving or continuing trustees or trustee", a term which includes a trustee who is retiring or refuses to act[19] but not a trustee removed against his will[20]; or if there is no such trustee,

---

[4] *Re Birchall* (1889) 40 Ch.D. 436.
[5] *Re Roche* (1842) 2 Dr. & War. 287 at 289; *Re Hopkins* (1881) 19 Ch.D. 61 at 63.
[6] *Re East* (1873) 8 Ch.App. 735; *Re Blake* [1887] W.N. 173.
[7] *Re Lemann's Trusts* (1883) 22 Ch.D. 633.
[8] T.A. 1925, s.36(3).
[9] An implied, resulting or constructive trust may make a minor a trustee, though he cannot be *appointed* one: *post*, para. 10–058.
[10] T.A. 1925, s.36(2).
[11] See *Re Wheeler and De Rochow* [1896] 1 Ch. 315.
[12] T.A. 1925, s.69(2).
[13] But the last surviving trustee cannot appoint by his will: *Re Parker's Trusts* [1894] Ch. 1.
[14] In the absence of a contrary intention, the power does not pass to the survivor of two or more nominees, unless the property is vested in them (see *Re Bacon* [1907] 1 Ch. 475; *Re Harding* [1923] 1 Ch. 183; Farwell, *Powers*, 514, 515) or they are trustees and hold the power as such: T.A. 1925, s.18(1); see *Re Smith* [1904] 1 Ch. 139.
[15] *Re Walker & Hughes' Contract* (1883) 24 Ch.D. 698.
[16] *Re Wheeler and De Rochow* [1896] 1 Ch. 315; *Re Sichel's Settlements* [1916] 1 Ch. 358.
[17] *Cradock v. Witham* [1895] W.N. 75.
[18] *Re Sheppard's S.T.* [1953] Ch. 59.
[19] T.A. 1925, s.36(8).
[20] *Re Stoneham S.T.* [1953] Ch. 59.

(iii) by the personal representatives of the last remaining (or sole[21]) trustee[22]; or, finally, if there is no such person,[23] or it is doubtful,[24]

(iv) by the court.[25]

10–058   *(c) Who may be appointed.* It is expressly provided that the person making the appointment may appoint himself.[26] Even if he appoints a person whom the court would not normally[27] appoint, such as a beneficiary,[28] or the solicitor to the trustees or beneficiaries,[29] the appointment will not as a result be rendered invalid. However, the appointment of a minor as a trustee, whether of realty or personalty, is void.[30]

2. Replacement under the Trusts of Land and Appointment of Trustees Act 1996

10–059   *(a) Power to appoint.* The Trusts of Land and Appointment of Trustees Act 1996 confers two distinct but limited powers to appoint trustees as a replacement for all or some of the existing trustees. What connects them, is that they are exercisable by the beneficiaries under the trust, but only in circumstances in which those beneficiaries could have terminated the trust. The powers may be excluded by a provision to that effect in the disposition creating the trust.[31]

10–060   (1) RETIREMENT AND REPLACEMENT AT THE BEHEST OF THE BENEFICIARIES. The first power is exercisable only where two conditions are satisfied.

(i) There is no person nominated for the purpose of appointing new trustees by the instrument, if any, creating the trust.[32] Where the trust instrument conferred a power of appointment on X who is now dead, there will be no person nominated and the condition will

---

[21] *Re Shafto's Trusts* (1885) 29 Ch.D. 247; but see *Nicholson v. Field* [1893] 2 Ch. 511.
[22] T.A. 1925, s.36(1).
[23] See *Re Higginbottom* [1892] 3 Ch. 132.
[24] See *Re May's W.T.* [1941] Ch. 109 (trustee in enemy territory).
[25] T.A. 1925, s.41. For the principles guiding the court, see *Re Tempest* (1866) 1 Ch.App. 485; *Re Northcliffe's Settlements* [1937] 3 All E.R. 804.
[26] T.A. 1925, s.36(1); contrast s.36(6); *post*, para. 10–065.
[27] For exceptional cases, see, *e.g. Re Clissold* (1864) 10 L.T. 642; *Re Marquis of Ailesbury and Lord Iveagh* [1893] 2 Ch. 345.
[28] *Forster v. Abraham* (1874) L.R. 17 Eq. 351 (tenant for life); *cf. ante*, para. 8–066.
[29] *Re Coode* (1913) 108 L.T. 94.
[30] L.P.A. 1925, s.20.
[31] T.L.A.T.A. 1996, s.21(5). For trusts in existence when the Act came into force, there is a power for the settlor (or if more than one, such of the settlors as are alive and of full capacity) to execute a deed (which is irrevocable) providing that the powers shall not apply: *ibid.*, s.21(6), (7).
[32] T.L.A.T.A. 1996, s.19(1)(a). A settlor or testator who wishes to exclude the power may readily do so by nominating the persons who may appoint new trustees.

be satisfied. It will be otherwise, however, if X is alive but lacks capacity.[33]

(ii) The beneficiaries under the trust are of full age and capacity and (taken together) are absolutely entitled to the property subject to the trust.[34] As such, they are able to determine the trust and to require the trustees to transfer the trust property to them or at their direction.[35]

The beneficiaries may then do either or both of the following—

(i) direct one or more of the trustees to retire[36];

(ii) direct the trustee or trustees for the time being (or if there are none, the personal representatives of the last person who was a trustee) to appoint by writing to be trustee or trustees the person or persons specified.[37]

In the latter case, the Act, by necessary implication, confers on the person or persons directed a power to appoint new trustees. In the limited circumstances in which it is exercisable, the effect of this statutory power is to reverse the rule that beneficiaries cannot direct trustees as to the exercise of their power to appoint new trustees.[38]

(2) REPLACEMENT OF AN INCAPABLE TRUSTEE. The second power may be **10–061** exercised where—

(i) a trustee is incapable by reason of mental disorder of exercising his functions as trustee;

(ii) there is no person who is both entitled to appoint a new trustee under the provisions of the Trustee Act 1925 explained above,[39] and is willing and able to do so; and

(iii) the beneficiaries under the trust are of full age and capacity and (taken together) are absolutely entitled to the property subject to the trust.[40]

---

[33] The suggestion made in C. Whitehouse and N. Hassall, *The Trusts of Land and Appointment of Trustees Act 1996*, para. 2.143, that the condition is satisfied if X lacks capacity is not justified by the wording of T.L.A.T.A. 1996, s.19(1)(a). *cf. ibid.*, s.20(1)(b); *infra.*
[34] *ibid.*, s.19(1)(b).
[35] Under the rule in *Saunders v. Vautier* (1841) 4 Beav. 115; *ante*, para. 7–169.
[36] Certain pre-conditions must be met before the trustee is obliged to retire. In particular, reasonable arrangements must be made for the protection of any rights he may have in connection with the trust (*e.g.* a right to be reimbursed for expenditure) and there must be at least two trustees or a trust corporation to perform the trust: T.L.A.T.A. 1996, s.19(3).
[37] *ibid.*, s.19(2).
[38] See *Re Brockbank* [1948] Ch. 206.
[39] s.36; *ante*, para. 10–056.
[40] T.L.A.T.A. 1996, s.20(1).

Where these circumstances occur, the beneficiaries may give a written direction to the person who can act on behalf of the incapable trustee[41] to appoint by writing the persons or persons specified in the direction to be the new trustee or trustees.[42] Once again, the Act impliedly confers on the person directed a power to appoint a new trustee.

10–062 *(b) Method of appointment.* In exercising the power, the beneficiaries may either give a joint direction, or each give a separate direction which specifies the appointment and retirement of the same person or persons.[43] Both the direction and the subsequent appointment must be made in writing,[44] though in practice a deed is likely to be employed for the latter.[45]

10–063 *(c) Who may be appointed.* There are no restrictions on who may be appointed as trustees, so that the beneficiaries may appoint one or more of their own number. There is, however, a general requirement that where there is a trust both of land and of the proceeds of sale of land, the same persons must be appointed as trustees of both, even though the appointments are required to be made by separate instruments.[46] This requirement also applies to the powers conferred by the 1996 Act.[47]

10–064 **3. Number.** Where a single trustee was originally appointed, the appointment of a single trustee in his place is valid.[48] In the case of settled land or land held on a trust of land, a sole trustee (not being a trust corporation) cannot be appointed under the statutory power if, after his appointment, he would be unable to give receipts for capital money,[49] as would be the case if there were no other trustee. There is never any obligation to appoint more than two trustees even if originally more than two were appointed.[50] The appointment may increase the number of trustees, provided that, in the case of settled land or land held on a trust of land, the number is not increased above four.[51] A separate set of trustees may be appointed for any part of the trust property held on distinct trusts.[52] The restrictions on the numbers of trustees apply whether

---

[41] Namely, a receiver, a person acting under a registered enduring power of attorney (*post*, para. 20–026), or a person authorised for the purpose by the authority having jurisdiction under Pt VII of the Mental Health Act 1983 (*post*, para. 20–024): T.L.A.T.A. 1996, s.20(2).

[42] *ibid.*, s.20(2).

[43] *ibid.*, s.21(1), (2).

[44] *ibid.*, ss. 19(2), 20(2).

[45] See T.A. 1925, s.40; *post*, para. 10–070.

[46] T.A. 1925, s.35(1) (as substituted by T.L.A.T.A. 1996, s.25(1); Sched. 3, para. 3); L.P.A. 1925, s.24 (as substituted by T.L.A.T.A. 1996, s.25(1); Sched. 3, para. 4).

[47] T.L.A.T.A. 1996, s.21(4).

[48] T.A. 1925, s.37(1)(c).

[49] *ibid.*, s.37(2). Even before the enactment of this provision, it was well established that a sole surviving trustee who, on retiring, appointed one trustee to succeed him rather than two, committed a breach of trust: *Hulme v. Hulme* (1833) 2 My. & K. 682; *Barnes v. Addy* (1873) 28 L.T. 398 (argued but not clearly decided on appeal: see (1874) 9 Ch.App. 244 at 250, 253).

[50] T.A. 1925, s.37(1)(c) (as amended by T.L.A.T.A. 1996, s.25(1), Sched. 3, para. 3).

[51] T.A. 1925, s.37(1)(a).

[52] *ibid.*, s.37(1)(b).

appointment is made under the Trustee Act 1925 or the Trusts of Land and Appointment of Trustees Act 1996.[53]

C. Additional Trustees

Even though no occasion has arisen for the appointment of new trustees, if there are not more than three trustees, one or more additional trustees may be appointed, provided that the effect of the appointment is not to increase the number above four.[54] The appointment must be made by the same persons and in the same way as an appointment of new trustees,[55] except that there is no provision for an appointment by the personal representatives of the last remaining trustees, or for the appointor to appoint himself.[56]

10–065

Section 2. Retirement and Removal of Trustees

1. Retirement. A trustee may retire—

10–066

(i) if another trustee is appointed in his place[57];

(ii) if no new trustee is being appointed in his place, provided that after his discharge there will be left either two or more persons or a trust corporation to act in the trust.[58] The retirement is effected by a deed declaring the trustee's desire to retire. This is executed by the retiring trustee, the continuing trustees and the person entitled to appoint new trustees, all of whom must concur in the retirement[59];

(iii) if authorised to do so by an express power in the trust instrument[60];

(iv) with the consent of all the beneficiaries if they are all of full age and capacity and between them absolutely entitled to the trust property[61];

---

[53] T.L.A.T.A. 1996, s.19(5).

[54] T.A. 1925, s.36(6) (as amended by T.L.A.T.A. 1996, s.25(1); Sched. 3, para. 3). The limit is not confined to trusts of land.

[55] *ibid*. After 1999, it will be possible for a person acting under a registered power of attorney to appoint an additional trustee: see T.A. 1925, s.36(6A) (inserted by the Trustee Delegation Act 1999, s.8).

[56] *Re Powers S.T.* [1951] Ch. 1074. This is an accident of drafting: see (1952) 68 L.Q.R. 19 (R.E.M.).

[57] *Ante*, para. 10–056.

[58] T.A. 1925, s.39(1) (as amended by T.L.A.T.A. 1996, s.25(1); Sched. 3, para. 3).

[59] *ibid*.

[60] *e.g. Lord Camoys v. Best* (1854) 19 Beav. 414.

[61] *cf. Wilkinson v. Parry* (1828) 4 Russ. 272 at 276.

(v) with the leave of the court.[62] This method should be employed only in cases of difficulty,[63] for if the trustee applies to the court without good cause he may have to pay his own costs.[64]

10–067   **2. Removal.** A trustee may be removed—

    (i) under the statutory powers to appoint new trustees considered above[65];

    (ii) under any express power to do so contained in the trust instrument[66];

    (iii) under the court's inherent jurisdiction to remove a trustee where it is necessary for the safety of the trust property or the welfare of the beneficiaries. Examples include—

        (a) where the trustee has been inactive for a long period[67];

        (b) where his interests conflict with those of the beneficiaries[68]; or

        (c) where there has been friction with the beneficiaries on the mode of administering the trust.[69]

Section 3. Vesting of Trust Property

10–068   Some trustees have no property vested in them, as is normally the case with trustees of settled land.[70] In such cases, no question of the devolution of trust property arises. But where property is vested in trustees, questions of the transfer of the trust property arise on their death, retirement or removal, or on the appointment of new trustees.

A. *On Death*

10–069   Trustees are always made joint tenants or joint owners of the trust property, whether it is real or personal. The advantage of this is that on the death of one trustee the estate or interest vested in him passes to the surviving trustees by the doctrine of survivorship.[71] Where a sole surviving trustee dies, any estate

---

[62] *Forshaw v. Higginson* (1855) 20 Beav. 485; *Gardiner v. Downes* (1856) 22 Beav. 395.

[63] See *Re Stokes' Trusts* (1872) L.R. 13 Eq. 333; *Re Chetwynd's Settlement* [1902] 1 Ch. 692.

[64] *Howard v. Rhodes* (1837) 1 Keen 581; *Porter v. Watts* (1852) 21 L.J.Ch. 211.

[65] See T.A. 1925, s.36 (*ante*, para. 10–056); T.L.A.T.A. 1996, ss.19, 20 (*ante*, paras 10–060, 10–061).

[66] *e.g. London and County Banking Co. v. Goddard* [1897] 1 Ch. 642.

[67] *Reid v. Hadley* (1885) 2 T.L.R. 12.

[68] *Passingham v. Sherborn* (1849) 9 Beav. 424.

[69] *Letterstedt v. Broers* (1884) 9 App.Cas. 371.

[70] *Ante*, para. 8–108.

[71] *Ante*, para. 9–003. Powers given to the trustees jointly also pass to the survivors: T.A. 1925, s.18(1).

or interest held by him on trust vests in his personal representatives notwith-standing any provision in his will.[72] Until new trustees are appointed, the personal representatives may exercise any power or trust exercisable by the former trustee,[73] without being obliged to do so.[74]

B. On Appointment of New Trustees

1. Vesting declaration. On an appointment of new trustees, the trust property has to be vested in the new trustees jointly with any continuing trustees. By the Trustee Act 1925,[75] if an appointment of new trustees is made by deed, a declaration therein by the appointor that the property shall vest in the trustees ("a vesting declaration") is sufficient to vest the property in them. Such a vesting declaration is implied in the absence of an express provision to the contrary.[76] It should be noted that these provisions apply even if the trust property is not vested in the appointor. He has a statutory power to transfer what he has not got.[77] Thus where A and B are trustees and X has the power to appoint new trustees, if A dies and X appoints C a trustee in his place, the deed of appointment will vest the trust property in B and C jointly.

10–070

2. Exceptions. In certain cases, however, the trust property cannot be transferred by a vesting declaration, either express or implied. These cases are when the property consists of—

10–071

(a) the benefit of a mortgage over land to secure trust money[78];

(b) land held under a lease with a provision against assigning or dispos-ing of the land without consent, unless—

    (i) the requisite consent has been obtained, or

    (ii) the vesting declaration would not be a breach of covenant or give rise to a forfeiture[79];

(c) any share, stock or other property which is transferable only in books kept by a company or other body, or in a way directed by statute[80]; or

---

[72] A.E.A. 1925, s.1.
[73] T.A. 1925, s.18(2): see *Re Waidanis* [1908] 1 Ch. 123; (1977) 41 Conv. (N.S.) 432 (P. W. Smith). Two or more personal representatives of a sole trustee may give valid receipts for capital money: see Wolst. & C. iv. 21.
[74] See *Re Ridley* [1904] 2 Ch. 774; *Re Benett* [1906] 1 Ch. 216.
[75] T.A. 1925, s.40(1)(a).
[76] *ibid.*, s.40(1)(b). The danger that an express declaration might be defective in form is met by T.A. 1925, s.40(3).
[77] See L.P.A. 1925, s.9(1).
[78] T.A. 1925, s.40(4)(a). Land conveyed on trust to secure debentures or debenture stock will vest in the new trustee under T.A. s.40(1): s.40(4)(a).
[79] T.A. 1925, s.40(4)(b).
[80] *ibid.*, s.40(4)(c).

(d) registered land.

In these excepted cases, the trust property must be transferred by the method appropriate to the subject-matter, *e.g* in the case of shares, by a duly registered transfer. The reason for (c) is apparent when the normal mode of transfer of such property is considered; (a) is included to avoid bringing the trusts on to the title,[81] for otherwise when the borrower sought to repay the loan, he would have to investigate the trust documents to see that he was paying the right persons; and (b) is included to avoid accidental breaches of the terms of the lease.[82] Where the trust property consists of registered land, the new trustee must be registered as a proprietor of the land.[83]

The court has a wide jurisdiction to make vesting orders where this is desirable.[84]

C. On Retirement or Removal

10–072 Where a trustee retires or is discharged from a trust without a new trustee being appointed, and the transaction is effected by deed, the trust property can be divested from the former trustee and vested solely in the continuing trustees by means of a vesting declaration.[85] This applies only if the deed is executed by the retiring trustee, the continuing trustees and any person with power to appoint new trustees.[86] There are the same exceptions in the case of vesting declarations on the appointment of new trustees.[87]

This special provision is necessary since the right of survivorship operates only on death and not on retirement.

Section 4. Procedure in the Case of Settled Land and Trusts of Land

A. Where the Title is Unregistered

10–073   **1. One instrument.** Although it is undesirable, an express trust of land may be created by only one instrument. In this case, where a new trustee is appointed, the appointment may be made by a single document. This may be merely in writing, but it should be made by deed so that the legal estate may be vested in the new and continuing trustees by virtue of the Trustee Act 1925,[88] thus avoiding the necessity of a separate conveyance. In addition, a memorandum must be endorsed on or annexed to the instrument creating the

---

[81] Lewin 435.
[82] Wolst. & C. iv. 67.
[83] Ruoff & Roper, 32-09; *post*, para. 10–075.
[84] T.A. 1925, ss.44–56.
[85] *ibid.*, s.40(2)(a). s.40(2) has been amended by T.L.A.T.A. 1996, s.25(1), Sched. 3, para. 3.
[86] Such a vesting declaration is now implied: *ibid.*, s.40(2)(b).
[87] See above.
[88] s.40; *ante*, para. 10–070.

trust of land, stating the names of those who are the trustees after the appointment is made,[89] and not merely the names of the new trustees.

2. Two instruments. Normally, however, an express trust of land is created by two documents.[90] In this case and in the case of settled land, the procedure is more complicated. There must be[91]—   **10–074**

> (i) an instrument to go with the conveyance on a trust of land or the vesting instrument;
>
> (ii) an appointment to go with the trust instrument;
>
> (iii) an endorsement of the conveyance on a trust of land or on the vesting instrument stating the names of those who are the trustees after the appointment.

In the case of settled land, the first document must be a deed. However, it merely states who are the trustees. In the case of a trust of land, it may be merely in writing, but, as before, should be by deed in order to take advantage of section 40 of the Trustee Act 1925. In either case it effects the actual appointment of the persons named in it as trustees of land. A similar procedure applies if a trustee of settled land is discharged without a new trustee being appointed.[92] The second document, both for settled land and trusts of land, is an appointment which may be made either in writing or by deed.

B. Where the Title is Registered ·

1. Trusts of land. Because the trustees will be registered as proprietors of any registered land held upon a trust of land, any new trustee must also be so registered. This may be done in one of two ways.[93] First, the existing trustees as registered proprietors may execute a transfer in the usual form in favour of all the new trustees. In the alternative, they may submit the deed of appointment to the registrar. This is deemed to be a conveyance of the land,[94] to which the registrar must give effect by means of the proper entry on the register.[95] In practice, the first method is employed because it is simpler and cheaper.   **10–075**

2. Settled land. Where the title to settled land is registered, any new trustees of the settlement will be appointed by deed in the usual way. An   **10–076**

---

[89] T.A. 1925, s.35(3) (substituted by T.L.A.T.A. 1996, s.25(1); Sched. 3, para. 3).
[90] *Ante*, para. 8–133.
[91] T.A. 1925, s.35 (as amended by T.L.A.T.A. 1996, s.25(1); Sched. 3, para. 3); S.L.A. 1925, s.35(1); *cf. ante*, para. 8–107.
[92] S.L.A. 1925, s.35(1): there is no corresponding provision for trusts of land.
[93] Ruoff & Roper, 32–18.
[94] T.A. 1925, s.40(5). The persons making the declaration are deemed to be parties to the conveyance.
[95] L.R.A. 1925, s.47(1) (by which the provisions of the Trustee Act 1925 relating to the appointment and discharge of trustees are made applicable to registered land).

application is then made to modify the existing restriction on the register[96] by substituting the names of the new and continuing trustees.[97]

Part 3

POWERS

10–077 The word "power" is normally used in the sense of an authority given to a person to dispose of property which is not his.[98] The person giving the power is called the donor and the person to whom it is given the donee.

Section 1. Classification

Powers may be classified as follows.

10–078 **1. Common law powers.** A common law power is a power which enables a legal estate to be transferred by a person in whom it is not vested. A common example is a power of attorney, under which one person authorises another to do certain acts on his behalf, such as convey land.[99]

10–079 **2. Statutory powers.** A number of statutes have given powers to convey legal estates. For example, the Law of Property Act 1925 gives a mortgagee a power to convey a legal estate not vested in him.[1]

10–080 **3. Equitable powers.** Unlike the powers mentioned above, equitable powers enable the donee to transfer only an equitable interest. A common example is a power of appointment.[2]

The 1925 legislation increased the number of equitable powers. The Law of Property Act 1925[3] provides that "every power of appointment over, or power to convey or charge land or any interest therein, whether created by a statute or other instrument or implied by law, and whether created before or after the commencement of this Act (not being a power vested in a legal mortgagee or an estate owner in right of his estate and exercisable by him or by another person in his name and on his behalf), operates only in equity". It will be seen

---

[96] *Ante*, paras 6–092, 6–093.

[97] Ruoff & Roper, 31–12. For the form of application, see L.R.R. 1925, Sched. 2, Form 77. The application should be made by the life tenant, the previous trustees and the new and continuing trustees.

[98] See *Freme v. Clement* (1881) 18 Ch.D. 499 at 504; *Re Armstrong* (1886) 17 Q.B.D. 521 at 531. For modern texts on powers, see Geraint Thomas, *Powers*; Halsb. vol. 36, pp. 529–631.

[99] Sugden, *Powers*, 45. They are now regulated by the Powers of Attorney Act 1971. See *Walia v. Michael Naughton Ltd* [1985] 1 W.L.R. 1115. After 1999, the law will be changed in a number of respects when the Trustee Delegation Act 1999 is brought into force.

[1] s.101; *post*, para. 19–057.

[2] *Post*, para. 10–081.

[3] s.1(7).

that this rule contains some exceptions. Others appear elsewhere in the 1925 legislation. Thus the following may still operate at law, and not only in equity—

> (i) a legal mortgagee's power of sale, by which he can convey a legal estate vested in the mortgagor[4];
>
> (ii) a power of attorney, enabling one person to convey a legal estate vested in another[5];
>
> (iii) the power of Settled Land Act trustees, acting in the name of the tenant for life and on his behalf, to convey the legal estate vested in him on certain special occasions.[6]

Apart from cases such as these, a legal estate can be conveyed only by the person in whom it is vested.

Section 2. Powers of Appointment

A. Introduction

1. Classification. Statutory powers are more conveniently considered under their appropriate heads, but powers of appointment, which are powers given under some settlement or trust authorising the donee to make an appointment of some or all of the trust property, must be discussed here. Such powers are usually classified as general, special or hybrid. **10–081**

(a) General power. A general power imposes no restrictions upon the donee's choice, allowing him, without obtaining the concurrence of any other person,[7] to appoint to anyone, including himself.[8] Thus a gift— **10–082**

> "to X for life, remainder as he shall appoint"

gives X a life interest and a general power of appointment. A general power may be created not only in an *inter vivos* settlement but also by will.[9]

(b) Special power. A special power fetters the donee's choice by providing that he can appoint the property only among a limited class of persons, known **10–083**

---

[4] *Post*, para. 19–057. See also L.P.A. 1925, s.22(1) (as amended) (persons suffering from a mental disorder).

[5] See the exception (in brackets) to L.P.A. 1925, s.1(7), *supra*; *cf.* s.7(4). For details see the Powers of Attorney Act 1971.

[6] *Ante*, para. 8–095.

[7] *Re Churston S.E.* [1954] Ch. 334; *ante*, para. 7–102.

[8] Farwell, *Powers*, 8; *Re Penrose* [1933] Ch. 793.

[9] *Re Beatty* [1990] 1 W.L.R. 1503 (rejecting the contention that there was any rule against testamentary delegation of which a general power fell foul). See too *Re Abrahams' W.T.* [1969] 1 Ch. 463. *cf.* (1991) 107 L.Q.R. 211 (J. D. Davies).

as "objects" of the power, as where X is given a power to appoint among his children.

10–084   *(c) Hybrid power.* A power to appoint to anyone except a named person or group of persons is perhaps best regarded as forming a third category,[10] sometimes called a "hybrid"[11] or "intermediate"[12] power. However, if the dichotomy of general and special powers is adopted, such a power may be classified as special for the purposes of section 27 of the Wills Act 1837,[13] as it now clearly is for the purposes of the rule against perpetuities.[14]

10–085   **2. Default of appointment.** Provision is usually made for some person or persons to take in default of appointment. If this is not done, the grantor is entitled in default of appointment. The effect of an appointment is to divest the interest of those entitled in default of appointment to the extent of the appointment.[15] Where, however, it appears that the objects of the power are intended to take in any event, the power is not a mere power, but "a power in the nature of a trust" (or, more simply, a trust), under which the objects take vested interests in the property in equal shares,[16] subject to being divested by any appointment.[17] It is often very difficult to determine whether a power is intended to be in the nature of a trust.[18] However, an express gift in default of appointment is conclusive against it, whereas the absence of such a gift is some indication of a trust, though not conclusive.[19]

10–086   **3. Certainty of objects.** A power must be sufficiently certain. It is now settled that a power will be valid only if it is possible to say with certainty whether any given individual is or is not a member of the class of objects.[20] If a power is void for uncertainty of objects, the gift takes effect in favour of those who take in default of appointment.

B. Formalities for Exercise of Powers

10–087   **1. Formalities.** The general rule is that any condition prescribed for the execution of a power must be observed, otherwise the appointment will be

---

[10] See *Re Jones* [1945] Ch. 105; *Re Harvey* [1950] 1 All E.R. 491; (1948) 13 Conv. (N.S.) 20 (J. G. Fleming); (1950) 66 L.Q.R. 304 (R.E.M.). See the discussion in *Re Lawrence's W.T.* [1972] Ch. 418. If the excepted person does not and cannot exist when the power comes to be exercised, it is a general power: *Re Harvey, supra.*

[11] See, *e.g. Re Triffitt's Settlement* [1958] Ch. 852.

[12] See, *e.g. Re Manisty's Settlement* [1974] Ch. 17; *Re Hay's S.T.* [1982] 1 W.L.R. 202.

[13] *Post*, para. 11–078.

[14] *Ante*, para. 7–104.

[15] *Re Brookes' S.T.* [1939] Ch. 993 at 996, 997.

[16] *Wilson v. Duguid* (1883) 24 Ch.D. 244.

[17] *Robinson v. Smith* (1821) 6 Madd. 194 at 198; *Faulkner v. Lord Wynford* (1845) 15 L.J.Ch. 8; *cf. ante*, para. 7–006.

[18] Contrast *Burrough v. Philcox* (1840) 5 My. & Cr. 72 with *Re Weekes' Settlement* [1897] 1 Ch. 289.

[19] *Re Mills* [1930] 1 Ch. 654; *Re Perowne* [1951] Ch. 785.

[20] *Re Gulbenkian's Settlements* [1970] A.C. 508.

void.[21] It is immaterial how absurd or unreasonable the conditions are.[22] But this position has been modified by statute.

(a) Wills. By the Wills Act 1837,[23] an appointment by will is valid so far as concerns execution and attestation, if it is executed with the formalities required for wills (*i.e.* signed or acknowledged by the testator in the presence of two witnesses who then sign their names or acknowledge their signatures in the presence of the testator[24]), even if the instrument creating the power requires other formalities, such as 10 witnesses.[25]   **10–088**

(b) Deeds. By the Law of Property Act 1925,[26] an appointment by deed is valid as regards execution and attestation if it is signed[27] in the presence of, and attested by, two witnesses, even if the instrument creating the power requires other formalities.   **10–089**

2. Substance. Deeds and wills are thus on a similar footing in this respect. But it must be noticed that these provisions apply only to formalities concerning execution and attestation, such as a requirement that the document should be executed in a certain place in the presence of three witnesses.[28] There is nothing in these provisions to make it unnecessary to comply with other requirements (*e.g.* as to obtaining the consent of specified persons[29]), and an appointment not made in accordance with such requirements is void.[30] Whether the power is general, special or hybrid, an appointment must also (apart from statute[31]) sufficiently indicate an intention to exercise the power.[32]   **10–090**

3. Relief in equity. In one limited class of such cases equity will intervene and treat a defective appointment as valid. This will be done only if both the following conditions are satisfied.   **10–091**

> (i) The defect is merely formal and not one of substance. Thus if under a power to appoint by deed the donee appoints by will, equity will grant relief.[33] But if there is a power exercisable only by will, equity will not aid an appointment by deed, for the power

---

[21] Farwell, *Powers*, 147 *et seq.*
[22] *Rutland v. Doe d. Wythe* (1843) 10 Cl. & F. 419 at 425. For an example of stringent requirements, see *Hawkins v. Kemp* (1803) 3 East 410.
[23] s.10.
[24] *Post*, paras 11–015—11–020.
[25] As to the operation of a will in exercising a power, see *post*, para. 11–078.
[26] s.159.
[27] L.P.(M.P.) A. 1989, s.1(3), replacing L.P.A. 1925, s.73. *Ante*, paras 5–073, 5–074.
[28] See *Hawkin v. Kemp* (1803) 3 East 410.
[29] See *e.g. Hulton v. Simpson* (1716) 2 Vern. 722.
[30] See, *e.g. Cooper v. Martin* (1867) 3 Ch.App. 47 (appointment to be made before a specified child was 25).
[31] See *post*, para. 11–078.
[32] *Re Lawrence's W.T.* [1972] Ch. 418.
[33] *Tollet v. Tollet* (1728) 2 P. Wms. 489.

was not intended to be exercised until the donee's death, and the donee was meant to be free to modify the appointment until then.[34]

(ii) The relief is sought by a purchaser, creditor or charity, or the wife or legitimate child of the donee of the power.[35]

It should be noted that although equity gives relief against the defective exercise of the power in these cases, it never gives relief against failure to exercise the power at all.[36]

C. Excessive Execution

10–092 An appointment which exceeds the limits set to the power either expressly or by law is said to be an excessive execution of the power. This may be illustrated by an appointment which infringes the rule against perpetuities[37] or appoints £8,000 under a power that authorises the appointment of only £7,000[38] or attaches an unauthorised condition to the interest appointed,[39] or an appointment to an illegitimate child which is made under a power to appoint to legitimate children.[40] In such cases the rule is that the appointment is valid so far as it is proper and void as to the excess only. However, if it is impossible to draw a clear boundary between what is proper and what is excessive, the whole appointment is bad.[41] Thus if under a power to appoint to children, an appointment is made to a child for life with remainder to a grandchild, the appointment is valid as to the life interest of the child only.[42] Again, a lease for 26 years granted under a power to lease for 21 years is valid for 21 years.[43] But if under a special power there is an appointment to a class of persons composed partly of persons who are not objects of the power, and the shares in which they are to take are not specified, the whole appointment fails, for it is impossible to sever the good from the bad.[44]

No appointment is bad merely because little or nothing is appointed to one or more of the objects, unless the power provides that each object shall receive some minimum amount at least and the donee does not comply with this

[34] *Reid v. Shergold* (1805) 10 Ves. 370; *Coffin v. Cooper* (1865) 13 W.R. 571 at 572; *secus*, it seems, if the deed was not to take effect until death, and was to be revocable until then.
[35] See Farwell, *Powers*, 385 *et seq.*
[36] *Holmes v. Coghill* (1806) 12 Ves. 206.
[37] *Re Brown and Sibly's Contract* (1876) 3 Ch.D. 156; *ante*, para. 7–110.
[38] *Parker v. Parker* (1714) Gilb.Eq. 168.
[39] *e.g. Re Neave* [1938] Ch. 793; *Re Morris's S.T.* [1951] 2 All E.R. 528 (appointment on protective and discretionary trusts held invalid on the ground that appointor's discretion could not be delegated); and see *Re Hunter's W.T.* [1963] Ch. 372.
[40] *Re Kerr's Trusts* (1877) 4 Ch.D. 600.
[41] See *Re Witty* [1913] 2 Ch. 666; Farwell, *Powers*, 343 *et seq.*
[42] *Doe d. Nicholson v. Welford* (1840) 12 A. & E. 61.
[43] *Campbell v. Leach* (1775) Amb. 740; but see Cru.Dig. iv, 202.
[44] *Harvey v. Stracey* (1852) 1 Drew. 73 at 117; *Re Brown's Trust* (1865) L.R. 1 Eq. 74.

requirement.[45] The law was once otherwise,[46] hence the phrase "cut off with a shilling".

D. Fraud on a Power

I. INVALIDITY OF APPOINTMENT

1. Bona fide. A special power of appointment must be exercised "bona fide **10–093** for the end designed, otherwise it is corrupt and void".[47] The donee must, in making the appointment, act in relation to the power as a trustee would act[48]; he must "act with good faith and sincerity, and with an entire and single view to the real purpose and object of the power, and not for the purpose of accomplishing or carrying into effect any bye or sinister object (I mean sinister in the sense of its being beyond the purpose and intent of the power) which he may desire to effect in the exercise of the power",[49] even if there is no "fraud" in the ordinary sense.[50] If an appointment does not satisfy these requirements, it is void as a fraud on the power; but the doctrine does not apply to a power to revoke an appointment.[51]

2. Fraud. An appointment may be deemed fraudulent and void on any of **10–094** three grounds.

(a) Corrupt purpose. The appointment was made with a corrupt purpose, as **10–095** by the donee appointing to one of his children who is seriously ill, expecting that the child would die and that he would take the property appointed as the child's next-of-kin.[52] "If a father . . . charges a portion for his child, not because the child wants it, but because the child is delicate in health, and likely to die, this court has authority to defeat such an act."[53]

(b) Foreign purpose. The appointment was made for purposes foreign to the **10–096** power. Thus where a mother appoints property to a child with the intent that

---

[45] L.P.A. 1925, s.158, replacing the Illusory Appointments Act 1830, and the Powers of Appointment Act 1874.

[46] Originally something more than a nominal sum had to be appointed to every object, unless the contrary was intended: *Thomas v. Thomas* (1705) 2 Vern. 513. Thus, an appointment would be set aside if nothing, or only a nominal sum such as five shillings, was appointed to one of the objects: *Gibson v. Kinven* (1682) 1 Vern. 66. The Illusory Appointments Act 1830 provided that the appointment of a nominal sum should not invalidate the exercise of the power, unless it directed otherwise. But until the Powers of Appointment Act 1874 the total exclusion of any object still prima facie invalidated the appointment: *Gainsford v. Dunn* (1874) L.R. 17 Eq. 405 at 407. "The Act of 1830 enabled an appointor to cut off any object of the power with a shilling: the Act of 1874 enables him to cut off the shilling also": Farwell, *Powers*, 427.

[47] *Aleyn v. Belchier* (1758) 1 Eden 132 at 138, *per* Henley L.K.

[48] See *Scroggs v. Scroggs* (1755) Amb. 272 at 273.

[49] *Duke of Portland v. Lady Topham* (1864) 11 H.L.C. 32 at 54, *per* Lord Westbury L.C.; and see *Henty v. Wrey* (1882) 21 Ch.D. 332 at 354.

[50] *Vatcher v. Paull* [1915] A.C. 372 at 378.

[51] *Re Greaves* [1954] Ch. 434.

[52] *Lord Hinchinbroke v. Seymour* (1789) 1 Bro.C.C. 395; *Lord Wellesley v. Earl of Mornington* (1855) 2 K. & J. 143; contrast *Henty v. Wrey* (1882) 21 Ch.D. 332 (appointment to healthy children not invalid merely because of their youth).

[53] *Keily v. Keily* (1843) 4 Dr. & War. 38 at 55, 56, *per* Sugden L.C.

the child should use it for the benefit of the father, who was not an object of the power, the appointment will be set aside even though the child was ignorant of the mother's intention.[54] But pressure on the appointee to settle the property on himself and his issue (who were not objects of the power) does not necessarily indicate a fraud on the power, for it may well be compatible with a genuine intention to benefit the appointee.[55]

10–097   *(c) Bargain to benefit non-objects.* The appointment was made in pursuance of a previous agreement with the appointee whereby persons who were not objects of the power obtained some benefit, as where the donee bargained for some advantage for himself[56] or a stranger[57] as a condition of making the appointment. In the case of a power to appoint to one person only, an appointment may be fraudulent and void under this head but not under the previous head, for there is no exercise of a power of selection among two or more objects which might be warped by the mere pressure of a foreign purpose, as distinct from a bargain.[58]

10–098   **3. Effect of fraud.** An appointment which is a fraud on the power under the above rules is usually treated as a whole even if the fraud affects only part; the entire appointment is thus bad.[59] But if the fraudulent part is clearly separable from the rest,[60] the court may hold only the fraudulent part void[61] and the rest valid.[62] Further, a fraudulent appointment is merely void, and does not stop the appointor subsequently making a fresh appointment[63]; but if this appointment is in favour of the same person, he must show that it is not tainted with the same fraud as the original appointment.[64]

II. POSITION OF A PURCHASER

10–099   **1. Before 1926.** Before 1926 the position of a purchaser of an interest which had been fraudulently appointed depended upon the question whether that interest was legal or equitable. If the interest was legal, the appointment was not void but voidable, *i.e.* it was good until set aside, so that if before the appointment was avoided the interest passed to a purchaser for value without notice of the fraud, he took a good title.[65] But if the interest was equitable, the

---

[54] *Re Marsden's Trusts* (1859) 4 Drew. 594; *Re Crawshay* [1948] Ch. 123 (family pressure); *Re Dick* [1953] Ch. 343 (request in memorandum left with will).

[55] *Re Burton's Settlements* [1955] Ch. 82.

[56] *Farmer v. Martin* (1828) 2 Sim. 502 (agreement to pay appointor's debts); *Cochrane v. Cochrane* [1922] 2 Ch. 230 (agreement to divorce appointor).

[57] *Birley v. Birley* (1858) 25 Beav. 299.

[58] *Re Nicholson's Settlement* [1939] Ch. 11 (see at 18, 19).

[59] See. *e.g. Agassiz v. Squire* (1854) 18 Beav. 431.

[60] See *Whelan v. Palmer* (1888) 39 Ch.D. 648 at 659.

[61] *Ranking v. Barnes* (1864) 33 L.J.Ch. 339.

[62] *Harrison v. Randall* (1852) 9 Hare 397.

[63] See *Topham v. Duke of Portland* (1869) 5 Ch.App. 40.

[64] *Re Chadwick's Trust* [1939] 1 All E.R. 850.

[65] *M'Queen v. Farquhar* (1805) 11 Ves. 467; *Cloutte v. Storey* [1911] 1 Ch. 18 at 24, 31. In other words, the appointment operated at law but the right to have it set aside for fraud was merely equitable.

appointment was void *ab initio*; even a purchaser without notice got no title, for he had not the security of the legal estate and was merely a subsequent equitable claimant.[66]

2. After 1925. Since 1925 all powers of appointment are equitable,[67] and so **10–100** the position of a purchaser is now more precarious. But the Law of Property Act 1925[68] gives a very limited measure of protection to purchasers and those deriving title under them.[69] The Act applies whenever the appointment was made, provided the purchase was made after 1925.[70] The purchaser must show—

    (i) that he bought for money or money's worth without notice of the fraud or circumstances from which it might have been discovered upon making reasonable inquiries[71]; and

    (ii) and that the appointee with whom he dealt was not less than 25 years of age.[71a]

Even if he proves this, he is protected only to the extent of the amount to which, at the time of the appointment, the appointee was presumptively entitled in default of appointment.[72] For example, if A has power to appoint £5,000 among his children and in default of appointment the children share equally, a purchaser from one of the children is protected to the extent of only £1,000 if A had five children at the date of the appointment; if A had two children at that time, £2,500 is the limit of the protection. This is so even if the whole £5,000 has been appointed to one child. A purchaser would have no protection if in default of appointment some third party was entitled to the property.

E. Determination of Powers

A power may be extinguished in two ways.

1. Expressly: by release, or by contract not to exercise it.[73] This rule now[74] **10–101** applies to all powers except a power coupled with a duty or in the nature of a trust, where a release would be a breach of that duty or trust.[75] Such a release

---

[66] *Cloutte v. Storey* [1911] 1 Ch. 18; *cf. ante*, para. 5–009.
[67] L.P.A. 1925, s.1(7); *ante*, para. 10–080.
[68] s.157.
[69] s.157(3).
[70] s.157(4).
[71] s.157(2).
[71a] *ibid.*
[72] s.157(1).
[73] L.P.A. 1925, s.155. A contract not to exercise a power operates as a release: Farwell, *Powers*, 19.
[74] See *ante*, para. 10–080.
[75] *Re Eyre* (1883) 49 L.T. 259; and see *Re Mills* [1930] 1 Ch. 654; *Re Wills' Trust Deed* [1964] Ch. 219, distinguished in *Muir v. I.R.C.* [1966] 1 W.L.R. 1269.

or contract may either totally extinguish the power, or be partial. A partial release may exclude part of the property from the operation of the power, leaving the rest subject to it,[76] or prevent the power being exercised in favour of one or more of the objects.[77] The rules relating to frauds on a power do not apply to the release of a power,[78] so that a bargain to release the power may be made by the donee of the power with those entitled to take in default.

The donee of a power may also disclaim it.[79] Disclaimer does not destroy the power but renders the donee who disclaims incapable of exercising it; it can still be exercised by any other donees.[80]

10–102   **2. Impliedly:** by any dealing inconsistent with the further exercise of the power.[81] Thus if a husband appoints one-quarter of the income to his wife for life, and subject thereto he appoints the property to his children, he cannot, after the death of his wife, appoint a life interest in one-fourth to his second wife, for he has exhausted the power.[82] There is also an implied release when all the purposes for which the power was created cease to exist.[83]

[76] *Re Evered* [1910] 2 Ch. 147 at 157.
[77] *Re Brown's Settlement* [1939] Ch. 944.
[78] *Re Somes* [1896] 1 Ch. 250.
[79] L.P.A. 1925, s.156.
[80] L.P.A. 1925, s.156(2).
[81] *Smith v. Death* (1820) 5 Madd. 371 at 374; *Foakes v. Jackson* [1900] 1 Ch. 807.
[82] *Re Hancock* [1896] 2 Ch. 173.
[83] See *Wolley v. Jenkins* (1856) 23 Beav. 53.

CHAPTER 11

WILLS AND INTESTACY

This chapter falls into four parts. The first three parts deal with wills, gifts **11–001** made in contemplation of death, and intestacy respectively, setting out the rules which determine who is beneficially entitled to property after the death of the owner. The fourth part deals with personal representatives, who hold the property of the deceased not for their own benefit but for the purpose of administering it (including the payment of debts and the like) and then vesting what is left in the persons beneficially entitled.

Part 1

WILLS

Section 1. Freedom of Testation

1. Historical development. For some while after the Norman Conquest it **11–002** was possible for a man to dispose of both his realty and his personalty by will. At first his powers of disposition over personalty were confined to a fixed proportion, his widow and children being entitled to the rest.[1] During the fourteenth century this restriction disappeared in nearly all parts of the country. However, in some places it survived until the seventeenth and eighteenth centuries, the last case being that of London, where it was abolished in 1725.[2] Realty, on the other hand, could at first be freely devised, but by the end of the thirteenth century all power of testamentary disposition had disappeared except in the case of local customs, such as gavelkind.[3] But this restriction was soon evaded by means of uses[4] and the general belief that the Statute of Uses 1535 had abolished this indirect power of testamentary disposition[5] provoked such an outcry that the Statute of Wills 1540[6] authorised the devise of all socage land and two-thirds of land held by knight

---

[1] P. & M. ii, 348; H.E.L. iii, 550. The fraction varied locally; often he was free to dispose of only a third if he left a widow and children, but a half if he left either a widow or children but not both.

[2] 11 Geo. I, c. 18 1724, ss.17, 18; and see H.E.L., iii, 552.

[3] *Ante*, paras 2–019, 3–043; H.E.L. iii, 75, 76.

[4] For the Statute of Uses, see the previous edition of this work, Appendix 3.

[5] This belief was probably unfounded: see 94 S.S. at p. 203 (J. H. Baker); and (1941) 7 C.L.J. 354 (R.E.M.).

[6] As explained by the Statute of Wills 1542.

service.[7] When the Tenures Abolition Act 1660 converted all land held by knight service into land of socage tenure, all land became devisable. But this power extended only to estates in fee simple: land held in tail could not be disposed of by will before the Law of Property Act 1925[8]; and land held *pur autre vie* did not become devisable until the Statute of Frauds was enacted in 1677.[9]

Copyhold land was not within the Statute of Wills 1540, and devises were effected by the testator in his lifetime making a surrender to the uses of his will.[10] If the testator was a joint tenant, this had the incidental effect of severing the joint tenancy.[11] But by Preston's Act 1815[12] a devise without a previous surrender was rendered effective, and the Wills Act 1837 applied to copyholds as well as to lands of other tenures. It is this latter Act, as amended, which governs wills of all property, real or personal, today.

2. Statutory restrictions on freedom of testation

11–003   *(a) Inheritance (Family Provision) Act 1938.* From the fourteenth century until 1939 there was, in general, no restriction upon a testator's power to dispose of property as he thought fit. He was under no obligation to provide for his family or dependants. The Inheritance (Family Provision) Act 1938 gave the court a limited power to modify the effect of a will in certain cases, and the Intestates' Estates Act 1952 gave the court power to modify the rules of succession on intestacy. Those powers were later extended by the Family Provision Act 1966 and the Family Law Reform Act 1969.[13]

(b) Inheritance (Provision for Family and Dependants) Act 1975[14]

11–004   (1) PROVISION UNDER THE ACT. The legislation explained above was replaced by the Inheritance (Provision for Family and Dependants) Act 1975, which conferred wider powers.[15] Its principal objects were to improve the provision for a surviving spouse, no longer confining it to maintenance; to include all children of the deceased even though not under a disability, together with non-relatives who were treated as children of the family or else were dependant on the deceased; and to extend the court's power to make orders. The purpose of

---

[7] See A. W. B. Simpson, *A History of the Land Law* (2nd ed.), p. 191.

[8] *Ante*, para. 3–089.

[9] s.12.

[10] Scriven 146.

[11] *Porter v. Porter* (1605) Cro.Jac. 100; *Gale v. Gale* (1789) 2 Cox Eq. 136; *Edwards v. Champion* (1847) 1 De G. & Sm. 75; (1853) 3 De G. M. & G. 202; and see *ante*, paras 9–003, 9–036 *et seq.*

[12] 55 Geo. 3, c. 192.

[13] For details of this legislation, see the previous edition of this work at p. 500.

[14] For a more detailed survey, see S. M. Cretney and J. M. Masson, *Principles of Family Law* (6th ed.), pp. 204–218.

[15] As recommended by the Law Commission ((1974) Law Com. No. 61). In view of the substantial changes made in the 1975 Act, decisions on the 1938 Act as to the exercise of the court's powers provide little guidance and must be approached with caution: *Moody v. Stevenson* [1992] Ch. 486. *Cf. Re Coventry* [1980] Ch. 461 at 474.

the Act is to make reasonable financial provision for an applicant who had either "some sort of moral claim" or some other reason to be maintained by the deceased beyond the mere fact of a blood relationship and for whom the deceased had failed to provide.[16] It is not the function of the Act "to provide legacies or rewards for meritorious conduct",[17] nor does it confer on a court a power "to reform the deceased's dispositions or those which statute makes of his estate to accord with what the court itself might have thought would be sensible if it had been in the deceased's position".[18]

(2) APPLICANTS. The persons for whom provision may now be made by the court are any of the following, provided that the deceased died after March 31, 1976 and was then domiciled in England and Wales[19]: **11–005**

    (a) the wife or husband of the deceased[20];

    (b) a former wife or husband who has not remarried[21];

    (c) a child, including an illegitimate child and a child *en ventre sa mère*[22] (an adopted child qualifies automatically)[23];

    (d) any other person treated by the deceased as a child of the family in relation to any marriage to which the deceased was at any time a party[24];

[16] *Re Coventry, supra*, at 475, *per* Oliver J. A moral claim or some other special factor will usually have to be shown if the claimant is an adult who is able to earn his own living: see *Re Jennings* [1994] Ch. 286 at 295. For recent examples where there was such a moral claim or special circumstances see *Re Goodchild* [1997] 1 W.L.R. 1216 (where the deceased inherited property from his first wife, who had left it to him under the mistaken belief that he was bound by a mutual wills agreement to make provision in his will for the claimant, their son); *Re Pearce* [1998] 2 F.L.R. 705 (claimant had worked unpaid for 10 years on his father's farm having been told that the farm would pass to him on his father's death). For cases where the successful applicant was also in straitened circumstances, see *Re Hancock* [1998] 2 F.L.R. 346 (where there was evidence that the deceased would have provided for her if he thought that he could, and where in fact the estate was very large); *Espinosa v. Burke* [1999] 1 F.L.R. 747 (deceased promised the claimant that he would leave her his wife's portfolio of shares).
[17] *Re Coventry, supra*, at 474, *per* Oliver J.
[18] *ibid.*, at 475.
[19] Inheritance (Provision for Family and Dependants) Act 1975, s.1.
[20] Including a wife by a polygamous marriage (*Re Sehota* [1978] 1 W.L.R. 1506) and a spouse from whom the deceased had long been separated: *Re Rowlands* [1984] F.L.R. 813 (parties separated for the last 43 years of their 62 years of marriage).
[21] See *Re Fullard* [1982] Fam. 42; *Cameron v. Treasury Solicitor* [1996] 2 F.L.R. 716 (divorced wife's application refused since her interests were settled in divorce proceedings). See too Inheritance (Provision for Family and Dependants) Act 1975, s.15 (as substituted).
[22] Inheritance (Provision for Family and Dependants) Act 1975, s.25(1).
[23] See *post*, para. 11–061. By contrast, if a child who would otherwise be entitled to make a claim under the Act has himself been adopted before proceedings are commenced, he will lose his right to make a claim. He is treated for all purposes as the child of the adopter under the Adoption Act 1976, s.39(2): *Re Collins* [1990] Fam. 56.
[24] It has been suggested, but never decided, that treatment of the claimant as a child of the family by the deceased even *before* the marriage ceremony would suffice: *Re Callaghan* [1985] Fam. 1 at 6. To fall within this paragraph, it is necessary that the deceased "has, *as wife or husband* (or widow or widower) under the relevant marriage, expressly or impliedly, assumed the position of a parent towards the applicant, with the attendant *responsibilities and privileges* of that relationship": *Re Leach* [1986] Ch. 226 at 237, *per* Slade L.J.

(e) any other person who was being maintained wholly or partly by the deceased immediately before the death.[25]

A further category has now been added where the deceased died after 1995:

(f) any person who had lived in the same household as the deceased as that person's husband or wife for two years immediately prior to his or her death.[26]

11–006   (3) APPLICATIONS. Application has to be made within six months of the first grant of representation,[27] but the court may extend the time.[28] A claim under the Act is personal to the applicant and will be extinguished by his death if no order has been made in his lifetime.[29] The ground of application must be that the deceased's will or the law of intestacy, or both in combination, do not make reasonable financial provision for the applicant.[30] In the case of a spouse in class (a), this means such provision as would be reasonable in all the circumstances for a spouse to receive, whether or not for maintenance.[31] In any other case the formula is the same except that it is confined to what is reasonably required[32] for that person's maintenance.[33] In the case of class (e),

---

[25] The words "immediately before the death of the deceased" are not construed literally, but "refer to the general arrangements for maintenance subsisting at the time of death": *Jelley v. Iliffe* [1981] Fam. 128 at 141, *per* Griffiths L.J.

[26] Law Reform (Succession) Act 1995, s.2, amending the Inheritance (Provision for Family and Dependants) Act 1975, s.1. This provision enables an application to be made by a surviving unmarried cohabitant even though he or she was not dependent on the deceased at the time of death. It implements the recommendations of the Law Commission: see (1989) Law Com. No. 187, Part IV. See *Re Watson* [1999] F.L.R. 878.

[27] The grant of representation must be a valid one. If a grant is revoked and a new grant made, time runs from the date of the latter grant: *Re Freeman* [1984] 1 W.L.R. 1419. No application under the 1975 Act will be entertained unless a grant of representation has been made: *Re McBroom* [1992] 2 F.L.R. 49.

[28] Inheritance (Provision for Family and Dependants) Act 1975, s.4. See *Re Salmon* [1981] Ch. 167 ($4\frac{1}{2}$ months extension refused, since estate distributed without warning of claim negligently deferred).

[29] *Whytte v. Ticehurst* [1986] Fam. 64.

[30] Inheritance (Provision for Family and Dependants) Act 1975, s.2. For the matters to which the court is required to have regard, see *ibid*. s.3. It is required to take into account the facts as known at the hearing: see *ibid*. s.3(5). Changes in circumstances (such as an increase or decrease in the size of the deceased's estate since his death) may, therefore, be relevant: *Re Hancock* [1998] 2 F.L.R. 346.

[31] See in particular *Re Besterman* [1984] Ch. 458 (court had to assess "what a reasonable provision would be in all the circumstances for the widow of a millionaire") and *Re Bunning* [1984] Ch. 480. See generally (1986) 102 L.Q.R. 445 (J. G. Miller).

[32] See *Re Coventry* [1980] Ch. 461 at 472; *Re Jennings* [1994] Ch. 286. In the latter case, a claim for provision by a son who was comfortably off, but whose father had abandoned him when a baby, failed. "It is not the purpose of the Act of 1975 to punish or redress past bad or unfeeling parental behaviour where that behaviour does not still impinge on the applicant's present financial situation" *ibid.*, at 301, *per* Henry L.J.

[33] Inheritance (Provision for Family and Dependants) Act 1975, s.1(2). The test for maintenance is whether the deceased made sufficient provision to enable the deceased "to live neither luxuriously nor miserably, but decently and comfortably according to his or her station in life": *Re Duranceau* [1953] 3 D.L.R. 714 at 720, *per* Roach J.A.; *Re Coventry, supra*, at 485; *Re Leach, supra*, at 240.

it must appear that the deceased had assumed responsibility for maintaining the applicant.[34] However, this will be presumed from the mere fact that the applicant was maintained by the deceased.[35] Furthermore, under that class, the applicant will be treated as having been maintained by the deceased, either wholly or partly, only if the latter was making a substantial contribution in money or money's worth (otherwise than for full valuable consideration) towards the applicant's reasonable needs.[36] The court will weigh the reciprocal benefits conferred by the deceased and the applicant upon each other. In the absence of an obvious imbalance, the applicant's case will fail *in limine*.[37] Examples of "substantial contribution" by the deceased have included the provision of free accommodation,[38] payment of living expenses,[39] and might include the education of a nephew at the expense of the deceased.[40]

(4) ORDERS. The Act sets out in detail the matters to which the court is to have regard in exercising its powers, such as financial resources and physical or mental disability.[41] Although the catalogue is apparently open-ended,[42] certain additional factors are required to be taken into account in relation to applications in specific classes.[43]   **11–007**

The court has wide discretion to order provision to be made for the applicant from the deceased's net estate by way of lump sum or periodical payments, transfer or settlement of specific property or of property to be acquired, or variation of a pre-existing marriage settlement.[44] The order may contain consequential or supplementary provisions as the court thinks necessary or expedient. It may direct the setting aside of a capital sum to produce periodical payments, thus allowing the rest of the estate to be distributed.[45]

---

[34] Inheritance (Provision for Family and Dependants) Act 1975, s.3(4).

[35] *Jelley v. Iliffe, supra*, not following on this point *Re Beaumont* [1980] Ch. 444.

[36] Inheritance (Provision for Family and Dependants) Act 1975, s.1(3). It is immaterial for the purposes of this subsection whether valuable consideration is provided pursuant to a contract or otherwise: *Jelley v. Iliffe, supra.* Domestic services which are attributable to mutual love and affection will not be regarded as "valuable consideration" for these purposes, so as to defeat the applicant's claim: *Bishop v. Plumley* [1991] 1 W.L.R. 582.

[37] *Jelley v. Iliffe, supra*, at 141; *Bishop v. Plumley, supra*, at 587. The unfortunate result of s.1(3) is therefore to reward "spongers and parasites" and penalise "industrious de facto spouses": [1991] C.L.J. 42 (S. Bridge).

[38] *Jelley v. Iliffe, supra*; *Bishop v. Plumley, supra*; *Graham v. Murphy* [1997] 1 F.L.R. 860.

[39] *Malone v. Harrison* [1979] 1 W.L.R. 1353 (applicant was the deceased's mistress).

[40] See Law Com. No. 61, para. 98.

[41] Inheritance (Provision for Family and Dependants) Act 1975, s.3(1).

[42] It includes "any other matter, including the conduct of the applicant or any other person, which in the circumstances of the case the court may consider relevant": s.3(1)(g).

[43] s.3(2), (2A) (inserted by the Law Reform (Succession) Act 1995, s.2(4)), (3) and (4). So, for example, in considering an application by a spouse the court will have regard to the provision that the applicant might reasonably have expected to receive if the marriage had been terminated by divorce rather than death: s.3(2); *Re Besterman, supra*; *Re Bunning, supra*; *Stead v. Stead* [1985] F.L.R. 16; *Moody v. Stevenson* [1992] Ch. 486; *Jessop v. Jessop* [1992] 1 F.L.R. 591. It is clear that this is only one element that the court will take into account in deciding whether appropriate provision has been made, and that it should not be given undue prominence. *Re Krubert* [1997] Ch. 97 (preferring *Re Besterman, supra*, to *Moody v. Stevenson, supra*).

[44] s.2. See (1986) 102 L.Q.R. 445 (J. G. Miller).

[45] s.2(3).

There are extensive powers also for later variation or discharge of orders for periodical payments, and for interim orders giving immediate financial assistance pending final decision of the case.[46] In addition, there are anti-avoidance provisions under which the court may order payments or transfers to be made by recipients under certain dispositions made by the deceased within six years before death for less than full valuable consideration and with intent to defeat the Act; and similarly for contracts to leave property by will, if made for insufficient consideration and with similar intent.[47]

11–008   (5) NET ESTATE. The deceased's net estate, out of which the provision has to be made, is defined so as to include property over which he had a general power of appointment at the time of his death; property ordered to be recovered under the anti-avoidance provisions mentioned above; property passing by statutory nomination[48] or by *donatio mortis causa*[49]; and the deceased's severable share under any beneficial joint tenancy, if the court so orders.[50]

Section 2. Nature of a Will

11–009   A will is an instrument that both contains and is made with the intention that it should be a revocable ambulatory disposition of the maker's property which is to take effect on death.[51] A document can be a will only if it is made with immediate testamentary intent. Its operation may be made subject to an express condition, but if it transpires that an apparently unconditional will was in fact subject to some condition that was expressed externally, it will be void and cannot be admitted to probate. The testator lacked the requisite *animus testandi* at the time when it was executed.[52]

11–010   **1. A will is ambulatory.** Until the death of the testator a will has no effect at all,[53] but operates as a mere declaration of his intention, which may be changed from time to time. For this reason, a will is said to be "ambulatory". This distinguishes a will from a conveyance, settlement or other dealing *inter vivos*, which operates at once or at some fixed time.[54]

A will is also ambulatory in that it "speaks from death", *i.e.* it is capable of disposing of all property owned by the testator at his death, even if acquired

---

[46] ss.6, 5.
[47] ss.10, 11. See *Re Dawkins* [1986] 2 F.L.R. 360.
[48] See *post*, para. 11–013.
[49] For such gifts in contemplation of death, see *post*, para. 11–083.
[50] s.25(1). See, *e.g. Jessop v. Jessop* [1992] 1 F.L.R. 591.
[51] *Re Berger* [1990] Ch. 118 at 129–130; 132.
[52] *Corbett v. Newey* [1998] Ch. 57 (deceased intended her will to be effective only when certain gifts of land had been completed, but these conditions were not expressed in the will).
[53] *Re Baroness Llanover* [1903] 2 Ch. 330 at 335; *Re Thompson* [1906] 2 Ch. 199 at 205.
[54] See Jarman 26. But a will may, as soon as made, rank as a "disposition" for certain statutory purposes: see *Re Gilpin* [1954] Ch. 1, and contrast *Berkeley v. Berkeley* [1946] A.C. 555 ("provision"), noted (1946) 62 L.Q.R. 340 (R.E.M.).

after the date of the will. Before 1838 this was true only of personalty: a will could not dispose of realty acquired between the making of the will and death. But by the Wills Act 1837,[55] unless a contrary intention appears, a will now speaks from death with regard to both real and personal property.

2. A will is revocable. Notwithstanding any declaration in the will itself or any other document, a will can be revoked at any time.[56] A binding contract not to revoke a will does not prevent its revocation,[57] though it gives a right of action for damages against the testator's estate if the will is revoked.[58] Such a contract will usually be construed as confined to acts of revocation performed as such, and not to the revocation that usually results automatically from marriage[59]; and even if the contract is wide enough to extend to marriage, it will be valid only so far as it is not in restraint of marriage.[60] In the case of land,[61] or where an implied trust arises from an agreement to make mutual wills,[62] the effect of a contract not to revoke the will is that the person to whom the assets have passed may be compelled to hold these on trust in accordance with the terms of the contract.[63]   **11–011**

3. Codicils. A codicil is similar to a will and is governed by the same rules. A testamentary document is usually called a codicil if it is supplementary to a will and adds to, varies or revokes provisions in the will: if it is an independent instrument, it is called a will. Although sometimes indorsed on a will, a codicil may be a separate document, and can stand by itself even if the will to which it is supplementary is revoked.[64] Codicils are construed in such a way as to disturb the provisions of a will no more than is absolutely necessary to give effect to the codicil.[65]   **11–012**

4. Minors. Since 1837 no minor can make a valid will,[66] except in the special cases of privilege (soldiers, sailors, marines and airmen) explained   **11–013**

---

[55] s.24; *post*, para. 11–071.
[56] *Vynior's Case* (1610) 8 Co. Rep. 8lb.
[57] *In b. Heys* [1914] P. 192.
[58] *Synge v. Synge* [1894] 1 Q.B. 466.
[59] *Re Marsland* [1939] Ch. 820; for revocation by marriage, see *post*, para. 11–029.
[60] *Robinson v. Ommanney* (1883) 23 Ch. D. 285; for restraint of marriage, see *ante*, para. 3–074.
[61] *i.e.* where the contract creates an equitable interest: *ante*, para. 4–025; *Goylmer v. Paddiston* (1682) 2 Ventr. 353; and see n. 63, below.
[62] *Ante*, para. 10–020.
[63] *Dufour v. Pereira* (1769) Dick. 419 and cases cited *ante*, para. 10–020. Where the title to the land is unregistered, the purchaser of a legal estate without notice, or against whom the contract is void for want of registration, will take free from it: *ante*, paras 5–002, 5–117. Yet *quaere* whether a contract to devise is an estate contract within the meaning of the L.C.A. 1972. For the statutory definition, see *ante*, para. 5–009. Where title is registered, such a contract would be a minor interest and could be protected by a notice or caution: see *ante*, paras 6–079, 6–083.
[64] *Black v. Jobling* (1869) L.R. 1 P. & D. 685; *In b. Savage* (1870) L.R. 2 P. & D. 78.
[65] *Doe d. Hearle v. Hicks* (1832) 1 Cl. & F. 20; Jarman 194.
[66] Wills Act 1837, s.7, as amended by Family Law Reform Act 1969, s.3(1), reducing the age of majority from 21 to 18 with effect from January 1, 1970.

later.[67] However, minors of 16 years or more have statutory power to make nominations of certain property (*e.g.* money in savings banks) to take effect on death.[68]

Section 3. The Formalities of a Will

A. History

11–014   The Statute of Wills 1540[69] required a will of realty to be made in writing, although it was unnecessary for it to be signed by the testator, or witnessed. Wills of personalty could be made by word of mouth. The Statute of Frauds 1677[70] required all wills of realty[71] not only to be in writing but also to be signed by the testator (or by some person in his presence and by his direction) and attested in his presence by at least three credible witnesses. The statute also laid down such stringent requirements for nuncupative (*i.e.* oral) wills of personalty over £30[72] that thereafter wills of personalty were usually made in writing. Written wills of personalty required no witnesses and did not need to be signed by the testator if written or acknowledged by him.[73]

The Wills Act 1837 repealed these provisions as regards all wills made after 1837[74] and substituted a uniform code for both realty and personalty. The rules have been amended several times, and in particular the Administration of Justice Act 1982 has made important changes.

B. Formal Wills

I. EXECUTION

11–015   The provision which governs the formal requirements for the execution of a will made by a testator dying after December 31, 1982, is section 9 of the Wills Act 1837, as reformulated with amendments by the Administration of Justice Act 1982.[75] It is as follows:

"No will shall be valid unless—
(a)   it is in writing, and signed by the testator, or by some other person in his presence and by his direction; and

---

[67] *Post*, para. 11–038.
[68] See Williams, Mortimer & Sunnucks, *Executors, Administrators and Probate*, 109; Administration of Estates (Small Payments) Act 1965 (and S.I. 1984 No. 539, raising the maximum amount for nominations to £5,000).
[69] s.1. This did not affect customary wills: Rob. Gav. 299.
[70] s.5. This expressly applied to land devisable by custom, *e.g.* gavelkind.
[71] Leaseholds and copyholds were not within the statute (Cru. Dig. vi, 69).
[72] ss.19, 20.
[73] See H.E.L. iii, 538; Bailey, *Wills*, 21, 22.
[74] ss.2, 34.
[75] s.17. This section was enacted in response to recommendations of the Law Reform Committee in *The Making and Revocation of Wills*, Cmnd. 7902 (1980).

(b) it appears that the testator intended by his signature to give effect to the will; and

(c) the signature is made or acknowledged by the testator in the presence of two or more witnesses present at the same time; and

(d) each witness either—

(i) attests and signs the will; or

(ii) acknowledges his signature,

in the presence of the testator (but not necessarily in the presence of any other witness),

but no form of attestation shall be necessary."[76]

1. Writing. The will must be in writing. Any form of writing, printing, typewriting and the like may be employed,[77] or a combination of these, *e.g.* a printed form completed in manuscript[78]; but pencil writing on a will made in ink is presumed to be merely deliberative, and will be excluded from probate unless it appears to be intended to be operative.[79] No special form of words need be used: all that is required is an intelligible document[80] which indicates an *animus testandi* (intention to make a will).[81]

11–016

2. Signature by testator. The will must be signed by the testator, or by someone else in his presence and by his direction.[82] The testator's signature may be made in any way, provided there is an intention to execute the will. Thus initials,[83] a stamped name,[84] a mark[85] (even if the testator could write[86]), or a signature in a former[87] or assumed[88] name all suffice.[89] But a seal is not enough for the will must be signed, and sealing is not signing.[90] Similar principles apply to signature by someone on behalf of the testator. Thus signature of his own name instead of that of the testator is sufficient.[91] But it

11–017

---

[76] The new elements in the amended version that were not found in the Wills Act 1837, s.9, as originally enacted are paragraphs (b) and (d)(ii) and the omission of the requirement that the testator's signature be "at the foot or end" of the will. In other respects the law remains as established under the Act of 1837.

[77] See, *e.g. In b. Usborne* (1909) 25 T.L.R. 519.

[78] *In b. Moore* [1892] P. 378.

[79] *In b. Adams* (1872) L.R. 2 P. & D. 367.

[80] *e.g. Thorn v. Dickens* [1906] W.N. 54 (entire will consisting of words "all for mother").

[81] In *Re Meynell* [1949] W.N. 273 probate was granted of written instructions to a solicitor, which had been duly witnessed because of fears that the testator might die suddenly. Where these formalities are observed there is a strong presumption of *animus testandi: ibid.*

[82] Wills Act 1837, s.9.

[83] *In b. Savory* (1851) 15 Jur. 1042.

[84] *Jenkins v. Gaisford* (1863) 3 Sw. & Tr. 93.

[85] *e.g.* a thumb-mark: *In b. Finn* (1936) 53 T.L.R. 153.

[86] *Baker v. Dening* (1838) 8 A. & E. 94.

[87] *In b. Glover* (1847) 11 Jur. 1022.

[88] *In b. Redding* (1850) 2 Rob. Ecc. 339.

[89] And see *In b. Chalcraft* [1948] P. 222 (testatrix too ill to complete more than part of her surname: held valid); *In b. Cook* [1960] 1 W.L.R. 353 ("your loving Mother": held valid).

[90] *Wright v. Wakeford* (1811) 17 Ves. 454.

[91] *In b. Clark* (1839) 2 Curt. 329.

is essential that the signature should be made in the testator's presence and authorised by him, either expressly or by implication.[92]

Where the testator died after 1982 it must appear that he intended by his signature to give effect to the will.[93] A signature in the normal place at the end of the will obviously fulfils this requirement, but questions may arise where the signature is in an abnormal place, as explained below.

11–018   **3. Position of signature.** Under the Act of 1837 the signature had to be at the "foot or end" of the will,[94] a provision that was the subject both of legislative amendment and considerable litigation.[95] The Act of 1982, as set out above, has now abolished the rule about the position of the testator's signature where he dies after 1982. The signature may now be placed in any position in the will,[96] provided that it appears that it is intended to give effect to it, and is not, for example, merely an indication that the document is the testator's property. Normally the testator will sign the instrument only after it has been written. However, the time at which the signature is appended is immaterial when the writing and signing of the will are all part of one operation.[97]

Effect will be given to dispositions contained in a document which has not been executed as a will if the document is incorporated in a will. For this to be the case—

>   (i) the will must clearly[98] identify the document to be incorporated[99];
>
>   (ii) the will must refer to the document as being already in existence[1] and not as one subsequently to be made[2]; and
>
>   (iii) the document must in fact be in existence when the will[3] (or a codicil confirming it[4]) is executed.

---

[92] *In b. Marshall* (1866) 13 L.T. 643.

[93] Wills Act 1837, s.9(b), *supra*, para. 11–015. It must be *by the act of signing* that he intended to give effect to the will, and not *e.g.* by presenting to witnesses a previously executed will which the testator had subsequently amended but had not re-signed: *Re White* [1991] Ch. 1 at 9.

[94] Wills Act 1837, s.9. Formerly the signature might be anywhere in the will (*Lemoyne v. Stanley* (1681) 3 Lev. 1), and a holograph will (*i.e.* one made in the testator's own handwriting) might be effective even if unsigned: *In b. Cosser* (1848) 1 Rob. Ecc. 633.

[95] For the law as it stood prior to 1983, see the previous edition of this work at p. 507.

[96] See *Wood v. Smith* [1993] Ch. 90 (opening words of will, "My Will by Percy Winterbone of 150, High Street, Margate", a sufficient signature); *Weatherhill v. Pearce* [1995] 1 W.L.R. 592 (attestation clause, "Signed by the said testator Doris Weatherhill . . . ", a sufficient signature); [1995] Conv. 256 (S. Grattan).

[97] *Re White* [1991] Ch. 1 at 8; *Wood v. Smith, supra*.

[98] But see *In b. Saxton* [1939] 2 All E.R. 418.

[99] *In b. Garnett* [1894] P. 90.

[1] *In b. Sutherland* (1866) L.R. 1 P. & D. 198.

[2] *University College of North Wales v. Taylor* [1908] P. 140.

[3] *Singleton v. Tomlinson* (1878) 3 App. Cas. 404.

[4] *In b. Hunt* (1853) 2 Rob. Ecc. 622. But the will, speaking from the date of the codicil, must here refer to the document as existing (*In b. Truro* (1866) L.R. 1 P. & D. 201); it is not enough that in fact the document was made before the codicil: *In b. Smart* [1902] P. 238.

4. Presence of witnesses. The testator must make the whole[5] of the signature (or acknowledge it) in the presence of two witnesses present at the same time.[6] Whether the signature to the will is made by the testator or by someone in his presence and by his direction, there is no need for witnesses to be present at the time of the signature if they are present when the testator subsequently makes a proper acknowledgment[7] of the signature. But either the signature or the acknowledgment must be made in the simultaneous presence of two witnesses. An express acknowledgment is desirable but not essential[8]; a gesture by the testator may suffice,[9] and an acknowledgment by a third party is effective if it can be shown that it should be taken to be the acknowledgment of the testator.[10] **11–019**

It is immaterial if the witnesses do not know that the document is a will[11]; it suffices if they see the testator write something (even if they do not know that it is his signature[12]) or if he asks them to sign a document on which they see his signature,[13] or could have seen it if they had looked.[14] But there is no signature in the presence of a witness if, although in the room, he had no knowledge that the testator was writing; a man cannot be a witness to an act of which he is unconscious.[15] Similarly, a blind person cannot witness a will.[16]

It is desirable but not essential[17] that the witnesses should be of full age and sound intelligence.

5. Signature by witnesses. The witnesses must then sign in the presence of the testator.[18] No form of attestation is necessary,[19] although a proper attestation clause showing that the will has been executed in accordance with the statutory requirements will facilitate the grant of probate. All that is necessary is that after the testator's signature has been made or acknowledged[20] in the **11–020**

---

[5] *Re Colling* [1972] 1 W.L.R. 1440.

[6] Wills Act 1837, s.9.

[7] See *Re Groffman* [1969] 1 W.L.R. 733 (will in testator's pocket: no sufficient acknowledgement).

[8] Except where the testator is acknowledging a signature made by someone else on his behalf: see *In b. Summers* (1850) 14 Jur. 791.

[9] *In b. Davies* (1850) 2 Rob. Ecc. 337.

[10] *Inglesant v. Inglesant* (1874) L.R. 3 P. & D. 172; but see *Morritt v. Douglas* (1872) L.R. 3 P. & D. 1.

[11] *Daintree v. Fasulo* (1888) 13 P.D. 102; *In b. Benjamin* (1934) 150 L.T. 417.

[12] *Smith v. Smith* (1866) L.R. 1 P. & D. 143.

[13] *Fischer v. Popham* (1875) L.R. 3 P. & D. 246; and see *Brown v. Skirrow* [1902] P. 3 at 5.

[14] *In b. Gunston* (1882) 7 P.D. 102 (see at 108); *secus* if the signature is covered up: *ibid.*

[15] *Brown v. Skirrow* [1902] P. 3.

[16] *In b. Gibson* [1949] P. 434.

[17] Wills Act 1837, s.14; Jarman 143, 144; *Smith v. Thompson* (1931) 146 L.T. 14 (effective attestation by infant).

[18] Wills Act 1837, s.9. The testator must be mentally as well as physically present, but latitude is allowed if a proper signature in the presence of witnesses has already been made: *In b Chalcraft* [1948] P. 222 (testatrix losing consciousness after signature and during attestation: will held valid).

[19] Wills Act 1837, s.9; and see *In b. Colver* (1889) 60 L.T. 368 (will executed in form of a deed held valid); *In b. Denning* [1958] 1 W.L.R. 462 (mere presence of two other signatures).

[20] See *Couser v. Couser* [1996] 1 W.L.R. 1301.

joint presence of two witnesses, they should sign their names in the testator's presence. It suffices that the testator knew that they were signing,[21] and either saw them sign,[22] or could have seen them if he had wished,[23] or if he had not been blind.[24]

Under the Act of 1837 there was no provision allowing a witness to acknowledge his signature. Thus, if the testator signed in the presence of A, who signed his name, and then B was called in and both the testator and A acknowledged their signature to B, who then signed, probate was refused.[25] But this difficulty has been removed in the case of testators dying after 1982 by the provision that a witness may acknowledge his signature "in the presence of the testator (but not necessarily in the presence of any other witness)".[26]

There is no need for the witnesses to sign in each other's presence,[27] although this is both usual and desirable. They may sign by a mark[28] or initials,[29] and the position of their signatures is immaterial, provided they are made with intent to attest the operative[30] signature of the testator.[31]

11–021   **6. International wills.** Any will that complies with Articles 2 to 5 of the Annex to the Convention on International Wills 1973 is valid as regards form, irrespective of the place where it is made, of the locality of the assets and of the nationality, domicile or residence of the testator.[32] The requirements of those Articles are generally similar to those of English law, but in addition the will is required to be acknowledged before "a person authorised to act in connection with international wills" who must attach to the will a certificate in the form of Article 10 certifying compliance with the formalities. The ordinary rules as to revocation are unaffected.

II. ALTERATIONS

11–022   "No obliteration, interlineation, or other alteration made in any will after the execution thereof[33] shall be valid or have any effect, except so far as the words

---

[21] *Jenner v. Finch* (1879) 5 P.D. 106.

[22] *e.g. Casson v. Dade* (1781) I Bro. C.C. 99 (view from carriage of witness signing in attorney's office).

[23] *In b. Trinnell* (1865) 11 Jur. (N.S.) 248.

[24] *In b. Piercy* (1845) 1 Rob. Ecc. 278.

[25] As in *Wyatt v. Berry* [1893] P. 5; *Re Colling* [1972] 1 W.L.R. 1440.

[26] A.J.A. 1982, s.17, quoted *ante*, para. 11–015.

[27] *In b. Webb* (1855) Dea. & Sw. 1.

[28] *In b. Amiss* (1849) 2 Rob. Ecc. 116. But a seal does not suffice: *In b. Byrd* (1842) 3 Curt. 117.

[29] *In b. Streatley* [1891] P. 172.

[30] *Phipps v. Hale* (1874) L.R. 3 P. & D. 166.

[31] *In b. Braddock* (1876) 1 P.D. 433 (witnesses to codicil signed on will to which it was pinned: held valid); *In b Streatley, supra.*

[32] A.J.A. 1982, s.27, Sched. 2 (setting out the Annex).

[33] See *In b. Campbell* [1954] 1 W.L.R. 516 (interlineation prior to execution).

or effect of the will before such alteration shall not be apparent, unless such alteration shall be executed in like manner as hereinbefore is required for the execution of the will[34] ... ". The same section of the Act goes on to provide that the signatures of the testator and the witnesses may be written either opposite or near to the alteration (*e.g.* in the margin) or else at the foot or end of, or opposite to a memorandum referring to the alteration. Signature by means of initials suffices.[35] A codicil confirming a will gives effect to any alterations of the will existing at the date of the codicil,[36] unless the codicil shows that the testator was treating the will as being unaltered.[37]

An obliteration or erasure of part of a will, even though unattested, has the **11–023** effect of revoking that part in so far as it makes it impossible to read ("not apparent"), provided that there was an intention to revoke.[38] The same applies to the pasting of paper over part of a will,[39] provided the words are not decipherable by any natural means, such as by the use of magnifying glasses or by holding the will up to the light.[40] The court will not permit physical interference with the will, as by using chemicals[41] or removing paper pasted over the words[42]; for they must be "apparent" on the will as it stands. Similarly, they are not "apparent" if they can be read only by making some other document, such as an infra-red photograph.[43] But intention to revoke is always necessary, and where paper is pasted over the amounts of legacies, but not the names of the recipients, the intention is evidently to revoke only by substituting new amounts. The doctrine of conditional revocation (explained below[44]) may then come to the rescue, so that the original amounts are unrevoked and can be proved by any means, including infra-red photography.[45]

III. REVOCATION

A will or codicil may be revoked by another will or codicil, by destruction, or **11–024** by marriage; and revocation may be conditional.

---

[34] Wills Act 1837, s.21. It is not enough that the witnesses attest the amendments to the will if the testator does not sign them or re-execute the will: *Re White* [1991] Ch. 1.

[35] *In b. Blewitt* (1880) 5 P.D. 116.

[36] *In b. Hall* (1871) L.R. 2 P. & D. 256 at 257, 258.

[37] *Re Hay* [1904] 1 Ch. 317 (unattested deletion of three legacies in will; codicil revoked one legacy: *held*, the other two stood).

[38] *Townley v. Watson* (1844) 3 Curt. 761. For revocation by destruction, see *post*, para. 11–026.

[39] *In b. Horsford* (1874) L.R. 3 P. & D. 211.

[40] *Ffinch v. Combe* [1894] P. 191; *In b. Brasier* [1899] P. 36.

[41] *Ffinch v. Combe, supra*, at 193.

[42] *In b. Horsford* (1874) L.R. 3 P. & D. 211. Where words illegible in 1874 had gradually become legible, they were admitted to probate in 1894: *Ffinch v. Combe* [1894] P. 191; and see *In b. Gilbert* [1893] P. 183 for removal of paper in order to ascertain whether an earlier will had been revoked, for the obliteration of the revoking words would not revive it: *post*, para. 11–035.

[43] *In b. Itter* [1950] P. 130.

[44] *Post*, para. 11–032.

[45] *In b. Itter, supra*.

11–025   **1. By another will or codicil.** A revocation clause expressly revoking all former wills is effective,[46] provided it is contained in a document[47] executed with the proper formalities.[48] This is so even if the testator had been misled as to the effect of the clause,[49] but not if the testator did not know of the presence of the clause.[50] A misapprehension may, however, admit the doctrine of conditional revocation, explained below.[51] A will is not revoked merely because a later will is entitled (as is usual) "This is the last will and testament of me" or some similar phrase.[52]

A will is revoked by implication if a later will is executed which merely repeats the former will[53] or is inconsistent with it[54]; but if the repetition or inconsistency is merely partial, those parts of the former will which are not repeated in the later will or inconsistent with it remain effective.[55] Any number of testamentary documents may be read together, each being effective except so far as subsequently varied or revoked. The sum total constitutes the testator's will.[56]

11–026   **2. By destruction.** A will is revoked "by the burning, tearing, or otherwise destroying the same by the testator, or by some person in his presence and by his direction, with the intention of revoking the same".[57] There are thus two elements: an act of destruction, and an *animus revocandi* (intention to revoke).

11–027   *(a) Destruction.* It is not necessary that the will should be completely destroyed; there must, however, be some burning, tearing or other destruction of the whole will or some essential part of it, as by cutting off[58] or obliterat-ing[59] the signature of the testator[60] or the witnesses.[61] It is not enough for the

---

[46] Including, in the absence of special circumstances (*Smith v. Thompson* (1931) 146 L.T. 14), the exercise of any power of appointment made thereby: *Re Kingdon* (1886) 32 Ch. D. 604; *Lowthorpe-Lutwidge v. Lowthorpe-Lutwidge* [1935] P. 151.

[47] See *Re Spracklan's Estate* [1938] 2 All E.R. 345 (duly executed letter directing destruction of will in recipient's custody held effective).

[48] Wills Act 1837, s.20.

[49] *Collins v. Elstone* [1893] P. 1; *Re Horrocks* [1939] P. 198 at 216; but see *Re Phelan* [1972] Fam. 33.

[50] *In b. Oswald* (1874) L.R. 3 P. & D. 162; *In b. Moore* [1892] P. 378.

[51] *Post*, para. 11–032.

[52] *Simpson v. Foxon* [1907] P. 54.

[53] *Re Hawksley's Settlement* [1934] Ch. 384: see at 397, 398. But consider *In b. Musgrave* (1932) [1934] Ch. 402 at 405.

[54] *In b. Bryan* [1907] P. 125.

[55] *Lemage v. Goodban* (1865) L.R. I P. & D. 57.

[56] *In b. Fenwick* (1867) L.R. 1 P. & D. 319; *cf. Townsend v. Moore* [1905] P. 66 (two inconsistent wills of uncertain priority: probate refused to each); *Re Robinson* [1930] 2 Ch. 332 (no revocation by ineffective disposition).

[57] Wills Act 1837, s.20.

[58] *In b. Gullan* (1858) 1 Sw. & Tr. 23.

[59] *In b. Morton* (1887) 12 P.D. 141; contrast *In b. Godfrey* (1893) 69 L.T. 22 (signature remaining legible). The courts apply the same test in cases involving the Wills Act 1837, s.20 as they do in cases of alteration under s.21 (para. 11–022, *ante*). If the signature is still "apparent", the will is taken to have been revoked: *Re Adams* [1990] Ch. 601.

[60] *In b. Gullan, supra.*

[61] *Williams v. Tyley* (1858) John. 530.

testator to draw a line through part of the will, indorse it "all these are revoked" and kick it into the corner.[62] Destruction of part of a will normally revokes that part alone,[63] unless the part destroyed is so important as to lead to the conclusion that the rest cannot be intended to stand alone.[64] Destruction by someone other than the testator is ineffective unless carried out both in his presence[65] and by his direction[66]; the testator cannot ratify an unauthorised destruction.[67]

If a will has been destroyed without being revoked (*e.g.* because an *animus revocandi* was lacking), it is proved by means of a draft or copy, or even by oral evidence.[68] A will kept in the testator's possession but which cannot be found at the testator's death is presumed to have been destroyed by him *animo revocandi* and cannot be proved[69] unless the presumption is rebutted by evidence of non-revocation.[70]

(b) *Intent to revoke.* The testator must have an *animus revocandi* at the time of the destruction. If a will is intentionally torn up by a testator who is drunk[71] or believes the will to be ineffective,[72] it is not revoked, for an intent to destroy the document is no substitute for the requisite intent to revoke the will.[73] "All the destroying in the world without intention will not revoke a will, nor all the intention in the world without destroying: there must be the two."[74]   **11–028**

3. By marriage. Marriage automatically revokes all wills made by the parties to the marriage.[75] This is so even where the marriage is voidable and is later annulled.[76] There are two exceptions, however.   **11–029**

(a) *Certain appointments.* An appointment by will under a power of appointment is not revoked by the marriage of the testator unless, in default of appointment, the property would pass to his personal representatives.[77] The general intention of this provision is that if the testator's new "family" will   **11–030**

---

[62] *Cheese v. Lovejoy* (1858) 2 P.D. 251.
[63] See *In b. Woodward* (1871) L.R. 2 P. & D. 206 (seven or eight lines out of a will written on seven sheets); *In b. Nunn* (1936) 105 L.J.P. 57 (part of will cut out and remaining parts stitched together; partial revocation only); *Re Everest* [1975] Fam. 44 (similar).
[64] *Leonard v. Leonard* [1902] P. 243 (two out of five sheets destroyed).
[65] *In b. Dadds* (1857) Dea. & Sw. 290; *In b. De Kremer* (1965) 110 S.J. 18 (solicitor burnt will on client's telephone instructions).
[66] *Gill v. Gill* [1909] P. 157.
[67] *ibid.*
[68] *In b. Dadds* (1857) Dea. & Sw. 290 (copy); *Sugden v. Lord St. Leonards* (1876) 1 P.D. 154 (oral evidence of a beneficiary: the leading case on this subject); *Mills v. Millward* (1889) 15 P.D. 20 (affidavit by executor); *Re Webb* [1964] 1 W.L.R. 509.
[69] *Eckersley v. Platt* (1866) L.R. 1 P. & D. 281; *Allan v. Morrison* [1900] A.C. 604.
[70] *Sugden v. Lord St. Leonards, supra.*
[71] *In b. Brassington* [1902] P. 1.
[72] *In b. Thornton* (1889) 14 P.D. 82; *cf. In b. Southerden* [1925] P. 177 at 185.
[73] See *Giles v. Warren* (1872) L.R. 2 P. & D. 401.
[74] *Cheese v. Lovejoy* (1877) 2 P.D. 251 at 253, *per* James L.J.
[75] Wills Act 1837, s.18, replaced as regards wills made after 1982 by A.J.A. 1982, s.18.
[76] *Re Roberts* [1978] 1 W.L.R. 653.
[77] Wills Act 1837, s.18(2).

get the property even if the will is revoked, there is no harm in allowing marriage to revoke it. But if in default of appointment the property would pass out of the "family", as defined by the rules of intestacy, or only partly to that family,[78] the will is allowed to stand so far as it exercises the power of appointment, though the rest of the will is revoked.[79]

11–031   *(b) Contemplation of marriage.* A will made after 1925 and expressed to be made in contemplation of a marriage was not revoked by the solemnisation of the marriage contemplated.[80] This exception applied only if the will referred to the particular marriage in fact celebrated; it was not enough for the testator to declare in the will that it was "made in contemplation of marriage",[81] though it sufficed if the will gave everything[82] to an identified beneficiary described as "my fiancée"[83] or possibly "my wife".[84] If the will was made after 1982 it is enough that it appears from the will that the testator was expecting to be married to a particular person and that he intended that the will, or a particular disposition in it, should not be revoked by the marriage. In the case of a particular disposition, that disposition is not revoked, nor is the remainder of the will revoked unless such an intention appears from it.[85]

Before 1983, if a testator's marriage was dissolved, annulled or declared void, his will was unaffected. If the testator died after 1982 but before 1996, there was a lapse of any devise or bequest to the former spouse, unless the will showed a contrary intention.[86] Where a life estate so lapsed, any remainder was accelerated.[87] However, in this context "lapse" meant no more than "fail". The former spouse was not deemed to have predeceased the testator.[88] In addition, in such cases the will took effect as if any appointment of the former spouse as an executor or trustee had been omitted from it.[89] Because of the anomalous results to which this interpretation of lapse gave rise,[90] the law was changed.[91] If the testator dies after 1995, then subject to any expression of contrary intention in the will, (i) any gift in the will to his former

---

[78] See *In b. McVicar* (1869) L.R. 1 P. & D. 671; *Re Paul* [1921] 2 Ch. 1.
[79] *In b. Russell* (1890) 15 P.D. 111; see also *In b. Gilligan* [1950] P. 32 at 38, which contains a helpful explanation of the enactment; (1951) 67 L.Q.R. 351 (J. D. B. Mitchell).
[80] L.P.A. 1925, s.177.
[81] *Sallis v. Jones* [1936] P. 43.
[82] *Re Coleman* [1976] Ch. 1 (gift of part not enough).
[83] *In b. Langston* [1953] P. 100, preferred on this point in *Re Coleman, supra*, to *Burton v. McGregor* [1953] N.Z.L.R. 487.
[84] *Pilot v. Gainfort* [1931] P. 103, doubted in *Re Coleman, supra*.
[85] A.J.A. 1982, s.18(1), inserting a new s.18 into the Wills Act 1837.
[86] Wills Act 1837, s.18A(1)(b) (as inserted by A.J.A 1982, s.18(2)).
[87] Wills Act 1837, s.18A(3). The lapse does not prejudice an application by the former spouse under the Inheritance (Provision for Family and Dependants) Act 1975: *ibid.* s.18A(2) (*ante*, para. 11–004).
[88] *Re Sinclair* [1985] Ch. 446 (overruling *Re Cherrington* [1984] 1 W.L.R. 446). In that case a husband, by his will, left his estate to his wife, and if she predeceased him, to a charity. When the husband predeceased the wife without having revoked the will, his estate passed on intestacy and not to the charity.
[89] Wills Act 1837, s.18(1)(a) (inserted by A.J.A. 1977, s.18(2)).
[90] See *Bromley's Family Law* (9th ed.), p. 870.
[91] See Law Reform (Succession) Act 1995, s.3, implementing recommendations in (1993) Law Com. No. 217, Pt III.

spouse shall pass; and (ii) any provision in the will appointing that former spouse as an executor or administrator shall take effect, as if that spouse had *died* on the termination of the marriage.[92] Thus a gift in an unrevoked will to X should the testatrix's spouse predecease her, will now take effect in favour of X if the parties are divorced before the testatrix's death, even though her former spouse is still alive at that time.

4. Conditional revocation. Revocation of a will may be conditional, in **11–032** which case the will remains unrevoked until the condition has been fulfilled.[93] One particular kind of conditional revocation is known as dependent relative revocation.[94] If revocation is relative to another will and intended to be dependent upon the validity of that will, the revocation is ineffective unless that other will takes effect. Four examples may be given.

(a) Destruction. If a will is destroyed by a testator who is about to make a **11–033** new will, and the evidence shows that he intended to revoke the old will only in order to make way for a new one, the old will remains valid if the new will is never executed.[95] No special declaration of intention is necessary, since the court will readily infer it from the fact that a new will was contemplated.[96] But if the evidence indicates an intention to revoke the will in any event, the fact that a new will was contemplated will not prevent the revocation from taking effect.[97]

(b) Revival. If Will No. 1 is revoked by Will No. 2, the revocation of Will **11–034** No. 2 is not sufficient to revive Will No. 1,[98] so that if the testator revokes Will No. 2 in the mistaken belief that he is thereby reviving Will No. 1, the doctrine of dependent relative revocation applies and the revocation of Will No. 2 is ineffective.[99]

---

[92] See respectively Wills Act 1837, ss.18A(1)(b), (1)(a) (inserted by the Law Reform (Succession) Act 1995, s.3(1)).

[93] *e.g. In b. Southerden* [1925] P. 177 (will destroyed in mistaken belief that testator's widow would take all his property on his intestacy; *held*, not revoked); *cf. Campbell v. French* (1797) 3 Ves. 321 (mistaken belief that legatee was dead); *In b. Greenstreet* (1930) 74 S.J. 188.

[94] A title "somewhat overloaded with unnecessary polysyllables. The resounding adjectives add very little, as it seems to me, to any clear idea of what is meant. The whole matter can be quite simply expressed by the word 'conditional' ": *In b. Hope Brown* [1942] P. 136 at 138, *per* Langton J.

[95] *Onions v. Tyrer* (1716) 2 Vern. 742; *Dixon v. Solicitor to the Treasury* [1905] P. 42 (testator gave instructions for new will, tore off his signature from old will and died before new will completed: old will admitted to probate); *In b. Hope Brown* [1942] P. 136 (new will incomplete by reason of omission of names of beneficiaries: both old and new wills admitted to probate); *In b. Bromham* [1952] 1 All E.R. 110 (will mutilated with intention (never completed) of making a new will: old will admitted to probate); *In b. Cocke* [1960] 1 W.L.R. 491; contrast *Re Feis* [1964] Ch. 106. For a full review of the authorities, see *Re Finnemore* [1991] 1 W.L.R. 793.

[96] *Re Jones* [1976] Ch. 200.

[97] *ibid.*

[98] For revival, see *post*, para. 11–037.

[99] *Powell v. Powell* (1866) L.R. 1 P. & D. 209; *In b. Bridgewater* [1965] 1 W.L.R. 416 (letter by testator admissible evidence both of destruction and of his intent).

11–035   *(c) Obliterations.*[1] If a testator obliterates a legacy and by unattested writing substitutes a new legacy,[2] or pastes over the amount of a legacy an unattested slip of paper bearing a new amount,[3] the old legacy remains effective if the court is satisfied that it was revoked only on the erroneous supposition that the new legacy would be effective.

11–036   *(d) Gifts to attesting witnesses.*[4] The doctrine also applies where a testator executes a will which expressly revokes an earlier one and each will contains a gift in similar terms to X who attests the second will. Under the Wills Act 1837[5] the legacy in the second will to X will be void if the first will is revoked in its entirety. In those circumstances the gift in the first will remains effective because the testator did not intend it to be invalidated by the execution of the second.[6]

IV. REVIVAL

11–037   A will revoked by destruction *animo revocandi* can never be revived.[7] Any other will can be revived, but only by re-execution with the proper formalities or by a codicil showing an intention to revive it.[8] If a will has been revoked by a subsequent will, the first will is thus not revived merely by the revocation of the later will.[9] If a will is first partially revoked, then wholly revoked, and then revived, the revival does not extend to the part partially revoked unless an intention to this effect is shown.[10]

C. Informal Wills

11–038   A long-standing dispensation from the rules of formality is confirmed by the Wills Act 1837 in the following words: "Provided always . . . that any soldier being in actual military service, or any mariner or seaman being at sea, may dispose of his personal estate as he might have done before the making of this Act".[11] Under this privilege completely informal dispositions are permitted,

---

[1] For obliterations, see *ante*, para. 11–023.

[2] *In b. Horsford* (1874) L.R. 3 P. & D. 211; *In b. McCabe* (1873) L.R. 3 P. & D. 94 (substitution of different legatee); *Sturton v. Whellock* (1883) 52 L.J.P. 29 (gifts to grandchildren at 21: "one" obliterated and unattested "five" substituted); *cf. In b. Hope Brown* [1942] P. 136; *ante*, para. 11–033, n.95.

[3] *In b. Itter* [1950] P. 130 (new amounts signed but not attested).

[4] *Post*, para. 11–055.

[5] s.15.

[6] *In b. Crannis* (1978) 122 S.J. 489; *Re Finnemore, supra.*

[7] *Rogers v. Goodenough* (1862) 2 Sw. & Tr. 342; *In b. Reade* [1902] P. 75.

[8] Wills Act 1837, s.22, see *Goldie v. Adam* [1938] P. 85; *In b. Davis* [1952] P. 279 (revival by duly attested inscription on envelope containing will; intention to revive inferred from facts); *Re Pearson* [1963] 1 W.L.R. 1358 (revival of will containing revocation clause revokes later will).

[9] *In b. Hodgkinson* [1893] P. 339. The law was otherwise before 1838: *Usticke v. Bawden* (1824) 2 Add. 116.

[10] Wills Act 1837. s.22.

[11] s.11, replacing Statute of Frauds 1677, s.22, which was in similar terms. Before 1677 anyone might make an informal will of personalty: *ante*, para. 11–014.

even by minors, and it has since been extended to realty as well as person-alty.[12] The underlying doctrine, borrowed from Roman law,[13] is that a soldier or sailor may at times be *inops consilii*, cut off from skilled advice and help; but the privilege is not lost merely because such advice and help is available, nor are the rules of Roman law incorporated.[14]

I. PRIVILEGED TESTATORS

1. A soldier in actual military service. It is not enough that the testator **11–039** was in an army; he must have been "in actual military service" when he made the will. This phrase means active service in the armed forces in connection with hostilities including insurrection,[15] whether past, present or believed to be imminent in the future; and it is interpreted liberally.[16] A soldier is deemed to be in actual military service from the moment he received mobilisation orders[17] until the full conclusion of the operations,[18] which may last for many years beyond the end of hostilities.[19] Thus the privilege extends to an escort for those delimiting a frontier after fighting is over,[20] and to a member of an army of occupation, even though fighting ended nine years earlier,[21] but not to a wounded soldier in a London hospital.[22]

"Soldier" includes both officers and other ranks, an army nurse,[23] and a member of the Air Force[24]; and in the Second World War it included members of the Women's Auxiliary Air Force,[25] Auxiliary Transport Service, and Home Guard.[26]

2. A mariner or seaman at sea.[27] This includes both members of the Royal **11–040** Navy[28] and merchant seamen; it has been held to extend to a typist employed on a liner.[29] It includes an admiral directing naval operations on a river,[30] and

---

[12] *Post*, para. 11–044.
[13] *Drummond v. Parish* (1843) 3 Curt. 522 at 531.
[14] *Re Booth* [1926] P. 118; *Re Wingham* [1949] P. 187.
[15] *Re Jones* [1981] Fam. 7 (soldier shot by "clandestine assassins and arsonists" in Northern Ireland).
[16] The leading case is *Re Wingham* [1949] P. 187, where an airman undergoing training in Canada was held to be privileged. It resolves some of the difficulties in the earlier cases: see (1941) 57 L.Q.R. 481 (R.E.M.), criticising *In b. Gibson* [1941] 2 All E.R. 91; disapproved in *Re Wingham, supra*.
[17] *Gattward v. Knee* [1920] P. 99; *Re Booth* [1926] P. 118.
[18] *Re Limond* [1915] 2 Ch. 240.
[19] *Re Colman* [1958] 1 W.L.R. 457.
[20] *Re Limond, supra*.
[21] *Re Colman, supra* (British army in Germany).
[22] *In b. Grey* [1922] P. 140.
[23] *In b. Stanley* [1916] P. 192.
[24] Wills (Soldiers and Sailors) Act 1918. s.5.
[25] *In b. Rowson* [1944] 2 All E.R. 36.
[26] See *Re Wingham* [1949] P. 187 at 196.
[27] Wills Acts 1837, s.11.
[28] The statutory restrictions on informal dispositions of wages, prize money, etc., by seamen in the Navy and Marines were repealed by the Navy and Marines (Wills) Act 1953.
[29] *In b. Hale* [1915] 2 I.R. 362.
[30] *In b. Austen* (1853) 2 Rob.Ecc. 611.

a master mariner in his ship lying in the Thames before starting on her voyage.[31] A seaman on shore leave is deemed to be at sea, if he is a member of a ship's crew[32] or has received orders to join a ship.[33] It makes no difference that his ship is in dock for refitting[34] or is permanently stationed in harbour,[35] provided that he has not been paid off.

11–041   **3. A member of Her Majesty's Naval or Marine Forces so circumstanced that, had he been a soldier, he would have been in actual military service.**[36] This enables a member of the navy or marines who has been called up to make an informal will even though he has not joined his ship.[37]

II. EXTENT OF THE PRIVILEGE

A testator within one of the above categories has the following privileges.

11–042   **1. He can make or revoke a will even if he is a minor.**[38]

11–043   **2. He can make or revoke a will informally.** The will may be in writing, with or without witnesses or signature, or it may be nuncupative, *i.e.* oral. Thus farewell words spoken at a railway station may constitute a valid will.[39] The testator need not know that he is making a will, provided he gives deliberate expression to his wishes as to the destination of his property on his death.[40] Those entitled to make informal wills are also entitled to revoke a will, even if it has been made formally, in an informal manner, as by an unattested letter to a relative asking that the will should be burned, "for I have already cancelled it"[41]; and marriage also effects revocation.[42]

A will properly made under the above conditions remains valid indefinitely unless revoked. This is so even after the military or other service is over[43]; but thereafter any revocation must be formal. It formerly seemed that a minor was

---

[31] *In b. Patterson* (1898) 79 L.T. 123.
[32] *In b. Newland* [1952] P. 71; but see *In b. Thomas* (1918) 34 T.L.R. 626, which seems not to have been cited.
[33] *In b. Wilson* [1952] P. 92. Contrast *Re Rapley* [1983] 1 W.L.R. 1069 (no orders received).
[34] *In b. Newland, supra.*
[35] *In b. M'Murdo* (1867) L.R. 1 P. & D. 540; *In b. Anderson* [1916] P. 49 at 52.
[36] Wills (Soldiers and Sailors) Act 1918, s.2.
[37] See *In b. Anderson* [1916] P. 49 at 52; *In b. Yates* [1919] P. 93.
[38] Wills (Soldiers and Sailors) Act 1918, s.1 (declaratory, removing doubts raised by *Re Wernher* [1918] 1 Ch. 339), as amended by Family Law Reform Act 1969, s.3(1) (reduction of age of majority from 21 to 18). This is contrary to the usual rule: *ante*, para. 11–013.
[39] *In b. Yates* [1919] P. 93.
[40] *Re Stable* [1919] P. 7 ("If I stop a bullet, everything of mine will be yours"); *In b. Spicer* [1949] P. 441. Contrast *In b. Donner* (1917) 34 T.L.R. 138 (soldier told, incorrectly, that on intestacy his mother would get all his property: "That is just what I want. I want my mother to have everything": *held* no will but rather a reason for making no will); similarly *In b. Knibbs* [1962] 1 W.L.R. 852.
[41] *In b. Gossage* [1921] P. 194.
[42] *In b. Wardrop* [1917] P. 54.
[43] *Re Booth* [1926] P. 118 (over 40 years); and see *In b. Coleman* [1920] 2 I.R. 352.

unable to revoke the will save by marriage, but in 1969 a general power of revocation was conferred.[44]

3. The will can dispose of all kinds of property. The statutory privileges **11–044** at first applied only to wills of personalty.[45] They were extended to realty by the Wills (Soldiers and Sailors) Act 1918.[46] However, as regards any testator who is a minor there seems to be ground for supposing that the latter enactment may have been unintentionally frustrated by the Administration of Estates Act 1925,[47] except in the case of a minor who is either married or dies leaving issue, or devises of interests *pur autre vie*. The Act of 1918 also allows a guardian for the testator's infant children to be appointed by a privileged will.[48]

Section 4. Operation of Wills

A. *Lapse*

I. GENERAL RULE

A legacy or bequest (*i.e.* a testamentary gift of personalty) or a devise (*i.e.* a **11–045** testamentary gift of realty) is said to lapse if the beneficiary dies before the testator.[49] In such a case, unless a contrary intention is shown, the gift fails and the property comprised in it falls into residue,[50] which means that it passes under any general or residuary gift in the will, such as "all the rest of my property I leave to X". If there is no residuary gift, or if the gift which lapses is itself a gift of all or part of the residue, there is a partial intestacy and the property passes to the persons entitled on intestacy.[51]

A special case of statutory lapse is where a gift to a spouse lapses as a consequence of the testator's marriage being dissolved, annulled or declared void.[52]

II. EXCLUSION OF THE GENERAL RULE

The general rule as to lapse is excluded in four classes of case, though one of these is now obsolete.

---

[44] Family Law Reform Act 1969, s.3(3).
[45] Wills Act 1837, s.11.
[46] s.3, giving power to dispose of real estate in England and Ireland.
[47] s.51(3) (as amended by T.L.A.T.A. 1996, Sched. 3, para. 6(4)): see *post*, para. 20–015.
[48] s.4, reversing *In b. Tollemache* [1917] P. 246.
[49] The term "lapse" is also sometimes applied to the failure of gifts through events which occur after the testator's death, such as failure to satisfy a contingency: see, *e.g. Smell v. Dee* (1707) 2 Salk. 415; *Re Parker* [1901] 1 Ch. 408; *Re Fox's Estate* [1937] 4 All E.R. 664; and see *ante*, para. 11–031.
[50] Wills Act 1837, s.25. Previously the same rule applied to personalty, but realty passed to the heir: *Wright v. Hall* (1724) Fort. 182.
[51] *Ackroyd v. Smithson* (1780) 1 Bro.C.C. 503; *Re Forrest* [1931] 1 Ch. 162; *Re Midgley* [1955] Ch. 576.
[52] *Ante*, para. 11–031.

11–046   **1. Moral obligation.** A legacy which is not mere bounty but is intended to satisfy some moral obligation recognised by the testator, whether legally enforceable or not, is outside the doctrine of lapse, so that even if the legatee predeceases the testator the legacy can be claimed by the legatee's personal representatives.[53] A legacy bequeathed in order to pay a debt barred by lapse of time[54] or by the bankruptcy law,[55] or intended to pay the debts of someone for whom the testator felt morally responsible[56] may thus be saved from lapse.

11–047   **2. Entails.** Under the Wills Act 1837, section 32, subject to any contrary intention in the will, there was no lapse if property was given to a person in tail and he predeceased the testator, leaving issue living at the testator's death capable of inheriting under the entail. In that case the gift took effect as if the legatee or devisee had died immediately after the testator. After 1996, entails can no longer be created and this provision has, therefore, been repealed.[56a]

11–048   **3. Gifts to issue.** Subject to any expression of contrary intention, where a will of a testator dying after 1982[57] makes a gift to the child or remoter descendant of the testator and that child or descendant predeceases him, leaving issue who survive him, the gift is "to take effect" as a gift to the issue directly, and the issue take in equal shares *per stirpes*.[58] A child or descendant *en ventre sa mère* at the testator's death and born alive thereafter is to be treated as having survived him, and illegitimates have the same rights as legitimates.

11–049   **4. Class gifts.** A class gift,[59] *e.g.* "to all my children", is normally construed as a gift only to those members of the class who are living at the testator's death. There is then no question of lapse in the case of a child who predeceases the testator, since nothing was ever given to him. However, where a testator dies after 1982,[60] and subject to any contrary intention in the will, a class gift to his children or remoter descendants will include the issue of a deceased member of the class who are living at the testator's death.[61] The

---

[53] *Stevens v. King* [1904] 2 Ch. 30; but see Theobald, *Wills* (15th ed., 1993), p. 783.
[54] *Williamson v. Naylor* (1838) 3 Y. & C.Ex. 208.
[55] *Re Sowerby's Trusts* (1856) 2 K. & J. 630.
[56] *Re Leach* [1948] Ch. 232 (bequest to pay son's debts).
[56a] T.L.A.T.A. 1996, s.25(2), Sched. 4. For the abolition of entails see *ante*, para. 3–037.
[57] For the position of a testator dying before 1983, see the previous edition of this work at p. 519.
[58] A.J.A. 1982, s.19, inserting a new s.33 into the Wills Act 1837. For *per stirpes*, see *post*, para. 11–103.
[59] For class gifts, see *ante*, para. 7–059.
[60] For the position of a testator dying before 1983, see the previous edition of this work at p. 521.
[61] As n.58, *supra*.

issue take in equal shares *per stirpes*.[62] Illegitimacy is disregarded, and children conceived before the testator's death but born alive after it are treated as being alive then.

5. Exceptions. In two cases the provisions of the Wills Act 1837[63] do not apply so as to prevent a lapse.   **11–050**

(a) Appointments under special powers. The Act does not apply to an appointment by will under a special power,[64] for it is confined to cases where there is a "devise or bequest" of property. It does, however, apply to appointments under general powers,[65] for the property is then construed as devisable by the appointor.[66]   **11–051**

(b) Interests terminable on donee's death and certain contingent gifts. Formerly the Act expressly excluded gifts of any estate or interest determinable at or before the testator's death, such as a gift of a mere life interest or in joint tenancy. This exclusion no longer appears in the Act, but it is unlikely that the position has changed. It seems improbable that issue of the donee of a life interest could contend that the gift should take effect as a bequest to him for his life.[67] The gift of a mere life interest is likely to be held to show a contrary intention, since it clearly indicates that after the death of the donee the gift is not intended to take effect at all. In any case the gift may fail as being a gift for the life of the father, "take effect" meaning merely "operate".[68] For similar reasons, it is thought that a bequest "to X as and when he is 25", where X predeceased the testator aged 20 leaving issue, would not take effect as a gift to the issue.[69]   **11–052**

III. COMMORIENTES

Where a devisee or legatee dies at nearly the same time as the testator, it is necessary to determine which of them survived the other in order to know whether the gift lapsed. Similar questions between *commorientes* (those dying together) arise on intestacy and in respect of joint tenancies. Before 1926 there was no means of settling the question if there was no evidence of the order of deaths. The estate of neither person could therefore benefit from that of the   **11–053**

---

[62] See *post*, para. 11–103.
[63] s.33, as substituted by A.J.A. 1982, s.19. Except as indicated, the position was the same for testators who died prior to 1983.
[64] *Holyland v. Lewin* (1883) 26 Ch.D. 266. For powers of appointment, see *ante*, para. 10–081.
[65] *Eccles v. Cheyne* (1856) 2 K. & J. 676.
[66] Wills Act 1837, s.27; *post*, para. 11–078.
[67] This question cannot arise in respect of gifts made by a testator who died before 1983: see the previous edition of this work at p. 521.
[68] *Re Butler* [1918] 1 I.R. 394.
[69] For the situation where the testator died before 1983 see the previous edition of this work at p. 521.

other. The Law of Property Act 1925 resolves this problem for deaths occurring after 1925 by providing that where it is uncertain which survived the other, for all purposes affecting the title to property the younger shall be deemed to have survived the elder, subject to any order of the court.[70] The section applies equally to cases of simple uncertainty, as where one of the parties is on a ship which founders with all hands on an uncertain date and the other dies at home during that period, and to common disasters, such as practically simultaneous deaths in an air-raid,[71] or deaths in an unknown sequence in a common shipwreck[72]; but it does not apply where one person is merely presumed to have died because he disappeared over seven years before the other died.[73]

11–054　　　This rule has now been modified as between husband and wife if one of them dies intestate.[74] Further, for the purposes of inheritance tax the old rule has been restored, and each of the deceased is deemed to have died simultaneously with the other.[75] It is still prudent to insert a survivorship clause in a will, making gifts by a husband to his wife conditional upon her surviving him for (say) a month.[76] Then if both are killed in an accident with all their issue and the wife actually or notionally survives the husband for a short while, the husband's property will pass to (for example) his own parents rather than to his wife's parents.

B. Gifts to Witnesses

11–055　　　**1. No benefit for witness.** The Wills Act[77] provides that the attestation of a beneficiary or his or her spouse should be valid, but that the beneficiary could claim no benefit under the will, as to either realty or personalty. Formerly this applied even if there were two other witnesses to the will, so that the beneficiary's signature was superfluous.[78] But where the testator dies after May 29, 1968, the attestations of any beneficiaries (or their spouses) are for this purpose to be disregarded if without them the will is duly executed.[79] Thus if one of the three witnesses is a legatee, the legacy is good; if two of them are legatees, both legacies fail.

---

[70] s.184. The last two words probably do not confer any general discretion on the court, *e.g.* to avoid hardship: see *Re Lindop* [1942] Ch. 377 at 382 (but the point was reserved in *Hickman v. Peacey* [1945] A.C. 304 (see at 337)).

[71] *Hickman v. Peacey* [1945] A.C. 304, the majority of the House of Lords rejecting the argument that the section is inapplicable where the deaths may have been simultaneous.

[72] *Re Rowland* [1963] Ch. 1.

[73] *Re Albert* [1967] V.R. 875.

[74] See *post*, para. 11–100.

[75] Inheritance Tax Act 1984, ss.4(2), 54(4). This point used to be important in the days of capital transfer tax, but is no longer so. Even if L.P.A. 1925, s.184 did apply, there would be no second charge to tax on the death of the notional survivor: Inheritance Tax Act 1984, s.141.

[76] For the statutory survivorship clause that applies in cases of intestacy, see A.E.A. 1925, s.46(2A); *post*, para. 11–101.

[77] s.15.

[78] *Randfield v. Randfield* (1863) 32 L.J.Ch. 668.

[79] Wills Act 1968, s.1.

2. Limits. The limits of the rule should be noticed. **11–056**

(i) It does not apply if no witnesses at all were necessary for the validity of the will, such as the will of a soldier in actual military service.[80]

(ii) It does not apply to a person who signs the will not as a witness but merely, for example, to show that he agrees with the testator's leaving him less than his brothers and sisters.[81]

(iii) A beneficiary who marries a witness after the date of the will is not disabled from claiming under it.[82]

(iv) The rule applies only to beneficial gifts and not to gifts to a person as trustee.[83] But the trustee cannot himself benefit; thus a solicitor trustee who attested the will cannot charge professional fees, although expressly so empowered by the will,[84] unless he is not appointed trustee until after the will has been made.[85]

(v) The rule does not apply if the gift is made or confirmed by any will or codicil not attested by the beneficiary.[86] Thus if there is a gift by will confirmed by codicil, a beneficiary who witnesses only one document is entitled to the gift since he can claim under the other document; this is so even where the residuary legatee under a will attested a codicil which, by revoking certain legacies, would swell the residue.[87]

(vi) The rule has no application where the testator leaves a gift to a legatee as secret trustee, and the will is witnessed by a beneficiary under that trust. The witness takes under the trust and not the will.[88]

(vii) In certain circumstances a gift to a legatee (or his spouse) who witnesses a will may be saved by the doctrine of dependant relative revocation, if there was a gift in similar terms to the same legatee in a previous will.[89]

3. Limited interests. The effect of the rule in the case of a limited interest **11–057**
is to accelerate the subsequent interests. Thus if property is given to A for life,

---

[80] *Re Limond* [1915] 2 Ch. 240.
[81] *Kitcat v. King* [1930] P. 266; *In b. Bravda* [1967] 1 W.L.R. 1080.
[82] *Thorpe v. Bestwick* (1881) 6 Q.B.D. 311.
[83] *Cresswell v. Cresswell* (1868) L.R. 6 Eq. 69; *Re Ray's W.T.* [1936] Ch. 520 (prior to testatrix's death witness becomes Abbess to whom property is given on trust: gift effective).
[84] *Re Pooley* (1888) 40 Ch.D. 1.
[85] *Re Royce's W.T.* [1959] Ch. 626.
[86] *Re Marcus* (1887) 56 L.J.Ch. 830; *Re Trotter* [1899] 1 Ch. 764.
[87] *Gurney v. Gurney* (1855) 3 Drew. 208.
[88] *Re Young* [1951] Ch. 344. For secret trusts, see *ante*, para. 10–045.
[89] See *Re Finnemore* [1991] 1 W.L.R. 793, *ante*, para. 11–033.

with remainder to B, the effect of A attesting the will is that B is entitled to the property as soon as the testator dies.[90] Similarly if property is given to X, Y and Z as joint tenants, and X attests the will, Y and Z are entitled to the whole of the property[91]; had they been tenants in common, X's third would have fallen into residue and passed on intestacy.[92]

C. Murder or Manslaughter of Testator[93]

11–058 At common law, as part of a wider rule of public policy that "no person can obtain, or enforce, any rights resulting to him from his own crime",[94] a person who is held to be guilty in criminal or civil proceedings[95] of a deliberate and intentional killing can take no benefit under the will or intestacy of his victim.[96] This is so whether the killing was in law murder, manslaughter, or aiding and abetting a suicide, and whether or not it involved acts or threats of violence.[97] Thus a killer's prospective share under his victim's intestacy devolves as if he did not exist, *e.g.* on his brothers and sisters, and not on the Crown.[98] There may however be great injustice in imposing what may be a severe civil sanction on a person who has either been acquitted, or whose moral culpability is such that a criminal court has not imposed a custodial sentence.[99] These considerations have prompted the further relaxation of the rule by statute. Under the terms of the Forfeiture Act 1982,[1] the court now has power to modify the rule in all cases of unlawful killing,[2] except where a person has been convicted of murder.[3] It may do so if it is satisfied that the

---

[90] *Jull v. Jacobs* (1876) 3 Ch.D. 703. Contrast *Re Doland's W.T.* [1970] Ch. 267 (substitutional or dependent gift falls with offending gift).

[91] *Young v. Davies* (1863) 2 Dr. & Sm. 167.

[92] *Hoare v. Osborne* (1864) 33 L.J.Ch. 586.

[93] See (1990) 10 O.J.L.S. 289 (S. M. Cretney); S. M. Cretney, *Law, Law Reform and the Family* (1999), p. 73.

[94] *In b. Crippen* [1911] P. 108 at 112, *per* Evans P. Although this general rule has often been affirmed (see, *e.g. Davitt v. Titcumb* [1990] Ch. 110), it is not now applied inflexibly. *Cf.* Forfeiture Act 1982, s.1(1).

[95] This rule may apply even if a person has been acquitted of a charge of murder or manslaughter, provided that in civil proceedings the court is satisfied on the balance of probabilities that he was guilty of a killing that fell within the scope of the rule: *Gray v. Barr* [1971] 2 Q.B. 554.

[96] The so-called "forfeiture rule": *In b. Hall* [1914] P. 1 (will: manslaughter); *Re Sigsworth* [1935] Ch. 89 (intestacy: murder). For the application of this rule to joint tenancies, see *ante*, para. 9–049.

[97] *Dunbar v. Plant* [1998] Ch. 412 (suicide pact); [1998] C.L.J. 31 (S. Bridge). The court disapproved *Re H* [1990] 1 F.L.R. 441, in which it had been held that, for the rule to apply, the killer had to have been guilty of violence or unlawful violence. See too *Jones v. Roberts* [1995] 2 F.L.R. 422 (manslaughter by reason of diminished responsibility).

[98] *Re Callaway* [1956] Ch. 559.

[99] *e.g.* a "battered wife" who has endured years of torment at the hands of her husband and is put on probation for his manslaughter: *Re K* [1985] Ch. 85.

[1] The Act began as a Private Member's Bill: (1990) 10 O.J.L.S. 289 (S. M. Cretney).

[2] s.2. Application to the court must be made within three months of any conviction for an offence of which an unlawful killing is an element: s.2(3).

[3] s.5.

justice of the case so requires,[4] *e.g.* in cases where the unlawful killing involves little moral blame.[5] The discretion will normally be exercised in cases of suicide pacts.[6] The forfeiture rule no longer precludes applications under the Inheritance (Provision for Family and Dependants) Act 1975 and the Matrimonial Causes Act 1973, or applications for social security benefits.[7]

Section 5. Construction of Wills

The construction of wills is a vast and difficult subject[8] of which only a few **11–059** of the more important rules can be mentioned here.

A. General Rule

1. Ascertaining intention. The cardinal rule of construction is that effect **11–060** must be given to the intention of the testator as expressed in the will, the words being given their natural meaning. The will alone must be looked at, and, in general,[9] no evidence can be received to contradict the meaning of the words used in the will. "The will must be in writing, and the only question is, what is the meaning of the words used in that writing."[10]

The words of the will must normally be given their natural meaning, or the most appropriate of their several natural meanings, except so far as that leads to absurdities or inconsistencies. But there is nothing to prevent words from being construed in some special sense if the will clearly shows that they are used in that sense; and in recent years the courts have been rather more ready to accept that the testator may have used words otherwise than in accordance with their "strict" meaning. Thus "money", in its strict legal meaning, comprises only cash and debts due, but a bequest in a home-made will of "all

---

[4] This does not empower the court to "do justice between the parties": *Dunbar v. Plant* [1998] Ch. 412 at 427. Phillips L.J. considered that the discretion under the Act should be exercised where the forfeiture rule appeared to "conflict with the ends of justice": *ibid.* at 436.

[5] s.2(2). See *Re K* [1985] Ch. 85; [1986] Ch. 180: *Re S* [1996] 1 W.L.R. 235.

[6] *Dunbar v. Plant, supra,* at 438.

[7] s.3. It was thought that the forfeiture rule was excluded in relation to the matters listed in s.3. However it has been held that applications under the Act of 1975 will still fail if the deceased had in fact made reasonable provision for the killer in his will: *Re Royse* [1985] Ch. 22. In such cases, the killer will therefore receive nothing unless the court exercises its discretion under the Forfeiture Act 1982, s.2. Presumably, in a case where the victim died intestate but where a court would not have exercised its discretion under s.2 had he left a will in favour of his killer, the court would decline to exercise its powers under the 1975 Act on an application by the killer. If this is not so, *Re Royse* creates an anomaly.

[8] "Wills and the construction of them do more perplex a man, than any other learning, and to make a certain construction of them, this *excedit juris prudentum artem*": *Roberts v. Roberts* (1613) 2 Bulstr. 123 at 130, *per* Coke C.J. Lord Eldon L.C. began one judgment: "Having had doubts upon this Will for 20 years . . . ": *Earl of Radnor v. Shafto* (1805) 11 Ves. 448 at 453; but see Megarry, *Miscellany-at-Law* (1955); p. 244. For the judicial tendency towards liberality and away from technicality, see (1976) 40 Conv. (N.S.) 66 (C. H. Sherrin).

[9] Contrast *Re Jones' W.T., infra,* and *Re Jebb* [1966] Ch. 666, (cases on "contrary intention").

[10] *Grey v. Pearson* (1857) 6 H.L.C. 61 at 106, *per* Lord Wensleydale.

moneys of which I die possessed" may be construed as including stocks and shares and personal property generally.[11] The court may invoke what is sometimes known as the "dictionary principle": the testator, by showing in the will that he has used a word in a particular sense, has made his own dictionary for the purposes of the will.[12]

11–061   **2. Illegitimate children.** It was a settled rule that "children" bore the natural meaning "legitimate children",[13] so that an illegitimate child was excluded even if he passed as legitimate.[14] Virtually all vestiges of this rule have now been removed by statute and illegitimate children are treated in almost all respects in the same way as those who are legitimate. In any will or codicil made after 1969, a provision for the benefit of a child, children or relations of any kind is to be construed as including those illegitimately related, unless the contrary intention appears.[15] The use of the word "heir" or of any expression which prior to 1997 was used to create an entailed interest does not show a contrary intention if it is contained in any disposition of property made on or after April 4, 1988.[16]

11–062   **3. Adopted children.** In the case of adopted children, if the adoption preceded the testator's death, the adopted children are treated as "children" of the adopter for purposes of dispositions of property,[17] unless a contrary intention appears from the will or the surrounding circumstances.[18]

11–063   **4. Mistakes and inept language.** Where the testator's intention is sufficiently clear from the will itself the court may be able to omit or supply words inserted or omitted by mischance.[19] The court may also strike out words if it is shown (*e.g.* from a draft) that the effect of the version signed by the testator was not known to and approved by him.[20] But this rule extends only to the deletion of words, not to their insertion. Vague expressions such as "X's relations" or "X's successors" may be construed as references to the persons who would be entitled on X's intestacy, so as to save the gift from being void

[11] *Perrin v. Morgan* [1943] A.C. 399.
[12] See *Hill v. Crook* (1873) L.R. 6 H.L. 265 at 285.
[13] *Wilkinson v. Adam* (1812) 1 V. & B. 422 at 462.
[14] *Re Pearce* [1914] 1 Ch. 254.
[15] Family Law Reform Act 1987, ss.1, 19, replacing the Family Law Reform Act 1969, s.15. The 1987 Act followed two Law Commission Reports: Law Com. Nos 118 and 157. See generally [1988] Conv. 410 (J. G. Miller). On the rights of legitimated children, see the Legitimacy Act 1976, ss.5, 6.
[16] Family Law Reform Act 1987, s.19(2). Prior to that date the rule had been otherwise: Family Law Reform Act 1969, s.15(2). The devolution of property along with a title of honour is unaffected by the 1987 Act: s.19(4). Entails cannot be created after 1996, *ante*, para. 3–037.
[17] Adoption Act 1976, ss.39, 42.
[18] *Re Jones' W.T.* [1965] Ch. 1124 (statement by testator admitted in evidence); *Re Brinkley's W.T.* [1968] Ch. 407.
[19] See, *e.g. Re Riley's W.T.* [1962] 1 W.L.R. 344; *Re Morris* [1971] P. 62; *Re Phelan* [1972] Fam. 33 (revocation clause omitted).
[20] *Re Reynette-James* [1976] 1 W.L.R. 161.

for uncertainty.[21] Meaningless and incongruous expressions may sometimes be disregarded.[22] Statute now allows extrinsic evidence, including evidence of the testator's intention, to be admitted to assist in the interpretation of any part of the will that is meaningless.[23]

Prior to 1983 the doctrine of rectification of mistakes in legal documents did not apply to wills,[24] and the court would not insert missing provisions, even where caused by mere miscopying of a draft[25] or by failing to provide for some obvious contingency.[26] But where the testator dies after 1982, the court has been given a limited statutory power to rectify his will if it is satisfied that it fails to carry out his intentions in consequence of a clerical error[27] or of a failure to understand his instructions.[28] Application must be made within six months from the date on which representation was first taken out, unless the court permits an extension of time. After the six months the personal representatives may distribute the estate without liability, regardless of the possibility of a later application being permitted, though without prejudice to any power to recover assets by virtue of the court's order.

B. Extrinsic Evidence

The general rule is that only the words of the will may be considered. **11–064**
Extrinsic evidence of the testator's intention (*i.e.* evidence not gathered from the will itself) is normally inadmissible. But the rule is subject to qualifications, and its rigour has been mitigated by statute.

1. Surrounding circumstances. Evidence of facts and circumstances exist- **11–065**
ing when the will was made is always admissible in order to explain its terms. "You may place yourself, so to speak, in [the testator's] armchair".[29] Thus extrinsic evidence is admissible to show that certain words had a peculiar meaning to the testator by the custom of the district or the usage of the class of persons to which he belonged,[30] or that a description was mistaken, in which case the testator's true intention is carried out; *falsa demonstratio non*

---

[21] *Rowland v. Gorsuch* (1789) 2 Cox Eq. 187; *Re Gansloser's W.T.* [1952] Ch. 30; *Re Kilvert* [1957] Ch. 388. As to the share taken, see *ante*, para. 9–020.

[22] *Re Macandrew's W.T.* [1964] Ch. 704.

[23] A.J.A. 1982, s.21, as recommended by the Law Reform Committee, Cmnd. 5301 (1973).

[24] For rectification generally see *post*, para. 12–122.

[25] *Re Reynette-James, supra.*

[26] *Re Hammersley* [1965] Ch. 481.

[27] A.J.A. 1982, s.20(1)(a), as recommended by the Law Reform Committee, above. A "clerical error" includes "an error made in the process of recording the intended words of the testator in the drafting or transcription of his will": *Wordingham v. Royal Exchange Trust Co. Ltd* [1992] Ch. 412 at 419, *per* Evans-Lombe, Q.C. (failure by solicitor to include exercise of a power of appointment in will: rectification ordered). It is not however confined to errors of transcription but also includes the case where the will contains a provision which is not in accordance with the testator's wishes: *Re Segelman* [1996] Ch. 171.

[28] A.J.A. 1982, s.20(1)(b). See *Re Segelman, supra*, at 180.

[29] *Boyes v. Cook* (1880) 14 Ch.D. 53 at 56, *per* James L.J.; but the testator is not to be assumed to have a well-stocked law library: *Re Follett* [1955] 1 W.L.R. 429; (1955) 71 L.Q.R. 17, 326 (R.E.M.).

[30] *Shore v. Wilson* (1839) 9 Cl. & F. 355 at 498 *et seq.*

nocet (a mistake in description does no harm).[31] Where the testator is under a misapprehension as to what he owns, however, the court is not at liberty to alter the language so as to make the gift apply to an altogether different asset, even though it may be satisfied that he would have done so had he appreciated the position.[32] Nicknames,[33] or symbols used by the testator in his trade,[34] may be explained by evidence; thus it may be shown that a gift for "mother" was intended for the testator's wife, whom he always described thus.[35]

2. Equivocations

11–066   *(a) Ambiguity.* Evidence of the testator's intention has always been admissible to explain an equivocation. There is said to be an equivocation or ambiguity in a will when there is a description of a person or thing which can apply equally well to two or more persons or things. Thus if a testator devises his close (enclosed land) "in the occupation of W" and he has two such closes, there is an equivocation.[36]

By statute,[37] extrinsic evidence, including evidence of the testator's intention, is admissible in so far as the language used in any part of his will is meaningless or is ambiguous on the face of it. The same applies also in so far as evidence, other than evidence of the testator's intention, shows that the language used in any part of his will is ambiguous in the light of surrounding circumstances.[38]

11–067   *(b) Effect of extrinsic evidence.* Once extrinsic evidence of the testator's intention is admitted, it will be given effect even if it shows that someone apparently outside the scope of the gift was intended to take. Thus, in one case[39] a testatrix gave part of her property "to my nephew Arthur Murphy". She had two legitimate nephews of that name and extrinsic evidence was admitted to explain this ambiguity. The evidence admitted showed that the testatrix intended to benefit an illegitimate nephew called Arthur Murphy, and it was held that he took to the exclusion of the two legitimate nephews. Had there been only one legitimate and one illegitimate nephew, there would have been no ambiguity, for "nephew" prima facie meant "legitimate nephew";

---

[31] See, *e.g. Re Ray* [1916] 1 Ch. 461; *Re Price* [1932] 2 Ch. 54; *Re Posner* [1953] P. 277 (bequest to "my wife R" upheld although R was not the testator's wife).

[32] *Re Lewis's W.T.* [1985] 1 W.L.R. 102 (gift of farm and stock did not refer to the testator's majority shareholding in the farm). See too *Re Tetsall* [1961] 1 W.L.R. 938.

[33] *Re Ofner* [1909] 1 Ch. 60.

[34] *Kell v. Charmer* (1856) 23 Beav. 195 (jeweller's bequest of "the sum of i.x.x." which was the trade symbol for £100).

[35] *Thorn v. Dickens* [1906] W.N. 54 (the entire will was "all for mother").

[36] *Richardson v. Watson* (1833) 4 B. & Ad. 787.

[37] A.J.A. 1982, s.21, as recommended by the Law Reform Committee, Cmnd. 5301 (1973). This section applies to persons dying after 1982. For the problems that formerly existed, see the previous edition of this work at p. 529.

[38] A.J.A. 1982, s.21, as recommended by the Law Reform Committee, Cmnd. 5301 (1973). See *Re Williams* [1985] 1 W.L.R. 905.

[39] *Re Jackson* [1933] Ch. 237.

consequently no extrinsic evidence would have been admitted and the legitimate nephew would have taken.[40]

(c) Uncertainty. If extrinsic evidence fails to resolve an ambiguity, the gift
is void for uncertainty.[41] The same applies where the description is on the face
of it indefinite, *e.g.* a gift by a testator "to one of the sons of X", X having at
the time several sons.[42]

11–068

C. Contradictions

1. Inconsistency. Extrinsic evidence is not admissible to explain a contradiction in a will, *e.g.* a gift of "one hundred pounds (£500) to X". In such a
case, the quaint[43] rule is that the second expression prevails over the first[44]
since it is the latest in the testator's mind. This contrasts with a deed, where
the former of two inconsistent expressions prevails, for what has once been
done cannot be undone.[45] Before resorting to such a rule of thumb, however,
the court tries to reconcile the two provisions in some way.[46]

11–069

A prevalent form of contradiction is where the testator makes inconsistent
gifts to his wife and children, as by saying "I leave everything to my wife and
then it shall be for our children". Where the testator dies after 1982 there is
now a statutory solution: a gift to a spouse in terms which in themselves
would give an absolute interest is to take effect as an absolute gift, notwithstanding any purported gift to the testator's issue in the same instrument.[47]

2. *Lassence v. Tierney.* A long-standing rule for the construction of a
certain type of contradictory gift is the rule in *Lassence v. Tierney*.[48] This
applies to deeds as well as to wills,[49] and to realty as well as to personalty.[50]
This rule has been stated as follows: "If you find an absolute gift to a legatee
in the first instance, and trusts are engrafted or imposed on that absolute
interest which fail, either from lapse or invalidity or any other reason, then the
absolute gift takes effect so far as the trusts have failed to the exclusion of the
residuary legatee or next of kin as the case may be".[51]

11–070

---

[40] *Re Fish* [1894] 2 Ch. 83.
[41] *Richardson v. Watson, supra.* n. 36 where the evidence showed that in fact the testator intended
both closes to pass.
[42] *Strode v. Russel* (1708) 2 Vern. 621 at 624, 625; *cf. Dowset v. Sweet* (1753) Amb. 175.
[43] See *ante*, para. 9–019.
[44] *Perkins v. Baynton* (1781) 1 Bro.C.C. 118; *Re Hammond* [1938] 3 All E.R. 308 (refusing to
apply the rule for commercial documents that the words control the figures).
[45] *Doe d. Leicester v. Biggs* (1809) 2 Taunt. 109 at 13; *Forbes v. Git* [1922] 1 A.C. 256 at 259;
cf. ante, para. 9–019.
[46] See *Wallop v. Darby* (1611) Yelv. 209 (gift to X in tail, followed by a separate gift of the same
property to Y in fee simple: *held*, Y took a remainder after X's entail); *Fyfe v. Irwin* [1939] 2
All E.R. 271 at 281.
[47] A.J.A. 1982, s.22: the rule is confined to spouses.
[48] (1849) 1 Mac. & G. 551.
[49] *Re Gatti's Voluntary S.T.* [1936] 2 All E.R. 1489; *Att.-Gen. v. Lloyds Bank Ltd* [1935] A.C.
382.
[50] *Moryoseph v. Moryoseph* [1920] 2 Ch. 33.
[51] *Hancock v. Watson* [1902] A.C. 14 at 22, *per* Lord Davey.

Thus, if there is a gift to X of a fee simple or an absolute interest in personalty, and later in the will[52] or in a codicil[53] there is a direction that the property given to X shall be held for X for life with remainder to his children, if the gift to the children fails, whether partly[54] or wholly (*e.g.* through there being no children[55] or through the perpetuity rule being infringed[56]), the gift of the fee simple or absolute interest to X takes effect instead of the property passing under a residuary gift or as on intestacy.[57]) For the rule to apply, there must be an initial absolute gift which is subsequently cut down[58]; one continuous limitation containing both gift and restrictions will normally not bring the doctrine into play,[59] nor will a gift in which the names of the beneficiaries are immediately followed by the words "subject to the provisions hereinafter contained".[60]

D. A Will Speaks from Death

A will speaks from death. There are two aspects of this rule. First, it is applied by statute to property. Secondly, the courts have applied it to certain persons.

I. AS TO PROPERTY

11–071 It has already been explained that a will is ambulatory.[61] By the Wills Act 1837,[62] a will, unless it shows a contrary intention—

    (i) speaks from death; and

    (ii) takes effect as if it had been executed immediately before the testator's death;

as regards all property comprised in it. This means that a will is capable of disposing of all property owned by the testator at his death even if he acquired it after making his will. Thus, a gift of "my shares in the Great Western Railway Company" includes not only those owned when the will was made but those acquired subsequently[63]; and a devise of "all the lands of which I am

---

[52] *Hulme v. Hulme* (1839) 9 Sim. 644.

[53] *Norman v. Kynaston* (1861) 3 De G.F. & J. 29.

[54] *Re Coleman* [1936] Ch. 528. See also *Re Litt* [1946] Ch. 154; *Re Atkinson's W.T.* [1957] Ch. 117.

[55] *Watkins v. Weston* (1863) 3 De G.J. & S. 434.

[56] *Ring v. Hardwick* (1840) 2 Beav. 352.

[57] *Whittell v. Dudin* (1820) 2 Jac. & W. 279.

[58] See, *e.g. Re Burton's S.T.* [1955] Ch. 348, on the distinction between a true gift and mere administrative direction.

[59] *Re Payne* [1927] 2 Ch. 1.

[60] *Re Cohen's W.T.* [1936] 1 All E.R. 103.

[61] *Ante*, para. 11–010.

[62] s.24; see *Re Bancroft* [1928] Ch. 577.

[63] *Trinder v. Trinder* (1866) L.R. 1 Eq. 695; contrast *Re Tetsall* [1961] 1 W.L.R. 938 ("my 750 shares").

seised" carries with it land acquired after the will was made,[64] together with all fixtures attached to the land, even if they were affixed after the will was made.[65]

This rule applies to all generic descriptions (*i.e.* descriptions of a class of objects which may increase or decrease[66]) and is not confined to general or residual gifts[67]; but it has no application to a gift of a specific object existing at the date of the will.[68] Thus if a testator makes a will giving "my piano" to X and subsequently sells that piano and buys another, X has no claim to it,[69] unless the will is confirmed by a codicil made after the purchase.[70] The bequest is said to have been adeemed, meaning that the gift has failed because the specified property ceased to exist, or ceased to belong to the testator, between the date of his will and his death.[71] A gift will also be adeemed if before his death the testator contracts to sell the property,[72] or if an option to purchase it granted by him before his death is exercised even after his death[73]; for in each case the specific asset had become a mere right to receive the purchase price.

II. AS TO PERSONS

1. Class gifts

(a) *The problem of distribution.* Class gifts[74] are construed on the ordinary **11–072** principle that the testator's intention shall govern the persons who are to take.[75] But a special problem arises where one member of the class becomes qualified to take before the maximum number of members can be fixed. Suppose, for example, that the testator leaves property "to all my grand-children who attain 21 in equal shares". As soon as a grandchild attains 21 he becomes entitled to a share. But to how much? If all future grandchildren are to be included, nothing can safely be paid out to him until all the parents, uncles and aunts are dead, so that the maximum number of shares is known. The essence of the problem, therefore, is an inconsistency in the testator's directions: *all* are to *take*, yet each is to take rather than have to await the completion of the class.

---

[64] *Doe* d. *York v. Walker* (1844) 12 M. & W. 591.

[65] For fixtures, see *post*, para. 14–311.

[66] *Re Slater* [1906] 2 Ch. 480 at 485. See *All Souls College v. Coddrington* (1719) 1 P.Wms. 597 (bequest of library "now in the custody" of X includes after-added books).

[67] *Re Ord* (1879) 12 Ch.D. 22 at 25.

[68] *Emuss v. Smith* (1848) 2 De G. & Sm. 722 at 733, 736.

[69] *Re Sikes* [1927] 1 Ch. 364.

[70] *Re Reeves* [1928] Ch. 351.

[71] See Bailey, *Wills*, 109, 113; *cf. Re Heilbronner* [1953] 1 W.L.R. 1254 and see *ante*, para. 11–010.

[72] *Re Edwards* [1958] Ch. 168.

[73] *Lawes v. Bennett* (1786) 1 Cox Eq. 167; *Re Isaacs* [1894] 3 Ch. 506; *Re Carrington* [1932] 1 Ch. 1; *Re Rose* [1948] Ch. 78.

[74] For definition, see *ante*, para. 7–059.

[75] Thus a gift, after a life interest to X (a spinster), to X's issue who attain 21 may be confined to issue born before X's death, without the aid of the rule in *Andrews v. Partington* (below): *Re Cockle's W.T.* [1967] Ch. 690.

11–073   (b) *Andrews v. Partington*. In order to expedite the distribution of the property, the courts have adopted the rule, already discussed in relation to the rule against perpetuities,[76] known as the rule in *Andrews v. Partington*.[77] This rule cuts down the class by confining it to persons in existence when the first capital[78] share becomes payable.[79] The interests of after-born members of the class are sacrificed for the purpose of fixing the maximum number of shares. Because this is unfair to them, the rule "has been repeatedly attacked over the two hundred years or so that it has survived",[80] and it has artificial limits. It may be generally stated as follows[81]:

> A class closes when the first member becomes entitled in possession; but where the shares of its members are to vest at birth, it will remain open indefinitely unless a member was born before the testator's death or before the end of some intermediate limitation. All persons born after the closing of the class are excluded from it.

The artificial element is the exception in the case of shares which vest at birth and not on some later contingency such as attainment of full age or marriage.

This is a rule of convenience for resolving the testator's contradictory directions.[82] He can therefore exclude it by expressing a contrary intention,[83] so that the contradiction disappears. He may exclude it by implication, as by giving trustees a power of advancement under which they can pay out presumptive shares.[84] For such an implication "the standard is high" and there must be "an inescapable incompatibility" with the operation of the rule.[85] Consequently the rule will not normally be excluded by expressions such as

---

[76] *Ante*, para. 7–063.

[77] (1791) 3 Bro.C.C. 401. It applies to both realty and personalty (see *Re Canney's Trust* (1910) 101 L.T. 905) and to settlements as well as wills: see *Re Knapp's Settlement* [1895] 1 Ch. 91; *Re Wernher's S.T.* [1961] 1 W.L.R. 136.

[78] The rule will not therefore apply to gifts of income only, *e.g.* for joint lives: *Re Stephens* [1904] 1 Ch. 322 (also holding that the closing of the class may be postponed by a period of accumulation of income); *Re Ward* [1965] Ch. 856 (discretionary trusts). But it is not excluded because land is held upon trust for sale and sale is postponed: *Re Edmondson's W.T.* [1972] 1 W.L.R. 183.

[79] *Re Emmet's Estate* (1880) 13 Ch.D. 484.

[80] *Re Harker's W.T.* [1969] 1 W.L.R. 1124 at 1127, *per* Goff J.

[81] The best general account of the rule and its various refinements is that given by J. H. C. Morris (1954) 70 L.Q.R. 61 *et seq.*, where he also deals with its effect on the operation of the perpetuity rule (already considered, *ante*, para. 7–063); and see Jarman, 1660 *et seq.* Helpful statements of the rule will be found in *Re Chartres* [1927] 1 Ch. 446 at 471, 472 and in [1958] C.L.J. 39 (S. J. Bailey).

[82] *Re Emmet's Estate*, *supra*, n. 79, at 490; *Re Stephens* [1904] 1 Ch. 322 at 328; *Re Chartres*, *supra*, at 474; [1958] C.L.J. 39 at 42 (S. J. Bailey). Yet in *Re Drummond* [1988] 1 W.L.R. 234 at 242, the rule was described as a rule of construction rather than of convenience.

[83] *Scott v. Earl of Scarborough* (1838) 1 Beav. 154 ("now born or who shall hereafter be born"); *Hodson v. Micklethwaite* (1854) 2 Drew. 294; *Re Ransome* [1957] Ch. 348; *Re Tom's Settlement* [1987] 1 W.L.R. 1021 ("each minor specified beneficiary who shall be living" at a specified date).

[84] *Re Henderson* [1969] 1 W.L.R. 651.

[85] *Re Clifford's S.T.* [1981] Ch. 63 at 67, *per* Megarry V.-C.

"all", "all and every", or "all or any"[86]; and if the class gift is in remainder or in the future even expressions like "born or to be born" may be taken as referring to persons born between the testator's death and the falling into possession of the remainder.[87] But the words "whenever born" have been held to exclude the rule, being emphatic and expressly unlimited as to time.[88]

(c) Examples. The operation of the rule is best explained by examples. **11–074**

(i) Devise "to all my sisters". Sisters alive at the testator's death take, and any sisters born afterwards are excluded. But if no sister was alive at the testator's death, the exception applies and any sister born subsequently can take.[89] Similarly a devise "to all A's children" or "to all my grandchildren" will benefit only those born before the testator's death, unless no member of the class has by then been born.[90] If only one member of the class was born before the testator's death, he or she takes the whole.

(ii) Devise "to all my grandchildren who attain 21". The class closes when the first grandchild attains 21,[91] whether or not he was born before the testator's death. When the class closes, all grandchildren then alive are included in it: those under 21 will obtain their shares on attaining 21; if any of them dies under 21, his potential share is divided among those who reach 21. Even if there is no grandchild alive at the testator's death, the class will nevertheless close when the first grandchild attains 21 (since the shares were not to vest at birth).[92] There is however some doubt on this last point.[93]

(iii) Devise "to A for life, remainder to all his grandchildren who attain **11–075** 21". Here the class closes at A's death, if by then any grandchild who survived the testator, or was born after his death, has attained 21.[94] As any such grandchild's interest will have vested, it will make no difference if he has predeceased A, for someone will be entitled to take his share under his will or intestacy,[95] and so the class must close. If at A's death there are no grandchildren,[96] or

[86] See *Re Emmet's Estate* (1880) 13 Ch.D. 484; *Re Edmondson's W.T.* [1972] 1 W.L.R. 183 at 187.
[87] *Scott v. Earl of Scarborough, supra,* at 168. *Re Chapman's S.T.* [1977] 1 W.L.R. 1163.
[88] *Re Edmondson's W.T., supra.*
[89] *Weld v. Bradbury* (1715) 2 Vern. 705.
[90] See *Re Chartres, supra.* Provided that the gift vests at once, it makes no difference that there are special trusts during minority: *Re Manners* [1955] 1 W.L.R. 1096.
[91] *Andrews v. Partington* (1791) 3 Bro.C.C. 401; *Re Deloitte* [1919] 1 Ch. 209, *Re Chartres, supra.* If a grandchild has attained 21 before the testator's death, the class closes at once: *Picken v. Matthews* (1878) 10 Ch.D. 264.
[92] *Pearse v. Catton* (1839) 1 Beav. 352; and see *Re Bleckly* [1951] Ch. 740 at 749.
[93] See Morris (1954) 70 L.Q.R. 61 at 68, 69.
[94] *Re Emmet's Estate* (1880) 13 Ch.D. 484; *Re Knapp's Settlement* [1895] 1 Ch. 91 at 96.
[95] *Greenwood v. Greenwood* [1939] 2 All E.R. 150.
[96] *Re Bleckly* [1951] Ch. 740.

only infant grandchildren,[97] the class closes when the first of them attains 21.[98]

Where the remainders are accelerated by the premature determination of the prior life interest (*e.g.* by disclaimer or release[99]) and a remainderman is already qualified to take, the rule will not apply unless, it seems, the limitation is one to which the rule would in any case apply. Thus if the gift is to A for life with remainder to his children who attain 21, no remainderman could be born after A's death, and so the premature determination of A's life interest will not bring within the rule a limitation which otherwise would stand outside it.[1] But had the remainder been to A's *grandchildren* who attain 21, the rule would apply to the limitation so as to exclude some remaindermen, as explained above, and so it has been held also to apply if A's life interest is prematurely determined.[2] Yet it seems contrary to principle for the class to be closed as a result of a disposition not made by the testator, and for the rule to be open to manipulation at the expense of the unborn.[3]

11–076   (d) *Individual gifts.* An even more drastic rule of convenience is applied where there is not one gift divisible among a class, but a series of gifts to each member of a class, for example, a gift of £100 to each of the children of X who attains 21. Here the class closes at the testator's death, and if X has then no living child the gift fails altogether.[4] The object of this rule is to enable the personal representatives to deal with the residue by fixing the maximum number of legacies at once. But the testator may exclude the rule by a sufficiently clear direction, and it will not be applied unless the circumstances require it.[5]

11–077   **2. Gifts to individuals.** In the case of gifts to existing individuals, the date of the will, and not the date of the testator's death, is normally the relevant time. Thus a gift "to the eldest son of my sister", there being such a son living at the date of the will, is a gift to him personally; if he dies before the testator, the gift lapses and the eldest son at the testator's death has no claim.[6] Similarly, a bequest "to Lord Sherborne" is a gift to the holder of the title at the date of the will.[7] But like all rules of construction, this yields to a contrary intention, and a legacy "to the Lord Mayor of London for the time being"

---

[97] See authorities cited in n. 94, *supra*.
[98] Similarly on a gift of a reversionary interest the class remains open until the reversion falls into possession: *Walker v. Shore* (1808) 15 Ves. 122.
[99] See [1958] C.L.J. 39 (S. J. Bailey); [1973] C.L.J. 246 (A. M. Prichard).
[1] *Re Kebty-Fletcher's W.T.* [1969] 1 Ch. 339; *Re Harker's W.T.* [1969] 1 W.L.R. 1124.
[2] *Re Davies* [1957] 1 W.L.R. 922, as explained in *Re Harker's W.T., supra.*
[3] See generally *Re Harker's W.T., supra.*
[4] *Rogers v. Mutch* (1878) 10 Ch.D. 25; *Re Belville* [1941] Ch. 414.
[5] *Re Belville, supra*. Presumably, therefore, if the residue is not distributable until some future date, *e.g.* after a life interest, all persons living at that date will be admitted.
[6] *Amyot v. Dwarris* [1904] A.C. 268.
[7] *Re Whorwood* (1878) 34 Ch.D. 446.

operates as a gift to the person holding that office at the testator's death,[8] while a gift "to the Mayor of Lowestoft for the benefit of poor and needy fishermen of Lowestoft" takes effect as a gift to the Mayor of Lowestoft for the time being, on the stated trusts, and not as a gift to a particular person who is Mayor at a particular time.[9]

E. Exercise of Powers of Appointment

A general devise or bequest (*e.g.* "I give all my property to X") operates to exercise a general power of appointment unless a contrary intention (and not merely an absence of intention[10]) is shown by the will,[11] or unless the general power is expressed to be exercisable only in some special way, *e.g.* by referring to the power[12] or the property.[13] On the other hand, a special power (which for this purpose includes a power, commonly known as a hybrid power, to appoint to "anyone except X"[14]) is not exercised by a general bequest or devise unless the will shows a contrary intention, as by referring expressly to the power or to the property.[15] **11–078**

F. "To A, but if He Die Without Issue, to B"

Where a gift is made "to A, but if he die without issue, to B", it has been provided by statute that the gift over to B becomes void as soon as any issue of A attains majority.[16] This did not apply where, in a will taking effect before 1997, an entail was given to A. It is not, however, excluded merely because A's "children" are specified instead of his "issue".[17] Where it applies, A's interest thus becomes absolute either if any issue attains full age (even if none survives A) or if A dies leaving any issue (even if none attains full age). **11–079**

G. "To A and his children": The Rule in Wild's Case

1. Before 1926. Under the Rule in *Wild's Case*[18] the effect of a devise "to A and his children" depended upon the facts existing when the will was made. Its peculiarity was that it continued to obey the old principle that the time of **11–080**

---

[8] *Re Daniels* (1918) 87 L.J.Ch. 661.
[9] *Re Pipe* (1937) 106 L.J.Ch. 252.
[10] *Re Thirlwell* [1958] Ch. 146; (1958) 74 L.Q.R. 21 (R.E.M.).
[11] Wills Act 1837, s.27; see, *e.g. Re Lawry* [1938] Ch. 318. For the rule apart from the section, see *ante*, para. 10–090.
[12] *Phillips v. Cayley* (1889) 43 Ch.D. 222; contrast *Re Lane* [1908] 2 Ch. 581 (reference to "any power" which the testator might have held sufficient).
[13] *Re Phillips* (1889) 41 Ch.D. 417.
[14] *Re Byron's Settlement* [1891] 3 Ch. 474.
[15] See *Re Ackerley* [1913] 1 Ch. 510; compare *Re Beresford's W.T.* [1938] 3 All E.R. 566 (mere use of "I appoint . . . " not enough).
[16] L.P.A. 1925, s.134, amended by the Family Law Reform Act 1969, s.1(3) and Sched. 1. This has been the rule for land since 1882 and for all property since 1925. For the law prior to 1882, see the previous edition of this work at p. 536.
[17] *Re Booth* [1900] 1 Ch. 768.
[18] (1599) 6 Co.Rep. 16b at 17a, 17b.

making the will was the significant time, even after the modern rule that the will speaks from death was adopted for other forms of gift.[19]

(i) If A had no children when the will was made, he took an estate tail, even if children had been born before the testator's death. "Children" was construed as a word of limitation, for the only way in which the testator could have intended to benefit A's children under an immediate gift was by their being entitled to succeed under A's entail.[20] Yet by barring the entail, A could of course prevent his children from taking anything.

(ii) If A had children living (and not merely *en ventre sa mère*[21]) when the will was made, the word "children" was treated as a word of purchase and A took jointly with all his children living at the testator's death, in accordance with the usual rules for class gifts.

11–081   **2. After 1925.** (i) If no children were living at the date of the will, then prior to 1997, A could not take an entail because it could not be created by informal words after 1925.[22] In such a case a fee simple interest passed and A was, it seems, solely entitled to it, even if children were born after the will was made but before the testator died.[23] However, it may have been that A took a life interest, with remainder to his children in fee simple.[24] Although after 1996 A cannot take an entail because it can no longer be created at all, the result should be the same.

(ii) The second branch of the rule has not been affected. As before, A takes jointly with all his children living at the testator's death.[25]

H. The Meaning of "Land"

11–082   A gift of "land" has always included freeholds,[26] though before the Wills Act 1837 it did not include leaseholds unless the testator had no freeholds[27] or showed an intention to include leaseholds.[28] Since the Act, "land" has included leaseholds unless a contrary intention appears in the will.[29] But a gift of "real estate" does not[30] include leaseholds, unless the testator had no freeholds.[31–32]

---

[19] See (1936) 6 C.L.J. 67 at 78 (S. J. Bailey).
[20] *Wild's Case, supra*, at 17a.
[21] *Roper v. Roper* (1867) L.R. 3 C.P. 32.
[22] *Ante*, para. 3–038.
[23] L.P.A. 1925, s.130(2) (repealed by T.L.A.T.A. 1996, s.25(2), Sched. 4); see (1956) 5 C.L.J. 46 (R.E.M.).
[24] See (1936) 6 C.L.J. 67 at 80; (1946) 9 C.L.J. 185 (S. J. Bailey).
[25] *ibid.*
[26] *Thompson v. Lady Lawley* (1800) 2 B. & P. 303.
[27] *Rose v. Bartlett* (1631) Cro.Car. 292.
[28] *Hobson v. Blackburn* (1833) 1 My. & K. 571.
[29] Wills Act 1837, s.26.
[30] *Butler v. Butler* (1884) 28 Ch.D. 66.
[31–32] *Re Holt* [1921] 2 Ch. 17.

Part 2

GIFTS IN CONTEMPLATION OF DEATH

1. Nature of a *donatio mortis causa.* [33] Although in general it is not **11–083** possible for a person to dispose of his property after his death except by an instrument that complies with the Wills Act 1837, there is an ancient and anomalous exception to this, the *donatio mortis causa*, which derives from the civil law.[34] It has been described as a gift "of an amphibious nature, being a gift which is neither entirely *inter vivos* nor testamentary".[35] It is a contingent gift made in contemplation of death that is recoverable by the donor if death does not in fact occur at that time.[36]

2. The essential elements of a *donatio mortis causa.* A *donatio mortis* **11–084** *causa* will be valid only if three conditions are satisfied.[37]

   (i) The gift must be made in contemplation, although not necessarily in expectation, of impending death: this means "not the possibility of death at some time or other, but death within the near future" or "death for some reason believed to be impending".[38]

  (ii) The gift must be made upon condition that it is absolute and perfected only on the donor's death.

 (iii) There must be delivery of the subject matter of the gift, or the essential indicia of title thereto, which amounts to a parting with dominion and not mere physical possession over the subject matter of the gift.[39]

3. The operation of a *donatio mortis causa.* If the donor effectively **11–085** transferred title to the donee, *e.g.* by delivery, the gift becomes unconditional on the donor's death and no further step is needed to perfect it. If the donor recovers or revokes the gift, the donee will then hold the property on trust for

---

[33] See generally Wh. & T., i, 341; Snell, *Equity*, Ch. 7; A. P. Bell, *Modern Law of Personal Property*, p. 420.

[34] See the leading case *Ward v. Turner* (1752) 2 Ves. Sen. 431; and Bl.Comm. ii, 514. For a statement of the civil law and a contrast with the position in Roman law, see J. Domat, *The Civil Law in its Natural Order*, Part II, 4.2.1.3.

[35] *Re Beaumont* [1902] 1 Ch. 889 at 892, *per* Buckley J. The phrase comes from Story's *Equity Jurisprudence*, para. 606.

[36] *Delgoffe v. Fader* [1939] Ch. 922 at 927.

[37] *Sen v. Headley* [1991] Ch. 425 at 431; *Woodard v. Woodard* [1992] R.T.R. 35 at 39; Snell, *Equity*, pp. 380–383.

[38] *Re Craven's Estate* [1937] Ch. 423 at 426, *per* Farwell J. Gifts made by persons who are seriously ill (*Cain v. Moon* [1896] 2 Q.B. 283); who have had an accident (*Birch v. Treasury Solicitor* [1951] Ch. 298); or who are about to have surgery (*Re Craven's Estate, supra*), are obvious examples. It is not necessary that death should in fact occur from the cause contemplated by the donor: *Wilkes v. Allington* [1931] 2 Ch. 104.

[39] *Birch v. Treasury Solicitor* [1951] Ch. 298 at 311 (gift of deposits at various banks: donee given the pass books); *Woodard v. Woodard, supra* (gift of car: one set of keys given to donee).

him.[40] If the act of delivery is not sufficient to transfer the title to the donee, the donor's personal representatives hold the property on trust for him and can be compelled to transfer it to him.[41] The trust is one which is "raised by operation of law",[42] that is to say a constructive trust.[43]

11–086   **4. The property which may be the subject matter of a *donatio mortis causa*.** In previous editions of this work there was no discussion of gifts made in contemplation of death. This was because it had always been assumed[44] that it was not possible to make a *donatio mortis causa* of land[45] but only of certain types of personalty.[46] It has now been held by the Court of Appeal in *Sen v. Headley*[47] that a valid *donatio mortis causa* may be made of land. The court accepted that the doctrine of gifts in contemplation of death was anomalous, but saw no reason why there should be anomalous exceptions to it. In that case transfer of the keys of a box which contained the title deeds was considered to satisfy the requirements of delivery. The trust raised by the gift was a constructive trust which was immune from the normal formal requirements applicable to trusts of land.[48]

Part 3

INTESTACY

11–087   The rules relating to intestacy must now be explained. If the deceased dies wholly intestate, leaving no effective will, these rules govern the devolution of all his property, while if he dies partly testate and partly intestate, they apply to all the property which does not pass under his will, unless the will directs otherwise.[49]

Before 1926 realty and personalty descended differently. All the realty vested in the heir; the personalty devolved through the personal representatives upon the next-of-kin. If a widower died intestate leaving three sons and four daughters, the eldest son was the heir and took all the realty, but all seven children shared the personalty equally. In the case of deaths occurring after

---

[40] *Staniland v. Willott* (1852) 3 Mac. & G. 664.
[41] *Re Beaumont, supra,* at 892.
[42] *Duffield v. Elwes* (1827) 1 Bli.(N.S.) 497 at 543.
[43] *Sen v. Headley, supra,* at 439.
[44] On the authority of certain remarks by Lord Eldon in *Duffield v. Elwes, supra,* at 535–543 (H.L.).
[45] In *Duffield v. Elwes, supra,* it was held that it was possible to make a *donatio mortis causa* of a mortgage of land which was in equity a mere security for money.
[46] The types of personal property that may or may not be the subject of a *donatio mortis causa* follow from the requirement that for there to be a valid gift there must be delivery of the property or of some indicia of title: see Snell, *Equity,* p. 383.
[47] *Supra.* For differing views on the case see [1991] C.L.J. 404 (J. W. A. Thornely); [1991] Conv. 307 (M. Halliwell); and (1992) 43 N.I.L.Q. 35 (P. Sparkes).
[48] L.P.A. 1925, s.53(2); *ante,* para. 10–044.
[49] A will providing only that nothing shall go to X excludes X from benefit under the intestacy rules: *Re Wynn* [1984] 1 W.L.R. 23.

1925, both realty and personalty devolve in the same way under a statutory code of intestacy; and for those dying after 1952, the Intestates' Estates Act 1952, as amended, has made some important modifications to the code. It is no longer necessary to consider the rules for the devolution of realty or personalty before 1926.[50] The rules relating to realty will govern certain rare situations, but those concerning personalty seldom arise.[51]

A. *The Present Rules of Intestacy*

Under the Administration of Estates Act 1925,[52] all property, whether real or personal, is held on trust by the deceased's personal representatives with power to sell it.[53] Out of any ready money of the deceased and any money arising from the disposition of any other part of his estate (after payment of costs) the personal representatives must pay all funeral, testamentary and administration expenses, debts and other liabilities, and set aside a fund to meet the pecuniary legacies (if any) bequeathed by the will of the deceased.[54] The residue must then be distributed to the persons beneficially entitled under the intestacy. The rules for ascertaining these persons are stated as amended by the Intestates' Estates Act 1952 and they apply in the case of persons who die intestate after 1952.[55] The Act of 1925 is still the primary Act, but the Act of 1952 has made important amendments to it, particularly by increasing the rights of a widower or widow. Certain fixed sums were increased by the Family Provision Act 1966 and the Family Provision (Intestate Succession) Orders of 1972, 1981, 1987 and 1993. The governing provision is now the 1993 Order, which applies where the intestate died after November 30, 1993.[56]

11–088

1. The surviving spouse. Widowers and widows have equal rights. But these rights vary greatly according to the state of the intestate's family. In the following summary[57] "specified relatives" means parent, brother or sister of the whole blood, or issue of a brother or sister of the whole blood. "Issue" is used in its normal meaning, as including children, grandchildren, or remoter

11–089

---

[50] For these rules, see the previous edition of this work at pp. 540 *et seq.*

[51] *Post*, paras 11–118 *et seq.*

[52] s.33(1) (as amended by T.L.A.T.A. 1996, Sched. 2, para. 5).

[53] This trust will apply to all those assets which fall to be administered according to English law under its conflict of laws rules (such as immovable property in England), even if the deceased died domiciled abroad. The consequences of this can be unfortunate: *Re Collens* [1986] Ch. 505.

[54] A.E.A. 1925, s.33(2) (as amended by T.L.A.T.A. 1996, Sched. 2, para. 5).

[55] The Law Commission was critical of the existing law: see *Distribution on Intestacy* (1989) Law Com. No. 187. However, only its subsidiary recommendations have been accepted and implemented: see Law Reform (Succession) Act 1995.

[56] S.I. 1993 No. 2906. The previous orders were respectively S.I. 1972 No. 916, S.I. 1981 No. 255 and S.I. 1987 No. 799.

[57] For full details see the Intestates' Estates Act 1952, s.1(2), and the table therein contained. The effect of the amendments on A.E.A. 1925, ss.46–49, may conveniently be seen from Sched. 1 to the I.E.A. 1952. These provisions must be read subject to the amendments made by the Law Reform (Succession) Act 1995, s.1, as regards persons dying intestate after 1995.

descendants, but references to "leaving issue" and "leaving no issue" refer only to issue who attain an absolutely vested interest.[58]

11–090   *(a) No issue and no specified relative.* If the intestate leaves no issue and no specified relative, the surviving spouse takes the whole residuary estate absolutely.

11–091   *(b) Issue.* If the intestate leaves issue (whether or not there are any specified relatives), the surviving spouse takes the following interests.

11–092   (1) THE "PERSONAL CHATTELS" ABSOLUTELY. These are elaborately defined.[59] They include furniture, horses, cars, plate, books, jewellery, wines and "articles of household or personal use or ornament", but exclude chattels used at the death of the intestate for business purposes, money and securities for money. Roughly speaking, the phrase includes everything that goes to make a home (though not the house itself), and more besides, such as a small yacht used for family purposes,[60] and a stamp collection kept as a hobby.[61] The phrase thus has a meaning quite distinct from "personalty" or "personal property".

11–093   (2) £125,000 ABSOLUTELY, free of taxes payable on death and costs, with interest on it at the rate of 6 per cent per annum from the date of death until payment.[62] Both the £125,000 and the interest on it are charged on the residuary estate and are therefore payable out of capital,[63] but the interest is *primarily* payable out of income.[64]

11–094   (3) A LIFE INTEREST in half of the residuary estate. Provision is made whereby the surviving spouse may call upon the personal representatives to purchase the life interest for a lump sum[65] (ascertained as prescribed by statutory order[66]), thus enabling the estate to be distributed forthwith. This right may be exercised only within 12 months from the first grant of representation, unless the court extends the time limit for special reasons[67] and it is exercisable only in so far as the property is in possession.[68] A written notice must be served on the personal representatives[69]; but if the surviving spouse is the sole personal representative, the right is effective only if written notice is given to the Senior Registrar of the Family Division of the High Court.[70]

---

[58] A.E.A. 1925, s.47(2)(b), (c); see *post*, para. 11–104.
[59] A.E.A. 1925, s.55(1)(x).
[60] *Re Chaplin* [1950] Ch. 507.
[61] *Re Reynold's W.T.* [1966] 1 W.L.R. 19; see (1966) 82 L.Q.R. 18 (R.E.M.). See also *Re Crispin's W.T.* [1975] Ch. 245 (collection of clocks and watches worth £50,000 included).
[62] The rate of interest is as specified by order of the Lord Chancellor under A.J.A. 1977, s.28. See S.I. 1977 No. 1491, as amended by S.I. 1983 No. 1374.
[63] *Re Saunders* [1929] 1 Ch. 674.
[64] I.E.A. 1952, s.1(4).
[65] *ibid.*, s.2.
[66] Administration of Justice Act 1977, s.28(3). S.I. 1977 No. 1491.
[67] A.E.A. 1925, s.47A(5).
[68] *ibid.*, s.47A(3)).
[69] *ibid.*, s.47A(6)).
[70] *ibid.* s.47A(7) (as amended by the Supreme Court Act 1981).

(c) No issue but specified relatives. If the intestate leaves no issue, but one **11–095**
or more of the specified relatives, the surviving spouse takes—

    (i) the "personal chattels" absolutely (as above);

    (ii) £200,000 absolutely (as above);

    (iii) half of the residuary estate absolutely.[71]

These provisions are subject to a number of rules.

(1) INCREASE OF FIXED SUMS. The Lord Chancellor may by order increase **11–096**
the sums mentioned above of £125,000 and £200,000.[72] Formerly they were
respectively £5,000 and £20,000 under the Intestates' Estates Act 1952 and
were increased in stages by the Family Provision Act 1966 and the orders
since made under it.

(2) MATRIMONIAL HOME. The surviving spouse has a special right to have **11–097**
appropriated to him or her any dwelling-house forming part of the residuary
estate in which he or she was resident at the intestate's death[73]; this will
usually be the matrimonial home. The spouse may require the personal
representatives (even if he or she is one of them[74]) to appropriate the house,
at a proper valuation, as part of the property to which he or she is entitled
absolutely[75]; and it must be exercised within 12 months of the first grant of
representation.[76] It applies to whatever interest the intestate had in the house,
even if only a leasehold; but it does not apply in the case of a leasehold which
would expire or be determinable within two years of the intestate's death.[77]
The mere right to call for an appropriation of the house does not, however,
give the surviving spouse even an equitable interest in it, or any right to retain
possession of it.[78] The Act contains a number of other provisions about the
details of this right.[79]

(3) PARTIAL INTESTACY. These rules apply equally to partial intestacies. **11–098**
The former rule by which the sum received as a statutory legacy[80] under the
intestacy was diminished by the value of any beneficial interest which the

---

[71] I.E.A. 1952, s.1(2), Table. Although the Law Commission proposed that a surviving spouse
should in all cases receive the whole estate (see (1989) Law Com. No. 187, Pt III), the
Government rejected the recommendation.
[72] Family Provision Act 1966, s.1.
[73] I.E.A. 1952, s.5 and Sched. 2.
[74] *ibid.*, Sched. 2, para.. 5(1).
[75] *ibid.*, para. 1(1); *Re Collins* [1975] 1 W.L.R. 309 (valuation to be at time of appropriation).
[76] I.E.A. 1952, Sched. 2, para. 3(1).
[77] *ibid.*, para. 1(2).
[78] *Lall v. Lall* [1965] 1 W.L.R. 1249.
[79] I.E.A. 1952, Sched. 2, para. 1(2). If the house is worth more than the surviving spouse's
absolute interest (which will be only £125,000 where there are issue and no personal chattels),
the spouse may pay the balance in cash: para. 5(2); *Re Phelps* [1980] Ch. 275.
[80] *i.e.* £125,000 or £200,000.

surviving spouse took under the deceased's will,[81] has been abolished as regards persons dying after 1995.[82]

11–099   (4) SEPARATION. If the spouses are separated by a judicial separation order and the separation is continuing, the property of either of them who dies intestate will devolve as if the other were already dead.[83]

11–100   (5) COMMORIENTES. If spouses die in circumstances which make it uncertain which survived the other (a phrase which is held to cover simultaneous deaths[84]) the statutory presumption that the younger survived the elder[85] is modified for the purposes of applying the rules of intestate succession. It is now always to be presumed that the spouse predeceased the intestate,[86] and so takes no benefit as a *surviving* spouse. Thus, if H (husband, aged 60) and W (wife, aged 50) are simultaneously killed in an accident and both die intestate, in distributing H's property W will be presumed to have predeceased H and so will have no rights in his intestacy, although she will be deemed to have survived him for other purposes. In distributing W's property, however, H will be presumed to have predeceased W,[87] and the same presumption will hold good for other purposes. It is only in the case of spouses that the normal presumption of the younger person's survival is modified: if H and his son are simultaneously killed, both intestate, the son can take under H's intestacy; but H cannot take under his son's, for H is presumed to have died first.

11–101   (6) SURVIVAL BY 28 DAYS. In the case of a spouse dying intestate after 1995, the survivor can only take if he or she survives the deceased for a period of 28 days beginning with the day on which the intestate died.[88]

11–102   **2. The issue.** Subject to the rights of the surviving spouse, if any, the property is held on special statutory trusts for the surviving issue.[89] Under these trusts the property is held upon trust for all the children of the deceased living at his death in equal shares, but qualified as follows.

---

[81] See A.E.A. 1925, ss.49(1)(a), (1)(aa), (2), (3). For this rule, see the previous edition of this work at p. 551.

[82] Law Reform (Succession) Act 1995, s.1(2)(b), implementing a recommendation in (1989) Law Com. No. 187, para. 55.

[83] Matrimonial Causes Act 1973, s.18(2).

[84] *Hickman v. Peacey* [1945] A.C. 304; *ante*, para. 11–053.

[85] L.P.A. 1925, s.184; *ante*, para. 11–053.

[86] A.E.A. 1925, s.46(3).

[87] This is by the operation of L.P.A. 1925, s.184; I.E.A. 1952, s.1(4) does not apply, since it is confined to cases where the L.P.A. 1925 would otherwise require the spouse to have survived the intestate.

[88] A.E.A. 1925, s.46(2A) (inserted by the Law Reform (Succession) Act 1995, s.1(1)); implementing recommendations in (1989) Law Com. No. 187, paras 56, 57. The Law Commission had recommended a survival period of 14 days, but this was increased to 28 days by Parliament. It is common for wills to contain an express survivorship clause having a similar effect.

[89] A.E.A. 1925, ss.46(1)(i), (ii), 47.

(a) Subject to representation. i.e. subject to the rule that surviving issue of **11–103** a deceased child stand in his shoes and take his share[90]; descent is thus *per stirpes.*

(b) Subject to the rule that no issue attains a vested interest until he is 18[91] **11–104** *years old or married.*[92] This in effect means that if a minor dies without having married, the property must be dealt with from that moment as if the minor had never existed.[93] Thus if X dies leaving a widow and infant son, the widow takes a life interest in half the residue. If the son dies before either marrying or attaining his majority, the widow forthwith takes either all or half the residue absolutely, just as if there had been no issue.

(c) Subject to hotchpot. In relation to deaths occurring prior to 1996, there **11–105** are elaborate rules as to hotchpot,[94] by which the following must be brought into account—

> (i) any money or property received by any children of the deceased by way of advancement or upon marriage; or

> (ii) in the case of a partial intestacy, any benefit received under the deceased's will by any children or remoter issue.[95]

For deaths after 1995, these rules are abolished.[96]

If no issue attains a vested interest, then, subject to any claim of a surviving spouse, the relatives of the deceased are entitled in the following order; any member of one class who takes a vested interest excludes all members of subsequent classes.

3. The parents of the deceased are entitled in equal shares absolutely[97]; if **11–106** one is dead, the survivor is entitled absolutely.[98]

4. The brothers and sisters of the whole blood, on the statutory trusts. A **11–107** division may be made here, for at this point the "specified relatives" end. Those included in the foregoing classes may take an interest even though the intestate left a surviving spouse; those in the subsequent classes cannot.

5. The brothers and sisters of the half blood, on the statutory trusts. **11–108**

6. The grandparents, if more than one in equal shares. **11–109**

[90] *ibid.,* s.47.
[91] Family Law Reform At 1969, s.3(2). For deaths prior to 1970 the prescribed age is 21.
[92] A.E.A. 1925, s.47 (as amended by the Family Law Reform Act 1969, s.3(2)).
[93] *ibid.,* s.47(2).
[94] For an account of these rules, see the previous edition of this work at p. 553.
[95] A.E.A. 1925, ss.47(1)(iii); 49(1)(a), (2), (3).
[96] Law Reform (Succession) Act 1995, s.1(2), implementing recommendations in (1989) Law Com. No. 187, para. 55.
[97] A.E.A. 1925, s.46(1)(iii).
[98] *ibid.,* s.46(1)(iv).

11–110   **7. The uncles and aunts of the whole blood,** on the statutory trusts.

11–111   **8. The uncles and aunts of the half blood,** on the statutory trusts.

11–112   **9. The Crown** (or the Duchy of Lancaster or Duke of Cornwall) as *bona vacantia* in lieu of any right to escheat.[99]

A number of points arise on the foregoing list.

11–113   (1) STATUTORY TRUSTS. The statutory trusts for the brothers, sisters, uncles and aunts are the same as those for the issue.[1] Thus deceased brothers, sisters, uncles and aunts are represented by their surviving descendants (*e.g.* nephews, nieces and cousins of the intestate),[2] and their interests in every case are contingent upon their attaining full age or marrying. "Uncles" and "aunts" include only blood relations; an aunt's husband, although bearing the courtesy title of uncle, has no claim.

11–114   (2) ILLEGITIMATE CHILDREN. As regards any person who dies on or after April 4, 1988, the status of illegitimacy either of the deceased himself or of any other person is irrelevant for the purposes of entitlement on intestacy. An illegitimate child is equated to one who was born legitimate.[3] However for these purposes there is a rebuttable presumption that the father of an illegitimate person (and those related to that person solely through his father) predeceased him.[4] Where the intestate died after 1969 but before April 4, 1988, an illegitimate child was treated as legitimate for the purposes of the rules of intestate succession only as regards his parents.[5] No disabilities attach to persons legitimated by the subsequent marriage of their parents.[6]

11–115   (3) ADOPTED CHILDREN. Adopted children are treated as children of their adopting (not their natural) parents, provided that the death occurred after the adoption.[7]

11–116   (4) CROWN DISCRETION. The Crown usually modifies its strict rights under head No. 9 by making provision for dependants of the deceased, whether related to him or not, and for others for whom he might reasonably have been expected to make provision. This purely discretionary power, which the Act

---

[99] *ibid.*, s.46(1)(vi).

[1] *ibid.*, s.47(3).

[2] *ibid.*, s.47(5), added by I.E.A. 1952. This contains a slip in drafting which appears to exclude the descendants unless one of the brothers, uncles, etc., also survives: but this is to be ignored: *Re Lockwood* [1958] Ch. 231; see (1958) 74 L.Q.R. 25 (R.E.M.).

[3] Family Law Reform Act 1987, ss.1, 18, replacing Family Law Reform Act 1969, s.14. See [1988] Conv. 410 (J. G. Miller).

[4] Family Law Reform Act 1987, s.18(2).

[5] Family Law Reform Act 1969, s.14. The rule that an illegitimate child could not succeed to an entail was however preserved by that section.

[6] Legitimacy Act 1976, s.5(3). There is an exception in relation to the descent of titles of honour: *ibid.*, Sched. 1, para. 4.

[7] Adoption Act 1976, s.39 (consolidating earlier legislation). Adoption does not affect the descent of any title of honour or of any property that devolves with that title: *ibid.*, s.44.

confirms,[8] is made all the more necessary by the increased prospects of the Crown of succeeding to property of an intestate.

(5) EXECUTOR'S CLAIM. On a partial intestacy the executor cannot take **11–117** undisposed of property beneficially unless an intention to this effect is shown by the will[9]; this rule now applies to an executor both as against the Crown and as against the statutory next-of-kin.

B. Survivals of the Old Rules

I. THE HEIR

In the case of all persons dying after 1925 the foregoing rules supersede the old rules relating to intestacy. But in the case of realty the old general law of descent still has to be applied in three cases.

1. Mental patient. If the deceased was a mental patient of full age at the **11–118** end of 1925 and dies without having recovered testamentary capacity, any realty as to which he died intestate descends according to the general law in force before 1926.[10]

2. Entail. An entail not disposed of by the will of the deceased[11] descends **11–119** in accordance with the general law in force before 1926.[12] Since entails were to be preserved, this could only be done by preserving their peculiar rules of devolution. Since entails were to be preserved, this could only be done by preserving their peculiar rules of devolution.[13] There was one statutory amendment to these rules that applied to any entail arising under either an *inter vivos* disposition or a will made after April 3, 1988. In the absence of an expression of contrary intention in the instrument which created it, such an entail is not limited (as were entails created prior to that date) to legitimate issue.[14] Such a contrary intention was not implied from the use of the words "heirs" or "in tail".[15]

3. Limitation to heir. If property is limited after 1925, whether *inter vivos* **11–120** or by will, to the heir of a deceased person, the "heir" is ascertained according to the general law in force before 1926.[16] This is not a case of descent on intestacy, for the heir takes as purchaser.

---

[8] A.E.A. 1925. s.46(1)(vi). For the practice, see N. D. Ing, *Bona Vacantia* (1971) Chap. 10.

[9] s.49(b). See *Re Skeats* [1936] Ch. 683.

[10] A.E.A. 1925, s.51(2).

[11] *Ante*, para. 3–089.

[12] L.P.A. 1925, s.130(4); A.E.A. 1925, ss.45(2), 51(4).

[13] As a result of the Trusts of Land and Appointment of Trustees Act 1996, it ceased to be possible to create new entails after 1996: see *ante*, para. 3–037.

[14] See the Family Law Reform Act 1987, ss.1(1) 19(1), (2).

[15] *ibid.*, s.19(2).

[16] L.P.A. 1925, s.132; A.E.A. 1925, s.51(1). By the former section the heir appears to take only an equitable interest, even in the (highly unlikely) event of an immediate conveyance by deed.

II. PERSONALTY

11–121   In the case of personalty, the old rules never apply to deaths occurring after 1925.[17] These rules still retain some of their importance, however, particularly in showing title to leaseholds, and in the practice of reversion conveyancing.

Part 4

DEVOLUTION OF LEGAL ESTATES

Section. 1. Introductory

11–122   **1. Vesting of property.** Hitherto we have examined only the beneficial devolution of property on death. We must now turn to the machinery by which the property becomes vested in those beneficially entitled. The general rule today is that all property first vests in the personal representatives of the deceased, who in due course transfer to the beneficiaries any of the property not required in the due administration of the estate, *e.g.* for payment of debts. In this context, "estate" is used not in the technical sense of an estate in land, but as a collective expression for the sum total of the assets and liabilities of the deceased.

11–123   **2. Executors.** "Personal representatives" is a phrase which includes both executors and administrators. If a person makes a will, he may (but need not) appoint one or more persons to be his executor or executors, with the duty of paying debts, taxes and funeral expenses, and ultimately of distributing the estate to those entitled. The executor derives his powers from the will, although he must obtain confirmation of his position by "proving the will", *i.e.* obtaining a grant of probate from the court.[18] If a sole or only surviving executor who has obtained probate dies having himself appointed an executor, the latter, on proving the original executor's will, becomes executor of the original testator also. This "chain of representation" may be continued indefinitely until broken by failure to appoint an executor, or failure of an executor to obtain a grant of probate.[19]

11–124   **3. Administrators.** If a person dies without having appointed an executor, or if none of the executors he has appointed is able and willing to act, application must be made to the court by some person or persons interested in the estate for "letters of administration" appointing an administrator or

---

[17] A.E.A. 1925, s.45(1).
[18] See, *e.g. Chetty v. Chetty* [1916] 1 A.C. 603; *Bainbridge v. I.R.C.* [1955] 1 W.L.R. 1329 at 1335; *Biles v. Caesar* [1957] 1 W.L.R. 156; *Re Crowhurst Park* [1974] 1 W.L.R. 583.
[19] A.E.A. 1925, s.7, replacing 25 Edw. 3, St. 5, c. 5, 1351. For criticism, see (1980) 77 *Law Society's Gazette* 265 (A. V. Barker).

administrators. The duties of an administrator are substantially the same as those of an executor. If the deceased left no will, simple administration is granted; if he left a will, administration *cum testamento annexo* ("with the will annexed") is granted.[20] The grant may be limited in any way the court thinks fit,[21] *e.g.* it may be confined to settled land, or may exclude settled land,[22] or may be *durante minore aetate* ("during the minority" of the sole executor).[23] There is no "chain of representation" for administrators. If a sole or last surviving administrator dies without completing the administration of the estate, application must be made for a grant of administration *de bonis non administratis* (more shortly, *de bonis non*), which is a grant "in respect of the goods left unadministered".

Applications for grants both of probate and of letters of administration are regulated by the Non-Contentious Probate Rules 1987 (as amended).[24]

Section 2. Devolution of Property on Personal Representatives

1. Vesting of property. Prior to 1897 a deceased's personal estate (including his leaseholds) devolved on his personal representatives, but his realty passed directly to his heir (on an intestacy) or to his devisee (under any will). Under the Land Transfer Act 1897, all property, whether real or personal, vested in the deceased's personal representatives.[25] The Administration of Estates Act 1925 substantially repeated the provisions of that Act. In the case of deaths after 1925, all land owned by the deceased, including leaseholds[26] and Crown lands,[27] vests in the personal representatives[28] with the following exceptions— **11–125**

(i) entails, unless disposed of by the deceased's will[29];

(ii) property to which the deceased was entitled as a joint tenant[30];

(iii) property to which the deceased was entitled as corporation sole[31]; and

(iv) interests which ceased on the death of the deceased, such as an interest for his life.[32]

---

[20] Supreme Court Act 1981, s.119.
[21] *ibid.*, s.113.
[22] See A.E.A. 1925, s.23; *ante*, para. 8–035.
[23] Supreme Court Act 1981, s.118.
[24] S.I. 1987 No. 2024 as amended by S.I. 1991 No. 1876.
[25] For an account of the law before 1926 see the previous edition of this work at pp. 559–561.
[26] A.E.A. 1925, s.3(1).
[27] *ibid.*, s.57; *e.g.* land passing as *bona vacantia*. The L.T.A. 1897, did not bind the Crown, so that land escheating to the Crown did not vest in the personal representatives: *In b. Hartley* [1899] P. 40.
[28] A.E.A. 1925, s.1(1).
[29] *ibid.*, s.3(3).
[30] *ibid.*, s.3(4).
[31] *ibid.*, s.3(5).
[32] *ibid.*, s.1(1).

Property subject to a general power of appointment exercised by the will of the deceased passes to his personal representatives.[33] On an intestacy, or where there are no executors to administer a will, the deceased's real and personal estate vests initially in the Public Trustee,[34] pending a grant of representation.[35]

2. Assents

11–126   *(a) Writing required.* If A dies leaving land, the title to which is unregistered, to B, and B wishes to sell the land to C, B establishes his title by proving—

> (i) the grant of representation to certain persons as A's personal representatives; and
>
> (ii) an assent or conveyance by those persons as personal representatives in favour of B.[36]

Where the assent or conveyance is made after March 1998, it triggers the requirement of compulsory registration[37] and should be registered within two months.[38] Where the title is registered, B will have to show merely that he is registered as proprietor. When a registered proprietor dies, his personal representatives may on production of the grant of probate or letters of administration either secure their own registration,[39] or transfer the land—

> (i) by way of transfer in favour of a purchaser; or
>
> (ii) by a vesting assent to the person entitled under the will or intestacy.[40]

---

[33] *ibid.*, s.3(2).

[34] Compare the situation where there are executors. The property vests in them at the moment of death and the grant of probate confirms their right to act: *ante*, para. 11–123.

[35] A.E.A. 1925, s.9 (as substituted by L.P.(M.P.)A. 1994, s.14(1)), implementing a recommendation in (1989) Law Com. No. 184, para. 2.23. Before July 1995, when this provision was brought into force, the deceased's property vested in the Probate Judge, who was the President of the Family Division: see A.E.A. 1925, s.55(1)(xv) (now repealed; *cf.* the previous edition of this work at p. 560.). The change to the Public Trustee (which was retrospective: see L.P.(M.P.)A. 1994, s.14(2)) was made because the President was not a corporation sole and obvious difficulties were foreseen should the President die in office. See Law Com. No. 184, para. 2.22; [1995] Conv. 476, 479 (L. Clements). For the functions of the Public Trustee in relation to the service of notices and documents concerning a deceased's estate, see L.P.(M.P.)A. 1994, s.19; and S.I. 1995 No. 1330. Prior to the Act of 1994, service of any notice in respect of an intestate's property before any grant of administration had been made, had to be on the President of the Family Division: see, *e.g. Edwards v. Strong* [1994] E.G.C.S. 182.

[36] Before 1926 B also had to prove A's will, showing that he was beneficially entitled.

[37] L.R.A. 1925, s.123 (substituted by L.R.A. 1997, s.1).

[38] L.R.A. 1925, s.123A (inserted by L.R.A. 1997, s.1).

[39] L.R.A. 1925, ss.37, 41(1); L.R.R. 1925, r. 168. See, *ante*, para. 6–107.

[40] L.R.A. 1925, s.41(3); L.R.R. 1925, r. 170.

An assent to the passing of an equitable interest requires no formality and may be inferred from conduct.[41]

(b) Documents of title: unregistered land. It has been explained above that, **11–127** where an assent of unregistered land is made after March 1998, the title to the land must be registered.[42] There will, however, be many cases where an assent of unregistered land was made prior to April 1998. In such cases the grant of probate[43] and the written assent[44] are essential documents of title. If the land is subsequently sold the assent has the effect of overreaching the equitable interests declared by the will.[45] In other words, a bona fide purchaser for value[46] from a devisee is not concerned with the terms of the will: he is concerned only to see that the legal estate has devolved upon the personal representatives, and that they have in turn vested it by assent or conveyance in the vendor.[47] Unless the purchaser has evidence to the contrary,[48] he cannot require the will to be disclosed[49]; and even if the assent is in favour of the wrong person the purchaser is protected, for the assent passes the legal estate,[50] and the purchaser will have no notice of the beneficiary's claim.[51] Interests arising under wills are therefore now kept off the title to the legal estate, just as are beneficial interests arising under trusts for sale and settlements.

(c) Precautions. Two supplemental provisions further illustrate the func- **11–128** tions of the grant of representation and of the personal representatives in the machinery of devolution.

(i) The person in whose favour an assent or conveyance of a legal estate is made may require notice of it to be indorsed on the grant of probate or letters of administration[52]; thus the grant of representation may be made a kind of register of dispositions,[53] indicating that some specified assent or conveyance is the right one.

---

[41] *Re Edwards' W.T.* [1982] Ch. 30 at 40.

[42] See L.R.A. 1925, s.123 (substituted by L.R.A. 1997, s.1).

[43] *Re Miller and Pickersgill's Contract* [1931] 1 Ch. 511 at 514. The same applies to letters of administration: *ibid.* Grants of representation, being orders of the court, cannot be invalidated against purchasers on account of lack of jurisdiction, or the absence of any consent, even though there was notice of the defect: L.P.A. 1925, s.204; *Hewson v. Shelley* [1914] 2 Ch. 13; *Re Bridgett and Hayes' Contract* [1928] Ch. 163.

[44] A.E.A. 1925, s.36(2), (4); Williams V. & P. 281, n. (g).

[45] A.E.A. 1925, s.39(1)(ii), giving personal representatives the overreaching powers of trustees for sale (for which see *ante*, para. 8–165); but a sole personal representative can receive purchase money: L.P.A 1925, s.27(2), as amended by L.P.(Am.)A. 1926, Sched.

[46] A.E.A. 1925, s.55(1)(xviii).

[47] *ibid.*, s.36(7).

[48] *Re Duce and Boots Cash Chemists (Southern) Ltd's Contract* [1937] Ch. 642.

[49] A.E.A. 1925, s.36(7).

[50] *ibid.*, s.36(4).

[51] See also *post*, paras 12–076, 12–077.

[52] A.E.A. 1925, s.36(4).

[53] See n. 43, *supra*.

(ii) A written statement by a personal representative that he has not disposed of a legal estate is sufficient evidence to a purchaser that no previous assent or conveyance has been made, unless notice is indorsed on the grant of representation as provided above[54]; thus a purchaser can obtain from the personal representative a document which acts as a curtain over all the personal representative's acts.

Both these provisions are permissive, not mandatory; but it is always advisable to employ them.

11–129　　*(d) Changes of capacity.* A personal representative is often given power to act in some other capacity, as where a will appoints X and Y both personal representatives and trustees of land. In such a case the legal estate will not vest in them as trustees of land unless as personal representatives they make a written assent in favour of themselves as trustees of land.[55] Where the title is unregistered, an assent therefore remains an essential link in the title to the legal estate, showing that the property is no longer subject to the personal representatives' powers of administration, even where it is to remain vested in the same persons. As has been explained, any such assent made after March 1998 triggers the requirement of compulsory registration of the land.[56] Where the title is already registered, the personal representatives will either be registered in their representative capacity,[57] or they may secure their registration as trustees of land subject to the appropriate restrictions (if any).[58] The registrar is required to assume that they are acting correctly and within their powers.[59]

11–130　　**3. Ownership of assets.** Although the personal representatives are in a fiduciary position, it is not right to regard them as holding only the legal estate in the assets, with the equitable interests in the beneficiaries. Not until there has been an assent can it be said whether any particular asset will be needed for the payment of debts or discharge of other liabilities, and so no beneficiary can assert that he has any interest in it, legal or equitable. Apart from any property specifically devised or bequeathed,[60] the personal representatives thus have the whole ownership of the assets vested in them, and the rights of the beneficiaries, whether under a will[61] or an intestacy,[62] are protected, not by vesting in them any equitable interest in any of the assets, but by the rule that

---

[54] A.E.A. 1925, s.36(5).
[55] *Re King's W.T.* [1964] Ch. 542, criticised in (1964) 80 L.Q.R. 328 (R. R. A. Walker), (1964) 28 Conv. (N.S.) 298 (J. F. Garner) and (1976) 29 C.L.P. 60 (E. C. Ryder); *cf. Re. Yerburgh* [1928] W.N. 208; *Re Edwards' W.T.* [1982] Ch. 30.
[56] L.R.A. 1925, s.123 (substituted by L.R.A. 1997, s.1); *ante*, para. 11–126.
[57] *Ante*, para. 11–126.
[58] L.R.R. 1925, r. 170 (as amended).
[59] *ibid.*, r. 170(5).
[60] *Kavanagh v. Best* [1971] N.I. 89.
[61] *Commissioner of Stamp Duties (Queensland) v. Livingston* [1965] A.C. 694. See too *Marshall v. Kerr* [1995] 1 A.C. 148 at 157, 165.
[62] *Eastbourne Mutual Benefit B.S. v. Hastings Corporation* [1965] 1 W.L.R. 861.

the court will control the personal representatives and ensure that the assets are duly administered in the interests of the beneficiaries and all other persons concerned.[63] A beneficiary prospectively entitled to any such asset can thus at most be said to have a species of "floating equity" in it which may or may not crystallise. Accordingly, even a beneficiary who is solely entitled under an intestacy cannot, for the purposes of a statutory right to compensation, claim to be "entitled to an interest" in a house which forms part of an unadministered estate[64]; and a surviving spouse with the right to call for the matrimonial home to be appropriated to her[65] has no *locus standi* to defend an action for possession of it.[66]

4. Powers of personal representatives. Personal representatives have joint   **11–131** and several powers over pure personalty but only joint authority in relation to the sale or conveyance of realty (including leaseholds).[67]

Personal representatives have in relation to any real estate comprised in the deceased's estate all the powers conferred by Part I of the Trusts of Land and Appointment of Trustees Act 1996,[68] and thus all the powers of an absolute owner.[69] Although they should sell the property only if that is necessary for the purposes of administration, *e.g.* to pay the deceased's debts, a conveyance to a purchaser for value in good faith is not invalidated merely because he knows that all the debts and other liabilities have been met.[70] Nor is a conveyance to a purchaser for value in good faith invalidated merely because the probate or letters of administration under which the personal representatives acted are subsequently revoked.[71]

Section 3. Number of Personal Representatives

A. Maximum

No grant of probate or letters of administration can be made to more than four   **11–132** personal representatives in respect of the same property.[72] If more than four executors are appointed by a testator, they must decide among themselves who shall apply for probate.

---

[63] See *Commissioner of Stamp Duties (Queensland) v. Livingston, supra*, at 712, 713, a passage of fundamental importance (not cited in *Williams v. Holland* [1965] 1 W.L.R. 739).
[64] *Eastbourne Mutual Benefit B.S. v. Hastings Corporation, supra*.
[65] See *ante*, para. 11–097.
[66] *Lall v. Lall* [1965] 1 W.L.R. 1249; and see Snell, *Equity*, 341, 342.
[67] A.E.A. 1925, s.2(2) (as amended by L.P.(M.P.)A. 1994, extending the provisions of s.2(2) to contracts to convey as well as to conveyances). The amendment implemented a recommendation in (1989) Law Com. No. 184, para. 2.13. For the background to the change, see *ibid.*, para. 2.11; [1995] Conv. 476, 478 (L. Clements).
[68] A.E.A. 1925, s.39 (as amended by T.L.A.T.A. 1996); T.L.A.T.A. 1996, s.18.
[69] T.L.A.T.A. 1996, s.6(1). For these powers, see *ante*, para. 8–137.
[70] A.E.A. 1925, ss.36(8), 55(1)(xviii).
[71] *ibid.*, ss.37, 55(1)(xviii), retrospectively confirming *Hewson v. Shelley* [1914] 2 Ch. 13.
[72] Supreme Court Act 1981, s.114(1). This is strictly construed: see *In b. Holland* (1936) 105 L.J.P. 113.

B. *Minimum*

11–133 A sole personal representative, whether original or by survivorship, has full power to give valid receipts for capital money or any other payments.[73] As has been explained, subject to certain exceptions, personal representatives are in the same position as trustees of land.[74] They have the same powers as such trustees,[75] but without their disability as to receiving capital money severally.[76] However, where any person interested in the estate is a minor or has a life interest in it, the court when granting administration, may not appoint a sole administrator (other than a trust corporation) unless it appears to the court to be expedient to do so.[77] A sole executor can act under such circumstances, but the court has power to appoint additional personal representatives.[78]

---

[73] L.P.A. 1925, s.27(2) (as amended by L.P.(Am)A. 1926, Sched.; T.L.A.T.A. 1996, s.25(1), Sched. 3, para. 4).
[74] *Ante*, para. 8–156.
[75] See T.L.A.T.A. 1996, s.6; *ante* para. 8–137.
[76] *Ante*, para. 8–166.
[77] Supreme Court Act 1981, s.114(2).
[78] *ibid.*, s.114(4).

CHAPTER 12

CONTRACTS OF SALE

A CONTRACT to sell or make any other disposition of any interest in land **12–001** differs from other contracts in three respects. First, since September 27, 1989, such a contract can only be made in writing in accordance with the formalities laid down by the Law of Property (Miscellaneous Provisions) Act 1989.[1] Secondly, the usual remedy for the enforcement of such contracts is specific performance rather than the normal award of damages,[2] and this has influenced many of the rules which apply to conveyancing contracts. Thirdly, and as a consequence of this, a purchaser, even before conveyance, acquires an immediate equitable interest in the property.[3]

Contracts for the sale of land are such an integral part of the whole system of conveyancing that they have many peculiarities drawn from land law. Such contracts invariably contain express terms which are called "conditions of sale".[4] However, the common law has evolved an extensive web of rules which regulate the affairs of vendors and purchasers in the absence of such conditions. To the extent that a matter is governed by them (rather than by a condition of sale), the contract is said to be "open".[5] Although it has never been conclusively settled whether these "open contract" rules are to be regarded as rights conferred by law or as terms which will as a matter of law be implied in the contract,[6] they are generally regarded as the latter because

---

[1] s.2, considered in detail, *post*, para. 12–018. For a brief summary of the law prior to September 27, 1989, see *post*, para. 12–015. Few contracts for sale arising under the previous law are now likely to be in issue, though equitable leases and options granted before the Act came into force and which will therefore remain subject to the previous law, are likely to arise for some considerable time to come.

[2] By contrast, specific performance of a contract for the sale of goods, although possible where the goods are specific or ascertained (see Sale of Goods Act 1979, s.52), is exceptional: *Re Wait* [1972] 1 Ch. 606.

[3] *Ante*, para. 4–025.

[4] "The word 'condition' is traditional rather than appropriate ... Shortly, they are no more than the terms of the contract": *Property & Bloodstock Ltd v. Emerton* [1968] Ch. 94 at 118, *per* Danckwerts L.J.

[5] See *post*, para. 12–046. It is very rare indeed for an entire contract to be open nowadays. For a case in which this did happen, see *Pips (Leisure Productions) Ltd v. Walton* (1980) 43 P. & C.R. 415.

[6] For the suggestion that they are rights conferred by law, see *Ogilvie v. Foljambe* (1817) 3 Mer. 53 at 63; *Want v. Stallibrass* (1873) 8 Exch. 175 at 185. *cf. Ellis v. Rogers* (1885) 29 Ch.D. 661 at 670, 671, where Cotton L.J. considered that they might be terms implied in the contract.

damages are recoverable for their breach.[7] Between the contract and either the conveyance (where title is unregistered) or the lodging of the transfer for registration (where title is registered),[8] which are respectively the first and last formal steps in a sale of land, many questions arise which have to be decided according to the settled practices of conveyancers. The performance of a contract is thus affected in numerous ways, and there is a body of rights which are applicable only to such contracts. Three issues are considered in this chapter:

(1) the types of contract that can exist for the sale or other disposition of land;

(2) the essentials that must be satisfied for there to be a valid contract for the sale of land; and

(3) the rights and duties created by contracts relating to land.

Part 1

TYPES OF CONTRACT

12–002　There are four principal types of contract for the sale or other disposition of land:

(1) an unconditional contract of sale;

(2) a contract that is subject to some form of condition;

(3) an option to purchase; and

(4) a right of pre-emption.[9]

In fact, both options and rights of pre-emption may be regarded as types of conditional contract at least for some purposes.[10] The usual form of binding contract is unconditional. Its principal elements are treated in the course of this chapter and no more need be said of it here.

---

[7] If such rules were merely rights conferred by law, the only consequence of their breach might be that the party in default would be unable to enforce the contract: see (1992) 108 L.Q.R. 280 at 282, 283 (C.H.).

[8] The latter is appropriate where the title to the land is registered: see *ante*, paras 6–096, 6–097.

[9] For the question whether a right of pre-emption can be properly characterised as a contract for the sale or other disposition of land, see *post*, para. 12–061.

[10] *Post*, para. 12–003.

Section 1. Conditional Contracts

1. Types of conditional contract. There are usually said to be four types of conditional contract,[11] and it is a matter of construction, based upon the characteristics of the particular arrangement, as to the category into which the agreement falls.[12]   **12–003**

(a) Condition precedent to a binding agreement. This is an arrangement   **12–004**
between V and P subject to a condition precedent to the making of any binding agreement at all. To describe such an arrangement as a conditional contract is a misnomer for there is no contract at all. The commonest example is an agreement "subject to contract",[13] and other phrases which have been held to have the same effect include "subject to the preparation and approval of a formal contract",[14] "subject to suitable agreements being arranged between your solicitors and mine"[15] and "subject to lease".[16] Such arrangements are of considerable importance and are considered in detail below.[17]

(b) Unilateral contract. In this situation, one party, A, assumes a unilateral   **12–005**
obligation to buy property from or sell property to the other, B, on the occurrence of a certain event, which neither is obliged to bring about. Although A cannot withdraw from the contract as long as it remains conditional, B is not bound by it unless and until he elects to become so.[18] Options and rights of pre-emption are probably best regarded as examples of such contracts,[19] but because they are subject to certain special rules, they are considered separately.[20] One form of such unilateral contracts that is some-

---

[11] See *Wood Preservation Ltd v. Prior* [1969] 1 W.L.R 1077 at 1090. See [1982] C.L.P. 151 (A. J. Oakley); [1992] Conv. 318 (C.H.).

[12] See [1992] Conv. 318 at 319 (C.H.).

[13] *Eccles v. Bryant* [1948] Ch. 93.

[14] *Wynn v. Bull* (1877) 7 Ch.D. 29. See too *Page v. Norfolk* (1894) 70 L.T. 781 ("subject to our approving a detailed contract to be entered into"). *cf. Branca v. Cobarro* [1947] K.B. 854 ("This is a provisional agreement until a fully legalized agreement, drawn up by a solicitor and embodying all the conditions herewith stated, is signed", held to create an immediate binding contract).

[15] *Lockett v. Norman-Wright* [1925] Ch. 56.

[16] Negotiations for the grant of a lease are nowadays often conducted on this basis (or indeed "subject to contract"). In such cases, the parties commonly do not enter into a formal contract to grant a lease nowadays, but proceed directly to the exchange of lease and counterpart: see *Longman v. Viscount Chelsea* (1989) 58 P. & C.R. 189; *Akiens v. Saloman* (1992) 65 P. & C.R. 364; *Enfield L.B.C. v. Arajah* [1995] E.G.C.S. 164. The principle of these cases will not be extended to unilateral acts, where the only question is whether or not the act has been done. Thus where a landlord agreed to the tenant making alterations to the leasehold premises subject to it entering into a formal licence agreement with the landlord, the latter was taken to have consented: *Mount Eden Land Ltd v. Prudential Assurance Co. Ltd* [1997] 1 E.G.L.R. 37. See too *Next Plc v. N.F.U. Mutual Insurance Co. Ltd* [1997] E.G.C.S. 181.

[17] *Post*, para. 12–010.

[18] See *Little v. Courage Ltd* (1994) 70 P. & C.R. 469 at 474. Because B is not bound, it is generally impossible to imply terms into a unilateral contract: *ibid.*

[19] *Wood Preservation Ltd v. Prior, supra*, at 1090.

[20] *Post*, para. 12–012 (options), para. 12–013 (pre-emptions).

times found is where A agrees to sell or purchase land if B performs certain conditions.[21]

12–006   *(c) Condition precedent.* This construction is appropriate where V enters into a bilateral contract to sell property to P subject to a condition precedent which one or other party is obliged to bring about. Although there is a binding contract between the parties it is not a contract for the sale of land until the condition precedent is fulfilled.[22] Neither party can waive the condition precedent, because the existence of the contract depends upon it.[23] For the same reason, if the condition is void for uncertainty, the whole contract fails *ab initio*.[24] Such contracts are in practice rare.[25] The only cases which are likely to fall into this category are those where it is for some reason impossible to enter into a contract for the sale of land unless and until some condition is fulfilled,[26] such as a contract by V to sell land which he does not yet own, that is contingent upon his acquiring it.[27] There is a tendency in the cases to characterise contracts in this way when in fact they fall into the fourth category.[28]

12–007   *(d) Condition subsequent.* The usual kind of conditional contract is where there is an immediate, binding contract for the sale of land which may be terminated by one or (sometimes) both parties if a condition to which it is subject is not performed.[29] The condition is one which either one or (in some cases) both parties are obliged to perform or use their best endeavours to bring

---

[21] See, *e.g. Daulia Ltd v. Four Millbank Nominees Ltd* [1978] Ch. 231; [1979] C.L.J. 31 (C. H. and D. L. Jones) (A undertook to sell land to B if B attended A's premises with the deposit and draft contract on a given date).

[22] For this reason, the doctrine of conversion (*post*, para. 12–059) does not operate until the condition is satisfied.

[23] [1982] C.L.P. 151 at 177 (A. J. Oakley). *cf. Ee v. Kakar* (1979) 40 P. & C.R. 223, where Walton J. held that a "condition precedent" could be waived. However, the condition was in fact a condition subsequent: see [1981] C.L.J. 23 (A. J. Oakley).

[24] *Lee-Parker v. Izzet (No. 2)* [1972] 1 W.L.R. 775 at 780. It has not been settled what the test of certainty is: see [1992] Conv. 318 at 320, 321 (C.H.).

[25] Unfortunately this is not always appreciated. Thus in *Lee-Parker v. Izzet (No. 2), supra*, a term that the sale was conditional upon the purchaser obtaining a satisfactory mortgage was treated as a condition precedent. Because the condition was held to be void for uncertainty, the contract was void *ab initio*. The Privy Council has declined to follow the decision: *Graham v. Pitkin* [1992] 1 W.L.R. 403.

[26] See *Property & Bloodstock Ltd v. Emerton* [1968] Ch. 94 at 116, doubting the analysis in *Aberfoyle Plantations Ltd v. Cheng* [1960] A.C. 115.

[27] *cf. Wylson v. Dunn* (1887) 34 Ch.D. 569. An example that was formerly common was a contract by a charity to sell its land on condition that it obtained the consent of the Charity Commissioners. Without such consent it could not enter into a contract of sale: see Charities Act 1960, s.29(1); *Michael Richards Properties Ltd v. Corporation of Wardens of St. Saviour's Parish* [1975] 3 All E.R. 416 at 421. The law is now different: see Charities Act 1993, ss.36–40; *post*, para. 20–030.

[28] See, *e.g. Mitchem v. Magnus Homes South West Ltd* (1996) 74 P. & C.R. 235 at 243.

[29] There is authority that the doctrine of conversion (*post*, para. 12–059) applies to such contracts: *Gordon Hill Trust Ltd v. Segall* [1941] 2 All E.R. 379. But see *Sainsbury Plc v. O'Connor* [1991] 1 W.L.R. 963 at 979; *Michaels v. Harley House (Marylebone) Ltd* [1997] 1 W.L.R. 967 at 975–978 (not considered on appeal: [1999] 3 W.L.R. 229).

about[30] within the time specified in the contract or implied by law.[31] If the party who is required to bring about the fulfilment of the condition fails to use his best endeavours to do so—

    (i) he cannot plead its non-fulfilment as a defence to any action for specific performance brought by the other[32]; and

    (ii) he will be liable to pay damages for loss of bargain if the other party does not or is unable to proceed with the sale.[33]

The contract will become unconditional in two circumstances. The first is if the condition is held to void for uncertainty.[34] The second is where the condition is waived by one party. Waiver is possible only if the condition is solely for his benefit.[35] If the performance of the condition affects both parties, as where the date for completion is linked to its fulfilment, neither party can waive it.[36] It is now clear that a court will consider the issue of waiver in deciding into which of the four categories a conditional contract falls, because only a condition subsequent is capable of waiver.[37]

Amongst the agreements which have been held to fall within this category **12–008** are contracts conditional upon the obtaining of—

    (i) the landlord's consent to the assignment of the lease (where the property to be conveyed was a lease)[38];

    (ii) planning permission[39];

    (iii) a satisfactory survey[40];

    (iv) vacant possession on completion[41]; and

---

[30] If neither party is obligated to perform the condition, the contract will be unilateral and therefore in the second category of conditional contracts explained *supra: Re Longlands Farm* [1968] 3 All E.R. 552 at 555. *cf. Tesco Stores Ltd v. William Gibson & Son Ltd* (1970) 214 E.G. 835.

[31] *Post*, para. 12–009.

[32] *Gordon Hill Trust Ltd v. Segall, supra*, at 387, 388.

[33] *Day v. Singleton* [1899] 2 Ch. 320.

[34] *cf. Graham v. Pitkin, supra*, at 405, 406. See [1992] Conv. 318 at 322 (C.H.), where the possible tests of certainty are also considered.

[35] *Bennett v. Fowler* (1840) 2 Beav. 302; *Batten v. White* (1960) 12 P. & C.R. 66; *Usanga v. Bishop* (1974) 232 E.G. 835; *Balbosa v. Ayoub Ali* [1990] 1 W.L.R. 914 at 919; *Graham v. Pitkin, supra*, at 405.

[36] *Heron Garage Properties Ltd v. Moss* [1974] 1 W.L.R. 148. For other conditions which could not be waived see *Federated Homes Ltd v. Turner* [1975] 1 E.G.L.R. 147 (condition that a right of access be obtained to property including land retained by the vendor); *Ganton House Investments Ltd v. Corbin* [1988] 2 E.G.L.R. 69 (contract to assign lease conditional on obtaining the landlord's consent).

[37] *Graham v. Pitkin, supra*, at 405, 406; [1992] Conv. 318 at 321, 322 (C.H.).

[38] *Lehmann v. McArthur* (1868) 3 Ch.App. 496.

[39] *Batten v. White, supra*,; *Heron Garage Properties Ltd v. Moss, supra. cf. Tesco Stores Ltd v. William Gibson & Son Ltd, supra*, where the condition was construed as a unilateral contract. *Sed quaere.*

[40] *Ee v. Kakar* (1979) 40 P. & C.R. 223. See n. 23, *supra*.

[41] *Usanga v. Bishop, supra*.

(v) a mortgage (or other finance).[42]

There is some doubt whether a contract which is expressed to be contingent upon the approval of the vendor's title by the purchaser's solicitor is a conditional contract at all. Although in some cases the provision has been treated as a condition subsequent,[43] it may do no more than express what is implied in the contract in any event,[44] namely that "the title must be investigated and approved of in the usual way, which would be by the solicitor of the purchaser".[45]

12–009   **2. The time for performance.** Where a conditional contract fixes a date either for the performance of the condition or for the completion of the sale, the condition must be performed by that date.[46] In each case, time is of the essence and will not be extended by reference to equitable principles.[47] If a party fails to perform the condition (whether precedent or subsequent) by the relevant date, the other is entitled to terminate the contract. In the absence of any factors giving rise to an estoppel, this is so even if the condition is in fact subsequently performed before the contract is determined.[48] If no date is fixed for completion, the condition must be fulfilled within a reasonable time determined objectively.[49]

3. "Subject to contract"

12–010   *(a) Meaning.* When an intending purchaser agrees to buy a property by private treaty,[50] that agreement is usually made "subject to contract". Where a document or preliminary agreement is expressed to be "subject to contract", it means that the parties do not intend to be contractually bound until another document embodying all the terms of the agreement between them is signed by the parties.[51] Normally this will occur on the exchange of formal written contracts in accordance with the usual conveyancing practice,[52] though it may take place at some other time is the parties so agree.[53] Once the parties have begun negotiations "subject to contract", that qualification governs their

---

[42] *Graham v. Pitkin* [1992] 1 W.L.R. 403. See too *Meehan v. Jones* (1982) 149 C.L.R. 571; (1983) 3 O.J.L.S. 438 (M. P. Furmston).

[43] See, *e.g. Caney v. Leith* [1937] 2 All E.R. 532; *Smallman v. Smallman* [1972] Fam. 25 at 32. The effect of such a condition subsequent would be that the opinion of the solicitor as to the title, if given in good faith, would be conclusive one way or the other. The matter could not be reopened by either party in court proceedings.

[44] *Post*, paras 12–072 *et seq.*

[45] *Hussey v. Horne-Payne* (1879) 4 App. Cas. 311 at 322, *per* Lord Cairns L.C.

[46] *Aberfoyle Plantations Ltd v. Cheng* [1960] A.C. 115 at 124.

[47] *ibid.*, at 125. For the equitable principles applicable to time stipulations in a contract for the sale of land, see, *post*, para. 12–091.

[48] *Millers Wharf Partnership Ltd v. Corinthian Column Ltd* (1990) 61 P. & C.R. 461.

[49] *Aberfoyle Plantations Ltd v. Cheng, supra*, at 124; *Re Longlands Farm* [1968] 3 All E.R. 552 at 556.

[50] For sales by auction see *post*, para. 12–023.

[51] *Tiverton Estates Ltd v. Wearwell Ltd* [1975] Ch. 146 at 159, 160.

[52] For the exchange of contracts see *post*, para. 12–036.

[53] *Eccles v. Bryant* [1948] Ch. 93 at 105.

subsequent dealings until contracts are exchanged, unless both agree expressly or by necessary implication that it should be expunged.[54] It is only in "a strong and exceptional case" that the words "subject to contract" will not be given their prima facie meaning.[55] This may, however, happen where the words are meaningless, as where the contract was complete and no further agreement was intended,[56] or where a detailed agreement replacing an existing contract was clearly intended to be binding.[57] It should be noted that a binding contract for the sale of land can no longer arise from a written offer and acceptance,[58] and that the main significance of the words "subject to contract" will now be in cases where draft contracts are exchanged.[59]

Although a party to negotiations which are "subject to contract" might be able to satisfy a court that the parties had subsequently agreed to convert the document into a contract or that some form of estoppel had arisen to prevent either of them from refusing to proceed with the transaction, such cases will necessarily be rare.[60] A party cannot usually claim to have been encouraged to act to his detriment in the course of negotiations "subject to contract".[61] If therefore he incurs expenditure in preparation for the anticipated contract, he will be unable to recover that sum if no contract is in fact concluded.[62]

(b) Effect. The effect of using the phrase "subject to contract" is that both **12–011** parties remain free to withdraw from the arrangement without incurring any legal liability.[63] If the purchaser has paid any deposit, he is entitled to its return should he decline to proceed.[64] Commonly either or both of the parties will be buying or selling another property. It has become usual to synchronise all such sales and purchases in what is known as a "chain".[65] This can be organised only if the parties are not contractually bound at the preliminary stage. Furthermore, the purchaser does not wish to be bound until he has arranged the necessary finance for the purchase and his solicitor has made the necessary

---

[54] *Sherbrooke v. Dipple* (1980) 41 P. & C.R. 173; *Cohen v. Nessdale Ltd* [1982] 2 All E.R. 97. See too *Henderson Group Plc v. Superabbey Ltd* [1988] 2 E.G.L.R. 155 at 157.

[55] *Chillingworth v. Esche* [1924] 1 Ch. 97 at 114, *per* Sargant L.J.

[56] *Michael Richards Properties Ltd v. Corporation of Wardens of St. Saviour's Parish, Southwark* [1975] 3 All E.R. 416. See too *Westway Homes Ltd v. Moores* (1991) 63 P. & C.R. 480 (exercise of option "subject to contract" held to be meaningless, because the terms of the contract were prescribed by the option agreement itself).

[57] *Alpenstow Ltd v. Regalian Properties Plc* [1985] 1 W.L.R. 721; [1985] C.L.J. 356 (C.H.).

[58] L.P.(M.P.)A. 1989, s.2; *Commission for the New Towns v. Cooper (Great Britain) Ltd* [1995] Ch. 259 at 287, 294; *post,* para. 12–037.

[59] *Commission for the New Towns v. Cooper (Great Britain) Ltd, supra,* at 293.

[60] *Att.-Gen. of Hong Kong v. Humphreys Estate (Queen's Gardens) Ltd* [1987] A.C. 114 at 127, 128. For proprietary estoppel, see *post,* Chap. 13.

[61] *Post,* para. 13–009.

[62] *Regalian Properties Plc v. London Docklands Development Corporation* [1995] 1 W.L.R. 212; [1995] C.L.J. 243 (G. Virgo); [1995] R.L.R. 100 (E. McKendrick).

[63] In *Goding v. Frazer* [1967] 1 W.L.R. 286 at 293, Sachs J. spoke of "this hybrid type of 'subject to contract' transaction, which is so often referred to as a gentleman's agreement, but which experience shows is only too often a transaction in which each side hopes the other will act like a gentleman and neither intends so to act if it is against his material interest".

[64] *Chillingworth v. Esche, supra.*

[65] See *Domb v. Isoz* [1980] Ch. 548 at 560, 561.

inquiries before contract.[66] One consequence of the parties' freedom to with-draw at will is that the vendor may (when property prices are rising) "gazump"[67] the purchaser by threatening to sell to another buyer unless a higher price is paid. Similarly, if property prices are falling, the purchaser may threaten to pull out of the agreement unless the vendor reduces the price, an abuse known as "gazundering". A number of devices have been employed to overcome these malpractices. The best-known is a so-called "lock-out" or "exclusivity" agreement by which V, for good consideration, agrees with P that, for a specified period of time, he will not negotiate with anyone except P in relation to the sale of his property.[68] It is essential to the validity of the agreement that it should be confined to a fixed period for otherwise it will be void for uncertainty as a mere agreement to negotiate.[69] Such an agreement is merely a negative agreement not to deal with anyone other than P. It is not a contract for the sale or other disposition of an interest in land and does not therefore have to comply with the formal requirements for such contracts.[70] The primary remedy for breach of a lock-out agreement is damages and the measure will be the amount which P has wasted in costs during the period of exclusivity.[71]

The conduct of conveyancing under the umbrella of "subject to contract" has arisen as a matter of custom and practice not because of any particular rule of law. It is quite unknown in Scotland where would-be purchasers submit sealed bids for the property offering both a price and terms for completion. The seller accepts the one which suits him best and the contract is then concluded. Chain sales do not exist and gazumping and gazundering are impossible. If desired, such a system could be readily adopted in England and Wales.[72]

Section 2. Options and Rights of Pre-emption

12–012   **1. Options.** An option is an undertaking by the grantor that he will sell certain property to the grantee if the latter wishes to purchase it within a specified period.[73] It may be created by a contract between the grantor and the

---

[66] *ibid.* See *ante*, para. 5–027.

[67] Described as a "verb of doubtful etymology": *Wroth v. Tyler* [1974] Ch. 30 at 55, *per* Megarry J.

[68] *Walford v. Miles* [1992] 2 A.C. 128 at 139; (1992) 108 L.Q.R. 405 (Sir Patrick Neill); *Pitt v. P.H.H. Asset Management Ltd* [1994] 1 W.L.R. 327. Unless the parties otherwise agree, a lock-out agreement will not found a claim for substantial damages or a long-term injunction: *Moroney v. Isofam Investments S.A.* [1997] E.G.C.S. 178.

[69] *Walford v. Miles, supra,* approving *Courtney & Fairburn Ltd v. Tolaini Brothers (Hotels) Ltd* [1975] 1 W.L.R. 297.

[70] *Pitt v. P.H.H. Asset Management Ltd, supra,* at 332, 334; [1993] C.L.J. 392 (C. MacMillan). *cf.* [1994] Conv. 58 (M. P. Thompson).

[71] See *Tye v. House* [1997] 2 E.G.L.R. 171; *Moroney v. Isofam Invesments S.A.* [1997] E.G.C.S. 178.

[72] See the Explanatory Guide, "House Selling the Scottish Way for England and Wales", produced by the Conveyancing Standing Committee of the Law Commission (1987).

[73] For the application of the rule against perpetuities to options see *ante*, para. 7–118.

grantee (which may stand by itself or be part of some other transaction such as a sale or lease), or it may be granted by will. It is only with the former that we are here concerned.[74] An option has been described as "a relationship *sui generis*".[75] It shares certain characteristics with other types of legal relationship but does not exactly correspond to any of them. First, it is "not the same juristic creature as a contract of sale",[76] because it binds only the grantor until it is exercised.[77] Secondly, it has been likened to an "irrevocable offer" to sell,[78] but it is really only from the grantee's standpoint that it can be so regarded.[79] In explaining the grantor's position, an option may be seen as analogous to a conditional contract.[80] However, the performance of the contingency lies within the sole power of the grantee[81] and the contract is not therefore "conditional" in the same sense as is a contract subject to a condition precedent or subsequent.[82] A court will adopt a purposive analysis in any given case to decide which of these analogies it is the most appropriate to apply to the issue which it is called upon to determine.[83] Thus an option has been treated as a conditional contract for the purposes of—

(i) the formalities required for a contract for the sale of an interest in land,[84] so that although the grant of the option has to comply with those requirements, its exercise does not[85]; and

(ii) registration as a land charge,[86] so that it is unnecessary to register as an estate contract the contract for sale that arises from the exercise of the option as well as the option itself.[87]

The grantor's undertaking to sell to the grantee will be enforceable even though the consideration for the option is only nominal, such as a payment of £1.[88] When the option is exercised in accordance with its terms, the original unilateral agreement which imposed no immediate obligations on either party

---

[74] For testamentary options see R. Castle, *Barnsley's Land Options* (3rd ed.), Chap. 6.

[75] *Spiro v. Glencrown Properties Ltd* [1991] Ch. 537 at 544, *per* Hoffmann J. See [1994] Conv. 483 (N. P. Gravells).

[76] *Chippenham Golf Club Trustees v. North Wiltshire D.C.* (1991) 64 P. & C.R. 527 at 531, *per* Scott L.J. (power to sell did not confer a power to grant an option).

[77] For the nature of the grantor's obligations see [1984] C.L.J. 55 (S. Tromans).

[78] *Stromdale & Ball Ltd v. Burden* [1952] Ch. 223 at 235; *Mountford v. Scott* [1975] Ch. 258 at 264; *United Scientific Holdings Ltd v. Burnley B.C.* [1978] A.C. 904 at 945. An "irrevocable offer" has been described as "juristically a contradiction in terms", because the word "irrevocable" implies the existence of an obligation, whereas "offer" implies none: *Varty v. British South Africa Co.* [1965] Ch. 508 at 523, *per* Diplock L.J.

[79] *Spiro v. Glencrown Properties Ltd, supra* at 543.

[80] *Griffith v. Pelton* [1958] Ch. 205 at 225.

[81] *Spiro v. Glencrown Properties Ltd, supra*, at 544.

[82] For these forms of conditional contract, see *ante*, paras 12–006, 12–007.

[83] *Spiro v. Glencrown Properties Ltd, supra* at 544. See too *Re Mulholland's W.T.* [1949] 1 All E.R. 460; *Chippenham Golf Club Trustees v. North Wiltshire D.C., supra*, at 531.

[84] See L.P.(M.P.)A. 1989, s.2; *post*, para. 12–018.

[85] *Spiro v. Glencrown Properties Ltd, supra*; *post*, para. 12–020.

[86] See L.C.A. 1972, s.2(4)(iv); *ante*, para. 5–099.

[87] *Armstrong & Holmes Ltd v. Holmes* [1993] 1 W.L.R. 1482.

[88] *Mountford v. Scott, supra.*

to do anything, is converted into a bilateral agreement which creates reciprocal rights and obligations on both parties.[89]

If the grantor of an option transfers the land in breach of the option, he will be liable in damages to the grantee.[90] The grantee may seek an injunction to restrain any such disposition.[91]

12–013   **2. Rights of pre-emption.** Where a landowner grants a right of pre-emption (or as it is often called, a right of first refusal), it imposes upon him for an agreed period[92] a negative obligation to refrain from selling the land, without first giving the grantee the opportunity to purchase it in preference to any other buyer. The grantor is under no obligation to sell the property, but should he decide to do so, he must first offer[93] it to the grantee, who is then free to accept or reject the proposal.[94] If the grantor decides to sell the property and offers it to the grantee, then unless the instrument creating the right of pre-emption otherwise provides,[95] that offer may be revoked before acceptance should the grantor reconsider his decision to sell.[96]

If the grantor disposes of the land without first offering it to the grantee he will be liable to the latter in damages.[97] Furthermore any such disposition can be restrained by injunction[98] and the grantor can be required to offer to sell the land to the grantee.[99]

The different effects of options and rights of pre-emption are explained later.[1]

Part 2

THE ESSENTIALS OF A VALID CONTRACT

12–014   It is no longer possible to distinguish the essential validity of a contract for the sale of land from its enforceability as it was prior to September 27, 1989, when section 2 of the Law of Property (Miscellaneous Provisions) Act 1989

---

[89] *Sudbrook Trading Estate Ltd v. Eggleton* [1983] 1 A.C. 444 at 477.

[90] *Midland Bank Trust Co. Ltd v. Green* [1980] Ch. 590 at 611 (not considered on appeal: [1981] A.C. 513).

[91] *Mason v. Schuppisser* (1899) 81 L.T. 147 at 148.

[92] The rule against perpetuities applies to rights of pre-emption as it does to options: Perpetuities and Accumulations Act 1964, s.9(2); *ante*, para. 7–118. But see *post*, para. 12–061.

[93] Whether or not a communication from the grantor amounts to an offer is a matter of construction of that document: *Churchman v. Lampon* [1990] 1 E.G.L.R. 211.

[94] See *Mackay v. Wilson* (1947) 47 S.R.(N.S.W.) 315 at 325; *Pritchard v. Briggs* [1980] Ch. 338 at 389, 423.

[95] As it did in *Pritchard v. Briggs, supra*.

[96] *Tuck v. Baker* [1990] 1 E.G.L.R. 195.

[97] *Gardner v. Coutts & Co.* [1968] 1 W.L.R. 173 (gift of land a breach of the right of pre-emption).

[98] *Coventry v. London, Brighton & South Coast Rly.* (1867) L.R. 5 Eq. 104; *Manchester Ship Canal Co. v. Manchester Racecourse Co.* [1901] 2 Ch. 37.

[99] *London & South Western Rly Co. v. Blackmore* (1870) L.R. 4 H.L. 610.

[1] *Post*, para. 12–061.

came into force.[2] Before examining the effect of that provision, a brief summary must be given of the former law.[3]

Section 1. Contracts made before September 27, 1989

1. Method of contracting. Before September 27, 1989, there were no constraints on the manner in which a contract for the sale or disposition of land or any interest might be made. Oral contracts were perfectly valid,[4] but were by statute unenforceable[5] in proceedings for specific performance or damages in the absence of "some memorandum or note thereof . . . in writing"[6] or some sufficient act of part performance. However, although no action could be brought upon an oral contract, the plaintiff could pursue any other remedy that he might have, *e.g.* by forfeiting any deposit he had received[7] or by suing to recover any money expended on the defendant's property because of a total failure of consideration.[8] The concept of a valid but unenforceable obligation was one of the strangest creations of English law.[9]

12–015

2. The requirement of written evidence. The effects of the statutory requirements as they came to be interpreted may be summarised as follows.

12–016

    (i) Either the agreement itself or a note or memorandum of it had to be made in writing and signed "by the party to be charged" or his authorised agent.[10] One effect of this was that if P had signed a memorandum of an oral contract, but V had not, V could enforce the contract against P, but not *vice versa*.

    (ii) The requirement of writing could be satisfied even by a document that was not intended for that purpose. Any document[11] signed by the defendant which recorded the terms of the contract sufficed.[12]

---

[2] L.P.(M.P.)A. 1989, s.5(3), (4).

[3] For a full account, see the previous edition of this work at pp. 571–599.

[4] Oral contracts had in fact become unusual. Because the parties usually intended to exchange written contracts, there was almost a presumption that an oral agreement was not intended to have contractual effect: *Damm v. Herrtage* [1975] 1 E.G.L.R. 107 at 110.

[5] See *e.g. Britain v. Rossiter* (1879) 11 Q.B.D. 123.

[6] L.P.A. 1925, s.40(1), replacing part of the Statute of Frauds 1677, s.4.

[7] *Monickendam v. Leanse* (1923) 39 T.L.R. 445. See too *Low v. Fry* (1931) 152 L.T. 585 (action brought on dishonoured cheque for the deposit).

[8] *Pulbrook v. Lawes* (1876) 1 Q.B.D. 284.

[9] One example still survives. A trust of land may be declared orally but is unenforceable in the absence of written evidence: L.P.A. 1925, s.53(1)(b); *ante*, para. 10–039. The matter is under review by the Law Commission.

[10] L.P.A. 1925, s.40.

[11] Examples from the cases include a letter, an entry in a diary, and a receipt or a telegram: see the previous edition of this work at p. 577.

[12] *Re Hoyle* [1893] 1 Ch. 84 at 99.

(iii) A memorandum might be made up of more than one document provided that they could be connected. If the document signed by the party to be charged contained some reference, express or implied, to another document or transaction, that sufficed. In such circumstances parol evidence was admissible to explain the transaction and to identify any document relating to it.[13]

(iv) A memorandum was valid only if it contained all the terms agreed between the parties.[14] If a term had been omitted, the memorandum was insufficient.[15] To this general rule there were two exceptions of somewhat uncertain ambit. A plaintiff might waive an omitted term if it was for his exclusive benefit,[16] or submit to it by performing (or offering to perform) the omitted term if it was for the benefit of the defendant.[17] There was some authority that a term could be waived only if it were "of no great importance",[18] but this view was by no means settled.[19]

12–017 **3. Part performance.** An oral contract for the sale of land might be specifically enforced in equity even if there was no sufficient memorandum to satisfy the statutory requirements. This would be the case where the party seeking relief had done a sufficient act of part performance of the contract.[20] This equitable doctrine[21] was the source of much difficulty because of its uncertain basis.[22] "What was in origin a rule of substantive law designed to vindicate conscientious dealing seems to have come in time sometimes to have been considered somewhat as a rule of evidence."[23] The substantive principle underlying the doctrine was that "if one party to an agreement stands by and lets the other party incur expense or prejudice his position on the faith of the agreement being valid he will not then be allowed to turn round and assert that the agreement is unenforceable. Using fraud in its older and less precise sense, that would be fraudulent on his part and it has become proverbial that courts of equity will not permit the statute to be made an instrument of fraud".[24] In such circumstances the defendant was in reality "charged" upon the equities resulting from the acts done in execution of the

---

[13] *Timmins v. Moreland Street Property Co. Ltd* [1958] Ch. 110 at 130; *Elias v. George Sahely & Co. (Barbados) Ltd* [1983] 1 A.C. 646.

[14] *Hawkins v. Price* [1947] Ch. 645; *Beckett v. Nurse* [1948] 1 K.B. 535.

[15] *Ram Narayan v. Shah* [1979] 1 W.L.R. 1349.

[16] *Morell v. Studd and Millington* [1913] 2 Ch. 648 at 660; *North v. Loomes* [1919] 1 Ch. 378 at 385, 386.

[17] *Martin v. Pycroft* (1852) 2 De G.M. & G. 785; *Scott v. Bradley* [1971] Ch. 850, not following *Burgess v. Cox* [1951] Ch. 383. See (1951) 67 L.Q.R. 299 (R.E.M.).

[18] *Hawkins v. Price* [1947] Ch. 646.

[19] See *Martin v. Pycroft, supra.*

[20] *cf.* L.P.A 1925, s.40(2).

[21] There was no equivalent at law: *O'Herlihy v. Hedges* (1803) 1 Sch. & Lef. 123 at 130. In *Morritt v. Wonham* [1993] N.P.C. 2, the fact that the doctrine was equitable was taken to give the court a wide power to do equity. *Sed quaere*: see [1994] Conv. 233 (M. P. Thompson).

[22] See [1979] Conv. 402 (M. P. Thompson).

[23] *Steadman v. Steadman* [1976] A.C. 536 at 559, *per* Lord Simon of Glaisdale.

[24] *ibid.*, at 540, *per* Lord Reid.

contract rather than on the contract itself.[25] However, it was also necessary that the acts of part performance should be of such a kind as to provide evidence of the agreement between the parties.[26]

By the time that the doctrine of part performance was abolished in 1989, there was considerable uncertainty as to the degree of particularity with which the agreement had to be proved.[27] The authorities were in conflict as to whether the acts had to be referable to a contract specifically concerning land,[28] though the trend was against it.[29] It was accepted however that the acts of part performance relied upon had to be "unequivocally, and in their own nature, referable to some such agreement as that alleged".[30] The paradigm was the case of a purchaser who, with the vendor's consent, took possession of the land which he had orally agreed to buy. Although there had to be an evidential connection between the acts of part performance and the contract, such acts were not regarded as a substitute for the written evidence required by the statute.[31] The acts did of course have to be performed by or on behalf of the plaintiff,[32] whereas under the statute, the written evidence had to be signed by the defendant.[33] Once acts of part performance were established, all the terms of the contract could be proved by oral evidence, including terms with which the acts of part performance had no connection.[34]

Section 2. Contracts made after September 26, 1989

For contracts made after September 26, 1989, section 2 of the Law of Property (Miscellaneous Provisions) Act 1989, which implemented the recommendations of the Law Commission,[35] has fundamentally changed the law.[36] Its   **12–018**

---

[25] *Maddison v. Alderson* (1883) 8 App. Cas. 467 at 475. There were obvious parallels between part performance and proprietary estoppel: *post*, para. 13–003. For consideration of their interrelationship, see (1990) 10 L.S. 325 (L. Bently and P. Coughlan); (1993) 13 O.J.L.S. 99 (C. Davis).

[26] *Maddison v. Alderson, supra*, at 478.

[27] The uncertainty arose as a result of the decision of the House of Lords in *Steadman v. Steadman, supra*, in which it was held that the mere payment of money might amount to an act of part performance. For criticism of the case see (1974) 90 L.Q.R. 433 (H.W.R.W.).

[28] Compare the view of Lord Reid and Viscount Dilhorne in *Steadman v. Steadman, supra*, at 542, 553 (the acts need not indicate a contract concerning land), with those of Lord Salmon: *ibid.*, at 570 (followed in *Re Gonin* [1979] Ch. 16 at 31). *cf.* [1979] Conv. 402 (M. P. Thompson).

[29] See *Du Boulay v. Raggett* (1988) 58 P. & C.R. 138 and 152.

[30] *Maddison v. Alderson, supra*, at 479, *per* Lord Selbourne L.C.

[31] *Steadman v. Steadman, supra*, at 542.

[32] *Williams v. Evans* (1875) L.R. 19 Eq. 547 (repairs and alterations executed by plaintiff's lessee).

[33] L.P.A. 1925, s.40(1).

[34] *Brough v. Nettleton* [1921] 2 Ch. 25.

[35] (1987) Law Com. No. 164. The draft Bill attached to the Law Commission's Report differs significantly from the wording of the final legislation: see *Pitt v. P.H.H. Asset Management Ltd* [1994] 1 W.L.R. 327 at 331; *Commission for the New Towns v. Cooper (Great Britain) Ltd* [1995] Ch. 259 at 287; *post*, para. 12–036.

[36] See *Firstpost Homes Ltd v. Johnson* [1995] 1 W.L.R. 1567 at 1571, where the main differences are succinctly summarised.

provisions are altogether more stringent than those of its precursor. The section has expressly repealed the requirement for written evidence of a contract for the sale of land.[37] It has provided instead that a contract for the sale or other disposition of an interest in land "can only be made in writing and only by incorporating all the terms which the parties have expressly agreed in one document or, where the contracts are exchanged, in each".[38] The terms may be incorporated in a document either by being set out in it or by reference to some other document.[39] The document incorporating the terms or, where contracts are exchanged, one of the documents incorporating them (but not necessarily the same one) must be signed by or on behalf of each party to the contract.[40]

There can no longer be a valid but unenforceable oral contract for the sale of land. In consequence the doctrine of part performance is necessarily abolished, because no contractual obligation exists that can be partly performed.[41] Unless an agreement is made in writing in accordance with the provisions of the section then, subject to the possibility of rectification in certain cases,[42] it is void. Furthermore, where there is a valid written contract, any subsequent agreement to vary its terms which does not itself comply with section 2 will be ineffective.[43]

12–019   The requirements of the Law of Property (Miscellaneous Provisions) Act 1989 must now be considered. Even where these are the same as those of its predecessor, it is by no means certain that much guidance is to be had from the authorities on the previous law.[43a] This is because—

(i) the underlying policy of the new Act is very different from that of its predecessor, requiring as it does a higher degree of certainty[44];

(ii) it is clear that the courts are adopting a purposive interpretation of its provisions[45]; and

(iii) some of the principles applicable under the former law were anomalous[46] and there is little reason to apply them to the new statute.

---

[37] ss.2(8), 4, Sched. 2.

[38] s.2(1).

[39] s.2(2); *post*, para. 12–027.

[40] s.2(3); *post*, paras 12–039–12–041.

[41] *Post*, para. 12–042.

[42] *Post*, para. 12–032.

[43] *McCausland v. Duncan Lawrie Ltd* [1997] 1 W.L.R. 38; [1996] Conv. 366 (M. P. Thompson). See too [1989] Conv. 431 at 436, 437 (P. H. Pettit). See *post*, para. 12–040.

[43a] See *Rudra v. Abbey National Plc* (1998) 76 P. & C.R. 537 at 541 (the old authorities were "not necessarily of much, if any, assistance" in interpreting s.2: *per* Robert Walker L.J.).

[44] See *Firstpost Homes Ltd v. Johnson* [1995] 1 W.L.R. 1567 at 1576, 1577; *United Bank of Kuwait Plc v. Sahib* [1997] Ch. 107 at 136, 138. The Act goes further than its predecessor in another significant respect. It requires that contracts for the sale of land should be made in a particular way: *post*, para. 12–036.

[45] See *Spiro v. Glencrown Properties Ltd* [1991] Ch. 537.

[46] See *post*, para. 12–026 for one example.

1. Contract for the sale or other disposition of an interest in land

(a) Types of transaction. Subject to certain exceptions considered below, the **12–020** provisions of the Act apply to "a contract for the sale or other disposition of an interest in land".[47] It follows from this that there must be a *contract*. Where the document, not being the grant of an option, takes the form of a mere offer to sell, without any promise by the addressee to purchase, it will not comply with the requirements of the section.[48] "Disposition" is widely defined to include a mortgage, charge, lease or indeed any other assurance of property.[49] It will therefore apply to contracts to sell a freehold; to grant, assign, or surrender a lease or sub-lease[50]; to mortgage freehold or leasehold land[51]; to grant an incorporeal hereditament, such as an easement or a *profit à prendre,*[52] or to devise particular land by will.[53] The grant of an option is also within the section, though its exercise is not, because an option is regarded for these purposes as a conditional contract.[54] The position both as to the grant and exercise of a right of pre-emption is much less clear. A right of pre-emption does not create an interest in land at the time when it is granted but it will do so should the grantor decide to sell the land. The right then becomes an option to purchase the land, and the grantor must offer to sell the property to the grantee.[55] A concluded contract for the sale of land is made when that offer is accepted.[56] There are in reality therefore two contracts—

(i) the grant of a right of pre-emption; and

(ii) its exercise.

The latter contract is certainly a contract for the sale or other disposition of an interest in land and should therefore have to comply with the formal requirements of the Act.[57] The former may also be, but this view is not universally shared.[58] A unilateral contract by X to enter into a contract to sell land to Y

---

[47] s.2(1).

[48] *Firstpost Homes Ltd v. Johnson* [1995] 1 W.L.R. 1567.

[49] L.P.(M.P.)A. 1989, s.2(6); L.P.A. 1925, s.205(1)(ii).

[50] *Commission for the New Towns v. Cooper (Great Britain) Ltd* [1995] Ch. 259 (contract to surrender an underlease within s.2).

[51] For the effect of the section on mortgages by deposit of title deeds, see *post*, para. 12–043.

[52] *cf. Webber v. Lee* (1882) 9 Q.B.D. 315 (contract to grant shooting rights fell within Statute of Frauds 1677, s.4).

[53] *Taylor v. Dickens* [1998] 1 F.L.R. 806 at 819.

[54] *Spiro v. Glencrown Properties Ltd* [1991] Ch. 537; [1991] C.L.J. 236 (A. J. Oakley). See too *Chippenham Golf Club v. North Wiltshire D.C.* (1991) 64 P. & C.R. 527 at 530, where Scott L.J. observed that "it was evident that the draftsman of this section did not take account of options".

[55] *Pritchard v. Briggs* [1980] Ch. 338 at 418, 423; *Kling v. Keston Properties Ltd* (1983) 49 P. & C.R. 212 at 217. For criticism, see *post*, paras 12–061–12–063.

[56] *Brown v. Gould* [1972] Ch. 53 at 58.

[57] R. Castle, *Barnsley's Land Options* (3rd ed.), pp. 163, 164, 168, 169. The grant of the pre-emption is unlikely to contain all the terms of any subsequent contract of sale: *Smith v. Morgan* [1971] 1 W.L.R. 803.

[58] Some consider that, as a right of pre-emption does not initially and may never create an interest in land, it is not within s.2.

if Y performs certain acts, has been held to be an agreement for some "other disposition" of an interest in land and it is therefore within the section.[59]

The section has no application to a transaction which is not a "sale or other disposition" even though it may concern land. For that reason the following transaction do not fall within it.

(i) A "sale" by a tenant to his landlord of fixtures (*i.e.* objects attached to land[60]) which he has a right to remove,[61] because in law this is no more than a waiver of his right to sever and take away what is legally part of the landlord's premises.[62]

(ii) A "lock-out" agreement by which a vendor agrees for a specific period *not* to sell to anyone save the purchaser.[63]

(iii) A compromise of possession proceedings between mortgagee and mortgagor.[64]

12–021 *(b) Transactions excluded.* The Act specifically excludes three categories of contract from the operation of section 2.[65]

12–022 (1) SHORT LEASES. As a lease for a term not exceeding three years at the best rent which can be reasonably obtained without taking a fine may be granted orally,[66] it is provided that a contract to grant such a lease may also be made orally.[67]

12–023 (2) SALES AT PUBLIC AUCTION. Under the previous law, a contract made in the course of a public auction was made on the fall of the hammer, and the auctioneer had authority to sign a memorandum on behalf of both the vendor[68] and the purchaser.[69] In this way, a contract made at auction was in practice always enforceable. Auction sales are excluded from the application of section 2 and there is a binding contract on the fall of the hammer even in the absence of any writing. This is to ensure that neither party can thereafter withdraw.[70]

---

[59] *Daulia Ltd v. Four Millbank Nominees Ltd* [1978] Ch. 231; [1979] C.L.J. 31 (C. H. and D. L. Jones). See too *Godden v. Merthyr Tydfil Housing Association* (1997) 74 P. & C.R. D1.

[60] See *post*, para. 14–311.

[61] For such "tenant's fixtures" see *post*, paras 14–318 *et seq.*

[62] *Hallen v. Runder* (1834) 1 Cr.M. & R. 266 at 276; *Lee v. Gaskell* (1876) 1 Q.B.D. 700. The same applies to an agreement by the landlord to extend the tenant's time for removing the fixtures: *Thomas v. Jennings* (1896) 66 L.J.Q.B. 5 at 8.

[63] *Pitt v. P.H.H. Asset Management Ltd* [1994] 1 W.L.R. 327. For lock-out agreements see *ante*, para. 12–011.

[64] *Kumah v. Osbornes* [1997] E.G.C.S. 1. For the mortgagee's right to possession, see *post*, para. 19–067.

[65] See s.2(5).

[66] L.P.A. 1925, s.54(2); *post*, para. 14–034.

[67] See (1987) Law Com. No. 164, para. 4.10; *post*, para. 14–037. See *Parc Battersea Ltd v. Hutchinson* [1999] 22 E.G. 149 at 154.

[68] *Beer v. London & Paris Hotel Co.* (1875) L.R. 20 Eq. 412 at 426.

[69] *Sims v. Landray* [1894] 2 Ch. 318 at 320.

[70] See (1987) Law Com. No. 164, para. 4.11.

(3) CONTRACTS REGULATED UNDER THE FINANCIAL SERVICES ACT 1986. To **12–024** avoid any possibility that a contract to sell an investment that was secured on or included an interest in land might fall within the Act,[71] it is provided that section 2 does not apply to a contract regulated under the Financial Services Act 1986.[72]

(c) Interest in land. "Interest in land" is defined by the Act to mean "any **12–025** estate, interest or charge in or over land".[73] The following have been held to be contracts for the sale of interests in land either under the Act or its predecessor—

(i) an indivisible contract for the sale of both land and chattels[74];

(ii) a contract to sell fixtures, even when they are sold separately from the land[75];

(iii) an agreement to sell building materials from a house, which the buyer was to demolish[76]; and

(iv) a contract to sell slag and cinders which had become part of the land.[77]

The mere fact that a contract concerns land will not bring it within the ambit of the section if it is not one for the disposition of an interest in land. Thus neither a contract to grant a licence nor a contractual licence itself is within the section because a licence creates no interest in property.[78]

The Act provides no definition of "land" as such, though it has been **12–026** assumed to have the same meaning as it had under the previous law.[79] However, in view of the courts' willingness to abandon the former law,[80] this is questionable. A court might consider it inappropriate that certain property which was regarded as "land" under the former law should be so for the

---

[71] *cf. Driver v. Broad* [1893] 1 Q.B. 744 (contract to sell debentures which were secured on the entirety of a company's property, including land, held to be within the Statute of Frauds 1677, s.4).

[72] See (1987) Law Com. No. 164, para. 4.12.

[73] s.2(6) (as amended by T.L.A.T.A. 1996, s.25(2); Sched. 4, to reflect the abolition of the doctrine of conversion by s.3 of that Act: see *ante,* para. 8–127.

[74] *Wright v. Robert Leonard Developments Ltd* [1994] E.G.C.S. 69 (a decision on L.P.(M.P.)A. 1989, s.2); [1995] Conv. 484 (M. P. Thompson). The parties are however at liberty "to hive off part of the terms of their composite bargain into a separate contract distinct from the written land contract that incorporates the rest of the terms": *Tootal Cleaning Ltd v. Guinea Properties Ltd* (1992) 64 P. & C.R. 452 at 456, *per* Scott L.J. See (1993) 109 L.Q.R. 191 (D. Wilde); and *post,* para. 12–034.

[75] *Jarvis v. Jarvis* (1893) 63 L.J.Ch. 10 at 13.

[76] *Lavery v. Pursell* (1888) 39 Ch.D 508.

[77] *Morgan v. Russell & Sons* [1909] 1 K.B. 357.

[78] *Ashburn Anstalt v. Arnold* [1989] Ch. 1.

[79] See *Benjamin's Sale of Goods* (5th ed., 1997), para. 1–091; and L.P.A. 1925, s.205(1)(ix).

[80] See *Firstpost Homes Ltd v. Johnson* [1995] 1 W.L.R. 1567; *ante,* para. 12–019.

purposes of the Act, given the more stringent formal requirements which it lays down.[81] This is particularly so where that earlier characterisation was irrational as, for example, in the case of certain growing crops.[82] Under the previous law, there was a distinction between "those crops which, broadly speaking, are produced in the year by the labour of the year, and crops such as fruit growing on trees, where the productive act is the planting of the trees, and where the fruit is produced by the trees year after year, primarily as the result of that initial productive act".[83] The former, which were known as *fructus industriales*, and included annual crops such as wheat, corn and potatoes, were never regarded as land but always as chattles.[84] The latter, called *fructus naturales*, such as grass, timber and fruit trees, were regarded as land unless—

(i) they were to be severed by the vendor and not by the purchaser[85]; or

(ii) the purchaser was bound by the contract to sever them as soon as possible.[86]

The justification for these rules was never apparent[87] and it was suggested that the statutory requirement of a written memorandum was inapposite in such cases and should have been confined to "such interests as are known to conveyancers".[88] Now that the formal requirements for contracts for the disposition of an interest in land have been made more rigorous, there is much to be said for rejecting these old distinctions and for treating all crops as chattels for the purposes of section 2. The same may be true as regards contracts to sell fixtures which are to be severed. This is particularly so because the Sale of Goods Act 1979[89] defines "goods" as including not only "industrial growing crops" but also "things attached to or forming part of the land which are agreed to be severed before sale or under the contract of sale". This last phrase would cover *fructus naturales* and such things as building materials or fixtures if sold separately, for then there must be a severance under the contract. Although under the previous law, a contract could at one and the same time, be a contract for the sale of both land within the Law of

---

[81] *Ante*, para 12–018.
[82] For a fuller consideration of this subject, see the previous edition of this work at pp. 573–575; and *Benjamin's Sale of Goods*, paras 1–092–1–094.
[83] *Saunders v. Pilcher* [1949] 2 All E.R. 1097 at 1104, *per* Jenkins L.J.
[84] See *Duppa v. Mayo* (1669) 1 Wms. Saund. 275; *Marshall v. Green* (1875) 1 C.P.D. 35 at 42.
[85] *Smith v. Surman* (1829) 9 B. & C. 561.
[86] *Marshall v. Green, supra.*
[87] See the criticisms in the previous edition of this work at p. 574.
[88] *Marshall v. Green, supra,* at 38, *per* Lord Coleridge C.J.
[89] s.61(1).

Property Act 1925 and goods within the Sale of Goods Act 1979, such an overlap has little to commend it.

2. All the terms

(a) The terms. The written terms of the contract must incorporate "all the **12–027** terms which the parties have expressly agreed".[90] If there is one contract for the sale of both land and chattels, it must include the terms relating to each.[91] It is clear that the Act was not in this respect intended to change the law materially.[92] Under the previous law, a memorandum was required to record all the terms agreed between the parties,[93] though omissions could sometimes be cured by submission to or waiver of a missing term.[94] However, because the Act of 1989 requires that all express terms must be made in writing, omissions can no longer be cured in this way,[95] though rectification may be possible in some cases.[96] The Act provides that the terms of the contract may be incorporated in a document either by being set out in it or by reference to some other document.[97] What is not clear is whether that incorporation must be express or whether, as under the previous law, it may be implied.[98] However, the principles of joinder of documents under the former law in cases where the connection was implied rather than express[99] were contrived and led to uncertainty. It would accord better with the policy of the Act of 1989 to confine the incorporation of documents to those referred to expressly or by necessary implication in the signed contract.[1]

There are three essential elements upon which the parties must expressly agree if there is to be a valid contract for the sale of land or of an interest in land.[2] These are—

    (i) the parties;

    (ii) the property;

    (iii) the consideration.

---

[90] L.P.(M.P.)A. 1989, s.2(1). There will be no contract if only the main terms are recorded: *Enfield L.B.C. v. Arajah* [1995] E.G.C.S. 164.

[91] *Wright v. Robert Leonard Developments Ltd* [1994] E.G.C.S. 69. The same was true under the former law: *Ram Narayan v. Shah* [1979] 1 W.L.R. 1349.

[92] See (1987) Law Com. No. 164, para. 4.7.

[93] *Hawkins v. Price* [1947] Ch. 645.

[94] *Ante*, para. 12–016.

[95] But see [1989] Conv. 431 at 438 (P. H. Pettit).

[96] *Post*, para. 12–032.

[97] L.P.(M.P.)A. 1989, s.2(2).

[98] The Law Commission intended to change the law: (1987) Law Com. No. 164, para. 4.6. However, the Act is much more specific than was the draft Bill attached to that report.

[99] See *ante*, para. 12–016.

[1] *cf. Record v. Bell* [1991] 1 W.L.R. 853 at 860, suggesting that incorporation must be express. See too *Firstpost Homes Ltd v. Johnson* [1995] 1 W.L.R. 1567 at 1573. In that case a letter offering to sell land referred to an enclosed plan. It was held that the letter and the plan were not one document.

[2] *Rossiter v. Miller* (1878) 3 App.Cas. 1124 at 1143, 1148.

If these elements have been determined with sufficient certainty[3] and incorporated into the written agreement, the requirements of the Act will be satisfied. This is so even though the parties have not agreed on other terms, such as the completion date,[4] whether a deposit should be taken,[5] or whether vacant possession should be given on completion.[6] Such lacunae will be regulated by the open contract rules implied by law.[7] Indeed, even if the parties have expressly agreed what would otherwise be implied by law, its omission from the written contract is unlikely to prove fatal.[8]

12–028   *(b) Certainty.* "If there is an essential term which has yet to be agreed and there is no express or implied provision for its solution, the result in point of law is that there is no binding contract."[9] In accordance with this principle, the three essential elements outlined above must be defined with sufficient certainty. However, this requirement is met if they fall within the maxim *id certum est quod certum reddi potest* (that is certain which can be made certain). As a contract for the sale of an interest in land must now be made in writing, cases of uncertainty should be less common. Under the previous law, a memorandum evidencing the contract between the parties could be construed out of a document which had been created for a quite different purpose, such as a receipt or a letter.[10] This is no longer possible. However, as the written contract is now intended to be a self-contained document providing "reliable uncontrovertible evidence of the existence and terms of a transaction" in order to minimise disputes,[11] the courts may insist upon a higher degree of certainty in identifying both the parties and the property sold than was formerly the case.[12] Some of the decisions on the previous law may need to be treated with caution therefore.[13]

---

[3] *Infra.*
[4] *Post*, paras 12–091, 12–092.
[5] *Post*, para. 12–107.
[6] *Post*, para. 12–088.
[7] *Perry v. Suffields Ltd* [1916] 2 Ch. 187. For the implication of the open contract rules, see *ante*, para. 12–032.
[8] See *Farrell v. Green* (1974) 232 E.G. 587. *cf.* [1989] Conv. 431 at 436 (P. H. Pettit). In such circumstances, the written agreement would probably be rectified even if it did not satisfy the section: L.P.(M.P.)A. 1989, s.2(4); *post*, para. 12–032.
[9] *British Bank for Foreign Trade Ltd v. Novinex Ltd* [1949] 1 K.B. 623 at 629, *per* Denning J. (cited with approval by Cohen L.J.). Although that case was not concerned with land, the principle there stated has been applied in conveyancing cases.
[10] See the previous edition of this work at p. 577.
[11] (1987) Law Com. No. 164, para. 2.7. See too *Firstpost Homes Ltd v. Johnson* [1995] 1 W.L.R. 1567.
[12] There has been a marked change of practice over the last century as to the degree of precision with which the property is described in conveyancing documents: (1994) 57 M.L.R. 361 (A. Pottage).
[13] This especially so after *Firstpost Homes Ltd v. Johnson, supra*; see above, 578. For a different view, see [1989] Conv. 431 at 434 (P. H. Pettit).

(1) PARTIES. It is essential that the parties (or their agents[14]) should be **12–029** stated,[15] but it is not necessary to give their names, provided that they are identifiable in such a way that "their identity cannot be fairly disputed".[16] Thus references to the "proprietor",[17] "mortgagees",[18] or "trustees"[19] of the property, or to "the legal personal representatives of X"[20] were held to suffice under the old law. Although such descriptions do not exclude all uncertainty, they may be more precise than the names of those concerned, for there may be more than one person of the same name.[21] A decision that "personal representatives" (without saying of whom) was adequate, must be open to doubt however.[22]

The following descriptions by themselves[23] have been held to be too indefinite—

    (i) "the vendor"[24];

    (ii) "landlord"[25];

    (iii) "proposing lender"[26];

    (iv) "my friend"[27]; or

    (v) "my clients".[28]

Land may be sold or let by many people other than the owner of the fee simple, *e.g.* by tenants, mortgagees or persons having a power of sale.[29] To allow parol evidence of the identity of one of the parties would defeat the purpose of the Act.[30] Conversely, it is not enough to give the names of the

---

[14] *Davies v. Sweet* [1962] 2 Q.B. 300.

[15] *Williams v. Lake* (1859) 2 E. & E. 349; *Williams v. Byrnes* (1863) 1 Moo.P. C.(N.S.) 154 at 196; *Stokell v. Niven* (1889) 61 L.T. 18.

[16] *Carr v. Lynch* [1900] 1 Ch. 613 at 615, *per* Farwell J.; *Potter v. Duffield* (1874) L.R. 18 Eq. 4 at 7; *Rossiter v. Miller* (1878) 3 App.Cas. 1124 at 1147, 1153; *Goldsmith Ltd v. Baxter* [1970] Ch. 85.

[17] *Sale v. Lambert* (1874) L.R. 18 Eq. 1; *Rossiter v. Miller, supra.*

[18] *Allen & Co. Ltd v. Whiteman* (1920) 89 L.J.Ch. 534 at 538.

[19] *Catling v. King* (1877) 5 Ch.D. 660 at 664.

[20] *Towle v. Topham* (1877) 37 L.T. 308; and see *Hood v. Lord Barrington* (1868) L.R. 6 Eq. 218.

[21] See *Catling v. King, supra*, at 664; *Donnison v. People's Cafe Co.* (1881) 45 L.T. 187 at 189.

[22] *Fay v. Miller Wilkins & Co.* [1941] Ch. 360, criticised (1941) 57 L.Q.R. 432 (R.E.M.).

[23] The circumstances may, however, narrow down the description so that they suffice: see *e.g. Commins v. Scott* (1875) L.R. 20 Eq. 11; *Sidle v. Bond-Cabell* (1885) 2 T.L.R. 44.

[24] *Potter v. Duffield, supra.*

[25] *Coombs v. Wilks* [1891] 3 Ch. 77.

[26] *Pattle v. Anstruther* (1893) 69 L.T. 175.

[27] *Rossiter v. Miller* (1878) 3 App.Cas. 1124 at 1141.

[28] *Lovesy v. Palmer* [1916] 2 Ch. 233.

[29] See *Donnison v. People's Cafe Co., supra*, at 189.

[30] See *Potter v. Duffield* (1874) L.R. 18 Eq. 4 at 8; *Jarrett v. Hunter* (1886) 34 Ch.D. 182 at 184, 185.

parties if the contract does not indicate their capacities,[31] *e.g.* which is vendor and which is purchaser.[32] But where there is an agent for an undisclosed principal, a contract in the name of that agent is good and binds both him and his principal, even if the other party knows that he is merely an agent.[33]

12–030   (2) PROPERTY. In relation to the property, two matters must be certain, namely the identity of the land which is to be sold and the estate which is to be granted.

As regard the identity of the land, the rule prior to the enactment of the 1989 Act was that the property had to be *described* with sufficient certainty in the contract, but parol evidence could then be adduced to *identify* the land.[34] For these purposes a general description sufficed.[35] On this basis, "Mr O's house",[36] "the house in Newport",[37] "my house"[38] and even "this place"[39] were all upheld with the aid of oral evidence, as descriptions.[40] In a case of a written contract the Court of Appeal went so far as to hold that "twenty-four acres of land, freehold, at Totmonslow" could be identified by oral evidence,[41] even in the absence of "my" or "the" or any other particular. It remains to be seen whether the courts will be so willing to strain language in cases arising under the 1989 Act. Indeed, it may no longer be permissible to adduce parol evidence to identify the land.[42] Although in one case such evidence was adduced, no reference was made to the 1989 Act and its possible effect.[42a]

Problems of uncertainty may arise where a sale of land is to be completed in instalments. If the particular tracts of land that are to be conveyed on payment of each instalment are not sufficiently identifiable, as where "a proportionate part" of the land is to be transferred when each payment is

---

[31] *Stokell v. Niven* (1889) 61 L.T. 18.

[32] *Vanderburgh v. Spooner* (1866) L.R. 1 Ex. 316 (vendor); *Dewar v. Mintoft* [1912] 2 K.B. 373 (purchaser).

[33] *Basma v. Weekes* [1950] A.C. 441 (purchaser's agent); *Davies v. Sweet* [1962] 2 Q.B. 300 (vendor's agent). Yet is the document the *true* contract?

[34] *Harewood v. Retese* [1990] 1 W.L.R. 333 at 341. See too *Plant v. Bourne* [1897] 2 Ch. 281.

[35] *Shardlow v. Cotterell* (1881) 20 Ch.D. 90 at 96, 98 ("property purchased at £420 at Sun Inn, Pinxton" on a specified day, sufficiently certain). These cases date from a time when descriptions of the property were vague. There has been a trend towards much greater precision in such descriptions since then: (1994) 57 M.L.R. 361 at 368 (A. Pottage).

[36] *Ogilvie v. Foljambe* (1817) 3 Mer. 53.

[37] *Owen v. Thomas* (1843) 3 My. & K. 353; and see *Bleakley v. Smith* (1840) 11 Sim. 150 ("the property in Cable Street"); *Wood v. Scarth* (1855) 2 K. & J. 33 ("the intended new public-house at Putney").

[38] *Cowley v. Watts* (1853) 17 Jur. 172.

[39] *Waldron v. Jacob* (1870) 5 I.R.Eq. 131.

[40] See *Sheers v. Thimbleby & Son* (1897) 76 L.T. 709 at 712.

[41] *Plant v. Bourne, supra.* This may be justified on the basis that a vendor is presumed to be selling his own property: *ibid.* at 290.

[42] See *Rudra v. Abbey National Plc* (1998) 76 P. & C.R. 537 at 541, 542. *cf.* (1989) 105 L.Q.R. 553 at 557 (R. E. Annand), suggesting that the assumption adopted in the old cases that a person was selling his own land should still apply.

[42a] *Freeguard v. Rogers* [1999] 1 W.L.R. 375 (grant of option to purchase "the property known as 9, Graffham Close, Chichester" coupled with an erroneous Land Registry title number: extrinsic evidence admissible to show that the property comprised both a freehold house and a leasehold garage under two separate title numbers). *Sed quaere.*

made, the contract as a whole will fail for uncertainty. This is so even though the identity of the totality of the land included in the agreement is certain.[43]

A contract will not be invalidated merely because it does not state the interest which the vendor intends to pass or that it is subject to incumbrances of which the purchaser knows or which are patent.[44] Where the contract is silent, it is presumed that the vendor is selling a fee simple subject to such incumbrances.[45] A contract to grant a lease, however, must specify or provide a means of determining[46] the date on which the term is to commence[47] and must state its duration.[48] "There must be a certain beginning and a certain ending, otherwise it is not a perfect lease, and a contract for a lease ... must contain those elements."[49] It will not be assumed that a term is to commence on the date of the agreement,[50] or when the tenant is to take possession,[51] or to begin paying rent.[52]

(3) CONSIDERATION. The contract must define with sufficient certainty the price to be paid, or, in the case of a contract to grant a lease, the rent or premium payable. The question whether the consideration has been expressed with sufficient certainty has generally arisen in the context of options to purchase land or renew a lease where the parties have attempted to retain some flexibility by postponing the determination of the price or rent until the option is exercised. Unless the parties make express provision for what is to happen in default of agreement,[53] there is a risk that such an arrangement will **12–031**

---

[43] *Bushwall Properties Ltd v. Vortex Properties Ltd* [1976] 1 W.L.R. 591. The decision does appear unnecessarily harsh: see [1976] C.L.J. 215 (C. T. Emery). The courts are generally reluctant to hold agreements void for uncertainty: *post*, para. 12–031. *cf. Hillreed Land Ltd v. Beautridge* [1994] E.G.C.S. 55 where the grantee of an option agreed to pay £x an acre for all the land for which he could obtain planning permission and £y an acre for the rest. No planning permission having been obtained, the option was void for uncertainty.

[44] For patent incumbrances, see *post*, para. 12–068.

[45] *Cox v. Middleton* (1854) 2 Drew. 209 at 216, 217; *Timmins v. Moreland Street Property Co. Ltd* [1958] Ch. 110 at 118, 119.

[46] See, *e.g. Trustees of National Deposit Friendly Society v. Beatties of London Ltd* [1985] 2 E.G.L.R. 59 at 61.

[47] *Blore v. Sutton* (1817) 3 Mer. 237; *Cartwright v. Miller* (1877) 36 L.T. 398; *Harvey v. Pratt* [1965] 1 W.L.R. 1025 at 1027.

[48] *Fitzmaurice v. Bayley* (1860) 9 H.L.C. 78; *Clarke v. Fuller* (1864) 16 C.B.(N.S.) 24. Thus an agreement to grant an underlease for the residue of the head lease "less a few days" was void for uncertainty: *Dolling v. Evans* (1867) 36 L.J.Ch. 474.

[49] *Marshall v. Berridge* (1881) 19 Ch.D. 233 at 245, *per* Lush L.J.

[50] *Marshall v. Berridge, supra.*

[51] *Edwards v. Jones* (1921) 124 L.T. 740; and see *Rock Portland Cement Co. Ltd v. Wilson* (1882) 52 L.J.Ch. 214. Prima facie, however, a renewed lease will run from the expiration of the existing lease: see *Verlander v. Codd* (1823) T. & R. 352; *Wood v. Aylward* (1888) 58 L.T. 667.

[52] *Humphrey v. Conybeare* (1899) 80 L.T. 40. This is particularly the case today when "rent-free" periods are often allowed for tenants to fit out the premises and commence trading: see *Trustees of National Deposit Friendly Society v. Beatties of London Ltd, supra* at 61.

[53] As in *Miller v. Lakefield Estates Ltd* (1988) 57 P. & C.R. 104; [1990] Conv. 288 at 289 (J. E. Martin).

be regarded as a mere agreement to negotiate "which is not recognised as an enforceable contract".[54] However, the courts are reluctant to hold an instrument void for uncertainty.[55] There are at least three types of option,[56] and an analysis of them demonstrates the various methods which the courts apply to save them from invalidity.

(i) The option may provide for a price or rent "to be agreed" with no formula for quantifying the consideration. Traditionally such arrangements have been regarded as void because they amount to mere agreements to contract.[57] However, there may now be a greater willingness to imply a formula for assessment in such cases.[58] Thus an option to renew a lease at a rent to be agreed, but not exceeding the existing rent, was upheld as valid. The court implied a term that the rent should be a fair rent agreed between the parties not exceeding the existing rent.[59] In one case of a right of pre-emption, the grantee was offered the first refusal to purchase certain land at "a figure to be agreed upon". The court implied a term that the grantor would offer to sell the land at the price at which she was willing to sell the land.[60] However, it has been suggested that the judge in that case "implied a substantial amount, perhaps too much",[61] and its authority is questionable. Where the parties provide some machinery for ascertaining the consideration, the courts will be very ready to imply a formula from that fact. Thus where the price is to be such as may be agreed upon by two valuers, that will necessarily imply that it should be a fair and reasonable one.[62]

(ii) The option may provide that the price is to be determined according to some stated formula, but without providing any machinery

---

[54] *Walford v. Miles* [1992] 2 A.C. 128 at 136, *per* Lord Ackner.

[55] *Brown v. Gould* [1972] Ch. 53 at 56.

[56] *ibid.*, at 58.

[57] *King's Motors (Oxford) Ltd v. Lax* [1970] 1 W.L.R. 426.

[58] In the past, the courts would imply a term only where the contract was valid and had been partially performed, as where there was a term in a lease that for the first five years the rent should be £1,250 per annum, and thereafter at such rent as should be agreed between the parties: *Beer v. Bowden* (1976) [1981] 1 W.L.R. 522n. See too *Trustees of National Deposit Friendly Society v. Beatties of London Ltd* [1985] 2 E.G.L.R. 59. For such rent review clauses, see *post*, para. 14–246.

[59] *Corson v. Rhuddlan B.C.* (1989) 69 P. & C.R. 185; [1990] Conv. 288 at 290 (J. E. Martin). The court doubted the correctness of *King's Motors (Oxford) Ltd v. Lax, supra,* suggesting that in that case a term could have been implied that the rent should be fair.

[60] *Smith v. Morgan* [1971] 1 W.L.R. 803. It is difficult to see how this implication overcame the vice of uncertainty.

[61] *Miller v. Lakefield Estates Ltd, supra,* at 198, *per* May L.J.

[62] *Sudbrook Trading Estates Ltd v. Eggleton* [1983] 1 A.C. 444 at 477. See too *Lear v. Blizzard* [1983] 3 All E.R. 662. *cf.* [1983] Conv. 76 (K. Hodkinson).

for the working out of that formula. In such a case, the court will supply whatever machinery is necessary for assessment.[63]

(iii) The option may provide both a formula and machinery for assessing the consideration.[64] If the machinery breaks down,[65] the court will supply its own, provided that it is merely subsidiary and inessential, but not where the personal qualities of the particular valuer are an essential element of the agreement.[66] Thus where a will conferred an option on the testator's son to purchase a farm "at the agricultural value thereof determined for probate purposes . . . as agreed with the district valuer" and the district valuer declined to make the valuation, the machinery was held to be an inessential element and an inquiry was directed to determine the value of the land.[67]

(c) Rectification. If there is "convincing proof"[68] that, by mistake, **12–032** either—

(i) the written "contract" does not in some way record the terms agreed between the parties[69]; or

(ii) the parts exchanged on an exchange of contracts do not in all respects correspond[70];

the court may order rectification of the contractual documents.[71] In these circumstances, there is necessarily no contract until the court makes its order

---

[63] *Brown v. Gould, supra* ("rent to be fixed having regard to the market value of the premises").

[64] One commonly used formula, "at a fair and reasonable market rent", has proved troublesome: see *ARC Ltd v. Schonfield* [1990] 2 E.G.L.R. 52.

[65] *cf. Harben Style Ltd v. Rhodes Trust* [1995] 1 E.G.L.R. 118, where the landlord refused to appoint a valuer to fix a rent under a rent review clause, because it was likely that the rent would be reduced. Under the lease the rent due prior to any review continued to be payable if no new rent was fixed. In those circumstances, the court held that there had been no failure of machinery and refused to imply any obligation on the part of the landlord to appoint a valuer.

[66] *Sudbrook Trading Estate Ltd v. Eggleton, supra*; (1982) 28 L.Q.R. 539 (J. Murdoch); *Royal Bank of Scotland Plc v. Jennings* [1997] 1 E.G.L.R. 101. *cf. Saipem Sp.A. v. Rafidain Bank* [1994] C.L.C. 253.

[67] *Re Malpass* [1985] Ch. 42. See too *Scottish Wholefoods Collective Warehouse Ltd v. Raye Investments Ltd* [1994] 1 E.G.L.R. 245 (option to sell "at the current market price" to be agreed upon between the parties not void where the parties could not agree).

[68] *Joscelyne v. Nissen* [1970] 2 Q.B. 86 at 98, *per* Russell L.J.

[69] As where it either omits terms that had been agreed by the parties or contains terms that had not been agreed.

[70] *Domb v. Isoz* [1980] Ch. 548 at 558 (provision concerning fixtures and fittings contained only in one of the signed parts). *cf. Harrison v. Battye* [1975] 1 W.L.R. 58 at 60 (parts differed as to amount of deposit payable, but there was no evidence to justify rectification).

[71] *Domb v. Isoz, supra*; *Wright v. Robert Leonard Developments Ltd* [1994] E.G.C.S. 69 (contract to sell a flat omitted the fixtures and fittings that were to be included; rectification was ordered to incorporate the term); [1995] J.B.L. 176 (M. Haley). Rectification is normally granted in cases of mutual mistake, but may exceptionally be given in cases where the mistake is unilateral: see *post*, para. 12–122.

because the documents do not satisfy the requirements of section 2 of the Act. The court is therefore given a discretion to declare in the order for rectification the time at which the contract shall come into being, or be deemed to have done so.[72]

12–033   *(d) Collateral contracts.* It often happens that one party enters into a contract to sell or purchase land on the strength of some assurance by the other.[73] In such circumstances there may in fact be two contracts—

> (i) the principal contract of sale; and
>
> (ii) the collateral undertaking.

The consideration for the latter is the making of the principal contract. In such cases, "the collateral contract may in substance be regarded as another way of enforcing a term omitted from what purports to be a contract in writing".[74] If the collateral contract is not itself a contract for the sale or other disposition of an interest in land,[75] it will not have to comply with section 2 of the Act of 1989. Thus in one case, V's solicitor was unable to obtain office copies of the register of V's title before contracts were due to be exchanged, but gave certain undertakings as to V's title in a side letter. P exchanged contracts on the basis of those promises (which were subsequently honoured) and V was able to enforce that contract against him. The undertakings in the side letter were not terms of the main contract but were collateral to it.[76]

12–034   *(e) Separate agreements.* It is always open to parties to break up a composite agreement that includes a sale of land into two or more separate contracts. Those contracts and their terms will then be regarded as discrete and not as one contract.[77] Furthermore, section 2 of the Act applies only to executory contracts. Once the parties have completed a sale of land it is irrelevant that the agreement which preceded the transfer was void because it did not comply with the section. In such circumstances, any other terms of the agreement that are not themselves a contract for the sale of land and which have not merged

---

[72] L.P.(M.P.)A. 1989, s.2(4); *Wright v. Robert Leonard Developments Ltd, supra* (contract deemed to have come into effect on exchange).

[73] The undertaking is commonly contained in a "side letter": see *e.g. Record v. Bell* [1991] 1 W.L.R. 853.

[74] (1987) Law Com. No. 164, para. 5.7.

[75] See, *e.g. Lotteryking Ltd v. AMEC Properties Ltd* [1995] 2 E.G.L.R. 13 (landlord's collateral undertaking to remedy damp did not have to comply with L.P.(M.P.)A. 1989, s.2); *Johnsey Estates Ltd v. Newport Marketworld Ltd* [1996] E.G.C.S. 87 (contract by A with B to guarantee lease to be granted by B to C outside s.2).

[76] *Record v. Bell, supra*; [1991] C.L.J. 399 (C.H.); (1992) 108 L.Q.R. 217 (R. J. Smith). There were cases of collateral contracts in similar circumstances under the previous law: *Jamieson v. Kinmell Bay Land Co. Ltd* (1931) 47 L.T. 593.

[77] *Tootal Clothing Ltd v. Guinea Properties Ltd* (1992) 64 P. & C.R. 452 at 456; (1993) 109 L.Q.R. 191 (D. Wilde). *cf.* (1993) 22 Anglo-American Law Review, 498 at 507 (M. Haley).

on completion,[78] may be enforceable. However, this will be so only where those terms are supported by consideration and can therefore be regarded as a "supplemental agreement".[79]

3. One document. The Act provides that "the document incorporating the terms or, where contracts are exchanged, one of the documents incorporating them (but not necessarily the same one) must be signed by or on behalf of each party to the contract".[80] This provision has two important effects each of which must be considered. First, it restricts the manner in which a contract for the sale of land may be made. Secondly, a valid contract will be mutually enforceable by both parties.   **12–035**

(a) Method of contracting

(1) METHODS LISTED IN THE ACT. The wording of the Act[81] suggests that there are now just two ways in which a written contract for the sale or other disposition of land may be made. First, each of the parties may sign one document incorporating all the agreed terms. This method was sometimes employed under the previous law.[82] Secondly, the parties may exchange contracts, which has long been the "customary way" of concluding contracts for the sale of land, particularly domestic sales.[83] The essential characteristic of exchange of contracts is "that each party shall have such a document signed by the other party in his possession or control", and it occurs when each party (or more usually his solicitor or licensed conveyancer) has the contract signed by the other in his actual or constructive possession.[84] This may be brought about in one of three ways.   **12–036**

   (i) There may be a physical exchange of the contracts by the parties' solicitors or licensed conveyancers, usually at the offices of one of them. Exchanges of this kind are usually impracticable in cases of chain sales.[85]

   (ii) The parts may be exchanged by post. It has never been settled whether the contract is concluded at the time when the second of

---

[78] For the doctrine of merger see *post*, para. 12–099.

[79] *Tootal Clothing Ltd v. Guinea Properties Ltd, supra*, at 455, *per* Scott L.J. (contract by landlord to pay tenant £30,000 for shop-fitting works after completion held to be enforceable). For criticism of the case see [1993] Conv. 89 (P. Luther).

[80] L.P.(M.P.)A. 1989, s.2(3).

[81] s.2(1), (3). These provisions differ significantly from those in the draft Bill attached to (1987) Law Com. No. 164, p. 24.

[82] *Smith v. Mansi* [1963] 1 W.L.R. 26.

[83] See *Eccles v. Bryant* [1948] Ch. 93 at 97, *per* Lord Greene M.R.

[84] *Domb v. Isoz* [1980] Ch. 548 at 557, *per* Buckley L.J. See too *Harrison v. Battye* [1995] 1 W.L.R. 58. For a detailed analysis of what constitutes an exchange of contracts, see *Commission for the New Towns v. Cooper (Great Britain) Ltd* [1995] Ch. 259 at 285, 286.

[85] *Domb v. Isoz, supra*, at 558, 564.

the two parts has been posted or only when it is received,[86] though the latter accords better with the essential characteristic of exchange of contracts outlined above. Exchange by post is inevitably uncertain and cannot achieve the synchronisation that is necessary in chain sales.

(iii) Exchange may be effected where the solicitor or licensed conveyancer for each of the parties unequivocally appropriates his client's part of the contract and holds it to the order of the other party. This forms the basis for the modern practice by which contracts are exchanged by telephone, telex or fax.[87] It provides the only effective method of bringing about an exchange of contracts where there is a chain of sales.[88] There are a number of different methods by which this can be done, as for example where each solicitor or licensed conveyancer, having in his possession the part of the contract signed by his client, agrees by telephone to hold it to the order of the other party.[89]

The Act has not affected the well-established practice for the exchange of contracts, nor was it intended to do so.[90]

12–037   (2) CONTRACTS BY CORRESPONDENCE. The wording of the Act suggests that no contract can arise from a mere exchange of letters between the parties unless that correspondence can be regarded as an "exchange of contracts".[91] It has indeed been held by the Court of Appeal that a simple offer and acceptance made by post or fax will not satisfy the requirements of section 2,[92] because there can be no exchange of contracts unless the parties have reached a prior written or oral agreement.[93] This was certainly not the intention of the Law Commission.[94] Although it has been suggested that

---

[86] See *Eccles v. Bryant, supra,* at 97, 98, where Lord Greene M.R. left the point open. It should be recalled that the so-called "postal rule", by which an offer is deemed to be accepted when that acceptance is posted (see *Henthorn v. Fraser* [1892] 3 Ch. 27 at 33), is an exception to the general principle that an acceptance must be communicated to the offeror: *Holwell Securities Ltd v. Hughes* [1974] 1 W.L.R. 155; *Brinkibon Ltd v. Stahag Stahl G.m.b.H.* [1983] 2 A.C. 34 at 41. Where an option can be exercised only by giving notice to the grantor, then the postal rule will not apply: *Holwell Securities Ltd v. Hughes, supra.*

[87] For the merits of exchange of contracts for fax, see (1988) 85/34 L.S.Gaz 11 (P. H. Kenny).

[88] It has been described as "a practice without which contracts could not be exchanged with the maximum of safety and the minimum of delay": *Domb v. Isoz, supra,* at 564, *per* Templeman L.J.

[89] The Law Society has produced three formulae which may be adopted for exchanging contracts by telephone, telex or fax: see (1986) 83 L.S.Gaz 2139; (1989) 86/11 L.S.Gaz. 26.

[90] "The present practice of exchanging contracts should not be inhibited": (1987) Law Com. No. 164, para. 4.6.

[91] See *Hooper v. Sherman* (unreported, CA, November 30, 1994), as explained in *Commission for the New Towns v. Cooper (Great Britain) Ltd* [1995] Ch. 259 at 288, 289, 295.

[92] *Commission for the New Towns v. Cooper (Great Britain) Ltd, supra*; [1995] C.L.J. 502 (A. J. Oakley).

[93] *ibid.,* at 295.

[94] See (1987) Law Com. No. 164, para. 4.15; and contrast cl. 1 of the draft Bill appended to that Report with L.P.(M.P.)A. 1989, s.2.

Parliament may have chosen to go further than the Law Commission recommendation "and required a greater degree of formality in this very important area of the law where it is crucial that the parties know for certain when they are bound and on what terms",[95] the reasons for the changes are not known.[96]

Not only does this interpretation significantly restrict the manner in which a contract for the sale of land can be made, but it means that section 2 of the 1989 Act conflicts with the provision of the Law of Property Act 1925 which regulates contracts by correspondence and the policy that lies behind it.[97] By that provision the Lord Chancellor may from time to time prescribe and publish forms of contracts and conditions of sale which shall apply to "contracts by correspondence" unless excluded or modified by the correspondence.[98] Conditions of sale have been prescribed[99] and these regulate matters such as the date and place of completion and the deduction of title. Their objective is "to supply the common forms for facilitating the carrying out of contracts by correspondence",[1] in order to meet the case where parties contract without taking legal advice. A "contract by correspondence" will not arise unless there has been an exchange of letters.[2] There will be no such contract where one party signs a copy of a letter already signed by the other.[3] In the light of this, it will only be in a very rare case that a contract by correspondence could now arise in a situation to which the provisions of section 2 of the 1989 Act were applicable,[4] and this seldom-used provision of the Law of Property Act 1925 appears to be largely redundant.

This restriction on the manner in which a contract for the sale of land can be made is hard to justify and is likely to cause difficulty in a number of common transactions, as where V, having granted P a right of pre-emption, offers in writing to sell the land to P. In such circumstances, a written acceptance by P of V's offer will not suffice. There will either have to be a

---

[95] *Commission for the New Towns v. Cooper (Great Britain) Ltd, supra*, at 287, *per* Stuart-Smith L.J. See too *McCausland v. Duncan Lawrie Ltd* [1997] 1 W.L.R. 38 at 44, 46, 49.

[96] It is understood that they were made when the Law Commission's Bill was redrafted in anticipation of its introduction into Parliament. The Parliamentary debates provide no clue as to why.

[97] This was acknowledged in *Commission for the New Towns v. Cooper (Great Britain) Ltd, supra*, at 287, 295. *cf. Hooper v. Sherman, supra*, where the Court of Appeal considered that it was still possible to create by correspondence a contract complying with L.P.(M.P.)A. 1989, s.2. See [1995] Conv. 317 (M. P. Thompson).

[98] s.46.

[99] S.R. & O. 1925, No. 779/L. 14.

[1] Wolst. & C. i, 405.

[2] *Stearn v. Twitchell* [1985] 1 All E.R. 631; *Fischer v. Toumazos* [1991] 2 E.G.L.R. 204 at 206.

[3] *Pips (Leisure Productions) Ltd v. Walton* (1980) 43 P. & C.R. 415 at 416; *Fischer v. Toumazos, supra*, at 206.

[4] In *Commission for the New Towns v. Cooper (Great Britain) Ltd* [1995] Ch. 259 at 287, 295, it was suggested that one might arise where there was a prior oral agreement between the parties and the exchange of correspondence was intended by the parties to be an "exchange of contracts". This has been criticised: see [1995] C.L.J. 502 (A. J. Oakley). A contract to grant a short lease within L.P.A. 1925, s.54(2) could still be made by correspondence as it is outside the ambit of L.P.(M.P.)A. 1989, s.2: *ante*, para. 12–022.

formal exchange of contracts, or both V and P will have to sign one contract.

12–038   *(b) Mutual enforceability.* There can be a valid contract only if it is signed by or on behalf of *both* parties.[5] Under the previous law, it was enough that the party to be charged had signed a memorandum, even if the claimant had not.[6] It follows that any valid contract must now be reciprocally enforceable by both parties. It is no longer possible for one party to be bound by the contract in circumstances where he cannot enforce it against the other.[7]

4. Signed

12–039   *(a) Signature.* The document incorporating the terms (or one of them where contracts are exchanged) "must be signed by or on behalf of each party to the contract".[8] The Act gives no guidance as to what constitutes a signature. However, as few contracts will now be made without legal advice, compliance with the requirement that the document must be signed is unlikely to be an issue very often.[9] This particularly so because both parties must sign the contract.

Under the previous law, the word "signed" was given an extended meaning by the courts.[10] Where the name of the party to be charged appeared in some part of the document[11] in some form, whether in writing, typewriting, print or otherwise,[12] there was a sufficient signature, provided that that party had shown in some way that he recognised the document as an expression of the contract.[13] However, this is no longer the law. The word "signed" is "to have the meaning which the ordinary man would understand it to have".[14] Therefore where a person typed his name and addressee on a letter,[15] he was held not to have signed it.[16]

12–040   *(b) Alterations.* Any alterations that are made to a concluded written contract must themselves comply with the requirements of section 2.[17] This

---

[5] L.P.(M.P.)A. 1989, s.2(3).
[6] *Ante,* para. 12–016.
[7] See [1989] Conv. 431 at 439 (P. H. Pettit).
[8] L.P.(M.P.)A. 1989, s.2(3). *cf. Enfield L.B.C. v. Arajah* [1995] E.G.C.S. 164 (no contract where only one of three purchasers signed solely on his own account).
[9] There seems no reason why a faxed signature should not be effective and it is certainly always treated as being so.
[10] For the old law, see the previous edition of this work at p. 584. It was initially thought the same principles would apply under the 1989 Act: see [1989] Conv. 431 at 439 (P. H. Pettit).
[11] *Caton v. Caton* (1867) L.R. 2 H.L. 127 at 142.
[12] *Tourret v. Cripps* (1879) 48 L.J.Ch. 567; *Halley v. O'Brien* [1920] 1 I.R. 330 at 339.
[13] *Evans v. Hoare* [1982] 1 Q.B. 593; *Leeman v. Stocks* [1951] Ch. 941; *Bilsland v. Terry* [1977] N.Z.L.R. 43.
[14] *Firstpost Homes Ltd v. Johnson* [1995] 1 W.L.R. 1567 at 1576, *per* Peter Gibson L.J.
[15] That was signed by the intending vendor.
[16] *Firstpost Homes Ltd v. Johnson, supra*; see [1996] C.L.J. 192 (A. J. Oakely).
[17] *McCausland v. Duncan Lawrie Ltd* [1997] 1 W.L.R. 38; [1996] Conv. 366 (M. P. Thompson).

cannot be achieved by an exchange of letters,[18] and the parties will therefore either have to exchange identical signed copies of the variation, or they will both have to sign one document which makes the change.[19] If they did not comply with section 2, the alteration will be a nullity and the original contract will remain enforceable because no binding agreement has superseded it.[20] However, the change which the parties agree may be so fundamental that it amounts to a rescission of the original contract.[21] In principle, an agreement to rescind a contract for the sale of land may be made orally because it is not a contract for the sale or other disposition of an interest in land within section 2.[22] Where the parties intend that the first contract for the sale of an interest in land should be rescinded and replaced by a second contract, it is by no means certain that rescission will always take place if that second contract fails to comply with section 2. The intention to rescind in such a case may be regarded as contingent upon the validity of the second contract.[23]

(c) Agents. The Act requires that the contract be signed "by or on behalf of" each contracting party.[24] There is no requirement that the agent should be given written authority to sign.[25] The same person may sign on behalf of both parties if has been authorised to do so by each of them.[26] Neither an estate agent[27] nor a solicitor[28] has implied authority to sign a contract. Such authority must be expressly given, though the principal may of course subsequently ratify any unauthorised signature.[29] **12–041**

5. Abolition of part performance. The doctrine of part performance, although not expressly abolished by the Act, can no longer apply.[30] Because an oral agreement to sell an interest in land cannot be a contract there is nothing that can be partly performed.[31] Given the uncertainties that had come to surround the doctrine of part performance, its abolition need not occasion much regret. Of rather greater concern is the manner in which the law may **12–042**

---

[18] *Ante*, para. 12–037.

[19] [1996] Conv. 366 at 368 (M. P. Thompson).

[20] *McCausland v. Duncan Lawrie Ltd, supra.*

[21] The test is whether the alteration goes "to the very root" of the original contract: *British & Benningtons Ltd v. N. W. Cachar Tea Co. Ltd* [1923] A.C. 48 at 68, *per* Lord Sumner. See, *e.g. Ginns v. Tabor* [1995] E.G.C.S. 182 (decided under the old law).

[22] G. H. Treitel, *The Law of Contract* (10th ed.), 172.

[23] See [1989] Conv. 431 at 436, 437 (P. H. Pettit).

[24] L.P.(M.P.)A. 1989, s.2(3).

[25] As there is in other formality provisions: see L.P.A. 1925, s.53(1)(c); *ante*, para. 10–049.

[26] *Gavaghan v. Edwards* [1961] 2 Q.B. 220.

[27] *Wragg v. Lovett* [1948] 2 All E.R. 968 at 969 (no authority to sign even where the estate agent is instructed to sell at a defined price). *cf. Kean v. Mear* [1920] 2 Ch. 574.

[28] *Smith v. Webster* (1876) 3 Ch.D. 49; *H. Clark (Doncaster) Ltd v. Wilkinson* [1965] Ch. 694 at 702.

[29] *Maclean v. Dunn* (1828) 4 Bing. 722.

[30] *Firstpost Homes Ltd v. Johnson* [1995] 1 W.L.R. 1567 at 1571.

[31] See (1987) Law Com. No 164, para. 4.13. This point was overlooked in *Singh v. Beggs* (1996) 71 P. & C.R. 120 at 122, where it was doubted that the doctrine had been abolished. For criticism, see [1997] Conv. 293 (S. J. A. Swann).

develop in the absence of the doctrine.[32] In this context, two aspects of the abolition of the doctrine of part performance are of some importance.

12–043   *(a) Informal mortgages by deposit of title deeds.* It was settled in 1783, that the deposit of the title deeds to property by way of security for money advanced created an equitable mortgage.[33] The deposit was taken both to show a contract to create a mortgage and to be part performance of that contract.[34] It was usual for such a mortgage to be accompanied by a memorandum recording the terms agreed between the parties and conferring on the mortgagee the power to sell and to appoint a receiver.[35] They were commonly employed in cases of temporary loans, *e.g.* to secure an overdraft at a bank. It has now been held that since the doctrine of part performance has been abolished, such mortgages are no longer possible. To be valid, any contract to grant a mortgage must now comply with the requirements laid down in the Act.[36]

12–044   *(d) Effect of non-compliance with section 2.* An agreement that does not comply with the provisions of the Act has no effect as a contract because it is void. However, the acts of the parties made pursuant to or in reliance upon such a void agreement may have legal consequences.[37] Those consequences fall under three possible heads.

     (i) ESTOPPEL. In some circumstances, one or other party may be able to invoke the principles of estoppel. This will be permitted only to the extent that it does not validate a transaction that the legislature requires to be treated as invalid on some ground of public policy.[38–39] Thus, the fact that the parties had waived the formal requirements of section 2 in earlier transactions will not mean that they are estopped by convention from insisting on compliance with

---

[32] It has been said that "the certainties of the past were preferable to the uncertainties of the new": [1994] Conv. 233 at 237 (M. P. Thompson).

[33] *Russel v. Russel* (1783) 1 Bro.C.C. 269. For a full account for this doctrine, see the previous edition of this work at p. 927.

[34] *Edge v. Worthington* (1786) 1 Cox Eq. 211; *Pryce v. Bury* (1853) 2 Drew. 41 (affd. L.R. 16 Eq. 153n.); *Carter v. Wake* (1877) 4 Ch.D. 605 at 606. The view that the doctrine was *sui generis* and was distinct from part performance has been rejected; *United Bank of Kuwait Plc v. Sahib* [1997] Ch. 107.

[35] For these powers, see *post*, paras 19–056, 19–079, 19–085, 19–090.

[36] *United Bank of Kuwait Plc v. Sahib, supra*; (1997) 113 L.Q.R. 533 (M. Robinson). For such contracts, see *post*, para. 19–039. The practice of mortgaging registered land by depositing a land certificate as security and then entering either a notice of deposit or a notice of intended deposit has been abrogated: see L.R.R. 1995, r. 4; *ante*, para. 6–114.

[37] See (1987) Law Com. No. 164, Pt V; Goff & Jones, *The Law of Restitution* (5th ed.), chap. 21; (1990) 10 L.S. 325 (L. Bently and P. Coughlan); (1993) 13 O.J.L.S. 99 (C. Davis). All of these commentaries must be read subject to *Godden v. Merthyr Tydfil Housing Association* (1997) 74 P. & C.R. D1; and *Yaxley v. Gotts* [1999] E.G.C.S. 92; and transcript.

[38–39] See *Westdeutsche Landesbank Girozentrale v. Islington L.B.C.* [1994] 4 All E.R. 890 at 929; *Godden v. Merthyr Tydfil Housing Association, supra*, at D3.

the section in later dealings.[40] However, there may be situations where the parties may be able to rely upon the doctrine of proprietary estoppel[41] without compromising the policy of the Act. This will be so where one of the parties (usually the purchaser) has acted to his detriment in reliance upon some agreement, arrangement or understanding between the parties, and where, in the circumstances, the court could have imposed a constructive trust.[42]

(ii) CONSTRUCTIVE TRUST. The 1989 Act provides expressly that nothing in section 2 "affects the creation or operation of resulting, implied or constructive trusts".[43] It follows that the imposition of a constructive trust to prevent unconscionable conduct[44] will not contravene the policy of the Act. This is most likely to arise in cases where the purchaser acts to his detriment in reliance on an informal agreement with the vendor that he shall acquire or have an interest in the land.[45] Thus, where a builder converted a property into flats on the basis of an oral agreement with the owner that he should be granted a long lease of one of them, the court gave effect to the transaction by imposing a constructive trust on the vendor.[46]

(iii) RESTITUTION. Where there is a void contract and one of the parties incurs expenditure in reliance upon it, he may be able to claim restitution. Thus, an intending purchaser who makes payments pursuant to the agreement, may be able to recover them on the basis that there has been a total failure of consideration.[47] If he improves the land he may recover the benefit conferred on the vendor if the latter freely accepts those improvements.[48] Similarly, a vendor who carried out works requested by the purchaser should be able to recover the cost of them.[49]

---

[40] *Godden v. Merthyr Tydfil Housing Association*, *supra*, at D3.
[41] The doctrine is explained, *post*, Chap. 13.
[42] *Yaxley v. Gotts*, *supra*; and see *infra*. For the interrelationship between proprietary estoppel and constructive trusts, see *ante*, para. 10–030; *post*, para. 13–036.
[43] L.P.(M.P.)A. 1989, s.2(5).
[44] See *ante*, para. 10–022.
[45] *Ante*, paras 10–023 *et seq.*
[46] *Yaxley v. Gotts*, *supra*.
[47] There may be no such total failure if the purchaser has entered into possession and enjoyed the land. *cf.* Goff & Jones, *The Law of Restitution* (5th ed.), p. 581, suggesting that, in such a case, recovery might in fact be allowed if a deduction were made for the fair rental value of the land for the period of the purchaser's occupancy. It is no longer an objection that the payments were made under a mistake of law: see *Kleinwort Benson Ltd v. Glasgow City Council* [1999] 1 A.C. 153.
[48] *Yaxley v. Gotts*, *supra*, *per* Robert Walker L.J.; Goff & Jones, *The Law of Restitution* (5th ed.), p. 581; (1993) 13 O.J.L.S. 99 at 124 (C. Davies).
[49] See *British Steel Corporation v. Cleveland Bridge and Engineering Co. Ltd* (1981) 1 All E.R. 504 at 511.

Part 3

CONTRACTS IN PRACTICE

Section 1. Cases Where it is Usual to have a Contract

12–045   Traditionally, whenever a transaction involves payment of a lump sum it has
been the practice for a contract to be made first and a conveyance or transfer
some time later. This is because the purchaser wishes to be sure of his bargain
and yet to have time to investigate the title fully before paying his money and
taking over the liabilities of ownership. Thus a formal contract is nowadays
normally made on—

    (i) a sale of a freehold;

    (ii) the grant of a lease of a flat by the freeholder; or

    (iii) an assignment by a tenant who holds under a lease at a ground rent
(a rent representing the value of the land without the buildings on
it.[50])

If, on the other hand, no capital payment is to be made, there is often no
contract, *e.g.* on the grant or assignment of a lease at a rack rent (a rent
representing the full value of the land and buildings). A mortgage, although
involving a capital payment, is rarely preceded by a contract; for it is in
essence an investment of money rather than a purchase of land, and it will
probably be no loss to the mortgagee if the deal falls through before completion. These statements are, however, no more than generalisations and they are
less true than once they were. Thus because of the widespread practice by
which the purchaser investigates the vendor's title before contracts are
exchanged, the time between contract and completion has steadily diminished,
and it is by no means unknown for both to take place on the same day.[51]
Furthermore, when a lease is granted, it is by no means uncommon to dispense
with a contract and to proceed directly to the exchange of lease and counterpart even when the consideration for the lease is a premium rather than the
payment of a rack rent.[52]

Section 2. Types of Contract

There are three main types of contract and something has already been said
about each.

---

[50] The capital sum paid for a lease is usually called a premium.
[51] In such a case, there are good reasons why the parties still enter into a contract before
completion: see *post*, para. 12–099.
[52] See, *e.g. Longman v. Viscount Chelsea* (1989) 58 P. & C.R. 189.

1. Open contracts. An open contract means a contract where only certain   **12–046**
terms have been expressly agreed, leaving others to be implied by the general
law. The simplest possible contract is where only the parties, property and
price are specified, *e.g.* where A agrees to buy Blackacre from B for
£100,000.[53] This is the most "open" contract of all and though it is unbusinesslike it is perfectly effective in law. It is implied that the vendor must show
a good title within a reasonable time and then complete the contract by the
appropriate conveyance or transfer. It is for the purchaser at his own expense
to prepare the draft conveyance or transfer for the vendor to execute.[54]

Contracts which are wholly open are in practice very rare nowadays,[55] and
they are likely to disappear because of the stricter formal requirements that
now apply to contracts for the sale of land.[56] However, the principles which
apply to open contracts form the bedrock upon which conveyancing law is
built.[57] As has already been explained, the open contract rules will regulate the
affairs of the parties to the extent that their contract does not do so expressly.[58]
The effect of these rules is considered below.[59]

2. Contracts made by correspondence. It has already been explained[60]   **12–047**
that in the case of "contracts by correspondence", the Law of Property Act
1925[61] provides that the Statutory Form of Conditions of Sale 1925[62] made by
the Lord Chancellor, shall govern the contract, subject to any modification or
contrary intention expressed in the correspondence. However, because contracts by correspondence can arise only by an exchange of letters,[63] they are
seldom likely to occur in future.[64]

3. Formal contracts. The wide range of matters which have to be dealt   **12–048**
with between contract and completion mean that in practice open contracts are
not employed. A contract will invariably contain conditions of sale which
modify the open contract position,[65] and this has been the practice for two
centuries.[66] Conditions of sale—which are "merely the terms of the sale and
purchase"[67]—are of two types. First, there are *special* conditions which
regulate the details of that particular transaction, specifying such matters as

---

[53] *Ante*, para. 12–027.
[54] Although the vendor prepares the draft contract, the purchaser bears the greater part of the costs
of a conveyancing transaction and must of course pay his own solicitor's costs.
[55] See *ante*, para. 12–001.
[56] Written contracts made in compliance with L.P.(M.P.)A. 1989, s.2 are in practice likely to be
made on legal advice: *ante*, para. 12–036.
[57] *Ante*, para. 12–001.
[58] *ibid.*
[59] *Post*, para. 12–049.
[60] *Ante*, para. 12–037.
[61] s.46.
[62] S.R. & O. 1925, No. 779/L. 14. For these Conditions, see Wolst & C., i, 405.
[63] *Stearn v. Twitchell* [1985] 1 All E.R. 631; *ante*, para. 12–037.
[64] *Ante*, para. 12–037.
[65] See *Tweed v. Mills* (1865) L.R. 1 C.P. 39 at 45; [1992] C.L.J. 263 at 281 (C.H.).
[66] For the history of such conditions see [1992] C.L.J. 263 at 264 (C.H.).
[67] *Property & Bloodstock Ltd v. Emerton* [1968] Ch. 94 at 112, *per* Danckwerts L.J.

the parties, the property, the price, the giving of vacant possession and any specific incumbrances to which the sale is made subject. Secondly, the contract will usually incorporate a set of *general* conditions. These are standard form conditions which regulate a wide range of matters which are likely to arise in most conveyancing transactions. These include the payment of a deposit, the timetable for the deduction of title and (if it is not the subject of a special condition) completion,[68] the responsibility for the property pending completion and the remedies for breach of the agreement. In practice, it is common to modify the general conditions in any particular case. Although such general conditions have been described as "very much part of the small print",[69] they are given their full status as contractual terms.[70] Sets of standard conditions were first developed by local law societies in the second half of the nineteenth century. There is now just one set of general conditions that is normally used, the Standard Conditions of Sale.[71] Under those conditions, it is expressly provided that the special conditions prevail over the general in the event of any conflict between the two. In the absence of such an express provision, the court will have to resolve any such conflict by determining which condition was intended by the parties to be the dominant one.[72]

Section 3. Terms of a Contract

12–049   The following are examples of the matters usually dealt with in the special or general conditions of a formal contract for the sale of land. Most of them are explained in greater detail below.

> (i) Provision for the payment of a deposit (usually 10 per cent of the purchase-money)[73] and for the payment of interest on the purchase-money if completion is delayed.
>
> (ii) Where the title is unregistered, the length and nature of the title to be shown by the vendor[74] and any special provisions, *e.g.* as to making no objection to some specified defect in title or flaw in the evidence of title.[75] Where title is registered, the title number of the

---

[68] Commonly the completion date is fixed by special condition. The general conditions provide a fall-back position.

[69] *Lyme Valley Squash Club Ltd v. Newcastle under Lyme B.C.* [1985] 2 All E.R. 405 at 410, *per* Blackett-Ord V.-C. *cf.* [1985] Conv. 243 (H. W. Wilkinson).

[70] *Squarey v. Harris-Smith* (1981) 42 P. & C.R. 118 at 128.

[71] Third edition, 1995, *ante*, para. 5–027.

[72] See [1988] Conv. 400 at 401 (C.H.). Compare *Korogluyan v. Matheou* (1975) 30 P. & C.R. 309 with *Topfell Ltd v. Galley Properties Ltd* [1979] 1 W.L.R. 446.

[73] For deposits, see *post*, para. 12–107.

[74] *Post*, para. 12–075.

[75] *Post*, para. 12–079.

property, the class of title and copies of any documents referred to on the register.[76]

(iii) The time within which the evidence of title,[77] requisitions on title and other matters must be dealt with.

(iv) The date and place for completion of the sale.[78]

(v) Power for either party to terminate the contract because the other has failed to perform his obligations under the agreement after service of a notice to complete.[79]

Until recently, it had been the practice for more than a century and a half to include in a contract a power for the vendor to rescind the agreement because of the purchaser's insistence on objections to title.[80] This power was employed because of "the intricacies of title, according to the law of real property"[81] that obtained until the present century and which also led the courts to restrict the recovery of damages in cases where a vendor was unable without fault to show title.[82] Today there are no longer the difficulties in making title that once existed, the restriction on the recovery of damages has been abolished[83] and the rescission clause has been deleted from the Standard Conditions of Sale.[84]

Section 4. Effect of a Contract

There is great deal of law peculiar to contracts for the sale of land, but it cannot be fully explained without opening up the wider subject of conveyancing, that is, the law which is concerned with the sale and transfer of land.   **12–050**

---

[76] Such as restrictive covenants. *cf. Faruqi v. English Real Estates Ltd* [1979] 1 W.L.R. 963, where the sale was made subject merely to "entries on the register". These related to restrictive covenants, the terms of which were unknown. The court declined to decree specific performance at the behest of the vendor because he had failed to make full and frank disclosure of the nature of the entries.

[77] Where title is unregistered, the evidence is in the form of an "abstract of title", see *post*, para. 12–075. For the position where title is registered, see *post*, para. 12–084.

[78] Under the Standard Conditions of Sale, this is "either at the seller's solicitor's office or at some other place which the seller reasonably specifies": c. 6.2.

[79] *Post*, para. 12–094.

[80] For a full account of such rescission clauses and the judicial limitations placed upon them, see [1990] Conv. 150 (C.H.). See too the previous edition of this work at p. 623.

[81] *Gray v. Fowler* (1873) L.R. 8 Exch. 249 at 282, *per* Blackburn J. For these difficulties see (1992) 108 L.Q.R. 280 at 292 (C.H.).

[82] The so-called Rule in *Bain v. Fothergill* (1874) L.R. 7 H.L. 158, which was abolished in 1989; *post*, para. 12–103. For the interrelationship of this Rule with rescission clauses, see [1990] Conv. 150 (C.H.).

[83] L.P.(M.P.)A. 1989, s.3; *post*, para. 12–103.

[84] It was abandoned in the Second Edition precisely because of the abolition of the Rule in *Bain v. Fothergill*: (1992) 89/38 L.S.Gaz 23 at 24 (T. Aldridge). It does not appear in the third edition.

There is of course no precise boundary between real property and conveyancing and the two subjects inevitably overlap. Although the detailed practice of conveyancing lies outside the scope of this book, some of the borderland must be explored in order to understand the special rights and liabilities which contracts for the sale of land create. For the purposes of this chapter, the rules which apply to contracts for sale are taken to include contracts for the grant or assignment of leases except where the contrary is stated.

A. The Purchaser at Once Becomes Owner in Equity

12–051   **1. The purchaser as owner.** If the purchaser is potentially entitled to the equitable remedy of specific performance,[85] he obtains an immediate equitable interest in the property contracted to be sold.[86] He is, or soon will be, in a position to call for it specifically. As equity "looks upon things agreed to be done as actually performed",[87] the purchaser becomes the owner in the eyes of equity from the date of contract.[88] It is therefore irrelevant that the date for completion (when the purchaser may pay the price and take possession of the land) has not arrived.[89] The purchaser becomes owner in equity through the operation of the doctrine of conversion.[90] However, conversion will operate only if—

>   (i) the contract between the parties is valid, *i.e.* one which is "sufficient in form and in substance, so that there is no ground whatever for setting it aside"[91]; and

>   (ii) title to the land is made by the vendor or is accepted by the purchaser.[92]

The purchaser's equitable ownership is, as has been seen, a proprietary interest, enforceable against third parties, though it must be registered to protect it against purchasers.

12–052   **2. The vendor as trustee.** As between the parties to it, the contract creates a relationship of trustee and beneficiary,[93] though it is one which does not

---

[85] *Ante*, para. 4–015; *post*, para. 12–115.

[86] *Ante*, paras 4–025, 4–064, 5–099.

[87] *Re Cary-Elwes' Contract* [1906] 2 Ch. 143 at 149, *per* Swinfen Eady J.

[88] See *Lysaght v. Edwards* (1876) 2 Ch.D. 499 at 506–510; Williams V. & P. 59, 545. *Aliter* if specific performance would not be granted: *Central Trust and Deposit Co. v. Snider* [1916] 1 A.C. 266 at 272.

[89] The purchaser does not of course become the legal owner of the land until it is conveyed to him or (where title is registered) he is registered as proprietor of it.

[90] *Lysaght v. Edwards, supra,* at 506.

[91] *ibid.,* at 507, *per* Jessel M.R.

[92] *ibid.* In such a case conversion then operates retrospectively to the date of the contract: *post*, para. 12–059. See A. J. Oakley, *Constructive Trusts* (3rd ed.), pp. 283–285. *cf.* (1960) 24 Conv. (N.S.) 47 (P. H. Pettit).

[93] See A. J. Oakley, *Constructive Trusts*, Chap. 6.

have all the incidents normally associated with a trust.[94] The vendor is said to be a trustee for the purchaser,[95] and the purchaser is regarded as the beneficial owner, at least for the purposes of disposition.[96] However, the nature of this trust must be carefully understood. Although as against third parties it creates an equitable interest,[97] the proprietary consequences between the parties themselves are limited, because the vendor retains his lien over the property for the price until it is paid.[98] It imposes obligations on the vendor[99] and transfers the risk of damage to or destruction of the property to the purchaser.[1]

The vendor's principal obligation under this curious form of trust is to manage[2] and preserve the property with the same care as is required of any other trustee.[3] Thus a vendor was held liable when between contract and conveyance a trespasser removed a large quantity of surface soil from the land, for with reasonable vigilance he should have observed and prevented the damage.[4] In another case, a vendor was held to be liable when, without the purchaser's knowledge, he withdrew an application for planning permission which had been made prior to contract.[5] But, provided that the vendor has acted with due care since the date of the contract, the purchaser cannot complain of the condition of the property which he has agreed to buy, even if (for example) a house turns out to be unfit for habitation.[6] The vendor's liability is that of a trustee in possession and ceases if the purchaser goes into possession before completion.[7]

3. Nature of trusteeship. It is necessary to distinguish the trusteeship that 12–053 arises from the existence of a specifically enforceable contract between

---

[94] *Berkley v. Poulett* [1977] 1 E.G.L.R. 86 at 93. Stamp L.J. there observed that "you may search the Trustee Act 1925 without obtaining much that is relevant to the relationship of vendor and purchaser". The nature of the vendor's trusteeship is explained *infra*.

[95] *Lysaght v. Edwards, supra*, at 506.

[96] *Baldwin v. Belcher* (1844) 1 Jo. & Lat. 18 at 26.

[97] Because of the doctrine of conversion, it may have consequences as regards inheritance: *post*, para. 12–059. Furthermore, in negotiations with potential sub-purchasers, the purchaser can describe himself without misrepresentation as owner of the land: *Gordon Hill Trust Ltd v. Segall* [1941] 2 All E.R. 379.

[98] "The purchaser has neither a legal nor an equitable right, as against the seller, until he pays the purchase price": *Baldwin v. Belcher, supra*, at 26, *per* Sugden L.C.; *Shaw v. Foster* (1872) L.R. 5 H.L. 321 at 349; *post*, para. 12–054.

[99] *Infra*.

[1] *Post*, para. 12–055.

[2] See *Earl of Egmont v. Smith* (1877) 6 Ch.D. 468; *Abdulla v. Shah* [1959] A.C. 124.

[3] *Phillips v. Silvester* (1872) 8 Ch.App. 173 at 177; *Raffety v. Schofield* [1897] 1 Ch. 937 at 944, 945. See [1995] Cambrian L.R. 33 (A. Dowling).

[4] *Clarke v. Ramuz* [1891] 2 Q.B. 456. See too *Phillips v. Lamdin* [1949] 2 K.B. 33 (removal of door by vendor: order for specific restitution); *Davron Estates Ltd v. Turnshire Ltd* (1982) 133 N.L.J. 937 (vendor liable for damage committed by squatters).

[5] *Sinclar-Hill v. Sothcott* (1973) 26 P. & C.R. 490.

[6] *Hoskins v. Woodham* [1938] 1 All E.R. 692; *Scott-Polson v. Hope* (1958) 14 D.L.R. (2d) 333; *cf. Miller v. Cannon Hill Estates Ltd* [1931] 2 K.B. 113 (where the general principle was accepted, but where there was either an express warranty or an implied term that a newly constructed house would be fit for habitation).

[7] *Phillips v. Silvester, supra*.

vendor and purchaser and that which arises from a payment of some or all of the purchase price by the purchaser.[8]

12–054   *(a) Trusteeship arising from specifically enforceable contract.* While he remains unpaid, the vendor's trusteeship arising from a specifically enforceable contract is of a peculiar kind,[9] because although a trustee, he has "a personal and substantial interest in the property, a right to protect that interest, and an active right to assert that interest if anything should be done in derogation of it".[10] He may occupy the land and take the rents and profits for himself up to the day fixed for handing over possession. Until the purchase price is paid he may stay in possession under his common law lien as vendor,[11] which arises at the date of contract.[12] Ordinarily both these rights will expire when the contract is completed by delivery of the conveyance or transfer, the purchase-money is paid, and the purchaser is let into possession. But if the vendor parts with possession of the land before he receives payment, he has an equitable lien on the land which entitles him, if he cannot obtain payment, to ask the court for an order for sale.[13] It has been held that an unpaid vendor's lien can arise only where the contract is one of which a court would order specific performance.[14] This limitation appears to be unjustified however, and the better view is that a valid contract between the parties is the only prerequisite.[15]

The vendor must pay all expenses properly attributable to his period of beneficial enjoyment, *e.g.* rates and taxes apportioned up to the date of completion, for in respect of these he has not the ordinary trustee's right of indemnity against the beneficiary.[16] Conversely he may take the benefit of statutory compensation falling due to the "owner" before completion.[17] But broadly speaking, "as between vendor and purchaser generally the powers of

---

[8] See [1984] C.L.J. 134 at 136–139 (C.H.).

[9] *Rayner v. Preston* (1881) 18 Ch.D. 1 at 6. In that case Brett L.J. doubted whether the vendor was ever trustee for the purchaser: *ibid.* at 11, but this goes too far. For more measured opinions, see *Berkley v. Poulett* [1977] 1 E.G.L.R. 86 at 93; *Chang v. Registrar of Titles* (1976) 137 C.L.R. 177 at 184, 189.

[10] *Shaw v. Foster* (1872) L.R. 5 H.L. 321 at 338, *per* Lord Cairns.

[11] *Phillips v. Silvester, supra,* at 176; *post,* para. 19–002.

[12] *Re Birmingham* [1959] Ch. 523.

[13] *Mackreth v. Symmons* (1808) 15 Ves. 329; Wh. & T. ii, 848; Snell, *Equity,* 464; *post,* para. 19–008. This is an equitable interest in land (*ante,* para. 5–012), registrable as a general equitable charge where the title is unregistered (*ante*) and as a notice or caution where title is registered (*ante,* paras 6–079, 6–083).The unpaid vendor's lien arises on the exchange of contracts: see *Barclays Bank Plc v. Estates & Commercial Ltd* [1997] 1 W.L.R. 415. See generally [1997] Conv. 336 (D. G. Barnsley).

[14] *Capital Finance Co. Ltd v. Stokes* [1969] 1 Ch. 261 at 278; *London & Cheshire Insurance Co. Ltd v. Laplagrene* [1971] Ch. 499 at 514; *Re Bond Worth* [1980] Ch. 228 at 251. But see to the contrary: *Ecclesiastical Commissioners v. Piney* [1899] 2 Ch. 729 (aff'd [1900] 2 Ch. 736).

[15] "The peculiar and discretionary grounds for resisting specific performance are simply not appropriate to be indiscriminately applied as criteria of exclusion": *Hewett v. Court* (1983) 46 A.L.R. 87 at 105, *per* Deane J. See [1997] Conv. 336 at 339 (D. G. Barnsley).

[16] *Re Watford Corporation and Ware's Contract* [1943] Ch. 82; Williams V. & P. 560.

[17] *Re Hamilton-Snowball's Conveyance* [1959] Ch. 308 (compensation on derequisition).

the vendor to act as owner of the property, and (*inter alia*) to change tenants and holdings, are suspended pending completion of the purchase."[18]

(b) Trusteeship arising from payment of the purchase price.[19] It has been **12–055** explained that the proprietary consequences of the trust arising from a specifically enforceable contract are in practice limited as between vendor and purchaser because of the vendor's lien for the price.[20] However, the purchaser does become in some sense the owner of the property in equity to the extent that he pays all or part of the price[21] (or furnishes other consideration[22]).[23] There is some uncertainty as to the nature of this ownership. It is often said that the purchaser has a lien over the property for the amount that he has paid,[24] but there is also authority that the vendor holds the property on trust for him,[25] and that he will hold it on a bare trust once the whole price has been paid.[26] The distinction between these two formulations could be important if the property were to increase or decrease in value, particularly if the vendor were insolvent.[27] The purchaser may assert his proprietary claim not only against the land, but should the vendor sell it to some third party in breach of contract, to the proceeds of that sale as well.[28]

For the lien or trust to arise there must be a valid contract between the parties[29] though it need not be specifically enforceable.[30] A purchaser can

---

[18] *Raffety v. Schofield* [1897] 1 Ch. 937 at 945, *per* Romer J.

[19] See [1994] C.L.J. 263 (S. Worthington); *Interests in Goods* (ed. N. Palmer and E. McKendrick), Chap. 25 (J. Phillips); [1977] Conv. 336 at 350 (D. G. Barnsley); (1997) 1 E.L.R. 437 at 457 (C.H.).

[20] *Ante*, para. 12–054.

[21] Payment must be to the vendor however. There is no lien if payment is made to a stakeholder, as commonly happens with a deposit: *Combe v. Lord Swaythling* [1947] Ch. 625.

[22] See *Lake v. Bayliss* [1974] 1 W.L.R. 1073 (where the consideration was the withdrawal of two writs and the assumption of liabilities under a planning application).

[23] The leading case is *Rose v. Watson* (1864) 33 L.J.Ch. 385 (a fuller report than 10 H.L.C. 672). See too *Wythes v. Lee* (1855) 3 Drew. 396; *Middleton v. Magnay* (1864) 2 H. & M. 233; *Levy v. Stogdon* [1898] 1 Ch. 478; *Whitbread & Co. Ltd v. Watt* [1902] 1 Ch. 835; *Combe v. Lord Swaythling, supra*; *Chattey v. Farndale Holdings Inc.* [1997] 1 E.G.L.R. 153.

[24] *e.g. Middleton v. Magnay, supra*; *Whitbread & Co. Ltd v. Watt, supra*; *Hewett v. Court* (1983) 46 A.L.R. 87. The issue usually arises in connection with a claim by the purchaser to recover his deposit: *post*, para. 12–108.

[25] *Rose v. Watson, supra*, at 390; *Shaw v. Foster* (1872) L.R. 5 H.L. 321 at 349.

[26] *Rose v. Watson, supra*, at 390; *Shaw v. Foster, supra*, at 356; *Re Pagani* [1892] 1 Ch. 236 at 238; *Chang v. Registrar of Titles* (1976) 137 C.L.R. 177 at 184, 189; *Coffey v. Brunel Construction Co. Ltd* [1983] I.R. 36 at 40, 43.

[27] It might be important for other reasons. If the property were let, the purchaser would be entitled to a proportion of the rents if he was beneficially entitled under a trust, but the same might not be true if he merely had a lien.

[28] *Lake v. Bayliss, supra*.

[29] *Whitbread & Co. Ltd v. Watt* [1901] 1 Ch. 911 at 915 (aff'd [1902] 1 Ch. 835); *Re Barrett Apartments Ltd* [1985] I.R. 350. The purchaser must have had a present, future or contingent right to the legal estate: *Chattey v. Farndale Holdings Inc.* [1997] 1 E.G.L.R. 153.

[30] *Chattey v. Farndale Holdings Inc., supra*; *Hewett v. Court, supra*. In the latter case, Deane J. explained that "an equitable lien to secure repayment of instalments of purchase price is only of real value if specific performance of the contract would not be decreed": (1983) 46 A.L.R. 87 at 106.

assert a lien only "where a purchase goes off by reason of some default on the part of the vendor".[31] The basis for the imposition of the lien is not wholly clear,[32] but it appears to arise out of the relationship of the parties by operation of equity[33] as a correlative of the unpaid vendor's lien.[34]

4. The risk passes

12–056   *(a) The position under open contract.* Under the trust that arises from a specifically enforceable contract, the property at once belongs to the purchaser in equity. In consequence the risk of damage or destruction to the property also passes to him as soon as conversion has operated.[35] Thus if a house has been sold and is, without the fault of the vendor, destroyed by fire before completion, the purchaser must nevertheless pay the full purchase-money and take the land as it is.[36] It is important for a purchaser of buildings to insure at once in his own name, since he undertakes the risk of accidents before he takes the property itself. He cannot take the benefit of any insurance maintained by the vendor in the vendor's name alone[37]; for insurance is normally only a personal indemnity against loss, and since the vendor is entitled to the whole purchase-money and so loses nothing he can recover nothing under his policy.[38] If the vendor does in fact obtain payment of the insurance money, the insurers can recover it.[39] Even if they do not, equity does not require the vendor to pay the money to the purchaser, for his qualified trusteeship extends only to the land, and not to the proceeds of a personal contract of insurance.[40]

---

[31] *Cornwall v. Henson* [1899] 2 Ch. 710 at 714, *per* Cozens-Hardy J. See too *Ridout v. Fowler* [1904] 1 Ch. 658 at 663; *Hedworth v. Jenwise Ltd* [1994] E.G.C.S. 133. A purchaser in default has no lien for his deposit or other part payments therefore: *ibid.*; *Dinn v. Grant* (1852) 5 De G. & Sm. 451.

[32] See (1993) 109 L.Q.R. 159 at 162 (W. M. C. Gummow).

[33] *Hewett v. Court, supra*, at 105.

[34] *Wythes v. Lee* (1855) 3 Drew. 396 at 403.

[35] The risk of defects in title which arise between contract and completion remains with the vendor, however, unless the parties have agreed otherwise: see *Wroth v. Tyler* [1974] Ch. 30. For defects in title, see *post*, para. 12–080.

[36] *Paine v. Meller* (1801) 6 Ves. 349; *Rayner v. Preston* (1881) 18 Ch.D. 1. The same principle applies if between contract and completion a building is listed as being of architectural or historical importance: there is no frustration, and the purchaser must take the land: *Amalgamated Investment & Property Co. Ltd v. John Walker & Sons Ltd* [1977] 1 W.L.R. 164; or a notice of intended compulsory purchase is served on the vendor: *E. Johnson & Co. (Barbados) Ltd v. N.S.R. Ltd* [1997] A.C. 400; *post*, para. 12–080. The doctrine of frustration *can* apply to contracts for the sale of land: see *Wong Lai-Ying v. Chinachem Investments Co. Ltd* [1978] H.K.L.R. 1, where the Privy Council held that a contract to purchase an interest in a block of flats was frustrated when the building was destroyed in a landslip.

[37] *Rayner v. Preston, supra.*

[38] See following note.

[39] *Castellain v. Preston* (1883) 11 Q.B.D. 380. Yet if the contract of insurance is framed not as an indemnity against loss but as a guarantee against fire, the vendor will be entitled to the insurance money: *Collingridge v. Royal Exchange Assurance Corp.* (1877) 3 Q.B.D. 173.

[40] *Rayner v. Preston* (1881) 18 Ch.D. 1.

By statute,[41] an insurance company can be required to lay out any insurance money in reinstating premises destroyed or damaged by fire at the request of a person interested. However, it now seems that this obligation may arise only where the assured was under an obligation to the person interested to reinstate the premises, as where a landlord has covenanted with a tenant to do so.[42] This is seldom likely to be the situation as between vendor and purchaser.

(b) Insurance by the purchaser. The position as to insurance is in practice **12–057** often regulated by conditions of sale and this is explained below. However, in the absence of any such agreement between vendor and purchaser, it is essential for the latter, if he wishes to insure the buildings, to take out insurance on his own account. In domestic conveyancing, the purchaser will in those circumstances commonly insure from the date of contract. Although this will lead to duplication of insurance by vendor and purchaser, the cost is not large because the period between contract and completion is normally short. To avoid such duplication the parties may arrange, with the consent of the insurers, for the vendor's existing insurance to be extended to cover the purchaser. Section 47 of the Law of Property Act 1925 provides that "where . . . money becomes payable" under the vendor's insurance policy in respect of damage to the property after the date of the contract, the vendor shall pay that money to the purchaser on completion. This is subject to: (a) the terms of the contract; (b) any requisite consent of the insurers; and (c) the payment by the purchaser of his share of the premium.[43] It has been assumed that, in consequence of this section, where the insurers consent to include the purchaser in the insurance, it is unnecessary to make further terms about the insurance money or premium. However, there must be a doubt as to whether the section achieves that effect. The vendor is entitled to receive from the purchaser the full contract price and will therefore suffer no personal loss if the property is damaged. It follows that on a literal interpretation of the section no insurance money will become payable under the policy and the purchaser will receive nothing.[44]

(c) Conditions of sale. The Law Commission, after reviewing this area of **12–058** the law, concluded that the law should be changed so that risk passed only on

---

[41] Fires Prevention (Metropolis) Act 1774, s.83. See *Vural Ltd v. Security Archives Ltd* (1989) 60 P. & C.R. 258 at 272.

[42] *Lonsdale & Thompson Ltd v. Black Arrow Group Plc* [1993] Ch. 361; [1993] C.L.J. 387 (A. J. Oakley). In that case the landlord had contracted to sell the reversion before the fire and made no claim on the policy. It was held that notwithstanding the contract of sale, he had an insurable interest beyond the value of his reversion and his insurers could be required by the tenant to reinstate the premises. *cf.* [1989] Conv. 1 at 5 (H. W. Wilkinson).

[43] Presumably these conditions must be satisfied *before* the loss occurs.

[44] This is almost certainly the case where the insurance is left in the vendor's name only, but the same conclusion would appear to follow even where the insurers have agreed to include the purchaser in the insurance: see Law Com. W.P. No. 109 (1988), paras 2.9–2.17; and *Ziel Nominees Pty Ltd v. V.A.C.C. Insurance Co. Ltd* (1975) 50 A.L.J.R. 106 (a case where the vendors had attempted to assign the benefit of the policy to the purchaser without the insurer's consent).

completion.[45] However, no proposals for legislation followed because the recommendation was incorporated in the Standard Conditions of Sale.[46] The relevant condition[47] provides that the vendor retains the risk of damage to or destruction of the property until completion. The purchaser may rescind the contract if at any time before then the physical state of the property makes it unusable for its purpose at the date of contract. The vendor may also rescind in such circumstances, but only if the damage is of a kind against which he could not reasonably have insured, or which it is not legally possible to make good, *e.g.* because of planning restrictions. The vendor is under no obligation to insure the premises and section 47 of the Law of Property Act 1925 is excluded.

12–059   **5. Conversion.** Another consequence of the change in beneficial ownership brought about by the contract is that the equitable doctrine of conversion applies.[48] If, for example, A contracts to sell land to B and then dies leaving all his land to X and all his other property to Y, Y will be entitled to the purchase-money when the contract is duly completed by the executors; for A's beneficial interest consisted of money due from B rather than of land.

12–060   **6. Specific enforceability.** The vendor's trusteeship, the passing of the risk and conversion (but not the lien or trust arising from a payment of the price) all flow from the fact that the contract is specifically enforceable. If it is not they are all excluded. For example, there might be a flaw in the vendor's title, so that the purchaser refused to complete. In that case the vendor would not be liable for negligent damage to the property, he could recover any insurance money payable for accidental damage, and the land would pass under a devise of real property.

12–061   **7. Options.** The nature of an option has already been explained.[49] It creates an immediate interest in the land, for the grantor has bound himself to enter into a contract of sale if and when the grantee exercises the option in accordance with its terms.[50] In this way, the grantee obtains a specifically enforceable right to secure the land in certain conditions, and the equitable interest which arises under the option is not "altered or superseded by some other and different interest on the exercise of the option".[51]

---

[45] (1988) Law Com. W.P. No. 109. See [1989] Conv. 1 (H. W. Wilkinson).
[46] (1990) See Law Com. No. 191.
[47] c. 5.1. See (1992) 89/38 L.S.Gaz 23 (T. Aldridge).
[48] See *ante*, paras 8–007, 8–118; Snell, *Equity*, 491; *Lysaght v. Edwards* (1876) 2 Ch.D. 499.
[49] *Ante*, para. 12–012.
[50] See *L. & S. W. Ry v. Gomm* (1882) 20 Ch.D. 562 at 581; *Griffith v. Pelton* [1958] Ch. 205 at 225; *Webb v. Pollmount Ltd* [1966] Ch. 584 at 597; *McCarthy & Stone Ltd v. Julian S. Hodge & Co. Ltd* [1971] 1 W.L.R. 1547; *First National Securities Ltd v. Chiltern D.C.* [1975] 1 W.L.R. 1075 at 1079, 1080; *Mountford v. Scott* [1975] Ch. 258 (consideration nominal: specific performance granted).
[51] *Armstrong & Holmes Ltd v. Holmes* [1993] 1 W.L.R. 1482 at 1488, *per* Judge Baker.

Whether the same is true of a right of pre-emption (or right of first refusal) is a question which the courts have not succeeded in answering satisfactorily.[52] This right differs from an ordinary option in that it entitles the holder to be offered the land on certain terms only if the owner decides to dispose of it. But this is merely an additional condition, and in principle it ought not to prevent the holder acquiring an immediate interest in the land, since here also he has secured to himself a specifically enforceable though contingent right to obtain it under a contract of sale.[53] Furthermore, the legislation of 1925 and later is replete with indications that rights of pre-emption were intended to take effect as interests in land which could bind purchasers if duly registered, on a par with other forms of option. The definition of estate contract in the Land Charges Act 1972, for example, includes "a valid option to purchase, a right of pre-emption or any other like right"[54]; and the Law of Property Act 1925 provides that "all statutory and other rights of pre-emption affecting a legal estate" shall, unless released, "remain in force as equitable interests only".[55]

Nevertheless the Court of Appeal has held that a right of pre-emption can take effect as an interest in land only from the time when it becomes exercisable, *i.e.* from the time when the owner decides to sell.[56] This was in a case where, in effect,[57] the owner of the land had granted a right of pre-emption exercisable during his own life to A and an option exercisable after his own death to B, so that B was to have the option only if A had not exercised his right. Although B was fully aware of A's right, which had been duly registered and under which A had in fact obtained the land before the

12–062

---

[52] In favour of an interest in land are *Birmingham Canal Co. v. Cartwright* (1879) 11 Ch.D. 421; *L & S.W. Ry v. Gomm, supra*, treating the *Birmingham Canal* case as correct on this point; *Halifax (City) v. Vaughan Construction Co. Ltd* [1961] S.C.R. 715; and the decisions at first instance in *Manchester Ship Canal Co. v. Manchester Racecourse Co.* [1900] 2 Ch. 352 and *Pritchard v. Briggs* [1980] Ch. 338. Against are the *Manchester Ship Canal* case [1901] 2 Ch. 37 (C.A.); *Murray v. Two Strokes Ltd* [1973] 1 W.L.R. 823; *Mackay v. Wilson* (1947) 47 S.R. (N.S.W.) 315; *Canadian Long Island Industries Ltd v. Irving Industries Ltd* [1975] 2 S.C.R. 715. The Court of Appeal's brief unreasoned statement in the *Manchester Ship Canal* case was *obiter*, since the land had not changed hands and injunctions were granted to prevent the original promisor and a would-be purchaser from acting inconsistently with the contract of first refusal.

[53] *Birmingham Canal Co. v. Cartwright, supra; cf.*, R. Castle, *Barnsley's Land Options* (3rd ed.), pp. 178, 179; (1973) 89 L.Q.R. 462 (M. J. Albery).

[54] s.2(4) Class C(iv), replacing the Land Charges Act 1925, s.10. For similar provisions see L.P.A. 1925, s.2(3)(iv); S.L.A. 1925, ss.58(2), 61(2); Perpetuities and Accumulations Act 1964, s.9(2); all clearly indicating that a right of pre-emption ranks as an interest in land. Another indication was the Housing Act 1957, s.104, which gave local authorities a right of pre-emption in the case of sale of a council house and provided for its registration so as to bind successors in title: see *First National Securities Ltd v. Chiltern D.C.* [1975] 1 W.L.R. 1075. The provisions which have since replaced the Housing Act 1957, s.104, have contained no similar provision for registration: see now the Housing Act 1985, s.33.

[55] s.186.

[56] *Pritchard v. Briggs* [1980] Ch. 338 (Templeman and Stephenson L.JJ., Goff L.J. holding that the right could not be an interest in land at all and that all the statutory indications to the contrary were merely mistaken assumptions). For criticism see (1980) 96 L.Q.R. 488 (H.W.R.W.).

[57] In fact the right of pre-emption had been granted by A's predecessors in title and A had acquired the benefit of it by assignment.

owner died, it was held that A must surrender the land to B at the option price (which was much lower than the pre-emption price paid by A) because B's option had been granted and registered before A's right of pre-emption became exercisable, so that B took priority. The result was unjust as well as technically questionable, violating the principle that a later purchaser with notice ought not to be able to defeat a prior third party right, and introducing the novel conception of a contingent interest in land which ranks as such not from its creation but only from the occurrence of the contingency.[58] The court stressed that the differentiating factor in a right of pre-emption was its dependence upon the owner's own violation, *i.e.* his willingness to sell; but it is difficult to see why that should make it so different from numerous other contingencies, volition-dependent or otherwise, which the law allows to be attached to interests in land.[59]

12–063   The legislation cited above implies distinctly that a right of pre-emption should rank as an interest in land from the time of its creation, like an ordinary option. By holding that it cannot do so until it becomes exercisable the court has in effect disqualified it as an interest in land, since nothing can be done to protect it against a successor in title until a time which in at least some situations will be too late.[60] If A grants to B a right of pre-emption in case A or his successors should wish to sell the land within 20 years and A then dies, his successor will not be bound by the mere contract, there being as yet no interest in land.[61] This hardly seems a suitable point at which to draw the line between special contracts which can bind third parties and ordinary contracts which cannot. It should be noted that, although the opinion expressed by the majority of the Court of Appeal as to the nature of rights of pre-emption has been followed at first instance,[62] those remarks were in fact *obiter* and the criticism to which they have been subjected has not escaped attention.[63]

---

[58] No authority for this strange proposition was cited. Goff L.J. rejected it on the ground that the right must from the start be one thing or the other. Templeman L.J. held that the right may be registered at once but takes priority only from the time when it becomes exercisable. See also *Haslemere Estates Ltd v. Baker* [1982] 1 W.L.R. 1109.

[59] It is not explained whether every volition-dependent condition is incompatible with an interest in land. If A gives to B an option to purchase A's land if A or his successors cease to reside on it within 20 years, cannot this bind the successor?

[60] But not in all. See *Kling v. Keston Properties Ltd* (1983) 49 P. & C.R. 212, where a purchaser of a garage with registered title was bound by a licensee's right of pre-emption. This crystallised into an option when the vendor contracted to sell the garage and took effect as an overriding interest because of the licensee's actual occupation: see *ante*, para. 6–052.

[61] B may have a remedy in damages against A's estate. During A's life he can obtain an injunction against A, or any third party with actual notice, dealing with the land inconsistently with his right: *Manchester Ship Canal Co. v. Manchester Racecourse Co.* [1901] 2 Ch. 37; *Swiss Bank Corp. v. Lloyds Bank Ltd* [1979] Ch. 548, reversed on other grounds [1982] A.C. 584.

[62] *Kling v. Keston Properties Ltd, supra.* See too *Homsey v. Murphy* (1996) 73 P. & C.R. 26 at 38, where Beldam L.J. accepted, *obiter*, the analysis of a right of pre-emption given in *Pritchard v. Briggs, supra.*

[63] See *London & Blenheim Estates Ltd v. Ladbrooke Retail Parks Ltd* [1994] 1 W.L.R. 31 at 38. *cf.* (1998) Law Com. No. 254, paras 3.29–3.32, recommending the reversal of *Pritchard v. Briggs, supra*, in relation to registered land.

A right of pre-emption implies a negative obligation to the owner not to part with the land so as to frustrate the right.[64] It may therefore be capable of binding successors in title as a restrictive covenant; but in order to do so it will have to obey the rules for such covenants, including the rule that the covenant must be for the protection of adjacent land of the covenantee.

B. *The Vendor must Convey the Land Described in the Contract*

1. The obligation. In the particulars of sale in the contract,[65] the vendor   **12–064**
must accurately describe the land which he intends to convey.[66] That description will usually encompass four matters—

(i)   the physical identity of the land[67];

(ii) the estate to be transferred[68];

(iii) proprietary rights which enure for the benefit of the land; and

(iv) any incumbrances which burden the property.

A vendor who misdescribes the land in the particulars commits a breach of contract. Examples of such misdescriptions have included—

(a)   erroneous statements as to the size of the land[69];

(b)   where land was registered merely with possessory title, a statement that it was "registered freehold property"[70]; and

(c)   a statement that land was leasehold when it was in fact held on an underlease,[71] but not a description of a "sub-underlease" as an underlease.[72]

---

[64] *Manchester Ship Canal Co. v. Manchester Racecourse Co., supra*; *Gardner v. Coutts & Co.* [1968] 1 W.L.R. 173.

[65] Although it has been said that "the proper office of the particulars is to describe the subject-matter of the contract, that of the conditions to state the terms on which it is sold" (*Torrance v. Bolton* (1872) L.R. 14 Eq. 124 at 130, *per* Malins V.-C.), the distinction between particulars and conditions of sale is one of practice rather than substance: J. T. Farrand, *Contract and Conveyance* (4th ed.), p. 50.

[66] *Swaisland v. Dearsley* (1861) 29 Beav. 430 at 436.

[67] Where title is registered, the description found in the property register is commonly adopted.

[68] A vendor is presumed to transfer the fee simple free from incumbrances unless either the contract states otherwise or the purchaser is aware that this is not the case: *Timmins v. Moreland Street Property Co. Ltd* [1958] Ch. 110 at 118.

[69] *Watson v. Burton* [1957] 1 W.L.R. 19 (land consisting of 2,360 square yards described as consisting of 3,920 square yards); *King Brothers (Finance) Ltd v. North Western British Road Services Ltd* [1986] 2 E.G.L.R. 253.

[70] *Re Brine and Davies' Contract* [1935] Ch. 388 (such a description implied that the vendor had an absolute title).

[71] *Re Russ and Brown's Contract* [1934] Ch. 34. An underlease is vulnerable to forfeiture for breach of covenant by the underlessor whereas a lease can be forfeited only for the lessee's own breach.

[72] *Becker v. Partridge* [1966] 2 Q.B. 155 at 170 where Danckwerts L.J. observed that "the term 'sub-underlease' is not really a conveyancing expression in current use".

Where the misdescription is substantial, the purchaser may either terminate the contract and sue the vendor for damages, or seek specific performance with compensation or damages in addition.[73] In this context, a misdescription will be substantial if the purchaser would not have entered into the contract but for it.[74] Where the misdescription is insubstantial, the vendor may specifically enforce the contract against the purchaser subject to an abatement of the price.[75] These remedies are explained later.[76]

12–065   **2. Conditions of sale.** If has long been common to include in contracts for the sale of land a condition of sale providing that in the event of any error, omission or misdescription in the particulars of sale, the purchaser shall not be able to terminate the contract, but shall complete it either with or (in some forms of the condition) without compensation.[77] However, where the misdescription is substantial in the sense explained above, the purchaser may terminate the contract and seek damages for its breach notwithstanding that the contract contains such a condition of sale.[78]

12–066   **3. Misdescription and misrepresentation.** A purchaser of land may be induced to enter into a contract because of the matters contained in the draft particulars of sale.[79] If those particulars are inaccurate, the purchaser will have remedies for both misrepresentation and breach of the subsequent contract of which the erroneous particulars become part.[80] In practice purchasers often pursue their remedies for misrepresentation (which are explained below)[81] in preference to a claim for breach of contract.

C. The Vendor must show a Good Title

12–067   A vendor is under a two-fold obligation as to the title of the property which he is selling. First, he must disclose to the purchaser prior to contracting all latent defects in title save those of which the purchaser is aware.[82] Secondly, by the contractual completion date he must both have the title which he has contracted to give and be able to prove that fact. It should be noted that the

---

[73] See [1981] C.L.J. 47 (C.H.).
[74] *Smith v. Tolcher* (1828) 4 Russ. 302 at 305; *Flight v. Booth* (1834) 1 Bing. (N.C.) 370 at 377; *Ridley v. Oster* [1939] 1 All E.R. 618 at 622. As to whether the test of substantiality is subjective, objective, or both, see [1992] C.L.J. 263 at 274 (C.H.).
[75] Conditions of sale may however exclude the entitlement to an abatement.
[76] *Post*, paras 12–102, 12–105 (damages), 12–117 (specific performance with compensation or damages).
[77] See [1992] C.L.J. 263 at 270 (C.H.). For the present version of the condition, see Standard Conditions of Sale (3rd ed.), c. 7.1.
[78] *Flight v. Booth, supra.*
[79] See *e.g. South Western General Property Co. Ltd v. Marton* [1982] 2 E.G.L.R. 19 (misstatement in auction particulars).
[80] A misrepresentation remains actionable even though it has become a term of the contract: Misrepresentation Act 1967, s.1(a).
[81] *Post*, paras 12–104, 12–112.
[82] See (1992) 108 L.Q.R. 280 (C.H.).

first of these obligations arises at the time of contracting[83] whereas the second must be satisfied at the date for completion.[84] Although the second of these obligations was established by the beginning of the nineteenth century, the first emerged only at the end of that century. Each of these obligations must now be explained.

1. Duty to disclose latent defects

(a) The obligation. A vendor is under a duty to disclose to the purchaser **12–068** before contracting any latent defects in title.[85] He is under no obligation to disclose any defect in title of which the purchaser is aware[86] or which is patent.[87] A defect is not patent merely because the purchaser has constructive notice of it.[88] It must be one "which arises either to the eye, or by necessary implication from something which is visible to the eye".[89] Thus an obvious right of way is likely to be patent,[90] but a tenancy,[91] a restrictive covenant[92] and a local land charge[93] are all latent incumbrances.[94]

The nature of the vendor's obligation to disclose latent defects prior to contract is obscure and cannot be regarded as finally settled. In some cases it has been explained on the basis that it is akin to fraud for a vendor not to reveal a defect in title of which he is aware.[95] In others, however, it is justified on the basis that the vendor's title is a matter exclusively within his knowledge and the purchaser therefore necessarily relies upon him to disclose any latent defects in it.[96] He must therefore disclose all latent defects in title, whether or not he knows of them. This may best be explained not as a pre-contractual duty of disclosure at all but as an implied term of a contract for the sale of land that the vendor has disclosed all latent defects in title.[97] The

---

[83] *Re Haedicke and Lipski's Contract* [1901] 2 Ch. 666 at 668.

[84] "The vendor must be prepared to make out a good title on the day when a purchase is to be completed": *Cornish v. Rowley* (1800) 1 Selwyn's *Nisi Prius* (13th ed.), 218 and 219, *per* Lord Kenyon C.J.

[85] *Reeve v. Berridge* (1880) 20 Q.B.D. 523; *Re White and Smith's Contract* [1896] 1 Ch. 637; *Re Haedicke and Lipski's Contract, supra*; *Molyneux v. Hawtrey* [1903] 2 K.B. 487. See too *Peyman v. Lanjani* [1985] Ch. 457 at 496, 497; Halsb. (4th ed. reissue) vol. 42, para. 55; (1992) 108 L.Q.R. 280 at 325 *et seq.* (C.H.).

[86] *Re Gloag and Miller's Contract* (1883) 23 Ch.D. 320 at 327; *McGrory v. Alderdale Estate Co. Ltd* [1918] A.C. 503 at 508; *post*, para. 12–081.

[87] *Bowles v. Round* (1800) 5 Ves. 508.

[88] *Caballero v. Henty* (1874) 9 Ch.App. 447, rejecting earlier authority to the contrary. See (1992) 108 L.Q.R. 280 at 321–324 (C.H.).

[89] *Yandle & Sons v. Sutton* [1922] 2 Ch. 199 at 210, *per* Sargant J.

[90] *Shonleigh Nominees Ltd v. Att.-Gen.* [1974] 1 W.L.R. 305 at 311, 315, 323. Not all rights of way will be patent: see *Ashburner v. Sewell* [1891] 3 Ch. 405.

[91] *Caballero v. Henty, supra; Pagebar Properties Ltd v. Derby Investment Holdings Ltd* [1972] 1 W.L.R. 1500.

[92] *Hone v. Gakstatter* (1909) 53 S.J. 286; *Re Stone and Saville's Contract* [1963] 1 W.L.R. 163.

[93] *Rignall Developments Ltd v. Halil* [1988] Ch. 190.

[94] For the meaning of "incumbrances", see *post*, para. 12–080.

[95] *Carlish v. Salt* [1906] 1 Ch. 335; *F & B Entertainment Ltd v. Leisure Enterprises Ltd* [1976] 2 E.G.L.R. 76 at 79; *Sakkas v. Donford Ltd* (1982) 46 P. & C.R. 290 at 302.

[96] *Yandle & Sons v. Sutton, supra*, at 210; *Peyman v. Lanjani* [1985] Ch. 457 at 496.

[97] See (1992) 108 L.Q.R. 280 at 332 (C.H.).

remedies available for failing to disclose latent defects in title suggest that this latter analysis is the correct one.

12–069   *(b) Remedies.* If a vendor contracts to sell land which he does not own or to which the title is bad,[98] the purchaser may at once treat the contract as repudiated and sue the vendor for damages.[99] He does not have to wait until the contractual completion date.[1] This can be justified only if the vendor is in breach of some contractual obligation that is distinct from his duty to convey the land with a good title on the contractual completion date. There is authority which suggests that it is the vendor's failure to disclose a defect in title that constitutes that breach.[2] Where the non-disclosure relates to either an insubstantial matter or a removable defect in title, the purchaser cannot terminate the contract.[3] In such circumstances either the vendor or the purchaser may seek specific performance of the contract subject to an abatement of the price in respect of any insubstantial but irremovable defect in title.[4]

12–070   *(c) Conditions of sale.* There are two types of condition of sale upon which vendors commonly rely in cases of non-disclosure. The first is the condition, considered above,[5] which purports to exclude the purchaser's right to terminate the contract in the event of any error, omission or misdescription in the particulars of sale. This condition will be inapplicable in cases where the non-disclosure relates to a substantial latent defect in title.[6] Secondly, a sale is often made with some general exclusion, such as "subject to any existing rights and easements of whatever nature".[7] However, it is a fundamental rule of equity that the vendor cannot rely on such a condition to cover a latent

---

[98] For what constitutes a bad title, see *post*, para. 12–073.

[99] *Bartlett v. Tuchin* (1815) 1 Marsh. 586; *Roper v. Coombs* (1827) 9 Dowl. & Ry. 562; *Brewer v. Broadhead* (1882) 22 Ch.D. 105; *Lee v. Soames* (1888) 36 W.R. 884; *Pips (Leisure Productions) Ltd v. Walton* (1980) 43 P. & C.R. 415; *Pinekerry Ltd v. Needs (Kenneth) (Contractors) Ltd* (1992) 64 P. & C.R. 245. See [1993] C.L.J. 22 (A. J. Oakley).

[1] *Forrer v. Nash* (1865) 35 Beav. 167 at 171. There was a view that in such circumstances the purchaser could only "rescind in equity": *Halkett v. Earl of Dudley* [1907] 1 Ch. 590; (1977) 41 Conv.(N.S.) 18 (C. T. Emery). This meant that he was no longer liable to an action for specific performance but could be sued for damages if the vendor perfected his title by the completion date. However this view was open to strong objections and has now been doubted: see *Pips (Leisure Productions) Ltd v. Walton, supra*, at 423–425; (1992) 108 L.Q.R. 280 at 301–313 (C.H.).

[2] *Stevens v. Adamson* (1818) 2 Stark. 422; *Peyman v. Lanjani, supra*, at 497.

[3] *Pips (Leisure Productions) Ltd v. Walton, supra*, at 424.

[4] *Dyer v. Hargrave* (1805) 10 Ves. 505 at 507; *Rutherford v. Acton-Adams* [1915] A.C. 866 at 869, 870. See [1981] C.L.J. 47 at 51; [1992] C.L.J. 263 and 270 (C.H.); *post*, para. 12–117. Obviously no question of abatement arises in respect of a removable defect which is discharged on or before completion.

[5] *Ante*, para. 12–065.

[6] *Re Puckett and Smith's Contract* [1902] 2 Ch. 258. Such a condition usually provides for compensation to be payable where there is an error, omission or misdescription. In cases where the non-disclosure is insubstantial, the vendor may enforce the contract subject to payment of compensation: *Re Belcham and Gawley's Contract* [1930] 1 Ch. 56.

[7] See *Heywood v. Mallalieu* (1883) 25 Ch.D. 357. For a modern example, see Standard Conditions of Sale (3rd ed.), c. 3.1.

defect in title of which he knew or ought to have known,[8] as where the defect is one which he ought to have discovered when he acquired the land.[9]

(d) Non-disclosure and misrepresentation. Mere non-disclosure of a defect **12–071** in title does not constitute a misrepresentation.[10] However, "suppression of the truth may contain a suggestion of falsity",[11] and a vendor may be liable to a purchaser for misrepresentation if his failure to disclose a latent defect in title misleads the latter.[12] Thus a negative answer to a precontractual inquiry as to the existence of any boundary disputes was held to be a misrepresentation where the vendor failed to disclose a long-standing boundary dispute which he erroneously believed to have been settled.[13]

The distinction between non-disclosure and misrepresentation has not always been clearly drawn. This has happened largely because of the now discredited use of the terminology of "rescission" in cases where one party to a contract treated it as discharged by the other's breach[14] rather than confining it to situations where the contract was rescinded *ab initio* for fraud or misrepresentation.[15]

2. Duty to prove good title. "In the absence of express stipulation to the **12–072** contrary . . . , a contract for the sale of land in fee simple obliges the vendor to make a good title to the whole legal and equitable interest in the freehold free from encumbrances."[16] This obligation is subject to two qualifications.

---

[8] *Edwards v. Wickwar* (1865) L.R. 1 Eq. 68 at 70; *Nottingham Patent Brick and Tile Co. v. Butler* (1885) 15 Q.B.D. 261 at 271; (1886) 16 Q.B.D. 778 at 786; *Re Turpin and Ahern's Contract* [1905] 1 I.R. 85 at 103; *Becker v. Partridge* [1966] 2 All E.R. 266 at 271 (a fuller report than [1966] 2 Q.B. 155); *Rignall Developments Ltd v. Halil* [1988] Ch. 190 at 197; *William Sindall Plc v. Cambridgeshire C.C.* [1994] 1 W.L.R. 1016 at 1023. See [1992] C.L.J. 263 at 298–305 (C.H.). For a case that is inconsistent with this principle and must be open to doubt, see *Beyfus v. Lodge* [1925] Ch. 350.

[9] *Becker v. Partridge, supra.*

[10] For a clear statement of the interrelationship between non-disclosure and misrepresentation, see *Atlantic Estates Plc v. Ezekiel* [1991] 2 E.G.L.R. 202 at 203.

[11] *McKeown v. Boudard Peveril Gear Co. Ltd* (1896) 74 L.T. 712 at 713, *per* Rigby L.J.

[12] Similar issues have arisen in relation to proof of title. Thus a condition of sale that required a purchaser to assume some fact as to the devolution of the vendor's title constituted an implied representation that the vendor knew nothing to make that fact untrue: *Re Banister* (1879) 12 Ch.D. 131 at 146, 147. The effect in that case was that the vendor could not rely on the condition of sale and had to prove his title in the usual way.

[13] *Walker v. Boyle* [1982] 1 W.L.R. 495. The existence of a boundary dispute makes the title doubtful rather than positively bad. However, a court will not force a purchaser to buy a law suit: *Nottingham Patent Brick and Tile Co. v. Butler* (1886) 16 Q.B.D. 778 at 789; *post*, paras 12–073, 12–116.

[14] *Post,* para. 12–106.

[15] For cases of non-disclosure where "rescission" was used in the now-discredited sense see, *e.g. Re Haedicke and Lipski's Contract* [1901] 2 Ch. 666; *Re Banister, supra*; *Becker v. Partridge, supra*. Prior to the abolition by L.P.(M.P.)A. 1989, s.3, of the Rule in *Bain v. Fothergill* (1874) L.R. 7 H.L. 158 (*post*, para. 12–103), which limited the damages which a vendor had to pay when, without fault on his part, he was unable to show title, there was little difference in effect in many cases between rescission *ab initio* and termination for breach. In either case the purchaser recovered his deposit and his conveyancing costs: see J. T. Farrand, *Contract and Conveyance* (4th ed.), p. 210.

[16] *Leominster Properties Ltd v. Broadway Finance Ltd* (1981) 42 P. & C.R. 372 at 380, *per* Slade J. See too *Re Ossemsley's Estates Ltd* [1937] 3 All E.R. 774 at 778.

The purchaser takes the land subject to irremovable defects in title which are either patent[17] or of which he knew when he contracted.[18] The manner in which a vendor of land discharges that obligation and proves that he has a good title to it depends upon whether the title to the property is registered or unregistered. With compulsory registration of title now applicable to the whole of England and Wales,[19] the latter method is rapidly decreasing in importance. It is estimated that two-thirds of all titles had been registered by the end of 1992 and that 90 per cent will be by the year 2000.[20]

12–073   (a) *Gradations of title.* Before examining these two methods of deducing title, something must be said as to the different gradations of title.[21] These cannot be measured or even defined precisely but are matters of degree. A *good title* is one which is free from incumbrances and which can be proved in the manner required by law. Such a title can be forced on an unwilling purchaser[22] without the need for any special condition of sale.[23] A *good holding title* is strictly a bad title, but one which is in fact perfectly marketable. It is a title which is imperfect in some way, but the holding under which is unlikely to be challenged successfully, normally because any adverse claims have been barred by lapse of time. It has been said that such titles although bad from a conveyancer's perspective are nonetheless "good in a business man's point of view".[24] A *bad title* is anything else, and includes a situation where the vendor has no title to the property at all, or only title to some lesser estate than he contracted to sell, or where the land is subject to some substantial but undisclosed latent defect in title. A *doubtful* title is one which the vendor cannot prove with certainty to be good,[25] and which is therefore in law bad.[26] A title is not necessarily doubtful merely because a doubt is raised with regard to it. Commonly the doubt will relate to a blot which has been cured by lapse of time so that any adverse claims have been barred.[27] In such a case, a court will attempt to resolve the doubt[28] and "if the facts and circumstances of a case are so compelling to the mind of the court that the

---

[17] *Yandle & Sons v. Sutton* [1922] 2 Ch. 199 at 210; *ante*, para. 12–068.

[18] *Timmins v. Moreland Street Property Co. Ltd* [1958] Ch. 110 at 132; *post*.

[19] *Ante*, para. 5–001. See too L.R.A. 1925, ss.123, 123A (inserted by L.R.A. 1997, s.1); *ante*, paras 5–001, 6–014.

[20] *Completing the Land Register in England & Wales* (Land Registry Consultation Paper, 1992), p. 7; and information supplied by the Land Registry.

[21] See *Barclays Bank Plc v. Weeks Legg & Dean* [1999] Q.B. 309 at 324–326.

[22] *Pyrke v. Waddington* (1852) 10 Hare 1 at 8.

[23] *Re Spollon and Long's Contract* [1936] Ch. 713 at 718. It appears that a "good marketable title" is not the same as a "good title" (or "open market title"), but is one that can be forced on the purchaser under *that particular* contract: *Barclays Bank Plc v. Weeks Legg & Dean, supra.*

[24] *Re Scott and Alvarez's Contract (No. 2)* [1895] 2 Ch. 603 at 613, *per* Lindley L.J.

[25] See, *e.g. Nottingham Patent Brick and Tile Co. v. Butler* (1886) 16 Q.B.D. 778 (title depended on whether the vendor had taken free of certain restrictive covenants when he acquired the land because he was a purchaser without notice).

[26] Such a title may in the end prove to be good, but it will be treated as bad until such proof is forthcoming: see, *e.g. Rignall Developments Ltd v. Halil* [1988] Ch. 190.

[27] See, *e.g. Re Atkinson and Horsell's Contract* [1912] 2 Ch. 1.

[28] See [1992] C.L.J. 263 at 291, 292 (C.H.).

court concludes beyond reasonable doubt that the purchaser will not be at risk of a successful assertion against him of the incumbrance, the court should declare in favour of a good title shown".[29]

(b) Unregistered title

(1) PROOF OF TITLE. Title to unregistered land is deduced by exhibiting to the purchaser the records of past transactions in the land, *e.g.* sales, mortgages and grants of probate, and by proving other relevant events such as deaths. This procedure has two main purposes: to persuade the purchaser that the vendor owns the land; and to give the purchaser his opportunity to inquire about the existence of equitable interests by which, if he made no inquiries, he would be bound. For the first purpose the vendor's title deeds are merely evidence; it is possible that owing to fraud, forgery or mistake he is not really the true owner, so that the purchaser will not obtain a good title.[30] For the second purpose the proof of title is conclusive: if the purchaser has made all reasonable inquiries and found nothing, he is safe from all equitable interests except such as are registered.[31] **12–074**

For the purpose of proving title the parties may agree on as much, or as little, disclosure of documents as they wish. For the purpose of searching for equities the purchaser is required to search back for a certain period. If he fails to do so, he has constructive notice of anything he would have discovered by doing so.[32]

(2) FIFTEEN YEARS' TITLE. If there is no agreement to the contrary, the period is now at least 15 years under the Law of Property Act 1969.[33] There are special rules in the case of leases, which are explained elsewhere.[34] The period is "at least" 15 years because the title must start from a document known as a good root of title, and it will only be by chance that such a document amongst the title deeds will be exactly 15 years old. Normally therefore only a document that is more than 15 years old will suffice. **12–075**

The period for which title has to be shown has been steadily reduced over the last 120 years,[35] largely without jeopardy to purchasers. That this has occurred is attributable to two main factors. The first is the reduction in the period of limitation. In most cases, title to land will be barred by 12 years' adverse possession.[36] The second factor is the simplification of conveyancing

---

[29] *M.E.P.C. Ltd v. Christian-Edwards* [1981] A.C. 205 at 220, *per* Lord Russell of Killowen. In that case, an unfulfilled sale contract of 1912 was held to have been necessarily abandoned, and the title therefore good.

[30] For relatives titles and "true owners", see *ante*, para. 3–122.

[31] See *ante*, paras 4–057, 5–018.

[32] *Ante*, para. 5–022.

[33] s.23.

[34] *Post*, para. 14–295.

[35] Prior to the enactment of the Vendor and Purchaser Act 1874, s.2, title was deduced for at least 60 years according to the custom of conveyancers. That Act reduced the period to 40 years, and it was further reduced to 30 years by L.P.A. 1925, s.44(1).

[36] *Post*, chap. 20. There has been a direct link between the limitation period and the period for which title has to be deduced. See *post*, para. 21–001.

that has followed the property legislation of 1925. It is noteworthy that although the reduction of the period of title to 15 years was accompanied by the scheme, explained earlier, for compensation purchasers affected by registered land charges which they could not discover from the title shown,[37] only two successful claims have been made.[38]

12–076 (3) GOOD ROOT OF TITLE. A good root of title is a document which describes the land sufficiently to identify it, which shows a disposition of the whole legal and equitable interest contracted to be sold, and which contains nothing to throw any doubt on the title.[39] Examples of documents which commonly serve as roots of title are—

(i) a conveyance on sale;

(ii) a legal mortgage[40];

(iii) an assent by a personal representative made after 1925 (after 1925 devises of land take effect not by force of the will but by force of the personal representatives' assent or conveyance,[41] which should describe the property[42]); and

(iv) a voluntary conveyance.[43]

Examples of documents which will not serve as roots of title on a sale of the fee simple are—

(i) a will taking effect after 1925[44];

(ii) a lease;

(iii) an equitable mortgage.

A squatter's title, *i.e.* a title obtained by adverse possession for 12 years or more,[45] must be proved from a good root of title, by showing the full title of the person from whom the squatter took the land and then proving the adverse possession.[46] This will often be difficult, and the vendor will generally try to

---

[37] L.P.A. 1969, s.25; *ante*, para. 5–113.
[38] The claims were for £20,000 and £375 respectively and each concerned a restrictive covenant.
[39] Williams V. & P. 124.
[40] Since 1925 a mortgage may no longer be made by a conveyance in fee simple (*post*, para. 19–019) and such a mortgage is not therefore in law a good root of title, though it may be accepted in practice.
[41] *Ante*, para. 11–126. An assent under seal by a person with no power to make an assent takes effect as a conveyance: *Re Stirrup's Contract* [1961] 1 W.L.R. 449.
[42] See examples given in Prideaux, vol. iii, 874 *et seq.*
[43] *Re Marsh and Earl Granville* (1883) 24 Ch.D. 11 at 24. See Williams V. & P. 127.
[44] The assent is now the effective disposition of the legal estate: *ante*, para. 11–126.
[45] See *ante*, para. 3–117.
[46] *Re Atkinson and Horsell's Contract* [1912] 2 Ch. 1; Williams V. & P. 122.

stipulate that the purchaser shall accept a title beginning with the adverse possession.

(4) DEDUCTION OF TITLE. Having established a good root of title of the **12–077** necessary age, the vendor must then prove all the later steps in the title which lead to himself. If the land has been in his ownership for more than 15 years there may be nothing more to prove. But more probably there will have been intervening transfers on sale, death or otherwise, which are necessary links in deducing the title to be proved. Statements in documents 20 years old or more are to be taken as sufficient evidence unless proved to be inaccurate.[47] If the proof is defective at any point, or if the title shown appears to be bad or doubtful,[48] The purchaser is entitled to terminate the contract on the ground that the vendor is unable to perform it.

(5) DEFECTS ANTERIOR TO THE ROOT OF TITLE. By statute, a purchaser may **12–078** not make any inquiry or objection about matters anterior to the root of title.[49] This provision, which is subject to certain exceptions,[50] has the same effect as a contractual condition in similar terms would have done.[51] Because it has this status, not only can it be ousted by an contrary provision in the contract,[52] but, in accordance with the general rule of equity,[53] it cannot be relied upon by a vendor to force on the purchase a pre-root defect in title of which the vendor knew or ought to have known.[54] In general, however, the purchaser must be content with a title starting with a good root in accordance with the contract. If he discovers *aliunde* (for example, from an accidental disclosure of older documents) that the earlier title is doubtful due to some technical defect, so that it is questionable whether the vendor is really owner at all, he must nevertheless take the property with the title as it stands.[55] This is consistent with the essential function of conditions of sale, which is "to protect the vendor from inquiries which he himself may be unable to satisfy, and against

---

[47] L.P.A. 1925, s.45(6).

[48] *e.g. Re Handman and Wilcox's Contract* [1902] 1 Ch. 599 (title dependent upon purchase without notice, insufficiently proved).

[49] L.P.A. 1925, s.45(1), replacing C.A. 1881, s.3(3), which confirmed earlier practice.

[50] L.P.A. 1925, s.45(1), proviso. This entitles the purchaser to see (i) any power of attorney under which an abstracted document is executed, (ii) any document creating a subsisting incumbrance, (iii) any document creating any limitation or trust by reference to which a disposition is made by a document appearing in the abstract (which is in fact confined to dispositions by trustees which are not overreaching dispositions).

[51] L.P.A. 1925, s.45(11); *Nottingham Patent Brick and Tile Co v. Butler* (1885) 15 Q.B.D. 261 at 272 (aff'd (1886) 16 Q.B.D. 778). See J. T. Farrand, *Contract and Conveyance* (4th ed.), p. 99; *Barnsley's Conveyancing Law and Practice* (4th ed.), pp. 27, 278; [1992] C.L.J. 263 at 303 (C.H.).

[52] L.P.A. 1925, s.45(10), proviso.

[53] *Ante*, para. 12–070.

[54] *Becker v. Partridge* [1966] 2 All E.R. 266. This limitation is necessarily preserved in relation to L.P.A. 1925, s.45(1) by s.45(11).

[55] See *Re Scott and Alvarez's Contract (No. 1)* [1895] 1 Ch. 596, where specific performance was decreed, so removing the doubt expressed in *Re National Provincial Bank and Marsh* [1895] 1 Ch. 190 at 192.

objections which he cannot explain away".[56] If, however, the purchaser can prove that the title is wholly bad, as where the vendor has no title at all to the land or where the property is subject to some undisclosed but irremovable latent incumbrance of a substantial character,[57] then specific performance will not be decreed against him.[58] This is because the court will not force a purchaser to take a title that will expose him to an immediate law suit.[59] However, unless the vendor knew or ought to have known of the defect, he will be able to rely upon the statutory provision that the purchaser is precluded from making any inquiry or objection as to matters before the root of title.[60] The purchaser will therefore be in breach of contract and the vendor may both forfeit his deposit[61] and sue him for damages.[62] The measure of damages will be the difference between the contract price and the market value of the land subject to the defect in title on the date on which the purchaser refuses to complete.[63] It follows therefore that the worse the vendor's title is, the greater the damages will be. The result has been acknowledged to be unsatisfactory,[64] and Parliament has attempted to ameliorate the position by providing that where a court refuses to grant specific performance, or in any action for the return of a deposit, it may, if it thinks fit, order the repayment of any deposit.[65] The weakness of this provision is that it does not bar the vendor's action against the purchaser for damages.[66] The court is therefore unlikely in practice to order the return of any deposit except in a case where its value exceeds the vendor's claim for damages.[67]

12–079   (6) AGREEMENT NOT TO INVESTIGATE. If a purchaser expressly agrees not to question the earlier title, or some intermediate step in the title to be shown

---

[56] *Edwards v. Wickwar* (1865) L.R. 1 Eq. 68 at 70, *per* Page Wood V.-C. See too *Re Sandbach and Edmondson's Contract* [1891] 1 Ch. 99.

[57] See *ante*, para. 12–068.

[58] *Re Scott and Alvarez's Contract (No. 2)* [1895] 2 Ch. 603, where fresh evidence turned a doubt as to the title into a certainty that it was bad.

[59] *ibid.*, at 613; *Pyrke v. Waddingham* (1852) 10 Hare 1 at 8; *Re Nichols' & Von Joel's Contract* [1910] 1 Ch. 43 at 46. For this rule, see [1990] C.L.J. 263 at 291 (C.H.); and *post*, para. 12–116.

[60] L.P.A. 1925, s.45(1), *supra.*

[61] *Re Scott and Alvarez's Contract (No. 2), supra.* For deposits, see *post*, para. 12–107.

[62] There is no reported case in which this has occurred, but it appears to be correct in principle. Although L.P.A. 1925, s.45(11) protects a purchaser against specific performance in any case in which it would not have been decreed in relation to a contract which contained a term similar to that found in s.45(1), it does not protect him against a damages claim: see J. T. Farrand, *Contract and Conveyance* (4th ed.), p. 99; *Barnsley's Conveyancing Law and Practice* (4th ed.), p. 278.

[63] See *Williams Bros v. E. T. Agius Ltd* [1914] A.C. 510.

[64] *Re Scott and Alvarez's Contract (No. 2), supra*, at 614.

[65] L.P.A. 1925, s.49(2). Although the sub-section was apparently passed to deal with this situation (see Wolst. & C, i, 125), its application is not confined to it: see *post*, para. 12–111.

[66] *Dimsdale Developments (South East) Ltd v. De Haan* (1983) 47 P. & C.R. 1. Compare the New South Wales Conveyancing Act 1919, s.55(1), which not only gives a purchaser the right to recover his deposit in a case in which specific performance is refused against him, but relieves him of any liability under the contract "whether at law or in equity". See [1984] C.L.J. 134 at 169–171 (C.H.).

[67] As was the case in *Dimsdale Developments (South East) Ltd v. De Haan, supra.*

under the contract, his position is similar to that outlined above in respect of pre-root defects in title. If it turns out that the vendor's title is bad owing to that part of the title into which he has agreed not to inquire—

(i) the vendor may rely upon the condition limiting his obligation unless he knew or ought to have known of the flaw in the title[68];

(ii) the court will not decree specific performance against the purchaser if to do so would expose him to a lawsuit[69]; and

(iii) the purchaser will be in breach of contract[70] and as such, will be liable both to forfeit any deposit that he has paid[71] and to pay damages to the vendor for his loss of bargain.

Thus the purchaser, by imprudently agreeing to accept the title in some respect unproved, has in effect become the vendor's insurer.

(7) FREEDOM FROM INCUMBRANCES. It has already been explained that a **12–080** good title means a title free from all incumbrances except those which are patent or are known to the purchaser at the time of contracting.[72] The term "incumbrances" covers all subsisting third party rights such as leases,[73] rentcharges, mortgages, easements and restrictive covenants.[74] It also includes statutory liabilities, if they are not merely potential[75] or imposed on property (or a particular class of property) generally.[76] Parliament has now expressly

---

[68] *Edwards v. Wickwar* (1865) L.R. 1 Eq. 68; *Else v. Else* (1872) L.R. 13 Eq. 196; *Re Marsh and Earl Granville* (1883) 24 Ch.D. 11.

[69] *Ante*, para. 12–078.

[70] *Re Scott and Alvarez's Contract (No. 2), supra*, at 612. This is because an express condition which prohibits the purchaser from raising objections (rather than merely exempting the vendor from answering them) amounts to an agreement that he will take the whole risk of the title turning out bad on account of the matters mentioned: *ibid.*

[71] Subject to the court's discretion under L.P.A. 1925, s.49(2) to order its repayment: *supra.*

[72] *Ante*, para. 12–067.

[73] Though see *District Bank Ltd v. Webb* [1958] 1 W.L.R. 148. The meaning of "incumbrance" can vary with the circumstances: see *Belvedere Court Management Ltd v. Frogmore Developments Ltd* [1997] Q.B. 858 at 877.

[74] It has been held that the service of a notice under a rent review clause in a lease is a defect in title because it may lead to a permanent alteration in the rights of the lessor and lessee: *F & B Entertainment Ltd v. Leisure Enterprises Ltd* [1976] 2 E.G.L.R. 76 at 79. However, the risk that a landlord may operate a break clause in a lease is not a defect in title: *Aslan v. Berkeley House Properties Ltd* [1990] 2 E.G.L.R. 202.

[75] *Re Allen and Driscoll's Contract* [1904] 2 Ch. 226 (street paving); *Re Farrer and Gilbert's Contract* [1914] 1 Ch. 125 (land improvement rentcharge not effective until resolution by local authority); *Re Forsey and Hollebone's Contract* [1927] 2 Ch. 379 (resolution by local authority to prepare a town planning scheme, held no incumbrance); and see *Manning v. Turner* [1957] 1 W.L.R. 91 (potential liability to estate duty: termination held valid).

[76] Such as rates or local taxes: see, *e.g. Barraud v. Archer* (1831) 9 L.J.Ch.(O.S.) 173 (liability to drainage taxes).

endorsed this definition.[77] There is some doubt as to whether statutory restrictions upon the user of property should be regarded as defects in title. On some occasions they have been so treated, but in each case the restriction placed the title at risk so that the property was liable either to demolition or to compulsory purchase.[78] However, as the fitness of the property for the purpose for which the purchaser intends it is generally a matter for him, such restrictions will not usually be regarded as a defect in title.[79] It follows that it is the purchaser and not the vendor who bears the risk that they may be imposed between contract and completion.[80] It should be noted that even though a statutory restriction on user may not be a defect in title, it may sometimes prevent the vendor from giving vacant possession on completion.[81]

Because the vendor must convey the land free from incumbrances, the purchaser may refuse to complete if any incumbrance comes to light or arises which he has not agreed to accept, and which will bind him if he takes the land.[82] Although there is some authority which suggests that a statutory liability must be borne by a purchaser if it attaches to the property after the date of the contract, this seems wrong in principle.[83] If a liability would have been an incumbrance if it had arisen before the contract, the same should be true if it arises in the period between contract and completion.[84] If the vendor has made title in accordance with the contract but completion is then delayed for reasons for which he is not to blame, the purchaser may not object to the

---

[77] See L.P.(M.P.)A. 1994, s.3(2), which was based upon this passage in the previous edition of this work at p. 611; HL Paper 62 (Session 1993–94), p. 28.

[78] *Sidney v. Buddery* (1949) 1 P. & C.R. 34; *Sakkas v. Donford* (1982) 46 P. & C.R. 46. It is suggested that the principle was correctly stated in *Harris v. Weaver* [1980] 2 N.Z.L.R 437 at 439, where Chilwell J. observed that planning restrictions "are matters of quality not of title unless they prevent the giving of title". *cf. James Macara Ltd v. Barclay* [1945] K.B. 148 where a vendor was in breach of his obligation to give vacant possession because the Crown had served a notice of requisition in respect of the premises: see *post*, para. 12–089.

[79] *Edler v. Auerbach* [1950] 1 K.B. 359 at 374; *Hill v. Harris* [1965] 2 Q.B. 601; *Gosling v. Anderson* (1971) 220 E.G. 1117 (revs'd on appeal on other grounds: (1972) 223 E.G. 1743). The vendor may of course be liable for misrepresentation if prior to contracting he leads the purchaser to believe that the property may be used for the purpose intended when this is not the case: *Laurence v. Lexourt Holdings Ltd* [1978] 1 W.L.R. 1128.

[80] *Amalgamated Investment & Property Co. Ltd v. John Walker & Sons Ltd* [1977] 1 W.L.R. 164 (building listed as being of architectural or historic interest). *cf. Aquis Estates Ltd v. Minton* [1975] 1 W.L.R. 1452.

[81] See *Topfell Ltd v. Galley Properties Ltd* [1979] 1 W.L.R. 446; *post*, para. 12–089.

[82] Objection may be made to incumbrances created between contract and completion even though the purchaser could have protected himself against them by registering his estate contract, for he is under no duty to register: *ante*, para. 5–122.

[83] *Re Farrer and Gilbert's Contract* [1914] 1 Ch. 125; *Hillingdon Estates Co. v. Stonefield Estates Ltd* [1952] Ch. 627. In the former case the point was conceded. In the latter, the purchaser would have borne the risk of the liability for other reasons: see *infra*. There is no doubt that a vendor will be in breach of his closely analogous obligation to give vacant possession if a statutory liability is imposed between contract and completion that precludes the giving of such possession: *Cook v. Taylor* [1942] Ch. 349; *James Macara Ltd v. Barclay* [1945] K.B. 148 (requisitioning notices); *Wroth v. Tyler* [1974] Ch. 30 (wife's statutory rights of occupation).

[84] In practice the parties often agree that the purchaser should bear the cost of compliance with any statutory liabilities which may arise between contract and completion: see Standard Conditions of Sale (3rd ed.), c. 3.1.4.

title on the ground of a defect in title that arose during the period of delay.[85]

A purchaser's concern is only with those incumbrances which are irremovable and will not be discharged on completion, such as restrictive covenants and easements. Although technically defects in title, incumbrances which are removable by the vendor as of right are regarded as "matters of conveyance" rather than matters of title and the vendor has until completion to secure their discharge.[86] Examples of matters of conveyance include—

(i) a mortgage that will be discharged on completion[87];

(ii) on the sale of settled land or land held upon a trust of land, the appointment of a co-trustee so that a valid receipt for the proceeds of sale can be given[88]; and

(iii) anomalously, on a sale of leasehold property, the obtaining of the landlord's licence to assign[89] where the terms of the lease require it.[90]

(8) WAIVER. A purchaser under an open contract is held to have waived his right to object to an incumbrance if (i) he knew that it was irremovable, and (ii) despite this, he contracted to purchase the property or took some other step inconsistent with his right to terminate the contract, such as entering into possession[91] or exercising some other right under the contract.[92] **12–081**

(9) LAND CHARGES. A serious stumbling-block was created in 1927 by the decision in *Re Forsey and Hollebone's Contract*[93] that an irremovable land charge (*e.g.* a restrictive covenant created since 1925) or a local land charge, unknown to the purchaser but already registered at the time of the contract, had to be accepted under the above doctrine, since registration is by statute **12–082**

---

[85] *Hillingdon Estates Co. v. Stonefield Estates Ltd, supra*; A. J. Oakley, *Constructive Trusts* (3rd ed.), p. 296.

[86] See, *e.g. Leominster Properties Ltd v. Broadway Finance Ltd* (1981) 42 P. & C.R. 372 at 380.

[87] *ibid.* Similarly, the concurrence of a mortgagee to a sale where the mortgage is immediately redeemable is a matter of conveyance: *Re Priestley's Contract* [1947] Ch. 469 at 477.

[88] *Hatten v. Russell* (1888) 38 Ch.D. 334.

[89] For the covenant against assigning without the landlord's consent, see *post*, para. 14–259.

[90] *Ellis v. Rogers* (1885) 29 Ch.D. 661. To treat the obtaining of the licence to assign as a matter of conveyance is anomalous because the vendor cannot compel the landlord to assent to the assignment. The reason for the anomaly is a practical one. Until the tenant contracts to assign, the landlord may not know the identity of the assignee and is not therefore in a position to give or withhold his consent. In practice a contract to sell a lease that is subject to this requirement is normally made conditional upon the obtaining of the landlord's consent: see *ante*, para. 12–008.

[91] *Re Gloag and Miller's Contract* (1883) 23 Ch.D. 320 at 327 (where a distinction is drawn between this situation and the case where the vendor expressly contracts to give a good title free from incumbrances, or where the objection to title is removable); *Ellis v. Rogers* (1888) 29 Ch.D. 61; *McGrory v. Aldersdale Estates Co.* [1918] A.C. 503. As to the question, there left unresolved, whether the right to a good title is founded on contract or on the general law, see *ante*, para. 12–001.

[92] *Aquis Estates Ltd v. Minton* [1975] 1 W.L.R. 1452.

[93] [1927] 2 Ch. 379 (Eve J.).

"deemed to constitute actual notice . . . to all persons and for all purposes connected with the land affected".[94] This violated conveyancing principles, since the proper time for searching the register is between contract and completion[95]; and in any case, as regards land charges, the purchaser could not usually make a full search before contract since he would not then know the names of previous owners on the title.[96] Nor did the decision appear to be right in law, since willingness to waive objection to the incumbrance could hardly be imputed to a purchaser who had no knowledge of it at all. Indeed this equation of a statutory form of notice with the knowledge required for waiver has been described as "deeply suspect",[97] because it was not the purpose of the statutory notice to affect the relationship between vendors and purchasers but to protect third party rights.[98] The decision led to an inconvenient change in conveyancing practice by which purchasers were (in effect) compelled to investigate title prior to the exchange of contracts, something that was impracticable in cases of sales by auction.[99] Fortunately two developments have occurred which have restored the law to what it was thought to be before 1927. First, the Law of Property Act 1969 removed the difficulty as regards land charges (but not local land charges).[1] Any question of the purchaser's knowledge of a registered land charge is to be determined by reference to his actual knowledge[2] and without regard to the statutory "deemed" notice. Furthermore, any stipulation to the contrary, or which restricts the purchaser's remedies in respect of such a charge is void.[3] Secondly, *Re Forsey and Hollebone's Contract*[4] has probably now received its quietus as a result of a subsequent case concerned with local land charges.[5] The earlier decision was doubted and its reasoning was criticised on the grounds set out in this paragraph.[6] A purchaser will probably now take subject to a local land charge which amounts to a defect in title only when he actually knows of it at the time of contracting.

---

[94] L.P.A. 1925, s.198(1). For notice by registration, see *ante*, para. 5–109.

[95] See *Re White and Smith's Contract* [1896] 1 Ch. 637. Until contracts have been exchanged, the purchaser has of course no right to see the vendor's title, though in practice he is usually permitted to do so.

[96] For these and other difficulties occasioned by the decision, see *Rignall Developments Ltd v. Halil* [1988] Ch. 190 at 201.

[97] *Rignall Developments Ltd v. Halil*, *supra*, at 201, *per* Millett J.

[98] *ibid.*, at 202.

[99] *ibid.*, at 201.

[1] s.24, which applies to contracts for the sale of unregistered land made after 1969. This reform was recommended by the Committee on Land Charges (1956) Cmd. 9825. For a fuller discussion, see [1954] C.L.J. 89 (H.W.R.W.); and contrast *Coles v. White City (Manchester) Greyhound Association Ltd* (1928) 45 T.L.R. 125, 230, noted *ante*, para. 5–109, n. 36.

[2] Or that of his counsel, solicitor or other agent: s.24(4).

[3] s.24(2).

[4] [1927] 2 Ch. 379.

[5] *Rignall Developments Ltd v. Halil*, *supra*; [1987] Conv. 291 (C.H.). The charge was a potential liability to repay an improvement grant. For local land charges, see *ante*, para. 5–132.

[6] Millett J. chose to distinguish *Re Forsey and Hollebone's Contract* on its facts rather than refuse to follow it: [1988] Ch. 190 at 202, 203.

(10) EXPRESS TERMS. It is only where the contract is open as to the title that **12–083** waiver can be implied from the making of the contract. If the vendor expressly contracts to show, for example, "a valid title"[7] or "a good marketable title",[8] he must carry out his promise and show a title entirely free from incumbrances. Even if the property is subject to an irremovable incumbrance which is patent or of which the purchaser knows, he is entitled to insist that the vendor should show a good title.[9] The vendor is in such circumstances obliged to find some means of removing the incumbrance by the completion date, *e.g.* by securing its release. But if, having discovered irremovable incumbrances, he takes some step indicating a desire to proceed (such as going into possession of the property or exercising some right conferred by the contract) without reserving his rights as to the title, this may amount to a waiver even of an express promise of a clear title.[10] The essence of the matter is that no waiver can be implied merely from the purchaser's entering into the contract if that is inconsistent with the express terms of the contract.[11]

Here again, it was held that the rule was different where the incumbrance was registered as a land charge or local land charge, and that even a sale "free from incumbrances" was made subject to incumbrances deemed to be known to the purchaser because of registration prior to the contract.[12] As explained above, this pitfall has now been removed by statute as regards land charges[13] and (probably) by judicial decision in relation to local land charges.[14]

(c) Registered title

(1) PROOF OF TITLE. The system of registration of title "eliminates the need **12–084** for the deduction by the vendor and the examination by the purchaser of proof of ownership originating from a satisfactory root of title at least 15 years old".[15] Instead the register provides proof of the title. As the register is now a public document,[16] a purchaser may search it without first obtaining the authority of the vendor (which was formerly required).[17] However, the Land Registration Act 1925 does make provision as to the proof which a purchaser can require from a vendor of registered land.[18]

---

[7] *Re Gloag and Miller's Contract* (1883) 23 Ch.D. 320.

[8] *Cato v. Thompson* (1882) 9 Q.B.D. 616.

[9] *Re Gloag and Miller's Contract, supra*, at 613; *McGrory v. Alderdale Estate Co. Ltd* [1918] A.C. 503 at 508.

[10] *Re Gloag and Miller's Contract, supra*; *Aquis Estates Ltd v. Minton* [1975] 1 W.L.R. 1452.

[11] *Re Gloag and Miller's Contract, supra*, at 327.

[12] *Re Forsey and Hollebone's Contract* [1927] 2 Ch. 379 at 387. See [1954] C.L.J. 89, 102, 103 (H.W.R.W.)

[13] L.P.A. 1969, s.24.

[14] *Rignall Developments Ltd v. Halil* [1988] Ch. 190; *ante*, para. 12–082.

[15] Ruoff & Roper, 2–01.

[16] L.R.A. 1925, s.112(1) (as substituted by L.R.A. 1988, s.1(1)); *ante*, para. 6–002.

[17] In cases of sale by private treaty, an intending purchaser will in practice usually search the register prior to contracting.

[18] The Law Commission and Land Registry have recommended the repeal of these provisions: (1998) Law Com. No. 254, paras 11.47, 11.48.

First, on a sale or other disposition of registered land to a purchaser other than a lessee[19] or chargee, the vendor must[20] at his own expense furnish the purchaser with a copy of—

    (i) the subsisting entries on the register;

    (ii) any filed plans; and

    (iii) copies or abstracts of any document (or parts of documents) noted on the register so far as they affect the land;

but not of charges or incumbrances which are to be discharged or overridden at or prior to completion.[21] This obligation, which cannot be ousted by any stipulation to the contrary,[22] is normally discharged by provision of office copies of the relevant matters,[23] though it is not settled whether the purchaser has a statutory right to evidence in this form.[24]

12–085   Secondly, the vendor is at his own expense also required to furnish the purchaser with copies, abstracts and evidence (if any) in respect of—

    (a) subsisting rights and interests appurtenant to the registered land as to which the register is not conclusive, such as the benefit of overriding interests; and

    (b) matters excepted from the effect of registration, such as the burden of overriding interests or evidence of defects in title where property is registered with a title that is less than absolute: these must be deduced in the same manner as they are where title is unregistered.[25]

This obligation can be ousted by an expression of contrary intention.[26] Except as stipulated by these two provisions and notwithstanding any agreement to the contrary, the vendor cannot be required to furnish the purchaser with any abstract or other written evidence of title, or any copy or abstract of the land

---

[19] Contracts to grant leases of registered land are subject to the same rules as to proof of title as are contracts in respect of unregistered land: see Ruoff & Roper, 21–05; *post*, para. 14–297. An intending lessor is under no statutory obligation as to the production of documents of title. An intending assignee of a lease is however entitled to see the lease that is to be assigned to him.

[20] Only "if required"—but it is inconceivable that a purchaser would not so require: Ruoff & Roper, 17–04.

[21] L.R.A. 1925, s.110(1). However, where the consideration is £1,000 or less, the purchaser must bear the costs: *ibid.*, s.110(1) proviso (a).

[22] *ibid.*, s.110(1).

[23] See Standard Conditions of Sale (3rd ed.), c. 4.2.1; *Wood v. Berkeley Homes (Sussex) Ltd* (1992) 64 P. & C.R. 311.

[24] See *Wood v. Berkeley Homes (Sussex) Ltd, supra*, at 321. *cf.* L.R.A. 1925, s.113.

[25] L.R.A. 1925, s.110(2). For overriding interests, see *ante*, para. 6–036. For titles other than absolute titles, see *ante*, paras 6–024–6–026.

[26] *ibid.*, s.110(2).

certificate, or of any charge certificate.[27] As between vendor and purchaser all filed documents are deemed to be both complete and correct, and any person who suffers loss by reason of any error or omission in them is entitled to indemnity from the Land Registry.[28] If the vendor is not himself registered as proprietor of the land or of the charge which gives him a power of sale over the land, he may be required by the purchaser, at his own expense and regardless of any contrary stipulation,[29] to procure the registration of himself as proprietor of the land or of the charge, or, in the alternative, to procure a disposition from the proprietor to the purchaser.[30] It is unclear whether the purchaser is entitled to decide which of these two alternatives should be met, or whether the choice lies with the vendor.[31]

(2) WHERE GROUNDS FOR RECTIFICATION EXIST. In the usual case where a **12–086** vendor is registered with absolute title, there is no root of title and therefore no possibility of defects anterior to the root. This would suggest that the provisions of the Law of Property Act 1925 which restrict inquiries and objections to matters lying behind the root of title have no application in such a case.[32] One feature of registered title which has no equivalent in unregistered conveyancing but which is somewhat analogous to a pre-root defect in title, is the possibility that the court or registrar may rectify the register.[33] The power to rectify is discretionary. If a ground for rectification exists,[34] it must therefore make the title doubtful rather than positively bad because there can be no certainty that rectification will be ordered.[35] Such a title could not therefore be forced on a purchaser in the absence of full disclosure prior to contract of the matter in respect of which rectification might lie, unless it was insubstantial.

In certain circumstances the registrar is required to amend the register, as where a squatter can demonstrate that he has barred the title of the registered proprietor and is therefore entitled to be registered as proprietor.[36] Where such circumstances exist the title will of course be bad.

---

[27] *ibid.*, s.110(3). Although this subsection invalidates any stipulation requiring documents which are outside the categories listed in s.110(1) and (2), it does not affect conditions of sale which define the type of copy of documents within those subsections which is to be provided: *Wood v. Berkeley Homes (Sussex) Ltd, supra.*

[28] L.R.A. 1925, s.110(4); Ruoff & Roper, 17–04.

[29] *Walia v. Michael Naughton Ltd* [1985] 1 W.L.R. 1115 at 1122.

[30] L.R.A. 1925, s.110(5). The contract may properly impose a time-limit within which the purchaser can request the vendor to make title in this way. Such a provision will not be a "stipulation to the contrary": see *Urban Manor Ltd v. Sadiq* [1997] 1 W.L.R. 1016; [1998] C.L.J 26 (A. J. Oakley).

[31] See [1979] Conv. 1 at 2 (J. T. Farrand).

[32] L.P.A. 1925, s.45(1) refers to the title "before the time prescribed by law": see [1992] C.L.J. 263 at 303 (C.H.). The point is devoid of authority.

[33] *Ante*, para. 6–119.

[34] See L.R.A. 1925, s.82(1).

[35] In cases in which rectification is ordered, an indemnity will be payable to the proprietor if he suffers loss in consequence unless his claim is barred by lapse of time: see *ante*, paras 6–132 *et seq.*

[36] L.R.A. 1925, s.75(3); *ante*, para. 6–116.

12–087   (3) MINOR INTERESTS AND LOCAL LAND CHARGES. The Land Registration Act 1925 contains no provision analogous to that found in the Law of Property Act 1925 in relation to the registration of land charges in unregistered land,[37] by which the registration of a minor interest constitutes notice to all persons for all purposes. Where a minor interest is protected in the usual way by a notice, registration constitutes notice to every proprietor of the land burdened by the incumbrance and the persons deriving title under him.[38] There is therefore no prospect that a purchaser of registered land will be taken to contract with knowledge of any minor interest merely because of its registration.[39]

Local land charges take effect as overriding interests in registered land.[40] The registration of such a charge in the local land charges register therefore constitutes actual notice to all persons for all purposes under the provisions of the Law of Property Act 1925[41] whether the title is registered or unregistered. However, the erroneous nature of the decision in *Re Forsey and Hollebone's Contract*[42] has now been made plain[43] and it is unlikely that it will be followed. A purchaser of registered land will therefore be entitled to object to any local land charge constituting a defect in title which has not been disclosed prior to contract.

D. The Vendor must give Vacant Possession on Completion

12–088   *(a) The obligation.* Under an open contract, a vendor impliedly contracts to give vacant possession on completion.[44] This implication will be rebutted—

> (i) by an express stipulation to the contrary[45]; or
>
> (ii) if at the time of contracting, the property was subject to some irremovable incumbrance or other impediment to vacant possession which was either known to the purchaser or patent.[46]

The purchaser's knowledge of a removable impediment to vacant possession is irrelevant.[47] It is usual for the parties to provide expressly that vacant

---

[37] s.198; *ante*, paras 5–109, 12–082.
[38] L.R.A. 1925, ss.48(1), 49(1), 50(2).
[39] See *Re Stone and Saville's Contract* [1963] 1 W.L.R. 163.
[40] L.R.A. 1925, s.70(1)(i): *ante*, para. 6–065.
[41] s.198. For local land charges, see *ante*, para. 5–132.
[42] [1927] 2 Ch. 379; *ante*, para. 12–082.
[43] *Rignall Developments Ltd v. Halil* [1988] Ch. 190; *ante*, para. 12–082.
[44] *Cook v. Taylor* [1942] 2 All E.R. 85 at 87 (a better report than [1942] Ch. 349); *Midland Bank Ltd v. Farmpride Hatcheries Ltd* [1981] 2 E.G.L.R. 147 at 151. See generally [1988] Conv. 324, 400 (C.H.); [1991] Conv. 185 at 188 (D. G. Barnsley).
[45] *Midland Bank Ltd v. Farmpride Hatcheries Ltd, supra* at 151. *cf. Re Crosby's Contract* [1949] 1 All E.R. 830 (grant of option on terms that the grantee would accept "without objection" the vendor's title, held not to enable grantor to grant a lease prior to the exercise of the grant).
[46] *Cook v. Taylor, supra*, at 87. See too *Timmins v. Moreland Street Property Co. Ltd* [1958] Ch. 110 at 118, 119. *cf. Farrell v. Green* (1974) 232 E.G. 587 at 589 (which was decided *per incuriam* on this point).
[47] See *Norwich Union Life Insurance Society v. Preston* [1957] 1 W.L.R. 813.

possession shall be given on completion (if that is to be the case).[48] Such an express provision will prevail even if, to the purchaser's knowledge, the property is not vacant at the time of contract and the impediment is an irremovable incumbrance.[49] It will be apparent that the obligation to give vacant possession is closely analogous to the vendor's obligation to convey the land free from incumbrances and is subject to similar rules,[50] and in particular, those which govern the extent to which it can be modified by conditions of sale.[51]

(b) The substance of the obligation. The meaning of "vacant possession"   **12–089** can vary according to the context.[52] However, the existence of any impediment which substantially prevents a purchaser from obtaining the quality of possession for which he had contracted, will constitute a breach of the obligation.[53] These have been held to include—

    (i) the presence on the premises of persons who are:

        (a) lawfully in possession such as tenants or licensees[54] (but not those whose rights are less extensive, such as those who merely have a *profit à prendre* over the land[55]); or

        (b) on the land unlawfully, for although the contrary has been held,[56] the better view is that it is the duty of the vendor to evict trespassers[57];

    (ii) removable physical impediments to vacant possession which substantially interfere with the enjoyment of the property[58]; and

    (iii) legal impediments to the enjoyment of the property such as a notice to requisition the land,[59] an order restricting the number of persons who can occupy the land,[60] or a notice to enter served as

---

[48] See Standard Conditions of Sale (3rd ed.), Special Condition 5.
[49] *Hissett v. Reading Roofing Co. Ltd* [1969] 1 W.L.R. 1757; *Sharneyford Supplies Ltd v. Edge* [1987] Ch. 305 (lease of maggot farm). *A fortiori* where the impediment to vacant possession is removable: *Cumberland Consolidated Holdings Ltd v. Ireland* [1946] K.B. 264.
[50] See [1988] Conv. 324 at 331 (C.H.).
[51] See [1988] Conv. 400 (C.H.) where the authorities are discussed.
[52] *Topfell Ltd v. Galley Properties Ltd* [1979] 1 W.L.R. 446 at 449.
[53] See *Cumberland Consolidated Holdings Ltd v. Ireland, supra,* at 271; *Korogluyan v. Matheou* (1975) 30 P. & C.R. 309 at 316.
[54] *Beard v. Porter* [1948] 1 K.B. 321; *Sharneyford Supplies Ltd v. Edge, supra.*
[55] *Horton v. Kurzke* [1971] 1 W.L.R. 769 (agricultural grazing tenancy). In such circumstances the vendor may be in breach of his obligations to show a good title: *ibid.*
[56] *Sheikh v. O'Connor* [1987] 2 E.G.L.R. 269 (*obiter*); criticised [1988] Conv. 324 (C.H.); [1991] Conv. 185, 191, 192 (D. G. Barnsley).
[57] *Cumberland Consolidated Holdings Ltd v. Ireland, supra,* at 271 (*obiter*).
[58] *ibid.* (large quantities of rubbish including solidified cement bags left on the premises). *cf. Hynes v. Vaughan* (1985) 50 P. & C.R. 444 (suggesting that outdoor rubbish may be different).
[59] See *Cook v. Taylor* [1942] 2 All E.R. 85; *James Macara Ltd v. Barclay* [1945] K.B. 148 (which must be taken to have overruled *Re Winslow Hall Estates Co. and United Glass Bottle Manufacturers Ltd's Contract* [1941] Ch. 503, the facts of which were identical).
[60] *Topfell Ltd v. Galley Properties Ltd, supra.* See H.A. 1985, ss.352–355.

part of the process of compulsory acquisition by a local authority.[61]

Because the vendor's obligation to give vacant possession necessarily arises at the time for completion, it can be broken by a matter that arises at any time before that date whether before or after the parties contracted.[62]

12–090 *(c) Remedies.* The position of a vendor who is in breach of his obligation to give vacant possession is as follows.

(i) He will be unable to obtain specific performance of the contract of sale against the purchaser.[63] However he may have the contract specifically enforced against him by the purchaser, and have to pay compensation for the impediment to vacant possession.[64]

(ii) The purchaser may refuse to complete and may both recover any deposit that he has paid[65] and sue the vendor for damages for the loss of his bargain.[66]

(iii) If the purchaser does complete even though vacant possession is not given, he may recover as damages the sum necessary to place him in the position in which he would have been had the contract been performed. Where the impediment to vacant possession is irremovable (as where the property is let to a tenant), the measure will be the difference between the purchase price and the market price of the property subject to the impediment, plus any consequential loss.[67] Where it is possible to remove the impediment, the purchaser may recover the cost of so doing.[68]

(iv) The purchaser will be able to terminate the contract *even after completion has taken place*, provided that he does not affirm the contract.[69]

---

[61] *Korogluyan v. Matheou* (1975) 30 P. & C.R. 309. By contrast, where the notice served as part of the process of compulsory purchase does not confer on the acquiring authority an immediate right to possession, the vendor will still be able to give vacant possession: see *Hillingdon Estates Co. v. Stonefield Estates Ltd* [1952] Ch. 627 at 633 (a mere notice to treat made by a local authority under its compulsory purchase powers); *E. Johnson & Co. (Barbados) Ltd v. N.S.R. Ltd* [1997] A.C. 400 (notice of intended compulsory purchase which did not give the Crown a right to immediate possession).

[62] For cases in which the impediment to vacant possession arose between contract and completion, see *Cook v. Taylor, supra*; *James Macara Ltd v. Barclay, supra*; *Wroth v. Tyler* [1974] Ch. 30.

[63] *Cook v. Taylor, supra.*

[64] *Topfell Ltd v. Galley Properties Ltd* [1979] 1 W.L.R. 446. For specific performance with compensation, see *post*, para. 12–118.

[65] *Cook v. Taylor, supra.*

[66] *Engell v. Fitch* (1869) L.R. 4 Q.B. 659; *Sharneyford Supplies Ltd v. Edge* [1987] Ch. 305.

[67] *Beard v. Porter* [1948] 1 K.B. 321 (costs arising from purchase of another property held recoverable).

[68] *Cumberland Consolidated Holdings Ltd v. Ireland* [1946] K.B. 264 (cost of removing rubbish recoverable).

[69] *Gunatunga v. De Alwis* (1995) 72 P. & C.R. 161. The obligation to give vacant possession does not merge in the conveyance, but remains actionable after completion: *post*, para. 12–099.

E. Stipulations as to Time

1. The general rule

(a) The position prior to the Judicature Act 1873. At common law, time was **12–091** "of the essence of the contract".[70] If either party failed to complete on time, he was in breach and the other party could treat the contract as terminated. But in equity the position was different.[71] Although it had once been held that time could *never* be of the essence in equity,[72] this view did not prevail.[73] It came to be recognised that time might be of the essence of a contract in equity "by express stipulation between the parties,[74] by the nature of the property,[75] or by surrounding circumstances, showing the intention of the parties that the contract was to be completed within a limited time".[76] Mere delay in completion did not bar a suit for specific performance in the absence of laches,[77] unless a notice was served on the party in delay requiring him to complete within a reasonable time.[78] However, it was only in connection with specific performance that this indulgence was shown, and it did not deprive the other party of his right to claim damages for any loss occasioned by the breach.[79] Even in equity, a court might decree specific performance with compensation for loss caused by the defendant's delay.[80]

(b) The effect of the Judicature Act 1873. Since the Judicature Act 1873, the **12–092** equitable doctrine has prevailed:

> "Stipulations in a contract, as to time or otherwise, which according to the rules of equity are not deemed to be or to have become of the essence of the contract, are also construed and have effect at law in accordance with the same rules."[81]

In the period following the Act, this provision was taken to mean that a party could not terminate a contract on the ground of delay in performance in

---

[70] See, *e.g. Beamish v. Owens* (1846) 7 L.T.O.S. 187; *Parkin v. Thorold* (1852) 16 Beav. 59 at 65.

[71] For the history see *Equity and Contemporary Legal Developments* (ed. S. Goldstein), 829 at 860 (C.H.); [1992] Conv. 318 at 324 (C.H.).

[72] *Gregson v. Riddle* (1784) unrep.: see *Seton v. Slade* (1802) 7 Ves. 265 at 268.

[73] See *Lloyd v. Collett* (1793) 4 Ves. 689.

[74] *Seton v. Slade* (1802) 7 Ves. 265 at 270; *Levy v. Lindo* (1817) 3 Mer. 81 at 84.

[75] Because it was of a wasting or fluctuating character: *Hudson v. Temple* (1860) 30 L.J.Ch. 251 (sale of 24-year residue of lease); *XEY S.A. v. Abbey Life Assurance Co. Ltd* (1994) 69 P. & C.R. D5 (contract to grant six-year underlease); *Newman v. Rogers* (1793) 4 Bro. C.C. 391 (sale of reversion); *Machbryde v. Weeks* (1856) 22 Beav. 533 (sale of lease of mines and minerals).

[76] *Roberts v. Berry* (1853) 3 De G.M. & G. 284 at 291, *per* Turner L.J.

[77] *Harrington v. Wheeler* (1799) 4 Ves. 686.

[78] See *Taylor v. Brown* (1839) 2 Beav. 180; *Wells v. Maxwell* (1863) 8 L.T. 713 at 714.

[79] A court of equity would if need be issue a common injunction restraining proceedings at law. Prior to the Judicature Act 1873, there does not in fact appear to have been any reported example of a claim at law for damages for delay by a plaintiff against whom the defendant had obtained a decree of specific performance in Chancery.

[80] *Gedye v. Duke of Montrose* (1858) 26 Beav. 45.

[81] L.P.A. 1925, s.41, replacing J.A. 1873, s.25(7).

circumstances where equity would before the Act have decreed specific performance.[82] However, it is now clear that this provision "places no ban upon further development of the rules by judicial decision".[83] In contracts for the sale of land, it remains the case that time will not be of the essence except in the circumstances outlined below.

If a vendor or purchaser fails to complete on the due date[84] he will still be in breach of contract even though time is not of the essence. The other party may therefore recover damages for any loss which he has suffered.[85] Thus, where the purchaser needed the property for professional purposes, and her practice was injured by the vendor's delay in completion, she recovered damages for this and other expenses.[86] In another case, the sales of one house by A to B and of another by B to C were due for completion on the same day. A failed to complete, causing B to default. C recovered the cost of this temporary accommodation as damages from B.[87]

12–093   *(c) Where time is of the essence.* However, time will be regarded as the essence in a number of circumstances. Where this is the case, the consequences of failure to perform the obligation on time will depend upon the nature of the term broken.[88] In the case where there is a failure to complete a contract for the sale of land, the party not in default may treat the contract as terminated and sue the other for damages.[89]

12–094   (1) EXPRESS PROVISION. Time will be of the essence in relation to a particular term[90] where a contractual provision makes it so.[91] Time is not normally of the essence for the completion of contracts for the sale of land under the

---

[82] *Stickney v. Keeble* [1915] A.C. 386 at 417.

[83] *United Scientific Holdings Ltd v. Burnley B.C.* [1978] A.C. 904 at 927, *per* Lord Diplock.

[84] Where the contract is silent as to the completion date, "the law implies that completion is to take place within a reasonable time" having regard to the conveyancing steps that have to be carried out: *Johnson v. Humphrey* (1946) 174 L.T. 324 at 326, *per* Roxburgh J. This is so, even where the parties have left the date for future agreement: *Walters v. Roberts* (1980) 41 P. & C.R. 210 at 216.

[85] *Raineri v. Miles* [1981] A.C. 1050, approving (at 1084, 1094) the statement in the 4th edition of this book that "whether time is of the essence or not, a party who is actually injured by breach of a time stipulation can recover damages". The Standard Conditions of Sale (3rd ed.) make provision for compensation for delay in completion: c. 7.3, but this condition may be invalid as a penalty: *cf. Newbery v. Turngiant Ltd* (1991) 63 P. & C.R 458.

[86] *Phillips v. Lamdin* [1949] 2 K.B. 33.

[87] *Raineri v. Miles, supra* (B also recovered from A).

[88] See *Re Olympia & York Canary Wharf Ltd (No. 2)* [1993] B.C.C. 159 at 173.

[89] See, *e.g. Harold Wood Brick Co. Ltd v. Ferris* [1935] 2 K.B. 198. In such a case, the court will not decree specific performance at the behest of the party in breach even if the delay is very slight: see *Union Eagle Ltd v. Golden Achievement Ltd* [1997] A.C. 514; *post*, para. 12–114.

[90] "There is . . . no general concept that time is of the essence of a contract as a whole: the question is whether time is of the essence of a particular term in question": *British and Commonwealth Holdings Plc v. Quadrex Holdings Ltd* [1989] Q.B. 842 at 856, *per* Browne-Wilkinson V.-C.

[91] Equivocal phrases such as "on or about" or "on or before" a certain date will probably not make time of the essence: see *Lock v. Bell* [1931] 1 Ch. 35 (where time was of the essence for other reasons, but where the use of that phrase provided a "little latitude"); *James Macara Ltd v. Barclay* [1945] K.B. 148 at 156.

general conditions of sale in ordinary use.[92] However, it is usual to provide in the contract that time may be made of the essence unilaterally if one party fails to complete on time by service upon him thereafter of a notice to complete.[93] No particular form is required for such a notice, but it must inform the recipient clearly and unambiguously of what he is required to do to fulfil his contractual obligations.[94] The notice once served is binding on both parties and if the party serving it is himself unable to complete on the date specified in the notice, the recipient may treat the contract as at an end.[95] It is usually provided that such a notice to complete can be served only if the server is himself "ready able and willing to complete" the contract.[96] There is a considerable (if not always consistent) body of authority as to when a party is or is not in such a position.[97] No notice can be served after specific performance has been decreed because the carrying out of the contract has by then become a matter for the court.[98]

The conditions of sale usually make express provision as to the remedies for failure to comply with a notice to complete.[99] Typically, these will involve the right to terminate the contract, to forfeit (or recover) any deposit, and to recover damages.

---

[92] See the Standard Conditions of Sale (3rd ed.), c. 6.1.1. It is of the essence for certain intermediate obligations, such as the raising of requisitions: *ibid.*, c. 4.1.1.

[93] *ibid.*, c. 6.8. Under this condition, the party who receives the notice can be required to complete within 10 working days: c. 6.8.3. The party serving the notice may specify a longer period than the condition allows: *Delta Vale Properties Ltd v. Mills* [1990] 1 W.L.R. 445. However, if he specifies a shorter period, he may himself commit a repudiatory breach of contract if he purports to terminate the contract at the end of it: *Rightside Properties Ltd v. Gray* [1975] Ch. 72. Under some conditions of sale (though not under the Standard Conditions of Sale), the express provision will have a saving for any other rights and remedies that the aggrieved party might have. In those circumstances, a notice that does not comply with the terms of the condition of sale may sometimes be valid under the general law, if the period which is specifies is reasonable: see *Dimsdale Developments (South East) Ltd v. De Haan* (1983) 47 P. & C.R. 1 at 10, as explained in *Country and Metropolitan Homes Surrey Ltd v. Topclaim Ltd* [1996] Ch. 307 at 314, 315. See further *post*, para. 12–097.

[94] *Delta Vale Properties Ltd v. Mills, supra*, at 452.

[95] *Quadrangle Development and Construction Co. Ltd v. Jenner* [1974] 1 W.L.R. 68. *cf. Oakdown Ltd v. Bernstein & Co.* (1984) 49 P. & C.R. 282 at 295.

[96] See Standard Conditions of Sale (3rd ed.), c. 6.8.1.

[97] A party will be "ready able and willing" even though he has sent an inaccurate completion statement (*Carne v. Debono* [1988] 1 W.L.R. 1107), has failed to produce a vacating receipt in respect of a discharged mortgage (*Edwards v. Marshall-Lee* [1975] 2 E.G.L.R. 149), is in breach of his obligations as vendor to take reasonable care of the property (*Prosper Homes Ltd v. Hambros Bank Executor & Trustee Co. Ltd* (1979) 39 P. & C.R. 395), or has substantially misdescribed the land to be sold (*Bechal v. Kitsford Holdings Ltd* [1989] 1 W.L.R. 105; *sed quaere*), but not where he has failed either to deduce a good title (*Walia v. Michael Naughton Ltd* [1985] 1 W.L.R. 1115) or disclose a latent defect in title (*Pagebar Properties Ltd v. Derby Investment Holdings Ltd* [1972] 1 W.L.R. 1500), or is unable to give vacant possession (*Eagleview Ltd v. Worthgate Ltd* [1998] E.G.C.S. 119). See too *Clowes Developments (U.K.) Ltd v. Mulchinock* [1998] 1 W.L.R. 42 (the validity of a notice to complete served by a developer who was alleged not to have complied with its obligations to construct roads on the estate, raised a serious issue to be tried).

[98] *Singh v. Nazeer* [1979] Ch. 474.

[99] See Standard Conditions of Sale (3rd ed.), cc. 7.5 (seller's remedies); 7.6 (buyer's remedies).

12–095   (2) SUBJECT-MATTER OF THE CONTRACT. Time may be of the essence of a contract because the nature of the subject-matter of the contract requires it. This will be the case for example on the sale of a wasting asset such as a leasehold,[1] or of a business such as a public-house sold as a going concern.[2] Although it has been held that time is of the essence in a contract for the sale of a house required for immediate occupation,[3] this view might not now be followed.[4] In any event, the general conditions of sale will often negative the inference that time is of the essence.[5]

12–096   (3) UNILATERAL AND CONDITIONAL CONTRACTS. Time is of the essence where a contract is unilateral, such as an option, under which it rests with one party to take action by a certain date if the other party is to be placed under an obligation.[6] Similarly time is of the essence where a contract is made conditional upon some act being done by a fixed date, or within a reasonable time.[7]

12–097   (4) UNREASONABLE DELAY. It remains the case that, where one party has unreasonably delayed either in completing the contract or in performing some intermediate obligation under it,[8] the other party may terminate the contract if the breach goes to the root of the contract.[9] However, the innocent party may do this only if he has first served on the party in delay a notice specifying a reasonable period for the performance of the obligation.[10] This is because in the absence of laches a notice to complete is required to bar a claim to specific performance.[11] However it is not apparent why if a delay in performance of a contractual obligation is a breach of contract,[12] an unreasonable delay should not be regarded as a repudiatory breach.[13] A notice to complete can be

---

[1] See, *e.g. Pips (Leisure Productions) Ltd v. Walton* (1980) 43 P. & C.R. 415 (15 years to run).

[2] *Day v. Luhke* (1868) L.R. 5 Eq. 336; *Lock v. Bell* [1931] 1 Ch. 35. In *Coslake v. Till* (1826) 1 Russ. 376, a delay of one day was held a breach.

[3] *Tilley v. Thomas* (1867) 3 Ch.App. 61 at 67.

[4] *Smith v. Hamilton* [1951] Ch. 174 at 179. See [1980] Conv. 238 (J. T. Farrand); *Barnsley's Conveyancing Law and Practice* (4th ed.), p. 424. *cf. Raineri v. Miles* [1981] A.C. 1050 at 1082.

[5] See Standard Conditions of Sale (3rd ed.), c. 6.1.1.

[6] *Finch v. Underwood* (1876) 2 Ch.D. 310; *United Scientific Holdings Ltd v. Burnley B.C.* [1978] A.C. 904 at 928, 945; *Di Luca v. Juraise (Springs) Ltd* [1998] 2 E.G.L.R. 125. See too *Chiltern Court (Baker Street) Residents Ltd v. Wallabrook Property Co. Ltd* [1989] 2 E.G.L.R. 207 at 208.

[7] *Aberfoyle Plantations Ltd v. Cheng* [1960] A.C. 115. For conditional contracts, see *ante*, para. 12–009.

[8] See *Behzadi v. Shaftesbury Hotels Ltd* [1992] Ch. 1 (notice to vendor to deduce title).

[9] *United Scientific Holdings Ltd v. Burnley B.C.* [1978] A.C. 904 at 946.

[10] *Graham v. Pitkin* [1992] 1 W.L.R. 403 at 406. For the view that the case was decided *per incuriam* and is contrary to *Howe v. Smith* (1884) 27 Ch.D. 89: [1994] Conv. 342; [1995] Conv. 84 (D. G. Barnsley). *Sed quaere*: see [1995] Conv. 83 (C.H.).

[11] *Graham v. Pitkin, supra*, at 406.

[12] *Raineri v. Miles* [1981] A.C. 1050; *ante*, para. 12–092.

[13] See [1992] Conv. 318 (C.H.). *cf. United Scientific Holdings Ltd v. Burnley B.C., supra*, at 945.

served as soon as one party fails to perform the obligation on time.[14] It is not necessary to wait until the delay is unreasonable.[15] The period specified must however be reasonable, but this is judged by reference to all the circumstances.[16] If it is plain that the party in default will not complete, that period may be very short.[17]

F. Discharge of the Contract

1. Completion. The principal obligations of both parties are discharged at completion.[18] Where title is unregistered completion takes place when the title has been accepted, the conveyance executed and delivered and the purchase-money paid.[19] Where title is registered, completion probably takes place on "payment of the price against delivery of the executed transfer"[20] rather than when that transfer is registered.[21] Should any defect in title arise after completion, the purchaser must rely on the covenants for title which are implied by the conveyance or when a transfer is registered.[22] These have already been explained.[23]

12–098

A purchaser, however, may have a conveyance set aside on grounds of fraud,[24] misrepresentation[25] or common mistake.[26] If a purchaser knows of a misrepresentation but chooses nonetheless to complete the contract, he

---

[14] For the view that a notice to complete can be served even *before* there has been a breach of contract, see *Bernard v. Williams* (1928) 139 L.T. 22 at 25; *Phillips v. Lamdin* [1949] 2 K.B. 33 at 42; [1978] Conv. 144 at 157 (C. T. Emery).

[15] *Behzadi v. Shaftesbury Hotels Ltd, supra*, overruling *Smith v. Hamilton* [1951] Ch. 174.

[16] *MacBryde v. Weeks* (1856) 22 Beav. 533 at 543. In determining what is reasonable, the court ignores any difficulty that the purchaser may experience in raising the price: *British and Commonwealth Holdings Plc v. Quadrex Holdings Ltd* [1989] Q.B. 842 at 860 (not following *Re Barr's Contract* [1956] Ch. 551).

[17] *Ajit v. Sammy* [1967] 1 A.C. 255 (six days held reasonable where the purchase had no prospect of raising the price).

[18] See [1991] Conv. 15, 81 and 185 (D. G. Barnsley).

[19] *Re Atkins' W.T.* [1974] 1 W.L.R. 761 and 766. Completion can take place even if part of the purchase-money is unpaid, provided that it is secured by a mortgage or charge: see [1991] Conv. 15 at 26–28; and perhaps even where it is paid by a cheque that is then dishonoured: *Redican v. Nesbitt* [1924] S.C.R. 135.

[20] *Abbey National B.S. v. Cann* [1991] 1 A.C. 56 at 85, *per* Lord Oliver.

[21] See L.R.A. 1925, s.110(6); *Dogma Properties Ltd v. Gale* (1984) 134 N.L.J. 453.

[22] Even if it transpires that the title is wholly bad, the conveyance cannot be set aside on the ground of total failure of consideration: *Clarke v. Lamb* (1875) L.R. 10 C.P. 334.

[23] *Ante*, paras 5–047, 6–102. In conveyances made after July 1, 1995, the covenants are implied only where the conveyance or transfer is made with either full or limited guarantee: see L.P.(M.P.)A. 1994, ss.2, 3.

[24] *Edwards v. M'Leay* (1815) G. Coop. 308; aff'd (1818) 2 Swans. 287 (vendor concealed from purchaser his lack of title to part of the land).

[25] Misrepresentation Act 1967, s.1(b). This is so even though the misrepresentation has become a term of the contract: *ibid.*, s.1(a). Where the misrepresentation was not fraudulent, a court may award damages in lieu of rescission: *ibid.*, s.2(2). For misrepresentation, see *post*, paras 12–104, 12–112.

[26] *Bingham v. Bingham* (1748) 1 Ves. Sen. 126 (purchaser was owner of the land that the vendor purported to convey to him). See *post*, para. 12–123.

thereby loses his right to seek rescission of the conveyance[27] but may still recover damages for negligent misrepresentation.[28]

12–099 **2. Merger.** On completion, many of the obligations in the contract of sale are merged in the conveyance or transfer.[29] They are presumed to have been superseded by the new agreement embodied in the deed.[30] Thus, for example, a purchaser loses any right to claim compensation in equity for misdescription[31] or because the vendor has no title to part of the land.[32] However, the presumption of merger is rebuttable. Completion does not bring about an automatic discharge of the whole contract if there are terms which are not intended to be so discharged. Some examples may be given. First, there are certain cases where the loss caused to the claimant by the defendant's breach of contract cannot be quantified until completion has taken place. This is the situation as regards damages for delay,[33] for breach of the vendor's fiduciary obligation to manage and preserve the property between contract and completion,[34] and for failure to give vacant possession on completion.[35] Secondly, certain conditions of sale survive completion. These include a condition that compensation shall be payable for any error, omission or misdescription in the particulars of sale,[36] an option for the vendor to buy back the property from the purchaser within a specified period,[37] and an undertaking by a purchaser of a freehold reversion to indemnify the vendor against any claims brought by the tenant.[38] Thirdly, a collateral warranty does not merge on completion because it is concerned with a matter that is not covered by the conveyance.[39]

---

[27] *Campbell v. Fleming* (1834) 1 Ad. & El. 40; *Gordon v. Selico Co. Ltd* [1986] 1 E.G.L.R. 71 at 77.

[28] Under the Misrepresentation Act 1967, s.2(1): *Production Technology Consultants Ltd v. Bartlett* [1988] 1 E.G.L.R. 182.

[29] *Knight Sugar Co. Ltd v. Alberta Railway & Irrigation Co.* [1938] 1 All E.R. 266 at 269. Where title is unregistered, merger operates on the execution of the conveyance. Although merger does apply to registered land, it is not settled whether it occurs on the execution of the transfer or on registration. The former seems preferable: [1991] Conv. 15 at 24 (D. G. Barnsley).

[30] *Leggott v. Barrett* (1880) 15 Ch.D. 306 at 311; *Re Cooper and Crondace's Contract* (1904) 90 L.T. 258 at 259; *Hissett v. Reading Roofing Co. Ltd* [1969] 1 W.L.R. 1757 at 1763; *International Press Centre v. Norwich Union Insurance Co* (1986) 36 B.L.R. 134 at 136, 137.

[31] *Greswolde-Williams v. Barneby* (1901) 83 L.T. 708. *cf. Hissett v. Reading Roofing Co. Ltd, supra*, at 1764.

[32] *Clayton v. Leech* (1889) 41 Ch.D. 103.

[33] *Phillips v. Lamdin* [1949] 2 K.B. 33 at 42; *Raineri v. Miles* [1981] A.C. 1050 at 1084.

[34] *Clarke v. Ramuz* [1891] 2 Q.B. 456 at 461, 462. If the purchaser completes without objection, knowing of the breach of duty, he will be taken to have waived his right to sue: *Berkley v. Poulett* [1977] 1 E.G.L.R. 86 at 93.

[35] *Hissett v. Reading Roofing Co. Ltd, supra*, at 1763, 1764; *Gunatunga v. De Alwis* (1995) 72 P. & C.R. 161.

[36] *Palmer v. Johnson* (1884) 13 Q.B.D. 351. *cf. Ex p. Riches* (1883) 27 S.J. 313. See [1992] C.L.J. 263 at 275, 276 (C.H.).

[37] *Mason v. Schuppisser* (1899) 81 L.T. 147.

[38] *Eagon v. Dent* [1965] 3 All E.R. 334. See Standard Conditions of Sale (3rd ed.), c. 3.3.2(d).

[39] *Lawrence v. Cassel* [1930] 2 K.B. 83; *Hancock v. B. W. Brazier (Anerley) Ltd* [1966] 1 W.L.R. 1317.

G. Certain Terms are Void

By the Law of Property Act 1925[40] certain terms are made void. This is partly **12–100**
to protect purchasers from having bad titles foisted upon them, and partly to
compel the use of the conveyancing machinery. Examples of void terms of the
former class are stipulations that the purchaser shall not employ his own
solicitor,[41] or that he shall accept a title which does not give him the legal
estate.[42] Examples of terms which are void for purely technical reasons are
terms requiring title to be made with the concurrence of the owner of an
interest which could be overreached,[43] or requiring the purchaser to pay the
costs of obtaining a vesting order or appointment of trustees.[44]

H. Remedies

One or more of the following remedies will be available to a vendor or **12–101**
purchaser in case of dispute about the effect of the contract.

1. Action for damages

(a) The general rule. An action for damages is the primary remedy under **12–102**
the law of contract, though it is less important in relation to contracts for the
sale of land than specific performance. The measure of damages is the loss to
the claimant from the non-performance of the contract.[45] A vendor, for
example, can recover the difference between the price agreed to be paid and
the net value of the property left on his hands.[46] A purchaser can claim for the
loss of a bargain, *i.e.* the amount by which the net value of the property when
conveyed to him at the due date would have exceeded the purchase price.[47]
But the court may order such damages to be assessed at some other date where

---

[40] L.P.A. 1925, ss.42, 48.
[41] s.48(1).
[42] s.42(3).
[43] s.42(1). An example would be where A held land on a trust of land for himself and B. A cannot
insist that a purchaser accept a title on the basis that B concurs in the sale. A must appoint a
co-trustee so that B's interest is overreached: see *ante*, para. 8–166. For overreaching see *ante*,
paras 4–078, 8–157.
[44] s.42(2).
[45] *Johnson v. Agnew* [1980] A.C. 367 at 400. The plaintiff cannot claim any gain that the
defendant has made in consequence of the breach: *Surrey C.C. v. Bredero Homes Ltd* [1993]
1 W.L.R. 1361. For criticism of this limitation see R. Goff & G. H. Jones, *The Law of
Restitution* (5th ed.), pp. 520–522.
[46] *Noble v. Edwards* (1877) 5 Ch.D. 378. Where the vendor resells the property, he can recover
both the loss on and the expenses of the resale: *Janred Properties Ltd v. E.N.I.T.* [1989] 2 All
E.R. 444 at 456.
[47] Together with damages in respect of any special circumstances known to the vendor: *Cottrill
v. Steyning and Littlehampton B.S.* [1966] 1 W.L.R. 753. Thus if at the time of contracting, a
vendor is unaware that the purchaser is negotiating a profitable sub-sale, and the vendor then
refuses to complete, he will not be liable for the loss of that sub-sale: *Seven Seas Properties Ltd
v. Al-Essa (No. 2)* [1993] 1 W.L.R. 1083. The purchaser need not accept an offer of repurchase
by the vendor: *Strutt v. Whitnell* [1975] 1 W.L.R. 870.

justice so requires[48]; this may be the date of the hearing if the property has risen in value meanwhile.[49] Where the purchaser claims damages for his loss of bargain he cannot in addition recover his costs, *e.g.* for investigation of title. If he is to be placed in the position in which he would have been had the contract been performed, he would necessarily have incurred those costs.[50]

Damages may be assessed on a "cost of cure" basis where the claimant can establish that his loss consists of or includes the cost of doing work that in breach of contract the defendant failed to do.[51] Thus where a vendor of land fails to carry out work that he contracted to do to the property prior to sale, the claimant may recover the cost of that work if either he does it himself or he can show that he intends to do so.[52] However, the court may refuse to award damages assessed on this basis if to do so would be unreasonable: the question in every case is to determine the loss that the claimant has actually suffered.[53]

12–103   *(b) The Rule in Bain v. Fothergill.* There was an exceptional rule which now applies only to contracts made before September 27, 1989,[54] Where a vendor failed to show a good title because of some irremovable defect, which was not due to his own fault, he was not liable to pay damages for the purchaser's loss of his bargain but merely for his wasted conveyancing expenses.[55] This anomalous rule, known as the Rule in *Bain v. Fothergill*, was said to be founded on "the peculiar difficulty of making a title to land in England".[56] The rule was much criticised[57] and could cause considerable hardship.[58] Following a recommendation by the Law Commission,[59] the rule was abolished as regards contracts made after September 26, 1989,[60] and few cases are now likely to arise in which it will still apply.

---

[48] *Johnson v. Agnew, supra*; *E. Johnson & Co. (Barbados) Ltd v. N.S.R. Ltd* [1997] A.C. 400 (land compulsorily acquired between commencement of proceedings and trial). The date selected can significantly affect the quantum of damages: see *Suleman v. Shahsavari* [1988] 1 W.L.R. 1181 (where in regard to a house sold for a price of £46,500, the difference between damages assessed at the breach date and those assessed at judgment was £20,000).

[49] *Suleman v. Sahsavari, supra.* See too *Wroth v. Tyler* [1974] Ch. 30; *Grant v. Dawkins* [1973] 1 W.L.R. 1406. In both these decisions damages were awarded in lieu of or in addition to specific performance under what is now the Supreme Court Act 1981, s.50 (*ante*, para. 4–015). Damages under that Act are awarded on the same basis as at common law: *Johnson v. Agnew, supra*.

[50] See *Cullinane v. British "Rema" Manufacturing Co. Ltd* [1954] 1 Q.B. 292 at 308.

[51] *Titto v. Waddell (No. 2)* [1977] Ch. 106 at 332. See too *Radford v. De Froberville* [1977] 1 W.L.R. 1262.

[52] *Dean v. Ainley* [1987] 1 W.L.R. 1729.

[53] *Ruxley Electronics and Construction Ltd v. Forsyth* [1996] A.C. 344.

[54] See *Newbery v. Turngiant Ltd* (1991) 63 P. & C.R. 458 at 470.

[55] *Flureau v. Thornhill* (1776) 2 W.Bl. 1078; *Bain v. Fothergill* (1874) L.R. 7 H.L. 158. For a fuller account of the rule, see the previous edition of this work at p. 617.

[56] *Elliott v. Pierson* [1948] Ch. 452 at 455, 456, *per* Harman J.

[57] See *Sharneyford Supplies Ltd v. Edge* [1987] Ch. 305 at 325; *Seven Seas Properties Ltd v. Al-Essa* [1988] 1 W.L.R. 1272 at 1275.

[58] See in relation to chain sales [1983] Conv. 435 (C.H.).

[59] (1987) Law Com. No. 166.

[60] L.P.(M.P.)A. 1989, s.3. Its abolition was "to the relief of all and in the interests of justice": *Newbery v. Turngiant Ltd, supra*, at 470, *per* Dillon L.J.

(c) Damages for misrepresentation. Damages will be awarded against a **12–104**
vendor for the tort of deceit if he induces a purchaser to contract by means of
a fraudulent misrepresentation.[61] Even if the misrepresentation is not fraudulent, the vendor will be liable in damages unless he can show that he had
reasonable grounds to believe and did believe up to the time of the contract
that the facts represented were true.[62] It has been held that the measure of
damages is the same as that for deceit.[63] According to that measure, the
vendor is liable to pay damages for all loss suffered by the purchaser in
consequence of having entered into the contract.[64] These include any difference between the price paid and the value of the land sold[65] plus any
consequential loss.[66] The claimant is, however, under a duty to mitigate his
loss once he has discovered the misrepresentation.[67] Where the misrepresentation has become a term of the contract, the purchaser may sue for damages for
breach of contract, and the quantum of damages will be such as to place him
in the position in which he would have been had the representation been
true.[68] In cases where the purchaser has entered into a contract after a
misrepresentation that was not fraudulent, the court or arbitrator may declare
the contract subsisting[69] and award damages in lieu of rescission if it would
be equitable to do so, having regard both to the nature of the misrepresentation
and to the loss that would be caused to the respective parties by upholding the
contract or rescinding it.[70] Such damages are assessed on a contractual basis

---

[61] *Doyle v. Olby (Ironmongers) Ltd* [1969] 2 Q.B. 158.
[62] Misrepresentation Act 1967, s.2(1), making innocent misrepresentation actionable on the same
basis as a fraudulent misrepresentation. The onus of proving reasonable belief rests on the
defendant: *Howard Marine and Dredging Co. Ltd v. A. Ogden & Sons (Excavations) Ltd* [1978]
Q.B. 574.
[63] *Royscot Trust Ltd v. Rogerson* [1991] 2 Q.B. 297; applied in *Bridgegrove Ltd v. Smith* [1997]
2 E.G.L.R. 40. This view is based upon a questionable interpretation of the Misrepresentation
Act 1967, s.2(1), by which if a defendant would be liable for damages had the misrepresentation been fraudulent, he "shall be so liable notwithstanding that the misrepresentation was not
made fraudulently". These words may have been intended only to remove the bar to damages
for non-fraudulent misrepresentations and not to import the same measure of damages: see
(1991) 107 L.Q.R. 547 (R. Hooley). The correctness of the decision was left open in *Smith New
Court Securities Ltd v. Citibank N.A.* [1997] A.C. 254 at 267, 282, 283. However, it is difficult
to reconcile with the long-established policy of "imposing more extensive liability on intentional wrongdoers than on merely careless defendants": *ibid.*, at 280, *per* Lord Steyn.
[64] *Smith New Court Securities Ltd v. Citibank N.A., supra*, at 267. See too *Cemp Properties (U.K.)
Ltd v. Dentsply Research & Development Corporation* [1991] 2 E.G.L.R. 197; *William Sindall
Plc v. Cambridgeshire C.C.* [1994] 1 W.L.R. 1016 at 1037, 1043.
[65] *Cemp Properties (U.K.) Ltd v. Dentsply Research & Development Corporation, supra*, at 200,
201. Although the court will normally value the land at the time when it is acquired this is not
an inflexible rule, and will not be applied, *e.g.* if the misrepresentation continued to operate
after the transaction so that the claimant was induced to retain the land, or if the circumstances
were such that he was "locked in" to the property: *Smith New Court Securities Ltd v. Citibank
N.A., supra*, at 267.
[66] *Doyle v. Olby (Ironmongers) Ltd, supra*; *East v. Maurer* [1991] 1 W.L.R. 461.
[67] *Smith New Court Securities Ltd v. Citibank N.A., supra*, at 267, 285.
[68] *Smith Kline & French Laboratories Ltd v. Long* [1989] 1 W.L.R. 1 at 6.
[69] Even if the contract has already been rescinded: *William Sindall Plc v. Cambridgeshire C.C.,
supra*, at 1044.
[70] Misrepresentation Act 1967, s.2(2). See *William Sindall Plc v. Cambridgeshire C.C., supra*, at
1036–1038.

and will not exceed the difference between the value of the property as received and its value if the representation had been true.[71]

2. Termination for breach

12–105   *(a) When termination occurs.* Although a claimant may always sue for damages for any breach of contract, he will not be entitled to treat a contract as discharged unless the breach is such as to render further performance by him purposeless.[72] This will be the case "where a party indicates either expressly or implicitly that he does not intend to complete his side of the contract or where, having regard to the contract as a whole, the obligation which is broken is of vital importance".[73] Once this happens, the contract is ended as regards further performance but remains alive for the awarding of damages.[74] These principles apply as much to contracts for the sale of land as they do to any other type of contract.[75] When the contract is brought to an end in this way—

>   (i) where the breach is by the vendor, the purchaser may sue for damages and recover any deposit or other part payments which he has paid (with interest); and

>   (ii) where it is the purchaser who is in breach, the vendor may forfeit any deposit and sue for damages for any loss that exceeds the value of that deposit.[76]

12–106   *(b) The "rescission" heresy.* Where a contract is voidable, for example on account of misrepresentation or fraud, the injured party may rescind the contract, treating it as non-existent, and claim *restitutio in integram, i.e.* to be put back into his original position, recovering any property transferred or payment made. This is commonly called rescission *ab initio.*[77] Where a claimant accepts a repudiation of the contract by the defendant and treats the contract as discharged, he is sometimes said to "rescind" the contract. This is not an apt term in this context, since the contract remains in force for some purposes as explained above. After much confusion both in judgments[78] and

---

[71] *William Sindall Plc v. Cambridgeshire C.C., supra,* at 1038, 1045. Such damages will be taken into account when assessing liability in any claim that is also made under the Misrepresentation Act 1967, s.2(1): *ibid.,* s.2(3).

[72] *Thompson v. Corroon* (1993) 66 P. & C.R. 445 at 459.

[73] *ibid.,* at 459, *per* Lord Lowry.

[74] *Heyman v. Darwins* [1942] A.C. 356 at 379.

[75] *Johnson v. Agnew* [1980] A.C. 367 at 392, 393. See too *Buckland v. Farmer & Moody* [1979] 1 W.L.R. 221; *Thompson v. Corroon, supra.*

[76] For deposits, see *post,* para. 12–107.

[77] *Johnson v. Agnew, supra,* at 393. For rescission *ab initio,* see *post,* para. 12–112.

[78] The line of erroneous decisions ran from *Henty v. Schröder* (1879) 12 Ch.D. 666 to *Horsler v. Zorro* [1975] Ch. 302.

textbooks[79] on this last point, the House of Lords has made it clear that acceptance of a repudiatory breach, despite being called "rescission", does not disqualify the injured party from claiming damages, even where he has already obtained an order for specific performance if that order proves abortive.[80]

(c) Return or forfeiture of deposit

(1) NATURE OF A DEPOSIT. A deposit "is an earnest for the performance of the contract; in the event of completion of the contract the deposit is applicable towards payment of the purchase price; in the event of the purchaser's failure to complete in accordance with the terms of the contract, the deposit is forfeit, equity having no power to relieve against forfeiture".[81] Although there is no obligation to pay a deposit in the absence of an express contractual provision, such a term is invariably included in a contract to sell land. Payment of a deposit is a fundamental term of the contract[82] and the vendor may treat the agreement as discharged if the purchaser by his conduct indicates his unwillingness or inability to pay it.[83] A deposit of 10 per cent of the purchase price is usually taken on the exchange of contracts.[84] It makes no difference to the function of a deposit that it is paid to a stakeholder rather than to the vendor or his agent.[85]

12–107

A vendor may forfeit a deposit if the purchaser defaults even though the amount bears no reference to his loss. Deposits are therefore an anomalous exception to the rule that such payments are unlawful as penalties.[86] A deposit that exceeds 10 per cent will regarded as a penalty in the absence of special circumstances. It will therefore be recoverable by the purchaser in full and the vendor will be left to his remedy in damages to recover his actual loss.[87]

---

[79] Especially Williams, V. & P. 1004, 1025 and Williams, *The Contract of Sale of Land*, 121, criticised in (1975) 91 L.Q.R. 337 (M. J. Albery), and providing "almost a perfect illustration of the dangers, well perceived by our predecessors but tending to be neglected in modern times, of placing reliance on textbook authority for an analysis of judicial decisions": *Johnson v. Agnew, supra*, at 395, *per* Lord Wilberforce.

[80] *Johnson v. Agnew* [1980] A.C. 367; and see *Biggin v. Minton* [1977] 1 W.L.R. 701; *Ogle v. Comboyuro Pty Ltd* (1976) 136 C.L.R. 444; [1980] C.L.J. 58 (A. J. Oakley).

[81] *Workers Trust & Merchant Bank Ltd v. Dojap Investments Ltd* [1993] A.C. 573 at 578, 579, *per* Lord Browne-Wilkinson. See too *Howe v. Smith* (1884) 27 Ch.D. 89 at 101; *Soper v. Arnold* (1889) 14 App. Cas. 429 at 435. For a full discussion of the modern law on deposits, see [1994] Conv. 41, 100 (A. J. Oakley).

[82] *Millichamp v. Jones* [1982] 1 W.L.R. 1422. Time is not usually of the essence of payment: *John Willmott Homes Ltd v. Read* (1985) 51 P. & C.R. 90. If the purchaser fails to pay a deposit, the vendor may sue him for it regardless of his actual loss: *Hinton v. Sparkes* (1868) L.R. 3 C.P. 161.

[83] *Millichamp v. Jones, supra*, at 1431, 1432.

[84] See Standard Conditions of Sale (3rd ed.), c. 2.2.1. Those conditions make provision for a "travelling deposit" where the sale is part of a chain, so that the vendor may use any deposit that he receives as a deposit on the property which he is purchasing in England and Wales as his residence: see c. 2.2.2. and [1994] Conv. 41 at 44 (A. J. Oakley).

[85] *Hall v. Burnell* [1911] 2 Ch. 551.

[86] *Linggi Plantations Ltd v. Jagatheesan* [1971] 1 M.L.J. 89 at 91.

[87] *Workers Trust & Merchant Bank Ltd v. Dojap Investments Ltd, supra*; (1993) 109 L.Q.R. 524 (H. Beale); [1993] C.L.J. 389 (C.H.). See too [1984] C.L.J. 134 at 161–166 (C.H.).

12–108   (2) RIGHTS OF THE PARTIES. Where the purchaser terminates a contract because of a breach by the vendor, he may recover his deposit and has an equitable lien over the land agreed to be sold to secure its repayment,[88] unless it was paid to a stakeholder rather than to the vendor or his agent.[89] If the vendor terminates the contract on account of the purchaser's default, he may forfeit the deposit, even though the contract makes no express provision for so doing.[90] If that does not adequately compensate him for his loss, he may recover any additional loss as damages.[91] However, the vendor must normally return any part payment that he has already received,[92] because such payments are usually regarded as conditional upon completion of the contract and cannot therefore be retained.[93]

12–109   (3) STAKEHOLDERS AND AGENTS. A stakeholder is a person who holds a sum of money as agent for both parties,[94] on terms requiring him to pay it either to the person who eventually becomes entitled to it under the contract,[95] or at the joint instructions of both parties even if the event upon which the stake is held has not occurred.[96] If the sale goes off by the purchaser's fault the stakeholder must pay over the deposit to the vendor, who may retain it, unless the contract provides otherwise. If the deposit is paid to a person who is merely the vendor's agent, rather than a stakeholder, any action to recover it must be brought against the vendor,[97] and the vendor can at any time require his agent to pay over the deposit to him.[98] A stakeholder resembles a banker in that he is not accountable for any interest earned by the deposit, whereas an agent must account for it to the vendor.[99] In the absence of any contractual provision, a solicitor or an estate agent who receives a deposit from a purchaser is deemed to do so as agent for the vendor, but an auctioneer

---

[88] *Whitbread & Co. Ltd v. Watt* [1902] 1 Ch. 835; *ante*, para. 12–055. For equitable liens, see *post*, para. 19–002.

[89] *Combe v. Lord Swaythling* [1947] Ch. 625.

[90] *Ex p. Barrell* (1875) 10 Ch.App. 512 at 514.

[91] *Icely v. Grew* (1836) 6 N. & M. 467; *Shuttleworth v. Clews* [1910] 1 Ch. 176.

[92] *Mayson v. Clouet* [1924] A.C. 980; *Hillel v. Christoforides* (1991) 63 P. & C.R. 301 at 306.

[93] *McDonald v. Dennys Lascelles Ltd* (1933) 48 C.L.R. 457 at 477–479. In some cases the payments may be unconditional and therefore irrecoverable: see (1981) 97 L.Q.R. 389 (J. Beatson).

[94] He is not a trustee of the money. His liability to account for it is contractual or quasi-contractual: *Potters v. Loppert* [1973] Ch. 399 at 406; *Hastingwood Property Ltd v. Saunders Bearman Anselm* [1991] Ch. 114 at 123; *Rockeagle Ltd v. Alsop Wilkinson* [1992] Ch. 47 at 52.

[95] *Collins v. Stimson* (1883) 11 Q.B.D. 142 at 144; *Skinner v. Reed's Trustee* [1967] Ch. 194. Once the event occurs on which the stake is payable, the stakeholder is not bound to retain the deposit but may pay it to the party whom he adjudges to be entitled to it. This is so even though there is a dispute between the vendor and the purchaser: *Hastingwood Property Ltd v. Saunders Bearman Anselm, supra.*

[96] *Rockeagle Ltd v. Alsop Wilkinson, supra.* The stakeholder has no lien over the deposit in such circumstances for money that is owed to him by either the vendor or the purchaser: *ibid.*

[97] *Ellis v. Goulton* [1893] 1 Q.B. 350.

[98] *Edgell v. Day* (1865) L.R. 1. C.P. 80.

[99] *Harington v Hoggart* (1830) 1 B. & Ad. 577 at 586, 587.

receives it as a stakeholder.[1] If an agent or a stakeholder defaults or becomes insolvent, it is the vendor and not the purchaser who must bear the loss.[2]

(4) PRE-CONTRACTUAL "DEPOSITS". Sometimes a person who has agreed to **12–110** purchase land "subject to contract" is asked to pay a pre-contractual deposit to the vendor's estate agent as an earnest of his seriousness.[3] This payment does not fulfil the ordinary function of the deposit unless and until the parties exchange contracts.[4] The purchaser can require its return at any time.[5] If the agent absconds or becomes insolvent, the loss will normally fall on the purchaser. The vendor is not liable to repay the deposit because the agent will not at that stage have his authority to receive the deposit.[6]

(5) DISCRETION OF COURT. Under the Law of Property Act 1925[7] the court **12–111** has discretion to order the return of a deposit in any case where specific performance is refused or the return of the deposit is claimed in an action.[8] It was the draftsman's intention that this section should apply in those cases where a vendor was unable to obtain specific performance because his title turned out to be wholly bad, but where the purchaser was in breach of contract by not completing because of a term in the contract.[9] But for this power, the purchaser would have no ground for the recovery of his deposit.[10] Although the discretion has been exercised in that situation,[11] it is not confined to it.[12] It may be used more widely "in mitigation of the vendor's right at law to forfeit the deposit",[13] not just in cases where the retention of the deposit would be unconscionable, but in any circumstances in which repayment is the fairest course between the parties.[14] Because an exercise of the discretion does

---

[1] *Tudor v. Hamid* [1988] 1 E.G.L.R. 251 at 255 (solicitor); *Ojelay v. Neosale Ltd* [1987] E.G.L.R. 167 at 168 (estate agent); *Harington v. Hoggart, supra*, at 589 (auctioneer).

[2] *Ojelay v. Neosale Ltd, supra*, at 168.

[3] For agreements "subject to contract" see *ante*, para. 12–010.

[4] *Chilliingworth v. Esche* [1924] 1 Ch. 97 at 115.

[5] *Chillingworth v. Esche, supra*.

[6] *Sorrell v. Finch* [1977] A.C. 728. See (1976) 92 L.Q.R. 484 (F. M. B. Reynolds).

[7] s.49(2).

[8] See [1984] C.L.J. 134 at 169 (C.H.); [1992] C.L.J. 263 at 293 (C.H.); [1994] Conv. 100 (A. J. Oakley).

[9] See Wolst. & C., i. 125 (repeating Sir Benjamin Cherry's own commentary on the sub-section found in the 11th and 12th editions). *cf. Safehaven Invesments Inc. v. Springbok Ltd* (1995) 71 P. & C.R. 59 at 70.

[10] See *Re Scott and Alvarez's Contract (No. 2)* [1895] 2 Ch. 603; *ante*, para. 12–078.

[11] See, *e.g. James Macara Ltd v. Barclay* [1944] 2 All E.R. 31 at 32; [1994] Conv. 100 at 101 (A. J. Oakley). In this situation, an order for repayment of the deposit may not always assist the purchaser because he remains liable damages to the vendor: *ante*, para. 12–078.

[12] *Universal Corporation v. Five Ways Properties Ltd* [1979] 1 All E.R. 552 at 554.

[13] *Schindler v. Pigault, supra*, at 336, *per* Megarry J., setting out criteria on which the discretion might be exercised.

[14] *Universal Corporation v. Five Ways Properties Ltd, supra*, where the Court of Appeal rejected a narrow view of the jurisdiction. See too *Maktoum v. South Lodge Flats, The Times*, April 22, 1980; [1984] C.L.J. 134 at 169 (C.H.). In *Safehaven Investments Inc. v. Springbok Ltd, supra* at 70, it was suggested that fairness to the parties required that the discretion should be exercised only where the vendor had acted inequitably or there were other special circumstances.

not bar the vendor's right to sue for damages,[15] a court is likely to order repayment principally in those cases where the retention of the deposit will overcompensate him.[16]

The court's statutory discretion may, it seems, be excluded by agreement between the parties.[17] Where this is the case and the contract is not completed, the normal common law rule applies by which the fate of the deposit depends upon which party is at fault.[18]

12–112   **3. Rescission *ab initio*.** Where one party has been induced to enter into a contract because the other has misled him[19] by some misrepresentation as to a material fact,[20] he may rescind the contract *ab initio*. In general, if a party seeks rescission, he must be able to effect restitution of what he has received under the contract.[21] Common law allowed either rescission or an action for damages if the misrepresentation was fraudulent.[22] Equity went further, and allowed rescission (but neither damages nor compensation[23]) even for innocent misrepresentation if it had both misled the other party and induced him to enter into the contract. Since the Judicature Act 1873, the equitable rules have prevailed.[24]

Rescission is a particularly important remedy for a purchaser.[25] If he has been induced to contract by the vendor's misrepresentation he may escape from a contract which might otherwise have bound him to complete or pay damages.[26] There were formerly two limitations on rescission for misrep-

---

[15] *Dimsdale Developments (South East) Ltd v. De Haan* (1983) 47 P. & C.R. 1; *ante*, para. 12–078. See too *Pratt v. Hawkins* (1991) 32 N.S.W.L.R. 319 at 323, 324. It had been suggested that an exercise of discretion under the section puts an end to the contract between the parties: *Schindler v. Pigault* (1975) 30 P. & C.R. 328 at 337; *Faruqi v. English Real Estates Ltd* [1979] 1 W.L.R. 963 at 969.

[16] [1994] Conv. 100 at 105 (A. J. Oakley); [1993] C.L.J. 389 at 390 (C.H.). *cf. Swingler v. Khosla* [1991] 1 E.G.L.R. 245 at 254.

[17] *Country and Metropolitan Homes Surrey Ltd v. Topclaim Ltd* [1996] Ch. 307.

[18] *ibid.*, at 316.

[19] There will be no misrepresentation if the vendor notifies the purchaser or his solicitor that he made an erroneous statement and corrects it before contracts are exchanged: *Strover v. Harrington* [1988] Ch. 390.

[20] It is enough if the misrepresentation "induces the person to whom it is made, whether solely or in conjunction with other inducements, to contract on the term on which he does contract": *Museprime Properties Ltd v. Adhill Properties Ltd* (1990) 61 P. & C.R. 111 at 124, *per* Scott J. For the nature of a misrepresentation, see *Atlantic Estates Plc v. Ezekiel* [1991] 2 E.G.L.R. 202 at 203.

[21] See G. H. Treitel, *The Law of Contract* (10th ed.), p. 350.

[22] The validity of a contract at law was not affected by an innocent misrepresentation unless there was a total failure of consideration: *Kennedy v. Panama, New Zealand and Australian Royal Mail Co. Ltd* (1867) L.R. 2 Q.B. 580 at 587.

[23] *Gilchester Properties Ltd v. Gomm* [1948] 1 All E.R. 493 (innocent misrepresentation as to rents of the property: purchaser's remedy held to be rescission, not specific performance with abatement of the price, as to which see *post*, para. 12–117.

[24] *Ante*, para. 4–020; *Pan Atlantic Insurance Co. Ltd v. Pine Top Insurance Co. Ltd* [1995] 1 A.C. 501 at 543, 544.

[25] It is not available to a sub-purchaser or successor in title: *Gross v. Lewis Hillman Ltd* [1970] Ch. 445.

[26] He may be able to seek specific performance with damages in addition under the Misrepresentation Act 1967, s.2(1): *Topfell Ltd v. Galley Properties Ltd* [1979] 1 W.L.R. 446 at 451; see [1981] C.L.J. 47 at 74 (C.H.) .

resentation but each has been removed by the Misrepresentation Act 1967. First, it was thought that a misrepresentation ceased to be actionable if it became a term of the subsequent contract.[27] However, a contract may now be rescinded even though the misrepresentation has become incorporated into the contract.[28] Secondly, the right to rescind for an innocent (but not a fraudulent) misrepresentation ceased on completion, and this was so even though the purchaser might have been unable to discover that he had been misled until after he had taken possession.[29] It is now provided that a person may rescind a contract, notwithstanding that it has been performed, if he would otherwise have been entitled to rescind without alleging fraud.[30] The Act does impose one restriction on rescission in cases of misrepresentations made otherwise than fraudulently. As already explained, the court is given a wide discretion to declare the contract subsisting and to award damages in lieu of rescission if this would be equitable, having regard (*inter alia*) to any loss that would be caused by upholding the contract or rescinding it.[31] The section was passed to remove the anomaly "by which a minor misrepresentation gave rise to a right of rescission whereas a warranty in the same terms would have grounded no more than a claim for modest damages".[32] Although the maxim *caveat emptor* has little application to defects in title,[33] it has always applied to other matters.[34] The Act substantially weakens that application so that vendors have to exercise a higher degree of caution than formerly.

The Act merely entitles the misled party "to rescind the contract", without **12–113** saying what is to happen to any executed conveyance, which may be a grant but not a contract. If the right to rescind after performance is to be effective, the grant must necessarily be set aside,[35] though the court may prefer to award damages in lieu of rescission.

Clauses which restrict the vendor's liability for misrepresentation, which are often included in standard forms of contract, are effective only in so far as the vendor can show that the restriction satisfies the requirement of reasonableness in the Unfair Contract Terms Act 1977.[36] The common clause that

---

[27] See *Compagnie Française de Chemin de Fer Paris–Orléans v. Leeston Shipping Co.* (1919) 1 Ll.L.R. 235; *Pennsylvania Shipping Co. v. Compagnie Nationale de Navigation* [1936] 2 All E.R. 1167.

[28] Misrepresentation Act 1967, s.1(a). On the interrelationship of remedies for misrepresentation and for breach of contract in such cases, see G. H. Treitel, *The Law of Contract* (10th ed.), p. 348; [1981] C.L.J. 47 at 74 (C.H.).

[29] *Angel v. Jay* [1911] 1 K.B. 666.

[30] Misrepresentation Act 1967, s.1(b).

[31] *ibid.*, s.2(2); *ante*, para. 12–104.

[32] *William Sindall Plc v. Cambridgeshire C.C.* [1994] 1 W.L.R. 1016 at 1038, *per* Hoffmann L.J.

[33] *Ante*, paras 12–067, 12–068.

[34] *Haywood v. Cope* (1858) 25 Beav. 140.

[35] For the court's power to do so, see *ante*, para. 5–079, *post*, para. 12–123. It is clear from the legislative history that the Act is intended to authorise the cancellation of conveyances and leases where *restitutio in integrum* is possible: see 277 H.L.Deb. cols 48–53 (October 18, 1966).

[36] Misrepresentation Act 1967, s.3, as amended by the Unfair Contract Terms Act 1977, s.8. See [1984] Conv. 12 (H. W. Wilkinson); [1992] C.L.J. 263 at 266 (C.H.).

"no error, mis-statement or omission in any preliminary answer shall annul the sale" fails to pass this test.[37] But a vendor may protect himself against misrepresentations made by his agent by stating that the agent has no authority to make representations of any kind.[38]

12–114   **4. Equitable relief.** The court's jurisdiction (rarely exercised) to grant relief against the consequences of a mistake is considered below in connection with rectification.[39] Relief against a forfeiture clause may also be granted, *e.g.* where instalments of purchase money are in arrear.[40] The doctrine does not extend to granting relief by way of an order for specific performance where the person seeking relief was in breach of an essential term of the contract.[41]

5. Specific performance

12–115   *(a) Right to specific performance.* An order of the court compelling specific performance of the contract is the remedy most commonly sought by vendors and purchasers of land. The performance which can be compelled is the due completion of the transaction in proper form according to the contract. This remedy is purely equitable, and in principle is confined to cases where the common law remedy of damages is inadequate.[42] But land is always treated as being of unique value, so that the remedy of specific performance is available to the purchaser as a matter of course[43]; and even though the vendor is merely concerned to obtain the purchase-money, so that he could be adequately compensated in damages for the purchaser's refusal to complete, the remedy of specific performance is equally available to him. A vendor can in fact "thrust the property down the purchaser's throat"[44]; and claims by vendors for specific performance are common, since it is often more convenient to them to get rid of the property than to resell it and claim damages.

---

[37] *Walker v. Boyle* [1982] 1 W.L.R. 495; and see *South Western General Property Co. Ltd v. Marton* [1982] 2 E.G.L.R. 19. *cf. Swingler v. Khosla* [1991] 1 E.G.L.R. 245 at 254.

[38] *Collins v. Howell-Jones* [1981] 2 E.G.L.R. 108, approving *Overbrooke Estates Ltd v. Glencombe Properties Ltd* [1974] 1 W.L.R. 1355. See too *Museprime Properties Ltd v. Adhill Properties Ltd* (1990) 61 P. & C.R. 111 at 120; (1981) 97 L.Q.R. 522 (J. Murdoch).

[39] *Post*, para. 12–123.

[40] *Starside Properties Ltd v. Mustapha* [1974] 1 W.L.R. 816.

[41] *Union Eagle Ltd v. Golden Achievement Ltd* [1977] A.C. 514 (time of the essence for completion of the contract: specific performance refused, even though the purchaser tendered the price 10 minutes' late). The Privy Council left open how it might deal with a situation where there was a penalty or in which the party terminating the contract might have been unjustly enriched by improvements made to the land by a purchaser in possession. *cf. Legione v. Hateley* (1983) 152 C.L.R. 406; *Stern v. McArthur* (1988) 165 C.L.R. 489; [1984] C.L.J. 134 (C.H.); *Equity and Contemporary Legal Developments* (ed. S. Goldstein), 829 at 863 (C.H.).

[42] However specific performance may be decreed even of agreements to create transient interests such as a contract for a short lease or to grant a licence: *Verrall v. Great Yarmouth Borough Council* [1981] Q.B. 202.

[43] *AMEC Properties Ltd v. Planning Research & Systems Plc* [1992] 1 E.G.L.R. 70 at 72.

[44] *Hope v. Walter* [1900] 1 Ch. 257 at 258, *per* Lindley L.J.

Specific performance is thus available to vendor and purchaser alike. However, this statement is subject to two qualifications. First, the view that was formerly held that the remedy is available to one of the parties only if it is available to the other (the supposed requirement of mutuality) is misconceived.[45] Secondly, the court will not decree specific performance where, at trial, the vendor is unable to convey the land.[46] It is of the essence of the remedy that the purchaser should obtain the land.[47]

(b) Remedy discretionary. Like other equitable remedies, specific performance is discretionary. However, the court's discretion is governed by settled principles.[48] Examples of where the remedy may be refused include the following— **12–116**

    (i) in proper cases where there is mistake or great hardship,[49] even though these do not invalidate the contract at law;

    (ii) where there has been delay causing injustice to the other party[50];

    (iii) where the vendor would be required to take hostile proceedings against his wife, in order to terminate her matrimonial home rights[51];

    (iv) where the property is being used for illegal purposes, which would make the purchaser liable to prosecution,[52] even though on this ground he has no right to terminate the contract; or

    (v) where the vendor's title is doubtful but he has failed to disclose the known cause of that doubt and the purchaser has agreed to accept any defects that there may be.[53]

---

[45] *Price v. Strange* [1978] Ch. 337, disapproving statements in Fry, *Specific Performance; Lyus v. Prowsa Developments Ltd* [1982] 1 W.L.R. 1044.

[46] *E. Johnson & Co. (Barbados) Ltd v. N.S.R. Ltd.* [1997] A.C. 400 at 409–411.

[47] *Re Scott and Alvarez's Contract* [1895] 2 Ch. 603 at 615.

[48] *AMEC Properties Ltd v. Planning Research & Systems Plc, supra,* at 72. The court's discretion cannot be fettered by any agreement between the parties: *Quadrant Visual Communications Ltd v. Hutchison Telephone (U.K.) Ltd* [1993] B.C.L.C. 442 at 451.

[49] Snell *Equity,* 602, 612. See *Patel v. Ali* [1984] Ch. 283 (personal hardship combined with delay). The mere fact that the vendor company has been placed in receivership is no defence to an action for specific performance: *Freevale Ltd v. Metrostore (Holdings) Ltd* [1984] Ch. 199; nor will a court take into account the effects of any such decree on the likely distribution of the assets of an insolvent company: *AMEC Properties Ltd v. Planning Research & Systems Plc, supra.*

[50] See *Lazard Brothers & Co. Ltd v. Fairfield Properties Co. (Mayfair) Ltd* (1977) 121 S.J. 793, not following *Milward v. Earl of Thanet* (1801) 5 Ves. 720n.; *Easton v. Brown* [1981] 3 All E.R. 278.

[51] *Wroth v. Tyler* [1974] Ch. 30.

[52] *Hope v. Walter* [1900] 1 Ch. 257.

[53] *Faruqi v. English Real Estates Ltd* [1979] 1 W.L.R. 963; [1992] C.L.J. 263 at 287 (C.H.). Where the vendor's title is bad but he knew only that it was doubtful, a purchaser who agreed to take the land subject to any defects but does not complete will be in breach of contract. In such a case, the court is unlikely to decree specific performance but will leave the vendor to his remedy in damages: *Warren v. Richardson* (1830) You. 1; *Re Scott and Alvarez's Contract (No. 2)* [1895] 2 Ch. 603; see [1992] C.L.J. 263 at 288 (C.H.); *ante,* para. 12–078. Where the vendor has failed to disclose a latent defect in title of which he knows or ought to have known,

In these cases the contract will remain binding at law, so that the party in default will be liable in damages, but equity will not assist with a decree of specific performance. On the other hand, specific performance may be decreed before the legal time for performance has arrived if there has been an anticipatory breach, *e.g.* by repudiation.[54]

12–117   *(c) Specific performance with abatement of the price or damages.* Specific performance may be decreed in cases where the vendor is unable to convey what he contracted to sell, either because he has misdescribed the land in the particulars of sale[55] or because the property is subject to some undisclosed incumbrance.[56]

12–118   (1) THE PURCHASER'S REMEDIES. In the absence of hardship,[57] the purchaser may always seek specific performance of the contract subject to an abatement of the price[58] for the deficiency.[59] Thus in one case, three legal tenants in common contracted to sell land, but one of them lacked capacity. The purchaser was able to obtain specific performance of the two shares that could be conveyed with compensation for the remainder.[60] The purchaser may in the alternative seek specific performance against the vendor with damages in addition.[61] The precise interrelationship between these alternative remedies is obscure.[62] Specific performance with compensation was developed by courts of equity in the eighteenth century, but is was only in 1858 that the Court of Chancery was given a general power to award damages in addition to a decree for specific performance.[63]

he cannot rely on a condition of sale in general terms to protect himself, and will therefore be in breach of his obligation to show a good title. The vendor will therefore be unable to obtain specific performance and will be liable to the purchaser in damages: *ante*, paras 12–069, 12–070. For the gradations of title, see *ante*, para. 12–073.

[54] *Hasham v. Zenab* [1960] A.C. 316. See (1960) 76 L.Q.R. 200 (R.E.M.).

[55] *Ante*, para. 12–064.

[56] *Ante*, para. 12–068.

[57] For a case of hardship see *Earl of Durham v. Legard* (1865) 34 Beav. 611 (no specific performance with abatement where the acreage given in the particulars of sale was nearly twice what it actually was but where the contract price had been agreed on the basis of the property's rental income not its acreage).

[58] The remedy is variously described as specific performance either with compensation or with abatement of the price. See [1981] C.L.J. 47 (C.H.).

[59] *Rutherford v. Acton-Adams* [1915] A.C. 866 at 870. The decision in *Rudd v. Lascelles* [1900] 1 Ch. 815, that a purchaser cannot obtain specific performance with compensation in cases where the property differs substantially from that which the vendor contracted to convey, appears to be based on an erroneous application of principles (considered *infra*) by which in *vendor* may obtain the remedy. See [1981] C.L.J. 47 at 59 (C.H.).

[60] *Basma v. Weekes* [1950] A.C. 441 (on appeal from Sierra Leone, where legal tenancies in common were still possible).

[61] See Supreme Court Act 1981, s.50; *ante*, para. 4–015.

[62] See [1981] C.L.J. 47 at 67 (C.H.). Where the purchaser seeks compensation he may be unable to recover any consequential loss. It has also been held that compensation can be recovered only up to the amount of the purchase price. For any additional sum, the purchaser must seek damages: *Grant v. Dawkins* [1973] 1 W.L.R. 1406. *Sed quaere.*

[63] Chancery Amendment Act 1858, s.2; see *ante*, para. 4–015. The Court of Chancery did on occasions award damages prior to that date: see (1992) 108 L.Q.R. 652 (P. McDermott).

(2) THE VENDOR'S REMEDY. A vendor who was unable to convey exactly **12–119** what he had contracted to transfer had no remedy at law against a purchaser who refused to complete,[64] though this strict rule has long been ameliorated by the employment of conditions of sale.[65] In equity however a breach of contract is not necessarily a bar to relief,[66] and a vendor may seek specific performance if he can comply substantially with the agreement, subject to an abatement of the price "for any small and immaterial deficiency".[67]

(d) Effect of a decree of specific performance. When a decree of specific **12–120** performance is made, the contract remains in force and is not merged in the judgment.[68] However, because the court is seised of the matter, it controls the working out, variation or cancellation of the order,[69] and it does so according to equitable principles.[70] It follows that neither party can act unilaterally thereafter without the leave of the court, *e.g.* by serving a notice to complete on the other[71] or by contracting to sell the property to a third party.[72] If the order is not complied with, the claimant may apply to the court either for its enforcement or to dissolve the order and put an end to the contract.[73] If the order is dissolved, he will then become entitled to damages.[74] He cannot claim such dissolution as of right and the court will not order it if to do so would be unjust in the circumstances then existing to the other party,[75] for equity "will not permit a party unconscionably to insist upon his legal rights".[76]

6. Injunction. This equitable remedy, the negative counterpart of specific **12–121** performance, is rarely appropriate in cases of vendor and purchaser, but it may

---

[64] *Tomkins v. White* (1806) 3 Smith's Rep. 435. The common law rule of strict compliance was subject to the exception of matters *de minimis*: *Belworth v. Hassell* (1815) 4 Camp. 140.

[65] See in particular the condition, in use since the beginning of the nineteenth century, that omissions and errors in description should not annul the sale and that the purchaser should complete with or (in some forms of the condition) without compensation. The vendor will not be able to rely on such a condition where the error or omission is substantial: *Flight v. Booth* (1834) 1 Bing. (N.C.) 370; *ante*, para. 12–065.

[66] "Equity does not need to expunge a breach of contract in order to award specific performance": *Raineri v. Miles* [1981] A.C. 1050 at 1063, *per* Templeman L.J. See *Equity and Contemporary Legal Developments* (ed. S. Goldstein), p. 829 at 855 (C.H.).

[67] *Rutherford v. Acton-Adams, supra*, at 869, 870, *per* Viscount Haldane; *ante*, para. 12–064. For the close interrelationship between the legal and equitable rules, see [1992] C.L.J. 263 at 270 (C.H.).

[68] *Austins of East Ham Ltd v. Macey* [1941] Ch. 338 at 341; *Johnson v. Agnew* [1980] A.C. 367 at 393.

[69] *Singh v. Nazeer* [1979] Ch. 474 at 480, 481. It is otherwise if the parties themselves come to an agreement: *ibid.*

[70] *Johnson v. Agnew, supra*, at 399.

[71] *Singh v. Nazeer, supra.*

[72] *G.K.N. Distributors Ltd v. Tyne Tees Fabrications Ltd* (1985) 50 P. & C.R. 403.

[73] *Johnson v. Agnew, supra*, at 394.

[74] *ibid.*, at 399.

[75] *ibid.*, at 399; *Hillel v. Christoforides* (1991) 63 P. & C.R. 301. This view has been criticised: see (1980) 96 L.Q.R. 403 (M. Hetherington). However it does seem correct in principle, for the defendant may have acted to his detriment in reliance upon the decree: see (1981) 97 L.Q.R. 26 (D. Jackson).

[76] *Hillel v. Christoforides, supra*, at 304, *per* Millett J.

be useful to prevent a breach of contract, *e.g.* if the vendor threatens to demolish a building while he is still in possession of the property.[77]

7. Rectification and setting aside. These are equitable remedies based on mistake.

12–122   *(a) Rectification.* Rectification may be sought where the agreement that the parties reached was not correctly recorded in their written contract by reason of a common mistake.[78] The court may then correct the mistake so that the terms of the contract accurately reproduce what the parties agreed[79]; and the court may order specific performance of the contract as so rectified, even in the same action.[80] This might be done, for example, where there was an agreement to build and let four houses but the written contract wrongly gave the number as six,[81] or where the rent agreed upon was wrongly stated.[82] The burden of proof in actions for rectification is heavy. The court requires "convincing proof" that the written words were contrary to the mutual intentions of the parties.[83] There is one qualification to the requirement of mutual mistake. A court may order rectification in a case of unilateral mistake, if—

(i) the circumstances make it inequitable to hold the mistaken party to the contract; and

(ii) the other party either knew of the mistake or turned a blind eye to it.[84]

---

[77] Williams V. & P. 558.

[78] *Domb v. Isoz* [1980] Ch. 548 at 559. For the requirement that the mistake must normally be mutual, see *Riverlate Properties Ltd v. Paul* [1975] Ch. 133, disapproving certain nineteenth-century authorities which suggested that a unilateral mistake might suffice. Rectification will not be ordered where there is no mistake as to the effect of the document in issue but only as to some other document: *London Regional Transport v. Wimpey Group Services Ltd* [1986] 2 E.G.L.R. 41.

[79] A contract for the sale of land must be made in writing and incorporate all the terms agreed between the parties: L.P.(M.P.)A. 1989, s.2(1); *ante*, para. 12–018. This does not preclude rectification if the written document does not record what the parties agreed. The court has power to specify the date when a contract comes into being in consequence of an order for rectification: L.P.(M.P.)A. 1989, s.2(4); *ante*, para. 12–032.

[80] *Craddock Brothers v. Hunt* [1923] 2 Ch. 136; *U.S.A. v. Motor Trucks Ltd* [1924] A.C. 196. For details of the remedy, see generally Snell, *Equity*, 626–636; *Riverlate Properties Ltd v. Paul, supra.*

[81] *Olley v. Fisher* (1886) 34 Ch.D. 367.

[82] *Garrard v. Frankel* (1862) 30 Beav. 445; but see *Riverlate Properties Ltd v. Paul, supra*, at 142.

[83] *Joscelyne v. Nissen* [1970] 2 Q.B. 86 at 98, *per* Russell L.J.; *Blacklocks v. J.B. Developments (Godalming) Ltd* [1982] Ch. 183 at 191, *per* Mervyn Davies J.

[84] *Commission for the New Towns v. Cooper (Great Britain) Ltd* [1995] Ch. 259; [1995] C.L.J. 502 (A. J. Oakley) (landlord mistakenly granted tenant a right to terminate the lease, having been misled into doing so by the tenant); *J.J. Huber Ltd v. The Private DIY Co. Ltd* (1995) 70 P. & C.R. D33 (mistake as to liability for rates in lease appreciated by the tenant); *Coles v. William Hill Organisation Ltd* [1998] E.G.C.S. 40 (break clause included by mistake of which tenants were aware). See too *Weeds v. Blaney* [1978] 2 E.G.L.R. 84; *Thomas Bates & Son Ltd v. Wyndham's (Lingerie) Ltd* [1981] 1 W.L.R. 505; *Kemp v. Neptune Concrete Ltd* [1988] 2 E.G.L.R. 87.

Where the title to land is unregistered, rectification may be used to correct mistakes in a conveyance, *e.g.* if it gives the purchaser more land,[85] or wider rights,[86] than he was entitled to have under the contract, or if it creates a joint tenancy when a tenancy in common was intended.[87] But, because it is an equitable remedy, it will not be available where there has been long delay, or where the land affected has passed into the hands of a bona fide purchaser who had no notice of the mistake in the conveyance.[88] Since the right to rectification is a "mere equity", such a purchaser need not necessarily acquire the legal estate.[89]

Where the title to land is registered, the court or registrar has a discretionary power to rectify the register in cases where, by reason of any entry made under a mistake, it may be deemed just to rectify the register.[90] If a person in actual occupation of registered land has the benefit of such a right to seek rectification, that right will constitute an overriding interest[91] binding on any third party who acquires the land.[92]

(b) Setting aside for mistake. At common law, a contract will be void if it was made under a mutual mistake the renders its subject-matter "essentially and radically different" from that which the parties believed to exist.[93] There is also an equitable jurisdiction to set aside or adjust transactions vitiated by mistake, even after execution of a conveyance or transfer. This applies not just to mistakes as to subject matter but to "a wider and perhaps unlimited category of 'fundamental' mistake".[94] In one case A took a lease of a fishery from B, both supposing it to be B's property when in fact it was A's property. The House of Lords set aside the lease in equity, subject to terms under which (*inter alia*) A was to reimburse B for his expenditure in obtaining a private Act of Parliament and in improving the fishery.[95] In another case A took a lease of a flat from B at a rent of £250, both believing that the former restricted rent of £140 did not apply, when in fact it did apply. The Court of Appeal set aside the lease on elaborate terms designed to protect the tenant but to allow the landlord to claim a statutory increase in rent.[96] There are however two prerequisites to the operation of the equitable jurisdiction. First, there must

12–123

---

[85] *Beale v. Kyte* [1907] 1 Ch. 564.
[86] *Clarke v. Barnes* [1929] 2 Ch. 368; *cf. post*, para. 18–120.
[87] *Re Colebrook's Conveyances* [1972] 1 W.L.R. 1397.
[88] Williams V. & P. 791; *Smith v. Jones* [1954] 1 W.L.R. 1089; *Taylor Barnard Ltd v. Tozer* [1984] 1 E.G.L.R. 21; *cf Garrard v. Frankel* (1862) 30 Beav. 445.
[89] *Ante*, para. 5–012.
[90] L.R.A. 1925, s.82(1)(h); *ante*, para. 6–125.
[91] Under L.R.A. 1925, s.70(1)(g); *ante*, para. 6–047.
[92] *Blacklocks v. J.B. Developments (Godalming) Ltd* [1982] Ch. 183; *Nurdin & Peacock Plc v. D. B. Ramsden & Co. Ltd* [1999] 1 E.G.L.R. 119 at 124–126; *ante*, para. 6–052.
[93] *Associated Japanese Bank (International) Ltd v. Credit du Nord S.A.* [1989] 1 W.L.R. 255 at 268, *per* Steyn J. (setting out the principles applicable to common law mistake); see (1988) 104 L.Q.R. 501 (G. H. Treitel).
[94] *William Sindall Plc v. Cambridgeshire C.C.* [1994] 1 W.L.R. 1016 at 1042, *per* Evans L.J.
[95] *Cooper v. Phibbs* (1867) L.R. 2 H.L. 149.
[96] *Solle v. Butcher* [1950] 1 K.B. 671 (Jenkins L.J. dissenting on the ground that the mistake was one of law against which the court could not at that time grant relief: but see now *Kleinwort Benson Ltd v. Glasgow City Council* [1999] 1 A.C. 153; *ante*, para. 12–044).

either be mutual mistake or inequitable conduct by one party.[97] Secondly, the matter must not be one where the parties have by their contract allocated the risk of the mistake. Thus where a purchaser takes land subject to all easements save those of which the vendor knows or has the means of knowledge, he cannot rescind the contract on grounds of mistake when an easement subsequently comes to light.[98]

12–124   **8. Declarations by the court (Vendor and Purchaser Summons).** In the nineteenth century, issues as to title were usually settled in specific performance proceedings, which were costly and cumbersome.[99] In a much expedited form, specific performance proceedings are once again the normal method for deciding disputes which may arise in the investigation of title (*e.g.* whether a good title has been shown according to the contract, or whether some incumbrance must be accepted by the purchaser). However, there are two alternative procedures available. The first is to ask the court to make a declaration.[1] The second is the Vendor and Purchaser Summons, introduced by the Vendor and Purchaser Act 1874[2] and now authorised by the Law of Property Act 1925.[3] This is a little used summary procedure[4] designed for the decision of particular points arising between contract and conveyance. It may not be used to question the existence or validity of the contract, but only for matters arising under it.[5] The court may make such order as it thinks just. This will normally be a declaration, but it may sometimes include an order for termination of the contract and repayment of deposit and conveyancing expenses.[6] What a purchaser cannot recover are damages over and above such expenses, such as damages for delay.[7] If a party wishes for a declaration as to the validity of the contract, or any other matter outside the scope of a Vendor and Purchaser Summons (including a claim for damages for loss of bargains), he must claim it in an ordinary action.

---

[97] *Riverlate Properties Ltd v. Paul* [1975] Ch. 133.
[98] *William Sindall Plc v. Cambridgeshire C.C.* [1994] 1 W.L.R. 1016 at 1035.
[99] For a detailed account see (1992) 108 L.Q.R. 280 at 292–301 (C.H.).
[1] CPR, Sched. 1, R15.16.
[2] s.9.
[3] s.49(1). Formerly a Vendor and Purchaser Summons was indicated by the title "*Re A's and B's contract*". This has now been abrogated: see Practice Direction (Chancery Procedure), para. 2, [1983] 1 W.L.R. 4.
[4] "This is nowadays a not altogether usual form of application": *Walia v. Michael Naughton Ltd* [1985] 1 W.L.R. 1115 at 1116, *per* Judge Finlay.
[5] L.P.A. 1925, s.49(1).
[6] *Re Hargreaves and Thompson's Contract* (1886) 32 Ch.D. 454. Claims for compensation are expressly within the scope of such a summons: L.P.A. 1925, s.49(1).
[7] *Re Wilsons and Steven's Contract* [1894] 3 Ch. 546. Since the Rule in *Bain v. Fothergill* (1874) L.R. 7 H.L. 158 was abolished by L.P.(M.P.)A. 1989, s.3 (*ante*, para. 12–103), this is likely to be a deterrent to using the Vendor and Purchaser Summons.

CHAPTER 13

PROPRIETARY ESTOPPEL

Section 1. The Nature of Proprietary Estoppel

1. The basis of the doctrine. Proprietary estoppel, which is also sometimes   **13–001**
referred to as "estoppel by acquiescence" or "estoppel by encouragement",[1]
is a means by which property rights may be affected or created.[2] The term
describes the equitable jurisdiction by which a court may interfere in cases
where the assertion of strict legal rights is found to be unconscionable.[3]
Although this jurisdiction is of ancient origin,[4] it has been much developed by
the courts in recent years[5] and some of its more "archaic and arcane" features
have been abandoned.[6] The flexibility of the jurisdiction is such that the
criteria for relief can be stated only in broad terms.[7] Without attempting to
provide a precise or comprehensive definition, it is possible to summarise the
essential elements of proprietary estoppel as follows.[8]

(i) An equity arises where—

[1] *Taylors Fashions Ltd v. Liverpool Victoria Trustees Co. Ltd* (1979) [1982] Q.B. 133n. at 151,
per Oliver J. The description "quasi-estoppel" (*Kammins Ballrooms Co. Ltd v. Zenith Investments (Torquay) Ltd* [1971] A.C. 850 at 884, *per* Lord Diplock; *J. Willis & Son v. Willis* [1986]
1 E.G.L.R. 62, *per* Parker L.J.), although in some senses accurate, has fortunately not become
widely used.
[2] *Western Fish Products Ltd v. Penwith D.C.* (1978) [1981] 2 All E.R. 204 at 217; *West
Middlesex Golf Club Ltd v. Ealing L.B.C.* (1993) 68 P. & C.R. 461 at 478. See too [1991] Conv.
36 (G. Battersby) (a particularly important contribution to the literature on estoppel). Rights
cannot be created by estoppel in favour of the general public: *CIN Properties Ltd v. Rawlins*
[1995] 2 E.G.L.R. 130 at 134; [1995] Conv. 332 at 336 (M. Haley).
[3] *Taylors Fashions Ltd v. Liverpool Victoria Trustees Co. Ltd, supra*, at 147. See too *Ward v.
Kirkland* [1967] Ch. 194 at 235. For a general account of the jurisdiction, see Snell, *Equity*,
pp. 573 *et seq.*
[4] See, *e.g. Edlin v. Battaly* (1675) 2 Lev. 152; *Short v. Taylor* (c.1693–1700), cited in *Anon* (1709)
2 Eq.Ca.Abr.522.
[5] "The doctrine is one of comparatively recent development (if not recent origin)": *Watson v.
Goldsbrough* [1986] 1 E.G.L.R. 265 at 267, *per* Browne-Wilkinson V.-C.
[6] See *Habib Bank Ltd v. Habib Bank A.G. Zurich* [1981] 1 W.L.R. 1265 at 1285, *per* Oliver
L.J.
[7] The courts are unwilling to define too exactly the ambit of the doctrine: *Amalgamated
Investment & Property Co. Ltd v. Texas Commerce International Bank Ltd* [1982] Q.B. 84 at
103; *Taylors Fashions Ltd v. Liverpool Victoria Trustees Co. Ltd, supra*, at 148.
[8] The best-known statement of the principles is found in Lord Kingsdown's dissenting judgment
in *Ramsden v. Dyson* (1866) L.R. 1 H.L. 129 at 170, 171. See too *Rochdale Canal Co. v. King
(No. 2)* (1853) 16 Beav. 630 at 633, 634; *Cairncross v. Lorimer* (1860) 3 Macq. 827 at 829, 830;
De Bussche v. Alt (1878) 8 Ch.D. 286 at 314; *Sarat Chunder Dey v. Gopal Chunder Laha*
(1892) L.R. 19 I.A. 203 at 215, 216; *Chalmers v. Pardoe* [1963] 1 W.L.R. 677 at 681, 682;

(*a*) the owner of land (O) induces, encourages or allows the claimant (C) to believe that he has or will enjoy some right or benefit over O's property;

(*b*) in reliance upon this belief, C acts to his detriment to the knowledge of O; and

(*c*) O then seeks to take unconscionable advantage of C by denying him the right or benefit which he expected to receive.

(ii) This equity gives C the right to go to court to seek relief. C's claim is an equitable one and subject to the normal principles governing equitable remedies.[9]

(iii) The court has a wide discretion as to the manner in which it will give effect to the equity, having regard to all the circumstances of the case and in particular to both the expectations and conduct of the parties.

(iv) The relief which the court may give may be either negative, in the form of an order restraining O from asserting his legal rights, or positive, by ordering O either to grant or convey to C some estate, right or interest in or over his land, to pay C appropriate compensation, or to act in some other way.

The issue in any given case is whether it would be unconscionable for O to deny that which he has allowed or encouraged C to assume to his detriment.[10] The courts no longer inquire (as once they did) whether the circumstances can be "fitted within the confines of some preconceived formula".[11]

The flexibility of proprietary estoppel, in terms both of the circumstances which may fall within its scope and the remedies that a court can give to satisfy any equity which arises, is its strength and its weakness. The court's freedom to mould the remedy to suit the circumstances very precisely, makes the outcome unpredictable. This is not conducive to the settlement of disputes and leads to costly litigation.[12]

Holiday Inns Inc. v. Broadhead (1974) 232 E.G. 951 at 1087; *Crabb v. Arun D.C.* [1976] Ch. 179 at 188; *Western Fish Products Ltd v. Penwith D.C.*, *supra*, at 217; *Watson v. Goldsbrough*, *supra*, at 267; *Roebuck v. Mungovin* [1994] 2 A.C. 224 at 235; *John v. George* (1996) 71 P. & C.R. 375 at 384.

[9] *Ante*, para. 4–014.

[10] *Taylors Fashions Ltd v. Liverpool Victoria Trustees Co. Ltd*, *supra*, at 151, 152, *per* Oliver J. See too *Crabb v. Arun D.C.*, *supra*, at 195; *John v. George*, *supra*, at 143; *Nationwide Anglia B.S. v. Ahmed* (1995) 70 P. & C.R. 381 at 390. For the meaning of unconscionability in this context, see [1995] L.M.C.L.Q. 538 at 540–542 (N. Bamforth).

[11] *Taylors Fashions Ltd v. Liverpool Victoria Trustees Co. Ltd*, *supra*, at 151, 152.

[12] Such litigation may turn on fine points of evidence: *cf. Wayling v. Jones* (1993) 69 P. & C.R. 170; [1996] Fam. Law 89 (R. Bailey-Harris).

Proprietary estoppel has some similarities with both common law estoppel and the now abolished equitable doctrine of part performance. Something must be said at the outset about its relationship with each of these.

2. Relationship with estoppel. It is perhaps unfortunate that proprietary **13–002** estoppel should be so called. Although the equitable doctrine shares some characteristics with estoppel at common law,[13] it differs fundamentally from it.[14] Estoppel in the strict sense is an aspect of the law of evidence by which a person may be precluded from denying something that he has asserted.[15] The principle is that when A, by his word or conduct, has led B to believe in a particular state of affairs, he will not be permitted to deny that assumption once B has acted to his prejudice upon it.[16] Estoppel is purely negative in its operation. It may provide a defence but it is not a cause of action.[17] By contrast, proprietary estoppel may operate positively and found a cause of action,[18] and this has long been recognised.[19]

3. Relationship with the former doctrine of part performance. Until the **13–003** Law of Property (Miscellaneous) Provisions Act 1989 came into force, there was no requirement that a contract for the sale of an interest in land should be made in writing.[20] An oral contract was valid, but was unenforceable in the absence of either a sufficient memorandum in writing or sufficient acts of part performance.[21] The basis of the doctrine of part performance was very similar to that of proprietary estoppel. It was that, "if one party to an agreement stands by and lets the other party incur expense or prejudice his position on the faith of the agreement being valid he will not then be allowed to turn round and assert that the agreement is unenforceable".[22] Not only was the close kinship between the two doctrines often acknowledged in the course of the

---

[13] *cf. Proctor v. Bennis* (1887) 36 Ch.D. 740 at 765.

[14] Snell, *Equity*, pp. 568 *et seq*. For the relationship between proprietary and promissory estoppel, see G.H. Treitel, *The Law of Contract* (10th ed.), pp. 135 *et seq*.; [1988] Conv. 346 (P. T. Evans).

[15] *London Joint Stock Bank v. Macmillan* [1918] A.C. 777 at 818; *Evans v. Bartlam* [1937] A.C. 473 at 484. See too *Sarat Chunder Dey v. Gopal Chunder Laha, supra*, at 210. The trend in more recent authorities has been to acknowledge that it is also a substantive rule of law: *Canadian and Dominion Sugar Co. Ltd v. Canadian National (West Indies) Steamship Ltd* [1947] A.C. 46 at 56.

[16] *Pickard v. Sears* (1837) 6 A. & E. 469 at 474; *Maclaine v. Gatty* [1921] 1 A.C. 376 at 386; *Moorgate Mercantile Co. Ltd v. Twitchings* [1976] Q.B. 225 at 241.

[17] *Seton, Laing & Co. v. Lafone* (1887) 19 Q.B.D. 68 at 70; *Low v. Bouverie* [1891] 3 Ch. 82 at 101.

[18] *Crabb v. Arun D.C., supra*, at 187.

[19] "The common-law doctrine of estoppel . . . is not the same as the equitable doctrine. You cannot found an action on it as you can in equity": *Williams v. Pinckney* (1897) 67 L.J.Ch. 34 at 37, *per* Vaughan Williams L.J.

[20] For the Law of Property (Miscellaneous Provisions) Act 1989, s.2, which came into force on September 27, 1989, see *ante*, para. 12–018.

[21] L.P.A. 1925, s.40, repealed by L.P.(M.P.)A. 1989, s.4. See the previous edition of this work at pp. 571 *et seq*.

[22] *Steadman v. Steadman* [1976] A.C. 536 at 540, *per* Lord Reid. For discussion, see *Yaxley v. Gotts* [1994] 2 A.C. 224 at 235.

nineteenth century, but in some cases the two were not clearly differentiated.[23] Indeed in the present century the very existence of the doctrine of proprietary estoppel was denied and the earlier authorities were explained as examples of the doctrine of part performance.[24] Such a view was inconsistent with earlier authority[25] and is now plainly untenable. The existence of a valid contract is not a prerequisite to an equity by estoppel.[26] Furthermore, it was an essential element of the doctrine of part performance that the acts relied upon should be referable to the contract.[27] There is no requirement in relation to proprietary estoppel that the detrimental acts should point to any arrangement between the parties because none may exist. The doctrine of part performance has now been abolished and all contracts for the sale of any interest in land must be made in writing.[28] This has not affected the operation of the doctrine of proprietary estoppel.[29]

Section 2. Historical Background

13–004   **1. The emergence of the doctrine.** The earliest cases of proprietary estoppel were principally concerned with two situations. The first was where C built on O's land in the mistaken belief either that it was his or that he had a right to do so,[30] as where a life tenant granted to C a lease that he had no power to grant, and the remainderman, O, knowing of the defect in title, stood by while C expended money on the premises.[31] No equity would arise if C was either aware of the defect in his title,[32] or acted to his detriment while the parties were still negotiating the terms of a formal agreement.[33] The second situation was where C was O's tenant and was encouraged to believe either

---

[23] See, *e.g. Gregory v. Mighell* (1811) 18 Ves. 328 at 333; *Dillwyn v. Llewelyn* (1862) 4 De G.F. & J. 517 at 521; *Nunn v. Fabian* (1865) 11 Jur. (N.S.) 868; *Ramsden v. Dyson* (1866) L.R. 1 H.L. 129 at 170, 171; *McManus v. Cooke* (1887) 35 Ch.D. 681 at 694 *et seq.*

[24] *Ariff v. Jadunath Majumdar* (1931) L.R. 58 I.A. 91 at 102; *Canadian Pacific Ry. Co. v. R.* [1931] A.C. 414 at 428, 429. The opinion of the Privy Council was in each case given by Lord Russell of Killowen. For an attempt to run together contract and proprietary estoppel, see *Vaughan v. Vaughan* [1953] 1 Q.B. 762 at 768.

[25] See, *e.g. Forbes v. Ralli* (1925) L.R. 52 I.A. 178 at 187.

[26] *Voyce v. Voyce* (1991) 62 P. & C.R. 290 at 296. For the relationship between proprietary estoppel and contract, see *post*, para. 13–034.

[27] *Maddison v. Alderson* (1883) 8 App. Cas. 467 at 479; and see the previous edition of this work at p. 591.

[28] L.P.(M.P.)A. 1989, s.2.

[29] *cf. Akiens v. Salomon* (1992) 65 P. & C.R. 364; and see (1987) Law. Com. No. 164 at paras 5.4 *et seq.*

[30] *Short v. Taylor* (c.1693–1700) 2 Eq.Cas.Abr. 522 at 523; *Steed v. Whitaker* (1740) Barn. C. 220; *Lord Cawdor v. Lewis* (1835) 1 Y. & C.Ex. 427.

[31] *Huning v. Ferrers* (1711) Gilb. Rep. 85; *Savage v. Foster* (1723) 9 Mod. 35; *Stiles v. Cowper* (1748) 3 Atk. 693.

[32] *Kenney v. Brown* (1796) 3 Ridgw. P.C. 462 at 518, 519; *Master, etc., of Clare Hall v. Harding* (1848) 6 Hare 273.

[33] *East India Co. v. Vincent* (1740) 2 Atk. 83.

that he would be granted some renewal or extension of his term,[34] or that O would not exercise some right which he had under the lease.[35] Such circumstances were often alleged by C, but seldom established.[36] Although in some of these earlier cases the relief given took the negative form of an injunction to restrain ejectment proceedings at common law brought by O against C,[37] in others it was of a positive character.[38] O might be ordered to pay compensation to C for his expenditure (secured if need be by a lien over O's land),[39] to execute a conveyance in C's favour[40] or to take some other step to perfect C's title.[41]

2. The principles defined. In the middle of the nineteenth century, the **13–005** doctrine of proprietary estoppel was rapidly developed in a series of decisions arising out of the activities of industrial entrepreneurs.[42] The cases commonly arose out of the construction of a railway or canal by C with the consent of O, but before O had granted C the appropriate legal right over his land (whether by a conveyance of land or the grant of an easement).[43] In all of these cases the court gave effect to C's equity, usually by ordering O to make the necessary grant to C[44] on terms that C paid O an appropriate sum for the right or interest obtained. These decisions provided the foundation for the modern

---

[34] Although this principle was always accepted (see, *e.g. Nunn v. Fabian* (1865) 11 Jur. (N.S.) 868; *Ramsden v. Dyson* (1866) L.R. 1 H.L. 129 at 140, 141, 170), there are few cases (if any) in which it was established. *Gregory v. Mighell* (1811) 18 Ves. 328, which is usually cited as illustrative, was a case of part performance.

[35] *Jackson v. Cator* (1800) 5 Ves. 688 (tenant beautified gardens with landord's assent; landlord could not then exercise his right to cut timber on the demised premises).

[36] *Att.-Gen. v. Baliol College, Oxford* (1744) 9 Mod. 407; *Dann v. Spurrier* (1802) 7 Ves. 231; *Pilling v. Armitage* (1805) 12 Ves. 78; *Ramsden v. Dyson, supra*. These decisions have their modern counterpart in cases where a business tenant negotiates with his landlord for a new lease and forgoes his statutory right to a new tenancy under L. & T.A. 1954, Pt II (*post*, para. 22–070). The tenant sometimes alleges that the landlord is estopped from refusing to grant him a new lease: see *J.T. Developments Ltd v. Quinn* (1990) 62 P. & C.R. 33 (where the claim succeeded).

[37] *e.g. Huning v. Ferrers, supra; Steed v. Whitaker, supra*. An injunction might also be granted to prevent O interfering with C's exercise of his right: *Cotching v. Bassett* (1862) 32 Beav. 101 (alteration to ancient lights by C with O's assent; O restrained from obstructing them).

[38] See *Lord Cawdor v. Lewis, supra*, at 433.

[39] *e.g. Neesom v. Clarkson* (1845) 4 Hare 97; *Unity Joint Stock Mutual Banking Association v. King* (1858) 25 Beav. 72.

[40] *e.g. Stiles v. Cowper, supra*.

[41] See *Savage v. Foster, supra*, where O was required to levy a fine to bar his rights under an entail.

[42] The cases reveal a strong judicial sympathy for these activities.

[43] *Powell v. Thomas* (1848) 6 Hare 300; *Duke of Devonshire v. Eglin* (1851) 14 Beav. 530; *Duke of Beaufort v. Patrick* (1853) 17 Beav. 60; *Somersetshire Coal Co. v. Harcourt* (1858) 2 De G. & J. 596; *Laird v. Birkenhead Rly. Co.* (1859) Johns. 500; *Mold v. Wheatcroft* (1859) 27 Beav. 510. See too *Rochdale Canal Co. v. King (No.2)* (1853) 16 Beav. 630 (construction of mill by C on understanding that water could be taken from O's canal); *Unity Joint Stock Mutual Banking Association v. King, supra* (father permitted sons to construct granaries and other buildings on his land).

[44] In one case a canal company was granted an injunction against the landowner on terms that it exercised its statutory powers of compulsory purchase to acquire the land: *Somersetshire Coal Co. v. Harcourt, supra*.

law of estoppel which subsequently emerged in a series of important decisions.[45] The circumstances which would give rise to an equity were clarified,[46]
and it was recognised that the court had a wide discretion as to how it could
most appropriately give effect to that equity.[47] "The court must look at the
circumstances in each case to decide in what way the equity can be satisfied."[48] This would commonly (but not necessarily) involve the grant of
some proprietary right or interest by O to C. Relief would often be given on
terms (*e.g.* as to payment), but the doctrine could be employed to perfect a
gift.[49] The courts clearly distinguished between the equity, which arose from
C's detrimental reliance, and the relief by which effect was given to it.
Although a court would (if need be) protect C in his possession pending the
grant of relief by the court,[50] C did not enjoy any defined property right in
consequence of his equity until the court made its final order.[51] That order
would be implemented by a conveyance or grant of the property right (if any)
to which C was adjudged to be entitled. C could enforce his equity against
both O and any person who acquired O's land with notice of it.[52] There is no
suggestion in the extensive corpus of nineteenth-century authority that proprietary estoppel was a means by which novel property rights might be created.[53]
It was however recognised that in giving effect to an equity arising by
estoppel, a court might declare a licence granted by O to C to be irrevocable,
as where C had acted to his detriment in the belief encouraged by O that he
might enjoy the premises on a permanent basis.[54]

13–006   **3. Licences by estoppel.** Although these principles were reaffirmed by the
Privy Council as late as 1963,[55] there was a divergence from them shortly
thereafter in some but not all[56] cases. There were two developments of
importance. First, the equity which arose by estoppel and the subsequent order
of the court giving effect to it came to be confused. If the court held that C was

[45] *Dillwyn v. Llewelyn* (1862) 4 De G.F. & J. 517; *Ramsden v. Dyson* (1866) L.R. 1 H.L. 129;
Plimmer v. Mayor, etc., of Wellington (1884) 9 App.Cas. 699. However, as will be apparent
from the foregoing analysis, the suggestion that the evolution of the doctrine of proprietary
estoppel "in the form in which we now know it cannot be dated before *Dillwyn v. Llewelyn*"
(*Sen v. Headley* [1991] Ch. 425 at 439, *per* Nourse L.J.) is incorrect.
[46] *Ramsden v. Dyson, supra,* at 170, 171.
[47] *Dillwyn v. Llewelyn, supra,* at 522; *Ramsden v. Dyson, supra,* at 171; *Plimmer v. Mayor, etc.,
of Wellington, supra,* at 713, 714.
[48] *Plimmer v. Mayor, etc., of Wellington, supra,* at 714, *per* Sir Arthur Hobhouse.
[49] C's detrimental reliance took the case out of the general principle that equity would not perfect
an imperfect gift: *Dillwyn v. Llewelyn, supra,* at 521.
[50] *Ramsden v. Dyson, supra,* at 171.
[51] In some of the cases C appears to have been no more than a licensee: see *e.g. Duke of
Devonshire v. Eglin, supra.*
[52] *Duke of Beaufort v. Patrick, supra; Plimmer v. Mayor, etc., of Wellington, supra.*
[53] Indeed the converse appears to have been the case. If the "right" visualised by the parties was
of too indefinite a character to be expressly granted, C's claim would fail: *Bankart v. Tennant*
(1870) L.R. 10 Eq. 141 at 148, 149.
[54] *Plimmer v. Mayor, etc., of Wellington, supra.* For the analogous doctrine of the executed
licence, see *post,* para. 13–037.
[55] *Chalmers v. Pardoe* [1963] 1 W.L.R. 677 at 683, 684.
[56] See, *e.g. Dodsworth v. Dodsworth* (1973) 228 E.G. 1115.

entitled to a particular right over O's land by estoppel, C would be regarded as having acquired this right from the time at which he had acted to his detriment and not merely from the time of the court's order.[57] Thus in one case concerned with unregistered land,[58] C was held to have an "equity which amounted to an equitable easement" over O's land.[59] However, that right was not in all respects the same as an equitable easement expressly granted because it was not registrable as a land charge and depended for its protection against third parties on the doctrine of notice.[60] Secondly, the doctrine of proprietary estoppel came to be employed to protect the rights of occupation of licensees.[61] If C, a licensee, acted to his detriment in reliance on an understanding that he could remain on O's land for as long as he wished, his licence became irrevocable.[62] That right of occupation—"a licence coupled with an equity"[63]—would be protected not only against O himself, but against any successor in title who took with notice.[64] It was immaterial whether that successor in title acquired the land before[65] or after[66] C had obtained an order of the court giving effect to his equity. In this way such "equitable licences"[67] or "licences by estoppel"[68] were in effect given the status of equitable proprietary rights.[69]

Although an equity arising by estoppel is probably best regarded as a species of equitable proprietary right,[70] it is questionable whether an estoppel licence can do so. There was no case prior to 1926 in which a licence made irrevocable by estoppel was held to bind a third party.[71] As the creation of novel equitable interests after 1925 appears to have been prohibited by

---

[57] See, *e.g. Ward v. Kirkland* [1967] Ch. 194 at 242, 243. For criticism, see [1988] Conv. 346 at 352, 353 (P. T. Evans).

[58] *E.R. Ives Investment Ltd v. High* [1967] 2 Q.B. 379. It is difficult to distil a ratio from the case: see (1967) 31 Conv. (N.S.) 332 (F.R. Crane); (1967) 30 M.L.R. 580 (H.W. Wilkinson); [1991] Conv. 36 at 39; (1995) 58 M.L.R. 637 at 643 (G. Battersby).

[59] *E.R. Ives Investment Ltd v. High, supra,* at 405, *per* Winn L.J. See too *Shiloh Spinners Ltd v. Harding* [1973] A.C. 691 at 721 (where Lord Wilberforce, in discussing the earlier decision, referred to "a right by estoppel—producing an effect similar to an easement").

[60] *Ante,* para. 5–104. The case might now be explained on the basis that the equity arising by estoppel may itself be a proprietary right which will bind a purchaser of unregistered land with notice: *post,* para. 13–031.

[61] *Inwards v. Baker* [1965] 2 Q.B. 29; *Jones v. Jones* [1977] 1 W.L.R. 438; *Williams v. Staite* [1979] Ch. 291. See too *Hussey v. Palmer* [1972] 1 W.L.R. 1286.

[62] *Re Sharpe* [1980] 1 W.L.R. 219 at 223.

[63] *Inwards v. Baker, supra,* at 37, *per* Lord Denning M.R.

[64] *ibid.*

[65] *ibid.*

[66] *Williams v. Staite, supra.*

[67] *Re Sharpe, supra,* at 225 *per* Browne-Wilkinson J.; *J. Willis & Son v. Willis* [1986] 1 E.G.L.R. 62 at 63, *per* Parker L.J.

[68] A phrase widely used by academic writers: see, *e.g.* [1981] Conv. 347 (P. Todd).

[69] See [1973] C.L.J. 123 at 125 *et seq.* (R.J. Smith). *cf. Pascoe v. Turner* [1979] 1 W.L.R. 431 at 439.

[70] *Post,* para. 13–029. This view is supported by nineteenth-century authority: see, *e.g. Duke of Beaufort v. Patrick* (1853) 17 Beav. 60.

[71] In *Plimmer v. Mayor, etc., of Wellington* (1884) 9 App.Cas. 699, an equity arising by estoppel, to which effect was subsequently given by an irrevocable licence, was held binding on a statutory successor in title. For the full facts of the case, see (1883) 1 N.Z.L.R. (C.A.) 229.

statute,[72] the correctness of treating an estoppel licence as an equitable proprietary right is open to doubt. Furthermore, not only has it now been settled that contractual licences do not create equitable interests in land,[73] but it has also been suggested that no licence of any kind may do so.[74] In any event, it is not obvious that a licence declared to be irrevocable by reason of estoppel should create an equitable interest in land when a contractual licence does not.[75]

Where a court is asked to give effect to an equity arising by estoppel, the fact that the claimant, C, is a licensee should of itself be irrelevant. The question in each case should be how best to give effect to the equity that has arisen in his favour.[76] The trend of modern decisions has been to adopt this approach.[77] Indeed, over the last decade or so there has been a reversion to the principles laid down in the nineteenth century.[78]

Section 3. The Elements of Estoppel

A. Establishing the Equity

A claimant who wishes to establish an equity arising by estoppel must satisfy the court on three matters.

13–007   **1. Encouragement or acquiescence.** The owner of the land, O must have encouraged C by words or conduct to believe that he has or will in the future enjoy some right or benefit over O's property. The mere fact that C acts to his detriment in the expectation of acquiring rights over O's land will not raise an equity in his favour unless O has encouraged that expectation.[79] O's conduct may be either active or passive.[80]

---

[72] L.P.A. 1925, s.4(1), proviso. See *ante*, para. 4–090.

[73] *Ashburn Anstalt v. Arnold* [1989] Ch. 1; *post*, para. 17–019. See too *Canadian Imperial Bank of Commerce v. Bello* (1991) 64 P. & C.R. 48 at 51; *I.D.C. Group Ltd v. Clark* [1992] 1 E.G.L.R. 187 at 189.

[74] *I.D.C. Group Ltd v. Clark, supra,* at 189.

[75] See (1988) 51 M.L.R. 226 (J. Hill); [1991] Conv. 36 (G. Battersby). cf. *Habermann v. Koehler* (1996) 73 P. & C.R. 515.

[76] For the forms of relief which the court may give, see *post*, para. 13–020.

[77] See, *e.g. Pascoe v. Turner* [1979] 1 W.L.R. 431; *Burrows v. Sharp* (1989) 23 H.L.R. 83.

[78] The starting point was the judgment of Scarman L.J. in *Crabb v. Arun D.C.* [1976] Ch. 179 at 192 *et seq.* which has been widely applied since: see, *e.g. Griffiths v. Williams* [1978] 2 E.G.L.R. 121; *Jones v. Jones* [1977] 1 W.L.R. 438 at 443; *Pascoe v. Turner, supra,* at 437; *Coombes v. Smith* [1986] 1 W.L.R. 808 at 815; *Roebuck v. Mungovin* [1994] 2 A.C. 224 at 235.

[79] *Att.-Gen v. Baliol College, Oxford* (1744) 9 Mod. 407; *Kenney v. Brown* (1796) 3 Ridgw. P.C. 462; *Pilling & Armitage* (1805) 12 Ves. 78; *Master, etc., of Clare Hall v. Harding* (1848) 6 Hare 273; *Ramsden v. Dyson* (1866) L.R. 1 H.L. 129; *Brinnand v. Ewens* (1987) 19 H.L.R. 415.

[80] *Russell v. Watts* (1883) 25 Ch.D. 559 at 576; *Plimmer v. Mayor, etc., of Wellington* (1884) 9 App.Cas. 699 at 712.

(a) Active encouragement. Active conduct has been held to include— **13–008**

(i) a request that C should act in a particular manner[81];

(ii) a written or oral assurance that C would have certain rights over O's land[82]; or

(iii) the giving of consent to C to undertake construction work either on O's land,[83] or on his own in a manner which would in some way affect O.[84]

In cases of active encouragement, it is no bar to an equity arising in favour of C that he was under no misapprehension as to his rights,[85] or that either O alone, or both O and C acted under a mistaken assumption as to their respective rights.[86]

(b) Passive encouragement. Passive encouragement occurs when O, an **13–009** owner of land stands by and allows C to act to his detriment knowing that he mistakenly believes that he has or will obtain an interest in or right over O's land.[87] In such a situation, "the circumstance of looking on is in many cases as strong as using terms of encouragement".[88] Thus an equity arose in C's favour where he constructed an engine shed on O's land and O both acquiesced in its construction and accepted rent for it.[89] In another case, in which a lease had been forfeited, the lessors knowingly allowed the underlessees to believe that their sub-leases were still subsisting. The underlessees having

---

[81] *e.g. Plimmer v. Mayor, etc., of Wellington, supra* (C constructed jetty and warehouse at O's request).

[82] *e.g. Dillwyn v. Llewelyn* (1862) 4 De G.F. & J. 517 (memordandum by O that he gave his lands to C); *Michaud v. City of Montreal* (1923) 129 L.T. 417 (written undertaking by O to give C certain land); *Forbes v. Ralli* (1925) L.R. 52 I.A. 178 (written assurance of "permanent lease"); *Veitch v. Caldicott* (1945) 173 L.T. 30 (oral assurance by trustee for creditors that he would not sell C's house); *Griffiths v. Williams, supra* (oral assurance by mother that daughter could live in her house for life); *Pascoe v. Turner, supra* (oral assurance by O to his former mistress that the house in which they lived was hers).

[83] *e.g. Ahmad Yar Khan v. Secretary of State for India* (1901) L.R. 28 I.A. 211 (construction of canal with government consent).

[84] *Cotching v. Bassett* (1862) 32 Beav. 101 (alteration by C to ancient lights with O's permission).

[85] *Plimmer v. Mayor, etc., of Wellington, supra; Veitch v. Caldicott, supra,* at 34; *Ward v. Kirkland* [1967] Ch. 194 at 238; *Taylors Fashions Ltd v. Liverpool Victoria Trustees Co. Ltd* (1979) [1982] Q.B. 133n. at 148.

[86] *Sarat Chunder Dey v. Gopal Chunder Laha* (1892) L.R. 19 I.A. 203 at 215, 216; *Re Eaves* [1940] Ch. 109 at 117, 118; *Taylors Fashions Ltd v. Liverpool Victoria Trustees Co Ltd, supra,* at 144 *et seq.* (where the authorities are fully reviewed).

[87] See, *e.g. Watson v. Goldsbrough* [1986] 1 E.G.L.R. 265 at 267.

[88] *Dann v. Spurrier* (1802) 7 Ves. 231 at 236 *per* Lord Eldon L.C. See too *De Bussche v. Alt* (1878) 8 Ch.D. 286 at 314 ("quiescence under such circumstances as that assent may be reasonably inferred from it": *per* Thesiger L.J.); *Ward v. Kirkland, supra,* at 239.

[89] *Mold v. Wheatcroft* (1859) 27 Beav. 510. See too *Powell v. Thomas* (1848) 6 Hare 300.

acted to their detriment in this belief, the lessors were estopped from denying the validity of the underleases.[90] Formerly the courts adopted defined criteria for establishing acquiescence,[91] and still sometimes do,[92] but the approach is now generally more flexible.[93] The trend of authority is that it is no longer necessary to force C's conduct "into a Procrustean bed constructed from some unalterable criteria",[94] but to consider whether in the circumstances it would be unconscionable for O to insist upon his strict legal rights.[95] The one element that is clearly essential is that O's conduct should have encouraged C to act as he did. Mere inaction by O in the face of an infringement of his rights cannot therefore amount to acquiescence because it does not induce C to act.[96] It is unlikely that O's conduct will be regarded as unconscionable unless he was aware of—

   (i) his proprietary rights[97];

   (ii) C's expenditure[98] or other detrimental acts[99]; and

   (iii) C's mistaken belief that he had or would acquire an interest in or over O's land.[1]

---

[90] *Hammersmith and Fulham L.B.C. v. Top Shop Centres Ltd* [1990] Ch. 237.

[91] The so-called "five probanda" set out by Fry J. in an unreserved judgment in *Willmott v. Barber* (1880) 15 Ch.D. 96 at 105, 106. See *Russell v. Watts* (1883) 25 Ch.D. 559 at 585; *Civil Service Musical Instrument Association v. Whiteman* (1899) 68 L.J.Ch. 484; *Kammins Ballrooms Co. Ltd v. Zenith Investments (Torquay) Ltd* [1971] A.C. 850 at 884; *Crabb v. Arun D.C.* [1976] Ch. 179 at 194; *E. & L. Berg Homes Ltd v. Grey* [1980] 1 E.G.L.R. 103 at 106; *Coombes v. Smith* [1986] 1 W.L.R. 808 at 817 (where the probanda were applied erroneously in a case of active encouragement).

[92] *e.g. Matharu v. Matharu* (1994) 68 P. & C.R. 93; criticised [1994] Fam. Law 625 (J. Dewar); (1995) 7 C.F.L.Q. 59 (G. Battersby); (1995) 58 M.L.R. 412 (P. Milne).

[93] *Electrolux Ltd v. Electrix Ltd* (1954) 71 P.R.C. 23 at 33; *Hopgood v. Brown* [1955] 1 W.L.R. 213 at 223; *Shaw v. Applegate* [1977] 1 W.L.R. 970 at 978; *H. P. Bulmer Ltd v. J. Bollinger S.A.* [1977] 2 C.M.L.R. 625 at 681; *Taylors Fashions Ltd v. Liverpool Victoria Trustees Co. Ltd, supra*, at 153, 154; *Lloyds Bank Plc v. Carrick* [1996] 4 All E.R. 630 at 640. Given the fine line between active and passive encouragement, some element of flexibility seems desirable.

[94] *Taylors Fashions Ltd v. Liverpool Victoria Trustees Co. Ltd, supra*, at 154, *per* Oliver J.

[95] See *Ward v. Kirkland, supra*, at 239; *Crabb v. Arun D.C., supra*, at 195; *Amalgamated Investment & Property Co. Ltd v. Texas Commerce International Bank Ltd* [1982] Q.B. 84 at 104.

[96] *Proctor v. Bennis* (1887) 36 Ch.D. 740 at 761; *Moorgate Mercantile Co. Ltd v. Twitchings* [1977] A.C. 890 at 902.

[97] *Armstrong v. Sheppard & Short Ltd* [1959] 2 Q.B. 384.

[98] *Swallow Securities Ltd v. Isenberg* [1985] 1 E.G.L.R. 132; *Barclays Bank Plc v. Zaroovabli* [1997] Ch. 321 at 330, 331.

[99] Notice of C's intention to act to his detriment will suffice: *Crabb v. Arun D.C., supra*, at 189, 198.

[1] "You cannot encourage a belief of which you do not have any knowledge": *Brinnand v. Ewens* (1987) 19 H.L.R 415 at 418, *per* Nourse L.J. (O was unaware that C, a tenant of part of a house, was undertaking repairs in the belief that he would acquire a tenancy of the whole house). See too *Barclays Bank Plc v. Zaroovabli, supra*, at 331. The extent of C's acts of detriment may be relevant in determining whether O must have known of C's mistake: see *Bibby v. Stirling* (1998) 76 P. & C.R. D36 (construction of large greenhouse by C only compatible with a belief that he might remain on the land indefinitely).

Where the parties are negotiating "subject to contract" or "subject to lease" there will usually be no room for estoppel.[2] The use of these conventional phrases is normally taken to negative any encouragement on O's part.[3]

(c) Agents. In considering whether O encouraged C to act as he did, the court will have regard not only to O's own knowledge and conduct, but to that of any agent of his.[4] In general, that agent will be taken to have the authority which he purports to exercise.[5] If O considers that he has exceeded his instructions, he can so inform C before C acts to his detriment.[6] In cases of acquiescence, only those matters which come to the knowledge of O's agent in the course of his agency will be imputed to O.[7]

13–010

(d) Right over property. For an equity to arise, C must have been led to believe that he had or would obtain some right or benefit in or over O's property.[8] A belief that he will acquire a right of a non-proprietary character will not suffice. Thus a local authority was not estopped from refusing C planning permission to build on his own land, because he had no expectation of acquiring rights over the property of the authority.[9] However, for these purposes the acquisition of property rights includes the release or non-enforcement by O of some right that he has over C's land, such as a covenant or easement. Thus where O had leased land to C, reserving a right to enter and cut timber, he was restrained from so doing after he had encouraged C to beautify the land by laying out gardens.[10] It has also been held that no equity can arise unless C's expectation that he will acquire some interest relates to specific property of O's.[11] This requirement will however be satisfied if the property is ascertainable, as where O leads C to believe that he will inherit his

13–011

---

[2] Similarly, if a person incurs expenditure in the hope of obtaining a contract relating to land (*e.g.* by preparing development plans), no equity will arise: *Haslemere Estates Ltd v. Baker* [1982] 1 W.L.R. 1109 at 1119. See too *Pridean Ltd v. Forest Taverns Ltd* (1996) 75 P. & C.R. 447.

[3] *Derby & Co. Ltd v. I.T.C. Pension Trust Ltd* [1977] 2 All E.R. 890 at 896; *Att.-Gen of Hong Kong v. Humphreys Estate (Queen's Gardens) Ltd* [1987] A.C. 114; *Akiens v. Salomon* (1992) 65 P. & C.R. 364 (but *cf.* Evans L.J., dissenting, at 372, 373). For a case in which an equity arose notwithstanding the use of the phrase "subject to contract", see *Salvation Army Trustee Co. Ltd v. West Yorkshire M.C.C.* (1980) 41 P. & C.R. 179.

[4] Thus if C acts to his detriment with the assent and co-operation of O's agent, that will be regarded as sufficient encouragement: *Rochdale Canal Co. v. King (No. 2)* (1853) 16 Beav. 630; *Laird v. Birkenhead Rly Co.* (1859) Johns 500.

[5] *Crabb v. Arun D.C., supra,* at 193.

[6] *ibid.*

[7] *Att.-Gen to the Prince of Wales v. Collom* [1916] 2 K.B. 193 (C's expenditure made with the knowledge of O's land agent imputed to O). *cf. Swallow Securities Ltd v. Isenberg, supra* (porter's knowledge of C's improvement to flat not imputed to O).

[8] *Western Fish Products Ltd v. Penwith D.C.* (1978) [1981] 2 All E.R. 204 at 217.

[9] *ibid.* See too *Lloyds Bank Plc v. Carrick* [1996] 4 All E.R. 630 at 641 (no equity arising by proprietary estoppel where O already held the land in question on a bare trust for C).

[10] *Jackson v. Cator* (1800) 5 Ves. 688. In that case it was enough for the court to grant an injunction, but in other cases it might be appropriate to require O to release the right.

[11] *Layton v. Martin* [1986] 2 F.L.R. 227 at 238 (representation by O that he would provide "financial security" for his mistress, C, not sufficient).

residuary estate,[12] and even where the property is not acquired until *after* C has acted to his detriment in reliance upon the expectation.[13]

13–012   **2. Detrimental reliance.** C must have acted to his detriment in reliance upon his belief that he has or will acquire some right over O's land. In the absence of detriment, it would seldom (if ever) be unconscionable for O to insist upon his strict legal rights.[14]

13–013   *(a) Detriment.* C must prove that he has acted to his detriment.[15] Detriment may take many forms, and the acts relied upon may be unconnected with either O or C's land.[16] Indeed it has been said that the categories of detriment are not closed.[17]

13–014   (1) EXPENDITURE. The most obvious examples of detriment have involved expenditure by C on O's land, as where he built a house,[18] constructed a garage wall,[19] or installed drains[20] on the property, or carried out improvements to it.[21] Expenditure by C on his own land will however suffice.[22] Thus in one case, the Salvation Army built a new hall on land which it had agreed to purchase, in reliance upon O compulsorily acquiring their existing premises.[23]

13–015   (2) OTHER FORMS OF DETRIMENT. There was sufficient detriment where C—

---

[12] *Re Basham* [1986] 1 W.L.R. 1498 at 1510. Although the decision in this case can be reconciled with *Layton v. Martin*, *supra* (which was not cited), the reasoning cannot. For criticism of *Re Basham* see [1987] C.L.J. 215 (D. J. Hayton); and *Taylor v. Dickens* [1998] 1 F.L.R. 806 (itself criticised in [1998] Conv. 210 (M. P. Thompson)). *cf. Gillett v. Holt* [1998] 3 All E.R. 917. It is clear that the courts will approach with caution a claim of proprietary estoppel based on a promise by O to make a will in favour of C: *ibid.*, at 929. This follows from the revocable nature of a will: see [1999] Conv. 46 (M. Dixon). In at least some cases, estoppel is pleaded because it is not possible to show a valid contract to leave the land by will that complies with the requirements of L.P.(M.P.)A. 1989, s.2, *ante*, para. 12–020. *cf. ante*, para. 12–044.

[13] *Wayling v. Jones* (1993) 69 P. &. C.R. 170. In that case O promised to leave his hotel business by will to C. O intended the promise to apply to the hotel which he owned when he died, not the one which he owned when C began to act to his detriment and which O subsequently sold. See [1995] Conv. 409 at 411 (C. Davies).

[14] *Watts v. Storey* (1984) 134 N.L.J. 631.

[15] *Stevens & Cutting Ltd v. Anderson* [1990] 1 E.G.L.R. 95 at 99, not following *Greasley v. Cooke* [1980] 1 W.L.R. 1306 at 1314. See too *Coombes v. Smith* [1986] 1 W.L.R. 808 at 821.

[16] See, *e.g. Greasley v. Cooke, supra.*

[17] *Watts v. Storey, supra, per* Dunn L.J.

[18] *Inwards v. Baker* [1965] 2 Q.B. 29.

[19] *Hopgood v. Brown* [1955] 1 W.L.R. 213.

[20] *Ward v. Kirkland* [1967] Ch. 194.

[21] *Dodsworth v. Dodsworth* (1973) 228 E.G. 1115; *Pascoe v. Turner* [1979] 1 W.L.R. 431 (home improvements and decorations); *Watson v. Goldsbrough* [1986] 1 E.G.L.R. 265 (stocking ponds with fish).

[22] *Rochdale Canal Co. v. King (No. 2)* (1853) 16 Beav. 630 (construction of mill); *Cotching v. Bassett* (1862) 32 Beav. 101 (alteration to ancient lights); *E.R. Ives Investment Ltd v. High* [1967] 2 Q.B. 379 (construction of garage).

[23] *Salvation Army Trustee Co. Ltd v. West Yorkshire M.C.C.* (1980) 41 P. & C.R. 179.

(i) sold off part of his land in the belief that he would obtain a right of access over property belonging to O[24];

(ii) looked after members of O's family without payment[25]; and

(iii) refused employment with tied accommodation and worked unpaid for O for many years.[26]

(3) COUNTERVAILING BENEFITS. In considering what detriment C has suf- **13–016** fered, the court will take into account any countervailing benefits that he has received from O.[27] In a number of cases, C's enjoyment of O's property rent-free has been considered to outweigh any detriment that he may have incurred, whether in expending money[28] or giving up alternative accommodation.[29] In such circumstances it is not unconscionable for O to insist upon his strict legal rights.[30]

(b) Reliance. C must have acted as he did in reliance upon O's active or **13–017** passive encouragement. However, such reliance will be readily inferred once it is shown that O encouraged C and C acted to his detriment.[31] In such circumstances, the onus will be on O to show that there was no such reliance.[32] If therefore O can prove that C would have acted as he did in any event,[33] that he acted on the basis of independent advice,[34] or that his conduct was motivated by some other factor,[35] no equity will arise. Thus in one case where C left her husband and became pregnant by O, it was held that she did

---

[24] *Crabb v. Arun D.C.* [1976] Ch. 179.

[25] *Greasley v. Cooke, supra.*

[26] *Re Basham* [1986] 1 W.L.R. 1498. See too *Wayling v. Jones* (1993) 69 P. & C.R. 170.

[27] *Watts v. Storey* (1984) 134 N.L.J. 631.

[28] *Lee-Parker v. Izzett (No. 2)* [1972] 1 W.L.R. 775; *E. & L. Berg Homes Ltd v. Grey* [1980] 1 E.G.L.R. 103; *Bostock v. Bryant* (1990) 61 P. & C.R. 23; *Sledmore v. Dalby* (1996) 72 P. &. C.R. 196.

[29] *Watts v. Storey, supra.*

[30] *Lovett v. Fairclough* (1990) 61 P. & C.R. 385 at 402, 403 (12 years' free fishing adequate compensation for modest expenditure on improvement of river bank).

[31] *Greasley v. Cooke, supra,* as explained in *Stevens & Cutting Ltd v. Anderson* [1990] 1 E.G.L.R. 95 at 97, and *Bostock v. Bryant, supra,* at 31. See too *Hammersmith and Fulham L.B.C. v. Top Shop Centres Ltd* [1990] Ch. 237 at 262; *Lim v. Ang* [1992] 1 W.L.R. 113 at 118; and Snell, *Equity,* 576.

[32] *Grant v. Edwards* [1986] Ch. 638 at 656; *Wayling v. Jones* (1993) 69 P. & C.R. 170. In the latter case, C was O's homosexual partner and worked for him, receiving only pocket money and living expenses on the understanding that O would leave to C in his will the hotel that he owned. It appears that C would have acted as he did if O had made *no* promise at all to him, but that, the promise having been made, C would have left O had he known that he had reneged on it: *ibid.,* at 175, 176. See (1995) 111 L.Q.R. 389 (E. Cooke).

[33] *Taylors Fashions Ltd v. Liverpool Victoria Trustees Co. Ltd* (1979) [1982] Q.B. 133n. at 155, 156 (installation of lift by tenants 18 years before expiry of term not undertaken in reliance upon option to renew).

[34] *cf. Western Fish Products Ltd v. Penwith D.C.* (1978) [1981] 2 All E.R. 204 at 217. (C acted in the belief that he had an existing legal right to build a factory rather than on the basis of any representation from the local planning authority).

[35] Such as natural love and affection: *cf. Re Basham, supra,* at 1505 (where on the facts, C's conduct went "well beyond what was called for by natural love and affection", *per* Nugee, Q.C.).

so out of affection for him rather than because of any expectation that she would acquire an interest in his property.[36]

13–018   **3. Unconscionability.** It must be unconscionable for O to take advantage of C by denying him the right or benefit which he expected to receive.[37] It is not however essential that O should also have been guilty of unconscionable conduct in permitting C to assume that he could act as he did.[38] In assessing whether such unconscionability exists, one factor that the court will take into account is the relative positions of O and C.[39]

This requirement of unconscionability is now regarded as the essential element of proprietary estoppel and it will not be treated lightly. The courts will not invoke proprietary estoppel "as a general jurisdiction in equity to relieve hardship resulting from the application of the general law",[40] or merely "because justice and good conscience" seem to require it.[41]

B. Bars to the Equity

13–019   No equity will arise if the owner lacks capacity at the time when the claimant is alleged to have been encouraged to act to his detriment. Thus not only can "nothing of acquiescence" be imputed to a minor,[42] but positive acts of encouragement by a person purporting to act on his behalf without authority will not bind him, though he may be taken to have adopted them by his conduct when he subsequently comes of age.[43] However, where the person under a disability himself makes the representation in circumstances where his conduct amounts to fraud, an equity may arise.[44] Although an equity can be asserted against the Crown[45] or a local authority,[46] this is subject to the important limitation that a public body cannot act outside its powers.[47] Therefore no estoppel can be raised "to prevent the exercise of a statutory

---

[36] *Coombes v. Smith* [1986] 1 W.L.R. 808.
[37] *Crabb v. Arun D.C.* [1976] Ch. 179 at 195; *Taylors Fashions Ltd v. Liverpool Victoria Trustees Co. Ltd, supra* at 151, 152. *cf. Lloyds Bank Plc v. Carrick* [1996] 4 All E.R. 630 at 641 (C's expectation that she was beneficial owner of the property she had contracted to purchase from O was defeated not by O subsequently mortgaging the property, but by C's failure to register her estate contract: *sed quaere*).
[38] *Lim v. Ang, supra*, at 117.
[39] See *Sledmore v. Dalby* (1996) 72 P. & C.R. 196 (C had lived on the property rent-free for 18 years, but his use of the premises had become minimal, whereas O had a pressing need for the property to accommodate her).
[40] *E. & L. Berg Homes Ltd v. Grey, supra*, at 108, *per* Ormrod L.J.
[41] *Haslemere Estates Ltd v. Baker* [1982] 1 W.L.R. 1109 at 1119, *per* Megarry V.-C.
[42] *Duke of Leeds v. Earl of Amherst* (1846) 2 Ph. 117 at 123, *per* Lord Cottenham L.C.
[43] *Somersetshire Coal Canal Co. Ltd v. Harcourt* (1858) 2 De G. & J. 596 (where O's steward purported to act on his behalf).
[44] *Savage v. Foster* (1723) 9 Mod. 35 at 37; Story's *Equity Jurisprudence*, § 385.
[45] *Plimmer v. Mayor, etc., of Wellington* (1884) 9 App.Cas. 699.
[46] *Crabb v. Arun D.C., supra*.
[47] *West Middlesex Golf Club Ltd v. Earling L.B.C.* (1993) 68 P. & C.R. 461 at 485.

discretion or to prevent or excuse the performance of a statutory duty".[48] It is also the case that no estoppel can be founded on an illegal user.[49]

C. The Form of Relief

1. Discretionary nature of relief. The court will look at the circumstances **13–020** in each case to determine how the equity can best be satisfied,[50] and it has a wide discretion as to the order which it may make.[51] This discretion is exercised according to equitable principles.[52] In some cases the court has done no more than restrain O from asserting his legal rights.[53] In others it has ordered O to grant to C a right over or an interest in his land,[54] or to convey the land to C either in fee simple[55] or for a term of years.[56] The court may order O to make a money payment to C by way of compensation,[57] which may be secured by a lien over O's property.[58] In a number of cases C has been granted a mere licence.[59] Relief may be and commonly is given on terms, *e.g.* C may be required to make some payment for the right which he is granted.[60]

---

[48] *Western Fish Products Ltd v. Penwith D.C.* (1978) [1981] 2 All E.R. 204 at 219, *per* Megaw L.J. See too *Southend-on-Sea Corporation v. Hodgson (Wickford) Ltd* [1962] 1 Q.B. 416; *Rootkin v. Kent C.C.* [1981] 1 W.L.R. 1186. For comment on and criticism of this rule, see H. W. R. Wade and C. F. Forsyth, *Administrative Law* (7th ed.) at pp. 270 *et seq.*; [1981] C.L.P. 1 (A.W. Bradley).

[49] *Hanning v. Top Deck Travel Group Ltd* (1993) 68 P. & C.R. 14 at 21 (illegal user of common land).

[50] *Plimmer v. Mayor, etc., of Wellington, supra,* at 714. See too *Lord Cawdor v. Lewis* (1835) 1 Y. & C.Ex. 427 at 433; *Roebuck v. Mungovin* [1994] 2 A.C. 224 at 235. For an analysis of the manner in which the discretion is exercised, see (1999) 115 L.Q.R. 438 (S. Gardner).

[51] *Holiday Inns Inc. v. Broadhead* (1974) 232 E.G. 951 at 1087; *Griffiths v. Williams* [1978] 1 E.G.L.R. 121 at 122; *Burrows v. Sharp* (1989) 23 H.L.R. 82 at 91.

[52] *Williams v. Staite* [1979] Ch. 291 at 301; *J. Willis & Son v. Willis* [1986] 1 E.G.L.R. 62 at 63.

[53] *e.g. Cotching v. Bassett* (1862) 32 Beav. 101; *Marharaj v. Chand* [1986] A.C. 898.

[54] *Crabb v. Arun D.C.* [1976] Ch. 179 (court ordered the grant of an easement); *Holiday Inns Inc. v. Broadhead, supra* (C granted a beneficial half share in O's property).

[55] *Dillwyn v. Llewelyn* (1862) 4 De G. F. & J. 517; *Pascoe v. Turner* [1979] 1 W.L.R. 431; *Voyce v. Voyce* (1991) 62 P. & C.R. 290; *Durant v. Heritage* [1994] E.G.C.S. 134. See too *Lim v. Ang, supra* (transfer of beneficial half share in property ordered).

[56] *Griffiths v. Williams, supra; Watson v. Goldsbrough* [1986] 1 E.G.L.R. 265; *J. T. Developments Ltd v. Quinn* (1990) 62 P. & C.R. 33.

[57] *Veitch v. Caldicott* (1945) 173 L.T. 30; *Dodsworth v. Dodsworth* (1973) 228 E.G. 1115; *Burrows v. Sharp, supra; Baker v. Baker* [1993] 2 F.L.R. 247; *Wayling v. Jones* (1993) 69 P. & C.R. 170. Both the reasons for awarding compensation and the quantification of the amount have varied, and will depend upon the circumstances, particularly, the nature of the expectation created: see [1995] Conv. 409 (C. Davies).

[58] *Unity Joint Stock Mutual Banking Association v. King* (1858) 25 Beav. 72; *Burrows v. Sharp, supra; Baker v. Baker, supra.*

[59] *Inwards v. Baker* [1965] 2 Q.B. 29; *Williams v. Staite, supra.* This form of relief is not without its difficulties: see *ante,* para. 13–006; and *post,* para. 13–033.

[60] *Duke of Devonshire v. Eglin* (1851) 14 Beav. 530; *Duke of Beaufort v. Patrick* (1853) 17 Beav. 60; *Lim v. Ang* [1992] 1 W.L.R. 113. See too *Crabb v. Arun D.C., supra,* where C would have been required to pay O for the easement which he was granted by the court, had O's conduct not been such that C's own land had been rendered useless for a number of years. In *Cameron v. Murdoch* (1986) 63 A.L.R. 575 at 596, the Privy Council gave effect to C's equity by allowing him to purchase land from O at a discount.

2. Factors relevant to the exercise of the discretion

13–021   *(a) Minimum equity.* In granting relief, the court will "analyse the minimum equity to do justice" to C.[61] It will not therefore give him a greater right or interest than he believed he had or expected to receive.[62] Prior to 1997, a particular problem had arisen when C had been encouraged to believe that he could occupy O's property indefinitely. If the court had granted him an indefinite licence to reside on the property, the effect of its order might have been to create a settlement under the Settled Land Act 1925[63] of which C would have been the life tenant.[64] Because such a life tenant has extensive powers of disposition under that Act,[65] C would thereby have acquired an interest in the property that would considerably have exceeded his expectations.[66] In such circumstances it became the practice for the court to make an order that more closely corresponds to C's expectations, such as by requiring O to grant him a long lease at a nominal rent determinable on C's death.[67] Since the Trusts of Land and Appointment of Trustees Act 1996 came into force,[68] these particular difficulties no longer exist, because new settlements cannot be created.[69]

Although C's expectations provide an upper limit to the relief which may be given, the court is not bound to give effect to them in the manner which C envisaged if circumstances have changed so as to make it inappropriate.[70] Thus if C has acted to his detriment in the belief that he can live with O and the parties subsequently become estranged, the court will not give C a right to reside on the premises but will find some other means of giving effect to the equity. This will commonly take the form of an order that O should pay C compensation for his expenditure,[71] or for the loss of the right of occupation which C expected to receive.[72] Furthermore, no relief of any kind will be given if the "right" which C claims is too indefinite to be adequately defined or granted.[73]

---

[61] *Crabb v. Arun D.C., supra,* at 198, *per* Scarman L.J. "One has to make up one's mind how far it is necessary to go to see that [C] has not suffered any wrong": *Veitch v. Caldicott, supra,* at 34, *per* Atkinson J.

[62] *Dodsworth v. Dodsworth* (1973) 228 E.G. 1115; *Watson v. Goldsbrough, supra,* at 267.

[63] The point is not free from doubt: see *ante,* para. 8–055.

[64] *Dodsworth v. Dodsworth, supra.* For there to be a settlement within S.L.A. 1925, s.1, there must be some "instrument", but the order of the court may satisfy this requirement: *Griffiths v. Williams* [1978] 1 E.G.L.R. 121 at 123. See *ante,* paras 8–055–8–057.

[65] *Ante,* paras 8–071 *et seq.*

[66] *Dodsworth v. Dodsworth, supra.*

[67] *Griffiths v. Williams, supra.*

[68] On January 1, 1997.

[69] *Ante,* para. 8–001.

[70] *Burrows v. Sharp* (1989) 23 H.L.R. 82 at 92. *cf.* (1984) 100 L.Q.R. 376 (S. Moriarty).

[71] *Dodsworth v. Dodsworth, supra; Burrows v. Sharp, supra.*

[72] *Baker v. Baker* [1993] 2 F.L.R. 247.

[73] *Bankart v. Tennant* (1870) L.R. 10 Eq. 141 at 148 (where the alleged "right" was to take surplus water from a canal); *Willis v. Hoare* (1998) 77 P. & C.R. D42 (undertaking to offer C a sub-lease without any indication of terms too uncertain).

(b) Conduct of the parties.[74] "In determining the relief appropriate the court must look at the conduct of the parties as well as the extent of the equity."[75] The jurisdiction to give relief is an equitable one and the conduct of both the claimant, C, and the owner of the land, O, is relevant to its exercise.

13–022

(1) CONDUCT OF THE CLAIMANT. A party seeking equitable relief must come with clean hands. Although trivial misconduct will not be fatal to his claim, the court will refuse relief if he has seriously misconducted himself,[76] as it did where C had submitted a fraudulent claim for improvements to O's property which had never been made.[77]

13–023

(2) CONDUCT OF THE LANDOWNER. The conduct of the owner of the land may influence both the extent of the relief granted and the terms upon which it is given.[78] In one case the court ordered O to transfer the fee simple in a house to C rather than merely giving her a licence to live there for her lifetime. Only in this way could it adequately protect C against O, who intended to evict her from the house by any means available.[79] In a case in which C's equity was satisfied by the grant of a right of way over O's property, the court did not require C to pay anything in return because O had rendered C's land sterile for several years by its high-handed conduct.[80]

13–024

(3) MISCONDUCT AFTER THE GRANT OF RELIEF. Once a court has given effect to C's equity, his subsequent conduct will not normally affect the right which he has been granted. Where C has been given some proprietary right over O's land which he then abuses, O has the usual tortious remedies of trespass and nuisance against him.[81] It has, however, been suggested that where C had been granted no more than a licence, O might be able to revoke it in a case of serious misconduct by C.[82] Even if this is the case (which is by no means certain[83]), the degree of impropriety that is required to justify the revocation of C's licence is greater than that which will bar his initial claim to relief.[84]

13–025

---

[74] See [1986] Conv. 406 (M. P. Thompson).
[75] *Baker v. Baker* [1993] 2 F.L.R. 247 at 258, *per* Roch L.J.
[76] *J. Willis & Son v. Willis* [1986] 1 E.G.L.R. 62. See too *Williams v. Staite* [1979] Ch. 291 at 301.
[77] *J. Willis & Son v. Willis, supra.*
[78] *Baker v. Baker, supra.*
[79] *Pascoe v. Turner* [1979] 1 W.L.R. 431. Could not the equity have been better satisfied by the grant of a long lease determinable on the death of C? *cf. Griffiths v. Williams* [1978] 1 E.G.L.R. 121 at 123; and see [1979] Conv. 379 at 381 (F. R. Crane).
[80] *Crabb v. Arun D.C.* [1976] Ch. 179.
[81] *Williams v. Staite, supra,* at 300.
[82] *ibid.,* at 298. See [1986] Conv. 406 at 412 *et seq.* (M. P. Thompson).
[83] *J. Willis & Son v. Willis, supra,* at 63.
[84] *ibid.*

(c) Other bars to relief

13–026　　(1) ENFORCEMENT CONTRARY TO STATUTE. The court will not give effect to C's equity if and to the extent that to do so would contravene some statute.[85] This latter principle is subject to two qualifications. First, the court will give such relief as does not conflict with the statute even if it cannot give the more extensive rights which C might otherwise have sought.[86] Secondly, it is not every statutory provision that is fatal to the enforcement of an equity. If the statute merely regulates the dealings between the parties to a transaction, rather than laying down some more general rule of a public character, the court may give effect to an equity in C's favour and O may be unable to rely on the statute.[87] O may therefore be estopped from relying on the provisions of—

> (i) a registration statute which would otherwise render void for non-registration some right or interest of C's[88]; or

> (ii) a statute requiring compliance with certain formalities for contracts[89] or trusts relating to land.[90]

13–027　　ENFORCEMENT INEQUITABLE. Other bars to equitable relief, such as laches, should in principle apply to C's claim. However, where C is either in possession of O's land or exercising the right over it which he believes that he has, mere delay will not bar his claim. In such circumstances C is not sleeping on his rights but is relying upon his equity.[91]

---

[85] *Chalmers v. Pardoe* [1963] 1 W.L.R. 677 (relief refused because its grant would have contravened a prohibition on dealing with land without the consent of a statutory body); *London & Associated Investment Trust Plc v. Calow* (1986) 53 P. & C.R. 340 at 354, 355 (party not estopped from relying on a statutory provision which prohibited contracting out). *cf. Ward v. Kirkland* [1967] Ch. 194 at 241, 242, where Ungoed-Thomas J., in giving effect to an equity, granted C a right which O had no capacity by statute to grant. *Sed quaere:* see (1966) 30 Conv. (N.S.) 233 at 236 (F. R. Crane).

[86] *Maharaj v. Chand* [1986] A.C. 898 (C granted an injunction to restrain eviction by O even though she could not claim an interest in the property by reason of a statutory prohibition). *cf.* Snell, *Equity*, 576, suggesting that the equity itself is barred, rather than merely the remedy.

[87] There is a close parallel with the doctrine that a court will not permit a statute to be used as an instrument of fraud: see, *ante*, para. 10–045. Although the precise basis of the doctrine is controversial, one possible explanation is that it is an aspect of equitable estoppel: see *Steadman v. Steadman* [1976] A.C. 536 at 540.

[88] See *Taylors Fashions Ltd v. Liverpool Victoria Trustees Co. Ltd* (1979) [1982] Q.B. 133n., where O was estopped from relying on L.C.A. 1925, s.13(2) (now L.C.A. 1972, s.4(6); *ante*, para. 5–118) when C had failed to register an estate contract as a land charge. *cf. Lyus v. Prowsa Developments Ltd* [1982] 1 W.L.R. 1044 at 1054, where the doctrine that a statute cannot be used as an instrument of fraud was applied to L.R.A. 1925, s.20(1).

[89] L.P.(M.P.)A. 1989, s.2: see *Yaxley v. Gotts* [1999] E.G.C.S. 92 and transcript, *ante*, para. 12–044.

[90] L.P.A. 1925, s.53(1)(b); *ante*, para. 10–045. *cf. Rochefoucauld v. Boustead* [1897] 1 Ch. 196 (where the doctrine that a statute may not be used as an instrument of fraud was applied to the precursor of this provision).

[91] *Voyce v. Voyce* (1991) 62 P. & C.R. 290 at 293. *cf. Williams v. Greatrex* [1957] 1 W.L.R. 31; *post*, para. 21–041.

D. The Nature of the Equity

1. The characteristics of the equity. The equity which arises by estoppel is an equitable right to go to a court to seek relief. The court has a wide discretion as to the manner in which it may satisfy the equity, which may or may not involve the grant to C of a proprietary right over O's land. If the court does order that C be granted a property right, that grant is not retrospective, but operates only from the time of the execution of the court's order.[92] There has been some controversy as to the nature of the equity[93] both because of its discretionary character and because it may not always lead to the grant of a property right. There are two principal views. The first is that it is a "mere equity" akin to a right to seek rectification or specific performance, but of an "inchoate" character.[94] As such, it is a proprietary right, the benefit of which will pass on a transfer by C of his land,[95] and which may in appropriate circumstances bind a third party who acquires O's land.[96] The second view is that the equity is a purely personal right enforceable only by C against O. This is because the "flexible claim does not seem certain or stable enough to qualify as a property interest".[97] This is questionable. The equity is a right to seek discretionary equitable relief and is not intrinsically different from a right to seek specific performance or rectification.[98] Although there are decisions which support the view that an equity is a personal right,[99] the weight of both authority and practice suggests that it is proprietary. The point cannot be regarded as finally settled, however.

13–028

2. The equity as proprietary right. In a number of decisions it has been assumed that the equity arising by estoppel is a proprietary right.[1] Thus where C constructed a canal on land owned by O, with O's encouragement, he was said to have "acquired a proprietary interest" in so much of O's land as was

13–029

[92] *Griffiths v. Williams* [1978] 1 E.G.L.R. 121 at 123; *Williams v. Staite* [1979] Ch. 291 at 300, 301. See [1992] Fam. Law 72 at 75 (P. J. Clarke).

[93] See [1992] Conv. 53 at 57 (J. E. Martin).

[94] See [1991] Conv. 15 (G. Battersby). See too (1976) 40 Conv. (N.S.) 156 at 158 (F. R. Crane) and [1986] Conv. 406 (M. P. Thompson). For mere equities, see *ante*, paras 5–012 *et seq.*

[95] *Boots the Chemist Ltd v. Street* [1983] 2 E.G.L.R. 51; *ante*, para. 5–013. There is some authority that the benefit of an equity arising by estoppel does indeed pass automatically on a conveyance of land: see *Brikom Investments Ltd v. Carr* [1979] Q.B. 467 at 484, 485 (where Lord Denning M.R.'s remarks, although made in relation to *promissory* estoppel, were intended to apply more generally).

[96] See, *infra*.

[97] (1990) 106 L.Q.R. 87 at 97 (D. J. Hayton); [1998] Conv. 502 (P. Critchley).

[98] See *Voyce v. Voyce, supra*, at 293, where Dillon L.J. drew an analogy between the grant of relief in a case of estoppel and the remedy of specific performance. The analogy is a close one. Where a party seeks specific performance, the court may make the decree, award damages in lieu under the Supreme Court Act 1981, s.50, or dismiss the action. Another possible analogy is with a pending land action: see (1995) 58 M.L.R. 637 at 642 (G. Battersby).

[99] See, *e.g. Ward v. Kirkland* [1967] Ch. 194 at 241, 242.

[1] If an equity arising by estoppel is proprietary, then not only may it be binding on third parties in certain circumstances (considered *infra*), but, as indicated *supra*, the benefit may be transmissible: *cf.* (1995) 7 C.F.L.Q. 59 at 63 (G. Battersby); [1995] Conv. 332 at 336 (M. Haley).

required for its construction and maintenance.[2] It has also been suggested that where C is in occupation of land pursuant to an equity, he can be regarded as "the equitable owner" against whom O may acquire a prescriptive right to light.[3] The courts have on occasions had to consider whether an equity was a proprietary interest for the purposes of a particular statute.[4] In one case, such an equity was held to be "an estate or interest" in land so as to entitle C to statutory compensation for the compulsory acquisition of his rights.[5] In another, however, it was held that there was no disposition of land where an equity arose which entitled C to have an indefinite right of drainage over O's land.[6] In one situation, C's equity arising by estoppel can only be a personal right against O. This is where O has not yet acquired the property in which C believes he is to have an interest.[7]

13–030   **3. Effect on third parties.** There is authority that an equity arising by estoppel may bind a third party who acquires the land affected by it.[8] The circumstances in which this may be so depend upon whether title to the land is unregistered or registered.[9]

13–031   *(a) Unregistered land.* It has been held on a number of occasions that where O conveys his land, the transferee is bound by an equity which affects the property. Two reasons have been given for this.

>   (i) At common law, an estoppel is binding on both the parties to it and their "privies".[10] For these purposes, "he who takes an estate under a deed, is privy in estate, and therefore never can be in a better situation than he from whom he takes it".[11] This principle has been applied in a number of modern cases where the estoppel arose

---

[2] *Ahmad Yar Khan v. Secretary of State for India* (1901) L.R. 28 I.A. 211 at 218, *per* Lord Macnaghten.

[3] *Voyce v. Voyce, supra,* at 294, *per* Dillon L.J. The remark was *obiter* because the interference with O's light was insufficient to justify an injunction.

[4] Such cases do of course turn on the wording of the particular statute and do not necessarily yield any wider principle: see, *e.g. Plimmer v. Mayor, etc., of Wellington* (1884) 9 App.Cas. 699 at 714.

[5] *Plimmer v. Mayor, etc., of Wellington, supra.* It is not entirely clear whether it was the equity arising by estoppel or the irrevocable licence to which C was entitled by reason of that equity that was regarded as the estate or interest in land: see 714, 715.

[6] *Ward v. Kirkland, supra,* at 241, 242. O was a rector, and any disposition by him would have required the consent of either the church commissioners (under the Ecclesiastical Leasing Act 1858) or the Ministry of Agriculture (under the Glebe Lands Act 1888). *cf.* (1966) 30 Conv. (N.S.) 233 at 236 (F.R. Crane); and see *ante,* para. 13–026.

[7] *Abbey National B.S. v. Cann* [1991] 1 A.C. 56 at 89. See [1991] Conv. 155 at 161 (P. T. Evans).

[8] In *J. T. Developments Ltd v. Quinn* (1990) 62 P. & C.R. 33 at 36, purchasers for value of land did not even dispute that they were bound by an equity affecting it. See generally (1994) 14 L.S. 147 (S. Baughen).

[9] In some cases it is not apparent whether the land was registered or unregistered: see, *e.g. J. T. Developments Ltd v. Quinn, supra.*

[10] Co.Litt 352a., 352b.

[11] *Taylor v. Needham* (1810) 2 Taunt. 278 at 283, *per* Mansfield C.J. This was in effect an application of the common law rule, *"nemo dat quod non habet"*.

from a representation made by O,[12] but never in case of acquiescence.

(ii) In accordance with the normal rules,[13] an equity is binding either on a purchaser with notice of it,[14] or on a donee irrespective of whether he has notice of it.[15] If, as seems likely, the equity is to be regarded as a mere equity, even a purchaser of an equitable interest without notice will take free of it.[16]

Given the equitable nature of an equity arising by estoppel, the latter explanation is the better one, particularly as it can be applied whether the equity rises by representation or acquiescence.

(b) Registered land. A purchaser of registered land takes it free of all rights **13–032** and interests except those which are protected by an entry on the register or which exist as overriding interests.[17] By contrast, a donee takes the land subject to all the minor interests which bound the transferor whether registered or not.[18] It is the practice of the Land Registry to treat an equity arising by estoppel as a proprietary right which may therefore be protected by a notice or caution.[19] However, an equity will seldom be so protected because the party in whose favour it arises is unlikely to appreciate the need to register his right. An equity arising by estoppel will be protected against a purchaser in most cases therefore only if it can exist as an overriding interest. To do so, it must both subsist "in reference" to the registered land and fall within one of the categories of overriding interest.[20] In practice the only relevant category is likely to be the rights of persons in actual occupation.[21] It has been accepted on a number of occasions that an equity arising by estoppel can be an overriding interest of this kind.[22] If indeed such an equity is a mere equity then

---

[12] *Hopgood v. Brown* [1955] 1 W.L.R. 213 at 255, 229, 231; *Brikom Investments Ltd v. Carr* [1979] Q.B. 467 at 484.

[13] *Ante,* paras 5–005 *et seq.*

[14] *Duke of Beaufort v. Patrick* (1853) 17 Beav. 60 at 78; *Gresham Life Assurance Society v. Crowther* [1914] 2 Ch. 219; *Inwards v. Baker* [1965] 2 Q.B. 29 at 37; *E.R. Ives Investment Ltd v. High* [1967] 2 Q.B. 379 at 400, 405. In *Lloyds Bank Plc v. Carrick* [1996] 4 All E.R. 630 at 642, Morritt L.J. inclined to the view that, in consequence of these earlier decisions, an equity arising by estoppel was a proprietary right. *cf. United Bank of Kuwait Plc v. Sahib* [1997] Ch. 107 at 142 (denying proprietary status to an equity arising by estoppel but without consideration of the relevant authorities).

[15] *Voyce v. Voyce* (1991) 62 P. & C.R. 290 at 294, 296.

[16] *Westminster Bank Ltd v. Lee* [1956] Ch. 7 at 18, 19; *National Provincial Bank Ltd v. Ainsworth* [1965] A.C. 1175 at 1238; (1955) 71 L.Q.R. 480 at 482 (R.E.M.); *ante,* para. 5–012.

[17] L.R.A. 1925, s.20(1); *ante,* para. 6–105.

[18] L.R.A. 1925, s.20(4); *ante,* para. 6–105.

[19] L.R.A. 1925, ss.49(1)(f) (notice), 54(1) (caution); Ruoff & Roper, 8–02, 35–33, 36–13.

[20] L.R.A. 1925, s.70(1); *ante,* para. 6–039.

[21] L.R.A. 1925, s.70(1)(g); *ante,* para. 6–047.

[22] *Lee-Parker v. Izzett (No. 2)* [1972] 1 W.L.R. 775 at 780; *Singh v. Sandhu* (unrep., May 4, 1995, CA); *Locobail (U.K.) Ltd v. Bayfield Properties Ltd* (unrep., March 9, 1999, Lawrence Collins, Q.C.); *ante,* para. 6–052. *cf. Canadian Imperial Bank of Commerce v. Bello* (1991) 64 P. & C.R. 48 at 52, where it was held that a *promissory* estoppel (which confers no proprietary rights) could not be an overriding interest.

this seems correct in principle.[23] However, the issue is not regarded as finally settled.[24]

13–033   **4. Effect after judgment.** The effect of any relief granted by a court to satisfy an equity arising by estoppel depends upon normal property principles. A right created by the court's order does not enjoy any special status but must be protected in the appropriate way if it is to bind third parties.[25] If the court orders O to grant some right, estate or interest to C, that conveyance should be executed (and if need be registered) in the usual manner.[26] The effect of the relief may be to give C no more than a personal right to occupy land, either because O is restrained from evicting him,[27] or because C is granted an irrevocable licence.[28] Although such a licence was until recently thought to be binding on a third party with notice of it,[29] the recognition that contractual licences do not create property rights[30] has cast serious doubt on the correctness of this conclusion.[31] C's position as a licensee will therefore be vulnerable against a third party purchaser. This is a factor that the court now takes into account when giving relief. It may grant C a proprietary right if a licence would not adequately protect his position.[32]

Section 4. Contrast with Other Forms of Relief

13–034   **1. Contract.** Although there is no reason why both a claim in contract and to an equity by proprietary estoppel should not normally arise from the same facts,[33] the existence of a valid contract is not a prerequisite to an equity by estoppel.[34] An estoppel may arise where—

---

[23] See *Blacklocks v. J. B. Developments (Godalming) Ltd* [1982] Ch. 183 (right to seek rectification could exist as an overriding interest under L.R.A. 1925, s.70(1)(g)); *ante*, para. 6–052.

[24] See *Habermann v. Koehler* (1996) 73 P. & C.R. 515. The Law Commission and H.M. Land Registry have recommended that, for the purposes of land registration, an equity arising by estoppel should be treated as a proprietary right: see (1998) Law Com. No. 254, paras 3.33–3.36.

[25] See [1991] Conv. 36 at 38; (1995) 58 M.L.R. 637 at 641; (1995) 7 C.F.L.Q. 59 at 63 (G. Battersby); (1994) 14 L.S. 147 (S. Baughen).

[26] See, *e.g.* the orders made in *Pascoe v. Turner* [1979] 1 W.L.R. 431 and *Voyce v. Voyce* (1991) 62 P. & C.R. 290.

[27] *e.g. Maharaj v. Chand* [1986] A.C. 898.

[28] *e.g. Williams v. Staite* [1979] Ch. 291.

[29] *ibid.*

[30] See *Ashburn Anstalt v. Arnold* [1989] Ch. 1; *post*, para. 17–019.

[31] See *ante*, para. 13–006.

[32] *Pascoe v. Turner, supra*, at 438, 439. *cf. Matharu v. Matharu* (1994) 68 P. & C.R. 93; [1995] Conv. 61 at 66 (M. Welstead).

[33] See [1983] Conv. 50 (M. P. Thompson). This is subject to one significant exception. No claim to an equity arising by estoppel will lie where a vendor holds the land in question for a purchaser on a bare trust arising from the specifically enforceable contract of sale: *Lloyds Bank Plc v. Carrick* [1996] 4 All E.R. 630 at 641.

[34] *Dillwyn v. Llewelyn* (1862) 4 De G.F. & J. 517; *Plimmer v. Mayor, etc., of Wellington* (1884) 9 App.Cas. 699; *Voyce v. Voyce* (1991) 62 P. & C.R. 290 at 296.

(a) there was no agreement of any kind between the parties[35];

(b) a gift was intended[36];

(c) the essentials for a valid contract were absent[37]; or

(d) a contract was void for uncertainty.[38]

Furthermore, the manner in which a court gives effect to an equity arising by estoppel differs substantially from the way in which it enforces a contract. A court will enforce a contract according to its terms and will award damages, assessed according to settled principles, for any breach that is committed. By contrast, where a claim is based upon estoppel—

(i) the rights of the parties are not fixed at the time when the claimant acts to his detriment, but may be varied by the court to take account of subsequent events[39];

(ii) the court has a wide discretion as to how best to give effect to the equity and is not obliged to give effect to the expectations of the parties in all circumstances[40]; and

(iii) in those cases in which the payment of compensation is considered to be the appropriate remedy, it does not "assess loss as though it were awarding damages", but maintains "a more flexible approach designed to achieve justice between the parties".[41]

2. Presumed resulting trusts.[42] Where a person has contributed all or   **13–035** some part of the purchase price of a property—

(i) he is presumed to have a beneficial interest in that property proportionate to his contribution unless that presumption is rebutted by evidence that he intended to make a gift or loan of the money; and

---

[35] This will commonly be the situation where the equity arises out of acquiescence by the party estopped: see, *e.g. Savage v. Foster* (1723) 9 Mod. 35. In such cases C acts to his detriment in a mistaken belief that he has a right to act as he does, not in reliance upon some express or implied agreement with O: *Willmott v. Barber* (1880) 15 Ch.D. 96 at 105.

[36] *Dillwyn v. Llewelyn, supra; Inwards v. Baker* [1965] 2 Q.B. 29; *Voyce v. Voyce, supra* (equity in favour of the donee); *Baker v. Baker* [1993] 2 F.L.R. 247 (equity in favour of the donor).

[37] *Crabb v. Arun D.C., supra.* See (1976) 92 L.Q.R. 342 (P. J. Millett) refuting the contrary suggestion in (1976) 92 L.Q.R. 174 (P. S. Atiyah).

[38] *Holiday Inns Inc. v. Broadhead* (1974) 232 E.G. 951 at 1087; *Lim v. Ang* [1992] 1 W.L.R. 113. See too *Ramsden v. Dyson* (1866) L.R. 1 H.L. 129 at 170; *Plimmer v. Mayor, etc., of Wellington* (1884) 9 App.Cas. 699 at 713; *Lee-Parker v. Izzett (No. 2)* [1972] 1 W.L.R. 775 at 780, 781.

[39] *Ante*, para. 13–021.

[40] *Ante*, para. 13–020.

[41] *Baker v. Baker, supra* at 258, *per* Roch L.J.

[42] For such trusts, see *ante*, para. 10–009.

(ii) his proportionate share under such a trust is fixed at the time when the property is acquired.

The operation of such a presumed resulting trust is not a matter for the discretion of the court. By contrast, where an equity by estoppel arises, the claimant's rights remain inchoate until such time as a court, exercising an equitable discretion, decides how best to give effect to his equity.[43] Furthermore, an equity may arise even where C has made a gift to O.[44]

13–036   **3. Constructive trusts based on common intention.** A constructive trust will be imposed when B acts to his detriment in reliance upon a common understanding that he will acquire an interest in A's property.[45] Both the close similarities and the differences between such a trust and proprietary estoppel have already been explained.[46] Such a constructive trust arises as soon as B acts to his detriment. From that moment he acquires an equitable interest in A's property. Where an equity arises by estoppel, however, the claimant C has no more than an inchoate right until the court decides how the equity should be satisfied. Relief may sometimes be given without granting C any property right over O's land.

Where it is alleged that an equity has arisen by estoppel, the court will take into account countervailing benefits that C has received from O.[47] However, such benefits have not been taken into account in cases where B has alleged that a constructive trust has arisen from his detrimental reliance on a common understanding with A. For this reason, proprietary estoppel may provide a better means of doing complete justice between the parties.

13–037   **4. Licences.** A licence is no more than permission to do on another's land what would otherwise be a trespass.[48] It is now settled that a contractual licence does not create a proprietary interest in land, and the same is probably true of other forms of licence.[49] Proprietary estoppel has no necessary connection with the law of licences. It is a means by which C may obtain relief (commonly in the form of the grant of some proprietary right) where he has acted to his detriment in reliance upon some expectation created by O. If C is in possession of O's land, an equity may arise in his favour even if he is a trespasser.[50] If C is a licensee, one form of relief which the court may give is of course to declare that his licence is thereafter irrevocable.[51]

---

[43] *Ante*, para. 13–028.
[44] *Baker v. Baker, supra* (gift by C to O of purchase price of house on the understanding that C could live there rent-free for life).
[45] *Ante*, para. 10–023.
[46] *Ante*, para. 10–030, where the differences between the two remedies are set out more fully.
[47] *Ante*, para. 13–016.
[48] For licences, see *post*, Chap. 17.
[49] *Ashburn Anstalt v. Arnold* [1989] Ch. 1; *Canadian Imperial Bank of Commerce v. Bello* (1991) 64 P. & C.R. 48 at 51; *I.D.C. Group Ltd v. Clark* [1992] 1 E.G.L.R. 187 at 189. See, *post*, para. 17–019.
[50] See, *e.g. Hopgood v. Brown* [1955] 1 W.L.R. 213.
[51] *Plimmer v. Mayor, etc., of Wellington, supra.*

There is a similarity between proprietary estoppel and one aspect of the law of licences. A licence once acted upon cannot be revoked.[52] Thus if A gives B permission to build his house in such a way that it interrupts A's right to light, A cannot thereafter revoke his licence and require B to demolish his house.[53] This doctrine differs from proprietary estoppel in that it is a common law and not an equitable doctrine, and it can operate even where A is unaware of his proprietary rights when he acquiesces in B's conduct.[54]

---

[52] "A licence executed is not countermandable; but only when it is executory": *Winter v. Brockwell* (1807) 8 East 308 at 310, *per* Lord Ellenborough C.J. See too *Armstrong v. Sheppard & Short Ltd* [1959] 2 Q.B. 384 at 399 *et seq.* For the analogy with proprietary estoppel, see *Plimmer v. Mayor, etc., of Wellington, supra,* at 714.

[53] *Liggins v. Inge* (1831) 7 Bing. 682 at 693.

[54] *Armstrong v. Sheppard & Short Ltd, supra.* In that case, A assented to B building a sewer on his land, even though he did not appreciate the land was his. B was not guilty of any trespass in constructing the sewer, but no equity arose in his favour because A was unaware of his ownership of the land.

CHAPTER 14

LEASES AND TENANCIES

Part 1

INTRODUCTORY

Section 1. Nature and History of Leases

14–001   A LEASE is both a contract and, in most cases, an estate.[1] It is "a contract for the exclusive possession and profit of land for some determinate period",[2] and any estate so created is called a term of years, but is commonly referred to as a lease or a leasehold interest.[3] The consideration for that contract is usually (but not necessarily) the payment of rent.[4] Although a lease must be created by a document in most cases,[5] there are certain tenancies which are not created by documents, or which are not for fixed periods. These are nevertheless part of the subject of leases.[6]

14–002   **1. Leases as interests in land.** Something has already been said of leases in relation to other estates in land[7]; and elsewhere will be found an account of the manner in which leases developed from mere personal contracts (rights *in personam*) into rights of property (rights *in rem*) after the invention of the action of ejectment in the fifteenth century.[8] Just as this development brought the term of years into the category of estates, so also, as has been seen, it brought it within the principle of tenure[9]; for the theory of tenure requires that all land which is held for any estate shall be held of a lord. It was in this way that the relationship of landlord and tenant for years, which had no place in the old feudal land law, came to be based upon tenure. Indeed, it is now the only

---

[1] *cf. Bradshaw v. Pawley* [1980] 1 W.L.R. 10 at 14. It will not create an estate capable of binding third parties if the grantor himself had no estate: see *Bruton v. London & Quadrant Housing Trust* [1999] 3 W.L.R. 150 at 156, 157. See *post*, paras 14–003, 14–026.
[2] *Prudential Assurance Co. Ltd v. London Residuary Body* [1992] 2 A.C. 286 at 390, *per* Lord Templeman. See too *Bruton v. London & Quadrant Housing Trust, supra*, at 155; *Javad v. Aqil* [1991] 1 W.L.R. 1007 at 1012; Bl. Comm. ii, 140.
[3] *Post*, para. 14–008.
[4] See Platt on *Leases*, i, 9; ii, 82; *post*, para. 14–003.
[5] *Post*, para. 14–034.
[6] For licences, see *post*, Chap. 17.
[7] *Ante*, para. 3–009.
[8] *Post*, Appendix.
[9] *Ante*, para. 3–015.

form of tenure which retains any practical importance after 1925. It is owing to the existence of tenure, for example, that the tenant's rent is properly called rent-service (as opposed to rentcharge)[10] and that the landlord has a remedy of distraint for rent owed to him.[11]

2. Leases as contracts. Although a lease is usually an estate, it is also a **14–003** contract.[12] The consideration for the grant of a lease is normally the payment of rent,[13] but it has long been settled that there can be a valid lease even though no rent is payable.[14] The consideration furnished by the tenant may take any form, including—

(i) the payment of a capital sum, called a premium;[15]

(ii) a right to live rent-free under a sale and lease-back arrangement[16];

(iii) the remission of interest on a debt owed to him by the landlord[17];

(iv) his undertaking to perform the covenants in the lease; or

(v) the mere acceptance of the lease by the tenant.[18]

The status of leases as contracts has been strongly emphasised in recent years.[19] First, it has been accepted that in exceptional circumstances a lease may be frustrated.[20] Secondly, a breach of covenant may amount to a wrongful

---

[10] Though the modern view is to regard rent as a contractual payment made in consideration of the grant of the lease: see *infra*.

[11] *Post*, para. 14–253.

[12] Bl. Comm. ii, 140. See *Hammersmith L.B.C. v. Monk* [1992] 1 A.C. 478 at 491.

[13] *Post*, para. 14–245. "Rent" is widely defined by L.P.A. 1925, s.205(1)(xxiii) and is taken to include the performance of services: see *Hornsby v. Maynard* [1925] 1 K.B. 514 at 525; *Montagu v. Browning* [1954] 1 W.L.R. 1039 at 1044, 1045. Thus in *Doe d. Tucker v. Morse* (1830) 1 B. & Ad. 365 the tenant was obliged to carry coal or culm for the landlord.

[14] *Knight's Case* (1588) 5 Co.Rep. 54b at 55a; L.P.A. 1925, s.205(1)(xxvii). In *Street v. Mountford* [1985] A.C. 809 at 816, 825, Lord Templeman appeared to suggest that the payment of rent was an essential element of a lease. This view was plainly wrong and has not been followed: see *Ashburn Anstalt v. Arnold* [1989] Ch. 1 at 9; *Birrell v. Carey* (1989) 58 P. & C.R. 184 at 187; *Canadian Imperial Bank of Commerce v. Bello* (1991) 64 P. & C.R. 48 at 53, 55; *Wrexham Maelor B.C. v. Macdougall* [1993] 2 E.G.L.R. 23 at 28. *cf. Prudential Assurance Co. Ltd v. London Residuary Body* [1992] 2 A.C. 386 at 390; *Bruton v. London & Quadrant Housing Trust* [1999] 3 W.L.R. 150 at 155 (grant of a lease was "usually in return for a periodic payment in money": *per* Lord Hoffmann).

[15] A premium is one example of a "fine" which is broadly defined by L.P.A. 1925, s.205(1)(xxiii); *post*, para. 14–270.

[16] *Skipton B.S. v. Clayton* (1993) 66 P. & C.R. 223.

[17] *Canadian Imperial Bank of Commerce v. Bello, supra*, at 55.

[18] *Anon* (1698) 2 Freeman 224 at 225. See Halsb. Vol. 27(1), para. 1.

[19] "This increasing 'contractualisation' of leases is a process that has been gathering pace in this country for the last 20 years": [1993] Conv. 71 (S. Bright).

[20] *National Carriers Ltd v. Panalpina (Northern) Ltd* [1981] A.C. 675; *post*, para. 14–189.

repudiation of the lease entitling the other party to terminate it.[21] Thirdly, rent is no longer regarded as "a thing issuing from the land",[22] but as a contractual payment for the use of the land.[23] Fourthly, it has been settled that one of a number of joint lessors or lessees of a periodic tenancy can unilaterally give an effective notice to terminate that tenancy even though the other lessors or lessees do not wish to end the lease.[24] Fifthly, the courts are willing to imply terms into a lease in the same manner as they do with any other contract.[25] Sixthly, a landlord's right to terminate a lease because of the tenant's denial of this title is now explained in terms of contractual repudiation rather than with regard to the feudal origins of the rule.[26] Seventhly, because of the inability of a person to contract with themselves, "a man cannot make himself his own tenant"[27] by granting a lease to himself.[28] Finally, a court may set aside a lease where it is induced by the fraud of one of the parties[29] or where it amounts to an unconscionable bargain.[30] This trend to regard leases primarily as contracts has potentially far-reaching consequences and a number of these will be mentioned.[31] Even the right to exclusive possession, which is the hallmark of a lease,[32] is now regarded as a product of the agreement between the parties rather than as a consequence of the ownership of the legal estate.[33]

14–004   **3. Duration of leases.** Leases came into common use long before they obtained full protection as interests in land[34]; they appear frequently from the

---

[21] *Hussein v. Mehlman* [1992] 2 E.G.L.R. 87 (tenant treated the lease as at an end because of landlord's failure to carry out repairing obligations); *Re Olympia & York Canary Wharf Ltd (No. 2)* [1993] B.C.C. 159 at 166; *Nynehead Developments Ltd v. R.H. Fibreboard Containers Ltd* [1999] 1 E.G.L.R. 7 at 12; [1995] Conv. 379 (M. Pawlowski); *post*, paras 14–191, 14–192.

[22] H.E.L. vii, 252.

[23] *Property Holding Co. Ltd v. Clark* [1948] 1 K.B. 630 at 648, 649; *C.H. Bailey Ltd v. Memorial Enterprises Ltd* [1974] 1 W.L.R. 728 at 732, 735; *United Scientific Holdings Ltd v. Burnley B.C.* [1978] A.C. 904 at 935; *Ingram v. I.R.C.* [1995] 4 All E.R. 334 at 340; *post*, para. 14–245.

[24] *Hammersmith L.B.C. v. Monk* [1992] 1 A.C. 478, where the House of Lords explicitly adopted the contractual as opposed to the property approach: *ibid.*, at 492; see *ante*, para. 9–006.

[25] *Liverpool C.C. v. Irwin* [1977] A.C. 239; *King v. South Northamptonshire D.C.* (1991) 64 P. & C.R. 35; *post*, para. 14–211.

[26] *W.G. Clark (Properties) Ltd v. Dupre Properties Ltd* [1992] Ch. 297.

[27] *Rye v. Rye* [1962] A.C. 496 at 512, *per* Lord Radcliffe.

[28] *Rye v. Rye, supra*; (1962) 78 L.Q.R. 175 (P. V. Baker). However, a valid lease may be granted to a nominee: *Ingram v. I.R.C.* [1999] 2 W.L.R. 90 at 98, 102.

[29] *Killick v. Roberts* [1991] 1 W.L.R. 1146 (tenancy induced by fraud of tenant set aside); [1992] C.L.J. 21 (L. Tee).

[30] *Boustany v. Pigott* (1993) 69 P. & C.R. 298 (where the Privy Council set aside a lease on this ground at the landlord's behest); (1993) 109 L.Q.R. 530 (J. Cartwright).

[31] *Post*, paras 14–119, 14–120, 14–146, 14–186, 14–191.

[32] *Post*, para. 14–013.

[33] But see *Bruton v. London & Quadrant Housing Trust* [1999] 3 W.L.R. 150 at 156, 157, 159, 160; *post*, para. 14–026. *cf. Ingram v. I.R.C.* [1997] 4 All E.R. 395 at 422, where Millett L.J. had suggested otherwise.

[34] For the history of leaseholders' remedies and the growth of leasehold interests in land, see *post*, Appendix.

early thirteenth century onwards.[35] There is a tradition that in ancient times leases might not exceed 40 years,[36] but there is no clear evidence that such a rule ever existed. A lease cannot be granted to endure in perpetuity,[37] but subject to this the law allows the creation of leases of any length. For example an ordinary mortgage now takes the form of a lease for 3,000 years[38]; and even a tenant for life, who at common law could not grant a lease which would continue after his death, may grant a building or forestry lease of 999 years under the Settled Land Act 1925.[39]

The system of farming under agricultural leases became widespread in the seventeenth century. Farming leases were generally granted for terms up to 21 years.[40] Much longer terms (*e.g.* 60 or 99 years) were used for building or mining leases, which were useful means for the development or exploitation of land. Under a building lease, for example, the land is let for a long term at a ground rent, the tenant puts up a building at his own expense, and at the end of the term this becomes the landlord's property[41]; such a lease is therefore a valuable long-term investment for the landlord. Leases of anything up to 999 years, or even more, are sometimes granted for similar purposes; here the reversion is too remote to have any value, but the advantage to the landlord is that he can control the use of the land by means of covenants in the lease, and a greater variety of covenants are enforceable under a lease than under an outright conveyance of the fee simple.[42] Such very long leases may therefore be useful when a landlord is developing an estate and wishes to keep control over its appearance and character.

4. Leases as conveyancing devices. Leases are also sometimes used as a mere conveyancing device, usually in order to provide security for the payment of money. For this purpose a long lease is granted, free of rent or other obligations, so that the lessee simply takes a valuable interest in the land which is a good security for money advanced by him. The most important example is one form of legal mortgage by which a lease is granted by a mortgagor to the mortgagee as security for the money lent.[43] It is unusual for

14–005

---

[35] P & M. ii, 110–112.

[36] Co.Litt. 45b, 46a.

[37] *Sevenoaks, Maidstone & Tunbridge Ry v. London, Chatham & Dover Ry* (1879) 11 Ch. D. 625 at 635.

[38] *Post*, para. 19–020.

[39] *Ante*, para. 8–076.

[40] See *Att.-Gen. v. Owen* (1805) 10 Ves. 55 at 560.

[41] But legislation has now in many cases expropriated the landlord's interest in the building in favour of the tenant and enabled the tenant to acquire the land compulsorily. In some cases, such as business tenancies, the tenant is given security of tenure: see *post*, paras 22–062, 22–063.

[42] *Post*, paras 15–003, 15–004, 15–080.

[43] For this form of mortgage, see *post*, para. 19–020. Usually a mortgage is created by means of a charge expressed to be by way of legal mortgage: see *post*, para. 19–025. Indeed where title is registered (as is normally the case today), the charge is presumed to take effect this way: L.R.A. 1925, s.27(1).

the lessee to take possession of the land except as a preliminary to exercising his power of sale.[44] This form of lease is dealt with under mortgages.[45] The leases discussed in this chapter are leases where the lessee has the right to occupy the land or to receive the rent from a sub-tenant.

14–006   **5. Leases for lives.** Formerly leases were often granted not for a term of years but for a life or lives[46] had the advantage of giving the lessee a freehold estate, instead of a mere term of years, so that even before the action of ejectment was invented he could recover the land itself.[47] Further, a lease for 21 years or three lives was formerly the longest term which could be granted by a tenant in tail or by an ecclesiastical or charitable corporation (*e.g.* a college).[48] By the middle of the nineteenth century wider leasing powers had been given to tenants in tail,[49] ecclesiastical corporations,[50] and certain universities and colleges,[51] and so the practice of granting leases for life had declined. A lease for life, like a lease for years, created tenure between the parties, so that rent or other services could be reserved. Such leases were usually commercial transactions which were quite distinct from tenancies for life under family settlements, where a beneficial interest was granted free of any rent or services. The scheme of the 1925 legislation required life interests to be merely equitable, and this, though suitable for settlements, was unsuitable for leaseholds. Accordingly, most leases for life have now been converted into terms of years, as will be seen later.[52]

14–007   **6. Law and equity.** Unlike life tenancies, leases are commonly legal estates, and any number of leases and sub-leases can exist as legal estates concurrently. A term of years can, of course, subsist as an equitable interest under a trust, or as a result of a failure to employ the formalities required for the grant of a legal term; but legal leases are much more common. In order to be capable of existing as a legal estate the leasehold interest must be a "term of years absolute" within the meaning of the Law of Property Act 1925, s.1(1). The wide meaning of this expression has already been explained[53] and should be borne in mind in reading this chapter.

---

[44] *Post*, para. 19–056.
[45] *Post*, para. 19–020.
[46] For this phrase, see Challis 65.
[47] *Ante*, para. 14–002.
[48] See *ante*, para. 3–085; Platt on *Leases*, i, 66, 67, 247.
[49] See Fines and Recoveries Act 1833; *ante*, para. 3–084.
[50] Ecclesiastical Leases Act 1842.
[51] Universities and College Estates Act 1858. The Universities and College Estates Acts, 1925 and 1964, continue the policy of the Universities and College Estates Act 1898 of giving these universities and colleges powers resembling those given to tenants for life under S.L.A. 1882 which are narrower than those given by S.L.A. 1925.
[52] *Post*, para. 14–086.
[53] *Ante*, para. 14–045.

Section 2. Terminology

It is important to be familiar with the terms used in the law of leases. The **14–008** grantor of a lease is known as the lessor, the person to whom it is granted as the lessee. On the grant of a lease, the lessor retains a reversion, which he may assign; similarly, the lessee may assign the lease. Instead of assigning the lease (*i.e.* transferring the property for the whole of the period for which it is held), the owner of the lease may grant a sub-lease (or underlease) for a period at least one day shorter than the lease, the parties to this sub-lease being known as the sub-lessor and the sub-lessee respectively. Where the original lessor and original lessee have both assigned their interests, the new owners of the reversion and the lease are sometimes referred to as the lessor and lessee, although it is better to reserve these expressions for the original parties to the lease, and refer to the owners for the time being of the reversion and the lease, whether original or by assignment, as the landlord and the tenant.

These expressions may be illustrated as follows. **14–009**

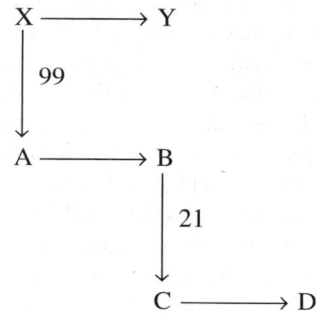

This diagram is the usual way of representing the following events. X grants a 99–year lease to A and then assigns the reversion to Y. B takes an assignment of A's lease and grants a sub-lease to C for 21 years, and C assigns his sub-lease to D. As to the 99 year lease, X is the "lessor," Y is the "assignee of the reversion" or "landlord", and A the "lessee". B is in a dual position: as to the 99 year lease, he is the "assignee" or "tenant"; as to the 21-year lease, he is "sub-lessor" or "landlord". The 99–year lease is then called the "head lease", so as to distinguish it from the sub-lease. C is the "sub-lessee", and D the "assignee" of the sub-lease, or the "sub-tenant". By annexing the dates of each transaction to each link in the diagram the sequence of events may be shown.

"Demise" is the technical term for "let" or "lease"; thus a lease may be referred to as a "demise" and the premises in question as the "demised premises". "Lease" and "term of years" are nearly synonymous terms today[54]; before 1926 a term of years could only be regarded as one kind of lease,[55] since leases for lives were by no means unknown. Today, leases for

---

[54] But see *Re Land and Premises at Liss, Hants.* [1971] Ch. 986.
[55] See *ante*, para. 14–006.

lives have nearly all disappeared.[56] "Lease" is often used interchangeably, either for the document or for the "term of years" or "leasehold interest" created by it, although primarily it means the document.[57]

Part 2

CREATION OF LEASES

Section 1. Essentials of a Lease

14–010   It has been explained that a lease is a bilateral contract.[58] The tenant is not only given an estate in land but also himself gives covenants, *e.g.* to pay rent and execute repairs. Leases must now be distinguished from other contracts concerning the use of land, for there is an infinite variety of such contracts which are not leases. Parties may make any bargain they like between themselves, and enforce it between themselves as a contract. But if one wishes to give the other an estate, that is to say a proprietary interest which will bind not only the grantor but also the rest of the world, then the interest must conform to the requirements by which the law limits the kinds of estates which can be created. For example, if A give B a mere licence[59] to use A's land, even though for payment, and then A sells the land to X, B can sue A for damages for breach of contract but he has no rights over the land as against X, for a licence creates no interest in the land.[60] But if A grants B a lease, then B has a legal estate subject to which X takes, so that B can enforce his rights against X as well as against A. It is therefore of great importance to know what transactions fall within the definition of a lease.

A. The Right to Exclusive Possession must be Given

1. Background

14–011   *(a) The traditional analysis.* It had always been of the essence of a lease that the tenant should be given the right to exclusive possession, that is the right to exclude all other persons from the premises.[61] A right to occupy certain premises for a fixed period cannot be a tenancy if the person granting the right remains in general control of the property. It will therefore take effect

---

[56] See *post*, para. 14–086.
[57] In the L.P.A. 1925 " lease" includes any tenancy: ss.154, 205(1)(xxiii). Further, the L.P.A. 1925, s.54(2), speaks of parol "leases" (and see s.52(2)(d)), and "oral lease" and its less correct relative "verbal lease" are common expressions.
[58] *Ante*, para. 14–001.
[59] See *post*, Chap. 17.
[60] *Street v. Mountford* [1985] A.C. 809 at 814.
[61] If the agreement between the parties confers exclusive possession, the arrangement will constitute a lease, even if it does not confer a legal estate on the tenant (because the lessor had none to grant): *Bruton v. London & Quadrant Housing Trust* [1999] 3 W.L.R. 150 at 155–157; *post*, para. 14–026.

as a licence. The typical case is where the landlord provides services for the occupant, such as cleaning.[62]

(b) The experiment with intention. These well-established and fundamental **14–012** principles were called into question in a series of decisions[63] in which the fact of exclusive possession ceased to be conclusive and was given "diminishing weight".[64] Instead, the court examined all the circumstances to determine whether the parties intended the occupier to have a "stake" in the property or merely a personal right of occupation.[65] Thus even where a person was granted exclusive possession the agreement might confer on him no more than a licence if that is what the parties actually intended.[66] These developments were prompted by the desire of landlords to avoid—

> (i) both the security of tenure and the benefit of rent control enjoyed by residential tenants under the Rent Acts[67]; and

> (ii) the security of tenure conferred on business tenants by Part II of the Landlord and Tenant Act 1954.[68]

The courts endeavoured to avoid "causing patently unintended injustice to landlords, whilst guarding against improper avoidance by the latter of the provisions of those Acts".[69] This approach was objectionable because it provided a means by which a well-advised landlord could "contract out" of the statutory protection given to tenants.[70] As the legal status of an occupier often turned on fine points of construction, the law was rendered both uncertain and difficult to administer.

(c) The return to exclusive possession. In *Street v. Mountford*,[71] a decision **14–013** that was much welcomed,[72] the House of Lords restored the law to its former

---

[62] For examples, see *post*, para. 14–015.

[63] Beginning with the judgment of Denning L.J. in *Errington v. Errington* [1952] 1 K.B. 290.

[64] *Barnes v. Barratt* [1970] 2 Q.B. 657 at 669, *per* Sachs L.J.

[65] See *Shell-Mex and B.P. Ltd v. Manchester Garages Ltd* [1971] 1 W.L.R. 612 at 615; *Marchant v. Charters* [1977] 1 W.L.R. 1181 at 1185.

[66] See *Somma v. Hazelhurst* [1978] 1 W.L.R. 1014.

[67] See *post*, para. 22–180. Lettings of residential accommodation made after January 14, 1989 have been subject to a different regime: see H.A. 1988, *post*, para. 22–131.

[68] See *post*, para. 22–063.

[69] *Barnes v. Barratt, supra*, at 669, *per* Sachs L.J. (a case concerned with the Rent Acts). Judicial attitudes to devices for circumventing this legislation have been equivocal: see *Kaye v. Massbetter Ltd* [1991] 2 E.G.L.R. 97 at 99 (Lord Donaldson M.R.); [1989] Conv. 128 at 133 (P. F. Smith).

[70] See, *e.g. Somma v. Hazelhurst, supra*. In reality such agreements were commonly not negotiated by parties at arm's length: *A.G. Securities v. Vaughan; Antoniades v. Villiers* [1990] 1 A.C. 417 at 458.

[71] [1985] A.C. 809. See too *Eastleigh B.C. v. Walsh* [1985] 1 W.L.R. 525, decided by the House of Lords shortly before *Street v. Mountford*.

[72] The House "sought to introduce some order into the law for the better administration of the law and guidance of the learned judges, particularly in the county court, who have to deal with this problem": *Brooker Settled Estates Ltd v. Ayers* (1987) 54 P. & C.R. 165 at 167, *per* O'Connor L.J. See too (1985) 101 L.Q.R. 467 (P. V. Baker); [1985] C.L.J. 351 (S. Tromans); (1985) 48 M.L.R. 712 (J. S. Anderson); [1985] All E.R. Rev. 190 (P. J. Clarke). The one dissentient voice was the unsuccessful claimant: [1985] Conv. 328 (R. Street).

more principled position.[73] Where as a matter of fact a person was granted exclusive possession of land for a fixed term that grant created a lease. This was so whatever label the parties might attach to the arrangement.[74] The test was one of fact not of form. Although there could be no tenancy in the absence of exclusive possession, an occupier who had exclusive possession would not be a tenant in three circumstances[75]—

(i) if there was no intention to create legal relations[76];

(ii) if his occupation was referable to some other legal relationship, as where he was a freeholder, a trespasser, a purchaser in possession under a contract of sale, an object of charity or where he occupied under a contract of employment or by reason of some office[77]; or

(iii) where the owner of the land had no power to grant a tenancy.[78]

The House accepted that "although the Rent Acts must not be allowed to alter or influence the construction of an agreement, the court should . . . be astute[79] to detect and frustrate sham devices and artificial transactions whose only object is to disguise the grant of a tenancy and to evade the Rent Acts".[80]

It should be noted that, as regards residential accommodation, disputes between the parties as to whether an arrangement has created a lease or licence are now less likely to arise. Since January 15, 1989, landlords have in practice been able to grant tenancies of dwellings at any rent that they may agree with the tenant.[81] As regards third parties the distinction between leases and licences remains of fundamental importance, because only the former can create proprietary rights.[82]

---

[73] The decision of the House confirmed the principles set out in the previous edition of this work at p. 633.

[74] "The manufacture of a five-pronged implement for manual digging results in a fork, even if the manufacturer . . . insists that he intended to make and did make a spade"; [1985] A.C. 809 at 819, *per* Lord Templeman. See *Addiscombe Garden Estates Ltd v. Crabbe* [1958] 1 Q.B. 513.

[75] See *Dellneed Ltd v. Chin* (1986) 53 P. & C.R. 172 at 187; *Camden L.B.C. v. Shortlife Community Housing Ltd* (1992) 90 L.G.R. 358 at 372.

[76] *Street v. Mountford, supra,* at 821.

[77] *ibid.,* at pp. 818, 827. Lord Templeman also included in this list the mortgagee in possession: *ibid.,* at 818. However such a mortgagee is in fact either a tenant (if the mortgage is by demise or subdemise) or has all the rights as if he were (if there is a charge by way of legal mortgage): *ante,* para. 14–005; *post,* paras 19–020, 19–025.

[78] *Street v. Mountford, supra,* at 821.

[79] A word that has been described as "rather emotive"; *Stribling v. Wickham,* (1989) 21 H.L.R. 381 at 390, *per* Sir Denys Buckley.

[80] *Street v. Mountford, supra,* at 825, *per* Lord Templeman. See too *A.G. Securities v. Vaughan; Antoniades v. Villiers* [1990] 1 A.C. 417 at 459.

[81] The matter is explained, *post,* Chap. 22.

[82] See *Ashburn Anstalt v. Arnold* [1989] Ch. 1; *Canadian Imperial Bank of Commerce v. Bello* (1991) 64 P. & C.R. 48; *ante,* para. 14–010; *post,* para. 17–001.

2. Exclusive possession

(a) Meaning. A tenant who has exclusive possession can exercise the rights **14–014** of a landowner.[83] He can exclude both strangers and the landlord[84] save where the landlord is entitled under the terms of the lease to inspect the premises and, *e.g.* carry out repairs.[85] Exclusive possession must be distinguished from exclusive occupation. Even if the grantee is exclusively entitled to occupy the premises, he may not have exclusive possession because the grantor may retain control of the premises.[86] Conversely, a grantee may have exclusive possession where he does not occupy the property himself but is in receipt of the rents and profits from it, as where he sublets it.[87]

(b) Residential accomodation. Persons who lawfully occupy residential **14–015** accommodation will either be tenants or licensees. Where they have exclusive possession they will be tenants unless they fall within one of the three exceptional circumstances explained below.[88] They will not have exclusive possession where—

(i) "the landlord provides attendance or services which require the landlord or his servants to exercise unrestricted access to and use of the premises[89], as will usually be the case with rooms in a hotel, hostel or boarding house[90];

(ii) they occupy shared accommodation other than as joint tenants; this is explained below[91]; or

---

[83] *Street v. Mountford* [1985] A.C. 809 at 816. The principles applicable to tenants apply equally to subtenants: *Monmouth B.C. v. Marlog* [1994] 2 E.G.L.R. 68 and 69.

[84] *Heslop v. Burns* [1974] 1 W.L.R. 1241 at 1247, 1249.

[85] *Street v. Mountford, supra,* at 816. The presence of such a term in the agreement between the parties is a strong indicator that the grantee has exclusive possession: *ibid.,* at 818; *Addiscombe Garden Estates Ltd v. Crabbe, supra,* at 524; *Dellneed Ltd v. Chin, supra,* at 184; *Vandersteen v. Agius* (1992) 65 P. & C.R. 266 at 273.

[86] *Luganda v. Service Hotels Ltd* [1969] 2 Ch. 209 at 219.

[87] *A.G. Securities v. Vaughan; Antoniades v. Villiers, supra,* at 455. However, if the grantee is *not* entitled to exclusive possession "he cannot acquire it merely by collecting the rents and profits from persons with no greater rights of occupation than he has himself": *Camden L.B.C. v. Shortlife Community Housing Ltd, supra,* at 381, *per* Millett J.

[88] *Post,* para. 14–023.

[89] The licensee will then be "a lodger": *Street v. Mountford, supra,* at 817, *per* Lord Templeman. However, "lodger" is not a term of art and has been understood in different ways at different times: see (1985) 48 M.L.R. 712 at 713 (J. S. Anderson). It may be doubted whether the dichotomy between tenant and lodger is particularly helpful: see (1987) 50 M.L.R. 226 (A. J. Waite). "While a lodger is necessarily a licensee, not a tenant, a licensee is not necessarily a lodger": [1989] All E.R. Rev. 184 (P. H. Pettit). See *Brooker Settled Estates Ltd v. Ayers* (1987) 54 P. & C.R. 165 at 168; *Hadjiloucas v. Crean* [1988] 1 W.L.R. 1006 at 1011, 1012. *cf. Aslan v. Murphy (Nos. 1 and 2); Duke v. Wynne* [1990] 1 W.L.R. 766 at 770.

[90] *Brillouet v. Landless* (1995) 28 H.L.R. 836. *cf. Mehta v. Royal Bank of Scotland* (1999) 78 P. & C.R. D11 January 25, 1999. It is not so much the quantum of the services as the need for unrestricted access; *Huwyler v. Ruddy* (1996) 72 P. & C.R. D3. If the landlord fails to provide services when he is obliged to do so, that failure does not convert the licence into a tenancy. The tenant's entitlement remains, whether or not he chooses to enforce it: *ibid.*

[91] *Post,* para. 14–016.

(iii) the nature of the accommodation is such that the landlord must retain control of it.[92]

An example of the third situation arose in a case where a local authority, in meeting its statutory obligations to house homeless persons, provided and ran a hostel for homeless men.[93] The authority had the right to move any occupant to another room, sharing it if need be with another person.[94] These arrangements did not give the occupant exclusive possession of his room. An occupant may have exclusive possession (and so be a tenant) even if the landlord provides some form of attendance or services if those are given under a separate and distinct agreement from the tenancy and could have been provided instead by some third party.[95]

14-016   *(c) Shared accommodation.* In a case of single occupancy of residential accommodation,[96] it is a comparatively straightforward question of fact whether or not the occupier has exclusive possession of the property. Where two or more persons share accommodation, the issues are more complex.[97] First, the property may have been granted to the parties as joint tenants, giving them collectively exclusive possession of it. This will be so only where the requirements for a joint tenancy are satisfied[98] so that there is unity of interest, title, time and possession between the occupants.[99] Secondly, although the occupants may not be joint tenants of the whole, they may be tenants of a particular part of the property of which they have exclusive possession, such as their own bedrooms.[1] Thirdly, the parties may be neither joint tenants of the

---

[92] As where the landlord has the power to reallocate the occupant to other accommodation and that power is a genuine one and not a sham. In relation to residential accommodation such cases are likely to be rare. They may be more common in dealings with business or agricultural property: see, *e.g. Dresden Estates Ltd v. Collinson* (1987) 55 P. & C.R. 47 (agreement to use a unit for storage under which the landowner could require the occupier to move to other adjoining premises); *McCarthy v. Bence* [1990] 1 E.G.L.R. 1 (agricultural sharemilking agreement under which the landowner could alter the fields in which the occupier grazed his cattle); [1991] Conv. 58 at 60 (C. Rodgers).

[93] *Westminster C.C. v. Clarke* [1992] 2 A.C. 288; [1992] Conv. 285 (D. S. Cowan). There was no suggestion in the case that the authority provided attendance or services. The case was not strictly concerned with whether the occupant was a tenant or a licensee (although the cases on the distinction were considered) but with whether he had exclusive possession for the purposes of H.A. 1985, s.79 (secure tenancies): see [1992] All E.R. Rev. 248 (P. H. Pettit). For a similar case in which an occupant of a hostel was held to be a licensee, see *Brennan v. Lambeth L.B.C.* (1997) 30 H.L.R. 481.

[94] There is little doubt that this power was necessary given the character of the occupants: *Westminster C.C. v. Clarke, supra,* at 296.

[95] *Vandersteen v. Agius* (1992) 65 P. & C.R. 266 at 274 (landlady provided cleaning for osteopath's surgery in her house and kept his appointment book).

[96] Such as in *Street v. Mountford* [1985] A.C. 809 itself.

[97] See *Hadjiloucas v. Crean, supra,* at 1022, 1023; [1988] All E.R. Rev. 171 (P. J. Clarke). For a thought-provoking commentary on the cases on shared accommodation, see R.J. Smith, *Property Law,* at pp. 350–356.

[98] *Ante,* para. 9–004.

[99] *A.G. Securities v. Vaughan; Antoniades v. Villiers* [1990] 1 A.C. 417 at 472, 474. This was the case in *Antoniades v. Villiers. cf.* (1989) 18 Anglo-American Law Review 151 (P. Sparkes).

[1] *A.G. Securities v. Vaughan; Antoniades v. Villiers, supra,* at 460, 466, 471, 473. *cf.* R.A. 1977, s.22; H.A. 1988, s.3. In such a case, the tenants would presumably be licensees of those shared parts of which they did not have exclusive possession.

shared property (because one or more of the four unities is absent) nor have exclusive possession of any defined part. In such circumstances, they will be merely licensees.[2] The landlord is not excluded from the property because he continues to enjoy possession of it through the other licensees whom he has permitted to occupy the premises.[3] This third construction will often be appropriate "given the informality of many sharing situations, and the obvious contemplation that they may terminate earlier than expected".[4] Although these three situations are theoretically distinct it can be difficult to differentiate them in practice, particularly where two or more persons simultaneously enter into individual agreements for the occupation of a flat, and each is severally liable for his share of the rent.[5] The issue has arisen because of the protection enjoyed by tenants in the first two situations under both the Rent Act 1977[6] and the Housing Act 1988.[7] In making its determination, the court will have to decide whether any of the terms are to be disregarded because they are a sham[8] and will consider "the surrounding circumstances including any relationship between the prospective occupiers, the course of negotiations and the nature and extent of the accommodation and the intended and actual mode of occupation of the accommodation".[9]

A fourth situation arises where two or more persons move into residential **14–017** property which has been let to just one of them as a tenant. Although it has been suggested that the court will presume that the tenant has granted the third party a contractual licence rather than a subtenancy (at least in the absence of a written agreement),[10] the matter should in principle depend upon whether the third party is granted exclusive possession of that part of the property which he occupies.

Finally, it sometimes happens that one of two persons who together occupy premises as licensees may depart. Normally that occurrence will not affect the status of the remaining occupant,[11] but if he then takes over the entirety of the premises with the landlord's consent, that arrangement may convert the licence into a tenancy because it may give him exclusive possession. However it has been suggested that it may be more difficult to establish that supervening events have converted a licence into a tenancy than to show that an agreement created a tenancy from its inception.[12]

---

[2] This was the case in *A.G. Securities v. Vaughan, supra.*

[3] *A.G. Securities v. Vaughan; Antoniades v. Villiers, supra,* at 471.

[4] *Hadjiloucas v. Crean* [1988] 1 W.L.R. 1006 at 1023, *per* Mustill L.J.

[5] Compare *Antoniades v. Villiers, supra,* with *Stribling v. Wickham* (1989) 21 H.L.R. 381 and *Mikeover Ltd v. Brady* [1989] 3 All E.R. 618. See (1990) 106 L.Q.R. 215 (J. Barton).

[6] s.22.

[7] See ss.3, 10; S. Bridge, *Residential Leases,* p. 21.

[8] This is explained *post,* para. 14–021.

[9] *A.G. Securities v. Vaughan; Antoniades v. Villiers, supra,* at 458, *per* Lord Templeman. See too *Stribling v. Wickham, supra,* at 386.

[10] *Monmouth B.C. v. Marlog* [1994] 2 E.G.L.R. 68 at 70.

[11] See, *e.g. Mikeover Ltd v. Brady, supra.*

[12] *Smith v. Northside Development Ltd* (1987) 55 P. & C.R. 164 at 167 (a case concerned with shop premises rather than residential accommodation).

14–018   *(d) Business and agricultural property.* The principles laid down in *Street v. Mountford*[13] in the context of residential accommodation apply equally to agreements concerning business premises[14] and agricultural land.[15]

14–019   (1) BUSINESS PREMISES. The test of whether the occupant has been granted exclusive possession for a term has been applied to situations as diverse as the provision of shop and office accommodation,[16] the right to use "gallops" for training racehorses,[17] the right to deposit refuse,[18] the use of rooms as an osteopath's surgery,[19] an agreement for the management of a Chinese restaurant[20] and a contract to run a petrol service station.[21] The issue in these cases has usually been whether the occupant enjoys the security of tenure conferred by Part II of the Landlord and Tenant Act 1954, which applies only to tenancies and not to licences.[22]

14–020   (2) AGRICULTURAL LAND. Subject to certain minor exceptions, lettings of agricultural land made on or after September 1, 1995 take effect as farm business tenancies under the Agricultural Tenancies Act 1995 and confer no security of tenure.[23] As regards lettings made before that date, not only a tenant but any licensee[24] will have security of tenure under the Agricultural Holdings Act 1986, provided that they have given valuable consideration[25] and have exclusive possession of the holding in the sense that "the grantee is entitled to prevent the grantor and any other person . . . from making any use of the land, at any rate for agricultural purposes, during the period of the grant".[26] There is some uncertainty as to the scope of this second limitation. On one interpretation of it virtually all the "licences" that fell within the ambit of the statute are in fact tenancies,[27] and the issue of exclusive possession

---

[13] [1985] A.C. 809.
[14] *London & Associated Investment Trust plc v. Calow* (1986) 53 P. & C.R. 340 at 352; [1987] Conv. 137 (S. Bridge); *Venus Investments Ltd v. Stocktop Ltd* [1996] E.G.C.S. 173. See too *Vandersteen v. Agius* (1992) 65 P. & C.R. 261. *cf. Dresden Estates Ltd v. Collinson* (1987) 55 P. & C.R. 47; criticised at (1987) 50 M.L.R. 655 (S. Bridge); [1987] Conv. 220 (P. F. Smith).
[15] *Colchester B.C. v. Smith* [1991] Ch. 448 at 483, 484 (on appeal [1992] Ch. 421).
[16] *Smith v. Northside Developments Ltd, supra* (shop); *London & Associated Investment Trust Plc v. Calow, supra* (office).
[17] *University of Reading v. Johnson–Houghton* [1985] 1 E.G.L.R. 113 (lease held to be granted even though under the terms of the agreement the grantor purported to retain some control over the land); [1986] Conv. 275 (C. P. Rodgers).
[18] *Hunts Refuse Disposals Ltd v. Norfolk Environmental Waste Services Ltd* [1997] 1 E.G.L.R. 16.
[19] *Vandersteen v. Agius, supra.*
[20] *Dellneed Ltd v. Chin* (1986) 53 P. & C.R. 172; [1987] Conv. 298 (S. Bridge).
[21] *Esso Petroleum Co. Ltd v. Fumegrange Ltd* [1994] 2 E.G.L.R. 90.
[22] See *post*, para. 22–063. *cf. Ashburn Anstalt v. Arnold* [1989] Ch. 1 (where the issue was whether a third party was bound by a right to occupy a shop).
[23] See *post*, para. 22–086.
[24] s.2(2)(b); *post*, para. 22–096.
[25] *Goldsack v. Shore* [1950] 1 K.B. 708.
[26] *Bahamas International Trust Co. Ltd v. Threadgold* [1974] 1 W.L.R. 1514 at 1527, *per* Lord Diplock.
[27] *McCarthy v. Bence* [1990] 1 E.G.L.R. 1 at 3; *Ashdale Land & Property Co. Ltd v. Manners* [1992] 2 E.G.L.R. 5 at 7, 8. There may be some genuine licences that will fall within the statute such as seasonal grazing licences: *ibid.*

therefore determines the availability of statutory protection.[28] It may be noted that a very similar issue has arisen in relation to secure tenancies granted by local authorities and other bodies.[29]

3. Shams or pretences. Although the parties will be presumed to mean **14–021**
what they say,[30] the court will be "astute" to detect provisions in the agreement between the parties that have been variously described as "sham devices and artificial transactions"[31] and "pretences",[32] whose only object is to disguise the grant of a tenancy and so evade the legislation that exists to protect residential, business and agricultural tenants.[33] The court seeks to ascertain whether the parties' true bargain is the same as that which appears on the face of the agreement, for it is the former to which effect will be given and which therefore determines whether the agreement is a lease or licence.[34] It may be evident on the face of the agreement that one or more of its terms is not genuine, such as a requirement that the occupant must vacate the premises between 10.30 a.m. and noon every day, or a provision empowering the landlord to remove furniture from the occupant's room without replacing it.[35] Even if this is not the case, the fact that a term is not genuine may be apparent either from the surrounding circumstances or from the conduct of the parties subsequent to the agreement.[36] Thus a provision by which the landlord could introduce an additional occupant to share the premises with the grantees was held to be a sham where—

---

[28] See *McCarthy v. Bence, supra* (share farming arrangement held to be outside the protection of the Agricultural Holdings Act 1986); *Sparkes v. Smart* [1990] 2 E.G.L.R. 245 at 253; [1991] Conv. 58 (C. Rodgers). For criticism of this limitation see [1991] Conv. 207 (M. Slatter).

[29] See H.A. 1985, s.79(3); *Westminster C.C. v. Clarke* [1992] 2 A.C. 288 at 299, 300.

[30] *Aslan v. Murphy (Nos 1 and 2); Duke v. Wynne* [1990] 1 W.L.R. 766 at 770.

[31] *Street v. Mountford* [1985] A.C. 821 at 825, *per* Lord Templeman.

[32] *A.G. Securities v. Vaughan; Antoniades v. Villiers* [1990] 1 A.C. 417 at 462, *per* Lord Templeman.

[33] Other devices have been employed to circumvent this legislation, such as a letting to a company to escape the provisions of the Rent Acts. Such transactions are also subject to scrutiny, often on similar principles, to determine whether they are "expressed in a form which do not truly reflect the parties' intentions": *Kaye v. Massbetter Ltd* [1991] 2 E.G.L.R. 97 at 99, *per* Nicholls L.J. See too *Estavest Investments Ltd v. Commercial Express Travel Ltd* [1988] 2 E.G.L.R. 91; *Hilton v. Plustitle Ltd* [1989] 1 W.L.R. 149; *Gisborne v. Burton* [1989] Q.B. 390; (1989) 105 L.Q.R. 167 (P. V. Baker); [1989] Conv. 196 (C. Rodgers); (1991) 11 O.J.L.S. 136 (S. Bright).

[34] *Aslan v. Murphy (Nos 1 and 2); Duke v. Wynne supra*, at 770, 771.

[35] *Crancour Ltd v. Da Silvaesa* [1986] 1 E.G.L.R. 80. See too *Aslan v. Murphy (No. 1), supra.*

[36] The court cannot look at subsequent conduct in construing an agreement, but it is admissible evidence as to whether the written agreement genuinely reflects the true intentions of the parties: *A.G. Securities v. Vaughan; Antoniades v. Villiers, supra*, at 469, 475; [1989] Conv. 128 (P. F. Smith); [1989] C.L.J. 19 (C.H.). As to whether a term will be regarded as a sham merely because the landlord chooses not to implement it, see [1988] All E.R. Rev. 175 (P. J. Clarke); and *infra.*

(i) the accommodation consisted respectively of a one-bedroomed flat furnished with a double bed in one case,[37] and a small room just 51 inches wide in another[38];

(ii) the landlord did not seriously contemplate introducing another occupant[39]; and

(iii) the arrangement was a sale by a couple of their home with a right to live in the property for the rest of their lives.[40]

14–022 However the subsequent conduct of the parties may demonstrate that the terms of an agreement were genuine. In one case two cohabitants entered into separate agreements with the landlord for the occupation of a flat by which each was severally liable for half the rent. One of them left and the landlord would accept only half the rent from the remaining occupant. The court held that these agreements were genuinely independent and therefore did not confer exclusive possession of the flat on the two occupants as joint tenants.[41]

Although the court must "keep a weather eye open for pretences",[42] the onus of proving that a term is a sham rests on the party asserting that it is.[43] The court does not "lean in favour of any particular approach to construction, or any particular inference from the facts of the case".[44] Even if a particular term has never been invoked by the landlord, it is open to him to justify it, *e.g.* as a matter of commercial practice.[45]

14–023 **4. Exceptional circumstances.** In three exceptional circumstances an occupier who has exclusive possession of premises will not be a tenant under a lease.[46] The scope of these exceptions has been narrowly construed and there is no open-ended exception for undefined "special circumstances".[47]

14–024 *(a) No intention to create legal relations.* Where the parties do not intend to create legal relations no tenancy will arise.[48] Such an agreement appears to create a licence rather than a tenancy at will.[49] Cases which fall within this

---

[37] *Antoniades v. Villiers, supra.*
[38] *Aslan v. Murphy (No. 1), supra.*
[39] *Nicolaou v. Pitt* (1989) 22 H.L.R. 487; *Duke v. Wynne, supra.*
[40] *Skipton B.S. v. Clayton* (1993) 63 P. & C.R. 223.
[41] *Mikeover Ltd v. Brady* [1989] 3 All E.R. 618.
[42] *Aslan v. Murphy (Nos 1 and 2); Duke v. Wynne* [1990] 1 W.L.R. 766, at 770, *per* Lord Donaldson M.R.
[43] *Mikeover Ltd v. Brady, supra,* at 626.
[44] *Stribling v. Wickham* (1989) 21 H.L.R. 381 at 390, *per* Sir Denys Buckley.
[45] *Esso Petroleum Co. Ltd v. Fumegrange Ltd* [1994] 2 E.G.L.R. 90 at 93.
[46] *Street v. Mountford, supra,* at 821; *ante,* para. 14–013.
[47] *Camden L.B.C. v. Shortlife Community Housing Ltd* (1992) 90 L.G.R. 358 at 372, *per* Millett J. See too *Dellneed Ltd v. Chin* (1986) 53 P. & C.R. 172 at 187; *Westminster C.C. v. Clarke* [1992] 2 A.C. 288 at 302.
[48] *Street v. Mountford, supra* at 819–822.
[49] *Cobb v. Lane* [1952] 1 T.L.R. 1037; *Colchester B.C. v. Smith* [1991] Ch. 448 at 485 (on appeal [1992] Ch. 421). *cf. Bostock v Bryant* (1990) 61 P. & C.R. 23 at 29. For tenancies at will and for the difference between such tenancies and licences, see *post,* para 14–075.

category will commonly come about as a result of some act of kindness or friendship,[50] or some family arrangement,[51] but they are not confined to such situations.[52] Thus where a local authority allowed an allotment holder to remain in possession of land rent-free at his own risk because it might wish to utilise the land at short notice, it was held that the arrangement created a licence and not a tenancy.[53] The mere fact that the occupier is a member of the grantor's family does not of itself preclude the existence of a tenancy.[54] If there is exclusive possession and rent is paid, the transaction is likely to be regarded as a lease.[55] Conversely, although there can be a tenancy without rent,[56] in a case of a family arrangement or act of friendship, its absence is likely to negative a tenancy.[57]

(b) Occupation referable to some other relationship. No tenancy will be **14–025** created if an occupant's exclusive possession is referable to some other legal relationship.[58] Thus there was no tenancy where a person occupied property because of her appointment as an "almsperson": she was the beneficiary of a charitable trust.[59] A trespasser who, on demand, paid sums to the owner for her unlawful use and occupation of the premises was not a tenant.[60] Nor was a purchaser who entered into possession under either a contract for the sale of land or an option to purchase the premises, because his occupation was "ancillary and referable to" his equitable interest in the property arising from the contract.[61] However there was no such referability as regards either a purchaser of the goodwill of a business conducted on the premises or a person

---

[50] See *Booker v. Palmer* [1942] 2 All E.R. 674 (evacuee allowed to occupy premises for the duration of the war rent-free); *Heslop v. Burns* [1974] 1 W.L.R. 1241 (family permitted to live rent-free in a cottage by former employer); *Sharp v. McArthur* (1986) 19 H.L.R. 364 (vendor permitted homeless person to occupy a house pending its sale).

[51] See *Cobb v. Lane, supra* (brother allowed to live rent-free on premises).

[52] See, *e.g. Holt v. Wellington* (1996) 71 P. & C.R. D40 ("sympathetic landlady scheme" for vulnerable persons: D.H.S.S. paid for the occupant's care and there was no contract with her).

[53] *Colchester B.C. v. Smith, supra* at 485.

[54] *Ward v. Warnke* (1990) 22 H.L.R. 496 at 500.

[55] *Nunn v. Dalrymple* (1989) 21 H.L.R. 569; *Ward v. Warnke, supra.*

[56] *Ante,* para. 14–003.

[57] *cf. Bostock v. Bryant, supra* (grant by "Uncle Joe" of exclusive possession of part of his house to the defendants, who paid no rent but contributed to the outgoings, held not to create a tenancy for the purposes of the Rent Acts).

[58] *Street v. Mountford* [1985] A.C. 809 at 826, 827.

[59] *Gray v. Taylor* [1998] 1 W.L.R. 1093.

[60] *Westminster C.C. v. Basson* (1990) 62 P. & C.R. 57. *cf. Tower Hamlets L.B.C. v. Ayinde* (1994) 26 H.L.R. 631 (where in the circumstances the claimants had by their conduct accepted the defendant as their tenant).

[61] *Essex Plan Ltd v. Broadminster* (1988) 56 P. & C.R. 353 at 356, *per* Hoffmann J. The status of a purchaser in possession is usually said to be that of a tenant at will rather than a licensee: see *Wheeler v. Mercer* [1957] A.C. 416 at 425; *post,* para. 14–075. A lease may arise if the purchaser or grantee makes payments for the use and occupation of the premises. If the property is residential, he will be protected as an assured tenant under H.A. 1988, s.1: *Francis Jackson Developments Ltd v. Stemp* [1943] 2 All E.R. 601 (a case on the Rent Acts). There was no such protection for a purchaser of agricultural property under the A.H.A. 1948 or 1986 (see *Walters v. Roberts* (1980) 41 P. & C.R. 210 at 219: and *post,* para. 22–086; after September 1, 1995 the point can no longer arise because there is no security of tenure for lettings under the A.T.A 1995) and there is probably none for a buyer of business premises (see *Wheeler v.*

who was merely contemplating the purchase of the property and who made payments in the nature of rent. Each was held to be a tenant.[62]

Perhaps the commonest example of this exception is service occupancy.[63] There is no tenancy but only a licence where an employee occupies his employer's premises because the nature of his duties requires it, such as a stockman or a gamekeeper.[64] The test is whether the employee is genuinely required to occupy the premises for the better performance of his duties rather than merely for his convenience,[65] and unless it is satisfied, the exception will not apply.[66]

14–026   *(c) No power to grant a tenancy.* There will be no tenancy where the grantor lacks the legal power or capacity to grant one,[67] as where it is a requisitioning authority.[68] It had been held that if a grantor had no estate in the land he could not grant a lease.[69] However, the House of Lords has now rejected this view.[70] Even if the grantor is himself a mere licensee, if he enters into a contract which gives the grantee the right to exclusive possession for a term, there will be a lease.[71] Although a lease usually creates a proprietary interest, it will not do so if the grantor had no estate out of which to grant one. It "is the fact that the agreement is a lease which creates the proprietary interest. It is putting the cart before the horse to say that whether the agreement is a lease depends upon whether it creates a proprietary interest".[72] A tenant who covenants not to assign or sublet the property without the landlord's consent will not fall within

---

Mercer, supra, at 425; *cf. Javad v. Aqil* [1991] 1 W.L.R. 1007). See generally [1987] Conv. 278 (P. Sparkes); [1991] C.L.J. 232 (S Bridge).

[62] See *Vandersteen v. Agius* (1992) 65 P. & C.R. 261 and *Bretherton v. Paton* [1986] 1 E.G.L.R. 172 respectively.

[63] For the effect of termination of service occupancy see *post,* para. 17–008.

[64] See *Dover v. Prosser* [1904] 1 K.B. 84 at 85; *Ramsbottom v. Snelson* [1948] 1 K.B. 473; *Glasgow Corporation v. Johnstone* [1965] A.C. 609.

[65] *Norris v. Checksfield* [1991] 1 W.L.R. 1241 at 1244 (where there was held to be a licence and not a tenancy of a bungalow provided so that a coach driver and mechanic would be available in emergencies). *cf. Hughes v. Greenwich L.B.C.* [1994] 1 A.C. 170.

[66] See, *e.g. Royal Philanthropic Society v. County* [1985] 2 E.G.L.R. 109 (no service occupancy where a teacher occupied a house two miles from the school).

[67] *Street v. Mountford, supra,* at 821; *Camden L.B.C. v. Shortlife Community Housing Ltd* (1992) 90 L.G.R. 358 at 372. In the latter case it was *ultra vires* the claimant authority to grant a tenancy without the consent of the Secretary of State.

[68] See, *e.g. Minister of Agriculture and Fisheries v. Matthews* [1950] 1 K.B. 148; *Finbow v. Air Ministry* [1963] 1 W.L.R. 697.

[69] *Camden L.B.C. v. Shortlife Community Housing Ltd, supra,* at 381; *Redbank Schools Ltd v. Abdullahzadeh* (1995) 28 H.L.R. 431; *Bruton v. London and Quadrant Housing Trust* [1998] Q.B. 834.

[70] *Bruton v. London & Quadrant Housing Trust* [1999] 3 W.L.R. 150; approving *Family Housing Association v. Jones* [1990] 1 W.L.R. 779.

[71] In *Bruton v. London & Quadrant Housing Trust,* a licensee was held to have granted a lease and was therefore liable to the implied obligation of repair under L.T.A. 1985, s.11 (*post,* para. 14–222).

[72] *Bruton v. London & Quadrant Housing Trust, supra,* at 157, *per* Lord Hoffmann.

this exception even though by granting a sublease he will be in breach of that covenant.[73]

5. Contrast with easements. The requirement of exclusive possession distinguishes leases not merely from licences but also from easements. An easement is merely a right over land, not a right to its possession.[74] If therefore a right by its nature does not confer exclusive possession on the grantee, such as a right to erect an advertising hoarding[75] or a right to pass and repass over another's land,[76] it may be a licence or an easement but it cannot be a tenancy.

14–027

B. *The Requirements as to Duration must be Satisfied*

A lease may fail because the estate is not clearly marked out, *e.g.* if it purports to be a lease for an indefinite period instead of for a fixed term. The various periods for which leases can validly be granted are treated separately below.[77]

14–028

C. *The Lease must be Created in the Proper Way*

I. FORMAL LEASES

In order to create a legal estate which can rank as a term of years absolute within section 1(1) of the Law of Property Act 1925[78] a lease must be made with the proper formalities. The present formal requirements can only be understood by reference to their historical evolution.[79] This took place in four stages.

14–029

1. Common law. At common law a lease of corporeal land could be granted in any way, even orally. This illustrates the ancient conception of a lease as a simple contract. But incorporeal rights which are within the definition of real property,[80] such as easements and profits, could be created at common law only by deed: they lay in grant, not in livery.[81] This rule was applied to leases, when they came to be considered estates in land, so that a lease of (for example) shooting or fishing rights had to be made by deed. But if land was leased to which such incorporeal rights were appurtenant, they could pass with the land without a deed.

14–030

---

[73] *Dellneed Ltd v. Chin* (1986) 53 P. & C.R. 172 at 186, 187.

[74] *Post*, para. 18–055.

[75] The contention that such a right could create a tenancy has been described as "misconceived and unarguable": *Kewal Investments Ltd v. Arthur Maiden* [1990] 1 E.G.L.R. 193 at 194, *per* Morison, Q.C.

[76] *IDC Group Ltd v. Clark* [1992] 2 E.G.L.R. 184 at 186 (right to use a fire escape).

[77] *Post*, paras 14–055 *et seq.*

[78] *Ante*, para. 4–045.

[79] See *Long v. Tower Hamlets L.B.C.* [1998] Ch. 197 at 204; [1992] Conv. 252; 337 (P. Sparkes).

[80] *Ante*, para. 4–037, *post*, para. 18–001.

[81] *Post*, para. 18–051.

14–031   **2. 1677–1845.** The common law rule that a lease could be established on oral evidence alone was a fertile source of fraud and perjury. The Court of Chancery manifested an unwillingness to enforce leases that had been granted orally. To remedy this, the Statute of Frauds 1677[82] required that every lease should be in writing (though not necessarily by deed) signed by the party creating it or his agent authorised in writing. In default of this, only a tenancy at will was created. An exception was made for a lease for a period not exceeding three years from its creation at a rent of at least two-thirds of the full improved value (*i.e.* the value taking into consideration any improvements to the property[83]). Such a lease could still be made orally. The rule that leases of incorporeal rights must be made by deed was not altered by the statute.[84]

14–032   **3. 1845–1926.** The Real Property Act 1845[85] required a deed in all cases in which the existing law required writing. The exception as to leases for three years or less therefore remained as before, but all other leases had to be made by deed. The Act said "a lease required by law to be in writing ... shall be void at law unless also made by deed".

4. Since 1925

14–033   *(a) The statute.* The provisions of the two previous Acts were repeated by the Law of Property Act 1925 but with certain alterations. No attempt was made to state the combined effect of the earlier Acts. Section 54 followed the Statute of Frauds 1677 and section 52 was modelled on the Real Property Act 1845, so that their differing provisions continue to stand side by side. This is presumably because they had become so familiar that it was thought best to preserve them.

14–034   *(b) The rule.* The present law may be stated as follows. A lease cannot create a legal estate unless it is made by deed; for all grants are "void for the purpose of conveyancing or creating a legal estate unless made by deed".[86] But no formality is required for a lease which—

> (i) takes effect in possession;
>
> (ii) is for a term not exceeding three years, whether or not the lessee is given power to extend the term; and
>
> (iii) is at the best rent reasonably obtainable without taking a fine.[87]

---

[82] s.1.

[83] s.2.

[84] *Duke of Somerset v. Fogwell* (1826) 5 B. & C. 875; *Bird v. Higginson* (1835) 6 A. & E. 824.

[85] s.3, replacing the Transfer of Property Act 1844, s.4.

[86] s.52(1); and see ss.54(1), 205(1)(ii).

[87] s.54(2). A "fine" in this sense is a lump sum payment made in consideration of a reduced rent. It is often called a "premium". Thus premises worth £5,000 per annum may be let for three years at £5,000 per annum (*i.e.* at a full "rack" rent) or at £500 per annum with a premium of £13,500.

Such a lease may be validly created either orally or in writing.[88] It will be seen that point (i) was new in 1925, and that point (iii) was a modification of the previous law.

(c) "Possession". To fall within the exception, the lease must take effect in **14–035** possession and not in reversion. Thus a three-month reversionary lease[89] granted today to take effect in 25 days' time cannot be created without a deed.[90] As many short leases are granted a few days in advance, this restriction may in practice seriously narrow the exception. This will defeat the whole purpose of exempting short leases from the statutory requirement of a deed.[91] "Possession" is not confined to physical possession, but includes receipt of rents and profits, *e.g.* from sub-tenants in physical possession.[92]

(d) "Three years". The phrase "a term not exceeding three years" includes **14–036** a monthly or other periodic tenancy,[93] even though it will continue indefinitely unless determined by notice,[94] for it is wholly uncertain that it will endure for more than three years. The phrase also includes a fixed term for three years or less which contains an option for the tenant to extend it beyond three years,[95] but not a fixed term for more than three years, even though it is determinable within that period.[96] The three years must be computed from the date of the grant.[97]

(e) Application. If all three conditions are complied with, a legal lease can **14–037** be created either orally or in writing. But the legislation seems to preserve the exception as to incorporeal rights, such as shooting or fishing, which therefore can be leased only by deed.[98] Further, an oral lease is not a "conveyance" within the Law of Property Act 1925,[99] and so it may be less effective than a lease by deed, *e.g.* for creating easements.[1] The concession in favour of the *grant* of an informal lease now applies equally to a *contract* for a lease, *i.e.* a promise to grant such a lease at a future date.[2] The usual requirement that a

---

[88] *Long v. Tower Hamlets L.B.C.* [1998] Ch. 197 at 210.

[89] Reversionary leases are considered *post*, para. 14–061.

[90] *Long v. Tower Hamlets L.B.C., supra* at 215–219.

[91] For criticism of the restriction, see [1992] Conv. 337 at 340 (P. Sparkes); (1995) 58 M.L.R. 637 at 639 (G. Battersby); [1998] Conv. 229 (S. Bright). If the lease is void for want of formality, it is likely to take effect as a periodic tenancy when the tenant enters and pays rent: see *Long v. Tower Hamlets L.B.C., supra* at 211, 219; *post*, para. 14–060. For the circumstances in which such a tenancy will now be inferred, see *post*, para. 14–065.

[92] L.P.A. 1925, s.205(1)(xix), *ante*, para. 4–044.

[93] *Ex p. Voisey* (1882) 21 Ch.D. 442; *Hammond v. Farrow* [1904] 2 K.B. 332 at 335.

[94] See *post*, para. 14–068.

[95] See *Hand v. Hall* (1877) 2 Ex.D. 355.

[96] *Kushner v. Law Society* [1952] 1 K.B. 264.

[97] See *Rawlins v. Turner* (1699) 1 Ld.Raym. 736.

[98] *Wood v. Leadbitter* (1845) 13 M. & W. 838 at 843; *Swayne v. Howells* [1927] 1 K.B. 385; *Mason v. Clarke* [1954] 1 Q.B. 460; [1955] A.C. 778; [1954] C.L.J. 189; *post*, para. 18–090.

[99] *Rye v. Rye* [1962] A.C. 496.

[1] *Post*, para. 18–108.

[2] L.P.(M.P.)A. 1989, s.2(5)(a); *ante*, para. 12–022. Prior to September 27, 1989, such contracts had either to comply with the formal requirements of L.P.A. 1925, s.40, or there had to be sufficient acts of part performance: see the previous edition of this work at p. 638.

contract for the sale or other disposition of land can only be made in writing[3] does not apply to such contracts, which may therefore be made orally.

14–038   *(f) Assignment.* Once a legal lease has been validly granted, a deed is required to effect its legal assignment, however short the term may be.[4] Thus the legal assignment of a yearly tenancy can only be made by deed,[5] even if the tenancy was created orally.[6] It follows from this, that a *contract* to assign such a lease must also be made in writing.[7] The result is anomalous and can lead to hardship.[8]

II. INFORMAL LEASES

14–039   **1. Informal lease void at law.** A lease which did not satisfy the above requirements was void at law and passed no legal estate. But a tenancy might arise independently of the lease. If a tenant took possession with the landlord's consent, a tenancy at will arose.[9] As the law formerly stood,[10] as soon as rent was paid and accepted, the tenancy at will was automatically converted into a yearly or other periodic tenancy, depending on the way in which the rent was paid.[11] Such a yearly tenancy was a legal estate, for the law implied an oral grant from one acceptance of rent by the landlord. Furthermore, it was held subject to any terms which the parties had agreed upon, so far as they were consistent with a yearly tenancy.[12]

An informal lease which was "void at law" under the Real Property Act 1845 was thus not entirely ineffective if a yearly tenancy later arose. If, for example, the tenant had covenanted to do repairs, this became one of the terms of the yearly tenancy. Other examples of such terms which are transferable to a yearly tenancy are given later.[13] Before 1875, therefore, the position *in a common law court* of a tenant who had entered and paid rent under a void lease was generally that of a yearly tenant subject to certain of the terms of the lease. The landlord was in a corresponding position. But both parties might have had other rights *in equity*, as will shortly be explained.

---

[3] L.P.(M.P.)A. 1989, s.2(1); *ante*, para. 12–020.

[4] Where a lease of registered land is registered with its own title, the legal estate will not pass until the transfer of the lease is registered: L.R.A. 1925, s.22(1); *post*, para. 14–108.

[5] L.P.A. 1925. s.52(1).

[6] *Crago v. Julian* [1992] 1 W.L.R. 372; [1992] Conv. 375 (P. Sparkes); [1992] Fam. Law 294 (S. Cretney); [1992] All E.R. Rev. 233 (P. Pettit). See too *Camden L.B.C. v. Alexandrou* (1997) 30 H.L.R. 534. *cf.* F.L.A. 1996, s.53; Sched. 7. As to the effect of informal assignment, see *post*, para. 14–108.

[7] To comply with L.P.(M.P.)A. 1989, s.2(1); *ante*, para. 12–020. The exception in s.2(5) is inapplicable.

[8] As it did in *Crago v. Julian, supra.* See (1995) 58 M.L.R. 637 at 638 (G. Battersby).

[9] Indeed it is provided by statute that an interest in land created without the formality required by law has the force and effect of an interest at will only: L.P.A. 1925, s.54(1); *Goodtitle d. Gallaway v. Herbert* (1792) 4 T.R. 680 at 681.

[10] The position is now different: *post*, para. 14–065.

[11] *Martin v. Smith* (1874) L.R. 9 Ex. 50.

[12] *Doe d. Rigge v. Bell* (1793) 5 T.R. 471; *Doe d. Thomson v. Amey* (1840) 12 A. & E. 476.

[13] *Post*, para. 14–066.

2. Effect as contract. Although such a lease failed to create any legal **14–040** estate, it might be treated as a contract to grant the lease agreed upon. A lease is clearly distinct from a contract to grant a lease: the difference is between "I hereby grant you a lease" and "I hereby agree that I will grant you a lease".[14] Nevertheless both law and equity concurred in treating an imperfect lease as a contract to grant a lease,[15] provided it was made for value and was sufficiently evidenced in writing or, in the case of equity, supported by a sufficient act of part performance.[16] The attitude of equity was particularly important, for under the doctrine of *Parker v. Taswell*[17] equity would first treat an imperfect lease of this kind as a contract to grant the lease, and then order specific performance of that contract.[18] Once a proper lease had been granted in pursuance of the decree of specific performance, the position of the parties was the same for the future as if the lease had been granted by deed in the first place.

3. *Walsh v. Lonsdale*[19]

(a) Effect of right to specific performance. The rights of the parties under an **14–041** imperfect lease sufficiently evidenced by writing or part performance were thus clear whenever specific performance had been decreed. What was not so clear was the position if, as was far more often the case, no decree of specific performance had been granted but the parties were entitled to obtain one. In equity the principle is "equity looks on that as done which ought to be done", so that the parties were treated as if the lease had been granted with proper formalities. But there was no such principle at law; for at law the transaction was void as a lease, and as a contract for a lease it was remediable only by an action for damages.

The difference in the position in equity is founded on the difference between damages and specific performance. A person entitled merely to damages has no rights in the land; but a person entitled to specific performance has the right to demand the land itself, and so in the eyes of equity such a person is the rightful occupant. Just as a purchaser becomes equitable owner

---

[14] The difference is often not so clear in practice, where the "agreement" made by the parties may be either a contract or a grant, depending on its language. In doubtful cases the court leans towards the interpretation which will give a greater validity to the transaction: *Browne v. Warner* (1807) 14 Ves. 156; *Rollason v. Leon* (1861) 7 H. & N. 73 ("A agrees to let and B agrees to take"); *cf. Wright v. Macadam* [1949] 2 K.B. 744 at 747 ("Agreement" held to be a lease).

[15] *Bond v. Rosling* (1861) 1 B. & S. 371; *Tiddey v. Mollett* (1864) 16 C.B. (N.S.) 298. An imperfect lease is not treated as an agreement for every purpose: see, *e.g. Harte v. Williams* [1934] 1 K.B. 201 (unsealed lease prepared by unqualified person).

[16] For the doctrine of part performance, see, *ante*, para. 12–017. The doctrine does not apply to contracts made after September 26, 1989.

[17] (1858) 2 De G. & J. 559; and see *Zimbler v. Abrahams* [1903] 1 K.B. 577; *Industrial Properties (Barton Hill) Ltd v. Associated Electrical Industries Ltd* [1977] Q.B. 580. *Cheshire Lines Committee v. Lewis* (1880) 50 L.J. Q.B. 121 is unsound on this point. As to incorporeal rights, see *Frogley v. Earl of Lovelace* (1859) John. 333.

[18] If the lease was void because it exceeded the lessor's power to grant it, it might similarly be treated as a contract for a properly limited lease; *cf.* L.P.A. 1925, s.152, *ante*, para. 8–078.

[19] (1882) 21 Ch.D. 9.

under a contract for sale,[20] so an intended lessee becomes equitable tenant under a contract for a lease. If a proper lease ought already to have been executed, he is in the same position as if it had been executed, with one important reservation, namely, that until he has obtained a proper lease his rights are equitable, not legal.

14–042   *(b) Fusion of courts.* A tenant holding under a mere contract for a lease, *i.e.* merely in equity, could, before 1875, always enforce his rights against the other party by recourse to the Court of Chancery. Here he could obtain a decree of specific performance, and he could meanwhile ask for an injunction to prevent the landlord interfering with the exercise of his equitable rights. After 1875 the tenant no longer needed to rely on the protection of one special court, for the result of the Judicature Act 1873–1875[21] was that "there is only one court, and the equity rules prevail in it".[22] This is shown in the leading case of *Walsh v. Lonsdale*,[23] which laid down that where there is a yearly tenancy at common law but a tenancy for years in equity, both parties can insist on their equitable rights against one another and that these prevail over their legal rights.

14–043   *(c) The decision.* The facts and decision in *Walsh v. Lonsdale*[24] were as follows. L agreed in writing to grant a seven year lease of a mill to T at a rent which was to vary with the number of looms run. One of the agreed terms was that on demand T would pay a year's rent in advance. No lease was executed, but T was let into possession and paid rent in arrears for a year and a half, thereby becoming a yearly tenant at law. L then demanded a year's rent in advance, and on T's refusal to pay, distrained for it. T then brought an action for damages for wrongful distress (in effect, for trespass), for an injunction and for specific performance of the agreement, and he applied for an interim injunction restraining the landlord's act meanwhile. It was upon this last application that the case was decided.

T's argument was that distress was a legal, and not an equitable, remedy, and that since at law he was only a yearly tenant and no obligation to pay rent in advance could be implied, especially in view of the variable nature of the rent, L could not distrain for the rent.[25] It was held, however, that since the distress would have been legal had the lease agreed upon been granted by deed, and since equity treated the parties as if this had been done, the distress was lawful in equity. In equity's eyes T was already tenant for seven years subject to all the terms of the agreement, not a yearly tenant subject to some terms only. Since 1875 the equitable rule prevailed over the rule at law in all courts and so T could not complain of the distress.

---

[20] *Ante*, para. 12–051.
[21] See J.A. 1873, s.25(11).
[22] *Walsh v. Lonsdale* (1882) 21 Ch.D. 9 at 14, *per* Jessel M.R.
[23] (1882) 21 Ch.D. 9.
[24] *ibid.*
[25] See *Manchester Brewery Co. v. Coombs* [1901] 2 Ch. 608 at 617, 618, *per* Farwell J.

The decision was novel and remains controversial,[26] though it has often been applied.[27] Prior to the Judicature Acts, distress was not available in respect of non-payment of rent under an agreement for a lease, because the relationship between the parties was entirely contractual.[28] Furthermore, a court of equity would never have ordered payment of rent or decreed performance of covenants.[29] If appropriate, it would have decreed specific performance of the agreement for a lease and left the parties to their remedy at law. But it was not the general practice to back-date decrees of specific performance except in very limited circumstances.[30]

(d) Extent of the principle. The doctrine of *Walsh v. Lonsdale* will operate **14–044** even where L does not hold the legal estate, provided that he has a specifically enforceable right to obtain it. There can thus be a chain of equitable interests, each in turn potentially effective. This is shown by a case where L was entitled to the legal fee simple under a contract of sale which, though the money had been paid, had never been completed by conveyance, in order to save stamp duty. L granted a "lease" to T which took effect as an agreement for a lease under *Parker v. Taswell* and as an effective lease under *Walsh v. Lonsdale*, even though L himself was not the legal owner. For either L or T could have enforced the "lease" by bringing in the owner of the outstanding legal estate and obtaining specific performance against him; and accordingly L was entitled to sue T for breach of the covenant to repair contained in the "lease".[31]

4. Differences between legal and equitable leases. The effect of *Walsh v.* **14–045** *Lonsdale* was often summed up in the words "a contract for a lease is as good as a lease."[32] For many purposes this is true, but as a generalisation it is misleading,[33] for it ignores the vital difference between legal and equitable interests. The difference between a contract for a lease and a lease is in reality substantial. The former falls short of the latter in the following respects.

(a) Dependence upon specific performance. The effect of *Walsh v. Lonsdale* **14–046** in equity depends upon the willingness of the court to grant the discretionary

---

[26] See (1987) 7 O.J.L.S. 60 (S. Gardner); (1988) 8 O.J.L.S. 350 (P. Sparkes); (1989) 10 J.L.H. 29 (P. Sparkes); R. P. Meagher, W. M. C. Gummow and J. R. F. Lehane, *Equity: Doctrines and Remedies* (3rd ed., 1992) paras 236–245; *Chan v. Cresdon Proprietary Ltd* (1989) 168 C.L.R. 242 at 250 *et seq.*

[27] See, *e.g. Re a Company, ex p. Tredegar Enterprises Ltd* [1992] 2 E.G.L.R. 39 (surety liable to pay rent under covenant to take a lease in the event of a tenant's insolvency).

[28] *Vincent v. Godwin* (1853) 1 Sm. & G. 384 at 394.

[29] *Cox v. Bishop* (1857) 8 De G.M. & G. 815 and 824.

[30] See *Chan v. Cresden Proprietary Ltd, supra* at 255; (1989) 10 J.L.H. 29 (P. Sparkes).

[31] *Industrial Properties (Barton Hill) Ltd v. Associated Electrical Industries Ltd* [1977] Q.B. 580. As to L's obligation to get in the legal estate, see at 610, *per* Roskill L.J. T was in any case liable by privity of contract, even if the lease itself was invalid.

[32] See *Re Maughan* (1885) 14 Q.B.D. 956 at 958; *Furness v. Bond* (1888) 4 T.L.R. 457; *Allhusen v. Brooking* (1884) 26 Ch.D. 551 at 565; *Lowther v. Heaver* (1889) 41 Ch.D. 248 at 264.

[33] See *Manchester Brewery Co. v. Coombs* [1901] 2 Ch. 608 at 617.

remedy of specific performance.[34] If for any reason an agreement for a lease is one of which the court cannot or will not grant specific performance the position under it is very different from that under a legal lease: the parties can have nothing more than a right to sue for damages under the agreement, though a yearly or other periodic tenancy may arise in the usual way. For example, there can normally be no specific performance in favour of a tenant whose tenancy agreement is subject to a condition precedent (*e.g.* to repair) which he has not performed,[35] or who is already in breach of one of the terms of the agreement,[36] or whose claim is to an underlease which can be granted to him only in breach of a covenant against sub-letting in the head lease.[37] He who comes to equity must come with clean hands, and he who seeks equity must do equity.[38] In such cases the tenant stands by his legal rights and remedies (if any). It is often said that a tenant who is in breach of one of the terms of an agreement for a lease cannot obtain specific performance,[39] but this seems too sweeping, for not every breach of contract will be a bar to specific performance.[40] Although the point is not settled, if the breach is one where the court would have granted relief against forfeiture had the lease been legal, then in principle specific performance should be decreed.[41] This is explained more fully in relation to the forfeiture of leases for breach of covenant.[42]

Limits to a court's jurisdiction may also create difficulties. Thus a claimant's right to specific performance in a county court is limited,[43] whereas a defendant's is not.[44]

---

[34] *ibid.*; *ante*, para. 12–115. At one time, the court would not decree specific performance of contracts for transient interests: see the previous edition of this work at p. 590. But now such contracts will be specifically enforced, provided that the action is heard before the agreed term has expired. Specific performance has even been decreed of an agreement to grant a licence for two days: *Verrall v. Great Yarmouth Borough Council* [1981] Q.B. 202; *post*, para. 7–009.

[35] *Greville v. Parker* [1910] A.C. 335; *Cornish v. Brook Green Laundry Ltd* [1959] 1 Q.B. 394; *Euston Centre Properties Ltd v. H. & J. Wilson Ltd* [1982] 1 E.G.L.R. 57; *Henry Smith's Charity Trustees v. Hemmings* [1983] 1 E.G.L.R. 94. See *post*, para. 14–301.

[36] *Coatsworth v. Johnson* (1886) 55 L.J.Q.B. 220.

[37] *Warmington v. Miller* [1973] Q.B. 877.

[38] See Snell, *Equity*, 30–32.

[39] See *e.g.* Pettit (1960) 24 Conv. (N.S.) 125 at 127; S. Bright and G. Gilbert, *Landlord and Tenant*, p. 215.

[40] See, *e.g. Parker v. Taswell* (1858) 2 De G. & J. 559; *Zimbler v. Abrahams* [1903] 1 K.B. 577 (both cases involving breaches of covenant by tenants under agreements for leases). For the circumstances in which equity will give relief to a party in breach of contract, see *Equity and Contemporary Legal Developments* (ed. S. Goldstein), p. 829 (C.H.).

[41] See (1987) 16 Anglo–American L.R. 160 at 170 (P. Sparkes); *Equity and Contemporary Legal Developments, supra,* at pp. 855–859 (C.H.); G. Jones & W. Goodhart, *Specific Performance* (2nd ed.), p. 84; and *post*, paras 14–169 *et seq.*

[42] *Post,* para. 14–168.

[43] *Foster v. Reeves* [1892] 2 Q.B. 255. It is confined to leases the value of which does not exceed £30,000: see C.C.A. 1984, s.23(d); S.I. 1981 No. 1123. It is remarkable that this figure has remained unchanged, given that Chancery business can normally be dealt with in either the High Court or the county court: *cf.* CPR 7PD–001, para. 2.5.

[44] *Kingswood Estates Co. Ltd v. Anderson* [1963] 2 Q.B. 169; and see *Cornish v. Brook Green Laundry Ltd* [1959] 1 Q.B. 394; (1959) 75 L.Q.R. 168 (R.E.M.); *Rushton v. Smith* [1976] Q.B. 480.

(b) Third parties. The effect in relation to third parties is different. A lease **14–047**
creates a legal estate, good against the world. A contract for a lease creates
only an equitable interest, namely the right to the equitable remedy of specific
performance. This suffers from the usual frailty of equitable interests that has
already been explained.[45] The position differs according to whether title to the
land is unregistered or registered.

(1) UNREGISTERED LAND. Where title to the land is unregistered, a contract **14–048**
for a lease is registrable as an estate contract. If it is not registered it is void
against a purchaser for money or money's worth of a legal estate in land.[46] If,
therefore, the tenant fails to register the contract against the landlord, he may
be defeated by a later purchaser (including a lessee) from the landlord, even
though the tenant is in possession of the land[47] or the purchaser knows of or
has notice of the contract.[48] It should be noted that, if the tenant does register
his estate contract, his interest will be protected even though he does not take
possession. Registration is deemed to be actual notice to all persons for all
purposes.[49]

In practice, agreements (especially for short terms) are often not registered,
even though this may leave the tenant with no remedy but an action for
damages (often worthless) if the lessor later grants another lease of the land,
or sells or mortgages it. As the tenant is under no duty to register, it is in the
interest of the landlord to see that the agreement is registered. This obviates
any risk of a damages claim against the landlord[50] should he make some
subsequent disposition to a third party that was intended to take effect subject
to the tenant's interest, but which in fact defeated it because it was not
registered.[51]

(2) REGISTERED LAND. Where title to the land is registered, a contract to **14–049**
grant a lease may be protected by the registration of either a notice or
caution.[52] However, even if the agreement is not registered, it will be protected against third parties as an overriding interest where the tenant is in
actual occupation of the property,[53] but not otherwise.[54]

---

[45] *Ante*, para. 4–056. Prior to 1926, such estate contracts could be defeated by a bona fide
purchaser of a legal estate for value without notice: *ante*, paras 4–011—4–013.
[46] L.C.A. 1972, s.4(6); *ante*, para. 5–117.
[47] L.P.A. 1925, s.14 is not in point: see *Lloyd's Bank Plc v. Carrick* [1996] 4 All E.R. 630 at 642;
ante, para. 5–121. Prior to 1926, any purchaser would be bound by the rights of a tenant in
possession under an agreement for a lease, because his possession was notice of his rights: *ante*,
para. 5–020.
[48] *Midland Bank Trust Co. Ltd v. Green* [1981] A.C. 513; *ante*, para. 5–119.
[49] L.P.A. 1925, s.198; *ante*, para. 5–109.
[50] See *ante*, para. 5–122.
[51] *cf. Hollington Bros Ltd v. Rhodes* [1951] 2 T.L.R. 691; *ante*, para. 5–118.
[52] See *ante*, paras 6–079 (notices), 6–083 (cautions).
[53] L.R.A. 1925, s.70(1)(g); *Ashburn Anstalt v. Arnold* [1989] Ch. 1 at 27; *ante*, para. 6–052.
[54] *City Permanent B.S. v. Miller* [1952] Ch. 840, holding that an agreement for a lease did not fall
within L.R.A. 1925, s.70(1)(k); *ante*, para. 6–067.

14–050   *(c) Assignment.* A further difference affecting third parties lies in the rules concerning assignment where the agreement for a lease was made prior to 1996.[55]

14–051   (1) AGREEMENTS MADE PRIOR TO 1996. In relation to a legal lease granted prior to 1996, an assignment of it passes to the assignee not only the lessee's rights but also his obligations to observe all the ordinary covenants, such as those to pay rent and to repair.[56] By contrast, a contract for a lease made before 1996 creates no legal estate with which the burden of such a covenant can run, *i.e.* there is no "privity of estate".[57] It is governed by the ordinary rule that the benefit but not the burden of a contract is assignable.[58] The lessee can therefore assign his right to specific performance and all other rights under the agreement, so that the assignee can sue the landlord to enforce them.[59] However for breach of any of the tenant's obligations the landlord can sue only the lessee and not the assignee,[60] even though the assignee has taken possession.[61]

Where the lessor assigns his reversion, the position has been simplified by statute.[62] The rules are the same whether the lessee holds under a legal lease or a mere contract.

14–052   (2) AGREEMENTS MADE AFTER 1995. The Landlord and Tenant (Covenants) Act 1995[63] has changed the law for leases and agreements for leases made after 1995. This has much simplified the law and has removed the distinction between leases and agreements for leases for the purposes of the transmission of the benefit and burden of covenants. The benefit and burden of all covenants, except those expressed to be personal, passes on an assignment of either a legal lease or an agreement for a lease, or on the assignment of the reversion on such a lease or agreement.[64]

14–053   *(d) Miscellaneous.* Several other differences flow from the fundamental distinction between a grant or contract, or from the wording of statutes. Five examples may be given.[65]

---

[55] For the rules governing assignments, see *post*, para. 14–108.

[56] As to the covenants in such leases which run with the land and with the reversion, see *post*, paras 15–004, 15–080.

[57] For the importance of privity of estate to the running of positive (but not restrictive) covenants in pre–1996 leases, see *post*, para. 15–004.

[58] The assignment takes effect in equity or under L.P.A. 1925, s.136. On the statutory assignment of equitable rights, see *Re Pain* [1919] 1 Ch. 38 at 44–46; Snell, *Equity*, 74.

[59] *Manchester Brewery Co. v. Coombs* [1901] 2 Ch. 608 at 616. The assignor must usually be made a party: *ibid.*

[60] *Camden v. Batterbury* (1859) 7 C.B. (N.S.) 864; *Purchase v. Lichfield Brewery Co.* [1915] 1 K.B. 184 (mortgagee by assignment held not liable for rent). But see *Boyer v. Warbey* [1953] 1 Q.B. 234; *post*, para. 15–031. The assignee may be liable for forfeiture, or to non-observance of restrictive covenants.

[61] *Cox v. Bishop* (1857) 8 De G.M. & G. 815 at 824.

[62] This is explained, para. 15–047.

[63] *Post*, para. 15–079.

[64] See L. & T.C.A. 1995, ss.3, 28(1).

[65] These do not exhaust the catalogue of differences. For example, a lease is not affected by the rule against perpetuities, but a contract for a lease sometimes is: *ante*, para. 7–119.

(i) Where title is unregistered, it is only under a lease, and not under a contract for a lease, that the tenant can plead purchase without notice against the owner of an unregistrable equitable interest[66] as opposed to a mere equity.[67] It is essential to this plea that the purchaser should obtain the legal estate before he is fixed with notice.[68]

(ii) Some important interests are void against a purchaser of unregistered land unless registered as land charges "before the completion of the purchase".[69] A person who has contracted to take a legal lease, but to whom it has not yet been granted, has not "completed the purchase", and is therefore presumably bound by such interests even though they are not registered.

(iii) Where title is registered, a contract for a lease takes effect either as a minor interest or, if the tenant is in actual occupation, as an overriding interest.[70] In either eventuality it will take effect subject to any prior minor interest (whether protected on the register or not) or overriding interest.[71] The grantee of a lease of registered land takes it subject only to entries on the register and overriding interests.[72]

(iv) A contract for a lease entitles the landlord to "the usual covenants", which oblige the tenant to repair and make the lease subject to forfeiture for non-payment of rent.[73] An executed legal lease implies no such covenants.

(v) A mere contract for a lease is not a "conveyance" within section 62 of the Law of Property Act 1925 so as to pass all the appurtenant rights listed in that section.[74]

D. Sub-leases

The same rules apply to sub-leases as apply to leases. **14–054**

Section 2. Types of Leases and Tenancies

A. Classification

Leases and tenancies may be classified under the five following heads.

---

[66] *e.g.* a pre–1926 restrictive covenant.
[67] *e.g.* a right to rescission.
[68] *Ante*, para. 5–009; *L. & S. W. Ry v. Gomm* (1882) 20 Ch.D. 562 at 583.
[69] L.C.A. 1972, s.4; *ante*, para. 14–049.
[70] *Ante*, para. 5–116.
[71] *Ante*, paras 6–073, 6–095.
[72] *Ante*, paras 6–031, 6–105.
[73] *Post*, para. 14–241.
[74] *Post*, para. 18–108.

1. Leases for a fixed period

14–055   *(a) Length of term.* A lease may be granted for any period of certain duration, no matter how long or short. Leases for a week or for 3,000 years are equally valid. A lease may be for discontinuous periods, *e.g.* for three successive bank holidays.[75] Discontinuous leases are becoming more common as they are sometimes used in the growing practice of time-sharing in holiday homes, as where a lump sum is paid for the right to occupy a cottage for one week in each year for 80 years. A lease on these terms has been held not to be "for a term certain exceeding 21 years" since although a single term is expressed to be granted, the interest in it is discontinuous.[76]

The term cannot begin before the lease itself is granted, but it may be defined by reference to an earlier date. A lease granted "for seven years from this day a year ago" will thus take effect as a lease for six years.[77]

(b) Certainty of term

14–056   (1) THE RULE. It has been settled by the House of Lords that both the commencement and the maximum duration of the term must be certain or capable of being rendered certain before the lease takes effect.[78] A lease granted until the landlord requires the land for road-widening purposes,[79] or so long as a company is trading,[80] will therefore be void. This rule does not invalidate leases granted for lives, because these, unlike leases for years, conferred a recognised *freehold* estate,[81] though virtually all are now converted into terms of years.[82]

If no time for commencement is stated, a grant of a tenancy usually takes effect at once,[83] provided that the date is clear.[84] But a contract for a future lease will be void, unless some definite time for the commencement of the lease can be inferred from it.[85] Where the term of a lease is to run "from" a particular date, there is a presumption that the specified date is not included in the period of the demise,[86] but this is rebuttable by evidence that it was

---

[75] *Smallwood v. Sheppards* [1895] 2 Q.B. 627.

[76] *Cottage Holiday Associates Ltd v. Customs and Excise Commissioners* [1983] Q.B. 735 (rating of lease for value added tax).

[77] *Bradshaw v. Pawley* [1980] 1 W.L.R. 10.

[78] *Prudential Assurance Co. Ltd v. London Residuary Body* [1992] 2 A.C. 386; [1993] C.L.J. 26 (S. Bridge); [1993] Conv. 461 (P.F. Smith). For application of the certainty rule to periodic tenancies, see *post*, para. 14–064.

[79] *Prudential Assurance Co. Ltd v. London Residuary Body, supra*, overruling expressly *Ashburn Anstalt v. Arnold* [1989] Ch. 1 (lease until landlord was ready to redevelop the property); and impliedly *Canadian Imperial Bank of Commerce v. Bello* (1991) 64 P. & C.R. 48 (lease until landlord returned to U.K.).

[80] *Birrell v. Carey* (1989) 58 P. & C.R. 184. *cf. Pocock v. Carter* [1912] 1 Ch. 663 (lease for the duration of a partnership erroneously assumed to be valid).

[81] See Platt on *Leases* (1847), Vol 1, p. 678; *Lace v. Chantler* [1944] K.B. 368 at 371, 372.

[82] *Post*, para. 14–086.

[83] *Doe d. Phillip v. Benjamin* (1839) 9 A. & E. 644 ("agrees to let" construed as grant rather than contract); *Furness v. Bond* (1888) 4 T.L.R. 457.

[84] *James v. Lock* [1978] 1 E.G.L.R. 1 at 2.

[85] *Harvey v. Pratt* [1965] 1 W.L.R. 1025.

[86] *Whelton Sinclair v. Hyland* [1992] 2 E.G.L.R. 158 at 161. The authorities are reviewed in [1993] Conv. 206 (E. Cooke).

intended to be.[87] By contrast, if the term is to commence "on" a specified day, that day is included within the term of the lease.[88]

As regards duration, a lease for 99 years from January 1 next, or a lease for seven years from the determination of an existing tenancy, are examples of terms which are valid under the above rule. A lease to take effect from January 1 next "for so many years as X shall name" will be valid if X names the term before January 1, but not otherwise.[89]

The court has sometimes succeeded in construing transactions as being **14–057** sufficiently certain. Thus a lease "for years" was interpreted to mean a lease for two years[90]; and an "option of a lease" (naming no period) was held to entitle the tenant to a lease for life.[91] Whether such indulgence would be shown now that the rule of certainty has been reaffirmed by the House of Lords is perhaps doubtful. There may however be cases where the lease may be saved by an application of principles of proprietary estoppel.[92] Thus where the lessor has only a limited power of disposition[93] and has agreed to grant an indefinite tenancy, the court may give effect to the tenant's equity (arising from his reliance upon the grant) by holding him entitled to the longest term which the lessor had power to grant.[94]

After some hesitation,[95] it was finally settled in 1944 that a lease granted during wartime "for the duration of the war" was void for uncertainty at common law.[96] But this would have led to so much inconvenience during the Second World War that such leases, and contracts to grant them, were converted by statute into terms, or contracts to grant terms, of 10 years determinable after the end of the war by (usually) one month's notice.[97] However the Act applied only to the Second World War[98] and it did not rescue tenancies granted for other uncertain periods.

It is important to note that the rule invalidating uncertain terms applies only **14–058** where the maximum duration is uncertain: if the maximum extent of the term is fixed, it may be made determinable on any uncertain event happening within the term.[99] Thus valid leases may be made "for 90 years if X shall so

---

[87] *Meadfield Properties Ltd v. Secretary of State for the Environment* [1995] 1 E.G.L.R. 39 (where the first and last date of the lease were specified, the term included both). See too *Whelton Sinclair v. Hyland, supra* (application of presumption would have meant that premises were unlet for one day).

[88] *Sidebotham v. Holland* [1895] 1 Q.B. 378 at 382.

[89] *Lace v. Chantler, supra,* at 370, 371; *cf.* Co.Litt. 45b.

[90] *Bishop of Bath's Case* (1605) 6 Co. Rep. 34b.

[91] *Austin v. Newham* [1906] 2 K.B. 167; contrast *Buck v. Howarth* (1947) 63 T.L.R. 195 (tenancy at will); and see *ante,* para. 3–039.

[92] *Ante,* Chap. 13.

[93] *e.g.* because his own interest was leasehold.

[94] *Siew Soon Wah v. Yong Tong Hong* [1973] A.C. 836, applying *Re King's Leasehold Estates* (1873) L.R. 16 Eq. 521; *Kusel v. Watson* (1879) 11 Ch.D. 129.

[95] *G.N. Ry v. Arnold* (1916) 33 T.L.R. 114; *Swift v. Macbean* [1942] 1 K.B. 375.

[96] *Lace v. Chantler* [1944] K.B. 368; approved and applied in *Prudential Assurance Co. Ltd v. London Residuary Body* [1992] 2 A.C. 386.

[97] Validation of War-Time Leases Act 1944.

[98] *ibid.,* s.7(2).

[99] *Prudential Assurance Co. Ltd v. London Residuary Body* [1992] 2 A.C. 386 at 390, 395. See too L.P.A. 1925, s.205(1)(xxvii).

long live"[1] or "for 21 years determinable if the tenant ceases to live on the premises". It is therefore perfectly possible to make a lease determinable upon some future uncertain event, provided that the device of a determinable fixed term is employed. Similarly the landlord may (and most commonly does) reserve a right of re-entry[2] to arise if some event happens during the term, *e.g.* if the tenant commits a breach of covenant. In that case the lease is subject to a condition subsequent and may be determined upon some quite uncertain event in the future.

14–059   (2) JUSTIFICATION FOR THE RULE. Although the rationale for both the genesis and the continuing purpose of the certainty requirement has been questioned,[3] the rule performs an essential function in the scheme of the law of property.[4] The certainty rule serves to distinguish a lease from a fee simple. The law does not recognise a lease in perpetuity.[5] But if a lease were granted at a rent until a particular event were to occur, and it subsequently became impossible for that determining event to happen,[6] that lease would indeed endure in perpetuity but for the certainty rule.[7] It would closely resemble a fee simple subject to a rent charge,[8] something which can no longer be created.[9] It would however differ significantly from such a fee in that the burden of positive covenants could run with the lease,[10] something which is impossible with a fee simple.[11] The operation of the certainty rule has been described as "arbitrary and crude".[12] However, it does at least avoid the injustice that could arise from the potentially perpetual continuation of a lease that the parties had implicitly intended to be of short duration, and where they had therefore made no provision for the periodic review of the rent.[13] The rule can of course be readily circumvented by creating a fixed term of years determinable on the earlier occurrence of a specified contingency.[14]

---

[1] See *post*, para. 14–087.

[2] *Post*, para. 14–122.

[3] *Prudential Assurance Co. Ltd v. London Residuary Body* [1992] 2 A.C. 386, 397, *per* Lord Browne–Wilkinson, suggesting that the Law Commission might examine the subject.

[4] For discussion of the rationale of the rule, see (1993) 109 L.Q.R. 93 (P. Sparkes); (1993) 13 L.S. 38 (S. Bright); [1993] Conv. 461 (P. F. Smith).

[5] *Sevenoaks, Maidstone and Tunbridge Ry. Co. v. London, Chatham and Dover Ry. Co.* (1879) 11 Ch.D. 625 at 635; *ante*, para. 14–004.

[6] As happened in *Prudential Assurance Co. Ltd v. London Residuary Body, supra*, where the lease was granted until the landlord required the land for road-widening purposes. The reversion subsequently came into the hands of a body that had no power to undertake road works.

[7] *cf. Prudential Assurance Co. Ltd v. London Residuary Body* [1992] 1 E.G.L.R. 47 at 52 (CA); [1992] 2 A.C. 386 at 394 (H.L.).

[8] *Ante*, para. 4–039.

[9] Rentcharges Act 1977, s.2; *post*, para. 18–018.

[10] See *post*, Chap. 15.

[11] See *Rhone v. Stephens* [1994] 2 A.C. 310; *post*, para. 16–017.

[12] (1993) 13 L.S. 38 at 48 (S. Bright).

[13] *Prudential Assurance Co. Ltd v. London Residuary Body* [1992] 2 A.C. 386 at 390; (1993) 109 L.Q.R. 93 at 112 (P. Sparkes); (1993) 13 L.S. 38 at 44 (S. Bright).

[14] *Prudential Assurance Co. Ltd v. London Residuary Body, supra*, at 390; ante, para. 14–058.

(3) CONSEQUENCES OF UNCERTAINTY. A person who enters into possession **14–060**
under a lease that is void because of its uncertain duration, will normally be
a tenant at will, at least initially, because he has exclusive possession.[15]
Although it has sometimes been assumed that he may be a licensee,[16] this will
be so only in exceptional circumstances because the grant of exclusive
possession of the land is the hallmark of a tenancy.[17] Where the tenant has
paid rent, however, the court is likely to infer the existence of a periodic
tenancy,[18] which may then be determined by either party on the giving of
notice in the usual way.[19] It will not be a term of that periodic tenancy that the
landlord can give notice to quit only on the occurrence of the specified event
that was to bring the void lease to an end.[20] Thus where a yearly periodic
tenancy was implied in place of a void lease granted until the land was
required for road-widening, the landlord could determine the lease on giving
six-months' notice even though it had no powers to carry out road works.

A much more difficult case would arise where the tenant paid no rent, but
a premium or some other consideration for the grant of the void lease.[21] As a
mere tenant at will,[22] his interest could be determined at the landlord's will.[23]
As a lease is a contract as well as being an estate,[24] normal contractual
principles should apply. Therefore, where a lease is void for uncertainty and
the tenant has received no part of what he bargained for (as where he has never
entered into possession), there is a total failure of consideration. He is then
entitled to restitution of the benefit he has conferred on the landlord.[25] By
contrast, where the tenant has received some part of what he had bargained for
(as where he had the use of the premises for a period before the lease was held
void), the general rule suggests that he can recover nothing.[26] In this latter
case, the tenant might sometimes be able to have recourse to the principles of

---

[15] *Denn d. Warren v. Fearnside* (1747) 1 Wils.K.B. 176; *Wheeler v. Mercer* [1957] A.C. 416 at
432; Halsb. Vol. 27(1), para. 170. Where a lease is void for non-compliance with the statutory
formal requirements, it also takes effect as a tenancy at will: L.P.A. 1925, s.54(1); *ante*, para.
14–039.

[16] *Ashburn Anstalt v. Arnold* [1989] Ch. 1 at 13; *Canadian Imperial Bank of Commerce v. Bello*
(1991) 64 P. & C.R. 48 at 51.

[17] *Colchester B.C. v. Smith* [1991] Ch. 448 at 483–485 (on appeal [1992] Ch. 421); *ante*, para.
14–013. See too *Onyx (U.K.) Ltd v. Beard* [1996] E.G.C.S. 55.

[18] *Prudential Assurance Co. Ltd v. London Residuary Body* [1992] 2 A.C. 386 at 392, 393. There
is no longer any presumption of a periodic tenancy where a tenant has exclusive possession and
pays rent: see *post*, para. 14–065. However, the court is likely to find the necessary intention
that there should be such a tenancy in these circumstances because the parties intended there
to be a lease.

[19] *Post*, paras 14–068, 14–073.

[20] *Prudential Assurance Co. Ltd v. London Residuary Body, supra*, at 392, reversing on this point
[1992] 1 E.G.L.R. 47, CA.

[21] *cf. Canadian Imperial Bank of Commerce v. Bello, supra* (lease granted because of money
owed to tenant).

[22] There can be no periodic tenancy without the payment and acceptance of rent: see *Prudential
Assurance Co. Ltd v. London Residuary Body* [1992] 1 E.G.L.R. 47, CA, at 51.

[23] *Post*, para. 14–076.

[24] *Ante*, para. 14–003.

[25] See Goff & Jones, *The Law of Restitution* (5th ed.), p. 602.

[26] See G.H. Treitel, *The Law of Contract* (10th ed.), pp. 977–978.

proprietary estoppel.[27] If he had been led to believe that he would have a lease until the occurrence of some event and, in reliance upon that expectation, had acted to his detriment, an equity would arise in his favour.[28] To satisfy that equity, the court might grant the tenant a lease for a term of years determinable on the earlier occurrence of the event.[29]

14–061   *(c) Reversionary leases.* Before 1926 there was no restriction upon the length of time that might elapse before the term began; a lease could thus be granted in 1917 to commence in 1946.[30] Such a lease was known as a reversionary lease.[31] For leases were not subject to the common law rule for freehold estates, based upon the need for livery of seisin in old times, that grants could not be made so as to take effect in the future.[32] The perpetuity rule was not infringed since the lessee took a vested interest forthwith; only the vesting in possession was postponed.[33] However, after 1925, any grant of a term at a rent or in consideration of a fine, limited to take effect more than 21 years from the date of the instrument creating it, is void; and the same applies to any contract to create such a term.[34]

This does not affect grants or contracts made before 1926 or leases taking effect in equity under a settlement.[35] Nor does it affect contracts for leases which, when eventually granted, will take effect in possession within 21 years of the grant; for these, subject to the perpetuity rule in certain cases after assignment,[36] are valid even after longer periods, as for example a contract to renew a 50-year lease at the tenant's option. The prohibition applies only to immediate grants the operation of which is suspended for more than 21 years, and to contracts for such grants.[37]

14–062   *(d) Interesse termini.* Before 1926 there was a common law rule that a lessee acquired no actual estate in the land until he had taken possession in accordance with the lease. Until he had exercised his right to take possession

---

[27] *Ante*, chap. 13. For the restitutionary character of proprietary estoppel, see *Sledmore v. Dalby* (1996) 72 P. & C.R. 196 at 208.

[28] As in *Siew Soon Wah v. Yong Tong Hong* [1973] A.C. 836, where a tenant paid $8,000 premium for a lease granted for as long as he wished to occupy the premises. This created an equity by estoppel in his favour, entitling him to remain there for 30 years. For the doctrine to apply, it will however be necessary to show detriment by the tenant in reliance upon the expectation created. *cf. Canadian Imperial Bank of Commerce v. Bello* (1991) 64 P. & C.R. 48, where the lease was granted *after* and because the tenant had incurred detriment.

[29] *cf. Griffiths v. Williams* [1978] 2 E.G.L.R. 121 at 123, 124.

[30] *Mann, Crossman & Paulin Ltd v. Registrar of the Land Registry* [1918] 1 Ch. 202.

[31] Contrast a lease of the reversion: *post*, para. 14–103; and see Preston, *Conveyancing*, ii. 145, 146; *Hyde v. Warden* (1877) 3 Ex. D. 72 at 83, 84.

[32] *Post*, Appendix.

[33] *Ante*, para. 7–001.

[34] L.P.A. 1925, s.149(3), excepting certain equitable terms. The reason for requiring a rent or fine is explained below: *post*, para. 14–088.

[35] L.P.A. 1925, s.149(3).

[36] *Ante*, para. 7–116.

[37] *Re Strand and Savoy Properties Ltd* [1960] Ch. 582; *Weg Motors Ltd v. Hales* [1962] Ch. 49, not following *Northchurch Estates Ltd v. Daniels* [1947] Ch. 117; see (1960) 76 L.Q.R. 352 (R.E.M.).

he had a legal proprietary right in the land which carried with it a right of entry and was called an *interesse termini*, an interest of a term.[38] This was an interest in land which could be freely assigned, and enabled the lessee to sue any person interfering with his entry on the land.[39] The doctrine of *interesse termini* was troublesome and could give rise to considerable difficulties.[40] It was abolished in respect of all leases, whether made before or after 1925.[41]

(e) Determination. A lease for a fixed period automatically determines when that period expires. There are certain statutory exceptions to this rule.[42]   **14–063**

2. Yearly tenancies

(a) Nature. A yearly tenancy is one which continues from year to year   **14–064**
indefinitely until determined by proper notice, notwithstanding the death of either party or the assignment of his interest. It is now clear that the requirement that a lease be of certain duration applies to all tenancies, including yearly and other periodic tenancies.[43] "A tenancy from year to year is saved from being uncertain because each party has power by notice to determine at the end of any year. The term continues until determined as if both parties made a new agreement at the end of each year for a new term for the ensuing year."[44] Although a new agreement is implied, such a tenancy continues only so long as it is the will of both parties that it should.[45] Traditionally the law treated each successive yearly term, when it took effect, as part and parcel of the original term, which therefore grew as time elapsed. Thus after 50 years, for example, the tenant's interest was regarded as a 50-year term, but as to the future as a yearly tenancy.[46] Now that periodic tenancies have been brought unequivocally within the ambit of the certainty rule, there must be some doubt

---

[38] Co. Litt. 270a.
[39] *Gillard v. Cheshire Lines Committee* (1884) 32 W.R. 943.
[40] See the previous edition of this work at p. 648.
[41] L.P.A. 1925, s.149(1), (2).
[42] See *post*, para. 14–116.
[43] *Prudential Assurance Co. Ltd v. London Residuary Body* [1992] 2 A.C. 386 at 394, overruling *Re Midland Railway Co.'s Agreement* [1971] Ch. 725 and *Ashburn Anstalt v. Arnold* [1989] Ch. 1 expressly, and *Canadian Imperial Bank of Commerce v. Bello* (1991) 64 P. & C.R. implicitly.
[44] *Prudential Assurance Co. Ltd v. London Residuary Body, supra*, at 394, *per* Lord Templeman.
[45] *A.G. Securities v. Vaughan* [1990] 1 A.C. 417 at 473; *Hammersmith L.B.C. v. Monk* [1992] 1 A.C. 478 at 484. Indeed where there are either joint tenants or joint landlords, the lease may be determined by any one of the parities: *ibid.*; *Harrow L.B.C. v. Johnstone* [1997] 1 W.L.R. 459 at 471. See *ante*, para. 9–006. A notice that one or more of the tenants does not wish the periodic tenancy to continue when it expires is not regarded as a disposition of property: see *Newlon Housing Trust v. Alsulaimen* [1999] 1 A.C. 313. See too *Crawley B.C. v. Ure* [1996] Q.B. 13.
[46] Preston, *Conveyancing*, iii, 76, 77; *Legg v. Strudwick* (1708) 2 Salk. 414; *Oxley v. James* (1844) 13 M. & W. 209 at 214; *Cattley v. Arnold* (1859) 1 J. & H. 651.

as to whether this analysis would still apply.[47] They might instead be regarded as a succession of one-year terms.

The characteristics of yearly tenancies were laid down by the courts principally in cases where such tenancies were held to arise by implication.[48] But they may equally well be created by express grant, *e.g.* to A "from year to year" or "as yearly tenant". A grant "to X for one year and thereafter from year to year" will give X a tenancy for at least two years. He has been given a definite term of one year followed by a yearly tenancy which cannot be determined before the end of its first year.[49]

14–065   *(b) Creation.* Formerly, there was a presumption that a yearly tenancy arose by implication when a person occupied land with the owner's consent and rent assessed on an annual basis was paid and accepted.[50] However, the issue was always to determine the likely intentions of the parties,[51] and the presumption was therefore rebuttable by evidence of those intentions.[52] It has more recently been said that the presumption "is unsound and no longer holds good",[53] or at best, will seldom apply.[54] This is because the statutory protection that is given in many cases to tenants is an important factor in determining whether or not the parties intended to create a tenancy or merely some more exiguous relationship, such as a tenancy at will or a licence.[55] The issue most commonly arises where, with the landlord's consent, a tenant holds over after the termination of a lease,[56] or a person enters into possession pending negotiations for a lease,[57] and in each case, pays rent assessed annually. The

---

[47] But see *A.G. Securities v. Vaughan, supra,* at 473, where Lord Jauncey spoke of "the continuance of the springing interest". See too (1993) 13 L.S. 38 at 39 (S. Bright).

[48] For their origin, see Smith's L.C. ii, 122, 123.

[49] *Re Searle* [1912] 1 Ch. 610.

[50] See, *e.g. Dougal v. McCarthy* [1893] 1 Q.B. 736; *Lewis v. M.T.C. (Cars) Ltd* [1975] 1 W.L.R. 457 at 462.

[51] *Doe d. Cheny v. Batten* (1775) Cowp. 243 at 245.

[52] *Doe d. Bastow v. Cox* (1847) 11 Q.B. 122.

[53] *Longrigg Burrough & Trounson v. Smith* [1979] 2 E.G.L.R. 42 at 43, *per* Ormrod L.J.

[54] *Javad v. Aqil* [1991] 1 W.L.R. 1007 at 1017. One situation in which the old presumption still holds good, as according with the likely intentions of the parties, is where the tenant enters under a void lease and pays rent annually: see *Prudential Assurance Co. Ltd v. London Residuary Body* [1992] 2 A.C. 386 at 392; *Inntrepreneur Estates Ltd v. Mason* (1993) 68 P. & C.R. 53 at 72.

[55] *Dealex Properties Ltd v. Brooks* [1966] 1 Q.B. 542; *Longrigg, Burrough & Trounson v. Smith, supra,* at 43. It should be noted that this statutory protection has now been partly dismantled: see H.A. 1988; A.T.A. 1995. See *post*, paras 22–139 and 22–086 respectively.

[56] In most of the modern cases where there was no intention to create a periodic tenancy, it was unnecessary to characterise the occupant's status: see, *e.g. Longrigg, Burrough & Trounson v. Smith, supra; Cardiothoracic Institute v. Shrewdcrest* [1986] 1 W.L.R. 368. Where the holding over is plainly consensual, as where the parties are negotiating a new lease, it is however likely to be regarded as a tenancy at will: *Dean and Chapter of Canterbury Cathedral v. Whitbread Plc* (1995) 72 P. & C.R. 9 at 13; *post*, para. 14–075. For the special position of a secure tenant under H.A. 1985, Pt IV, against whom an order for possession has been obtained, see *Burrows v. Brent L.B.C.* [1996] 1 W.L.R. 1448.

[57] In some cases, the person has been held to be a tenant at will: see *Javad v. Aqil, supra;* and in others a mere licensee; see *P. Dunwell v. Hunt* (1996) 72 P. & C.R. D6. *cf.* [1991] C.L.J. 232 (S. Bridge).

court will look to the intentions of the parties,[58] having regard to what was agreed and all the surrounding circumstances.[59] Although the matter is always one of intention, it is, however, unlikely that a periodic tenancy will arise where the occupant has entered as a trespasser and the land owner has subsequently accepted payment from him for his use and occupation of the premises.[60]

(c) Terms. In those now unusual cases where a tenant holds over and a **14–066** yearly tenancy is implied, the tenancy will be subject to such of the terms of the expired or informal lease or agreement as are not inconsistent with a yearly holding.[61] The same applies to a tenant who enters and pays yearly rent under a mere agreement or an informal lease: he is tenant from year to year at law, although he may have other rights in equity.[62] Covenants to repair,[63] to pay rent in advance,[64] to carry on some specified trade on the premises,[65] and provisos for re-entry by the landlord on non-payment of rent or breach of covenant,[66] may all be implied in a yearly tenancy. But a covenant to paint every three years[67] or a provision for two years' notice to quit[68] are inconsistent with a yearly tenancy and cannot be implied in this way.[69]

(d) Frequency of rent days. The payment of rent at more frequent intervals **14–067** than a year will not prevent a yearly tenancy from arising by implication.[70] The test is the period by reference to which the parties calculated the rent. Thus an agreement for "£5,200 per annum payable weekly" prima facie creates a yearly tenancy. Had the agreement been for "£100 per week", a weekly tenancy would be presumed, even though in each case the tenant

---

[58] See, *e.g. Vaughan–Armatrading v. Sarsah* (1995) 27 H.L.R. 631 at 635; *Greenwich L.B.C. v. Regan* (1996) 72 P. & C.R. 507 at 512; *Burrows v. Brent L.B.C., supra,* at 1454. Whether the parties' intentions are to be determined subjectively or objectively has not yet been determined: compare *Land v. Sykes* [1992] 1 E.G.L.R. 1 at 4 (favouring an objective view) with *Longrigg, Burrough & Trounson v. Smith* [1979] 2 E.G.L.R. 42 and 43 (adopting a subjective approach); and see *Dreamgate Properties Ltd v. Arnot* (1997) 76 P. & C.R. 25 (where the point was left open). See Halsb. Vol. 27(1), para. 179.

[59] *Longrigg, Burrough & Trounson v. Smith, supra,* at 43; *Javad v. Aqil* [1991] 1 W.L.R. 1007 at 1012.

[60] See, *e.g. Westminster City Council v. Basson* (1990) 62 P. & C.R. 57; *Brent L.B.C. v. O'Bryan* (1992) 65 P. & C.R. 258; *Vaughan–Armatrading v. Sarsah, supra.* A landowner is entitled to be compensated for the use of his property, even where the occupant is a trespasser: see *post,* Appendix.

[61] *Hyatt v. Griffiths* (1851) 17 Q.B. 505 (holding over after a term of four years); *Dougal v. McCarthy* [1893] 1 Q.B. 736 (holding over after term of one year).

[62] *Ante,* para. 14–040.

[63] *Felnex Central Properties Ltd v. Montague Burton Properties Ltd* [1981] 2 E.G.L.R. 73.

[64] *Lee v. Smith* (1854) 9 Exch. 662.

[65] *Sanders v. Karnell* (1858) 1 F. & F. 356.

[66] *Thomas v. Packer* (1857) 1 H. & N. 669.

[67] *Pinero v. Judson* (1829) 6 Bing. 206; contrast *Martin v. Smith* (1874) L.R. 9 Ex. 50 (tenant under unsealed lease held liable on covenant to paint in seventh year, since he had stayed for seven years).

[68] *Tooker v. Smith* (1857) 1 H. & N. 732.

[69] *cf. Re Leeds & Batley Breweries Ltd and Bradbury's Lease* [1920] 2 Ch. 548 (option to purchase reversion not implied).

[70] *Shirley v. Newman* (1795) 1 Esp. 266.

would in fact have made precisely the same payments, namely, £100 every week.[71] The same principle applies in the case of other periods, *e.g.* months or quarters.[72] But every case may be affected by its own special facts, if any contrary intention can be inferred from them. The question is sometimes difficult where a tenant holds over after the expiry of a lease for a fixed term of years at a weekly rent, and continues to pay rent weekly as before.[73] If, in such a case, the court considers that the parties intended there to be a periodic tenancy, it will infer a weekly tenancy unless there is evidence that the weekly payments were instalments of an annual rent.[74]

14–068   *(e) Determination.* A yearly tenancy is determinable by notice.[75] The parties may agree on any period of notice,[76] and the landlord's period may be different from the tenant's.[77] A term that the landlord shall not give notice—

    (i) at all[78];

    (ii) as long as the tenant observes his undertakings[79]; or

    (iii) on the occurrence of some contingency which may never occur[80];

is void as being repugnant to the nature of a tenancy.[81] Yet a provision that the landlord is not to give notice to the tenant during a fixed period unless he requires the premises for some specified purpose (*e.g.* his own occupation, or redevelopment), has been held valid.[82] Such a provision would however be

---

[71] *Ladies Hosiery and Underwear Ltd v. Parker* [1930] 1 Ch. 304 at 328, 329, where, however, it is pointed out that the days in a year are not precisely divisible into 52 weeks.

[72] The statement of Chambre J. in *Richardson v. Langridge* (1811) 4 Taunt. 128 at 132 that payment of rent measured by any aliquot part of a year is evidence of a yearly tenancy must not be read as extending Mansfield C.J.'s phrase (at 131) "a yearly rent, though payable half-yearly or quarterly".

[73] See *Ladies Hosiery and Underwear Ltd v. Parker, supra*; *cf. Richardson v. Langridge* (1811) 4 Taunt. 128 at 132.

[74] *Adler v. Blackman* [1953] 1 Q.B. 146, overruling *Covered Markets Ltd v. Green* [1947] 2 All E.R. 140. For the implication of express terms in yearly tenancies, see *Godfrey Thornfield Ltd v. Bingham* [1946] 2 All E.R. 485, and n. 67 above.

[75] For notices given by one of two or more joint tenants, see *ante*, para. 9–006.

[76] *Re Threlfall* (1880) 16 Ch.D. 274 at 281, 282; *Allison v. Scargall* [1920] 3 K.B. 443.

[77] *Breams Property Investment Co. Ltd v. Stroulger* [1948] 2 K.B. 1; *Wallis v. Semark* [1951] 2 T.L.R. 222.

[78] *Centaploy Ltd v. Matlodge* [1974] Ch. 1.

[79] *Warner v. Browne* (1807) 8 East 165; and see *Cheshire Lines Committee v. Lewis & Co.* (1880) 50 L.J.Q.B. 121 at 124, 128 (landlord not to give notice until premises required for demolition).

[80] *Prudential Assurance Co. Ltd v. London Residuary Body* [1992] 2 A.C. 386.

[81] For the possibility that the tenant may sometimes have a remedy in such circumstances by recourse to the principles of proprietary estoppel, see *ante*, paras 14–057, 14–060.

[82] *Breams Property Investment Co. Ltd v. Stroulger* [1948] 2 K.B. 1; *Prudential Assurance Co. Ltd v. London Residuary Body, supra*, at 395.

void if it were not confined to a definite period because it would offend the
rule that the maximum duration of a lease must be certain.[83]

In default of agreement, a yearly tenancy can be determined by at least half   **14–069**
a year's notice expiring at the end of a completed year of the tenancy.[84] It is
desirable but not essential that the notice should be in writing.[85] It cannot, it
seems, be given before the tenancy begins.[86] But once a valid notice is given,
it automatically terminates the tenancy on the date stated, and cannot be
withdrawn or waived; even a purported agreement to withdraw it cannot
prevent it operating, though the agreement may create a new tenancy in place
of the old.[87]

The notice to quit may specify either the last day of a year of the tenancy
(*i.e.* the day *before* the anniversary of the commencement of the year) or the
following day.[88] In either case the tenancy actually terminates at the stroke of
midnight which ends the year.[89] It is also possible to employ a general formula
in the notice to quit, such as "at the expiration of the year of your tenancy
which will expire next after the end of one half year from the service of this
notice".[90] If the tenancy began on one of the usual quarter days (Lady Day
(March 25), Midsummer Day (June 24), Michaelmas (September 29) or
Christmas (December 25)), "half a year" means "two quarters"; otherwise
"half a year" means 182 days.[91] Thus the period of the notice is not necessarily six months,[92] although of course the parties may agree that such shall
be the notice required.

It was formerly the rule that when giving notice to determine a tenancy the
requisite period of notice had to be stated accurately. The court would not

---

[83] *Prudential Assurance Co. Ltd v. London Residuary Body, supra; ante,* paras 14–056, 14–064.

[84] *Sidebotham v. Holland* [1895] 1 Q.B. 378.

[85] *Doe d. Lord Macartney v. Crick* (1805) 5 Esp. 196. Notice may be given or received in his own name by an agent of either the landlord or the tenant who has general authority in relation to the property: *Jones v. Phipps* (1868) L.R. 3 Q.B. 567; *Townsends Carriers Ltd v. Pfizer Ltd* (1977) 33 P. & C.R. 361; *Peel Developments (South) Ltd v. Siemens Plc* [1992] 2 E.G.L.R. 85. However, such cases are uncommon because "a general agency is an unusual commercial relationship". In the absence of express authority, it requires clear evidence to support it: see *Lemmberbell Ltd v. Britannia LAS Direct Ltd* [1998] 3 E.G.L.R. 67 at 70, *per* Peter Gibson L.J.

[86] *Lower v. Sorrell* [1963] 1 Q.B. 959; but the decision on this point may be confined to agricultural holdings. See generally (1963) 79 L.Q.R. 178 (R.E.M.).

[87] *Dagger v. Shepherd* [1946] K.B. 215 at 221; *Clarke v. Grant* [1950] 1 K.B. 104 (payment and acceptance of rent immaterial); *Lower v. Sorrell, supra.*

[88] *Sidebotham v. Holland* [1895] 1 Q.B. 378; *Manorlike Ltd v. Le Vitas Travel Agency & Consultancy Services Ltd* [1986] 1 E.G.L.R. 79; *Yeandle v. Reigate and Banstead B.C.* [1996] 1 E.G.L.R. 20. This is a special rule that applies only to periodic tenancies and not to break clauses in fixed-term leases: *Mannai Investment Co. Ltd v. Eagle Star Life Assurance Co. Ltd* [1995] 1 W.L.R. 1508 at 1514 (decision reversed on appeal but expressly affirmed on this point: [1997] A.C. 749).

[89] *Crate v. Miller* [1947] K.B. 946 at 948.

[90] *Addis v. Burrows* [1948] 1 K.B. 444.

[91] *Anon* (1575) 3 Dy. 345a. The odd half-day is ignored.

[92] The phrase "six months" should be avoided, since "half a year" is the proper expression (*Doe d. Williams v. Smith* (1836) 5 A. & E. 350 at 351) although "six months" is sometimes used in judgments where the point is not material. Six months may be more than two quarters or 182 days, or less, depending on the quarters or months.

grant relief against the consequences of forgetfulness or mistake.[93] However, this approach has now been rejected by the House of Lords.[94] The courts will now adopt a commercial construction, and the test is an objective one. What would a reasonable person placed in the actual circumstances of the recipient have understood by the notice? If the meaning of the notice was plain, so that the recipient was in no doubt as to its intended effect, it will not be vitiated because it contains a mistake, *e.g.* as to the date on which it is to operate[95] or the description of the property.[96] In this regard, notices to quit and notices under break clauses are not *sui generis*, but "belong to the general class of unilateral notices served under contractual rights reserved, *e.g.* notices to determine licences and notices to complete".[97]

In general, a notice to quit must be brought to the attention of the tenant, though in the absence of contrary evidence this will be presumed if it is delivered to his spouse, employee or agent.[98] The statutory provisions as to service of notices[99] do not apply to notices to quit unless the parties have expressly provided that they should.[1]

14–070   *(f) Commencement.* Where a yearly tenancy is created by a tenant under a lease for a fixed period holding over and paying rent, the yearly tenancy is calculated from the end of the original tenancy, so that where a tenant held over after a tenancy from November 11, 1915, to December 25, 1916, his yearly tenancy was terminable on Christmas Day, 1917, or any subsequent Christmas Day.[2]

---

[93] See *e.g. Hankey v. Clavering* [1942] 2 K.B. 326 (December 21 stated by mistake for December 25); where the notice was held invalid.

[94] *Mannai Investment Co. Ltd v. Eagle Star Life Assurance Co. Ltd* [1997] A.C. 749, overruling *Hankey v. Clavering, supra*, and approving the approach in *Carradine Properties Ltd v. Aslam* [1976] 1 W.L.R. 442 (notice given in 1974 specified expiry date as in 1973 by mistake for 1975: notice valid) and *Micrografix v. Woking 8 Ltd* (1995) 71 P. & C.R. 43 (notice specifying March 23 instead of June 23 held valid). For an application of the "reasonable recipient" principle, see *Garston v. Scottish Widow's Fund and Life Assurance Society* 1 W.L.R. 1583 (July 9 stated in error for June 24). The principle applies as much to statutory notices as it does to contractual ones: see *York v. Casey* [1998] 2 E.G.L.R. 25 (notice under H.A. 1988).

[95] *Mannai Investment Co. Ltd v. Eagle Star Life Assurance Co. Ltd, supra.* In that case a notice by the tenant to terminate the lease one day earlier than authorised was held to be valid and took effect as if it had specified the first moment of the following day. See too *York v. Casey, supra.*

[96] *Doe d. Cox v. Rea* (1803) 4 Esp. 185; *Mannai Investment Co. Ltd v. Eagle Star Life Assurance Co. Ltd, supra,* at 775. *cf. Lemmerbell Ltd v. Britannia LAS Direct Ltd* [1998] 3 E.G.L.R. 67 at 71 (failure by A to explain how it could give notice on behalf of B vitiated the notice and was not a mere slip).

[97] *Mannai Investment Co. Ltd v. Eagle Star Life Assurance Co. Ltd, supra* at 768, per Lord Steyn.

[98] See, *e.g. Tanham v. Nicolson* (1872) L.R. 5 H.L. 561; Halsb. Vol. 27(1), para. 198. There are certain specific statutory provisions as to service of notices in relation to certain types of tenancies, see, *e.g.* A.H.A. 1986, s.93.

[99] See L.P.A. 1925, s.196, providing for notices to be left at or posted to the last known place of abode or business of the person.

[1] *Wandsworth L.B.C. v. Attwell* (1995) 27 H.L.R. 536; *Enfield L.B.C. v. Devonish* (1996) 29 H.L.R. 691.

[2] *Croft v. William F. Blay Ltd* [1919] 2 Ch. 343.

(g) Agricultural holdings and farm business tenancies. There are special **14–071** statutory rules for the determination of yearly tenancies of agricultural holdings and farm business tenancies. These are explained in a later chapter.[3]

3. Weekly, monthly and other periodic tenancies

(a) Creation. A tenancy from week to week, month to month, quarter to **14–072** quarter, or other period less than a year,[4] can be created in a similar way to a yearly tenancy, namely—

    (i) by express agreement;

   (ii) by inference, such as that arising from the payment and acceptance of rent measured by reference to a week, month, quarter or other period,[5] in circumstances where the parties intended there to be a periodic tenancy and not a mere tenancy at will or a licence[6]; or

  (iii) by an express provision that the tenancy is to be determinable by some specific period of notice, *e.g.* a quarter's notice.[7]

(b) Termination. In general the position of the parties under any such **14–073** tenancy is similar to that under a yearly tenancy, save that notice of termination is not half a period but a full period, expiring at the end of a completed period.[8] The period is computed in the usual way, so that for a weekly tenancy, unless otherwise agreed,[9] the notice need not be seven *clear* days (reckoned by excluding both the day on which it is given and the day on which it expires, *e.g.* notice given on Sunday to quit on the following Monday week). Thus a weekly tenancy commencing on a Monday can be determined by notice given on or before one Monday[10] to expire at midnight on the following Sunday. In accordance with the special rule application to periodic tenancies,[11] the notice may be given either for "Sunday" or "Monday". Provided no other time is specified, this will be construed as referring to the midnight that divides the two days and the notice will therefore be effective.[12] A notice to quit "on or before", or "by", the proper date is valid if given by the landlord[13] but void

---

[3] *Post*, paras 22–091, 22–101.

[4] *e.g.* for successive periods of 364 days: *Land Settlement Association Ltd v. Carr* [1944] K.B. 657.

[5] *Cole v. Kelly* [1920] 2 K.B. 106 at 132. See, *e.g. Huffell v. Armistead* (1835) 7 C. & P. 56.

[6] *Ante*, para. 14–065. For cases where there was no such intention notwithstanding such periodical payments, see *e.g. Cardiothoracic Institute v. Shrewdcrest Ltd* [1986] 1 W.L.R 368; *Javad v. Aqil* [1991] 1 W.L.R. 1007.

[7] *Kemp v. Derrett* (1814) 3 Camp. 510. This is subject to any contrary indication, as in a yearly tenancy with a special period of notice.

[8] *Lemon v. Lardeur* [1946] K.B. 613.

[9] *Weston v. Fidler* (1903) 88 L.T. 769.

[10] *Crate v. Miller* [1947] K.B. 946; *Newman v. Slade* [1926] 2 K.B. 328.

[11] *Mannai Investment Co. Ltd v. Eagle Star Life Assurance Co. Ltd* [1995] 1 W.L.R. 1508 at 1514; *ante*, para. 14–069.

[12] *Crate v. Miller, supra. cf. Bathavon R.D.C. v. Carlile* [1958] 1 Q.B. 461 (notice to quit "by noon on Monday" invalid).

[13] *Dagger v. Shepherd* [1946] K.B. 215; *Eastaugh v. Macpherson* [1954] 1 W.L.R. 1307.

if given by the tenant[14]; for in the former case the tenant knows when he must go, though he can go earlier, whereas in the latter case the landlord is left uncertain when the tenant will go. Both the length of notice and the date of expiration are subject to any contrary agreement.[15] Furthermore, by statute, in the case of premises genuinely let as a dwelling,[16] at least four weeks,[17] notice is required,[18] unless both the landlord and the tenant agree to some lesser period.[19]

14–074   Similarly, and again subject to any contrary agreement, a monthly tenancy requires a month's notice expiring at the end of a month of the tenancy.[20] In the case of a lease made by deed or in writing, a month normally means a calendar month[21] ending on the corresponding day of the following month, except that where there is no corresponding day (*e.g.* under a month's notice is given on March 31), the month naturally ends on its last day.[22] A quarterly tenancy requires a quarter's notice expiring at the end of one of the quarters of the tenancy.[23] A quarterly tenancy commencing on October 29 could therefore be determined only on 29 January, April, July or October, in default of any contrary agreement.[24]

4. Tenancies at will

14–075   *(a) Creation.* A tenancy at will arises whenever a tenant, with the consent of the owner, occupies land as tenant (and not merely as a servant or agent[25])

---

[14] *Perduzzi v. Cohen* [1942] L.J.N.C.C.R. 136; *Dagger v. Shepherd, supra,* at 224.

[15] *Re Threlfall* (1880) 16 Ch.D. 274; *H. & G. Simonds Ltd v. Haywood* [1948] 1 All E.R. 260. Express words in the lease are required for this purpose: *Harler v. Calder* [1989] 1 E.G.L.R. 88 (notice to comply with statutory requirement but that "no other formality will be required" held insufficient).

[16] Thus excluding a mere formal tenancy under an attornment clause (see *post,* para. 19–077): *Alliance B.S. v. Pinwill* [1958] Ch. 788. Where a property is let as an agricultural holding, it is not within the statutory provisions, even though the letting includes a dwelling house: *National Trust v. Knipe* [1998] 1 W.L.R. 230.

[17] See *Schnabel v. Allard* [1967] 1 Q.B. 627 (notice given on Friday to expire on Friday valid).

[18] P.E.A. 1977, s.5 (as amended by H.A. 1988, s.32), also requiring the notice to contain the information prescribed by S.I. 1988 No. 2201. These provisions do not apply to "excluded tenancies": see P.E.A. 1977, s.3A (added by H.A. 1988, s.31); *post,* para. 14–229. The four-week requirement applies to a notice to quit given by either the tenant or the landlord: *Hounslow L.B.C. v. Pilling* [1993] 1 W.L.R. 1242 at 1247.

[19] The lesser period will not be valid however if, *e.g.* only one of two joint tenants has agreed to it: *Hounslow L.B.C. v. Pilling, supra. cf. ante,* para. 9–006.

[20] *Precious v. Reedie* [1942] 2 K.B. 149. Although there is apparently no authority in point, in the case of a dwelling, the common law period should prevail over the requirements of P.E.A. 1977, s.5, *supra*) where the former is longer than the latter (as it will be except where notice is given on January 31).

[21] L.P.A. 1925, s.61. At common law, a month meant a lunar month: see *P. Phipps & Co. (Northampton and Towcester Breweries) Ltd v. Rogers* [1925] 1 K.B. 14 and 23. Query whether the common law rule applies to *oral* tenancies, which are not within s.61. *cf.* [1992] Conv. 263 (E. Cooke).

[22] *Dodds v. Walker* [1981] 1 W.L.R. 1027. A statutory month is similar: *ibid.*; Interpretation Act 1978, Sched. 1.

[23] *Kemp v. Derrett* (1814) 3 Camp. 510.

[24] *ibid.*

[25] *Mayhew v. Suttle* (1854) 4 E. & B. 347.

on the terms that either party may determine the tenancy at any time. This kind of tenancy may be created either expressly[26] or by implication. Common examples are where a tenant whose lease has expired holds over with the landlord's permission[27]; where a person is allowed into possession while the parties negotiate the terms of a lease[28]; where a tenant takes possession under a void lease, or under a mere agreement for lease and no periodic tenancy has arisen from the payment of rent[29]; where a person is allowed to occupy a house rent-free and for an indefinite period; and (usually) where a purchaser has been let into possession pending completion.[30] Unless the parties agree that the tenancy shall be rent-free, or the tenant has some other right to rent-free occupation,[31] the landlord is entitled to compensation for the "use and occupation" of the land,[32] which will be the ordinary market value of the premises.[33] If the rent has been agreed upon, it may be distrained for as such in the usual way.[34]

(b) Determination. The essence of the tenancy is that either party can determine it at will, even if it is made determinable at the will of the landlord only, for the law will imply that it is to be determinable at the will of the tenant also.[35] A tenancy at will also comes to an end when either party does any act incompatible with the continuance of the tenancy, as where the tenant commits voluntary waste,[36] or the landlord enters the land and cuts trees or carries away stone,[37] or serves a writ claiming possession of the land,[38] or either party gives notice to the other determining the tenancy.[39] The tenancy is likewise

14–076

---

[26] *e.g. Manfield & Sons Ltd v. Botchin* [1970] 2 Q.B. 612.

[27] See *e.g. Dean and Chapter of Canterbury Cathedral v. Whitbread Plc* (1995) 72 P. & C.R. 9 at 13. Where the tenant pays rent, it is a question of intention whether or not a periodic tenancy arises: see, *e.g. Cardiothoracic Institute v. Shrewdcrest* [1986] 1 W.L.R. 368; *ante*, para. 14–065.

[28] See, *e.g. Uzun v. Ramadan* [1986] 2 E.G.L.R. 255. In *Hagee (London) Ltd v. A.B. Erikson and Larson* [1976] Q.B. 209 at 217, Scarman L.J. referred to the "classic circumstances" in which a tenancy at will arose of "holding over or holding pending negotiation".

[29] *Ante*, para. 14–065. In this situation, a periodic tenancy is likely to arise if rent is paid and accepted, because it will accord with the probable intentions of the parties: *ante*, para. 14–060.

[30] *Howard v. Shaw* (1841) 8 M. & W. 118; *Wheeler v. Mercer* [1957] A.C. 416 at 425; Tudor L.C. 16–18. But the trend of recent decisions is to regard the purchaser as a licensee: *Street v. Mountford* [1985] A.C. 809 at 827; *Essex Plan Ltd v. Broadminster* (1988) 56 P. & C.R. 353 at 355, 356; *ante*, para. 14–025. Furthermore, under the Standard Conditions of Sale (3rd ed.), the purchaser occupies expressly as a licensee: c. 5.2.

[31] *e.g.* a purchaser in possession under a contract of sale (if he is indeed still to be regarded as a tenant at will).

[32] *Howard v. Shaw, supra*; *post*, para. 14–251.

[33] *Dean and Chapter of Canterbury Cathedral v. Whitbread Plc* (1995) 72 P. & C.R. 9.

[34] Litt. 72; *Anderson v. Midland Ry* (1861) 3 E. & E. 614.

[35] Co. Litt. 55a.

[36] *Countess of Shrewsbury's Case* (1600) 5 Co. Rep. 13b. But note the doubts expressed in Halsb. vol. 27(1), para. 348.

[37] *Turner v. Doe d. Bennett* (1842) 9 M. & W. 643.

[38] *Martinali v. Ramuz* [1953] 1 W.L.R. 1196 (a writ is not a notice to quit).

[39] See *Crane v. Morris* [1965] 1 W.L.R. 1104 at 1108 (such a notice is not within Protection from Eviction Act 1977, s.5: *ante*, para. 10–073).

determined if either party dies,[40] or assigns his interest in the land.[41] But the tenant may not be ejected until he has knowledge of the act or event which has determined the tenancy.[42]

14-077   *(c) Conversion.* Where a person occupies land as a tenant at will and rent is paid and accepted on some regular periodic basis, there is no longer any presumption of a periodic tenancy as there was formerly.[43] The matter is one of the likely intentions of the parties.[44] While the payment of rent on a periodic basis is one important factor from which these may be inferred, it is not conclusive and a court will consider all the circumstances, not least the statutory protection that the tenant may have if there is a periodic tenancy.[45]

14-078   *(d) Nature.* The precise nature of a tenancy at will has never been definitively settled.[46] Probably the best analysis of it is that it is a form of tenure but one that confers no estate. Although an estate cannot exist without tenure, there seems no reason why tenure should not exist without any estate. A may hold land of B, but for no fixed period and merely for so long as B may allow. If it is remembered that tenure by itself is a purely personal relationship when unconnected with any estate or interest which can exist as a right *in rem*, this may explain why a tenancy at will cannot survive death or alienation; and it may also explain why tenancy at will is possible despite the rule which requires every leasehold estate to be for a term certain.

5. Tenancies at sufferance

14-079   *(a) Creation.* A tenancy at sufferance arises where a tenant, having entered under a valid tenancy, holds over without the landlord's assent or dissent.[47] Such a tenant differs from a trespasser in that his original entry was lawful, and from a tenant at will in that his tenancy exists without the landlord's consent. A tenancy at sufferance can arise only by operation of law,[48] and not by express grant, for it assumes an absence of agreement between landlord and tenant. Indeed, it is strictly incorrect to call it "tenancy" at all, for there is no "privity", *i.e.* tenure, between the parties.[49] But since it normally arises between parties who have been landlord and tenant it has acquired the title of tenancy; and the tenant is liable to a claim for "use and occupation",[50] which

---

[40] *Turner v. Barnes* (1862) 2 B. & S. 435; *James v. Dean* (1805) 11 Ves. 383 at 391.
[41] *Doe d. Davies v. Thomas* (1851) 6 Exch. 854 at 857; *Pinhorn v. Souster* (1853) 8 Exch. 763 at 772.
[42] *Doe d. Davies v. Thomas, supra.*
[43] See *ante*, para. 14–065.
[44] *Longrigg, Burrough & Trounson v. Smith* [1979] 2 E.G.L.R. 42; *Javad v. Aqil* [1991] 1 W.L.R. 1007.
[45] *Longrigg, Burrough & Trounson v. Smith, supra,* at 43; *Javad v. Aqil, supra,* at 1012, 1013.
[46] See the previous edition of this work at p. 655, where the point is more fully considered, and *ante*, para. 4–045. The matter is unlikely to have many practical consequences today.
[47] Co.Litt. 57b; *Remon v. City of London Real Property Co. Ltd* [1921] 1 K.B. 49 at 58.
[48] Tudor L.C. 8; Halsb. vol. 27(1), para. 176.
[49] Co.Litt. 270b, Note by Butler, and 271a.
[50] See *post*, para. 14–251.

properly lies against a tenant,[51] rather than to an action for damages for trespass or for mesne profits.[52] There can, of course, be no claim for rent as such, for rent is a *service* which depends upon a proper tenure by consent.[53] The landlord may eject the tenant, or sue for possession, at any time, and the tenant will have no right to emblements.[54]

(b) Nature.[55] A tenant at sufferance is in a position akin to that of a squatter, **14–080** *i.e.* an adverse claimant.[56] It has already been explained that a squatter's interest may be a legal estate.[57]

(c) Conversion. A tenancy at sufferance will be converted into a tenancy at **14–081** will if the landlord subsequently assents to the tenant's occupation. The circumstances in which such a tenancy at will may be converted into a yearly or other periodic tenancy have already been explained.[58]

(d) Holding over. There are statutory penalties for tenants who wrongfully **14–082** hold over after giving or receiving notice to quit.

(1) DOUBLE VALUE. If the landlord gives the tenant *written* notice to quit and **14–083** the tenant is a tenant *for life or for years*, the tenant is liable to pay the landlord a sum calculated at double the annual value of the land in respect of the period for which he wilfully[59] holds over after the notice expires; this can be enforced by action but not otherwise, *e.g.* not by distress.[60] This provision applies to tenancies from year to year[61] as well as to tenancies for fixed terms of years or for a year certain, [62] but not to weekly[63] or, it seems, other similar periodic tenancies.[64]

(2) DOUBLE RENT. If the tenant gives the landlord *written or oral*[65] notice to **14–084** quit, then whatever the type of tenancy (provided it is determinable by notice[66]), the tenant is liable to pay double rent in respect of the period for

---

[51] *Bayley v. Bradley* (1848) 5 C.B. 396 at 406; *Leigh v. Dickeson* (1884) 15 Q.B.D. 60; *post*, para. 14–251.

[52] See *post*, Appendix. This may now be a distinction without a difference: *Dean and Chapter of Canterbury Cathedral v. Whitbread Plc* (1995) 72 P. & C.R. 9 at 16.

[53] *Post.*

[54] *Doe d. Bennett v. Turner* (1840) 7 M. & W. 226 at 235. But as to ejection, see *post*, para. 14–226. For emblements, see *ante*, para. 3–114.

[55] For fuller consideration of this point, see the previous edition of this work at p. 656.

[56] This was not so for the purpose of acquiring title by limitation before 1833; but the doctrine of adverse possession upon which the distinction was founded was abolished by the Real Property Limitation Act 1833; Tudor L.C. 9; *post*, para. 21–016.

[57] *Ante*, para. 3–122.

[58] *Ante*, para. 14–077.

[59] Which means "as a trespasser": see *Oliver Ashworth (Holdings) Ltd v. Ballard* [1999] 3 W.L.R. 57; *infra*. See, *e.g. French v. Elliott* [1960] 1 W.L.R. 40; *Dun & Bradstreet Software Services (England) Ltd v. Provident Mutual Life Assurance Association* [1996] E.G.C.S. 62.

[60] Landlord and Tenant Act 1730, s.1.

[61] See *Ryal v. Rich* (1808) 10 East. 48.

[62] *Cobb v. Stokes* (1807) 8 East 358.

[63] *Lloyd v. Rosbee* (1810) 2 Camp. 453.

[64] See *Williamson v. Hall* (1837) 3 Bing.N.C. 508.

[65] *Timmins v. Rowlison* (1764) Wm.Bl. 533.

[66] *Johnstone v. Hudlestone* (1825) 4 B. & C. 922.

which he holds over after the notice expires; payment can be enforced by action or distress.[67]

The differing terms of these aged provisions will be noticed. The rent and the annual value may be the same, but they often differ, as where premises have been let at a reduced rent in consideration of a fine. However, notwith-standing these differences, it is now clear that the courts will read the two provisions together as a single code. They will apply only where the tenant is a trespasser and is treated as such by the landlord.[68]

B. Statutory Modifications

14–085 Although leases can in general be created for such periods as the parties think fit, there are special statutory rules for some cases, which sometimes produce surprising results.

1. Leases for lives or until marriage

14–086 *(a) Conversion to 90-year terms.* By the Law of Property Act 1925[69] a lease[70] at a rent or a fine[71] "for lives or for any term of years determinable with life or lives or on the marriage of the lessee", is converted into a term of 90 years.[72] A contract for such a lease is treated in a similar way; but a term "taking effect in equity under a settlement or created out of an equitable interest under a settlement for mortgage, indemnity, or other like purposes" is excluded, even if a rent is reserved. For the statute to apply, the lease must determine automatically on the death or marriage of the lessee. A lease which may be determined by the giving of notice *after* such death or marriage is outside the statute.[73]

When a lease falls within the statute neither death nor marriage determines the lease, but "on the death or marriage (as the case may be) of the original lessee" either party may determine it by serving on the other at least one month's written notice to expire on one of the quarter days applicable to the tenancy, or, if no special quarter days are applicable, on one of the usual quarter days. If the lease is determinable with "the lives of persons other than or besides the lessees", the notice is "capable of being served" on the dropping of their lives, "instead of after the death of the original lessee".

14–087 *(b) Operation of the statute.* For example, leases at a rent or fine granted—

---

[67] Distress for Rent Act 1737, s.18.
[68] *Oliver Ashworth (Holdings) Ltd v. Ballard, supra.*
[69] s.149(6).
[70] Whether granted before 1926 or after 1925.
[71] A fine has been held to include a discount on the price paid by a purchaser on a sale and leaseback to the vendors for their joint lives: *Skipton B.S. v. Clayton* (1993) P. & C.R. 233 at 231, 232.
[72] Where neither rent nor a premium is payable under the lease, the section is inapplicable: *Binions v. Evans* [1972] Ch. 359 at 366.
[73] *Bass Holdings Ltd v. Lewis* [1986] 2 E.G.L.R. 40.

"to A for life",
"to B for 10 years if he so long lives", and
"to C for 99 years if he so long remains a bachelor",

are all converted into terms which will continue for 90 years unless by the proper notice they are determined on a quarter day (not necessarily the first) after the event has occurred. In most cases this position will cause little change in the effective rights of the parties. But it may drastically cut down the lessor's reversion if, in a case like the second of the above examples, he wishes to grant only a short term, conditional upon the lessee remaining alive or unmarried.[74] And the drafting of the statute seems ill-adapted for leases such as "to A during B's life",[75] or "to C for 50 years if D so long remains unmarried", or "to E until he remarries".

(c) Contrast with life interests. The general object of these provisions is to **14–088** bring leases for life within the general scheme of the 1925 legislation, and to distinguish between leases for life which involve the relationship of landlord and tenant[76] and beneficial life tenancies under a settlement. Normally the former are commercial transactions, whereas the latter are family transactions. This distinction is usually marked by whether or not a premium or rent is payable; and this is the test adopted by the statute. Life interests of a family character are subject to the law governing either settled land (if created before 1997) or trusts of land (if created after 1996), but are in either case equitable. Life tenancies of a commercial character are converted into true terms of years, unaffected by the principles of the law of settled land or trusts of land.

The distinction is, however, not always clear cut. Thus, where a testator gives one of his relations the right to be granted a tenancy for life at a nominal rent,[77] or at less than the market rent,[78] the transaction, though at a rent, is also partly of a beneficial or family nature. On the other hand, a commercial transaction in which there is no beneficial or family element may create a tenancy for life which prior to 1997 made the land settled land[79] and will now create a trust of land.[80] Further, the statute itself provides for the exclusion of certain leases even though granted at a rent, *e.g.* those taking effect in equity under a settlement.[81] Nevertheless, in most cases the distinction is valid.[82]

---

[74] *cf.* Wolst. & C. i, 278. The difficulty can be readily overcome by making the lease determinable by the landlord on giving notice after the tenant's death or marriage: see *Bass Holdings Ltd v. Lewis, supra.*

[75] For it seems that a notice could be served after the death of A even if B is still living.

[76] For these, see *ante*, para. 14–006.

[77] *Re Catling* [1931] 2 Ch. 359 (£1 a year).

[78] *Blamires v. Bradford Corporation* [1964] Ch. 585 (30s. a week).

[79] As in *Binions v. Evans* [1972] Ch. 359. In some cases there has, however, been a family relationship of some kind, as in *Bannister v. Bannister* [1948] 2 All E.R. 133 (sale of land at reduced price to brother-in-law in return for life interest); *Costello v. Costello* (1994) 27 H.L.R. 12 (purchase at discounted price by son but subject to life interest for parents).

[80] See T.L.A.T.A. 1996, ss.1, 2; *ante*, para. 8–125.

[81] *Re Catling, supra*, seems to be an example of this.

[82] See, *e.g. Kingswood Estate Co. Ltd v. Anderson* [1963] 2 Q.B. 169 (clearly commercial).

2. Perpetually renewable leases

14–089 *(a) Renewability.* A perpetually renewable lease is a lease which gives the tenant the right to renew it for another period as often as it expires. Such leases are seldom deliberately created today.[83] But they may be created inadvertently by unrestricted renewal clauses, as by an option giving the tenant a right of renewal "on the same terms and conditions, including this clause",[84] or "on identical terms and conditions".[85] The lease is then held to be perpetually renewable even though the parties may have had no such intention: "the courts have manoeuvred themselves into an unhappy position"[86] in these decisions. However the courts lean against perpetual renewals. Thus where a lease contained a covenant to renew on terms which conferred a further right of renewal, that was held to give the tenant a right to renew the lease twice but not perpetually.[87]

14–090 *(b) Conversion.* By the Law of Property Act 1922,[88] perpetually renewable leases take effect as terms of 2,000 years from the date fixed for the commencement of the term. Any perpetually renewable sub-lease created out of a perpetually renewable lease is converted into a term of 2,000 years less one day.[89]

14–091 *(c) Terms.* The 2,000-year lease is subject to the same terms as the original lease, with the following modifications.

(i) The tenant (but not the landlord) may terminate the lease on any date upon which, but for the conversion by the Act, the lease would have expired if it had not been renewed, provided he gives at least 10 days' written notice to the landlord.[90]

(ii) Every assignment or devolution of the lease must be registered with the landlord or his solicitor or agent within six months, and a fee of one guinea paid.[91]

(iii) A tenant who assigns the lease is not liable for breaches of covenant committed after the assignment.[92] The general rule for leases granted before 1996 is that the original lessee remains liable for all breaches occurring during the term, even if he parts with the

---

[83] They used to be common in Ireland: see *Swinburne v. Milburn* (1884) 9 App.Cas 844 at 855.

[84] *Hare v. Burges* (1857) 4 K. & J. 45; *Parkus v. Greenwood* [1950] Ch. 644; *Caerphilly Concrete Products Ltd v. Owen* [1972] 1 W.L.R. 372.

[85] *Northchurch Estates Ltd v. Daniels* [1947] Ch. 117 (tenancy for a year becomes a term of 2,000 years).

[86] *Caerphilly Concrete Products Ltd v. Owen*, supra, at 376, *per* Sachs L.J.

[87] *Marjorie Burnett Ltd v. Barclay* [1981] 1 E.G.L.R. 41.

[88] s.145 and Sched. 15.

[89] L.P.A. 1922, Sched. 15, paras 2, 5.

[90] *ibid.*, para. 10(1)(i).

[91] *ibid.*, para. 10(1)(ii). This operates by way of covenant and is subject to any proviso for forfeiture for breach of covenants of the lease: *ibid.* As to forfeiture, see *post*, para. 14–118.

[92] L.P.A. 1922, Sched. 15, para. 11.

lease.[93] Perpetually renewable leases were made an exception to that rule, because otherwise the original lessee's liability might last for ever.

(d) Right to determine. It should be noted that the landlord has no right to determine the lease at the renewal dates. If L has granted T a lease for 21 years with a perpetual right of renewal, the lease continues after the expiry of each 21-year period unless T elects to determine it.[94]   **14–092**

3. Over-lengthy renewals. A contract to renew a lease for over 60 years from its termination is void.[95] This is aimed at single renewals, not perpetual renewals.   **14–093**

4. Reversionary leases. A lease at a rent or a fine cannot be granted to commence at too distant a future date. This has already been explained.[96]   **14–094**

C. Tenancy by Estoppel

1. Estoppel between landlord and tenant. There is a general rule that a tenant is estopped from denying his landlord's title, and a landlord from denying his tenant's.[97] Estoppel is a principle of the law of evidence and, in this context, it may arise in one of two ways.[98]   **14–095**

  (i) *By deed.* It is an ancient principle that a grantor is precluded from disputing the validity or effect of his grant, often called estoppel by deed.[99]

  (ii) *By representation.* A landlord may be estopped by an unambiguous and material representation as to his title (usually in a recital) on the strength of which the tenant takes a lease.[1]

---

[93] See *post*, para. 15–008. The rule has been alleviated by certain provisions of the L. & T.C.A. 1995; *post*, para. 15–014. For leases granted after 1995, see *post*, para. 15–064.

[94] Prior to 1926, renewal was not automatic: T had to give notice to L.

[95] L.P.A. 1922, Sched. 15, para. 7.

[96] *Ante*, para. 14–061.

[97] *Cooke v. Loxley* (1792) 5 T.R. 4; *Cuthbertson v. Irving* (1859) 4 H. & N. 742; (1860) 6 H.& N. 135, as explained in *Industrial Properties (Barton Hill) Ltd v. Associated Electrical Industries Ltd* [1977] Q.B. 580. See also *Mackley v. Nutting* [1949] 2 K.B. 55. For a general survey, see (1968) 32 Conv. (N.S.) 249 (C. J. W. Allen).

[98] See the leading modern case, *First National Bank Plc v. Thompson* [1996] Ch. 231, which follows closely the reasoning in (1964) 80 L.Q.R. 370 (A.M. Prichard). The two types of estoppel have different effects: *post*, paras 14–099, 14–100.

[99] *Goodtitle v. Bailey* (1777) 2 Cowp. 597 at 600, 601; *Bruton v. London and Quadrant Housing Trusts* [1998] Q.B. 834 at 844 (CA). *cf. ibid.*, [1999] 3 W.L.R. 150 (HL), reversing the Court of Appeal, where Lord Hoffmann emphasised (at 157) that it was "not the estoppel which creates the tenancy, but the tenancy which creates the estoppel". For the circumstances in which an oral lease can found an estoppel, see Co.Litt. 352a; (1964) 80 L.Q.R. 370 at 395 (A. M. Prichard).

[1] *First National Bank Plc v. Thompson, supra*, at 237, 243.

In either case,[2] the landlord cannot question the validity of his own grant, nor can the tenant question it once he is in possession[3] and has the benefit of the lease, "for so long as a lessee enjoys everything which his lease purports to grant, how does it concern him what the title of the lessor, or the heir or assignee of his lessor, really is?"[4] It is otherwise if the lessee is disturbed by title paramount, *i.e.* if some title superior to the lessor's is made good against him; for then he may be liable for mesne profits to the adverse claimant, and he can reclaim rent paid to the lessor.[5] But in the absence of an adverse title he cannot repudiate his obligations under the lease. He can therefore be sued for breach of a repairing covenant after he has given up possession, even though he can show that the lessor was not the legal owner when the lease was granted.[6] This is an example of the proposition that *jus tertii* cannot be pleaded against a prior possessory title.[7] Even if the landlord was not the true owner when he granted the lease, the tenant may not deny his title to grant it if in fact he has the benefit of it. But the tenant is estopped only from denying the landlord's title to put him into possession: he may always show, if he can, that the landlord's title has subsequently come to an end.[8] Thus if the landlord has conveyed the reversion to X, but sues the tenant for rent, the tenant can of course plead that the rent is now due to X and so deny the landlord's title.[9] Likewise if the landlord's title is a lease which has expired, the tenant can withhold the rent even though no third party is claiming it.[10]

14–096   This estoppel applies to all types of tenancy, including periodic tenancies, tenancies at will and at sufferance,[11] and statutory tenancies under the Rent Acts[12]; and business tenancies under the Landlord and Tenant Act 1954.[13] It applies similarly to licences.[14] It operates whether the tenancy was created by deed, in writing or orally.[15] It is a general rule, being part of the doctrine of

[2] It is not confined to cases where there is a recital in the grant of the lessor's legal title: *First National Bank Plc v. Thompson, supra.*

[3] See *Hall v. Butler* (1839) 10 A. & E. 204; *Doe d. Marlow v. Wiggins* (1843) 4 Q.B. 367.

[4] *Cuthbertson v. Irving* (1859) 4 H. & N. 742 at 758, *per* Martin B.

[5] See the *Industrial Properties case, supra,* at 596, *per* Lord Denning M.R.

[6] *ibid.* For this case, see *ante,* para. 14–044. The Court of Appeal rejected its decision in *Harrison v. Wells* [1967] 1 Q.B. 263 as made *per incuriam.*

[7] As explained *ante,* para. 3–124. See *Bell v. General Accident Fire & Life Assurance Corporation Ltd* [1998] 1 E.G.L.R. 69 at 71.

[8] *Mountnoy v. Collier* (1853) 1 E. & B. 630; *Serjeant v. Nash, Field & Co.* [1903] 2 K.B. 304; *National Westminster Bank Ltd v. Hart* [1983] Q.B. 773; [1984] Conv. 64 (J. W. Price); Foa L. & T. 474.

[9] *Harmer v. Bean* (1853) 3 C. & K. 307.

[10] *National Westminster Bank Ltd v. Hart, supra.* The authorities indicate, inconsistently, that as against an assignee of the reversion the tenant must be able to show a valid adverse title in a third party: *ibid.*

[11] *Doe d. Bailey v. Foster* (1846) 3 C.B. 215 at 229.

[12] See *Stratford v. Syrett* [1958] 1 Q.B. 107. For statutory tenancies, see *post,* para. 22–186.

[13] See *Bell v. General Accident Fire & Life Assurance Corporation Ltd* [1998] 1 E.G.L.R. 69. For business tenancies, see *post,* para. 22–063.

[14] *Doe. d. Johnson v. Baytup* (1835) 3 A. & E. 188*; Terunnanse v. Terunnanse* [1968] A.C. 1086*; Government of Penang v. Bang Hong Oon* [1972] A.C. 425; *Sze To Chun Keung v. Kung Kwok Wai David* [1997] 1 W.L.R. 1232; compare *Tadman v. Henman* [1893] 2 Q.B. 168 at 171.

[15] *E.H. Lewis & Son Ltd v. Morelli* [1948] 2 All E.R. 1021. The limits stated in Co.Litt. 47b no longer apply: see *e.g. Mackley v. Nutting* [1949] 2 K.B. 55.

possessory titles as pointed out earlier.[16] Subject to one exception, those claiming through the parties are also estopped, so that the estoppel binds the successors in title to both landlord and tenant.[17] The exception is that, where the tenancy by estoppel arises by deed,[18] a bona fide purchaser for value from the grantor without notice of the transaction takes free of it.[19] But where the estoppel is by representation, the grantee's title is good, even against a bona fide purchaser.[20]

2. Tenancy by estoppel. Where the landlord's title is defective but the parties are bound by the estoppel just described, there is said to be a tenancy by estoppel.[21] This may occur where, for example, the landlord has contracted to purchase the freehold but where it has not yet been transferred to him. Even though it is apparent to the parties that the landlord's title is defective,[22] then subject to the exception mentioned above, both they and their successors in title will be estopped from denying that the grant was effective to create the tenancy that it purported to create.[23] Thus, in effect, there is brought into being a tenancy under which the parties and their successors in title have (as against one another) most of the rights and liabilities of a legal estate. The tenancy by estoppel will devolve and may be alienated in the same way as any other tenancy,[24] and the landlord may distrain for rent in the ordinary way.[25] But since estoppels do not bind strangers, he cannot exercise his normal right[26] to distrain goods not owned by the tenant.[27]

14–097

3. Feeding the estoppel

(a) Where the landlord subsequently acquires a legal estate. If after creating a tenancy by estoppel the landlord later acquires a legal estate out of which the tenancy could be created (as where he purchases the fee simple), this is said to "feed the estoppel": the tenant then at once acquires a tenancy based upon

14–098

---

[16] *Ante*, para. 3–126.

[17] *Webb v. Austin* (1844) 7 Man. & G. 701; *Cuthbertson v. Irving* (1859) 4 H. & N. 742 at 758 (aff'd (1860) 6 H. & N. 135).

[18] For the distinction between estoppel by deed and estoppel by representation, see *ante*, para. 14–095.

[19] *General Finance, Mortgage and Discount Co. v. Liberator Permanent Benefit* B.S. (1878) 10 Ch.D. 15; *First National Bank Plc v. Thompson* [1996] Ch. 231 at 239, 240, 244. This is a rule of law, not equity; *ibid.*, at 240.

[20] *First National Bank Plc v. Thompson, supra*, at 239.

[21] The doctrine is discussed in (1964) 80 L.Q.R. 370 (A.M. Prichard).

[22] *Morton v. Woods* (1869) L.R. 4 Q.B. 293.

[23] See *Cuthbertson v. Irving, supra*, at 757, 758.

[24] *Gouldsworth v. Knights* (1843) 11 M. & W. 337; *Webb v. Austin* (1844) 7 Man. & G. 701; *Cuthbertson v. Irving, supra*, at 758; *Mackley v. Nutting* [1949] 2 K.B. 55.

[25] *Gouldsworth v. Knights, supra*.

[26] See *post*, para. 14–254.

[27] *Tadman v. Henman* [1893] 2 Q.B. 168. In principle this seems questionable, since the tenancy by estoppel is probably a possessory legal estate of the kind discussed *ante*, para. 3–117.

the newly acquired estate in place of his tenancy by estoppel.[28] Similarly, if a tenant dies or leaves the premises and another tenant occupies them and pays rent to the landlord, the second tenant has an implied lease by estoppel while the first tenancy remains in existence, and a true tenancy as from its determination[29]; for upon its determination the landlord recovers his immediate legal title, and that feeds the estoppel.

(b) Where the landlord has a legal estate at the time of the grant

14–099 (1) ESTOPPEL BY DEED. Where the estoppel is by deed and not by representation,[30] the grantor is estopped merely from denying that he has a legal title.[31] No tenancy by estoppel can therefore arise in such circumstances if the lessor did in fact have any present legal estate (as distinct from a mere equitable interest[32]) in the land when he granted the lease.[33] If the lessor's interest was a freehold, or a leasehold which would outlast the lease which he granted, the lease takes effect in the ordinary way; if it was a leasehold equal to[34] or smaller than[35] the subsequent lease, the grant of that lease operates as an assignment of the lessor's interest.[36] Thus if L grants T a lease for 99 years and subsequently acquires the fee simple (*e.g.* under his father's will), T will take a lease for 99 years by estoppel if L had no interest in the land when the lease was granted. But if L had a lease for 10 years at that time, the lease for 99 years will operate only as an assignment to T of L's lease for 10 years,[37] and L will not be estopped from recovering the land when the 10-year term expires.

14–100 (2) ESTOPPEL BY REPRESENTATION. Where, by contrast, the estoppel arises from an unequivocal representation of the grantor's title, he is estopped from denying that he has that particular title.[38] Therefore, the estoppel is "not excluded by the ownership of some lesser estate".[39]

---

[28] *Rawlin's Case* (1587) Jenk. 254; 4 Co.Rep. 52a; *Webb v. Austin* (1844) 7 Man. & G. 701 at 724; *Sturgeon v. Wingfield* (1846) 15 M. & W. 224; *Rajapakse v. Fernando* [1920] A.C. 892 at 897; *cf.* L.P.A. 1925, s.152(2), *ante*, para. 8–078. The doctrine of feeding the estoppel is not confined to the creation of tenancies, but applies whenever "a grantor has purported to grant an interest in land which he did not at the time possess, but subsequently acquires": *Rajapakse v. Fernando, supra,* at 897, *per* Lord Moulton.

[29] *Edward H. Lewis & Son Ltd v. Morelli* (1948) 65 T.L.R. 56; *Mackley v. Nutting* [1949] 2 K.B. 55; *Moses v. Warsop* (1949) 100 L.J.News. 51.

[30] See *ante*, para. 14–095.

[31] *First National Bank Plc v. Thompson* [1996] Ch. 231 at 239.

[32] *Universal Permanent B.S. v. Cooke* [1952] Ch. 95 at 102 (tenancy by estoppel where the lessor had contracted to buy the property let but had not completed the purchase). A lease by a mortgagor may also take effect by estoppel despite the equity of redemption still vested in him; *post*, paras 19–112, 19–121.

[33] Co.Litt. 47b; *Doe d. Strode v. Seaton* (1835) 2 C.M. & R. 728 (lease granted by tenant for life not binding on successors in title); *Cuthbertson v. Irving* (1859) 4 H. & N. 742, affirmed (1860) 6 H. & N. 135.

[34] *Beardman v. Wilson* (1868) L.R. 4 C.P. 57; *Hallen v. Spaeth* [1923] A.C. 684 at 687.

[35] *Wollaston v. Hakewill* (1841) 3 Man. & G. 297 at 323 (not a case of estoppel).

[36] For this rule, see *post*, para. 14–110.

[37] See *post*, para. 14–110.

[38] *First National Bank Plc v. Thompson* [1996] Ch. 231 at 239.

[39] *ibid., per* Millett L.J.

(c) Effect on third parties. The effect of an estoppel on the grantor's **14–101** successor in title where the estoppel has been fed by the acquisition of the legal estate is the same as where it has not.[40] The same rules apply whether the title to the land is unregistered or registered.[41] The tenant will of course acquire a legal estate by estoppel. Where the estoppel is by representation, that estate will bind any third party who derives title through or under the grantor regardless of notice.[42] But where the estoppel is by deed, a bona fide purchaser without notice of the earlier transaction takes free of the tenancy.[43] It is at first sight strange both that a purchaser in good faith should take free of a *legal* estate[44] and that questions of notice[45] can arise in relation to registered land.[46] However, this is because the issue is not whether the third party is bound by the estate or interest arising by estoppel, but whether he is bound by the estoppel itself upon which the estate or interest depends. It should be noted, however, that where title is registered, the grantee by estoppel is entitled either to register or to protect by registration his estate or interest.[47] If he does, any purchaser is likely to have notice of his rights.[48]

4. Purchaser in possession before completion. Sometimes a purchaser of **14–102** land is allowed to go into possession before completion. If he then grants a tenancy of the land, and subsequently, on completion, mortgages the land in order to raise the purchase-money, the question arises whether the lease (which, until it was "fed" by completion of the purchase, was a mere lease by estoppel) is binding upon the mortgagee.[49] This is in fact part of a wider question as to whether the mortgage takes effect simultaneously with the conveyance or only subsequent to it. This affects not just tenancies granted by a purchaser who has gone into possession prior to completion, but other rights, *e.g.* those of a spouse or relative who contributes part of the purchase price and who claims a commensurate interest in the property under a resulting trust.[50] After a period of uncertainty, the Court of Appeal held that the purchase and the mortgage were two distinct transactions and that the legal estate had to be vested in the purchaser before any mortgage could become

---

[40] This has already been explained: *ante,* para. 14–099.
[41] See *First National Bank Plc v. Thompson, supra,* at 240. For the application of the doctrine of feeding the estoppel to registered land, see *ibid.,* (legal charge); *Woolwich Equitable B.S. v. Marshall* [1952] Ch. 1 (tenancy).
[42] *First National Bank Plc v. Thompson, supra,* at 239.
[43] *ibid.,* at 239, 240, 244.
[44] *Ante,* para. 4–011.
[45] At common law in this context, not in equity.
[46] The doctrine of notice is inapplicable to dealings with registered land: *ante,* paras 4–072, 6–077.
[47] *First National Bank Plc v. Thompson, supra.*
[48] *ibid.,* at 244.
[49] Obviously where the mortgage is executed after the conveyance to the purchaser, there can be no doubt that the estoppel will be fed in the interval so as to give priority to the tenant: see *Universal Permanent B.S. v. Cooke* [1952] Ch. 95 (mortgage executed one day after completion).
[50] See *ante,* para. 10–016.

effective.[51] There was considered to be a *scintilla temporis* between the purchaser's acquisition of the legal estate and the creation of the mortgage during which the estoppel could be fed. This doctrine was always controversial[52] because the legal estate could never have been acquired at all without the mortgage. Nor could it be readily reconciled with the authorities on debentures, where no such *scintilla temporis* was recognised.[53]

The House of Lords has subsequently dismissed the *scintilla temporis* as "no more than a legal artifice".[54] It has held that where the acquisition of the legal estate is dependent upon the provision of funds by a mortgagee, the transfer of legal title to the purchaser and the mortgage occur simultaneously.[55] Strictly speaking, this rule does no more than determine the time at which interests are considered to have been created. However, its effect is to ensure that a mortgagee will always take priority, not only over a tenant by estoppel in possession but even as against some other person who provides a substantial part of the purchase price.[56]

D. Concurrent Leases

14–103   **1. Grant.** If a landlord who has granted a lease subsequently grants another lease of the same land for some or all of the period of the existing lease, so that there are concurrent leases, he is said to have granted a lease of the reversion.[57] The effect of the second grant depends upon when the first lease was granted. Leases granted before 1996 are governed by rules of common law, whereas those granted after 1995 are subject to the provisions of the Landlord and Tenant (Covenants) Act 1995 which has changed the law for new leases.[58] Both must be considered.

---

[51] *Church of England B.S. v. Piskor* [1954] Ch. 553, following *Woolwich Equitable B.S. v. Marshall* [1952] Ch. 1 and *Universal Permanent B.S. v. Cooke, supra*, and overruling on this point *Coventry Permanent B.S. v. Jones* [1951] 1 All E.R. 901. See [1954] C.L.J. 192 (H.W.R.W.).

[52] It was held not to apply where a new mortgage was executed to replace an existing one, but on somewhat different terms: *Walthamstow B.S. v. Davies* (1989) 60 P. & C.R. 99. See too *Equity & Law Home Loans Ltd v. Prestidge* [1992] 1 W.L.R. 137 at 144.

[53] In these cases, a purchaser who had contracted to acquire land with the aid of a mortgage, granted a debenture prior to completion of the purchase. The mortgage took priority over the debenture: see *Re Connolly Brothers Ltd (No. 2)* [1912] 2 Ch. 25; *Security Trust Co. v. Royal Bank of Canada* [1976] A.C. 503; and *Lloyds Bank Plc v. Rosset* [1989] Ch. 350 at 388–393.

[54] *Abbey National B.S. v. Cann* [1991] 1 A.C. 56 at 93, *per* Lord Oliver.

[55] *Abbey National B.S v. Cann, supra*. For different views on the case see (1990) 106 L.Q.R. 545 (R. J. Smith); [1990] C.L.J. 397 (A. J. Oakley). See too *Nationwide Anglia B.S. v. Ahmed* (1995) 70 P. & C.R. 381 (unpaid vendor remained in occupation: no *scintilla temporis* in which his lien could gain priority over the mortgagee).

[56] As was the case in *Abbey National B.S. v. Cann, supra*.

[57] Contrast a reversionary lease: *ante*, para. 14–061.

[58] For the L. & T.C.A. 1995, see *post*, para. 15–064. For what constitutes a new lease for these purposes, see *post*, para. 15–007.

(a) Leases granted before 1996. Where the first lease was granted before **14–104** 1996, the second grant is *pro tanto* a disposition of the reversion,[59] and so creates the relationship of landlord and tenant between the second and first lessee respectively,[60] with all the rights and liabilities as to rent and other matters which are capable of running with the tenancy.[61] This supplants the relationship of landlord and tenant between the landlord and the first lessee.[62] Thus if L granted a lease of Blackacre to T for 21 years in 1994, and then granted a lease of Blackacre to X for 30 years in 1995, X became and remains the immediate reversioner upon T's lease so long as it continues, and is therefore T's landlord. When T's lease determines in 2015, X will become entitled to possession of Blackacre. The result would be the same if X's lease had been granted for a term shorter than T's,[63] except of course, that X's lease would normally expire before he had become entitled to take possession. X could collect rent and enforce covenants against T,[64] and if T's lease prematurely determined before X's term expired, X would be entitled to possession of the land.[65] Statute has expressly preserved this rule that a legal term (whether or not a mortgage term) may be created to take effect in reversion expectant upon a longer term.[66]

(b) Leases granted after 1995. Where a lease has been granted after 1995, **14–105** a lease of the reversion no longer operates as a partial disposition of the reversion but as a genuine lease of the reversion. This is because where L grants a lease to T and then a lease of the reversion to X, he retains the right to sue T on the covenants of the first lease.[67] In many cases L will in fact be estopped from doing so by his grant of a lease of the reversion to X. He could hardly lease to X the right to receive the rents and profits from T and then claim them himself. However, there may be circumstances in which L may have a good reason for wishing to enforce a covenant directly against T. This is explained more fully later.[68]

2. Effect

(a) Leases granted before 1996. Because a lease of the reversion on a lease **14–106** granted before 1996 is *pro tanto* an assignment of it, it must obey the rules

---

[59] Shep. Touch. 275, 276; *Neale v. Mackenzie* (1836) 1 M. & W. 747; *Harmer v. Bean* (1853) 3 C. & K. 307; *Wordsley Brewery Co. v. Halford* (1903) 90 L.T. 89; *Cole v. Kelly* [1920] 2 K.B. 106.

[60] *Birch v. Wright* (1786) 1 T.R. 378 at 384. *cf.* the apparent dictum to the contrary in *Cole v. Kelly, supra,* at 120, which seems wrong.

[61] *Burton v. Barclay* (1831) 7 Bing. 754; *Horn v. Beard* [1912] 3 K.B. 181; *Cole v. Kelly, supra*; Preston, *Conveyancing,* ii, 145, 146.

[62] See *Wordsley Brewery Co. v. Halford, supra* (notice to quit by landlord to first lessee bad).

[63] *Neale v. Mackenzie, supra; Re Moore & Hulm's Contract* [1912] 2 Ch. 105.

[64] *Burton v. Barclay, supra.*

[65] *Stephens v. Bridges* (1821) 6 Madd. 66 at 67; *Re Moore & Hulm's* Contract [1912] 2 Ch. 105.

[66] L.P.A. 1925, s.149(5). The statement in Wolst & C. i, 277, that this and s.149(2) overrule *Neale v. Mackenzie, supra,* is puzzling.

[67] L. & T.C.A. 1995, s.15(1)(a).

[68] *Post,* para. 15–084.

governing assignments of reversions explained below.[69] Such a lease can therefore have no effect at law unless made by deed. If, in the above example of a lease granted in 1994, X's lease was created orally, it was wholly void at common law during the full term of T's lease, even if T's lease determined prematurely.[70] And this was equally true if the term of X's lease did not exceed three years.[71] But once T's term had expired, X's lease (if still in being) could take effect as a lease of the land, not as a disposition of the reversion, and so be valid as a reversionary lease if it conformed to the rules for the creation of such leases.[72] It is not clear, however, whether the relationship between L and X during T's term is that of landlord and tenant or that of assignor and assignee,[73] or whether there is a lease by estoppel between them.[74] Nor is it clear whether the Law of Property Act 1925 has made it possible for X's lease to be created orally if its term does not exceed three years.[75]

14–107   *(b) Leases granted after 1995.* As regards a lease granted after 1995, any subsequent lease of the reversion does not operate as an assignment. If, therefore, L grants a lease to T and then a lease of the reversion to X, the relationship of landlord and tenant and the reciprocal right to enforce the covenants of the relevant lease exists between—

      (i) L and T;

      (ii) X and T; and

      (iii) L and X.[76]

The same doubt mentioned above exists as to whether the lease from L to X could be granted if it were for a term not exceeding three years.

Part 3

ASSIGNMENT OF LEASES AND REVERSIONS

Section 1. Assignment of leases

14–108   **1. Lease assignable by deed.** A lease, like other forms of property, is freely transferable. Even if, as is common, the lease contains a covenant against

---

[69] *Post*, para. 14–113.
[70] *Neale v. Mackenzie* (1836) 1 M. & W. 747 (where the lease was held void only as to the part of the land already leased).
[71] *Brawley v. Wade* (1824) M'Clel. 664 (tenancy from year to year).
[72] *Doe d. Thomas v. Jenkins* (1832) 1 L.J.K.B. 190.
[73] The authorities appear to be silent on this point.
[74] Bacon's *Abridgement* (7th ed., 1832), iv, 848; Platt on *Leases*, ii, 59. For tenancy by estoppel, see *ante*, para. 14–095.
[75] s.54(2) (*ante*, para. 14–034) requires the lease to take effect in possession, but X's lease can take effect only in reversion upon T's lease. By s.205(1)(xix) "possession" includes the right to receive rents and profits. But presumably this right can pass only under a grant by deed, *i.e.* as incident to the reversion.
[76] L. & T.C.A. 1995, s.15(1)(a); (2); *post*, paras 15–084, 15–085.

assignment, this will not prevent an assignment from taking effect, though it may expose the assignor to proceedings for forfeiture or damages for breach of covenant.[77]

A legal lease, once created, can be transferred *inter vivos* only by deed, in accordance with the general rule.[78] This applies to all tenancies, even those created orally, *e.g.* a yearly tenancy.[79] However, on principles similar to those applicable to the creation of leases, an assignment will be effective in equity as between the assignor and the assignee as a contract to assign, provided that it is made in writing and contains all the terms expressly agreed between the parties.[80] Where such an assignment is made of a lease granted before 1996, the assignee will not be liable to the landlord on the covenants of the lease,[81] even if he enters and pays rent, though in special cases he may be estopped from denying liability.[82] Where the lease was granted after 1995, however, the burden of the covenants will pass on such an equitable assignment.[83]

Where, in the case of registered land, the lease assigned is registered with its own title, the assignment[84] will not be effective to transfer the legal estate unless it is registered.[85] This may mean that the assignor can exercise a break clause in the lease even after he has executed the transfer of the lease, if it has not then been registered.[86]

2. Contrast with sub-lease. The difference between an assignment of a **14–109** lease and the grant of a sub-lease has already been mentioned. As will appear later,[87] this is of fundamental importance to the question of liability for breaches of covenant, if the original tenant has made some disposition of the land. If he assigns his lease, he grants his whole estate to the assignee, thus putting the assignee in his shoes as immediate tenant of the head landlord. If he grants a sub-lease, he does not cease to be tenant, for he retains his estate: he has merely carved out of it a lesser estate, in respect of which he owns the immediate reversion. The assignment of a lease transfers an estate but creates

---

[77] See *post*, para. 14–259.

[78] L.P.A. 1925, s.52, *ante*, para. 14–038.

[79] *Crago v. Julian* [1992] 1 W.L.R. 372 (where this statement was approved at 377); *Camden L.B.C. v. Alexandrou* (1997) 30 H.L.R. 534. But see [1992] Conv. 375 (P. Sparkes); (1995) 58 M.L.R. 637 at 638 (G. Battersby); *ante*, para. 14–038.

[80] *Ante*, para. 14–039; *Parc Battersea Ltd v. Hutchinson* [1999] 22 E.G. 149 at 153. Prior to September 27, 1989, an oral or written assignment was effective in equity if it was evidenced by writing or there were sufficient acts of part performance: see the previous edition of this work at p. 665.

[81] There was no privity of estate: see *ante*, para. 14–051; *post*, para. 15–033.

[82] *Rodenhurst Estates Ltd v. W.H. Barnes Ltd* [1936] 2 All E.R. 3, where the landlord had granted a licence for a legal assignment which had been acted upon in all respects except for the execution of a formal assignment. See [1978] C.L.J. 98 at 116 (R. J. Smith). Compare *Official Trustee of Charity Lands v. Ferriman Trust Ltd* [1937] 3 All E.R. 85; and see *Richmond v. McGann* [1954] 1 W.L.R. 1282.

[83] L. & T.C.A. 1995, ss.3(1), (2), 28(1); *post*, paras 15–065, 15–079.

[84] See L.R.R. 1925, rr. 115, 116.

[85] L.R.A. 1925, s.22(1).

[86] *Brown & Root Technology Ltd v. Sun Alliance & London Assurance Co. Ltd* (1996) 75 P. & C.R. 223 (a case on the construction of the word "assignment" in break clause).

[87] *Post*, paras 15–004, 15–005.

no new tenure; the grant of a sub-lease creates a new tenure between sub-lessor and sub-lessee.

14–110   **3. Sub-lease as assignment.** Since the distinction between an assignment and a sub-lease is one of substance, not one of form, it follows that if the tenant disposes of the whole residue of his estate, the transaction must operate as an assignment even though the parties intend it to operate as a sub-lease.[88] For example, if three years ago L granted a lease to A for seven years, and A now purports to grant a sub-lease to B for 10 years, the sub-lease operates as an assignment despite its terms, and any covenants and conditions contained in it (*e.g.* as to rent, repair or forfeiture) have such operation as they may have under an assignment.[89] A is then no longer tenant of L; there is direct tenure between L and B. A cannot therefore distrain for rent due to him from B under the so-called sub-lease,[90] although it has the legal quality of being rent, and can be sued for.[91] And if the so-called sub-lease is followed by a yearly or other periodic tenancy (*e.g.* to B for five years and thereafter from year to year), A cannot give B notice to quit under the periodic tenancy since A is not B's landlord.[92] But if A had granted to B a sub-lease for the residue of A's term less one day, this would have been a valid sub-lease.

This rule applies only where the tenant creates an interest which is certain to last as long as, or longer than, his own. Therefore, where a tenant from year to year granted a sub-lease of 34 years, this took effect as a sub-lease, not as an assignment; for the yearly tenancy might have outlasted the sub-lease, and so left a reversion in the sub-lessor.[93] Similarly a tenant from year to year can create a sub-lease from year to year[94]; and it would seem that a tenant for a fixed term may grant a sub-lease of a yearly or other periodic kind, provided that the head lease will outlast at least the initial period of the sub-lease; for there is then always a potential reversion in case the periodic sub-tenancy should be determined by notice.

14–111   **4. Formalities.** Assignments which result from "sub-leases" of the tenant's whole interest are brought about by operation of law, and are excepted from the rule that they must be made by deed.[95] Thus if a tenant with less than three

---

[88] *Hicks v. Downing* (1696) 1 Ld.Raym. 99; *Palmer v. Edwards* (1783) 1 Doug. K.B. 187; *Wollaston v. Hakewill* (1841) 3 Man. & G. 297; *Milmo v. Carreras* [1946] K.B. 306; *Parc Battersea Ltd v. Hutchinson, supra.* See (1967) 31 Conv.(N.S.) 159 (P. Jackson); *post*, para. 19–039.

[89] As between L and A there is no longer privity to estate (*post*, para. 15–004); but a forfeiture clause may still operate: *Doe d. Freeman v. Bateman* (1818) 2 B. & Ald. 168.

[90] For distress, see *post*, para. 14–253.

[91] *Williams v. Hayward* (1859) 1 E. & E. 1040.

[92] *Milmo v. Carreras* [1946] K.B. 306.

[93] *Oxley v. James* (1844) 13 M. & W. 209. See likewise *William Skelton & Son Ltd v. Harrison & Pinder Ltd*, (1974) 29 P. & C.R. 113 (head lease extended indefinitely by Landlord and Tenant Act 1954, Pt II: see *post*, para. 22–070).

[94] *Pike v. Eyre* (1829) 9 B. & C. 909.

[95] L.P.A. 1925 s.52(2)(g), excepting "conveyances which take effect by operation of law". *Parc Battersea Ltd v. Hutchinson* [1999] 22 E.G. 149. See *Preece v. Corrie* (1828) 5 Bing. 24; *Milmo v. Carreras* [1946] K.B. 306. But this point has not yet been finally settled.

years of his term unexpired purports to grant an informal sub-lease for three years at a rack-rent, this operates as an assignment of the residue of the term. This doctrine produces a paradox in situations such as that just given. If described correctly as an assignment, an informal disposition of a lease is void at law and can operate only in equity; but if described incorrectly as a sub-lease, it takes effect as a valid assignment by operation of law.

Assignments of only part of the demised land are treated later.[96]

5. Covenants and conditions. The assignment may contain covenants by either or both parties, and covenants by the assignee may be reinforced by a forfeiture clause entitling the assignor to resume the lease in case of breach. Such a clause creates an equitable right of entry,[97] and where the clause merely provides security for the attainment of a primary purpose which can still be achieved, the court has jurisdiction to grant relief.[98]   **14–112**

Section 2. Assignment of Reversions

1. Need for deed. The landlord's reversion is freely assignable by him, but in order to take effect at law the assignment must be made by deed.[99] This was always the rule at common law, since a reversion was regarded as analogous to an incorporeal hereditament which "lay in grant".[1] The rule is now part of the general rule enacted by the Law of Property Act 1925, that legal estates in land can be conveyed or created only by deed.[2]   **14–113**

2. Effect. An absolute assignment of the reversion, if validly made by deed, transfers the assignor's fee simple or leasehold legal estate to the assignee, subject to the subsisting lease, so that the assignee becomes the landlord.[3] The effect of the assignment on the enforceability of the covenants in the lease is explained in the next chapter, as is also the effect of a partial assignment.[4] Assignment for a term of years, often called a lease of the reversion or a concurrent lease, has been discussed above.[5]   **14–114**

---

[96] *Post*, paras 15–037, 15–087.
[97] *Ante*, para. 4–054.
[98] *Shiloh Spinners Ltd v. Harding* [1973] A.C. 691. For relief against forfeiture, see *post*, paras 14–136, 14–152.
[99] *Brawley v. Wade* (1824) M'Clel. 664.
[1] *ibid.*, Challis 48 (but see also 53); and see *post*, para. 18–051.
[2] L.P.A. 1925, s.52.
[3] If the property includes a dwelling, it is an offence if the assignee fails to give the tenant written notice of the assignment and his name and address within (usually) two months: L. & T.A. 1985, s.3; *post*, para. 14–251. The landlord who assigns the lease remains liable on the covenants in such circumstances until the tenant is notified of the name and address of the new landlord: *ibid.*, s.3(3A) (as substituted by L. & T.A. 1987, s.50). Where the assigning landlord had granted the lease, he would remain liable for such breaches of covenant in any event: see *post*, paras 15–012, 15–070.
[4] *Post*, paras 15–048, 15–087.
[5] *Ante*, para. 14–103.

Part 4

DETERMINATION OF TENANCIES

14–115   A lease or tenancy may come to an end in the following ways.

(1) By expiry.
(2) By notice.
(3) By forfeiture.
(4) By surrender.
(5) By merger.
(6) By enlargement.
(7) By disclaimer.
(8) By frustration.
(9) By termination for breach.

The first three of these methods of determination, and probably the ninth, are subject to statutory restrictions on the landlord's right to recover possession, as mentioned later.[6] All nine must now be explained successively.

Section 1. By Expiry

14–116   At common law, as has already been mentioned,[7] a lease or tenancy for a fixed period automatically determines when the fixed period expires. There are, however, important statutory exceptions under which the existing tenancy is automatically prolonged, with further provision for the grant of a new tenancy,[8] or a statutory periodic tenancy may arise to protect the tenant.[9]

It has also been explained[10] how a lease for a fixed period may be made determinable upon the happening of some event within that period, *e.g.* a death. In that case, at common law, the lease automatically ended when the event happened; but such tenancies, in so far as they belong to the law of landlord and tenant, are converted by statute into long terms determinable by notice after the event.[11] But in the case of other events, *e.g.* if the tenant parts with possession of the property,[12] the lease will still determine automatically if limited so as to last only until the condition is fulfilled.[13] Yet a lease until the tenant commits a breach of covenant falls within the provision of the Law

---

[6] *Post*, paras 14–134 *et seq.*, 14–193, 14–226.
[7] *Ante*, para. 14–063.
[8] *Post*, paras 22–070 *et seq.* (business tenancies); 22–185 *et seq.* (regulated tenancies).
[9] *Post*, paras 22–144 *et seq.* (assured tenancies).
[10] *Ante*, para. 14–058.
[11] *Ante*, para. 14–086.
[12] *Doe d. Lockwood v. Clarke* (1807) 8 East 185.
[13] See, however, (1963) 27 Conv.(N.S.) 111 (F. R. Cane).

of Property Act 1925 relating to forfeiture and relief therefrom in the same way as if the lease were determinable under a proviso for re-entry.[14]

Such determinable terms must be distinguished from terms made subject to some proviso or condition subsequent,[15] for in the latter case the lease does not end until the landlord re-enters; this is explained below in connection with forfeiture.[16]

Section 2. By Notice

A lease or tenancy for a fixed period cannot be determined by notice unless this is expressly agreed upon. Thus a lease for a substantial term such as 21 years often contains provisions enabling the tenant to determine it, *e.g.* at the end of the seventh or fourteenth year, in which case the length of the notice required, the time when it is to be given, and other matters of this kind, depend on the terms of the lease.[17] In the absence of any such provision the lease will continue for the full period. **14–117**

Yearly, weekly, monthly and other periodic tenancies can be determined by notice. These rules, and those for the determination of tenancies at will and at sufferance, have already been explained.[18] As in the case of tenancies for a fixed term, there are important statutory exceptions to the rules which prevent a landlord from determining the tenancies, or entitle the tenants to remain after the tenancies have been determined.[19]

Section 3. By Forfeiture

A. Right to Forfeit

The landlord may become entitled to re-take the premises, and so prematurely put an end to the lease, either under the terms of the lease or by operation of law. The former reason is by far the more common, and must be treated in detail. The latter is to be seen in the rules relating to the denial of title, which will be considered first. **14–118**

---

[14] L.P.A. 1925, s.146(7); for these provisions, see *post*, para. 14–146.

[15] In principle the distinction is similar to that between determinable and conditional fees: *ante*, para. 3–064.

[16] *Post*, para. 14–121.

[17] It is commonly provided that the tenant can terminate the tenancy only if he has complied with the covenants of the lease. This will generally be construed as a condition precedent, and while past breaches of covenant that have been remedied will not bar the giving of a valid notice, subsisting breaches will: see *Trane (U.K.) Ltd v. Provident Mutual Life Assurance* [1995] 1 E.G.L.R. 33. In the past, a landlord would often not insist upon compliance with the condition, so that he could be rid of an unsatisfactory tenant: (1987) 103 L.Q.R. 504 at 505 (P. V. Baker). With the fall in rents, this may no longer be the case. *cf., post*, para. 14–301.

[18] *Ante*, paras 14–068, 14–073, 14–076, 14–081.

[19] *Post*, paras 22–005, *et seq.*

14–119   **1. Denial of title.** The rule is that a tenant who denies his landlord's title is automatically made liable to forfeit his lease,[20] a rule derived from the feudal principle that repudiation of the lord destroys the tenure.[21] The doctrine has now been detached from its feudal foundation and justified on a new basis. It is an implied condition of the lease that the tenant will do nothing to prejudice the title of the landlord.[22] The tenant's denial of title is therefore akin to a repudiation of a contract.[23] The denial must be clear and unambiguous and demonstrate an intention by the tenant no longer to be bound by the relationship of landlord and tenant.[24] Thus a denial of title as to part only of the property comprised in the lease will not usually suffice.[25] The tendency to treat the doctrine in this comparatively narrow way is a modern one. At one time it was even held to apply where the tenant inadvertently denied the landlord's title in a pleading in a action.[26] However, a mere pleader's general denial which sets up no adverse title has since been held to be innocuous.[27] In any event, the tenant may sometimes save himself if leave is given to amend his pleading before the landlord claims forfeiture.[28] Amendment will not assist the tenant in the more common case where the landlord has already forfeited the lease by commencing proceedings for possession.[29] In the case of a tenancy for years an oral denial of title will not produce forfeiture.[30] It will, however, do so in the case of a yearly (or other periodic) tenancy. This is because the tenant, by denying that he has a tenancy, is taken to waive any notice to quit. The landlord can claim possession at once.[31]

It may be doubted whether forfeiture by denial of title should be regarded any longer as taking effect by operation of law at all. If it is in reality based

---

[20] See Woodfall L. & T. 17.302; Foa L. & T. 589. As to relief, see *post*, paras 14–136, 14–152.

[21] *Doe d. Ellerbrock v. Flynn* (1834) 1 C.M. & R. 137; *Wisbech St Mary Parish Council v. Lilley* [1956] 1 W.L.R. 121. The same applies if a tenant assists another person to deny the landlord's title: *Doe d. Ellerbrock v. Flynn, supra.*

[22] *W. G. Clarke (Properties) Ltd v. Dupre Properties Ltd* [1992] Ch. 297 at 308. See [1993] Conv. 299 (J. Martin).

[23] *W. G. Clarke (Properties) Ltd v. Dupre Properties Ltd, supra*, at 302. This is one more instance of the increasingly contractual view that is now taken of the relationship of landlord and tenant: see *ante*, para. 14–003.

[24] *W. G. Clarke (Properties) Ltd v. Dupre Properties Ltd, supra* at 303.

[25] *ibid.*, at 305. It might be otherwise if the denial related to a physically distinct part of those premises which could be forfeited separately from the rent of the property comprised in the lease: *ibid.*

[26] *Kisch v. Hawes Bros Ltd* [1935] Ch. 102; *cf. Barton v. Reed* [1932] at 367. The forfeiture in each case was brought about by a Rule of the Supreme Court that has since been revoked. These decisions were overruled in *Warner v. Sampson* [1959] 1 Q.B. 297.

[27] *Warner v. Sampson, supra.*

[28] *ibid.*

[29] *W. G. Clarke (Properties) Ltd v. Dupre Properties Ltd, supra*, at 307 (but *cf. post*, para. 14–124). Because denial of title is a breach of an implied condition, it has been suggested (*obiter*) that the landlord is required to serve on the tenant a notice under L.P.A. 1925, s.146 requiring him to remedy the breach if this is possible: *ibid.*, at 309 (not following the decision at first instance in *Warner v. Sampson* [1958] 1 Q.B. 404 at 422); *post*, paras 14–146, 14–155.

[30] *Doe d. Graves v. Wells* (1839) 10 A. & E. 427.

[31] *Wisbech St Mary Parish Council v. Lilley* [1956] 1 W.L.R. 121. However, the landlord must presumably first serve a notice on the tenant under L.P.A. 1925, s.146: *supra.*

on an implied term in the lease that the tenant will do nothing to prejudice the title of the landlord, it may be better to treat such cases in the same way as breach of any other implied covenant. The Law Commission has recommended that the implied condition that the tenant shall not deny the landlord's title should be abolished.[32]

2. Covenants. In other cases the traditional view has been that the lease is subject to forfeiture only if there is some provision to that effect in the lease. Nearly every lease contains a list of things which the tenant shall and shall not do, and these may be framed as conditions or covenants. If, as is normally the case, they are framed as covenants (*e.g.* "The tenant hereby covenants with the landlord as follows . . . "), it was thought until recently that the landlord had no right to determine the lease if they were broken unless the lease contained an express provision for forfeiture on breach of a covenant.[33] There were in fact a number of authorities which established that a lease could be determined by *a tenant* where there was a repudiatory breach of covenant by the landlord.[34] In the light of these decisions and of the fact that it is now recognised that the doctrine of frustration applies to leases,[35] it has been accepted that leases are subject to the doctrine of repudiatory breach.[36] Although the doctrine has only been applied in this country to the termination of a lease by a tenant for breach of covenant by the landlord,[37] there seems to be no reason why it should not be equally applicable in the converse situation. Both the applicability to leases of the doctrine of repudiatory breach and the extent to which a landlord may thereby circumvent statutory restrictions on the termination of tenancies are considered later in this Chapter.[38] Notwithstanding this development, it remains the practice to include a forfeiture clause in every lease.

14–120

3. Conditions. Instead of framing the tenant's obligations as covenants, they may instead be worded as conditions, as, for example, where the lease is granted "upon condition that" or "provided always that" certain things are done or not done. In this case the term created by the lease becomes liable to forfeiture if the condition is broken, even if—

14–121

---

[32] See (1994) Law Com. No. 221; Draft Bill, cl. 49; and see (1985) Law Com. No. 142, paras 5.32–5.35.

[33] *Doe d. Wilson v. Phillips* (1824) 2 Bing. 13; *Total Oil Great Britain Ltd v. Thompson Garages (Biggin Hill) Ltd* [1972] 1 Q.B. 318.

[34] See, *e.g. Smith v. Marrable* (1843) 11 M. & W. 5; *Wilson v. Finch Hatton* (1877) 2 Ex.D. 336. The authorities are reviewed in *Hussein v. Mehlman* [1992] 2 E.G.L.R. 87 at 89, at 90.

[35] *National Carriers Ltd v. Panalpina (Northern) Ltd* [1981] A.C. 675; post, para. 14–189.

[36] *Hussein v. Mehlman, supra*; *Re Olympia & York Canary Wharf Ltd (No. 2)* [1993] B.C.C. 159 and 166. See too *National Carriers Ltd v. Panalpina (Northern) Ltd, supra*, where the House of Lords cited with apparent approval the decision in *Highway Properties Ltd v. Kelly, Douglas & Co. Ltd* (1971) 17 D.L.R. (3d) 710 (S.C.C.) that the doctrine of wrongful repudiation applied to leases.

[37] But see *W. G. Clark (Properties) Ltd v. Dupre Properties Ltd* [1992] Ch. 297 at 302, 303 (tenant's denial of landlord's title a repudiatory breach of lease).

[38] *Post*, paras 14–146, 14–191.

   (i) there is no forfeiture clause[39]; or

   (ii) the lease is made in writing and not by deed.[40]

In such a case the continuance of the lease has been made conditional upon the tenant performing his obligations. On breach of one of them the lease becomes voidable at the landlord's option. It does not become void automatically, even if the proviso expressly declares that it shall: the tenant will not be allowed to set up his breach of condition as determining the lease unless the landlord chooses to determine it by re-entry or by claiming possession.[41] In one case, where it was "stipulated and conditioned that the lessee should not underlet", these words were held to create a condition subsequent, so that the landlord was entitled to re-enter upon breach of the covenant, even though there was no other forfeiture clause.[42]

14–122   **4. Forfeiture clauses.** A forfeiture clause is a provision which is exercisable only in the event of some default by the tenant and which operates to bring a lease to an end earlier than it would otherwise terminate.[43] Rather than making the lease conditional upon the performance of the tenant's obligations, the more common practice is to set out the tenant's duties in the form of covenants and then add a forfeiture clause on the following lines: "provided always that if the tenant commits a breach of covenant or becomes bankrupt it shall be lawful for the lessor to re-enter upon the premises and immediately thereupon the term shall absolutely determine". Under this sort of proviso the lessor reserves to himself a right of re-entry[44] and the lease continues unless and until he exercises it. As in the case of a condition, even if a proviso for re-entry also states that the lease shall determine or become void immediately upon the breach, it is settled that the lease remains valid until the lessor re-enters[45] or, perhaps, otherwise indicates his unequivocal intention to determine the lease.[46] The lease is thus not void but merely voidable[47] by the lessor (not by the lessee[48]).

---

[39] *Doe d. Lockwood v. Clarke* (1807) 8 East 185.
[40] *Doe d. Henniker v. Watt* (1828) 8 B. & C. 308 at 315.
[41] For the similar rule governing conditional fees, see *ante*, para. 3–066. Formerly this principle did not apply to leases (Co.Litt. 214b); but the law appears to have changed: *Doe d. Bryan v. Bankes* (1821) 4 B. & Ald. 401; *Roberts v. Davey* (1833) 4 B. & Ad. 664.
[42] *Doe d. Henniker v. Watt* (1828) 8 B. & C. 308.
[43] *Clays Lane Housing Co-operative Ltd v. Patrick* (1984) 49 P. & C.R. 72 (power to give weekly tenant a month's notice to quit if she failed to pay the rent not a forfeiture clause). For these purposes, a lease is taken to terminate at the end of the fixed period for which it is granted or, if it is a periodic tenancy, the date on which it could be terminated by a notice to quit: *ibid.*
[44] A proprietary interest, not merely a contractual right: *cf.* L.P.A. 1925, s.1(2)(e), *ante*, para. 4–054. For its application against third parties, *e.g.* underlessees, see *post*, para. 15–057.
[45] *Arnsby v. Woodward* (1827) 6 B. & C. 519; *Davenport v. R.* (1877) 3 App.Cas. 115 at 128; *Quesnel Forks Gold Mining Co. Ltd v. Ward* [1920] A.C. 222; *Smith's L.C.* i, 45, 46.
[46] *Moore v. Ullcoats Mining Co. Ltd* [1908] 1 Ch. 575 at 588; *quaere* how far this view can stand with the authorities in n. 45, *supra*.
[47] *Quesnel Forks Gold Mining Co. Ltd v. Ward, supra*, at 227.
[48] *Rede v. Farr* (1817) 6 M. & S. 121.

5. Forfeiture

(a) Peaceable re-entry or possession action. If a landlord is entitled to **14–123** re-enter,[49] he can enforce his right either by making peaceable entry on the land[50] or by commencing an action for possession.[51] In relation to residential property, however, it is usually inadvisable for a landlord to adopt the first method,[52] because if force is used, he may be criminally liable under the Criminal Law Act 1977.[53] It is possible that in such circumstances his conduct may also be actionable under the Housing Act 1988 as constituting unlawful eviction.[54] Although peaceable re-entry is still used in relation to business premises, it is generally undertaken outside office hours to avoid possible criminal liability under the 1977 Act.[55] In any case, if the premises are let as a dwelling, it is unlawful to enforce a forfeiture otherwise than by proceedings in court while any person is lawfully residing on any part of the premises.[56] In consequence the normal method of enforcing a forfeiture is by issuing and serving a writ for possession.

To constitute peaceable re-entry by the landlord there must be some unequivocal act or words, as where he changes the locks[57] or grants a new tenancy.[58] Where a sub-tenant is in possession, the landlord may peaceably re-enter by making an arrangement by which he holds under a new tenancy from the landlord.[59] There will be no such re-entry if the landlord allows the sub-tenant to remain in possession under the existing tenancy.[60]

---

[49] It has been held that a landlord could peaceably re-enter in respect of non-payment of rent, even though he had assigned the right to recover that rent to his predecessor in title: see *Kataria v. Safeland Plc* [1998] 1 E.G.L.R. 39.

[50] *Aglionby v. Cohen* [1955] 1 Q.B. 558. Merely re-letting does not suffice: *Parker v. Jones* [1910] 2 K.B. 32; but see, *contra, Edward H. Lewis & Son Ltd v. Morelli* [1948] 1 All E.R. 433, reversed on other grounds, [1948] 2 All E.R. 1021.

[51] Proceedings will nowadays usually be in the county court which has unlimited jurisdiction in forfeiture cases: *cf.* C.C.A. 1984, ss.21(1) and 138 (as amended); and see High Court and County Courts Jurisdiction Order 1991, art. 2 (S.I. 1991 No. 724). It should be noted that where the defaulting tenant is bankrupt, the landlord requires the leave of the court to commence forfeiture proceedings: I.A. 1986, s.285(3). By contrast, he may peaceably re-enter without such leave: *Razzaq v. Pala* [1997] 1 W.L.R. 1336 (where this anomaly is noted); *Re Lomax Leisure Ltd* [1999] 3 All E.R. 22.

[52] Described as a "dubious and dangerous method of determining a lease": *Billson v. Residential Apartments Ltd* [1992] 1 A.C. 494 at 536, *per* Lord Templeman. *cf. Khar v. Delbounty Ltd* (1996) 75 P. & C.R. 232.

[53] s.6; *post*, para. 14–228. This section replaced the old Forcible Entry Acts 1381–1623.

[54] ss.27, 28; *post*, para. 14–201.

[55] As we explain *post*, para. 14–152, a court may grant the tenant relief against forfeiture in such a case. Although this ought to have lessened the attractions of this means of terminating a tenancy, in practice its use has increased in recent years.

[56] Protection from Eviction Act 1977, s.2. The occasional presence of nightwatchmen does not constitute residence for these purposes: *Billson v. Residential Apartments Ltd* (1990) 60 P. & C.R. 392 at 408 (on appeal [1992] 1 A.C. 494).

[57] See, e.g. *Billson v. Residential Apartments Ltd* [1992] 1 A.C. 494.

[58] See, *e.g. Re AGB Research Plc* [1995] B.C.C. 1091. Mere acceptance of rent from a third party will not, without more, be sufficient: see *Cromwell Developments Ltd v. Godfrey* [1998] 2 E.G.L.R. 62.

[59] *London and County (A. & D.) Ltd v. Wilfred Sportsman Ltd* [1971] Ch. 764.

[60] *Ashton v. Sobelman* [1987] 1 W.L.R. 177.

In cases where the tenant wishes either to challenge the landlord's right to re-enter or to seek relief against forfeiture,[61] he will commonly seek an interlocutory injunction to restore him to possession pending the outcome of the proceedings.[62] This can ameliorate the often serious consequences for the tenant of peaceable re-entry.[63]

14–124 *(b) Rights of the parties after commencement of proceedings for possession.* Where a landlord has commenced proceedings against a tenant[64] which unequivocally claims possession (as distinct from one which includes alternative claims for injunctions based on the continued existence of the lease and its covenants[65]), he is taken to have elected to treat the lease as forfeited.[66] It has been said that "there is room for argument"[67] as to the precise relationship between the landlord and tenant during the "twilight period"[68] after commencement of proceedings but before the court's final decision on whether to order forfeiture of the lease.[69] If the action is dismissed or the court grants relief against forfeiture,[70] the lease is reinstated retrospectively.[71] It is only when the landlord either obtains an unconditional judgment for possession[72] or the tenant admits the forfeiture[73] that the tenancy is extinguished. Some authorities suggest that the lease is regarded as having been determined during the twilight period, subject to the possibility that it may be restored.[74] The

---

[61] *Post.*

[62] It has been held that sub-tenants do not have *locus standi* to seek such relief, because they become trespassers on re-entry, and even if they are given relief, it will not be retrospective: *Pellicano v. M.E.P.C. Plc* [1994] 1 E.G.L.R. 104. Since that decision, it has been held that retrospective relief *is* available to sub-tenants as well as tenants: see *Escalus Properties Ltd v. Dennis* [1996] Q.B. 231; *post*, para. 14–165. The outcome might now be different therefore.

[63] *cf. Kataria v. Safeland Plc* [1998] 1 E.G.L.R. 39 (where the tenant did not seek interlocutory relief and was out of possession for nearly a year).

[64] Under the new Civil Procedure Rules, proceedings are commenced (whether in the High Court or the county court) when the court issues a claim form at the request of the claimant: CPR Pt 7, r. 2. The distinction that formerly existed between the *issue* of a writ and its *service* no longer obtains. Under the old law, the issue of the writ was not an election to forfeit the lease: it had to be served on the tenant: see *Canas Property Co. Ltd v. K.L. Television Services Ltd* [1970] 2 Q.B. 433.

[65] See *Calabar Properties Ltd v. Seagull Autos Ltd* [1969] 1 Ch. 451; G.S. *Fashions Ltd v. B. & Q. Plc* [1995] 1 W.L.R. 1088 at 1095.

[66] See *Jones v. Carter* (1846) 15 M. & W. 718; *Moore v. Ullcoats Mining Co. Ltd* [1908] 1 Ch. 575 at 584; *Associated Deliveries Ltd v. Harrison* (1984) 50 P. & C.R. 91; *Hynes v. Twinsectra Ltd* (1995) 28 H.L.R. 183; *Ivory Gate Ltd v. Spetale* [1998] 2 E.G.L.R. 43 at 46.

[67] *Kingston-upon-Thames Royal L.B.C. v. Marlow* [1996] 1 E.G.L.R. 101 at 102, *per* Simon Brown L.J.

[68] *Meadows v. Clerical Medical and General Life Assurance Society* [1981] Ch. 70 at 78, *per* Megarry V.-C.

[69] "The tenancy has a trance-like existence *pendente lite*; none can assert with assurance whether it is alive or dead": *ibid.*, at 75, *per* Megarry V.-C. It has been said that the intervening position in this "period of limbo" is "one of very considerable complexity": *Liverpool Properties Ltd v. Oldbridge Investments Ltd* [1985] 2 E.G.L.R. 111 at 112, *per* Parker L.J. See too *Maryland Estates Ltd v. Joseph* [1999] 1 W.L.R. 83 at 87.

[70] *Post*, paras 14–136, 14–152.

[71] *Howard v. Fanshawe* [1895] 2 Ch. 581; *Dendy v. Evans* [1910] 1 K.B. 263.

[72] See, *e.g. Borzak v. Ahmed* [1965] 2 Q.B. 320 at 326.

[73] *G.S. Fashions Ltd v. B. & Q. Plc* [1995] 1 W.L.R. 1088.

[74] See, *e.g. Dendy v. Evans, supra; Driscoll v. Church Commissioners for England* [1957] 1 Q.B. 330.

inference from others is that the lease is not finally terminated until there is judgment for possession.[75] In practice, each view may be correct for particular purposes. Thus the tenant has no title to the lease which he can sell under an open contract.[76] But he is a "tenant" for the purposes of both Part II of the Landlord and Tenant Act 1954[77] and the Leasehold Reform Act 1967,[78] and a "person interested" in land within section 84 of the Law of Property Act 1925.[79] Similarly, the liability of a surety who has guaranteed the performance of the covenants in the lease does not end when possession proceedings are commenced, but continues until the lease is actually determined.[80]

Because the issue of possession proceedings constitutes a decisive election on the part of the landlord to put an end to the lease,[81] he is taken to treat the tenant as a trespasser thereafter.[82] There are a number of consequences of this. First, the tenant is liable to pay mesne profits[83] to the landlord to compensate him until he obtains possession.[84] Those will normally be assessed at the ordinary letting value of the premises.[85] Secondly, the landlord can no longer enforce the covenants in the lease pending the outcome of the proceedings.[86] Thirdly, the lease will be finally determined if the tenant accepts the forfeiture,[87] thereby terminating all future rights and liabilities under the lease and for the property.[88] The landlord cannot thereafter dispute the validity of the forfeiture, *e.g.* in order to claim rent.[89] By contrast, if the tenant does not

[75] "The lease is potentially good and the process of forfeiture is not complete until the proceedings are determined:" *Hynes v. Twinsectra Ltd, supra,* at 195, *per* Aldous L.J.; [1996] Conv. 55 (M. Pawlowski). See too *Meadows v. Clerical Medical and General Life Assurance Society, supra,* at 75.

[76] *Pips (Leisure Productions) Ltd v. Walton* (1980) 43 P. & C.R. 415. The tenant's right to relief has been described as "an equity": *Fuller v. Judy Properties Ltd* (1991) 64 P. & C.R. 176 at 184, *per* Dillon L.J. See *post,* para. 14–145.

[77] He can therefore apply for a new tenancy: *Meadows v. Clerical Medical and General Life Assurance Society, supra.* For Pt II of the Landlord and Tenant Act 1954, see *post,* para. 22–063.

[78] And may therefore acquire the freehold: *Hynes v. Twinsectra Ltd, supra.* For the Leasehold Reform Act 1967, see *post,* para. 22–232.

[79] He may therefore apply for the discharge or modification of a restrictive covenant: *Driscoll v. Church Commissioners for England, supra.* For L.P.A. 1925, s.84, see *post,* para. 16–085.

[80] *Ivory Gate Ltd v. Spetale* [1998] 2 E.G.L.R. 43.

[81] *Peninsular Maritime Ltd v. Padseal Ltd* [1981] 2 E.G.L.R. 43 at 45.

[82] *Jones v. Carter* (1846) 15 M. & W. 718 at 726; *Billson v. Residential Apartments Ltd* [1992] 1 A.C. 494 at 534.

[83] *Post,* Appendix.

[84] Pending the outcome of the claim, the court may order the tenant to make interim payments to the landlord on account of mesne profits (if the landlord succeeds) or of rent (if the tenant succeeds), since some payment will be due to the landlord in either event: CPR Pt 25, r. 7; *Old Grovebury Manor Farm Ltd v. W. Seymour Plant Sales & Hire Ltd* [1979] 1 W.L.R. 263.

[85] *Viscount Chelsea v. Hutchinson* [1994] 2 E.G.L.R. 61 (tenant who had sub-let house was liable for the letting value of the whole property from the issue of proceedings because the forfeiture terminated the underleases as well).

[86] *Associated Deliveries Ltd v. Harrison* (1984) 50 P. & C.R. 91.

[87] *G.S. Fashions Ltd v. B. & Q. Plc,* [1995] 1 W.L.R. 1088; [1995] Conv. 161 (M. Haley).

[88] *Kingston-upon-Thames Royal L.B.C. v. Marlow* [1996] 1 E.G.L.R. 101 (on vacating the premises, the tenant ceases to be liable to pay rates).

[89] *G.S. Fashions Ltd v. B. & Q. Plc, supra.*

treat the lease as determined, he is not, it seems, barred from enforcing the landlord's covenants,[90] which remain "potentially good".[91]

Where a landlord has obtained a judgment for possession, he may assert his title and eject squatters. This is so, even though his judgment against the tenant is conditional and the tenant will escape forfeiture if he complies with the conditions.[92]

There can be a partial forfeiture where the breach affects only part of the premises which can be treated separately from the rest.[93]

B. Waiver of Breach

14–125   **1. Waiver.** If a landlord waives the breach of covenant he will be unable to proceed with the forfeiture of the lease. This is so whether the waiver takes place before or after he has shown that he is treating the lease as forfeited. Waiver may be express or implied. It will be implied only if two conditions are satisfied.

First, the landlord must be aware[94] of the acts or omissions of the tenant which make the lease liable for forfeiture. He need not know all the facts, as long as he appreciates enough to put him on inquiry as to the nature of the breach.[95] Mere suspicion, if it is strong enough, may amount to knowledge for these purposes.[96] Deemed official notification does not.[97]

Secondly, the landlord must do some unequivocal act which, objectively considered,[98] recognises the continued existence of the lease.[99] There will be

---

[90] *ibid.*, at 1093; *Peninsular Maritime Ltd v. Padseal Ltd* [1981] 1 E.G.L.R. 43. But see *Associated Deliveries Ltd v. Harrison, supra,* at 101.

[91] *Peninsular Maritime Ltd v. Padseal Ltd, supra,* at 46, *per* Stephenson L.J.

[92] *City of Westminster Assurance Co. Ltd v. Ainis* [1975] 1 E.G.L.R. 49. It is by no means clear that a landlord could eject a squatter if he had merely commenced proceedings against the tenant but had not obtained judgment: *ibid.,* at 49, 50.

[93] *G.M.S. Syndicate Ltd v. Gary Elliott Ltd* [1982] Ch.1 (basement used for immoral purposes: forfeiture of basement only and relief refused). *cf. W. G. Clark (Properties) Ltd v. Dupre Properties Ltd* [1992] Ch. 297 at 305; *ante,* para. 14–119.

[94] Knowledge of an employee or agent may be imputed to the landlord: *Metropolitan Properties Co. Ltd v. Cordery* [1979] 2 E.G.L.R. 78 (porters of block of flats knew of sub-letting in breach of covenant).

[95] *Cornillie v. Saha* (1996) 72 P. & C.R. 147.

[96] *Van Haarlam v. Kasner* (1992) 64 P. & C.R. 214; [1993] Conv. 298 (J. Martin). There, the tenant, who was arrested for spying, had conducted his activities on the demised premises in breach of a covenant against using them for illegal purposes. The landlord, although aware of the circumstances, demanded rent after the arrest but before conviction and was held to have waived the breach. *cf. Chrisdell Ltd v. Johnson* (1987) 54 P. & C.R. 257; [1988] Conv. 139 (J. Martin) (landlord considered that he had insufficient proof of breach: no waiver).

[97] *Official Custodian for Charities v. Parway Estates Developments Ltd* [1985] Ch. 151 at 163 (notification of insolvency through publication in the *London Gazette* not actual knowledge).

[98] *Central Estates (Belgravia) Ltd v. Woolgar (No. 2)* [1972] 1 W.L.R. 1048 at 1054; *Expert Clothing Service & Sales Ltd v. Hillgate House Ltd* [1986] Ch. 340 at 360.

[99] *Matthews v. Smallwood* [1910] 1 Ch.777 at 786, approved in *Fuller's Theatre & Vaudeville Co. Ltd v. Rofe* [1923] A.C. 435. But a transaction with a third party, not communicated to the tenant, does not imply waiver: *post,* para. 15–052.

no waiver therefore if the landlord, knowing of the breach, adopts a merely passive attitude unaccompanied by any such act.[1] Nor will there be a waiver where the landlord, with knowledge of the breach—

    (i) serves a notice on the tenant who is in arrears with the rent, calling on him to remedy a breach of another covenant[2];

    (ii) sues for rent that fell due prior to peaceable re-entry or the issue of possession proceedings[3]; or

    (iii) sends a letter in the course of negotiations which does not unequivocally indicate that he regards the lease as subsisting.[4]

By contrast, a waiver will be implied when a landlord[5] with knowledge of **14–126** the breach—

    (i) demands,[6] sues for[7] or accepts[8] rent falling due after the breach[9];

    (ii) distrains for rent, whether due before or after the breach[10];

    (iii) agrees to grant a lease to the tenant to commence from the normal determination of the existing lease[11];

    (iv) offers to purchase the tenant's interest in the property[12]; or

---

[1] *Perry v. Davis* (1858) 3 C.B.(N.S.) 769.

[2] *Church Commissioners for England v. Nodjoumi* (1985) 51 P. & C.R. 155. Service of such a notice (under L.P.A. 1925, s.146; *post*, para. 14–146) is a statutory prerequisite to forfeiture and cannot therefore affirm the existence of the lease.

[3] *Kapur v. Houghton* (1995) 70 P. & C.R. D27. See too *Re A Debtor* [1995] 1 W.L.R. 1127 at 1131 (where re-entry was subsequent to the commencement of proceedings for the recovery of rent arrears).

[4] *Expert Clothing Service & Sales Ltd v. Hillgate House Ltd, supra*, at 360, 361; *Re National Jazz Centre Ltd* [1988] 2 E.G.L.R. 57. See too *Yorkshire Metropolitan Properties Ltd v. Co-operative Retail Services Ltd* [1997] E.G.C.S. 57 (sending invoice for insurance premiums not a waiver of other breaches of covenant).

[5] Or his agent, having actual or ostensible authority: see *John Lewis Plc v. Viscount Chelsea* (1993) 67 P. & C.R. 120 at 138. In that case receipt by the landlord's bankers of rent that had not been demanded was held not to amount to waiver. On discovering the payment, the landlord had returned it.

[6] *Segal Securities Ltd v. Thoseby* [1963] 1 Q.B. 887. For the special position of a statutory tenant under the Rent Act 1977, see *Trustees of Henry Smith's Charity v. Willson* [1983] Q.B. 316.

[7] *Dendy v. Nicholl* (1854) 4 C.B.(N.S.) 376.

[8] *Doe d. Gatehouse v. Rees* (1838) 4 Bing. N.C. 384. This will be so even though (as is commonly the case) the landlord's acceptance of the rent is accidental: *Greenwich L.B.C. v. Discreet Selling Estates Ltd* (1990) 61 P. & C.R. 405 at 409.

[9] *Goodright d. Charter v. Cordwent* (1795) 6 T.R. 219.

[10] *Doe d. David v. Williams* (1835) 7 C. & P. 322.

[11] *Ward v. Day* (1864) 5 B. & S. 359.

[12] *Bader Properties Ltd v. Linley Property Investments Ltd* (1967) 19 P. & C.R. 620 at 641.

(v) begins proceedings to enforce a particular provision of the lease.[13]

Although there will be waiver if the landlord demands or accepts rent after he has served a notice[14] requiring the tenant to remedy the breach,[15] there will be none if such acts occur *after* the landlord has commenced proceedings for possession or re-entered.[16] That initiation of proceedings is "such a final election by the landlord to determine the tenancy that subsequent receipt of rent is no waiver of the forfeiture".[17] However, a waiver by demand or acceptance of rent is not excluded merely because—

(i) the lease provided that any waiver must be in writing[18];

(ii) the rent was accepted "without prejudice"[19]; or

(iii) the demand and acceptance were due to a clerical error[20] or were in some other way accidental.[21]

Although it is a question of fact whether money has been tendered and accepted as rent, such acceptance once proved is in law a waiver, regardless of the intention with which it was demanded or received.[22] However, cases of acceptance of rent "fall into a special category", and in other situations the court is less rigid in its approach. It is "free to look at *all* the circumstances of the case" to determine whether the act alleged to constitute a waiver was unequivocal.[23]

14–127   **2. Extent of waiver.** As might be expected, the waiver of a covenant or condition extends only to the particular breach in question and does not operate as a general waiver of all future breaches.[24] The same applies to a licence granted to the tenant to do any act.[25] A waiver of the right to forfeit

---

[13] *Cardigan Properties Ltd v. Consolidated Property Investments Ltd* [1991] 1 E.G.L.R. 64 at 68 (proceedings to compel production of insurance policies); *Cornillie v. Saha* (1996) 72 P. & C.R. 147 (proceedings to enforce right to enter and inspect premises under the terms of the lease).

[14] Under L.P.A. 1925, s.146; *post*, para. 14–146.

[15] *Greenwich L.B.C. v. Discreet Selling Estates Ltd* (1990) 61 P. & C.R. 405 at 409.

[16] *Evans v. Enever* [1920] 2 K.B. 315. The same is true where he distrains after service or re-entry: *Grimwood v. Moss* (1872) L.R. 7 C.P. 360.

[17] *Civil Service Co-operative Society Ltd v. McGrigor's Trustee* [1923] 2 Ch. 347 at 358, *per* Russell J.

[18] *R. v. Paulson* [1921] 1 A.C. 271.

[19] *Davenport v. R.* (1877) 3 App.Cas. 115; *Segal Securities Ltd v. Thoseby* [1963] 1 Q.B. 887.

[20] *Central Estates (Belgravia) Ltd v. Woolgar (No. 2)* [1972] 1 W.L.R. 1048; *John Lewis Plc v. Viscount Chelsea* (1993) 67 P. & C.R. 120 at 138.

[21] *Greenwich L.B.C. v. Discreet Selling Estates Ltd, supra*, at 409.

[22] *Segal Securities Ltd v. Thoseby, supra*, at 898; *Central Estates (Belgravia) Ltd v. Woolgar (No. 2), supra; David Blackstone Ltd v. Burnetts (West End) Ltd* [1973] 1 W.L.R. 1487.

[23] *Expert Clothing Service & Sales Ltd v. Hillgate House Ltd* [1986] Ch. 340 at 360, *per* Slade L.J.

[24] L.P.A. 1925, s.148.

[25] *ibid.*, s.143.

the tenancy is not also a waiver of the right to sue for damages for its breach.[26] Nor does a waiver make lawful *ab initio* an unlawful act done before the waiver.[27] But once the waiver has become effective it is not personal to the tenant but will also benefit any assignee from him.[28]

3. Continuing breaches. Where the breach is of a continuing nature,[29] as, **14–128** for example, breach of a covenant to repair[30] or of a covenant to use the premises in a particular manner,[31] a waiver will extend at most to the time for which the landlord knew that the breaches would continue.[32] Breaches which continue after the date of the waiver will normally give a fresh right of forfeiture.[33] But waiver of the breach of one covenant will extend to a consequential continuing breach of another covenant which the tenant cannot discontinue. Thus where property was sub-let in breach of covenant and used by the sub-tenant for purposes prohibited by the lease, the waiver of the covenant against sub-letting was also a waiver of the breach of the user covenant.[34]

C. Conditions for Forfeiture

The law leans against forfeiture, and a landlord suing for it is put to strict **14–129** proof of his case. Moreover, both equity and statute have intervened so as to allow tenants to rescue themselves from liability to forfeiture in certain cases. There are different sets of rules for forfeiture for non-payment of rent[35] and forfeiture for other cases. This is because equity would very commonly relieve a tenant against forfeiture for failure to pay rent, but as a general rule refused relief in all other cases.[36] Accordingly, relief in cases of non-payment of rent

---

[26] *Stephens v. Junior Army and Navy Stores Ltd* [1914] 2 Ch. 516; *Norman v. Simpson* [1946] K.B. 158 at 160.

[27] *Muspratt v. Johnston* [1963] 2 Q.B. 383.

[28] See *Brikom Investments Ltd v. Carr* [1979] Q.B. 467 (not a forfeiture case).

[29] A breach of covenant is not a continuing breach merely because the breach can be remedied. It means the breach of a continuing obligation: *Farimani v. Gates* [1984] 2 E.G.L.R. 66 and 68, 69.

[30] *Coward v. Gregory* (1866) L.R. 2 C.P. 153; *Spoor v. Green* (1874) L.R. 9 Ex. 99 at 111, *per* Bramwell B. ("the covenant is broken afresh every day the premises are out of repair"); *Greenwich L.B.C. v. Discreet Selling Estates Ltd* (1990) 61 P. & C.R. 405 at 412. *cf. Farimani v. Gates, supra* (breach of covenant to lay out insurance monies on repairs not a continuing breach).

[31] *Marsden v. Edward Heyes Ltd* [1927] 2 K.B. 1; *Creery v. Summersell* [1949] Ch. 751.

[32] *Segal Securities Ltd v. Thoseby* [1963] 1 Q.B. 887 at 901.

[33] *Doe d. Ambler v. Woodbridge* (1829) 9 B. & C. 376; *Cooper v. Henderson* [1982] 2 E.G.L.R. 42. The fact that rent is payable in advance is immaterial.

[34] *Downie v. Turner* [1951] 2 K.B. 112.

[35] Rent does not for these purposes include the payment of service charges unless, as is common, the lease expressly provides that such charges are deemed to be payable as additional rent: see *Escalus Properties Ltd v. Dennis* [1996] Q.B. 231 at 243, 244; *Khar v. Delbounty Ltd* (1996) 75 P. & C.R. 232 at 236.

[36] For discussion, see *Billson v. Residential Apartments Ltd* [1992] 1 A.C. 494 at 512 (Browne–Wilkinson V.-C.); *Equity and Contemporary Legal Developments* (ed. S. Goldstein), pp. 844–854 (C.H.); [1994] J.B.L. 37 (P. Luxton).

is given by the equitable jurisdiction as amended by statute.[37] In other cases there is a purely statutory jurisdiction, which is quite distinct. The extent to which there is a residual equitable discretion to give relief where the statutory jurisdiction is for some reason inapplicable, is both controversial and uncertain, though it may now be of little consequence.[38]

I. FORFEITURE FOR NON-PAYMENT OF RENT

14–130   A landlord who according to the lease has the right to re-enter for non-payment of rent must sometimes nevertheless make a formal demand for the rent before he may re-enter; and on complying with certain conditions the tenant may be able to have the proceedings for forfeiture terminated, or obtain relief against the forfeiture.

14–131   **1. Landlord's formal demand.** The landlord must either have made a formal demand for the rent, or else be exempted from making such a demand.

14–132   *(a) Formal demand.* To make a formal demand, the landlord or his authorised agent must demand the exact sum due on the day when it falls due at such convenient hour before sunset as will give time to count out the money, the demand being made upon the demised premises and continuing until sunset.[39]

14–133   *(b) Exemption from formal demand.* In order to avoid the technicalities of a formal demand, every well-drawn lease provides that the lease may be forfeited if the rent is a specified number of days in arrear, "whether formally demanded or not". The words quoted exempt the landlord from making a formal demand. Even if a lease contains no such clause, there is no need for such a formal demand in any forfeiture action, whether in the High Court[40] or the county court,[41] if—

  (i) half a year's rent is in arrear, and

  (ii) any goods to be found upon the premises available for distress[42] are not sufficient to satisfy all the arrears due.[43]

---

[37] See C.L.P.A. 1852, ss.210–212; Supreme Court Act 1981, s.38; *Billson v. Residential Apartments Ltd, supra,* at 510–512. The county court has no inherent equitable jurisdiction unlike the High Court. It can give relief only where authorised by statute: *Di Palma v. Victoria Square Property Co. Ltd* [1986] Ch. 150 at 160, 161.

[38] *Post,* para. 14–144.

[39] See 1 Wms.Saund. (1871) 434 *et seq.,* being notes to *Duppa v. Mayo* (1669).

[40] C.L.P.A. 1852, s.210.

[41] C.C.A. 1984, s.139(1).

[42] See *post,* para. 14–253. If the premises are locked, no distress can be "found" and the Act is satisfied: *Hammond v. Mather* (1862) 3 F. & F. 151.

[43] "All arrears": not merely half a year's rent, if more is due: *Cross v. Jordan* (1853) 8 Exch. 149.

2. Tenant's right to stay proceedings

(a) Tenant's statutory right. If the landlord brings an action for possession, **14–134** the tenant has a statutory right[44] to have the action discontinued (*i.e.* terminated) by himself[45] paying all arrears of rent and costs—

(i) at any time before trial in the High Court[46]; or

(ii) not less than five clear days before trial in the county court.[47]

Where proceedings are in the High Court, the ill-drafted provisions of the Common Law Procedure Act 1852 have been held[48] to confine this right to cases where at least half a year's rent is in arrear.[49] Presumably, in other cases, the decision to stay proceedings lies at the discretion of the court[50] and is not automatic.[51] No such restriction applies to proceedings in the county court.[52] Furthermore, in county court proceedings the court cannot require the tenant to give the landlord possession until at least four weeks from the date of its order.[53] That order will not take effect if within that time, or any extension of it,[54] the tenant pays into court or to the landlord all arrears of rent due and the costs of the action.[55] The tenant's automatic right to have proceedings discontinued is therefore greater in the county court than it is in the High Court.

Where proceedings are stayed, the tenant holds the land according to the existing lease without the need to grant any new term.[56]

---

[44] The court has no discretion in the matter: see *U.D.T. Ltd v. Shellpoint Trustees Ltd* [1993] 4 All E.R. 310 at 316.

[45] See *Matthews v. Dobbins* [1963] 1 W.L.R. 227 (payment by stranger insufficient under C.C.A. 1959, s.191(1) (now C.C.A. 1984, s.138(5)). Payment may, however, be made by underlessees or those with derivative interests under the lease: *post*, para. 14–135.

[46] C.L.P.A. 1852, s.212.

[47] C.C.A. 1984, s.138(2).

[48] *Standard Pattern Co. Ltd v. Ivey* [1962] Ch. 432; but see (1962) 78 L.Q.R. 168 (R.E.M); [1994] J.B.L. 37 at 39 (P. Luxton).

[49] Presumably when proceedings are commenced.

[50] Apart from its inherent jurisdiction, the High Court has a statutory power to grant relief against forfeiture in summary manner in any action for the forfeiture of a lease for non-payment of rent: Supreme Court Act 1981, s.38(1). After judgment for forfeiture s.38 is inapplicable, and recourse must be had instead to the inherent jurisdiction: see, *e.g. Ladup Ltd v. Williams & Glyn's Bank Plc* [1985] 1 W.L.R. 851 and 854.

[51] (1962) 78 L.Q.R. 168 (R.E.M.). This produces the absurdity that "a tenant with small arrears may be less well off than one with large arrears": *ibid.*

[52] See C.C.A. 1984, s.138(2). The county court has power to extend the time for payment: *ibid.*, s.138(3)–(5). These provisions do not apply where a landlord has obtained a possession order against an assured tenant: *Artesian Residential Investments Ltd v. Beck* [1999] 3 All E.R. 113. For assured tenancies under H.A. 1988, see *post*, para. 22–131.

[53] *ibid.*, s.138(3).

[54] *ibid.*, s.138(4).

[55] *ibid.*, s.138(3). For these purposes, "the rent in arrears" means the rent due at the time of the summons seeking forfeiture, together with mesne profits for use and occupation due at the time when the court makes its order for possession: *Maryland Estates Ltd v. Joseph* [1999] 1 W.L.R. 83.

[56] C.L.P.A. 1852, s.212 (High Court); C.C.A. 1984, s.138(5) (as amended by A.J.A. 1985) (county court).

14–135   *(b) Rights of underlessees and mortgagees.* Where the landlord has begun possession proceedings against a tenant, any underlessees or mortgagees have the same rights to seek a stay as does the tenant, if they pay the arrears of rent and costs due to the landlord from the tenant.[57] This is so whether the action is in the High Court or the county court and even though the underlessees or mortgagees are not parties to the proceedings against the tenant.[58] Furthermore, in such circumstances and "somewhat remarkably",[59] the lease is retrospectively reinstated and is vested in the underlessee or mortgagee instead of the tenant.[60] Because relief takes the form of the retrospective reinstatement of the lease in the underlessee or mortgagee, the landlord cannot claim mesne profits[61] for the period between the service of the proceedings and the date of judgment, but only the rent due. Where the property is held on a long lease at a low ground rent, the differences between these sums can be considerable.[62]

14–136   **3. Tenant's claim to relief.** Even where the tenant has no other defence, he may still be able to escape forfeiture by claiming relief. This jurisdiction is much used. It is of great importance to tenants, and it greatly qualifies the landlord's common law right of forfeiture.

14–137   *(a) The claim.* Equity considered that a right of re-entry, in whatever form it was reserved,[63] was merely security for payment of the rent,[64] so that if—

  (i) the tenant paid the rent due; and

  (ii) the tenant paid any expenses to which the landlord had been put; and

  (iii) it was just and equitable to grant relief,

equity would restore the tenant to his position despite the forfeiture of the lease.[65] This equitable jurisdiction to grant relief was of course discretionary.[66] It was not given as of right as is the case where proceedings are discontinued as explained above.

---

[57] C.L.P.A. 1852, s.212; Supreme Court Act 1981, s.38(2); C.C.A. 1984, ss.138(5), 140.
[58] *Doe d. Wyatt v. Byron* (1845) 1 C.B. 623; *U.D.T. Ltd v. Shellpoint Trustees Ltd* [1993] 4 All E.R. 310 at 317, 318; *Escalus Properties Ltd v. Robinson* [1996] Q.B. 231 at 244; [1986] Conv. 187 at 190, 191 (S. Tromans).
[59] *Bank of Ireland Home Mortgages v. South Lodge Developments* [1996] 1 E.G.L.R. 91 at 93, *per* Lightman J. Yet the outcome follows naturally from the wording of the statutory provisions.
[60] *Escalus Properties Ltd v. Robinson, supra.*
[61] These will normally be assessed as the ordinary letting value of the premises: *ante*, para. 14–124.
[62] *Escalus Properties Ltd v. Robinson, supra*, at 242.
[63] *Richard Clarke & Co. Ltd v. Widnall* [1976] 1 W.L.R. 845 (right to determine tenancy by giving notice).
[64] See, *e.g. Ladup Ltd v. Williams & Glyn's Bank Plc* [1985] 1 W.L.R. 851 at 860.
[65] See *Howard v. Fanshawe* [1895] 2 Ch. 581; *Belgravia Insurance Co. Ltd v. Meah* [1964] 1 Q.B. 436.
[66] See, *e.g. Silverman v. A.F.C.O. (U.K.) Ltd* (1988) 56 P. & C.R. 185; and *post*, para. 14–141.

(b) Time-limit. Originally there was no limit to the time within which **14–138** application for relief had to be made,[67] apart from the general principle that equity would give no assistance to stale claims. But this was inconvenient[68] and in 1730 the power to give relief was curtailed.[69]

(1) HIGH COURT PROCEEDINGS. The position today as regards proceedings in **14–139** the High Court is that where the landlord has obtained judgment for possession in the circumstances which dispense him from making a formal demand for rent,[70] an application for relief must be made within six months of execution of the judgment.[71] In other cases[72] the equitable jurisdiction to grant relief is unimpaired.[73] Although the court may adopt a similar time limit[74] "as a guide",[75] it will not "boggle at a matter of days".[76] Where relief is given, the lease is retrospectively reinstated.[77]

(2) COUNTY COURT PROCEEDINGS. Where a landlord has peaceably **14–140** re-entered for non-payment of rent, the county court has a statutory power to grant relief to the tenant if he applies at any time within six months from the date of re-entry.[78] Formerly, where there were forfeiture proceedings, the court had no power to give relief after its order for possession was effective.[79] Nor could a tenant seek relief in the High Court in such circumstances,[80] because he was "barred from all relief".[81] However, in 1985 the law was changed and the county court may now give relief at any time within six months from the date on which the landlord recovers possession.[82] Where relief is given, the tenant holds under the original lease.[83] A tenant who fails to apply within six

---

[67] *Hill v. Barclay* (1811) 18 Ves. 56 at 59, 60. For the historical background, see [1994] J.B.L. 37 at 38 (P. Luxton).

[68] See *Platt on Leases* (1847), vol. 2, p. 475.

[69] L. & T.A. 1730, ss.2, 4.

[70] For these, see *ante*, para. 14–133.

[71] C.L.P.A. 1852, ss.210–212 (replacing the provisions of L. & T.A. 1730).

[72] As where forfeiture proceedings are taken where less than six months' rent is in arrears, or the landlord re-enters peaceably.

[73] *Lovelock v. Margo* [1963] 2 Q.B. 786; *Di Palma v. Victoria Square Property Co. Ltd* [1984] Ch. 346 at 366 (on appeal [1986] Ch. 150).

[74] *Howard v. Fanshawe* [1895] 2 Ch. 581 at 589.

[75] *Di Palma v. Victoria Square Property Co. Ltd, supra, per* Scott J.

[76] *Thatcher v. C.H. Pearce & Sons (Contractors) Ltd* [1968] 1 W.L.R. 748 at 756, *per* Simon P. (non-contentious re-entry; relief granted on application made six months and four days later).

[77] This is so whether relief is given under the statutory or inherent jurisdiction: see C.L.P.A. 1852, s.212; Supreme Court Act 1981, s.38(2); *Howard v. Fanshawe* [1895] 2 Ch. 581 at 592.

[78] C.C.A. 1984, s.139(2), (3).

[79] *Di Palma v. Victoria Square Property Co. Ltd* [1986] Ch. 150.

[80] *ibid.*, overruling *Jones v. Barnett* [1984] Ch. 500 (which had held that the High Court could give relief). The tenant's subsequent proceedings before the European Commission of Human Rights, alleging breach of E.C.H.R., Art. 8; Art. 1 of Protocol 1, were unsuccessful: see *Di Palma v. U.K.* (1988) 10 E.H.R.R. 149.

[81] C.C.A. 1984, s.138(7).

[82] *ibid.*, s.138(9A) (inserted by A.J.A. 1985).

[83] *ibid.*, s.138(9B) (inserted by A.J.A. 1985).

months is barred from all relief whether in the county court or the High Court.[84]

14–141   *(c) Discretion.* Save in very exceptional circumstances, the court will grant the tenant relief against forfeiture if it is sought within the six-month period, on payment of all arrears of rent and costs.[85] Relief will be granted to the tenant even though he is insolvent,[86] he has been a bad payer in the past,[87] or the landlord has other grounds of complaint against him.[88] This approach follows from the fact that equity regards the right of re-entry as mere security for payment of the rent.[89] There are, however, limits to equity's indulgence, as where the conduct of the tenant has been sufficiently shocking to disqualify him from claiming any relief or assistance whatever,[90] or where no rent has been paid for years and the tenancy has been treated as at an end.[91] Furthermore, the court may refuse relief if the landlord has granted a third party an interest in the property within the six-month period if their conduct was reasonable and not precipitate and the grant of relief would cause either or both of them injustice.[92] This situation is most likely to arise where the tenant has in some way led the landlord to believe that relief will not be sought but then applies towards the end of the six-month period.[93] In such cases two questions arise. First, if the transaction in favour of the purchaser has been completed, was the purchaser bound by the tenant's claim to relief? The circumstances in which that will be so are considered below.[94] Even if the purchaser is not bound, the court may still give relief as between the landlord and the tenant, *e.g.* by granting the tenant a reversionary lease.[95] Secondly, if the transaction has not been completed, or if the purchaser took subject to the tenant's claim to relief, then the reasonableness of the parties' conduct will largely depend upon their knowledge.[96] Thus, if the intending purchaser was (or ought to have been) aware that the six-month period for relief had not

---

[84] *U.D.T. Ltd v. Shellpoint Trustees Ltd* [1993] 4 All E.R. 310. For a valuable comment on this important case, see (1994) 110 L.Q.R. 15 (N. Gravells).

[85] *Gill v. Lewis* [1956] 2 Q.B. 1; *Re Brompton Securities (No. 2)* [1988] 3 All E.R. 677 at 680.

[86] *Re Brompton Securities (No. 2), supra.*

[87] *Gill v. Lewis, supra,* at 17. This particular indulgence is rightly regarded as a source of grievance by many landlords.

[88] *Gill v. Lewis, supra,* at 13.

[89] *Chandless-Chandless v. Nicholson* [1942] 2 K.B. 321 at 323; and see *ante,* para. 14–137.

[90] *Gill v. Lewis, supra,* at 13, 14, where Jenkins L.J. instanced a tenant who was notoriously using the premises "as a disorderly house". But in that case, the court granted relief even though the tenant was in prison for indecently assaulting two boys on the premises.

[91] *Public Trustee v. Westbrook* [1965] 1 W.L.R. 1160 (bombed site: no rent paid for 22 years). *cf. Re Brompton Securities (No. 2), supra,* at 680.

[92] *Silverman v. A.F.C.O. (U.K.) Ltd* (1988) 56 P. & C.R. 185 at 192, 193, *per* Slade L.J.

[93] See *Stanhope v. Haworth* (1886) 3 T.L.R. 34; *Silverman v. A.F.C.O. (U.K.) Ltd, supra.*

[94] *Post,* para. 14–145.

[95] See *Bank of Ireland Home Mortgages v. South Lodge Developments* [1996] 1 E.G.L.R. 91 at 93. *cf. Bhojwani v. Kingsley Investment Trust Ltd* [1992] 2 E.G.L.R. 70 and 74.

[96] *Bank of Ireland Home Mortgages v. South Lodge Developments, supra,* at 94.

expired, but failed to make any enquiries, the court might grant relief to the tenant.[97]

Because relief is discretionary, in addition to requiring payment of all arrears and costs, the court may impose further terms on the tenant, *e.g.* that he should execute outstanding repairs.[98]

(d) Derivative interests. Where a lease is forfeited, any derivative interests **14–142** created out of it, such as mortgages and underleases, automatically come to an end.[99] This is because "every subordinate interest must perish with the superior interest on which it is dependent".[1] But an underlessee or mortgagee has the same right to apply for relief against forfeiture of the head lease as has the tenant who holds under it.[2] The existence of a number of overlapping (and not always consistent) statutory provisions does, however, mean that the law is needlessly complex.

The form of relief sought is likely to depend on whether the applicant is a mortgagee or an underlessee.[3] Where a mortgagee[4] applies for relief, he will almost invariably seek to have the defaulting lessee's term vested in him. He will hold it by way of substituted security[5] and subject therefore both to the lessee's equity of redemption and to his obligations to account to subsequent mortgagees should he realise the security.[6] This could lead to the curious result that the defaulting lessee could redeem the mortgage, and the landlord might find himself once again with an undesirable tenant whose lease he had previously forfeited.[7]

The position is even more difficult where an underlessee seeks relief. His lease will necessarily be of shorter duration than the defaulting lessee's, perhaps substantially so. It may also comprise only part of the property demised by the superior lease. In some cases therefore an underlessee may seek to have the lessee's lease vested in him. In others, he may seek a new

---

[97] *ibid.*

[98] *Newbolt v. Bingham* (1895) 72 L.T. 852; *Belgravia Insurance Co. Ltd v. Meah* [1964] 1 Q.B. 436.

[99] *G.W. Ry v. Smith* (1876) 2 Ch.D. 235 at 253; *Viscount Chelsea v. Hutchinson* [1994] 2 E.G.L.R. 61 and 62. There are two statutory exceptions to this rule: see Rent Act 1977, s.137; H.A. 1988, s.18 (sub-tenancy continues where protected, statutory or assured tenancy terminated).

[1] *Bendall v. McWhirter* [1952] 2 Q.B. 466 at 487, *per* Romer L.J. The position may be different in relation to statutory tenancies that arose under the Rent Acts: *Jessamine Investments Ltd v. Schwartz* [1978] Q.B. 64.

[2] For an illuminating analysis, see [1986] Conv. 187 (S. Tromans).

[3] *ibid.*, at pp. 197 *et seq.*

[4] Who for these purposes includes an equitable chargee: *Ladup Ltd v. Williams & Glyn's Bank Plc* [1985] 1 W.L.R. 851; *Croydon (Unique) Ltd v. Wright* [1999] 4 All E.R. 257 (in each case the applicant had obtained a charging order). The decision to the contrary in *Bland v. Ingrams Estates Ltd* [1999] 25 E.G. 185, is now in doubt: see *Croydon (Unique) Ltd v. Wright* at 266.

[5] *Chelsea Estates Investment Trust Co. Ltd v. Marche* [1955] Ch. 328; *Official Custodian for Charities v. Parway Estates Developments Ltd* [1985] Ch. 151 at 164.

[6] For the mortgagor's equity of redemption, see *post*, para. 19–017. For the obligations of a mortgagee to account to any subsequent mortgagees for the proceeds of sale of the mortgaged property, see *post*, paras 19–063, 19–064.

[7] For the anomalies that arise in this situation, see *Chelsea Estates Investment Trust Co. Ltd v. Marche, supra,* at 338, 339; (1955) 18 M.L.R. 301 (L. A. Sheridan).

lease that is of lesser duration, of part only of the property, or both. In the former case, if the court grants such relief, the term will be assigned to the underlessee. In some circumstances this would appear to be excessively generous to him, as where the term is a long lease granted at a premium with a ground rent and the underlease is for a short term at a rack rent. In such circumstances, the underlessee should in principle be required to make some payment to the landlord for the value of the lease as well as meeting the outstanding arrears and costs. Yet the court does not have power to impose terms in all cases where relief against forfeiture for non-payment of rent is given.

14–143   During the course of forfeiture proceedings, whether in the High Court[8] or the county court,[9] relief may be given to any underlessee or mortgagee on payment of arrears of rent and costs. In the county court the right to obtain relief is automatic and not discretionary[10] and continues until possession is given, which must be not less than four weeks from the court's order.[11] The form of relief in either court will be an order retrospectively vesting the lease in the applicant.[12] It is also the case that where a lessor is proceeding by action or otherwise[13] to enforce a right of re-entry for non-payment of rent, an underlessee or mortgagee may seek relief under the provisions of the Law of Property Act 1925 which are explained in more detail later.[14] On such an application, the court may prospectively[15] grant a new lease of the property or any part of it for the whole term of the lease or for a lesser term. Such relief may be given on such terms and conditions[16] as the court in the circumstances of each case may think fit. In practice these will be the payment of the outstanding rent until the proceedings for forfeiture were commenced and mesne profits thereafter, together with costs.[17]

Where relief is sought within six months of the landlord peaceably re-entering, the underlessee or mortgagee may seek an order retrospectively vesting the lease in him.[18] In the High Court relief is given on payment of arrears of rent and costs. In the county court relief may be given on such terms

---

[8] Supreme Court Act 1981, s.38; *Escalus Properties Ltd v. Robinson* [1996] Q.B. 231 at 245. The section has no application after judgment has been given: *Ladup Ltd v. Williams & Glyn's Bank Plc, supra*, at 854.

[9] C.C.A. 1984, ss.138(5), 140; *U.D.T. Ltd v. Shellpoint Trustees Ltd* [1993] 4 All E.R. 310 at 315–318.

[10] See *U.D.T. Ltd v. Shellpoint Trustees Ltd, supra*, at 316.

[11] C.C.A. 1984, s.138(3).

[12] Supreme Court Act 1981, s.38(2); C.C.A. 1984, s.138(5).

[13] For the meaning of this expression, see *post*, para. 14–152.

[14] s.146(4); *post*, para. 14–162.

[15] See *Cadogan v. Dimovic* [1984] 1 W.L.R. 609 at 613, 616; *Official Custodian for Charities v. Mackey* [1985] Ch. 168.

[16] As to "execution of any deed or other document, payment of rent, costs, expenses, damages, compensation, giving security, or otherwise": L.P.A. 1925, s.146(4).

[17] *Escalus Properties Ltd v. Robinson, supra*, at 242.

[18] As regards the High Court, see C.L.P.A. 1852, s.212 (which applies to those with derivative interests: *U.D.T. Ltd v. Shellpoint Trustees Ltd, supra*, at 317, 318); *Howard v. Fanshawe* [1895] 2 Ch. 581 at 591. The county court is governed by C.C.A. 1984, s.139(2), (3) (s.139(3) was inserted by A.J.A. 1985).

and conditions as the court thinks fit,[19] which in practice is also likely to mean in most cases on payment of arrears of rent and costs.[20]

Where the underlessee or mortgagee applies for relief in the High Court within six months of the landlord executing an order for possession made in forfeiture proceedings, the court may make an order retrospectively vesting the lease in the applicant.[21] In proceedings in the county court the position is the same, except that the court may vest the lease in the applicant either for the remainder of the term *or for any lesser period.*[22] Relief will not usually be granted where an application is made more than six months after the execution of an order for possession.[23] This is so whether the proceedings are brought in the High Court[24] or the county court.[25]

A person who has no legal interest in the term created by the lease, such as an adverse possessor (a squatter) of unregistered land,[26] cannot seek relief.[27]

(3) DUTY TO NOTIFY. Prior to 1986, a landlord was under no obligation to **14–144** notify any person having a derivative interest in the lease that he was taking proceedings to forfeit it.[28] There was therefore a real risk that the person with the derivative interest (generally a mortgagee) might not discover the forfeiture until after the time allowed by law for an application for relief[29] had expired.[30] It remains controversial whether in those circumstances the court has any residual jurisdiction to grant relief.[31] In view of subsequent procedural

---

[19] C.C.A. 1984, s.139(2).

[20] No doubt there could be other terms if the justice of the case demanded it.

[21] C.L.P.A. 1852, s.210.

[22] C.C.A. 1984, s.138(9C) (inserted by A.J.A. 1985).

[23] But see *infra.*

[24] C.L.P.A. 1852, s.210.

[25] C.C.A. 1984, s.138(7); *U.D.T. Ltd v. Shellpoint Trustees Ltd* [1993] 4 All E.R. 310.

[26] A squatter who adversely possesses against a registered leasehold is entitled to be registered as proprietor of that lease once the limitation period has elapsed. He will then become an assignee of the lease by operation of law and, as such, entitled to relief against forfeiture. *cf. Central London Commercial Estates Ltd v. Kato Kagaku Ltd* [1998] 4 All E.R. 948; *post,* para. 21–056.

[27] *Tickner v. Buzzacott* [1965] Ch. 426. A squatter has a freehold regardless of the estate of the person against whom he takes adverse possession: see *Rosenberg v. Cook* (1881) 8 Q.B.D. 162 at 165. Where the title to the lease is registered and the squatter, having barred the estate of the registered proprietor, is registered as the new proprietor of it, his freehold estate is, apparently, extinguished: *cf. Central London Commercial Estates Ltd v. Kato Kagaku Ltd, supra,* at 959, 960; (1999) 115 L.Q.R. 187 (C.H.).

[28] *Hammmersmith and Fulham L.B.C. v. Tops Shop Centres Ltd* [1990] Ch. 237 at 252, 253.

[29] Explained *supra.*

[30] See *Abbey National B.S. v. Maybeech* [1985] Ch. 190, where the landlord deliberately did not notify the tenant's mortgagee.

[31] For conflicting views compare *Abbey National B.S. v. Maybeech, supra,* and *Billson v. Residential Apartments Ltd* [1992] 1 A.C. 494 at 527–531 (Nicholls L.J.), which favour of relief, with *Official Custodian for Charities v. Parway Estates Developments Ltd* [1985] Ch. 151 at 164–166; *Smith v. Metropolitan City Properties Ltd* [1986] 1 E.G.L.R. 52 (a case where the *tenant* sought to re-open the forfeiture); and *Billson v. Residential Apartments Ltd* [1992] 1 A.C. 494 at 516–519 (Browne-Wilkinson V.-C.) 520–522 (Parker L.J.), which are against it. See [1992] C.L.J. 216 (S. Bridge).

development, however, the existence or otherwise of any such discretion may now be of little practical importance.

In 1986 the rules of court were amended and now require the landlord—

    (i) to state in the particulars of claim[32–33] in any forfeiture proceedings, the name and address of any underlessee or mortgagee entitled to claim relief against forfeiture of whom he knows[34];

    (ii) file the particulars of claim for service by the court on the mortgagee or under-lessee.[35]

If the landlord fails to do so, he commits a clear breach of the rules of court[35a] and any judgment that he obtains against the tenant would be liable to be set aside on the application of the underlessee or mortgagee as irregular.[36] Even if no copy of the process is served on the mortgagee or underlessee because the landlord is unaware of his interest, so that any judgment is perfectly regular, he may seek to set aside that judgment, provided he has a good claim to relief against forfeiture.[37] By contrast, where the landlord does serve a copy of the process on the holder of a derivative interest, who then fails to take any steps to intervene in the judgment,[38] the court will not set aside the judgment in the absence of special circumstances.[39] In the light of these developments, it is of course now the normal practice for a mortgagee or underlessee to inform the head lessor of his interest when it is granted.[40]

[32–33] Under the Civil Procedure Rules, proceedings in both the High Court and the county court are commenced when the court issues a claim form at the request of the claimant: CPR Pt 7, r. 2; *ante*, para. 14–124. The particulars of claim must either be contained in or served with the claim form or served on the defendant by the claimant within 14 days after service of the claim form: CPR Pt 7, r. 4.

[34] CPR 16 PD–002, para. 6.8; Sched. 2, C6.3(2).

[35] This is clear in relation to proceedings in the county court: CPR, Sched. 2, C6.3(2). It is less so as regards proceedings in the High Court, where there is apparently no express provision to this effect: *cf.* CPR 16PD–002, para. 6.8. Presumably, where the particulars are included with the claim form, the court will serve a copy on the underlessee or mortgagee. In other cases, the claimant should, in principle, serve a copy of the particulars on the underlessee or mortgagee, but the rules fail to make this explicit.

[35a] At least in the county court. But see n.33, *supra*, for the doubt that now exists in relation to proceedings in the High Court as a result of the new CPR.

[36] *Rexhaven Ltd v. Nurse* (1995) 28 H.L.R. 241 at 255, 256. See too *Billson v. Residential Apartments Ltd, supra*, at 543. For the jurisdiction to set aside, see *Craig v. Kanssen* [1943] K.B. 256 at 262; *Fleet Mortgage & Investment Co. Ltd v. Lower Maisonette 46 Eaton Place Ltd* [1972] 1 W.L.R. 765. In principle, the new Civil Procedure Rules should not have affected this.

[37] *Rexhaven Ltd v. Nurse, supra*, at 256.

[38] Or, where relevant, to apply for relief within six months after execution of the judgment under C.L.P.A. 1852, s.210; or C.C.A. 1984, s.138(9C); *ante*, para. 14–143.

[39] *Rexhaven Ltd v. Nurse, supra* (copy of proceedings served on mortgagee but inadvertently filed: application to set aside proceedings dismissed).

[40] Actions for negligence against solicitors and licensed conveyancers who have failed to inform the lessor of their client's interest are a regrettable commonplace.

(e) The rights of third parties. The possibility that a tenant, underlessee or **14–145** mortgagee may obtain relief after a lease has been forfeited for non-payment of rent,[41] creates a potential hazard for any third party who acquires an interest in the land—typically under a new lease—during the period in which relief might be granted. Proceedings for relief which are commenced after forfeiture will be a pending land action[42] and should be protected by the appropriate registration.[43] Where title is unregistered, a purchaser who has express notice of the proceedings will be bound by them even though no pending land action has been registered.[44] The right to seek relief against forfeiture has itself been characterised as an equity, even if no proceedings are pending.[45] Where the lessor's title is unregistered, any bona fide purchaser of a legal estate without notice of the equity will take free of it.[46] Where the lessor's title is registered and the lease is either itself registered or noted on the lessor's title,[47] the registrar is required to amend the register in the appropriate manner when he is satisfied that the lease has determined.[48] Where a lease has been forfeited for non-payment of rent, he will not in practice entertain an application to amend the register until six months after the date of re-entry, because of the possibility of a claim for relief against forfeiture.[49] Once the register has been amended, any purchaser will of course take free of any rights that might still exist to claim relief.[50]

II. FORFEITURE FOR BREACH OF OTHER COVENANTS OR CONDITIONS

The general rule is that the right to re-enter for breach of any covenant or **14–146** condition[51] other than for payment of rent is subject to—

---

[41] Whether by peaceable re-entry or in legal proceedings.

[42] *i.e.* any action or proceeding pending in court relating to land or any interest in or charge on land: L.C.A. 1972, s.17(1); *ante*, para. 5–088. *cf. Selim Ltd v. Bickenhall Engineering Ltd* [1981] 1 W.L.R. 1318 at 1322 (forfeiture proceedings would be a pending land action).

[43] As a land charge where title is unregistered: L.C.A. 1972, s.5; and by lodging a caution where title is registered: L.R.A. 1925, s.59.

[44] L.C.A. 1972, s.5(7). No similar rule exists where title is registered: *cf.* L.R.A. 1925, s.59(1) (caution the only form of protection).

[45] *Fuller v. Judy Properties Ltd* (1991) 64 P. & C.R. 176 at 184. This result seems preferable to the suggestion that a purchaser's knowledge should merely be one factor relevant to the exercise of the court's discretion: *cf.* [1993] Conv. 297 (J. Martin).

[46] *Fuller v. Judy Properties Ltd, supra; Bank of Ireland Home Mortgages v. South Lodge Developments* [1996] 1 E.G.L.R. 91 and 93.

[47] A lease of 21 years or less takes effect as an overriding interest: L.R.A. 1925, s.70(1)(k); and cannot be noted on the register: L.R.A. 1925, ss.19(2), 22(2): *ante*, para. 6–066.

[48] L.R.A. 1925, s.46; L.R.R. 1925, rr. 200, 201. The registrar has no discretion. He must amend the register once satisfied by the production of appropriate evidence: *Abbey National B.S. v. Maybeech* [1985] Ch. 190 at 205.

[49] Ruoff & Roper, 21–32.

[50] *Bank of Ireland Home Mortgages v. South Lodge Developments, supra,* at 93 (where the title to the forfeited lease was cancelled less than six months after re-entry). This is because a purchaser of registered land takes it free of all interests other than overriding interests and entries on the register: L.R.A. 1925, ss.20(1), 23(1). For these purposes, the grant of a lease or sub-lease of 21 years or less is regarded as a registered disposition: *ibid.*, ss.19(2), 22(2).

[51] Even if involuntary, as on bankruptcy: *Halliard Property Co. Ltd v. Jack Segal Ltd* [1978] 1 W.L.R. 377.

(i) the landlord's obligation to serve a notice in the statutory form requiring the tenant to remedy the breach (if possible)[52]; and

(ii) the tenant's right to relief.

It has been explained that relief against forfeiture for non-payment of rent must normally be sought before re-entry or within six months thereafter.[53] Relief in other cases must be sought while the landlord is proceeding by action or otherwise to forfeit the lease, though this restriction has been held not to preclude an application for relief after peaceable re-entry.[54] The procedure of serving a preliminary notice gives the tenant an opportunity to apply for relief if he is not otherwise able to comply with its requirements.[55]

Both the obligation to serve a notice and the tenant's consequent right to apply for relief prevail over any stipulation to the contrary.[56] They cannot be defeated by framing the lease so that it continues only so long as the lessee abstains from committing a breach of covenant[57] or by devices such as an undated surrender executed by the tenant as a guarantee against breach.[58] There is some concern however that there may be other ways of determining a tenancy for breach without giving either the tenant or those with derivative interests in the lease an opportunity to seek relief against forfeiture. Of these, two deserve specific mention. First, in a case where a tenant, in breach of covenant, sub-let without the landlord's consent, the court granted a mandatory injunction requiring the sub-lessee (who was aware of the breach) to surrender the sub-lease on the grounds that there was a conspiracy between the tenant and the sub-lessee.[59] As there was nothing unusual about the facts, this outcome is surprising.[60] Secondly, the doctrine of repudiatory breach can apply where the tenant is in breach of covenant.[61] It has yet to be determined whether the landlord must serve a statutory notice on the tenant, or whether he may simply treat the lease as terminated by the breach.[62]

---

[52] L.P.A. 1925, s.146(1); *infra.*
[53] *Ante*, para. 14–141.
[54] *Post*, para. 14–152.
[55] See *Horsey Estate Ltd v. Steiger* [1899] 2 Q.B. 79 at 91. Although there is a statutory requirement that the landlord must serve a notice on the tenant before he can enforce a right of re-entry, it is unnecessary that the tenant should be aware that re-entry has actually taken place: *Capital and City Holdings Ltd v. Dean Warburg Ltd* (1988) 58 P. & C.R. 346 at 354.
[56] L.P.A. 1925, s.146(12).
[57] *ibid.*, s.146(7).
[58] *Plymouth Corporation v. Harvey* [1971] 1 W.L.R. 549. A power to give the tenant notice to quit in the event of a breach of covenant would presumably suffer the same fate: *cf. Richard Clarke & Co. Ltd v. Widnall* [1976] 1 W.L.R. 845 (a case on non-payment of rent).
[59] *Hemingway Securities Ltd v. Dunraven Ltd* [1995] 1 E.G.L.R. 61. There is nothing to suggest that a notice under L.P.A. 1925, s.146 was served. *cf. Old Grovebury Manor Farm Ltd v. W. Seymour Plant Sales and Hire Ltd* [1979] 1 W.L.R. 1397 (assignment of lease in breach of covenant effective: landlord required to serve notice under L.P.A. 1925, s.146(1) on assignee).
[60] See the telling criticisms of the case in [1995] Conv. 416 (P. Luxton and M. Wilkie).
[61] *Post*, para. 14–191.
[62] *ibid., cf. W. G. Clark (Properties) Ltd v. Dupre Properties Ltd* [1992] Ch. 297 at 309; *ante*, para. 14–119.

We explain in detail the general rule, the exceptions to it and the special provisions for those with derivative interests, such as underlessees and mortgagees.

1. General rule

(a) Service of notice

(1) THE NOTICE. Before proceeding to enforce forfeiture either by action or **14–147** re-entry, the landlord must serve the statutory notice on the tenant under the Law of Property Act 1925, s.146,[63] or else the forfeiture will be void.[64] The notice must—

> (i) specify the breach complained of[65]; and
>
> (ii) require it to be remedied, if this is possible; and
>
> (iii) require the tenant to make compensation in money for the breach if the landlord requires such compensation.

A landlord who fails to comply with these requirements and who re-enters the premises is a trespasser. He is liable in damages accordingly.[66]

(2) TERMS OF THE NOTICE. The subsection says that money compensation **14–148** shall be required "in any case", but it has been held that the landlord need not ask for it if he does not want it.[67] Thus if the breach cannot be remedied and no compensation is desired, a notice merely specifying the breach will suffice.[68] Reasonable details of the breach must be given, so that the tenant may know what is required of him.[69] A notice is not invalidated merely because it includes more than the landlord is entitled to require.[70]

The requirement that the notice must direct the tenant to remedy the breach if it is capable of remedy has caused some difficulty. The authorities have not always distinguished between three quite distinct issues—

> (i) whether the covenant is one the breach of which is irremediable as a matter of law;
>
> (ii) whether the breach of covenant is irremediable on the particular facts; and

---

[63] Replacing C.A. 1881, 2. 14; C.A. 1892, ss.2, 4.

[64] *Re Riggs* [1901] 2 K.B. 16.

[65] If there is no breach, plainly the notice is of no effect: see *Hagee (London) Ltd v. Co-operative Insurance Society Ltd* (1991) 63 P. & C.R. 362 (no breach of covenant where the act in question was carried out by an independent contractor without instructions from or knowledge of the tenant).

[66] *Cardigan Properties Ltd v. Consolidated Property Investments Ltd* [1991] 1 E.G.L.R. 64.

[67] *Lock v. Pearce* [1893] 2 Ch. 271.

[68] *Rugby School (Governors) v. Tannahill* [1935] 1 K.B. 87.

[69] *Fletcher v. Noakes* [1897] 1 Ch. 271; and see *Fox v. Jolly* [1916] 1 A.C. 1; *Adagio Properties Ltd v. Ansari* [1998] 2 E.G.L.R. 69.

[70] *Blewett v. Blewett* [1936] 2 All E.R. 188; *Silvester v. Ostrowska* [1959] 1 W.L.R. 1060.

(iii) if the breach is irremediable, whether the case is one where the court should give relief against forfeiture.

The third issue is considered separately below.[71] It now appears that there is only one covenant the breach of which cannot be remedied as a matter of law, namely the covenant not to assign or underlet without the landlord's consent.[72] If any other covenant is broken, it is a question of fact and not law whether the breach is remediable,[73] and this is so whether the covenant is positive or negative.[74] The issue in each case is whether compliance within a reasonable time with a notice served under section 146 coupled with payment of any appropriate monetary compensation would effectively remedy the harm which the landlord had suffered or was likely to suffer.[75] Because virtually all covenants are in principle remediable, a landlord will in practice usually require in his notice that the breach be remedied "if it is capable of remedy", so that he can proceed with his action for forfeiture if in fact the breach is not remedied within a reasonable time.[76]

14–149   Breaches of a positive covenant will usually be remediable, albeit out of time,[77] though not in all cases.[78] The extent to which breaches of negative covenants against an immoral or illegal user are remediable has been a source of considerable discussion. Normally such a breach of covenant will be irremediable.[79] Mere cesser of the user will not remedy the breach,[80] because the reputation or "stigma" that attaches to the premises does not terminate because the activity ceases even for a reasonable period.[81] In every case the issue must be one of fact. Thus use of premises for immoral purposes by a

---

[71] *Post*, para. 14–152.
[72] *Scala House & District Property Co. Ltd v. Forbes* [1974] Q.B. 575. The prediction that this case would lead to the view that the breach of *any* negative covenant was in law incapable of remedy (see (1973) 89 L.Q.R. 462 (P. V. Baker)) has not been fulfilled, and the correctness of the decision must now be open to doubt.
[73] *Savva v. Houssein* (1996) 73 P. & C.R. 150, disapproving *Billson v. Residential Apartments Ltd* (1990) 60 P. & C.R. 392 at 406, 407, and holding that a covenant not to put up signs or make alterations to the property without the landlord's consent was remediable.
[74] *Savva v. Houssein, supra*. In logic "a covenant not to do something, once broken, is broken for ever": *Bass Holdings Ltd v. Morton Music Ltd* [1988] Ch. 493, 541, *per* Bingham L.J. However, in practice, the distinction between positive and negative obligations may not be easily drawn: *ibid*.
[75] *Expert Clothing Service & Sales Ltd v. Hillgate House Ltd* [1986] Ch. 340 at 358.
[76] *Glass v. Kencakes Ltd* [1966] 1 Q.B. 611 at 629.
[77] *Expert Clothing Service & Sales Ltd v. Hillgate House Ltd, supra*, at 355.
[78] As where there has been a breach of the covenant to insure the premises which have already burned down: *ibid*.
[79] Immoral user may not however constitute a breach of a covenant not to cause a nuisance to the neighbours: *Burfort Financial Investments Ltd v. Chotard* [1976] 2 E.G.L.R. 53 (brothel in Soho).
[80] *Hoffmann v. Fineberg* [1949] Ch. 245 at 257 (gambling); *Van Haarlam v. Kasner* (1992) 64 P. & C.R. 214 at 223 (spying).
[81] See *Rugby School (Governors) v. Tannahill* [1935] 1 K.B. 87; *Egerton v. Esplanade Hotels London Ltd* [1947] 2 All E.R. 88; *Ropemaker Properties Ltd v. Noonhaven Ltd* [1989] 2 E.G.L.R. 50. See *Expert Clothing Service & Sales Ltd v. Hillgate House Ltd, supra*, at 357.

sub-tenant may not amount to an irremediable breach on the part of the tenant provided that he does not know of it[82] and he takes prompt steps both to stop it and to seek forfeiture of the sub-lease.[83]

(3) MODE OF SERVICE. The notice may be served under the general provisions governing all notices under the Act, *i.e.* by a written notice being left at the tenant's last known abode or business address, or being left on the demised premises.[84] It is sufficient service to despatch the written notice to his last known abode or business address by registered letter or recorded delivery[85] (but not ordinary post[86]), provided it is not returned as undelivered.[87] But if a repairing covenant is broken, the landlord must prove that the tenant[88] had knowledge of the service of the notice,[89] and service by registered post is only prima facie proof of this[90]; in other cases service by registered post or recorded delivery suffices by itself, and is deemed to have been made when in the ordinary course the letter would have been delivered.[91]

14–150

If there are several tenants, the notice must be served on all of them.[92] The definition of "lessee" for this purpose includes successors in title[93]; and where the lease has been assigned, even though in breach of covenant, the notice must be served on the assignee.[94] But a sub-lessee or mortgagee need not be served.[95] Nor need an assignee who takes after proper service on the tenant for the time being.[96] However, although there is no obligation to serve the notice on such persons, there is a requirement[97] in the particulars of claim in forfeiture proceedings for the landlord to give the name and address of any

---

[82] A tenant who deliberately shuts his eyes to the conduct will be taken to know of it: *British Petroleum Pension Trust v. Behrendt* (1985) 52 P. & C.R. 117.

[83] *Glass v. Kencakes Ltd* [1966] 1 Q.B. 611.

[84] Such service will be good even though the landlord knows that the tenant is not in residence and has made arrangements for all documents to be received by an agent: *Van Haarlam v. Kasner* (1992) 64 P. & C.R. 214 at 221.

[85] Recorded Delivery Services Act 1962, s.1.

[86] *Holwell Securities Ltd v. Hughes* [1973] 1 W.L.R. 757.

[87] L.P.A. 1925, s.196.

[88] Or an undertenant holding under a sub-lease nearly as long as the lease, or the person who last paid rent.

[89] L. & T.A. 1927, s.18(2).

[90] *ibid.*

[91] L.P.A. 1925, s.196(4).

[92] *Blewett v. Blewett* [1936] 2 All E.R. 188.

[93] L.P.A 1925, s.146(5).

[94] *Old Grovebury Manor Farm Ltd v. W. Seymour Plant Sales and Hire Ltd (No. 2)* [1979] 1 W.LR. 1397. In *Fuller v. Judy Properties Ltd* (1991) 64 P. & C.R. 176, a landlord failed to serve a s.146 notice on the assignee, peaceably re-entered and then served a further notice on the assignee. Remarkably, the Court of Appeal upheld the validity of the second notice. But query whether a landlord in possession can serve a s.146 notice: see *ibid.*, at 185; [1992] Conv. 343 (J. Martin).

[95] *Egerton v. Jones* [1939] 2 K.B. 702; *Church Commissioners for England v. Ve-Ri-Best Manufacturing Co. Ltd* [1957] 1 Q.B 238.

[96] *Kanda v. Church Commissioners for England* [1958] 1 Q.B. 323. See also *post,* para. 14–287.

[97] *Ante,* para. 14–144.

underlessee or mortgagee whom he knows to be entitled to claim relief against forfeiture.[98]

14–151   *(b) Time for compliance.* The landlord must then allow the tenant a reasonable time in which to comply with the notice.[99] The Act does not define what is a reasonable time. The issue is one of fact in every case, having regard to the circumstances that actually exist.[1] The nature of the covenant broken and any work that has to be done to remedy it, and the effect of the harm suffered by the landlord, are all factors to be taken into account.[2] Even where the breach cannot be remedied, whether in law or in fact (as where the provision is for forfeiture on the bankruptcy of the tenant), reasonable notice must be given so as to enable the tenant to consider his position.[3] In such cases two days' notice has been held inadequate[4] and 14 days' has sufficed.[5]

(c) Relief

14–152   (1) CIRCUMSTANCES IN WHICH RELIEF MAY BE SOUGHT. If within a reasonable time the notice has not been complied with, the landlord may proceed to enforce the forfeiture. This he may do by peaceable re-entry or by action. While the landlord "is proceeding", by action or otherwise, to enforce the forfeiture, the tenant[6] may apply to the court for relief, either in any action by the landlord enforcing the forfeiture or by a separate action of his own.[7] It is now settled that for these purposes a landlord "is proceeding" at any time after he has served a notice under section 146[8] until he has actually entered pursuant to a judgment of the court.[9] It is not enough that judgment for possession has been given, if the landlord has not retaken possession.[10]

---

[98] CPR 16PD–002, para. 6.8; Sched. 2, C6.3(2). Where the lease had been assigned after the service of the notice under L.P.A. 1925, s.146, the particulars would of course have to be served on the assignee as defendant.

[99] L.P.A. 1925, s.146(1).

[1] *Expert Clothing Service & Sales Ltd v. Hillgate House Ltd* [1986] Ch. 340 at 356; *Cardigan Properties Ltd v. Consolidated Property Investments Ltd* [1991] 1 E.G.L.R. 64 at 67.

[2] *ibid.*, In a case of repairing covenants, "times of up to a year or more have been considered reasonable": *Cardigan Properties Ltd v. Consolidated Property Investments Ltd, supra,* at 67, *per* Deputy Judge Cox, Q.C.

[3] *Horsey Estate Ltd v. Steiger* [1899] 2 Q.B. 79 at 90.

[4] *ibid.*, at 92.

[5] *Civil Service Co-operative Society Ltd v. McGrigor's Trustee* [1923] 2 Ch. 347; *Scala House & District Property Co. Ltd v. Forbes* [1974] Q.B. 575.

[6] Which includes a person deriving title under the tenant, such as an equitable assignee: see L.P.A. 1925, s.146(5); *High Street Investments Ltd v. Bellshore Property Investments Ltd* [1996] 2 E.G.L.R. 40; *post*, para. 14–161. If the premises are held by joint tenants, the application must be made by all of them: *Fairclough & Sons Ltd v. Berliner* [1931] 1 Ch. 60.

[7] L.P.A. 1925, s.146(2). Formerly application could be by originating summons: *High Street Investments Ltd v. Bellshore Property Investments Ltd, supra* (not following on this point *Lock v. Pearce* [1893] 2 Ch. 271). Presumably, if there were no substantial dispute of fact Part 8 procedure (which has replaced originating summonses) might now be employed: *cf.* CPR Pt 8, r. 1.

[8] *Pakwood Transport Ltd v. 15, Beauchamp Place Ltd* (1977) 36 P. & C.R. 112.

[9] *Quilter v. Mapleson* (1882) 9 Q.B.D. 672; *Rogers v. Rice* [1892] 2 Ch. 170; *Billson v. Residential Apartments Ltd* [1992] 1 A.C. 494 at 540.

[10] See *West v. Rogers* (1888) 4 T.L.R. 229; and see *Egerton v. Jones* [1939] 2 K.B. 702.

Furthermore, where he re-enters peaceably, he is still "proceeding"[11] so that the tenant may seek relief at least until lapse of time debars any such claim.[12] Even where judgment has been given against the tenant and the landlord has re-entered, relief may be granted to the tenant if the judgment is set aside or successfully appealed.[13]

(2) FACTORS RELEVANT TO THE GRANTING OF RELIEF. The court may grant **14–153** relief on such terms as it thinks fit,[14] and if relief is granted the effect is as if the lease had never been forfeited.[15] The statutory discretion is a very wide one and gives the power, *e.g.* to order a sale of the lease as a condition of relief.[16] If the breach has been remedied, relief is nearly always granted in the absence of exceptional circumstances.[17] It is, however, always discretionary, and it may be refused if, *e.g.* the tenant's personal qualifications are of importance and he has proved to be an unsatisfactory tenant.[18] The discretion conferred by the section is a wide one and the courts have declined to lay down rigid rules for its exercise.[19] Amongst the factors that the court will consider are the conduct of the tenant, the nature and gravity of the breach, and its relation to the value of the property forfeited.[20] The wilfulness of the breach is relevant to the exercise of discretion but does not of itself bar relief, even in the absence of exceptional circumstances.[21] However, while the court may give relief in a case of immoral user,[22] it will do so "only in the rarest and most exceptional circumstances".[23] Where the breach consists of a failure to pay a sum of money, such as a service charge, the court will apply the same

---

[11] *Billson v. Residential Apartments Ltd, supra*: [1992] C.L.J. 216 (S. Bridge); [1992] Conv. 273 (P. F. Smith). This decision has had a considerable practical impact, and has made peaceable re-entry less attractive for landlords (though it is still widely used).

[12] *Billson v. Residential Apartments Ltd, supra*, at 543.

[13] *ibid.*, at 540. In such a case, the court "will take into account any consequences of the original order and repossession and the delay of the tenant": *ibid., per* Lord Templeman.

[14] L.P.A. 1925, s.146(2). For an example of an elaborate order made on different terms for different parties, see *Duke of Westminster v. Swinton* [1948] 1 K.B. 524.

[15] *Dendy v. Evans* [1910] 1 K.B. 263; *Driscoll v. Church Commissioners for England* [1957] 1 Q.B. 330; *Cadogan v. Dimovic* [1984] 1 W.L.R. 609 and 617.

[16] *Khar v. Delbounty* (1996) 75 P. & C.R. 232 (sale ordered because tenants had a bad record for paying maintenance charges).

[17] *Cremin v. Barjack Properties Ltd* [1985] 1 E.G.L.R. 30 at 31, 32, giving as examples of exceptional circumstances gross and wilful breaches, or where the tenant was unlikely to fulfil his obligations in future.

[18] *Bathurst (Earl) v. Fine* [1974] 1 W.L.R. 905.

[19] *Hyman v. Rose* [1912] A.C. 623 at 621; *Darlington B.C. v. Denmark Chemists Ltd* [1993] 1 E.G.L.R. 62 at 64.

[20] *Cremin v. Barjack Properties Ltd, supra*, at 31. If the advantage to the landlord of the forfeiture is out of proportion to any damage he has suffered, the court is likely to give relief: *Southern Depot Co. Ltd v. British Railways Board* [1990] 2 E.G.L.R. 39 at 44. The courts have not so far developed any principle of unjust enrichment by which a tenant may claim compensation in a case where relief against forfeiture has been refused: *Darlington B.C. v. Denmark Chemists Ltd, supra*, at 64, 65.

[21] *Southern Depot Co. Ltd v. British Railways Board, supra*, at 43, 44; *Crown Estate Commissioners v. Signet Group Plc* [1996] 2 E.G.L.R. 200 at 208–210.

[22] *Central Estates (Belgravia) Ltd v. Woolgar (No. 2)* [1972] 1 W.L.R. 1048.

[23] *Ropemarker Properties Ltd v. Noonhaven Ltd* [1989] 2 E.G.L.R. 50 at 56, *per* Millett J. (night club used for prostitution: relief granted because activity had ceased, the tenant was in poor health and the lease was very valuable).

considerations as it does in cases of non-payment of rent, and will generally give relief on payment of the sums due.[24]

14–154   (3) EFFECT OF RELIEF. Where relief is granted, the lease is retrospectively reinstated together with any derivative interests, such as mortgages and underleases.[25]

14–155   **2. Exceptional cases.** In general, the provisions of section 146 concerning the landlord's notice and the tenant's right to apply for relief govern all covenants and conditions (other than those for payment of rent), even in cases of forfeiture for denial of title.[26] However, there are two cases where, for the benefit of the tenant, a landlord cannot proceed without satisfying certain conditions. By contrast, there are also two situations in which the section may have no application at all.[27] In these cases, no notice need be served on the tenant to terminate the lease and the court has no power to grant relief.

14–156   *(a) Where conditions have to be satisfied.* Where there has been a breach of a covenant or condition to repair or to pay a service charge, any notice served under section 146 may be ineffective unless it contains certain additional information. First, in the case of certain leases,[28] a notice served in a case of disrepair must inform the tenant of his right to serve a counter-notice claiming the benefit of the Leasehold Property (Repairs) Act 1938.[29] If such a counter-notice is served, the landlord can take no steps to forfeit the lease by re-entry or action without the leave of the court.[30] This is explained later.[31] Secondly, in relation to leases other than business tenancies, tenancies of agricultural holdings or farm business tenancies, the Housing Act 1996 has made provision to protect tenants from landlords who make unreasonable demands for service charges. A landlord may not exercise his right to re-enter or forfeit the lease for failure to pay a service charge unless its amount has been—

   (i) agreed or admitted by the tenant; or

   (ii) determined by a court or arbitral tribunal and 14 days have subsequently elapsed.[32]

---

[24] *Khar v. Delbounty* (1996) 75 P. & C.R. 232; see *ante*, para. 14–141.
[25] *Dendy v. Evans* [1910] 1 K.B. 263. But note the court's wide powers to impose conditions on the grant of relief: *cf. Khar v. Delbounty, supra.*
[26] *W.G. Clark (Properties) Ltd v. Dupre Properties Ltd* [1992] Ch. 297 at 308, 309, not following *Warner v. Sampson* [1958] 1 Q.B. 404 at 422.
[27] For a third exception, now obsolete, see L.P.A. 1925, s.146(8)(i) (pre-1926 breach of covenant against assignment or underletting).
[28] For these, see *post*, para. 14–285.
[29] Leasehold Property (Repairs) Act 1938, s.1(1), (4).
[30] *ibid.*, s.1(3), (5).
[31] *Post*, para. 14–286.
[32] H.A. 1996, s.81. For the meaning of "service charge", see L. & T.A. 1985, s.18. A consideration of service charges lies outside the scope of this book and reference should be made to Woodfall, L. & T. 7.162–7.234.

This will be the case whether the obligation to pay the service charge takes the form of a free-standing covenant or is part of the obligation to pay rent.[33] In the former case, a notice served under section 146 of the Law of Property Act 1925 in respect of non-payment of service charge must set out the applicability and effect of these restrictions.[34] In cases of dispute, the tenant may have the service charge determined by a leasehold valuation tribunal.[35]

(b) Mining leases. Section 146 has no application where there has been a **14–157** breach of a covenant in a mining lease which provides for inspection of the books, accounts, weighing machines or other things, or the mine itself.[36] Since the rent reserved by such a lease usually varies with the quantity of minerals mined, such a covenant is most important to the landlord. There is consequently no restriction upon the landlord forfeiting the lease without serving a notice, and no provision enabling the tenant to obtain relief.

(c) Bankruptcy or execution. Section 146 is in certain circumstances inap- **14–158** plicable where there has been a breach of a condition against the bankruptcy of the tenant (which includes the winding-up of a corporation[37]) or the taking of the lease in execution.[38] This must be divided into two heads.

(1) SECTION 146 EXCLUDED. In five specified cases,[39] on breach of such a **14–159** condition, section 146 has no application at all; the lease can thus be forfeited at once without service of notice and without possibility of relief.[40] These cases are those where the lease is of—

    (i) agricultural or pastoral land, or

    (ii) mines or minerals, or

    (iii) a public house or beershop, or

    (iv) a furnished house, or

    (v) property with respect to which the personal qualifications of the tenant are of importance for the preservation of the value or character of the property, or on the ground of neighbourhood to the landlord or to any person holding under him.[41]

---

[33] Whether it is reserved as rent or is merely deemed payable as additional rent. See the definition of "service charge" in L. & T.A. 1985, s.18(1). *cf. Escalus Properties Ltd v. Robinson* [1996] Q.B. 231 at 243, 244.

[34] H.A. 1996, s.82.

[35] *ibid.*, s.83. Prior to this Act, it had usually been necessary to take court proceedings to challenge the assessment of any service charge.

[36] L.P.A. 1925, s.146(8)(ii).

[37] L.P.A. 1925, s.205(1)(i).

[38] L.P.A. 1925, s.146(9), (10).

[39] L.P.A. 1925, s.146(9). See *Hockley Engineering Co. Ltd v. V & P Midlands Ltd* [1993] 1 E.G.L.R. 76.

[40] *Official Custodian for Charities v. Parway Estates Developments Ltd* [1985] Ch. 151 at 165.

[41] In determining whether a case falls within this paragraph, the court adopts an objective approach. The importance must arise from the special qualities of the demised premises and be such as to justify the quick eviction of the bankrupt: *Hockley Engineering Co. Ltd v. V & P Midlands Ltd, supra,* at 79.

14–160   (2) SECTION 146 APPLIES FOR ONE YEAR. In all other cases, on breach of such a condition, the protection of section 146 applies for one year from the bankruptcy[42] or taking in execution. If during that year the landlord wishes to forfeit the lease, he must serve the notice and the tenant can apply for relief.[43] The period of a year gives the trustee in bankruptcy time to fulfil his obligation to dispose of the bankrupt's assets whilst ensuring that the landlord is not indefinitely saddled with an insolvent tenant.[44] Once the year has elapsed, the tenant is no longer protected. The landlord can enforce the forfeiture of the lease (provided the breach has not been waived) without serving notice and the court has no power to grant relief.[45] Any inherent jurisdiction to do so is ousted by the express legislative provision.[46]

In one case under this head, however, the provisions as to notice and relief apply without limit of time. If the tenant's lease is sold during the year, the protection of section 146 continues indefinitely.[47] This allows the trustee in bankruptcy or, in the case of execution, the sheriff, to dispose of the lease to a purchaser at a reasonable price. If the lease were liable to be forfeited after the year without service of the notice or the chance of relief, not only would its value be reduced but it would also be difficult to find a purchaser.

14–161   **3. Sub-tenants and mortgagees.** It has been explained that where a lease is forfeited, any derivative interests come to an end with it.[48] It is therefore provided that where the landlord "is proceeding, by action or otherwise"[49] to enforce a right of re-entry or forfeiture against the lessee, any sub-tenant or mortgagee[50] may seek relief against forfeiture in one of two ways,[51] either in the lessor's action against the tenant or in proceedings specifically initiated for relief. In outline these two forms of relief, which are explained below, are—

> (i) the prospective grant to the claimant of a wholly new lease on such terms as the court thinks fit[52]; or

---

[42] Probably the date of adjudication.

[43] L.P.A. 1925, s.146(10); *Civil Service Co-operative Society Ltd v. McGrigor's Trustees* [1923] 2 Ch. 347 at 355.

[44] *Official Custodian for Charities v. Parway Estates Developments Ltd, supra*, at 166.

[45] L.P.A. 1925, s.146(10).

[46] *Official Custodian for Charities v. Parway Estates Developments Ltd, supra*, at 165.

[47] L.P.A. 1925, s.146(10); *Civil Service Co-operative Society Ltd v. McGrigor's Trustees, supra*, at 355.

[48] *Ante*, para. 14–142.

[49] For the meaning of this expression, see *ante*, para. 14–152.

[50] But not a squatter, at least where title to the lease is unregistered, or, where registered, when the rights of the lessee have not been barred. In such circumstances, an adverse possessor has no interest in the term and has no right to apply for relief: see *Tickner v. Buzzacott* [1965] Ch. 426; *ante*, para. 14–143. Where title is registered and the squatter has barred the rights of the lessee, he is entitled to be registered as proprietor of the lease: see *post*, para. 21–056.

[51] Under respectively L.P.A. 1925, s.146(2) and (4): see *Escalus Properties Ltd v. Dennis* [1996] Q.B. 231.

[52] L.P.A. 1925, s.146(4).

(ii) the retrospective vesting of the tenant's lease in the claimant.[53]

The circumstances in which the latter form of relief is available are more limited than for the former, but it may be more advantageous for the applicant. Where either form of relief may be granted, the court has a discretion as to which it may grant.[54]

(a) Relief under section 146(4)

(1) WHEN RELIEF MAY BE GRANTED. Under section 146(4) of the Law of Property Act 1925,[55] a sub-tenant (including a mortgagee[56]) may apply for relief against the forfeiture of his landlord's lease on whatever ground that forfeiture is being enforced.[57] A sub-tenant has this right whether the head lease is being forfeited for non-payment of rent,[58] for one of the exceptional matters mentioned above or for any other reason, even if the tenant himself cannot claim relief.[59] Thus even if a mining lease is forfeited for breach of a covenant for inspection, a sub-tenant (but not the tenant) can ask for relief.

14–162

(2) FORM OF RELIEF. The court may make an order vesting the whole or any part of the demised premises in the sub-tenant "for the whole term of the lease or any less term" on such conditions as it thinks fit, but the sub-tenant is in no case "entitled to require a lease to be granted to him for any longer term than he had under his original sub-lease".[60] The latter of these conflicting provisions prevails, and the court will not grant the sub-tenant a longer term than his sub-lease.[61] Conditions may be imposed requiring, for example, the sub-tenant to pay a higher rent to the head landlord,[62] to covenant with him to

14–163

---

[53] *ibid.*, s.146(2).
[54] *Escalus Properties Ltd v. Dennis, supra,* at 251; *Rexhaven Ltd v. Nurse* (1995) 28 H.L.R. 241 and 249; *post,* para. 14–165.
[55] As amended by L.P.(Am.)A. 1929, s.1, restoring the law as first enacted by C.A. 1892, s.4, and inadvertently altered by L.P.A. 1925, s.146(8)–(10).
[56] If the mortgage is by sub-demise or legal charge: *Re Good's Lease* [1954] 1 W.L.R. 309; *Grand Junction Co. Ltd v. Bates* [1954] 2 Q.B. 160; *Chelsea Estates Investments Trust Co. Ltd v. Marche* [1955] Ch. 328 (vesting order in favour of mortgagee held not to extinguish right of redemption).
[57] Before the C.A. 1892, a sub-tenant could not obtain relief if the tenant's lease was forfeited otherwise than for non-payment of rent: *Burt v. Gray* [1891] 2 Q.B. 98.
[58] This jurisdiction is then as described, *ante,* para. 14–137: *Belgravia Insurance Co. Ltd v. Meah* [1964] 1 Q.B. 436.
[59] See *Imray v. Oakshette* [1897] 2 Q.B. 218; *Official Custodian for Charities v. Parway Estates Developments Ltd* [1985] Ch. 151 at 164 (where a lease could be forfeited on the insolvency of the tenant, a sub-tenant was entitled to seek relief more than a year after the insolvency).
[60] L.P.A. 1925, s.146(4).
[61] *Ewart v. Fryer* [1901] 1 Ch. 499 at 515, *per* Romer L.J., *obiter* (in H.L. [1902] A.C. 187). The point seems to have been expressly decided in *Ellerman v. Lillywhite* (1923) unrep.: see *Factors (Sundries) Ltd v. Miller* [1952] 2 All E.R. 630 at 634. The term of the sub-lease may be extended by statutory security of tenure: *Cadogan v. Dimovic* [1984] 1 W.L.R. 609.
[62] *Chatham Empire Theatre (1955) Ltd v. Ultrans Ltd* [1961] 1 W.L.R. 817.

perform the covenants of the forfeited lease,[63] and to make good any subsisting breaches.[64]

14–164   (3) THE EFFECT OF RELIEF. When the court grants "relief" by making a vesting order under section 146(4),[65] it does not reinstate the former sub-lease, but grants a wholly new lease to the sub-tenant.[66] This has a number of important consequences. First, the new lease need not be on the same terms as the lease that was held prior to the forfeiture of the head lease.[67] Secondly, the grant of the new lease is not retrospective, but takes effect from the date of the order.[68] Thirdly, where the sub-tenant had himself created derivative interests out of his sub-lease, as where he had granted an underlease, such interests are not automatically reinstated on the grant of the new lease under section 146(4).[69] Fourthly, in the period between the forfeiture of the lease[70] and the grant of relief, the sub-tenant is regarded as a trespasser.[71] As such, he is liable to pay mesne profits to the landlord and not rent (which may cause considerable hardship where the lease was granted for a premium and a ground rent).[72] He cannot, however, be compelled to account to the landlord for any sums that he has received by way of rent from any underlessee,[73] even though he had no right to receive such sums and may therefore be compelled to repay them to the underlessees as money paid under a mistake of fact.[74]

14–165   *(b) Relief under section 146(2).* Until the recent decision of the Court of Appeal in *Escalus Properties Ltd v. Dennis*,[75] it had not been appreciated that a sub-tenant could seek relief against forfeiture under section 146(2) of the Law of Property Act 1925. The basis of the decision was that relief could be given to a "lessee" under the sub-section and "lessee" was defined to include an underlessee. This conclusion was clearly prompted by the fact that relief

---

[63] *Gray v. Bonsall* [1904] 1 K.B. 601 at 608.

[64] See *Ewart v. Fryer* [1901] 1 Ch. 499.

[65] There is no mention of "relief" in L.P.A. 1925, s.146(4), whereas there is in s.146(2).

[66] *Official Custodian for Charities v. Mackey* [1985] Ch. 168 at 183; *Hammersmith and Fulham L.B.C. v. Tops Shop Centres Ltd* [1990] Ch. 237 at 250. The fact that it is a new lease may now have a significant effect on the enforceability of covenants if the lease that had been forfeited was granted before 1996: see L. & T.C.A. 1995; *post*, para. 15–064.

[67] *Hammersmith and Fulham L.B.C. v. Tops Shop Centres Ltd, supra,* at 250–253.

[68] *Cadogan v. Dimovic* [1984] 1 W.L.R. 609 at 617; *Official Custodian for Charities v. Mackey, supra; Viscount Chelsea v. Hutchinson* [1994] 2 E.G.L.R. 61 and 62.

[69] "Such reinstatement would require agreement between sub-lessees and the relevant lessor although a measure of reinstatement could be effected by s.146(4) vesting orders made on the application of the sub-lessees"; *Official Custodian for Charities v. Mackey, supra,* at 188, *per* commences proceedings Scott J.; *Hammersmith and Fulham L.B.C. v. Tops Shop Centres Ltd, supra.*

[70] *i.e.* when the landlord either peaceably re-enters or commences proceedings for forfeiture: *ante*, para. 14–123.

[71] *Official Custodian for Charities v. Mackey, supra,* at 181; *Pellicano v. M.E.P.C. Plc* [1994] 1 E.G.L.R. 104 at 106, 107; *Viscount Chelsea v. Hutchinson, supra.*

[72] *ibid. Escalus Properties Ltd v. Dennis* [1996] Q.B. 231 at 242; *ante.*

[73] *Official Custodian for Charities v. Mackey (No. 2)* [1985] 1 W.L.R. 1308. The sums received might not be the same as the mesne profits which the sub-tenant was liable to pay to the landlord: *ibid.,* at 1315.

[74] *ibid.,* at 1315.

[75] *Supra.*

under that sub-section is retrospective to the time of the forfeiture[76] and not merely prospective, as it is when a new lease is granted under section 146(4).[77] However, the sub-tenant[78] cannot seek relief under section 146(2)—as he can under section 146(4)—where the head lease is forfeited for non-payment of rent or in those other situations where the provisions of section 146 are excluded.[79] The grant of relief under section 146(2) to a mortgagee is unlikely to cause any difficulty. It is settled that he will take the lease by way of substituted security and therefore subject to the former tenant's equity of redemption.[80] By contrast, there is a risk that a sub-tenant might be unjustly enriched as against the landlord, for reasons already explained.[81] However, as the court can grant relief on such terms as it thinks fit,[82] the sub-tenant could be required to pay a capital sum for the lease in an appropriate case.

(c) Duty to notify. The landlord's duty to give the names and addresses of **14–166** any underlessees or mortgagees of whom he knows in the particulars of claim in any proceedings for forfeiture, and the consequences of any failure to do so have already been explained.[83]

D. Reform

It will be apparent from the account that has been given, that the law **14–167** governing the forfeiture of tenancies is both exceptionally complex and thoroughly unsatisfactory in its operation. In two reports, the Law Commission has recommended its complete replacement with a new scheme for the termination of tenancies by court order in cases of breach of covenant.[84] The essentials of the Law Commission's scheme are as follows.

(i) The present law on forfeiture, including the landlord's right of peaceable re-entry,[85] would be abolished.

---

[76] *Ante*, para. 14–154.

[77] *Escalus Properties Ltd v. Dennis, supra*, at 242.

[78] Including a mortgagee.

[79] See L.P.A. 1925, s.146(8), (9); *ante*, paras 14–157—14–159.

[80] *Chelsea Estates Investment Trust Co. Ltd v. Marche* [1955] Ch. 328; *Official Custodian for Charities v. Parway Estates Developments Ltd* [1985] Ch. 151 at 164; *ante*, para. 14–142.

[81] *Ante*, para. 14–142.

[82] L.P.A. 1925, s.146(2). By contrast, in some (but not all) cases of non-payment of rent, the court has no power to impose terms on the grant relief.

[83] *Ante*, para. 14–144. See *Rexhaven Ltd v. Nurse* (1995) 28 H.L.R. 241.

[84] See Report on Forfeiture of Tenancies (1985) Law Com. No. 142 and the subsequent Termination of Tenancies Bill (1994) Law Com. No. 221, comprising a draft Bill to implement part of the first report. The proposals in the first report for a tenant's termination scheme (to enable tenants to terminate a lease on breach of covenant by a landlord) were not included in the draft Bill. For comment, see [1986] Conv. 165 (P. F. Smith); [1994] Conv. 177 (H. W. Wilkinson).

[85] Because peaceable re-entry is widely employed, its abolition would be controversial. In 1998, the Law Commission reconsidered its proposals on peaceable re-entry and issued a Consultative Document provisionally recommending the retention of a limited statutory form of peaceable re-entry.

   (ii) There would instead be a power to bring termination order proceedings to determine the lease.[86] This power would arise where a "termination order event" took place, namely a breach of any of the tenant's obligations,[87] or where it was provided that the lease should terminate on the happening of some event,[88] such as the insolvency of the tenant.[89]

   (iii) The court would have power to make either an absolute or a remedial termination order. The latter order would normally be made and would require the tenant to take specified steps to set matters right relating to the tenancy. An absolute order could be made (*inter alia*) in cases of serious or persistent breaches of a tenant's obligations, his insolvency or where he was unwilling or unable to comply with a remedial order. The lease would remain on foot unless and until it was determined pursuant to an absolute termination order.

   (iv) A landlord would only waive his right to rely on a termination order event if, knowing of it, his conduct would have led a reasonable tenant to believe that he would not rely on it, and the tenant did in fact so believe. Mere acceptance of rent by the landlord would not therefore suffice.

   (v) Provision is made for the protection and preservation of derivative interests and to cover cases where the tenant has abandoned the premises. One novelty would be the relief that might be given to a mortgagee. The court could order the landlord to grant a lease to himself subject to the mortgage. That lease would, contrary to the normal rule,[90] be valid. The mortgagee could then exercise his power of sale and, if there was any surplus, would account for it to the landlord.[91]

This scheme would be a very considerable improvement on the present law and would remove most of the difficulties to which it has given rise.

---

[86] Subject to the allocation of business under the Courts and Legal Services Act 1990, s.1, the scheme would apply equally to the High Court and the county court.

[87] Non-payment of rent would only be a termination order event at the end of a period specified in the lease or, if none were specified, 21 days. In relation to a lease granted before the coming into force of the legislation, only a breach of covenant or condition for which the landlord could re-enter or forfeit the lease would be a termination order event. In leases granted after any legislation came into force, no proviso for forfeiture would be required.

[88] This would catch "disguised breaches of covenant", as where a tenant undertakes to surrender the lease on the occurrence of a particular event.

[89] This alternative is intended to prevent obvious devices for circumventing the termination order scheme.

[90] A person may not grant a lease to himself: *Rye v. Rye* [1962] A.C. 496; *ante*, para. 14–003.

[91] Not as at present to the former tenant: see *Chelsea Estates Investment Trust Co. Ltd v. Marche* [1955] Ch. 328; *ante*, paras 14–142, 14–165.

E. Forfeiture and Equitable Leases

Where the tenant holds under a mere agreement for a lease and breaches its **14–168** terms, the issue will not be whether the court should order the forfeiture of the lease and grant or refuse the tenant relief, but whether it should decree specific performance of the agreement in the tenant's favour.[92] The extent to which the principles applicable to the forfeiture of legal leases are relevant to the grant or otherwise of specific performance is in fact remarkably uncertain.[93]

1. The law prior to the Conveyancing Act 1881. Prior to the Convey- **14–169** ancing Act 1881, the position was clear. In the case of a legal lease, the court would grant relief against forfeiture for non-payment of rent but not for breach of any other covenant in the absence of factors justifying equitable intervention, such as fraud, accident or mistake.[94] Where there was a mere agreement for a lease and the tenant was in breach of its terms, specific performance would be refused if the breach would have led to the forfeiture of the lease had it been legal.[95] It followed therefore that where the lease would have contained a forfeiture clause had it been executed, specific performance would not normally be granted except in cases of non-payment of rent.[96] If the court was in doubt, it would decree specific performance retrospectively to the date of the contract, leaving the landlord to his remedy (if any) at law.[97] Where there would have been no forfeiture clause had the lease been executed, the tenant's conduct became relevant to the issue. Specific performance would generally be granted unless the breaches were gross and wilful and could not be compensated by an award of damages at law.[98]

2. The effect of the Conveyancing Act 1881. The present law governing **14–170** the forfeiture of a lease for breaches of any covenant other than for payment of rent, was first introduced by the Conveyancing Act 1881,[99] and has already been explained.[1] One effect of that legislation is that the court has power (which it previously lacked) to relieve against forfeiture in relation to any such

---

[92] *cf. ante*, para. 14–046. Although where the landlord has peaceably re-entered the issue could arise in trespass proceedings brought by the tenant (as in *Coatsworth v. Johnson* (1886) 55 L.J.Q.B. 220), the outcome will depend on whether specific performance would have been decreed.

[93] See (1987) 16 Anglo-American L.R. 160 (P. Sparkes); *Equity and Contemporary Legal Developments* (ed. S. Goldstein), 829 at 855 (C.H.).

[94] *Hill v. Barclay* (1811) 18 Ves. 56; *Barrow v. Isaacs & Son* [1891] 1 Q.B. 417 at 425; and see *Shiloh Spinners Ltd v. Harding* [1973] A.C. 691 at 722; *Billson v. Residential Apartments Ltd* [1992] 1 A.C. 494 at 512. The point was not uncontroversial: see *Equity and Contemporary Legal Developments, supra*, at pp. 844 *et seq.* (C.H.).

[95] *Hare v. Burges* (1857) 5 W.R. 585; *Rankin v. Lay* (1860) 2 De G.F. & J. 65 at 71, 72.

[96] See *e.g. Gregory v. Wilson* (1852) 9 Hare 683 (no specific performance where there were breaches of repairing and insurance covenants).

[97] *Parker v. Taswell* (1858) 2 De G. & J. 559 at 573; *Lillie v. Legh* (1858) 3 De G. & J. 204.

[98] *Gourlay v. Duke of Somerset* (1812) 1 V. & B. 68 at 72; *Parker v. Taswell, supra*, at 573.

[99] s.14; re-enacted (with certain amendments) as L.P.A. 1925, s.146.

[1] *Ante*, para. 14–146.

covenant. In two cases decided shortly after the 1881 Act came into force, the Court of Appeal held that it was inapplicable as a matter of construction to an agreement for a lease, and refused specific performance.[2] The Act was then amended by extending the definition of a lease to include "an agreement for a lease where the lessee has become entitled to have his lease granted".[3] It has been assumed that this provision reversed those earlier decisions, so that agreements for leases are now subject to the provisions of section 146 of the Law of Property Act 1925 as much as are legal leases.[4] Although this seems correct in principle, the point cannot be regarded as finally settled.[5]

14–171 **3. Non-payment of rent.** In cases of non-payment of rent due under an agreement for a lease, a court of equity would normally have granted the tenant specific performance on payment of arrears and costs, because a court would have granted relief against forfeiture had the lease been legal.[6] This practice continued after the Judicature Act 1873.[7] As the jurisdiction of the High Court to decree specific performance is inherent and has not been curtailed, the law should in principle have remained unchanged, though some doubt has been cast upon this.[8] The county court has the same jurisdiction to grant specific performance as the High Court where the value of the property does not exceed the county court limit,[9] and so the same practice should apply there. In any event, the statutory provisions applicable in the county court to the forfeiture of a legal lease for non-payment of rent and the grant of relief in such cases,[10] apply equally to "an agreement for a lease where the lessee has become entitled to have a lease granted".[11] If these words have any meaning,[12] the relief may be given.

Section 4. By Surrender

14–172 **1. Effect of surrender.** If a tenant surrenders his lease to his immediate landlord, who accepts the surrender, the lease merges in the landlord's reversion and is extinguished. The surrender must be to the immediate landlord; the

---

[2] *Coatsworth v. Johnson* (1886) 55 L.J.Q.B. 220 (breach of husbandry covenant); *Swain v. Ayres* (1888) 21 Q.B.D. 289 (breach of repairing covenant). In neither case would specific performance have been decreed prior to C.A. 1881.

[3] C.A. 1892, s.5; see now L.P.A. 1925, s.146(5)(a).

[4] *Sport International Bussum B.V. v. Inter-Footwear Ltd* [1984] 1 W.L.R. 777 at 789, 790 (not considered on appeal to the H.L.: *ibid.*, at 790).

[5] It has been suggested that the tenant never becomes entitled to have his lease granted (within L.P.A. 1925, s.146(5)(a)) because of his breach of covenant: (1960) 24 Conv.(N.S.) 125 (P. H. Pettit). But if this is correct, the amendment made in 1892 had no effect.

[6] *Ante*, para. 14–169.

[7] See *Zimbler v. Abrahams* [1903] 1 K.B. 577 (CA).

[8] See *Sport International Bussum B.V. v. Inter–Footwear Ltd, supra*, at 790 (CA); criticised (1984) 100 L.Q.R. 369 at 372 (C.H.). The relevant authorities were neither cited nor considered.

[9] C.C.A. 1984, s.23(d). The limit is £30,000.

[10] C.C.A. 1984, ss.138, 139; *ante*, para. 14–134, 14–136.

[11] C.C.A. 1984, s.140.

[12] *cf.* L.P.A. 1925, s.146(5)(a); *supra*.

transfer of the lease to a superior landlord does not work a surrender but operates merely as an assignment of the lease. Thus if A leases land to B for 99 years and B sub-leases it to C for 21 years, C's lease will be extinguished by surrender if he transfers it to B but not if he transfers it to A.

Where, before the surrender, the tenant has granted an underlease or created some other incumbrance, the landlord is bound by it for so long as it would have bound the tenant had the lease not been surrendered. To return to the above example, if B surrendered his lease to A before C's sub-lease expired, A would take subject to C's sub-lease, for during the residue of the 99-year period A's title is derived from B and is subject to such other interests as B validly created before surrendering his lease to A.[13] This principle does not apply where instead of surrendering the lease, B, the tenant, terminates the lease by serving on A an upwards notice to quit. C's sub-lease then determines with B's lease,[14] unless the notice is given collusively by agreement between A and B.[15]

Surrender discharges the parties (and their sureties) from all future obligations under the lease but not from liabilities already incurred.[16]

2. Express surrender. Surrender may be either express or by operation of law. For an express surrender, a deed is required by the Law of Property Act 1925,[17] even though the lease was created orally.   **14–173**

3. Surrender by operation of law. Surrender by operation of law requires some act by the parties that is inconsistent with the continuation of the lease, in circumstances such that it would be inequitable for them to rely on the fact that there has been no surrender by deed.[18] The matter is determined objectively. The conduct of the parties must point unequivocally to the termination of the tenancy, but their intentions are irrelevant.[19] The basis of this doctrine is the law of estoppel,[20] which operates at the determination of a tenancy   **14–174**

---

[13] Co.Litt. 338a: "having regard to strangers . . . the estate surrendered hath in consideration of law a continuance"; *David v. Sabin* [1893] 1 Ch. 523, explained *ante*, para. 5–063. *Phipos v. Callegari* (1910) 54 S.J. 635; *E.S. Schwab & Co. Ltd v. McCarthy* (1975) 31 P. & C.R. 196.

[14] *Pennell v. Payne* [1995] Q.B. 192; [1995] Conv. 263 (P. Luxton and M. Wilkie).

[15] See *Sparkes v. Smart* [1990] 2 E.G.L.R. 245. A notice to quit that is given by agreement is treated as a surrender: *Barrett v. Morgan* [1999] 1 W.L.R. 1109.

[16] *Torminster Properties Ltd v. Green* [1983] 1 W.L.R. 676 (liability for increased rent not yet quantified).

[17] s.52.

[18] *Nicholas v. Atherstone* (1847) 10 Q.B. 944; *Glynn v. Coghlan* [1918] 1 I.R. 482 at 485; *Foster v. Robinson* [1951] 1 K.B. 149; *Proudreed Ltd v. Microgen Holdings Plc* (1996) 72 P. & C.R. 388; [1996] J.B.L. 274 (M. Haley).

[19] *Zionmor v. Islington L.B.C.* (1997) 30 H.L.R. 822 at 827, 828; *Mattey Securities Ltd v. Ervin* [1998] 2 E.G.L.R. 66 at 68.

[20] *Lyon v. Reed* (1844) 13 M. & W. 285; *Wallis v. Hands* [1893] 2 Ch. 75; *Foster v. Robinson, supra*; *Gibbs Mew Plc v. Gemmell* [1999] 1 E.G.L.R. 43 at 45. However, "surrender by operation of law is commensurate with what is necessary to give validity to the transaction the surrenderer is estopped from disputing", and, in a particular case, the surrender may only operate in relation to part of the property subject to the lease: *Allen v. Rochdale B.C.* [1999] 3 All E.R. 443 at 451, *per* Morritt L.J.

much as at the creation of one.[21] It is only the landlord and tenant and those deriving title under them who are bound by the estoppel. It does not bind third parties,[22] though it may affect them.[23]

Surrender by operation of law can occur in a number of ways, as where the parties agree that the tenancy shall cease but the tenant shall in future occupy the property rent-free as a licensee,[24] or the landlord grants a lease to a third party with the agreement of the tenant.[25] However, such surrender normally occurs where the tenant accepts a new (and valid[26]) lease from his immediate reversioner. This is so even if the new lease is granted for a shorter term than the original[27] or to take effect at a future date.[28] It is not always easy to distinguish between the grant of a new lease which amounts to a surrender and a mere variation of the terms of the existing lease which does not.[29] The issue is whether in substance the parties intended the tenant to have a new lease on different terms from the former tenancy.[30] A lease has been held to have been surrendered by operation of law where either the length of the term has been increased[31] or the area of the holding has been extended.[32] There was no such surrender and regrant however where—

(i) an additional party was added to the lease[33];

(ii) one rent was fixed for two parcels of land held under different leases on different terms[34];

---

[21] *Ante*, para. 14–095.

[22] See, *e.g. Barclays Bank Ltd v. Stasek* [1957] Ch. 28 (*post*, para. 19–124). In that case the reversion had been mortgaged. The landlord granted the tenant a new lease which operated as between the landlord and tenant as a surrender by operation of law. The new lease was granted contrary to the terms of the mortgage. As between the mortgagee and the tenant, the new tenancy was ineffective and the original tenancy remained on foot. See too *Re Arkwright* [1945] Ch. 195.

[23] Thus surrender of the tenant's lease will release any surety who had guaranteed performance of the covenants: *Proudreed Ltd v. Microgen Holdings Plc* (1996) 72 P. & C.R. 388 at 389.

[24] *Foster v. Robinson* [1951] 1 K.B. 149; *Scrimgeour v. Waller* [1981] 1 E.G.L.R. 68.

[25] *Metcalfe v. Boyce* [1927] 1 K.B. 758.

[26] *Corporation of Canterbury v. Cooper* (1908) 99 L.T. 612; 100 L.T. 597; *Rhyl U.D.C. v. Rhyl Amusements Ltd* [1959] 1 W.L.R. 465.

[27] *Dodd v. Acklom* (1843) 6 Man. & G. 672.

[28] *Ive's Case* (1597) 5 Co. Rep. 11a.

[29] "There must be something in the nature of an agreement and that agreement must amount to more than a mere variation of the terms of an existing tenancy": *Smirk v. Lyndale Developments Ltd* [1975] Ch. 317 at 339, *per* Lawton L.J. See [1995] Conv. 124 (A. Dowling). For a discussion of whether, in the case of a periodic tenancy, the withdrawal of a notice to quit given by either party amounts to a surrender, see [1994] Conv. 437 (A. Dowling).

[30] *Take Harvest Ltd v. Liu* [1993] A.C. 552 at 565. See, *e.g. Joseph v. Joseph* [1967] Ch. 78 (new lease where the parties, rent and term were altered).

[31] *Baker v. Merckel* [1960] 1 Q.B. 657; *Jenkin R. Lewis & Son Ltd v. Kerman* [1971] Ch. 477 at 496; *Bush Transport Ltd v. Nelson* [1987] 1 E.G.L.R. 71. A landlord may of course grant a tenant a reversionary lease for a further term of years to take effect on the expiry of the existing term, and this does not operate as a surrender.

[32] *Jenkin R. Lewis & Son Ltd v. Kerman, supra*, at 496.

[33] *Trustees of Saunders dec'd v. Ralph* [1993] 1 E.G.L.R. 1.

[34] *J.W. Childers Trustees v. Anker* [1996] 1 E.G.L.R. 1.

(iii) the rent was increased by agreement[35];

(iv) rent was received from a third party (who was trading on the premises under the same name as the tenant had done) in the mistaken belief that he was the tenant[36]; or

(v) a new landlord issued the tenant with a rent book containing terms that were inconsistent with the terms under which he held the property.[37]

A clear case of surrender by operation of law will arise where— **14–175**

(a) the tenant gives up possession of the premises[38]; and

(b) the landlord accepts it.

The landlord's acceptance estops him from asserting that the lease continues even though the tenant's act may be in breach of its terms.[39] His acceptance will not be inferred merely because, to protect his interest, he enters the premises and takes steps to secure them.[40] Abandonment of the premises by the tenant without more (even if rent is unpaid) is not a surrender, because the landlord may wish the tenant's liability to continue.[41] Nor is the delivery of the key of the premises to the landlord enough by itself.[42] Even if he accepts it, it must be shown that he did so with the intention of determining the tenancy[43] and not merely because he had no alternative, *e.g.* because the tenant has left the country.[44] What is normally required is evidence that the landlord

---

[35] *Jenkin R. Lewis & Son Ltd v. Kerman, supra; Friends' Provident Life Office v. British Railways Board* [1996] 1 All E.R. 336.

[36] *Mattey Securities Ltd v. Ervin* [1998] 2 E.G.L.R. 66.

[37] *Smirk v. Lyndale Developments Ltd* [1975] Ch. 317.

[38] The tenant must have given up possession completely. There will therefore be no surrender if his wife remains in occupation under her statutory rights: *Hoggett v. Hoggett* (1979) 39 P. & C.R. 121 (wife protected by Matrimonial Homes Act 1967; *cf. Sanctuary Housing Association v. Campbell* [1999] 1 W.L.R. 1279); or allows a friend to live on the premises: *Zionmor v. Islington L.B.C.* (1997) 30 H.L.R. 822.

[39] *Oastler v. Henderson* (1877) 2 Q.B.D. 575.

[40] *Bird v. Defonvielle* (1846) 2 Car. & K. 415 at 421; *McDougalls Catering Foods Ltd v. BSE Trading Ltd* [1997] 2 E.G.L.R. 65 at 69. The onus lies on the tenant to prove that the landlord's conduct went beyond this: *Relvok Properties Ltd v. Dixon* (1972) 25 P. & C.R. 1 at 5.

[41] *Preston B.C. v. Fairclough* (1982) 8 H.L.R. 70; *aliter* if the absence was longer and a substantial sum of rent was owed: *ibid.* It has never been suggested that the landlord is under any duty to mitigate his loss by re-letting the premises. The law is otherwise elsewhere, *e.g.* Ontario and British Columbia: see S. Bright and G. Gilbert, *Landlord and Tenant* (1995), p. 89.

[42] *Cannan v. Hartley* (1850) 9 Q.B. 634; *Oastler v. Henderson, supra; Proudreed Ltd v. Microgen Holdings Plc* (1996) 72 P. & C.R. 388 at 393; *Borkorat v. Ealing L.B.C.* [1996] E.G.C.S. 67.

[43] See *e.g. Filering Ltd v. Taylor Commercial Ltd* [1996] E.G.C.S. 95 (surrender of the lease the only real explanation for the handing over of the keys); *Bolnore Properties Ltd v. Cobb* (1996) 75 P. & C.R. 127 (clear evidence of intention to surrender by tenant and acceptance by landlord pursuant to a written agreement).

[44] *Oastler v. Henderson* (1877) 2 Q.B.D. 575.

entered into "profitable occupation",[45] usually by re-letting the premises.[46] Even if there is such a surrender, the tenant may remain liable in damages to the landlord, if the premises are let at a lower rent than the tenant was himself paying.[47]

A contract by the tenant to purchase the reversion does not normally bring about a surrender,[48] though the terms of the contract may have this effect.[49]

Section 5. By Merger

14–176   **1. Effect of merger.** Merger is the converse of surrender. A surrender occurs where the landlord acquires the lease; merger occurs where the tenant retains the lease and acquires the reversion, or a third party acquires both lease and reversion. The principle is the same in both surrender and merger: the lease is absorbed by the reversion and destroyed.

14–177   **2. Requirements.** For merger to be effective, the lease and the reversion must be vested in the same person in the same right with no vested estate intervening. If he holds the lease and reversion in different capacities, *e.g.* if he holds the lease as his own, and the reversion as executor or administrator, there is no merger.[50] There was formerly a difference between merger at common law and in equity.[51] At law merger was automatic, by operation of law. In equity merger was a matter of intention. It did not occur unless intended by the person who acquired the two estates.[52] Indeed, there was a presumption against merger if it was against that person's interest.[53] The common law rules have now been amended by statute so as to follow the equitable doctrine: "there is no merger by operation of law only of any estate the beneficial interest in which would not be deemed to be merged or extinguished in equity."[54] Thus there is no merger either at law or in equity if it is intended that there shall be none.[55]

The position of a sub-tenant where the head lease has been surrendered or has become merged is discussed below.[56]

---

[45] *Bird v. Defonvielle, supra,* at 421, *per* Erle J.
[46] *Hall v. Burgess* (1826) 5 B. & C. 332. Merely advertising the premises does not suffice: *Oastler v. Henderson, supra.*
[47] *Gray v. Owen* [1910] 1 K.B. 622.
[48] *Nightingale v. Courtney* [1954] 1 Q.B. 399.
[49] See *Turner v. Watts* (1928) 97 L.J.Q.B. 403 (interest payable on the balance of the price from the date of contract instead of rent: held to be a surrender). *cf.* Standard Conditions of Sale (3rd ed.), c. 5.2.1. (which obviates this problem).
[50] *Chambers v. Kingham* (1878) 10 Ch.D. 743.
[51] For a fuller account, see the previous edition of this work at p. 686.
[52] See *Capital and Counties Bank Ltd v. Rhodes* [1903] 1 Ch. 631.
[53] *Ingle v. Vaughan Jenkins* [1900] 2 Ch. 368.
[54] L.P.A. 1925, s.185.
[55] See *Re Fletcher* [1917] 1 Ch. 339.
[56] *Post*, para. 15–055.

Section 6. By Enlargement

1. The power. Under certain conditions, not often encountered in practice, a lease may be enlarged into a fee simple by the tenant executing a deed of enlargement. Under the Law of Property Act 1925[57] this can be done only if— **14–178**

(i) there is no less than 200 years of the lease unexpired; and

(ii) the lease was originally granted for at least 300 years; and

(iii) no trust or right of redemption[58] exists in favour of the reversioner; and

(iv) the lease is not liable to be determined by re-entry for condition broken; and

(v) no rent of any money value is payable. A rent of "one silver penny if lawfully demanded" is rent of no money value,[59] but a rent of three shillings is not.[60] A rent in such a lease which does not exceed one pound per annum and which has not been paid for a continuous period of 20 years (five having elapsed since 1925) is deemed to have ceased to be payable[61] and can no longer be recovered.[62]

For a sub-lease to be capable of enlargement under the section, it must, in addition, be derived out of a lease which is itself capable of enlargement.[63] A tenant of a lease that may be enlarged in this way may acquire an easement against his landlord by prescription,[64] contrary to the normal rule.[65] **14–179**

2. The resulting fee. A fee simple acquired by enlargement is subject to all the same covenants, provisions and obligations as would have applied to the lease had it not been enlarged.[66] The lessor's reversion, however, presumably disappears, for the existence of a fee simple absolute in possession excludes the possibility of any estate in reversion. **14–180**

3. Effect of enlargement. This statutory power has been little used, and its possibilities have not yet been worked out. Of these, the one that has been **14–181**

---

[57] s.153.
[58] This excludes mortgages: *post*, paras 19–014 *et seq.*
[59] *Re Chapman and Hobbs* (1885) 29 Ch.D. 1007.
[60] *Re Smith and Stott* (1883) 29 Ch.D. 1009. Similarly, it seems, one shilling a year: see *Blaiberg v. Keeves* [1906] 2 Ch. 175.
[61] L.P.A. 1925, s.153(4).
[62] *ibid.*, subs.(5).
[63] *ibid.*, subs.(2).
[64] *Bosomworth v. Faber* (1992) 69 P. & C.R. 288 at 293; *post*, para. 18–139.
[65] *Post*, para. 18–128.
[66] L.P.A. 1925, s.153(8).

most canvassed is that the power may provide a means of making positive covenants run with freehold land.[67] In principle, if long leases followed by enlargements can be deliberately used as conveyancing devices to bring about such results, the boundaries between freehold and leasehold principles may be liable to break down in important respects. However, there is little evidence of their use for such purposes. If commonhold is introduced,[68] it is likely to remove such vestigial significance as they may presently have.

Section 7. By Disclaimer

14–182   **1. The term.** The term *disclaimer* is sometimes used as meaning repudiation of the tenancy in cases where the tenant denies the landlord's title. This type of disclaimer, which can bring about the termination of a lease, has already been explained under the heading of forfeiture.[69]

14–183   **2. Statute.** A right to end a lease by disclaimer sometimes arises by statute. Thus tenants whose premises were rendered unfit by war damage were given a statutory power to disclaim their tenancies; the effect of a valid disclaimer was the same as if there had been a surrender.[70] Similar rights were given to certain tenants of premises which had been requisitioned.[71]

14–184   **3. Insolvency.** There is a rather different form of disclaimer under the Insolvency Act 1986.[72] This Act authorises a liquidator of a company or a trustee in bankruptcy to disclaim onerous property belonging to the company or the bankrupt which has become vested in the trustee under its provisions. Leaseholds are often onerous. This may be because they are near to expiry and subject to liabilities, *e.g.* to repair, or, as is now commonly the case, because the rental liability in respect of the premises makes the lease uneconomic.[73] There is no longer any requirement that disclaimer can be made only with the leave of the court.[74] Disclaimer, if properly made, brings to an end the rights and liabilities in the lease of the company or of the bankrupt and his trustee,[75]

---

[67] See further, *post*, para. 16–023. For other possibilities, see the previous edition of this work at p. 688 and (1958) 22 Conv.(N.S.) 101 (T. P. D. Taylor).

[68] See *ante*, para. 3–041; *post*, para. 16–029.

[69] *Ante*, para. 14–119. In reality, it may be more accurately characterised as an example of termination for breach: *ibid.*

[70] Landlord and Tenant (War Damage) Acts, 1939 and 1941.

[71] Landlord and Tenant (Requisitioned Land) Acts 1942 and 1944.

[72] ss.178 (liquidator of a company); 315 (trustee in bankruptcy). For the meaning of disclaimer in this context see *Allied Dunbar Assurance Plc v. Fowle* [1994] 1 E.G.L.R. 122 at 126.

[73] This has been the effect of many upwards-only rent review clauses: see, *e.g. Christopher Moran Holdings Ltd v. Bairstow* [1999] 2 W.L.R. 396. For rent review clauses, see *post*, para. 14–246.

[74] See *Re Hans Place Ltd* [1992] B.C.C. 737. Prior to the Act leave was required in the case of company insolvency: Companies Act 1948, s.323; and in some but not all cases of bankruptcy: Bankruptcy Act 1914, s.54(3); Bankruptcy Rules 1952, r. 278.

[75] I.A. 1986, ss.178(4), 315(3).

thereby determining the lease and accelerating the landlord's reversion.[76] It does not, however, affect the rights or liabilities of any third party except in so far as it is necessary to release from any liability the company or the bankrupt and his trustee.[77] Notwithstanding the determination of the lease, the effect of the statute is to deem the rights and liabilities of third parties to remain as if the lease had continued.[78] The court may make a vesting order in favour of any person interested in the property,[79] *e.g.* a mortgagee. In such a case, the lease, although determined, is re-created.[80] If no vesting order is made and the landlord chooses to re-enter the premises, he will thereby determine the liability of both the tenant and anyone else to perform the obligations under the lease thereafter.[81] Any person sustaining loss or damage in consequence of the operation of disclaimer is deemed to be a creditor and may prove for his loss in the winding up or bankruptcy.[82]

The effect of these provisions has recently been reviewed by the House of Lords,[83] and their operation is as follows. **14–185**

    (a)   Where a surety has guaranteed the performance of the obligations under the lease, disclaimer of the term does not release him from further liability.[84] For nearly a century, the contrary rule had applied,[85] thereby depriving the lessor of the benefit of the surety's guarantee in one of the situations in which it was most likely to be required.[86]

    (b)   Where it is an assignee of the lease who becomes insolvent and the lease is disclaimed, the assignee is released from further liability,[87]

---

[76] *Hindcastle Ltd v. Barbara Attenborough Associates Ltd* [1997] A.C. 70.

[77] I.A. 1986, ss.178(4); 315(3). It should be noted that a trustee in bankruptcy who disclaims a lease is not thereby precluded from claiming any surplus realised on its disposal. The matter then lies in the court's discretion under *ibid.*, s.320, *infra*: see *Lee v. Lee* [1998] 1 F.L.R. 1018; [1998] Fam. Law 312 (S. Cretney).

[78] *Hindcastle Ltd v. Barbara Attenborough Associates Ltd, supra*, at 88.

[79] I.A. 1986, ss.181, 320. The disclaimer of a lease does not take effect unless a copy of it has been served on any person claiming as underlessee or mortgagee of the company or bankrupt, and either no application or no successful application is made by such person for a vesting order: *ibid.*, ss.179, 317. For restrictions on the power to make vesting orders see *ibid.*, ss.182, 321.

[80] *Hindcastle Ltd v. Barbara Attenborough Associates Ltd, supra*, at 89.

[81] *ibid.* But there must be a taking of possession for this to occur: see *Cromwell Developments Ltd v. Godfrey* [1998] 2 E.G.L.R. 62.

[82] I.A. 1986, ss.178(6), 315(5). For the principles upon which a landlord's loss is determined on such a disclaimer, see *Christopher Moran Holdings Ltd v. Bairstow* [1999] 2 W.L.R. 396.

[83] *Hindcastle Ltd v. Barbara Attenborough Associates Ltd, supra.* Many earlier decisions must now be regarded as superseded.

[84] *ibid.*, overruling *Stacey v. Hill* [1901] 1 Q.B. 660.

[85] *Stacey v. Hill, supra.*

[86] The rule was much criticised: see *W.H. Smith Ltd v. Wyndham Investments Ltd* (1994) 70 P. & C.R. 21 at 27. It has not been followed in Ireland: see *Maurice Tempany v. Royal Liver Trustees Ltd* [1984] B.C.L.C. 568. See [1995] C.L.J. 253 (S. Bridge).

[87] *M.E.P.C. Ltd v. Scottish Amicable Life Assurance Society* [1993] 2 E.G.L.R. 93. The liquidator or trustee in bankruptcy cannot disclaim liability under the licence to assign unless he also disclaims the lease: *ibid.*

but his surety is not.[88] Furthermore, where the lease was granted prior to 1996, the original tenant remains liable on all the covenants in the lease[89] as does any surety of his.[90] Where the lease was granted after 1995, the tenant who assigned the lease may in certain circumstances be liable to the landlord under an authorised guarantee agreement. This is explained later.[91] In either eventuality, the tenant who is called upon to meet the liability may be able to call for an overriding lease of the premises.[92]

(c) Where the lessee is a company which is struck off the register of companies, its property will vest in the Crown as *bona vacantia*.[93] If the Crown disclaims the lease,[94] but the company is then restored to the register, the effect is as if the property had never vested in the Crown at all.[95]

(d) Any sub-lease remains in being[96] and the landlord may distrain on the sub-tenant for rent due under the head lease or re-enter for breach of covenant.[97] Furthermore, if the landlord forfeits the head lease, the sub-tenant may seek relief against forfeiture.[98] However, although the sub-lease subsists, the covenants in the sub-lease are no longer directly enforceable by or against the sub-tenant.[99] It is for that reason that it is provided that if a sub-tenant is not willing to take an order vesting the lease in him,[1] he is thereafter excluded from any interest in the property.[2]

---

[88] *Murphy v. Sawyer-Hoare* [1993] 2 E.G.L.R. 61, which held to the contrary on the authority of *Stacey v. Hill*, *supra*, is no longer good law.

[89] *Hill v. East and West India Dock Co.* (1884) 9 App. Cas. 448; *Warnford Investments Ltd v. Duckworth* [1979] Ch. 127. See too *W.H. Smith Ltd v. Wyndham Investments Ltd, supra*; and *post*, para. 15–008.

[90] *Hill v. East and West India Dock Co., supra; Hindcastle Ltd v. Barbara Attenborough Associates Ltd* [1997] A.C. 70.

[91] L. & T.C.A. 1995, s.16; *post*, para. 15–067.

[92] L. & T.C.A. 1995, s.19; *post*, para. 15–017.

[93] Companies Act 1985, s.654.

[94] Which it may: *ibid.*, s.656.

[95] Prior to the decision in *Hindcastle Ltd v. Barbara Attenborough Associates Ltd, supra*, the liability of any surety would have determined when the company was struck off the register, only to be revived (with retrospective effect from the moment of the company's dissolution) when the company was restored to the register: *Allied Dunbar Assurance Plc v. Fowle* [1994] 1 E.G.L.R. 122. The surety's liability would not now determine with the insolvency of the company.

[96] *Re Thompson & Cottrell's Contract* [1943] Ch. 97. See generally *Hindcastle Ltd v. Barbara Attenborough Associates Ltd, supra*, at 89.

[97] *Ex p. Walton* (1881) 17 Ch.D. 746.

[98] *Barclays Bank Plc v. Prudential Assurance Co. Ltd* [1998] 1 E.G.L.R. 44 (relief granted to mortgagee of the head lease, where, after disclaimer, that lease had been forfeited for non-payment of rent and service charge).

[99] *Re A.E. Realisations Ltd* [1988] 1 W.L.R. 200 at 211.

[1] An application can be made by the lessor to seek such an order: I.A. 1985, ss.181, 320.

[2] I.A. 1985, ss.182(4), 321(4); *Re A.E. Realisations Ltd, supra*, at 211. Where an underlessee declines to take a vesting order, the freeholder is not entitled to have the head lease vested in him in order to keep the underlease alive: *Sterling Estates v. Pickard (U.K.) Ltd* [1997] 2 E.G.L.R. 33.

Section 8. By Frustration

1. General rule. The doctrine of frustration is part of the law of contract, **14–186** and may sometimes be invoked to discharge a party from contractual liability when some unforeseen event has made performance impracticable. As a general rule the doctrine does not apply to executed leases; for a lease creates an estate which vests in the lessee, and cannot be divested except in one or other of the ways enumerated above. In other words, the lessor's principal obligation is executed when he grants the lease and puts the tenant into possession. Normally the doctrine of frustration can apply only to obligations which are executory and which can therefore be rendered futile or impossible by later events. But the courts are now inclined to stress the contractual as opposed to the proprietary character of leases, and to accept that there may occasionally be frustration even of the lease itself on the same basis as frustration of a contract.[3]

2. Covenants. A covenant in a lease may accordingly be suspended or **14–187** discharged by impossibility of performance if it creates a continuing or future obligation. If the impossibility ceases before the time for performance is past, the covenant is merely suspended until performance is possible.[4] If the impossibility continues throughout the time for performance, the covenant is discharged. For example, under a building lease the landlord may let the site to the tenant for 99 years at a fixed rent, the tenant undertaking to erect a building which at the end of the term will pass to the landlord. If, after the grant of the lease, the building is prevented by some unforeseen cause such as wartime regulations or requisitioning, the lease continues and the rent remains payable.[5] However the existence of a doctrine of lawful excuse for the non-performance of covenants in a lease[6] means that the landlord will probably have no remedy in damages against the tenant for failure to build.[7] Even if he has reserved a power to re-enter for breach of the building covenant, he will not be able to exercise it.[8] The supervening impossibility destroys the tenant's obligations and there is therefore no breach.[9] There is no hard-and-fast rule, since every covenant must be interpreted according to the intention of the

---

[3] See *National Carriers Ltd v. Panalpina (Northern) Ltd* [1981] A.C. 675, *post*, para. 14–189. For the contractual nature of leases, see *ante*, para. 14–003.

[4] *John Lewis Properties Plc v. Viscount Chelsea* (1993) 67 P. & C.R. 120 at 133.

[5] *Cricklewood Property and Investment Trust Ltd v. Leighton's Investment Trust Ltd* [1945] A.C. 221.

[6] *John Lewis Properties Plc v. Viscount Chelsea, supra*, at 132; [1995] Conv. 74 (J. Morgan).

[7] *cf. Baily v. De Crespigny* (1869) L.R. 4 Q.B. 180. That case concerned a covenant by a tenant that neither he nor his assigns would build on certain land. That land was acquired by a railway company under compulsory purchase powers for building a railway station. The tenant was held not liable in damages. Contrast n.16, *infra*. *Baily's* case may turn merely on the construction of "assigns" and so not apply to the case in the text.

[8] *Doe d. Marquis of Anglesea v. Churchwardens of Rugeley* (1844) 6 Q.B. 107; *John Lewis Properties Plc v. Viscount Chelsea, supra* (no breach of covenant to build when listed building consent unobtainable: landlord not entitled to re-enter).

[9] *Brewster v. Kitchell* (1698) 1 Salk. 198; *John Lewis Properties Plc v. Viscount Chelsea, supra*, at 133.

parties to it, and it is quite possible to frame it so that the landlord may re-enter for non-fulfilment of some condition even if its performance is impossible.[10]

14–188   **3. Mere difficulty.** An obligation to pay money (*e.g.* rent) is never regarded as impossible of performance, unless prohibited by statute. Rent accordingly remains payable even if the tenant is evicted by armed forces of the Crown,[11] or is prohibited by legislation from occupying the land,[12] or if the property is destroyed by fire.[13] For similar reasons tenants who have covenanted to repair are not relieved of liability if a building is accidentally destroyed by fire[14] or by enemy action,[15] for it is still possible to repair it, at whatever cost. Even legislation which prohibits the effecting of repairs without a licence does not relieve a tenant who is sued for damages for not repairing. Should he be refused a licence he is not prevented by the legislation from paying damages.[16] But all these instances are now subject to the reservation that in an exceptional case the court may hold the whole transaction to be frustrated.

14–189   **4. Leases.** The question whether the doctrine of frustration could ever apply to a lease itself, as distinct from the covenants contained in it, was resolved by the House of Lords after a period of doubt.[17] The House held that in principle a lease was capable of being frustrated, though cases are likely to be rare.[18] In fact the House rejected the tenant's plea of frustration and held that rent remained payable where a local authority had closed the only road giving access to the property (a warehouse), thus rendering it useless for a period likely to last for 20 months in the middle of a 10-year lease. The question was treated as one of degree, so that a longer interruption might have produced frustration.[19] The rival arguments were fully debated, the majority upholding the view that a lease might be frustrated not only by physical catastrophe ("if, for example, some vast convulsion of nature swallowed up the property

---

[10] *cf. Moorgate Estates Ltd v. Trower* [1940] Ch. 206 (a case of mortgagor and mortgagee); *Edward H. Lewis & Son Ltd v. Morelli* [1948] 1 All E.R. 433, reversed on other grounds [1948] 2 All E.R. 1021.

[11] *Paradine v. Jane* (1647) Aleyn 26; *Whitehall Court Ltd v. Ettlinger* [1920] 1 K.B. 680; and see *Cyprus Cinema & Theatre Co. Ltd v. Karmiotis* [1967] 1 Cy.L.R. 42.

[12] *London & Northern Estates Co. v. Schlesinger* [1916] 1 K.B. 20.

[13] *Belfour v. Weston* (1786) 1 T.R. 310.

[14] *Matthey v. Curling* [1922] 2 A.C. 180; and see para. 14–190, n. 26, *infra*.

[15] *Redmond v. Dainton* [1920] 2 K.B. 256. But for the possibility of disclaimer under statute, see *ante*, para. 14–183.

[16] *Maud v. Sandars* [1943] 2 All E.R. 783; *Eyre v. Johnson* [1946] K.B. 481. These cases appear to interpret the covenant as a covenant either to repair or to pay compensation.

[17] *National Carriers Ltd v. Panalpina (Northern) Ltd* [1981] A.C. 675. There were conflicting opinions in *Cricklewood Property and Investment Trust Ltd v. Leighton's Investment Trust Ltd* [1945] A.C. 221.

[18] *National Carriers Ltd v. Panalpina (Northern) Ltd, supra*, holding that it was a matter of "hardly ever" rather than "never".

[19] *cf. Prince v. Robinson* (1998) 31 H.L.R. 89 at 93 (the doctrine of frustration applied to leases "only in wholly exceptional circumstances", and it was doubtful that it could apply to a weekly or other periodic tenancy where fire damage could be repaired in a matter of weeks).

altogether, or buried it in the depths of the sea"[20]) but also by supervening events so far beyond the contemplation of the parties that it would be unjust to enforce the lease.[21] The primary argument to the contrary is that under settled principles of land law the risk of accidents passes to the purchaser, and that this should apply just as much where he takes a lease (especially if it is a long one) as where he buys the fee simple outright. Another consideration is that the termination of an estate, unlike the discharge of a contract, may affect the rights of third parties, such as sub-lessees or mortgagees, whose titles depend upon the lease.[22] Various problems of this kind await solution.[23] Nor is it clear whether frustration depends upon some implied term or upon the fact that the whole basis of the transaction between landlord and tenant has been altered beyond recognition.[24]

5. Destruction of subject-matter. If there is a lease of land and buildings, **14–190** the destruction of the buildings does not affect the continuance of the lease, so that the lessee remains entitled to possession of the land and any buildings that may subsequently be erected on it.[25] But the complete destruction of the whole of the demised premises, as where an upper-floor flat is destroyed by fire, or where the demised land disappears beneath the sea, would raise problems of a different kind.[26] The correct answer may be that the tenancy would come to an end, and with it liability on the covenants,[27] for there would no longer be any physical entity which the tenant could hold of his landlord for any term.[28] and there can hardly be tenure without a tenement.[29] In the case of a flat destroyed by fire it might be contended that the tenancy (and with it liability on the covenants) would endure in the vacant air space[30] and would thus attach to the corresponding flat in any building erected to replace the building destroyed. This would be an equitable solution if the landlord had covenanted to reinstate the building in the case of damage by fire, particularly if the tenant had paid a premium for the lease; but the theoretical difficulties may well be insuperable. Now that the House of Lords has opened the door to the doctrine of frustration, the courts may be able to use it to escape from

---

[20] *Cricklewood* case, *supra*, at 229, *per* Lord Simon L.C.; and see at 239–241, *per* Lord Wright.

[21] The doctrine is "an expedient to escape from injustice": *per* Lord Simon in the *National Carriers* case, *supra*, at 701.

[22] *Cricklewood case, supra*, at 244, 245, *per* Lord Goddard; similarly Lord Russell of Killowen at 233, 234.

[23] The court has powers to adjust the rights of the parties, within limits, under the Law Reform (Frustrated Contracts) Act 1943.

[24] Both theories are favoured in the *National Carriers* case, *supra*.

[25] *Simper v. Coombs* [1948] 1 All E.R. 306; *Denman v. Brise* [1949] 1 K.B. 22.

[26] Suggestions in Rolle's and Bacon's *Abridgements* that rent abates in case of partial loss or destruction seem to be based on no authority: see Foa L. & T. 111, n.(g).

[27] See *National Carriers Ltd v. Panalpina (Northern) Ltd* [1981] A.C. 675 at 709, *per* Lord Russell of Killowen, dissenting.

[28] Contrast *Izon v. Gorton* (1839) 5 Bing.N.C. 501; but that was a case of partial, not total, destruction.

[29] For the dependence of leases upon tenure, see *ante*, para. 14–002.

[30] See *Izon v. Gorton, supra*, at 507; and see 14 Vin.Abr. 320.

such problems. It may be noted that a contract to purchase a share in a leasehold block of flats then under construction was held to be frustrated when the building was destroyed by a landslip.[31]

Section 9. By Termination for Breach

14–191   **1. Application to leases.** One result of the emphasis on the contractual nature of a lease[32] is the recognition, both in this country[33] and in other states in the Commonwealth,[34] that in appropriate circumstances, a lease may be terminated by the breach of its terms by one of the parties to it.[35] Although there was authority against this view,[36] it was based on the now discredited assumption that a lease could not be frustrated. There was in any event an earlier body of authority in which it had been accepted that a lease could be terminated for breach.[37] A lease will be terminated by breach if a party to the lease "evinces an intention not to be bound by the contract or . . . intends to fulfil the contract in a manner substantially inconsistent with his obligations and not in any other way".[38] To have this result, the breach must probably be one which vitiates "the central purpose of the contract of letting".[39] Clearly both the length and the terms of the lease will be relevant to whether there has been a breach that will justify treating it as terminated. The longer the lease, the more artificial it is to regard it other than as an estate in land. It is therefore only in relation to shorter lettings that an allegation of discharge by breach is normally likely to be successful.[40]

14–192   **2. Examples.** The application of the principles of termination for breach to leases has yet to be fully worked out in this country. To date, the right to terminate a lease for breach of its terms has been recognised in a number of situations,[41] which include the following—

---

[31] *Wong Lai-ying v. Chinachem Investment Co. Ltd* [1980] H.K.L.R. 1 (P.C.); *ante*, para. 12–056.

[32] *Ante*, paras 14–003, 14–186.

[33] *Hussein v. Mehlman* [1992] 2 E.G.L.R. 87; *Re Olympia & York Canary Wharf Ltd (No. 2)* [1993] B.C.C. 159 at 166; *Nynehead Developments Ltd v. R.H. Fibreboard Containers Ltd* [1999] 1 E.G.L.R. 7 at 12. See too *National Carriers Ltd v. Panalpina (Northern) Ltd* [1981] A.C. 675 at 696.

[34] See *Highway Properties Ltd v. Kelly, Douglas & Co. Ltd* (1971) 17 D.L.R. (3d) 710 (Canada); *Proprietary Mailing House Pty Ltd v. Tabali Pty Ltd* (1985) 157 C.L.R. 17 (Australia).

[35] *Ante*, para. 14–119. See [1993] Conv. 71 (S. Bright); [1993] C.L.J. 212 (C.H.); [1995] Conv. 379 (M. Pawlowski).

[36] *Total Oil Great Britain Ltd v. Thompson Garages (Biggin Hill) Ltd* [1972] Ch. 318 at 324.

[37] See *infra*.

[38] *Proprietary Mailing House Pty Ltd v. Tabali Pty Ltd, supra*, at 33, *per* Mason J.

[39] *Hussein v. Mehlman, supra*, at 91, *per* Sedley, Q.C. See too *Nynehead Developments Ltd v. R.H. Fibreboard Containers Ltd, supra*, at 12.

[40] It has therefore been suggested that it would be rare to find that a long lease granted at a small ground rent had been repudiated by the tenant unless he had abandoned the premises: *Proprietary Mailing House Pty Ltd v. Tabali Pty Ltd, supra*, at 34, 53. See [1993] Conv. 71 at 73 (S. Bright).

[41] Most of the cases concerned short lettings of three years or less.

(i) where a tenant purported to terminate the lease pursuant to a break clause in circumstances in which he was not entitled to do so[42];

(ii) where a landlord let a furnished property in breach of the implied condition that it was fit for human habitation[43];

(iii) where a landlord failed to restrain a nuisance by one tenant of a shopping mall which was seriously impeding the business of another[44];

(iv) where a landlord's breach of a repairing covenant rendered the property uninhabitable[45]; and

(v) where a landlord purported to forfeit a lease for breach of covenant when the tenant was not in breach.[46]

A landlord's right to terminate a lease because of a tenant's denial of title may also now be best explained in terms of termination for breach.[47]

3. Termination for breach and forfeiture. One particular difficulty about   **14–193** the application of the doctrine of repudiation for breach to leases lies in its uncertain relationship with the landlord's right of forfeiture.[48] It has been suggested that the right to terminate may be limited or modified by the express terms of the letting, including in particular any forfeiture clause, so that the landlord could terminate for breach only if he complied with the requirements[49] for forfeiture.[50] Indeed, the right to forfeit a lease under an express right of re-entry and the right to terminate the lease for breach have been equated, so that the latter may in any event be subject to the same statutory requirements as the former.[51] Where a lease is forfeited, the tenant ceases to be liable to pay rent.[52] However, a tenant's repudiatory breach of the terms of the lease may not deprive the landlord of his right to sue for damages for the loss of his bargain because he forfeits the lease for that breach.[53] As part of its

---

[42] *Gray v. Owen* [1910] 1 K.B. 622 (landlord entitled to claim damages from tenant for his loss when he re-let at a lower rental); *ante*, para. 14–175.

[43] *Wilson v. Finch Hatton* (1877) 2 Ex.D. 336; see *post*, para. 14–212.

[44] *Chartered Trust Plc v. Davies* [1997] 2 E.G.L.R. 83; *post*, para. 14–209.

[45] *Hussein v. Mehlman* [1992] 2 E.G.L.R. 87 (which contains a valuable analysis of the earlier authorities).

[46] *cf. G.S. Fashions Ltd v. B. & Q. Plc* [1995] 1 W.L.R. 1088, 1093 (*obiter*).

[47] *W. G. Clark (Properties) Ltd v. Dupre Properties Ltd* [1992] Ch. 297 at 302, 303; *ante*, para. 14–119.

[48] For forfeiture, see *ante*, para. 14–118.

[49] Including the statutory requirements: see L.P.A. 1925, s.146; *ante*, para. 14–146.

[50] *Hussein v. Mehlman, supra*, at 90.

[51] *W. G. Clark (Properties) Ltd v. Dupre Properties Ltd, supra*, at 309; *ante*, paras 14–119, 14–146. *cf. G.S. Fashions Ltd v. B. & Q. Plc, supra*, at 1093.

[52] *Ante*, para. 14–124.

[53] This is the law in Australia: *Proprietary Mailing House Pty Ltd v. Tabali Pty Ltd* (1985) 157 C.L.R. 17; [1986] Conv. 262 (J. W. Carter and J. Hill).

proposals for the termination of tenancies,[54] the Law Commission has recommended that it should not be possible for the landlord to circumvent the scheme by having recourse to repudiatory breach.[55]

Part 5

RIGHTS AND DUTIES OF THE PARTIES UNDER A LEASE OR TENANCY

14–194   The rights and duties of the landlord and tenant under a lease or tenancy fall under four heads. First, the lease may be silent as to everything except the essential terms as to parties, premises, rent and duration. This is not infrequently the case with weekly and other periodic tenancies. Secondly, the parties may have agreed to be bound by the "usual covenants". Thirdly, the lease may provide in the orthodox way not only for the matters dealt with by the "usual covenants" but also for a number of other matters. Fourthly, there are a number of statutory provisions relating to the rights and duties of the parties to a lease, which at this stage can only be mentioned briefly.

Although in 1975 the Law Commission recommended a new scheme of statutory obligations as part of their project for the codification of the law of landlord and tenant,[56] this scheme has never been implemented. The Commission has subsequently made further proposals in relation to the obligations of landlord and tenant, but these have been more limited.[57]

The question how far covenants in a lease can be enforced between persons other than the original lessor and original lessee is considered separately.[58]

Section 1. Position of the Parties in the Absence of Express Provision

14–195   Except so far as the lease or tenancy agreement otherwise provides, the position of the parties is as set out below.

A. Position of the Landlord

1. Implied covenant for quiet enjoyment

14–196   *(a) Implication.* The relationship of landlord and tenant automatically implies a covenant for quiet enjoyment by the lessor.[59] This position has been established only after much conflict of judicial opinion, for it was long thought

---

[54] *Ante*, para. 14–167.
[55] (1994) Law Com. No. 221, draft Bill, cl. 5(2).
[56] (1975) Law Com. No. 67. For a subsequent overview of the reform of landlord and tenant law, see (1987) Law Com. No. 162. Because of the lack of implementation, the Law Commission has since ceased work on landlord and tenant law: see (1995) Law Com. No. 234, p. 30.
[57] See *post*, paras 14–215, 14–221, 14–237, 14–258, 14–262.
[58] *Post*, paras 15–022, 15–079.
[59] *Budd-Scott v. Daniel* [1902] 2 K.B. 351; *Markham v. Paget* [1908] 1 Ch. 697.

that the covenant was implied only if the word "demise" was used in the grant.[60] The covenant is thus not linked with any form of words, as it may now be on the grant of a lease.[61]

(b) Effect. The covenant gives the tenant the right to be put into possession **14–197** of the whole of the premises demised,[62] and to recover damages from the landlord if the landlord, or any other person to whom the covenant extends, physically interferes with the tenant's enjoyment of the land.[63] The obligation which the lessor undertakes under the covenant is that the tenant will be free from disturbance by the exercise of adverse rights over the property or over other neighbouring land occupied by the lessor or some person for whom he was responsible.[64] Whether the covenant can be broken in other circumstances is less clear. Although it is not a prerequisite to the landlord's liability on the covenant that the conduct complained of should constitute a nuisance,[65] there are conflicting decisions as to whether it can also be broken by the commission of a nuisance by him or by some person for whom he was responsible.[66] The issue has arisen in the context of inadequately soundproofed flats where ordinary day-to-day noise interferes with the reasonable enjoyment of the flats by the tenants.[67] If the landlord can be liable in such circumstances, he may be required to install adequate soundproofing, thereby improving the property. The balance of authority is against liability[68] and indeed it has also been held that a landlord is not liable in the tort of nuisance for the noise from his tenants.[69]

Examples of where a landlord has been held to be in breach of the covenant include where—

[60] *Baynes & Co. v. Lloyd & Sons* [1895] 2 Q.B. 610; *cf. Jones v. Lavington* [1903] 1 K.B. 253; *Hart v. Windsor* (1843) 12 M. & W. 68 at 85. See Woodfall L. & T. 11.026.

[61] *Post,* para. 14–205 ("with full title guarantee" or "with limited title guarantee").

[62] *Ludwell v. Newman* (1795) 6 T.R. 458; *Miller v. Emcer Products Ltd* [1956] Ch. 304.

[63] See *Jaeger v. Mansions Consolidated Ltd* (1903) 87 L.T. 690.

[64] *Hudson v. Cripps* [1896] 1 Ch. 265 at 268. On the extent of a landlord's liability for other tenants, compare *Celsteel Ltd v. Alton House Holdings Ltd (No. 2)* [1987] 1 W.L.R. 291 (express covenant of quiet enjoyment given by a landlord to a tenant in respect of the acts of those "claiming under" the landlord did not include the actions of other tenants whose rights derived from a title paramount to the landlord's) with *Queensway Marketing Ltd v. Associated Restaurants Ltd* [1988] 2 E.G.L.R. 49 (sub-underlessor liable for acts of superior lessor on an express covenant of quiet enjoyment against interruption by the "landlord" which was defined to include superior lessors).

[65] *Southwark L.B.C. v. Mills* [1999] 2 W.L.R. 409 at 413.

[66] Compare *Sampson v. Hodson-Pressinger* [1981] 3 All E.R. 710 at 714; *Baxter v. Camden L.B.C.* (1997) 30 H.L.R. 501 (which support breach of the covenant) with *Southwark L.B.C. v. Mills, supra* (holding that there is no such liability). *cf. Toff v. McDowell* (1993) 69 P. & C.R. 535.

[67] Until recently, the view had generally been that the covenant is not one for "quiet" enjoyment in the acoustic sense: see *Jenkins v. Jackson* (1888) 40 Ch.D. 71; *Matania v. National Provincial Bank Ltd* [1936] 2 All E.R. 633.

[68] See *Southwark L.B.C. v. Mills, supra* (where the authorities are reviewed). As Mantell L.J. explained in that case (at 414), the view that the landlord is not liable is consistent with the rules: (i) that a landlord does not impliedly covenant that an unfurnished house is fit for human habitation (*post,* para. 14–210); and (ii) that an obligation to repair is not generally an obligation to improve (*post,* para. 14–275).

[69] *Baxter v. Camden L.B.C. (No. 2)* [1999] 2 W.L.R. 566.

(i) he has reserved the right to work the minerals under the land demised and causes a subsidence of the land by his mining activities[70];

(ii) he constructs an access way across the tenant's land without his consent[71];

(iii) he tries to drive out the tenant by persistent threats or violent behaviour[72];

(iv) he inflicts physical discomfort on the tenant by cutting off his water, gas or electricity or depriving him of proper washing facilities[73];

(v) he causes loss of business to the tenant by obscuring his shop with scaffolding.[74]

There is, however, no breach of the covenant where the landlord re-enters the premises pursuant to an order of the court forfeiting the lease, even if that order is subsequently reversed on appeal.[75]

14–198   *(c) Interference with enjoyment.* Usually there is no breach of the covenant unless the tenant suffers some physical interference with his enjoyment of the property. Thus where a landlord erected an external staircase which passed the tenant's bedroom windows and so destroyed his privacy, the tenant's action for damages failed.[76]

14–199   *(d) Damages.* An award of damages for breach of the implied covenant is assessed according to normal contractual principles.[77] A court will not therefore award the tenant either aggravated damages for his distress and inconvenience[78] or exemplary damages to punish his landlord.[79] The tenant may of

---

[70] *Markham v. Paget* [1908] 1 Ch. 697.

[71] *Branchett v. Beaney* [1992] 3 All E.R. 910.

[72] *Kenny v. Preen* [1963] 1 Q.B. 499; *Sampson v. Floyd* [1989] 2 E.G.L.R. 49.

[73] *Perera v. Vandiyar* [1953] 1 W.L.R. 672; *Guppys (Bridport) Ltd v. Brookling* [1984] 1 E.G.L.R. 29.

[74] *Owen v. Gadd* [1956] 2 Q.B. 99; *Queensway Marketing Ltd v. Associated Restaurants Ltd* [1988] 2 E.G.L.R. 49 (affirming [1984] 2 E.G.L.R. 73, a judgment that contains a valuable statement of the law); *Lawson v. Hartley-Brown* (1995) 71 P. & C.R. 242. See too *Mira v. Aylmer Square Investments Ltd* [1990] 1 E.G.L.R. 45 (damages awarded for loss of opportunity to sub-let due to construction of penthouses on roof of block of flats).

[75] *Hillgate House Ltd v. Expert Clothing Services & Sales Ltd (No. 2)* [1987] 1 E.G.L.R. 65.

[76] *Browne v. Flower* [1911] 1 Ch. 219; contrast *Owen v. Gadd* [1956] 2 Q.B. 99 (scaffolding).

[77] *Branchett v. Beaney* [1992] 3 All E.R. 910 at 917.

[78] *Branchett v. Beaney, supra* (not following on this point *Sampson v. Floyd, supra*, because it was decided *per incuriam*).

[79] *Perera v. Vandiyar, supra; Kenny v. Preen, supra; Guppys (Bridport) Ltd v. Brookling, supra*, at 34. For the distinction between aggravated and exemplary damages, see *Ramdath v. Oswald Daley (t/a D. & E. Auto Spares)* [1993] 1 E.G.L.R. 82 at 84.

course seek an injunction to restrain the breach of covenant. In many cases these limitations on the damages that the court may award will be of little consequence because the tenant will have other remedies against the landlord in tort for nuisance or trespass, or by statute under the Housing Act 1988.[80] These are commonly sought in the alternative in proceedings on the implied covenant. Something must be said both about them and about a landlord's criminal liability in cases of harassment.

(e) Tortious, statutory and criminal liability

(1) CLAIMS IN TORT. The tenant may be able to bring proceedings for trespass **14–200** (including trespass to goods), nuisance or harassment[81] against a landlord. Trespass proceedings are commonly brought in cases where the landlord improperly evicts the tenant,[82] or where he undertakes works on the premises in an attempt to encourage the tenant to leave.[83] Proceedings for nuisance have been brought where the landlord disconnects essential services such as water or electricity.[84] They may also lie where the tenant suffers discomfort as a result of a nuisance, not deliberately created, which emanates from property in the landlord's possession.[85]

In proceedings in trespass or nuisance, both aggravated damages for distress and inconvenience[86] and exemplary damages for "monstrous behaviour"[87] may be awarded against the landlord.[88] The latter will be given only where the landlord's conduct is calculated to make him a profit that may exceed any compensation that he has to pay to the tenant.[89] It will not necessarily be a bar to an award of such damages that the landlord has been prosecuted for the conduct in question.[90] Indeed in relation to offences of

---

[80] s.27; explained *post*, para. 14–201.

[81] Although attempts to develop tort of harassment at common law have proved abortive (see *Hunter v. Carnary Wharf Ltd* [1997] A.C. 655), there is now a statutory tort: see Protection from Harassment Act 1997, s.3.

[82] Typically, the landlord changes the locks, enters the tenant's room in his absence, and either damages his property or throws it out of the premises: see *e.g. Drane v. Evangelou* [1978] 1 W.L.R. 455; *Asghar v. Ahmed* (1984) 17 H.L.R. 25; *McMillan v. Singh* (1984) 17 H.L.R. 120; *Murray v. Aslam* (1994) 27 H.L.R. 284.

[83] *e.g. Branchett v. Beaney, supra; Sampson v. Wilson* [1996] Ch. 39.

[84] *e.g. Guppys (Bridport) Ltd v. Brookling, supra.*

[85] As in *Sharpe v. Manchester City Council* (1977) 5 H.L.R. 71 (landlord liable for cockroach infestation via the service ducts from the common parts). *cf. Habinteg Housing Association v. James* (1994) 27 H.L.R. 299 (landlord not liable for a cockroach infestation where the source was not under his control).

[86] *Branchett v. Beaney* [1992] 3 All E.R. 910 at 914.

[87] *Drane v. Evangelou, supra,* at 457, *per* Lord Denning M.R.

[88] For exemplary damages for nuisance, see *Guppys (Bridport) Ltd v. Brookling* [1984] 1 E.G.L.R. 29. But see *AB v. South West Water Services Ltd* [1993] Q.B. 507 at 522, 531.

[89] *Broome v. Cassell & Co. Ltd* [1972] A.C. 1027 at 1079; *McMillan v. Singh* (1984) 17 H.L.R. 120 at 124; *Ramdath v. Oswald Daley (t/a D. & E. Auto Spares)* [1993] 1 E.G.L.R. 82 at 83; *AB v. South West Water Services Ltd, supra; Mehta v. Royal Bank of Scotland Plc* (1999) 78 P. & C.R. D11 at D13.

[90] See *Asghar v. Ahmed* (1984) 17 H.L.R. 25 at 29 (where there was other outrageous conduct by the landlord in addition to the matters that had led to his prosecution).

unlawful eviction and harassment, any civil liability to which the landlord may be subject is expressly preserved.[91]

14–201   (2) STATUTORY LIABILITY. The Housing Act 1988[92] has created "what is in effect a new statutory tort of unlawful eviction".[93] The landlord[94] can commit the tort—either by his own acts or by a person acting on his behalf—in one of three ways.[95] The first is where he unlawfully deprives the residential occupier[96] of any premises of his occupation of the whole or part of those premises.[97] The second is where the occupier gives up his occupation because the landlord has unlawfully attempted to deprive him of it.[98] The third is where the occupier abandons his occupation because the landlord has interfered with his peace or comfort (or that of members of his household), or has persistently withdrawn or withheld services reasonably required for the occupation of the premises as a residence. To be liable under this third head the landlord must know or have reasonable cause to believe that his conduct is likely to cause the occupier either to give up his occupation of all or part of the premises or to refrain from exercising any right or pursuing any remedy in respect of the premises.[99] It is defence to any action for the landlord to show either that he had reasonable cause to believe that the tenant had ceased to reside on the premises when he did the act complained of, or that he had reasonable grounds for acting as he did.[1]

Damages are awarded for the loss of the right to occupy[2] and are intended to deprive the landlord of any financial gain that may have been obtained from the eviction.[3] The landlord[4] is liable to pay the difference between the value of the premises if the occupier's interest had been determined and its value

---

[91] P.E.A. 1977, s.1(5).

[92] ss.27, 28. See generally, S. Bridge, *Residential Leases*, pp. 276–281.

[93] *Sampson v. Wilson* (1994) 26 H.L.R. 486 at 500, *per* Judge Roger Cooke (on appeal [1996] Ch. 39). The Act expressly makes the liability tortious: s.27(4)(a). For the retrospective effect of the provisions, see *Jones v. Miah* [1992] 2 E.G.L.R. 50.

[94] Which means both the person who, but for the occupier's right to occupy, would be entitled to occupy the premises, and any superior landlord under whom that person derives title: H.A. 1988, s.27(9)(c). Although a person who has contracted to purchase the reversion may be the landlord for these purposes (see *Jones v. Miah, supra*), a person who merely expects to enter into such a contract cannot: *Francis v. Brown* (1997) 30 H.L.R. 143.

[95] The three forms of the tort are modelled upon the *criminal* liability of a landlord for unlawful harassment or eviction under P.E.A. 1977, s.1; see *post*, para. 14–203.

[96] Which means a person occupying the premises as a residence, whether under a contract, or by virtue of some enactment or rule of law giving him the right to remain in occupation or restricting the right of any other person to recover possession of the premises: H.A. 1988, s.27(9)(a); P.E.A. 1977, s.1(1).

[97] H.A. 1988, s.27(1).

[98] *ibid.*, s.27(2)(a).

[99] *ibid.*, s.27(2)(b). An example would be where a landlord cuts off the water supply of a protected tenant who seeks to have a fair rent registered under R.A. 1977, s.67. *cf. Drane v. Evangelou* [1978] 1 W.L.R. 455.

[1] H.A. 1988, s.27(8). See *Osei-Bonsu v. Wandsworth L.B.C.* [1999] 1 W.L.R. 1011.

[2] H.A. 1988, s.27(5).

[3] *Sampson v. Wilson* [1996] Ch. 39 at 49.

[4] Only the landlord can be liable to pay damages under the Act. A person acting on his behalf cannot: *Sampson v. Wilson, supra*.

subject to that interest.[5] This will obviously reflect the period of time for which the tenant would have been entitled to remain on the premises had the eviction not occurred.[6] There will be no liability if the occupier is reinstated in his occupation before the date of proceedings or if the court makes an order which has the effect of reinstating the occupier.[7] The court may reduce the damages payable if before proceedings[8] were begun, the landlord offered to reinstate the occupier and it was unreasonable for the former residential occupier to refuse that offer, or it would have been had he not obtained alternative accommodation in the meantime.[9] A tenant must elect at trial whether he wishes to claim statutory damages for eviction or a declaration that his tenancy continues. He cannot have both.[10]

Statutory liability for unlawful eviction is in addition to any other liability **14–202** to which the landlord may be subject, whether in contract, tort or otherwise.[11] Nevertheless, although the occupier can pursue his other remedies, he cannot recover twice over damages for loss of the right to occupy.[12] There has been some uncertainty as to what additional damages may be recovered at common law.[13] However, it is now established that exemplary damages cannot be awarded in addition to such statutory damages because the latter deprive the landlord of any financial gain from the eviction, thereby leaving no role for the former.[14] By contrast, in an appropriate case, aggravated damages may be awarded in addition to an award of statutory damages.[15] Damages both for harassment amounting to a breach of the covenant for quiet enjoyment and for trespass to goods have also been recovered in addition to statutory damages.[16]

---

[5] H.A. 1988, s.28(1). The damages may be reduced if the conduct of the tenant (or any person living with him) was such that it is reasonable for the court to mitigate them: H.A. 1988, s.27(7)(a). This is to cover the case where the tenant has "in some measure ... brought the problem on his head": *Tagro v. Cafane* [1991] 1 W.L.R. 378 at 384, *per* Lord Donaldson M.R. This may include a failure to pay the rent: *Regalgrand Ltd v. Dickerson* (1996) 74 P. & C.R. 312. See too *Osei-Bonsu v. Wandsworth L.B.C.* [1999] 1 W.L.R. 1011 at 1021.

[6] See *Regalgrand Ltd v. Dickerson, supra* (tenant would have left a week later); *King v. Jackson* (1997) 30 H.L.R. 541 (tenant would have left six days later: no award under the Act, but damages given for breach of the covenant for quiet enjoyment).

[7] H.A. 1988, s.27(6). Reinstatement means allowing the tenant to resume his occupation fully: *Tagro v. Cafane, supra*, at 385.

[8] *i.e.* under H.A. 1988, ss.27, 28: *Tagro v. Cafane, supra*, at 385.

[9] H.A. 1988, s.27(7)(b).

[10] *Osei-Bonsu v. Wandsworth L.B.C.* [1999] 1 W.L.R. 1011.

[11] *ibid.*, s.27(4)(a).

[12] *ibid.*, s.27(5).

[13] See [1994] Conv. 411 (S. Bridge). The suggestion by Hollis J. in *Mason v. Nwokorie* [1994] 1 E.G.L.R. 59 at 62, that the occupier can recover either statutory damages or damages at common law but not both, is incorrect: see H.A. 1988, s.27(5).

[14] *Francis v. Brown* (1997) 30 H.L.R. 143. Awards of damages under the Act are in fact substantially higher than the sums conventionally given by way of exemplary damages: see (1993) L.C.C.P. No. 132, para. 3.46.

[15] *Francis v. Brown, supra*, distinguishing *Mason v. Nwokorie, supra*; where an award was refused: *cf.* [1994] Conv. 411 (S. Bridge).

[16] See respectively *Kaur v. Gill, The Times*, June 15, 1995, *Tagro v. Cafane* [1991] 1 W.L.R. 378.

14–203 (3) CRIMINAL LIABILITY. The Protection from Eviction Act 1977[17] creates three offences relating to unlawful eviction or harassment. These constitute the criminal law analogues of the statutory tort of unlawful eviction. First, it is a criminal offence for any person unlawfully to deprive the residential occupier of his occupation of any of the premises unless he proves that he believed, with reasonable cause, that the residential occupier had ceased to reside on the premises.[18] The deprivation of occupation must have the character of an eviction.[19] Secondly, a person commits a crime if he does acts likely to interfere with the peace or comfort of a residential occupier[20] or his household or he withdraws services reasonably required for residential occupation if his intention is either—

(i) to cause him to give up his occupation of the premises; or

(ii) to prevent him from exercising his rights in respect of them.[21]

The offence is not committed where the landlord persuades a tenant to leave temporarily, *e.g.* to enable the property to be refurbished,[22] but it may be committed where the tenant loses his key and the landlord refuses to replace it.[23] Although a landlord may be guilty of this particular offence even though his acts are not such as to subject him to civil liability,[24] such cases will now be rare since the creation of the statutory tort of unlawful eviction.[25] Thirdly, it is a crime for a landlord of a residential occupier to do acts likely to interfere with the peace or comfort of that occupier or his household or to withdraw services reasonably required for residential occupation, knowing or having reasonable cause to believe that that conduct is likely to cause the occupier either—

(i) to give up his occupation of all or part of the premises; or

(ii) to refrain from exercising any right or to pursue any remedy in respect of the premises[26];

unless he can prove that he had reasonable grounds for doing the acts or withdrawing or withholding the services in question.[27]

---

[17] s.1, as amended by H.A. 1988, s.29.
[18] P.E.A. 1977, s.1(2).
[19] *R. v. Yuthiwattana* (1984) 80 Cr.App.Rep. 55 (locking tenant out for a day and a night insufficient).
[20] And not, say, a mere squatter: see *R. v. Phekoo* [1981] 1 W.L.R. 1117 at 1127.
[21] P.E.A. 1977, s.1(3). The subsection creates one offence which can be committed with one of two possible intentions: *Schon v. Camden L.B.C.* (1983) 53 P. & C.R. 361.
[22] *Schon v. Camden L.B.C., supra.*
[23] *R. v. Yuthiwattana, supra.*
[24] *R. v. Burke* [1991] 1 A.C. 135.
[25] H.A. 1988, s.27; *ante*, para. 14–201.
[26] P.E.A. 1977, s.1(3A) (inserted by H.A. 1988, s.29). The subsection was added because of the difficulties of showing the necessary intent under s.1(3).
[27] P.E.A. 1977, s.1(3B) (inserted by H.A. 1988, s.29).

(f) Acts of others and eviction by title paramount

(1) LEASES GRANTED PRIOR TO JULY 1995. In leases granted prior to July 1, **14–204**
1995, there are no implied covenants for title.[28] The tenant may have remedies
against the landlord for the acts of third parties in nuisance, for derogating
from his grant, or for breach of the covenant for quiet enjoyment implied in
the lease.[29] The covenant for quiet enjoyment extends to the landlord's own
acts, whether rightful or wrongful. It also extends to the rightful acts of those
claiming under him, such as other tenants, because it is through him that they
are able to disturb the tenant. Traditionally, the landlord has not been held
liable for the wrongful acts of those claiming under him. The tenant was
expected to proceed against them directly.[30] However, this approach has now
been called into question. A landlord who is in a position to control the
conduct of other tenants, whether by enforcing covenants in the lease or by
proceedings for nuisance, will be expected to do so, and will be held responsible for his failure to do so.[31] For example, where a landlord of a tenant of a
shop in a shopping mall failed to control a nuisance by another tenant, the
tenant was entitled to treat the lease as repudiated.[32]

The covenant for quiet enjoyment gives the tenant no remedy if he is
evicted by title paramount, at all events if the word "demise" is not used,[33]
and probably even if it is.[34] It follows that, in relation to leases granted before
July 1995, the tenant will usually have no remedy against the landlord if his
title turns out to be bad.[35]

(2) LEASES GRANTED AFTER JUNE 1995. For leases granted after June 1995, the **14–205**
provisions of the Law of Property (Miscellaneous Provisions) Act 1994 have
changed the law.[36] In consequence of that Act, covenants may be implied into

---

[28] *Ante*, para. 5–050. Even if the landlord purported to grant a lease "as beneficial owner", the
covenants for title would not have been implied: L.P.A. 1925, s.76(5).

[29] See *Hilton v. James Smith & Sons (Norwood) Ltd* [1979] 2 E.G.L.R. 44. The courts do not
attach much significance as to the "label" given to the action in such cases: *ibid*. For the
principle that a landlord must not derogate from his grant, see *post*, para. 14–028.

[30] See *Malzy v. Eichholz* [1916] 2 K.B. 308 (no breach of the covenant where other tenants of the
lessor caused nuisance without his concurrence); *Matania v. National Provincial Bank Ltd*
[1936] 2 All E.R. 633. *cf. ante*, para. 14–197.

[31] See *Hilton v. James Smith & Sons (Norwood) Ltd, supra* (landlord liable for failing to control
parking by tenants and their visitors on a private right of way); *Sampson v. Hodson-Pressinger*
[1981] 3 All E.R. 710 (landlord liable for nuisance caused by the lawful use of an inadequately
insulated flat by another of his tenants); *Chartered Trust Plc v. Davies* [1997] 2 E.G.L.R. 83,
infra.

[32] *Chartered Trust Plc v. Davies, supra. cf. Hussain v. Lancaster City Council* [1999] 2 W.L.R.
1142.

[33] *Jones v. Lavington* [1903] 1 K.B. 253; *Markham v. Paget* [1908] 1 Ch. 697.

[34] See *Baynes & Co. v. Lloyd & Sons* [1895] 2 Q.B. 610. But contrast an express covenant for
quiet enjoyment: *Williams v. Burrell* (1845) 1 C.B. 402.

[35] For examples, see *Baynes & Co. v. Lloyd & Sons, supra* (lessee mistakenly granted a sub-lease
for longer than his lease: the sub-lessee had no remedy when evicted by the freeholder); *Jones
v. Lavington, supra* (tenant had no remedy against landlord when it transpired that the property
was subject to a restrictive covenant against the carrying on of a business on the premises
which was enforced against him).

[36] See *ante*, para. 5–067.

any instrument effecting or purporting to effect a disposition of property.[37] This will be the case in relation to a lease if it is expressed to be granted either "with full title guarantee" or "with limited title guarantee".[38] The covenants that are implied by these words have already been explained[39] and need only be considered to the extent that they relate to the grant of leases.

Where the lease is granted with full title guarantee, the landlord impliedly covenants that—

(a) he has the right to dispose of the property;

(b) he will at his own cost do all that he reasonably can to give the tenant the title which he purports to give;

(c) the property is free from all charges, incumbrances and third party rights other than those of which the landlord neither knows nor could reasonably be expected to know; and

(d) where the grant is of a sub-lease, the lease out of which the sub-lease is created is subsisting at the time of the disposition, and that there is no subsisting breach of any term of that lease which would render it liable to forfeiture.[40]

As regards (a), (c) and (d), the landlord is not liable for matters to which the disposition was made expressly subject or for anything of which the tenant actually knew or which was patent.[41]

14–206   Where the landlord grants the lease with limited guarantee, his obligations are the same except as regards (c). He covenants merely that, since the last disposition of the property for value, he has neither created any subsisting charge, incumbrance or third party right nor suffered the property to be subjected to any such rights.[42]

Because the covenants for title implied under the 1994 Act are absolute and are not confined to the acts of the grantor and certain others through whom he derived title, there will be a breach of the covenant that he has a good right to dispose of the property if the tenant is evicted by title paramount. Similarly, the landlord may find himself liable under the covenant that the property is free from incumbrances because of some undisclosed latent incumbrance affecting the property. The position of the tenant is therefore much strengthened.

14–207   *(g) Lease not by deed.* Where the lease is not granted by deed, there cannot be any covenant in the technical sense, for the essence of a covenant is that it

---

[37] L.P.(M.P.)A. 1994, s.1(1). It was expressly intended that covenants for title should apply to leases: see (1991) Law Com. No. 199, paras 4.4, 4.5.
[38] Or their Welsh equivalents: L.P.(M.P.)A. 1994, s.8(4).
[39] *Ante*, para. 5–068.
[40] L.P.(M.P.)A. 1994, ss.2–4.
[41] *ibid.*, s.6.
[42] *ibid.*, s.3(3).

should be entered into by deed; but there will be corresponding contractual obligations.[43]

2. Obligation not to derogate from his grant

(a) The obligation. It is a principle of general application that a grantor must **14–208** not derogate from his grant[44]; he must not seek to take away with one hand what he has given with the other. This obligation binds not only the grantor himself but persons claiming under him[45]; and the right to enforce it passes to those who claim under the grantee.[46] In the cases of leases, the covenant for quiet enjoyment will extend to many of the acts which might be construed as a derogation from the lessor's grant; but acts not amounting to a breach of the covenant or to a tort may nevertheless be restrained as being in derogation of the grant. Thus if land is leased for the express purpose of storing explosives, the lessor and those claiming under him will be restrained from using adjoining land so as to endanger the statutory licence necessary for the storage of explosives.[47] Again, if land is leased to a timber merchant for use for his business, the landlord and his assigns will be restrained from building on adjoining land so as to interrupt the flow of air to sheds used for drying timber.[48] In neither case would there have been any remedy against such acts by strangers, for they were not torts. There will be no derogation from grant if the landlord's activities were clearly contemplated by the parties,[49] unless that permitted activity was carried out in an unreasonable manner that had not been envisaged by them.[50]

(b) Extent of the obligation. To constitute a derogation from grant there **14–209** must be some act rendering the premises substantially less fit for the purposes for which they were let.[51] The act giving rise to liability will commonly be executed on property in the possession of the grantor at the time of the grant,[52] but in exceptional circumstances, it may even take place on land which he had had no plans to acquire at the time of the grant but which he subsequently

---

[43] *Baynes & Co. v. Lloyd & Sons* [1895] 1 Q.B. 820 at 826 (in C.A. [1895] 2 Q.B. 610).

[44] *Palmer v. Fletcher* (1663) 1 Lev. 122; and see *post*, para. 18–075; (1964) 80 L.Q.R. 244 (D.W. Elliott); (1965) 81 L.Q.R. 28 (M.A. Peel).

[45] *Aldin v. Latimer Clark, Muirhead & Co.* [1894] 2 Ch. 437; *Johnston & Sons Ltd v. Holland* [1988] 1 E.G.L.R. 264 at 268.

[46] This statement was approved in *Molton Builders Ltd v. Westminster L.B.C.* (1975) 30 P. & C.R. 182 at 186, *per* Lord Denning M.R.

[47] *Harmer v. Jumbil (Nigeria) Tin Areas Ltd* [1921] 1 Ch. 200. This was an extension of the principle, for the landlord's act had no direct physical effect on the premises: see *Port v. Griffith* [1938] 1 All E.R. 295 at 298.

[48] *Aldin v. Latimer Clark, Muirhead & Co.* [1894] 2 Ch. 437.

[49] *Lyttelton Times Co. Ltd v. Warners Ltd* [1907] A.C. 476.

[50] See, *e.g. Yankwood Ltd v. Havering L.B.C.* [1998] E.G.C.S. 75 (land adjacent to property let for equestrian pursuits to be used for recreational and social purposes; derogation from grant when those activities were conducted unreasonably).

[51] *Aldin v. Latimer Clark, Muirhead & Co., supra.*

[52] See *e.g. Lyme Valley Squash Club Ltd v. Newcastle-under-Lyme B.C.* [1985] 2 All E.R. 405 (construction of building so as to interfere with grantee's right to light).

acquired.[53] The construction of additional floors on top of a property which had been let without any reservation of the right to do so may amount to a derogation from grant.[54] It is now clear that a failure by the landlord to stop a nuisance by another tenant may itself constitute a derogation.[55] No action will lie if the tenant's business is abnormally sensitive to interference and its abnormality was unknown to the landlord when the lease was granted,[56] or if the landlord, having let the premises for some particular trade, *e.g.* for use as a wool shop only, lets adjoining premises for a similar trade which competes with it: for the original premises are still fit for use as a wool shop even if the profit will be diminished.[57] Nor, as in the case of the covenant for quiet enjoyment, will mere invasion of privacy amount to a breach of the obligation, even though the property is let for residential purposes.[58] But interference with the stability of the house by vibrations caused by powerful engines on adjoining land may be restrained on this ground[59]; and so may excessive noise, such as that caused in altering another flat in the same building,[60] or a substantial interference with the light reaching the tenant's windows.[61]

The rule against derogation from grant may therefore give the tenant a wider protection against his landlord than he has against strangers under the ordinary law. However, it will not prevent a landlord from barring the tenant's title by adverse possession.[62]

3. Implied condition of safety or fitness in certain cases

14–210   *(a) General rule: no liability for state and condition of the premises.* In general, a landlord is under no contractual liability to the tenant for the state of the demised premises in the absence of any express undertaking to repair or maintain them.[63] He gives no implied undertaking that the premises are or will be fit for human habitation, or for any particular use,[64] or that any

---

[53] *Johnston & Sons Ltd v. Holland* [1988] 1 E.G.L.R. 264 (construction by landlord of hoarding on land acquired after the grant of the lease to obscure wall which tenant used for advertising purposes).

[54] *Lawson v. Hartley-Brown* (1995) 71 P. & C.R. 242.

[55] *Chartered Trust Plc v. Davies* [1997] 2 E.G.L.R. 83; *ante*, para. 14–204.

[56] *Robinson v. Kilvert* (1889) 41 Ch.D. 88.

[57] *Port v. Griffith* [1938] 1 All E.R. 295; *Romulus Trading Co. Ltd v. Comet Properties Ltd* [1996] 2 E.G.L.R. 70; *cf. O'Cedar Ltd v. Slough Trading Co.* [1927] 2 K.B. 123 (adjoining premises let for purposes increasing fire insurance premiums of the original premises: no derogation); *Molton Builders Ltd v. City of Westminster L.B.C.* (1975) 30 P. & C.R. 183 (Crown Lands Commissioners, as lessors, authorised enforcement of planning control: no derogation).

[58] *Browne v. Flower* [1911] 1 Ch. 219; *Kelly v. Battershell* [1949] 2 All E.R. 830.

[59] *Grosvenor Hotel Co. v. Hamilton* [1894] 2 Q.B. 836.

[60] *Newman v. Real Estate Debenture Corpn. Ltd* [1940] 1 All E.R. 131.

[61] *Coutts v. Gorham* (1829) Moo. & M. 396; *Cable v. Bryant* [1908] 1 Ch. 259.

[62] *Sze To Chun Keung v. Kung Kwok Wai David* [1997] 1 W.L.R. 1232 at 1235; *post*, para. 21–031.

[63] *Chappell v. Gregory* (1863) 34 Beav. 250 at 253.

[64] *Hart v. Windsor* (1843) 12 M. & W. 68; *Cheater v. Cater* [1918] 1 K.B. 247; *Stokes v. Mixconcrete (Holdings) Ltd* (1978) 38 P. & C.R. 488 (right of way).

particular use is lawful,[65] or that he will do any repairs[66] or rebuild the premises (*e.g.* if destroyed by fire), even if he has covenanted for quiet enjoyment.[67] Furthermore he owes no duty of care to the tenant, his family or his lawful visitors[68] except where—

> (i) he is under an express or implied obligation to repair or maintain the demised premises or has a right to enter them for that purpose[69]; or
>
> (ii) he was responsible for the design and construction.[70]

These principles are subject to certain qualifications, both common law and statutory.

(b) Implied contractual terms. In certain circumstances, an obligation to repair may be implied as a term of the lease. Whether or not such an implication is to be made "is dependant upon the same considerations that apply to any other contract".[71] There are two types of term which may be implied into a contract. The first is where a term is implied as an incident of a particular type of contract.[72] In relation to repairing liabilities there are two such categories of contract, furnished lettings and leases of buildings where the landlord retains the essential access to the properties. The second is where the implication is necessary to give business efficacy to the agreement. **14–211**

(1) FURNISHED LETTINGS. Where a house is let furnished, it is an implied condition of the letting by the landlord that it is fit for human habitation at the time when it is let.[73] If this is not the case, the tenant may both treat the **14–212**

---

[65] *Edler v. Auerbach* [1950] 1 K.B. 601 (covenant to carry on profession forbidden by Defence Regulations); *Hill v. Harris* [1965] 2 Q.B. 601 (user by sub-tenant in accordance with sub-lease but prohibited by covenant in head lease); *Molton Builders Ltd v. City of Westminster L.B.C., supra.*

[66] *Gott v. Gandy* (1853) 2 E. & B. 845; *Sleafer v. Lambeth B.C.* [1960] 1 Q.B. 43 (landlord not liable for failure to repair dangerous door, where landlord in practice did repairs and knew of the defect). See too *Tennant Radiant Heat Ltd v. Warrington Development Corporation* [1988] 1 E.G.L.R. 41 and 43.

[67] *Brown v. Quilter* (1764) Amb. 619.

[68] *Cavalier v. Pope* [1906] A.C. 428; *McNerny v. Lambeth L.B.C.* [1989] 1 E.G.L.R. 81. For criticism, see [1989] Conv. 216 (P. F. Smith).

[69] See Defective Premises Act 1972, s.4; *post*, para. 14–225.

[70] *Rimmer v. Liverpool City Council* [1985] Q.B. 1. In such a case, the landlord owes a duty to take reasonable care to see that the property is free from any defect likely to cause injury: *Targett v. Torfaen B.C.* [1992] 3 All E.R. 27 at 34.

[71] *Hafton Properties Ltd v. Camp* [1994] 1 E.G.L.R. 67 at 69, *per* Judge Fox-Andrews, Q.C.. See too *Barrett v. Lounova (1982) Ltd* [1990] 1 Q.B. 348 at 356. In accordance with normal contractual principles, a court will ignore the conduct of the parties subsequent to the contract in determining whether any repairing obligation is to be implied: *Demetriou v. Poolaction Ltd* [1991] 1 E.G.L.R. 100 at 104.

[72] *Liverpool City Council v. Irwin* [1977] A.C. 239 at 257, 258; *Duke of Westminster v. Guild* [1985] Q.B. 688, 698.

[73] *Smith v. Marrable* (1843) 11 M. & W. 5 (bugs); *Wilson v. Finch Hatton* (1877) 2 Ex.D. 336 (drains); *Bird v. Lord Greville* (1884) Cab. & E. 317; (measles); *Collins v. Hopkins* [1923] 2 K.B. 617 (tuberculosis).

tenancy as repudiated[74] and recover damages for any loss that he has suffered.[75] The landlord's obligation is satisfied if the premises are fit for human habitation when they are let. He is not required to keep them in this condition for the duration of the term.[76] Unfitness in this context appears to be confined to matters which are a danger to health, due to disease or infestation.[77] A landlord who lets a property that is unsafe on grounds of disrepair is not in breach of this condition.[78] The implied undertaking has no application to unfurnished premises.[79] Furthermore, there is no corresponding implied undertaking by the tenant that he is a suitable tenant, *e.g.* that he is not infected by some contagious disease.[80]

14–213   (2) WHERE THE LANDLORD RETAINS ESSENTIAL MEANS OF ACCESS. Where—

(a) flats or other multiple units within a building are separately let; or

(b) individual properties which are let are part of an estate;

and the landlord retains either—

(i) the necessary means of access (such as staircases, lifts or paths); or

(ii) other facilities essential to the use of the property (such as rubbish ducts);

without the tenants undertaking any liability for them, it may be implied in the lease that the landlord will take reasonable care to keep them in repair.[81] This principle is subject to two qualifications. First, it applies only to rights which are *essential* to the enjoyment of the tenancy. Where the tenant has other rights over property retained by the landlord, such as an easement of drainage, then in the absence of special circumstances, the tenant must bear the cost of

---

[74] *Wilson v. Finch Hatton, supra.* Although this is because the implied covenant is also a condition, the modern approach is to regard covenants as a contractual term, so that a tenant may treat the contract as repudiated if a breach of the covenant by the landlord goes to the root of the contract of letting: see *Hussein v. Mehlman* [1992] 2 E.G.L.R. 87 at 90; *ante,* para. 14–003.

[75] *Charsley v. Jones* (1889) 53 J.P. 280.

[76] *Sarson v. Roberts* [1895] 2 Q.B. 395. It was there suggested that to extend the obligation for the duration of the lease would be "most unreasonable": *ibid.,* at 398, *per* A. L. Smith L.J. *cf.* L. & T.A. 1985, s.8; *post,* para. 14–216.

[77] See the cases cited, *supra,* n. 73.

[78] *Maclean v. Currie* (1884) Cab. & E. 361 (no breach where plasterwork was in a dangerous state). *cf.* L. & T.A. 1985, s.8; *post,* para. 14–216.

[79] *Hart v. Windsor* (1843) 12 M. & W. 68, correcting *Smith v. Marrable, supra; Cruse v. Mount* [1933] Ch. 278; *Adami v. Lincoln Grange Management Ltd* [1998] 1 E.G.L.R. 58 at 60. See (1974) 37 M.L.R. 377 (J. I. Reynolds).

[80] *Humphreys v. Miller* [1917] 2 K.B. 122 (leprosy).

[81] *Liverpool City Council v. Irwin* [1977] A.C. 239 (block of flats); *King v. South Northampton D.C.* (1991) 64 P. & C.R. 35 (housing estate).

keeping the drain in repair,[82] in accordance with the usual rule that the servient owner is not obliged to keep the servient tenement in repair.[83] Secondly, there will only be a breach of the implied obligation if the landlord is negligent. If, for example, the landlord is unable to prevent the means of access from being persistently vandalised even though he has taken reasonable care, he will not be liable.[84]

(3) TO GIVE BUSINESS EFFICACY TO THE LEASE. A term will be implied into a **14–214** contract where to do so is necessary to give business efficacy to the agreement, a process that is akin to rectification.[85] Only where it is manifest that the agreement is incomplete will such an implication normally be appropriate.[86] This is because it has never been considered necessary to imply a repairing covenant by the landlord to give business efficacy to a contract of letting.[87] Indeed there may be situations where neither party is under any express or implied obligation to repair all or some part of the premises.[88] The more comprehensive the terms of the agreement therefore, the less likely it is that a term will be implied.[89]

The cases suggest that a repairing obligation on the part of the landlord may be implied because of a correlative obligation on the part of the tenant,[90] as where he is obliged to pay a specified sum for such service, whether as part of his rental[91] or at fixed intervals.[92] On the same basis, an obligation by the landlord to repair the exterior of the property has been implied where the tenant was required under the lease to repair the interior.[93] Such an implication will not necessarily be made where the tenant's obligation to pay arises only as and when the landlord carries out the work.[94] Nor will an obligation by the landlord be implied merely because he reserves a right to inspect the state of

---

[82] *Duke of Westminster v. Guild* [1985] Q.B. 688; [1985] Conv. 66 (P. Jackson).

[83] *Post*, para. 18–194; *Liverpool City Council v. Irwin, supra*, at 259; *Stokes v. Mixconcrete (Holdings) Ltd* (1978) 38 P. & C.R. 488 (tenant responsible for surfacing of right of way).

[84] *Liverpool City Council v. Irwin, supra* (landlord's vain attempts to keep them in order in a 15-storey tower block).

[85] *ibid.*, at 258.

[86] *Gordon v. Selico Co. Ltd* [1986] 1 E.G.L.R. 71 at 77.

[87] *Tennant Radiant Heat Ltd v. Warrington Development Corporation* [1988] 1 E.G.L.R. 41 at 43. "Special facts may no doubt justify a departure from the general rule": *Duke of Westminster v. Guild, supra*, at 697, *per* Slade L.J. For the right of a tenant holding under a long lease of a flat to apply to the court in a case where the lease fails to make satisfactory provision with respect to repair and maintenance, see L. & T.A. 1987, s.35.

[88] *Demetriou v. Poolaction Ltd* [1991] 1 E.G.L.R. 100 at 104. *cf. Barrett v. Lounova (1982) Ltd* [1990] 1 Q.B. 348 at 358; [1988] Conv. 448 (P. F. Smith); but see *Crédit Suisse v. Beegas Nominees Ltd* [1994] 4 All E.R. 803 at 819.

[89] *Gordon v. Selico Co. Ltd, supra*, at 77, 78.

[90] For a useful summary, see *Hafton Properties Ltd v. Camp* [1994] 1 E.G.L.R. 67 at 69.

[91] *Barnes v. City of London Real Property Co.* [1918] 2 Ch. 18 at 32.

[92] *Edmonton Corporation v. W.M. Knowles & Son Ltd* (1961) 60 L.G.R. 124.

[93] *Barrett v. Lounova (1982) Ltd, supra*. However, this decision "must be taken as decided upon the special facts of that case": *Adami v. Lincoln Grange Management Ltd* [1998] 1 E.G.L.R. 58 at 61, *per* Sir John Vinelott.

[94] *Duke of Westminster v. Guild* [1985] Q.B. 688 at 697.

repair of the premises,[95] though in such circumstances he must take reasonable care to ensure that the premises are safe.[96] A covenant by a landlord to insure against specific risks implies an obligation by him to lay any insurance money in making good the damage, but not to undertake repairs not covered by the policies.[97]

14–215   (4) REFORM. The Law Commission has recommended that there should be implied into many leases,[98] a term that the landlord shall keep in repair both the property let and any other parts of the building under his control.[99] This implied term would apply unless either—

    (a) an obligation was imposed on a party to the lease (whether by the lease or by statute) to keep that property in repair; or

    (b) the parties agreed that it should not.

The proposal would exclude any possibility of an implied repairing obligation in a lease. It would also mean that a situation in which neither party was under an obligation to repair could only occur by the parties' deliberate choice and not by reason of an oversight.

(c) Implied obligation of fitness in houses let at low rents

14–216   (1) HUMAN HABITATION. Under the Landlord and Tenant 1985,[1] if a house is let at a very low rent there is an implied condition that the house[2] is fit for human habitation at the commencement of the tenancy, and an implied undertaking by the landlord that he will keep it in this condition throughout the tenancy. This provision, which cannot be excluded by any stipulation to the contrary,[3] applies to houses let on or after July 6, 1957 at an annual rent not exceeding £80 in London and £52 elsewhere.[4] In this context "rent" means the gross rent payable to the landlord, without deduction for any taxes or other outgoings for which the land is liable.[5] These sums have remained substantially unaltered since 1957[6] and the implied covenant, which formerly

---

[95] *ibid., Sleafer v. Lambeth B.C.* [1960] 1 Q.B. 43.

[96] Defective Premises Act 1972, s.4(4); *post*, paras. 14–225, 14–278, 14–279.

[97] *Adami v. Lincoln Grange Management Ltd, supra.*

[98] There are significant exceptions, notably oral leases, leases of agricultural holdings, farm business tenancies and leases of dwellings granted for less than seven years.

[99] (1996) Law Com. No. 238, Pt VII.

[1] s.8(1) replacing provisions of the earlier Housing Acts, dating from 1885 onwards. See (1962) 26 Conv. (N.S.) 132 (W. A. West); (1974) 37 M.L.R. 377 (J. I. Reynolds); W. R. Cornish & G. de N. Clark, *Law and Society in England 1750–1950*, pp. 151–166; 179–184.

[2] Defined to include both a part of a house and any yard, garden, outhouses and appurtenances belonging to the house or usually enjoyed with it: L. & T.A. 1985, s.8(6).

[3] *ibid.*, s.8(1).

[4] *ibid.*, s.8(3), (4). For the meaning of "London", see *ibid.*, s.8(4) n.2.

[5] *Rousou v. Photi* [1940] 2 K.B. 379. This situation will not often arise now in view of the way in which liability to pay council tax is determined: see Local Government Finance Act 1992, s.6.

[6] A minor amendment was made by the London Government Act 1963, Sched. 8, Pt 1, para. 2.

encompassed a very considerable proportion of rented housing,[7] has in consequence little (if any) application today.[8] The implied covenant was introduced to correct the anomaly that on the letting of a furnished dwelling there was an implied condition that it was fit for human habitation,[9] but where the property was unfurnished there was no equivalent implication.[10]

(2) NOTICE. The undertaking is confined to defects of which the landlord has **14–217** notice.[11] However this principle is now subject to the qualification that, if the landlord ought to have known of a defect which might make the premises unsafe, he will be in breach of a statutory duty of care if injury to person or property results.[12]

(3) EXTENT OF DEFECTS. A small defect such as a broken sashcord may **14–218** constitute a breach of the statute, for the test is not how difficult it is to repair the defect but whether the state of repair of the house "is such that by ordinary user damage may naturally be caused to the occupier, either in respect of personal injury to life or limb or injury to health".[13] There is now a statutory list of the matters to be considered (including repair, freedom from damp, natural lighting and drainage) in determining whether a house is unfit for human habitation.[14] But the obligation is limited to cases where the house is capable of being made fit for human habitation at reasonable expense.[15]

(4) CONTRACT. Since this statutory duty operates by way of implying a term **14–219** into the contract,[16] it makes the landlord contractually liable only to the tenant personally.[17] But in certain cases he may be liable to visitors and others for breach of a statutory duty of care.[18]

---

[7] From 1885 until at least 1958, the prescribed rental limits were well above average rentals.

[8] See *R. v. Cardiff City Council, ex p. Cross* (1982) 6 H.L.R. 1 at 13; *Quick v. Taff Ely B.C.* [1986] Q.B. 809 at 817; *McNerny v. Lambeth B.C.* [1989] 1 E.G.L.R. 81 at 84.

[9] *Ante*, para. 14–212. Because of Parliament's unwillingness to change the rent limits, the courts have declined to extend the implied term at common law to unfurnished premises: *McNerny v. Lambeth B.C., supra*, at 84.

[10] See *Hansard* (H.L.), July 16, 1885, vol. 299, col. 892 (Marquess of Salisbury, the then Prime Minister).

[11] *McCarrick v. Liverpool Corporation* [1947] A.C. 219; *Morgan v. Liverpool Corporation* [1927] 2 K.B. 131. For this doctrine, see *post*, para. 14–277.

[12] Defective Premises Act 1972, s.4(1); *post*, paras 14–225, 14–278. Both *McCarrick v. Liverpool Corporation, supra*, and *Morgan v. Liverpool Corporation, supra*, would probably now be decided differently in consequence, because the landlord ought to have known of the defect which caused the injury to the claimant.

[13] *Summers v. Salford Corporation* [1943] A.C. 283 at 289, *per* Lord Atkin.

[14] L. & T.A. 1985, s.10. It should be noted that local authorities have powers to make repair, closing and demolition orders in respect of properties that are not fit for human habitation: see H.A. 1985, ss.189, 264, 265. The standard by which unfitness is judged is no longer the same as that in L. & T.A. 1985, s.10: see H.A. 1985, s.604 (as substituted by the Local Government and Housing Act 1989, s.165(1); Sched. 9, Pt V, para. 83). These powers are widely used *by* local authorities, but cannot be used against them by local authority tenants; *R. v. Cardiff City Council, ex p. Cross* (1982) 6 H.L.R. 1.

[15] *Buswell v. Goodwin* [1971] 1 W.L.R. 92; (1976) 39 M.L.R. 43 (M.J. Robinson).

[16] See *McCarrick v. Liverpool Corporation, supra*, discussed in *O'Brien v. Robinson* [1973] A.C. 912.

[17] *Ryall v. Kidwell* [1914] 3 K.B. 135.

[18] See *post*, para. 14–225.

14–220   (5) EXCEPTIONS. There are two principal exceptions to the application of this implied covenant. First, it does not apply to tenancies of houses for less than three years, which are not determinable by option within three years, and which provide that the lessee is to put the house into a condition fit for human habitation.[19] Secondly, it is not binding on the Crown.[20]

14–221   (6) REFORM. The Law Commission has recommended that the implied covenant of fitness for human habitation should apply to all leases of houses granted for a period of less than seven years, and that it should cease to be subject to rent limits.[21] There would be certain exceptions to enable property acquired for development by bodies having powers of compulsory purchase to be used as "shortlife" accommodation.

(d) Implied repairing obligations in houses let for a short term

14–222   (1) THE OBLIGATION. The Landlord and Tenant Act 1985[22] provides that in any lease of a dwelling-house[23] granted after October 1961[24] for a term of less than seven years[25] there shall be an implied covenant by the landlord—

> (1) to keep in repair[26] the structure and exterior[27] (including drains, gutters and external pipes); and

---

[19] L. & T.A. 1985, s.8(5). For the curious omission of building leases from the exceptions, see the previous edition of this work at p. 698.

[20] *Department of Transport v. Egoroff* [1986] 1 E.G.L.R. 89.

[21] (1996) Law Com. No. 238, Pt VIII. This would make the obligation parallel to the implied obligation on the landlord to keep in repair dwellings let for a term of less than seven years: L. & T.A. 1985, s.11; *infra. cf. Issa v. Hackney L.B.C.* [1997] 1 W.L.R. 956 at 964–965 (supporting the Commission's proposals). For comment see [1996] Conv. 324 (S. Bridge); [1998] Conv. 189 (P. F. Smith).

[22] s.11, replacing H.A. 1961, s.32. For similar provisions applicable to long leases granted as a result of the exercise by public sector tenants of their right to buy, see H.A. 1985, s.139, Sched. 6, para. 14.

[23] Which means a lease by which a building or part of a building is let wholly or mainly as a private residence: L. & T.A. 1985, s.16(b).

[24] *ibid.*, s.13. Certain leases are excluded from the ambit of s.11, *e.g.* new business tenancies, agricultural holdings and agricultural tenancies: *ibid.*, ss.13(3), 14. The implied obligation is not binding on the Crown: *Department of Transport v. Egoroff* [1986] 1 E.G.L.R. 89.

[25] See *Brikom Investments Ltd v. Seaford* [1981] 1 W.L.R. 863.

[26] The standard of repair is determined by having regard to the age, character and prospective life of the dwelling-house and the locality in which it is situated: L. & T.A. 1985, s.11(3). This is similar to the test applied at common law (see *Proudfoot v. Hart* (1890) 25 Q.B.D. 42 at 55) except that it requires the prospective life of the property to be taken into account as well: see *Newnham L.B.C. v. Patel* (1978) 13 H.L.R. 77 at 85. For the meaning of repair, see *post*, para. 14–275.

[27] "The structure of the dwelling-house consists of those elements of the overall dwelling-house which give it its essential appearance": *Irvine v. Moran* [1991] 1 E.G.L.R. 261 at 262, *per* Thayne Forbes, Q.C. The structure need not be load-bearing and includes the windows: *ibid.*; *Quick v. Taff Ely B.C.* [1986] Q.B. 809 (but *cf. Holiday Fellowship Ltd v. Hereford* [1959] 1 W.L.R. 211). As to internal plasterwork, compare *Irvine v. Moran, supra* (plasterwork not part of structure) with *Quick v. Taff Ely B.C., supra; Staves v. Leeds City Council* [1992] 2 E.G.L.R. 37 (plasterwork assumed to be part of the structure). The exterior may include the means of access to the premises (*Brown v. Liverpool Corporation* [1969] 3 All E.R. 1345), but not a back yard (*Hopwood v. Cannock Chase D.C.* [1975] 1 W.L.R. 373), steps to a back garden (*McAuley v. Bristol City Council* [1992] Q.B. 134), or a rear access path not included in the lease (*King v. South Northamptonshire D.C.* (1991) 64 P. & C.R. 35).

(2) to keep in repair and proper working order[28] the installations in the house—

    (i) for the supply of water, gas and electricity and for sanitation (including basins, sinks, baths and sanitary conveniences[29] but not other fixtures, fittings and appliances for making use of water, gas and electricity); and

    (ii) for space heating or heating water.

(2) EXTENSION TO OTHER PARTS OF THE BUILDING. These provisions were restrictively interpreted and were confined to the exterior, structure and installations comprised within the lease.[30] The obligations did not therefore apply to a boiler in the basement of a block of flats which provided the hot water for the whole block, or (except as regards a top floor flat) to the roof. To remedy this deficiency, the implied repairing covenant has been extended in cases where the dwelling-house forms part only of the building.[31] The obligation to repair the structure and the exterior now applies to any part of the building in which the landlord has an estate or interest. The obligations in relation to installations apply to those which directly or indirectly serve the dwelling-house and which either form part of the building in which the landlord has an estate or interest or are owned by him or under his control.[32] The landlord is under no liability, however, unless the disrepair or failure to maintain in working order is such as to affect the tenant's enjoyment of the dwelling-house or of those common parts which he is entitled to use.[33] **14–223**

(3) OTHER MATTERS. Contracting out is forbidden except to the extent that the county court may authorise as reasonable.[34] Furthermore, any covenant by the tenant to repair or pay money in lieu of repair is modified accordingly.[35] But the tenant remains liable to use the premises in a tenant-like manner,[36] and the landlord is not required to rebuild or reinstate after fire or other inevitable accident or to repair tenant's fixtures.[37] The tenant must also allow the **14–224**

---

[28] This means in good *mechanical* condition. There was therefore no breach where the landlord had failed to lag water pipes: *Wycombe Health Authority v. Barnett* (1982) 47 P. & C.R. 394.

[29] The landlord will be in breach of his obligation if the installations are defective in their design: *Liverpool City Council v. Irwin* [1977] A.C. 239 at 269, 270 (cistern overflowed due to bad design).

[30] *Campden Hill Towers Ltd v. Gardner* [1977] Q.B. 823; *Douglas-Scott v. Scorgie* [1984] 1 W.L.R. 716.

[31] L. & T.A. 1985, s.11(1A) (inserted by H.A. 1988, s.116).

[32] *ibid.*, It is a defence for the landlord to show that he used all reasonable endeavours to gain access to the part of the premises to carry out the necessary works, but was unable to do so: see *ibid.*, s.11(3B). This could happen if he needed access to part of the premises let by him to another tenant. See however Access to Neighbouring Land Act 1992, *post*, para. 18–225.

[33] L. & T.A. 1985, s.11(1B) (inserted by H.A. 1988, s.116).

[34] *ibid.*, s.12.

[35] *ibid.*, s.11(4), (5). See *Irvine v. Moran* [1991] 1 E.G.L.R. 261 at 262.

[36] See *post*, para. 14–234.

[37] L. & T.A. 1985, s.11(2). For tenant's fixtures, see *post*, para. 14–317.

landlord to enter and view the premises at reasonable times after 24 hours' notice in writing to the occupier.[38]

The landlord's obligation takes effect as a repairing covenant in the lease.[39] This has three consequences. First, the landlord is liable only for defects of which he has notice.[40] However, if there is a defect in the premises of which he ought to have known and which makes them unsafe, he will be in breach of a statutory duty of care[41] should that defect injure a person or damage their property.[42] Secondly, the obligation is one of repair.[43] The landlord will not therefore be liable if the property is subject to an inherent defect which causes no damage within the scope of the covenant.[44] Thirdly, the tenant has the usual contractual remedies to enforce the covenant. Three points merit particular mention in this regard—

(i) The tenant can seek specific performance of the covenant.[45] In practice this remedy is now commonly granted, and is available even in claims which have been allocated to the small claims track under the Civil Procedure Rules.[46]

(ii) If the breach of covenant is such as to make the premises uninhabitable, the tenant may treat the lease as repudiated.[47] In such circumstances, not only will the tenant be able to terminate the lease, but the landlord will be liable in damages for the breach.

(iii) The court may award damages for inconvenience and distress.[48]

For the purposes of this implied obligation, "lease" includes an agreement for a lease, a sub-lease and any other tenancy,[49] but does not include a mortgage term.[50] If the landlord can[51] determine the lease within seven years it is treated

---

[38] L. & T.A. 1985, s.11(6).
[39] *O'Brien v. Robinson* [1973] A.C. 912 at 927.
[40] *O'Brien v. Robinson, supra,* applying the same approach as for the statutory obligation to keep fit for habitation: *ante,* para. 14–217. For the requirement of notice, see *post,* para. 14–277.
[41] See Defective Premises Act 1972, s.4; *post,* paras. 14–225, 14–278.
[42] See, *e.g. Clarke v. Taff Ely B.C.* (1980) 10 H.L.R. 44.
[43] *Post,* para. 14–275.
[44] *Quick v. Taff Ely B.C.* [1986] Q.B. 809 (premises unfit for human habitation due to condensation caused by the design of the windows: landlord not liable for damage to tenant's property). This is a serious drawback given that the implied covenant of fitness under L. & T.A. 1985, s.8 is now virtually redundant: *ante,* para. 14–216.
[45] See L. & T.A. 1985, s.17; *post,* para. 14–280.
[46] *Joyce v. Liverpool City Council* [1996] Q.B. 252 (decided under the old CCR, O. 19). For the small claims track, see CPR 26PD–004; and Pt 27.
[47] *Hussein v. Mehlman* [1992] 2 E.G.L.R. 87; [1993] Conv. 71 (S. Bright); [1993] C.L.J. 212 (C.H.).
[48] *Chiodi (Personal Representatives) v. Marney* [1988] 2 E.G.L.R. 64. Breach of a repairing covenant is one of the exceptions to the general rule that damages for inconvenience and distress will not be awarded for a breach of contract: see *Watts v. Morrow* [1991] 1 W.L.R. 1421 at 1445.
[49] L. & T.A. 1985, s.36.
[50] *ibid.,* s.16(a).
[51] A right to do so in certain events is not enough: *Parker v. O'Connor* [1974] 1 W.L.R. 1160.

as a lease for less than seven years, but it is not so treated if the tenant can extend it to seven years or more.[52] The rent payable under the lease is irrelevant.

(e) Duty of care for safety. In certain cases a landlord owes to all persons[53] who might reasonably be expected to be affected by defects in the premises a statutory duty to take reasonable care to see that they and their property are reasonably safe from injury or damage.[54] This duty arises when under the tenancy the landlord is either— **14–225**

(i) under an obligation to the tenant (whether statutory,[55] express[56] or implied[57]) for the maintenance or repair of the premises[58]; or

(ii) has a right to enter the premises to carry out any description of maintenance or repair of them.[59]

The duty is owed only if the defect falls within the landlord's obligation or right to maintain or repair,[60] and he knows or ought to have known of the defect.[61] This rule applies to all types of tenancy, including statutory tenancies and tenancies at will or sufferance, but not to mortgage terms or tenancies under attornment clauses in mortgages.[62] It also applies to mere rights of occupation given by contract or statute, which for this purpose are treated as if they were tenancies.[63] No contracting out of this duty is possible.[64]

4. Statutory restrictions on the recovery of possession. When a lease or tenancy comes to an end, whether by effluxion of time or by notice to quit, the landlord's right at common law to recover possession is subject to certain statutory restrictions. **14–226**

(a) Statutory security. Many tenancies are protected by statutory systems of control which either prolong the tenancy or else restrict to a greater or lesser extent the landlord's right to recover possession. These systems include— **14–227**

---

[52] L. & T.A. 1985, s.13(2).

[53] Including the tenant: see *Smith v. Bradford Metropolitan Council* (1982) 44 P. & C.R. 171; *Barrett v. Lounova (1982) Ltd* [1990] 1 Q.B. 348 at 359.

[54] Defective Premises Act 1972, s.4, replacing Occupiers' Liability Act 1957, s.4. See [1975] C.L.J. 48 at 62 (J.R. Spencer); and *post*, para. 14–278.

[55] Defective Premises Act 1972, s.4(5). An example is the landlord's implied obligation to repair under L.T.A. 1985, s.11; *ante*, para. 14–222.

[56] See, *e.g. Smith v. Bradford Metropolitan Council* (1982) 44 P. & C.R. 171.

[57] See, *e.g. McAuley v. Bristol City Council* [1992] Q.B. 134.

[58] Defective Premises Act 1972, s.4(1).

[59] *ibid.*, s.4(4), not benefiting a tenant who has failed in his own express obligations. The existence of such a right to enter has to be proved: *McAuley v. Bristol City Council, supra*, at 150. See generally, *Hamilton v. Martell Securities Ltd* [1984] Ch. 266 at 271.

[60] Defective Premises Act 1972, s.4(3); *McNerny v. Lambeth L.B.C.* [1989] 1 E.G.L.R. 81, 83; *McAuley v. Bristol City Council, supra*, at 145.

[61] Defective Premises Act 1972, s.4(2); see *post*, para. 14–278.

[62] *ibid.*, s.6(1); see *post*, para. 19–077.

[63] *ibid.*, s.4(6).

[64] *ibid.*, s.6(3).

(i) for most dwellings, either the Rent Act 1977 or the less restrictive Housing Act 1988; and

(ii) for most business tenancies, the Landlord and Tenant Act 1954, Part II.

They are discussed later.[65]

14–228   *(b) Forcible entry.* Under the Criminal Law Act 1977 it is a criminal offence for any person without lawful authority to use or threaten violence for the purpose of securing entry into any premises for himself or any other person, if he knows that someone present on the premises is opposed to the entry; and a right to possession or occupation is not lawful authority for this purpose.[66] But there is an exception in favour of a person excluded from his residence by a trespasser, provided that he was not a trespasser himself.

14–229   *(c) Dwellings.* The Protection from Eviction Act 1977[67] restricts the recovery of possession of premises which have been let as dwellings and which are neither protected[68] nor excluded tenancies.[69] This protection has now been extended to licences other than excluded licences.[70] When such a tenancy[71] or licence comes to an end but any person lawfully residing in the premises continues to reside in any part of them, it is unlawful for the person entitled to possession to enforce his right of possession otherwise than by proceedings in the county court or, if it has no jurisdiction, the High Court.[72] If the landlord or licensor fails to comply with the requirements of the Act, he may be guilty of both the offence[73] and the statutory tort of unlawful eviction.[74] The court has some discretion in fixing the date for the surrender of possession.[75] The

---

[65] See *post*, paras 22–005 *et seq*.

[66] ss.6, 12(3). s.13 abolishes common law offences of forcible entry and forcible detainer and repealed the Forcible Entry Acts 1381–1623.

[67] s.3, as amended by H.A. 1980 and H.A. 1988. See S. Bridge, *Residential Leases*, pp. 268–271.

[68] For such tenancies, see P.E.A. 1977, s.8. They include a protected occupancy or statutory tenancy under the Rent (Agriculture) Act 1976, a protected tenancy under the Rent Act 1977 (but not a statutory tenancy: see *Haniff v. Robinson* [1993] Q.B. 419 at 426), an assured tenancy or assured agricultural occupancy under the Housing Act 1988, and a tenancy of an agricultural holding under the Agricultural Holdings Act 1986. See *National Trust v. Knipe* [1998] 1 W.L.R. 230.

[69] For such tenancies, see P.E.A. 1977, s.3A (inserted by H.A. 1988, s.31). They include tenancies of accommodation shared with the landlord or a member of his family as his or their only or principal home, holiday lettings and property let otherwise than for money or money's worth. See *West Wiltshire D.C. v. Snelgrove* (1997) 30 H.L.R. 57.

[70] P.E.A. 1977, s.3(2B) (inserted by H.A. 1988, s.30). Licences are excluded: (i) on the same ground as are tenancies; and (ii) if they confer rights of occupation in hostels provided by certain bodies: P.E.A. 1977, s.3A.

[71] A service occupancy is treated as a tenancy for these purposes: P.E.A. 1977, s.8(2).

[72] *ibid.*, ss.3(1), 9(1). Even if the landlord obtains an order for possession from the court, he cannot peaceably re-enter. The order must be executed by the bailiff: *Haniff v. Robinson, supra*.

[73] P.E.A. 1977, s.1(2); *ante*, para. 14–203.

[74] H.A. 1988, s.27; *ante*, para. 14–201. See *e.g. Haniff v. Robinson, supra.*

[75] *McPhail v. Persons Unknown* [1973] Ch. 447 at 459, 460.

Act does not, however, affect the jurisdiction of the High Court in proceedings for forfeiture of a lease, or to enforce a mortgagee's right to possession where there is a tenancy not binding on him.[76] The Act also makes special provision for the court to suspend the execution of any order for possession of an agricultural "tied dwelling", *i.e.* a dwelling occupied by an agricultural worker under the terms of his employment.[77]

B. *Position of the Tenant*

1. Obligation to pay rent. This is discussed below.[78]   **14–230**

2. Obligation to pay rates and taxes. The tenant is under an obligation to   **14–231**
pay all rates and taxes except those for which the landlord is liable. A landlord is liable to pay income tax under Schedule A in respect of profits and gains arising in respect of rents under leases of land.[79] By contrast, the tenant is liable to pay—

    (i) rates where he is the occupier of non-domestic property[80]; or

    (ii) council tax where he is a resident of a dwelling house.[81]

3. Obligation not to commit waste

(a) Tenants for years. The law of voluntary and permissive waste has   **14–232**
already been explained in connection with freehold estates.[82] Under the ancient common law it had no application to leaseholds.[83] But since 1267 it has been laid down by statute that a tenant for a fixed term of years is liable for both voluntary and permissive waste, unless there is a contrary agreement.[84] This means that if the terms of the tenancy make no provision about

---

[76] P.E.A., s.9(3) (reversing the effect of *Borzak v. Ahmed* [1965] 2 Q.B. 320, a case on forfeiture); and see *Bolton B.S. v. Cobb* [1966] 1 W.L.R. 1 (tenancy not binding on mortgagee; for such tenancies, see *post*, para. 19–121).

[77] P.E.A. 1977, s.4. See, *e.g. Crane v. Morris* [1965] 1 W.L.R. 1104.

[78] *Post*, para. 14–245.

[79] See Income and Corporation Taxes Act 1988, s.15 and Pt II.

[80] See Local Government Finance Act 1988, Pt III. The burden of payment falls on the occupier. *ibid.*, s.43. For the definition of a "non-domestic hereditament", see *ibid.*, s.66.

[81] See Local Government Finance Act 1992, Pt I. It is the person who resides on the premises who is obliged to pay: *ibid.*, s.6.

[82] *Ante*, para. 3–098.

[83] At common law only tenants whose estates arose by operation of law, such as by curtesy or dower, were liable for waste. Tenants who estates arose by act of parties were not liable unless the grantor had imposed this liability upon them.

[84] Statute of Marlbridge 1267, making lessees for life or years liable for waste; *Yellowly v. Gower* (1855) 11 Exch. 274; *Davies v. Davies* (1888) 38 Ch.D. 499 at 504. The severe penalties imposed by the Statute of Gloucester, 1278, were repealed by the Civil Procedure Acts Repeal Act 1879.

repairs,[85] the tenant is liable for them and must maintain the property in the condition in which he took it.[86]

14–233   *(b) Yearly tenancies.* Under yearly and other periodic tenancies, the tenant must use the premises in a tenant-like manner.[87] Thus he will be liable for voluntary waste,[88] and he must not alter the character of the property, as by converting premises let as a shop and dwelling into one large shop.[89] As regards permissive waste, a yearly tenant is merely liable to keep the premises wind- and water-tight,[90] fair wear and tear excepted.[91]

14–234   *(c) Weekly tenancies.* A weekly tenant is, it seems, normally absolved from any liability for permissive waste by the implied understanding that "the house will be kept in reasonable and habitable condition . . . by the landlord and not by the tenant".[92] This does not make the landlord liable to repair[93]; it merely absolves the tenant. But the tenant is under a duty to use the premises in a tenant-like manner[94]: he must "take proper care of the place. He must, if he is going away for the winter,[95] turn off the water and empty the boiler. He must clean the chimneys, when necessary, and also the windows. He must mend the electric light when it fuses. He must unstop the sink when it is blocked by his waste. . . . But apart from such things, if the house falls into disrepair through fair wear and tear or lapse of time, or for any reason not caused by him, then the tenant is not liable to repair it".[96] The position of a monthly or quarterly tenant, though uncertain, is probably similar.

14–235   *(d) Tenancies at will and at sufferance.* A tenant at will is not liable for permissive waste[97]; but if he commits voluntary waste his tenancy is thereby terminated and he is liable to an action for damages.[98] A tenant at sufferance is liable for voluntary waste[99] but probably not for permissive waste.

14–236   *(e) Third parties.* A person who directs or procures a tenant to commit waste may himself be liable in tort for so doing. Thus where a company was

---

[85] There are conflicting views as to whether, if there is a repairing covenant, the landlord can sue the tenant in tort for waste rather than on the covenant: see *Mancetter Developments Ltd v. Garmanson Ltd* [1986] Q.B. 1212 at 1218 (where Dillon L.J. suggested that he could) and 1223 (where Kerr L.J. took a contrary view). The earlier authorities firmly support the former view: see *Kinlyside v. Thornton* (1776) 2 W.Bl. 1111; *Marker v. Kenrick* (1853) 13 C.B. 188.

[86] Contrast the statement by Denning L.J. in *Warren v. Keen* [1954] 1 Q.B. 15 at 20 that a tenant is prima facie not liable for repair. This branch of the law is strangely uncertain: see (1954) 70 L.Q.R. 9 (R.E.M.); [1954] C.L.J. 71 (H.W.R.W.).

[87] *Marsden v. Edward Heyes Ltd* [1927] 2 K.B. 1; *Warren v. Keen* [1954] 1 Q.B. 15.

[88] See *Warren v. Keen, supra*, at 21.

[89] *Marsden v. Edward Heyes Ltd, supra.*

[90] *Wedd v. Porter* [1916] 2 K.B. 91; but the test is doubtful: see *Warren v. Keen, supra.*

[91] See *Warren v. Keen, supra*; for fair wear and tear, see *post*, para. 14–276.

[92] *Mint v. Good* [1951] 1 K.B. 517 at 522, *per* Somervell L.J.

[93] *Mint v. Good, supra*, at 522; *Sleafer v. Lambeth B.C.* [1960] 1 Q.B. 43 (weekly tenancy).

[94] *Warren v. Keen, supra.*

[95] But not if for two nights: *Wycombe Area Health Authority v. Barnett* (1982) 47 P. & C.R. 394.

[96] *Warren v. Keen, supra*, at 20, *per* Denning L.J.

[97] *Harnett v. Maitland* (1847) 16 M. & W. 257.

[98] *Countess of Shrewsbury's Case* (1600) 5 Co.Rep. 13b.

[99] *Burchell v. Hornsby* (1808) 1 Camp. 360.

a tenant and, on the instruction of its managing director, its employees removed the tenant's fixtures without making good the consequent damage, both the company and the director were held liable in waste.[1]

(f) Reform. The Law Commission has recommended that the tort of waste should be abolished to the extent that it applies to tenants for years, at will or at sufferance and to licensees.[2] There would instead be implied covenants by a tenant for years—   **14–237**

    (a)   to take proper care of the premises as a good tenant;

    (b)   to make good damage wilfully done by the tenant, any sub-tenant or lawful visitor to the premises; and

    (c)   not to carry out any alterations or other works which might destroy or alter the character of the premises to the landlord's detriment.

Similar covenants would be implied on the part of a licensee or tenants at will or sufferance.[3]

4. Landlord's right to view. The tenant is under an obligation to permit the landlord to enter and view the state of repair of the premises in cases where the landlord is liable to repair them.[4] The landlord may also have a statutory right to enter and view the premises in certain other cases.[5] But apart from these, unless he has reserved a right of entry, he has no right to enter the premises during the term, however good his reason (*e.g.* to do necessary repairs),[6] for he has given the tenant the right of exclusive possession as long as the tenancy endures.   **14–238**

5. Right to estovers. A tenant for years has the same right to estovers and botes as a tenant for life.[7]   **14–239**

Section 2. Position of the Parties under a Lease containing the Usual Covenants

1. Contracts for leases. The rights and duties set out above are those which arise when a lease is granted and there is no agreement to the contrary. But   **14–240**

---

[1] *Mancetter Developments Ltd v. Garmanson Ltd* [1986] Q.B. 1212.

[2] (1996) Law Com. No. 238, Pt X. Liability for waste would remain as regards those with limited interests in possession under a trust.

[3] To overcome the problem that such relationships are commonly gratuitous, the tenant or licensee would be deemed to have covenanted for valuable consideration for the purpose of assessing damages for breach of the implied obligations.

[4] See *Saner v. Bilton* (1878) 7 Ch.D. 815 (express covenant); *Mint v. Good* [1951] 1 K.B. 517 (implied obligation).

[5] See, *e.g.* A.H.A. 1986, s.23; L. & T.A. 1927, s.10; L. & T.A. 1985, s.11(6).

[6] *Stocker v. Planet B.S.* (1879) 27 W.R. 877; *Regional Properties Ltd v. City of London Real Property Co. Ltd* [1981] 1 E.G.L.R. 33.

[7] Co.Litt. 41b: *ante*, para. 3–105.

where, as occasionally happens, the lease is preceded by a contract that such a lease shall be granted,[8] the position of the parties is usually rather different, even where the contract is silent as to the covenants to be included. For the rule is that it is an implied term in a contract for a lease that the lease shall contain "the usual covenants".[9] If nevertheless the lease does not contain them, owing to the mistake of both parties when drawing it up, the lease may be rectified so as to accord with the contract.[10]

Where the "usual covenants" are to be included, they do not weaken the ordinary implied obligations of both parties, which have already been explained. In some instances they merely make express provision for what would otherwise be implied; in others they impose rather more extensive liabilities.[11]

14–241   **2. The usual covenants.** The following covenants and conditions are always "usual".[12]

(a) On the part of the landlord—

a covenant for quiet enjoyment in the usual qualified form,[13] *i.e.* extending only to the acts of the lessor or the rightful acts of anyone claiming from or under him.

(b) On the part of the tenant—

(i) a covenant to pay rent;

(ii) a covenant to pay tenant's rates and taxes, *i.e.* all rates and taxes except those which statute requires the landlord to bear[14];

(iii) a covenant to keep the premises in repair and deliver them up in repair at the end of the term;

(iv) (if the landlord has undertaken any obligation to repair) a covenant to permit the landlord to enter and view the state of repair;

(v) a condition of re-entry for non-payment of rent, but not for breach of any other covenant.[15]

---

[8] For the distinction between lease and contract, see *ante*, para. 14–040.

[9] *Propert v. Parker* (1832) 3 My. & K. 280; *Morrall v. Krause* [1994] E.G.C.S. 177.

[10] For rectification, see *ante*, para. 12–122.

[11] For criticism of the basis on which the usual covenants are implied, see [1992] Conv. 18 (L. Crabb).

[12] See *Hampshire v. Wickens* (1878) 7 Ch.D. 555.

[13] *Hampshire v. Wickens, supra.*

[14] See *ante*, para. 14–231.

[15] *Hodgkinson v. Crowe* (1875) 10 Ch.App. 662; *Re Anderton & Milner's Contract* (1890) 45 Ch.D. 476. This is so even in the case of a lease of a public-house: *Re Lander and Bagley's Contract* [1892] 3 Ch. 41.

3. Other usual covenants. In addition to the above provisions, which are **14–242** always "usual", other covenants may be "usual" in the circumstances of the case, by virtue, for example, of the custom of the neighbourhood or normal commercial usage[16]; in each case this is a question of fact for the court. "It may very well be that what is usual in Mayfair or Bayswater is not usual at all in other parts of London, such, for instance, as Whitechapel."[17] Under an agreement for a commercial lease of garage workshops in London for 14 years from 1971 it was held that the usual covenants included tenants' covenants not to alter the appearance or user of the building (consent not to be unreasonably withheld), not to obstruct lights or allow encroachments, and not to allow nuisances; and a right of re-entry for breach of any covenant.[18]

4. Covenants commonly inserted. Many covenants which in practice are **14–243** usually inserted in leases and are therefore literally "usual" may nevertheless not be deemed to be "usual" in the technical sense of the word. Examples are covenants against assignment,[19] covenants against carrying on specified trades,[20] and provision for forfeiture for breaches of any covenant, whether for payment of rent or otherwise.[21] Such provisions are frequently inserted when no contract to take a lease has been made and the terms of the lease are a matter for negotiation between the parties. But if a contract for a lease has been made, no covenant can be inserted in the lease without the concurrence of both parties unless either the contract provides for it or the covenant is technically a "usual" covenant.

Section 3. Position under Certain Covenants Commonly Found in Leases

In addition to the covenants already considered there are a number of others **14–244** which are very often agreed upon and need brief explanation.

1. Covenant to pay rent

(a) Nature of rent. Rent has been described as: "(i) a periodical sum, **14–245** (ii) paid in return for the occupation of land, (iii) issuing out of the land, (iv)

---

[16] See *Flexman v. Corbett* [1930] 1 Ch. 672 at 678, *per* Maugham J.: "if it is established that (to put a strong case) in nine cases out of ten the covenant would be found in a lease of premises of that nature for that purpose and in that district, I think the court is bound to hold that the covenant is usual".

[17] *ibid.*, at 678, *per* Maugham J. See too *Charalambous v. Ktori* [1972] 1 W.L.R. 951.

[18] *Chester v. Buckingham Travel Ltd* [1981] 1 W.L.R. 96; (1981) 97 L.Q.R. 385 (G. Woodman).

[19] *Lady De Soysa v. De Pless Pol* [1912] A.C. 194.

[20] *Propert v. Parker* (1832) 3 My. & K. 280.

[21] *Re Anderton & Milner's Contract* (1890) 45 Ch.D. 476. Contrast *Chester v. Buckingham Travel Ltd, supra,* See Woodfall L. & T. 4.031 for other examples.

for the non-payment of which a distress[22] is leviable".[23] This description reflects the fact that, under a normal form of written lease, the landlord has two rights to rent. The first is by reservation of the rent-service in the terms of the grant. The second is under the tenant's express or implied covenant to pay the rent reserved. In practice rent is nowadays normally regarded as a contractual payment.[24] Unless the lease provides otherwise, rent is payable in arrear.[25] Sometimes a service charge is expressed to be payable as rent and will be so treated.[26] However, as already explained, the restrictions on forfeiting a lease for non-payment of service charge will apply to that element of the rent.[27]

A rent may be made to vary with circumstances (as was done in *Walsh v. Lonsdale*[28]), and there is nothing to prevent rent being reserved in kind,[29] *e.g.* bottles of wine,[30] or in services, *e.g.* the doing of team work[31] or cleaning the parish church.[32] In one case an ill-drafted "gold clause" reserving an annual rent equivalent to £1,900 in gold sterling was said to entitle the lessor only to £1,900 in bank notes, one ground being a variable rent linked to the price of gold was contrary to public policy.[33] But this surprising decision has not been followed.[34]

A provision in a lease entitling the landlord to increase or reduce the rent to any sum that he wishes is not void for uncertainty.[35] What is required is that the rent should be ascertained or ascertainable at the time when payment is due.[36] Once a lease has been granted the court will strive to give meaning to indefinite provisions about rent. Thus it sometimes happens that the lease

---

[22] *Post*, para. 14–253.
[23] *Escalus Properties Ltd v. Robinson* [1996] Q.B. 231, 243, *per* Nourse L.J. Rent reserved by a lease is properly called rent-*service*, because there is tenure and privity of estate: Litt. 113, 214, 215; see *ante*, para. 3–015. It is said to be "incident to the reversion" of the landlord: Co.Litt. 143a. In this way it is distinguished from a rent *charge* (*post*, para. 18–014), which is a rent reserved out of land but not attached to any reversion.
[24] "In modern law rent is no longer thought of as a thing issuing out of land and recoverable by distraint but as a payment which a tenant is bound by his contract to make to his landlord for the use of the land": *Ingram v. I.R.C.* [1995] 4 All E.R. 334 at 340, *per* Ferris J. summarising the effect of the authorities (*ante*, para. 14–003). In practice, distress for rent is more common than this statement might suggest: *post*, para. 14–253.
[25] *Coomber v. Howard* (1845) 1 C.B. 440.
[26] *Escalus Properties Ltd v. Robinson, supra*, at 243, 244; L. & T.A. 1985, s.18.
[27] H.A. 1996, s.81; *ante*, para. 14–156.
[28] *Ante*, para. 14–043. See also *Selby v. Greaves* (1868) L.R. 2 C.P. 594 at 602; *Smith v. Cardiff Corporation (No. 2)* [1955] Ch. 159 at 173; (1957) 21 Conv. (N.S.) 265 (B. Hargrove).
[29] Co.Litt. 142a.
[30] *Pitcher v. Tovey* (1692) 4 Mod. 71.
[31] *Duke of Marlborough v. Osborn* (1864) 5 B. & S. 67.
[32] *Doe d. Edney v. Benham* (1845) 7 Q.B. 976. Contrast *Barnes v. Barratt* [1970] 2 Q.B. 657 (services not "rent" for purposes of Rent Acts).
[33] *Treseder-Griffin v. Co-operative Insurance Society Ltd* [1956] 2 Q.B. 127 at 145, *per* Denning L.J.
[34] *Multiservice Bookbinding Ltd v. Marden* [1979] Ch. 84, holding that mortgage payments linked to the Swiss franc were enforceable. See too *Nationwide B.S. v. Registry of Friendly Societies* [1983] 1 W.L.R. 1226.
[35] *Greater London Council v. Connolly* [1970] 2 Q.B. 100 (increase of council house rent).
[36] *ibid.*

stipulates the initial rent for a fixed period and then provides that the rent thereafter is to be agreed or determined. If no formula is given for its assessment, the rent will be determined according to what it would be reasonable for the particular parties to the lease to agree.[37] By contrast, where a formula is given, the assessment is likely to be an objective one, as where the rent was to be "a reasonable rent for the demised premises".[38] The difficult case of "a fair and reasonable market rent" has been held to mean an open market rental.[39]

(b) Rent review clauses

(1) NATURE. In the absence of any express provision in the lease or statutory right, the landlord cannot increase the rent except by giving the tenant notice to quit.[40] It has therefore long been the practice for landlords, when granting leases for any length of time (especially commercial leases), to insert rent review clauses.[41] The general purpose of these provisions "is to enable the landlord to obtain from time to time the market rental which the premises would command if let on the same terms on the open market at the review dates", and "to reflect the changes in the value of money and real increases in the value of the property during a long term".[42] In practice rent review clauses are of the greatest importance and often influence the other terms of the lease such as the responsibility for repairs and the ability of the tenant to assign and sublet. However, a full account of them lies beyond the scope of this book.[43]

14–246

(2) CONTENTS. A rent review clause will, typically, make provision for—

14–247

    (i) the timing of both the review and the date on which the new rent will become payable;

---

[37] See *ARC Ltd v. Schofield* [1990] 2 E.G.L.R. 52 and 54. For examples, see *Thomas Bates & Son Ltd v. Wyndham's (Lingerie) Ltd* [1981] 1 W.L.R. 505; *Central & Metropolitan Estates Ltd v. Compusave* [1983] 1 E.G.L.R. 60; *Lear v. Blizzard* [1983] 3 All E.R. 662. See too *Beer v. Bowden* (1976) [1981] 1 W.L.R. 522 n. (such rent as was agreed between landlord and tenant but disregarding any tenant's improvements).

[38] *Ponsford v. H.M.S. Aerosols Ltd* [1979] A.C. 63 (taken to mean the premises together with the tenant's improvements). *cf. English Exporters (London) Ltd v. Eldonwall Ltd* [1973] Ch. 415 ("a rent which would be reasonable for a tenant to pay" may mean that the tenant's improvements are ignored).

[39] *ARC Ltd v. Schofield, supra.*

[40] *Greater London Council v. Connolly, supra*, at 108. For a statutory right to increase the rent see, *e.g.* H.A. 1988, s.13; *post*, para. 22–172.

[41] For the statutory rent review procedure applicable to farm business tenancies, see A.H.A. 1995, Pt II; *post*, para. 22–092.

[42] *British Gas Corporation v. Universities Superannuation Scheme Ltd* [1986] 1 W.L.R. 398 at 401, *per* Browne-Wilkinson V.-C. See too *M.F.I. Properties Ltd v. B.I.C.C. Group Pension Trust Ltd* [1986] 1 All E.R. 974 at 975; *Basingstoke and Deane B.C. v. Host Group Ltd* [1988] 1 W.L.R. 348 at 353.

[43] The case law is extensive. Reference should be made to specialist works, such as R. Bernstein, K. Reynolds and M. Rodger, *Handbook of Rent Review*; D. Clarke and J. Adams, *Rent Reviews and Variable Rents* (3rd ed.); Woodfall, L. & T. chap. 8.

    (ii) the machinery for initiating the review and for agreeing the new rent;

    (iii) the method of calculating the new rent[44]; and

    (iv) the resolution of disputes.[45]

14–248   (3) TIME. It is now settled that as a general rule time is not of the essence for the various steps that have to be taken to initiate the rent review and during the course of it.[46] The presumption is a strong one[47] that will be rebutted only by a compelling contra-indication.[48] Even where the delay is unreasonable or such as will cause hardship to the tenant, the landlord may still claim a rent review which will be retrospective to the relevant date.[49] Time will be of the essence if the agreement so provides, expressly or impliedly,[50] as where the same timetable is set both for the review and for the tenant's right to determine the tenancy, for which time is of the essence.[51] However, the fact that time expressly is of the essence for certain of the steps does not mean that it will be for others.[52] Where the tenant has no right to initiate the review, he may serve a notice on the landlord requiring him to do so within a specified time.[53] If the landlord then fails to do so, he will lose his right to a review.[54]

14–249   (4) CONSTRUCTION. A rent review clause usually postulates a hypothetical letting of the premises at an open market rental between a willing landlord and

---

[44] Usually some formula for determining an open market rental together with various assumptions and disregards.

[45] Dispute resolution is either by arbitrator or by expert. It is more difficult to challenge an expert's decision than it is an arbitrator's. An arbitrator is subject to the provisions of the Arbitration Act 1996.

[46] *United Scientific Holdings Ltd v. Burnley B.C.* [1978] A.C. 904 (99-year lease provided for rent review in the year preceding each 10-year period of the term: landlord entitled to have the rent reviewed after the stipulated time); *Bickenhall Engineering Co. Ltd v. Grandmet Restaurants Ltd* [1995] 1 E.G.L.R. 110.

[47] *Panavia Air Cargo Ltd v. Southend-on-Sea B.C.* [1988] 1 E.G.L.R. 124.

[48] *Phipps-Faire Ltd v. Malbern Construction Ltd* [1987] 1 E.G.L.R. 129 at 131.

[49] *London & Manchester Assurance Co. Ltd v. G.A. Dunn & Co.* [1983] 1 E.G.L.R. 111 at 118; *Amherst v. James Walker Goldsmith & Silversmith Ltd* [1983] Ch. 305. The landlord might be estopped from exercising his right (*ibid.*, at 316), as where he represented in some way that he would not activate the clause and the tenant acted to his detriment in reliance upon it, *e.g.* by not exercising a break clause.

[50] Contrast *Drebbond Ltd v. Horsham D.C.* (1978) 37 P. & C.R. 237 ("and not otherwise") with *Touche Ross & Co. v. Secretary of State for the Environment* (1982) 46 P. & C.R. 187.

[51] *United Scientific Holdings, supra* at 962; *Al Saloom v. Shirley James Travel Service Ltd* (1982) 42 P. & C.R. 181; *Coventry City Council v. J. Hepworth & Son Ltd* [1983] 1 E.G.L.R. 119; *Legal & General Assurance (Pension Management) Ltd v. Cheshire County Council* (1982) 46 P. & C.R. 160. The authorities are reviewed in *Central Estates Ltd v. Secretary of State for the Environment* (1995) 72 P. & C.R. 482.

[52] *cf. Kings (Estate Agents) Ltd v. Anderson* [1992] 1 E.G.L.R. 121.

[53] If the tenant can initiate the review, he cannot serve such a notice: *Factory Holdings Group Ltd v. Leboff International Ltd* [1987] 1 E.G.L.R. 135.

[54] See *London & Manchester Assurance Co. Ltd v. G.A. Dunn & Co.* [1983] 1 E.G.L.R. 111 at 118; *Amherst v. James Walker Goldsmith & Silversmith Ltd* [1983] Ch. 305 at 318.

a willing tenant.[55] In construing a particular clause a court will not generally rely on previous decisions as an aid to construction,[56] though they have accepted some guidelines.[57] The courts will however have regard to the commercial purpose of a rent review clause.[58] There is therefore a "presumption of reality" by which, in the absence of contrary provision or necessary implication, "it is assumed that the hypothetical letting required by the clause is of the premises as they actually were, on the terms of the actual lease and in the circumstances as they actually existed".[59] If the language employed is capable of more than one meaning, the court will select the one that accords with the commercial purpose of the clause.[60] There is no presumption that a rent review clause is upward only.[61]

(c) Other rules. The tenant ceases to be liable to the landlord for the rent **14–250** where the amount owing has been paid by a third party under a contract of guarantee.[62] This is so even if that sum has been paid by the surety to secure his release from the guarantee.[63] Furthermore, a husband or wife with statutory rights of occupation may pay rent on behalf of the other spouse.[64] If the landlord refuses to accept rent from the tenant, so that the tenant cannot make title to an assignee, the tenant may obtain a declaration from the court, at the landlord's expense in costs, that the lease is not liable to forfeiture.[65]

If the tenant is wrongfully evicted from any part of the premises by the landlord[66] or by any person claiming under the landlord,[67] the whole of the

---

[55] There is, however, no assumption as to the state of the market in which these hypothetical parties operate: see *Dennis & Robinson Ltd v. Kiossos Establishment* [1987] 1 E.G.L.R. 133 at 135.

[56] See *Equity & Law Life Assurance Society Plc v. Bodfield Ltd* [1987] 1 E.G.L.R. 124 at 125; *Prudential Assurance Co. Ltd v. 99 Bishopsgate Ltd* [1992] 1 E.G.L.R. 119 at 120.

[57] See *British Gas Corporation v. Universities Superannuation Scheme Ltd* [1986] 1 W.L.R. 398 at 403.

[58] *Basingstoke and Deane B.C. v. Host Group Ltd* [1988] 1 W.L.R. 348 at 353.

[59] *Co-operative Wholesale Society Ltd v. National Westminster Bank Plc* [1995] 1 E.G.L.R. 97 at 99, *per* Hoffmann L.J. See too *Basingstoke and Deane B.C. v. Host Group Ltd, supra* at 354; *Ocean Accident & Guarantee Corporation v. Next Plc* [1996] 2 E.G.L.R. 84 at 86; *Braid v. Walsall M.B.C.* (1998) 78 P. & C.R. 94.

[60] *M.F.I. Properties Ltd v. B.I.C.C. Group Pension Trust Ltd* [1986] 1 All E.R. 974 at 976.

[61] *Philpots (Woking) Ltd v. Surrey Conveyancers Ltd* [1986] 1 E.G.L.R. 97 at 98.

[62] *Milverton Group Ltd v. Warner World Ltd* [1995] 2 E.G.L.R. 28, applying *Re Hawkins* [1972] Ch. 714 at 724–729, and holding that remarks to the contrary in *London and County (A. & D.) Ltd v. Wilfred Sportsman Ltd* [1971] Ch. 764 at 780 were inconsistent with *P. & A. Swift Investments v. Combined English Stores Group Plc* [1989] A.C. 632 at 638, 642. However a tender of rent by a third party will not otherwise discharge the tenant unless made by him as the tenant's agent with prior authority or subsequent ratification: *Richards v. De Freitas* (1974) 29 P. & C.R. 1; *Bessa Plus Plc v. Lancaster* (1997) 30 H.L.R. 48.

[63] *Milverton Group Ltd v. Warner World Ltd, supra.* The landlord is however entitled to appropriate the payments to the sums owed to him and may defer so doing until it becomes necessary: *ibid.,* at 31, 32.

[64] F.L.A. 1996, s.30(3), applying also to mortgage payments and other outgoings. For this Act, see *post,* para. 17–023.

[65] *Preston v. Lindlands Ltd* [1976] 2 E.G.L.R. 50 (ground rent refused).

[66] *Morrison v. Chadwick* (1849) 7 C.B. 266.

[67] *Neale v. Mackenzie* (1836) 1 M. & W. 747. See *ante,* para. 14–204.

rent (but not liability under the other covenants) is suspended while the eviction lasts. But if the eviction is by some person lawfully claiming by title paramount, only an apportioned part of the rent is suspended[68]; and if the landlord is the Crown, the requisitioning of the land under statutory powers is not an unlawful eviction and the rent is not suspended.[69]

No rent is recoverable if the tenancy was granted for an immoral purpose,[70] or for some illegal purpose, such as deceiving the rating authorities.[71]

14–251   Where the premises let consist of or include a dwelling,[72] the landlord is required to provide by written notice[73] an address in England and Wales at which notices may be served on him by the tenant.[74] If he fails to do so, any rent (or service charge) otherwise due is treated as not being due at any time before the landlord does comply with this requirement.[75] Once that happens, however, any arrears of rent are recoverable by him.[76]

Where a weekly rent is payable for a residence the landlord is required to provide a rent book containing the landlord's name and address and a variety of information in prescribed form.[77] Failure to provide a proper rent book is a criminal offence, but it does not prevent the landlord from recovering rent due.[78]

Where there is no agreement either for a rent or for a rent-free tenancy the landlord may recover from the tenant a reasonable sum, assessed at the ordinary market value,[79] for the use and occupation of the land.[80] This right is based upon implied contract reinforced by statute,[81] and it applies to all forms of tenancy, including tenancy at sufferance.[82] It is to be distinguished

---

[68] *Neale v. Mackenzie, supra*, at 758, 759.

[69] *Commissioners of Crown Lands v. Page* [1960] 2 Q.B. 274.

[70] *Upfill v. Wright* [1911] 1 K.B. 506. Contrast *Heglibiston Establishment v. Heyman* (1977) 36 P. & C.R. 351 (unmarried cohabitation no longer regarded as immoral purpose).

[71] *Alexander v. Rayson* [1936] 1 K.B. 169.

[72] Which for these purposes include agricultural lettings but not business tenancies: see L. & T.A. 1987, s.46; *Lindsey Trading Properties Inc. v. Dallhold Estates (U.K.) Pty Ltd* (1993) 70 P. & C.R. 332; [1994] Conv. 325 (M. Haley).

[73] An oral communication will not suffice: see *Rogan v. Woodfield Building Services Ltd* (1994) 27 H.L.R. 78; [1995] Conv. 154 (M. Haley).

[74] L. & T.A. 1987, s.48(1). The obligation will be satisfied by a statement of the landlord's name and address in the lease: *Rogan v. Woodfield Building Services Ltd, supra*. If there is any change of landlord the tenant must be notified in any event: L. & T.A. 1985, s.3. *cf. Lindsey Trading Properties Inc. v. Dallhold Estates (U.K.) Pty Ltd, supra*. A notice under s.48 is not necessarily invalid because it gives more than one address for service: see *Marath v. MacGillivray* (1996) 28 H.L.R. 484 at 495.

[75] L. & T.A. 1987, s.48(2). This means, *e.g.* that the landlord cannot take steps to forfeit the lease for non-payment of rent: see *Hussain v. Singh* [1993] 2 E.G.L.R. 70 at 71.

[76] *Lindsey Trading Properties Inc. v. Dallhold Estates (U.K.) Pty Ltd, supra*.

[77] L. & T.A. 1985, s.4(1); S.I. 1982 No. 1474; S.I. 1988 No. 2198; S.I. 1990 No. 1067.

[78] *Shaw v. Groom* [1970] 2 Q.B. 504.

[79] *Dean and Chapter of Canterbury Cathedral v. Whitbread Plc* (1995) 72 P. & C.R. 9. In assessing this, the court will "look at the actual parties in their actual situation": *ibid.*, at 17, *per* Judge Cooke.

[80] *Gibson v. Kirk* (1841) 1 Q.B. 850; Foa, L. & T. 403.

[81] Distress for Rent Act 1737, s.4.

[82] *Ante*, para. 14–079.

from the right of action to recover mesne profits, which lies against a trespasser and is mentioned later.[83]

(d) Enforcement. The landlord may enforce payment of the rent—

14–252

    (a)   directly, by—

        (i) an action for the money, or

        (ii) distress, *i.e.* seizing the tenant's goods[84];

    (b)   indirectly, by the threat of forfeiture if the lease contains a forfeiture clause.

Forfeiture has already been dealt with[85] and there is no need to discuss an action for the money. But distress must be considered in outline.

(e) Distress

(1) NATURE OF DISTRESS. "Distress for rent is a remedy which enables **14–253** landlords to recover arrears of rent, without going to court,[86] by taking goods from the demised property and selling them.[87] In essence distress is the ancient feudal remedy by which a lord could coerce his tenant into rendering his services.[88] The right to distrain for rent arises automatically only where there is the relationship of landlord and tenant (legal or equitable).[89] Distress may therefore be levied against a tenant at will,[90] but not against a tenant at sufferance.[91] Although distress had fallen into disuse,[92] it has undergone a modern revival.[93]

In general, the right to distress arises as soon as rent is overdue. The landlord himself or his bailiff acting on his behalf[94] may then enter the premises[95] without formal demand and seize and impound any chattels that are found there.[96] He may take only enough property to provide reasonable security for the outstanding rent and expenses.[97] To levy distress there must be

---

[83] *Post,* Appendix.

[84] Suing or distraining will normally waive any right of forfeiture (*ante,* para. 14–126), so that they are alternative and not additional remedies to forfeiture. But in actions for forfeiture arrears of rent may be claimed (see, *e.g. Evans v. Enever* [1920] 2 K.B. 315).

[85] *Ante,* para. 14–118.

[86] Because the levying of distress is not a process involving court proceedings, it is not barred by an interim order made under I.A. 1986, s.252 to protect a tenant against (*inter alia*) "execution or other legal process" without the leave of the court: *McMullen & Sons Ltd v. Cerrone* [1994] 1 B.C.L.C. 152; *Re a Debtor* [1995] 1 W.L.R. 1127 at 1137, 1138. This is anomalous because the right to distress is conterminous with the right to recover rent by action (see *infra*).

[87] *Rhodes v. Allied Dunbar Pension Service* [1989] 1 W.L.R. 800 at 803, *per* Nicholls L.J.

[88] It might be employed in other situations, *e.g.* by an owner of a market for tolls. The lawfulness of distress could be tested by proceedings for replevin: *post,* para. 14–256.

[89] See *ante,* paras 14–002, 14–043.

[90] Co.Litt. 142b; *Turner v. Barnes* (1862) 2 B. & S. 435.

[91] *Williams v. Stiven* (1846) 9 Q.B. 14; Woodfall L. & T. 9.006.

[92] *Abingdon R.D.C. v. O'Gorman* [1968] 2 Q.B. 811 at 819.

[93] See (1991) Law Com. No. 194 para. 1.12.

[94] See *post,* para. 14–257 and (1986) L.C.C.P. No. 97, paras 2.7–2.11.

[95] The power to levy distress "is not dependent on an express right of re-entry, but is a remedy which the law confers on the landlord for the recovery of rent": *T. & E. Homes Ltd v. Robinson* [1979] 1 W.L.R. 452 at 458, *per* Templeman L.J.

[96] Statute of Marlbridge 1267, c. 15.

[97] *ibid.,* c. 4.

actual entry[98] on the premises save perhaps in exceptional circumstances.[99] Posting a notice of distress through the letter box does not suffice.[1] Seizure may be actual or constructive. Actual seizure occurs where the goods are identified and a declaration made that they are taken for distress. The nature of constructive seizure is uncertain, but it probably occurs where the landlord makes his intention to distrain apparent by his actions.[2] Impounding is the process by which the goods are placed in the custody of the law as a prelude to their sale.[3] It is not necessary that they should be actually retained by the party distraining them.[4]

The landlord's right to levy distress exists only where rent is due to him. He can recover no more by distress therefore than he can by action.[5] It follows that he may not distrain if his claim to rent will be defeated by a cross-claim by the tenant,[6] or if it is in respect of rent unpaid by a previous tenant before the lease was assigned.[7]

14-254   (2) THIRD PARTIES. Formerly a landlord could take in distress chattels found on the land[8] and sell them, even if they belonged to third parties,[9] *e.g.* lodgers. The Law of Distress Amendment Act 1908[10] provided some relief. Most third parties[11] can now protect their goods by making a written declaration in a prescribed form to the landlord.[12] There are also statutory provisions as to

---

[98] Which must be lawful. There is no right to forcible entry: *Evans v. South Ribble B.C.* [1992] Q.B. 757 at 764. Where possession has once been taken, forcible *re-entry* can only be justified if the bailiff is forcibly expelled or excluded: see *McLeod v. Butterwick* [1998] 1 W.L.R. 1603. The case contains a valuable explanation of distress for rent.

[99] *Evans v. South Ribble B.C., supra,* at 768, explaining *Cramer & Co. Ltd v. Mott* (1870) L.R. 5 Q.B. 357; *Werth v. London and Westminster Loan Co.* (1889) 5 T.L.R. 320.

[1] *Evans v. South Ribble B.C., supra* (a case involving distress in respect of unpaid community charge, but the principles are of general applicability: *ibid.,* at 763); [1993] Conv. 77 (J.E.M. Sulek).

[2] *Swann v. Earl of Falmouth* (1828) 8 B. & C. 456; *Evans v. South Ribble B.C., supra,* at 764; (1986) L.C.C.P. No. 97, para. 2.50.

[3] Originally a landlord had no right to sell the chattels: distress was merely coercive, not compensatory. However, the Distress for Rent Act 1689, s.1, gave a right of sale after five days, provided that notice was given to the tenant.

[4] *Jones v. Biernstein* [1899] 1 Q.B. 470. Distress is completed once the goods are impounded, though the goods may subsequently be abandoned: *Evans v. South Ribble B.C., supra,* at 765.

[5] *Eller v. Grovecrest Investments Ltd* [1995] Q.B. 272 at 278, 280.

[6] *Eller v. Grovecrest Investments Ltd, supra.* A tenant of an agricultural holding has a statutory right to set off any compensation against rent due to the landlord, and the latter may only distrain for the balance: A.H.A. 1986, s.17.

[7] *Wharfland Ltd v. South London Co-operative Building Co. Ltd* [1995] 2 E.G.L.R. 21.

[8] Or elsewhere, if fraudulently removed: Distress for Rent Act 1737, s.1.

[9] *Lyons v. Elliott* (1876) 1 Q.B.D. 210.

[10] Which itself replaced and extended the Lodgers' Goods Protection Act 1871.

[11] Including lodgers, certain undertenants and persons having no interest in the property, but excluding (*inter alia*) goods in the tenant's reputed ownership (which have been held not to include a van hired by the tenant: *Salford Van Hire (Contracts) Ltd v. Bocholt Developments Ltd* [1995] 2 E.G.L.R. 50), goods belonging to the tenant's spouse and goods comprised in a hire-purchase, consumer hire or conditional sale agreement with the tenant: Law of Distress Amendment Act 1908, ss.1, 4(1), 4A (added by the Consumer Credit Act 1974).

[12] *ibid.,* s.1. It may be signed by an agent: *Lawrence Chemical Co. Ltd v. Rubinstein* [1982] 1 W.L.R. 284.

stock and machinery on agricultural holdings,[13] but not in relation to farm business tenancies.[14]

(3) PRIVILEGED GOODS. Many classes of goods, even if they belong to the tenant, are privileged against distress.[15] For example, things in actual use[16] and perishable may not be taken at all.[17] By statute the following are excepted from distress—

14–255

> (i) those tools, books, vehicles and other items of equipment which are necessary to the tenant for use personally by him in his employment, business or vocation[18]; and
>
> (ii) clothing, bedding, furniture, household equipment and provisions which are necessary to satisfy the basic domestic needs of the person.[19]

Fixtures may not be taken even though they may be removable as tenant's fixtures, since in law they are land, not chattels.[20] Similarly growing crops could not be distrained at common law,[21] nor could sheaves of corn, which could not be returned in the same state[22]; but both these privileges were taken away by statute.[23] In the case of agricultural holdings distress must be made within a year of the default.[24] And there are general rules, some of ancient origin, as to time: distress may not be levied between dusk and dawn, or on a Sunday.

(4) POUND-BREACH, RESCUE AND REPLEVIN. The landlord may impound the goods (*i.e.* secure them for safe custody) either on the premises[25] or elsewhere. If the tenant interferes with them he commits "pound-breach" and becomes liable to an action for treble damages.[26] But if the distress is illegal[27]

14–256

---

[13] A.H.A. 1986, s.18(1).

[14] Under A.T.A. 1995.

[15] See Woodfall L. & T. 9.046–9.085; A.H.A. 1986, ss.18, 19.

[16] Otherwise a breach of the peace would be probable: see *Storey v. Robinson* (1795) 6 T.R. 138.

[17] *e.g.* the carcasses of pigs (*Morley v. Pincomb*) (1848) 2 Exch. 101), for they could not be returned in the same condition if the tenant subsequently paid the rent.

[18] *e.g.* a piano used by a music teacher: *Boyd Ltd v. Bilham* [1909] 1 K.B. 14.

[19] C.C.A. 1984, s.89(1)(a) (as amended by the Courts and Legal Services Act 1990, s.15(2)).

[20] *Provincial Bill Posting Co. v. Low Moor Iron Co.* [1909] 2 K.B. 344.

[21] Co.Litt. 47a.

[22] *ibid.*

[23] Distress for Rent Acts 1689 and 1737.

[24] A.H.A. 1986, s.16. As indicated above, there are no equivalent provisions in relation to farm business tenancies.

[25] This is the more usual. It was authorised by the Distress for Rent Act 1737, s.10; before that, the tenant's consent was required before the goods could be impounded on the premises.

[26] Distress for Rent Act 1689, s.3. Once the goods have been distrained, it is a "rescue" to take them out of the custody of the distrainer, and treble damages can be recovered, (*ibid*). Pound-breach is also an indictable offence: Woodfall L. & T. 9.170. No action will lie against someone who innocently assists in the removal of the goods after the pound has been broken: *Lavell & Co. Ltd v. O'Leary* [1933] 2 K.B. 200.

[27] *i.e.* wrongful from the start, as where no rent is due.

or irregular[28] or excessive[29] the landlord is liable as for a trespass. In the case of illegal (but not irregular or excessive) distress the tenant has two other remedies: he may "rescue", *i.e.* re-take his goods, provided they are not yet impounded[30]; or he may "replevy", *i.e.* obtain in the county court an order for the return of the goods on his giving security for the rent and costs due, and undertaking to bring an action against the landlord.

14–257   (5) LEVY. A landlord who does not distrain in person is now required to employ a certificated bailiff, and it is by such a bailiff that distress is ordinarily levied.[31] It may be done by taking "taking possession", *i.e.* by leaving the goods impounded *in situ* on the premises under an agreement with the tenant.[32] But a third party who removes his goods without knowing that they are thus impounded does not commit pound-breach.[33] The court's leave to levy distress is required in the case of certain types of tenancy.[34]

The remedy of distress is not available for breach of any covenant except a covenant to pay rent.[35]

14–258   (6) REFORM. The law of distress is arcane and obscure[36] and "appears to have outlived its usefulness as a just remedy".[37] The Law Commission has recommended its abolition, describing it as "wrong in principle".[38]

2. Covenant against assignment, underletting or parting with possession

14–259   *(a) Rights of tenants.* If the lease is silent on the matter, the tenant may assign or underlet without the landlord's consent.[39] Accordingly a covenant against assignment, underletting or parting with possession of all or any part of the property is often inserted in leases. This cannot by itself invalidate an

---

[28] *i.e.* where the distress was lawful initially, but the procedure required by law has not been complied with, as where the goods are sold before the five days have expired.

[29] *i.e.* where more goods are seized than are reasonably necessary to satisfy the rent and costs.

[30] Once impounded they are "in the custody of the law".

[31] Law of Distress Amendment Act 1888, s.7. Certificates are granted by the county court and must be produced when distress is levied: Distress for Rent Rules 1988 (S.I. 1988 No. 2050).

[32] The bailiff has a right to charge for taking "walking possession": Distress for Rent Rules 1988 (S.I. 1988 No. 2050), App. 1.

[33] *Abingdon R.D.C. v. O'Gorman* [1968] 2 Q.B. 811.

[34] Namely, a protected occupancy or statutory tenancy under the Rent (Agriculture) Act 1976, s.8; a protected or statutory tenancy under the Rent Act 1977, s.147; and an assured tenancy under the Housing Act 1988, s.19.

[35] Not every sum described as rent in the lease will be distrainable rent. It will not, it seems, include fluctuating sums (such as service charge payments) which are often included as "rent" in the lease: *cf. United Scientific Holdings Ltd v. Burnley B.C.* [1978] A.C. 904 at 935, 947; (1986) L.C.C.P. No. 97, paras 2.13–2.16.

[36] See (1991) Law Com. No. 194, para. 2.17, where the criticisms of the remedy are listed; and [1992] C.L.P. 81 at 111 (A. Clarke). *cf.* [1991] Conv. 246 (H.W. Wilkinson).

[37] *Salford Van Hire (Contracts) Ltd v. Bocholt Developments Ltd* [1995] 2 E.G.L.R. 50 at 54, *per* Sir Ralph Gibson. See too Hirst L.J. at 54.

[38] (1991) Law Com. No. 194, para. 3.1.

[39] See *Doe d. Mitchinson v. Carter (No. 1)* (1798) 8 T.R. 57 at 60; *Leith Properties Ltd v. Byrne* [1983] Q.B. 433.

assignment or sub-lease as against the grantee,[40] for the tenant has an estate which is always alienable property.[41] However, there will be a breach of covenant which, if reinforced by a forfeiture clause, may result in the determination of the lease, and the landlord may in any case sue the assignor for damages. If, however, the landlord accepts rent from an assignee or sub-lessee, that amounts to an implied consent to the transaction.[42]

(b) Withholding consent. A covenant against assignment may be either **14–260** absolute or qualified. An absolute covenant forbids any assignment or under-letting. Although the landlord is free to waive it in any particular instance, he cannot be compelled to do so, even if his attitude is entirely unreasonable.[43] A qualified covenant is one against assigning, sub-letting or parting with possession without the landlord's licence or consent.[44] In theory the distinction between the two types of covenant of this kind is one of form, given the landlord's power to waive even an absolute covenant. The reality is otherwise. In practice, few tenants are likely to be willing to take a lease of any length subject to an absolute covenant against assignment. Furthermore, such a covenant is likely to have an adverse impact on any rent review.[45] In law, a qualified covenant is subject to significant statutory regulation,[46] whereas an absolute covenant is subject to none.

(c) Statutory restrictions on qualified covenants

(1) LANDLORD AND TENANT ACT 1927. The Landlord and Tenant Act 1927[47] **14–261** requires that, notwithstanding any contrary provision, a qualified covenant[48] shall be deemed to be subject to a proviso that the licence or consent is not to

---

[40] Even if the consent is obtained by fraud: *Sanctuary Housing Association v. Baker* [1998] 1 E.G.L.R. 42.

[41] *Parker v. Jones* [1910] 2 K.B. 32 at 38; *Property & Bloodstock Ltd v. Emerton* [1968] Ch. 94 at 110; *Old Grovebury Manor Farm Ltd v. W. Seymour Plant Sales and Hire Ltd (No. 2)* [1979] 1 W.L.R. 1397; *Peabody Donation Fund (Governors of) v. Higgins* [1983] 1 W.L.R. 1091. Contrast *Elliott v. Johnson* (1866) L.R. 2 Q.B. 120 at 126, 127.

[42] *Hyde v. Pimley* [1952] 2 Q.B. 506. For waiver implied from acceptance of rent, see *ante*, para. 14–126.

[43] See *Lilley and Skinner v. Crump* (1929) 73 S.J. 366; *F.W. Woolworth & Co. Ltd v. Lambert* [1937] Ch. 37 at 58, 59; but note *Property & Bloodstock v. Emerton, supra*, at 119.

[44] There may be occasions where, in the case of such qualified covenant, more than one consent may be needed to an assignment or sub-letting. If the tenant is granted a licence to sub-let on condition that the sub-lessee covenants not to assign without the consent of both the tenant and the head landlord, the tenant impliedly covenants not to approve an assignment without the head landlord's consent: *Drive Yourself Hire Co. (London) Ltd v. Strutt* [1954] 1 Q.B. 250; or the landlord may be made a covenantee under the L.P.A. 1925, s.56; see *post*, para. 16–006.

[45] For rent reviews, see *ante*, para. 14–246.

[46] L. & T.A. 1927, s.19 (as amended, most notably by L. & T.C.A. 1995, s.22); L. & T.A. 1988; considered *infra*.

[47] s.19(1). This section does not apply to agricultural holdings or farm business tenancies: s.19(4) (as amended). But it applies to leases whether granted before or after the Act.

[48] Although the point is not wholly free from doubt, the better view is that the subsection has no application to an absolute covenant against assignment: see *Bocardo S.A. v. S. & M. Hotels Ltd* [1980] 1 W.L.R. 17 at 22, 26; *Vaux Group Plc v. Lilley* (1990) 61 & P. & C.R. 446 and 453; 454. *cf. Property & Bloodstock Ltd v. Emerton* [1968] Ch. 94 at 119, 120.

be unreasonably withheld.[49] The effect of the section is to write the words into the covenant in the lease.[50] The section does not affect the form of covenant, still sometimes employed,[51] that the tenant shall offer to surrender his tenancy to the landlord before assigning or underletting.[52] Even where the section does apply, it does not permit the tenant to assign or sub-let without seeking the landlord's consent. If he does so, he has committed a breach of covenant even if the landlord could not properly have refused his consent if it had been asked.[53] If he seeks consent and it is unreasonably withheld, he may then assign or sub-let without the consent,[54] or seek a declaration from the court[55] of his right to do so.[56]

14–262   (2) LANDLORD AND TENANT ACT 1988. This Act, which implements recommendations by the Law Commission,[57] is intended to ensure that landlords deal expeditiously with applications for consent to assign.[58] It applies to any tenancy containing a qualified covenant against assigning, underletting, charging or parting with possession.[59] Where a tenant serves a written application for permission on the person who under the covenant may consent to a proposed transaction[60]—who will usually be the landlord—he must give his consent within a reasonable time except where it is reasonable for him not to.[61] He in turn must serve written notice of his decision on the tenant

---

[49] For the meaning of reasonableness in this context, see below.

[50] *F. W. Woolworth & Co. Ltd v. Lambert, supra*, at 60; *Vaux Group Plc v. Lilley, supra*, at 452.

[51] The covenant was described as novel and burdensome in *Cardshops Ltd v. Davies* [1971] 1 W.L.R. 591 at 595. It subsequently became common, but intending tenants will not now usually accept it. For the position of such a covenant under L. & T.A. 1954, s.38(1), see *Allnatt London Properties Ltd v. Newton* [1981] 2 All E.R. 290 (aff'd [1984] 1 All E.R. 423). For the background to this form of covenant, see [1983] Conv. 158 (C. Blake).

[52] *Bocardo S.A. v. S. & M. Hotels Ltd, supra*, following *Adler v. Upper Grosvenor Street Investment Ltd* [1957] 1 W.L.R. 227, discussed in (1957) 73 L.Q.R. 157 (R.E.M.); see likewise *Creer v. P. & O. Lines of Australia Pty Ltd* (1971) 125 C.L.R. 84. Contrast *Greene v. Church Commissioners for England* [1974] Ch. 467.

[53] *Eastern Telegraph Co. Ltd v. Dent* [1899] 1 Q.B. 835.

[54] *Treloar v. Bigge* (1874) L.R. 9 Ex. 151.

[55] The county court has jurisdiction to make such a declaration: L. & T.A. 1954, s.53(1) (as amended).

[56] *Young v. Ashley Gardens Properties Ltd* [1903] 2 Ch. 112. For the tenant's right to seek damages in such a case, see *infra*.

[57] (1987) Law Com. No. 161; [1988] Conv. (H.W. Wilkinson).

[58] For the difficulties that arose prior to the Act, see *29 Equities Ltd v. Bank Leumi (U.K.) Ltd* [1986] 1 W.L.R. 1490 at 1494. For a valuable statement of the law after the Act, see *Kened Ltd v. Connie Investments Ltd* (1995) 70 P. & C.R. 370 at 373, 374.

[59] L. & T.A. 1988, s.1(1).

[60] *ibid.*, s.1(2). *cf. Dong Bang Minerva (U.K.) Ltd v. Davina Ltd* [1995] 1 E.G.L.R. 41 at 45 (landlord's mortgagee not such a person whose consent was required *under the covenant*: the point did not arise on appeal: [1996] 2 E.G.L.R. 31). The Act has no application to freehold covenants: *cf. Estates Governors of Alleyn's College v. Williams* (1994) 70 P. & C.R. 67.

[61] L. & T.A. 1988, s.1(3). The tenant is not obliged to give an undertaking to meet all the landlord's costs, whether reasonable or not, as a pre-condition to the landlord making any decision: *Dong Bang Minerva (U.K.) Ltd v. Davina Ltd* [1996] 2 E.G.L.R. 31. Once a reasonable time has elapsed, the landlord cannot raise objections to the assignment or sub-letting that he has not hitherto raised: *Norwich Union Life Insurance v. Shopmoor Ltd* [1999] 1 W.L.R. 531; *Footwear Corp. Ltd v. Amplight Properties Ltd* [1999] 1 W.L.R. 551.

specifying the reasons for withholding consent[62] or any conditions subject to which it is given.[63] The onus of proof is on the landlord to show that he consented within a reasonable time, that any conditions for the consent were reasonable, or if he withheld consent, that it was reasonable for him to do so.[64] Similar obligations are imposed on a head landlord whose consent is required to a disposition by the sub-tenant.[65] There may be occasions where, under the covenant, the consent of more than one person is required to a transaction by a tenant, such as a superior landlord or a mortgagee of the reversion. If the tenant applies to the landlord (or the person who may consent), the Act imposes a duty on the recipient to pass on applications within a reasonable time where he believes that the consent of some other person may be required to the transaction.[66] An action for damages in tort for breach of statutory duty may be brought against any person who has broken any duty imposed by the Act.[67]

(3) LANDLORD AND TENANT (COVENANTS) ACT 1995. In leases granted prior to **14–263** 1996, the parties to a lease could not stipulate in advance what was to be regarded as a reasonable ground for the landlord's refusal of consent to an assignment. It was said that reasonableness must be determined objectively,[68] for otherwise the purpose of the Landlord and Tenant Act 1927 might be stultified.[69] However, for some leases granted after 1995, the 1927 Act has been amended by the Landlord and Tenant (Covenants) Act 1995.[70] The amendment applies only to a "qualifying lease", which means a "new tenancy" under the 1995 Act[71] of any property other than—

---

[62] The Act "requires a landlord to give his reasons for a refusal and limits him to those reasons in justifying his refusal": *Southern Depot Co. Ltd v. British Railway Board* [1990] 2 E.G.L.R. 39 at 44, *per* Morritt J.

[63] L. & T.A. 1988, s.1(3). Any condition must itself be reasonable: *ibid.*, s.1(4).

[64] *ibid.*, s.1(6); *Midland Bank Plc v. Chart Enterprises Inc* [1990] 2 E.G.L.R. 59; *Air India v. Balabel* [1993] 2 E.G.L.R. 66. Prior to the Act, the burden of proving unreasonableness lay on the tenant: *Shanly v. Ward* (1913) 29 T.L.R. 714. Where a *freehold* covenant requires the consent of a third party to some act, such consent not to be unreasonably withheld, the burden of proving unreasonableness remains with the covenantor: *Estates Governors of Alleyn's College v. Williams, supra.*

[65] L. & T.A. 1988, s.3. See *Mount Eden Land Ltd v. Straudley Investments Ltd* (1996) 74 P. & C.R. 306.

[66] L. & T.A. 1988, s.2(1).

[67] *ibid.*, s.4; see *e.g. CIN Properties Ltd v. Gill* [1993] 2 E.G.L.R. 97. Prior to the Act, a landlord who unreasonably withheld his consent was not liable in damages: *Treloar v. Bigge* (1874) L.R. 9 Exch. 151; unless he had expressly covenanted not to withhold consent arbitrarily: *Ideal Film Renting Co. Ltd v. Nielsen* [1921] 1 Ch. 575.

[68] But compare *Lovelock v. Margo* [1963] 2 Q.B. 786 at 789. For the extent to which the test of reasonableness is objective, see *post*, para. 14–265.

[69] *Re Smith's Lease* [1951] 1 All E.R. 346.

[70] s.22, inserting s.19(1A)–(1E) L. & T.A. 1927. For the Landlord and Tenant (Covenants) Act 1995 see chap. 15. Its principal purpose is to abrogate the rule that the original tenant remains liable on the covenants for the duration of the term notwithstanding the assignment of the lease: see *post*, para. 15–014. This abolition of privity of contract by a Private Member's Bill was made possible by an agreement that had been reached between representatives of the property industry. The amendment of L. & T.A. 1927, s.19 was an important element of that agreement: see *post*, para. 15–064.

[71] See L. & T.C.A. 1995, s.1(3)–(6); *post*, para. 15–007.

(i) a lease of an agricultural holding or a farm business tenancy[72];
   or

(ii) a residential lease.[73]

The parties to such a lease may enter into an agreement in relation to an assignment,[74] specifying either—

(i) any circumstances in which the landlord may withhold his licence or consent to that assignment; or

(ii) any conditions subject to which any such licence or consent may be granted.[75]

14–264 The landlord will not then be regarded as unreasonably withholding his licence or consent if he does so on the grounds that such circumstances exist and in fact they do exist. Nor will he be regarded as imposing unreasonable conditions if he gives his consent subject to such conditions.[76] One condition that is likely to be imposed in virtually all cases is that the assignor should guarantee the performance of the covenants by the assignee until the time when the lease is next assigned.[77] It is also likely to become normal practice to prescribe conditions that will have to be satisfied as to the financial standing of any assignee. There are, however, certain limitations on the conditions or circumstances that may be validly specified. They cannot be framed by reference to—

(i) any matter that falls to be determined by the landlord[78]; or

(ii) any matter that falls to be determined by a third party unless he has to exercise that determination reasonably or his decision can be reviewed by an independent third person.[79]

Because these provisions are contained in the Landlord and Tenant (Covenants) Act 1995, they are subject to the anti-avoidance provisions of that Act.[80] Any agreement that attempts to restrict or frustrate their operation will in consequence be void.

[72] L. & T.A. 1927, s.19(4) (as amended).
[73] *ibid.*, s.19(1E).
[74] The provisions apply on to an assignment and not to a sub-letting or a charging of the premises: *ibid.*, s.19(1A). The agreement need not be contained in the lease and can be made at any time before the application is made for the landlord's consent to the assignment: *ibid.*, s.19(B).
[75] *ibid.*, s.19(1A).
[76] *ibid.* In practice this has made L. & T.A. 1988, s.1(4), *supra*, virtually redundant in relation to business leases.
[77] For such "authorised guarantee agreements" see L. & T.C.A. 1995, s.16; *post*, para. 15–067.
[78] L. & T.A. 1927, s.19(1C). Thus a condition that the tenant could not assign to any person who, in the landlord's opinion, was not creditworthy, would not be valid.
[79] L. & T.A. 1927, s.19(1C).
[80] s.25; *post*, para. 15–096.

(d) Reasonableness

(1) OBJECTIVE OR SUBJECTIVE? It has never been finally determined whether **14–265** the grounds for a landlord's refusal of consent to an assignment or subletting must be objectively or subjectively reasonable.[81] It has been said that the test is "not a purely objective one".[82] The reasonableness of the decision will be judged according to the circumstances existing and known to the landlord at the time when he withheld his consent.[83] He cannot rely on reasons which did not influence his decision.[84] If he gives a valid reason for refusing consent, that refusal will not be vitiated merely because he gave other reasons which would not have justified his decision.[85] As a landlord must now give his reasons for any refusal,[86] there is no possibility that he might be able to rely on a reason which he failed to give in writing within a reasonable time but which nevertheless influenced his decision.[87]

(2) PRINCIPLES OF LAW. The principles of law which are applicable in **14–266** determining whether a landlord has unreasonably refused his consent have been summarised by the Court of Appeal.[88]

> (i) The purpose of a qualified covenant is to protect a landlord from having his premises used or occupied either in an undesirable way or by an undesirable tenant.[89]
>
> (ii) A landlord is not entitled to refuse his consent to an assignment on grounds which have nothing whatever to do with the relationship

---

[81] This issue will not arise in leases granted after 1995 in relation to any matters which the parties have themselves stipulated will be regarded as a reasonable ground for refusing consent.

[82] *Bromley Park Garden Estates Ltd v. Moss* [1982] 1 W.L.R. 1019 at 1034, *per* Slade L.J.

[83] *Leeward Securities Ltd v. Lilyheath Properties Ltd* (1983) 17 H.L.R. 35; *Rossi v. Hestdrive Ltd* [1985] 1 E.G.L.R. 50; *CIN Properties Ltd v. Gill* [1993] 2 E.G.L.R. 97 at 98; [1994] Conv. 316 (L. Crabb).

[84] *Bromley Park Garden Estates Ltd v. Moss, supra*, at 1034; *Blockbuster Entertainment Ltd v. Leakcliff Properties Ltd* [1997] 1 E.G.L.R. 28 at 31.

[85] *British Bakeries (Midlands) Ltd v. Michael Testler & Co. Ltd* [1986] 1 E.G.L.R. 64. This is the position both at common law and under L. & T.A. 1988: *BRS Northern Ltd v. Templeheights Ltd* [1997] E.G.C.S. 180.

[86] L. & T.A. 1988, s.1(3); *ante*, para. 14–262. It is necessarily implicit in this requirement that he may only rely upon the reasons which he gives for such a refusal.

[87] See *Norwich Union Life Insurance v. Shopmoor Ltd* [1999] 1 W.L.R. 531 at 545; *Footwear Corp. Ltd v. Amplight Properties Ltd* [1999] 1 W.L.R. 551 at 559. It was never resolved prior to the 1988 Act whether the landlord could rely on such unarticulated reasons: see (1963) 79 L.Q.R. 479 (R.E.M.), where the conflicting authorities are considered. See too *Searle v. Burroughs* (1966) 110 S.J. 248; *Bromley Park Gardens Estates Ltd v. Moss, supra* at 1034.

[88] *International Drilling Fluids Ltd v. Louisville Investments (Uxbridge) Ltd* [1986] Ch.513 at 519–521; [1986] Conv. 287 (L. Crabb). These principles, which have been frequently applied since, are stated as they stand in the light of subsequent developments.

[89] *Bates v. Donaldson* [1896] 2 Q.B. 241 at 247; *Houlder Brothers & Co. Ltd v. Gibbs* [1925] Ch. 575. The landlord will not therefore be precluded from refusing consent to an assignment merely because he is offered a guarantee. A guarantee "is not a satisfactory substitute for a satisfactory and responsible tenant": *Warren v. Marketing Exchange Ltd* [1988] 2 E.G.L.R. 247 at 252, *per* Judge Finlay, Q.C. *cf. Venetian Glass Gallery Ltd v. Next Properties Ltd* [1989] 2 E.G.L.R. 42 and 46.

of landlord and tenant in regard to the subject-matter of the lease,[90] as where a landlord refused consent in order to achieve a collateral purpose[91] unconnected with the lease.[92]

(iii) It is not necessary for the landlord to prove that the conclusions which led him to refuse consent were justified, if they were conclusions which might be reached by a reasonable person in the circumstances.[93] It is only if no reasonable landlord could have refused consent for the reasons stated that the decision to withhold consent will be unreasonable. The court is not entitled to substitute its own judgement for that of the landlord.[94]

(iv) It may be reasonable for the landlord to refuse his consent to an assignment on the ground of the purpose for which the proposed assignee intends to use the premises, even though that purpose is not forbidden by the lease.[95] However, it will not be reasonable to withhold consent where the terms of the lease contemplate the particular user, and the assignee intends to use them for that purpose.[96]

(v) While a landlord need usually only consider his own relevant interests,[97] there may be cases where there is such a disproportion between the benefit to the landlord and the detriment that the tenant will suffer if the landlord withholds his consent to assignment, that such a refusal of consent will be unreasonable.[98] Thus it

---

[90] *Houlder Brothers & Co. Ltd v. Gibbs, supra; Norwich Union Life Insurance v. Shopmoor Ltd, supra.* It is clear that this principle must be read together with (i) above, and not in isolation: The landlord's objections must relate to the reasonably anticipated consequences of the proposed assignment as well as to the matters listed in (ii): see *Jaison Property Development Co. Ltd v. Roux Restaurants Ltd* (1996) 74 P. & C.R. 357.

[91] An "uncovenanted advantage": *Bromley Park Garden Estates Ltd v. Moss* [1982] 1 W.L.R. 1019 at 1031, *per* Cumming–Bruce L.J. See too *Mount Eden Land Ltd v. Straudley Investments Ltd* (1996) 74 P. & C.R. 306 at 310.

[92] *Bromley Park Garden Estates Ltd v. Moss, supra* (where the landlord told the tenant that it was not his practice to permit assignments of residential tenancies, but that he would accept a surrender of the tenancy); [1983] Conv. 140 (L. Crabb).

[93] *Pimms Ltd v. Tallow Chandlers Company* [1964] 2 Q.B. 547 at 564; *Estates Governors of Alleyn's College v. Williams* (1994) 70 P. & C.R. 67 at 72; *Kened Ltd v. Connie Investments Ltd* (1995) 70 P. & C.R. 370 at 374. This principle is unaffected by L. & T.A. 1988, s.1 (*ante*, para. 14–262): *Air India v. Balabel* [1993] 2 E.G.L.R. 66 at 69.

[94] *Kened Ltd v. Connie Investments Ltd, supra*, at 374.

[95] *Bates v. Donaldson, supra*, at 244. This will be so if the purpose is one to which the landlord may reasonably object: *ibid.*

[96] *Rayburn v. Wolf* [1985] 2 E.G.L.R. 235 (qualified covenant against assigning or underletting: refusal of consent to assignment on the ground that the assignee intended to sub-let held to be unreasonable).

[97] *West Layton Ltd v. Ford* [1979] Q.B. 593 at 605; *Ponderosa International Development Inc. v. Pengap Securities (Bristol) Ltd* [1986] 1 E.G.L.R. 66 at 68; *Venetian Glass Gallery Ltd v. Next Properties Ltd* [1989] 2 E.G.L.R. 42 at 46.

[98] *International Drilling Fluids Ltd v. Louisville Investments (Uxbridge) Ltd* [1986] Ch. 513 at 521, attempting to reconcile divergent lines of authority. In that case the diminution in the paper value of the landlord's reversion (which it had no plans to sell) because of the assignee's intended user, was outweighed by the hardship to the tenant, who could find no other assignee.

may be reasonable for a landlord to refuse his consent to an assignment if the assignee would acquire statutory protection under the Rent Acts,[99] or the right to acquire the freehold under the Leasehold Reform Act 1967,[1] when in either case the assignor could not claim or did not want such rights. However, there may be circumstances where the refusal of consent may be unreasonable,[2] even though it may lead to the creation of a tenancy that enjoys some form of statutory protection.[3]

(vi) Subject to these propositions, it is in each case a question of fact depending upon all the circumstances, whether or not the landlord has unreasonably withheld his consent,[4] and the onus of showing that he acted reasonably now rests on the landlord.[5]

(3) OPERATION OF THE PRINCIPLES. The operation of these principles can be **14–267** illustrated in relation to two particular issues.[6] The first is the extent to which it is reasonable for the landlord to take into account the risk that a proposed assignee may commit a breach of covenant, particularly as to the user of the premises.[7] It has been held that a landlord may reasonably refuse his consent to an assignment or underletting where—

(i) under the terms of a proposed underlease, the underlessee was to use the premises in breach of a user covenant in the head lease[8];

(ii) there were long-standing and serious breaches of a repairing covenant and the landlord was not satisfied that the proposed assignee would remedy them[9]; or

(iii) the tenant was in breach of a positive covenant to keep open a store for retail trade and the proposed assignee was unlikely to take steps to re-open a store.[10]

By contrast, a refusal will be unreasonable where—

---

[99] *Lee v. K. Carter Ltd* [1949] 1 K.B. 85; *Swanson v. Forton* [1949] Ch. 143; *West Layton Ltd v. Ford, supra; Leeward Securities Ltd v. Lilyheath Properties Ltd, supra.*

[1] *Norfolk Capital Group Ltd v. Kitway Ltd* [1977] Q.B. 506; *Bickel v. Duke of Westminster* [1977] Q.B. 517.

[2] *Leeward Securities Ltd v. Lilyheath Properties Ltd, supra,* at 47.

[3] *Deverall v. Wyndham* (1988) 58 P. & C.R. 12.

[4] *International Drilling Fluids Ltd v. Louisville Investments (Uxbridge) Ltd, supra,* at 521.

[5] L. & T.A. 1988, s.1(6); *ante,* para. 14–262.

[6] See [1988] Conv. 45 (G. Kodilinye).

[7] See [1987] Conv. 381 (L. Crabb).

[8] *Packaging Centre Ltd v. Poland Street Estate Ltd* (1961) 178 E.G. 189; *Granada T.V. Network Ltd v. Great Universal Stores Ltd* (1963) 187 E.G. 391.

[9] *Orlando Investments Ltd v. Grosvenor Estate Belgravia* [1989] 2 E.G.L.R. 74; [1989] Conv. 371 (P. F. Smith).

[10] *F. W. Woolworth Plc v. Charlwood Alliance Properties Ltd* [1987] 1 E.G.L.R. 53. A "keep open" covenant of his kind cannot be enforced by a mandatory injunction: *Co-operative Insurance Society Ltd v. Argyll Stores (Holdings) Ltd* [1998] A.C. 1.

    (i) there has been no breach of a user covenant by the assignor and the intending assignee will not necessarily be in breach of it, even though he wishes to use the premises for purposes that are not permitted[11]; or

    (ii) there are continuing but insubstantial breaches of a repairing covenant.[12]

14–268   The second issue concerns the degree to which it is reasonable for the landlord to safeguard his financial position. In general the courts regard such concerns as a reasonable ground for the refusal of consent. It has been held accordingly that a landlord is entitled to refuse his consent to an assignment where—

    (i) the proposed assignee's references were unsatisfactory[13];

    (ii) the landlord who had developed the site was intending to sell his reversion to an investor (as the tenant knew) and the financial standing of the proposed assignee was not as strong as that of the tenant thereby reducing the value of the reversion[14]; and

    (iii) the then tenant wished to re-assign the lease to the original tenant to enable the latter to exercise a break clause and terminate the tenancy.[15]

However, where a tenant sought consent to sub-let at a market rent, it was held to be unreasonable for a landlord to refuse consent on the basis that the market was depressed and that the tenant should wait until it improved.[16]

14–269   *(e) Racial objections.* Under the Race Relations Act 1976 it is unlawful for any person to discriminate against another on grounds of colour, race, nationality or ethnic or national origins by withholding licence or consent to an assignment, sub-letting or parting with possession of any premises comprised

---

[11] *Killick v. Second Covent Garden Property Co. Ltd* [1973] 1 W.L.R. 658. As the assignee will be bound by the user covenant, the landlord may prevent a breach of it by injunction. If the landlord agrees to an assignment to an assignee knowing that he will breach the user covenant, he may be estopped from enforcing the covenant unless he reserves his right to do so: *ibid.*, at 662.

[12] *Beale v. Worth* [1993] E.G.C.S. 135.

[13] *Shanly v. Ward* (1913) 29 T.L.R. 714.

[14] *Ponderosa International Development Inc. v. Pengap Securities (Bristol) Ltd* [1986] 1 E.G.L.R. 66. The landlord would have been willing to consent to a sub-lease to the proposed assignee instead.

[15] *Olympia & York Canary Wharf Ltd v. Oil Property Investment Ltd* (1994) 69 P. & C.R. 43. The tenant was paying twice the open market rental, hence its desire to be rid of the lease. It has since been held on similar facts that had there been a re-assignment, the original tenant would not have been able to terminate the lease, because the break clause was spent once he had assigned: *Max Factor Ltd v. Weslyan Assurance Society* [1996] 2 E.G.L.R. 210.

[16] *Blockbuster Entertainment Ltd v. Leakcliff Properties Ltd* [1997] 1 E.G.L.R. 28.

in a tenancy.[17] There is an exception for small premises where the person withholding consent or a near relative of his will continue to reside on the premises and shares other accommodation on them with persons who are not members of his household.[18]

(f) Fines. Covenants to which the Landlord and Tenant Act 1927 applies are **14–270** subject to a further restriction under the Law of Property Act 1925,[19] namely a proviso that no "fine" or similar sum shall be payable in respect of any licence or consent unless the lease expressly provides for it. "Fine" is defined in wide terms[20] which include any valuable consideration given in circumstances such that, if it were money, it would be what is commonly known as a fine.[21] It will therefore include a stipulation in a lease of a public-house which makes it a house "tied" to the landlord, a brewer.[22] However the section preserves the landlord's right to require the payment of a reasonable sum in respect of any legal or other expenses incurred in relation to the licence or consent.[23] If a fine which a tenant need not pay is in fact paid without protest, the tenant cannot recover it, for the payment is not unlawful but merely unnecessary.[24]

(g) Building leases. In one case no consent is required, namely where a **14–271** building lease (*i.e.* a lease granted in consideration wholly or partially of the erection, or the substantial improvement, addition or alteration of buildings) is granted for more than 40 years. If that lease contains a covenant against assigning, underletting or parting with possession without the landlord's consent, there is implied a proviso (notwithstanding any contrary provision) that no consent is required to an assignment, underlease or parting with possession made more than seven years before the end of the term, provided that written notice is given to the landlord within six months.[25] This provision does not apply—

    (i) where the lessor is one of certain public and statutory authorities[26]; or

---

[17] Race Relations Act 1976, ss.1–3, 24, replacing in amended form provisions of the Race Relations Acts 1965 and 1968.

[18] *ibid.*, defining "small premises" as those not normally containing more than two additional households or six additional persons.

[19] s.144. A similar (but not identical) provision exists in relation to covenants against the alteration of the user of the premises without consent: see L. & T.A. 1927, s.19(3). See *Barclays Bank Plc v. Daejan Investments (Grove Hall) Ltd* [1995] 1 E.G.L.R. 68.

[20] L.P.A. 1925, s.205(1)(xxiii).

[21] *Waite v. Jennings* [1906] 2 K.B. 11 at 18.

[22] *Gardner & Co. Ltd v. Cone* [1928] Ch. 955. See also *Comber v. Fleet Electrics Ltd* [1995] 1 W.L.R. 566.

[23] L.P.A. 1925, s.144. It has not been finally decided whether the section confers the right to recover such costs even if no licence or consent is in fact granted: see *Goldman v. Abbott* [1989] 2 E.G.L.R. 78 at 79, 81.

[24] *Andrew v. Bridgman* [1908] 1 K.B. 596.

[25] L. & T.A. 1927, s.19(1)(b).

[26] *ibid.*

(ii) in the case of a mining or agricultural lease or a farm business tenancy[27]; or

(iii) to a "qualifying lease" within the Landlord and Tenant Act 1927.[28]

In practice this third exception has removed the significance of this provision for most leases granted after 1995. This is because qualified covenants against assignment are generally found in business leases, which will be qualifying leases.

14–272　　*(h) Breaches.* To amount to a breach of a covenant against assignment, underletting, or parting with possession there must in general be some voluntary dealing with the property *inter vivos.* Thus a bequest of the lease is no breach,[29] nor is the involuntary vesting of the lease in the trustee in bankruptcy[30] upon the tenant's bankruptcy[31] (as distinct from a voluntary sale by the trustee in bankruptcy[31]), or the compulsory sale of the lease under statutory provisions,[32] or the vesting of the lease in new trustees under an order of the court.[33] Loss of the lease by the execution of a judgment is not regarded as a breach, even where the covenant extends to parting with possession,[34] unless the action and judgment were collusive and designed solely to evade the covenant.[35] A mortgage made by the grant of a sub-lease is a breach,[36] but a declaration of trust made by the tenant for the benefit of his creditors is not.[37] It is neither an assignment[38] nor a parting with possession[39] if the tenant merely allows other persons to share in the use of the premises, or grants a licence for the limited use of part of the premises. But allowing a company formed by the tenant to occupy the premises is parting with possession.[40]

---

[27] *ibid.,* s.19(4) (as amended).
[28] *ibid.,* s.19(1D) (inserted by L. & T.C.A. 1995, s.22); *ante,* para. 14–263. A "qualifying lease" must be a "new tenancy" granted after 1995: see *ibid.,* s.19(1E); L. & T.C.A. 1995, s.1; *post,* para. 15–007. Agricultural leases, farm business tenancies and residential leases are not qualifying leases: see *ante,* para. 14–263.
[29] *Fox v. Swann* (1655) Sty. 482; *Doe d. Goodbehere v. Bevan* (1815) 3 M. & S. 353; Woodfall L. & T. 11.166 (but see *Berry v. Taunton* (1594) Cro.Eliz. 331). *Quaere* as to an assent giving effect to a bequest: see Williams on *Assents* 130. *Re Wright* [1949] Ch. 729 suggests that consent is needed; and see (1963) 27 Conv. (N.S.) 159 (D. G. Barnsley).
[30] *Re Riggs* [1901] 2 K.B. 16.
[31] *Re Wright* [1949] Ch. 729.
[32] *Slipper v. Tottenham & Hampstead Junction Ry* (1867) L.R. 4 Eq. 112.
[33] *Marsh v. Gilbert* [1980] 2 E.G.L.R. 44.
[34] *Doe d. Mitchinson v. Carter (No. 1)* (1798) 8 T.R. 57.
[35] *Doe d. Mitchinson v. Carter (No. 2)* (1799) 8 T.R. 300.
[36] *Serjeant v. Nash, Field & Co.* [1903] 2 K.B. 304; *cf.* a legal charge (*post,* para. 19–025).
[37] *Gentle v. Faulkner* [1900] 2 Q.B. 267.
[38] *Glan Singh & Co. v. Devraj Nahar* [1965] 1 W.L.R. 412 (premises shared with partners); *Edwardes v. Barrington* (1901) 85 L.T. 650 (licence to use refreshment bar, etc., in theatre).
[39] *Chaplin v. Smith* [1926] 1 K.B. 198 (company permitted to run demised garage): *Stening v. Abrahams* [1931] 1 Ch. 470 (advertisement hoarding).
[40] *Lam Kee Ying Snd. Bhd. v. Lam Shes Tong* [1975] A.C. 247.

A covenant merely against underletting is perhaps not broken by an assignment[41] or by letting lodgings.[42] A covenant against parting with possession is broken by assignment[43]; and it would presumably be broken by allowing a squatter to obtain a title under the Limitation Act 1980. Underletting or parting with possession of a part of the property is no breach of a general covenant not to underlet or part with possession[44]; but it is of course otherwise if the covenant is worded (as it usually is) so as to extend to the property "or any part thereof". A covenant which prohibits the assignment or sub-letting of "any part" of the premises without the landlord's consent, is however broken by a sub-letting of the whole of the property.[45]

3. Covenant to use the premises as a private dwelling-house only. This   **14–273** covenant is broken if the house is divided into two, or if part of the house is sub-let, even though for private use, since it is implicit in the covenant that the premises shall be used as one single dwelling-house.[46] The question, which is one of fact and degree, is whether the premises are used as a private household.[47] Thus taking a paying guest will normally be no breach,[48] but using a property to provide supervised housing for a group of former mental patients will be.[49] There will also be a breach where the premises are used by the tenant to provide a house for an employee so that he is better able to perform his duties.[50] There is a statutory jurisdiction for the county court to authorise the division of a house in certain circumstances.[51]

4. Covenant to repair

(a) The covenant. In long leases the tenant often covenants to do all repairs.   **14–274** In short leases the landlord commonly assumes liability for external and structural repairs and, in some cases, is required to do so by statute.[52] In every case, except those where statute implies an obligation to repair,[53] the matter is one for negotiation. There may be situations in which there is no repairing

---

[41] *Re Doyle & O'Hara's Contract* [1899] I.R. 113 (no breach); *Greenaway v. Adams* (1806) 12 Ves. 395 (breach).

[42] *Doe. d. Pitt v. Laming* (1814) 4 Camp. 73, doubted in *Greenslade v. Tapscott* (1834) 1 Cr.M. & R. 55.

[43] *Marks v. Warren* [1979] 1 All E.R. 29.

[44] *Wilson v. Rosenthal* (1906) 22 T.L.R. 233; *Cottell v. Baker* (1920) 36 T.L.R. 208; *Cook v. Shoesmith* [1951] 1 K.B. 752; *Esdaile v. Lewis* [1956] 1 W.L.R. 709 (see (1956) 72 L.Q.R. 325: R.E.M.).

[45] *Field v. Barkworth* [1986] 1 W.L.R. 137; *Troop v. Gibson* [1986] 1 E.G.L.R. 1 at 5.

[46] *Barton v. Keeble* [1928] Ch. 517; *Dobbs v. Linford* [1953] 1 Q.B. 48, distinguishing *Downie v. Turner* [1951] 2 K.B. 112; and see *Re Endericks' Conveyance* [1973] 1 All E.R. 843.

[47] See *Segal Securities Ltd v. Thoseby* [1963] 1 Q.B. 887 at 894; *Heglibiston Establishment v. Heyman* (1977) 36 P. & C.R. 351 at 360; *C. & G. Homes Ltd v. Secretary of State for Health* [1991] Ch. 365 at 383 (where the relevant considerations are set out).

[48] *Segal Securities Ltd v. Thoseby, supra.*

[49] *C. & G. Homes Ltd v. Secretary of State for Health, supra.*

[50] *Methodist Secondary Schools Trust Deed Trustees v. O'Leary* [1993] 1 E.G.L.R. 105.

[51] H.A. 1985, s.610; *post*, para. 16–092.

[52] See L. & T.A. 1985, s.11, *ante*, para. 14–222.

[53] *ibid.*

obligation imposed either expressly or impliedly on either the landlord or tenant.[54] In those circumstances the tenant may sometimes be liable for them because of the general law relating to waste,[55] though recourse to this form of liability is now rare.[56]

14–275   (1) "REPAIR." "Repair" has in law its ordinary meaning,[57] and the extent of the liability of any party under a repairing covenant therefore depends upon the construction of the particular covenant.[58] Relevant factors in deciding whether work can be regarded as "repair" include the nature of the building, the terms of the lease, the state when let, the character of the defect, the nature and cost of the remedial work and who is to do it, its effect on the value and lifespan of the building, the comparative cost of alternative remedial works and their impact on the use and enjoyment of the building by the occupants. The weight given to each of these factors varies from case to case.[59]

Where a party is liable to repair the property, he is not required to undertake the reconstruction of substantially the whole of the subject-matter of the property let, but only the renewal or replacement of subsidiary parts.[60] There is no obligation "to make a new and different thing."[61] However, by virtue of an ancient and anomalous rule, if the premises have been destroyed by a calamity, such as a fire, the whole of the premises must be rebuilt.[62] Nor is an obligation to repair an obligation to improve the premises,[63] though it may be that the repair of a property will necessarily improve it.[64] The question is one

---

[54] *Demetriou v. Poolaction Ltd* [1991] 1 E.G.L.R. 100 at 104. See too *Tennant Radiant Heat Ltd v. Warrington Development Corporation* [1988] 1 E.G.L.R. 41 at 43.

[55] *Ante*, paras 14–232—14–237, where the exceptions are also stated.

[56] See *Mancetter Developments Ltd v. Garmanson Ltd* [1986] Q.B. 1212 at 1218.

[57] *Post Office v. Aquarius Properties Ltd* [1985] 2 E.G.L.R. 105 at 107 (aff'd [1987] 1 All E.R. 1055).

[58] For a useful summary of the tests to be applied in determining whether work falls within the scope of a covenant to repair, see *McDougall v. Easington D.C.* (1989) 58 P. & C.R. 201 at 207.

[59] *Holding and Management Ltd v. Property Holding and Investment Trust Plc* [1990] 1 All E.R. 938 at 945 (omitted from the report at [1989] 1 W.L.R. 1313, 1321).

[60] *Lurcott v. Wakely* [1911] 1 K.B. 905 at 924 (obligation to rebuild wall); *Minja Properties Ltd v. Cussins Property Group Plc* [1998] 2 E.G.L.R. 52 (replacement of window units).

[61] *Lister v. Lane* [1893] 2 Q.B. 212 at 217, *per* Lord Esher M.R. See, *e.g. Halliard Property Co. Ltd v. Clarke Investments Ltd* [1984] 1 E.G.L.R. 45 (no obligation to replace "jerry-built" structure with properly constructed building).

[62] *Bullock v. Dommitt* (1796) 6 T.R. 650. As regards war damage there is now no such liability: see Landlord and Tenant (War Damage) Act 1939, s.1 (reversing the effect of *Redmond v. Dainton* [1920] 2 K.B. 256, where there was liability to repair serious bomb damage); *ante*, para. 14–183.

[63] Neither party is obliged "to provide the other with a better house than there was to start with": *Quick v. Taff Ely B.C.* [1986] Q.B. 809 at 821, *per* Lawton L.J. See, *e.g. Wainwright v. Leeds City Council* (1984) 82 L.G.R. 657 (no obligation to install damp course in old house); *Mullaney v. Maybourne Grange (Croydon) Management Co. Ltd* [1986] 1 E.G.L.R. 70 (replacement of wooden-framed windows with double-glazed units was improvement not repair). *cf. Elmcroft Developments Ltd v. Tankersley–Sawyer* [1984] 1 E.G.L.R. 47 (obligation to replace defective slate damp-proof course in flat in a "high-class fashionable residential area" with a silicone injection course was a repair).

[64] *Quick v. Taff Ely B.C., supra*, at 823; *Sutton (Hastoe) Housing Association v. Williams* [1988] 1 E.G.L.R. 56 at 58.

of degree.[65] A party who is under an obligation to repair is not absolved from liability because the disrepair has been caused by an inherent defect in the design or construction of the building demised.[66] Indeed, the inherent defect must be corrected if that is the only practicable method of remedying the disrepair.[67] However, there will be no liability to repair if the inherent defect causes no damage within the scope of the covenant.[68] A party who is under an obligation to repair must also make good any consequential damage[69] and pay compensation for any consequential loss.[70]

Expressions such as "tenantable repair", "sufficient repair", or "good and substantial repair" seem to add little to the meaning of the word "repair",[71] and indicate "such repair as, having regard to the age, character and locality of the house, would make it reasonably fit for the occupation of a reasonably-minded tenant of the class who would be likely to take it".[72] The tenant must keep the premises in substantially the same state as they were at the time of the demise.[73] The standard will not diminish merely because the tenant's failure to repair the premises makes them unattractive,[74] or because of changes in the character of the neighbourhood.[75] A covenant to "keep" the premises in good repair imposes an obligation on the covenantor— **14–276**

    (i) to put the premises into repair even if they are in a state of disrepair at the start of the term[76]; and

    (ii) to ensure that they do not thereafter fall into a state of disrepair.[77]

---

[65] *Brew Brothers Ltd v. Snax (Ross) Ltd* [1970] 1 Q.B. 612; *Ravenseft Properties Ltd v. Davstone (Holdings) Ltd* [1980] Q.B. 12.

[66] *Ravenseft Properties Ltd v. Davstone (Holdings) Ltd, supra* (tenant liable for inherent defects in walls); *Smedley v. Chumley & Hawke Ltd* (1981) 44 P. & C.R. 50 (landlord liable for defective foundations under covenant to keep main walls and roof in good structural repair and condition).

[67] *Ravenseft Properties Ltd v. Davstone (Holdings) Ltd, supra,* (insertion of expansion joints); *Stent v. Monmouth D.C.* (1987) 54 P. & C.R. 193 (replacement of door); *Creska Ltd v. Hammersmith & Fulham L.B.C.* [1998] 3 E.G.L.R. 35 (replacement of underfloor heaters with improved features).

[68] *Quick v. Taff Ely B.C., supra; Post Office v. Aquarius Properties Ltd* [1987] 1 All E.R. 1055.

[69] Such as damage to the decorative state of the property: *McGreal v. Wake* [1984] 1 E.G.L.R. 42; *Bradley v. Chorley B.C.* [1985] 2 E.G.L.R. 49.

[70] Including, where necessary, the cost of temporarily re-housing the tenant: *McGreal v. Wake, supra.*

[71] *Proudfoot v. Hart* (1890) 25 Q.B.D. 42 at 50, 51; *Anstruther–Gough–Calthorpe v. McOscar* [1924] 1 K.B. 716 at 722, 723, *per* Bankes L.J.; 729, *per* Scrutton L.J. *cf.* at 731, 732, *per* Atkin L.J.

[72] *Proudfoot v. Hart, supra,* at 55, *per* Lopes L.J.; *Crédit Suisse v. Beegas Nominees Ltd* [1994] 4 All E.R. 803 at 821.

[73] *Gutteridge v. Munyard* (1934) 7 C. & P. 129 at 133.

[74] *Ladbroke Hotels Ltd v. Sandhu* [1995] 2 E.G.L.R. 92 at 95.

[75] *Anstruther-Gough-Calthorpe v. McOscar, supra.*

[76] *Payne v. Haine* (1847) 16 M. & W. 541 at 545; *Proudfoot v. Hart, supra,* at 50; *Crédit Suisse v. Beegas Nominees Ltd, supra,* at 821, 822.

[77] *Proudfoot v. Hart, supra,* at 50.

A covenant to "repair, amend, renew ... and otherwise keep in good and tenantable condition" may require the covenantor to undertake work, such as the correction of an inherent defect that is not a repair strictly so called.[78]

The insertion into the covenant of words such as "fair wear and tear excepted" relieve the tenant from liability for any disrepair which he can show has resulted from the reasonable use of the premises and the ordinary operation of natural forces. However he remains liable for any consequential damage, such as damage to the interior resulting from the tenant's failure to prevent rain entering where tiles have slipped from the roof or a skylight has become defective.[79]

14–277   (2) NOTICE OF DISREPAIR. In general, a covenantor is in breach of covenant to keep in repair as soon as the disrepair occurs even though he is unaware of it.[80] It is now clear that this is the general rule and not, as was previously thought, the exception to it.[81] It has not been settled whether this rule applies—

    (i) where the covenant is merely to repair and not to keep in repair[82]; or

    (ii) where the breach is caused by an occurrence wholly outside the covenantor's control.[83]

However, even where the rule is applicable, the covenantee is well advised to inform the covenantor of the breach in order to mitigate his loss.[84]

To this general rule, there is an important exception. Where a landlord has covenanted to repair the actual premises leased, he is not liable for any breach until he has been given notice of the disrepair[85] and has had a reasonable time

---

[78] *Crédit Suisse v. Beegas Nominees Ltd, supra,* at 821, 822; [1994] All E.R. Rev. 258 (P. H. Pettit). See too *Norwich Union Life Insurance Society v. British Railways Board* [1987] 2 E.G.L.R. 137 (covenant "when necessary to rebuild, reconstruct or replace" in a 150-year lease might require the tenant to rebuild the premises).

[79] *Regis Property Co. Ltd v. Dudley* [1959] A.C. 370.

[80] *British Telecommunications Plc v. Sun Life Assurance Society Plc* [1996] Ch. 69 (breach of landlord's covenant to keep the building in repair broken, when the wall below the demised premises began to bulge) [1997] Conv. 59 (P. F. Smith); *Passley v. Wandsworth L.B.C.* (1996) 30 H.L.R. 165 (landlord liable for burst pipe in the roof of a block of flats). See too *Melles & Co. v. Holme* [1918] 2 K.B. 100; *Bishop v. Consolidated London Properties Ltd* (1933) 102 L.J.K.B. 257; *Loria v. Hammer* [1989] 1 E.G.L.R. 249; *Ladsky v. TSB Bank Plc* (1996) 74 P. & C.R. 372 at 375. cf. *Trane (U.K.) Ltd v. Provident Mutual Life Assurance* [1995] 1 E.G.L.R. 33 at 37.

[81] *British Telecommunications Plc v. Sun Life Assurance Society Plc, supra,* at 48.

[82] The point was left open in *British Telecommunications Plc v. Sun Life Assurance Society Plc, supra,* at 629, 630, though in principle, the rule should be equally applicable.

[83] *British Telecommunications Plc v. Sun Life Assurance Society Plc, supra,* at 629, where it was suggested, *obiter,* that it did not. The contrary is however arguable. The covenantor who has undertaken the obligation might be expected to bear the risk rather than the covenantee, in accordance with normal contractual principles.

[84] *Minchburn Ltd v. Peck* [1988] 1 E.G.L.R. 53 at 55.

[85] *Makin v. Watkinson* (1870) L.R. 6 Ex. 25; *Torrens v. Walker* [1906] 2 Ch. 166; *McCarrick v. Liverpool Corporation* [1947] A.C. 219.

to remedy it.[86] These conditions are implied into the covenant both because of the unreasonableness of expecting the landlord to do something of which he lacks notice and because the tenant is likely to be in a better position to know of the defect than is the landlord.[87] It applies not only to those defects of which the tenant knows, so that he is in a position to give the landlord notice, but also to latent defects where such notice is impossible.[88] It is not necessary that the landlord should be informed by the tenant.[89] It is enough if notice of the disrepair comes to the landlord's attention from a responsible source,[90] or if he has information that would place a reasonable landlord on inquiry.[91] The mere fact that the building is visibly out of repair,[92] or that the landlord has reserved a right to enter and view the state of repair,[93] is not however enough.

The Defective Premises Act 1972[94] has substantially qualified the require- **14–278** ment that a landlord is not liable for any disrepair to the demised premises until he receives notice of it. If a landlord is under an obligation to maintain or repair the premises,[95] or has a right to enter them to carry out repairs or maintenance,[96] he owes a duty of care to all persons who are likely to be affected by his failure to do so. That duty arises when he either knows (from whatever source) or ought in all the circumstances to have known of the relevant defect.[97] He will be liable therefore for any injury to such a person or to their property where—

    (i) he was negligent in not discovering the defect that caused the harm, even though he was given no notice of that defect; and

    (ii) that defect was one which fell within the scope of his repairing obligations or which he had a right to enter to rectify.[98]

---

[86] *Calabar Properties Ltd v. Stitcher* [1984] 1 W.L.R. 287 at 298; *Morris v. Liverpool City Council* [1988] 1 E.G.L.R. 47.

[87] *Murphy v. Hurly* [1922] 1 A.C. 369 at 375, 376, 383.

[88] *O'Brien v. Robinson* [1973] A.C. 912 (tenant injured by collapse of bedroom ceiling). For criticism of this rule, see *McGreal v. Wake* [1984] 1 E.G.L.R. 42 at 43; (1974) 37 M.L.R. 377 (J. I. Reynolds).

[89] *Dinefwr B.C. v. Jones* [1987] 2 E.G.L.R. 58 at 59; *Hall v. Howard* (1988) 57 P. & C.R. 226 at 230.

[90] *ibid.*

[91] *Griffin v. Pillet* [1926] 1 K.B. 17 at 21; *O'Brien v. Robinson, supra,* at 930; *Hall v. Howard, supra,* at 230.

[92] *Torrens v. Walker, supra.*

[93] *Hugall v. M'Lean* (1885) 53 L.T. 94; *Torrens v. Walker, supra; McCarrick v. Liverpool Corporation* [1947] A.C. 219.

[94] See *ante*, para. 14–225; and *infra.*

[95] Defective Premises Act 1972, s.4(1).

[96] *ibid.*, s.4(4).

[97] *ibid.*, s.4(2); see, *e.g. Clarke v. Taff Ely B.C.* (1980) 10 H.L.R. 44 (reasonably foreseeable that floors might rot due to dampness, but landlord failed to carry out inspections).

[98] There is no liability if it was outside that scope: *McNerny v. Lambeth L.B.C.* [1989] 1 E.G.L.R. 81, 83; *McAuley v. Bristol City Council* [1992] Q.B. 134, 145.

It remains the case that the landlord will not be liable for injury or damage caused by a latent defect of which he had no reason to know.

14–279   (3) EXTENSION OF LIABILITY. The wide duty of care imposed by the Defective Premises Act 1972[99] abrogates the former rule[1] that the landlord's obligation to repair, being contractual, did not cover injury to the tenant's family or visitors.[2] It also extends the landlord's repairing obligations, for it converts a mere right to enter to carry out repairs and maintenance into a duty to do so in so far as they are necessary to ensure the safety of those who might be injured by reason of the disrepair.[3] That duty is owed to the tenant himself except where the disrepair has arisen because of his failure to carry out an express repairing obligation in the tenancy.[4]

(b) Remedies

14–280   (1) WHERE THE LANDLORD IS IN BREACH OF COVENANT. Where it is the landlord who breaks a repairing covenant, damages may not be an adequate remedy for the tenant, particularly if the breach concerns property not comprised in the lease and so not accessible to the tenant. Specific performance may be and often is[5] decreed against him, either under the court's inherent jurisdiction[6] or, in the case of dwellings, by statute.[7] A court may exceptionally even grant a mandatory injunction in interlocutory proceedings to require the performance of a landlord's obligation to repair or maintain.[8]

In a case where damages are appropriate, the measure will depend upon whether the tenant—

> (i) remains in possession, when it will be the loss of comfort and convenience that results from the disrepair; or

---

[99] *Supra.* The duty is confined to the premises let and does not include other property of the landlord's over which the tenant is permitted to have access: *King v. South Northamptonshire D.C.* (1991) 64 P. & C.R. 35 at 40. The landlord may however owe the tenant and his visitors a duty of care in respect of such property under the Occupiers' Liability Act 1957, s.2.

[1] See *Cavalier v. Pope* [1906] A.C. 428; *Ryall v. Kidwell* [1914] 3 K.B. 135.

[2] See *Rimmer v. Liverpool City Council* [1985] Q.B. 1 at 11. *Cavalier v. Pope* itself would not be decided differently, because the obligation to repair in that case arose under a collateral agreement and not under the tenancy as s.4(1) of the 1972 Act requires. The Act leaves intact the other limb of the decision in *Cavalier v. Pope, supra,* that in the absence of any relevant repairing obligation, a landlord is under no liability for letting a dangerous house: *Rimmer v. Liverpool City Council, supra,* at 11; *McNerny v. Lambeth L.B.C.* [1989] 1 E.G.L.R. 81.

[3] Defective Premises Act 1972, s.4(4); *Smith v. Bradford Metropolitan Council* (1982) 44 P. & C.R. 171; *Hamilton v. Martell Securities Ltd* [1984] Ch. 266 at 271; *Barrett v. Lounova (1982) Ltd* [1990] 1 Q.B. 348 at 359.

[4] Defective Premises Act 1972, s.4(4).

[5] See *Joyce v. Liverpool City Council* [1996] Q.B. 252.

[6] *Jeune v. Queens Cross Properties Ltd* [1974] Ch. 97 (balcony not part of the demised premises); *Francis v. Cowlcliffe Ltd* (1976) 33 P. & C.R. 368 at 374 (lift); *Tustian v. Johnston* [1993] 2 All E.R. 673 at 680. For a possible objection, see *Gordon v. Selico Co. Ltd* [1985] 2 E.G.L.R. 79 at 84; on appeal: [1986] 1 E.G.L.R. 71 at 75.

[7] L. & T.A. 1985, s.17, replacing H.A. 1974, s.125.

[8] See, *e.g. Peninsular Maritime Ltd v. Padseal Ltd* [1981] 2 E.G.L.R. 43; *Parker v. Camden L.B.C.* [1986] Ch. 162 at 173.

(ii) disposes of his interest, when it will be the diminution in the value of the lease (if he assigns his interest) or the rental (if he sub-lets) caused by the landlord's breach of covenant.[9]

If, after giving notice of the default of the landlord, the tenant does the repairs himself, he may deduct his expenditure from his payments of rent, exercising his right of set-off at common law.[10] Even if he does not undertake the repairs, the tenant may withhold any rent payable to the landlord. In proceedings brought by the landlord to forfeit the lease or to recover the rent, the tenant may then claim an equitable set-off in respect of his claim against the landlord for the disrepair.[11] The existence of such a right of set-off is also a defence to any claim by the landlord to levy distress for unpaid rent.[12] That right to set-off may be excluded by the terms of the lease,[13] but only by a clear and explicit provision.[14]

(2) WHERE THE TENANT IS IN BREACH OF COVENANT. Apart from forfeiture, **14–281** the remedies for breach of a tenant's repairing covenant are damages, or in appropriate cases, a decree of specific performance.[15] Until recently, it was though that specific performance would not be decreed against a tenant,[16] but the reasons for that limitation was questionable.[17] However, "it will be a rare

---

[9] *Wallace v. Manchester City Council* [1998] 3 E.G.L.R. 38.

[10] *Lee–Parker v. Izzet* [1971] 1 W.L.R. 1688; *Asco Developments Ltd v. Gordon* [1978] 2 E.G.L.R. 41 (where the possibility of an equitable set-off for an unliquidated claim was deliberately not explored).

[11] *Melville v. Grapelodge Developments Ltd* [1980] 1 E.G.L.R. 42; *British Anzani (Felixstowe) Ltd v. International Marine Management (U.K.) Ltd* [1980] Q.B. 137. Provided that the claim is made in good faith, the landlord's claim for possession will be stayed pending trial: *British Anzani (Felixstowe) Ltd v. International Marine Management (U.K.) Ltd, supra; Haringey L.B.C. v. Stewart* (1991) 23 H.L.R. 557 at 559. See generally [1981] Conv. 137 (A. Waite). Because the right to a set-off is in these circumstances equitable, it is subject to equitable defences, *e.g.* want of clean hands by the tenant: *Televantos v. McCulloch* [1991] 1 E.G.L.R. 123 (where the defence was not established).

[12] *Eller v. Grovecrest Investments Ltd* [1995] Q.B. 272. For distress, see *ante*, para. 14–253.

[13] *Electricity Supply Nominees Ltd v. I.A.F. Group Ltd* [1993] 1 W.L.R. 1059; *Star Rider Ltd v. Inntrepreneur Pub Co.* [1998] 1 E.G.L.R. 53. In those cases it was held that such terms are not subject to the provisions of the Unfair Contract Terms Act 1977. It is uncertain whether the Unfair Contract Terms Directive (S.I. 1994 No. 3159) applies to such terms: see (1995) 111 L.Q.R. 655 (S. & C. Bright).

[14] *Connaught Restaurants Ltd v. Indoor Leisure Ltd* [1994] 1 W.L.R. 501 (landlord's right to payment of rent "without deduction" did not exclude tenant's equitable right of set-off in respect of repairs).

[15] *Rainbow Estates Ltd v. Tokenhold Ltd*; [1998] J.B.L. 564 (P. Luxton); [1999] Ch. 64; [1999] C.L.J. 283 (S. Bridge). The trend of modern authority is to decree specific performance if it is appropriate: *cf. Tito v. Waddell (No. 2)* [1977] Ch. 106 at 321; *Posner v. Scott–Lewis* [1987] Ch. 27; [1987] C.L.J. 21 (G. H. Jones).

[16] Based on the authority of *Hill v. Barclay* (1810) 16 Ves. 402 at 405.

[17] One of the main justifications was lack of mutuality: *Hill v. Barclay, supra*, at 405. However, as a tenant can seek specific performance of a landlord's repairing obligations (*infra*), the force of this objection had been "much weakened": *Regional Properties Ltd v. City of London Real Property Co. Ltd* [1981] 1 E.G.L.R. 33 at 34, *per* Oliver J. Prior to *Rainbow Estates v. Tokenhold Ltd, supra*, the Law Commission had recommended that a landlord should be able to obtain specific performance of a tenant's repairing covenants: (1996) Law Com. No. 238, Pt IX.

case in which the remedy of specific performance will be the appropriate one," because the landlord will either have power under the lease to enter the premises to do the repairs at the tenant's expense, or to seek the forfeiture of the lease.[18]

The measure of damages recoverable for the breach of a tenant's repairing covenant formerly varied according to the time of the breach.[19] If the breach occurred during the term, the damages were calculated on the decrease in the value of the reversion caused by the breach.[20] The longer the lease had to run, the less would be the damages. But if the breach occurred at the end of the term, the cost of repairing the premises was recoverable by the landlord[21]; and (by way of exception to the ordinary rule that the measure of damages is the loss actually suffered) it was held to make no difference that the landlord did not propose to carry out the repairs but intended to demolish the premises instead.[22]

14–282   However, by the Landlord and Tenant Act 1927,[23] damages for breach of a repairing covenant are not to exceed the diminution in the value of the reversion,[24] *i.e.* the difference between the value of the reversion with the repairs done and its value without.[25] In normal cases when repairs are likely to be done (and in some cases, perhaps even where they are not[26]) the cost of executing them provides the best guide to the diminution in the value of the reversion,[27] at least where the term has come to an end.[28] The landlord's claim is not reduced merely because he has let the premises to a new tenant who has

---

[18] *Rainbow Estates Ltd v. Tokenhold Ltd, supra*, at 74, *per* Lawrence Collins, Q.C. In that case, the lease contained neither a forfeiture clause nor a power for the landlord to enter to execute repairs.

[19] For a useful summary of the principles, see *Crown Estate Commissioners v. Town Investments Ltd* [1992] 1 E.G.L.R. 61 and 63.

[20] *Doe d. Worcester Trustees v. Rowlands* (1841) 9 C. & P. 734; *Ebbetts v. Conquest* [1895] 2 Ch. 377, affirmed, *Conquest v. Ebbetts* [1896] A.C. 490. This principle is unaffected by L. & T.A. 1927, s.18 (*infra*): see *Crewe Services & Investment Corporation v. Silk* [1998] 2 E.G.L.R. 1.

[21] *Joyner v. Weeks* [1891] 2 Q.B. 31.

[22] *ibid.*, at 44, 45. But this exception does not apply to a covenant to reinstate after alterations: *James v. Hutton* [1950] 1 K.B. 9. As to the effects of L. & T.A. 1927, s. 19(2), in such a case, *quaere: ibid.*

[23] s.18.

[24] *Smiley v. Townshend* [1950] 2 K.B. 311; *Family Management v. Gray* [1980] 1 E.G.L.R. 46.

[25] *Hanson v. Newman* [1934] Ch. 298; *Shortlands Investments Ltd v. Cargill Plc* [1995] 1 E.G.L.R. 51 at 56.

[26] See *Shortlands Investments Ltd v. Cargill Plc, supra*, at 56; but *cf. Haviland v. Long* [1952] 2 Q.B. 80 at 84. In the *Shortlands* case, the fact that the landlords had a reversion with a negative value did not deprive them of their claim for dilapidations, because the disrepair increased the amount of the reverse premium that they had to pay to an incoming tenant.

[27] *Jones v. Herxheimer* [1950] 2 K.B. 106; *Culworth Estates Ltd v. Society of Licensed Victuallers* [1991] 2 E.G.L.R. 54 at 56. If the cost of carrying out the repairs exceeds the diminution in the value of the reversion, it will be reduced accordingly: *Shortlands Investments Ltd v. Cargill Plc, supra*.

[28] See *Crewe Services & Investment Corporation v. Silk* [1998] 2 E.G.L.R. 1, holding that the cost of repairs was not the appropriate measure where the landlord sought damages during the currency of the term. It was incumbent on the landlord in such a case to lead evidence as to the diminution of the value of the reversion caused by the breach.

covenanted to repair them,[29] or because his reversion is of very short duration.[30] But no damages at all are recoverable if the premises are to be demolished, or structurally altered in such a way as to make the repairs valueless, at or soon after the end of the term.[31] This is so even if in the event no demolition is carried out.[32] But damages will be recoverable if the reason for the demolition is merely the tenant's breach of his repairing obligations.[33] These rules relate only to repairing covenants. Damages for breach of other covenants (*e.g.* against making alterations) are recoverable in the usual way.[34] It should be noted, however, that developments in the law of damages mean that the rule embodied in the 1927 Act may do no more than reflect what is now the common law. It appears that a claimant can only recover the cost of remedying a breach of contract if it is reasonable for him to do so, which will not normally be the case unless he intends to do the work (and not always then).[35]

(c) Appointment of a receiver or manager. A problem that has often arisen **14–283** in recent years is of a landlord of a block of flats who, although receiving rent and service charge from the tenants, fails to carry out his repairing obligations under the lease.[36] In these circumstances, the court has a wide jurisdiction[37] to appoint a receiver and manager if it is just and convenient to do so.[38] The receiver, once appointed, collects the payments from the tenants and applies them in carrying out the repairs.[39] However, this jurisdiction can no longer be exercised in relation to blocks of flats[40] but only as regards other forms of leasehold properties. Part II of the Landlord and Tenant Act 1987 makes provision for a tenant of a flat to apply to the court for the appointment of a manager.[41] He may be appointed to carry out such functions in connection with the management of the premises and of a receiver as the court thinks fit.[42] The court will appoint a manager only where it is satisfied that—

---

[29] *Haviland v. Long, supra.*

[30] *Jaquin v. Holland* [1960] 1 W.L.R. 258; *Lloyds Bank Ltd v. Lake* [1961] 1 W.L.R. 884.

[31] See, *e.g. Cunliffe v. Goodman* [1950] 2 K.B. 237; *Mather v. Barclays Bank Plc* [1987] 1 E.G.L.R. 254; (1988) 104 L.Q.R. 372 (D. N. Clarke).

[32] *Keats v. Graham* [1960] 1 W.L.R. 30.

[33] *Hibernian Property Co. Ltd v. Liverpool Corporation* [1973] 1 W.L.R. 751, also holding that the intention to demolish must be that of the landlord: *sed quaere.*

[34] *Eyre v. Rea* [1947] K.B. 567.

[35] *Ruxley Electronics and Construction Ltd v. Forsyth* [1996] A.C. 344.

[36] See *Clayhope Properties Ltd v. Evans* [1986] 1 W.L.R. 1223 at 1231; *Blawdziewicz v. Diadon Establishment* [1988] 2 E.G.L.R. 52 at 53.

[37] Under Supreme Court Act 1981, s.37.

[38] *Hart v. Emelkirk Ltd* [1983] 1 W.L.R. 1289; *Daiches v. Bluelake Investments Ltd* (1985) 51 P. & C.R. 51. The court will not appoint a receiver to carry out duties imposed by statute on a particular body (such as a local authority): *Parker v. Camden L.B.C.* [1986] Ch. 162.

[39] When such an order is made in interlocutory proceedings, the receiver can only carry out the repairs from receipts. The court will not order the landlord to meet his expenses: *Evans v. Clayhope Properties Ltd* [1988] 1 W.L.R. 358.

[40] L. & T.A. 1987, s.21(6). For the definition of a "flat" for these purposes, see *ibid.*, s.60(1).

[41] *ibid.*, s.21(1). The building must contain two or more flats: *ibid.*, s.21(2).

[42] *ibid.*, s.24(1).

(i) the landlord is (and is likely to continue to be) in breach of his obligations to manage the property; and

(ii) it is just and convenient to do so.[43]

Part III of the Act enables tenants of flats to acquire compulsorily their landlord's reversionary interest in certain cases where he is in breach of his obligations of repair, maintenance, insurance or management of the premises.[44]

14–284   *(d) Internal decorative repairs.* The Law of Property Act 1925[45] enables the court in certain cases to relieve the tenant from liability for internal decorative repairs if the landlord acts unreasonably. But there are a number of exceptions, *e.g.* when the tenant has never performed a contract to put the property into decorative repair. This power of the court is not confined to proceedings for forfeiture but extends to actions for damages.

(e) The Leasehold Property (Repairs) Act 1938

14–285   (1) OBJECT OF ACT. This Act was passed in order to protect tenants of small houses under long leases from having to pay heavy bills for dilapidations under the threat of forfeiture for breach of covenant. This mischief which the Act was designed to remedy was that speculators could buy the reversion of dilapidated house property for a small price, enforce forfeiture of the lease on account of non-repair, and so get the residue of the term for nothing.[46] As now extended,[47] the Act applies to all types of property (except agricultural holdings) where the tenancy was granted for a term certain of not less than seven years, and has at least three years unexpired.[48] However, its applicability is limited to cases where there has been a breach by the tenant of a covenant to keep or put in repair, and not, *e.g.* of a covenant to cleanse the premises[49] or to lay out insurance monies in the reinstatement of the premises.[50]

14–286   (2) LEAVE OF COURT. Where the Act applies, the landlord may neither sue for damages nor enforce forfeiture for failure to repair unless he first serves on the

---

[43] *ibid.*, s.24(2). The section contains detailed provisions as to the powers that may be conferred upon the manager.

[44] The pre-conditions for the grant of an acquisition order are strict: see L. & T.A. 1987, s.29. For a fuller account, see P. F. Smith, *West's Law of Dilapidations* (10th ed.), pp. 156–164.

[45] s.147.

[46] See *National Real Estate and Finance Co. Ltd v. Hassan* [1939] 2 K.B. 61 at 78.

[47] By the Landlord and Tenant Act 1954, s.51, removing (*inter alia*) the former limits as to rateable value.

[48] Leasehold Property (Repairs) Act 1938, ss.1, 7. The Act applies to leases created before or after the Act (s.5).

[49] *Starrokate Ltd v. Burry* [1983] 1 E.G.L.R. 56.

[50] *Farimani v. Gates* [1984] 1 E.G.L.R. 66.

tenant a notice under section 146 of the Law of Property Act 1925,[51] which informs the tenant of his right to serve a counter-notice, and one month elapses thereafter.[52] Within 28 days after service of the notice the tenant may serve a counter-notice claiming the benefit of the Act. The result of this is that the landlord can take no further proceedings without leave of the court. This will be given only if he can prove on the balance of probabilities[53] that the immediate remedying of a breach of the repairing covenant is required in order to save the landlord from substantial loss or damage which he would otherwise sustain.[54] In granting or refusing leave, the court may impose such conditions on either party as it thinks fit.[55] It has been said that "the battle between landlord and tenant must be fought at some stage".[56] It is now fought on the application for leave and not, as was formerly the case, in any subsequent forfeiture proceedings. If the landlord fails, the threat of forfeiture is lifted. If he succeeds, the tenant "will know what steps he must take to avoid forfeiture".[57]

One important feature of the Act is that, where it applies, it shifts the onus of applying to the court from the tenant to the landlord. But it does not apply where the landlord is reclaiming from the tenant the cost of tenant's repairs which the landlord has himself carried out under a clause in the lease empowering him to do so, since this is a claim in debt and not in damages.[58]

(3) SERVICE OF NOTICE. There is no need to serve a notice under the Act on **14–287** a mortgagee of the lease[59]; and if a notice was properly served on the tenant

---

[51] For this, see *ante*, para. 14–147. It has been held that where the landlord executed the repairs himself, he could not then serve a notice under s.146, because the breach had already been remedied: *S.E.D.A.C. Investments Ltd v. Tanner* [1982] 1 W.L.R. 1342. The landlord was therefore unable to recover the cost of the repairs from the tenant. Not only is the result unjust, but it is based on a very questionable reading of s.146: see [1986] Conv. 85 (P. F. Smith). *cf Hamilton v. Martell Securities Ltd* [1984] Ch. 266 at 281.

[52] Leasehold Property (Repairs) Act 1938, ss.1(2), (4), 3. A notice that does not comply with the requirements of s.1(4) will be invalid: *BL Holdings Ltd v. Marcolt Investments Ltd* [1979] 1 E.G.L.R. 97.

[53] *Associated British Ports v. C.H. Bailey Plc* [1990] 2 A.C. 703, overruling *Sidnell v. Wilson* [1966] 2 Q.B. 67 (where it was held that the landlord had only to show a prima facie case). For criticism, see [1990] C.L.J. 401 (S. Bridge), but compare [1990] Conv. 305 (P. F. Smith).

[54] Leasehold Property (Repairs) Act 1938, s.1(5) listing five possible grounds on which leave may be given. See *Phillips v. Price* [1959] Ch. 181; *Re Metropolitan Film Studio Ltd's Application* [1962] 1 W.L.R. 1315.

[55] Leasehold Property (Repairs) Act 1938, s.1(6).

[56] *Associated British Ports v. C.H. Bailey Plc, supra*, at 713, *per* Lord Templeman.

[57] *ibid.* The decision has led to a marked change in practice: see [1990] C.L.J. 401 (S. Bridge).

[58] *Jervis v. Harris* [1996] Ch. 195, overruling *Swallow Securities Ltd v. Brand* (1981) 45 P. & C.R. 328 (where McNeill J. had held that the Act applied), and approving *Hamilton v. Martell Securities Ltd* [1984] Ch. 266; *Colchester Estates (Cardiff) v. Carlton Industries Plc* [1986] Ch. 80; and *Elite Investments Ltd v. T. I. Bainbridge Silencers Ltd* [1986] 2 E.G.L.R. 43 at 49.

[59] *Church Commissioners for England v. Ve–Ri–Best Manufacturing Co. Ltd* [1957] 1 Q.B. 238. If leave is given to the landlord to proceed with forfeiture proceedings and he subsequently commences an action for possession, the landlord should furnish the names and addresses of any mortgagee or underlessee of whom he knows in the particulars of claim to ensure that they are served with copies of those particulars: see *ante*, para. 14–144.

for the time being, no notice need be served on a subsequent assignee, though if the tenant served a counter-notice leave to proceed against the assignee must be obtained.[60] The Act does not protect the original lessee after he has assigned, even though by privity of contract he remains liable on the repairing covenant.[61]

14–288   **5. Covenant to insure.** A covenant to insure against fire is broken if the premises are uninsured for any period, however short, even if no fire occurs.[62] If the covenant is to insure with a named company, or with some other responsible company with the landlord's approval, the landlord, who may wish to have all his properties insured with one company, can withhold his approval of an alternative company without giving any reasons.[63] A covenant to insure with a named company binds the tenant to take out such policy of the company as is usual at the time, so that if such a policy excepts some specified risks, the tenant is not liable under this covenant if the house is destroyed in one of the excepted ways.[64]

14–289   The respective rights of the landlord and the tenant in relation to the proceeds of any insurance that may have been effected in respect of the leased premises depend upon the terms of both the lease and the policy of insurance.[65] A landlord is entitled to insure the premises demised against destruction to its full reinstatement value. This is so notwithstanding that he has a limited interest in the property and even though the tenant's interest is not noted on the policy.[66] Commonly, the landlord undertakes to insure the premises and the tenant pays him an additional rent to cover that portion of the premiums that is attributable to the leasehold interest. Where in such circumstances the lease contains no obligation on either party to reinstate the premises, the tenant can require the landlord to apply any insurance monies for that purpose.[67] Where the insurance is taken for the benefit of the interests of both landlord and tenant and insurance monies become payable under the policy because of its damage or destruction—

> (i) those monies are apportioned between them by reference to the values of their respective interests if through no fault of the parties

---

[60] *Kanda v. Church Commissioners for England* [1958] 1 Q.B. 332.
[61] See *Cusack–Smith v. Gold* [1958] 1 W.L.R. 611; but see *Baker v. Sims* [1959] 1 Q.B. 114 at 129. A tenant will be liable on grounds of privity only in leases granted prior to 1996: see *post*, paras 15–014, 15–064.
[62] *Penniall v. Harborne* (1848) 11 Q.B. 368.
[63] *Viscount Tredegar v. Harwood* [1929] A.C. 72.
[64] *Upjohn v. Hitchens* [1918] 2 K.B. 48. It is otherwise if no company is named: see *Enlayde Ltd v. Roberts* [1917] 1 Ch. 109.
[65] *Beacon Carpets Ltd v. Kirby* [1985] Q.B. 755 at 768.
[66] See *Mumford Hotels Ltd v. Wheler* [1964] Ch. 117; *Mark Rowlands Ltd v. Berni Inns Ltd* [1986] Q.B. 211 at 226. A stranger to the lease has no insurable interest however: see *Sadlers v. Clements* [1995] E.G.C.S. 197.
[67] This is either because the landlord is regarded as insuring for the joint benefit of both parties (see *Mumford Hotels Ltd v. Wheler, supra*, at 125) or because the court will imply a term that the landlord will exercise the rights conferred by the policy in such a way as to preserve the tenant's interests: *Vural Ltd v. Security Archives Ltd* (1989) 60 P. & C.R. 258 at 273.

it becomes impossible to reinstate the premises[68] or if the parties agree that it should not be reinstated[69];

> (ii) the landlord cannot sue the tenant for negligence if that was the cause of the damage and was a risk covered by the policy[70]; and

> (iii) the tenant may require the insurer to apply the monies in reinstating the premises even though the landlord has sold the reversion and has no claim against the insurer in respect of his own interest.[71]

Where, by contrast, the tenant is required to insure the premises and reinstate them, he will be entitled to the entirety of the proceeds if the premises are destroyed and if without fault on his part it becomes impossible to reinstate them.[72]

Section 4. Statutory Protection of Tenants

Until comparatively recently, Parliament had tended to make special statutory **14–290** provisions to protect tenants from landlords, irrespective of any agreement between the parties. The movement was from contract to status. Some instances of this have already been given. Another example is that anyone who demands or receives rent or acts as agent for a landlord of a dwelling must comply with a written request by the tenant of the dwelling for his landlord's name and address.[73] Other, more far-reaching examples lie beyond the scope of this book. In particular, tenancies of agricultural holdings granted prior to September 1995, under the Agricultural Holdings Act 1986, most tenancies of dwelling houses granted before January 15, 1989, under the Rent Act 1977,[74] and tenancies of business premises under Part II of the Landlord and Tenant Act 1954, are all governed by extensive codes, one primary purpose of which is to restrict the landlord's right to recover possession. More recently, there has been a move back to freedom of contract. It is now possible

---

[68] *Beacon Carpets Ltd v. Kirby, supra* at 769, distinguishing *Re King* [1963] Ch. 459; considered *infra*.

[69] *Beacon Carpets Ltd v. Kirby, supra.*

[70] *Mark Rowlands Ltd v. Berni Inns Ltd, supra*, [1986] C.L.J. 22 (M.A. Clarke). The insurer cannot therefore sue the tenant in exercise of his rights of subrogation. The landlord will be unable to sue the tenant only where the parties intended that the insurance should enure for the benefit of both. This will not be inferred merely because the landlord covenanted to insure the premises: such insurance may be taken for his benefit only. It is not necessary that the lease itself should demonstrate a common intention to insure for the benefit of both parties. Regard may be had, *e.g.* to correspondence between the parties. See *Lambert v. Keymood Ltd* [1997] 1 E.G.L.R. 70 at 74.

[71] Under the Fires Prevention (Metropolis) Act 1774, s.83: *Lonsdale & Thompson Ltd v. Black Arrow Group Plc* [1993] Ch. 361; *ante*, para. 12–056.

[72] *Re King, supra.*

[73] L. & T.A. 1985, s.1(1). Failure to comply without reasonable excuse is an offence: *ibid.*, s.1(2).

[74] Or earlier legislation having similar effect.

for landlords to grant leases of residential property under the Housing Act
1988 without giving security of tenure to tenants. Nor is there any such
extended security of tenure in relation to farm business tenancies granted after
August 1995 under the Agricultural Tenancies Act 1995. A detailed consideration of this legislation would require another book. It is therefore best
regarded as a separate subject, and is summarised in a later chapter.[75]

Part 6

LEASEHOLD CONVEYANCING

14–291 The rules governing contracts for the sale of land have been explained, and
brief accounts given of unregistered and registered conveyancing, though
primarily with reference to the sale of a fee simple. Many of the same
principles apply to the creation and assignment of leases. For example, we
have already seen that a contract to grant or assign a lease must be made in
writing in the same way as a contract for sale, and that its operation in equity
is similar.[76] On the other hand, the rules as to the formalities necessary when
granting (but not assigning) legal leases are in some ways different from the
rules for freehold conveyances. The following paragraphs explain the main
points of both similarity and divergence between the rules governing freehold
and leasehold dispositions.

A. Contracts

14–292   **1. Formality.** A contract to grant or assign a lease requires the same
formalities as any other contract for the disposition of an interest in land.[77]
There is however an exception in respect of a contract to grant (but not assign)
a lease that may be made orally.[78]

14–293   **2. Effect in equity.** A contract to grant or assign a lease creates an equitable
interest, analogous to that created by a contract to sell a freehold. It is
registrable as an estate contract where title is unregistered and may be
protected by means of a notice or caution where title is registered. This has
been explained in connection with *Walsh v. Lonsdale.*[79]

14–294   **3. Duty to disclose latent defects in title.** Where a person contracts to
grant or assign a lease, he is under the same obligation to disclose latent
defects in title prior to contracting as is a vendor of freehold land.[80] If he fails

---

[75] See *post*, paras 22–062 *et seq.*
[76] *Ante*, para. 12–018.
[77] *ibid.*
[78] *Ante*, paras 12–022, 14–037.
[79] *Ante*, paras 14–047—14–049.
[80] *Ante*, para. 12–068.

to do so, the grantee or assignee may terminate the contract at once, even before the date for the commencement of the term or the completion of the assignment.[81] In the case of a contract to assign a lease, an onerous or unusual covenant is regarded as a defect in title for these purposes, and must be disclosed.[82] The obligation is normally satisfied by giving the purchaser a copy of the lease to inspect prior to contract.[83]

4. Duty to prove good title

(a) Unregistered land. The title which may be called for under an open contract by an intending lessee or assignee of unregistered land differs from that to which a purchaser of the freehold is entitled.[84] The Law of Property Act 1925[85] provides that in default of any express provision to the contrary— **14–295**

> (i) under a contract for the grant or assignment of a lease or sub-lease, there is no right to call for the title to the freehold[86];
>
> (ii) under a contract for the assignment of a sub-lease, there is no right to call for the title to the superior lease[87]; and
>
> (iii) under a contract to grant a sub-lease, there is no right to call for the title to the head lease.[88]

These provisions are obscurely worded. It is assumed in practice that the "title to" a lease or sub-lease includes the lease or sub-lease itself.[89] The effect of these rules may then be conveniently summarised by saying that an intending tenant or assignee may always inspect any lease under which the other contracting party holds. There is no right to inspect the title to the freehold. It should be noted however that, subject to these restrictions, there is an obligation to deduce title in the normal way, with a good root of title that is at least

---

[81] See, *e.g. Roper v. Coombes* (1827) 9 Dowl. & Ry. 562 (lessee contracted to grant sub-lease longer than his term); *Pips (Leisure Productions) Ltd v. Walton* (1980) 43 P. & C.R. 415 (lessee contracted to assign its lease after it had been forfeited).

[82] *Reeve v. Berridge* (1888) 20 Q.B.D. 523; *Re Haedicke and Lipski's Contract* [1901] 2 Ch. 666; see (1992) 108 L.Q.R. 280 at 325 (C.H.). For the covenants that will not be regarded as "usual", see *ante*, para. 14–241.

[83] See, *e.g.* Standard Conditions of Sale (3rd ed.), cc. 3.2, 8.1.

[84] See *ante*, paras 12–074 *et seq.*

[85] s.44(2)–(4), replacing V. & P.A. 1874, s.2 (as amended). For the law prior to the 1874 Act, see the previous edition of this work at p. 724.

[86] s.44(2).

[87] s.44(3).

[88] s.44(4).

[89] The dictum to the contrary in *Gosling v. Woolf* [1893] 1 Q.B. 39 at 41 is thought to be wrong, and is not supported by the report in (1892) 68 L.T. 89, indicating that the case concerned the grant (not the assignment) of a sub-lease. See Wolst. & C. i, 111.

15 years old.[90] An example might be where L granted a 60-year lease in 1950 to T and that lease was assigned by T to A in 1965, by A to B in 1978 and by B to C in 1989. If C now enters into an open contract to assign it to D, the title which C must deduce will be the lease from L to T; and the assignments from A to B and from B to C. C will not have to deduce L's freehold title, nor the assignment of the lease from T to A.[91]

Since these rules yield to contrary provision in the contract, the intending tenant may (and commonly does) stipulate for fuller disclosure, particularly if the lease is granted for more than 21 years and will therefore be registered.[92] Furthermore, even though an intending tenant or assignee may be precluded from seeing a superior title, he may still object to the title if he discovers *aliunde* that it is defective.[93]

14–296 These statutory limitations on the purchaser's right to inspect the title have created a difficulty in relation to those few equitable incumbrances which still bind a purchaser with notice, such as restrictive covenants created before 1926. The lessee or assignee is fixed with notice of everything that he would have discovered had he stipulated for and made a full investigation of title. This has been held to be the case even though he is deprived by statute of the right to make such an investigation.[94] To meet this difficulty, the Law of Property Act 1925 provides that where, by reason of the statutory restrictions, an intending lessee or assignee is unable to make a full investigation of title, "he shall not be deemed to be affected with notice of any matter or thing of which, if he had contracted that such title should be furnished, he might have had notice".[95] The effect of this provision is however merely to shift the hardship from the shoulders of the lessee to the owner of the equitable incumbrance. His interest is void against the lessee as a purchaser of a legal estate for value without notice.[96]

The Act protects a purchaser only from the consequences of his inability to investigate title fully. It does not protect him if he acquired notice in some other way, *e.g.* where he actually knew of the incumbrance.[97] This may be important where the equitable incumbrance is registered as a land charge, since registration is deemed to be actual notice.[98] Registered incumbrances will therefore in any case bind a lessee or sub-lessee or the assignee of a sub-lease.[99] Furthermore, because of the defects of the registration machinery

---

[90] L.P.A. 1969, s.23; *ante*, paras 5–021, 12–075.

[91] See *Williams v. Spargo* [1893] W.N. 100.

[92] See Standard Conditions of Sale (3rd ed.), c. 8.2.4 (grantor to deduce a title that will enable lessee to be registered with absolute title).

[93] *Jones v. Watts* (1890) 43 Ch.D. 574.

[94] *Patman v. Harland* (1881) 17 Ch.D. 353; and see *ante*, paras 5–021, 5–022. For a fuller account of this problem, see the previous edition of this work at p. 725.

[95] s.44(5).

[96] As in *Shears v. Wells* [1936] 1 All E.R. 832.

[97] The burden of proving notice is on the person seeking to enforce the adverse interest: *Shears v. Wells, supra.*

[98] *Ante*, para. 5–109.

[99] *White v. Bijou Mansions Ltd* [1937] Ch. 610 (in C.A. [1938] Ch. 351).

discussed earlier,[1] it may be impossible for a purchaser to discover a registered incumbrance which is binding on him.[2] Unless he has access to all the title deeds he cannot discover the names of the owners against which he must search, with the exception of the immediate vendor and of persons named in such documents as he is allowed to see.

(b) Registered land. Where the superior title is registered, the difficulties **14–297** outlined above in relation to unregistered land do not arise.[3] This is because the register is a public document which can be inspected without the authority of the registered proprietor.[4] An intending lessee or assignee can therefore discover any defects in the landlord's title that appear on the register and will usually be registered with an absolute title.[5] However, the statutory restrictions on the title which an intending tenant or assignee is entitled to call for apply as much to registered as to unregistered land.[6] Furthermore, the obligations as to proof of title imposed on a vendor of registered land, have no application to the grant of a lease.[7]

Where a lease is granted for a term exceeding 21 years, or an existing unregistered lease having more than 21 years to run is assigned, the lease must be registered with its own title.[8] If the lessee then contracts to assign the lease, he must prove his title in the usual way applicable to registered land.[9] By contrast, a lease of registered land granted for 21 years or less cannot be registered with its own title or even noted on the superior title, but must take effect as an overriding interest.[10] Such leases are therefore treated as unregistered land[11] and, on an assignment, title is deduced in accordance with the principles of unregistered conveyancing.[12]

(c) Particular problems. Certain problems arise as to title that are peculiar **14–298** to leases, of which two may be mentioned.

(1) VENDOR IN BREACH OF COVENANT. The first is where a tenant, holding **14–299** under a lease which contains a proviso for re-entry for breach of covenant, contracts to assign the term at a time when he is in breach of covenant. The courts appear to treat all breaches of covenant as irremovable defects in title,

---

[1] *Ante*, para. 5–110.

[2] In certain cases the tenant may be entitled to compensation: L.P.A. 1969, s.25; *ante*, para. 5–113. There have been just two successful claims for compensation under this Act (neither of which involved a lease), suggesting that the problems are more apparent than real.

[3] They *will* however arise in relation to a lease granted for more than 21 years and which has therefore been registered (see *infra*), but where the superior title remains unregistered.

[4] L.R.A. 1925, s.112(1) (substituted by L.R.A. 1988, s.1(1)); *ante*, para. 6–002.

[5] Ruoff & Roper, 21–05.

[6] *ibid.*

[7] L.R.A. 1925, s.110; *ante*, para. 12–084.

[8] L.R.A. 1925, s.123(1); *ante*, para. 6–015.

[9] See L.R.A. 1925, s.110; *ante*, para. 12–084.

[10] See L.R.A. 1925, ss.19(2), 22(2), 48(1); *ante*, para. 6–066.

[11] *e.g.* equitable incumbrances affecting such leases are registered as land charges under L.C.A. 1972.

[12] *Ante*, para. 14–295.

even though most such breaches are in law capable of remedy.[13] It is by statute provided that on a sale of a lease, the purchaser is to assume, unless the contrary appears—

    (i) that the lease was duly granted; and

    (ii) on the production of the receipt for the last payment of rent due under the lease prior to completion, that all the covenants in the lease have been performed and observed up to the actual completion date.[14]

The basis of the second assumption is that, by accepting rent, the landlord waives the breach.[15] However, waiver will not always protect a purchaser because there will normally be a period of time between the rent payment and completion. Where the breach is of a continuing nature[16] it is considered to arise afresh after the waiver,[17] thereby placing the purchaser at risk that the lease will be forfeited. The authorities establish that, if the purchaser is either—

    (i) unaware of the breach of covenant at the time of contracting; or

    (ii) aware of the breach, but the vendor has expressly contracted to show a good title;

he is not precluded by the statutory assumption from showing the vendor is in breach of covenant.[18] The purchaser may therefore either repudiate the contract or require the vendor to remedy the breach.

14–300   (2) LANDLORD'S CONSENT TO ASSIGNMENT. It has been explained that many leases require the landlord's consent to any assignment.[19] Compliance with the requirement is, anomalously, regarded as a matter of conveyance rather than of title, and the assignor has therefore until completion to obtain it.[20] He

---

[13] If they are remedied, the landlord cannot forfeit the lease: *ante*, paras 14–147—14–149. Normally a purchaser's knowledge of a removable defect in title at the time of contracting does not affect the vendor's obligation to discharge the incumbrance prior to completion: *ante*, paras 12–080, 12–081. However, this principle is apparently not applied to breaches of leasehold covenants. *cf* [1988] Conv. 400 at 408 (C.H.).

[14] L.P.A. 1925, s.45(2). See, *e.g. Clarke v. Coleman* [1895] W.N. 114; *Lockharts v. Bernard Rosen & Co.* [1922] 1 Ch. 433. For the analogous provision applicable to the sale of an underlease, see *ibid.*, s.45(3). Both provisions may be ousted if a contrary intention appears from the contract: *ibid.*, s.45(10).

[15] For waiver, see *ante*, para. 14–125.

[16] *e.g.* a breach of a repairing covenant.

[17] *Ante*, para. 14–128.

[18] See *Re Taunton and West of England Perpetual Benefit B.S. and Roberts' Contract* [1912] 2 Ch. 381; *Re Highett and Bird's Contract* [1903] 1 Ch. 287 as explained in *Re Allen and Driscoll's Contract* [1904] 2 Ch. 226 at 231.

[19] *Ante*, para. 14–259.

[20] *Ante*, para. 12–080. All other matters of conveyance involve incumbrances that the vendor can remove as of right, such as mortgages.

will be in breach of contract if consent has not been given by then,[21] unless the landlord withholds it unreasonably. In the latter case, the parties are entitled to proceed with the assignment without it,[22] though a court will not compel the assignee to take an assignment because the vendor's title will be doubtful.[23]

It has long been usual for such contracts to be made conditional upon obtaining the landlord's consent.[24] If consent is not forthcoming—

(i) the purchaser need not complete and may recover any deposit that he has paid; but

(ii) the vendor will not be in breach of contract provided that he has used his best endeavours to secure the consent.[25]

Such conditions provide a simple means of escape for a vendor without first having to determine in court proceedings whether or not the landlord had acted unreasonably.[26]

5. Options to renew. A lease will often contain an option for renewal or for the purchase of the freehold.[27] It has been the practice for more than two centuries for such options to be subject to the proviso that the tenant has complied with all covenants at a specified date, *e.g.* the exercise of the option.[28] The general rule in relation to options is that there must be no subsisting actionable breaches of covenant at the specified date,[29] and this is so even though only nominal damages would be awarded for the breach of covenant.[30] However, the fact that there have been breaches in the past is no bar to the enforcement of the option, provided that—

14–301

---

[21] *Bain v. Fothergill* (1874) L.R. 5 H.L. 158. The measure of damages in such a case would now be different: see L.P.M.P.A. 1989, s.3; *ante*, para. 12–103.

[22] *Treloar v. Bigge* (1874) L.R. 9 Ex. 151 at 157.

[23] *Re Marshall and Salt's Contract* [1900] 2 Ch. 202. The court would have to determine the issue of the lessor's unreasonableness in proceedings to which he would not be a party and by whose decree he would not therefore be bound.

[24] See, *e.g.* Standard Conditions of Sale (3rd ed.), c. 8.3. For conditional contracts of this kind, see *ante*, paras 12–007—12–008.

[25] *Lehmann v. McArthur* (1868) L.R. 3 Ch.App. 496. The vendor will be liable if he does not use his best endeavours: *Day v. Singleton* [1899] 2 Ch. 320.

[26] See *Bickel v. Courtenay Investments (Nominees) Ltd* [1984] 1 W.L.R. 795.

[27] Or a break clause to enable a tenant to terminate the lease prematurely: see *ante*, para. 14–117. The principles explained in this section apply to both: see *Reed Personnel Services Plc v. American Express Ltd* [1997] 1 E.G.L.R. 229.

[28] *Bass Holdings Ltd v. Morton Music Ltd* [1988] Ch. 493 at 517, 528. For the principles applicable where there are preconditions to the exercise of options, see *Little v. Courage Ltd* (1994) 70 P. & C.R. 469 at 474.

[29] *Bass Holdings Ltd v. Morton Music Ltd, supra* (reviewing earlier authorities); (1987) 103 L.Q.R. 504 (P. V. Baker); *West Middlesex Golf Club Ltd v. Ealing L.B.C.* (1993) 68 P. & C.R. 461 and 486 (disrepair, but not actionable).

[30] *Bairstow Eves (Securities) Ltd v. Ripley* (1992) 65 P. & C.R. 220. See too *Kitney v. Greater London Properties Ltd* [1984] 2 E.G.L.R. 83.

(i) any breach (whether of a positive or a negative covenant) has ceased; and

(ii) there are no subsisting causes of action in respect of it.[31]

14–302   **6. Remedies.** These are generally the same as under contracts for the sale of a freehold.[32] It used to be thought that equity would not grant specific performance of agreements for short leases, *e.g.* leases of a year or less, but the modern authorities indicate that there is no such rule.[33]

B. Conveyances

14–303 The grant or assignment of a lease by deed is a "conveyance" within the meaning of the Law of Property Act 1925,[34] except where provision is made to the contrary.[35]

14–304   **1. Form.** A specimen of a simple lease is given in the next section. The rules governing the creation and assignment of leases have already been explained. The notable difference from freehold conveyancing is, of course, that certain leases may be granted[36] (but not assigned[37]) orally or in writing.

2. Covenants for title

14–305 *(a) Leases granted or assigned before July 1995.* The *grant* of a lease prior to July 1995 was outside the provisions of the Law of Property Act 1925 which implied certain covenants from the use of certain words.[38] It has already been explained that the tenant of such a lease has only the benefit of the landlord's qualified covenant for quiet enjoyment. This is implied not from the use of any particular words or by statute, but from the relationship of landlord and tenant.[39]

By contrast, the *assignment* of a lease before July 1995, was within the provisions for statutory covenants, and the assignor would normally have conveyed "as beneficial owner". These words imported not only the usual statutory covenants for title,[40] but also a covenant that the lease was valid and

---

[31] *Bass Holdings Ltd v. Morton Music Ltd, supra.*
[32] *Ante*, para. 12–101.
[33] *Ante*, para. 14–046.
[34] s.205(1)(ii).
[35] As in s. 77(3).
[36] *Ante*, para. 14–043.
[37] *Ante*, para. 14–108.
[38] L.P.A. 1925, s.76(5).
[39] *Ante*, para. 14–196.
[40] *Ante*, para. 5–048.

in full force at the time of the assignment, and that all the rent had been paid and all covenants observed.[41]

(b) Leases granted or assigned after June 1995. In relation to leases granted **14–306** after June 1995, not only does the tenant have the benefit of the landlord's qualified covenant for quiet enjoyment, but covenants for title will also be implied if the landlord grants the lease with either full or limited title guarantee. This has already been explained.[42]

Where a lease is assigned after June 1995 and the disposition is made with either full or limited title guarantee, there will be imported into that assignment—

(i) the covenants for title imported into every disposition by such words[43]; and

(ii) a covenant that the lease is subsisting at the time of the disposition and that there is no subsisting breach of a condition or tenant's obligation nor anything which at that time would render the lease liable to forfeiture.[44]

3. Indemnity. As regards the assignee's obligations (if any) to indemnify **14–307** the assignor, it is necessary to distinguish between leases granted before 1996 and those granted thereafter. In relation to the former, the assignee may be required to execute the deed of assignment. He will as a result (and without the need for special words) covenant that he will pay the rent and observe all the covenants in the lease and will indemnify the assignor against the consequences of any breach.[45] The covenant by the assignee is explained more fully below.[46] Where a lease granted after 1995 is assigned, the assignor is released from the covenants in the lease and is not therefore liable for any default by the assignee after the assignment.[47] In consequence no indemnity covenant by the assignee is required and none is implied.[48] If the assignor enters into an authorised guarantee agreement with the landlord at the time of the assignment,[49] he has the usual rights of a surety to be recouped by the assignee (as principal debtor) should he be called upon to discharge that assignee's liability.[50]

---

[41] L.P.A. 1925, s. 76(1)(B) and Sched. 2 Pt II (unregistered); L.R.A. 1925, s.24(1)(a) (registered land).

[42] *Ante*, para. 14–205.

[43] For these, see *ante*, paras 5–068, 14–205.

[44] L.P.(M.P.)A. 1994, s.4.

[45] L.P.A. 1925, s.77(1)(c) and (D), and Sched. 2, Pts IX and X (unregistered land); L.R.A. 1925, s.24(1)(b), (2) (registered land). These provisions do not apply to mortgages.

[46] *Post*, para. 15–043.

[47] L. & T.C.A. 1995, s.5; *post*, para. 15–066.

[48] L.P.A. 1925, s.77(1)(C) and (D) and L.R.A. 1925, s.24(1)(b) and (2) do not apply: L. & T.C.A. 1995, s.14.

[49] L. & T.C.A. 1995, s.16; *post*, para. 15–067. The usual rules of suretyship apply to such guarantees: L. & T.C.A. 1995, s.16(8).

[50] See, *e.g. Rowlatt on Principal and Surety* (4th ed.), p. 134.

C. Precedent of a lease

14–308 Commencement and date. Parties

THIS LEASE made the 1st day of January, 1997, between William Woodfall of No. 15 Cherry Street Wolstenholme in the County of Sussex solicitor (hereinafter called "the landlord") of the one part and Thomas Platt of No. 4 Stewart Court Brickdale in the County of Gloucester bookseller (hereinafter called "the tenant") of the other part

Testatum

WITNESSETH as follows:—

Demise.

1. The landlord hereby demises unto the tenant ALL THAT messuage or dwelling-house with the yard gardens offices and outbuildings thereto belonging known as "West Hill" Manthorpe in the County of Surrey Title Number S 0672345[51]

Habendum.

which premises for purposes of identification and not of limitation are coloured pink on the plan annexed to these presents TO HOLD the same unto the tenant from the 25th day of December, 1996, for the term of five years PAYING therefor

Reddendum.

the net yearly rent of £6000 clear of all deductions (except only such as the tenant may by law be entitled to make notwithstanding any agreement to the contrary) by equal quarterly instalments commencing on the 25th day of March next and thereafter on the usual quarter days.

Tenant's covenants

2. The tenant hereby covenants with the landlord as follows:—

(i) To pay the rent hereby reserved on the days hereinbefore mentioned.

(ii) To pay all rates taxes assessments charges and outgoings now or hereafter legally payable in respect of the property hereby demised (save only as aforesaid) whether payable by the owner or occupier thereof.

[*Then follow other covenants by the tenant, e.g. to repair, to insure, not to assign, underlet or part with possession of the premises.*]

---

[51] Any lease of registered land is required to refer to the land by its title number and meet certain other requirements: L.R.R. 1925, r. 113.

Landlord's
covenants.

3. The landlord hereby covenants with the tenant as follows:—

(i) That the tenant paying the rent hereby reserved and observing and performing the covenants on his part herein contained shall peaceably hold and enjoy the premises hereby demised during the said term without any interruption or disturbance[52-53] by the landlord or any person rightfully claiming under or in trust for him.

[*Then follow any other covenants by the landlord, e.g. to execute certain classes of repairs or improvements, or to renew the lease at the tenant's request.*]

14–309

Provisos.

4. PROVIDED ALWAYS and it is hereby expressly agreed and declared as follows:—

Forfeiture clause.

(i) that if the rent hereby reserved or any part thereof shall remain unpaid for twenty-one days after becoming payable (whether formally demanded or not) or if any covenant on the part of the tenant herein contained shall not be performed or observed or if the tenant shall become bankrupt or enter into any composition with his creditors or suffer any distress or execution upon his goods then and in any of the said cases it shall be lawful for the landlord at any time thereafter to re-enter upon the demised premises or any part thereof in the name of the whole and thereupon this demise shall absolutely determine.

[*Then follow any other previsos, e.g. that the tenant may determine the lease by giving notice.*]

SIGNED AS A DEED etc.

(signatures and witnesses)

The PLAN above referred to.

This short form of lease may be compared with the brief precedents of a conveyance in fee simple of unregistered land and a transfer in fee simple of registered land given earlier.[54]

Subject to any written agreement to the contrary,[55] no party to a lease or tenancy agreement is now liable to pay any legal costs of any other party.[56]

14–310

[52-53] The word "lawful" is often (but inaccurately) inserted before "interruption or disturbance", It does not absolve the landlord from unlawful disturbance of the tenant (*Crosse v. Young* (1685) 1 Show.K.B. 425; *Lloyd v. Tomkies* (1787) 1 T.R. 671), and it merely duplicates "rightfully claiming" in the case of third parties.

[54] *Ante*, paras 5–035, 6–098.

[55] Which in practice there usually is nowadays.

[56] Costs of Leases Act 1958.

Formerly the tenant was usually liable for the costs of both parties, save that the landlord bore the cost of his counterpart (*i.e.* duplicate) if he had one.[57] The normal practice is for the landlord to take a counterpart executed by the tenant, in order to facilitate the enforcement of the tenant's covenants.

Part 7

FIXTURES

14–311   The question whether an object affixed to the land by a tenant can be removed by him or his representatives at the end of the term is one on which there has been much litigation. Similar problems arise, though less frequently, in the case of mortgages, sales, devises and settlements,[58] and these also will be considered here.

The meaning of "real property" in law extends, as has been seen, to a great deal more than "land" in everyday speech.[59] It comprises, for instance, incorporeal hereditaments; and it also includes fixtures. The general rule as to fixtures is "*quicquid planatur solo, solo cedit*"[60] (whatever is attached to the soil becomes part of it). Thus if a building is erected on land and objects are permanently attached to the building, then the soil, the building and the objects affixed to it are all in law "land," *i.e.* they are real property, not chattels. They will become the property of the owner of the land, unless otherwise granted or conveyed.[61] This is so, notwithstanding that it was the common intention of the parties that there should be no merger or ownership.[62] "The subjective intention of the parties cannot affect the question whether the chattel has, in law, become part of the freehold . . . ".[63]

In general, the word "fixture" means anything which has become so attached to land as to form in law part of the land.[64] This is however subject to two qualifications. First, the context may restrict this meaning. Thus if part

---

[57] Foa, L. & T. 339.

[58] Whether an object has become part of the land or remains a chattel can be important in many other contexts as well, *e.g.* for the purposes of listed building consent (see *Kennedy v. Secretary of State for Wales* [1996] E.G.C.S. 17); in a claim for capital allowances against corporation tax (see *Melluish v. B.M.I. (No. 3) Ltd* [1996] A.C. 454); or whether a tenancy is of a dwelling house for the purposes of the Rent Act 1977 (*Elitestone Ltd v. Morris* [1997] 1 W.L.R. 687).

[59] *Ante*, para. 4–037; *post*, para. 18–001.

[60] *Minshall v. Lloyd* (1837) 2 M. & W. 450 at 459.

[61] *Royco Homes Ltd v. Eatonwill Construction Ltd* [1979] Ch. 276 at 289; *Melluish v. B.M.I. (No. 3) Ltd, supra*, at 473.

[62] *Melluish v. B.M.I. (No. 3) Ltd, supra*, overruling in part *Simmons v. Midford* [1969] 2 Ch. 415.

[63] *Elitestone Ltd v. Morris* [1997] 1 W.L.R. 687 at 693, *per* Lord Lloyd.

[64] *Hulme v. Brigham* [1943] K.B. 152 at 154; and see *Reynolds v. Ashby & Son* [1904] A.C. 466.

of a house is leased, a covenant to repair the interior "including all landlord's fixtures" does not extend to the windows, which in relation to what was demised, are not fixtures but part of the original structure.[65] Secondly, there are signs that the courts may be moving away from the traditional distinction between fixtures and chattels in favour of threefold division between a chattel, a fixture, and an object that has become part and parcel of the land. The term "fixture" may in future be confined more to its everyday meaning, so that a building which does not remain a chattel will be regarded as part of the land rather than as a fixture.[66]

A. Distinction between Fixtures and Chattels

A physical object will usually be either land or a chattel, but its nature may change according to the use made of it. The materials used for building a house are thereby converted from chattels into land, and so automatically pass out of the ownership of the person who owned them as chattels and become the property of the owner of the land to which they are attached; and it makes no difference whether the person who attached them had a right to do so or not.[67] Conversely, when a house is pulled down, the person who severs the materials from the building converts them from land into chattels. The question whether an object has become a fixture, and so is part of the land to which it has been fixed, will therefore often determine the question of ownership as between competing claimants. A tenant, for example, who attaches fixtures to the demised premises may thereby make them the property of his landlord; and a purchaser of land may claim as part of his purchase all objects which were fixtures at the date of the contract, for they form part of the land sold to him. The first need, therefore, is to be able to decide what is a fixture and what is not. In borderline cases this is often difficult; but in principle it depends upon two tests, namely—   **14–312**

    (1) the degree of annexation, and

    (2) the purpose of annexation.

1. Degree of annexation. An article is prima facie a fixture if it has some substantial connection with the land or a building on it. An article which merely rests on the ground by its own weight, such as a cistern[68] or a free-   **14–313**

---

[65] *Boswell v. Crucible Steel Co.* [1925] 1 K.B. 119, discussed in *Holiday Fellowship Ltd v. Hereford* [1959] 1 W.L.R. 211; and see *Pole–Carew v. Western Counties and General Manure Co. Ltd* [1920] 2 Ch. 97.

[66] *Elitestone Ltd v. Morris, supra*, at 690–692; [1997] C.L.J. 498 (S. Bridge); [1998] Conv. 418 (H. Conway). For a further reason for adopting this threefold division, see *post*, para. 14–314.

[67] See *post*, para. 14–327.

[68] *Mather v. Fraser* (1856) 2 K. & J. 536.

standing greenhouse,[69] is prima facie not a fixture. On the other hand a chattel attached to the land or a building on it in some substantial manner, *e.g.* by nails or screws, will prima facie be a fixture even if it would not be difficult to remove it. Examples in this category are fireplaces, panelling, wainscot, and a conservatory on a brick foundation.[70] It has been said that "if an object cannot be removed without serious damage to, or destruction of, some part of the realty, the case for its having become a fixture is a strong one".[71] Buildings will therefore generally be regarded as part of the land unless they are constructed in such a way as to be removable.[72] Although the degree of annexation was formerly the primary test, "today so great are the technical skills of affixing and removing objects to land or buildings", that it has become subordinate to the test of purpose,[73] except perhaps in relation to buildings. A building that can be removed as a unit or in sections may remain a chattel, but this will not be the case if it can be removed only by destroying it.[74]

14–314   **2. Purpose of annexation.** The original common law rule was that everything substantially attached to the land became the property of the landowner. The severity of this rule was ameliorated by two exceptions. First, certain kinds of chattels were held to remain chattels even after annexation, if the purpose of the annexation was for the better enjoyment of the object as a chattel rather than to improve the land permanently.[75] Secondly, even though an object was clearly a fixture, and therefore part of the land, a tenant for years or for life was allowed to sever and remove it if he had annexed it to the land for certain purposes.

In principle the distinction is plain. Objects of the first class are removable because they never cease to be the property of the person who affixed them. By contrast, objects of the second class are fixtures properly so called, and become the property of the owner of the land, but the law confers a special power of removal on the person who was the owner of the object while it was a chattel. In practice, although the distinction between these two exceptions

---

[69] *H.E. Dibble Ltd v. Moore* [1970] 2 Q.B. 181; *Deen v. Andrews* (1985) 52 P. & C.R. 17 (where the facts were similar); *Hynes v. Vaughan* (1985) 50 P. & C.R. 444 at 457 (chrysanthemum growing frame held to be a chattel).

[70] *Buckland v. Butterfield* (1820) 2 Brod. & B. 54. As regards buildings themselves, see *infra*.

[71] *Berkley v. Poulett* [1977] 1 E.G.L.R. 86 at 88, *per* Scarman L.J.

[72] *Elitestone Ltd v. Morris* [1997] 1 W.L.R. 687 at 692, 693. *cf. Potton Developments Ltd v. Thompson* [1998] N.P.C. 49 (where, on the facts, a prefabricated building remained a chattel).

[73] *Berkley v. Poulett, supra,* at 89. See too *Hamp v. Bygrave* [1983] 1 E.G.L.R. 174 at 177 ("the purpose of the annexation is now of first importance": *per* Boreham J.); *TSB Bank Plc v. Botham* (1996) 73 P. & C.R. D1 at D2.

[74] *Elitestone Ltd v. Morris, supra,* at 692–693.

[75] In this context, the "purpose" is determined objectively from the evidence. It does not mean the subjective purpose of the person who annexed the chattel: see *ante*, para. 14–311 and *Deen v. Andrews, supra,* at 22.

can have important consequences,[76] it is often blurred.[77] This confusion has been criticised by the House of Lords, and was one reason why it chose to restrict the term "fixture" to situations which the word more literally described.[78]

The distinction between chattels on the one hand and fixtures and other objects that become part and parcel of the land was authoritatively stated in a leading case. "Perhaps the true rule is, that articles not otherwise attached to the land than by their own weight are not to be considered as part of the land, unless the circumstances are such as to show that they were intended to be part of the land, the onus of showing that they were so intended lying on those who assert that they have ceased to be chattels, and that, on the contrary, an article which is affixed to the land even slightly is to be considered as part of the land, unless the circumstances are such as to show that it was intended all along to continue a chattel, the onus lying on those who contend that it is a chattel."[79] "Thus blocks of stone placed one on top of another without any mortar or cement for the purpose of forming a dry stone wall would become part of the land, though the same stones, if deposited in a builder's yard and for convenience' sake stacked on top of each other in the form of a wall, would remain chattels."[80] Again, "the anchor of a large ship must be very firmly fixed in the ground . . . yet no one could suppose that it became part of the land".[81] Yet material such as piles of abandoned spoil from a slate quarry may become a permanent accretion to the land.[82]

These examples are clear, but others are less so. Looms in a worsted mill, **14–315** fixed by nails to wooden beams and plugs in the floor, have been held to be part of the land,[83] although they were easily removable without damage to the building, and by the test "is there any more fixing than was necessary for the

---

[76] See *Crossley v. Lee* [1908] 1 K.B. 86; *post*, para. 14–317.

[77] Compare the treatment of certain tapestries in *Re De Falbe* [1901] 1 Ch. 523 in the Court of Appeal and on appeal to the House of Lords, *sub nom. Leigh v. Taylor* [1902] A.C. 157. A life tenant displayed certain tapestries by fixing them to a framework of wood and canvas nailed to the walls. Each tapestry was then surrounded with a moulding which was also fastened firmly to the wall. When the life tenant died, the issue was whether the tapestries passed with the settled land or with the life tenant's personal estate. The Court of Appeal appears to have regarded them as tenant's fixtures which could therefore be removed by the life tenant and those entitled to her estate after her death. The House of Lords, by contrast, appears to have considered that the tapestries had never lost their character as chattels. There was no other way that the tapestries could be enjoyed except by fixing them to the walls.

[78] *Elitestone Ltd v. Morris, supra*, at 691–692; *ante*, para. 14–311.

[79] *Holland v. Hodgson* (1872) L.R. 7 C.P. 328 at 335, *per* Blackburn J. (cited with approval in *Elitestone Ltd v. Morris* [1997] 1 W.L.R. 687 at 692). In *Bradshaw v. Davey* [1952] 1 All E.R. 350 this dictum was applied to a yacht's mooring (a movable arrangement of anchors and chains) which was held to be a chattel and not a hereditament for rating purposes.

[80] *Holland v. Hodgson, supra*, at 335, *per* Blackburn J.

[81] *ibid.*

[82] *Mills v. Stokman* (1967) 116 C.L.R. 61.

[83] *Holland v. Hodgson, supra* (as between mortgagor and mortgagee); *cf. Reynolds v. Ashby & Son* [1904] A.C. 466 (machinery fixed by bolts passed to mortgagee with land); *Jordan v. May* [1947] K.B. 427 (electric light generating engine fixed by bolts held a fixture, but batteries held to be chattels).

enjoyment of the chattel as such?"[84] they might have been thought to be chattels. But machinery standing merely by its own weight remains personalty,[85] unless (perhaps) it can be shown to be installed for the permanent improvement of the premises. Statues, figures, vases and stone garden seats have been held to become part of the land because they were essentially part of the design of a house and grounds, even though standing merely by their own weight.[86] But the contrary has been held in the case of a statue standing on a plinth and a sundial resting on a pedestal.[87] Movable dog grates, substituted for fixed grates, have been held to be fixtures,[88] and so have some temporary structures, such as a corrugated iron shed bolted to metal straps fixed in concrete foundations.[89]

Similar articles may remain chattels or become fixtures depending on the circumstances of their annexation, *e.g.* tip-up seats fastened to the floor of a cinema or theatre.[90]

B. Right to Remove Fixtures

14–316 If according to the above rules an article is not a fixture, it can be removed by the person bringing it onto the land or by his successors in title, though not by a subsequent tenant who takes a fresh tenancy from the landlord.[91] But if the article is a fixture, prima facie it cannot be removed from the land and must be left for the fee simple owner, Nevertheless, as already mentioned, there are some exceptional cases where something which is undeniably part of the land may be removed by the person who affixed it: the object is a fixture, but the person who affixed it has a power to sever and remove it. This power arises in certain cases if the object has been affixed for certain purposes. The test of "purpose of annexation" therefore applies again here, although in a different

---

[84] *Re De Falbe* [1901] 1 Ch. 523 at 536, *per* Vaughan Williams L.J.

[85] *Hulme v. Brigham* [1943] K.B. 152 (mortgagor and mortgagee).

[86] *D'Eyncourt v. Gregory* (1866) L.R. 3 Eq. 382. Although the correctness of part of the decision in this case has been doubted on its facts (see *Re De Falbe* [1901] 1 Ch. 523 at 531, 532), the principle that an object resting on its own weight can be a fixture if it is part of the overall design of the property has been approved: *Berkley v. Poulett* [1977] 1 E.G.L.R. 86 at 89, 90. See too *Kennedy v. Secretary of State for Wales* [1996] E.G.C.S. 17 (carillon clock which rested on its own weight a fixture, as it was part of the design of a historic house). "White goods" (oven, refrigerator, dish washer, etc.) are not fixtures, even if they are part of the overall design of the kitchen, because they do not permanently improve it: *TSB Bank Plc v. Botham* (1996) 73 P. & C.R. D1.

[87] *Berkley v. Poulett, supra* (purchaser's claim failed). Contrast *Hamp v. Bygrave* [1983] 1 E.G.L.R. 174, where *Berkley v. Poulett, supra,* was not cited.

[88] *Monti v. Barnes* [1901] 1 Q.B. 205 (they were the only means of heating the house). *cf. TSB Bank Plc v. Botham, supra* (mock coal gas fires held not to be fixtures).

[89] *Webb v. Frank Bevis Ltd* [1940] 1 All E.R. 247 (tenant's fixture), not cited in *Billing v. Pill* [1954] 1 Q.B. 70 (army hut similarly attached held a mere chattel and so the subject of larceny). *cf. L.C.C. v. Wilkins* [1957] A.C. 362.

[90] Contrast *Lyon & Co. v. London City & Midland Bank* [1903] 2 K.B. 135 (seats hired for temporary use: held, not fixtures) with *Vaudeville Electric Cinema Ltd v. Muriset* [1923] 2 Ch. 74 (seats owned by cinema owner: held, fixtures).

[91] *Re Thomas* (1881) 44 L.T. 781; and see *Leschallas v. Woolf* [1908] 1 Ch. 641; *Smith v. City Petroleum Co. Ltd* [1940] 1 All E.R. 260.

way. It is best to consider separately the classes of cases in which the power of removal can and cannot arise.

1. Landlord and tenant. Prima facie, all fixtures attached by the tenant are **14–317** "landlord's fixtures", *i.e.* must be left for the landlord.[92] But important exceptions to this rule have arisen, and fixtures which can be removed under these exceptions are known as "tenant's fixtures". This expression must not be allowed to obscure the fact that the legal title to the fixture is in the landlord until the tenant chooses to exercise his power and sever it.[93] The tenant may do so only during the tenancy or (except in cases of forfeiture or surrender[94]) within such reasonable time thereafter as may properly be attributed to his lawful possession *qua* tenant.[95]

Where the tenancy is determinable by a week's notice, for example, and the fixtures cannot reasonably be removed within a week,[96] the tenant will be allowed a reasonable time after the notice has expired. Once that time has elapsed, the tenant loses his right of removal and the landlord's title to the fixture is absolute[97]; any extension of time that he grants to the tenant binds only him and not, *e.g.* a mortgagee who has taken possession.[98] But a tenant retains his right of removal if, when his tenancy ends, he remains in possession as tenant, whether under some statutory right (*e.g.* the Rent Act 1977) or because he has been granted a new tenancy.[99] In general, a tenant is under no obligation to remove anything that he has lawfully affixed to the land.[1] A tenant who fails to make good any damage when tenants' fixtures are removed may be liable for voluntary waste, even though that failure is in the nature of an omission.[2]

The following are tenants' fixtures.

(a) Trade fixtures. Fixtures attached by the tenant for the purpose of his **14–318** trade or business have long been removable by the tenant at any time during

---

[92] See, *e.g. Stokes v. Costain Property Investments Ltd* [1984] 1 W.L.R. 763 (lifts and other plant installed by tenant were landlord's fixtures).

[93] A neat illustration of the position is *Crossley v. Lee* [1908] 1 K.B. 86 at 90 (tenant's fixtures may not be taken on a distress (*ante*, para. 14–253), since they are not chattels but part of the demised premises).

[94] *Pugh v. Arton* (1869) L.R. 8 Eq. 626; *Ex p. Brook* (1878) 10 Ch.D. 100. But contrast surrender by operation of law: n. 99, *infra*.

[95] See *Ex p. Stephens* (1877) 7 Ch.D. 127 at 130. The exact limits of the rule are rather obscure: see *Ex p. Brook, supra*, at 109; [1987] Conv. 253 (G. Kodilinye).

[96] *Smith v. City Petroleum Co. Ltd, supra.*

[97] *Lyde v. Russell* (1830) 1 B. & Ad. 394; *Smith v. City Petroleum Co. Ltd, supra.*

[98] *Thomas v. Jennings* (1896) 66 L.J.Q.B. 5.

[99] *New Zealand Government Property Cpn. v. H.M. & S. Ltd* [1982] Q.B. 1145, overruling earlier authority that the right of removal was lost if there was a surrender by operation of law when an existing tenancy was replaced by a new tenancy: see *ante*, para. 14–174.

[1] See *Never–Stop Railway (Wembley) Ltd v. British Empire Exhibition (1924) Incorporated* [1926] Ch. 877 (licensee).

[2] *Mancetter Developments Ltd v. Garmanson Ltd* [1986] Q.B. 1212. In that case, the director of the company which committed the tort was held personally liable for waste as well because he instructed its commission: see *ante*, para. 14–236.

the term, but not after it has come to an end.[3] Vats, fixed steam engines and boilers,[4] a shed for making varnish,[5] shrubs planted by a market gardener,[6] the fittings of a public house,[7] floor coverings and light fittings[8] and petrol pumps affixed to tanks embedded in the ground[9] have all been held to come within this category.

14–319　　(b) *Ornamental and domestic fixtures.* This exception appears to be rather more limited than the previous one, and seems to extend only to chattels perfect in themselves which can be removed without substantial injury to the building.[10] An article which can be moved entire is more likely to fall within this exception than one which cannot.[11] Thus a conservatory on brick foundations has been held not to be removable[12]; but looking glasses,[13] ornamental chimney pieces,[14] panelling,[15] window blinds,[16] stoves, grates and kitchen ranges,[17] pumps and coppers,[18] and bells,[19] have all been held to be removable during the tenancy.

14–320　　(c) *Agricultural fixtures.* At common law agricultural fixtures were not regarded as falling within the exception of trade fixtures.[20] Market gardeners were regarded as being engaged primarily in trade, not agriculture, and so could remove their fixtures[21]; but farmers were liable in damages if they removed sheds, sties and the like erected by them, even if they removed them before the end of the term and did no damage.[22] The matter has however been regulated by statute for many years.[23] There are different rules for—

　　　　(i) tenancies of agricultural holdings under the Agricultural Holdings Act 1986; and

[3] *Poole's Case* (1703) 1 Salk. 368.
[4] *Climie v. Wood* (1869) L.R. 4 Ex. 328.
[5] *Penton v. Robart* (1801) 2 East 88.
[6] *Wardell v. Usher* (1841) 3 Scott N.R. 508.
[7] *Elliott v. Bishop* (1854) 10 Exch. 496.
[8] *Young v. Dalgety Plc* [1987] 1 E.G.L.R. 116 (these items were installed by the tenant under a contractual obligation, and were to be disregarded in fixing an open market rent under a rent review clause). This is open to doubt, because such items lack the necessary quality of permanence to be fixtures: see *TSB Bank Plc v. Botham* (1996) 73 P. & C.R. D1.
[9] *Smith v. City Petroleum Co. Ltd* [1940] 1 All E.R. 260.
[10] See *Martin v. Roe* (1857) 7 E. & B. 237 at 244; *Spyer v. Phillipson* [1931] 2 Ch. 183; *Young v. Dalgety Plc, supra,* at 119.
[11] *Grymes v. Boweren* (1830) 6 Bing. 437.
[12] *Buckland v. Butterfield* (1820) 2 Brod. & B. 54.
[13] *Beck v. Rebow* (1706) 1 P. Wms. 94.
[14] *Leach v. Thomas* (1835) 7 C. & P. 327.
[15] *Spyer v. Phillipson* [1931] 2 Ch. 183.
[16] *Colegrave v. Dias Santos* (1823) 2 B. & C. 76 at 77.
[17] *Darby v. Harris* (1841) 1 Q.B. 895.
[18] *Grymes v. Boweren* (1830) 6 Bing. 437 at 439.
[19] *Lyde v. Russel* (1830) 1 B. & Ad. 394.
[20] *Elwes v. Maw* (1802) 3 East 38.
[21] *Wardell v. Usher* (1841) 3 Scott N.R. 508 (shrubs and young trees); *Mears v. Callender* [1901] 2 Ch. 388 (glass-houses).
[22] *Elwes v. Maw, supra.*
[23] For earlier legislation see, *e.g.* L. & T.A. 1851, s.3; A.H.A. 1923, s.22; and A.H.A. 1948, s.13.

(ii) farm business tenancies under the Agricultural Tenancies Act 1995.[24]

In each case, the tenant is given a qualified right to remove *any* fixture that he has attached to the land, whether or not it would otherwise be characterised as a tenant's fixture.

(1) TENANCIES OF AGRICULTURAL HOLDINGS. A tenant of an agricultural holding may remove any fixture (whether agricultural or not) that he has attached to the land at any time before, or within two months of, the termination of the tenancy.[25] Contrary to the general rule that has already been explained, the fixture remains his property for as long as he has a right to remove it.[26] Certain fixtures may not be removed, such as ones which were attached in pursuance of some obligation or to replace the landlord's.[27] Furthermore, the following conditions must be observed— **14–321**

(i) one month's written notice must be given to the landlord;

(ii) all rent due must be paid and all the tenant's obligations under the tenancy satisfied by him;

(iii) no avoidable damage may be done in the removal and any damage done must be made good; and

(iv) the landlord may retain the fixtures if he serves a written counter-notice and pays the tenant their fair value to an incoming tenant.[28]

However, the landlord has no right to retain any trade or ornamental fixtures if the tenant is unwilling to sell them. This is because the tenant's common law right to remove such fixtures is expressly preserved and overrides the landlord's option to purchase them.[29]

(2) FARM BUSINESS TENANCIES. A farm business tenant has the same statutory right to remove a fixture as does a tenant of an agricultural holding,[30] but any common law rights to remove tenant's fixtures are abrogated.[31] The fixture remains his property so long as he remains in possession as a tenant.[32] The tenant may not remove any fixtures— **14–322**

---

[24] For these tenancies, see *post*, para. 22–087.
[25] A.H.A. 1986, s.10(1).
[26] *ibid.*
[27] *ibid.*, s.10(2).
[28] *ibid.*, s.10(3)–(5).
[29] *ibid.*, s.10(8).
[30] A.T.A. 1995, s.8(1).
[31] *ibid.*, s.8(7). A farm business tenancy differs from a tenancy of an agricultural holding in this respect.
[32] *ibid.*, s.8(1). A farm business tenancy continues from year to year after the initial term has expired, but may be determined by notice by either party.

(i) that were attached in pursuance of some obligation or to replace those of the landlord;

(ii) for which he has obtained compensation[33]; or

(iii) for which the landlord gave his consent on condition that the tenant agreed not to remove them.[34]

Thus instead of giving the landlord an option to purchase a tenant's fixtures, the Act provides for a system of compensation for improvements instead. In removing any fixture, the tenant must do no avoidable damage to the holding and must make good all damage done.[35]

14–323   **2. Tenant for life and remainderman.** If land is held in trust for A for life with remainder to B, on the death of A the question arises whether fixtures which A has attached to the land can be removed and treated as part of A's estate or whether they must be left for B. The position here is similar to that between landlord and tenant. Prima facie all the fixtures must be left for B, with the common law exception of trade, ornamental and domestic fixtures, which applies to a tenant for life in the same way as to a tenant for years[36]; but the statutory exception of agricultural fixtures does not apply.

14–324   **3. Devisee and personal representative.** If land is given by will the rule is that all fixtures pass under the devise; the testator's personal representatives are not entitled to remove them for the benefit of the testator's estate, whether they are ornamental, trade or any other kind of fixture.[37] For the devise naturally carries with it everything which can fairly be said to be part of the land[38]; and there is no question of hardship upon a limited owner, as in the case of a lessee or life tenant. The same rule applied to descent to the heir on intestacy.[39]

14–325   **4. Vendor and purchaser.** Without exception, all fixtures attached to the land at the time of a contract of sale must be left for the purchaser unless otherwise agreed.[40] The conveyance will be effective to pass the fixtures to the

---

[33] For the tenant's entitlement to compensation, see A.T.A. 1995, ss.15–17.

[34] *ibid.*, s.8(2).

[35] *ibid.*, s.8(3), (4).

[36] *Lawton v. Lawton* (1743) 3 Atk. 13; *Re Hulse* [1905] 1 Ch. 406 at 410; but it has been said that a tenant for life is less favoured than a tenant for years: see *Norton v. Dashwood* [1896] 2 Ch. 497 as 500.

[37] *Bain v. Brand* (1876) 1 App.Cas. 762 (machinery); *Re Whaley* [1908] 1 Ch. 615 (tapestry so fixed as to improve the premises as such held not to be removable even though ornamental); *Re Lord Chesterfield's S.E.* [1911] 1 Ch. 237 (wood carvings).

[38] See *Re Hulse* [1905] 1 Ch. 406 at 410.

[39] See *Norton v. Dashwood* [1896] 2 Ch. 497 at 500.

[40] *Colegrave v. Dias Santos* (1823) 2 B. & C. 76; *Phillips v. Lamdin* [1949] 2 K.B. 33; *Berkley v. Poulett* [1977] 1 E.G.L.R. 86; *Hamp v. Bygrave* [1983] 1 E.G.L.R. 174. For the effect of hire-purchase agreements, see (1963) 27 Conv. (N.S.) 30 (A. G. Guest and J. Lever).

purchaser without express mention.[41] The statutory "general words" also operate to convey all buildings, erections and fixtures along with the land, in default of contrary intention[42]; but they will not convey structures which are not fixtures, such as greenhouses merely resting on the land and not attached to it.[43]

5. Mortgagor and mortgagee. If land is mortgaged, all fixtures on it are included in the mortgage without special mention[44]; the exceptions as between landlord and tenant do not apply.[45] The mortgagor is not even entitled to remove fixtures which he has attached after the date of the mortgage.[46]   **14–326**

C. Rights of Third Parties

It has already been seen that the primary rule governing fixtures, namely, that they become the property of the owner of the land, applies irrespective of the title of the person who affixed them: "the title to chattels may clearly be lost by being affixed to real property by a person who is not the owner of the chattels".[47] If, for example, X steals Y's bricks and builds them into a house on Z's land, the owner of the bricks is not Y but Z; there is no room for the principle that a man cannot give a better title than he has (*nemo dat quod non habet*), since the title to the object as a chattel is extinguished entirely when it is turned into land.[48]   **14–327**

Likewise if A hires machinery from B and fixes it to the floor of A's factory, and the factory is mortgaged (whether prior to the fixing or not), the machinery becomes subject to the mortgage as against B.[49] But if the machinery is hired under a hire-purchase agreement which entitles B to enter and retake it if A fails to pay the instalments, this creates an equitable interest in land (apparently a right of entry[50]) which, where title is unregistered, will bind all later takers except a bona fide purchaser of a legal estate for value without notice. In such a case, therefore, B can enforce his rights against a subsequent equitable mortgagee of the land,[51] or a purchaser who has not yet taken his conveyance. Such an equitable interest does not appear to be registrable as a land charge.[52] Where, however, the title is registered, the equitable right of   **14–328**

---

[41] *Colegrave v. Dias Santos, supra.*
[42] L.P.A. 1925, s.62, *ante*, para. 5–045.
[43] *H.E. Dibble Ltd v. Moore* [1970] 2 Q.B. 181; *Deen v. Andrews* (1985) 52 P. & C.R. 17.
[44] L.P.A. 1925, ss.62(1), 205(1)(ii). As to hire-purchase, see n. 40, *supra.*
[45] *Monti v. Barnes* [1901] 1 Q.B. 205; *Climie v. Wood* (1869) L.R. 4 Ex. 328 at 330 (trade fixtures); *cf. Lyon & Co. v. London City & Midland Bank* [1903] 2 K.B. 135.
[46] *Reynolds v. Ashby & Son* [1904] A.C. 466.
[47] *Reynolds v. Ashby & Son, supra,* at 475, *per* Lord Lindley; see also *Gough v. Wood* [1894] 1 Q.B. 713 at 718, 719; *Crossley v. Lee* [1908] 1 K.B. 86.
[48] But, of course, Y may have a personal remedy against X in tort (conversion).
[49] *Hobson v. Gorringe* [1897] 1 Ch. 182 (before); *Reynolds v. Ashby & Son* [1904] A.C. 466 (after).
[50] *Re Morrison, Jones & Taylor Ltd* [1914] 1 Ch. 50 at 58; *ante*, para. 4–054.
[51] *Re Samuel Allen & Sons Ltd* [1907] 1 Ch. 575; *Re Morrison, Jones & Taylor Ltd* [1914] 1 Ch. 50.
[52] *Poster v. Slough Estates Ltd* [1969] 1 Ch. 495; *Shiloh Spinners Ltd v. Harding* [1973] A.C. 691; *ante*, para. 5–104. See also (1963) 27 Conv. (N.S.) 30 (A.G. Guest and J. Lever).

entry can be protected by registration either as a notice[53] if the land certificate is produced,[54] or as a caution if it is not.[55] A person who lets out goods on hire may thus be able to protect himself to some extent against the consequences of the law of fixtures if he reserves a right of entry against the owners of the land on which the goods are used.

[53] L.R.A. 1925, s.49(1)(f); Ruoff & Roper, 35–32A; see *ante*, para. 6–080. In *Poster v. Slough Estates Ltd, supra*, at 507, 508, Cross J. suggested *obiter* that such a right was neither registrable nor an overriding interest. However, his attention was not drawn to s.49(1)(f), *supra*.

[54] See *ante*, para. 6–078.

[55] L.R.A. 1925, s.54; *ante*, para. 6–083.

Chapter 15

LEASEHOLD COVENANTS

THIS chapter is concerned with the running of covenants in leases and of **15–001**
guarantees given as security for the performance of such covenants. A fundamental distinction now exists between leases granted before and after January
1, 1996. The former are governed largely by common law rules which are of
long standing, extended by statute. By contrast, the principles applicable to the
latter are found almost exclusively in a code laid down by the Landlord and
Tenant (Covenants) Act 1995. This statute, which is of some complexity,
creates a new and fundamentally different regime that rests on principles quite
distinct from those that apply to leases in existence when it came into force.
The rules governing the transmissibility of guarantees continue to be a matter
for the common law, whether the obligations guaranteed are found in leases
granted before or after January 1, 1996. However, the position of guarantors
has been affected in a number of ways by the Act of 1995.

Part 1

COVENANTS IN LEASES GRANTED BEFORE 1996: GENERAL
PRINCIPLES

A covenant is a promise under seal, *i.e.* contained in a deed. Such a promise **15–002**
is enforceable, according to the ordinary law of contract, between the persons
who are parties to it or their personal representatives. But certain kinds of
covenants are so much part of the system of transactions in land that they are
enforceable in cases which the law of contract does not cover: they partake,
so to speak, of the nature of the estates in connection with which they are
made, so that like those estates they may benefit and bind third parties.
Therefore they belong to the category of interests in land as well as to the law
of contract, and two sets of rules have to be considered together. Common
examples of these kinds of covenants are covenants in a lease, *e.g.* to repair,
and restrictive covenants taken on a sale, *e.g.* binding the purchaser and future
occupiers not to carry on a business on the property sold. The rules which
govern such covenants also apply, in general, to contractual promises not
made under seal, such as "covenants" contained in a mere agreement for a
lease.[1]

---

[1] See, *e.g. post*, para. 15–031.

The primary question is, how far are covenants made in connection with transactions in land enforceable outside the law of contract. The fundamental principles applicable to leases granted before 1996 are as follows.[2]

15–003 **1. If there is privity of contract, all covenants are enforceable.** There is said to be privity of contract when the parties are in direct contractual relations, *i.e.* bound to one another by the ordinary law of contract. Clearly, if two people have agreed to do or not to do certain things, their obligations bind them whether their contract has anything to do with land or not. Contractual liability is enforceable by or against the estate of a party who is dead; and in general the benefit, but not the burden, of the contract is assignable, so that assignees of the benefit can sue the original promisor or his personal representatives without the aid of the law of property.

The covenant can be enforced both at law, by an action for damages, and in equity, by an injunction or specific performance.

15–004 **2. If there is privity of estate, but not privity of contract, only covenants which touch and concern the land are enforceable.** Privity of estate means that there is tenure between the parties, *i.e.* that the relationship of landlord and tenant exists between them[3]; cases in this category are thus confined to leases and tenancies.[4] If L grants a lease to T and then T assigns it to A, there is no privity of contract between L and A since there has been no direct transaction between them; but there is privity of estate, for A has become L's tenant by acquiring the estate which L created and which is held of L as the immediate landlord. Similarly, if L assigns his reversion to R, there is privity of estate between R and A. In such cases any covenants in the lease which "touch and concern" the land, *e.g.* repairing covenants, are enforceable both at law and in equity. They have become "imprinted on the estate".[5]

Covenants which do not relate to the land are not enforceable under this head, for they have nothing to do with the relationship of landlord and tenant on which this right to enforce covenants against third parties is founded. Nor do all covenants in leases "touch and concern" the land for this purpose, even though they concern the land in a general sense. For we are here outside the bounds of the law of contract, and the law of property as usual sets limits to the kinds of interests which can be made to bind all comers. For example, as will be seen shortly, an option to purchase the freehold is not a covenant which

---

[2] See *Manchester Brewery Co. v. Coombs* [1901] 2 Ch. 608 at 614; (1991) 11 L.S. 47 (R. Thornton). For the definition of a lease granted prior to 1996, see *post*, para. 15–007.

[3] *Milmo v. Carreras* [1946] K.B. 306; *ante*, para. 14–002. Privity of estate is a legal relationship, not equitable: *Cox v. Bishop* (1857) 8 De G. M. & G. 815 at 824. For its meaning in this context, see *Manchester Brewery Co. v. Coombs, supra*, at 613, 614; *Purchase v. Lichfield Brewery Co.* [1915] 1 K.B. 184.

[4] "Privity of estate" was, however, also used to describe the relationship of grantor and grantee of the fee simple, where the grantee claimed the *benefit* of a covenant (running with land) as a successor in title to the grantor: see *David v. Sabin* [1893] 1 Ch. 523 at 537, 545; *Campbell v. Lewis* (1820) 3 B. & Ald. 392; Co. Litt. 271a.

[5] *City of London Corporation v. Fell* [1993] Q.B. 589 at 604, *per* Nourse L.J.; approved [1994] 1 A.C. 458 at 465.

"touches and concerns" the land, though it may bind an assignee as an estate contract."[6]

3. If there is privity neither of contract nor of estate, then with two exceptions, no covenants are enforceable. There is privity neither of contract nor of estate between a lessor and a sub-lessee, or between the vendor of freehold land and a person who buys it from the purchaser. In such cases the general rule is that covenants concerning the land are not enforceable between the parties mentioned. To this rule there are two important exceptions.   **15–005**

First, even the common law allowed the *benefit* of a covenant (*i.e.* the right to sue on it) to be assigned with land for the benefit of which it was made, provided that the covenant was one which "touched and concerned" that land. One example already mentioned[7] is that of a grantor's covenants for title in a conveyance: the benefit of these runs with the land conveyed so that whoever is entitled to the land is entitled to the benefit of the covenants. Equity went further, and enforced assignments of the *benefit* of contracts generally, whether or not connected with land; and there is now a statutory procedure for assignment which takes effect at law.[8] Thus it has become the general rule that the benefit of a contract is assignable. But the burden of a contract (*i.e.* the liability to be sued on it) has never been assignable by itself: assignment applies only to rights, not to duties. Nevertheless the burden of certain covenants concerning land can pass with the land affected under the rules of the law of property: either at law, because there is privity of estate, as already mentioned; or in equity, under the next following exception.

Secondly, equity allows the transmission of both the benefit and the burden of restrictive covenants. A restrictive covenant is a covenant imposing a negative obligation (*e.g.* not to build) as opposed to a positive covenant (*e.g.* to build); and the benefit and burden of a restrictive covenant can run in equity only if there is both land which is benefited and land which is burdened. As usual, however, in cases where the doctrine of notice is still relevant, a purchaser of a legal estate without notice takes free from the burden.[9]   **15–006**

These three principles should always be borne in mind in considering the enforceability of covenants. They should be applied in the given order: if there is privity of contract, there is no need to look further; and if there is privity of estate, there is no need to consider whether the covenant is restrictive.

4. For leases granted after 1995 privity of contract and estate are irrelevant. For leases granted after 1995 the general principles of privity of contract and estate set out in this Part have no application. The Landlord and   **15–007**

---

[6] *Post*, para. 15–027.

[7] *Ante*, paras 5–047, 5–053, 5–071.

[8] L.P.A. 1925, s.136.

[9] See *ante*, para. 4–011. For the application of the doctrine to covenants in leases and the position where title is registered, see *post*, paras 16–045, 16–055.

Tenant (Covenants) Act 1995 provides a discrete statutory code which governs such leases and which supersedes the previous common law and statutory provisions.[10]

A number of provisions of that Act are applicable to both existing leases and those granted after January 1, 1996.[11] However, most apply only to new tenancies granted after that date.[12] A new tenancy is for these purposes one that is granted[13] on or after January 1, 1996,[14] unless it is a tenancy granted in pursuance of—

(i) an agreement (including an option or right of pre-emption) entered into before 1996[15]; or

(ii) an order of the court made before 1996.[16]

A tenancy is defined to mean any lease or other tenancy and includes a sub-tenancy and an agreement for a lease, but not a mortgage term.[17]

Part 2

PRIVITY: COVENANTS IN LEASES GRANTED PRIOR TO 1996

Section 1. Privity of Contract: Liability of the Original Covenantors

1. Liability of the original tenant throughout the term

15–008   *(a) Liability notwithstanding assignment.* In a lease granted prior to 1996 by L to T, there is privity of contract between them. The effect is that L may enforce all the covenants in the lease against T throughout the term, provided

---

[10] The Act expressly provides that the statutory provisions which apply to leases granted prior to January 1, 1996 (*sc.* L.P.A. 1925, ss.78, 79, 141 and 142) are inapplicable to leases granted thereafter: L. & T.C.A. 1995, s.30(4). See *post*, para. 15–064.

[11] See L. & T.C.A. 1995, ss.1(2), 17–20.

[12] *ibid.*, ss.1(1), 3–16, 21.

[13] Although a "grant" has been taken to denote the grant of a *legal* lease (see *City Permanent B.S. v. Miller* [1952] Ch. 840), it is not used in that technical sense here, but includes the creation of an agreement for a lease as well: see n.17, *infra*. If this were not so, the provisions of the Act could be readily circumvented by the creation of equitable leases.

[14] *ibid.*, s.1(3). It includes a tenancy that arises where, as a result of a variation of the lease, there is a deemed surrender and regrant of the lease: *ibid.*, s.1(5). For variations which amount to a surrender, see *ante*, para. 14–174.

[15] L. & T.C.A. 1995, s.1(3)(a), 1(6), 1(7). A tenancy granted under the statutory right to buy (see H.A. 1995, s.118) will not fall within the exception, because it is not in the nature of an option.

[16] *ibid.*, s.1(3)(b).

[17] *ibid.*, s.28(1). Although that definition applies "unless the context otherwise requires" (*ibid.*), the purpose of the Act would be defeated if it did not apply here. See n.13, *supra*.

that L retains the reversion.[18] Subject to two statutory exceptions,[19] T's liability continues notwithstanding any assignment of the lease by him to A.[20] T cannot divest himself of his personal contractual liability by parting with the land, and the fact that A may also be liable to L by reason of privity of estate is no defence to T if L prefers to sue T on the contract.[21] L may sue T for unpaid rent, or for damages if a covenant to repair is not observed by the assignee. The extent of T's liability can be onerous. He remains liable even if after assignment—

   (i) the rent is increased under a rent review clause[22];

   (ii) A has become insolvent and his trustee in bankruptcy[23] has disclaimed the lease[24]; or

   (iii) the breach is committed not by A but by some subsequent assignee over whose selection T had no control[25];

   (iv) he could not have secured performance of the covenant himself because he had no right of re-entry as against A.[26]

Two different persons may therefore be liable for one breach of covenant, one   **15–009**
by privity of contract and the other by privity of estate. The nature of T's liability is not that of a surety for A.[27] He is severally liable with A for any

---

[18] The rule is an ancient one: see *Walker's Case* (1587) 3 Co.Rep. 22a. It applied only to express covenants: *Barnard v. Goodscall* (1612) Cro.Jac. 309; *Bachelour v. Gage* (1631) Cro.Car. 188. If the obligation to pay rent was merely implied and not express, and T assigned the lease to A with L's consent, T was not liable for rent unpaid by A because the obligation to pay rent depended upon possession of the land: *March v. Brace* (1614) 2 Bulst. 151 at 153; *Wadham v. Marlowe* (1784) 4 Doug. 54 at 70; *Auriol v. Mills* (1790) 4 T.R. 94 at 98; *John Betts & Sons Ltd v. Price* (1924) 40 T.L.R. 589 at 590. L's consent to an assignment was implied if he accepted rent from A, but not if T merely informed L of the assignment: *Wadham v. Marlowe, supra*, at 70; *Mayor of Swansea v. Thomas* (1882) 10 Q.B.D. 48 at 50. T remained liable if L did not accept the assignee: *Orgill v. Kemshead* (1812) 4 Taunt. 642. These cases on implied covenants to pay rent may be no more than examples of rent service (see *ante*, para. 14–245), by which the payment of rent was a condition of tenure. This would explain why it was only the tenant for the time being who was liable for the rent.

[19] See L.P.A. 1922, s.145; Sched. 15, para. 5 (perpetually renewable leases); *ante*, para. 14–089; Matrimonial Causes Act 1973, Sched. 1, para. 2(2) (transfer of leases on divorce).

[20] See, *e.g. Walker's Case, supra*, at 23a; *Hill v. East and West India Dock Co.* (1884) 9 App.Cas. 448 at 453.

[21] T's continuing liability on a covenant does not depend upon his covenanting both for himself and for his assigns, though this is now implied by statute in order to overcome an inconvenient rule at common law: see Law of Property Act 1925, s.79; *post*.

[22] *Centrovincial Estates Plc v. Bulk Storage Ltd* (1983) 46 P. & C.R. 393; *Selous Street Properties Ltd v. Oronel Fabrics Ltd* [1984] 1 E.G.L.R. 50.

[23] Or, where A is a company, its liquidator.

[24] *W. H. Smith Ltd v. Wyndham Investments Ltd* (1994) 70 P. & C.R. 21; *Hindcastle Ltd v. Barbara Attenborough Associates Ltd* [1997] A.C. 70.

[25] Even though L's consent is required to the assignment, he owes no duty of care to T to assess the creditworthiness of any proposed assignee: *Norwich Union Life Insurance Society v. Low Profile Fashions Ltd* (1991) 64 P. & C.R. 187; [1992] C.L.J. 425 (S. Bridge).

[26] *Thames Manufacturing Co. Ltd v. Perrots (Nichol & Peyton) Ltd* (1985) 50 P. & C.R. 1.

[27] *Baynton v. Morgan* (1888) 22 Q.B.D. 74. He cannot therefore avail himself of the defences that would have been open to a surety.

breach.[28] It is entirely a matter for L therefore whether he sues T, A, or both of them.[29] T will be discharged from liability by—

(a) performance of the covenants, whether by T or A,[30] or by any person who has guaranteed the obligations in the lease[31];

(b) surrender of the whole of the lease[32]; or

(c) an accord and satisfaction by L with A under which L is precluded from enforcing the debt against T.[33]

T's personal covenant operates independently of the estate granted and is enforceable even though—

(i) the legal term has not yet begun[34]; or

(ii) owing to some defect in L's title, no legal term is in fact created.[35]

If T becomes insolvent,[36] L can prove for the loss of his covenant.[37] The measure of that loss is the difference between the market value of the reversion with and without the covenant.[38]

---

[28] *Deanplan Ltd v. Mahmoud* [1993] Ch. 151 at 159, 160; *Burford Midland Properties Ltd v. Marley Extrusions Ltd* [1995] 1 B.C.L.C. 102 at 115.

[29] *Norwich Union Life Insurance Society v. Low Profile Fashions Ltd, supra,* at 192. L cannot of course have double satisfaction.

[30] *Allied London Investments Ltd v. Hambro Life Assurance Ltd* [1984] 1 E.G.L.R. 16 at 19.

[31] See *Milverton Group Ltd v. Warner World Ltd* [1995] 2 E.G.L.R. 28; [1995] J.B.L. 181 (M. Haley). In that case A failed to pay the rent. It was held that L must give T credit for any payments received from sureties, even where those sums were paid in consideration for their discharge from their liabilities as guarantors. However, L was entitled to appropriate the sums so received against future liabilities that were unquantified at the time when L sued T for the arrears of rent. L could not be compelled to appropriate them to the existing arrears of rent.

[32] *Allied London Investments Ltd v. Hambro Life Assurance Ltd, supra,* at 46. Surrender of part of the lease will not discharge T: *Baynton v. Morgan, supra* (though query whether T is discharged *pro tanto*). Surrender may take place by operation of law, as where L grants A a new lease on different terms from the old tenancy: *Take Harvest Ltd v. Liu* [1993] A.C. 552; see *ante,* para. 14–174.

[33] This will be determined from the surrounding circumstances and any express or implied terms of that agreements: *Johnson v. Davies* [1999] Ch. 117. It is a matter of construction whether or not the agreement is an accord and satisfaction. The view that T would not be discharged merely because A came to an arrangement with his creditors (see *R. A. Securities Ltd v. Mercantile Credit Co. Ltd* [1995] 3 All E.R. 581), was rejected in *Johnson v. Davies.* Such an arrangement is treated in the same way as a consensual agreement: *ibid.,* at 137, 138.

[34] *Bradshaw v. Pawley* [1980] 1 W.L.R. 10.

[35] *Industrial Properties (Barton Hill) Ltd v. Associated Electrical Industries Ltd* [1977] Q.B. 580. This was a secondary ground of decision, the primary ground being that the tenant was estopped: *ante,* para. 14–095.

[36] Or, if T is a company, is wound up.

[37] *James Smith & Sons (Norwood) Ltd v. Goodman* [1936] Ch. 216.

[38] *Re House Property and Investment Co. Ltd* [1954] Ch. 576 at 592. *cf. Stanhope Pension Trust Ltd v. Registrar of Companies* [1993] 2 E.G.L.R. 118.

(b) Extensions of the term. It sometimes happens that the term of a lease is **15–010**
extended, *e.g.* under the Landlord and Tenant Act 1954.[39] Where T has
assigned the lease before it is extended, he will not be liable for breaches of
covenant committed by A during any such extension[40] unless and to the extent
that he has undertaken that liability.[41] Thus where a lease contains an option
for renewal which is exercised by A, the new lease will normally be a new
contract which will not involve T in liability.[42] But T's liability will continue
where the old lease is merely extended under its own terms.[43]

(c) Liability to the assignee of the reversion. At common law, the benefit of **15–011**
a covenant did not pass on an assignment of L's reversion to R.[44] Therefore
R could sue T neither for his own breaches nor for those of A. The Grantees
of Reversions Act 1540[45] changed the law[46] and gave R the same rights to sue
T for breach of covenants as L had had.[47] It was thereby considered to create
privity of contract between those who had privity of estate.[48] Despite some
decisions to the contrary,[49] it became established that T was liable to R for
breaches of covenant committed by A, because L's privity of contract passed
under the statute to R.[50]

Although the Act of 1540 remained in force until the end of 1925,[51] its
provisions were extended but not superseded by the Conveyancing Acts
1881–1911.[52] The Conveyancing Acts did not expressly confer on R the same
rights of suit for breach of covenant as L would have had, but instead annexed
the benefit of covenants touching and concerning the land to the reversion so

---

[39] s.24; *post*, para. 22–070.
[40] *City of London Corporation v. Fell* [1994] 1 A.C. 458; [1994] C.L.J. 28 (S. Bridge). It has not
been decided whether T remains liable on the covenants where the lease is extended *before* he
assigns it to A.
[41] "Everything depends on the contract between the parties": *Herbert Duncan Ltd v. Cluttons*
[1993] Q.B. 589 at 608, *per* Nourse L.J.
[42] Generally an alteration to the length of a lease beyond its original term operates as a surrender
of the old lease and the grant of a new one: *Re Savile S.E.* [1931] 2 Ch. 210 at 217; *Jenkin R.
Lewis Ltd v. Kerman* [1971] Ch. 477 at 496.
[43] *Baker v. Merckel* [1960] 1 Q.B. 657 (lease for seven years to be extended to 11 years on notice
from the tenant).
[44] *Post*, para. 15–046; see *Webb v. Russell* (1789) 3 T.R. 393 at 394 (*arguendo*); *Bickford v. Parson*
(1848) 5 C.B. 920 at 929, 931; *Re King* [1963] Ch. 459 at 479.
[45] 32 Hen. 8, c. 34, s.1; *post*, para. 15–046. There were analogous provisions in s.2 of that Act
relating to the burden of the covenants in the lease.
[46] *Isherwood v. Oldknow* (1815) 3 M. & S. 382 at 394; *P. & A. Swift Investments v. Combined
English Stores Group Plc* [1989] A.C. 632 at 640.
[47] The right was confined to covenants which touched and concerned the land: *post*, para.
15–046.
[48] *Thursby v. Plant* (1670) 1 Wms.Saund. 230 at 240; *Bickford v. Parson, supra,* at 930.
[49] *Humble v. Glover* (1594) Cro.Eliz. 328 (*sub nom. Humble v. Oliver* (1594) Poph. 55); *Overton
v. Sydal* (1595) Cro.Eliz. 555; Platt on *Leases*, ii, 386.
[50] *Brett v. Cumberland* (1617) Cro.Jac. 521; *Thursby v. Plant, supra*; *Edwards v. Morgan* (1685)
3 Lev. 229. The statute applied only to leases under seal (*post* para. 15–047), and in those cases
where it was inapplicable, R had no remedy against T: *Allcock v. Moorhouse* (1882) 9 Q.B.D.
366.
[51] It was repealed by L.P.A. 1925, s.207; Sched. 7.
[52] 1881, s.10; 1911, s.2; *post*, para. 15–046. The 1540 Act was still employed: see, *e.g. Stuart v.
Joy* [1904] 1 K.B. 362 (a case concerned with the transmission of the burden of L's
covenants).

that the reversioner for the time being might enforce them.[53] Those provisions, as amended,[54] were re-enacted by section 141 of the Law of Property Act 1925, and are now interpreted by the courts without regard to the law prior to 1881.[55] It is generally assumed that after an assignment of the reversion R (and not L) can enforce T's continuing liability[56] and that the right to do so passes to R automatically, without the need for an express assignment, under section 141 of the Law of Property Act 1925.[57] There is however no decision in which this conclusion has been reached as a matter of construction of the section.[58]

15–012　　**2. Liability of the original landlord throughout the term.** On principles similar to those explained above, L remains liable on his covenants for the whole term, notwithstanding any assignment of the reversion to R.[59] Furthermore L is liable not only for his own breaches of covenant, but for those committed by R.[60] It has been suggested that in such circumstances, that liability can be enforced by A if T has assigned the lease to him.[61] This is said to be the effect of section 142 of the Law of Property Act 1925,[62] by which the burden of covenants in the lease passes on an assignment of the reversion.[63]

15–013　　**3. Liability of an assignee on a direct covenant.** It is explained below that an assignee of a lease is liable only for breaches of covenant committed while the lease is vested in him.[64] Commonly, however, a lease can be assigned only with the landlord's consent.[65] It is now usual in commercial leases for L to

---

[53] C.A. 1881, s.10.

[54] See C.A. 1911, s.2.

[55] *Re King* [1963] Ch. 459 at 490, 491, 494.

[56] See, *e.g. W. H. Smith Ltd v. Wyndham Investments Ltd* (1994) 70 P. & C.R. 21; *Milverton Group Ltd v. Warner World Ltd* [1995] 2 E.G.L.R. 28 (where, in each case, R successfully sued T for A's breach but no argument was addressed as to his right to do so). *cf. Centrovincial Estates Plc v. Bulk Storage Ltd* (1983) 46 P. & C.R. 393 at 394, where Harman J. was prepared to assume that it was so in the absence of contrary argument.

[57] See *Burford Midland Properties Ltd v. Marley Extrusions Ltd* [1995] B.C.L.C. 102 at 105. Query whether the right might pass under L.P.A. 1925, s.78 (which applies to covenants in leases granted before 1996: *Caerns Motor Services Ltd v. Texaco Ltd* [1994] 1 W.L.R. 1249); *post*, para. 16–063.

[58] Some support is perhaps provided by *Arlesford Trading Co. Ltd v. Servansingh* [1971] 1 W.L.R. 1080, in which it was held that R could sue T for a breach of covenant committed before L assigned the reversion to R (see *post*, para. 15–054). However, there was in that case privity of estate between R and T at the time of the action (though not at the time of breach). Furthermore, the wording of L.P.A. 1925, s.141(3) implies that rights of action in respect of pre-existing breaches of covenant pass to R.

[59] *Stuart v. Joy* [1904] 1 K.B. 362 (where L was liable to T for a breach of covenant committed before the assignment of the reversion).

[60] *Wright v. Dean* [1948] Ch. 686 (R took free of T's option to purchase the reversion, which T had failed to register as a land charge).

[61] *Celsteel Ltd v. Alton House Holdings Ltd (No. 2)* [1986] 1 W.L.R. 666 at 672; aff'd on this point: [1987] 1 W.L.R. 291 at 296. The remarks were *obiter*.

[62] Replacing Grantees of Reversions Act 1540, s.2.

[63] *Post*, para. 15–046.

[64] *Post*, para. 15–039.

[65] See, *ante*, para. 14–259.

require A to enter into a direct covenant with him to observe all the terms of the lease as a condition of L's licence to assign. In the absence of contrary provision, A's liability to L on this direct covenant will not be confined to the period that the lease is vested in him[66] but will continue until it expires.[67] This will be so even though A's covenant is not made specifically for the residue of the term.[68]

It has not been settled whether, on an assignment of the reversion, the benefit of L's direct covenant with A passes to R automatically or only on an express assignment.[69] As it cannot pass under section 141 of the Law of Property Act 1925,[70] any automatic transmission would either have to be at common law[71] or under some other statutory provision.[72] Analogous situations provide little guidance. Although the benefit of a covenant by a surety guaranteeing the performance of covenants in the lease passes with the reversion at common law,[73] as has been explained,[74] the benefit of a tenant's covenants in a lease did not.[75]

4. Reform: the Landlord and Tenant (Covenants) Act 1995. The con-   **15–014**
tinued liability of an original covenantor[76] throughout the term can cause considerable hardship.[77] The widespread use of upward only rent review clauses[78] may mean that T is called upon to discharge obligations substantially more onerous than those he had originally undertaken. Furthermore, although it is reasonable to expect T to choose an assignee who is financially responsible, he has no control over subsequent assignments. There was considerable pressure to restrict T's liability,[79] and in 1988 the Law Commission recommended that—

> (i) on an assignment of a lease, a tenant should generally cease to be liable on the covenants and should also cease to have the benefit of the lease; and

---

[66] An assignee's liability on grounds of privity of estate is so limited: *post*, para. 15–039.

[67] *J. Lyons & Co. Ltd v. Knowles* [1943] K.B. 366.

[68] *Estates Gazette Ltd v. Benjamin Restaurants Ltd* [1994] 1 W.L.R. 1528.

[69] Whether a statutory written assignment under L.P.A. 1925, s.136 or an equitable assignment. In practice, express assignments are widely employed.

[70] Because that section applies only to covenants in the lease itself: s.141(1); *P. & A. Swift Investments v. Combined English Stores Group Plc* [1989] A.C. 632 at 639.

[71] *Post*, para. 16–056.

[72] See L.P.A. 1925, s.78(1); *post*, para. 16–063.

[73] *Kumar v. Dunning* [1989] Q.B. 193; *P. & A. Swift Investments v. Combined English Stores Group Plc.*, *supra*; *post*, paras 15–024, 15–056.

[74] *Ante*, para. 15–011.

[75] See *P. & A. Swift Investments v. Combined English Stores Group Plc*, *supra*, at 640.

[76] Who for these purposes also includes an assignee of a lease who enters into a direct covenant with the landlord: see *ante*, para. 15–013.

[77] For a summary of the criticisms of the law, see (1988) Law Com. No. 174, para. 3.1.

[78] For rent review clauses, see *ante*, para. 14–246.

[79] Not least because the recession prompted many landlords to have recourse to the original tenant, which came as a surprise to many: see *Mytre Investments Ltd v. Reynolds* [1995] 3 All E.R. 588 at 590. For the change in the nature of the relationship of landlord and tenant that made first tenant liability a major issue, see (1996) 59 M.L.R. 78 at 81 (M. Davey).

(ii) where the landlord's consent to any assignment is necessary, he would be able to require the tenant to guarantee the performance of the covenants by the immediate assignee as a condition for giving his consent (an "authorised guarantee agreement"), but that liability would cease on a further assignment.[80]

These recommendations have been implemented in substantially modified form (as part of a much larger series of measures) by the Landlord and Tenant (Covenants) Act 1995, but only as regards leases granted after 1995.[81] However, that Act has also introduced three provisions which are applicable to both new and existing leases and which alleviate the position of original tenants under the latter.[82] These provisions, which cannot be excluded,[83] are as follows.

15–015 *(a) Restriction on liability.* At common law L was under no obligation to notify T that A was in arrears with payments of rent, service charge or any other fixed amount. Substantial sums might therefore become due before T was aware of his liability. The Act of 1995 now makes provision for the case where A owes L—

(a) rent;

(b) any service charge[84]; or

(c) any sum payable under a liquidated damages clause for breach of covenant.[85]

If L wishes to recover any such fixed charge from T he must now serve on him, within six months of the sum becoming due, a notice informing him both that the charge is now due and that he intends to recover from T the amount specified in the notice with interest (if payable).[86] If L fails to serve such a notice, T is not liable to pay the sum. Furthermore, L can recover no more than the sum specified in the notice unless—

(i) T's liability is subsequently determined to be greater;

(ii) the notice had warned him of the possibility that this might be so[87]; and

---

[80] (1988) Law Com. No. 174; [1989] Conv. 145; [1992] Conv. 393 (H. W. Wilkinson).

[81] *Post*, para. 15–064.

[82] These provisions are the result of proposals made by the property industry: *post*, para. 15–064.

[83] See L. & T.C.A. 1995, s.25(1); *post*, para. 15–096.

[84] For the meaning of service charge, see L. & T.A. 1985, s.18.

[85] L. & T.C.A. 1995, s.17(6).

[86] *ibid.*, s.17(2). Where a fixed charge had become payable before January 1, 1996, the sum is treated as if it had become due on that date provided that no proceedings for its recovery had been instituted by then: *ibid.*, s.17(5). A notice under s.17 is not invalidated merely because it includes items to which the landlord is not entitled: *Commercial Union Life Assurance Co. Ltd v. Moustafa* [1999] 24 E.G. 155 at 159, 160.

[87] An obvious example would be if a rent review was pending.

(iii) a further notice is served on T within three months of that determination informing him that L intends to recover that greater amount (including interest, if applicable).[88]

These provisions will be of primary importance as regards leases granted before 1996. They will be of relevance to leases granted after 1995 in two situations. These are explained below.[89]

There are similar provisions which restrict the liability of a guarantor who has guaranteed performance by A of the covenants explained above.[90] There is no requirement however that L must first serve a notice on A and seek payment from him.[91]

(b) Variations of covenants. At the time when the 1995 Act was passed, it **15–016** was thought that T was liable on the covenants in the lease even though their terms had been subsequently varied by an agreement between L and A to which T was not a party.[92] It was not easy to see any logical basis for a rule so productive of injustice, and the authorities on which it was based have in fact since been disapproved.[93] In any event, the Act places the matter beyond doubt for any variations made after 1995.[94] T is not liable to pay any amount that is referable to any variation of the tenant covenants that is made after T has assigned the lease.[95] The variation must be one which either—

(i) L had an absolute right to refuse to allow at the time when it was made[96]; or

(ii) was one L would have had an absolute right to refuse if T had sought his consent immediately before he assigned the lease to A.[97]

---

[88] L. & T.C.A. 1995, s.17(4).

[89] The first situation is where T is liable on an "authorised guarantee agreement": *post*, para. 15–067. The second is where the assignment from T to A is an "excluded assignment": *post*, para. 15–074.

[90] L. & T.C.A. 1995, s.17(3).

[91] *Cheverell Estates Ltd v. Harris* [1998] 1 E.G.L.R. 27.

[92] See *Centrovincial Estates Plc v. Bulk Storage Ltd* (1983) 46 P. & C.R. 393 at 396; *Selous Street Properties Ltd v. Oronel Fabrics Ltd* [1984] 1 E.G.L.R. 50; *GUS Property Management Ltd v. Texas Homecare Ltd* [1993] 2 E.G.L.R. 63. *cf. Burford Midland Properties Ltd v. Marley Extrusions Ltd* [1995] 1 B.C.L.C. 102 at 114 (casting doubt on these decisions).

[93] *Friends' Provident Life Office v. British Railways Board* [1996] 1 All E.R. 336 (decided by the Court of Appeal six days after the Act had received the Royal Assent). See too *Beegas Nominees Ltd v. BHP Petroleum Ltd* [1998] 2 E.G.L.R. 57.

[94] L. & T.C.A. 1995, s.18. The Act does not apply to variations made before 1996: *ibid.*, s.18(6).

[95] *ibid.*, s.18(2).

[96] Where L has merely a *qualified* right to refuse (as where his consent is required to any such variation), T will be bound by the clause as amended. In such circumstances T is taken to be aware that the lease may be varied at some future date.

[97] L. & T.C.A. 1995, s.18(4).

It follows that T cannot object to a variation for which the lease made specific provision and to which he was a party (such as the increase of the rent under a rent review clause).

The situation which the Act seeks to remedy is of course where the variation makes A's financial obligations more onerous than were T's. Its provisions should therefore be confined to that situation. If the variation reduces the burden on A, who subsequently defaults, T's liability to L should be limited to the amount which L could have claimed from A.[98]

(c) Right to overriding lease

15–017 (1) THE NATURE OF AN OVERRIDING LEASE. At common law there is no means by which T can limit his liability for repeated breaches of covenant committed by A, for although a lease invariably contains a forfeiture clause, T cannot compel L to exercise it and terminate the lease.[99] The Act now gives T a remedy in many, but not all circumstances. Where T has had to pay the full amount of a demand made in respect of any fixed charge unpaid by A,[1] he is entitled to be granted an overriding lease by L.[2] An overriding lease is a lease of the reversion.[3] It is granted for a term equal to the remainder of the term of A's lease plus three days[4] and contains the same covenants as those in A's lease, unless a particular covenant was expressed to be personal between L and A,[5] or has ceased to be binding.[6] Once T has been granted an overriding lease,[7] he can of course exercise any right of re-entry and take steps to forfeit A's tenancy. T's overriding lease will then take effect in possession and he may either assign the lease or sub-let the premises.[8] In this way, not only can T terminate A's breaches of covenant (thereby limiting his liability for them), but he may also be able to recoup the amount he has been compelled to pay to L.[9]

---

[98] *cf. Mytre Investments Ltd v. Reynolds* [1995] 3 All E.R. 588 at 592. L can be regarded as releasing A *pro tanto* from the covenant to the extent that obligation is reduced.

[99] If A is insolvent and his trustee in bankruptcy disclaims, T can seek to have the lease vested in him: I.A. 1986, s.320; *ante*, para. 14–184.

[1] See L. & T.C.A. 1995, s.17; *ante*, para, 15–015.

[2] L. & T.C.A. 1995, s.19(1).

[3] *ibid.*, s.19(2). For leases of the reversion, see *ante*, para. 14–103.

[4] Or, where L is himself a leaseholder, the longest period (less than three days) that will not wholly displace L's reversion.

[5] L. & T.C.A. 1995, ss.19(2), 19(3). If any covenant in the original tenancy operates in some way by reference to its commencement (such as a covenant to repaint the exterior of the premises after three years), the corresponding covenant in the overriding lease also operates by reference to the commencement of the original lease: *ibid.* s.19(4).

[6] *ibid.*

[7] T can seek an overriding lease, even though he is himself a tenant under an overriding lease: *ibid.*, s.19(11).

[8] Subject to any requirement that he first obtains L's consent.

[9] It is uncertain what effect the grant of an overriding lease may have on T's rights of indemnity against any intermediate assignee. In principle, if T is fully recouped from such a grant he should be debarred from such a claim, but not if he is only partially recouped. If he does obtain an indemnity, the intermediate assignee cannot claim an overriding lease. It is only where payment is made to the landlord of the defaulting tenant that such a right arises: L. & T.C.A. 1995, s.19(1).

(2) COMPETING CLAIMS. Where A has defaulted under a covenant in the **15–018** lease to pay one or more fixed sums, L may have had recourse not only to T, but to others who are also liable, such as a guarantor or an intermediate assignee. It is therefore possible that there may be more than one person entitled to an overriding lease. Priority is given to the first person to apply for such a lease.[10] Where L receives two applications on the same day, preference is given—

    (i) to a former tenant over a guarantor; and

    (ii) as between former tenants, to the one whose liability commenced earlier.[11]

(3) GRANT. To seek the grant of an overriding lease, T must apply to L in **15–019** writing within a year of making the payment that entitles him to the lease, specifying that payment.[12] L must then grant and deliver a lease in favour of T[13] unless—

    (i) L has already determined A's lease[14];

    (ii) L has granted an overriding lease to, or received a request for such a lease from, another person[15]; or

    (iii) T has withdrawn his application in writing or abandoned it.[16]

A request by T for such a lease is registrable as an estate contract under the Land Charges Act 1972 where title is unregistered,[17] or as a minor interest where it is registered.[18] A failure by L to grant T an overriding lease is a breach of statutory duty for which T may recover damages in tort.[19]

(4) MISCELLANEOUS PROVISIONS. To meet the case where L's reversion is **15–020** mortgaged on terms that restrict his power to grant further leases,[20] the grant of an overriding lease is deemed to be authorised as against, and binding upon, the mortgagee.[21] Similarly, because the overriding lease contains the same terms as the original tenancy, it may include a covenant against sub-letting or

---

[10] *ibid.*, s.19(7).
[11] *ibid.*, s.19(8).
[12] *ibid.*, s.19(5).
[13] *ibid.*, s.19(6). T must in turn deliver an executed counterpart of the lease to L, and meet his reasonable costs: *ibid.*
[14] *ibid.*, s.19(7).
[15] *ibid.*
[16] *ibid.*, s.19(9).
[17] For the registration of estate contracts, see *ante*, para. 5–099.
[18] L. & T.C.A. 1995, s.20(6). The right cannot be an overriding interest: *ibid.* For minor interests, see *ante*, para. 6–075. For overriding interests, see *ante*, para. 6–036.
[19] L. & T.C.A. 1995, s.20(3).
[20] See *post*, para. 19–120.
[21] L. & T.C.A. 1995, s.20(4). L is obliged to deliver the counterpart of the overriding lease to the mortgagee within a month, and a failure to do so is deemed to be a breach of the terms of the mortgage: *ibid.*

parting with possession. In such a case, T is not in breach of the covenant merely because his overriding lease necessarily takes effect subject to A's lease.[22]

15–021   (5) OLD AND NEW TENANCIES. All overriding leases must state that they have been granted under section 19 of the 1995 Act and also whether or not they are new tenancies.[23] Where T exercises his right to claim an overriding lease in respect of a lease granted before 1996, that overriding lease is not a new tenancy. It is therefore subject to the rules of law applicable to all leases granted before 1996,[24] including the rules of privity of contract. Where L grants the lease after 1995, both the lease and any overriding lease that may be granted subsequently will of course be a new tenancy and therefore subject to the provisions of the Act. These are explained below.[25]

There are two circumstances in which T can seek an overriding lease where the original lease to him was granted after 1995. These are explained below.[26]

Section 2. Privity of Estate: Position of Assignees

A. Covenants Touching and Concerning Land

15–022   **1. The meaning of "touching and concerning".** The rights and liabilities of assignees, either of the lease or of the reversion, depend upon two things: whether there is privity of estate[27] between the claimant and the defendant, and whether the covenant in question "touches and concerns the land"[28] or, to use more modern phraseology, "has reference to the subject-matter of the lease".[29] These are technical expressions which bear the same meaning,[30] and refer to the limited class of covenants which can be made to bind third parties so that the right to enforce them is a proprietary interest as well as a merely contractual right. A covenant which does not "touch and concern" the land cannot run with the land by reason of privity of estate.

15–023   **2. Uncertainty of the test.** The requirement that a covenant must touch and concern the land rests upon the idea that obligations that are intended to be personal to the parties to the lease should not run with the lease or reversion. The distinction between personal and proprietary covenants is superficially

---

[22] *ibid.*, s.20(5).
[23] *ibid.*, s.20(2). See *ante*, para. 15–007.
[24] L. & T.C.A. 1995, s.20(1).
[25] *Post*, para. 15–064.
[26] The first situation is where T has entered into an authorised guarantee agreement: *post*, paras 15–067, 15–068. The second is where the assignment from T to A was an excluded assignment so that T remains liable on the covenants: *post*, paras 15–074, 15–075.
[27] *Ante*, para. 15–004.
[28] *Spencer's Case* (1583) 5 Co.Rep. 16a.
[29] L.P.A. 1925, ss.141, 142.
[30] *Davis v. Town Properties Investment Corporation Ltd* [1903] 1 Ch. 797.

attractive, but in practice it is one that is not easily drawn. It is impossible to reason by analogy, for the rules concerning it "are purely arbitrary, and the distinctions for the most part, quite illogical".[31]

An attempt was made to formulate a "satisfactory working test"[32] in a series of decisions in which it was held that the benefit of a covenant by a surety to guarantee the performance of a tenant's obligations under the lease touched and concerned the land and passed with the lessor's reversion when it was assigned.[33] A covenant would touch and concern the land if it—

    (i) benefited only the owner for the time being of the covenantee's land, and if separated from that land ceased to benefit that covenantee;

    (ii) affected the nature, quality, mode of user or value of the land of the covenantee; and

    (iii) was not expressed to be personal (neither being given to a specific covenantee nor in respect of the obligations of a specific covenantor).[34]

A covenant to pay a sum of money (such as a surety covenant or a covenant to pay rent) could touch and concern the land if it satisfied these three requirements.[35]

However, doubts have arisen both as to the applicability of this test and its **15–024** content. First, it may apply only to the transmission of the benefit of surety covenants. These pass at common law. The benefit of leasehold covenants passes on an assignment of the reversion under section 141 of the Law of Property Act 1925, and it has been suggested that to determine which of them touch and concern the land regard should be had to the authorities on that section rather than to the test devised for surety covenants.[36] By contrast, it has been assumed that the test applies to the passing of the burden of covenants on an assignment of the reversion under section 142 of the Law of Property Act 1925.[37] Secondly, it is clear that the transmission of the benefit

---

[31] *Grant v. Edmondson* [1931] 1 Ch. 1 at 28, *per* Romer L.J. (giving examples of the illogicalities at 28, 29).

[32] "Without claiming to expound an exhaustive guide": *P. & A. Swift Investments v. Combined English Stores Group Plc* [1989] A.C. 632 at 642, *per* Lord Oliver.

[33] *Kumar v. Dunning* [1989] Q.B. 193; *P. & A. Swift Investments v. Combined English Stores Group Plc, supra; Coronation Street Industrial Properties Ltd v. Ingall Industries Plc* [1989] 1 W.L.R. 304.

[34] *P. & A. Swift Investments v. Combined English Stores Group Plc, supra*, at 642. See too *Kumar v. Dunning, supra*, at 204.

[35] *ibid.*

[36] *Caerns Motor Services Ltd v. Texaco Ltd* [1994] 1 W.L.R. 1249. The correctness of this suggestion must be open to question. In *Kumar v. Dunning, supra*, no distinction was drawn in the analysis of the authorities between cases which involved leases and those which did not.

[37] *Systems Floors Ltd v. Ruralpride Ltd* [1995] 1 E.G.L.R. 48. The court did note that it had been formulated in cases in which L.P.A. 1925, ss.141 and 142 were inapplicable: *ibid.*, 50.

of a covenant does not depend on the transmissibility of the burden, and vice versa.[38] Thus a covenant may touch and concern the land even though—

(i) the benefit is personal to the covenantee if the burden is intended to pass[39]; or

(ii) the burden is personal to the covenantor if the benefit is intended to pass.[40]

Whether or not a covenant touches and concerns the land all too often appears to be purely arbitrary. Thus although a covenant by a surety to guarantee performance of covenants in the lease touches and concerns the land,[41] a covenant by L to repay to T a security deposit does not.[42] This is so, even though the objective of each covenant is to provide L with security for the performance of the obligations in the lease.

15–025   **3. Examples.** The present law can be best understood by examples in addition to the ones given above. The covenants in the left-hand column below have been held to touch and concern the land, while those in the right-hand column have been held not to do so.

---

[38] *Systems Floors Ltd v. Ruralpride Ltd, supra,* at 50, 51.

[39] *Systems Floors Ltd v. Ruralpride Ltd, supra.* In that case L had granted T by side letter a right to surrender the lease after a rent review, and that right was to be personal to T alone. When L assigned to R, the burden of L's undertaking passed to R.

[40] This is the case where a surety guarantees the performance of the covenants in the lease.

[41] *Kumar v. Dunning* [1989] Q.B. 193; *P. & A. Swift Investments v. Combined English Stores Group Plc, supra; Coronation Street Industrial Properties Ltd v. Ingall Industries Plc* [1989] 1 W.L.R. 304; [1988] C.L.J. 180 (C.H.).

[42] *Hua Chiao Commercial Bank Ltd v. Chiaphua Industries Ltd* [1987] A.C. 99. The decision seems wrong in principle.

(a) Covenants by a lessee

TOUCHING AND CONCERNING	NOT TOUCHING AND CONCERNING
To pay rent.[43]	To pay an annual sum to a third person.[48]
To repair the property or fixtures on it.[44]	To pay rates in respect of other land.[49]
To pay £40 towards redecoration on quitting.[45]	Not to employ persons living in other parishes to work in the demised mill (the landlord's motive being to benefit his other property in the parish).[50]
To insure against fire.[46]	
To use as a private dwellinghouse only.[47]	
Not to assign the lease without the landlord's consent.[51]	To repair and renew the tools of a smithy standing on the land (the tools were movable chattels, not fixtures).[55]
Not to let X be concerned in the conduct of the business carried on upon the promises.[52]	
To buy beer for a public-house[53] or petrol for a filling station[54] only from the lessor.	

[43] *Parker v. Webb* (1693) 3 Salk. 5.

[44] *Matures v. Westwood* (1598) Cro.Eliz. 599; *Williams v. Earle* (1868) L.R. 3 Q.B. 739.

[45] *Boyer v. Warbey* [1953] 1 Q.B. 234; and see *Moss' Empires Ltd v. Olympia (Liverpool) Ltd* [1939] A.C. 544 (covenant to spend specified sum on repairs or pay the sum to the landlord).

[46] *Vernon v. Smith* (1821) 5 B. & Ald. 1.

[47] *Wilkinson v. Rogers* (1864) 2 De G.J. & S. 62.

[48] *Mayho v. Buckhurst* (1617) Cro.Jac. 438.

[49] *Gower v. Postmaster-General* (1887) 57 L.T. 527.

[50] *Congleton Corporation v. Pattison* (1808) 10 East 130.

[51] *Goldstein v. Sanders* [1915] 1 Ch. 549; *Cohen v. Popular Restaurants Ltd* [1917] 1 K.B. 480; cf. *Re Robert Stephenson & Co. Ltd* [1915] 1 Ch. 802.

[52] *Lewin v. American & Colonial Distributors Ltd* [1945] Ch. 225, where there is a useful review of the authorities.

[53] *Clegg v. Hands* (1890) 44 Ch. D. 503; *Manchester Brewery Co. v. Coombs* [1901] 2 Ch. 608.

[54] *Regent Oil Co. Ltd v. J. A. Gregory (Hatch End) Ltd* [1966] Ch. 402; *Caerns Motor Services Ltd v. Texaco Ltd* [1994] 1 W.L.R. 1249.

[55] *Williams v. Earle* (1868) L.R. 3 Q.B. 739.

15–027

(b) Covenants by a lessor

TOUCHING AND CONCERNING	NOT TOUCHING AND CONCERNING
To renew the lease[56] (the inclusion of this is somewhat anomalous).[57]	To sell the reversion at a stated price, at the tenant's option.[62]
To supply the demised premises with water[58]	To pay at the end of the lease for chattels not amounting to fixtures.[63]
Not to build on a certain part of the adjoining land.[59]	To pay the tenant £500 at the end of the lease unless a new lease is granted.[64]
Not to determine a periodic (quarterly) tenancy during its first three years.[60]	Not to open another public house within half a mile (in a lease of a public house).[65]
To accept a surrender of the lease from the tenant after a rent review.[61]	To allow the tenant to display advertising signs on other premises.[66]

Although it has been held that a covenant does not touch and concern the land merely because its non-performance may cause a lease of the land to be forfeited,[67] this decision is unlikely to be followed. It is inconsistent with the principle that a convenant will touch and concern the land if it affects its value.[68]

15–028   **4. Reform.** The Law Commission recommended the abolition of the requirement that covenants should pass only if they touch and concern the land.[69] These proposals have now been implemented as regards leases granted after 1995.[70] In general, the benefit and burden of all covenants passes on an

---

[56] *Richardson v. Sydenham* (1703) 2 Vern. 447; *Muller v. Trafford* [1901] 1 Ch. 54 at 60; *Weg Motors Ltd v. Hales* [1962] Ch. 49.

[57] *Woodall v. Clifton* [1905] 2 Ch. 257 at 279.

[58] *Jourdain v. Wilson* [1821] 4 B. & Ald. 266.

[59] *Ricketts v. Enfield Churchwardens* [1909] 1 Ch. 544.

[60] *Breams Property Investment Co. Ltd v. Stroulger* [1948] 2 K.B. 1.

[61] *Systems Floors Ltd v. Ruralpride Ltd* [1995] 1 E.G.L.R. 48.

[62] *Woodall v. Clifton, supra;* see *post,* para. 15–063, n.56. Similarly, a right of pre-emption over adjoining land: *Collison v. Lettson* (1815) 6 Taunt. 224.

[63] *Gorton v. Gregory* (1862) 3 B. & S. 90.

[64] *Re Hunter's Lease* [1942] Ch. 124.

[65] *Thomas v. Hayward* (1869) L.R. 4 Ex. 311. The correctness of this decision has been doubted: *Kumar v. Dunning* [1989] Q.B. 193 at 205. In principle a covenant which benefits the business of the lessee should be capable of touching and concerning the land. Not only will a freehold covenant touch and concern the land if it benefits a business conducted on the land (see *Newton Abbot Co-operative Society Ltd v. Williamson & Treadgold Ltd* [1952] Ch. 286 at 293), but an easement may accommodate the dominant tenement if it is for the benefit of a business carried on on the premises: *Moody v. Steggles* (1879) 12 Ch.D. 261; *post* para. 18–045.

[66] *Re No. 1, Albemarle Street* [1959] Ch. 531.

[67] *Dewar v. Goodman* [1909] A.C. 72 (covenant by sub-lessor to observe covenants in the head lease held not to touch and concern the land).

[68] *Kumar v. Dunning* [1989] Q.B. 193 at 205, holding *Dewar v. Goodman, supra,* to be inconsistent with *Dyson v. Foster* [1909] A.C. 98.

[69] (1988) Law Com. No. 174.

[70] L. & T.C.A. 1995, s.2(1). This is subject to certain limited exceptions: *ibid.,* s.2(2); see *post,* para. 15–080.

assignment of such a lease or its reversion unless the covenant is expressed to be personal to one or both of the parties.[71]

B. Principles of Transmission

Having seen which covenants touch and concern the land, we must now examine the rights and liabilities of assignees. As in every other case of enforcing rights of property, two separate points must be considered: **15–029**

(i) is the defendant liable? and

(ii) is the plaintiff entitled to sue?

In the case of the rights and liabilities of assignees under covenants concerning land, it is more usual to put these questions as follows:

(i) has the burden of the covenant passed? and

(ii) has the benefit of the covenant passed?

In discussing these questions it will be convenient to deal first with assignments of leases, then with assignments of reversions, then with the transfer of the benefit of surety covenants and the rights of sureties, and finally with forfeiture clauses.[72] The rules which govern the transmissibility of covenants are neither rational nor coherent.[73] For leases granted after 1995, they are replaced with a statutory code that attempts to remove the inconsistencies and anomalies that apply to leases granted before 1996.[74]

I. WHERE THE LESSEE ASSIGNS HIS LEASE

If L leases land to T, and T assigns the lease to A, the common law rule laid down in *Spencer's Case*[75] is that A is entitled to the benefit, and subject to the burden, of all covenants and conditions touching and concerning the land, because there is privity of estate between L and A. Where there is privity of estate, both the benefit and the burden of the covenants run with the land demised.   **15–030**

The details of this fundamental rule must now be studied.

1. The lease must be in due form. It used to be held that only a lease made by deed would carry the benefit or burden of special stipulations to an assignee, since they could not otherwise be annexed to the estate.[76] But if the   **15–031**

---

[71] *ibid.*, s.3; *post*, paras 15–080, 15–081.

[72] For the transfer of the benefit and burden of covenants with a lease of a right in the nature of an incorporeal hereditament, see the previous edition of this work at p. 756.

[73] For an admirable account of their operation, see (1991) 11 L.S. 47 (R. Thornton).

[74] *Post*, paras 15–080, 15–081.

[75] (1583) 5 Co.Rep. 16a.

[76] *Elliott v. Johnson* (1866) L.R. 2 Q.B. 120 at 127.

assignee of an informal lease went into possession and paid rent the court would readily infer a new agreement on the same terms as the old, so that the assignee would become bound by privity of contract[77]; and under equitable doctrines, if there was a specifically enforceable agreement for a lease the benefit, but not the burden, of its terms could be assigned.[78] The Court of Appeal has, however, held that the burden (and presumably also the benefit) of a stipulation can pass on the assignment of a lease for three years or less made merely in writing[79]; and dicta in the same case would apparently extend the concession to mere agreements for a lease,[80] thus conflicting with the rule that the burden of a mere agreement is not assignable. The very reasonable decision to hold the assignee bound by the terms of a legal lease not made by deed is rather strangely attributed to "the fusion of law and equity" made by the Judicature Act 1873 which is said to have largely obliterated the distinction between agreements under hand and covenants made by deed.[81] Whether the doctrine extends to tenancies for three years or less which are made merely orally (*i.e.* without writing) is uncertain.[82]

2. There must be a legal assignment of the whole term

15–032   *(a) Legal assignment.* The benefit and burden of covenants run with the lease only in the case of a legal assignment of the whole of the remainder of the term.[83] Where instead of an assignment there has been a sub-lease, the sub-lessee takes neither the benefit nor the burden of the covenants in the lease,[84] even if his sub-lease is only one day shorter than the head lease. Thus if L leases land to T for 99 years, T assigns the lease to A, and A sub-leases the land to S for the residue of the term of 99 years less one day, S is not an assignee and there is privity neither of contract nor of estate between L and S. A is still the tenant under the lease for 99 years and remains liable upon it. Consequently if S does some act which is contrary to a covenant in the 99 years' lease, L cannot sue S but can sue A. If the lease contains a forfeiture

---

[77] *Buckworth v. Johnson* (1835) 1 Cr.M. & R. 833; *Cornish v. Stubbs* (1870) L.R. 5 C.P. 334 at 338, 339.

[78] *Ante.* para. 14–051.

[79] *Boyer v. Warbey* [1953] 1 Q.B. 234 (lease of a flat for three years made in writing and not by deed, with a term that the tenant on quitting would pay £40 towards cost of redecoration: held, this term was binding on an assignee of the lease); *cf. Weg Motors Ltd v. Hales* [1962] Ch. 49 (burden of covenant written but not by deed running with reversion).

[80] *Boyer v. Warbey, supra*, at 246 (Denning L.J.). Any such agreement would now have to comply with the formal requirements of L.P.(M.P.)A. 1989, s.2. See *ante*, paras 12–018, 14–040.

[81] *Boyer v. Warbey, supra*, at 246. See [1978] C.L.J. 98 at 105 (R. J. Smith).

[82] *Boyer v. Warbey, supra*, appears to overrule *Elliott v. Johnson, supra*, where there was a mere oral agreement implied in the case of a tenant who had held over after the expiration of a lease for 14 years. There are obvious difficulties for an assignee in ascertaining the terms of an oral tenancy unless, as in that case, they are contained in an earlier lease.

[83] *West v. Dobb* (1869) L.R. 4 Q.B. 634.

[84] *South of England Dairies Ltd v. Baker* [1906] 2 Ch. 631; but it is possible that the sub-lessee can now take the benefit by virtue of L.P.A. 1925, s.78: see *Smith v. River Douglas Catchment Board* [1949] 2 K.B. 500, *post*, para. 16–015. A sub-lessee may be bound by restrictive covenants: *post*, para. 16–045. For the difference between an assignment and a sub-lease, see *ante*, para. 14–008.

clause, L can also take proceedings for forfeiture and so put an end to both head lease and sub-lease together. In practice the covenants inserted in a sub-lease are made at least as stringent as those in the head lease, so that the sub-lessor may have a remedy against the sub-lessee in case the sub-lessee's acts render the sub-lessor liable to the head landlord.

(b) Other assignments. Since the covenants run only where there is privity **15–033** of estate, a mere equitable assignment (*e.g.* under a contract to assign) cannot pass the burden of covenants.[85] But the benefit may itself be assigned as such; and if the covenant creates an interest in land (*e.g.* a restrictive covenant, or an option), the burden will affect subsequent occupiers in accordance with the ordinary rules governing legal and equitable interests. These cases are explained more fully below.[86]

(c) Squatters. Where title is unregistered, a squatter, *i.e.* a person who bars **15–034** the lessee's interest by adverse possession for 12 years under the Limitation Act 1980, is not an assignee of the lease, at least where the title to the land is unregistered. He cannot therefore sue or be sued on covenants in the lease which run only where there is privity of estate.[87] But if he claims some advantage under the lease, *e.g.* a reduction of rent which is conditional on observance of the covenants, he may estop himself from denying that he is bound by the lease.[88] Where title to land is registered the position is quite different. A squatter who bars the rights of a lessee by adverse possession is entitled to be registered as proprietor of the lease in place of the former tenant. The squatter is, therefore, the successor in title to the former tenant so that there is privity of estate with the landlord. The squatter therefore takes both the benefit and the burden of the covenants in the lease.[89]

(d) Personal representatives. A personal representative of the tenant is an **15–035** assignee by operation of law, for when the tenant dies the lease devolves automatically upon his executor or administrator.[90] But the extent of a personal representative's liability varies. If he takes possession of the land, he is personally liable to the same extent as an ordinary assignee,[91] though by proper pleading he may limit his liability to the annual value of the land.[92] If he does not take possession, he is liable only[93] in his representative capacity,

---

[85] *Cox v. Bishop* (1857) 8 De G.M. & G. 815; *Friary, Holroyd & Healey's Breweries Ltd v. Singleton* [1899] 1 Ch. 86, reversed on other grounds [1899] 2 Ch. 261. See [1978] C.L.J. 98 (R. J. Smith). There may be facts which estop the assignee from denying liability: see *ante,* paras 14–095–14–097.
[86] See *post,* paras 15–061–15–063.
[87] *Tichborne v. Weir* (1892) 67 L.T. 735; *post,* para. 21–067.
[88] *Ashe v. Hogan* [1920] 1 I.R. 159; *post,* para. 21–067.
[89] See *Central London Commercial Estates Ltd v. Kato Kagaku Ltd* [1998] 4 All E.R. 948; *post,* paras 21–056, 21–068.
[90] *Ante,* para. 11–125.
[91] *Tilny v. Norris* (1700) 1 Ld.Raym. 553; *Stratford-upon-Avon Corpn. v. Parker* [1914] 2 K.B. 562 at 567.
[92] *Rendall v. Andreae* (1892) 61 L.J.Q.B. 630.
[93] *Wollaston v. Hakewill* (1841) 3 Man. & G. 297 at 320.

i.e. to the extent of the deceased tenant's assets.[94] The representative liability of an original lessee's estate endures for the whole term of the lease, despite any assignment by him[95] or by his personal representatives.[96]

This representative liability formerly made it unsafe for a personal representative to distribute the assets to the persons beneficially entitled so long as any liability might arise under the covenants in the lease.[97] However, a personal representative is now protected by statute against his representative liability if he has first satisfied any existing claims, set aside any *fixed* sum agreed to be laid out on the land, and assigned the lease to a beneficiary or purchaser.[98] But this provides no protection if the personal representative or trustee has taken possession and so is liable as an assignee; in such cases he may set aside a fund for his protection,[99] though this will be distributable when all possible claims have been paid or barred by lapse of time.[1]

15–036   *(e) Several assignees.* If the tenancy is vested in two or more assignees, each is liable for the full amount of any damages for breach of covenant and not merely a proportionate share, even if in equity they are not joint tenants but tenants in common.[2]

15–037   **3. Partial assignment.** It is possible for part only of the demised land to be assigned separately from the rest. In that case covenants capable of running with the land will bind the assignee in so far as they relate to the part assigned to him,[3] whether or not that assignment is made with the landlord's consent.[4] In an action for rent the assignee is liable only for the proportion attributable to his part,[5] which in default of agreement,[6] may be determined by the court,[7] or by the appropriate Secretary of State if application is made to him.[8] But although the landlord can sue only for this proportion, the ancient right of

---

[94] *Helier v. Casebert* (1665) 1 Lev. 127; *Youngmin v. Heath* [1974] 1 W.L.R. 135 (weekly tenancy).
[95] *Brett v. Cumberland* (1619) Cro.Jac. 521; and see *Matthews v. Ruggles-Brise* [1911] 1 Ch. 194.
[96] *Pitcher v. Tovey* (1692) 4 Mod. 71 at 76.
[97] See *Davis v. Blackwell* (1832) 9 Bing. 6; *Collins v. Crouch* (1849) 13 Q.B. 542.
[98] T.A. 1925, s.26; re-enacting legislation first introduced by L.P.(Am.)A. 1859, s.27.
[99] *Re Owers* [1941] Ch. 389; compare *Re Bennett* [1943] 1 All E.R. 467, a curious case.
[1] *Re Lewis* [1939] Ch. 232.
[2] See *United Dairies Ltd v. Public Trustee* [1923] 1 K.B. 469 (repair: legal tenancy in common before 1926); *cf. ante,* paras 9–031–9–034.
[3] *Congham v. King* (1631) Cro.Car. 221 (repair), approved in *Stevenson v. Lambard* (1802) 2 East 575. For a valuable review of the authorities, see *Lester v. Ridd* [1990] 2 Q.B. 430 at 438.
[4] *Lester v. Ridd, supra,* at 438.
[5] *Curtis v. Spitty* (1835) 1 Bing. N.C. 756. Although some doubt was expressed as to this principle in *Whitham v. Bullock* [1939] 2 K.B. 81 at 86, "the law has continued to be stated in the text books on the subject as being that an assignee of part of the land cannot be sued for the whole of the rent, but only for a proportionate part thereof": *Lester v. Ridd, supra,* at 438, *per* Dillon L.J. *cf.* Slade L.J. at 442.
[6] Such an agreement will not bind persons not parties to it: *Bliss v. Collins* (1822) 5 B. & Ald. 876 (severance of reversion). See L.P.A. 1925, s.190(3) (which is declaratory of the law); and *Lester v. Ridd, supra,* at 442.
[7] See *Whitham v. Bullock, supra,* at 86, citing *Bliss v. Collins, supra.*
[8] L. & T. A. 1927, s.20.

distress is available against every part of the demised land for the whole of the rent.[9] If the assignee of part is thus compelled to pay the whole rent, he can claim contribution from the tenant of the other part, on the principle which gives a right of indemnity to persons compelled to pay a debt for which some other person is primarily liable.[10]

4. Covenants relating to things *in posse*. If a covenant made before 1926   **15–038**
imposed an obligation upon the tenant to do some entirely new thing, such as to erect a building, the burden of the covenant ran with the land only if the lessee expressly covenanted for himself *and for his assigns* that the covenant would be performed.[11] This rule did not apply to covenants relating to things *in esse* (in existence) nor even to covenants relating only conditionally to something *in posse* (not in existence), such as a covenant to repair a new building if it is erected[12]; in such cases it was immaterial whether or not the covenant mentioned assigns. This unreasonable distinction between covenants relating to things *in posse* and those relating to things *in esse* is still in force as regards all leases granted before 1926; but by the Law of Property Act 1925[13] it does not apply to leases made after 1925.

5. Duration of liability. The original lessee is liable for all breaches of   **15–039**
covenant throughout the term of the lease, even after assignment, because there is still privity of contract.[14] But, in the absence of a direct covenant with the landlord,[15] an assignee is liable only for breaches of covenant committed while the lease is vested in him,[16] for privity of estate exists only while the estate is held.[17] An assignee is under no liability for breaches committed before the lease was assigned to him[18] unless they are continuing breaches (as of a covenant to repair),[19] nor is he liable for breaches committed after he has assigned the lease.[20] But if a covenant is broken while the lease is vested in him, his liability for this breach continues despite any assignment.[21] Thus while the original lessee of an onerous lease cannot divest himself of liability

---

[9] *Whitham v. Bullock, supra*, at 86; *Lester v. Ridd, supra*, at 438, 442.

[10] *Whitham v. Bullock, supra* (payment under threat of distress). For another example of this principle, see *post, para.* 15–042.

[11] *Spencer's Case* (1583) 5 Co.Rep. 16a, second resolution; though see *Minshull v. Oakes* (1858) 2 H. & N. 793; *Re Robert Stephenson & Co. Ltd* [1915] 1 Ch. 802 at 807.

[12] *Minshull v. Oakes, supra.*

[13] s.79; see *Rhone v. Stevens* [1994] 2 A.C. 310 at 322; *post, para.* 16–016.

[14] *Ante, para.* 15–008.

[15] *Ante, para.* 15–013.

[16] *Eaton v. Jaques* (1780) 2 Doug.K.B. 455 at 460; *Chancellor v. Poole* (1781) 2 Doug.K.B. 764.

[17] *Johnsey Estates Ltd v. Lewis and Manley (Engineering) Ltd* (1987) 54 P. & C.R. 296 at 299, 300.

[18] *Grescott v. Green* (1700) 1 Salk. 199. The point has arisen in recent cases concerning unpaid rent: see *Parry v. Robinson-Wyllie Ltd* [1987] 2 E.G.L.R. 133 at 134; *Wharfland Ltd v. South London Co-operative Building Co. Ltd* [1995] 2 E.G.L.R. 21.

[19] *Granada Theatres Ltd v. Freehold Investment (Leytonstone) Ltd* [1959] Ch. 592.

[20] *Paul v. Nurse* (1828) 8 B. & C. 486.

[21] *Harley v. King* (1835) 2 Cr.M. & R. 18.

for future breaches, an assignee can do so by assigning the lease, even if the assignee is a pauper.[22] For this reason, it has become the usual practice in business leases to require an assignee to enter into a direct covenant with the landlord, undertaking to observe all the covenants and conditions in the lease for the duration of the term. This has already been explained.[23]

15–040　　**6. Right to sue for breach of covenant.** When a lease is assigned, the assignor retains the right to sue for breaches of covenant committed by the landlord prior to that assignment.[24] That right does not pass to the assignee unless it is expressly assigned,[25] though he can of course enforce any continuing breach of covenant by the landlord.[26] In this respect, an assignment of a lease differs from an assignment of the reversion, where the right to sue for a pre-existing breach of covenant passes with the reversion.[27] For leases granted after 1995, the law has been changed.[28]

15–041　　**7. Indemnities by assignee.** If a covenant which runs with the land has been broken, the lessee and the assignee entitled to the lease at the time of the breach are each liable to be sued by the lessor.[29] But although the lessor may obtain judgment against either or both, he can only have one satisfaction[30]; he has no right to recover twice. The same rule applies to all the other cases in the examples given below where one person may sue more than one defendant in respect of one liability: both may be sued, but the money may be recovered only once. The value of alternative rights of enforcement is that if one defendant is inaccessible or insolvent, satisfaction may be had from the other.

15–042　　*(a) Implied indemnity.* The primary liability is that of the assignee, since he has the exclusive benefit of the lease.[31] If the lessee is sued, he may claim indemnity from the assignee in whom the lease was vested at the time of the breach, whether that assignee obtained the lease from the lessee directly or from some intermediate assignee.[32] The principle here is a branch of restitution "independent of contract",[33] by which the law implies an obligation between joint debtors to repay money paid by one of them for the exclusive

---

[22] *Valliant v. Dodemede* (1742) 2 Atk. 546.

[23] *Ante,* para. 15–013.

[24] *City and Metropolitan Properties Ltd v. Greycroft Ltd* [1987] 1 W.L.R. 1085; [1987] Conv. 374 (P. F. Smith).

[25] The assignment of a right to sue that is ancillary to a property right is not champertous: *Trendtex Trading Corporation v. Credit Suisse* [1982] A.C. 679 at 703.

[26] *City and Metropolitan Properties Ltd v. Greycroft Ltd, supra,* at 1087, 1088.

[27] *ibid.; post,* para. 15–051.

[28] *Post,* para. 15–092.

[29] Unless liability for other persons' acts is expressly restricted, as in *Wilson v. Twamley* [1904] 2 K.B. 99 (a covenant not to do or to suffer to be done certain acts was not infringed by the acts of sublessee, who was not the tenant's agent).

[30] See, *e.g. Brett v. Cumberland* (1619) Cro.Jac. 521 at 523.

[31] *Moule v. Garrett* (1872) L.R. 7 Ex. 101; *Selous Street Properties Ltd v. Oronel Fabrics Ltd* [1984] 1 E.G.L.R. 50 at 61, 62.

[32] *Moule v. Garrett, supra; Wolveridge v. Steward* (1833) 1 Cr. & M. 644.

[33] *Becton Dickinson U.K. Ltd v. Zwebner* [1989] Q.B. 208 at 217, *per* McNeill L.J.

benefit of the other, when both were legally liable to a common creditor.[34] Since the assignee is solely entitled to enjoy the lease, the satisfaction of the lessor's claim enures to the assignee's benefit alone. The lessee has, in fact, paid the assignee's debt for him, and has the same right of indemnity as has a surety.[35] Where performance of the obligations in the lease by the assignee has been guaranteed by a surety, the lessee can also seek reimbursement from that surety.[36]

(b) Express indemnity. It is also usual practice for an assignor to require a   **15–043** covenant of indemnity by the assignee against liability for future breaches of covenant, whoever might commit them. The common form of covenant is now implied by statute—

> (i) on a conveyance for valuable consideration[37] of the entirety of the land comprised in a lease[38]; and

> (ii) on the transfer of any leasehold interest in registered land otherwise than by way of underlease.[39]

This covenant is purely personal and cannot, of course, run with the land. The assignor can enforce the covenant only against the immediate assignee. He cannot compel that assignee (if insolvent) to enforce any rights of indemnity that he might have against a subsequent (solvent) assignee.[40] Where the immediate assignee is in breach, the assignor can still enforce his implied common law right of restitution[41] against the assignee, even if the implied covenant has been expressly excluded in the assignment.[42]

(c) Effect. The effect of these rights of indemnity may be illustrated thus: **15–044**

```
        A
        |  99 years
        B — C — D — E
                    |  21 years
                    F
```

---

[34] *Electricity Supply Nominees Ltd v. Thorn EMI Ltd* (1991) 63 P. & C.R. 143.

[35] *Moule v. Garrett, supra*; at 104; *cf. ante,* para. 15–037.

[36] *Becton Dickinson U.K. Ltd v. Zwebner, supra.*

[37] A conveyance will be for valuable consideration simply by virtue of the assignee assuming the obligation to pay rent and observe the other covenants in the lease, even though the assignment is otherwise for nominal consideration: *Johnsey Estates Ltd v. Lewis and Manley (Engineering) Ltd* (1987) 54 P. & C.R. 296 (assignment of lease for £1).

[38] L.P.A. 1925, s.77(1)(C); Sched. 2, Pt IX. This covenant includes liability for continuing breaches (*e.g.* of a repairing covenant) existing when the lease was assigned: *Middlegate Properties Ltd v. Bilbao* (1972) 24 P. & C.R. 329.

[39] L.R.A. 1925, s.24(1)(b).

[40] *R.P.H. Ltd v. Mirror Group Newspapers Plc* (1992) 65 P. & C.R. 252.

[41] *Supra.*

[42] *Re Healing Research Trustee Co. Ltd* [1992] 2 All E.R. 481; [1992] C.L.J. 425 (S. Bridge). It was assumed in that case that the implication of the covenant *could* be expressly excluded. However, L.P.A. 1925, s.77(6) provides merely that such covenants can be "varied or extended by deed". By contrast, where title is registered, L.R.A. 1925, s.24(1) envisages the exclusion of the implication of the covenant.

A has leased land to B for 99 years; by successive assignments E has become entitled to the lease and has granted a sub-lease to F for 21 years. If F does some act which is contrary to a covenant in the head lease, A can sue either B (privity of contract) or E (privity of estate), but has no right to recover twice.[43] A cannot sue C, D or F, for he has no privity of any kind with them. Nor can A compel B to pursue any claim for indemnity which B may have against C.[44] If A sues B, B has an implied restitutionary right of indemnity against E, but not against F.[45] Alternatively, if on the assignment to C a covenant of indemnity was given to B (either expressly or by the statutory implication), B may claim indemnity (contractual) from C. C in turn may claim a similar indemnity from D, and D from E, provided in each case that the covenant for indemnity was given on the assignment.

15–045　　If B took a covenant of indemnity from C, and either—

　　　(i) C failed to take one from D as did D from E; or

　　　(ii) C prefers to sue E rather than D,

C and D may presumably claim an indemnity by way of restitution from E for anything which they have been compelled to pay. This is because E is liable in restitution to B. He is therefore also similarly liable to C if C is compelled to discharge this liability for E's sole benefit. By parity of reasoning, as E is liable to indemnify C, he is also liable to indemnify D if D is compelled to pay C under a covenant for indemnity. Apart from the rules relating to restrictive covenants,[46] F incurs no liability to anyone except so far as his act was a breach of a covenant in the sub-lease. This makes him liable to E, because it is only with E that F has any privity of any kind.

II. WHERE THE LESSOR ASSIGNS HIS REVERSION

15–046　　The common law rule was that covenants touching and concerning the land could run with the lease, but not with the reversion.[47] If L, a tenant in fee simple, leased his land to T, and then L sold his fee simple, subject to the lease, to R, R was neither able to sue nor liable to be sued on the covenants in the lease. But R could sue and be sued on the obligations (often called implied covenants[48]) inherent in the relationship of landlord and tenant, since these arose automatically from the privity of estate (*i.e.* tenure) between R and

---

[43] *Ante*, para. 15–041.

[44] *ibid.* If A has taken a direct covenant from C or D as a condition of the licence to assign, he will of course be able to sue them: see *ante*, para. 15–013.

[45] *Bonner v. Tottenham & Edmonton Permanent Investment B.S.* [1899] 1 Q.B. 161; this is because F is not jointly liable with B to A, and payment by B to A does not relieve F of any liability. The principle of *Moule v. Garrett* (1872) L.R. 7 Ex. 101; *ante*, para. 15–042, does not therefore apply.

[46] *Post*, para. 16–030.

[47] *Ante*, para. 15–011., *Thursby v. Plant* (1670) 1 Wms. Saund. 230 at 240, n.3. Distinguish the cases where the benefit of a covenant could run with other land belonging to the reversioner (not with the reversion itself): *post*, para. 16–011.

[48] *Ante*, para. 14–195.

T.[49] Thus R could sue T for the rent, for rent was due not merely under a personal covenant but as a service incident to the tenant's estate.[50] The same applied to any services analogous to rent, *e.g.* grinding corn at the lessor's mill.[51]

But before *Spencer's Case* laid down the principles upon which covenants could run with leases, statute enabled them to run with reversions. When the monastic lands were seized and distributed it was necessary to enable grantees to enforce the terms of leases, and the Grantees of Reversions Act 1540[52] altered the law generally.

The effect of the Act was that the benefit and burden of all covenants, provisions and conditions contained in a lease which touched and concerned the land[53] (or, in the modern phrase, had reference to the subject-matter of the lease[54]) passed with the reversion. The meaning of "touching and concerning the land" was here the same as in *Spencer's Case*, discussed above.[55] The subsequent legislative history of these provisions has already been explained.[56] An extended and significantly different version of them, first introduced by the Conveyancing Acts 1881–1911,[57] is now found in the Law of Property Act 1925, ss.141 (benefit) and 142 (burden).

The following points must be observed.

1. The lease must be in due form. The Act of 1540 applied only to leases **15–047** made by deed,[58] but that of 1881 applied also to leases evidenced in writing,[59] though not to mere oral tenancies.[60] Since 1925 it appears that even a mere oral tenancy is sufficient, for by section 154 of the Law of Property Act 1925, sections 141 and 142 extend to an underlease "or other tenancy"[61]; and "covenant" is not confined to promises made by deed.[62]

By a liberal construction it has been held that even a contract for a lease, provided that it satisfies the formal requirements for such a contract[63] and is

---

[49] *Wedd v. Porter* [1916] 2 K.B. 91 at 100, 101; and see Platt on *Covenants*, 532.

[50] *cf.* Co.Litt. 215a (rent payable to lord who took reversion by escheat).

[51] *Vyvyan v. Arthur* (1823) 1 B. & C. 410.

[52] 32 Hen. 8, c. 34.

[53] This qualification was added by judicial legislation, by analogy to the principle of *Spencer's Case* (*ante*, paras 15–022–15–027): see Smith's L.C. i, 59.

[54] See L.P.A. 1925, ss.141, 142; *Davis v. Town Properties Investment Corporation* [1903] 1 Ch. 797.

[55] *Ante*, para. 15–022.

[56] *Ante*, para. 15–011.

[57] 1881, ss.10, 11; 1911, s.2.

[58] *Smith v. Eggington* (1874) L.R. 9 C.P. 145 (burden); *Standen v. Chrismas* (1847) 10 Q.B. 135 (benefit).

[59] *Cole v. Kelly* [1920] 2 K.B. 106; *Rye v. Purcell* [1926] 1 K.B. 446.

[60] *Blane v. Francis* [1917] 1 K.B. 252.

[61] See also the dictum of Denning L.J. in *Boyer v. Warbey, ante*, para. 15–031. That case concerned the assignment of a lease, but the dictum extends to assignment of the reversion.

[62] *Weg Motors Ltd v. Hales* [1962] Ch. 49 at 73. It is unclear whether a collateral undertaking not to enforce a particular obligation in the lease is itself an "obligation under a condition or of a covenant", the burden of which will pass with the reversion under L.P.A. 1925, s.142(1): see *Systems Floors Ltd v. Ruralpride Ltd* [1995] 1 E.G.L.R. 48 at 51.

[63] See L.P.(M.P.)A. 1989, s.2; *ante*, para. 12–018.

specifically enforceable, is "a lease", and the intending lessor's interest a "reversionary estate", within the Acts of 1881 and 1925.[64] This implies an extension of the doctrine of *Walsh v. Lonsdale*[65] so as to affect third parties: not only the benefit but also the burden of the stipulations becomes assignable by the proposed lessor, although as has been seen only the benefit is assignable by the proposed lessee.[66] The decisions so far given concern only the benefit of the lessor's covenants, but their reasoning applies equally to the burden. This difference between the lessor's and lessee's positions under a mere contract may perhaps rest in principle on the fact that the burden of an estate contract can run with the land of the lessor as an equitable burden of a proprietary kind, carrying with it the burden of covenants[67]; but the lessee's obligations are purely contractual until a lease is executed, and therefore they cannot be assigned.

Sections 141 and 142 of the Law of Property Act apply only to covenants made between lessor and lessee.[68] The benefit and burden of covenants made by strangers to the lease such as sureties[69] or subsequent assignees[70] do not therefore fall within the ambit of the sections. The benefit of the lessee's covenants will pass with the reversion only if they are contained in the lease.[71] By contrast, the burden of the lessor's covenants will pass even if they are contained in some other document, such as a collateral option agreement,[72] a collateral contract to execute repairs[73] or a side letter,[74] provided that they were "entered into by a lessor with reference to the subject matter of the lease".[75] There is no obvious reason for this difference.

15–048   **2. The reversion may have been assigned in whole or in part.** The assignee of the entire reversion takes the benefit and burden of the provisions in the lease; and if the reversion is held on trust, it is the trustee, as legal reversioner, and not the beneficiaries who can enforce the covenants.[76] Where the reversion is not assigned in its entirety, the position is not so simple. Two separate cases must be considered.

15–049   *(a) Severance as regards the estate.* Where the assignee has part of the reversion, *e.g.* where a fee simple reversioner grants a lease of his reversion

---

[64] Doubted in *Manchester Brewery Co. v. Coombs* [1901] 2 Ch. 608 at 619, but so held in *Rickett v. Green* [1910] 1 K.B. 253 and *Rye v. Purcell* [1926] 1 K.B. 446.
[65] *Ante*, para. 14–041.
[66] *Ante*, para. 14–051.
[67] *Ante*, para. 14–025.
[68] *Kumar v. Dunning* [1989] Q.B. 193 at 200; *P. & A. Swift Investments v. Combined English Stores Group Plc* [1989] A.C. 632 at 639.
[69] *ibid.*
[70] For direct covenants by an assignee of the lease with the landlord, see *ante*, para. 15–013.
[71] L.P.A. 1925, s.141(1).
[72] *Weg Motors Ltd v. Hales* [1962] Ch. 49 at 73.
[73] *Lotteryking Ltd v. AMEC Properties Ltd* [1995] 2 E.G.L.R. 13.
[74] *Systems Floors Ltd v. Ruralpride Ltd* [1995] 1 E.G.L.R. 48.
[75] L.P.A. 1925, s.142(1); *Systems Floors Ltd v. Ruralpride Ltd, supra*, at 50.
[76] See *Schalit v. Joseph Nadler Ltd* [1933] 2 K.B. 79.

to X (whether for a shorter or longer period than the existing lease), the reversion is severed as regards the estate.[77] The benefit and burden of all covenants and conditions touching and concerning the land pass to the assignee under sections 141 and 142 of the Law of Property Act 1925.[78] That is to say, the covenants run with the *immediate* reversion, for it is the person entitled to the next immediate reversion upon the lease who has privity of estate with the tenant.[79] This explains why the benefit and burden of the covenants pass to a mere lessee of the reversion, but do not pass to a sub-lessee of the lease.

(b) Severance as regards the land. Where the assignee has the reversion of   **15–050** part, *e.g.* where a fee simple reversioner grants the fee simple of half the land to X, the reversion is severed as regards the land. It has been held that this does not sever the tenancy, so that although there is a severed reversion, there is still a single tenancy.[80] Provision is made by statute for the apportionment of both the benefit and the burden of the covenants in the lease.[81] As regards the benefit of covenants, all conditions and rights of re-entry are apportioned on the severance of the reversion and are annexed to the severed parts of the reversion.[82] The burden of covenants is expressly annexed to "the several parts" of the reversionary estate notwithstanding the severance of that estate.[83] These provisions apply only to a genuine severance of the reversion and not, *e.g.* to a conveyance to a bare trustee for the assignor.[84]

There is a statutory rule about a notice to quit which is served after a severance of the reversion and so applies to part of the demised land only. The tenant may elect to quit the whole, provided that within one month he serves on the other reversioner a counter-notice expiring at the same time as the original notice.[85]

---

[77] For this see *ante*, para. 14–104.
[78] As was also the case under the Grantees of Reversions Act 1540: Co.Litt. 215a, 215b, and notes by Butler; *Wright v. Burroughes* (1846) 3 C.B. 685. L.P.A. 1925, s.141(2) expressly provides that covenants can be enforced by "the person from time to time entitled, subject to the term, to the income of the whole or any part . . . of the land leased".
[79] Preston, *Conveyancing*, ii, 145, 146; *ante*, para. 14–104.
[80] *Jelley v. Buckman* [1974] Q.B. 488.
[81] For the law that is applicable in cases where a lease was both made before 1882 and where the reversion was severed before 1926, see the previous edition of this work at pp. 754, 755.
[82] L.P.A. 1925, s.140(1) replacing earlier legislation: L.P.(Am.)A. 1859, s.3 (non-payment of rent); C.A. 1881, s.12 (other conditions). It is not necessary that the right should be *expressly* contained in the lease: *Persey v. Bazley* (1983) 47 P. & C.R. 37 at 45 (implied right to serve notice to quit on periodic tenant apportioned on severance).
[83] L.P.A. 1925, s.142(1).
[84] *Persey v. Bazley, supra. cf. John v. George* [1995] 1 E.G.L.R. 9 (bona fide transfer to trustees to hold for third party a genuine severance).
[85] L.P.A. 1925, s.140(2).

3. Effect of assignment of reversion on liability for previous breaches

15–051   *(a) Assignee's right to sue for previous breaches.* An assignee of the reversion acquires the right to sue for breaches of covenant committed before the assignment, and the assignor loses this right.[86] This has been held to be the result of section 141 of the Law of Property Act 1925,[87] which provides that rent and the benefit of leasehold covenants (if they touch and concern the land) and conditions shall be "annexed and incident to *and shall go with*" the reversion.[88] As has been explained,[89] the position of an assignee of the reversion differs in this regard from that of an assignee of the lease, who does not acquire the right to sue for prior breaches of covenant by the landlord.[90] The legislation has in this respect changed the previous law, which was that the assignor of the reversion and not the assignee could sue for rent due and other breaches of covenant committed before the assignment, not being breaches of a continuing character.[91] Thus in a case where, at the time of the assignment of the reversion, there were outstanding breaches of covenants to repair and reinstate the property, the assignee and not the assignor is the person entitled to sue.[92] But this rule will, it seems, yield to any contrary intention in the assignment.[93]

15–052   *(b) Assignee's right to enforce right of re-entry for previous breach.* A right of re-entry for breach of covenant could not be assigned at common law, so that if a reversion was assigned after a covenant had been broken, the new reversioner could not take advantage of a forfeiture clause.[94] By the Law of Property Act 1925,[95] such rights of re-entry are enforceable by the new reversioner provided they have not been waived.[96] Although the court will often imply waiver,[97] it will not do so merely because the reversion is

---

[86] *Re King* [1963] Ch. 459; *London and County (A. & D.) Ltd v. Wilfred Sportsman Ltd* [1971] Ch. 764.

[87] For the history of this section, see *ante*, para. 15–011.

[88] subs. (1); and see subss (2), (3). The words in italics were particularly emphasised in *Re King*, *supra*, at 497 by Diplock L.J. It has not been resolved whether on the termination of a head lease, the head lessor or the lessee can sue the underlessee for breach of covenant committed prior to that termination: *Electricity Supply Nominees Ltd v. Thorn EMI Ltd* (1991) 63 P. & C.R. 143. *cf.* Fox L.J. at 147, suggesting that s.141(3) might be wide enough to allow recovery by the head lessor.

[89] *Ante*, para. 15–040.

[90] In *City and Metropolitan Properties Ltd v. Greycroft Ltd* [1987] 1 W.L.R. 1085 at 1087, the argument that the right to sue passed under L.P.A. 1925, s.142(1) was rejected. The section "does not say that the right to take advantage of the landlord's covenants is annexed or incident to the term, or 'shall go with' it": *ibid.*, at 1087, *per* Mowbray, Q.C.

[91] *Flight v. Bentley* (1835) 7 Sim. 149 (rent); *Re King*, *supra* (where Lord Denning M.R., dissenting, was of opinion that the previous law remained unaltered).

[92] *Re King*, *supra*.

[93] *Re King*, *supra*, at 488.

[94] *Hunt v. Bishop* (1853) 8 Exch. 675; *Hunt v. Remnant* (1854) 9 Exch. 635. The Real Property Act 1845, s.6 (*ante*, para. 3–076), did not apply: *ibid.*

[95] s.141(3).

[96] *Rickett v. Green* [1910] 1 K.B. 253; *London and County (A. & D.) Ltd v. Wilfred Sportsman Ltd* [1971] Ch. 764.

[97] For waiver generally, see *ante*, para. 14–125.

conveyed to a third party "subject to the lease", since this is *res inter alios acta* and the reference to the lease is a conveyancing formality.[98]

(c) No liability for assignor's breach. Where L assigns the reversion to R, **15–053** R is not liable to T for breaches of covenant committed by L prior to the assignment.[99] Section 142(1) of the Law of Property Act does not transmit the consequences of past breaches of covenant. Where there is a continuing breach of covenant, the assignee of the reversion is liable for his own breach but not for the damage that has accrued prior to assignment.[1]

This general rule is subject to a statutory exception. Where a landlord of premises which consist of or include a dwelling house assigns the lease, the assignee is required to give notice in writing of the assignment, and of his name and address, to the tenant within two months.[2] If the assignee fails to do so,[3] the assignor remains liable for any breach of covenant that is committed by the assignee after the assignment.[4]

4. Relevance of privity of estate. The benefit of covenants run with the **15–054** reversion by force of the statute, and not because of the doctrine of privity of estate. Thus if the original lessee assigns the lease and later the landlord assigns the reversion, the new landlord can sue the original lessee for rent previously due from him, even though there has never been privity of estate between them.[5] By contrast, the burden of covenants passes with the reversion only where there is privity of estate.[6]

5. Merger or surrender of the reversion. At common law, if the reversion **15–055** disappeared,[7] no covenants could run with it, for privity of estate was destroyed. Thus the surrender of a head lease would—

(i) extinguish that lease;

(ii) leave the sub-lease in existence and binding on the freeholder; but

(iii) render unenforceable all the covenants in the sub-lease.[8]

---

[98] *London and County (A. & D.) Ltd v. Wilfred Sportsman Ltd, supra,* overruling *Davenport v. Smith* [1921] 2 Ch. 270, which had treated the phrase as recognising that the lease still existed.

[99] *Duncliffe v. Caerfelin Properties Ltd* [1989] 2 E.G.L.R. 38.

[1] *ibid.,* at 39, 40; [1990] Conv. 126 (J. E. Martin).

[2] L. & T.A. 1985, s.3(1).

[3] Such failure constitutes a criminal offence: *ibid.,* s.3(3).

[4] *ibid.,* s.3(3A), (3B) (inserted by L. & T.A. 1987, s.50), making the assignor jointly and severally liable for the breach with the assignee.

[5] *Arlesford Trading Co. Ltd v. Servansingh* [1971] 1 W.L.R. 1080.

[6] *Duncliffe v. Caerfelin Properties Ltd* [1989] 2 E.G.L.R. 38 at 39.

[7] For merger and surrender, see *ante,* paras 14–172–14–177.

[8] *Webb v. Russell* (1789) 3 T.R. 393. See *Electricity Supply Nominees Ltd v. Thorn EMI Ltd* (1991) 63 P. & C.R. 143 at 145, 146.

By statute however, the benefit and burden of covenants have been preserved from destruction in this way.[9]

III. SURETY COVENANTS AND THE RIGHTS OF SURETIES

15–056   It is now common practice in a lease of business premises to require a third party to guarantee the performance of the tenant's obligations in the lease either directly or by undertaking to take a lease in place of the tenant in the event that the tenant becomes insolvent and his trustee in bankruptcy[10] disclaims the lease.[11] After a period of doubt it has now been settled that such surety covenants touch and concern the land[12] and pass on an assignment of the reversion at common law.[13]

A surety who guarantees the performance of the covenants and conditions in the lease has been described as "a quasi tenant who volunteers to be a substitute or twelfth man for the tenant's team and is subject to the same rules and regulations as the player he replaces".[14] His obligations are, at least for some purposes, conterminous with those of the tenant.[15] If the surety pays the tenant's debts to the landlord, he is entitled to have assigned to him "every judgment, specialty, or other security" held by the landlord, and may enforce them to the extent of the payment that he has been compelled to make.[16] This will not entitle the surety to an assignment of the landlord's right to distrain

---

[9] L.P.A. 1925, s.139, replacing Real Property Act 1845, s.9. For examples see *Phipos v. Callegari* (1910) 54 S.J. 635; *Plummer v. David* [1920] 1 K.B. 326. The covenants are similarly preserved where the head lease expires and the sub-lease continues under the provisions of L. & T.A. 1954, Pt II: see s.65(2) of that Act. L.P.A. 1925, s.139 does not apply in such circumstances: *Electricity Supply Nominees Ltd v. Thorn EMI Ltd, supra*, at 146.

[10] Or, if the tenant is a company, its liquidator.

[11] The reason for this latter form of the covenant was that until recently, on such a disclaimer of the lease, the surety ceased to be liable on his guarantee under the much-criticised rule in *Stacey v. Hill* [1901] 1 Q.B. 660: see *Re A.E. Realisations Ltd* [1988] 1 W.L.R. 200 at 203. *Stacey v. Hill* has now been overruled by *Hindcastle Ltd v. Barbara Attenborough Associates Ltd* [1997] A.C. 70. See *ante*, para. 14–185.

[12] *Ante*, para. 15–023.

[13] *Kumar v. Dunning* [1989] Q.B. 193; *P. & A. Swift Investments v. Combined English Stores Group Plc.* [1989] A.C. 632 (direct covenant to guarantee performance); *Coronation Street Industrial Properties Ltd v. Ingall Industries Plc* [1989] 1 W.L.R. 304 (covenant to take lease).

[14] *P. & A. Swift Investments v. Combined English Stores Group Plc, supra*, at 638, *per* Lord Templeman. Pursuing the sporting analogy further (though changing the game), Lord Templeman observed that where the surety was obliged to take a lease due to the tenant's insolvency and the disclaimer of the lease, "the tenant retires mortally wounded and the surety is the substitute": *Coronation Street Industrial Properties Ltd v. Ingall Industries Plc, supra*, at 309.

[15] "There is a single set of obligations, to pay the rent and perform the covenants, owed by both tenant and guarantor": *Milverton Group Ltd v. Warner World Ltd* [1995] 2 E.G.L.R. 28 at 31, *per* Hoffmann L.J. But see *Romain v. Scuba T.V. Ltd* [1997] Q.B. 887 at 892–894. One consequence of this is that when the lease is determined by forfeiture, then in the absence of explicit provision, the surety is not liable to the landlord if he claims thereafter for mesne profits in trespass for the tenant's continued possession: *Associated Dairies Ltd v. Pierce* (1981) 43 P. & C.R. 208.

[16] Mercantile Law Amendment Act 1856, s.5.

on the tenant's chattels, because a right to distress is not a security for a debt.[17] Nor may a surety enforce the landlord's right to forfeit the lease for non-payment of rent,[18] even though that right has sometimes been regarded for some purposes as a security for payment.[19]

A surety's liability differs from that of the original tenant who, as has been explained, remains liable on the covenants in the lease for the duration of the term.[20] It is apparently the law that any material variation in the terms of the lease will discharge the surety,[21] but not the original tenant.[22]

IV. OPERATION OF FORFEITURE CLAUSES

1. Lack of privity. An occupier of leasehold land (*e.g.* a sub-tenant) may be in neither privity of contract nor privity of estate with the head landlord, and so not be bound by the covenants of the head lease; yet he may have to observe them under penalty of forfeiture. This question can arise only where there is an express forfeiture clause.[23] Normally this will be found in the head lease, but it may also be one of the terms of an assignment of a lease[24] or of a grant in fee simple.[25] It creates a conditional right of re-entry that is a proprietary interest[26] and is not merely the benefit of a covenant. Where the right of re-entry is reserved by the landlord in a legal lease, the right will be legal and will therefore bind any occupant of the property.[27] However, where

15–057

---

[17] *Re Russell* (1885) 29 Ch.D. 254.

[18] *BSE Trading Ltd v. Hands* [1996] 2 E.G.L.R. 214 at 216. In that case S, one of three co-sureties, was a party to an agreement by which T (who was in arrears with the rent) surrendered the lease to L in consideration of S paying a premium to L. It was held that S could not claim any contribution towards the cost of the premium from the co-sureties. "There is no security in the form of the lease to which the surety and co-surety might have recourse if payment of the rent is made by a surety": *ibid.*, at 216, *per* Peter Gibson L.J.

[19] *Howard v. Fanshawe* [1895] 2 Ch. 581 at 588 ("simply a security for the rent", *per* Stirling J.); *Exchange Travel Agency Ltd v. Triton Property Trust Plc* [1991] 2 E.G.L.R. 50 at 51. For a full analysis of the extent to which such a right can be regarded as a security; see *Razzaq v. Pala* [1997] 1 W.L.R. 1336. The weight of authority is now against treating a right to forfeit as a security: see *Re Lomax Leisure* [1999] 3 All E.R. 22.

[20] *Ante*, para. 15–008.

[21] *Holme v. Brunskill* (1878) 3 Q.B.D. 495. Although doubts have been expressed as to the correctness of this decision: *Wardens etc. of the Mystery of Mercers of the City of London v. New Hampshire Insurance Co.* [1992] 1 W.L.R. 762 n.; transcript, p. 30 (where Scott L.J. suggested, *obiter*, that discharge might not be absolute but *pro tanto*), it continues to be applied: see *Howard de Walden Estates Ltd v. Pasta Place Ltd* [1995] 1 E.G.L.R. 79; *Metropolitan Properties Co. (Regis) Ltd v. Bartholomew* [1996] 1 E.G.L.R. 82. The mere fact that the cost of complying with the terms of the lease, *e.g.* where the intensity of occupation leads to an increase in service charges, will not discharge the surety: *Metropolitan Properties Co. (Regis) Ltd v. Bartholomew, supra*, at 83.

[22] *Baynton v. Morgan* (1888) 22 Q.B.D. 74.

[23] *Ante*, para. 14–122.

[24] As in *Shiloh Spinners Ltd v. Harding* [1973] A.C. 691 (right of re-entry reserved by assignor of lease to enforce covenants given by assignee).

[25] *i.e.* a conditional fee: *ante*, para. 3–064.

[26] L.P.A. 1925, s.1(2)(e); *ante*, para. 4–054.

[27] Where title is registered, a grantee or transferee for valuable consideration takes the land subject to all obligations and incidents to the estate transferred, which necessarily includes any right of re-entry: L.R.A. 1925, s.23(1)(a).

it is reserved by a tenant on an assignment of the lease, it will be equitable.[28] Where title is unregistered, this equitable right will be binding on any assignee of the lease with notice of it,[29] but where title is registered, an assignee will take subject to it only if it is registered as a minor interest.[30] The fact that the occupier of the land may not be bound by the covenants themselves is immaterial.[31] It may indeed be just for this reason that a forfeiture clause is employed.

For example, L demises property to T, T covenanting to repair and L reserving a right of re-entry for breach of this covenant. If T sub-demises to S, and S fails to repair, L can then re-enter and determine both T's and S's estates, subject to the statutory restrictions on enforcing forfeiture and the provisions for relief against forfeiture.[32-33] T could give S no better rights against L than T had himself, and T's rights were subject to forfeiture. S's failure to repair places T in breach of his covenant.

15–058   **2. Covenants not touching and concerning the land.** The law is less clear where the covenant which precipitates the forfeiture is a covenant of the kind which does not "touch and concern the land". In the first place, section 79 of the Law of Property Act 1925 does not apply to such covenants, so that they only apply to the covenantor personally: he is not liable for the acts of his successors in title unless the covenant expressly so provides. Prior to 1926 a right of re-entry could not be exercised in respect of such a covenant. At common law, the right of re-entry did not pass on an assignment of the reversion, but it was made to do so by the Grantees of Reversions Act 1540.[34] That Act dealt with covenants and conditions in similar terms, so that when the courts engrafted on to it the qualification that it applied only to covenants which touched and concerned the land,[35] this restriction was applied equally to conditional rights of re-entry. Accordingly, an assignee of the reversion could enforce a forfeiture clause only in respect of a breach of a covenant which touched and concerned the land.[36]

15–059   But the statutory provision which has superseded the Act of 1540 (now section 141 of the Law of Property Act 1925) gives to the assignee of a reversion the benefit of "every covenant or provision therein contained,

---

[28] *Semble*; see [1973] C.L.J. 218 (P. Fairest). The remarks of Lord Wilberforce in *Shiloh Spinners Ltd v. Harding, supra*, at 719 are ambiguous on this point (in that case, the right of re-entry had been reserved by the assignor for a perpetuity period and not for the residue of the lease). It is uncertain whether a right of entry that was reserved for the unexpired residue of a lease would be one that was "exercisable over or in respect of a term of years absolute" within L.P.A. 1925, s.1(2)(e). *cf. ante*, para. 4–054.

[29] *ibid.*

[30] L.R.A. 1925, s.101.

[31] *Shiloh Spinners Ltd v. Harding, supra.*

[32-33] See *ante*, paras 14–152 *et seq.*

[34] *Ante*, para. 15–046.

[35] *Ante*, para. 15–046.

[36] *Stevens v. Copp* (1868) L.R. 4 Ex. 20 (proviso for re-entry in case of offence against game laws; breach by sub-tenant of an assignee of the lease; action for possession brought by an assignee of reversion failed).

having reference to the subject-matter thereof . . . and every condition of re-entry and other condition therein contained". This wording, it will be noticed, qualifies covenants but not conditions, and appears to intend that the assignee shall be entitled to re-enter even where the condition is something unrelated to the land. This seems reasonable, for now that rights of re-entry are freely assignable[37] there would seem to be no reason why the assignee should not take all the assignable rights of the assignor, and take advantage of a condition that (for example) the lease should be determinable "when X returns from Rome". The House of Lords appears to favour this view.[38]

3. Assignment or sub-lease. There remain the cases where the lease is   **15–060**
assigned, or a sub-lease is granted. The latter case presents no difficulty: the sub-lease depends upon the head lease, and shares its fate if it is determined by forfeiture, unless the sub-tenant succeeds in obtaining relief.[39] The more difficult question is whether an assignee of a lease is subject to forfeiture for non-observance of a covenant which does not touch and concern the land. On principle, a right of re-entry for breach of covenant should be exercisable against any assignee of the lease, as well as against any other third party, whether or not the covenant touches and concerns the land; for a right of re-entry is a proprietary interest in its own right,[40–41] and may be made exercisable on any event, *e.g.* "when X returns from Rome". In the only direct decision in which the point has been considered, it was suggested that a condition of re-entry would run with the lease at law only if the condition touched and concerned the land.[42] However, there must be considerable doubt as to the correctness of this dictum.[43] A right to re-enter for breach of covenant should in principle be exercisable whenever there is a breach of covenant.[44] If an assignee of a lease acts in a manner that is contrary to a covenant in the lease that does not touch and concern the land, he incurs no liability himself on that covenant, but he does nonetheless place the original tenant in breach of it.[45] The landlord should therefore be able to forfeit the lease.

---

[37] L.P.A. 1925, s.4(2); *ante*, para. 3–076.

[38] See *Shiloh Spinners Ltd v. Harding* [1973] A.C. 691 at 717, disparaging *Stevens v. Copp, supra,* n. 36.

[39] *Ante*, para. 14–161. See, *e.g. Cresswell v. Davidson* (1887) 56 L.T. 811; *Westminster (Duke) v. Swinton* [1948] 1 K.B. 524.

[40–41] L.P.A. 1925, s.1(2)(e); *ante*, paras 4–054, 15–057.

[42] *Horsey Estate Ltd v. Steiger* [1899] 2 Q.B. 79 at 88, 89, where however, the difference between conditions and covenants was not observed, and the condition (against the tenant company's liquidation) in any case touched and concerned the land. The only authority relied on related to assignments of reversions, which are governed by the special construction of the Act of 1540; *ante*, para. 15–058.

[43] See the hostile references to *Horsey Estate Ltd v. Steiger, supra,* in *Shiloh Spinners Ltd v. Harding, supra,* at 717.

[44] A right of re-entry is normally stated to be exercisable in respect of *any* breach of covenant: see, *e.g. The Encyclopaedia of Forms and Precedents* (5th ed., 1986), vol. 22, para. 750.

[45] *cf. Wright v. Dean* [1948] Ch. 686 at 693–695, dealing with the converse case, where L assigned the reversion and R acted contrary to a covenant in the lease that did not touch and concern the land. L was held liable to T.

C. Transmission by Other Means

15–061   In certain cases benefits and burdens which will not be transmitted under the rules set out above will nevertheless pass to assignees. This is of special importance in relation to options in a lease to purchase the freehold,[46] which do not touch and concern the land.[47]

15–062   **1. Benefit.** The general principle is that the benefit of any contract is assignable.[48] Accordingly, the benefit of a covenant in a lease is assignable as such, even though it does not touch and concern the land and so run with the land automatically under the rules explained above. For example, a lease may contain an option to purchase the freehold, which will not run automatically[49]; but the benefit of the option will pass to an assignee of the lease if the assignment is construed as extending to the benefit of the option as such. The benefit does not cease to be separately assignable merely because the option is contained in a lease, or because it is assigned along with the lease.[50] Even the conventional definition in the lease of "lessee" as including successors in title has been treated as evidence that an ordinary assignment of the lease was intended to carry also the benefit of the option.[51] There must however be some doubt as to the correctness of this conclusion.[52]

15–063   **2. Burden.** Leases may contain covenants of the kind which, under principles explained elsewhere, create interests in land, so that the burden will run with the land. Thus restrictive (as opposed to positive) covenants are equitable interests which are capable of binding assignees and others,[53] and their effect is not reduced merely because they occur in a lease.[54] Similarly an equitable interest will normally arise if the owner of land binds himself to sell it or let it, or grants an option for sale or lease.[55] Subject to the rules as to purchase without notice and registration as land charges (where title is unregistered) or

---

[46] On the nature of options, see *Spiro v. Glencrown Properties Ltd* [1991] Ch. 537; *ante*, para. 12–012.

[47] *Ante*, para. 15–058.

[48] *Ante*, para. 14–051.

[49] *Ante*, para. 15–027.

[50] *Griffith v. Pelton* [1958] Ch. 205; *Re Button's Lease* [1964] Ch. 263.

[51] *ibid.* Yet provided the lease does not indicate that the option is purely personal, it should be the terms of the assignment rather than of the lease that are decisive: see [1957] C.L.J. 148 (H.W.R.W.). See also *Re Adams and the Kensington Vestry* (1883) 24 Ch.D. 199 at 206 (on appeal, (1884) 27 Ch.D. 394); *Batchelor v. Murphy* [1926] A.C. 63; (1957) 73 L.Q.R. 452 (R.E.M.); (1958) 74 L.Q.R. 242 (W. J. Mowbray). *County Hotel and Wine Co. Ltd v. L.N.W. Ry* [1918] 2 K.B. 251 at 256, 257 (on appeal [1919] 2 K.B. 29; [1921] 1 A.C. 85) seems to show the right approach.

[52] Although *Griffith v. Pelton, supra*, was applied in *Coastplace Ltd v. Hartley* [1987] Q.B. 948 (holding that the benefit of a surety covenant passes on assignment of the reversion), Browne-Wilkinson V.-C. subsequently stated that he had "considerable difficulty in understanding what *Griffith v. Pelton* did decide": *Kumar v. Dunning* [1989] Q.B. 193 at 207 (holding that a surety covenant touched and concerned the land and was thereby annexed to the reversion). See [1988] C.L.J. 180 (C.H.).

[53] *Post*, para. 16–032.

[54] But for a difference as to registration, see *ante*, para. 5–103.

[55] *Ante*, paras 4–025, 5–099, 12–051.

protection on the register (where title is registered), such covenants will accordingly bind any assignee or other person interested in the land.[56] Even legal interests can sometimes be created by what in form are mere covenants, for example by covenants creating rentcharges[57] and covenants creating easements, such as rights of way.[58]

Part 3

STATUTORY LIABILITY: COVENANTS IN LEASES GRANTED AFTER 1995

Section 1. The Abolition of Privity of Contract: Position of the Original Parties

1. Introduction

(a) The Landlord and Tenant (Covenants) Act 1995. In leases granted after   **15–064** 1995,[59] both the liability of the parties under the covenants of the tenancy and the circumstances in which the benefit and burden of those covenants will pass on an assignment of the lease or reversion are determined according to the provisions of the Landlord and Tenant (Covenants) Act 1995.[60] That Act consists of three elements.[61] First, it implements in modified form the recommendations of the Law Commission[62] for the abolition of the rule that the original tenant remains liable throughout the duration of the lease for the performance of the covenants of the tenancy.[63] Secondly, it gives effect to the unpublished recommendations of the Law Commission for modernising and rationalising the rules on the transmission of the benefit and burden of covenants in tenancies and for integrating the proposals for the abolition of

---

[56] Consider *Woodall v. Clifton* [1905] 2 Ch. 257, where the option, had it not been void for perpetuity, would have bound the reversion in equity, even though it did not touch and concern the land and so run at law. The reason why the court decided that it did not run at law was because it had been argued that all covenants capable of running at law were exempt from the perpetuity rule. See the fuller explanation at (1955) 19 Conv. (N.S.) 255 (H.W.R.W.).

[57] *Post*, para. 18–014.

[58] *Post*, para. 18–092.

[59] For the meaning of leases granted after 1995, see L. & T.C.A. 1995, s.1; *ante*, para. 15–007.

[60] For an interesting account of the legislative history of the Act, see (1996) 59 M.L.R. 78 (M. Davey). For a valuable survey of the Act and its effect, see [1996] C.L.J. 313 (S. Bridge).

[61] When introduced as a Private Members' Bill under the Ten Minute Rule by Peter Thurnham M.P., it contained only the first of the three elements of the Act. The Bill received government support, but to secure its passage, it was substantially amended in its course through Parliament, and the second and third elements were thereby introduced. For the relevant Parliamentary debates, see *Hansard* (H.L.), June 21, 1995, vol. 565 cols 354–400; July 5, 1995, vol. 565, cols 1104–1109; *Hansard* (H.C.), July 14, 1995, vol. 263, cols 1236–1269.

[62] See (1988) Law Com. No. 174; *ante*, para. 15–014.

[63] For this rule, see *ante*, para. 15–008.

privity of contract into the law on covenants.[64] Thirdly, it incorporates the results of an agreement made between representatives of the property industry which were thought to be necessary to make the abolition of privity of contract acceptable to landlords.[65] The components of this third element, which have already been explained, are—

> (i) the power of a landlord to impose conditions on the giving of consent to an assignment[66];
>
> (ii) the requirement that the original tenant be notified within six months where an assignee defaults on the payment of some fixed charge[67];
>
> (iii) the prohibition on increasing the original tenant's liability by variation of the covenants in the lease[68]; and
>
> (iv) the right of an original tenant in certain circumstances to the grant of an overriding lease.[69]

15–065   *(b) Applicability of the Act.* The provisions of the Act that deal with its first and second elements apply to all tenancies granted after 1995.[70] The general principle that underlies these two elements is that a party to a lease should be subject to the burdens and should enjoy the benefits only for the time that he is respectively the tenant or the landlord.[71] There are three concepts which are fundamental to the Act, and all are broadly defined. First, the Act applies to a "tenancy", which means any lease or tenancy, including a sub-tenancy and an agreement for a lease, but not a mortgage term.[72] Secondly, the Act is concerned with the rights and liabilities of the parties under a "covenant" of the tenancy. A covenant is defined to include any term, condition and obligation, and a covenant of the tenancy includes a covenant contained in a collateral agreement (whether that agreement is made before or after the tenancy).[73] A covenant may be express or implied, or one imposed by law.[74] The Act distinguishes between "landlord" and "tenant" covenants which are

---

[64] The Law Commission had intended to consult on these proposals and had prepared a consultation paper for this purpose. The introduction of the Bill in Parliament precluded its publication. The Commission's proposals would have codified and clarified the law for existing leases as well as making proposals for new leases. It was not thought appropriate to include the former proposals in the Bill, given its curious legislative path.

[65] This agreement, between the British Property Federation and the British Retail Consortium, was the subject of public consultation by the Lord Chancellor's Department.

[66] *Ante*, para. 14–263.

[67] *Ante*, para. 15–015.

[68] *Ante*, para. 15–016.

[69] *Ante*, para. 15–017.

[70] L. & T.C.A. 1995, ss.1, 31; S.I. 1995 No. 2963.

[71] See Law Com. No. 174, para. 4.1; *ante*, para. 15–014.

[72] L. & T.C.A. 1995, s.28(1).

[73] *ibid*. This could therefore include covenants undertaken by an assignee in a licence to assign: *post*, para. 15–069.

[74] L. & T.C.A. 1995, s.2(1). For an example of a covenant imposed by law, see L. & T.A. 1985, s.11; *ante* para. 14–222.

covenants that fall to be complied with by the landlord and by the tenant respectively.[75] Thirdly, the transaction that is fundamental to the operation of the Act is an "assignment", whether of the lease or of the reversion. It is widely defined to include an equitable assignment and an assignment in breach of covenant or by operation of law.[76] Although the Act refers to assignments by "the landlord" or "the tenant", those expressions are taken to include any assignment by which the whole of the party's interest is transferred, even if it is not effected by him but by some third party, *e.g.* a mortgagee in exercise of his power of sale.[77] It should be noted that a lease of the reversion does not operate as a *pro tanto* assignment of a lease by operation of law as it does in relation to leases granted before 1996.[78]

The effect of these provisions is that, in relation to leases granted after 1995, no distinction is drawn between either legal and equitable leases or legal and equitable assignments.[79] The reasons for adopting this course were—

(i) to simplify the law by having just one set of rules for the transmission of the benefit and burden of covenants[80]; and

(ii) to prevent an obvious means of evading the provisions of the Act.[81]

2. Liability of the original tenant

(a) Release from liability on assignment. Subject to exceptions applicable to assignments made in breach of covenant or by operation of law,[82] the Act abolishes the liability of the original tenant for breaches of the covenants in the tenancy committed by any assignee after the lease has been assigned. Where a tenant assigns the whole of the premises let to him, he is released from the tenant covenants in the tenancy and can no longer enforce the landlord covenants.[83] Where the assignment is of part only of the premises let, then to the extent that the tenant covenants fall to be complied with in relation to the part assigned, he is released from them and can no longer enforce the

15–066

---

[75] L. & T.C.A. 1995, s.28(1).

[76] *ibid.* There are however special provisions applicable to such assignments: see *post*, para. 15–074.

[77] L. & T.C.A. 1995, s.28(6).

[78] This is explained *post*, para. 15–084.

[79] Compare the position as regards leases granted prior to 1996: see *ante*, paras 15–033, 15–047.

[80] This was thought to be desirable not least because of the uncertainty as to the applicable rules where an equitable lease is assigned or there is an equitable assignment of a legal lease: see [1978] C.L.J. 98 (R. J. Smith); *ante*, para. 15–047. In theory, the effect of treating an equitable assignment as a completed assignment could mean that a person who had merely contracted to purchase a lease could find himself liable on the covenants of the lease. However, in those circumstances, the purchaser would have a right to indemnity against the vendor and could in many cases terminate the sale on the ground that the vendor had failed to show a good title (because a breach of covenant might lead to a forfeiture of the lease).

[81] For the anti-avoidance provisions of the Act, see s.25; *post*, para. 15–096.

[82] For these, see L. & T.C.A. 1995, s.11; *post*, para. 15–074.

[83] L. & T.C.A. 1995, s.5(2).

landlord covenants.[84] Where a tenant is released from the tenant covenants, any person who has guaranteed the performance of those covenants will also be released.[85] Any provision by which a guarantor undertook to remain liable even after the release of the tenant would be void under the anti-avoidance provisions of the Act.[86]

15–067   *(b) Authorised guarantee agreements.* Although the Act abolishes the privity rule, the tenant may be obliged to guarantee the performance of the tenant covenants by the assignee until the next assignment.[87] This will be the case where—

> (i) on an assignment the tenant is to any extent released from a tenant covenant[88]; and

> (ii) the tenancy contains a covenant against assignment, whether absolute or qualified.[89]

If the covenant against assignment is absolute, the landlord is entitled in these circumstances to require the tenant to enter into an authorised guarantee agreement as a condition of his consent to any assignment.[90] However, where the covenant is merely qualified, the landlord will be able to do this only if he has stipulated in the lease that the entry into such an authorised guarantee agreement will be a condition of the giving of consent to any assignment,[91] or if he has not, if it is reasonable to require the tenant to enter into such an agreement.[92] The application of these provisions in the case of excluded assignments is explained below.[93]

An authorised guarantee agreement may impose on the assigning tenant all or any of the following—

> (a) liability as sole or principal debtor for the obligations owed by the assignee under the tenancy[94];

---

[84] *ibid.,* s.5(3).
[85] *ibid.,* s.24(2).
[86] *ibid.,* s.25(1); *post,* para. 15–096.
[87] L. & T.C.A. 1995, s.16.
[88] *ibid.,* s.16(1).
[89] See *ante,* para. 14–259. This is most likely to be the case in business rather than residential tenancies.
[90] L. & T.C.A. 1995, s.16(3). If these pre-conditions for an authorised guarantee agreement are not satisfied, any such agreement entered into by the tenant on an assignment will be void: *ibid.,* s.25; *post,* para. 15–096.
[91] L. & T.A. 1927, s.19(1A) (inserted by L. & T.C.A. 1995, s.22); *ante,* para. 14–263. It is anticipated that this is likely to be the situation in almost every case.
[92] L. & T.A. 1988, s.1; *ante,* paras 14–263, 14–264. This requirement is imported because L. & T.C.A. 1995, s.16(3)(b) provides that the condition must be one that is lawfully imposed.
[93] *Post,* para. 15–074.
[94] The advantage of this form of guarantee from a landlord's perspective is that the surety is not released by any material variation in the terms of the lease, as would otherwise be the case: *ante,* para. 15–056.

(b) liability as guarantor in respect of the assignee's performance of the covenants, provided that it is no more onerous than liability under (a) would be;

(c) in the event that the lease is disclaimed,[95] an obligation to take a new lease on terms not more onerous as to duration and covenants than the lease which he had assigned.[96]

An authorised guarantee agreement is subject to the rules of law applicable to **15–068** guarantees, and in particular those relating to the release of the surety.[97] Furthermore, the tenant will be liable for any fixed charge under such an agreement only if he is informed of it by notice within six months of the charge falling due.[98] If he makes full payment of any amount which he is required to meet under the guarantee, he is entitled to call for the grant of an overriding lease.[99]

The Act makes provision to ensure that a tenant's liability ceases when the assignee himself assigns. It provides that an agreement will not be an authorised guarantee agreement if it purports to impose on the tenant either—

(i) any requirement to guarantee performance of any tenant covenant by anybody other than the assignee; or

(ii) any liability, restriction or requirement after the assignee is released from any tenant covenant under the provision of the Act.[1]

Any such agreement will be void.[2] It has been explained that if, prior to the assignment, performance of the tenant covenants is guaranteed by a third party, that surety will be released on assignment.[3] If the landlord purports to require a surety to guarantee performance by the assignee, that agreement will not be an authorised guarantee agreement (which may be made only with a tenant[4]) and it may be void because it frustrates the operation of provisions of

---

[95] On the insolvency of the assignee: see *ante*, para. 14–185.

[96] L. & T.C.A. 1995, s.16(5). The agreement may also make incidental or supplementary provisions: *ibid.* Where the lease was either granted to the tenant in pursuance of his obligations under an authorised guarantee agreement or had revested in him following disclaimer by an assignee, he may still be required to enter into an authorised guarantee agreement: *ibid.* s.16(7).

[97] *ibid.*, s.16(8). Thus a material variation in the terms of the lease will discharge the tenant from his guarantee: see *ante*, para. 15–056. Furthermore, if the tenant is required to discharge the assignee's indebtedness, he will have a right of recoupment against that assignee: *ante*.

[98] L. & T.C.A. 1995, s.17; *ante*, para. 15–015.

[99] L. & T.C.A. 1995, s.19; *ante*, para. 15–017.

[1] L. & T.C.A. 1995, s.16(4).

[2] *ibid.*, s.25; *post*, para. 15–096.

[3] L. & T.C.A. 1995, s.24(2); *ante*, para. 15–066.

[4] L. & T.C.A. 1995, s.16(1).

the Act for the release of a surety on assignment by the tenant.[5] However, in practice, landlords may grant leases to tenants and sureties jointly, so that on an assignment, both parties could be required to enter into an authorised guarantee agreement.[6]

15–069   **3. Liability of an assignee on a direct covenant.** In the absence of any express agreement with the landlord, an assignee of a lease ceases to be liable on the covenants in the lease after he has further assigned it.[7] He has no need to resort to the provisions of the Act to be released from the tenant covenants, and cannot be required to enter into an authorised guarantee agreement even if the landlord's consent to assignment is needed.[8] However, it has been explained that an assignee of a commercial lease is commonly required to enter into a direct covenant with the landlord to observe all the terms of the tenancy as a condition of the landlord's licence to assign.[9] In this way he becomes subject to the tenant covenants of the tenancy,[10] and but for the Act, that liability would continue after a further assignment by him. In these circumstances, the provisions of the Acts[11] relating to the release of covenants and to authorised guarantee agreements will apply to the assignee in the same way as they apply to the original tenant.

4. The liability of the original landlord

15–070   *(a) Release on first assignment.* Where a landlord assigns his reversion in whole or part, his position is different from that of the tenant.[12] He not only retains his right to enforce the tenant covenants[13] but he also remains liable on the landlord covenants in the lease. However, except in those cases where the assignment is by operation of law,[14] he may apply to the tenant to be released from the landlord covenants of the tenancy,[15] whereupon he loses his right to enforce the tenant covenants as from the assignment.[16] If the landlord assigns only part of the reversion, these provisions apply to the part in question. To secure such a release, the landlord must serve a notice[17] on the tenant either

---

[5] *ibid.*, s.25(1); *post*, para. 15–096. Prior to the 1995 Act, there was no practice of requiring that guarantees should themselves be guaranteed.

[6] *cf.* [1996] C.L.J. 313 at 340 (S. Bridge).

[7] *Ante*, para. 15–039.

[8] That obligation arises only if the tenant is to any extent released from a tenant covenant by virtue of the Act; *ante*, para. 15–067. If the assignee did enter into such an agreement, it would be void under L. & T.C.A. 1995, s.25; *post*, para. 15–096.

[9] *Ante*, para. 15–013.

[10] Even though these are contained in the licence to assign. That licence is, for the purposes of the Act, a collateral agreement, and the covenants in it are therefore tenant covenants: L. & T.C.A. 1995, s.28(1); *ante*, para. 15–065.

[11] See *ante*, paras 15–066, 15–067.

[12] The reason for this difference is that a tenant has no control over an assignment by his landlord, although the landlord may require his consent to the assignment of the lease: see Law Com. No. 174, para. 4.16.

[13] This is unlikely to be a right of any consequence: see *post*, para. 15–074, n.35.

[14] For such excluded assignments, see L. & T.C.A. 1995, s.11; *post*, para. 15–074.

[15] L. & T.C.A. 1995, s.6(2).

[16] *ibid.*

[17] For the form of notice, see *ibid.*, s.27; S.I. 1995 No. 2964.

before or within four weeks of the assignment.[18] This must inform the tenant of both the actual or intended assignment and the request that the covenant be released.[19] The covenant will then be released unless the tenant serves a written counter-notice on the landlord within four weeks of service objecting to the release. In those circumstances there will be no release unless either—

> (i) the landlord applies to the county court for, and obtains, a declaration that it is reasonable for the covenant to be released; or

> (ii) the tenant in writing withdraws his objection.[20]

Any release is effective from the date of the assignment.[21]

(b) Agreements to release in advance void. Although either party to a **15–071** tenancy may release the other from a covenant,[22] any provision in the lease by which a tenant binds himself to release the landlord on an assignment of the reversion, will be void as contravening the anti-avoidance provisions of the Act.[23] The expressed intention of the provisions is that a tenant should be able to object to the release of landlord covenants in cases where it is unreasonable for the landlord to seek it.[24] For a tenant to undertake in advance to give such a release on an assignment by the landlord, regardless of the circumstances that might then prevail, would plainly frustrate that purpose.

(c) Release on subsequent assignment. There may be occasions where a **15–072** landlord is not released from the landlord covenants when he assigns the reversion, either because he did not seek or was unable to obtain a release on that occasion, or because the assignment was by operation of law and therefore outside the scope of the release provisions.[25] If this happens, the landlord may apply to be released from the covenants on any subsequent assignment of the reversion.[26] To obtain such a release, the landlord must apply to the tenant for the time being[27] in the way that has already been explained.[28]

5. Effect of release. Where any person is released from a covenant by **15–073** virtue of the provisions of the Act, his liability for any breach of covenant

---

[18] It was originally proposed that the notice should pre-date the assignment: see Law Com. No. 174, Draft Bill, cl. 6. This was changed in the Act because of concerns raised by landlords who often wish to keep negotiations about the assignment of the reversion confidential.

[19] L. & T.C.A. 1995, s.8(1).

[20] *ibid.*, s.8(2).

[21] *ibid.*, s.8(3).

[22] *ibid.*, s.26(1).

[23] *ibid.*, s.25(1)(a); *post*, para. 15–096.

[24] *cf.* L. & T.C.A. 1995, s.8(2)(b). An example of an unreasonable request for a release would be where the landlord was under onerous repairing obligations in the lease and was proposing to assign the reversion to an assignee who lacked the means to comply with them.

[25] *Post*, para. 15–074.

[26] L. & T.C.A. 1995, s.7(1), (2).

[27] See the definition of "tenant" in L. & T.C.A. 1995, s.28(1).

[28] *ibid.*, s.8; *supra*.

committed before the release remains unaffected.[29] Conversely, where under the Act a person ceases to be entitled to the benefit of a covenant, he retains his right to sue for the breach of any covenant that occurred before he ceased to be entitled,[30] though he is free to assign that right.[31]

6. Excluded assignments

15–074   *(a) No release until next assignment.* The provisions of the Act by which the tenant is automatically released from the tenant covenants on an assignment of the lease, and a landlord may be released from the landlord covenants on application to the tenant where a reversion is assigned, have no application to excluded assignments.[32] An excluded assignment is one that is either made in breach of covenant or takes effect by operation of law.[33] In practice, the former will apply only to assignments of leases.[34] Where a party makes an excluded assignment, he remains bound by his covenants of the tenancy but retains his right to enforce those of the other party.[35] It is only on the next assignment that is not an excluded assignment that the Act's provisions for the release from covenants are operative.[36] Two examples will demonstrate their operation.

> (i) If T transfers the lease to A in breach of a qualified covenant against assignment, T remains liable on the tenant covenants in the lease and can enforce the landlord covenants unless and until A assigns the lease to B with L's consent. T is then automatically released and loses his rights of enforcement.

> (ii) Where L dies and his reversion passes to R under L's will, L's estate cannot apply to be released from the landlord covenants, but can continue to enforce the tenant covenants of the lease. It is only when R assigns the reversion, that L's estate can apply to T to be released from the landlord covenants and will, on release, lose their rights to enforce the tenant covenants.

Because T remains liable on the tenant covenants under the lease, he is entitled to be notified by L of any demand for a fixed charge within six months

---

[29] L. & T.C.A. 1995, s.24(1).
[30] *ibid.*, s.24(4).
[31] *ibid.*, s.23(2); *post*, para. 15–093.
[32] L. & T.C.A. 1995, s.11.
[33] *ibid.*, s.11(1).
[34] *i.e.* where the tenant assigns a lease in breach of a qualified or absolute covenant against assignment. For such covenants, see *ante*, para. 14–259.
[35] L. & T.C.A. 1995, s.11(2)–(4). The continuing right to enforce the other party's covenants is likely to be of little practical importance. Once a lease or reversion has been assigned, the assignor is unlikely to suffer any loss from any subsequent breach of covenant by the landlord or the tenant (as the case may be). A former landlord will be unable to sue the tenant for arrears of rent falling due after the assignment of the reversion, because he has assigned the right to the rents and profits of the land and will be estopped by his deed from claiming them.
[36] Where the next assignment is only of part of the lease or reversion, it is only in relation to that part that the provisions apply: L. & T.C.A. 1995, s.11(7).

of it falling due,[37] and, if he is obliged to pay it in full, may call for an overriding lease.[38]

(b) Authorised guarantee agreements. No obligation to enter into an author-   **15–075**
ised guarantee agreement can arise on an excluded assignment of a tenancy, because the original tenant remains liable on the tenant covenants.[39] However, on the next assignment of the lease that is not an excluded assignment, that tenant is released. If the tenancy contains an absolute or qualified covenant against assignment the landlord may then be able to require him to enter into an authorised guarantee agreement on that next assignment. This will be so even if the landlord also requires the assignor of the lease to enter into an authorised guarantee agreement as well. Thus if T assigns a lease to A in breach of a covenant to assign without L's consent, and A subsequently assigns the lease to B with L's consent, L may then require both T and A to enter into authorised guarantee agreements. There is no injustice in this. L might reasonably have objected to the assignment to A, *e.g.* because of his weak financial position. A's guarantee may therefore be of little value. T must therefore guarantee the performance of the covenants until B assigns the lease with L's consent.

7. Management companies. It is not uncommon for properties which are   **15–076**
leased to be managed for the landlord by a management company.[40] The management company, which will be a party to the lease, will be obliged to perform certain services. The cost of these is likely to be met by a service charge payable by the tenant or by a management fee payable by the landlord. It was obviously necessary to bring such companies within the scheme of the Act to ensure (in particular) that after a tenant had assigned his lease, he could no longer enforce the company's obligations, and equally, that he should be under no liabilities to the company for any defaults by the assignee.[41] The Act therefore makes specific provision in this regard for any third party[42] who is liable as principal under a covenant of the tenancy to discharge any function that has to be carried out in relation to all or any of the premises which have been let.[43]

The Act achieves its objective by employing a fiction. A covenant of the tenancy which confers rights that are exercisable by or against the third party

---

[37] *ibid.,* s.17; *ante,* para. 15–015.
[38] L. & T.C.A. 1995, s.19; *ante,* para. 15–017.
[39] It is only where the tenant is released that the obligation can arise: see L. & T.C.A. 1995, s.16(1); *ante,* para. 15–067.
[40] *cf. Hafton Properties Ltd v. Camp* [1994] 1 E.G.L.R. 67 (the court would not imply a term in a lease that the landlord would carry out repairs which the management company had failed to execute).
[41] Had provision not been made for such bodies, landlords would have been able to circumvent the provisions of the Act abolishing first tenant liability by the simple expedient of using a management company.
[42] Other than a guarantor or a person who has undertaken some financial liability referable to the performance or otherwise of a covenant of the tenancy by another party to it: L. & T.C.A. 1995, s.12(1)(b).
[43] *ibid.,* s.12(1)(a).

is to be treated for the purpose of transmitting the benefit or burden of it as if it were—

    (i) a tenant covenant, where those rights are exercisable by the landlord or against the tenant; and

    (ii) a landlord covenant, where those rights are exercisable by the tenant or against the landlord.[44]

The effect is as follows. First, on an assignment of the lease or the reversion, the benefit and burden of any covenant with the third party will pass to the assignee under the provisions of the Act which regulate transmission.[45] Secondly, where a tenant assigns his lease, he is thereby released from the burden, but also loses the benefit, of any covenant with the third party, in the same way as he would as regards the landlord. Thirdly, where the landlord assigns his reversion, he remains liable on any covenant made with, but can continue to enforce any covenant that falls to be performed by, the third party. However he is entitled to apply to the third party for release from the covenant in the same way as he can apply to a tenant for release from a landlord covenant.[46]

It was not intended that the Act should make provision for the situation where the management company wishes to transfer its rights and obligations to some other body. Such a transfer would require a novation just as it does in relation to leases granted before 1996.

15–078   **8. Indemnity.** The situations in which an assignor of either a tenancy or a reversion may require an indemnity from the assignee are much more limited than is the case in relation to leases granted before 1996. It is only where the assignor is not released on assignment or where he enters into an authorised guarantee agreement that such an indemnity may be required. The Act abolishes the implied statutory indemnity covenant by the assignee[47] as regards leases granted after 1995.[48] In those situations where the assignor remains liable after assignment, he has an implied right to restitution from the assignee should he be called upon to meet the latter's default.[49]

Section 2. Position of Assignees

15–079   **1. A statutory code.** It has been explained that, for leases granted after 1995, the Landlord and Tenant (Covenants) Act 1995 lays down a self-

---

[44] *ibid.*, s.12(2), (3).
[45] *ibid.*, s.3; *post*, paras 15–079 *et seq.*
[46] *ibid.*, s.12(3)–(5); see *ante*, para. 15–070. The rules governing apportionment (*post*, para. 15–089.) also apply: *ibid.*, s.12(4).
[47] L.P.A. 1925, s.77(1)(C) and (D); L.R.A. 1925, s.24(1)(b); *ante*, para. 15–043.
[48] L. & T.C.A. 1995, s.14.
[49] See *Moule v. Garrett* (1872) L.R. 7 Ex. 101; *ante*, para. 15–042.

contained code[50] for the transmission of the benefit and burden of landlord and tenant covenants that supersedes the existing law.[51] The concept of privity of estate as traditionally understood[52] has no place in the statutory scheme, for the rules apply even where the lease is equitable or where there has been an equitable assignment of a legal lease.[53]

2. Covenants which are transmissible. The Act abrogates the requirement **15–080** that the benefit or burden of a leasehold covenant will pass on an assignment of the lease or of the reversion only if it touches and concerns the land.[54] The objective of that requirement was to prevent purely personal covenants passing on an assignment. This is now achieved more simply under the provisions of the Act. It lays down a general rule that the benefit and burden of *all* landlord and tenant covenants are transmissible.[55] However, if a covenant is expressed to be personal (in whatever terms) to any person, it will not be enforceable by or against any other person.[56] This does not necessarily mean that such a covenant will be wholly untransmissible, for it may be expressed to be personal merely to one of the parties and not to both.[57] The new rule has two advantages over the previous law. First, it allows the parties to make their own bargain and determine for themselves which covenants should pass. Secondly, it leads to certainty. Transmissibility will no longer depend on the vagaries of the touching and concerning requirement.[58] There are two exceptions to these general rules.

(a) The burden of a landlord or a tenant covenant will not pass on an assignment of a lease or reversion if it has ceased to be binding on the assignor prior to the assignment,[59] as where it has been released, or being limited to a specific duration, has expired. It often happens that one party to a lease agrees to waive the performance of a particular covenant in the lease by the other, commonly on the understanding that the waiver should be personal to the party to whom it is given. If the latter assigns the lease or reversion, that waiver will not preclude the transmission of the

---

[50] See *Hansard* (H.C.), July 14, 1995, vol. 263, col. 1241.
[51] *Ante*, para. 15–007. Thus L.P.A. 1925, ss.78, 79, 141 and 142 are inapplicable to such leases: L. & T.C.A. 1995, s.30(4), though the disapplication of L.P.A. 1925, ss.78 and 79 would appear to be confined to their application to covenants between landlord and tenant, and not, *e.g.* to a restrictive covenant entered into for the benefit of leasehold land by a neighbour. The common law rules on transmission are also replaced: see *infra*.
[52] *Ante*, para. 15–003.
[53] *Ante*, para. 15–065.
[54] L. & T.C.A. 1995, s.2(1); *ante*, para. 15–022.
[55] L. & T.C.A. 1995, ss.2(1), 3(1).
[56] L. & T.C.A. 1995, s.3(6)(a).
[57] *cf.* Leases granted before 1996, in which a covenant may touch and concern the land even though it is personal to one of the parties: *ante*, para. 15–024.
[58] See *ante*, para. 15–023.
[59] L. & T.C.A. 1995, ss.3(2), (3).

burden of the covenant if the waiver is expressed (in whatever terms) to be personal to the assignor.[60]

(b) The benefit or burden of a landlord or a tenant covenant will not pass on an assignment of a lease or reversion if it falls to be complied with in relation to any demised premises not comprised in the assignment.[61] Thus, for example, if there is a partial assignment of property leased, the burden of a tenant covenant to repair a building on the part not transferred would not pass to the assignee. The practical application of the covenant is attributable to the part of the land retained by the assignor.[62]

In relation to leases granted after 1995, the Act abolishes, to the extent that it remains in force, the ancient rule[63] that the burden of a covenant whose subject-matter is not in existence at the time when it is made (such as a covenant to build a wall), does not run with the land unless it is made on behalf of the covenantor and his assigns.[64]

3. Principles of transmission

15–081   *(a) Annexation of covenants and rights of re-entry.* The benefit and burden of all transmissible landlord and tenant covenants are annexed and incident to the whole, and to each and every part of the premises let by the tenancy and of the reversion in them.[65] They will pass accordingly on an assignment of the whole or any part of those premises or of that reversion.[66] The benefit of a landlord's right of re-entry under a tenancy is similarly annexed to the reversion, so as to pass on an assignment of the whole or any part of it.[67]

---

[60] L. & T.C.A. 1995, s.3(4).

[61] *ibid.*, ss.3(2), (3). The Act lays down the circumstances in which a covenant falls to be complied with in relation to a particular part of the premises: *ibid.* ss.28(2), (3). These include, *e.g.* where the covenant in its terms applies to that part or, in the case of a money covenant, where the amount payable is determinable specifically by reference to that part.

[62] See L. & T.C.A. 1995, s.28(2)(b).

[63] See *Spencer's Case* (1583) 5 Co.Rep. 16a, second resolution; *ante*, para. 15–038. It is circumvented (rather than abolished) in relation to leases granted after 1925 but before 1996, by L.P.A. 1925, s.79.

[64] L. & T.C.A. 1995, s.3(7).

[65] The benefit of the landlord's right to receive rent passes under these provisions, reflecting the modern view of rent as a contractual payment for the use of the land: see *ante*, para. 14–245. The Act deliberately makes no mention of "rent reserved by the lease", the expression used in L.P.A. 1925, s.141(1) (which governs assignments of reversions on leases granted before 1996).

[66] L. & T.C.A. 1995, s.3(1).

[67] *ibid.* s.4. Where, as regards part of the land leased, the lease is surrendered or otherwise terminated, it is thought that the benefit of any right of re-entry and the burden of the tenant covenants will remain annexed to the severed part of the reversion and the lease respectively. Even if L. & T.C.A. 1995, ss. 3, 4, do not have this effect, L.P.A. 1925, s.140 (*ante*, para. 15–050), expressly does so. That section, unlike L.P.A. 1925, ss.141, 142, is not repealed for leases granted after 1995.

By way of an exception, the Act preserves the rule that a purchaser of a lease or reversion takes free of those covenants which are unenforceable by reason of non-registration.[68]

(b) Right to sue former landlord or tenant who has not been released from   **15–082**
his covenants. It has been explained above that there may be occasions where a landlord or a tenant is not released from a covenant on an assignment of the reversion or the lease respectively and therefore remains liable on the covenants of the lease.[69] Thus, for example, if—

> (i) L assigns his reversion to R, but does not seek (or cannot obtain) a release of the landlord covenants from T, the tenant, L's liability on those covenants continues and he is jointly and severally liable with R[70] for any breach that R may commit; and

> (ii) T assigns his lease to A in breach of a covenant not to assign without L's consent, T is similarly liable to L for any breach of covenant that A may commit.

If in (i), T subsequently assigns the lease to A and in (ii), L assigns his reversion to R, the right to sue L or A will pass to A and R respectively. The terms "landlord covenant" and "tenant covenant" include covenants that are binding not just on the landlord or tenant for the time being,[71] but on any former landlord or tenant who has not been released.[72] The right to enforce them must therefore pass on an assignment of the lease or reversion.[73]

(c) Enforcement. The Act lays down detailed rules both as to who can   **15–083**
enforce a transmissible covenant[74] that has been annexed to the lease or reversion and as against whom. The rules differ in a number of respects from those applicable to leases granted before 1996.

(1) RIGHT TO ENFORCE ANY TENANT COVENANTS OR RIGHT OF RE-ENTRY. The   **15–084**
Act provides that the following persons can enforce against both the tenant

---

[68] L. & T.C.A. 1995, ss.3(6), 15(5). The usual case will be an option to renew a lease of unregistered land which is void against an assignee of the reversion for non-registration under L.C.A. 1972, s.4(6): *Phillips v. Mobil Oil Co. Ltd* [1980] 1 W.L.R. 88; *ante*, paras 5–099, 5–115, 5–117. An option to renew a lease of registered land will usually bind a purchaser of the reversion as an overriding interest: *ante*, para. 6–052.

[69] *Ante*, para. 15–070.

[70] For joint and several liability in this context, see L. & T.C.A. 1995, s.13(1).

[71] The Act provides that, unless the context otherwise requires, "landlord" means the person for the time being entitled to the reversion immediately expectant on the term; and "tenant" means the person entitled to the term: L. & T.C.A. 1995, s.28(1). Here, the context plainly does require that "landlord" and "tenant" have a different meaning.

[72] This can be deduced from L. & T.C.A. 1995, ss.5(2), 7(1), 11(2).

[73] Under L. & T.C.A. 1995, s.3(1); *ante*, para. 15–081.

[74] A covenant that is expressed to be personal to any person cannot be enforced by or against any other person: L. & T.C.A. 1995, s.15(5)(a). A covenant that is void for non-registration is not enforceable: *ibid.*, s.15(5)(b).

and any mortgagee in possession of the premises comprised in the lease[75] the tenant covenants and any right of re-entry in the lease—

    (i) the landlord who granted the lease[76]; and

    (ii) a lessee of the reversion[77]; and

    (iii) a mortgagee in possession of the reversion.[78]

This marks a departure from the previous law, though the difference may be more apparent than real. In relation to leases granted before 1996, a landlord ceases to be entitled to enforce the tenant covenants if and to the extent that some other person (such as a lessee of the reversion or a mortgagee in possession of the reversion) becomes entitled to the income of all or part of the land leased.[79] Furthermore, as regards any lease granted before 1996, any subsequent grant of a lease of the reversion operates as a *pro tanto* assignment of the reversion.[80] By contrast, the grant of a lease of the reversion on a lease granted after 1995 must take effect *as a lease* and not as an assignment,[81] because the landlord retains his right to enforce the tenant covenants in the lease. Subject to any estoppel arising from the grant of the lease of the reversion, both the landlord *and* any lessee of the reversion may in principle enforce the tenant covenants or any right of re-entry in the original lease.[82] While it will almost always be the latter who will wish to exercise these rights, there may be occasions where the tenant's breach of covenant causes loss not only to the interest of the lessee of the reversion but to the landlord's ultimate reversion as well.[83] As each can only recover for the distinct injury to his own reversion, the tenant will not be required to pay damages twice over. If both the landlord and the lessee of the reversion wish to exercise the right of re-entry, the former will have priority.[84] However, he is seldom likely to exercise that right because the effect of terminating the original lease will be that the lessee of the reversion becomes entitled in possession.

    The position is similar where a mortgagee of the reversion is in possession. He becomes entitled to enforce the tenant covenants and any right of re-entry

---

[75] *ibid.*, s.15(4).

[76] *ibid.*, s.15(1), (6).

[77] *ibid.*, s.15(1)(a). Leases of the reversion are likely to be more common after 1995, because of the overriding lease provisions of the Act: see *ibid.* s.19; *ante*, para. 15–017.

[78] L. & T.C.A. 1995, s.15(1)(b).

[79] L.P.A. 1925, s.141(2); *ante*, para. 15–049.

[80] *Ante*, para. 14–106.

[81] This was to avoid the possibility that on an assignment of a lease of the reversion the landlord might be able to obtain a release from the landlord covenants of the original lease as a result of L. & T.C.A. 1995, ss.7, 11; *ante*, para. 15–072.

[82] The landlord will be estopped by his grant from enforcing rights against the tenant that he had leased to the lessee of the reversion, such as the right to claim rent.

[83] As where the tenant is in serious breach of his repairing obligations and the lease of the reversion is about to expire.

[84] The lessee of the reversion necessarily takes subject to the landlord's pre-existing right of re-entry against the tenant.

and in practice it is he who is likely to do so, rather than the landlord (who retains his rights of enforcement).

(2) RIGHT TO ENFORCE ANY LANDLORD COVENANTS. Any landlord covenant   **15–085** may be enforced by—

(i) the tenant; or

(ii) any mortgagee in possession of any premises comprised in the lease[85];

but not by any sub-lessee (as is apparently the case in relation to leases granted before 1996[86]). The covenant is enforceable against—

(a) the landlord;

(b) any lessee of the reversion; and

(c) any mortgagee in possession of the reversion.[87]

Where, as a result of these provisions, the tenant can sue more than one person, the defendants will be jointly and severally liable.[88] However, a landlord who has to pay damages to the tenant for a breach of the landlord covenants by either a lessee of the reversion or a mortgagee in possession, will be entitled to an indemnity from the party in breach.[89]

(3) RESTRICTIVE COVENANTS. Any landlord or tenant covenant that is a   **15–086** restrictive covenant is enforceable against any assignee of the reversion or lease and any owner or occupier of the premises to which the covenant relates, even though there is no express provision in the tenancy to that effect.[90] This means that any sub-lessee, licensee or even squatter, will be bound automatically by any restrictive covenant in the head lease.[91]

4. Partial assignments

(a) Attribution of the burden of covenants. Where there has been a partial   **15–087** assignment of the lease or of the reversion, then whether and to what extent a particular assignee is subject to the burden of such a covenant depends upon whether it is attributable to a particular part of the property or whether it is

---

[85] L. & T.C.A. 1995, s.15(3).

[86] This is the apparently fortuitous effect of L.P.A. 1925, s.78; *ante*, para. 15–032. There is no good reason why a sub-lessee should be able to enforce covenants against the head lessor when the converse is not the case except as regards restrictive covenants.

[87] L. & T.C.A. 1995, s.15(2).

[88] *ibid*. s.13(1).

[89] Under the principle that where A is compelled to pay a sum for which B is ultimately liable, A has a right to be indemnified by B: see *Moule v. Garrett* (1872) L.R. 7 Ex. 101 at 104; *Brook's Wharf and Bull Wharf Ltd v. Goodman Bros.* [1937] 1 K.B. 534 at 544.

[90] L. & T.C.A. 1995, s.3(5).

[91] In practice this replicates the effect of the law applicable to leases granted before 1996: see *post*, para. 16–054.

applicable to the whole of the premises that are the subject of the lease.[92] No issue of apportionment will arise where a covenant falls to be complied with or performed in relation to either the part retained or the part assigned. The burden of the covenant will bind only the part to which it relates.[93] For example, where L leases a house and a field to T, covenanting to keep the exterior of the house in repair, and L then assigns the reversion on the house but not the field to R, T can enforce the repairing covenant against R but not L.

15–088   *(b) Joint and several liability for non-attributable covenants.* A covenant that is not attributable to any premises comprised in the partial assignment of the lease or reversion is charged on the whole of the property. An example is a tenant covenant to pay rent or service charge. In such a case, in the absence of any apportionment, both landlords or (as the case may be) both tenants will be jointly and severally liable for any breach of the covenant.[94] If one of the covenantors is held liable, he may however seek contribution from the other.[95]

15–089   *(c) Apportionment.* Where there is a non-attributable landlord or tenant covenant, the burden of it may be apportioned in one of two ways. First, the Act permits apportionment where the relevant parties to the tenancy, namely the landlord, the tenant and the assignee of the lease or the reversion, all agree to it.[96] Secondly, in the absence of any such agreement, the Act creates a means by which the assignor and assignee can agree an apportionment and make it binding upon the landlord or the tenant respectively.[97] Thus, if T assigns to A part of the premises that are leased to him by L, and T and A agree an apportionment of the rent payable in respect of their respective parts,[98] they may apply to L[99] for that apportionment to be made binding on him.[1] That application must be in the form of a notice,[2] served on L before or within four weeks of the assignment.[3] This must inform L of the proposed or actual assignment, provide prescribed particulars of the agreement, and request that the apportionment should become binding on him.[4] The apportionment will then become binding on L unless he serves a written counter-notice on T and A within four weeks of service objecting to the

---

[92] See L. & T.C.A. 1995, s.9(6).
[93] See L. & T.C.A. 1995, s.3(2), (3); *ante*, para. 15–080.
[94] L. & T.C.A. 1995, s.13(1).
[95] *ibid.* s.13(3), adapting the provisions of the Civil Liability (Contribution) Act 1978.
[96] L. & T.C.A. 1995, s.26(1).
[97] *ibid.* s.9.
[98] The parties may agree that one of them is to be exonerated from all liability under the covenant: *ibid.* s.9(3).
[99] As the "appropriate person": *ibid.* s.9(7). It may be necessary to make the apportionment binding on some other party, *e.g.* a management company, and the Act makes provision for this: *ibid.* s.9(5).
[1] *ibid.* s.9(1), (4). For the converse case, where an apportionment is made on the assignment of the reversion, see *ibid.* s.9(2), (4).
[2] See *ibid.* s.27.
[3] *ibid.* s.10(1).
[4] *ibid.*

apportionment. In those circumstances there will be no apportionment unless either—

(i) T and A apply to the county court for, and obtain, a declaration that it is reasonable for the apportionment to become binding; or

(ii) L in writing withdraws his objection.[5]

Any apportionment is effective from the date of the partial assignment.[6] Once it has become binding, the apportionment cannot be affected by any subsequent order or decision made under any other statutory power of apportionment.[7]

(d) Excluded assignments. Where the partial assignment is in breach of **15–090** covenant or by operation of law,[8] the parties to it cannot apply for an agreed apportionment to become binding on the landlord or tenant (as the case may be).[9] Such an application can be made only on the next assignment that is not an excluded assignment.[10]

(e) Forfeiture and disclaimer. If a lease containing a right to re-enter for **15–091** breach of covenant is assigned in part, the landlord can forfeit only that part held by the tenant who is in breach and not the whole of the premises to which the right relates.[11] Similarly, where a tenant of part becomes insolvent, the liquidator or trustee in bankruptcy can exercise his power of disclaimer[12] only in respect of that part.[13]

5. Assignee's position in relation to previous breaches of covenant

(a) No liability for breaches by assignor. The Act preserves the rule[14] that **15–092** the assignee of a lease or reversion incurs no liability for breaches of covenant committed by the assignor.[15]

(b) Right to sue for previous breaches does not pass. It has been explained **15–093** that on an assignment of a lease granted before 1996, the right to sue for breaches of covenant committed by the landlord prior to the assignment does not pass on the assignment.[16] By contrast, where the landlord assigns the reversion on such a lease, the right to sue for pre-existing breaches of

---

[5] *ibid.*, s.10(2). In the converse case, where L has assigned part of the reversion to R, L and R would of course serve the notice on T, and T would serve any counter-notice on L and R.
[6] L. & T.C.A. 1995, s.10(3).
[7] *ibid.*, s.26(3). There are many such statutory provisions: see *e.g.* A.H.A. 1986, s.33.
[8] And therefore an excluded assignment, see *ante*, para. 15–074.
[9] L. & T.C.A. 1995, s.11(5)(a).
[10] *ibid.*, s.11(5)(b), (6).
[11] *ibid.*, s.21(1).
[12] See *ante*, para. 14–184.
[13] L. & T.C.A. 1995, s.21(2).
[14] *Ante*, para. 15–039.
[15] L. & T.C.A. 1995, s.23(1).
[16] *Ante*, para. 15–040.

covenant does pass to the assignee.[17] As regards leases granted after 1995, the Act lays down one rule which applies equally to the assignment of both the tenancy and the reversion. Consistently with the underlying principle of the Act that rights and liabilities under the lease should go together,[18] it is provided that—

(i) the right to sue for any pre-existing breach of covenant does not pass on an assignment of either the lease or the reversion[19]; but

(ii) such a right may be expressly assigned to the assignee.[20]

In practice it is likely that such express assignments will be the norm, particularly on an assignment of a reversion.

15–094   *(c) Right to re-enter for breach prior to assignment.* Although the right to sue for the breach of a covenant committed by the tenant prior to the assignment of the reversion does not pass in the absence of an express assignment, the assignee of the reversion is entitled to exercise any right of re-entry in the lease in respect of such a breach, unless there had been a waiver or release of that breach prior to assignment.[21] If the assignee were not entitled to do this, a tenant who was in breach of covenant might escape the forfeiture of his lease simply because of the fortuitous circumstance that the reversion had been assigned. If, as is likely, the breach occurred shortly before the assignment, the assignor may have had no opportunity to take steps to forfeit the lease.

15–095   The interaction of the principles that, in respect of a breach of covenant committed before the assignment of the reversion, the assignee can forfeit the lease but only the assignor can sue the tenant on the covenant, can be demonstrated by three examples. In each case L, the landlord of a lease containing a right of re-entry, has assigned the reversion to R. Prior to that assignment, T, the tenant, has committed a breach of covenant which was not waived or released by L. L has not assigned to R his rights of action against T.

(i) In the simplest case, R forfeits the lease and T fails to obtain relief. L can still sue T for any loss which he has suffered. This may be for the diminution in the value of the reversion at the time of the sale to R (*e.g.* because of T's failure to repair), or in the case of non-payment of rent or service charge, for the sum unpaid at the time the reversion was assigned to R.

---

[17] *Ante*, para. 15–051.
[18] See Law Com. No. 174, paras 4.1, 4.49; *ante*, para. 15–065.
[19] L. & T.C.A. 1995, s.23(1).
[20] *ibid.* s.23(2).
[21] *ibid.* s.23(3). For waiver, see *ante*, para. 14–125. The commonest example of waiver is where a landlord accepts rent from the tenant in the knowledge that he is in breach of covenant. In many cases therefore, the breach will have been waived before the reversion is assigned.

(ii) In the second case, T has committed a breach of a positive covenant such as a repairing obligation. Under threat of forfeiture, T remedies the breach. L may still sue T for damages for the breach of the covenant and can recover the loss that he has suffered. That will be the amount by which the value of his reversion was diminished by T's breach of covenant at the time of the sale.[22]

(iii) In the third example, T is in arrears of rent at the time when L assigns the reversion to R. If R commences forfeiture proceedings against T, T is in practice likely to pay the arrears either to R or into court in order to secure relief.[23] In either eventuality, it is suggested that the payment should discharge T,[24] and that L will be entitled to claim the sum paid by T because R has no right to retain it. L may seek restitution either on the basis of the developing law of unjust enrichment,[25] or through the imposition of a constructive trust on the basis that it is unconscionable for R to retain the sum.[26]

6. Attempts to exclude the operation of the Act. The Act contains   **15–096**
sweeping anti-avoidance provisions by which any agreement relating to a tenancy[27] is void to the extent that it either purports to have certain effects or places specified obligations upon the tenant.[28]

First, an agreement is void in so far as it would have the effect of excluding, modifying or otherwise frustrating the operation of any provision of the Act.[29] This is, and was intended by Parliament to be, a provision of considerable breadth.[30] It enables a court to examine the purpose of any given term of the lease in the light of the policy of the Act as a whole or of a particular section. It can reasonably be assumed that the courts will make full use of this power

---

[22] *cf.* L. & T.A. 1927, s.18(1); *ante*, para. 14–282. The amount will obviously depend on how much the sale of the reversion had been discounted because of T's breach.

[23] See Common Law Procedure Act 1852, s.212; County Courts Act 1984, s.138(3) (as amended); *ante*, para. 14–134. Each statute requires that, for T to obtain relief, he must pay the monies either into court or to the *landlord*, who would be R not L.

[24] Because of his compliance with the statutory requirements for obtaining relief against forfeiture.

[25] See *Lipkin Gorman v. Karpnale Ltd* [1991] 2 A.C. 548; *Banque Financière de la Cité v. Parc (Battersea) Ltd* [1999] 1 A.C. 221.

[26] If R was aware of T's arrears and paid less for the reversion because L did not assign to him the benefit of the right to sue for them, the case for imposing a constructive trust would be strong: *cf. Ashburn Anstalt v. Arnold* [1989] Ch. 1; *ante*, para. 10–022.

[27] Whether or not the agreement is contained in the tenancy or was made before the creation of that tenancy: L. & T.C.A. 1995, s.25(4).

[28] *ibid.*, s.25(1).

[29] For example, a provision in a lease which required a tenant who wished to dispose of his lease to sub-let for a term exceeding his term, would be void under s.25(1). Such a sub-lease operates by way of an assignment by operation of law: *ante*, para. 14–110. The tenant would not therefore be released from the covenants: L. & T.C.A. 1995, s.11; *ante*, para. 15–074. See *Hansard* (H.C.), July 14, 1995, vol. 263, col. 1266.

[30] See *Hansard* (H.C.), July 14, 1995, vol. 263, cols 1265, 1266; and Law Com. No. 174 paras 4.57, 4.58.

where it is necessary to defeat sham terms whose principal objective is to circumvent the Act.[31]

Secondly, an agreement will be void to the extent that it provides for—

> (i) the termination or surrender of the tenancy; or

> (ii) imposes on the tenant any penalty, disability or liability,

in the event of, in connection with, or in consequence of the operation of any provision of the Act. This is intended to catch obvious devices for circumventing the Act, such as a term which requires a tenant to pay a large premium to the landlord on assignment. Certain transactions, such as absolute or qualified covenants against assignment, and authorised guarantee agreements, are not rendered void by the anti-avoidance provisions.[32]

---

[31] See *Hansard* (H.C.), July 14, 1995, vol. 263, col. 1266. For shams, see *ante*, para. 14–021.
[32] L. & T.C.A. 1995, s.25(2), (3).

Chapter 16

FREEHOLD COVENANTS

THIS chapter is concerned with the running of covenants with freehold land. **16–001**
Much of this topic consists of the law of restrictive covenants, a nineteenth-
century development which was the creature of equity.

1. Classification. A freehold covenant resembles an incumbrance. The **16–002**
covenant creates a right over land in favour of someone who is a stranger to
it, and the occupier is bound by it just as by any other third party right such
as an easement or mortgage. There is some overlapping with the law on
leasehold covenants. First, we have already examined the principles governing covenants made by third parties guaranteeing the performance of obligations in leases. These are subject to the rules relating to freehold rather than
leasehold covenants.[1] Secondly, a landlord may be able to sue a sub-tenant on
a covenant in the head lease if it qualifies as a restrictive covenant and is
binding on the sub-tenant under the rules explained in this chapter.

2. Divergence of law and equity. At common law it has always been **16–003**
possible for the benefit, as opposed to the burden, of a covenant to run with
the land automatically, even where the parties do not stand in the relationship
of landlord and tenant. If P, on buying a plot of land from V, enters into a
covenant with V for the benefit of V's other land (*e.g.* if P covenants to clean
annually the ditches on V's side of the boundary), the benefit of this covenant
may pass at law to P.[2] By contrast, the burden of P's covenant does not run
with his land so as to bind his successors in title.[3] The covenant binds only P
himself and (after his death) his estate.[4]

In equity the rules are of more recent origin, and are much wider. First,
equity allowed the benefit of a contract or covenant to be assigned, whether or
not it concerned land, as a chose in action.[5] Express assignments may now

---

[1] *Ante*, para. 15–056.
[2] *Post*, para. 16–009.
[3] *Austerberry v. Corporation of Oldham* (1885) 29 Ch.D. 750 at 781–785; *Smith v. Colbourne*
[1914] 2 Ch. 533 at 542; *E. & G.C. Ltd v. Bate* (1935) 97 L.J. News 203 (covenant to build
road; assignee of benefit failed against devisee of covenantor); *Cator v. Newton* [1940] 1 K.B.
415; *Jones v. Price* [1965] 2 Q.B. 618; *Rhone v. Stephens* [1994] 2 A.C. 310; *post*, para.
16–017.
[4] See, *e.g. Hall v. National Provincial Bank Ltd* [1939] L.J.N.C.C.R. 185.
[5] For this reason a right to specific performance is assignable: *ante*, para. 14–051.

have legal as well as equitable effect if they comply with the Law of Property Act 1925.[6] Secondly, equity followed the law in allowing the benefit of certain covenants to be annexed to the land so as to run with the land without express assignment. Thirdly, however, the revolutionary contribution of equity was to recognise that, subject to certain conditions, the *burden* of restrictive (*i.e.* negative or prohibitory) covenants, such as covenants not to build or to carry on a particular activity on the land, could run with the land that was subject to them.[7]

This transformed the law of covenants in cases where there was neither privity of contract nor privity of estate. The effectiveness of a covenant concerning the covenantor's land was no longer confined to the period for which the original covenantor retained his land, but might continue indefinitely. Once it could be shown that the necessary conditions had been satisfied, a restrictive covenant might continue to burden one plot of land for the benefit of another irrespective of the number of times each plot changed hands. The position must now be examined in some detail. For the sake of completeness, the position of the original parties to the covenant will be considered as well, though this is simply a matter of privity of contract.

Section 1. At Law

A. The Benefit of the Covenant

I. THE ORIGINAL COVANANTEE

16–004 **1. Enforcement.** The original covenantee can always enforce any express[8] covenant against the original covenantor, provided that the covenantee has not expressly assigned the benefit to some other person. But if the covenant was made for the benefit of land belonging to the covenantee, and the covenantee has parted with the land before the breach occurred, he may only recover nominal damages, for the loss is likely to fall not on him but on the assignee of the land. The assignee himself may or may not be able to sue, as is explained below.

16–005 **2. Parties to the deed.** Normally the original covenantee will be a party to the deed containing the covenant. At common law it was a strict rule that no one could sue on a deed made *inter partes* who was not a party to it.[9] This rule was never applied to a deed poll, *i.e.* a deed executed by one party alone as

---

[6] s.136; see Snell, *Equity*, 72.
[7] *Tulk v. Moxhay* (1848) 2 Ph. 774; *post*, para. 16–033.
[8] Implied covenants may be sued upon only where there is a present relationship of landlord and tenant, *ante*, para. 14–196.
[9] *Lord Southampton v. Brown* (1827) 6 B. & C. 718.

a unilateral act, so that any person with whom he purported to contract could enforce the contract.[10]

3. Non-parties. The rule for deeds *inter partes* has been qualified by the Law of Property Act 1925, s.56, under which a person may take an interest in "land or other property" or the benefit of any condition, covenant or agreement respecting land or other property, "although he may not be named as a party to the conveyance or other instrument". "Land or other property" may mean "land or other real property" or it may extend to personal property as well[11]; but on any footing the section appears to apply only to agreements which relate to some pre-existing property and not, *e.g.* to contracts for personal services.[12] To this extent this provision has abolished the common law rule requiring anyone claiming any benefit under a deed to be named as a party to it, and so it extends in an important way the class of persons who can be brought within the benefit of a covenant. For example, if V sells land to P, and P enters into a covenant with V "and also with the owners for the time being" of certain adjacent plots of land, the persons who are the adjoining owners at the time of the covenant can sue, for although they are not named as parties to the conveyance, they are covenantees just as much as is V[13]; and if the benefit of the covenant is capable of running with land (as explained below), it can benefit the successors in title of the adjoining owners.

Ambit of section 56. The true aim of section 56 seems to be not to allow a third party to sue on a contract merely because it is made for his benefit; the contract must purport to be made *with* him.[14] Just as, under the first part of the section, a person cannot benefit by a conveyance unless it purports to be made *to* him (as grantee), so he cannot benefit by a covenant which does not purport

16–006

16–007

---

[10] *Chelsea & Walham Green B.S. v. Armstrong* [1951] Ch. 853: registered transfer (see *ante*, para. 6–096) held equivalent to deed poll, so that a covenant therein could be enforced by the covenantee, even though not a party to the transfer.

[11] See the differing views in *Beswick v. Beswick* [1968] A.C. 58, where the majority took the former view and the minority took the latter (and preferable) view: see at 76, 81, 87, 94, 105.

[12] But see *Beswick v. Beswick, supra*, at 76.

[13] *Westhoughton U.D.C. v. Wigan Coal & Iron Co. Ltd* [1919] 1 Ch. 159; *Re Ecclesiastical Commissioners for England's Conveyance* [1936] Ch. 430. The suggestion that the section is confined to covenants running with the land is denied at 438; but there is the authority of the Court of Appeal for it in *Forster v. Elvet Colliery Co. Ltd* [1908] 1 K.B. 629 (aff'd *sub nom. Dyson v. Forster* [1909] A.C. 98) and *Grant v. Edmondson* [1931] 1 Ch. 1. Since s.56 may now extend to property other than land the suggestion seems difficult to justify.

[14] *Beswick v. Beswick, supra*, at 106 *per* Lord Upjohn, Lord Pearce concurring. Though said (at 105) to be "obiter and tentative", this judgment confirms what has long been the better opinion: see *White v. Bijou Mansions Ltd* [1937] Ch. 610 at 624 (in C.A. [1938] Ch. 351); *Re Sinclair's Life Policy* [1938] Ch. 799; *Re Foster* [1938] 3 All E.R. 357 at 365; *Re Miller's Agreement* [1947] Ch. 615. For Lord Denning's opinions to the contrary see *Drive Yourself Hire Co. (London) Ltd v. Strutt* [1954] 1 Q.B. 250 (*cf. Smith v. River Douglas Catchment Board* [1949] 2 K.B. 500); *Beswick v. Beswick* [1966] Ch. 538. These cases were criticised (see [1954] C.L.J. 66 (H.W.R.W.), and have not been followed because they are inconsistent with *Beswick v. Beswick, supra*: see *Amsprop Trading Ltd v. Harris Distribution Ltd* [1997] 1 W.L.R. 1025, also disapproving *Re Shaw's Application* (1994) 68 P. & C.R. 591 at 598.

to be made *with* him (as covenantee).[15] On this view, if A covenants with B that A will convey land to C, B can enforce the covenant but C cannot; for B is a covenantee, but C is merely a third party. But if A's covenant is expressed to be made with B and C, C can enforce it as well as B, even though B was a party to the deed and C was not.[16] This interpretation follows the sound principle that a promisor should be liable only to those to whom he chooses to engage himself.

The Court of Appeal, however, has asserted that section 56 enables a mere third party, not being a promisee, to enforce a contract made for his benefit.[17] Although the House of Lords rejected this proposition, the opinion of the majority was that section 56 was inapplicable because it was confined to real property,[18] not because it could not benefit a mere third party. On this footing, it is conceiveable that the Court of Appeal's revolutionary doctrine may still be operative as regards real property.[19] However, two opinions were given to the contrary,[20] after a review of the history and true purpose of the section, and these are altogether more convincing. These opinions have now been followed at first instance.[21]

16–008   **5. Non-existent persons.** It seems to be clear that a person cannot be a covenantee within the scope of section 56 unless he is in existence and identifiable at the time when the covenant is made.[22] Thus in the example given,[23] the covenant cannot be made to benefit future purchasers of plots directly; but they may obtain the benefit of if through V or one of the previous plot-owners under the rules relating to assignees. In the same way, if a covenant is expressed to be made with an owner of land and his successors in

---

[15] s.56 of the L.P.A. 1925 "can be called in aid only by a person who, although not a party to the conveyance or other instrument in question, is yet a person to whom that conveyance or other instrument purports to grant something or with whom some agreement or covenant is thereby purported to be made": *Re Foster, supra*, at 365, *per* Crossman J., summarising earlier cases; and similarly *White v. Bijou Mansions Ltd, supra*, at 625, *per* Simonds J.; *Lyus v. Prowsa Developments Ltd* [1982] 1 W.L.R. 1044 at 1049, *per* Dillon J.

[16] *Stromdale & Ball Ltd v. Burden* [1952] Ch. 223 is a borderline case.

[17] *Beswick v. Beswick* [1966] Ch. 538 (C.A.); [1968] A.C. 58 (HL). A coal merchant transferred his business to his nephew, the nephew promising to pay an annuity of £5 a week to the merchant's widow; held (by the Court of Appeal), the widow could enforce the promise under s.56. The House of Lords upheld her claim, but only *qua* the merchant's administratrix, representing the promisee personally. The House surmounted the difficulty that the merchant's estate suffered no loss by granting specific performance. If the Contracts (Rights of Third Parties) Bill, presently before Parliament, is enacted, a person who is not a party to a contract will usually be able to enforce it if there is either a term to that effect or if the contract purports to confer a benefit on him: see *ante*, para. 10–022.

[18] See *Beswick v. Beswick* [1968] A.C. 58; *ante*, para. 16–006; *Southern Water Authority v. Carey* [1985] 2 All E.R. 1077 at 1083.

[19] Lords Hodson and Guest seem to support this: *Beswick v. Beswick, supra*, at 80, 85, 87.

[20] *Per* Lords Pearce and Upjohn: *ibid.* at 94, 106; *ante*, para. 16–007. For the uncertain scope of s.56 after *Beswick v. Beswick* see G. H. Treitel, *The Law of Contract* (10th ed.), p. 617.

[21] *Amsprop Trading Ltd v. Harris Distribution Ltd* [1997] 1 W.L.R. 1025.

[22] *Re Ecclesiastical Commissioners for England's Conveyance* [1936] Ch. 430 at 437; *Lyus v. Prowsa Developments Ltd* [1982] 1 W.L.R. 1044 at 1049; *Pinemain Ltd v. Welbeck International Ltd* [1984] 2 E.G.L.R. 91 at 93, 94; *Re Distributors & Warehousing Ltd* [1986] 1 E.G.L.R. 90 at 94.

[23] *Ante*, para. 16–006.

title, only the present owner is an original covenantee; successors in title can claim the benefit only as assignees.

II. ASSIGNEES OF THE LAND

Where a covenantee disposes of his land, the benefit of the covenant may pass at law to the transferee in one of two ways. First, it may be expressly assigned as a chose in action. Secondly, in certain circumstances it may run automatically with the land.

16–009

1. Express assignment as a chose in action. The benefit of a covenant may be expressly assigned as a chose in action. This will usually be by means of a statutory assignment under section 136 of the Law of Property Act 1925.[24] As such it must be made in writing with written notice to the covenantor. There are two relevant limitations on this statutory power to assign. First, the covenant must not be of a purely personal nature.[25] Secondly, the assignment must, by the section, be absolute. This means that it can only be assigned once. If therefore the covenantee were to sell part of his land and to assign the benefit of the covenant as a chose in action under section 136, he would no longer be able to enforce the covenant himself and would be unable to assign the benefit to any purchaser of the remainder.

16–010

2. The covenant may run with the land

(a) Introduction. The benefit of a covenant may run with the covenantee's land at law in certain circumstances. When it does, the person entitled to the benefit of covenant may sue for damages for its breach or otherwise enforce it[26] in the same way as the original covenantee could have done. Before examining the circumstances in which the benefit will run, it is important to note two matters. Although neither of them is relevant to the transmissibility of a covenant at law, each is important in relation to restrictive covenants in equity.[27]

16–011

> (i) It is immaterial whether the covenant is negative (not to do something) or positive (to do something). Thus the common law doctrine applies equally to a covenant not to build on the land purchased by P or a covenant to supply pure water to the land retained by V.[28]
>
> (ii) There is no requirement either that the covenant should have any relevance to land belonging to the covenantor, or indeed that he should have any land at all. Three examples may be taken to

---

[24] See Snell, *Equity*, 72. The benefit of the chose could also be transferred by means of an equitable assignment: *ibid.*, 76.

[25] See G. H. Treitel, *The Law of Contract* (10th ed.), p. 639.

[26] *e.g.* by injunction.

[27] *Post*, paras 16–040, 16–044.

[28] *Sharp v. Waterhouse* (1857) 7 E. & B. 816; *Shayler v. Woolf* [1946] 1 All E.R. 464 at 467 (aff'd [1946] Ch. 320).

illustrate this. First, in an ancient case a prior covenanted with the lord of the manor that he and his convent would sing divine service in the chapel of the manor. It was held that the lord's successors in title could sue the prior for non-performance.[29] Secondly, in a more recent decision, a river catchment board entered into a covenant with a farmer to repair and maintain the banks of a river that abutted his property. The board was held liable in damages to the farmer's successors in title when, due to the inadequacy of the work, a field was flooded.[30] Thirdly, the benefit of the covenants for title implied in a conveyance ran with land conveyed at common law.[31]

16–012   *(b) Requirements for the benefit to run.* For the benefit of a covenant to run at common law, two conditions must be satisfied.[32] First, the covenant must "touch and concern" the land. Secondly, both the covenantee and the assignee must have a legal estate in the land benefited. There is a suggestion in some cases that there may be a third condition, namely that the parties must have intended that the benefit should run with the land.[33] However, it is far from certain that there ever was such a requirement,[34] and the House of Lords has recently restated the requirements for a covenant to run at common law without reference to this supposed requirement.[35] In any event, as regards covenants entered into after 1925, annexation both at law and in equity is effected automatically without proof of intention to annex under the provisions of section 78 of the Law of Property Act 1925.[36] This is explained fully later.[37]

16–013   (1) THE COVENANT MUST TOUCH AND CONCERN THE LAND OF THE CONVE-NANTEE. The traditional words "touch and concern" are adopted from the

---

[29] *The Prior's Case* (also known as *Pakenham's Case*) Y.B. 42 Edw. 3, Hil., pl. 14 (1368); Co.Litt. 385a; Smith's L.C. i, 55; *post*, para. 16–014.

[30] *Smith v. River Douglas Catchment Board* [1949] 2 K.B. 500. See too *Williams v. United Construction Co. Ltd* (1951) 19 Conv.(N.S.) 262.

[31] Smith's L.C. i, 73; *ante*, para. 5–047. These covenants now run by force of L.P.A. 1925, s.76(6) (if entered into prior to July 1, 1995); and L.P.(M.P.)A. 1994, s.7 (if entered into after June 30, 1995). Each of these provisions applies to transfers of registered land: L.R.A. 1925, s.38(2) (as amended): *ante*, para. 6–102.

[32] *Rogers v. Hosegood* [1900] 2 Ch. 388 at 395; *P. & A. Swift Investments v. Combined English Stores Group Plc* [1989] A.C. 632 at 639, 640. See too (1984) Law Com. No. 127, paras 3.17–3.19.

[33] "Every covenant which has those characteristics does not necessarily run with the land. That is a question of intention in each case"; *Rogers v. Hosegood, supra*, at 396, *per* Farwell J. see too *Smith v. River Douglas Catchment Board, supra*, at 506, 511; *Williams v. Unit Construction Co. Ltd, supra*, at 265. cf. (1982) 2 L.S. 53 at 57 (D. J. Hurst).

[34] There is no reference to it in either *Dyson v. Forster* [1909] A.C. 98 (on appeal from *Forster v. Elvet Colliery Co. Ltd* [1908] 1 K.B. 629) or *Westhoughton U.D.C. v. Wigan Coal & Iron Co. Ltd* [1919] 1 Ch. 159.

[35] *P. & A. Swift Investments v. Combined English Stores Group Plc, supra*, at 639, 640.

[36] *Federated Homes Ltd v. Mill Lodge Properties Ltd* [1980] 1 W.L.R. 594. It is clear from that case that statutory annexation applies as much to the transmission of covenants at law as in equity, because at 605, the Court of Appeal relied on two cases on assignment at law, *Smith v. River Douglas Catchment Board, supra*, and *Williams v. Unit Construction Co. Ltd, supra*.

[37] *Post*, para. 16–063.

rules for covenants in leases.[38] In the present context they signify that the covenant must be made for the benefit of land owned by the covenantee (*i.e.* V in the above examples) at the time of the covenant, in the sense that it is designed to benefit both V and his successors in title, and not V alone.[39] This sense will readily be inferred if the circumstances indicate that the covenant will be of importance to successive owners and will enhance the value of the land. A covenant by a catchment board to keep river banks in repair will touch and concern the covenantee's adjacent farmland which is liable to be flooded if repair is neglected,[40] and a covenant to keep a road in repair will touch and concern the covenantee's land reached by the road, if the land will be more valuable on that account.[41] Where the covenant is to keep something in repair, or to do other recurrent acts, the benefit to the land and the identity of that land are usually obvious from the circumstances in which the covenant was taken, so that no special words to this effect need be included in it.[42] The facts themselves show that the benefit is annexed to the land.[43]

Where the covenant is made between landlord and tenant the lessor's reversion alone will not rank as "land" for this purpose, for it will be recalled that the benefit of covenants could not run with the reversion at common law, before the Grantees of Reversion Act 1540.[44] But some incorporeal hereditaments rank as "land". Thus the benefit of a covenant to repair a footpath may run with an easement of way over the path.[45]

It is now clear that where the covenant runs with the land, there is a rebuttable presumption that it is annexed both to the whole and to each and every part of the land.[46] This applies to annexation of covenants at law as much as it does in equity.[47]

(2) THE COVENANTEE AND THE ASSIGNEE MUST EACH HAVE A LEGAL ESTATE IN THE LAND BENEFITED. A common law court could take no cognisance of an **16–014**

---

[38] *Ante*, paras 15–022–15–024, *Rogers v. Hosegood, supra*; *Kumar v. Dunning* [1989] Q.B. 193; *P. & A. Swift Investments v. Combined English Stores Group Plc, supra.*

[39] Co.Litt. 385a; *Rogers v. Hosegood, supra*, at 395; *Formby v. Barker* [1903] 2 Ch. 539 at 554; *Dyson v. Forster, supra*, at 102; *Smith v. River Douglas Catchment Board, supra*, at 506; *Williams v. Unit Construction Co. Ltd, supra*, at 264, 265; *Re Gadd's Land Transfer* [1966] Ch. 56 at 66; *P. & A. Swift Investments v. Combined English Stores Group Plc, supra*, at 640–642.

[40] As in *Smith v. River Douglas Catchment Board, supra.*

[41] As in *Williams v. Unit Construction Co. Ltd, supra* (company covenanted with lessee of building land to make up and maintain roads and footpaths; sub-lessee of one plot who was injured by disrepair of footpath recovered damages from company).

[42] *Smith v. River Douglas Catchment Board, supra.*

[43] *Westhoughton U.D.C. v. Wigan Coal & Iron Co. Ltd* [1919] 1 Ch. 159 at 170 where Swinfen Eady M.R. said: " . . . the covenant touches and concerns the land. The covenant is, therefore, to be deemed to be annexed to the land; the benefit of it runs at law with the land; and the assignee can sue upon it".

[44] *Ante*, para. 15–046.

[45] *Gaw v. Coras Iompair Eireann* [1953] I.R. 232. However *Grant v. Edmondson* [1931] 1 Ch. 1 (holding that a covenant to pay a rentcharge will not run with the rentcharge) was not cited. See *post*, para. 18–028.

[46] *Federated Homes Ltd v. Mill Lodge Properties Ltd* [1980] 1 W.L.R. 594 at 606.

[47] *Williams v. Unit Construction Co. Ltd*, (1951) 19 Conv.(N.S.) 262; *Federated Homes Ltd v. Mill Lodge Properties Ltd, supra*, at 606.

equitable interest before 1875,[48] and if the covenantee was merely an equitable owner (*e.g.* a mortgagor, prior to 1926) the benefit of a covenant could not
run with his interest at law.[49]

During the medieval period the circumstances in which some person other
than the original covenantee might sue at law on a covenant were obscure.[50]
Some covenants could be enforced only by the covenantee's heirs,[51] whilst
others were enforceable by whoever had the land.[52] It was not until the
sixteenth century that it was finally settled that a covenant might run with the
land so that it could be enforced by a stranger to whom the land had been
conveyed.[53]

It appears to have become customary for covenants to be made with the
covenantee, his heirs and assigns, even though those additional words were
not necessary in order that the benefit should run.[54] However, these words
may have limited the range of persons who might enforce the covenant. There
was some authority that an assignee who sought to enforce the covenant had
to have the same estate as the original covenantee.[55]

By the Conveyancing Act 1881,[56] a covenant relating to land was deemed
to be made "with the covenantee, his heirs and assigns" and was to take effect
as if those persons were expressed, thereby shortening the wording of covenants.[57] It was held that those who derived title under but did not take the
same estate as the covenantee (such as his lessees) were not his "assigns" and
could not therefore enforce the covenant.[58] However, doubts were expressed
as to the correctness of this conclusion.[59]

---

[48] *Ante*, paras 4–016–4–017.

[49] *Webb v. Russell* (1789) 3 T.R. 393; *Rogers v. Hosegood* [1900] 2 Ch. 388 at 404.

[50] See A. W. B. Simpson, *A History of the Common Law of Contract*, pp. 37–40.

[51] Who might not have the same estate as the covenantee. Thus the plaintiff in *The Prior's Case*,
   Y.B. 42 Edw. 3, Hil., pl. 14 (1368), was a tenant in tail but the covenantee had been the owner
   in fee simple.

[52] *The Prior's Case, supra*; quoted in Holmes, *The Common Law*, p. 397. "Precisely what was
   decided in the case is not at all clear"; A. W. B. Simpson, *op. cit.*, at p. 38.

[53] *Spencer's Case* (1583) 5 Co.Rep. 16a at 17b, 18a; A. W. B. Simpson *op cit.*, at p. 39.

[54] *Lougher v. Williams* (1673) 2 Lev. 92. The rule derived from the principles applicable to
   covenants in leases. These would run with the landlord's reversion even though the word
   "assigns" was not used: *Kitchen v. Buckly* (1663) 1 Lev. 109.

[55] *Webb v. Russell* (1789) 3 T.R. 393 at 402, 403; *Rogers v. Hosegood* [1900] 2 Ch. 388 at
   404.

[56] s.58.

[57] It appears to have been erroneously thought that such words were necessary to make the benefit
   of a covenant run: see *Wolstenholme's Conveyancing and Settled Land Acts* (10th ed., 1913),
   p. 129.

[58] *Westhoughton U.D.C. v. Wigan Coal & Iron Co. Ltd* [1919] 1 Ch. 159 (lessee could not enforce
   covenant made with the freeholder); *South of England Dairies Ltd v. Baker* [1906] 2 Ch. 631
   (underlessee unable to enforce covenant made with the lessee).

[59] See *Westhoughton U.D.C. v. Wigan Coal & Iron Co. Ltd, supra*, at 176 (Duke L.J.); (1980) 43
   M.L.R. 445 at 449 (D. J. Hayton). In *Taite v. Gosling* (1879) 11 Ch.D. 273, Fry J. held that a
   lessee was an "assign" for the purposes of enforcing a *restrictive* covenant that had been
   granted to a freeholder. In so doing he relied on *Wright v. Burroughes* (1846) 3 C.B. 685, a
   decision at law, which held that a lessee of the reversion was an "assignee" for the purposes
   of the Grantees of Reversions Act 1540.

As regards covenants entered into after 1925, the provisions of the Act of **16–015** 1881 have been replaced by the Law of Property Act 1925, s.78. It provides that "a covenant relating to any land of the covenantee shall be deemed to be made with the covenantee and his successors in title and the persons deriving title under him or them,[60] and shall have effect as if such successors and other persons were expressed". The change in the wording is explained in part because the term "heirs" became obsolete under the 1925 legislation.[61] However, it is likely that it was also intended to resolve the doubts as to who could enforce a covenant which ran with the land so as to make it clear that it included lessees, sub-lessees and mortgagees.[62] The courts have certainly interpreted it in this way.[63] Thus, in a case where a catchment board covenanted to maintain the banks of a river, and the land was later sold to a purchaser who let it to a tenant, both the purchaser and the tenant were able to recover damages for injury to their respective interests (the reversion and the tenancy) after the land had been inundated due to breach of covenant.[64] The result of this change is welcome even though the reasoning behind it has been questioned by some.[65] The provisions of the 1881 Act, with the attendant doubts as to their precise scope, will continue to apply to covenants entered into before 1926.[66]

(c) Relationship between sections 78 and 79. Doubts have been expressed **16–016** as to the interpretation of section 78 of the Law of Property Act 1925[67] because it is worded in similar terms to its partner section 79, which has been held to be much more limited in its effect. Section 79(1) provides that "a covenant relating to any land of the covenantor or capable of being bound by him, shall, unless a contrary intention is expressed, be deemed to be made by

[60] Subject to what is said in relation to registered land, *post*, para. 16–063, n. 77, in relation to *positive* covenants, these words will not include squatters and licensees. The former are not "successors in title" and the latter have no "title". By contrast, squatters and licensees *will* be able to enforce *restrictive* covenants because, as regards such covenants, the owners and occupiers for the time being are deemed to be successors in title by the section: see n.62, *infra*.

[61] *Ante*, para. 11–087. Two amendments were made to C.A. 1881, by L.P.A. 1922, s.96(2)–(4), and by L.P.(Am.)A. 1924, Sched. 3, Pt I, cl. 11. The words "his successors in title and the persons deriving title under him or them" appeared for the first time in L.P.A. 1925, s.78. The Act of 1925 was a consolidating Act, and while there is a presumption that such an Act is not intended to change the law, "this prima facie view must yield to plain words to the contrary": *Grey v. I.R.C.* [1960] A.C. 1 at 13, *per* Viscount Simonds. Whether the clarification of a point of doubt should be regarded as a change in the law is debatable. *cf.* (1981) 97 L.Q.R. 32 at 40 (G. H. Newsom, Q.C.).

[62] The view that L.P.A. 1925, s.78 was intended to clarify who could enforce covenants which ran with the land gains further support from the fact that, for the purposes of enforcing *restrictive* covenants, the section deems to be "successors in title" the owners and occupiers of the land for the time being of the land of the covenantee intended to be benefited. This extension of the section was clearly intended: see L.P.(Am.)A. 1924, Sched. 3, Pt I, cl. 11. See *post*, para. 16–063.

[63] *Smith v. River Douglas Catchment Board* [1949] 2 K.B. 500, especially at 516. See similarly *Williams v. Unit Construction Co. Ltd* (1951) 19 Conv.(N.S.) 262 at 265–267.

[64] *Smith v. River Douglas Catchment Board, supra.*

[65] See (1956) 20 Conv.(N.S.) 43 at 53 (D. W. Elliott).

[66] *cf. J. Sainsbury Plc v. Enfield L.B.C.* [1989] 1 W.L.R. 590.

[67] See, *e.g.* (1981) 97 L.Q.R. 32 at 34, 47 (G. H. Newsom Q.C.).

the covenantor on behalf of himself, his successors in title and the persons deriving title under him or them, and, subject as aforesaid, shall have effect as if such successors and other persons were expressed". The sub-section expressly extends "to a covenant to do some act relating to the land, notwithstanding that the subject-matter may not be in existence when the covenant is made". It has recently been held by the House of Lords that this provision "has always been regarded as intended to remove conveyancing difficulties with regard to the form of covenants and to make it unnecessary to refer to successors in title".[68] The principal "conveyancing difficulties" are as follows.

(i) The *burden* of a *restrictive* covenant will run with the covenantor's land only if the parties so intend.[69] The effect of the section is that such an intention will be presumed unless the contrary is expressed.[70]

(ii) By an old rule (if and in so far as it existed), the burden of a covenant in a lease obliging the tenant to do some entirely new thing (such as building a wall) did not run with the reversion unless the covenant was made expressly with the lessee and his assigns.[71] The section overcomes that difficulty.[72]

The House of Lords has now held that section 79 does not cause the *burden* of a positive covenant to run with the land.[73] The House reached this conclusion "without casting any doubt" on the decisions, explained above,[74] by which section 78 has been held to annex the benefit of a covenant to the land and to be enforceable not only by successors in title, but also by those with derivative interests.[75]

B. The Burden of the Covenant

16–017 **1. The general rule: the burden does not run.** The rule at law is that the burden of a covenant will not pass with freehold land.[76] This is of particular

---

[68] *Rhone v. Stephens* [1994] 2 A.C. 310 at 322, *per* Lord Templeman.

[69] *Post*, para. 16–049.

[70] See *Tophams Ltd v. Earl of Sefton* [1967] 1 A.C. 50 at 81. The contrary expression need not take the form of an express provision but may be "sufficiently contained in the wording and context of the instrument": *Re Royal Victoria Pavilion, Ramsgate* [1961] Ch. 581 at 589, *per* Pennycuick J.

[71] *Spencer's Case* (1583) 5 Co. Rep. 16a, second resolution. See *ante*, para. 15–038.

[72] For another possible function of s.79, see *post*, para. 16–038. For the abolition of this rule for leases granted after 1995, see L. & T.C.A. 1995, s.3(7); *ante*, para. 15–080.

[73] *Rhone v. Stephens*, *supra*, at 322. See too *Tophams Ltd v. Earl of Sefton*, *supra*, at 81.

[74] *Smith v. River Douglas Catchment Board* [1949] 2 K.B. 500; *Williams v. Unit Construction Co. Ltd* (1951) 19 Conv.(N.S.) 262; *Federated Homes Ltd v. Mill Lodge Properties Ltd* [1980] 1 W.L.R. 594.

[75] *Rhone v. Stephens*, *supra*, at 322, *per* Lord Templeman. The House noted that in *Federated Homes Ltd v. Mill Lodge Properties*, *supra*, at 606, Brightman L.J. had considered that s.79 involved "quite different considerations" and did not provide "a helpful analogy".

[76] *Austerberry v. Corporation of Oldham* (1885) 29 Ch.D. 750; *ante*, paras 15–005, 16–003.

relevance to *positive* covenants, for the burden of *restrictive* covenants may run in equity. The rationale for the distinction between positive and restrictive covenants was explained by the House of Lords in *Rhone v. Stephens*.[77] "Equity cannot compel an owner to comply with a positive covenant entered into by his predecessors in title without flatly contradicting the common law rule that a person cannot be made liable upon a contract unless he is a party to it. Enforcement of a positive covenant lies in contract; a positive covenant compels an owner to exercise his rights. Enforcement of a negative covenant lies in property; a negative covenant deprives the owner of a right over property."[78] In that case, the common owner of a house and cottage sold the cottage and covenanted "for himself and his successors in title" with the purchaser to maintain part of the roof of the house which also covered part of the cottage. The House held that the purchaser's successor in title could not enforce the covenant against the vendor's successor in title, and declined to overrule the earlier authority which held that the burden of positive covenants would not run with the land. To have done so would have retrospectively imposed liabilities on many property owners who had entered into positive covenants on the basis of a clearly settled rule of law. Any solution lay in the hands of Parliament.[79]

The rule that the burden of positive covenants does not run with freehold **16–018** land is in sharp contrast to the position in relation to leasehold property where such covenants are enforceable if, in the case of leases granted before 1996, they touch and concern the land and there is privity of estate, or, in leases granted after 1995, the covenants are not expressed to be personal.[80] The "ill-consequences" of the rule have often been noted.[81] Two of the most obvious are as follows.

(i) Two neighbours cannot enter into agreements for such everyday matters as the maintenance of a wall or the pruning of trees in such a way that the burden will run with the land.

(ii) Flying freeholds[82] cannot in practice be granted because of the difficulties of ensuring rights of support for the upper floors and for the maintenance of the roof. Flats are therefore granted by means

---

[77] [1994] 2 A.C. 310; noted (1994) 110 L.Q.R. 346 (N. P. Gravells); [1994] Conv. 477 (J. Snape). See too *Thamesmead Town Ltd v. Allotey* [1998] 3 E.G.L.R. 97.

[78] [1994] 2 A.C. 310 at 318, *per* Lord Templeman. For criticism of this reasoning (but not of the actual decision in the case), see [1995] C.L.J. 60 at 63 (S. Gardner).

[79] [1994] 2 A.C. 310 at 321.

[80] *Ante*, paras 15–004, 15–079.

[81] See, *e.g.* (1984) Law Com. No. 127, para. 4.4 (from which the two examples below are drawn); [1972B] C.L.J. 157 (H.W.R.W.); (1995) 58 M.L.R. 486 (D.N. Clarke). In *Rhone v. Stephens* (1993) 67 P. & C.R. 9 at 14 (C.A.), Nourse L.J. commented that the discovery of this rule had "shocked more than one eminent judge unversed in the subtleties of English real property law".

[82] *Ante*, para. 3–041.

of a lease so that the necessary covenants can be both imposed and enforced.

Although there have been a number of proposals for reform (of which the most recent are considered below),[83] to date "nothing has been done".[84]

There are already certain important statutory exceptions to the rule that the burden of positive covenants does not run with the land. For example, under the Town and Country Planning Act 1990 (as amended),[85] any person interested in land may, by agreement or otherwise, enter into a planning obligation with the local authority, enforceable by injunction,[86] requiring specified operations or activities to be carried out in, on, under or over the land.[87] This obligation, which is registrable as local land charge,[88] is enforceable against both the person entering into the obligation and any person deriving title from him.[89]

16–019   **2. Indirect methods of transmitting the burden.** Although the burden of a positive covenant does not run with the land, it is possible to circumvent this rule to some extent by the use of certain devices.[90] None of them provides an effective general solution to the problem however.[91]

16–020   *(a) Chain of covenants.* If V sells land to P, and P covenants, for example, to erect and maintain a fence, P will remain liable to V on the covenant by virtue of privity of contract even if P sells the land to Q. P will accordingly protect himself by extracting from Q a covenant of indemnity against future breaches of the covenant to fence. If Q then fails to maintain the fence, V cannot sue Q, but he can sue P, and P can then sue Q on the covenant for indemnity.[92] Similarly if P dies without having parted with the land, P's

---

[83] *Post*, para. 16–027. See The Report on the Committee on Positive Covenants Affecting Land (1965) Cmnd. 2719; The Law of Positive and Restrictive Covenants (1984) Law Com. No. 127; Commonhold: A Consultation Paper (1990) Cm. 1345.

[84] *Rhone v. Stephens* [1994] 2 A.C. 310 at 321, *per* Lord Templeman. See too *TRW Steering Systems Ltd v. North Cape Properties Ltd* (1993) 69 P. & C.R. 265 at 266.

[85] s.106 (substituted by Planning and Compensation Act 1991, s.12); *post*, para. 16–094. This replaces and considerably extends earlier legislation: see T. & C.P.A. 1971, s.52. It does not have retrospective effect: *Good v. Epping Forest D.C.* [1994] 1 W.L.R. 376 at 380. For another example, see the Local Government (Miscellaneous Provisions) Act 1982, s.33.

[86] T. & C.P.A. 1990, s.106(5).

[87] *ibid.*, s.106(1). Other planning obligations may restrict the development or use of land, require the land to be used in any specified way, or pay a sum or sums to the local authority.

[88] *ibid.*, s.106(11).

[89] *ibid.*, s.106(3). The local authority has power in certain circumstances to enter the land to carry out the operations if the landowner defaults: *ibid.*, s.106(6).

[90] See Law Com. No. 127, paras 3.31–3.42; (1973) 37 Conv.(N.S.) 194 (A. Prichard); (1995) 58 M.L.R. 486 (D. N. Clarke).

[91] Law Com. No. 127, para. 3.42.

[92] Although in practice such an express covenant of indemnity is invariably taken (see *Rhone v. Stephens* (1993) 67 P. & C.R. 9 at 14 (C.A.)), there is in fact an implied right to indemnity: *TRW Steering Systems Ltd v. North Cape Properties Ltd* (1993) 69 P. & C.R. 265 at 272. All actions may be heard together by bringing in indemnifiers as third parties: in accordance with CPR Pt 20. This makes no difference to the substantive law.

personal representatives remain liable in damages, and may require an indemnity from anyone to whom P may have left the land by his will.[93] But a chain of purely personal covenants is unsatisfactory for many reasons. The longer it grows, the more liable it is to be broken by the insolvency or disappearance of one of the parties, or by the neglect of one of them to take a covenant of indemnity from his successor; and the remedy can only be in damages, whereas a mandatory injunction is the remedy usually desired.

(b) Right of entry annexed to rentcharge.[94] Since a right of entry annexed **16–021** "for any purpose" to a legal rentcharge is a legal interest in land,[95] it will be enforceable against successors in title to the land charged even though its primary purpose is to secure the performance of positive covenants rather than the payment of money.[96] It has the further advantages that it is exempt from the perpetuity rule[97] and that it avoided complications under the Settled Land Act 1925.[98] Consequently a device commonly used in practice for securing the performance of covenants to build, repair, and so on, is to reserve a rentcharge, and to annex to it a right of entry allowing its proprietor to enter and make good any default in the observance of the covenants, charging the cost to the owner in possession.[99] Such covenants will usually relate to the rentcharge since they will improve the security, but the words "for any purpose" suggest that no particular connection is necessary; and in practice the rentcharge may be of a nominal amount and may serve merely as a peg on which to hang enforcement of the covenants.[1] This device, though untested judicially,[2] has received the implied blessing of Parliament in the Rentcharges Act 1977, which permits the continued use of rentcharges imposed for the purpose of making covenants enforceable against successive owners.[3]

(c) Rights of re-entry. It would appear to be possible for the vendor of a **16–022** freehold to reserve a right of re-entry as a means of enforcing a positive covenant without creating a rentcharge. This device has been employed by a lessee who assigned a lease[4] and should in principle be available to a freeholder as well. It suffers from two drawbacks. First, the right of re-entry

---

[93] A.E.A. 1925, s.36(10).

[94] See [1988] Conv. 99 (S. Bright).

[95] *Ante*, para. 4–054.

[96] It is immaterial that the covenant does not itself bind successors: *Shiloh Spinners Ltd v. Harding* [1973] A.C. 691 at 717. The court may grant relief: L.P.A. 1925, s.146(5); *ante*, para. 3–067.

[97] L.P.A. 1925, s.4(3); Perpetuities and Accumulations Act 1964, s.11.

[98] *Ante*, paras 4–040, 4–041, 8–053.

[99] For a description see (1975) Law Com. No. 68, para. 49. For a precedent see Prideaux, i, 719.

[1] Law. Com. No. 68, as *supra*.

[2] But Lindley L.J. described it as "means known to conveyancers" whereby the result could be achieved "with comparative ease": *Austerberry v. Corporation of Oldham* (1885) 29 Ch.D. 750 at 783.

[3] *Post*, para. 18–019.

[4] See *Shiloh Spinners Ltd v. Harding* [1973] A.C. 691.

can be reserved only for the period allowed by the rule against perpetuities.[5] Secondly, such a right of entry will be equitable and not legal.[6] Although such equitable rights of entry are not registrable as land charges where title is unregistered,[7] they need to be protected by notice or caution where title is registered.[8]

16-023 *(d) Enlarged long lease.* A more artificial device, of untested validity and subject to difficulties, is to insert the covenant in a long lease which can be enlarged into a fee simple under the statutory power.[9] If the lease is enlarged, the resultant fee simple is by statute made subject to all the same covenants, provisions and obligations as the lease would have been subject to had it not been enlarged.[10] It seems that a fee simple may by these means be made subject to any covenant which touches and concerns the land, *e.g.* a covenant to repair.[11] It should, however, be noted that not all rules that are applicable to leases which cannot be enlarged will apply to those which can be.[12]

16-024 *(e) Condition of taking benefits.* Since it is the general rule that the benefit but not the burden of a contract is assignable, it is normal for the burden to remain with the assignor although the benefit passes to the assignee.[13] But it is possible for acceptance of the burden to be made a condition of enjoyment of the benefit, and thus for the burden to pass. If A conveys land to B reserving the mining rights "so that compensation in money be made" for any damage done, the liability to pay compensation is a condition of the exercise of the mining rights and will run with them so as to bind A's successors in title,[14] against whom B or his successors can claim both compensation under the condition and an injunction to forbid future mining unless compensation is paid.[15] If the provision for compensation is expressed as a covenant separately from the grant or reservation of the covenantor's rights, it may still operate as a condition if it is held, as a matter of construction, that "the benefit and the burden have been annexed to each other *ab initio*".[16]

---

[5] *Ante*, para. 7–096. A royal lives clause was employed in *Shiloh Spinners Ltd v. Harding*, *supra*.

[6] *Shiloh Spinners Ltd v. Harding*, *supra*.

[7] *ibid.*

[8] *Ante*, paras 6–080, 6–086.

[9] L.P.A. 1925, s.153, for which see *ante*, para. 14–178; and see *Re M'Naul's Estate* [1902] 1 I.R. 114. See generally (1958) 22 Conv.(N.S.) 101 (T. P. D. Taylor).

[10] L.P.A. 1925, s.153(8).

[11] Challis 334, 335; Hood & Challis, 282.

[12] See *Bosomworth v. Faber* (1992) 69 P. & C.R. 288 at 292, 293, where it was held that the rule that a tenant cannot acquire a lease by prescription against his own landlord or another tenant of his landlord (*post*, para. 18–128) does not apply to a tenant under a lease which he could at any any time unilaterally enlarge into the fee simple.

[13] As illustrated *ante*, paras 14–051, 15–032–15–034.

[14] *Aspden v. Seddon (No. 2)* (1876) 1 Ex.D. 496; *Chamber Colliery Co. v. Twyerould* (1893) reported in [1915] 1 Ch. 268n. (HL).

[15] *Westhoughton U.D.C. v. Wigan Coal & Iron Co. Ltd* [1919] 1 Ch. 159 at 171, 172.

[16] *Tito v. Waddell (No. 2)* [1977] Ch. 106 at 290, *per* Megarry V.-C., discussing in detail the cases here cited.

Even if the burden is imposed by a separate covenant, as distinct from a **16–025** condition, it may still bind successors in title under a doctrine which has been evolved with the aid of an old rule relating to deeds: "it is ancient law that a man cannot take benefit under a deed without subscribing to the obligations thereunder".[17] This proposition was invoked in a case where purchasers of plots on a building estate were entitled under a trust deed to use private roads and other amenities, and each on purchasing his plot covenanted to pay a just proportion of the cost of their maintenance. It was held that the purchasers' successors were liable for their due contribution while they made use of the roads.[18] That decision was approved by the Court of Appeal in enforcing an informal agreement between neighbours under which one was to have a right of way across the other's yard in exchange for withdrawing objection to a small encroachment on his land by the foundations of the other's building: so long as the encroachment was permitted, the right of way could not be withdrawn.[19]

However, there must now be some doubt both as to the correctness of this **16–026** decision and as to the precise extent of the principle of mutual benefit and burden. The House of Lords has rejected any "pure" principle of benefit and burden,[20] by which "any party deriving any benefit from a conveyance must accept any burden in the same conveyance".[21] Although the House accepted that conditions could be attached expressly or impliedly to the exercise of a power, this was so only where the condition was "relevant to the exercise of the right".[22] The party must, "at least in theory", be able to elect between enjoying the right and performing his obligation or renouncing the right and freeing himself of the burden.[23] On that basis, the House held that the fact that A's roof was supported by B's property did not mean that B could enforce

[17] *Halsall v. Brizell* [1957] Ch. 169 at 172, *per* Upjohn J. The decision was approved in *Rhone v. Stephens* [1994] 2 A.C. 310 at 322.

[18] *Halsall v. Brizell, supra.* It was unnecessary in that case for Upjohn J. to explain how the obligation to pay might be enforced. It has been suggested that it could not be enforced by action as such, but only by withholding from the purchasers' successors the right to use the road unless and until they paid the charges due: *IDC Group Ltd v. Clark* [1992] 1 E.G.L.R. 187 at 190 (aff'd [1992] 2 E.G.L.R. 184). See too *Four Oaks Estates Ltd v. Hadley* (1986) 83 L.S.Gaz. 2326 (estate management company could not apportion cost of maintaining the roads over the whole estate when house owners had only covenanted to contribute to the maintenance of roads adjacent to their houses).

[19] *E.R. Ives Investment Ltd v. High* [1967] 2 Q.B. 379; there were other grounds for this decision for which see *ante*, para. 13–006. See similarly *Hopgood v. Brown* [1955] 1 W.L.R. 213 (reciprocal licences to use drains); *ante*, paras 13–014, 13–031. In *Parkinson v. Reid* (1966) 56 D.L.R. (2d) 315 the Supreme Court of Canada held that when the benefit (use of a party wall) ceased to be enjoyed, the covenantor's successor was freed from the burden (to maintain a staircase), even assuming that such a burden could run.

[20] Such a principle had been distilled from the authorities in *Tito v. Waddell (No. 2), supra*, at 302. See the previous edition of this work at p. 769.

[21] *Rhone v. Stephens, supra*, at 322, *per* Lord Templeman.

[22] *ibid.*

[23] *ibid.* See too *Thamesmead Town Ltd v. Allotey* [1998] 3 E.G.L.R. 97 (emphasising that the doctrine was only applicable where the successor in title had a choice whether or not to take the benefit.

against A a positive covenant made by A's predecessor in title with B's to repair the roof. This approach provides little guidance as to when a party will be regarded as having a genuine choice whether or not to renounce the benefits in order to be relieved of the burdens.[24] In the case mentioned above,[25] it seems improbable that the neighbour who enjoyed the benefit of the right of way could in reality give it up so as to require the removal of the foundations of his neighbour's building from his land.[26]

The policy underlying the decision of the House seems to be to restrict the ambit of the doctrine of benefit and burden as a means of circumventing the rule that the burden of positive covenants does not run. The intention would seem to be to prompt the abolition of the rule by legislation that had been drafted with careful regard to the consequences.[27]

16–027   **3. Proposals for reform.** Those consequences have been considered on more than one occasion, and proposals made for reform.[28] Two of these proposals—the creation of land obligations and a system of "commonhold"— are still under active consideration.

16–028   *(a) Land obligations.* The Law Commission has recommended a scheme of "land obligations".[29] Under this scheme, the details of which are explained below,[30] there would be a new interest in land, which could be legal and which would embrace both positive and restrictive obligations. Such an obligation would be akin to an easement and there would have to be both land benefited and land burdened by it. The burden of a land obligation would run with the land. The following positive obligations would be capable of subsisting as a land obligation—

    (i) to carry out on either the servient or dominant land works which would benefit the whole or any part of the dominant land;

    (ii) to provide services for the benefit of the whole or any part of the dominant land; and

---

[24] See (1994) 110 L.Q.R. 346 at 348 *et seq.* (N. P. Gravells); [1994] Conv. 477 at 480 *et seq.* (J. Snape). *cf. Amsprop Trading Ltd v. Harris Distribution Ltd* [1997] 1 W.L.R. 1025 at 1034.

[25] *E.R. Ives Investment Ltd v. High, supra*; para. 16–025.

[26] See *Rhone v. Stephens, supra,* at 323. *E.R. Ives Investment Ltd v. High* was not cited to the House.

[27] Lord Templeman warned that "social injustice can be caused by logic", citing the difficulties that the enforcement of positive covenants had given rise to in relation to leases: *Rhone v. Stephens, supra,* at 321.

[28] *Ante,* para. 16–018.

[29] (1984) Law Com. No. 127. The scheme presented there has in fact been modified as a result of subsequent developments. In particular, the proposal for the creation of "development obligations" has been abandoned in the light of the commonhold proposals: see Commonhold: A Consultation Paper (1990) Cm. 1345, para. 3.49.

[30] *Post,* para. 16–081.

(iii) to pay in a specified manner for expenditure that is incurred in performing an obligation under (i) or (ii).[31]

The present rules by which the benefit of a positive covenant may run with the land would be abolished, though it would still be possible to assign them in accordance with the usual contractual rules.[32] The doctrine of mutual benefit and burden—presumably in its now attenuated form—would be unaffected.[33]

(b) Commonhold. A system of "commonhold" has been put forward by the **16–029** Lord Chancellor's Department[34] as a means of creating freehold strata titles,[35] a practice which, for reasons explained above,[36] is at present inadvisable. The proposed scheme is necessarily very elaborate but its main features may be summarised as follows.[37]

(i) A commonhold would consist of two or more units (such as a block of flats) which because of their shared facilities and services would require a system of communal management.

(ii) The units making up the commonhold would have to be structurally independent of any building outside the scheme.

(iii) Each unit owner would own the freehold in his unit and that ownership would automatically carry with it the right to essential facilities and any communal services.

(iv) Ownership of the common parts would be vested in a commonhold association, a corporate body run exclusively by the unit owners. The common parts, facilities and services would all be managed by the association.

---

[31] Law Com. No. 127, paras 6.3–6.6. In a case in which there was land benefited by the positive covenant but none burdened, such as *Smith v. River Douglas Catchment Board* [1949] 2 K.B. 500 (*ante*, paras 16–011, 16–013), the benefit would therefore have to be expressly assigned.

[32] Law Com. No. 127, paras 24.8, 24.9.

[33] *ibid.*, paras 24.31–24.33.

[34] See Commonhold, Freehold Flats and Freehold Ownership of Other Interdependent Buildings (1987), Cm. 179 (report of a working group chaired by T. Aldridge); Commonhold: A Consultation Paper (1990) Cm. 1345; [1991] Conv. 170 (H. W. Wilkinson). For a detailed examination of the commonhold proposals and its relationship with leasehold enfranchisement, see (1995) 58 M.L.R. 486 (D. N. Clarke); [1998] Conv. 283 (L. Crabb).

[35] Other countries have made statutory provision for this, including elaborate schemes of management which can be adopted for blocks of flats and similar developments. This is known in North America as the law of condominium, and in Australasia as that of strata titles.

[36] *Ante*, paras 16–017, 16–018.

[37] See Commonhold: A Consultation Paper (1990) Cm. 1345, pp. 1–18, and draft Bill; Commonhold—The Way Ahead (Lord Chancellor's Department, 1993). A draft Bill, that was intended to give effect to these proposals, was not, in the end, introduced in the 1996–97 Session of Parliament.

(v) A commonhold could be wound up. The freehold in the individual units would then vest automatically in the commonhold association and the rights of unit owners would be converted into a share in the net assets of the association.

(vi) The title to all commonholds would have to be registered at the Land Registry.[38]

Commonhold has been devised against the background of the proposals on land obligations and it is intended that the two systems would complement each other. It seems likely that further work will be undertaken on each and that revised proposals may be forthcoming.

Section 2. In Equity: Restrictive Covenants

16–030   **1. Law and equity.** The relationship between the divergent rules of common law and of equity is best understood by imagining the two separate jurisdictions which existed before 1875.[39] Equity's jurisdiction had, furthermore, two distinct aspects of its own. First, equity followed the law and provided better remedies than damages. Secondly, equity broke away from the rule that the burden of a covenant affecting land can only run with a lease, and allowed *restrictive* covenants to be enforced even against later owners of a freehold.

16–031   **2. Equitable remedies.** The special equitable remedies may be disposed of shortly. The value of a covenant affecting land is generally of a "real" character; that is to say, it lies in continued observance rather than in monetary compensation for a breach. Therefore an injunction, an equitable remedy, is usually more valuable than damages, at any rate where the obligation is merely negative. An injunction would normally be awarded[40] in a court of equity (and since 1875 in any Division of the High Court[41]) in any case where a covenant was enforceable at law.

16–032   **3. Restrictive covenants.** In inventing special rules about restrictive covenants equity added a new chapter to the law of property. The essentials of a restrictive covenant are that it is negative, and made for the benefit of land belonging to the covenantee. An example is where V, having two adjacent houses, sells one of them to P, and P covenants not to carry on any trade or business in the house he has bought, in order to preserve the residential value

---

[38] For the possible limits on the powers of commonholders to lease and mortgage their units, see (1995) 58 M.L.R. 486 at 500, 501 (D. N. Clarke).

[39] *Ante*, paras 4–015, 4–016.

[40] *Doherty v. Allman* (1878) 3 Ap.Cas. 709 at 719.

[41] *Ante*, para. 4–016.

of V's other house.[42] The real starting point, after some doubts[43] and precursors,[44] was the decision in *Tulk v. Moxhay*[45] in 1848, a time when the full effect of the vast expansion in industrial and building activities was being felt. It was held that a restrictive covenant could be enforced against a later purchaser unless (as always, in equity) he bought without notice of the covenant. A corpus of detailed rules evolved around this equitable doctrine. First, the circumstances in which the burden of a covenant would pass were defined. Subsequently, rules were developed as to when the benefit might be transmitted. Somewhat surprisingly, the latter caused greater difficulties than the former, but these problems have now been overcome. Each must be examined in turn.

A. The Burden of the Covenant

1. The decision. *Tulk v. Moxhay,*[46] decided in 1848, laid the first foundations of the modern doctrine of restrictive covenants. Previously the burden of a covenant (not made in a lease) would no more run in equity than it would at law. But in that case it was held by Lord Cottenham L.C., affirming Lord Langdale M.R.,[47] that a covenant to maintain the garden at Leicester Square uncovered with any buildings would be enforced by injunction against a purchaser of the land who bought with notice of the covenant. Thus was invented a new interest in land,[48] purely equitable in nature. No longer was a negative covenant enforceable only against the covenantor or his personal

16–033

---

[42] Such covenants are not in unlawful restraint of trade when given on the acquisition of new property. It may be otherwise when the property already belonged to the covenantor: *Esso Petroleum Co. Ltd v. Harper's Garage (Stourport) Ltd* [1968] A.C. 269; *Cleveland Petroleum Co. Ltd v. Dartstone Ltd* [1969] 1 W.L.R. 116. The remarkable operation of this distinction, suggested for the first time during the argument in the *Esso* case in the House of Lords, is illustrated by the example put in argument at p. 289 of that case. It is perhaps significant that, in a subsequent sale and leaseback case, the Court of Appeal upheld a tying covenant: *Alec Lobb (Garages) Ltd v. Total Oil (Great Britain) Ltd* [1985] 1 W.L.R. 173. Such tying covenants may now be vulnerable under Art. 85 of the Treaty of Rome, which prohibits certain anti-competitive agreements and which can apply to such covenants even though both parties are within, and performance is to take place in, the same Member State of the European Union. See *Inntrepreneur Estates Ltd v. Mason* (1993) 68 P. & C.R. 53; *Inntrepreneur Estates (G.L.) Ltd v. Boyes* (1993) 68 P. & C.R. 77; *Star Rider Ltd v. Inntrepreneur Pub Co.* [1998] 1 E.G.L.R. 53; and for a valuable commentary, [1994] Conv. 150 (T. Frazer). *cf. Gibbs Mew Plc v. Gemmell* [1999] 1 E.G.L.R. 43. It should be noted that even if a covenant is void under Art. 85 against the landlord who granted it, it may be valid and enforceable by an assignee of the reversion: see *Passmore v. Morland Plc* [1999] 1 E.G.L.R. 51 (tying covenant could be enforced by assignee of the reversion, which was a small regional brewer, even though it might have been void as regards the assignor, a major brewery group).

[43] The doctrine was denied in *Keppell v. Bailey* (1834) 2 My. & K. 517 at 546, 547 (on which see Challis 185) and treated as still unsettled in *Bristow v. Wood* (1844) 1 Coll.C.C. 480.

[44] *Whatman v. Gibson* (1838) 9 Sim. 196; *Mann v. Stephens* (1846) 15 Sim. 377.

[45] 2 Ph. 774.

[46] (1848) 2 Ph. 774. For a sequel see *Tulk v. Metropolitan Board of Works* (1868) 16 W.R. 212.

[47] (1848) 11 Beav. 571. The appeal was decided a mere 16 days after the decision below.

[48] *cf. ante*, para. 4–026. See the survey at (1971) 87 L.Q.R. 539 (D. J. Hayton).

representatives as a mere contract: it was now enforceable against his successors in title as an incumbrance, a right over some other person's land.

16–034   **2. Original basis.** For some while the question was thought to depend on two things only: the character of the covenant, and the fact of notice. A person who took land with notice that it was bound by some restriction could not, it was thought, disregard that restriction. On this footing it was immaterial whether the restriction had been imposed to benefit other land or merely the covenantee personally.[49] In fact, the suit in *Tulk v. Moxhay* had been brought by the original covenantee, who had other property in Leicester Square, and Lord Cottenham had relied on the argument that if the covenant did not run "it would be impossible for an owner of land to sell part of it without incurring the risk of rendering what he retains worthless".[50]

16–035   **3. Dominant tenement.** The argument relied upon by Lord Cottenham in fact became the foundation of the doctrine; and since 1903 it has been settled that equity will enforce a restrictive covenant against a purchaser only if it was made for the protection of other land.[51] Restrictive covenants came to resemble easements as being rights over one plot of land ("the servient tenement") existing for the benefit of another plot of land ("the dominant tenement"). It was said that the new principle was "either an extension in equity of the doctrine of *Spencer's Case* to another line of cases, or else an extension in equity of the doctrine of negative easements; such, for instance, as a right to the access of light, which prevents the owner of the servient tenement from building so as to obstruct the light".[52] But in reality the rule was a new departure, and eventually it was recognised that a new type of equitable interest had been created.[53]

16–036   **4. Essentials.** It was accordingly established that this new liability could run with land only where: (i) the covenant was restrictive, *i.e.* negative, in nature; (ii) two plots of land were concerned, one bearing the burden and the other receiving the benefit; and (iii) the defendant could not set up the overriding defence in equity of purchase of the legal estate for value without notice. We consider first the special position of the person who originally entered into the covenant, and then deal with these three conditions in order.

---

[49] *Catt v. Tourle* (1869) 4 Ch.App. 654 and *Luker v. Dennis* (1877) 7 Ch.D. 227 are two examples which are no longer good law.

[50] *Tulk v. Moxhay, supra,* 2 Ph. at 777. For more recent litigation concerning another covenant entered into in 1874 on a sale of land in Leicester Square by a member of the Tulk family, see *R. v. Westminster City Council, ex p. Leicester Square Coventry Street Association* (1989) 87 L.G.R. 675.

[51] *Formby v. Barker* [1903] 2 Ch. 539; *L.C.C. v. Allen* [1914] 3 K.B. 642 at 659, 660. There are certain exceptions to this rule; *post,* para. 16–045.

[52] *London and South Western Ry v. Gomm* (1882) 20 Ch.D. 562 at 583, *per* Jessel M.R. For discussion and criticism of the principles evolved in the decisions of this period, see (1982) 98 L.Q.R. 279 at 293 (S. Gardner). See also [1978] Conv. 24 (J. D. A. Brooke-Taylor).

[53] *Re Nisbet and Potts' Contract* [1905] 1 Ch. 391 at 396 (on appeal, [1906] 1 Ch. 386).

I. THE ORIGINAL COVENANTOR

The original covenantor normally remains liable on the covenant, even if there **16–037** is no dominant tenement, and even if he has parted with the servient tenement. This is because his liability is purely contractual and exists quite apart from the law of property, just as in the case of an original tenant under a lease granted before 1996 who has assigned his lease.[54] In the absence of an expression of contrary intention, a person is, by statute, deemed to covenant on behalf of himself, his successors in title and those deriving title under him.[55] There is some dispute as to the significance of these words. There appear to be two possible interpretations of them.

(i) The words are included merely to show an intention that the **16–038** burden of the covenant should run with the land and not to make the covenantor personally liable for the acts of his successors in title.[56] This view must be open to serious doubt. In the analogous case of leaseholds granted before 1996, it is clear that the original lessee cannot escape from liability on his covenants by assigning the lease, and it seems to be immaterial whether he has covenanted on behalf of his successors in title or not.[57]

(ii) The covenantor is in effect taken to give a personal warranty that neither he nor any of his successors in title will infringe the terms of the covenant.[58] If that is so, the words are, in one sense, mere surplusage. The original covenantor is liable for the acts of his successors in title simply by virtue of privity of contract, and this has always been perceived to be the reason why the first tenant under a lease granted before 1996 remains liable on the covenants throughout the duration of the term.[59] However, the words implied by the statute do preclude any ambiguity as to the extent of the original covenantor's liability. By covenanting on behalf of his successors in title, he makes it apparent that he will remain liable on the basis of privity of contract for the acts of his successors in title notwithstanding that he may have parted with the land.[60] If he

---

[54] *Ante*, para. 15–008. For leases granted after 1995, see *ante*, paras 14–280, 14–281.

[55] L.P.A. 1925, s.79(1); *ante*, para. 16–016. As regards restrictive covenants, "successors in title" is deemed to include the owners for the time being of the land: *ibid.*, s.79(2). Prior to 1926, a person would commonly covenant expressly "for himself, his heirs and assigns, and other persons claiming under him".

[56] *Powell v. Hemsley* [1909] 1 Ch. 680 at 688 (Eve J.); *cf.* [1909] 2 Ch. 252 at 256, 258 (CA).

[57] *cf. Walker's Case* (1587) 3 Co.Rep. 22a at 23a. In the case of a lease, the natural inference is that parties intended to contract for the duration of the term. In relation to a freehold covenant the inference that a covenantor intends to bind himself in perpetuity is perhaps less obvious.

[58] *cf. Baily v. De Crespigny* (1869) L.R. 4 Q.B. 180 at 186.

[59] *Ante*, para. 15–008.

[60] A covenantor could in principle *limit* his liability by covenanting only on behalf of successors in title and not on behalf of all owners and occupiers for the time being of the land (as he is deemed to do under L.P.A. 1925, s.79(2) in relation to restrictive covenants). *cf. Baily v. De Crespigny, supra,* at 186, 187.

wishes to limit his liability to his own acts, he must covenant expressly to that effect.

In practice there is little authority on the liability of the original covenantor for breach of a restrictive covenant after he has disposed of the burdened land. This is not surprising. The owner of the land benefited by the restrictive covenant is likely to wish to restrain by injunction any act that contravenes the covenant, rather than merely seeking damages for its breach.[61] The appropriate defendant will therefore be the person who presently owns or occupies the land and not the original covenantor.

II. ASSIGNEES

16–039 An assignee of the original covenantor's land is bound by the covenant only if four conditions are fulfilled.

1. The covenant must be negative in nature

16–040 *(a) Negativity.* After a few cases in which the court was prepared to enforce a positive covenant,[62] the rule was settled in 1881 that only a negative covenant would be enforced by equity.[63] The equitable interest created by the covenant is one primarily enforceable by injunction, and whereas a negative injunction restraining the commission or continuance of specified acts normally presents no difficulties of enforcement, equity has long been chary of making orders to perform a series of acts requiring supervision,[64] even though it has the necessary jurisdiction to decree specific performance or grant a mandatory injunction,[65] ordering specified acts to be done. The doctrine is confined to negative covenants because effect can be given to these "by means of the land itself".[66]

16–041 *(b) Substance.* The question is whether the covenant is negative in nature: it is immaterial whether the wording is positive or negative. Thus the covenant in *Tulk v. Moxhay*[67] was positive in wording (to maintain the Leicester Square garden "in an open state, uncovered with any buildings") but negative in

---

[61] *Post*, para. 16–051. The court may award damages in lieu of an injunction under the Supreme Court Act 1981, s.50. The original covenantor will invariably take an indemnity covenant from any transferee of the land burdened: see Standard Conditions of Sale, c. 4.5.3.

[62] *Morland v. Cook* (1868) L.R. 6 Eq. 252; *Cooke v. Chilcott* (1876) 3 Ch.D. 694. For differing interpretations of these cases see [1981] Conv. 55 (C. D. Bell); [1983] Conv. 29 (R. Griffith); 327 (C. D. Bell). For the enforcement of positive covenants today, see *ante*, paras 16–017 *et seq.*

[63] *Haywood v. Brunswick Permanent Benefit B.S.* (1881) 8 Q.B.D. 403. This principle has been reaffirmed by the House of Lords: *Rhone v. Stephens* [1994] 2 A.C. 310.

[64] But this is less so than formerly: *cf. ante*, paras 14–280, 14–281.

[65] See *Jackson v. Normanby Brick Co.* [1899] 1 Ch. 438 (order to demolish buildings erected in breach of covenant).

[66] *Re Nisbet & Potts' Contract* [1905] 1 Ch. 391 at 397, *per* Farwell J. "To enforce a positive covenant would be to enforce a personal obligation against a person who has not covenanted. To enforce negative covenants is only to treat the land as subject to a restriction": *Rhone v. Stephens, supra*, at 321, *per* Lord Templeman.

[67] (1848) 2 Ph. 774; *ante*, para. 16–033.

nature, for it merely bound the covenantor to refrain from building, without requiring him to do any positive act. A test which is often applied is whether the covenant requires expenditure of money for its performance; if the covenant requires the covenantor "to put his hand into his pocket", it is not negative in nature.[68] But the converse does not necessarily follow; a covenant that can be performed without expense may still require some positive act and so not be restrictive. A covenant to use the premises as a private dwelling-house only is negative in nature, for really it is a prohibition against use for other purposes[69]; and the same applies to a covenant to give the first refusal of a plot of land,[70] for in effect it is a covenant not to sell to anyone else until the covenantee has had an opportunity of buying. But a covenant "not to let the premises fall into disrepair", despite its apparently negative form, is in substance positive, for it can be performed only by the expenditure of money on repairs.

(c) Severance. If a covenant has both positive and negative elements in it, the negative element may bind the land even though the positive cannot.[71] Even a positive obligation may be binding if it is no more than a condition of a negative one; thus a covenant to submit plans before building may be enforceable against a purchaser as a covenant not to build without first submitting plans.[72]   **16–042**

(d) Common covenants. Some examples may be given of the restrictive covenants that are most frequently encountered in practice, particularly in transfers or leases of urban property. They include covenants against—   **16–043**

    (i) building on land[73];

    (ii) carrying on any trade or business (or certain specified trades or businesses) on the premises[74];

---

[68] *Haywood v. Brunswick Permanent Benefit B.S.*, *supra*, at 409, 410. See too *Bedwell Park Quarry Co. Ltd v. Hertfordshire County Council* [1993] J.P.L. 349 (obligation by quarry company to restore quarry to agriculture: "it was hard to think of an obligation that was more positive in substances as well as form": *per* Sir Christopher Slade at 352).

[69] *e.g. German v. Chapman* (1877) 7 Ch.D. 271.

[70] See *Manchester Ship Canal Co. v. Manchester Racecourse Co.* [1901] 2 Ch. 37; *Lange v. Lange* [1966] N.Z.L.R. 1057.

[71] *Shepherd Homes Ltd v. Sandham (No. 2)* [1971] 1 W.L.R. 1062 (approved in *Bedwell Park Quarry Co. Ltd v. Hertfordshire County Council*, *supra*, at 351). Thus in *Tulk v. Moxhay* (*ante*, para. 16–033) the covenant was to maintain the garden as well as not to build upon it.

[72] *Powell v. Hemsley* [1909] 1 Ch. 680; 2 Ch. 252; and see *Westhoughton U.D.C. v. Wigan Coal & Iron Co. Ltd* [1919] 1 Ch. 159 (not to let down surface without paying compensation).

[73] *Wrotham Park Estate Co. Ltd v. Parkside Homes Ltd* [1974] 1 W.L.R. 798; *R. v. Westminster City Council, ex p. Leicester Square Coventry Street Association* (1989) 87 L.G.R. 675 (covenant not infringed by the mere sale of the property to a third party who intended to build).

[74] See, however, *Petrofina (Gt Britain) Ltd v. Martin* [1966] Ch. 146. It has now been held that a covenant restraining alienation is within the doctrine: see *Hemingway Securities Ltd v. Dunraven Ltd* [1995] 1 E.G.L.R. 61 at 62. *cf. ante*, para. 3–071. The covenant is breached only if the trade or business is undertaken on the land burdened by it and not if the property is used merely as a means of access to other land on which such trade or business is carried on: *Elliott v. Safeway Stores Plc* [1995] 1 W.L.R. 1396.

(iii) carrying on any activity that constitutes a nuisance, or is offensive or dangerous[75]; and

(iv) using the premises for any purpose other than as a private dwelling-house.[76]

16–044   **2. The covenant must be made for the protection of land retained by the covenantee.**[77] It is axiomatic that the justification for converting a personal covenant into an equitable incumbrance is to enable the covenantee to preserve the value of other land of his in the neighbourhood.[78] As with easements,[79] therefore, there must be two plots of land in the case: the doctrine depends on a relation of "dominancy" and "serviency" of lands.[80] Whether this relationship exists is a question of fact in each case, and proof of the facts may make the relationship plain.[81] Proximity is essential: covenants binding land in Hampstead will be too remote to benefit land in Clapham.[82] A covenantee similarly ceases to be able to enforce a covenant (except as against the original covenantor) if he parts with all the land for the benefit of which the covenant was taken,[83] or if it ceases to be reasonably possible to regard the covenant as being for the benefit of the land.[84] And a covenant made for the protection of a leasehold interest ceases to be enforceable when the lease determines, *e.g.* by merger in the freehold.[85]

To this rule requiring the covenantee to hold adjacent land there are the following exceptions and qualifications.

---

[75] *Hall v. Ewin* (1887) 37 Ch.D. 74 (covenant infringed by user of house in Edgware Road to display lions); *Tod-Heatley v. Benham* (1888) 40 Ch.D. 80 (covenant infringed by user of house as hospital treating over 50 persons each day). *cf. National Schizophrenia Fellowship v. Ribble Estates S.A.* [1994] 1 E.G.L.R. 181 (covenant not infringed by acquisition of house to accommodate elderly mental patients).

[76] *C. & G. Homes Ltd v. Secretary of State for Health* [1991] Ch. 365 (covenant infringed by use of house to provide supervised housing for a group of mental patients). See too *Brown v. Heathlands Mental Health NHS Trust* [1996] 1 All E.R. 133 at 135. This form of covenant is narrower than a covenant against carrying on a trade or business: see [1991] Conv. 388 (P. Devonshire). See too *Jaggard v. Sawyer* [1995] 1 W.L.R. 269 (covenant not to use land except as a private garden contravened by construction of a driveway). In rural areas there may be a covenant against using the premises for any save agricultural purposes: *Holdom v. Kidd* (1990) 61 P. & C.R. 456 (covenant infringed by user of land to accommodate gypsy caravans: it was irrelevant that many of the gypsies worked on local farms).

[77] *Millbourn v. Lyons* [1914] 2 Ch. 231 (the relevant date is that of the covenant, not the contract therefor); *L.C.C. v. Allen* [1914] 3 K.B. 642.

[78] *Ante*, para. 16–032.

[79] *Post*, para. 18–045.

[80] *Formby v. Barker* [1903] 2 Ch. 539 at 552 (Vaughan Williams L.J.). For a detailed account of the evolution of this rule, see *L.C.C. v. Allen, supra*, at 664 *et seq*. For comment see (1982) 98 L.Q.R. 279 at 306 (S. Gardner).

[81] In other words, it need not appear from the covenant itself: *Tulk v. Moxhay* (1848) 2 Ph. 774; *Marten v. Flight Refuelling Ltd* [1962] Ch. 115.

[82] *Kelly v. Barrett* [1924] 2 Ch. 379 at 404.

[83] *Chambers v. Randall* [1923] 1 Ch. 149 at 157, 158.

[84] *Wrotham Park Estate Co. Ltd v. Parkside Homes Ltd* [1974] 1 W.L.R. 798.

[85] *Golden Lion Hotel (Hunstanton) Ltd v. Carter* [1965] 1 W.L.R. 1189. L.P.A. 1925, s.139 (*ante*, para. 15–055) does not cover this situation.

(a) Leases and mortgages. The doctrine of *Tulk v. Moxhay* applies equally **16–045** to covenants contained in leases. Moreover, the landlord enjoys an important dispensation: his reversion is apparently a sufficient interest to enable him to sue a sub-lessee in equity on a restrictive covenant contained in the lease. There is therefore no need for any other land which could be called a dominant tenement.[86] In relation to leases granted before 1996, this is an important extension of the reversioner's rights, for where the covenant is negative he may have a remedy against someone, such as a sub-tenant, with whom he has neither privity of contract nor privity of estate.[87] A similar dispensation appears to apply to mortgages, so that the mortgagee's interest in the mortgaged land likewise suffices.[88]

(b) Scheme of development. The meaning of "scheme of development" will **16–046** shortly be explained.[89] When, under such a scheme, the common vendor disposes of the last of the plots laid out for development, he may retain no adjacent land. But even though the owners of the other plots are not expressly made covenantees,[90] the last purchaser's covenants are enforceable by them against both the last purchaser himself and his successors in title, so that the rule in *Tulk v. Moxhay* applies.

(c) Statutory exceptions. The rules applied to private landowners have been **16–047** modified by numerous statutes for the benefit of public bodies. These statutes enable such bodies to enforce covenants in gross.[91] For example, under the Town and Country Planning Act 1990 (as amended) any person interested in land may (by agreement or otherwise) enter into a planning obligation with a local authority restricting the land in any specified way.[92] Such an agreement is enforceable against both the person entering into the obligation and his successor in title.[93] Where, in carrying out its obligations in relation to housing under the Housing Act 1985, a local authority enters into a covenant on the disposal of land held by it for housing purposes, or with any landowner, that covenant is enforceable against the covenantor and his successors in title even though it was not taken for the benefit of any land owned by the authority.[94] The National Trust may enforce a covenant made with it against the successor in title of the covenantor as if it had been made for the benefit

---

[86] *Hall v. Ewin* (1887) 37 Ch.D. 74, decided before the requirement of benefited land was firmly settled, but approved by Harman L.J. in *Regent Oil Co. Ltd v. J.A. Gregory (Hatch End) Ltd* [1966] Ch. 402 at 433; and see *Teape v. Douse* (1905) 92 L.T. 319.

[87] *cf. ante*, para. 15–005. For leases granted after 1995, see *ante*, para. 15–086.

[88] *John Brothers Abergarw Brewery Co. v. Holmes* [1900] 1 Ch. 188; *Regent Oil Co. Ltd v. J.A. Gregory (Hatch End) Ltd, supra, per* Harman L.J.

[89] *Post*, para. 16–075.

[90] *Ante*, para. 16–006.

[91] Such statutes have been employed for many years: see *Governors of Peabody Donation Fund v. London Residuary Body* (1987) 55 P. & C.R. 355 (Artisans and Labourers Dwellings Improvement Act 1875).

[92] s.106(1) (substituted by the Planning and Compensation Act 1991, s.12); *ante*, para. 16–018. This section replaces with a different and much more extensive regime, so-called "s.52 agreements": see the now repealed T. & C.P.A. 1971, s.52.

[93] T. & C.P.A. 1990, s.106(3).

[94] H.A. 1985, s.609.

of the Trust's land.[95] Likewise local authorities can enforce agreements made with landowners against their successors under the Ancient Monuments Act 1979[96] and the Wildlife and Countryside Act 1981.[97]

16–048   *(d) Remedies in contract and tort.* It has been held[98] that where there is a covenant not to "cause or permit" land to be used otherwise than for specified purposes, it will be no breach of the covenant for the covenantor to agree to sell the land to a purchaser whom he knows to intend to use it for other purposes, and to assist him in obtaining planning permission for that use. For the vendor, on selling, loses control of the property, and "one cannot permit that which one does not control".[99] But if the covenant had been framed so as to prohibit parting with control in such circumstances, it appears that both the vendor and the purchaser could have been restrained by injunction from completing the sale, and that the covenantee, if he suffered damage, could have sued the purchaser in tort for wrongfully inducing a breach of contract,[1] and perhaps also for conspiracy.[2] In one case where the covenantor and the purchaser were companies controlled by a third company and the land was transferred in conspiracy with the object of breaking the covenant, the court granted a mandatory injunction requiring the land to be reconveyed to the covenantor.[3] A purchaser must therefore remember that even when a covenant will not bind him as a successor in title,[4] he may yet become implicated in a breach of contract by the vendor.

16–049   **3. The burden of the covenant must have been intended to run with the covenantor's land.** A covenant may be so worded as to bind the covenantor alone, and of course in such a case assignees of the covenantor's land will not be bound by the covenant.[5] But if the covenant is made by the covenantor for himself, his heirs and assigns, the burden will normally run with his land. Covenants relating to the covenantor's land which are made after 1925 are deemed to have been made by the covenantor on behalf of himself, his successors in title, and the persons deriving title under him or them, unless a

---

[95] National Trust Act 1938, s.8. See, *e.g. Gee v. National Trust* [1966] 1 W.L.R. 170; *Re Whitting's Application* (1988) 58 P. & C.R. 321.
[96] s.17(5).
[97] s.39(3).
[98] *Tophams Ltd v. Earl of Sefton* [1967] 1 A.C. 50 (proposal to build houses on Aintree Racecourse).
[99] *ibid.* at 65, *per* Lord Hodson.
[1] *Sefton v. Tophams Ltd* [1965] Ch. 1140 (C.A.); reversed, *supra*, n. 98. But there was no appeal against this part of the decision. See (1977) 41 Conv.(N.S.) 318 (R. J. Smith); (1982) 45 M.L.R. 241 (N. Cohen-Grabelsky). *cf. ante*, para. 4–093.
[2] *Midland Bank Trust Co. Ltd v. Green (No. 3)* [1982] Ch. 529. This tort requires concerted action with the dominant purpose of causing injury, and can be committed by husband and wife: *ibid.*
[3] *Esso Petroleum Co. Ltd v. Kingswood Motors (Addlestone) Ltd* [1974] Q.B. 142 (covenant to buy all motor fuel from plaintiffs and to procure similar covenant from any transferee; damages held inadequate remedy).
[4] In the *Sefton* case, *supra*, the vendor retained no land benefited by the covenant.
[5] *Re Fawcett and Holmes' Contract* (1889) 42 Ch.D. 150; *Re Royal Victoria Pavilion, Ramsgate* [1961] Ch. 581.

contrary intention appears.[6] The burden of a covenant restricting the use of land and made since 1925 will therefore prima facie run with the land.[7]

4. The burden of the covenant runs only in equity. There are two   **16–050**
principal consequences of the rule that the burden of the covenant runs only in equity.

(a) Only equitable remedies are available

(1) INJUNCTION. Only equitable remedies are available and this means in   **16–051**
practice that the case must be remediable by injunction, which is the only equitable remedy appropriate to a negative covenant. This is in keeping with the nature of a restrictive covenant as an equitable interest: it is not intended as a subject for monetary compensation, but as a means of preserving the value of land specifically. A mandatory injunction may be granted if necessary, *e.g.* for the removal of a building erected in breach of covenant,[8] or to order the surrender of a sub-lease granted in breach of a covenant in the head lease.[9]

Like other equitable remedies, an injunction lies in the discretion of the court. This does not mean that it will not be granted as a matter of course in an ordinary case. But it will be refused if it would be inequitable to grant it, as it may be where, for example, the claimant has known of the breach for five years and taken no action[10]; and in some cases the court may award damages while refusing an injunction.[11] Although failure to enforce a covenant against one person does not necessarily waive it as against others,[12] an injunction may be refused if the claimant has exhibited such inactivity in the face of open breaches of covenant as to justify a reasonable belief that he no longer intends to enforce the covenant.[13] It is also possible for an injunction to be refused because the character of the neighbourhood has been so completely changed that the covenant has become valueless.[14] But otherwise a restrictive covenant remains enforceable indefinitely, even after the perpetuity period has run.[15]

(2) DAMAGES IN LIEU OF AN INJUNCTION. Since the Chancery Amendment   **16–052**
Act 1858[16] the court has been empowered to award damages in any case

---

[6] L.P.A. 1925, s.79, explained *ante*, para. 16–038.

[7] The burden of positive covenants cannot run with the land, irrespective of the intentions of the parties, and s.79 has not altered this rule: *ante*, para. 16–016.

[8] As in *Wakeham v. Wood* (1981) 43 P. & C.R. 40 (building obstructed plaintiff's sea view), where the Court of Appeal explained the practice in granting such orders.

[9] *Hemingway Securities Ltd v. Dunraven Ltd* [1995] 1 E.G.L.R. 61.

[10] *Gaskin v. Balls* (1879) 13 Ch.D. 324.

[11] As in *Shaw v. Applegate* [1977] 1 W.L.R. 970.

[12] *German v. Chapman* (1877) 7 Ch.D. 271.

[13] See *Chatsworth Estates Co. v. Fewell* [1931] 1 Ch. 224.

[14] *Chatsworth Estates Co. v. Fewell, supra*; and see *Westripp v. Baldock* [1939] 1 All E.R. 279. In the former case (at 227, 228), it was doubted whether it was legitimate to consider (as was done in *Sober v. Sainsbury* [1913] 2 Ch. 513) changes in property outside the district. For the discharge of obsolete covenants, see *post*, para. 16–086.

[15] *Mackenzie v. Childers* (1889) 43 Ch.D. 265 at 279.

[16] s.2. See now Supreme Court Act 1981, s.50.

where an injunction or specific performance could have been awarded. Such damages are not awarded as of right to a claimant who makes out his case unlike damages at common law.[17] Nor will they be awarded if no injunction could have been granted.[18] An award of damages in lieu of an injunction is intended as a substitute for loss arising from future wrongs, a situation for which no remedy exists at common law.[19] Where a claimant seeks damages in lieu of an injunction for breach of a restrictive covenant,[20] then even if the breach would cause no diminution in the value of his land,[21] the court may award him damages measured by the amount which he could have obtained for the release of the covenant.[22]

16–053   *(b) Effect on third parties.* Because a restrictive covenant is only equitable it must usually be protected by the appropriate form of registration if it is to bind third parties who purchase a legal estate. A restrictive covenant will always be enforceable against a donee, a devisee or a squatter because none of them is a purchaser.[23]

16–054   (1) UNREGISTERED LAND. Where title to the land is unregistered, any restrictive covenants will be registrable as land charges under the Land Charges Act 1972 except those entered into before 1926 or made between a lessor and lessee.[24] A covenant which is registrable but not registered will be void against a subsequent purchaser for money or money's worth of a legal estate in the land charged with it.[25] Registration of a covenant constitutes actual

---

[17] See *Kelly v. Barrett* [1924] 2 Ch. 379.

[18] As where the defendant had sold the houses it had built in breach of covenant and the purchasers had not been joined as parties to the action: *Surrey County Council v. Bredero Homes Ltd* [1993] 1 W.L.R. 1361. The question, which is "effectively one of jurisdiction", is "whether at the date of the writ the court *could* have granted an injunction, not whether it *would* have done": *Jaggard v. Sawyer* [1995] 1 W.L.R. 269 at 285, *per* Millett L.J.

[19] *ibid.*, at 290. Damages may of course be awarded in addition for any loss that has already been suffered before the matter is adjudicated.

[20] The typical case is where the defendant has constructed a building in contravention of a restrictive covenant and the claimant took no steps to seek an interlocutory injunction to restrain him: see, *e.g. Jaggard v. Sawyer, supra.* For an analogous situation where damages may be awarded in lieu of an injunction where a person builds so as to obstruct an easement, see *Snell & Prideaux Ltd v. Dutton Mirrors Ltd* [1995] 1 E.G.L.R. 259.

[21] So that if the court could not have awarded an injunction any damages that might have been awarded at common law against the original covenantor would have been nominal: *Surrey County Council v. Bredero Homes Ltd, supra.*

[22] *Wrotham Park Estate Co. Ltd v. Parkside Homes Ltd* [1974] 1 W.L.R. 798. Although doubts have been expressed as to the correctness of this decision (see *e.g. Surrey County Council v. Bredero Homes Ltd, supra,* at 1386), it has now been approved: see *Jaggard v. Sawyer, supra.* Although there has been considerable debate as to whether in *Wrotham Park Estate Co. Ltd v. Parkside Homes Ltd, supra,* the court was awarding the plaintiff compensation for his loss (*i.e.* the right to extract payment for the release of the covenant) or granting him in part at least the defendant's gain, the former has now been established: *Jaggard v. Sawyer, supra; cf. Wrotham Park S.E. v. Hertsmere B.C.* [1993] 2 E.G.L.R. 15 at 18. See generally Goff & Jones, *The Law of Restitution,* (5th ed.), pp. 518–523.

[23] *Re Nisbet and Potts' Contract* [1906] 1 Ch. 386 (squatter).

[24] L.C.A. 1972, s.2(5)(ii); *ante*, para. 5–103.

[25] L.C.A. 1972, s.4(6); *ante*, para. 5–117.

notice of it to all persons and for all purposes.[26] As regards covenants that are within the two classes which are not registrable, the position is as follows.

(i) Covenants entered into before 1926 or made between lessor and lessee where the lease was granted before 1996 still depend upon the doctrine of notice. They will not therefore be binding on a bona fide purchaser for value of a legal estate[27] without notice of the covenant, or someone claiming through such a person.[28] In a lease granted prior to 1996, a restrictive covenant in a head lease will be binding on a sub-lessee who took with notice of it.[29] As the sub-lessee will have the right to see the head lease, he will in practice be fixed with notice of any restrictive covenant in it.[30]

(ii) In a lease granted after 1995,[31] a restrictive covenant is enforceable against the assignee and any other person who is the owner or occupier of any demised premises to which the covenant relates.[32] A sub-lessee will be bound by the covenant therefore even though there is no express provision in the sub-lease to that effect.[33]

(2) REGISTERED LAND. Where title is registered, a restrictive covenant[34] **16–055** takes effect as a minor interest and may be protected either as a notice[35] if the land certificate is produced to, or deposited with, the registrar,[36] or as a caution if it is not.[37] Where a notice is entered, both the proprietor of the land affected by it and the persons subsequently deriving title under him are deemed to be affected with notice of the covenant.[38] A covenant between a lessor and lessee is not registrable as a notice.[39] However, any restrictive covenant in a lease will bind a sub-lessee because he takes the land subject to all implied and express covenants, obligations, and liabilities incident to the estate created.[40] In any event, a restrictive covenant in a lease granted after 1995 is binding on

---

[26] L.P.A. 1925, s.198(1) *ante*, para. 5–109. For the difficulties which arise for a tenant who cannot investigate the freehold title, but who will nevertheless be bound by any covenant registered against a previous owner of the reversion, see *ante*, para. 14–296.

[27] Not a mere equitable interest: *London & South Western Ry. v. Gomm* (1882) 20 Ch.D. 562 at 583; *Osborne v. Bradley* [1903] 2 Ch. 446 at 451.

[28] *ibid.*

[29] *Hall v. Ewin* (1887) 37 Ch.D. 74 at 79 (the remarks were *obiter* as the injunction was sought against the tenant rather than the sub-tenant).

[30] *Ante*, para. 14–295.

[31] For the leases in question, see L. & T.C.A. 1995, s.1; *ante*, para. 15–007.

[32] L. & T.C.A. 1995, s.3(5).

[33] *ibid.*, ss.3(5), 28(1).

[34] For the powers of a registered proprietor to create or discharge a restrictive covenant, see L.R.A. 1925, s.40.

[35] L.R.A. 1925, s.50(1); L.R.R. 1925, r. 212. The notice should, where practicable refer to the land (whether registered or not) for the benefit of which the covenant is taken: L.R.A. 1925, s.50(4).

[36] *Ante*, paras 6–078, 6–079.

[37] L.R.A. 1925, s.54 *ante*, paras 6–083, 6–084.

[38] L.R.A. 1925, s.50(2).

[39] *ibid.*, s.50(1).

[40] *ibid.*, s.23(1)(a).

any sub-lessee under the provisions of the Landlord and Tenant (Covenants) Act 1995.[41]

B. The Benefit of the Covenant

16–056   In order to enforce a covenant, the plaintiff must show that he is entitled to the benefit of it. The original covenantee can of course sue the original covenantor, and he can also sue successors in title of the original covenantor, if the burden has passed to them. But he cannot sue the successors in title if he has parted with all the land for the benefit of which the covenant was taken,[42] for equity would not enforce the doctrine of *Tulk v. Moxhay* where the covenant was divorced from the land it was intended to protect.[43]

As for successors in title of the original covenantee, it should be remembered that the benefit of a restrictive covenant could, and still can, run with the covenantee's land at common law, without the help of equity, under the rules already stated.[44] In order to succeed at law the plaintiff must be legal owner of the land to which the covenant relates. But in equity he can succeed if he has some lesser estate,[45] or is merely an equitable owner, such as a successor under the covenantee's will or intestacy who has not yet obtained a legal title,[46] or a person for whom the benefit of the covenant is otherwise held upon trust.[47] The benefit is regarded as an interest in property which devolves on death in the ordinary way.[48]

16–057   Since 1875 it ought to make no practical difference whether the benefit passes under the rules of law or of equity, since the same court can enforce both. In one leading case the court was prepared to allow the benefit to run with the benefited land at law even where the defendant, being a successor of the covenantor, was liable only in equity.[49] Equity here merely followed the law. But more complicated rules developed which were assumed to apply in all actions against such defendants, so making the law follow equity.[50] However, since the end of 1979, many of these rules have become irrelevant. This is because of the effect of the decision of the Court of Appeal in *Federated Homes Ltd v. Mill Lodge Properties Ltd,*[51] which has greatly simplified the

---

[41] ss.3(5), 28(1); *supra.*
[42] *Chambers v. Randall* [1923] 1 Ch. 149.
[43] See *ibid.*, at 157, 158; *post*, para. 16–066.
[44] *Ante*, para. 16–011.
[45] *Taite v. Gosling* (1879) 11 Ch.D. 273 (tenant of purchaser from covenantee).
[46] *Lord Northbourne v. Johnston* [1922] 2 Ch. 309; *Newton Abbot Co-operative Society Ltd v. Williamson & Treadgold Ltd* [1952] Ch. 286; *Earl of Leicester v. Wells-next-the-Sea U.D.C.* [1973] Ch. 110.
[47] *Lord Northbourne v. Johnston, supra*; *Marten v. Flight Refuelling Ltd* [1962] Ch. 115.
[48] *Ives v. Brown* [1919] 2 Ch. 314.
[49] *Rogers v. Hosegood* [1900] 2 Ch. 388 at 394, 404.
[50] See *Re Union of London and Smith's Bank Ltd's Conveyance* [1933] Ch. 611 at 630, saying that equity prescribed special rules.
[51] [1980] 1 W.L.R. 594; *post*, para. 16–063.

rules governing the transmission of the benefit of restrictive covenants entered into since 1925.[52] The rules may be stated as follows.

1. The covenant must touch and concern land of the covenantee. This is the same as the rule at common law.[53] The benefit of a covenant can run only with land to which the covenant in fact relates; and in the case of a restrictive covenant the essential object, on which the doctrine of *Tulk v. Moxhay* depends,[54] is to preserve the value of the covenantee's other land. A covenant will satisfy this requirement if it benefits a business conducted on the dominant land.[55] Whether that land is in fact benefited must be established by extrinsic evidence.[56]

16–058

2. The benefit of the covenant must have passed to the plaintiff in one of three ways: by annexation; by assignment; or under a scheme of development. In principle this rule is the same as the preceding one.[57] Under that rule the benefit of a covenant could run at law, and equity needed only to follow the law. But in the case of negative covenants, which assumed a new importance when the burden of them was allowed to run in equity, the rule was held to require further elaboration.[58] The examples of the benefit running at law were mostly cases of positive covenants where it was obvious from the facts that identifiable land of the covenantee was to be benefited, as explained earlier.[59] But a restrictive covenant, which merely prohibits the covenantor from some kind of activity on his own land, does not ordinarily indicate that it is intended to benefit any land, still less any particular land, of the covenantee.[60] It was considered that if the benefit of a restrictive covenant was to run with the covenantee's land, something further was required to identify the land. This could be done in one of three ways—

16–059

(i) by showing that the benefit was annexed to that land; or

---

[52] The decision does not affect covenants entered into prior to 1926: *post*, para. 16–064.

[53] *Rogers v. Hosegood* [1900] 2 Ch. 388; *Re Union of London & Smith's Bank Ltd's Conveyance* [1933] Ch. 611; *Re Ballard's Conveyance* [1937] Ch. 473; see *ante*, para. 16–013.

[54] *Ante*, para. 16–031.

[55] *Newton Abbot Co-operative Society Ltd v. Williamson & Treadgold Ltd* [1952] Ch. 286 at 293; *Re Quaffers Ltd's Application* (1988) 56 P. & C.R. 142 at 152. *cf.* the requirement that an easement must accommodate the dominant tenement, where the same rule applies: *post*, para. 18–045.

[56] See, *e.g. Re Ballard's Conveyance*, *supra*.

[57] In *Rogers v. Hosegood*, *supra*, Farwell J. spoke (at 395) of the covenant touching and concerning the land, while the Court of Appeal spoke (at 407) of the benefit being annexed to it. The meaning appears to be the same, although the former decision was based on the rules of common law and the latter on the rules of equity, it having transpired in the Court of Appeal that the legal estate was outstanding in a mortgagee.

[58] For criticism of this exposition, see (1982) 2 L.S. 53 (D. J. Hurst). But the difference here stressed is not that between the rules of law and of equity, but that between positive and negative covenants.

[59] *Ante*, para. 16–013.

[60] Though sometimes the covenant itself may make it plain, as in *Westhoughton U.D.C. v. Wigan Coal & Iron Co. Ltd* [1919] 1 Ch. 159 (covenant not to let down surface of land).

(ii) by expressly assigning the benefit; or

(iii) by showing that the land lies within a scheme of development.

In fact most restrictive covenants entered into after 1925 will be automatically annexed by statute to the covenantee's land benefited by them. Other forms of annexation are now relevant only to restrictive covenants entered into before 1926 and are therefore treated only in outline.[61] The circumstances in which the benefit of a covenant will require assignment are now very limited. Schemes of development remain of considerable importance for reasons that are explained later.[62] Details of the three alternative methods of transmitting the benefit are as follows.

I. ANNEXATION

16–060   *(a) Annexation in equity.* A covenant may be made for the benefit of the covenantee personally or for the benefit of land which he owns. It might have been thought that if a covenant touched and concerned the land so that it was not merely personal to the covenantee, it could be regarded as having been taken for the benefit of the covenantee's land.[63] However this is not so. It has long been established that it is necessary to show in addition that it was the intention of the parties that the covenant should be annexed to the covenantee's land.[64] This may be established either from the express words of the covenant or from a construction of the instrument creating it, having regard to the surrounding circumstances.[65]

16–061   (1) EXPRESS ANNEXATION.[66] The benefit will be effectively annexed to the land so as to run with it if in the instrument the land is sufficiently indicated and the covenant is either stated to be made for the benefit of the land, or stated to be made with the convenantee in his capacity as owner of the land[67]; for then in either case it is obvious that future owners of that land are intended to benefit. A classic formula is "with intent that the covenant may enure to the benefit of the vendors their successors and assigns and others claiming under them to all or any of their lands adjoining".[68] It will be noted that this formula

---

[61] For a fuller exposition, see the previous edition of this work at pp. 782–785.

[62] *Post,* para. 16–075.

[63] Compare the position in relation to leases granted prior to 1996 where, if the covenant touches and concerns the land, it is annexed to the estate of the covenantee: see *ante,* para. 15–022.

[64] *Renals v. Cowlishaw* (1878) 9 Ch.D. 125 at 129; aff'd (1879) 11 Ch.D. 866; *Rogers v. Hosegood* [1900] 2 Ch. 388 at 396; *Sainsbury Plc v. Enfield L.B.C.* [1989] 1 W.L.R. 590 at 595. The test is whether the covenant was intended to enure for the benefit of the particular land of the covenantee: *Re Union of London and Smith's Bank Ltd's Conveyance* [1933] Ch. 611 at 628.

[65] *Renals v. Cowlishaw* (1878) 9 Ch.D. 125 at 129; *Shropshire County Council v. Edwards* (1982) 46 P. & C.R. 270 at 276; *Sainsbury Plc v. Enfield L.B.C., supra,* at 597.

[66] See *R. v. Westminster City Council, ex p. Leicester Square Coventry Street Association* (1989) 87 L.G.R. 675 at 681.

[67] See *Osborne v. Bradley* [1903] 2 Ch. 446 at 450; *Drake v. Gray* [1936] Ch. 451 at 466.

[68] *Rogers v. Hosegood* [1900] 2 Ch. 388.

indicates the benefited land only in general terms,[69] so that precise definition is not required. On the other hand, to covenant merely with "the vendors their heirs executors administrators and assigns" is insufficient, for no reference is made to any land, and the reference to executors and others is so wide that it indicates no particular purpose.[70]

(2) IMPLIED ANNEXATION.[71] It has now been clearly recognised that annexa- **16–062** tion may be implied rather than express.[72] Although express words of annexation are highly desirable, they are not necessary.[73] "If, on the construction of the instrument creating the restrictive covenant, both the land which is intended to be benefited and an intention to benefit that land, as distinct from benefiting the covenantee personally, can be clearly established, then the benefit of the covenant will be annexed to that land and run with it, notwithstanding the absence of express words of annexation."[74] However, an intention to annex will not be implied merely from the surrounding circumstances. It must be manifested in the instrument containing the covenant when construed in the light of those attendant circumstances.[75]

(b) Statutory annexation

(1) SECTION 78. These rules on express and implied annexation are now **16–063** relevant only to covenants made prior to 1926. As regards any covenants made since 1925, they will be annexed, if at all, by statute. In relation to such covenants it is no longer necessary to show an intention to annex. By section 78(1) of the Law of Property Act 1925, "a covenant relating to any land of the covenantee shall be deemed to be made with the covenantee and his successors in title and the persons deriving title under him or them, and shall have

---

[69] Reliance should not be placed on unduly strict statements in *Renals v. Cowlishaw* (1879) 11 Ch.D. 866 at 868; *Re Union of London and Smith's Bank Ltd's Conveyance* [1933] Ch. 611 at 625; *Newton Abbot Co-operative Society Ltd v. Williamson & Treadgold* [1952] Ch. 286 at 289. See [1972B] C.L.J. 157 at 166 (H.W.R.W.).

[70] *Renals v. Cowlishaw* (1878) 9 Ch.D. 125; aff'd (1879) 11 Ch.D. 866. "Assigns" has been said to be ambiguous, for it may mean assigns of the benefit of the covenant as well as assigns of the land benefited: see *Rogers v. Hosegood* [1900] 2 Ch. 388 at 396. "Heirs and assigns" sufficed in *Mann v. Stephens* (1846) 15 Sim. 377, though this was before it had been settled that there must be dominant land (*ante*, para. 16–044).

[71] For a fuller treatment of this subject, see the previous edition of this work at p. 784; and [1972B] C.L.J. 157 at 169 (H.W.R.W.). The doubts raised in (1968) 84 L.Q.R. 22 at 30 (P. V. Baker) as to the existence of implied annexation as a distinct category, have now been dispelled by authority.

[72] *Shropshire County Council v. Edwards* (1982) 46 P. & C.R. 270 at 277; *Sainsbury Plc v. Enfield L.B.C.* [1989] 1 W.L.R. 590 at 597; *Re W. & S. (Long Eaton) Ltd* (1989) [1994] J.P.L. 840. *cf. Jamaica Mutual Life Assurance Society v. Hillsborough Ltd* [1989] 1 W.L.R. 1101 at 1105, 1106.

[73] Where the connection with the benefited land is obvious, to insist upon express words would involve "not only an injustice but a departure from common sense": *Marten v. Flight Refuelling Ltd* [1962] Ch. 115 at 133, *per* Wilberforce J.

[74] *Shropshire County Council v. Edwards, supra*, at 277, *per* Judge Rubin.

[75] *Sainsbury Plc v. Enfield L.B.C., supra*, at 595–597; *Jamaica Mutual Life Assurance Society v. Hillsborough Ltd, supra*, at 1105; [1991] Conv. 52 (S. Goulding).

effect as if such successors and other persons were expressed".[76] As regards restrictive (but not positive) covenants, the words "successors in title" are given a wider meaning than they would normally have, and are deemed to include the owners and occupiers for the time being of the covenantee's land.[77] The wording of section 78 is "significantly different"[78] from that of its predecessor, section 58 of the Conveyancing Act 1881. This has already been explained.[79]

The wording of section 78 strongly suggests that it was intended to annex to the land of the covenantee the benefit of any covenant which touched and concerned it. If the words of the section were used expressly in a covenant,[80] there seems little doubt that they would be effective to annex it.[81] The reference in it to successors in title, to derivative owners and to owners and occupiers for the time being of the land, could not more clearly show that the covenant was intended to be for the benefit of the covenantee's land and not for the covenantee personally. However, the possibility that the section might have this effect remained unconsidered until the decision of the Court of Appeal in *Federated Homes Ltd v. Mill Lodge Properties Ltd*[82] in 1979.

In that case it was held that a covenant against erecting more than 300 dwellings on the covenantor's land was enforceable by successors in title of the covenantor. The lack of any express words of annexation was made good by section 78 since it was clear from the facts that the covenant related to the covenantee's adjoining land. The court pointed out, approving suggestions in

---

[76] For an interesting illustration of the operation of the section, see *Caerns Motor Services Ltd v. Texaco Ltd* [1994] 1 W.L.R. 1249 at 1267.

[77] L.P.A. 1925, s.78(2). The words will therefore embrace squatters (other than a squatter who has been registered as the proprietor of registered land which he has adversely possessed, who is a successor in title: see *post*, para. 21–056) and licensees, who may in consequence enforce an annexed restrictive covenant even though they could not enforce an annexed positive covenant: see *ante*, para. 16–015. This is logical. A restrictive covenant has been described as "an extension in equity of the doctrine of negative easements": *London & South Western Ry. v. Gomm* (1882) 20 Ch.D. 562 at 583, *per* Jessel M.R. The owner or occupier for the time being of land would be entitled to enjoy the benefit of any easement which was appurtenant to and therefore part of it.

[78] *Federated Homes Ltd v. Mill Lodge Properties Ltd* [1980] 1 W.L.R. 594 at 604, *per* Brightman L.J.

[79] *Ante*, para. 16–015.

[80] By the section they are of course deemed to be.

[81] See *ante*, para. 16–016.

[82] [1980] 1 W.L.R. 594; (1980) 43 M.L.R. 445 (D. J. Hayton); [1980] Conv. 216 (A. Sydenham). There were no words of annexation; the benefit had been expressly assigned to the first successor in title but not by that successor to the plaintiff. The judgment of Brightman L.J., unlike so many in this area, is clear and straightforward, and firmly based on realities. For comment, criticism and legislative history see (1981) 97 L.Q.R. 32; (1982) 98 L.Q.R. 202; [1982] J.P.L. 295 (G. H. Newsom Q.C.); (1982) 2 L.S. 53 (D. J. Hurst). The articles by G. H. Newsom Q.C. attack the decision from the orthodox conveyancer's standpoint, but do not consider the opposing arguments. The strongest argument *against* the interpretation of s.78 adopted in *Federated Homes* is that there are a number of provisions in the Act by which the benefit of a covenant is annexed by the words, "shall be annexed and incident to and shall go with" a particular estate: see L.P.A. 1925, ss.76(6), 77(5), 141(1). However, each of those provisions (unlike s.78) was carried forward from C.A. 1881, and the words "shall go with" appear to have an effect that is additional to the annexation of the covenant: see *Re King* [1963] Ch. 459 at 497.

a previous edition of this book and elsewhere,[83] that it was deciding consistently with the cases on the running of the benefit of positive covenants, in which section 78 had played some part.[84]

(2) LIMITS ON STATUTORY ANNEXATION. Although some commentators have **16–064** suggested that the decision in the *Federated Homes* case can be interpreted narrowly,[85] it was decided on the basis of the broad principle that "if the condition precedent of section 78 is satisfied—that is to say, there exists a covenant which touches and concerns the land of the covenantee—that covenant runs with the land for the benefit of his successors in title, persons deriving title under him or them and other owners and occupiers".[86] On this basis the rules for positive and negative covenants are largely assimilated[87] and simplified,[88] and much of the unnecessary mystique and semantics which had accumulated round negative covenants is swept away. The law has in consequence become altogether simpler and more reasonable.[89]

However, it is clear that there are a number of limitations on annexation under section 78. First, it remains the case that the land benefited by the covenant must be identifiable in the appropriate manner.[90] Secondly, statutory annexation applies only to covenants made since 1925. It has been held that the predecessor of section 78, the differently worded section 58 of the Conveyancing Act 1881,[91] did not annex the benefit of a covenant without proof of intention that the covenant should run.[92] Thirdly, annexation under

---

[83] (1941) 57 L.Q.R. 203 at 205 (G. R.Y. Radcliffe); [1972B] C.L.J. 157 at 173 (H.W.R.W.); this book, 4th ed., p. 765.

[84] For these cases see *ante*, para. 16–015.

[85] See particularly [1985] Conv. 177 (P. N. Todd).

[86] [1980] 1 W.L.R. 594 at 605, *per* Brightman L.J. See too *Sainsbury Plc v. Enfield L.B.C.* [1989] 1 W.L.R. 590 at 598.

[87] But the assimilation is not complete. The range of persons who can enforce an annexed *restrictive* covenant includes the owners and occupiers for the time being of the land of the covenantee: L.P.A. 1925, s.78(2); n. 77, *supra*. Only successors in title (in the strict sense) and derivative owners can enforce positive covenants: *ante*, para. 16–015.

[88] *cf. Rhone v. Stephens* [1994] 2 A.C. 310 at 327, where Lord Templeman was careful not to cast doubt on the decisions, considered *ante*, para. 16–015, in which "it was held by the Court of Appeal that section 78 . . . had the effect of making the benefit of a positive covenant run with the land".

[89] The decision has been applied in *Jalarne Ltd v. Ridewood* (1989) 61 P. & C.R. 143 at 152; *Robins v. Berkeley Homes (Kent) Ltd* [1996] E.G.C.S. 75. It was referred to without any suggestion of doubt by Lord Templeman in *Rhone v. Stephens* [1994] 2 A.C. 310 at 322.

[90] In *Federated Homes Ltd v. Mill Lodge Properties Ltd, supra,* at 604, Brightman L.J. left it open whether the benefited land had to be identified by the deed of covenant or whether it sufficed if it was identifiable from the surrounding circumstances. For reasons that have been explained, the latter view is to be preferred: see *ante*, para. 16–061.

[91] *Ante*, para. 16–014.

[92] *Sainsbury Plc v. Enfield L.B.C., supra,* at 601. See too *Federated Homes Ltd v. Mill Lodge Properties Ltd, Supra,* at 604. Compare however [1972B] C.L.J. 157 at 173 (H.W.R.W.). It should also be noted that L.P.A. 1925, s.78 does not apply to new tenancies granted after 1995 under L. & T.C.A. 1995: see *ibid.*, s.30(4); *ante*, para. 15–079. However, this disapplication is restricted to covenants in the lease. Thus a tenant under a lease granted after 1995 could take advantage of a covenant that was annexed to the freehold under L.P.A. 1925, s.78 (as in *Smith v. River Douglas Catchment Board* [1949] 2 K.B. 500; *ante*, para. 16–015). The section would also apply to a covenant entered into with the tenant for the benefit of his leasehold estate by a neighbour.

section 78 will occur only where the covenant is unqualified. Although the section makes no provision for its exclusion by an expression of contrary intention,[93] a covenant will not be annexed by it if it is clear that it is only to pass by express assignment.[94] Indeed this is implicit in the *Federated Homes* decision itself, for Brightman L.J. acknowledged that "a covenantee may expressly or by necessary implication retain the benefit of a covenant wholly under his own control, so that the benefit will not pass unless the covenantee chooses to assign".[95]

In the light of these limitations, the effect of statutory annexation may be summarised as follows.

> (i) A restrictive covenant entered into after 1925 which touches and concerns the land will be annexed to the covenantee's land, unless either expressly or by necessary implication, the covenant is intended to pass only by express assignment.

> (ii) A restrictive covenant entered into prior to 1926 will pass only if it has been expressly or impliedly annexed to the covenantee's land or if it is expressly assigned by a landowner who has the benefit of it.

It will be apparent from this that the benefit of restrictive covenants will nowadays seldom need to be expressly assigned.

16–065   (3) SECTION 62. It has been suggested that the benefit of a restrictive covenant might pass on any conveyance of the benefited land under the general words implied by section 62 of the Law of Property Act 1925.[96] Although this was the basis of the decision at first instance in the *Federated Homes* case,[97] it has since been held by the Court of Appeal that "a right under covenant cannot appertain to the land[98] unless the benefit is in some way annexed to the land. If the benefit of a covenant passes under section 62 even if not annexed to the land, the whole modern law of restrictive covenants would have been established on an erroneous basis".[99]

16–066   *(c) Area.* If the benefit of a covenant is annexed to the covenantee's land, then prima facie it is taken to be annexed both to the whole of the land and

---

[93] Unlike L.P.A. 1925, s.79: see *ante*, para. 16–016. That section has been said to involve "quite different considerations" from s.78: *Federated Homes Ltd v. Mill Lodge Properties Ltd, supra*, at 606, *per* Brightman L.J.

[94] *Roake v. Chadha* [1984] 1 W.L.R. 40; [1984] Conv. 68 (P. N. Todd).

[95] [1980] 1 W.L.R. 594 at 606.

[96] See (1971) 87 L.Q.R. 539 at 570 (D. J. Hayton). For L.P.A. 1925, s.62, see *post*, para. 18–018.

[97] The decision is unreported, but see [1980] 1 W.L.R. 594 at 601. *cf. Shropshire County Council v. Edwards* (1982) 46 P. & C.R. 270 at 279.

[98] As the section requires.

[99] *Kumar v. Dunning* [1989] Q.B. 193 at 198, *per* Browne-Wilkinson V.-C. See too *Roake v. Chadha, supra*, at 47.

to each and every part of it, unless the contrary clearly appears.[1] This means that anyone who subsequently acquires some part of the benefited land can enforce the covenant, as can the person who retains the remainder. It is possible that a covenant may be annexed to the whole of the land only and not to every part of it,[2] but this will now have to be clearly shown.[3]

A covenant will be annexed only if, at the time when it is imposed, it benefits the land for which it is taken.[4] However, such benefit will be presumed in the absence of either exceptional circumstances[5] or contrary evidence.[6] Furthermore, even if the covenant purports to be taken for an area that is greater than can reasonably be benefited by it, the owner of any part of that land which is in fact so benefited may be able to enforce it.[7] This will be so where the covenant is annexed to each and every part of the land (which is now presumed) and not to the whole only.[8]

(d) Transmission. Once the benefit of the covenant is annexed to land, it passes with the land to each successive owner, tenant or occupier,[9] even if he knew nothing of it when he acquired the land,[10] "a hidden treasure which may be discovered in the hour of need".[11]   **16–067**

II. ASSIGNMENT

Even if the benefit of the covenant has not been annexed to the land to be benefited, an assignee of the land may nevertheless succeed in enforcing the covenant if the benefit of the covenant has also been assigned to him. However, since the *Federated Homes* decision,[12] the circumstances in which it will be necessary to have recourse to assignment are likely to be rare.[13] It will be necessary to do so in three cases—   **16–068**

---

[1] *Federated Homes Ltd v. Mill Lodge Properties Ltd* [1980] 1 W.L.R. 594 at 606. Prior to this decision, it appears to have been thought that a covenant was annexed to the whole of the land only, in the absence of evidence to the contrary, and that on a sale of part of the property the benefit could pass only if it was expressly assigned: see, *e.g. Re Jeff's Transfer (No. 2)* [1966] 1 W.L.R. 841 (a case that would probably now be decided differently). The reversal of the presumption has brought about a welcome simplification of the law.

[2] See *Re Union of London and Smith's Bank Ltd's Conveyance* [1933] Ch. 611 at 628; *Re Ballard's Conveyance* [1937] Ch. 473.

[3] "I find the idea of the annexation of a covenant to the whole of the land but not to part of it a difficult conception fully to grasp": *Federated Homes Ltd v. Mill Lodge Properties Ltd, supra,* at 606, *per* Brightman L.J.

[4] *Marquess of Zetland v. Driver* [1939] Ch. 1 at 8.

[5] As "where the covenant was on the face of it taken capriciously or not bona fide": *Marten v. Flight Refuelling Ltd* [1962] Ch. 115 at 136, *per* Wilberforce J.

[6] *Earl of Leicester v. Wells-next-the-Sea U.D.C.* [1973] Ch. 110 at 124, 125.

[7] *Marquess of Zetland v. Driver, supra,* at 10.

[8] *cf. Re Ballard's Conveyance, supra* (a case which on its facts might now be decided differently).

[9] L.P.A. 1925, s.78, *ante,* para. 16–063; *Taite v. Gosling* (1879) 11 Ch.D. 273.

[10] *Rogers v. Hosegood* [1900] 2 Ch. 388; *R. v. Westminster City Council, ex p. Leicester Square Coventry Street Association* (1989) 87 L.G.R. 675 at 682.

[11] *Lawrence v. South County Freeholds Ltd* [1939] Ch. 656 at 680, *per*, Simonds J.

[12] [1980] 1 W.L.R. 594; *ante,* para. 16–063.

[13] See *ante,* para. 16–064. For a fuller treatment of assignment see the previous edition of this work at p. 787.

(i) where the covenant was entered into prior to 1926, the benefit was not expressly or impliedly annexed to the covenantee's land, and the intending assignor is either the original covenantee[14] or has acquired the benefit by an unbroken chain of assignments[15];

(ii) where the covenant, at whatever date it was entered into, was expressly taken for the benefit of and annexed to the whole of the covenantee's land only, and where the covenantee wished to dispose of some part of that land with the benefit of the covenant; and

(iii) where by the terms of the covenant (at whatever date it was entered into), the benefit was to pass only by express assignment.

16–069   *(a) Form of assignment.* Although the assignment must ordinarily be made expressly, the assignment will be effective provided that there is a distinct agreement between the vendor and the purchaser that the covenant shall pass to the assignee.[16] The benefit will not run with the land in the absence of such an agreement unless the covenant is annexed.[17]

16–070   *(b) Assignment with land.* It has already been explained that if the assignee is suing the original covenantor or his personal representative (who are liable at law), he has only to prove that the benefit of the covenant has been properly assigned to him as a chose in action.[18] He may then seek either damages or an injunction. However, if he is suing some successor in title to the covenantor's land (who can be liable only in equity under the rule in *Tulk v. Moxhay*), he must also prove that the benefit was assigned to him with the land benefited as part of the same transaction. It appears to be the case that the covenant must be assigned together with all or part of the land.[19] The primary purpose of the covenant is to preserve the value of the land retained by the vendor, and "if he has been able to sell any particular part of his property without assigning to the purchaser the benefit of the covenant, there seems no reason why he should at a later date and as an independent transaction be at liberty to confer upon the purchaser such benefit".[20] This special rule of equity applies only for the purposes of an action brought against a successor in title to the covenantor's land. There is no objection to a later assignment which merely gives effect to an existing equitable right to the benefit of the covenant, as where the

---

[14] Which is unlikely to be the case nowadays unless the covenantee is a corporation.

[15] For a doubt as to whether an unbroken chain of assignments is in fact necessary or whether the first express assignment annexes the benefit of the covenant, see *post*, para. 16–073.

[16] *Renals v. Cowlishaw* (1878) 9 Ch.D. 125 at 129–131; aff'd (1879) 11 Ch.D. 866; *Re Union of London and Smith's Bank Ltd's Conveyance* [1933] Ch. 611 at 628; *Drake v. Gray* [1936] Ch. 451 at 455.

[17] *Renals v. Cowlishaw*, *supra*.

[18] *Ante*, para. 16–010.

[19] A vendor who has disposed of whole of the benefited land can no longer assign the benefit of the covenant in equity: *Chambers v. Randall* [1923] 1 Ch. 149; *Re Union of London and Smith's Bank Ltd's Conveyance*, *supra*.

[20] *Re Union of London and Smith's Bank Ltd's Conveyance*, *supra*, at 632, *per* Romer L.J. See too *Re Rutherford's Conveyance* [1938] Ch. 396.

benefited land is conveyed by trustees to a beneficiary and they later assign the benefit of the covenant to him.[21]

(c) Assignment with part. In those rare cases in which annexation of the covenant was only to the benefited land as a whole, the benefit may nevertheless be assigned with part only of the land. Although at law the benefit cannot be assigned in pieces, equity allows the benefit to be assigned with any part or parts of the benefited land.[22] **16–071**

(d) Intention to benefit. Where there has been an express assignment of the benefit of a covenant, the purchaser will be able to sue on it only if he can show that the covenant was intended to benefit the land which he has purchased. However, it is unnecessary to prove the connection from the deed of covenant. It may be proved instead from the surrounding circumstances.[23] **16–072**

(e) Chain of assignments. It has been held that where the benefit of a covenant has not been annexed to the land, the benefit will pass to subsequent owners of it only if there is an unbroken chain of assignments.[24] However, the older authorities had suggested that when the benefit was once assigned it became annexed to the land,[25] because the assignment demonstrated that the benefit of the covenant was intended to pass with the land and not remain a separate right.[26] Although on principle the view taken in these older cases is to be preferred, it may not apply in all situations, as where the covenant was on its face to pass only by express assignment.[27] **16–073**

(f) Assignor. It is not always necessary that the assignment should be made by the original covenantee: it may be made by anyone in whom the land and the benefit of the covenant are both vested. If, for example, the original covenantee dies, and under his will or intestacy his son becomes entitled both to the benefited land and to the benefit of the covenant (two separate assets of the deceased), the son can effectively assign the benefit of the covenant if he subsequently sells the land.[28] The benefit of the covenant will pass to him **16–074**

---

[21] *Lord Northbourne v. Johnston* [1922] 2 Ch. 309 (assignment to devisee of beneficiary). This decision appears to assume that the benefit ran in equity without either annexation or assignment.

[22] *Re Union of London and Smith's Bank Ltd's Conveyance, supra,* at 630.

[23] *Newton Abbot Co-operative Society Ltd v. Williamson & Treadgold Ltd* [1952] Ch. 286 at 297. See too *Marten v. Flight Refuelling Ltd* [1962] Ch. 115 at 130–133.

[24] *Re Pinewood Estate, Farnborough* [1958] Ch. 280, where the authorities to the contrary were not cited: see [1957] C.L.J. 146 (H.W.R.W.); (1968) 84 L.Q.R. 22 at 31 (P. V. Baker). See also *Federated Homes Ltd v. Mill Lodge Properties Ltd* [1980] 1 W.L.R. 594 at 603 ("delayed annexation by assignment" not accepted at first instance).

[25] It has been suggested that "express assignment is delayed annexation": (1968) 84 L.Q.R. 22 at 29 (P. V. Baker).

[26] *Renals v. Cowlishaw* (1878) 9 Ch.D. 125 at 130, 131 (aff'd (1879) 11 Ch.D. 866); *Rogers v. Hosegood* [1900] 2 Ch. 388 at 408; *Reid v. Bickerstaff* [1909] 2 Ch. 305 at 320, 326, 328.

[27] As in *Roake v. Chadha* [1984] 1 W.L.R. 40.

[28] *Newton Abbot Co-operative Society Ltd v. Williamson & Treadgold Ltd, supra.*

automatically with the benefited land if it is clear from the facts that the covenant was intended to protect the land.[29]

III. SCHEMES OF DEVELOPMENT

16–075   *(a) An independent equity.* Building and other development schemes have special rules of their own, which derive from the wider principle that the benefit of covenants runs in equity according to the common intention and common interest of the original parties.[30] Where land is to be sold or let in lots according to a plan, restrictions are often imposed on the purchasers of each lot for the benefit of the estate generally, such as covenants restraining trading on the estate, or prohibiting the erection of cheap buildings. Much of the purpose of the covenants given by a purchaser of one lot would be lost if they could not be enforced—

    (i) by those who have previously bought lots, and

    (ii) by those who subsequently buy the unsold lots.

Both these results could be achieved without any special rules for schemes of development. The first could be achieved if the purchaser's covenants were expressed to be made with the owners of the lots previously sold as well as with the vendor.[31] The second could be achieved by framing the covenants expressly for the benefit of the whole or any part of the land retained by the vendor, and so annexing the benefit of them to each lot to be sold in the future, or by express assignment to the later purchasers, as already described.

16–076   The special character of schemes of development makes it possible to dispense with these formalities. If such a scheme exists, the covenants given on the sale of each plot are enforceable by the owner for the time being of any plot on the estate. "Community of interest necessarily ... requires and imports reciprocity of obligation."[32] The covenants in effect form a sort of local law for the estate.[33] They give rise to "an equity which is created by

---

[29] *Earl of Leicester v. Wells-next the-Sea U.D.C.* [1973] Ch. 110. The personal representatives hold the benefit of the covenant upon trust for him, so that he can sue in equity: *ibid.* Alternatively they themselves can sue: *Ives v. Brown* [1919] 2 Ch. 314.

[30] *Re Dolphin's Conveyance* [1970] Ch. 654. The doctrine can be traced back to *Whatman v. Gibson* (1838) 9 Sim. 196, thus antedating *Tulk v. Moxhay* (1848) 2 Ph. 774. It was approved by the House of Lords in *Spicer v. Martin* (1888) 14 App.Cas. 12; see *Lawrence v. South County Freeholds Ltd* [1939] Ch. 656 at 675. And see (1938) 6 C.L.J. 363, 364 (S. J. Bailey).

[31] L.P.A. 1925, s.56, replacing R.P.A. 1845, s.5, discussed *ante*, para. 16–006. But the possibility of this was not fully understood until *Forster v. Elvet Colliery Co. Ltd* [1908] 1 K.B. 629 (aff'd *sub nom. Dyson v. Forster* [1909] A.C. 98), and the rules relating to schemes had by then been settled.

[32] *Spicer v. Martin* (1888) 14 App.Cas. 12 at 25, *per* Lord Macnaghten.

[33] *Reid v. Bickerstaff* [1900] 2 Ch. 305 at 319; *Brunner v. Greenslade* [1971] Ch. 993 at 1004.

circumstances and is independent of contractual obligation",[34] thus transcending ordinary restrictions. In particular:

    (i) the annexation of the benefit of the covenants to every plot still unsold proves itself from the surrounding facts,[35] so that no special formula for annexation need be used;

    (ii) the owners of plots sold previously are shown by the facts to be within the benefit of the covenants, even though not expressly mentioned as covenantees[36];

    (iii) no unsold plot may later be disposed of by the vendor without his requiring the purchaser to enter into the covenants of the scheme; and

    (iv) the vendor is himself bound by the covenants of the scheme, even if he has not himself entered into them.

As soon as the first disposition under the scheme has been made, the scheme crystallises, and all the land within the scheme is bound.[37] The vendor himself is in the position of a trustee, and is not at liberty to authorise breaches of the covenants.[38]

Whether or not a scheme of development exists is a question of fact which may depend upon extraneous circumstances as well as upon the terms of the conveyances.[39]

(b) Elements of a scheme

(1) INTENTION. The classic statement of the facts to be proved required that **16–077** there should have been a common vendor who first laid out the property for sale in lots subject to restrictions consistent only with a scheme of development; that the common vendor should have intended the restrictions to benefit all the lots to be sold; and that the purchasers from the common vendor should have purchased on the footing that the restrictions were for the benefit of the other lots.[40] Although this statement of the requirements is still accepted as a starting point,[41] it has never been treated as a comprehensive statement of the

---

[34] *Lawrence v. South County Freeholds Ltd* [1939] Ch. 656 at 682 (Simonds J.); *Brunner v. Greenslade* [1971] Ch. 993.

[35] *Ante*, paras 16–061, 16–064.

[36] *Spicer v. Martin* (1888) 14 App.Cas. 12.

[37] *Brunner v. Greenslade, supra*, at 1003, summarising the first principles of schemes; and see *post*, para. 16–079.

[38] *Brunner v. Greenslade, supra*, at 1003.

[39] *Texaco Antilles Ltd v. Kernochan* [1973] A.C. 609.

[40] *Elliston v. Reacher* [1908] 2 Ch. 374 at 384 (Parker J.); aff'd [1908] 2 Ch. 655.

[41] See *Page v. Kings Parade Properties Ltd* (1967) 20 P. & C.R. 710 at 716; *Emile Elias & Co. Ltd v. Pine Groves Ltd* [1993] 1 W.L.R. 305 at 309.

law nor has it inhibited further development. Later decisions have emphasised two pre-requisites of a building scheme.[42] The first is that there must be reciprocity of obligation between the purchasers of the various lots.[43] There must be an intention to impose a scheme of mutually enforceable restrictions in the interest of all the purchasers and their successors,[44] which must be known to them.[45] The second is that the area affected by the scheme should be clearly defined.[46] It is not sufficient that the common vendor has himself defined the area. It must also be known to the purchasers.[47] If these two requirements are satisfied, neither a common vendor nor laying out in lots is indispensable.[48] The present tendency is to relax formal requirements and to give effect to the manifest intention of the transaction.

16–078   (2) EVIDENCE. It is not necessary to prove an express undertaking by each purchaser that the covenants given by him are to be enforceable by the owners of all the other lots, provided the circumstances show that he must have realised it.[49] This will be so if before his purchase he saw some plan of the estate with the restrictions indorsed on it. But the absence of a proper plan may prove fatal,[50] if the intention to impose a scheme of mutually enforceable restrictions does not otherwise appear.[51] The evidence must, of course, show that the vendor intended to do more than merely benefit himself.[52] A building scheme will not be implied merely from "a common vendor and the existence of common covenants".[53]

Although "a common code of covenants" is "one of the badges of an enforceable building scheme",[54] the following matters will not negative the existence of such a scheme—

---

[42] *Jamaica Mutual Life Assurance Society v. Hillsborough Ltd* [1989] 1 W.L.R. 1101 at 1106.
[43] *Kingsbury v. L.W. Anderson Ltd* (1979) 40 P. & C.R. 136 at 142, 143; *Jamaica Mutual Life Assurance Society v. Hillsborough Ltd, supra,* at 1106; *Emile Elias & Co. Ltd v. Pine Groves Ltd, supra,* at 311, 312.
[44] This is lacking, for example, if the covenants on one side are merely for indemnifying the vendor: *Kingsbury v. L.W. Anderson Ltd, supra.*
[45] *White v. Bijou Mansions Ltd* [1938] Ch. 351 at 362; *Re Shaw's Application* (1994) 68 P. & C.R. 591 at 597.
[46] *Reid v. Bickerstaff* [1909] 2 Ch. 305; *Jamaica Mutual Life Assurance Society v. Hillsborough Ltd* [1989] 1 W.L.R. 1101 at 1106, 1107.
[47] *Lund v. Taylor* (1975) 31 P. & C.R. 167; *Emile Elias & Co. Ltd v. Pine Groves Ltd, supra,* at 310.
[48] *Baxter v. Four Oaks Properties Ltd* [1965] Ch. 816 (no lotting: size of plots variable); *Re Dolphin's Conveyance* [1970] Ch. 654 (two successive vendors; no lotting; no plan).
[49] As where this was made clear in the advertisements for the sale of the properties: *cf. Jamaica Mutual Life Assurance Society v. Hillsborough Ltd, supra,* at 1108.
[50] *e.g. Osborne v. Bradley* [1903] 2 Ch. 446; *Kelly v. Barrett* [1924] 2 Ch. 379; *Re Wembley Park Estate Co. Ltd's Transfer* [1968] Ch. 491; *cf. Hodges v. Jones* [1935] Ch. 657 (plan with no restrictions on it not enough).
[51] As in *Re Dolphin's Conveyance, supra; Lund v. Taylor, supra.*
[52] *Tucker v. Vowles* [1893] 1 Ch. 195; *Willé v. St. John* [1910] 1 Ch. 325.
[53] *Re Wembley Park Estate Co. Ltd's Transfer, supra,* at 503, *per* Goff J.; *Jamaica Mutual Life Assurance Society v. Hillsborough Ltd, supra,* at 1108.
[54] *Emile Elias & Co. Ltd v. Pine Groves Ltd* [1993] 1 W.L.R. 305 at 311, *per* Lord Browne-Wilkinson.

(i) the reservation of a power by the vendor either to release all or part of the land from the restrictions,[55] or to vary the details of the scheme or the restrictions imposed on later purchasers[56];

(ii) the employment of an express formula of annexation in the conveyances or transfers[57]; or

(iii) the fact that the restrictions imposed on each plot are not identical.[58]

But if the agreement provides for the covenants to be enforced by the vendor on behalf of all parties, that is inconsistent with mutual enforceability.[59]

(3) SUB-SCHEMES. If one of the plots is later subdivided, the covenants of the scheme will be mutually enforceable between the sub-purchasers *inter se*, so far as they are applicable, as well as between them and the occupiers of the other plots, even though none of the sub-purchasers themselves gave covenants.[60] If the sub-purchasers themselves entered into "scheme of development" covenants differing from those of the main scheme, they can enforce only their own sub-scheme *inter se*, but can still enforce the head scheme against others.[61] The covenants of the head scheme thus remain operative unless some contrary intention appears.[62] This illustrates the special operation of such covenants as "a local law for the area of the scheme".[63] Another illustration is that if two plots come into common ownership but are later separated, the covenants are not discharged by unity of ownership but will continue to operate.[64]

(c) Extent of principle. The law for schemes of development originated with building schemes, but the principle applies to numerous other types of schemes of development involving uniform covenants; the term "scheme of development" is the genus and "building scheme,' is merely a species.[65] If an estate already fully built upon is disposed of in sections, whether freehold or

16–079

16–080

---

[55] *Elliston v. Reacher* [1908] 2 Ch. 665 at 672; *Pearce v. Maryon-Wilson* [1935] Ch. 188 (leaseholds); *Newman v. Real Estate Debenture Corpn Ltd* [1940] 1 All E.R. 131; *Re Wembley Park Estate Co. Ltd's Transfer, supra.*

[56] *Re 6, 8, 10 and 12 Elm Avenue, New Milton* [1984] 1 W.L.R. 1398 at 1406. The inclusion of such a power points to the existence of a building scheme because it would be unnecessary in the absence of such a scheme: *ibid.* See too *Re Beechwood Homes Ltd's Application* [1994] 2 E.G.L.R. 178 (power to vary layout of estate).

[57] *Texaco Antilles Ltd v. Kernochan* [1973] A.C. 609.

[58] *Collins v. Castle* (1887) 36 Ch.D. 243 at 253, 254; *Reid v. Bickerstaff* [1909] 2 Ch. 305 at 319; *Emile Elias & Co. Ltd v. Pine Groves Ltd* [1993] 1 W.L.R. 305 at 311.

[59] *White v. Bijou Mansions Ltd* [1938] Ch. 351 at 363.

[60] *Brunner v. Greenslade* [1971] Ch. 993.

[61] On sub-schemes see *Knight v. Simmonds* [1896] 1 Ch. 653; *Lawrence v. South County Freeholds Ltd* [1939] Ch. 656; *Brunner v. Greenslade, supra.*

[62] *Brunner v. Greenslade, supra,* at 1006.

[63] *ibid.* at 1004.

[64] *Brunner v. Greenslade, supra*; *Texaco Antilles Ltd v. Kernochan, supra.* See (1977) 41 Conv. (N.S.) 107 at 115 (J. D. A. Brooke-Taylor).

[65] *Brunner v. Greenslade, supra,* at 999.

leasehold, and the appropriate conditions for schemes of development are satisfied, the covenants will be enforceable as in building schemes.[66] The principle of such schemes can apply to a block of residential flats let on similar leases,[67] so that the landlord will be restrained from letting[68] or using[69] any of them otherwise than for residential purposes, even though it was only the tenants, and not the landlord, who entered into any express covenant as to user.

If the parties to a scheme modify it by releasing the covenants and substituting new covenants, it seems that the new covenants will not have the benefit of the rules as to schemes.[70]

Covenants under a scheme of development enjoy no dispensation from the requirement of registration, so that the "local law" principle depends upon due registration against all the purchasers if the land is freehold and developed after 1925.[71] Registration governs the running of the burden of the covenant, whereas the development scheme rules govern the running of the benefit.

C. Reform

16–081 **1. Land obligations.** The present law of restrictive covenants has been criticised on the grounds of both its complexity and its uncertainty.[72] The Law Commission has proposed the replacement of the present system for the future by a scheme of land obligations,[73] of which something has already been said in relation to positive covenants.[74] The Commission originally proposed the creation of two types of land obligation on the model of easements, neighbour obligations and development obligations.[75] However, in the light of the subsequent proposals, already explained,[76] to introduce a system of commonhold, the need for development obligations is considered to have been obviated.[77]

16–082 **2. Assimilation of positive and restrictive covenants.** A land obligation would be created between two neighbouring landowners, and there would be both land benefited by the obligation and land burdened by it. The obligation

---

[66] *Nottingham Patent Brick & Tile Co. v. Butler* (1886) 16 Q.B.D. 778; *Spicer v. Martin* (1888) 14 App.Cas. 12 (leasehold); *Torbay Hotel Ltd v. Jenkins* [1927] 2 Ch. 225.

[67] *Hudson v. Cripps* [1896] 1 Ch. 265; *Alexander v. Mansions Proprietary* (1900) 16 T.L.R. 431; *Gedge v. Bartlett* (1900) 17 T.L.R. 43; *Jaegar v. Mansions Consolidated Ltd* (1903) 87 L.T. 690; *cf. Kelly v. Battershell* [1949] 2 All E.R. 830 (no scheme found).

[68] *Gedge v. Barlett, supra.*

[69] *Newman v. Real Estate Debenture Corpn Ltd* [1940] 1 All E.R. 131 ("the high watermark of cases where a scheme can be inferred": *Kelly v. Battershell, supra,* at 841, *per* Cohen L.J.).

[70] *Re Pinewood Estate Farnborough* [1985] Ch. 280. This seems questionable: see [1957] C.L.J. 146 (H.W.R.W.).

[71] *Ante*, paras 16–053–16–055.

[72] (1984) Law Com. No. 127, para. 4.8.

[73] Law Com. No. 127, Pt V.

[74] *Ante*, para. 16–028.

[75] Law Com. No. 127, para. 6.2.

[76] *Ante*, para. 16–029.

[77] See Commonhold: A Consultation Paper (1990) Cm. 1345, para. 3.49.

might be restrictive or positive, or it might involve reciprocal payment. The proposals as to positive obligations and those involving reciprocal payment have already been explained.[78] A restrictive obligation would be one which imposed a restriction that benefited the whole or part of the dominant land.[79] A land obligation could only be created by deed or in writing by a servient owner who had a legal estate in the servient land. The obligation would be a legal interest in land if it was created by deed for an interest equivalent to a fee simple absolute in possession or a term of years, and an equitable interest in any other case.[80] The instrument would have to—

(i) state that the obligation created was a land obligation;

(ii) describe both the dominant and servient land in sufficient detail to identify them, and

(iii) identify (expressly or impliedly) the legal estates in the dominant and servient land which are respectively benefited and burdened by the covenant.[81]

The benefit of a land obligation would be appurtenant to the dominant land and the burden would be capable of running with every part of the burdened land.[82] However, land obligations would be binding on a purchaser of the servient tenement only if registered as a Class C land charge where the title was unregistered,[83] or protected in the same manner as an easement where title was registered.[84] Because land obligations would be analogous to easements, the only person who would be liable for breach of the obligation (whether positive or negative) would be the landowner (or occupier of the land) for the time being bound by the obligation.

Section 3. Declaration as to Restrictive Covenants

In the case of freehold land (or certain long leaseholds[85]) it is now possible to apply to the court for a declaration stating whether the land is or would be affected by any restriction, and if so, the nature, extent and enforceability of it.[86] If the court declares that the land is not subject to restrictive covenants, **16–083**

---

[78] *Ante*, para. 16–028.

[79] Law Com. No. 127, para. 6.6.

[80] *ibid.*, paras 8.7–8.10.

[81] *ibid.*, paras 8.13–8.24.

[82] *ibid.*, paras 10.2–10.6; 11.4–11.6.

[83] *ibid.*, paras 9.4–9.6. Such obligations would constitute a new class C(v) land charge. For such land charges, see *ante*, paras 5–095 *et seq.*

[84] Law Com. No. 127, paras 9.7–9.16. This would entail the entry of a notice against the land burdened by the covenant (see *ante*, para. 6–080). The benefit would be noted as an appurtenance to the dominant land (see *post*, para. 18–096). Land obligations, unlike some easements (see *ante*, para. 16–090), would not be capable of existing as overriding interests.

[85] See *post*, para. 6–042.

[86] L.P.A. 1925, s.84(2), as amended by L.P.A. 1969, s.28(4). See *e.g. Re Freeman-Thomas Indenture* [1957] 1 W.L.R. 560; *Re Gadd's Land Transfer* [1966] Ch. 56; *Griffiths v. Band* (1974) 29 P. & C.R. 243.

its effect is *in rem* and the court will therefore only make such a declaration if it is clear from the evidence that the property is not burdened by restrictions.[87] This provision is a convenience to intending purchasers or lessees who wish to find out whether some long-standing restriction is really operative or not. It is often used to test the many nineteenth-century covenants which may today be unenforceable through non-compliance with the rules governing the transfer of the benefit.

Section 4. Discharge of Restrictive Covenants

16–084   **1. Unity of ownership.** If the land benefited and the land burdened come into common ownership the covenant can no longer have effect and is therefore permanently discharged.[88] But this may not be the case where there is a scheme of development, as already mentioned.

2. Statutory modification or discharge

16–085   *(a) The power.* Restrictive covenants, being free from any perpetuity rule, may last indefinitely, but changes in the environment may render them obsolete or may make their enforcement anti-social. As the court has no inherent power to declare that a covenant is obsolete and thereby unenforceable,[89] a discretionary[90] power has been given to the Lands Tribunal (subject to appeal on a point of law to the Court of Appeal[91]) to modify or discharge the restrictive covenant[92] with or without the payment of compensation.[93] The applicant must satisfy the Lands Tribunal that one of the following four grounds exists.

16–086   (1) OBSOLETE. That by reason of changes in the character of the property or the neighbourhood or other material circumstances the restriction ought to be deemed obsolete.[94] This requirement is not satisfied if the covenant still provides real protection to persons entitled to enforce it.[95]

---

[87] *Re 6, 8, 10 and 12 Elm Avenue, New Milton* [1984] 1 W.L.R. 1398 at 1407.
[88] *Texaco Antilles Ltd v. Kernochan* [1973] A.C. 609 at 626; *Re Tiltwood, Sussex* [1978] Ch. 269.
[89] *Westminster City Council v. Duke of Westminster* [1991] 4 All E.R. 138 at 142.
[90] *Driscoll v. Church Commissioners for England* [1957] 1 Q.B. 330.
[91] Lands Tribunal Act 1949, s.3.
[92] The Lands Tribunal has no jurisdiction to modify *positive* covenants: *Westminster City Council v. Duke of Westminster, supra,* at 147.
[93] L.P.A. 1925, s.84(1) as extended by L.P.A. 1969, s.28. Procedure is now prescribed by S.I. 1996 No. 1022 (consolidating earlier orders). See Preston & Newsom, *Restrictive Covenants* (9th ed.), chap. 15.
[94] L.P.A. 1925, s.84(1)(a). See, *e.g. Re Quaffers Ltd's Application* (1988) 56 P. & C.R. 142 (amenity diminished due to motorway construction); *Re Wards Construction (Medway) Ltd's Application* (1994) 67 P. & C.R. 379 (change in neighbourhood and need for some redevelopment of the site in any event).
[95] The typical case is where the covenants made under a building scheme still preserve the character of the estate: see, *e.g. Re Truman, Hanbury, Buxton & Co. Ltd's Application* [1956] 1 Q.B. 261; *Re Sheehy's Application* (1991) 63 P. & C.R. 95.

(2) OBSTRUCTIVE. That its continued existence would impede some reason- **16–087** able use of the land for public or private purposes, in a case where either it confers no practical benefit of substantial value or is contrary to the public interest and (in either case) any loss can be adequately compensated in money.[96] The "practical benefit" may include the enjoyment of a fine view,[97] or the preservation of the peaceful character of a neighbourhood.[98] It need not necessarily be enjoyed on the land benefited by the covenant. It may be, for example, a beautiful view enjoyed from land nearby.[99] However, the mere loss of a bargaining position is not regarded as a practical benefit.[1]

(3) AGREEMENT. That the persons of full age and capacity entitled to the **16–088** benefit of the restrictions have agreed, either expressly or by implication by their acts and omissions, to the discharge or modification sought.[2]

(4) NO INJURY. That the discharge or modification will not injure the persons **16–089** entitled to the benefit of the covenant.[3]

The Lands Tribunal must take into account the development plan and any declared or ascertainable planning policy for the area[4] and any other material circumstances, *e.g.* permissions granted by those entitled to enforce the covenant.[5] As a condition of modification or discharge the Tribunal may require the applicant to compensate those persons in money either for any loss on their part or for any reduction in the price of the land due to the imposition of the covenant. They may also require him to accept reasonable alternative restrictions. The respective jurisdictions to discharge or modify a restriction are not always co-extensive. Thus, if the Tribunal finds that the reasonable user of the land will be impeded unless the restriction is discharged, it has no power to order its modification.[6]

---

[96] L.P.A. 1925, ss.84(1)(aa); 84(1A). Compare *Re Lloyd's Application* (1993) 66 P. & C.R. 112 (contrary to public interest to impede user of a residential house as rehabilitation centre for mental patients for which there was a "desperate" local need) with *Re Solarfilms (Sales) Ltd's Application* (1993) 67 P. & C.R. 110 (no similar pressing need for the "Puddleduck's Children's Nursery" in a residential estate).

[97] *Re Bushell's Application* (1987) 54 P. & C.R. 386.

[98] *Stannard v. Issa* [1987] A.C. 175 at 188 (covenant restricting the number of dwellings in the neighbourhood).

[99] *Gilbert v. Spoor* [1983] Ch. 27 (view enjoyed by a number of owners within development scheme).

[1] *Stockport M.B.C. v. Alwiyah Developments* (1983) 52 P. & C.R. 278; *Re Bennett's and Tamarlin Ltd's Application* (1987) 54 P. & C.R. 378; *Re Hydeshire Ltd's Application* (1993) 67 P. & C.R. 93.

[2] L.P.A. 1925, s.84(1)(b).

[3] See *Re Freeman-Thomas Indenture* [1957] 1 W.L.R. 560 (estate broken up and no one entitled to benefit); *Ridley v. Taylor* [1965] 1 W.L.R. 611 at 622 (discouragement of frivolous objections); contrast *Gee v. The National Trust* [1966] 1 W.L.R. 170

[4] L.P.A. 1925, s.84(1B). However, the grant of planning permission is merely a circumstance that will be taken into account by the Lands Tribunal. It has no wider effect: *Re Martins' Application* (1988) 57 P. & C.R. 119 at 125; *Re Beech's Application* (1990) 59 P. & C.R. 502; [1990] Conv. 455 (N. D. M. Parry).

[5] See *Re Ghey and Galton's Application* [1957] 2 Q.B. 650.

[6] See *Re University of Westminster* [1998] 3 All E.R. 1014 at 1023, 1024.

16–090   *(b) Covenants within the power.* These provisions as to discharge, and the provisions mentioned above as to declarations, apply to restrictions whenever made and of whatever kind, even if they are not capable of running with land[7] and even if made under statutory authority and not benefiting any land[8]; but they do not apply to restrictions imposed on a disposition made either gratuitously or for a nominal consideration for public purposes.[9] They apply as between the original contracting parties as well as between successors in title,[10] though discretion may be exercised against an original covenantor who himself accepted the restriction not long previously.[11] They apply to restrictions on freehold land, and to restrictions on leasehold land if the lease was made for more than 40 years and at least 25 years have expired; but they do not apply to mining leases.[12] The court may be less willing to modify or discharge covenants affecting leaseholds than covenants affecting freeholds, because of the landlord's interest in the future of the property.[13]

16–091   *(c) Stay of proceedings.* A defendant in an action to enforce a restrictive covenant may apply for a stay of proceedings in order that he may apply to the Lands Tribunal for an order of discharge or modification[14]; but there is no similar power to stay proceedings for forfeiture of a lease for breach of a restrictive covenant.[15]

16–092   *(d) Conversion of houses.* There is also provision for the county court, on such terms as the court thinks fit, to authorise the conversion of a house into two or more tenements in contravention of a restrictive covenant or a provision in a lease if owing to changes in the neighbourhood the house cannot readily be let as a whole, or if planning permission for the conversion has been granted.[16]

16–093   *(e) Reform.* As part of its work in preparing a scheme of land obligations to replace for the future the existing law of positive and restrictive covenants,[17] the Law Commission considered the position of existing covenants (to which any legislation will not apply).[18] Covenants that cease to confer any practical benefits of substantial value or benefit impede the process of conveyancing.

---

[7] *Shepherd Homes Ltd v. Sandham (No. 2)* [1971] 1 W.L.R. 1062; *Gilbert v. Spoor, supra.*

[8] *Gee v. The National Trust, supra*; see *e.g. Re Beecham Group Ltd's Application* (1980) 41 P. & C.R. 369 (agreement with local planning authority).

[9] L.P.A. 1925, s.84(7).

[10] *Ridley v. Taylor* [1965] 1 W.L.R. 611.

[11] *Cresswell v. Proctor* [1968] 1 W.L.R. 906 (two years). But the time factor is not necessarily decisive, even where only a few months have elapsed: *Jones v. Rhys-Jones* (1974) 30 P. & C.R. 451.

[12] L.P.A. 1925, s.84(12) as amended by L.T.A. 1954, s.52.

[13] *Ridley v. Taylor, supra.*

[14] See L.P.A. 1925, s.84(9); *Fielden v. Byrne* [1926] Ch. 620; *Richardson v. Jackson* [1954] 1 W.L.R. 447; *Shepherd Homes Ltd v. Sandham (No. 2), supra.*

[15] *Iveagh v. Harris* [1929] 2 Ch. 281.

[16] H.A. 1985, s.610 (replacing earlier legislation). See Preston & Newsom, *Restrictive Covenants* (8th ed.), App. VI. For the limits of this, see *Josephine Trust Ltd v. Champagne* [1963] 2 Q.B. 160.

[17] *Ante*, para. 16–081.

[18] (1991) Law Com. No. 201.

Furthermore, application to the Lands Tribunal for the discharge or modification of covenants is expensive. In an attempt to meet these difficulties, the Commission recommended that all restrictive covenants should lapse 80 years after their creation, but that an application could be made to the Lands Tribunal by a party who considered that the covenant was not in fact obsolete. If the application was successful, the covenant would be replaced by a land obligation. Although the objective of this proposed scheme was laudable, it was not without its difficulties.[19] It has now been rejected by the Lord Chancellor.

Section 5. Restrictive Covenants and Planning

The extension of planning control has somewhat reduced the importance of **16–094** restrictive covenants. The effect of this control[20] is to impose restrictions throughout England and Wales on any change in the use of any land, subject to various exceptions. Restrictive covenants need no longer be employed so widely and their scope can be more limited. Nevertheless, restrictive covenants have not been superseded by planning control. A landowner must see that what he proposes to do will contravene neither the private system of restrictive covenants nor the public system of planning control. Restrictive covenants sometimes extend to matters not covered by the planning legislation, as for example a change of the business carried on on the premises. Not only may it be better to be able to enforce a restrictive covenant as of right than to be dependent on the local planning authority enforcing planning control,[21] but the covenant may enable the covenantee or his successor in title to achieve greater control over the use of the servient land.[22]

The grant of planning permission does not by itself authorise the breach of a restrictive covenant.[23] But there are special provisions where a local authority has acquired land, or appropriated its own land,[24] for planning purposes. The erection, construction or carrying out, or maintenance, of any building or work on land in accordance with planning permission is then authorised by statute even though this involves a breach of restrictive covenants or interference with easements and similar rights of third parties.[25] This provision extends both to the local authority and to their successors in title, but statutory

---

[19] Age alone may not make a covenant obsolete. Nor does it seem entirely just that the person enjoying the benefit of a covenant should be required to take proceedings before the Lands Tribunal to prevent its extinction.

[20] *Ante*, para. 3–049; and *post*, para. 22–009.

[21] For further discussion see (1964) 28 Conv.(N.S.) 190 (A. R. Mellows).

[22] *Re Jones' and White & Co.'s Application* (1989) 58 P. & C.R. 512 at 516 (a case concerned with a planning agreement under T. & C.P.A. 1971, s.52).

[23] *Re Martins' Application* (1988) 57 P. & C.R. 119 at 124.

[24] *cf. Sutton L.B.C. v. Bolton* [1993] 2 E.G.L.R. 181.

[25] T. & C.P.A. 1990, s.237(1).

undertakers are excepted from its effect.[26] Where any such expropriation occurs, the owners of such rights may claim compensation.[27]

Planning authorities make much use of their statutory power to enter into planning obligations[28] with landowners for the purpose of restricting or regulating the development or use of land.[29] It has already been explained that such authorities do not need to possess adjacent land in order to enforce restrictions taken for this purpose.[30]

Section 6. Restrictive Covenants and Compulsory Acquisition

16–095 Where land which is subject to a restrictive covenant is acquired compulsorily[31] by a public authority under statutory powers, no action lies for breach of the covenant if what is done on the land is validly done in the exercise of statutory powers.[32] The authority of Parliament then overrides the contractual restriction, and the covenantee's only remedy is to claim compensation for the injurious affection of his own land which was previously benefited by the covenant.[33] "The remedy is given because Parliament, by authorising the works, has prevented damages caused by them from being actionable, and the compensation is given as a substitute for damages at law."[34] Such an award of compensation does not extinguish the covenant, which continues to bind the acquired land as regards any use not authorised by statute. Thus where the Air Ministry compulsorily purchased agricultural land for use as an aerodrome and later let it to a firm for use for commercial flying, an injunction was granted to prevent the firm from so using the land in

---

[26] *ibid.*, s.237(3).

[27] *ibid.*, s.237(4). See *infra*.

[28] Formerly there was a system of planning *agreements* under T. & C.P.A. 1971, s.52, re-enacted as T. & C.P.A. 1990, s.106. Since October 25, 1991, it has not been possible to enter into such agreements. Instead a new and very different system of planning *obligations* has applied: Planning and Compensation Act 1991, s.12, substituting a new T. & C.P.A. 1990, s.106, and inserting new ss.106A, 106B. Although planning agreements were consensual, this is not always true of planning obligations which may be imposed on a local authority, *e.g.* on an appeal against a refusal to grant planning permission to a planning inspector or to the Secretary of State. To modify or discharge planning agreements application was made to the Lands Tribunal under L.P.A. 1925, s.84 (*ante*, para. 16–085). A planning obligation can be modified or discharged either by agreement with the local authority or at a determination made by the authority on application to it: T. & C.P.A. 1990, s.106A. Appeal lies to the Secretary of State: T. & C.P.A. 1990, s.106B.

[29] T. & C.P.A. 1990, s.106 (as substituted). Planning obligations may also impose positive obligations: *ante*, para. 16–018.

[30] *Ante*, para. 16–047.

[31] As to purchase by agreement under statutory powers, see *Kirby v. Harrogate School Board* [1896] 1 Ch. 437.

[32] *Kirby v. Harrogate School Board, supra*; *Marten v. Flight Refuelling Ltd* [1962] Ch. 115.

[33] *Long Eaton Recreation Grounds Co. Ltd v. Midland Ry* [1902] 2 K.B. 574. *cf. Hawley v. Steele* (1877) 6 Ch.D. 521.

[34] *Horn v. Sunderland Corporation* [1941] 2 K.B. 26 at 43, *per* Scott L.J. On the measure of compensation in such a case, see *Wrotham Park S.E. v. Hertsmere B.C.* [1993] 2 E.G.L.R. 15.

breach of a covenant restricting it to agricultural use; but an injunction to prevent them for using it for Air Ministry work was refused.[35]

Section 7. Restrictive Covenants and Race Relations

Under the Race Relations Act 1976 it is unlawful for a person disposing of or managing any premises to discriminate against another person on grounds of colour, race, nationality or ethnic or national origins.[36] There is an exception for the provision of accommodation in, or the disposal of "small premises" in which the proprietor or manager (or a near relative) resides and which are shared with other persons not members of his household.[37]   **16–096**

The Act does not directly prohibit restrictive covenants requiring racial discrimination. Plainly such covenants are void in so far as they require discrimination prohibited by the Act, but it seems that they may be effective in requiring discrimination that is permitted by the exception for "small premises".

[35] *Marten v. Flight Refuelling Ltd, supra.*
[36] ss.1–3, 21.
[37] s.22. For "small premises" see *ante*, para. 14–269.

CHAPTER 17

LICENCES

Section 1. Nature of a Licence

17–001 A licence is a mere permission which makes it lawful for the licensee to do what would otherwise be a trespass.[1] Such rights are an everyday commonplace, and examples include lodging in a person's house,[2] going onto his land to play cricket,[3] storing goods on his premises,[4] or advertising on a hoarding on his wall.[5] Such a licence is merely a defence to an action in tort and confers no estate or interest in land.[6] "A licence in connection with land while entitling the licensee to use the land for the purposes authorised by the licence does not create an estate in land."[7] A licence cannot therefore bind a successor in title of the licensor. Furthermore, at common law, a licensor might always revoke his licence,[8] though he might have to pay damages for breach of contract.

The boundary of the law of property is drawn between leases and licences. Where the requirements for a tenancy are not satisfied, the interest can be no more than a licence.[9] If A owns a lodging house and sells it, B, the purchaser, can recover possession from the lodgers,[10] who are in law mere licensees, notwithstanding their agreements,[11] unless in the circumstances B's conduct is sufficiently unconscionable to warrant the intervention of equity.[12] In the usual

---

[1] See *Thomas v. Sorrell* (1673) Vaugh. 330 at 351.
[2] *Ante*, para. 14–015.
[3] *Frank Warr & Co. Ltd v. L.C.C.* [1904] 1 K.B. 713 at 723.
[4] *Morris-Thomas v. Petticoat Lane Rentals* (1986) 53 P. & C.R. 238 (storage of antiques in a former bacon curing oven).
[5] *Kewal Investments Ltd v. Arthur Maiden Ltd* [1990] 1 E.G.L.R. 193; *Arthur Maiden Ltd v. Patel* [1990] 1 E.G.L.R. 269.
[6] *Ashburn Anstalt v. Arnold* [1989] Ch. 1 at 22. In *IDC Group Ltd v. Clark* [1992] 2 E.G.L.R. 184 at 186, Nourse L.J. stated that "a licence properly so called is a permission to do something on or over land which creates no interest in it".
[7] *Street v. Mountford* [1985] A.C. 809 at 814, *per* Lord Templeman. See too *Wettern Electric Ltd v. Welsh Development Agency* [1983] Q.B. 796 at 805; *Camden L.B.C. v. Shortlife Community Housing Ltd* (1992) 90 L.G.R. 358 at 373.
[8] For the position in equity, see *post*, para. 17–009.
[9] *Ante*, para. 14–010.
[10] B will have to obtain a court order: see P.E.A. 1977, s.3(1), (2B) (inserted by H.A. 1988, s.30). There is however an exception from this requirement in the case of certain "excluded licences" (which are licences of accommodation shared in some way with the landlord or which fall within certain other specified categories): see P.E.A. 1977, s.3A (added by H.A. 1988, s.31).
[11] *Clore v. Theatrical Properties Ltd* [1936] 3 All E.R. 483.
[12] *Post*, para. 17–019.

case, the lodger's only remedy is to sue A for damages.[13] Although there was an attempt to elevate licences into interests in land, the traditional nature of licences has since been reasserted.[14]

Section 2. Types of Licences

Licences can be granted in a wide variety of forms. At one end of the scale is an occupational licence which confers a right of occupation but not of exclusive possession,[15] such as the licence of a lodger in a lodging-house.[16] At the other end of the scale are all kinds of miscellaneous licences for temporary purposes, such as the hire of a concert hall for a few days,[17] permission to erect an advertisement hoarding[18] or electric sign,[19] permission to use pleasure boats on a canal,[20] the grant of the right to use refreshment rooms in a theatre,[21] and permission to view a race on a racecourse[22] or a film in a cinema.[23] There is no limit to the possible variety of licences; yet three main varieties require consideration.   **17–002**

1. Bare licence. This is the simplest form of licence. A bare licence is a licence which is not supported by any contract, such as a gratuitous permission to enter a house or to cross a field. Such a licence may be expressly given or it may be implied. Thus a person with lawful business may enter a householder's garden gate and proceed to the door of the house,[24] or he may go into a shop that is open.[25] A bare licence can be revoked at any time[26] on   **17–003**

---

[13] *King v. David Allen & Sons (Billposting) Ltd* [1916] 2 A.C. 54.
[14] *Post*, paras 17–016–17–019.
[15] *Ante*, para. 14–015. A person may be in exclusive possession but not in actual occupation, as where a tenant sub-lets the premises leased to him: *Camden L.B.C. v. Shortlife Community Housing Ltd* (1992) 90 L.G.R. 358 at 381.
[16] *Allen v. Liverpool Overseers* (1874) L.R. 9 Q.B. 180 at 190, 191. An occupier is a lodger "if the landlord provides attendance or services which require the landlord or his servants to exercise unrestricted access to and use of the premises": *Street v. Mountford* [1985] A.C. 809 at 818, *per* Lord Templeman.
[17] *Taylor v. Caldwell* (1863) 3 B. & S. 826.
[18] *Wilson v. Tavener* [1901] 1 Ch. 578.
[19] *Walton Harvey Ltd v. Walker and Homfrays Ltd* [1931] 1 Ch. 274.
[20] *Hill v. Tupper* (1863) 2 H. & C. 121.
[21] *Frank Warr & Co. Ltd v. L.C.C.* [1904] 1 K.B. 713; *Clore v. Theatrical Properties Ltd* [1936] 3 All E.R. 483. Similarly in *Isaac v. Hotel de Paris Ltd* [1960] 1 W.L.R. 239 the right to use one floor of a hotel as a night bar at a monthly rent was held to be a licence.
[22] *Wood v. Leadbitter* (1845) 13 M. & W. 838.
[23] *Hurst v. Picture Theatres Ltd* [1915] 1 K.B. 1.
[24] *Robson v. Hallett* [1967] 2 Q.B. 939 at 953, 954.
[25] *Davis v. Lisle* [1936] 2 K.B. 434 at 440.
[26] There is an ancient common law doctrine that a licence is irrevocable after being acted upon: see, *e.g. Webb v. Paternoster* (1619) 2 Roll. 152, Palm. 71 at 74; *Feltham v. Cartwright* (1839) 5 Bing. N.C. 569; *Hounslow L.B.C. v. Twickenham Garden Developments Ltd* [1971] Ch. 233 at 255; *ante*, para. 13–037; *post*, para. 17–012.

reasonable notice without rendering the licensor liable in damages,[27] but the licensee will not be a trespasser until he has had reasonable time to withdraw.[28] Even a licence granted by deed may be revocable,[29] provided that there is no covenant not to revoke it. A revocable licence is automatically determined by the death of the licensor or the assignment of the land.[30]

Under the rule already explained,[31] a licensee in possession is estopped from denying the title of the licensor, so that he cannot resist making any agreed payment by pleading that the licensor is not the true owner[32]; but under the same rule the estoppel ceases to operate when he gives up possession.[33]

17–004   **2. Contractual licence.** A licence will often be granted under the terms of some contract which restricts the licensor's right to revoke it. The contract is normally express but it may sometimes be implied.[34] Examples include a lodger in a lodging-house and a ticket-holder at a cricket match or on the railway.

Contractual licences are subject to the same rules which govern all contracts, as three examples will demonstrate. First, in appropriate circumstances a court will imply terms into a licence to give it business efficacy,[35] such as a term that the licensor will not disturb the quiet enjoyment of a residential licensee.[36] Such terms are not necessarily the same as those which would be implied into a lease even where the licence is for the use and occupation of land.[37] Secondly, a person who knowingly induces the breach of a contractual licence may commit the tort of inducing breach of contract.[38] Thirdly, the licensor or licensee may commit a breach of the terms of a contractual licence that will entitle the other to treat it as at an end. If, however, a licensee elects

---

[27] *Aldin v. Latimer Clark, Muirhead & Co.* [1894] 2 Ch. 437 (where the licensor gave no reasonable notice and so was liable in damages); *Armstrong v. Sheppard and Short Ltd* [1959] 2 Q.B. 384.

[28] *Cornish v. Stubbs* (1870) L.R. 5 C.P. 334; *Mellor v. Watkins* (1874) L.R. 9 Q.B. 400; *Aldin v. Latimer Clark, Muirhead & Co., supra* (damages awarded but injunction refused); *Canadian Pacific Ry. v. The King* [1931] A.C. 414; *Minister of Health v. Bellotti* [1944] K.B. 298; *Australian Blue Metal Ltd v. Hughes* [1963] A.C. 74.

[29] *Wood v. Leadbitter* (1845) 13 M. & W. 838 at 845.

[30] *Terunnanse v. Terunnanse* [1968] A.C. 1086.

[31] *Ante*, para. 14–095.

[32] *Terunnanse v. Terunnanse, supra*; *Sze To Chun Keung v. Kung Kwok Wai David* [1997] 1 W.L.R. 1232 at 1235.

[33] *Government of Penang v. Beng Hong Oon* [1972] A.C. 425.

[34] *Tanner v. Tanner* [1975] 1 W.L.R. 1346; *Chandler v. Kerley* [1978] 1 W.L.R. 693. See too *Horrocks v. Forray* [1976] 1 W.L.R. 230 at 239.

[35] *Winter Garden Theatre (London) Ltd v. Millennium Productions Ltd* [1948] A.C. 173; *Smith v. Nottinghamshire C.C., The Times*, November 13, 1981; *Wettern Electric Ltd v. Welsh Development Agency* [1983] Q.B. 796.

[36] *Smith v. Nottinghamshire C.C., supra* (injunction granted to restrain building work during examination period at a students' hall of residence).

[37] *Wettern Electric Ltd v. Welsh Development Agency, supra* (obligation implied that newly constructed factory premises were fit for the purposes of the licensee, even though no such obligation would have been implied into a lease: see *ante*, para. 14–210). *cf. Morris-Thomas v. Petticoat Lane Rentals* (1986) 53 P. & C.R. 238 at 249, 255 (no such implied term where the licensee knew the state of the property when she took the licence).

[38] *Binions v. Evans* [1972] Ch. 359 at 371; *Arthur Maiden Ltd v. Patel* [1990] 1 E.G.L.R. 269. See *ante*, para. 4–093.

to affirm the contract, he will remain liable to pay the licence fee as long as he occupies the premises.[39]

3. **Licence coupled with an interest.** The one form of licence which caused **17–005** no problems at common law was a licence coupled with a recognised interest in property. A right to enter another man's land to hunt and take away the deer killed, or to enter and cut down a tree and take it away, involves two things, namely, a licence to enter the land (and) the grant of an interest (a *profit à prendre*[40]) in the deer or tree.[41] At common law such a licence is both irrevocable[42] and assignable,[43] but only as an adjunct of the interest with which it is coupled. It therefore has no independent existence merely as a licence. It may be reinforced by the principle that a person may not derogate from his grant,[44] which is explained further below.[45] In any case such a licence is not only irrevocable but is enforceable by and against successors in title of the grantee and grantor respectively, as part and parcel of the interest granted.

The interest in question must, of course, have been validly created. If the **17–006** licence was to go upon land to take game or dig for materials, these rights, being *profits à prendre*, must have been duly granted by deed[46] or acquired by prescription.[47] An interest in chattels, however, can be created with less formality, as where there is a sale of hay or timber already cut, coupled with a licence to the purchaser to cart them away.[48] An interest in standing timber or growing crops can be created, it seems, only by the formalities appropriate for land.[49] In equity, as usual, effect will be given to a specifically enforceable agreement to grant an interest; and thus a licence coupled with a *profit à prendre* granted for value but merely in writing[50] can be enforced by injunction.[51]

---

[39] *Dudley Port Warehousing Co. Ltd v. Gardner Transport & Distribution Ltd* [1995] E.G.C.S. 5.

[40] For such interests see *post*, paras 18–079, 18–213.

[41] See *Thomas v. Sorrell* (1673) Vaugh. 330 at 351; *Wood v. Leadbitter* (1845) 13 M. & W. 838 at 845.

[42] *James Jones & Sons Ltd v. Earl of Tankerville* [1909] 2 Ch. 440 at 442 (sale of timber); *Doe d. Hanley v. Wood* (1819) 2 B. & Ald. 724 at 738 (sale of hay); *Wood v. Manley* (1839) 11 A. & E. 34; *Wood v. Leadbitter* (1845) 13 M. & W. 838 at 845.

[43] *Muskett v. Hill* (1839) 5 Bing. N.C. 694 at 707, 708.

[44] *cf. Wood v. Manley* (1839) 11 A. & E. 34 at 37, 38.

[45] *Post*, para. 18–075; and see *ante*, para. 14–208.

[46] *Duke of Somerset v. Fogwell* (1826) 5 B. & C. 875 at 886 (fishing lease).

[47] *Post*.

[48] See n. 42 above.

[49] Although a sale of timber to be cut forthwith is not a contract for the sale of an interest in land (*semble*, see *ante*, para. 12–026), the property in the timber cannot pass until it is cut, *i.e.* no proprietary interest can be created informally so long as the timber is in fact part of the land: *Morison v. Lockhart*, 1912 S.C. 1017, followed in *Kursell v. Timber Operators and Contractors Ltd* [1927] 1 K.B. 298. "Timber trees cannot be felled with a goose quill": *Liford's Case* (1614) 11 Co. Rep. 46b at 50a.

[50] A contract to grant such an interest is void unless it is made in writing, contains all the terms agreed, and is signed by each party to it: *ante*, para. 12–018.

[51] *Frogley v. Earl of Lovelace* (1859) John 333: *cf. Duke of Devonshire v. Eglin* (1851) 14 Beav. 530; *McManus v. Cooke* (1887) 35 Ch.D. 681; *cf. ante*, para. 14–040.

Licences have occasionally been held to be coupled with an interest, and so irrevocable, even though no recognisable interest was involved.[52] But the better view must be that some kind of proprietary interest is necessary.[53]

Licences of this class may be compared with rights of entry, which are recognised interests in land.[54]

Section 3. Revocability of Licences

17–007 At common law, a licence, unless coupled with an interest, was always revocable, for the licence had no estate or interest in the land that would entitle him to remain there. But this simple position has been modified in important respects.

1. Revocation restricted by contract

17–008 *(a) Revocability a matter of construction.* Except in those cases which are governed by statute,[55] then whether or not a contractual licence is revocable is a question of construction of the contract.[56] If the contract makes no express provision for determination, the court will imply a term that is appropriate in the circumstances.[57] Thus in cases of service occupancy,[58] the licence will normally be granted for the duration of the licensee's employment.[59] It is implicit therefore that it will terminate when that employment ceases,[60] even if the licensee has been wrongfully dismissed.[61] With most contractual licences the court usually implies a term that reasonable notice shall be given.[62] If the licensor purports to terminate the licence without giving

---

[52] As in *Vaughan v. Hampson* (1875) 33 L.T. 15 (successful action for assault by licensee ejected from meeting); *Hurst v. Picture Theatres Ltd, infra.*

[53] *Hounslow L.B.C. v. Twickenham Garden Developments Ltd* [1971] Ch. 233.

[54] *Ante*, para. 4–054.

[55] *Infra.*

[56] *Millennium Productions Ltd v. Winter Garden Theatre (London) Ltd* [1946] 1 All E.R. 678 at 680; [1948] A.C. 173 at 196, 198 (*sub nom. Winter Garden Theatre (London) Ltd v. Millennium Productions Ltd*). In construing the contract the court has regard to the circumstances existing when the contract is made: *Australian Blue Metal Ltd v. Hughes* [1963] A.C. 74 at 99.

[57] *Winter Garden Theatre (London) Ltd v. Millennium Productions Ltd, supra.*

[58] A service occupancy will exist where the licensee's occupation of the premises is either necessary for the performance of his duties, or is required by his employer for the better performance of those duties: *Norris v. Checksfield* [1991] 1 W.L.R. 1241 at 1244. *cf. Hughes v. Greenwich L.B.C.* [1994] 1 A.C. 170 at 178.

[59] *Ivory v. Palmer* [1975] I.C.R. 340; *Burgoyne v. Griffiths* [1991] 1 E.G.L.R. 14 at 16.

[60] *Norris v. Checksfield* [1991] 1 W.L.R. 1241 at 1248.

[61] *Ivory v. Palmer, supra.*

[62] *Winter Garden Theatre (London) Ltd v. Millennium Productions Ltd, supra*; *Greater London Council v. Jenkins* [1978] 1 W.L.R. 155 at 158; *Smith v. Northside Developments Ltd* [1987] 2 E.G.L.R. 151 at 152. What is reasonable is determined in the light of curcumstances existing at the time when the notice is given: *Australian Blue Metal Ltd v. Hughes, supra*, at 99. See too *Governing Body of Henrietta Barnett School v. Hampstead Garden Suburb* [1995] E.G.C.S. 55.

reasonable notice, that notice will be effective, but only after a reasonable time has elapsed.[63] If the contract specifies the period of notice, however, any purported determination that is not in accordance with the contract is a nullity.[64] On the termination of the licence, the licensee is permitted a reasonable time to vacate the premises.[65]

Under the Protection from Eviction Act 1977, the licensor must give the licensee not less than four weeks' written notice to quit in the case of certain "periodic licences"[66] of a dwelling.[67] This requirement does not however apply to excluded licences.[68]

(b) Remedies for improper revocation. In *Wood v. Leadbitter*[69] a ticket-holder was wrongfully turned off the Doncaster racecourse, but failed in an action for assault even though he would have succeeded in an action for breach of contract. The defect of the common law remedy in contract is that the plaintiff can merely recover the price of the ticket; he cannot insist on his right to remain on the land. But if the contract is specifically enforceable in equity, *e.g.* by an injunction against wrongful interference with the licensee, the licensee has then a specific equitable right to remain on the land: an injunction will be granted to restrain a threatened revocation of the licence and also to restrain a wrongful revocation from being enforced.[70] Specific performance may also be granted, as it was where a local authority, after a change of political control, repudiated an agreement for the hire of a hall for a two-day conference of the National Front.[71] Equity may thus protect the licensee effectively, at least before and during the period of the licence. Even if he cannot seek an equitable remedy until afterwards, the fact that it was due to

17–009

---

[63] *Minister of Health v. Bellotti* [1944] Q.B. 298. This has been criticised: see [1996] C.L.J. 229 (T. Kerbel), where it is suggested that a notice that fails to specify a period that is in fact reasonable ought to be invalid. *cf. Canadian Pacific Ry. v. The King* [1931] A.C. 414.

[64] *Wallshire Ltd v. Advertising Sites Ltd* [1988] 2 E.G.L.R. 167.

[65] The "packing-up period": *Winter Garden Theatre (London) Ltd v. Millennium Productions Ltd, supra,* at 206, *per* Lord MacDermott; *Minister of Health v. Bellotti, supra,* at 305, 306.

[66] A term not defined by P.E.A. 1977, and described by Woolf L.J. in *Norris v. Checksfield* [1991] 1 W.L.R. 1241 at 1246 as "a new animal". It is apparently a licence granted on a periodic basis in a similar manner to a periodic tenancy: *ibid.*

[67] P.E.A. 1977, s.5(1A) (added by H.A. 1988, s.23). For the prescribed information that the notice to quit must contain, see S.I. 1988 No. 2201.

[68] *ibid.,* s.5(1B) (added by H.A. 1988, s.32). For "excluded licences", see P.E.A. 1977, s.3A; *ante,* para. 17–001.

[69] (1845) 13 M. & W. 838. Contrast *Feltham v. Cartwright* (1829) 5 Bing.N.C. 569, where a contractual licence was held irrevocable after being acted upon (*ante,* para. 17–003, n. 26), and *Butler v. Manchester, Sheffield & Lincolnshire Ry* (1888) 21 Q.B.D. 207, where the Court of Appeal allowed an action for assault to a ticket-holder who was wrongfully turned off a railway train.

[70] *Winter Garden Theatre (London) Ltd v. Millennium Productions Ltd* [1946] 1 All E.R. 678 at 684 (reversed on other grounds, *infra*) *per* Lord Greene M.R.; and see *Errington v. Errington* [1952] 1 K.B. 290; *Hounslow L.B.C. v. Twickenham Garden Developments Ltd* [1971] Ch. 233.

[71] *Verrall v. Great Yarmouth Borough Council* [1981] Q.B. 202, rejecting the contention that specific performance is not granted for short lettings. It is not clear why an injunction was not the more suitable remedy.

him at the time of the wrongful revocation may entitle him to sue for assault if ejected.[72]

17–010 But what if equity will not assist, so that the question is one of common law? In one case the owners of two schools agreed to share premises owned by one of them, and after revocation of the licence the licensee re-entered forcibly. The Court of Appeal held that he was a trespasser, even if the revocation was a breach of contract.[73] Equity would not assist him, since "the court cannot specifically enforce an agreement for two people to live peaceably under the same roof".[74] This affirmed the old doctrine that at common law a licensor has a *power* to eject his licensee even though he has no *right* to do so. Shortly afterwards this doctrine was repudiated in the House of Lords, but in a case where the question did not really arise, for it was held that the contract impliedly permitted revocation of the licence, which was for the use of a theatre for the production of plays.[75]

Since then the Court of Appeal has adopted the views of the House of Lords, though again in a case where the question did not arise since the licensee was entitled to the assistance of equity and was granted an order of specific performance when the licensor purported to revoke the licence.[76] The judicial consensus is now to the effect that a licensor has no right to eject a licensee in breach of contract, even where equity will not assist the licensee, and that if he does so forcibly the licensee can sue for assault.[77] It seems to follow that the licensor is equally liable for assault if he forcibly and in breach of contract resists the licensee's entry, though in most cases the licensee's natural remedy will be an injunction against the breach of contract. A licensor acting in breach of contract is himself unlikely to be awarded equitable remedies.[78]

17–011 *(c) Informal family arrangements.* In a number of cases of informal family arrangements the court has found an implied contract which prevented or restricted the revocation of a licence.[79] Where a man bought a house and installed his mistress and their children in it, the mistress having given up her

---

[72] This appears to be the explanation of *Hurst v. Picture Theatres Ltd* [1915] 1 K.B. 1 (successful action for assault by ticket-holder ejected from cinema).

[73] *Thompson v. Park* [1944] K.B. 408; (interlocutory injunction against licensee granted).

[74] *Thompson v. Park, supra,* at 409, *per* Goddard L.J.

[75] *Winter Garden Theatre (London) Ltd v. Millennium Productions Ltd* [1948] A.C. 173, *per* Lord Simon, holding that the mere contract gives the licensee a right to remain. His explanation of *Wood v. Leadbitter, supra,* was not accepted by Lord Porter. Lord Porter and Lord Uthwatt, however, speak only of cases where equity will assist.

[76] *Verrall v. Great Yarmouth Borough Council, supra,* disapproving *Thompson v. Park, supra,* and approving the comment on that case in the *Hounslow case, supra.*

[77] As suggested in (1948) 64 L.Q.R. 57 (H.W.R.W.).

[78] *Hounslow L.B.C. v. Twickenham Garden Developments Ltd, supra* (injunction against contractor remaining on building site refused). Contrast *Thompson v. Park, supra* (injunction granted to expel violent intruder). In each case the decision preserved the *status quo*: see the *Hounslow case* at 250.

[79] These cases date from the late 1970s. In more recent decisions the courts have shown a reluctance to find such implied contracts: see *Coombes v. Smith* [1986] 1 W.L.R. 808 at 814, 815.

rent-controlled flat, a contractual licence was inferred under which the mistress and children were entitled to retain the house so long as the children were of school age and reasonably required it.[80] Where a mother bought a house for her son and his wife, asking them to pay £7 per week, and the son deserted the wife, the court imputed a contractual licence under which the mother could not evict the wife provided that she made the stipulated payments and that nothing occurred to justify revocation of the licence, a proviso which the court did not further explain.[81] It was admitted that the parties never in fact formed the intention imputed to them: the contractual licence was employed as a flexible device for achieving an equitable result. But the mere fact that a man installs his mistress and their child in a house will not give her an irrevocable licence if the court sees no reason for inferring that the arrangement was contractual.[82]

An irrevocable licence does not become revocable merely because the licensee harasses or obstructs the licensor or his successors in title, since the licensor should pursue his ordinary remedies in trespass or nuisance.[83] But grave misconduct may amount to a breach of an implied term in a contractual licence and so prevent the licensee from relying on equity to restrain revocation.[84]

2. No revocation of a licence acted upon. It has already been explained **17–012** that it is a long-established rule of the common law that a licence once acted upon cannot usually be revoked.[85] "If A gives authority to B for the doing of an act on A's land, and the act is done and completed, then, whatever be the strict description of the authority . . . it is, generally speaking at any rate, too late for A, who gave the authority, to complain of it."[86] The principle which underlies this rule is similar to the equitable doctrine of proprietary estoppel.[87] It is unreasonable for B to incur expense in reliance upon A's licence, and for A then to revoke that licence and treat B as a trespasser.[88] Thus where A, with B's permission, lowers a river bank and diverts part of the flow of a river over a weir which he has constructed, that licence cannot be revoked so as to make A's conduct tortious.[89] Similarly, if B has an easement of light and permits A to build a wall against B's window, B cannot complain of the infringement of

---

[80] *Tanner v. Tanner* [1975] 1 W.L.R. 1346. In fact, the plaintiff had been rehoused, and so was awarded damages. *cf. Chandler v. Kerley* [1978] 1 W.L.R. 693 (mistress held to have contractual licence revocable on 12 months' notice).

[81] *Hardwick v. Johnson* [1978] 1 W.L.R. 683. See similarly *Re Sharpe* [1980] 1 W.L.R. 219, *post*, para. 17–018.

[82] *Horrocks v. Forray* [1976] 1 W.L.R. 230 (gift of house intended but not effected because of conveyancing costs).

[83] *Williams v. Staite* [1979] Ch. 291.

[84] *Brynowen Estates Ltd v. Bairne* (1981) 131 N.L.J. 1212; and see *Williams v. Staite, supra*, at 298; *Hardwick v. Johnson, supra*, at 689, *per* Lord Denning M.R.

[85] *Ante*, para. 13–037. "A licence executed is not countermandable, but only when it is executory": *Winter v. Brockwell* (1807) 8 East 308 at 310, *per* Lord Ellenborough C.J.

[86] *Armstrong v. Sheppard & Short Ltd* [1959] 2 Q.B. 384 at 399, *per* Lord Evershed M.R.

[87] For the diffferences between the two doctrines, see *ante*, para. 13–037.

[88] *Winter v. Brockwell, supra*, at 310.

[89] *Liggins v. Inge* (1831) 7 Bing. 682.

his right to light.[90] The doctrine applies even where A has merely started to perform the act authorised by B and has not completed it.[91] The doctrine has been overlooked on occasions,[92] and has in any event been largely eclipsed by the equitable doctrine of proprietary estoppel.

17–013 **3. Revocation restricted by estoppel.** The doctrine of proprietary estoppel has already been explained.[93] It has no necessary connection with the law of licences, though the converse was once thought to be true.[94] If A has a licence over B's land, and B encourages him to act to his detriment in the belief that he will acquire certain rights over B's property, an equity may arise in A's favour. One way in which the court may satisfy that equity arising by estoppel is by declaring A's licence to be irrevocable, either in perpetuity[95] or only on the occurrence of certain events.[96]

Section 4. Licences and Third Parties

A. Transmission of the Benefit

17–014 Whether or not the benefit of a licence is assignable must depend upon the circumstances of its grant. If the licence was intended to be personal to the licensor it will not be assignable. This is clearly settled in relation to contractual licences: it is a matter of construction of the contract.[97] It is more difficult to see how a bare licence is capable of assignment. It is neither a contractual nor a proprietary right but only bare permission. In practice, any "assignment" of a bare licence may be better explained either as a renewal to the assignee of the licence,[98] or as a case where the permission given by the licensor was intended to include not only the original licensee but also his assigns.

B. Transmission of the Burden

17–015 **1. General.** In principle, the burden of a licence should not be transmissible because it creates no interest in land.[99] This is certainly true of a bare licence

---

[90] *ibid.*, at 693; *Armstrong v. Sheppard & Short Ltd, supra,* at 399, 400.

[91] *Winter Garden Theatre (London) Ltd v. Millennium Productions Ltd* [1948] A.C. 173 at 194; *Hounslow L.B.C. v. Twickenham Garden Developments Ltd* [1971] Ch. 233 at 255.

[92] See the criticism of *Wood v. Leadbitter* (1845) 13 M. & W. 838 in *Hounslow L.B.C. v. Twickenham Garden Developments Ltd, supra,* at 255.

[93] *Ante,* Chap. 13.

[94] *Ante,* paras 13–006, 13–037.

[95] *Plimmer v. Mayor, etc., of Wellington* (1884) 9 App.Cas. 699.

[96] *Inwards v. Baker* [1965] 2 Q.B. 29 (licence for A to remain as long as he wished).

[97] See, *e.g. Clapman v. Edwards* [1938] 2 All E.R. 507; *Shayler v. Woolf* [1946] Ch. 320. An assignment of a contractual licence must be made in writing with notice to the licensor: see L.P.A. 1925, s.136.

[98] *E.R. Ives Investment Ltd v. High* [1967] 2 Q.B. 379 at 404.

[99] *Ante,* para. 17–001. Licences coupled with an interest are of course a special case. The licence is no more than ancillary to the proprietary interest. If the proprietary interest binds a transferee of the land then so too does the licence.

which, as has been explained, is "automatically determined by the death of the licensor or by the assignment of the land over which the licence is exercised".[1] However the position of contractual licences has until recently been uncertain and calls for fuller explanation.

2. Contractual licences

(a) The orthodox position. The law for long set its face firmly against the **17–016** notion that a contractual licence could be binding upon the licensor's successors in title, on the principle that licences were personal transactions which created no proprietary interests in land. A purchaser of the licensor's land therefore had no concern with any mere licence, even when he bought with express notice of it.[2] Thus, where a licence had been granted to sellers of refreshments giving them the exclusive use of the refreshment rooms of a theatre, a purchaser of the theatre was able to prevent an assignee of the licensee from enforcing his rights, and the Court of Appeal held that the proper remedy was in damages against the licensor.[3]

(b) Contractual licences as equitable interests. The first sign of a new **17–017** attitude appeared in *Errington v. Errington.*[4] The Court of Appeal held that a contractual licence for the occupation of a dwelling-house will bind a person to whom the licensor leaves the house by will; and it was said that a contractual licence created an equitable interest in land which would bind all comers except a purchaser without notice. Not only was this view contrary to earlier House of Lords and Court of Appeal authority,[5] but the creation of new equitable interests appears to have been prohibited by the Law of Property Act 1925.[6] In that case a father bought a house, raising part of the money on mortgage, and allowed his son and daughter-in-law to live in it, saying that if they paid off the mortgage instalments the house would become theirs. Before the instalments had all been paid the father died, having by his will left the house to his widow. The widow failed in an action to recover the house, on the

---

[1] *Terunnanse v. Terunnanse* [1968] A.C. 1086 at 1095, *per* Lord Devlin; *ante*, para. 17–003. See too *Wallis v. Harrison* (1838) 4 M. & W. 528 at 543, 544.

[2] *King v. David Allen & Sons, Billposting Ltd* [1916] 2 A.C. 54 (agreement for licence to display advertisements on a building held not binding on tenant to whom licensor later demised the land); *Clore v. Theatrical Properties Ltd, infra; cf. Plimmer v. Mayor, etc., of Wellington* (1884) 9 App.Cas. 699 at 714; contrast *Webb v. Paternoster* (1619) Poph. 151, *per* Montague C.J.

[3] *Clore v. Theatrical Properties Ltd* [1936] 3 All E.R. 483.

[4] [1952] 1 K.B. 290; amplified in *Bendall v. McWhirter* [1952] 2 Q.B. 466 at 474 *et seq.* and repeated by Lord Denning M.R. in *Binions v. Evans* [1972] Ch. 359; criticised in (1952) 68 L.Q.R. 337 (H.W.R.W.) and (1953) 69 L.Q.R. 466 (A.D. Hargreaves); approved in (1953) 16 M.L.R. 1 (G.C. Cheshire). *cf. Kelaghan v. Daly* [1913] 2 I.R. 328, and contrast *Wallace v. Simmers*, 1960 S.C. 225.

[5] *Daly v. Edwardes* (1900) 83 L.T. 548; *King v. David Allen & Sons, Billposting Ltd, supra; Clore v. Theatrical Properties Ltd, supra.* See too *Millennium Productions Ltd v. Winter Garden Theatre (London) Ltd* [1946] 1 All E.R. 678 at 680 ("a licence created by contract is not an interest": *per* Lord Greene M.R.).

[6] s.4(1) (proviso); *ante*, para. 4–090. *cf.* (1988) 51 M.L.R. 226 at 229 (J. Hill).

ground that it was occupied under a licence which was binding upon her. For reasons which are hard to understand the court rejected the argument that the transaction was a contract to convey the house on completion of the payments, which would have created an equitable interest (an estate contract) of a familiar type:[7]

17–018   *(c) Contractual licences and constructive trusts.* The next stage began when the Court of Appeal declared that a contractual licence may give rise to a constructive trust and so take effect as an equitable interest. The case in which this innovation appeared concerned the purchaser of a cottage who had agreed in the contract to take it subject to a contractual licence previously granted by the vendor to an employee's widow, entitling her to live in it for life, and who had paid a reduced price on that account. On those facts it was easy to hold that the purchaser had made himself a constructive trustee for the licensee.[8] But later there emerged a broader proposition, that "a contractual licence (under which a person has the right to occupy premises indefinitely) gives rise to a constructive trust, under which the legal owner is not allowed to turn out the licensee".[9] The case did not involve successors in title, but it designated contractual licences as equitable interests which would necessarily bind successors according to the ordinary rules. This result duly occurred where a man had bought a house with the aid of a loan from his aunt and had told her that she could live in it for so long as she liked. It was held that the aunt had an irrevocable licence until the loan was repaid and that this was binding upon the nephew's trustee in bankruptcy, "whether it be called a contractual licence or an equitable licence or an interest under a constructive trust".[10] The judge observed, with some understatement, that the law was "very confused and difficult to fit in with established equitable principles".[11]

17–019   *(d) Return to orthodoxy.* Fortunately the Court of Appeal has now restored the law to some semblance of principle. In *Ashburn Anstalt v. Arnold*,[12] it held

---

[7] *Ante*, para. 12–051. A written contract would not have been necessary, since the taking of possession would at that time have amounted to part performance: see the previous edition of this work at p. 594. Nor would non-registration have mattered, for the plaintiff was not a purchaser. The court rejected this interpretation on the ground that there is no equitable interest where there is no obligation to complete the transaction. But this is contrary to well-recognised authority, *e.g.* in the case of options: see *ante*, paras 12–061–12–063. See the criticism in *National Provincial Bank Ltd v. Ainsworth* [1965] A.C. 1175 at 1239, *per* Lord Upjohn and at 1251, *per* Lord Wilberforce; *Re Solomon* [1967] Ch. 573 at 585, *per* Goff J.

[8] *Binions v. Evans* [1972] Ch. 359. Compare *Lyus v. Prowsa Development Ltd* [1982] 1 W.L.R. 1044, *ante*, para. 10–022, where this type of constructive trust is discussed.

[9] *D.H.N. Food Distributors Ltd v. Tower Hamlets L.B.C.* [1976] 1 W.L.R. 852 at 859 *per* Lord Denning M.R. (company occupying premises under irrevocable licence held entitled to full compensation for disturbance on compulsory acquisition by local authority on the ground (among others) that it owned an equitable interest).

[10] *Re Sharpe* [1980] 1 W.L.R. 219 at 224, *per* Browne-Wilkinson J.

[11] *ibid.*, at 226, *per* Browne-Wilkinson J.

[12] [1989] Ch. 1 at 13 *et seq.* See [1988] C.L.J. 353 (A.J. Oakley); (1988) 104 L.Q.R. 175 (P. Sparkes); (1988) 51 M.L.R. 226 (J. Hill); [1988] Conv. 201 (M.P. Thompson).

that a contractual licence did not create an interest in land. Although the court did not doubt the correctness of the actual decision in *Errington v. Errington*,[13] it considered that the reasoning conflicted with earlier decisions of the House of Lords[14] and should not therefore be followed. The court also held that although a constructive trust might be imposed on a transferee of land in respect of an interest affecting that land which would not otherwise bind him, it would do so only where the transferee's conscience was affected.[15] The mere fact that land was conveyed "subject to" a right such as a contractual licence was not sufficient.[16] This has already been explained.[17] Although the comments in the *Ashburn* case were *obiter*,[18] they have been widely endorsed.[19] It has been said that the case "finally repudiated the heretical view that a contractual licence creates an interest in land capable of binding third parties".[20] and that it "put the *quietus* to the heresy that parties to a contractual licence necessarily become constructive trustees".[21]

3. Licences irrevocable by estoppel. If a contractual licence is a purely **17–020** personal right, then in principle the same should be true of a licence held to be irrevocable in satisfaction of an equity arising by proprietary estoppel.[22] It has already been explained that there has in the past been some confusion between the equity which arises by estoppel[23] and the right eventually conferred by the court in giving effect to that equity.[24] If the right so conferred is a property right, it will bind third parties if appropriately protected. If however the right is merely a licence, it does not cease to be personal merely because

---

[13] [1952] 1 K.B. 290. The court offered three explanations of the case: [1989] Ch. 1 at 17.

[14] *Edwardes v. Barrington* (1901) 85 L.T. 650; *King v. David Allen & Sons, Billposting Ltd* [1916] 2 A.C. 54.

[15] [1989] Ch. 1 at 25.

[16] *ibid.* There will have to be "very special circumstances showing that the transferee of the property undertook a new liability to give effect to provisions for the benefit of third parties": *IDC Group Ltd v. Clark* [1992] 1 E.G.L.R. 187 at 190, *per* Browne-Wilkinson V.-C. (on appeal [1992] 2 E.G.L.R. 184). See too *Kewal Investments Ltd v. Arthur Maiden Ltd* [1990] 1 E.G.L.R. 193 at 194; *Sparkes v. Smart* [1990] 2 E.G.L.R. 245 at 249, 250.

[17] *Ante*, paras 4–094, 10–022.

[18] The actual decision in the case has now been overruled: *Prudential Assurance Co. Ltd v. London Residuary Body* [1992] 2 A.C. 386; *ante*, para. 14–056.

[19] See *Kewal Investments Ltd v. Arthur Maiden Ltd, supra*, at 194; *Canadian Imperial Bank of Commerce v. Bello* (1991) 64 P. & C.R. 48 at 51, 52; *IDC Group Ltd v. Clark, supra*, at 189, 190; *Camden L.B.C. v. Shortlife Community Housing Ltd* (1992) 90 L.G.R. 358 at 373; *Nationwide Anglia B.S. v. Ahmed* (1995) 70 P. & C.R. 381 at 387–389.

[20] *Camden L.B.C. v. Shortlife Community Housing Ltd, supra*, at 373, *per* Millett J. See too *Nationwide Anglia B.S. v. Ahmed, supra*, at 389.

[21] *IDC Group Ltd v. Clark, supra*, at 189, *per* Browne-Wilkinson V.-C. However, in eliminating one heresy, the courts may have created another: see (1997) 1 E.L.R. 437 at 451 (C.H.); *ante*, para. 10–022. If the Contracts (Rights of Third Parties) Bill, presently before Parliament, is enacted, these cases may in future be dealt with on a contractual basis: *ante*, para. 10–022.

[22] *Ante*, para. 13–006. See [1991] Conv. 36 (G. Battersby). *cf. Habermann v. Koehler* (1996) 73 P. & C.R. 515 at 520.

[23] That equity itself may bind third parties: *ante*, paras 13–030–13–032.

[24] *Ante*, para. 13–006.

the licensor loses his power to revoke it through the operation of proprietary estoppel.[25]

Section 5. Matrimonial Homes

17–021   **1. The short-lived "deserted wife's equity".** Another revolution in the law of licences was the appearance of the "deserted wife's equity". This was based on the notion of a matrimonial rather than a contractual licence.[26] Despite authority to the contrary,[27] it was held that a wife who had been deserted by her husband had an irrevocable licence enforceable in equity against third parties, such as her husband's trustee in bankruptcy[28] or a purchaser with notice of her situation.[29] This right was held to be at most a "mere equity",[30] and not an equitable interest,[31] and to be determinable at the discretion of the court.[32] Unless otherwise agreed it became revocable on divorce[33] or, apparently, on commission of a matrimonial offence by the wife.[34]

All this new law, which was the subject of much criticism,[35] was summarily swept away by the House of Lords in 1965. The case was one where the husband had deserted his wife and then conveyed the matrimonial home to a company, whereupon the company charged it to a bank as security for money owed. The House of Lords held that the bank could enforce its security and take possession of the property, and that the wife must vacate it.[36] It was made clear that a wife was not a licensee in her husband's house, and that if it was his sole property she had no sort of proprietary interest in it, even if she had been deserted. She had rights against her husband personally which flowed from her status as wife, and she might be able to obtain an injunction restraining him from dealing with the matrimonial home in a way which

---

[25] "Once the interest has come into existence, the fact that it arose by estoppel becomes irrelevant": [1991] Conv. 36 at 39 (G. Battersby).

[26] See *Re Solomon* [1967] Ch. 573 at 581–586 (husband's undertaking to court not contractual).

[27] See *Thompson v. Earthy* [1951] 2 K.B. 596; *Bradley-Hole v. Cusen* [1953] 1 Q.B. 300 at 306.

[28] *Bendall v. McWhirter* [1952] 2 Q.B. 466, *per* Denning L.J.

[29] *Ferris v. Weaven* [1952] 2 All E.R. 233; *Street v. Denham* [1954] 1 W.L.R. 624.

[30] See *ante*, paras 5–012, 5–013.

[31] *Westminster Bank Ltd v. Lee* [1956] Ch. 7; see (1955) 71 L.Q.R. 481 (R.E.M.); [1955] C.L.J. 158 (H.W.R.W.).

[32] *Jess B. Woodcock and Sons Ltd v. Hobbs* [1955] 1 W.L.R. 152; *Churcher v. Street* [1959] Ch. 251.

[33] *Vaughan v. Vaughan* [1953] 1 Q.B. 762.

[34] *Wabe v. Taylor* [1952] 2 Q.B. 735; but contrast *Short v. Short* [1960] 1 W.L.R. 833.

[35] See (1952) 68 L.Q.R. 379 (R.E.M.). See generally (1953) 16 M.L.R. 215 (O. Kahn-Freund); (1952) 16 Conv. (N.S.) 323 (F. R. Crane); (1953) 17 Conv. (N.S.) 440 (L. A. Sheridan); see also *Brennan v. Thomas* [1953] V.L.R. 111; *Dickson v. McWhinnie* [1958] S.R.(N.S.W.) 179 (a full survey); (1956) 72 L.Q.R. 477 (R.E.M.).

[36] *National Provincial Bank Ltd v. Ainsworth* [1965] A.C. 1175, approving *Thompson v. Earthy, supra*, and overruling *Bendall v. McWhirter, supra*, *Street v. Denham, supra*, and *Jess B. Woodcock & Sons Ltd v. Hobbs, supra*.

infringed these rights.[37] But she could enforce them against her husband alone, and not against his successors in title or other third parties.

2. Statutory rights to occupy the matrimonial home. The collapse of the **17–022** "deserted wife's equity" admittedly left an unsatisfactory situation. The solution was to give statutory "matrimonial home rights"[38] to husbands and wives alike.[39] These rights are more properly described as matrimonial rights than as licences, but arise automatically[40] from the fact of marriage[41] in cases where one spouse is entitled[42] to the home and the other is not. This far-reaching change was effected by the Matrimonial Homes Act 1967. The legislation has now been recast in amended form in the Family Law Act 1996 as part of a statutory code that deals with the family home and domestic violence.[43] The purpose of the legislation is to confer on the spouse "a judicially protected right of occupation".[44] The courts will not countenance its use for any ulterior purpose (*e.g.* to apply financial pressure to the other spouse).[45]

(a) Matrimonial home rights. The statutory "matrimonial home rights" are **17–023** given to a spouse who either has no right to occupy the home by virtue of any estate, interest, contract or statute, or has only an equitable interest in it,[46] and does not have the legal fee simple or a legal term of years in it, either solely

---

[37] *Lee v. Lee* [1952] 2 Q.B. 489. *cf. Short v. Short* [1960] 1 W.L.R. 833.

[38] This term was introduced by F.L.A. 1996, s.30(2) instead of "rights of occupation" which had been used in the legislation which that Act replaced: see M.H.A. 1983, s.1(1). See too F.L.A. 1996, Sched. 9, para. 11–15.

[39] It should be noted that although the legislation applies to both spouses, "its primary purpose was . . . to protect the occupational rights of the deserted wife, as the so-called equity of the deserted wife had done until that doctrine was disapproved": *Kashmir Kaur v. Gill* [1988] Fam. 110 at 117, *per* Bingham L.J.

[40] But they can be released: F.L.A. 1996, Sched. 4, para. 5(1).

[41] Even if polygamous: *ibid.*, s.63(5).

[42] *i.e.* is entitled to occupy by virtue of a beneficial interest, contract or statute: F.L.A. 1996, s.30(1). It will therefore include a right to occupy under either the Rent Acts or H.A. 1988 (see *Penn v. Dunn* [1970] 2 Q.B. 686 at 692). Property held by the spouse on trust is excluded unless he is also beneficially interested in it. In determining whether a spouse is entitled to occupy a property, a right to possession which he has as mortgagee is disregarded: F.L.A. 1996, s.54(1).

[43] For a discussion of the legislation, which is not without its difficulties, see *Wroth v. Tyler* [1974] Ch. 30. In 1978 the Law Commission considered M.H.A. 1967 and made recommendations for its amendment: Law Com. No. 86, Book 2. These were enacted in the Matrimonial Homes and Property Act 1981. The legislation was consolidated by M.H.A. 1983. The Law Commission recommended further changes in 1992: see Law Com. No. 207, Pt IV. These were enacted in F.L.A. 1996, Pt IV. These changes include the extension of occupation rights to cohabitants and former spouses. However, such rights are not capable of binding a purchaser, unlike those of a spouse.

[44] *Richards v. Richards* [1984] A.C. 174 at 211, *per* Lord Scarman.

[45] *Barnett v. Hassett* [1981] 1 W.L.R. 1385.

[46] F.L.A. 1996, s.30(9) adds "or in its proceeds of sale". However, following the abolition of the doctrine of conversion by T.L.A.T.A. 1996, s.3(1), these words will be otiose except in relation to the two transitional situations excepted from that abolition: *ibid.*, ss.3(2); 18(3). See *ante*, para. 8–128.

or jointly.[47] Thus if the husband is the sole owner, or if he holds the legal estate in trust for himself and his wife jointly or in common, the wife but not the husband has the statutory matrimonial home rights.

The statutory matrimonial home rights are the right—

(i) not to be evicted or excluded from occupation; and

(ii) to enter and occupy with leave of the court.[48]

These rights will be brought to an end only by—

(i) the death of the other spouse;

(ii) the termination (otherwise than by death) of the marriage; or

(iii) the determination of the spouse's entitlement to occupy the property.[49]

17–024 However the court has power to extend the statutory matrimonial home rights even after the termination of the marriage by death or otherwise,[50] in any case where it considers that in all circumstances it is just and reasonable to do so.[51] On the application of *either* spouse,[52] the court has power to enforce those rights as against the other spouse and may also in some way restrict or terminate that other spouse's rights of occupation.[53] In deciding whether to exercise its discretion, the court is required to have regard to all the circumstances including the housing needs and resources of each party and any relevant child,[54] the financial resources of each spouse, and the likely effect of any order (or decision not to make an order) on the health and well-being of the parties and on any relevant child.[55]

The provisions of the Family Law Act 1996 may apply to any dwelling-house which either is or at any time has been the home of the person having the matrimonial home rights and the other spouse or was intended by them to

---

[47] F.L.A. 1996, s.30(1), (9). Until M.H.A. 1967 was amended by M.P.P.A. 1970, s.38, it protected only what Lord Denning M.R. memorably described as a "bare" wife, having no proprietary, contractual or statutory right in the home: *Gurasz v. Gurasz* [1970] P. 11 at 17.

[48] F.L.A. 1996, s.30(2).

[49] *ibid.*, ss.30(8), 31(8).

[50] *ibid.*, s.33(5).

[51] *ibid.*, s.33(8).

[52] See *ibid.*, s.33(1)(a).

[53] *ibid.*, s.33(3).

[54] For the meaning of "relevant child", see *ibid.*, s.62(2).

[55] *ibid.*, s.33(6). The court *must* make an order if it appears that the applicant or any relevant child is likely to suffer significant harm attributable to the conduct of the other spouse if such an order is not made: *ibid.*, s.33(7).

be their home.[56] Where the matrimonial home is leasehold and one of the spouses is the tenant, the extent to which he can determine the tenancy so as to deprive the other spouse of her occupation is not finally settled. Thus one spouse's occupation is treated as that of the other for the purposes of the Rent Act 1977 and the Housing Act 1988,[56a] and it has been held that a tenant cannot validly surrender a tenancy protected under the Rent Act so as to defeat the rights of the other spouse.[57] By contrast, a surrender by a tenant of a contractual tenancy under the Housing Act 1985 was effective as against her spouse.[58]

(b) *Successors in title.* Successors in title may be bound by these matrimo- **17–025** nial home rights, but only where the owning spouse's rights are founded on an estate or interest, as opposed to a contract or statute.[59] In the former case the non-owning spouse's rights are a charge on the estate or interest and have "the same priority as if it were an equitable interest" created on January 1, 1968, on marriage, or on the acquisition of the estate or interest, whichever is the latest.[60] The charge is registrable.[61] It follows that, so long as the owning spouse is alive, the marriage lasts or the rights are extended by court notwith-standing the termination of the marriage by death or otherwise,[62] the non-owning spouse can enforce the charge against third parties,[63] provided that, in the case of a purchaser, it has been duly registered.[64] However in exercising its discretion, the court is entitled to take into account the circumstances of the

---

[56] *ibid.,* s.33(1)(b). A person may therefore have matrimonial home rights in more than one property, including a property that was acquired as a common home even though the parties never lived there, *e.g.* because the relationship terminated before they could move in. This is a change in the law (*cf.* M.H.A. 1983, s.1(10)) and implements a recommendation in (1992) Law Com. No. 207, para. 4.4. The Act does not apply to a property that never was nor was ever intended to be a matrimonial home: F.L.A. 1996, s.30(7).

[56a] See F.L.A. 1996, s.30(4). For the protection conferred by R.A. 1977 and H.A. 1988, see *post,* paras 22–185 *et seq.;* and 22–144 *et seq.* respectively.

[57] This was a common law rule: see *Old Gate Estates Ltd v. Alexander* [1950] 1 K.B. 311; *Penn v. Dunn* [1970] 2 Q.B. 686 at 691; *Hoggett v. Hoggett* (1979) 39 P. & C.R. 121. The authorities are reviewed in *Hall v. King* (1987) 55 P. & C.R. 307 at 309, 310; *Griffiths v. Renfree* [1989] 2 E.G.L.R. 46 at 48, 49.

[58] *Sanctuary Housing Association v. Campbell* [1999] 1 W.L.R. 1279, distinguishing *Hoggett v. Hoggett, supra,* and casting doubt on the common law authorities cited in the previous note on which it was based. For secure tenancies under H.A. 1985, see *post,* paras 22–263 *et seq.*

[59] F.L.A. 1996, s.31(1). Rights under a contract for sale or lease, which creates an equitable interest, ought in principle to count as an interest rather than as a contract, but the position is not clear.

[60] *ibid.,* s.31(2), (3). "The charge seems to be neither legal nor equitable, but a pure creature of statute, with a priority (though not a nature) defined by reference to equity": *Wroth v. Tyler* [1974] Ch. 30 at 43, *per* Megarry J.

[61] Where title is unregistered, it is registrable as a Class F land charge: *ante,* para. 5–107. Where title is registered, it is registrable as a notice: F.L.A. 1996, s.31(10)(a); *ante* para. 00. It cannot be protected by lodging a caution: *ibid.,* s.31(11). Nor can the charge take effect as an overriding interest if unregistered: *ibid.,* s.31(10)(b); *ante,* para. 6–051.

[62] F.L.A. 1996, ss.31(8), 33(5).

[63] *ibid.,* s.31(9) also protects it against merger, *e.g.* where the owning spouse acquires the freehold of a leasehold home.

[64] A spouse not in occupation may register effectively: *Watts v. Waller* [1973] Q.B. 153. The right of one spouse to enforce a right of occupation against the other is not dependent on registration: *Hoggett v. Hoggett* (1979) 39 P. & C.R. 121 at 127.

purchaser,[65] and may decline to make an order against him.[66] Successors in title may in any event apply to the court to have the spouse's rights of occupation restricted or terminated in the same manner as may the owning spouse.[67] Where the spouse's rights extend to two or more dwelling-houses, they are registrable as a charge against only one of them at any one time. If they have been registered against more than one property, only the last registration may stand.[68]

17–026   *(c) Bankruptcy of the owning spouse.* Where a spouse's matrimonial home rights exist prior to the bankruptcy of the owning spouse,[69] they will bind his trustee in bankruptcy,[70] and any application for an order under the Family Law Act 1996 must be made to the bankruptcy court.[71] On such an application,[72] the court is required to make such order as it thinks just and equitable having regard to a number of factors including "all the circumstances of the case other than the needs of the bankruptcy".[73] Once a year has elapsed since the vesting of the bankrupt's estate, the court is required to assume, unless the circumstances of the case are exceptional, that the interests of the bankrupt's creditors outweigh all other considerations.[74] The trustee in bankruptcy is therefore likely to apply to have any rights of occupation terminated so that the matrimonial home can be sold.

17–027   *(d) Conveyancing implications.* The power to register a charge naturally makes it possible for the non-owning spouse to impede transactions with the property by the owning spouse, even if the non-owner is in no danger of being left homeless and merely objects to moving. The non-owner can, indeed, register a charge without the knowledge of the owner,[75] so rendering the owner liable in damages by frustrating a prior contract of sale.[76] However, the

---

[65] F.L.A. 1996, ss.33(6), 34. The court has power to make an order under s.33 against a successor in title of the owning spouse if it considers that it is just and reasonable to do so: *ibid.*, s.34(2).

[66] *Kashmir Kaur v. Gill* [1988] Fam. 110; [1988] C.L.J. 355 (C.H.). *cf.* [1988] Conv. 295 (M. Welstead). The decision is in effect codified by F.L.A. 1996, s.34(2).

[67] *ibid.*, s.34; *Kashmir Kaur v. Gill, supra.*

[68] F.L.A. 1996, Sched. 4, para. 2.

[69] Matrimonial home rights cannot be acquired in the period between the presentation of a bankruptcy petition against an owning spouse until the time when his estate vests in his trustee in bankruptcy, if the matrimonial home is part of the bankrupt's estate: I.A. 1986, s.336(1) (as amended by F.L.A. 1996, Sched. 8, para. 57).

[70] Formerly the charge was void against the trustee: M.H.A. 1983, s.2(7) (repealed by I.A. 1985, s.235(3); Sched. 10).

[71] I.A. 1986. s.336(2) (as amended by F.L.A. 1996, Sched. 8, para. 57).

[72] Which may be made by the other spouse or by the owning spouse's trustee in bankruptcy. The trustee has the right to apply because he derives title under the owning spouse: F.L.A. 1996, s.34.

[73] I.A. 1986, s.336(4) (as amended by F.L.A. 1996, Sched. 8, para. 57).

[74] I.A. 1986, s.336(5). See, *e.g. Re Bremner* [1999] 1 F.L.R. 912. *cf. ante,* para. 9–072.

[75] It is not the practice of the Land Registry to notify the owning spouse of the registration by the other spouse of her rights of occupation: Ruoff & Roper, 39–11.

[76] *Watts v. Waller, supra; Wroth v. Tyler* [1974] Ch. 30. Where rights of occupation have been registered and the owning spouse then contracts to sell the house with vacant possession, it is an implied term of the contract that he will procure the cancellation of that charge prior to completion: F.L.A. 1996, Sched. 4, para. 3.

vast majority of these charges are in practice left unregistered, so that the conveyancing proceeds on the curious basis of the mass invalidation of the charges for want of registration.[77] The registration of adverse interests in relation to the matrimonial home is both inappropriate and, in the words of a former Master of the Rolls, "precious little use".[78]

---

[77] See *Wroth v. Tyler, supra*, at 46. For the conveyancing implications of the decision, see (1974) 38 Conv. (N.S.) 110 (D.J. Hayton). In practice most spouses will rely for their protection on the beneficial interest that they will commonly have in the home. It is not unknown for spouses in that position also to frustrate a contract of sale by virtue of their interests: see *Watts v. Spence* [1976] Ch. 165.

[78] *Williams & Glyn's Bank Ltd v. Boland* [1979] Ch. 312 at 328, *per* Lord Denning M.R. See too at 339, *per* Ormrod L.J., pointing out that registration is an essentially hostile proceeding, not well suited to married couples living on good terms.

CHAPTER 18

INCORPOREAL HEREDITAMENTS

18–001   **1. Meaning of term.** Incorporeal hereditaments are rights of property of certain special classes. Their distinguishing feature is that the law of real property applies to them, just as it applies to corporeal land.[1] But since the property owned is a mere right, and not a physical object, it is called incorporeal. The list of incorporeal hereditaments is a varied one, and it includes several curiosities; for it was for historical rather than logical reasons that certain rights were treated as real property instead of personal property. Most of them are, indeed, closely connected with land. But there is no logic in treating a rentcharge (the right to an income charged upon land) as real property and a lease as personal property; yet so it is.

18–002   **2. Rules governing realty.** There are a number of consequences of designating some particular right as a hereditament and therefore real property, of which two may be given as examples.[2] First, it can be conveyed only by deed because it "lies in grant".[3] Secondly, a will leaving "all my real property to X and all my personal property to Y" will pass a rentcharge to X but a lease to Y. Although some incorporeal hereditaments such as tithes are now of little significance, others such as easements and profits are amongst the most important property rights.

18–003   **3. Contrast with corporeal hereditaments.** Corporeal and incorporeal hereditaments together make up what is "real property" in the wide sense.[4] Corporeal hereditaments are physical objects, not rights, and they are of only one type: land, including buildings and other fixtures.[5] Incorporeal hereditaments are rights, not physical objects, and are of many types. This classification of *rights* and *things* as if they were similar has been ridiculed on theoretical grounds in Austin's *Jurisprudence*,[6] but in reality it is the inevitable outcome of having two separate systems of property law. A line has to be

---

[1] *Ante*, para. 1–011; *cf.* L. P. A. 1925, s.205(1)(ix).
[2] The distinction was formerly of some importance when land devolved on intestacy in a different manner from personalty: see the previous edition of this work at p. 813.
[3] *Post*, para. 18–051.
[4] *Ante*, para. 1–011. But "real property" and "hereditaments" were not exactly coterminous. An annuity of inheritance was a hereditament but not real property, since real property was property recoverable by a real action: *cf.* Wolst. & C. i, 337.
[5] For fixtures, see *ante*, para. 14–311.
[6] i. 372. *cf.* Cheshire and Burn, *Modern Law of Real Property*, (15th ed.), p. 142.

drawn between real and personal property in terms of the *things* which are governed by each set of rules. But there are many species of property which are not physical things but yet must be governed by property law. Personal property must include, for example, choses in action, *e.g.* debts, money in a bank, stocks and shares; real property must equally necessarily include certain special interests of an intangible kind. The illogical part of the subject is not the inclusion of mere rights, but the kinds of rights which have been allotted to realty and personalty respectively. The early tendency to treat all rights as proprietary if that was at all possible made our law "rich with incorporeal things": this is "the most medieval part of medieval law".[7]

The distinction between corporeal and incorporeal hereditaments is not always easily drawn in practice. Thus the right to graze beasts on a piece of land, known as "cattlegate",[8] can exist either as an incorporeal grazing right or as a form of co-ownership of the land in common with other "stint-holders".[9] It can be difficult to distinguish between these two forms of the right.[10]

4. Principal incorporeal hereditaments. The following are the most important incorporeal hereditaments to be found nowadays.[11]   **18–004**

(a) Rentcharges. A rentcharge is an annuity secured on some specified land.[12] Although the circumstances in which rentcharges can now be created are circumscribed by statute, and most will be abolished in due course,[13] they remain of some importance and are considered below.[14]   **18–005**

(b) Annuities. An annuity differs from a rentcharge in not being secured upon or connected with land. An annuity, *e.g.* £10,000 a year, could be granted or devised to a person and his heirs and would then devolve as a hereditament, like land.[15]   **18–006**

(c) Advowsons. An advowson is the perpetual right of presentation to an ecclesiastical living.[16] The owner of an advowson is known as the patron and has the right, when the living becomes vacant, to nominate the clergyman who shall next hold it. However, the exercise of this right is now much restricted.[17] An advowson is an incorporeal hereditament and therefore, somewhat curiously, real property. However, although the patron has an estate in land, an   **18–007**

---

[7] P. & M. ii, 124, 149.
[8] Also known as "stint", "beastgate" and "pasturegate". For "shackage" (the right to graze after the taking of arable crops), see *R. v. Suffolk C.C., ex p. Steed* (1995) 70 P. & C.R. 487 at 496.
[9] *Brackenbank Lodge Ltd v. Peart* (1993) 67 P. & C.R. 249 at 255.
[10] See *Brackenbank Lodge Ltd v. Peart, supra.*
[11] For a fuller account, see the previous edition of this work at pp. 814 *et seq.*
[12] Litt. 218.
[13] Under the provisions of the Rentcharges Act 1977, considered *post*, paras 18–018 *et seq.*
[14] *Post*, para. 18–014.
[15] H.E.L. iii, 152; Wolst. & C. v, 79; Challis 46. Such a "personal hereditament" could not be entailed (*ibid.*); it was enforceable only against the grantor or his estate.
[16] Co. Litt. 17b.
[17] By the Patronage (Benefices) Measure 1986.

advowson cannot be sold,[18] and it is no longer regarded as land for the purposes of the Land Registration Act 1925.[19] The functions of a patron cannot be exercised unless the advowson was registered with the registrar of the diocese by the beginning of 1989.[20]

18–008   *(d) Tithes.[21]* A tithe was the right of a rector to a tenth part of the produce of all the land in his parish. The right to tithes has been almost entirely dismantled by a series of statutes,[22] and little vestige remains of it today, except the anachronistic liability of certain landowners ("lay rectors") to repair chancels. This remains a potential conveyancing trap and must be explained.

18–009   (1) THE BASIS OF LIABILITY.[23] On the dissolution of the monasteries in the reign of Henry VIII many rectories passed into royal hands and were granted to lay landowners. The right to tithes thus passed into lay hands in many cases and was said to be "impropriated" by the lay rector. This carried with it (*inter alia*) the rector's common law liability to repair the chancel of the church.[24] In certain circumstances that liability became attached to the ownership of certain land.[25] The liability is a legal right which binds all purchasers, and where the title is registered, it takes effect as an overriding interest.[26] Liability is not limited to the profits of the land, and where more than one impropriator is liable, is several and not joint.[27] When an impropriator sells his land he ceases to be liable for repairs which arise thereafter.[28]

18–010   (2) REFORM. The incidence of liability for chancel repairs is entirely capricious and depends upon factors such as whether the church was founded before the dissolution of the monasteries[29] and whether particular land became burdened by it, *e.g.* because of an inclosure award.[30] Not only can the liability prove to be heavy,[31] but because records are incomplete, its incidence may be

---

[18] *ibid.*, s.3.

[19] *ibid.*, s.6(2). The right can no longer be registered therefore: *ibid.*, s.6(1). See Ruoff & Roper, 9–03.

[20] Patronage (Benefices) Measure 1986, s.1(1).

[21] See the previous edition of this work at p. 830.

[22] See, *e.g.* Tithe Acts 1836, 1918, 1925, 1936, 1951; Statute Law (Repeals) Act 1998.

[23] For a full account of the history of this form of liability, see (1985) Law Com. No. 152, App. B. See too the previous edition of this work at pp. 830–833.

[24] See *Wickhambrook Parochial Church Council v. Croxford* [1935] 2 K.B. 417; *Chivers & Sons Ltd. v. Air Ministry* [1955] Ch. 585; Millard, *Tithes*, pp. 143–145; Chancel Repairs Act 1932. For an admirable summary of the law, see (1984) 100 L.Q.R. 181 (J. H. Baker).

[25] See (1984) 100 L.Q.R. 181 at 183; Law Com. No. 152, paras 2.2–2.7 and App. B; *Tithe Records in the Public Record Office* (P.R.O. Leaflet 13, 1981), para. 14.

[26] L.R.A. 1925, 70(1)(c); *ante*, para. 6–045.

[27] *Wickhambrook Parochial Church Council v. Croxford, supra.*

[28] *Chivers & Sons Ltd v. Air Ministry, supra.*

[29] It cannot apply to those which were founded thereafter: Law Com. No. 152, para. 1.2. One estimate is that 3,785,000 acres of land may be subject to this form of liability: *ibid.*

[30] See Law Com. No. 152, App. B, paras 2.11, 2.12.

[31] See the case cited in Law Com. No. 152, para. 1.3, of a landowner, who although unaware of his liability, had to pay over £10,000. There are more recent examples of liability for more than £100,000, some of them exceeding the value of the land burdened.

virtually impossible for a purchaser to discover.[32] Chancel repair liability is therefore precisely the kind of encumbrance that any rational system of conveyancing should seek to avoid. The Law Commission recommended that it should either be abolished after a period of 10 years or become registrable as a local land charge if this cannot be done.[33] However, the Government has rejected the recommendations. Although retention of such liability might contravene the provisions of the European Convention on Human Rights, so too might its abolition.[34]

(e) Easements. It is only in modern times that easements have been recognised as incorporeal hereditaments,[35] though they are now the most important of such rights. Examples include private rights of way and rights of light. Easements are considered in detail later in this chapter.[36]   **18–011**

(f) Profits à prendre. A profit is a right to take something off another's land, such as a right of common or of shooting or fishing. Such rights are of considerable importance and are therefore considered more fully later in this chapter.[37]   **18–012**

(g) Franchises. A franchise is "a royal privilege or branch of the royal prerogative subsisting in the hands of a subject, by grant from the King".[38] In the early Middle Ages they were of many kinds, such as fairs, markets, the right to wrecks and treasure trove,[39] and free fisheries.[40] Today, the most important franchise is that of market.[41] Where such a franchise exists, no rival market[42] may be set up within six and two-thirds miles.[43] Breach of the franchise is actionable in tort as a nuisance,[44] and damages are awarded without proof of loss.[45]   **18–013**

We now examine in detail the principal incorporeal hereditaments that remain important today: rentcharges, easements and profits.

---

[32] See Law Com. No. 152, Pt III.

[33] *ibid.*, Pt VII.

[34] See Hansard (H.L.), vol. 592, WA 202.

[35] *Post*, para. 18–040.

[36] *ibid.*

[37] *Post*, paras 18–040, 18–079.

[38] *Spook Erection Ltd v. Secretary of State for the Environment* [1989] Q.B. 300 at 305, *per* Nourse L.J. See P. & M. i, 571; H.E.L. i, 87; iii, 169; Bl. Comm. i, 302.

[39] For details of treasure trove at common law, see the previous edition of this work at p. 65. For the Treasure Act 1996, which now governs treasure trove, see *ante*, para. 3–053.

[40] See *post*, para. 18–086.

[41] For the regime of rights affecting a franchise market, see *Gloucester C.C. v. Williams* (1990) 88 L.G.R. 853 at 857, 858.

[42] Which may include a "car boot sale": *Newcastle–upon–Tyne C.C. v. Noble* (1990) 89 L.G.R. 618. On what constitutes a rival market, see *Kingston upon Hull C.C. v. Greenwood* (1984) 82 L.G.R. 586.

[43] See *Birmingham C.C. v. Anvil Fairs* [1989] 1 W.L.R. 312. The same rule applies to a statutory market: *Manchester C.C. v. Walsh* (1985) 84 L.G.R. 1.

[44] *Sevenoaks D.C. v. Pattullo & Vinson Ltd* [1984] Ch. 211.

[45] *Stoke–on–Trent C.C. v. W. & J. Wass Ltd* (1989) 87 L.G.R. 129 (discussing the measure of damages).

Part 1

RENTCHARGES

Section 1. Nature of Rentcharges

18–014   **1. Rentcharges and rent services.** Periodical payments in respect of land fall under the two main heads of rentcharges and rent services. Where the relationship of lord and tenant exists between the parties, any rent payable by virtue of that relationship by the tenant to the lord is a rent service.[46] If there is no relationship of lord and tenant, the rent is a rentcharge. Thus if L grants a lease to T at £100 per annum and X charges his fee simple estate with the payment of £200 per annum to Y, L has a rent service and Y a rentcharge. Since the Statute *Quia Emptores* 1290 it has been impossible for a grantor to reserve any services on a conveyance of freehold land in fee simple, for the grantee holds of the grantor's lord, and not of the grantor.[47] Consequently no rent reserved on a conveyance of freehold land in fee simple after 1290 can be a rent service.

The only rent service met with in practice is thus the rent reserved upon the grant of a lease for a term of years. A rent reserved by a lease is annexed to a reversion in land, while a rentcharge stands on its own as an incorporeal hereditament.

18–015   **2. Legal and equitable rentcharges.** A rentcharge is real property. Prior to 1926, both at law and in equity it could be held for any of the usual estates or interests.[48] However, since 1925, an interest in a rentcharge can be legal only if it is—

    (a) in possession,[49] and

    (b) either perpetual or for a term of years absolute.[50]

Further, a legal rentcharge cannot be created at law without certain formalities.[51] A mere contract for a rentcharge may however create an equitable interest in the usual way.[52]

18–016   **3. Rentcharge on a rentcharge.** At common law a rentcharge could be charged only upon a corporeal hereditament. There could be no rentcharge

---

[46] *Ante*, para. 14–245.
[47] *Ante*, para. 2–040.
[48] Such as an estate tail: *Chaplin v. Chaplin* (1733) 3 P.Wms. 229; or a term of years: *Re Fraser* [1904] 1 Ch. 726.
[49] As to when a rentcharge is deemed to be in possession, see *ante*, para. 4–049.
[50] L.P.A. 1925, s.1(2)(b); *ante*, para. 4–048.
[51] See *infra*.
[52] *Jackson v. Lever* (1792) 3 Bro.C.C. 605; *cf. ante*, para. 14–040.

charged upon another rentcharge[53] or other incorporeal hereditament,[54] since obviously there could then be no right of distress. But this technical obstacle was removed both for the past and for the future by the Law of Property Act 1925,[55] which validates rentcharges charged on other rentcharges and provides special machinery for enforcing payment.

4. Rentcharges in conveyancing. In certain parts of the country, especially   **18–017** in the areas of Manchester, Bristol and Bath, rentcharges were long used as a substitute for capital payments on the sale of land.[56] Instead of a capital sum the vendor either took a perpetual rentcharge charged on the land, or he took the purchase price in the form partly of a capital sum and partly of a rentcharge. These freehold rentcharges were known as chief rents or fee farm rents. These rentcharges complicated conveyancing, particularly where they were of long standing and the land in question had been subdivided, and were unpopular with land owners because they were "repugnant to the concept of freehold ownership".[57] Since they had ceased to play any useful part in the financing of the purchase of property, they were abolished for the future by the Rentcharges Act 1977, as explained below.

Rentcharges are more suitably employed in connection with schemes of development, particularly where plots or flats are sold freehold and the purchasers contribute to the cost of maintaining the common parts of the buildings or grounds. In this context they have proved useful as a device for circumventing the rule that the burden of positive covenants cannot run with freehold land.[58] Consequently such rentcharges have not been abolished by the Rentcharges Act 1977.

Section 2. Abolition of Rentcharges

1. Rentcharges abolished. In accordance with recommendations of the   **18–018** Law Commission, the Rentcharges Act 1977 made provision for the abolition of those rentcharges which were inconvenient and unpopular, while exempting those which were useful. It defines a rentcharge as "any annual or other periodic sum charged on or issuing out of land, except rent reserved by a lease or tenancy, or any sum payable by way of interest".[59] It then provides as follows.[60]

---

[53] Co.Litt. 47a; *Earl of Stafford v. Buckley* (1750) 2 Ves.Sen. 170 at 178.
[54] *Re The Alms Corn Charity* [1901] 2 Ch. 750 at 759.
[55] s.122; *post*, para. 18–032.
[56] For a full survey, see (1975) Law Com. No. 68, on which the Rentcharges Act 1977 was based.
[57] Law Com. No. 68, para. 26.
[58] *Ante*, para. 16–021.
[59] s.1.
[60] ss.2, 3, 18(2).

(i) No rentcharge, whether legal or equitable, may be created after August 21, 1977.

(ii) A pre-existing rentcharge shall be extinguished at the end of 60 years from July 22, 1977 or 60 years from the date when it first became payable, whichever is the later; but in the case of a variable rentcharge the period of 60 years runs only from the date, if any, on which it ceases to be variable.

(iii) Certain rentcharges are exempted from the above provisions.

18–019   **2. Rentcharges exempted.** The rentcharges which are exempted from the Rentcharges Act 1977 are the following.[61]

(i) Those which give effect to family charges under Schedule 1 to the Trusts of Land and Appointment of Trustees Act 1996.[62] These charges, which are imposed voluntarily or in consideration of marriage or by way of family arrangement, have been explained in connection with settled land and trusts of land.[63]

(ii) "Estate rentcharges", meaning those created for the purpose of—

   (a) making covenants enforceable (by the device mentioned earlier),[64] or
   (b) meeting expenses incurred by the rent owner in performing covenants for services, maintenance, repairs or insurance, or for any payment for the benefit of the burdened land.

If created for purpose (a), the rentcharge must be of a nominal amount only, and if created for purpose (b), its amount, if not nominal, must be reasonable in relation to the covenanted services, etc.[65] The object of this restriction is to prevent the exemptions being used to create substantial rentcharges which ought to be abolished. But pre-existing rentcharges created for these purposes are exempt from the provisions for extinguishment regardless of their amount.[66]

(iii) Rentcharges payable in lieu of tithes.[67]

(iv) Statutory rentcharges created in connection with the execution of works on land or the commutation of any obligation to do them.

---

[61] s.2(3) (as amended by T.L.A.T.A. 1996, Sched. 3, para. 15); 2(4).
[62] Para. 3.
[63] *Ante*, para. 8–125.
[64] *Ante*, para. 16–021.
[65] s.2(5).
[66] s.3(3)(b).
[67] s.3(3)(a), applying for purposes of extinguishment only. Tithe redemption annuities were extinguished in 1977, but corn rents do still exist (and continue to be collected): see (1998) Law Com. No. 254, para. 5.40, and the previous edition of this work at p. 833.

(v) Rentcharges created under an order of the court.

The last two heads can be illustrated from the provisions of the Settled Land Act 1925 for the repayment by instalments of capital money expended on improvements to settled land, under which a rentcharge may be created by the tenant for life or by a court order.[68]

Section 3. Creation and Transfer of Rentcharges

1. Creation. When permitted by the Rentcharges Act 1977, a rentcharge may be created by statute, by an instrument *inter vivos*, or by will.   **18–020**

(a) By statute. A rentcharge may be created by statute, or by virtue of powers conferred thereby.[69]   **18–021**

(b) By instrument inter vivos. Apart from statute, a legal rentcharge can be created *inter vivos* only by a deed,[70] although it has always been possible for a person disposing of land to reserve a rentcharge to himself, without the grantee of the land executing the deed.[71]   **18–022**

An equitable rentcharge may be created merely by contract[72] or by signed writing.[73]

(c) By will. A will operates only in equity[74]; therefore, if a rentcharge is created or devised by will, the beneficiary gets no legal interest until the personal representatives have assented to the gift. The assent must be in writing, but need not be by deed.[75]   **18–023**

2. Words of limitation

(a) Transfer. The words of limitation required for the transfer of an existing rentcharge are governed by the ordinary rules for dispositions of land,[76] so that a will made after 1837 or a deed executed since 1925 will pass the whole interest in the rentcharge unless a contrary intention is shown.[77]   **18–024**

---

[68] s.85; and see n. 69, *infra*.

[69] See, *e.g.* Improvement of Land Acts, 1864 and 1899, which empowered a landowner (*e.g.* a tenant for life) to obtain an order from the Ministry of Agriculture, Fisheries and Food charging the land with repayment of money borrowed to finance improvements. These Acts were in general superseded by the Settled Land Acts 1882 and 1925 (*ante*, para. 8–001), but the Act of 1864 is still occasionally resorted to because (by s.59) it may give the rentcharge priority over other incumbrances.

[70] *Hewlins v. Shippam* (1826) 5 B. & C. 221 at 229. The usual exceptions apply: see L.P.A. 1925, s.52.

[71] Co.Litt. 143a.

[72] Above, n. 52.

[73] L.P.A. 1925, s.53.

[74] L.P.(Am.)A. 1924, Sched. IX.

[75] A.E.A. 1925, s.36; *ante*, para. 11–127.

[76] *Ante*, paras 3–023 *et seq*.

[77] Wills Act 1837, s.28; L.P.A. 1925, s.60(1).

18–025   *(b) Creation.* On the creation of a new rentcharge the Wills Act 1837, s.28, has been held not to apply; it is confined to the transfer of an existing interest.[78] Accordingly the devisee of a rentcharge created by the will can take it only for life unless a contrary intention appears.[79]

It is not so clear whether the Law of Property Act 1925, s.60[80] applies to the creation of rentcharges by deed, though the better view is that it does.[81] If that is correct, a perpetual rentcharge will need no special words of limitation when created by deed.

18–026   **3. Rentcharges charged upon registered land.**[82] In those circumstances in which a rentcharge may still be created after the Rentcharges Act 1977,[83] a registered freehold proprietor may either—

(i) grant[84]; or

(ii) transfer the registered land subject to the reservation of,[85]

a rentcharge in possession that is either perpetual or for a term of years. A registered leasehold proprietor has the same power, save that he may only grant a rentcharge to the extent of his estate.[86] The grant or reservation of a rentcharge is a registered disposition.[87] A legal rentcharge should be registered with its own title,[88] and also noted against the title affected.[89]

Section 4. Means of Enforcing Payment of Rentcharges

A. Rentcharge Charged on Land

18–027   There are four remedies available to the owner of a rentcharge if it is not paid. The first is the common law action for the money. The other three are implied into every rentcharge by statute,[90] subject to any expression of contrary

---

[78] *Nichols v. Hawkes* (1853) 10 Hare 342.
[79] *Ante,* para. 3–032.
[80] *Ante,* para. 3–030; *cf. post,* para. 18–092, n. 32.
[81] For a fuller treatment of this point, see the previous edition of this work at p. 823.
[82] See Ruoff & Roper, Chap. 26.
[83] *Ante,* para. 18–018.
[84] L.R.A. 1925, s.18(1)(b); L.R.R. 1925, r. 113.
[85] L.R.A. 1925, s.18(1)(d); L.R.R. 1925, r. 113.
[86] L.R.A. 1925, s.21(1)(b), (d).
[87] *Ante,* para. 6–031.
[88] L.R.R. 1925, rr. 50, 108 (as amended).
[89] L.R.A. 1925, ss.19(2); 22(2); Ruoff & Roper, 26–17.
[90] L.P.A. 1925, s.121. Formerly, the powers in question were often expressly conferred by the deed creating the rentcharge.

intention in the instrument creating the rentcharge.[91] These statutory remedies
do not extend the law, because they confer no greater powers than would an
express stipulation to the same effect.[92]

1. Action for the money. A personal action for the rent (as for a debt) will   **18–028**
lie against the "terre tenant" (the freehold tenant for the time being of the land
upon which the rent is charged), even if the rent was not created by him[93] and
even if it exceeds the value of the land.[94] If the land charged has been divided,
the terre tenant of any part is liable for the full amount.[95] A mere lessee for
a term of years is not liable,[96] for the action is the modern successor of one
of the ancient real actions,[97] which lay only against the person seised of the
land, *i.e.* the freeholder in possession. Its "real" nature is attested by the fact
that though nominally a personal action it lies against assignees of the land. In
truth, "the land is the debtor",[98] and the action asserts title to an incorporeal
hereditament.

Although the right to sue and the liability to be sued run with the rentcharge
and the land respectively, the benefit of an express covenant for payment does
not run with the rentcharge without express assignment.[99] Thus if a rentcharge
created by A in favour of X is conveyed to Y and the land to B, Y cannot sue
A on his covenant for payment if B fails to pay: A is liable to Y only while
A is entitled in possession, unless Y is an express assignee of X's rights under
the covenant to pay. This is another illustration of the medieval view of a rent
as a thing rather than a promise.

2. Distress. If an express power of distress is given by the instrument   **18–029**
creating the rentcharge, the extent of the right is a question of construction. If
there is no such express power, the rentcharge owner can distrain as soon as
the rent or any part of it is 21 days in arrear.[1]

3. Entry into possession. In the absence of any expression of contrary   **18–030**
intention in the instrument creating the rentcharge, the rentcharge owner may,
when the rent or any part of it is 40 days in arrear, enter and take possession

---

[91] *ibid.*, s.121(5), (7).
[92] *ibid.*, s.121(1).
[93] *Thomas v. Sylvester* (1873) L.R. 8 Q.B. 368.
[94] *Pertwee v. Townsend* [1896] 2 Q.B. 129.
[95] *Christie v. Barker* (1884) 53 L.J.Q.B. 537.
[96] *Re Herbage Rents* [1896] 2 Ch. 811. A mortgagee is therefore not liable since 1925, for he
holds a mere term of years; previously he was liable if he took a freehold estate: *Cundiff v.
Fitzsimmons* [1911] 1 K.B. 513.
[97] *Post*, Appendix.
[98] *Thomas v. Sylvester, supra*, at 372, *per* Quain J.
[99] *Grant v. Edmondson* [1931] 1 Ch. 1, where the rentcharge was created before 1926; for
rentcharges created after 1925, see Halsb. vol. 39(2), para. 876. For criticism of *Grant v.
Edmondson* see (1931) 47 L.Q.R. 380 (W. Strachan).
[1] L.P.A. 1925, s.121(2), (5), (7).

of the land without impeachment of waste and take the income until he has paid himself all rent due with costs.[2]

18–031   **4. Demise to a trustee.** If the rentcharge shows no contrary intention, the rentcharge owner may, if the rent or any part of it is 40 days in arrear, demise the land to a trustee for a term of years, with or without impeachment of waste, on trust to raise the money due, with all costs and expenses, by creating a mortgage, receiving the income or any other reasonable means.[3] If a rentcharge owner has only an equitable interest, he can grant only an equitable lease to the trustee,[4] but the estate owner can be compelled to clothe the equitable lease with the legal estate.[5]

These last three remedies are expressly excepted from the law relating to perpetuities, together with like powers conferred by any instrument for enforcing payment of a rentcharge.[6] This provision is perhaps not wide enough to cover a clause which is sometimes inserted entitling the rentcharge owner to effect a permanent forfeiture of the land if the rent is unpaid for a specified period, properly called a right of re-entry as opposed to a right of entry.[7] The general rule that such a power is void unless confined to the perpetuity period[8] probably applies in such a case.[9] However, if the rentcharge was created after July 15, 1964, the rule against perpetuities does not apply to any powers or remedies for recovery or enforcing payment, whether statutory or otherwise.[10]

B. Rentcharge Charged on Another Rentcharge

18–032   Instead of the statutory remedies of distress, entry into possession, and demise to a trustee, the owner of a rentcharge charged upon another rentcharge may appoint a receiver if the rent or any part of it is 21 days in arrear.[11] The receiver has all the powers of a receiver appointed by a mortgagee.[12] Thus if Blackacre is charged with a rent of £1,000 per annum and that rentcharge is charged with a rent of £250 per annum in favour of X, a receiver of the £1,000 can be appointed by X if the £250 is unpaid for 21 days.

There is no provision for any personal action against an assignee of the rentcharge upon which the second rentcharge is charged; but since the latter can be created "in like manner as the same could have been made to issue out

---

[2] *ibid.*, s.121(3), (5), (7).
[3] *ibid.*, s.121(4), (5), (7).
[4] *ibid.*, s.121(4).
[5] L.P.A. 1925, ss.3(1), 8(2); S.L.A. 1925, s.16.
[6] L.P.A. 1925, s.121(6) (amended by the Perpetuities and Accumulations Act 1964, s.11(2)).
[7] *Ante*, para. 4–040.
[8] *Ante*, para. 7–096, discussing *Re Hollis' Hospital Trustees & Hague's Contract* [1899] 2 Ch. 540.
[9] The combined effect of L.P.A. 1925, ss.4(3), 121(6), 162, 190(8), is not at all plain: see Law Reform Committee's Fourth Report, 1956, Cmnd. 18, paras 42, 43.
[10] Perpetuities and Accumulations Act 1964, ss.11(1), 15(5); *ante*, para. 7–131.
[11] L.P.A. 1925, s.122.
[12] *ibid.*; and see *post*, para. 19–081, for such a receiver's powers.

of land"[13] it may be that the right to such a rentcharge is implicitly accompanied by the usual common law remedy.[14]

Section 5. Apportionment of Rentcharges

1. Voluntary apportionment. If land which is subject to a rentcharge is   **18–033**
divided, the owner of each part of it is liable for the full amount, as already
explained. The owner of the rentcharge may, however, agree to an apportionment, in which case the liability of each part will be limited accordingly. If the
landowners make an apportionment among themselves without the agreement
of the owner of the rentcharge, the owner will not be bound by it, and it will
merely entitle one landowner to reclaim from the others if compelled to pay
more than his agreed proportion. Apportionments which do and do not bind
the owner are known as legal and equitable apportionments respectively,[15]
though the latter are not technically based on principles of equity. Equitable
apportionments are given statutory force by the Law of Property Act 1925 so
as to bind and benefit successors in title and to give remedies of distress and
appropriation of income which are exempt from the perpetuity rule.[16]

2. Compulsory apportionment. Under the Rentcharges Act 1977 the   **18–034**
Secretary of State[17] may authorise compulsory legal apportionment so as to
bind the owner of the rentcharge.[18] An owner of part or all of the burdened
land may apply for an apportionment order, so that an owner about to divide
his land may apply as well as an owner of a part already divided. But no
application may be made in respect of statutory rentcharges or rentcharges in
lieu of titles,[19] or where a part already divided has been charged with the
whole liability to the exoneration of the remaining land. A draft of the order
must be served on the owner of the rentcharge who may object on the ground
that it will be inadequately secured; but unless the Secretary of State modifies
the order in the light of the objection, he must apportion the rentcharge in the
way proposed by the owner or owners of the burdened land, or as he thinks
fit if there are several such owners who have not agreed. Where an apportioned amount is £5 or less per annum, it may be ordered to take effect only
for the purpose of being redeemed. An apportionment order is subject to
appeal to the Lands Tribunal.

[13] L.P.A. 1925, s.122(1).
[14] *Ante*, para. 18–028.
[15] See Rentcharges Act 1977, s.13(1).
[16] s.190.
[17] For the Environment, or for Wales.
[18] ss. 4–7.
[19] *i.e.* those exempted from the Act (*ante* para. 18–019, classes (iii) and (iv)).

Section 6. Extinguishment of Rentcharges

18–035 A rentcharge may be extinguished by release, merger, lapse of time or statutory redemption.

18–036 **1. Release.** The owner of a rentcharge may by deed release the land from the rent, either wholly or in part. A partial release may take the form of releasing all of the land from part of the rent,[20] or releasing part of the land from the whole of the rent.[21] An informal release may be valid in equity.

A limited owner, *e.g.* a life tenant, of a rentcharge cannot release more than his own interest, except under the powers conferred by the Settled Land Act 1925.[22] Nor can the owner of a rentcharge charged upon several different properties increase the liability on one of them by releasing another, unless the owner of the property to be burdened concurs in the release.[23] Thus if a rent of £1,000 is charged on five plots of land owned by five different people, and one plot is released, the rentcharge owner can recover £1,000 in respect of the four remaining plots if the owners concurred in the release,[24] but only £800 if they did not concur.[25]

18–037 **2. Merger.** At common law, if a rentcharge became vested in the same person as the land upon which it was charged, the rentcharge became extinguished by merger, even if this was not the intention.[26] For this to occur, both the rent and the land must have been vested in the same person at the same time and in the same right.[27] This automatic rule of the common law no longer applies, for by the Law of Property Act 1925[28] there is to be no merger at law except in cases where there would have been a merger in equity, and the equitable rule is that merger depends upon the intention of the parties.[29] Even if an intention that there should be no merger cannot be shown, there will be a presumption against merger if it is to the interest of the person concerned to prevent it.[30]

18–038 **3. Lapse of time.** If a rentcharge is not paid for 12 years and no sufficient acknowledgment of the owner's title is made, it is extinguished.[31] It is also

---

[20] Co.Litt. 148a.
[21] L.P.A. 1925, s.70.
[22] *Ante*, para. 8–042.
[23] L.P.A. 1925, s.70.
[24] *Price v. John* [1905] 1 Ch. 774.
[25] *Booth v. Smith* (1884) 14 Q.B.D. 318.
[26] *Capital and Counties Bank Ltd v. Rhodes* [1903] 1 Ch. 631 at 652, 653.
[27] *Re Radcliffe* [1892] 1 Ch. 227 at 231.
[28] s.185.
[29] *Ingle v. Vaughan Jenkins* [1900] 2 Ch. 368.
[30] *Re Fletcher* [1917] 1 Ch. 339; but see *Re Attkins* [1913] 2 Ch. 619.
[31] L.A. 1980, ss.15, 38; *Shaw v. Crompton* [1910] 2 K.B. 370; *post*, para. 21–034.

extinguished, unless exempt, on the expiry of the 60-year period under the Rentcharges Act 1977, as explained above.[32]

4. Statutory redemption. Under the Rentcharges Act 1977,[33] replacing the Law of Property Act 1925,[34] the owner of land which is subject to a rentcharge is entitled to redeem it by paying an equivalent capital sum to the owner of the rentcharge or into court. The Act of 1977 grants this right only in respect of rentcharges which are subject to the provisions for extinguishment in 60 years, already explained[35]; thus it strengthens the position of "estate rentcharges" and the other exempted classes, which formerly were liable to redemption under the Act of 1925. The capital sum is computed according to a statutory formula which takes account of the fact that the rentcharge is now a wasting asset. When this sum has been duly paid under the statutory procedure the Secretary of State issues a redemption certificate which discharges the land from the rentcharge, but without prejudice to the recovery of arrears.

18–039

Part 2

EASEMENTS AND PROFITS

The common law recognised a limited number of rights which one landowner could acquire over the land of another; and these rights were called easements and profits. Examples of easements are rights of way, rights of light and rights of water. Examples of profits are rights to dig gravel, or cut turf, or to take game or fish.

18–040

Nowadays both these classes of rights are incorporeal hereditaments.[36] But before the eighteenth century easements were not properly so described, because an easement could exist only if it was "appurtenant" (*i.e.* annexed) to some piece of land (the dominant tenement) so as to benefit it. It was therefore said that easements were not incorporeal hereditaments, but rights appurtenant to corporeal hereditaments[37]; or, in other words, that an easement was not an object of property in itself, but was a privilege which could be obtained for the benefit of corporeal land. The same could be said of a profit when it was attached to and passed with some particular parcel of land. But profits, unlike

---

[32] *Ante*, paras 18–018, 18–019.

[33] ss.8–10. Payment into court may be authorised in case of difficulty, *e.g.* if the owner of the rentcharge cannot be found.

[34] s.191.

[35] *Ante*, para. 18–019.

[36] *Hewlins v. Shippam* (1826) 5 B. & C. 221 at 229; *Hill v. Midland Ry.* (1882) 21 Ch. D. 143; *Great Western Ry. v. Swindon Ry.* (1882) 22 Ch.D. 677, 9 App.Cas. 787; *Jones v. Watts* (1890) 43 Ch.D. 574 at 585; contrast *Re Brotherton's and Markham's S.E.* (1907) 97 L.T. 880 at 882, on appeal 98 L.T. 547; Sweet's note to Challis 55, 56.

[37] Challis 51, 52, 55.

easements, could also exist "in gross", that is to say without any dominant tenement. For example, rights of mining or of shooting are often held by persons who are not adjacent landowners; but rights of way or rights of light are not. Rights held in gross were clearly incorporeal hereditaments.

18–041   In modern times the attempt to distinguish rights which are merely appurtenances has been abandoned, and easements and profits are classed together indiscriminately as incorporeal herteditaments.[38] This is convenient, for they have many common points and both should fall within the definition of land. Logically, no doubt, restrictive covenants[39] should also be included. But they, being a recent innovation and purely equitable, have a quite separate history and many different characteristics, and therefore stand apart from the older interests which are hereditaments in themselves.[40]

Section 1. Nature of Easements

18–042   An easement is "either a right to do something or a right to prevent something".[41] In order to explain what rights can and cannot exist as easements we must examine—

    (a) the essentials of an easement, and

    (b) the distinction between easements and certain analogous rights.

A. Essentials of an Easement

18–043   It is now settled that four essentials must be satisfied before there can be an easement.[42] First, there must be a dominant and a servient tenement. Secondly, the easement must confer a benefit on (or "accommodate") the dominant tenement. Thirdly, the dominant and servient tenements must not be owned and occupied by the same person. Fourthly, the easement must be capable of forming the subject-matter of a grant. Each of these requirements must now be examined.

18–044   **1. There must be a dominant and a servient tenement.** If X owns Blackacre and grants a right to use a path across Blackacre to the owner for

---

[38] n.36. *supra.*
[39] *Ante*, para. 16–030.
[40] For general accounts of the law of easements, see *Gale on Easements* (16th ed.); P. Jackson, *Law of Easements and Profits*; C. Sara, *Boundaries and Easements* (2nd ed.).
[41] Gale, 1–69.
[42] *Re Ellenborough Park* [1956] Ch. 131 at 163; *London & Blenheim Estates Ltd v. Ladbroke Retail Parks Ltd* [1994] 1 W.L.R. 31 at 36.

the time being of the neighbouring plot Whiteacre, Blackacre is the servient tenement and Whiteacre the dominant tenement. Had X granted the right to A who owned no land at all, A would have acquired a licence to walk over Blackacre, but his right could not exist as an easement, for a dominant tenement was lacking. Put technically, according to the distinction already explained, an easement cannot exist in gross[43] but only as appurtenant to a dominant tenement. The reason for this requirement is said to lie in the policy of the law against encumbering land with burdens of uncertain extent.[44] On any transfer of the dominant tenement, the easement will pass with the land, so that the occupier for the time being can enjoy it,[45] even if he is a mere lessee.[46] Where the dominant tenement is severed, the benefit of the easement will pass with each and every part of it,[47] subject to two restrictions.[48] First, the severed part of the dominant tenement must itself be accommodated by the easement. Secondly, the severance must not increase the burden on the servient tenement. A dominant tenement may be wholly incorporeal,[49] or partly corporeal and partly incorporeal, as where it consists of the whole undertaking of a waterworks company and thus comprises both physical land and rights over the land of others, such as the right to lay pipes.[50]

Where an easement is created by an express grant there is no legal necessity for it to specify or refer to the dominant tenement. The court will consider all the relevant facts known to the grantor and the grantee at the time of the grant[51] to see whether there was in fact a dominant tenement for the benefit of which the easement was granted,[52] and what its extent and identity were.[53] Documentary evidence to identify the dominant tenement is certainly desirable in practice,[54] but it is not required by law. It is however essential that

---

[43] *Rangeley v. Midland Ry.* (1868) 3 Ch.App. 306 at 310; *Hawkins v. Rutter* [1892] 1 Q.B. 668; *London & Blenheim Estates Ltd v. Ladbroke Retail Parks Ltd, supra,* at 36 (where Peter Gibson L.J. described the proposition as "trite law"). The authorities said to establish this proposition have been questioned and the rule criticised in (1980) 96 L.Q.R. 557 (M. F. Sturley). See too (1982) 98 L.Q.R. 279 at 305, 306 (S. Gardner); Challis 54, 55. *cf.* Gale, 1–78.

[44] *London & Blenheim Estates Ltd v. Ladbroke Retail Parks Ltd, supra,* at 37; but see (1980) 96 L.Q.R. 557 at 564–567 (M. F. Sturley).

[45] *Leech v. Schweder* (1874) 9 App.Cas. 463 at 474, 475; L.P.A. 1925, s.187(1).

[46] *Thorpe v. Brumfitt* (1873) 8 Ch.App. 650.

[47] *Newcomen v. Coulson* (1877) 5 Ch.D. 133 at 141.

[48] *Semble.* See *Gallagher v. Rainbow* (1994) 68 A.L.J.R. 512 at 516 (High Court of Australia). There is a remarkable dearth of English authority on the severance of the dominant tenement.

[49] *Hanbury v. Jenkins* [1901] 2 Ch. 401 at 422 (several profit of piscary).

[50] *Re Salvin's Indenture* [1938] 2 All E.R. 498.

[51] *Johnstone v. Holdway* [1963] 1 Q.B. 601 at 611; *Hamble P.C. v. Haggard* [1992] 1 W.L.R. 122 at 130.

[52] *Thorpe v. Brumfitt* (1873) 8 Ch.App. 650; *Johnstone v. Holdway, supra; London & Blenheim Estates Ltd v. Ladbroke Retail Parks Ltd* [1992] 1 W.L.R. 1278 at 1283 (on appeal [1994] 1 W.L.R. 31). *cf. Callard v. Beeney* [1930] 1 K.B. 353.

[53] *The Shannon Ltd v. Venner Ltd* [1965] Ch. 682 (easement held appurtenant not only to land acquired when it was granted but also to land previously acquired).

[54] For the position in the parallel case of restrictive covenants, see *ante,* paras 16–061, 16–064.

there should be an identifiable dominant tenement in existence at the time that the easement is granted.[55]

2. The easement must accommodate the dominant tenement

18–045   *(a) Benefit to land.* A right cannot exist as an easement unless it confers a benefit on the dominant tenement as such.[56] It is not sufficient that the right should give the owner for the time being some personal advantage; the test is whether the right makes the dominant tenement a better and more convenient property. This may be done not only by improving its general utility, as by giving means of access or light, but also by benefiting some trade which is carried on on the dominant tenement, at least if the trade is one long established. For example, a public house may have an easement to fix a signboard to the house next door,[57] and a shop may have an easement to put out a stall in the street on market day.[58]

18–046   *(b) Propinquity.* The servient tenement must be close enough to the dominant tenement to confer a practical benefit on it. Thus if X owns land in Northumberland, he cannot burden it with an easement of way in favour of land in Kent, for although it may be very convenient for the owner of the Kentish land to walk across X's Northumberland estate when he goes north, the right of way does not improve the Kentish land.[59] This does not mean that a right cannot exist as an easement unless the dominant and servient tenements are contiguous; even if they are separated by other land, an easement can still exist, provided that they are near enough for the dominant tenement to receive some benefit as such.[60] For example, a right to use a cart track may be appurtenant to a farm even though the track crosses properties lying at some little distance from the farm and does not lead directly to it. And the use of a pew in a church may belong to the owners of a house in the parish.[61] Nor will a right be any less an easement merely because it benefits other land as well as the dominant tenement.[62]

18–047   *(c) Disconnected user.* In *Ackroyd v. Smith*[63] it was held that a right of way granted "for all purposes" to the tenant of Blackacre and his successors in title

---

[55] *London & Blenheim Estates Ltd v. Ladbroke Retail Parks Ltd* [1994] 1 W.L.R. 31; *Voice v. Bell* (1993) 68 P. & C.R. 441 (in each case a right had been granted or reserved for a dominant tenement that had neither been acquired nor identified at the time of the grant or reservation).

[56] See *Mason v. Shrewsbury and Hereford Ry.* (1871) L.R. 6 Q.B. 578 at 587.

[57] *Moody v. Steggles* (1879) 12 Ch.D. 261 (and see the examples given by Fry J. at 266); *William Hill (Southern) Ltd v. Cabras Ltd* (1986) 54 P. & C.R. 42 at 46.

[58] *Ellis v. Mayor, etc., of Bridgnorth* (1863) 15 C.B. (N.S.) 52.

[59] See *Bailey v. Stephens* (1862) 12 C.B. (N.S.) 91 at 115.

[60] *Todrick v. Western National Omnibus Co. Ltd* [1934] Ch. 561; *Pugh v. Savage* [1970] 2 Q.B. 373.

[61] *Philipps v. Halliday* [1891] A.C. 228. This easement is of an exceptional kind.

[62] *Simpson v. Mayor, etc., of Godmanchester* [1897] A.C. 696 (right to open sluice gates to protect dominant tenement from flooding: held, this could be an easement even though it protected other land as well).

[63] (1850) 10 C.B. 164.

was not an easement, for the grant permitted the way to be used for purposes not connected with Blackacre. Had the grant been worded "for all purposes connected with Blackacre" it could have created an easement; and probably the words used in *Ackroyd v. Smith* would today be construed in this sense, as they were in the later case of *Thorpe v. Brumfitt.*[64]

(d) Personal advantage. In *Hill v. Tupper*[65] the owner of a canal leased land   **18–048**
on the bank of the canal to Hill and granted him the sole and exclusive right of putting pleasure boats on the canal. Tupper, without any authority, put rival pleasure boats on the canal. The question was whether Hill could successfully sue Tupper. If Hill's right amounted to an easement, he could sue anyone who interfered with it, for it was a right of property enforceable against all the world. If it was not an easement, then it could only be a licence,[66] *i.e.* a mere personal permission given to Hill by the canal owner, and not a proprietary interest which Hill could defend against third parties in his own right. It was held that the right to put out pleasure boats was not an interest in property which the law could recognise as being appurtenant to land. The monopoly which Hill had obtained was therefore a merely personal or commercial advantage, not connected with the use of his land as such.[67] The result would have been different if the right granted had been to cross and re-cross the canal to get to and from Hill's land, and Tupper's boats had been so numerous as to interfere with it. If Hill had taken a lease of the canal itself he could, of course, have sued Tupper for trespassing on it.[68] Similarly Tupper could have been sued, on the facts as they were, by the owner of the canal.

**3. The dominant and servient tenements must not be both owned and   18–049
occupied by the same person.** An easement is essentially a right *in alieno solo* (in the soil of another). A man cannot have an easement over his own land.[69] "When the owner of Whiteacre and Blackacre passes over the former to Blackacre, he is not exercising a right of way in respect of Blackacre; he is merely making use of his own land to get from one part of it to another."[70] As this observation implies, the same person must not only own both tenements but also occupy both of them before the existence of an easement is rendered

---

[64] (1873) 8 Ch.App. 650 at 655–657; and see *Todrick v. Western National Omnibus Co. Ltd* [1934] Ch. 561 at 583; *Gaw v. Coras Iompair Eireann* [1953] I.R. 232 at 243; contrast *Clapman v. Edwards* [1938] 2 All E.R. 507 ("for advertising purposes" held not restricted to user for the benefit of the business carried on upon the dominant tenement, and therefore not an easement).

[65] (1863) 2 H. & C. 121. *cf. Manchester Airport Plc v. Dutton* [1999] 3 W.L.R. 524 (licensee with contractual right to possession able to bring possession proceedings against squatters); *post,* Appendix.

[66] For licences see *ante,* chap. 17.

[67] For another aspect of this case, see *post,* para. 18–053.

[68] *Lord Chesterfield v. Harris* [1908] 2 Ch. 397 at 412 (a river or canal is treated as land covered with water, and the trespass is to the land underlying the water).

[69] *Metropolitan Ry v. Fowler* [1892] 1 Q.B. 165 at 171; *Sovmots Investments Ltd v. Secretary of State for the Environment* [1979] A.C. 144 at 169; *London & Blenheim Estates Ltd v. Ladbroke Retail Parks Ltd* [1992] 1 W.L.R. 1278 at 1283 (on appeal [1994] 1 W.L.R. 31).

[70] *Roe v. Siddons* (1888) 22 Q.B.D. 224 at 236, *per* Fry L.J.

impossible. Thus there is no difficulty about the existence of an easement in favour of a tenant against his own landlord, or another tenant of his landlord, although the landlord owns the freehold of both dominant and servient tenements.[71]

The rule is therefore really no more than the self-evident proposition that a man cannot have rights against himself. When an easement has once come into existence as between two different landowners, and both their properties later come into the hands of a single person, *e.g.* under a lease,[72] the question arises whether the easement is extinguished or merely suspended while the two properties are in one hand. This question is dealt with later in connection with the extinguishment of easements.[73]

18–050   Rights habitually exercised by a man over part of his own land which, if the part in question were owned and occupied by another would be easements, are often called quasi-easements.[74] The term is sometimes also used to include other rights similar to easements, such as customary rights of way[75]; but in this book it is used only in the stricter sense. Quasi-easements are of some importance, for they may sometimes become true easements if the land is subsequently sold in separate parcels.[76]

18–051   **4. The easement must be capable of forming the subject-matter of a grant.** All easements "lie in grant"; that is to say, no right can exist as an easement unless it could have been granted by deed. The principles underlying this rule are that only certain kinds of rights are capable of being rights of property which one person can convey to another,[77] and that every easement in theory owes its existence to a grant by deed; although in practice many easements are established by long user, the presumption always is that a grant was once made.[78]

This assumption that an easement must have been created by deed leads to the following rules.

(a) The right must be within the general nature of rights capable of being created as easements

18–052   (1) THE LIST IS NOT CLOSED. Although most easements fall under one of the well-known heads of easements, such as way, light, support or water, the list of easements is not closed.[79] "The category of servitudes and easements must alter and expand with the changes that take place in the circumstances of

---

[71] See, *e.g. Borman v. Griffith* [1930] 1 Ch. 493, *post*, para. 18–118. See also *Richardson v. Graham* [1908] 1 K.B. 39; *Buckby v. Coles* (1814) 5 Taunt. 311 at 315. There are difficulties about acquiring such easements by prescription: *post*, para. 18–129.

[72] See, *e.g. Thomas v. Thomas* (1835) 2 Cr.M. & R. 34.

[73] *Post*, para. 18–191.

[74] See, *e.g. Wheeldon v. Burrows* (1879) 12 Ch.D. 31 at 49.

[75] *Brocklebank v. Thompson* [1903] 2 Ch. 344 at 348.

[76] See *post*, para. 18–104.

[77] *cf. ante*, para. 15–004.

[78] For prescription see *post*, para. 18–121. Exceptions to the presumption of a lost grant occur under the Prescription Act 1832: *post*, para. 18–169.

[79] See the 35 varieties of easement listed by Gale, 1–65.

mankind."[80] An example of this might be a right for a house to have telephone lines running across a neighbour's land. There has as yet been no decision that this can be an easement. But a right to use a clothes line is probably capable of being one,[81] and the analogy may be close enough for the purpose.

(2) LIMITS. There are, however, limits. "It must not therefore be supposed **18–053** that incidents of a novel kind can be devised and attached to property, at the fancy or caprice of any owner."[82] This expresses the overriding principle that the various kinds of proprietary interests are fixed by the law, and finite in number.[83] Even though the list of easements is not closed, it is not open to interests which do not conform to the rules about the general nature of easements.[84] For example, a right to an unspoilt view[85] cannot exist as an easement. Nor can a right to have the wall of a house protected from the weather by an adjoining house.[86] Such a right is too uncertain in its ambit to be an easement,[87] and might in any event require expenditure by the servient owner,[88] something which is generally fatal to the acceptance of a right as an easement.[89] However the right of support which often exists in favour of semi-detached houses is well-recognised as an easement.

It used to be said that a right to use a path or a garden merely for taking walks, being a mere *jus spatiandi*, is incapable of being an easement[90]; but this right, which is of value to many houses adjacent to parks and gardens, has now been admitted into the company of easements,[91] and the same may apply to a right to boat on a neighbouring lake.[92] The law of easements may protect projecting buildings, or even the projecting bowsprits of ships using a dock[93];

---

[80] *Dyce v. Lady James Hay* (1852) 1 Macq. 305 at 312, 313, *per* Lord St Leonards.

[81] *Drewell v. Towler* (1832) 3 B. & Ad. 735; *cf.* the right to run a timber "traveller" (aerial tramway) over other land: *Harris v. De Pinna* (1886) 33 Ch.D. 238 at 251, 260, 261.

[82] *Keppell v. Bailey* (1834) 2 My. & K. 517 at 535, *per* Lord Brougham L.C.

[83] *Ante*, para. 18–051.

[84] *London & Blenheim Estates Ltd v. Ladbroke Retail Parks Ltd* [1994] 1 W.L.R. 31 at 37 (a right intended to be an easement and attached to a servient tenement before the dominant tenement was acquired could not exist as an easement).

[85] *Post*, para. 18–057.

[86] *Phipps v. Pears* [1965] 1 Q.B. 76. The reason for the decision was that "the law has been chary of creating new negative easements" because they unduly restrict what the servient owner may do on his land: *ibid.*, at 83, *per* Lord Denning M.R. This reasoning has been criticised: (1964) 80 L.Q.R. 318 (R.E.M.); (1964) 28 Conv. (N.S.) 450 at 451 (M. A. Peel). A right to protection from the weather has been held to exist as between owners of a party wall: *Upjohn v. Seymour Estates Ltd* [1938] 1 All E.R. 614.

[87] See (1964) 80 L.Q.R. 318 at 320 (R.E.M.).

[88] This would certainly have been the case in *Phipps v. Pears, supra*. The defendant had been compelled to demolish his property by the local authority. He would necessarily have had to expend money to weatherproof the wall thereby exposed.

[89] *Post*, para. 18–054. The possibility that a right to protection in the horizontal plane by means of a roof might be an easement has been canvassed: see *Sedgwick Forbes Bland Payne Group Ltd v. Regional Properties Ltd* [1981] 1 E.G.L.R. 33 at 36.

[90] *International Tea Stores Co. v. Hobbs* [1903] 2 Ch. 165 at 172.

[91] *Re Ellenborough Park* [1956] Ch. 131. For the position of a *jus spatiandi* as a public right, see *R. v. Doncaster B.C., ex p. Braim* (1986) 57 P. & C.R. 1; [1988] Conv. 369 at 371 (J. Hill).

[92] *Re Ellenborough Park, supra*, at 175. Contrast a mere commercial right to hire out boats on the water: *ante*, para. 18–048.

[93] *Suffield v. Brown* (1864) 4 De G.J. & S. 185.

but it will not extend to overhanging trees.[94] More examples of the various species of easements are given below.[95]

18–054   (3) EXPENDITURE. "A right to have something done is not an easement."[96] It is therefore most unlikely that a right would be accepted as an easement if it involved the servient tenant in the expenditure of money.[97] None of the recognised easements does so,[98] except the obligation to fence land in order to keep out cattle (which has been described as "in the nature of a spurious easement"[99]) and, perhaps, certain obligations to repair sea-walls, river banks and gutters (though the status of such rights as easements is questionable).[1] Thus a right of way to cross a bridge, for example, imposes no obligation on the servient owner to keep the bridge in repair.[2] Where positive action is needed to maintain an easement, the general principle is that the dominant owner may enter and execute repairs upon the servient land, *e.g.* to a pipe or pump which he is entitled to use; all this is implicit in the concept of grant.[3] The servient owner's only obligation is to refrain from any action of his own which impedes the enjoyment of the easement. In the case of an easement of support, he may allow the supporting structure to fall into decay and collapse,[4] but he may not himself pull it down[5]; and the dominant owner is entitled to enter and repair it as soon as this is necessary to protect his own building.[6] Nor may the servient owner do anything which might prevent the dominant owner from executing repairs.[7]

18–055   (4) THE RIGHT MUST NOT BE TOO EXTENSIVE. An easement is no more than a right over land and not a right to either possession or joint user of it.[8] "There

---

[94] *Lemmon v. Webb* [1895] A.C. 1.

[95] *Post,* paras 18–192 *et seq.*

[96] Gale, 1–69.

[97] *Regis Property Co. Ltd v. Redman* [1956] 2 Q.B. 612 (covenant to supply hot water creates no easement, being a right to services); *Rance v. Elvin* (1983) 49 P. & C.R. 65 (where Nicholls J. held that the grant of right to metered water supply paid for by the servient owner created no easement since it involved a positive obligation. The Court of Appeal reversed the decision on a different ground: (1985) 50 P. & C.R. 9, but affirmed that "a positive obligation to pay such charges was quite inconsistent with the existence of an easement giving a right to a supply of water": *ibid.,* at 13, *per* Browne-Wilkinson L.J.). *cf.* [1985] C.L.J. 458 (A. J. Waite), where the generality of this rule is questioned.

[98] See *Pomfret v. Ricroft* (1669) 1 Wms.Saund. 321.

[99] *Lawrence v. Jenkins* (1873) L.R. 8 Q.B. 274 at 279, *per* Archibald J.; *post,* para. 18–211. There are certain statutory duties to fence: *e.g.* under the Railway Clauses Consolidation Act 1845; see *R. Walker & Sons v. British Railways Board* [1984] 1 W.L.R. 805.

[1] See *e.g. Hudson v. Tabor* (1876) 2 Q.B.D. 290; *R. v. Commissioners for Sewers for Essex* (1885) 14 Q.B.D. 561; (1964) 28 Conv. (N.S.) 450 at 451 (M. A. Peel); [1985] C.L.J. 458 at 461 (A. J. Waite).

[2] *Jones v. Pritchard* [1908] 1 Ch. 630 at 637.

[3] Gale 1–82; 1–83; *Goodhart v. Hyett* (1883) 25 Ch.D. 182; *Jones v. Pritchard, supra.*

[4] *Bond v. Nottingham Corporation* [1940] Ch. 429 at 438. He may be liable independently in nuisance: *Bradburn v. Lindsay* [1983] 2 All E.R. 408. See [1984] Conv. 54 (P. Jackson). *cf.* [1987] Conv. 47 (A. J. Waite).

[5] See *post,* para. 18–209.

[6] *Bond v. Nottingham Corporation, supra.*

[7] *Goodhart v. Hyett, supra* (injunction against servient owner building over water pipe).

[8] *Copeland v. Greehalf* [1952] Ch. 488 at 498.

is no easement known to law which gives exclusive and unrestricted use of a piece of land."[9] This principle has been in issue in a number of cases where A has claimed an easement to store goods or park vehicles on B's land.[10] It is now established that easements to store[11] or to park[12] are known to the law. Whether or not the right is an easement is a question of degree.[13] "If the right granted in relation to the area over which it is to be exercisable is such that it would leave the servient owner without any reasonable use of his land, whether for parking or anything else, it could not be an easement though it might be some larger or different grant."[14] Thus a right to store coal in a shed in a garden was held to be an easement,[15] but a wheelwright's claim to park an unlimited number of vehicles on a strip of his neighbour's land was unsuccessful because it went "wholly outside any normal idea of an easement".[16] However, the fact that the exercise of a right involves the temporary exclusion of the servient owner is not incompatible with its status as an easement.[17] *Miller v Emcer products Ltd 1956 right to use lavatory easement*

(5) NEW EASEMENTS. New rights not involving the servient owner in expenditure have from time to time been recognised as easements. Thus in 1896 the courts recognised as an easement the right to go upon the land of another to open sluice gates,[18] in 1915 the right to store casks and trade produce on land,[19] in 1955 the right to use a neighbour's lavatory,[20] in 1973 the right to use an airfield,[21] and in 1982 the right to park cars anywhere in a defined area, *e.g.* round a block of flats.[22]   **18–056**

(b) The right must be sufficiently definite. The extent of the right claimed   **18–057**
must be capable of reasonably exact definition, for otherwise it could not be granted at all. This rule is really a corollary of the preceding one, but it helps

---

[9] *Reilly v. Booth* (1890) 44 Ch.D. 12 at 26, *per* Lopes L.J.
[10] The authorities are reviewed in *London & Blenheim Estates Ltd v. Ladbroke Retail Parks Ltd* [1992] 1 W.L.R. 1278 at 1285 *et seq.*
[11] *Att.–Gen. of Southern Nigeria v. John Holt & Co. (Liverpool) Ltd* [1915] A.C. 599 at 617.
[12] *Newman v. Jones* [1982] March 22 (unrep., Megarry V.–C); see at 35, 36 of the transcript; *London & Blenheim Estates Ltd v. Ladbroke Retail Parks Ltd, supra,* at 1288 (on appeal [1994] 1 W.L.R. 31). See too *Patel v. W.H. Smith (Eziot) Ltd* [1987] 1 W.L.R. 853 at 859; *Pavledes v. Ryesbridge Properties Ltd* (1989) 58 P. & C.R. 459 at 481.
[13] *Grigsby v. Melville* [1972] 1 W.L.R. 1355 at 1364 (on appeal [1974] 1 W.L.R. 80); *London & Blenheim Estates Ltd v. Ladbroke Retail Parks Ltd, supra,* at 1288.
[14] *London & Blenheim Estates Ltd v. Ladbroke Retail Parks Ltd supra,* at 1288, *per* Judge Baker. The definition of what constitutes the servient tenement is therefore of some importance.
[15] *Wright v. Macadam* [1949] 2 K.B. 744.
[16] *Copeland v. Greenhalf, supra,* at 498, *per* Upjohn J. See too *Grigsby v. Melville, supra* (claim to exclusive use of a cellar probably too extensive to be an easement).
[17] *Miller v. Emcer Products Ltd* [1956] Ch. 304 at 316 (right to use a lavatory held to be an easement).
[18] *Simpson v. Mayor, etc., of Godmanchester* [1896] 1 Ch. 214; [1897] A.C. 696.
[19] *Att.–Gen. of Southern Nigeria v. John Holt & Co. (Liverpool) Ltd, supra,* at 617 (*post*, para. 18–074). See too *Smith v. Gates* [1952] C.P.L. 814.
[20] *Miller v. Emcer Products Ltd, supra.*
[21] *Dowty Boulton Paul Ltd v. Wolverhampton Corporation (No. 2)* [1976] Ch. 13.
[22] *Newman v. Jones, supra,* at 35, 36 of the transcript. See too *London & Blenheim Estates Ltd v. Ladbroke Retail Parks Ltd supra; Handel v. St. Stephens Close Ltd* [1994] 1 E.G.L.R. 70 at 71, 72.

to explain the exclusion of certain kinds of rights. Thus, although there can be an easement of light where a defined window receives a defined amount of light,[23] there can be no easement of indefinite privacy[24] or prospect (*i.e.* the right to a view).[25] Again, an easement may exist for the passage of air through a defined channel[26]; but there can be no easement for the general flow of air over land to a windmill,[27] chimney,[28] drying shed for timber,[29] or otherwise.[30] A catalogue of recognised species of easements and profits will be found at the end of this chapter.[31]

Of course, it is often possible to secure by way of contract rights which are too indefinite to be easements; and a restrictive covenant properly framed may be used to confer a right of amenity, *e.g.* an unspoilt view, upon one piece of land as against another,[32] so as in substance to create a right of property to that effect. Another doctrine which may sometimes circumvent the limits of easements is the rule against "derogation from grant", explained below.[33]

18–058   *(c) There must be a capable grantor.* There can be no claim to an easement if at the relevant time the servient tenement was owned by someone incapable of granting an easement, *e.g.* a statutory corporation with no power to grant easements,[34] an incumbent who has not obtained a faculty to grant a right of way over a churchyard,[35] or a tenant under a lease who has no power to bind the reversion.[36] Where the claim is based on an express grant, the grantor must, of course, have been capable of granting the easement: thus an easement over a common cannot be granted by some only of the commoners.[37]

18–059   *(d) There must be a capable grantee.* An easement can be claimed only by a legal person capable of receiving a grant.[38] Thus a claim by a company with no power to acquire easements must fail.[39] A fluctuating body of persons, such as "the inhabitants for the time being of the village of X", cannot claim an easement, for no grant can be made to them. But they may have similar rights if there is a valid custom to that effect,[40] such as a customary right of way

---

[23] *Post*, para. 18–202.
[24] *Browne v. Flower* [1911] 1 Ch. 219 at 225.
[25] *William Aldred's Case* (1610) 9 Co.Rep. 57b at 58b, *per* Wray C.J.: "for prospect, which is a matter only of delight, and not of necessity, no action lies for stopping thereof . . . the law does not give an action for such things of delight".
[26] *Bass v. Gregory* (1890) 25 Q.B.D. 481 (ventilation shaft for cellar); *Cable v. Bryant* [1908] 1 Ch. 259 (aperture in stable).
[27] *Webb v. Bird* (1862) 13 C.B. (N.S.) 841.
[28] *Bryant v. Lefever* (1879) 4 C.P.D. 172.
[29] *Harris v. De Pinna* (1886) 33 Ch.D. 238.
[30] *Chastey v. Ackland* [1895] 2 Ch. 389.
[31] *Post*, paras 18–212 *et seq.*
[32] *Ante*, para. 16–030; *post*, para. 18–072.
[33] *Post*, para. 18–075.
[34] *Mulliner v. Midland Ry.* (1879) 11 Ch.D. 611.
[35] *Re St Clement's, Leigh–on–Sea* [1988] 1 W.L.R. 720 at 728.
[36] *Derry v. Sanders* [1919] 1 K.B. 223 at 231.
[37] *Paine & Co. Ltd v. St. Neots Gas & Coke Co.* [1939] 3 All E.R. 812.
[38] See *Re Salvin's Indenture* [1938] 2 All E.R. 498.
[39] *National Guaranteed Manure Co. Ltd v. Donald* (1859) 4 H. & N. 8.
[40] For custom see *post*, para. 18–078.

across land to reach the parish church,[41] or a customary right to take water from a spout,[42] or to water cattle at a pond,[43] or for recreation on a common,[44] or to play games[45] or dry nets[46] on certain land.

B. Distinctions between Easements and Certain Analogous Rights

It will have been gathered that the attempt to define an easement leads to a list of miscellaneous examples rather than to a precise definition. Some further help may be had from contrasting easements with certain other rights which are distinct from them.

18–060

I. NATURAL RIGHTS

1. Support for land. The most obvious difference between an easement and a natural right is that a natural right exists automatically but an easement must be acquired. A "natural right" is, in fact, simply a right protected by the law of tort, *i.e.* the right to damages or an injunction for nuisance. In addition to his rights over his own land[47] every landowner has a natural right[48] of support. The law in relation to the removal of rights of support is not wholly rational. An action in nuisance will lie against a neighbour if he deliberately removes the support (as by quarrying),[49] or removes the subjacent strata of minerals,[50] or if the support is damaged by natural causes occurring on the neighbour's land.[51] By contrast, no action lies when the support is removed by the neighbour's abstraction of water.[52] There is a similar right of support where the surface of the land and the soil underneath are owned by different persons; the owner of the surface has a natural right to have it supported by the subjacent soil, and even if he has let or sold minerals lying below the

18–061

---

[41] *Brocklebank v. Thompson* [1903] 2 Ch. 344.
[42] *Harrop v. Hirst* (1868) L.R. 4 Ex. 43.
[43] *Manning v. Wasdale* (1836) 5 A. & E. 758.
[44] *R. v. Doncaster B.C., ex p. Braim* (1986) 57 P. & C.R. 1.
[45] *New Windsor Corporation v. Mellor* [1975] Ch. 380.
[46] *Mercer v. Denne* [1905] 2 Ch. 538.
[47] *e.g.* to walk over his land to reach his house. Such rights are for certain purposes called "quasi-easements"; see *ante*, para. 18–050.
[48] *Backhouse v. Bonomi* (1861) 9 H.L.C. 503; *Dalton v. Angus & Co.* (1881) 6 App.Cas. 740 at p. 791.
[49] *Redland Bricks Ltd v. Morris* [1970] A.C. 652 (support removed by excavation of clay; damages awarded but mandatory injunction refused). *cf. Holbeck Hall Ltd v. Scarborough B.C.* [1997] 2 E.G.L.R. 213 at 215.
[50] *Lotus Ltd v. British Soda Co. Ltd* [1972] Ch. 123 (subsidence due to brine pumping: damages and an injunction awarded).
[51] *Leakey v. National Trust* [1980] Q.B. 485 (not following *Rouse v. Gravelworks Ltd* [1940] 1 K.B. 489).
[52] *Stephens v. Anglian Water Authority* [1987] 1 W.L.R. 1381 (there is a useful summary of the law at 1384, 1385). See too *Brace v. S.E. Regional Housing Association Ltd* [1984] 1 E.G.L.R. 144 at 145, 146; [1988] Conv. 175 (M. Harwood). *cf. Home Brewery Co. Ltd v. William Davis & Co. (Leicester) Ltd* [1987] Q.B. 339; [1987] C.L.J. 205 (J. R. Spencer).

surface he can sue if the mining causes subsidence,[53] provided of course that he has not agreed to the surface being let down.[54]

The cause of action for the tort of interference with a natural right of support does not arise until damage has been suffered, though the court may grant a *quia timet* injunction if it is anticipated. If remedial work is carried out by the landowner in anticipation of subsidence, that expenditure will therefore be irrecoverable.[55]

18–062   **2. No support for buildings.** This natural right, however, extends only to land in its natural state[56]; there is no natural right to support for buildings or for the additional burden on land which they cause.[57] "The owner of the adjacent soil may with perfect legality dig that soil away, and allow his neighbour's house, if supported by it, to fall in ruins to the ground."[58] But if withdrawing support would have caused actionable damage even if nothing had been built, the damages recoverable include any damage to the buildings.[59] Similarly there is no natural right to have buildings supported by neighbouring buildings.[60] If no more damage is done than is necessary, a man may pull down his house without having to provide support for his neighbour's house.[61] The right to have buildings supported by land or by other buildings can, however, be acquired as an easement[62]; and the provision of statutory rights of this kind, subject to safeguards, has been suggested.[63]

18–063   **3. Light and water.** "No natural right exists to a single ray of light."[64] This is, no doubt, because land in its natural state must always receive light through the air-space above it, which is protected by the law of trespass.[65] There are no natural rights in respect of buildings. But there is a natural right to water, where it flows naturally in a definite channel. Therefore if the stream is dammed or diverted the riparian owners can sue.[66] The right to dam or divert

---

[53] *L. & N.W. Ry. v. Evans* [1893] 1 Ch. 16 at 30.
[54] See, *e.g. Butterknowle Colliery Co. Ltd v. Bishop Auckland Industrial Co-operative Co. Ltd* [1906] A.C. 305 at 309.
[55] *Midland Bank Plc v. Bardgrove Property Services Ltd* (1992) 65 P. & C.R. 153.
[56] *Hunt v. Peake* (1860) Johns. 705.
[57] *Wyatt v. Harrison* (1832) 3 B. & Ad. 871.
[58] *Dalton v. Angus & Co.* (1881) 6 App.Cas. 740 at 804, *per* Lord Penzance.
[59] *Stroyan v. Knowles* (1861) 6 H. & N. 454; *Lotus Ltd v. British Soda Co. Ltd* [1972] Ch. 123 (where, however, the real injury was abstraction of the plaintiff's own subsoil); *Ray v. Fairway Motors (Barnstaple) Ltd* (1968) 20 P. & C.R. 261.
[60] *Peyton v. The Mayor & Commonalty of London* (1829) 9 B. & C. 725.
[61] *Southwark & Vauxhall Water Co. v. Wandsworth District Board of Works* [1898] 2 Ch. 603 at 612, 613.
[62] *Post*, para. 18–209.
[63] Law Reform Committee, 14th Report, Cmnd. 3100 (1966), paras 89, 90; Law Commission Working Paper No. 36 (1971), para. 82.
[64] Gale, 12th ed., 6. An easement of light can be acquired for a building, however: *post*, para. 18–202.
[65] *Ante*, para. 3–051.
[66] *Swindon Waterworks Co. Ltd v. Wilts and Berks Canal Navigation Co.* (1875) L.R. 7 H.L. 697; and see *ante*, para. 3–057.

it, on the other hand, may be acquired as an easement.[67] There is no natural right to water percolating underground, for there is then no definite channel.[68]

II. PUBLIC RIGHTS

An easement must always be appurtenant to land; it is a right exercisable by the owner for the time being by virtue of his estate in the land.[69] A public right, on the other hand, is a right[70] exercisable by anyone, whether he owns land or not, merely by virtue of the general law.[71] Thus there is a public right to fish and navigate over the foreshore (the area between the ordinary high and low water marks) when it is covered with water, but no right of bathing, walking or beachcombing on it.[72]

18–064

The public rights which most closely resemble easements are public rights of way.[73] The land over which a public right of way exists is known as a highway[74]; and although most highways have been made up into roads, and most easements of way exist over footpaths, the presence or absence of a made road has nothing to do with the distinction. There may be a highway over a footpath, while a well-made road may be subject only to an easement of way, or may exist only for the landowner's benefit and be subject to no easement at all. A highway may exist as such even if it does not lead to another highway or any public place.[75] If it is maintainable at public expense under the Highways Act 1980 it vests in the statutory highway authority,[76] which then holds the surface of the land affected, together with so much of the land below and the air-space above as is required by their statutory duties, for "a determinable statutory fee simple interest".[77]

1. Creation. A public right of way may be created in the following ways.

18–065

---

[67] Gale, 1–65, 6–44.
[68] *Acton v. Blundell* (1843) 12 M. & W. 324; *Chasemore v. Richards* (1859) 7 H.L.C. 376; *Bradford Corporation v. Pickles* [1895] A.C. 587. See too *Stephens v. Anglian Water Authority* [1987] 1 W.L.R. 1381.
[69] *Ante*, para. 18–044.
[70] The user must be *as of right* and not merely tolerated: *Ministry of Defence v. Wiltshire C.C.* [1995] 4 All E.R. 931 at 934, 935.
[71] This definition was approved by the Court of Appeal in *Overseas Investment Services Ltd v. Simcobuild Construction Ltd* (1995) 70 P. & C.R. 322 at 328, 330.
[72] *Brinckman v. Matley* [1904] 2 Ch. 313; *Alfred F. Beckett Ltd v. Lyons* [1967] Ch. 449. Such activities are enjoyed not as of right but by tolerance.
[73] See [1993] Conv. 129 (M. Welstead).
[74] At common law highways are of three kinds: (i) a full highway or cartway (right of passage on foot, with beasts of burden, or with vehicles and cattle); (ii) a bridleway (right of passage on foot and with beasts of burden); and (iii) a footpath (right of passage on foot only): *Suffolk C.C. v. Mason* [1979] A.C. 705 at 709, 710.
[75] *Williams-Ellis v. Cobb* [1935] 1 K.B. 310.
[76] s.263.
[77] *Foley's Charity Trustees v. Dudley Corporation* [1910] 1 K.B. 317 at 322; and see *Tithe Redemption Commission v. Runcorn U.D.C.* [1954] Ch. 383; *Wiltshire C.C. v. Frazer* (1983) 47 P. & C.R. 69 at 72.

18–066   *(a) By statute.* The Highways Act 1980 makes provision for the adoption of an existing highway and for the adoption and dedication of one that is to be constructed.[78]

(b) By dedication and acceptance.

18–067   (1) AT COMMON LAW. To establish a highway at common law by dedication and acceptance it must be shown—

(i) that the owner of the land dedicated the way to the public, and

(ii) that the public accepted that dedication, the acceptance normally being shown by user by the public.[79]

Dedication may be formal, although this is comparatively infrequent.[80] It is usually inferred from long user by the public, so that user is thus effective to prove both dedication and acceptance.[81] But in order to raise a presumption of dedication there must have been open user as of right[82] for so long a time and in such a way that the landowner must have known that the public were claiming a right.[83] User with the landowner's permission or tolerance is not user as of right,[84] and the court is slow to find a claim of right where the user is attributable to the landowner's indulgence.[85] The user must also have been without interruption by the owner. A practice frequently adopted to disprove any intention to dedicate is to close the way for one day in each year, for this asserts the landowner's right to exclude the public at will.[86]

18–068   The length of the enjoyment to be shown depends on the circumstances of the case. Where the circumstances have pointed to an intention to dedicate, 18 months has been held to be enough[87]; where the circumstances are against dedication, a substantially greater period may be insufficient,[88] especially if in recent years there has been no occupier capable of dedicating a highway in perpetuity.[89]

At common law it is possible for an occupier of adjoining land to be liable for repair of the highway under the conditions of tenure of the land, *ratione tenurae*.[90] This liability is in effect a burden running with land,[91] since it falls

---

[78] s.38.
[79] See *Cubitt v. Lady Caroline Maxse* (1873) L.R. 8 C.P. 704 at 715.
[80] *Simpson v. Att.-Gen.* [1904] A.C. 476 at 494.
[81] *Cubitt v. Lady Caroline Maxse, supra.*
[82] See *Hue v. Whiteley* [1929] 1 Ch. 440 at 445; and see *post*, para. 18–123.
[83] *Greenwich District Board of Works v. Maudslay* (1870) L.R. 5 Q.B. 397 at 404.
[84] *R. v. Broke* (1859) 1 F. & F. 514; *cf. post*, para. 18–126.
[85] *Att.-Gen. v. Antrobus* [1905] 2 Ch. 188 (no public right of access to Stonehenge).
[86] *British Museum Trustees v. Finnis* (1833) 5 C. & P. 460.
[87] *North London Ry. v. Vestry of St. Mary's, Islington* (1872) 27 L.T. 672.
[88] *R. v. Hudson* (1732) 2 Stra. 909 (4 years).
[89] See *Williams-Ellis v. Cobb* [1935] 1 K.B. 310.
[90] See *Pratt & Mackenzie on Highways*, 21st ed., 76.
[91] Where the title is registered it is an overriding interest: L.R.A. 1925, s. 70(1)(a). See *ante*, para. 6–039.

on successive owners and occupiers, though it seems that they bear only personal liability. In theory, the tenure must have been created before 1290,[92] but in practice liability is proved by showing that the occupier and his predecessors have repaired the highway over a long period of time.

(2) UNDER THE HIGHWAYS ACT 1980. The object of section 31 of the Highways **18–069** Act 1980[93] is to simplify proof of dedication by laying down a definite period of use which will suffice to show that a right of way exists. The public can still claim a right of way based on use for a shorter period than that laid down by the Act if an intent to dedicate can be inferred.[94] As will appear later, the legislation was modelled upon the Prescription Act 1832.[95]

The Act provides[96] that a right of way can be established by 20 years' enjoyment of a way over land[97] by the public as of right[98] and without interruption, unless the landowner can show[99] that during that period there was no intention to dedicate a way.[1] Where user of a way is merely incidental to some other activity, such as recreation, it will not give rise to a presumption of dedication as a highway.[2] "Without interruption" means "without physical obstruction", and not merely "not contentious"[3]; and even a physical obstruction at times when nobody was likely to use the way is no interruption.[4] A mere restriction on the user of the way may not amount to an interruption.[5] The absence of any intention to dedicate can be shown either in one of the usual ways, as by closing the way for one day in each year,[6] or in one of the special statutory ways namely, by exhibiting a notice visible to those using

---

[92] *Ante*, para. 2–040.

[93] Which replaced the Rights of Way Act 1932 and later legislation.

[94] s.31(9).

[95] *Post*, para. 18–140; and see *R. v. Oxfordshire C.C., ex p. Sunningwell P.C.* [1999] 3 W.L.R. 160 at 168.

[96] Highways Act 1980, s.31(1).

[97] Although "land" is defined to include "land covered with water" (*ibid.*, s.31(11)), the section does not apply to rights of navigation over a river or canal: *Att.-Gen. ex rel. Yorkshire Derwent Trust Ltd v. Brotherton* [1992] 1 A.C. 425. The definition is included *ex abundanti cautela* to cover cases where the way passes through a ford or is subjected to flooding: *ibid.*, at 437, 442. "I cannot . . . think that any reader of Alfred Lord Tennyson would have regarded the Lady of Shalott, as she floated down to Camelot through the noises of the night, as exercising a right of way over the subjacent soil": *ibid.*, at 435, *per* Lord Oliver.

[98] This has the same meaning as in the case of easements, namely user which is *nec vi, nec clam, nec precario*: see *R. v. Oxfordshire C.C., ex p. Sunningwell P.C., supra*, reviewing the authorities; and *post*, paras 18–123 *et seq.* User under a licence will not therefore suffice: *R. v. Secretary of State for the Environment, ex p. Billson* [1999] Q.B. 374.

[99] And the onus is on him to do so: *Ward v. Durham C.C.* (1994) 70 P. & C.R. 585 at 589.

[1] He does not have to prove that he did not dedicate the land, merely that he had no intention to do so: *Jacques v. Secretary of State for the Environment* [1994] J.P.L. 1031.

[2] *Dyfed C.C. v. Secretary of State for Wales* (1989) 59 P. & C.R. 275 at 279 (where user of a path may have been merely ancillary to the use of a lake for fishing, swimming, sunbathing and picnicking).

[3] See *Merstham Manor Ltd v. Coulsdon and Purley U.D.C.* [1937] 2 K.B. 77.

[4] *Lewis v. Thomas* [1950] 1 K.B. 438.

[5] *Gloucestershire C.C. v. Farrow* [1985] 1 W.L.R. 741 at 747 (right of way subject to restriction twice a year due to the holding of a fair).

[6] *Merstham Manor Ltd v. Coulsdon and Purley U.D.C., supra*, at 85.

the way,[7] or by depositing a map with the local authority with a statement of what ways the landowner admits to be highways, and lodging statutory declarations at intervals of not more than six years stating whether any other ways have been dedicated.[8]

The 20-year period is to be calculated as that next before the time when the right to use the way was brought into question by a notice exhibited to the public negativing the dedication or otherwise.[9] Enjoyment prior to the date of the Act suffices.[10]

18–070   A reversioner or a remainderman is at risk that a public right of way may be acquired by 20 years' user against the tenant for life or years. The Highways Act 1980 therefore provides that—

> (i) where the land is let on lease, the reversioner may exhibit a notice rebutting dedication[11]; and

> (ii) where it is held by a tenant for life, the reversioner or remainderman may take proceedings for trespass as if he were already in possession.[12]

Local authorities are required to maintain definitive maps and statements, subject to the determination of objections, of public footpaths and bridleways in their areas.[13] These maps are conclusive as to the rights shown,[14] but the local authority is under a duty to keep them under continuous review and to amend them accordingly.[15] Not only is the conclusiveness of the maps without prejudice to the question of whether greater rights exist,[16] but rights erroneously included on them may be either deleted or reclassified as a lesser form of right, as where a bridleway is reclassified as a mere footpath.[17]

18–071   **2. Extinguishment.** Once a highway has been established, it can be extinguished only—

---

[7] Highways Act 1980, s.31(3). If this is torn down or defaced, a written notice to the local council will be effective: s.31(4). If the land is leased, the landlord is entitled to enter and erect a notice: s.31(5).

[8] *ibid.*, s.31(6).

[9] *ibid.*, s.34(2); *cf. post*, paras 18–144–18–146.

[10] *Att.-Gen. and Newton Abbot R.D.C. v. Dyer* [1947] Ch. 67; *Fairey v. Southampton C.C.* [1956] 2 Q.B. 439. See [1956] C.L.J. 172 (R. N. Gooderson).

[11] s.31(4).

[12] s.33.

[13] Wildlife and Countryside Act 1981, Pt III, replacing (with amendments) earlier legislation. This duty was introduced by the National Parks and Access to the Countryside Act 1949, Pt IV.

[14] Wildlife and Countryside Act 1981, s.56(1).

[15] *ibid.*, s.53(2)(b).

[16] *ibid.*, s.56, reversing *Suffolk C.C. v. Mason* [1979] A.C. 705. See (1979) 95 L.Q.R. 21 (L. H. Hoffmann).

[17] Wildlife and Countryside Act 1981, s.53; *R. v. Secretary of State for the Environment, ex p. Burrows and Simms* [1991] 2 Q.B. 354, overruling *Rubinstein v. Secretary of State for the Environment* (1989) 57 P. & C.R. 111.

(i) by natural causes, such as inroads of the sea or landslips[18]; or

(ii) if it is closed or diverted by an order made under certain statutory provisions[19]; or

(iii) if closing orders have extinguished all ways leading to it.[20]

The mere obstruction of the highway or the failure of the public to use it will not destroy the rights of the public, for "once a highway always a highway".[21] A mere closing order for a highway leaves unaffected any easement over the route of the highway,[22] while the statutory extinguishment of an easement may not affect a highway over the route.[23]

III. RESTRICTIVE COVENANTS

Easements and restrictive covenants[24] are similar in that an easement, like a restrictive covenant, may entitle a landowner to restrict the use that his neighbour makes of his land; thus the owner of an easement of light may prevent the servient owner from obstructing his light by erecting a building on the adjoining land. There are other similarities, such as the need for dominant and servient tenements. In general it is possible to say that the law of restrictive covenants is an equitable extension of the law of easements.[25] But, historically, this was not a case of equity following the law. The enforcement of restrictive covenants against purchasers with notice was really a new departure, founded on equitable principles. It will be seen from the section on restrictive covenants[26] that although they have some elements in common with easements they are a fundamentally different kind of interest. Unlike restrictive covenants, easements may exist at law as well as in equity, and they may be acquired by prescription (*i.e.* long enjoyment). **18–072**

There is some overlap, nevertheless. Certain rights of a negative kind, such as rights to light, air, support, or water, may be either acquired as easements or secured by restrictive covenants. But more often restrictive covenants are used for some purpose outside the scope of easements, such as preserving the amenity of a neighbourhood. On the other hand a restrictive covenant cannot confer a positive right like a right of way. **18–073**

---

[18] *R. v. Secretary of State for the Environment, ex p. Burrows and Simms, supra*, at 363.

[19] *e.g.* Highways Act 1980, s.116; Town and Country Planning Act 1990, Pt X. On these provisions, see respectively *Ramblers Association v. Kent C.C.* (1990) 60 P. & C.R. 464 and *Vasiliou v. Secretary of State for Transport* [1991] 2 All E.R. 77 (decided under the equivalent provisions of the Town and Country Planning Act 1971).

[20] See *Bailey v. Jamieson* (1876) 1 C.P.D. 329.

[21] *Dawes v. Hawkins* (1860) 8 C.B. (N.S.) 848 at 858, *per* Byles J.; *Suffolk C.C. v. Mason* [1979] A.C. 705 at 710, *per* Lord Diplock.

[22] *Walsh v. Oates* [1953] 1 Q.B. 578.

[23] *Att.-Gen. v. Shonleigh Nominees Ltd* [1974] 1 W.L.R. 305.

[24] For restrictive covenants generally, see *ante*, para. 16–030.

[25] See *ante*, para. 16–035.

[26] See n. 24, above.

IV. LICENCES

18–074 Here again there is some overlap. If A permits B to use a path across A's land, this may simply be a licence[27] given by A to B. But if the requirements for an easement are satisfied, the same right may be an easement (an easement of way). Yet not all licences have their counterparts in the law of easements. In general the categories of easements are old and restricted, whereas the categories of licences are new and flexible. In particular, there are the following differences.

(i) An easement requires a dominant tenement, a licence does not.

(ii) There are rules of formality for the creation of easements,[28] but not of licences.[29]

(iii) An easement cannot give a general right to occupy land.[30] A licence may do so.[31] For example, the right to occupy lodgings in a lodging-house is a licence, but cannot be an easement.

Whether or not a particular grant creates an easement or a licence is a matter of construction.[32] However, the use of the term "licence" and not the words usually employed to grant an easement in a professionally drafted deed will strongly suggest that a licence was intended.[33]

V. RIGHTS RESULTING FROM THE RULE AGAINST DEROGATION FROM GRANT

18–075 **1. Derogation.** A person who sells or lets land, knowing that the purchaser intends to use it for a particular purpose, may not do anything which hampers the use of the purchaser's land for the purpose which both parties contemplated at the time of the transaction. A grantor may not derogate from his grant.[34] Although this principle "conjures up images of parchment and sealing wax, of copperplate handwriting and fusty title deeds",[35] it "merely embodies

---

[27] For licences see *ante*, para. 17–001.

[28] *Post*, para. 18–092.

[29] But see *ante*, para. 17–006.

[30] *Ante*, para. 18–005.

[31] *Ante*, para. 14–015. In *Att.-Gen. of Southern Nigeria v. John Holt & Co. (Liverpool) Ltd* [1915] A.C. 599, *ante*, para. 18–055, a claim to occupy foreshore failed as an easement but succeeded as a licence.

[32] *IDC Group Ltd v. Clark* [1992] 2 E.G.L.R. 184. Contrast the position where the issue is whether a right of occupation creates a lease or a licence: *ante*, para. 14–013. There is no logical reason why the distinction between a licence and an easement should be one of construction while that between a lease and a licence is a matter of law.

[33] *ibid.*

[34] *cf. ante*, paras 14–208, 14–209, where examples are given. See generally (1964) 80 L.Q.R. 244 (D. W. Elliott).

[35] *Johnston & Sons Ltd v. Holland* [1988] 1 E.G.L.R. 264 at 267, *per* Nicholls L.J. The case contains an important discussion of the principle.

in a legal maxim a rule of common honesty".[36] "A grantor having given a thing with one hand is not to take away the means of enjoying it with the other."[37] "If A lets a plot to B, he may not act so as to frustrate the purpose for which in the contemplation of both parties the land was hired."[38]

2. A right of property. In so far as this doctrine restricts the grantor's freedom to use any of his neighbouring land which he may have retained, it is really part of the law of property, since the rights which it creates bind not only the grantor but also all who claim title through him; so that, in effect, the grantee and his successors in title have a proprietary interest of a special kind against the grantor's land, into whosesoever hands it may pass.[39] For example, where a lease was granted to a timber merchant who required a free flow of air to his stacks of drying timber, it was held that a purchaser of the lessor's adjoining land could not build upon it so as to obstruct the ventilation required by the lessee.[40] The right claimed was one which could not exist as an easement since the air did not flow through any definable channel or aperture.[41] "The implications usually explained by the maxim . . . do not stop short with easements."[42] It is in this that the importance of the doctrine lies. Paradoxically, the law will allow a grant made for a particular purpose to create rights which are really proprietary and which yet, according to the rules for easements, do not lie in grant. **18–076**

3. Application. The doctrine is not confined to cases of landlord and tenant: it may apply as well to a sale as to a lease.[43] Indeed it applies to all forms of grant[44] and is not confined to real property.[45] It is sometimes said to rest upon an implied promise[46]; but it is in truth an independent rule of law, and has nothing to do with restrictive covenants or the equitable doctrine of notice.[47] **18–077**

---

[36] *Harmer v. Jumbil (Nigeria) Tin Areas Ltd* [1921] 1 Ch. 200 at 225, *per* Younger L.J.
[37] *Birmingham Dudley & District Banking Co. v. Ross* (1888) 38 Ch.D. 295 at 313, *per* Bowen L.J.
[38] *Lyttelton Times Co. Ltd v. Warners Ltd* [1907] A.C. 476 at 481, *per* Lord Loreburn L.C.
[39] *Johnston & Sons Ltd v. Holland, supra*, at 268.
[40] *Aldin v. Latimer Clark, Muirhead & Co.* [1894] 2 Ch. 437; *cf. Thomas v. Owen* (1887) 20 Q.B.D. 225.
[41] *Ante*, para. 18–057.
[42] *Browne v. Flower* [1911] 1 Ch. 219 at 225, *per* Parker J. See too *Johnston & Sons Ltd v. Holland, supra*, at 267.
[43] *Cable v. Bryant* [1908] 1 Ch. 259, where the maxim was resorted to because the adjoining land was in lease at the time of the sale, and it was said that a reversionary easement could not be granted; *Woodhouse & Co. Ltd v. Kirkland (Derby) Ltd* [1970] 1 W.L.R. 1185.
[44] *Johnston & Sons Ltd v. Holland, supra*, at 267.
[45] It has been applied to the sale of a car by the manufacturer: *British Leyland Motor Corporation Ltd v. Armstrong Patents Ltd* [1986] A.C. 577 at 641.
[46] *North Eastern Ry. v. Elliot* (1860) 1 J. & H. 145 at 153.
[47] *Cable v. Bryant, supra*, at 264. This statement was approved by Lord Denning M.R. in *Molton Builders Ltd v. City of Westminster L.B.C.* (1975) 30 P. & C.R. 182 at 186. See too *Johnston & Sons Ltd v. Holland, supra*, at 267.

VI. CUSTOMARY RIGHTS OF FLUCTUATING BODIES

18–078   We have already seen examples of customary rights, *e.g.* for parishioners to use a path to the church, or to water cattle at a pond.[48] Such rights differ from easements in that they are exercisable by all who are included within the custom, independently of ownership of a dominant tenement and independently of any grant. They differ from public rights in that they are exercisable only by members of some local community,[49] not by members of the public generally. The user must be as of right and, as such, linked to a particular locality.[50] For these purposes, the locality must, it seems, be some unit recognised in law, such as a parish or town.[51]

A custom really amounts to a special local law, a local variation of the common law. The common law recognises such variations only if they are ancient, certain, reasonable and continuous.[52] To be "ancient" a custom must date back to the year 1189, the beginning of legal memory; but ancient origin may be presumed if there has been long enjoyment and there is no proof of a later origin.[53] Nor is it a fatal objection that the nature of the custom has changed with the times; for example, an ancient custom to play games has been held to cover cricket, "although it is reasonably certain that cricket was unknown until long after the time of Richard I".[54] Customs have been proved for the holding of a fair or wake[55]; for the fishermen of a parish to dry their nets on private land[56]; and for inhabitants of a parish "to enter upon certain land in the parish, erect a maypole thereon, and dance round and about it, and otherwise enjoy on the land any lawful and innocent recreation at any times in the year".[57] Such rights are not lost by disuse or waiver.[58] Special customs of many kinds were also to be found in manors.

---

[48] *Ante*, para. 18–059.

[49] *Manning v. Wasdale* (1836) 5 A. & E. 758 (parish); *Race v. Ward* (1855) 4 E. & B. 702 (town); *New Windsor Corporation v. Mellor* [1975] Ch. 380 (town). It suffices if the land is used predominantly by the inhabitants of the locality, even if others may also use it: *R. v. Oxfordshire C.C., ex p. Sunningwell P.C.* [1999] 3 W.L.R. 160 at 173.

[50] *R. v. Suffolk C.C., ex p. Steed* (1995) 70 P. & C.R. 487 at 503, 504 (enjoyment of right by persons who happen to come from a particular geographical area insufficient). Aff'd on a different ground: [1997] 1 E.G.L.R. 131 at 134.

[51] *Ministry of Defence v. Wiltshire C.C.* [1995] 4 All E.R. 931 at 937 (residents of three streets did not constitute a locality). *cf. R. v. Suffolk C.C., ex p. Steed* (1995) 70 P. & C.R. 487 at 504. These two cases, which raised very similar issues, were decided only two days apart and in ignorance of the other.

[52] *Lockwood v. Wood* (1844) 6 Q.B. at 64; and see the discussion of such rights in *Mercer v. Denne* [1904] 2 Ch. 534 at 552–554; [1905] 2 Ch. 538.

[53] See *Simpson v. Wells* (1872) L.R. 7 Q.B. 214 (custom to have stalls in statutory hiring fair held bad because origin of fair was statute of Edward III or later); *Mercer v. Denne* [1904] 2 Ch. 534, [1905] 2 Ch. 538.

[54] *Mercer v. Denne* [1904] 2 Ch. 534 at 553, *per* Farwell J. (aff'd [1905] 2 Ch. 538). See too *R. v. Oxfordshire C.C., ex p. Sunningwell P.C., supra*, at 172.

[55] *Wyld v. Silver* [1963] Ch. 243 (discussing the mode of enforcement of such rights).

[56] *Mercer v. Denne* [1905] 2 Ch. 538.

[57] *Hall v. Nottingham* (1875) 1 Ex.D. 1, headnote.

[58] *Wyld v. Silver, supra; New Windsor Corporation v. Mellor, supra* (right of inhabitants to use town green for sports and pastimes).

Section 2. Nature of a *Profit à Prendre*

A *profit à prendre* has been described as "a right to take something off another **18–079** person's land".[59] This it is, but not all such rights are profits. If the right is to be a profit, the thing taken must be either part of the land,[60] *e.g.* minerals or crops, or the wild animals existing on it[61]; and the thing taken must at the time of taking be susceptible of ownership.[62] A right to "hawk, hunt, fish and fowl" may thus exist as a profit,[63] for this gives the right to take creatures living on the soil which, when killed, are capable of being owned.[64] But a right to take water from a spring or a pump,[65] or the right to water cattle at a pond,[66] may be an easement but cannot be a profit; for the water, when taken, was not owned by anyone[67] nor was it part of the soil.[68]

Rights exercised by a person over part of his own land which, if that part were owned and occupied by another, would be profits, are sometimes called quasi-profits; and similar principles apply to them as apply to quasi-easements.[69]

A. Classification of Profits à Prendre

I. AS TO OWNERSHIP

A *profit à prendre* may be enjoyed— **18–080**

    (i) by one person to the exclusion of all others: this is known as a several profit; or

    (ii) by one person in common with others: this is known as a profit in common, or a common.

---

[59] *Duke of Sutherland v. Heathcote* [1892] 1 Ch. 475 at 484, *per* Lindley L.J.

[60] *Manning v. Wasdale* (1836) 5 A. & E. 758 at 764.

[61] Halsb. vol. 14, p. 116.

[62] *Race v. Ward* (1855) 4 E. & B. 702 at 709; *Lowe v. J.W. Ashmore Ltd* [1971] Ch. 545 at 557.

[63] *Wickham v. Hawker* (1840) 7 M. & W. 63.

[64] *Case of Swans* (1592) 7 Co.Rep. 15b at 17b; *Blades v. Higgs* (1865) 11 H.L.C. 621; *Lord Fitzhardinge v. Purcell* [1908] 2 Ch. 139 at 168. There is no established meaning to the word "game". The scope of a grant or reservation of a right to take game is therefore a matter of construction: *Inglewood Investment Co. Ltd v. Forestry Commissioners* [1988] 1 W.L.R. 1278 (reservation of "all game woodcocks snipe and other wild fowl hares rabbits and fish" did not include deer). See too *Pole v. Peake* [1998] E.G.C.S. 125.

[65] See *Polden v. Bastard* (1865) L.R. 1 Q.B. 156.

[66] *Manning v. Wasdale, supra.* As to water stored in a tank, see (1938) 2 Conv. (N.S.) 203 (J. S. Fiennes); but the authorities seem unsatisfactory.

[67] *Embrey v. Owen* (1851) 6 Exch. 353 at 369. Game becomes the subject of ownership as soon as killed (see n. 64, *supra*), *i.e.* sometimes before being taken; water is reduced into ownership only at the time of taking. Yet the difference between taking fish in a net and taking water in a bucket seems slight.

[68] *Manning v. Wasdale, supra*, at 764; *Race v. Ward, supra*, at 709.

[69] See *ante*, para. 18–050.

II. IN RELATION TO LAND

18–081   Unlike an easement, a profit is not necessarily appurtenant to land. It may exist in the following forms.

18–082   **1. A profit appurtenant.** This is a profit, whether several or in common, which by act of parties, actual or presumed,[70] is annexed to some nearby dominant tenement and runs with it. In general there must be compliance with the four conditions necessary for the existence of an easement, which is always appurtenant.[71] Thus a profit of piscary appurtenant cannot be exploited for commercial purposes; the number of fish taken must be limited to the needs of the dominant tenement.[72] There may, however, be cases where the profit is one of pasture and is defined not by reference to the specific needs of the dominant tenement but as a right to graze a specific number of animals. In such a case, the profit is alienable apart from the dominant tenement and thereupon becomes a profit in gross.[72a]

18–083   **2. A profit appendant.** This is a profit annexed to land by operation of law; probably it exists only in the form of a common of pasture.[73] If before the Statute *Quia Emptores* 1290[74] the lord of a manor subinfeudated arable land to a freeholder, the freeholder obtained as appendant to the arable land the right to pasture, on the waste land of the manor, animals to plough and manure the land granted to him[75]; for "he must have some place to keep such cattle in whilst the corn is growing on his own arable land".[76] This right was known as a common of pasture appendant and was limited both as to the kind and number of animals which could be depastured. It extended only to horses and oxen (to plough the land) and cows and sheep (to manure it),[77] and only to the number of these "levant and couchant" on the land to which the right was appendant, *i.e.* the number which the dominant tenement was capable of maintaining by its produce during the winter, including the hay and other crops obtained from it in the other seasons of the year.[78] It was immaterial that the land was at any particular time used for purposes temporarily rendering the maintenance of cattle impossible, for the test was not the number actually supported but the number which the land could be made to support.[79] Where

---

[70] *i.e.* by prescription. See *White v. Taylor* [1969] 1 Ch. 150 at 158.

[71] *Ante,* para. 18–043.

[72] *Harris v. Earl of Chesterfield* [1911] A.C. 623; and see *post,* para. 18–222.

[72a] *Bettison v. Langton* [1999] 3 W.L.R. 39. For profits in gross, see *post,* para. 18–085.

[73] See Halsb., vol. 6, p. 220. Tudor L.C.R.P. states that other profits appendant exist, *e.g.* piscary (713), estovers (714) and turbary (716), but authority for this seems to be lacking.

[74] *Ante,* para. 2–040.

[75] *Earl of Dunraven v. Llewellyn* (1850) 15 Q.B. 791 at 810.

[76] *Bennett v. Reeve* (1740) Willes 227 at 231, *per* Willes C.J.

[77] *Tyrringham's Case* (1584) 4 Co.Rep. 36b at 37a.

[78] *Robertson v. Hartopp* (1889) 43 Ch.D. 484 at 516; *Re Ilkley and Burley Moors* (1983) 47 P. & C.R. 324 at 329.

[79] *Robertson v. Hartopp, supra,* at 516, 517.

rights of pasture are registered under the Commons Registration Act,[79a] levancy and couchancy are abolished. Instead the registration must be for a fixed number of animals.[79b]

No common appendant could be created after 1290, for a conveyance of freehold land in a manor after that date resulted in the feoffee holding of the feoffor's lord, and the land passed out of the manor altogether.[80]

3. A profit pur cause de vicinage. This also exists only in the form of a common of pasture. It is a true right of common and not merely a defence to an action of trespass.[81] If two adjoining commons are open to each other, there is a common *pur cause de vicinage* if the cattle put on one common by the commoners have always been allowed to stray to the other common and *vice versa*.[82] The claim fails if in the past the cattle have been driven off one common by the commoners thereof,[83] or if the commons have been fenced off (as may be done from either side at any time[84]), or if the two commons are not contiguous to each other, even if they are separated only by a third common.[85]

18–084

4. A profit in gross. This is a profit, whether several or in common, exercisable by the owner independently of his ownership of land; there is no dominant tenement.[86] Thus a right to take fish from a canal without stint (*i.e.* without limit) can exist as a profit in gross,[87] but not, as already seen,[88] as a profit appurtenant. A profit in gross is an interest in land which will pass under a will or intestacy or can be sold or dealt with in any of the usual ways,[89] being an incorporeal hereditament.[90]

18–085

B. Distinctions between Profits à Prendre and Certain Analogous Rights

I. PUBLIC RIGHTS

The public right which most closely resembles a profit is the right of the public to fish in the sea and all tidal waters.[91] In theory the right is the Crown's, and it was formerly possible for the Crown to grant to an individual

18–086

[79a] s.15; *post*, para. 18–219. For the Commons Registration Act 1965, see *post*, paras 18–179 *et seq.*

[79b] *Bettison v. Langton, supra.*

[80] *Baring v. Abingdon* [1892] 2 Ch. 374 at 378; *ante*, para. 2–040.

[81] *Newman v. Bennett* [1981] Q.B. 726.

[82] *Pritchard v. Powell* (1845) 10 Q.B. 589 at 603; *Newman v. Bennett, supra.*

[83] *Heath v. Elliott* (1838) 4 Bing.N.C. 388.

[84] *Tyringham's Case* (1584) 4 Co.Rep. 36b.

[85] *Commissioners of Sewers of the City of London v. Glasse* (1874) L.R. 19 Eq. 134.

[86] *Lord Chesterfield v. Harris* [1908] 2 Ch. 397 at 421 (in H.L. [1911] A.C. 623).

[87] *Staffordshire and Worcestershire Canal Navigation v. Bradley* [1912] 1 Ch. 91.

[88] *Ante*, para. 18–082.

[89] *e.g.* leased (*Staffordshire and Worcestershire Canal Navigation v. Bradley, supra.*)

[90] *Webber v. Lee* (1882) 9 Q.B.D. 315; *Lovett v. Fairclough* (1990) 61 P. & C.R. 385 at 396.

[91] The right to fish includes the ancillary rights to cross the foreshore in order to fish and to take worms from the foreshore to be used as bait for that fishing: *Anderson v. Alnwick D.C.* [1993] 1 W.L.R. 1156.

the exclusive right to fish in a specified part of the sea or tidal waters. Such a franchise[92] was known as a free fishery.[93] The public may therefore fish in all tidal waters except a free fishery. But it has been held that the effect of *Magna Carta* 1215 was to prevent the Crown from creating any new free fisheries,[94] although any already existing remain valid and transferable to this day[95]; and a lawful origin may be inferred from long-continued enjoyment.[96]

The right of fishery in non-tidal waters is dealt with below.[97]

II. RIGHTS OF FLUCTUATING BODIES

18–087　There can be no custom for a fluctuating body of persons to take a profit.[98] The reason is said to be that otherwise the subject-matter would be destroyed, "and such a claim, which might leave nothing for the owner of the soil, is wholly inconsistent with the right of property in the soil".[99] Neither can such rights exist as profits, for a profit lies in grant just like an easement[1] and a fluctuating body is not a capable grantee.

Yet if such a right has in fact been enjoyed for a long time, as of right[2] and not merely by toleration,[3] the courts will strive to find a legal origin for it. "The first thing the court looks at as the criterion of property is usage and enjoyment . . . . Very high judges have said they would presume any thing in favour of a long enjoyment and uninterrupted possession."[4] Upon this principle two methods have been evolved for circumventing the rule against these customs, which in modern times finds little favour with the courts.

18–088　**1. Presumed incorporation by Crown grant.** The Crown is able to incorporate any body of persons and so endow them, as a corporation, with a single legal personality. Thus the Crown could grant a charter to a village making it a city or borough. Consequently there is nothing to prevent the Crown from making a grant of a profit to the inhabitants of a district and providing therein that for the purposes of the grant they should be treated as a corporation, though for other purposes they remain unincorporated. The obstacle that there is no definite person or persons in whose favour a grant

---

[92] A franchise is an incorporeal hereditament: *ante*, para. 18–013.

[93] Cru.Dig. iii, 261; see, *e.g. Stephens v. Snell* [1939] 3 All E.R. 622.

[94] *Malcolmson v. O'Dea* (1863) 10 H.L.C. 593 at 618, criticised in Theobald, *Law of Land* (2nd ed.), pp. 58 *et seq.*

[95] *Neill v. Duke of Devonshire* (1882) 8 App.Cas. 135 at 180.

[96] *Malcolmson v. O'Dea, supra: Loose v. Castleton* (1978) 41 P. & C.R. 19.

[97] *Post*, para. 18–222.

[98] *Gateward's Case* (1607) 7 Co.Rep. 59b; *Commissioners of Sewers of the City of London v. Glasse* (1872) 7 Ch.App. 456 at 465; *Alfred F. Beckett Ltd v. Lyons* [1967] Ch. 449.

[99] *Race v. Ward* (1855) 4 E. & B. 702 at 709, *per* Lord Campbell C.J.; and see *Chesterfield v. Fountaine* (1895) [1908] 1 Ch. 243n.

[1] *Ante*, para. 18–051.

[2] See *post*, para. 18–123.

[3] *Alfred F. Beckett Ltd v. Lyons, supra.*

[4] *Att.-Gen. v. Lord Hotham* (1823) T. & R. 209 at 217, 218, *per* Plumer M.R.

could be presumed[5] is thus surmounted by presuming the existence of a corporation created ad hoc in a grant from the Crown. In fact such grants have been made but rarely.[6] Their chief importance is that the court will presume such a grant to have been made[7] provided that—

(i) long enjoyment is proved; and

(ii) the right claimed derives from the Crown; and

(iii) those claiming the grant and their predecessors have always regarded themselves as a corporation and acted as such as regards the right, as by holding meetings or appointing some officer to supervise the right.[8]

2. Presumed charitable trust. Even when the claimants are destitute of   **18–089**
any sign of corporate capacity,[9] the difficulty may not be insuperable. If long enjoyment[10] is shown the court may succeed in finding a legal origin for the right by presuming a grant of the profit to some existing corporation, subject to a trust or condition that the corporation should allow the claimants to exercise the right claimed. This in *Goodman v. Mayor of Saltash*[11] the free inhabitants of certain ancient tenements had for 200 years enjoyed an oyster fishery from Candlemas (February 2) to Easter Eve each year. This right had been shared by the local corporation, which had enjoyed the right all the year round from time immemorial. The House of Lords refused to presume a grant incorporating the inhabitants for the purpose of the grant, but by "a splendid effort of equitable imagination"[12] held that the corporation was entitled to a profit subject to a trust or condition in favour of the free inhabitants. More recently, a court applying these principles has been prepared to presume that a right of recreation over Doncaster Common, in favour of the general public, had a lawful origin.[13] Such a trust is charitable, since it exists to benefit the inhabitants of a particular place, as a section of the public, and so it is not subject to the rule against trusts of perpetual duration.[14] But enjoyment as of right is essential. Local inhabitants claiming to be entitled to collect coal on

[5] *Fowler v. Dale* (1594) Cro.Eliz. 362.
[6] See, *e.g. Willingale v. Maitland* (1866) L.R. 3 Eq. 103, explained in *Chilton v. Corporation of London (No. 2)* (1878) 7 Ch.D. 735.
[7] *Re Free Fishermen of Faversham* (1887) 36 Ch.D. 329.
[8] See *Lord Rivers v. Adams* (1878) 3 Ex.D. 361 at 366, 367 (where the claim failed for want of corporate acts).
[9] See *e.g. Harris v. Earl of Chesterfield* [1911] A.C. 623 at 639.
[10] *e.g. Haigh v. West* [1893] 2 Q.B. 19 (claim to pasturage by roadside succeeded on proof of 115 years' user). Examples of unsuccessful claims under this doctrine are *Lord Fitzhardinge v. Purcell* [1908] 2 Ch. 139; *Harris v. Earl of Chesterfield* [1911] A.C. 623.
[11] (1882) 7 App.Cas. 633. For a discussion of the problems of reconciling the *Goodman* case with general principles of the law of charity, see *Peggs v. Lamb* [1994] Ch. 172 at 193 *et seq.*
[12] *Harris v. Earl of Chesterfield* [1911] A.C. 623 at 633, *per* Lord Ashbourne, dissenting.
[13] *R. v. Doncaster B.C., ex p. Braim* (1986) 57 P. & C.R. 1; [1988] Conv. 369 (J. Hill). Doncaster Common is used (*inter alia*) as the site of the St. Leger.
[14] *Ante*, para. 7–151.

the foreshore therefore failed when they could show only a practice sufficiently explained by mere toleration.[15] A trust is not normally presumed against a landowner who can show a documentary title bearing no trace of it.[16] This is not an absolute rule, however, and the facts may be such that the court can presume the express creation of a trust by the landowner by a document since lost.[17]

Section 3. Acquisition of Easements and Profits

18–090   An easement or profit can exist as a legal interest in land only if it is—

(i) held for an interest equivalent to a fee simple absolute in possession or term of years absolute[18]; and

(ii) created either by statute, deed or prescription.

A document that is not a deed cannot create a legal[19] easement or profit, not even (it seems) for a term of three years or less.[20] But if made for value it may create a valid equitable easement[21] or profit.[22] Although formerly an oral agreement for value for such a right might create a valid equitable easement or profit if supported by sufficient acts of part performance,[23] that will no longer be the case, unless the circumstances are such as to merit the imposition of a constructive trust.[24]

The various methods of acquisition must now be considered.

---

[15] *Alfred F. Beckett Ltd v. Lyons* [1967] Ch. 449. See similarly *Mahoney v. Neenan* [1966] I.R. 559 (seaweed).

[16] *Goodman v. Mayor of Saltash* (1882) 7 App. Cas. 633 at 647; *Att.-Gen. v. Antrobus* [1905] 2 Ch. 188.

[17] *R. v. Doncaster B.C., ex p. Braim, supra*, at 11 (court prepared to presume grant where land had been acquired by Doncaster Corporation in 1505).

[18] L.P.A. 1925, s.1(2); *ante*, para. 4–047. Although the subsection does not mention profits expressly, it is almost beyond argument that they are covered by the words "easement, right, or privilege". In any case, a profit would fall within the definition of "land" in s.205(1)(ix), and would thus come within s.1(1). Section 62, which is manifestly intended to include profits, also does not mention them expressly, but is content to use words similar to those in s.1(2).

[19] L.P.A. 1925, s.52; *Hewlins v. Shippam* (1826) 5 B. & C. 221 (easement); *Duke of Somerset v. Fogwell* (1826) 5 B. & C. 875 (profit); *Armstrong v. Sheppard and Short Ltd* [1959] 2 Q.B. 384.

[20] *Hewlins v. Shippam, supra*, at 229; *Wood v. Leadbitter* (1845) 13 M. & W. 838 at 843; *Mason v. Clarke* [1954] 1 Q.B. 460 at 468, 471, reversed on other grounds, [1955] A.C. 778. L.P.A. 1925, s.54(2), will not assist interests which could not validly be created by parol at common law: *Rye v. Rye* [1962] A.C. 496, *ante*, para. 14–037.

[21] *May v. Belleville* [1905] 2 Ch. 605. For a valuable analysis of the cirumstances in which an equitable easement may now arise, see (1999) 115 L.Q.R. 89 (D. G. Barnsley). *cf. ante*, paras 5–104, 5–105.

[22] *Frogley v. Earl of Lovelace* (1859) John 333. But if for any reason the court would refuse specific performance of the contract (*e.g.* because it is tainted with fraud) there is no such equitable right: see *Mason v. Clarke, supra*. For this principle, see *ante*, para. 12–060.

[23] For the former doctrine of part performance, see *ante*, para. 12–017.

[24] See L.P. (M.P.)A. 1989, s.2(1)–(3), (5); *ante*, para. 12–044.

A. By Statute

Easements and profits created by statute are most frequently found in the case **18–091**
of local Acts of Parliament, *e.g.* an Act giving a right of support to a canal
constructed under statutory powers,[25] or an Inclosure Act giving the lord of
the manor shooting rights over land allotted to the commoners.[26] But statutory
rights analogous to easements are also often created by general Acts, *e.g.* Acts
giving rights to public utility undertakings in respect of electric cables, gas
pipes, water pipes, sewers and similar things.[27]

B. By Express Grant or Reservation

1. Grant The simplest way to create an easement or profit is by an express **18–092**
grant by deed. No special words are needed for a grant, so that a covenant or
agreement, if contained in a deed, will have the same effect.[28] The provisions
of section 62 of the Law of Property Act 1925, discussed below,[29] often cause
a conveyance to operate as an express grant of easements and profits which
are not expressly mentioned in the conveyance.

Before 1926 it was uncertain whether a grant of an easement without words
of limitation created more than an easement for the life of the grantee[30]; but
such a grant made after 1925 seems to give the grantee an easement in fee
simple under the ordinary rule,[31] provided that the grantor is able to create
such an interest, and that no contrary intention appears.[32]

It has been argued, but not decided, that an easement cannot be granted in
reversion, *i.e.* to take effect at some future time.[33] Since a grant requires a
grantee, a developer selling off plots of land cannot create easements in
advance of each sale.[34]

2. Reservation. Reservation is the converse of grant. When a landowner **18–093**
disposes of part of his land and retains the rest, he may wish to reserve
easements or profits over the part sold. Although this can now be achieved
quite simply, there were formerly difficulties. Before 1926 a legal easement or
profit could not be created by a simple reservation in favour of the grantor.
Any part of the land, or any pre-existing right over it, could be *excepted* from

---

[25] See, *e.g. London & North Western Ry. v. Evans* [1893] 1 Ch. 16.
[26] Halsb. Vol. 14, p. 122.
[27] See (1956) 20 Conv. (N.S.) 208 (J. F. Garner).
[28] *Russell v. Watts* (1885) 10 App.Cas. 590 at 611; *Dowty Boulton Paul Ltd v. Wolverhampton Corporation (No. 2)* [1976] Ch. 13.
[29] See *post,* para. 18–108.
[30] See *Hewlins v. Shippam* (1826) 5 B. & C. 221 at 228, 229, for some indication that words of limitation were necessary; and see the controversy between Underhill, Sweet and Williams (1908) 24 L.Q.R. 199, 259, 264.
[31] *Ante,* para. 3–030.
[32] L.P.A. 1925, s.60(1), as read with s.205(1)(ii), (ix) defining "conveyance" and "land". The wording of s.60(1) is not wholly appropriate to the creation of new interests as distinct from the transfer of existing interests (see *ante,* para. 3–030), but it would be inconvenient to hold it inapplicable to grants *de novo.*
[33] *Cable v. Bryant* [1908] 1 Ch. 259; *ante,* para. 18–077.
[34] Law Commission Working Paper No. 36, para. 112.

the grant, as, for example, minerals[35]; and some new right could be *reserved* if it was to issue out of the land granted, as did a rentcharge.[36] But an easement or profit created on a sale fell outside both these rules. It was not a pre-existing right, and it lay only in grant. Before 1926 a person could not grant to himself.[37] Devices were however devised to overcome this obstacle.[38]

The situation was rectified, at least in part, by the Law of Property Act 1925. It provides[39] that the reservation of a legal estate or interest "shall operate at law without execution of the conveyance by the grantee . . . or any regrant by him".

18–094 **3. Effect of grant or reservation.** The effect of a grant or reservation is a question of construction, which must be approached in the light of the rules that a grant is in general construed against the grantor[40] and that a person may not derogate from his grant.[41] Examples of the latter rule have already been given,[42] and examples of the former are given below.[43]

These rules governing grants ought also equally to govern reservations. The principle is that in case of doubt a man's legal acts should be construed against him, since the person who dictates the terms of the transaction cannot complain of not being given the benefit of any doubt.[44] But it has several times been said that the creation of easements by reservation under the Law of Property Act 1925 (explained above) represents a mere change of machinery, and that a reservation is to be construed as if it were a regrant.[45] Yet these statements conflict not only with the principle but also with express words in the Act ("shall operate at law without . . . any regrant . . . "), which do not seem to have been given their full effect.[46] The Court of Appeal has conceded that there is "much force in this reasoning"[47]; but it holds itself bound (though only *obiter*) by its earlier decision that a vendor's reservation is to be

---

[35] See Co.Litt. 47a; *Durham & Sunderland Ry. v. Walker* (1842) 2 Q.B. 940 at 967.
[36] Co.Litt. 143a.
[37] *Durham & Sunderland Ry. v. Walker, supra*, at 967.
[38] For an explanation of these, see the previous edition of this work at p. 857.
[39] s.65(1). The Act also provides that a conveyance of a legal estate expressed to be made subject to another legal estate not in existence immediately before the date of the conveyance, shall operate as a reservation, unless a contrary intention appear: s.65(2). A conveyance of land subject to an easement not yet in existence falls within this subsection, and takes effect as a reservation: see *Wiles v. Banks* (1984) 50 P. & C.R. 80.
[40] *Williams v. James* (1867) L.R. 2 C.P. 577 at 581; *Neill v. Duke of Devonshire* (1882) 8 App.Cas. 135 at 149.
[41] *Ante*, para. 18–075.
[42] *ibid*.
[43] *Post*, paras 18–100, 18–197.
[44] Thus at common law reservations (*e.g.* of rent or other services) and exceptions are construed against the person making them: *Lofield's Case* (1612) 10 Co.Rep. 106a; *Savill Bros. Ltd v. Bethell* [1902] 2 Ch. 523; Shep. Touch. 100.
[45] *Bulstrode v. Lambert* [1953] 1 W.L.R. 1064; *Mason v. Clarke* [1954] 1 Q.B. 460, reversed on other grounds, [1955] A.C. 778; *Johnstone v. Holdway* [1963] 1 Q.B. 601. See [1954] C.L.J. 191 (H.W.R.W.).
[46] *Cordell v. Second Clanfield Properties Ltd* [1969] 2 Ch. 9, holding that the reservation should be construed against the vendor.
[47] See *St Edmundsbury and Ipswich Diocesan Board of Finance v. Clark (No. 2)* [1975] 1 W.L.R. 468 at 479.

construed against the purchaser, contrary to the general rule for other reservations and exceptions.[48]

The judicial addiction to the anomaly of the pre-1926 law has even been **18–095** carried beyond questions of construction. Where land held upon trust was sold and conveyed by a deed which both the legal and the equitable owners executed, and in which the equitable owner reserved a right of way, it was held that this took effect in law as a regrant by the purchaser (to the equitable owner) of a legal easement, so that it did not create a mere equitable easement requiring registration as a land charge.[49]

4. Registered land. The grant or reservation of an easement by a registered **18–096** proprietor is a registered disposition that should be completed by registration of the burden of the right against the servient tenement.[50] The benefit of the easement is appurtenant to the dominant tenement and may be registered as such on the application of the registered proprietor.[51]

C. By Implied Reservation or Grant

1. Implied reservation. The general rule, as explained above, is that a grant **18–097** is construed in favour of the grantee. Therefore normally no easements will be implied in favour of a grantor; if he wishes to reserve any easements he must do so expressly.[52] To this rule there are two exceptions.

(a) Easements of necessity

(1) NECESSITY. If a grantor grants a plot of land in such circumstances as to **18–098** cut himself off completely from some other part of his own land (*e.g.* if a plot retained in the middle is completely surrounded by the part granted) there is implied in favour of the part retained a way of necessity over the part granted, for otherwise there would be no means of access to the land retained.[53] This rule is one of construction of the relevant grant, depending upon the intention of the parties as implied from the circumstances and not upon public policy.[54]

---

[48] *St Edmundsbury and Ipswich Diocesan Board of Finance v. Clark (No. 2), supra,* treating the point as concluded by *Johnstone v. Holdway, supra.* See too *Trailfinders Ltd v. Razuki* [1988] 2 E.G.L.R. 46 at 48.

[49] *Johnstone v. Holdway, supra.*

[50] L.R.A. 1925, ss.18(1), (2), 19(2), 21(1), 22(2); Ruoff & Roper, 9–13; *ante,* para. 6–031.

[51] L.R.R. 1925, rr. 252, 254, 257. The registrar is required to give such notice to the owner of the servient land as may seem advisable, and may enter a notice against the title of such land: *ibid.,* r. 253. If the registrar is not satisfied that the right claimed is appurtenant, he may make a qualified entry on the register of the alleged dominant tenement, or he may merely enter notice that the right is claimed by the proprietor: *ibid.,* r. 254.

[52] *Wheeldon v. Burrows* (1879) 12 Ch.D. 31 at 49 (a leading case on reservation of easements, reviewing the authorities); *Liddiard v. Waldron* [1934] 1 K.B. 435. For a neat illustration of the different positions of grantor and grantee, see Williams V. & P. 661, 662.

[53] *Pinnington v. Galland* (1853) 9 Exch. 1; *Manjang v. Drammeh* (1990) 61 P. & C.R. 194 at 197 (where Lord Oliver lists the essentials for the implication of such an easement of necessity). See (1981) 34 C.L.P. 133 (P. Jackson).

[54] *Nickerson v. Barraclough* [1981] Ch. 426; *Manjang v. Drammeh, supra,* at 197. Consequently there could be no such easement where land was acquired by escheat (*Proctor v. Hodgson* (1855) 10 Exch. 824) or by adverse possession (*Wilkes v. Greenway* (1890) 6 T.L.R. 449).

Whether the former owner of both plots of land retains or parts with the landlocked close, he may select the particular way to be enjoyed,[55] provided it is a convenient way[56]; and once selected, the route cannot subsequently be changed.[57] A way of necessity will be implied even if some of the surrounding land belongs to third parties[58]; but it is essential that the necessity should exist at the time of the grant and not merely arise subsequently.[59]

If some other way exists, even if it is by water rather than over land,[60] no way of necessity will be implied unless that other way is merely precarious and not as of right,[61] or unless, perhaps, it would be a breach of the law to use that other way for the purpose in question.[62] Nor will there be a way of necessity if the other way is merely inconvenient,[63] as where the land abuts on a highway in a cutting 20 feet below[64]; for the principle is that an easement of necessity is one "without which the property retained cannot be used at all, and not one merely necessary to the reasonable enjoyment of that property".[65] Thus if a man grants land and retains an adjoining house, no easement of light is implied in his favour, for the house is not unusable without the easement.[66] Yet where a landowner grants away the subsoil of his land (*e.g.* for mining), but retains the surface, an easement of support is implied in his favour.[67]

18–099   (2) CESSATION OF NECESSITY. It has not been conclusively settled whether an easement of necessity once acquired ceases when the necessity ceases.[68] Although there is some authority which suggests that it does,[69] the weight of English authority is now against it.[70] This seems correct in principle. A grant

---

[55] *Bolton v. Bolton* (1879) 11 Ch.D. 968 at 972. On a simultaneous grant of both plots (*e.g.* by devise) it seems that in the absence of any indication from the terms of the grant, any existing way which is used at the time will constitute the way of necessity: *Pearson v. Spencer* (1861) 1 B. & S. 571 at 585; aff'd. (1863) 3 B. & S. 761.

[56] *Pearson v. Spencer, supra.*

[57] *Deacon v. South Eastern Ry.* (1889) 61 L.T. 377.

[58] *Barry v. Hasseldine* [1952] Ch.835.

[59] *Midland Ry. v. Miles* (1886) 33 Ch.D. 632.

[60] *Manjang v. Drammeh* (1990) 61 P. & C.R. 194 (no easement of necessity where there was water-borne access to premises over the River Gambia); [1992] C.L.J. 220 (C.H.).

[61] *Barry v. Hasseldine, supra.*

[62] See *Hansford v. Jago* [1921] 1 Ch. 322 at 342, 343, where it was suggested but not decided that a way of necessity might arise when the only alternative way of emptying earth closets was by carrying the contents through cottages in breach of a by-law.

[63] *Dodd v. Burchell* (1862) 1 H. & C. 113.

[64] *Titchmarsh v. Royston Water Co. Ltd* (1899) 81 L.T. 673. See too *M.R.A. Engineering Ltd v. Trimster Co. Ltd* (1987) 56 P. & C.R. 1 (no easement of necessity where there was pedestrian but not vehicular access to a house). cf. [1989] Conv. 355 at 356 (J. E. Martin).

[65] *Union Lighterage Co. v. London Graving Dock Co.* [1902] 2 Ch. 557 at 573, *per* Stirling L.J. See too *M.R.A. Engineering Ltd v. Trimster Co. Ltd, supra,* at 6.

[66] *Ray v. Hazeldine* [1904] 2 Ch. 17.

[67] *Richards v. Jenkins* (1868) 18 L.T. 437.

[68] See [1981] C.L.P. 133 at 145 (P. Jackson); [1990] Conv. 292 at 294 (G. Kodilinye).

[69] *Holmes v. Goring* (1824) 2 Bing. 76; better reported on this point at 9 Moo.C.P. 166. The remarks were *obiter.*

[70] See *Procter v. Hodgson* (1855) 10 Exch. 824; *Barkshire v. Grubb* (1881) 18 Ch.D. 616 at 620; *Huckvale v. Aegean Hotels Ltd* (1989) 58 P. & C.R. 163 at 168, 169. In Scotland, Canada and the USA the opposite rule prevails: see [1981] C.L.P. 133 at 146 (P. Jackson).

once implied should not be "affected by the chance subsequent acquisition of other property" by the grantee.[71]

(b) Intended easements. Easements required to carry out the common **18–100** intention of the parties will be implied in favour of the grantor even though not expressed in the conveyance. Thus on the grant of one of two houses supported by each other, the mutual grant and reservation of easements of support will be implied (as is usual) such an intention can be inferred.[72] It is, however, essential in such cases that the parties should intend that the servient tenement should be used in the particular way claimed as an easement: an intent that there should be user which might or might not involve the user claimed as an easement is not enough.[73] A grantor alleging an intended reservation of an easement bears a heavy burden of proof.[74]

2. Implied grant. In favour of a grantee easements are implied much more **18–101** readily, on the principle that a grant must be construed in the amplest rather than in the narrowest way. An express grant of the land is therefore often accompanied by the implied grant of easements.[75] Rights which will arise by implied grant are as follows.

(a) Easements of necessity,[76] and **18–102**

(b) Intended easements. The rules which apply in these two cases are similar to those in the case of implied reservation, except that the court is readier to imply easements in favour of the grantee than in favour of the grantor.[77] Indeed in cases of implied grant, the authorities suggest that there is little difference between easements of necessity and intended easements.[78] The grantee must show that at the date of the grant, the parties had a common intention that the property should be used in some definite and particular manner, and that the easement claimed was necessary to give effect to this

---

[71] *Maude v. Thornton* [1929] I.R. 454 at 458, *per* Meredith J.

[72] *Richards v. Rose* (1853) 9 Exch. 218 at 221; *cf. Shubrook v. Tufnell* (1882) 46 L.T. 886, which treats such rights as easements of necessity. For other examples, see *Jones v. Pritchard* [1908] 1 Ch. 630 (common flue); *Cory v. Davies* [1923] 2 Ch. 95 (use of drive); *Simpson v. Weber* (1925) 133 L.T. 46 (right to let creeper climb neighbour's wall, and support for gate); *Peckham v. Ellison* (1998) 77 P. & C.R. D27 (rear access to house); contrast *Pwllbach Colliery Co. Ltd v. Woodman* [1915] A.C. 634 at 647; *Re Webb's Lease* [1951] Ch. 808; *Chaffe v. Kingsley* (1997) 77 P. & C.R. 281. Where a party wall notice has been served under the Party Wall, etc., Act 1996 (*ante*, para. 9–109), the rights conferred by that Act supersede any common law rights arising from an implied easement of support: see *e.g. Selby v. Whitbread* [1917] 1 K.B. 736.

[73] *Pwllbach Colliery Co. Ltd v. Woodman, supra*, at 647.

[74] *cf. Re Webb's Lease, supra.*

[75] *Phillips v. Low* [1892] 1 Ch. 47 at 50.

[76] *Pinnington v. Galland* (1853) 9 Exch. 1 at 12.

[77] *Richards v. Rose* (1853) 9 Exch. 218; *Pwllbach Colliery Co. Ltd v. Woodman, supra*, at 646; *Stafford v. Lee* (1992) 65 P. & C.R. 172 at 175; and see *Wheeldon v. Burrows* (1879) 12 Ch.D. 31; *Barry v. Hasseldine, supra.*

[78] Compare *Wong v. Beaumont Property Trust Ltd* [1965] 1 Q.B. 173 at 180 with *Stafford v. Lee, supra*, at 175.

purpose.[79] In one case a landlord let cellars to a tenant who covenanted to use them as a restaurant, to eliminate smells and to comply with health regulations. In fact, unknown to the parties, this could not lawfully be done without installing a proper ventilation system, and so it was held that the tenant had an easement of necessity to construct such a system (partly on the landlord's part of the premises) and use it.[80] Similarly, easements necessary for the enjoyment of some right expressly granted will be implied, *e.g.* a right to use stairs, lifts and rubbish chutes on the letting of a maisonette in a tower block,[81] or a right of way to a spring, on the grant of an easement to draw water from it.[82] But a squatter can claim no way of necessity.[83]

(c) Easements within the rule in Wheeldon v. Burrows

18–103   (1) SCOPE OF THE RULE. *Wheeldon v. Burrows*[84] determines what easements are implied in favour of the grantee of one part of a holding against the owner of the remainder. It is really a branch of the general rule against derogation from grant.[85] It relates not to the transmission of existing easements over the land of third parties (these, being already appurtenant to the land granted, naturally pass with it) but to the translation into easements of rights over the grantor's retained land which are necessary to the proper enjoyment of the land granted. It is natural for this purpose to look at the grantor's previous use of the land, and to allow the grantee to take easements corresponding to the facilities which the grantor himself found necessary.[86] Before the grant they cannot have been easements because of the common ownership. They are therefore called "quasi-easements", *i.e.* rights which are potential easements in case of a division of the land.[87]

18–104   (2) THE RULE. *Wheeldon v. Burrows*[88] was a case where a long line of earlier authorities was summed up in a general rule.[89] It laid down that upon the grant of part of a tenement, there would pass to the grantee as easements all quasi-easements over the land retained which—

(i) were continuous and apparent,

---

[79] *Stafford v. Lee, supra.* In the absence of extrinsic evidence of the parties' intentions at that time, the court will construe the grant in the light of surrounding circumstances: *ibid.*

[80] *Wong v. Beaumont Property Trust Ltd, supra.*

[81] *Liverpool City Council v. Irwin* [1977] A.C. 239.

[82] *Pwllbach Colliery Co. Ltd v. Woodman, supra*, at 646.

[83] *Wilkes v. Greenway* (1890) 6 T.L.R. 449; *ante*, para. 3–126.

[84] (1879) 12 Ch.D. 31.

[85] *ibid.*, at 49; *M.R.A. Engineering Ltd v. Trimster Co. Ltd* (1987) 56 P. & C.R. 1 at 7. For that rule, see *ante*, para. 18–075. Consequently no such easements arise on a compulsory purchase: *Sovmots Investments Ltd v. Secretary of State for the Environment* [1979] A.C. 144.

[86] Regard may be had to issues such as safety in determining what is necessary: see *Millman v. Ellis* (1995) 71 P. & C.R. 158 at 163 (egress on to main road unsafe without right of way).

[87] See *ante*, para. 18–050.

[88] *Supra.*

[89] The decision itself, however, was concerned with implied reservation rather than with implied grant. The rules for implied grant were set out by way of contrast.

(ii) were necessary for the reasonable enjoyment of the land granted,[90] and

(iii) had been, and were at the time of the grant,[91] used by the grantor for the benefit of the part granted.

Although it is by no means clear how far requirements (i) and (ii) are distinct,[92] the most recent decision of the Court of Appeal has treated them as separate requirements, both of which must be met.[93-94] The distinction between "continuous and apparent" easements and others was unknown to English law until 1839, when it seems to have been imported by a text-writer from the French law of prescription.[95] It then became a source of confusion, since it did not fit easily into the older and wider English rule against derogation from grant[96]; nor was it always insisted upon, or correctly understood. However, the history of the rule provides justification for the view that the Court of Appeal has now taken, as it tends to suggest that the two requirements were intended to have distinct functions.[97]

Because the rule rests on the principle of non-derogation from grant, it can apply even though the conveyance of the dominant tenement includes the express grant of a more limited easement.[98] But the implication of an easement will not be made if it is inconsistent with the terms of the express grant.[99]

(3) "CONTINUOUS AND APPARENT". A "continuous" easement is one which is enjoyed passively, such as a right to use drains or a right to light, as opposed

18–105

---

[90] This does not mean that it must be an easement of necessity, *i.e.* an easement without which the property cannot be enjoyed *at all*, but merely that *reasonable* enjoyment of the property cannot be had without the easement: see *Wheeler v. J.J. Saunders Ltd* [1996] Ch. 19 at 25, 31. The easement must of course do more than merely accommodate the dominant tenement: see [1995] Conv. 239 at 240 (M. P. Thompson).

[91] See *Re St. Clement's, Leigh-on-Sea* [1988] 1 W.L.R. 720 at 729 (no implied grant where use of way had ceased long before the relevant conveyance).

[92] In *Wheeldon v. Burrows* (1879) 12 Ch.D. 31 they are treated in one place as synonymous at (49) and in another as alternative at (58). See *Squarey v. Harris-Smith* (1981) 42 P. & C.R. 118; (1967) 83 L.Q.R. 240 at 245 (A. W. B. Simpson); (1977) 41 Conv. (N.S.) 415 (C.H.).

[93-94] *Millman v. Ellis* (1995) 71 P. & C.R. 158; [1995] Conv. 346 (J. West). *cf. Wheeler v. J.J. Saunders Ltd, supra,* at 31; and [1995] Conv. 239 at 240 (M. P. Thompson).

[95] *Gale on Easements* (1st ed., 1839), p. 53; see *Dalton v. Angus & Co.* (1881) 6 App.Cas. 740 at 821, where Lord Blackburn explains the origins of this expression. In *Suffield v. Brown* (1864) 4 De G.J. & S. 185 at 195 Lord Westbury criticises it as "a mere fanciful analogy, from which rules of law ought not to be derived"; and see at 199 (though at 194 he appears to accept the doctrine for grants as distinct from reservations). In *Wheeldon v. Burrows, supra,* the Court of Appeal applied his distinction between grants and reservations, thus rejecting the principle of the French law which applied to both equally. Why the French terminology was nevertheless preserved is a mystery.

[96] The English rule goes back at least to 1663: *Palmer v. Fletcher* (1663) 1 Lev. 122.

[97] See *Watts v. Kelson* (1870) 6 Ch.App. 166 at 172; [1979] Conv. 113 at 117 (C.H.).

[98] *Millman v. Ellis, supra,* at 165. *cf. Gregg v. Richards* [1926] Ch. 521; *post,* para. 18–117.

[99] *Millman v. Ellis, supra,* at 164.

to one requiring personal activity for its enjoyment, such as a right of way.[1] An "apparent" easement is one which is evidenced by some sign on the dominant tenement[2] (or perhaps the servient tenement[3]) discoverable on "a careful inspection by a person ordinarily conversant with the subject".[4] Thus an underground drain into which water from the eaves of a house runs may be both continuous and apparent. Other examples are a watercourse running through visible pipes,[5] windows enjoying light[6] and a building enjoying support. On the other hand, a right to take water from a neighbour's pump from time to time[7] or a right to project the bowsprits of ships when in dock over the land of another[8] have been held to be outside the meaning of "continuous and apparent" easements.

Despite their adoption of these unsuitable terms, the courts have not applied them rigidly. Thus a right of way over a made road,[9] or one which betrays its presence by some indication such as a worn track[10] or its obvious use in connection with the land granted,[11] will pass under the rule in *Wheeldon v. Burrows*; and the court will, it seems, turn a blind eye to the obstacle that a right of way is not "continuous".[12] The rule against derogation from grant is a flexible doctrine, capable, indeed, of creating rights which cannot be easements at all.[13]

18–106   (4) SIMULTANEOUS GRANTS. The rules relating to implied grant apply also to cases where the grantor, instead of retaining any land himself, makes simultaneous grants to two or more grantees. Each grantee obtains the same easements over the land of the other as he would have obtained if the grantor had retained it.[14]

---

[1] Code Civil, Art. 688. See (1967) 83 L.Q.R. 240 (A. W. B. Simpson). *Suffield v. Brown* (1864) 4 De G.J. & S. 185 at 199, holding that "continuous" requires incessant use, is evidently erroneous. Gale in his 1st ed., 1839, at 53, confined his doctrine to "those easements only which are attended by some alteration which is in its nature obvious and permanent; or, in technical language, to those easements only which are apparent and continuous". He thus apparently equated "continuous" with "permanent".

[2] Code Civil, Art. 689; *Schwann v. Cotton* [1916] 2 Ch. 120 at 141 (aff'd at 459); *Ward v. Kirkland* [1967] Ch. 194 at 225 (right to go on neighbour's land to maintain wall on edge of dominant land held not continuous and apparent).

[3] See *Ward v. Kirkland, supra,* at 225.

[4] *Pyer v. Carter* (1857) 1 H. & N. 916 at 922, *per* Watson B. In so far as this case applied the same rule to implied reservation it cannot now be good law: *Wheeldon v. Burrows* (1879) 12 Ch.D. 31.

[5] *Watts v. Kelson* (1870) 6 Ch.App. 166.

[6] *Phillips v. Low* [1892] 1 Ch. 47 at 53.

[7] *Polden v. Bastard* (1865) L.R. 1 Q.B. 156; and see *Ward v. Kirkland* [1967] Ch. 194.

[8] *Suffield v. Brown* (1864) 4 De G.J. & S. 185.

[9] *Brown v. Alabaster* (1887) 37 Ch.D. 490.

[10] *Hansford v. Jago* [1921] 1 Ch. 322; *Borman v. Griffith* [1930] 1 Ch. 493; *Millman v. Ellis* (1995) 71 P. & C.R. 158.

[11] *Borman v. Griffith, supra.*

[12] *ibid.,* at 499.

[13] *Ante,* para. 18–076.

[14] *Swansborough v. Coventry* (1832) 2 Moo. & Sc. 362 (a better report than that in 9 Bing. 305: see *Broomfield v. Williams* [1897] 1 Ch. 602 at 616); *Hansford v. Jago, supra.*

(5) WILLS. Gifts by will are treated no differently from grants by deed for   **18–107**
purposes of implied easements.[15] Thus on a devise of adjoining houses to
different devisees, mutual rights of way over a connecting passage running
behind the houses have been implied.[16] The rules are rules of common law
and do not depend upon the grantee giving valuable consideration.

I. IMPLIED GRANT AND SECTION 62 OF THE LAW OF PROPERTY ACT 1925

1. Section 62. The operation of the rules relating to implied grant has been   **18–108**
considerably modified by the Law of Property Act 1925, s.62. This provision,
which dates from 1881[17] and so applies to all conveyances executed since
then,[18] is designed to make it unnecessary to set out the full effect of every
conveyance by "general words" extending it to all kinds of particulars. Now,
if no contrary intention is expressed, every conveyance of land passes with it
(*inter alia*) "all . . . liberties, privileges, easements, rights, and advantages
whatsoever, appertaining or reputed to appertain to the land, or any part
thereof, or, at the time of conveyance, . . . enjoyed with . . . the land or any
part thereof".[19] "Conveyance" includes, *inter alia*, mortgages, leases, and
assents,[20] but not a mere contract, *e.g.* for a lease for over three years[21] or for
the sale of the fee simple.[22] But a contract for sale may be relevant in
providing some evidence of what rights exist which can fall within the
statutory language when the conveyance is made.[23]

2. Creation of easements and profits

(a) No application to existing appurtenances. Section 62 has no effect on   **18–109**
existing easements or profits appurtenant to the land conveyed, which pass
with it automatically and without express mention.[24] Indeed where a person is
registered as proprietor of registered land (whether as first or subsequent
proprietor), such appurtenances vest in him by statute.[25]

(b) Creation of easements and profits

(1) APPLIES TO ALL QUASI-EASEMENTS AND QUASI-PROFITS. Section 62 has the   **18–110**
important effect of creating new easements and profits, by way of express

---

[15] *Phillips v. Low* [1892] 1 Ch. 47.
[16] *Milner's Safe Co. Ltd v. Great Northern & City Ry.* [1907] 1 Ch. 208.
[17] It replaces C.A. 1881, s.6.
[18] L.P.A. 1925, s.62(6).
[19] L.P.A. 1925, s.62(1); and see subs. (2) for conveyances of land with buildings on it. A right
    enjoyed with part of the land conveyed may benefit the whole: *Graham v. Philcox* [1984] Q.B.
    747.
[20] L.P.A. 1925, s.205(1)(ii).
[21] *Borman v. Griffith* [1930] 1 Ch. 493.
[22] *Re Peck and the School Board for London's Contract* [1892] 2 Ch. 315.
[23] See *White v. Taylor (No. 2)* [1969] 1 Ch. 160.
[24] *Godwin v. Schweppes Ltd* [1902] 1 Ch. 926 at 932.
[25] L.R.A. 1925, ss.5, 9, 20, 23.

grant,[26] out of all kinds of quasi-easements and quasi-profits.[27] It therefore goes beyond the rule in *Wheeldon v. Burrows*, which applies only to continuous and apparent quasi-easements and may not apply at all to quasi-profits. A quasi-easement which is not reasonably necessary to the enjoyment of the property granted but merely convenient (*e.g.* an alternative way of access through another person's house) can become an easement under section 62,[28] although it cannot under *Wheeldon v. Burrows*.

18–111   (2) NATURE OF RIGHTS CONVERTED. Section 62 will convert into full easements or profits (*inter alia*) the following rights—

> (i) a licence[29];
>
> (ii) a right that was accustomed to be exercised but the origin of which was perhaps unknown[30];
>
> (iii) a right that was reputed to be exercised with a particular property[31];
>
> (iv) a continuous and apparent quasi-easement[32];

provided that such right was enjoyed at the time when the conveyance was made.[33] "It matters not . . . whether the user is continuous and permanent or permissive and precarious."[34] It is remarkable that the section has been interpreted as having these surprising effects and the outcome has not escaped criticism.[35]

18–112   **3. Operation of the section.** Illustrations of the wide operation of section 62 are to be found in cases where the grantee has previously been tenant of the quasi-dominant tenement and has enjoyed certain additional rights by permission of the landlord. In one case, for example, the tenant had been allowed to use a roadway leading into a yard belonging to his landlord; the tenant eventually purchased the reversion, and it was held that he acquired an easement to use the roadway, even though his previous user was purely

---

[26] *Gregg v. Richards* [1926] Ch. 521 at 534, 535.

[27] *White v. Williams* [1922] 1 K.B. 727 (quasi-profit of sheepwalk); *Crow v. Wood* [1971] 1 Q.B. 77 (quasi-easement).

[28] *Goldberg v. Edwards* [1950] Ch. 247.

[29] *International Tea Stores Co. v. Hobbs* [1903] 2 Ch. 247.

[30] *White v. Williams, supra.* In the case of a quasi-easement of fencing, "it is immaterial that a party has voluntarily fenced his premises simply for . . . his own protection": *Crow v. Wood, supra*, at 87, *per* Edmund Davies L.J.

[31] *Newman v. Jones* [1982] March 22 (unrep., Megarry V.-C.); applied in *Handel v. St. Stephens Close Ltd* [1994] 1 E.G.L.R. 70 at 71, 72 (where tenants in a block of flats habitually parked their cars within the curtilage, the right was reputed to appertain to the flats and it was irrelevant that a previous tenant of a particular flat had not in fact had a car); *Pretoria Warehousing Co. Ltd v. Shelton* [1993] E.G.C.S. 120.

[32] *Bayley v. G.W.R.* (1884) 26 Ch.D. 434; *post*, para. 18–114.

[33] *Post*, para. 18–113.

[34] *White v. Williams, supra*, at 740, *per* Younger L.J.

[35] See [1998] Conv. 115 (L. Tee).

precarious.[36] A mere renewal of the tenant's lease would have had the same result, for a lease is equally a "conveyance" within the meaning of section 62, and nonetheless so because it was made informally,[37] provided that it was made in writing and not merely by word of mouth.[38] A landlord about to renew a lease should therefore take care first to revoke any licences which he has given to the tenant and prevent any further enjoyment of them, or else insert some provision in the new lease to exclude the application of section 62; otherwise section 62 may turn them into easements and give the tenant a right to enjoy them indefinitely.[39] Again, if a landlord lets a tenant into possession before granting a lease, and permits him to pass through a passage in the landlord's other property, the subsequent grant of the lease will turn this revocable licence into an irrevocable easement; for section 62 operates at the date of conveyance, and not at the date appointed by the conveyance for the beginning of the lessee's term.[40] Not surprisingly, the justice of this doctrine has been doubted.[41]

4. Limits of the section

(a) Right must be capable of existing as an easement. Section 62 cannot 18–113 create as an easement or profit a right which is incapable of being an easement or profit.[42] The object of the section is to shorten conveyances, not to extend the categories of interests known to the law. Thus the section cannot confer an easement for the protection of one house by another against weather,[43] or for a precarious right such as a right to take water from an artificial watercourse and pond if and when the landowner chooses to let water into them[44]; for such rights cannot exist as easements. Since section 62 operates by way of express grant, it will not create a right which the grantor had no power to grant,[45] as where he did not own the servient tenement.[46] Nor will it create a right out of

---

[36] *International Tea Stores Co. v. Hobbs* [1903] 2 Ch. 165, not cited in *White v. Taylor (No. 2)* [1969] 1 Ch. 160 at 185, which appears to assume the contrary. See too *Handel v. St Stephens Close Ltd, supra* (easement to park cars claimed by tenants following the renewal of their leases).

[37] *Wright v. Macadam* [1949] 2 K.B. 744.

[38] *Rye v. Rye* [1962] A.C. 496. For informal leases, see *ante*, para. 14–039.

[39] The automatic continuance of a weekly or other periodic tenancy for each new period would not be a "conveyance", but merely a continuance of the original grant: see *ante* para. 14–064; *Cattley v. Arnold* (1859) 1 J. & H. 651. See also (1962) 106 S.J. 483.

[40] *Goldberg v. Edwards* [1950] Ch. 247.

[41] *Wright v. Macadam, supra*, at 755; *Green v. Ashco Horticulturist Ltd* [1966] 1 W.L.R. 889 at 897; Law Commission Working Paper No. 36, para. 92, suggesting reform.

[42] *International Tea Stores Co. v. Hobbs* [1903] 2 Ch. 165 at 172; *Bartlett v. Tottenham* [1932] 1 Ch. 114; *Regis Property Co. Ltd v. Redman* [1956] 2 Q.B. 612; *Anderson v. Bostock* [1976] Ch. 312.

[43] *Phipps v. Pears* [1965] 1 Q.B. 76.

[44] *Burrows v. Lang* [1901] 2 Ch. 502; and see *Green v. Ashco Horticulturist Ltd, supra* (right of way exercisable only when convenient to landlord).

[45] *Quicke v. Chapman* [1903] 1 Ch. 659; *Re St Clement's, Leigh-on-Sea* [1988] 1 W.L.R. 720 at 728. See too L.P.A. 1925, s.62(5).

[46] *M.R.A. Engineering Ltd v. Trimster Co. Ltd* (1987) 56 P. & C.R. 1.

some facility which was not being enjoyed at the time of the grant, or was being enjoyed with land other than the land granted.[47] "Section 62 is apt for conveying existing rights, but it does not resurrect mere memories of past rights."[48] However, a right may be "reputed to appertain" within section 62 even if it was not being enjoyed at the time of the grant, but had been shortly before the conveyance.[49]

18–114   *(b) Diversity of occupation or continuous and apparent.* Section 62 does not apply unless at the time of the grant there was either—

> (i) prior diversity of occupation of the dominant and servient tenements; or
>
> (ii) the "right" was continuous and apparent.[50]

The section applies only to "easements, rights and advantages" which appertain to or are enjoyed with the land. Therefore "when land is under one ownership one cannot speak in any intelligible sense of rights, or privileges, or easements being exercised over one part for the benefit of another. Whatever the owner does, he does as owner and, until a separation occurs, of ownership or at least of occupation, the condition for the existence of rights, etc., does not exist".[51] It follows therefore that if A conveys to B part of his land which B has previously occupied (whether as a tenant or as a licensee[52]), then any right which B had enjoyed over A's land prior to the conveyance which is capable of being an easement will become one. If however A owns and occupies all of his land and sells part of it to B, the section will not operate to pass to B as an easement any quasi-easements enjoyed by A.[53] This principle is apparently subject to two important exceptions however. It is settled by Court of Appeal authority that both quasi-easements of light[54] and

---

[47] *Nickerson v. Barraclough* [1981] Ch. 426; *Re Broxhead Common Whitehill, Hampshire* (1977) 33 P. & C.R. 451. A right may be "enjoyed with" the land even if there is no actual user at the time of the conveyance: *Re Yateley Common, Hampshire* [1977] 1 W.L.R. 840 at 850, 851.

[48] *Penn v. Wilkins* (1974) 236 E.G. 203, *per* Megarry J.

[49] *Castagliola v. English* (1969) 210 E.G. 1425 at 1429, 1431; approved in *Pretoria Warehousing Co. Ltd v. Shelton* [1993] E.G.C.S. 120 (right to free use of shopping-centre concourse which terminated six months before conveyance held to pass under the section); [1994] Conv. 238 (A. Dowling).

[50] *Long v. Gowlett* [1923] 2 Ch. 177; [1979] Conv. 113 (C.H.).

[51] *Sovmots Investments Ltd v. Secretary of State for Environment* [1979] A.C. 144 at 169, *per* Lord Wilberforce; *Payne v. Inwood* (1996) 74 P. & C.R. 42. See too *Bolton v. Bolton* (1879) 11 Ch.D. 968 at 970, 971; *Roe v. Siddons* (1888) 22 Q.B.D. 224 at 236; *Metropolitan Ry v. Fowler* [1892] 2 Q.B. 165 at 171.

[52] Such as a purchaser who is allowed into possession prior to completion: *Lyme Valley Squash Club Ltd v. Newcastle under Lyme B.C.* [1985] 2 All E.R. 405.

[53] *Sovmots Investments Ltd v. Secretary of State for Environment, supra; Payne v. Inwood, supra.*

[54] *Broomfield v. Williams* [1897] 1 Ch. 602; *Sovmots Investments Ltd v. Secretary of State for Environment, supra,* at 176.

continuous and apparent quasi-easements[55] (such as a watercourse which runs through a man-made culvert,[56] or a made up road[57]) will pass under the general words. The easement of light is an exception to many rules.[58] The reasons for the exception of continuous and apparent quasi-easements are largely historical. Although it was always acknowledged that a person could not have an easement over his own land, continuous and apparent quasi-easements were regarded as an exception to this.[59] Such "rights" are considered to pass under the general words either because they are enjoyed with the land or because they appertain or are reputed to appertain to it.[60]

If this exception does exist,[61] and A conveys part of his land to B, there will pass to B all those continuous and apparent quasi-easements that were enjoyed by A at the time of the conveyance. This will be so even if the rights were merely convenient and not necessary for the reasonable enjoyment of the land granted. In such cases therefore, it will be unnecessary to have recourse to the rule in *Wheeldon v. Burrows*.[62] Where section 62 does not apply, as where it is expressly excluded,[63] there may nevertheless be an implied grant under that rule, provided that the criteria for its application are satisfied.

5. Contrary intention. Section 62 applies "only if and as far as a contrary   **18–115** intention is not expressed in the conveyance".[64] An express grant of a more limited right of way than section 62 would carry does not by itself amount to a contrary intention for this purpose.[65] But the section is also subject to any contrary intention which may be implied from circumstances existing at the time of the grant. If, for example, the plot sold and the plot retained are both subject to a building scheme, the purchaser of a house standing on the plot sold will not be able to prevent the plot retained from being built upon so as to diminish his light; for the light was enjoyed "under such circumstances as to show that there could be no expectation of its continuance".[66]

---

[55] *Watts v. Kelson* (1870) 6 Ch.App. 166; *Bayley v. G.W.R.* (1883) 26 Ch.D. 434 at 456, 457. See too *Barkshire v. Grubb* (1881) 18 Ch.D. 616.

[56] *Watts v. Kelson, supra.*

[57] *Barkshire v. Grubb, supra.*

[58] *Sovmots Investments Ltd v. Secretary of State for Environment, supra,* at 176. However quasi-easements of light may be merely one example of continuous and apparent quasi-easements and so fall within the second exception rather than being a distinct exception in themselves: see *Broomfield v. Williams, supra,* at 615, 617.

[59] See [1979] Conv. 113 at 114 *et seq* (C.H.); [1995] Conv. 239 at 241 (M. P. Thompson).

[60] *cf. Bayley v. G.W.R., supra,* at 457.

[61] The cases supporting it have not been considered in any modern decision. Compare the previous edition of this work at p. 865.

[62] There is a suggestion in *M.R.A. Engineering Ltd v. Trimster Co. Ltd* (1987) 57 P. & C.R. 1 at 7 that section 62 has superseded the rule in *Wheeldon v. Burrows* and applies to quasi-easements. But see *ibid.,* at 5.

[63] See *infra.*

[64] L.P.A. 1925, s.62(4).

[65] *Gregg v. Richards* [1926] Ch. 521; *Snell & Prideaux Ltd v. Dutton Mirrors Ltd* [1995] 1 E.G.L.R. 259 at 264.

[66] *Birmingham, Dudley & District Banking Co. v. Ross* (1888) 38 Ch.D. 295 at 307, *per* Cotton L.J.

II. IMPLIED RESERVATION AND GRANT WHERE TITLE IS REGISTERED

18–116   The Land Registration Act 1925 provides that the general words implied into conveyances by section 62 of the Law of Property Act 1925 shall apply to dispositions of registered land.[67] Any easement so created takes effect as an overriding interest unless and until it is registered.[68] Apart from this provision, the Act has nothing to say about the implied grant and reservation of easements, rights and privileges on a disposition of registered land.[69] Although the Land Registration Act 1925 requires that the grant or reservation of all easements should be completed by registration,[70] it is unlikely that those which arise by implied grant or reservation will be so registered.[71] However, it is provided by the Land Registration Rules 1925 that easements which appertain to or are enjoyed with land and which adversely affect registered land take effect as overriding interests.[72] It has been held in reliance upon this rule that any easement which is openly exercised and enjoyed as appurtenant to land may be an overriding interest,[73] and this is likely to encompass most implied easements.[74] The benefit of an easement impliedly granted or reserved may be noted on the register of the dominant title on the application of the registered proprietor in the same way as a right expressly created.[75]

III. DIFFERENCE BETWEEN EFFECTS OF CONTRACT AND OF GRANT

18–117   **1. Contract and grant.** In the great majority of cases, conveyances of a freehold are intended to give effect to some previous contract for a sale. It is important to realise that the rules which determine the operation of a conveyance do not in any way affect the interpretation of a contract.[76] The rule in *Wheeldon v. Burrows*[77] presupposes a grant and proceeds on the principle that a person who has made a grant may not derogate from it. Section 62 of the Law of Property Act 1925 applies only to a "conveyance", which, although widely defined,[78] does not include a contract.[79] The rules which govern the operation of conveyances merely say what the result will be if the conveyance is made without reservations. But a vendor of land, even under an open contract, is not necessarily under any obligation to make such a conveyance: his obligation is to convey what he has contracted to sell; and while he may not convey less, he need not convey more.

---

[67] L.R.A. 1925, ss.19(3), 22(3). See L.R.R. 1925, r. 251.
[68] L.R.A. 1925, s.70(1)(a); L.R.R. 1925, r. 258; *ante*, para. 6–042.
[69] See Gale, 5–06, 5–07; Ruoff & Roper, 6–07.
[70] ss.18(1); 19(2); 21(1); 22(2).
[71] See (1987) Law Com. No. 158, para. 2.28.
[72] r. 258.
[73] *Celsteel Ltd v. Alton House Holdings Ltd* [1985] 1 W.L.R. 204 at 221; *Thatcher v. Douglas* (1996) 146 N.L.J. 282; *ante*, paras 6–033, 6–042.
[74] See Law Com. No. 158, para. 2.28.
[75] *Ante*, para. 18–096.
[76] *Re Peck and the School Board for London's Contract* [1893] 2 Ch. 315 at 318.
[77] *Ante*, para. 18–103.
[78] L.P.A. 1925, s.205(1)(ii); see *ante*, para. 18–108.
[79] *Borman v. Griffith* [1930] 1 Ch. 493.

2. Scope of contract. A purchaser of land is ordinarily entitled by the contract to existing easements or profits which are appendant or appurtenant to the land sold.[80] As regards quasi-easements, he is entitled to such rights as may fairly be implied into the contract.[81] "When a property with a particular mode of access apparently and actually constructed as a means of access to it is contracted to be sold the strong presumption is that the means of access is included in the sale."[82] Thus in *Borman v. Griffith*[83] there was an agreement to let a house in a large park which stood close to a driveway leading to a larger house, and it was held that the agreement included the right to use the driveway for general purposes. This was plainly within the scope of the contract, since the lease stated that the house was let to the tenant for his trade of poultry and rabbit farming, and he proved that the only other way of access existing at the time of the contract was quite impracticable for many purposes of this trade. In another case, where there was a contract to sell house property in London which was approached by made-up private roads both from the east and west, the purchaser was held entitled to the use of one of them only, as a way of necessity, and not to the use of the other.[84] In such a case, subject to allowing for the reasonable convenience of the purchaser, the vendor is entitled to select the way.[85]

18–118

3. Scope of grant. It therefore seems that there is no general rule that a contract entitles the purchaser to all the rights which an unrestricted conveyance would pass to him.[86] He is rather entitled only to existing easements, and such quasi-easements as are necessary or intended[87]; and by an action for specific performance he cannot compel the vendor to convey more. The vendor may therefore insert limitations into the conveyance so as to make it accord with the contract.[88] In *Borman v. Griffith*[89] it was held that the tenant was entitled by the contract to such rights as would have passed to him under a conveyance executed before 1882, *i.e.* including quasi-easements within the rule in *Wheeldon v. Burrows*[90]; for he was held to be entitled to the same rights as if specific performance had been decreed in his favour before 1882 and the conveyance had made no mention of rights of way.

18–119

---

[80] *Re Walmsley & Shaw's Contract* [1917] 1 Ch. 93.
[81] This statement was adopted by Forbes J. in *Sovmots Investments Ltd v. Secretary of State for the Environment* [1977] Q.B. 411 at 441 (on appeal [1979] A.C. 144).
[82] *Re Walmsley & Shaw's Contract, supra,* at 98, *per* Eve J.
[83] [1930] 1 Ch. 493.
[84] *Bolton v. Bolton* (1879) 11 Ch.D. 968.
[85] See *Re Peck and the School Board for London's Contract, supra*; *Re Walmsley and Shaw's Contract, supra.* The words "and the appurtenances" do not narrow the scope of a contract but may enlarge the scope of a conveyance: *Hansford v. Jago* [1921] 1 Ch. 322.
[86] *Sovmots Investments Ltd v. Secretary of State for the Environment* [1977] Q.B. 411 at 441.
[87] See Williams V. & P. 658.
[88] *Re Peck and the School Board for London's Contract, supra* (the object and limitations of the statutory formula are well explained by Chitty J. at 318); *Re Hughes and Ashley's Contract* [1900] 2 Ch. 595; *Re Walsley and Shaw's Contract, supra.*
[89] [1930] 1 Ch. 493; see the text, *ante,* para. 18–118.
[90] *Ante,* para. 18–104.

The reasoning (though not the result) of this case is somewhat difficult. As explained above, a contract to grant land will prima facie comprise only such quasi-easements as are necessary or intended; and it should make no difference to assume specific performance, for a vendor need never convey more than he has contracted to sell. But since the rule governing contracts is so similar in its scope to the rule which governed grants without special words made before 1882, it is not always perceived that they are really two distinct rules. The first rule, for contracts, is still unaltered. The second rule, for grants, has been widened by statute, so that a conveyance may easily transfer more extensive rights than the purchaser is entitled to demand, unless the vendor takes care to make the proper reservations. A way of convenience over the vendor's other land is an example of a quasi-easement which may fall outside a contract for sale but within the wide general words of section 62.[91]

18–120   **4. Rectification.** Even if the vendor mistakenly makes an unrestricted conveyance, and so conveys more rights than he has agreed to sell, there is the possibility of rectification.[92] The court has an equitable jurisdiction to rectify the conveyance, and so make it accord with the contract, if by the common mistake of both parties it has been wrongly worded. The common intention of the parties appears from the contract, so that a mistake in the conveyance is a common mistake. For example, where a conveyance of a plot of land operated by reason of section 62 to create (unintentionally, as regards the vendor) a right of way over a track across the vendor's other land, because the track had in fact been used in connection with the land sold, the court rectified the conveyance by expressly excluding this right of way, even though the purchaser alleged that he agreed to buy the land on the assumption that he would get the right of way.[93] But there are limits to the use of rectification, and it by no means nullifies the operation of section 62. Since it is an equitable remedy, it will not be awarded to a vendor who has misled the purchaser, or who has unduly delayed claiming it; nor will it be awarded against a bona fide purchaser for value who had no notice of the discrepancy between the contract and the conveyance.[94]

D. By Presumed Grant, or Prescription

18–121   The basis of prescription is that if long enjoyment of a right is shown, the court will strive to uphold the right by presuming that it had a lawful origin.[95] Thus the court may presume, on proof of the fact of long enjoyment, that there

---

[91] *Bolton v. Bolton* (1879) 11 Ch.D. 968; *Re Peck and the School Board for London's Contract, supra*; *Re Walmsley and Shaw's Contract, supra*; *Clark v. Barnes* [1929] 2 Ch. 368 at 380 (purchaser under open contract (but subject to an express oral agreement excluding the right of way in question: see at 382) held not entitled to a reputed way which fell within s.62).

[92] *Ante*, para. 12–122.

[93] *Clark v. Barnes, supra*; *cf. Barkshire v. Grubb* (1881) 18 Ch.D. 616 (rectification in favour of purchaser).

[94] For this purpose the right to rectification is a "mere equity": *ante*, para. 5–012.

[95] *Clippens Oil Co. Ltd v. Edinburgh and District Water Trustees* [1904] A.C. 64 at 69, 70. See (1975) 38 M.L.R. 640 (S. Anderson).

once was an actual grant of the right, even though it is impossible to produce any direct evidence of such a grant.[96] It is then "the habit, and in my view the duty, of the court, so far as it lawfully can, to clothe the fact with right".[97] "The court is endowed with a great power of imagination for the purpose of supporting ancient user."[98] This policy extinguishes stale claims, quiets titles, and preserves established property, while at the same time paying lip service to the doctrine that every easement must owe its origin to a grant.

Today it is questionable whether this policy should be preserved; undoubt- **18–122** edly it has produced far too complex a body of law. The Law Reform Committee reported "that the law of prescription is unsatisfactory, uncertain and out of date, and that it needs extensive reform". A majority of the committee recommended its total abolition; but a strong minority recommended that in lieu of all existing forms of prescription there should be an improved Prescription Act for easements, though not for profits, based on a 12-year period of user.[99]

For a claim by prescription it is not enough to show long user by itself; there must have been continuous user "as of right" before the court will go so far as to presume a grant, and even then the court will not presume a grant except in fee simple. These fundamental conditions must first be discussed before considering the three methods of prescription, namely, at common law, by lost modern grant, and under the Prescription Act 1832.

1. User as of right. The claimant must show that he has used the right as **18–123** if he were entitled to it, for otherwise there is no ground for presuming that he enjoys it under a grant. From early times English authorities have followed the definition of Roman law[1]: the user which will support a prescriptive claim must be user *nec vi, nec clam, nec precario* (without force, without secrecy, without permission).[2] The essence of this rule is that the claimant must prove not only his own user but also circumstances which show that the servient owner acquiesced in it as in an established right.[3] Since the necessary conditions are negative, it is usually the servient owner who alleges that the user was either forcible, secret or permissive; but the burden of proof on these matters nevertheless rests on the claimant.[4]

(a) Vi. Forcible user (*vi*) extends not only to user by violence, as where a **18–124** claimant to a right of way breaks open a locked gate, but also to user which

---

[96] *Gardner v. Hodgson's Kingston Brewery Co. Ltd* [1903] A.C. 228 at 239.
[97] *Moody v. Steggles* (1879) 12 Ch.D. 261 at 265, *per* Fry J.
[98] *Neaverson v. Peterborough R.D.C.* [1902] 1 Ch. 557 at 573, *per* Collins M.R.
[99] 14th Report, Cmnd. 3100 (1966).
[1] Dig. 8.5.10; 43.17.1; Bracton lib. 2 fo. 51b, 52a, 222b; Co.Litt. 114a. For modern authorities, see Gale, paras 4–62 *et seq.*, and the paragraphs below.
[2] *Solomon v. Mystery of Vintners* (1859) 4 H. & N. 585 at 602 (common law prescription); *Sturges v. Bridgman* (1879) 11 Ch.D. 852 at 863 (lost modern grant); *Tickle v. Brown* (1836) 4 A. & E. 369 at 382 (prescription under the Prescription Act 1832; and see ss.1, 2).
[3] *Sturges v. Bridgman, supra,* at 863.
[4] *Gardner v. Hodgson's Kingston Brewery Co. Ltd* [1903] A.C. 229; *Patel v. W.H. Smith (Eziot) Ltd* [1987] 1 W.L.R. 853.

is contentious or allowed only under protest.[5] User is considered to be forcible "once there is knowledge on the part of the person seeking to establish prescription that his user is being objected to and that the use which he claims has become contentious".[6] Thus if there is a state of "perpetual warfare" between the parties there can obviously be no user as of right; and if the servient owner chooses to resist not by physical but by legal force, as by making unmistakable protests or taking legal proceedings,[7] the claimant's user will not help a claim by prescription. Nor will user which is prohibited by statute,[8] for "the court will not recognise an easement established by illegal activity".[9]

18–125   (*b*) *Clam.* As the basis of a prescriptive claim is acquiescence by the owner of the servient tenement,[10] he "must have knowledge or the means of knowledge that the act is done".[11] Secret user (*clam*) will not therefore found a prescriptive claim. It is illustrated by cases where the right claimed is exercised underground, *e.g.* by discharging waste fluid from a factory intermittently and secretly (though without active concealment) into a local authority's sewers,[12] or by fixing the sides of a dock to the adjacent land by underground rods.[13] The same objection may be made to a claim for support of one building by another if the degree of support required for the dominant building is abnormally great because of some peculiarity not apparent to the servient owner.[14] But the servient owner cannot make the user secret by shutting his own eyes: it must be "of such a character that an ordinary owner of the land, diligent in the protection of his interests, would have, or must be taken to have a reasonable opportunity of becoming aware of that enjoyment".[15] Thus a plea of *clam* failed where an outbuilding in a yard had for many years been supported by the wall of a dye-works, even though the outbuilding could not be seen from the servient tenement, for the servient owner should have had sufficient opportunity to discover its existence.[16]

---

[5] *Eaton v. Swansea Waterworks Co.* (1851) 17 Q.B. 267; *Dalton v. Angus & Co.* (1881) 6 App.Cas. 740 at 786.

[6] *Newnham v. Willison* (1987) 56 P. & C.R. 8 at 19, *per* Kerr L.J.

[7] *Eaton v. Swansea Waterworks Co., supra; Dalton v. Angus & Co., supra.*

[8] *Cargill v. Gotts* [1981] 1 W.L.R. 441 (abstraction of water contrary to Water Resources Act 1963).

[9] *ibid.*, at 446, *per* Templeman L.J.

[10] *Dalton v. Angus* (1881) 6 App.Cas. 740 at 773.

[11] *Diment v. N.H. Foot Ltd* [1974] 1 W.L.R. 1427 at 1433, *per* Pennycuick V.-C., discussing the circumstances in which an agent's knowledge or means of knowledge might suffice.

[12] *Liverpool Corporation v. H. Coghill & Sons Ltd* [1918] 1 Ch. 307.

[13] *Union Lighterage Co. v. London Graving Dock Co.* [1902] 2 Ch. 557.

[14] *Dalton v. Angus & Co.* (1881) 6 App.Cas. 740.

[15] *Union Lighterage Co. v. London Graving Dock Co., supra*, at 571, *per* Romer L.J.

[16] *Lloyds Bank Ltd v. Dalton* [1942] Ch. 466; contrast *Davies v. Du Paver* [1953] 1 Q.B. 184, where the plaintiff claimed a profit of sheepwalk over part of a hill farm in Wales in country where there had been little fencing; the owner lived some distance away and had only recently bought the farm: held, despite some evidence that the enjoyment was "common knowledge" in the district, the plaintiff had failed to show user with the owner's knowledge and his claim failed. This decision creates difficulties: see *post*, para. 18–160, n. 62.

(c) Precario. Permissive user *(precario)* is the most common kind of   **18–126**
enjoyment which will vitiate a claim by prescription. Prescriptive rights are
necessarily established because of the acquiescence or tolerance of the landowner over whose property they are exercised.[17] If a reasonable person would
appreciate that A was asserting a continuous right of enjoyment over B's land,
and B did nothing to resist it, he would be taken to have assented to A's
conduct, and his acquiescence or tolerance would not make the exercise of
that right permissive.[18] User under licence is of course permissive, whether or
not there is a contract or annual payment.[19–20] The advantage of a periodic
payment is that it shows that permission is regularly sought and renewed;
otherwise user which was at first permissive may in time become user as of
right if the circumstances indicate that the original permission is no longer
relied upon.[21] The right to receive an artificial flow of water is often permissive by its very nature, since it frequently depends upon the servient owner
being willing to continue it. Thus where waste water pumped from mines had
flowed to the claimant's land for over 60 years he had no right to its
continuance, since he enjoyed it at all times only because the servient owner
chose to supply it.[22]

(d) User qua easement or profit. User during unity of possession, *i.e.* while   **18–127**
the claimant was in possession of both dominant and servient tenements,
cannot be user as of right[23]; nor can user enjoyed in the mistaken belief that
the claimant was entitled to the servient tenement[24] or that he had the
temporary permission of the landlord.[25] But proof that the claimant exercised
his right in the mistaken belief that a valid easement or profit had already been
granted to him will not prevent the user from being as of right.[26] The principle
is that the right must have been exercised *qua* easement or profit and not, for
example, under any actual or supposed right of an occupant of both tenements.

---

[17] *Sturges v. Bridgman* (1879) 11 Ch.D. 852 at 863.
[18] *Mills v. Silver* [1991] Ch. 271, rejecting earlier dicta which had suggested otherwise; [1992]
C.L.J. 220 at 221 (C.H.). See too *R. v. Oxfordshire C.C., ex p. Sunningwell P.C.* [1999] 3
W.L.R. 160 at 173.
[19–20] *Monmouth Canal Co. v. Harford* (1834) 1 Cr.M. & R. 614; *Tickle v. Brown* (1836) 4 Ad. &
E. 369 at 382; *Mills v. Colchester Corporation* (1867) L.R. 2 C.P. 476, 486; *Gardner v.
Hodgson's Kingston Brewery Co. Ltd* [1903] A.C. 229. It has been suggested that user will be
by the licence of the landowner if he merely puts up a notice to that effect, even though his
permission is not asked: *Rafique v. Trustees of the Walton Estate* (1992) 65 P. & C.R. 356 at
357. This seems wrong both in principle and on authority: see [1994] Conv. 196 at 207 *et seq.*
(H. Wallace).
[21] This is a question of fact: *Gaved v. Martyn* (1865) 19 C.B. (N.S.) 732.
[22] *Arkwright v. Gell* (1839) 5 M. & W. 203; *cf. Wood v. Waud* (1849) 3 Ex. 748; *Bartlett v.
Tottenham* [1932] 1 Ch. 114; and see *ante*, para. 18–113.
[23] *Bright v. Walker* (1834) 1 Cr.M. & R. 211 at 219; *Outram v. Maude* (1881) 17 Ch.D. 391
(dominant owner holding servient land under lease); and see *Clayton v. Corby* (1842) 2 Q.B.
813 (profit), and *Battishill v. Reed* (1856) 18 C.B. 696 and *Damper v. Bassett* [1901] 2 Ch. 350
(easements), decided under the Prescription Act 1832.
[24] *Lyell v. Lord Hothfield* [1914] 3 K.B. 911 (profit); *Att.-Gen. of Southern Nigeria v. John Holt
& Co. (Liverpool) Ltd* [1915] A.C. 599 at 617, 618 (easement).
[25] *Chamber Colliery Co. v. Hopwood* (1886) 32 Ch.D. 549 (easement).
[26] *Earl de la Warr v. Miles* (1881) 17 Ch.D. 535 (profit); *Bridle v. Ruby* [1989] Q.B. 169
(easement). *cf.* [1989] Conv. 261 (G. Kodilinye).

"The whole law of prescription ... [rests] upon acquiescence ... I cannot imagine any case of acquiescence in which there is not shown to be in the servient owner: 1, a knowledge of the acts done; 2, a power in him to stop the acts or to sue in respect of them; and 3, an abstinence on his part from the exercise of such power."[27]

2. User in fee simple

18–128   *(a) User by and against the fee.* The user must be by or on behalf of a fee simple owner against a fee simple owner.[28] "The whole theory of prescription at common law is against presuming any grant or covenant not to interrupt, by or with anyone except an owner in fee."[29] An easement or profit for life or for years, for example, may be expressly granted but cannot be acquired by prescription,[30] for the theory of prescription presumes that a permanent right has been duly created at some unspecified time in the past. A claim by prescription must therefore fail if user can be proved only during a time when the servient land was occupied by a tenant for life[31] or for years,[32] for then the fee simple owner may never have been in a position to contest the user.[33] But if it can be shown that user as of right began against the fee simple owner, it will not be less effective because the land was later settled or let[34]; and user against the fee simple will be presumed, unless the servient owner can show the contrary.[35]

---

[27] *Dalton v. Angus & Co.* (1881) 6 App.Cas. 740 at 773, 774, *per* Fry J.; and see at 803, *per* Lord Penzance. See also *Oakley v. Boston* [1976] Q.B. 270, discussing the problem of establishing acquiescence by persons in a fiduciary position whose consent to any grant is requisite.

[28] *Bright v. Walker* (1834) 1 Cr.M. & R. 211 at 221 (prescription at common law); *Simmons v. Dobson* [1991] 1 W.L.R. 720 at 724 (lost modern grant); *Kilgour v. Gaddes* [1904] 1 K.B. 457 at 460 (Prescription Act 1832). It might have been expected that this rule would not apply to cases of lost modern grant, although it is now clear that it does. For lost modern grant: see *post*, para. 18–136.

[29] *Wheaton v. Maple & Co.* [1893] 3 Ch. 48 at 63, *per* Lindley L.J. (lost modern grant).

[30] *Wheaton v. Maple & Co., supra*, n. 29, at 63; *Kilgour v. Gaddes, supra*, n. 28 at 460 (Prescription Act 1832); *Simmons v. Dobson, supra*, at 724. These decisions of the Court of Appeal appear to be decisive. For contrary opinions, see *Bright v. Walker* (1834) 1 Cr.M. & R. 211 at 221 (suggestion that before the Prescription Act 1832, a grant by a termor could be presumed from long user); *East Stonehouse U.D.C. v. Willoughby Bros Ltd* [1902] 2 K.B. 318 at 332. In Ireland the law is otherwise: *Flynn v. Harte* [1913] 2 I.R. 326; *Tallon v. Ennis* [1937] I.R. 549.

[31] *Roberts v. James* (1903) 89 L.T. 282; *Baker v. Richardson* (1821) 4 B. & Ald. 579. For the question whether any change was brought about because a tenant for life was empowered to grant easements in fee simple under the Settled Land Act 1925, see *post*, para. 18–139, n. 92. After 1996, no new settlements may be created: *ante*, para. 8–001.

[32] *Daniel v. North* (1809) 11 East 372.

[33] *Pugh v. Savage, infra.*

[34] *Palk v. Shinner* (1852) 18 Q.B. 215; *Pugh v. Savage* [1970] 2 Q.B. 373, in effect approving this passage, and suggesting that it remains correct even if the tenancy, though granted after the user commenced, began before the 20 years' period next before action under the Prescription Act 1832 began to run.

[35] *Davis v. Whitby* [1973] 1 W.L.R. 629, aff'd [1974] Ch. 186; contrast *Diment v. N.H. Foot Ltd* [1974] 1 W.L.R. 1427 (onus discharged).

It will be seen, accordingly, that the theory of prescription does not deal properly with cases where the servient land is in the hands of a limited owner. It seems irrational to allow prescription against land if occupied by an owner in fee simple but not if occupied under a 999-year lease, for example.[36] The law in Ireland, where prescription against limited owners is allowed, seems more satisfactory.[37]

(b) *User by lessee.* Where it is the dominant tenement that is let, a tenant **18–129** cannot make a claim by prescription to an easement as annexed to his limited estate; if he claims an easement on the strength of his own user, he must necessarily claim it for his landlord as well as for himself. If follows that a tenant cannot prescribe for an easement over his landlord's adjacent land, for the landlord can have no right against himself.[38] For the same reason, if A leases two plots of his land to two tenants, one tenant cannot prescribe for an easement against the other, for otherwise the result would be that A would acquire an easement over his own land.[39]

(c) *Exceptions.* There are certain modifications of this rule. First, profits in **18–130** gross may be acquired by prescription at common law[40] (though not under the Prescription Act 1832[41]), which is then known as "prescription in gross". In this case the right is not claimed in respect of any dominant tenement but on behalf of the claimant personally. The claimant must show enjoyment by himself and his predecessors in title to the profit,[42] instead of by himself and his predecessors in title to the dominant tenement. In technical terms, prescription in gross is contrasted with prescription "in the *que* estate"[43] where the claimant used to plead user by himself and "*ceux que estate il ad*"[44] (*i.e.*, those whose estate he has). There can be no prescription in gross for easements, which cannot exist in gross.[45] Secondly, certain exceptions arise under the Prescription Act 1832, as is explained below.[46]

---

[36] Although this was acknowledged in *Simmons v. Dobson* [1991] 1 W.L.R. 720 at 724, the Court of Appeal extended the rule against prescription by tenants to cases of lost modern grant. For criticism, see [1992] Conv. 167 (P. Sparkes). However, for the case of a long lease which may be enlarged into a freehold under L.P.A. 1925, s.153 (*ante*, para. 14–178), see now *Bosomworth v. Faber* (1992) 69 P. & C.R. 288 at 293, *post*, para. 18–139.

[37] See (1958) 74 L.Q.R. 82 (V.T.H. Delany).

[38] *Gayford v. Moffat* (1868) 4 Ch.App. 133.

[39] *Kilgour v. Gaddes* [1904] 1 K.B. 457. Here again the law is different in Ireland: *Flynn v. Harte* [1913] 2 I.R. 326; *Tallon v. Ennis* [1937] I.R. 549.

[40] *Johnson v. Barnes* (1873) L.R. 8 C.P. 527; *Lovett v. Fairclough* (1990) 61 P. & C.R. 385 at 396.

[41] *Shuttleworth v. Le Fleming* (1865) 19 C.B. (N.S.) 687.

[42] *Welcome v. Upton* (1840) 6 M. & W. 536. There can therefore be no prescriptive claim to a profit in gross unless the claimant can show that either he or those through whom he derived title by inheritance or by assignment had exercised the right for the requisite period. The claimant cannot add his period of user to that of some stranger who happened to have exercised the same right before him: *Lovett v. Fairclough, supra*, at 399.

[43] *Austin v. Amhurst* (1877) 7 Ch.D. 689 at 692.

[44] Litt. 183; and see Y.B. 1 & 2 Edw. 2 (17 S.S.), p. xlviii.

[45] *Ante*, para. 18–045.

[46] *Post*, para. 18–167.

18–131   **3. Continuous user.** The claimant must show continuity of enjoyment.[47] This is interpreted reasonably; in the case of easements of way it is clearly not necessary to show ceaseless user by day and night.[48] User whenever circumstances require it is normally sufficient,[49] provided the intervals are not excessive, but not merely casual or occasional user.[50] A claim which clearly fell on the wrong side of the line was where a right of way had been exercised only on three occasions at intervals of 12 years.[51] But continuity is not broken merely by some agreed variation in the user, as by the parties altering the line of a right of way for convenience.[52]

The requirement of continuity of user must be distinguished both from the special rule under the Prescription Act 1832 as to user "without interruption", and from the degree of disuse that may extinguish an easement or profit after it has been acquired.[53]

The three methods of prescription must now be described.

I. PRESCRIPTION AT COMMON LAW

18–132   **1. Presumption of grant.** Prescription and limitation are in many ways similar principles, but as the law has developed they have become quite distinct subjects.[54] By *limitation* one person may acquire the land of another by adverse possession for a period which is now generally 12 years. By *prescription* one person may acquire rights such as easements and profits over the land of another. One important difference is that limitation is extinctive but prescription is acquisitive: that is to say, adverse possession of land for 12 years extinguishes the previous owner's title, leaving the adverse possessor with a title based on his own actual possession[55]; but prescription creates a new right, an incorporeal hereditament, which no one possessed previously. Prescription therefore must have positive operation, so as to create a new title. This is brought about by presuming a grant. "Every prescription presupposes a grant to have existed.[56]

---

[47] *Dare v. Heathcote* (1856) 25 L.J.Ex. 245 (common law); *Att.-Gen. v. Simpson* [1901] 2 Ch. 671 at 698 (lost modern grant); *Hollins v. Verney* (1884) 13 Q.B.D. 304 at 314, 315 (Prescription Act 1832).

[48] *Hollins v. Verney, supra*, at 308.

[49] *Dare v. Heathcote, supra* (easement); see *Earl de la Warr v. Miles* (1881) 17 Ch.D. 535 at 600 (profit). But see *Parker v. Mitchell* (1840) 11 A. & E. 788 (easement: user shown from 50 years before action down to four years before action, but no user shown during the last four years: claim failed). Compare *Carr v. Foster* (1842) 3 Q.B. 581 (profit: 30 years' user shown, except for two years near the middle of the 30, when the claimant had no commonable cattle: claim succeeded).

[50] *Ironside v. Cook* (1978) 41 P. & C.R. 326 (intermittent encroachments on verge of track merely for enabling two vehicles to pass: claim failed).

[51] *Hollins v. Verney* (1884) 13 Q.B.D. 304.

[52] *Davis v. Whitby* [1974] Ch. 186.

[53] *Smith v. Baxter* [1900] 2 Ch. 138 at 143, 146; *post*, paras 18–144, 18–186.

[54] For limitation, see *post*, para. 21–001. For discussion of the development of prescription, see *R. v. Oxfordshire C.C., ex p. Sunningwell P.C.* [1999] 3 W.L.R. 160 at 165 *et seq.*

[55] *Ante*, para. 3–117. For the application of the Statutes of Limitation to incorporeal hereditaments, see Co.Litt. 115a and notes by Hargrave.

[56] Bl.Comm. ii, 265.

2. Time immemorial. At common law a grant would be presumed only **18–133** where user as of right had continued from time immemorial, "from time whereof the memory of men runneth not to the contrary".[57] For this purpose the year 1189 was fixed as the limit of legal memory, so that any right enjoyed at that date was unchallengeable. This date was first fixed by statute in 1275,[58] and applied primarily to limitation; but it was also adopted for prescription. Yet although the law of limitation was changed by later statutes,[59] they were held not to alter the limit of legal memory for purposes of prescription. A claimant by prescription at common law must therefore have the boldness to claim that he and his predecessors have enjoyed the right since 1189.[60]

3. Twenty years' user. It is clearly impossible in most cases to show **18–134** continuous user since 1189, and so the courts have adopted the rule that if user as of right for 20 years or more is shown, the court will presume that the user has continued since 1189.[61] The period of 20 years was probably adopted by analogy with the limitation period laid down by the Limitation Act 1623.[62] Such user for less than 20 years requires supporting circumstances to raise the presumption[63]; and if there is evidence of user as far back as the period of living memory, it is immaterial that no continuous period of 20 years is covered.[64] This rule reduced to reasonable proportions a burden of proof which in theory was absurdly onerous.

4. Defects. Serious obstacles remained, however. The worst was that the **18–135** presumption of user from time immemorial could be rebutted by showing that at some time since 1189 the right could not or did not exist.[65] Thus an easement of light cannot be claimed by prescription at common law for a building which is shown to have been erected since 1189.[66] Consequently it was very difficult to establish a claim to light at common law, and many claims based on enjoyment lasting for centuries were liable to be defeated by evidence that there could have been no enjoyment of the light in 1189. Again, if it could be shown that at any time since 1189 the dominant and servient tenements had been in the same ownership and occupation, any easement or profit would have been extinguished[67] and so any claim at common law would fail. Yet again, a person could not prescribe for a right contrary to custom.[68]

---

[57] Litt. 170.
[58] Statute of Westminster I, 1275, c. 39; *post,* para. 21–003.
[59] *Post,* para. 21–003.
[60] See the account of this rule given by Cockburn C.J. in *Bryant v. Foot* (1867) L.R. 2 Q.B. 161 at 180, 181.
[61] *Darling v. Clue* (1864) 4 F. & F. 329 at 334.
[62] *Bright v. Walker* (1834) 1 Cr.M. & R. 211 at 217; *post,* para. 21–003.
[63] *Bealey v. Shaw* (1805) 6 East 208 at 215.
[64] *R.P.C. Holdings Ltd v. Rogers* [1953] 1 All E.R. 1029.
[65] *Hulbert v. Dale* [1909] 2 Ch. 570 at 577.
[66] *Bury v. Pope* (1588) Cro.Eliz. 118; *Duke of Norfolk v. Arbuthnot* (1880) 5 C.P.D. 390.
[67] See *post,* para. 18–191; *Keymer v. Summers* (1769) Bull.N.P. 74.
[68] *Perry v. Eames* [1891] 1 Ch. 658 at 667.

To remedy these failings the courts invented the "revolting fiction"[69] of the lost modern grant.

II. LOST MODERN GRANT

18–136   **1. Nature of doctrine.** The weakness of common law prescription was the liability to failure if it was shown that user had begun after 1189. The doctrine of lost modern grant avoided this by presuming from long user that an easement or profit had been actually granted after 1189 but prior to the user supporting the claim,[70] and that the deed of grant had been lost. The doctrine was an entirely judge-made fiction.[71] It is therefore really a variety of pre-scription at common law, but was a fairly late and distinct development[72] and is always classified separately. It has been described as "in the nature of an estoppel by conduct".[73]

18–137   **2. Presumption of grant.** "Juries were first told that from user, during living memory, or even during 20 years, they might presume a lost grant or deed; next they were recommended to make such presumption; and lastly, as the final consummation of judicial legislation, it was held that a jury should be told, not only that they might, but also that they were bound to presume the existence of such a lost grant, although neither judge nor jury, nor anyone else, had the shadow of belief that any such instrument had ever really existed".[74] In their anxiety to find a legal origin for a right of which there had been open and uninterrupted enjoyment for a long period, unexplained in any other way,[75] the courts presumed that a grant had been made, and so made it immaterial that enjoyment had not continued since 1189. "Grant" is not confined to dispositions nor to the creation of easements and profits, but to other rights such as licences[76] or franchises.[77] Thus the court may be willing to presume a lost faculty from an ecclesiastical authority,[78] a lost Crown charter, a lost ministerial consent,[79] and even a lost port authority's regula-tion,[80] though it is very difficult to presume a lost statute.[81] Twenty years' user

---

[69] *Angus & Co. v. Dalton* (1877) 3 Q.B.D. 85 at 94, *per* Lush J.

[70] See, *e.g. Dalton v. Angus & Co.* (1881) 6 App.Cas. 740 at 813.

[71] *Bridle v. Ruby* [1989] Q.B. 169 at 173.

[72] The earliest case in the reports is said to be *Lewis v. Price* (1761), noted in 2 Wms.Saund., 16th ed., 175; 85 E.R. 926: see *Dalton v. Angus & Co., supra,* at 812.

[73] *Angus & Co. v. Dalton* (1878) 4 Ch.D. 162 at 173, *per* Thesiger L.J.

[74] *Bryant v. Foot* (1867) L.R. 2 Q.B. 161 at 181, *per* Cockburn C.J.

[75] *Att.-Gen. v. Simpson* [1901] 2 Ch. 671 at 698.

[76] *Re St Martin le Grand, York* [1990] P. 63 (no easement could be created over consecrated ground, but the court found an indefinite licence).

[77] *Dysart (Earl of) v. Hammerton* [1914] 1 Ch. 822; *General Estates Co. v. Beaver* [1914] 3 K.B. 918 (franchise of ferry). See Gale, 4–14.

[78] *Phillips v. Halliday* [1891] A.C. 228; *Re St Martin le Grand, York, supra.*

[79] *Re Edis's Declaration of Trust* [1972] 1 W.L.R. 1135.

[80] *Att.-Gen. v. Wright* [1897] 2 Q.B. 318.

[81] *Harper v. Hedges* [1924] 1 K.B. 151.

will normally raise such presumptions,[82] but that is perhaps the minimum period.[83]

3. Improbability of grant. Presuming the existence of grants which had **18–138** probably never been made was frequently felt to be objectionable, particularly when it fell to juries who were required to find it as a fact upon oath. But the doctrine was elaborately considered and indorsed by the House of Lords in *Dalton v. Angus & Co.*,[84] and is now unquestionable. Certain rules survive as relics of judicial reluctance to strain the consciences of juries more than necessary. In the first place, rather stronger evidence of user is required to induce the court to presume a lost modern grant than is required for prescription at common law.[85] Although it is said that the doctrine can be invoked only if something excludes common law prescription,[86] in practice the common law claim is regarded as adding nothing in most cases to the claim based on lost modern grant: "they stand or fall together".[87] Since the doctrine is admittedly a fiction, the claimant will not be ordered to furnish particulars of the fictitious grant, *e.g.* as to the parties,[88] though he must plead whether the grant is alleged to have been made before or after a particular date.[89]

4. Impossibility of grant. It is now settled that the presumption cannot be **18–139** rebutted by evidence that no grant was in fact made.[90] But it is a good defence that during the entire period when the grant could have been made there was nobody who could lawfully have made it.[91] Thus the court has refused to presume a lost grant of a way where the land had been in strict settlement (under which there was no power to grant in fee simple) from the time when the user began down to the time of action.[92] When no grant could be made without some authority's consent, the court has refused to presume that

---

[82] *Penwarden v. Ching* (1829) Moo. & M. 400; *Dalton v. Angus & Co.* (1881) 6 App.Cas. 740, *e.g.* at 812.
[83] *Mann v. R.C. Eayrs Ltd* (1973) 231 E.G. 843.
[84] *Supra.*
[85] *Tilbury v. Silva* (1890) 45 Ch.D. 98 at 123.
[86] *Bryant v. Lefever* (1879) 4 C.P.D. 172 at 177.
[87] *Mills v. Silver* [1991] Ch. 271 at 278, *per* Dillon L.J.
[88] *Palmer v. Guadagni* [1906] 2 Ch. 494.
[89] *Tremayne v. English Clays Lovering Pochin & Co. Ltd* [1972] 1 W.L.R. 657; contrast *Gabriel Wade & English Ltd v. Dixon & Cardus Ltd* [1937] 3 All E.R. 900.
[90] *Tehidy Minerals Ltd v. Norman* [1971] 2 Q.B. 528; *Bridle v. Ruby* [1989] Q.B. 169 (party acting under a mistaken belief that an easement had been reserved, when in fact the reservation had been deleted from the conveyance). This proposition was for long controversial: see the previous edition of this work at p. 878.
[91] *Neaverson v. Peterborough R.D.C.* [1902] 1 Ch. 557; *Tehidy Minerals Ltd v. Norman, supra,* at 552.
[92] *Roberts v. James* (1903) 89 L.T. 282, where it was also held that an intervening resettlement made no difference; this leaves little, if anything, of *Williams v. Ducat* (1901) 65 J.P. 40. The question whether the court could presume a grant under the Settled Land Act (*ante,* para. 8–074) was not raised and may still be open. Similar cases where lost grants were not presumed are *Barket v. Richardson* (1821) 4 B. & Ald. 579 (user against glebe land over which the rector could not grant an easement); *Rochdale Canal Co. v. Radcliffe* (1852) 18 Q.B. 287 (corporation with limited power of grant); *Daniel v. North* (1809) 11 East 372 (user against leaseholder).

consent without evidence of the authority's acquiescence in the user.[93] Naturally the court has refused to presume a lost grant which would be contrary to statute[94] or custom.[95] However, although the law in England is now firmly settled to the contrary,[96] there seems nothing in principle that necessarily excludes a lost modern grant by or to a person owning less than a fee simple.[97] It has at least been held that a lessee, who has a unilateral right by statute to enlarge his leasehold interest into a fee simple,[98] may acquire an easement by lost modern grant over other land belonging to his landlord.[99]

III. UNDER THE PRESCRIPTION ACT 1832

18–140 The Prescription Act 1832 was designed to reduce the difficulties and uncertainties of prescription, and in particular the difficulty of persuading juries to presume grants to have been made when they knew this was not true.[1] In many cases it has substituted certainty for uncertainty and thus simplified a claimant's position. It makes special provisions for easements of light; and these have now been supplemented by the Rights of Light Act 1959. Accordingly, other easements will be treated first, together with profits, and then easements of light.

The Act of 1832 is notorious as "one of the worst drafted Acts on the Statute Book".[2] It is perhaps best explained by giving a summary of the effect of the principal sections and annotating the sections in groups. The elements of the Act are as follows.

1. Easements (other than light) and profits

18–141 *(a) The statutory periods*

SECTIONS 1 AND 2:

(i) An easement enjoyed for 20 years as of right and without interruption cannot be defeated by proof that user began after 1189.[3]

(ii) An easement enjoyed for 40 years as of right and without interruption is deemed "absolute and indefeasible" unless enjoyed by written consent.[3a]

---

[93] *Oakley v. Boston* [1976] Q.B. 270 (grant of right of way over glebe land required consent of Ecclesiastical Commissioners). *Sed quaere. cf. Re St Martin le Grand, York* [1990] P. 63.

[94] *Neaverson v. Peterborough R.D.C., supra; Hulley v. Silversprings Bleaching and Dyeing Co. Ltd* [1922] 2 Ch. 268; *Hanning v. Top Deck Travel Group Ltd* (1993) 68 P. & C.R. 14.

[95] *Wynstanley v. Lee* (1818) 2 Swans. 33; *Perry v. Eames* [1891] 1 Ch. 658 at 667 (City of London custom against prescription for light, except under s.3 of the Prescription Act 1832; *post*, para. 18–165); *Bowring Services Ltd v. Scottish Widows' Fund & Life Assurance Society* [1995] 1 E.G.L.R. 158 at 160.

[96] *Simmons v. Dobson* [1991] 2 W.L.R. 720; *ante*, para. 18–128.

[97] See (1958) 74 L.Q.R. 82 (V.T.H. Delaney); [1992] Conv. 167 (P. Sparkes).

[98] Under L.P.A. 1925, s.153 (or earlier legislation having like effect); *ante*, para. 14–178.

[99] *Bosomworth v. Faber* (1992) 69 P. & C.R. 288 at 293.

[1] *Mounsey v. Ismay* (1865) 3 H. & C. 486 at 496.

[2] Law Reform Committee, 14th Report, Cmnd. 3100 (1966), para. 40.

[3] s.2.

[3a] *ibid.*

(iii) The same rules apply to profits, except that the periods are 30 and 60 years respectively.[4]

SECTION 3: This section, which lays down special rules for the easement of light, is dealt with below.[5]

SECTION 4:

(i) All periods of enjoyment under the Act are those periods next before some suit or action in which the claim is brought into question.

(ii) No act is to be deemed an interruption until it has been submitted to or acquiesced in for one year after the party interrupted had notice both of the interruption and of the person making it.

(b) Shorter and longer periods. The shorter periods (20 and 30 years for **18–142** easements and profits respectively) operate negatively, *i.e.* they assist prescription at common law by prohibiting one kind of defence. The longer periods operate positively, for then the Act declares the right to be "absolute and indefeasible". This important distinction is further discussed below, in the light of other provisions of the Act.[6]

(c) "Next before some suit or action". The Act does not say that an **18–143** easement or profit comes into existence after 20, 30, 40 or 60 years' user in the abstract; all periods under the Act are those next before some action in which the right is questioned. Thus until some action is brought, there is no right to any easement or profit under the Act, however long the user.[7] It is sometimes said that the right remains merely inchoate until action is brought.[8] The important point is that the fruits of the Act can be reaped only by a litigant. Any person who wishes to consolidate an inchoate right under the Act can issue a writ against the servient owner claiming a declaration that he is entitled to an easement or profit.[9] He need not wait for some interference with it by the servient owner.

Even if there has been user for longer than the statutory periods, the vital period remains the period next before action. Thus if user commenced 50 years ago but ceased five years ago, a claim to an easement will fail if the action is commenced today, for during the 20 or 40 years next before the action there has not been continuous user.[10] Similarly a claim under the Act will fail if there has been unity of possession for a substantial time during the

---

[4] s.1. The Act does not apply to profits in gross: *ante*, para. 18–130.

[5] *Post*, para. 18–164.

[6] *Post*, paras 18–159, 18–160.

[7] *Colls v. Home and Colonial Stores Ltd* [1904] A.C. 179 at 189, 190; *Hyman v. Van den Bergh* [1908] 1 Ch. 167.

[8] *Newnham v. Willison* (1987) 56 P. & C.R. 8 at 12, 17.

[9] If the case is plain the servient owner will not defend and the plaintiff will obtain judgment on satisfying the court of his claim.

[10] *Parker v. Mitchell* (1840) 11 Ad. & El. 788.

period immediately before the action, for then there has not been user as an *easement* during the whole of the vital period.[11]

(d) "Without interruption"

18–144   (1) ONE YEAR'S ACQUIESCENCE. The user must be "without interruption"; but a special meaning is given to "interruption". If D has used a way over S's land for over 20 years, and then a gate is locked or a barrier erected barring his way, D can still succeed in establishing an easement provided that, at the time an action is brought, he has not submitted to or acquiesced in the obstruction for one year after he has known both of the obstruction and of the person responsible for it.[12] Acquiescence occurs where D is eventually satisfied to submit to the interruption. Submission occurs when D is not willing to submit, but fails to make his opposition apparent to S.[13] While the best way for D to prove that he did not acquiesce in or submit to the interruption is by commencing an action, protests will do as well if they can be proved[14]; and protests may continue to have effect for some while after they are made so that protests prior to the year may negative acquiescence during the year.[15]

18–145   (2) "INTERRUPTION". "Interruption" means some hostile obstruction[16] (even though by a stranger) and not mere non-user,[17] or natural occurrences, such as the drying up of a stream.[18] Prolonged non-user, however, may mean that there has been insufficient enjoyment to support a claim[19]; and, conversely, an interruption may be too intermittent to be effective.[20] It is important to realise that "interruption" does not mean user by permission, which is to be contrasted with user "as of right" rather than with user "without interruption".[21] Interruption means some interference with enjoyment or cessation of enjoyment[21a]; enjoyment by permission, or subject to protest,[22] is not interrupted, but rather continuing.

18–146   (3) NINETEEN YEARS AND A DAY. The special meaning of "interruption" is illustrated by the case of a claimant who has used an easement for 19 years

---

[11] *Damper v. Bassett* [1901] 2 Ch. 350, discussing earlier authorities.

[12] Both elements are essential: *Seddon v. Bank of Bolton* (1882) 19 Ch.D. 462.

[13] *Dance v. Triplow* (1991) 64 P. & C.R. 1 at 5; [1992] Conv. 197 (J.E. Martin).

[14] *Bennison v. Cartwright* (1864) 5 B. & S. 1; *Glover v. Coleman* (1874) L.R. 10 C.P. 108; *Newnham v. Willison* (1987) 56 P. & C.R. 8.

[15] The question is one of fact: *Davies v. Du Paver* [1953] 1 Q.B. 184 (claim to a profit of sheepwalk).

[16] *Davies v. Williams* (1851) 16 Q.B. 546. In certain cases there are special rules for commons: see *post*, para. 18–158.

[17] *Smith v. Baxter* [1900] 2 Ch. 138 at 143; *Carr v. Foster* (1842) 3 Q.B. 581 (non-user of right of pasture for two years owing to lack of cattle: claim upheld).

[18] *Hall v. Swift* (1838) 4 Bing.N.C. 381.

[19] For examples of this, see *Parker v. Mitchell* (1840) 11 A. & E. 788 (non-user for four or five years next before action); *Hollins v. Verney* (1884) 13 Q.B.D. 304 (intervals of 12 years between each act of user).

[20] *Presland v. Bingham* (1889) 41 Ch.D. 268 (piles of packing cases obstructing light to varying extents from time to time).

[21] *Plasterers' Co. v. Parish Clerks' Co.* (1851) 6 Exch. 630.

[21a] *ibid.*

[22] *Reilly v. Orange* [1955] 1 W.L.R. 616; see the text, *infra*.

and a day, and is then interrupted. For the remainder of the twentieth year he has no right to contest the interruption, for he cannot show 20 years' enjoyment.[23] But there will come one day (the first day of the twenty-first year) when, if he issues his writ on that day, he will succeed; for he can then show 20 years' enjoyment before action brought, the interruption being disregarded since it is one day less than a year. A writ issued on the following day will be too late, for the interruption will then have lasted a full year.[24] But if instead the servient owner starts proceedings disputing the right, he can effectively defeat the claim to the easement; for his action is not an "interruption",[25] as defined, and the dominant owner cannot complete 20 years' enjoyment as of right.

(e) User "as of right"

(1) MEANING. Sections 1 and 2 provide that the enjoyment must be by a **18–147**
"person claiming the right thereto", and section 5 provides that it is sufficient to plead enjoyment "as of right". Claims under the Act must be based on user of the same character as is required at common law.[26] Under the Act, the requisite user "as of right" means not only user *nec vi, nec clam, nec precario*, but also user by or on behalf of one fee simple owner against another.[27]

(2) PRECARIO. At common law any consent or agreement by the servient **18–148**
owner, whether oral or written, rendered the user *precario*; it made no difference how long ago the permission was given provided that user was in fact enjoyed under it and not under a claim to use as of right. Under the Act this rule applies to the shorter periods (20 years for easements, 30 years for profits). But a dilemma arises in the case of the longer periods (40 years for easements, 60 years for profits) because of the provision that the right shall be absolute unless enjoyed by written consent or agreement.[28] This clearly implies that enjoyment by oral consent shall be effective; but what then becomes of the rule that enjoyment must be as of right?

(3) ORAL PERMISSION. The House of Lords has partially solved this puzzle **18–149**
by deciding that a right enjoyed by oral permission renewed every year cannot be acquired as an easement by user, however long, for it is not enjoyed "as of

---

[23] *Lord Battersea v. Commissioners of Sewers for the City of London* [1895] 2 Ch. 708; *Barff v. Mann, Crossman & Paulin Ltd* (1905) 49 S.J. 794 (writ issued after 19 years and 352 days held premature).

[24] See *Flight v. Thomas* (1840) 11 Ad. & E. 688 at 771; 8 Cl. & F. 231. Perhaps the claimant could save himself by proving that he had contested the interruption, and so had not "submitted to or acquiesced in" it for a full year; see *ante*, para. 18–144. But non-acquiescence is presumably effective only in the period after the 20 years have expired. Before the expiration of the 20 years the claimant has no right to contest the interruption: therefore he can be compelled to submit to it, and whether he protests or not can hardly matter. As soon as he acquired an enforceable right to contest the interruption, his acquiescence or non-acquiescence becomes important, as in *Glover v. Coleman* (1874) L.R.10 C.P. 108.

[25] *Reilly v. Orange, supra.*

[26] *Tickle v. Brown* (1836) 4 Ad. & E. 369 at 382; *Gardner v. Hodgson's Kingston Brewery Co. Ltd* [1903] A.C. 229 at 238, 239.

[27] *Kilgour v. Gaddes* [1904] 1 K.B. 457; and see *ante*, para. 18–128.

[28] ss.1 and 2.

right" in any sense.[29] Even a single oral consent given during the period will vitiate the user, since there is no difference in principle between permission given once or more often.[30] But if the only oral permission given was given before the period began to run and not later renewed, it is probable that the Act will prevail; that is to say, the claim will succeed because the original licence was not made in writing.[31] If it were otherwise the provision about written permission would be meaningless. The position can be summarised as follows.

(i) Any consents, whether oral or written, which have been given from time to time during the period make the user *precario* and defeat a claim based on either the shorter or longer periods.[32]

(ii) A written consent given at the beginning of the user (and extending throughout) defeats a claim based on either the shorter or longer periods.

(iii) An oral consent given at the beginning of the user (and extending throughout) defeats a claim based on the shorter periods but not a claim based on the longer periods.[33]

If user commences by consent, the question whether it continues by consent is one of fact.[34]

18–150   (4) POWER TO CONSENT. The person competent to give consent is the occupier of the servient tenement, for it is by his sufferance that the claimant's enjoyment continues.[35] Similarly, the occupier of the dominant tenement, who in fact enjoys the right, also may make enjoyment precarious by acknowledging that he has no indefeasible right.[36] It is a question of fact who is occupier: he may be the fee simple owner, or a tenant for life or years, or even

---

[29] *Gardner v. Hodgson's Kingston Brewery Co. Ltd* [1903] A.C. 229 (user of a way for at least 70 years, 15 shillings being paid each year for the user; held, no easement. The result would have been the same if no money had been paid, but annual consents had been given by word of mouth; the payment is merely evidence of the consent); and see *Monmouth Canal Co. v. Harford* (1834) 1 Cr.M. & R. 614 at 630, 631 (20 years' period).

[30] *Tickle v. Brown* (1836) 4 Ad. & E. 369; and see *Ward v. Kirkland* [1967] Ch. 194 (period of permissive user).

[31] *Tickle v. Brown, supra,* at 383; *cf. Gardner v. Hodgson's Kingston Brewery Co. Ltd* [1901] 2 Ch. 198 at 215; [1903] A.C. 229 at 236.

[32] This will include the case where user continues on a common understanding that it is to be permissive: *Jones v. Price* (1992) 64 P. & C.R. 404.

[33] *Healey v. Hawkins* [1968] 1 W.L.R. 1967 (approving this sentence). As to the shorter period, see *Tickle v. Brown, supra,* at 383. But Alderson B. gave a contrary opinion in *Kinloch v. Nevile* (1840) 6 M. & W. 795 at 806; and see *Gardner v. Hodgson's Kingston Brewery Co. Ltd* [1900] 1 Ch. 592 at 599 (reversed [1901] 2 Ch. 198; [1903] A.C. 229). Perhaps the question is one of fact in which it is hard to draw the inference that user in such a case is user as of right: see *Gaved v. Martyn* (1865) 19 C.B. (N.S.) 732 at 744, 745; (1968) 32 Conv. (N.S.) 40 (P. S. Langan).

[34] *Gaved v. Martyn* (1865) 19 C.B. (N.S.) 732; *Healey v. Hawkins, supra.*

[35] See, *e.g. Lowry v. Crothers* (1871) I.R. 5 C.L. 98 (tenant for life).

[36] *Bewley v. Atkinson* (1879) 13 Ch.D. 283; *Hyman v. Van den Bergh* [1908] 1 Ch. 167.

a squatter; but a mere lodger or servant is not an occupier. A tenant may thus frustrate his landlord's claim to an easement under the Act by acknowledging that his user is permissive; for then the period immediately before action brought is not a period of continuous user as of right.[37] But if the landlord can make out a case by prescription at common law or lost modern grant, his rights so acquired cannot be given away by a tenant or other occupier of the dominant land, for they are vested rights in fee simple which a tenant has no power to dispose of.[37a]

(*f*) *Statutory provisions as to the periods.* The remaining sections of the Act **18–151** may now be summarised.

SECTION 5 deals with pleadings.

SECTION 6 provides that no presumption is to be made in support of a claim by showing enjoyment for less than the statutory periods. This deals with presumptions, not inferences, and so does not prevent inferences being drawn from user for less than the statutory periods.[38] Thus such user may be taken into account with other circumstances in establishing an easement.[39]

SECTION 7 provides that any period during which the servient tenant has been a minor, mental patient or tenant for life shall automatically be deducted from the shorter periods; and despite the changes made by the 1925 legislation it seems that the periods of minorities and life tenancies will still be deducted.[40] Further, the period during which an action is pending and actively prosecuted is also to be deducted.[41]

SECTION 8 provides that if the servient tenement has been held under a "term of life, or any term of years exceeding three years from the granting thereof", the term shall be excluded in computing the 40 years' period in the case of a "way or other convenient [*sic*] watercourse or use of water", provided the claim is resisted by a reversioner upon the term within three years of its determination.

No more need be said about sections 5 and 6. Sections 7 and 8 are complicated and can conveniently be dealt with together.

(*g*) *Effect of deductions.* Where either section 7 or 8 applies, the period **18–152** deducted is excluded altogether when calculating the period next before action. Thus if there has been enjoyment of a profit for 45 years in all, consisting of 25 years' user against the fee simple owner, then 19 years

---

[37] See the discussion of these points in *Hyman v. Van den Bergh* [1907] 2 Ch. 516 at 531 (Parker J.) and [1908] 1 Ch. 167 at 179 (Farwell L.J.). This decision concerned the easement of light, but its principle seems applicable to all claims made under the Act. Lost modern grant was not pleaded in the alternative, and conflicting opinions were expressed as to the possibility of pleading it successfully in a case where a defence provided by the Act had been made out. As to pleading claims in the alternative, see *post*, para. 18–162.

[37a] *Hyman v. Van den Bergh* [1907] 2 Ch. 516 at 531; [1908] 1 Ch. 167 at 179.

[38] *Hollins v. Verney* (1884) 13 Q.B.D. 304 at 308.

[39] *Hamer v. Chance* (1865) 4 De G.J. & S. 626 at 631.

[40] See L.P.A. 1925, s.12.

[41] The same deduction would probably be allowed in the case of the longer periods; but the Act makes no provision for it.

against a life tenant, and then a further year against the fee simple owner, the claim fails, for by section 7 the period of the life tenancy is deducted when calculating the period next before action brought, and thus less than 30 years' user is left. But if the user continues for another four years, the claim will then succeed, for there is 30 years' user consisting of 25 years before and five years after the life tenancy; since the period of the life tenancy is disregarded, the 30-year period is, for the purposes of the Act, next before action within section 4.[42] The sections in effect connect the periods immediately before and after the period deducted, but they will not connect two periods separated in any way, *e.g.* by a period of unity of possession.[43] Nor will events that have occurred during the life tenancy, such as an interruption, be disregarded; the provision is for the benefit not of the claimant but of those resisting the claim,[44] and it appears to operate not as a cloak of oblivion but merely mathematically.

18–153   *(h) Rights within the sections.* Section 7 applies to the shorter periods both for easements and profits; but section 8 does not apply to profits at all, and applies to the longer period only in the case of easements of way "or other convenient watercourse or use of water". The word "convenient" is "not unreasonably supposed to be a misprint for 'easement' ",[45] so that the phrase should read "or other easement, watercourse or use of water", thus corresponding with the phrase used in section 2. If so, section 8 may apply to all easements; but the point is unsettled.[46]

(i) Disabilities within the sections

18–154   (1) THE DISABILITIES. Section 7 applies if the servient owner is a minor, mental patient or tenant for life; section 8 applies where the servient tenement has been held under a term for over three years, or for life. Thus a life tenancy is the only disability which applies to both the longer and the shorter periods. Infancy and mental illness affect only the shorter periods, and leases affect only the longer periods for the claims mentioned in section 8. Thus if D enjoys a way against S's land for 25 years, but S has been mentally ill for the last 15 of those years, section 7 defeats D's claim. If D continues his user for another 15 years, however, his claim succeeds, even though S remains mentally ill throughout.

18–155   (2) LEASES FOR YEARS. It is curious that leases for years, unlike life tenancies, may be deducted only under section 8 and not under section 7. Thus where there had been user of a way for 20 years, the servient land being under lease for 15 of the 20 years, but free from any lease at the beginning of the

---

[42] *Clayton v. Corby* (1842) 2 Q.B. 813.
[43] *Onley v. Gardiner* (1838) 4 M. & W. 496.
[44] *Clayton v. Corby, supra,* at 825.
[45] *Laird v. Briggs* (1880) 50 L.J.Ch. 260 at 261, *per* Fry J. (omitted from the report in 16 Ch.D. 440 at 447); and see *Wright v. Williams* (1836) Tyr. & G. 375 at 390, by counsel in argument.
[46] In *Laird v. Briggs, supra,* the point was reserved on appeal: see (1881) 19 Ch.D. 22 at 33, 36, 37.

period, an easement was established[47]: for section 7 makes no mention of leaseholds, and section 8 does not apply to the 20-year period. Such user began against a fee simple owner who, by leasing the land, voluntarily put it out of his power to resist the user. Had the lease been granted before the user began and continued throughout, the position would have been different, for there (unlike the case when the servient owner had granted a number of successive tenancies[48]) no user as against a fee simple owner able to resist it could have been shown.[49] It will also be seen that even if there had been user for 40 years, the claim would have succeeded only on the last 20 years' user; a claim based on 40 years' user would make the lease deductible, leaving a period of 25 years' user only. In such a case, therefore, a claim based on the short period may succeed where one based on the long period will fail.

(3) EFFECT OF LEASE. A lease may therefore affect a claim in two ways: **18–156**

    (i) by showing that there has been no user against a fee simple owner who knows of it and can resist it; and

    (ii) by falling within the provisions of section 8 allowing deduction.

The first of these is a common law rule not affected by the Act[50]; the second is a creature of the statute and can apply only to claims under the Act.

(j) Right to deduct. In section 7 the provision for deduction is absolute; in   **18–157** section 8 it is subject to the condition that the reversioner resists the claim within three years of the determination of the term of years or life.[51] Thus if the reversioner fails to resist the claim within the three years, he has no right of deduction at all. Another peculiarity of section 8 is that it extends only to a reversioner and not to a remainderman,[52] so that it will rarely apply to land held by a tenant for life under the usual kind of settlement.

It will be seen that section 7 is wide in its scope, giving an absolute right of deduction from the shorter periods for both easements and profits; section 8, on the other hand, is very narrow, giving only a reversioner a conditional right of deduction from the 40 years' period in the case of (possibly) only two classes of easements.

(k) Rights of common. Under the Commons Registration Act 1965, special   **18–158** rules apply to rights of common where during any period the right was not exercised, but for the whole or part of that period the servient tenement was

---

[47] *Palk v. Shinner* (1852) 18 Q.B. 568.
[48] See *Bishop v. Springett* (1831) 1 L.J.K.B. 13.
[49] *Daniel v. North* (1809) 11 East 372; *Bright v. Walker* (1834) 1 Cr.M. & R. 211.
[50] Unless it is unnecessary to presume a grant in the case of the longer period: see *post*, para. 18–160.
[51] *Wright v. Williams* (1836) 1 M. & W. 77 at 100.
[52] *Symons v. Leaker* (1885) 15 Q.B.D. 629 (remainderman held unable to deduct life tenancy of 55 years). But see *Holman v. Exton* (1692) Carth. 246 (remainderman held to be "within the equity" of a statute applicable to reversioners).

requisitioned (*i.e.* in the possession of a government department under emergency powers), or for reasons of animal health (*e.g.* restrictions to prevent the spread of animal diseases) the right, being a right to graze animals, could not be or was not exercised.[53] In such cases, that period or part of a period is to be left out of account—

> (i) in determining whether there has been an "interruption" within the Act of 1832, and

> (ii) in computing the 30 or 60 years' period under that Act.[54]

Further, any objection to the registration of a right of common under the Act of 1965[55] is to be treated as a suit or action within section 4 of the Act of 1832.[56]

(l) Difference between shorter and longer periods

18–159   (1) SHORTER PERIODS. In the case of the shorter periods, the only benefits which the Act of 1832 confers upon a claimant are that the period for which he must show user is clearly laid down, and that he cannot be defeated by proof that his enjoyment began after 1189. The nature of the user required is still substantially the same, so that the claimant must show continuous uninterrupted user as of right by or on behalf of a fee simple owner against a fee simple owner who both knew of the user and could resist it, at least at the time when user began.[57] The effect of the Act is merely to facilitate prescription at common law, by eliminating the objection to user which is not of immemorial antiquity. Apart from that, the Act provides that a claim based on the shorter period "may be defeated in any other way by which the same is now liable to be defeated".[58] "The Act was an Act 'for shortening the time of prescription in certain cases'. And really it did nothing more."[59]

18–160   (2) LONGER PERIODS. User as of right is equally necessary in the case of the longer periods. But here the language of the Act is positive: the right becomes "absolute and indefeasible". This is held not to alter the fundamental rule that prescription must operate for and against a fee simple estate. "An easement for a term of years may, or course, be created by grant; but such an easement cannot be gained by prescription [*sc.* at common law], and, not being capable of being so acquired, it does not fall within the scope of the statute."[60] A

---

[53] Commons Registration Act 1965, s.16(1), (3), (4).
[54] *ibid.*, s.16(1).
[55] See *post*, para. 18–179.
[56] Commons Registration Act 1965, s.16(2).
[57] *Ante*, paras 18–123—18–128.
[58] Prescription Act 1832, ss.1, 2.
[59] *Gardner v. Hodgson's Kingston Brewery Co. Ltd* [1903] A.C. 229 at 236, *per* Lord Macnaghten.
[60] *Wheaton v. Maple* [1893] 3 Ch. 48 at 64, *per* Lindley L.J.; that was a case about light, but its principle was applied to other easements in *Kilgour v. Gaddes* [1904] 1 K.B. 457.

tenant cannot therefore prescribe against his own landlord, or against another tenant of his own landlord.[61]

One difference, however, arises from the positive words of the Act: it is no defence that user began against a mere tenant or other occupier. Thus by 40 years' user against a tenant for years or for life the claimant can acquire an easement against the fee simple, even though the fee simple owner was in no position to contest the user, provided that a defence is not available under section 8.[62] In principle also it should be possible under the longer periods to prescribe against corporations which have no power of grant; for the positive right conferred by the Act should require no presumption of a grant by the servient owner. But on this last point the authorities are conflicting.[63]

(m) Limitations. The Prescription Act 1832 does not create easements or profits which could not exist as such at common law.[64] Thus a claim by the freemen and citizens of a town to enter land and hold races thereon on Ascension Day cannot be established under the Act.[65] Nor, it is held, does it apply to the acquisition of profits in gross, which can therefore be prescribed for only at common law or by lost modern grant.[66] **18–161**

(n) Alternative claims. One of the many uncertainties raised by the Act was whether it had abolished the other methods of prescription. It is now clearly settled that it did not.[67] The doctrine of lost modern grant is therefore still available, even in the case of light.[68] Consequently all three methods of prescription may be relied upon in the alternative,[69] without pleading them individually.[70] It has been said that lost modern grant should be pleaded last,[71] but in fact the order of pleading seems immaterial. **18–162**

---

[61] *Kilgour v. Gaddes, supra* (unsuccessful claim to use of a pump, habitually used for over 40 years, by one tenant against another tenant of the same landlord).

[62] *Wright v. Williams* (1836) 1 M. & W. 77, not cited in *Davies v. Du Paver* [1953] 1 Q.B. 184, where the contrary was held: see (1956) 72 L.Q.R. 32 (R.E.M.).

[63] Against the claim: *The Proprietors of the Staffordshire and Worcestershire Canal Navigation v. The Proprietors of the Birmingham Canal Navigations* (1866) L.R. 1 H.L. 254 at 268, 278. For the claim: *Lemaitre v. Davis* (1881) 19 Ch.D. 281 at 291. In the special case of the easement of light there is clearly no presumption of grant: *post*, para. 18–169.

[64] *Wheaton v. Maple & Co.* [1893] 3 Ch. 48 at 65.

[65] *Mounsey v. Ismay* (1865) 3 H. & C. 486.

[66] See *ante*, para. 18–085.

[67] *Aynsley v. Glover* (1875) 10 Ch.App. 283; *Healey v. Hawkins* [1968] 1 W.L.R. 1967. See also (1958) 74 L.Q.R. at 86, 87 (V.T.H. Delany) and cases cited below.

[68] *Tisdall v. McArthur & Co. (Steel & Metal) Ltd* [1951] I.R. 228; *Marine & General Mutual Life Assurance v. St James' Real Estate Co. Ltd* [1991] 2 E.G.L.R. 178; *Marlborough (West End) Ltd v. Wilks Head & Eve* (Lightman J., unreported, December 20, 1996). This seems the better view. Although in *Tapling v. Jones* (1865) 11 H.L.C. 290 at 304, Lord Westbury suggested that the right to ancient lights rested on the provisions of the Prescription Act 1832 and "ought not to be rested on any presumption of grant or fiction of a licence", those remarks, properly understood, do not contradict the view in the text: see *Tisdall v. McArthur & Co. (Steel & Metal) Ltd, supra*, at 235–242.

[69] See *Bass v. Gregory* (1890) 25 Q.B.D. 481; *Aynsley v. Glover, supra*, at 284.

[70] *Pugh v. Savage* [1970] 2 Q.B. 373 (claim to right of way "by prescription": lost modern grant presumed). The comments in that case were specifically in the context of pleadings in the county court, "where ideal pleadings are not to be expected": *per* Harman L.J. (at 386), but it is thought that the same would now apply in the High Court as well: *cf.* CPR Pt 7.

[71] *Gardner v. Hodgson's Kingston Brewery Co. Ltd* [1903] A.C. 229 at 240.

Claims at common law or by lost modern grant therefore remain of great importance, since in many cases a claim under the Act may be defeated by some technicality, *e.g.* an interruption, or a consent by a tenant of the dominant land, or unity of possession.[72] Thus in one case[73] a claim by lost modern grant succeeded where a right of way of modern origin had been subject to unity of possession for 16 out of the last 20 years, so that neither common law nor the Act were of any help. In a comparable case the court presumed a lost modern grant of a right of grazing although the servient land had been under requisition, thus preventing user, for 19 of the 30 years next before action.[74] In the case of profits, lost modern grant has the substantial advantage that 20 years' user suffices, whereas the Act requires at least 30.[74a]

The Court of Appeal has commented on the unnecessary complication and confusion caused by the co-existence of three separate methods of prescription,[75] but a much better Act will be required before the judge-made methods can be eliminated.[76]

18–163   **2. The easement of light.** There are special provisions for facilitating claims to light, both under the Prescription Act 1832 and the Rights of Light Act 1959.

(a) Under the Prescription Act 1932

18–164   (1) THE STATUTE. The easement of light, having been perhaps the most difficult easement to acquire by prescription before the Act of 1832,[77–78] has now become the easiest. Section 3 provides that the actual enjoyment of the access of light to a "dwelling-house, workshop or other building" for 20 years without interruption shall make the right absolute and indefeasible unless enjoyed by written consent or agreement. "Building" here includes a

---

[72] See *Healey v. Hawkins, supra* (lost modern grant where user not continuous to time of action brought). In *Hyman v. Van den Bergh* [1908] 1 Ch. 167 at 176–178, Farwell L.J. expressed the opinion that a plea of lost modern grant would not succeed in a case where one of the defences provided by the Prescription Act had been made out; but later decisions impose no such retriction.

[73] *Hulbert v. Dale* [1909] 2 Ch. 570.

[74] *Tehidy Minerals Ltd v. Norman* [1971] 2 Q.B. 528 (user as of right, 1920–1941; requisition, 1941–1960; user by consent, 1960–1966). See too *Mills v. Silver* [1991] Ch. 271 at 278.

[74a] *Tehidy Minerals Ltd v. Norman, supra.*

[75] *ibid.*, at 543. See the recommendations of the Law Reform Committee, *ante*, para. 18–122.

[76] It should be noted that, for all its shortcomings, prescription under the Prescription Act 1832 is, from a conveyancing point of view, preferable to prescription by lost modern grant. Because it has to be exercised without interruption "next before some suit or action", it may be easier for any purchaser of the servient tenement to discover. If an easement has been acquired by lost modern grant, it will not be lost by mere non-user (*post*, para. 18–186). A purchaser may be bound by it even though he could not have discovered its existence. For this reason, the Law Commission and Land Registry have recommended that, for the future, the only form of prescription applicable to registered land should be that under the Prescription Act 1832: (1998) Law Com. No. 254, para. 10.91.

[77–78] *Ante*, para. 18–135.

church,[79] a greenhouse,[80] and a cowshed,[81] but not a structure for storing timber.[82] A right acquired under the section is an easement for the access of light to a building, not to a particular room within it.[83]

(2) EFFECT. The general effect of section 3, therefore, is that 20 years' enjoyment of light is equivalent to 40 years' enjoyment of any other easement.[84] But there are three important differences. **18–165**

    (i) Section 3 says nothing of user as of right. Enjoyment by itself suffices, even though precarious,[85] unless the consent is in writing.

    (ii) Sections 7 and 8 are inapplicable, so that there are no disabilities which can be pleaded against a claim to light.

    (iii) No easement of light can be acquired over Crown land, for unlike sections 1 and 2, section 3 is not expressed to bind the Crown.[86]

In other respects light is governed by the same rules as other easements: the 20 years' period is that next before action,[87] and subject to the Rights of Light Act 1959,[88] "interruption" has the same special meaning as in other cases.[89]

(3) USER AS A RIGHT UNNECESSARY. The fact that user as of right is unnecessary in claims to light under the Act has far-reaching implications, for the whole basis of prescription is thus changed. For instance, the provision that written consent defeats the claim is the only fragment of *nec vi, nec clam, nec precario* which is left in claims to light under the Act; oral consent is no bar,[90] even though evidenced by annual payments.[91] From this there arises a crop of peculiarities connected with tenants. A tenant can acquire a right to light against his own landlord,[92] or against another tenant of his own landlord,[93] though in each case the landlord's reservation in the lease of a right to rebuild **18–166**

---

[79] *Ecclesiastical Commissioners for England v. Kino* (1880) 14 Ch.D. 213.
[80] *Clifford v. Holt* [1899] 1 Ch. 698: *Allen v. Greenwood* [1980] Ch. 119.
[81] *Hyman v. Van den Bergh* [1908] 1 Ch. 167.
[82] *Harris v. De Pinna* (1886) 33 Ch.D. 238.
[83] *Carr-Saunders v. Dick McNeil Associates Ltd* [1986] 1 W.L.R. 922 at 928.
[84] *Dalton v. Angus & Co.* (1881) 6 App.Cas. 740 at 800.
[85] *Colls v. Home and Colonial Stores Ltd* [1904] A.C. 179 at 205.
[86] *Wheaton v. Maple & Co.* [1893] 3 Ch. 48. This includes land held under Crown Leases: *ibid.* The wording also makes s.3 prevail against any custom to the contrary, *e.g.* against prescriptive rights of light in the City of London: *Perry v. Eames* [1891] 1 Ch. 658 at 667; *ante,* para. 18–139.
[87] *Hyman v. Van den Bergh* [1908] 1 Ch. 167.
[88] See *post,* para. 18–170.
[89] *Smith v. Baxter* [1900] 2 Ch. 138.
[90] *London Corporation v. Pewterers' Co.* (1842) 2 Moo. & R. 409.
[91] *Plasterers' Co. v. Parish Clerks' Co.* (1851) 6 Exch. 630.
[92] *Foster v. Lyons & Co. Ltd* [1927] 1 Ch. 219 at 227.
[93] *Morgan v. Fear* [1907] A.C. 425. The older authorities were discussed in the Court of Appeal: *Fear v. Morgan* [1906] 2 Ch. 406.

the adjoining property may amount to a consent in writing that will defeat the claim.[94] Where the easement is acquired against another tenant, and the lease of the servient land expires first, the easement binds the landlord and all subsequent occupiers.[95]

18–167   (4) EASEMENTS ONLY IN FEE. Nevertheless, an easement for a term of years cannot be acquired even in the case of light. Thus where there was 20 years' enjoyment against a tenant of the Crown it was held that since the Crown could not be bound, so neither could the tenant.[96] It therefore seems that light must be acquired, if at all, in fee simple, even though user is against a tenant. Thus a common landlord will not only be bound if the lease of the servient land expires first: he will also benefit if the lease of the dominant land expires first. It is of course paradoxical that easements can arise both for and against the same fee simple reversion, but that is attributable to the strength of the words "absolute and indefeasible" when freed from the requirement of user as of right.

18–168   (5) UNITY OF POSSESSION. Another divergence appears, though somewhat darkly, in cases where there is unity of possession during the statutory period. In the case of easements other than light we have seen that this vitiates any claim under the Act.[97] In the case of light it has been said that unity of possession merely suspends the running of the period, so that enjoyment for 25 years can be successfully pleaded even though during that time there was five years' unity of possession.[98] The principle on which this distinction rests is obscure[99]; and it is difficult to see how it can be reconciled with section 4, requiring all periods to be those next before action.

18–169   (6) NO GRANT. It is clear that there is no presumption of a grant in the case of light.[1] Thus it may be acquired under the Act against a corporation having no power of grant.[2] It now seems unlikely that the Act has by implication abolished claims to light under the doctrine of lost modern grant.[3]

18–170   *(b) Under the Rights of Light Act 1959.* This Act changed the law in a number of respects.[4] It extends to Crown land, though it preserves the Crown's immunity against claims to light under the Prescription Act 1832.[5]

---

[94] *Willoughby v. Eckstein* [1937] Ch. 167 (landlord and tenant); *Blake & Lyons Ltd v. Lewis, Berger & Sons Ltd* [1951] 2 T.L.R. 605 (tenant and tenant).

[95] *Morgan v. Fear, supra.*

[96] *Wheaton v. Maple & Co.* [1893] 3 Ch. 48.

[97] *Ante,* para. 18–143.

[98] *Ladyman v. Grave* (1871) 6 Ch.App. 763.

[99] According to *Ladyman v. Grave, supra,* the same rule applies to all easements; but according to *Damper v. Bassett* [1901] 2 Ch. 350 it is confined to light.

[1] *Tapling v. Jones* (1865) 11 H.L.C. 290 at 304, 318.

[2] *Jordeson v. Sutton, Southcoates & Drypool Gas Co.* [1898] 2 Ch. 614 at 626 (aff'd [1899] 2 Ch. 217).

[3] *Marine & General Mutual Life Assurance v. St James' Real Estate Co. Ltd* [1991] 2 E.G.L.R. 178; *ante,* para. 18–162.

[4] It was enacted in response to the Report of the Committee on Rights of Light, 1958, Cmnd. 473. For a clear explanation of the origin and scheme of the Act, see *Bowring Services Ltd v. Scottish Widows' Fund and Life Assurance Society* [1995] 1 E.G.L.R. 158 at 159, 160.

[5] Rights of Light Act 1959, s.4; and see *ante,* para. 18–165.

The interruption of light by screens and hoardings has always been cumbrous, and is now subject to planning controls.[6] The Act provides that instead, a servient owner may now register a notice as a local land charge, provided the Lands Tribunal has certified either that due notice has been given to those likely to be affected or that a temporary notice should be registered on grounds of exceptional urgency.[7] The notice must identify the servient land and the dominant building, and specify the position and size of an obstruction on the servient land to which the notice is intended to be equivalent. It then takes effect, both under the Act of 1832 and otherwise, as if the access of light had in fact been so obstructed, and as if the obstruction had been both known to and acquiesced in by all concerned.[8]

The notice remains effective for one year unless before then it is cancelled or, being temporary, expires.[9] While it is in force the dominant owner may sue for a declaration as if his light had actually been obstructed, and may claim cancellation or variation of the registration; and for this purpose the dominant owner may treat his enjoyment as having begun one year earlier than it did, thus avoiding the problem of interruption during the final year of the period.[10]

Section 4. Remedies for Infringement of Easement and Profits

1. Easement. The remedy is either by abatement or by action.[11]

(a) *Abatement.* Provided that no more force is used than is reasonably **18–171** necessary,[12] that there is no injury to innocent third parties or the public,[13] and that the circumstances are not likely to lead to a breach of the peace,[14] the owner of the easement may abate any obstruction to its exercise without notice to the servient owner,[15] *e.g.* by breaking open a locked gate or removing boards interfering with his light. But the law does not favour abatement.[16]

---

[6] See *post*, para. 22–009.
[7] Rights of Light Act 1959, s.2. See also Lands Tribunal Rules 1975 (S.I. 1975 No. 299), Pt VI; Local Land Charges Rules 1977 (S.I. 1977 No. 985), r. 10; and see *ante*, para. 5–132.
[8] Rights of Light Act 1959, s.3; and see *ante*, para. 18–144.
[9] *ibid.*, s.3. See *Bowring Services Ltd v. Scottish Widows' Fund and Life Assurance Society, supra*, at 161.
[10] Rights of Light Act 1959, s.3.
[11] *Lane v. Capsey* [1891] 3 Ch. 411.
[12] *Hill v. Cock* (1872) 26 L.T. 185 at 186.
[13] *Roberts v. Rose* (1865) L.R. 1 Ex. 82 at 89.
[14] *Davies v. Williams* (1851) 16 Q.B. 546 (*e.g.* demolition of an occupied dwelling-house).
[15] See *Perry v. Fitzhowe* (1846) 8 Q.B. 757. This and the previous case were cases on profits, but in this respect the same law applies to easements: see *Lane v. Capsey, supra*. In practice it will always be prudent to give notice first.
[16] *Lagan Navigation Co. v. Lambeg Bleaching, Dyeing and Finishing Co. Ltd* [1927] A.C. 226 at 244.

18–172   *(b) Action.* The plaintiff may seek damages, an injunction,[17] a declaration,[18] or a combination of these.[19] Trivial or temporary infringements will not justify an injunction.[20] But in other cases an injunction is a valuable remedy, for otherwise the servient owner could in effect make a compulsory purchase of the easement.[21] If damages are sought, some substantial interference with the enjoyment of the easement must be shown, and not merely injury to the servient land[22]; but proof of actual damage is not essential.[23]

Since the owner of an easement does not occupy the servient tenement in any sense, he has not the occupier's right of protection against third parties without proof of title. In other words, in an action for infringement he must be prepared to prove his title even against a third party. If, for example, an artificial watercourse is polluted by someone other than the servient owner, it is a defence that there was no capable grantor of the right.[24] This is a case where title rests upon the concept of absolute ownership, not possessory rights, and where therefore the defendant may plead *jus tertii*.[25] This applies to the title to the easement, not to the title to the dominant tenement. Any occupier of the land to which an easement (already duly acquired) is appurtenant (*e.g.* a tenant for life[26] or years[27]) may sue for disturbance of his right without having to prove his title to the land,[28] unless the defendant himself claims title to that land. A reversioner may also sue if the interference is such as to injure the reversion, *e.g.* by withdrawal of support to a building, or obstruction of light.[29]

18–173   **2. Profits.** Here also the remedy is either by abatement or by action.

18–174   *(a) Abatement.* This remedy (*e.g.* pulling down a fence or house which has been erected to the detriment of a profit of pasture) is governed by the same principles as in the case of easements.[30]

---

[17] Which may be mandatory, requiring the defendant to demolish a building that he has erected: *Pugh v. Howells* (1984) 48 P. & C.R. 298.

[18] *Litchfield-Speer v. Queen Anne's Gate Syndicate (No. 2) Ltd* [1919] 1 Ch. 407.

[19] *Leeds Industrial Co-operative Society Ltd v. Slack* [1924] A.C. 851 at 857.

[20] *Cowper v. Laidler* [1903] 2 Ch. 341; *Pettey v. Parsons* [1914] 1 Ch. 704 (reversed on another point [1914] 2 Ch. 653), where an injunction was refused, but £5 damages awarded for a "petty" infringement.

[21] *Dent v. Auction Mart Co.* (1866) L.R. 2 Eq. 238 at 246; *Pugh v. Howells, supra*, at 304.

[22] *Weston v. Lawrence Weaver Ltd* [1961] 1 Q.B. 402; *Saint v. Jenner* [1973] Ch. 275.

[23] *Nicholls v. Ely Beet Sugar Factory Ltd (No. 2)* [1936] Ch. 343 at 349.

[24] *Paine & Co. Ltd v. St Neots Gas & Coke Co.* [1939] 3 All E.R. 812. But see cases noted *ante*, para. 3–122, n. 37, which were not cited.

[25] For the rule against this defence in other cases, see *ante*, para. 3–124, and contrast the rule as to profits given below.

[26] *Simper v. Foley* (1862) 2 J. & H. 555.

[27] *Fishenden v. Higgs & Hill Ltd* (1935) 153 L.T. 128.

[28] Gale 14–17; *cf. William Aldred's Case* (1610) 9 Co.Rep. 57b. n. A.

[29] Gale 14–20. Similarly where the death of a witness might make a future claim more difficult to prove: see *Shadwell v. Hutchinson* (1829) 2 C. & P. 615 at 617; (1831) 2 B. & Ad. 97 at 98, 99.

[30] *Arlett v. Ellis* (1827) 7 B. & C. 346, (1829) 9 B. & C. 671; *Davies v. Williams* (1851) 16 Q.B. 546.

(b) Action. The rules are the same as in the case of easements,[31] with one   **18–175**
notable exception. This is that a profit, by conferring a right to take something
from the servient land, is held to give a sufficient degree of possession to
enable the possessor to sue a third party for infringement without proving his
title to the profit. Thus where a "several fishery" was injured by the discharge
from a factory some miles upstream, it was held that the defendant could not
dispute the plaintiff's title and so plead *jus tertii*.[32] This exception is connected with the doctrine that a profit, unlike an easement, may exist in gross.[33]
Had the action been against the servient owner, it would have been open to
him to contest the title; but a mere stranger cannot contest the title of a person
in possession.[34]

Section 5. Extinguishment of Easements and Profits

A. By Statute

There is no statutory procedure for the discharge or modification of obsolete   **18–176**
or obstructive easements, as there is in the case of restrictive covenants,[35]
though it might be equally desirable.[36] The only statutes of general application
relate to commons, which may be extinguished by approvement, by inclosure,
and under the Commons Registration Act 1965.[37]

1. Approvement. The lord of a manor had a common law right to   **18–177**
"approve" the manorial waste over which the tenants exercised rights of
pasture. Approvement was effected by the lord taking part of the waste for his
separate enjoyment. The Statutes of Merton 1235[38] and Westminster II 1285[39]
confirmed this practice, but obliged the lord to leave sufficient land for the
commoners. The onus of proving sufficiency was on the lord, and there had to
be enough pasture for all the animals which the commoners were entitled to
turn out, and not merely for those in fact turned out in recent years.[40] Since the
Commons Act 1876[41] a person seeking to approve a common otherwise than

---

[31] See *e.g. Fitzgerald v. Firbank* [1897] 2 Ch. 96 at 102 (damages); *Peech v. Best* [1931] 1 K.B. 1 (declaration).
[32] *Nicholls v. Ely Beet Sugar Factory Ltd (No. 1)* [1931] 2 Ch. 84. For *jus tertii*, see *ante*, para. 3–124.
[33] See *Paine & Co. Ltd v. St Neots Gas & Coke Co.* [1939] 3 All E.R. 812 at 823, *per* Luxmoore L.J. In *Mason v. Clarke* [1954] 1 Q.B. 460 at 470, Denning L.J. appears to deny that a claim to a profit may be based on a possessory title, but the decision was reversed by the House of Lords: [1955] A.C. 778, esp. at 794, *per* Viscount Simonds.
[34] See *ante*, para. 3–122, for discussion of this principle.
[35] *Ante*, para. 16–085.
[36] (1971) Law Commission Working Paper No. 36, para. 121.
[37] See generally G. D. Gadsden, *The Law of Commons* (1988). For a valuable summary of the legal history of common land, see *Hampshire C.C. v. Milburn* [1991] 1 A.C. 325 at 338–341, *per* Lord Templeman.
[38] c. 4.
[39] c. 46.
[40] *Robertson v. Hartopp* (1889) 43 Ch.D. 484.
[41] s.31.

under the Act must advertise his intention in the local press on three successive occasions; and the Law of Commons Amendment Act 1893[42] makes the consent of the appropriate Secretary of State, given after holding a local inquiry, essential to approvement.

18–178   **2. Inclosure.** Inclosure involves the discharge of the whole manorial waste from all rights of common, whereas approvement applies only to commons of pasture appendant or appurtenant, and discharges only part of the land. From the middle of the eighteenth century onwards a large number of private inclosure Acts were passed. The policy of Parliament was to encourage the efficient production of food, which was hardly possible under the medieval system of communal agriculture. The Inclosure (Consolidation) Act 1801 and the Inclosure Act 1845 further facilitated inclosures; but public opinion was aroused by the disappearance of open spaces, and the Inclosure Act 1852[43] prevented inclosures being made without the consent of Parliament. The procedure is now governed by the Commons Act 1876. An application must first be made to the appropriate Secretary of State, and if a prima facie case is made out, regard being had to the benefit of the neighbourhood, a local inquiry is held.[44–45]

3. The Commons Registration Act 1965

18–179   *(a) Object.* With the passage of time and changed social and economic conditions, there were many uncertainties about what lands were subject to rights of common, and what rights of common existed over these lands.[46] In order to lay a foundation for further legislation to govern the management and improvement of common land (which amounts to over 4 per cent of the total area of England and Wales), the Commons Registration Act 1965 enacted a scheme for ascertaining what rights were claimed to be still in existence, and for extinguishing the others.[47] The intended further legislation has not yet been forthcoming.[48]

18–180   *(b) Registrable rights.* The Act made registrable—

(i) common land;

(ii) rights of common over common land; and

---

[42] ss.2, 3.

[43] s.1 (now partially repealed); *cf.* Inclosure Act 1845, s.12, which had made the consent of Parliament essential in some, but not in all, cases.

[44–45] Commons Act 1876, ss.10, 11, 12. Most of this Act, together with substantial portions of the remaining inclosure legislation, was repealed by the Statute Law (Repeals) Act 1998.

[46] See Report of Royal Commission on Common Land, 1955–1958 (Cmnd. 462).

[47] For a survey of the working of the Act, see [1985] Conv. 24 (A. Samuels). For a powerful commentary on the "deficiencies of the 1965 commons legislation", see *R. v. Suffolk C.C., ex p. Steed* (1995) 70 P. & C.R. 487 at 489–494, *per* Carnwath J. (on appeal [1997] 1 E.G.L.R. 131).

[48] See *Hampshire C.C. v. Milburn* [1991] 1 A.C. 325 at 341; *R. v. Suffolk C.C., ex p. Steed* (1995) 70 P. & C.R. 487 at 493.

(iii) persons claiming to be, or found to be owners of common land.[49]

"Common land" means land that is subject to rights of common, and also waste land of a manor which is not subject to rights of common.[50] After considerable controversy it has now been settled that waste land of the manor means "waste land now or formerly of a manor" or "waste land of manorial origin".[51] It follows from this that land will not cease to be common land merely because the owner conveys the lordship of the manor to a third party while retaining the land (or *vice versa*).[52] To be waste, land must be open, uncultivated and unoccupied.[53] Rights of common cannot be registered if they are merely held for a term of years or from year to year.[54]

(c) Registration. The Act and the regulations made under it required **18–181** registration to be made with county and county borough councils. Registration had to be effected before August 1970[55]; and all applications for registration had to be made before January 3, 1970.[56] Any person might apply for registration of any land as common land.[57] Registration was merely provisional,[58] pending the determination of any objection, which had to be lodged before August 1972[59]; and provisional registration was of itself no evidence of the existence of the right registered.[60] If an objection was made, the validity

---

[49] s.1(1) Town and village greens were also registrable (*ibid.*): see *New Windsor Corporation v. Mellor* [1975] Ch. 380; *Re The Rye, High Wycombe, Buckinghamshire* [1977] 1 W.L.R. 1316; *Ministry of Defence v. Wiltshire C.C.* [1995] 4 All E.R. 931; *R. v. Suffolk C.C., ex p. Steed* [1997] 1 E.G.L.R. 131. The three-part definition of "town or village green" in s.22(1) of the Act gives rise to difficulties: see *Ministry of Defence v. Wiltshire C.C., supra*, at 937, 938; *R. v. Suffolk C.C., ex p. Steed* (1995) 70 P. & C.R. 487 at 491–493 (Carnwath J.). The definition includes land on which the inhabitants have indulged in lawful sports and pastimes as of right for not less than 20 years. It has been held that "as of right" means no more than *nec vi, nec clam, nec precario* (*cf. ante*, paras 18–123 *et seq.*). It is unnecessary to prove subjective belief as to that right by the inhabitants: see *R. v. Oxfordshire C.C., ex p. Sunningwell P.C.* [1999] 3 W.L.R. 160, overruling on this point *R. v. Suffolk C.C., ex p. Steed* [1997] 1 E.G.L.R. 131.
[50] s.22(1).
[51] *Hampshire C.C. v. Milburn* [1991] 1 A.C. 325, where the House of Lords approved *Re Chewton Common* [1977] 1 W.L.R. 1242, at 1249, 1250, in which Slade J. defined waste land of the manor as land "which was once waste land of a manor in the days when copyhold tenure still existed".
[52] *Hampshire C.C. v. Milburn, supra*, overruling *Re Box Hill Common* [1980] Ch. 109; *Lewis v. Mid Glamorgan C.C.* [1995] 1 W.L.R. 313. There had been an earlier attempt to reverse the *Box Hill* decision by a Private Member's Bill in 1980.
[53] *Re Britford Common* [1977] 1 W.L.R. 39.
[54] s.22(1).
[55] ss.1–4; S.I. 1970 No. 383.
[56] s.4(6); S.I. 1966 No. 1470; but see *post*, para. 18–182.
[57] s.4(2).
[58] s.4(5). See *Cooke v. Amey Gravel Co. Ltd* [1972] 1 W.L.R. 1310.
[59] S.I. 1968 No. 989; S.I. 1970 No. 384.
[60] *Cooke v. Amey Gravel Co. Ltd, supra.* Such provisional registration is not without effect however: see *Dynevor (Lord) v. Richardson* [1995] Ch. 173 (provisional registration of an expressly granted grazing right precluded any further claim to an equivalent right arising by lost modern grant in the period pending determination of the claim).

of the registration was decided by a Commons Commissioner, the burden of proof being on the person making the registration.[61] An objection to the registration of part only of the land in a registered unit put in issue the registration of the whole.[62] In determining whether land was or was not common land, the commissioner was required to have regard to the situation at the time of the hearing, not at the date of registration. If the land had ceased to be common land in the interim, the registration could not be confirmed.[63] There was a right of appeal to the High Court on a point of law[64]; and after the commissioners were appointed, their jurisdiction excluded that of the courts in all save cases of bad faith.[65]

18–182   Registration became final if no objection was duly lodged, or if after determining the objection the Commissioner or the court ordered confirmation.[66] There are provisions for rectification or amendment of the register in case of fraud or change of circumstances,[67] such as where land ceases to be common land, or becomes common land, or where registered rights are extinguished, varied or transferred. Otherwise final registration is conclusive evidence as to the land being common land and as to the registered rights of common over it as at the date of registration,[68] even where an entry is clearly wrong.[69] However, the position has been temporarily ameliorated by the provisions of the Common Land (Rectification of Registers) Act 1989. This is considered below.

After July 1970 no land capable of being registered is to be deemed to be common land unless it is so registered; and no rights of common "shall be exercisable" over any such land unless they are either registered under the Act or have been registered previously[70] under the Land Registration Acts, 1925 and 1936.[71] These provisions accordingly operate to extinguish all existing unregistered rights,[72] including statutory rights of common derived from

---

[61] *Re Sutton Common, Wimborne* [1982] 1 W.L.R. 647; *Re Ilkley and Burley Moors* (1983) 47 P. & C.R. 324 at 328; *Re West Anstey Common* [1985] Ch. 330. Thus the inquiry was not merely into the objection.

[62] *Re West Anstey Common, supra.*

[63] *Re Merthyr Mawr Common* [1989] 1 W.L.R. 1014.

[64] ss.6, 17, 18. For the procedure before the commissioners, see S.I. 1971 No. 1727; S.I. 1973 No. 815.

[65] *Thorne R.D.C. v. Bunting* [1972] Ch. 470 (court's jurisdiction before any commissioners were appointed); *Wilkes v. Gee* [1973] 1 W.L.R. 742.

[66] ss.6, 7, 10. For the registers and procedure, see S.I. 1966 No. 1471; S.I. 1980 No. 1195; S.I. 1982 Nos. 209, 210.

[67] ss.13, 14. These provisions cannot be used as a means of challenging a registration that should not have been made in the first place: *R. v. Norfolk County Council, ex p. Perry* (1996) 74 P. & C.R. 1.

[68] s.10.

[69] *Corpus Christi College Oxford v. Gloucestershire County Council* [1983] Q.B. 360, where the Court of Appeal criticised these provisions.

[70] See s.1(1).

[71] s.1(2); S.I. 1970 No. 383. In this context, "registered" includes both provisional and final registration: *Dynevor (Lord) v. Richardson* [1995] Ch. 173.

[72] *Central Electricity Generating Board v. Clwyd County Council* [1976] 1 W.L.R. 151.

enclosure awards,[73] and public rights of access.[74] By themselves, they would have prevented any new rights from arising; but elaborate provisions have been made for the registration of any land becoming common land (or a town or village green) after January 2, 1970, and also for the registration of rights of common over such land, and rights of ownership.[75] The general procedure is similar to that for existing rights.

(d) *Exemptions.* Certain land is outside these provisions, such as the New Forest and Epping Forest, and any other land exempted by ministerial order[76]; and provision is also made for the vesting and protection of land which has been registered as common land but which has no registered owner.[77]   **18–183**

(e) *Removal from the register under the Common Land (Rectification of Registers) Act 1989.*[78] A major defect of the Commons Registration Act 1965 was that property could be provisionally registered as common land without notification to the owner. He then lost his property when that registration became absolute.[79] The Common Land (Rectification of Registers) Act 1989[80] was therefore enacted "to rectify the injustice caused by the inadvertent expropriation of private property by an Act the purpose of which was the preservation of customary rights and public rights".[81] It was a limited measure, now spent, which provided that any person might, within a three-year period,[82] object to the registration as common land of property which, at all times since August 5, 1945, had been a dwelling-house and/or land which was ancillary to it.[83] "Dwelling-house" has been widely interpreted to include a property constructed or adapted for dwelling in, even though derelict and uninhabitable.[84] Land ancillary to a dwelling-house is defined as a garden, private garage or outbuildings used and enjoyed with the dwelling-house.[85] Land may be a garden although it is not cultivated,[86] and even if it is separated from the dwelling-house and held under a different title.[87] But fields of pasture are not within the definition.[88] Objections are determined by a commons   **18–184**

---

[73] *Re Turnworth Down, Dorset* [1978] Ch. 251.
[74] *R. v. Doncaster M.B.C., ex p. Braim* (1986) 57 P. & C.R. 1 at 7, 8; [1988] Conv. 369 at 370 (J. Hill). For public rights over common land, see L.P.A. 1925, s.193.
[75] S.I. 1969 No. 1843. See *R. v. Suffolk C.C., ex p. Steed* [1997] 1 E.G.L.R. 131.
[76] s.11. See S.I. 1965 Nos. 2000, 2001.
[77] ss.8, 9.
[78] See [1989] Conv. 384 (A. Samuels); [1992] 24 L.S.G. 18 (A. Favell).
[79] *Cresstock Investments Ltd v. Commons Commissioner* [1992] 1 W.L.R. 1088 at 1089.
[80] It was introduced as a Private Member's Bill. For regulations under the Act, see S.I. 1990 No. 311.
[81] *Storey v. Commons Commissioner* (1993) 66 P. & C.R. 206 at 216, *per* Vinelott J.
[82] Which began on July 21, 1989 and ended on July 20, 1992: s.1(1).
[83] s.1(2).
[84] *Re 1–4, White Row Cottages, Bewerley* [1991] Ch. 441.
[85] s.1(3).
[86] *Cresstock Investments Ltd v. Commons Commissioner, supra.*
[87] *Storey v. Commons Commissioner, supra.* It has been held to include land used for car parking: *Re Fox Barn, part of Hawridge and Cholesbury Commons* [1994] E.G.C.S. 149.
[88] *Re Land at Freshfields* (1993) 66 P. & C.R. 9; *Re Land at Mooredge Farm* [1994] E.G.C.S. 82.

commissioner who is required to modify the register by excluding from the register any land that satisfies the criteria laid down by the Act.[89]

B. By Release

18–185   **1. Express release.** At law a deed is required for an express release of an easement of profit.[90] In equity, however, an informal release will be effective provided it would be inequitable for the dominant owner to claim that the right still exists,[91] as where he has orally consented to his light being obstructed and the servient owner has spent money on erecting the obstruction.[92] A release of a portion of a common appurtenant extinguishes the whole common,[93] but this does not apply to a several profit appurtenant.[94]

2. Implied release

18–186   *(a) Abandonment.* Abandonment of an easement or profit will not be lightly inferred.[95] An owner of property does not normally wish to divest himself of it even though he may have no present use for it.[96] Mere non-user will not of itself suffice therefore,[97] even if accompanied by a mistaken belief that the right has been extinguished.[98] It is now clear that non-user for a period of 20 years will not raise a presumption of abandonment,[99] despite earlier authority which suggested otherwise.[1] It must be proved[2] that the person having the right intends to abandon it,[3] that is, that neither he nor any of his successors

---

[89] s.1(4).

[90] Co. Litt. 264b; *Lovell v. Smith* (1857) 3 C.B. (N.S.) 120 at 127; but see *Norbury v. Meade* (1821) 3 Bli. 211 at 241, 242 (easement).

[91] *Davies v. Marshall* (1816) 10 C.B. (N.S.) 697 at 710.

[92] *Waterlow v. Bacon* (1866) L.R. 2 Eq. 514.

[93] *Miles v. Etteridge* (1692) 1 Show.K.B. 349.

[94] *Johnson v. Barnes* (1873) L.R. 8 C.P. 527.

[95] *Huckvale v. Aegean Hotels Ltd* (1989) 58 P. & C.R. 163 at 171, 173; *Snell & Prideaux Ltd v. Dutton Mirrors Ltd* [1995] 1 E.G.L.R. 259 at 261, 262. Abandonment, where it is established, may be partial and not total (*semble*): *ibid.*, at 261. For the view that the true basis of abandonment is a form of estoppel, see [1995] Conv. 291 (C. J. Davis).

[96] *Gotobed v. Pridmore* (1971) 217 E.G. 759 at 760; *Benn v. Hardinge* (1992) 66 P. & C.R. 246 at 257, 262; *Bosomworth v. Faber* (1992) 69 P. & C.R. 288 at 294, 295.

[97] *Ward v. Ward* (1852) 7 Exch. 838 at 839; *Re Yateley Common* [1977] 1 W.L.R. 840 at 845. For an extreme case, see *Treweeke v. 36 Wolseley Road Pty Ltd* (1973) 128 C.L.R. 274 (way survives despite vertical rock faces, impenetrable bamboo plantations, swimming pool and fence).

[98] *Obadia v. Morris* (1974) 232 E.G. 333.

[99] *Benn v. Hardinge, supra,* rejecting a statement to the contrary in the previous edition of this work at p. 898. In that case, 175 years' non-user was held not to amount to abandonment when there was no substantial physical change to the servient tenement and no obstacle to the exercise of the right. See too *Gotobed v. Pridmore, supra* (abandonment not inferred from 65 years' non-user). The Law Commission and Land Registry have recommended that where title is registered, this presumption should be reinstated in respect of easements which take effect as overriding interests: (1998) Law Com. No. 254, paras 5.21–5.24.

[1] *Crossley & Sons Ltd v. Lightowler* (1867) 2 Ch.App. 478 at 482.

[2] The onus lies on the party asserting abandonment: *Re Yateley Common, supra,* at 845.

[3] *Swan v. Sinclair* [1924] 1 Ch. 254, aff'd [1925] A.C. 227; but see *post,* para. 18–189, n. 17.

in title intends thereafter to exercise it.[4] "It is one thing not to assert an intention to use a way, and another thing to assert an intention to abandon it."[5]

(b) Intention. It is a question of fact whether an act was intended as an   **18–187** abandonment.[6] Grazing rights have been held not to be abandoned merely by the commoners making temporary arrangements for regulating their rights, even if this is accompanied by payments to the servient owner[7]; and the bricking-up of a door for over 30 years was held no abandonment of a right of way.[8] On the other hand, replacing a wall containing windows by a blank wall was held to be an abandonment of light after 17 years,[9] but the servient owner had meanwhile erected buildings which would have obstructed the former lights, and the presumption of abandonment is naturally stronger where the dominant owner has allowed the servient owner to incur expense without any protest.[10] However, the court will be reluctant to find such an intention unless there has been some fundamental change to the dominant tenement.[11]

(c) Altering dominant tenement. Alterations to the dominant tenement   **18–188** which make the enjoyment of an easement or profit impossible or unnecessary may show an intent to abandon the right. Thus, if a mill to which an easement of water is appurtenant is demolished without any intent to replace it, the easement is released[12]; and a profit of pasture appurtenant will be extinguished if the dominant land becomes part of a town, or a reservoir, but not if the land could easily be turned to the purpose of feeding cattle.[13] Again, the demolition of a house to which an easement of light is appurtenant may amount to an implied release, but not if it is intended to replace the house by another building.[14] It is not essential that the new windows should occupy exactly the same positions as the old, provided they receive substantially the same light[15]; the test is identity of light, not identity of aperture.[16]

---

[4] *Gotobed v. Pridmore, supra,* at 760; *Tehidy Minerals Ltd v. Norman* [1971] 2 Q.B. 528 at 553; *Williams v. Usherwood* (1981) 45 P. & C.R. 235 at 256; *Lovett v. Fairclough* (1990) 61 P. & C.R. 385 at 400; *Snell & Prideaux Ltd v. Dutton Mirrors Ltd, supra.*

[5] *James v. Stevenson* [1893] A.C. 162 at 168, *per* Sir Edward Fry.

[6] *Cook v. Mayor and Corporation of Bath* (1868) L.R. 6 Eq. 177 at 179.

[7] *Tehidy Minerals Ltd v. Norman* [1971] 2 Q.B. 528.

[8] *Cook v. Mayor and Corporation of Bath* (1868) L.R. 6 Eq. 177. See too *Carder v. Davies* (1998) 76 P. & C.R. D33 (right to use roadway with no limit as to point of access not abandoned when one entry point was built over).

[9] *Moore v. Rawson* (1824) 3 B. & C. 332.

[10] *Cook v. Mayor and Corporation of Bath, supra,* at 179; *cf. Waterlow v. Bacon* (1866) L.R. 2 Eq. 514.

[11] *Re Yateley Common* [1977] 1 W.L.R. 840 at 848.

[12] *Liggins v. Inge* (1831) 7 Bing. 682 at 693; and see *National Guaranteed Manure Co. Ltd v. Donald* (1859) 4 H. & N. 8 (canal converted into railway: right to water for canal extinguished).

[13] *Carr v. Lambert* (1866) L.R. 1 Ex. 168.

[14] *Ecclesiastical Commissioners for England v. Kino* (1880) 14 Ch.D. 213.

[15] *Scott v. Pape* (1886) 31 Ch.D. 554.

[16] *Andrews v. Waite* [1907] 2 Ch. 500 at 510. These rules apply equally to alterations made while the light is being acquired: *ibid.,* at 509.

18–189   *(d) Effect of excessive user.* It has been suggested that if the burden of the easement is substantially increased, the right may be extinguished altogether.[17] However, although this is true for continuous easements such as rights of light or support,[18] it has been doubted in relation to discontinuous rights, such as rights of way. The owner of a servient tenement is entitled to an injunction to restrain excessive user of the easement,[19] but this does not extinguish or suspend the right.[20] "Provided that the owner of the dominant tenement subsequently reverts to lawful use of the easement, his prior excessive use of it is then irrelevant."[21] There may be cases of excessive user which are such that the servient owner may obstruct the exercise of the easement. However, this will be the case only where "it is impossible to sever the good user from the excessive user",[22] as where a person discharges sewage into a surface water drain.[23]

18–190   *(e) Altering servient tenement.* An alteration of the servient tenement may bring about an extinguishment if it is acquiesced in by the dominant owner[24] or if it is made to give effect to an agreement between the dominant and servient owners to replace the existing right with a new one.[25]

C. By Unity of Ownership and Possession

18–191   If the dominant and servient tenements come into the ownership and possession of the same person, any easement or profit is extinguished.[26] Unity of possession without unity of ownership is not enough[27]; and unity of ownership means acquisition of both tenements for a fee simple absolute.[28] If there is only unity of possession the right is merely suspended until the unity of possession ceases.[29] If there is only unity of ownership the right continues

---

[17] "An easement is extinguished when its mode of user is so altered as to cause prejudice to the servient tenement": *Ray v. Fairway Motors (Barnstaple) Ltd* (1968) 20 P. & C.R. 261 at 266, *per* Willmer L.J. (easement of support extinguishable, irrespective of intention, by greatly increasing weight on dominant land—though this was not proved on the facts). See too *Ankerson v. Connelly* [1906] 2 Ch. 544, aff'd [1907] 1 Ch. 678 (easement of light for aperture in partly-open shed extinguished by enclosing shed and shutting out all other light).

[18] But see *Woodhouse v. Consolidated Property Corporation Ltd* (1992) 66 P. & C.R. 234 at 243 (material alteration to the nature of use required to extinguish easement of support).

[19] *Jelbert v. Davis* [1968] 1 W.L.R. 589; *Hamble P.C. v. Haggard* [1992] 1 W.L.R. 122 at 134.

[20] *Graham v. Philcox* [1984] Q.B. 747.

[21] *ibid.,* at 756, *per* May L.J.

[22] *Hamble P.C. v. Haggard, supra,* at 134, *per* Millett J.

[23] *e.g. Charles v. Finchley Local Board* (1883) 23 Ch.D. 767 at 775; Gale 12–82.

[24] *Scrutton v. Stone* (1893) 9 T.L.R. 478 (pasture claimed over land which had become covered with buildings).

[25] *Bosomworth v. Faber* (1992) 69 P. & C.R. 288 (new tank and pipes for taking water from the plaintiff's land pursuant to a written licence held to extinguish existing easement).

[26] *Tyrringham's Case* (1584) 4 Co. Rep. 36b at 38a (profit); *Buckby v. Coles* (1814) 5 Taunt. 311 (easement). See (1977) 41 Conv. (N.S.) 107 (J. D. A. Brooke-Taylor). *cf. Re Tiltwood, Sussex* [1978] Ch. 269 (restrictive covenants), *ante,* para. 16–084.

[27] *Canham v. Fisk* (1831) 2 Cr. & J. 126; and see *Thomas v. Thomas* (1835) 2 Cr.M. & R. 34 at 40.

[28] Gale 12–02; *R. v. Inhabitants of Hermitage* (1692) Carth. 239 at 241 (union of base fee with fee simple absolute works no extinguishment).

[29] *Canham v. Fisk, supra.*

until there is also unity of possession.[30] Thus if both dominant and servient tenements are under lease, the easement or profit will not be extinguished merely because both leases are assigned to X,[31] or both reversions to Y[32]; but if both leases and both reversions become vested in Z, the right is gone. Similarly, if the fee simple owner of one tenement takes a lease of the other, the right is merely suspended during the lease.[33]

A common appurtenant has been held to be wholly extinguished if the dominant owner acquires any part of the servient tenement, since otherwise the remainder of the servient tenement would be unduly burdened.[34] But in the case of a common appendant the burden was apportioned,[35] and much may be said for extending this more liberal rule to commons appurtenant.[36]

Section 6. Species of Easements

A. Rights of Way

1. Extent of easements of way

(a) General or limited. An easement of way may be either general or limited. A general right of way is one which may be used by the owner of the dominant tenement and his visitors[37] at any time and in any way. A limited right of way is one which is restricted in some way. The restriction may be as to time, *e.g.* a way which can be used only in the daytime,[38] or it may be as to the mode in which the way can be used, *e.g.* a way limited to foot passengers,[39] or to cattle and other animals in charge of a drover,[40] or to wheeled traffic,[41] and the like.

18–192

(b) Other land. A right of way can normally be used only as a means of access to the dominant tenement. A right to pass over Plot A to reach Plot B

18–193

---

[30] *Richardson v. Graham* [1908] 1 K.B. 39. For this reason "unity of seisin" is not a satisfactory term for the unity of both ownership and possession which is required.

[31] *Thomas v. Thomas, supra.*

[32] *Richardson v. Graham, supra.* This was a case on light, and it is not clear whether the decision was founded on the peculiar nature of the easement of light, or the doctrine of non-derogation from grant (*ante*, para. 18–075). In principle the rule should be the same for all easements. *cf. Buckby v. Coles* (1814) 5 Taunt. 311 at 315, 316.

[33] *Simper v. Foley* (1862) 2 J. & H. 555 at 563, 564.

[34] *White v. Taylor* [1969] 1 Ch. 150.

[35] *Wyat Wyld's Case* (1609) 8 Co.Rep. 78b.

[36] Consider *Benson v. Chester* (1799) 8 T.R. 396 at 401.

[37] *Jalnarne Ltd v. Ridewood* (1989) 61 P. & C.R. 143 at 160; *Re St Martin le Grand, York* [1990] Fam. 63 at 78–81.

[38] *Collins v. Slade* (1874) 23 W.R. 199; *cf. Hollins v. Verney* (1884) 13 Q.B.D. 304 (right of way to remove timber cut every 12 years).

[39] *Cousens v. Rose* (1871) L.R. 12 Eq. 366.

[40] *Brunton v. Hall* (1841) 1 Q.B. 792.

[41] *Ballard v. Dyson* (1808) 1 Taunt. 279.

cannot be used as a means of access to Plot C lying beyond Plot B,[42] unless Plot B is itself used as a means of access to Plot C at the time of the grant.[43] But the mere fact that Plot C is added to Plot B, so that the dominant tenement is enlarged, will not destroy a right of way previously appurtenant to Plot B,[44] provided that the user is not excessive,[45] or is merely ancillary to the user of Plot B.[46] Furthermore, the grant of a right of way to part of the dominant tenement may be construed as a grant for the benefit of the whole of that tenement.[47]

18–194   *(c) Construction and repair.* In the absence of contrary agreement,[48] or special circumstances,[49] it is for the grantee of a way, not the grantor, to construct the way[50] and to repair it when constructed: the grantee may enter the servient tenement for these purposes.[51] The benefit of a covenant by the grantor to repair the way may run with the easement[52]; but as such a covenant is positive, the burden cannot of course run with the servient land.[53] If the way becomes impassable, there is no right to deviate from it[54] unless the servient owner has obstructed it.[55] A limited right of way cannot be converted into a general right of way by improving it.[56]

18–195   *(d) Interference.* Although any obstruction of a public way is actionable *per se*, no action will lie in respect of a private right of way unless the interference

---

[42] *Skull v. Glenister* (1864) 16 C.B. (N.S.) 81; *Colchester v. Roberts* (1839) 4 M. & W. 769 at 774; *Harris v. Flower* (1904) 74 L.J.Ch. 127 (building standing partly on B and partly on C); *Bracewell v. Appleby* [1975] Ch. 408; *Alvis v. Harrison* (1990) 62 P. & C.R. 10 at 15, 16; *Jobson v. Record* [1998] 1 E.G.L.R. 113. *cf. Britel Developments (Thatcham) Ltd v. Night-freight (G.B.) Ltd* [1998] 4 All E.R. 432.

[43] *Nickerson v. Barraclough* [1980] Ch. 325 at 336, not affected on appeal [1981] Ch. 426 (implied grant under L.P.A. 1925, s.62).

[44] *Graham v. Philcox* [1984] Q.B. 747; but see *National Trust v. White* [1987] 1 W.L.R. 907 at 913, treating *Graham v. Philcox* as an authority only on L.P.A. 1925, s.62(2) (by which a conveyance includes all easements appertaining to the land "or any part thereof"); [1987] Conv. 363 (J. E. Martin).

[45] *Graham v. Philcox, supra.*

[46] *National Trust v. White, supra* (car park merely ancillary to right of way to iron age hill fort).

[47] *Callard v. Beeney* [1930] 1 K.B. 353.

[48] *Taylor v. Whitehead* (1781) 2 Doug.K.B. 745 at 749. The contrary agreement may be implied rather than express: *Liverpool City Council v. Irwin* [1977] A.C. 239; *King v. South North-amptonshire D.C.* (1991) 64 P. & C.R. 35.

[49] *Miller v. Hancock* [1893] 2 Q.B. 177, not affected on this point by *Fairman v. Perpetual Investment B.S.* [1923] A.C. 74.

[50] *Ingram v. Morecraft* (1863) 33 Beav. 49 at 51.

[51] *Newcomen v. Coulson* (1877) 5 Ch.D. 133; *Stokes v. Mixconcrete (Holdings) Ltd* (1978) 38 P. & C.R. 488. Lord Upjohn's denial of this right in *Redland Bricks Ltd v. Morris* [1970] A.C. 652 at 665 seems to have been *per incuriam.*

[52] *Gaw v. Coras Iompair Eireann* [1953] I.R. 232; contrast *Grant v. Edmondson* [1931] 1 Ch. 1 (rentcharge: *ante*, para. 18–030).

[53] *Ante*, para. 16–017.

[54] *Bullard v. Harrison* (1815) 4 M. & S. 387.

[55] *Selby v. Nettlefold* (1873) 9 Ch.App. 111.

[56] *Mills v. Silver* [1991] Ch. 271. The dominant owner may "not substantially alter the nature of the road nor otherwise prejudice the servient tenement": *Alvis v. Harrison* (1990) 62 P. & C.R. 10 at 15, *per* Lord Jauncey.

with its exercise is substantial.[57] This will be the case only where the act or conduct interferes with the reasonable user of the right.[58] The servient owner has no right to alter the route of a right of way unless such a right has been expressly or impliedly conferred on him either by the grant or reservation of the easement or by subsequent agreement.[59] Whether such a realignment will in all cases be an actionable interference, even if it is equally convenient to the servient owner, has not been settled.[60]

2. Effect of mode of acquisition. The extent of an easement of way **18–196** depends upon the manner of its acquisition.

(a) Express grant or reservation. Here the question is primarily one of **18–197** determining the intention of the parties as a matter of construction from the words of grant[61] read in the light of the surrounding circumstances.[62] The rules of construction, as already explained,[63] are that in case of doubt—

> (i) the grant of an easement is construed against the person making it in accordance with the general rule[64]; but

> (ii) the reservation of an easement is treated as if it were still made by means of a grant and regrant and is construed against the owner of the servient tenement.[65]

Rights of way are often granted in very wide terms, *e.g.* "at all times and for all purposes". But even without such words the right, if granted in general terms, is not confined to the purpose for which the land is used at the time of the grant, but may be used for any other lawful purpose.[66] A right of way for general purposes granted as appurtenant to a house can be used (though not enlarged[67]) for the business of a hotel if that house is subsequently converted

---

[57] *Pettey v. Parsons* [1914] 2 Ch. 653 at 662. "The plaintiff cannot complain, unless he can prove an obstruction which injures him": *Thorpe v. Brumfitt* (1873) 8 Ch.App. 650 at 656, *per* James L.J. See too *Clifford v. Hoare* (1874) L.R. 9 C.P. 362.

[58] *Keefe v. Amor* [1965] 1 Q.B. 334 at 347, *per* Russell L.J.; *Celsteel Ltd v. Alton House Holdings Ltd* [1985] 1 W.L.R. 204 at 216, 217.

[59] *Greenwich Healthcare N.H.S. Trust v. London and Quadrant Housing Trust* [1998] 1 W.L.R. 1749.

[60] *ibid.*, at 1754, 1755.

[61] *cf. Jobson v. Record* [1998] 1 E.G.L.R. 113 (right of way for agricultural purposes did not include removal of felled timber).

[62] *Robinson v. Bailey* [1948] 2 All E.R. 791. The surrounding circumstances may include both the physical characteristics of the way (*White v. Richards* (1993) 68 P. & C.R. 105) and the terms of an existing planning consent (*Scott v. Martin* [1987] 1 W.L.R. 841).

[63] *Ante*, para. 18–094.

[64] *Williams v. James* (1867) L.R. 2 C.P. 577 at 581.

[65] See *ante*, paras 18–094, 18–095 for criticism.

[66] *South Eastern Ry v. Cooper* [1924] 1 Ch. 211; *Alvis v. Harrison, supra*, at 15; *Jalnarne Ltd v. Ridewood* (1989) 61 P. & C.R. 143 at 157, 158; *Pole v. Peake* [1998] E.G.C.S. 125.

[67] *White v. Grand Hotel, Eastbourne, Ltd* [1913] 1 Ch. 113 at 116.

into a hotel.[68] A right of way over a strip of land 20 feet wide approached by a narrow gap may be exercisable over the whole width when later the gap is widened[69]; and a right "to pass and repass" along a way may include a right to halt and load or unload vehicles,[70] with a right to adequate space overhead and perhaps a little latitude alongside.[71] A right to cross a railway line "with all manner of cattle" may be a right of way for all purposes and not confined to agricultural purposes.[72] But where the servient owner is liable to repair the way, user may not be increased so as to add to that liability.[73] A way granted as appurtenant to an open space *as such* cannot be used as a means of access to a cottage subsequently built on it.[74] Nor, of course, can a way be used so as to infringe the rights of others entitled to use it.[75] Where a right of way is granted "for all purposes" in common with other persons, the exercise of that right must not interfere unreasonably with the use by the others so entitled.[76]

18–198   If a way is granted "as at present enjoyed", prima facie these words refer to the quality of the user (*e.g.* on foot or with vehicles) and do not limit the quantity of the user to that existing at the time of the grant.[77] In case of difficulty, as where there is a simple grant or reservation of "a right of way", the surrounding circumstances must be considered[78]: thus both the condition of the way (*e.g.* whether it is a footpath or a metalled road) and the nature of the dominant tenement (*e.g.* whether it is a dwelling-house or a factory) may be of assistance in determining whether any vehicles, and if so, which, may use the way.[79]

18–199   *(b) Implied grant or reservation.* A way of necessity is limited to the necessity existing at the time the right arose; thus if an encircled plot is used for agricultural purposes at the time of the grant, the way of necessity over the

---

[68] *White v. Grand Hotel, Eastbourne, Ltd, supra* (aff'd 84 L.J.Ch. 938). See also *Robinson v. Bailey* [1948] 2 All E.R. 791 (way to building plot held to cover business user).

[69] *Keefe v. Amor* [1965] 1 Q.B. 334.

[70] *Bulstrode v. Lambert* [1953] 1 W.L.R. 1064; *McIlraith v. Grady* [1968] 1 Q.B. 468; but see *Todrick v. Western National Omnibus Co. Ltd* [1934] Ch. 561 (user by omnibuses excessive). *cf. London and Suburban Land and Building Co. (Holdings) Ltd v. Carey* (1991) 62 P. & C.R. 480.

[71] *V.T. Engineering Ltd v. Richard Barland & Co. Ltd* (1968) 19 P. & C.R. 890 ("swing space" for loading and unloading vehicles).

[72] *British Railways Board v. Glass* [1965] Ch. 538.

[73] *T.R.H. Sampson Associates Ltd v. British Railways Board* [1984] Q.B. 747 (Board liable for repair of bridge).

[74] *Allan v. Gomme* (1840) 11 A. & E. 759. Contrast *Graham v. Philcox* [1984] Q.B. 747.

[75] *Jelbert v. Davis* [1968] 1 W.L.R. 589 (user of way for 200-caravan site).

[76] *Rosling v. Pinnegar* (1986) 54 P. & C.R. 124 (use of way by coaches bringing visitors to see mansion excessive).

[77] *Hurt v. Bowmer* [1937] 1 All E.R. 797.

[78] *St Edmundsbury & Ipswich Diocesan Board of Finance v. Clark (No. 2)* [1975] 1 W.L.R. 468.

[79] *Cannon v. Villars* (1878) 8 Ch.D. 415 at 420. See also *Att.-Gen. v. Hodgson* [1922] 1 Ch. 429 (carriageway granted in 1861 held to extend to motor cars); *Kain v. Norfolk* [1949] Ch. 163 (grant for use by "carts" held to cover use by motor-lorries). There is a general discussion in *St Edmundsbury & Ipswich Diocesan Board of Finance v. Clark (No. 2), supra.*

surrounding land is limited to agricultural purposes and cannot be used for the carting of building materials.[80]

In other cases of implied grant the circumstances of the case must be considered. Thus where a testator devised adjoining plots of land to different persons, and one plot was bought by a railway company for conversion into a railway station, it was held that a way which had been used in the testator's lifetime for domestic purposes and for the purposes of warehouses on the land could not be used as a public approach to the station.[81]

(c) Prescription. Where an easement of way is acquired by long user, "the right acquired must be measured by the extent of the enjoyment which is proved".[82] Thus a way acquired by long user for farming purposes cannot be used for mineral purposes,[83] or for a camping ground,[84] or for the cartage of building materials.[85] It has been held that user during the prescriptive period as a carriageway does not authorise user for cattle[86]; but it covers user as a footway[87] (since prima facie the greater includes the less[88]) and it extends to user for motor traffic even if the user proved was for horse-drawn vehicles alone, for the right is essentially a right for vehicles, and the mode of propulsion is immaterial.[89] Apart from any radical change in the dominant tenement, the user of the way is not limited by reference to numbers or frequency during the prescriptive period, so that a way acquired for a sparsely occupied caravan site may still be used when the site holds more caravans,[90] and user of a way acquired for business purposes may expand with the expansion of the business.[91]   **18–200**

B. Rights of Light

1. No natural right. There is no natural right to light[92]; a landowner may so build on his land as to prevent any light from reaching his neighbour's   **18–201**

---

[80] *Corp. of London v. Riggs* (1880) 13 Ch.D. 798.
[81] *Milner's Safe Co. Ltd v. Great Northern & City Ry* [1907] 1 Ch. 208.
[82] *Williams v. James* (1867) L.R. 2 C.P. 577 at 580, *per* Bovill C.J. See too *United Land Co. v. Great Eastern Ry* (1875) 10 Ch.App. 586 at 590; *Ironside v. Cook* (1978) 41 P. & C.R. 326 at 336; *Mills v. Silver* [1991] Ch. 271 at 287.
[83] *Bradburn v. Morris* (1876) 3 Ch.D. 812.
[84] *R.P.C. Holdings Ltd v. Rogers* [1953] 1 All E.R. 1029.
[85] *Wimbledon & Putney Commons Conservators v. Dixon* (1875) 1 Ch.D. 362. The fact that there has been occasional user for the cartage of materials to enlarge the farm house and rebuild a cottage on the farm does not enable the dominant owner to cart materials to build new houses: *ibid.*
[86] *Ballard v. Dyson* (1808) 1 Taunt. 279. This seems to have turned to some extent on the danger offered by horned cattle (see at 286). And see *British Railways Board v. Glass* [1965] Ch. 538.
[87] *Davies v. Stephens* (1836) 7 C. & P. 570.
[88] See Gale 9–02.
[89] *Lock v. Abercester Ltd* [1939] Ch. 861.
[90] *British Railways Board v. Glass* [1965] Ch. 538.
[91] *Woodhouse & Co. Ltd v. Kirkland (Derby) Ltd* [1970] 1 W.L.R. 1185.
[92] *Ante*, para. 18–063.

windows,[93] unless his neighbour has an easement of light or some other right such as a restrictive covenant against building. The access of light to windows is sometimes deliberately obstructed to prevent an easement of light being acquired by prescription.[94] Long established rights to light are sometimes called "ancient lights".

18–202   **2. Quantum of light.** An easement of light can exist only in respect of a building which receives it through a window[95] or other aperture such as a skylight,[96] or through transparent panels as in the case of a greenhouse.[97] The amount of light to which the dominant owner is entitled was determined by the House of Lords in *Colls v. Home and Colonial Stores Ltd*.[98] This amount is enough light according to the ordinary notions of mankind for the comfortable use of the premises as a dwelling, or, in the case of business premises, for the beneficial use of the premises as a warehouse, shop or other place of business. The same test applies, *mutatis mutandis*, to any other premises, *e.g.* a church,[99] a greenhouse,[1] or a photographic studio.[2] The measure is thus "ordinary user"; the dominant owner is not entitled to object even to a substantial diminution in his light, provided enough is left for ordinary purposes. The test is not "How much light has been taken away?", but "How much light is left?"[3] But the light needed for ordinary user depends upon the nature of the building, so that the high level of light required for a greenhouse can be acquired as an easement either by grant or by prescription.[4]

18–203   An easement of a greater amount of light than that required for ordinary purposes can, it seems be granted and also be acquired by prescription if for 20 years the dominant owner has both needed and enjoyed it to the knowledge of the servient owner.[5] On the other hand, the quantum of light to which the dominant owner is entitled is not affected by the fact that he has used the room for purposes which only require a little light.[6] A right of light is a right to have

---

[93] *Tapling v. Jones* (1865) 11 H.L.C. 290.
[94] See *e.g. Mayor, etc., of Paddington v. Att.-Gen.* [1906] A.C. 1.
[95] *Levet v. Gas Light & Coke Co.* [1919] 1 Ch. 24.
[96] *Easton v. Isted* [1903] 1 Ch. 405.
[97] *Allen v. Greenwood* [1980] Ch. 119.
[98] [1904] A.C. 179.
[99] *Newham v. Lawson* (1971) 22 P. & C.R. 852.
[1] *Allen v. Greenwood, supra.*
[2] *ibid.*, at 133.
[3] See *Higgins v. Betts* [1905] 2 Ch. 210 at 215, *per* Farwell J.; *Carr-Saunders v. Dick McNeil Associates Ltd* [1986] 1 W.L.R. 922 at 928. The Prescription Act 1832 has made no change in this rule: *Kelk v. Pearson* (1871) 6 Ch.App. 809.
[4] *Allen v. Greenwood, supra* (claim under Prescription Act 1832 succeeded). The Court of Appeal left open the question of claims involving heat only, *e.g.* for solar heating. For the problems which can arise where a room is so badly lit that any deprivation of light will render it unfit for ordinary use, see [1984] Conv. 408 (A. H. Hudson).
[5] *Allen v. Greenwood, supra*, as the secondary ground of decision, following *Lanfranchi v. Mackenzie* (1867) L.R. 4 Eq. 421 in preference to *Ambler v. Gordon* [1905] 1 K.B. 417. The requirement of acquiescence seems to be a gloss on the Act.
[6] *Price v. Hilditch* [1930] 1 Ch. 500 (scullery).

access of light for all ordinary purposes to which the room may be put,[7] which may include a subdivision of the space into smaller units if this is an ordinary and reasonable use of it.[8]

3. Infringement. If the dominant owner alters the user of his premises,[9] or the size or position of the windows,[10] the burden on the servient tenement is not increased. An obstruction which would not have been actionable before the alteration will therefore not be actionable even if it deprives the altered window of most of its light[11]; the test is identity of light, not identity of aperture.[12] If the alterations to the dominant tenement render it impossible for the court to determine the extent to which the light received by the old windows is received by the new, the easement is lost.[13] Yet if an easement of light for one set of windows is infringed, and another set of windows (for which no easement exists) is deprived of light by the same obstruction, the dominant owner can recover damages in respect of both sets of windows, for the obstruction is illegal and the damage to both sets of windows is the direct and foreseeable consequence of it.[14] But such "parasitic damages" may be recoverable only in respect of windows which would necessarily benefit from an injunction protecting the dominant windows.[15]

18–204

4. Standard of light. The standard of light varies to some extent from neighbourhood to neighbourhood,[16] the test in each case being that laid down in *Colls'* case. There is no "45 degrees" rule, *i.e.* no rule that an interference with light is actionable only if the obstruction arises above a line drawn upwards and outwards from the centre of the window at an angle of 45 degrees,[17] at the most, this test provides a very slight presumption.[18] Scientific methods today permit accurate measurement of light, and tests which have been propounded are whether the whole room, or half of it,[19] receives light not below a factor called the "grumble point".[20] But these are not reliable guides,

18–205

---

[7] *Yates v. Jack* (1866) 1 Ch.App. 295.

[8] *Carr-Saunders v. Dick McNeil Associates Ltd, supra*; [1987] C.L.J. 26 (S. Bridge).

[9] *Colls v. Home and Colonial Stores Ltd* [1904] A.C. 179 at 204.

[10] *Smith v. Evangelization Society (Incorporated) Trust* [1933] Ch. 515.

[11] *Ankerson v. Connelly* [1907] 1 Ch. 678.

[12] *Andrews v. Waite* [1907] 2 Ch. 500 at 510; *ante*, para. 18–188.

[13] *Ankerson v. Connelly* [1906] 2 Ch. 544 at 548, 549 (aff'd [1907] 1 Ch. 678); *News of the World Ltd v. Allan Fairhead & Sons Ltd* [1931] 2 Ch. 402 at 407.

[14] *Re London, Tilbury & Southend Ry and the Trustees of the Gower's Walk Schools* (1889) 24 Q.B.D. 326; *Griffith v. Richard Clay & Sons Ltd* [1912] 2 Ch. 291. Contrast *Scott v. Goulding Properties Ltd* [1973] I.R. 200.

[15] See (1975) 39 Conv. (N.S.) 116 (A. H. Hudson).

[16] *Fishenden v. Higgs & Hill Ltd* (1935) 153 L.T. 128; *Ough v. King* [1967] 1 W.L.R. 1547. But see *Horton's Estate Ltd v. James Beattie Ltd* [1927] 1 Ch. 75.

[17] *Colls v. Home and Colonial Stores Ltd* [1904] A.C. 179 at 210; *Fishenden v. Higgs & Hill Ltd, supra*.

[18] *Ecclesiastical Commissioners for England v. Kino* (1880) 14 Ch.D. 213 at 220.

[19] *Fishenden v. Higgs & Hill Ltd, supra*.

[20] See *Charles Semon & Co. Ltd v. Bradford Corpn.* [1922] 2 Ch. 737 at 747, 748.

since the court may take account not only of the locality but of the higher standard which may reasonably be required in present times.[21]

18–206   **5. Other sources of light.** In considering whether an easement of light has been obstructed, other sources of light of which the dominant owner cannot be deprived must be taken into account, such as vertical light through a sky-light[22]; and if this has been blocked up by the dominant owner during the prescriptive period, his rights will be assessed on the footing of it being unobstructed.[23] In one case[24] a room was lit through two sets of windows, one set facing A's land and the other facing B's land. It was held that the light received by both sets of windows had to be considered, but that A could not obscure the greater part of the light passing over his land in reliance upon B supplying a larger quantity of light. Neither servient owner could build to a greater extent than, assuming a building of like height on the other servient tenement, would still leave the dominant tenement with sufficient light according to the test in *Colls'* case.

18–207   **6. Precarious light.** Light which the dominant tenement receives from other sources but of which it may be deprived at any time must be ignored.[25] Nor is it a sufficient answer for the servient owner to offer to provide glazed tiles or mirrors to reflect the light,[26] for no provision can be made which will effectively bind future owners of the servient tenement to keep the tiles or mirrors clean.[27] An easement to receive reflected light apparently cannot exist[28]; but in considering whether an easement of light has been infringed, reflected or diffused light entering from ordinary sources cannot be disregarded.[29]

C. Rights of Water

18–208   A variety of easements may exist in connection with water,[30] such as rights—

> (i) to take water from a river,[31] a spring[32] or a pump[33];

---

[21] *Ough v. King, supra*; *Deakins v. Hookings* [1994] 1 E.G.L.R. 190; and see the criticisms in *McGrath v. Munster & Leinster Bank Ltd* [1959] I.R. 313.

[22] *Smith v. Evangelization Society (Incorporated) Trust* [1933] Ch. 515.

[23] *ibid.*

[24] *Sheffield Masonic Hall Co. Ltd v. Sheffield Corpn.* [1932] 2 Ch. 17.

[25] *Colls v. Home and Colonial Stores, Ltd, supra*, at 211.

[26] *Black v. Scottish Temperance Life Assurance Co.* [1908] 1 I.R. 541 (H.L.).

[27] *Dent v. Auction Mart Co.* (1866) L.R. 2 Eq. 238 at 251, 252.

[28] *Goldberg v. Waite* [1930] E.G.D. 154.

[29] *Sheffield Masonic Hall Co. Ltd v. Sheffield Corpn., supra*, at 24, 25.

[30] See Gale 6–37.

[31] *Cargill v. Gotts* [1981] 1 W.L.R. 441 (right to take water from mill pond for ordinary farming purposes allows increased abstraction for crop-spraying).

[32] *Race v. Ward* (1855) 4 E. & B. 702.

[33] *Polden v. Bastard* (1865) L.R. 1 Q.B. 156.

(ii) to water cattle at a pond[34];

(iii) to take water from a stream running through the dominant tenement for purposes which the natural rights of ownership[35] do not permit[36];

(iv) to receive water through a pipe on the servient land[37];

(v) to pollute the waters of a stream or river[38];

(vi) to discharge water on to the land of another[39];

(vii) to receive the discharge of water from the land of another[40];

(viii) to enter the land of another to open sluice gates[41];

(ix) to permit rainwater to drop from a roof onto a neighbour's land ("easement of eavesdrop").[42]

These rights must be distinguished from the natural rights which a landowner may have in respect of water,[43] which have already been mentioned.[44]

D. Rights of Support

As already mentioned,[45] a landowner's natural right of support for his land extends only to his land in its natural state; it does not include buildings. But a right of support for buildings may be acquired as an easement. Thus where one of two adjoining houses was converted into a coach factory which threw more pressure upon the other house, and was so used for over 20 years, the House of Lords held that an action lay for demolishing the other house and so

18–209

---

[34] *Manning v. Wasdale* (1836) 5 A. & E. 758.

[35] For these, see *ante*, para. 18–063.

[36] *McCartney v. Londonderry & Lough Swilly Ry* [1904] A.C. 301 at 313.

[37] *Goodhart v. Hyett* (1883) 25 Ch.D. 182; *Rance v. Elvin* (1985) 50 P. & C.R. 9. See too *Duffy v. Lamb* (1997) 75 P. & C.R. 364 (right to receive electricity via a cable).

[38] *Baxendale v. McMurray* (1867) 2 Ch.App. 790.

[39] *Mason v. Shrewsbury & Hereford Ry* (1871) L.R. 6 Q.B. 578 at 587.

[40] *Ivimey v. Stocker* (1866) 1 Ch.App. 396. It is harder to obtain this by prescription than the previous right, which is complementary to it; for it is difficult to contend that because a man's pump had dripped onto the land of another for 20 years, the latter had a right to say that the pump must go on leaking: *Chamber Colliery Co. v. Hopwood* (1886) 32 Ch.D. 549 at 558. See also *Arkwright v. Gell* (1839) 5 M. & W. 203 and *Burrows v. Lang* [1901] 2 Ch. 502 for the difficulties which may lie in the way of a claim to continue to receive water temporarily flowing from another person's land.

[41] *Simpson v. Mayor, etc. of Godmanchester* [1897] A.C. 696.

[42] *Harvey v. Walters* (1873) L.R. 8 C.P. 162.

[43] See Gale 6–01 *et seq*.

[44] *Ante*, para. 18–063.

[45] *Ante*, para. 18–062.

causing part of the factory to collapse.[46] Where adjoining buildings support one another it is therefore difficult for their owners to preserve their liberty to demolish them for more than 20 years. Probably their only course is to issue a writ claiming a declaration that no easement as yet subsists, so preventing user as of right. Although there is no natural right for a landowner to have the surface of his land supported by water but only by subjacent strata of minerals,[47] there is no such limitation as regards an easement of support. Removal of support is actionable even if it is caused by the draining of water from the subsoil.[48]

Where an easement of support exists, it entitles the dominant owner to enter and execute repairs to the servient tenement; but it does not put the servient owner under any obligation to keep the supporting building in repair, since the easement cannot entail a positive obligation.[49]

E. Rights of Air

18–210   These have already been mentioned.[50]

F. Right of Fencing

18–211   The right to require a neighbouring landowner to repair his fences has been called a "spurious easement",[51] and even a "quasi-easement".[52] In fact it appears to be an easement,[53] though exceptional in requiring positive action by the servient owner. It lies in grant[54]; it will pass under section 62 of the Law of Property Act 1925[55]; and it can be acquired by prescription.[56] In order to establish the right it must be shown that the servient owner repaired his fence not merely to keep his cattle in or the dominant owner's out, but as a matter of obligation to the dominant owner, e.g. by habitually repairing the

---

[46] *Dalton v. Angus & Co.* (1881) 6 App.Cas. 740. This is the leading case on easements of support, and contains a great many important observations about easements generally. A local authority cannot exercise compulsory powers to demolish the servient house without providing equivalent support: *Bond v. Nottingham Corporation* [1940] Ch. 429.

[47] *Stephens v. Anglia Water Authority* [1987] 1 W.L.R. 1381; *ante*, para. 18–063.

[48] *Brace v. S.E. Regional Housing Association Ltd* [1984] 1 E.G.L.R. 144.

[49] *Ante*, para. 18–062.

[50] *Ante*, para. 18–063.

[51] *Coaker v. Willcocks* [1911] 2 K.B. 124 at 131, *per* Farwell L.J.; and see *ante*, para. 18–054. The obligation binds the landowner "to put up such fence that a pig not of a peculiarly wandering disposition, nor under any excessive temptation, will not get through it" (*Child v. Hearn* (1874) L.R. 9 Ex. 176 at 182, *per* Bramwell B.); but the fence need not be sufficient to exclude sheep of a "peculiarly wandering and saltative disposition" (*Coaker v. Willcocks* [1911] 1 K.B. 649 at 654, *per* Darling J.), nor need it to be "so close and strong that no pig could push through it, or so high that no horse or bullock could leap it" (*Child v. Hearn, supra*, at 181, *per* Bramwell B.). For a discussion of this obligation, see (1971) 87 L.Q.R. 13 (P. V. Baker); Sara, *Boundaries and Easements* (2nd ed.), chap. 22; G. L. Williams, *Liability for Animals*, p. 208; North, *The Modern Law of Animals*, p. 157

[52] *Jones v. Price* [1965] 2 Q.B. 618; for the normal meaning of this term, see *ante*, paras 18–050, 18–103.

[53] *Crow v. Wood* [1971] 1 Q.B. 77.

[54] *ibid.*

[55] *Ante*, para. 18–108.

[56] *Lawrence v. Jenkins* (1873) L.R. 8 Q.B. 274; *Jones v. Price, supra.*

fence on his demand.[57] The servient owner cannot be required to repair fences on the dominant owner's land.[58] A corresponding right may also be acquired by custom.[59] There are certain statutory obligations which require a land-owner to fence his property.[60]

G. Miscellaneous Easements

There are many miscellaneous easements, such as rights—   **18–212**

    (i) to create a nuisance by the discharge of gases, fluids or smoke,[61] or perhaps even by making noises[62] or vibrations[63];

    (ii) to hang clothes on a line passing over another's land[64];

    (iii) to fix a signboard on a neighbouring house[65];

    (iv) to mix manure on the servient tenement for the benefit of the adjoining farm[66];

    (v) to place stones on the servient tenement to prevent sand or earth from being washed away by the sea[67];

    (vi) to use a wall for nailing trees to it[68] or for supporting a creeper[69];

    (vii) to extend the bowsprits of ships over a wharf[70];

    (viii) to store casks and trade products on the servient tenement[71];

---

[57] *Hilton v. Ankesson* (1872) 27 L.T. 519.

[58] *Jones v. Price, supra; Egerton v. Harding* [1975] Q.B. 62.

[59] *Egerton v. Harding, supra* not following *Crow v. Wood, supra.*

[60] See Halsb., vol. 4(1), p. 432.

[61] *Crump v. Lambert* (1867) L.R. 3 Eq. 409 at 413 (dictum by Romilly M.R.); but see n. 63, below.

[62] *Elliotson v. Feetham* (1835) 2 Bing.N.C. 134; *Ball v. Ray* (1873) 8 Ch.App. 467 at 471, 472; but see next note.

[63] *Sturges v. Bridgman* (1879) 11 Ch.D. 852. This and the cases cited in the previous two footnotes are unsatisfactory authorities, for in none did the plaintiff succeed. If 20 years' user as of right could have been shown, the question would have arisen whether such rights can lie in grant. This seems highly questionable: there is no direct authority; *contra, Lemmon v. Webb* [1895] A.C. 1, *ante*, para. 18–053.

[64] *Drewell v. Towler* (1832) 3 B. & Ad. 735.

[65] *Moody v. Steggles* (1879) 12 Ch.D. 261.

[66] *Pye v. Mumford* (1848) 11 Q.B. 666 (the right was claimed as a *profit à prendre*).

[67] *Philpot v. Bath* (1905) 21 T.L.R. 634.

[68] *Hawkins v. Wallis* (1763) 2 Wils.K.B. 173.

[69] *Simpson v. Weber* (1925) 133 L.T. 46.

[70] *Suffield v. Brown* (1864) 4 De. G.J. & S. 185.

[71] *Att.-Gen. of Southern Nigeria v. John Holt & Co. (Liverpool) Ltd* [1915] A.C. 599; *ante*, para. 18–055.

(ix) to use a coal shed on the servient tenement[72];

(x) to park a car[73];

(xi) to use an airfield[74];

(xii) to let down the surface of land by mining operations under it[75];

(xiii) to use a kitchen[76] or a lavatory[77];

(xiv) to use a letter-box[78];

(xv) to use a pew in a church.[79]

Section 7. Species of *Profits à Prendre*

18–213 The following are the main types of *profits à prendre*. They are more often met with as commons than as several profits.

A. *Profits of Pasture*

18–214 A profit of pasture is a true profit; the taking and carrying away is effected by means of the mouths and stomachs of the cattle in question.[80]

1. Forms of profit. A profit of pasture may exist in the following forms.

18–215 *(a) Appendant.* A profit of pasture appendant is limited to horses, oxen, cows and sheep. The numerical test is that of levancy and couchancy.[81]

18–216 *(b) Appurtenant.* A profit of pasture appurtenant is not confined to any particular animals, but depends on the terms of the grant or, in the case of prescription, the animals habitually turned out to pasture.[82] Thus it may extend

---

[72] *Wright v. Macadam* [1949] 2 K.B. 744.
[73] *Newman v. Jones*, March 22, 1982 (unrep., Megarry V.-C); *London & Blenheim Estates Ltd v. Ladbroke Retail Parks Ltd* [1992] 1 W.L.R. 1278 (on appeal [1994] 1 W.L.R. 31).
[74] *Dowty Boulton Paul Ltd v. Wolverhampton Corporation (No. 2)* [1976] Ch. 13.
[75] *Rowbotham v. Wilson* (1860) 8 H.L.C. 348 at 362. But see *Newcastle-under-Lyme B.C. v. Wolstanton Ltd* [1939] 3 All E.R. 597 (aff'd [1940] A.C. 860) as to the acquisition of such a right by prescription; and see (1940) 56 L.Q.R. 438 (R.E.M.).
[76] See *Heywood v. Mallalieu* (1883) 25 Ch.D. 357.
[77] *Miller v. Emcer Products Ltd* [1956] Ch. 304; and see *Simmons v. Midford* [1969] 2 Ch. 415 (exclusive right to use a drain).
[78] *Goldberg v. Edwards* [1950] Ch. 247.
[79] *Philipps v. Halliday* [1891] A.C. 228. But see *Brumfitt v. Roberts* (1870) L.R. 5 C.P. 224 at 233.
[80] See Preston, *Estates*, i, 15.
[81] *Ante*, para. 18–083.
[82] Hall, *Profits à Prendre*, (1871) 263.

to sheep, when it is known as a "foldcourse"[83] or "sheepwalk".[84] The number of animals may either be limited by levancy and couchancy, or be fixed; it cannot be unlimited.[85]

(c) Pur cause de vicinage. Under a common of pasture *pur cause de* **18–217** *vicinage*,[86] the commoners of one common may not put more cattle upon it than it will maintain; thus, if Common A is 50 acres in extent and Common B 100 acres, the commoners of A must not put more cattle on A than 50 acres will support in reliance upon their cattle straying to B.[87]

(d) In gross. A profit of pasture in gross[88] may exist for a fixed number of **18–218** animals or *sans nombre*. The last phrase means literally "without number" (an alternative form is "without stint"), but such a right is limited to not more cattle than the servient tenement will maintain in addition to any existing burdens.[89]

2. Quantification of commons. For the purpose of registration under the **18–219** Commons Registration Act 1965[90] rights of common which consist of or include a right, not limited by number, to graze animals must be registered for a definite number of animals. When such registration has become final, the right is exercisable only in relation to the number so registered.[91] Where these provisions apply, they replace levancy and couchancy as a test,[91a] as well as the test for a profit *sans nombre*; and commoners may license others to graze their beasts up to the registered number.[92]

B. Profit of Turbary

A profit of turbary is the right to dig and take from the servient tenement peat **18–220** or turf for use as fuel in a house on the dominant tenement. It may exist as appurtenant, or, where it is limited to some specified quantity, in gross.[93] Where it is appurtenant, the turves can be used only for the benefit of the dominant tenement and not, *e.g.* for sale,[94] even if the dominant owner is entitled to a fixed quantity.[95]

---

[83] *Robinson v. Duleep Singh* (1878) 11 Ch.D. 798. For the distinction between this and a grant of the herbage, see *ibid.*, at 820.
[84] *White v. Williams* [1922] 1 K.B. 727.
[85] *Benson v. Chester* (1799) 8 T.R. 396 at 401; *Anderson v. Bostock* [1976] Ch. 312; *ante*, para. 18–083. A profit of pasture "without stint" or "*sans nombre*" means a profit for animals *levant et couchant*: Halsb. vol. 6, p. 226; 1 Wm. Saund., 6th ed., 28, n. (4).
[86] *Ante*, para. 18–084.
[87] *Sir Miles Corbet's Case* (1585) 7 Co.Rep. 5a.
[88] *Ante*, para. 18–085.
[89] Halsb. vol. 6, p. 229.
[90] For registration, see *ante*, paras 18–181 *et seq.*
[91] Commons Registration Act 1965, s.15. See *ante*, para. 18–083.
[91a] *Bettison v. Langton* [1999] 3 W.L.R. 39 at 54 *et seq.*
[92] *Davies v. Davies* [1975] Q.B. 172.
[93] *Mellor v. Spateman* (1669) 1 Wms.Saund. 339 at 346.
[94] *Valentine v. Penny* (1605) Noy 145.
[95] *Hayward v. Cunnington* (1668) 1 Lev. 231.

C. Profit of Estovers

18–221   A profit of estovers is the right to take wood from the land of another as hay-bote, house-bote, or plough-bote.[96] It may exist as appurtenant, or, if limited to a specified quantity, in gross.[97] If it is appurtenant to a house, the right will not be increased if the house is enlarged.[98] It sometimes includes the right to cut timber,[99] but may be limited to trees of small value.[1] It may extend to furze, gorse, heather, fern or long grass for fuel, manure or litter.[2] In every case the profit must be limited in some way as to quantity, either by reference to some defined quantity or by reference to the needs of the dominant tenement.[3]

Similar rights to profits of estovers are rights of lopwood, *i.e.* to lop wood for fuel at certain periods of the year,[4] and pannage, *i.e.* to send pigs onto the servient tenement in order to eat acorns or beech-mast which have fallen to the ground.[5]

D. Profit of Piscary and Other Sporting Rights

18–222   A profit of piscary is a right to catch and take away fish. It can exist in gross (when it may be unlimited)[6] or as appurtenant (when it must be limited to the needs of the dominant tenement).[7] Other sporting rights, such as a right of hunting (venery), shooting, fowling (auceptary), and the like, may also exist as *profits à prendre*.[8] Unless the grant otherwise indicates, rights of fishing[9] are exclusive but other rights of this kind are not.[10] It is no infringement of a right to take game if the servient owner merely cuts timber in the ordinary way, even if he thereby drives away game[11]; but it is otherwise if fundamental changes in the land are made, as where the whole or a substantial part of the

---

[96] *Ante*, para. 3–105. This must be distinguished from the similar rights a tenant for life has over the land of which he is tenant, for a profit of estovers is exercised over the land of another.

[97] Halsb. vol. 6, pp. 236, 262.

[98] *Brown & Tucker's Case* (1610) 4 Leon. 241.

[99] *Russel & Broker's Case* (1587) 2 Leon. 209.

[1] *Anon* (1572) 3 Leon. 16.

[2] *Warrick v. Queen's College, Oxford* (1871) 6 Ch.App. 716; *Earl de la Warr v. Miles* (1881) 17 Ch.D. 535.

[3] *Clayton v. Corby* (1843) 5 Q.B. 415 at 419, 420.

[4] *Chilton v. Corporation of London (No. 2)* (1878) 7 Ch.D. 735.

[5] *Chilton v. Corporation of London (No. 1)* (1878) 7 Ch.D. 562. The servient owner may nevertheless lop the trees in the ordinary course of management, and fell the trees when ripe: *ibid.*

[6] *Staffordshire and Worcestershire Canal Navigation v. Bradley* [1912] 1 Ch. 91; *Lovett v. Fairclough* (1990) 61 P. & C.R. 385 at 396: *ante*, para. 18–085.

[7] *Harris v. Earl of Chesterfield* [1911] A.C. 623; *ante*, para. 18–082.

[8] *Ewart v. Graham* (1859) 7 H.L.C. 331 at 345. See the extensive rights claimed in *Thorne R.D.C. v. Bunting* [1972] Ch. 470.

[9] *Lady Dunsany v. Bedworth* (1979) 38 P. & C.R. 546 (reservation: but a grant may be different: see at 548).

[10] *Duke of Sutherland v. Heathcote* [1892] 1 Ch. 475.

[11] *Gearns v. Baker* (1875) 10 Ch.App. 355.

land is built upon or converted into racing stables.[12] Such a right imposes no obligation to keep down the numbers of birds or animals.[13]

E. Profit in the Soil

A profit in the soil is the right to enter the servient tenement and take sand,[14] **18–223** stone,[15] gravel,[16] brick-earth,[17] coal,[18] minerals[19] and the like.[20] It may exist as appurtenant or in gross.

Section 8. Rights of Access

1. No right of access at common law. It is often the case that one **18–224** landowner, A, cannot carry out works of repair or improvement to his own property without going onto the land of his neighbour, B, to execute them. There is however no right at common law[20a] for A to enter B's land unless—

    (i) he has an easement to go onto B's property to carry out the works[21]; or

    (ii) B has consented to his so doing.

Any unauthorised entry by A is a trespass which may be restrained by injunction, and this is so even though A is required to carry out the works by the local authority because the premises are in a dangerous condition.[22] In such a case, A is caught between "the Scylla of the dangerous building" and "the Charybdis of trespassing on the plaintiff's land".[23] To provide a partial solution to this problem, Parliament has enacted the Access to Neighbouring

---

[12] *Peech v. Best* [1931] 1 K.B. 1.

[13] *Seligman v. Docker* [1949] Ch. 53.

[14] *Blewett v. Tregonning* (1835) 3 A. & E. 544 at 575.

[15] *Heath v. Deane* [1905] 2 Ch. 86.

[16] *Constable v. Nicholson* (1863) 14 C.B. (N.S.) 230 at 239.

[17] *Church v. The Inclosure Commissioners* (1862) 11 C.B. (N.S.) 664.

[18] See *Duke of Portland v. Hill* (1866) L.R. 2 Eq. 765.

[19] *Duke of Sutherland v. Heathcote* [1892] 1 Ch. 475 at 483.

[20] Co.Litt. 122a. As to a right to take ice from a canal, see *Newby v. Harrison* (1861) 1 J. & H. 393; (1938) 2 Conv. (N.S.) 203 at 204 (J. S. Fiennes).

[20a] There is a *statutory* right to enter a neighbour's land to repair a party wall under the Party Walls, etc., Act 1996, s.2: *ante*, para. 9–109.

[21] Such an easement is known to the law: *Ward v. Kirkland* [1967] Ch. 194.

[22] *John Trenberth Ltd v. National Westminster Bank Ltd* (1979) 39 P. & C.R. 104; [1980] Conv. 308 (H. Street). For the powers of the local authority in relation to dangerous buildings, see the Building Act 1984, s.77.

[23] *John Trenberth Ltd v. National Westminster Bank Ltd, supra*, at 106, *per* Walton J.

Land Act 1992,[24] which came into force on January 31, 1993.[25] The provisions of this Act, which are of limited effect, must now be considered.

2. Access orders under the Access to Neighbouring Land Act 1992

(a) Access orders

18–225   (1) GROUNDS ON WHICH AN ORDER MAY BE MADE. If A wishes to carry out works that are reasonably necessary for the preservation of the whole or any part of his land,[26] and it is either impossible or substantially more difficult[27] for him to do so without access to B's adjacent or adjoining property, A may apply to the court for an access order, should B's consent be needed but not forthcoming.[28] Although the Act does not attempt to define comprehensively what works will be reasonably necessary for the preservation of the land, it does provide that (without prejudice to the generality of that requirement) certain works will be so. These are as follows.

> (a) Specified "basic preservation works" (such as the maintenance, repair or renewal of any part of a building or structure on A's land).[29]
>
> (b) Works which otherwise satisfy the requirements but incidentally involve—
>
> > (i) the making of some alteration, adjustment or improvement to A's land; or
> > (ii) the demolition of the whole or part of some building or structure upon it.[30]
>
> (c) Anything that is a necessary incident of carrying out the works,[31] including the right to enter B's land for certain purposes of inspection.[32]

The court shall not make an access order if it is satisfied that the making of it would either—

---

[24] The Act was based upon (but does not in all respects follow) the recommendations of the Law Commission: (1985) Law Com. No. 151. See [1992] Conv. 225 (H.W. Wilkinson).

[25] S.I. 1992 No. 3349.

[26] For these purposes, "land" includes a party wall: *Dean v. Walker* (1996) 73 P. & C.R. 366. For party walls, see *ante*, para. 9–104. It is no longer necessary to rely on the Access to Neighbouring Land Act 1992 in relation to the repair of party walls because of the Party Walls, etc., Act 1996: see *ante*, para. 9–109.

[27] In many cases it may be more expensive for A to carry out the works without access to B's land. Query whether this makes it "more difficult" within the meaning of the Act.

[28] s.1(1), (2). All actions must be commenced in the county court but may be transferred to the High Court: s.7.

[29] s.1(4).

[30] s.1(5).

[31] s.1(6).

[32] s.1(7).

(i) interfere with or disturb the enjoyment of B's land by the occupant; or

(ii) cause that person hardship,

to such a degree that it would be unreasonable.[33]

(2) TERMS AND EFFECT OF THE ORDER. An access order made by the court **18–226** must define certain matters (such as both the works to be carried out and the time within which they must be executed),[34] and may be made subject to terms and conditions if the court considers that it is reasonably necessary to do so to avoid or restrict any loss, damage, injury, inconvenience or loss of privacy that might otherwise be caused to B (or any other person).[35] If the works which A undertakes on B's property lead to an increase in its value and that land is not residential, the court may require him to make a payment for the privilege of entering B's land.[36]

The access order will authorise A or any or his "associates"[37] to enter the land and to bring onto it materials for the specified works or waste from carrying them out.[38] It will also require him to remove waste from and make good B's land, and to indemnify B for any damage caused in the execution of the order.[39] B is required to permit A or any of his associates (so far as he has power to do so) to do anything which the order authorises or requires A to do.[40] The court may order any person who contravenes or fails to comply with any requirement imposed upon him by or under the Act to pay damages to any other person affected by that breach.[41] The court also has wide powers to suspend the order or to vary the terms and conditions upon which it was given.[42]

(b) Effect on third parties. The benefit of an access order is apparently **18–227** personal to the applicant, A.[43] There is nothing in the Act which makes the right appurtenant to his land so that it can be enforced by a successor in title.[44]

---

[33] s.1(3).

[34] s.2(1).

[35] s.2(2), (3). A may be required to pay compensation for any such loss, damage or inconvenience: s.2(4).

[36] s.2(5), (6). "Residential land" is widely defined: s.2(7).

[37] Defined by the Act to include any persons whom A may reasonably authorise to enter the land to carry out the works (whether or not they are his servants or agents): s.3(7).

[38] s.3(2).

[39] s.3(3).

[40] s.3(1).

[41] s.6(2). The right to seek damages is not confined to A or B. If the breach affected a neighbour, he could seek damages. The statutory power to award damages is without prejudice to any other remedy available, such as an injunction.

[42] s.6(1).

[43] The Act throughout refers to the "applicant", which is never defined to include successors in title.

[44] It is understood that the Land Registry will not therefore register the benefit of an access order as appurtenant to registered land under L.R.R. 1925, r. 257, and this appears correct in principle.

By contrast, an access order will both bind and be enforceable by any person—

(i) who is a successor in title to B; or

(ii) who has acquired an estate, interest or right in or over B's land subsequent to the making of the access order;

provided that the order has been registered as provided by the Act.[45] Where the title to B's land is unregistered, the order is registrable as a land charge in the register of writs and orders affecting land.[46] Where the title is registered, the order may be registered as a notice[47] without the need to produce B's land certificate,[48] but the rights conferred by the order are not capable of constituting an overriding interest.[49]

18–228   *(c) Limited effect of access orders.* The Access to Neighbouring Land Act 1992 provides no mechanism for A to go onto B's land to improve or redevelop his own property. An access order can be granted only in respect of works that are reasonably necessary for the preservation of A's property, and only incidental improvements or demolition works may be sanctioned. Even where the works are reasonably necessary for the preservation of A's property, no order can be made unless it is substantially more difficult for A to carry them out without entry onto B's land. All that the Act provides therefore is "a very restricted and temporary form of compulsory acquisition of an easement".[50]

---

[45] s.4(1), (2). The application for an access order is treated as a pending land action: *ibid.*, s.5(6).

[46] s.5(1), amending L.C.A. 1972, s.6(1); see *ante*, para. 5–088.

[47] s.5(2), amending L.R.A. 1925, s.49(1).

[48] s.5(3), amending L.R.A. 1925, s.64; see *ante*, para. 6–080.

[49] s.5(5); *ante*, para. 6–051.

[50] [1992] Conv. 225 at 230 (H. W. Wilkinson). Contrast the sweeping powers enjoyed in relation to party walls under the Party Walls, etc., Act 1996; *ante*, para. 9–109.

CHAPTER 19

MORTGAGES

Part 1

NATURE OF A MORTGAGE

WHEN one person lends money to another, he may be content to make the loan **19–001** without security, or he may demand some security for the payment of the money. In the former case, the lender has a right to sue for the money if it is not duly paid, but that is all; if the borrower becomes insolvent, the lender may lose part or all of his money. But if some security of adequate value is given for the loan, the lender is protected even if the borrower becomes insolvent, for the lender has a claim to the security which takes precedence over other creditors.

The most important kind of security is the mortgage. The essential nature of a mortgage is that it is a conveyance of a legal or equitable interest in property, with a provision for redemption, *i.e.* that upon repayment of a loan or the performance of some other obligation the conveyance shall become void or the interest shall be reconveyed.[1] The borrower is known as the "mortgagor", the lender as the "mortgagee".

A mortgage must be distinguished from a lien, a pledge and a charge.[2]

1. Lien. A lien may arise at common law, in equity or under certain statutes. **19–002** A common law lien is the right to retain possession of the property of another until a debt is paid; thus a garage proprietor has a common law lien upon a motor-car repaired by him.[3] This lien is a mere passive right of retention, giving no right to sell[4] or otherwise deal with the property, and is extinguished if the creditor parts with possession to the debtor or his agent.[5] It is therefore merely a means of coercing the debtor into payment, rather than a security against payment not being made.

---

[1] *Santley v. Wilde* [1899] 2 Ch. 474, *per* Lindley M.R., approved in *Noakes & Co. Ltd v. Rice* [1902] A.C. 24 at 28; and see *Swiss Bank Corporation v. Lloyds Bank Ltd* [1982] A.C. 584 at 595, *per* Buckley L.J.

[2] See *Haliday v. Holgate* (1868) L.R. 3 Ex. 299 at 302.

[3] *Green v. All Motors Ltd* [1917] 1 K.B. 625.

[4] *Mulliner v. Florence* (1878) 3 Q.B.D. 484.

[5] *Pennington v. Reliance Motor Works Ltd* [1923] 1 K.B. 127.

19–003   An equitable lien is not dependent upon continued possession of the property[6] and in this respect resembles a mortgage. It is also within the definition of "mortgage" in the Law of Property Act 1925.[7] But it differs from a mortgage (*inter alia*) in that a mortgage is intentionally created by contract whereas an equitable lien arises automatically under some doctrine of equity.[8] Thus a vendor of land has an equitable lien on it until the full purchase price is paid, even if he has conveyed the land to the purchaser and put him into possession.[9] This lien gives him no right to possession of the land, but enables him to apply to the court for a declaration of charge and for an order for sale of the land, under which he will be paid the money due.[10] If he is paid off by a third party, the third party can claim the benefit of the lien by subrogation.[11] An equitable lien is therefore a species of equitable charge arising by implication of law.[12]

A statutory lien is the creature of the statute under which it arises, and the rights which it confers depend on the terms of that statute. For example, railway companies,[13] solicitors[14] and airports[15] have been given such rights.

19–004   **2. Pledge.** A pledge or pawn is a loan of money secured by the possession of chattels delivered to the lender. Although the lender has certain powers of sale, the general property in the goods remains in the borrower and the lender has possession[16]; in a mortgage, on the other hand, the lender acquires ownership and the borrower usually retains possession. The great advantage of a mortgage, as opposed to a pledge, is that the borrower can thus keep possession of his property for the time being. Land, being immovable, is naturally mortgaged, not pledged; chattels may be either pledged or mortgaged.[17]

19–005   **3. Charge.** For most practical purposes a charge should be regarded as a species of mortgage, and it is so dealt with in this chapter. Nevertheless there is an essential difference between a mortgage and a charge. A mortgage is a conveyance of property subject to a right of redemption, whereas a charge conveys nothing and merely gives the chargee certain rights over the property as security for the loan.[18]

---

[6] *Wrout v. Dawes* (1858) 25 Beav. 369.
[7] s.205(1)(xvi).
[8] See *Mackreth v. Symmons* (1808) 15 Ves. 329 at 340; *Re Beirnstein* [1925] Ch. 12 at 17.
[9] *Ante*, para. 12–054. There is also a purchaser's lien: *ante*, paras 12–055, 12–108.
[10] Williams V. & P. 988.
[11] *Coptic Ltd v. Bailey* [1972] Ch. 446; *Orakpo v. Manson Investments Ltd* [1978] A.C. 95 (subrogation displaced by specific charge; contrast *Bank of Ireland Finance Ltd v. D. J. Daly Ltd* [1978] I.R. 83).
[12] *Re Birmingham* [1959] Ch. 523.
[13] Railways Clauses Consolidation Act 1845, s.97.
[14] Solicitors Act 1974, s.73.
[15] Civil Aviation Act 1982, s.88.
[16] See *Re Morritt* (1886) 18 Q.B.D. 222.
[17] Mortgages of chattels are effected by bills of sale, which are outside the scope of this book.
[18] See *post*, para. 19–040.

Part 2

CREATION OF MORTGAGES

Section 1. Methods of Creating Legal Mortgages and Charges

The methods of creating a legal mortgage differ for freehold and leaseholds. **19–006**
In each case it is necessary to understand the history of the subject before
considering the effect of the legislation of 1925.

A. *Freeholds*

I. HISTORY BEFORE 1926

1. Twelfth and thirteenth centuries. In the twelfth and thirteenth centuries **19–007**
the forms of mortgage were influenced by the laws against usury, which was
both a crime and a sin.[19] Since lending money at a fixed rate of interest was
prohibited, other transactions were resorted to which escaped the usury laws
but which were sufficiently profitable to the lender, the mortgagee. Most
commonly the mortgagor leased the land to the mortgagee, who went into
possession.[20] This therefore resembled a pledge rather than a mortgage. If the
income from the land was used to discharge the mortgage debt, the transaction
was known as *vivum vadium* (a live pledge), since it was self-redeeming. If the
mortgagee kept the income, it was known as *mortuum vadium* (a dead
pledge).[21] This latter form was not unlawful; but the Church regarded it as
sinful, for the income was taken by way of interest. In either case, if the
money was not repaid by the time the lease expired, the mortgagee's lease was
enlarged into a fee simple by a condition subsequent expressed in the
mortgage.

2. Fifteenth century. By the middle of the fifteenth century the usual form **19–008**
of mortgage had changed. Even in the thirteenth century a form of mortgage
by conveyance of the fee simple had been known and this form gradually
ousted the others, for it gave seisin, and therefore impregnable security, to the
mortgagee.[22] The mortgagor conveyed the land to the mortgagee in fee
simple, subject to a condition that the mortgagor might re-enter and determine
the mortgagee's estate if the money lent was repaid on a named date.[23] The
mortgagee still took possession forthwith. The condition was construed

---

[19] H.E.L. viii, 102; Glanvil, Bk. 7, 16.
[20] H.E.L. iii, 130.
[21] H.E.L. iii, 128; Glanvil, Bk. 10, pp. 6, 8. Hence the name "mortgage"; mort (dead) gage
(pledge).
[22] H.E.L. iii, 129, 130; (1967) 83 L.Q.R. 229 (J. L. Barton). Doubts had also arisen as to the
validity of the idea that a term of years could swell into a fee simple: *ibid.*
[23] H.E.L. iii, 129, 130. A variant of this form was a conveyance of the fee simple subject to a
condition that the conveyance should be void if the money was paid on the named date.

strictly; if the mortgagor was a single day late in offering to repay the money, he lost his land for ever and yet remained liable for the debt.[24]

3. Seventeenth century onwards

19–009   *(a) Form of mortgage.* By the beginning of the seventeenth century two changes had taken place. First, the form of a mortgage was usually a conveyance in fee simple with a covenant to reconvey the property if the money was paid on the fixed date. This was the modern form before 1926, and it simplified proof of title; whether the fee simple was vested in the mortgagor or not no longer depended merely upon whether the money had been paid within the fixed time, but depended upon whether a reconveyance had been executed by the mortgagee.[25] Mortgages made by granting leases of the property were, however, equally possible,[26] and were employed where there were special reasons for preferring them.[27]

19–010   *(b) Intervention of equity.* Secondly, a far more important change had been made by the intervention of equity. By this time loans at interest were no longer illegal, but a maximum rate of interest was from time to time fixed by statute.[28] This greatly altered the function of a mortgage; for instead of providing both security for capital and a source of profit in lieu of interest, the mortgage ought henceforth to be a security only, and should not yield profit to the mortgagee over and above the interest permitted by law. The Court of Chancery, at this time expanding its jurisdiction and concerned as always to prevent unconscionable dealing, now undertook to enforce this policy. No longer might the mortgagee reap any benefit from his fee simple. If he took possession, equity held him liable to account for a full rent to the mortgagor.[29] Thus it was no longer an advantage to the mortgagee to occupy the land; and there emerged the modern type of mortgage where the mortgagor remains in possession and conveys the fee simple to the mortgagee merely by way of security.[30]

19–011   *(c) Mortgages as securities.* Equally important, it was repugnant to every idea of equity that the mortgagor should lose his property merely because he was late in repaying the loan. At first equity intervened in cases of accident,

---

[24] *Kreglinger v. New Patagonia Meat and Cold Storage Co. Ltd* [1914] A.C. 25 at 35.
[25] See *Durham Brothers v. Robertson* [1898] 1 Q.B. 765 at 772.
[26] See *e.g. Horne v. Darbyshire* (1619) Ritchies's Bac.Cac. 188; *Aldrige v. Duke* (1679) Rep.t.Finch 439.
[27] *e.g.* for raising portions in family settlements. For portions, see the previous edition of this work at pp. 412 *et seq.* where a leasehold interest left the other limitations of the settlement undisturbed.
[28] The Usury Acts of 1545 (37 Hen. 8, c. 9) and 1571 (13 Eliz. 1, c. 8) allowed 10 per cent; this was reduced to 8 per cent in 1623 (21 Jac. 1, c. 17) and to 5 per cent in 1714 (13 Ann. c. 15; Ruff., 12 Ann., St. 2, c. 16). The usury laws were finally repealed by the Usury Laws Repeal Act 1854. For their history, see H.E.L. viii, 100. The court now has wide powers to modify or set aside extortionate transactions: see *post*, para. 19–158.
[29] *Holman v. Vaux* (c. 1616) Tot. 133; *Pell v. Blewet* (1630) Tot. 133; H.E.L. v. 331.
[30] But as to "Welsh mortgages", see Coote, *Mortgages*, chap. III.

mistake, special hardship and the like; but soon relief was given in all cases.[31] Even if the date fixed for repayment had long passed, equity compelled the mortgagee to reconvey the property to the mortgagor on payment of the principal with interest and costs. The mortgagor was thus given an equitable right to redeem at a time when the agreement between the parties provided that the mortgagee was to be the absolute owner.[32] No longer, therefore, did the mortgagee stand to gain by obtaining a property which might be worth much more than the debt. Equity compelled him to treat the property as no more than a security for the money actually owed to him. This equity of redemption became a valuable interest vested in the mortgagor: the measure of its value was the difference between the amount of the debt and the value of the mortgaged property. Since it was an equitable interest in the land,[33] the mortgagor could enforce it not only against the mortgagee personally but against anyone to whom the mortgagee transmitted his fee simple, save only a bona fide purchaser without notice of the mortgage.[34]

(d) Foreclosure. There had, of course, to be some limit to the equitable right **19–012** to redeem, for otherwise the security would not have fulfilled its purpose of enabling the mortgagee to recover his capital when required. Equity therefore devised the decree of foreclosure, which was an order of the court, made on the mortgagee's application, declaring that the equitable right to redeem was at an end, and thus leaving the mortgagee with an unhampered fee simple.[35] But if the property was much more valuable than the debt the court would order a sale of the property, out of which the mortgagee would receive only the balance due to him, and the mortgagor would take the rest. Foreclosure could not therefore be used oppressively, and in any case a mortgagee who sought it had to come before the court.

(e) Date for redemption. These revolutionary changes made mortgages into **19–013** fair and convenient commercial transactions instead of instruments of extortion. The day fixed for repayment by the mortgage deed (the *legal* date for redemption) became unimportant, for the *equitable* right of redemption extended far beyond it. It therefore became customary to fix the initial legal redemption date very early, commonly six months after the mortgage, so that the mortgagee might have the right to call in his loan, and if necessary start foreclosure proceedings, at any time thereafter. This was no hardship to the mortgagor, who had his equity of redemption, and was convenient to the mortgagee, for his investment was then in a liquid form.

(f) The two rights to redeem. The result was to make the legal effect of a **19–014** mortgage much less intimidating than its appearance. An ordinary mortgage

---

[31] H.E.L. v. 330–332. This may have been due to "the piety" or else to the "love of fees of those who administered equity": *Salt v. Marquess of Northampton* [1892] A.C. at 19, *per* Lord Bramwell.

[32] See *Salt v. Marquess of Northampton* [1892] A.C. 1 at 18.

[33] See *e.g. Casborne v. Scarfe* (1738) 1 Atk. 603 at 605.

[34] *Ante*, paras 4–011, 4–012.

[35] *How v. Vigures* (1628) 1 Ch.Rep. 32; H.E.L. v. 331, 332.

deed would recite the loan, and then convey the fee simple to the mortgagee subject only to a proviso for redemption in six months' time (a date when neither party, probably, would have the least wish for redemption). This legal redemption date would soon pass by, and then according to the terms of the deed the property would belong absolutely to the mortgagee. But the mortgagor would be fully protected by equity, which would enforce his rights in defiance of the terms of the deed. Mortgages are still frequently made in a similar and no less cryptic form. "No one ... by the light of nature ever understood an English mortgage of real estate."[36]

It will be seen that the two rights to redeem are quite distinct.

19–015   (1) LEGAL RIGHT TO REDEEM. This is a contractual right at law to redeem on the precise day fixed by the mortgage, neither before nor after. This is exercisable as of right, irrespective of any equitable considerations.

19–016   (2) EQUITABLE RIGHT TO REDEEM. This is a right conferred by equity to redeem at any time after[37] the stipulated day; but this is exercisable only on terms considered proper by equity, for "he who seeks equity must do equity".[38]

19–017   *(g) The equity of redemption.* The equitable right to redeem must be distinguished from the "equity of redemption",[39] in its wider sense, although sometimes the terms are used interchangeably. First, the equitable right to redeem does not arise until the contractual date for redemption has passed,[40] whereas the equity of redemption arises as soon as the mortgage is made.[41] Secondly, and more important, the equitable right to redeem is a particular right,[42] whereas the equity of redemption is an equitable interest in the land consisting of the sum total of the mortgagor's rights in the property. Although at law he has parted with his land and has only a limited right to recover it, in equity he is the owner of the land, though subject to the mortgage[43]; the mortgagee, on the other hand, is at law the owner but in equity a mere incumbrancer.

19–018   The mortgagor's equity of redemption, in the wider sense of the term, is thus an interest in the land[44] which includes his right to redeem it, but is much more than a mere right of redemption. It is an interest in the land which the mortgagor can convey, devise, settle, lease or mortgage, just like any other

---

[36] *Samuel v. Jarrah Timber and Wood Paving Corporation Ltd* [1904] A.C. 323 at 326, *per* Lord Macnaghten. And Maitland called a mortgage "one long *suppressio veri* and *suggestio falsi*": *Equity*, 2nd ed., 182. For an example, see *post*, para. 19–041.

[37] Or before, if the mortgagee has demanded payment, *e.g.* by taking possession: *post* para. 19–148.

[38] The doctrine of consolidation is an example: see *post*, para. 19–096.

[39] See *Kreglinger v. New Patagonia Meat & Cold Storage Co. Ltd* [1914] A.C. 25 at 48.

[40] *Brown v. Cole* (1845) 14 Sim. 427.

[41] *Kreglinger v. New Patagonia Meat & Cold Storage Co. Ltd, supra,* at 48.

[42] Perhaps a "mere equity" (for which see *ante*, para. 5–012).

[43] *Re Wells* [1933] Ch. 29 at 52.

[44] He has "an equitable right inherent in the land": *Pawlett v. Att.-Gen.* (1667) Hardres 465 at 469, *per* Hale C.B.

interest in land.[45] If, for example, a property worth £50,000 is mortgaged to secure a debt of £10,000, the value of the equity of redemption is obvious; and the mortgagor must clearly be at liberty to deal with it like any other property which is subject to incumbrances. He may wish to sell the property (which subject to the mortgage would be worth about £40,000) or to raise a further loan on it by a second mortgage. But since before 1926 the mortgagee usually held the legal fee simple, any such dealings must necessarily have been equitable. Before 1926 a second mortgage was therefore usually an equitable mortgage, *i.e.* a mortgage of the equity of redemption.

II. AFTER 1925   **19–019**

By the Law of Property Act 1925 freeholds can no longer be mortgaged by conveyance of the fee simple. Two methods only are permitted by the Act[46] for effecting legal mortgages of freeholds—

(i) a demise for a term of years absolute, subject to a provision for cesser on redemption; or

(ii) a charge by deed expressed to be by way of legal mortgage.

A legal mortgage can therefore be created only by deed.

1. Demise for a term of years absolute

(a) Form of mortgage. The term of years granted to the mortgagee is   **19–020** usually a long term, *e.g.* 3,000 years. The provision for cesser on redemption is a clause providing that the term of years shall cease when the loan is repaid; it is really unnecessary, for on repayment the term becomes a satisfied term and automatically ceases.[47] In other respects the position is much as it was before 1926. A fixed redemption date is still named, and it is still usually six months after the date of the mortgage; thereafter the mortgagor has an equitable right to redeem in lieu of his legal right. The difficulty that a mortgagee by demise has no right to the title deeds is obviated by an express provision giving a first mortgagee the same right to the deeds as if he had the fee simple.[48]

(b) Retention of fee. The principal change brought about by the 1925   **19–021** legislation is that the mortgagor retains the legal fee simple. This brings the legal position rather more into accord with reality, for now the mortgagor

---

[45] *Casborne v. Scarfe* (1738) 1 Atk. 603 at 605; and see *Fawcett v. Lowther* (1751) 2 Ves. Sen. 300 at 303 (descent of equity of redemption according to custom of gavelkind).
[46] s.85(1). For criticism of the variety of forms of mortgage and suggestions for reform, see (1978) 94 L.Q.R. 571 (P. Jackson). See *post*, para. 19–266.
[47] See *Knightsbridge Estates Trust Ltd v. Byrne* [1939] Ch. 441 at 461 (in H.L. [1940] A.C. 613); and *post*, para. 19–192.
[48] See *post*, para. 19–035.

remains owner at law as well as in equity, and the mortgagee has an incumbrance only. The change is one of form rather than of substance, for it does not alter the rights of mortgagor and mortgagee; it merely makes the conveyancing machinery more logical.[49]

19–022   *(c) Equity of redemption.* In particular, the equity of redemption has in no way lost its importance. A fee simple giving the right to possession of land only when a lease for 3,000 years has expired is of little value compared with the right to insist that the fee simple shall forthwith be freed from the term of 3,000 years on payment of the money due. Indeed, the term "equity of redemption" is sometimes used as including the mortgagor's legal estate, for it is the equity of redemption which is the substantial interest, and the legal estate which is the shadow.

19–023   *(d) Successive legal mortgages.* As the mortgagor now retains the legal fee simple, he can grant further legal terms of years. Consequently second, third and subsequent mortgages may all be legal after 1925. Thus A, the fee simple owner of Blackacre, may create successive legal mortgages in favour of X, Y and Z. The term he grants to each mortgagee is usually[50] at least one day longer than the previous mortgage. Thus X may be given 2,000 years, Y 2,000 years and a day, and Z 2,000 years and two days, so that each mortgagee has a reversion upon the prior mortgage term. Here again the change is purely formal.[51] The rights of Y and Z *at law* are quite nebulous: no one would lend money on the security of one day's reversion at 2,000 years' distance. What is valuable security to Y and Z is their interest in the equity of redemption; subject to X's mortgage, they have the next prior claims to the property in equity.[52]

19–024   *(e) Purported conveyance.* A purported conveyance of a fee simple which in fact[53] is made by way of mortgage now operates as a grant of a term of 3,000 years without impeachment of waste but subject to cesser on redemption.[54] An attempt to create a second or subsequent mortgage in the same way takes effect as the grant of a term one day longer than the preceding term.[55] The system is thus foolproof.

---

[49] Save that on a sale by the mortgagee the estate that he conveys is no longer one that is vested in him but one vested in the mortgagor that the mortgagee conveys by virtue of a statutory power; see *post*, para. 19–065.

[50] This is not essential: *post* para. 19–031.

[51] Perhaps there is this substantial difference, that the mortgagor's covenants which touch and concern the land (*e.g.* his covenants to repair, insure, etc., but not his covenant to repay the loan) will run with the reversion if the mortgagor assigns his interest: see *ante*; *post*, para. 19–182.

[52] See *post*, para. 19–141.

[53] See *Grangeside Properties Ltd v. Collingwoods Securities Ltd* [1964] 1 W.L.R. 139 (on the similar wording of L.P.A. 1925, s.86(2): *post*, para. 19–032).

[54] L.P.A. 1925, s.85(2).

[55] L.P.A. 1925, s.85(1).

2. Charge by deed expressed to be by way of legal mortgage. This was **19–025** introduced by the Law of Property Act 1925[56] and is sometimes for brevity called a "legal charge". The importance of this innovation also is mainly formal. The "legal charge" is a statutory form of legal mortgage which is shorter and simpler than the accustomed form. It states merely that the property has been charged with the debt by way of legal mortgage. There is no conveyance of any estate to the mortgagee. The "legal charge" is intended to provide an optional alternative to the ordinary form of mortgage which, although equally uninformative, is at least not positively misleading to a lay reader.

This statutory legal charge must be—

    (i) made by deed[57]; a charge merely in writing will have no effect at law[58]; and

    (ii) expressed to be by way of legal mortgage[59]; the deed must contain a statement that the charge is made by way of legal mortgage.

The effect of such a charge of freeholds is that the chargee (whether first or **19–026** subsequent) gets "the same protection, powers and remedies" as if he had a term of 3,000 years without impeachment of waste.[60] Although he gets no actual legal term of years, he is as fully protected as if he had one,[61] so that he is as able to create tenancies and enforce covenants relating to the land (whether or not they are connected with the charge) as if he had an actual term vested in him.[62] The name "charge" is thus a little misleading, because although a legal charge is by nature a charge and not a mortgage,[63] for all practical purposes it takes effect as a mortgage.

The advantages of a legal charge are considered below,[64] and a precedent of such a charge is also given.[65]

B. Leaseholds

I. BEFORE 1926

The intervention of equity in the case of mortgages of leaseholds produced the **19–027** same results in matters of substance as in the case of freeholds.[66] As to form,

---

[56] L.P.A. 1925, s.87(1).
[57] L.P.A. 1925, s.87(1).
[58] But it may sometimes take effect in equity as a contract to grant a mortgage: see *post*, para. 19–039.
[59] L.P.A. 1925, s.87(1).
[60] *ibid.*
[61] See *Grand Junction Co. Ltd v. Bates* [1954] 2 Q.B. 160; *Weg Motors Ltd v. Hales* [1962] Ch. 49 at 74; *Cumberland Court (Brighton) Ltd v. Taylor* [1964] Ch. 29.
[62] *Regent Oil Co. Ltd v. J. A. Gregory (Hatch End) Ltd* [1966] Ch. 402.
[63] *Ante*, para. 19–005.
[64] *Post*, para. 19–034.
[65] *Post*, para. 19–041.
[66] *Ante*, para. 19–010.

a legal mortgage of leaseholds could be made before 1926 in either of two ways:

> (i) by assignment of the lease to the mortgagee with a covenant for reassignment on redemption; or
>
> (ii) by the grant to the mortgagee of a sub-lease at least one day shorter than the lease, with a proviso for cesser on redemption.

19–028　　**1. Liability under the lease.** The first method was rarely employed, for it brought the mortgagee into privity of estate with the landlord, and so made the mortgagee liable for the rent and for the performance of such other covenants in the lease as ran with the land.[67] This was not so under the second method, for then the mortgagee was only an underlessee and there was privity neither of contract nor of estate between him and the lessor.[68] In either case the mortgage normally contained the usual provision for redemption on a fixed date six months ahead, and thereafter the mortgagor had an equitable right to redeem.

19–029　　**2. Subsequent mortgages.** Where a mortgage had been made by assignment, second and subsequent mortgages were made by a mortgage of the mortgagor's equity of redemption. Where the prior mortgage had been made by a sub-lease, subsequent mortgages were made by the grant of other sub-leases, each normally being longer than the previous one. By the second, and usual, method it was therefore possible to create several legal mortgages of a leasehold property. It was desirable to leave a space of, say, 10 days between the end of the first sub-lease and the end of the lease, so as to leave room for further mortgage terms, each longer by one day than the preceding sub-lease.[69]

II. AFTER 1925

19–030　　By the Law of Property Act 1925[70] leaseholds can no longer be mortgaged by assignment. Two methods only are possible at law:

> (i) by a subdemise for a term of years absolute, subject to a provision for cesser on redemption, the term being at least one day shorter than the term vested in the mortgagor; or
>
> (ii) by a charge by deed expressed to be by way of legal mortgage.

19–031　　**1. Subdemise for a term of years absolute.** The term of the sub-lease must be at least one day shorter than the term of the lease which is being mortgaged,

---

[67] *Ante*, para. 15–003.
[68] *Ante*, para. 15–005.
[69] The extra day was not essential to the creation of a legal estate (*ante*, para. 14–104), but it made it clear beyond doubt that the second or later mortgagee was the immediate reversioner.
[70] s.86(1).

otherwise it would operate as an assignment.[71] If the lease requires the tenant to obtain the landlord's licence before a subdemise by way of mortgage is made, the licence cannot be unreasonably refused.[72] It is usual to make the sub-term 10 days shorter than the lease, so as to allow room for second and subsequent mortgages. Thus if T's 50 years' lease is mortgaged, a first mortgage will be secured by a lease for 50 years less 10 days, a second by 50 years less nine days and so on. But this is not essential, for the old rule that a lease may take effect in reversion upon another lease of the same or greater length[73] was confirmed by the Law of Property Act 1925.[74] Thus if the first mortgage was made by a sub-term of 50 years less one day, the second mortgage could be secured by a sub-term of the same length and so on; each mortgage would then take effect in its proper order.

A purported assignment of a lease which in fact[75] is made by way of mortgage since 1925 operates as a subdemise for a term of years absolute subject to cesser on redemption.[76] A first or only mortgagee takes a term 10 days shorter than the lease mortgaged. Second and subsequent mortgagees take terms one day longer than the previous mortgagee if this is possible; in every case, however, the sub-term must be at least one day shorter than the term mortgaged.[77]   **19–032**

If the mortgaged lease is subject to forfeiture, a mortgagee by subdemise (or by legal charge) has the same right to relief as any other subtenant.[78]

2. Charge by way of legal mortgage. A charge by deed expressed to be by way of legal mortgage gives the mortgagee (whether first or subsequent) the same rights and remedies as if he had a sub-term one day shorter than the term vested in the mortgagor.[79] As in the case of freeholds, he gets no actual term of years but is as fully protected as if he had one.   **19–033**

C. Advantages of a Legal Charge

There is nothing in the Law of Property Act 1925 which suggests any reason why a statutory legal charge, either of freeholds or leaseholds, should be preferred to an ordinary mortgage. But there seem to be three practical advantages in using a legal charge.   **19–034**

(i) It is a convenient way of mortgaging freeholds and leaseholds together; the deed is shortened by stating that all the properties

---

[71] *Beardman v. Wilson* (1868) L.R. 4 C.P. 57 *ante*, para. 14–110.
[72] L.P.A. 1925, s.86(1); *cf. ante*, para. 14–259.
[73] *Re Moore & Hulm's Contract* [1912] 2 Ch. 105; *ante*, para. 14–104.
[74] L.P.A. 1925, s.149(5).
[75] *Grangeside Properties Ltd v. Collingwoods Securities Ltd* [1964] 1 W.L.R. 139, holding that the assignment need not be *expressed* to be by way of mortgage.
[76] L.P.A. 1925, s.86(2).
[77] *ibid*. Thus if more mortgages are made than spare days are available, the last mortgagees each take a term of one day less than the term mortgaged.
[78] *Ante* para. 14–162.
[79] L.P.A. 1925, s.87(1).

specified in the Schedule are charged by way of legal mortgage, instead of setting out the length of the various mortgage terms in each case.

(ii) It is probable that the grant of a legal charge on a lease does not amount to a breach of any covenant in that lease against subletting, for the charge creates no actual sub-lease in favour of the mortgagee but merely gives him the same rights as if he had a sub-lease.[80]

(iii) The form of a legal charge is short and simple.

The charge by way of legal mortgage is now invariably employed.[81] Indeed, it has been said that "it is difficult to justify the continued existence of the mortgage by demise, given that it is no longer used in practice".[82]

D. Custody of Title Deeds

19–035 In the case of land with unregistered title, it has always been to the mortgagee's advantage to take into his custody the title deeds of the property,[83] for then any person to whom the mortgagor might try to convey or re-mortgage it would soon discover from the absence of the deeds that there was a prior mortgage. This precaution was of particular importance in the case of equitable mortgages (discussed below), in order to prevent a purchase of the legal estate without notice of the mortgagee's rights. But a legal mortgagee will also wish to have the deeds deposited with him. When mortgages were made by a grant of the fee simple, this automatically entitled the mortgagee to take the deeds. Now that legal mortgages are made by legal charge,[84] the first mortgagee has been given a statutory right to possession of the documents of title,[85] for he would not otherwise be entitled to demand them.[86]

19–036 In the rare case of a legal mortgage of a leasehold by *assignment* before 1926, the mortgagee was automatically entitled to possession of the lease. In the more common case of mortgage by *subdemise* he was not so entitled, but

---

[80] See Wolst. & C. i, 178; *Gentle v. Faulkner* [1900] 2 Q.B. 267; *Matthews v. Smallwood* [1910] 1 Ch. 777; *Grand Junction Co. Ltd v. Bates* [1954] 2 Q.B. 160 at 168. However, where the covenant in question also prohibits the tenant from parting with possession of the property (as it usually will), there will be a breach if the mortgagee enforces his right to possession.

[81] Where title to land is registered (as it usually will be), there is, in effect, a rebuttable presumption that a registered charge take effect as a charge by way of legal mortgage: see L.R.A. 1925, s.27(1). It is possible to create expressly a charge by demise or sub-demise, or provide that the charge is to take effect as such. For registered charges, see *ante*, para. 6–074.

[82] (1991) Law Com. No. 204, para. 2.13. For the Law Commission's proposals for the reform of the law on mortgages, see *post*, para. 19–266.

[83] "Title deeds" is used in a wide sense, so as to include all documents necessary to prove the mortgagor's title, *e.g.* assents by personal representatives made in writing but not by deed: *ante* para. 11–126. For limits on what amount to title deeds, see *Clayton v. Clayton* [1930] 2 Ch. 12 at 21.

[84] And may (at least in theory) be made by a long lease.

[85] L.P.A. 1925, s.85(1).

[86] *Ante*, para. 19–020.

he would usually stipulate expressly for it to be handed over. This stipulation is no longer necessary, for a first mortgagee of leaseholds has now, by statute,[87] the same right to possession of documents as if he were mortgagee by assignment.

A legal mortgage of unregistered freehold land or of a lease with more than 21 years to run, which is protected by a deposit of title deeds and is executed after March 1998, triggers the requirement of compulsory registration.[88] The underlying legal estate must be registered and the mortgage will then be registered as a registered charge over that estate.

Where title is registered, there are of course no title deeds of which any registered chargee can have custody. However, the registered proprietor's land certificate must be deposited with the registry until the charge is cancelled.[89] The registry will issue the chargee with a charge certificate.[90] In this way, the registered proprietor is effectively precluded from making any disposition of the land that requires registration without the chargee's consent.

Section 2. Methods of Creating Equitable Mortgages and Charges

The fundamental difference between a mortgage and a charge is that a mortgage is a conveyance of property, legal or equitable, subject to a right of redemption, whereas a charge conveys nothing but merely gives the chargee certain rights over the property charged.[91] Only mortgages could be created at common law; but in equity both mortgages and charges were possible. Equitable charges are still occasionally created, but the remedies of an equitable chargee are inferior to those of a mortgagee.[92] **19–037**

A. *Equitable Mortgages*

1. Mortgage of an equitable interest. If the mortgagor has no legal estate but only an equitable interest, any mortgage he effects must necessarily be equitable. Thus the beneficiaries under a trust of land have mere equitable interests and can create only equitable mortgages. **19–038**

The 1925 legislation did not affect the form of equitable mortgages of equitable interests.[93] Such mortgages are still made by a conveyance of the whole equitable interest with a proviso for reconveyance. The actual form of

---

[87] L.P.A. 1925, s.86(1).
[88] L.R.A. 1925, ss.123(2), 123A(1) (inserted by L.R.A. 1997, s.1); *ante* para. 6–015.
[89] L.R.A. 1925, s.65. In practice the registry does not issue a land certificate at all in such circumstances. There is no question of certificates being stored at the registry.
[90] *ibid.*, s.63(1).
[91] *Jones v. Woodward* (1917) 116 L.T. 378 at 379; *London County and Westminster Bank Ltd v. Tompkins* [1918] 1 K.B. 515 (esp. at 528). Yet a charge by way of legal mortgage is in substance a mortgage, not merely a charge, since the chargee has all the rights of a mortgagee.
[92] See *post*, para. 19–091.
[93] It is true that L.P.A. 1925, ss.85(2), 86(2), unlike ss.85(1), 86(1), are not in terms confined to mortgages effected "at law"; yet such a restriction would probably be implied.

words employed is immaterial, provided the meaning is plain.[94] Nor need the mortgage be made by deed, as is essential for a legal mortgage; but it must either be made (and not merely evidenced[95]) in writing signed by the mortgagor or his agent authorised in writing.[96] It is wise, though not essential, for the mortgagee to give notice of his mortgage to the trustees in whom the legal estate is vested, both to prevent the trustees from paying the mortgagor, and to preserve priority.[97]

19–039 **2. Contract to create a mortgage.** A contract to create a legal mortgage, like other contracts to create legal estates, gives an equitable interest to any party entitled to specific performance.[98] But an equitable mortgage of this type is more than a mere preliminary to a legal mortgage: equity treats it as an actual mortgage,[99] for in the great majority of cases the execution of a legal mortgage is never intended and never carried out. In theory the mortgagee may call for a legal mortgage, but in practice he is content to rest upon his equitable rights.

A contract for a mortgage must comply with the formal requirements of section 2 of the Law of Property (Miscellaneous Provisions) Act 1989. It must be made in writing, signed by both parties and incorporate all the terms agreed.[1] This has had a very significant consequence which has already been explained.[2] For two centuries before the 1989 Act came into force on September 27, 1989, it had been possible to create a mortgage informally, without even a written memorandum, by depositing the title deeds to a property as security for a loan.[3] Although the basis of such mortgages was contractual, they were enforceable on the basis of the doctrine of part performance.[4] Such mortgages were in common commercial use, and lenders purported to create them even after the passing of the 1989 Act. However, it has now been decided that a mortgage supported by a deposit of title deeds is ineffective unless it complies with the requirements of section 2 of that Act.[5] This is because the doctrine of part performance has been abrogated by the 1989 Act.

Where the title to the land is registered and a contract to mortgage the land is supported by a deposit of the land certificate, the mortgagee should protect

---

[94] *William Brandt's Sons & Co. v. Dunlop Rubber Co. Ltd* [1905] A.C. 454 at 462.
[95] See *ante*, para. 10–046.
[96] L.P.A. 1925, s.53(1)(c).
[97] See *post*, paras 19–208, 19–233.
[98] See *ante*, para. 4–025.
[99] See *Ex p. Wright* (1812) 19 Ves. 255 at 258.
[1] *Ante*, para. 12–018.
[2] *Ante*, para. 12–043.
[3] See *Russel v. Russel* (1783) 1 Bro. C.C. 269. For an account of such mortgages, see the previous edition of this work at p. 927.
[4] See *Re Alton Corporation* [1985] B.C.L.C. 27 at 33. For the doctrine of part performance see *ante*, para. 12–017.
[5] *United Bank of Kuwait Plc v. Sahib* [1997] Ch. 107; *ante*, para. 12–043.

his interest by the entry of a notice.[6] It is no longer possible to enter a notice of deposit.[7]

B. Equitable Charges

An equitable charge is created by appropriating specific property to the discharge of some debt or other obligation without there being any change in ownership either at law or in equity.[8] No special form of words is required: it is sufficient if the parties have made plain their intention that the property should constitute a security.[9] Thus, if A signs a written contract agreeing that he thereby charges his land with the payment of £500 to B, an equitable charge is created.[10] The same applies where a will or voluntary settlement charges land with the payment of a sum of money.[11]

19–040

Section 3. Form of Legal Charge

THIS LEGAL CHARGE[12] is made the first day of January 1998 between William Fisher of etc. ("the borrower") of the one part and Lightwood Finance Plc. of etc. ("the lender") of the other part
WHEREAS—

19–041

(1) The borrower is the estate owner in respect of the fee simple absolute in possession of the property described in the Schedule ("the mortgaged property")

(2) The lender has agreed to lend the borrower the sum of £120,000 upon having the repayment thereof with interest thereon secured in the manner hereinafter appearing

NOW THIS DEED made in pursuance of the said agreement and in consideration of the sum of £120,000 now paid to the borrower by the lender (the receipt of which the borrower hereby acknowledges)
WITNESSETH as follows:—

1. The borrower hereby covenants with the lender to pay the lender on the first day of July next the said sum of £120,000 with interest thereon from the

---

[6] See Ruoff & Roper, 25–07.

[7] *Ante*, para. 6–114.

[8] *Carreras Rothmans Ltd v. Freeman Mathews Treasure Ltd* [1985] Ch. 207 at 227; *Re Cosslett (Contractors) Ltd* [1998] Ch. 495 at 508; and see *ante*, para. 19–005.

[9] *Cradock v. Scottish Provident Institution* (1893) 69 L.T. 380, aff'd 70 L.T. 718; *National Provincial and Union Bank of England v. Charnley* [1924] 1 K.B. 431 at 440, 445, 459.

[10] *Matthews v. Goodday* (1861) 31 L.J.Ch. 282 at 282, 283.

[11] *Re Owen* [1894] 3 Ch. 220; *Matthews v. Goodday, supra.*

[12] In the previous edition of this work at p. 929, a precedent was given of a legal mortgage by demise. As such mortgages are seldom if ever used, this has not been included in the present edition. In practice, charges by way of legal mortgage are now usually made on the lender's standard form and by reference to its mortgage conditions, rather than in the form given in the text.

date of this deed at the rate of £8 per cent per annum and further if the said moneys shall not be so paid to pay the lender interest at the rate aforesaid by equal monthly payments on the first day of every month in each year on the moneys for the time being remaining due on this security.

2. The borrower charges ALL THAT the mortgaged property by way of legal mortgage with full title guarantee with the payment to the lender of the principal money, interest, and other money hereby covenanted to be paid by the borrower under this deed.

3. The borrower hereby covenants with the lender:

[There will then be set out covenants by the mortgagor to repair, insure, etc., and any other terms agreed upon]

SIGNED AS A DEED etc.

Schedule

C. Statutory Requirements

19–042   **Consumer Credit Act 1974.** This Act introduced an elaborate scheme of safeguards for the purpose of consumer protection in credit transactions of widely varying kinds. It applies to certain mortgages, but only to those where the credit provided does not exceed £25,000[13] and where none of the exemptions apply. The exemptions include transactions where the creditor is a building society, an institution authorised under the Banking Act 1987 or a local authority and numerous other cases specified by ministerial order.[14] The financial limit means that most ordinary mortgages for house purchase or commercial finance are exempt. The provisions are aimed at second mortgages by which house-owners may be tempted to borrow improvidently for personal needs.

19–043   Where the Act applies, the agreement must be in the form prescribed by regulations so as to make the mortgagor aware of his rights and duties, the amount and rate of the total charge for credit, and the protection and remedies provided by the Act.[15] It must contain all the agreed terms, except implied terms, and must be signed by both parties.[16] In addition, the mortgagee must supply the mortgagor with a copy of the proposed agreement seven days in advance and refrain from approaching him in the meantime, in order to give him an opportunity to withdraw.[17] An agreement which fails to comply with these requirements is improperly executed and enforceable only on an order of the court.[18] A mortgage within the Act is in any case enforceable only on

---

[13] S.I. 1983 No. 1878, as amended by S.I. 1998 No. 996.

[14] s.16; S.I. 1989 No. 869.

[15] ss.60, 61. See the Consumer Credit (Agreements) Regulations 1983 (S.I. 1983 No. 1553) (as amended).

[16] s.61.

[17] ss.58, 61(2).

[18] ss.61, 65.

a court order,[19] but the court may take account of improper execution in assessing any prejudice caused and the degree of culpability for it.[20]

Part 3

RIGHTS OF THE PARTIES UNDER A MORTGAGE OR CHARGE

The rights of the parties under a mortgage or charge will be considered under three heads— **19–044**

    (i) the rights of the mortgagee or chargee;

    (ii) rights common to both parties; and

    (iii) the rights of the mortgagor or chargor.

Section 1. Rights of the Mortgagee or Chargee

A. Remedies for Enforcing his Security

Unless the parties have otherwise agreed, a mortgagee or chargee has certain standard remedies. First of all, he may of course sue for the money due, so soon as the date fixed for repayment has arrived, though not before.[21] But the remedies peculiar to mortgages and charges are the remedies for enforcing the security, though these may be and nowadays often are sought in addition to a money judgment for the sums due under the mortgage.[22] These remedies may be classified as follows. **19–045**

    (a) *Remedies primarily for recovery of capital*

        (i) Foreclosure
        (ii) Sale.

    (b) *Remedies primarily for recovery of interest*

        (i) Taking possession
        (ii) Appointment of receiver.

---

[19] s.126. No order is necessary if the mortgagor consents: s.173(3).
[20] s.127.
[21] See, *e.g. Bolton v. Buckenham* [1891] 1 Q.B. 278. A mortgagor's obligation to repay is presumed in the absence of express provision from the receipt of the loan: see *Sutton v. Sutton* (1882) 22 Ch.D. 511 at 515; and for registered land, L.R.A. 1925, s.28. For the rebuttal of the presumption where the mortgagor's property was security for a loan to a third party, see *Fairmile Portfolio Management Ltd v. Davies Arnold Cooper* [1998] E.G.C.S. 149.
[22] See *Cheltenham and Gloucester B.S. v. Grattidge* (1993) 25 H.L.R. 454; *Cheltenham and Gloucester B.S. v. Grant* (1994) 26 H.L.R. 703 at 708; *Cheltenham and Gloucester B.S. v. Johnson* (1996) 73 P. & C.R. 293 (money judgment sought in addition to order for possession); *post*, para. 19–074.

19–046 The first two remedies are necessarily final remedies, since they put an end to the whole transaction. The other two remedies are useful if the mortgagee wishes to keep the mortgage alive, as where there is a favourable rate of interest, and to enforce punctual payment of the interest. The rights to foreclose and to take possession arise from the very nature of the security. The powers to sell and to appoint a receiver are improvements designed by conveyancers and now incorporated by statute in the great majority of mortgages. They may usually be exercised out of court, whereas in most cases the mortgagee can enforce payment of the money due, foreclose or obtain possession only by proceedings in court. The jurisdictional position in relation to such proceedings is as follows—

(a) in claims for the payment of moneys secured by a mortgage—

   (i) the jurisdiction of the county court is confined to cases where the amount owing is less than £30,000, *except* where possession is also sought where its jurisdiction is unlimited[23]; and

   (ii) in other cases the matter must be heard by the Chancery Division of the High Court[24];

(b) in claims for foreclosure,[25] the jurisdiction of the county court is confined to cases where the amount owing is less than £30,000[26]: in other cases the matter must be heard by the Chancery Division of the High Court[27];

(c) in claims for possession, subject to (b) above, the county court has exclusive jurisdiction in relation to dwelling-houses outside London, and concurrent jurisdiction with the Chancery Division of the High Court as regards all other types of property.[28]

19–047 It is no longer possible for a mortgagee to obtain a judgment in default of defence.[29] Prior to the introduction of the Civil Procedure Rules 1998, such a

---

[23] C.C.A. 1984, ss.21 (as amended), 23(c). £30,000 is the present county court limit.
[24] C.P.R. Sched. 1, R88.2(a).
[25] The mortgagee must genuinely seek foreclosure, and must not have added it "as a mere colourable claim": *Trustees of Manchester Unity Life Insurance Collecting Society v. Sadler* [1974] 1 W.L.R. 770 at 773, *per* Walton J. (a decision on earlier legislation).
[26] C.C.A. 1984, s.23(c). The parties may agree to proceedings in the county court where the sum is greater than £30,000: *ibid.*, s. 24(1), (2)(g).
[27] Supreme Court Act 1981, s.61(1); Sched. 1, para. 1.
[28] C.C.A. 1984, s.21(1) (3); C.P.R. Sched. 1, R88.2. Where a claim for possession of a dwelling-house outside London has been commenced in the county court, there is no jurisdiction to transfer it to the High Court: see *Yorkshire Bank Plc v. Hall* [1999] 1 W.L.R. 1713.
[29] C.P.R. 12.2(c); 12PD–001, para. 1.2(3) (though the reference to C.P.R. Sched. 2, C24 as involving "mortgage claims" seems misplaced).

judgment was possible, but only with the leave of the court. However, this restriction was narrowly interpreted and did not apply—

    (i) if the mortgaged property had already been sold by a prior mortgagee, so that the money was no longer secured on any property[30];

    (ii) to an action brought for the repayment of a loan that happened to be secured by a mortgage, but without reference to or reliance upon it.[31]

The same restrictions will almost certainly be applied to the new rule precluding any judgment in default of defence in mortgage actions.

All the above remedies are available to a legal mortgagee or chargee, and his position will be considered first. An equitable mortgagee or chargee has more restricted remedies, which are considered later.

Where the mortgage is regulated by the Consumer Credit Act 1974,[32] it is enforceable only on an order of the court, which has wide discretion to extend time limits or impose conditions or suspend the operation of the order[33]; and it may not be enforced so as to give the creditor a benefit greater than the debt.[34]

I. LEGAL MORTGAGE OR LEGAL CHARGE

A legal mortgagee or legal chargee has the following remedies for enforcing his security.   **19–048**

1. To foreclose

(a) The right of foreclosure

(1) EQUITY'S INTERVENTION. By giving the mortgagor an equitable right to redeem after he had lost his legal right of redemption, equity interfered with the bargain made between the parties. But equity prescribed limits to the equitable right to redeem which it created. Thus, before 1926, a legal first mortgagee of freeholds had the fee simple vested in him, and once the legal date for redemption had passed, the mortgagor's right to redeem was merely equitable. "Foreclosure" was the name given to the process whereby the mortgagor's equitable right to redeem was declared by the court to be extinguished and the mortgagee was left owner of the property, both at law and in equity. Equity had interfered to prevent the conveyance by way of mortgage from having its full effect; but there had to be some final point at   **19–049**

---

[30] *Newnham v. Brown* [1966] 1 W.L.R. 875.

[31] *National Westminster Bank Plc v. Kitch* [1996] 1 W.L.R. 1316 (judgment in default of defence validly obtained in the Queen's Bench Division of the High Court).

[32] *Ante*, para. 19–042.

[33] ss.126, 129, 135. See *post.* para. 19–073.

[34] s.113. This may rule out foreclosure unless the court orders the mortgagee to account for any surplus value.

which the mortgagee could enforce his security, and therefore by foreclosure "the court simply removes the stop it has itself put on".[35] The mortgagee was from the first entitled to the property at law; and when he obtained the necessary order of the court, foreclosure made him an absolute owner in equity as well.[36]

19–050   (2) ORDER OF COURT. An order of the court is essential for foreclosure. "Foreclosure is done by the order of the court, not by any person."[37] Since 1925 a mortgagee does not have the whole legal estate of the mortgagor vested in him,[38] but only a long term of years in the case of freeholds and an underlease in the case of leaseholds. Consequently it is no longer sufficient for a decree of foreclosure merely to destroy the mortgagor's equity of redemption; and the Law of Property Act 1925 provides that a foreclosure decree absolute shall vest the mortgagor's fee simple[39] or term of years[40] in the mortgagee.

In practice, "foreclosure actions are almost unheard of today and have been for many years".[41] This is both because of the lack of finality of a foreclosure decree,[42] and because mortgagees prefer to exercise other remedies, such as sale or the appointment of a receiver.[43]

19–051   (3) RIGHT TO FORECLOSE. The right to foreclose does not arise until repayment has become due at law,[44] for until the equitable right to redeem has arisen, it cannot be extinguished by foreclosure. Repayment is due at law when the legal date for redemption has passed, or, if the mortgage has made the money fall due on breach of any term of the mortgage, on the occurrence of any such breach, such as failure to make due payment of interest[45] or of an instalment of principal.[46] Once this has occurred, the mortgagee may begin foreclosure proceedings unless he has agreed not to do so[47]; and the mere acceptance of a late payment will not by itself waive the right to foreclose for a breach.[48] In practice the mortgagee sometimes contracts not to enforce the security by foreclosure or other means until he has given some specified

---

[35] *Carter v. Wake* (1877) 4 Ch.D. 605 at 606, *per* Jessel M.R.
[36] *Heath v. Pugh* (1881) 6 Q.B.D. 345 at 360.
[37] *Re Farnol Eades Irvine & Co. Ltd* [1915] 1 Ch. 22 at 24, *per* Warrington J.
[38] But see *ante*, para. 19–038, as to equitable mortgages of equitable interests.
[39] s.88(2).
[40] s.89(2).
[41] *Palk v. Mortgage Services Funding Plc* [1993] Ch. 330 at 336, *per* Nicholls V.-C.
[42] *Post*. para. 19–055.
[43] *Palk v. Mortgage Services Funding Plc, supra*, at 336. See too *Halifax B.S. v. Thomas* [1996] Ch. 217 at 226.
[44] *Williams v. Morgan* [1906] 1 Ch. 804.
[45] *Keene v. Biscoe* (1878) 8 Ch.D. 201; *Twentieth Century Banking Corporation Ltd v. Wilkinson* [1977] Ch. 99; contrast *Burrowes v. Molloy* (1845) 2 Jo. & Lat. 521.
[46] *Kidderminster Mutual Benefit B.S. v. Haddock* [1936] W.N. 158.
[47] *Ramsbottom v. Wallis* (1835) 5 L.J. Ch. 92.
[48] See *Keene v. Biscoe, supra*, and contrast *Re Taaffe's Estate* (1864) 14 Ir.Ch.R. 347.

notice or until the mortgagor has broken one of his covenants in the mortgage.[49] If no redemption date is fixed[50] or if the loan is repayable on demand,[51] the right to foreclose arises when a demand for repayment has been made and a reasonable time thereafter has elapsed.[52]

(b) Parties to a foreclosure action. An action for foreclosure can be brought **19–052** by any mortgagee of property, whether he is the original mortgagee or an assignee,[53] and whether he is a first or subsequent mortgagee.[54] The effect of a foreclosure order absolute in an action brought by the first mortgagee is to make him the sole owner both at law and in equity, free from any subsequent mortgages; if the action is brought by a second or subsequent mortgagee, he will hold the property subject to prior incumbrances[55] but free from all subsequent incumbrances. These are the natural results of extinguishing the equity of redemption.

As will be seen shortly,[56] a foreclosure action gives the mortgagor and all others interested in the equity of redemption an opportunity of redeeming the mortgage or of applying for a sale in lieu of foreclosure. Consequently all persons interested in the equity of redemption must be made parties to the action.[57] Thus if X has made successive mortgages of his property to A, B and C, and B starts foreclosure proceedings,[58] A will not be affected by them and so need not be made a party to the action.[59] But if the action is successful, C will lose his mortgage and X his equity of redemption, and so both must be made parties to the action.[60] The same may apply to X's spouse and to certain other "connected persons".[61]

(c) Procedure. Foreclosure proceedings may be commenced by claim form **19–053** or (as is likely in most cases) under the Civil Procedure Rules Part 8 procedure (which is akin to the old originating summons). The court then makes a foreclosure order nisi.[62] This directs the taking of the necessary accounts and provides that if the mortgagor pays the money due by a fixed day (usually six months from the accounts being settled by the master), the mortgage shall be discharged; but that if this is not done the mortgage shall be foreclosed. If there are several mortgagees and the first mortgagee is foreclosing, each

---

[49] See *Seaton v. Twyford* (1870) L.R. 11 Eq. 591.
[50] *Fitzgerald's Trustee v. Mellersh* [1892] 1 Ch. 385.
[51] *Balfe v. Lord* (1842) 2 Dr. & War. 480.
[52] *Brighty v. Norton* (1862) 3 B. & S. 305; *Toms v. Wilson* (1862) 4 B. & S. 442. But see Coote, *Mortgages*, chap. III, for "Welsh mortgages".
[53] *Platt v. Mendel* (1884) 27 Ch.D. 246 at 247.
[54] *Rose v. Page* (1829) 2 Sim. 471.
[55] See *Slade v. Rigg* (1843) 3 Hare 35 at 38.
[56] See *post*, para. 19–054.
[57] *Brisco v. Kenrick* (1832) 1 Coop.t.Cott. 371; *Westminster Bank Ltd v. Residential Properties Improvement Co. Ltd* [1938] Ch. 639 (need to join debenture holders of company).
[58] As in *Rose v. Page* (1829) 2 Sim. 471.
[59] *Richards v. Cooper* (1842) 5 Beav. 304.
[60] *Tylee v. Webb* (1843) 6 Beav. 552 at 557.
[61] *Post*, para. 19–142.
[62] *i.e.* the mortgage will be foreclosed unless (nisi) the mortgagor redeems.

mortgagee is given the alternative of either losing his security or else redeeming the first mortgage, *i.e.* buying it up. Sometimes the court will give the mortgagees successive periods (*e.g.* of six months) to effect this redemption,[63] but usually there will be only one period between them.[64]

In the special case of instalment mortgages of dwellinghouses the court has wide discretionary power to adjourn the proceedings or to suspend its order, as explained below.[65]

19–054   (d) *Sale.* At the request of the mortgagee or of any person interested (*e.g.* a later mortgagee or the mortgagor) the court may order a sale of the property instead of foreclosure. It may do so notwithstanding that any person dissents. This jurisdiction[66] has always existed, but it is now statutory.[67] It is an important safeguard where the property mortgaged is (as is usual) worth substantially more than the mortgage debt. If, for example, X borrows £20,000 from A on a first mortgage of a property worth £50,000, and then borrows £10,000 from B on a second mortgage, foreclosure by A will be manifestly unjust. For A will obtain far more than is due to him, X will lose far more than he owes, and B will lose his security altogether. X or B will therefore apply for a sale by order of the court (a "judicial sale"), and though the court has a free discretion, an order for sale will almost certainly be made in such a case.[68] When the sale has taken place, each incumbrancer is paid what is due to him according to his priority, and the balance belongs to the mortgagor.[69]

19–055   (e) *Opening the foreclosure.* If no order for sale is made and the property is not duly redeemed, a foreclosure order absolute is made. This destroys the mortgagor's equity of redemption and transfers his fee simple[70] or term of years[71] to the mortgagee, who thus becomes sole owner at law and in equity, subject only to prior incumbrances. But even the order of foreclosure absolute is not necessarily final, for the court will sometimes "open[72] the foreclosure".[73] Circumstances which may influence the court to do this are an accident at the last moment preventing the mortgagor from raising the money, any special value which the property had to the mortgagor (*e.g.* if it was an old family estate), a marked disparity between the value of the property and the

---

[63] *Smithett v. Hesketh* (1890) 44 Ch.D. 161.
[64] *Platt v. Mendel* (1884) 27 Ch.D. 246.
[65] *Post*, para. 19–074.
[66] Which may now be exercised by the county court where the amount owing at the commencement of proceedings does not exceed £30,000: L.P.A. 1925, s.91(8) (as inserted).
[67] L.P.A. 1925, s.91(2). See *Twentieth Century Banking Corporation Ltd v. Wilkinson* [1977] Ch. 99, not deciding whether the applicant, if the mortgagee, need show that he is entitled to foreclose. It would seem not, since any person interested may apply for sale under the wide terms of the subsection.
[68] In *Silsby v. Holliman* [1955] Ch. 552 special circumstances made a sale inequitable.
[69] Waldock, *Mortgages*, 366, 367.
[70] L.P.A. 1925, s.88(2).
[71] *ibid.*, s.89(2).
[72] Or "reopen".
[73] See *Campbell v. Holyland* (1877) 7 Ch.D. 166 at 172–175.

amount lent, and the promptness of the application.[74] Even if the mortgagee has sold the property after foreclosure absolute, the court may still open the foreclosure. This is unlikely, however, if the purchaser bought the property some time after foreclosure and without notice of circumstances which might induce the court to interfere.[75] It is the lack of finality in foreclosure proceedings which sometimes leads mortgagees, as well as mortgagors, to apply for judicial sale instead.

2. To sell

(a) History. There is no right, either at common law or in equity, for a **19–056** mortgagee to sell the mortgaged property free from the equity of redemption. He can freely transfer the estate which is vested in him subject to the equity of redemption, that is to say, he can transfer or assign the mortgage. But he cannot rely upon being able to realise his security in this way, for it may be difficult to find a willing transferee. Yet he desires a better remedy than foreclosure, for foreclosure requires elaborate proceedings before the court and is in many ways an unsatisfactory remedy.

The solution was found by inserting an express power in mortgage deeds enabling the mortgagee to sell the property out of court and free from the equity of redemption.[76] This power was carefully drafted so as to allow the mortgagee to take only what was due to him out of the proceeds of sale, and only to exercise the power in proper circumstances, for otherwise equity would have intervened. The power has long enjoyed statutory approval, and need no longer be inserted expressly. The power is now contained in the Law of Property Act 1925,[77] though a limited power was first granted by Lord Cranworth's Act 1860.[78]

(b) The power

(1) POWER ARISING. In the absence of an expression of contrary intention in **19–057** the mortgage,[79] every mortgagee has a power of sale, provided that—

> (i) the mortgage was made by deed[80] (and all legal mortgages must be made in this way); and

---

[74] *ibid., per* Jessel M.R.; and see *Lancashire & Yorkshire Reversionary Interest Co. Ltd v. Crowe* (1970) 114 S.J. 435.

[75] See *Campbell v. Holyland, supra.*

[76] This did not become the usual practice until about 1820 or 1830: see *Stevens v. Theatres Ltd* [1903] 1 Ch. 857 at 860; *Clarke v. Royal Panopticon* (1857) 4 Drew. 26 at 30.

[77] L.P.A. 1925, ss.101–107. These provisions have no application to ship mortgages: see *The Maule* [1997] 1 W.L.R. 528 at 532, 533; [1997] L.M.C.L.Q. 329 at 333, 334 (A. Clarke).

[78] 23 & 24 Vict. c. 145, ss.11–16. See Sugden, *Powers*, 877–883. The power was extended by both C.A. 1881, s.19 and C.A. 1911.

[79] L.P.A. 1925, s.101(4).

[80] *ibid.*, s.101(1).

(ii) the mortgage money is due,[80a] *i.e.* the legal date for redemption has passed; if the mortgage money is payable by instalments, the power of sale arises as soon as any instalment is in arrear.[81]

19–058   (2) POWER EXERCISABLE. When the foregoing conditions have been fulfilled, the statutory power of sale *arises*; nevertheless, the power does not become *exercisable* unless one of the three following conditions has been satisfied—

(i) notice requiring payment of the mortgage money has been served on the mortgagor and default has been made in payment of part or all of it for three months thereafter[82]; or

(ii) some interest under the mortgage is two months or more in arrear[83]; or

(iii) there has been a breach of some provision contained in the Act[84] or in the mortgage deed[85] (other than the covenant for payment of the mortgage money or interest) which should have been observed or performed by the mortgagor or by someone who concurred in making the mortgage.[86]

A mortgagee's power to sell is unaffected by any disclaimer of the estate mortgaged by the mortgagor's liquidator or trustee in bankruptcy. This is so, even though, if the estate is a fee simple, it is terminated when it escheats to the Crown on such disclaimer.[87]

19–059   *(c) Protection of purchaser.* The difference between the power of sale arising and becoming exercisable is that if the power has not arisen, the mortgagee has no statutory power of sale at all; he can only transfer his mortgage. But if the power of sale has arisen, he can make a good title to a purchaser free from the equity of redemption even if the power has not become exercisable. The purchaser's title is not impeachable merely because none of the three specified events has occurred or the power of sale has in some way been irregularly or improperly exercised.[88] Any person injured by an unauthorised, improper or irregular exercise of the power has a remedy in

---

[80a] *ibid.*

[81] *Payne v. Cardiff R.D.C.* [1932] 1 K.B. 241. Contrast *Twentieth Century Banking Corporation Ltd v. Wilkinson* [1977] Ch. 99 (interest in arrear but principal not yet due: no power of sale).

[82] L.P.A. 1925, s.103(i). Alternatively the notice may demand payment in three months' time, and the mortgagee, if unpaid, may then sell at once: *Barker v. Illingworth* [1908] 2 Ch. 20.

[83] L.P.A. 1925, s.103(ii).

[84] See *Public Trustee v. Lawrence* [1912] 1 Ch. 789 (failure to deliver counterpart of lease as required by s.99(11); see *post* para. 19–117).

[85] *e.g.* breach of covenant to repair or insure.

[86] L.P.A. 1925, s.103(iii).

[87] *Scmlla Properties Ltd v. Gesso Properties (B.V.I.) Ltd* [1995] B.C.C. 793 at 799, 810. For escheat of freeholds, see *ante*, para. 2–050.

[88] L.P.A. 1925, s.104(2). It is unnecessary to state that the sale is made in exercise of the statutory power, for that is presumed: s.104(3).

damages against the person exercising it.[89] Thus while a purchaser from a mortgagee must satisfy himself that the power of sale has arisen, he need not inquire whether it has become exercisable.[90] Proof of title is thereby simplified, for the existence of the power of sale is proved by the form of the mortgage and the redemption date specified in it. The purchaser's title does not depend on the fact of some later default by the mortgagor.

If, however, the purchaser in fact "becomes aware . . . of any facts showing that the power of sale is not exercisable,[91] or that there is some impropriety in the sale" (as there would be if the mortgagee is selling even though the mortgagor has tendered principal and interest[92]), then notwithstanding the statutory provision that the purchaser's title is not to be impeachable "he gets no good title on taking the conveyance".[93] To hold otherwise, it has been said, would be to convert the provisions of the statute into an instrument of fraud.[94] Yet the purchaser need not make the inquiries which a suspicious man would make, though he should not shut his eyes to suspicious circumstances.[95]

(d) Mode of sale

(1) THE MORTGAGEE'S RIGHTS. In general, the statutory power of sale is **19–060** exercisable without any order of the court.[96] This is its principal advantage over foreclosure. The mortgagee may sell by public auction or private contract and has a wide discretion as to the terms and conditions upon which the sale is made,[97] and as to making the sale subject to restrictions.[98] The power is exercised as soon as a contract for sale is made, even if it is merely conditional; thereafter the mortgagor's equity of redemption is suspended while the contract subsists, and he cannot stop the sale by tendering the money due.[99] Before entering into such a contract, the mortgagee should first obtain and execute an order for possession (if he is not already in possession).[1] If he does not, he may be unable to give the purchaser vacant possession on completion, and is therefore likely to be in breach of contract.[2] The risk is particularly

---

[89] L.P.A. 1925, s.104(2).

[90] *Bailey v. Barnes* [1894] 1 Ch. 25 at 35.

[91] See *Selwyn v. Garfit* (1888) 38 Ch.D. 273 (decided on an express power of sale).

[92] *Jenkins v. Jones* (1860) 2 Giff. 99 (decided on an express power of sale).

[93] *Lord Waring v. London and Manchester Assurance Co. Ltd* [1935] Ch. 310 at 318, *per* Crossman J.

[94] *Bailey v. Barnes* [1894] 1 Ch. 25 at 30, *per* Stirling J., impliedly confirmed by the Court of Appeal. For an analogous construction of a different statute, see *Le Neve v. Le Neve* (1747) Amb. 436.

[95] See *Bailey v.Barnes* [1894] 1 Ch. 25 at 30, 34. This seems to lay down a somewhat different standard from that usually applied under the doctrine of notice: see *ante* para. 5–018.

[96] An exceptional case arises under L.P.A. 1925, s.110, in cases where a mortgage provides that a power of sale shall be exercisable in case of bankruptcy. Leave of the court is there required, but a purchaser is not concerned: L.P.A. 1925, s.104(2).

[97] L.P.A. 1925, s.101(1)(i).

[98] *ibid.*, s.101(2).

[99] *Lord Waring v. London & Manchester Assurance Co. Ltd* [1935] Ch. 310; *Property & Bloodstock Ltd v. Emerton* [1968] Ch. 94.

[1] For possession proceedings, see *post*, para. 19–067.

[2] For a vendor's obligation to give vacant possession on completion, see *ante*, para. 12–088.

acute where the mortgage is of a dwellinghouse. If the mortgagee seeks an order for possession only after contracting to sell, the court has power to suspend or adjourn the order.[3] Any purchaser will take subject to the mortgagor's rights in such circumstances.[4]

A disposition or contract to sell made by the mortgagor has no effect on the mortgagee's power of sale.[5]

19–061   (2) NO TRUSTEESHIP. There is some uncertainty as to whether a mortgagee's conduct in relation to his power of sale is governed exclusively by principles of equity or whether he may also be under a duty of care in tort both to the mortgagor and to other persons who may have an interest in the mortgaged property.[6] The trend of recent authority has been to regard the duties as arising in equity from the relationship between the mortgagor and mortgagee.[7] However, although this now seems settled, the content of any obligations in equity are flexible and will be adjusted to "fit the requirements of the time".[7a] The mortgagee is under a general duty, both to the mortgagor and to any others interested in the equity of redemption (such as subsequent encumbrancers or guarantors), to act in good faith and to use his powers only for proper purposes,[7b] but he is not a trustee for the mortgagor of his power of sale.[8] That power is given to the mortgagee for his own benefit to enable him to realise his security more effectively,[9] and his interest in the property has priority over the mortgagor's.[10] However, the mortgagor is both interested in the proceeds of sale in so far as they exceed the debt, and liable for any shortfall if they are insufficient to discharge his indebtedness. His interests must not be sacrificed.[11] In all matters relating to the power, the mortgagee must therefore act in good faith and behave fairly towards the mortgagor.[12] The mortgagee is not under any general duty of care to the mortgagor.[13] He is therefore free to

---

[3] Under A.J.A. 1970, s.36; *post*, para. 19–074. The hope when the court exercises its discretion is that the mortgagor will retain possession, pay off any arrears (or remedy any other default), and ultimately redeem the mortgage.

[4] *National and Provincial B.S. v. Ahmed* [1995] 2 E.G.L.R. 127 at 129.

[5] *Duke v. Robson* [1973] 1 W.L.R. 267.

[6] See [1990] Conv. 431 (L. Bently); (1995) 46 N.I.L.Q. 182 (P. Devonshire).

[7] See *China and South Sea Bank Ltd v. Tan* [1990] 1 A.C. 536 at 543; *Parker-Tweedale v. Dunbar Bank Plc* [1991] Ch. 12 at 18, 19; *Downsview Nominees Ltd v. First City Corporation Ltd* [1993] A.C. 295 at 315; *AIB Finance Ltd v. Debtors* [1998] 2 All E.R. 929; *Yorkshire Bank Plc v. Hall* [1999] 1 W.L.R. 1713 at 1728.

[7a] *Medforth v. Blake* [1999] 3 All E.R. 97 at 111, *per* Scott V.-C.

[7b] *Burgess v. Auger* [1998] 2 B.C.L.C. 478 at 482; *Yorkshire Bank Plc v. Hall, supra*, at 1728.

[8] *Colson v. Williams* (1889) 58 L.J.Ch. 539 at 540; *Kennedy v. De Trafford* [1897] A.C. 180; *Cuckmere Brick Co. Ltd v. Mutual Finance Ltd* [1971] Ch. 949 at 965; *Bishop v. Bonham* [1988] 1 W.L.R. 742 at 749.

[9] *Warner v. Jacob* (1882) 20 Ch.D. 220 at 224.

[10] *Palk v. Mortgage Services Funding Plc* [1993] Ch. 330 at 337. Such duties as the mortgagee owes are "qualified by being subordinated to the protection of his own interests": *Re Potters Oils Ltd* [1986] 1 W.L.R. 201 at 206, *per* Hoffmann J.

[11] *Cuckmere Brick Co. Ltd v. Mutual Finance Ltd, supra*, at 969.

[12] *Kennedy v. De Trafford, supra*, at 185, 192; *Palk v. Mortgage Services Funding Plc, supra*, at 337.

[13] *Downsview Nominees Ltd v. First City Corporation Ltd* [1993] A.C. 295 at 315. This decision has been criticised in relation to receivers under a floating charge: see G. Lightman and

choose the time at which he sells,[14] even though this (or any of the terms of the sale) may be disadvantageous to the mortgagor.[15] Indeed, he is not obliged to exercise the power at all.[16] If he does not, and the value of the security declines, he incurs no liability to the mortgagor,[17] and he still has his remedy on the personal covenant against the mortgagor and any surety.[18]

Although his general duty is to act in good faith, the mortgagee is, in certain circumstances, under a specific duty of care.[18a] If he decides to sell, he must take reasonable care to obtain what has variously been described as "the true market value"[19] and "the best price reasonably obtainable at the time".[20] Where the mortgage security includes a business conducted on the premises charged, the mortgagee must "ensure that the value of the combined asset is maximised".[21] However, his obligation to do so arises only if he takes possession of those premises.[22] Although this duty of care has been treated as tortious in a number of cases,[23] the better view is that it arises in equity as an incident of the relationship between mortgagor and mortgagee.[24] A similar duty is owed by the mortgagee to a guarantor[25] and to a subsequent mortgagee,[26] but not to a beneficiary under a trust of which the mortgagor is

---

G. Moss, *The Law of Receivers of Companies* (2nd ed.) pp. 7–13; (1994) 45 N.I.L.Q. 61 (M. Fealy); [1996] J.B.L. 113 at 119 (Lightman J.).

[14] *Parker-Tweedale v. Dunbar Bank Plc, supra,* at 18.

[15] *Cuckmere Brick Co. Ltd v. Mutual Finance Ltd, supra,* at 965; *Downsview Nominees Ltd v. First City Corporation Ltd, supra,* at 315. See too *Tse Kwong Lam v. Wong Chit Sen* [1983] 1 W.L.R. 1349 at 1355.

[16] *Palk v. Mortgage Services Funding Plc, supra,* at 337.

[17] *China and South Sea Bank Ltd v. Tan, supra,* at 545. This is the case even if he is professionally advised to do so: *Lloyds Bank Plc. v. Bryant* (1996, Lightman J., unreported).

[18] *ibid.*

[18a] *Yorkshire Bank Plc v. Hall* [1999] 1 W.L.R. 1713 at 1728; *Medforth v. Blake* [1999] 3 All E.R. 97 at 107, 108.

[19] *Cuckmere Brick Co. Ltd v. Mutual Finance Ltd, supra,* at 966, *per* Salmon L.J. See too *Palk v. Mortgage Services Funding Plc, supra,* at 338.

[20] *Tse Kwong Lam v. Wong Chit Sen, supra,* at 1355; *per* Lord Templeman. A building society is, by statute, under a similar duty to ensure that the price is the best reasonably obtainable: Building Societies Act 1986, Sched. 4, para. 1(a), replacing earlier legislation: see *Reliance Permanent B.S. v. Harwood-Stamper* [1944] Ch. 362.

[21] *AIB Finance Ltd v. Debtors* [1997] 4 All E.R. 677 at 687, *per* Carnwath J.

[22] *AIB Finance Ltd v. Debtors* [1998] 2 All E.R. 929 (C.A.) (no liability where business had closed down before the mortgagee took possession).

[23] See, *e.g. Knight v. Lawrence* [1993] B.C.L.C. 215 at 221.

[24] See, *e.g. AIB Finance Ltd v. Debtors* [1998] 2 All E.R. 929. The duty is closely analogous to the mortgagee's equitable duty when in possession to maximise his return from the property: see *Palk v. Mortgage Services Funding Plc, supra,* at 338; *Downsview Nominees Ltd v. First City Corporation Ltd* [1993] A.C. 295 at 315.

[25] *Standard Chartered Bank Ltd v. Walker* [1982] 1 W.L.R. 1410; followed in *American Express International Banking Corporation v. Hurley* [1985] 3 All E.R. 564. The duty was in each case treated as tortious. However, "equity intervenes to protect a surety": *China and South Sea Bank Ltd v. Tan* [1990] 1 A.C. 536 at 544, *per* Lord Templeman. A surety may be required by a mortgagee to pay the debt, and if that is so, will be subrogated to the mortgage. In principle, the equitable duty to sell at the market price should therefore be owed to a surety as well as to the mortgagor: *cf. China and South Sea Bank Ltd v. Tan, supra,* at 545. See too *Medforth v. Blake* [1999] 3 All E.R. 97 at 109.

[26] By virtue of his interest in the equity of redemption: see *Tomlin v. Luce* (1889) 43 Ch.D. 191.

trustee,[27] nor to a tenant at will of the property.[28] Suggestions that a mortgagee's selling agent owes a duty of care in tort to the mortgagor must now be doubted.[29] Although a mortgagee may exclude liability for loss caused to the mortgagor on any sale, such clauses are narrowly construed.[30]

19–062   The authorities provide some indication of the circumstances in which a mortgagee will be liable for breach of his duty.[31] Examples include—

    (i) where the mortgagee advertised the property without mentioning that the land had valuable planning permission[32];

    (ii) where the mortgagee sold at a "crash sale valuation" to obtain an immediate sale rather than exposing the property properly to the open market[33]; and

    (iii) where the mortgagee's receiver failed to serve notices on tenants of the mortgaged property to trigger a rent review, thereby making the reversion less valuable when sold.[34]

It has not been finally settled whether a mortgagee discharges his duty by employing a competent agent. However, the tenor of the authorities is against it.[35] Some of the earlier cases suggested that the mortgagee's duties in relation to any sale were not onerous because he was at liberty to decide when (if at all) he would exercise his power of sale. However, these may no longer be good law.[36]

---

[27] *Parker-Tweedale v. Dunbar Bank Plc* [1991] Ch. 12. *cf. Hayim v. Citibank N.A.* [1987] A.C. 730 at 748.

[28] *Jarrett v. Barclays Bank Ltd* [1947] Ch. 187. Such a person has no interest in the property charged.

[29] See *Cuckmere Brick Co. Ltd v. Mutual Finance Ltd* [1971] Ch. 949 at 973; *Garland v. Ralph Pay & Ransom* [1984] 2 E.G.L.R. 147 at 151. *cf. Routestone Ltd v. Minories Finance Ltd* [1997] 1 E.G.L.R. 123 at 124.

[30] *Bishop v. Bonham* [1988] 1 W.L.R. 742 (authority to the mortgagee to sell on such terms as he saw fit, meant in accordance with the duty to take reasonable care imposed by law).

[31] The burden lies on the mortgagor or guarantor to prove lack of proper care: *Haddington Island Quarry Co. Ltd v. Huson* [1911] A.C. 722.

[32] *Cuckmere Brick Co. Ltd v. Mutual Finance Ltd, supra.* See too *American Express International Banking Corporation v. Hurley* [1985] 3 All E.R. 564 (receiver liable when he failed either to take specialist advice or to advertise in specialist journals when selling lighting and sound equipment for pop concerts).

[33] *Predeth v. Castle Phillips Finance Co. Ltd* [1986] 2 E.G.L.R. 144; [1986] Conv. 442 (M. P. Thompson). It was accepted in that case that the mortgagee could sell at such time as he saw fit and was not obliged to wait for the market to pick up. However, the decision inevitably casts some doubt on the extent to which a mortgagee can proceed with a "forced sale", despite previous recognition of the legitimacy of such sales: see *Farrar v. Farrars Ltd* (1888) 40 Ch.D. 395 at 398.

[34] *Knight v. Lawrence* [1993] B.C.L.C. 215. For rent review clauses, see *ante*, para. 14–126. For receivers, see *post*, para. 19–079.

[35] *Tomlin v. Luce* (1889) 43 Ch.D. 191; *Cuckmere Brick Co. Ltd v. Mutual Finance Ltd, supra*, at 969, 973, 980. *cf. Routestone Ltd v. Minories Finance Ltd, supra*, at 124.

[36] See the previous edition of this work at p. 939.

In any case the sale must be a true sale; a "sale" by the mortgagee to himself, either directly[37] or through an agent,[38] is no true sale and may be set aside[39] or ignored.[40] Thus if the mortgagee sells to himself and later purports to sell as absolute owner, the first sale will be disregarded and so the second will operate as a sale by a mortgagee as such.[41] But there is nothing to prevent a sale to one of two mortgagors being a true sale, and not a mere redemption of the mortgage, even if the price is the exact sum due under the mortgage.[42] Nor is a sale to a company in which the mortgagee holds shares necessarily irregular, provided that it is proper in other respects.[43]

(e) Proceeds of sale. Although the mortgagee is not a trustee of his power   **19–063**
of sale,[44] he is a trustee of the proceeds of sale.[45] These must be employed in the following order[46]—

    (i) in discharge of any prior incumbrances free from which the property was sold;

    (ii) in discharge of the expenses of the sale or any attempted sale;

    (iii) in discharge of the money due[47] to the mortgagee under the mortgage[48]; and

    (iv) by paying the balance to the next subsequent incumbrancer or, if none, to the mortgagor.[49]

If the balance is paid to a subsequent incumbrancer, he in turn will hold it on   **19–064**
trust to pay his own claim, and pass on the balance, if any. Where title is unregistered, a mortgagee who has a surplus should therefore search the Land

---

[37] *Farrar v. Farrars Ltd* (1888) 40 Ch.D. 395 at 409.

[38] *Downes v. Grazebrook* (1817) 3 Mer. 200.

[39] And see *Hodson v. Deans* [1903] 2 Ch. 647 (sale by auction by mortgagee Friendly Society to one of its trustees who had been concerned with conduct of sale: sale set aside).

[40] *Henderson v. Astwood* [1894] A.C. 150; *Williams v. Wellingborough Borough Council* [1975] 1 W.L.R. 1327 (council house sold to tenant with purchase money left on mortgage; purported sale by council to itself held void). But councils are now empowered to take back such houses with leave of the county court and with due adjustment of accounts: H.A. 1985, s.452; Sched. 17, para. 1 (as amended by the Housing and Planning Act 1986).

[41] *Henderson v. Astwood, supra.*

[42] *Kennedy v. De Trafford* [1896] 1 Ch. 762 at 776; [1897] A.C. 180.

[43] *Tse Kwong Lam v. Wong Chit Sen* [1983] 1 W.L.R. 1349.

[44] *Ante*, para. 19–061.

[45] L.P.A. 1925, s.105, and See *Banner v. Berridge* (1881) 18 Ch.D. 254 at 269; *Thorne v. Heard* [1895] A.C. 495.

[46] L.P.A. 1925, s.105. See *Re Thompson's Mortgage Trusts* [1920] 1 Ch. 508.

[47] Including statute-barred arrears of interest: *post*, para. 21–073.

[48] Despite any cross-claim against him by the mortgagor: *Samuel Keller (Holdings) Ltd v. Martins Bank Ltd* [1971] 1 W.L.R. 43; *Inglis v. Commonwealth Trading Bank of Australia Ltd* (1972) 126 C.L.R. 161 (no injunction to restrain sale).

[49] s.105 makes the surplus payable "to the person entitled to the mortgaged property". Literally this means the purchaser, but plainly the phrase must be read as "to the person *who immediately before the sale* was entitled to the mortgaged property", *i.e.* the next mortgagee or the mortgagor: see *British General Insurance Co. Ltd v. Att.-Gen.* [1945] L.J.N.C.C.R. 113 at 115.

Charges Register[50] to discover the existence of any subsequent mortgagees because registration is equivalent to notice.[51] If the mortgagee pays the money to the mortgagor he will be liable to any subsequent mortgagee who is thereby prejudiced.[52] In the case of registered land, by contrast, registration does not confer notice. In principle therefore, a mortgagee of registered land should not have to search the register, but should be entitled to pay any surplus to the mortgagor unless he has been notified of the existence of any other mortgage (as will usually be the case).[53] If the rights of all subsequent incumbrancers and the mortgagor have become barred by lapse of time,[54] the mortgagee may retain the money himself.[55] In cases of difficulty the money may be paid into court.[56]

The rules explained above apply even in the case where the mortgage was obtained by fraud. A mortgagee who, in such circumstances decides to affirm the mortgage (rather than seeking to avoid it) and exercise his power of sale, must account for any surplus to the mortgagor notwithstanding the latter's fraud.[57]

19–065 *(f) Effect of sale.* A sale by a mortgagee under his statutory powers vests the whole estate of the mortgagor, whether it is a fee simple[58] or a term of years,[59] in the purchaser, subject to any prior mortgages, but free from the mortgage of the vendor and all subsequent mortgages, and free from the mortgagor's equity of redemption, which is extinguished. For example, if X has mortgaged his freehold property successively to A, B and C, and B sells, the purchaser will take the fee simple subject to A's mortgage but free from the claims of B, C and X, which are overreached,[60] *i.e.* transferred to the purchase-money.

---

[50] *Post*, para. 19–220.

[51] L.P.A. 1925, s.198(1). *cf. Rignall Developments Ltd v. Halil* [1988] Ch. 190 at 202.

[52] *West London Commercial Bank v. Reliance Permanent B.S.* (1885) 29 Ch.D. 954.

[53] If a beneficiary under a trust has assigned his equitable interest, the trustees are not liable for breach of trust if they continue to make payments to him from the trust, unless they have notice of the assignment: see, *e.g. Phipps v. Lovegrove* (1873) L.R. 16 Eq. 80 at 88; *Ward v. Duncombe* [1893] A.C. 369 at 392.

[54] See *post*, paras 21–035, 21–036.

[55] *Young v. Clarey* [1948] Ch. 191.

[56] T.A. 1925, s.63.

[57] *Halifax B.S. v. Thomas* [1996] Ch. 217; [1996] R.L.R. 92 (P. Jaffey). Because the mortgagee affirms the mortgage, there is no constructive trust in his favour: [1996] Ch. 217 at 228. If, instead, the mortgagee avoided the mortgage for fraud, the mortgagor might be a constructive trustee of the property acquired with the money advanced on account of his fraud. The mortgagee might then be able to trace the fund into the proceeds and assert a proprietary claim to the property: *ibid.* Some of the remarks in *Halifax B.S. v. Thomas, supra,* as to the availability of a constructive trust may be too narrow: *cf. Lonrho Plc. v. Fayed (No. 2)* [1992] 1 W.L.R. 1 at 11, 12; *Westdeutsche Landesbank Girozentrale v. Islington L.B.C.* [1996] A.C. 669 at 716.

[58] L.P.A. 1925, ss.88(1), 104(1). But see *post*, para. 19–085.

[59] L.P.A. 1925, ss.89(1), 104(1). See s.89(6) as to a sale where the mortgage includes only part of the land which has been leased.

[60] L.P.A. 1925, s.2(1)(iii).

The mortgagee now conveys a fee simple or leasehold that is vested in the mortgagor by virtue of his statutory power.[61] Where the property is a leasehold and the landlord's licence is required for any assignment, it must not be unreasonably refused.[62]

(g) Order for sale. Quite apart from the mortgagee's power of sale, the **19–066** court has jurisdiction to order a sale of the mortgaged property on the application of anyone interested either in the mortgage money or in the equity of redemption.[63] Something has already been said about this provision in the context of foreclosure,[64] but it has been employed in two very different situations in recent years.

First, the court has sanctioned a sale by a mortgagee even though the statutory power of sale had become exercisable.[65] The purchaser's title could not therefore be impeached by the mortgagor. An order of this kind is exceptional. It will be justified only where the mortgagee reasonably fears that the sale may be lost, because the mortgagor is likely to threaten proceedings in an attempt to spoil the transaction, even though there is little prospect of his successfully impeaching it.[66]

Secondly, the court has exercised the jurisdiction, on the application of a mortgagor, to order a mortgagee to sell the mortgaged property, even though the proceeds would be insufficient to discharge the mortgage debt.[67] The circumstances were, however, exceptional. The mortgagee was seeking possession in order to let the property until there was a sufficient upturn in the property market to justify a sale. Any rental was likely to fall far short of the interest that would accrue on the debt. A sale would, by contrast, substantially reduce the mortgagor's indebtedness. The mortgagee intended to reserve its right to sue the mortgagor on the personal covenant should an upturn in the market not occur. A major factor in the court's decision to order a sale was that the mortgagee was gambling on the possibility of a rise in property prices at the mortgagor's expense.[68]

A court will seldom order a sale under this power where the proceeds will not pay off the mortgage debt.[69] In particular, it will not do so if the mortgagee can show that there is a real possibility that a postponement of sale may be

---

[61] On a sale before 1926, a first mortgagee conveyed the fee simple that was vested in him.
[62] L.P.A. 1925, s.89(1).
[63] *ibid.,* s.91.
[64] *Ante,* para. 19–054.
[65] *Arab Bank Plc v. Mercantile Holdings Ltd* [1994] Ch. 71.
[66] *ibid.,* at 90.
[67] *Palk v. Mortgage Services Funding Plc* [1993] Ch. 330.
[68] Although such a sale would deprive the mortgagee of its security, it was open to it to purchase the property and then take advantage of any increase in value that might subsequently occur: *ibid.,* at 340, 345.
[69] But see *Polonski v. Lloyds Bank Mortgages Ltd* [1998] 1 F.L.R. 896 (sale ordered where the mortgage debt exceeded the price to enable the mortgagor to move to a safer area where her employment prospects were better).

beneficial,[70] or if the mortgagee is himself seeking possession with a view to sale.[71] Furthermore, where the mortgagee is seeking possession in the county court,[72] the mortgagor will often have to apply to the High Court to obtain such an order for sale.[73] However, he will be unable to seek a suspension of the court's order for possession to enable him to make such an application if the sale is unlikely to meet the sums due under the mortgage.[74]

3. To take possession

19–067   *(a) The right.* Since a legal mortgage gives the mortgagee a legal estate in possession, he is entitled, subject to any agreement to the contrary, to take possession of the mortgaged property as soon as the mortgage is made, even if the mortgagor is guilty of no default.[75] A legal chargee has a corresponding statutory right.[76] The mortgagee "may go into possession before the ink is dry on the mortgage".[77] He may do so without a court order, even in those cases where the mortgaged property includes a dwelling-house and a court may grant relief to a mortgagor.[77a] If the property was already let to a tenant before the mortgage was made, or if a subsequent lease is binding on the mortgagee,[78] the mortgagee cannot take physical possession; but he may take possession by directing the tenants to pay their rents to him instead of to the mortgagor.[79] After entry by a mortgagee his right to possession dates back to the time at which his legal right to enter accrued. He can therefore bring an action for trespass committed before the entry.[80]

---

[70] *e.g.* because of a likely rise in property prices or because of the revenue that the property may generate. The court will give the mortgagee the benefit of the doubt: *Palk v. Mortgage Services Funding Plc, supra,* at 343.

[71] *Cheltenham and Gloucester Plc v. Krausz* [1997] 1 W.L.R. 1558, disapproving *Barrett v. Halifax B.S.* (1995) 28 H.L.R. 634 (which had suggested that, in *all* cases of so-called "negative equity", the mortgagor could resist possession proceedings and seek an order under L.P.A. 1925, s.91, that he and not the mortgagee should be able to sell the property).

[72] As will often be the case: see *ante* para. 19–046.

[73] The county court can only make an order under L.P.A. 1925, s.91, where the amount due under the mortgage does not exceed £30,000: *ibid.,* s.91(8); *ante,* para. 19–054.

[74] *Cheltenham and Gloucester Plc v. Krausz, supra,* at 1567; *post,* para. 19–075. But *cf.* (1998) 18 L.S. 279 (M. Dixon).

[75] *Birch v. Wright* (1786) 1 T.R. 378 at 383; *Four-Maids Ltd v. Dudley Marshall (Properties) Ltd* [1957] Ch. 317. The mortgagor thereupon becomes entitled to redeem forthwith without notice: *post,* para. 19–148. The mortgagee must be sure of his right, since unlawful eviction of a residential occupier is a criminal offence: P.E.A. 1977, s.1. His right may also be restricted by A.J.A. 1970, s.36; *post,* para. 19–074: *cf. Ropaigealach v. Barclays Bank Plc* [1999] 2 W.L.R. 17, *infra*; and *post,* para. 19–074.

[76] L.P.A. 1925, s.87(1).

[77] *Four-Maids Ltd v. Dudley Marshall (Properties) Ltd, supra,* at 320, *per* Harman J.; and see *Westminster City Council v. Haymarket Publishing Ltd* [1980] 1 W.L.R. 683 at 686 ("the well-established rule": *per* Dillon J.).

[77a] *Ropaigealach v. Barclays Bank Plc, supra;* reluctantly rejecting the contrary view advanced in [1983] Conv. 293 (A. Clarke). For the statutory jurisdiction to grant relief, see A.J.A. 1970, s.36; *post,* para. 19–074. *cf.* P.E.A. 1977, s.1, *supra.*

[78] See *post,* para. 19–114.

[79] *Horlock v. Smith* (1842) 6 Jur. 478; and see *Heales v. M'Murray* (1856) 23 Beav. 401; *cf. Kitchen's Trustee v. Madders* [1949] Ch. 588, aff'd [1950] Ch. 134.

[80] *Ocean Accident and Guarantee Corporation Ltd v. Ilford Gas Co.* [1905] 2 K.B. 493.

An agreement restricting the mortgagee's right to take possession may be **19–068** either express or implied. It will more readily be implied where the principal is repayable by instalments, as is common in building society mortgages[81]; but that fact by itself is not sufficient, and the court will not lightly restrict the mortgagee's right.[82]

A mortgagee must exercise his right to possession in good faith and for the purpose of enforcing the security.[83] In consequence, a mortgagee will not normally be granted possession against just one of two joint mortgagors where that is of no benefit to the mortgagee.[84] Nor will a mortgagee be allowed to exercise this right collusively for purposes other than the protection or enforcement of his security. Thus where a mortgagor arranged for his wife to pay off the mortgage and so become the mortgagee, she was held to be acting as his agent so that she could not assert the paramount rights of the original mortgagee and evict tenants of the mortgagor.[85] It was said that "equity has ample power to restrain any unjust use of the right to possession"[86] and that a mortgagee's rights are only vested in him to protect his position as a mortgagee and to enable him to obtain repayment.[87]

(b) Mortgagee's liability to account strictly. A mortgagee's object in taking **19–069** possession may be to protect his security by carrying out repairs or preventing waste or vandalism.[88] But his usual object is to enforce the security by either selling or intercepting the net rents and profits and so securing punctual payment of interest. The mortgagee may, if he wishes, apply any surplus to paying off the principal debt; but he may, if he prefers, hand it over to the mortgagor, for he cannot be compelled to accept repayment in parts.[89] What he may not do is to reap any personal advantage beyond what is due to him under the mortgage; for he is liable to account in equity for any such advantage.[90] He is liable to account strictly, "on the footing of wilful default". This means that he must account not only for all that he receives but also for all that he ought to have received, had he managed the property with due

---

[81] See *Birmingham Citizens Permanent B.S. v. Caunt* [1962] Ch. 883, where a term entitling the mortgagees to take possession if any instalment was one month in arrear implied that they could not do so otherwise.

[82] *Esso Petroleum Co. Ltd v. Alstonbridge Properties Ltd* [1975] 1 W.L.R. 1474; *Western Bank Ltd v. Schindler* [1977] Ch. 1. See [1979] Conv. 266 (R. J. Smith).

[83] *Quennell v. Maltby* [1979] 1 W.L.R. 318 at 322; *Albany Home Loans Ltd v. Massey* [1997] 2 All E.R. 609 at 612, 613. See too *Palk v. Mortgage Services Funding Plc* [1993] Ch. 330 at 337, 338. For the power of sale, see *ante*, para. 19–056. For the power to appoint a receiver, see *post*, para. 19–079.

[84] *Albany Home Loans Ltd v. Massey, supra.* This is especially the case where the mortgagors are spouses: *ibid.*

[85] *Quennell v. Maltby, supra.* For the rules about transfer and "keeping alive", see *post*, para. 19–143.

[86] *Quennell v. Maltby, supra,* at 323, *per* Lord Denning M.R., who relied upon equity, not agency.

[87] *ibid.,* at 324, *per* Templeman L.J.

[88] See *Western Bank Ltd v. Schindler, supra.*

[89] *Nelson v. Booth* (1858) 3 De G. & J. 119; *Wrigley v. Gill* [1905] 1 Ch. 241.

[90] *Ante,* para. 19–010.

diligence.[91] Indeed, he "must take reasonable care to maximise his return from the property".[92] However, this does not mean that he is bound or allowed to enter into speculation and adventure,[93] but merely that he will be liable for negligence amounting to wilful default.[94]

For example, where the mortgagee was a brewer and the mortgaged property a "free" house, a mortgagee who took possession and let the property as a "tied" house was held liable for the additional rent he would have obtained if he had let the property as a "free" house.[95] If the mortgagee occupies the property himself instead of letting it, he is liable for a fair occupation rent.[96] More usually he will wish to let it; his power to grant binding leases is explained below.[97] The most convenient situation for the mortgagee is where the property is already let, so that he has no responsibility for the amount of the existing rents.

19–070   *(c) Powers of mortgagee in possession.* While in possession, a mortgagee whose mortgage was made by deed has a statutory power to cut and sell timber and other trees ripe for cutting which were not planted or left standing for shelter or ornament, or contract for this to be done within 12 months of the contract.[98] Although he is not liable for waste,[99] he will be liable if he improperly cuts timber[1]; and despite his right to work mines already opened,[2] he may not open new mines.[3] But if the property becomes insufficient security for the money due, the court will not interfere if he cuts timber and opens mines, provided he is not guilty of wanton destruction.[4] He must effect reasonable repairs[5] and may without the mortgagor's consent effect reasonable improvements,[6] though not excessive improvements which might cripple the mortgagor's power to redeem[7]; for the cost of the repairs and improvements will be charged to the mortgagor in the accounts.

19–071   *(d) Irrelevance of any counterclaim.* The mortgagee's right to possession is unaffected by the existence of a cross-claim, even if it exceeds the amount of

---

[91] *Chaplin v. Young (No. 1)* (1863) 33 Beav. 330 at 337, 338. See (1979) 129 N.L.J. 334 (H. E. Markson). *cf. Medforth v. Blake* [1999] 3 All E.R. 97 at 108.

[92] *Palk v. Mortgage Services Funding Plc* [1993] Ch. 330 at 338, *per* Nicholls V.-C. See too *Downsview Nominees Ltd v. First City Corporation Ltd* [1993] A.C. 295 at 315.

[93] *Hughes v. Williams* (1806) 12 Ves. 493.

[94] *ibid.*, at 495.

[95] *White v. City of London Brewery Co.* (1889) 42 Ch.D. 237. The "tie" was to the mortgagee, but he was held not accountable for the profit on beer sold to the tenant.

[96] *Marriott v. Anchor Reversionary Co.* (1861) 3 De G.F. & J. 177 at 193; thus he need pay no rent if the property is too ruinous to be capable of beneficial occupation: *Marshall v. Cave* (1824) 3 L.J. (o.s.) Ch. 57.

[97] *Post*, para. 19–114.

[98] L.P.A. 1925, s.101(1).

[99] L.P.A. 1925, ss.85(2), 86(2), 87(1).

[1] *Withrington v. Banks* (1725) Ca.t.King 30.

[2] *Elias v. Snowden Slate Quarries Co.* (1879) 4 App.Cas. 454.

[3] *Millett v. Davey* (1863) 31 Beav. 470 at 475.

[4] *ibid.*, at 476.

[5] *Richards v. Morgan* (1753) 4 Y. & C. Ex. 570.

[6] *Shepard v. Jones* (1882) 21 Ch.D. 469 at 479.

[7] *Sandon v. Hooper* (1843) 6 Beav. 246; aff'd 14 L.J. Ch. 120.

the mortgage debt.[8] This will be so whether the claim is liquidated or unliquidated.[9] Although the results can be harsh,[10] the principle is sound. The mortgagor has no right to appropriate the amount of the cross-claim unilaterally,[11] because the mortgagee might have good reasons for keeping the mortgage alive, however large that cross-claim might be.[12] Furthermore, there is an obvious risk that specious cross-claims could be brought to impede the mortgagee's rights.[13] The only possible exception to this principle may be where there is a right of equitable set-off in respect of a sum that is equal to or greater than the mortgage debt. In that situation, the claim might discharge the mortgage.[14] However, the point remains undecided.[15]

(e) Relief of mortgagor

(1) THE POSITION AT COMMON LAW. Formerly a mortgagee could obtain **19–072** summarily an order for possession in the Queen's Bench Division of the High Court without the matter coming before a judicial officer.[16] But since 1936, when the jurisdiction to hear mortgagees' claims for possession was transferred from the King's Bench to the Chancery Division,[17] the High Court has assumed a limited discretionary jurisdiction to refuse an immediate order for possession, whether the proceedings were commenced by writ (or now, a claim form) or originating summons (or now Part 8 procedure under the Civil Procedure Rules).[18] Although the point has not been explicitly decided, it appears that the county court has a similar power in proceedings begun by plaint.[19] Under this jurisdiction, a short adjournment may be granted in order to give the mortgagor a chance of paying off the mortgagee in full or

---

[8] *Mobil Oil Co. Ltd v. Rawlinson* (1981) 43 P. & C.R. 221 (cross-claim for breach of supply and loan agreements); *Citibank Trust Ltd v. Ayivor* [1987] 1 W.L.R. 1157 (cross-claim for negligence and breach of warranty); *National Westminster Bank Plc v. Skelton* (1989) [1993] 1 W.L.R. 72n (cross-claim for breach of banker's duty of confidence); *Ashley Guarantee Plc v. Zacaria* [1993] 1 W.L.R. 62 (cross-claim for passing off etc.); *Midland Bank Plc v. McGrath* [1996] E.G.C.S. 61 (cross-claim for breach of contract, negligence and conspiracy); *Albany Home Loans Ltd v. Massey* [1997] 2 All E.R. 609 (cross-claim for unfair dismissal). See [1993] Conv. 459 (J. E. Martin).

[9] *Mobil Oil Co. Ltd v. Rawlinson, supra,* at 226.

[10] See *Ashley Guarantee Plc v. Zacaria, supra,* at 70.

[11] *Mobil Oil Co. Ltd v. Rawlinson, supra,* at 226.

[12] *e.g.* an attractive rate of interest or fiscal considerations: *Samuel Keller (Holdings) Ltd v. Martins Bank Ltd* [1971] 1 W.L.R. 43 at 48, 51.

[13] *ibid.,* at 51; *National Westminster Bank Plc v. Skelton, supra,* at 78.

[14] *National Westminster Bank Plc v. Skelton, supra,* at 78; *Ashley Guarantee Plc v. Zacaria, supra,* at 66.

[15] *National Westminster Bank Plc v. Skelton, supra,* at 78.

[16] *Redditch Benefit B.S. v. Roberts* [1940] Ch. 415 at 420.

[17] For the reasons behind this change, see *National Westminster Bank Plc v. Kitch* [1996] 1 W.L.R. 1316.

[18] See C.P.R. Sched. 1, R88.2. For a survey of the inherent and statutory powers to grant relief, see (1997) 17 L.S. 483 (M. Haley).

[19] See *Cheltenham and Gloucester Plc v. Booker* (1996) 73 P. & C.R. 412. It would be anomalous if the county court lacked such a power, given its exclusive jurisdiction in a significant class of mortgage possession actions: see *ante,* para. 19–046.

otherwise satisfying him. If there is no reasonable prospect of this, an adjournment will be refused.[20] Nor will the courts extend this jurisdiction to allow an adjournment in other situations.[21] The precise limits of the court's inherent jurisdiction have not been fully clarified,[22] though it retains a residual role.[23]

19–073 (2) STATUTORY RELIEF. There are two situations in which the court has statutory powers to postpone or suspend the mortgagee's right to possession in some way.

(i) Agreements regulated under the Consumer Credit Act 1974. In those cases where the mortgage is subject to the Consumer Credit Act 1974,[24] if it appears just to the court to do so, it may—

(i) suspend an order for possession[25]; and/or

(ii) make a "time order" providing for payment of any sums owed by such instalments, payable at such times as it considers reasonable, having regard to the means of the debtor.[26]

It is not a prerequisite to the exercise of (i) that the mortgagor should be able to repay the instalments within a reasonable time. However, in deciding whether it is just to make an order under either of these provisions, the court will consider the creditor's position as well as the debtor's,[27] and it might refuse to exercise its powers, therefore, if there was no prospect of repayment within a reasonable time.

---

[20] *Hinckley and South Leicestershire Permanent Benefit B.S. v. Freeman* [1941] Ch. 32; *Robinson v. Cilia* [1956] 1 W.L.R. 1502; *Braithwaite v. Winwood* [1960] 1 W.L.R. 1257; *Birmingham Citizens Permanent B.S. v. Caunt* [1962] Ch. 883 (reviewing the authorities). See (1962) 78 L.Q.R. 171 (R.E.M.).

[21] *Cheltenham and Gloucester Plc v. Krausz* [1997] 1 W.L.R. 1558 at 1566, 1567 (no power for the High Court to adjourn proceedings where a mortgagor, defending an action for possession in the county court, wished to apply to the High Court for an order for sale under L.P.A. 1925, s.91). See *ante*, para. 19–066.

[22] In particular, it has been suggested that such adjournments can be granted only in cases where the capital is repayable by instalments concurrently with interest, and the mortgagee undertakes not to go into possession so long as the payments are punctually made: *Four Maids Ltd v. Dudley Marshall (Properties) Ltd* [1957] Ch. 317; (1957) 73 L.Q.R. 300 (R.E.M.); *cf. ante*, para. 19–066. Later decisions have thrown doubt on this notion: see *Braithwaite v. Winwood*, *supra*; *Birmingham Citizens Permanent B.S. v. Caunt*, *supra*.

[23] *Post*, para. 19–075.

[24] This will be the case only where the credit provided does not exceed £25,000: See *ante*, para. 19–042.

[25] s.135.

[26] s.129. The court is empowered to amend any agreement or security in consequence of any term of the order that it makes: *ibid.*, s.136.

[27] *First National Bank Plc v. Syed* [1991] 2 All E.R. 250 at 256 ("time order" refused where there was a history of default and where the instalments that the debtor could afford did not even meet the interest falling due); (1994) 110 L.Q.R. 221 (N. Hickman).

(ii) Dwelling-houses. In cases where the mortgagee of property, which **19–074** consists of or includes a dwelling-house,[28] brings proceedings for possession[29] against the mortgagor,[30] the court has a wide statutory discretion under the Administration of Justice Act 1970 to adjourn those proceedings, suspend the execution of any order it makes for possession, or postpone the date for delivery of possession for such period[31] as it thinks fit.[32] This discretion may be exercised whether or not the mortgagor is in default.[33] There is a major (and unsatisfactory) restriction on the statutory discretion. If the mortgagee (or his successor) takes possession without a court order, it is inapplicable.[33a] Where it is exercisable, the court's statutory power applies to all types of mortgage[34] except one which secures a regulated agreement under the Consumer Credit Act 1974,[35] where the court has the powers conferred by that Act.[36] Where an order for possession has been suspended under the 1970 Act, the court may entertain an application by the mortgagee at any time for leave to enforce that order.[37] There are limits on the court's discretion. Once an order for possession has been executed, there is no jurisdiction either—

  (i) to order its suspension; or

  (ii) to set it aside, make a new order for possession, and then suspend that order.[38]

---

[28] See, *e.g. Lord Marples of Wallasey v. Holmes* (1975) 31 P. & C.R. 94 (hotel containing a residential flat). See too A.J.A. 1970, s.39(2) (a property will be a dwelling-house for the purposes of s.36, even if part of it is used as a shop or for business, trade or professional purposes).

[29] Other than a foreclosure action. But see A.J.A. 1973, s.8(3); *infra.*

[30] For these purposes, "mortgagor" and "mortgagee" include any person deriving title under the original mortgagor or mortgagee: A.J.A. 1970, s.39. However, a statutory tenant under the Rent Act 1977 does not derive title under the mortgagor and cannot invoke s.36: *Britannia B.S. v. Earl* [1990] 1 W.L.R. 422. Nor could any tenant whose lease was a breach of the mortgage agreement, and so not binding on the mortgagor: *ibid.*, at 430. See [1990] Conv. 450 (S. Bridge). Query whether a purchaser who purchased from a mortgagee would be bound, or whether the mortgagor's rights would have been overreached by the sale: *cf. Ropaigealach v. Barclays Bank Plc* [1999] 2 W.L.R. 17 at 36, 37; [1999] C.L.J. 281 at 282, 283 (M. Dixon).

[31] Which must be "a stretch of time ending with some specified or ascertainable date": *Royal Trust Co. of Canada v. Markham* [1975] 1 W.L.R. 1416 at 1421, *per* Sir John Pennycuick. For the difficulties in determining such a period where the mortgagor is not in default, see *Western Bank Ltd v. Schindler* [1977] Ch. 1.

[32] A.J.A. 1970, s.36.

[33] *Western Bank Ltd v. Schindler, supra* (but the contrary opinion of Goff L.J. is preferable). See (1977) 40 M.L.R. 356 (C.H.).

[33a] *Ropaigealach v. Barclays Bank Plc, supra*; [1999] C.L.J. 281 (M. Dixon); *ante*, para. 19–067. In that case, Clarke L.J. commented that it was "very curious that mortgagors should only have protection in the case where the mortgagee chooses to take legal proceedings and not in the case where he chooses simply to enter the property": *supra*, at 35.

[34] *Royal Trust Co. of Canada v. Markham, supra*, at 1421.

[35] A.J.A. 1970, s.38A. This limitation was overlooked in *First National Bank Plc v. Syed* [1991] 2 All E.R. 250. The decision is therefore *per incuriam*: see (1994) 110 L.Q.R. 221 (N. Hickman).

[36] *Supra.*

[37] *Abbey National Mortgages Plc v. Bernard* (1995) 71 P. & C.R. 257 at 261.

[38] *National and Provincial B.S. v. Ahmed* [1995] 2 E.G.L.R. 127. Once such an order has been executed, the mortgagee can safely contract to sell the property without any risk that the ⸲

The court may only exercise its powers where it appears that "the mortgagor is likely to be able within a reasonable period to pay any sums due under the mortgage"[39] or to remedy any default. To resolve a difficulty that arose soon after the statutory power was first conferred, it is now provided by the Administration of Justice Act 1973 that, in the case of an instalment mortgage, or of a mortgage which otherwise permits deferred repayment,[40] the "sums due" are merely any instalments or payments in arrear and not the whole capital sum.[41] This is so, even if (as is usual) the mortgage makes this payable on any default by the mortgagor.[42] But the court's powers under the 1970 Act are then exercisable only if there is a likelihood that, at the end of the "reasonable period", the mortgagor will be able to pay any further amounts then due under the mortgage.[43] Where the mortgage falls within the 1973 Act the court's discretionary powers extend also to foreclosure actions,[44] whether or not possession is sought in the same proceedings.[45]

In determining what amounts to a "reasonable period" under both the 1970 and 1973 Acts, the court will take into account the interests of both mortgagor and mortgagee.[46] The starting point will normally be the full term of the mortgage, and the court will consider the mortgagor's ability to pay off all the arrears over that time.[47] However, a shorter period is likely to be imposed where the mortgagor cannot discharge the arrears by periodical payments but

---

might be defeated by an application under A.J.A. 1970, s.36: *ibid.* See too *Mortgage Agency Services Number Two Ltd v. Bal* (1998) 77 P. & C.R. D7.

[39] The payment must be one which the mortgagor can afford and which will be sufficient to pay off the arrears within the period: *First National Bank Plc v. Syed* [1991] 2 All E.R. 250 at 255.

[40] This has been held to include a traditional mortgage which could be kept alive indefinitely: *Centrax Trustees Ltd v. Ross* [1979] 2 All E.R. 952; and an interest-only endowment mortgage where the capital was repayable at the end of a specified number of years: *Governor and Company of the Bank of Scotland v. Grimes* [1985] Q.B. 1179; *Citibank Trust Ltd v. Ayivor* [1987] 1 W.L.R. 1157. It did not include a mortgage to secure a bank overdraft repayable on demand in writing, because the mortgagor was not permitted to defer payment: *Habib Bank Ltd v. Taylor* [1982] 1 W.L.R. 1218; [1982] All E.R. Rev. 177 (P. J. Clarke). See [1984] Conv. 91 (S. Tromans).

[41] A.J.A. 1973, s.8(1). The courts will not lay down rigid guidelines as to how the discretion under this section and A.J.A. 1970, s.36, should be exercised: see *Cheltenham and Gloucester B.S. v. Grant* (1994) 26 H.L.R. 703. *cf.* [1995] Conv. 51 (M. P. Thompson).

[42] This was the difficulty that was brought to light in *Halifax B.S. v. Clark* [1973] Ch. 307 and which prompted the enactment of A.J.A. 1973, s.8. It was assumed in that case that a "reasonable period" was a short one, and that there was no likelihood that the mortgagor could repay the whole capital sum within that time. However, it was subsequently held in *First Middlesborough Trading and Mortgage Co. Ltd v. Cunningham* (1973) 28 P. & C.R. 69 that a reasonable period might be the whole term of the mortgage.

[43] A.J.A. 1973, s.8(2).

[44] Which is not the case in respect of mortgages which fall exclusively within A.J.A. 1970, s.36; *supra.*

[45] A.J.A. 1973, s.8(3). There is no discretion in other cases: see *Lord Marples of Wallasey v. Holmes* (1975) 31 P. & C.R. 94.

[46] *Cheltenham and Gloucester B.S. v. Norgan* [1996] 1 W.L.R. 343 at 356.

[47] *Cheltenham and Gloucester B.S. v. Norgan, supra*; (1996) 112 L.Q.R. 553 (J. Morgan). On this basis a number of earlier cases might now be decided differently: see, *e.g. Citibank Trust Ltd v. Ayivor* [1987] 1 W.L.R. 1157 (24-year mortgage term: no relief where proposed repayment of arrears would take $8\frac{1}{2}$ years).

only by a sale of the property,[48] or where there has been a breach of some term other than that for payment.[49]

The county court has a statutory power to suspend on terms any money judgment against a debtor who is unable to pay it, until such time as his inability ceases.[50] In a case in which the 1970 Act is applicable, and a mortgagee seeks both possession and a judgment for the moneys due under the mortgage, the court may (and usually will) suspend any money judgment on the same terms as any order which it makes for possession.[51] The court may however depart from this practice in special circumstances.[52] There is no equivalent power for the High Court to suspend a money judgment: the most that the court can do is to stay its execution.[53]

(3) EXERCISE OF DISCRETION WHERE A SALE IS CONTEMPLATED. One situation **19–075** in which the court is often asked to exercise its discretion to suspend an order for possession (whether under its common law or statutory powers) is where it is proposed to sell the property to discharge the mortgagor's liabilities. The real issue in such a case is whether the mortgagor or mortgagee should have the conduct of the sale. Where the mortgagee's power of sale has become exercisable,[54] the mortgagee has a right to sell the property if and when he chooses.[55] But a repossession sale by a mortgagee with vacant possession is likely to yield a lower price than a sale by a mortgagor in possession.[56] However, if an order for possession is adjourned to enable the mortgagor to sell, there is an obvious danger that he will prevaricate.[57] The court undoubtedly has power to suspend an order for possession, under either its inherent jurisdiction or the 1970 Act (if applicable), to enable the *mortgagor* to sell the property, provided that the value is likely to be sufficient to discharge his indebtedness.[58] It may even exercise its powers so as to allow the mortgagor

---

[48] *Bristol and West B.S. v. Ellis* (1996) 73 P. & C.R. 158. That case makes clear that although a period of six months to a year is likely to be the maximum in such a case (see *National and Provincial B.S. v. Lloyd* [1996] 1 All E.R. 630), there is no fixed rule to that effect: see (1996) 73 P. & C.R. at 162, 163, where the relevant criteria for selecting the length of the period are set out. A short suspension is probable if there is likely to be a considerable delay in selling or if the value of the property is close to the total of the mortgage debt.

[49] *e.g.* if the mortgagor had let the premises to a tenant in breach of covenant.

[50] C.C.A. 1984, s.71(2).

[51] *Cheltenham and Gloucester B.S. v. Grattidge* (1993) 25 H.L.R. 454; *Cheltenham and Gloucester B.S. v. Grant* (1994) 26 H.L.R. 703 at 708; *Cheltenham and Gloucester B.S. v. Johnson* (1996) 73 P. & C.R. 293.

[52] *Cheltenham and Gloucester B.S. v. Grattidge, supra,* at 458; *Cheltenham and Gloucester B.S. v. Johnson, supra,* at 302.

[53] By writ of *fieri facias*: C.P.R. Sched. 1, R47.1. There is as yet no authority as to what the High Court would do in such a case.

[54] Which will almost always be the case.

[55] *China and South Sea Bank Ltd v. Tan* [1990] 1 A.C. 536; *ante,* para. 19–061.

[56] *cf. Target Homes Ltd v. Clothier* [1994] 1 All E.R. 439 at 448.

[57] See *Cheltenham and Gloucester Plc v. Krausz* [1997] 1 W.L.R. 1558 at 1564.

[58] Inherent jurisdiction: *Cheltenham and Gloucester Plc v. Booker* (1996) 73 P. & C.R. 412 at 415; *Royal Trust Co. of Canada v. Markham* [1975] 1 W.L.R. 1416 at 1420; A.J.A. 1970, s.36: *ibid.,* at 1422; *Bristol and West B.S. v. Ellis* (1996) 73 P. & C.R. 158 at 162. For the factors that will influence the court in selecting the length of any suspension under s.36, see *ibid.,* at 162, 163; *ante,* para. 19–074.

to remain in possession where the property is to be sold by the *mortgagee*.[59] However, that will seldom be appropriate, and possession will normally be given to the party having the conduct of the sale.[60]

There is no power, under either the 1970 Act or the court's inherent jurisdiction, to suspend an order for possession to enable a sale to take place at a price that will not discharge the mortgagor's indebtedness.[61]

19–076   *(f) Procedure.* A summons for possession need be served only on the mortgagor and any other person in possession who claims a right to possession against the mortgagee.[62] There is also a statutory duty to serve notice of the action on persons who have registered their matrimonial home rights under the Family Law Act 1996 (or earlier equivalent legislation).[63]

19–077   *(g) Attornment clause.* At one time, many mortgages contained an attornment clause by which the mortgagor attorned, or acknowledged himself to be, a tenant at will or from year to year of the mortgagee, usually at a nominal rent such as a peppercorn or five pence.[64] This practice grew up to enable mortgagees to take advantage of a speedy procedure for recovering possession that was available to landlords but not at that time to mortgagees.[65] However, as mortgagees have in their own right enjoyed a similar speedy procedure for more than 60 years, there is now no substantial advantage in an attornment clause and they are no longer much used.[66]

Despite earlier doubts, it is established that an attornment clause still effectually creates the relationship of landlord and tenant.[67] Nevertheless, the substance of the transaction is a mortgage to which the attornment clause is merely ancillary. The resultant tenancy has therefore been held to be outside a number of statutes which are intended to protect those who in substance are tenants.[68] But in other respects the general law of landlord and tenant applies. Thus if the mortgagee wishes to take possession, he must first determine the tenancy by proper notice,[69] unless (as is often the case) the attornment clause creates a mere tenancy at will, or makes the tenancy determinable without notice, *e.g.* upon default being made by the mortgagor.[70] Similarly a mere

---

[59] *Cheltenham and Gloucester Plc v. Booker, supra*, at 415.

[60] *ibid.*, at 416.

[61] See A.J.A. 1970, s.36(1); *Cheltenham and Gloucester Plc v. Krausz, supra*, at 1567. See *ante*, para. 19–066.

[62] Despite the repeal of RSC, 1883, Ord. 55, r. 55A, *Alliance B.S. v. Yap* [1962] 1 W.L.R. 857 and *Brighton and Shoreham B.S. v. Hollingdale* [1965] 1 W.L.R. 376 (deserted wife) are probably still good law.

[63] F.L.A. 1996, s.56; *post*, para. 19–142.

[64] See *Woolwich Equitable B.S. v. Preston* [1938] Ch. 129.

[65] See the previous edition of this work at p. 946.

[66] See *Ingram v. I.R.C.* [1997] 4 All E.R. 395 at 422.

[67] *Regent Oil Co. Ltd v. J.A. Gregory (Hatch End) Ltd* [1966] Ch. 402.

[68] *See, e.g. Portman B.S. v. Young* [1951] 1 All E.R. 191 (Rent Acts); *Peckham Mutual B.S. v. Registe* (1980) 42 P. & C.R. 186 (P.E.A. 1977); *Steyning and Littlehampton B.S. v. Wilson* [1951] Ch. 1018 (A.H.A. 1948).

[69] *Hinckley and Country B.S. v. Henny* [1953] 1 W.L.R. 352.

[70] See, *e.g. Woolwich Equitable B.S. v. Preston* [1938] Ch. 129, where it is said that the issue of a summons for possession takes effect as a re-entry and turns the tenancy into a tenancy at will, and the service of the summons terminates the tenancy at will.

tenancy at will determines automatically as soon as the mortgagor assigns his interest.[71] But in other cases the assignee will be bound by the tenancy and by covenants which run with it under the ordinary rules.[72] There is, in fact, a duality of positions: under the tenancy arising from the mortgage or charge the mortgagor is the landlord and the mortgagee the tenant, whereas under the subtenancy created by the attornment clause their positions are reversed. Nevertheless, any covenants by the mortgagor in the mortgage are enforceable against the assignee from the mortgagor if they relate to the premises (*e.g.* covenants to repair them, or not to use them for certain purposes).[73] They will therefore bind the assignee, whether the mortgagee is enforcing them *qua* tenant or *qua* sub-landlord.[74]

(h) Limitation. If a mortgagee remains in possession of the mortgaged land **19–078** for 12 years without acknowledging the mortgagor's title or receiving any payment of principal or interest from him, the right to redeem the land is extinguished[75] and the mortgagee acquires a title to the land.

4. To appoint a receiver

(a) History. In order to avoid the responsibilities of taking possession and **19–079** yet achieve substantially the same result, well-drawn mortgages used to provide for the appointment of a receiver with extensive powers of management of the mortgaged property. Thus the mortgagee, without taking possession himself, could ensure that the property was efficiently managed and that his claim for interest was made a first charge on the net rents and profits. At first the appointment was made by the mortgagor at the request of the mortgagee; but subsequently mortgagees began to reserve a power for themselves, acting in theory as agents for the mortgagor, to appoint a receiver.[76] In such circumstances the receiver was, by the terms of the power, deemed the agent of the mortgagor,[77] and the mortgagee was not liable to account strictly in the same way as would have been the case if he had taken possession or the receiver had been his agent.[78] Lord Cranworth's Act 1860[79] gave a somewhat unsatisfactory statutory power to appoint a receiver, but the Conveyancing

---

[71] *Regent Oil Co. Ltd v. J. A. Gregory (Hatch End) Ltd* [1966] Ch. 402 at 429, 438; *ante*, para. 14–076.

[72] *Regent Oil Co. Ltd v. J. A. Gregory (Hatch End) Ltd, supra.*

[73] This is so whether the mortgage was made before 1996 or after 1995. The rules laid down in L. & T.C.A. 1995 for the transmission of covenants (*ante*, para. 15–079) do not apply to mortgage terms: see the definition of "tenancy" in L. & T.C.A. 1995, s.28(1).

[74] *Regent Oil Co. Ltd v. J. A. Gregory (Hatch End) Ltd, supra.*

[75] Limitation Act 1980, s.16 (and see s.29(4) as to the date from which time runs); *Young v. Clarey* [1948] Ch. 191: see *post*, para. 21–035.

[76] *Gaskell v. Gosling* [1896] 1 Q.B. 669 at 692. See too *Medforth v. Blake* [1999] 3 All E.R. 97 at 103.

[77] *Jefferys v. Dickson* (1866) 1 Ch.App. 183 at 190; and see *Lever Finance Ltd v. Needlemans' Trustee* [1956] Ch. 375 at 382.

[78] *Ante*, para. 19–069. See *Saffron Walden Herts & Essex B.S. v. Bunbury* (1998) 77 P. & C.R. D22 at D23.

[79] 23 & 24 Vict. c. 145, ss.17–23.

Act 1881[80] (replaced by the Law of Property Act 1925[81]) conferred a power which satisfies most mortgagees.

Compared with taking possession, the appointment of a receiver has one minor disadvantage: lapse of time may confer a title to the land upon a mortgagee in possession,[82] but not upon a mortgagee who has appointed a receiver.

19–080   *(b) The power.* The statutory power to appoint a receiver arises and becomes exercisable in the same circumstances as the power of sale.[83] A mortgagee has power to appoint a receiver provided—

(i) his mortgage was made by deed; and

(ii) the mortgage money is due.[84]

But this power is not exercisable until one of the three events set out earlier[85] has occurred,[86] although persons paying money to the receiver are not bound to see that his appointment has been thereby justified.[87] A mortgagee who is in possession is not thereby debarred from appointing a receiver.[88]

In deciding whether or not to exercise the power, the mortgagee must act in good faith, but owes no duty of care to the mortgagor (or to any guarantor).[89] However, where he does appoint a receiver, he may owe a duty to select one who is competent.[90]

The statutory power to appoint a receiver usually makes it unnecessary to apply to the court for a receiver, although the court has long had jurisdiction to make the appointment on such terms as it thinks just in all cases in which it appears to be just and convenient to do so.[91]

19–081   *(c) Procedure.* The mortgagee must make the appointment by writing,[92] and may remove or replace the receiver in the same way.[93] Though appointed by, and for the benefit of the mortgagee,[94] the receiver is deemed to be the agent of the mortgagor, who is solely responsible for his acts.[95] This will not be the

---

[80] s.19.
[81] s.101(1)(iii).
[82] *Supra.*
[83] *Ante*, paras 19–057, 19–058.
[84] L.P.A. 1925, s.101(1)(iii).
[85] *Ante*, para. 19–058.
[86] *ibid.*, s.109(1).
[87] *ibid.*, s.109(4).
[88] *Refuge Assurance Co. Ltd v. Pearlberg* [1938] Ch. 687.
[89] *Shamji v. Johnson Matthey Bankers Ltd* [1991] B.C.L.C. 36.
[90] *ibid.*, at 42.
[91] Supreme Court Act 1981, s.37 (replacing legislation dating back to 1873).
[92] L.P.A. 1925, s.109(1).
[93] *ibid.*, s.109(5).
[94] See *Re B. Johnson & Co. (Builders) Ltd* [1955] Ch. 634 at 644.
[95] L.P.A. 1925, s.109(2), confirming the general rule: see *Jeffreys v. Dickson* (1866) L.R. 1 Ch. App. 183 at 190.

case if the mortgage otherwise provides[96]; or if the mortgagee either represents the receiver as being his agent,[97] or directs or interferes with his activities.[98] The agency also ceases if the mortgagor becomes insolvent.[99] If the receiver continues to act thereafter, he does so as principal,[1] unless the mortgagee by his conduct constitutes him as his agent.[2] Where a receiver is the mortgagee's agent, the latter will be liable for his conduct, as where he sells the mortgaged property and fails to obtain the true market price.[3]

Although a receiver is under a general duty to act in good faith and to exercise his powers for proper purposes,[3a] he is under specific duties to take reasonable care and act with due diligence in conducting any sale of, or in managing any business on, the mortgaged property.[3b] The receiver has power to recover the income of the property by action, distress or otherwise, and to give valid receipts for it.[4] If the mortgagee so directs in writing, the receiver must insure the property against fire to the same extent as the mortgagee might have insured,[5] and the mortgagee may by writing delegate his powers of leasing[6] and accepting surrenders of leases.[7]

(d) Application of receipts. The money received by the receiver must be applied in the following order.[8]   **19–082**

    (i) In discharge of rents, rates and taxes.

    (ii) In keeping down annual sums and the interest on principal sums having priority to the mortgage.

    (iii) In payment of his commission and insurance premiums and, if so directed in writing by the mortgagee, the cost of repairs. His commission is 5 per cent on the gross sum received unless his appointment specifies less or the court otherwise directs.[9]

    (iv) In payment of the interest under the mortgage.

    (v) If the mortgagee so directs in writing, towards the discharge of the principal money lent; otherwise it must be paid to the person who

---

[96] L.P.A. 1925, s.109(2).

[97] *Chatsworth Properties Ltd v. Effiom* [1971] 1 W.L.R. 144.

[98] *American Express International Banking Corporation v. Hurley* [1985] 3 All E.R. 564 at 571.

[99] *Gosling v. Gaskell* [1897] A.C. 575.

[1] See R. P. Meagher, W. M. C. Gummow & J. R. F. Lehane, *Equity: Doctrines and Remedies* (3rd ed.), §2842. *cf Sowman v. David Samuel Trust Ltd* [1978] 1 W.L.R. 22 at 27–30.

[2] *American Express International Banking Corporation v. Hurley, supra,* at 568.

[3] *American Express International Banking Corporation v. Hurley, supra.* See too *Circuit Systems Ltd v. Zuken-Redac (U.K.) Ltd* [1997] 1 W.L.R. 721 at 739.

[3a] *Downsview Nominees Ltd v. First City Corporation Ltd* [1993] A.C. 295 at 315.

[3b] *Medforth v. Blake* [1999] 3 All E.R. 97. *cf. ante,* para. 19–061.

[4] L.P.A. 1925, s.109(3).

[5] *ibid.,* s.109(7).

[6] *ibid.,* s.99(19).

[7] *ibid.,* s.100(13). For these powers, see *post,* paras 19–112, 19–122.

[8] L.P.A. 1925, s.109(8).

[9] L.P.A. 1925, s.109(6).

would have received it if the receiver had not been appointed, *i.e.* normally the mortgagor.

19–083   **The mortgagee's remedies are cumulative.** A mortgagee is not bound to select any one of his remedies and pursue that exclusively: subject to his not recovering more than is due to him, he may employ any or all of the remedies to enforce payment.[10] If he sells the property for less than the mortgage debt, he may still sue the mortgagor upon the personal covenant for payment of the balance,[11] and the same applies on a sale by the court, even if the mortgagee, with the leave of the court, has bought the property at the sale and later resold it at an increased price.[12] If he takes possession, he is not thereby prevented from appointing a receiver.[13]

Foreclosure, however, puts an end to other remedies, since if the mortgagee takes the whole security he cannot also claim payment. He may therefore sue on the personal covenant only if he opens the foreclosure, so that the mortgagor, if he can pay, may also redeem.[14] The mortgagor thus has the option of either paying the whole of the mortgage debt and recovering his property, or paying the difference between the mortgage debt and the value of the property and losing the property. If by disposing of the property after foreclosure (*e.g.* by selling it) the mortgagee has put it out of his power to reopen the foreclosure, he can no longer sue the mortgagor[15] (or a guarantor[16]) upon the personal covenant,[17] even though the proceeds of sale are less than the amount of the debt.[18] Further, a foreclosure order nisi suspends the power of sale, and the mortgagee must obtain the leave of the court if he wishes to sell.[19] Unless the proceedings have been registered as a pending land action,[20] the order will not bind a purchaser of unregistered land without express notice.[21] Where the title is registered, a purchaser acquiring title under a registered disposition would take free of the order regardless of notice, unless the proceedings had been protected by lodging a caution.[22]

II. EQUITABLE MORTGAGEE

The extent to which the foregoing remedies are exercisable by an equitable mortgagee is as follows.

---

[10] *Palmer v. Hendrie* (1859) 27 Beav. 349 at 351.
[11] *Rudge v. Richens* (1873) L.R. 8 C.P. 358.
[12] *Gordon Grant & Co. Ltd v. Boos* [1926] A.C. 781.
[13] *Refuge Assurance Co. Ltd v. Pearlberg* [1938] Ch. 687.
[14] *Perry v. Barker* (1806) 13 Ves. 198.
[15] *Palmer v. Hendrie* (1859) 27 Beav. 349.
[16] *Lloyds & Scottish Trust Ltd v. Britten* (1982) 44 P. & C.R. 249.
[17] *Palmer v. Hendrie, supra.*
[18] *Lockhart v. Hardy* (1846) 9 Beav. 349.
[19] *Stevens v. Theatres Ltd* [1903] 1 Ch. 857.
[20] *ibid.,* at 863.
[21] L.C.A. 1972, s.5(7); *ante,* para. 5–088.
[22] L.R.A. 1925, s.59(6); *ante,* para. 6–087. In the absence of some error, no disposition *could* be registered if a caution had been lodged: *ante,* para. 6–086.

1. To foreclose. Foreclosure is the primary remedy of an equitable mort-   **19–084**
gagee. Since he has no legal estate the court's order absolute will direct the
mortgagor to convey the land to the mortgagee unconditionally, *i.e.* free from
any right to redeem.[23–25]

2. To sell. The statutory power of sale[26] applies only where the mortgage   **19–085**
was made by deed[27]; other mortgagees have no power of sale. For this reason,
as already mentioned, many equitable mortgages are made by deed. But even
then there may be a difficulty, for it has been held that the statutory power to
sell "the mortgaged property"[28] enables the mortgagee to sell only the interest
which he has, *i.e.* the equitable interest.[29] In other words, the power is a power
over the equity of redemption and not a power over the legal estate if vested
in some other person. But this narrow interpretation has been doubted.[30] Since
of course the power of sale is of little value unless it extends to the legal estate,
it is often so extended by either or both of two conveyancing devices.

(a) Power of attorney. A power of attorney[31] is inserted in the deed   **19–086**
empowering the mortgagee or his assigns[32] to convey the legal estate.[33] This
power, being given for value, may be made irrevocable in perpetuity in favour
of a purchaser, and so will not be affected by any act of the mortgagor, or by
his death.[34]

(b) Declaration of trust. A clause is inserted in the deed whereby the
mortgagor declares that he holds the legal estate on trust for the mortgagee
and empowers the mortgagee to appoint himself or his nominee as trustee in
place of the mortgagor.[35] The mortgagee can in this way vest the legal estate
in himself or a purchaser.[36]

In the case of an equitable mortgage not made by deed (for example, a
written contract for a mortgage) there is no power of sale out of court. But the
court has the power to order a sale[37] on the application of either party, and to

---

[23–25] *James v. James* (1873) L.R. 16 Eq. 153.
[26] *Ante,* para. 19–056.
[27] L.P.A. 1925, s.101(1).
[28] *ibid.,* s.101(1)(i).
[29] *Re Hodson & Howes' Contract* (1887) 35 Ch.D. 668.
[30] *Re White Rose Cottage* [1965] Ch. 940 at 951 *per* Lord Denning M.R., invoking the contrast
   in wording between C.A. 1881, s.21(1) and L.P.A. 1925, s.104(1). Yet the phrase relied on
   ("the subject of the mortgage") is the same in each subsection.
[31] These powers are now regulated by the Powers of Attorney Act 1971, as amended by the
   Supreme Court Act 1981, s.152(4) and Sched. 7.
[32] L.P.A. 1925, s.128.
[33] In *Re White Rose Cottage, supra,* the property was in fact sold by the mortgagor, with a release
   of the mortgage by the mortgagee; the conveyance was validly executed by the mortgagee but
   as attorney for the mortgagor.
[34] L.P.A. 1925, s.126.
[35] See *London & County Banking Co. v. Goddard* [1897] 1 Ch. 642.
[36] Under T.A. 1925, s.40; see *ante,* para. 10–070.
[37] L.P.A. 1925, s.91(2); *ante,* para. 19–054; *Oldham v. Stringer* (1884) 51 L.T. 895.

vest a legal term of years in the mortgagee, so that he can sell as if he were a legal mortgagee.[38]

3. To take possession

19–087   *(a) The right.* It is generally said that an equitable mortgagee has no right to take possession.[39] Certainly he has none at law, for he has no legal estate. But in equity he should be entitled to the same rights as if he had a legal mortgage, and there would seem to be no reason why he should not take possession under the doctrine of *Walsh v. Lonsdale*,[40] for the basis of an equitable mortgage is the creation of the relationship of mortgagor and mortgagee forthwith, rather than a mere contract for a future mortgage.[41] The court may, in any case, award him possession[42]; and there is some authority which indicates that he may take possession in his own right,[43] as in principle one would expect. He may certainly do so if the agreement so provides.[44]

19–088   *(b) Collection of rents.* What the mortgagee cannot do without an order of the court[45] is to collect the rents if the land is let[46]; but the true reason for this disability is that rent is payable to the legal reversioner and that—at least where the lease was granted prior to 1996—an equitable assignment of the reversion does not create the legal relationship of landlord and tenant (*i.e.* privity of estate, or tenure) upon which the right to receive rent depends.[47] It does not follow that because an equitable mortgagee is not entitled to demand

---

[38] L.P.A. 1925, ss.90, 91(7).

[39] Coote, *Mortgages*, 832; Waldock, *Mortgages*, 235; Halsb. vol. 32, para. 673; and see *Barclays Bank Ltd v. Bird* [1954] Ch. 274 at 280. But no satisfactory authority is cited; see (1954) 70 L.Q.R. 161 (R.E.M.) *Garfitt v. Allen* (1887) 37 Ch.D. 48 is a case of charge, not mortgage, and a chargee plainly has no right to take possession. Since the Judicature Acts, 1873–1875, an action for the recovery of land will not be defeated merely for want of the legal estate: *General Finance Mortgage and Discount Co. v. Liberator Permanent Benefit B.S.* (1878) 10 Ch.D. 15 at 24; *Re O'Neill* [1967] N.I. 129. For fuller discussion, see (1955) 71 L.Q.R. 204 (H.W.R.W.).

[40] (1882) 21 Ch.D. 9; *ante*, para. 14–041.

[41] See *ante*, para. 19–039.

[42] *Barclays Bank Ltd v. Bird*, *supra*; *Re O'Neill*, *supra*.

[43] *Ex p. Bignold* (1834) 4 Deac. & Ch. 259, *per* Erskine C.J. (*contra* the opinion of Sir G. Rose); *Re Gordon* (1889) 61 L.T. 299; *Tichborne v. Weir* (1892) 67 L.T. 735; *Antrim County Land Building and Investment Co. Ltd v. Stewart* [1904] 2 I.R. 357 (the judgment of Palles C.B. is particularly helpful); *Spencer v. Mason* (1931) 75 S.J. 295. See (1955) 71 L.Q.R. 204 (H.W.R.W.).

[44] *Ocean Accident & Guarantee Corporation Ltd v. Ilford Gas Co.* [1905] 2 K.B. 493.

[45] The court's order is for the appointment of a receiver by way of equitable execution: *Vacuum Oil Co. Ltd v. Ellis* [1914] 1 K.B. 693 at 703. For the appointment of a receiver, see *post*, para. 19–090.

[46] *Re Pearson* (1838) 3 Mont. & A. 592; *Finck v. Tranter* [1905] 1 K.B. 427; *Vacuum Oil Co. Ltd v. Ellis* [1914] K.B. 693, where the dicta should probably be limited to the points which were before the court, *i.e.* that there was no right to possession as against a prior tenant in possession, and no legal title to the rents.

[47] *Cox v. Bishop* (1857) 8 De G.M. & G. 815; *Friary Holroyd & Healey's Breweries Ltd v. Singleton* [1899] 1 Ch. 86 at 90 (reversed on the facts [1899] 2 Ch. 261); and see *ante*, para. 15–033. Where a lease has been granted after 1995, the benefit of a covenant passes on both a legal and an equitable assignment of the reversion: see L. & T.C.A. 1995, ss.3; 28(1); *ante*, paras 15–065, 15–080.

rent as against a tenant, he is not entitled to possession as against the mortgagor. For the effect of the contract in equity, as between the contracting parties, is something quite different from its effect upon third parties such as tenants.[48]

(c) Possible implied term. The only possible basis for the rule, as commonly **19–089** stated, that an equitable mortgagee has no right to possession would seem to be an implied term in the contract. It might be said that a contract for a mortgage does not contemplate giving possession to the mortgagee, as contrasted with a contract for a lease, which contemplates possession by the tenant. But there seems to be no authority, and no evident necessity, for implying such a term, nor would it accord with the decisions.[49]

4. To appoint a receiver. An equitable mortgagee has always had the right **19–090** to have a receiver appointed by the court in a proper case,[50] *e.g.* when interest is in arrear.[51] If his mortgage is by deed he has also the statutory power,[52] which is more convenient since there is no need to apply to the court.

III. EQUITABLE CHARGEE

The primary remedies of an equitable chargee are to apply to the court for an **19–091** order for sale[53] or for the appointment of a receiver.[54] But since the statutory definition of a mortgage extends to a charge,[55] an equitable chargee *by deed* is in the same position as an equitable mortgagee as regards sale or the appointment of a receiver out of court. An equitable chargee can neither foreclose[56] nor take possession,[57] since he has neither a legal estate nor the benefit of a contract to create one.[58]

B. Other Rights of a Mortgagee

Certain other rights of a mortgagee must now be considered. The law is in **19–092** general the same for both mortgages and charges, whether legal or equitable, and "mortgage" will accordingly be used hereafter to include all such incumbrances unless the contrary is indicated.

1. Right to fixtures. It is a question of construction to decide what property **19–093** is included in a mortgage. Subject to any contrary intention, a mortgage

---

[48] *Ante,* para. 14–047.
[49] See n. 43, *supra.*
[50] Supreme Court Act 1981, s.37.
[51] *Shakel v. Duke of Marlborough* (1819) 4 Madd. 463.
[52] L.P.A. 1925, s.101(1)(iii); *ante,* para. 19–080.
[53] The court has power under L.P.A. 1925, s.90 (*ante* para. 19–086) to vest in the chargee a legal term of years so that he can sell as if he were a legal mortgagee; *Ladup Ltd v. Williams & Glyn's Bank Plc* [1985] 1 W.L.R. 851 at 855.
[54] *Tennant v. Trenchard* (1869) 4 Ch.App. 537; *Re Owen* [1894] 3 Ch. 220.
[55] L.P.A. 1925, s.205(1)(xvi).
[56] *Tennant v. Trenchard, supra,* at 542; *Re Lloyd* [1903] 1 Ch. 385 at 404.
[57] *Garfitt v. Allen* (1887) 37 Ch.D. 48 at 50.
[58] See *Carreras Rothmans Ltd v. Freeman Mathews Treasure Ltd* [1985] Ch. 207 at 227; *Ladup Ltd v. Williams & Glyn's Bank Plc, supra,* at 855.

includes all fixtures attached to the land either at the date of the mortgage or thereafter.[59] A mortgagor does not have the same power to remove certain fixtures that is enjoyed by tenants.[60]

19–094   **2. Right to possession of the title deeds.** As already mentioned, where title to the land is unregistered, a first mortgagee has the same right to the title deeds as if he had the fee simple or an assignment of the lease which has been mortgaged, as the case may be.[61] The introduction of the new triggers for compulsory registration of title[62] means that this right will seldom arise in future. Where it does still apply, then notwithstanding any contrary agreement, the mortgagor is entitled to inspect and make copies of the deeds at reasonable times and on payment of the mortgagee's costs.[63] As long as the mortgage exists the mortgagee is not liable for negligent loss of the deeds,[64] but if at redemption he fails to deliver them to the mortgagor he may be ordered to pay him compensation.[65] Upon redemption the mortgagee must deliver the deeds to the mortgagor,[66] unless he has notice of some subsequent incumbrance, in which case the deeds should be delivered to the incumbrancer next in order of priority of whom the mortgagee has notice.[67]

Contrary to the general rule that registration is notice, registration under the Land Charges Act 1972 or in a local register is not deemed to be notice for this purpose.[68] The mortgagee accordingly need not make a search before returning the deeds, although, as has been seen, a mortgagee is bound to search before he distributes any surplus after a sale.[69] If a mortgage becomes statute-barred by lapse of time,[70] the mortgagee must return the deeds even if no part of the mortgage debt has been or will be paid.[71]

19–095   **3. Right to insure against fire at the mortgagor's expense.** This enables the mortgagee to protect the value of his security. It used to be incorporated expressly, but is now imported[72] by the Law of Property Act 1925[73] into every

---

[59] *Ante*, para. 14–326.
[60] *Ante*, para. 14–317.
[61] *Ante*, paras 19–035, 19–036.
[62] *Ante*, para. 19–036. After March 1998, any first legal mortgage of an unregistered freehold or of a lease having more than 21 years to run, which is supported by documents of title triggers the requirement to register the underlying freehold or lease: L.R.A. 1925, s.123(2) (as substituted by L.R.A. 1997, s.1).
[63] L.P.A. 1925, s.96(1).
[64] *Browning v. Handiland Group Ltd* (1976) 35 P. & C.R. 345. L.P.A. 1925, s.13, preserves the (questionable) principle of the pre-1926 law, which was that the mortgagee, being owner of the land, was also owner of the deeds and could not be liable for losing his own property.
[65] *ibid.*
[66] See *James v. Rumsey* (1879) 11 Ch.D. 398.
[67] See *Corbett v. National Provident Institution* (1900) 17 T.L.R. 5.
[68] L.P.A. 1925, s.96(2), added by L.P.(Am.)A. 1926, Sched. For another case where registration does not constitute notice, see *post*, para. 19–260.
[69] *Ante*, para. 19–064.
[70] See *post*, para. 21–036.
[71] *Lewis v. Plunket* [1937] Ch. 306.
[72] Subject to the provisions of the mortgage: L.P.A. 1925, s.101(3), (4).
[73] L.P.A. 1925, ss.101(1)(ii), 108.

mortgage made by deed. The mortgagee is empowered to insure the mortgaged property against fire and charge the premiums on the property in the same way as the money lent.[74] The power is exercisable as soon as the mortgage is made.[75] The amount of the insurance must not exceed the amount specified in the deed, or, if none, two-thirds of the amount required to restore the property in case of total destruction.[76] But the mortgagee cannot exercise his power if—

(i) the mortgage deed declares that no insurance is required; or

(ii) the mortgagor keeps up an insurance in accordance with the mortgage deed (as is very often stipulated); or

(iii) the mortgage deed is silent as to insurance and the mortgagor keeps up an insurance to the amount authorised by the Act with the mortgagee's consent.[77]

If the mortgagor insures on his own account and not under these provisions, the mortgagee has no right to the policy money.[78] Where, however, the mortgagor insures pursuant to a covenant in the mortgage, that covenant operates to give the mortgagee a charge over the proceeds, and this is so even if the insurance is in the name of the mortgagor.[79] Because the charge operates by way of a partial equitable assignment, the mortgagee should notify the insurer accordingly.[80]

4. Right to consolidate

(a) The right. Consolidation may be described as the right of a person in **19–096** whom two or more mortgages are vested to refuse to allow one mortgage to be redeemed unless the other or others are also redeemed. If A has mortgaged both Blackacre and Whiteacre to X, each property being worth £15,000 and each loan being £10,000, it would be unfair, if the value of Blackacre subsequently sinks to £5,000 and the value of Whiteacre doubles, to allow A to redeem Whiteacre and leave Blackacre unredeemed. In such a case equity permits X to consolidate, and so oblige A to redeem both mortgages or neither. In seeking redemption after the legal date for redemption has passed, A is asking for the assistance of equity, and equity puts its own price upon its interference[81]: he who seeks equity must do equity.[82] This is a notable case of equity restricting rather than extending the right to redeem. Even more

---

[74] The premiums are only a charge on the property; they cannot be recovered from the mortgagor as a debt: Halsb. vol. 25, para. 560.
[75] L.P.A. 1925, s.101(1)(ii).
[76] *ibid.*, s.108(1).
[77] *ibid.*, s.108(2).
[78] *Halifax B.S. v. Keighley* [1931] 2 K.B. 248.
[79] *Colonial Mutual General Insurance Co. Ltd v. ANZ Banking Group (New Zealand) Ltd* [1995] 1 W.L.R. 1140.
[80] Under the rule in *Dearle v. Hall* (1828) 3 Russ. 1; *post*, para. 19–209.
[81] *Cummins v. Fletcher* (1880) 14 Ch.D. 699 at 708.
[82] *Willic v. Lugg* (1761) 2 Eden 78 at 80.

remarkably, the mortgagee is allowed to consolidate even though each property is still sufficient security for its debt. What was originally a principle of equity is now an automatic right. Even a mortgagee who is foreclosing may insist upon it.[83]

19–097 *(b) Conditions of exercise.* The principle of consolidation has been elaborated to some extent, particularly with regard to third parties, *e.g.* where one of the properties is sold subject to its mortgage, or one of the mortgages is transferred. The rules on the subject are now that there can be no consolidation unless each of the following four conditions is satisfied.

19–098 (1) RESERVATION OF RIGHT. One or both of the mortgage deeds must show an intent[84] to allow consolidation.[85] The Law of Property Act 1925 excludes consolidation unless a contrary intention is expressed in "the mortgage deeds or one of them".[86] These words may confine consolidation to cases where each mortgage (or possibly one of them) is by deed.

Where the title to the land is registered, there is some doubt as to whether it is possible to exclude the provision of the Law of Property Act 1925 explained above, and thereby reserve the right to consolidate.[87] However, as the Land Registration Rules 1925 make provision for consolidation,[88] the practice of the Land Registry is to allow it.[89]

19–099 (2) REDEMPTION DATES PASSED. In the case of both mortgages, the legal dates for redemption must have passed.[90] Consolidation is an equitable doctrine and does not override the legal right to redeem on the date agreed.

19–100 (3) SAME MORTGAGOR. Both mortgages must have been made by the same mortgagor.[91] Mortgages made by different mortgagors can never be consolidated, even if both properties later come into the same hands. This is so even if X makes one mortgage and Y, as trustee for X, makes the other,[92] or if A makes one mortgage and A and B jointly make the other.[93] But it is immaterial whether or not the mortgages were made to the same mortgagees.

19–101 (4) SIMULTANEOUS UNIONS OF MORTGAGES AND EQUITIES. There must have been a time when both the mortgages were vested in one person and simultaneously both the equities of redemption were vested in another.[94] If this state

---

[83] *Cummins v. Fletcher* (1880) 14 Ch.D. 699.
[84] See *Hughes v. Britannia Permanent Benefit B.S.* [1906] 2 Ch. 607.
[85] L.P.A. 1925, s.93(1) (re-enacting in substance C.A. 1881, s.17); *Re Salmon* [1903] 1 K.B. 147.
[86] s.93(1).
[87] This is because of the wording of an obscure provision, L.R.A. 1925, s.25(3)(ii): see Ruoff & Roper, 23–41.
[88] r. 154.
[89] See Ruoff & Roper, 23–41, where the procedure is explained. See *post*, para. 19–109.
[90] *Cummins v. Fletcher, supra.*
[91] *Sharp v. Rickards* [1909] 1 Ch. 109.
[92] *Re Raggett* (1880) 16 Ch.D. 117 at 119.
[93] *Thorneycroft v. Crockett* (1848) 2 H.L.C. 239; *Cummins v. Fletcher* (1880) 14 Ch.D. 699 at 710.
[94] See *Pledge v. White* [1896] A.C. 187 at 198.

of affairs once existed, it is immaterial that the equities of redemption have subsequently become vested in different persons. The one exception is where consolidation is based on an express contractual right to consolidate, and not merely on the equitable doctrine. In such a case, a purchaser of the equity of redemption takes subject to the risk of the consolidation of mortgages subsequently created by the mortgagor,[95] except where the mortgagee had notice of the purchase before making the subsequent loans.[96] As for the mortgagee, both mortgages must be vested in him when he seeks to consolidate, so that there can be no consolidation if one is vested in him solely and the other jointly.[97]

(c) Examples. There is no need to illustrate (1) and (2), but the following **19–102** examples may be given of the operation of (3) and (4).

(i)

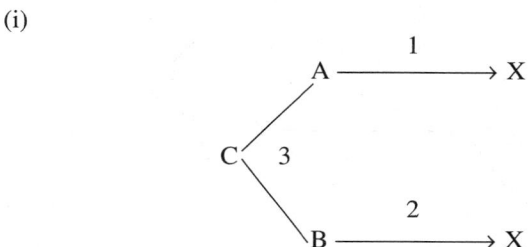

This represents the following steps.

(a)   A mortgages one property to X.

(b)   B mortgages another property to X.

(c)   C purchases the equities of redemption of both properties.

There can be no consolidation here, even though condition (4) is satisfied, for the mortgages were made by different mortgagors.

(ii)   **19–103**

A ———1———→ X
                              3 Z
A ———2———→ Y

(a)   A mortgages one property to X.

---

[95] *Andrew v. City Permanent Benefit B.S.* (1881) 44 L.T. 641; *sed quaere.*
[96] *Hughes v. Britannia Permanent Benefit B.S.* [1906] 2 Ch. 607, borrowing from the law of tacking (*post,* para. 19–246).
[97] *Riley v. Hall* (1898) 79 L.T. 244.

(b) A mortgages another property to Y.

(c) Z purchases both mortgages.

Here Z can consolidate, provided conditions (1) and (2) are satisfied. Condition (3) is satisfied, and so is condition (4). Similarly X could consolidate if he acquired Y's mortgage, or Y if he acquired X's.

19–104   (iii)

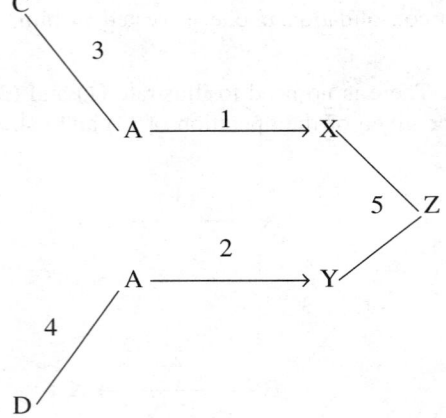

(a) A mortgages one property to X.

(b) A mortgages another property to Y.

(c) C purchases the first property.

(d) D purchases the second property.

(e) Z purchases both mortgages.

There can be no consolidation here, for condition (4) is not satisfied. It is true that at one stage (after step (b)), both equities were in one person's hands, and that at another stage (step (e)) both mortgages were in another person's hands; but at no one moment have both these conditions obtained. The equities of redemption separated before the mortgages came together.[98] The result would be the same if only one of the properties had been sold (*e.g.* if step (d) were omitted), since it would be equally true that the equities were separated before the mortgages were united.

    If C instead of D had purchased the second property, Z could have consolidated, even though at the time of C's purchase no right to consolidate had arisen; the purchaser of two or more properties from a single mortgagor takes

---

[98] *Harter v. Coleman* (1882) 19 Ch.D. 630; *Minter v. Carr* [1894] 3 Ch. 498. *Beevor v. Luck* (1867) L.R. 4 Eq. 537 is no longer law.

subject to the risk of the mortgages coming into the same hands and so permitting consolidation.[99]

(iv)

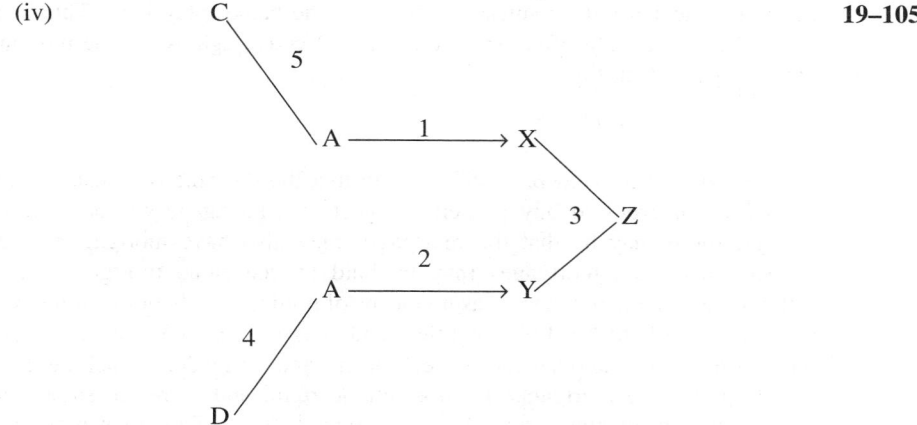

19–105

This represents the same position as the previous example, except that steps (c) and (e) have changed places. As Z has now purchased both mortgages *before* A parted with either equity, Z may consolidate the mortgages provided conditions (1) and (2) are satisfied. In this event, if C seeks to redeem his mortgage, Z can refuse redemption unless C purchases the mortgage on D's property as well as redeeming his own mortgage.[1] Here again it would make no difference if A had disposed of only one of the properties, *e.g.* by omitting step (e): Z can consolidate against the owner of either property provided that he acquired both mortgages while both equities of redemption were still in A's hands.[1]

(d) Three or more mortgages. These rules of consolidation apply equally when it is sought to consolidate more than two mortgages. Sometimes it will be found that while mortgage I can be consolidated with mortgages II and III, there is no right to consolidate mortgages II and III with each other, *e.g.* if only mortgage I contains a consolidation clause. Examples containing more than two mortgages are best worked out by taking the mortgages in pairs and applying the rules to each pair in turn.

19–106

(e) Application of doctrine. The nature of the mortgages or of the property mortgaged is immaterial. There can be consolidation even if one mortgage is legal and one equitable,[2] or if both are equitable,[3] or if one mortgage is of personalty and the other of realty,[4] or if both are mortgages of personalty.[5] The

19–107

[99] *Vint v. Padget* (1858) 2 De G. & J. 611 at 613; *Pledge v. White* [1896] A.C. 187.
[1] *Jennings v. Jordan* (1880) 6 App.Cas 698 at 701.
[2] *Cracknall v. Janson* (1879) 11 Ch.D. 1 at 18.
[3] *Tweedale v. Tweedale* (1857) 23 Beav. 341.
[4] *Tassel v. Smith* (1858) 2 De G. & J. 713.
[5] See *Watts v. Symes* (1851) 1 De G.M. & G. 240.

doctrine has even been applied, though probably wrongly, to two mortgages on the same property.[6] It is immaterial whether the equity of redemption has been conveyed outright or whether it has merely been mortgaged,[7] or has devolved under a will or intestacy, or under the bankruptcy law.[8] Thus if a mortgagee has a right of consolidation, it is effective against all the mortgagor's successors in title.

(f) Danger to purchaser

19–108   (1) UNREGISTERED LAND. It will be seen that the doctrine of consolidation makes it dangerous to buy property subject to a mortgage without careful inquiry, for it may be that the mortgagor may also have mortgaged other property and both mortgages may be held by the same mortgagee. The difficulty is that the purchaser has no means of finding out about this if the two properties are held by different titles; and it is no defence that he bought without notice of the other mortgage,[9] for the right to redeem which he must assert against the mortgagee is an equitable right, and therefore subject to prior equitable interests, irrespective of notice.[10] Even if his own mortgage reserves no right to consolidate, the other mortgage may well do so and that will suffice.[11] If he redeems the other mortgage he of course becomes a transferee and takes the benefit of it.[12] But, unreasonable as it seems, he may then have to pay the penalty of the mortgagee's imprudence as a lender, since consolidation is most likely to be enforced where the security for the other mortgage is insufficient.

19–109   (2) REGISTERED LAND. The potential danger to a purchaser of registered land subject to a registered charge is marginally less than it is where the title is unregistered. This is because where the right to consolidate relates to a specified charge, the registrar will require the production of the land certificates of all the titles affected, and will then note on the register that the specified charges are consolidated.[13]

19–110   *(g) Value of doctrine.* In practice, the right to consolidate causes less trouble than might be supposed. But as a source of risk to an innocent purchaser it is a freak of equity; it is "not one of those doctrines of the Court of Chancery

---

[6] *Re Salmon* [1903] 1 K.B. 147. *Pace* Waldock, *Mortgages*, 285, this is not a question of tacking, *i.e.* of priority, but of the right to redeem. But *Re Salmon* is not a convincing case. A mortgagor who redeems cannot keep the mortgage alive to the prejudice of a mortgagee (*post*, para. 19–144), and if he redeems the earlier mortgage (*i.e.* that which is the better secured) he improves the mortgagee's security for the later mortgage. How the principle of consolidation (that redemption of one property alone may impair the security given by the other) can then fit the case is inexplicable.

[7] *Beevor v. Luck* (1867) L.R. 4 Eq. 537 at 546.

[8] *Selby v. Pomfret* (1861) 3 De G.F. & J. 595.

[9] *Ireson v. Denn* (1796) 2 Cox Eq. 425.

[10] The legal estate obtained from the mortgagor is of no avail, since it is subject to the mortgage term and that can only be cleared off by exercising the equitable right to redeem.

[11] *Ante*, para. 19–098.

[12] *Post*, para. 19–143.

[13] L.R.R. 1925, r. 154(2). See Ruoff & Roper, 23–41.

which has met with general approbation".[14] There may well be doubts as to the wisdom of equity in allowing a mortgagee who has made two distinct bargains, one good and one bad, to use the success of one to rescue him from the failure of the other. But the doctrine has existed almost as long as the equity of redemption itself,[15] and is too well settled to be questioned.[16]

5. Right to tack. This is considered below,[17] since it is part of the subject of priorities.   **19–111**

Section 2. Rights Common to Both Parties

A. Power of Leasing

1. The mortgagor. The most important right common to both parties is the right of leasing the mortgaged property. Apart from any statutory or contractual provisions, the position of the mortgagor as soon as he has executed a mortgage is that he has (or, in the normal case of a charge by way of legal mortgage, is deemed to have) granted a long term of years to the mortgagee and retains merely the reversion on the lease together with an equity of redemption. But since the mortgagor is usually left in possession of the land he needs an owner's usual powers of management. Any lease which he purports to grant will at least be binding as between him and his tenant, as a lease by estoppel,[18] and so the mortgagor may sue or distrain for the rent.[19] But this is subject to the paramount rights of the mortgagee.[20] The mortgagee is always entitled to take possession or to require the rent (including even arrears[21]) to be paid to himself,[22] though in the latter case he must make an effective demand for payment in order to defeat the claim of the mortgagor.[23] The mortgagor cannot, of course, fetter the mortgagee's right to take possession[24]; against the mortgagee therefore the tenant has no defence.[25] Similarly the statutory provisions about protection from eviction after a tenancy has ended do not fetter the mortgagee.[26]   **19–112**

---

[14] *Pledge v. White* [1896] A.C. 187 at 192, *per* Lord Davey.
[15] It first appeared in *Bovey v. Skipwith* (1671) 1 Ch.Cas. 201.
[16] *Pledge v. White, supra.*
[17] *Post.* para. 19–249.
[18] *Webb v. Austin* (1844) 7 Man. & G. 701; *Cuthbertson v. Irving* (1859) 4 H. & N. 742 at 754 (aff'd (1860) 6 H. & N. 135); presumably also it is a good lease in equity. For leases by estoppel, see *ante*, para. 14–102.
[19] *Trent v. Hunt* (1853) 9 Exch. 14.
[20] L.P.A. 1925, s.98. The difficulties arising from the language of this provision, discussed in *Fairclough v. Marshall* (1878) 4 Ex.D. 37 and *Matthews v. Usher* [1900] 2 Q.B. 535, are perhaps best explained by Farwell L.J. in *Turner v. Walsh* [1909] 2 K.B. 484 at 495.
[21] *Moss v. Gallimore* (1779) 1 Doug.K.B. 279.
[22] *Pope v. Biggs* (1829) 9 B. & C. 245; *Underhay v. Read* (1887) 20 Q.B.D. 209.
[23] See *Kitchen's Trustee v. Madders* [1950] Ch. 134, *post*, para. 19–157.
[24] See *Thunder d. Weaver v. Belcher* (1803) 3 East 449.
[25] *Rogers v. Humphreys* (1835) 4 A. & E. 299 at 313; *Dudley & District Benefit B.S. v. Emerson* [1949] Ch. 707; *Rust v. Goodale* [1957] Ch. 33.
[26] *Bolton B.S. v. Cobb* [1966] 1 W.L.R. 1. For these provisions, see *ante*, para. 14–226.

19–113   **2. The mortgagee.** The mortgagee always has the legal right to possession and the power to grant leases; but such leases, like the mortgage itself, will usually be subject to the equity of redemption.[27] Again, therefore, the tenant will have no security against the other party to the mortgage.

19–114   **3. The statutory power.** It will be seen from this that once property has been mortgaged, a satisfactory lease could be made only with the concurrence of both mortgagor and mortgagee. The mortgagee's concurrence might be implied from some later act[28]; but it would not be implied from his mere knowledge of the lease, even though the mortgagor was in default at the time.[29] The only satisfactory solution was for the mortgage to confer upon either or both of the parties a power to grant binding leases.[30] The Law of Property Act 1925[31] confers such a power, though subject to contrary agreement.[32] It provides as follows.

19–115   *(a) Power to lease.* A power to grant leases and to make agreements for leases[33] which will be binding on both mortgagor and mortgagee is exercisable—

> (1) by the mortgagee if he is in possession[34] or has appointed a receiver who is still acting[35] (in which case the mortgagee may by writing delegate his powers of leasing to the receiver[36]); otherwise,
>
> (2) by the mortgagor, being in possession.[37]

In fact, when a mortgagee grants a lease, he thereby takes possession of the land.[37a] It follows therefore that a lease granted by a first mortgagee will be binding on any subsequent mortgagee, even if, under the terms of a subsequent mortgage, no lease may be granted without that mortgagee's consent.[37b] Were this not so, the priority enjoyed by the first mortgagee would be meaningless.[37c]

---

[27] See *Franklinski v. Ball* (1864) 33 Beav. 560 at 563, 564; *Chapman v. Smith* [1907] 2 Ch. 97 at 102.

[28] See *Parker v. Braithwaite* [1952] 2 All E.R. 837; *Stroud B.S. v. Delamont* [1960] 1 W.L.R. 431, approved in *Chatsworth Properties Ltd v. Effiom* [1971] 1 W.L.R. 144. For a recent example, see *Mann v. Nijar* [1998] E.G.C.S. 188.

[29] *Taylor v. Ellis* [1960] Ch. 368; and see *Barclays Bank Ltd v. Kiley* [1961] 1 W.L.R. 1050; *Mann v. Nijar, supra.*

[30] See *e.g. Carpenter v. Parker* (1857) 3 C.B. (N.S.) 206.

[31] L.P.A. 1925, s.99.

[32] These provisions apply as much where title is registered as where it is unregistered: see L.R.A. 1925, s.104; L.R.R. 1925, r. 141.

[33] L.P.A. 1925, s.99(17); see *post*, para. 19–118.

[34] *ibid.*, s.99(2).

[35] *ibid.*, s.99(19).

[36] *ibid.*; *ante*, para. 19–081.

[37] *ibid.*, s.99(1).

[37a] *Mexborough U.D.C. v. Harrison* [1964] 1 W.L.R. 733 at 736.

[37b] *Berkshire Capital Funding Ltd v. Street* [1999] 25 E.G. 191.

[37c] *ibid.*, at 193.

(b) Term of lease. If the mortgage was made after 1925, a lease may be **19–116**
granted for not more than—

    (i) 50 years for agricultural or occupation purposes;

    (ii) 999 years for building.[38]

(c) Conditions of lease. To fall within the statutory powers, any lease **19–117**
granted must comply with the following conditions.

    (1) It must be limited to take effect in possession not later than 12
        months after its date.[39]

    (2) It must reserve the best rent reasonably obtainable, and with certain
        qualifications, no fine may be taken.[40] But in a building lease the
        rent may be nominal for not more than the first five years,[41]
        although the lessee must (whether the rent is nominal or not) agree
        to erect, improve or repair buildings within five years if he has not
        done so already.[42]

    (3) It must contain a covenant by the lessee for payment of rent and a
        condition of re-entry on the rent not being paid for a specified
        period not exceeding 30 days.[43]

    (4) A counterpart of the lease must be executed by the lessee and
        delivered to the lessor.[44] A counterpart of any lease granted by the
        mortgagor must be delivered within one month to the mortgagee;
        but the lessee is not concerned to see that this is done,[45] and non-
        compliance does not invalidate the lease, although it makes the
        power of sale exercisable.[46]

These regulations, however, do not prevent informal transactions, since the **19–118**
definition of "lease" here extends, "as far as circumstances admit . . . to an
agreement, whether in writing or not, for leasing or letting".[47] An oral lease
or agreement may thus be a valid exercise of the power. However, it is not
certain whether the conditions, mentioned above, as to covenants and conditions of re-entry apply in such a case.[48] A lease by the mortgagor is not

---

[38] *ibid.*, s.99(3). The subsection lays down different periods in respect of mortgages granted
    before 1926.
[39] L.P.A. 1925, s.99(5).
[40] *ibid.*, s.99(6).
[41] *ibid.*, s.99(10).
[42] *ibid.*, s.99(9).
[43] *ibid.*, s.99(7).
[44] *ibid.*, s.99(8).
[45] *ibid.*, s.99(11).
[46] *Public Trustee v. Lawrence* [1912] 1 Ch. 789 (*ante*, para. 19–058); and see *Rhodes v. Dalby*
    [1971] 1 W.L.R. 1325.
[47] L.P.A. 1925, s.99(17).
[48] *Pawson v. Revell* [1958] 2 Q.B. 360. Wolst. & C. i, 200, retains unchanged the passage doubted
    in the case at p. 370 and *Rhodes v. Dalby* [1971] 1 W.L.R. 1325 now supports the book in
    saying that the conditions do not apply.

invalidated merely because it includes furniture and sporting rights not comprised in the mortgage[49]; but it will not bind the mortgagee if it includes other land at a single inclusive rent.[50]

19–119   *(d) Non-compliance.* By statute,[51] if a lease does not comply with the statutory requirements but is made in good faith, and the tenant has entered under it, it may nevertheless take effect in equity as a contract for a lease, varied so as to comply with the requirements. This provision for assisting defective leases made under powers has already been encountered elsewhere.[52]

19–120   *(e) Contrary agreement.* The statutory power may be either excluded[53] or extended[54] by agreement of the parties expressed in the mortgage or otherwise in writing. It could not, however, be excluded in any mortgage of agricultural land that was made after March 1, 1948 but before September 1, 1995.[55] Nor can its exclusion hamper the power of the court to order the grant of a new lease of business premises under the Landlord and Tenant Act 1954.[56] In practice, most mortgages expressly exclude the power, and in addition the mortgagor is often required to covenant not to make any letting without the mortgagee's consent.

19–121   **4. Leases not under the statutory power.** If the power is excluded and the mortgagor nevertheless grants an unauthorised lease, the lease is void as against the mortgagee and his successors in title[57] (unless they are estopped from asserting this[58]), but valid as between the parties to it. The statutory powers of leasing do not deprive the parties of their common law rights to create leases not binding upon each other. For example, if a mortgage contains a covenant by the mortgagor not to exercise the statutory power of leasing without the mortgagee's written consent, the mortgagor may nevertheless grant a yearly tenancy which binds the mortgagor under the principle of estoppel but which does not bind the mortgagee.[59]

---

[49] *Brown v. Peto* [1900] 1 Q.B. 346 at 354 (aff'd [1900] 2 Q.B. 653).
[50] *King v. Bird* [1909] 1 K.B. 837.
[51] L.P.A. 1925, s.152. See *Pawson v. Revell* [1958] 2 Q.B. 360 (omission of condition of re-entry).
[52] *Ante*, para. 8–078.
[53] L.P.A. 1925, s.99(13) ("as far as a contrary intention is not expressed"). Where title is registered, any exclusion of the powers should be noted on the register: see L.R.R. 1925, r. 141(1). This rule is more honoured in the breach than in the observance: see (1998) 114 L.Q.R. 354 (M. Robinson).
[54] L.P.A. 1925, s.99(14).
[55] L.P.A. 1925, s.99(13A) (inserted by A.T.A. 1995, s.31). Mortgages of agricultural land made after August 1995 may therefore exclude the statutory power.
[56] L.T.A. 1954, s.36(4). For the Act, see *post*, para. 22–063.
[57] *Rust v. Goodale* [1957] Ch. 33; *Quennell v. Maltby* [1979] 1 W.L.R. 318 at 323; *Britannia B.S. v. Earl* [1990] 1 W.L.R. 422.
[58] *Lever Finance Ltd v. Needlemans' Trustee* [1956] Ch. 375. See (1978) 128 N.L.J. 773 (A. Walker).
[59] See *Iron Trades Employers Insurance Association Ltd v. Union Land and House Investors Ltd* [1937] Ch. 313.

Where a lease has been granted prior to the mortgage, the mortgagee will of course take subject to it, even if the mortgage prohibits any further letting.[60] In some cases, the tenant may agree to waive his priority,[61] but this cannot be validly done where the tenancy is protected under the Rent Act 1977.[62]

B. Power of Accepting Surrenders of Leases

If the parties have not expressed a contrary intention, either in the mortgage **19–122** or otherwise in writing,[63] the Law of Property Act 1925[64] enables a surrender of any lease or tenancy to be effected, binding the parties to the mortgage, on the following terms.

1. Power to accept. The surrender may be accepted— **19–123**

    (i) by the mortgagee, if he is in possession[65] or has appointed a receiver who still acts[66] (in which case the mortgagee may by writing delegate his powers of accepting surrenders to the receiver[67]); or

    (ii) by the mortgagor, if he is in possession.[68]

2. Conditions of surrender. For the surrender to be valid— **19–124**

    (i) an authorised lease of the property must be granted to take effect in possession within one month of the surrender;

    (ii) the term of the new lease must not be shorter than the unexpired residue of the surrendered lease; and

    (iii) the rent reserved by the new lease must not be less than the rent reserved by the surrendered lease.[69]

The statutory power of accepting a surrender is thus exercisable only for the purpose of replacing one lease by another; and a surrender which does not

---

[60] *Barclays Bank Plc v. Zaroovabli* [1997] Ch. 321 (tenancy granted *after* the charge was executed but *before* it was registered held binding on the mortgagee); see [1997] C.L.J. 496 (D. G. Barnsley). For a survey of the rights of such tenants as against a mortgagee who seeks possession, see [1991] J.S.W.L. 220 (D. G. Barnsley).
[61] There is no direct authority on this point, but it seems correct in principle. *cf. Skipton B.S. v. Clayton* (1993) 66 P. & C.R. 223 at 228, 229.
[62] *Woolwich B.S. v. Dickman* [1996] 3 All E.R. 204; [1997] Conv. 402 (J. Morgan). This conclusion follows from R.A. 1977, s.98(1) (restricting the grounds on which possession can be given against a protected or statutory tenant). *cf. Appleton v. Aspin* [1988] 1 W.L.R. 410.
[63] L.P.A. 1925, s.100(7).
[64] s.100.
[65] L.P.A. 1925, s.100(2).
[66] *ibid.*, s.100(13).
[67] *ibid.*
[68] *ibid.*, s.100(1).
[69] *ibid.*, s.100(5).

comply with these conditions is void.[70] But the power may be extended by an agreement in writing, whether in the mortgage or not.[71]

Section 3. Rights of the Mortgagor

A. *Right of Redemption*

I. PROTECTION OF THE MORTGAGOR

19–125 The distinction between the mortgagor's legal right to redeem and his equitable right to redeem has already been considered.[72] The latter right, being the creature of equity, must be protected by equity; for otherwise the mortgagee, who often can bring pressure to bear on a prospective mortgagor by threatening to withhold the loan,[73] might be able to defeat the whole purpose of a mortgage, *i.e.* that it should provide security and nothing more. The mortgagor's equity of redemption is inviolable; the maxim is "once a mortgage, always a mortgage".[74] The principle is applied in two ways.

19–126 **1. The test of a mortgage is in substance, not form.** If a transaction is in substance a mortgage, equity will treat it as such, even if it is dressed up in some other guise,[75] as by the documents being cast in the form of an absolute conveyance.[76] Thus if a mortgage is expressed in the form of a conveyance with an option for the mortgagor to repurchase the property in a year's time, the mortgagor is entitled to redeem it even after the year has expired.[77] "In all these cases the question is what was the real intention of the parties?",[78] and parol evidence is admissible to show what it was.[79]

19–127 **2. No clogs on the equity.** There must be no clog or fetter on the equity of redemption. This means both that the mortgagor cannot be prevented from eventually redeeming his property on repayment of the sum advanced together with interest due and the mortgagee's proper costs, and also that, after

---

[70] See, *e.g. Barclays Bank Ltd v. Stasek* [1957] Ch. 28; (1957) 73 L.Q.R. 14 (R.E.M.).

[71] L.P.A. 1925, s.100(10).

[72] *Ante*, para. 19–014.

[73] "For necessitous men are not, truly speaking, free men, but, to answer a present exigency, will submit to any terms that the crafty may impose upon them": *Vernon v. Bethell* (1762) 2 Eden 110 at 113, *per* Lord Henley L.C.

[74] *Seton v. Slade* (1802) 7 Ves. 265 at 273, *per* Lord Eldon L.C.

[75] See *Williams v. Owen* (1840) 5 My. & Cr. 303 at 306; *Re Watson* (1890) 25 Q.B.D. 27.

[76] *England v. Codrington* (1758) 1 Eden 169; *Barnhart v. Greenshields* (1853) 9 Moo.P.C. 18.

[77] See *Danby v. Read* (1675) Rep.t.Finch 226; *Muttylol Seal v. Annundochunder Sandle* (1849) 5 Moo.Ind.App. 72; *Croft v. Powel* (1738) 2 Com. 603; *Waters v. Mynn* (1850) 15 L.T. (o.s.) 157; *cf. Salt v. Marquess of Northampton* [1892] A.C. 1 (Lord Bramwell's attack on the equity of redemption as an interference with freedom of contract is entertaining).

[78] *Manchester, Sheffield and Lincolnshire Ry v. North Central Wagon Co.* (1888) 13 App. Cas. 554 at 568, *per* Lord Macnaghten.

[79] *Lincoln v. Wright* (1859) 4 De G. & J. 16; *Barton v. Bank of New South Wales* (1890) 15 App.Cas. 379.

redemption, he is free from all the conditions of the mortgage. This will be considered under the two heads.

(a) No irredeemability[80]

(1) REDEMPTION. "Redemption is of the very nature and essence of a mortgage, as mortgages are regarded in equity."[81] The right exists whether or not it has been expressly reserved in the mortgage.[82] It is inconsistent with the very nature of a mortgage that it shall be totally irredeemable[83] or that the right of redemption shall be confined to certain persons (such as the mortgagor and the heirs male of his body[84]) or to a limited period (such as the joint lives of the mortgagor and mortgagee[85] or the life of the mortgagor alone[86]), or to part only of the mortgaged property.[87] Thus if the property mortgaged is a lease together with an option to renew it, or to purchase the freehold, and the mortgagee exercises the option, the mortgagor is entitled on redemption not only to the lease but also, on paying the cost of acquisition, to the fruits of exercising the option.[88]

19–128

(2) EXCLUSION OF REDEMPTION. Any express stipulation which is inconsistent with the right of redemption will be ineffective. No mortgagee can secure, as a condition of the mortgage, that the property shall become his absolutely when some specified event occurs.[89] In all such cases the owner of the equity of redemption may redeem as if there had been no such restriction. If, for example, the mortgage agreement gives the mortgagee an option to purchase the mortgaged property, that term is void, as repugnant to the equity of redemption, even though the transaction is not in itself oppressive to the mortgagor.[90] But a mere right of pre-emption (*i.e.* of first refusal) is probably unobjectionable if its terms are fair, since the mortgagor cannot be compelled to sell.[91]

19–129

Once the mortgage has been made, equity will not intervene if the mortgagor, by a separate and independent transaction, gives the mortgagee an interest

---

[80] *Fairclough v. Swan Brewery Co. Ltd* [1912] A.C. 565 at 570.
[81] *Noakes & Co. Ltd v. Rice* [1902] A.C. 24 at 30, *per* Lord Macnaghten.
[82] *National Westminster Bank Plc v. Powney* (1989) 60 P. & C.R. 420 at 438 (omitted from the report in [1991] Ch. 339).
[83] *Re Wells* [1933] Ch. 29 at 52.
[84] *Howard v. Harris* (1683) 1 Vern. 190.
[85] *Spurgeon v. Collier* (1758) 1 Eden 55.
[86] *Newcomb v. Bonham* (1681) 1 Vern. 7; *Salt v. Marquess of Northampton* [1892] A.C. 1.
[87] See *Re Wells, supra*; *Salt v. Marquess of Northampton, supra*.
[88] *Nelson v. Hannam* [1943] Ch. 59.
[89] *Toomes v. Conset* (1745) 3 Atk. 261.
[90] *Samuel v. Jarrah Timber and Wood Paving Corporation Ltd* [1904] A.C. 323, where the House of Lords expressed a distaste for the rule in the case of a fair commercial bargain, but felt bound to apply it. *cf. J. A. Pye (Oxford) Estates Ltd v. Ambrose* [1994] N.P.C. 53 (21-year option to purchase granted in return for £8,000, secured by a mortgage. The loan was only repayable if the option was not exercised. There was no clog on the equity, because the mortgage was only enforceable if the option was spent).
[91] See *Orby v. Trigg* (1722) 9 Mod. 2, where the only objection to a right of pre-emption was that the mortgagee exercised it too late and misled the mortgagor.

in the property, even if it may wholly or partly destroy the equity of redemption, such as an option to purchase[92] or a long lease.[93] Equity will protect the mortgagor while he is in the defenceless position of one seeking a loan; once he has obtained his loan, this protection is not needed. But where a mortgagor seeks to escape from his mortgagee by procuring a transfer of the mortgage to a new mortgagee, there is in effect a new loan, and any option obtained by the new mortgagee will be subject to the rules stated above.[94]

19–130   (3) POSTPONEMENT OF REDEMPTION. A provision postponing the date of redemption until some future period longer than the customary six months may be valid, provided the mortgage as a whole is not so oppressive and unconscionable that equity would not enforce it,[95] and provided it does not make the equitable right to redeem illusory.[96] The question here is one of degree. An excessive postponement of the redemption date may in itself be oppressive and thus a clog on the equity of redemption. In one case a lease for 20 years was mortgaged on conditions which prevented its redemption until six weeks before the end of the term. Such a provision rendered the equitable right to redeem illusory; for it prohibited redemption until the lease was nearly valueless and redemption was not worth having. The mortgagor was accordingly allowed to redeem after only three years.[97]

19–131   In the case of a wasting security, therefore, any long postponement of the right to redeem is likely to be objectionable. But in other cases it is often not so. In *Knightsbridge Estate Trust Ltd v. Byrne*,[98] the Knightsbridge company had mortgaged a large number of properties to an insurance company on terms that repayment should be made by half-yearly instalments over a period of 40 years. The mortgagees, for their part, agreed not to call in the money in advance of the due dates. Six years later the Knightsbridge company sought a declaration that the company was entitled to redeem the mortgage, claiming, *inter alia*, that it was oppressive that they should be unable to redeem their properties for 40 years. But on this ground their action failed, for it was held that in the circumstances the agreement was a perfectly fair one and the contractual right of redemption was in no way illusory. The court is concerned

---

[92] *Reeve v. Lisle* [1902] A.C. 461.

[93] *Alex Lobb (Garages) Ltd v. Total Oil Great Britain Ltd* [1983] 1 W.L.R. 87 at 98, 99 (51-year lease of part of property). This point was not considered on appeal: [1985] 1 W.L.R. 173.

[94] *Lewis v. Frank Love Ltd* [1961] 1 W.L.R. 261. For transfer of mortgages, see *post* para. 19–183.

[95] *Knightsbridge Estates Trust Ltd v. Byrne* [1939] Ch. 441 at 463 (aff'd on other grounds [1940] A.C. 613).

[96] *ibid.*, at 456.

[97] *Fairclough v. Swan Brewery Co. Ltd* [1912] A.C. 565; *cf. Davis v. Symons* [1934] Ch. 442, as explained in the *Knightsbridge case, supra*, at 460–462 (same principle applied to mortgage of insurance policies due to mature before redemption date 20 years distant). Contrast *Santley v. Wilde* [1899] 2 Ch. 474, where it was held by the Court of Appeal that a 10-year lease of a theatre was irredeemable because part of the mortgagee's security was a covenant by the mortgagor to pay one-third of the profits to the mortgagee during the whole remainder of the lease. The decision proceeded on the ground that without the covenant there would have been insufficient security. It has been criticised in the House of Lords: *Noakes & Co. Ltd v. Rice* [1902] A.C. 24 at 31, 34.

[98] [1939] Ch. 441; aff'd on other grounds [1940] A.C. 613.

to see that the essential requirements of a mortgage are observed, and that oppressive or unconscionable terms are not enforced.[99] But it is naturally reluctant to interfere with a contract made as a matter of business by parties well able to look after themselves. "The directors of a trading company in search of financial assistance are certainly in a very different position from that of an impecunious landowner in the toils of a crafty money-lender."[1] Even though a business contract is unlikely to be struck down as being oppressive or unconscionable, it may, however, be in unlawful restraint of trade.[2] The test in such cases is whether the restraint is—

(i) reasonable between the parties; and

(ii) not contrary to the public interest.[3]

If one element in the transaction is a mortgage which is to be irredeemable during the period of unlawful restraint, the fetter on redemption may be held inoperative.[4] A significant factor in determining whether the tie is unlawful is, in practice, its length.[5] For the future, it is possible that the validity of such tied-house arrangements may be challenged under Article 85 of the Treaty of Rome rather than on grounds of restraint of trade.[6]

(4) DEBENTURES. The decision of the Court of Appeal in *Knightsbridge* **19–132** *Estates Trust Ltd v. Byrne*[7] is now the leading case on postponement of redemption. It was affirmed by the House of Lords,[8] but on the ground that the security was a debenture. A debenture is a written acknowledgment of indebtedness made by a company, and it is usually secured by a mortgage or charge on some property of the company. A factory building may, for example, be mortgaged to trustees for the debenture holders; and even an ordinary mortgage by a company appears to be a debenture. Mortgages created to secure

---

[99] *Knightsbridge Estates Trust Ltd v. Byrne* [1939] Ch. 441 at 457.

[1] *Samuel v. Jarrah Timber and Wood Paving Corporation Ltd* [1904] A.C. 323 at 327, *per* Lord Macnaghten.

[2] It should be emphasised that this is a distinct ground of invalidity that is unconnected with the equitable doctrine of clogs and fetters.

[3] See, *e.g. Esso Petroleum Co. Ltd v. Harper's Garage (Stourport) Ltd* [1968] A.C. 269 at 300.

[4] *Esso Petroleum Co. Ltd v. Harper's Garage (Stourport) Ltd, supra,* (mortgagor to sell only mortgagee's brand of petrol for 21 years and to redeem only by instalments over 21 years: restraint held excessive and mortgage held redeemable; a similar agreement in relation to another garage for less than five years was, by contrast, upheld as valid).

[5] See *Alec Lobb (Garages) Ltd v. Total Oil (Great Britain) Ltd* [1985] 1 W.L.R. 173 at 178, where Dillon L.J. accepted that the *Esso* case had laid down a "rule of thumb" that an agreement was not in restraint of trade if it lasted no longer than five years (but the court there upheld a tie that would last for at least seven years). See, *e.g. Texaco Ltd v. Mulberry Filling Station Ltd* [1972] 1 W.L.R. 814. *cf.* [1985] Conv. 141 (P. Todd).

[6] See [1994] Conv. 150 (T. Frazer); (1998) 49 N.I.L.Q. 202 (N. Hopkins); *ante,* para. 16–032. It should be noted that the European Commission often gives exemptions from Art. 85 in respect of such solus agreements.

[7] [1939] Ch. 441.

[8] [1940] A.C. 613.

debentures form a statutory exception to the general rule prohibiting irredeemability,[9] since it is provided by the Companies Act 1985[10] that debentures may be made irredeemable, or redeemable only on the happening of a contingency or the expiration of a period of time.

19–133   (5) REGULATED MORTGAGES. In the relatively few cases where the mortgage is regulated by the Consumer Credit Act 1974,[11] the mortgagor is entitled to repay the loan at any time, even before the due date; and any term of the mortgage is void to the extent that it is inconsistent with this right.[12] Thus the mortgagor has an overriding right of redemption exercisable at any time.

19–134   *(b) Redemption free from conditions in the mortgage.* The mortgagor cannot be prevented from redeeming the property free from all the conditions of the mortgage. Redemption must be complete redemption, so that the mortgagor is restored to his original position and all the liabilities of the mortgage transaction are ended.

19–135   (1) COLLATERAL ADVANTAGES. The essence of a mortgage is a loan of a certain sum of money upon security. Sometimes terms are inserted in a mortgage which give the mortgagee some other advantage in addition to his security and interest. For example, in the case of a mortgage of a public house to a brewery company the mortgagee will usually stipulate that the mortgagor shall sell only the mortgagee's beer. And in business transactions, which include an investment of money secured by mortgage, there may be other provisions giving some commercial advantage to the mortgagee. These "collateral advantages" were at one time held void,[13] for before the repeal of the usury laws in 1854[14] any such advantage was an evasion of the law limiting the rate of interest. But since 1854 the attitude has changed,[15] and it is clear that collateral advantages are objectionable only if they are unconscionable[16] or clog the equity of redemption.

An example of an unconscionable advantage is an excessive premium imposed unfairly. In one case a property company sold a house to one of its tenants, advancing £2,900 under a mortgage which made no provision for interest but which required repayment of £4,553. This premium of £1,653 was held to be an unreasonable and unconscionable collateral advantage, since it was far more than a fair rate of interest and, by making the charge exceed the value of the house, it rendered the equity of redemption worthless. The

---

[9] Strictly, however, an irredeemable debenture "is not a mortgage at all": *Samuel v. Jarrah Timber and Wood Paving Corporation Ltd* [1904] A.C. 323 at 330, *per* Lord Lindley.
[10] s.193, replacing earlier legislation.
[11] *Ante*, para. 19–042.
[12] ss.94, 173.
[13] *Jennings v. Ward* (1705) 2 Vern. 520 at 521.
[14] *Ante*, para. 19–010.
[15] *Biggs v. Hoddinott* [1898] 2 Ch. 307 at 316; *Kreglinger v. New Patagonia Meat & Cold Storage Co. Ltd* [1914] A.C. 25 at 54, 55; and see at 46, *per* Lord Mersey ("an unruly dog").
[16] See *Barrett v. Hartley* (1866) L.R. 2 Eq. 789 at 795; *James v. Kerr* (1889) 40 Ch.D. 449.

mortgagor was therefore entitled to redeem by paying £2,900 with reasonable interest fixed by the court.[17]

The court declined to intervene, on the other hand, where a company had mortgaged its business premises upon terms which deferred redemption for 10 years and indexed both principal and interest to the Swiss franc.[18] At the end of the 10 years the pound sterling had fallen to a third of its original value against the Swiss franc, so that in terms of sterling the mortgagee obtained a very large premium. But this was held in the circumstances to be neither unfair nor oppressive, even though it might be unreasonable by the standard which the court would adopt if it had to settle the terms itself.[19] The court resolved the ambiguity in the earlier decisions by holding that a collateral advantage was not objectionable merely because it was unreasonable. It would be condemned only if it was unfair and unconscionable, being imposed in a morally reprehensible manner; and that could not be said of such a transaction between businessmen acting with their eyes open, even though it was a hard bargain. It is where there is some inequality of bargaining power or undue influence that the court is most disposed to grant relief. The Court of Appeal has subsequently endorsed this view.[20]   **19–136**

(2) INVALIDITY AFTER REDEMPTION. A collateral advantage which is not unconscionable is valid until redemption but not afterwards. The principle is illustrated by a mortgage of a public house under which the mortgagor covenants to sell only the mortgagee's beer. While the mortgage is still on foot the mortgagor is bound by the covenant.[21] But so soon as he redeems he is free from it,[22] even though it was intended to bind him for a fixed period, for otherwise he could not redeem his property completely; he mortgaged a "free house", and if he could redeem only a "tied house" he would still be fettered by the terms of the mortgage after redemption. The same principle appears in *Bradley v. Carritt*,[23] where the mortgagor mortgaged to a tea broker the shares which gave him a controlling interest in a tea company. As a condition of the loan he guaranteed that the mortgagee should always remain broker to the company thereafter. The mortgagor, having paid off the mortgage, was held to be free from this apparently unlimited guarantee. Had it been otherwise he could never have disposed of his shares after redemption, for he would have been compelled to keep control of the company.   **19–137**

---

[17] *Cityland and Property (Holdings) Ltd v. Dabrah* [1968] Ch. 166.
[18] *Multiservice Bookbinding Ltd v. Marden* [1979] Ch. 84. As to obligations linked to foreign currencies, see *ante*, para. 14–245.
[19] Certain other onerous terms were taken into account.
[20] *Alec Lobb (Garages) Ltd v. Total Oil (Great Britain) Ltd* [1985] 1 W.L.R. 173 at 183. The case involved a lease-back agreement rather than a mortgage. Dillon L.J. there explained that "the courts would only interfere in exceptional cases where as a matter of common fairness it was not right that the strong should be allowed to push the weak to the wall".
[21] *Biggs v. Hoddinott* [1898] 2 Ch. 307.
[22] *Noakes & Co. Ltd v. Rice* [1902] A.C. 24 (covenant to buy mortgagee's beer during whole residue of mortgagor's lease: House of Lords unanimous).
[23] [1903] A.C. 253 (House of Lords divided 3–2).

19–138   (3) VALIDITY AFTER REDEMPTION. In some cases the courts, in their desire not to unsettle commercial contracts for doctrinal reasons, have allowed collateral stipulations in mortgages to remain binding even after redemption. The leading case is *Kreglinger v. New Patagonia Meat and Cold Storage Co. Ltd*,[24] where the meat company had raised a loan from a firm of woolbrokers on a mortgage by way of a floating charge[25] on the company's undertaking. It was made a condition that for five years the company should not sell any sheepskins to any other person without first offering them to the woolbrokers at the best price obtainable elsewhere, and that the woolbrokers should have a commission on all sheepskins sold by the company to other persons. The company redeemed the property after two years and claimed to be freed from the option[26] and commission clauses. But the House of Lords held that they remained bound, on the ground that these clauses were in truth a separate agreement, part of the consideration for the mortgage but not part of the mortgage itself, and therefore no impediment to complete redemption. These principles have been applied to an exclusive sale agreement and mortgage between a garage and its supplier, on the basis that it was a commercial transaction of which the mortgage was merely a part, and therefore outside the clogs and fetters doctrine.[27]

19–139   (4) DISTINCTIONS. The reasons given for these decisions are, as a matter of logic, not entirely easy to reconcile. There is clearly a distinction between a case where the parties negotiate a loan, and the mortgagee then succeeds in getting the mortgagor to agree to a stipulation giving the mortgagee some additional advantage, and a case where from the outset the bargain is for some advantage in return for a loan.[28] In the former situation there is likely to be equality of bargaining power, whereas in the latter there is not. A condition which restricts the alienability of the mortgaged property after redemption, as in *Bradley v. Carritt*, is also clearly distinguishable. It may in addition be important whether, as in *Bradley v. Carritt*, specific property is bound, or whether, as in the *Kreglinger* case, there is merely a floating charge.[29]

A distinction that is perhaps even more important—though it is less clearly stated—is whether the borrower is a private individual or a person or company engaged in commerce. The former may require the protection of the law, the latter may not. A collateral advantage that is a term of a personal loan, is more

---

[24] [1914] A.C. 25 (House of Lords unanimous); applied in *Re Cuban Land & Development Co. (1911) Ltd* [1921] 2 Ch. 147; and *cf. De Beers Consolidated Mines Ltd v. British South Africa Co.* [1912] A.C. 52; *post*, para. 19–140.

[25] *i.e.* a charge on such assets as the company had from time to time, which would "crystallize" on certain specified events occurring, and attach to the company's then assets.

[26] *Quaere* whether the right was not merely a right of pre-emption; and see *ante*, para. 19–129.

[27] *Re Petrol Filling Station, Vauxhall Bridge Road, London* (1968) 20 P. & C.R. 1. The possibility that the agreement might have been in unlawful restraint of trade was held over for subsequent proceedings.

[28] See, *e.g. Biggs v. Hoddinott* [1898] 2 Ch. 307 at 316, 317; *Kreglinger v. New Patagonia Meat & Cold Storage Co. Ltd*, *supra*, at 39, 45, 61.

[29] See *Kreglinger's Case*, *supra*, at 41, 42.

difficult to regard as an independent transaction than one which forms part of an elaborate commercial agreement. In the former case the advantage can generally be terminated on redemption without hardship to the mortgagee. In the latter case, if the court interferes with a commercial contract, it may deprive the mortgagee of the valuable fruits of a careful investment. The test of "severability", which *Kreglinger's* case introduced, provides a convenient but indefinable rule for dealing with such cases on their merits. "The question is one not of form but of substance, and it can be answered in each case only by looking at all the circumstances, and not by mere reliance on some abstract principle, or upon the dicta which have fallen *obiter* from judges in other and different cases."[30]

It is also important to consider what has been included in the mortgage. **19–140** Thus where a company agreed to grant a perpetual licence for mining on its land, and later mortgaged the land to the licensee, it was held that after redemption the agreement to grant the licence still bound the company. This was so even though the agreement for the licence expressly contemplated the subsequent mortgage, for the two transactions were substantially independent of each other.[31] When the property was mortgaged, it had already been "burdened and encumbered with the prior obligation, superior to the mortgage security, to grant the licence",[32] and so there was no clog on the equity; for on redemption "everything which had been charged was restored to the mortgagor".[33]

It should perhaps be noted that recourse to the technical doctrines of clogs and fetters has become increasingly rare. In part at least, this may be due to their uncertain application.

II. WHO CAN REDEEM

1. Persons interested. Redemption is usually sought by the mortgagor; but **19–141** the right to redeem is not confined to him and may be exercised by any person interested in the equity of redemption,[34] however small his interest.[35] Once the mortgagor has parted with his whole interest in the property he ceases to be able to redeem[36]; but if he is subsequently sued on the covenant for payment he acquires a fresh right of redemption.[37] The right to redeem extends to assignees of the equity of redemption (even if the assignment was voluntary[38]), subsequent mortgagees,[39] unless they are statute-barred,[40] and even a

---

[30] *Kreglinger's Case, supra*, at 39 *per* Lord Haldane: his speech is analysed in *Re Petrol Filling Station, Vauxhall Bridge Road, London* (1968) 20 P. & C.R. 1.
[31] *De Beers Consolidated Mines Ltd v. British South Africa Co.* [1912] A.C. 52. Compare the principle explained in connection with options: *ante*, para. 19–129.
[32] *ibid.*, at 66, *per* Lord Atkinson.
[33] *ibid.*, at 73, *per* Earl Loreburn L.C.
[34] *Pearce v. Morris* (1869) 5 Ch.App. 227 at 229.
[35] *Hunter v. Macklew* (1846) 5 Hare 238.
[36] Consider *Moore v. Morton* [1886] W.N. 196.
[37] *Kinnaird v. Trollope* (1888) 39 Ch.D. 636.
[38] *Howard v. Harris* (1683) 1 Vern. 190.
[39] *Fell v. Brown* (1787) 2 Bro.C.C. 276.
[40] *Cotterell v. Price* [1960] 1 W.L.R. 1097.

lessee under a lease granted by the mortgagor but not binding on the mortgagee.[41]

If several persons simultaneously seek to redeem a mortgage the first in order of priority has the first claim.[42]

19–142   **2. Spouses and "connected persons".** A spouse who has statutory matrimonial home rights under the Family Law Act 1996,[43] will be entitled to redeem a mortgage of the matrimonial home as being a person interested in the equity of redemption, as explained above.[44] In addition, the spouse is expressly empowered to make mortgage payments due from the other spouse in respect of the home.[45] The spouse is also entitled to be made a party to any action brought by the mortgagee to enforce his security,[46] and if a Class F land charge has been registered, to be served with notice of the action.[47]

The Family Law Act 1996 has extended some of these rights to certain "connected persons", namely former spouses, cohabitants and former cohabitants,[48] but only in the circumstances prescribed by the Act.[49] These are the rights to make mortgage payments due from the mortgagor,[50] and to be made a party to any action brought by the mortgagee to enforce his security.[51]

III. EFFECT OF REDEMPTION

19–143   **1. Discharge or transfer.** Where redemption is effected by the only person interested in the equity of redemption, and the mortgage redeemed is the only incumbrance on the property, the effect of redemption is to discharge the mortgage and leave the property free from incumbrances. But in other cases, as where a second mortgagee redeems the first mortgage, the effect of redemption will normally be that the person paying the money takes a transfer of the mortgage[52]; for, of course, the redemption enures to the benefit of the person redeeming, and the second mortgagee must be able to maintain the first mortgage as against the mortgagor.

19–144   **2. Redemption by mortgagor.** By contrast, if the mortgagor himself redeems a mortgage which has priority over one or more subsequent mortgages, this discharges the mortgage, and the mortgagor cannot claim to have it kept alive to the prejudice of the subsequent mortgagees.[53] He "cannot

[41] *Tarn v. Turner* (1888) 39 Ch.D. 456.
[42] *Teevan v. Smith* (1882) 20 Ch.D. 724 at 730.
[43] *Ante*, para. 17–023.
[44] See *Hastings and Thanet B.S. v. Goddard* [1970] 1 W.L.R. 1544.
[45] F.L.A. 1996, s.30(3).
[46] Subject to the court being satisfied that this may affect the outcome: *ibid.*, s.55.
[47] *ibid.*, s.56; see *ante*, para. 19–076.
[48] See F.L.A. 1996, s.54(5).
[49] For those conditions, see *ibid.*, ss.35, 36.
[50] *ibid.*, ss.35(13), 36(15).
[51] *ibid.*, s.55.
[52] *cf.* L.P.A. 1925, s.115(2).
[53] *Otter v. Lord Vaux* (1856) 6 De G.M. & G. 638 (purported sale by mortgagee to mortgagor under power of sale, intended to give mortgagor a title free from claims of later mortgagees, held ineffective for this purpose); and see L.P.A. 1925, s.115(3), recognising the rule.

derogate from his own bargain by setting up the mortgage so purchased against a second mortgagee".[54] This is so even if some third party provided him with the money.[55] Thus if the property proves insufficient to satisfy all the claims the mortgagor cannot claim priority for the amount due on the first mortgage. If the mortgagor redeems a first mortgage he therefore improves the security for any later mortgagees.

3. Subsequent purchaser. The above rule applies only to the mortgagor,   **19–145**
and not to later purchasers of the equity of redemption. Thus if Blackacre has been mortgaged first to A and then to B, and is then sold or mortgaged (subject to the mortgages) to X, X may pay off A's mortgage but keep it alive against B.[56] Similarly, if the sale is made not to X but to A, A can keep his mortgage alive against B. It will be presumed in such cases, in the absence of contrary evidence, that there is no intention of a merger of the two interests if it is to the advantage of the purchaser that merger should not take place.[57]

4. Right to compel transfer. Instead of redeeming, a person who is entitled   **19–146**
to redeem a mortgage may usually insist upon the mortgagee transferring the mortgage to a nominee of the person paying the money.[58] This right exists notwithstanding any stipulation to the contrary, and applies irrespective of the date of the mortgage,[59] though it is exercisable only upon the same terms as the right of redemption.[60] If there are competing claims they take effect in order of priority,[61] as in the case of redemption. The right is excluded, however, if the mortgagee is or has been in possession,[62] for he thereby became liable to account strictly[63] despite any transfer of the mortgage and is liable for any defaults of the transferee[64] unless he transferred under an order of the court.[65] It would thus be unfair if the mortgagor could compel him to make a transfer.[66]

IV. TERMS OF REDEMPTION

1. Method. A mortgage may be redeemed either in court or out of court; the   **19–147**
latter is the more usual except in complicated cases. The mortgage remains in

---

[54] *Whiteley v. Delaney* [1914] A.C. 132 at 145, *per* Lord Haldane L.C.
[55] *Parkash v. Irani Finance Ltd* [1970] Ch. 101.
[56] *Adams v. Angell* (1877) 5 Ch.D. 634; *Thorne v. Cann* [1895] A.C. 11; *Whiteley v. Delaney* [1914] A.C. 132.
[57] *Ante*, para. 14–177; L.P.A. 1925, s.185. The decision in *Toulmin v. Steere* (1817) 3 Mer. 210, to the effect that merger will not be presumed if the purchaser has notice of later mortgages at the time he redeems, is of doubtful authority: see *Whiteley v. Delaney, supra*, at 144, 145.
[58] L.P.A. 1925, s.95(1), (2); and see Hood and Challis, pp. 190, 191.
[59] L.P.A. 1925, s.95(5).
[60] *ibid.*, s.95(1). Thus it may be subject to a right of consolidation.
[61] L.P.A. 1925, s.95(2); see *Teevan v. Smith* (1882) 20 Ch.D. 724.
[62] L.P.A. 1925, s.95(3).
[63] See *ante*, para. 19–069.
[64] *Hinde v. Blake* (1841) 11 L.J. Ch. 26; and see 1 Eq.Ca.Abr. 328, pl. 2.
[65] *Hall v. Heward* (1886) 32 Ch.D. 430.
[66] But see Hood and Challis, pp. 190, 191.

being until the money due has actually been paid and accepted.[67] The mortgagor remains liable for interest under it until either he duly tenders repayment and, if it is not accepted, sets the money aside,[68] or else the mortgagee waives tender, *e.g.* by unequivocally refusing a proposed repayment.[69] If a mortgagee unreasonably refuses to accept a proper tender of the money due and so makes an action for redemption necessary, he may be penalised in costs.[70]

19–148   **2. Notice.** The mortgagor may redeem on the legal date for redemption (or before, if the mortgagee has sought payment, *e.g.* by taking possession[71]) without giving notice of his intention to do so.[72] After that date,[73] when (as is usual) he is forced to rely upon his equitable right to redeem, it is a rule of practice[74] that he must either—

> (i) give the mortgagee reasonable[75] notice (*i.e.* normally, or, in the absence of express provision, perhaps always,[76] six months) of his intention to redeem[77]; or
>
> (ii) pay him six months' interest instead.[78]

It is only fair that the mortgagee should have a reasonable opportunity to find investment for his money.[79] But the mortgagee is not entitled to any notices or interest instead—

> (i) if the mortgage is merely of a temporary nature[80]; or
>
> (ii) if he has taken steps to enforce his security,[81] as by taking possession,[82] or starting foreclosure proceedings,[83] or giving the mortgagor notice to repay the loan so as to entitle the mortgagee to sell on default being made,[84] "It is said, 'You have demanded payment by

---

[67] *Samuel Keller (Holdings) Ltd v. Martins Bank Ltd* [1971] 1 W.L.R. 43.

[68] *Barratt v. Gough-Thomas (No. 3)* [1951] 2 All E.R. 48.

[69] *Chalikani Venkatarayanim v. Zamindar of Tuni* (1922) L.R. 50 Ind.App. 41.

[70] *Graham v. Seal* (1918) 88 L.J. Ch. 31.

[71] *Bovill v. Endle* [1896] 1 Ch. 648; 65 L.J. Ch. 542.

[72] See *Crickmore v. Freeton* (1870) 40 L.J. Ch. 137.

[73] Which is usually six months after the execution of the mortgage: see *ante*, para. 19–013.

[74] *Smith v. Smith* [1891] 3 Ch. 550; *Centrax Trustees Ltd v. Ross* [1979] 2 All E.R. 952 at 955. Nowadays mortgages normally contain express provisions to deal with redemption.

[75] *Browne v. Lockhart* (1840) 10 Sim. 420 at 424.

[76] See *Cromwell Property Investment Co. Ltd v. Western & Toovey* [1934] Ch. 322, where, at 332, Maugham J. calls the rule "harsh".

[77] *Shrapnell v. Blake* (1737) West.t.Hard. 166.

[78] *Johnson v. Evans* (1889) 61 L.T. 18.

[79] *Browne v. Lockhart, supra*, at 424.

[80] *Fitzgerald's Trustee v. Mellersh* [1892] 1 Ch. 385. That case was concerned with an equitable mortgage by deposit of title deeds. Such mortgages must now take the form of a contract to grant a mortgage that complies with L.P.(M.P.)A. 1989, s.2: see *ante*, para. 19–039.

[81] *Re Alcock* (1883) 23 Ch.D. 372 at 376.

[82] *Bovill v. Endle* [1896] 1 Ch. 648.

[83] *Hill v. Rowlands* [1897] 2 Ch. 361 at 363.

[84] *Edmonson v. Copland* [1911] 2 Ch. 301.

your proceedings, and here is payment: you cannot decline what you have demanded'."[85]

If the mortgagor gives six months' notice and fails to pay on the proper day, he must usually give a further six months' notice or pay six months' interest instead,[86] unless he can give a reasonable explanation of his failure to pay. If he can, it is enough if he gives reasonable notice, *e.g.* three months.[87]

3. Interest and costs. Even if the mortgage makes no provision for interest, the mortgagor, on redeeming, must pay interest on the loan, and the rate will, if necessary, be fixed by the court.[88] If a redemption action is brought the mortgagor must also pay the mortgagee's proper costs, including any expenses incurred for protecting his security.[89]   **19–149**

V. SALE IN LIEU OF REDEMPTION

Any person entitled to redeem may apply to the court for an order for sale, and is apparently entitled to such an order as of right.[90]   **19–150**

VI. "REDEEM UP, FORECLOSE DOWN"

1. Parties to action. The maxim "Redeem up, foreclose down" applies where there are several incumbrancers and one of them seeks by action to redeem a superior mortgage. The effect is best shown by an example. X has mortgaged his property successively to A, B, C, D and E, the mortgages ranking in that order; X thus ranks last, *e.g.* in claiming any surplus if the property is sold. Suppose that D wishes to redeem B, and owing to the complexity of the accounts or some other circumstance an action for redemption is begun. Before B can be redeemed, the exact amount due to him must be settled by the court. This amount, however, does not affect only B and D, for C, E and X are all concerned with the amount which has priority to their interests. Thus if the property were to be sold, C, E and X would all wish to know whether what B was entitled to was, say, £6,000 or £16,000, for upon that figure might depend their chances of receiving anything from the proceeds of sale. Consequently the court will insist upon their being made parties to D's action for redemption, so that they can be represented in the taking of the accounts between B and D and thus be bound by the final result.[91]   **19–151**

---

[85] *Bovill v. Endle, supra*, at 651, *per* Kekewich J.

[86] *Re Moss* (1885) 31 Ch.D. 90 at 94.

[87] *Cromwell Property Investment Co. Ltd v. Western & Toovey* [1934] Ch. 322.

[88] See *Cityland and Property (Holdings) Ltd v. Dabrah* [1968] Ch. 166. Even statute-barred interest must be paid: *post*, para. 21–073.

[89] See *Sinfield v. Sweet* [1967] 1 W.L.R. 1489. Though a charge on the property, the mortgagor is not personally liable for these expenses: *ibid.*

[90] L.P.A. 1925, s.91(1). See *Clarke v. Pannell* (1884) 29 S.J. 147; and see *ante*, paras 19–054, 19–086.

[91] This also protects B against a further taking of his account if a later incumbrancer should offer to redeem both B and D: *Johnson v. Holdsworth* (1850) 1 Sim. (N.S) 106 at 109.

19–152   **2. Rights of the parties.** It would, however, be unfair to give C, E and X
the trouble and expense of taking part in the action merely to watch accounts
being taken,[92] with the risk of a similar event taking place in the future. The
court therefore insists that the rights of all parties concerned in the action shall
be settled once and for all. A is not concerned[93]; it is immaterial to him what
is due to B, for A's mortgage has priority to B's. A, therefore, need not be
joined in the action,[94] and will be left undisturbed in his position of first
mortgagee.[95] But all the other parties are concerned, and the order of the court
will be that D shall redeem not only B, but also C, for both their mortgages
have priority to D's. E and X must also be disposed of, and that can be done
only by foreclosure: that is, each of them will have the opportunity of saving
his rights by paying off the prior mortgages concerned in the action, or of
asking for a sale, but if he does neither, he will be foreclosed.[96] "The natural
decree is, that the second mortgagee shall redeem the first mortgagee, and that
the mortgagor shall redeem him or stand foreclosed."[97] Thus if E and X fail
to redeem and are foreclosed, the final result will be that D, at the price of
redeeming B and C, now holds the equity of redemption subject only to the
first mortgage in favour of A.

19–153   **3. The principle.** The principle may be stated thus: a mortgagee who seeks
to redeem a prior mortgage by action must not only redeem any mortgages
standing between him and that prior mortgage,[98] but must also foreclose all
subsequent mortgagees and the mortgagor.[99] In short, "redeem up, foreclose
down".

19–154   **4. Limits to the principle.** It is important to notice that this principle has
no application to redemptions made out of court.[1] And there is no converse
rule "foreclose down; redeem up": a mortgagee who forecloses is under no
obligation to redeem any prior mortgages,[2] although he must foreclose all
subsequent mortgagees as well as the mortgagor.[3] In other words, for foreclosure the rule is simply "foreclose down": a mortgagee cannot foreclose a
subsequent mortgagee or the mortgagor unless he forecloses everyone beneath
him.[4]

---

[92] *Ramsbottom v. Wallis* (1835) 5 L.J. Ch. 92.
[93] *Slade v. Rigg* (1843) 3 Hare 35 at 38.
[94] *Rose v. Page* (1829) 2 Sim. 471; *Slade v. Rigg, supra.*
[95] *Brisco v. Kenrick* (1832) 1 L.J. Ch. 116; 1 Coop.t.Cott. 371.
[96] *Fell v. Brown* (1787) 2 Bro.C.C. 276 at 278.
[97] *ibid.*, at 278, *per* Lord Thurlow L.C.
[98] *Teevan v. Smith* (1882) 20 Ch.D. 724 at 729.
[99] *Farmer v. Curtis* (1829) 2 Sim. 466.
[1] See *Smith v. Green* (1844) 1 Coll.C.C. 555.
[2] *Richards v. Cooper* (1842) 5 Beav. 304.
[3] *Bishop of Winchester v. Beavor* (1797) 3 Ves. 314; *Anderson v. Stather* (1845) 2 Coll.C.C.
   209.
[4] *Cockes v. Sherman* (1676) Free.Ch. 13.

VII. TERMINATION OF EQUITY OF REDEMPTION

An equity of redemption may be extinguished against the mortgagor's   **19–155**
will—

(i) by foreclosure[5];

(ii) by sale[6]; or

(iii) by lapse of time.[7]

In addition, the mortgagor may himself extinguish it by releasing it to the
mortgagee,[8] or by redeeming.

B. Right to Bring Actions

1. Mortgagor's right to sue. A mortgagor's right to bring actions of   **19–156**
various kinds needs special consideration, since he is normally left in possession of the property but has not immediate legal title to possession as against
the mortgagee. As against third parties, *e.g.* trespassers or neighbours committing nuisances, the mortgagor, like any other person lawfully in possession of
land, could sue at common law to protect that possession,[9] and thus, *e.g.*
recover the land from anyone other than the mortgagee or someone claiming
through him. In equity, he was regarded as owner of the land, subject to the
mortgage, and so could obtain equitable remedies (such as an injunction[10])
against any person, *e.g.* to prevent injury to the property,[11] or to enforce a
restrictive covenant.[12]

2. Action as landlord. Difficulties arose, however, when the right of action   **19–157**
depended on the legal relationship of landlord and tenant, for example in the
case of actions for rent or to enforce covenants against tenants to whom the
land had been let before the date of the mortgage.[13] In such cases the mortgage
was of course an assignment of the reversion, and thereafter the covenants
became enforceable by the mortgagee only.[14] Moreover the court would only
allow the mortgagor to sue in the mortgagee's name if the mortgagor offered

---

[5] *Ante*, para. 19–049.

[6] *Ante*, para. 19–056.

[7] *Post*, para. 21–035.

[8] *e.g. Knight v. Marjoribanks* (1849) 2 Mac. & G. 10; *Reeve v. Lisle* [1902] A.C. 461; see *ante*,
para. 19–129.

[9] See *ante*, paras 3–117, 3–118, where the possessory nature of title to land is explained.

[10] *Van Gelder, Apsimon & Co. v. Sowerby Bridge United District Flour Society* (1890) 44 Ch.D.
374.

[11] *Matthews v. Usher* [1900] 2 Q.B. 535 at 538; *Turner v. Walsh* [1909] 2 K.B. 484 at 487.

[12] *Fairclough v. Marshall* (1878) 4 Ex.D. 37.

[13] If the mortgage was made before the lease the mortgagor could of course sue: *Turner v. Walsh,
supra*, at 495. As to the nature and effect of such leases, which operate by estoppel, see *ante*,
paras 14–102, 19–112.

[14] *Turner v. Walsh, supra*, at 495; *Matthews v. Usher* [1900] 2 Q.B. 535. For the general law, see
ante, paras 15–004, 15–007.

to redeem,[15] though without doing this he could distrain for rent as agent of the mortgagee.[16]

This difficulty is now remedied by statute.[17] Provided that the mortgagee has not given effective notice of his intention to take possession or enter into receipt of the rents and profits,[18] the mortgagor in possession may—

(i) sue in his own name for possession or for the rent and profits;

(ii) bring an action to prevent, or recover damages for, any trespass or other wrong[19]; and

(iii) enforce all covenants and conditions in leases of the property.[20]

C. Rights to Relief and Other Rights

I. EXTORTIONATE CREDIT BARGAINS

19–158   The mortgagor has the right to seek relief from an extortionate credit bargain.[21] This right is conferred by the Consumer Credit Act 1974, which defines an extortionate credit bargain as one which requires the debtor or a relative of his to make payments which are "grossly exorbitant", or which otherwise "grossly contravenes ordinary principles of fair dealing".[22] The court must have regard to all relevant considerations, including prevailing rates of interest,[23] the mortgagor's age, experience, state of health and business capacity and any financial pressure upon him.[24] This definition is a comprehensive one, and in determining whether a bargain is extortionate, the courts will not look outside the Act to the equitable jurisdiction to relieve against unconscionable bargains.[25] A transaction will not be set aside merely because it is unwise. "The jurisdiction seems to . . . contemplate at least a substantial imbalance in bargaining power of which one party has taken

---

[15] *Turner v. Walsh, supra,* at 495, 496.
[16] *Trent v. Hunt* (1853) 9 Exch. 14.
[17] L.P.A. 1925, ss.98, 141 (where the lease was granted prior to 1996), L. & T.C.A. 1995, s.15 (where the lease was granted after 1995).
[18] Proceedings for possession which by a technical defect are a nullity do not suffice: *Kitchen's Trustee v. Madders* [1949] Ch. 588, aff'd [1950] Ch. 134.
[19] L.P.A. 1925, s.98(1). For the limits of this, see *Turner v. Walsh, supra.*
[20] L.P.A. 1925, s.141(2) (leases granted prior to 1996); L. & T.C.A. 1995, s.15 (leases granted after 1995).
[21] See [1989] Conv. 164; 234 (L. Bently and G. G. Howells).
[22] s.138. For the jurisdiction to set aside an extortionate credit bargain entered into within three years of the commencement of: (i) a corporation's winding up; and (ii) an individual's bankruptcy, see respectively I.A. 1986, ss.244, 343.
[23] See *Davies v. Directloans Ltd* [1986] 1 W.L.R. 823 at 834–836. In examining the rate of interest, the court will have regard to the credit record of the debtor and the risk to the lender: see, *e.g. Woodstead Finance Ltd v. Petrou (sub nom. Petrou v. Woodstead Finance Ltd)* 1986 F.L.R. 158 (42 per cent not extortionate given the debtor's "appalling record").
[24] Consumer Credit Act 1974, s.138.
[25] *Davies v. Directloans Ltd, supra,* at 831. For this equitable jurisdiction, see *post,* para. 19–176.

advantage."[26] If found extortionate, the agreement may be reopened by the court at the instance of the debtor or a surety,[27] and the court may relieve either of them from any payment in excess of what is fairly due and reasonable[28] and may alter the terms of the agreement or the security.[29] These provisions are not restricted by any financial limit such as the Act imposes for other purposes.[30] The only exemption is where the debtor is a corporation.[31] The burden of proof is on the creditor.[32]

Because a mortgage involves the provision of financial services, certain terms may not be enforceable against the mortgagor if they are "unfair" for the purposes of the Unfair Terms in Consumer Contracts Regulations 1994.[32a] A detailed consideration of these Regulations lies outside the scope of this book.[32b] However, it may be noted here that they will apply to terms in a mortgage which have not been individually negotiated[32c] where—

> (i) the mortgagee supplies financial services whilst acting for purposes relating to his business; and

> (ii) the mortgagor, in making the contract, is acting for purposes which are outside his business.[32d]

II. MORTGAGES VITIATED BY NOTICE OF FRAUD, MISREPRESENTATION OR UNDUE INFLUENCE

A mortgagor may have a right to have the mortgage set aside because it was induced by fraud or undue influence. The issue commonly arises nowadays in   **19–159**

---

[26] *Wills v. Wood* [1984] C.C.L.R. 7 at 15, *per* Donaldson M.R. If the lender has been implicated in any fraudulent conduct, this may constitute a gross contravention of the principles of fair dealing: *Coldunell Ltd v. Gallon* [1986] Q.B. 1184 at 1211.

[27] In *Castle Phillips Finance Co. Ltd v. Williams* [1986] C.C.L.R. 13, the debtor failed to plead an extortionate credit bargain, but the court referred the papers to the Director General of Fair Trading for him to consider whether any action was required against the lender under the Consumer Credit Act 1974 (including revocation of its licence).

[28] The court has no power under this provision to relieve a person from an obligation to convey property: *J.A. Pye (Oxford) Estates Ltd v. Ambrose* [1994] N.P.C. 53 (transcript, p. 41).

[29] Consumer Credit Act 1974, ss.137, 139. In *A. Ketley Ltd v. Scott* [1981] I.C.R. 241, the court refused relief where the debtor was an experienced businessman, legally advised, who wanted to complete a house purchase the same day and agreed to pay interest at 12 per cent for three months, equivalent to 48 per cent. The debtor's application for the loan had in fact been deceitful. A credit bargain may be extortionate even if the rate of interest does not exceed 48 per cent: *Castle Phillips Finance Co. Ltd v. Williams, supra*, at 20.

[30] *Ante*, para. 19–042.

[31] Consumer Credit Act 1974, s.137(2). However, where a corporation was in receipt of credit under an extortionate credit bargain within three years of its being wound up, the court has similar powers to those conferred by the 1974 Act: see I.A. 1986, s.244.

[32] Consumer Credit Act 1974, s.171(7). See *Coldunell Ltd v. Gallon* [1986] Q.B. 1184.

[32a] S.I. 1994 No. 3159, implementing EC Council Directive 93/13. It is now clear that mortgages are within the scope of the Regulations: see (1999) 115 L.Q.R. 360 (S. Bright). See too (1995) 111 L.Q.R. 655 (S. and C. Bright). For what constitutes unfairness, see reg. 4.

[32b] For a detailed consideration, see G. H. Treitel, *The Law of Contract* (10th ed.), pp. 244–258.

[32c] reg. 3(1).

[32d] reg. 2(1).

a case where the mortgagor has been induced to agree to its execution by the fraud, misrepresentation or undue influence of the debtor whose liability is secured by the mortgage. The same problem arises where a person either guarantees a debt, or cedes priority to a mortgagee over his rights in the property charged, having been similarly induced to act. The typical situation is where the matrimonial home is jointly owned, the husband seeks to mortgage it as security for his business debts, and induces his wife to agree to the charge.[33] When the mortgagee comes to enforce its security, the question arises as to whether the wife is bound by the charge. The legal principles governing this situation were in some confusion until two decisions of the House of Lords, delivered at the same time, *Barclays Bank Plc v. O'Brien*[34] and *C.I.B.C. Mortgages Plc v. Pitt*[35] in which the earlier authorities were largely rejected and the law was restated according to first principles.[36]

19–160   **1. The basis of liability.** In those two cases, the House of Lords established that a mortgage[37] or guarantee could not be enforced against the surety if it had been procured by the fraud, misrepresentation or undue influence of the principal debtor[38] and either—

(i) the principal debtor was acting as agent for the creditor in securing the agreement of the surety; or

(ii) the facts were such as to put the creditor on notice of the risk of such wrongdoing, and it failed to take adequate steps to ensure that the surety received independent legal advice as to the risks that he was running.[39]

In a number of cases prior to *O'Brien* and *Pitt*, it had been held that a creditor was liable if the principal debtor had been acting in some sense as its agent

---

[33] These cases are, in a sense, a sequel to the decision in *Williams & Glyn's Bank Ltd v. Boland* [1981] A.C. 487; *ante*, para. 6–061. It has been the practice of mortgagees since that case to require that any person who has (or may have) a beneficial interest in the property should either be a party to the mortgage or agree to subordinate their rights to the lender.

[34] [1994] 1 A.C. 180 ("*O'Brien*").

[35] [1994] 1 A.C. 200 ("*Pitt*"). The cases are noted at (1994) 110 L.Q.R. 167 (J. R. F. Lehane); [1994] C.L.J. 21 (M. Dixon); (1995) 15 O.J.L.S. 119 (S. H. Goo). There is an important summary of the law and practice as it has since developed in *Royal Bank of Scotland Plc v. Etridge (No. 2)* [1998] 4 All E.R. 705 at 710 *et seq*.

[36] There is a considerable literature on this subject: see especially (1995) 15 L.S. 35 (G. Battersby); [1995] L.M.C.L.Q. 346 (R. Hooley); (1995) 7 C.F.L.Q. 104 (M. Oldham); [1995] C.L.J. 280 (A. Lawson); [1997] C.L.J. 60 (M. Chen-Wishart); and [1998] J.B.L. 355 (M. Haley).

[37] Or a waiver of prior proprietary rights in favour of the mortgagee, to which the same principles apply: see *Banco Exterior Internacional v. Mann* [1995] 1 All E.R. 936 at 942; *Halifax B.S. v. Brown* [1996] 1 F.L.R. 103 at 112–115.

[38] It is not necessary that the principal debtor who is responsible for the wrongdoing should be a party to the transaction between the surety and the creditor: see *Banco Exterior Internacional S.A. v. Thomas* [1997] 1 W.L.R. 221 at 229. It is therefore immaterial whether the mortgage is of property owned by the surety alone or concurrently with the principal debtor.

[39] For a clear summary of the principles, see *National Bank of Abu Dhabi v. Mohamed* (1997) 30 H.L.R. 383 at 391.

when he improperly obtained the surety's consent.[40] Such a finding of agency was contrary to the true position, namely that the creditor required the principal debtor to provide a surety, and the principal debtor acted for himself in procuring the concurrence of that surety.[41] It is clear from *O'Brien* that although there *may* be situations where the principal debtor was indeed acting for the creditor in procuring the surety's assent, "such cases will be of very rare occurrence".[42] The security will usually be impugned because the creditor had notice of the principal debtor's improper conduct in securing it.

2. Undue influence, fraud or misrepresentation. The first element that   **19–161**
must be established is that the surety was induced to execute the mortgage (or to agree to subordinate his rights in favour of the mortgagee) by undue influence, fraud or misrepresentation.[43] In a number of cases, the principal debtor has either failed to disclose or has misrepresented to the surety the extent of his liability.[44] In most, however, the surety's consent has been obtained by undue influence. There are two types of undue influence, presumed and actual.

(a) Presumed undue influence. Undue influence will be presumed—   **19–162**

    (i) as a matter of law from certain relationships such as doctor and patient, solicitor and client, religious superior and inferior; and

    (ii) as a matter of fact where one person reposed trust and confidence in another[45];

provided that the party alleging undue influence can show that the transaction was to his manifest disadvantage.[46] This last requirement is, however, controversial.[47] The presumption of undue influence can be rebutted by showing that the party alleged to have been influenced had entered into the transaction freely and as an exercise of independent will.[48]

---

[40] See *B.C.C.I. International S.A. v. Aboody* [1990] 1 Q.B. 923, where the authorities are reviewed.

[41] *O'Brien* [1994] 1 A.C. 180 at 194.

[42] *ibid.*, at 195, *per* Lord Browne-Wilkinson. See too *Bradford & Bingley B.S. v. Chandock* (1996) 72 P. & C.R. D28 at D29.

[43] *O'Brien, supra*, at 198.

[44] See, *e.g. O'Brien, supra; T.S.B. Bank Plc v. Camfield* [1995] 1 W.L.R. 430; *Bank Melli Iran v. Samadi-Rad* [1995] 2 F.L.R. 367.

[45] See *Steeples v. Lea* [1998] 1 F.L.R. 138 at 141.

[46] *National Westminster Bank Plc v. Morgan* [1985] A.C. 686 at 706. *cf. Goldsworthy v. Brickell* [1987] Ch. 378 at 401; *Petrou v. Woodstead Finance Ltd* 1986 F.L.R. 158.

[47] See (1985) 48 M.L.R. 579 (D. Tiplady). See *B.C.C.I. International S.A. v. Aboody* [1990] 1 Q.B. 923 at 962–964; *Pitt* [1994] 1 A.C. 200 at 209 for the difficulties of reconciling the requirement of manifest disadvantage with the authorities on abuse of confidence. See too *Royal Bank of Scotland Plc v. Etridge (No. 2)* [1998] 4 All E.R. 705 at 713.

[48] Commonly this will be shown by proving that the complainant received independent advice: see *Inche Noriah v. Shaik Allie Bin Omar* [1929] A.C. 127 at 135. However, "taking independent advice is neither always necessary nor always sufficient to rebut the presumption of undue influence": *Claughton v. Price* (1997) 30 H.L.R. 396 at 408, *per* Nourse L.J.

19–163   *(b) Actual undue influence.* In cases where there is no presumption of undue influence, the party influenced will have to prove actual undue influence by showing that—

      (i) the party who induced the transaction had the capacity to influence him;

      (ii) influence was exercised;

      (iii) it was undue; and

      (iv) its exercise brought about the transaction.[49]

Actual undue influence is a species of fraud. If, therefore, these four elements are established, the party influenced is entitled to have the transaction set aside. He does not have to show additionally that the transaction was manifestly disadvantageous to him.[50]

19–164   **3. Notice of the wrongdoing.** The second element that must be shown to make the creditor liable is that he had notice of the fraud, misrepresentation or undue influence. This will depend upon three closely interconnected factors.

19–165   *(a) The nature of the transaction.* In general, the creditor will not be put on inquiry unless, by the transaction, the surety makes himself responsible in some way to the creditor for the debts of the principal debtor.[51] By contrast, where a lender makes a joint advance to A and B on the security of their co-owned property, the transaction is not usually of a kind to put him on notice that A may have acted improperly to induce B to agree to it.[52] However, even in the case of a joint advance, the circumstances may be such as to put the lender on inquiry.[53]

19–166   *(b) Whether the transaction was to the financial disadvantage of the surety.* The creditor will be put on inquiry if "the transaction is on its face not to the financial advantage" of the surety,[54] as where the surety guarantees the debts of the principal debtor[55] or subordinates his rights in the property to those of

---

[49] *B.C.C.I. International S.A. v. Aboody, supra,* at 967.

[50] *Pitt, supra,* at 208, 209, overruling (on this point) *B.C.C.I. International S.A. v. Aboody, supra.* There cannot be both actual *and* presumed undue influence: the situations in which they arise are mutually exclusive: *Bank of Scotland v. Bennett* (1998) 77 P. & C.R. 447 at 465.

[51] *Pitt, supra,* at 211.

[52] *ibid.*

[53] *Infra.*

[54] *O'Brien* [1994] 1 A.C. 180 at 196, *per* Lord Browne-Wilkinson. In determining whether this is so, the court must necessarily look at the transaction through the eyes of the creditor, having regard to the facts known to it: see *Bank of Scotland v. Bennett, supra,* at 469. In other words, the transaction must *in fact* be manifestly disadvantageous (which, according to *Bank of Cyprus (London) Ltd v. Markou* [1999] 2 All E.R. 707 at 717, is determined by reference to the positions of the debtor and the surety) *and* must also appear to the creditor to be so on its face. Only then will a creditor be put on inquiry: see *Bank of Scotland v. Bennett, supra,* at 470.

[55] See, *e.g. Bank of Baroda v. Rayarel* [1995] 2 F.L.R. 376.

the creditor.[56] Where, by contrast, the transaction is a joint loan for a purpose that is apparently for the benefit of both the borrowers, the creditor will not be put on inquiry.[57] In a number of cases, a wife has made herself liable in some way for a loan made to a family company in which she has a shareholding. Where the family income is derived from the company, the provision of security by the wife "cannot be said to be extravagantly or even necessarily improvident".[57a] However, the transaction may, nonetheless, be to her financial disadvantage if it is a particularly hazardous one,[58] or if her liability is disproportionate to her interest in the company.[59] In such circumstances, the creditor will not be exonerated from inquiry.[60]

The creditor will not be under any liability if the transaction is not in fact to the surety's financial disadvantage even if on its face it appeared to be, and so should have put the creditor on inquiry.[61]

(c) The relationship between the principal debtor and the surety. The **19–167** creditor will be put on inquiry if the character of the transaction is such that there is a substantial risk that the principal debtor has committed a legal or equitable wrong in procuring a person to act as surety, and that wrong is one that entitles the surety to set aside the transaction.[62] If the two preceding factors are present, it will be the nature of the relationship that will determine whether or not that risk exists. In *O'Brien*, the House of Lords was concerned with the position of a wife who acted as surety for her husband's debts (as have most subsequent decisions). The House indicated that "the same principles are applicable to all other cases where there is an emotional relationship between cohabitees".[63] This was because of "the underlying risk of one cohabitee exploiting the emotional involvement and trust of the other".[64] In

---

[56] See, *e.g. Banco Exterior Internacional v. Mann* [1995] 1 All E.R. 936; *Halifax B.S. v. Brown* [1996] 1 F.L.R. 103.

[57] *Pitt* [1994] 1 A.C. 200 at 211; *Britannia B.S. v. Pugh* (1996) 29 H.L.R. 423; *Birmingham Midshires Mortgage Services v. Mahal* (1996) 73 P. & C.R. D7; *Dunbar Bank Plc v. Nadeem* [1998] 3 All E.R. 876; *Davies v. Norwich Union Life Insurance Society* (1998) 78 P. & C.R. 119. See too *Society of Lloyd's v. Khan* [1999] 1 F.L.R. 246 (wife became a name at Lloyd's on her husband's direction: transaction not manifestly disadvantageous).

[57a] *Bank of Scotland v. Bennett, supra*, at 469, *per* Chadwick L.J.

[58] *Nightingale Finance Ltd v. Scott* [1997] E.G.C.S. 161 (the creditor also knew that the wife relied entirely on her husband).

[59] Compare *Goode Durrant Administration v. Biddulph* (1994) 26 H.L.R. 625 (wife had 2.5 per cent interest in the company, but was potentially liable for more than £300,000: transaction not for her financial benefit) with *Barclays Bank Plc v. Sumner* [1996] E.G.C.S. 65 (wife had 50 per cent interest in the company, and was jointly liable on an unlimited guarantee: transaction not disadvantageous). *cf.* [1994] Fam. Law 675 (S. Cretney) and see *Bank of Scotland v. Bennett, supra*.

[60] *Bank of Scotland v. Bennett* [1997] 1 F.L.R. 801 at 832. The decision in that case was, however, reversed on appeal on its facts: see (1998) 77 P. & C.R. 447.

[61] *Scotlife Home Loans (No. 2) Ltd v. Hedworth* (1995) 28 H.L.R. 771 (loan granted for husband's "business purposes" in fact used to discharge existing mortgages on the family home).

[62] *O'Brien* [1994] 1 A.C. 180 at 196. This will be judged according to the circumstances known to the creditor at the time of the transaction: *Scottish Equitable Life Plc v. Virdee* [1999] 1 F.L.R. 863 at 866.

[63] *O'Brien, supra*, at 198, *per* Lord Browne-Wilkinson.

[64] *ibid.* Lord Browne-Wilkinson made it clear that the cohabitation might be heterosexual or homosexual.

fact, in subsequent authorities, the principles have been applied where there was no cohabitation and where the relationship between the parties was one of trust rather than an emotional one. Apart from the usual case where a wife acted as surety for her husband's debts, other relationships which have been either held or alleged to put a creditor on inquiry include the following—

(i) where a husband acted as surety for his wife's debts[65];

(ii) where a woman charged her house as surety for her (male) lover with whom she did not cohabit[66];

(iii) where a woman charged her house as surety for the borrowings of a close (male) friend[67];

(iv) where a junior employee mortgaged her house as security for her employer's indebtedness[68];

(v) where a father charged his property to secure a loan to his son[69]; and

(vi) where a sister mortgaged her home as principal debtor to secure a loan for her brother.[69a]

It is clear from these cases that a creditor will now be put upon inquiry whenever he knows that the surety had such trust and confidence in the principal debtor that undue influence would be presumed between them.[70] The creditor's obligation to make inquiry is not confined to cases where he knows that the relationship between surety and principal debtor is a sexual one.[71]

4. The effect of notice

(a) Ensuring informed consent to the transaction

19–168   (1) WHERE THERE IS A POSSIBILITY OF FRAUD OR UNDUE INFLUENCE. Where the creditor has notice that the surety's consent to the proposed transaction may be obtained by fraud or undue influence, he is not expected to inquire of the surety whether he has in fact been unduly influenced or misled by the

---

[65] *Barclays Bank Plc v. Rivett* (1997) 29 H.L.R. 893.
[66] *Massey v. Midland Bank Plc* [1995] 1 All E.R. 929.
[67] *Banco Exterior Internacional S.A. v. Thomas* [1997] 1 W.L.R. 221 (the relationship "was neither a romantic nor a sexual one": *ibid.*, at 224, *per* Scott V.-C.).
[68] *Credit Lyonnais Bank Nederland N.V. v. Burch* [1997] 1 All E.R. 144; *Steeples v. Lea* [1998] 1 F.L.R. 138.
[69] *UCB Bank Plc v. Sharif* [1997] E.G.C.S. 52 (creditor not fixed with notice of any undue influence on the facts). See too *Avon Finance Co. Ltd v. Bridger* (1979) [1985] 2 All E.R. 281 (elderly parents induced by misrepresentation to stand surety for their son); approved in *O'Brien* [1994] 1 A.C. 180 at 198.
[69a] *Northern Rock B.S. v. Archer* (1998) 78 P. & C.R. 65.
[70] See *ante*, para. 19–162.
[71] *Credit Lyonnais Bank Nederland N.V. v. Burch, supra*, at 155.

principal debtor.[72] He must instead seek to neutralise the effect of any such fraud or undue influence by taking reasonable steps to ensure that the surety enters into the transaction freely and with full knowledge of the true facts.[73] If he does not do this, he will be unable to enforce his security against the surety.[74] As regards any transaction entered into after the decision in *O'Brien*, the House of Lords has made it clear what is expected of a creditor. He must—

(i) warn the surety (at a meeting not attended by the principal creditor) of the amount of his potential liability and of the risks involved, and

(ii) advise him to obtain independent legal advice.[75]

The House was mindful of the need to balance the protection of the vulnerable against the danger of making the matrimonial home unacceptable as security for financial institutions.[76]

As regards transactions that had taken place prior to the *O'Brien* decision, their validity is judged according to whether the creditor had taken reasonable steps to bring home to the surety the risks that he was running, and had advised him to take independent advice.[77]

(2) WHERE THERE IS A PROBABILITY OF UNDUE INFLUENCE. Whether the transaction took place before or after *O'Brien*, the House accepted that there might be exceptional cases where the creditor knew that undue influence was probable rather than merely possible. In such a case, the creditor would have to insist that the surety took separate advice.[78] This may be the best explanation of two cases in each of which a junior employee guaranteed the debts of her employer without independent legal advice, and the mortgage was set aside.[79] Indeed there may be some cases so extreme that even where the surety receives independent legal advice, the creditor will still be regarded as having **19–169**

---

[72] *O'Brien* [1994] 1 A.C. 180 at 196. To make such an inquiry would be "plainly impossible": *per* Lord Browne-Wilkinson.

[73] See [1995] L.M.C.L.Q. 346 at 356 (R. Hooley); [1995] C.L.J. 536 (J. Mee).

[74] *O'Brien, supra,* at 196, 198. This reflected recommended practice for banks and building societies in the Code of Banking Practice (1992). The current version of the Code was issued in 1997.

[75] *O'Brien, supra,* at 196, 197, 199. In fact, creditors do not hold a private meeting with the surety, but insist that he obtains independent legal advice and that this is confirmed in writing. This goes beyond what was required in *O'Brien*, and is therefore acceptable: see *Royal Bank of Scotland Plc v. Etridge (No. 2)* [1998] 4 All E.R. 705 at 720.

[76] *O'Brien, supra,* at 188. See too *Pitt* [1994] 1 A.C. 200 at 211; *Scotlife Home Loans (No. 2) Ltd v. Hedworth* (1995) 28 H.L.R. 771 at 782.

[77] *O'Brien, supra,* at 196.

[78] *ibid.,* at 197.

[79] *Credit Lyonnais Bank Nederland N.V. v. Burch* [1997] 1 All E.R. 144; *Steeples v. Lea* [1998] 1 F.L.R. 138.

constructive notice of the undue influence.[80] This will be the case if the transaction is one into which no competent solicitor could advise the surety to enter.[80a]

19–170   *(b) Independent legal advice.* In all the cases that have arisen to date, the transactions have pre-dated the *O'Brien* decision, and the issue has been whether, on the facts as they appeared to the creditor,[81] he had taken sufficient steps to warn the surety and to encourage him to take independent advice.[82] He will have done if he has ensured that the surety received independent legal advice.[83] A creditor will not be absolved from liability even if the surety does take independent legal advice if either he is in possession of material information not available to the solicitor advising the surety.[84] However, the creditor is not required either—

   (i) to inquire into the relationship between the principal debtor and the surety and the latter's motives for agreeing to guarantee the debt[85]; or

   (ii) to ensure that the surety actually *takes* independent advice even though urged to do so,[86] except in those rare cases where there is a *probability* of undue influence.[87]

Where the surety does take legal advice, it will be regarded as independent even when it is given by the solicitor acting for the creditor or the principal debtor.[88] The creditor is entitled to assume that appropriate advice has been properly given.[89] The courts have rejected the view that, in such cases, the

---

[80] See *Credit Lyonnais Bank Nederland N.V. v. Burch, supra,* at 156; *Barclays Bank Plc v. Caplan* [1998] 1 F.L.R. 532 at 545 (where Deputy Judge Sumption, Q.C., characterised such cases as those where "no chargor who understood the transaction could possibly enter into it".

[80a] *Royal Bank of Scotland Plc v. Etridge (No. 2)* [1998] 4 All E.R. 705 at 722.

[81] This is the test: see *Banco Exterior Internacional v. Mann* [1995] 1 All E.R. 936 at 944.

[82] The absence of a private meeting between the surety and creditor, although not good practice, was held not to be fatal where the surety obtained independent legal advice: see *Massey v. Midland Bank Plc* [1995] 1 All E.R. 929 at 934. In transactions after *O'Brien,* such a meeting is in practice unusual. The creditor insists instead that the surety obtain independent legal advice: *Royal Bank of Scotland Plc v. Etridge (No. 2), supra,* at 720; *ante,* para. 19–168.

[83] *National Bank of Abu Dhabi v. Mohamed* (1997) 30 H.L.R. 383. Independent advice means advice in relation to the surety's own position *vis-à-vis* both the creditor and the debtor: see *Northern Rock B.S. v. Archer* (1998) 78 P. & C.R. 65 at 76.

[84] *Royal Bank of Scotland Plc v. Etridge (No. 2)* [1998] 4 All E.R. 705 at 722.

[85] *Banco Exterior Internacional S.A. v. Thomas* [1997] 1 W.L.R. 221 at 230.

[86] *Massey v. Midland Bank Plc, supra,* at 934, 935; *Birmingham Midshires Mortgage Services v. Mahal* (1996) 73 P. & C.R. D7; *Turner v. Barclays Bank Plc* [1997] 2 F.C.R. 151.

[87] *Supra.*

[88] See *Midland Bank Plc v. Serter* (1995) 71 P. & C.R. 264; *Bradford & Bingley B.S. v. Chandock* (1996) 72 P. & C.R. D28; *Barclays Bank Plc v. Thomson* [1997] 4 All E.R. 816. *cf.* [1997] Conv. 216 (M. P. Thompson).

[89] *Bank of Baroda v. Shah* [1988] 3 All E.R. 24 at 29, 31; *Massey v. Midland Bank Plc, supra,* at 935; *Bank of Baroda v. Rayarel* [1995] 2 F.L.R. 376; *Bank of Scotland v. Bennett* [1997] 1 F.L.R. 801 at 833, 834. This is so even if the confirmation that independent advice has been given comes from the creditor's solicitor rather then directly from the surety's: see *Scottish Equitable Life Plc v. Virdee* [1999] 1 F.L.R. 863 at 866.

solicitor may still be regarded as the creditor's agent.[90] The creditor will not therefore be fixed with notice of anything that the solicitor discovers while advising the surety, because the matter does not come to the solicitor's notice while acting as the creditor's agent.[91] This approach has not escaped criticism.[92] The Court of Appeal has now issued detailed guidance as to the steps that should be taken to ensure that the risks are brought home to the surety.[93] This guidance highlights the difficult position that now faces any solicitor who is asked to give independent advice to an intending surety. For example, if the solicitor considers that the transaction is one into which the surety should not enter, he should so advise the client. He should then inform the creditor that he has given "certain advice" and has declined to act further for the surety.[93a] The creditor is unlikely to proceed with the transaction in those circumstances.

5. The function of notice. It is the creditor's actual or constructive notice   **19–171** "of the facts on which the equity to set aside the transaction is founded" that will vitiate the mortgage or waiver of rights in his favour.[94] Such notice implicates him in the principal debtor's undue influence or other wrongdoing.[95] In other words, where C (the creditor) enters into a transaction[96] with B (the surety) where he has notice that B was induced to do so by the wrongdoing of A (the principal debtor), the transaction will be voidable by B.[97] That is, of course, very different from the situation where A transfers property to C who claims to take free of B's rights in the property as a purchaser without notice.[98] The distinction is an important one but it was not

---

[90] *Barclays Bank Plc v. Thomson, supra; National Westminster Bank Plc v. Beaton* (1997) 30 H.L.R. 99; *Royal Bank of Scotland Plc v. Etridge, supra*, at 721; [1997] J.B.L. 220 (M. Haley).

[91] See L.P.A. 1925, s.199(1)(ii)(b) (*ante*, para. 5–023); *Halifax Mortgage Services Ltd v. Stepsky* [1996] Ch. 207; *Birmingham Midshires Mortgage Services v. Mahal, supra; Barclays Bank Plc v. Thomson, supra*, at 828, 829; *National Westminster Bank Plc v. Beaton, supra; Leamington Spa B.S. v. Verdi* (1997) 75 P. & C.R. D16. This approach is preferable to but not easy to reconcile with earlier authority: see *Dryden v. Frost* (1838) 3 My. & Cr. 670; *Kennedy v. Green* (1834) 3 My. & K. 699; *Lloyds Bank Ltd v. Marcan* [1973] 1 W.L.R. 339 at 348; *ante*, para. 5–023.

[92] It has been said that creditor's assumption that the surety has received adequate legal advice is one which the creditor "almost always knows to be false": (1998) 114 L.Q.R. 214 at 220 (Sir Peter Millett).

[93] [1998] 4 All E.R. 705. See [1998] Fam. Law 665 (S. Cretney); [1999] C.L.J. 28 (S. Bridge).

[93a] *Royal Bank of Scotland Plc v. Etridge (No. 2), supra*, at 715. This notionally respects the confidentiality of the advice while in fact telling the creditor that he has advised against the transaction.

[94] *Barclays Bank Plc v. Boulter* [1998] 1 W.L.R. 1 at 11, *per* Mummery L.J. As explained *ante*, para. 19–168, the effect of such notice can be neutralised if the creditor takes reasonable steps to ensure that the surety seeks independent advice.

[95] *O'Sullivan v. Management Agency and Music Ltd* [1985] Q.B. 428 at 464.

[96] Whether a mortgage or a waiver of rights.

[97] *Post*, para. 19–173.

[98] This distinction was made in [1994] Conv. 421 (M. Dixon and C.H.); (1995) 15 L.S. 35 (G. Battersby). See too *Barclays Bank Plc v. Boulter, supra*, at 8, 9.

appreciated by some commentators. It was initially suggested that the principle in the *O'Brien* case could not apply to registered land, where the doctrine
of the purchaser for value without notice has no application.[99] However, it has
now been settled that the analysis given above is the correct one, and "it is
irrelevant whether the land is registered or unregistered".[1]

19–172   6. Pleading and burden of proof. The surety must adequately plead, and
bears the burden of proving, that the creditor had notice of the undue influence
or other wrongdoing.[2] The onus of proof will be discharged by the surety
showing that the creditor knew of the relationship between the surety and the
debtor, that the transaction was to the surety's financial disadvantage, and that
there was, therefore, a risk that the surety's consent had been obtained
improperly.[3]

7. Relief

19–173   (a) Rescission ab initio where the surety receives no benefit. Where a
creditor is held to have notice of the principal debtor's fraud or undue
influence, then subject to the usual discretionary bars (such as delay or
acquiescence), a surety who has gained no benefit from the transaction is
entitled to rescind it.[4] Thus where a wife agreed to a mortgage of the
matrimonial home on the basis of a misrepresentation by her husband that the
maximum liability would be £15,000, when it was in fact unlimited, the wife
was able to rescind the mortgage and was not liable even for £15,000.[5]
Because this principle applies only where the surety has received no benefits
from the transaction, there are none which he has to restore to the creditor to
achieve *restitutio in integrum*.[6]

There may, however, be exceptional cases where it is possible to sever one
part of an agreement that is not vitiated by fraud or undue influence from
another part that is, so that only the latter is struck down. This could happen
where an existing and valid charge is subsequently extended to cover further

---

[99] See [1994] Conv. 140 (M. P. Thompson). For the inapplicability of the doctrine of notice to
registered land, see *ante*, paras 4–072, 5–006. *cf.* [1995] Conv. 250 (P. Sparkes).

[1] *Barclays Bank Plc v. Boulter, supra*, at 11, *per* Mummery L.J., preferring the view expressed
in [1994] Conv. 421.

[2] *Barclays Bank Plc v. Boulter*, HL, unreported, October 21, 1999, affirming the Court of Appeal
([1998] 1 W.L.R. 1) on the facts but reversing it on the law.

[3] *Barclays Bank Plc v. Boulter, supra*, where Lord Hoffmann illustrated the point by reference
to the common case where a wife acts as surety for her husband's indebtedness.

[4] *T.S.B. Bank Plc v. Camfield* [1995] 1 W.L.R. 430 (resolving conflicting decisions at first
instance); (1995) 111 L.Q.R. 555 (P. Ferguson).

[5] *ibid.* See too *O'Brien* [1994] 1 A.C. 180 (husband misrepresented to wife that liability on the
mortgage was limited to £60,000, whereas it was unlimited).

[6] *cf. T.S.B. Bank Plc v. Camfield, supra*, at 434; *MacKenzie v. Royal Bank of Canada* [1934] A.C.
468 at 476 (a case in which there had been a misrepresentation by the *creditor* to the
surety).

indebtedness and where that extension is vitiated by fraud or undue influence of which the creditor has notice.[7]

(b) Rescission on terms where the surety has received some benefit. Where **19–174** the surety has received some benefit from the transaction, rescission will be given on the usual basis that the surety makes counter restitution.[8] Thus, where a husband applied part of a loan from the creditor to discharge an earlier mortgage of the matrimonial home to which his wife had been a willing party, the creditor was subrogated to that earlier mortgage, notwithstanding the husband's misrepresentation of which the creditor had notice.[9]

(c) Where rescission is impossible. Circumstances could arise in which **19–175** rescission might be impossible, as where the surety raised the issue of fraud or undue influence by the principal debtor only after the creditor had enforced his security by selling the property charged by the surety.[10] There are two possible answers to this problem. First, the courts may no longer regard the sale of property as a bar to rescission,[11] not least because of their willingness to make elaborate financial adjustments on rescission to effect *restitutio in integrum*.[12] Secondly, even if this is not the case, the court might order the creditor to make a monetary payment to the surety. There are two possible bases for this. First, there is an equitable jurisdiction to award compensation for breach of duty arising out of a confidential relationship,[13] and it has been exercised against a person who acquired property from another through the exercise of undue influence.[14] However, not every case of undue influence will involve a breach of fiduciary duty, and in any event, it seems unlikely that the jurisdiction could be extended so that compensation could be awarded against a creditor who merely had notice of the principal debtor's undue influence. The second (and better) approach would be to treat the surety's claim as one in restitution to prevent the creditor's unjust enrichment.[15]

8. Unconscionable bargains. There may be situations where the surety can **19–176** set aside the charge directly as against the creditor because it constitutes an

---

[7] *Barclays Bank Plc v. Caplan* [1998] 1 F.L.R. 532.

[8] *Dunbar Bank Plc v. Nadeem* [1998] 3 All E.R. 876 at 884. The case demonstrates the necessity to determine what benefit the surety received and which he must restore.

[9] *Castle Phillips Finance v. Piddington* [1995] 1 F.L.R. 783. The case was in fact one of *double* subrogation. The first mortgage was valid. The second mortgage (which discharged the first) was tainted by misrepresentation. The third mortgage (which discharged the second) was obtained by the husband forging his wife's signature. The third mortgagee was, by double subrogation, able to enforce the first mortgage against the wife.

[10] For a mortgagee's power of sale, see *ante*, para. 19–057.

[11] See *Smith New Court Securities Ltd v. Citibank N.A.* [1997] A.C. 254 at 262. *cf.* [1994] 1 W.L.R. 1271 at 1280 (C.A., *sub nom. Smith New Court Securities Ltd v. Scrimgeour Vickers (Asset Management) Ltd*).

[12] See, *e.g. O'Sullivan v. Management Agency and Music Ltd* [1985] Q.B. 428.

[13] See *Nocton v. Lord Ashburton* [1914] A.C. 932.

[14] *Mahoney v. Purnell* [1996] 3 All E.R. 61 at 86–91. See (1997) 113 L.Q.R. 8 (J. D. Heydon).

[15] See [1997] R.L.R. 72 (P. Birks). The amount of the surety's claim would presumably be determined by the value of the property when it was sold, even though the property had declined in value since the date of the charge: *cf. Cheese v. Thomas* [1994] 1 W.L.R. 129.

unconscionable bargain,[16] rather than indirectly, on the ground that the creditor is implicated by notice in the principal debtor's undue influence. Although unconscionable conduct is well-recognised as a vitiating factor,[17] the principles governing its operation are not yet firmly settled.[18] The adoption of this alternative approach has been seen by some to be preferable to the principles laid down in the *O'Brien* case because the latter has "substituted an inappropriate bright line rule for proper investigation of the facts" and has "failed the vulnerable in the process".[19] However, it is likely that a transaction will be set aside on grounds of unconscionability only in extreme cases. In most situations, the *O'Brien* principles may be the only applicable ones.[20]

19–177　　**9. O'Brien in Scotland.** The principles laid down in the *O'Brien* case have been imported into Scottish law by the House of Lords, but on a different basis.[21] There was some unease about imposing liability on a creditor on the basis that he had constructive notice of the principal debtor's fraud or undue influence. Although a creditor could be regarded as having constructive notice of undue influence between a husband and wife, it had never been suggested that "any particular class of persons is more likely to misrepresent in relation to a contract than any other class".[22] The House therefore based its decision not on notice (or indeed any other concept of equity) but on the duty of good faith that was required of a creditor in a contract of cautionry (suretyship). It held that a creditor owed a duty to give advice to a potential cautioner (surety) "where the creditor should reasonably suspect that there may be factors bearing on the participation of the cautioner which might undermine the validity of the contract through his or her intimate relationship with the debtor".[23] If the creditor wished to enforce the contract, he should warn the cautioner of the consequences of entering into the transaction and advise him to take independent advice.[24]

　　The Scottish approach is both simpler and more direct than the English one. A creditor is under an explicit duty to warn a surety where there is a risk that

---

[16] See *Credit Lyonnais Bank Nederland N.V. v. Burch* [1997] 1 All E.R. 144. In that case, Millett L.J. described the transaction (by which a junior employee entered into an unlimited guarantee charged on her house as surety for her employer) as one that "shocks the conscience of the court": *ibid.*, at 152. See (1997) 113 L.Q.R. 10 (H. Tjio); [1997] L.M.C.L.Q. 17 (R. Hooley and J. O'Sullivan).

[17] See *Hart v. O'Conner* [1985] A.C. 1000 at 1018. For the circumstances in which relief may be given in respect of a collateral advantage in a mortgage that is unconscionable, see *ante*, paras 19–135, 19–136.

[18] The fullest statement is to be found in *Boustany v. Pigott* (1993) 69 P. & C.R. 198 at 303. For a valuable review of the authorities, see [1995] L.M.C.L.Q. 538 (N. Bamforth). See too (1998) 114 L.Q.R. (D. Capper).

[19] (1998) 114 L.Q.R. 214, 220 (Sir Peter Millett). *cf. Credit Lyonnais Bank Nederland N.V. v. Burch, supra*, at 152–157.

[20] For a valuable analysis of the extent to which principles of unconscionability underlie the *O'Brien* decision, see [1997] C.L.J. 60 (M. Chen-Wishart).

[21] *Smith v. Bank of Scotland* 1997 S.L.T. 1061. See (1998) 114 L.Q.R. 17 (C. E. F. Rickett).

[22] 1997 S.L.T. 1061, at 1064, *per* Lord Jauncey.

[23] *ibid.*, at 1068, *per* Lord Clyde.

[24] *ibid.*

the surety may have been induced to act by some impropriety on the part of the principal debtor. English law reaches the same conclusion but by the much more circuitous (and potentially misleading) route of constructive notice.[25]

III. OTHER RIGHTS

The mortgagor's rights to have the property sold under an order of the court,[26]   **19–178**
to inspect the title deeds,[27] and to compel a transfer of the mortgage,[28] have been explained in an earlier section.

Part 4

TRANSFER OF RIGHTS

Section 1. Death of Mortgagor

In relation to all deaths after 1925,[29] the Administration of Estates Act 1925,   **19–179**
replacing an earlier patchwork of provisions, provides that property (whether real or personal) mortgaged or charged shall, as between the different persons claiming through a deceased person, be primarily liable to answer the debt, unless the deceased has signified a contrary intention in some document.[30] A general direction to pay debts out of personal estate or out of residue is not by itself to be deemed to show contrary intention.[31] Such an intention may be shown in any document (*e.g.* a letter[32]), and it may be partial, *e.g.* applying to mortgages but not to liens.[33] A direction to pay mortgages out of a special fund suffices,[34] though only to the extent of that fund[35]; but it is not enough merely to make a specific devise of part of the mortgaged land, as distinct from the whole.[36]

---

[25] English law was for some time equivocal as to whether contracts of guarantee were contracts *uberrimae fidei*. However, it was eventually held that they were not, and that only a non-disclosure that amounted to implied misrepresentation entitled the surety to avoid the guarantee: see *North British Insurance Co. v. Lloyd* (1854) 10 Exch. 523; *Seaton v. Heath* [1899] 1 Q.B. 782 at 792. The principles laid down in *O'Brien* have effectively created an exception to this in cases where there is a risk of fraud or undue influence: *ante*, para. 19–160.

[26] *Ante*, para. 19–054.

[27] *Ante*, para. 19–094.

[28] *Ante*, para. 19–146.

[29] For the position prior to 1926, see the previous edition of this work at p. 979.

[30] A.E.A. 1925, ss.35, 55(1)(xvii). See, *e.g. Re Turner* [1938] Ch. 593 (bequest of shares subject to lien of company).

[31] s.35(2).This slightly modifies the earlier provisions.

[32] See, *e.g. Re Wakefield* [1943] 2 All E.R. 29 (letter to solicitors directing them to complete a purchase held to show no intention that the devisee should take the property free from the vendor's lien for unpaid purchase-money); and see *Re Birmingham* [1958] Ch. 523.

[33] *Re Beirnstein* [1925] Ch. 12.

[34] *Allie v. Katah* [1963] 1 W.L.R. 202.

[35] *Re Fegan* [1928] Ch. 45.

[36] *Re Neeld* [1962] Ch. 643, overruling *Re Biss* [1956] Ch. 243.

These provisions do not affect any rights the mortgagee may have against the estate of the mortgagor; they merely ensure that as between the person taking the mortgaged property and the other beneficiaries, the burden of the mortgage should fall primarily upon the former. They do not apply to a person who is given by a will the right to purchase part of the estate, even at a favourable price; for he is a purchaser and not a devisee or legatee.[37]

Section 2. Death of Mortgagee

A. Death of Sole Mortgagee

19–180   When a sole legal mortgagee dies, the mortgage vests in his personal representatives in the usual way.[38] Prior to the Conveyancing Act 1881,[39] the legal estate (which was realty) and the right to the money lent (which was personalty) had devolved in different ways.[40]

B. Death of One of Several Mortgagees

19–181   Where two or more persons lend money on mortgage and one of them dies the legal title to the mortgage vests in those surviving by virtue of the right of survivorship.[41] In equity there is a presumption of a tenancy in common where two or more together lend on mortgage.[42] Formerly, in the absence of any provision to the contrary, when one of the mortgagees died his equitable share passed to his personal representatives. If the mortgagor redeemed they would have to join in the transaction.[43] If they did not the mortgagor would not obtain a good receipt for the money from the persons entitled to receive it, and the reconveyance would not give him a good title.[44] To overcome this difficulty, it is provided by statute[45] that as between the mortgagor and the mortgagees, the mortgagees are deemed to have advanced the money on a joint account unless a contrary intention appears from the mortgage. As a result, the survivor or survivors can give a complete discharge for all monies due notwithstanding any notice of severance which the mortgagor may have.[46]

---

[37] *Re Fison's W.T.* [1950] Ch. 394.
[38] A.E.A. 1925, ss.1(1), 3(1); *ante*, para. 11–125.
[39] s.30.
[40] See the previous edition of this work at p. 981.
[41] *Ante*, para. 9–003.
[42] *Rigden v. Vallier* (1751) 2 Ves.Sen. 252 at 258: *ante*, para. 9–028.
[43] *Vickery v. Cowell* (1839) 1 Beav. 529.
[44] A similar problem arose where the mortgagees were trustees investing trust money; see the previous edition of this work at pp. 981–982, where these points are more fully considered.
[45] L.P.A. 1925, s.111. By s.112, a purchaser is absolved from notice of trusts merely because a transfer of the mortgage is stamped 50p instead of *ad valorem*. By s.113, trusts of the mortgage money do not concern a person dealing in good faith with the mortgagee, or with the mortgagor after discharge.
[46] L.P.A. 1925, s.111(1).

This is, of course, mere conveyancing machinery, enabling the surviving mortgagees to overreach the beneficial interests in the mortgaged property. It does not affect the rights of the mortgagees *inter se*; if they are beneficially entitled and not trustees, the survivors must account to the personal representatives of the deceased mortgagee for his share. The joint account clause by itself does not alter the presumption as to a tenancy in common.[47]

Section 3. Transfer of Equity of Redemption *Inter Vivos*

A mortgagor may at any time without the mortgagee's consent make a conveyance of his property subject to the mortgage. Notwithstanding any such conveyance, and even if the transferee undertakes personal liability to the mortgagee,[48] the mortgagor remains personally liable on the covenant to pay the money.[49] He therefore usually takes an express covenant for indemnity from the transferee, but even if he does not[50] a transferee for value[51] will be under an implied obligation to indemnify him.[52] **19–182**

A mortgagor who wishes to sell free from the mortgage may do so—

(i) if he redeems; or

(ii) if the mortgagee consents (as he may well do if the security is adequate or if some other property is substituted for the property in question); or

(iii) if the mortgagor takes advantage of the statutory provision enabling the court to declare property free from an incumbrance upon sufficient money being paid into court.[53]

An assignee of the equity of redemption in general steps into the shoes of the mortgagor; but he does not merely by the assignment become personally liable to the mortgagee to pay the mortgage debt to him.[54]

Section 4. Transfer of Mortgage *Inter Vivos*

A. In General

1. Mortgages of unregistered land. A mortgagee may transfer his mortgage at any time.[55] He may do so by a simple form of transfer. Since 1925 a **19–183**

---

[47] *Re Jackson* (1887) 34 Ch.D. 732.
[48] *West Bromwich B.S. v. Bullock* [1936] 1 All E.R. 887.
[49] *Kinnaird v. Trollope* (1888) 39 Ch.D. 636.
[50] *Mills v. United Counties Bank Ltd* [1912] 1 Ch. 231 (implied obligation excluded by express but limited obligation).
[51] But not a volunteer: see *Re Best* [1924] 1 Ch. 42.
[52] *Bridgman v. Daw* (1891) 40 W.R. 253.
[53] L.P.A. 1925, s.50(1), (2). This provision is particularly useful if the legal right to redeem has not arisen.
[54] *Re Errington* [1894] 1 Q.B. 11.
[55] See, *e.g. Turner v. Smith* [1901] 1 Ch. 213.

deed executed by a mortgagee purporting to transfer his mortgage, or the benefit of it, transfers to the transferee the estate in the land together with the right to the money and the benefit of all covenants, powers and securities therefor, unless a contrary intention appears.[56] The transfer can be made without the concurrence of the mortgagor, but he should always be made a party if possible,[57] for then he admits the state of accounts, *i.e.* he acknowledges that some specified sum is still due under the mortgage. If he does not join in the transfer, the transferee gets the benefit only of that sum which is actually due,[58] even if the transferor represents that more is owing.[59]

Once the transfer has been made, the transferee should give notice of it to the mortgagor, unless the mortgagor has notice already, *e.g.* because he was a party to the transfer. If the mortgagor has no actual or constructive notice, the transferee cannot complain if the mortgagor pays to the transferor money due under the mortgage.[60]

19–184   **2. Registered charges.** Where registered land is subject to a registered charge, the proprietor of that charge has a right[61] to transfer it in the prescribed manner.[62] The transfer is completed only when it is registered and, until then, the transferor remains proprietor.[63] A registered transferee for valuable consideration takes the charge free of any irregularity or invalidity in it of which he did not have notice.[64]

B. Sub-mortgages

19–185   **1. Meaning.** A sub-mortgage is a mortgage of a mortgage. A mortgagee may, instead of transferring his mortgage outright, borrow money upon the security of it. A well-secured debt is in itself a good security for another loan. Thus if X has lent £100,000 upon a mortgage made by B, and X then wishes to raise a temporary loan of £10,000 himself, it would clearly be inadvisable for X to call in the whole of his loan. Consequently, X would raise the money by mortgaging his mortgage, *i.e.* by making a sub-mortgage.

2. Creation

19–186   *(a) Unregistered land.* Where unregistered land has been mortgaged, a sub-mortgage may be created—

---

[56] L.P.A. 1925, s.114.
[57] Fisher & Lightwood, *Mortgage*, p. 263.
[58] *Bickerton v. Walker* (1885) 31 Ch.D. 151 at 158. He cannot add the costs of the transfer to the mortgage debt: *Re Radcliffe* (1856) 22 Beav. 201.
[59] *Turner v. Smith, supra.*
[60] *Dixon v. Winch* [1900] 1 Ch. 736 at 742.
[61] That cannot be excluded: L.R.A. 1925, s.25(3).
[62] *ibid.*, s.33(1); L.R.R. 1925, r. 153. See Ruoff & Roper, 24–05.
[63] L.R.A. 1925, s.33(2).
[64] *ibid.*, s.33(3).

(i) in the case of an equitable mortgage or a legal charge, by assigning the mortgage debt to the sub-mortgagee subject to a proviso for redemption[65];

(ii) in the case of a legal mortgage by demise or sub-demise, by grant of a sub-term or by a legal charge[66]; or

(iii) in the case of a legal charge or a legal mortgage by demise or sub-demise, by an equitable contract to sub-mortgage.

(b) Registered land.[67] Where registered land is subject to a registered **19–187** charge, the proprietor of that charge may create a sub-charge in the same form and manner as a registered charge.[68] The sub-charge must be completed by registration.[69] He may also sub-mortgage the charge by deed or otherwise, in any manner that would have been permissible if the land had not been registered.[70] Such a sub-mortgage takes effect in equity as a minor interest and will be capable of being overridden unless protected by the entry of a notice or caution.[71]

3. Powers. In general, where title is unregistered, the sub-mortgagee takes **19–188** over the mortgagee's rights of enforcing payment under the original mortgage. He may, for example, sell the property under a power of sale. Alternatively he may exercise his remedies against the mortgage. If the sub-mortgage confers a power of sale, he may sell the mortgage or charge itself.

Where title is registered, the proprietor of the sub-charge has the same powers as the proprietor of the principal charge.[72]

Section 5. Discharge of Mortgage

A. Unregistered Land

1. Indorsed receipt. In the case of any mortgage of unregistered land **19–189** discharged after 1925,[73] a receipt indorsed on or annexed to the mortgage deed, signed[74] by the mortgagee and stating the name of the person paying the money, normally operates as a surrender of the mortgage term or a reconveyance, as the case may be, and discharges the mortgage.[75] The mortgagor may, if he prefers, have a reassignment, surrender, release or transfer executed

---

[65] Fisher & Lightwood, *Mortgage*, p. 272.
[66] See L.P.A. 1925, s.86(1), (3).
[67] See Ruoff & Roper, 24–10.
[68] For sub-charges, see L.R.R. 1925, rr. 163–166, made pursuant to L.R.A. 1925, s.36. Certificates of sub-charge are issued and dealt with in the same manner as charge certificates: see L.R.R. 1925, r. 166. For registered charges, see *ante*, para. 6–112.
[69] L.R.R. 1925, r. 164(1).
[70] L.R.A. 1925, s.106.
[71] *ibid.*
[72] L.R.R. 1925, r. 163(2).
[73] See L.P.A. 1925, s.115(8), (10).
[74] *Simpson v. Geoghegan* [1934] W.N. 232.
[75] L.P.A. 1925, s.115(1).

instead.[76] This is necessary if only part of the debt is being paid and part of the property redeemed.[77]

19–190   **2. Transfer.** If the receipt shows that the person paying the money was not entitled to the immediate equity of redemption and makes no provision to the contrary, it operates as a transfer of the mortgage to him.[78] Thus where a third mortgagee pays off the first mortgage, the statutory receipt will transfer the mortgage to him. But this does not enable the mortgagor, on paying off a mortgage, to keep it alive against a subsequent mortgagee.[79]

19–191   **3. Building societies.** A building society may use either a reconveyance or else a special form of statutory receipt. This receipt does not state who paid the money and cannot operate as a transfer of the mortgage; but otherwise it takes effect under these provisions.[80]

19–192   **4. Satisfied term.** Apart from these provisions, once a mortgage by sub-demise has been redeemed, the sub-term becomes a satisfied term and ceases forthwith.[81] Under this provision an ordinary receipt (*i.e.* one not complying with the conditions relating to indorsed receipts) might be thought to operate as a sufficient discharge. However, conveyancers do not in practice rely upon such a receipt, because it is only prima facie proof of payment.[82]

B. Registered Land

19–193   The provisions governing the discharge of mortgages of unregistered land are inapplicable where title is registered.[83] Discharge of a registered charge (whether in whole or part) is made by notification on the register,[84] either on the application of the registered proprietor of the charge[85] or by the registrar where there is proof that the charge has been satisfied.[86] There is no special form of discharge where the registered proprietor of the charge is a building society[87] as there is where title is unregistered,[88] though in practice the

---

[76] *ibid.*, s.115(4).

[77] Fisher & Lightwood, *Mortgage*, p. 572.

[78] L.P.A. 1925, s.115(2).

[79] *Otter v. Lord Vaux* (1856) 6 De G.M. & G. 638; L.P.A. 1925, s.115(3); see *Cumberland Court (Brighton) Ltd v. Taylor* [1964] Ch. 29; and see *ante*, para. 19–144.

[80] Building Societies Act 1986, s.13(7), Sched. 4, para. 2, replacing earlier legislation.

[81] L.P.A. 1925, ss.5, 116; *cf. supra.* This now applies to terms created out of leaseholds as well as those created out of freeholds.

[82] Wolst. & C. i, 225.

[83] L.P.A. 1925, s.115(10).

[84] L.R.A. 1925, s.35. Any provision which purports to take away the right of the registered proprietor of the land to have the cessation of the charge notified on the register is void: *ibid.*, s.25(3) (the subsection mistakenly refers to the proprietor *of the charge*: see Ruoff & Roper, 24–17).

[85] L.R.R. 1925, r. 151; Sched., Form 53.

[86] L.R.A. 1925, s.35(1); Ruoff & Rope, 24–17. Discharge extinguishes the charge without any surrender: L.R.A. 1925, s.35(2); Ruoff & Roper, 24–20.

[87] For the appropriate form, see L.R.R. 1925, r. 151(c).

[88] *Ante*, para. 19–189. See Building Societies Act 1986, s.13(7), Sched. 4, para. 2(4) (which restricts the statutory receipt to unregistered land).

registrar will accept a receipt in statutory form subject to certain conditions.[89]

Where a legal or equitable mortgage is not registered as a charge but is noted on the register, that notice will be cancelled on production of satisfactory evidence that the mortgage has been discharged.[90]

Part 5

PRIORITY OF MORTGAGES

Where there is more than one mortgage on the same property, it is sometimes **19–194** necessary to determine the priority of the mortgages, *e.g.* if the property is sold by one mortgagee and there is not enough money to satisfy all. There is no question of the various mortgagees sharing the loss. Each mortgagee takes his full claim in order of priority, and it is for a later mortgagee to satisfy himself as to the security before he takes his mortgage. Cases of dispute as to priority are most likely to arise where, perhaps because of the fraud of the mortgagor, a later mortgagee advances his money in ignorance of an earlier mortgage. "It happens with unfortunate frequency that a man having title to land contrives by means of fraudulent concealment to get money from a number of different persons on the security of the land—then disappears—and the lenders are left to dispute among themselves as to the order in which they are to be paid out of the value of the land which is insufficient to pay all of them."[91] This particular malpractice, however, seems to have been commoner in the past than it is today.

Fundamentally the rules which govern priority are general rules about the **19–195** relationship of estates, both legal and equitable. Thus the question whether a first equitable mortgage takes priority over a second legal mortgage is essentially the same as the question whether an equitable mortgage binds a later purchaser of the fee simple. The rules are not peculiar to mortgages, but it is in connection with mortgages that they are most likely to present problems. The question whether a lease takes priority over a mortgage, in a case where a purchaser of land lets it before completion and mortgages it at the time of completion, has been considered elsewhere.[92] It has also been explained that some statutory charges may have an overriding priority of their own, regardless of the ordinary rules.[93]

As regards unregistered land, the general rules for determining priority will be discussed first, followed by the rules relating to tacking, which is a method

---

[89] Ruoff & Roper, 24–19. A system by which registered charges may be discharged electronically is presently undergoing trials.

[90] L.R.A. 1925, s.106(4); Ruoff & Roper, 24–22.

[91] Maitland, *Equity*, 125.

[92] It is now settled that the mortgage takes priority: see *ante*, para. 14–102.

[93] *Ante*. The possibility of such charges being incurred by the mortgagor can impair the mortgagee's security: see *Westminster City Council v. Haymarket Publishing Ltd* [1980] 1 W.L.R. 683 (rating surcharge takes priority over earlier legal mortgage).

of altering the priorities that is settled by general rules. In each case it is first necessary to explain the rules as they stood before 1926. Those rules remain the essential foundation, but their operation in relation to unregistered land is radically affected by the system of registration of land charges introduced in 1925 and by other amendments. The position where the title is registered, which has already been explained,[94] is then briefly summarised.

It should be noted that where there are two mortgages of the same property, the mortgagees can agree to alter the priority of those charges without the mortgagor's consent. If a mortgagor wishes to prevent this happening, he must ensure that the mortgage contains a specific contractual provision precluding such alteration.[95]

Section 1. Unregistered Land: General Rules

A. Priority Before 1926

19–196 Before 1926 there was one set of rules for determining priorities where the property mortgaged was an interest in land and a separate set of rules for cases where the property mortgaged was an interest in pure personalty, *i.e.* personalty other than leaseholds.[96] Since the latter affected interests under trusts for sale of land, both sets of rules require explanation.

I. MORTGAGES OF AN INTEREST IN LAND

19–197 Two main rules applied to mortgages of land, including sub-mortgages, *i.e.* mortgages of a mortgage of land.[97] These rules applied whether the interest was legal or equitable[98] and whether the land was freehold or leasehold.[99]

    (i) *"Qui prior est tempore, potior est jure"* (he who is first in time is stronger in law); mortgages primarily ranked in the order of their creation, or "first made, first paid"; but

    (ii) *"Where the equities are equal, the law prevails"*; if, apart from the order of their creation, a legal and an equitable mortgage had equal claims to be preferred, the legal mortgage would have priority.[1]

19–198 A conflict between two mortgages accordingly fell into one of four classes:

    (i) where both mortgages were legal;

---

[94] *Ante*, para. 6–112.
[95] *Cheah v. Equiticorp Finance Group Ltd* [1992] 1 A.C. 472.
[96] See *post*, para. 19–197.
[97] *Taylor v. London & County Banking Co.* [1901] 2 Ch. 231.
[98] *Wilmot v. Pike* (1845) 5 Hare 14; *Wiltshire v. Rabbits* (1844) 14 Sim. 76.
[99] *Rooper v. Harrison* (1855) 2 K. & J. 86; *Union Bank of London v. Kent* (1888) 39 Ch.D. 238.
[1] *Bailey v. Barnes* [1894] 1 Ch. 25 at 36. "Equality means the non-existence of any circumstance which affects the conduct of one of the rival claimants, and makes it less meritorious than that of the other": *ibid.*, *per* Lindley L.J.

(ii) where the first was legal and the second equitable;

(iii) where the first was equitable and the second legal; and

(iv) where both were equitable.

These will be considered in order.

1. Both mortgages legal. Conflicts where both mortgages were legal rarely **19–199** came before the courts, since most mortgages of freeholds were effected by a conveyance of the fee simple, which made the creation of subsequent legal mortgages impossible. Successive legal mortgages could, however, be created by the grant of successive terms of years,[2] and a lease might be mortgaged by the grant of two successive subleases.[3] In any such cases, where two or more legal mortgages were created in succession, priority normally[4] depended on the order of creation, for after the grant of one lease, the second lease must take effect in reversion upon the first, and a legal estate in reversion was postponed to one in possession.[5]

2. Legal mortgage followed by equitable mortgage. Where a legal mort- **19–200** gage was followed by an equitable mortgage, the legal mortgagee had a double claim to priority, both as being prior in point of time and as being a legal mortgagee in competition with a mere equitable mortgagee. But this natural priority might be displaced in a number of ways.

(a) By fraud. If the legal mortgagee was party to some fraud whereby the **19–201** equitable mortgagee was deceived into believing that there was no legal mortgage on the property, the legal mortgagee was postponed to the equitable mortgagee.[6]

(b) By estoppel. If the legal mortgagee either expressly or by implication **19–202** made some misrepresentation by which the equitable mortgagee was deceived, the legal mortgagee might be estopped from asserting his priority.[7] Thus if the legal mortgagee indorsed a receipt for his money on the mortgage and somebody was thereby induced to lend money on an equitable mortgage of the property, the legal mortgagee could not afterwards claim priority for his loan if in fact it had not been discharged.[8] Again, if the legal mortgagee returned the deeds to the mortgagor in order to enable him to raise a further

---

[2] *Aldridge v. Duke* (1697) Rep.t.Finch 439.

[3] *Jones v. Rhind* (1869) 17 W.R. 1091.

[4] As explained later (see *infra*), a legal mortgagee could lose priority by negligently parting with the title deeds (see *Jones v. Rhind, supra*), and no doubt also by failure to obtain them, or by fraud.

[5] Coote, *Mortgages,* p. 1240. See *Ex p. Knott* (1806) 11 Ves. 609; *Hurst v. Hurst* (1852) 16 Beav. 372. See also *Re Russell Road Purchase-Moneys* (1871) L.R. 12 Eq. 78 (lease mortgaged first by the grant of a legal sub-term and then by legal assignment; the mortgagee by assignment claimed priority over an intervening equitable mortgage of which he had no notice, but the case was compromised before the Court of Appeal could give judgment).

[6] *Peter v. Russel* (1716) 1 Eq.Ca.Abr. 321.

[7] *Dixon v. Muckleston* (1872) 8 Ch.App. 155 at 160.

[8] *Rimmer v. Webster* [1902] 2 Ch. 163; *cf. Rice v. Rice* (1853) 2 Drew. 73 (two equitable incumbrances).

loan, he was postponed to any subsequent mortgagee who lent money without notice of the first mortgage, even if the mortgagor had agreed to inform the second mortgagee of the first mortgage,[9] or had agreed to borrow only a limited amount which in fact he exceeded.[10] Once the mortgage had clothed the mortgagor with apparent authority to deal with the property freely, he could not afterwards claim the protection of any undisclosed limits set to this authority.[11]

19–203   *(c) By gross negligence in relation to the title deeds.* It was held in one case that an earlier legal mortgagee could never lose his priority by mere carelessness or want of prudence, falling short of fraud.[12] But the law appears rather to have been that by gross negligence in failing to obtain the title deeds,[13] or, perhaps, to retain them,[14] he could lose priority as against a later equitable mortgagee who exercised due diligence himself.[15] "Gross negligence" is an indefinable expression, but it was used to indicate a degree of negligence which made it unjust to enforce the natural order of priority.[16] A legal mortgagee who failed to ask for the deeds at all[17] would certainly be postponed. But a legal mortgagee might claim the benefit of the doctrine, explained below,[18] which preserves priority for mortgagees who ask for the deeds and are given a reasonable excuse for their non-production.[19] Further, where the mortgagee knew that the deeds were in the hands of a prior equitable mortgagee but gave him no notice, so that when the mortgagor paid off the equitable mortgage the mortgagor recovered the deeds and was enabled to create a later equitable mortgage,[20] he was held not guilty of such gross

[9] *Briggs v. Jones* (1870) L.R. 10 Eq. 92; and see *Martinez v. Cooper* (1826) 2 Russ. 198.

[10] *Perry Herrick v. Attwood* (1857) 2 De G. & J. 21.

[11] *Brocklesby v. Temperance Permanent B.S.* [1895] A.C. 173; *Rimmer v. Webster, supra*, at 173; *Abigail v. Lapin* [1934] A.C. 491.

[12] *Northern Counties of England Fire Insurance Co. v. Whipp* (1884) 26 Ch.D. 482.

[13] *Colyer v. Finch* (1856) 5 H.L.C. 905; *Clarke v. Palmer* (1882) 21 Ch.D. 124; *Walker v. Linom* [1907] 2 Ch. 104. In the last case W conveyed land to trustees, handing over a bundle of title deeds but keeping the last previous deed, a conveyance to himself; later he made, or purported to make, a mortgage with the help of this deed: held, that the mortgagee took priority over the trustees, and that a beneficiary under the trust was in no better position than the trustees. It might have been thought that the mortgagee, who saw only one deed (seven years old) and cannot have investigated the title properly, had little claim in equity against the legal owner. But this point does not appear to have arisen. For this case, see further *post*, para. 19–204.

[14] This is less certain. In *Northern Counties of England Fire Insurance Co. v. Whipp, supra*, the manager of a company mortgaged his property to the company. Later he took back the deeds, which had been placed in a safe to which he had a key, and gave them to X under a mortgage. Held, that the company had priority over X. A distinction between failure to obtain deeds and failure to retain them is difficult to justify, and the Court of Appeal's decision is probably open to question in the light of *Derry v. Peek* (1889) 14 App.Cas. 337: see Waldock, *Mortgages*, p. 397.

[15] *Hunt v. Elmes* (1860) 2 De G.F. & J. 578 at 586, 587. See *Walker v. Linom* [1907] 2 Ch. 104 at 114.

[16] See *Oliver v. Hinton* [1899] 2 Ch. 264 at para. 19–206.

[17] *Clarke v. Palmer* (1882) 21 Ch.D. 124; *Walker v. Linom, supra.*

[18] *Post*, para. 19–205.

[19] *Manners v. Mew* (1885) 29 Ch.D. 725. *Quaere* whether the excuse given there would be treated as reasonable today; but the case can perhaps be supported on the relationship between the parties: see, *e.g. Hewitt v. Loosemore* (1851) 9 Hare 449; *post*, para. 19–206.

[20] *Grierson v. National Provincial Bank of England Ltd* [1913] 2 Ch. 18.

negligence as would postpone him. Nor was the legal mortgagee postponed merely because he failed to obtain all the title deeds: if he obtained some of them reasonably believing them to be all, he was not postponed.[21]

The postponement of an earlier legal to a later equitable incumbrancer for **19–204** any of the above three reasons is explicable only as an intervention by equity against the ordinary rules governing estates, in particular against the rule that no one can convey what he has not got. The later equitable mortgagee could obtain from the mortgagor only a mortgage of the equity of redemption: the legal estate was outstanding in the first mortgagee, and could be obtained only by redeeming. Nevertheless, if the conduct of the first mortgagee raised a case of fraud, estoppel or gross negligence, the second mortgagee could enforce a prior equitable right to the legal estate, and so ultimately obtain it without redemption. If, for example, his mortgage gave him a power of sale, he could give a good title to a purchaser, free from the earlier mortgage which in law stood first but which in equity stood second.[22] Conversely, it seems probable that if the earlier legal mortgagee transferred his mortgage to a transferee for value who took without notice of the circumstances, *e.g.* of fraud, the transferee would take free from the equitable liability to postponement.

3. Equitable mortgage followed by legal mortgage

(a) Purchaser without notice. Where an equitable mortgage was followed **19–205** by a legal mortgage, the primary rule that the mortgages rank in the order of creation might be displaced by the superiority of a legal estate. For this to occur, the legal mortgagee had to show that he was a bona fide purchaser[23] for value of a legal estate without notice[24] of the prior equitable mortgage.[25] In

---

[21] *Cottey v. The National Provincial Bank of England Ltd* (1904) 20 T.L.R. 607. *Contra, Walker v. Linom, supra.*

[22] *Walker v. Linom* [1907] 2 Ch. 104; *ante*, para. 19–203. In a note to Maitland, *Equity*, 138, the editor (J. W. Brunyate) draws attention to the second incumbrancer's lack of title in that case. The facts were striking, since the prior disposition was an outright conveyance, not a mere mortgage. But a mere mortgage would have had the same effect before 1926, as regards the legal estate. In fact the peculiarity seems to apply equally to all the cases in this class. The legal estate remains vested in the person to whom it was first conveyed (*Walker v. Linom*, at 110), but presumably the person entitled to priority in equity can compel a transfer of it. He is said to have "a subsequent equitable estate" (at 114), but this seems to arise from an intervention of the court rather than from any interest which the mortgagor had power to create.

[23] "Purchaser" includes a mortgagee: *Brace v. Duchess of Marlborough* (1728) 2 P. Wms. 491; *Pilcher v. Rawlins* (1872) 7 Ch.App. 259.

[24] It was only when the equities were equal that the law prevailed, and "he that has Notice has no Equity at all"; *Oxwith v. Plummer* (1708) Gilb.Ch. 13 at 15, *per* Lord Cowper L.C.

[25] *Ante*, para. 5–011. As there mentioned, a better equitable right to an outstanding legal estate would do; see the case put in *Wilmot v. Pike* (1845) 5 Hare 14 at 21, 22, which may be paraphrased thus: successive mortgages are made to A (legal), B (equitable) and C (equitable); A joins in the mortgage to C and (neither A nor C then knowing of B's mortgage) declares himself trustee for C subject to A's own mortgage. C then takes priority to B because of his better title to the legal estate; but not if either A or C knew of B's mortgage at the time of the declaration of trust. This shows the importance of B giving notice to A. C could not secure priority merely by giving notice to A before B did so, for the rule in *Dearle v. Hall* (1828) 3 Russ. 1 (see *post*, para. 19–208) did not apply to realty; therefore a declaration of trust was essential to C's claim.

general, a failure to inquire for the deeds at all,[26] or the inability of the mortgagor to produce the title deeds, would amount to constructive notice to the legal mortgagee that some prior mortgage or conveyance had already been made.[27] But there might be good reason for the absence of the deeds (_e.g._ that they had been destroyed in a fire), and if the later legal mortgagee accepted a "reasonable excuse" for the non-production of the deeds, he was held to have no notice of the prior mortgage.

19–206   _(b) Excuses for not producing deeds._ The courts have, however, been satisfied by surprisingly frail excuses, imperfectly investigated. The excuse that the deeds also relate to other property has been held insufficient[28]; but prior equitable mortgagees, in possession of the deeds, have lost priority over later legal mortgagees who have been told by the mortgagor that he was busy then, but would produce the deeds later,[29] or that the deeds were in Ireland, where the property was.[30] Such cases appear to deviate from the ordinary principle of notice, which absolves a purchaser of a legal estate only if he has taken all the steps which a prudent man of business, properly advised, would be expected to take[31]; a mere story invented by the mortgagor and not investigated may deprive the first mortgagee of his priority.

This rule probably owes its origin to a doctrine about "gross negligence" which has caused some confusion. It has often been said that the later legal mortgagee is entitled to priority if he has not been fraudulent or grossly negligent.[32] But in this class of case, unlike the class previously discussed, the rule contradicts the principle that an equitable interest should bind a purchaser who does not investigate the title. The exception is, however, firmly established.

19–207   **4. Both mortgages equitable.** Where both mortgages were equitable, the primary rule was that priority depended upon the order in which the mortgages were created.[33] This, however, was subject to the equities being in other

---

[26] _Berwick & Co. v. Price_ [1905] 1 Ch. 632.

[27] That, indeed, is a primary object in depositing the deeds: see _ante_, para. 19–035.

[28] _Oliver v. Hinton_ [1899] 2 Ch. 264.

[29] _Hewitt v. Loosemore_ (1851) 9 Hare 449, and earlier cases there cited; _cf. Ratcliffe v. Barnard_ (1871) 6 Ch.App. 652 (receipt by legal mortgagee of some only of the deeds, in reasonable belief that they were all).

[30] _Agra Bank Ltd v. Barry_ (1874) L.R. 7 H.L. 135.

[31] _Ante_, para. 5–017.

[32] See _Hewitt v. Loosemore, supra; Oliver v. Hinton_ [1899] 2 Ch. 264; _Hudston v. Viney_ [1921] 1 Ch. 98. In _Oliver v. Hinton_ there was first an equitable mortgage by deposit, followed by an outright sale of the legal estate to a purchaser who had no actual notice of the mortgage but who accepted an inadequate excuse for non-production of the deeds (_viz._ that they related also to other property). It was held that the purchaser took subject to the mortgage. On general grounds it should have sufficed to say that the purchaser had constructive notice, and the case was so decided by Romer J. at first instance, at 268 (this was also the view of Parker J. in _Walker v. Linom_ [1907] 2 Ch. 104 at 114). But the Court of Appeal held the purchaser liable not because of notice but because of his "gross negligence": see Lindley M.R.'s judgment at 273, 274. Why this doctrine was needed, or how, if at all, it differs from the doctrine of notice, is not explained.

[33] _Rice v. Rice_ (1853) 2 Drew. 73 at 78.

respects equal,[34] so that although the vested interest of the prior mortgagee would not lightly be displaced,[35] the order might be altered by the inequitable behaviour of the prior mortgagee.[36] Accordingly, a first mortgagee who failed to ask for the title deeds,[37] or who, having obtained them, redelivered them to the mortgagor without pressing for their early return,[38] might be postponed to a second mortgagee who took all proper precautions but who was nevertheless deceived. But a first mortgagee who accepted some only of the title deeds, on the mortgagor's written assurance that they were all, did not lose his priority.[39]

II. MORTGAGES OF AN EQUITABLE INTEREST IN PURE PERSONALTY

1. The rule in *Dearle v. Hall*. Legal mortgages of chattels fall under the   **19–208** head of bills of sale and are outside the scope of this book; so also are mortgages of choses in action. Prior to 1997, equitable interests in pure personalty, on the other hand, included the rights of those interested under a trust for sale of land,[40] and so must be dealt with here. Mortgages of such interests were governed by the rule in *Dearle v. Hall*.[41] This laid down that priority depended upon the order in which notice of the mortgages or other dealings was received by the owner of the legal estate or interest (the trustees, in the case of a trust for sale); but that a mortgagee who, when he lent his money, had actual or constructive notice of a prior mortgage could not gain priority over it by giving notice first.

2. Basis of the rule. The rule in *Dearle v. Hall* is a general principle of   **19–209** equity governing dealings with equitable interests in pure personalty. Various explanations of the basis of the rule have been given.[42] The "leading consideration" is that as between two equally innocent incumbrancers, priority should be given to the one who, by giving notice, had prevented the mortgagor from representing himself to be the unincumbered owner of the property and

---

[34] *ibid.*

[35] *Cory v. Eyre* (1863) 1 De G.J. & S. 149 at 167.

[36] Whether priority will be lost only by the same degree of gross negligence as will displace a legal mortgagee is doubtful: see *Taylor v. Russell* [1891] 1 Ch. 8 at 14–20 where the authorities are reviewed. See also the decision of the House of Lords in that case ([1892] A.C. 244 at 262) and *National Provincial Bank of England v. Jackson* (1886) 33 Ch.D. 1, for the view that a smaller degree of negligence may suffice to displace an equitable mortgagee. See R. P. Meagher, W. M. C. Gummow & J. R. F. Lehane, *Equity: Doctrines and Remedies* (3rd ed), §§ 806–818.

[37] *Farrand v. Yorkshire Banking Co.* (1888) 40 Ch.D. 182.

[38] *Waldron v. Sloper* (1852) 1 Drew. 193; *Dowle v. Saunders* (1864) 2 H. & M. 242.

[39] *Dixon v. Muckleston* (1872) 8 Ch.App. 155.

[40] *Lee v. Howlett* (1856) 2 K. & J. 531. This was because of the doctrine of conversion, explained, *ante*, para. 8–118. Since T.L.A.T.A. 1996 came into force on January 1, 1997, trusts for sale have become trusts of land and the doctrine of conversion has been abolished: see *ante*, paras 8–127, 8–128. Interests under a trust of land are necessarily an interest *in land*.

[41] (1828) 3 Russ. 1, approved by the House of Lords in *Foster v. Cockerell* (1835) 3 Cl. & F. 456; and see *Ward v. Duncombe* [1893] A.C. 369.

[42] See. *e.g. Ward v. Duncombe*, *supra*, at 392.

so defrauding third parties.[43] The rule may also be based on an analogy with chattels, where title passes by delivery of possession. An assignee of an equitable interest in personalty must, it was held, take steps to obtain the equivalent to possession by giving notice to the trustee, and so perfecting his title.[44] An imperfect title would not prevail over a later assignee's perfected title; and the earlier assignee's equity was all the weaker for his own negligence in allowing the trustees to suppose that the later assignee was the first.

Although the rule was founded on equitable principles, it soon crystallised into a rigid rule[45] and by the beginning of this century it was settled that it would not be extended.[46]

19–210   **3. Loan without notice.** It will be noticed that for a second mortgagee to claim priority over a first mortgagee by giving notice first, he must be able to show that at the time of lending his money he had no notice of the first mortgage.[47] If at that time he had notice, and yet he lent his money, it would be inequitable for him subsequently to claim priority merely because he gave notice first, for the failure of the first mortgagee to give notice had in no way prejudiced him; he lent his money knowing of the first mortgage. But if he lent his money without notice of the first mortgage, it was immaterial that he had notice of the first mortgage at the time when he gave notice to the trustees.[48] Indeed, such knowledge is just what would impel him to give notice.[49]

19–211   **4. Details of the rule.** The details of the rule were worked out in a series of cases, which may be summarised under three main heads.

19–212   *(a) Priority depended upon notice being received, not given.* Although it was both usual and advisable for a mortgagee to give express notice, the test was not whether the mortgagee had taken active steps to give notice but whether the trustees had received knowledge of the mortgage from any reliable source. For example, where one chargee left written notice with the legal owner, a bank, after closing hours, and other chargees gave notice the next day, as soon as the bank opened, it was held that the bank must be treated

---

[43] *ibid.*, at 378.
[44] But see Lord Macnaghten's criticisms in *Ward v. Duncombe, supra*; *cf.* Lord Herschell's speech at 378. The House of Lords discussed the rule in *B.S. Lyle Ltd v. Rosher* [1959] 1 W.L.R. 8.
[45] See, *e.g. Re Dallas* [1904] 2 Ch. 385 (X charged a legacy he was expecting under the will of a living testator, who had become insane, first to A and then to B: the testator then died and A and B each gave notice to the administrator as soon as they knew of his appointment, B's notice being received first: held B had priority).
[46] *Ward v. Duncombe, supra*, at 394; *Hill v. Peters* [1918] 2 Ch. 273.
[47] *Re Holmes* (1885) 29 Ch.D. 786.
[48] *Mutual Life Assurance Society v. Langley* (1886) 32 Ch.D. 460.
[49] *cf. Wortley v. Birkhead* (1754) 2 Ves.Sen. 571 at 574. *cf. post*, para. 19–246, for a somewhat similar situation in the old law of tacking.

as having received all notices simultaneously, and consequently that the charges ranked in the order of creation.[50]

Clear and distinct oral notice sufficed,[51] but a statement made in a casual conversation with a trustee did not.[52] Knowledge received through reading a notice in a paper,[53] and knowledge acquired by a trustee before his appointment which continued to operate on his mind after his appointment,[54] have both been held sufficient to protect a mortgagee against a later mortgagee who gave express notice, although neither would obtain priority for a later mortgagee over a prior mortgagee[55]; stronger measures are needed to upset the natural order of the mortgages than are needed to maintain it.

(b) *It was advisable to give notice to all the trustees.* This was because of the following.   **19–213**

    (i) Notice given to all the existing trustees remained effective even though they all retired or died without communicating the notice to their successors.[56]

    (ii) Notice given to one of several trustees was effective against all incumbrances created during his trusteeship, and for this purpose remained effective after his death or retirement.[57]

    (iii) But notice given to one of several trustees was not effective against incumbrancers who advanced money after the death or retirement of that trustee, unless he had communicated the notice to one or more of the continuing trustees.[58]

    (iv) If the mortgagor was a trustee, the mere fact that he knew of the transaction would not affect priorities for such notice afforded no protection to subsequent mortgagees.[59] But if the mortgagee was a trustee, his knowledge of the transaction did affect priorities; for to protect his mortgage he would readily disclose its existence to any prospective incumbrancers.[60]

---

[50] *Calisher v. Forbes* (1871) 7 Ch.App. 109; and see *Johnstone v. Cox* (1880) 16 Ch.D. 571 (aff'd 19 Ch.D. 17). *Re Dallas* [1904] 2 Ch. 385 at 405 must, it seems, be taken to refer to simultaneous notices.

[51] *Browne v. Savage* (1859) 4 Drew. 635 at 640; *Re Worcester* (1868) 3 Ch.App. 555 (statement at directors' meeting); compare the simultaneous notices in *Calisher v. Forbes, supra.*

[52] *Re Tichener* (1865) 35 Beav. 317.

[53] *Lloyd v. Banks* (1868) 3 Ch.App. 488.

[54] *Ipswich Permanent Money Club Ltd v. Arthy* [1920] 2 Ch. 257.

[55] *ibid.,* at 271; *Arden v. Arden* (1885) 29 Ch.D. 702.

[56] *Re Wasdale* [1899] 1 Ch. 163.

[57] *Ward v. Duncombe* [1893] A.C. 369.

[58] *Timson v. Ramsbottom* (1836) 2 Keen 35, criticised by Lord Macnaghten in *Ward v. Duncombe, supra,* at 394, but accepted by Lord Herschell at 381, 382, and followed in *Re Phillips' Trusts* [1903] 1 Ch. 183.

[59] *Lloyds Bank v. Pearson* [1901] 1 Ch. 865. To hold otherwise would make the rule in *Dearle v. Hall* "a mere trap": *ibid.,* at 873, *per* Cozens-Hardy J.

[60] *Browne v. Savage* (1859) 4 Drew. 635 at 641.

19–214　　*(c) A mortgagee who lent his money with notice of a prior mortgage could not gain priority over it by giving notice first.* This has been discussed above.[61]

19–215　　**5. Protection on distribution.** In addition to securing priority, notice to the trustees, though not essential to the validity of the mortgage,[62] safeguarded the mortgagee by ensuring that his claims would not be disregarded when the funds were distributed. Trustees were bound to give effect to all claims of which they knew,[63] but were not liable if they distributed the trust funds to the prejudice of a mortgagee of whom they did not know.[64] Nor were they bound to answer inquiries either by the beneficiary or a prospective mortgagee as to the extent to which the beneficiary's share was incumbered: "it is no part of the duty of a trustee to assist his *cestui que trust* in selling or mortgaging his beneficial interest and in squandering or anticipating his fortune."[65]

B. Priority After 1925

19–216　　The general scheme of the 1925 legislation called for some amendment of the rules relating to priority. In particular, the old rule of the superiority of the legal estate was clearly inappropriate to a system which encouraged the creation of more than one legal mortgage of the same property; and since the interests of beneficiaries under strict settlements could no longer be legal, for the purposes of priority they could conveniently be classed with interests arising under a trust for sale.

Before 1926 the line of cleavage was the line between interests in land and interests in pure personalty: if the former, the case was governed by the rules relating to the order of creation and the superiority of the legal estate; if the latter, by the rule in *Dearle v. Hall.* Since 1925 the question is whether the interest mortgaged is legal or equitable. A mortgage of a legal estate in land now depends for its priority upon possession of the title deeds, or, in default, upon registration; a mortgage of an equitable interest in realty or personalty depends upon the rule in *Dearle v. Hall.* Thus if an equitable interest in settled land was mortgaged before 1926, priority depended on the order in which the mortgages were created; if it is mortgaged after 1925, priority is governed by the rule in *Dearle v. Hall.*

I. MORTGAGES OF A LEGAL ESTATE

19–217　　This title includes all mortgages of a legal estate, whether the mortgage itself is legal or equitable. The question is "Has a legal estate been mortgaged?", not "Is the mortgage legal or equitable?" Legal and equitable mortgages need

---

[61] *Ante*, para. 19–210.
[62] *Burn v. Carvalho* (1839) 4 My. & Cr. 690; *Gorringe v. Irwell India Rubber & Gutta Percha Works* (1886) 34 Ch.D. 128.
[63] *Hodgson v. Hodgson* (1837) 2 Keen 704.
[64] *Phipps v. Lovegrove* (1873) L.R. 16 Eq. 80.
[65] *Low v. Bouverie* [1891] 3 Ch. 82 at 99, *per* Lindley L.J.

no longer be separated, since the legislation of 1925 treats them both on the same lines.[66]

1. Categories of mortgages

(a) The scheme. The scheme of the legislation is to divide all mortgages of **19–218** a legal estate into two classes—

    (i) mortgages protected by deposit of deeds; and

    (ii) mortgages not so protected;

and to make class (ii) registrable as land charges under the Land Charges Act 1972 (replacing the Land Charges Act 1925).[67] The aim is to make all mortgages readily ascertainable. If a mortgagee has possession of the deeds, their absence will proclaim his mortgage to all other persons seeking to deal with the land. If he has not, he can proclaim his interest to the world by registration. Protection by deposit of deeds is in practice so effective that there is no need to require the registration of mortgages belonging to class (i).[68] However, there is some risk that this scheme may have been unsettled because of the manner in which informal mortgages by deposit of title deeds have been held to operate.[69]

(b) Unregistrable mortgages. If the doubt just mentioned is disregarded for **19–219** the moment, it is clear that protected mortgages (class (i) above) are intended to be outside the registration machinery and are governed, as regards priority, by the same rules as applied before 1926. They are defined as mortgages "protected" (or "secured") by a "deposit of documents relating to the legal estate affected". There is no positive enactment about them; they are simply excluded (as will shortly be seen) from the classes of land charges among which unprotected mortgages are intended to be registered. Although it is not clear, probably "protected" (or "secured") means *originally* protected or secured, rather than *continuously* protected or secured, for otherwise the mortgage would fluctuate between being registrable and unregistrable as often as the mortgagee parted with the deeds and regained them.[70]

(c) Registrable mortgages. Unprotected mortgages (class (ii) above), if **19–220** made after 1925, are registrable in the following classes.

    (i) If legal, as "puisne mortgages". A puisne mortgage is defined as a legal mortgage not "protected by a deposit of documents relating to the legal estate affected".[71]

---

[66] There is a general survey of priorities of such mortgages at (1940) 7 C.L.J. 243 (R.E.M.).

[67] For the rules where the title to the land is registered, see *ante*, para. 6–112; *post*, para. 19–263.

[68] But see *post*, para. 19–231, for the risk of "reasonable excuse".

[69] *Post*, para. 19–222.

[70] See (1940) 7 C.L.J. 249 (R.E.M.).

[71] L.C.A. 1972, s.2(4).

(ii) If equitable, as "general equitable charges". A general equitable charge is any equitable charge which, not being "secured by a deposit of documents relating to the legal estate affected", does not arise under a trust of land or a settlement; and is not included in any other class of land charge.[72]

As will shortly be explained, there is a possibility that a contract to grant a mortgage may have to be registered as an "estate contract", even if it is supported by a deposit of title deeds.[73]

19–221   *(d) Failure to register.* The penalty for failing to register a registrable mortgage is loss of priority over a later purchaser or incumbrancer. The mortgage remains valid as between mortgagor and mortgagee, but as against a later purchaser from the mortgagor (including a later mortgagee) it is void. There are two provisions to be applied—

(i) section 97 of the Law of Property Act 1925, which provides that every such mortgage "shall rank according to its date of registration as a land charge pursuant to the Land Charges Act, 1925 or 1972"[74]; and

(ii) section 4(5) of the Land Charges Act 1972, which provides that a puisne mortgage or general equitable charge created after 1925 shall "be void as against a purchaser of the land charged therewith, or of any interest in such land, unless the land charge is registered in the appropriate register before the completion of the purchase". In the Act, unless the context otherwise requires, "purchaser" means "any person (including a mortgagee or lessee) who, for valuable consideration, takes any interest in land or in a charge on land".[75] Thus a registrable but unregistered mortgage is void against a later mortgagee, even if he had actual knowledge if it; for where an interest is void for non-registration as against a purchaser, he is not prejudicially affected by notice of it.[76]

19–222   *(e) Equitable mortgages as estate contracts.* Before the operation of these rules is illustrated, one problem must be faced. It is plain that the design of the Land Charges Acts is to exempt all protected mortgages from registration.[77] However, it has now been held that an equitable mortgage by deposit of title deeds takes effect as a contract to grant a mortgage and not as something *sui generis*.[78] It would therefore appear to fall within the definition of an "estate

---

[72] L.C.A. 1972, s.2(4); *ante*, para. 5–096.
[73] L.C.A. 1972, s.2(4); *ante*, para. 5–098.
[74] L.C.A. 1972, s.18(6) in effect inserts the last two words.
[75] L.C.A. 1972, s.17(1).
[76] L.P.A. 1925, s.199(1); *ante*, paras 4–085, 5–117.
[77] The usual view is that they are not registrable: see, *e.g.* Cheshire & Burn's *Modern Law of Real Property*, (15th ed), p. 721; Waldock, *Mortgages*, p. 410.
[78] *United Bank of Kuwait Plc v. Sahib* [1997] Ch. 107; *ante*, paras 12–043, 19–039. The decision was in the context of the formal requirements of L.P.(M.P.)A. 1989, s.2.

contract" (any contract "to convey or create a legal estate"[79]), which contains nothing to exclude equitable mortgages by deposit.[80] The difficulty with this view is that it "was plainly not envisaged"[81] when the Land Charges Act was drafted, and would upset the scheme of the Act. It would also destroy the security of many equitable mortgages.[82] The point remains unresolved[83] and, for the future, the only safe course is to register such a mortgage as an estate contract. However, it has been acknowledged that in the scheme of the Land Charges Act 1972, "all mortgages must be registered unless protected by deposit of title deeds".[84] It is to be hoped that the courts will be willing to interpret the provisions of the 1972 Act purposively to give effect to this scheme, even though such an approach is not easy to reconcile with the express words of that Act.[85]

The examples that follow are given on the assumption that such equitable mortgages are not registrable, but they must be read subject to the caveat that this may prove not to be the case.[86]

2. Operation of the rules. The rules can operate in four possible combinations of mortgages.

(a) Both mortgages protected by a deposit of deeds. There is nothing to **19–223** require the deposit of all the deeds; therefore it may be possible for two or more mortgages of the same property to be exempted from registration provided that the deeds deposited do in fact "protect" or "secure" the mortgage. For example, A may make a mortgage to X and hand over all the existing deeds; A may then sell the property to B, subject to the mortgage; and B may then mortgage it to Y and deposit with Y the conveyance from A to B. In such a case registration is inapplicable and the old law applies. The 1925 legislation has not altered the basic principle that prima facie mortgages rank in the order of their creation,[87] subject to the rules as to loss of priority, *e.g.* by fraud, gross negligence, or the plea of purchaser without notice.[88] In this

---

[79] L.C.A. 1972, s.2(4)(iv); *ante*, para. 5–099.
[80] See (1930) 69 L.J. News 227 (J.M.L.); (1940) 7 C.L.J. 250, 251 (R.E.M.); (1949) 10 C.L.J. 245 (S. J. Bailey); (1962) 26 Conv. (N.S.) 445 (R. F. Rowley).
[81] *United Bank of Kuwait Plc v. Sahib, supra,* at 139, *per* Peter Gibson L.J.
[82] Many such informal mortgages created since L.P.(M.P.)A. 1989, s.2, was brought into force, will in fact have been invalidated by the decision in *United Bank of Kuwait Plc v. Sahib, supra,* because they did not comply with s.2. See *ante,* para. 12–043.
[83] *United Bank of Kuwait Plc v. Sahib, supra,* at 139.
[84] *ibid.,* at 138, *per* Peter Gibson L.J.
[85] The suggestion in the previous edition of this work (at pp. 998, 999) that even if a mortgage by deposit of title deeds were invalid as an estate contract, it could be valid as a mere charge is precluded by the decision in *United Bank of Kuwait Plc v. Sahib, supra,* at 128.
[86] It should be noted that, by L.C.A. 1972, s.4(6), an unregistered estate contract is void "as against a purchaser for money or money's worth . . . of a legal estate in the land charged with it". An unregistered estate contract enjoys greater protection than an unregistered puisne mortgage or general equitable charge. See *ante,* para. 5–117.
[87] See *Roberts v. Croft* (1857) 2 De G. & J. 1; *Beddoes v. Shaw* [1937] Ch. 81; [1936] 2 All E.R. 1108.
[88] See *Dixon v. Muckleston* (1872) 8 Ch.App. 155; *ante,* paras 19–200 *et seq.*

class of case it may therefore still matter whether the mortgages are legal or equitable.

(b) Neither mortgage protected by a deposit of deeds

19–224   (1) BOTH MORTGAGES REGISTRABLE. In this case both mortgages are registrable. No difficulty arises if the first mortgage is duly registered before the second is made. Even if the first is equitable and the second legal the first prevails, for the provision that registration amounts to notice prevents the legal mortgagee from claiming to be a purchaser without notice.[89] Nor is there any difficulty if neither mortgage is registered. Even if the first mortgage is legal and the second equitable, under section 4(5) the first is void against the second for want of registration and so the second has priority. Indeed, if there are several successive registrable mortgages, none of which has been registered, the maxim *"qui prior est tempore, potior est jure"* is now reversed, for the last will rank first and so on.

19–225   (2) CONFLICT OF STATUTES. The more difficult case is where the first mortgage was registered after the creation of the second mortgage. For example:

January 1	A grants a registrable mortgage to X
February 2	A grants a registrable mortgage to Y
March 3	X registers
March 4	Y registers

Here the provisions of the Law of Property Act 1925 (s.97) and the Land Charges Act 1972 (s.4(5)) are in apparent conflict. According to section 4(5) the order of priority is plainly Y, X, for X's mortgage is void against Y. According to a simple reading of section 97 the order should be X, Y, for the section requires every such mortgage to "rank according to its date of registration".[90] How this conflict would be resolved is uncertain, but it might well be that section 4(5) would be held to prevail, despite the argument (not a strong one[91]) that section 97 would then be meaningless. If X's mortgage is void as against Y, it is difficult to see how the subsequent registration of X's mortgage can give priority to something which, *ex hypothesi*, has no existence as regards Y.[92] Against that, section 4(5) applies to mortgages only by reason of the statutory definition of "purchaser", which applies only unless the

---

[89] *Ante*, para. 5–109.

[90] An argument for this solution, and for the rejection of s.4(5), is put forward in (1950) 13 M.L.R. at pp. 534–535 (A. D. Hargreaves). It depends on a distinction between mortgages and other purchases which is not convincing.

[91] This could equally well be said of s.199(1)(i) for the same reason. Overlapping provisions are by no means rare.

[92] See (1926) 61 L.J.News. 398 (J.M.L.); (1940) 7 C.L.J. 255 (R.E.M.); *Hollington Bros Ltd v. Rhodes* [1951] 2 T.L.R. 691 at 696. And technically L.C.A. 1925 (the predecessor of L.C.A. 1972), was a later statute than L.P.A. 1925, and should prevail in the case of irreconcilable conflict. Of two conflicting provisions in the same Act, the later prevails: *Eastbourne Corporation v. Fortes Ice Cream Parlour (1955) Ltd* [1959] 2 Q.B. 92 at 107.

context otherwise requires,[93] whereas section 97 is patently intended to regulate the priority of mortgages; and *generalia specialibus non derogant.*[94]

(3) AVOIDANCE OF CONFLICT. A possible interpretation of section 97 which **19–226** avoids any conflict is that it merely refers to the machinery of the Land Charges Act and accords with it. The section says that an unprotected mortgage "shall rank according to its date of registration as a land charge pursuant to the Land Charges Act", 1925 or 1972. The operation of section 4(5) is governed, of course, by the date of registration, but it does not necessarily follow that the mortgage first registered stands first in priority in all cases. Section 97 does not say, to quote the language of another Act of 1925,[95] that registrable charges shall "rank according to the order in which they are entered on the register"; and it might have been more natural to say this had it been intended.[96] On this interpretation section 97 merely provides that registrable mortgages shall rank for priority according to the provisions of the Land Charges Act, *i.e.* according to section 4(5).

The argument that the two sections conflict draws its strength from the evident intention of section 97 to deal with the question of priority. Precedents can be found for similar forms of words in Acts requiring registration,[97] and section 97 may have been modelled upon them. If it was intended as a mere reference to the Land Charges Act, it seems both redundant and contradictory. The argument against conflict, on the other hand, has the merit that this argument should always prevail in case of doubt. The presumption against Parliament simultaneously enacting two contradictory systems is strong, especially where one of the two supposedly conflicting Acts expressly makes reference to the other.[98]

(4) THREE OR MORE MORTGAGES. Where there are three or more registrable **19–227** mortgages it is possible to construct insoluble problems. For example:

January 1	A grants a registrable mortgage to X
February 2	A grants a registrable mortgage to Y
March 3	X registers
April 4	A grants a registrable mortgage to Z

---

[93] L.C.A. 1972, s.17(1).
[94] General provisions do not derogate from special provisions.
[95] L.R.A. 1925, s.29.
[96] *cf.* Bills of Sale Act 1878, s.10: "shall have priority in the order of the date of their registration".
[97] *cf.* Merchant Shipping (Registration etc.) Act 1993, s.8(1) (the priority of mortgages of ships is to be determined "by the order in which the mortgages were registered"); and see the repealed Yorkshire Registries Act, 1884, s.14 ("shall have priority according to the date of registration thereof"). The Middlesex Registry Act 1708 (also repealed) provided with exemplary clarity that an unregistered assurance was void against a subsequent purchaser unless registered before the registration of the subsequent purchaser's assurance.
[98] "All this property legislation must be construed together; and obviously a result which would make the sections . . . mutually conflict must be avoided, unless there is no escape": *Northchurch Estates Ltd v. Daniels* [1947] Ch. 117 at 123, *per* Evershed J. in another context.

Here Y has priority to X and Z has priority to Y; but X has priority to Z, so that the priorities run not in a series but in a circle. There is some authority for solving such problems by recourse to the doctrine of subrogation, by which one creditor is allowed to stand in the shoes of another on equitable grounds.[99] The court's order then might be to pay Z to the extent of Y's claim against X; then to pay X in full; then to pay any balance due to Z on his own claim; and finally to pay any balance to Y. It is easy to find fault with any such solution, for the problem of the *circulus inextricabilis* is in fact insoluble. Here Y is sacrificed to X, whereas Y should be paid before X. Subrogation produces an arbitrary result, for there is no logical point at which to break the circle and begin the process; and if begun at a different point it gives a different solution. The cases so far reported seem to suggest that the court would elect to take the mortgages in order of date of creation and begin by subrogating the latest mortgagee to the earliest, as in the above example.[1]

19–228   (5) PRIORITY NOTICES AND OFFICIAL SEARCHES. Since it was physically impossible to register a land charge the instant after it had been created, there was at first a dangerous gap between the creation of a mortgage and its registration. Further, even if a search for prior incumbrances was made, the mortgagee could not be sure that no incumbrance had been registered between the time of his search and the completion of the mortgage. These difficulties have been met by the devices of the priority notice and the official search which have been dealt with in the chapter on registration.[2]

19–229   *(c) First but not second mortgage protected by a deposit of deeds.* In this case the first mortgage, by taking its priority from the date of its creation, will normally have priority over the second mortgage, subject to the established rules as to loss of priority, *e.g.* by fraud or gross negligence.[3]

19–230   *(d) Second but not first mortgage protected by a deposit of deeds.* Here section 4(5) and section 97 must work in harmony, however section 97 is interpreted. If the first mortgage is registered before the second is made, the first ranks for priority "according to its date of registration" (s.97), *i.e.* prior to the second mortgage, and section 4(5) has no application. If the first mortgage is not registered when the second mortgage is made, the first mortgage is void against the second for want of registration; and even if it is

---

[99] See *Benham v. Keane* (1861) 1 J. & H. 685; 3 De G.F. & J. 318; and see *Re Wyatt* [1892] 1 Ch. 188 at 209 (a puzzle suggested by the rule in *Dearle v. Hall, ante,* para. 19–208; *Re Armstrong* [1895] 1 I.R. 87; *Re Weniger's Policy* [1910] 2 Ch. 291. For discussion, see (1968) 32 Conv. (N.S.) 325 (W. A. Lee).
[1] See generally (1961) 71 Yale L.J. 53 (G. Gilmore).
[2] *Ante,* paras 5–127—5–130.
[3] *Ante,* paras 19–201—19–204.

subsequently registered, it takes priority from the date of registration and therefore ranks second.

3. Summary

(a) Deeds. A mortgage protected by a deposit of deeds ranks according to the date on which it was created. The mortgagee may lose priority— **19–231**

- (i) by conduct which before 1926 would have had this effect; or

- (ii) if his mortgage is equitable, by a legal mortgage being made to a mortgagee for value without notice, or to a mortgagee who accepts a "reasonable excuse" for non-production of the deeds.[4]

(b) No deeds. A mortgage not protected by deposit of deeds should be protected by registration. If the mortgagee fails to do this, he will not be protected against a subsequent mortgagee (s.4(5)), even if (as it seems) he registers before him (section 97 notwithstanding). If he does register, he will be protected against all mortgages made thereafter. **19–232**

Since an equitable mortgagee who has custody of the title deeds may through no fault of his own lose priority to a later legal mortgagee to whom the mortgagor makes some excuse for non-production of the deeds,[4a] it seems in theory to be safer for the first mortgagee to refuse to take the title deeds, and to register a general equitable charge. But in fact mortgagees prefer the practical security of having the title deeds to the theoretical advantage of refusing them.

II. MORTGAGES OF AN EQUITABLE INTEREST

A mortgage of an equitable interest under a trust of any property, whether land or pure personalty, now takes priority according to the rule in *Dearle v. Hall*,[5] as amended by the Law of Property Act 1925.[6] That is to say, the rule in *Dearle v. Hall* has now been amended, and extended from the realm of personalty to that of land; but as regards land it applies only to dealings with an equitable interest under a trust, *e.g.* mortgages of the beneficial interest of a tenant for life under a settlement, whether in the land itself or in the capital money representing it. Mortgages of such interests are therefore now governed by the principle that priority depends upon the order in which notice of the mortgages is received by the appropriate trustee or trustees. **19–233**

This principle "does not apply until a trust has been created".[7] The meaning of this restriction is not entirely clear, but it appears to be designed to exclude

---

[4] *Ante*, para. 19–206.
[4a] *ibid.*
[5] *Ante*, para. 19–208.
[6] ss.137, 138. See [1993] Conv. 22 (J. Howell).
[7] L.P.A. 1925, s.137(10).

equitable interests which fall outside the ordinary categories of trusts, such as the interest of a purchaser under a contract of sale or lease.[8]

The amendments made by the Law of Property Act 1925 are as follows.

19–234 **1. Notice in writing.** No notice given or received can affect priority unless it is in writing.[9] Apart from this, no alteration has been made in the rules relating to notice.[10]

19–235 **2. Persons to be served.** The persons to be served with notice are:

(i) in the case of settled land,[11] the trustees of the settlement;

(ii) in the case of a trust of land, the trustees;

(iii) in the case of any other land, the estate owner[12] of the land affected.[13]

Thus the person to be served is normally the owner of the legal estate, except in the case of settled land, where notice to the tenant for life might well be no protection, *e.g.* if it was his life interest which had been mortgaged. In cases other than the three mentioned above, no special provision has been made, so that notice must be given to the legal owner as before 1926. Nor has any alteration been made to the law relating to notice received by one of several trustees.[14]

19–236 **3. Indorsement of notice.** If for any reason a valid notice cannot be served (*e.g.* where there are no trustees), or can be served only at unreasonable cost or delay, a purchaser[15] may require that a memorandum be indorsed on or permanently annexed to the instrument creating the trust, and this has the same effect as notice to the trustees.[16] He may also require the instrument to be produced in order to prove proper indorsement.[16a] The document to be used for this purpose is—

(i) in the case of settled land, the trust instrument; and

---

[8] As, for example, in *Property Discount Corpn. Ltd v. Lyon Group Ltd* [1981] 1 W.L.R. 300, where an equitable charge of a building contractor's rights to obtain leases took priority under different rules: *ante*, para. 5–108.

[9] L.P.A. 1925, s.137(3). *Quaere* whether the notice in *Lloyd v. Banks* (1868) 3 Ch.App. 488 (*ante*, para. 19–212) would not still be sufficient, for it was "received" by the trustee in printed form. Yet L.P.A. 1925, s.137(2), speaks of the persons "to be *served* with notice".

[10] *Ante*, paras 19–211—19–214.

[11] Including capital money or securities representing capital money.

[12] *i.e.* the owner of a legal estate: L.P.A. 1925, s.205(1)(v); *ante*, para. 4–038.

[13] L.P.A. 1925, s.137(2) (as amended by T.L.A.T.A. 1996, Sched. 3, para. 15).

[14] *Ante*, paras 19–211—19–214.

[15] Including, of course, a mortgagee.

[16] L.P.A. 1925, s.137(4).

[16a] *ibid.*

(ii) the case of a trust of land, the instrument creating the equitable interest.[17]

If the trust is created by statute or by operation of law, or there is no instrument creating the trust, the document to be used is that under which the equitable interest is acquired or which evidences its devolution, *e.g.* in the case of an intestacy, the probate or letters of administration in force when the dealing was effected.[18]

4. Notice to trust corporation. The instrument creating the trust, the trustees, or the court, may nominate a trust corporation to receive notices instead of the trustees.[19] In such cases, only notice to the trust corporation affects priority; notice to the trustees has no effect until they deliver it to the trust corporation, which they are bound to do forthwith.[20] Provision is made for—   **19–237**

(i) the indorsement of notice of the appointment on the instrument upon which notices may be indorsed[21];

(ii) the keeping of a register of notices[22];

(iii) the inspection of the register[23];

(iv) the answering of inquiries[24]; and

(v) the payment of fees for performing these functions.[25]

This is in effect machinery for setting up a private register of charges. In practice little use is made of these provisions.

5. Production of notices. On the application of any person interested in the equitable interest, the trustees or estate owner must now produce any notices served on them or their predecessors.[26] This reverses what had previously been the law.[27]   **19–238**

C. Summary

A summary of the principal divisions of the rules relating to the priority of mortgages may be useful.

[17] *ibid.*, s.137(5) (as amended by T.L.A.T.A. 1996, Sched. 3, para. 15).
[18] *ibid.*, s.137(6).
[19] *ibid.*, s.138(1).
[20] *ibid.*, s.138(3), (4).
[21] *ibid.*, s.138(2).
[22] *ibid.*, s.138(7).
[23] *ibid.*, s.138(9).
[24] *ibid.*, s.138(10).
[25] *ibid.*, s.138(9), (10), (11).
[26] *ibid.*, s.137(8), (9).
[27] See *Low v. Bouverie* [1891] 3 Ch. 82; *ante*, para. 19–215. In that case, it had been held that the trustees were under no duty to disclose notices to third parties, so that a prospective mortgagee might not be able to discover previous incumbrances.

1. Before 1926

19–239   *(a) Legal or equitable interests in land.* Priority was governed by the order of creation, subject to the doctrine of purchaser without notice, and to special rules as to fraud, estoppel, gross negligence, and "reasonable excuse" for non-production of title deeds.

19–240   *(b) Equitable interests in pure personalty. Dearle v. Hall* applied.

2. After 1925

19–241   *(a) Legal estates in land.* Priority is governed by the same rules as before 1926, subject to the rules requiring registration of mortgages not protected by deposit of documents.

19–242   *(b) Equitable interests in any property. Dearle v. Hall* applies.

Section 2. Unregistered Land: Tacking

19–243   Tacking is a special way of obtaining priority for a secured loan by amalgamating it with another secured loan of higher priority. It may apply both to realty and to personalty.[28] Before 1926 there were two forms of tacking:

> (i) what was called the *tabula in naufragio* ("the plank in the shipwreck"); and

> (ii) the tacking of further advances.

The 1925 legislation abolished the first kind of tacking and amended the law as to the second. The first will be briefly explained for the sake of its intrinsic interest,[29] and the second as the necessary prologue to the amendments of 1925.

A. Before 1926

I. THE *TABULA IN NAUFRAGIO*

19–244   **1. The doctrine.** In a contest between two equitable mortgagees, the later could sometimes gain priority over the earlier by acquiring a legal mortgage which had priority to both.[30] The insufficiency of the security was the "shipwreck", and the legal estate was the "plank" which any equitable mortgagee might seize without concern for the others.[31] The metaphor implies a disaster where someone must lose, and each party may save himself as best

---

[28] Coote, *Mortgages*, p. 1245.

[29] For a recent case in which the doctrine had to be considered, see *Macmillan Inc. v. Bishopsgate Investment Trust Plc* [1995] 1 W.L.R. 978 at 1002, 1003.

[30] *Marsh v. Lee* (1671) 2 Vent. 337; *Peacock v. Burt* (1834) 4 L.J. Ch. 33.

[31] The phrase is Hale C.J.'s: see *Brace v. Duchess of Marlborough* (1728) 2 P.Wms. 491, *per* Jekyll M.R.

he can. There is no moral equity in the doctrine, which has often been criticised,[32] and "could not happen in any other country but this".[33] It is a curious example of the deference paid by equity to the legal estate.[34] Where, apart from the order of creation, the equities between the mortgagees were equal, the holder of the legal estate had priority[35]; "where the equities are equal, the law prevails", and so upsets the natural equitable order of priority.

The opportunity for this master-stroke occurred when there was first a legal   **19–245** and then two equitable mortgages, all made to different mortgagees, and the mortgagor managed to conceal the second mortgage at the time when he created the third.[36] Thus if A mortgaged his property to X by a legal mortgage and then to Y and Z by successive equitable mortgages, Z's mortgage could be given priority over Y's if Z bought X's mortgage, provided Z had no notice of Y's mortgage when he advanced his money.[37] X's legal mortgage was the plank in the shipwreck, and if Z could secure it before Y, he could throw onto Y the loss which would otherwise have fallen upon himself. Since Z knew nothing of Y's mortgage when he took his own mortgage, he might naturally have lent more than the security would satisfy. A property worth £100,000 might for example have been mortgaged first to X for £20,000, then to Y for £60,000, and then again to Z for £60,000, Z knowing nothing of Y's mortgage. Thus when the mortgagor defaulted a shipwreck was inevitable.

2. No notice. The mortgagee seeking to tack must have had no notice of the   **19–246** prior equitable mortgage when he advanced his money[38]; if he had notice, he could not tack, for obviously his equity was then not equal to Y's.[39] But if he had no notice at that time, it was immaterial that he obtained notice later, before he acquired the legal estate.[40] Indeed, on a principle similar to the rule in *Dearle v. Hall*[41] notice of the prior equitable mortgage before the later mortgagee acquired the legal estate was "the very occasion, that shews the necessity of it".[42] The natural time for tacking was when the third mortgagee, who when he made his loan imagined that he was taking a second mortgage, discovered later that there was an intervening mortgage, and then took a transfer of the first legal mortgage in order to secure priority. Notice to the first mortgagee (who held the legal estate) was immaterial, so that the second mortgagee could not protect himself against tacking by giving him notice.[43] Such circumstances "look very like a conspiracy between the first and third

---

[32] See Waldock, *Mortgages*, p. 391.
[33] *Wortley v. Birkhead* (1754) 2 Ves.Sen. 571 at 574, *per* Lord Hardwicke L.C.
[34] *Bailey v. Barnes* [1894] 1 Ch. 25 at 36.
[35] *Wortley v. Birkhead* (1754) 2 Ves.Sen. 571 at 574.
[36] See *Phillips v. Phillips* (1862) 4 De G.F. & J. 208 at 216.
[37] *Brace v. Duchess of Marlborough, supra.*
[38] *Bates v. Johnson* (1859) Johns. 304 at 313.
[39] *Lacey v. Ingle* (1847) 2 Ph. 413.
[40] *Taylor v. Russell* [1892] A.C. 244 at 259.
[41] *ante*, para. 19–208.
[42] *Wortley v. Birkhead* (1754) 2 Ves.Sen. 571 at 574, *per* Lord Hardwicke L.C.
[43] *Peacock v. Burt* (1834) 4 L.J. Ch. 33.

mortgagees to cheat the second, which cannot be right".[44] But such was the law.

19–247   A legal estate which was already held on trust for the intervening mortgagee would not be used against him by a later mortgagee who took it with notice of the trust,[45] for the trust would then bind the later mortgagee.[46] He "must not, to get a plank to save himself, be guilty of a breach of trust".[47] Thus if a third mortgagee took the legal estate from the first mortgagee with notice that the first mortgage had already been paid off (so that the legal estate was held by the first mortgagee merely as trustee for those entitled to it, including the second mortgagee), tacking was impossible.[48] But while the first mortgage was still unredeemed, notice that the second mortgagee wished to redeem did not, it seems, make it a breach of trust for the first mortgagee to give priority to the third mortgagee by transferring the legal estate to him,[49] although he might thus have been able to sell it to the highest bidder.

19–248   **3. Legal estate.** It was of the essence of tacking that the mortgagee should secure a legal estate. Any prior[50] legal estate would do, *e.g.* an outstanding term of years,[51] or even a judgment giving legal rights against the land[52]; but an equitable interest would not suffice.[53] Nevertheless, in accordance with the doctrine that the better right to the legal estate may rank as possession of it,[54] an express declaration of trust by the owner of the legal estate in favour of the mortgagee seeking to tack, or a transfer of the legal estate to a trustee for him, might be sufficient.[55] In all cases the mortgage and the legal estate had to be held in the same right, and not one on trust and the other beneficially.[56] Further, if the mortgagee parted with the legal estate he thereupon lost his right to tack.[57]

[44] *West London Commercial Bank v. Reliance Permanent B.S.* (1885) 29 Ch.D. 954 at 963, *per* Lindley L.J.; and see *Bates v. Johnson, supra*, at 314.

[45] *Sharples v. Adams* (1863) 32 Beav. 213; *Mumford v. Stohwasser* (1874) L.R. 18 Eq. 556 at 562; *cf. Taylor v. London & County Banking Co.* [1901] 2 Ch. 231 at 256.

[46] *Saunders v. Dehew* (1692) 2 Vern. 271.

[47] *ibid., per* Lords Commissioners.

[48] See *Bates v. Johnson* (1859) Johns 304 at 315–317; *Prosser v. Rice* (1859) 28 Beav. 68 at 74; *Harpham v. Shacklock* (1881) 19 Ch.D. 207; *Macmillan Inc. v. Bishopsgate Investment Trust Plc* [1995] 1 W.L.R. 978 at 1003.

[49] *Bates v. Johnson, supra*, at 313, 314, criticised in *West London Commercial Bank v. Reliance Permanent B.S.* (1885) 29 Ch.D. 954 at 960; the point is reserved at 961.

[50] In *Cooke v. Wilton* (1860) 29 Beav. 100 the first (equitable) mortgagee had a right to a legal mortgage, which was in fact executed after the intervening mortgage; this was held to relate back to the date of the original mortgage, and so to be effective for tacking.

[51] *Willoughby v. Willoughby* (1756) 1 T.R. 763; and see *Maundrell v. Maundrell* (1804) 10 Ves. 246.

[52] *Morret v. Paske* (1740) 2 Atk. 52.

[53] *Brace v. Duchess of Marlborough* (1728) 2 P.Wms. 491 at 495, 496.

[54] See *ante*, para. 5–011.

[55] See *Wilkes v. Bodington* (1707) 2 Vern. 599 at 600; *Earl of Pomfret v. Lord Windsor* (1752) 2 Ves.Sen. 472 at 486; *Pease v. Jackson* (1868) 3 Ch.App. 576; *Crosbie-Hill v. Sayer* [1908] 1 Ch. 866 at 875, 876.

[56] *Morret v. Paske, supra*, at 53; *Harnett v. Weston* (1806) 12 Ves. 130.

[57] *Rooper v. Harrison* (1855) 2 K. & J. 86.

Although tacking usually took place when a later mortgagee acquired the legal estate, the principle extended also to a legal incumbrancer who acquired a later mortgage without notice of an intervening incumbrance, *e.g.* where a first legal mortgagee took a transfer of a third mortgage without notice of the second.[58]

II. TACKING OF FURTHER ADVANCES

1. The doctrine. The tacking of further advances was the more important   **19–249**
branch of the doctrine of tacking. It often happened that a mortgagee would wish to lend more money on the same security at some later date. If, then, the borrower had mortgaged the property to another mortgagee between the dates of the first and second loans from the original mortgagee, the question was whether the last loan could be tacked to the first so as to take priority over the second. This question arose very commonly in banking, where a mortgage was made to secure an overdraft which might be increased as further cheques were cashed.

2. Forms of tacking. Before 1926 there were two cases where tacking of   **19–250**
this kind was allowed.

(a) Agreement of intervening incumbrancer. The mortgagee could tack if   **19–251**
the intervening incumbrancer agreed; here it was immaterial whether the first mortgage was legal or equitable. Building estates sometimes provided examples of this, when the owner required more money to build on his estate and thus make it a better security. The second mortgagee, not wishing to lend any more money, might agree to the first mortgagee making a further advance to be expended on further building and to rank in priority to the second mortgage. In this case priority was secured simply by contract between the mortgagees.

(b) No notice of intervening incumbrance. If a further advance was made   **19–252**
without notice of the intervening mortgage, it might be tacked if either of the following conditions was satisfied.

(1) LEGAL ESTATE. The further advance was made either by a legal mort-   **19–253**
gagee,[59] or by an equitable mortgagee with the best right to the legal estate (as where A advanced money and had the legal estate conveyed to a trustee).[60] Priority here resulted from the strength of the legal estate.

(2) CONTRACT. The prior mortgage expressly provided that the security   **19–254**
should extend to any further advances, whether or not it was obligatory for the mortgagee to make them. A bank, for example, might take a mortgage to

---

[58] *Morret v. Paske, supra*, at 53.
[59] *Wyllie v. Pollen* (1863) 3 De G.J. & S. 596.
[60] See *ante*, paras 5–011, 19–248; and see *Wilmot v. Pike* (1945) 5 Hare 14, explained *ante*, para. 19–205. See also *Wormald v. Maitland* (1866) 35 L.J. Ch. 69, where this point received perfunctory treatment.

secure an overdraft, with a clause stating that the security should cover any further overdraft which the bank might allow. Such tacking was said to be available to any mortgagee, legal or equitable; for it was tacking not by virtue of a legal estate but by virtue of the contract whereby the equity of redemption was potentially charged with any further advances, so that an intervening mortgagee took it subject to this right.[61]

19–255   **3. Effect of notice.** It was an invariable rule that a further advance could not be tacked if at the time of making it the mortgagee had notice of the intervening mortgage.[62] This was a suitable rule for tacking in class (1), for the law should prevail only where the equities are equal. But, after some hesitation, the courts extended it to class (2),[63] whereas it might have been thought that if a paramount right to tack was secured by the terms of the first mortgage, it could not be taken away by a later mortgagee giving notice of his charge. The rule was applied even to the case where the first mortgage obliged the mortgagee to make further advances,[64] though the mortgagee was protected by the rule that he was released from the obligation to make the further advances as soon as the mortgagor, by creating a later incumbrance, prevented any further advance from having the priority of the original mortgage.[65]

The effect of these rules was that a mortgagee with notice of a subsequent incumbrance could never tack further advances against it, and an equitable mortgagee without notice could tack only if his mortgage made provision for further advances, or if he was one of the rare examples of an equitable mortgagee who had some prior claim on the legal estate.[66]

B. After 1925

19–256   The law as to tacking is now to be found in section 94 of the Law of Property Act 1925. The position is as follows.

I. THE *TABULA IN NAUFRAGIO*

19–257   Without prejudice to any priority gained before 1926, the right to tack, except in respect of further advances, was abolished at the end of 1925.[67] That was the end of the *tabula in naufragio*.

---

[61] See Fisher and Lightwood, *Mortgage*, p. 486 citing *Calisher v. Forbes* (1871) 7 Ch.App. 109 and *Re Weniger's Policy* [1910] 2 Ch. 291 at 295; but see below, n. 64.
[62] *Hopkinson v. Rolt* (1861) 9 H.L.C. 514, explained in *Bradford Banking Co. Ltd v. Henry Briggs, Son & Co. Ltd* (1886) 12 App.Cas. 29, and *Union Bank of Scotland v. National Bank of Scotland* (1886) 12 App.Cas. 53.
[63] *Hopkinson v. Rolt, supra*, where opinions in the House of Lords were divided.
[64] *West v. Williams* [1899] 1 Ch. 132. Having reached this point, the authorities had become inconsistent with the notion that an equitable mortgagee could tack at all. The doctrine that an agreement for further advances created a potential charge was denied in *West v. Williams* at 143, 146, and this struck at the root of an equitable mortgagee's power to tack.
[65] See *West v. Williams, supra*, at 143, 146.
[66] See *ante*, para. 19–253.
[67] L.P.A. 1925, s.94(3).

II. TACKING OF FURTHER ADVANCES

The tacking of further advances has been modified so as to make it immaterial **19–258** whether any of the mortgages concerned are legal or equitable,[68] and so as to make the rules more reasonable where the first mortgage expressly contemplates further advances. After 1925 a prior mortgagee may tack further advances so as "to rank in priority to subsequent mortgagee"[69] in the three cases set out below. As this exemption from the general abolition of tacking is confined to mortgages, it seems that further advances cannot be tacked so as to take priority over other intervening interests such as estate contracts.[70] The three cases are as follows.

1. Agreement of intervening incumbrancer. The position is **19–259** unchanged.[71]

2. No notice of intervening incumbrance. A further advance can be **19–260** tacked if it was made without notice of the intervening mortgage.[72] Where the intervening mortgage is protected by a deposit of deeds and is thus not registrable as a land charge, the normal rules as to notice operate.[73] If the mortgage is not protected in this way and is accordingly registrable (as will usually be the case), the rule that registration amounts to notice[74] will normally apply and so protect it if it is registered. But, by a special exception, if the prior mortgage was made expressly for securing further advances (*e.g.* in the case of an overdraft at a bank, where the debt is increased or decreased as sums are drawn out or paid in), mere registration of a later mortgage as a land charge is not deemed to be notice, unless that mortgage was registered when the last search was made by the prior mortgagee.[75] The same applies to a spouse's matrimonial home rights under the Family Law Act 1996 which are registered after a mortgage has been made. Even if the spouse's charge arose before the mortgage, the charge is deemed for this purpose to be a subsequent mortgage.[76]

An example may make this clearer. Mortgages have been made to A (who **19–261** took the deeds) and B, in that order, and A has made further advances. If when A made his further advances he had actual, constructive or imputed notice of B's mortgage, he cannot tack under this head even if his mortgage, without obliging him to make further advances, was stated to be security for any

---

[68] L.P.A. 1925, s.94(1).
[69] *ibid.*
[70] See Maitland, *Equity*, 214 (J. W. Brunyate); (1958) 22 Conv. (N.S.) 44 at 56 (R. G. Rowley); this is probably a failure in drafting.
[71] L.P.A. 1925, s.94(1)(a).
[72] *ibid.*, s.94(1)(b).
[73] *Ante*, para. 5–015.
[74] L.P.A. 1925, s.198(1).
[75] L.P.A. 1925, s.94(2), as amended by L.P.(Am.)A. 1926. The amendment safeguards a mortgage registered (presumably by priority notice: *ante*, para. 5–129) before the principal mortgage was created.
[76] s.31(12), replacing earlier legislation. See *ante*, para. 17–023.

further advances he might choose to make.[77] If he had no such notice of B's mortgage when he made his further advances, but B's mortgage was registered at that time, then if A's mortgage is silent as to further advances, the registration amounts to notice and prevents A from tacking. But if A's mortgage was expressed to be security for any further advances he might make, the registration will not prevent him from tacking, and thus he need not search before making each further advance. It would be unreasonable, in particular, to require banks to make a search before cashing each cheque on a secured overdraft.

This highlights a practical point. Even if a second mortgage has been duly registered, the mortgagee should still give express notice of his mortgage to the first mortgagee, for this—

    (i) prevents tacking under this head; and

    (ii) compels the first mortgagee to hand over the deeds to him when the first mortgage is discharged.[78]

In these two respects registration by itself is not notice.

19–262   **3. Obligation to make further advances.** A further advance may be tacked if the prior mortgage imposes an obligation on the mortgagee to make it.[79] In this case, not even express notice will prevent tacking.[80] If in return for a mortgage a bank binds itself to honour a customer's cheques up to an overdraft of £10,000, there is no question of the bank losing priority, for not even express notice will prevent the bank from tacking each further advance.[81] The principle of this is, of course, that the later mortgagee has clear warning that the prior mortgagee has further claims on the security.

Section 3. Registered Land: Priority

The priority of mortgages and charges where title is registered has already been explained.[82] It may be summarised as follows.

19–263   **1. Priority of registered charges.** Registered charges rank in priority according to the date on which they are registered and not according to the order of their creation.[83]

---

[77] This confirms *Hopkinson v. Rolt* (1861) 9 H.L.C. 514; *ante*, para. 19–255.

[78] *Ante*, para. 19–094.

[79] L.P.A. 1925, s.94(1)(c).

[80] This reverses *West v. Williams*, *ante*, para. 19–255.

[81] *Quaere* whether this affects *Deeley v. Lloyds Bank Ltd* [1912] A.C. 756 (payments into the account prima facie go in reduction of the bank's prior charge, thus improving the later mortgagee's position).

[82] *Ante*, paras 6–095, 6–112.

[83] L.R.A. 1925, s.29; *ante*, para. 6–112.

2. Priority of mortgages which take effect as minor interests. The **19–264** priority of mortgages which are not registered charges is determined by the rules which govern the priority of minor interests generally. First, where an interest under a trust is mortgaged, priority is preserved by giving notice to the trustees under the rule in *Dearle v. Hall*[84] as it has been applied by the Law of Property Act 1925.[85] Secondly, in other cases, because minor interests take effect in equity, the priority of competing mortgages is determined by the date on which such rights are created, subject to the exceptions of gross carelessness and inequitable behaviour.[86] Such priority is unaffected by the fact that one or other mortgage is protected by the entry on the register of a notice or caution.[87] However, where a mortgage which has taken effect as a minor interest is subsequently registered as a registered charge, that may affect priorities. For example:

January 1	A executes a charge in favour of X: the charge is not registered, but takes effect as a minor interest
February 2	A executes a charge in favour of Y: Y does not initially register the charge, which therefore takes effect subject to X's
March 3	Y registers his charge as a registered charge. A registered charge takes effect as a registered disposition and, as such, the chargee takes free of unregistered minor interests.[88] Y therefore ceases to be bound by X's charge

3. Tacking. It has already been explained that the provisions of the Law of **19–265** Property Act 1925 which relate to the tacking of further advances[89] are inapplicable to registered land,[90] and that where title is registered, the Land Registration Act 1925 limits the circumstances in which further advances may be tacked.[91]

Part 6

REFORM

There is little doubt that the law of mortgages is in need of reform. It is **19–266** needlessly complicated and "has achieved a state of artificiality and complexity that is now difficult to defend".[92] The Law Commission undertook an

---

[84] (1828) 3 Russ. 1.
[85] s.137; *ante*, paras 6–094, 19–233.
[86] *Ante*, paras 5–013, 19–207.
[87] *Ante*, para. 6–095.
[88] L.R.R. 1925, r. 148; Ruoff & Roper, 24–11.
[89] s.94; *ante*, para. 19–258.
[90] L.P.A. 1925, s.94(4).
[91] L.R.A. 1925, s.30; *ante*, para. 6–112.
[92] (1991) Law Com. No. 204, para. 2.1.

ambitious review of the law and made sweeping recommendations for the simplification of the law.[93] For example, it was proposed that there should be just two ways of creating a mortgage, one formal and the other informal. Restrictions would have been imposed on the exercise by mortgagees of their powers in respect of residential property. The doctrine of clogs and fetters on the equity of redemption[94] would have been abolished and the court would have had a power to set aside and vary the terms of a mortgage. The Government has declined to accept the proposals in their present form (because there was insufficient support for them) and it seems likely that they will be reconsidered by the Law Commission at some future date.

---

[93] Law Com. No. 204; see [1992] Conv. 69 (H. W. Wilkinson).
[94] *Ante.*

CHAPTER 20

DISABILITIES

CERTAIN persons are subject to disabilities as to the interests in land which **20–001** they can hold, create or alienate. Formerly the range of persons subject to disability was much greater than it is now,[1] and included married women,[2] traitors and felons,[3] aliens[4] and corporations.[5] The three principal categories of persons still subject to some form of disability, and which are considered in this chapter, are minors, mental patients and charities. The last of these— charities—are in fact now largely free of restrictions on their capacity, and are therefore treated briefly.

Section 1. Minors

A minor is a person who has not attained full age.[6] A person attains the age **20–002** of majority at the first moment of the eighteenth anniversary of his birth.[7] The following are the main principles governing a minor's rights in land.

1. Ownership of land. Before 1926 a minor was capable of holding both **20–003** legal estates and equitable interests in land. After 1925 a minor cannot hold a legal estate in land, whether registered or unregistered,[8] though he may still hold an equitable interest.[9]

2. Attempted conveyance to a minor. The effect of an attempted convey- **20–004** ance of a legal estate to a minor after 1925 depends upon whether it was made before 1997 or after 1996.[10]

---

[1] Reference should be made to the previous edition of this work for an account of the former law.

[2] See the previous edition of this work at p. 1020.

[3] *ibid.*, at p. 1026.

[4] *ibid.*, at p. 1027.

[5] *ibid.*, at p. 1027.

[6] The term "minor" is now generally employed instead of "infant" in legal usage.

[7] Family Law Reform Act 1969, s.9. This has been the law since January 1, 1970: *ibid.*, s.1. Prior to that date a person attained majority at the first moment of the day *preceding* the 21st anniversary of his birth. For an explanation of this, see the previous edition of this work at p. 1015.

[8] L.P.A. 1925, s.1(6); L.R.A. 1925, s.3(iv).

[9] See S.L.A. 1925, s.26(6); T.L.A.T.A. 1996, s.2(6); Sched. 1, para. 1.

[10] Where title to the land is registered there are corresponding provisions: (i) to identify the person or persons who should be the registered proprietor; and (ii) to ensure that no minor is registered as proprietor: see L.R.A. 1925, s.111(1)–(3).

20–005   *(a) Attempted conveyance prior to 1997.* An attempt made prior to 1997 to convey a legal estate to a minor either alone or jointly with other minors operated as contract for value by the intending transferor to make a proper settlement under the Settled Land Act 1925 by means of a vesting deed and trust instrument. In the meantime, the party making the conveyance held the land on trust for the minor or minors.[11] Any such contract that was still in existence when the Trusts of Land and Appointment of Trustees Act came into force at the beginning of 1997 ceased to have effect. Instead the conveyance operated as a declaration that the land was held in trust for the minors.[12] An attempted conveyance of a legal estate to a minor jointly with a person of full age vested the legal estate in the person of full age on a statutory trust for sale for himself and the minor.[13] Any such trust that was subsisting on January 1, 1997 became a trust of land.[14] These rules did not apply to a conveyance to a minor as mortgagee or trustee, for which special provision was made.[15]

20–006   *(b) Attempted conveyance after 1996.* After 1996, an attempted conveyance to one or more minors does not pass the legal estate but operates as a declaration that the transferor holds the property in trust for those minors.[16] An attempted conveyance to one or more minors together with another person or persons of full age, vests the land in the adult transferees in trust for both the minors and adults.[17] These rules apply as much to any purported attempt to create a mortgage of a legal estate as they do to an attempted outright conveyance of a freehold or leasehold or the grant of a lease.[18]

20–007   **3. Mortgages.** A minor cannot be a legal mortgagee or chargee. Prior to 1997, an attempt to grant or transfer a legal mortgage to one or more minors operated as an agreement for value to execute a proper mortgage or transfer when the minor or minors came of age. In the meantime the grantor or transferor held any beneficial interest in the mortgage debt in trust for the persons intended to benefit.[19] But a mortgage to a minor and other persons of full age operated, so far as the legal estate was concerned, as if the minor were not named, although any beneficial interest of his in the mortgage debt was not affected.[20]

---

[11] L.P.A. 1925, s.19(1); S.L.A. 1925, s.27(1). Both provisions have now been repealed. See too (in relation to registered land) L.R.A. 1925, s.111(1).

[12] T.L.A.T.A. 1996, Sched. 1, para. 1(3).

[13] L.P.A. 1925, s.19(2) (now repealed). See too (in relation to registered land) L.R.A. 1925, s.111(1), proviso (a) (providing that the minor shall not be registered as proprietor until he attains full age).

[14] T.L.A.T.A. 1996, s.1(2).

[15] L.P.A. 1925, s.19(3) (now repealed). For mortgages, see *infra*.

[16] See T.L.A.T.A. 1996, s.2(6); Sched. 1 para. 1(1); and (in relation to registered land) L.R.A. 1925, s.111(1).

[17] T.L.A.T.A. 1996, Sched. 1, para. 1(2).

[18] This follows from the definition of "conveyance": see T.L.A.T.A. 1996, s.23(2); L.P.A. 1925, s.205(1)(ii).

[19] L.P.A. 1925, s.19(6) (now repealed).

[20] *ibid.*

It has been explained above that, after 1996, any purported grant or transfer of a mortgage or charge to one or more minors either alone or jointly with adult transferees operates in the same way as an attempted conveyance of the legal estate.

4. Personal representatives. A minor can be neither an executor[21] nor an **20–008** administrator.[22] If a minor would be entitled to be an administrator but for his minority, or is appointed sole executor, he cannot take a grant until he is of full age. In the meantime a grant may be taken by someone on his behalf, *e.g.* his guardian. In the case of administration, the grant must normally be made to at least two persons or a trust corporation on the minor's behalf, since a minor is interested in the estate.[23] If a minor is appointed one of several executors, the remainder of whom are of full age, he must wait until he attains his majority, when he can join in the grant of probate previously made to the others.

5. Trustees. No minor can be appointed a trustee after 1925.[24] This applies **20–009** to trusts of any property, real or personal. The effect of a purported conveyance of a legal estate in land to a minor as trustee, although governed by different (and not identically worded) statutory provisions, is in substance the same whether it was made before 1997 or after 1996.

(i) If the minor is a sole trustee, the conveyance operates as a declaration of trust by the grantor in favour of the intended beneficiaries and no legal estate passes. The effect is the same if the conveyance is to two or more trustees, all of whom are minors.[25]

(ii) If the minor is one of two or more trustees, at least one of whom is of full age, the conveyance operates to vest the land in the adult transferee (or transferees) in trust for the intended beneficiaries.[26]

These provisions do not prevent a minor from becoming a trustee of property other than a legal estate in land[27] in other ways, *e.g.* under a constructive trust.[28]

---

[21] Supreme Court Act 1981, s.118.

[22] *In b. Manuel* (1849) 13 Jur. 664.

[23] Supreme Court Act 1981, s.114(2).

[24] L.P.A. 1925, s.20.

[25] Pre-1997: L.P.A. 1925, s.19(4) (now repealed); post-1996: T.L.A.T.A. 1996, s.2(6), Sched. 1, para. 1(1).

[26] Pre-1997: L.P.A. 1925, s.19(5) (now repealed); post-1996: T.L.A.T.A. 1996: Sched. 1, para. 1(2).

[27] See *ante*, para. 20–003.

[28] *Ante*, para. 10–017.

6. Beneficial ownership of land

20–010   *(a) Land acquired prior to 1997.* Land to which a minor became entitled in possession prior to 1997 was deemed to be settled land.[29] This was so even if the minor was absolutely entitled. The purpose of applying the Settled Land Act 1925 machinery to minors was to make the land freely alienable.[30] The legal estate and statutory powers were, in such a case, vested in the statutory owners.[31]

20–011   *(b) Land acquired after 1996.* After 1996, no settlement may be created under the Settled Land Act 1925.[32] If a minor now becomes entitled to a legal estate in land[33] other than by a purported conveyance, *e.g.* under a will or intestacy, it is held in trust for him until he comes of age.[34] In practice the trustees are likely to be the personal representatives, at least initially.[35]

7. Dispositions by minors

20–012   *(a) Voidable.* Any disposition by a minor of an interest in land is voidable at the option of the minor (but not of the grantee[36]) on the minor attaining his majority,[37] or within a reasonable time thereafter.[38] If the minor dies under age, his personal representatives may avoid the disposition within a reasonable time.[39] This is a long established rule of common law. As the disposition is voidable and not void, it is binding if the minor fails to repudiate it within a reasonable time after attaining his majority.[40]

20–013   *(b) Statutory owner.* It has been explained that where a minor became entitled in possession to a fee simple absolute or term of years in land prior to 1997, the land became settled land.[41] Under the Settled Land Act 1925 the statutory owner has power to make a binding disposition of the minor's land and is not handicapped by his privilege of revocation.[42] The Act permits sales,

---

[29] S.L.A. 1925, s.1(1); *ante*, para. 8–051.
[30] See the previous edition of this work at p. 318.
[31] S.L.A. 1925, s.26; *ante*, para. 8–015. For the position where the title was registered, see L.R.A. 1925, ss.91, 111(1) proviso (c).
[32] T.L.A.T.A. 1996, s.2(1); *ante*, para. 8–001.
[33] Including the benefit of a legal charge.
[34] T.L.A.T.A. 1996, Sched. 1, para. 2.
[35] Where title to the land is registered, the personal representatives cannot transfer the title to the minor until he comes of age: L.R.A. 1925, s.111(2). They could of course transfer it to other trustees to hold on trust for the minor. *cf.* T.A. 1925, s.36.
[36] *Zouch d. Abbot v. Parsons* (1765) 3 Burr. 1794.
[37] *Ashfeild v. Ashfeild* (1628) W.Jo. 157 (lease). See *Chaplin v. Leslie Frewin (Publishers) Ltd* [1966] Ch. 71.
[38] *Carnell v. Harrison* [1916] 1 Ch. 328.
[39] Cru.Dig. iv, 69.
[40] *Edwards v. Carter* [1893] A.C. 360.
[41] S.L.A. 1925, s.1(1); *ante*, para. 8–051.
[42] See the previous edition of this work at p. 318.

exchanges, leases and mortgages on certain terms; but in general it does not permit gifts or marriage settlements.

(c) Trustees of land. In a case where a minor becomes entitled to an estate in land after 1996, so that the land is held by trustees on a trust of land,[43] the trustees have in relation to the land all the powers of an absolute owner.[44] Those powers are conferred for the purposes of exercising their functions as trustees.[45] If, under the express terms of a trust of land, the consent of a person who is a minor is required to the exercise of any function relating to the land— **20–014**

> (i) in favour of a purchaser, his consent is not required; but
>
> (ii) the trustees are required to obtain the consent of either a parent who has parental responsibility for him[46] or a guardian.[47]

8. Transfer on death. A minor cannot make a will,[48] except if he is privileged as a soldier or mariner, as already explained.[49] **20–015**

Normally, therefore, any interest vested in a minor will pass on his death by intestacy. But there is one statutory complication. The relevant provision[50] has been altered as regards any minor who dies after 1996.[51] The law is therefore stated as it applies both to deaths before 1997 and after 1996. It can be most readily understood in tabular form.

(a) Deemed entail or life estate **20–016**

DATE OF DEATH OF THE MINOR:	PRIOR TO 1997	AFTER 1996
PROVISION APPLIES:	(i) Where the minor died without having been married; and	(i) Where the minor dies without having been married *and* without issue; and

---

[43] *Ante*, paras 8–125, 20–011.
[44] T.L.A.T.A. 1996, s.6(1); *ante*, para. 8–136.
[45] *ibid.*
[46] For the meaning of this expression, see Children Act 1989, s.3.
[47] T.L.A.T.A. 1996, s.10(3). In the absence of any express requirement of consent, trustees of land, when exercising their powers, are obliged to consult (so far as practicable) only the beneficiaries *of full age* who are beneficially entitled to an interest in possession in the land: *ibid.*, s.11(1); *ante*, para. 8–147.
[48] Wills Act 1837, s.7.
[49] *Ante*, para. 11–039.
[50] A.E.A. 1925, s.51(3).
[51] By T.L.A.T.A. 1996, Sched. 3, para. 4.

20–016 *(a) Deemed entail or life estate—cont.*

DATE OF DEATH OF THE MINOR:	PRIOR TO 1997	AFTER 1996
	(ii) where he would, but for the provision, have been entitled at his death under a settlement[52] (including a will or intestacy[53]) to a vested estate in fee simple,[54] or an absolute interest in property settled to devolve with such land as freehold land.	(ii) he would, but for the provision, have been entitled at his death under a trust or settlement (including a will or intestacy) to a vested estate in fee simple in freehold land or in any property to devolve with that estate as freehold land.
EFFECT:	The minor was deemed to have an *entailed interest* and the settlement was construed accordingly.	The minor is deemed to have a *life interest* and the trust or settlement is construed accordingly.

The reason for the change after 1996 is that an entail can no longer be created.[55] A life estate is therefore substituted.

20–017 *(b) Purpose.* The objects of this somewhat strange provision appear to be—

(i) to make it unnecessary always to take out a grant of administration to the infant's estate; and

(ii) to make the land revert to the donor.

That was certainly the way in which the provision operated before April 4, 1988 and how it operates after 1996, though in the intervening period, the effect could be different as an example will demonstrate. If D settled land on A for life with remainder to B (a minor) in fee simple, and B died a minor without having married, the position may be summarised as follows.

---

[52] As defined by S.L.A. 1925, ss.1(1), 117(1)(xxiv); A.E.A. 1925, s.55(1)(xxiv); *ante,* para. 20–010.
[53] *Re Taylor* [1931] 2 Ch. 242; but see (1932) 76 S.J. 227.
[54] Including perhaps, a fee simple in remainder: see (1932) 76 S.J. 227.
[55] T.L.A.T.A. 1996, Sched. 1, para. 5; *ante,* para. 3–037.

WHERE B DIED BEFORE APRIL 4, 1988:	WHERE B DIED AFTER APRIL 3, 1988 BUT BEFORE 1997:	WHERE B DIES AFTER 1996:
(i) B was deemed to have an entail. Since he could have no legitimate children, the notional entail came to an end. (ii) D was entitled in fee simple subject to A's life estate.[57]	(i) B was deemed to have an entail. If B had any issue the entail would take effect and devolve on the relevant child.[56] (ii) If B had issue, there was an entail in remainder, subject to A's life interest. In the absence of issue D was entitled in fee simple subject to A's life estate.	(i) B is deemed to have a life interest in the absence of any issue. If B has issue, the provision is inapplicable. (ii) In the absence of issue D is entitled in fee simple subject to A's life estate.

It is not apparent why in 1925 the draftsman adopted the device of an entail rather than a life estate to achieve his purpose. The entail would never take effect because B, who would only fall within the provision if he died unmarried, could never leave legitimate issue who could take in tail.[58] Once it became possible to create an entail in favour of an illegitimate child in 1988,[59] the result could be different (as the above example demonstrates). The changes that were made in 1996 restrict the rule to cases where the minor dies both unmarried *and* childless, and achieve with greater simplicity the apparent objectives of the provision.

9. Leases. The effect of an attempted grant of a legal term of years to a **20–019** minor depends on whether it was made prior to 1997 or after 1996. In the former case it operated merely as a covenant by the lessor to make a settlement on the minor, and in the meantime to hold the term in trust for him.[60] If the grant is made after 1996, it operates as a declaration that the transferor holds the property in trust for the minor.[61] In either case, the minor can only take an equitable interest. He may disclaim this interest within a

---

[56] After April 3, 1988, an entail could arise in favour of an illegitimate child: Family Law Reform Act 1987, ss.1(1); 19(1), (2); see *ante*, para. 11–119.

[57] If B was solely entitled on D's intestacy, a perpetual oscillation of the land between B's estate and D's estate was avoided by carrying the land from D's estate to the person who, after B, would be entitled on D's intestacy: *Re Taylor* [1931] 2 Ch. 242.

[58] The consequences of this (including the grotesque result of a conveyance for value) are more fully explored in the previous edition of this work at p. 1019. The difficulties canvassed there are now unlikely ever to be in issue.

[59] *Ante*, para. 11–119.

[60] *Ante*, para. 20–005; *Davies v. Beynon-Harris* (1931) 47 T.L.R. 424.

[61] *Ante*, para. 20–006.

reasonable time after attaining full age.[62] If he does so, this will discharge him from liability for future rent but not from liability in respect of his past use and occupation of the premises.[63] Nor will disclaimer enable him to recover rent that he has already paid.[64] If he does not then disclaim, he is bound by the terms of the tenancy even though he was a minor when he entered into it.[65] Although there is some authority that during his minority a minor is liable to pay for the use and occupation of property of the premises only if they can be said to be "necessary",[66] this may not represent the law. The preferable view is that an infant is liable to pay for use and occupation even if the lease is disadvantageous to him, unless he disclaims it on coming of age.[67] If the lease is set aside by the landlord because the minor obtained it by fraudulently representing himself to be of full age, he cannot also make the infant liable for use and occupation.[68]

Section 2. Mental Patients

20–020 Where a person is suffering from a mental disorder someone must be appointed to manage his property, because he is himself incapacitated.

1. Control over property

20–021 *(a) The jurisdiction.* Under statutes dating from the fourteenth-century *De Prerogativa Regis*[69] and later the Lunacy Act 1890, the Crown had jurisdiction over the property of persons then called "lunatics". This was exercised by the Lord Chancellor and certain judges. Today, under the Mental Health Act 1983, jurisdiction is still exercisable by the Lord Chancellor and nominated judges.[70] However, in practice, subject to appeal to a nominated judge, the jurisdiction is usually exercised by the Master, Deputy Master or a nominated judge of the Court of Protection, which is an office of the Supreme Court.[71] The jurisdiction arises when it is established that "a person is incapable, by reason of mental disorder, of managing and administering his property and

---

[62] *Ketsey's Case* (1613) Cro.Jac. 320; and see *Edwards v. Carter* [1893] A.C. 360 (settlement).
[63] *Blake v. Concannon* (1870) I.R. 4 C.L. 323.
[64] *Valentini v. Canali* (1889) 24 Q.B.D. 166. *cf.* R. Goff & G.H. Jones, *The Law of Restitution* (5th ed.), p. 641.
[65] *Davies v. Beynon-Harris, supra.*
[66] *Lowe v. Griffith* (1835) 4 L.J.C.P. 94.
[67] *North Western Ry v. M'Michael* (1850) 5 Ex. 114 at 128.
[68] *Lemprière v. Lange* (1879) 12 Ch.D. 675. *cf.* G.H. Trietel, *The Law of Contract* (10th ed.), p. 514.
[69] Of uncertain date, printed as 17 Ed. II, St. 1, cc. 9, 10; 1324 (Ruff).
[70] The ancient prerogative of the Crown to act as *parens patriae* in relation to the person and property of those of unsound mind no longer exists: *Re F (Mental Patient: Sterilisation)* [1990] 2 A.C. 1 at 57, 58.
[71] Mental Health Act 1983, ss.93, 105. The Chancery Division may also exercise jurisdiction in certain cases of small trusts: see *Re K's S.T.* [1969] 2 Ch. 1. The Law Commission has recommended the creation of a new superior court of record called the Court of Protection to replace the existing arrangements: see (1995) Law Com. No. 231, Pt X.

affairs".[72] The person concerned is now called "the patient". The present system was introduced by the Mental Health Act 1959, which is now consolidated in the Mental Health Act 1983.

(b) Powers. There are very wide powers of ordering or authorising dispositions and other transactions concerning the patient's property, whether for the benefit of the patient himself or his family or other persons for whom he might have been expected to provide.[73] In cases of emergency these powers may even be exercised before the question of incapacity has been determined.[74] The powers extend, for example, to the making of settlements[75] and wills,[76] the management of a business, and the conduct of litigation, and include the power, commonly exercised, to appoint a receiver[77] who may exercise any of the powers under the court's directions.[78] But there is no power to make a disposition which the patient could not himself have made if of sound mind.[79] Where property of the patient has been disposed of, those who would have taken it under the patient's will or intestacy may claim corresponding interests in the property which represents it.[80]

20–022

2. Patient's incapacity. The principles that govern a patient's capacity differ according to whether or not the court has taken control of his affairs.[81] It may be that a patient will be regarded as being under the court's control as the result of any intervention by it, but it will certainly be the case where the court has appointed a receiver.

20–023

(a) Where the court has taken control of the patient's affairs. Once a patient has been placed under the jurisdiction of the Court of Protection, he cannot make any valid disposition of his property *inter vivos*, even in a lucid interval.[82] Any other rule "would raise a conflict with the court's control of

20–024

---

[72] Mental Health Act 1983, s.94(2).

[73] *ibid.*, ss.95, 96. The powers conferred under these sections apply only to "business matters, legal transactions and other dealings of a similar kind" and not to wider issues, such as medical treatment: *Re F (Mental Patient: Sterilisation), supra,* at 59, *per* Lord Brandon. Where the patient has never enjoyed a rational mind, the court will assume that he "would have been a normal decent person, acting in accordance with contemporary standards of morality": *Re C (a patient)* [1991] 3 All E.R. 866 at 870, *per* Hoffmann J. What the court does will be determined according to the circumstances of the individual patient: see *Re S (Gifts by Mental Patient)* [1997] 1 F.L.R. 96.

[74] Mental Health Act 1983, s.98.

[75] See *e.g. Re D.M.L.* [1965] Ch. 1133; *Re L. (W.J.G.)* [1966] Ch. 135.

[76] Mental Health Act 1983, ss.96, 97, not applying to patients who are minors, and substituting special formalities for those of the Wills Act 1837, s.9. See *Re Davey* [1981] 1 W.L.R. 164. *Re D. (J.)* [1982] Ch. 237 and *Re C (a patient), supra,* examine the principles for making such wills.

[77] Or some named person.

[78] Mental Health Act 1983, s.99. See, *e.g. Re E.* [1985] 1 W.L.R. 245.

[79] *Pritchard v. Briggs* [1980] Ch. 339 at 409.

[80] Mental Health Act 1983, s.101.

[81] The principles have not been affected by the Mental Health Acts 1959 and 1983.

[82] *Re Beaney* [1978] 1 W.L.R. 770 at 772, summarising the effect of *Re Walker* [1905] 1 Ch. 160 and *Re Marshall* [1920] 1 Ch. 284.

his affairs",[83] and would mean that his affairs would be under both his own control and the receiver's.[84] By contrast, a will made by a patient in a lucid interval would be valid, because "a will does not take effect until death, at which time the Court of Protection has no further concern for his affairs".[85]

Where the patient is a proprietor of registered land, the receiver (or other person authorised to manage his property and affairs) may exercise all of the powers that the patient could have done if he had been free from disability.[86] No restriction will be entered on the register unless the receiver either so requests or is himself registered as proprietor.[87]

20–025   *(b) Where the court has not intervened.* Where either—

    (i) the court has not intervened; or

    (ii) the validity of a will is in issue after a patient's death;

any disposition or any will made during mental incapacity is voidable at the instance of those who would otherwise be entitled.[88] However it cannot be set aside either where the incapacity was unknown to the other party,[89] or at the instance of the person making it, unless he can prove that the other party knew of the incapacity.[90]

It has been held that "capacity to perform a juristic act exists when the person who purported to do the act had at the time the mental capacity, with the assistance of such explanation as he may have been given, to understand the nature and effect of that particular transaction".[91] The degree of under-standing required to uphold the disposition is therefore relative to the partic-ular transaction.[92] In the case of a will the degree required is always high.[93] In the case of a contract or a gift the degree varies with the circumstances, and

---

[83] *Re Beaney, supra,* at 772, *per* Nourse, Q.C.
[84] *Re Marshall, supra,* at 289.
[85] *Re Beaney, supra,* at 772, *per* Nourse, Q.C. See too *In b. Walker* (1912) 28 T.L.R. 466.
[86] L.R.A. 1925, s.111(5) (as amended by the Mental Health Acts 1959 and 1983). A copy of the court order must be filed with the registrar: *ibid.*
[87] See Ruoff & Roper, 10–06.
[88] *Re Beaney, supra (inter vivos* gift of house); *Hart v. O'Connor* [1985] A.C. 1000 at 1018, 1019 (contract); *Simpson v. Simpson* [1992] 1 F.L.R. 601 *(inter vivos* transfers of shares and bank deposits).
[89] *Hart v. O'Connor, supra.* A transaction will of course be voidable if there are other distinct grounds for setting the transaction aside as unconscionable: *ibid.*, at 1021. For the relevant principles, see *Boustany v. Pigott* (1993) 69 P. & C.R. 298 at 303. The plea that the other party knew of the incapacity appears only in cases where the patient is sued on a contract. But since its basis is that the other party fraudulently took advantage of the patient (*Browne v. Joddrell* (1827) Moo. & M. 105), it should in principle be equally applicable to dispositions.
[90] See *Imperial Loan Co. v. Stone* [1892] 1 Q.B. 599.
[91] *Re K (Enduring Power of Attorney)* [1988] Ch. 310 at 313, *per* Hoffmann J.
[92] *Re Beaney* [1978] 1 W.L.R. 770 at 774; *Simpson v. Simpson, supra,* at 613.
[93] For the matters which must be understood by the testator, see *Banks v. Goodfellow* (1870) L.R. 5 Q.B. 549 at 565.

it will be as high as it is for a will if a patient is disposing of all or most of his assets.[94]

3. Enduring powers of attorney. It is now possible to avoid the necessity   **20–026**
of court proceedings and the appointment of a receiver in many cases by
employing an enduring power of attorney.[95] The Enduring Powers of Attorney
Act 1985 "was intended to provide an inexpensive method by which a person
could confer power to manage his affairs on a person of his own choice which
would remain effective notwithstanding any change in his mental capacity".[96]
Prior to the Act this was not possible because the authority of a donee acting
under a power of attorney was revoked by the donor's loss of mental
capacity.[97] A person has capacity to create such a power provided that he
understands its nature and effect, even though he may no longer be able to
manage his property and affairs.[98] Such a power will therefore be valid in the
common case where it is created by the donor after he has shown the first
signs of mental incapacity.[99] The enduring power must be executed in the
prescribed form and manner by both the donor of the power and the attorney.[1]
It may either confer a general authority on the attorney or it may be confined
to specified matters.[2] There may be more than one attorney.[3] An enduring
power can only be granted in relation to "the property and affairs" of the
donor,[4] which does not extend to matters such as healthcare or welfare.[5]

An enduring power cannot be exercised once the donor becomes incapable
(except by order of the court[6]) until the attorney registers the power with
the Court of Protection.[7] If, therefore, the attorney has reason to believe that

---

[94] *Re Beaney, supra*, at 774 (gift of house to daughter declared void since donor did not appreciate claims of her other children and had no other assets).

[95] What follows is only the barest summary. Reference should be made to specialist commentaries, such as S. Cretney and D. Lush, *Enduring Powers of Attorney* (4th ed.).

[96] *Re K (Enduring Power of Attorney), supra*, at 311, *per* Hoffmann J. See too *Re R (Enduring Power of Attorney)* [1990] Ch. 647 at 650. The Trustee Delegation Act 1999, which comes into force on January 1, 2000, will make some amendments to the Enduring Powers of Attorney Act 1985.

[97] *Re K (Enduring Power of Attorney), supra*, at 312, 313; *Yonge v. Toynbee* [1910] 1 K.B. 215 at 228. If, after the donor becomes incapable, the attorney enters into a transaction which is invalid as a result, he may be liable for breach of his warranty of authority, even though he did not know of the incapacity: *ibid.*

[98] *Re K (Enduring Power of Attorney), supra*, particularly at 316, where the requirements are explained in detail.

[99] *ibid.*, at 315.

[1] Enduring Powers of Attorney Act 1985, s.2(1)–(3).

[2] *ibid.*, s.3(1).

[3] For the power to be an enduring power of attorney, the attorneys must be appointed either jointly, or jointly and severally: *ibid.*, s.11(1).

[4] *ibid.*, s.3(1).

[5] *cf. Re F (Mental Patient: Sterilisation)* [1990] 2 A.C. 1 at 59; *ante*, para. 20–022. An enduring power cannot therefore be employed to empower the donee to make decisions as to the medical treatment which the donor is to receive, or where he should live.

[6] Enduring Powers of Attorney Act 1985, s.1(1).

[7] *ibid.*, s.6. It has been said that an enduring power of attorney "has very limited effect until it is registered. When registered, it takes effect according to its terms": *Re R (Enduring Power of Attorney)* [1990] Ch. 647 at 651, *per* Vinelott J.

the attorney is becoming mentally incapable, he should apply to register the power.[8] Before making the application, he is required to give notice to the relatives of the donor,[9] and they may object to the registration on certain specified grounds.[10]

20–027   Subject to conditions or restrictions contained in the power, the attorney is given authority to act so as to benefit himself or other persons by providing for his or their needs if and to the extent that the donor might have been expected to do so.[11] The court has wide supervisory powers after registration to ensure that the attorney exercises his powers of management and administration properly,[12] *e.g.* it may give directions as to the management or disposal of the donor's property.[13]

The Law Commission has proposed the replacement of the enduring power of attorney with a "continuing power of attorney".[14] This would not be limited to the property and business affairs of the patient (as is an enduring power),[15] but would extend to all (or to any specified) matters relating to the donor's personal welfare, health care, property or affairs.

Section 3. Charities

20–028   Charities were formerly subject to restrictions both as to the gifts of land that they might receive[16] and as to their powers to dispose of lands which they held.[17] The former were abolished by the Charities Act 1960,[18] and nothing further need be said about them. The latter restrictions have been largely removed by the Charities Act 1992 (the relevant provisions of which are now consolidated in the Charities Act 1993) and the Trusts of Land and Appointment of Trustees Act 1996. These changes require some explanation.

20–029   **1. Powers of disposition of charity trustees.** Prior to 1997 land held upon charitable trusts was deemed for some but not all purposes to be settled land, and in consequence charity trustees had the powers conferred on the life

---

[8] Enduring Powers of Attorney Act 1985, s.4(1), (2).

[9] *ibid.*, s.4(3); Sched. 1 (which lists the relatives for this purpose and prescribes the content of the notices).

[10] *ibid.*, s.6(5).

[11] *ibid.*, s.3(4). There are also powers to make seasonal, birthday and anniversary gifts to persons related or connected to the donor, and to make gifts to charities to which the donor might have been expected to make gifts: *ibid.*, s.3(5).

[12] *cf. Re K (Enduring Power of Attorney)* [1988] Ch. 310 at 316, where Hoffmann J. commented that the power was "hedged about on all sides with statutory protection for the donor".

[13] *ibid.*, s.8. See *Re R (Enduring Power of Attorney), supra*, where it was held that s.8(2) did not give the court power to direct the disposal of the donor's property by way of gift.

[14] (1995) Law Com. No. 231, Pt VII.

[15] *Ante*, para. 20–026.

[16] See the previous edition of this work at p. 1028.

[17] *ibid.*, at pp. 1028, 1029.

[18] ss.38, 48, Sched. 7.

tenant and the trustees of a settlement by the Settled Land Act 1925.[19] After 1996, charity trustees hold any land upon a trust of land.[20] As such they have in relation to the land and for the purposes of exercising their functions as trustees, all the powers of an absolute owner,[21] subject only to the restrictions on their exercise laid down in the Charities Act 1993.[22]

Certain university and college lands are dealt with separately by the Universities and College Estates Acts 1925 and 1964.[23]

2. Restrictions on disposition. Prior to 1993, there were restrictions on the **20–030** powers of most charities to make dispositions of land which formed part of their permanent endowment or which were or had been occupied for the purposes of the charity. No such dispositions could be made without the order of the court or the Charity Commissioners,[24] except by an exempt charity.[25] In practice such consent was given on conditions that were intended to ensure that the trustees acted in the best interests of the charity. Under the Charities Act 1993,[26] these rules no longer apply,[27] and charity trustees may sell or lease land held by the charity subject to certain conditions.[28] Those conditions are generally[29] that the trustees obtain a written report from qualified independent surveyor, advertise the proposed disposition to the extent that he advises, and decide that they are satisfied that the terms on which the disposition is to be made are the best that can reasonably be obtained by the charity.[30] There are also corresponding restrictions on the mortgaging powers of charity trustees.[31] There are supplementary provisions which are intended to ensure that the restrictions on a charity's powers of disposition are brought to the attention of—

(i) any purchaser or mortgagee of the charity's land; and

---

[19] S.L.A. 1925, s.29(1) (repealed by T.L.A.T.A. 1996, s.25(2); Sched. 4; there is a limited exemption from this repeal in respect of the Chequers and Chevening Estates: *ibid.*, s.25(3)).

[20] T.L.A.T.A. 1996, ss.1(1), 2 (5).

[21] *ibid.*, s.6(1). See *ante*, para. 8–136.

[22] Part V, *infra*. The powers conferred by T.L.A.T.A. 1996, s.6(1) are made subject to restrictions imposed by other statutes: *ibid.*, s.6(6).

[23] T.L.A.T.A. 1996 does not apply to such lands: *ibid.*, s.1(3).

[24] Charities Act 1960, s.29 (repealed by Charities Act 1992, s.78(2), Sched. 7).

[25] For exempt charities, see *infra*.

[26] Part V, consolidating changes made by the Charities Act 1992, ss.32–37.

[27] Except in relation to dispositions to a connected person or a trustee for a connected person (generally a relative or an associate of the donor or trustee): Charities Act 1993, s.36(1), (2); Sched. 5.

[28] *ibid.*, s.36(2). The conditions are similar to those which were formerly imposed by the court or by the Charity Commissioners when consenting to a disposition.

[29] Less stringent requirements apply to leases granted for seven years or less except where the lease is granted wholly or partly for a fine: *ibid.*, s.36(5).

[30] *ibid.*, s.36(3).

[31] *ibid.*, s.38. The charity trustees are required to obtain and consider proper advice on the necessity for the mortgage to enable them to pursue the course of action for which the loan is sought, the reasonableness of the terms of the mortgage and the ability of the charity to repay the loan: *ibid.*, s.38(2), (3).

(ii) recorded on the title or, as will now usually be the case, the register of title, of any land acquired by the charity.[32]

These restrictions do not apply to dispositions by exempt charities. The charities designated as exempt include many universities and a number of other bodies such as the Boards of Trustees of the principal London museums.[33] There are also certain other exceptions, *e.g.* dispositions under statutory authority.[34]

---

[32] See *ibid.*, ss.37, 39 (as amended by T.L.A.T.A. 1996, Sched. 4; L.R.A. 1997, Sched. 1, para. 6); T.L.A.T.A. 1996, Sched. 1, para. 4. See too L.R.R. rr. 60–62; 122–124; Ruoff & Roper, Chap. 33.

[33] The list of exempt charities is to be found in the Charities Act 1993, Sched. 2, with subsequent additions by Order in Council: see Ruoff & Roper, paras 33–08, 33–18.

[34] Charities Act 1993, s.36(9).

CHAPTER 21

ADVERSE POSSESSION AND LIMITATION

Part 1

GENERAL PRINCIPLES

1. Limitation and prescription. "Limitation" means the extinction of stale **21–001**
claims and obsolete titles. Rights of action are limited in point of time, and are
lost if not pursued within due time. Some such principle is necessary to every
system of law; but in English law it depends wholly on statute, since limitation
was unknown to the common law. Different periods of limitation have been
laid down for different kinds of action. In relation to land (for which the
period is now in general 12 years) it is in the public interest that a person who
has long been in undisputed possession should be able to deal with the land
as owner. It is more important that an established and peaceable possession
should be protected than that the law should assist the agitation of old claims.[1]
A statute which effects this purpose is "an act of peace. Long dormant claims
have often more cruelty than of justice in them".[2]

Limitation also fulfils another important function. It facilitates the investigation of title to unregistered land.[3] The period of title which a purchaser of
land must investigate (at present 15 years[4]) is directly related to the limitation
period and this has long been the case.[5] The statutes of limitation have
therefore provided "a kind of qualified guarantee that any possible outstanding claims to ownership by third parties are time-barred".[6]

Limitation must be distinguished from prescription, for although similar in **21–002**
result they are different in principle. Prescription is primarily a common law

---

[1] *Cholmondeley v. Lord Clinton* (1820) 2 Jac. & W. 1 at 140; (1821) 4 Bli. 1 at 106; *Manby v.
Berwicke* (1857) 3 K. & J. 342 at 352.

[2] *A'Court v. Cross* (1825) 3 Bing. 329 at 332, *per* Best C.J.

[3] See [1985] Conv. 272 (M. Dockray).

[4] L.P.A. 1969, s.23, *ante*, para. 5–021.

[5] [1985] Conv. 272 at pp. 278 *et seq.*

[6] *ibid.*, at 278. Where title to the land is registered this justification is absent: see (1998) Law
Com. No. 254, Pt X. It was originally impossible to acquire title to registered land by adverse
possession: L.T.A. 1875, s.21. However this rule was abandoned: L.R.A. 1925, s.75. The basis
of title to registered land is not possession (as it is where title is unregistered) but the fact of
registration: see *ibid.*, s.69(1). It should be noted, however, that the register is not normally
conclusive as to boundaries: L.R.R. 1925, r. 278; *ante*, para. 6–010; and that leases of 21 years
or less cannot be protected by registration but take effect only as overriding interests: L.R.A.
1925, ss.19(2), 22(2), 70(1)(k); *ante*, para. 6–066.

doctrine, though extended by statute, by which certain rights (easements and profits) can be acquired over the land of others.[7] Fundamentally it is a rule of evidence, leading to a presumption of a grant from the owner of the land and therefore of a title derived through him. Limitation is the antithesis of prescription and rests on wrongful possession rather than on any presumption of right.[8] It is wholly statutory, and is concerned with the title to the land itself.

The contrast between limitation and prescription is most apparent where the title to the land is unregistered. In such a situation, limitation simply extinguishes a former owner's right to recover possession of the land, leaving some other person with a title based on adverse possession of the land. Prescription operates positively like a conveyance, whereas limitation operates negatively, by eliminating the claim of a person having a superior title, without any "parliamentary conveyance" or transfer from that person.[9] It has already been explained how this negative operation helps to reveal the possessory character of title to land at common law.[10]

The contrast is less marked where the title is registered. The registered proprietor, whose title has been extinguished, is deemed to hold the property on a bare trust for the adverse possessor until the latter is registered as proprietor instead.[11] It is now clear that, unlike the position where title is unregistered, the effect of adverse possession is to give the squatter the right to be substituted by registration for the registered proprietor. There is, in truth, a parliamentary conveyance.[12]

21–003   **2. Statutes of limitation.** We must now turn to the details of the modern system. Statutes of limitation have a long history. At first, periods of limitation were fixed from time to time in relation to particular events or dates of public knowledge, such as the death of Henry I or the last voyage of Henry II into Normandy.[13] Ultimately the Statute of Westminster I 1275[14] laid down a prohibition against disputing rights enjoyed in 1189, a date that is still of significance in relation to prescription.[15] For two-and-a-half centuries this remained the law, so that there gradually ceased to be any effective system of limitation.

The modern type of limitation, which, instead of selecting fixed dates, sets a preclusive period to rights of action as from the time they arise, was introduced by a statute of 1540,[16] which fixed periods of 60 years or less for

---

[7] *Ante,* paras 18–121 *et seq.*

[8] *Buckinghamshire County Council v. Moran* [1990] Ch. 623 at 644; *Sze To Chun Keung v. Kung Kwok Wai David* [1997] 1 W.L.R. 1232 at 1235.

[9] *Ante,* para. 3–117.

[10] *Ante,* chap. 3.

[11] L.R.A. 1925, s.75; *ante,* para. 6–116; *post,* paras 21–058—21–064.

[12] *Central London Commercial Estates Ltd v. Kato Kagaku Ltd* [1998] 4 All E.R. 948.

[13] See, *e.g. Glanvill,* XIII, 32; ed. G.D.G. Hall, p. 167.

[14] Chapter 39 forbade writs of right based on seisin obtained prior to 1189, and fixed 1216 and 1242 as the corresponding dates for other real actions.

[15] See *ante,* para. 18–133.

[16] 32 Hen. 8, c. 2 (periods of 60, 50 and 30 years.).

the various real actions.[17] In 1623 rights of entry were limited to 20 years,[18] and this period therefore governed the action of ejectment. A 20-year limitation period for actions for land generally was fixed by the Real Property Limitation Act 1833.[19] However, the period was reduced to 12 years by the Real Property Limitation Act 1874.[20] The earlier statutes were repealed by the Limitation Act 1939.[21] That Act was in turn amended by the Limitation Amendment Act 1980[22] and the law was then consolidated in the Limitation Act 1980.[23]

The provisions of the Limitation Act 1980 will be treated in three sections:

(1) the length of the limitation period;

(2) when time starts to run; and

(3) the effect of lapse of time.

Part 2

THE LENGTH OF THE LIMITATION PERIOD

1. Three main periods. The Limitation Act 1980 lays down three main periods of limitation which are relevant to the law of real property. **21–004**

(a) Six years. A period of six years applies for actions on simple contracts,[24] for arrears of rent[25] and on any judgment.[26] The same period applies to actions in tort,[27] except that a three-year period, subject to special provisions for extension, has been imposed for actions for personal injuries.[28] **21–005**

(b) Specialties. A period of 12 years applies for actions on a specialty.[29] A specialty[30] includes a covenant in a deed, *e.g.* a covenant contained in a conveyance or in a lease.[31] **21–006**

---

[17] See the historical sketch in *Bryant v. Foot* (1867) L.R. 2 Q.B. 161 at 179–181, *per* Cockburn C.J.; and see P. & M. ii, 81.
[18] Limitation Act 1623.
[19] s.2.
[20] s.1.
[21] Based on the recommendations in Cmd. 5334 (1936).
[22] Based upon a report of the Law Reform Committee, Cmnd. 6923 (1977).
[23] Repealing the earlier Acts. It came into force on May 1, 1981: L.A. 1980, s.41(2).
[24] L.A. 1980, s.5.
[25] *ibid.*, s.19.
[26] *ibid.*, s.24.
[27] *ibid.*, s.2.
[28] *ibid.*, ss.11, 12, 33.
[29] *ibid.*, s.8. The obligation must be created or secured by the specialty, not merely acknowledged or evidenced by it: *Re Compania de Electricidad de la Provincia de Buenos Aires Ltd* [1980] Ch. 146.
[30] A statute is also a specialty (*Cork & Brandon Ry. v. Goode* (1853) 13 C.B. 826), but claims to sums recoverable under statute are barred in six years: L.A. 1980, s.9. See, *e.g. Swansea C.C. v. Glass* [1992] Q.B. 844.
[31] Any contract made by deed will be a specialty for the purposes of s.8: see *Aiken v. Stewart Wrightson Members Agency Ltd* [1995] 1 W.L.R. 1281 at 1291–1293.

21–007   *(c) Land.* A period of 12 years applies for the recovery of land.[32] The same period is prescribed for the recovery of money charged on land, *e.g.* by a mortgage, or the proceeds of sale of land, *e.g.* where trustees of land have exercised their power of sale.[33] "Land" for this purpose includes rentcharges and tithes, but not other incorporeal hereditaments such as *profits à prendre* or advowsons[34] and it includes any legal or equitable interest in land.[35]

21–008   **2. Special cases.** Longer periods are provided in the following special cases.

21–009   *(a) Crown lands.* For actions for the recovery of Crown lands the period is 30 years.[36] Before the Act of 1929 it was 60 years,[37] a period which has been retained in the one case of foreshore owned by the Crown.[38] Claims by subjects to recover lands from the Crown are barred after the ordinary period of 12 years.

21–010   *(b) Corporations sole.* The title of a spiritual or eleemosynary (*i.e.* charitable) corporation sole, such as a bishop, or the master of a hospital, is barred after 30 years.[39]

21–011   *(c) Advowsons.* A claim to an advowson is barred after the period during which three successive incumbencies have been held adversely to the owner of the advowson, or 60 years of adverse possession, whichever is the longer, but subject to a maximum period of 100 years.[40]

21–012   **3. Reform.** The Law Commission has provisionally recommended that the different limitation periods in relation to all types of action should be rationalised.[41] As regards actions for the recovery of land, it has been suggested that the limitation period should be 10 years (in place of the present 12), and that the special periods that presently apply to Crown lands and corporations sole should cease to do so.

The Law Commission and HM Land Registry have jointly recommended that, in relation to registered land, a wholly new set of principles should apply in cases of adverse possession.[42] Adverse possession would of itself not bar the title of the registered proprietor (whatever its duration), and in most cases,

---

[32] L.A. 1980, s.15.
[33] *ibid.*, s.20(1).
[34] *ibid.*, s.38(1).
[35] *ibid.*
[36] *ibid.* Sched. 1, para. 10. For successors in title to the Crown see *post*, para. 00.
[37] Crown Suits Acts 1769, 1861, called the "Nullum Tempus Acts", from the maxim *nullum tempus occurrit regi.* The Limitation Act 1623 had fixed 1564 as the limitation date for Crown actions.
[38] L.A. 1980, Sched. 1, para. 11.
[39] *ibid.* Sched. 1, para. 10. For successors in title the rule is the same as for successors to Crown land: *ibid.*, para. 12.
[40] *ibid.*, s.25.
[41] (1998) L.C.C.P. No. 151.
[42] (1998) Law Com. No. 254, Pt X.

the fact of registration would protect the proprietor against the claims of an adverse possessor. The proposed scheme has already been explained.[43]

Part 3

THE RUNNING OF TIME

In order to find the moment when a right of action becomes barred, three 21–013 questions must be considered: first, when time begins to run; secondly, what will postpone this date; and thirdly, what will start time running afresh.[44]

Section 1. When Time Begins to Run

In the case of actions for the recovery of land or capital sums charged on land, 21–014 time begins to run in accordance with the following rules.

1. Owner entitled in possession

(a) Dispossession, discontinuance and adverse possession. When the owner 21–015 of land is entitled in possession, time begins to run as soon as both—

(i) the owner has been dispossessed, or has discontinued his possession[45]; and

(ii) adverse possession has been taken by some other person.[46]

"Dispossessed" merely means that the owner has been driven out of possession by another,[47] whereas "discontinued" means that the owner has abandoned possession.[48] It is thus not necessary that the owner should have been driven out of possession. If the owner abandons possession,[49] or if he dies and

---

[43] *Ante*, para. 6–117.

[44] In general once time has begun to run, it runs continuously: *Prideaux v. Webber* (1661) 1 Lev. 31; *Rhodes v. Smethurst* (1840) 6 M. & W. 351; but see *Bowring-Hanbury's Trustee v. Bowring-Hanbury* [1943] Ch. 104, discussed at (1943) 59 L.Q.R. 117 (R.E.M.). Disability or fraud may postpone the date when time begins to run, and an acknowledgment or part payment may start time running afresh. There has been, however, one instance in which statutory provision was made for the running of time to be suspended for a period and then resumed: Limitation (Enemies and War Prisoners) Act 1945.

[45] L.A. 1980, Sched. 1, para. 1.

[46] *ibid.*, para. 8.

[47] *Rains v. Buxton* (1880) 14 Ch.D. 537 at 539.

[48] *ibid.*; *Rimington v. Cannon* (1853) 12 C.B. 18 at 33; *M'Donnell v. M'Kinty* (1847) 10 Ir.L.R. 514 at 526; *Smith v. Lloyd* (1854) 9 Exch. 526 at 572. Mere non-user is not enough: *Tecbild Ltd v. Chamberlain* (1969) 20 P. & C.R. 633.

[49] Abandonment will not however be lightly presumed, and the slightest acts done by the owner will negative discontinuance: *Powell v. McFarlane* (1977) 38 P. & C.R. 452 at 472. Cases of abandonment are therefore uncommon. For a modern example, see *Red House Farms (Thorndon) Ltd v. Catchpole* [1977] 2 E.G.L.R. 125.

the person next entitled (*e.g.* as devisee or remainderman) does not take possession, time will begin to run as soon as adverse possession is taken by another. Whether or not the owner knows that he has been dispossessed is immaterial.[50] But it is essential that there should be adverse possession by another, for until there is, there is nobody against whom the owner is failing to assert his rights.

21–016 (b) *Adverse possession.* Before 1833, "adverse possession" bore a highly technical meaning.[51] Today it merely means possession inconsistent with the title of the true owner,[52] and not, *e.g.* possession under a licence from him[53] or under some contract or trust.[54] There is a presumption that the owner of the land with the paper title is in possession of the land.[55] To establish adverse possession, a squatter must prove that he had both factual possession of the land and the requisite intention to possess (*animus possidendi*).[56] If a person is in possession of land with the permission of the true owner, his possession cannot be adverse.[57]

21–017 (1) FACTUAL POSSESSION. To establish adverse possession, the squatter must demonstrate that by his acts he has taken a sufficient degree of exclusive physical control.[58] Whether he has done so is a matter of fact, depending on all the circumstances, in particular the nature of the land and the manner in which such land is commonly enjoyed.[59] "The type of conduct which indicates possession must vary with the type of land."[60] In the case of open land, absolute physical control is normally impracticable.[61] There are obvious difficulties in establishing a squatter's title to part of a swamp[62]; but where marshy land is virtually useless except for shooting, shooting over it may

---

[50] *Rains v. Buxton, supra; Powell v. McFarlane, supra,* at 480.

[51] See Lightwood, *Time Limit on Actions,* p. 6; Lightwood, *Possession,* p. 180. Thus before the Real Property Limitation Act 1833, possession by a younger brother was deemed possession by the heir (Co.Litt. 242a); possession by one co-owner was deemed possession by all; possession by a tenant at will or at sufferance was deemed possession by the lessor.

[52] *Wilson v. Martin's Exors* [1993] 1 E.G.L.R. 178 at 179, 180. L.A. 1980, Sched. 1, para. 8(1) requires merely possession by "some person in whose favour the period of limitation can run". Adverse possession is not further defined by the Act.

[53] *Hughes v. Griffin* [1969] 1 W.L.R. 23; *Buckinghamshire County Council v. Moran* [1990] Ch. 623 at 636. Contrast the position of a tenant at will, *post,* para. 21–032.

[54] *Hyde v. Pearce* [1982] 1 W.L.R. 560 (purchaser in possession under contract of sale for 14 years: possession not adverse since referable to the contract).

[55] *Powell v. McFarlane, supra,* at 470; *R. v. Secretary of State for the Environment, ex p. Davies* (1990) 61 P. & C.R. 487 at 493.

[56] *Buckinghamshire County Council v. Moran, supra,* at 636; *Marsden v. Miller* (1992) 64 P. & C.R. 239 at 242, 243.

[57] See, *e.g. Moses v. Lovegrove* [1952] 2 Q.B. 533 at 540, 544; *Smith v. Lawson* (1997) 74 P. & C.R. D34.

[58] *Powell v. McFarlane, supra,* at 471; *Marsden v. Miller, supra,* at 243.

[59] *Powell v. McFarlane, supra,* at 471.

[60] *Wuta-Ofei v. Danquah* [1961] 1 W.L.R. 1238 at 1243, *per* Lord Guest.

[61] *Powell v. McFarlane, supra,* at 471. Acts of possession undertaken on parts of a piece of land to which possessory title is claimed, may be evidence of possession of the whole: *Higgs v. Nassauvian Ltd* [1975] A.C. 464 at 474.

[62] *West Bank Estates Ltd v. Arthur* [1967] 1 A.C. 665; and see *Higgs v. Nassauvian Ltd, supra* (rotational farming).

amount to adverse possession.[63] In many cases adverse possession cannot in the nature of things be continuous from day to day.[64] "Enclosure is the strongest possible evidence of adverse possession, but is not indispensable",[65] nor, it may be added, is it necessarily conclusive.[66] But where the adverse possessor performs clear acts of ownership, he does not have to show that they inconvenienced or otherwise affected the owner.[67] The adverse possessor need not himself be in physical possession of the land. If he grants a tenancy or licence, the tenant or licensee possesses on his behalf and is estopped from denying the licence or tenancy.[68]

Both because exclusive control is essential to establish adverse possession **21–018** and because of the presumption that the paper owner remains in possession of the land, trivial acts will rarely suffice to establish adverse possession,[69] unless the adverse possessor can demonstrate that the land has been abandoned by the paper owner.[70] Once factual possession has been established, it will not be terminated merely because the true owner sends a letter to the squatter requiring him to vacate the premises. Time will continue to run in favour of the squatter unless and until he vacates the premises or acknowledges the true owner's title.[71]

It has been suggested that "adverse possession must be peaceable and open",[72] but this seems incorrect in principle. Although such requirements must be satisfied in relation to a claim to an incorporeal hereditament founded on prescription,[73] such a claim rests upon a presumption that the enjoyment

---

[63] *Red House Farms (Thorndon) Ltd v. Catchpole* [1977] 2 E.G.L.R. 125.

[64] *Bligh v. Martin* [1968] 1 W.L.R. 804.

[65] *Seddon v. Smith* (1877) 36 L.T. 168 at 169, *per* Cockburn C.J. For a recent example, see *Hughes v. Cork* [1994] E.G.C.S. 25.

[66] See *Littledale v. Liverpool College* [1900] 1 Ch. 19; *George Wimpey & Co. Ltd v. Sohn* [1967] Ch. 487 (fencing of gardens equivocal as excluding public as well as owner); *Marsden v. Miller, supra* (fence erected but removed by paper owner within 24 hours); [1982] Conv. 256, 345 (M. Dockray).

[67] *Treloar v. Nute* [1976] 1 W.L.R. 1295 (land fenced off and levelled for building); see similarly *Williams v. Usherwood* (1981) 45 P. & C.R. 235 (land fenced, driveway paved and cars parked).

[68] *Sze To Chun Keung v. Kung Kwok Wai David* [1997] 1 W.L.R. 1232 at 1235. For tenancies and licences by estoppel, see *ante*, paras 14–095, 17–003.

[69] See *Boosey v. Davis* (1987) 55 P. & C.R. 83 (occasional grazing of goats and clearance of scrub); *Pavledes v. Ryesbridge Properties Ltd* (1989) 58 P. & C.R. 459 (parking of cars on a small scale on a large site); *Wilson v. Martin's Exors* [1993] 1 E.G.L.R. 178 (cutting timber and repairing fences).

[70] *Wuta-Ofei v. Danquah, supra*, at 1243; *Red House Farms (Thorndon) Ltd v. Catchpole, supra*.

[71] *Mount Carmel Investments Ltd v. Peter Thurlow Ltd* [1988] 1 W.L.R. 1078. It has been held that the unilateral grant by the true owner to a squatter of a licence to occupy, which is not repudiated by the latter, is effective to make the squatter a licensee and so stop time running: *B.P. Properties Ltd v. Buckler* (1987) 55 P. & C.R. 337 at 345, 346. This conclusion is questionable because the grant affects neither the nature of the squatter's possession nor his *animus possidendi*. It rests on the now discredited view (considered *infra*) that the true owner's intention could be relevant to the issue of adverse possession. See [1994] Conv. 196 (H. Wallace).

[72] *Browne v. Perry* [1991] 1 W.L.R. 1297 at 1302, *per* Lord Templeman.

[73] *Ante*, paras 18–123–18–126.

has been as of right.[74] Adverse possession is, by contrast, "possession as of wrong"[75] and there seems no reason to restrict its operation to instances where possession was taken without force and was apparent.[76]

21–019   (2) *ANIMUS POSSIDENDI.*[77] The squatter must have "an intention for the time being to possess the land to the exclusion of all other persons, including the owner with the paper title".[78] An intention to own or acquire the ownership of the land is not required, nor is it necessary that the squatter should intend to exclude the true owner in all circumstances.[79] The *animus* can be sufficiently established even if both the true owner and the squatter mistakenly believe that the land belongs to the latter,[80] or where a squatter did not realise that he was trespassing on another's land.[81] The intention to possess must be manifested clearly, so that it is apparent that the squatter was not merely a persistent trespasser, but was seeking to dispossess the true owner.[82] If the squatter's acts are equivocal then he will not be treated as having the requisite *animus possidendi*.[83] Any form of acknowledgment of the true owner's title will of course negative any intention to possess.[84]

The true owner's intention is, in contrast to that of the squatter, "irrelevant in practice".[85] It follows that a squatter may be in adverse possession even though his acts do not substantially interfere with the true owner's future plans.[86] There will be no presumption in such circumstances that he is a

---

[74] *Gardner v. Hodgson's Kingston Brewery Co. Ltd* [1903] A.C. 229 at 239.

[75] *Buckinghamshire County Council v. Moran* [1990] Ch. 623 at 644, *per* Nourse L.J. See too *Sze To Chun Keung v. Kung Kwok Wai David* [1997] 1 W.L.R. 1232 at 1235.

[76] See *Rains v. Buxton* (1880) 14 Ch.D. 537 at 540, 541. *Aliter* if there is deliberate concealment: *post*, para. 21–048.

[77] See (1980) 96 L.Q.R. 333 (P. Jackson); [1989] Conv. 211 (G. McCormack); [1990] C.L.J. 23 (C.H.).

[78] *Buckinghamshire County Council v. Moran, supra,* at 643, *per* Slade L.J.; *R. v. Secretary of State for the Environment, ex p. Davies* (1990) 61 P. & C.R. 487 at 495.

[79] *Buckinghamshire County Council v. Moran, supra,* at 643.

[80] *Pulleyn v. Hall Aggregates (Thames Valley) Ltd* (1992) 65 P. & C.R. 276 at 282; *Hughes v. Cork* [1994] E.G.C.S. 25.

[81] *Prudential Assurance Co. Ltd v. Waterloo Real Estate Inc.* [1999] 17 E.G. 131.

[82] *Powell v. McFarlane* (1977) 38 P. & C.R. 452, at 480; *R. v. Secretary of State for the Environment, ex p. Davies, supra,* at 497; *Prudential Assurance Co. Ltd v. Waterloo Real Estate Inc., supra,* at 133. The intention must, in practice, be determined objectively, because evidence of the squatter's subjective intention is likely to be self-serving: *Bolton Metropolitan B.C. v. Musa* (1998) 77 P. & C.R. D36.

[83] *Tecbild Ltd v. Chamberlain* (1969) 20 P. & C.R. 633 at 642 (grazing ponies and allowing children to play on the land insufficient); *Powell v. McFarlane, supra,* at 472 (grazing a cow, shooting, and taking pasturage by a 14-year-old boy regarded as a taking of profits from the land rather than as evidence of an intention to dispossess); *Buckinghamshire County Council v. Moran, supra,* at 642.

[84] *Pavledes v. Ryesbridge Properties Ltd* (1989) 58 P.&C.R. 459 at 480 (request to paper owners to exclude other trespassers); *R. v. Secretary of State for the Environment, ex p. Davies, supra* (offer to pay rent).

[85] *Buckinghamshire County Council v. Moran* [1990] Ch. 623 at 645, *per* Nourse L.J.

[86] *Buckinghamshire County Council v. Moran, supra,* rejecting the existence of such a supposed rule (said to derive from remarks attributed to Bramwell L.J. in *Leigh v. Jack* (1879) 5 Ex.D 264 at 273, but which are omitted from all other reports of the case). See too *Hounslow L.B.C. v. Minchinton* (1997) 74 P. & C.R. 221.

licensee unless the actual facts of the case warrant it.[87] The squatter's knowledge of the true owner's future plans will however place a heavier onus upon him to prove by unequivocal conduct the necessary intention to possess.[88]

(3) PROPERTY WHICH MAY BE ADVERSELY POSSESSED. There can be adverse **21–020** possession of a subterranean building or of sub-soil even though the true owner remains in possession of the surface.[89] There may also be adverse possession of a party wall.[90] A squatter's title may be subject to rights similar to easements in favour of the dispossessed owner if they have been exercised by the latter during the period of dispossession, such as a right to trim a hedge and clean a drain[91] or a right of entry for repairing an adjacent house.[92]

2. Successive squatters

(a) Dispositions by squatter. As already explained, a squatter has a title **21–021** based on his own possession, and this title is good against everyone except the true owner.[93] Accordingly, if a squatter who has not barred the true owner sells the land he can give the purchaser a right to the land which is as good as his own. The same applies to devises, gifts or other dispositions by the squatter, and to devolution on his intestacy; in each case the person taking the squatter's interest can add the squatter's period of possession to his own.[94] Thus if X, who has occupied A's land for eight years, sells the land to Y, A will be barred after Y has held the land for a further four years.

(b) Squatter dispossessed by squatter. If a squatter is himself dispossessed **21–022** the second squatter can add the former period of occupation to his own as against the true owner. This is because time runs against the true owner from the time when adverse possession began,[95] and so long as adverse possession continues unbroken it makes no difference who continues it.[96] But as against the first squatter, the second squatter must himself occupy for the full period before his title becomes unassailable. This has already been explained,[97] but a simple example may be useful here. If land owned by A has been occupied by X for eight years and Y dispossesses X, A will be barred when 12 years

---

[87] L.A. 1980, Sched. 1, para. 8(4) controverting the opinion of Lord Denning M.R. in *Wallis's Cayton Bay Holiday Camp Ltd v. Shell-Mex and B.P. Ltd* [1975] Q.B. 94, at 103 and of the Court of Appeal in *Gray v. Wykeham-Martin* [1977] C.L.Y. (Unreported Cases) §537: see *Powell v. McFarlane, supra,* at 484.

[88] *Buckinghamshire County Council v. Moran, supra,* at 645; *Pulleyn v. Hall Aggregates (Thames Valley) Ltd, supra,* at 283.

[89] *Rains v. Buxton* (1880) 14 Ch.D. 537 (cellar).

[90] *Prudential Assurance Co. Ltd v. Waterloo Real Estate Inc.* [1999] 17 E.G. 131.

[91] *Marshall v. Taylor* [1895] 1 Ch. 641.

[92] *Williams v. Usherwood* (1981) 45 P. & C.R. 235, holding that such rights are implied by law where necessary.

[93] *Ante,* para. 3–118.

[94] *Ante,* para. 3–122; *Asher v. Whitlock* (1865) L.R. 1 Q.B. 1; *Mount Carmel Investments Ltd v. Peter Thurlow Ltd* [1988] 1 W.L.R. 1078.

[95] L.A. 1980, Sched. 1, para. 8(1), governing para. 1.

[96] See *Willis v. Earl Howe* [1893] 2 Ch. 545.

[97] *Ante,* para. 3–122.

have elapsed from X first taking possession. But although at the end of that time A is barred, X will not be barred until 12 years from Y's first taking possession; for Y cannot claim to be absolutely entitled until he can show that everybody with any claim to the land has been barred by the lapse of the full period.

21–023   (*c*) *Possession abandoned.* There is no right to add together two periods of adverse possession if a squatter abandons possession before the full period has run and some time passes before someone else takes adverse possession of the land. During the gap between the two squatters, the owner has possession in law, and there is no person whom he can sue. The land therefore ceases to be in adverse possession; and when adverse possession is taken by the second squatter a fresh right of action accrues to the true owner, who has the full period within which to enforce it.[98]

3. Future interests. Future interests are governed by two rules.

21–024   (*a*) *Alternative periods.* If adverse possession began before the reversion or remainder fell into possession, the 12-year period runs against the reversioner or remainderman from the beginning of the adverse possession; but he has an alternative period of six years from the falling into possession of his interest. In other words, he must sue within 12 years of the previous owner's dispossession, or within six years of his own interest vesting in possession, whichever is the longer period.[99] Thus, if land is held by A for life with remainder to B in fee simple, and X dispossesses A 20 years before A's death, B still has six years from A's death in which to recover the land. If X had dispossessed A three years before A's death, B would have 12 years from the dispossession of A, *i.e.* nine years from A's death. But if X had not taken adverse possession until after A's death, the ordinary period of 12 years from the taking of possession would apply, for B's interest would have ceased to be a future interest before time began to run.[1]

21–025   (*b*) *Entails.* A reversioner or remainderman expectant upon an entail in possession is not entitled to the alternative six-year period if his interest could have been barred by the tenant in tail.[2] Thus if B has granted land to A in tail,[3] retaining the fee simple reversion, and X dispossesses A or the heirs of his body, B's reversion is barred 12 years after the dispossession, even though B himself had no right to the land during the period. This rule emphasises again the precarious nature of an interest expectant upon an entail: it may be barred

---

[98] L.A. 1980, Sched. 1, para. 8(2) (making statutory the decision in *Trustees, Executors and Agency Co. Ltd v. Short* (1883) 13 App.Cas. 793).

[99] Limitation Act 1980, s.15(2). His trustees may also sue on his behalf: s.18(4).

[1] See Sched. 1, paras 4, 8.

[2] This is the combined effect of ss.5(1), (3) and 38(5), requiring the reversioner or remainderman to be treated as a person claiming through the tenant in tail in such cases, and so to be barred together with him.

[3] No new entails can be created after 1996: see T.L.A.T.A. 1996, Sched. 1, para. 5; *ante*, para. 3–037.

by limitation, as well as by disentailment, and the owner is powerless to intervene.

4. Leaseholds

(a) Reversioner on a lease. The above provisions do not apply to a reversioner on a lease when the tenant has been ousted. No matter when the dispossession occurred, time does not run against the reversioner until the lease expires.[4] Thus, if L grants T a lease for 99 years and T is dispossessed by X, the 12-year period runs against T from the dispossession but against L only from the determination of the lease. X can therefore retain the land as against T during the rest of the term, but L can recover it from X at the end of the term, provided L takes proceedings within 12 years of that date.[5] If, at the end of the term, L, instead of evicting X, grants a new lease, the new tenant can recover the land from X because he claims through L. This is so even if that new tenant is T, whose title X had barred.[6] Where, however, that new lease was granted pursuant to an option in the lease, T will be unable to recover the land from X because his rights under the original lease are barred.[7]

21–026

(b) Title acquired by tenant. A tenant cannot acquire a title against his landlord during the currency of the lease; for occupation by a tenant is never adverse to the landlord's title, which the tenant is estopped from denying.[8] Any encroachments by the tenant on land belonging to third parties will enure for the landlord's benefit,[9] unless a different intention is shown by the conduct of the landlord or tenant.[10] If the tenant occupies other land belonging to the landlord but not included in the demise, that land is presumed to be an addition to the land demised to the tenant ("a mere extension of the *locus* of his tenancy"[11]), so that it becomes subject to the terms of the tenancy,[12] and although the tenant may acquire a title to it against the landlord for the remainder of the term, he must give it up to him when the tenancy ends.[13] But

21–027

---

[4] s.15(2); the words "not being a term of years absolute" confirm *Walter v. Yalden* [1902] 2 K.B. 304 on this point. See *Chung Ping Kwan v. Lam Island Development Co. Ltd* [1997] A.C. 38 at 46.

[5] See further *post*, para. 21–061.

[6] *Chung Ping Kwan v. Lam Island Development Co. Ltd*, *supra*, at 46, 47. See (1998) 28 H.K.L.J. 329 (C.H.).

[7] *Chung Ping Kwan v. Lam Island Development Co. Ltd*, *supra*, at 48, 49. This outcome has been described as "a little incongruous": (1997) 71 A.L.J. 98 at 99 (P. Butt). A tenant who finds himself in this position, is likely to seek the grant of a new lease from the landlord instead of exercising the option.

[8] *Ante*, paras 3–125, 14–095.

[9] *Whitmore v. Humphries* (1871) L.R. 7 C.P. 1; *Att.-Gen. v. Tomline* (1880) 5 Ch.D. 150; *East Stonehouse U.D.C. v. Willoughby Bros. Ltd* [1902] 2 K.B. 318; *King v. Smith* [1950] 1 All E.R. 553; *ante*, para. 3–122, n. 42.

[10] *Kingsmill v. Millard* (1855) 11 Exch. 313; *Smirk v. Lyndale Developments Ltd* [1975] Ch. 317, approving (at 337) the analysis of the law made by Pennycuick V.-C.; *Long v. Tower Hamlets L.B.C.* [1998] Ch. 197 at 203.

[11] *Lord Hastings v. Saddler* (1898) 79 L.T. 355 at 356, *per* Lord Russell C.J.

[12] *J. F. Perrott & Co. Ltd v. Cohen* [1951] 1 K.B. 705 (repairing covenant).

[13] *Tabor v. Godfrey* (1895) 64 L.J.Q.B. 245; *Smirk v. Lyndale Developments Ltd*, *supra*.

the presumption may be rebutted, *e.g.* by the tenant conveying the land to a third party and informing the landlord of this while the tenancy is still running.[14]

21–028   *(c) Non-payment of rent.* Failure to pay rent merely bars the landlord's claim to recover any particular instalment of rent after six years from its falling due[15]; it has no effect on the landlord's title to the land.

21–029   *(d) Right of re-entry.* A right of re-entry under a forfeiture clause (*e.g.* for non-payment of rent) is a right to recover land,[16] and is therefore barred if not exercised for 12 years. But this does not affect the landlord's title to the reversion, for he will have a fresh right of action when the lease expires.[17] A fresh right of entry arises every time the forfeiture clause is brought into play, *e.g.* by non-payment of rent falling due subsequently. In the case of continuing breaches of covenant,[18] such as failure to repair or user for a prohibited purpose, time continually begins running afresh, and forfeiture can be claimed at any time.

21–030   *(e) Adverse receipt of rent.* A landlord's title may, indeed, be barred if adverse possession is taken not of the land but of the rent from it. The rule is that if a tenant who holds under a written lease pays a rent of at least £10 per annum for 12 years to some person who wrongfully claims the reversion, this bars the landlord's rights altogether.[19] Adverse receipt of rent by a third party is equivalent to adverse possession of the reversion by him,[20] and after 12 years it will extinguish the reversion, even if the true owner of it is also the tenant who paid the rent.[21]

21–031   *(f) Adverse possession by landlord.* Although a tenant cannot acquire title against his landlord during the term of his lease because he is in possession with the landlord's consent,[22] there is no similar constraint on the landlord. He can therefore bar the leasehold title of his own tenant by adverse possession, notwithstanding the rule that he must not derogate from his grant. This is because adverse possession is "possession as of wrong".[23]

---

[14] *Kingsmill v. Millard, supra*; *Smirk v. Lyndale Developments Ltd, supra*, not following *Lord Hastings v. Saddler, supra*.

[15] See *post.* para. 21–072.

[16] L.A. 1980, s.38(7).

[17] *ibid.*, Sched. 1, para. 7(2).

[18] See *ante*, para. 14–128.

[19] L.A. 1980, Sched. 1, para. 6. Payment of rent to the true reversioner will stop time running: *ibid.*; *Nicholson v. England* [1926] 2 K.B. 93. These rules do not apply to any lease granted by the Crown: para. 6(2).

[20] L.A. 1980, Sched. 1, para. 8(3).

[21] *Bligh v. Martin* [1968] 1 W.L.R. 804.

[22] *Ante*, paras 21–016, 21–027.

[23] *Sze To Chun Keung v. Kung Kwok Wai David* [1997] 1 W.L.R. 1232 at 1235, *per* Lord Hoffmann (Crown in adverse possession to its lessee). See *ante*, paras 21–002, 21–018. For non-derogation from grant, see *ante*, para. 14–208.

5. Tenants at will and at sufferance. Time begins to run in favour of a   **21–032**
tenant at will only from the determination of the tenancy.[24] In the case of a
tenancy at sufferance, time begins to run from the commencement of the
tenancy. This is because a tenancy at sufferance is really not a tenancy at all,
but is adverse possession.[25]

6. Yearly or periodic tenants. A tenant under a yearly or other periodic   **21–033**
tenancy who does not hold under a lease in writing[26] is in a stronger position
than other tenants. Time runs from the end of the first year or other period of
the tenancy,[27] subject to extension by payment of rent[28] or written acknowledgment. An oral tenancy will thus in time ripen into ownership if the rent is
not paid.[29] If there is a lease in writing, time runs from the determination of
the tenancy.

7. Rentcharges. In the case of a rentcharge[30] in possession, time runs from   **21–034**
the last payment of rent to the owner of the rentcharge.[31] Thus the owner's
rights are barred—

    (i) if no rent is paid for 12 years, in which case the rentcharge is
        extinguished; or

    (ii) if the rent is paid to a stranger for 12 years, in which case the
        rentcharge remains enforceable against the land but the former
        owner's claim to it is extinguished in favour of the stranger.

The definition of rentcharge excludes rent service.[32] Rent due under a lease
(which is rent service) is dealt with elsewhere.[33]

---

[24] This follows because L.A. 1980 (unlike L.A. 1939) contains no provision deeming a tenancy
at will to terminate after a specified period: *Colchester B.C. v. Smith* [1991] Ch. 448 at 481 (in
C.A. [1992] Ch. 421). For the former position, see the previous edition of this work at p.
1039.

[25] *Ante*, para. 14–080.

[26] A document that merely evidences the terms of an agreement for a lease is not a lease in writing
for these purposes because it does not create the term: see *Long v. Tower Hamlets L.B.C.* [1998]
Ch. 197.

[27] L.A. 1980, Sched. 1, para. 5.

[28] Time then runs from the last receipt of rent: L.A. 1980, Sched.1, para. 5(2); see *Price v. Hartley*
[1995] E.G.C.S. 74.

[29] *Moses v. Lovegrove* [1952] 2 Q.B. 533, holding that the Rent Acts did not prevent time from
running, and that a rent book is not a "lease in writing"; *Hayward v. Chaloner* [1968] 1 Q.B.
107, where there was disagreement whether there was adverse possession; *Jessamine Investment Co. v. Schwartz* [1978] Q.B. 264, following *Moses v. Lovegrove*, *supra*. Time will run in
favour of the tenant even though he thinks he is paying rent when this is not in fact the case:
Lodge v. Wakefield Metropolitan C.C. [1995] 2 E.G.L.R. 124.

[30] Defined as "land": L.A. 1980, s.38(1).

[31] *ibid.*, s.38(8).

[32] *ibid.*, s.38(1), also excluding mortgage interest.

[33] Mentioned *ante*, and discussed *post*, para. 21–072.

8. Mortgages

21–035   *(a) The mortgagor's right to redeem.* The right to redeem, whether legal or equitable, is barred if the mortgagee remains in possession of the mortgaged land for 12 years without giving any written acknowledgment of the title of the mortgagor or of his equity of redemption and without receiving any payment on account of principal or interest[34] made by or on behalf of the mortgagor; the mere receipt of rents and profits while in possession does not count for this purpose,[35] although the mortgagee is accountable to the mortgagor for them.[36] The rule that a mortgagee in possession can bar the mortgagor's title is an exception to the general rules that time runs only where there is adverse possession, and that a lessee (here, a mortgagee having a long term of years[37]) may not bar his lessor's title.[38]

When a second mortgagee's rights against the mortgagor are barred, he can no longer exercise his right to redeem the first mortgagee[39]; for his interest in the property is at an end.[40]

21–036   *(b) Mortgagee's right to enforce the mortgage.* The mortgagee's rights to foreclose,[41] to sue for possession,[42] and to sue for the principal[43] all become barred after 12 years from the date when repayment became due under the mortgage[44]; and his title is then extinguished.[45] But time begins to run afresh if during the period the mortgagor makes any written acknowledgment or if he or the person in possession of the land makes any payment of interest or of capital which complies with the Act.[46]

21–037   **9. Claims through Crown or corporation sole.** It has been seen that the Crown is entitled to a period of 30 years instead of the usual 12.[47] If a person against whom time has started to run conveys his land to the Crown, the only change is that the limitation period becomes 30 years from the dispossession instead of 12.[48] But in the converse case where time has started to run against the Crown and the Crown then conveys the land to X, the rule is that X is barred at the expiration of 30 years from the original dispossession or 12 years

---

[34] L.A. 1980, ss.16, 29(4); *Young v. Clarey* [1948] Ch. 191 (mortgagor and second mortgagee barred by mortgagee in possession); and see *post*, para. 21–051.
[35] *Harlock v. Ashberry* (1882) 19 Ch.D. 539; and see *Re Lord Clifden* [1900] 1 Ch. 774.
[36] *Ante*, para. 19–069.
[37] See *ante*, para. 19–020.
[38] *Ante*, para. 21–027.
[39] See *ante*, para. 19–152.
[40] *Cotterell v. Price* [1960] 1 W.L.R. 1097.
[41] L.A. 1980, s.20(4), treating this as an action to recover land.
[42] L.A. 1980, s.17; *Cotterell v. Price, supra.*
[43] L.A. 1980, s.20(1). For interest, see *post*, para. 21–073.
[44] See *Lloyds Bank Ltd v. Margolis* [1954] 1 W.L.R. 644 (charge to secure bank overdraft with covenant to pay "on demand": time runs from demand).
[45] See *Lewis v. Plunket* [1937] 1 All E.R. 530 at 534 (omitted from [1937] Ch. 306); *Cotterell v. Price, supra.*
[46] L.A. 1980, s.29; for the details of acknowledgments, see *post*, para. 21–052.
[47] *Ante*, para. 21–009.
[48] L.A. 1980, Sched. 1, para. 10.

from the conveyance to him, whichever is the shorter.[49] Thus X is entitled to 12 years from the date of the conveyance unless at that time there were less than 12 years of the Crown period unexpired, in which case X merely has the residue of that period.

Similar rules apply to the longer periods for a spiritual or eleemosynary corporation sole.[50]

10. Equitable titles, trusts and remedies

(a) Adverse possession by a stranger. In general, the 12-year period for the recovery of land applies as much to equitable interests in land as to legal estates.[51] But adverse possession of trust property by a stranger does not bar the trustee's title to the property until all the beneficiaries have been barred.[52] Thus if land is held on trust for the benefit of A for life with remainder to B, 12 years' adverse possession of the land by X bars A's equitable interest and, but for the provision just mentioned, would bar the trustees' legal estate. But time will not start to run against B's equitable interest until A's death,[53] and the same accordingly applies to the trustees' legal estate. Consequently, after the 12 years have run, the trustees will hold the legal estate on a future trust for B as from A's death.[54] This is so even if A is the trustee, as will normally be the case if the land is settled land.

21–038

(b) Adverse possession by a trustee. It is a general principle that a trustee can never obtain a title by adverse possession against his beneficiaries. There is, indeed, a limitation period of six years for actions to recover trust property or in respect of breach of trust, in cases where no other period of limitation is prescribed.[55] However, it does not apply to a beneficiary's action against a trustee—

21–039

(i) for any fraud or fraudulent breach of trust to which the trustee was a party or privy; or

(ii) for recovery of the trust property or its proceeds in the possession of the trustee, or previously received by him and converted to his own use.[56]

In these cases, subject to one exception, the trustee can never bar the claims of his beneficiaries. The exception is where the trustee is also a beneficiary

---

[49] *ibid.*, Sched. 1, para. 12.
[50] *ibid.*, Sched. 1, paras 10, 12.
[51] *ibid.*, ss.18(1) (as amended by T.L.A.T.A. 1996, Sched. 4), 20(1).
[52] *ibid.*, s.18(2), (3), (4).
[53] *Ante*, para. 21–024.
[54] As to X's interest, see *post*, paras 21–057, 21–058.
[55] L.A. 1980, s.21(3). This subsection applies only to "an action by a beneficiary". An action brought by the Attorney-General in respect of a charitable trust is not within the subsection and is subject to no limitation period: *Att.-Gen. v. Cocke* [1988] Ch. 414.
[56] L.A. 1980, s.21(1).

and acted honestly and reasonably in distributing the property. In that case, once the appropriate period has expired, his liability to restore either the property or its proceeds is limited to the excess over his own proper share.[57]

Personal representatives are trustees for this purpose.[58] The limitation period for claims to a deceased person's estate is 12 years,[59] even where the claim is made against a third party, *e.g.* someone to whom the estate has been wrongly distributed.[60] But personal representatives are often expressly given the duties of trustees, and claims against them in the latter capacity are governed by the rules as to trustees, explained above.[61]

For these purposes, persons are "trustees" if their trusteeship precedes the breach of trust complained of, namely where they are either expressly appointed or they take it upon themselves to act as trustees.[61a] However, persons whose trusteeship does not precede but is a direct consequence of the unlawful transaction which is impeached by the claimant,[62] do not fall within these provisions.[63]

21–040   *(c) Adverse possession by a beneficiary.* Under the Limitation Act 1980[64] time will not run against a trustee in favour of a beneficiary in possession, except where the beneficiary in possession is solely and absolutely entitled, and it will not run against a co-beneficiary.[65] Where a purchaser is in possession under an uncompleted contract of sale and the vendor has been paid, time will run against the vendor,[66] who is in effect a bare trustee.[67] However, if the vendor has not been paid, it seems that time does not run against him, at least if the purchaser acknowledges that he is in possession under the contract and not as a trespasser, since his possession is not then adverse.[68]

21–041   *(d) Equitable remedies.* Except where, as explained above, the Limitation Act specifically imposes periods of limitation, there are no statutory time-limits for claims for specific performance or for an injunction or for other

---

[57] *ibid.*, s.21(2).
[58] *ibid.*, s.38(1); T.A. 1925, s.68(17). And see *ante*, para. 11–125.
[59] *Ante*, para. 21–007 (land); L.A. 1980, s.22 (personalty).
[60] *Ministry of Health v. Simpson* [1951] A.C. 251.
[61] See *Re Oliver* [1927] 2 Ch. 323.
[61a] Such as an executor *de son tort*: see *James v. Williams* [1999] 3 W.L.R. 451.
[62] Such as those who dishonestly procure or assist in a breach of trust or knowingly receive trust property transferred in breach of trust: see *ante*, para. 10–019.
[63] See *Paragon Finance Plc v. D.B. Thakerar & Co.* [1999] 1 All E.R. 400 at 407–414. At 414, Millett L.J. doubted whether such cases were cases of constructive trusteeship at all. See too *Coulthard v. Disco Mix Club Ltd* [1999] 2 All E.R. 457 at 475 *et seq.*
[64] For the former position, see the previous edition of this work at p. 1042.
[65] L.A. 1980, Sched. 1, para. 9; see *Earnshaw v. Hartley* [1999] 3 W.L.R. 709.
[66] *Bridges v. Mees* [1957] Ch. 457, where Harman J. rejected the argument that the vendor had no right of action which could be barred. See also n. 71, *infra.*
[67] *Ante*, para. 12–055.
[68] *Hyde v. Pearce* [1982] 1 W.L.R. 560. The explanation may be that the purchaser remains a licensee or tenant at will: *cf, ante*, paras 14–025, 14–075. But *Bridges v. Mees, supra,* was not cited to the Court of Appeal, and the reconciliation is conjectural.

equitable relief.[69] These remedies are expressly exempted from the time-limits applicable in actions based on tort or simple contract or on a specialty.[70] If beneficial interests are not affected, such remedies may be awarded after long intervals of time, for example for the purpose of getting in an outstanding legal estate.[71] But other cases are subject to the long established doctrine that equity, following the law, adopts a time-limit by analogy with any comparable statutory period.[72] Before fixed periods were imposed upon claims based on equitable titles and trusts, equitable claims to recover land were dismissed if not brought within the 20-year period then prescribed for similar actions at law[73]; and equitable money claims, if analogous to claims at law for money had and received, were limited by the same six-year period.[74] As there are now fixed periods for many equitable claims, there is little scope left for the doctrine of analogy. It will, of course, not apply where the Limitation Act deliberately excludes some particular case, such as liability for fraudulent breach of trust.

On the other hand, there is the equitable doctrine of laches, which requires that remedies be sought without unreasonable delay.[75] In cases governed specifically by the Act the court will not refuse relief within the statutory period on the ground of delay alone.[76] However, it may do so where the delay is coupled with circumstances indicating acquiescence or abandonment, so making it inequitable to prosecute the claim.[77] Mere delay by itself may be fatal where the case is omitted from the Act,[78] and probably also where the Act is followed by analogy.[79] The Act expressly preserves the equitable jurisdiction to refuse relief "on the ground of acquiescence or otherwise".[80]

An action for an account leads to an equitable remedy, since the corresponding action at common law has long been obsolete.[81] It is now subject to

---

[69] *e.g.* rectification (*ante*, para. 12–122) or relief from mistake (*post*, para. 21–050).

[70] L.A. 1980, s.36(1). The same applies in actions for statutory debts and actions to enforce judgments and certain arbitration awards: *ibid.*

[71] *Shepheard v. Walker* (1875) L.R. 20 Eq. 659; (1876) 34 L.T. 230 (specific performance awarded after 18 years); *Williams v. Greatrex* [1957] 1 W.L.R. 31 (specific performance awarded after 10 years).

[72] *Smith v. Clay* (1763) 3 Bro.C.C. 639n. See generally Brunyate, *Limitation of Actions in Equity*, Ch. 1.

[73] *Cholmondely v. Clinton* (1821) 4 Bli. 1.

[74] *Re Robinson* [1911] 1 Ch. 502.

[75] See Brunyate, *op. cit.*, chap. 7; Snell, *Equity*, 35.

[76] *Re Pauling's S.T. (No. 1)* [1964] Ch. 303.

[77] "The test is whether, in the circumstances, it has become unconscionable for the plaintiff to rely upon his legal right": *Shaw v. Applegate* [1977] 1 W.L.R. 970 at 980, *per* Goff L.J. See too *Frawley v. Neill* [1999] 5 C.L. §531. *cf. ante*, chap. 13; and see Brunyate, *op. cit.* chap. 7; Lightwood, *The Time Limit on Actions*, p. 252.

[78] Thus insufficiently explained delays of one year (*Watson v. Reid* (1830) 1 Russ. & M. 236), or three-and-a half years (*Eads v. Williams* (1854) 4 De G.M. & G. 674) have been held to bar specific performance. Contrast *Wroth v. Tyler* [1974] Ch. 30 at 53.

[79] Brunyate, *op. cit.*, 258; contrast Lightwood, *op. cit.*, 254.

[80] s.36(2).

[81] See *Tito v. Waddell (No. 2)* [1977] Ch. 106 at 250, discussing the problems of L.A. 1939, s.2(2), (7) before the amendments made by Limitation Amendment Act 1980, Sched. 1, paras 2, 8.

the same time-limit as applies to the claim which is the basis of the duty to account.[82]

11. Co-ownership

21–042   *(a) Ouster.* At common law, the unity of possession between co-owners meant that if one joint tenant or tenant in common occupied the whole of the land, or took the whole of the rents and profits, this by itself was not adverse possession which would start time running. Some further act, such as ouster of the co-owners was needed.[83] However, a presumption of ouster might arise from long exclusive enjoyment by one co-owner.[84] After 1833, by statute,[85] time normally began to run as between co-owners as soon as one enjoyed more than his share of the land or of the rents and profits, to the exclusion of the other.[86]

21–043   *(b) After 1925.* Since 1925 the law has been changed, perhaps unintentionally, by the imposition of what is now the statutory trust of land which operates in all cases of tenancy in common and beneficial joint tenancy.[87] This brings into play the rules relating to trusts, mentioned above,[88] in particular the rules that a trustee cannot bar his beneficiary, and that one beneficiary cannot bar another beneficiary. Thus in a case[89] where one of two tenants in common took all the rents and profits from 1925 for over 12 years, the other tenant's claim failed in respect of the years 1923–1925, when the old law applied. However, it succeeded in respect of the later years, for after 1925 the legal estate was vested in the two tenants as trustees for sale[90] on their own behalf, and so neither could plead the Limitation Act against the other. Since 1940, moreover, the position would be the same even if other persons were trustees,[91] because of the provision that one beneficiary cannot bar another.[92]

---

[82] L.A. 1980, s.23. As the obligation to account in equity arises not from the breach of any duty but simply from the existence of a fiduciary relationship, s.23 may have very little application: *Att.-Gen. v. Cocke* [1988] Ch. 414.

[83] See Carson's *Real Property Statutes* (2nd ed.), p. 149.

[84] See *Doe d. Fishar v. Taylor* (1774) 1 Cowp. 217. *cf. Doe d. Hellings v. Bird* (1809) 11 East 49.

[85] Real Property Limitation Act 1833, s.12.

[86] See *Paradise Beach Co. Ltd v. Price-Robinson* [1968] A.C. 1072.

[87] *Ante*, para. 9–051.

[88] *Ante*, 21–038 *et seq.* See too *Earnshaw v. Hartley* [1999] 3 W.L.R. 709, where (at 714), Nourse L.J. noted "the reintroduction of the doctrine of non-adverse possession among beneficial co-owners of land".

[89] *Re Landi* [1939] Ch. 828, rejecting the argument that the old law is preserved by L.P.A. 1925, s.12 (a saving clause for the operation of statutes and the general law of limitation). *cf. Re Milking Pail Farm Trusts* [1940] Ch. 996; and see (1941) 57 L.Q.R. 26 (R.E.M.); (1971) 35 Conv. (N.S.) 6 (G. Battersby).

[90] They would now be trustees of land.

[91] For example if the legal estate were vested in personal representatives under L.P.A. 1925, s.34(3); *ante*, para. 9–051.

[92] L.A. 1980, Sched. 1, para. 9 (as amended by T.L.A.T.A. 1996, Sched. 3, para. 18, and Sched. 4); *ante*, para. 21–040.

Section 2. Postponement of the Period

The date from which time begins to run may be postponed on account of **21–044** disability, fraud, deliberate concealment, or (in certain special cases) mistake.

A. Disability

1. Alternative periods. If the owner of an interest in land is under a **21–045** disability when the right of action accrues, he is allowed an alternative period of six years from the time when he ceases to be under a disability or dies, whichever happens first, with a maximum period in the case of land of 30 years from the date when the right of action first accrued.[93] Thus if X takes possession of A's land at a time when A is a mental patient, A will have 12 years from the dispossession or six years from his recovery from mental disability in which to bring his action, whichever is longer. However, in no case can A sue after 30 years from the dispossession. The following rules should be noted.

2. Disability. A person is under a disability for this purpose if he is a minor **21–046** or of unsound mind.[94] A disability is immaterial unless it existed at the time when the cause of action accrued.[95] Thus if A becomes insane the day before he is dispossessed, the provisions for disability apply, whereas if he becomes insane the day after he has been dispossessed, they do not.[96]

3. Successive disabilities. In the case of successive disabilities, if a person **21–047** is under one disability and before that ceases another disability begins, the period is extended until both disabilities cease, subject to the 30 years' maximum.[97] But if one disability comes to an end before another starts, or if the person under disability is succeeded by another person under disability, time runs from the ceasing of the first disability. For example, A is a minor when the cause of action accrues. If later, during his minority, he becomes mentally ill, the six-year period does not start to run until he ceases to be ill and is also of full age.[98] But if he reaches full age before he becomes mentally ill, or if he dies a minor and B, a mental patient becomes entitled to the land, the six-year period runs from A's majority in the first case and his death in the second. In no case can the right of action survive for more than 30 years after it accrued.

B. Fraud, Concealment and Mistake

1. Fraud or deliberate concealment. Where— **21–048**

    (i) an action is based on the fraud of the defendant or his agent (or any person through whom he claims, or his agent), or

---

[93] L.A. 1980, s.28.
[94] *ibid.*, s.38(2)–(4).
[95] *ibid.*, s.28(1); see, *e.g. Garner v. Wingrove* [1905] 2 Ch. 233.
[96] *Goodhall v. Skerratt* (1855) 3 Drew. 216.
[97] L.A. 1980, s.28(1).
[98] See, *e.g. Borrows v. Ellison* (1871) L.R. 6 Ex. 128 (infancy and coverture).

(ii) a fact relevant to the right of action has been deliberately concealed by the fraud of any such person,

time does not begin to run until the claimant discovers the fraud or concealment or could with reasonable diligence have discovered it.[99] A person will have shown reasonable diligence if he takes those steps which a prudent person would have taken in the circumstances. He is not required to do everything possible.[1] Deliberate concealment extends to a deliberate breach of duty in circumstances which make it unlikely to be discovered for some time.[2] The relevant concealment may occur after the cause of action has accrued and time had therefore begun to run. In such a case, in accordance with the wording of the Limitation Act 1980, time does not run until the fact is discovered by the claimant.[3]

21–049   These rules are a restatement of the previous law, substituting "deliberately concealed" for the former words "concealed by fraud".[4] The latter term had become misleading, since in contrast to "fraud", which here as elsewhere necessarily implies dishonesty,[5] "fraudulent concealment" has been carried far beyond its natural meaning, and dishonesty or moral turpitude were not indispensable elements.[6] A clandestine act such as surreptitious abstraction of underground minerals could amount to a fraudulent concealment,[7] as could also the subsequent concealment of the act.[8] Similarly there might be fraudulent concealment if title deeds were destroyed,[9] or if a builder covered up what he knew to be defective foundations without saying anything to the purchaser.[10] Where a vendor employed a builder as an independent contractor, the builder might for this purpose be treated as the vendor's "agent".[11] But there was no fraudulent concealment in the open occupation of land, even if it was subterranean and the owner had no knowledge of the occupation.[12]

The plea of fraud or concealment will not postpone the beginning of the ordinary period of limitation if the defendant is or claims through a purchaser for value who was not a party to the fraud or concealment and at the time of

---

[99] L.A. 1980, s.32(1).

[1] *Peco Arts Inc. v. Hazlitt Gallery Ltd.* [1983] 1 W.L.R. 1315 at 1323.

[2] L.A. 1980, s.32(2).

[3] *Sheldon v. R.H.M. Outhwaite (Underwriting Agencies) Ltd* [1996] A.C. 102. As Lord Nichols explained in that case, although time has started to run, "in the case of subsequent concealment the clock is turned back to zero": *ibid.*, at 152.

[4] The change was made by the Limitation Amendment Act 1980, s.7.

[5] See *Beaman v. A.R.T.S. Ltd* [1949] 1 K.B. 550 at 558.

[6] *Kitchen v. R.A.F. Association* [1958] 1 W.L.R. 563; *Clark v. Woor* [1965] 1 W.L.R. 650; *Tito v. Waddell (No. 2)* [1977] Ch. 106 at 204; and see *Bartlett v. Barclays Bank Trust Co. Ltd (No. 1)* [1980] Ch. 515 at 537 ("unconscionable").

[7] *Bulli Coal Mining Co. v. Osborne* [1899] A.C. 351; compare *Trotter v. Maclean* (1879) 13 Ch.D. 574.

[8] *Beaman v. A.R.T.S. Ltd, supra*, at 559; and see *Eddis v. Chichester Constable* [1969] 2 Ch. 345 (mere silence).

[9] *Lawrence v. Lord Norreys* (1890) 15 App. Cas. 210.

[10] *Applegate v. Moss* [1971] 1 Q.B. 406; *King v. Victor Parsons & Co.* [1973] 1 W.L.R. 29.

[11] *Applegate v. Moss, supra*, perhaps straining the words of the Act in the interests of justice.

[12] *Rains v. Buxton* (1880) 14 Ch.D. 537.

his purchase neither knew nor had reason to believe that it had been committed.[13] This now statutory rule derives from the older law under which relief against fraud was given only in equity.[14]

2. Relief from mistake. Similar provisions apply to an action "for relief   **21–050**
from the consequences of a mistake".[15] This rule has a narrow scope, and applies only where the mistake is the gist of the action, *i.e.* where it is the mistake itself that gives a right to apply to the court for relief. An example is an action for the recovery of money paid under a mistake[16] (whether of fact or law).[17] In the case of land, most claims for relief against mistake are based on equitable grounds, *e.g.* to set aside a conveyance executed under a misapprehension,[18] or by way of rectification,[19] or rescission.[20] These are not subject to any period of limitation,[21] and so nothing would be gained by providing that the period shall not begin to run until some later date. There is no general rule that mistake stops time from running,[22] *e.g.* where a landowner allows his neighbour to take adverse possession of a strip of land owing to a mistake about his boundary. Nor does mere ignorance stop time from running.[23]

Section 3. Starting Time Running Afresh

1. Acknowledgment or payment. Time may be started running afresh—   **21–051**

    (i) by a written and signed acknowledgment of the claimant's title[24]; or

---

[13] L.A. 1980, s.32(3), (4).
[14] See *Oelkers v. Ellis* [1914] 2 K.B. 139.
[15] L.A. 1980, s.32(1), (3), (4).
[16] See *Phillips-Higgins v. Harper* [1954] 1 Q.B. 411. A person who has mistakenly paid too much has an extension of time, whereas one who has mistakenly received too little has not. In an action to recover money paid by mistake, the mistake is the gist of the action, whereas the remedy for an underpayment is merely to sue for the balance, and mistake has nothing to do with that.
[17] Money paid under a mistake of law is now recoverable: see *Kleinwort Benson Ltd v. Lincoln C.C.* [1999] 1 A.C. 153; *Nurdin & Peacock Plc. v. D.B. Ramsden & Co. Ltd (No. 2)* [1999] 1 W.L.R. 1249.
[18] *Cooper v. Phibbs* (1867) L.R. 2 H.L. 149; *cf. ante*, para. 12–123.
[19] *Ante*, para. 12–122.
[20] *Ante*, para. 12–112.
[21] *Ante*, para. 21–041.
[22] See *Phillips-Higgins v. Harper, supra.*
[23] See *Cartledge v. E. Jopling & Sons Ltd* [1963] A.C. 758. L.A. 1980 (as amended by the Latent Damage Act 1986 and the Consumer Protection Act 1987), ss.11, 11A, 12, 14, 14A, 14B, allows (under certain conditions) an extension of time for ignorance in actions for damages for personal injuries and in respect of defective products and other cases of latent damage. See Preston and Newsom's *Limitation of Actions* (4th ed), chap. 5.
[24] L.A. 1980, ss.29(1), (2), 30. The requirement of writing provides certainty and rules out fraud, mistake or failure of memory: see *Browne v. Perry* [1991] 1 W.L.R. 1297.

(ii) by payment of part of the principal or interest due in respect of a debt.[25]

The acknowledgment or payment must be—

(a) made by or on behalf of the person in whose favour time is running;

(b) to or for the account of the person whose title is being barred[26]; and

(c) signed by the person making it.[27]

An acknowledgment signed by a solicitor authorised by a mortgagor to "clear up" his affairs binds the mortgagor.[28] However, an acknowledgment to some third party, such as the Inland Revenue, will not satisfy the Act,[29] and interrogatories cannot be used so as to wring an acknowledgment out of a litigant.[30]

21–052 **2. Sufficiency of acknowledgment of payment.** The acknowledgment must be of an existing liability, and not merely of a possible liability[31]; but any statement recognising the claimant's right to sue is enough.[32] Accordingly, statements in a company's balance sheets which relate to past periods will not suffice[33] unless they are put forward as showing the existing position.[34] No special form is required, nor need there be any intention to make an acknowledgment. Thus a letter by a squatter to the owner offering, subject to contract, to buy the land may be sufficient, by recognising that the owner has the better title[35]; and an acknowledgment of unquantified indebtedness (*e.g.* the "amount I owe you") suffices, for extrinsic evidence is admissible to quantify it.[36] But the statement must acknowledge that there is a debt and not merely that there may be a claim. It is not therefore enough to state that "the question of outstanding rent can be settled as a separate agreement as soon as you present your account".[37]

---

[25] L.A. 1980, s.29(3)–(6).

[26] *ibid.*, s.30(2); *Re Compania de Electricidad de la Provincia de Buenos Aires Ltd* [1980] Ch. 146 (balance sheet effective acknowledgement if received by creditor).

[27] L.A. 1980, s.30(1).

[28] *Wright v. Pepin* [1954] 1 W.L.R. 635.

[29] *Bowring-Hanbury's Trustees v. Bowring-Hanbury* [1943] Ch. 104.

[30] *Lovell v. Lovell* [1970] 1 W.L.R. 1451.

[31] *Re Flynn (No. 2)* [1969] 2 Ch. 403; *Kamouh v. Associated Electrical Industries International Ltd* [1980] Q.B. 199.

[32] *Moodie v. Bannister* (1859) 4 Drew. 432.

[33] *Consolidated Agencies Ltd v. Bertram Ltd* [1965] A.C. 470.

[34] *Jones v. Bellgrove Properties Ltd* [1949] 2 K.B. 700; *Re Overmark Smith Warden Ltd* [1982] 1 W.L.R. 1195.

[35] *Edginton v. Clark* [1964] 1 Q.B. 367; the question is one of construing the words used: see at 377.

[36] *Dungate v. Dungate* [1965] 1 W.L.R. 1477; and see *Wright v. Pepin, supra.*

[37] *Good v. Parry* [1963] 2 Q.B. 418, as construed in *Dungate v. Dungate, supra.*

3. Expiration of period. A current period of limitation may be repeatedly   **21–053**
extended by further acknowledgments or payments.[38] Furthermore, where a
landowner's claim for possession has been compromised, the squatter will be
estopped by the agreement from subsequently asserting title by adverse
possession.[39] But when once the full period has run, no payment or acknowledgment can revive any right to recover land,[40] for the lapse of time will have
extinguished not only the owner's remedies for recovering the land but also
his right to it.[41]

4. Judgment for possession. After a judgment for possession has been   **21–054**
obtained against a squatter, the true owner cannot enforce it without the leave
of the court if more than six years has elapsed since it was entered.[42] This will
be so even though the squatter may have been in adverse possession for more
than 12 years by the time that the judgment is actually enforced.[43] Conversely,
if enforcement does not take place within six years, the true owner may begin
new proceedings for possession, provided that at the time of their commencement, his right of action has not been barred by 12 years' adverse
possession.

Part 4

THE EFFECT OF THE LAPSE OF TIME

Section 1. Title to Land

A. Effect on Owner's Title

The effect of adverse possession upon the title of the paper owner depends
upon whether the land is unregistered or registered.

1. Unregistered land. Before 1833 the effect of the Statutes of Limitation   **21–055**
was merely to bar rights of action. They extinguished remedies not rights.[44]
Thus a person whose right to recover land had been barred might, if he could
recover it peaceably, reassert his old title.[45] This principle still applies to pure

---

[38] L.A. 1980, s.29(7).

[39] *Colchester B.C. v. Smith* [1992] Ch. 421. Such compromises are in a wholly different position
from the subsequent acknowledgments or payments caught by s.29(7): *ibid.*, at 435.

[40] L.A. 1980, s.29(7); *Sanders v. Sanders* (1881) 19 Ch.D. 373; *Nicholson v. England* [1926] 2
K.B. 93.

[41] *Post*, para. 21–055.

[42] CPR Sched. 1, R46.2(a); Sched.2, C26.5(a). L.A. 1980, s.24(1) only bars a subsequent action
brought on the judgment: see *Lowsley v. Forbes* [1999] 1 A.C. 329.

[43] *B.P. Properties Ltd v. Buckler* (1987) 55 P. & C.R. 337 (decided under L.A. 1939).

[44] See *Wainford v. Barker* (1697) 1 Ld.Raym. 232; *Hunt v. Burn* (1703) 2 Salk. 422.

[45] See *Doe d. Burrough v. Reade* (1807) 8 East 353 (possession peaceably taken when the land
was vacant after a death).

personalty, other than chattels[46]; but as regards land it was abolished by the Real Property Limitation Act 1833.[47] The rule now is that, at the end of the limitation period, both the right of action to recover the land and the claimant's title to it are extinguished.[48] This applies equally to redemption and foreclosure actions.

When title to land has been extinguished by adverse possession, the rights which that title carried are also extinguished. The former owner cannot thereafter sue the squatter either for rent that fell due before title was extinguished or for damages for trespass.[49]

21–056   **2. Registered land.** Although the Limitation Act 1980 applies to registered land in the same manner and to the same extent as it does to unregistered land,[50] this principle is subject to an important exception. The registered proprietor's estate is not extinguished by adverse possession, but is deemed to be held by him (or by his successors in title) on trust for the squatter, but without prejudice to the estates or interests of any person whose rights have not been extinguished.[51] The squatter who claims to have acquired a title may then apply to be registered as proprietor of that estate,[52] and must be so registered provided that the registrar is satisfied as to his claim.[53]

Although the trust has been described as mere machinery for applying the Limitation Acts to registered land, which "does not alter the substantive position very materially",[54] it has become clear that the two systems are different.[55] First, it is now recognised that the squatter acquires his estate by means of a "parliamentary conveyance",[56] which is not the case where the title is unregistered.[57] Secondly, it has been suggested that until he is registered as proprietor, the squatter's title is merely equitable, so that any interest granted by him in the interim will therefore also be equitable.[58] This has been criticised[59] and the better view is that the squatter has a legal fee simple in the

---

[46] See L.A. 1980, s.3(2).

[47] s.34.

[48] L.A. 1980, s.17.

[49] *Re Jolly* [1900] 2 Ch. 616; *Mount Carmel Investments Ltd v. Peter Thurlow Ltd* [1988] 1 W.L.R. 1078.

[50] L.R.A. 1925, s.75(1).

[51] *ibid.* See *ante*, para. 6–116.

[52] L.R.A. 1925, s.75(2). It should be noted that the squatter is registered with the estate which the registered proprietor formerly had is his successor in title: see *Central London Commercial Estates Ltd v. Kato Kagaku Ltd* [1998] 4 All E.R. 948.

[53] *ibid.*, s.75(3). The squatter may not be registered with the same class of title as the former proprietor: *ibid.*

[54] *St Marylebone Property Co. Ltd v. Fairweather* [1963] A.C. 510 at 548, *per* Lord Denning. See too *Jessamine Investment Co. v. Schwartz* [1975] Q.B. 264 at 274, 275.

[55] *Spectrum Investment Co. v. Holmes* [1981] 1 W.L.R. 221 at 229, 230; Ruoff & Roper, 29–02.

[56] *Central London Commercial Estates Ltd v. Kato Kagaku Ltd* [1998] 4 All E.R. 948; *post*, para. 21–064; and see L.R.A. 1925, s.75(2). *cf. Spectrum Investment Co. v. Holmes*, *supra*, at 229, where the point was left open.

[57] *Ante*, paras 3–126, 21–002.

[58] Ruoff & Roper, 29–02.

[59] *Central London Commercial Estates Ltd v. Kato Kagaku Ltd*, *supra*, at 953 ("surely wrong").

usual way by virtue of his adverse possession until he bars the title of the registered proprietor.[60] When he becomes a beneficiary under the statutory trust this has the effect of nullifying the squatter's common law freehold.[61] Thirdly, the incidents of this statutory trust are by no means clear.[62]

It should be noted that these provisions apply only where there has been adverse possession against a registered estate.[63] They have no application therefore to those leases of registered land granted for 21 years or less which can exist only as overriding interests.[64] Such estates will be extinguished by adverse possession in the same way as if the title to the land were unregistered.

B. The Squatter's Title

1. Rights of third parties

(a) Unregistered land. The general character of a title acquired by limitation has already been discussed.[65] The squatter[66] holds a new estate of his own, founded on his adverse possession and the absence of any better title, but he holds it subject to any third party rights which run with the land and have not themselves been extinguished. Thus a squatter will be bound by easements or restrictive covenants affecting the land. It makes no difference whether such incumbrances are legal or equitable, or whether (if registrable as land charges) they are registered. If they are legal, they bind all comers, including squatters. If they are equitable (and even if they are registrable as land charges but unregistered[67]) they bind all persons who are not purchasers for value, and a squatter gives no value.[68]

21–057

(b) Registered land. Where the proprietor of a registered estate holds it on trust for the squatter, he does so without prejudice to the estates and interests of any other persons whose rights have not been barred by adverse possession.[69] Where the squatter is registered as proprietor of the registered estate—

21–058

---

[60] See *ante*, para. 3–122; *post*, para. 21–059.

[61] *Central London Commercial Estates Ltd v. Kato Kagaku Ltd, supra,* at 959. *cf.* (1999) 115 L.Q.R. 187 at 189, 190 (C.H.).

[62] For discussion, see *Central London Commercial Estates Ltd v. Kato Kagaku Ltd, supra.*

[63] L.R.A. 1925, s.75(1), (2). For the definition of "registered estate", see *ibid.,* s.3(xxiii).

[64] L.R.A. 1925, ss.19(2), 22(2), 70(1)(k); *ante*, para. 6–066.

[65] *Ante*, paras 3–117 *et seq.*

[66] Meaning a true adverse possessor and not a mere trespasser, as explained *ante*, para. 21–016.

[67] See *ante*, para. 5–117.

[68] *Re Nisbet & Potts' Contract* [1906] 1 Ch. 386 (squatter bound by restrictive covenant: *ante* para. 4–013); *Scott v. Scott* (1854) 4 H.L.C. 1065 (squatter bound by trusts of a settlement). Contrast *Bolling v. Hobday* (1882) 31 W.R. 9, *ante*, para. 4–013; and an equitable title to *possession* may be barred: *ante*, para. 21–038.

[69] L.R.A. 1925, s.75(1).

(i) it is without prejudice to any estate or interest protected by entry on the register which has not been extinguished under the Limitation Acts[70];

(ii) the registrar has a discretion as to the class of title which is given to the property[71]; and

(iii) the registration has the same effect as the registration of a first proprietor,[72] and the squatter therefore takes subject to overriding interests.[73]

The squatter is entitled to be registered with the same title as the previous registered proprietor, and becomes subject to the same incidents as that proprietor.[74]

21–059   **2. Progressive improvement.** A squatter's estate is normally a fee simple absolute,[75] though it may be cut down by the unextinguished rights of other persons. If, for example, land is held by trustees of land on trust for A for life with remainder to B in fee simple, and S occupies it for 12 years during A's lifetime, A's life interest is extinguished, but B will have at least six years from A's death in which to assert his rights.[76] Meanwhile S, who has extinguished A's equitable life interest but not the legal estate which is held on trust,[77] has an independent legal estate based on his own occupation, but subject to B's future right when it accrues. S's estate is in effect an estate *pur autre vie*. However, it is more correct to call it a fee simple subject to an adverse title, and therefore a legal estate[78]; for unless B sues within the time allowed his title will also be barred. In other words, S's title is not one which comes to a sudden stop at A's death. It continues indefinitely, until someone having a superior title contests it. The interest gained by S is therefore not necessarily commensurate with the interest lost by A.[79] The principle is that S's title may progressively improve as each successive adverse claimant becomes barred.

---

[70] *ibid.*, s.75(3).

[71] *ibid.* For the classes of title, see *ante*, paras 6–021 *et seq.*

[72] L.R.A. 1925, s.75(3). For the effect of first registration, see *ante*, para. 6–022.

[73] L.R.A. 1925, ss.5, 9.

[74] Thus in the case of a registered leasehold title, the squatter "becomes entitled, without regard to merits to be placed in the same relationship with the freeholder as had been enjoyed by the leaseholder" and is subject to the rights and liabilities of that lease: *Central London Commercial Estates Ltd v. Kato Kagaku Ltd* [1998] 4 All E.R. 948 at 959, *per* Sedley J.

[75] See, *e.g. Leach v. Jay* (1878) 9 Ch.D. 42 at 44, 45; *Rosenberg v. Cook* (1881) 8 Q.B.D. 162 at 165; *Central London Commercial Estates Ltd v. Kato Kagaku Ltd, supra,* at 951; (1998) Law Com. No. 254, paras 10.22–10.24; and *ante*, para. 21–024.

[76] *Ante*, para. 3–122.

[77] *Ante*, para. 21–038.

[78] *Ante*, para. 3–123.

[79] See *Taylor v. Twinberrow* [1930] 2 K.B. 16 at 23. Earlier dicta to the contrary are attributable to the "parliamentary conveyance" heresy: see *ante*, para. 21–002.

3. Effect on third parties. Time runs in favour of the adverse possessor **21–060**
throughout successive ownerships of the paper title. Any action is barred after
the expiry of the limitation period, whether it accrued to the claimant himself
or to some predecessor in title.[80] Where the title is registered, rights acquired
or in the course of being acquired under the Limitation Acts take effect as
overriding interests and will therefore bind any successor in title to the
registered proprietor.[81]

4. Leases

(a) Landlord not barred. Interesting questions can arise where a squatter **21–061**
bars a leasehold tenant. If L leases land to T for 99 years and S occupies the
land adversely to T for 12 years, S has extinguished T's title. But this has no
effect on L's title.[82] L has disposed of his right to possession for the term of
the lease, and nothing done by third parties in the meantime will give it back
to him. L cannot therefore eject S, since apart from any right of forfeiture,[83]
no right of action to recover the land will accrue to L until the expiry of the
term of T's lease[84]; and S being in possession, has the best immediate
title.[85]

(b) Unregistered land

(1) SURRENDER OF LEASE. Where the title to land is unregistered,[86] if T **21–062**
surrenders his lease to L after time has run in S's favour, it has been held by
the House of Lords that L is then entitled to eject S.[87] Thus T, whose title

---

[80] L.A. 1980, s.15(1).
[81] L.R.A. 1925, s.70(1)(f); Ruoff & Roper, 6–14, 29–02; *ante*, para. 6–046.
[82] See *Chung Ping Kwan v. Lam Island Development Co. Ltd* [1997] A.C. 38 at 47.
[83] *e.g.* for breach of covenant against parting with possession (see *infra*), or if T denies L's title:
  see *ante*, paras 14–118, 15–057.
[84] See *Jessamine Investment Co. v. Schwartz* [1978] Q.B. 264, where the tenant's title was barred
  by a sub-tenant but when the head lease expired the sub-tenant was protected by the Rent Act
  1968; *Spectrum Investment Co. v. Holmes* [1981] 1 W.L.R. 221, where the landlord was unable
  to eject the squatter who had barred the tenant during a 99-year lease.
[85] *Ante*, para. 3–122. This can perhaps be made clear by comparison with the barring of a fee
  simple. If A is fee simple owner and sells to B, and B's title is extinguished by S (a squatter),
  obviously A can assert no title against S. The same is true in the case of a reversioner as regards
  any time before the reversion is due to fall into possession.
[86] The same rules apply where the title is registered, but where the lease is granted for a term of
  21 years or less and so takes effect as an overriding interest under L.R.A. 1925, s.70(1)(k).
  Such leases are dealt with in the same way as unregistered land: *ante*, para. 6–072.
[87] *St. Marylebone Property Co. Ltd v. Fairweather* [1963] A.C. 510, overruling *Walter v. Yalden*
  [1902] 2 K.B. 304, and approving *Taylor v. Twinberrow* [1930] 2 K.B. 16; and applied (though
  without violation of principle) in *Jessamine Investment Co. v. Schwartz, supra.* For further
  criticism, see (1962) 78 L.Q.R. 541 (H.W.R.W.). The *St Marylebone* case has not been followed
  in Ireland: *Perry v. Woodfarm Homes Ltd* [1975] I.R. 104, and the Privy Council has left open
  its correctness in the light of the "powerful critique" mentioned *ante*: see *Chung Ping Kwan
  v. Lam Island Development Co. Ltd* [1997] A.C. 38 at 47, *per* Lord Nicholls. It has been held
  not to apply to registered land: see *Central London Commercial Estates Ltd v. Kato Kagaku Ltd*
  [1998] 4 All E.R. 948 at 959; *post*, para. 21–064. For a defence of the *St. Marylebone* case, see
  (1994) 14 L.S. 1 at 7 (E. Cooke), where it is suggested that "the tenant no longer has a key to
  the door, but he can stand out of the way so that the landlord can use his own key". As the
  tenant's interest has been extinguished, it is not clear how he can do this.

against S is bad, can nevertheless confer upon L a good title against S, and thus accelerate L's right to possession. This is said to follow from the fact that the lease remains valid as between L and T. But this reasoning seems unsound,[88] since it ignores the fact that T has lost all power to eject S and cannot therefore confer any such power upon L. As against S, T's lease is no longer a good title, whether pleaded by T or by L, and to allow it to be so pleaded violates the fundamental principle that no one can confer a better title than he has himself (*nemo dat quod non habet*).[89] It would be different if L had a present right to determine T's lease, for he could then assert an immediate paramount title of his own without relying upon any right derived through T.[90] The House of Lords' decision gravely impairs the squatter's statutory title, by putting it into the power of the person barred (T) to enable a third party (L) to eject the squatter. The operation of the Limitation Act 1980 in respect of leaseholds is thus substantially curtailed. It is otherwise in the case of registered land, as explained below.

21–063   (2) ACQUISITION OF THE REVERSION. If T acquires L's reversion after S has taken adverse possession, T has the same rights as L. Thus in one case, where the reversion was purchased by T, a yearly tenant whose title as such had already been barred by another person, it was held that T acquired a fresh right of action at once by stepping into the landlord's shoes. The lease merged in the freehold forthwith, for it was determined by notice and T could not give notice to himself.[91] The result is held to be the same even if the lease is for a fixed term of years which L could not determine, so that L could not eject S.[92] L's conveyance of the reversion thus gives T a power which L does not possess, against violating the principle *nemo dat quod non habet*.

21–064   (c) *Registered land.*[93] The situations discussed in the two preceding paragraphs are resolved in a different and more satisfactory manner where the title to the land is registered and where the lease is a registered estate.[94] In that case a squatter who has barred a tenant is entitled to be registered as proprietor of

---

[88] See (1998) Law Com. No. 254, at para. 10.25, where it is pointed out: (i) that, *as a contract*, the lease remains on foot between L and T and T can therefore surrender his contractual liabilities (see *post*, para. 21–065); but (ii) that this cannot affect the leasehold *estate* which continues to exist, even though nobody actually owns it or can deal with it.

[89] A principle to which there have been no exceptions (apart from statute) since the abolition of the old tortious conveyances: *ante*, para. 3–115.

[90] *Taylor v. Twinberrow, supra.*

[91] *ibid.* For merger, see *ante*, para. 14–176.

[92] See dicta in *St. Marylebone Property Co. Ltd v. Fairweather* [1963] A.C. 510 at 541, 555. The House of Lords treated *Taylor v. Twinberrow, supra,* as inconsistent with *Walter v. Yalden* [1902] 2 K.B. 304, despite the significance of the landlord's power in the former case to determine the tenancy by notice and so eject the squatter.

[93] See Ruoff &Roper, 29–05.

[94] Only a lease with more than 21 years to run can be registered as a registered estate: L.R.A. 1925, s.8. A lease of 21 years or less can be neither a registered estate nor a minor interest, but only an overriding interest: L.R.A. 1925, ss.19(2), 22(2), 48(1), 70(1)(k); *ante*, paras 6–031, 6–066. Such leases are subject to the same principles as leases of unregistered land: *ante*, para. 21–062.

the tenant's leasehold estate[95] and thus obtains that same estate by a "parliamentary conveyance", contrary to the rules which govern unregistered conveyancing.[96] Consequently where S, having barred the title of T, had been registered with possessory title, and T then surrendered his interest to L in the hope of defeating S, the surrender was ineffective and L was unable to eject S.[97] Where S's title had not been registered, and the leasehold interest was surrendered, L took that lease impressed by the statutory trust.[98] S's interest therefore prevailed as an overriding interest to which any disposition by T was necessarily subject.[99]

(d) Continuing liability of tenant

(1) UNREGISTERED LAND. Where a tenant has lost his title to an interloper by **21–065** adverse possession, he may still remain liable to the landlord on the covenants in the lease (*e.g.* for rent) because of the continuing privity of contract. It has been held that, since the leasehold estate is extinguished, there is no longer any privity of estate, so that if the tenant were an assignee of the lease rather than the original tenant he would cease to be liable on the covenants when his title became barred.[1] But the better view is that the leasehold estate is extinguished only as against the squatter, and that privity of estate remains as between the landlord and the tenant.[2]

(2) REGISTERED LAND. Where title is registered the position is different. **21–066** From the time when the registered proprietor of the lease is barred by adverse possession, he holds the lease on trust for the squatter, who is entitled to be placed in the same relationship with the freeholder as had previously been enjoyed by the leaseholder.[3] Until the squatter has been registered, there continues to be privity of estate between the landlord and the registered leaseholder,[4] though the squatter is obliged to indemnify the leaseholder against outgoings.[5] However, the registration of the squatter as proprietor appears to operate as "a statutory conveyance of the entire leasehold interest".[6] Thereafter there is privity of estate between the landlord and the squatter rather than the former registered leaseholder.

---

[95] L.R.A. 1925, s.75(2); *ante*, para. 6–116.
[96] *Ante*, para. 21–002.
[97] *Spectrum Investment Co. v. Holmes* [1981] 1 W.L.R. 221, rejecting unconvincing dicta in *St. Marylebone Property Co. Ltd v. Fairweather, supra,* to the effect that registration of title should make no difference. It appears that in the latter case the land was in fact registered, but this was argued so late that leave to plead the necessary facts was refused: see [1963] A.C. at 541, *per* Lord Radcliffe, and (1962) 78 L.Q.R. at p. 557.
[98] For the statutory trust, see L.R.A. 1925, s.75(1); *ante*, paras 6–116, 21–058.
[99] *Central London Commercial Estates Ltd v. Kato Kagaku Ltd* [1998] 4 All E.R. 948. See L.R.A. 1925, s.70(1)(f) and (g).
[1] *Re Field* [1918] 1 I.R. 140.
[2] *Spectrum Investment Co. v. Holmes, supra,* at 226; *Taylor v. Twinberrow* [1930] 2 K.B. 16.
[3] *Central London Commercial Estates Ltd v. Kato Kagaku Ltd, supra,* at 959.
[4] *cf. Brown & Root Technology Ltd v. Sun Alliance & London Assurance Co. Ltd* (1996) 75 P. & C.R. 223; *ante,* para. 6–032.
[5] *Central London Commercial Estates Ltd v. Kato Kagaku Ltd, supra,* at 959.
[6] *ibid.,* at 959, *per* Sedley J.

(e) Liability of squatter

21–067   (1) UNREGISTERED LAND. The position of S, in our example, is that he has a legal fee simple,[7] subject to L's right of entry at the end of the period of the original term. Having no privity of estate with L, S is not liable on the covenants in T's lease,[8] except so far as they may be enforceable in equity as restrictive covenants.[9] But if T's lease was determinable by notice, or contained a forfeiture clause, L can enforce these terms against S,[10] and so by threat of notice or forfeiture compel S to perform the covenants. In such case, S has no right to apply for relief against forfeiture.[11] The reason why such a clause is enforceable against S, even where the covenant itself is not, is that a covenant creates a purely personal obligation unless it is a restrictive covenant or there is privity of estate. However, a clause which reserves to the lessor a conditional right of entry gives him a proprietary right (a right of entry for condition broken)[12] and therefore binds a squatter just like any other successor in title. Furthermore, although a squatter may not be liable to be sued on the covenant for the rent, he may be liable to distress if he does not pay it.[13] This is because distress is a tenurial remedy enforceable against all occupiers of the land if the rent-service is not paid, with certain statutory exceptions.[14]

It follows that an adverse occupant of unregistered leasehold land will almost always have to pay the rent. Although the matter depends on the intentions of the parties in any case, the trend of modern authority is, however, to treat those who have entered as trespassers but from whom the landlord has accepted rent, as tenants at will rather than periodic tenants.[15] However, if the squatter takes advantage of the previous tenant's lease he may estop himself from denying that he holds under it. In this way—but only in this way—he may become bound by the covenants. The principle here is that a person who claims the benefit of a deed is estopped from denying that he has accepted all its terms.[16] Mere payment of the rent reserved by the former lease raises no

---

[7] See *Central London Commercial Estates Ltd v. Kato Kagaku Ltd, supra,* at 951.

[8] *Tichborne v. Weir* (1892) 67 L.T. 735 (unsuccessful action for damages on repairing covenant against assignee of a mortgage of a lease who had taken possession and barred the tenant's equity of redemption; the action was brought after the term had expired). Nor will a squatter be bound by "implied covenants", for they arise from the relationship of landlord and tenant, *i.e.* from privity of estate; *ante,* para. 14–195.

[9] *Re Nisbet & Potts' Contract* [1906] 1 Ch. 386; *ante* para. 21–057.

[10] *Humfrey v. Damion* (1612) Cro.Jac. 300 (forfeiture); and *cf. Taylor v. Twinberrow supra.*

[11] *Tickner v. Buzzacott* [1965] Ch. 426. For the question whether T can deliberately bring about a forfeiture, *e.g.* by not paying rent, and so enable L to eject S, see *St Marylebone Property Co. Ltd v. Fairweather* [1963] A.C. 510 at 547; and (1962) 78 L.Q.R. 541 at 555 (H.W.R.W.).

[12] L.P.A. 1925, ss.1(2)(e), 4(2)(b); *ante,* para. 4–054. For the operation of forfeiture clauses against third parties, see *ante,* paras 15–057, 15–058.

[13] *Humfrey v. Damion, supra.* But *quaere* whether a squatter's goods are protected by the Law of Distress Amendment Act 1908, s.1, as he might be said to be a person "not being a tenant of the premises . . . and not having any beneficial interest in any tenancy of the premises".

[14] *Ante,* para. 14–253.

[15] See *ante,* para. 14–065.

[16] Litt. 374, and authorities cited in *Norton on Deeds,* 26, 27. However, this principle is a limited one: see [1998] C.L.J. 522 at 523–525 (C. Davies); and *ante,* paras 16–024—16–026.

estoppel against a squatter,[17] for he is not claiming any benefit from the lease but merely performing one of the conditions of tenure. But it was held that an estoppel arose where the squatter took advantage of a clause in the lease that the rent should be halved so long as the covenants were observed. Having paid rent at the half rate, he was said to be precluded from denying that he was bound by the covenants.[18]

(2) REGISTERED LAND. Where the title to the lease is registered and the squatter has been registered as proprietor of the lease in place of the former registered proprietor, S's position is that of an assignee of the lease by operation of law, and is as follows— **21–068**

    (i) S, as tenant, becomes subject to the burdens and obtains the benefit of the covenants in the lease to the extent that they pass on the transfer,[19] and these covenants may therefore be enforced by or against L;

    (ii) T remains liable to the landlord on the covenants in the lease either on grounds of privity of contract (where the lease was granted before 1996)[20] or because the assignment, taking effect as it does by operation of law, is an excluded assignment which does not terminate T's liability (where the lease was granted after 1995)[21];

    (iii) where the lease contains a right of re-entry for breach of covenant, L may forfeit the lease for any breach by S in the usual way, but because S is L's tenant, he is entitled to seek relief against for-feiture; and

    (iv) S is liable to distress for unpaid rent.

C. Proof of Title

1. Long possession not enough. As between vendor and purchaser, a good title cannot be shown under open contract[22] merely by proving adverse possession of land, however long the period.[23] If A and his predecessors in title have been in possession for 20, 50 or 100 years, that does not prove that A is entitled to it, for the true owner— **21–069**

---

[17] *Tichborne v. Weir* (1892) 67 L.T. 735.
[18] *Ashe v. Hogan* [1920] 1 I.R. 159 (999-year lease at rent of £8 reducible to £4 so long as covenants observed); and see *O'Connor v. Foley* [1906] 1 I.R. 20. Yet it is not easy to see what other course is open to the squatter than to pay such rent as is legally due, or why by paying the one and only correct amount he makes any representation which estops him.
[19] For the rules governing the transmission of the benefit and the burden of leasehold covenants in leases, see *ante*, paras 15–022 *et seq.* (leases granted before 1996); 15–079 *et seq.* (leases granted after 1995).
[20] *Ante*, para. 15–008.
[21] See L. & T.C.A. 1995, s.11; *ante*, para. 15–074.
[22] See *ante*, para. 12–001.
[23] *Moulton v. Edmonds* (1859) 1 De G.F. & J. 246 at 250; *Jacobs v. Revell* [1900] 2 Ch. 858.

(i) might have been under disability at the time of dispossession; or

(ii) might have been the Crown; or

(iii) might have been the reversioner or remainderman under a settlement; or

(iv) might be the reversioner on a long lease.

21–070 **2. Proving owner barred.** Consequently, in order to establish a good title by operation of the Limitation Act, the vendor must prove—

(i) the title of the former owner of the interest in land in question; and

(ii) the extinction of that title in the vendor's favour.

This is a heavy burden of proof, particularly since, if the title is unregistered, the vendor will often not have access to the title deeds of the land acquired by limitation.[24] But if the vendor can discharge the burden of proof, he can force the purchaser to accept his title.[25] Where the land is registered, the vendor can of course apply to be registered as proprietor of the property,[26] and can then convey the land with such title as he has been given by the Chief Land Registrar.[27]

D. Exclusion of Limitation

21–071 In specified cases statute precludes the acquisition of a title by limitation. Thus no right adverse to the title of the Coal Authority to any coal or mine of coal can be acquired by limitation.[28]

Section 2. Arrears of Income

21–072 **1. Rent.** The recovery of arrears of income is a matter distinct from the recovery of the land or capital money which produces it. The arrears of rent which a landlord or the owner of a rentcharge may recover, whether by action or distress, are limited to the arrears accrued due during the preceding six

---

[24] But he may be able to demand them under the rule that the deeds belong to the owner of the land: *ante*, para. 5–034.

[25] *Scott v. Nixon* (1843) 3 Dr. & War. 388; *Games v. Bonnor* (1884) 54 L.J.Ch. 517; *Re Atkinson & Horsell's Contract* [1912] 2 Ch. 1. Contrast *George Wimpey & Co. Ltd v. Sohn* [1967] Ch. 487. Unless he has been registered with an absolute title, a vendor will in practice always sell such land subject to a special condition of sale.

[26] L.R.A. 1925, s.75(2).

[27] For the Registrar's discretion, see L.R.A. 1925, s.75(3); *ante*, para. 6–116.

[28] Coal Industry Act 1994, s.10(2). For earlier legislation, see Coal Act 1938, s.17(2); Coal Industry Nationalisation Act 1946, s.49(3); Coal Industry Act 1987, s.1.

years,[29] whether or not the rent is payable under a deed.[30] Each time a gale of rent falls due, a new cause of action accrues,[31] and so the six years' period begins to run in respect of it. Even if the rent has not been paid for, say, 20 years, a landlord whose title has not become barred[32] may at any time enforce payment of the last six years' arrears of rent, and future rent as it falls due. With the exception of a nominal rent payable under a lease capable of enlargement into a fee simple,[33] mere non-payment of rent never extinguishes the liability for future rent[34]; but it is otherwise with rentcharges.[35] However, in the case of agricultural holdings, the landlord's right of distress is restricted to rent which fell due, or would normally have been paid, in the year preceding the distress[36]; and there are special rules for bankruptcy.[37]

2. Mortgage interest. There is also a six years' period for any action for arrears of mortgage interest.[38] But a mortgagee who exercises his power of sale may retain all arrears of interest, however old, out of the proceeds of sale, for this is not recovery by action[39]; and if the first mortgagee sells, the second mortgagee is similarly entitled to all his arrears of interest out of the surplus proceeds of sale.[40] Further, a mortgagor who seeks to redeem can do so only on the equitable terms of paying all arrears of interest.[41] **21–073**

3. Part payment. Though payment of part of any arrears of rent or interest may start time running again in respect of the land or the capital,[42] it does not extend the period for claiming the rest of the arrears.[43] **21–074**

---

[29] Limitation Act 1980, s.19. This rule applies not only to the tenant but to any guarantor who has expressly undertaken the same obligations as the tenant: *Romain v. Scuba TV Ltd* [1997] Q.B. 887.

[30] L.A. 1980, s.8(2).

[31] *Re Jolly* [1900] 2 Ch. 616.

[32] See *ante*, para. 21–026. It is otherwise if the title of the landlord has been barred: see *Re Jolly, supra*; *Mount Carmel Investments Ltd v. Peter Thurlow Ltd* [1988] 1 W.L.R. 1078 at 1088; *ante*, para. 21–055.

[33] L.P.A. 1925, s.153; see *ante*, para. 14–178. In such cases a rent of £1 a year or less becomes irrecoverable if unpaid for a continuous period of 20 years, of which at least five have elapsed since 1925; *ibid*.

[34] *Ante*, para. 21–028.

[35] *Ante*, para. 21–034.

[36] A.H.A. 1986, s.16 (replacing earlier legislation). It does not affect an action for the rent, as distinct from distress. There is no equivalent provision in relation to farm business tenancies under A.T.A. 1995.

[37] I.A. 1986, s.347 (six months' rent due before commencement of bankruptcy).

[38] L.A. 1980, s.20(5); but see subs. (6) for the position where a prior incumbrancer has been in possession; and see subs. (7) as regards capitalisation of arrears of interest.

[39] *Re Marshfield* (1887) 34 Ch.D. 721; *Re Lloyd* [1903] 1 Ch. 385. *Secus* if the mortgage itself is barred: *Re Hazeldine's Trusts* [1908] 1 Ch. 34.

[40] *Re Thomson's Mortgage Trusts* [1920] 1 Ch. 508; compare *Young v. Clarey* [1948] Ch. 191, where the right of redemption was barred.

[41] *Elvy v. Norwood* (1852) 5 De G. & Sm. 240; *Dingle v. Coppen* [1899] 1 Ch. 726. *Holmes v. Cowcher* [1970] 1 W.L.R. 834 (approving this statement).

[42] *Ante*, para. 21–051.

[43] L.A. 1980, s.29(6).

CHAPTER 22

THE SOCIAL CONTROL OF LAND

Part 1

THE AMBIT OF SOCIAL CONTROL

22–001   During the twentieth century great changes have been made in the law governing the use and enjoyment of land. These changes are distinct from the changes made by the property legislation of 1925 and its subsequent amendments, for the latter primarily concerned the ownership of estates and interests in land, rather than the fruits of enjoyment; and unlike that legislation the changes have been piecemeal and unsystematic.

22–002   **1. Social control of land.** Two series of statutes may be regarded as having achieved the social control of land by giving effect to two allied views. First, it is against the interests of the public at large for landowners to have an unfettered power to develop their land as they wish. Second, it is also socially undesirable that when a tenancy expires the landlord should be uncontrolled in his power to refuse to renew the tenancy and to demand whatever rent he chooses.

22–003   **2. Growth of social control.** A modest start in social control was made by an Act in 1875 which gave some protection to agricultural tenants. After that, there was nothing until some degree of planning control was imposed by an Act of 1909; but then, within 20 years, the main systems for protecting tenants had all been initiated. The twentieth century also saw heavy increases in the burden of taxation. Stated broadly, in 1900 the standard rate of income tax had been increased to 5 per cent, whereas in 1999 the rate was 40 per cent, apart from about 22.5 per cent on the first £27,100. On death, an estate worth a million pounds bore estate duty at the rate of 7.5 per cent in 1900, whereas in 1999 the rate of inheritance tax was over four times as much. One result of such increases is that many transactions in land have to be moulded with the object of mitigating or avoiding taxation; and for some, that is the main object.

Increased taxation has also led to the break up of many large estates; but it is no direct part of the social control of land, and will not be dealt with here.

3. Development of planning control. Planning control developed in three **22–004** distinct stages. First, the 1909 Act imposed a system of control which initially applied only to urban areas but was extended by the Act of 1932 to the whole country. The system was based on making a scheme for each area; but progress was slow. By 1943, only 4 per cent of the country was subject to a scheme. Of the rest, 26 per cent was subject to no control, and the remaining 70 per cent was subject to an ineffective system of interim control under which no enforcement action could be taken against unauthorised development until a scheme had come into force. The second stage came when the 1943 Act enabled enforcement proceedings to be taken forthwith against any unauthorised development, without waiting for a scheme. This transformed the position by subjecting the whole country to an effective though simple form of planning control. The third stage came when the 1947 Act swept away the old law and substituted an elaborate and comprehensive system which, as subsequently amended and re-enacted, applies today.[1]

4. Growth in the protection of tenants. There is much diversity in the **22–005** history of the statutory protection of tenants.

(a) Business tenants. Business tenants were first protected by a somewhat **22–006** ineffective Act of 1927. This gave them the right to a new tenancy or compensation, but only if they had attached goodwill to the premises which increased their value. This concept effectively restricted the right to tenancies of shops, and not all of them. The 1954 Act abandoned this concept, and created an effective and comprehensive system for business premises generally, including shops, offices and factories.[2]

(b) Agricultural holdings. The statutory protection of farming tenants has a **22–007** history of rise and fall. The 1875 Act gave tenants a right to compensation for improvements, and, under the 1923 Act, for dispossession without good cause. The 1947 Act gave tenants security of tenure and protection as to rent, but for tenancies beginning on or after September 1, 1995 the 1995 Act substituted a much more limited form of protection.[3]

(c) Dwellings. The statutory protection of tenants of dwelling began with an **22–008** Act of 1915.[4] Protection depended on the rateable value of the dwelling not

---

[1] Housing, Town Planning, &c Act 1909; Town and Country Planning Act 1932; Town and Country Planning (Interim Development) Act 1943; Town and Country Planning Act 1947.

[2] Landlord and Tenant Act 1927, Pt I; Landlord and Tenant Act 1954.

[3] Agricultural Holdings (England) Act 1875; Agriculture Act 1947, later Agricultural Holdings Act 1948; Agricultural Tenancies Act 1995.

[4] Increase of Rent and Mortgage Interest (War Restrictions) Act 1915. The other Acts cited are the Increase of Rent and Mortgage Interest (Restrictions) Act 1920; Rent and Mortgage Interest Restrictions (Amendment) Act 1933; Increase of Rent and Mortgage Interest (Restrictions) Act 1938; Rent and Mortgage Interest Restrictions Act 1939; Rent Act 1957; Rent Act 1965; Rent Act 1977. (The titles shortened as complexity increased.).

exceeding certain amounts; but these amounts later rose and fell under successive Acts: 1920 (increase); 1933, 1938 (successive decreases); 1939 (increase); 1957 (decrease); and 1965 (increase). Throughout, security of tenure was mainly based on preventing the landlord from evicting the tenant except on certain specified grounds. Protection as to rent, however, suffered many changes. Initially, the system based the maximum rent on the rent being paid when the Acts first applied to the dwelling, together with specified permitted increases. But the 1957 Act substituted rents based on the rateable value, and the 1965 Act replaced these with "fair rents" that were independently assessed and then registered. There are now substantial variations in the form of protection afforded under different classes of tenancy, including the right of some tenants to buy the reversion.[5]

Part 2

PLANNING CONTROL OVER THE USE OF LAND

Section 1. Introduction

22–009   **1. Historical development.** A system of comprehensive planning control was introduced in England and Wales in 1948,[6] and it imposed a significant limitation on the freedom which the common law allowed for landowners to build on their land, or to change the use to which their land and buildings were put. The Town and Country Planning Act 1947 was part evolutionary and part revolutionary. It built upon machinery that had been steadily evolving through successive Acts of Parliament going back to 1909,[7] but it added some wholly new elements and it introduced a draconian tax on land values. Its basic features, except for that tax, remain intact today in the Town and Country Planning Act 1990.[8]

22–010   They key characteristics of the British approach to town and country planning are that it is:

> (1) highly centralised: planning and the control of development are functions for local authorities, but they act within a tight framework of supervision by national government;
>
> (2) comprehensive in its controls: as a general rule, no development of any land may lawfully be carried out without planning permission;

---

[5] See *post*, para. 21–131.
[6] By the Town and Country Planning Act 1947, which came into force on July 1, 1948.
[7] Housing, Town Planning &c Act 1909. For a summary of the effects of the legislation of the intervening years, see the 5th edition, pp. 1059–1061, and *ante*, para. 22–004.
[8] Hereafter "the Act of 1990". Planning legislation has been much amended, and there have been three consolidations (1962, 1971 and 1990). The 1990 consolidation also gave rise to the Planning (Listed Buildings and Conservation Areas) Act 1990 and the Planning (Hazardous Substances) Act 1990.

(3) broad in its coverage: it is a system not just of town planning, but of town and country planning; and its objectives today extend as much to urban regeneration and historic conservation, as to environmental protection, the containment of urban sprawl and sustainable development;

(4) highly discretionary and administrative in character: although local authorities are required to prepare and adopt land-use plans, these are indicative rather than legally binding. Landowners' substantive common law rights are translated into statutory procedural rights. Safeguards against abuse of discretion are maintained primarily through administrative procedures, such as rights of objection and appeal, rather than through the conferment of substantive rights;

(5) uncompensated in its effects: planning decisions can have a dramatic impact upon the value of land, yet there is no longer any differential taxation of any uplift in value,[9] and no right to claim compensation[10] for any loss of value.

Section 2. The Institutional Framework

1. Central–local relations. Planning controls substitute State objectives for private choice. But the State power is not monolithic. It is exercised through a special relationship between central and local government. National government has the responsibility of setting national spatial planning objectives, of promulgating national policies to achieve them, of supervising the performance of local authorities in pursuing those policies and of providing an independent review for the protection of landowners. An example is the objective which emerged in the 1950s of containing the growth of towns and cities and preventing urban sprawl. The national policy response was to encourage local authorities to designate green belts around the major conurbations, within which new development was to be discouraged. The areas proposed by the local authorities were approved by central government. Although the green belt did not of itself prohibit development, it would be powerful a factor for the local authority when determining an application by a landowner for planning permission to build houses there, as it would for the Secretary of State if the landowner were to appeal against the local authority's decision.

22–011

2. Functions of central government. Within central government, responsibility for the planning system in England resides with the Secretary of State

22–012

---

[9] The 1948 tax was repealed in 1953: see below, para. 22–054.
[10] With only minor exceptions which are outlined below, para. 22–060.

for the Environment, Transport and the Regions.[11] These responsibilities are not as extensive as they were originally. At one time, the Secretary of State's approval was required for every development plan prepared by local authorities, but this created a burden which proved impossible to discharge efficiently.[12] Today, the formal powers are of three principal types:

(1) a jurisdiction to determine appeals and objections;

(2) power to call-in planning applications and development plans, taking them out of the hands of the local authority concerned and reserving them for central decision; and

(3) reserve powers, rarely used in practice, to intervene in cases of local default.

22–013   **3. The nature of national policy.** These formal powers are not, however, exercised in a vacuum, but in the context of national policy. They provide the Secretary of State with the ability to make and enforce planning policy, and this is done through a variety of means. The most common statement of policy historically was the ministerial circular, which was simply a letter to all local authorities announcing the Secretary of State's policy. From 1988 onwards policy statements have been issued in the more sophisticated format of a series of Planning Policy Guidance notes (PPGs).[13] There are presently 24 titles in this series. Two parallel series provide guidance respectively on minerals planning (MPGs) and regional planning (RPGs). These provide guidance on the approach which local authorities should take on such important matters as the preparation of development plans,[14] planning and transport,[15] housing,[16] and the protection of the green belt.[17]

22–014   **4. The regional dimension.** Spatial choices arise at the regional as well as the national and local levels: for example, for promoting regional economic development and for ensuring an adequate supply of land for new housing. Until recently, the only institutional structures at regional level were the Government Offices for the Regions and, in some regions, voluntary groupings of local authorities coming together as regional planning conferences. Their function was to participate in the preparation of regional planning guidance (RPG). A new dimension was added with the creation from April

---

[11] For Wales, responsibility has since 1965 resided with the Secretary of State for Wales, but was transferred in 1999, by the Government of Wales Act 1998, to the Welsh Assembly. Within England, certain functions respecting historic buildings and conservation areas reside with the Secretary of State for Culture, Sport and the Media.

[12] *The Future of Development Plans*: Report of the Planning Advisory Group 1965.

[13] All policy guidance is reproduced, along with current legislation, in Grant, M.(ed.), *Encyclopedia of Planning Law and Practice* (6 vols loose-leaf, Sweet and Maxwell).

[14] PPG 12, *Development Plans and Regional Planning Guidance* (1992).

[15] PPG 13, *Transport* (1994).

[16] PPG 3, *Housing* (1992); a revised consultative draft was published in April 1999.

[17] PPG 2, *Green Belts* (1993).

1999 of Regional Development Agencies for nine regions in England.[18] The RDAs are required to prepare economic strategies for their regions, which will run alongside the regional planning guidance which is being prepared by the regional planning conferences.

5. Local planning authorities. Day to day responsibility for the planning system resides with elected local authorities. Theirs is the responsibility for preparing development plans for their areas, for receiving and determining planning applications, and for taking other steps in furtherance of their spatial and environmental objectives. In many parts of the country, there is only one tier of local government. These unitary councils are to be found in Wales,[19] in London[20] and in the six other metropolitan areas of England,[21] and also in certain other areas of England.[22] In the remainder of England, there are two tiers of local government: the county councils and district councils. When exercising its functions under planning legislation, a council is known as the local planning authority. In the two-tier areas, a county council is the local planning authority for some functions (such as structure planning and controls over minerals and waste) and the district council is the local planning authority for all other functions. In the National Parks the responsibility resides with special National Park authorities.[23]

22–015

Section 3. Development Plans

1. Background. Development plans lie at the heart of the planning system, yet they have consistently proved to be one of its weakest characteristics. A major change effected by the 1947 Act was the severance of the link between plan and permission. Where the old development schemes prepared under earlier legislation had allowed development defined in them to be carried out without further permission, the new plans were to have no direct legal effect. Planning permission was henceforth required for all development, and in granting or refusing it the local planning authority need do no more than

22–016

---

[18] Regional Development Agencies Act 1998. Special arrangements are in effect in Wales, where control over the Welsh Development Agency was transferred from July 1999 to the Welsh Assembly; and in London, where it is proposed (by the Greater London Authority Bill 1999) that responsibility for the London Development Agency will reside with the Mayor of London.

[19] As a result of the Local Government (Wales) Act 1994, which created 22 new unitary councils.

[20] Though subject to the proposed Greater London Authority.

[21] The former Greater London Council (created in 1965 by the London Government Act 1963) and the metropolitan county councils for the West Midlands, Tyne and Wear, Greater Manchester, Merseyside, West Yorkshire and South Yorkshire (created by the Local Government Act 1972) were abolished from April 1986 by the Local Government Act 1985.

[22] Following recommendations to that effect by the Local Government Commission for England under the Local Government Act 1992.

[23] Created by the Environment Act 1995, s.65.

"have regard to" the development plan, alongside all other "material considerations".[24] It was clear, however, that the Government had intended that the new development plans, once approved, should be complied with. Indeed, a procedural requirement was introduced to require local authorities to notify central government before granting permission for any development which did not comply with their development plan.

22–017   This aspiration was to prove simply unrealistic. The production of development plans has always proved particularly controversial and time-consuming, with the consequence that the assumptions upon which their detailed norms and guidance are based (such as forecasts of economic growth and demographic change) will quickly have been overtaken by events in the real world—perhaps even by the time the plan has been adopted. Local planning authorities have therefore needed flexibility to use the plan as a general framework for decision-making, but to depart from it on a case-by-case basis. There is a clear tension between the need to respect the political commitments contained in the formal development plan, based upon an open process involving public participation, and the desire to respond to the expediency of the moment.

22–018   **2. The plan-led system.** The balance between formal plan-making and discretionary development control has shifted significantly over the past 50 years. The low point came in the 1980s when outdated development plans were believed to be impeding economic growth, and the Government proved willing to use its planning appeal powers to override local authority decisions and allow a higher rate of development. But the pendulum swung back, to the extent that by the end of the decade the same Government was urging greater reliance upon development plans, and through the Planning and Compensation Act 1991 introduced a requirement that every local planning authority should have an area-wide development plan, and that the system should henceforth be "plan-led".

22–019   **3. The strategic level of plan-making.** "Strategic" is used loosely in this context, primarily to distinguish its objectives from the detailed land allocation that occurs in local plans, but also to signify that the issues involved will often transcend local authority boundaries and therefore cannot be readily addressed in individual local plans. Strong economic growth that brings employment benefits to one local authority area will often generate demand for housing land and for new highways works in the areas of its neighbours. In 1948 there was to be only one development plan for each main town and county, but citizens' rights of objections and hearings meant that the approval process focused more on detail than on broad strategy, and that time scales became long drawn-out. The Town and Country Planning Act 1968 therefore split development plans into two tiers: the structure plan, which provides the broad framework for planning and development control over a wide territorial

---

[24] See now the Act of 1990, s.70(2).

area, usually a whole county; and the local plan, which takes the next step of reflecting those proposals in detailed land allocations and policies guiding development control. Following local government reorganisation in 1974, the preparation of structure plans fell to the county councils, and local plans principally to the district councils. These arrangements changed again in 1986 in areas where the two-tier local government system in London and the metropolitan areas yielded to unitary authorities.[25] Here there is once again a single planning instrument, the unitary development plan, Part I of which is strategic in its focus, and Part II is detailed.

There is now full coverage of structure plans. They are updated by amend-   **22–020** ments (or, occasionally, by the repeal and replacement of the whole plan). In drafting an amendment or a new plan, the local planning authority are required to have regard to national policy and to the relevant Regional Planning Guidance for the region.[26] The draft, together with an accompanying explanatory memorandum, must be made available for public inspection.[27] An opportunity must be provided for public objection, and the authority may not adopt the plan until after they have considered objections.[28] The proposals are subjected to a special scrutiny process, an Examination in Public, conducted by a Panel appointed by the Secretary of State. The Panel prepares a report which must then be considered by the local planning authority who may, in light of it, prepare modifications to their proposals. They are not required to accept the Panel's recommendations, but they must act fairly in relation to them. Their response is scrutinised by the Secretary of State, who may direct them to modify their proposals,[29] and may call-in the plan for his own approval.[30]

4. The local level of plan-making. Every area in England and Wales must   **22–021** have a district-wide development plan. This is a local plan in the case of the two-tier district councils in England, and a unitary development plan elsewhere. A local plan must be in general conformity with the structure plan.

Section 4. Development Control

1. Development. Planning control is an important process which an author-   **22–022** ity is able to employ to implement its development plan. It is the point at which planning cuts directly across the rights that flow at common law from land ownership. Planning control is exercised primarily over changes in the

---

[25] Though not generally in the unitary authorities created in England under the Local Government Act 1992, where the new authorities have mainly been kept within the structure plan framework, preparing the plans jointly with the other authorities.

[26] Act of 1990, s.31(6)(a).

[27] Act of 1990, s.33(2).

[28] Act of 1990, s.33(6).

[29] Act of 1990, s.35(2).

[30] Act of 1990, s.35A (inserted by the Planning and Compensation Act 1991, Sched. 4, para. 17).

use of land. A local planning authority may interfere with a lawful use of land only by making a discontinuance order,[31] but will be liable to pay compensation for any loss or damage incurred by the owner as a result. Similarly if they revoke or modify an extant planning permission.[32] Special rules apply to mineral planning permissions, which are often extant for decades while the extraction of minerals continues, and where the legislation now permits the imposition of tighter environmental standards on the basis of the industry sharing a proportion of the cost.[33]

22–023   **2. Definition of "development".** The starting point is the definition of development, for which planning permission is required. It is defined as: "the carrying out of building, engineering, mining or other operations in, on, over or under land, or the making of any material change in the use of any buildings or other land".[34] This comprehensive definition covers two types of land-use change: that which involves operations leading to some physical change in the character of the land; and that involving a change in its use. In many cases, both elements are involved: the construction of a house on agricultural land involves a building operation and a change of use from agricultural to residential. But the two categories are conceptually distinct,[35] and planning permission granted solely for a change in use will not authorise any operational development.[36]

22–024   *(a) Operational development.* The definition is broad enough to catch almost all human activity in relation to land. In practice, its scope is reduced by so-called "permitted development rights"[37] which permit a wide range of development activity, much of it minor in impact, by classes of developers such as householders and public utilities. Operational development is that which results in some physical change in land.[38] It does not, for example, arise if a residential caravan is simply stationed on land without being attached to it.[39] But if what has resulted from an operation is the construction of a building, then the court "should want a great deal of persuading that the erection of it had not amounted to a building or other operation",[40] even if it

[31] Act of 1990, s.102.
[32] Act of 1990, s.97.
[33] Town and Country Planning (Compensation for Restrictions on Mineral Working and Mineral Waste Depositing) Regulations 1997 (S.I. 1997 No. 1111).
[34] Act of 1990, s.55(1).
[35] *Parkes v. Secretary of State for the Environment* [1978] 1 W.L.R. 1308.
[36] *Wivenhoe Port Ltd v. Colchester Borough Council* [1985] J.P.L. 396.
[37] Under the Town and Country Planning (General Permitted Development) Order 1995 (S.I. 1995 No. 418): see further below.
[38] Hence, there is no operational development involved in a proposal to establish a heliport on a vessel navigating up and down a 10-mile stretch of the Thames, stopping from time to time to allow helicopters to take off, though it might involve a material change in use of the river: *Thames Heliport Ltd v. Tower Hamlets London Borough Council* (1996) 74 P. & C.R. 159.
[39] *Wealden District Council v. Secretary of State for the Environment* [1988] J.P.L. 268.
[40] *Barvis Ltd v. Secretary of State for the Environment* (1971) 22 P. & C.R. 710 at 715: erection of large scale tower crane running along rails involved a building operation, notwithstanding that it was capable of being dismantled and erected elsewhere.

is a very small building.[41] The demolition of a building has not been regarded by the courts as a "building operation",[42] but that position has been reversed by legislation, subject to wide-ranging exemptions and exceptions.[43]

(b) Material change in use. Whether there is a material change in use of **22–025** land tends to depend upon the level of abstraction at which the old and new use are defined. If the appropriate level is "residential", for example, there is no change in use when a private dwelling-house comes to be used as a hotel; but there would be if "use as a private dwelling" were to be the definition of the existing use. The Act provides no guidance on this, so the courts have developed their own principles. In many cases, a high-level abstraction is in any event provided by the Town and Country Planning (Use Classes) Order 1987,[44] because this instrument deems there to be no material change in use involved when the use of land for a purpose within any given class of the Order changes to use for another purpose within the same class. For example, the business class, Class B1, covers use as an office (otherwise than for financial and professional services[45]), use for research, and use for light industrial purposes.[46] This not only permits change between different commercial uses, but also allows light industrial units to be used as offices.[47] Similarly (though with some specified exceptions) a shop may be used for the sale of any goods[48] and different general industrial uses may be substituted for each other without attracting planning control.[49]

In cases where the Use Classes Order does not apply, the courts have been **22–026** reluctant to prescribe *a priori* classifications, preferring to rely upon the approach that this is a question "of fact and degree" for the primary decision-maker, normally the local planning authority or the Secretary of State.[50] The change must be "material", which means material in terms of its impact for

---

[41] *Buckingham County Council v. Callingham* [1952] 2 Q.B. 515: model village.

[42] *Cambridge City Council v. Secretary of State for the Environment* [1992] 3 P.L.R. 4.

[43] Planning and Compensation Act 1991, s.13.

[44] S.I. 1987 No. 764.

[45] These fall instead within Class A2, "where the services are provided principally to visiting members of the public".

[46] Change is permitted by the Order only to or from a use "which can be carried on in any residential area without detriment to the amenity of the area by reason of noise, vibration, smell, fumes, smoke, soot, ash, dust or grit".

[47] That was the objective of the introduction of the business class in 1987, following the 1985 report of the Property Advisory Group, *Review of the Use Classes Order* DOE 1985.

[48] UCO, Class A1. Use for the sale of food and drink for on-site consumption, or hot food for off-site consumption, is in a separate Class A3; and there is a list in art. 3(6) of so-called "*sui generis*" uses which are outside the provisions altogether.

[49] UCO, Class B2. Planning permission is also granted by the Town and Country Planning (General Permitted Development) Order 1995, Sched. 2, Pt 3, for change from this class to Class B1.

[50] See *e.g. London Residuary Body v. Secretary of State for the Environment* (1989) 58 P. & C.R. 370, where the Court of Appeal accepted that the office use of County Hall, formerly the seat of the Greater London Council, was ancillary to the primary "London governmental use", and that planning permission would therefore be required for the building to be put to commercial office use. An appeal to the House of Lords succeeded on other grounds: [1990] 1 W.L.R. 744.

planning purposes.[51] Applying this principle, the courts have accepted that a change merely in the identity of the person carrying out an activity, without a change in the activity itself, cannot amount to a material change in use[52]; that change from single-family occupation to a house used for holiday lettings on a limited basis is not necessarily material,[53] and that a significant intensification of an existing use may constitute a material change in use.[54]

22–027　　　*(c) Primary and ancillary uses.* The starting point in all cases of material change in use is to establish what is the primary use of the unit of occupation under consideration. That primary use will often comprise a number of different activities which would, if each were considered on its own, be a different use. For example, activities comprised in a private dwelling use might include the provision of sleeping accommodation, catering, a study, laundering, horticulture and car maintenance and repair. There is no material change in the primary use as these various activities start up or cease, but there is if they develop to the point where they develop a separate identity of their own, perhaps even supplanting the primary use. Their lawfulness depends upon their continuing to be part of or ancillary to the primary use itself.[55]

22–028　　　*(d) The planning unit.* It is necessary also to define the physical unit to which the test applies. The general rule is that the materiality of change should be assessed against the whole of the unit of occupation or ownership, though this is inadequate as a universal rule because the larger the unit the less likely is the change in use of part of it to result in a material change in use of the unit as a whole. This approach would therefore result in an unequal application of planning control between large and small units. To overcome this problem, the courts have developed the doctrine of the planning unit. This holds that where, within a single unit of occupation, there are two or more physically separate and distinct units which are occupied for substantially different and unrelated purposes, each area used for a different primary use ought to be considered as a separate planning unit.[56] For example, there may be no material change in use if a flat is provided in a block of offices as accommodation for a caretaker, because that use is ancillary to the primary use of the building as a whole. But there will be a material change in use if the flat comes to be occupied by someone with no ancillary link to the primary use of the building. In this case, the planning unit is the flat, not the building as a whole. Adopting this approach, it is appropriate to regard each of the retail units in a large shopping mall as a separate planning unit.[57]

[51] *Thames Heliport Ltd v. Tower Hamlets London Borough Council* (1996) 74 P. & C.R. 159.
[52] *Lewis v. Secretary of State for the Environment* (1971) 23 P. & C.R. 125; *Westminster City Council v. British Waterways Board* [1985] A.C. 676.
[53] *Blackpool Borough Council v. Secretary of State for the Environment* [1980] J.P.L. 527.
[54] *Brooks and Burton Ltd v. Secretary of State for the Environment* [1977] 1 W.L.R. 1294.
[55] See, *e.g. London Residuary Body v. Secretary of State for the Environment, supra.*
[56] *Burdle v. Secretary of State for the Environment* [1972] 1 W.L.R. 1207.
[57] *Church Commissioners v. Secretary of State for the Environment* (1995) 71 P. & C.R. 73 (Metro Centre at Gateshead).

(e) Statutory exclusions and exceptions. The Act of 1990 furnishes a   **22–029**
number of exceptions to, and exclusions from, its broad definition of "development". In addition to changes of use within one of the classes defined by the
Use Classes Order[58] they include works affecting only the interior of a
building,[59] and the use of land or buildings within the curtilage of a dwelling-
house for purposes "incidental to the enjoyment of the dwelling-house as
such".[60] "Enjoyment" is not a purely subjective matter at the whim of the
occupier. It excludes the extravagant and the unreasonable, such as keeping 44
dogs in a dwelling-house,[61] or keeping a large wooden replica of a Spitfire
aircraft in the garden of a house which already had a 14-foot replica of a fish
springing out of its roof.[62] The statutory exceptions also include use for
agricultural or forestry purposes.[63] These purposes include fox farming[64] and
the grazing of horses[65]; but not non-agricultural activities such as the breeding
and keeping of horses otherwise than for use on the farm,[66] the keeping of
non-agricultural ponies,[67] hobby use as leisure plots,[68] or wine-making.[69]

(f) When planning permission is required. Planning permission is required   **22–030**
for the carrying out of any development of land.[70] It is not required for the
continuance of the lawful existing use of the land. Hence, whether it is
required in any given case depends upon the existence and scope of the
existing use rights. A use of land is lawful if it was instituted prior to the
introduction of comprehensive planning control in 1948[71]; or if the change to
that use was made with the benefit of planning permission and its continuance
remains in accordance with that permission; or if, having been instituted
unlawfully, the lapse of time means that enforcement action can no longer be
taken in respect of it. The right to use land for a purpose which has planning

---

[58] See the discussion above of the Town and Country Planning (Use Classes) Order 1987.
[59] Provided they do not "materially affect the external appearance of the building": Act of 1990,
s.55(2)(a).
[60] Act of 1990, s.55(2)(d).
[61] *Wallington v. Secretary of State for Wales* (1990) 62 P. & C.R. 150.
[62] *Croydon London Borough Council v. Gladden* [1994] 1 P.L.R. 30: large replicas of a military
tank and of a rocket-like missile and a large inflatable figure of Winston Churchill had already
been removed from the garden following enforcement action applying the same principles.
[63] Act of 1990, s.55(2)(e):
[64] *North Warwickshire Borough Council v. Secretary of State for the Environment* [1984] J.P.L.
434.
[65] *Sykes v. Secretary of State for the Environment* [1981] J.P.L. 285.
[66] *Belmont Farm Ltd v. Minister of Housing and Local Government* (1962) 13 P. & C.R. 417.
[67] *South Oxfordshire District Council v. Secretary of State for the Environment* [1987] J.P.L.
868.
[68] *Pitman v. Secretary of State for the Environment* [1989] J.P.L. 831.
[69] *Millington v. Secretary of State for the Environment, Transport and the Regions* [1998]
E.G.C.S. 154. However, this was reversed by the Court of Appeal, *The Times*, June 29,
1999.
[70] Act of 1990, s.57(1).
[71] Town and Country Planning Act 1971, Sched. 24, para. 12 (continued in effect by the Planning
(Consequential Provisions) Act 1990, Sched. 3, para. 3). Special provision is also made by the
Act of 1990, s.57, in respect of temporary uses in 1948, and in respect of the resumption of the
normal use following temporary use for another purpose.

permission continues even if operations have ceased for some years,[72] provided there has been no intervening use physically inconsistent with its
continuance[73]; but an existing use right arising otherwise than by permission
(*e.g.* a pre-1948 use) is capable of being abandoned if the use has ceased with
no apparent intention that it should be resumed.[74]

22–031   **2. Obtaining planning permission.** Planning permission is granted in two
principal ways: by a general grant of permission, for example, the permitted
development rights conferred by the Town and Country Planning (General
Permitted Development) Order 1995,[75] and by a specific grant of permission
in response to a planning application.

22–032   (*a*) *Permitted development.* A great variety of permissions is contained in
the Town and Country Planning (General Permitted Development) Order
1995. It is through this instrument that the Government is able to lift planning
controls over activity which is relatively minor or temporary in its effects[76];
which it is deemed economically desirable to promote rather than restrict,[77] or
which is the subject of other controls.[78] Many of the permitted development
rights conferred by the Order are specially restricted in environmentally
sensitive areas, such as conservation areas,[79] National Parks[80] and areas of
outstanding natural beauty.[81] Planning permission may also be granted by
Special Development Orders, applicable only to such land or descriptions of
land as are specified in the order,[82] enterprise zone schemes[83] and simplified

---

[72] *Pioneer Aggregates (UK) Ltd v. Secretary of State for the Environment* [1985] A.C. 132.
[73] *Petticoat Lane Rentals Ltd v. Secretary of State for the Environment* [1971] 1 W.L.R. 1112.
[74] *Hartley v. Minister of Housing and Local Government* [1970] 1 Q.B. 413; *White v. Secretary of State for the Environment* [1989] 2 P.L.R. 29.
[75] S.I. 1995 No. 418.
[76] One example is so-called "householder development", for which the Order grants rights to extend dwelling-houses, and to erect garages and other buildings: Town and Country Planning (General Permitted Development) Order 1995 (hereafter GPDO), Sched. 2, Pt 1.
[77] *e.g.* development for agricultural or forestry purposes (GPDO, Sched. 2, Pts 6 and 7), and various types of development by local authorities or public utilities (GPDO, Sched. 2, Pts 12–18).
[78] *e.g.* development by telecommunications code system operators (GPDO, Sched. 2, Pts 24 and 25).
[79] Designated under the Planning (Listed Buildings and Conservation Areas) Act 1990, s.69.
[80] Designated under the National Parks and Access to the Countryside Act 1949, s.5.
[81] Designated by the Countryside Agency (formerly the Countryside Commission), or the Countryside Council for Wales, under the National Parks and Access to the Countryside Act 1949.
[82] Act of 1990, s.58. These have been used in practice to grant permission for development in new towns and urban development areas, and also for nationally controversial schemes (including atomic energy establishments and exploratory works to identify sites suitable for long-term storage of radioactive waste).
[83] An enterprise zone scheme (designated under the Local Government, Planning and Land Act 1980) will normally grant planning permission for a 10-year period for any development within the scheme (subject to specified limitations and exceptions). The largest office development in Europe, Canary Wharf in London Docklands, was constructed in accordance with an EZ permission: as to the significance of this, see *Hunter v. Canary Wharf Ltd* [1997] A.C. 653.

planning zone schemes.[84] Permitted development rights may be withdrawn by planning condition[85] on the grant of express permission; or by special direction by the local planning authority,[86] which may give rise to compensation liability.[87]

(b) *Application for planning permission.* Application for express planning **22–033** permission is made to the local planning authority (the district council, borough, city, or London borough council where the land is situated). Although application may be made by any person, a certificate must be provided to the effect that the owner[88] of the land has been notified of the application.[89] Where the proposed development comprises the erection of a building, the application may be for outline planning permission, allowing the local planning authority to grant approval to the development in principle, but to reserve the details of the scheme for subsequent approval. "Reserved matters" include the "siting, design, external appearance, means of access and landscaping",[90] but one of these matters can be regarded as being "reserved" only if details of it were not provided in the application. The prescribed list is definitive, and the size or scale of the development is not capable of being a reserved matter.[91] Application for approval of the reserved matters must be made within three years of the grant of outline permission,[92] and whatever is then approved must fall within the parameters of the outline permission.[93]

A fee is payable for a planning application.[94] All applications must be **22–034** publicised, either by a site notice or by notification to neighbours, and, in some cases, by advertisement in a local newspaper.[95] Applications must also be notified to consultees, such as other local authorities and public agencies, according to the type and scale of the development proposed.[96] Applications involving a material departure from the development plan must be notified to

---

[84] Act of 1990, ss.82–87. An SPZ is a local model of an enterprise zone, designated by the local planning authority and conferring a broad grant of planning permission, but without the fiscal incentives to development which were available in enterprise zones. They have been very rarely used.

[85] See further below, para. 22–043.

[86] GPDO, art. 4.

[87] If planning permission is subsequently refused for development which had previously been permitted by the order: Act of 1990, s.108.

[88] This includes the fee simple owner, a person entitled to a tenancy granted or extended for a term of which not less than seven years remain unexpired, agricultural tenants and the owners of certain minerals rights.

[89] Act of 1990, s.65, and Town and Country Planning (General Development Procedure) Order 1995 (hereafter GDPO), art. 8.

[90] GDPO, art. 1(2).

[91] *R. v. Newbury District Council, ex p. Chieveley Parish Council* [1999] P.L.C.R. 51.

[92] Unless the local planning authority specify a different period: Act of 1990, s.92(2).

[93] *R. v. Secretary of State for the Environment, ex p. Slough Borough Council* [1995] J.P.L. 1128; *R. v. Ashford Borough Council, ex p. Shepway District Council* [1999] P.L.C.R. 12.

[94] Town and Country Planning (Fees for Applications and Deemed Applications) Regulations 1989 (S.I. 1989 No. 193).

[95] Act of 1990, s.65; GDPO, art. 8.

[96] The requirements are specified in the GDPO, art. 10.

the Secretary of State,[97] with a view to his exercising his powers of call-in.[98] There is a duty in all cases for the local planning authority to take resultant representations into account when determining the application.[99]

22–035   *(c) Environmental assessment.* Special procedural requirements apply to applications for development which is likely to have a significant impact on the environment, under regulations[1] made in transposition of obligations imposed by European law.[2] Under the regulations, certain development, listed in Schedule 1, must always be subject to environmental assessment; other development, listed in Schedule 2, must be subject to environmental assessment where it is to be carried out in a "sensitive area", or if it is above a threshold specified in that Schedule.[3] There are four main steps in environmental assessment:

(1) the pre-application stage, when a prospective applicant may apply to the local planning authority for a ruling as to whether an application for the proposed development would be an EIA application, and, if so, what information should be furnished in the environmental statement[4];

(2) the submission of an application, preceded by public advertisement and the posting of a site notice,[5] and accompanied by an environmental statement[6];

(3) consultation on the environmental statement[7]; and

---

[97] Town and Country Planning (Development Plans and Consultation) Direction 1992 (Annex 3 to DOE Circular 19/92).

[98] Act of 1990, s.77: see further below.

[99] GDPO, art. 10(5), art. 19.

[1] Town and Country Planning (Assessment of Environmental Effects) (England and Wales) Regulations 1999 (S.I. 1999 No. 293) (hereafter "EA Regs").

[2] Council Directive 85/337 on the assessment of the effects of certain public and private projects on the environment, as amended by Council Directive 97/11 (effective from March 3, 1999).

[3] EA Regs, reg. 3.

[4] EA Regs, reg. 6. There is a right to appeal to the Secretary of State against the local planning authority's ruling under reg. 7.

[5] EA Regs, reg. 13.

[6] EA Regs, reg. 14. An environmental statement is intended to provide, *inter alia*, a detailed description of the physical characteristics of the whole development and the main characteristics of the proposed production processes; an estimate, by type and quantity, of expected residues and emissions; an outline of the main alternatives studied by the applicant and an indication of the main reasons for his choice, taking into account the environmental effects; a description of the aspects of the environment likely to be significantly affected by the proposed development (population, fauna, flora, soil, water, air, climatic factors, material assets, including the architectural and archaeological heritage, landscape and the inter-relationship between the above factors); a description of the likely significant effects of the proposed development on the environment (direct effects and any indirect, secondary, cumulative, short, medium and long-term, permanent and temporary, positive and negative effects); and the measures envisaged to prevent, reduce and where possible offset any significant adverse effects on the environment.

[7] EA Regs, Pt V.

(4) the determination of the application, taking into account the environmental statement and the consultation on it.[8]

(d) Determining planning applications. Each planning application falls to **22–036** be determined by the local planning authority, though should they fail to do so within eight weeks of the date of the application[9] the applicant is entitled to appeal to the Secretary of State as if the application had been refused.[10] An application may be called-in by the Secretary of State for his own determination at any time prior to it being determined by the local planning authority.[11] This is a broad but not unfettered discretion.[12] However, call-in is rare, and is confined as a matter of policy to applications raising issues of more than purely local significance.[13]

(e) The criteria for determining planning applications. Both the local **22–037** planning authority and, on appeal or call-in, the Secretary of State, have a broad discretion. Permission may be granted or refused, whether or not the development accords with the provisions of the development plan. The obligation is one to "have regard to the provisions of the development plan, so far as material to the application, and to any other material considerations".[14] The obligation has been further qualified by the introduction of a requirement that "the determination shall be made in accordance with the development plan unless material considerations indicate otherwise".[15] However, although that provision heightens the role of the development plan, and indeed introduces a presumption in favour of the plan, the matter is still one of judgment, and the courts have resisted attempts to have them second-guess, by way of judicial review, the weight that may be properly attached by decision-makers respectively to the plan and to other material considerations.[16]

They have similarly resisted attempts to restrict the categories of "other **22–038** material considerations", taking the approach that: "[I]n principle ... any consideration which relates to the use and development of land is capable of being a planning consideration. Whether a particular consideration falling within that broad class is material in any given case will depend on the circumstances".[17] Hence, in addition to the normal planning considerations such as highways access, public open space and the design of the buildings to

---

[8] EA Regs, reg. 3(2).

[9] Or such longer period as may be agreed in writing between the authority and the applicant: GDPO, art. 20(2). The period is extended to 16 weeks in the case of an EIA application (EA Regs, reg. 32(2)).

[10] Act of 1990, s.78(2).

[11] Act of 1990, s.77(1).

[12] *Rhys Williams v. Secretary of State for Wales* [1985] J.P.L. 29; *Asda Stores Ltd v. Secretary of State for Scotland* [1998] P.L.C.R. 233.

[13] *Planning: Appeals, Call-in and Major Public Inquiries* Cm. 43 (1986), paras 50–51.

[14] Act of 1990, s.70(2).

[15] Act of 1990, s.54A, inserted by the Planning and Compensation Act 1991, s.26.

[16] See, *e.g. City of Edinburgh v. Secretary of State for Scotland* [1997] 1 W.L.R. 1447; *R. v. Leominster District Council, ex p. Pothecary* (1997) 76 P. & C.R. 346.

[17] *Stringer v. Minister of Housing and Local Government* [1971] 1 All E.R. 65 at 77, *per* Cooke J.

be built, the courts have held that, although planning control should be concerned only with the development and use of land,[18] it may nonetheless be a material consideration to consider the need to protect private interests of other landowners[19]; or the personal circumstances of occupiers[20]; or even public fears, perhaps unjustified, about the adverse consequences of the proposed development.[21] A bald financial inducement offered to the local planning authority in order to encourage them to grant planning permission would not be a material consideration, because planning permission is not to be bought and sold; but it is capable of being a material consideration if its purpose is to provide the means of overcoming a legitimate planning objection,[22] even if the need for it is not primarily generated by the development itself.[23]

22–039   *(f) Appeal to the Secretary of State.* An applicant may appeal to the Secretary of State against a decision of the local planning authority,[24] or their failure to decide within the time specified or agreed.[25] In determining an appeal, the Secretary of State has all the powers of the local planning authority.[26] Both the appellant and the local planning authority are entitled to appear before and be heard by a "person appointed by the Secretary of State for the purpose"[27] (in practice a planning inspector). However, the right to be heard is waived by both parties in almost 80 per cent of planning appeals, in favour of having the matter dealt with by written representations,[28] which provides a procedure that is swifter and cheaper. Where a party insists upon being heard, it may be, at the option of the Planning Inspectorate, through the holding of a hearing or through a public local inquiry.[29] A public local inquiry,

[18] *East Barnet U.D.C. v. British Transport Commission* [1962] 2 Q.B. 484.
[19] *Stringer v. Minister of Housing and Local Government (supra)*: need to protect operation of Jodrell Bank radio telescope from interference which might result from housing development nearby.
[20] *Great Portland Estates plc v. Westminster City Council* [1985] A.C. 885.
[21] *West Midlands Probation Committee v. Secretary of State for the Environment* [1998] J.P.L. 388; *Newport County Borough Council v. Secretary of State for Wales* [1998] J.P.L. 377; [1998] 1 P.L.R. 47.
[22] *R. v. Plymouth City Council, ex p. Plymouth and South Devon Co-operative Society* (1993) 67 P. & C.R. 78 (contribution to various on-site and off-site facilities, including the servicing of alternative sites for light industrial development to off-set the effect of allocating the development site to superstore development).
[23] *Tesco Stores Ltd v. Secretary of State for the Environment* [1995] 1 W.L.R. 759 (financial contribution offered towards provision of town by-pass).
[24] Act of 1990, s.78(1).
[25] Act of 1990, s.78(2). The prescribed period is eight weeks (GDPO, art. 20), extended to 16 weeks in a case requiring an environmental statement (new EIA Regs, reg. 32(2)).
[26] Act of 1990, s.79(1).
[27] Act of 1990, s.79(2).
[28] Planning Inspectorate Agency, *Statistical Report 1997/98*, Chart 1: 79% of appeals were determined on the basis of written representations; 16.3% following a hearing; and 7.7% following a public local inquiry.
[29] The Inspectorate decides whether a hearing or inquiry should be held, taking into account the preferences of the parties: DOE Circular 15/96, *Planning Appeal Procedures*, para. 15. An informal hearing is simpler and cheaper, but there is an inquisitorial duty on the inspector to investigate the facts in order that the statutory right to be heard should not be nullified (*Dyason v. Secretary of State for the Environment* (1998) 75 P. & C.R. 506).

now usually held only for appeals raising matters of policy significance or contested facts, is a quasi-judicial hearing, conducted in accordance with formal rules of procedure,[30] and with opportunity for participation by third parties.

Jurisdiction actually to determine planning appeals is now transferred to planning inspectors[31] in 99 per cent of cases. An inspector acts on behalf of the Secretary of State, and within the policy framework established by him. Any person aggrieved by the decision on the grounds that it is outside the statutory powers, or that relevant procedural requirements have not been complied with, may apply within six weeks to the High Court to have it set aside.[32]

22–040

(g) The effect of planning permission. Planning permission enures in perpetuity for the benefit of the land and of all persons for the time being interested in the land,[33] unless it provides otherwise.[34] It effects a crystallisation of development rights, and it may be subsequently modified or revoked[35] only upon payment of compensation for any loss or damage.[36] It authorises the carrying out of the development permitted by it,[37] but it does not confer statutory immunity from an action in nuisance in respect of that development,[38] nor does it authorise interference with other private rights.[39] If granted for the erection of a building, it includes permission to use the building for the purpose for which it was designed.[40]

22–041

Section 5. Planning Conditions and Planning Obligations

1. The powers. Two further instruments are available to local planning authorities when determining planning applications. They may impose "such

22–042

---

[30] Town and Country Planning (Inquiries Procedure) Rules 1992 (S.I. 1992 No. 2038); Town and Country Planning Appeals (Determination by Inspectors) (Inquiries Procedure) Rules 1992 (S.I. 1992 No. 2039).

[31] Act of 1990, Sched. 6, para. 1; Town and Country Planning (Determination of Appeals by Appointed Persons) Regulations 1997 (S.I. 1997 No. 420).

[32] Act of 1990, s.288.

[33] Act of 1990, s.75(1).

[34] It may provide otherwise in two cases: a personal permission, limited to a named individual; and a planning permission granted for a limited period (Act of 1990, s.72(1) and (2)), which requires an express condition for that purpose and not merely words of limitation (*I'm Your Man Ltd v. Secretary of State for the Environment* [1999] P.L.C.R. 109).

[35] Act of 1990, ss.97–100.

[36] That entitlement does not arise if the permission is set aside on a statutory application to the High Court, or on an application for judicial review (*R. v. Bassetlaw District Council, ex p. Oxby* [1998] P.L.C.R. 283).

[37] If the permitted development involves a material change in use, the permission is spent once the use has changed, and will not authorise any further changes between uses: *Cynon Valley Borough Council v. Secretary of State for Wales* [1986] J.P.L. 760.

[38] *Wheeler v. JJ Saunders Ltd* [1995] 1 P.L.R. 55; *Hunter v. Canary Wharf Ltd* [1997] A.C. 665.

[39] *Delyn Borough Council v. Solitaire (Liverpool) Ltd* (1995) 93 L.G.R. 614.

[40] Unless the permission specifies the purpose for which it may be used: Act of 1990, s.75(2), (3).

conditions as they think fit" when granting planning permission,[41] and they may enter into planning obligations with landowners.

22–043　　**2. Planning conditions.** The courts have insisted that, to be valid, a planning condition must be imposed only for a planning purpose, must fairly and reasonably relate to the permitted development, and must not be manifestly unreasonable.[42] A condition in a permission for a private housing scheme which required that the units be first let to tenants on the council's housing waiting list was held not to have been imposed for a planning purpose.[43] A condition requiring the applicants to construct a road on their industrial estate and to make it available for use by neighbouring occupiers was held in 1963 to be manifestly unreasonable,[44] on the assumption that it was for the State to provide such public benefits; but a different conclusion might well be reached in the different economic conditions of today.[45] A condition may validly postpone the commencement of the development, or the occupation of the units to be constructed, until some pre-condition has been satisfied, even though it is not exclusively within the power of the applicant to satisfy it,[46] and even if there might appear to be no reasonable prospect of satisfying it.[47]

22–044　　If a condition is found to be invalid, the court will be reluctant to sever it and to allow the permission to stand, unless the condition deals only with some ulterior, trivial or collateral matter.[48] The preferred course will be to quash the permission and allow the application to be redetermined. The most common method by which a landowner or applicant will seek to challenge a condition is therefore by appeal on the merits to the Secretary of State.[49] The Secretary of State has power to set aside, replace or modify a condition in the light of policy criteria and guidance adopted by him.[50]

22–045　　**3. Planning obligations.** Planning legislation has long contained a power for the local planning authority to enter into an agreement with a landowner

---

[41] Act of 1990, s.70(2).

[42] *Pyx Granite Co. Ltd v. Minister of Housing and Local Government* [1958] 1 Q.B. 554 (in H.L. [1960] A.C. 260); *Newbury District Council v. Secretary of State for the Environment* [1981] A.C. 578.

[43] *R. v. Hillingdon London Borough Council, ex p. Royco Homes Ltd* [1974] 1 Q.B. 720.

[44] *Hall & Co. Ltd v. Shoreham-by-Sea Urban District Council* [1964] 1 W.L.R. 240.

[45] See *Tesco Stores Ltd v. Secretary of State for the Environment* [1995] 1 W.L.R. 759 at 776, *per* Lord Hoffmann.

[46] *Grampian Regional Council v. City of Aberdeen* (1984) 47 P. & C.R. 633: such conditions are known as "Grampian conditions".

[47] *British Railways Board v. Secretary of State for the Environment* [1994] J.P.L. 32.

[48] *Kingsway Investment (Kent) Ltd v. Kent County Council* [1971] A.C. 72; *Hall & Co. Ltd v. Shoreham-by-Sea Urban District Council* [1964] 1 W.L.R. 240.

[49] This may be by appeal against the original decision (though that may put the permission itself at risk), by applying afresh for permission to carry out the development without compliance with the disputed condition (Act of 1990, s.73), or by appealing against an enforcement notice requiring compliance with the condition.

[50] DOE Circular 11/95, *The Use of Conditions in Planning Permissions*, which establishes the policy tests that a condition should be: necessary; relevant to planning; relevant to the development to be permitted; enforceable; precise; and reasonable in all other respects.

respecting the development or use of the land.[51] Those provisions were revised and extended by the Planning and Compensation Act 1991,[52] which introduced a power to enter into a planning obligation, so-called because it may be created not only by agreement, but also unilaterally by the landowner. Planning obligations are widely used in order to give effect to requirements that cannot validly be imposed by planning conditions, such as to provide, or to contribute towards the cost of, off-site infrastrutures such as highway improvements or schools.

(a) The legal character of planning obligations. Planning obligations are a **22–046** legal hybrid: they are in effect covenants affecting the use of land, but the power to enforce them is vested exclusively[53] in the local planning authority named in the instrument,[54] against the person entering into the obligation and against any person deriving title from that person.[55] Hence, there is no requirement of benefited land, and obligations may contain requirements that are positive in character. They may restrict the development or use of land; or require specified actions to be carried out; or require the land to be used in a particular way; or require sums of money to be paid.[56]

(b) The use and validity of planning obligations: planning gain. In practice, **22–047** the use of planning obligations has proved controversial, because of the fear, on the one hand, that local planning authorities may use their powers coercively to obtain benefits from developers that are unnecessary for the development to proceed; and, on the other hand, that developers may offer unnecessary financial inducements to local planning authorities in return for the grant of planning permission. Government advice counsels that obligations should be used only where they are relevant to planning, directly related to the permitted development, and necessary to make a proposal acceptable in land-use planning terms.[57] However, these are policy tests and not tests of legal validity: questions of necessity and proportionality are matters for the planning authorities, not for the courts.[58] Questions of validity arise only where an obligation is beyond the powers conferred by the section, or where regard is had, in granting planning permission, to an obligation which bears no relationship to the proposed development and hence could not be considered a material consideration.

---

[51] A planning agreement power was contained in the Town and Country Planning Act 1932, s.34, but an amended version was introduced in the Act of 1947, which in due course became s.52 of the consolidating Act of 1971, and s.106 of the 1990 Act.

[52] Section 12, substituting new ss.106, 106A and 106B in the Act of 1990.

[53] *Attorney General (ex rel Scotland) v. Barratt Manchester Ltd* (1991) 63 P. & C.R. 179.

[54] Act of 1990, s.106(6), (9).

[55] Planning obligations are local land charges: Act of 1990, s.106(11).

[56] Act of 1990, s.106(1).

[57] Circular 01/97, *Planning Obligations*, para. B.12.

[58] *R. v. Plymouth City Council, ex p. Plymouth and South Devon Co-operative Society Ltd* (1993) 67 P. & C.R. 78; *Tesco Stores Ltd v. Secretary of State for the Environment* [1995] 1 W.L.R. 759.

22–048 *(c) Variation of planning obligations.* A planning obligation is a consensual instrument, executed by the owner of the relevant interest in the land, and there is therefore no right of appeal to the Secretary of State. Nor does the Secretary of State have power to enter into or enforce a planning obligation. However, an obligation may be varied at any time by agreement between the parties; and any person against whom an obligation is enforceable may apply to the local planning authority to modify or discharge it, with a right to appeal to the Secretary of State.[59] No such application may be made within five years from the date the obligation was entered into, and an obligation may be discharged only if it no longer serves a useful purpose.[60] The primary purpose of a unilateral obligation (to which the same principles apply) is to allow a landowner to overcome a refusal by the local planning authority to enter into an agreement if, on appeal, the Secretary of State proves willing to grant permission subject to an obligation.

Section 6. Enforcement of Planning Control

22–049 **1. The character of planning enforcement.** The enforcement of planning control has proved difficult in practice, and the law has had to be reviewed and reformed comprehensively on no fewer than three occasions since 1947.[61] The fundamental principle remains largely unchanged: it is that a breach of planning control[62] is not in itself an offence. Where it appears to a local planning authority that such a breach has occurred,[63] they may serve an enforcement notice on the owner and occupier of the land specifying the alleged breach, and specifying what steps they require to be taken, within a specified time, to remedy it.[64] It is only a failure to comply with the requirements of the notice that is an offence. An appeal may be made to the Secretary of State at any time before the notice takes effect,[65] and it is then of no effect pending the final determination of the appeal.[66]

---

[59] Act of 1990, s.106A.

[60] Act of 1990, s.106A(3), (6).

[61] By the Caravan Sites and Control of Development Act 1960, following the Report by Sir John Arton Wilson, *Caravans as Homes* Cmnd. 872 (1959); by the Local Government, Planning and Land (Amendment) Act 1981; and by the Planning and Compensation Act 1991, implementing certain of the recommendations of the Carnwath Report, *Enforcing Planning Control* (HMSO, 1989).

[62] The expression includes carrying out development without the required permission, and failing to comply with a planning condition: Act of 1990, s.171A(1).

[63] The breach must have occurred within the 10 years preceding the notice, or four years in the case of operational development or change of use to use as a dwelling-house (Act of 1990, s.171B). Unauthorised development against which enforcement action has not been taken within the specified time becomes lawful.

[64] Act of 1990, s.172.

[65] Act of 1990, s.174: the Secretary of State has wide power to vary the terms of the notice, or to grant planning permission for the breach complained of.

[66] Act of 1990, s.175(4). The suspension continues if a further appeal is made from the Secretary of State to the High Court under s.289, unless the court otherwise directs (s.289(4A)).

2. Urgent cases. This implies a somewhat leisurely approach to remedying   **22–050**
planning breaches, which is not always appropriate. There are therefore
supplementary powers allowing the local planning authority to serve a stop
notice in certain cases,[67] thereby insisting that the breach stop immediately on
pain of criminal liability, but laying the local planning authority open to a
claim for compensation should their allegations prove to be wrong in law.[68] A
1991 amendment to the 1990 Act confirmed and extended the power of local
planning authorities to apply directly to the court for an injunction to restrain
breaches of planning control,[69] which has proved a powerful and flexible
remedy.[70]

3. Breach of planning condition. Summary action may be taken where the   **22–051**
breach comprises a failure to observe a planning condition. The local planning
authority may serve a "breach of condition" notice requiring the owner or
occupier to secure compliance, and failure to do so within the specified time
is an offence.[71]

4. Continuing effect of enforcement notice. An enforcement notice con-   **22–052**
tinues to have effect, even after it has been complied with,[72] until it is
withdrawn by the local planning authority[73] or superseded by a grant of
planning permission to the extent that the requirements of the notice are
inconsistent with the permission.[74]

5. Certification of lawfulness of use or development. It is not always easy   **22–053**
to determine whether the existing use or development of land is lawful. It is
commonly a mixed question of law and fact. The Act of 1990 therefore
provides machinery for an owner to apply for a certificate of the lawfulness of
any existing use or development, whose effect is to provide a conclusive
presumption of the lawfulness of any development specified in it.[75] A similar
procedure is available in respect of any proposed use or development,[76] and
the usual rights of appeal to the Secretary of State exist in both cases against
the decision (or failure to decide) of the local planning authority.[77]

Section 7. The Financial Framework

1. The 1947 scheme and its successors. By influencing the supply and   **22–054**
location of land for development, regulatory planning control inevitably has

[67] Act of 1990, s.183.
[68] Act of 1990, s.186.
[69] Act of 1990, s.187B.
[70] See, *e.g. Runnymede Borough Council v. Harwood* (1994) 92 L.G.R. 561; *Croydon London Borough Council v. Gladden* [1994] 1 P.L.R. 30.
[71] Act of 1990, s.187A.
[72] Act of 1990, s.180(3).
[73] Or its requirements are relaxed or waived, under the Act of 1990, s.173A.
[74] Act of 1990, s.180.
[75] Act of 1990, s.191.
[76] Act of 1990, s.192.
[77] Act of 1990, s.195.

an effect on market values. Whether, and if so how, the State should compensate for adverse effects, and recover so-called "betterment" effects, has proved politically controversial throughout the life of the British comprehensive planning system. The financial scheme of the 1947 legislation was significantly more controversial than its planning provisions. It introduced a development charge, which was levied at a 100 per cent rate on increases in land value above the value of the land in its existing use ("current use value"). Hence it sought to tax any increase in value due to the land's development potential ("development value"). It was repealed by the incoming Conservative administration in 1951. A second attempt to tax development values was made by the Labour Government in 1967 with the introduction of a betterment levy, administered by a new Land Commission. It, too, was repealed upon the return of a Conservative Government in 1970. The third attempt came with the Labour Government of 1974, with the complementary legislation of the Community Land Act 1975 and the Development Land Tax Act 1976. Although the Community Land Act was repealed in 1980, development land tax remained on the statute book until 1985.

22–055　　**2. Planning gain and infrastructure contributions.** There is today no differential taxation of increases in the value of development land, although they fall within the reach of capital gains tax. There has, however, been a shift in responsibility for the provision of public good relating to new development, from the State to landowners and developers, through the planning gain process described above.

Section 8. The Compulsory Acquisition of Land

22–056　　**1. Authorisation.** Title to land may be acquired compulsorily by the State, or by any other public or private body[78] upon which legislation confers such a power. The process is compulsory, but not confiscatory: landowners' rights to their land are converted into rights to claim compensation for their loss. Much of the land required by these bodies is bought through market transactions, albeit under the shadow of compulsion. The use of compulsory powers is commonly reserved for cases where negotiation has failed, and for instances of multiple ownership, particularly along the line of proposed linear infrastructures such as a railway or highway, where failure to acquire just one interest might defeat the whole project. The acquiring body will be required in all cases to justify its need for the land, and to demonstrate why that need should outweigh the claim of the owner to remain there.

22–057　　**2. Procedure.** The first formal step in compulsory acquisition is the making and service of a draft compulsory purchase order, which has no effect until

---

[78] Bodies authorised to acquire land compulsorily include privatised public utilities such as electricity generating companies and water companies.

confirmed by the relevant "confirming authority", normally the Secretary of State.[79] Any owner, lessee or occupier is entitled to object to the order, and to be heard by a person appointed by the Secretary of State for that purpose before determining whether to confirm the order.[80] Planning permission may already have been granted for the development for which the land is required, or the two procedures may be combined. There are special authorisation arrangements for certain railway and other transport projects under the Transport and Works Act 1992,[81] which allow for the making of an order for the compulsory acquisition of land, the granting of planning permission and the overriding of other rights.

The acquiring authority have three years from the confirmation of a compulsory purchase order[82] in which to give notice to all persons interested in the land stating that they "are willing to treat for the purchase of the land"[83] (a "notice to treat"), and they are thereafter, upon giving not less than 14 days' notice, entitled to take physical possession of the land.[84]

3. Compensation. The basic measure by which compensation for land **22–058** compulsorily acquired is assessed is its market value,[85] ignoring the fact that the acquisition is compulsory, and ignoring the actual impact on market values of the scheme underlying the acquisition.[86]

4. Development of acquired land. An acquiring authority is entitled to put **22–059** the land to the purpose for which it was acquired. Where land is acquired by a local planning authority using the broad powers conferred by the 1990 Act,[87] it may be used for any other purpose for which it has compulsory acquisition powers[88]; it may be disposed of[89]; or it may be developed.[90] The acquisition

---

[79] Acquisition of Land Act 1981, Pt II.
[80] Acquisition of Land Act 1981, s.13.
[81] The purpose of the Act was to set aside the requirement for private Parlimentary legislation for authorising such schemes, and to confer in its place an order-making power on the executive government.
[82] Compulsory Purchase Act 1965, s.4.
[83] Compulsory Purchase Act 1965, s.5.
[84] Compulsory Purchase Act 1965, s.11.
[85] Land Compensation Act 1981, s.5.
[86] *Pointe Gourde, etc. Co. Ltd v. Sub-Intendent of Crown Lands* [1947] A.C. 565, which was given statutory expression in the Land Compensation Act 1961, s.6. The valuer (ultimately the Lands Tribunal in cases of dispute) is required to take into account various assumptions about planning permission (Land Compensation Act 1961, ss.14–21), and the parties may apply for a certificate of what development would have been appropriate for the land were it not for the acquisition (*ibid.*, s.17).
[87] Act of 1990, s.226, which authorises the compulsory acquisition of land "suitable for and required in order to secure the carrying out of development, redevelopment or improvement", or for "the proper planning of the area".
[88] Act of 1990, s.232.
[89] Act of 1990 s.233: indeed, the land may be acquired for the purposes of such disposal, for example to assemble land from multiple ownerships into a single ownership in order to promote its development.
[90] Act of 1990, s.235.

of the land in itself overrides certain private rights in it,[91] and any development of it which is in accordance with planning permission overrides existing easements and restrictive covenants.[92] The right extends equally to a subsequent redevelopment of the site,[93] and compensation is payable for loss or damage caused.[94]

22–060   **5. Inverse compulsory acquistion.** Planning legislation confers two remedies on landowners which enable them to require a public authority to acquire their land. A landowner may serve a blight notice where the value of land is so adversely affected by proposals for public works that it has become impossible to sell it except at a price substantially lower than it would have reached were it not for the planning blight.[95] The procedure for purchase notices has a similar outcome, but it is designed for cases where land has become incapable of reasonably beneficial use in its existing state, and planning permission has not been forthcoming to allow it to be rendered capable of reasonably beneficial use.[96] However, since even a quite unremunerative use is held to be capable of being "reasonably beneficial",[97] the purchase notice remedy provides a relatively fragile system of compensation for planning restrictions.

Section 9. Special Cases

22–061   Separate planning controls are exercised in respect of listed buildings and conservation areas,[98] scheduled monuments and areas of archaeological importance[99] and tree preservation.[1] The procedures are similar in respect of each. There is a designation process, through which the building or tree or area is identified in accordance with the statutory criteria. Thereafter, works or activities which are deemed potentially harmful[2] are prohibited, on pain of criminal sanctions, unless they are permitted by a specific or general consent. Application for consent is made to the local planning authority or Secretary of State,[3] and must be publicly advertised. Consent may be refused, or granted

---

[91] Act of 1990, s.236.
[92] Act of 1990, s.237.
[93] *R. v. City of London Corporation, ex p. Mystery of the Barbers of London* (1996) 73 P. & C.R. 59.
[94] Act of 1990, s.237(4).
[95] Act of 1990, ss.149, 150.
[96] Act of 1990, s.37.
[97] *Colley v. Secretary of State for the Environment and Canterbury City Council* [1998] C.A. Trans. 98–1294.
[98] Planning (Listed Buildings and Conservation Areas) Act 1990.
[99] Ancient Monuments and Archaeological Areas Act 1979.
[1] Act of 1990, ss.197–214.
[2] *e.g.* "works for the demolition of a listed building or for its alteration or extension in any manner which would affect its character as a building of special architectural or historic interest" (Planning (Listed Buildings and Conservation Areas) Act 1990, s.7).
[3] The Secretary of State is the primary consenting authority for scheduled monument consent (Ancient Monuments and Archaeological Areas Act 1979, s.3).

subject to conditions, including conditions as to the period within which the consent may be implemented. There is a right for the applicant to appeal to the Secretary of State against an adverse decision of the local planning authority, and there are remedial enforcement provisions in addition to the direct criminal sanctions.

A similar procedure is adopted in the special additional controls relating to the outdoor display of advertisements[4] and the storage on land of hazardous substances,[5] except that there is no prior designation process.

Part 3

PROTECTION OF TENANTS

Section 1. Business Premises

Business premises have been protected since the enactment of the Landlord **22–062** and Tenant Act 1927.[6] This gave the tenant the right to a new lease (or compensation in lieu) provided he could establish that by reason of the carrying on of a business at the premises for not less than five years, goodwill had become attached to them whereby they could be let at a higher rent than they would otherwise have realised.[7] It was essential to show goodwill which remained adherent to the premises after the tenant had gone,[8] a formidably difficult task. Some tenancies of shops were thus protected, but tenancies of professional premises were outside the provisions altogether. These relatively ineffectual provisions were replaced by the much more far-reaching and well-drafted[9] terms of the Landlord and Tenant Act 1954, Part II.[10] These contain no requirement of adherent goodwill, and contracting out of the statute (*e.g.* by means of a contract for the surrender of the tenancy[11]) is prohibited, except where the court gives its express sanction prior to the commencement of the

---

[4] Act of 1990, ss.220–225; Town and Country Planning (Control of Advertisements) Regulations 1992 (S.I. 1992 No. 666).

[5] Planning (Hazardous Substances) Act 1990.

[6] They were protected for nearly a year under the Rent Acts: Increase of Rent and Mortgage Interest (Restrictions) Act 1920, s.13. For the history of the statutory regulation of business tenancies, see Haley, (1999) 19 L.S. 207.

[7] Landlord and Tenant Act 1927, ss.4, 5.

[8] See, *e.g. Whiteman Smith Motor Co. Ltd v. Chaplin* [1934] 2 K.B. 35.

[9] See *Scholl Mfg Co. Ltd v. Clifton (Slim–Line) Ltd* [1967] Ch. 41 at 49.

[10] The Act has only been substantially amended once, by the Law of Property Act 1969, but it is currently the subject of reform proposals by the Law Commission: Law Com. 208 (November 1992).

[11] *Joseph v. Joseph* [1967] Ch. 78; *Tarjomani v. Panther Securities Ltd* (1983) 46 P. & C.R. 32. An instrument of surrender is itself effective unless it is executed before the tenant has been in occupation for one month: L.T.A. 1954, s.24(2).

tenancy.[12] A closely restricted right for business tenants to claim compensation for improvements subject to certain conditions, which was introduced by the Landlord and Tenant Act 1927, continues in amended form.[13]

22–063　　**1. Tenancies within Part II of the Landlord and Tenant Act 1954.** Part II applies to "any tenancy where the property comprised in the tenancy is or includes premises which are occupied[14] by the tenant and are so occupied for the purposes of a business carried on by him or for those and other purposes".[15] These terms are widely defined. " 'Business' includes a trade, profession or employment, and includes any activity carried on by a body of persons, whether corporate or unincorporate."[16] Thus shops, offices, factories, clubs,[17] hospitals,[18] surgeries, laboratories, schools and government offices[19] are all included, but not a residence where the tenant carries on a voluntary Sunday school,[20] or takes in a few lodgers,[21] nor premises used for dumping waste materials from the tenant's shops during reconstruction.[22] "Premises" can include bare land, such as a public open space,[23] or gallops for training racehorses.[24] Occupation must be "by the tenant". Although occupation by a company which the tenant controls will not suffice,[25] the tenant may occupy premises by means of those (possibly including companies[26]) who are genuinely his servants.[27] A tenant of a block of flats who sub-lets the flats does not thereafter "occupy" the premises for business purposes, unless the degree of

---

[12] L.T.A. 1954, s.38, as amended by the L.P.A. 1969, s.5; see *Hagee (London) Ltd v. A. B. Erikson and Larsen* [1976] 1 Q.B. 209; *Essexcrest Ltd v. Evenlex Ltd* [1988] 1 E.G.L.R. 69. If the court purports to make an order outside its jurisdiction, the agreement will be ineffective to exclude the operation of Part II: *Nicholls v. Kinsey* [1994] Q.B. 600 (agreement not "for a term of years certain").

[13] *Post*, para. 22–085.

[14] Thus Part II does not apply to business user of a right of way: *Land Reclamation Co. Ltd v. Basildon D.C.* [1979] 1 W.L.R. 767; *cf. Nevill Long & Co. (Boards) Ltd v. Firmenich & Co.* (1984) 47 P. & C.R. 59.

[15] L.T.A. 1954, s.23(1). On insignificant business use, see *Cheryl Investments Ltd v. Saldanha* [1978] 1 W.L.R. 1329; *Gurton v. Parrott* [1991] 1 E.G.L.R. 98; *Wright v. Mortimer* (1996) 28 H.L.R. 719.

[16] L.T.A. 1954, s.23(2).

[17] *Addiscombe Garden Estates Ltd v. Crabbe* [1958] 1 Q.B. 513 (lawn tennis club).

[18] *Hills (Patents) Ltd v. University College Hospital Board of Governors* [1956] 1 Q.B. 90; *Groveside Properties Ltd v. Westminster Medical School* (1984) 47 P. & C.R. 507 (flats provided for hospital's medical students).

[19] *Town Investments Ltd v. Department of the Environment* [1978] A.C. 359.

[20] *Abernethie v. A, M. & J. Kleiman Ltd* [1970] 1 Q.B. 10.

[21] *Lewis v. Weldcrest Ltd* [1978] 1 W.L.R. 1107.

[22] *Hillil Property and Investment Co. Ltd v. Naraine Pharmacy Ltd* (1979) 39 P. & C.R. 67.

[23] *Wandsworth L.B.C. v. Singh* (1991) 62 P. & C.R. 219.

[24] *Bracey v. Read* [1963] Ch. 88.

[25] *Cristina v. Seear* [1985] 2 E.G.L.R. 128. Where the tenancy is held on trust, occupation by all or any of the beneficiaries under the trust will be treated as equivalent to that of the tenant: L.T.A. 1954, s.41; *Frish Ltd v. Barclays Bank Ltd* [1955] 2 Q.B. 541; *Trustees of the Methodist Schools Trust Deed v. O'Leary* (1992) 66 P. & C.R. 364 at 376.

[26] *Nozari–Zadeh v. Pearl Assurance Plc.* [1987] 2 E.G.L.R. 91 at 93.

[27] *Teasdale v. Walker* [1958] 1 W.L.R. 1076; *cf. Chapman v. Freeman* [1978] 1 W.L.R. 1298.

his control and provision of services suffices to constitute occupation.[28] An intention to continue occupying the premises suffices for a tenant who is physically absent owing to events over which he has no control,[29] but not for the tenant who voluntarily absents himself or ceases trading.[30] "Tenancy" is widely defined.[31] It includes any tenancy created by a tenancy agreement,[32] and also a tenancy by estoppel,[33] though other provisions of Part II of the Act indicate that a tenancy at will is not included.[34]

2. Exceptions. Certain tenancies are expressly excluded from Part II of the Act. Tenancies of licensed premises (*i.e.* public houses and similar establishment), many of which were so excluded, have now been brought within its scope.[35] The remaining exceptions are as follows.[36]   **22–064**

(a) Tenancies of agricultural holdings.[37]   **22–065**

(b) Farm business tenancies.[38]   **22–066**

(c) Mining leases.[39]   **22–067**

(d) Service tenancies. These are tenancies granted by reason of the tenant holding an office, appointment or employment, and ending or terminable with it. Unless the tenancy was granted prior to the commencement of the Act, it must have been granted by a written instrument which expressed the purpose for which the tenancy was granted.   **22–068**

(e) Short tenancies. This means any tenancy granted for a term certain not exceeding six months unless it contains provisions for renewing the term or extending it beyond six months from the commencement, or the tenant and any predecessor in his business have been in occupation for more than 12 months in total.[39a]   **22–069**

---

[28] *Bagettes Ltd v. G.P. Estates Ltd* [1956] Ch. 290; *cf. Lee–Verhulst (Investments) Ltd v. Harwood Trust* [1973] Q.B. 204. If the sub-tenant is in "occupation" himself, the tenant cannot also be in occupation: *Graysim Holdings Ltd v. P. & O. Property Holdings Ltd* [1996] A.C. 329.

[29] *Morrisons Holding Ltd v. Manders Property (Wolverhampton) Ltd* [1976] 1 W.L.R. 533 (severe fire damage); *cf. Demetriou v. Robert Andrews (Estate Agencies) Ltd* (1991) 62 P. & C.R. 536 (premises uninhabitable due to tenant's failure to repair).

[30] *Pulleng v. Curran* (1982) 44 P. & C.R. 58; *Aspinall Finance Ltd v. Viscount Chelsea* [1989] 1 E.G.L.R. 102.

[31] It appears to be agreed, after initial doubt, that *Street v. Mountford* principles (see *ante*, para. 14–013) are to be applied in determining whether commercial premises are subject to a tenancy: *London & Associated Investment Trust Plc v. Calow* [1986] 2 E.G.L.R. 80; *Vandersteen v. Agius* (1993) 65 P. & C.R. 266; *cf. Dresden Estates Ltd v. Collinson* [1987] 1 E.G.L.R. 45.

[32] L.T.A. 1954, s.69(1).

[33] *Bell v. General Accident Fire & Life Assurance Corporation Ltd* [1998] 1 E.G.L.R. 69.

[34] *Wheeler v. Mercer* [1957] A.C. 416; *Hagee (London) Ltd v. A. B. Erikson and Larsen* [1976] Q.B. 209; *Javad v. Aqil* [1991] 1 W.L.R. 1007.

[35] With effect from July 11, 1992: Landlord and Tenant (Licensed Premises) Act 1990, repealing L.T.A. 1954, s.43(1)(d).

[36] L.T.A. 1954, s.43, as amended (*inter alia*) by L.P.A. 1969, s.12.

[37] Agricultural Holdings Act 1986, s.1(1); Agriculture Act 1958, Sched. 1, para. 29.

[38] See Agricultural Tenancies Act 1995: *post*, para. 22–086.

[39] As defined in L.T.A. 1927, s.25(1): see L.T.A. 1954, s.46.

[39a] *Cricket Ltd v. Shaftesbury Plc* [1999] 3 All E.R. 283.

22–070   **3. Security of tenure.** Security of tenure is conferred by the simple provision that a tenancy within Part II "shall not come to an end unless terminated in accordance with the provisions of this Part of this Act".[40] An ordinary notice to quit given by the landlord thus has no effect, and a tenancy for a fixed term will continue indefinitely after the expiration of the term. A tenancy may still be determined by a notice to quit given by the tenant, or by a surrender or forfeiture, or by the forfeiture of a superior tenancy,[41] but in all other cases the special machinery of the Act must be used. "Landlord" is for these purposes defined as the next immediate reversioner who for the time being has either the fee simple or a tenancy which will not come to an end within 14 months.[42] Where a business tenancy is assigned, the tenancy becomes that of the assignee.[43] Thus if, following assignment, the tenancy continues by virtue of Part II of the 1954 Act, the original tenant will not be liable for the rent or under the covenants of the lease unless express contrary provision has been made.[44]

22–071

The statutory machinery falls under two heads.

(a) Determination by landlord. The landlord may determine the tenancy by giving not less than six[45] nor more than 12 months' notice in the statutory form,[46] to expire not earlier than the date[47] when, apart from the Act, the tenancy could have been determined by notice to quit, or would have expired.[48] The date of expiration of the statutory notice thus need not be an anniversary or the end of a complete period of the tenancy; it merely must not be too early. On receiving such a notice, the tenant may claim a new tenancy if[49]:

---

[40] L.T.A. 1954, s.24(1).

[41] L.T.A. 1954, s.24(2). A tenant's notice to quit, or surrender, is ineffective if given or executed in the first month of occupation by the tenant. See also *Meadows v. Clerical Medical and General Life Assurance Society* [1981] Ch. 70 (no determination while claim for relief against forfeiture subsists); *Cadogan v. Dimovic* [1984] 1 W.L.R. 609; *Hill v. Griffin* [1987] 1 E.G.L.R. 81.

[42] L.T.A. 1954, s.44; *Bowes–Lyon v. Green* [1963] A.C. 420; *Shelley v. United Artists Corporation* (1990) 60 P. & C.R. 241. For special provisions for joint tenancies, see s.41A, added by L.P.A. 1969, s.9.

[43] *City of London Corporation v. Fell* [1993] Q.B. 589 at 604 (C.A.).

[44] *City of London Corporation v. Fell* [1994] 1 A.C. 458 (H.L.). For an example of contrary provision, see *Herbert Duncan Ltd v. Cluttons* [1993] Q.B. 589 at 605 *et seq.* If the business tenancy was granted on or after January 1, 1996, the Landlord and Tenant (Covenants) Act 1995 will apply to protect the original tenant further: see *ante*, para. 15–066.

[45] *Hogg Bullimore & Co. v. Co-operative Insurance Society Ltd* (1985) 50 P. & C.R. 105.

[46] S.I. 1957 No. 1157, S.I 1983 No. 133, S.I. 1989 No. 1548. The name of the landlord must be correctly stated: *Morrow v. Nadeem* [1986] 1 W.L.R. 1381; *Pearson v. Alyo* [1990] 1 E.G.L.R. 114 (joint landlords). The notice must relate to the whole of the land comprised in the tenancy: *Southport Old Links Ltd v. Naylor* [1985] 1 E.G.L.R. 66.

[47] Errors of date will be benevolently construed: *Mannai Investment Co. Ltd v. Eagle Star Life Assurance Co. Ltd* [1997] A.C. 749, applied to L.T.A. 1954, Pt II, in *Garston v. Scottish Widows Fund & Life Assurance Society* [1998] 1 W.L.R. 1583.

[48] L.T.A. 1954, s.25; *cf. Lewis v. M.T.C. (Cars) Ltd* [1975] 1 W.L.R. 457.

[49] L.T.A. 1954, ss.25(5), 29(2), (3). Failure to make application to the court within the time-limit is critical, as the court has no power to extend time: see, *e.g. Hodgson v. Armstrong* [1967] 2 Q.B. 299.

(i) within two months he gives or serves[50] on the landlord notice in writing, however informal,[51] that he is not willing to give up possession of the premises; and also

(ii) not less than[52] two nor more than[53] four months after receiving the notice he applies to the county court or Chancery Division[54] for a new tenancy.

(b) Determination by the tenant. A tenant who wishes to leave the premises   **22–072**
may determine the tenancy by an ordinary notice to quit, as at common law,[55] or, if the tenancy is for a fixed term, by three months' notice in writing to expire at the end of the term, or on any quarter day thereafter.[56] Where the tenant gives up occupation on or before expiry of a fixed term, Part II of the 1954 Act will cease to apply and no statutory continuation will occur.[57] If, on the other hand, the tenant wishes to have a new tenancy in place of his existing tenancy, he must serve on the landlord a request for a new tenancy in the statutory form.[58] This must specify a date for the commencement of the new tenancy not less than six nor more than 12 months ahead, and not earlier than the date on which the existing tenancy would expire or could be determined.[59] The tenant must also apply to the court for the new tenancy not less than two nor more than four months after he has served the request on the landlord.[60] These provisions are confined to tenancies for a term certain exceeding a year, or for a term certain and thereafter from year to year[61]; a tenant under an ordinary periodic tenancy cannot make a request for a new tenancy, although he may claim a new tenancy if the landlord serves notice on him under the previous head.

4. Opposition to a new tenancy. The court is bound to grant a new tenancy   **22–073**
unless the landlord establishes one or more of the statutory grounds of opposition. The landlord may only rely on such grounds as are stated (or

---

[50] *Chiswell v. Griffon Land and Estates Ltd* [1975] 1 W.L.R. 1181.

[51] *Lewington v. Trustees of the Society for the Protection of Ancient Buildings* (1983) 45 P. & C.R. 336; *cf. Mehmet v. Dawson* [1984] 1 E.G.L.R. 74.

[52] *E. J. Riley Investments Ltd v. Eurostile Holdings Ltd* [1985] 2 E.G.L.R 124. The landlord may waive his right to object to a premature notice: *Kammins Ballrooms Co. Ltd v. Zenith Investments (Torquay) Ltd* [1971] A.C. 850; *cf. Stevens & Cutting Ltd v. Anderson* [1990] 1 E.G.L.R. 95.

[53] A day late is too late: *Dodds v. Walker* [1981] 1 W.L.R. 1027.

[54] The jurisdiction of the county court is unlimited: S.I. 1991 No. 724, amending L.T.A. 1954, s.63(2); CPR 1998, Sched. 1, RSC O. 97; CPR 1998, Sched. 2, CCR O. 43.

[55] L.T.A. 1954, s.24(2).

[56] L.T.A. 1954, s.27. But see *ante*, n. 41.

[57] *Esselte AB v. Pearl Assurance plc* [1997] 1 W.L.R. 891, not following *Long Acre Securities Ltd v. Electro Acoustic Industries Ltd* (1991) 61 P. & C.R. 177.

[58] S.I. 1983 No. 133, S.I. 1989 No. 1548, S.I. 1991 No. 724.

[59] L.T.A. 1954, s.26(2). Where a tenancy is granted for a term of years (and not for a term of years and thereafter from year to year), the tenant cannot seek a new tenancy commencing on a date earlier than the date on which the tenancy expires by effluxion of time: *Garston v. Scottish Widows Fund & Life Assurance Society* [1998] 1 W.L.R. 1583.

[60] L.T.A. 1954, s.29(3); *Akiens v. Solomon* (1993) 65 P. & C.R. 364.

[61] L.T.A. 1954, s.26(1).

indicated[62]) in a notice to determine the tenancy given by him or his predecessor in title,[63] or in a notice opposing the grant of a new tenancy served on the tenant within two months of receiving his request.[64] The seven grounds are as follows.[65]

22–074   *(a) Disrepair.* The tenant ought not to be granted a new tenancy in view of the state of repair of the "holding" (*i.e.* the premises let, excluding any part not occupied by the tenant or a service tenant of his[66]) due to the tenant's failure to comply with his repairing obligations.

22–075   *(b) Delay in paying rent.* The tenant ought not to be granted a new tenancy in view of his persistent delay in paying the rent.[67]

22–076   *(c) Breach of obligation.* The tenant ought not to be granted a new tenancy in view of other substantial breaches by him of his obligations under the tenancy, or for any other reason connected with his use or management of the holding.[68]

22–077   *(d) Alternative accommodation.* The landlord has offered and is willing to provide or secure the provision of suitable alternative accommodation on reasonable terms.

22–078   *(e) Premises more valuable as a whole.* The premises are part of larger premises held by the landlord under a tenancy and the tenant ought not to be granted a new tenancy because the landlord could obtain a substantially greater rent for the property as a whole than for the parts separately.

22–079   *(f) Demolition or reconstruction.* "On the termination of the current tenancy[69] the landlord intends to demolish or reconstruct[70] the premises comprised in the holding or a substantial part[71] of those premises or to carry out substantial work of construction[72] on the holding or part thereof and that he could not reasonably do so without obtaining possession of the holding."[73]

---

[62] *Bolton's (House Furnishers) Ltd v. Oppenheim* [1959] 1 W.L.R. 913.

[63] *A. D. Wimbush & Son Ltd v. Franmills Properties Ltd* [1961] Ch. 419; *Marks v. British Waterways Board* [1963] 1 W.L.R. 1008.

[64] L.T.A. 1954, ss.25(6), 26(6), 30(1).

[65] L.T.A. 1954, s.30(1).

[66] L.T.A. 1954, s.23(3).

[67] The court has a discretion: see, *e.g. Betty's Cafés Ltd v. Phillips Furnishing Stores Ltd* [1957] Ch. 67 at 82; *Hurstfell Ltd v. Leicester Square Property Co. Ltd* [1988] 2 E.G.L.R. 105.

[68] This may include conduct during the tenancy, and also any intention to use the premises illegally in the future: *Eichner v. Midland Bank Executor & Trustee Co. Ltd* [1970] 1 W.L.R. 1120; *Turner & Bell v. Searles (Stanford–le–Hope) Ltd* (1977) 33 P. & C.R. 208.

[69] *Edwards v. Thompson* (1990) 60 P. & C.R. 222.

[70] *Percy E. Cadle Ltd v. Jacmarch Properties Ltd* [1957] 1 Q.B. 323; *Joel v. Swaddle* [1957] 1 W.L.R. 1094; *Romulus Trading Company Ltd v. Trustees of Henry Smith's Charity* (1990) 60 P. & C.R. 62.

[71] *Bewlay (Tobacconists) Ltd v. British Bata Shoe Co. Ltd* [1959] 1 W.L.R. 45.

[72] *Botterill v. Bedfordshire County Council* [1985] 1 E.G.L.R. 82.

[73] *i.e.* as of right, and not merely by the tenant's permission: *Whittingham v. Davies* [1962] 1 W.L.R. 142.

The landlord cannot establish this ground if he has a contractual right to enter and do the intended work,[74] or if the tenant is willing to enable the landlord to carry out the intended work[75] (without interfering with the tenant's business to a substantial extent or for a substantial time[76]) by including such right in the new tenancy or by accepting a new tenancy of only part of the holding.[77] Provided that the landlord retains control of the demolition or reconstruction, it does not matter that it is carried out by some other person, *e.g.* by employees, independent contractors, or even by a new tenant on his behalf.[78]

(g) Own occupation. "On the termination of the current tenancy the land-　**22–080** lord intends to occupy the holding[79] for the purposes, or partly for the purposes, of a business to be carried on by him therein, or as his residence." The landlord may occupy the premises vicariously,[80] or share occupation with another.[81] The occupier may be a company controlled by the landlord[82] or, where the landlord is a company, a company in the same group of companies.[83] But this ground is not available to a landlord whose interest[84] was purchased[85] or created less than five years before the termination of the current tenancy.[86]

5. Intention. The last two grounds both depend on what the landlord　**22–081** "intends". Proof of such intention requires that at the date of the hearing[87] there should be not a mere hope or aspiration, or an exploration of possibilities, but a genuine, firm and settled intention, not likely to be changed, to do something which the landlord has a reasonable prospect of bringing about.[88] The intention of a corporate landlord must be ascertained by considering all

---

[74] *Heath v. Drown* [1973] A.C. 498.

[75] *Decca Navigator Co. Ltd v. G.L.C.* [1974] 1 W.L.R. 748.

[76] These phrases are to be read conjunctively: *Cerex Jewels Ltd v. Peachey Property Corporation Plc* [1986] 2 E.G.L.R. 65.

[77] L.T.A. 1954, s.31A, added by L.P.A. 1969, s.7; *Redfern v. Reeves* (1978) 37 P. & C.R. 364.

[78] *Gilmour Caterers Ltd v. St Bartholomew's Hospital Governors* [1956] 1 Q.B. 387; *Spook Erection Ltd v. British Railways Board* [1988] 1 E.G.L.R. 76; *Turner v. Wandsworth L.B.C.* (1994) 69 P. & C.R. 433.

[79] *Method Development Ltd v. Jones* [1971] 1 W.L.R. 168; *Cam Gears Ltd v. Cunningham* [1981] 1 W.L.R. 1011; *Leathwoods v. Total Oil Great Britain Ltd* (1985) 51 P. & C.R. 20; *J. W. Thornton Ltd v. Blacks Leisure Group Plc* [1986] 2 E.G.L.R. 61; *cf. Nursey v. P. Currie (Dartford) Ltd* [1959] 1 W.L.R. 273.

[80] *Teesside Indoor Bowls Ltd v. Stockton-on-Tees B.C.* [1990] 2 E.G.L.R. 87.

[81] *Willis v. Association of Universities of the British Commonwealth* [1965] 1 Q.B. 140.

[82] L.T.A. 1954, s.30(1), added by L.P.A. 1969, s.6.

[83] L.T.A. 1954, s.42(3), added by L.P.A. 1969, s.10.

[84] *Artemiou v. Procopiou* [1966] 1 Q.B. 878.

[85] *H. L. Bolton (Engineering) Co. Ltd v. T. J. Graham & Sons Ltd* [1957] 1 Q.B. 159.

[86] L.T.A. 1954, s.30(2); *Diploma Laundry Ltd v. Surrey Timber Co. Ltd* [1955] 2 Q.B. 604.

[87] *Betty's Cafés Ltd v. Phillips Furnishing Stores Ltd* [1959] A.C. 20.

[88] *Cunliffe v. Goodman* [1950] 2 K.B. 237; *Reohorn v. Barry Corporation* [1956] 1 W.L.R. 845; *Gregson v. Cyril Lord Ltd* [1963] 1 W.L.R. 41; *Westminster City Council v. British Waterways Board* [1985] A.C. 676.

the relevant circumstances: a formal resolution by the board of directors is neither essential nor conclusive.[89] However, an undertaking to the court to take the requisite steps (*e.g.* to demolish or reconstruct the premises, or occupy them for business purposes) will, if given by a responsible person or body, normally establish the intention required.[90] A landlord who cannot rely upon the final ground (own occupation) because of the five years rule may still succeed on the previous ground (demolition or reconstruction) if his intention is genuine and not merely colourable; for the existence of one ground does not exclude all others,[91] and an intention to demolish or reconstruct (or both) is not necessarily inconsistent with an intention to occupy.

22–082   **6. Terms of new tenancy.** When premises are first let to a business tenant there are no restrictions on the rent or other terms of the tenancy which the landlord requires, nor is there any power, except by contract,[92] to revise those terms during the currency of the original tenancy. But when a new tenancy is granted under the Act, the rent and other terms are in default of agreement determined by the court. The rent is to be that at which the holding might reasonably be expected to be let in the open market by a willing lessor, disregarding any effect of the occupation of the holding by the tenant or his predecessors, any goodwill due to them, and certain tenant's improvements.[93] In default of agreement,[94] the duration of the new tenancy is whatever the court considers reasonable in all the circumstances, not exceeding 14 years[95]; and the other terms are such as the court may determine having regard to the terms of the current tenancy and to all relevant circumstances,[96] *e.g.* including a rent review clause,[97] a break clause,[98] a right to display advertisements on neighbouring premises,[99] or a provision requiring a guarantor.[1] In determining

---

[89] *H. L. Bolton (Engineering) Co. Ltd v. T. J. Graham & Sons Ltd* [1957] 1 Q.B. 159; *Fleet Electrics Ltd v. Jacey Investments Ltd* [1956] 1 W.L.R. 1027.

[90] *Espresso Coffee Machine Co. Ltd v. Guardian Assurance Co. Ltd* [1959] 1 W.L.R. 250.

[91] *Fisher v. Taylors Furnishing Stores Ltd* [1956] 2 Q.B. 78; *Betty's Cafés Ltd v. Phillips Furnishing Stores Ltd* [1959] A.C. 20.

[92] *e.g.* a rent review clause.

[93] L.T.A. 1954, s.34, as amended by L.P.A. 1969, ss.1, 2. The improvements to be disregarded are those made by any tenant, otherwise than under an obligation to the landlord, within the previous 21 years if the holding has been continuously let under the Act since they were made.

[94] An agreement "subject to contract" or "without prejudice" is not effective: *Derby & Co. Ltd v. ITC Pension Trust Ltd* [1977] 2 All E.R. 890.

[95] L.T.A. 1954, s.33: *Upsons Ltd v. E. Robins Ltd* [1956] 1 Q.B. 131; *London and Provincial Millinery Stores Ltd v. Barclays Bank Ltd* [1962] 1 W.L.R. 510; *Chipperfield v. Shell (U.K.) Ltd* (1980) 42 P. & C.R. 136; *Becker v. Hill Street Properties Ltd* [1990] 2 E.G.L.R. 78.

[96] L.T.A. 1954, s.35; *Cardshops Ltd v. Davis* [1971] 1 W.L.R. 591.

[97] L.T.A. 1954, s.34(3).

[98] *McCombie v. Grand Junction Co. Ltd* [1962] 1 W.L.R. 581; *J. H. Edwards & Sons Ltd v. Central London Commercial Estates Ltd* [1984] 2 E.G.L.R. 103.

[99] *Re No. 1 Albemarle Street* [1959] Ch. 531; *cf. G. Orlik (Meat Products) Ltd v. Hastings & Thanet Building Society* (1974) 29 P. & C.R. 126; *Kirkwood v. Johnson* (1979) 38 P. & C.R. 392.

[1] *Cairnplace Ltd v. C.B.L. (Property Investment) Co. Ltd* [1984] 1 W.L.R. 696.

the rent and other terms, the court must also take account of the effect of the Landlord and Tenant (Covenants) Act 1995 on rent levels and the standard terms of commercial tenancies.[2] At least in so far as changes in market conditions are not attributable to the operation of that statute, the burden will rest on the party seeking to change the existing terms (usually the landlord).[3] The property to be included in the new tenancy is "the holding",[4] although where the holding is only part of the premises included in the current tenancy the landlord may require the whole of those premises to be included.[5]

The landlord may apply to the court for an interim rent to be fixed for the **22–083** period until the new tenancy begins.[6] An interim rent takes effect from the date of the application or the date specified for the end of the former tenancy, whichever is the later.[7]

These provisions give effect to the basic principle of Part II of the Act, namely, that a business tenant has a prima facie right to continue his business indefinitely in his premises on reasonable terms. There is no limit to the number of times a tenancy may be renewed.

7. Compensation for eviction. On quitting the holding, the tenant is **22–084** entitled to compensation from the landlord if the only grounds on which the landlord opposed the grant of a new tenancy were one or more of the last three grounds listed above,[8] and either the court is thereby precluded from granting a new tenancy or else the tenant does not apply for a new tenancy or withdraws his application.[9]

8. Compensation for improvements. Under the Landlord and Tenant Act **22–085** 1927,[10] if a tenant of premises used for a trade, business or profession carries out improvements to the premises which add to their letting value, the tenant may recover compensation from the landlord on leaving. But the tenant must satisfy a number of conditions: in addition to making his claim at the right time and in due form, he must give the landlord three months' notice of his intention to make the improvement. The landlord may then exclude the

---

[2] Landlord and Tenant (Covenants) Act 1995, Sched. 1, paras 3, 4, amending L.T.A. 1954, ss.34, 35.
[3] *O'May v. City of London Real Property Co. Ltd* [1983] 2 A.C. 726.
[4] See *ante*, para. 22–074.
[5] L.T.A. 1954, s.32(2).
[6] L.T.A. 1954, s.24A; *English Exporters (London) Ltd v. Eldonwall Ltd* [1973] Ch. 415; *Fawke v. Viscount Chelsea* [1980] Q.B. 441; *Halberstam v. Tandalco Corporation NV* [1985] 1 E.G.L.R. 90.
[7] *Stream Properties Ltd v. Davis* [1972] 1 W.L.R. 645.
[8] See *ante*, paras 22–078—22–080 (*i.e.* grounds (e), (f) and (g)).
[9] For calculation of compensation, see L.T.A. 1954, s.37(1), as amended by L.P.A. 1969, s.11; Local Government, Planning and Land Act 1980, s.193, Sched. 33; Local Government and Housing Act 1989, s.149, Sched. 7; S.I. 1990 No. 363.
[10] Sections 1–3, as amended by L.T.A. 1954, Pt III. Proposals for reform were made by the Law Commission in 1989, but have yet to be acted upon: Law Com. No. 178.

tenant's right to compensation if he successfully objects to the improvement, or carries it out himself in return for a reasonable increase in rent.

Section 2. Agricultural Tenancies[11]

22–086   Agricultural tenancies have been regulated by Parliament for longer than any other form of tenancy.[12] Initially, the Acts provided compensation for the tenant who had made improvements to the holding, or, latterly, had been dispossessed without good cause. In 1947, statutory security of tenure (and rent protection) was conferred upon many agricultural tenants, the most recent such code being contained in the Agricultural Holdings Act 1986. Statutory security led to a decline in the use of the lease for agricultural property, as well as to widespread invocation of the various methods of letting outside the legislation which were available and sanctioned by the courts.[13] These methods, essentially short-term arrangements which did not reflect the realities of farming in the late twentieth century,[14] resulted in pressure for reform from within the industry, which in turn led to the enactment of the Agricultural Tenancies Act 1995. This important statute has effectively removed statutory security with respect to tenancies entered into after it came into force, and allowed the parties the freedom to contract on their own terms. It is hoped that this legislation, together with fiscal incentives to letting enacted to take effect contemporaneously,[15] will revive the rented sector of agricultural land. The result is that there are two parallel statutory systems. The 1986 Act broadly applies to tenancies which began before September 1, 1995; the 1995 Act to those which have begun subsequently.[16] As the definitional provisions of the two statutes are by no means identical, it is important in each case to examine closely the statutory terminology.

A. Farm Business Tenancies

I. TENANCIES WITHIN THE AGRICULTURAL TENANCIES ACT 1995

22–087   **1. Definition.** A tenancy[17] is a "farm business tenancy" within the 1995 Act if[18]:

---

[11] See further Muir Watt & Moss, *Agricultural Holdings*, (14th ed., 1998); Scammell & Densham's *Law of Agricultural Holdings* (8th ed., 1997).

[12] The first statute was the Agricultural Holdings (England) Act of 1875.

[13] See, *e.g.* the *Gladstone v. Bower* tenancy: *post*, para. 22–096.

[14] See Cardwell [1993] Conv. 138.

[15] Landowners can claim 100% relief from inheritance tax on let agricultural land where it is subject to a new letting after September 1, 1995: Finance Act 1995, s.155, amending Inheritance Tax Act 1984, s.116 (as itself amended by Finance (No. 2) Act 1992, Sched. 14, paras 4, 8).

[16] A tenancy "begins" on the date when the tenant is entitled to go into possession: A.T.A. 1995, s.38(4).

[17] "Tenancy" includes sub-tenancy, and an agreement for a tenancy or sub-tenancy, but not a tenancy at will: A.T.A. 1995, s.38(1).

[18] A.T.A. 1995, s.1(1).

(i) all or part of the land comprised in the tenancy is farmed for the purposes of a trade or business,[19] and has been at all times since the beginning of the tenancy[20]; and

(ii) *either* the character of the tenancy is primarily or wholly agricultural[21] (having regard to the terms of the tenancy, the use of the land, the nature of any commercial activities carried on upon that land, and any other relevant circumstances)[22]

or at the beginning of the tenancy, the character of the tenancy was primarily or wholly agricultural as above, and on or before that date[23] the landlord and tenant exchanged written notices identifying the land in question and stating their intention that the tenancy was to be (and remain) a farm business tenancy.[24]

2. Exceptions. A tenancy cannot be a farm business tenancy if it began **22–088** before September 1, 1995, or if it is a tenancy of an agricultural holding within the 1986 Act.[25] Certain tenancies beginning on or after September 1, 1995 will be subject to the earlier legislation.[26]

II. RECOVERY OF POSSESSION

The general effect of the 1995 Act is to require notice of not less than 12 nor **22–089** more than 24 months in order to determine the farm business tenancy. No prescribed form of notice is required, and no contracting out is permitted.[27] However, where the farm business tenancy is a fixed-term tenancy of two years or less, or a periodic tenancy other than a tenancy from year to year, the 1995 Act allows termination in accordance with the terms of the lease.[28] For example, a landlord will be entitled to recover possession when a farm business tenancy granted for a fixed term of one year expires by effluxion of time.

1. Continuation of tenancies for more than two years. A farm business **22–090** tenancy may be a fixed-term tenancy or a periodic tenancy.[29] There is no

---

[19] "Farmed" is partially defined as including "the carrying on in relation to land of any agricultural activity": A.T.A. 1995, s.38(2).
[20] The "business conditions": A.T.A. 1995, s.1(2).
[21] Defined as in the Agricultural Holdings Act 1986 (see *post*, para. 22–095): A.T.A. 1995, s.38(1).
[22] The "agricultural condition": A.T.A. 1995, s.1(3).
[23] Or the date, if earlier, on which the written tenancy agreement was entered into.
[24] The "notice conditions": A.T.A. 1995, s.1(4). Compliance with the notice conditions is waived in certain cases of surrender and re-grant: see A.T.A. 1995, s.3(1). For service provisions, see A.T.A. 1995, s.36.
[25] A.T.A. 1995, s.2(1).
[26] A.T.A. 1995, s.4. See further *post*, para. 22–094.
[27] A.T.A. 1995, s.5(4).
[28] *cf.* the so-called *Gladstone v. Bower* tenancies in relation to the 1986 Act: *post*, para. 22–096.
[29] For the purposes of the 1995 Act, a "fixed-term tenancy" means any tenancy other than a periodic tenancy: A.T.A. 1995, s.38(1).

minimum or maximum length imposed by statute. If it is a tenancy for a term of more than two years, on expiry of that term it will continue as a tenancy from year to year, in other respects on the same terms as the original fixed-term tenancy, unless either party has given to the other written notice of his intention to terminate the tenancy at least 12 months (but less than 24 months) before the term was due to expire.[30]

22–091   **2. Notices to quit.** The "aggregate" of the land comprised in a farm business tenancy is known as the "holding".[31] A notice to quit the holding or part of it will be invalid unless it is in writing, and is given at least 12 but less than 24 months before the date on which it is to take effect. If the tenancy is a tenancy from year to year, the notice must take effect at the end of a year of the tenancy.[32] If the tenancy is for a term of more than two years, any such notice must be given pursuant to provision in the tenancy itself.[33] There is no security provided for farm business tenants over and above these requirements.

III. PROTECTION AS TO RENT

22–092   To a limited extent, the parties to a farm business tenancy are free to contract concerning rent. If the tenancy contains a provision that the rent is not to be reviewed during the tenancy, or that the rent is to be varied either by or to a specified amount or in accordance with a specified formula which does not preclude reduction or require or permit the exercise of any judgment or discretion in relation to its determination (but otherwise is to remain fixed), then such provision will be effective to avoid the application of Part II of the 1995 Act.[34] Otherwise, and notwithstanding any agreement to the contrary, either party to a farm business tenancy may, by service of a statutory review notice, refer the rent to be payable to arbitration.[35] Any variation in the rent will have effect from the "review date", which must be not less than 12, and not more than 24, months from the date when the notice is given, and which, in the absence of agreement to the contrary, must be an anniversary of the beginning of the tenancy. The review date must be at least three years from the beginning of the tenancy, or, if later, the date when any previous variation of the rent as a result of arbitration, review, or agreement took effect.[36] On a statutory rent review, the arbitrator has jurisdiction to increase or reduce the rent payable or leave it unchanged. The rent payable is that at which the holding might reasonably be expected to be let on the open market by a

---

[30] A.T.A. 1995, s.5(1).
[31] A.T.A. 1995, s.38(1).
[32] A.T.A. 1995, s.6(1).
[33] A.T.A. 1995, s.7(1).
[34] A.T.A. 1995, s.9. Thus, "upwards only" rent review clauses will be ineffective.
[35] A.T.A. 1995, s.10(1).
[36] See generally A.T.A. 1995, s.10(2)–(6).

willing landlord to a willing tenant, taking account of all relevant circumstances, and disregarding certain tenant's improvements, and certain other matters.[37]

IV. COMPENSATION FOR IMPROVEMENTS

Whilst the 1995 Act seriously reduces the security of tenure of agricultural **22–093** tenants, the recoupment of the tenant's investment on giving up possession remains an important component of legislative policy. Thus there are complex provisions contained in Part III of the 1995 Act entitling a farm business tenant to be compensated for improvements on quitting the holding. "Improvements" are widely defined so as to include not only physical improvements but also "intangible advantages" (such as milk quotas and planning permissions).[38] The landlord must have consented to the improvements in question[39] (the tenant being entitled to refer a refusal of consent to arbitration[40]), and there are exclusions. The tenant is entitled to be paid an amount equal to the increase attributable to the improvement in the value of the holding at the termination of the tenancy.[41]

B. Agricultural Holdings

I. AGREEMENTS WITHIN THE 1986 ACT

1. Agreements beginning on or after September 1, 1995. The 1986 Act **22–094** does not apply to tenancies[42] beginning on or after September 1, 1995. There are certain limited exceptions, namely, tenancies of agricultural holdings[43]—

(i) granted by a written contract of tenancy entered into before that date which indicates that the 1986 Act is to apply to the tenancy; or

(ii) obtained by virtue of certain directions of an Agricultural Land Tribunal on the death or retirement of the previous tenant[44]; or

(iii) granted on an agreed succession[45] by a written contract of tenancy indicating that Part IV of the 1986 Act is to apply to the tenancy; or

---

[37] A.T.A. 1995, s.13.
[38] For definition of "tenant's improvement", see A.T.A. 1995, s.15.
[39] A.T.A. 1995, s.17.
[40] A.T.A. 1995, s.19.
[41] A.T.A. 1995, s.20. Different principles are applied where the improvement consists of a planning permission: A.T.A. 1995, ss.18, 21.
[42] Whilst it is expressly stated that this includes agreements to which A.H.A. 1986, s.2 (see *post*, para. 22–096) would otherwise apply, it is not clear whether such agreements may come within the exceptional circumstances which are then listed.
[43] A.T.A. 1995, s.4(1).
[44] See A.H.A. 1986, ss.39, 53; *post*, para. 22–112.
[45] Defined in A.T.A. 1995, s.4(2).

(iv) created by the previous tenant's acceptance of certain compensation provisions[46]; or

(v) granted by a purported variation of a previous tenancy with the tenant of the holding[47] which takes effect as a new tenancy by reason of the operation of the doctrine of "surrender and re-grant".[48] However, an agreement which is expressed to take effect as a new tenancy between the parties will not be subject to the 1986 Act.

22–095

2. "Agricultural holding"

(a) The definition. "Agricultural holding" is defined as meaning "the aggregate of the land (whether agricultural land or not) comprised in a contract of tenancy which is a contract for an agricultural tenancy"[49]; and there is a contract for an agricultural tenancy if, having regard to the terms of the tenancy, the actual and contemplated use of the land, and all other relevant circumstances, "the whole of the land" (apart from any insubstantial exceptions) "is let for use as agricultural land".[50] "Agricultural land" is "land used for agriculture which is so used for the purposes of a trade or business"[51]; and "agriculture" has a wide definition which includes horticulture, fruit growing, seed growing, market gardening,[52] and even grazing the horses of a riding school.[53]

22–096

(b) "Contract of tenancy". The term "contract of tenancy" is restricted to "a letting of land, or agreement for letting land, for a term of years or from year to year".[54] However, an agreement for value[55] whereby land is let (or a licence is granted "to occupy" the land[56]) for use as agricultural land for an "interest less than a tenancy from year to year", in circumstances which otherwise would make the land an agricultural holding, takes effect (with the necessary modifications) as if it were an agreement for a tenancy from year to

---

[46] The so-called "Evesham custom": A.H.A. 1986, s.80(3)–(5).

[47] Or any agricultural holding which comprised the whole or a substantial part of the land comprised in the holding.

[48] See further *ante*, para. 14–174.

[49] A.H.A. 1986, s.1(1), which provision excludes service tenancies.

[50] A.H.A. 1986, s.1(2).

[51] A.H.A. 1986, s.1(4). The Minister may designate land as "agricultural land": Agriculture Act 1947, s.109(1).

[52] A.H.A. 1986, s.96(1). Thus a letting of a garden centre, at least where a substantial part of the produce is "home-grown", may comprise an agricultural holding: *Short v. Greeves* [1988] 1 E.G.L.R. 1.

[53] *Rutherford v. Maurer* [1962] 1 Q.B. 16.

[54] A.H.A. 1986, s.1(5).

[55] *Goldsack v. Shore* [1950] 1 K.B. 708; *Collier v. Hollinshead* (1984) 272 E.G. 941. The agreement must be made on or after March 1, 1948: A.H.A. 1986, Sched. 12, para. 1.

[56] Occupation must be exclusive: *Harrison-Broadley v. Smith* [1964] 1 W.L.R. 456; *Bahamas International Trust Co. Ltd v. Threadgold* [1974] 1 W.L.R. 1514; *McCarthy v. Bence* [1990] 1 E.G.L.R. 1.

year.[57] Thus, most agricultural tenancies, and many licences, appear to fall within the 1986 Act. A fixed-term tenancy for more than one year but less than two is, however, excluded from the security of tenure and succession provisions.[58] A tenancy for one year is within the Act.[59]

The statutory extension to lettings for an interest less than a tenancy from year to year does not apply to[60]— **22–097**

> (i) a letting or a grant which had the prior approval of the Minister of Agriculture, Fisheries and Foods[61];

> (ii) an agreement for the letting of the land (or the grant of a licence to occupy it) made "in contemplation[62] of the use of the land only for grazing or mowing during some specified period of the year".[63] Such a period need not be fixed by dates; it will include any period which is so named or described as to be identifiable by persons versed in agricultural matters.[64] Although 364 days may be such a period,[65] one year cannot[66]; or

> (iii) a sub-tenancy or sub-licence granted by a person having less than a tenancy from year to year.[67]

(c) Contracting out.[68] An agreement between landlord and tenant that the **22–098** 1986 Act is not to apply to their tenancy will be of no effect.[69] However, if before the grant of a tenancy of not less than two nor more than five years, on an application made by both parties jointly, the Minister gave his approval, no further tenancy will arise on expiry of the fixed term by operation of law, and the landlord will be entitled to repossession. This provision will only operate if the contract of tenancy is in writing, contains a statement that section 3 of the 1986 Act is not to apply to it, and is within the terms of the ministerial approval.[70]

---

[57] A.H.A. 1986, s.2(1). See, *e.g. Calcott v. J. S. Bloor (Measham) Ltd* [1998] 3 E.G.L.R. 1.

[58] *Gladstone v. Bower* [1960] 2 Q.B. 384; *E.W.P. Ltd v. Moore* [1992] Q.B. 460 (letting for 23 months); *cf. Keen v. Holland* [1984] 1 W.L.R. 251 ("back-dating" ineffective). The tenancy is, however, a tenancy of an agricultural holding for other purposes, such as tenant compensation, and the tenancy will be excluded from protection as a business tenancy pursuant to L.T.A. 1954, Pt II: *E.W.P. Ltd v. Moore, ante.*

[59] *Bernays v. Prosser* [1963] 1 Q.B. 592.

[60] See Cardwell [1993] Conv. 138.

[61] A.H.A. 1986, s.2(1). See, *e.g. Finbow v. Air Ministry* [1963] 1 W.L.R. 697; *Ashdale Land & Property Co. Ltd v. Manners* [1992] 2 E.G.L.R. 5.

[62] *Scene Estate Ltd v. Amos* [1957] 2 Q.B. 205; *cf. Rutherford v. Maurer* [1962] 1 Q.B. 16.

[63] A.H.A. 1986, s.2(3).

[64] *Mackenzie v. Laird* 1959 S.C. 266; *Watts v. Yeend* [1987] 1 W.L.R. 323 ("seasonal" grazing licences).

[65] *Reid v. Dawson* [1955] 1 Q.B. 214; *South West Water Authority v. Palmer* (1983) 268 E.G. 357; *cf. Lory v. Brent L.B.C.* [1971] 1 W.L.R. 823.

[66] *Rutherford v. Maurer* [1962] 1 Q.B. 16; *Brown v. Tiernan* (1992) 65 P. & C.R. 324.

[67] A.H.A. 1986, s.2(3).

[68] See Scammell & Densham (8th ed., 1997), Chap. 4.

[69] *Johnson v. Moreton* [1980] A.C. 37.

[70] A.H.A. 1986, s.5; *Pahl v. Trevor* [1992] 1 E.G.L.R. 22.

22–099   *(d) Mixed lettings.* Where agricultural land is let with non-agricultural land, the Act will either apply to the tenancy as a whole or not at all; there is no segregation of the agricultural from the non-agricultural.[71]

II. SECURITY OF TENURE

22–100   The general scheme of security contained in the Act is as follows.[72] First, a notice to quit of one year in length, such notice expiring at the end of a year of the tenancy, is required to terminate every agricultural tenancy, including fixed-term tenancies which have expired. Secondly, the Act prevents any such notice to quit from operating at all except in certain specified cases. Agricultural tenancies accordingly continue indefinitely until determined on one of the grounds specified in the Act, or until agricultural use is abandoned.[73]

22–101   **1. Determination of tenancies.**

(a) Notice to quit. The Act of 1986 makes 12 months' notice to quit requisite in almost every case. This is effected by the following means. First, as has been seen, certain short tenancies and licences are treated as yearly tenancies. Secondly, a tenancy for two years or upwards is continued as a tenancy from year to year[74] from the end of the fixed term unless (not less than one year nor more than two years before the date fixed for the expiration of the term) either party has given to the other written notice of his intention to terminate the tenancy.[75] Thirdly, and with some exceptions, the Act invalidates a notice to quit[76] an agricultural holding if it purports to terminate the tenancy before the expiration of 12 months from the end of the then current year of the tenancy[77]; and this is so even if the notice is given by the tenant.[78]

22–102   *(b) Types of notice.* A landlord's notice to quit may take one of two forms.[79]

The landlord's notice may refer to one or more of eight "Cases", set out in Schedule 3 to the 1986 Act,[79a] which the landlord alleges entitles him to

---

[71] See A.H.A. 1986, s.1(2); *Howkins v. Jardine* [1951] 1 K.B. 614.
[72] Common law methods of termination (notably surrender, forfeiture and disclaimer) remain available despite the Act.
[73] *Wetherall v. Smith* [1980] 1 W.L.R. 1290.
[74] But if the tenant under a tenancy granted after September 12, 1984, dies, the tenancy will expire at its contractual end, or one year later if he dies in the last year of the term: A.H.A. 1986, s.4(1), (2).
[75] A.H.A. 1986, s.3(1).
[76] Including a notice exercising an option of termination contained in the tenancy agreement: *Edell v. Dulieu* [1924] A.C. 38.
[77] A.H.A. 1986, s.25(1). For exceptions, see s.25(2), (3) and S.I. 1987 No. 710, arts 7 and 14.
[78] *Flather v. Hood* (1928) 44 T.L.R. 698. But the recipient of a shorter notice may agree to treat it as being valid: *Elsden v. Pick* [1980] 1 W.L.R. 898.
[79] A.H.A. 1986, s.26. See generally *Carradine Properties Ltd v. Aslam* [1976] 1 W.L.R. 442; *Land v. Sykes* [1991] 1 E.G.L.R. 18. For the effect of a fraudulent statement in the notice, see *Earl of Stradbroke v. Mitchell* [1991] 1 E.G.L.R. 1.
[79a] See *post*, paras 22–105—22–114.

enforce the notice to quit. If the tenant wishes to contest a landlord's claim based on Cases A, B, D, or E, he must within one month serve notice on the landlord requiring the question to be determined by arbitration[80] or, where a notice to quit was given under Case D, serve a counter-notice[81]; otherwise he cannot challenge the claim. Cases C, F, G and H cannot be referred to arbitration (which would not in any event be appropriate).

Alternatively, the landlord may serve an ordinary "unqualified" notice to quit which does not specify any of the "Cases". This will enable the tenant to serve a counter-notice claiming security of tenure. On service of such a counter-notice, the landlord will be unable to enforce his notice to quit by repossession unless he obtains the consent of the Agricultural Lands Tribunal on proof of certain grounds.

The notice must make it plain which type of notice it is,[82] and which Case, **22–103** if any, is relied upon.[83] If it specifies a Case which the landlord fails to establish on arbitration, the landlord cannot then argue that the notice was effective as an ordinary "unqualified" notice which the tenant should have met with a counter-notice.[84]

2. Recovery of possession. It can thus be seen that in relation to a 1986 Act **22–104** tenancy, the landlord has two routes to repossession, which can be compared in some respects with the distinction between "mandatory" and "discretionary" grounds relevant to residential tenancies.[85] If the landlord can establish one of the Cases in Schedule 3, the tenant's security will disappear. If, however, he has to rely on the Tribunal consenting to the operation of his notice to quit, the landlord is on far weaker ground, as repossession is dependent on the exercise of discretion in his favour.

(a) Schedule 3. Where the landlord serves a notice to quit specifying one or **22–105** more of the Cases under Schedule 3, the tenant can serve a counter-notice only where the landlord bases his claim on the failure of the tenant to comply with a notice to do work under Case D.[86] The notice to quit will accordingly operate unless the tenant refers the landlord's notice to arbitration within one month, a course that is possible only if the notice is based on Cases A, B, D or E. If a notice based on any other Case is contested by the tenant, he must either seek a declaration from the court that the landlord's notice is invalid, or raise his arguments in the course of the landlord's possession proceedings. The Cases in Schedule 3 are as follows.

---

[80] S.I. 1987 No. 710, art. 9; *Att.-Gen. (Duchy of Lancaster) v. Simcock* [1966] Ch. 1; *Magdalen College, Oxford v. Heritage* [1974] 1 W.L.R. 441.
[81] A.H.A. 1986, s.28.
[82] *Cowan v. Wrayford* [1953] 1 W.L.R. 1340; *Mills v. Edwards* [1971] 1 Q.B. 379.
[83] *Budge v. Hicks* [1951] 2 K.B. 335; *Magdalen College, Oxford v. Heritage* [1974] 1 W.L.R. 441.
[84] *Cowan v. Wrayford* [1953] 1 W.L.R. 1340; *Mills v. Edwards* [1971] 1 Q.B. 379.
[85] See *post*, para. 22–148.
[86] For which, see A.H.A. 1986, s.28.

22–106   CASE A: COMPULSORY RETIREMENT OF SMALLHOLDERS.[87] On or after September 12, 1984, a smallholdings authority or the Minister may let a smallholding subject to the provisions of this Case. Such land can be repossessed once the tenant has attained the age of 65, and suitable alternative accommodation[88] is available for him.

22–107   CASE B: PLANNING PERMISSION. The land is required[89] (even if not by the landlord[90]) for some non-agricultural use for which planning permission has been given or (in certain restricted circumstances) is not required.[91]

22–108   CASE C: BAD HUSBANDRY. Not more than six months before the notice to quit was given the Tribunal certified that the tenant was not farming in accordance with the rules of good husbandry.[92]

22–109   CASE D: UNREMEDIED BREACH. The tenant has committed a breach of any term of his tenancy (other than a term inconsistent with good husbandry) and has failed to comply fully[93] with a written notice by the landlord in the prescribed form[94] requiring compliance within two months (in the case of rent) or (in other cases) a specified reasonable time, being not less than six months if works of repair, maintenance or replacement have to be done.[95]

22–110   CASE E: IRREPARABLE BREACH. The landlord's interest in the holding has been materially prejudiced by an irreparable breach[96] by the tenant of a valid[97] term of the tenancy (other than a term inconsistent with good husbandry).

22–111   CASE F: BANKRUPTCY The tenant is insolvent.[98]

22–112   CASE G: DEATH. This Case is closely related to the provisions for statutory succession to agricultural holdings[99] which were severely limited by the

---

[87] See further Agriculture Act 1970, Pt III.
[88] A.H.A. 1986, Sched. 3, Pt II, paras 1–7.
[89] *Jones v. Gates* [1954] 1 W.L.R. 222.
[90] *Rugby Joint Water Board v. Foottit* [1973] A.C. 202.
[91] In *Bell v. McCubbin* [1990] 1 Q.B. 976, a Case B notice to quit was held valid although the landlord, wishing to sub-let for residential purposes, did not seek or require planning permission. Case B was subsequently amended to reverse this ruling, but the amendment applies only to notices served on or after July 29 1990: Agricultural Holdings (Amendment) Act 1990.
[92] A.H.A. 1986, s.96(3), Sched. 3, para. 9; Agriculture Act 1947, ss.10, 11.
[93] *Price v. Romilly* [1960] 1 W.L.R. 1360; *Stoneman v. Brown* [1973] 1 W.L.R. 459.
[94] S.I. 1987 No. 711. Where the landlord specifies what he requires the tenant to do, he must do so accurately: *Pickard v. Bishop* (1975) 31 P. & C.R. 108; *Dickinson v. Boucher* (1983) 269 E.G. 1159. But a misdescription of the landlord which is not likely to mislead the tenant may not be critical: *Divall v. Harrison* [1990] 1 E.G.L.R. 16.
[95] See, *e.g. Lloyds Bank Ltd v. Jones* [1955] 2 Q.B. 298; *Sumnall v. Statt* (1985) 49 P. & C.R. 367; *Jones v. Lewis* (1973) 25 P. & C.R. 375. For forms and procedure, see S.I. 1987 No. 710, 711.
[96] Although a covenant may have been broken, the landlord may be estopped from relying on it where the parties had acted on the assumption that no such covenant existed (or, presumably, where the landlord has waived it): *Troop v. Gibson* [1986] 1 E.G.L.R. 1.
[97] *Johnson v. Moreton* [1977] E.G.D. 1, affirmed [1980] A.C. 37.
[98] A.H.A. 1986, s.96(2).
[99] Themselves only introduced eight years earlier: Agriculture (Miscellaneous Provisions) Act 1976.

Agricultural Holdings Act 1984.[1] With certain exceptions,[2] where a tenancy was granted before July 12, 1984, any "eligible person" may within three months of the death[3] apply to the Tribunal for a tenancy.[4] An "eligible person" is any surviving close relative[5] of the deceased who is not himself the occupier of a commercial unit of agricultural land[6] and who, at the death of the tenant and for at least five of the previous seven years, derived his only or principal source of livelihood from agricultural work on the holding.[7] If the Tribunal consider him suitable, he is entitled to a tenancy.[8] However, where the tenancy was granted on or after July 12, 1984,[9] then, with certain exceptions,[10] no statutory succession will take place on the death of the tenant.[11]

Case G enables the landlord to give a notice to quit within three months of **22–113** notice[12] of the death of the sole (or sole surviving) tenant being served on him by the tenant's personal representatives or (if sooner) notice being given to him of an "eligible person" under the above provisions. Such notice to quit, if given "by reason of the tenant's death", will deprive the tenant's estate of security. However, such notice to quit will not have effect unless no application has been made under the statutory succession provisions, or application has been made but the Tribunal has either refused to determine that the applicant is a suitable successor, or consented to the operation of the notice to quit.[13]

CASE H: MINISTERIAL CERTIFICATE. The notice to quit is given by the **22–114** Minister, and he certifies that it is given to enable him to effect an amalgamation (within the meaning of the Agriculture Act 1967) or the reshaping of any agricultural unit. This, however, applies only if in the tenancy agreement the tenant agreed that it was subject to Case H.

(b) Security depending on reasonableness. There is no security of tenure **22–115** (and the court cannot grant relief[14]) if within one month the tenant[15] fails to

---

[1] Now see A.H.A. 1986, Pt IV.

[2] A.H.A. 1986, ss.36–38. In particular, there could be only two succession tenancies.

[3] The three-month period begins on the day after the death.

[4] A.H.A. 1986, s.39(1). A tenant may retire and nominate an "eligible person" as his successor, thereby occasioning *inter vivos* statutory succession to pre-1984 Act tenancies: A.H.A. 1986, ss.49–58.

[5] A.H.A. 1986, s.35(2).

[6] A.H.A. 1986, s.36(3)(b), Sched. 6, para. 3.

[7] A.H.A. 1986, s.36(3)(a); *Welby v. Casswell* [1995] 2 E.G.L.R. 1; S.I. 1984 No. 1301. The Tribunal may treat as an "eligible person" someone who satisfies section 36(3)(a) "to a material extent": A.H.A. 1986, s.41; *Littlewood v. Rolfe* [1981] 2 All E.R. 51; *Wilson v. Earl Spencer's Settlement Trusts* [1985] 1 E.G.L.R. 3.

[8] A.H.A. 1986, s.39(5), (6).

[9] The day the 1984 Act came into force.

[10] A.H.A. 1986, s.34(1)(b).

[11] Although the tenancy will devolve as part of the tenant's estate.

[12] A.H.A. 1986, Sched. 3, Pt II, para. 12; *B.S.C. Pension Fund Trustees Ltd v. Downing* [1990] 1 E.G.L.R. 4; *Lees v. Tatchell* [1990] 1 E.G.L.R. 10.

[13] A.H.A. 1986, s.43(1).

[14] *Parrish v. Kinsey* (1983) 268 E.G. 1113.

[15] Where there are joint tenants, normally all must concur in the counter-notice: *Featherstone v. Staples* [1986] 1 W.L.R. 469.

serve a counter-notice requiring section 26(1) of the 1986 Act to apply[16] to an ordinary "unqualified" notice to quit. If the tenant serves a valid counter-notice, the landlord may within one month[17] apply to the Agricultural Lands Tribunal for consent to the operation of the notice to quit. However, the discretion of the Tribunal is fettered. They must give consent to the landlord's notice to quit taking effect if (and only if) they are satisfied as to one or more of the "matters" listed in section 27(3). Even if they are so satisfied, they must not give consent if in all the circumstances it appears to them that a fair and reasonable landlord would not insist on possession.[18] The cases in which the tenant's security of tenure depends on the reasonableness of his being evicted (the section 27(3) "matters") are as follows.

22–116   (1) GOOD HUSBANDRY. The landlord proposes to terminate the tenancy for a purpose that is desirable in the interests of good husbandry as respects the land to which the notice relates, treated as a separate unit.

22–117   (2) SOUND MANAGEMENT. The landlord proposes to terminate the tenancy for a purpose that is desirable in the interests of sound management of the land concerned (physically, and not merely financially for the landlord[19] or the tenant[20]) or of the estate of which it forms part.

22–118   (3) RESEARCH. Carrying out the purpose for which the landlord proposes to terminate the tenancy is desirable for the purposes of agricultural research, education, experiment or demonstration, or for the purposes of the statutes relating to smallholdings or allotments.

22–119   (4) GREATER HARDSHIP. Considering all who might be affected,[21] greater hardship would be caused by withholding consent than by granting it.

22–120   (5) NON-AGRICULTURAL USE. The landlord proposes to terminate the tenancy for the purpose of the land being used for some non-agricultural use not falling within Case B.

Where consent is given to the operation of the notice to quit, the Tribunal may impose conditions to secure that the land is used for the purposes stated by the landlord; and the Tribunal may subsequently vary or revoke the conditions.[22]

22–121   **3. Sub-tenants.** These provisions apply as between a tenant and any sub-tenant of his,[23] but not as between the sub-tenant and the head landlord. Thus

---

[16] The counter-notice need not be in prescribed form: it suffices if it evinces a clear intention to invoke the tenant's rights under the Act: *Mountford v. Hodkinson* [1956] 1 W.L.R. 422; *Frankland v. Capstick* [1959] 1 W.L.R. 204.

[17] S.I. 1978 No. 259, Sched. 1, r. 2(2).

[18] A.H.A. 1986, s.27(2). As circumstances are likely to change, issue estoppel will not bar the service of successive notices to quit: *Wickington v. Bonney* (1984) 47 P. & C.R. 655.

[19] *National Coal Board v. Naylor* [1972] 1 W.L.R. 908.

[20] *Evans v. Roper* [1960] 1 W.L.R. 814.

[21] *Purser v. Bailey* [1967] 2 Q.B. 500.

[22] A.H.A. 1986, s.27(4), (5).

[23] See, however, S.I. 1987 No. 710, art. 16.

where a landlord's notice to quit takes effect it determines not only the tenancy but also any sub-tenancies; no provision has been made[24] to exclude the common law rule that a sub-tenancy falls with the tenancy out of which it was created.[25] However, the courts will be astute to detect, and to strike down, collusive arrangements between landlord and tenant or artificial transactions using nominees as intermediaries, which in either case are designed to prevent the effective tenant from exercising his statutory rights.[26] Where the tenant has served a counter-notice on the landlord, the sub-tenant can make representations to the Tribunal, for he must be made a party to the proceedings[27]; and the sub-tenant may be entitled to compensation.[28]

III. PROTECTION AS TO RENT

When an agricultural tenancy is first granted, the parties are free to agree   **22–122**
whatever rent they please. However, not more frequently than once in every three years, either party may require the amount of the rent to be submitted to arbitration by an arbitrator appointed either by agreement or in default by (usually) the President of the RICS, on the basis of the open market rent.[29] Any increase or decrease awarded by the arbitrator takes effect as from the next day on which the tenancy could be determined by a notice to quit given when the reference to arbitration was demanded, provided the arbitrator has been duly appointed before that day.[30] Thus unless otherwise provided, no revision of rent is possible during a tenancy for a fixed term which is not determinable by notice to quit. In addition, the landlord may increase the rent in respect of certain improvements carried out by him.[31]

IV. COMPENSATION

The tenant's rights to compensation may be put under three heads. None of   **22–123**
them can be excluded by any agreement to the contrary[32]; and any provision which would even by implication exclude a claim for compensation (*e.g.* a provision for determination at such short notice as to leave no time to claim compensation) is void.[33]

1. Compensation for disturbance. A tenant not in default who quits the   **22–124**
holding in consequence of a notice to quit given by the landlord (whether or

---

[24] The Lord Chancellor's power to provide protection for sub-tenants (A.H.A. 1986, s.29, Sched. 4, para. 7) has not been exercised; but see *infra.*
[25] *Lord Sherwood v. Moody* [1952] 1 All E.R. 389; *Pennell v. Payne* [1995] Q.B. 192 (tenant's "upwards" notice to quit).
[26] *Sparkes v. Smart* [1990] 2 E.G.L.R. 245; *Barrett v. Morgan* [1999] 1 W.L.R. 1109; *Gisborne v. Burton* [1989] Q.B. 390.
[27] S.I. 1978 No. 259, Sched. 1, r. 13.
[28] A.H.A. 1986, s.63.
[29] A.H.A. 1986, s.12; for supplementary provisions (factors, disregards, etc.), see Sched. 2.
[30] *Sclater v. Horton* [1954] Q.B. 1; *University College, Oxford v. Durdy* [1982] Ch. 413.
[31] A.H.A. 1986, s.13.
[32] A.H.A. 1986, s.78(1).
[33] *Coates v. Diment* [1951] 1 All E.R. 890; *Parry v. Million Pigs Ltd* (1980) 260 E.G. 281.

not the notice is valid[34]) is usually entitled to compensation for disturbance.[35]

22–125   2. Compensation for improvements. When an agricultural tenant quits his holding at the end of his tenancy, he is entitled to compensation for certain improvements carried out by him, provided he has observed the necessary conditions. Such improvements fall into three main categories. First, there are certain long-term improvements (*e.g.* planting orchards) for which the landlord's consent is required. Secondly, there are other long-term improvements (*e.g.* the erection of buildings) for which either the landlord's consent or the Tribunal's approval is necessary. Thirdly, there are some short-term improvements (*e.g.* the chalking or liming of land) for which neither consent nor approval is needed. The measure of compensation is the increase in value of the holding, or, in the case of a short-term improvement, the value of the improvement to an incoming tenant.[36]

22–126   3. Other compensation. The tenant may claim compensation for any increase in the value of the holding due to his having adopted a more beneficial system of farming than that required by his tenancy agreement, or, if none, than that practised on comparable holdings.[37] He may also be able to claim compensation in respect of a milk quota.[38] The landlord, on the other hand, may recover from a tenant who has quitted the holding compensation in respect of dilapidation or deterioration of the holding, or damage to it caused by failure to farm in accordance with the rules of good husbandry,[39] having due regard to the landlord's contractual obligations[40] and the condition of the property when the tenancy was granted.[41]

22–127   4. Fixed equipment. Compensation apart, a tenant may benefit by being provided with fixed equipment on the holding. In continuation of war-time regulations, the Agriculture Act 1947 gave the Minister of Agriculture, Fisheries and Food substantial powers to enforce efficient farming by owners and tenants alike. Most of these powers disappeared with the Agriculture Act 1958, but there is still power (now under the Agricultural Holdings Act 1986[42]) for an Agricultural Lands Tribunal to direct a landlord to provide, alter or repair fixed equipment on the holding which is needed in order to avoid contravening statutory requirements, *e.g.* for producing clean milk. If the landlord fails to do so, the tenant may do it himself at the landlord's

---

[34] *Kestell v. Langmaid* [1950] 1 K.B. 233.
[35] A.H.A. 1986, ss.60–63.
[36] A.H.A. 1986, ss.64–69, Scheds 7–9.
[37] A.H.A. 1986, s.70.
[38] Agriculture Act 1986, s.13, Sched. 1.
[39] A.H.A. 1986, ss.71–73.
[40] *Barrow Green Estates Co. v. Walker's Executors* [1954] 1 W.L.R. 231.
[41] *Evans v. Jones* [1955] 1 Q.B. 58.
[42] Section 11.

expense. "Fixed equipment" includes buildings, structures affixed to land, and works on land.

Section 3. Dwellings[43]

The protection of private sector residential tenancies began modestly over 75 years ago. The first "Rent Act", the Increase of Rent and Mortgage Interest (War Restrictions) Act 1915, was a mere six pages long; but from it grew a highly complex set of systems laid down in hundreds of pages of detailed legislation and interpreted in thousands of cases. The general pattern of the earlier legislation was that rent control was imposed and expanded in order to meet war-time shortages, and was then gradually attenuated as days of peace brought relief. Since the Second World War, social and political pressures have intervened. The Rent Act 1957 released many tenancies from control, and whilst the ensuing years saw a gradual reversal of that policy of deregulation, the Acts being finally consolidated in the Rent Act 1977, more recent developments have promoted the freedom of the lettings market. **22–128**

Part I of the Housing Act 1988 can be equated to the Rent Act 1957 in that it comprised an attempt to remove rent control from the private sector (to "deregulate"). It sought to phase out the Rent Acts by stipulating that from January 15, 1989 (the date the 1988 Act came into force) new residential lettings would no longer be subject to their control. The Rent Act "regulated" tenancy was replaced by the "assured" tenancy, a form of letting which permits the landlord to charge a commercial rent, whilst at the same time giving the tenant some security in his own home. The Housing Act 1996 confers still greater autonomy on the private sector landlord by providing that, unless the parties agree otherwise, any assured tenancy granted on or after February 28, 1997 will be an assured shorthold tenancy. This form of tenancy, first created in the 1988 Act, enables the landlord to recover possession on giving notice, and thereby denies the tenant any significant security. **22–129**

In this field, dates have always been important, and January 15, 1989 and February 28, 1997 are of central importance. A private sector residential tenancy created before the former date will normally be regulated under the Rent Act 1977; one created between the two dates will normally be assured (unless the specific criteria for a shorthold have been satisfied); and one created on or after the latter date will normally be an assured shorthold tenancy. But these are rules of thumb only. Great care needs to be taken to ensure that the relevant statutory provisions are consulted in each case. **22–130**

The seven different systems of control may broadly be indicated as follows. **22–131**

---

[43] See generally *Megarry on the Rent Acts* (11th ed., 1988).

(1) *Assured tenancies*: tenancies created on or after January 15, 1989, which confer security of tenure and protection as to rent, though only for increases under periodic tenancies.[44]

(2) *Shorthold tenancies*: tenancies created on or after January 15, 1989, which confer no security of tenure but protection as to rent.[45]

(3) *Regulated tenancies*: tenancies created before January 15, 1989, which still confer security of tenure and protection as to rent under the Rent Act 1977, the consolidating Act.[46]

(4) *Agricultural tied cottages*: tenancies or licences held by agricultural tenants which confer protection similar to that given by assured tenancies and give special rights to alternative accommodation.[47]

(5) *Residential long tenancies*: long tenancies at a low rent with protection as to possession and the right to buy the freehold or to be granted a new tenancy.[48]

(6) *Tenancies of flats*: long leases and certain other tenancies of flats with a collective statutory right of pre-emption for the tenants if the landlord proposes to dispose of the building.[49]

(7) *Secure tenancies*: tenancies held from a local authority or other public body which confer protection as to possession (but not rent) and the right to buy the freehold or a long lease at a low rent.[50]

22–132   It will be seen that it is the first three categories which provide the present general system of control, the first two for "new" tenancies and the third for "old". The fourth is narrowly restricted, and the other three are mainly concerned with rights for the tenant to buy the freehold. The seven categories are not all mutually exclusive, and there is some overlap.

A. Assured Tenancies

I. TENANCIES WITHIN PART I OF THE HOUSING ACT 1988

22–133   **1. Introduction.** An assured tenancy is a contractual tenancy upon which Part I of the Housing Act 1988 confers additional security of tenure. Although the parties to the tenancy can agree any rent which they wish, there are statutory restrictions on rent increases under assured periodic tenancies.

---

[44] *Infra.*
[45] *Post*, para. 22–174.
[46] *Post*, para. 22–180.
[47] *Post*, para. 22–218.
[48] *Post*, para. 22–226.
[49] *Post*, para. 22–248.
[50] *Post*, para. 22–262.

2. Definition. Every tenancy under which a dwelling-house is let as a   **22–134**
separate dwelling is an assured tenancy if and so long as (a) the tenant (or each
of the joint tenants) is an individual[51]; (b) the tenant (or at least one of the joint
tenants) occupies the dwelling-house as his only or principal home; and (c) the
tenancy is not excluded from assured tenancy status by express statutory
provision.[52] In particular, tenancies entered into before, or pursuant to a
contract made before, January 15, 1989, cannot be assured tenancies.[53]

(a) "Dwelling-house". A dwelling-house may be a house or a part of a   **22–135**
house.[54] What is structurally a single dwelling-house often contains many
"dwelling-houses" for the purposes of the Act, even if it has not been
physically divided into self-contained flats. Thus one or two rooms, with a
right to share the bathroom and lavatory, may for this purpose constitute a
dwelling-house.

(b) "Let as a separate dwelling". The premises must be "let", so that   **22–136**
although any form of tenancy suffices (even a tenancy at will or at sufferance),
mere licences do not.[55] Whether the premises are let "as" a dwelling depends
upon the use provided for or contemplated by the tenancy agreement, or, in
default, by the *de facto* user at the time.[56] The letting must be as "a" (*i.e.* a
single) dwelling, and not for use as two or more dwellings.[57] Although the
dwelling must be "separate", the tenant who shares certain living accommodation with other occupiers will be protected by the Act as long as he has
exclusive occupation of his own room.[58] If such a tenant shares with the
landlord, however, he is likely to be excluded from protection.[59] Finally, the
premises must be let as a "dwelling", and not, *e.g.*, for business or agricultural
purposes.[60] Premises let partly for business and partly as a residence are
treated as being business premises within Part II of the Landlord and Tenant
Act 1954.[61]

(c) "Occupation as his only or principal home". An assured tenant will lose   **22–137**
his statutory protection (and no longer be assured) if he ceases to occupy the
premises as his home, or, where he has more than one, his principal home.

[51] Lettings to companies cannot be assured tenancies: see, *e.g. Hiller v. United Dairies Ltd* [1934]
1 K.B. 57; *Hilton v. Plustitle Ltd* [1989] 1 W.L.R. 149; *Kaye v. Massbetter Ltd* (1992) 24 H.L.R.
28.
[52] Housing Act 1988, s.1(1).
[53] H.A. 1988, Sched. 1, para. 1. Such tenancies are likely to be regulated under the Rent Acts: see
post, para. 22–180. Note also H.A. 1988, s.38, as amended by Local Government and Housing
Act 1989, s.194(1), Sched. 11.
[54] H.A. 1988, s.45(1).
[55] See *ante*, para. 14–010.
[56] *Wolfe v. Hogan* [1949] 2 K.B. 194; *Russell v. Booker* (1982) 263 E.G. 513.
[57] *Langford Property Co. Ltd v. Goldrich* [1949] 1 K.B. 511; *cf. Kavanagh v. Lyroudias* [1985] 1
All E.R. 560.
[58] H.A. 1988, ss.3, 10.
[59] See *post*, para. 22–143.
[60] It is a matter of construing the contractual purpose: *Andrews v. Brewer* (1997) 30 H.L.R.
203.
[61] L.T.A. 1954, s.23(1); H.A. 1988, Sched. 1, para. 4; see, *e.g. Cheryl Investments Ltd v. Saldanha*
[1978] 1 W.L.R. 1329, *ante*, para. 22–063.

Mere temporary absences are immaterial. However, should the absent tenant lose his *animus revertendi* (intention of returning) or his *corpus possessionis* (a visible indication of his continuing *animus*, such as the presence on the premises of a caretaker, or perhaps furniture), then he will no longer be an assured tenant.[62] A tenant who sub-lets the whole of the premises (even for a relatively short time) is unlikely to preserve continuity of occupation of the premises as his principal home.[63] A tenant who finally departs premises which comprise the matrimonial home,[64] leaving his spouse in occupation, will remain an assured tenant, as the occupation of the spouse will be deemed to be that of the absentee.[65]

22–138   **3. Exceptions.** Certain tenancies which would otherwise be assured tenancies are nevertheless excluded from the protection of the Act, on a variety of grounds.

22–139   *(a) Personal.* In some cases, the exception is personal to the landlord. Thus, a tenancy cannot be assured if the landlord is the Crown or a government department,[66] or a public body such as local authorities, the Commission for the New Towns, urban development corporations, and housing action trusts.[67] While tenancies of "fully mutual" housing associations cannot be assured, tenancies of other housing associations can.[68]

22–140   *(b) Nature of tenancy.* Other exceptions depend on the nature of the tenancy. Thus, a tenancy is not assured if the letting is rent-free, or the rent payable is £1,000 or less per annum in Greater London or £250 or less elsewhere.[69] Nor is a tenancy assured if it was granted in order to confer on the tenant the right to occupy the dwelling-house for a holiday,[70] or if the tenant is pursuing or intends to pursue a course of study provided by a specified educational institution and the tenancy was granted either by that institution or by another such institution or body of persons.[71] A protected or secure tenancy[72] cannot be an assured tenancy.[73]

---

[62] *Brown v. Brash* [1948] 2 K.B. 247; *Tickner v. Hearn* [1960] 1 W.L.R. 1406; *Gofor Investments Ltd v. Roberts* (1975) 29 P. & C.R. 366; *Hampstead Way Investments Ltd v. Lewis-Weare* [1985] 1 W.L.R. 164.

[63] *Ujima Housing Association v. Ansah* (1997) 30 H.L.R. 831.

[64] *Hall v. King* [1988] 1 F.L.R. 376.

[65] Family Law Act 1996, s.30(4); *cf.* post-divorce, *Metropolitan Properties Ltd v. Cronan* (1982) 44 P. & C.R. 1.

[66] H.A. 1988, Sched. 1, para. 11.

[67] H.A. 1988, Sched. 1, para. 10. Tenancies by such public bodies tend to be "secure tenancies", and subject to a distinct code of protection altogether: see *post*, para. 22–262.

[68] H.A. 1988, Sched. 1, para. 10.

[69] H.A. 1988, Sched. 1, para. 3A, a provision which does not apply if the tenancy was granted before April 1, 1990. In such a case, the rent must not exceed two-thirds of the rateable value of the house on March 31, 1990: H.A. 1988, Sched. 1, para. 3B.

[70] H.A. 1988, Sched. 1, para. 9.

[71] H.A. 1988, Sched. 1, para. 8; S.I. 1998 No. 1967.

[72] On which, see *post*, paras 22–183 and 22–262 respectively.

[73] H.A. 1988, Sched. 1, para. 13.

(c) Nature of premises. Other exceptions depend upon the nature and status 22–141
of the premises themselves. Thus tenancies of public houses are excluded,[74]
and few agricultural lettings will be assured tenancies.[75] Normally, where the
main purpose of a letting is the provision of a home for the tenant, any land
"let together with" a dwelling-house is treated as being part of it: but the
tenancy will not be assured if more than two acres of agricultural land are let
together with the house.[76]

(d) High rent or rateable value. The abolition of the domestic rating system 22–142
led to complicated amendments of the exclusion from assured tenancy status
of dwelling-houses with high rateable values.[77] Where the tenancy was
entered into before April 1, 1990, or subsequently in pursuance of a contract
made before that date, then it cannot be assured if the dwelling-house had a
rateable value on March 31, 1990 in excess of £1,500 in Greater London or
£750 elsewhere.[78] However, where the tenancy commenced on or after April
1, 1990, the test is the level of the rent. If the rent payable exceeds £25,000
per annum (wherever the premises are situated), the tenancy cannot be
assured.[79]

(e) Resident landlords. In order to obviate the "social embarrassment" 22–143
which may arise out of "close proximity",[80] Part I of the Housing Act 1988
excludes certain tenancies granted by resident landlords from statutory protection. The term "resident landlord" is used to denote a landlord where the
dwelling that is let forms part of a building, and throughout the tenancy, with
minor qualifications, the landlord for the time being (or one of two or more
joint landlords) has occupied as his only or principal home another dwelling
in the same building.[81] The provisions do not apply to a purpose-built block
of flats[82] unless the dwelling let is part of a flat in the block and the landlord
occupies as his home another dwelling in that flat. Nor does it apply if the
tenant was immediately prior to the letting an assured tenant of the dwelling,
or of another dwelling in the same building.[83]

II. SECURITY OF TENURE

The general law sufficiently protects an ordinary tenant against eviction as 22–144
long as his tenancy exists.[84] But once it has ended, whether by notice to quit,
effluxion of time or otherwise, his dwelling-house is liable to repossession by

---

[74] H.A. 1988, Sched. 1, para. 5.
[75] H.A. 1988, Sched. 1, para. 7. They will normally be subject to either the Agricultural Holdings
Act 1986 or the Agricultural Tenancies Act 1995: see *ante*, para. 22–086.
[76] H.A. 1988, s.2; Sched. 1, para. 6.
[77] References to Rating (Housing) Regulations, S.I. 1990 No. 434.
[78] H.A. 1988, Sched. 1, para. 2A (as amended).
[79] H.A. 1988, Sched. 1, para. 2 (as amended).
[80] *Bardrick v. Haycock* (1976) 31 P. & C.R. 420 at 424, *per* Lord Scarman.
[81] H.A. 1988, Sched. 1, para. 10, and Pt III.
[82] See, *e.g. Barnes v. Gorsuch* (1981) 43 P. & C.R. 294.
[83] H.A. 1988, Sched. 1, para. 10(3), an anti-avoidance device.
[84] See further *ante*, paras 14–200—14–203.

the landlord unless statute otherwise provides. Part I of the Housing Act 1988 gives protection in relation to periodic assured tenancies by rendering the service of a notice to quit ineffective and in relation to fixed-term assured tenancies by imposing a statutory periodic tenancy on the expiry of the term. Although the tenant can terminate an assured tenancy by exercising such rights as the contract confers (*e.g.* by giving notice of the appropriate length), the landlord can recover possession only by obtaining an order of the court on proof of one of the statutory grounds for possession. The distinction between fixed-term tenancy and periodic tenancy is central to the machinery of the Act.

22–145   **1. Fixed-term tenancy.** For the purpose of the 1988 Act, a fixed-term tenancy is any tenancy other than a periodic tenancy.[85] The court cannot make an order for possession of a dwelling-house currently being let on a fixed-term assured tenancy unless:

> (a)   the landlord proves one of Grounds 2, 8 and 10 to 15 in Schedule 2 to the Act[85a]; and
>
> (b)   the terms of the tenancy make provision for it to be brought to an end on the ground in question.[86]

The landlord may terminate an assured fixed-term tenancy by exercising a power reserved in the lease to determine the tenancy in certain circumstances (as under a break clause, though not a proviso for re-entry for breach of covenant[87]), but this will not normally entitle the landlord to possession.[88] On termination of an assured fixed-term tenancy otherwise than by court order or by the tenant's action, the tenant's right to possession will be preserved under a periodic tenancy arising by virtue of statute: a statutory periodic tenancy.[89]

22–146   **2. Periodic tenancy.** An assured periodic tenancy, whether it be contractual (*i.e.* where the parties initially agreed upon a periodic tenancy) or statutory, cannot be brought to an end by the landlord except by obtaining an order of the court.[90] A court order can only be obtained on proof of one of Grounds 1 to 17 set out in Schedule 2 to the Act.[91]

---

[85] H.A. 1988, s.45(1).
[85a] See *post*, paras 22–151—22–166.
[86] H.A. 1988, s.7(6).
[87] H.A. 1988, s.45(4).
[88] H.A. 1988, s.5(1).
[89] H.A. 1988, s.5(2), (3). See also s.6, which contains the machinery whereby the terms of a statutory periodic tenancy other than rent can be varied.
[90] H.A. 1988, s.5(1).
[91] H.A. 1988, s.7(1): see *post*, paras 22–150–22–168. The rights of a mortgagee to bring possession proceedings are expressly preserved by this provision.

3. Grounds for possession. Proof of a ground for possession is therefore **22–147** essential, whether the assured tenancy is fixed-term or periodic. The landlord and tenant cannot contract out of the protection given by the Act.[92] Unless the tenant voluntarily gives notice, surrenders his interest, or ceases to be an assured tenant altogether (*e.g.* by ceasing to occupy the house as his principal home), the landlord must seek a court order. However, the assured tenant's security does not prevent the recovery of possession by local authorities seeking to exercise their public law powers,[93] or by the tenant's mortgagees seeking to exercise their contractual or statutory powers.[94]

There are two kinds of ground for possession. On proof of a "mandatory **22–148** ground" (Grounds 1 to 8), the court must make a possession order, and it has limited flexibility in stipulating the time when the tenant must leave. On proof of a "discretionary ground" (Grounds 9 to 17), the court may make a possession order if it considers it reasonable to do so. Should the court decide to make an order on a discretionary ground, it has a wide discretion to stay or suspend possession, or postpone the date for delivering up possession.

It is an implied term of every assured periodic tenancy[95] that the tenant shall not assign, in whole or in part, or sub-let or part with possession of the whole or any part of the dwelling-house without the consent of the landlord.[96] If a dwelling-house is lawfully sub-let[97] by an assured tenant, the head landlord who recovers possession against him will remain bound by the interest of the sub-tenant, the sub-tenant becoming the assured tenant of the head landlord.[98] In such circumstances, the landlord will have to prove a ground for possession as against any other assured tenant.

(a) Mandatory grounds. If the landlord establishes a mandatory ground, the **22–149** court must order possession, whether or not it is reasonable to do so.[99] The court cannot postpone the date for possession for more than 14 days, or six weeks if "exceptional hardship" would otherwise be caused.[1] The grounds are as follows.[2]

GROUND 1: OWNER–OCCUPIER. This ground comprises two discrete **22–150** alternatives:

---

[92] H.A. 1988, s.5(5).
[93] See, *e.g.* H.A. 1985, s.612.
[94] Reserved by H.A. 1988, s.7(1).
[95] Save where express prohibition is made, or a premium is required to be paid on the grant or renewal of the tenancy: H.A. 1988, s.15(3).
[96] H.A. 1988, s.15(1). The landlord need not have reasonable grounds for withholding consent, unless the tenancy expressly indicates otherwise: H.A. 1988, s.15(2).
[97] This will include sub-leases where the head landlord has waived the breach of covenant which they occasioned: see, *e.g. Oak Property Co. Ltd v. Chapman* [1947] K.B. 886.
[98] Unless the tenancy is precluded from being an assured tenancy by Schedule 1 to the Housing Act 1988. See H.A. 1988, s.18(1), (2).
[99] H.A. 1988, s.7(3).
[1] H.A. 1980, s.89. See also the accelerated possession procedure: *post*, para. 22–169.
[2] See generally H.A. 1988, Sched. 2.

(i) the landlord[3] who is now seeking possession occupied the dwelling-house as his only or principal home at some time before the beginning of the tenancy. It is not necessary for the landlord to show an intention to resume occupation, so that Ground 1 can be used to obtain vacant possession merely with a view to sale; or

(ii) the landlord[4] who is now seeking possession requires the dwelling-house as his or his spouse's only or principal home. In this case, neither the landlord nor any predecessor of his must have become landlord by acquiring the reversion for money or money's worth.[5]

Whenever (i) or (ii) above is relied upon, the landlord must have given notice to the tenant, not later than the beginning of the tenancy, that possession might be recovered under this ground. The court has power to dispense with this requirement of prior written notice where it is of opinion that it is just and equitable to do so.[6]

22–151   GROUND 2: MORTGAGEE SEEKING POSSESSION. The dwelling-house is subject to a mortgage granted before the beginning of the tenancy, and the mortgagee, being entitled to exercise a power of sale conferred by the mortgage or by statute, requires possession of the house for the purpose of disposing of it with vacant possession in exercise of that power. As long as notice was given as under Ground 1 (or the court dispenses with such notice), then the court must order possession.

22–152   GROUND 3: SHORT LETTING OF HOLIDAY HOME. The tenancy was granted for a fixed term not exceeding eight months, and at some time within the 12 months prior to the letting, the dwelling was occupied under a right to occupy it for a holiday. The landlord must have given written notice, not later than the beginning of the tenancy, that possession might be recovered under this ground. The court has no apparent power to dispense with notice.

22–153   GROUND 4: SHORT LETTING OF STUDENT RESIDENCE. The tenancy was granted for a fixed term not exceeding 12 months, and at some time within the 12 months previous to the letting the dwelling was let on a tenancy within paragraph 8 of Schedule 1 to the 1988 Act (*i.e.* a letting to a student by a specified educational institution). The landlord must have given written notice, not later than the beginning of the tenancy, that possession might be recovered under this ground, the court having no power to dispense with this requirement.

---

[3] Or, in the case of joint landlords seeking possession, one of them.
[4] See n. 3 *ante.*
[5] See *ante*, para. 22–080.
[6] For guidelines on the use of such a dispensation power, see *Bradshaw v. Baldwin-Wiseman* (1985) 49 P. & C.R. 382 at 388. Giving oral notice at the time of grant may be an important factor, but it is not a prerequisite to exercising the power of dispensation: *Boyle v. Verrall* [1997] 1 E.G.L.R. 25.

GROUND 5: MINISTER OF RELIGION. The dwelling is held for the purpose of   **22–154**
being available for occupation by a minister of religion as a residence from
which to perform the duties of his office, and the dwelling is now required for
this purpose. As with Grounds 3 and 4, prior written notice must have been
given to the tenant.

GROUND 6: DEMOLITION OR RECONSTRUCTION. The landlord seeking posses-   **22–155**
sion[7] intends to demolish or reconstruct the whole or a substantial part of the
dwelling-house, or to carry out substantial works on the dwelling-house or any
part thereof or any building of which it forms part, and all the following
conditions are fulfilled:

(a)   the work cannot reasonably be carried out without the tenant giving
      up possession, for one of four reasons (the tenant is not willing to
      agree to a variation of the terms of his tenancy; the nature of the
      work is such that no such variation is practicable; the tenant is not
      willing to accept an assured tenancy of a reduced part of the
      dwelling so that the landlord could then carry out the works; or the
      nature of the works is such that no such tenancy of a reduced part is
      practicable); and

(b)   either the landlord seeking possession acquired his interest in the
      dwelling before the grant of the tenancy, or, if he acquired his
      interest subsequently, such acquisition was not for money or
      money's worth; and

(c)   the assured tenancy did not arise by virtue of the succession provi-
      sions of the Rent Act 1977[8] or the Rent (Agriculture) Act 1976.[9]

Proof of the landlord's intention will depend on the same factors as the like
ground contained in the business tenancy code, on which this provision was
modelled.[10]

GROUND 7: DEATH OF PERIODIC TENANT. Where an assured periodic tenancy   **22–156**
devolves by will or on intestacy (and not by statute[11]), the landlord has a
12-month period of grace during which he can decide whether he wishes to
recover possession. If in that period (which runs from the date of the death, or,
if the court so orders, from the date the landlord became aware of the death)
the landlord seeks possession, the court must make the order.

---

[7] Or, if that landlord is a registered social landlord or a charitable housing trust, a superior
landlord.
[8] See *post*, para. 22–188.
[9] See *post*, para. 22–220.
[10] L.T.A. 1954, s.30(1)(f); see *ante*, para. 22–081.
[11] H.A. 1988, s.17: see *post*, para. 22–170.

22–157   GROUND 8: NON-PAYMENT OF RENT. At least two months' rent[12] is lawfully due but unpaid both at the date of the service of the notice seeking possession[13] and at the date of the hearing. If the landlord is unable to prove Ground 8, he may choose to claim possession on discretionary Grounds 10 or 11 below.

22–158   *(b) Discretionary grounds.* If the overriding requirement of reasonableness is satisfied, the court may make an order for possession in the following cases.[14] There is a wide discretion to adjourn the proceedings, or to stay, suspend, or postpone possession, which, when exercised, will often be subject to terms (*e.g.* as to payment of rent arrears).[15]

22–159   GROUND 9: SUITABLE ALTERNATIVE ACCOMMODATION.[16] Suitable alternative accommodation is available for the tenant, or will be when the order for possession takes effect. The accommodation must be either on an assured tenancy (neither a shorthold nor a tenancy in respect of which notices under Grounds 1 to 5 have been served) or on terms which afford reasonably equivalent security to the tenant. In addition, it must be reasonably suitable to the needs of the tenant and his family as regards proximity to place of work and either similar as regards rental and extent to houses provided in the neighbourhood by a local housing authority for those with similar needs as regards extent, or else reasonably suitable to the tenant's means and his and his family's needs as regards extent and character. If furniture has been provided, furniture must be provided in the alternative accommodation which either is similar or is reasonably suitable to the needs of the tenant and his family. But the accommodation need not be as good, or as cheap,[17] as the existing accommodation, and it may even consist of part of it[18]: the question is whether it is "reasonably suitable", not "as suitable".[19] A certificate of the local housing authority that it will provide suitable alternative accommodation for the tenant by a specified date is conclusive.[20]

22–160   GROUND 10: NON-PAYMENT OF RENT. Some rent lawfully due from the tenant is unpaid on the date proceedings are begun, and was also in arrears at the date the landlord served the notice seeking possession[21] (save where the court dispenses with service of such a notice).

---

[12] For the precise method of calculating the rent arrears required, see H.A. 1988, Sched. 2, Ground 8, as amended by H.A. 1996, s.101.

[13] See *post*, para. 22–169, and for the effect of non-compliance, *Mountain v. Hastings* (1993) 25 H.L.R. 427.

[14] H.A. 1988, s.7(4).

[15] H.A. 1988, s.9.

[16] See further H.A. 1988, Sched. 2, Pt III.

[17] *Cresswell v. Hodgson* [1951] 2 K.B. 92.

[18] *Mykolyshyn v. Noah* [1970] 1 W.L.R. 1271.

[19] *Warren v. Austin* [1947] 2 All E.R. 185 at 188.

[20] H.A. 1988, Sched. 2, Pt III, para. 1.

[21] See *post*, para. 22–169.

GROUND 11: PERSISTENT DELAY IN PAYMENT OF RENT. The tenant has persis- **22–161**
tently delayed in paying rent which has become lawfully due. It does not
matter that no rent is in arrear at the date proceedings are begun or heard: the
object is to give the court power to remove a persistent defaulter.

GROUND 12: BREACH OF OBLIGATION. Any obligation of the tenancy (other **22–162**
than one related to the payment of rent) has been broken or not performed.

GROUND 13: DETERIORATION OF DWELLING-HOUSE. The tenant, or any other **22–163**
person residing in the dwelling-house, is responsible, through acts of waste,
neglect, or default, for the deterioration of the condition of the dwelling or any
of the common parts. Where the waste, neglect or default was that of a lodger
or sub-tenant of his, the tenant must have failed to take reasonable steps to
remove him.

GROUND 14[22]: NUISANCE. The tenant or any person residing in or visiting **22–164**
the dwelling-house has been guilty of conduct causing or likely to cause a
nuisance or annoyance to a person residing, visiting, or otherwise engaging in
a lawful activity in the locality, or has been convicted either of using the
dwelling-house, or allowing it to be used, for immoral or illegal purposes[23] or
of an arrestable offence committed in, or in the locality of, the dwelling-
house.

GROUND 14A[24]: DOMESTIC VIOLENCE. The dwelling-house was occupied by **22–165**
a married couple or a couple living together as husband and wife, and one
partner has left the house, and is unlikely to return because of violence or
threats of violence by the other towards that partner or a member of that
partner's family residing with that partner. This ground may only be invoked
by a landlord who is a registered social landlord[25] or a charitable housing
trust.[26]

GROUND 15: DETERIORATION OF FURNITURE. The tenant or any other person **22–166**
residing with him is responsible, through ill-treatment, for the deterioration of
the condition of furniture provided under the tenancy. As with Ground 13
above, the tenant must have failed to take reasonable steps for the removal of
such other person who is a lodger or sub-tenant.

GROUND 16: EMPLOYEES' LETTINGS. The dwelling was let to the tenant in **22–167**
consequence of his employment by the landlord seeking possession or a
previous landlord, and the tenant has ceased to be in that employment.

---

[22] As amended by H.A. 1996, s.148.
[23] *S. Schneiders & Sons v. Abrahams* [1925] 1 K.B. 301; *Abrahams v. Wilson* [1971] Q.B. 88.
[24] Added by H.A. 1996, s.149. There are additional notice requirements in relation to this ground:
see H.A. 1996, s.150, amending H.A. 1988, s.8.
[25] Defined in H.A. 1996, Pt I, Chap. I.
[26] Defined as a housing trust (see Housing Associations Act 1985, s.2) which is a charity (see
generally Charities Act 1993).

22–168   GROUND 17[27]: FALSE STATEMENT BY TENANT. The landlord was induced to grant the tenancy by a false statement made knowingly or recklessly by the tenant (that tenant being the current tenant, or one of them) or a person acting at the tenant's instigation.

22–169   **4. Possession proceedings.**[28] Before beginning proceedings, the landlord must serve a notice in prescribed form[29] on the tenant informing him that he intends to bring possession proceedings on one or more grounds specified in the notice, and that those proceedings will not begin earlier than a date specified in the notice. The minimum notice is two weeks (applicable where possession is to be sought on Grounds 3, 4, 8, and 10 to 15 inclusive): otherwise the notice must be no less than two months, and, in the case of a periodic tenancy requiring a longer notice, must be a notice of that length. The court has a discretion to dispense with service of the notice where it considers it just and equitable to do so,[30] but this power cannot be exercised where the landlord seeks to recover possession on Ground 8. There is an "accelerated" procedure for the recovery of possession which may be invoked where the landlord is proceeding on the basis of Grounds 1, 3, 4, or 5.[31]

22–170   **5. Succession to assured tenancies.** Where an assured tenant has a fixed-term tenancy, the term will pass on the death of the tenant to the person entitled under the tenant's will or intestacy.[32] Where the assured tenancy is periodic, however, succession provisions in the 1988 Act[33] take precedence over the will or the intestacy rules. By these provisions, an assured periodic tenancy will vest in the tenant's "spouse" (defined so as to include a person living with the tenant as his or her wife or husband) on his death, provided three conditions are satisfied:

(1) the tenant was the sole tenant. If the tenancy was held jointly with another or others, then survivorship will operate;

(2) the spouse was occupying the dwelling as his only or principal home immediately before the death of the tenant; and

(3) the tenant was not himself a "successor". He will be a successor for these purposes if the tenancy became vested in him by virtue of the Rent Act 1977 or the Housing Act 1988 under the will or on the intestacy of a previous tenant, or by right of survivorship. It is

---

[27] Added by H.A. 1996, s.102.
[28] H.A. 1988, s.8, as amended by H.A. 1996, s.151.
[29] S.I. 1997 No. 194, Form 3; see *Mountain v. Hastings* (1993) 25 H.L.R. 427; *Marath v. MacGillivray* (1996) 28 H.L.R. 484.
[30] See *Kelsey Housing Association v. King* (1995) 28 H.L.R. 270.
[31] S.I. 1993 No. 2175.
[32] See *ante*, Chap. 11.
[33] H.A. 1988, s.17.

immaterial that the landlord has granted a new tenancy to him since the succession took place.

6. Protection as to rent. The only jurisdiction enjoyed by rent assessment **22–171** committees over assured tenancies (excluding assured shorthold tenancies[34]) concerns rent increases in periodic tenancies. This jurisdiction is essential for the protection of the landlord as much as the tenant. The landlord is in a weak negotiating position, as he cannot effectively terminate an assured periodic tenancy by service of a notice to quit when faced by a tenant who is unwilling to accept a rent increase. The landlord may have been sufficiently perspicacious to insert a rent review clause into the tenancy agreement: in so far as such a provision remains binding on the tenant, the statutory procedure will not apply.[35]

The procedure provided by the 1988 Act[36] requires the landlord to serve **22–172** notice in prescribed form[37] on the tenant proposing a new rent to take effect at the beginning of a new period of the tenancy. Save where the tenancy is yearly, or based on periods of less than a month (notices of six months and one month are then respectively required), the landlord must give notice no shorter than the length of a period of the tenancy. Where the periodic tenancy is contractual, a landlord cannot attempt to obtain an increased rent in the first year of the tenancy. Where the periodic tenancy is statutory (*i.e.* taking effect following expiry of a fixed term), there is no such restriction.

If the tenant wishes to object to the rent proposed, he refers the notice to the **22–173** rent assessment committee by an application in prescribed form.[38] The committee then determines the rent at which they consider the dwelling-house might reasonably be expected to be let on the open market by a willing landlord under an assured tenancy, disregarding such factors as the tenancy being granted to a sitting tenant, increases in the value of the dwelling attributable to certain tenant's improvements, and reductions in its value attributable to the tenant's failure to comply with the terms of the tenancy.[39] The rent determined will then become the rent payable under the tenancy with effect from the date specified in the landlord's notice, although the committee has a discretion to set a later date where undue hardship would be caused to the tenant.[40] A rent assessment committee has jurisdiction to set a rent above

---

[34] See *post*, para. 22–179.

[35] H.A. 1988, s.13(1)(b).

[36] H.A. 1988, s.13. The landlord was also able, for a year commencing April 1, 1993, to propose an increased rent to take account of the assured tenant's liability to make payments to the landlord in respect of council tax: H.A. 1988, ss.14A, 14B, added by S.I. 1993 No. 651.

[37] S.I. 1997 No. 194, Form 4.

[38] S.I. 1997 No. 194, Form 5. For rent assessment committee regulations, see S.I. 1971 No. 1065, as amended by, *inter alia*, S.I. 1988, No. 2200.

[39] H.A. 1988, s.14; *cf.* disrepair for which the tenant's predecessor was responsible: *N. & D. (London) Ltd v. Gadsdon* [1992] 1 E.G.L.R. 112.

[40] H.A. 1988, s.14(7).

the £25,000 limit for assured tenancies, although the effect of such a determination will be to render the tenancy no longer assured.[41]

B. Shorthold Tenancies

22–174   In order to encourage the grant of residential tenancies, the Housing Act 1980 permitted landlords to grant, on fulfilling numerous tightly prescribed conditions, a "protected shorthold tenancy". This gave the tenant the same rent control as any other Rent Act regulated tenant, but without the security of tenure. In essence, on termination of the contractual tenancy, the landlord of a protected shorthold tenant could obtain possession as of right. Part I of the Housing Act 1988 phased out the protected shorthold tenancy in much the same way as other regulated tenancies, replacing it in the new regime with the assured shorthold tenancy. Devoid of statutory security of tenure, the assured shorthold tenant has, at least in theory, a little more protection as to rent than the "standard" (*i.e.* non-shorthold) assured tenant. Until the Housing Act 1996, the landlord had to satisfy relatively strict conditions to create an effective shorthold, most significantly by serving a notice on the tenant informing him of his occupational status. But now the assured shorthold tenancy has become the default tenancy. Unless the parties expressly contract otherwise (or certain exceptions apply) any assured tenancy entered into on or after February 28, 1997 will be an assured shorthold.

22–175   **1. Definition.** There are several ways whereby an assured shorthold tenancy may have been created.

(1) A grant of a new tenancy to a *protected* shorthold tenant[42] on or after January 15, 1989 will have conferred an assured shorthold tenancy on the tenant, even though no notice was served on him to that effect.[43]

(2) An assured tenancy entered into before February 28, 1997, created an assured shorthold tenancy if it satisfied the following conditions[44]:

(i) it was a fixed-term tenancy granted for a term certain of not less than six months[45];

(ii) it gave the landlord no power to determine the tenancy at any time earlier than six months from the beginning of the tenancy

---

[41] *R. v. London Rent Assessment Panel, ex p. Cadogan Estates Ltd* [1997] 2 E.G.L.R. 134.

[42] Or a statutory tenant to whom R.A. 1977, Case 19 applies, *i.e.* a former protected shorthold tenant holding over following expiry of his fixed term.

[43] H.A. 1988, s.34(3): unless before the new tenancy began the landlord served notice on the tenant that it was not to be a shorthold.

[44] H.A. 1988, s.20(1)–(3).

[45] Despite the word "shorthold", there is no maximum duration. A tenancy granted on December 18, 1990 expiring on June 17, 1991, is a term of not less than six months: *Bedding v. McCarthy* (1993) 27 H.L.R. 103.

(otherwise than by means of re-entry or forfeiture for breach of covenant[46]);

(iii) before the tenancy began, a notice in prescribed form[47] was served by the landlord on the tenant stating that the tenancy was to be an assured shorthold tenancy; and

(iv) the grant was not made to an existing standard assured tenant of the dwelling.

The grant of a new tenancy to an existing assured shorthold tenant takes effect as an assured shorthold tenancy, whether or not the above conditions or any of them are satisfied.[48]

(3) Where any assured tenancy is entered into on or after February 28, 1997 (otherwise than pursuant to a contract made before that date) it will be an assured shorthold tenancy unless it falls within one of a number of statutory exceptions[49]:

(i) the landlord served a notice on the tenant before the tenancy was entered into stating that the tenancy was not to be an assured shorthold;

(ii) the landlord served a notice on the tenant after it was entered into stating that the tenancy was no longer to be an assured shorthold[50];

(iii) the tenancy itself contains provision to the effect that the tenancy is not an assured shorthold;

(iv) the assured tenancy has arisen by succession to a Rent Act regulated tenancy (other than a protected shorthold or a tenancy to which Case 19 of the 1977 Act applies);

(v) the tenancy became assured on ceasing to be a secure tenancy;

(vi) the assured tenancy arose by virtue of Schedule 10 to the Local Government and Housing Act 1989[51];

(vii) the assured tenancy was granted to an existing assured tenant, unless the tenant serves notice in prescribed form[52] on the landlord before the tenancy is entered into stating that the

---

[46] See H.A. 1988, s.45(4).

[47] S.I. 1988 No. 2203, Form 7, as amended by S.I. 1990 No. 1532 and S.I. 1993 No. 654 (all now revoked by S.I. 1997 No. 194, r. 4, with savings for notices served before February 28, 1997). Where, notwithstanding an obvious or evident error in the notice, a reasonable recipient would be left in no reasonable doubt as to its terms, the notice will be valid: *York v. Casey* [1998] 2 E.G.L.R. 25, applying *Mannai Investment Co. Ltd v. Eagle Star Life Assurance Co. Ltd* [1997] A.C. 749.

[48] H.A. 1988, s.20(4): but not if the landlord serves notice on the tenant that his new tenancy is not a shorthold: s.20(5).

[49] H.A. 1988, s.19A, inserted by H.A. 1996, s.96(1). The exceptions are listed in H.A. 1988, Sched. 2A, inserted by H.A. 1996, Sched. 7.

[50] Such a notice cannot prejudice the rights of a tenant who has an application for rent reduction pending before a rent assessment committee: H.A. 1988, s.22(5A), inserted by H.A. 1996, Sched. 8, para. 2(6).

[51] See *post*, para. 22–229.

[52] S.I. 1997 No. 194, Form 8.

tenancy is to be an assured shorthold. Thus a landlord cannot by the simple expedient of granting a new tenancy to a non-shorthold tenant on or after February 28, 1997, create an assured shorthold tenancy;

(viii) the tenancy comes into being when a non-shorthold tenancy comes to an end (*i.e.* as a statutory periodic tenancy); and

(ix) certain assured agricultural occupancies.

22–176   **2. Security of tenure.** On expiry of the fixed term, the assured shorthold tenant on whom no notice seeking possession has been served will hold over as statutory periodic tenant. This statutory periodic tenancy is itself an assured shorthold tenancy.[53] The assured shorthold tenant has no statutory right to terminate the tenancy by notice during the fixed term, and thus his right to terminate prematurely will depend on the parties' agreement.

22–177   The landlord who wishes to recover possession of a dwelling let on assured shorthold tenancy may use any of the grounds for possession relevant to assured tenancies, and where the fixed term is still current, he will be restricted to such grounds.[54] Once the fixed term has expired, however, he can recover possession as of right. The landlord must serve a notice in writing on the tenant stating that he requires possession of the dwelling.[55] It does not appear that the notice has to take any particular form (none is prescribed) nor need it comply with the statutory requirements for a "notice seeking possession".[56] The minimum period of notice is two months, and where at the time of service the tenant is already holding over as a statutory periodic tenant, the date of possession must not be earlier than the earliest day on which a periodic tenancy of that length could be terminated under the general law.[57] It is not necessary for the notice to record the exact date on which possession is to be given up provided that the tenant knows or can easily ascertain it from the information given.[58] Nor does it have to show the date on which it was served.[59] Landlords seeking to recover possession from most assured shorthold tenants may invoke an accelerated form of proceedings for possession.[60]

22–178   There are obvious differences which arise from the methods of creation of assured shorthold tenancies. An assured shorthold tenant created under (3) above has the statutory right to require the landlord to provide him with a written statement of certain important terms of the tenancy (the commencement date, the rent, the dates for payment, any rent review, and the length of

---

[53] H.A. 1988, ss.5(2), 20(4).
[54] Only a limited number are available during the currency of the fixed term: H.A. 1988, s.7(6).
[55] H.A. 1988, s.21(1), as amended by H.A. 1996, s.98.
[56] *Panayi v. Roberts* (1993) 25 H.L.R. 421.
[57] H.A. 1988, s.21(4), as amended by H.A. 1996, s.98. For the "general law", see *ante*, paras 14–068, 14–073.
[58] *Lower Street Properties Ltd v. Jones* (1996) 28 H.L.R. 877.
[59] *ibid.*
[60] S.I. 1993 No. 2175.

a fixed term) which are not evidenced in writing.[61] Such a tenant may hold on periodic tenancy from the outset. In such a case, the court may not make a possession order to take effect earlier than six months from the beginning of the tenancy. Where the tenancy has come into being when an earlier assured shorthold tenancy has ended (*e.g.* when a fixed term expires, and the tenant holds over as a statutory periodic tenant), this six-month period dates from the commencement of the earlier tenancy.[62]

3. Protection as to rent. Unlike other assured tenants, the assured short-   **22–179** hold tenant can refer (by application in prescribed form[63]) the amount of the rent to a rent assessment committee even though he has agreed that rent with the landlord.[64] The application must be made within the fixed term of an assured shorthold tenancy falling within (2) above,[64a] or within six months of the beginning of an assured shorthold tenancy within (3).[65] The committee is to determine the rent which the landlord might reasonably be expected to obtain under the assured shorthold tenancy.[66] If the rent agreed by the parties exceeds the rent so determined, the excess is irrecoverable from the tenant.[67] However, the committee must not intervene unless they consider:

    (i) that there is a significant number of similar dwelling-houses in the locality let on assured tenancies; and

    (ii) that the rent payable is significantly higher than the rent which the landlord might reasonably be expected to obtain under the tenancy.[68]

The Secretary of State has power to disapply the rent reduction provisions in such cases, areas or circumstances as he specifies by order.[69]

C. Regulated Tenancies

I. TENANCIES WITHIN THE RENT ACTS

1. Definition. Although legislation has considerably reduced the signifi-   **22–180** cance of the Rent Acts in recent years, there remain many tenancies which fall within their ambit. The major attributes of a Rent Act regulated tenancy are protection as to both rent and possession. In addition, there is a statutory bar on premiums. The residual form of statutory protection pursuant to a "restricted contract" (for certain residential occupiers who did not qualify as

---

[61] H.A. 1988, s.20A, inserted by H.A. 1996, s.97.
[62] H.A. 1988, s.21(5)–(7), inserted by H.A. 1996, s.99.
[63] S.I. 1997 No. 194, Form 6.
[64] H.A. 1988, s.22.
[64a] See para. 22–175.
[65] See para. 22–175. H.A. 1988, s.22(2), as amended by H.A. 1996, s.100.
[66] H.A. 1988, s.22(1).
[67] H.A. 1988, s.22(4).
[68] H.A. 1988, s.22(3).
[69] H.A. 1988, s.23.

regulated tenants) has now been almost entirely phased out.[70] Control of certain "regulated mortgages" is also virtually obsolete.[71]

22–181 There are two categories of "regulated tenancy". The "protected tenancy" is an ordinary contractual tenancy under which the tenancy itself, whilst it continues, protects the tenant's possession, the 1977 Act providing rent control. The "statutory tenancy", on the other hand, is a creature of statutory implication, arising when a protected tenancy ends, and based upon the tenant's continued occupation of the dwelling as his residence. The 1977 Act prevents the statutory tenant from being evicted save by an order of the court on specified grounds, as well as providing control of the rent.

22–182 As a result of Part I of the Housing Act 1988, contractual tenancies entered into on or after January 15, 1989 cannot, subject to exceptions, be protected tenancies.[72] The 1977 Act continues to apply to those tenancies which remain protected, and on the termination of such a protected tenancy, a statutory tenancy will arise as before. The exceptional circumstances in which tenancies may still be "protected" although entered into on or after the above date are as follows.[73]

> (i) Where a contract was made prior to January 15, 1989, for a tenancy beginning on or after that date.

> (ii) Where a new tenancy is entered into by a landlord with an existing protected or statutory tenant of his. Thus, a landlord cannot, merely by granting new tenancies to his Rent Act regulated tenants, deprive them of Rent Act protection.

> (iii) If the landlord obtains possession of a dwelling held on a protected or statutory tenancy by virtue of suitable alternative accommodation being provided for the tenant,[74] the court may order, if it decides that an assured tenancy under the 1988 Act would not give the tenant the required security, that the new accommodation is to be held on a protected tenancy.

> (iv) Certain tenancies where the landlord was at the time of grant a new town corporation.[75]

22–183 **2. Protected tenancies.** Every tenancy under which a dwelling-house (which may be a house or a part of a house) is let as a separate dwelling is a protected tenancy[76] unless:

---

[70] H.A. 1988, s.36. For the effect of restricted contract protection, see the 5th edition of this book, at p. 1118.

[71] See the 5th edition of this book, at p. 1118.

[72] H.A. 1988, s.34.

[73] H.A. 1988, s.34(1).

[74] R.A. 1977, s.98(1)(a); see *post*, para. 22–200.

[75] See further H.A. 1988, ss.34(1)(d), 38(4).

[76] R.A. 1977, s.1. For interpretation of the terminology of this provision, see para. 22–134.

(a) subject to the above exceptions, it is entered into on or after January 15, 1989; or

(b) it falls within one of the exceptions listed in the 1977 Act.[77]

The 1977 Act exceptions are similar, although not identical, to those relevant to assured tenancies.[78] Thus lettings by the Crown or government departments, or public bodies such as local authorities, are excluded, as are lettings at a low rent, holiday lets, lettings by resident landlords, and accommodation provided by educational institutions for their students. Tenancies of most housing associations and housing cooperatives are outside Rent Act protection.[79] Further exclusions are agricultural holdings occupied by the farmer, farm business tenancies, public houses and Church of England parsonage houses. A tenancy where the rent includes payments in respect of board or attendance cannot be a protected tenancy, provided that in the case of attendance the amount of rent attributable to it, having regard to its value to the tenant, forms a "substantial part" of the whole rent.[80]

3. Property value. There have been many changes in the levels of rateable value which sufficed to exclude a dwelling from Rent Act control,[81] and these, together with the necessary reforms following the abolition of the domestic rating system in 1990, have contrived to make the exercise of determining whether a given dwelling is subject to the protection of the Acts a difficult one. Tenancies entered into on or after April 1, 1990 (unlikely to be protected in any event) will be excluded if the rent payable exceeds £25,000 per annum.[82] Tenancies entered into prior to that date[83] will not be protected if on "the appropriate day" (*i.e.* the date on which the rateable value for the dwelling was first shown in the valuation list, or, if that was before March 23, 1965, that date[84]) and also on certain subsequent dates, the rateable value exceeded certain amounts.[85]

22–184

II. SECURITY OF TENURE

Unlike the assured tenancy, which the landlord cannot unilaterally terminate without an order of the court, the protected tenancy is terminable by the

22–185

---

[77] R.A. 1977, ss.4–16A.

[78] See *ante*, para. 22–138.

[79] See R.A. 1977, s.15. However, a form of rent control is provided for many such tenancies in R.A. 1977, Part VI.

[80] R.A. 1977, s.7; *Palser v. Grinling* [1948] A.C. 291; *Otter v. Norman* [1989] A.C. 129.

[81] See the 4th edition of this book, pp. 1130–32; 5th edition, p. 1108.

[82] R.A. 1977, s.4(4)–(7), as inserted by the References to Rating (Housing) Regulations 1990, (S.I. 1990 No. 434).

[83] Or entered into on or after April 1, 1990 pursuant to a contract made before that date, the dwelling-house having a rateable value on March 31, 1990.

[84] R.A. 1977, s.25(3).

[85] R.A. 1977, s.4(1)–(3), as amended by S.I. 1990 No. 434. If the appropriate day was before March 22, 1973, the amounts are £200 for the appropriate day, £300 for March 22, 1973, and £750 for April 1, 1973. If the appropriate day was between March 21 and April 1, 1973, the amounts are £300 for the appropriate day and £750 for April 1, 1973. If the appropriate day was after March 31, 1973, the amount is £750 for the appropriate day. In each case these figures are doubled for dwellings in Greater London.

landlord exercising such rights reserved to him under the lease, *e.g.* notice to quit, or forfeiture for breach of covenant. However, the termination of the protected tenancy will not entitle the landlord to repossess the premises. The Rent Act 1977 provides protection when a protected tenancy ends by prohibiting the court from making an order for possession except on specified grounds, and by giving the tenant the right to remain in possession as a "statutory tenant" despite the termination of his contractual tenancy.

22–186 **1. Statutory tenancy.** A statutory tenancy is the right of a protected tenant[86] who occupies the dwelling as his residence when the contractual tenancy ends to remain in possession under the Act, despite the termination of his contractual tenancy.[87] He holds on all the terms of the contractual tenancy that are not inconsistent with the Act,[88] unless and until the court makes an order for possession against him. A statutory tenancy is not really a tenancy at all, in the common law sense of the word: the tenant has no estate or interest in the land, but instead a mere personal right of occupation which has been termed a "status of irremovability".[89] The tenant cannot dispose of his interest by assignment or by will,[90] and it will not vest in his trustee in bankruptcy.[91] However, the tenant has a limited statutory power, exercisable only with the landlord's consent, to substitute another tenant in his place without thereby creating another contractual tenancy,[92] and the court has power to order the transfer of a statutory tenancy in matrimonial proceedings.[93]

22–187 **2. Determination.** A statutory tenancy will cease to exist[94] if the tenant ceases to occupy the premises as his home,[95] or as one of his homes.[96] If he has two or more homes, it is not necessary for the dwelling in question to be his principal home.[97] A protected or statutory tenancy may also be determined by a housing authority in the exercise of its public law powers,[98] or by the exercise of a mortgagee's contractual or statutory powers.[99]

---

[86] Including one of two or more joint tenants: *Lloyd v. Sadler* [1978] Q.B. 774; see also *Daejan Properties Ltd v. Mahoney* (1996) 28 H.L.R. 498 at 510.

[87] R.A. 1977, s.2.

[88] R.A. 1977, s.3.

[89] *Keeves v. Dean* [1924] 1 K.B. 685 at 686, *per* Lush J.; and see *Roe v. Russell* [1928] 2 K.B. 117 at 131.

[90] *Lovibond & Sons Ltd v. Vincent* [1929] 1 K.B. 687.

[91] *Sutton v. Dorf* [1932] 2 K.B. 304.

[92] R.A. 1977, s.3(5), Sched. 1, paras 13, 14.

[93] Family Law Act 1996, Sched. 7, para.1.

[94] *John M. Brown Ltd v. Bestwick* [1951] 1 K.B. 21.

[95] *Skinner v. Geary* [1931] 2 K.B. 546; *cf. Haines v. Herbert* [1963] 1 W.L.R. 1401.

[96] *Hallwood Estates Ltd v. Flack* (1950) 66(2) T.L.R. 368; *Herbert v. Byrne* [1964] 1 W.L.R. 519; *Regalian Securities Ltd v. Scheuer* (1982) 47 P. & C.R. 362.

[97] *cf.* the assured tenancy, *ante*, para. 22–137.

[98] See, *e.g.* H.A. 1985, s.612; R.A. 1977, s.101 (overcrowding).

[99] By virtue of the mortgagee's paramountcy of title: *Dudley & District Building Society v. Emerson* [1949] Ch. 707; *Britannia Building Society v. Earl* [1990] 1 W.L.R. 422. Where the mortgage post-dates the tenancy, or does not bind the tenant due to non-registration, the tenant will normally have priority over the mortgagee: *Woolwich Building Society v. Dickman* [1996] 3 All E.R. 204; *Barclays Bank plc v. Zaroovabli* [1997] Ch. 321.

3. Succession. If a protected or statutory tenant dies, his or her spouse,[1] if   **22–188**
residing in the dwelling-house at that time, or otherwise any other member of
his family[2] residing with him then becomes statutory tenant in his place.[3] If
the tenant died before January 15, 1989, the family member (although not the
spouse) must prove six months' residence with the tenant. If the tenant dies on
or after that date, the period of residence becomes two years, and the family
member becomes entitled to an assured tenancy "by succession" rather than
a statutory tenancy.[4] Where the deceased tenant was a protected (and so
contractual) tenant, that contractual tenancy will devolve under the general
law, though it will be suspended while the statutory tenancy lasts.[5]

Second successions may occur, although amendments made by the 1988
Act make the criteria difficult to satisfy in the event of a "first successor"
dying on or after January 15, 1989.[6] In such circumstances, the second
successor must have been a member of the family both of the original tenant
and of the first successor, and have been residing in the dwelling-house with
the first successor both at the date of his or her death and for the previous two
years. A second successor under these provisions becomes an assured tenant
by succession.

4. Grounds for possession. The Rent Acts have always been restrictive   **22–189**
rather than enabling. If a protected tenancy still exists, the landlord must first
establish that he is entitled to possession under the terms of the tenancy, *e.g.*
by virtue of a forfeiture clause or by notice to quit. However, even if he is, or
if the tenant is merely a statutory tenant, the 1977 Act still prevents the court
from making an order for possession against the tenant except in specified
cases. The grounds for possession are either "discretionary" or
"mandatory".[7]

(a) Discretionary grounds. An order for possession can only be made if the   **22–190**
court considers that in all the circumstances it is reasonable to make such an
order. Some of the "Cases" are identical with grounds for possession for
assured tenancies, and cross references have accordingly been made in the
following text.

---

[1] If the tenant dies on or after January 15, 1989, "spouse" includes a person living with the tenant
as his or her wife or husband: R.A. 1977, Sched. 1, para. 2(2), inserted by H.A. 1988, Sched.
4, para. 2. A homosexual partner of the tenant cannot succeed as a spouse: *Fitzpatrick v.
Sterling Housing Association Ltd* [1998] Ch. 304.
[2] *Carega Properties S.A. v. Sharratt* [1979] 1 W.L.R. 928; *Fitzpatrick v. Sterling Housing
Association Ltd* [1998] Ch. 304.
[3] R.A. 1977, s.2(1)(b); Sched. 1, Pt I.
[4] R.A. 1977, Sched. 1, para. 3, as amended by H.A. 1988, s.39(2), (3); Sched. 4, Pt I.
[5] *Moodie v. Hosegood* [1952] A.C. 61; *cf.* the assured tenant: H.A. 1988, s.17, *ante*, para.
22–170.
[6] R.A. 1977, Sched. 1, para. 6, as substituted by H.A. 1988, Sched. 4, para. 6.
[7] R.A. 1977, s.98(1), (2). See *ante*, paras 22–149, 22–158. The grounds are set out in R.A. 1977,
Sched. 13, Pts 1 and 2 respectively.

22–191   CASE 1: BREACH OF COVENANT. Rent lawfully due has not been paid, or some other obligation of the tenancy which is consistent with the Act has been broken.

22–192   CASE 2: NUISANCE.[8]

22–193   CASE 3: DETERIORATION OF DWELLING-HOUSE.[9]

22–194   CASE 4: DETERIORATION OF FURNITURE.[10]

22–195   CASE 5: TENANT'S NOTICE TO QUIT. The tenant has given notice to quit, and the landlord has acted on it so as to be seriously prejudiced if he cannot obtain possession.

22–196   CASE 6: ASSIGNMENT OR SUB-LETTING. The tenant, without the landlord's consent,[11] has (after certain specified dates) assigned or sub-let the whole of the premises, or has sub-let part, the remainder being already sub-let.[12]

22–197   CASE 8[13]: REQUIRED FOR LANDLORD'S EMPLOYEE. The premises are reasonably required as a residence for a person engaged (or with whom a conditional contract has been made) in the whole-time employment of the landlord or some tenant of his, and the premises were let to the tenant in consequence of[14] his employment[15] by the landlord (or a former landlord), which has come to an end.

22–198   CASE 9: REQUIRED FOR LANDLORD OR FAMILY. The landlord reasonably requires the premises for occupation as a residence for himself,[16] a child of his over 18 years old, or one of his parents or parents-in-law. This Case is not available:

> (i) to a landlord who became landlord by purchasing[17] any interest in the premises after March 23, 1965, or certain other specified dates; or
>
> (ii) if the tenant satisfies the court that in all the circumstances "greater hardship" would be caused by granting the order for possession than by refusing to grant it.[18]

22–199   CASE 10: EXCESSIVE RENT. The tenant has sub-let part of the premises at a rent in excess of that recoverable having regard to the 1977 Act.

22–200   CASE AA: SUITABLE ALTERNATIVE ACCOMMODATION.[19] Suitable alternative accommodation is available for the tenant, or will be when the order for

---

[8] See H.A. 1988, Ground 14, *ante*, para. 22–164.
[9] See H.A. 1988, Ground 13, *ante*, para. 22–163.
[10] See H.A. 1988, Ground 15, *ante*, para. 22–166.
[11] *Hyde v. Pimley* [1952] 2 Q.B. 506.
[12] *Leith Properties Ltd v. Byrne* [1983] Q.B. 433.
[13] Case 7 has been repealed.
[14] *Braithwaite & Co. Ltd v. Elliot* [1947] K.B. 177.
[15] *Duncan v. Hay* [1956] 1 W.L.R. 1329.
[16] *Richter v. Wilson* [1963] 2 Q.B. 426.
[17] *Powell v. Cleland* [1948] 1 K.B. 262; *Thomas v. Fryer* [1970] 1 W.L.R. 845.
[18] R.A. 1977, Sched. 15, Pt III; *Harte v. Frampton* [1948] 1 K.B. 73.
[19] R.A. 1977, s.98(1), Sched. 15, Pt IV. The Act does not number the Case, but Case AA seems better than nothing.

possession takes effect. The first element of "suitability" requires the alternative accommodation to be let on a protected tenancy, or let as a separate dwelling on terms affording a reasonably equivalent security of tenure. The court has jurisdiction to order that the alternative accommodation is to be held on a protected tenancy, even though the tenancy is entered into on or after January 15, 1989, where it is satisfied that an assured tenancy would not afford the required security.[20] Otherwise, this ground for possession is practically identical with Ground 9 of the 1988 Act, to which reference should be made.[21]

(b) Mandatory grounds. On the landlord establishing a mandatory ground, **22–201** the court must order possession, and has as little scope for giving the protected or statutory tenant time as it has in relation to assured tenants when a mandatory ground is proved under the 1988 Act.[22] For each of the mandatory grounds which follow, the landlord must have given the tenant written notice, normally before the tenancy began, that possession might be recovered under the particular Case. In Cases 11, 12 and 20, however, if the court considers it just and equitable to make an order for possession, it may dispense with this requirement, and also with the further requirement of these Cases that there should have been no previous letting of the dwelling on a protected tenancy after certain dates without such a notice.[23]

CASE 11: OWNER-OCCUPIER.[24] The owner, having at any time previously had **22–202** occupied the dwelling as his residence, let it on a regulated tenancy, and one of the following conditions is satisfied[25]:

(i) the dwelling is genuinely required[26] as a residence for the owner[27] or any member of his family who resided with him when he last lived in it;

(ii) the owner has died, and the dwelling is required as a residence for a member of his family who was residing with him when he died;

(iii) the owner has died, and the dwelling is required by a successor in title as his residence or for disposal with vacant possession;

(iv) the dwelling is subject to a mortgage by deed granted before the grant of the tenancy, and the mortgagee requires it for sale with vacant possession under a contractual or statutory power; or

---

[20] H.A. 1988, s.34(1)(c).
[21] See *ante*, para. 22–159.
[22] See *ante*, para. 22–149.
[23] R.A. 1977, Sched. 15, Pt II; Housing Act 1980, s.67; *Bradshaw v. Baldwin-Wiseman* (1985) 49 P. & C.R. 382.
[24] The landlord cannot rely on this Case if after December 8, 1965, or certain other dates, the dwelling has been let on a protected tenancy without the tenant having been given the requisite written notice.
[25] R.A. 1977, Sched. 15, Pt II; Housing Act 1980, s.66, Sched 7.
[26] Reasonableness is not needed: *Kennealy v. Dunne* [1977] Q.B. 837.
[27] One of two or more joint owners will do: *Tilling v. Whiteman* [1980] A.C. 1.

(v) the dwelling is not reasonably suitable to the owner's needs in relation to his place of work, and he requires it for sale with vacant possession in order to use the proceeds to acquire a dwelling more suitable to those needs.

22–203   CASE 12: RETIREMENT HOME.[28] The landlord, although intending to occupy the dwelling as his residence on his retirement from regular employment, has let it on protected tenancy before such retirement, and either now has retired and requires the dwelling as a residence, or one of the conditions set out in paragraphs (ii) to (iv) above is satisfied.

22–204   CASE 13: SHORT LETTING OF HOLIDAY HOME.[29]

22–205   CASE 14: SHORT LETTING OF STUDENT RESIDENCE.[30]

22–206   CASE 15: MINISTER OF RELIGION.[31]

22–207   CASE 16: AGRICULTURAL WORKER.

22–208   CASE 17: FARMHOUSE REDUNDANT ON AMALGAMATION.

22–209   CASE 18: OTHER REDUNDANT FARMHOUSES. The general purpose of the complex provisions of Cases 16–18 is to enable a landlord to obtain possession of an agricultural holding for a farm worker of his from a tenant who lacks sufficient agricultural justification for retaining it.

22–210   CASE 19: PROTECTED SHORTHOLD TENANCY. This category of protected tenancy has now been superseded by the assured shorthold tenancy of Part I of the Housing Act 1988.[32]

22–211   CASE 20: SERVICEMEN.[33] The landlord was a member of the regular armed forces both at the time when he acquired the dwelling and when he let it, and either he requires the dwelling as his residence or one of the conditions set out in paragraphs (ii) to (v) above is satisfied. However, a landlord cannot rely on this Case if after November 28, 1980 the dwelling has been let on a protected tenancy without the tenant having been given the requisite written notice.

III. PROTECTION AS TO RENT

22–212   The great advantage traditionally enjoyed by regulated tenants over assured tenants is rent control. Not only is there a system which imposes and enforces a maximum rent, but there are also prohibitions on premiums.

22–213   **1. No registered rent.** The control of rents is based on the determination and registration of a "fair rent" for the dwelling. Until this has been done, there is generally no restriction on the rent that may be charged. But if a

---

[28] The landlord cannot rely on this Case if after December 8, 1965, or certain other dates, the dwelling has been let on a protected tenancy without the tenant having been given the requisite written notice.

[29] See H.A. 1988, Ground 3, *ante*, para. 22–152.

[30] See H.A. 1988, Ground 4, *ante*, para. 22–153.

[31] See H.A. 1988, Ground 5, *ante*, para. 22–154.

[32] See *ante*, para. 22–174.

[33] Added by Housing Act 1980, s.67, Sched. 7.

protected tenancy is granted to an existing tenant, or to someone who could succeed him as a statutory tenant, the rent must not exceed the existing rent unless the parties have signed a special form of "rent agreement", which states, *inter alia*, that the tenant can apply for registration of a fair rent; and the same applies to any increase of rent under an existing tenancy.[34] Further, the rent payable by a statutory tenant is limited to the rent recoverable at the end of the previous protected tenancy.[35] There are provisions for adjusting the rent for changes in the landlord's provision of furniture or services.[36]

2. Registered rent. Once a rent for a dwelling is registered, it will govern every subsequent regulated tenancy, provided it is of substantially the same type for substantially the same dwelling. The registered rent for an unfurnished tenancy will thus not apply if the premises are let furnished, or have had a room added or subtracted.[37] No rent may exceed the registered rent, and if it does, any excess paid is recoverable by the tenant within two years.[38] If the rent is less than the registered rent, the landlord may by notice increase it up to the registered rent.[39]

22–214

3. Registration of fair rent.

22–215

(a) Applications. Under a regulated tenancy, either the landlord or the tenant may apply to the rent officer for the area for the registration of a rent, and each is entitled to be heard.[40] The rent officer registers the rent, if he thinks it fair, or, if not, determines the fair rent and registers it; and within 28 days of receiving notice of this, either landlord or tenant may make an objection requiring the matter to be referred to a rent assessment committee.[41] After giving the parties an opportunity of being heard, the committee must either confirm the rent, or determine a fair rent which will be registered. Unless otherwise ordered, all registrations take effect from the date of application for registration; and for two years neither party can apply for the registration of a different rent unless there has been a change in the condition of the dwelling or in other circumstances which make the registered rent no longer a fair rent.[42] The registered rent constitutes the rent limit which must not be exceeded.[43]

---

[34] R.A. 1977, ss.51, 54.
[35] R.A. 1977, s.45.
[36] R.A. 1977, s.47.
[37] *Kent v. Millmead Properties Ltd* (1982) 44 P. & C.R. 353.
[38] R.A. 1977, ss.44, 57.
[39] R.A. 1977, s.45.
[40] R.A. 1977, ss.66, 67, Sched. 11; S.I. 1980 Nos 1696, 1697; *Druid Development Co. (Bingley) Ltd v. Kay* (1982) 44 P. & C.R. 76.
[41] R.A. 1977, Sched. 11; S.I. 1971 No. 1065, as amended. Rent assessment committees are "tribunals" for the purposes of the Tribunals and Inquiries Act 1971, Sched. 1.
[42] R.A. 1977, s.67, as amended by Housing Acts 1980 and 1988; *London Housing and Commercial Properties Ltd v. Cowan* [1977] Q.B. 148.
[43] R.A. 1977, ss.44, 45. For cancellation of registration, see s.73; S.I. 1980 No. 1698.

22–216   *(b) Fair rent.* In determining a fair rent, regard must be had "to all the circumstances (other than personal circumstances[44]) and in particular to the age, character, locality and state of repair of the dwelling-house", and the quantity, quality and condition of any furniture that is provided.[45] But the effect of local shortages of housing accommodation (the "scarcity" element) must be disregarded.[46] So too must voluntary improvements carried out by the tenant or his predecessors in title; any disrepair or other defects due to his or their failure to comply with the terms of the tenancy; any improvement to the furniture by the tenant or his predecessor in title; and any deterioration in its condition due to ill-treatment by the tenant, persons residing with him, or his sub-tenants.[47] It is important to realise that the determination of a fair rent will usually involve the committee considering rents of comparable properties in the locality. Some such properties will be let on regulated, and some on assured, tenancies. Assured tenancy rents should not be discounted on the ground that such rents might be higher, as a "fair rent" must not be interpreted as a "reasonable rent".[48] Application of this reasoning may ultimately lead to registered rents being brought into line with assured tenancy rents, and the gradual disappearance of any disparity between the rents of the two types of tenancy.[49]

22–217   **4. Premiums.** There have long been wide provisions which prohibit any person[50] from requiring a premium as a condition of the grant, renewal, continuance or assignment of any protected tenancy,[51] or in connection therewith; and these prevent a statutory tenant (who has no assignable interest) from asking for or receiving any consideration from anyone except the landlord as a condition of giving up possession, or in connection therewith. Rent payable before the relevant rental period begins, and excessive prices for furniture, are treated as being premiums. It is an offence to require a premium; and, if paid, the money is recoverable.[52]

D. Agricultural Tied Cottages

22–218   Many agricultural workers who are housed by their employers, usually on or close to a farm, were for long outside the Rent Acts because even if they were

---

[44] *Mason v. Skilling* [1974] 1 W.L.R. 1437; *Palmer v. Peabody Trust* [1975] Q.B. 604; *Spath Holme Ltd v. Greater Manchester & Lancashire Rent Assessment Committee* [1995] 2 E.G.L.R. 80.

[45] R.A. 1977, s.70; *Black v. Oliver* [1978] Q.B. 870.

[46] *Metropolitan Property Holdings Ltd v. Finegold* [1975] 1 W.L.R. 349; *Western Heritable Investment Co. Ltd v. Husband* (1983) 47 P. & C.R. 300.

[47] R.A. 1977, s.70(3). See generally *Metropolitan Properties Co. (F.G.C.) Ltd v. Lannon* [1968] 1 W.L.R. 815 (reversed on the issue of bias at [1969] 1 Q.B. 577).

[48] *Spath Holme Ltd v. Greater Manchester & Lancashire Rent Assessment Committee* [1995] 2 E.G.L.R. 80; *Curtis v. London Rent Assessment Committee* [1999] Q.B. 92.

[49] *B.T.E. v. Merseyside & Cheshire Rent Assessment Committee* (1991) 24 H.L.R. 514; *Spath Holme Ltd v. Greater Manchester & Lancashire Rent Assessment Committee* [1995] 2 E.G.L.R. 80.

[50] *Farrell v. Alexander* [1977] A.C. 59 (not confined to landlord).

[51] There are no restrictions on premiums in connection with assured tenancies.

[52] R.A. 1977, Pt IX, Sched. 1, Pt II.

tenants and not licensees, they paid little or no rent: the cottage or other dwellings "went with the job". In such cases, the loss of the job meant the loss of the home, for it would be needed for a new farm worker. The general scheme of the Rent (Agriculture) Act 1976[53] was to give such workers much of the protection of regulated tenancies, and yet to protect the farmer by imposing a special obligation on housing authorities to provide alternative accommodation for the occupier when agricultural efficiency required it. Part I of the Housing Act 1988 phased out the "protected occupier" status created in the 1976 Act, replacing it by assured agricultural occupancies, which have similar security to assured tenancies. The term "tied cottage" is traditional and convenient, but the Act is in no way limited to cottages.

1. Rent (Agriculture) Act 1976: protected occupiers

(a) *Definition.* A person is a "protected occupier" if he is a "qualifying   **22–219**
worker", or is incapable of whole-time work in agriculture in consequence of a qualifying injury or disease, and under a "relevant licence or tenancy" is in occupation of a dwelling in "qualifying ownership".[54] A person is a qualifying worker if he has worked whole-time in agriculture[55] for at least 91 out of the previous 104 weeks.[56] A relevant licence is one that gives exclusive occupation of a separate dwelling and would, if a tenancy, have been a protected tenancy under the Rent Act 1977 but for the low rent or certain other matters; and a relevant tenancy is correspondingly defined.[57] It follows that a licence or tenancy entered into on or after January 15, 1989, cannot be a relevant licence or tenancy under the 1976 Act, unless it is entered into pursuant to a contract made before that date, or it is granted to an existing protected occupier or statutory tenant (within the 1976 Act) of the landlord.[58]

(b) *Security of tenure.* Even if he has only a licence, the occupier becomes   **22–220**
a statutory tenant after his protected occupancy has determined, unless the landlord is the Crown, a local authority, or one of certain other public or housing bodies.[59] When a protected occupier dies, his or her spouse,[60] or a member of his or her family, if resident, can succeed the occupier (the spouse

---

[53] Amended by, although not consolidated in, the Rent Act 1977; further amendments were made by the Housing Acts of 1980 and 1988.

[54] R.A.A. 1976, s.2, and Sched. 3: a dwelling is in qualifying ownership if the occupier is employed in agriculture and his employer either owns the dwelling or has arranged for his agricultural workers to live in it.

[55] Very widely defined: R.A.A. 1976, s.1; but see *Earl of Normanton v. Giles* [1980] 1 W.L.R. 28.

[56] R.A.A. 1976, Sched. 3, Pt I.

[57] R.A.A. 1976, Sched. 2, as amended by R.A. 1977, Sched. 23.

[58] H.A. 1988, s.34(4).

[59] R.A.A. 1976, ss.4, 5. For the terms of the statutory tenancy, see R.A.A. 1976, Sched. 5.

[60] Including a person living with the occupier as his wife or her husband: R.A.A. 1976, s.4(5A), inserted by H.A. 1988, Sched. 4.

as statutory tenant, any other family member as assured tenant by succession).[61] No order for possession can be made against a protected occupier or statutory tenant except on certain specified grounds which closely resemble the discretionary and mandatory grounds for regulated tenancies, save that the mandatory grounds are limited to lettings by owner-occupiers, retirement homes, and cases of over-crowding.[62]

22–221   *(c) Rents.* With some modifications, the system of registered rents applies to a protected occupier.[63] But if he becomes a statutory tenant, no rent is payable until the parties agree upon one or the landlord serves a notice of increase on the tenant.[64] The rent must not then in either case exceed the registered rent, or, if none is registered, an amount calculated in accordance with a statutory formula.[65]

2. Assured agricultural occupancies

22–222   *(a) Definition.* Where a licence or tenancy is entered into on or after February 28, 1989, it cannot, subject to exceptions, be protected by the 1976 Act.[66] However, a tenancy or licence conferring exclusive occupation of a separate dwelling which would, if a tenancy, have been an assured tenancy under the Housing Act 1988 but for the low rent or certain other matters,[67] will be an "assured agricultural occupancy" provided that the "agricultural worker condition" is for the time being fulfilled. This requires the tenant or licensee to be either a "qualifying worker" as defined in the 1976 Act,[68] or a person incapable of whole-time work in agriculture in consequence of a qualifying injury or disease.[69] The dwelling must also be in "qualifying ownership".[70] A tenancy will not be an assured agricultural occupancy if it is an assured shorthold tenancy.[71] However, where the agricultural worker condition is fulfilled with respect to a dwelling-house which is subject to an assured tenancy entered into on or after February 28, 1997, that tenancy will only be a shorthold if a notice in prescribed form has been served on the tenant prior to the tenancy.[72] Thus, the adoption of the assured shorthold tenancy as

---

[61] R.A.A. 1976, ss.3, 4. A member of the occupier's family must have resided with him in the dwelling for two years before his death in order to qualify: R.A.A. 1976, s.4(4), as amended by H.A. 1988, Sched. 4.

[62] R.A.A. 1976, ss.6, 7, Sched. 4; and see *ante*, paras 22–202, 22–203.

[63] R.A.A. 1976, s.13; *ante*, para. 22–212.

[64] R.A.A. 1976, s.10.

[65] R.A.A. 1976, ss.11, 12, as amended by S.I. 1990 No. 434.

[66] H.A. 1988, s.34(4).

[67] The tenancy is comprised in an agricultural holding, or the holding is held under a farm business tenancy, and is occupied by the person responsible for the control or management of the holding. However, if the tenancy is itself a tenancy of an agricultural holding, or a farm business tenancy, it will be excluded: H.A. 1988, s.24, as amended by H.A. 1996, s.103.

[68] See *ante*, para. 22–219.

[69] H.A. 1988, Sched. 3.

[70] R.A.A. 1976, Sched. 3, applied by H.A. 1988, Sched. 3.

[71] H.A. 1988, s.24(2)(a).

[72] See further H.A. 1996, Sched. 7, para. 9; S.I. 1997 No. 194, Form 9.

the default method of tenure by the Housing Act 1996[73] does not apply in the context of agricultural occupancies.

(b) Security of tenure. The assured agricultural occupancy confers a secu- **22–223** rity of tenure identical with that enjoyed by the assured tenant in all respects but one: the discretionary ground available where an assured tenant's employment has ceased (Ground 16) may not be used.[74] The spouse[75] or other members of the worker's family may succeed on his death to the occupancy.[76]

(c) Rents. The rent payable under an assured agricultural occupancy will be **22–224** determined by the agreement of the parties. The system of registered rents does not apply. A landlord who wishes to increase rent under a periodic occupancy may serve notice as for any other assured periodic tenancy,[77] and the occupant may refer the notice to a rent assessment committee for a determination of the market rent.[78]

3. Re-housing. A local housing authority must use its "best endeavours" to **22–225** provide suitable alternative accommodation for assured agricultural occupants, protected occupiers and statutory tenants (or similarly protected or statutory agricultural tenants under the Rent Act 1977) if the owner satisfies the authority on three matters, namely:

(1) he cannot himself by any reasonable means provide suitable alternative accommodation;

(2) he requires vacant possession of the dwelling for an agricultural worker of his; and

(3) in the interests of efficient agriculture the authority ought to provide such accommodation.[79]

This obligation does not apply if, when the alternative accommodation is available, the owner is still employing the person for whom it is to be provided in the same capacity, and will continue to do so if that accommodation is provided.[80]

E. Residential Long Tenancies

The long lease is a widely used device for holding land in English law. It is **22–226** a property interest of considerable value, and on the assignment of a long

---

[73] See *ante*, para. 22–174.
[74] H.A. 1988, ss.24(3), 25(2).
[75] Including a person living with the occupier as his wife or her husband: H.A. 1988, Sched. 3, para. 3(2).
[76] Subject to conditions of prior residence: H.A. 1988, Sched. 3, para. 3.
[77] See *ante*, para. 22–172.
[78] H.A. 1988, ss.13, 14, 24(4).
[79] R.A.A. 1976, ss.27, 28, as amended by H.A. 1988, s.26 and Sched. 17.
[80] R.A.A. 1976, s.28(9).

lease the price paid by the purchaser may not be significantly less than the price which would be paid on a disposal of the freehold. The origin of many long leases lies in the building lease. The lessee takes an interest, commonly for 99 years, at a mere ground rent representing the undeveloped value of the land, and builds a house upon it at his own expense. He and his successors then have a long period of enjoyment at this low rent; but at the expiry of the lease, the house, being part of the land, reverts to the landlord or his successors, whose object in the bargain, long-term capital gain, is thereby achieved. Moreover, the disposition of property on a long lease carries advantages in the imposition and enforceability of obligations on the tenant which the alienation of freeholds does not: thus positive obligations to pay service charges and observe repairing covenants, which pose serious difficulties in relation to freeholders, can be enforced by virtue of the doctrine of privity of estate.[81]

22–227   However, the long lease poses problems for the tenant. It is a depreciating asset, and as the fixed term comes towards its end the leasehold interest will prove difficult to alienate, not least because lending institutions will be reluctant to take it as security. Long leaseholders have also experienced difficulties with landlords who fail to comply with repairing or service obligations expeditiously or at all. The last 40 years have seen considerable statutory intervention designed to improve the leaseholder's lot. No doubt there is more to come, particularly the much-heralded inception of commonhold, which will, it is hoped, provide a workable regime between dwellers in flats who acquired their landlord's interest by negotiation or enfranchisement.[82]

22–228   The legislation to date can be summarised as follows. By Part I of the Landlord and Tenant Act 1954, long leaseholders were given security of tenure. The Leasehold Reform Act 1967 conferred on long leaseholders of lower value houses the right to "enfranchise", *i.e.* the opportunity to buy the freehold, or the right to extend their leases. The Landlord and Tenant Act 1987, a statute which is not confined to long leaseholders,[83] gave certain tenants of flats the right of first refusal on the landlord's disposal of his interest, and provided remedies for tenants dissatisfied with their landlord's failure to comply with his obligations under the lease.[84] Finally, the Leasehold Reform, Housing and Urban Development Act 1993 extended enfranchisement rights to houses of higher value, and conferred both collective and individual enfranchisement rights on long leaseholders of flats.

There are four heads:

(1) Security of tenure;

(2) Individual enfranchisement of houses;

---

[81] See *ante*, Chap. 15.
[82] The commonhold proposals emanate from the Law Commission: see *Commonhold, Freehold Flats and Freehold Ownership of other Independent Buildings*, Cm. 179, and *Commonhold: A Consultation Paper*, Cm. 1345.
[83] See *post* para. 22–258.
[84] Landlord and Tenant Act 1987, Pts II and III.

(3) Collective enfranchisement of flats; and

(4) Individual enfranchisement of flats.

I. SECURITY OF TENURE

1. Introduction: the two regimes. Since 1954, a statutory security of **22–229** tenure has been conferred on those tenants who but for the lowness of the rent would have been entitled to retain possession of the premises under the Rent Acts.[85] This analogy ceased to be effective on January 15, 1989, as a tenancy entered into on or after that date could not, subject to exceptions, be a protected tenancy.[86] As a result, a new code, contained in Schedule 10 to the Local Government and Housing Act 1989, was enacted (some time after the Housing Act 1988 came into force) so as to apply to any long tenancy at a low rent which but for the low rent would have been an assured tenancy under Part I of the Housing Act 1988.[87] Since January 15, 1989, all qualifying long tenancies have been subject to the 1989 Act, and the 1954 Act has been phased out, save in transitional circumstances. Where a long tenancy was granted between January 15, 1989 and March 30, 1990, it is arguable that the 1989 Act has no application, an unfortunate result of Parliament's apparent failure, when enacting the Housing Act 1988, to appreciate its effect on the security of long tenancies at a low rent.

2. " Long tenancy at a low rent". The 1989 Act applies to a "long tenancy **22–230** at a low rent". A tenancy is "long" if it is granted for a term of years certain exceeding 21 years[88] whether or not subsequently extended by act of the parties or by any enactment; but any tenancy which is, or may become, terminable before the end of the term by notice given to the tenant is excluded.[89] Such a tenancy is at a "low rent" if either no rent is payable or the rent payable does not exceed certain limits equivalent to those set by Part I of the Housing Act 1988.[90]

3. Protection. The tenancy continues by operation of law after the date on **22–231** which the fixed term expires ("the term date").[91] While during the fixed term

---

[85] Landlord and Tenant Act 1954, Pt I (see in particular s.2); R.A. 1977, s.5.
[86] H.A. 1988, s.34(1).
[87] See H.A. 1988, Sched. 1, para. 3.
[88] "Back-dating" the tenancy will be ineffective: see *Roberts v. Church Commissioners for England* [1972] 1 Q.B. 278. However, where there has been a term exceeding 21 years, subsequent grants for a shorter term at a low rent will be deemed to be long tenancies: see L.G.H.A. 1989, Sched. 10, para. 16.
[89] L.G.H.A. 1989, Sched. 10, para. 2(3).
[90] L.G.H.A. 1989, Sched. 10, para. 2(4), (5), as amended by the References to Rating (Housing) Regulations 1990 (S.I. 1990 No. 434).
[91] L.G.H.A. 1989, Sched. 10, para. 3.

the tenant can rely on his rights under the lease, after its expiry he is protected by statute. However, on or after the term date, the landlord can (following service of certain notices[92]) either, on proof of statutory grounds, obtain a court order entitling him to possession, or transform the tenancy into an assured tenancy. The landlord must give not less than six nor more than 12 months' notice,[93] and such notice must take one of two forms. A "landlord's notice to resume possession" states that if the tenant is not willing to give up possession by the specified date, the landlord proposes to apply to the court for possession on one or more specified grounds.[94] The landlord then has four months in which to apply to the court for possession on statutorily prescribed grounds.[95] If the tenant formally intimates his intention to retain possession by notice, the landlord's application must be made within two months of the "election to retain possession".[96] Alternatively, the landlord may serve a notice proposing an assured tenancy.[97] The terms of the tenancy are at the outset those of the long tenancy from which it derives, with obvious differences such as the length of the term, but the Act contains provision for subsequent variation by agreement with reference to a rent assessment committee[98] in case of dispute.

The tenant may terminate a tenancy which is continuing by virtue of the protective code by one month's written notice.[99]

II. INDIVIDUAL ENFRANCHISEMENT FOR TENANTS OF HOUSES: THE LEASEHOLD REFORM ACT 1967

22–232   **1. Introduction.** The Leasehold Reform Act 1967 granted to certain tenants occupying houses under long leases at a low rent the right to enfranchisement (*i.e.* to purchase the freehold) or to extend the lease (for 50 years) on paying a price or rent based on the value of the land alone, ignoring the house itself. This never applied to flats. The Act of 1967 has survived amendment of its valuation provisions and challenge before the European Court of Human Rights based on its allegedly confiscatory nature,[1] and recent statutes have widened the availability of enfranchisement (but not extension of the lease) to leaseholders who were previously excluded.[2]

---

[92] On the tenant, on which see *Galinski v. McHugh* [1989] 1 E.G.L.R. 109.
[93] L.G.H.A. 1989, Sched. 10, para. 4. For forms, see S.I. 1997 Nos 3005, 3008.
[94] L.G.H.A. 1989, Sched. 10, para. 4(5)(b).
[95] For the grounds, see L.G.H.A. 1989, Sched. 10, para. 5.
[96] L.G.H.A. 1989, Sched. 10, para. 4(7), para. 13(1), (2).
[97] L.G.H.A. 1989, Sched. 10, para. 4(5)(a).
[98] See Sched. 10, paras 9–12.
[99] L.G.H.A. 1989, Sched. 10, para. 8.
[1] See the fifth edition of this work at p. 1127. The European Court of Human Rights has ruled that the Act does not breach Art. 1 of the First Protocol to the European Convention on Human Rights ("no-one shall be deprived of his possessions except in the public interest"): *James v. United Kingdom* [1986] 26 R.V.R. 139.
[2] See *post*, para. 22–238.

2. Qualifying tenancies. The Act of 1967[3] applies to any "long tenancy" **22–233** at a "low rent" which satisfies three statutory conditions.[4] A "long tenancy" is a tenancy granted for a term of more than 21 years, even if determinable during the term.[5] The definition of "low rent" is now very complex, as subsequent statutes have added glosses to the 1967 Act. The Acts must themselves be consulted, but their effect can be briefly summarised, at considerable risk of over-simplification, as follows.

    (i) A tenancy is at a "low rent" if either:

        (a) it was entered into before April 1, 1990 (or later, pursuant to an earlier contract), and the current yearly rent is less than two-thirds of the rateable value of the property on the appropriate day",[6] (or, if later, the first day of the term); or

        (b) where the tenancy does not fall within the above provision, the current yearly rent does not exceed £1,000 in Greater London, or £250 elsewhere.[7]

    (ii) The "low rent" test will also be satisfied *for enfranchisement purposes only* where in the initial year of the tenancy *either* no rent was payable *or* the aggregate amount of rent payable did not exceed certain limits.[8]

    (iii) Schedule 9 to the Housing Act 1996 confers additional rights of enfranchisement (only) in relation to certain long tenancies which would otherwise fail the low rent test.[9]

The Act applies equally to a sub-tenancy, where there are elaborate provisions **22–234** for extinguishing or adjusting intermediate tenancies and compensating their owners to a limited extent.[10] There are three statutory conditions.

---

[3] *i.e.* the Leasehold Reform Act 1967, as amended by (*inter alia*) the Rent Acts 1968 and 1977, the Housing Acts 1974, 1980 and 1985, the Leasehold Reform Act 1979, the Housing and Planning Act 1986, the References to Rating (Housing) Regulations 1990, the Leasehold Reform, Housing and Urban Development Act 1993, and the Housing Act 1996 (L.R.A. 1967).

[4] L.R.A. 1967, ss.1–4. Certain shared ownership leases granted by public bodies or housing associations are excluded from the operation of the Act: s.33A, Sched. 4A, added by Housing and Planning Act 1986, s.18, Sched. 4, paras 5, 11. So too are tenancies of agricultural holdings: see L.R.A. 1967, s.1(3), and *Lester v. Ridd* [1990] 2 Q.B. 430.

[5] L.R.A. 1967, s.3, which also provides for certain perpetually renewable leases, leases terminable by notice on death or marriage, and tenants holding over after expiry of their long fixed terms.

[6] *i.e.* the day on which a rateable value for the dwelling-house was first shown in the valuation list, or if that was before March 23, 1965, that date: L.R.A. 1967, s.1(4); Rent Act 1977, s.25(3); *Dixon v. Allgood* [1987] 1 W.L.R. 1689.

[7] L.R.A. 1967, s.4(1), as amended by H.A. 1996, s.105(1).

[8] L.R.A. 1967, s.4A, as amended by H.A. 1996, s.105(2). See further *post*, para. 22–238.

[9] H.A. 1996, s.106.

[10] L.R.A. 1967, s.5, Sched. 1. The price for enfranchisement cannot be increased by making alterations in any interests in the reversion, *e.g.* as to rent: Leasehold Reform Act 1979, s.1, dealing with a problem identified in *Jones v. Wrotham Park Settled Estates* [1980] A.C. 74.

22–235 *(a) House.* The premises must consist of a house, as defined.[11] This includes semi-detached and terrace houses, but not flats or maisonettes. If the premises are part of a larger building, the division must in effect be vertical.[12] It suffices if the premises can reasonably be called a house (*e.g.* where part is a shop and the rest a dwelling) even though they can reasonably be described as something else. The question is one of law, not fact.[13]

22–236 *(b) Residence.* When the tenant gives his notice of enfranchisement or extension, he must have been occupying part[14] or all of the house under a long tenancy at a low rent as his only or main residence[15] for the last three years, or for periods amounting to three years out of the last 10.[16] It thus suffices if the house has been divided into flats and he has occupied one of them for three years; and it is immaterial if he also uses the house for other purposes. If the tenant dies and a member of his family succeeds him as tenant, the successor can, if the house was his main residence before the death, include in the period of three years his period of residence before the death.[17]

22–237 *(c) Property value.* The Act of 1967 imposed certain limits on the value of property which could be the subject of a claim. In effect, the rateable value of the premises had to be less than a certain amount on "the appropriate day".[18] The abolition of domestic rates in 1990 meant that a new means of value assessment was necessary, and this was provided by the introduction of a statutory formula, to be used where tenancies were entered into on or after April 1, 1990.[19]

22–238 **3. Extension of right to enfranchise only.** The Leasehold Reform, Housing and Urban Development Act 1993 extended the right to enfranchise to houses with a value exceeding the property limits of the Act of 1967, and to certain tenancies (granted before April 18, 1980) terminable by notice after death or marriage.[20] However, the extended right does not apply where the tenant's immediate landlord is a charitable housing trust and the house forms part of the housing accommodation provided by the trust in pursuit of its charitable purposes.[21] With regard to the leases for which claims arise as a

---

[11] L.R.A. 1967, s.2.

[12] The Act does not apply to a house "which is not structurally detached and of which a material part lies above or below a part of the structure not comprised in the house": s.2(2). See *Parsons v. Viscount Gage* [1974] 1 W.L.R. 435; *Gaidowski v. Gonville and Caius College, Cambridge* [1975] 1 W.L.R. 1066; *Sharpe v. Duke Street Securities Ltd* [1987] 2 E.G.L.R. 106; *Duke of Westminster v. Birrane* (1994) 27 H.L.R. 321.

[13] L.R.A. 1967, s.2(1); *Lake v. Bennett* [1970] 1 Q.B. 663; *Tandon v. Trustees of Spurgeon's Homes* [1982] A.C. 755.

[14] L.R.A. 1967, s.1(2)(a); *Harris v. Swick Securities Ltd* [1969] 1 W.L.R. 1604 (some parts sub-let).

[15] *Poland v. Earl Cadogan* [1980] 3 All E.R. 544 is the leading authority.

[16] L.R.A. 1967, s.1, as amended by Housing Act 1980, Sched. 21.

[17] L.R.A. 1967, s.7.

[18] L.R.A. 1967, s.1.

[19] References to Rating (Housing) Regulations 1990 (S.I. 1990 No. 434).

[20] L.R.H.U.D.A. 1993, ss.63, 64.

[21] L.R.H.U.D.A. 1993, s.67.

consequence, an alternative rent limit is applied, based on the initial year of the tenancy; and where a claim is made out, the price payable by the tenant on enfranchisement is calculated on a slightly different basis, with further allowance for compensation to the landlord.[22] Provision is also made for landlords to retain powers of management under estate management schemes by making application to a leasehold valuation tribunal within two years of the coming into force of the relevant section, or subsequently, with the consent of the Secretary of State.[23]

4. Claim. A tenant who wishes to claim either enfranchisement or extension must do so by serving on his landlord a written notice to this effect in the prescribed form.[24] He may do this at any time while his long tenancy exists under the lease itself or while it is being automatically continued on the original terms under Schedule 10 to the Local Government and Housing Act 1989.[25] But if under these statutes the landlord serves a notice seeking to terminate the tenancy, the tenant will lose his rights under the Act of 1967 unless he serves his notice within two months.[26] When served, the tenant's notice takes effect as a contract "freely entered into" for the landlord to convey the freehold of the "house and premises" (*i.e.* the house and any premises let and used with it), or to grant the new tenancy of them, as the case may be[27]; and it is registrable as an estate contract or, for registered land, protected by a notice or caution.[28] In default of agreement on the price or rent, these and the other terms will be determined by the Leasehold Valuation Tribunal, or, on appeal, by the Lands Tribunal[29]; otherwise the terms are a matter for the county court, which has general jurisdiction over claims under the Act.[30] For enfranchisement (but not for extension) there is a right for the tenant to withdraw within a month of the price being agreed or determined[31]; and there is also a special procedure where the landlord is unknown or cannot be found.[32]

22–239

5. Completion.

22–240

(a) Extension. If the tenant's notice seeks an extension of his tenancy, he is entitled to the grant of a tenancy for 50 years from the expiry of his existing

---

[22] L.R.H.U.D.A. 1993, ss.65, 66.
[23] L.R.H.U.D.A. 1993, ss.69–75.
[24] L.R.A. 1967, s.22, Sched. 3, para. 6; S.I. 1997 No. 640.
[25] L.R.A. 1967, s.3(2). For the relationship with forfeiture proceedings, see *Twinsectra Ltd v. Hynes* (1995) 28 H.L.R. 183.
[26] L.R.A. 1957, Sched. 3, para. 2.
[27] L.R.A. 1967, s.5.
[28] L.R.A. 1967, s.5(5).
[29] L.R.A. 1967, s.21; Housing Act 1980, s.142, Sched. 22; S.I. 1981 No. 271. Rent assessment committees sit as Leasehold Valuation Tribunals.
[30] L.R.A. 1967, s.20.
[31] L.R.A. 1967, s.9(3), as amended by Housing Act 1980, Sched. 21. He must compensate the landlord, and no new notice may be given for three years.
[32] L.R.A. 1967, s.27; *Re Robertson's Application* [1969] 1 W.L.R. 109.

lease, on corresponding terms.[33] The rent is to be a ground rent representing the letting value of the site when the new tenancy begins, disregarding the value of the buildings on it, though after 25 years the landlord may require the rent to be raised to the then current letting value of the site; and the tenant must pay the landlord's reasonable costs of the transaction. The tenant cannot claim enfranchisement, or a further extension, during a term thus extended, and both during the extension and on its expiry further statutory rights to security of tenure are excluded.[34]

22–241   *(b) Enfranchisement.* If the tenant's notice seeks enfranchisement, he is entitled to a conveyance in fee simple subject to his tenancy and any incumbrances on it, but otherwise free from most incumbrances on the freehold such as mortgages.[35] There are two bases of assessment of the purchase price, depending on whether the value of the house and premises exceeds certain limits.[36]

    (1) If the value does not exceed these limits, the price is the value of the freehold of the house and premises on the open market (excluding from that market the tenant and members of his family residing in the house), on the assumption that the tenancy will be extended under the Act.[37] The price will thus be based on the capitalised value of the ground rents payable during the existing and extended terms, with the right to possession of the house and premises deferred until those terms have expired.[38]

    (2) If the value exceeds these limits, the price is the value of the freehold of the house and premises on the open market (including the tenant and his family), subject to the tenancy and the right of the tenant to remain in possession pursuant to Schedule 10 to the Local Government and Housing Act 1989, but on the assumption that the tenant has no right to enfranchisement or extension under the 1967 Act.[39] A reduction is made for any tenant's improvements, and it is assumed that the tenant has no liability to carry out repairs, maintenance or redecorations during any statutory continuation.[40] In this case, the price will reflect more of the value of the house.

---

[33] L.R.A. 1967, ss.14, 15.

[34] L.R.A. 1967, s.16.

[35] But not redeemable rentcharges: L.R.A. 1967, s.8, as amended by Rentcharges Act 1977, Sched. 1.

[36] L.R.A. 1967, s.9. Where the house and premises had a rateable value on March 31, 1990, the limit (adjusted to take account of tenant's improvements) is a rateable value of £1,000 in Greater London, and £500 elsewhere, on that date. Where the property had no rateable value on that date, a statutory formula is applied.

[37] L.R.A. 1967, s.9(1).

[38] *Farr v. Millersons Investments Ltd* (1971) 22 P. & C.R. 1055.

[39] L.R.A. 1967, s.9(1A), added by Housing Act 1974, s.118(4), and subsequently amended by Housing and Planning Act 1986, s.23 and Local Government and Housing Act 1989, s.194(1), Sched. 11, para. 10.

[40] L.R.A. 1967, s.9(1A), (1B), added by Housing Act 1974, s.118(4), and subsequently amended as above: see *Norfolk v. Trinity College, Cambridge* (1976) 32 P. & C.R. 147.

Under either head, the tenant must pay the landlord's reasonable costs of the transaction.[41]

6. Modifications. No contract can exclude or modify the tenant's right to **22–242** enfranchisement or extension, or to compensation as mentioned below[42]; but the Act itself limits the provisions for enfranchisement or extension in certain cases.

(a) Required for residence by landlord. A tenant's right to enfranchisement **22–243** or extension will be defeated if, after he has given notice claiming it, the landlord obtains an order for possession of the house for occupation as the only or main residence for himself or for an adult member of his family; but no order will be made if to make it would cause greater hardship than to refuse it.[43] A tenant whose claim is defeated in this way is entitled to compensation (determined by the Leasehold Valuation Tribunal in default of agreement) equal to the open market value of a tenancy of the house as extended under the Act, though with nothing for losing the right of enfranchisement.[44]

(b) Redevelopment. Not more than a year before the contractual term **22–244** expires, the landlord, if the tenant has claimed an extension or it has been granted, may apply for an order for possession on the ground that for purposes of redevelopment he proposes to demolish or reconstruct the house or a substantial part of it. If this ground is established, the court must declare that the landlord is entitled to possession and the tenant to compensation. Such a declaration will determine any extended tenancy that has already been granted and defeat any claim to an extension, though the tenant will be entitled to compensation as above.[45] A claim for enfranchisement cannot normally be defeated on this ground.[46]

(c) Development by public bodies.[47] If a Minister certifies that a public body **22–245** will require the property within 10 years for development for the purposes of that body, a tenant cannot effectively claim either enfranchisement or extension under the Act. But if before the certificate is served, or within two months thereafter, the tenant claims enfranchisement or extension, the tenancy is treated as having been extended; and if the public body wishes to obtain possession, it must apply to the court as under the provisions for redevelopment in the last paragraph. On such an application, the Minister's certificate is conclusive as to the required purposes. The term "public body" includes

---

[41] L.R.A. 1967, s.9(4); but see Housing Act 1980, Sched. 22, para. 5.
[42] L.R.A. 1967, s.23. An agreement between the landlord and a third party may be affected by this provision: see *Rennie & Rennie v. Proma & Byng* (1989) 22 H.L.R. 129. However, an agreement which has the effect of making enfranchisement more expensive to the tenant is not, although certain agreements of this kind are invalidated by the Leasehold Reform Act 1979, s.1: see further *Jones v. Wrotham Park Settled Estates* [1980] A.C. 74.
[43] L.R.A. 1967, s.18.
[44] L.R.A. 1967, s.21(1), Sched. 2, para. 5.
[45] L.R.A. 1967, s.17.
[46] L.R.A. 1967, s.17.
[47] L.R.A. 1967, s.28.

local authorities, universities (or colleges of universities), certain health authorities and nationalised industries.

22–246   *(d) The Crown.*[48] A tenant holding directly from the Crown cannot claim either enfranchisement or extension under the Act; but usually the Crown will, as of grace, agree to grant one or the other on the terms of the Act.

22–247   *(e) Management.* Where there was an area occupied by tenants under one landlord, the appropriate Minister could certify, on application made to him before 1970,[49] that in order to maintain standards it was in the general interest that the landlord should retain powers of management and control over the development and use of houses in the area. A scheme for this purpose (*e.g.* regulating the redevelopment or use of enfranchised property, and providing for repairs) could then subsequently be submitted to the High Court and, if approved, take effect.[50] However, although such schemes may regulate enfranchised property in many matters of detail, they do not prevent enfranchisement or extension. Application for a scheme can be made not only by a landlord but also by a tenants' association approved by the Minister, the scheme conferring on the association rights or powers which might otherwise have been conferred on the landlord.[51] As the landlord's interest will usually be expropriated, the provisions for management schemes are particularly useful to tenants' associations.

III. COLLECTIVE ENFRANCHISEMENT FOR TENANTS OF FLATS: THE LEASEHOLD
REFORM, HOUSING AND URBAN DEVELOPMENT ACT 1993[52]

22–248   **1. Introduction.** The 1993 Act conferred on "qualifying tenants" a right of collective enfranchisement in respect of certain premises.[53] The premises must consist of a self-contained building or part of a building, and contain two or more flats[54] held by qualifying tenants. The total number of flats held by qualifying tenants must be not less than two-thirds of the total number of flats contained in the premises.[55] Where more than 10 per cent of the internal floor area of the premises is occupied otherwise than for residential purposes or is comprised in common parts, or where the premises contain no more than four

---

[48] L.R.A. 1967, s.33. For other exclusions, see L.R.A. 1967, ss.31, 32, 32A (added by Leasehold Reform, Housing and Urban Development Act 1993, s.68), and 33A.
[49] Before July 31, 1976, for tenancies brought within the Act solely by the higher rateable values of the Housing Act 1974: see s.118.
[50] L.R.A. 1967, s.19. See *e.g. Re Sherwood Close (Barnes) Management Co. Ltd* [1972] Ch. 208; *Eton College v. Nassar* [1991] 2 E.G.L.R. 271.
[51] L.R.A. 1967, s.19(3). The landlord and a tenants' association can make a joint application: see *Re Abbots Park Estate* [1972] 1 W.L.R. 598; *Re Abbots Park Estate (No. 2)* [1972] 1 W.L.R. 1597.
[52] See Bright [1994] Conv. 211; Clarke [1994] Conv. 223; Davey (1994) 57 M.L.R. 773.
[53] L.R.H.U.D.A. 1993, s.1.
[54] "Flat" means a separate set of premises (whether or not on the same floor) which forms part of a building, and is constructed or adapted for use as a dwelling, and either the whole or a material part of it lies above or below some other part of the building: L.R.H.U.D.A. 1993, s.101(1).
[55] L.R.H.U.D.A. 1993, s.3, which further defines "building".

units and have a resident landlord, they are excluded from the right of enfranchisement.[56] Premises where different persons own the freehold of different parts of the premises are also excluded, provided that any of those parts is a self-contained part of a building.[57]

2. Qualifying tenants. A "qualifying tenant" is a tenant of a flat under a **22–249** "long lease" at a "low rent".[58] A "long lease" is a lease granted for a term exceeding 21 years, even if determinable during the term.[59] Certain tenancies for a "particularly long term" are deemed without more to be long tenancies at a low rent for the purposes of collective enfranchisement.[60] In other cases, the definition of "low rent" depends on the date the lease was entered into.[61] If it was before April 1, 1963, the rent in the initial year of the tenancy must not have exceeded two-thirds of the letting value of the flat on the date of commencement of the lease. If the lease was entered into between March 31, 1963 and April 1, 1990, the rent in the initial year must not have exceeded two-thirds of the rateable value on the "appropriate date".[62] Otherwise, the rent in the initial year must not have exceeded £1,000 (in Greater London) or £250 (elsewhere). There are three important exclusions:

(1) business leases;

(2) flats let by charitable housing trusts in pursuit of their charitable purposes; and

(3) "unlawful" sub-leases unless the superior lease was itself a long lease at a low rent.[63]

If a tenant qualifies in respect of three or more flats in the premises, there is taken to be no qualifying tenant of any of those flats.[64]

3. The right to collective enfranchisement. The right to collective enfran- **22–250** chisement conferred on qualifying tenants is the right to have the freehold of the premises in which their flats are contained acquired on their behalf by a person or persons (usually a company formed for this purpose) appointed by them, at a price determined in accordance with the statute.[65] They are also entitled to acquire the freehold of appurtenant property and "common parts",

---

[56] L.R.H.U.D.A. 1993, s.4. "Resident landlord" is widely defined in s.10 so as to include members of the landlord's family.
[57] L.R.H.U.D.A. 1993, s.4(3A), added by H.A. 1996, s.107.
[58] L.R.H.U.D.A. 1993, s.5(1).
[59] See further L.R.H.U.D.A. 1993, s.7, a lengthy provision which contains a complex definition.
[60] Tenancies for a term of years certain exceeding 50 years, and other analogous tenancies: see L.R.H.U.D.A. 1993, s.8A, added by H.A. 1996, Sched. 9, para. 3.
[61] L.R.H.U.D.A. 1993, s.8.
[62] For definitions of "initial year", "appropriate date", "rent", and "letting value", see L.R.H.U.D.A. 1993, s.8(2), (3).
[63] L.R.H.U.D.A. 1993, s.5(2).
[64] L.R.H.U.D.A. 1993, s.5(5).
[65] L.R.H.U.D.A. 1993, s.1(1).

whether or not contained in the premises as such.[66] However, the freeholder may require the purchaser to grant a leaseback of such flats in the premises as are not occupied by qualifying tenants (and of such parts of the premises as are not flats); and in the case of flats let on secure tenancies and certain lettings by housing associations such leaseback is mandatory, and not therefore dependent on the freeholder serving a notice of his claim. The leaseback to the freeholder is for a term of 999 years at a peppercorn rent.[67] The freeholder may prevent the acquisition of his property altogether if the court is satisfied that not less than two-thirds of the long leases of the flats in the premises are due to terminate within five years, that the freeholder intends on termination of the leases to demolish, reconstruct, or carry out substantial works of construction (for the purposes of redevelopment) of the whole or a substantial part of the premises, and that he could not reasonably do so without obtaining possession of the premises demised by those leases.[68]

22–251   **4. The price.** The price to be paid by the purchaser to the freeholder is calculated by aggregating three elements.[69]

> (1) *The value of the freeholder's interest in the premises.*[70] This is the amount that might be expected to be obtained for the interest by a willing seller on the open market, with neither the nominee purchaser nor any tenant in the premises nor any owner of an interest which the purchaser is to acquire, buying or seeking to buy. In other words, this element is based on the capitalised value of the ground rents during the existing (and any extended) term, and the value of the reversion on expiry of the term. Various assumptions are made.
>
> (2) *The freeholder's share of the "marriage value".*[71] The "marriage value" is the difference between:
>
> > (i)   the aggregate value of the freehold and intermediate leasehold interests in the premises prior to the acquisition; and
> > (ii) the aggregate value of those interests after acquisition. The marriage value is thus the increase in value attributable to the participating tenants' potential ability, subsequent to acquisition, to grant themselves new leases without payment of premiums and without restrictions as to the length of the term.
>
> The freeholder's share of the marriage value is no less than 50 per cent of this difference, and may be greater if on a sale on the open

---

[66] L.R.H.U.D.A. 1993, s.1(2), (3), as amended by H.A. 1996, s.105(3). By granting "permanent rights" over the common parts the purchaser may acquit his obligation to transfer the freehold of such property: s.1(4).
[67] L.R.H.U.D.A. 1993, s.36, Sched. 9, Pts II and III.
[68] L.R.H.U.D.A. 1993, s.23.
[69] L.R.H.U.D.A. 1993, s.32, Sched. 6, as amended by H.A. 1996, s.107.
[70] L.R.H.U.D.A. 1993, Sched. 6, para. 3, as amended by H.A. 1996, s.109.
[71] L.R.H.U.D.A. 1993, Sched. 6, para. 4.

market a greater proportion would have been determined by agreement between the parties.

(3) *Compensation for loss resulting from enfranchisement.*[72] The freeholder is entitled to reasonable compensation for loss or damage suffered by virtue of any diminution in the value of any interest he has in other property resulting from the acquisition, and also any loss of development value in the property being acquired.

The reasonable costs of acquisition (as listed in the statute) are to be met by the nominee purchaser.[73] The purchaser may also have to pay for any intermediate leasehold interests, and indeed other interests, which are acquired.[74]

5. Claim. A claim is initiated by notice to "the reversioner", who will **22–252** normally be the freeholder of the premises.[75] This "initial notice" must be given by not less than two-thirds of the qualifying tenants, representing not less than one-half of the total number of flats in the premises. In turn, not less than one-half of these "participating tenants" must have occupied their flat as their only or principal home for the last 12 months or for periods amounting to three years in the last 10 years.[76] The notice must designate the nominee purchaser, and contain detailed particulars of the claim.[77] The reversioner then has a period of not less than two months in which to give a counter-notice to the nominee purchaser admitting or denying the right claimed, or claiming an intention to redevelop.[78] Where the reversioner contests entitlement to enfranchise in a counter-notice, and the nominee purchaser wishes to proceed, he should apply to the court within two months, and seek a declaration of entitlement.[79] Where an intention to redevelop is claimed, any appropriate landlord should apply to the court within the same period for a declaration that the right to collective enfranchisement is not exercisable in relation to those premises.[80] Where the counter-notice accepts that the right exists and is exercisable, any remaining disputes as to the terms of acquisition (including the price payable by the nominee purchaser) should be referred to a leasehold valuation tribunal.[81]

---

[72] L.R.H.U.D.A. 1993, Sched. 6, para. 5.
[73] L.R.H.U.D.A. 1993, s.33.
[74] L.R.H.U.D.A. 1993, Sched. 6, Pts III and IV.
[75] L.R.H.U.D.A. 1993, s.9.
[76] L.R.H.U.D.A. 1993, s.13(2). The "residence condition" is set out in s.6, as amended by H.A. 1996, s.111.
[77] L.R.H.U.D.A. 1993, s.13, as amended by H.A. 1996, s.108.
[78] L.R.H.U.D.A. 1993, s.21. For intention to redevelop, see s.23, *ante*, para. 22–250. In the event of a failure to give a counter-notice within the requisite period, the court has power to determine the terms of acquisition: s.25.
[79] L.R.H.U.D.A. 1993, s.22.
[80] L.R.H.U.D.A. 1993, s.23.
[81] L.R.H.U.D.A. 1993, s.24.

22–253   **6. Estate management schemes.** The 1993 Act contains provisions analogous to those in the Leasehold Reform Act 1967 enabling landlords to apply to leasehold valuation tribunals (within a period of two years from the provisions coming into force[82]) for approval of an estate management scheme.[83] On such approval being given, the landlord will retain powers of management in respect of the house or premises, and have rights against the property in question arising from the exercise elsewhere of his powers of management.[84]

IV. INDIVIDUAL ENFRANCHISEMENT FOR TENANTS OF FLATS: LEASEHOLD REFORM HOUSING AND URBAN DEVELOPMENT ACT 1993

22–254   **1. Extended leases.** A tenant who is a "qualifying tenant" within the Act of 1993[85] may not wish to, or may not be able to, benefit from collective enfranchisement. He may, however, choose to assert his individual right to a new lease of 90 years on payment of a premium. To do so, he must satisfy the residence condition, *i.e.* have occupied the flat as his only or principal home for the last three years, or for three years out of the last 10 (whether or not he has used it for other purposes).[86] There is no exclusion relating to user of the premises, or occupation by a resident landlord.

22–255   **2. The claim.** The tenant's claim is made by notice to his landlord,[87] particularising the property, the lease, and the premium which the tenant proposes to pay.[88] The landlord replies by counter-notice, admitting or denying the tenant's claim, and the court has power to determine whether the claim is valid.[89] In cases of dispute over terms, leasehold valuation tribunals have jurisdiction, and there are provisions for vesting orders if the landlord proves unco-operative or untraceable.[90] If the landlord establishes an intention to redevelop and the tenant's lease is due to terminate within five years of the relevant date, the court may make an order declaring that the tenant's right to acquire a new lease should not be exercisable.[91]

22–256   **3. The lease.** The tenant who establishes his claim is entitled to be granted, in substitution for the existing lease, a new lease of the flat[92] for a peppercorn

---

[82] Where the right to collective enfranchisement arose by virtue of the amendments in the H.A. 1996, Sched. 9, para. 1, the period of two years runs from April 1, 1997. H.A. 1996, s.118; S.I. 1997 No. 618.
[83] L.R.H.U.D.A. 1993, ss.69–75, as amended by H.A. 1996, s.118.
[84] L.R.H.U.D.A. 1993, s.69(1).
[85] See *ante*, para. 22–249.
[86] L.R.H.U.D.A. 1993, s.39, as amended by H.A. 1996, s.112 (dealing also with leases vested in trustees).
[87] Defined in L.R.H.U.D.A. 1993, s.40.
[88] L.R.H.U.D.A. 1993, s.42.
[89] L.R.H.U.D.A. 1993, ss.45, 46.
[90] L.R.H.U.D.A. 1993, ss.48–51.
[91] L.R.H.U.D.A. 1993, s.47.
[92] "Flat" includes any garage, outhouse, garden, yard and appurtenances belonging to or usually enjoyed with the flat and let with it to the tenant: L.R.H.U.D.A. 1993, s.62(2); *Cadogan Viscount Chelsea v. McGirk* (1996) 29 H.L.R. 294.

rent for a term expiring 90 years after the term date of the existing lease.[93] The tenant must pay a premium comprising[94]:

(i) *the diminution in value of the landlord's interest in the flat*, being the difference between the value of the landlord's interest in the tenant's flat prior to the grant of the new lease and the value of his interest once the new lease is granted, various assumptions being made;

(ii) *the landlord's share of the marriage value*, being 50 per cent thereof or such greater proportion as the parties agree or the leasehold valuation tribunal determines to be the proportion that would have been agreed on a sale on the open market; and

(iii) *such compensation as is payable to the landlord* in relation to loss suffered by any resultant diminution in value in any other property or resulting from the landlord's ownership of such interest (including loss of development value).

The landlord is not obliged to execute the lease until the premium, together with any sums payable to owners of intermediate leasehold interests,[95] and any other sums and costs then payable, including rent arrears, have been tendered.[96] Where a lease has been granted pursuant to the 1993 Act, any future tenant may claim a further statutory extension, but none of the statutory provisions conferring security of tenure will apply to the lease or to derivative sub-leases.[97]   **22–257**

F. Tenancies of Flats within the Landlord and Tenant Act 1987, Part I

1. Introduction. Prior to the introduction of the more radical measures of collective and individual enfranchisement conferred on long leaseholders occupying flats under the Leasehold Reform, Housing and Urban Development Act 1993, Part I of the Landlord and Tenant Act 1987 had granted to certain tenants, not necessarily long leaseholders, rights of first refusal on a disposal of the landlord's interest in the property.[98] The Act remains of   **22–258**

---

[93] L.R.H.U.D.A. 1993, s.56.
[94] See generally L.R.H.U.D.A. 1993, Sched. 13, as amended by H.A. 1996, s.110.
[95] L.R.H.U.D.A. 1993, Sched. 13, Pt III.
[96] L.R.H.U.D.A. 1993, s.56(3).
[97] L.R.H.U.D.A. 1993, s.59.
[98] The Landlord and Tenant Act 1987 was enacted in response to the Report of the Nugee Committee, *The Management of Privately Owned Blocks of Flats.* See further Percival (1988) 51 M.L.R. 97; Rodgers [1988] Conv. 122. Following trenchant judicial criticism of the drafting, which, *per* Hobhouse L.J. in *Belvedere Court Management Ltd v. Frogmore Developments Ltd* [1997] Q.B. 858 at 882, "does not disclose a clear and consistent policy and . . . falls between the two stools of being both excessively and inadequately detailed", it has been significantly amended by the Housing Act 1996.

importance, as it is in some respects wider in ambit than the more recent provisions. However, the right of first refusal which it confers is only activated by the landlord's decision to dispose of the property, and the tenants can only buy at the price which he has agreed with the third party purchaser. The Act applies to premises which consist of the whole or part of a building, and which contain two or more flats held by qualifying tenants. The number of flats held by qualifying tenants must exceed 50 per cent of the total number of flats contained in the premises.[99] However, the Act does not apply where more than 50 per cent of the internal floor area of the premises is occupied otherwise than for residential purposes (disregarding the common parts), or the landlord's interest is held by an "exempt landlord" or a "resident landlord"[1]

22–259   **2. Qualifying tenants.** A qualifying tenant is a tenant of a flat under a tenancy *other than* an assured tenancy[2] (or assured agricultural occupancy), a business tenancy, a tenancy terminable on the cessation of his employment, or a protected shorthold tenancy.[3] Thus, most long leaseholders will qualify,[4] as will Rent Act protected or statutory tenants. There is no residence requirement, but a person is not a qualifying tenant of any flat contained in any particular premises consisting of the whole or part of a building if by virtue of one or more tenancies (none of which is excluded as above) he is the tenant not only of the flat in question but also of at least two other flats contained in the premises.[5]

22–260   **3. Machinery.** When the landlord proposes to make a "relevant disposal" (*i.e.* a disposal of any legal or equitable interest in the premises, subject to a lengthy list of exceptions[6]), he must serve an "offer notice" to this effect on the qualifying tenants of the flats contained in the premises.[7] The tenants are given a minimum period of two months in which to decide whether to accept or reject the offer, or to make a counter-offer of their own. If the parties reach agreement, then a binding contract will arise.[8] If the landlord does not inform the qualifying tenants of his disposal (or otherwise contravenes the provisions

---

[99] L.T.A. 1987, s.1(2).

[1] L.T.A. 1987, s.1(3), (4). For the definition of "exempt landlord" (mainly public bodies) and "resident landlord", see L.T.A. 1987, s.58.

[2] Which expression includes assured shorthold tenancies: see Housing Act 1988, s.20(1).

[3] L.T.A. 1987, s.3(1).

[4] As the rent is low, it is unlikely that they will be assured tenants: Housing Act 1988, Sched. 1, para. 3.

[5] L.T.A. 1987, s.3(2), as amended by H.A. 1988, s.119 (with savings: see S.I. 1988 No. 2152).

[6] L.T.A. 1987, s.4, as amended by H.A. 1996, s.90. A disposal takes place on completion of the transfer of the reversion: *Mainwaring v. Trustees of Henry Smith's Charity* [1998] Q.B. 1.

[7] L.T.A. 1987, ss.1(1), 5(1). Failure to serve a notice without reasonable excuse is a criminal offence: L.T.A. 1987, s.10A, added by H.A. 1996, s.91.

[8] See, for the detailed procedure, L.T.A. 1987, ss.5–10, as amended by H.A. 1996, s.92, Sched. 6.

as to notice), then the tenants can enforce their rights against the transferee ("the new landlord") by serving a purchase notice on him[9]; and similar provisions operate against subsequent purchasers of the landlord's interest.[10] The new landlord is obliged to give notice not only of the assignment of the landlord's interest[11] but also of the rights to which it has given rise.[12] The qualifying tenants are entitled to a transfer of the landlord's reversionary interest to them although the building may be comprised in separate titles, and although the statute does not expressly say that the tenants have this right against the new landlord.[13]

4. Price. The price to be paid by the qualifying tenants on their acquisition **22–261** of the landlord's interest is the price at which the disposal which had been proposed would have been made. The rent assessment committee is given jurisdiction to determine questions relating to purchase notices,[14] but this does not entitle the committee to determine the amount of consideration *de novo* as between landlord and tenants.[15]

G. Secure Tenancies

Until Part I of the Housing Act 1980[16] came into force on October 3, 1980, a **22–262** tenant had virtually no statutory protection if his landlord was a local authority or one of various other public bodies, as the Rent Acts had long been excluded in such cases.[17] Since 1945, the number of tenants who for this reason were unprotected had greatly increased, and so the changes made by the 1980 Act were highly significant. Public sector tenants were given the right to buy their dwellings or take a long lease of them on advantageous terms, together with a form of protection as to possession (but not rent) that resembled the provisions for regulated tenancies. In subsequent years, further measures promoted the transfer of housing away from the public sector, and there has been a resultant decline in the public housing stock.[18]

---

[9] L.T.A. 1987, s.12.
[10] L.T.A. 1987, s.16.
[11] L.T.A. 1985, s.3.
[12] L.T.A. 1985, s.3A, added by H.A. 1996, s.93. Failure to give such notice is a criminal offence: *ibid.*
[13] *Belvedere Court Management Ltd v. Frogmore Developments Ltd* [1997] Q.B. 858; *Kay Green v. Twinsectra Ltd* [1996] 1 W.L.R. 1587.
[14] L.T.A. 1987, s.13.
[15] *Cousins v. Metropolitan Guarantee Ltd* [1989] 2 E.G.L.R. 223; *Gregory v. Saddiq* [1991] 1 E.G.L.R. 237.
[16] Amended by the Housing and Building Control Act 1984 and consolidated in Pts IV and V of the Housing Act 1985. Further amendments have been made by, *e.g.*, the Housing and Planning Act 1986 and the Housing Acts of 1988 and 1996.
[17] Rent Act 1977, s.14.
[18] The public sector percentage of the housing stock in Great Britain was 17% in 1951, had risen to 31% by 1981, and fallen again to 17% by 1997: *Housing & Construction Statistics*, HMSO.

I. TENANCIES WITHIN PART IV OF THE 1985 ACT

22–263   1. Secure tenancies

(a) Definition. Subject to exceptions, a secure tenancy is a tenancy under which a dwelling-house is let as a separate dwelling[19] at any time when the "landlord condition" and the "tenant condition" are both satisfied.[20] The landlord condition is satisfied if the landlord's interest belongs to one of a number of public bodies, including local authorities, development corporations, and certain housing co-operatives.[21] As a result of the Housing Act 1988, lettings by housing associations which were entered into on or after January 15, 1989, cannot (subject to certain exceptions) be secure tenancies, but those which commenced prior to this date may well be.[22] The tenant condition is satisfied if the tenant is an individual who occupies the dwelling as his only or principal home; for joint tenants, it suffices if they are all individuals and at least one occupies the dwelling as his home.[23] Part IV also applies to a licence which, had it been a tenancy, would have been a secure tenancy.[24]

22–264   *(b) Exceptions.* There is a long list of exceptions.[25] Some of these correspond to exceptions for protected tenancies under the Rent Act 1977 or assured tenancies under the Housing Act 1988, such as long tenancies, agricultural holdings, farm business tenancies, licensed premises, student lettings and business tenancies. Others meet the special needs of the public sector, such as the tenancies of certain employees whose employment is linked to the dwelling (including the police and fire services), various forms of short-term accommodation, *e.g.* for homeless persons, those who come to the area seeking employment and permanent accommodation, those holding "introductory tenancies"[26] and certain licences granted by almshouse charities.

22–265   *(c) Cessation.* A secure tenancy may cease to be a secure tenancy, as where the landlord condition or the tenant condition is no longer satisfied.[27] Assignment of secure tenancies is generally prohibited.[28] The exceptions to this general rule are "assignments by way of exchange", property adjustment orders made in connection with matrimonial proceedings, and assignments to

---

[19] See *ante*, para. 22–136; *Central YMCA Housing Association Ltd v. Saunders* (1990) 23 H.L.R. 212; *Tyler v. Royal Borough of Kensington & Chelsea* (1991) 23 H.L.R. 380.

[20] H.A. 1985, s.79(1).

[21] H.A. 1985, s.80, as amended by H.A. 1988, ss.83, 140, Sched. 17, para. 106, Sched. 18.

[22] H.A. 1988, s.35(4). Lettings by housing associations on or after January 15, 1989, are usually assured tenancies.

[23] H.A. 1985, s.81; *e.g. Crawley Borough Council v. Sawyer* (1987) 20 H.L.R. 98.

[24] H.A. 1985, s.79(3). The licence must confer exclusive possession: *City of Westminster v. Clarke* [1992] 2 A.C. 288. Licences granted as a "temporary expedient" to those who entered as trespassers are excluded: Housing Act 1985, s.79(4).

[25] H.A. 1985, Sched.1.

[26] See *post*, para. 22–288.

[27] H.A. 1985, ss.80, 81.

[28] H.A. 1985, s.91. Secure tenancies for a term certain granted before November 5, 1982, may be assigned, but this will normally lead to the tenancy ceasing to be secure.

potential successors.[29] Where a tenant sub-lets the whole of the dwelling, or, having sub-let part, sub-lets the remainder, the tenancy will cease to be secure.[30] Where a secure tenancy for a fixed term is ended by a termination order or by effluxion of time, without the tenant being granted another secure tenancy, a periodic tenancy automatically arises in his favour.[31]

2. Succession on death. When the tenant under a secure tenancy dies, there may be a "person qualified to succeed him", *i.e.* a person who at the death was occupying the dwelling as his only or principal home, and was either the tenant's spouse, or else another member of the tenant's family[32] who had resided with him throughout the 12 months ending with his death.[33] If there are two or more qualified persons, the spouse is preferred to the others, and as between the others, the selection, in default of agreement, is made by the landlord.[34] If the secure tenancy is a periodic tenancy, it vests in the qualified person and remains a secure tenancy, whereas if it is a tenancy for a fixed term it vests in the tenant's personal representatives; it then remains a secure tenancy if it is vested in a qualified person, but ceases to be a secure tenancy if it is vested in somebody else or if it is known that on vesting it will not be a secure tenancy.[35] There can be only one such succession: these provisions do not apply where the deceased tenant was himself a successor.[36]

22–266

II. SECURITY OF TENURE

1. Order of court. A secure tenant can terminate the tenancy according to its terms, by giving notice to quit, or by surrendering the lease.[37] However, the termination of a secure tenancy by the landlord, and the consequent recovery of possession of the dwelling, can only be effected by an order for possession made by the court on one of the grounds specified in Part IV of the 1985 Act.[38] A secure tenancy which is either a periodic tenancy or is determinable by the landlord (*e.g.* under a "break" clause) continues until the date on which the tenant is to give up possession under the order.[39] If the landlord seeks to enforce a proviso for forfeiture or re-entry in a fixed-term secure tenancy, the

22–267

---

[29] H.A. 1985, ss.91(3), 92.

[30] H.A. 1985, s.95.

[31] H.A. 1985, s.86. For such orders, see *post*, para. 22–267.

[32] The wide definition in Housing Act 1985, s.113, includes most of those who would take on an intestacy (*ante*, para. 11–088), as well as "unmarried spouses".

[33] H.A. 1985, s.87. Residence need not have been in the premises to which succession is claimed: *Waltham Forest L.B.C. v. Thomas* [1992] 2 A.C. 198.

[34] H.A. 1985, s.89(2).

[35] H.A. 1985, ss.89, 90. Compare regulated tenancies, *ante*, para. 22–180.

[36] H.A. 1985, s. 88.

[37] *Greenwich L.B.C. v. McGready* (1982) 6 H.L.R. 36; *Hammersmith & Fulham L.B.C. v. Monk* [1992] 1 A.C. 478; *R. v. Croydon L.B.C., ex p. Toth* (1986) 20 H.L.R. 576; *City of Westminster v. Peart* (1991) 24 H.L.R. 389.

[38] H.A. 1985, s.82(1). For the position of the secure tenant who remains in possession with the landlord's consent after the termination of the tenancy, see *Greenwich L.B.C. v. Regan* (1996) 28 H.L.R. 469; *Burrows v. Brent L.B.C.* [1996] 1 W.L.R. 1448.

[39] H.A. 1985, s.82(2).

usual provisions for relief apply,[40] and if the court would otherwise have made an order for possession, it must instead make an order terminating the secure tenancy on a specified date, whereupon a periodic tenancy will automatically arise.[41] Neither order can be made unless the landlord has first served a notice in the prescribed form[42] on the tenant, particularising the grounds on which possession is sought. If the tenancy is periodic, the notice must also specify the date after which proceedings may be begun; and this must not be earlier than the date when the notice, if a notice to quit, could have determined the tenancy, apart from the Act.[43] The notice ceases to be effective 12 months after the specified date.[44]

22–268   **2. Grounds for possession.** Part IV of the Act specifies 18 grounds for possession.[45] Many of these are closely similar to the grounds for possession for assured and regulated tenancies considered above,[45a] and so are not detailed here. There are three categories. The court cannot make an order:

   (i) on Grounds 1 to 8 unless the court considers it reasonable to make the order;

   (ii) on Grounds 9 to 11, unless the court is satisfied that suitable alternative accommodation[46] will be available for the tenant when the order takes effect; or

   (iii) on Grounds 12 to 16, unless both these requirements are satisfied.

22–269   Further, no order can be made on any grounds not specified in the landlord's notice, although with the leave of the court those grounds may be added to or altered.[47] Unless the order for possession is made on Grounds 9 to 11, the court has wide powers to adjourn the proceedings, or to stay or suspend execution of the order, or to postpone the date for possession; but on doing

---

[40] *Ante*, para. 14–129.
[41] H.A. 1985, ss.82(3), 86.
[42] S.I. 1987 No. 755, as amended by S.I. 1997 Nos 71, 377; *Torridge D.C. v. Jones* (1985) 18 H.L.R. 107; *Dudley Metropolitan Council v. Bailey* (1990) 22 H.L.R. 424; *Camden L.B.C. v. Oppong* (1996) 28 H.L.R. 701. The court has power to dispense with the notice where it is just and equitable to do so: H.A. 1985, s.83, as amended by H.A. 1996, s.147.
[43] There are modifications where the landlord is invoking Ground 2 or 2A: see H.A. 1996, s.147, amending H.A. 1985, s.83, and adding H.A. 1985, s.83A.
[44] H.A. 1985, s.83, as amended. There is no need to serve an additional notice in relation to the "automatic" periodic tenancy which arises on termination of a secure term certain: *ibid.*, s.83(6).
[45] H.A. 1985, s.84, Sched. 2, as amended by Housing and Planning Act 1986, s.9(1), H.A. 1988, Sched. 17, and H.A. 1996, s.147(2).
[45a] See *ante*, paras 22–150 *et seq.*, and 22–190 *et seq.*
[46] Although this is similar to "suitable alternative accommodation" for assured and regulated tenancies the 1985 Act is rather more detailed: see Sched. 2, Pt IV thereof.
[47] H.A. 1985, s.84(3).

this the court must impose terms as to making payments for occupation and paying any arrears of rent, unless this would cause "exceptional hardship" to the lessee, or otherwise be unreasonable.[48] In Grounds 9 to 11, however, the court cannot postpone the date for possession for more than 14 days, or six weeks if "exceptional hardship" would otherwise be caused.[49]

(a) Reasonableness.

GROUND 1: RENT UNPAID OR BREACH OF COVENANT. **22–270**

GROUND 2: NUISANCE.[50] **22–271**

GROUND 2A: DOMESTIC VIOLENCE.[51] **22–272**

GROUND 3: DETERIORATION OF DWELLING-HOUSE. **22–273**

GROUND 4: DETERIORATION OF FURNITURE. **22–274**

GROUND 5: FALSE STATEMENT.[52] **22–275**

GROUND 6: PREMIUM. The tenancy has been assigned for a premium. **22–276**

GROUND 7: MISCONDUCT. A service tenant is guilty of misconduct. **22–277**

GROUND 8: TEMPORARY ACCOMMODATION. The tenant became a temporary **22–278** tenant of the dwelling while works were being carried out on another dwelling which he occupied as his only or principal home on a secure tenancy, and after completion of the works that other dwelling is again available for him on a secure tenancy.

(b) Suitable alternative accommodation available. **22–279**

GROUND 9: OVERCROWDING. The dwelling is over-crowded in circumstances that render the occupier guilty of an offence.[53]

GROUND 10: DEMOLITION OR RECONSTRUCTION. The landlord intends, within **22–280** a reasonable time of obtaining possession of the dwelling, to demolish or reconstruct some or all of the premises comprising the dwelling, or to do other works on it, and he cannot reasonably do this without obtaining possession of the dwelling.

GROUND 10A: REDEVELOPMENT.[54] The landlord wishes to dispose of the **22–281** dwelling in accordance with an approved redevelopment scheme.[55]

GROUND 11: CHARITY. The landlord is a charity and the tenant's continued **22–282** occupation of the dwelling conflicts with the charity's objects.

---

[48] H.A. 1985, s.85.
[49] H.A. 1980, s.89(1); and see *ante*, para. 22–149.
[50] Amended by H.A. 1996, s.144.
[51] Added by H.A. 1996, s.145.
[52] Amended by H.A. 1996, s.146.
[53] Under H.A. 1985, Pt X.
[54] Added by the Housing and Planning Act 1986, s.9(1).
[55] See further H.A. 1985, Sched. 2, Pt V, added by the Housing and Planning Act 1986, s.9(2).

22–283 GROUND 12: SERVICE TENANT. In certain cases either the dwelling is reasonably required for an employee or the tenant is a service tenant whose employment has ended.

22–284 *(c) Reasonableness, and suitable alternative accommodation available.*

GROUND 13: DISABLED PERSON'S HOME. Features of the dwelling designed to make it suitable for occupation by a physically disabled person differ substantially from those of ordinary dwellings, but no such person lives there, and the landlord requires it for occupation by such a person.

22–285 GROUND 14: SPECIAL NEEDS. The landlord is a housing association or housing trust which lets dwellings only to those whose circumstances (other than merely financial) make it especially difficult for them to satisfy their housing needs, but no such person lives in the dwelling (or else a local authority has offered the tenant a separate dwelling on a secure tenancy), and the landlord requires it for occupation by such a person.

22–286 GROUND 15: SPECIAL FACILITIES. The dwelling is one of a group of dwellings which the landlord habitually lets to those with special needs, and some social service or special facility is provided nearby in order to assist such persons, but no such person lives in the dwelling, and the landlord requires it for occupation by such a person.

22–287 GROUND 16: OVER-EXTENSIVE ACCOMMODATION. The dwelling provides more extensive accommodation than the tenant normally requires, and not only did the tenant succeed to the tenancy when the previous tenant died (as a member of the family, but not as his spouse), but also notice of the proceedings for possession was given more than six but less than 12 months after the death.[56]

III. INTRODUCTORY TENANCIES

22–288 Part V of the Housing Act 1996, titled "Conduct of Tenants", permits local housing authorities and housing action trusts to operate, by election, an "introductory tenancy regime". Such a scheme enables the landlord to give new tenants a trial or "probationary" period, during which recovery of possession may be effected expeditiously, without proof of a ground for possession. Thus, where a landlord elects to operate an introductory tenancy scheme, every periodic tenancy[57] entered into by the landlord which would otherwise have been a secure tenancy will, subject to limited exceptions, be an introductory tenancy for a 12-month period from the date the tenancy was entered into.[58] While the tenancy is introductory, the landlord has an absolute right to a possession order from the court, provided proper notice is given to

---

[56] Where no notice is served, and the court dispenses with service, the possession proceedings must be begun within this time: H.A. 1996, s.147(3).

[57] "Tenancy" includes most licences to occupy: see H.A. 1996, s.126.

[58] For calculation of period, and counting of earlier time as a tenant, see H.A. 1996, s.125.

the tenant, together with reasons for the landlord's decision to claim possession.[59] The tenant has the right to have the decision reviewed by the landlord,[60] and although there is no statutory right to an independent review,
judicial review is available to a tenant who considers that the decision to
terminate was not based on reasonable grounds.[61] If no proceedings are
brought within the 12-month period, the tenancy will automatically become
secure within Part IV of the Housing Act 1985. Provision is made for
succession to an introductory tenancy on death. An introductory tenancy
cannot be assigned, save by virtue of a property adjustment order on divorce,
or an *inter vivos* assignment to the prospective successor.[62]

IV. NO CONTROL OF RENT

Part IV of the Housing Act 1985 provides security of tenure, but imposes no
system of rent control. When dwellings are owned by local authorities, they
may make "such reasonable charges as they may determine for the tenancy or
occupation of their houses".[63] In so doing, they must have particular regard to
the principle that the rents of houses of any class or description should bear
broadly the same proportion to private sector rents[64] as the rents of houses of
any other class or description.[65] A tenant may challenge the rent set by his
local authority landlord by judicial review, although the courts have proved to
be somewhat reluctant to intervene.[66]

22–289

V. THE RIGHT TO BUY

Part V of the Housing Act 1985[67] confers on many secure tenants the right to
buy, at discounted prices, either the freehold of the dwelling or a long lease of
it at a low rent. The practical result is that tenants who exercise this statutory
right will become owners, and although they will normally continue to make
regular payments much as they did while they were tenants, these can go
towards discharging a mortgage instead of being mere rent. The tenant's right
to a mortgage from the landlord, part of the original statutory bundle of rights,
has been abolished.[68]

22–290

---

[59] H.A. 1996, ss.127, 128.
[60] See further Introductory Tenants (Review) Regulations 1997 (S.I. 1997 No. 72).
[61] H.A. 1996, s.129. The tenant cannot, however, defend an action for possession on this ground:
Manchester City Council v. Cochrane [1999] 1 W.L.R. 809.
[62] H.A. 1996, ss.131–134. See also provisions requiring publication of information, and for
consultation with tenants: H.A. 1996, ss.136, 137.
[63] H.A. 1985, s.24(1).
[64] *i.e.* rents of houses let on assured tenancies under the Housing Act 1988: H.A. 1985, s.24(4),
added by Local Government and Housing Act 1989, s.162.
[65] H.A. 1985, s.24(3), added by Local Government and Housing Act 1989, s.162.
[66] *Luby v. Newcastle under Lyme Corporation* [1965] 1 Q.B. 214; *Wandsworth L.B.C. v. Winder
(No. 2)* (1987) 19 H.L.R. 204.
[67] Consolidating, *inter alia*, Pt I of the Housing Act 1980.
[68] L.R.H.U.D.A. 1993, s.107.

22–291 **1. Conditions**

(a) *The tenant.*[69] A secure tenant has the right to buy only if he has been a "public sector tenant" for a total of at least two years. Such a tenant is closely similar to a secure tenant, although the list of landlords who satisfy the "landlord condition" is longer. Different periods can be added together to make up the two years, and so may periods when the tenant would have been a public sector tenant if Part V or its predecessor had been in force, together with any periods of a public sector tenancy of his or her deceased spouse if they occupied the same dwelling as their only or principal home. Neither the landlord nor the dwelling need have been the same throughout, though any period when the landlord was exempt from the tenant's right to buy is excluded. The tenant cannot exercise the right if during the course of his application he ceases to be a secure tenant, if a possession order has been made against him, or if he is the subject of bankruptcy proceedings.[70]

22–292 (b) *The landlord.*[71] There is no right to buy if the landlord is a charitable housing trust or a housing association that is charitable, co-operative or unsubsidised.[72] However, a tenant of a registered social landlord[73] is entitled to acquire the dwelling if he is an assured tenant (but not an assured shorthold tenant or long tenant) or a secure tenant, if the dwelling was provided with public money,[74] and has remained in the social rented sector since that time, subject to satisfying any further qualifying conditions.[75] Such tenants do not enjoy the right to buy on "rent to mortgage terms", or the "preserved right to buy".[76]

22–293 (c) *The dwelling-house.*[77] Certain types of dwelling are exempt. These include certain sheltered or adapted accommodation for physically disabled, mentally disordered, or elderly persons. Dwellings let to service tenants by local authorities, development corporations and certain other public bodies are also exempt if they are held mainly for non-housing purposes.

22–294 **2. Freehold or long lease.**[78] If the dwelling is a "house" and the landlord is the freeholder, the right is to buy the freehold or a long lease. If the dwelling

---

[69] H.A. 1985, ss.118, 119, Sched. 4.

[70] H.A. 1985, s.121; *Sutton L.B.C. v. Swann* (1985) 18 H.L.R. 140; *Muir Group Housing Association Ltd v. Thornley* (1993) 25 H.L.R. 89. On the effect of a concurrent application for a possession order and initiation of the right to buy procedure, see *Bristol City Council v. Lovell* [1998] 1 W.L.R. 446, overruling *Dance v. Welwyn Hatfield D.C.* [1990] 1 W.L.R. 1097.

[71] H.A. 1985, Sched. 4, paras 7, 8.

[72] H.A. 1985, s.120, Sched. 5, paras 1–3.

[73] H.A. 1996, ss.1, 2.

[74] H.A. 1996, s.16(2). This definition requires the dwelling to have been acquired by the landlord after the commencement of the relevant provision (April 1, 1997).

[75] H.A. 1996, ss.16, 17.

[76] S.I. 1997 No. 619, which contains further exclusions and qualifications; and see *post*, paras 22–299, 22–301.

[77] H.A. 1985, s.120, Sched. 5, paras 4–12, as amended by H.A. 1988, s.123 and L.R.H.U.D.A. 1993, s.106.

[78] H.A. 1985, s.118.

is a "flat", the right is to buy a long lease. If the dwelling is a house, and the landlord is not the freeholder, the tenant may still have the right to buy the freehold if those who hold interests superior to those of the landlord are themselves public sector bodies.[79] For these purposes, every dwelling that is not a "house" is a "flat".[80] If a building is divided horizontally, the flats or other units are not "houses", but if it is divided vertically the units may be houses, though no unit can be a house if a material part of it lies above or below the rest of the structure. The tenant may require any land used with the dwelling to be included, if this is reasonable.[81]

3. The price. The price payable is the value of the dwelling when the right to buy is exercised, less the discount.[82] **22–295**

(a) Value.[83] The value of the dwelling is the price that it would fetch if sold **22–296** with vacant possession by a willing seller on the open market, on the assumption that neither the tenant nor any member of his family living with him wants to buy it. For these purposes, any improvements made by the tenant or certain predecessors of his are to be disregarded, and so is any failure by them to keep the dwelling in good internal repair. What is valued is the interest obtained by the tenant, namely, the fee simple, or, if he buys a lease, a lease at a ground rent not exceeding £10 a year for not less than 125 years, or for the whole of the landlord's term (less five days) if the landlord has only a shorter leasehold. In each case there are various specified terms as to easements, covenants, and so on.

(b) Discount.[84] From the value so ascertained, a discount based on the **22–297** length of the discount period is deducted. In broad terms, the discount period is the total of the periods for which the tenant (or his spouse or deceased spouse) has been a public sector tenant or has been occupying service accommodation as a member of the regular armed forces of the Crown. In the case of a house,[85] the discount is 32 per cent of the value plus 1 per cent for each year by which the discount period exceeds two years. But the discount may not exceed either 60 per cent or £50,000, nor may it reduce the price below an amount determined by the Secretary of State as being the costs incurred in respect of the dwelling over the last eight years; and the discount will be reduced by the amount of certain previous discounts given.

---

[79] See S.I. 1993 No. 2240.
[80] H.A. 1985, s.183.
[81] H.A. 1985, s.184. (Land let together with the dwelling, in so far as it is not agricultural land exceeding two acres, is automatically treated as part of the dwelling).
[82] H.A. 1985, s.126.
[83] H.A. 1985, s.127; s.139, Sched. 6.
[84] H.A. 1985, ss.129–131, Sched. 4, as amended by Housing Act 1988, s.122; S.I. 1989 No. 513.
[85] In the case of a flat, the discount is 44%, plus 2% for each year over the two years, with a ceiling of £70,000.

22–298   *(c) Repayment of discount.*[86] If within three years the freehold or lease is disposed of, the tenant or his successors in title must pay the landlord the whole of the discount, less one-third for each year that has elapsed since the conveyance or grant. The conveyance or lease must contain a covenant to this effect, and the liability will be a registrable charge on the dwelling. But certain disposals are exempted, *e.g.* disposals within the family or under a will or intestacy.

22–299   **4. Acquisition on "rent to mortgage terms".** A tenant who does not wish to exercise his right to buy immediately (perhaps because he cannot obtain a sufficient mortgage) may choose to acquire the freehold or leasehold interest in his dwelling on "rent to mortgage terms".[87] The statutory provisions are complex.[88] On the tenant making an "initial payment", the landlord is obliged to convey the freehold or grant the lease, retaining a "share" representing the sum left outstanding by the tenant. The tenant's "rent" gradually pays off the landlord's share, and the tenant is free to redeem the landlord's interest by making a "final payment" at any time.

22–300   **5. Procedure.** The tenant claims his right to buy by serving a notice in the prescribed form[89] on the landlord.[90] Within four weeks the landlord must serve on the tenant a notice in the prescribed form either admitting the tenant's right to buy, or denying it and stating the reasons.[91] When the right has been admitted or established, the landlord must within eight weeks (or 12, if a lease is being bought) serve a notice on the tenant, describing the dwelling (including structural defects known to the landlord), stating the price and how it was computed, estimating service charges or improvement contributions, and stating the terms to be contained in the conveyance or lease, with certain other matters.[92] If the value or the discount are disputed, the tenant may then have them determined by the District Valuer or the county court respectively.[93] When all matters relating to the grant have been agreed or determined, the landlord is bound to convey the fee simple or grant the lease to the tenant, unless his rent is four weeks in arrear; and this duty is enforceable by

---

[86] H.A. 1985, ss.155, 156, 159, 160, as amended by Housing and Planning Act 1986, s.2, Sched. 5.

[87] Acquisition on "rent to mortgage terms" has replaced the strange and complex "shared ownership leases", for which see the fifth edition of this work, at p. 1140.

[88] L.R.H.U.D.A. 1993, ss.108–118, Sched. 16, amending H.A. 1985, s.143 *et seq.*

[89] Forms prescribed for the right to buy procedure are to be found in S.I. 1986 No. 2194, as amended by S.I. 1993 No. 2246.

[90] H.A. 1985, s.122. The tenant may elect to "share" the right to buy with any members of his family (up to a maximum of three) who are occupying the dwelling-house as their only or principal home. Such persons are then treated as joint tenants for the purposes of the application, and can, in the event of the death of the tenant, insist on completion of the acquisition: H.A. 1985, s.123; *Harrow L.B.C. v. Tonge* (1992) 25 H.L.R. 99.

[91] H.A. 1985, s.124.

[92] H.A. 1985, ss.125, 125A–C, added by Housing and Planning Act 1986, s.4(2).

[93] H.A. 1985, ss.128, 181.

injunction.[94] If the tenant defaults after receiving successive notices to complete, his notice to buy is deemed to be withdrawn.[95] The county court has a general jurisdiction in these matters[96]; and if one or more tenants have difficulty in exercising their right to buy effectively and expeditiously, the Secretary of State may carry out the landlord's duties, with power to make vesting orders.[97]

6. Preserved right to buy. Recent government policy, exemplified by the tenant's right to buy itself, has been to promote a transfer of housing away from the public sector.[98] Tenants who do not exercise their right to buy may well lose a public sector landlord in the event of an assignment of the reversion to a private sector landlord. In such circumstances, the tenant's right to buy will, subject to exceptions, be "preserved" in favour of the tenant and certain successors.[99] The tenant should register this right, as it cannot be treated as an overriding interest even though the tenant may be in actual occupation.[1]   **22–301**

Part 4

THE EFFECT OF SOCIAL CONTROL OF LAND

During the twentieth century Parliament has been increasingly active in curtailing and restricting the rights of landowners where this has appeared to be necessary and desirable in order to promote perceived social and public values. Planning control and the protection of tenants have been by far the most important products of these activities; but they do not stand alone. A good example is the provision of public rights of access to the countryside under the National Parks and Access to the Countryside Act 1949.[2]   **22–302**

Under this Act, the public may, for the purpose of open-air recreation (but not organised games), be given access to any open country that predominantly consists of mountains, moors, heaths, downs, cliffs or foreshore; but this is subject to wide prohibitions against interfering with the land in its natural state

---

[94] H.A. 1985, s.138; *Dance v. Welwyn Hatfield D.C.* [1990] 1 W.L.R. 1097; *Taylor v. Newham L.B.C.* [1993] 1 W.L.R. 444.

[95] H.A. 1985, ss.140, 141. The burden is on the landlord to establish the validity of notices to complete: *Milne-Berry v. Tower Hamlets L.B.C.* (1995) 28 H.L.R. 225.

[96] H.A. 1985, s.181.

[97] H.A. 1985, s.164; *R. v. Secretary of State for the Environment, ex p. Norwich City Council* [1982] Q.B. 808.

[98] See, *e.g.* H.A. 1985, ss.32, 43; H.A. 1988, Pts III and IV.

[99] H.A. 1985, ss.171A–171H, added by Housing and Planning Act 1986, s.8(1), and subsequently amended by Housing Act 1988, s.127. For details of the present law, see S.I. 1993 No. 2241.

[1] H.A. 1985, Sched. 9A, added by Housing and Planning Act 1986, s.8(2), Sched. 2.

[2] National Parks and Access to the Countryside Act 1949, replacing and amplifying the Access to Mountains Act 1939.

or damaging it or anything on it.[3] These rights may be provided under an agreement made by the local planning authority with the owners of interests in the land, or, if no adequate agreement can be made, by a compulsory order confirmed by the Secretary of State, subject to compensating any persons whose interests in the land are depreciated in value by the order.[4] Such access may also be provided by the local planning authority or the Secretary of State acquiring the land compulsorily.[5] A wider "right to roam" has yet to be enacted.

22–303   The general effect of the growth of social control has been to create a shift of emphasis. Formerly, the conveyancer was concerned to see that his client obtained a good title to his land and that his client's instructions as to any dispositions by will, settlement or other transactions were carried out as suitably and effectively as possible. These objects remain; and the extension of registration of title and other improvements have to some extent simplified the task. But social control, on the other hand, has increased the burden. The client must not only obtain a good title to the land but also be assured that he will be able to use it as he wishes, without being frustrated by planning control or the rights of protected tenants. Often "use" stands side by side with title as a matter for investigation, and sometimes it overshadows it.

The general tendency has been for the ambit of social control to increase, though in 85 years of protecting tenants there have been many fluctuations both in the extent and in the content of control, with periods of expansion and contraction alternating. Unlike land law in general, social control is especially responsive to political views, the pressure of public opinion, and changes in economic conditions: and the future is unpredictable.

---

[3] National Parks and Access to the Countryside Act 1949, ss.59, 60, 114.
[4] *ibid.*, ss.64, 65, 70.
[5] *ibid.*, ss.76, 77.

EXPLANATORY NOTES

1. Style

In printing the statutes, the Queen's Printer's copies of the Acts and statutory instruments have been departed from to the following extent only:

(a) The formal words of enactment of the Act have been omitted.

(b) Marginal notes have been set in bold type and moved into the text.

(c) Marginal and other references to the year and chapter number of Acts cited in the text of the Act have been omitted.

2. Repeals and amendments

Square brackets are used in the text of the statutes to indicate provisions that have been inserted or substituted; italic is used to indicate provisions that have been repealed.

3. S.I. Standard forms

Statutory instruments, which provide standard forms requiring to be completed often, use italic and square brackets as a guide to filling up the forms. These forms are here printed in accordance with the style, and so italic and square brackets here do not always have their usual significance.

ACTIONS FOR RECOVERY OF LAND

THE substantive law of real property has been deeply marked by the remedies which the law has provided, at various periods of history, for the recovery of land. The purpose of this Appendix is to give a short account of the way in which these remedies have influenced the character of real property law and the concept of title. Of no branch of our law can it be more truly said that it developed on the principle *ubi remedium, ibi jus*: rights result from remedies. The story begins with the ancient real actions and ends with modern reforms.

Section 1. The Real Actions

1. The writ of right. The real actions began as remedies to enforce feudal customs.[1] Originally feudal lords were sovereign in their own courts baron. If they chose to depart from the customs of their courts, *e.g.* as to inheritance of a tenant's fee, no redress was available to the disappointed claimant. The first attempt by the Crown to meet this grievance was by the writ of right. This commanded the lord to "do full right" to the claimant, with the threat that if he did not, the sheriff would.[2] As the lord was often unable to grant the land to the claimant, because he had accepted another's homage for it,[3] the action was transferred to the county court,[4] where it was originally tried by battle. In or about 1179, Henry II introduced a new procedure, the Grand Assize, by which the defendant could claim trial before royal justices.[5] Various forms of the writ were in time adapted to different cases, including claims to incorporeal hereditaments. Procedure was extremely cumbersome, with numerous

---

[1] For an authoritative modern treatment of these actions, see S. F. C. Milsom, *Historical Foundations of the Common Law* (2nd ed.), chap. 6. For more detail, see S. F. C. Milsom, *The Legal Framework of English Feudalism.*

[2] For the form of writ see *Glanvill* (ed. G. D. G. Hall), I, 6 (p. 5); J. H. Baker, *An Introduction to English Legal History* (3rd ed.), p. 613. The writ emerged in the mid-twelfth century.

[3] The person who had given homage was the notional defendant to the action, and was known as "the tenant". The real defendant was, however, often the lord, because if the claimant succeeded, the lord could be compelled to find other land for the ousted tenant (*escambium*). By taking his homage the lord undertook to protect the tenant in his holding.

[4] By a process called "*tolt*".

[5] Either in eyre or on special commission. The action was transferred from the county court by writ of *pone*.

pretexts for making essoins (excuses for non-appearance and other defaults) and other dilatory pleas.

The writ of right developed at a time when land was heritable but not freely alienable. The only effective method of alienating land in the twelfth century was by subinfeudation, rather than, as now, by substitution.[6]

2. The possessory assizes. In origin, the four possessory assizes, like the writ of right, were intended to provide speedy remedies against lords who departed from the customs of their feudal courts. They were tried by royal justices with a jury. Two of the assizes must be mentioned.[7] The first is the assize of *mort d'ancestor*,[8] which in origin was probably intended to prevent feudal lords from taking a deceased tenant's land into their own hands and then excluding the heir until he agreed to pay an exorbitant relief.[9] It enabled the heir to recover the land from the lord swiftly and leave the appropriate relief to subsequent agreement. The other is *novel disseisin*. The wording of the writ suggests that it originally provided a means by which a tenant could recover his land when it had been taken from him by his feudal lord without proper observance of his feudal customs, as for example in a dispute (real or contrived) about services due from the tenant.[10]

In time, particularly after the statute *Quia Emptores* 1290 had prohibited alienation by subinfeudation,[11] these assizes came to be used against third parties who had wrongly taken the land than against lords who had abused their feudal rights. The actions therefore came to protect possession, whether rightful or wrongful.

Novel disseisin, as its name implies, was intended at first to be a speedy remedy. But no new limitation date was prescribed after the Statute of Westminster I 1275 appointed the year 1242, at the same time as it appointed the year 1189 for the writ of right and other purposes.[12] Thus the action lost its "novel" aspect and became merely one form of proprietary action for trying title.[13]

3. Writs of entry. The writs of entry were developed in the thirteenth century as a means by which lords could recover land from tenants "who had been admitted under earlier grants which were either invalid or no longer

---

[6] *Ante*, para. 2–039.

[7] The others were *darrein presentment*, which was to resolve disputes as to the right to present to a living, and *utrum*, which was to determine whether land had been given in free alms to the church, without feudal service to the lord.

[8] Introduced by the Assize of Northampton 1176, c. 4. For specimen writs, see *Glanvill*, XIII, 3 (p. 150); J. H. Baker, *An Introduction to English Legal History*, p. 617.

[9] S. F. C. Milsom, *Historical Foundations of the Common Law*, p. 135. For reliefs, see *ante*, para. 2–012.

[10] S. F. C. Milsom, *Historical Foundations of the Common Law*, p. 140. For specimen writs, see *Glanvill*, XIII, 33 (p. 167); J. H. Baker, *An Introduction to English Legal History*, p. 619.

[11] *Ante*, para. 2–040.

[12] D. W. Sutherland, *The Assize of Novel Disseisin*, p. 139.

[13] *ibid.*, at pp. 153 *et seq.*; S. F. C. Milsom, *Historical Foundations of the Common Law*, p. 157.

availed them".[14] These writs eventually covered many cases for which the older actions were not adapted.[15] Their common feature was that the plaintiff claiming the land averred that the defendant or his predecessor in title "had no entry" thereto save through some wrongful act or event. This put in issue that act or event alone, and not the whole title. The Statute of Marlbridge 1267 allowed writs of entry "in the *post*", in which the defendant's wrongful title, if complicated, did not have to be pleaded precisely, but it was enough to claim that he came in after (*post*) the wrongful act or event.[16] This rounded off the system of the real actions, which would then meet any case. But they became a "hopeless tangle"[17] and better remedies were therefore badly needed. Indeed, for a while, freeholders resorted to the action of trespass when seeking to recover land, even though it was not a real action but gave only a remedy in damages.[18]

All the real actions were in essence demands for seisin, and could not therefore be used by leaseholders or copyholders.[19]

Section 2. The Action of Ejectment

1. Origin. The action of ejectment[20] was originally invented for the protection of leaseholders, but was later allowed to copyholders also.[21] Since it was a species of the action of trespass (its proper title was "trespass in ejectment"), it belonged to a group of actions which were of later invention than the real actions, and were free from most of their archaisms. It was therefore pressed into service by freeholders as well, at a period when the real actions had become intolerable. This was done with the aid of John Doe and Richard Roe and some elaborate legal fictions.

2. Recovery of leaseholds. As leases grew in popularity, it became necessary to protect tenants by some better remedy than a mere action of trespass for damages. The action *Quaere ejecit infra terminum*, introduced about 1235, did allow a tenant to recover his land specifically, but it was held to be confined to actions against the lessor and his successors.[22] It was not until the second half of the fifteenth century that the common law courts, fearing competition from the specific remedies available in the Chancery, abandoned

---

[14] J. H. Baker, *An Introduction to English Legal History*, p. 268. For a specimen writ, see *ibid.*, p. 615.

[15] For some of the advantages enjoyed by such writs over the writ of right, see D. W. Sutherland, *The Assize of Novel Disseisin*, p. 82.

[16] Maitland, *Forms of Action*, p. 42.

[17] *ibid.*, 43.

[18] See D. W. Sutherland, *The Assize of Novel Disseisin*, chap. V.

[19] See *ante*, para. 3–018; S. F. C. Milsom, *Historical Foundations of the Common Law*, chap. 7; A. W. B. Simpson, *A History of the Land Law* (2nd ed.), pp. 71–77; chap. 7.

[20] For the action of ejectment, see A. W. B. Simpson, *A History of the Land Law*, chap. 7; Bl.Comm. iii, 200, and appendix No. II.

[21] *Melwich v. Luter* (1588) 4 Co.Rep. 26a; H.E.L. iii, 209; vii, 9.

[22] H.E.L. iii, 214; A. W. B. Simpson, *A History of the Land Law*, p. 74.

their scruples and allowed a leaseholder to recover his land specifically from any wrongful claimant.[23] By awarding a writ of possession to a leaseholder, and by strengthening the remedy in other ways, a personal action of trespass was "licked into the form of a real action".[24] The result was the action of trespass in ejectment,[25] or, for short, "ejectment". Once the leaseholder was able to recover his land from all comers, it could no longer be denied that he had an estate in the land (a right *in rem*), or that he held it in tenure.

3. Procedure. By 1600, a century after its invention, ejectment was in common use by freeholders; and by about 1650 its form for this purpose had been perfected.[26] A full description need not be given, but the essence of the action was that the nominal plaintiff was John Doe, asserting that he was tenant of the true plaintiff and that he (Doe) had entered upon the land and had thence been ejected by Richard Roe. In the perfected form of the action Doe and Roe were imaginary characters, Roe being known as "the casual ejector". The first real step in the proceedings was that the plaintiff's solicitor sent to the defendant the declaration (or statement of claim) in Doe's action against Roe, under cover of a letter advising the defendant to apply for leave to defend the action in Roe's place and ending "otherwise I shall suffer judgment to be entered against me and you will be turned out of possession. Your loving friend, Richard Roe".[27] It was then essential for the true defendant to appear as such, but the court would allow him to do so only if he confessed the lease, entry and ouster: that is to say, if he undertook not to dispute any of the fictitious allegations. Thus, when the action came to trial, the only question left was whether Doe had a good claim to the land, and this was merely the question whether the plaintiff, as Doe's lessor, had a better title than the defendant. The action was then entitled *Doe d. A v. B*, meaning *Doe on the demise of A v. B.*[28]

4. Limitations. This piece of make-believe rapidly put the real actions out of business. But it did not supplant them completely. In the first place, ejectment was subject to a 20-year period of limitation; but longer periods were appointed for the real actions, so that after 20 years a plaintiff might find that only a real action was open to him.[29] Secondly, ejectment was also barred if the plaintiff had lost his right of entry upon the land, for then he had no title

---

[23] Bl.Comm. iii, 200; H.E.L. vii, 8, n. 7. Specific restitution in ejectment was finally allowed in 1499, after a period of uncertainty: H.E.L. iii, 216; A. W. B. Simpson, *A History of the Land Law*, p. 144.

[24] *Goodtitle v. Tombs* (1770) 3 Wils. K.B. 118 at 120 *per* Wilmot C.J. For details see H.E.L. vii, 13.

[25] Its Latin title was a trespass *de ejectione firmae*.

[26] For details, see H.E.L. vii, 10.

[27] The common forms of these documents are printed in Sutton, *Personal Actions at Common Law*, pp. 53, 54, and in Bl.Comm. iii, appendix, No. II.

[28] The plaintiff could, however, use any names he pleased, and sometimes the causal ejector was named as the defendant; thus cases were tendentiously entitled *Fairclaim d. Fowler v. Shamtitle* (1762) 3 Burr. 1290 and *Goodtitle d. Pye v. Badtitle* (1800) 8 T.R. 638.

[29] H.E.L. vii, 20, 22.

to grant an effective lease in possession to Doe; and there were certain occasions when, for technical reasons derived from the medieval law, a right of entry was "tolled" (taken away), and all that remained was a right of action.[30] In those cases the plaintiff would be driven to fall back on the real actions, for although he had a title, he could not sue in ejectment. These cases, like novel disseisin in its early days, provide examples of a wrongful possessor being protected against the true owner. Thirdly, ejectment would not lie for incorporeal hereditaments such as advowsons, where the fictions of lease, entry and ouster broke down.[31]

5. Titles relative. The theory that the action of ejectment introduced a new concept of "ownership" into English law, in the sense that a plaintiff had to prove a title that was absolutely good rather than one that was relatively better than the defendant's, was a fallacy. The issue in ejectment was a purely relative one, and the relativity of all titles, which all depend in the last resort upon possession, has already been explained.[32] Far from requiring a plaintiff to prove absolute ownership, the action of ejectment preserved the conception of relative titles which had been part of English law from the time of the writ of right, while at the same time avoiding the difficulties which surrounded the real actions. What it did was to shift the basis of title from the feudal concept of seisin to the modern concept of adverse possession.

Section 3. Statutory Reforms

1. Abolition of real actions. The real actions were abolished by the Real Property Limitation Act 1833.[33] The only exceptions were the old actions for dower and advowsons, for which there were no satisfactory substitutes.[34] At the same time the old rules about "tolling" rights of entry were abolished.[35] Thus the action of ejectment was left without competitors. The action itself underwent no reform, and Doe and Roe still had to play their old parts in actions by freeholders.

2. Abolition of forms of action. Finally the Common Law Procedure Act 1852 abolished the forms of action in general and ejectment in particular.[36] Thereafter a plaintiff merely had to institute his action for the recovery of land by pleading his claim to it in ordinary language. But this did not bring about any change in the substantive law: an action for the recovery of land would

---

[30] *ibid.*; Lightwood, *Possession of Land*, p. 44; Co.Litt. 237a, 325a. The old law was very complex.

[31] H.E.L. vii, 21.

[32] *Ante*, para. 3–122.

[33] s.36, naming the various actions.

[34] *ibid.* These exceptions were abolished by the Common Law Procedure Act 1860, ss.26, 27; this was the final disappearance of real actions.

[35] Real Property Limitation Act 1833, s.39.

[36] ss.168–221.

meet with the same success or failure as an action of ejectment would have done before the Act. Similarly, when new rules of court were introduced by the Judicature Acts 1873–1875,[37] the new procedure made no change in the substantive law relating to titles. But the amalgamation of legal and equitable jurisdiction[38] meant that the same form of proceedings could be used to assert either a legal or an equitable title,[39] thus consummating a reform which Lord Mansfield had unsuccessfully attempted in the eighteenth century, when the action of ejectment was confined to claims at law.[40]

3. Modern law

(a) Title to land. The law of title to land remains as it was in the latter days of the action of ejectment. An action for recovery of land is still in essence an action of trespass. However, as is explained below, the scope of the action has recently been widened.

(b) Remedies

(1) SUMMARY POSSESSION PROCEEDINGS. Under the Civil Procedure Rules there are two swift remedies against a person who occupies land without the consent of a person who has a right to possession of them. It has recently been held that these remedies are available not only to an estate owner (whether or not he is in possession of the land), but also to a licensee, whether he is in possession or merely has a contractual right to possession.[41] The result is striking. Not only will possession be protected against all save those who have a better right to possess the land, but the mere *right* to possess will also be, even where the person having that right has no estate in or title to the land.[41a]

First, the claimant may issue a claim form seeking possession even if he cannot discover the names of the squatters. The court may make an order for possession a specified number of clear days[42] after it has been served.[43] On proof of the case, the court must make the order. There is no power to suspend

---

[37] Judicature Act 1873, Sched. There is now one code of procedure governing both the High Court and the county court: see the Civil Procedure Rules, made pursuant to the Civil Procedure Act 1997, s.1.

[38] *Ante*, para. 4–017.

[39] See *General Finance Mortgage and Discount Co. v. Liberator Permanent Benefit Building Society* (1878) 10 Ch.D. 15 at 24; *Antrim County Land Building and Investment Co. Ltd v. Steward* [1904] 2 I.R. 357; *cf. ante*, para. 19–087.

[40] H.E.L. vii, 19, 23. See, *e.g. Doe d. Lloyd v. Passingham* (1827) 6 B. & C. 305; *Doe d. Butler v. Lord Kensington* (1846) 8 Q.B. 429 at 449; Cole on *Ejectment*, pp. 66, 287.

[41] *Manchester Airport Plc v. Dutton* [1999] 3 W.L.R. 524 (licensees who had been granted the right to occupy a wood to carry out work preparatory to the extension of an airport runway could bring proceedings against environmental protesters who had set up camps in the wood). *cf. Hill v. Tupper* (1863) 2 H. & C. 121 at 127, 128 (licensee of canal had no right of action against third parties for infringement of his rights under the licence, and could only sue with the consent and in the name of the canal company; *ante*, para. 18–048).

[41a] *cf. ante*, para. 3–118.

[42] Five for residential property and two for other land.

[43] CPR Sched. 1, R113 (High Court); Sched. 2, C24 (county court). Most cases are now brought in the county court.

its operation,[44] though the court has a discretion to grant a stay of execution if the defendant seeks to appeal.[45] This procedure is not available against a tenant holding over after the determination of his tenancy.[46] It may however be used to eject an unlawful sub-tenant where the head lease contained an absolute covenant against sub-letting,[47] or to eject a licensee whose licence has expired.[48] An order for possession may be obtained which authorises the sheriff to evict all persons found on the premises, whether bound by the judgment or not.[49] The order may extend to—

(i) the whole of the premises, even though only part of them had been wrongfully occupied[50]; and

(ii) other premises on which there has not yet been any trespass, but where there is a real danger of such violation.[51]

The second remedy available against squatters is an interim possession order.[52] This is a particularly expeditious form of summary proceedings that is enforced by criminal sanctions.[53] A squatter who fails to leave within 24 hours of the order, or re-enters as a trespasser within a year thereafter, commits a criminal offence.[54]

(2) MESNE PROFITS. As against a trespasser the owner—or indeed a licensee, whether in possession or having a contractual right to possession under the licence[54a]—may claim damages for the trespass. In making such a claim for "mesne profits", as it is traditionally called,[55] the owner may elect to seek

---

[44] *McPhail v. Persons, Names Unknown* [1973] Ch. 447; *Swordheath Properties Ltd v. Floydd* [1978] 1 W.L.R. 550. Because the procedure is summary, the court has a discretion to order that the matter be adjourned for a full hearing in cases which raise disputed factual or legal issues: see *Filemart Ltd v. Avery* [1989] 2 E.G.L.R. 177.

[45] *Bibby v. Partap* [1996] 1 W.L.R. 931 (decided on the identical provisions in Trinidad and Tobago).

[46] CPR Sched. 1, R113.1; Sched. 2, C24.1.

[47] *Moore Properties (Ilford) Ltd v. McKeon* [1976] 1 W.L.R. 1278.

[48] *Greater London Council v. Jenkins* [1975] 1 W.L.R. 155. cf. *Markou v. Da Silvaesa* (1986) 52 P. & C.R. 204 (allegation that the terms of a licence were a sham was a triable issue that should not be tried on summons).

[49] *R. v. Wandsworth County Court, ex p. Wandsworth L.B.C.* [1975] 1 W.L.R. 1314; *Wiltshire County Council v. Frazer* (1983) 47 P. & C.R. 69; para. 3–121 *ante*.

[50] *University of Essex v. Djemal* [1980] 1 W.L.R. 1301 (sit-in students); *Wiltshire County Council v. Frazer, supra* ("new age travellers" who parked their caravans on, but without obstructing, an ancient highway).

[51] *Ministry of Agriculture, Fisheries and Food v. Heyman* (1989) 59 P. & C.R. 48 ("roving bands of nomadic-like persons" who were likely to move from one site to another).

[52] This order, which was first introduced in 1995, is granted only in the county court: see CPR Sched. 2, C24.8–C24.15. It only lies against a person who has throughout been a trespasser and not against one who holds over after lawful occupation. Furthermore, the claimant must have had an immediate right to possession at the time of the claim and throughout the period of unlawful possession of which he complains.

[53] See Criminal Justice and Public Order Act 1994, ss.75, 76.

[54] See *ibid.*, s.76(2)–(4).

[54a] See *Manchester Airport Plc v. Dutton* [1999] 3 W.L.R. 524 at 536–539.

[55] See *Goodtitle v. Tombs* (1770) 3 Wils. K.B. 118, *per* Wilmot C.J.

either restitution of the benefit which the defendant has received or damages for the loss he has suffered.[56]

(i) Usually the owner will claim compensation for having been deprived of the use and occupation of the land. This is assessed according to the current value of the land, normally the ordinary letting value.[57] The landowner is entitled to this sum "whether or not he can show that he would have let the property to anybody else, and whether or not he would have used the property himself".[58] This claim is distinct from the claim for compensation for use and occupation which lies where there is some kind of tenancy between the parties, as explained earlier.[59]

(ii) A landowner may seek restitution for the benefit received by the defendant where he cannot claim the ordinary letting value, because, *e.g.* the property is not available for letting on the open market.[60]

The court may make an interim award to the owner in respect of—

(i) mesne profits;

(ii) use and occupation (where a tenant holds over)[61]; or

(iii) rent;

where it is certain that he will be entitled under one or other of these heads at the end of the proceedings.[62]

---

[56] *Ministry of Defence v. Ashman* (1993) 66 P. & C.R. 195; *Ministry of Defence v. Thompson* [1993] 2 E.G.L.R. 107; *Dean and Chapter of Canterbury Cathedral v. Whitbread Plc* (1995) 72 P. & C.R. 9 at 16. The two forms of claim are mutually exclusive: *Ministry of Defence v. Ashman, supra*, at 201. For fuller consideration of the issues raised by these cases: see, *e.g.* (1994) 110 L.Q.R. 420 (E. Cooke); (1996) 112 L.Q.R. 39 (P. Watts).

[57] *Clifton Securities Ltd v. Huntley* [1948] 2 All E.R. 283; *Swordheath Properties Ltd v. Tabet* [1979] 1 W.L.R. 285. For a discussion of this so-called "user principle" in assessing damages, see *Stoke-on-Trent City Council v. W. & J. Wass Ltd* [1988] 1 W.L.R. 1406.

[58] *Inverugie Investments Ltd v. Hackett* [1995] 1 W.L.R. 713 at 717, *per* Lord Lloyd (tenant's claim for mesne profits against his trespassing landlord in respect of loss-making hotel).

[59] *Ante*, para. 14–079.

[60] As in *Ministry of Defence v. Ashman, supra; Ministry of Defence v. Thompson, supra* (property available only to members of the armed services).

[61] *Ante*, para. 14–079.

[62] CPR Pt 25, r. 7(d). See *Old Grovebury Manor Farm Ltd v. W. Seymour Plant Sales & Hire Ltd* [1979] 1 W.L.R. 263.

INDEX